# CLASSZONE.COM

D1195312

## Looking for ways to integrate the Web into your curriculum?

ClassZone, McDougal Littell's
textbook-companion Web site, is the solution!
Online teaching support for you and engaging,
interactive content for your students!

**ClassZone** is your online guide to
*The Americans*

- Links provide updated connections to relevant Web sites.
- Quizzes check comprehension with self-scoring assessment.
- Activities offer students a fun and engaging way to study history.
- Current Events check students' knowledge of the weekly news.
- Teacher Center provides lesson planning support and teaching ideas.

**Log on to ClassZone at**
www.classzone.com
With the purchase of *The Americans* you
have immediate access to ClassZone.

**Teacher Access Code**

# MCD359YAU76RT

Use this code to create your own user name
and password. Then access both teacher and
student resources.

McDougal Littell

*The* AMERICANS

*Reconstruction to the 21st Century*

TEXAS TEACHER'S EDITION

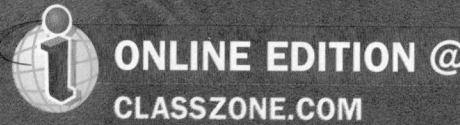

ONLINE EDITION @
CLASSZONE.COM

# Texas Advisers and Reviewers

**TEXAS TEACHER
REVIEWER PANEL**
The following educators participated in planning, reviewed
prototypes, reviewed content
outlines, reviewed manuscript,
or wrote classroom activities.

**PATRICIA BRISON**
Bellaire High School
Bellaire, Texas

**DEBRA BROWN**
Eisenhower High School
Houston, Texas

**SHERRY BURGIN**
Garland High School
Garland, Texas

**GWEN CASH**
Clear Creek High School
League City, Texas

**AL CELAYA**
Robert E. Lee High School
Tyler, Texas

**MARCI SMITH DEAL**
Hurst-Euless-Bedford
Independent School District
Bedford, Texas

**KENWARD GOODE**
Robert E. Lee High School
Tyler, Texas

**KYLE HOWARD**
Cooper High School
Lubbock, Texas

**MELODY KENNEY**
Turner High School
Carrollton, Texas

**JIM LEE**
Lamar High School
Arlington, Texas

**JANIE MALDONADO**
Lanier High School
Austin, Texas

**TERRY MCRAE**
Robert E. Lee High School
Tyler, Texas

**PEYTON MULLINS**
Robert E. Lee High School
Tyler, Texas

**LEANNA MORSE**
Memorial High School
McAllen, Texas

**GLORIA REMIJIO**
Del Valle High School
El Paso, Texas

**ALICE WHITE**
Bryan Adams High School
Dallas, Texas

**PATTIE WILLBANKS**
Robert E. Lee High School
Tyler, Texas

The following educators
reviewed the Pupil's Edition
section entitled *Strategies for
Taking TAKS.*

**CAROL MCCREE**
DeBakery Health Professional
High School
Houston, Texas

**SUZANNE COOK**
Scarborough High School
Houston, Texas

**PAM MAYFIELD**
Pasadena, High School
Houston, Texas

**JAMES BOYCE**
Performing and Visual Arts
High School
Houston, Texas

Keep your students current with today's events! Subscribe to USA TODAY®.
Call 1 (800) 757-TEACH for further information.

The USA TODAY® service mark has been licensed by USA TODAY® for use for certain purposes by
McDougal Littell Inc. USA TODAY® charts, articles, and photographs incorporated in these reading
materials are displayed for informational and promotional purposes only. The USA TODAY® charts,
articles, and photographs incorporated herein are solely for private, personal, and noncommercial use.
Any other use of the USA TODAY® charts, articles, and photographs incorporated herein, without prior
express written permission of USA TODAY®, is strictly prohibited.

ISBN 0-618-18405-8

Printed in the United States of America.

# Table of Contents

# A Pupil's Edition Customized for Texas

*The Americans: Reconstruction to the 21st Century* is customized for Texas with a special section called *Strategies for Taking TAKS,* which teaches your students test-taking strategies that will help them to improve performance on the Texas Assessment of Knowledge and Skills.

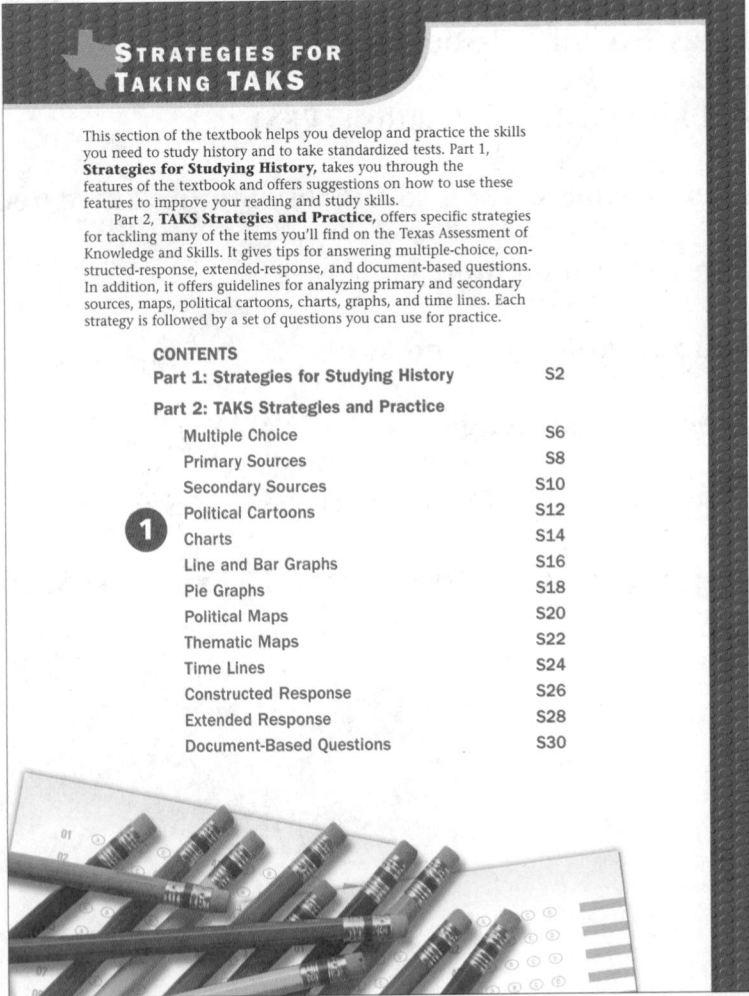

## STRATEGIES FOR TAKING TAKS

This section of the textbook helps you develop and practice the skills you need to study history and to take standardized tests. Part 1, **Strategies for Studying History,** takes you through the features of the textbook and offers suggestions on how to use these features to improve your reading and study skills.

Part 2, **TAKS Strategies and Practice,** offers specific strategies for tackling many of the items you'll find on the Texas Assessment of Knowledge and Skills. It gives tips for answering multiple-choice, constructed-response, extended-response, and document-based questions. In addition, it offers guidelines for analyzing primary and secondary sources, maps, political cartoons, charts, graphs, and time lines. Each strategy is followed by a set of questions you can use for practice.

### CONTENTS

**1 TAKS ITEM TYPES**
Strategies for Taking TAKS includes strategies and practice in the item types found on the Grade 11 Exit Level Social Studies TAKS exam. Included are multiple-choice items, map-based items, chart-based items, primary source questions, items based on political cartoons, and more.

**2 STRATEGIES**
For every item type, strategies are presented in a step-by-step format that helps students think through the correct answer. Each numbered strategy corresponds to a number on the model that is provided.

**3 CRITICAL THINKING**
The strategies emphasize higher order thinking skills. Call-outs that accompany the models help students see how to think through the correct answer.

## Political Cartoons

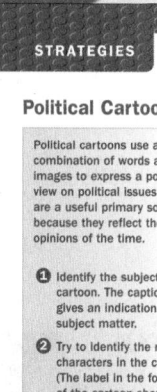

Political cartoons use a combination of words and images to express a point of view on political issues. They are a useful primary source, because they reflect the opinions of the time.

**1** Identify the subject of the cartoon. The caption often gives an indication of the subject matter.

**2** Try to identify the main characters in the cartoon. (The label in the foreground of the cartoon shows that they are members of the Tammany Ring, New York's Democratic political machine. "Boss" Tweed, the leader, is on the left.)

**3** Identify any important symbols—ideas or images that stand for something else.

**4** Review labels and any other written information in the cartoon.

**5** Analyze the point of view. The use of caricature—the exaggeration of physical features—often signals the cartoonist's attitude.

**6** Interpret the cartoonist's message.

The cartoonist uses a diamond stickpin to symbolize Tweed's excesses.

The labels identify other members of the Tweed Ring.

WHO STOLE THE PEOPLES MONEY? – DO TELL. KTYMES.    'TWAS HIM.

The Granger Collection, New York.

Tweed's physical appearance is exaggerated, making him look grossly overweight. This suggests that the cartoonist had a low opinion of Tweed and his followers.

**1** Which sentence best summarizes the way members of the Tammany Ring would answer the question in the caption?

A They did not, and would not, steal the people's money.

B They accept responsibility for stealing the people's money.

C They do not know who stole the people's money.

D They each blame someone else for stealing the people's money.

**2** Based on the cartoon, what word do you think the cartoonist might use to describe the Tammany Ring?

F Lazy

G Corrupt

H Honest

J Hard-working

Since you know that the cartoon is critical of the Tammany Ring, you can eliminate the two positive choices—H and J.

answers: 1 (D), 2 (G)

For more test practice online . . .
**TEST PRACTICE**
CLASSZONE.COM

**4**

**Directions:** Use the political cartoon and your knowledge of United States history to answer the following questions.

FIRST DOLLAR    FIRST 59¢

Doug Marlette, *Charlotte Observer*, 1981.

**1** According to the cartoon, for every dollar that working men earned, working women earned —

A 49 cents

B 59 cents

C 69 cents

D 79 cents

**2** Which of the following **BEST** summarizes the point of the cartoon?

F Men are happier than women are.

G Working men have bigger offices than working women.

H Working women earn less than working men.

J Working women do the real work in an office.

**3** What phrase summarizes feminists' solution to the problem illustrated in the cartoon?

A "We Shall Overcome"

B "Equal Pay for Equal Work"

C "ERA Now"

D "Our Bodies, Ourselves"

**4** Today, women make up nearly 50 percent of the workforce. However, they still encounter problems in the workplace, including —

F the "glass ceiling"

G lack of quality child care

H sexual harassment

J All of the above

### TEKS and TAKS

| | Item Number | TEKS | TAKS |
|---|---|---|---|
| **STRATEGY** | 1, 2, 3, 4. | (6)(B): analyze major issues and events of World War II | (US6)(B): analyze major issues and events of World War II |
| | 2. | (6)(C): explain the roles played by significant military leaders of World War II | |
| **PRACTICE** | 1. | (3)(A): explain significant events of the Spanish-American War | |
| | 2. | (1)(B): apply chronology through the sequencing of significant events | (US1)(B): apply chronology through the sequencing of significant events |
| | 3. | (2)(A): analyze political issues in the U.S. from 1877 to 1898<br>(2)(B): analyze economic issues in the U.S. from 1877 to 1898 | (US2): understand political changes in the U.S. from 1877 to 1898<br>(US2)(B): analyze economic issues in the U.S. from 1877 to 1898 |
| | 4. | (22)(A): explain the effects of technological innovations on economic development in the U.S. | (US22)(A): explain the effects of technological innovations on economic development in the U.S. |

**4 PRACTICE**
For each item type, a page of practice immediately follows the page that explains the strategies.

**5 TAKS FORMAT**
All practice items are in the multiple-choice format that students will find on the TAKS exam.

**6 CORRELATION TO TEKS AND TAKS**
In the Teacher's Edition, a chart shows how every item Strategies for Taking TAKS correlates to a TEKS objective and a TAKS objective for Grade 11 Exit Level Social Studies.

# Using the Texas Teacher's Edition

The Texas Teacher's Edition provides the information you need to coordinate your teaching with Texas curriculum standards and assessments. Special Texas resources will help you meet state requirements. Complete information about how *The Americans: Reconstruction to the 21st Century* meets the requirements of Texas Essential Knowledge and Skills (TEKS) and Texas Assessment of Knowledge and Skills (TAKS) will help you select materials to meet your teaching goals.

## CHAPTER 11 CORRELATION

### CORRELATION TO THE TEXAS ESSENTIAL KNOWLEDGE AND SKILLS

Chapter 11 addresses the following standards of the Texas Essential Knowledge and Skills for U.S. History.

| TEKS | Instruction | Student Question/Activity |
|---|---|---|
| (3B) Identify the reasons for U.S. involvement in World War I. | PE 378–380—explanation of the events that prompted America to enter the war, including unrestricted submarine warfare by Germany | TE 379—skillbuilder mini-lesson about evaluation America's decision to declare war |
| (3C) Analyze the impact of significant individuals including John J. Pershing, during World War I. | PE 384—examination of General John J. Pershing's life and the significant role he played in the war | TE 384—question about what made Pershing such an effective military leader |
| (3D) Analyze major issues raised by U.S. involvement in World War I, Wilson's Fourteen Points, and the Treaty of Versailles. | PE 398–403—analysis of the post-war peace efforts, including Wilson's Fourteen Points and the Treaty of Versailles | PE 403—critical thinking questions regarding various issues surrounding the Treaty of Versailles |
| (9B) Identify and explain reasons for changes in political boundaries such as international conflicts. | PE 400—dual map showing the dramatic change in political boundaries in Europe as a result of World War I | PE 400—questions that require students to interpret information about the map |
| (10A) Analyze the effects of changing demographic patterns resulting from migration within the United States. | PE 393–394—discussion of the causes and effects of the Great Migration, which brought thousands of Southern African Americans to the North | TE 394—writing activity examining the experiences of African Americans who migrated to the North |
| (12E) Describe the economic effects of international military conflicts on the United States. | PE 389—chart examining the ways in which the war impacted the U.S. economy | PE 389—questions that require students to interpret information about the chart |
| (15B) Explain the impact of significant international events such as World War I on changes in the role of the federal government. | PE 388–392—examination of how the federal government took a greater role in the economy and society during World War I | PE 395—critical thinking question about how the war affected the power of the federal government |
| (21D) Identify the political, social, and economic contributions of women to American society. | PE 394—discussion of the significant role American women played in the war effort | PE 395—question about efforts by women during the war |

### TAKS MINI-LESSONS

1. **Social Studies Skills: Objective 1 (US3.B):** Identify the reasons for U.S. involvement in World War I **Activity** Have students consider the significance of Germany's unrestricted submarine warfare in prompting the United States to enter the war.

2. **Social Studies Skills: Objective 2 (US10.A):** Analyze the effects of changing demographic patterns resulting from migration within the United States **Activity** Have students complete the writing activity on TE page 394 regarding the Great Migration.

3. **Social Studies Skills: Objective 1 (US3.C):** Analyze major issues raised by U.S. involvement in World War I **Activity** Have students summarize President Wilson's Fourteen Points as well as the debate in American over the Treaty of Versailles.

4. **English Language Arts Skills: Objective 1 (7.F):** Produce summaries of texts by identifying main ideas and their supporting details. **Activity** Have students summarize the weaknesses of the Treaty of Versailles.

5. **English Language Arts Skills: Objective 3 (19.B):** Analyze ideas as represented in various media **Activity** Have students answer the questions regarding the political cartoon on page 391.

---

### HISTORY from VISUALS

**Interpreting the Illustration**
Ask the students to discuss how the artist portrays the sinking of the *Lusitania*. (Students may notice that there are a lot of women on the lifeboats, the two hands coming out of the water in center foreground, and a man climbing onto the raft. Some students may say the ad would have kept them from sailing for fear of being attacked.)

### More About . . .

**Blockade vs. Submarines**
The British naval blockade of Germany was a far more effective weapon than Germany's submarine warfare. The naval blockade of Germany reduced shipping into Germany to almost nothing. By contrast, German subs were only capable of preventing a small percentage of ships bound for Britain from reaching their destination. For example, in March 1915, roughly 6,000 ships sailed for Britain. The Germans sank only 21 of them. Meanwhile, German submarines were constantly harassed by new anti-submarine measures. For instance, the British invented depth charges, which were canisters dropped from ships. These charges exploded under water in the vicinity of a sub. The shock waves usually damaged the subs, forcing them to the surface where a British ship's guns would fire on the sub.

▲ This image of a U-boat crew machine-gunning helpless survivors of the *Lusitania* was clearly meant as propaganda. In fact, U-boats seldom lingered after an attack.

### The War Hits Home ③

Although the majority of Americans favored victory for the Allies rather than the Central Powers, they did not want to join the Allies' fight. By 1917, however, America had mobilized for war against the Central Powers for two reasons: to ensure Allied repayment of debts to the United States and to prevent the Germans from threatening U.S. shipping.

**THE BRITISH BLOCKADE** As fighting on land continued, Britain began to make more use of its naval strength. It blockaded the German coast to prevent weapons and other military supplies from getting through. However, the British expanded the definition of contraband to include food. They also extended the blockade to neutral ports and mined the entire North Sea.

The results were two fold. First, American ships carrying goods for Germany refused to challenge the blockade and seldom reached their destination. Second, Germany found it increasingly difficult to import foodstuffs and fertilizers for crops. By 1917, famine stalked the country. An estimated 750,000 Germans starved to death as a result of the British blockade.

Americans had been angry at Britain's blockade, which threatened freedom of the seas and prevented American goods from reaching German ports. However, Germany's response to the blockade soon outraged American public opinion.

**GERMAN U-BOAT RESPONSE** Germany responded to the British blockade with a counterblockade by U-boats (from *Unterseeboot*, the German word for a submarine). Any ship found in the waters around Britain would be sunk—and it would not always be possible to warn crews and passengers of an attack.

One of the worst disasters occurred on May 7, 1915, when a U-boat sank the British liner *Lusitania* (lōṓ'sĭ-tā'nē-ə) off the southern coast of Ireland. Of the 1,198 persons lost, 128 were Americans. The Germans defended their action on the grounds that the liner carried ammunition. Despite Germany's explanation, Americans became outraged with Germany because of the loss of life. American public opinion turned against Germany and the Central Powers.

③ ⟁ TAKS
Mini-Lesson 1:
SS11 1(US3.B)

378 CHAPTER 11

▲ A newspaper ad for the *Lusitania* included a warning from the German Embassy.

---

### DIFFERENTIATING INSTRUCTION     STUDENTS ACQUIRING ENGLISH/ESL

**Understanding Main Ideas**
Write the heading "The War Hits Home" on the board. Explain to students that this phrase refers to the fact that even though the war was being fought in distant countries, it still had an impact on the people in the United States. Ask students to create a list of the ways the war affected life in the United States. Read the section "The War Hits Home" with students. Then ask them to point out the statements in the text that support the heading.

Some of the statements they might write include:
- "American ships carrying goods for Germany refused to challenge the blockade and seldom reached their destination."
- "Of the 1,198 persons lost, 128 were Americans."
- "Americans became outraged with Germany because of the loss of life."

▣ Integrated Assessment
· Rubric 2

---

**① TEKS CORRELATIONS**
This chart lists TEKS objectives emphasized in the chapter and explains where in the Pupil's Edition and Teacher's Edition you will find instruction and activities relevant to the objective.

**② TAKS MINI-LESSONS**
For every chapter, five mini-lessons are recommended that are based on activities in the Pupil's Edition and Teacher's Edition. Three mini-lessons focus on social studies, while two focus on English language arts or reading.

**③ TAKS MINI-LESSON REFERENCES**
Each of the TAKS mini-lessons is referenced with the Teacher's Edition or Pupil's Edition activity that serves as the basis for the mini-lesson.

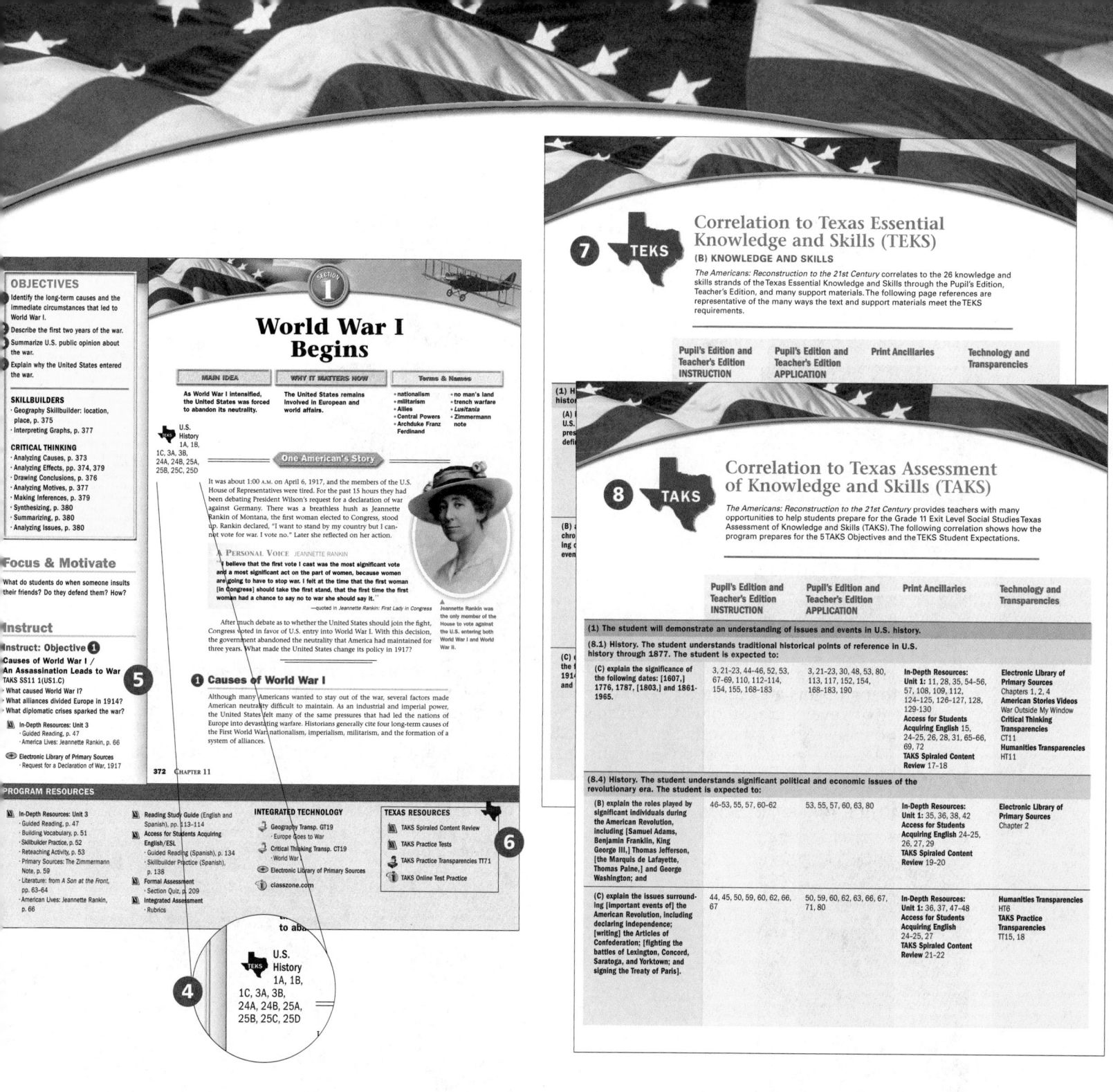

**4 SECTION-BY-SECTION REFERENCES**
At the beginning of every section of the text, you will find a list of the Texas Essential Knowledge and Skills (TEKS) covered in the section.

**5 TAKS REFERENCES WITH EVERY HEAD**
A TAKS objective is referenced with every blue head in the textbook.

**6 TEXAS RESOURCES**
This page always includes a list of the Texas Resources that you can use in teaching that section.

**7 TEKS CORRELATIONS (PAGES TX18–TX51)**
An easy-to-read chart provides a detailed correlation of *The Americans* with the Texas Essential Knowledge and Skills (TEKS) for United States History Studies Since Reconstruction. This correlation provides specific page references to the Pupil's Edition, Teacher's Edition, print ancillaries, transparencies, and technology.

**8 TAKS CORRELATIONS (PAGES TX58–TX84)**
Another chart provides a detailed correlation of *The Americans* to the Texas Assessment of Knowledge and Skills (TAKS) exam for Grade 11 Exit Level Social Studies. This correlation provides specific page references to the Pupil's Edition, Teacher's Edition, print ancillaries, transparencies, and technology.

# Additional Texas Teaching Resources

McDougal Littell has created a number of publications and technology resources to help you coordinate your teaching of *The Americans: Reconstruction to the 21st Century* with Texas curriculum standards and to help prepare your students for TAKS.

### TAKS SPIRALED CONTENT REVIEW

This book provides a review of the social studies content that students are required to know for the Grade 11 Exit Level Social Studies TAKS exam. The book thoroughly reviews the tested content of U.S. History in Grades 8 and 11, World Geography, and World History.

### TAKS PRACTICE TRANSPARENCIES

One transparency for each section of the textbook familiarizes students with the types of items on TAKS and provides a review of the content of each section. Each transparency is correlated to a TAKS objective and includes a TAKS content review question.

### LESSON PLANS FOR TEXAS

These lesson plans give you a two-page lesson plan for each section in the Pupil's Edition. The lesson plans include TEKS and TAKS objectives and options for teaching students acquiring English, for integrating technology, for block schedules, and more.

### ONLINE LESSON PLANNER

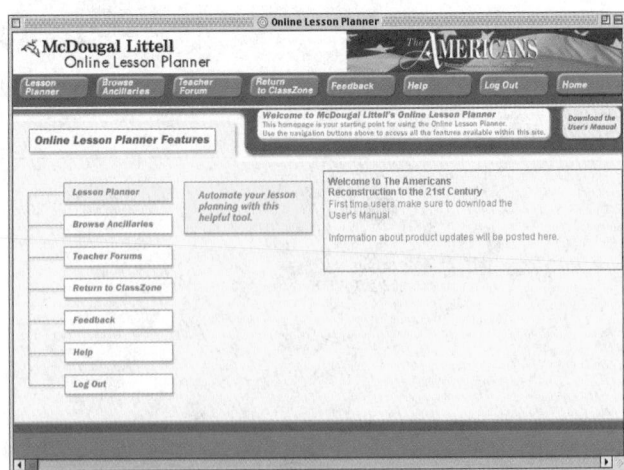

This innovative planning tool allows teachers to create, edit, and customize lesson plans, using all of their resources. A correlation feature allows the plans to be correlated to TEKS and TAKS.

## TAKS PRACTICE TESTS

This book gives your students practice in answering the types of questions they will see on the Grade 11 Exit Level Social Studies TAKS exam. The book provides diagnostic items and feedback for students. A complete practice test in the format of the Grade 11 Exit Level Social Studies TAKS exam is also included.

## TAKS ONLINE TEST PRACTICE

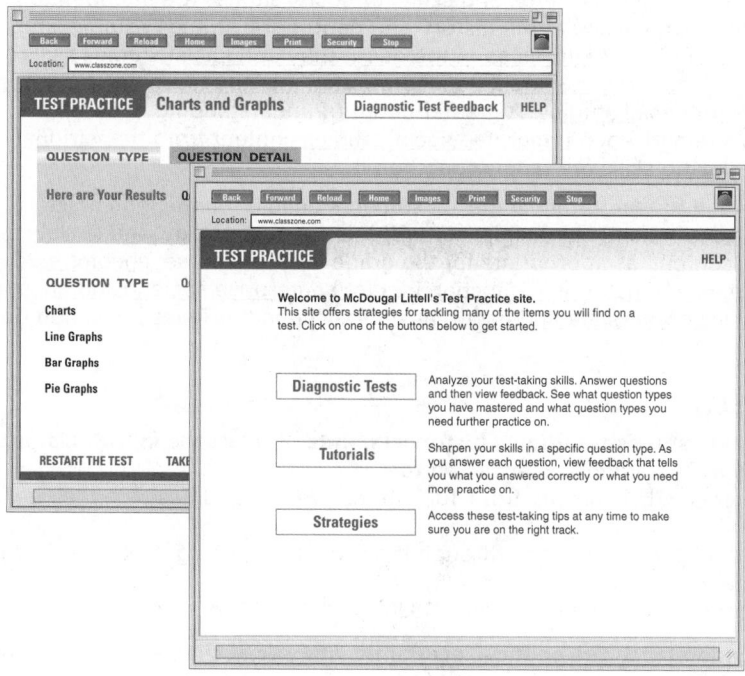

Online practice in TAKS can be accessed through McDougal Littell's companion Web site—ClassZone. Diagnostics and feedback help students see what test-taking skills and strategies they need to improve on for TAKS. Tutorials provide instruction and practice in test-taking skills needed on TAKS.

## TEST GENERATOR CD-ROM

The Test Generator contains quizzes for every section and three tests for every chapter. Questions are provided in three levels: basic, average, and advanced. The quiz and test items are correlated to TEKS and TAKS, as well as national standards.

## TEXAS ELECTRONIC TEACHER TOOLS CD-ROM

All of the print ancillaries for *The Americans: Reconstruction to the 21st Century*, including those designed specifically for Texas teachers, are located on this convenient CD-ROM. View, search, and print the ancillaries, which are organized by resource and chapter.

TEKS

# Texas Essential Knowledge and Skills (TEKS)

§113.32. United States History Studies Since Reconstruction

## (A) INTRODUCTION

(1) In this course, which is the second part of a two-year study of U.S. history that begins in Grade 8, students study the history of the United States since Reconstruction to the present. Historical content focuses on the political, economic, and social events and issues related to industrialization and urbanization, major wars, domestic and foreign policies of the Cold War and post-Cold War eras, and reform movements including civil rights. Students examine the impact of geographic factors on major events and analyze causes and effects of the Great Depression. Students examine the impact of constitutional issues on American society, evaluate the dynamic relationship of the three branches of the federal government, and analyze efforts to expand the democratic process. Students describe the relationship between the arts and the times during which they were created. Students analyze the impact of technological innovations on the American labor movement. Students use critical-thinking skills to explain and apply different methods that historians use to interpret the past, including points of view and historical context.

(2) To support the teaching of the essential knowledge and skills, the use of a variety of rich primary and secondary source material such as biographies and autobiographies; landmark cases of the U.S. Supreme Court; novels; speeches, letters, and diaries; and poetry, songs, and artworks is encouraged. Selections may include a biography of Dwight Eisenhower, Upton Sinclair's *The Jungle*, and Martin Luther King's letter from the Birmingham City Jail. Motivating resources are also available from museums, historical sites, presidential libraries, and local and state preservation societies.

(3) The eight strands of the essential knowledge and skills for social studies are intended to be integrated for instructional purposes with the history and geography strands establishing a sense of time and a sense of place. Skills listed in the geography and social studies skills strands in subsection (c) of this section should be incorporated into the teaching of all essential knowledge and skills for social studies. A greater depth of understanding of complex content material can be attained when integrated social studies content from the various disciplines and critical-thinking skills are taught together.

(4) Throughout social studies in Kindergarten-Grade 12, students build a foundation in history; geography; economics; government; citizenship; culture; science, technology, and society; and social studies skills. The content, as appropriate for the grade level or course, enables students to understand the importance of patriotism, function in a free enterprise society, and appreciate the basic democratic values of our state and nation as referenced in the Texas Education Code, §28.002(h).

## (B) KNOWLEDGE AND SKILLS

(1) **History. The student understands traditional historical points of reference in U.S. history from 1877 to the present. The student is expected to:**
  (A) identify the major eras in U.S. history from 1877 to the present and describe their defining characteristics;
  (B) apply absolute and relative chronology through the sequencing of significant individuals, events, and time periods; and
  (C) explain the significance of the following dates: 1898, 1914-1918, 1929, 1941-1945, and 1957.

(2) **History. The student understands the political, economic, and social changes in the United States from 1877 to 1898. The student is expected to:**
  (A) analyze political issues such as Indian policies, the growth of political machines, and civil service reform;
  (B) analyze economic issues such as industrialization, the growth of railroads, the growth of labor unions, farm issues, and the rise of big business; and
  (C) analyze social issues such as the treatment of minorities, child labor, growth of cities, and problems of immigrants.

# Texas Essential Knowledge and Skills (TEKS)

(3) **History. The student understands the emergence of the United States as a world power between 1898 and 1920. The student is expected to:**
- **(A)** explain why significant events and individuals, including the Spanish-American War, U.S. expansionism, Henry Cabot Lodge, Alfred Thayer Mahan, and Theodore Roosevelt, moved the United States into the position of a world power;
- **(B)** identify the reasons for U.S. involvement in World War I, including unrestricted submarine warfare;
- **(C)** analyze significant events such as the battle of Argonne Forest and the impact of significant individuals including John J. Pershing during World War I; and
- **(D)** analyze major issues raised by U.S. involvement in World War I, Wilson's Fourteen Points, and the Treaty of Versailles.

(4) **History. The student understands the effects of reform and third party movements on American society. The student is expected to:**
- **(A)** evaluate the impact of Progressive Era reforms including initiative, referendum, recall, and the passage of the 16th and 17th amendments;
- **(B)** evaluate the impact of reform leaders such as Susan B. Anthony, W.E.B. DuBois, and Robert LaFollette on American society; and
- **(C)** evaluate the impact of third parties and their candidates such as Eugene Debs, H. Ross Perot, and George Wallace.

(5) **History. The student understands significant individuals, events, and issues of the 1920s. The student is expected to:**
- **(A)** analyze causes and effects of significant issues such as immigration, the Red Scare, Prohibition, and the changing role of women; and
- **(B)** analyze the impact of significant individuals such as Clarence Darrow, William Jennings Bryan, Henry Ford, and Charles A. Lindbergh.

(6) **History. The student understands the impact of significant national and international decisions and conflicts from World War II and the Cold War to the present on the United States. The student is expected to:**
- **(A)** identify reasons for U.S. involvement in World War II, including the growth of dictatorships and the attack on Pearl Harbor;
- **(B)** analyze major issues and events of World War II such as fighting the war on multiple fronts, the internment of Japanese-Americans, the Holocaust, the battle of Midway, the invasion of Normandy, and the development of and Harry Truman's decision to use the atomic bomb;
- **(C)** explain the roles played by significant military leaders during World War II, including Omar Bradley, Dwight Eisenhower, Douglas MacArthur, George Marshall, and George Patton;
- **(D)** describe U.S. responses to Soviet aggression after World War II, including the Truman Doctrine, the Marshall Plan, the North Atlantic Treaty Organization, and the Berlin airlift;
- **(E)** analyze the conflicts in Korea and Vietnam and describe their domestic and international effects;
- **(F)** describe the impact of the GI Bill, the election of 1948, McCarthyism, and Sputnik I;
- **(G)** analyze reasons for the Western victory in the Cold War and the challenges of changing relationships among nations; and
- **(H)** identify the origins of major domestic and foreign policy issues currently facing the United States.

(7) **History. The student understands the impact of the American civil rights movement. The student is expected to:**
- **(A)** trace the historical development of the civil rights movement in the 18th, 19th, and 20th centuries, including the 13th, 14th, 15th amendments;
- **(B)** identify significant leaders of the civil rights movement, including Martin Luther King, Jr.;
- **(C)** evaluate government efforts, including the Civil Rights Act of 1964, to achieve equality in the United States; and
- **(D)** identify changes in the United States that have resulted from the civil rights movement such as increased participation of minorities in the political process.

# Texas Essential Knowledge and Skills (TEKS)

**TEKS**

(8) **Geography. The student uses geographic tools to collect, analyze, and interpret data. The student is expected to:**
(A) create thematic maps, graphs, charts, models, and databases representing various aspects of the United States; and
(B) pose and answer questions about geographic distributions and patterns shown on maps, graphs, charts, models, and databases.

(9) **Geography. The student understands the impact of geographic factors on major events. The student is expected to:**
(A) analyze the effects of physical and human geographic factors on major events including the building of the Panama Canal; and
(B) identify and explain reasons for changes in political boundaries such as those resulting from statehood and international conflicts.

(10) **Geography. The student understands the effects of migration and immigration on American society. The student is expected to:**
(A) analyze the effects of changing demographic patterns resulting from migration within the United States; and
(B) analyze the effects of changing demographic patterns resulting from immigration to the United States.

(11) **Geography. The student understands the relationship between population growth and modernization on the physical environment. The student is expected to:**
(A) identify the effects of population growth and distribution and predict future effects on the physical environment; and
(B) trace the development of the conservation of natural resources, including the establishment of the National Park System and efforts of private nonprofit organizations.

(12) **Economics. The student understands domestic and foreign issues related to U.S. economic growth from the 1870s to 1920. The student is expected to:**
(A) analyze the relationship between private property rights and the settlement of the Great Plains;
(B) compare the purpose of the Interstate Commerce Commission with its performance over time;
(C) describe the impact of the Sherman Antitrust Act on businesses;
(D) analyze the effects of economic policies including the Open Door Policy and Dollar Diplomacy on U.S. diplomacy; and
(E) describe the economic effects of international military conflicts, including the Spanish-American War and World War I, on the United States.

(13) **Economics. The student understands significant economic developments between World War I and World War II. The student is expected to:**
(A) analyze causes of economic growth and prosperity in the 1920s;
(B) analyze the causes of the Great Depression, including the decline in worldwide trade, the stock market crash, and bank failures;
(C) analyze the effects of the Great Depression on the U.S. economy and government;
(D) evaluate the effectiveness of New Deal measures in ending the Great Depression; and
(E) analyze how various New Deal agencies and programs such as the Federal Deposit Insurance Corporation, the Securities and Exchange Commission, and Social Security continue to affect the lives of U.S. citizens.

(14) **Economics. The student understands the economic effects of World War II, the Cold War, and increased worldwide competition on contemporary society. The student is expected to:**
(A) describe the economic effects of World War II on the home front, including rationing, female employment, and the end of the Great Depression;
(B) identify the causes and effects of prosperity in the 1950s;
(C) describe the impact of the Cold War on the business cycle and defense spending;
(D) identify actions of government and the private sector to expand economic opportunities to all citizens; and
(E) describe the dynamic relationship between U.S. international trade policies and the U.S. free enterprise system.

# Texas Essential Knowledge and Skills (TEKS)

**(15) Government. The student understands changes in the role of government over time. The student is expected to:**
  (A) evaluate the impact of New Deal legislation on the historical roles of state and federal governments;
  (B) explain the impact of significant international events such as World War I and World War II on changes in the role of the federal government;
  (C) evaluate the effects of political incidents such as Teapot Dome and Watergate on the views of U.S. citizens concerning the role of the federal government; and
  (D) predict the effects of selected contemporary legislation on the roles of state and federal governments.

**(16) Government. The student understands the changing relationships among the three branches of the federal government. The student is expected to:**
  (A) evaluate the impact of events, including the Gulf of Tonkin Resolution and the War Powers Act, on the relationship between the legislative and executive branches of government; and
  (B) evaluate the impact of events, including Franklin Roosevelt's attempt to increase the number of U.S. Supreme Court justices, on the relationships among the legislative, executive, and judicial branches of government.

**(17) Government. The student understands the impact of constitutional issues on American society in the 20th century. The student is expected to:**
  (A) analyze the effects of 20th-century landmark U.S. Supreme Court decisions such as *Brown* v. *Board of Education, Regents of the University of California* v. *Bakke, and Reynolds* v. *Sims*;
  (B) analyze reasons for the adoption of 20th-century constitutional amendments.

**(18) Citizenship. The student understands efforts to expand the democratic process. The student is expected to:**
  (A) identify and analyze methods of expanding the right to participate in the democratic process, including lobbying, protesting, court decisions, and amendments to the U.S. Constitution;
  (B) evaluate various means of achieving equality of political rights, including the 19th, 24th, and 26th amendments; and
  (C) explain how participation in the democratic process reflects our national identity.

**(19) Citizenship. The student understands the importance of effective leadership in a democratic society. The student is expected to:**
  (A) describe qualities of effective leadership;
  (B) evaluate the contributions of significant political and social leaders in the United States such as Andrew Carnegie, Shirley Chisholm, and Franklin D. Roosevelt; and
  (C) identify the contributions of Texans who have been President of the United States.

**(20) Culture. The student understands the relationship between the arts and the times during which they were created. The student is expected to:**
  (A) describe how the characteristics and issues of various eras in U.S. history have been reflected in works of art, music, and literature such as the paintings of Georgia O'Keeffe, rock and roll, and John Steinbeck's *The Grapes of Wrath*;
  (B) describe the impact of significant examples of cultural movements in art, music, and literature on American society, including the Harlem Renaissance;
  (C) identify examples of American art, music, and literature that transcend American culture and convey universal themes;
  (D) analyze the relationship between culture and the economy and identify examples such as the impact of the entertainment industry on the U.S. economy; and
  (E) identify the impact of popular American culture on the rest of the world.

**(21) Culture. The student understands how people from various groups, including racial, ethnic, and religious groups, adapt to life in the United States and contribute to our national identity. The student is expected to:**
  (A) explain actions taken by people from racial, ethnic, and religious groups to expand economic opportunities and political rights in American society;
  (B) explain efforts of the Americanization movement to assimilate immigrants into American culture;

# Texas Essential Knowledge and Skills (TEKS)

**TEKS**

    **(C)** analyze how the contributions of people of various racial, ethnic, and religious groups have helped to shape the national identity; and

    **(D)** identify the political, social, and economic contributions of women to American society.

**(22)** **Science, technology, and society. The student understands the impact of science and technology on the economic development of the United States. The student is expected to:**

    **(A)** explain the effects of scientific discoveries and technological innovations such as electric power, the telegraph and telephone, petroleum-based products, medical vaccinations, and computers on the development of the United States;

    **(B)** explain how scientific discoveries and technological innovations such as those in agriculture, the military, and medicine resulted from specific needs; and

    **(C)** analyze the impact of technological innovations on the nature of work, the American labor movement, and businesses.

**(23)** **Science, technology, and society. The student understands the influence of scientific discoveries and technological innovations on daily life in the United States. The student is expected to:**

    **(A)** analyze how scientific discoveries and technological innovations, including those in transportation and communication, have changed the standard of living in the United States; and

    **(B)** explain how technological innovations in areas such as space exploration have led to other innovations that affect daily life and the standard of living.

**(24)** **Social studies skills. The student applies critical-thinking skills to organize and use information acquired from a variety of sources including electronic technology. The student is expected to:**

    **(A)** locate and use primary and secondary sources such as computer software, databases, media and news services, biographies, interviews, and artifacts to acquire information about the United States;

    **(B)** analyze information by sequencing, categorizing, identifying cause-and-effect relationships, comparing, contrasting, finding the main idea, summarizing, making generalizations and predictions, and drawing inferences and conclusions;

    **(C)** explain and apply different methods that historians use to interpret the past, including the use of primary and secondary sources, points of view, frames of reference, and historical context;

    **(D)** use the process of historical inquiry to research, interpret, and use multiple sources of evidence;

    **(E)** evaluate the validity of a source based on language, corroboration with other sources, and information about the author;

    **(F)** identify bias in written, oral, and visual material;

    **(G)** support a point of view on a social studies issue or event; and

    **(H)** use appropriate mathematical skills to interpret social studies information such as maps and graphs.

**(25)** **Social studies skills. The student communicates in written, oral, and visual forms. The student is expected to:**

    **(A)** use social studies terminology correctly;

    **(B)** use standard grammar, spelling, sentence structure, and punctuation;

    **(C)** transfer information from one medium to another, including written to visual and statistical to written or visual, using computer software as appropriate; and

    **(D)** create written, oral, and visual presentations of social studies information.

**(26)** **Social studies skills. The student uses problem-solving and decision-making skills, working independently and with others, in a variety of settings. The student is expected to:**

    **(A)** use a problem-solving process to identify a problem, gather information, list and consider options, consider advantages and disadvantages, choose and implement a solution, and evaluate the effectiveness of the solution; and

    **(B)** use a decision-making process to identify a situation that requires a decision, gather information, identify options, predict consequences, and take action to implement a decision.

# Correlation to Texas
# Essential Knowledge and Skills (TEKS)

## (A) INTRODUCTION

The following material will help you identify the ways in which *The Americans: Reconstruction to the 21st Century* correlates to the Introduction to the Social Studies content requirements of the Texas Essential Knowledge and Skills (see underscored material on page TX10). The boldfaced items below match the underscores on page TX10. Pages cited are representative.

**(1)  Students examine the impact of geographic factors on major events.**

The importance of geography in U.S. history is made clear throughout the text. Scores of maps along with the basic narrative help accomplish this. From the lure of open land in helping to settle the Great Plains, pages **214–216**, to the role of America's natural resources in fueling the country's rapid industrialization, pages **230–232**, to the difficulties that U.S. troops faced in the jungle terrain of Vietnam, pages **738–739**, the significance of geographic factors is emphasized time and again. Two-page features entitled *Geography Spotlight* also help highlight the important part geography has played in the nation's development. Example titles include *Industry Changes the Environment*, pages **234–235**, and *The Movement of Migrant Workers*, pages **684–685**.

**(1)  Students analyze causes and effects of the Great Depression.**

The Great Depression was one of the most significant events of the 20th century, one that touched the lives of nearly every American and transformed the country in fundamental ways. The text devotes two chapters to this most important period in American history. In particular, the book analyzes both the long-term causes of the Great Depression, such as a gradual decline in various industries and the farming sector, page **465**, a decline in consumer spending, pages **465–466**, uneven distribution of income, page **466,** and the high-risk practices of speculation and buying on margin, page **467**, and the immediate causes, including the stock market crash, pages **467–469**, as well as widespread bank and business failures, page **469**. The text also provides an in-depth analysis of the effects of the Great Depression, including the many hardships people suffered, pages **472–477** and the efforts taken by the Roosevelt administration to address the crisis under the New Deal, pages **486–519**.

**(1)  Students examine the impact of constitutional issues on American society.**

As the driving force behind the nation's democratic system, the U.S. Constitution has been at the center of numerous social, political, and legal issues throughout America's development. The text examines many such issues, including the rights of people living in U.S. territories, page **353**, the abridgement of civil liberties during World War I, pages **391–392**, the internment of Japanese Americans during World War II, page **594–595**, and the suppression of freedoms during the anti-Communist hysteria of the 1950s, pages **620–621**, just to name a few.

**(1)  Students evaluate the dynamic relationship of the three branches of the federal government.**

Throughout the nation's history, the three branches of the federal government have converged, for the purpose of working together as well as serving as a check on each other's power. The text highlights numerous examples of this relationship. Among them is the historic duel between President Woodrow Wilson and the Senate over the Treaty of Versailles, pages **400–403**, President Franklin Roosevelt's attempt to influence the Supreme Court, page **493**, the Gulf of Tonkin Resolution, which handed President Johnson broad military powers in Vietnam, page **735**, the recommendation by the House Judiciary Committee to impeach President Richard Nixon, page **806**, the congressional investigation into the Iran-Contra scandal, pages **852–853**, and the impeachment and Senate trial of President Bill Clinton, page **865**.

# Correlation to Texas Essential Knowledge and Skills (TEKS)

**(1) Students analyze efforts to expand the democratic process.**

Throughout its history, the United States has witnessed many efforts to expand the democratic process—mainly by different groups that have sought a greater voice in the country's political process. The text chronicles their struggles and achievements, examining among other topics the political reforms of the Progressive Era, page **312,** the success of the woman suffrage movement, page **334,** the historic civil rights movement of the 1950s and 1960s, pages **698–723,** the efforts by Hispanic Americans and Native Americans during the 1960s and 1970s to strengthen their political and social standing, pages **768–773,** and the establishment of the 26th amendment, which extended voting rights to Americans over the age of 18, page **798.**

**(1) Students describe the relationship between the arts and the times during which they were created.**

In telling the story of history, the text examines the world of the arts—and pays particular attention to the ways in which art reflected the times in which it was created. Examples of this include a look at the rise of newspapers and popular fiction that accompanied the growth of literacy rates during the turn of the 20th century, pages **294–296,** the writers and artists of the 1920s Jazz Age, pages **450–451,** Depression-era paintings, songs, and literature, pages **512–514,** the growth of science fiction during the Cold War, pages **628–629,** the emergence of the beat movement and rock 'n' roll in reaction to the quiet and comfortable 1950s, page **655–657,** and the rise of diverse writers as an indication of the nation's growing multiculturalism at the beginning of the 21st century, pages **874–875.**

**(1) Students analyze the impact of technological innovations on the American labor movement.**

Ingenuity and innovation are an important part of the nation's history. The text details the various inventions, discoveries, and innovations that helped to shape the United States. The book also analyzes the effects of technology on the working men and women of the country, including how rapid industrialization—and the difficult working conditions it prompted—led to the emergence of labor unions, pages **244–247,** as well as how the rise of the computer-driven service economy impacted workers and trade unions at the end of the 20th century, pages **869–872.**

**(1) Students use critical-thinking skills to explain and apply different methods that historians use to interpret the past, including points of view and historical context.**

As they read the text, students are called on to use a variety of critical thinking skills—in inner column questions, and in every section and chapter assessment. See, for example, pages **209, 351, 630, 826.** In addition, the text offers a feature entitled Point/Counterpoint, which enables students to examine different points of view about a particular issue. These features address a number of important topics, including the League Of Nations, page **401,** and the legacy of the Great Society, page **692.**

**(2) The use of a variety of rich primary and secondary source material such as biographies and autobiographies; landmark cases of the U.S. Supreme Court; novels; speeches, letters, and diaries; and poetry, songs, and artworks is encouraged.**

The book contains an in-depth discussion of landmark cases of the U.S. Supreme Court in two-page features entitled *Historic Decisions of the Supreme Court.* Examples include *Schenck* v. *United States,* pages **396–397,** *Korematsu* v. *United States,* pages **596–597,** and *Brown* v. *Board of Education of Topeka,* pages **708–709.** In addition, the widest possible variety of primary and secondary sources is factored systematically into the student text. Included are excerpts from articles, journals, sermons, essays, decrees, and other documents such as Upton Sinclair's *The Jungle,* page **317,** and Martin Luther King, Jr.'s "Letter from a Birmingham City Jail," page **712.** Quotes are used from histories and other nonfiction works as well as from biographies and autobiographies such as those on pages **372** and **848,** novels, pages **450** and **762–763,** speeches, pages **372** and **670,** among others, letters, pages **332** and **631,** diaries, page **472,** poetry, page **459,** songs, page **745,** and works of art, page **435.**

# Correlation to Texas Essential Knowledge and Skills (TEKS)

**(2)** **Motivating resources are also available from museums, historical sites, presidential libraries, and local and state preservation societies.**

End-of-chapter activities and projects consistently encourage students to use a variety of motivating sources in addition to their textbook program. These include the Internet, if available, libraries, museums, and local sites of geographical and historical interest. See, for example, pages **115**, **201**, and **225**.

**(3)** **Geography and social studies skills strands should be incorporated into the teaching of all essential knowledge and skills for social studies. Integrated social studies content from the various disciplines and critical-thinking skills are taught together.**

The teachers' lesson plans that accompany this textbook include annotations that correlate the Texas Essential Knowledge and Skills to each section of every chapter. The annotations are organized according to eight strands of essential knowledge and skills: history, geography, economics, government, citizenship, culture, science/technology/society, and social studies skills. A look at several of these section annotations will confirm that geography and social studies skills are, in fact, incorporated into the teaching of all essential knowledge and skills; see, for example, pages **31**, **202**, **359**, and **478**.

**(4)** **Students will be enabled to understand the importance of patriotism.**

Patriotism is a theme that runs throughout U.S. history, and the text makes sure to note the achievements of the country's many patriots. Discussed in the text are patriots from the Revolutionary War period, including Samuel Adams, page **47**, and Thomas Paine, page **52**, to name only a few. Patriots such as George Washington, John Adams, and Thomas Jefferson continued as leaders during the nation's early years, pages **74–79** and **112–114**. Among the many other patriots mentioned in the text are Sam Houston, who led the effort by Texas to achieve independence, page **135**, and Sergeant Alvin York, a hero of World War I, page **386**.

In addition, biographical vignettes entitled *Key Players* appear throughout the book and deal with numerous Americans considered patriots.

**(4)** **Students are enabled to function in a free enterprise society.**

The free enterprise system is introduced to students on page **140**. From there, students examine the various economic issues the nation faced throughout its history, including the market revolution, pages **139–142**, the growth of industrialization and big business, pages **230–244**, the Great Depression, pages **462–519**, the transformation from a manufacturing-based to a service-based economy, page **814,** and the emergence of a global economy, pages **869–873**. In addition, the book offers an Economics Handbook, pages **R38–R47,** and a number of features entitled *Economic Background* that provide students with background information on the workings of the nation's economic system. The topics analyzed in the features include among others, what is a recession, page **680**, and the 1980s Texas oil boom, page **813**.

**(4)** **Students are enabled to appreciate the basic democratic values of our state and nation.**

The democratic concepts that are critical to our society appear in discussion of the American Revolution and the formation of the United States along with the documents: The Declaration of Independence, pages **54–57**, and the U.S. Constitution with its Bill of Rights, pages **84–103**. The expansion of democracy during the 1820s—in which more Americans gained the right to vote—is discussed on page **123**. Civil War-related democratic values such as the Emancipation Proclamation, pages **172–173**, and the rights guaranteed by the 13th, 14th, and 15th Amendments, pages **183**, **185–186**, are also discussed. Pages **334–335** examine the 19th Amendment, which gave women the right to vote. Furthermore, the text highlights the actions taken by our nation to promote democratic values, from joining World War I to help make the world "safe for democracy," page **380**, to helping guide Japan from an autocratic regime to a democracy after World War II, page **587**.

# Correlation to Texas Essential Knowledge and Skills (TEKS)

## (B) KNOWLEDGE AND SKILLS

*The Americans: Reconstruction to the 21st Century* correlates to the 26 knowledge and skills strands of the Texas Essential Knowledge and Skills through the Pupil's Edition, Teacher's Edition, and many support materials. The following page references are representative of the many ways the text and support materials meet the TEKS requirements.

| | Pupil's Edition and Teacher's Edition INSTRUCTION | Pupil's Edition and Teacher's Edition APPLICATION | Print Ancillaries | Technology and Transparencies |
|---|---|---|---|---|
| **(1) History. The student understands traditional historical points of reference in U.S. history from 1877 to the present. The student is expected to:** | | | | |
| **(A) identify the major eras in U.S. history from 1877 to the present and describe their defining characteristics;** | S14, S28, 230–233, 262–266, 342–344, 434–451, 452–457, 464–471, 488–503, 528–535, 602–629, 641–652, 698–725, 728–763, 766–787 | S25, S29, 223, 250, 266, 272, 345, 380, 451, 457, 471, 494, 501, 535, 604, 608, 621, 627, 649, 707, 716, 723, 735, 741, 747, 753, 761, 773, 780, 785 | **In-Depth Resources:** **Unit 1:** 35, 72, 73, 100 **Unit 2:** 19, 20, 40, 60 **Unit 3:** 1, 2, 3, 4, 5 **Unit 4:** 1, 2, 3, 18, 19, 20, 21, 36, 37, 38, 53, 54, 55, 56, 57 **Unit 5:** 22, 39, 40, 41, 42 **Unit 6:** 2, 3, 18, 19, 20, 39, 56, 57, 58 **Unit 7:** 1, 2, 3, 4 | **TAKS Practice Transparencies** TT65, 67, 106 |
| **(B) apply absolute and relative chronology through the sequencing of significant individuals, events, and time periods; and** | 200, 201, 228, 229, 252, 253, 274, 275, 304, 305, 340, 341, 357, 358, 370, 371, 410, 411, 432, 433, 449, 462, 463, 486, 487, 500, 508, 517, 526, 527, 560, 561, 580, 581, 600, 601, 613, 618, 619, 632, 633, 668, 669, 675, 691, 698, 699, 714, 728, 729, 766, 767, 773, 787, 792, 793, 828, 829, 851, 858, 859, US2–US15 | S7, 200, 228, 232, 252, 274, 337, 341, 349, 357, 358, 364, 371, 486, 500, 517, 523, 541, 547, 557, 574, 577, 632, 668, 673, 696, 715, 716, 728, 731, 753, 764, 766, 773, 780, 792, 804, 807, 817, 849, 856, 858, 868, 890 | **In-Depth Resources:** **Unit 2:** 1 **Unit 3:** 13-14, 24 **Unit 5:** 2, 3, 4, 11, 23, 24 **Unit 6:** 1, 20, 21, 39 **Unit 7:** 2 **Access for Students Acquiring English** 81, 103, 130, 144, 188, 189, 190, 197, 198, 225, 233, 234, 241, 262 | **Critical Thinking Transparencies** CT58 **Geography Transparencies** GT18, 19, 30, 33 **TAKS Practice Transparencies** TT68, 120 |
| **(C) explain the significance of the following dates: 1898, 1914–1918, 1929, 1941–1945, and 1957.** | 340, 341, 348–351, 352, 353, 355, 358, 368, 370, 371, 462, 467–469, 526, 527, 554–557, 560, 561, 569–587, 600, 601, 626, 627, 643, 644, 703, 704 | S25, 340, 349–351, 358, 365, 368, 370, 372, 406, 471, 484, 526, 556–558, 560, 570–577, 579–581, 583, 587, 598, 626, 632, 644, 707 | **In-Depth Resources:** **Unit 3:** 47, 48 **Unit 5:** 4, 14, 23, 24 **Unit 6:** 1 **Access for Students Acquiring English** 128, 130, 131, 132, 139, 144, 165, 169 | **Electronic Library of Primary Sources** Chapters 10, 14 **American Stories Videos** Ace of Aces **Critical Thinking Transparencies** CT58 **Geography Transparencies** GT18, 19 |

# Correlation to Texas Essential Knowledge and Skills (TEKS)

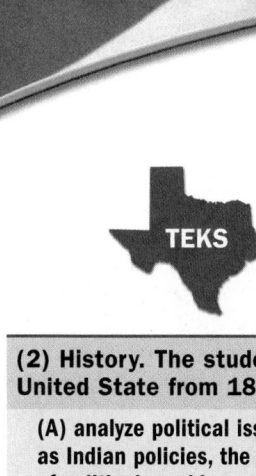

**TEKS**

| | Pupil's Edition and Teacher's Edition INSTRUCTION | Pupil's Edition and Teacher's Edition APPLICATION | Print Ancillaries | Technology and Transparencies |
|---|---|---|---|---|
| **(2) History. The student understands the political, economic, and social changes in the United State from 1877 to 1898. The student is expected to:** | | | | |
| **(A)** analyze political issues such as Indian policies, the growth of political machines, and civil service reform: | S12, 204–208, 219–223, 238, 267–271, 309–312, 317–320, 324, 325, 327, 328, 332–334, 350, 351 | S7, 204–206, 208, 211, 219–221, 223, 225, 226, 238, 267–272, 304–307, 309–312, 319, 324, 327, 329, 333, 350, 351 | **In-Depth Resources:** **Unit 2:** 1, 12, 14, 18, 41, 60 **Unit 3:** 1, 2, 3, 4, 5, 13–14, 17, 18 **Access for Students Acquiring English** 79–80, 81, 99, 102, 103, 118–119, 120, 122, 123, 128–129, 130, 131, 133 | **Electronic Library of Primary Sources** Chapters 5, 7 **American Stories Videos** A Walk in Two Worlds, From China to Chinatown **Critical Thinking Transparencies** CT13, 14 **Geography Transparencies** GT13, 17 |
| **(B)** analyze economic issues such as industrialization, the growth of railroads, the growth of labor unions, farm issues, and the rise of big business; and | S22, 208–210, 216–221, 230–249, 271, 281, 313, 314, 320, 323, 324, 328, 329, 332, 334, 354, 355 | S7, 208, 209, 211, 214–223, 226, 229–250, 270, 271, 304, 305, 309, 320, 325, 327, 333, 334, 354 | **In-Depth Resources:** **Unit 2:** 2, 3, 19, 20, 21, 22, 28–29, 31, 32, 33, 37, 38, 40, 48–49 **Unit 3:** 1 **Access for Students Acquiring English** 89–90, 91, 92, 93, 94, 96–97, 98–99, 101 | **Electronic Library of Primary Sources** Chapter 6 **American Stories Videos** Gusher!, A Child on Strike **Critical Thinking Transparencies** CT13, 14, 15, 17, 48, 49 **Humanities Transparencies** HT14, 35 **Geography Transparencies** GT13, 14, 17 **TAKS Practice Transparencies** TT51, 52, 53, 54 |
| **(C)** analyze social issues such as the treatment of minorities, child labor, growth of cities, and problems of immigrants. | 234, 235, 245, 246, 254–259, 260, 261, 262–266, 284, 285, 286–289, 306–309, 310–312, 313, 314–316, 317, 320–327, 334–337 | 234, 235, 238, 245, 252, 253, 256, 257, 259, 261, 264–266, 282, 283, 287–290, 300, 304–312, 314–316, 322, 327, 335, 337 | **In-Depth Resources:** **Unit 2:** 1, 12, 18, 31, 37, 39, 40, 46, 48–49, 50–51, 53, 54, 55, 56–58, 59, 62, 63, 71–72, 75, 76, 80 **Unit 3:** 1, 2, 3, 7, 15, 16, 17, 19–21, 22, 23 **Access for Students Acquiring English** 79, 81, 98–99, 100, 101, 107–108, 109–110, 112, 113, 118–119, 121 **Historic Supreme Court Decisions** 67–72 | **Electronic Library of Primary Sources** Chapters 6, 7, 9 **American Stories Videos** A Walk in Two Worlds, From China to Chinatown, A Child on Strike **Critical Thinking Transparencies** CT14, 15, 17, 49, 50, 51 **Humanities Transparencies** HT15, 16 **TAKS Practice Transparencies** TT56, 60 |

# Correlation to Texas Essential Knowledge and Skills (TEKS)

| TEKS | Pupil's Edition and Teacher's Edition INSTRUCTION | Pupil's Edition and Teacher's Edition APPLICATION | Print Ancillaries | Technology and Transparencies |
|---|---|---|---|---|
| **(3) History. The student understands the emergence of the United States as a world power between 1898 and 1920. The student is expected to:** | | | | |
| **(A)** explain why significant events and individuals, including the Spanish-American War, U.S. expansionism, Henry Cabot Lodge, Alfred Thayer Mahan, and Theodore Roosevelt, moved the United States into the position of a world power; | 91, 340, 342–344, 348–351, 353, 354, 356, 357, 359–363, 365, 366–377, 404, 405 | S7, 344, 346, 348–350, 351, 352, 354, 356, 358–360, 363, 365, 368, 369, 404, 405 | **In-Depth Resources:** **Unit 3:** 24, 25, 26, 27, 36–37, 40, 41, 42–44, 46 **Access for Students Acquiring English** 128–129, 130, 131, 132, 133, 135, 137–138 | **Electronic Library of Primary Sources** Chapters 10, 11 **Critical Thinking Transparencies** CT18, 19 **Humanities Transparencies** HT37, 38 **Geography Transparencies** GT18 **TAKS Practice Transparencies** TT69 |
| **(B)** identify the reasons for U.S. involvement in World War I, including unrestricted submarine warfare; | 372–380 | S25, 371–373, 377–380, 406, 407 | **In-Depth Resources:** **Unit 3:** 47, 59 **Access for Students Acquiring English** 139, 141 | **Electronic Library of Primary Sources** Chapter 11 **American Stories Videos** Ace of Aces **Critical Thinking Transparencies** CT19 **Geography Transparencies** GT19 **TAKS Practice Transparencies** TT71 |
| **(C)** analyze significant events such as the battle of Argonne Forest and the impact of significant individuals including John J. Pershing during World War I; and | 372–376, 383, 384, 386, 387 | 373, 375, 386, 387 | **In-Depth Resources:** **Unit 3:** 48 | **American Stories Videos** Ace of Aces |
| **(D)** analyze major issues raised by U.S. involvement in World War I, Wilson's Fourteen Points, and the Treaty of Versailles. | 390, 391, 398–402 | 390, 391, 399–401, 403, 406 | **In-Depth Resources:** **Unit 3:** 50, 57–58 **Access for Students Acquiring English** 140, 144 | **Electronic Library of Primary Sources** Chapter 11 **American Stories Videos** Ace of Aces **Critical Thinking Transparencies** CT19 **TAKS Practice Transparencies** TT74 |

# Correlation to Texas Essential Knowledge and Skills (TEKS)

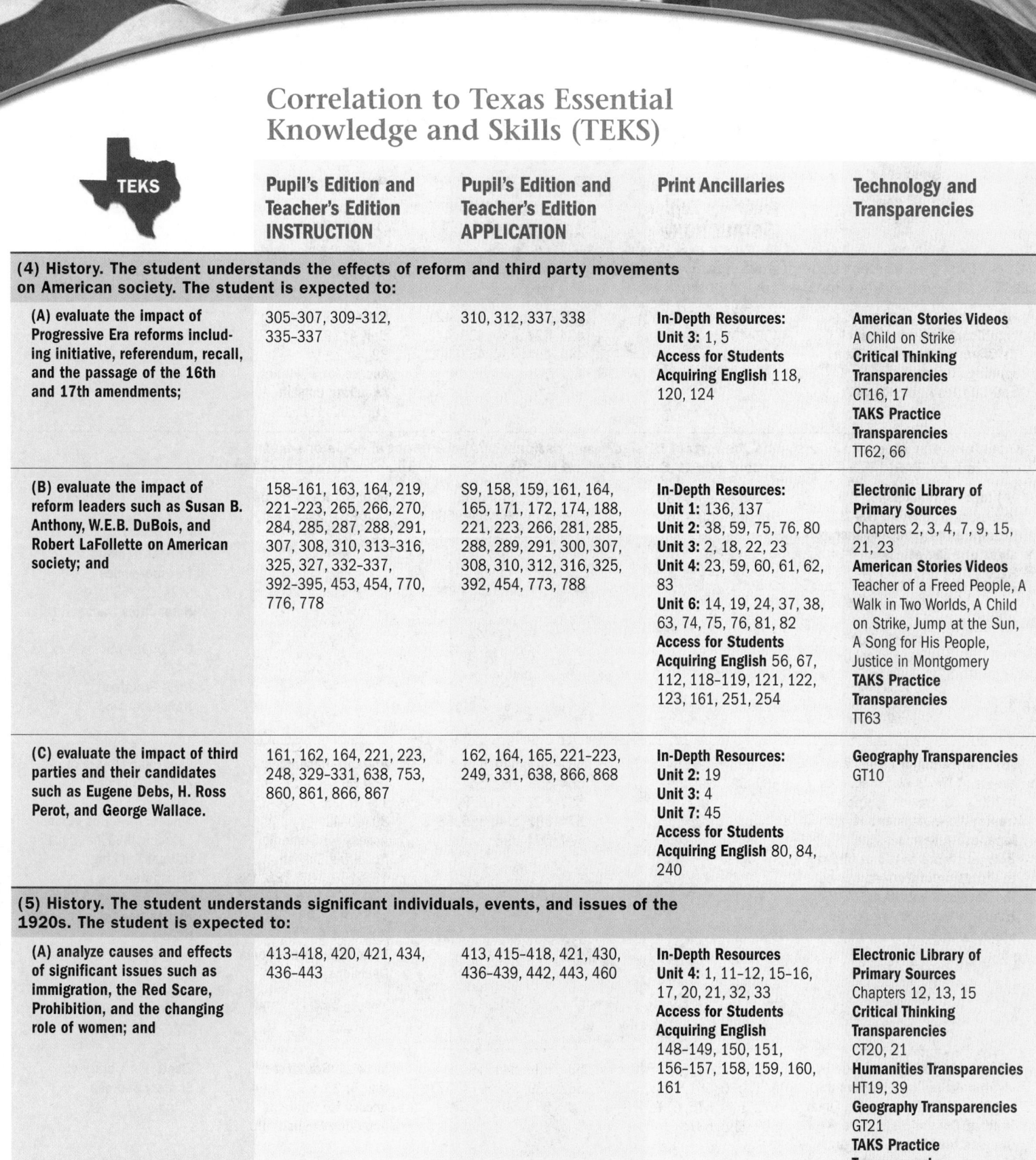

| TEKS | Pupil's Edition and Teacher's Edition INSTRUCTION | Pupil's Edition and Teacher's Edition APPLICATION | Print Ancillaries | Technology and Transparencies |
|---|---|---|---|---|
| **(4) History. The student understands the effects of reform and third party movements on American society. The student is expected to:** | | | | |
| **(A)** evaluate the impact of Progressive Era reforms including initiative, referendum, recall, and the passage of the 16th and 17th amendments; | 305–307, 309–312, 335–337 | 310, 312, 337, 338 | **In-Depth Resources:** **Unit 3:** 1, 5 **Access for Students Acquiring English** 118, 120, 124 | **American Stories Videos** A Child on Strike **Critical Thinking Transparencies** CT16, 17 **TAKS Practice Transparencies** TT62, 66 |
| **(B)** evaluate the impact of reform leaders such as Susan B. Anthony, W.E.B. DuBois, and Robert LaFollette on American society; and | 158–161, 163, 164, 219, 221–223, 265, 266, 270, 284, 285, 287, 288, 291, 307, 308, 310, 313–316, 325, 327, 332–337, 392–395, 453, 454, 770, 776, 778 | S9, 158, 159, 161, 164, 165, 171, 172, 174, 188, 221, 223, 266, 281, 285, 288, 289, 291, 300, 307, 308, 310, 312, 316, 325, 392, 454, 773, 788 | **In-Depth Resources:** **Unit 1:** 136, 137 **Unit 2:** 38, 59, 75, 76, 80 **Unit 3:** 2, 18, 22, 23 **Unit 4:** 23, 59, 60, 61, 62, 83 **Unit 6:** 14, 19, 24, 37, 38, 63, 74, 75, 76, 81, 82 **Access for Students Acquiring English** 56, 67, 112, 118–119, 121, 122, 123, 161, 251, 254 | **Electronic Library of Primary Sources** Chapters 2, 3, 4, 7, 9, 15, 21, 23 **American Stories Videos** Teacher of a Freed People, A Walk in Two Worlds, A Child on Strike, Jump at the Sun, A Song for His People, Justice in Montgomery **TAKS Practice Transparencies** TT63 |
| **(C)** evaluate the impact of third parties and their candidates such as Eugene Debs, H. Ross Perot, and George Wallace. | 161, 162, 164, 221, 223, 248, 329–331, 638, 753, 860, 861, 866, 867 | 162, 164, 165, 221–223, 249, 331, 638, 866, 868 | **In-Depth Resources:** **Unit 2:** 19 **Unit 3:** 4 **Unit 7:** 45 **Access for Students Acquiring English** 80, 84, 240 | **Geography Transparencies** GT10 |
| **(5) History. The student understands significant individuals, events, and issues of the 1920s. The student is expected to:** | | | | |
| **(A)** analyze causes and effects of significant issues such as immigration, the Red Scare, Prohibition, and the changing role of women; and | 413–418, 420, 421, 434, 436–443 | 413, 415–418, 421, 430, 436–439, 442, 443, 460 | **In-Depth Resources** **Unit 4:** 1, 11–12, 15–16, 17, 20, 21, 32, 33 **Access for Students Acquiring English** 148–149, 150, 151, 156–157, 158, 159, 160, 161 | **Electronic Library of Primary Sources** Chapters 12, 13, 15 **Critical Thinking Transparencies** CT20, 21 **Humanities Transparencies** HT19, 39 **Geography Transparencies** GT21 **TAKS Practice Transparencies** TT75, 76, 78, 79 |

# Correlation to Texas Essential Knowledge and Skills (TEKS)

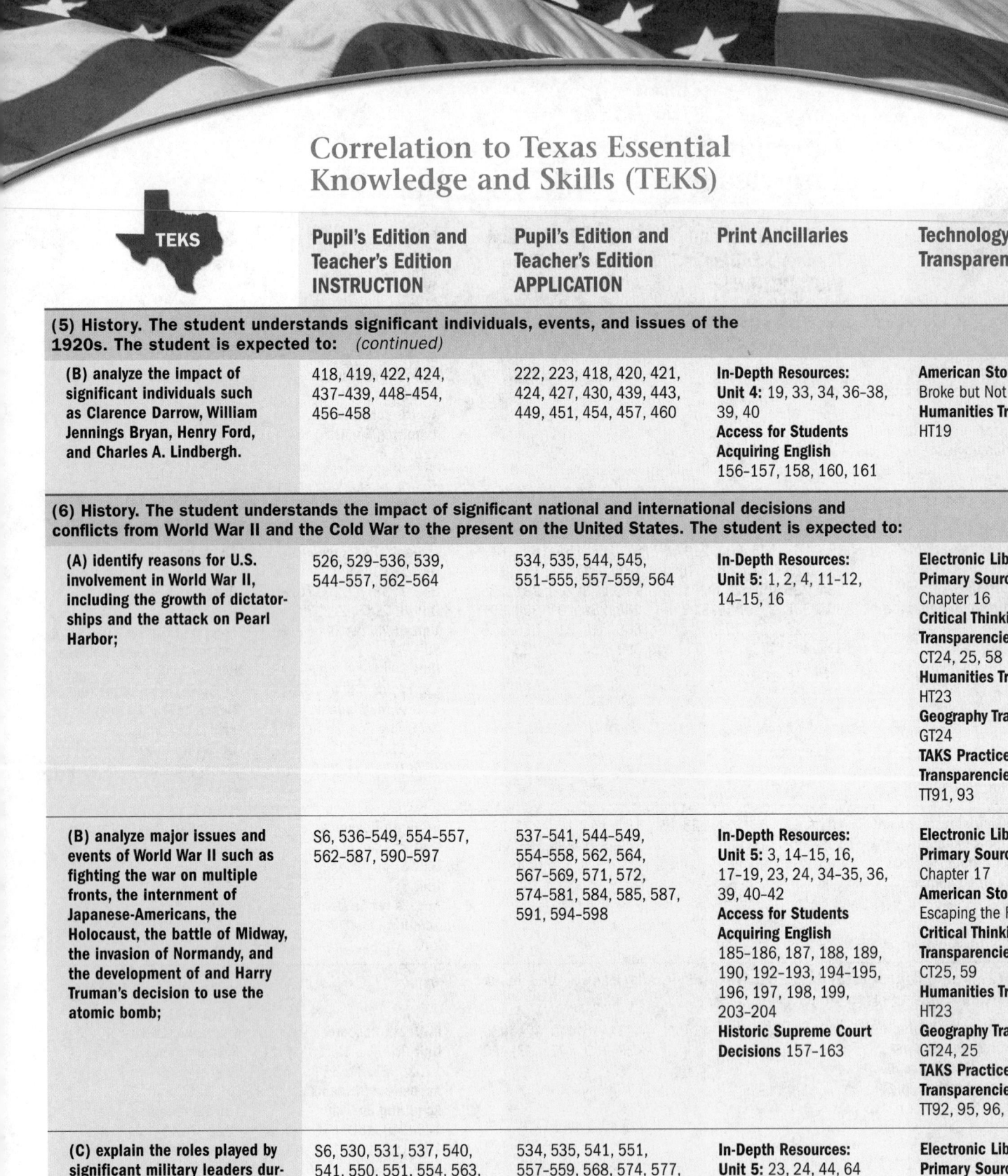

| TEKS | Pupil's Edition and Teacher's Edition INSTRUCTION | Pupil's Edition and Teacher's Edition APPLICATION | Print Ancillaries | Technology and Transparencies |
|---|---|---|---|---|
| **(5) History. The student understands significant individuals, events, and issues of the 1920s. The student is expected to:** *(continued)* | | | | |
| **(B) analyze the impact of significant individuals such as Clarence Darrow, William Jennings Bryan, Henry Ford, and Charles A. Lindbergh.** | 418, 419, 422, 424, 437–439, 448–454, 456–458 | 222, 223, 418, 420, 421, 424, 427, 430, 439, 443, 449, 451, 454, 457, 460 | **In-Depth Resources:** **Unit 4:** 19, 33, 34, 36–38, 39, 40 **Access for Students Acquiring English** 156–157, 158, 160, 161 | **American Stories Videos** Broke but Not Broken **Humanities Transparencies** HT19 |
| **(6) History. The student understands the impact of significant national and international decisions and conflicts from World War II and the Cold War to the present on the United States. The student is expected to:** | | | | |
| **(A) identify reasons for U.S. involvement in World War II, including the growth of dictatorships and the attack on Pearl Harbor;** | 526, 529–536, 539, 544–557, 562–564 | 534, 535, 544, 545, 551–555, 557–559, 564 | **In-Depth Resources:** **Unit 5:** 1, 2, 4, 11–12, 14–15, 16 | **Electronic Library of Primary Sources** Chapter 16 **Critical Thinking Transparencies** CT24, 25, 58 **Humanities Transparencies** HT23 **Geography Transparencies** GT24 **TAKS Practice Transparencies** TT91, 93 |
| **(B) analyze major issues and events of World War II such as fighting the war on multiple fronts, the internment of Japanese-Americans, the Holocaust, the battle of Midway, the invasion of Normandy, and the development of and Harry Truman's decision to use the atomic bomb;** | S6, 536–549, 554–557, 562–587, 590–597 | 537–541, 544–549, 554–558, 562, 564, 567–569, 571, 572, 574–581, 584, 585, 587, 591, 594–598 | **In-Depth Resources:** **Unit 5:** 3, 14–15, 16, 17–19, 23, 24, 34–35, 36, 39, 40–42 **Access for Students Acquiring English** 185–186, 187, 188, 189, 190, 192–193, 194–195, 196, 197, 198, 199, 203–204 **Historic Supreme Court Decisions** 157–163 | **Electronic Library of Primary Sources** Chapter 17 **American Stories Videos** Escaping the Final Solution **Critical Thinking Transparencies** CT25, 59 **Humanities Transparencies** HT23 **Geography Transparencies** GT24, 25 **TAKS Practice Transparencies** TT92, 95, 96, 97 |
| **(C) explain the roles played by significant military leaders during World War II, including Omar Bradley, Dwight Eisenhower, Douglas MacArthur, George Marshall, and George Patton;** | S6, 530, 531, 537, 540, 541, 550, 551, 554, 563, 572, 574, 575, 577, 579, 583, 584, 587 | 534, 535, 541, 551, 557–559, 568, 574, 577, 583, 587, 598 | **In-Depth Resources:** **Unit 5:** 23, 24, 44, 64 **Access for Students Acquiring English** 196, 197 | **Electronic Library of Primary Sources** Chapter 17 |

# Correlation to Texas Essential Knowledge and Skills (TEKS)

**TEKS**

| | Pupil's Edition and Teacher's Edition INSTRUCTION | Pupil's Edition and Teacher's Edition APPLICATION | Print Ancillaries | Technology and Transparencies |
|---|---|---|---|---|
| **(6) History. The student understands the impact of significant national and international decisions and conflicts from World War II and the Cold War to the present on the United States. The student is expected to:** *(continued)* | | | | |
| **(D) describe U.S. responses to Soviet aggression after World War II, including the Truman Doctrine, the Marshall Plan, the North Atlantic Treaty Organization, and the Berlin airlift;** | S28, 405, 602-608, 621-627 | 405, 603-608, 623-625, 627, 630 | **In-Depth Resources:** **Unit 5:** 45, 55-56 **Access for Students Acquiring English** 205-206, 207, 210, 212-213 | **Electronic Library of Primary Sources** Chapter 18 **Critical Thinking Transparencies** CT26 **Humanities Transparencies** HT25 **Geography Transparencies** GT26 **TAKS Practice Transparencies** TT98 |
| **(E) analyze the conflicts in Korea and Vietnam and describe their domestic and international effects;** | S10, 405, 611-615, 621, 639, 688, 730-763, 781 | 405, 611-615, 630, 631, 728, 729, 731-735, 737-741, 743-747, 749, 751-753, 755-761, 763, 764 | **In-Depth Resources:** **Unit 5:** 46, 58-59, 60 **Unit 6:** 39, 40, 41, 42, 43, 45, 51-52, 53-54, 55, 56, 57, 58, 59-61, 62, 63 **Access for Students Acquiring English** 239-240, 241, 242, 243, 244, 245, 247-248, 249-250 | **Electronic Library of Primary Sources** Chapter 22 **American Stories Videos** Matters of Conscience **Critical Thinking Transparencies** CT30, 62, 64 **Humanities Transparencies** HT28, 45 **Geography Transparencies** GT30 **TAKS Practice Transparencies** TT99 |
| **(F) describe the impact of the GI Bill, the election of 1948, McCarthyism, and Sputnik I;** | S28, 589, 592, 616-621, 626, 627, 635, 638, 639 | 589, 595, 617-621, 626, 627, 630, 631, 634, 635, 637, 638, 640, 664 | **In-Depth Resources:** **Unit 5:** 47 **Access for Students Acquiring English** 206 | **Electronic Library of Primary Sources** Chapter 20 **American Stories Videos** The Cold War Comes Home **Critical Thinking Transparencies** CT26, 60 **Humanities Transparencies** HT41 **TAKS Practice Transparencies** TT100, 101, 102 |

# Correlation to Texas Essential Knowledge and Skills (TEKS)

| TEKS | Pupil's Edition and Teacher's Edition INSTRUCTION | Pupil's Edition and Teacher's Edition APPLICATION | Print Ancillaries | Technology and Transparencies |
|---|---|---|---|---|
| **(6) History. The student understands the impact of significant national and international decisions and conflicts from World War II and the Cold War to the present on the United States. The student is expected to:** *(continued)* | | | | |
| **(G)** analyze reasons for the Western victory in the Cold War and the challenges of changing relationships among nations; and | 405, 676-678, 848-855, 863, 864, 872, 873 | 405, 677, 678, 849, 850-857, 863, 864, 873 | **In-Depth Resources:** **Unit 7:** 25 | **Geography Transparencies** GT33 |
| **(H)** identify the origins of major domestic and foreign policy issues currently facing the United States. | 374, 405, 438, 439, 499-501, 515-519, 615, 623, 625, 640, 660-663, 673, 674, 676-678, 680, 684, 685, 689-695, 717-719, 722, 723, 761, 768-772, 774, 777-780, 785, 798-801, 803, 806, 807, 811, 813, 815-825, 830, 831, 833-836, 839-845, 848-855, 861-865, 868-873, 876, 878, 883-886, US2-US15 | 405, 439, 499, 518, 519, 522, 623, 660-662, 664, 674, 678, 681, 682, 685, 690, 692, 693, 695, 696, 717, 722, 723, 726, 761, 764, 770-773, 776-779, 785, 788, 797-800, 803, 807, 811, 816, 817, 819, 821-826, 831, 835, 836, 838, 840-845, 849-857, 861-864, 866-868, 871-873, 883, 886, 890, 891 | **In-Depth Resources:** **Unit 5:** 69, 76-77 **Unit 6:** 14, 19, 20, 21, 22, 28-29, 30, 31, 32, 33, 34-36, 37, 38, 43, 66, 72-73, 74, 75, 76, 81, 82 **Unit 7:** 1, 3, 4, 11-12, 16, 22, 24, 25, 32-33, 34-35, 38, 45, 46, 47, 48, 49, 53, 55-56, 58, 59, 60, 61, 62, 63, 64, 65 **Access for Students Acquiring English** 227, 231-232, 233, 234, 235, 251-252, 253, 254, 255, 257-258, 260, 264, 268-269, 271, 272, 273, 274, 275-276, 279-280, 282, 283, 284, 286-287, 289, 290, 291, 292, 293, 294, 295 | **Electronic Library of Primary Sources** Chapters 19, 20, 21, 23, 24, 25, 26 **American Stories Videos** Escaping the Final Solution, Justice in Montgomery **Critical Thinking Transparencies** CT34, 62, 66 **Humanities Transparencies** HT48 **Geography Transparencies** GT32 |
| **(7) History. The student understands the impact of the American civil rights movement. The student is expected to:** | | | | |
| **(A)** trace the historical development of the civil rights movement in the 18th, 19th, and 20th centuries, including the 13th, 14th, 15th amendments; | S24, S26, 33, 36, 39, 46, 47, 64, 65, 69-71, 82, 85, 86, 97, 98-100, 104, 105, 145-149, 158-165, 183, 185, 186, 221, 286-291, 324, 325, 335, 337, 391-395, 413, 429, 453, 454, 566, 592, 593, 637, 638, 640, 662, 663, 671, 682, 690-695, 698-725, 768-780, 818, 819, 842-845 | 33, 36, 39, 42, 47, 65, 69-71, 99, 100, 105, 146-149, 152, 158, 159, 165, 185, 186, 189, 190, 221, 287-291, 300, 301, 324, 336, 337, 391, 392, 394, 395, 406, 413, 429, 454, 592, 593, 595, 637, 638, 640, 662, 663, 682, 691, 693, 695, 696, 701-707, 709, 711-716, 719-723, 725-727, 768-773, 777, 778, 780, 788, 789, 818, 819, 842-845, 856 | **In-Depth Resources:** **Unit 1:** 34, 49, 72, 81, 100, 137, 138 **Unit 2:** 63, 75, 76 **Unit 3:** 3, 5, 62 **Unit 4:** 18 **Unit 5:** 25, 40-42, 69 **Unit 6:** 20, 21, 22, 28-29, 30, 31, 32, 33, 34-36, 37, 38 **Unit 7:** 38 **Access for Students Acquiring English** 38, 110, 112, 113, 157, 161, 215, 219, 227, 231-232, 233, 234, 235, 237-238, 251-252, 253, 254, 255, 257-258 | **Electronic Library of Primary Sources** Chapters 1-4, 18-21, 23 **American Stories Videos** Teacher of a Freed People, A Walk in Two Worlds, Jump at the Sun, A Song for His People, Justice in Montgomery **Critical Thinking Transparencies** CT4, 11, 12, 29 **Humanities Transparencies** HT10, 11, 12, 27 **Geography Transparencies** GT29 **TAKS Practice Transparencies** TT111 |

# Correlation to Texas Essential Knowledge and Skills (TEKS)

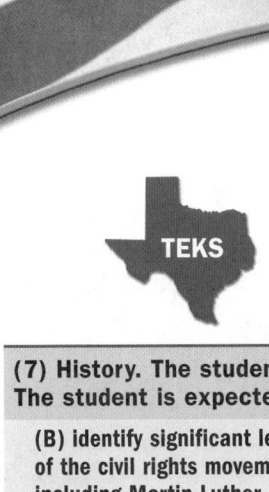

| TEKS | Pupil's Edition and Teacher's Edition INSTRUCTION | Pupil's Edition and Teacher's Edition APPLICATION | Print Ancillaries | Technology and Transparencies |
|---|---|---|---|---|
| **(7) History. The student understands the impact of the American civil rights movement. The student is expected to:** *(continued)* | | | | |
| **(B) identify significant leaders of the civil rights movement, including Martin Luther King, Jr.;** | S24, 85, 145–146, 148–149, 172, 173, 177, 324, 325, 335–337, 392, 393, 453, 454, 566, 593, 671, 702, 704–706, 712, 714, 716, 718–722, 750, 770, 776, 843–845 | 149, 173, 325, 454, 701, 705–707, 719–721, 723, 726, 727, 770, 771, 773, 780, 788, 845 | **In-Depth Resources:** **Unit 1:** 34, 72, 81, 100, 104, 136, 137 **Unit 2:** 75, 76, 80 **Unit 3:** 62 **Unit 4:** 18, 23 **Unit 6:** 37, 38 **Access for Students Acquiring English** 52, 56, 112, 231–232, 234, 251–252 | **Electronic Library of Primary Sources** Chapters 3, 4, 21, 23 **American Stories Videos** Teacher of a Freed People, A Walk in Two Worlds, Jump at the Sun, A Song for His People, Justice in Montgomery **Humanities Transparencies** HT10, 11, 12 **TAKS Practice Transparencies** TT110 |
| **(C) evaluate government efforts, including the Civil Rights Act of 1964, to achieve equality in the United States; and** | S24, S26, 64, 65, 70, 71, 104, 105, 172, 183, 185, 186, 506, 637, 638, 691, 711, 714–716, 722, 723, 772, 773, 774–775, 779, 844 | 64, 65, 71, 105, 172, 173, 183, 185, 186, 189, 190, 506, 638, 640, 691, 714, 716, 722, 723, 726, 775, 779, 788, 845 | **In-Depth Resources:** **Unit 1:** 62, 106, 107, 121, 138 **Unit 6:** 21 **Access for Students Acquiring English** 231–232, 234 | **Electronic Library of Primary Sources** Chapters 4, 19, 20 **American Stories Videos** Teacher of a Freed People **Critical Thinking Transparencies** CT12, 29, 45 **Humanities Transparencies** HT11, 12 |
| **(D) identify changes in the United States that have resulted from the civil rights movement such as increased participation of minorities in the political process.** | 64, 65, 70, 71, 104, 105, 188, 505–507, 692, 714–716, 720, 722–725, 768–773, 843–845, 885–887 | 65, 71, 99, 105, 188, 505, 507, 509, 692, 716, 722, 723, 725–727, 770–773, 788, 789, 845 | **In-Depth Resources:** **Unit 1:** 72, 109, 133–135, 138 **Unit 6:** 28–29, 34–36, 64 | **Critical Thinking Transparencies** CT29 **Humanities Transparencies** HT12 **Geography Transparencies** GT29 |

# Correlation to Texas Essential Knowledge and Skills (TEKS)

| TEKS | Pupil's Edition and Teacher's Edition INSTRUCTION | Pupil's Edition and Teacher's Edition APPLICATION | Print Ancillaries | Technology and Transparencies |
|---|---|---|---|---|
| **(8) Geography. The student uses geographic tools to collect, analyze, and interpret data. The student is expected to:** | | | | |
| **(A) create thematic maps, graphs, charts, models, and databases representing various aspects of the United States; and** | 416, 423, 520, 521, R25–R26, R27, R28, R30, R31, R32, R33 | 13, 20, 30, 42, 53, 63, 71, 73, 79, 80, 91, 96, 100, 115, 117, 122, 127, 133, 135, 138, 149, 151, 152, 161, 162, 164, 165, 170–174, 181–183, 189, 190, 210, 215, 218, 225, 226, 232, 233, 235, 240, 242, 244, 245, 248, 249, 255, 263, 266, 272, 281, 345, 351, 358, 365, 380, 387, 395, 397, 403, 406, 407, 416–418, 421, 424, 427, 435, 439, 443, 453, 454, 457, 460, 471, 477, 483, 484, 491, 494, 501, 509, 514, 519, 521, 522, 529–531, 535, 539, 541, 555–559, 565, 567, 568, 577, 587, 595, 598, 608, 611, 613, 615, 621, 623, 627, 636, 540, 649, 651, 657, 663, 664, 678, 683, 685, 693, 696, 707, 715, 721, 726, 733, 735, 738, 741, 743, 747, 751, 759, 761, 764, 769, 770, 773, 780, 784, 785, 788, 801, 804, 809, 813, 817, 824–826, 832, 833, 835, 838, 847, 849, 851, 852, 855, 856, 865, 868, 872, 873, 881, 887, 890, R30, R31, R32, R33 | **In-Depth Resources:**<br>**Unit 1:** 9, 10, 11, 12, 19, 35, 36, 37, 38, 40, 41, 42, 52, 77, 78, 79, 80, 86, 92, 106, 107, 108, 109, 138<br>**Unit 2:** 1, 2, 3, 12, 20, 21, 22, 39, 40, 41, 61, 62, 63, 64, 71<br>**Unit 3:** 1, 2, 3, 4, 5, 7, 24, 25, 26, 27, 29, 37, 47, 48, 49, 50, 51<br>**Unit 4:** 1, 2, 3, 20, 21, 22, 23, 24, 41, 42, 43, 44, 60, 61, 62, 63, 64, 66<br>**Unit 5:** 1, 2, 3, 22, 23, 24, 25, 27, 35–36, 42, 45, 46, 47, 48, 49, 50, 66, 67, 68, 69, 71, 80<br>**Unit 6:** 1, 2, 3, 17, 20, 21, 22, 39, 40, 41, 42, 43, 54, 64, 65, 66, 68, 75<br>**Unit 7:** 1, 3, 4, 22, 23, 24, 25, 38, 39, 45, 46, 47, 48, 58, 59, 60, 61, 62, 63, 64, 65, 67, 68<br>**Access for Students Acquiring English** 81–86, 91–95, 100–104, 111–115, 120–125, 130–134, 137, 138, 141–145, 150–152, 158–162, 167–170, 175–180, 184, 187–190, 196–200, 207–211, 216–219, 225–227, 233–235, 241–245, 250, 253–256, 261–265, 270–274, 278, 281–285, 288–295, 297, 298 | **American Stories Videos** Teacher of a Freed People, From China to Chinatown, Jump at the Sun, Broke but Not Broken, A Song for His People, Escaping the Final Solution, The Cold War Comes Home, Justice in Montgomery, Matters of Conscience, Poisoned Playground |

# Correlation to Texas Essential Knowledge and Skills (TEKS)

| TEKS | Pupil's Edition and Teacher's Edition INSTRUCTION | Pupil's Edition and Teacher's Edition APPLICATION | Print Ancillaries | Technology and Transparencies |
|---|---|---|---|---|
| **(8) Geography. The student uses geographic tools to collect, analyze, and interpret data. The student is expected to:** *(continued)* | | | | |
| **(B)** pose and answer questions about geographic distributions and patterns shown on maps, graphs, charts, models, and databases. | S16, S18, S20, S22, 69, 72, 73, 151, 159, 160, 169–171, 176, 179, 205, 209, 226, 231, 235, 239, 255, 263, 323, 344, 345, 349, 357, 375, 386, 400, 416, 423, 474, 520, 521, 651, 685, 701, 816, 827, 846, 847, 866, 885 | S15, S17, S19, S21, S23, 7, 15, 17, 25, 29, 32, 38, 41, 42, 59, 62, 69, 73, 115, 116, 125, 132, 134, 136, 147, 151, 159, 160, 167, 169, 170, 171, 176, 179, 190, 205, 209, 226, 231, 235, 239, 255, 263, 323, 344, 345, 349, 357, 375, 376, 383, 386, 400, 416, 423, 430, 474, 484, 521, 530, 532, 538, 545, 556, 572, 575, 580, 591, 594, 604–606, 613, 624, 651, 675, 681, 685, 701, 733, 749, 775, 816, 827, 844, 847, 866, 885, 890 | **In-Depth Resources:**<br>**Unit 1:** 1, 2, 3, 4, 5, 6, 7, 8, 26, 27, 29, 48, 64, 92, 93, 94–95, 119, 120<br>**Unit 2:** 11, 29, 49, 72<br>**Unit 3:** 14, 35, 36, 58<br>**Unit 4:** 31, 50, 73, 74<br>**Unit 5:** 12, 33<br>**Unit 6:** 10, 29, 51, 73<br>**Unit 7:** 33, 34, 56<br>**Access for Students Acquiring English** 19, 21, 22, 34, 41, 62, 63, 75, 76, 85, 88, 97, 127, 136, 137, 147, 155, 164, 172, 182, 193, 201, 203, 213, 229, 238, 248, 249, 258, 276, 277, 287 | **TAKS Practice Transparencies**<br>TT9, 12, 13, 14, 17, 18, 23, 39, 103, 131 |
| **(9) Geography. The student understands the impact of geographic factors on major events. The student is expected to:** | | | | |
| **(A)** analyze the effects of physical and human geographic factors on major events including the building of the Panama Canal; and | S8, 38, 59, 62, 136, 170, 171, 176, 179, 203, 204, 208–218, 236–240, 359–363, 366, 367, 375, 386, 416, 422–424, 449, 453, 474, 520, 521, 528–533, 538–541, 556, 572, 575, 580, 605, 613, 673–678, 733, 738–740, 749 | 38, 59, 62, 80, 136, 170, 176, 179, 190, 203, 208, 209, 211, 212, 216, 218, 226, 236–240, 359–361, 366–368, 375, 386, 416, 423, 449, 474, 477, 484, 521, 530, 532, 538, 556, 558, 572, 575, 580, 598, 605, 613, 675, 677, 678, 696, 733, 738–740, 749 | **In-Depth Resources:**<br>**Unit 1:** 7, 21, 47–48, 69–70, 118–119, 138<br>**Unit 2:** 2, 3, 50–51<br>**Unit 3:** 26, 27, 34–35, 36–37, 41<br>**Unit 4:** 49–50, 53<br>**Unit 5:** 11–12, 32–33<br>**Access for Students Acquiring English** 79–80, 82, 83, 87–88, 89, 92, 99, 128–129, 135–136, 192–193, 194–195, 197, 198, 247 | **Electronic Library of Primary Sources**<br>Chapters 20, 22<br>**American Stories Videos**<br>Gusher!, Broke but Not Broken, Matters of Conscience<br>**Critical Thinking Transparencies**<br>CT9, 11, 13<br>**Humanities Transparencies**<br>HT14<br>**Geography Transparencies**<br>GT18<br>**TAKS Practice Transparencies**<br>TT70 |

# Correlation to Texas Essential Knowledge and Skills (TEKS)

| TEKS | Pupil's Edition and Teacher's Edition INSTRUCTION | Pupil's Edition and Teacher's Edition APPLICATION | Print Ancillaries | Technology and Transparencies |
|---|---|---|---|---|
| **(9) Geography. The student understands the impact of geographic factors on major events. The student is expected to:** *(continued)* | | | | |
| **(B) identify and explain reasons for changes in political boundaries such as those resulting from statehood and international conflicts.** | S20, 37–39, 62, 67, 116, 117, 134–137, 157–158, 160, 344–351, 353–358, 400, 529–533, 605, 613, 625, 688, 815, 863, 864 | 38, 39, 42, 116, 117, 134, 135, 138, 152, 157, 160, 165, 344, 345, 347, 349, 350, 354, 356, 358, 400, 530, 605, 613, 615, 624, 630, 815, 863, 864 | **In-Depth Resources:** **Unit 1:** 1, 2, 3, 4, 5, 6, 7, 8, 26, 27, 29, 48, 64, 92, 93, 94–95, 119, 120 **Unit 3:** 26, 36, 40, 42–44, 57–58 **Access for Students Acquiring English** 19, 21, 22, 34, 41, 62, 63, 75, 76, 128–129, 130, 131, 132, 133, 134, 208 | **Critical Thinking Transparencies** CT18, 19 **Geography Transparencies** GT18 |
| **(10) Geography. The student understands the effects of migration and immigration on American society. The student is expected to:** | | | | |
| **(A) analyze the effects of changing demographic patterns resulting from migration within the United States; and** | 72, 73, 77, 122–126, 130–133, 137, 138, 160, 203, 204, 212–216, 238, 257, 262–265, 276–278, 288, 313, 314, 392–395, 422–424, 428, 434–437, 452–457, 474, 475, 590–592, 660, 661, 684, 685, 701, 702, 768, 769, 846, 847, 882–884, 888, 889 | S15, 73, 77, 125, 127, 131, 132, 137, 138, 152, 159, 160, 203, 211–217, 226, 238, 262–264, 266, 272, 278, 392–395, 423, 429, 435, 453, 460, 474, 484, 591, 685, 701, 702, 769, 775, 844, 847, 883, 887, 889 | **In-Depth Resources:** **Unit 1:** 79, 94–95, 101–102, 118–119, 138 **Unit 2:** 1, 2, 3, 28, 40, 48–49, 50–51, 53, 55 **Unit 4:** 49–50 **Unit 5:** 67, 69, 78, 79, 81, 82–83 **Unit 7:** 32–33, 48 **Access for Students Acquiring English** 63–64, 79–80, 81, 82, 83, 98–99, 101, 284 | **Electronic Library of Primary Sources** Chapter 17 **American Stories Videos** A Walk in Two Worlds, Jump at the Sun, Broke but Not Broken **Critical Thinking Transparencies** CT9, 12, 13, 15, 37, 47, 49, 55, 61 **Humanities Transparencies** HT15, 16, 42 **Geography Transparencies** GT7, 8, 9, 31, 38 **TAKS Practice Transparencies** TT27, 47, 81 |
| **(B) analyze the effects of changing demographic patterns resulting from immigration to the United States.** | 34, 78, 137, 138, 254–259, 261, 277, 284, 289, 344, 345, 392–395, 414–417, 428, 446–448, 506, 507, 543, 544, 660, 661, 768, 769, 885–889 | 42, 137, 138, 252, 254–256, 259–261, 272, 284, 344, 393, 414, 416, 429, 447, 474, 484, 507, 543, 544, 661, 663, 664, 769, 885–887, 889–891 | **In-Depth Resources:** **Unit 2:** 39, 40 **Unit 7:** 48, 49, 50–51, 59 **Access for Students Acquiring English** 98, 100, 275–276, 289 | **Electronic Library of Primary Sources** Chapter 17 **American Stories Videos** From China to Chinatown, A Child on Strike, A Song for His People **Critical Thinking Transparencies** CT47, 69, 70, 71 **Geography Transparencies** GT15, 31 **TAKS Practice Transparencies** TT55 |

# Correlation to Texas Essential Knowledge and Skills (TEKS)

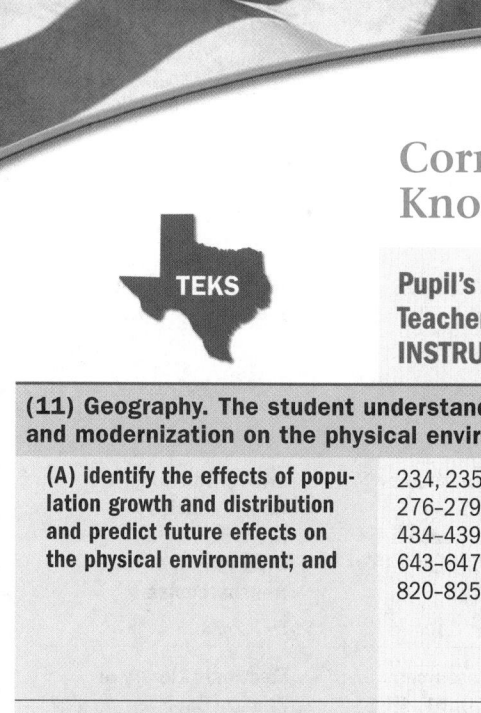

| TEKS | Pupil's Edition and Teacher's Edition INSTRUCTION | Pupil's Edition and Teacher's Edition APPLICATION | Print Ancillaries | Technology and Transparencies |
|---|---|---|---|---|
| **(11) Geography. The student understands the relationship between population growth and modernization on the physical environment. The student is expected to:** | | | | |
| (A) identify the effects of population growth and distribution and predict future effects on the physical environment; and | 234, 235, 264–266, 276–279, 322–324, 434–439, 452–454, 643–647, 650, 651, 820–825, 881, 883 | S15, S19, 208, 234, 235, 252, 253, 262, 264–266, 272, 279, 323, 324, 452, 453, 643, 646, 649, 651, 664, 820, 822, 825, 881, 883 | **In-Depth Resources:** **Unit 2:** 20, 40 **Unit 4:** 30–31 **Access for Students Acquiring English** 214–215, 217, 260, 264 | **American Stories Videos** Broke but Not Broken **Critical Thinking Transparencies** CT13, 47 **TAKS Practice Transparencies** TT1, 50 |
| (B) trace the development of the conservation of natural resources, including the establishment of the National Park System and efforts of private nonprofit organizations. | 278, 322–324, 328, 329, 475, 491, 492, 519–521, 690, 691, 825 | 323, 324, 329, 491, 519, 521, 522, 691, 820–822, 825–827 | **In-Depth Resources:** **Unit 2:** 71–72 **Unit 3:** 3 **Unit 6:** 14, 19 **Unit 7:** 4 **Access for Students Acquiring English** 260, 264 | **Electronic Library of Primary Sources** Chapter 24 **American Stories Videos** Poisoned Playground **Humanities Transparencies** HT13 |
| **(12) Economics. The student understands domestic and foreign issues related to U.S. economic growth from the 1870s to 1920. The student is expected to:** | | | | |
| (A) analyze the relationship between private property rights and the settlement of the Great Plains; | 214–216, 428 | 214, 215, 226, 429 | **In-Depth Resources:** **Unit 2:** 3 **Access for Students Acquiring English** 80, 83 | **Critical Thinking Transparencies** CT12, 47 |
| (B) compare the purpose of the Interstate Commerce Commission with its performance over time; | 239–240, 320, 711 | 240, 250, 320 | **In-Depth Resources:** **Unit 2:** 21 **Unit 3:** 3 **Access for Students Acquiring English** 89, 92 | **Critical Thinking Transparencies** CT13, 14, 17 |
| (C) describe the impact of the Sherman Antitrust Act on businesses; | 244, 249, 319, 320 | 249, 319 | **In-Depth Resources:** **Unit 2:** 22 **Unit 3:** 3 **Access for Students Acquiring English** 90, 93 | **American Stories Videos** Gusher! **Critical Thinking Transparencies** CT13, 14, 17 **Humanities Transparencies** HT35 |
| (D) analyze the effects of economic policies including the Open Door Policy and Dollar Diplomacy on U.S. diplomacy; and | 356–358, 362–363 | 358, 363, 368 | **In-Depth Resources:** **Unit 3:** 26 | **Critical Thinking Transparencies** CT18, 52 |
| (E) describe the economic effects of international military conflicts, including the Spanish-American War and World War I, on the United States. | 350, 351, 354, 355, 377, 388–395, 403 | 377, 390, 394, 395, 403, 406 | **In-Depth Resources:** **Unit 3:** 48 **Access for Students Acquiring English** 128, 131, 139–140, 143 | **Critical Thinking Transparencies** CT18, 53 |

# Correlation to Texas Essential Knowledge and Skills (TEKS)

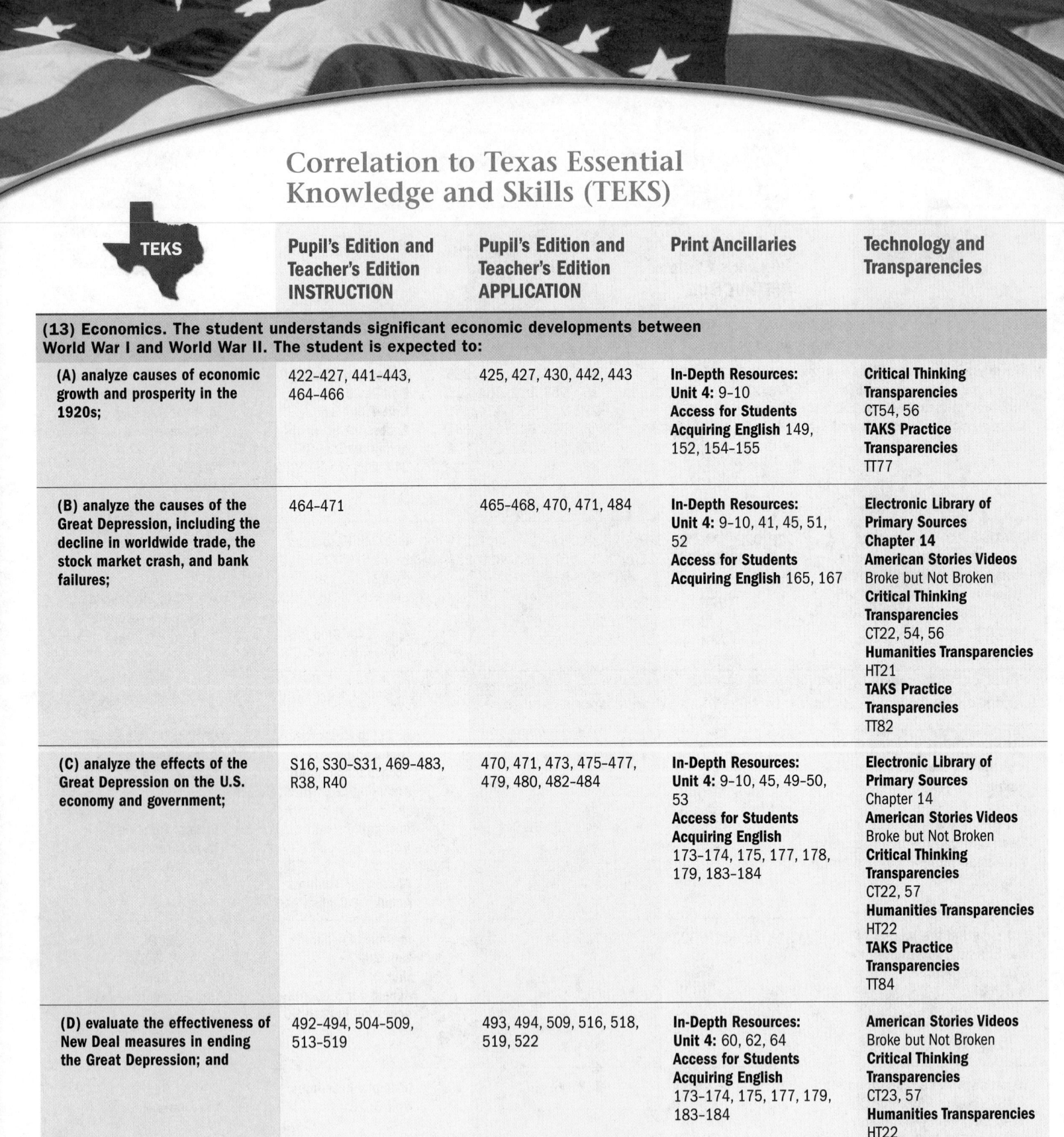

| TEKS | Pupil's Edition and Teacher's Edition INSTRUCTION | Pupil's Edition and Teacher's Edition APPLICATION | Print Ancillaries | Technology and Transparencies |
|---|---|---|---|---|
| **(13) Economics. The student understands significant economic developments between World War I and World War II. The student is expected to:** | | | | |
| **(A)** analyze causes of economic growth and prosperity in the 1920s; | 422–427, 441–443, 464–466 | 425, 427, 430, 442, 443 | **In-Depth Resources: Unit 4:** 9–10 **Access for Students Acquiring English** 149, 152, 154–155 | **Critical Thinking Transparencies** CT54, 56 **TAKS Practice Transparencies** TT77 |
| **(B)** analyze the causes of the Great Depression, including the decline in worldwide trade, the stock market crash, and bank failures; | 464–471 | 465–468, 470, 471, 484 | **In-Depth Resources: Unit 4:** 9–10, 41, 45, 51, 52 **Access for Students Acquiring English** 165, 167 | **Electronic Library of Primary Sources** Chapter 14 **American Stories Videos** Broke but Not Broken **Critical Thinking Transparencies** CT22, 54, 56 **Humanities Transparencies** HT21 **TAKS Practice Transparencies** TT82 |
| **(C)** analyze the effects of the Great Depression on the U.S. economy and government; | S16, S30–S31, 469–483, R38, R40 | 470, 471, 473, 475–477, 479, 480, 482–484 | **In-Depth Resources: Unit 4:** 9–10, 45, 49–50, 53 **Access for Students Acquiring English** 173–174, 175, 177, 178, 179, 183–184 | **Electronic Library of Primary Sources** Chapter 14 **American Stories Videos** Broke but Not Broken **Critical Thinking Transparencies** CT22, 57 **Humanities Transparencies** HT22 **TAKS Practice Transparencies** TT84 |
| **(D)** evaluate the effectiveness of New Deal measures in ending the Great Depression; and | 492–494, 504–509, 513–519 | 493, 494, 509, 516, 518, 519, 522 | **In-Depth Resources: Unit 4:** 60, 62, 64 **Access for Students Acquiring English** 173–174, 175, 177, 179, 183–184 | **American Stories Videos** Broke but Not Broken **Critical Thinking Transparencies** CT23, 57 **Humanities Transparencies** HT22 **Geography Transparencies** GT23 |

# Correlation to Texas Essential Knowledge and Skills (TEKS)

**TEKS**

| | Pupil's Edition and Teacher's Edition INSTRUCTION | Pupil's Edition and Teacher's Edition APPLICATION | Print Ancillaries | Technology and Transparencies |
|---|---|---|---|---|
| **(13) Economics. The student understands significant economic developments between World War I and World War II. The student is expected to:** *(continued)* | | | | |
| **(E)** analyze how various New Deal agencies and programs such as the Federal Deposit Insurance Corporation, the Securities and Exchange Commission, and Social Security continue to affect the lives of U.S. citizens. | 488–490, 496, 497, 499–501, 504–506, 513–519, 884–885, R42–R43, R45 | S32–S33, 490, 491, 500, 501, 509, 516, 518, 519, 522, 884 | **In-Depth Resources: Unit 4:** 60, 62, 64 **Access for Students Acquiring English** 175, 177, 179 | **American Stories Videos** Broke but Not Broken **Critical Thinking Transparencies** CT23 **Geography Transparencies** GT23 **TAKS Practice Transparencies** TT89 |
| **(14) Economics. The student understands the economic effects of World War II, the Cold War, and increased worldwide competition on contemporary society. The student is expected to:** | | | | |
| **(A)** describe the economic effects of World War II on the home front, including rationing, female employment, and the end of the Great Depression; | 550, 554–557, 564–568, 590–592, 910, 911 | 557, 562, 564, 565, 568, 590, 592, 595, 598 | **In-Depth Resources: Unit 5:** 22, 25, 37 **Access for Students Acquiring English** 194–195, 196, 199, 288 | **Electronic Library of Primary Sources** Chapter 17 **Critical Thinking Transparencies** CT24, 27 |
| **(B)** identify the causes and effects of prosperity in the 1950s; | 551, 634–663, R44 | 551, 632, 634, 636, 640–643, 646, 648, 649, 651–654, 657–661, 663, 664 | **In-Depth Resources: Unit 5:** 67 **Access for Students Acquiring English** 214–215, 217, 218, 221–222 | **Critical Thinking Transparencies** CT27, 61 **Geography Transparencies** GT27 |
| **(C)** describe the impact of the Cold War on the business cycle and defense spending; | 626, 673, 834–836, R38 | 626, 835, 836, 857 | **In-Depth Resources: Unit 7:** 23 **Access for Students Acquiring English** 205–206, 268–269 | **Critical Thinking Transparencies** CT26, 33, 62 |
| **(D)** identify actions of government and the private sector to expand economic opportunities to all citizens; and | 429, 680, 682, 688, 689–690, 723, 771–773, 795, 796, 862, 869–871, R41 | 681, 683, 688, 693, 773, 795, 796, 862, 871 | **In-Depth Resources: Unit 6:** 20 **Access for Students Acquiring English** 279–280, 292 | **Electronic Library of Primary Sources** Chapter 25 **Critical Thinking Transparencies** CT67 |
| **(E)** describe the dynamic relationship between U.S. international trade policies and the U.S. free enterprise system. | 799, 872, 873, R46, R47 | 872, 873, 890 | **In-Depth Resources: Unit 7:** 55, 56 **Access for Students Acquiring English** 279–280, 282, 286–287, 296–298 | **Critical Thinking Transparencies** CT40 **TAKS Practice Transparencies** TT122 |

# Correlation to Texas Essential Knowledge and Skills (TEKS)

| TEKS | Pupil's Edition and Teacher's Edition INSTRUCTION | Pupil's Edition and Teacher's Edition APPLICATION | Print Ancillaries | Technology and Transparencies |
|---|---|---|---|---|
| **(15) Government. The student understands changes in the role of government over time. The student is expected to:** | | | | |
| **(A) evaluate the impact of New Deal legislation on the historical roles of state and federal governments;** | S30–S31, 492–499, 501–503, 507–509, 512–513, 515–519 | 493, 494, 499, 501, 503, 509, 513, 516, 519, 522 | **In-Depth Resources:** **Unit 4:** 60, 64 **Access for Students Acquiring English** 174, 175, 176, 179 | **Electronic Library of Primary Sources** Chapter 15 **American Stories Video** Broke But Not Broken **Critical Thinking Transparencies** CT23 **Geography Transparencies** GT23 **Humanities Transparencies** HT21, 22 |
| **(B) explain the impact of significant international events such as World War I and World War II on changes in the role of the federal government;** | 118, 119, 381, 382, 388, 389, 390–392, 400–402, 551, 567, 568, 623, 624 | 382, 395, 406, 551, 567, 568, 598, 624 | **In-Depth Resources:** **Unit 3:** 48, 49 **Access for Students Acquiring English** 194, 196 | **Electronic Library of Primary Sources** Chapter 17 **Critical Thinking Transparencies** CT19 |
| **(C) evaluate the effects of political incidents such as Teapot Dome and Watergate on the views of U.S. citizens concerning the role of the federal government; and** | 189, 420, 421, 620, 621, 627, 757, 772, 806, 807, 864–867, US2–US15 | 189, 420, 421, 430, 621, 630, 631, 761, 806, 807, 826, 827, 866, 868 | **In-Depth Resources:** **Unit 4:** 2 **Unit 5:** 58–59, 60 **Unit 7:** 2, 14 **Access for Students Acquiring English** 148–149, 151, 259–260, 262 | **Electronic Library of Primary Sources** Chapter 12 **Critical Thinking Transparencies** CT32 **Humanities Transparencies** HT46 |
| **(D) predict the effects of selected contemporary legislation on the roles of state and federal governments.** | 794–796, 861, 862, 868, 885, US2–US15 | 795, 796, 819, 861, 868 | **Access for Students Acquiring English** 279–280, 282 | **Critical Thinking Transparencies** CT23, 39 |
| **(16) Government. The student understands the changing relationships among the three branches of the federal government. The student is expected to:** | | | | |
| **(A) evaluate the impact of events, including the Gulf of Tonkin Resolution and the War Powers Act, on the relationship between the legislative and executive branches of government; and** | 75, 185, 186, 189, 310–312, 534, 535, 550–554, 616–621, 734, 735, 737, 761, 797, 802–807, 865, US2–US15 | 75, 189, 312, 535, 551, 552, 554, 557, 558, 621, 735, 764, 797, 803, 806, 807, 868, 890 | **In-Depth Resources:** **Unit 6:** 39 | **Electronic Library of Primary Sources** Chapter 22 |
| **(B) evaluate the impact of events, including Franklin Roosevelt's attempt to increase the number of U.S. Supreme Court justices, on the relationships among the legislative, executive, and judicial branches of government.** | 74, 75, 118, 119, 185, 186, 312, 332–334, 492–494, 503, 796–798, 867 | 118, 119, 189, 333, 493, 494, 503, 796, 798, 867 | **In-Depth Resources:** **Unit 1:** 77, 96–97 **Access for Students Acquiring English** 173 | **Electronic Library of Primary Sources** Chapter 2 |

# Correlation to Texas Essential Knowledge and Skills (TEKS)

| TEKS | Pupil's Edition and Teacher's Edition INSTRUCTION | Pupil's Edition and Teacher's Edition APPLICATION | Print Ancillaries | Technology and Transparencies |
|---|---|---|---|---|
| **(17) Government. The student understands the impact of constitutional issues on American society in the 20th century. The student is expected to:** | | | | |
| **(A)** analyze the effects of 20th-century landmark U.S. Supreme Court decisions such as *Brown v. Board of Education, Regents of the University of California v. Bakke,* and *Reynolds v. Sims;* | S26, 83, 97, 93, 99, 286, 287, 290, 291, 310–312, 334, 335, 353, 396, 397, 502, 503, 596, 597, 640, 690–693, 695, 696, 702–704, 708, 709, 774, 775, 779, 806, 814, 818, 819, 898, 899, 901 | 99, 290, 291, 397, 502, 503, 596, 597, 640, 691–693, 695, 696, 702, 703, 707, 709, 726, 774, 775, 779, 788, 807, 818, 819 | **In-Depth Resources:** **Unit 6:** 3, 20, 28–29 **Access for Students Acquiring English** 227, 231–232, 233, 237–238 **Historic Supreme Court Decisions** 73–78 | **Electronic Library of Primary Sources** Chapters 9, 21 **Humanities Transparencies** HT27 **TAKS Practice Transparencies** TT109 |
| **(B)** analyze reasons for the adoption of 20th-century constitutional amendments. | 83, 97, 100–103, 105, 312, 334, 335, 434, 436, 437, 716, 798 | 100–103, 105, 106, 312, 335, 436, 437, 439, 460, 716, 798 | **In-Depth Resources:** **Unit 3:** 2, 5, 13–14 **Unit 4:** 20, 32 **Access for Students Acquiring English** 118, 156 | **Electronic Library of Primary Sources** Chapter 9 |
| **(18) Citizenship. The student understands efforts to expand the democratic process. The student is expected to:** | | | | |
| **(A)** identify and analyze methods of expanding the right to participate in the democratic process, including lobbying, protesting, court decisions, and amendments to the U.S. Constitution; | S26, 23, 24, 34, 35, 64, 65, 98, 100–105, 109, 145–149, 182–186, 291, 312, 314–316, 334–335, 392–395, 429, 482, 483, 504–506, 508, 509, 592, 593, 596, 597, 640, 662, 663, 705–707, 710–716, 725, 744–747, 750–752, 769–774, 776–780, 798, 842, 843 | S9, 23, 24, 35, 39, 65, 99–103, 105, 109, 146, 147, 149, 152, 183, 186, 190, 291, 312, 316, 335, 429, 483, 505, 509, 593, 596, 597, 640, 662, 663, 705–707, 711, 713–716, 725, 726, 745, 747, 752, 770–774, 777, 780, 788, 826, 842, 843 | **In-Depth Resources:** **Unit 1:** 49–50, 62, 72, 100, 104, 107, 108, 109, 121, 137, 138 **Unit 2:** 80 **Unit 3:** 2, 5, 13–14 **Unit 6:** 21, 22, 28–29, 31, 32, 33, 37, 38, 74, 75, 81 **Access for Students Acquiring English** 24–25, 26, 27, 28, 35–41, 66, 160, 195, 231–232, 233, 234, 235, 237–238, 251–252, 253, 254, 257–258 | **Electronic Library of Primary Sources** Chapters 2, 3, 4, 9 **American Stories Videos** Teacher of a Freed People, A Walk in Two Worlds, From China to Chinatown, A Song for His People, Justice in Montgomery **Critical Thinking Transparencies** CT4, 5, 12 **Humanities Transparencies** HT12 |
| **(B)** evaluate various means of achieving equality of political rights, including the 19th, 24th, and 26th amendments; and | S24, 98, 100–105, 182, 183, 186, 314–316, 334, 335, 395, 429, 504–506, 705–707, 710–716, 725, 769–774, 776–780, 798 | 101–105, 183, 316, 335, 429, 505, 506, 509, 705–707, 711, 713–716, 725, 726, 770–774, 777, 780, 788, 826 | **In-Depth Resources:** **Unit 1:** 62, 100, 104, 107, 108, 109, 121, 137, 138 **Unit 3:** 2, 5, 13–14 **Unit 6:** 21, 22, 28–29, 31, 32, 33, 37, 38, 74, 75, 81 **Access for Students Acquiring English** 35–41, 66, 231–232, 233, 234, 235, 237–238, 251–252, 253, 254, 257–258 | **Electronic Library of Primary Sources** Chapter 4 **American Stories Videos** Teacher of a Freed People, A Walk in Two Worlds, Justice in Montgomery **Critical Thinking Transparencies** CT12 **TAKS Practice Transparencies** TT73, 119 |

# Correlation to Texas Essential Knowledge and Skills (TEKS)

| TEKS | Pupil's Edition and Teacher's Edition INSTRUCTION | Pupil's Edition and Teacher's Edition APPLICATION | Print Ancillaries | Technology and Transparencies |
|---|---|---|---|---|
| **(18) Citizenship. The student understands efforts to expand the democratic process. The student is expected to:** *(continued)* | | | | |
| **(C) explain how participation in the democratic process reflects our national identity.** | 776–780, 784, 785, 830–833 | 664, 775, 785, 831–833 | **In-Depth Resources:** **Unit 1:** 69–70 | **American Stories Videos** Teacher of a Freed People **Critical Thinking Transparencies** CT4, 5 |
| **(19) Citizenship. The student understands the importance of effective leadership in a democratic society. The student is expected to:** | | | | |
| **(A) describe qualities of effective leadership;** | 10, 36, 52, 53, 60, 68, 74–76, 85, 91, 99, 102, 105, 158, 163, 164, 307, 310, 316–319, 332–334, 345, 352, 360, 400–402, 418, 424, 452–454, 466, 480, 483, 489–501, 504, 505, 507–509, 515–519, 529–535, 540, 541, 550–557, 569–574, 578–580, 603, 612, 614, 639, 640, 672, 704–706, 719, 720, 731, 811, 812, 832, 833, 848, 849 | S11, 36, 39, 52, 53, 75, 79, 165, 319, 401, 418, 427, 454, 480, 483, 489, 490, 492–494, 496, 501, 509, 519, 522, 523, 531, 535, 541, 557–559, 598, 608, 613, 614, 639, 640, 659, 669, 672, 676, 687, 705, 707, 720, 723, 726, 735, 773, 788, 807, 811, 812, 826, 827, 832–834, 838, 842, 843, 849, 856 | **In-Depth Resources:** **Unit 1:** 54–56, 72, 77, 78, 104, 137 **Unit 2:** 18, 31, 37, 38, 59, 75, 80 **Unit 3:** 3, 5, 39 **Unit 4:** 19, 59, 83 **Unit 5:** 13, 44, 60 **Unit 7:** 20 **Access for Students Acquiring English** 25, 50–51, 52, 53, 119, 122, 124, 129, 139–140, 144 | **Electronic Library of Primary Sources** Chapters 2, 17 **American Stories Videos** War Outside My Window, A Walk in Two Worlds, Ace of Aces, Broke but Not Broken |
| **(B) evaluate the contributions of significant political and social leaders in the United States such as Andrew Carnegie, Shirley Chisholm, and Franklin D. Roosevelt; and** | 52, 53, 59, 60, 68, 69, 74–76, 85, 91, 95, 99, 102, 105, 112–114, 116, 117, 122–127, 134, 135, 145, 146, 148, 149, 156–161, 163–166, 171–174, 176, 177, 180, 184–186, 188, 221–223, 241, 242, 245, 246, 248, 266, 270, 284, 285, 307, 313–319, 332, 334–337, 359–365, 384, 398, 399, 418, 424, 466, 478–483, 489–501, 504, 505, 507–509, 515–521, 534, 535, 550–557, 569, 570, 574–577, 583, 585–587, 603, 605, 606, 614, 620, 621, 623, 636–640, 679–682, 689–693, 702–706, 714, 719, 719–722, 732, 734–738, 740, 744, 745–747, 750–755, 758, 770, 776–779, 784, 794–801, 810–817, 820, 821, 832–837, 852–855, 860–865 | S11, 52, 53, 60, 75, 76, 79, 80, 113, 116, 117, 126, 127, 149, 152, 157, 158, 163, 165, 173, 177, 183, 185, 189, 190, 222, 223, 226, 242, 249, 266, 272, 285, 300, 316, 319, 363, 365, 399, 421, 427, 479, 480, 482–484, 489–494, 496, 500, 501, 509, 519, 522, 523, 534, 553, 554, 557–559, 569, 577, 585, 587, 598, 603, 606, 608, 614, 621, 636, 638–640, 664, 689, 690, 692, 696, 701, 705–707, 719–721, 723, 726, 727, 732, 734–738, 745–747, 750, 751, 753–755, 758, 770, 773, 780, 788, 795–799, 811–816, 837, 855, 856, 861, 865, 868 | **In-Depth Resources:** **Unit 1:** 49–50, 54–56, 58, 71, 72, 77, 78, 98, 104, 105, 126–127, 121, 136, 137 **Unit 2:** 19, 31, 37, 38, 54, 59, 75, 76, 80 **Unit 3:** 3, 5, 18, 22, 23, 39, 50, 62 **Unit 4:** 18, 59, 83, 60, 61, 62, 64, 74–75 **Unit 5:** 13, 23, 24, 44, 55–56, 57, 58–59, 60, 64 **Unit 6:** 1, 2, 3, 32, 37, 38, 40, 58, 74, 75, 81 **Unit 7:** 23, 25 **Access for Students Acquiring English** 25, 26, 50–51, 52, 54, 67, 69, 70, 81, 90, 94, 101, 110, 112, 113, 115, 118–119, 121, 122, 123, 157, 173, 175, 176, 177, 231–232, 234, 239–240, 241, 242, 244, 245, 251–252, 259–260, 261, 263, 264, 268–269, 271, 272, 279–280, 281, 282, 291 | **Electronic Library of Primary Sources** Chapters 1–7, 9–11, 15, 19–26 **American Stories Videos** War Outside My Window, Teacher of a Freed People, A Walk in Two Worlds, Gusher!, A Child on Strike, Ace of Aces, Jump at the Sun, Broke but Not Broken, A Song for His People, Justice in Montgomery, Poisoned Playground **Critical Thinking Transparencies** CT33 **Humanities Transparencies** HT44 |

# Correlation to Texas Essential Knowledge and Skills (TEKS)

TEKS

| | Pupil's Edition and Teacher's Edition INSTRUCTION | Pupil's Edition and Teacher's Edition APPLICATION | Print Ancillaries | Technology and Transparencies |
|---|---|---|---|---|
| **(19) Citizenship. The student understands the importance of effective leadership in a democratic society. The student is expected to:** *(continued)* | | | | |
| **(C) identify the contributions of Texans who have been President of the United States.** | S14, 571–573, 574–577, 623, 625, 686–693, 734–738, 745–747, 750, 838, 851, 853–855, 867, 868, US2–US15 | 577, 598, 627, 688, 690, 692, 693, 696, 697, 734–737, 750, 764, 836, 838, 852–854, 856, 868, 890 | **In-Depth Resources:** **Unit 5:** 60 **Unit 7:** 23 **Access for Students Acquiring English** 268–269, 271 | **Electronic Library of Primary Sources** Chapter 22 **American Stories Videos** Matters of Conscience **Critical Thinking Transparencies** CT28 **Humanities Transparencies** HT44 |
| **(20) Culture. The student understands the relationship between the arts and the times during which they were created. The student is expected to:** | | | | |
| **(A) describe how the characteristics and issues of various eras in U.S. history have been reflected in works of art, music, and literature such as the paintings of Georgia O'Keeffe, rock and roll, and John Steinbeck's The Grapes of Wrath;** | 52, 53, 138, 158, 160, 178, 210, 224, 225, 294, 296, 326, 327, 364, 382, 393, 402, 414, 435, 444, 445, 450–459, 467, 481, 496, 510–514, 628, 629, 642, 645, 655–659, 745, 762, 763, 783–787, 874, 875 | 52, 53, 138, 158, 159, 165, 178, 210, 224, 225, 294–296, 327, 364, 393, 402, 414, 435, 445, 451, 454, 459, 460, 467, 481, 512–514, 523, 628, 629, 645, 652, 655–657, 659, 664, 762, 763, 783, 784, 787, 788, 875 | **In-Depth Resources:** **Unit 1:** 29, 54–56, 101–103, 133–135 **Unit 2:** 15–17, 34–36, 56–58, 77–79 **Unit 3:** 19–21, 42–44, 63–65 **Unit 4:** 15, 17, 35, 36–38, 55–57, 80–82 **Unit 5:** 68 **Unit 6:** 14, 15–17, 31, 34–36, 59–61, 76, 78–80 **Access for Students Acquiring English** 157, 161, 174, 178 | **Electronic Library of Primary Sources** Chapter 6 **American Stories Videos** War Outside My Window, Teacher of a Freed People, A Walk in Two Worlds, From China to Chinatown, Jump at the Sun, A Song for His People **Humanities Transparencies** HT1–21, 26, 27, 29 |
| **(B) describe the impact of significant examples of cultural movements in art, music, and literature on American society, including the Harlem Renaissance;** | 52, 53, 210, 224, 225, 296, 326, 327, 444, 445, 448–451, 454–459, 512–514, 628, 629, 655–657, 783–787 | 52, 53, 210, 224, 225, 296, 327, 445, 451, 454, 456, 457, 459, 460, 514, 629, 655–657, 664, 783–789 | **In-Depth Resources:** **Unit 2:** 64, 77–79 **Unit 4:** 23, 35 **Access for Students Acquiring English** 157, 161, 174, 178, 215, 218 | **American Stories Videos** Jump at the Sun |
| **(C) identify examples of American art, music, and literature that transcend American culture and convey universal themes;** | 52, 53, 210, 224, 225, 296, 402, 448–451, 454–459, 496, 512–514, 628, 629, 655–657, 783–787, 874, 875 | 52, 53, 158, 210, 224, 225, 402, 454, 459, 460, 512, 513, 629, 655–657, 783–789, 874, 875 | **In-Depth Resources:** **Unit 1:** 59–62, 100 **Unit 4:** 55–57 **Unit 5:** 68 **Unit 6:** 14, 31 **Access for Students Acquiring English** 157, 161, 174, 178 | **American Stories Videos** War Outside My Window, Jump at the Sun **Humanities Transparencies** HT5, 10, 11, 12, 13, 15, 18, 19, 22 |

# Correlation to Texas Essential Knowledge and Skills (TEKS)

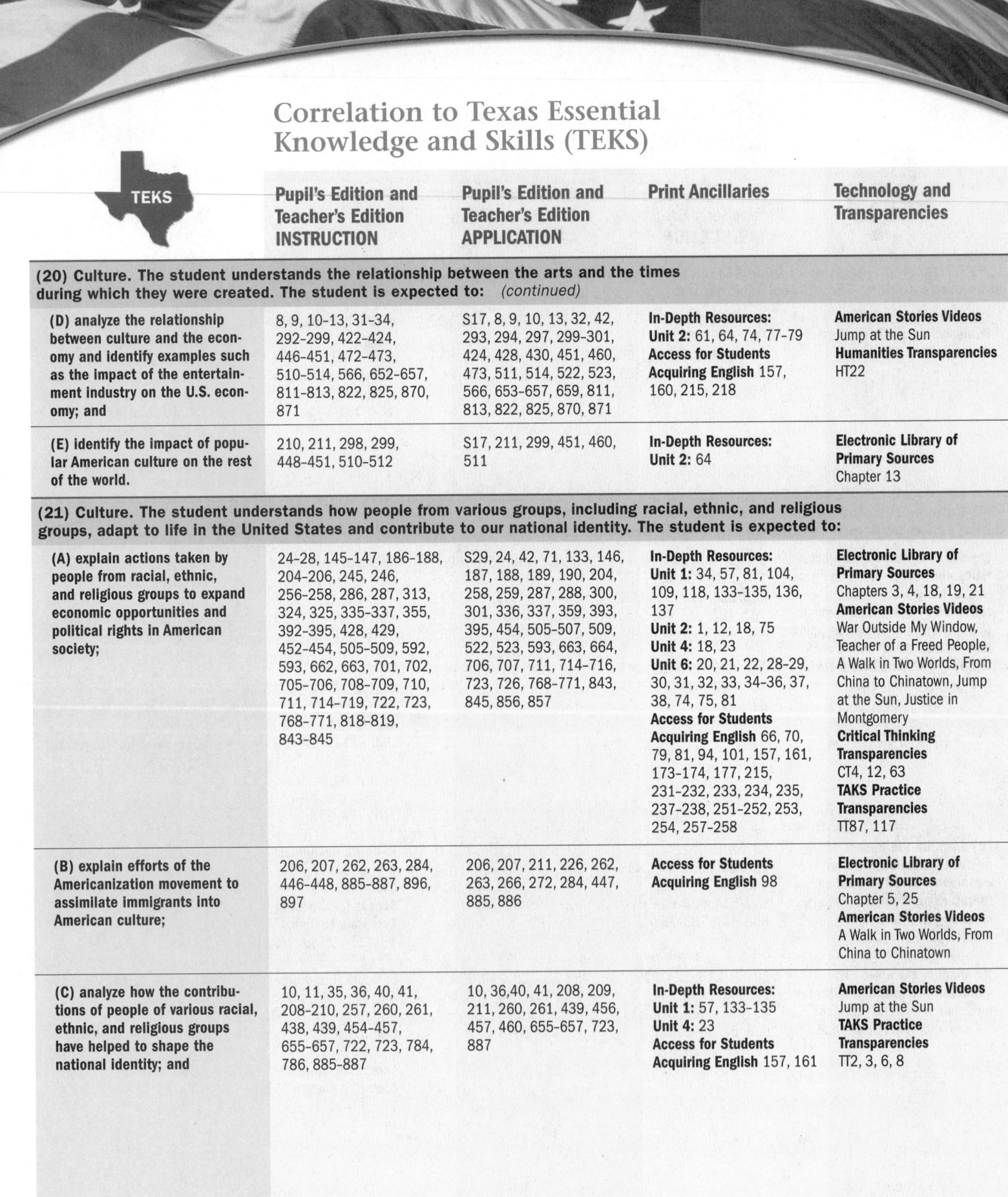

| TEKS | Pupil's Edition and Teacher's Edition INSTRUCTION | Pupil's Edition and Teacher's Edition APPLICATION | Print Ancillaries | Technology and Transparencies |
|---|---|---|---|---|
| **(20) Culture. The student understands the relationship between the arts and the times during which they were created. The student is expected to:** *(continued)* | | | | |
| **(D)** analyze the relationship between culture and the economy and identify examples such as the impact of the entertainment industry on the U.S. economy; and | 8, 9, 10–13, 31–34, 292–299, 422–424, 446–451, 472–473, 510–514, 566, 652–657, 811–813, 822, 825, 870, 871 | S17, 8, 9, 10, 13, 32, 42, 293, 294, 297, 299–301, 424, 428, 430, 451, 460, 473, 511, 514, 522, 523, 566, 653–657, 659, 811, 813, 822, 825, 870, 871 | **In-Depth Resources:** **Unit 2:** 61, 64, 74, 77–79 **Access for Students Acquiring English** 157, 160, 215, 218 | **American Stories Videos** Jump at the Sun **Humanities Transparencies** HT22 |
| **(E)** identify the impact of popular American culture on the rest of the world. | 210, 211, 298, 299, 448–451, 510–512 | S17, 211, 299, 451, 460, 511 | **In-Depth Resources:** **Unit 2:** 64 | **Electronic Library of Primary Sources** Chapter 13 |
| **(21) Culture. The student understands how people from various groups, including racial, ethnic, and religious groups, adapt to life in the United States and contribute to our national identity. The student is expected to:** | | | | |
| **(A)** explain actions taken by people from racial, ethnic, and religious groups to expand economic opportunities and political rights in American society; | 24–28, 145–147, 186–188, 204–206, 245, 246, 256–258, 286, 287, 313, 324, 325, 335–337, 355, 392–395, 428, 429, 452–454, 505–509, 592, 593, 662, 663, 701, 702, 705–706, 708–709, 710, 711, 714–719, 722, 723, 768–771, 818–819, 843–845 | S29, 24, 42, 71, 133, 146, 187, 188, 189, 190, 204, 258, 259, 287, 288, 300, 301, 336, 337, 359, 393, 395, 454, 505–507, 509, 522, 523, 593, 663, 664, 706, 707, 711, 714–716, 723, 726, 768–771, 843, 845, 856, 857 | **In-Depth Resources:** **Unit 1:** 34, 57, 81, 104, 109, 118, 133–135, 136, 137 **Unit 2:** 1, 12, 18, 75 **Unit 4:** 18, 23 **Unit 6:** 20, 21, 22, 28–29, 30, 31, 32, 33, 34–36, 37, 38, 74, 75, 81 **Access for Students Acquiring English** 66, 70, 79, 81, 94, 101, 157, 161, 173–174, 177, 215, 231–232, 233, 234, 235, 237–238, 251–252, 253, 254, 257–258 | **Electronic Library of Primary Sources** Chapters 3, 4, 18, 19, 21 **American Stories Videos** War Outside My Window, Teacher of a Freed People, A Walk in Two Worlds, From China to Chinatown, Jump at the Sun, Justice in Montgomery **Critical Thinking Transparencies** CT4, 12, 63 **TAKS Practice Transparencies** TT87, 117 |
| **(B)** explain efforts of the Americanization movement to assimilate immigrants into American culture; | 206, 207, 262, 263, 284, 446–448, 885–887, 896, 897 | 206, 207, 211, 226, 262, 263, 266, 272, 284, 447, 885, 886 | **Access for Students Acquiring English** 98 | **Electronic Library of Primary Sources** Chapter 5, 25 **American Stories Videos** A Walk in Two Worlds, From China to Chinatown |
| **(C)** analyze how the contributions of people of various racial, ethnic, and religious groups have helped to shape the national identity; and | 10, 11, 35, 36, 40, 41, 208–210, 257, 260, 261, 438, 439, 454–457, 655–657, 722, 723, 784, 786, 885–887 | 10, 36, 40, 41, 208, 209, 211, 260, 261, 439, 456, 457, 460, 655–657, 723, 887 | **In-Depth Resources:** **Unit 1:** 57, 133–135 **Unit 4:** 23 **Access for Students Acquiring English** 157, 161 | **American Stories Videos** Jump at the Sun **TAKS Practice Transparencies** TT2, 3, 6, 8 |

# Correlation to Texas Essential Knowledge and Skills (TEKS)

| TEKS | Pupil's Edition and Teacher's Edition INSTRUCTION | Pupil's Edition and Teacher's Edition APPLICATION | Print Ancillaries | Technology and Transparencies |
|---|---|---|---|---|
| **(21) Culture. The student understands how people from various groups, including racial, ethnic, and religious groups, adapt to life in the United States and contribute to our national identity. The student is expected to:** *(continued)* | | | | |
| **(D)** identify the political, social, and economic contributions of women to American society. | 32, 34, 56, 61, 64-65, 147-149, 158-160, 173, 174, 216-219, 248, 249, 266, 286, 306-309, 313, 314, 332, 334, 335, 372, 388, 392-395, 440-443, 474-477, 489, 495-498, 504-506, 562-567, 591, 644, 645, 700-702, 704, 705, 722, 744, 776-780, 820, 821, 836, 842, 843, 874, 875 | 32, 56, 61, 64-65, 147, 148, 158, 165, 172, 174, 190, 249, 250, 307, 314, 335, 394, 441, 443, 460, 476, 477, 497, 498, 509, 522, 562, 565, 595, 645, 649, 707, 716, 744, 776-780, 788, 821, 842, 843, 874, 875 | **In-Depth Resources:** **Unit 1:** 81, 100, 136, 138 **Unit 2:** 13, 19, 54, 59, 76 **Unit 3:** 2, 13-14, 15, 17, 18, 23, 66 **Unit 4:** 21, 39, 61, 84 **Unit 5:** 22, 43, 65 **Unit 6:** 19, 30, 37 **Unit 7:** 21, 43, 64, 73 **Access for Students Acquiring English** 67, 78, 84, 94, 101, 118, 121, 156, 159, 161, 194, 196, 231, 233, 234, 251-252, 254, 271, 281 | **Electronic Library of Primary Sources** Chapters 3-9, 15, 17, 19, 26 **American Stories Videos** War Outside My Window, A Walk in Two Worlds, A Child on Strike, Jump at the Sun, Justice in Montgomery, Poisoned Playground **Critical Thinking Transparencies** CT8, 31, 65 **Humanities Transparencies** HT10 **TAKS Practice Transparencies** TT31, 118, 129 |
| **(22) Science, technology, and society. The student understands the impact of science and technology on the economic development of the United States. The student is expected to:** | | | | |
| **(A)** explain the effects of scientific discoveries and technological innovations such as electric power, the telegraph and telephone, petroleum-based products, medical vaccinations, and computers on the development of the United States; | 34, 35, 121, 140, 141, 211, 214, 215, 217, 230-233, 264, 276-281, 299, 306-309, 310-312, 314, 372-380, 384, 385, 422-425, 429, 438, 439, 441-443, 446-451, 480, 482, 510-512, 520, 521, 588, 589, 618, 619, 622, 623, 626, 627, 644, 646. 647, 652-655, 679-681, 808, 809, 811-813, 822-825, 870, 871, 876-881 | S7, S27, 35, 39, 121, 140, 152, 211, 215, 217, 231, 233, 250, 277-281, 299, 300, 309, 311, 376, 387, 406, 423-425, 427, 429, 430, 439, 442, 448, 449, 451, 460, 482, 511, 521, 522, 588, 589, 618, 623, 626, 646, 649, 652-654, 657, 664, 681, 683, 809, 811, 813, 817, 825-827, 871, 877-881, 891 | **In-Depth Resources:** **Unit 1:** 29, 80, 138 **Unit 2:** 3, 20, 30, 48-49, 61 **Unit 3:** 34-35, 41 **Unit 4:** 3, 9-10, 30-31 **Unit 5:** 39 **Unit 7:** 48, 52 **Access for Students Acquiring English** 89-90, 91, 92, 93, 149, 152, 157, 160, 163-164, 194, 214-215, 217, 266-267, 280, 282, 283, 286-287 | **Electronic Library of Primary Sources** Chapters 8, 17 **American Stories Videos** Gusher!, From China to Chinatown, A Child on Strike, Ace of Aces **Critical Thinking Transparencies** CT7, 8, 13, 35, 60 **Humanities Transparencies** HT18, 24, 41, 42 **Geography Transparencies** GT13, 14, 16, 17, 22, 27 **TAKS Practice Transparencies** TT33, 80 |

# Correlation to Texas Essential Knowledge and Skills (TEKS)

| TEKS | Pupil's Edition and Teacher's Edition **INSTRUCTION** | Pupil's Edition and Teacher's Edition **APPLICATION** | Print Ancillaries | Technology and Transparencies |
|---|---|---|---|---|
| **(22) Science, technology, and society. The student understands the impact of science and technology on the economic development of the United States. The student is expected to:** *(continued)* | | | | |
| **(B)** explain how scientific discoveries and technological innovations such as those in agriculture, the military, and medicine resulted from specific needs; and | 12, 24, 121, 182, 211, 217, 231, 281, 308, 309, 359-361, 383-385, 449, 520, 521, 552, 553, 567, 583, 584, 588, 589, 622, 623, 626, 627, 644, 681, 738-740, 880 | 12, 24, 121, 152, 182, 211, 217, 281, 308, 309, 361, 383-385, 521, 522, 553, 567, 589, 623, 626, 627, 649, 681, 738, 739, 741, 881 | **In-Depth Resources:** **Unit 1:** 80, 138 **Unit 2:** 3, 20, 30, 48-49, 61 **Unit 3:** 34-35, 41 **Unit 4:** 3, 30 **Unit 5:** 39 **Access for Students Acquiring English** 194, 215-216, 217 | **Electronic Library of Primary Sources** Chapter 17 **American Stories Videos** Ace of Aces, Broke but Not Broken, Matters of Conscience **Critical Thinking Transparencies** CT8, 36, 60 **Humanities Transparencies** HT18, 24, 41 |
| **(C)** analyze the impact of technological innovations on the nature of work, the American labor movement, and businesses. | 12, 121, 142, 143, 233, 279-281, 308, 309, 313, 314, 392-395, 422-426, 441-443, 510-512, 520, 521, 618, 619, 641-643, 646, 648, 649, 814, 869-871, 876-878 | 12, 121, 142, 143, 152, 233, 281, 309, 314, 394, 424, 425, 430, 442, 443, 511, 521, 522, 641-643, 649, 664, 814, 873, 877, 878, 890 | **In-Depth Resources:** **Unit 1:** 80 **Unit 2:** 3, 20, 48-49, 61 **Unit 4:** 19 **Unit 7:** 48, 52 **Access for Students Acquiring English** 89-90, 91, 93, 94 | **American Stories Videos** A Child on Strike **Critical Thinking Transparencies** CT5, 8 **TAKS Practice Transparencies** TT130 |
| **(23) Science, technology, and society. The student understands the influence of scientific discoveries and technological innovations on daily life in the United States. The student is expected to:** | | | | |
| **(A)** analyze how scientific discoveries and technological innovations, including those in transportation and communication, have changed the standard of living in the United States; and | 120, 121, 139-141, 208-210, 214, 215, 232, 233, 236-238, 264, 276-281, 359, 361, 366, 367, 425-427, 435, 447, 448, 465, 510-512, 626, 627, 646, 647, 650-655, 869-873, 876-881 | 121, 140, 141, 152, 209, 211, 215, 218, 233, 237, 240, 250, 266, 277-279, 281, 300, 367, 425, 427, 430, 435, 448, 465, 511, 522, 626, 646, 651, 653, 654, 664, 870, 871, 873, 878, 880, 881, 890 | **In-Depth Resources:** **Unit 1:** 80 **Unit 2:** 3, 20, 48-49, 61 **Unit 4:** 9-10, 30-31 **Unit 7:** 48, 52 **Access for Students Acquiring English** 89-90, 91, 92, 93, 280, 282, 283, 286-287 | **American Stories Videos** Gusher!, From China to Chinatown **Critical Thinking Transparencies** CT5, 13 **Humanities Transparencies** HT42 **TAKS Practice Transparencies** TT104, 105 |
| **(B)** explain how technological innovations in areas such as space exploration have led to other innovations that affect daily life and the standard of living. | 425, 426, 429, 441-443, 446-448, 588, 589, 646, 647, 650-655, 679, 681, 796, 841, 876-881 | 426, 429, 430, 443, 448, 460, 588, 589, 646, 651, 653, 654, 664, 681, 683, 877, 878, 880, 881, 890 | **In-Depth Resources:** **Unit 1:** 80 **Unit 2:** 3, 20, 48-49, 61 **Unit 4:** 9-10, 30-31 | **Electronic Library of Primary Sources** Chapter 8 **American Stories Videos** Gusher! **Critical Thinking Transparencies** CT5, 13 |

# Correlation to Texas Essential Knowledge and Skills (TEKS)

| TEKS | Pupil's Edition and Teacher's Edition INSTRUCTION | Pupil's Edition and Teacher's Edition APPLICATION | Print Ancillaries | Technology and Transparencies |
|------|---------------------------------------------------|---------------------------------------------------|-------------------|-------------------------------|
| **(24) Social studies skills. The student applies critical-thinking skills to organize and use information acquired from a variety of sources including electronic technology. The student is expected to:** | | | | |
| (A) locate and use primary and secondary sources such as computer software, databases, media and news services, biographies, interviews, and artifacts to acquire information about the United States; | S8, S10, S12, S30–S31, 3, 4, 14, 18, 21, 30, 31, 36, 39, 40, 45, 46, 52, 54–58, 60, 64, 66, 70, 72, 74, 79, 82–87, 108–109, 111, 112, 117, 118, 120, 124, 128, 130, 139, 142, 144, 149, 156, 160, 165, 166, 168, 172, 175, 177, 184, 187, 201, 202, 206, 208, 212, 214, 216, 219, 223, 224, 229, 230, 234, 236, 241, 244, 245, 247, 253, 254, 256, 257, 260, 262, 265, 267, 268, 275–279, 282, 283, 286, 288, 290, 292, 298, 305, 306, 308, 313, 315, 317, 325, 326–328, 331, 332, 337, 341, 342, 346, 352, 355, 358, 359, 364, 366, 371, 372, 374, 380, 381, 383, 385, 387, 388, 391, 392, 394, 396, 398, 404, 411–415, 419, 420, 422, 427, 428, 433–435, 437, 439, 440, 443, 444, 446, 449, 450, 452–454, 456–459, 463, 464, 469, 470, 472, 473, 476, 478, 479, 483, 487, 488, 490, 492, 494–497, 499, 502, 504, 506, 508, 510, 513, 515, 516, 527, 528, 535, 536, 538, 541, 542, 544, 548, 549, 550, 554, 555, 560–563, 565, 566, 569, 570, 572, 576–578, 581, 582, 584, 586, 588, 590, 593, 595, 596, 601, 602, 605, 609, 616, 619, 620, 622, 627–629, 633, 634, 636, 639, 641, 642, 644, 649, 650, 652, 654–658, 660, 661, 666–667, 669, 670, 672, 673, 676, 679, 681, 684, 687, 689, 699, 700, 705, 708, 710, 712, 714, 715, 717, 719–721, 724, | S9, S11, S13, S27, 2, 3, 4, 8, 11, 14, 16, 17, 21, 22, 24, 25, 27, 31, 32, 40, 42, 44, 45, 46, 48, 50, 54, 58, 64–66, 71–73, 78, 80, 107, 108, 110, 111, 113, 119, 121, 126, 129, 132, 134, 137, 140, 141, 145, 147, 154, 155, 157–159, 161, 164, 166–170, 173–175, 177–182, 184, 187–189, 201, 202, 210, 213, 220, 225, 229, 230, 235, 240, 250, 253, 261, 269, 275, 278, 280, 283, 291, 295, 299, 311, 319, 325, 327, 341, 354, 387, 397, 402, 405, 407, 411, 433, 435, 436, 443, 445, 459–461, 463, 467, 468, 481, 486, 489, 490, 492, 493, 497–501, 505, 508, 511, 513, 517, 520, 523, 526, 529, 543, 544, 546, 552, 554, 555, 557, 559, 561, 566, 568, 577, 582, 589, 597, 600, 601, 603, 607, 608, 610, 611, 613, 616–618, 620, 621, 625, 626, 629, 631–633, 637, 638, 644, 645, 647, 649, 651, 653–656, 659, 664, 665, 666–667, 668, 669, 675, 677, 678, 680, 681, 688, 689, 691, 693, 695, 697, 699, 700, 702, 703, 706, 709, 711–716, 718, 719, 723, 728, 729, 731–734, 738, 739, 743, 745–747, 749, 750, 752, 758, 759, 763, 766, 767, 770, 773, 775, 783, 784, 787–789, 792, 793, 795, 798, 800, 805, 806, 809, 811, 813, 816, 819, 820, 824–829, 836, 838, 844, 849, 851, 852, 854, 857–859, 862–868, 871, 872, 875, 877–880, 883, | **In-Depth Resources:** **Unit 1:** 15, 16, 25, 26–27, 28, 29, 30–32, 49–50, 51, 52, 53, 54–56, 59–63, 96–97, 98, 99, 100, 101–103, 121, 122, 123, 126–127, 130, 133–135 **Unit 2:** 12, 13, 14, 15–17, 30, 31, 32, 33, 34–36, 43, 53, 54, 55, 56–58, 73, 74, 75, 76, 77–79 **Unit 3:** 15, 16, 17, 18, 19–21, 22, 23, 38, 39, 40, 41, 42–44, 45, 46, 59, 60, 61, 62, 63–65, 66, 67 **Unit 4:** 11–12, 13, 14, 15–16, 17, 32, 33, 34, 35, 36–38, 51, 52, 53, 54, 55–57, 76, 77, 78, 79, 80–82 **Unit 5:** 13, 14–15, 16, 17–19, 20, 21, 36, 37, 38, 39, 40–42, 43, 44, 57, 58, 59, 60, 61–63, 64, 65, 78, 79, 80, 81, 82–83, 84, 85, 86 **Unit 6:** 11–12, 13, 14, 15–17, 18, 19, 30, 31, 32, 33, 34–36, 37, 38, 55, 56, 57, 58, 59–61, 74, 75, 76, 77, 78–90 **Unit 7:** 13, 14, 15, 16, 17–19, 20, 21, 36, 37, 38, 39, 40–41, 42, 43, 44, 46, 47, 48, 49, 50–51, 52, 53 | **Electronic Library of Primary Sources** Chapters 1–26 **American Stories Videos** War Outside My Window, Teacher of a Freed People, A Walk in Two Worlds, Gusher!, From China to Chinatown, A Child on Strike, Ace of Aces , Jump at the Sun, Broke but Not Broken, A Song for His People, Escaping the Final Solution, The Cold War Comes Home , Justice in Montgomery, Matters of Conscience, Poisoned Playground **TAKS Practice Transparencies** TT124, 127 |

# Correlation to Texas Essential Knowledge and Skills (TEKS)

| TEKS | Pupil's Edition and Teacher's Edition **INSTRUCTION** | Pupil's Edition and Teacher's Edition **APPLICATION** | Print Ancillaries | Technology and Transparencies |
|---|---|---|---|---|
| **(24) Social studies skills. The student applies critical-thinking skills to organize and use information acquired from a variety of sources including electronic technology. The student is expected to:** *(continued)* | | | | |
| **(A) locate and use primary and secondary sources such as computer software, databases, media and news services, biographies, interviews, and artifacts to acquire information about the United States;** *(continued)* | 729, 730, 736, 737, 739, 740, 742, 743, 745–748, 751, 752, 754, 755, 759, 762, 763, 767, 768, 772, 774, 776–779, 781, 783, 786, 787, 793, 794, 797, 800, 802, 804, 808, 810, 812, 818, 820, 821, 824, 829, 830, 832, 834, 835, 839, 842, 843, 846, 848, 853, 856, 860, 862, 864, 867, 869, 870, 876, 879, 882, US2–US15, R2–R10, R22, R23, R24, R29 | 885, 886, 890,R2–R10, R22, R23, R24, R29 | | |
| **(B) analyze information by sequencing, categorizing, identifying cause-and-effect relationships, comparing, contrasting, finding the main idea, summarizing, making generalizations and predictions, and drawing inferences and conclusions;** | S14, S16, S18, S24, S28, S30–S31, R2, R3, R4, R7, R8, R10, R13, R14, R18, R20, R21 | S17, S19, S21, S23, S25, S26, S29, 2–18, 20, 22–28, 30, 32, 33, 35–39, 41, 42, 45, 47–53, 59–63, 65, 67–71, 73, 75–80, 82–104, 106, 107, 110, 111, 113–125, 127, 128, 131, 132, 134–143, 145–148, 152, 155–167, 169–171, 173–183, 185–190, 201, 203–206, 208–211, 213, 215, 217, 218, 220–223, 225, 226, 229, 231–233, 235, 237–241, 243–247, 249, 250, 253, 255–257, 259, 261, 263, 264, 266, 268–270, 272, 273, 277–279, 281, 283, 284, 285, 287–289, 291, 293–297, 299–301, 307, 308, 310, 312, 315, 316, 319, 322–325, 327, 329, 331, 333–337, 341, 343–345, 347–351, 353–358, 360, 361, 363, 365, 373, 374, 377, 379, 380, 382–384, 386, 387, 389, 390, 391–395, 397, 399, 400, 403, 405, 406, 415, 418, 420, 424–427, 429, 430, 433, 435–437, 439, 441, 442, 443, 445, 448–451, 453, 457, 459, 460, 463, 465, 466, 467, | **In-Depth Resources:** **Unit 1:** 1, 2, 3, 4, 5, 6, 7, 8, 9, 10, 11, 12, 13, 22, 23, 25, 27, 28, 29, 32, 33, 34, 35, 36, 37, 38, 40, 41, 42, 48, 50, 51, 52, 53, 56, 57, 58, 64, 70, 71, 72, 73, 74, 76, 75, 77, 78, 79, 80, 81, 82, 83, 84, 85, 86, 93, 94, 97, 98, 99, 100, 103, 104, 105, 106, 107, 108, 109, 112, 113, 119, 121, 122, 123, 124, 127, 130, 135, 136, 137, 138 **Unit 2:** 2, 3, 5, 6, 11, 12, 13, 14, 17, 18, 19, 20, 21, 22, 24, 29, 30, 31, 32, 33, 36, 37, 38, 39, 40, 41, 43, 44, 46, 48, 49, 50, 53, 54, 55, 58, 59, 60, 61, 62, 63, 64, 66, 71, 72, 73, 74, 75, 76, 79, 80, 81 **Unit 3:** 1, 2, 3, 4, 5, 7, 14, 15, 16, 17, 18, 21, 22, 23, 24, 25, 26, 27, 29, 35, 36, 37, 38, 39, 40, 41, 44, 45, 46, 47, 48, 49, 50, 52, 58, 59, 60, 61, 62, 65, 66, 67 | **American Stories Videos** War Outside My Window, Teacher of a Freed People, A Walk in Two Worlds, Gusher!, From China to Chinatown, A Child on Strike, Ace of Aces, Jump at the Sun, Broke but Not Broken, A Song for His People, Escaping the Final Solution, The Cold War Comes Home , Justice in Montgomery, Matters of Conscience, Poisoned Playground **Critical Thinking Transparencies** CT38, 39, 40, 41, 42, 43, 44, 45, 46, 47, 49, 50, 51, 52, 53, 54, 55, 56, 57, 62, 63, 65, 66, 68, 69, 70, 71 **TAKS Practice Transparencies** TT21, 22, 24, 29, 35, 36, 43, 44, 48, 49, 128 |

## Correlation to Texas Essential Knowledge and Skills (TEKS)

| | Pupil's Edition and Teacher's Edition INSTRUCTION | Pupil's Edition and Teacher's Edition APPLICATION | Print Ancillaries | Technology and Transparencies |
|---|---|---|---|---|
| **(24) Social studies skills. The student applies critical-thinking skills to organize and use information acquired from a variety of sources including electronic technology. The student is expected to:** *(continued)* | | | | |
| **(B)** analyze information by sequencing, categorizing, identifying cause-and-effect relationships, comparing, contrasting, finding the main idea, summarizing, making generalizations and predictions, and drawing inferences and conclusions; *(continued)* | | 468–471, 473–477, 482–484, 486, 487, 489–494, 496, 497, 499, 501, 505–509, 511–514, 516, 518, 519, 521, 522, 526–538, 540–544, 546, 547, 550–558, 561, 564–581, 585–598, 600, 601, 603–608, 610–618, 620, 621, 623–630, 632–636, 638–649, 651–664, 668, 669, 671–678, 680–685, 687–693, 695, 696, 698, 699, 701–704, 706, 707, 709, 711–721, 723, 725–747, 749–761, 763, 764, 766–775, 777–785, 787, 792, 793, 795–801, 803–807, 809, 811–817, 820–826, 828, 829, 831–833, 835, 836–838, 840–845, 847, 849, 850–855, 857–859, 861, 862, 864–873, 877, 879–881, 883–890 | **Unit 4:** 1, 3, 5, 10, 12, 14, 17, 18, 19, 20, 21, 22, 25, 31, 32, 33, 34, 35, 38, 39, 40, 41, 42, 43, 45, 50, 52, 53, 54, 58, 59, 60, 61, 62, 64, 66, 73, 74, 77, 82, 83, 84 **Unit 5:** 1, 2, 3, 4, 6, 12, 13, 15, 16, 19, 20, 21, 27, 32, 33, 34–35, 36, 37, 38, 39, 42, 43, 44, 45, 46, 47, 48, 50, 56, 57, 59, 60, 63, 64, 65, 66, 67, 68, 69, 71, 77, 78, 79, 80, 81, 83, 84, 85, 86 **Unit 6:** 1, 2, 3, 5, 10, 12, 13, 14, 17, 18, 19, 20, 21, 22, 24, 29, 30, 31, 32, 33, 36, 37, 38, 39, 40, 41, 42, 43, 45, 52, 54, 55, 56, 57, 58, 61, 68, 69, 64, 65, 66, 68, 73, 74, 75, 76, 77, 80, 81, 82 **Unit 7:** 1, 2, 3, 4, 6, 12, 13, 14, 15, 16, 19, 20, 21, 22, 23, 24, 25, 32, 33, 34, 35, 36, 37, 38, 39, 41, 42, 43, 44, 45, 46, 47, 48, 56, 46, 47, 48, 49, 51, 52, 53, 58, 59, 60, 61, 62, 63, 64, 65, 66, 67, 68 **Access for Students Acquiring English** 15, 16, 19, 30, 32, 54, 58, 59, 72, 80–86, 88, 90–95, 97, 99–103, 106, 107, 110–115, 117, 119–125, 127, 129–133, 136, 137, 141–145, 147, 149–153, 155, 157–162, 164, 166–170, 172, 174–180, 182, 183, 186–191, 193, 195–200, 202, 203, 206–211, 213, 224–228, 230, 232–236, 238, 240–246, 248, 249, 252–257, 260–265, 267, 269–274, 276, 277, 280–285, 287–298 | |

# Correlation to Texas Essential Knowledge and Skills (TEKS)

**TEKS**

| | Pupil's Edition and Teacher's Edition **INSTRUCTION** | Pupil's Edition and Teacher's Edition **APPLICATION** | Print Ancillaries | Technology and Transparencies |
|---|---|---|---|---|

**(24) Social studies skills. The student applies critical-thinking skills to organize and use information acquired from a variety of sources including electronic technology. The student is expected to:** *(continued)*

| | Pupil's Edition and Teacher's Edition **INSTRUCTION** | Pupil's Edition and Teacher's Edition **APPLICATION** | Print Ancillaries | Technology and Transparencies |
|---|---|---|---|---|
| **(C)** explain and apply different methods that historians use to interpret the past, including the use of primary and secondary sources, points of view, frames of reference, and historical context; | S12, 302–303, 408–409, 410, 411, 413, 432, 433, 435, 436, 438, 439, 452, 565–567, 570, 572–576, 581, 583–585, 587, 588, 593–597, 601, 602, 609, 616, 622, 628, 642, 644, 645, 649, 653–658, 661, 662, 666–667, 790–791, 793, 794, 802, 808, 810, 818, 820, 829, 830, 832, 834, 839, 846, 848, 859, 860, 869, 882, 888, R3, R5–R21 | S13, S27, S29, S32–S33, 2, 3, 8, 9, 11, 14–16, 19, 21, 22, 24, 26, 27, 31, 33–36, 40–42, 44–50, 52, 55–62, 64, 65, 67, 71–73, 75, 77, 78, 80–113, 115–121, 123–134, 136–145, 147–149, 154, 155, 157–159, 161–167, 169–190, 201, 202, 210, 215, 216, 220, 225, 226, 229, 236–238, 240, 241, 250, 253, 254, 261, 266, 275, 278, 280, 282, 283, 286, 291, 295, 297, 299, 302–303, 312, 319, 324, 325, 327, 331, 336, 337, 354, 361, 387, 392, 403, 406, 408–409, 411, 421, 433, 435–437, 439, 443, 445, 459, 463, 477, 481, 482, 486, 487, 489, 490, 492, 493, 497, 498, 500, 502, 503, 505, 506, 508, 511, 513, 517, 519, 520, 523, 526, 529, 531–535, 537–541, 543, 544, 546, 548, 549, 554, 555, 557, 560, 561, 563, 568–570, 577, 582–584, 586, 589–593, 596, 597, 600, 601, 603, 604, 607, 608, 610, 611, 613–615, 617, 618, 620, 621, 625, 626, 629, 631, 632, 635, 637, 638, 640, 644, 645, 647, 649, 651, 653–657, 659, 660, 664, 666–667, 669, 670, 672, 679, 682, 684, 687, 688, 693, 699, 700, 708, 710, 712, 717, 724, 729, 730, 735, 736, 742, 747, 748, 753, 754, 762–764, 773, 775, 780, 787, 790–791, 792–798, 800, 802, 803, 805–809, 811–816, 819–822, 824–829, 831–833, 836, 838, 840–844, 849–853, 857, 858, 860–875, 877–880, R3, R5–R21 | **In-Depth Resources:** **Unit 1:** 10, 11, 12, 15, 16, 25, 26, 27, 28, , 29, 30–32, 33, 34, 42, 49–50, 51, 52, 53, 54–56, 57, 58, 59–63, 74, 78, 79, 83, 85, 96–97, 98, 99, 100, 101–103, 104, 106 121, 122, 123, 126–127, 130, 133–135, 136, 137, 138 **Unit 2:** 12, 13, 14, 15–17, 18, 19, 30, 31, 32, 33, 34–36, 37, 38, 39, 40, 43, 46, 53, 54, 55, 56–58, 63, 64, 73, 74, 75, 76, 77–79 **Unit 3:** 2, 13, 15, 16, 17, 18, 19–21, 22, 23, 34–35, 36, 38, 39, 40, 41, 42–44, 45, 46, 47, 48, 57–58, 59, 60, 61, 62, 63–65, 66, 67 **Unit 4:** 2, 12, 13, 14, 15–16, 17, 18, 19, 21, 23, 30–31, 32, 33, 34, 35, 36–38, 39, 40, 42, 51, 52, 53, 54, 55–57, 58, 76, 77, 78, 79, 80–82, 83, 84 **Unit 5:** 1, 2, 3, 4, 6, 12, 13, 14–15, 16, 17–19, 20, 21, 23, 24, 33, 36, 37, 38, 39, 40–42, 43, 44, 47, 48, 50, 55–56, 57, 58, 59, 60, 61–63, 64, 65, 68, 69, 71, 76–77, 78, 79, 80, 81, 82–83, 84, 85, 86 **Unit 6:** 1, 3, 9–10, 11–12, 13, 14, 15–17, 18, 19, 20, 21, 22, 30, 31, 32, 33, 34–36, 37, 38, 39, 41, 42, 51–52, 55, 56, 57, 58, 58–61, 64, 65, 66, 68, 74, 75, 76, 77, 78–90 **Unit 7:** 2, 3, 4, 6, 11–12, 13, 14, 15, 16, 17–19, 20, 21, 23, 36, 37, 38, 39, 40–41, 42, 43, 44, 46, 47, 48, 49, 50–51, 52, 53 **Access for Students Acquiring English** 13, 14, 15, 18, 20, 22, 24–25, 26, 27, 35–38, 40–41, 45, 47, 49, 50–51, 52, 53, 54, 55, 56, 63–64, 65–66 | **Electronic Library of Primary Sources** Chapters 1–26 **American Stories Videos** War Outside My Window, Teacher of a Freed People, A Walk in Two Worlds, Gusher!, From China to Chinatown, A Child on Strike, Ace of Aces , Jump at the Sun, Broke but Not Broken, A Song for His People, Escaping the Final Solution, The Cold War Comes Home, Justice in Montgomery, Matters of Conscience, Poisoned Playground **TAKS Practice Transparencies** TT10, 15, 19, 26, 30, 38, 41, 42, 57, 61, 90, 112 |

# Correlation to Texas Essential Knowledge and Skills (TEKS)

| TEKS | Pupil's Edition and Teacher's Edition INSTRUCTION | Pupil's Edition and Teacher's Edition APPLICATION | Print Ancillaries | Technology and Transparencies |
|---|---|---|---|---|
| **(24) Social studies skills. The student applies critical-thinking skills to organize and use information acquired from a variety of sources including electronic technology. The student is expected to:** *(continued)* | | | | |
| **(D) use the process of historical inquiry to research, interpret, and use multiple sources of evidence;** | 198–199, 432–433, 669, 670, 672, 678, 679, 684, 699, 700, 708, 710, 712, 717, 724, 729, 730, 736, 742, 748, 754, 762, 767, 768, 774, 776, 778, 781, 786, 829, 836, 838, 857, 859, 860, 869, 882, 888, R1–R29 | 2, 3, 7, 8, 11, 12, 15–17, 22, 24, 25, 27, 29, 32–34, 42, 44, 45, 47, 49, 57, 59, 62, 65, 67, 73, 76, 82–113, 118, 120, 121, 128, 130, 132, 134, 137, 139, 140, 141, 144, 145, 147, 154, 157–161, 164, 167, 170, 171, 173, 174, 176–179, 182, 187, 189, 190, 198–199, 201, 205, 209, 210, 213, 220, 225, 229, 235, 240, 253, 255, 259, 263, 269, 275, 278, 280, 283, 291, 295, 297, 299, 300, 305, 319, 333, 336, 337, 377, 387, 397, 400, 405, 407, 433, 435, 443, 463, 465, 486, 489, 490–493, 497, 498, 500, 501, 503, 505, 508, 511, 513, 517, 519, 520, 523, 533, 534, 540, 560, 561, 563, 567, 570, 572, 573, 575, 577, 580, 582, 586, 589, 591, 597, 601, 620, 621, 629, 631, 649, 651, 659, 666–667, 668, 669, 672, 675, 677, 678, 681, 685, 688, 689, 691–693, 701–703, 706, 709, 711–716, 718, 719, 723, 725–729, 731–734, 738, 739, 743, 746, 747, 750, 752, 753, 755, 758, 759, 763, 766, 770–773, 775, 779, 783, 784, 787, 792, 793, 795, 796, 798, 800, 805, 806, 809, 811, 813, 814, 816, 819, 823–829, 836, 838, 841, 844, 849, 851, 852, 857–859, 862–868, 871, 872, 875, 878–880, 883, 885, 886, 890, R1–R29 | **In-Depth Resources:**<br>**Unit 1:** 22, 25, 27, 28, 41, 51, 56, 64, 74, 84, 85, 103, 104, 124, 135, 137, 138<br>**Unit 2:** 17, 30, 54, 74, 75<br>Unit 3: 15, 16, 17, 18, 19–21, 38, 39, 40, 41, 42–44, 59, 60, 61, 62, 63–65<br>**Unit 4:** 12, 13, 14, 16, 17, 31, 32, 33, 34, 35, 38, 50, 51, 52, 53, 54, 57, 73, 74, 76, 77, 78, 79, 82<br>**Unit 5:** 13, 14–15, 16, 17–19, 36, 37, 38, 39, 40–42, 57, 58–59, 60, 61–63, 78, 79, 80, 81, 82–83, 84<br>**Unit 6:** 11–12, 13, 14, 15–17, 30, 31, 32, 33, 34–36, 55, 56, 57, 58, 59–61, 74, 75, 76, 77, 78–90<br>**Unit 7:** 12, 13, 14, 15, 16, 17–19, 20, 21, 36, 37, 38, 39, 40–41, 42, 43, 44, 46, 47, 48, 49, 50–51, 52, 53 | **Electronic Library of Primary Sources**<br>Chapters 1–26<br>**American Stories Videos**<br>War Outside My Window, Teacher of a Freed People, A Walk in Two Worlds, Gusher!, From China to Chinatown, A Child on Strike, Ace of Aces, Jump at the Sun, Broke but Not Broken, A Song for His People, Escaping the Final Solution, The Cold War Comes Home , Justice in Montgomery, Matters of Conscience, Poisoned Playground |

# Correlation to Texas Essential Knowledge and Skills (TEKS)

| TEKS | Pupil's Edition and Teacher's Edition INSTRUCTION | Pupil's Edition and Teacher's Edition APPLICATION | Print Ancillaries | Technology and Transparencies |
|---|---|---|---|---|
| **(24) Social studies skills. The student applies critical-thinking skills to organize and use information acquired from a variety of sources including electronic technology. The student is expected to:** *(continued)* | | | | |
| **(E) evaluate the validity of a source based on language, corroboration with other sources, and information about the author;** | 108, R15, R17, R22, R24 | 405, 552, R22, R23, R24 | **In-Depth Resources:** **Unit 1:** 25, 26, 27, 28, 29, 30–32, 49–50, 51, 52, 53, 54–56, 59–63, 96–97, 98, 99, 100, 101–103, 121, 122, 123, 126–127, 130, 133–135 **Unit 3:** 16, 18, 19, 38, 39, 40, 59, 62, 63 **Unit 5:** 13, 14, 36, 38, 39, 57, 58, 60, 71, 80, 81 **Unit 6:** 13, 31, 55, 57, 58, 74, 76 **Unit 7:** 14, 15, 16, 37, 38, 39, 46, 47, 48, 50 | **American Stories Videos** War Outside My Window, Teacher of a Freed People, A Walk in Two Worlds, Gusher!, From China to Chinatown, A Child on Strike, Ace of Aces , Jump at the Sun, Broke but Not Broken, A Song for His People, Escaping the Final Solution, The Cold War Comes Home , Justice in Montgomery, Matters of Conscience, Poisoned Playground |
| **(F) identify bias in written, oral, and visual material;** | 11, 48, 78, 108, 126, 127, 187, 189, 240, 250, 290, 339, 426, 524–525, 582, 666, R15, R23, R24 | 11, 48, 50, 78, 108, 126, 131, 161, 187, 189, 240, 250, 291, 312, 319, 351, 354, 361, 362, 371, 387, 395, 405–407, 414, 426, 467, 524–525, 534, 551, 564, 582, 585, 593, 655, 712, 732, 737, 795, 806, 825, R15, R23, R24 | **In-Depth Resources:** **Unit 1:** 28, 51, 85–99, 122, 123, 130, 133–135 **Unit 2:** 12, 18, 19, 30, 31, 32, 37, 38, 53, 54, 55, 56–58, 59, 74, 75, 76, 80 **Unit 4:** 14, 32, 52, 53, 58, 77 **Unit 5:** 27 **Unit 6:** 45 **Unit 7:** 6 | **American Stories Videos** War Outside My Window, Teacher of a Freed People, A Walk in Two Worlds, Gusher!, From China to Chinatown, A Child on Strike, Ace of Aces , Jump at the Sun, Broke but Not Broken, A Song for His People, Escaping the Final Solution, The Cold War Comes Home , Justice in Montgomery, Matters of Conscience, Poisoned Playground **TAKS Practice Transparencies** TT85, 115 |

# Correlation to Texas Essential Knowledge and Skills (TEKS)

| TEKS | Pupil's Edition and Teacher's Edition INSTRUCTION | Pupil's Edition and Teacher's Edition APPLICATION | Print Ancillaries | Technology and Transparencies |
|---|---|---|---|---|
| **(24) Social studies skills. The student applies critical-thinking skills to organize and use information acquired from a variety of sources including electronic technology. The student is expected to:** *(continued)* | | | | |
| **(G) support a point of view on a social studies issue or event; and** | S34-1, 410, 411, 436, 818, 819, R34–R35, R36 | S32–S33, S34-1, 11, 30, 52, 67, 71, 73, 78, 81, 84–86, 88, 94, 95, 98, 99, 101–104, 108, 120, 121, 125, 126, 129, 138, 143, 144, 146, 155, 158, 160, 165, 180, 183, 186, 189, 249, 259, 275, 301, 325, 329, 331, 341, 345, 351, 365, 371, 387, 395, 406, 407, 411, 418, 421, 427, 433, 436, 439, 482, 516, 519, 523, 527, 534, 544, 552, 553, 563, 584, 585, 587, 601, 614, 615, 624, 627, 633, 640, 649, 657, 659, 662, 674, 682, 685, 686, 689, 690, 695, 699, 707, 712, 727, 745–747, 753, 758, 765, 768, 776, 779, 802, 805, 811, 817–820, 823, 840, 841, 853, 855, 868, 873, 885, 886 | **In-Depth Resources:**<br>**Unit 1:** 74, 122, 138<br>**Unit 2:** 32, 59<br>**Unit 3:** 16, 22<br>**Unit 4:** 12, 54, 76<br>**Unit 5:** 39<br>**Unit 6:** 56<br>**Unit 7:** 56, 46, 49 | **Electronic Library of Primary Sources**<br>Chapters 4, 5, 6, 7, 9, 14, 15, 17, 18, 19, 20, 21, 22, 23, 24, 25<br>**American Stories Videos**<br>From China to Chinatown, The Cold War Comes Home, Justice in Montgomery |
| **(H) use appropriate mathematical skills to interpret social studies information such as maps and graphs.** | S18, S20, 7, 72, 73, 115, 132, 147, 169, 179, 182, 205, 213, 247, 255, 283, 300, 416, 425, 427, 532, 545, 556, 564, 575, 580, 606, 613, 626, 627, 636, 638, 643, 653, 659, 661, 813, 833, 842, 847, 857, 871, 884 | S19, 7, 73, 90, 115, 121, 132, 147, 159, 169, 179, 182, 188, 205, 213, 247, 255, 283, 300, 334, 349, 377, 389, 406, 407, 416, 425, 427, 468, 470, 492, 517, 532, 545, 556, 564, 575, 580, 606, 613, 626, 627, 636, 638, 643, 653, 659, 661, 675, 697, 700, 708, 723, 725, 743, 753, 775, 777, 787, 813, 814, 833, 842, 847, 853, 857, 865, 871, 884 | **In-Depth Resources:**<br>**Unit 1:** 21–22, 69–70, 92–93, 94–95, 118–119, 124<br>**Unit 2:** 29, 49, 50<br>**Unit 4:** 10, 31, 50, 73<br>**Unit 5:** 56, 77, 80<br>**Unit 7:** 12, 67, 68 | **Geography Transparencies**<br>GT1–38 |

# Correlation to Texas Essential Knowledge and Skills (TEKS)

| TEKS | Pupil's Edition and Teacher's Edition INSTRUCTION | Pupil's Edition and Teacher's Edition APPLICATION | Print Ancillaries | Technology and Transparencies |
|---|---|---|---|---|
| **(25) Social studies skills. The student communicates in written, oral, and visual forms. The student is expected to:** | | | | |
| (A) use social studies terminology correctly; | 4, 14, 21, 31, 46, 58, 66, 74, 112, 120, 139, 144, 156, 168, 175, 184, 202, 214, 219, 230, 236, 241, 254, 262, 267, 276, 282, 286, 292, 306, 313, 317, 328, 332, 342, 346, 352, 359, 372, 381, 388, 398, 412, 419, 422, 434, 440, 446, 452, 472, 478, 488, 495, 504, 510, 515, R38–R47, R53–R66 | 13, 20, 30, 39, 42, 51, 53, 63, 71, 79, 80, 86, 89, 96, 107–109, 117, 119, 127, 129, 138, 143, 149, 165, 174, 183, 189, 190, 208, 211, 218, 223, 226, 233, 240, 249, 250, 259, 266, 272, 281, 285, 289, 297, 300, 355, 380, 386, 403, 405–407, 418, 421, 427, 430, 439, 443, 451, 457, 460, 471, 477, 481, 483, 484, 494, 501, 507, 509, 514, 519, 522, 535, 541, 549, 557, 558, 568, 577, 587, 595, 598, 608, 612, 615, 621, 627, 630, 640, 643, 649, 657, 661, 663, 664, 676, 678, 683, 693, 697, 705–707, 716, 723, 726, 735, 741, 747, 753, 761, 764, 773, 778, 780, 785, 788, 797, 801, 807, 817, 825, 826, 833, 838, 843, 845, 855, 856, 868, 870, 873, 881, 887, 890, R35 | **In-Depth Resources:**<br>**Unit 1:** 35, 36, 37, 38, 77, 78, 79, 80, 81, 106, 107, 109<br>**Unit 2:** 4, 23, 42, 65<br>**Unit 3:** 1, 2, 3, 4, 24, 25, 26, 27, 47, 48, 49<br>**Unit 4:** 2, 3, 21, 22, 41, 42, 60, 61, 62, 64<br>**Unit 5:** 1, 2, 3, 22, 23, 24, 25, 45, 46, 47, 48, 66, 67, 68, 69<br>**Unit 6:** 1, 2, 21, 22, 39, 42, 43<br>**Unit 7:** 1, 3, 4, 22, 23, 24, 46, 47, 48, 62, 63, 64, 65<br>**Access for Students Acquiring English** 13, 14, 26–29, 52–56, 67, 68, 70, 81–84, 92, 94, 100–103, 111–114, 120–123, 130–133, 141–143, 150–152, 159, 160, 167–169, 175–177, 179, 187–189, 196, 197–199, 207–210, 216–219, 225, 226, 234, 235, 241, 244, 245, 261, 263, 264, 270–272, 281–284, 292-298 | **TAKS Practice Transparencies**<br>TT20<br>**American Stories Videos**<br>War Outside My Window, Teacher of a Freed People, A Walk in Two Worlds, Gusher!, From China to Chinatown, A Child on Strike, Ace of Aces, Jump at the Sun, Broke But Not Broken, A Song for His People, Escaping the Final Solution, The Cold War Comes Home, Justice in Montgomery, Matters of Conscience, Poisoned Playground |

# Correlation to Texas Essential Knowledge and Skills (TEKS)

| TEKS | Pupil's Edition and Teacher's Edition INSTRUCTION | Pupil's Edition and Teacher's Edition APPLICATION | Print Ancillaries | Technology and Transparencies |
|---|---|---|---|---|
| **(25) Social studies skills. The student communicates in written, oral, and visual forms. The student is expected to:** *(continued)* | | | | |
| **(B) use standard grammar, spelling, sentence structure, and punctuation;** | S34-1, R34–R35 | S34-1, 13, 20, 22, 26, 28, 30, 39, 42, 49, 51-53, 55, 57, 59, 63, 65, 67, 71, 79, 80, 89, 93, 103, 107, 108, 109, 115, 117, 119, 125, 127, 129, 136–138, 140, 142, 143, 145, 146, 149, 155, 157, 158, 160, 165, 167, 174, 178, 179, 184, 189, 211, 213, 218, 223, 225, 226, 229, 233, 235, 240, 249, 250, 259, 266, 271, 272, 281, 285, 289, 291, 297, 300, 301, 312, 316, 325, 327, 331, 345, 351, 358, 365, 368, 380, 386, 403, 405–407, 418, 421, 427, 430, 439, 443, 451, 457, 459, 460, 468, 471, 477, 483, 484, 492, 494, 497, 501, 508, 509, 514, 516, 519, 522, 534, 535, 541, 549, 557, 558, 564, 566, 568, 576, 577, 584, 587, 589, 595, 597, 598, 604, 608, 615, 621, 627, 630, 635, 640, 647, 649, 651, 657, 659, 663–665, 674, 678, 683, 685, 693, 695–697, 702, 706, 707, 716, 719, 720, 723, 725–727, 731, 735, 739–741, 743, 747, 752, 758, 761, 763, 764, 773, 780, 785, 787, 788, 795, 801, 803, 805, 807, 809, 815, 817, 819, 825–827, 833, 838, 845, 847, 855–857, 859, 868, 873, 875, 881, 887, 890, 891, R34–R35 | **In-Depth Resources:** **Unit 1:** 1, 2, 3, 4, 5, 6, 7, 8, 9, 10, 11, 12, 13, 14, 22, 23, 29, 32, 33, 34, 35, 36, 37, 38, 39, 40, 41, 42, 44, 50, 51, 52, 53, 56. 64, 63, 70, 74, 76, 77, 78, 79, 80, 81, 82, 83, 84, 85, 86, 93, 94, 97, 98, 99, 100, 103, 106, 107, 108, 109, 110, 113, 119, 121, 123, 130, 124, 127, 135, 138 **Unit 2:** 2, 3, 5, 6, 11, 12, 13, 14, 17, 18, 19, 20, 21, 22, 24, 29, 30, 31, 32, 33, 36, 37, 38, 39, 40, 41, 43, 44, 46, 48, 49, 50, 53, 54, 55, 58, 59, 60, 61, 62, 63, 64, 66, 71, 72, 73, 74, 75, 76, 79, 80, 81 **Unit 3:** 16, 41, 44 **Unit 4:** 13, 52 **Unit 5:** 38, 84 **Unit 6:** 36 **Unit 7:** 14, 39, 56 **Access for Students Acquiring English** 149, 153, 155, 157, 164, 166, 172, 174, 182, 183, 186, 191, 193, 195, 202, 203, 206, 213, 215, 220, 222, 224, 228, 230, 232, 236, 238, 240, 248, 249, 252, 258, 260, 264, 267, 269, 276, 277, 280, 283, 287, 288, 292, 296–298 | **American Stories Videos** War Outside My Window, Teacher of a Freed People, A Walk in Two Worlds, Gusher!, From China to Chinatown, A Child on Strike, Ace of Aces, Jump at the Sun, Broke but Not Broken, A Song for His People, Escaping the Final Solution, The Cold War Comes Home, Justice in Montgomery, Matters of Conscience, Poisoned Playground |

# Correlation to Texas Essential Knowledge and Skills (TEKS)

| TEKS | Pupil's Edition and Teacher's Edition INSTRUCTION | Pupil's Edition and Teacher's Edition APPLICATION | Print Ancillaries | Technology and Transparencies |
|------|------|------|------|------|
| **(25) Social studies skills. The student communicates in written, oral, and visual forms. The student is expected to:** *(continued)* | | | | |
| **(C)** transfer information from one medium to another, including written to visual and statistical to written or visual, using computer software as appropriate; and | R30, R31, R32, R33, R37 | 2, 7, 10-13, 15, 17, 19, 20, 22, 25-27, 29, 30, 32, 34, 36-39, 41, 42, 47-50, 53, 56, 59-63, 65, 67-71, 73, 75-81, 85-87, 90, 91, 96, 99, 105, 110, 113, 115, 116, 117, 122, 125-127, 132-138, 143, 147, 149, 152, 154, 159-162, 164, 165, 169-174, 176, 178, 179, 181-183, 187, 189, 190, 205, 209, 211, 213, 218, 220, 223, 225, 226, 231-233, 235, 239, 240, 247, 249, 250, 255, 259, 263, 266, 269, 271, 272, 278, 281, 283, 285, 289, 291, 297, 299-301, 319, 323, 333, 336, 344, 345, 349, 351, 357, 364, 375, 386, 389, 391, 397, 402, 405, 407, 414, 416, 423, 426, 430, 435, 439, 443, 451, 457, 460, 467, 470, 471, 474, 477, 483, 484, 486, 491-494, 497, 501, 508, 509, 512-514, 517, 519, 521, 522, 526, 529-532, 534, 538, 539, 543-547, 552, 555-560, 564, 566, 567, 570, 572, 575, 577, 580, 582, 591, 594, 600-603, 605-607, 609-611, 613, 616-618, 620, 622, 625, 626, 628, 631, 632, 635, 636, 638, 640, 642, 643, 646, 647, 649, 651, 653, 657, 659, 661, 663, 664, 668, 672, 673, 675, 677, 678, 681, 685, 688, 690, 691, 693, 697, 698, 701, 703, 712-715, 721, 723, 726-728, 732, 733, 738, 740, 743, 747, 749, 751, 753, 755, 757, 759, 766, 769, 770, 773, 777, 784, 792, 795, 801, 804, 807, 809, 813, 814, 816, 817 | **In-Depth Resources:**<br>**Unit 1:** 1, 2, 3, 4, 5, 6, 7, 8, 21, 23-24, 47-48, 51, 69-70, 92-93, 94-95, 99, 118-119, 124-125<br>**Unit 2:** 6, 11, 12, 14, 24, 29, 36, 43, 44, 46, 49, 50, 58, 66, 72, 74, 79<br>**Unit 3:** 1, 2, 3, 4, 5, 7, 13, 17, 24, 25, 26, 27, 29, 35, 37, 44, 47, 48, 49, 50, 51, 58, 61, 64<br>**Unit 4:** 1, 2, 3, 10, 14, 20, 21, 22, 23, 32, 41, 42, 43, 45, 50, 52, 60, 61, 63, 64, 74, 78<br>**Unit 5:** 1, 2, 3, 4, 12, 16, 22, 23, 24, 25, 27, 33, 34, 37, 45, 46, 47, 48, 50, 56, 66, 67, 68, 69, 77, 78<br>**Unit 6:** 1, 2, 3, 10, 12, 13, 14, 17, 20, 21, 22, 29, 30, 31, 32, 33, 39, 40, 41, 42, 43, 52, 53, 55, 56, 57, 58, 64, 65, 66, 68, 73, 74, 75, 77, 80<br>**Unit 7:** 1, 3, 4, 12, 22, 23, 24, 25, 33, 34, 36, 38, 41, 45, 46, 47, 48, 56, 58, 59, 60, 61, 62, 63, 64, 65, 67, 68<br>**Access for Students Acquiring English** 13-16, 19-22, 26-32, 34, 52-56, 59, 60, 62, 63, 67-72, 75, 76, 125, 127, 134, 135, 138, 147, 150-152, 155, 158-162, 164, 167-170, 172, 175-181, 183, 187-190, 193, 196-200, 202, 203, 207-211, 213, 216-219, 222, 225-227, 229, 233-235, 238, 241-245, 248, 249, 253-256, 258, 261-265, 267, 270-274, 276-278, 281-285, 287-295, 297, 298 | **American Stories Videos**<br>War Outside My Window, Teacher of a Freed People, A Walk in Two Worlds, Gusher!, From China to Chinatown, A Child on Strike, Ace of Aces, Jump at the Sun, Broke but Not Broken, A Song for His People, Escaping the Final Solution, The Cold War Comes Home, Justice in Montgomery, Matters of Conscience, Poisoned Playground |

# Correlation to Texas Essential Knowledge and Skills (TEKS)

| TEKS | Pupil's Edition and Teacher's Edition INSTRUCTION | Pupil's Edition and Teacher's Edition APPLICATION | Print Ancillaries | Technology and Transparencies |
|---|---|---|---|---|
| **(25) Social studies skills. The student communicates in written, oral, and visual forms. The student is expected to:** *(continued)* | | | | |
| **(C) transfer information from one medium to another, including written to visual and statistical to written or visual, using computer software as appropriate; and** *(continued)* | | 824, 826, 828, 833, 835, 838, 842, 844, 845, 847, 851, 852, 854–856, 858, 865, 866, 868, 871–873, 875, 877, 881, 883–885, 887, 890 | | |
| **(D) create written, oral, and visual presentations of social studies information.** | S34-1, 108–109, 198–199, 302–303, 408–409, 521–524, 666–667, 790–791, R34, R36, R37 | 3, 5–13, 15–20, 22–30, 32–34, 36–39, 41, 42, 47–50, 53, 56, 59–63, 65, 67–71, 73, 75–83, 85–95, 99–103, 105, 107–111, 113–129, 131–143, 145–147, 149, 152, 153, 155–190, 201, 203–206, 208–211, 213, 215–218, 220–223, 225, 226, 229, 231–233, 235, 237, 238, 240, 242–247, 249, 250, 253–255, 257–259, 261, 263, 264, 266, 268–273, 275, 277–281, 283–285, 287–289, 291, 293–297, 299–301, 311, 312, 316, 325, 327, 331, 334, 335, 337, 338, 345, 349, 351, 357, 358, 361, 364, 365, 368, 375, 377, 379, 380, 382, 383, 385–387, 389–391, 393–395, 397, 399–401, 403, 406, 407, 418, 421, 427, 430, 433, 435–437, 439, 441–443, 445, 447, 449–451, 453, 457, 459–461, 467, 468, 471, 477, 483, 484, 489–501, 503–509, 511–514, 516, 518, 519, 521, 522, 529, 531–535, 537–541, 543, 547, 548, 551–559, 561, 563–568, 570–577, 579–587, 589, 591, 593–595, 597, 598, 601, 603–608, 610–615, 617, 618, 621, 623–627, 629, 630, 632–636, 638–649, 651, 653–657, 659, 661–664, 669, 671–675 | **In-Depth Resources:** **Unit 1:** 1, 2, 3, 4, 5, 6, 7, 8, 9, 10, 11, 12, 13, 22, 23, 25, 27, 28, 29, 32, 33, 34, 35, 36, 37, 38, 40, 41, 42, 48, 50, 51, 52, 53, 56, 57, 58, 64, 70, 71, 72, 73, 74, 75, 76, 77, 78, 79, 80, 81, 82, 83, 84, 85, 86, 93, 94, 97, 98, 99, 100, 103, 104, 105, 106, 107, 108, 109, 112, 113, 119, 121, 122, 123, 124, 127, 130, 135, 136, 137, 138 **Unit 2:** 1, 2, 3, 6, 10, 11, 12, 13, 14, 17, 18, 19, 20, 21, 22, 24, 29, 30, 31, 32, 33, 36, 37, 38, 39, 40, 41, 43, 44, 46, 49, 50, 53, 54, 55, 58, 59, 60, 61, 62, 63, 64, 66, 72, 73, 74, 75, 76, 79, 80, 81 **Unit 3:** 1, 2, 3, 4, 5, 7, 14, 15, 16, 17, 18, 21, 22, 23, 24, 25, 26, 27, 29, 35, 36, 37, 38, 39, 40, 41, 44, 45, 46, 47, 48, 49, 50, 52, 58, 59, 60, 61, 62, 65, 66, 67 **Unit 4:** 1, 2, 3, 5, 10, 12, 13, 14, 16, 17, 18, 19, 20, 21, 22, 23, 25, 31, .32, 33, 34, 35, 38, 39, 40, 41, 42, 43, 45, 50, 51, 52, 53, 54, 57, 58, 59, 60, 61, 62, 63, 64, 66, 73, 74, 77, 78, 79, 82, 83, 84 **Unit 5:** 1, 2, 3, 4, 6, 12, 13, 15, 16, 19, 20, 21, 27, 32, 33, 34–35, 36, 37, 38, 39, 42, 43, 44, 45, 46, 47, 48, 50, 56, 57, 59, 60, 63, 64 | **American Stories Videos** War Outside My Window, Teacher of a Freed People, A Walk in Two Worlds, Gusher!, From China to Chinatown, A Child on Strike, Ace of Aces, Jump at the Sun, Broke but Not Broken, A Song for His People, Escaping the Final Solution, The Cold War Comes Home, Justice in Montgomery, Matters of Conscience, Poisoned Playground **TAKS Practice Transparencies** TT16 |

## Correlation to Texas Essential Knowledge and Skills (TEKS)

| TEKS | Pupil's Edition and Teacher's Edition INSTRUCTION | Pupil's Edition and Teacher's Edition APPLICATION | Print Ancillaries | Technology and Transparencies |
|---|---|---|---|---|
| **(25) Social studies skills. The student communicates in written, oral, and visual forms. The student is expected to:** *(continued)* | | | | |
| **(D) create written, oral, and visual presentations of social studies information.** *(continued)* | | 677, 678, 680–683, 685, 687–693, 695–697, 701–707, 709, 711–716, 718–723, 725–727, 729–735, 737–741, 743–747, 749, 750–753, 755–759, 761, 763, 764, 767, 769–771, 773, 775, 777–780, 782–785, 787–789, 792, 793, 795–801, 803–807, 809, 811–817, 819–827, 829, 831–833, 835–838, 840–845, 847, 849–859, 861–868, 870–873, 875, 877, 878, 880, 881, 887, 890 | 65, 66, 67, 68, 69, 71, 77, 78, 79, 80, 81, 83, 84, 85, 86 **Unit 6:** 1, 2, 3, 5, 10, 12, 13, 14, 17, 18, 19, 20, 21, 22, 24, 29, 30, 31, 32, 33, 36, 37, 38, 39, 40, 41, 42, 43, 45, 52, 54, 55, 56, 57, 58, 61, 68, 69, 64, 65, 66, 68, 73, 74, 75, 76, 77, 80, 81, 82 **Unit 7:** 1, 2, 3, 4, 6, 12, 13, 14, 15, 16, 19, 20, 21, 22, 23, 24, 25, 32, 33, 34, 35, 36, 37, 38, 39, 41, 42, 43, 44, 45, 46, 47, 48, 49, 51, 52, 53, 56, 58, 59, 60, 61, 62, 63, 64, 65, 66, 67, 68 **Access for Students Acquiring English** 14–19, 21, 22, 26–32, 39, 41–49, 52–60, 62, 63, 67–73, 75–77, 80–86, 88, 90–95, 97, 99–103, 106, 107, 110–115, 117, 119–125, 127, 129–133, 136, 137, 141–145, 147, 149–153, 155, 157–162, 164, 166–170, 172, 174–180, 182, 183, 186–191, 193, 195–200, 202, 203, 206–211, 213, 215–220, 222, 224–228, 230, 232–236, 238, 240–246, 248, 249, 252–257, 260–265, 267, 269–274, 276, 277, 280–285, 287–298 | |

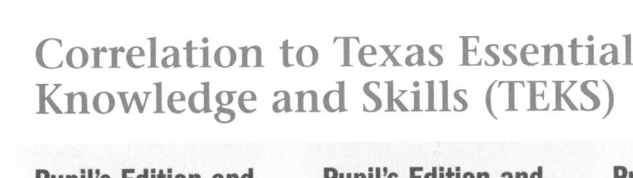

# Correlation to Texas Essential Knowledge and Skills (TEKS)

| TEKS | Pupil's Edition and Teacher's Edition INSTRUCTION | Pupil's Edition and Teacher's Edition APPLICATION | Print Ancillaries | Technology and Transparencies |
|---|---|---|---|---|
| **(26) Social studies skills. The student uses problem-solving and decision-making skills, working independently and with others, in a variety of settings. The student is expected to:** | | | | |
| **(A)** use a problem-solving process to identify a problem, gather information, list and consider options, consider advantages and disadvantages, choose and implement a solution, and evaluate the effectiveness of the solution; and | 108–109, 410, 411, 428, 429, 436, 746, R5, R16 | 22, 71, 73, 87, 94, 109, 146, 169, 183, 189, 250, 264, 266, 281, 289, 329, 359, 360, 401, 411, 418, 421, 427, 429, 436, 439, 443, 451, 457, 460, 461, 468, 482, 484, 514, 516, 556, 559, 577, 585, 587, 595, 601, 615, 627, 692, 727, 746, 769, 815, 827, 841, 845, 853, 857, 873, 887, 883 | **In-Depth Resources:** **Unit 2:** 12, 14 **Unit 6:** 12 **Unit 7:** 46 | **Electronic Library of Primary Sources** Chapters 1, 2, 3, 4, 5, 6, 7, 9, 11, 12, 14, 15, 16, 17, 18, 19, 20, 21, 22, 23, 24, 25, 26 |
| **(B)** use a decision-making process to identify a situation that requires a decision, gather information, identify options, predict consequences, and take action to implement a decision. | 108–109, 428–429, 436, R16, R18, R20 | 71, 73, 101, 102, 129, 138, 160, 163, 180, 181, 261, 291, 329, 341, 344, 345, 360, 365, 379, 386, 395, 402, 407, 418, 421, 427, 429, 436, 439, 443, 451, 457, 460, 503, 523, 532, 534, 541, 544, 552, 555, 559, 563, 577, 584, 585, 587, 595, 601, 615, 627, 692, 695, 697, 709, 746, 759, 775, 801, 805, 811, 817, 823, 841, 853, 867 | **In-Depth Resources:** **Unit 1:** 86 **Unit 2:** 37, 58, 59 **Unit 6:** 12 **Unit 7:** 46 | **Electronic Library of Primary Sources** Chapters 3, 4, 6, 9, 11, 14, 16, 17, 25 |

**TAKS**

# Texas Assessment of Knowledge and Skills (TAKS)

**Grade 11 Exit Level Social Studies**
**TAKS Objectives and TEKS Student Expectations**

---

**TAKS Objective 1** The student will demonstrate an understanding of issues and events in U.S. history.

**(8.1)** **History. The student understands traditional historical points of reference in U.S. history through 1877. The student is expected to:**

    **(C)** explain the significance of the following dates: [1607,] 1776, 1787, [1803,] and 1861–1865.

**(8.4)** **History. The student understands significant political and economic issues of the revolutionary era. The student is expected to:**

    **(B)** explain the roles played by significant individuals during the American Revolution, including [Samuel Adams, Benjamin Franklin, King George III,] Thomas Jefferson, [the Marquis de Lafayette, Thomas Paine,] and George Washington; and

    **(C)** explain the issues surrounding [important events of] the American Revolution, including declaring independence; [writing] the Articles of Confederation, [fighting the battles of Lexington, Concord, Saratoga, and Yorktown; and signing the Treaty of Paris].

**(8.16)** **Government. The student understands the American beliefs and principles reflected in the U.S. Constitution and other important historic documents. The student is expected to:**

    **(C)** identify colonial grievances listed in the Declaration of Independence and explain how those grievances were addressed in the U.S. Constitution and the Bill of Rights.

**(US1)** **History. The student understands traditional historical points of reference in U.S. history from 1877 to the present. The student is expected to:**

    **(A)** identify the major eras in U.S. history from 1877 to the present and describe their defining characteristics;

    **(B)** apply absolute and relative chronology through the sequencing of significant individuals, events, and time periods; and

    **(C)** explain the significance of the following dates: 1898, 1914–1918, 1929, 1941–1945, [and 1957].

**(US3)** **History. The student understands the emergence of the United States as a world power between 1898 and 1920. The student is expected to:**

    **(A)** explain why significant events and individuals, including the Spanish-American War, U.S. expansionism, [Henry Cabot Lodge, Alfred Thayer Mahan,] and Theodore Roosevelt, moved the United States into the position of a world power;

    **(B)** identify the reasons for U.S. involvement in World War I, including unrestricted submarine warfare; and

    **(D)** analyze major issues raised by U.S. involvement in World War I, Wilson's Fourteen Points, and the Treaty of Versailles.

**(US5)** **History. The student understands significant individuals, events, and issues of the 1920s. The student is expected to:**

    **(A)** analyze causes and effects of significant issues such as immigration, the Red Scare, Prohibition, and the changing role of women; and

    **(B)** analyze the impact of significant individuals such as Clarence Darrow, William Jennings Bryan, Henry Ford, and Charles A. Lindbergh.

# Texas Assessment of Knowledge and Skills (TAKS)

**(US6)** **History. The student understands the impact of significant national and international decisions and conflicts from World War II and the Cold War to the present on the United States. The student is expected to:**

**(A)** identify reasons for U.S. involvement in World War II, including the growth of dictatorships and the attack on Pearl Harbor;

**(B)** analyze major issues and events of World War II such as fighting the war on multiple fronts, the internment of Japanese-Americans, the Holocaust, the battle of Midway, the invasion of Normandy, and the development of and Harry Truman's decision to use the atomic bomb;

**(D)** describe U.S. responses to Soviet aggression after World War II, including the Truman Doctrine, the Marshall Plan, the North Atlantic Treaty Organization, [and the Berlin airlift];

**(E)** analyze the conflicts in Korea and Vietnam and describe their domestic and international effects; and

**(F)** describe the impact of the GI Bill, [the election of 1948,] McCarthyism, and Sputnik I.

**TAKS Objective 2** The student will demonstrate an understanding of geographic influences on historical issues and events.

**(US8)** **Geography. The student uses geographic tools to collect, analyze, and interpret data. The student is expected to:**

**(B)** [pose and] answer questions about geographic distributions and patterns shown on maps, graphs, charts, models, [and databases].

**(US9)** **Geography. The student understands the impact of geographic factors on major events. The student is expected to:**

**(A)** analyze the effects of physical and human geographic factors on major events including the building of the Panama Canal.

**(US10)** **Geography. The student understands the effects of migration and immigration on American society. The student is expected to:**

**(A)** analyze the effects of changing demographic patterns resulting from migration within the United States; and

**(B)** analyze the effects of changing demographic patterns resulting from immigration to the United States.

**(US11)** **Geography. The student understands the relationship between population growth and modernization on the physical environment. The student is expected to:**

**(A)** identify the effects of population growth [and distribution and predict future effects] on the physical environment.

**(WG1)** **History. The student understands how geographic contexts (the geography of places in the past) and processes of spatial exchange (diffusion) influenced events in the past and helped to shape the present. The student is expected to:**

**(A)** analyze the effects of physical and human geographic patterns and processes on events in the past [and describe their effects on present conditions, including significant physical features and environmental conditions that influenced migration patterns in the past and shaped the distribution of culture groups today] (correlates with WH12B); and

**(B)** trace the spatial diffusion of a phenomenon and describe its effects on regions of contact such as the spread of bubonic plague, the diffusion and exchange of foods between the New and Old Worlds, [or the diffusion of American slang] (correlates with WH11B).

# Texas Assessment of Knowledge and Skills (TAKS)

**TAKS**

**(WG6) Geography. The student understands the types and patterns of settlement, the factors that affect where people settle, and processes of settlement development over time. The student is expected to:**

**(A)** [locate settlements and] observe patterns in the size and distribution of cities using maps, graphics, and other information (correlates with WH26C).

**(WH23) Science, technology, and society. The student understands how major scientific and mathematical discoveries and technological innovations have affected societies throughout history. The student is expected to:**

**(A)** give examples of [major mathematical and scientific discoveries and] technological innovations that occurred at different periods in history and describe the changes produced by these discoveries and innovations (correlates with WG19A and WG20A).

**TAKS Objective 3** The student will demonstrate an understanding of economic and social influences on historical issues and events.

**(US2) History. The student understands the political, economic, and social changes in the United States from 1877 to 1898. The student is expected to:**

**(B)** analyze economic issues such as industrialization, the growth of railroads, the growth of labor unions, farm issues, and the rise of big business; and

**(C)** analyze social issues such as the treatment of minorities, child labor, growth of cities, and problems of immigrants.

**(US4) History. The student understands the effects of reform and third party movements on American society. The student is expected to:**

**(B)** evaluate the impact of reform leaders such as Susan B. Anthony, W.E.B. DuBois, [and Robert LaFollette] on American society.

**(US7) History. The student understands the impact of the American civil rights movement. The student is expected to:**

**(B)** identify significant leaders of the civil rights movement, including Martin Luther King, Jr.

**(US13) Economics. The student understands significant economic developments between World War I and World War II. The student is expected to:**

**(A)** analyze causes of economic growth and prosperity in the 1920s;

**(B)** analyze the causes of the Great Depression, including the decline in worldwide trade, the stock market crash, and bank failures;

**(C)** analyze the effects of the Great Depression on the U.S. economy and government; and

**(E)** analyze how various New Deal agencies and programs such as the Federal Deposit Insurance Corporation, [the Securities and Exchange Commission,] and Social Security continue to affect the lives of U.S. citizens.

**(US14) Economics. The student understands the economic effects of World War II, the Cold War, and increased worldwide competition on contemporary society. The student is expected to:**

**(A)** describe the economic effects of World War II on the home front, including rationing, female employment, and the end of the Great Depression; and

**(E)** describe the dynamic relationship between U.S. international trade policies and the U.S. free enterprise system.

# Texas Assessment of Knowledge and Skills (TAKS)

**(US21)** **Culture. The student understands how people from various groups, including racial, ethnic, and religious groups, adapt to life in the United States and contribute to our national identity. The student is expected to:**

**(A)** explain actions taken by people from racial, ethnic, and religious groups to expand economic opportunities and political rights in American society; and

**(D)** identify the political, social, and economic contributions of women to American society.

**(US22)** **Science, technology, and society. The student understands the impact of science and technology on the economic development of the United States. The student is expected to:**

**(A)** explain the effects of scientific discoveries and technological innovations such as electric power, the telegraph and telephone, petroleum-based products, medical vaccinations, and computers on the development of the United States; and

**(C)** analyze the impact of technological innovations on the nature of work, the American labor movement, and businesses.

**(US23)** **Science, technology, and society. The student understands the influence of scientific discoveries and technological innovations on daily life in the United States. The student is expected to:**

**(A)** analyze how scientific discoveries and technological innovations, including those in transportation and communication, have changed the standard of living in the United States.

**(WG5)** **Geography. The student understands how political, economic, and social processes shape cultural patterns and characteristics in various places and regions. The student is expected to:**

**(B)** analyze political, economic, social, and demographic data to determine the level of development and standard of living in nations (correlates with WH14C).

**(WG10)** **Economics. The student understands the distribution and characteristics of economic systems throughout the world. The student is expected to:**

**(C)** compare the ways people satisfy their basic needs through the production of goods and services such as subsistence agriculture versus market-oriented agriculture or cottage industries versus commercial industries (correlates with WH14C).

**TAKS Objective 4** The student will demonstrate an understanding of political influences on historical issues and events.

**(8.3)** **History. The student understands the foundations of representative government in the United States. The student is expected to:**

**(A)** explain the reasons for the growth of representative government and institutions during the colonial period.

**(8.16)** **Government. The student understands the American beliefs and principles reflected in the U.S. Constitution and other important historic documents. The student is expected to:**

**(A)** identify the influence of ideas from historic documents including the Magna Carta, the English Bill of Rights, [the Mayflower Compact,] the Declaration of Independence, the Federalist Papers, [and selected anti-federalist writings] on the U.S. system of government; and

**(D)** analyze how the U.S. Constitution reflects the principles of limited government, republicanism, checks and balances, federalism, separation of powers, popular sovereignty, and individual rights.

# Texas Assessment of Knowledge and Skills (TAKS)

**(8.17)** **Government. The student understands the process of changing the U.S. Constitution and the impact of amendments on American society. The student is expected to:**

**(B)** describe the impact of 19th-century amendments including the 13th, 14th, and 15th amendments on life in the United States.

**(8.18)** **Government. The student understands the dynamic nature of the powers of the national government and state governments in a federal system. The student is expected to:**

**(B)** describe historical conflicts arising over the issue of states' rights, including the Nullification Crisis and the Civil War.

**(8.20)** **Citizenship. The student understands the rights and responsibilities of citizens of the United States. The student is expected to:**

**(A)** define and give examples of unalienable rights; and
**(B)** summarize rights guaranteed in the Bill of Rights.

**(8.22)** **Citizenship. The student understands the importance of the expression of different points of view in a democratic society. The student is expected to:**

**(B)** describe the importance of free speech and press in a democratic society.

**(US4)** **History. The student understands the effects of reform and third party movements on American society. The student is expected to:**

**(A)** evaluate the impact of Progressive Era reforms including [initiative, referendum, recall, and] the passage of the 16th and 17th amendments.

**(US7)** **History. The student understands the impact of the American civil rights movement. The student is expected to:**

**(A)** trace the historical development of the civil rights movement in the 18th, 19th, and 20th centuries, including the 13th, 14th, 15th amendments; and
**(C)** evaluate government efforts, including the Civil Rights Act of 1964, to achieve equality in the United States.

**(US17)** **Government. The student understands the impact of constitutional issues on American society in the 20th century. The student is expected to:**

**(A)** analyze the effects of 20th-century landmark U.S. Supreme Court decisions such as *Brown* v. *Board of Education*, [*Regents of the University of California* v. *Bakke, and Reynolds* v. *Sims*].

**(US18)** **Citizenship. The student understands efforts to expand the democratic process. The student is expected to:**

**(B)** evaluate various means of achieving equality of political rights, including the 19th, 24th, and 26th amendments.

# Texas Assessment of Knowledge and Skills (TAKS)

**TAKS Objective 5** The student will use critical thinking skills to analyze social studies information.

**(US24)** **Social studies skills. The student applies critical-thinking skills to organize and use information acquired from a variety of sources including electronic technology. The student is expected to:**

**(A)** [locate and] use primary and secondary sources [such as computer software, databases, media and news services, biographies, interviews, and artifacts] to acquire information about the United States (correlates with 8.30A and WH25B);

**(B)** analyze information by sequencing, categorizing, identifying cause-and-effect relationships, comparing, contrasting, finding the main idea, summarizing, making generalizations [and predictions], and drawing inferences and conclusions (correlates with 8.30B and WH25C);

**(C)** explain and apply different methods that historians use to interpret the past, including the use of primary and secondary sources, points of view, frames of reference, and historical context (correlates with 8.30D and WH25D); and

**(F)** identify bias in written, [oral,] and visual material (correlates with 8.30F and WH25G).

**(WG8)** **Geography. The student understands how people, places, and environments are connected and interdependent. The student is expected to**

**(B)** compare ways that humans depend on, adapt to, and modify the physical environment using [local,] state, national, and international human activities in a variety of cultural and technological contexts (correlates with WH12B and WH12C).

**(WG21)** **Social studies skills. The student applies critical-thinking skills to organize and use information acquired from a variety of sources including electronic technology. The student is expected to:**

**(C)** [construct and] interpret maps to answer geographic questions, infer geographic relationships, and analyze geographic change (correlates with WH11B and WH12C).

**(WH26)** **Social studies skills. The student communicates in written, oral, and visual forms. The student is expected to:**

**(C)** interpret [and create databases, research outlines, bibliographies, and] visuals including graphs, charts, timelines, and maps (correlates with WG21C).

# Correlation to Texas Assessment of Knowledge and Skills (TAKS)

*The Americans: Reconstruction to the 21st Century* provides teachers with many opportunities to help students prepare for the Grade 11 Exit Level Social Studies Texas Assessment of Knowledge and Skills (TAKS). The following correlation shows how the program prepares for the 5 TAKS Objectives and the TEKS Student Expectations.

| | Pupil's Edition and Teacher's Edition INSTRUCTION | Pupil's Edition and Teacher's Edition APPLICATION | Print Ancillaries | Technology and Transparencies |
|---|---|---|---|---|
| **(1) The student will demonstrate an understanding of issues and events in U.S. history.** | | | | |
| **(8.1) History. The student understands traditional historical points of reference in U.S. history through 1877. The student is expected to:** | | | | |
| **(C)** explain the significance of the following dates: [1607,] 1776, 1787, [1803,] and 1861-1965. | 3, 21-23, 44-46, 52, 53, 67-69, 110, 112-114, 154, 155, 168-183 | 3, 21-23, 30, 48, 53, 80, 113, 117, 152, 154, 168-183, 190 | **In-Depth Resources: Unit 1:** 11, 28, 35, 54-56, 57, 108, 109, 112, 124-125, 126-127, 128, 129-130 **Access for Students Acquiring English** 15, 24-25, 26, 28, 31, 65-66, 69, 72 **TAKS Spiraled Content Review** 17-18 | **Electronic Library of Primary Sources** Chapters 1, 2, 4 **American Stories Videos** War Outside My Window **Critical Thinking Transparencies** CT11 **Humanities Transparencies** HT11 |
| **(8.4) History. The student understands significant political and economic issues of the revolutionary era. The student is expected to:** | | | | |
| **(B)** explain the roles played by significant individuals during the American Revolution, including [Samuel Adams, Benjamin Franklin, King George III,] Thomas Jefferson, [the Marquis de Lafayette, Thomas Paine,] and George Washington; and | 46-53, 55, 57, 60-62 | 53, 55, 57, 60, 63, 80 | **In-Depth Resources: Unit 1:** 35, 36, 38, 42 **Access for Students Acquiring English** 24-25, 26, 27, 29 **TAKS Spiraled Content Review** 19-20 | **Electronic Library of Primary Sources** Chapter 2 |
| **(C)** explain the issues surrounding [important events of] the American Revolution, including declaring independence; [writing] the Articles of Confederation; [fighting the battles of Lexington, Concord, Saratoga, and Yorktown; and signing the Treaty of Paris]. | 44, 45, 50, 59, 60, 62, 66, 67 | 50, 59, 60, 62, 63, 66, 67, 71, 80 | **In-Depth Resources: Unit 1:** 36, 37, 47-48 **Access for Students Acquiring English** 24-25, 27 **TAKS Spiraled Content Review** 21-22 | **Humanities Transparencies** HT6 **TAKS Practice Transparencies** TT15, 18 |

# Correlation to Texas Assessment of Knowledge and Skills (TAKS)

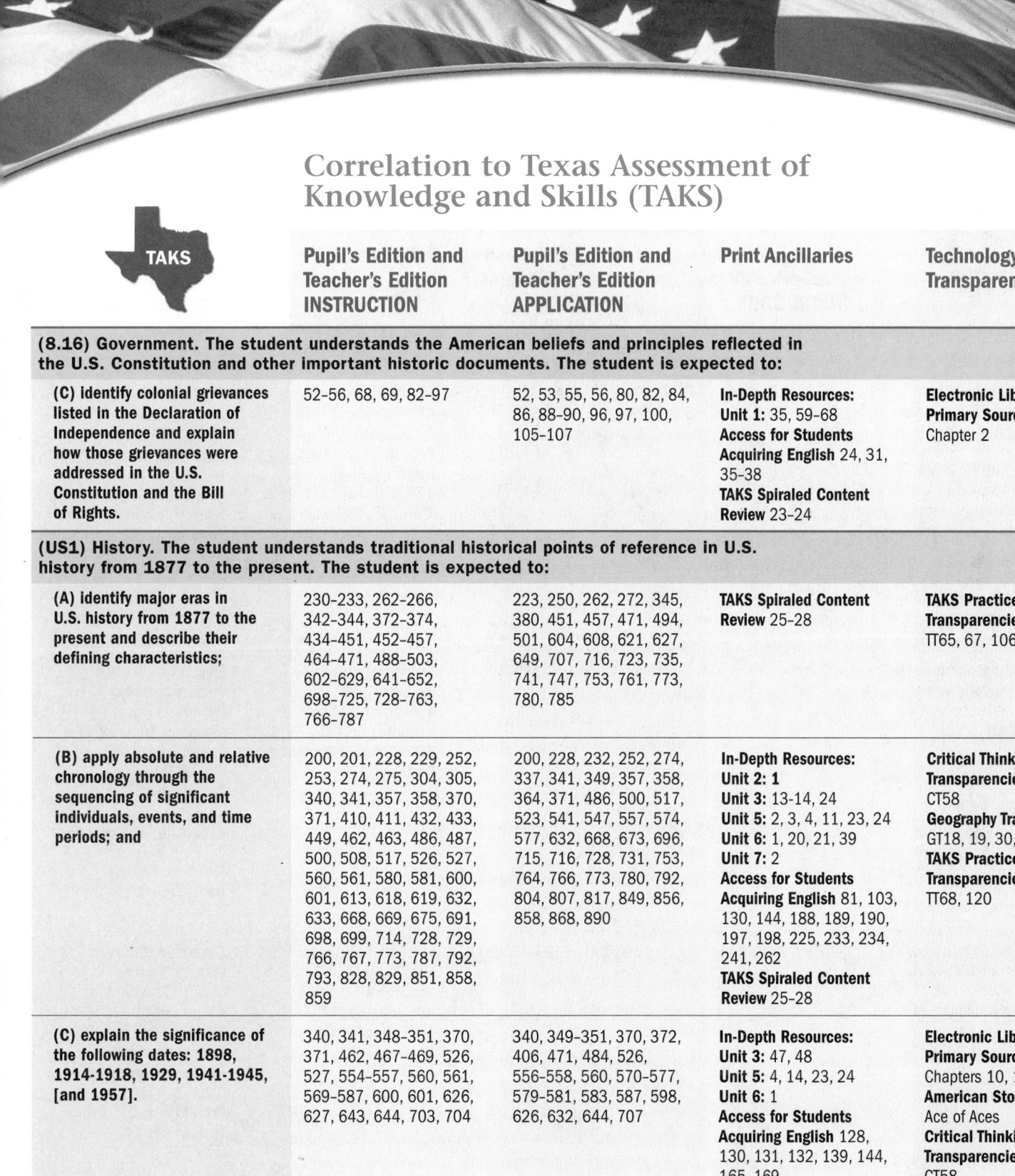

| TAKS | Pupil's Edition and Teacher's Edition INSTRUCTION | Pupil's Edition and Teacher's Edition APPLICATION | Print Ancillaries | Technology and Transparencies |
|---|---|---|---|---|
| **(8.16) Government. The student understands the American beliefs and principles reflected in the U.S. Constitution and other important historic documents. The student is expected to:** | | | | |
| **(C) identify colonial grievances listed in the Declaration of Independence and explain how those grievances were addressed in the U.S. Constitution and the Bill of Rights.** | 52-56, 68, 69, 82-97 | 52, 53, 55, 56, 80, 82, 84, 86, 88-90, 96, 97, 100, 105-107 | **In-Depth Resources:** **Unit 1:** 35, 59-68 **Access for Students Acquiring English** 24, 31, 35-38 **TAKS Spiraled Content Review** 23-24 | **Electronic Library of Primary Sources** Chapter 2 |
| **(US1) History. The student understands traditional historical points of reference in U.S. history from 1877 to the present. The student is expected to:** | | | | |
| **(A) identify major eras in U.S. history from 1877 to the present and describe their defining characteristics;** | 230-233, 262-266, 342-344, 372-374, 434-451, 452-457, 464-471, 488-503, 602-629, 641-652, 698-725, 728-763, 766-787 | 223, 250, 262, 272, 345, 380, 451, 457, 471, 494, 501, 604, 608, 621, 627, 649, 707, 716, 723, 735, 741, 747, 753, 761, 773, 780, 785 | **TAKS Spiraled Content Review** 25-28 | **TAKS Practice Transparencies** TT65, 67, 106 |
| **(B) apply absolute and relative chronology through the sequencing of significant individuals, events, and time periods; and** | 200, 201, 228, 229, 252, 253, 274, 275, 304, 305, 340, 341, 357, 358, 370, 371, 410, 411, 432, 433, 449, 462, 463, 486, 487, 500, 508, 517, 526, 527, 560, 561, 580, 581, 600, 601, 613, 618, 619, 632, 633, 668, 669, 675, 691, 698, 699, 714, 728, 729, 766, 767, 773, 787, 792, 793, 828, 829, 851, 858, 859 | 200, 228, 232, 252, 274, 337, 341, 349, 357, 358, 364, 371, 486, 500, 517, 523, 541, 547, 557, 574, 577, 632, 668, 673, 696, 715, 716, 728, 731, 753, 764, 766, 773, 780, 792, 804, 807, 817, 849, 856, 858, 868, 890 | **In-Depth Resources:** **Unit 2:** 1 **Unit 3:** 13-14, 24 **Unit 5:** 2, 3, 4, 11, 23, 24 **Unit 6:** 1, 20, 21, 39 **Unit 7:** 2 **Access for Students Acquiring English** 81, 103, 130, 144, 188, 189, 190, 197, 198, 225, 233, 234, 241, 262 **TAKS Spiraled Content Review** 25-28 | **Critical Thinking Transparencies** CT58 **Geography Transparencies** GT18, 19, 30, 33 **TAKS Practice Transparencies** TT68, 120 |
| **(C) explain the significance of the following dates: 1898, 1914-1918, 1929, 1941-1945, [and 1957].** | 340, 341, 348-351, 370, 371, 462, 467-469, 526, 527, 554-557, 560, 561, 569-587, 600, 601, 626, 627, 643, 644, 703, 704 | 340, 349-351, 370, 372, 406, 471, 484, 526, 556-558, 560, 570-577, 579-581, 583, 587, 598, 626, 632, 644, 707 | **In-Depth Resources:** **Unit 3:** 47, 48 **Unit 5:** 4, 14, 23, 24 **Unit 6:** 1 **Access for Students Acquiring English** 128, 130, 131, 132, 139, 144, 165, 169 **TAKS Spiraled Content Review** 25-28 | **Electronic Library of Primary Sources** Chapters 10, 14 **American Stories Videos** Ace of Aces **Critical Thinking Transparencies** CT58 **Geography Transparencies** GT18, 19 |

# Correlation to Texas Assessment of Knowledge and Skills (TAKS)

| TAKS | Pupil's Edition and Teacher's Edition INSTRUCTION | Pupil's Edition and Teacher's Edition APPLICATION | Print Ancillaries | Technology and Transparencies |
|------|------|------|------|------|
| **(US3) History. The student understands the emergence of the United States as a world power between 1898 and 1920. The student is expected to:** | | | | |
| **(A)** explain why significant events and individuals, including the Spanish-American War, U.S. expansionism, [Henry Cabot Lodge, Alfred Thayer Mahan,] and Theodore Roosevelt, moved the United States into the position of a world power; | 91, 340, 342–344, 348–351, 356, 359–363, 404, 405 | 344, 346, 348–350, 352, 354, 356, 358–360, 365, 368, 404, 405 | **In-Depth Resources:** **Unit 3:** 24, 25, 26, 27, 36–37, 40, 41, 42–44, 46 **Access for Students Acquiring English** 128–129, 130, 131, 132, 133, 135, 137–138 **TAKS Spiraled Content Review** 29–30 | **Electronic Library of Primary Sources** Chapters 10, 11 **Critical Thinking Transparencies** CT18, 19 **Humanities Transparencies** HT37, 38 **Geography Transparencies** GT18 **TAKS Practice Transparencies** TT69 |
| **(B)** identify the reasons for U.S. involvement in World War I, including unrestricted submarine warfare; and | 372–380 | 371–373, 377–380, 406, 407 | **In-Depth Resources:** **Unit 3:** 47, 59 **Access for Students Acquiring English** 139, 141 **TAKS Spiraled Content Review** 31–32 | **Electronic Library of Primary Sources** Chapter 11 **American Stories Videos** Ace of Aces **Critical Thinking Transparencies** CT19 **Geography Transparencies** GT19 **TAKS Practice Transparencies** TT71 |
| **(D)** analyze major issues raised by U.S. involvement in World War I, Wilson's Fourteen Points, and the Treaty of Versailles. | 390, 391, 398–402 | 390, 391, 399–401, 403, 406 | **In-Depth Resources:** **Unit 3:** 50, 57–58 **Access for Students Acquiring English** 140, 144 **TAKS Spiraled Content Review** 31–32 | **Electronic Library of Primary Sources** Chapter 11 **American Stories Videos** Ace of Aces **Critical Thinking Transparencies** CT19 **TAKS Practice Transparencies** TT74 |

# Correlation to Texas Assessment of Knowledge and Skills (TAKS)

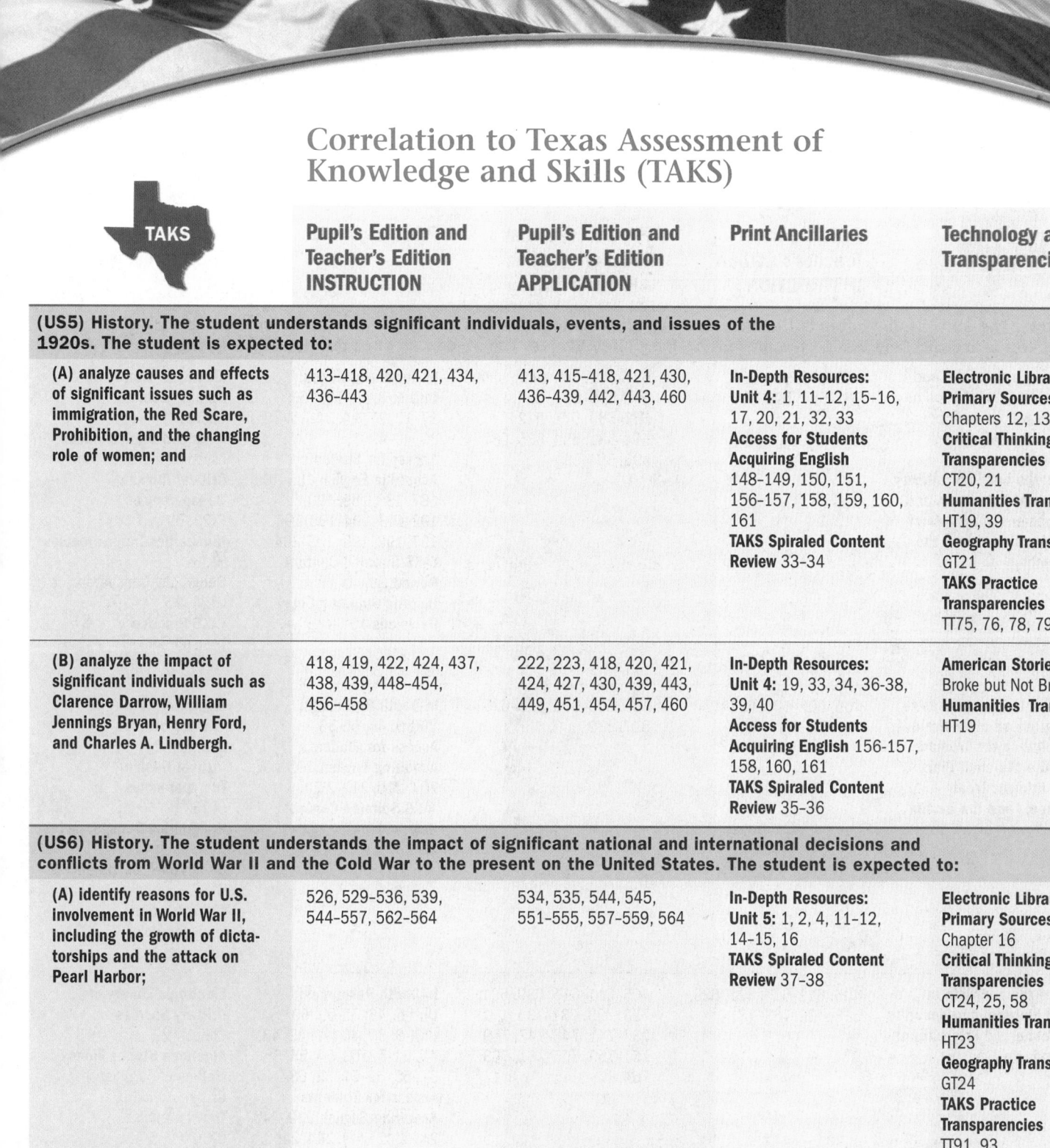

| TAKS | Pupil's Edition and Teacher's Edition INSTRUCTION | Pupil's Edition and Teacher's Edition APPLICATION | Print Ancillaries | Technology and Transparencies |
|---|---|---|---|---|
| **(US5) History. The student understands significant individuals, events, and issues of the 1920s. The student is expected to:** | | | | |
| **(A) analyze causes and effects of significant issues such as immigration, the Red Scare, Prohibition, and the changing role of women; and** | 413–418, 420, 421, 434, 436–443 | 413, 415–418, 421, 430, 436–439, 442, 443, 460 | **In-Depth Resources:** Unit 4: 1, 11–12, 15–16, 17, 20, 21, 32, 33 **Access for Students Acquiring English** 148–149, 150, 151, 156–157, 158, 159, 160, 161 **TAKS Spiraled Content Review** 33–34 | **Electronic Library of Primary Sources** Chapters 12, 13, 15 **Critical Thinking Transparencies** CT20, 21 **Humanities Transparencies** HT19, 39 **Geography Transparencies** GT21 **TAKS Practice Transparencies** TT75, 76, 78, 79 |
| **(B) analyze the impact of significant individuals such as Clarence Darrow, William Jennings Bryan, Henry Ford, and Charles A. Lindbergh.** | 418, 419, 422, 424, 437, 438, 439, 448–454, 456–458 | 222, 223, 418, 420, 421, 424, 427, 430, 439, 443, 449, 451, 454, 457, 460 | **In-Depth Resources:** Unit 4: 19, 33, 34, 36–38, 39, 40 **Access for Students Acquiring English** 156–157, 158, 160, 161 **TAKS Spiraled Content Review** 35–36 | **American Stories Videos** Broke but Not Broken **Humanities Transparencies** HT19 |
| **(US6) History. The student understands the impact of significant national and international decisions and conflicts from World War II and the Cold War to the present on the United States. The student is expected to:** | | | | |
| **(A) identify reasons for U.S. involvement in World War II, including the growth of dictatorships and the attack on Pearl Harbor;** | 526, 529–536, 539, 544–557, 562–564 | 534, 535, 544, 545, 551–555, 557–559, 564 | **In-Depth Resources:** Unit 5: 1, 2, 4, 11–12, 14–15, 16 **TAKS Spiraled Content Review** 37–38 | **Electronic Library of Primary Sources** Chapter 16 **Critical Thinking Transparencies** CT24, 25, 58 **Humanities Transparencies** HT23 **Geography Transparencies** GT24 **TAKS Practice Transparencies** TT91, 93 |

# Correlation to Texas Assessment of Knowledge and Skills (TAKS)

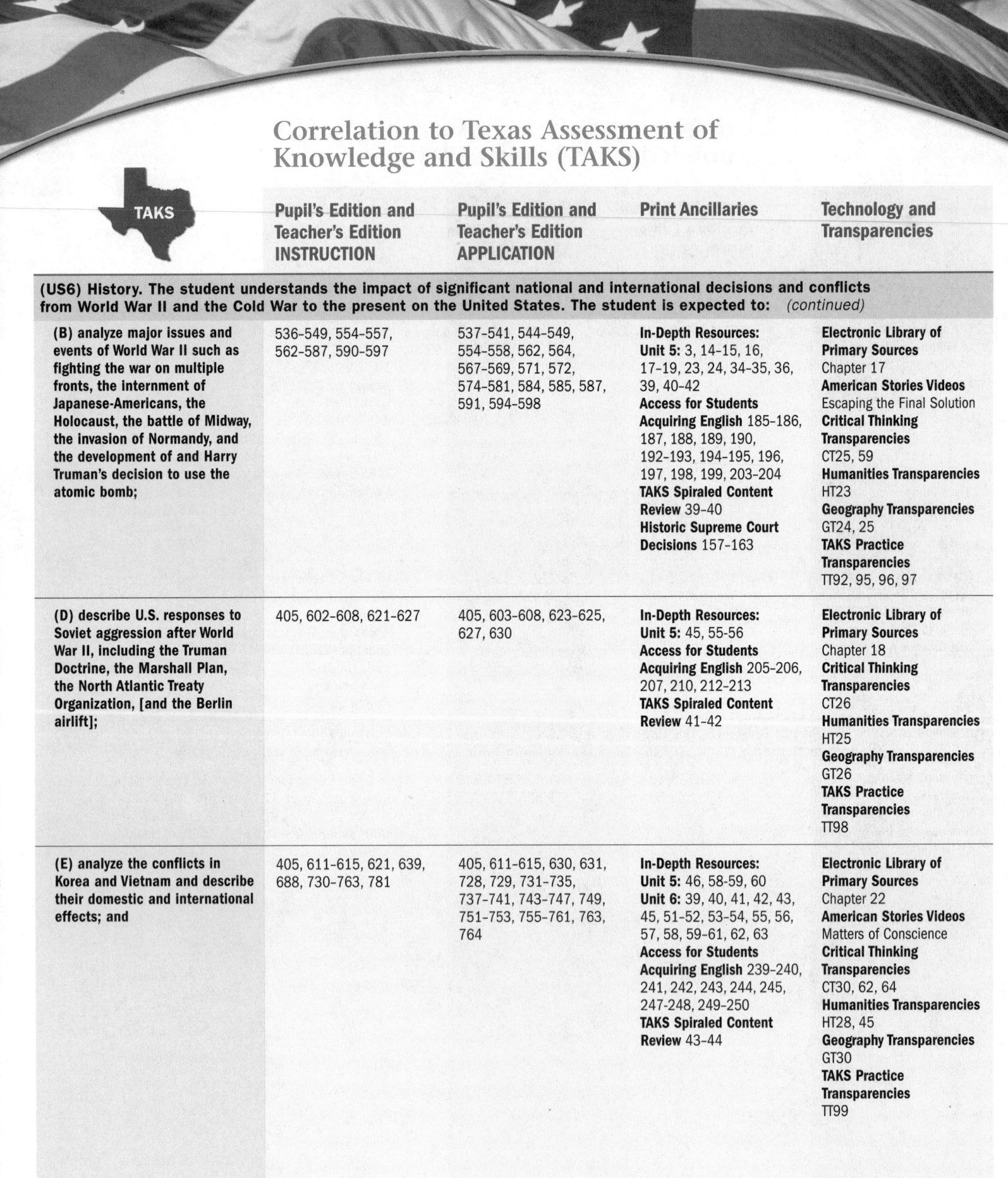

| TAKS | Pupil's Edition and Teacher's Edition INSTRUCTION | Pupil's Edition and Teacher's Edition APPLICATION | Print Ancillaries | Technology and Transparencies |
|---|---|---|---|---|
| **(US6) History. The student understands the impact of significant national and international decisions and conflicts from World War II and the Cold War to the present on the United States. The student is expected to:** *(continued)* | | | | |
| **(B) analyze major issues and events of World War II such as fighting the war on multiple fronts, the internment of Japanese-Americans, the Holocaust, the battle of Midway, the invasion of Normandy, and the development of and Harry Truman's decision to use the atomic bomb;** | 536–549, 554–557, 562–587, 590–597 | 537–541, 544–549, 554–558, 562, 564, 567–569, 571, 572, 574–581, 584, 585, 587, 591, 594–598 | **In-Depth Resources:** Unit 5: 3, 14–15, 16, 17–19, 23, 24, 34–35, 36, 39, 40–42 **Access for Students Acquiring English** 185–186, 187, 188, 189, 190, 192–193, 194–195, 196, 197, 198, 199, 203–204 **TAKS Spiraled Content Review** 39–40 **Historic Supreme Court Decisions** 157–163 | **Electronic Library of Primary Sources** Chapter 17 **American Stories Videos** Escaping the Final Solution **Critical Thinking Transparencies** CT25, 59 **Humanities Transparencies** HT23 **Geography Transparencies** GT24, 25 **TAKS Practice Transparencies** TT92, 95, 96, 97 |
| **(D) describe U.S. responses to Soviet aggression after World War II, including the Truman Doctrine, the Marshall Plan, the North Atlantic Treaty Organization, [and the Berlin airlift];** | 405, 602–608, 621–627 | 405, 603–608, 623–625, 627, 630 | **In-Depth Resources:** Unit 5: 45, 55–56 **Access for Students Acquiring English** 205–206, 207, 210, 212–213 **TAKS Spiraled Content Review** 41–42 | **Electronic Library of Primary Sources** Chapter 18 **Critical Thinking Transparencies** CT26 **Humanities Transparencies** HT25 **Geography Transparencies** GT26 **TAKS Practice Transparencies** TT98 |
| **(E) analyze the conflicts in Korea and Vietnam and describe their domestic and international effects; and** | 405, 611–615, 621, 639, 688, 730–763, 781 | 405, 611–615, 630, 631, 728, 729, 731–735, 737–741, 743–747, 749, 751–753, 755–761, 763, 764 | **In-Depth Resources:** Unit 5: 46, 58–59, 60 Unit 6: 39, 40, 41, 42, 43, 45, 51–52, 53–54, 55, 56, 57, 58, 59–61, 62, 63 **Access for Students Acquiring English** 239–240, 241, 242, 243, 244, 245, 247–248, 249–250 **TAKS Spiraled Content Review** 43–44 | **Electronic Library of Primary Sources** Chapter 22 **American Stories Videos** Matters of Conscience **Critical Thinking Transparencies** CT30, 62, 64 **Humanities Transparencies** HT28, 45 **Geography Transparencies** GT30 **TAKS Practice Transparencies** TT99 |

# Correlation to Texas Assessment of Knowledge and Skills (TAKS)

**TAKS**

| | Pupil's Edition and Teacher's Edition **INSTRUCTION** | Pupil's Edition and Teacher's Edition **APPLICATION** | Print Ancillaries | Technology and Transparencies |
|---|---|---|---|---|
| **(US6) History. The student understands the impact of significant national and international decisions and conflicts from World War II and the Cold War to the present on the United States. The student is expected to:** *(continued)* | | | | |
| **(F) describe the impact of the GI Bill, [the election of 1948,] McCarthyism, and Sputnik I.** | 589, 592, 616–621, 626, 627, 635, 638, 639 | 589, 595, 617–621, 626, 627, 630, 631, 634, 635, 637, 638, 640, 664 | **In-Depth Resources: Unit 5:** 47 **Access for Students Acquiring English** 206 **TAKS Spiraled Content Review** 45–46 | **Electronic Library of Primary Sources** Chapter 20 **American Stories Videos** The Cold War Comes Home **Critical Thinking Transparencies** CT26, 60 **Humanities Transparencies** HT41 **TAKS Practice Transparencies** TT100, 101, 102 |
| **(2) The student will demonstrate an understanding of geographic influences on historical issues and events.** | | | | |
| **(US8) Geography. The student uses geographic tools to collect, analyze, and interpret data. The student is expected to:** | | | | |
| **(B) [pose and] answer questions about geographic distributions and patterns shown on maps, graphs, charts, models, [and databases].** | 69, 72, 73, 159, 160, 169–171, 176, 179, 205, 209, 226, 231, 239, 255, 263, 323, 344, 345, 349, 357, 375, 386, 400, 416, 423, 474, 520, 521, 701, 816, 827, 846, 847, 866, 885 | 7, 15, 17, 25, 29, 32, 38, 41, 42, 59, 62, 69, 73, 115, 116, 125, 132, 134, 136, 147, 159, 160, 167, 169, 170, 171, 176, 179, 190, 205, 209, 226, 231, 239, 255, 263, 323, 344, 345, 349, 357, 375, 376, 383, 386, 400, 416, 423, 430, 474, 484, 521, 530, 532, 538, 545, 556, 572, 575, 580, 591, 594, 604–606, 613, 624, 675, 681, 685, 701, 733, 749, 775, 816, 827, 844, 847, 866, 885, 890 | **In-Depth Resources: Unit 1:** 1, 2, 3, 4, 5, 6, 7, 8, 26, 27, 29, 48, 64, 92, 93, 94–95, 119, 120 **Unit 2:** 11, 29, 49, 72 **Unit 3:** 14, 35, 36, 58 **Unit 4:** 31, 50, 73, 74 **Unit 5:** 12, 33 **Unit 6:** 10, 29, 51, 73 **Unit 7:** 33, 34, 56 **Access for Students Acquiring English** 19, 21, 22, 34, 41, 62, 63, 75, 76, 85, 88, 97, 127, 136, 137, 147, 155, 164, 172, 182, 193, 201, 203, 213, 229, 238, 248, 249, 258, 276, 277, 287 **TAKS Spiraled Content Review** 47–50 | **TAKS Practice Transparencies** TT13, 39, 103, 131 |

# Correlation to Texas Assessment of Knowledge and Skills (TAKS)

| TAKS | Pupil's Edition and Teacher's Edition INSTRUCTION | Pupil's Edition and Teacher's Edition APPLICATION | Print Ancillaries | Technology and Transparencies |
|---|---|---|---|---|
| **(US9) Geography. The student understands the impact of geographic factors on major events. The student is expected to:** | | | | |
| (A) analyze the effects of physical and human geographic factors on major events including the building of the Panama Canal. | 38, 59, 62, 136, 170, 171, 176, 179, 203, 204, 208–218, 236–240, 359–363, 366, 367, 375, 386, 416, 422–424, 449, 453, 474, 520, 521, 528–533, 538–541, 556, 572, 575, 580, 605, 613, 673–678, 733, 738–740, 749 | 38, 59, 62, 80, 136, 170, 176, 179, 190, 203, 208, 209, 211, 212, 216, 218, 226, 236–240, 359–361, 366–368, 375, 386, 416, 423, 449, 474, 477, 484, 521, 530, 532, 538, 556, 558, 572, 575, 580, 598, 605, 613, 675, 677, 678, 696, 733, 738–740, 749 | **In-Depth Resources:** **Unit 1:** 7, 21, 47–48, 69–70, 118–119, 138 **Unit 2:** 2, 3, 50–51 **Unit 3:** 26, 27, 34–35, 36–37, 41 **Unit 4:** 49–50, 53 **Unit 5:** 11–12, 32–33 **Access for Students Acquiring English** 79–80, 82, 83, 87–88, 89, 92, 99, 128–129, 135–136, 192–193, 194–195, 197, 198, 247 **TAKS Spiraled Content Review** 51–52 | **Electronic Library of Primary Sources** Chapters 20, 22 **American Stories Videos** Gusher!, Broke but Not Broken, Matters of Conscience **Critical Thinking Transparencies** CT9, 11, 13 **Humanities Transparencies** HT14 **Geography Transparencies** GT18 **TAKS Practice Transparencies** TT70 |
| **(US10) Geography. The student understands the effects of migration and immigration on American society. The student is expected to:** | | | | |
| (A) analyze the effects of changing demographic patterns resulting from migration within the United States; and | 72, 73, 77, 122–126, 130–133, 137, 138, 160, 203, 204, 212–216, 238, 257, 262–265, 276–278, 288, 313, 314, 392, 395, 422–424, 428, 434–437, 452–457, 474, 475, 590–592, 660, 661, 684, 685, 701, 702, 768, 769, 846, 847, 882–884, 888, 889 | 73, 77, 125, 127, 131, 132, 137, 138, 152, 159, 160, 203, 211–217, 226, 238, 262–264, 266, 272, 278, 392–395, 423, 429, 435, 453, 460, 474, 484, 591, 685, 701, 702, 769, 775, 844, 847, 883, 887, 889 | **In-Depth Resources:** **Unit 1:** 79, 94–95, 101–102, 118–119, 138 **Unit 2:** 1, 2, 3, 28, 40, 48–49, 50–51, 53, 55 **Unit 4:** 49–50 **Unit 5:** 67, 69, 78, 79, 81, 82–83 **Unit 7:** 32–33, 48 **Access for Students Acquiring English** 63–64, 79–80, 81, 82, 83, 98–99, 101, 284 **TAKS Spiraled Content Review** 53–54 | **Electronic Library of Primary Sources** Chapter 17 **American Stories Videos** A Walk in Two Worlds, Jump at the Sun, Broke but Not Broken **Critical Thinking Transparencies** CT9, 12, 13, 15, 37, 47, 49, 55, 61 **Humanities Transparencies** HT15, 16, 42 **Geography Transparencies** GT7, 8, 9, 31, 38 **TAKS Practice Transparencies** TT27, 47, 81 |

# Correlation to Texas Assessment of Knowledge and Skills (TAKS)

| TAKS | Pupil's Edition and Teacher's Edition **INSTRUCTION** | Pupil's Edition and Teacher's Edition **APPLICATION** | **Print Ancillaries** | **Technology and Transparencies** |
|---|---|---|---|---|
| **(US10) Geography. The student understands the effects of migration and immigration on American society. The student is expected to:** *(continued)* | | | | |
| **(B)** analyze the effects of changing demographic patterns resulting from immigration to the United States. | 34, 78, 137, 138, 254–259, 261, 277, 284, 289, 344, 345, 392, 395, 414–417, 428, 446–448, 506, 507, 543, 544, 660, 661, 768, 769, 885–889 | 42, 137, 138, 252, 254–256, 259–261, 272, 284, 344, 393, 414, 416, 429, 447, 474, 484, 507, 543, 544, 661, 663, 664, 769, 885–887, 889–891 | **In-Depth Resources:** **Unit 2:** 39, 40 **Unit 7:** 48, 49, 50–51, 59 **Access for Students Acquiring English** 98, 100, 275–276, 289 **TAKS Spiraled Content Review** 55–56 | **Electronic Library of Primary Sources** Chapter 17 **American Stories Videos** From China to Chinatown, A Child on Strike, A Song for His People **Critical Thinking Transparencies** CT47, 69, 70, 71 **Geography Transparencies** GT15, 31 **TAKS Practice Transparencies** TT55 |
| **(US11) Geography. The student understands the relationship between population growth and modernization on the physical environment. The student is expected to:** | | | | |
| **(A)** identify the effects of population growth [and distribution and predict future effects] on the physical environment. | 234, 235, 264–266, 276–279, 322–324, 434–439, 452–454, 643–647, 650, 651, 820–825, 881, 883 | 208, 234, 235, 252, 253, 262, 264–266, 272, 279, 323, 324, 452, 453, 643, 646, 649, 651, 664, 820, 822, 825, 881, 883 | **In-Depth Resources:** **Unit 2:** 20, 40 **Unit 4:** 30–31 **Access for Students Acquiring English** 214–215, 217, 260, 264 **TAKS Spiraled Content Review** 57–58 | **American Stories Videos** Broke but Not Broken **Critical Thinking Transparencies** CT13, 47 **TAKS Practice Transparencies** TT1, 50 |

# Correlation to Texas Assessment of Knowledge and Skills (TAKS)

| TAKS | Pupil's Edition and Teacher's Edition INSTRUCTION | Pupil's Edition and Teacher's Edition APPLICATION | Print Ancillaries | Technology and Transparencies |
|---|---|---|---|---|
| **(WG1) History. The student understands how geographic contexts (the geography of places in the past) and processes of spatial exchange (diffusion) influenced events in the past and helped to shape the present. The student is expected to:** | | | | |
| (A) analyze the effects of physical and human geographic patterns and processes on events in the past [and describe their effects on present conditions, including significant physical features and environmental conditions that influenced migration patterns in the past and shaped the distribution of culture groups today]; and | 21-23, 31-34, 37, 38, 50, 116, 117, 125, 131-138, 156-161, 170, 175-177, 180, 181, 186, 188, 203-206, 214-216, 230-232, 234-239, 255-258, 262, 263, 322-324, 342-350, 353, 357, 360, 361, 366, 367, 375, 376, 378, 379, 403, 423, 424, 434, 452, 453, 473, 474, 538, 571-576, 578-580, 591, 605, 607, 635, 660, 738-740, 869, 870, 872, 873, 882, 883, 885, 886, US2-US15 | 25, 30, 37, 42, 59, 62, 115-117, 125, 131-134, 138, 150, 159, 160, 165, 168-170, 176, 177, 180, 187, 190, 204, 205, 207, 215, 218, 226, 231, 235, 237-240, 250, 255, 263, 266, 272, 323, 341, 343-345, 349, 353, 357, 361, 367, 375, 376, 379, 380, 406, 423, 427, 474, 484, 538, 572, 575, 580, 591, 598, 605, 607, 608, 630, 738, 739, 741, 764, 872, 873, 883, 885 | **In-Depth Resources:** **Unit 1:** 47-48, 79, 92-93, 101-103 **Unit 2:** 2, 3, 12, 20, 21, 39, 40 **Unit 3:** 30, 31, 32, 33, 34-35, 36-37, 41, 48, 49, 57-58 **Unit 4:** 42, 49-50, 74-75 **Unit 5:** 1, 2, 4, 11-12, 14-15, 32-33, 45, 46, 67, 78 **Unit 6:** 9-10, 39, 40, 51-52, 53-54 **Unit 7:** 4, 32-33, 46, 48, 55-56, 67 **Access for Students Acquiring English** 12, 17, 33-34, 51, 54, 61-62, 66, 74-75, 76-77, 83, 98, 100, 107-108, 128-129, 130, 131, 132, 133, 135-136, 137-138, 146-147, 168, 171-172, 183-184, 192-193, 195, 198, 201-202, 206, 210, 231, 240, 244, 247-248, 249-250, 260, 264, 275-276 **TAKS Spiraled Content Review** 59-60 | **Electronic Library of Primary Sources** Chapters 3, 7, 10, 12, 17 **American Stories Videos** From China to Chinatown Broke But Not Broken **Critical Thinking Transparencies** CT1, 3, 6, 9, 13, 14, 15, 18, 36, 43, 49 **Humanities Transparencies** HT18 **Geography Transparencies** GT2, 12, 13, 18, 24, 25, 30, 36 **TAKS Practice Transparencies** TT6, 34, 83 |
| (B) trace the spatial diffusion of a phenomenon and describe its effects on regions of contact such as the spread of bubonic plague, the diffusion and exchange of foods between the New and Old Worlds, [or the diffusion of American slang]. | 15, 130-133, 203, 204, 211, 214-216, 445, 456, 457, 532, 533, 706, 707, 782, US2-US15 | 15, 133, 211, 215, 218, 456, 457, 532 | **In-Depth Resources:** **Unit 1:** 79 **Unit 2:** 3 **Unit 4:** 4, 11-12 **Unit 6:** 20, 21, 66 **Access for Students Acquiring English** 14, 54, 83, 231, 234, 240 | **TAKS Spiraled Content Review** 61-62 **Electronic Library of Primary Sources** Chapter 5 **American Stories, Videos** Justice in Montgomery **Critical Thinking Transparencies** CT9, 29, 47 **Humanities Transparencies** HT27 **TAKS Practice Transparencies** TT4, 5 |

# Correlation to Texas Assessment of Knowledge and Skills (TAKS)

| TAKS | Pupil's Edition and Teacher's Edition INSTRUCTION | Pupil's Edition and Teacher's Edition APPLICATION | Print Ancillaries | Technology and Transparencies |
|---|---|---|---|---|
| **(WG6) Geography. The student understands the types and patterns of settlement, the factors that affect where people settle, and processes of settlement development over time. The student is expected to:** | | | | |
| **(A) [locate settlements and] observe patterns in the size and distribution of cities using maps, graphics, and other information.** | 21-23, 25, 216, 238, 239, 263, 264-266, 434, 635 | 22, 25, 238, 239, 263, 264, 266 | **In-Depth Resources:** **Unit 1:** 48-49, 55 **Access for Students Acquiring English** 89, 98-99, 108, 109 **TAKS Spiraled Content Review** 63-64 | **Critical Thinking Transparencies** CT7, 15, 49, 61 **Geography Transparencies** GT9 **TAKS Practice Transparencies** TT12, 58 |
| **(WH23) Science, technology, and society. The student understands how major scientific and mathematical discoveries and technological innovations have affected societies throughout history. The student is expected to:** | | | | |
| **(A) give examples of [major mathematical and scientific discoveries and] technological innovations that occurred at different periods in history and describe the changes produced by these discoveries and innovations.** | 12, 24, 34, 35, 120, 121, 139-141, 211, 214, 215, 217, 231-233, 264, 274, 276-281, 299, 306-314, 359, 360, 361, 372-380, 383-385, 392, 395, 422-426, 438, 439, 441-443, 446, 447-451, 510-512, 520, 521, 588, 589, 618, 619, 622, 623, 626, 627, 641-643, 646, 647, 650-655, 679-681, 738-740, 796, 808, 809, 811-814, 822-825, 841, 869-871, 876-881 | 12, 24, 35, 39, 121, 140, 141, 152, 211, 215, 217, 230-233, 236-238, 250, 277-281, 299, 300, 308, 309, 311, 314, 321, 361, 376, 383-385, 387, 394, 406, 422-425, 427, 430, 438, 439, 442, 443, 448, 449, 451, 460, 511, 521, 522, 567, 588, 589, 623, 626, 641-643, 646, 649, 651, 653, 654, 657, 664, 681, 683, 738, 739, 741, 809, 811, 813, 814, 817, 825-827, 841, 870, 871, 873, 877-881, 890, 891 | **In-Depth Resources:** **Unit 1:** 29, 80, 138 **Unit 2:** 3, 20, 30, 48-49, 61 **Unit 3:** 34-35, 41 **Unit 4:** 3, 9-10, 19, 30-31 **Unit 5:** 39 **Unit 7:** 48, 52 **Access for Students Acquiring English** 89-90, 91, 92, 93, 94, 149, 152, 157, 160, 163-164, 266-267, 280, 282, 283, 286-287 **TAKS Spiraled Content Review** 65-66 | **Electronic Library of Primary Sources** Chapters 8, 17 **American Stories Videos** Gusher!, From China to Chinatown, A Child on Strike, Ace of Aces, Broke but Not Broken, Matters of Conscience **Critical Thinking Transparencies** CT5, 7, 8, 13, 35, 36, 60 **Humanities Transparencies** HT18, 24, 41, 42 **Geography Transparencies** GT13, 14, 16, 17, 22, 27 **TAKS Practice Transparencies** TT25, 107 |

# Correlation to Texas Assessment of Knowledge and Skills (TAKS)

TAKS

| | Pupil's Edition and Teacher's Edition INSTRUCTION | Pupil's Edition and Teacher's Edition APPLICATION | Print Ancillaries | Technology and Transparencies |
|---|---|---|---|---|
| **(3) The student will demonstrate an understanding of economic and social influences on historical issues and events.** | | | | |
| **(US2) History. The student understands the political, economic, and social changes in the United States from 1877 to 1898. The student is expected to:** | | | | |
| **(B) analyze economic issues such as industrialization, the growth of railroads, the growth of labor unions, farm issues, and the rise of various big business; and** | 208-210, 216-221, 230-249, 271, 281, 313, 314, 320, 323, 324, 328, 329, 332, 334, 354, 355 | 208, 209, 211, 214-223, 226, 229-250, 270, 271, 304, 305, 309, 320, 325, 327, 333, 334, 354 | **In-Depth Resources:** **Unit 2:** 2, 3, 19, 20, 21, 22, 28-29, 31, 32, 33, 37, 38, 40, 48-49 **Unit 3:** 1 **Access for Students Acquiring English** 89-90, 91, 92, 93, 94, 96-97, 98-99, 101 **TAKS Spiraled Content Review** 67-68 | **Electronic Library of Primary Sources** Chapter 6 **American Stories Videos** Gusher!, A Child on Strike **Critical Thinking Transparencies** CT13, 14, 15, 17, 48, 49 **Humanities Transparencies** HT14, 35 **Geography Transparencies** GT13, 14, 17 **TAKS Practice Transparencies** TT51, 52, 53, 54 |
| **(C) analyze social issues such as the treatment of minorities, child labor, growth of cities, and problems of immigrants.** | 234, 235, 245, 246, 254-259, 260-266, 284-289, 306-317, 320-327, 334-337 | 234, 235, 238, 245, 252, 253, 256, 257, 259, 261, 264-266, 282, 283, 287-290, 300, 304-312, 314-316, 322, 327, 335, 337 | **In-Depth Resources:** **Unit 2:** 1, 12, 18, 31, 37, 39, 40, 46, 48-49, 50-51, 53, 54, 55, 56-58, 59, 62, 63, 71-72, 75, 76, 80 **Unit 3:** 1, 2, 3, 7, 15, 16, 17, 19-21, 22, 23 **Access for Students Acquiring English** 79, 81, 98-99, 100, 101, 107-108,109-110, 112, 113, 118-119, 121 **TAKS Spiraled Content Review** 69-70 **Historic Supreme Court Decisions** 67-72 | **Electronic Library of Primary Sources** Chapters 6, 7, 9 **American Stories Videos** A Walk in Two Worlds, From China to Chinatown, A Child on Strike **Critical Thinking Transparencies** CT14, 15, 17, 49, 50, 51 **Humanities Transparencies** HT15, 16 **TAKS Practice Transparencies** TT56, 60 |

# Correlation to Texas Assessment of Knowledge and Skills (TAKS)

| TAKS | Pupil's Edition and Teacher's Edition INSTRUCTION | Pupil's Edition and Teacher's Edition APPLICATION | Print Ancillaries | Technology and Transparencies |
|---|---|---|---|---|
| **(US4) History. The student understands the effects of reform and third party movements on American society. The student is expected to:** | | | | |
| (B) evaluate the impact of reform leaders such as Susan B. Anthony, W.E.B. DuBois, [and Robert LaFollette] on American society. | 158–161, 163, 164, 219, 221–223, 265, 266, 270, 284, 285, 287, 288, 291, 307, 308, 310, 313–316, 325, 327, 332–337, 392–395, 453, 454, 770, 776, 778 | 158, 159, 161, 164, 165, 171, 172, 174, 188, 221, 223, 266, 281, 285, 288, 289, 291, 300, 307, 308, 310, 312, 316, 325, 392, 454, 773, 788 | **In-Depth Resources:** **Unit 1:** 136, 137 **Unit 2:** 38, 59, 75, 76, 80 **Unit 3:** 2, 18, 22, 23 **Unit 4:** 23, 59, 60, 61, 62, 83 **Unit 6:** 14, 19, 24, 37, 38, 63, 74, 75, 76, 81, 82 **Access for Students Acquiring English** 56, 67, 112, 118–119, 121, 122, 123, 161, 251, 254 **TAKS Spiraled Content Review** 71–72 | **Electronic Library of Primary Sources** Chapters 2, 3, 4, 7, 9, 15, 21, 23 **American Stories Videos** Teacher of a Freed People, A Walk in Two Worlds, A Child on Strike, Jump at the Sun, A Song for His People, Justice in Montgomery **TAKS Practice Transparencies** TT63 |
| **(US7) History. The student understands the impact of the American civil rights movement. The student is expected to:** | | | | |
| (B) identify significant leaders of the civil rights movement, including Martin Luther King, Jr. | 85, 145, 146, 148, 149, 172, 173, 177, 324, 325, 335–337, 392, 393, 453, 454, 566, 593, 671, 702, 704–706, 712, 714, 716, 718–722, 750, 770, 776, 843–845 | 149, 173, 325, 454, 701, 705–707, 719–721, 723, 726, 727, 770, 771, 773, 780, 788, 845 | **In-Depth Resources:** **Unit 1:** 34, 72, 81, 100, 104, 136, 137 **Unit 2:** 75, 76, 80 **Unit 3:** 62 **Unit 4:** 18, 23 **Unit 6:** 37, 38 **Access for Students Acquiring English** 52, 56, 112, 231–232, 234, 251–252 **TAKS Spiraled Content Review** 73–74 | **Electronic Library of Primary Sources** Chapters 3, 4, 21, 23 **American Stories Videos** Teacher of a Freed People, A Walk in Two Worlds, Jump at the Sun, A Song for His People, Justice in Montgomery **Humanities Transparencies** HT10, 11, 12 **TAKS Practice Transparencies** TT110 |
| **(US13) Economics. The student understands significant economic developments between World War I and World War II. The student is expected to:** | | | | |
| (A) analyze causes of economic growth and prosperity in the 1920s; | 422–427, 441–443, 464–466 | 425, 427, 430, 442, 443 | **In-Depth Resources** **Unit 4:** 9–10 **Access for Students Acquiring English** 149, 152, 154–155 **TAKS Spiraled Content Review** 75–76 | **Critical Thinking Transparencies** CT54, 56 **TAKS Practice Transparencies** TT77 |

# Correlation to Texas Assessment of Knowledge and Skills (TAKS)

| TAKS | Pupil's Edition and Teacher's Edition INSTRUCTION | Pupil's Edition and Teacher's Edition APPLICATION | Print Ancillaries | Technology and Transparencies |
|---|---|---|---|---|
| **(US13) Economics. The student understands significant economic developments between World War I and World War II. The student is expected to:** *(continued)* | | | | |
| **(B) analyze the causes of the Great Depression, including the decline in worldwide trade, the stock market crash, and bank failures;** | 464–471 | 465–468, 470, 471, 484 | **In-Depth Resources: Unit 4:** 9–10, 41, 45, 51, 52 **Access for Students Acquiring English** 165, 167 **TAKS Spiraled Content Review** 77–78 | **Electronic Library of Primary Sources** Chapter 14 **American Stories Videos** Broke but Not Broken **Critical Thinking Transparencies** CT22, 54, 56 **Humanities Transparencies** HT21 **TAKS Practice Transparencies** TT82 |
| **(C) analyze the effects of the Great Depression on the U.S. economy and government; and** | 469–483 | 470, 471, 473, 475–477, 479, 480, 482–484 | **In-Depth Resources: Unit 4:** 9–10, 45, 49–50, 53 **Access for Students Acquiring English** 173–174, 175, 177, 178, 179, 183–184 **TAKS Spiraled Content Review** 77–78 | **Electronic Library of Primary Sources** Chapter 14 **American Stories Videos** Broke but Not Broken **Critical Thinking Transparencies** CT22, 57 **Humanities Transparencies** HT22 **TAKS Practice Transparencies** TT84 |
| **(E) analyze how various New Deal agencies and programs such as the Federal Deposit Insurance Corporation, [the Securities and Exchange Commission,] and Social Security continue to affect the lives of U.S. citizens.** | 488–490, 496, 497, 499–501, 504–506, 513–519, 884–885 | 490, 491, 500, 501, 509, 516, 518, 519, 522, 884 | **In-Depth Resources: Unit 4:** 60, 62, 64 **Access for Students Acquiring English** 175, 177, 179 **TAKS Spiraled Content Review** 79–80 | **American Stories Videos** Broke but Not Broken **Critical Thinking Transparencies** CT23 **Geography Transparencies** GT23 **TAKS Practice Transparencies** TT89 |

# Correlation to Texas Assessment of Knowledge and Skills (TAKS)

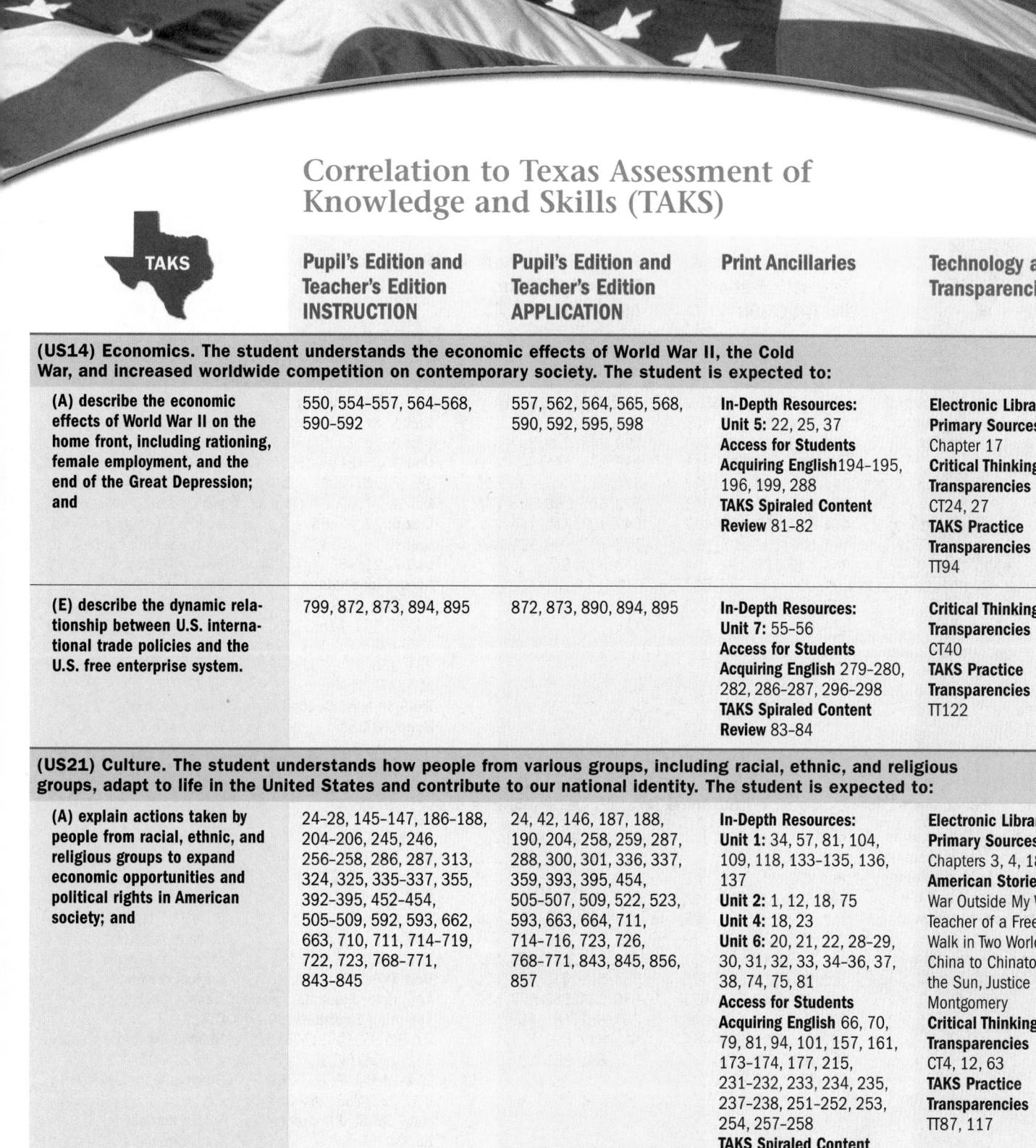

| TAKS | Pupil's Edition and Teacher's Edition INSTRUCTION | Pupil's Edition and Teacher's Edition APPLICATION | Print Ancillaries | Technology and Transparencies |
|---|---|---|---|---|
| **(US14) Economics. The student understands the economic effects of World War II, the Cold War, and increased worldwide competition on contemporary society. The student is expected to:** | | | | |
| **(A) describe the economic effects of World War II on the home front, including rationing, female employment, and the end of the Great Depression; and** | 550, 554-557, 564-568, 590-592 | 557, 562, 564, 565, 568, 590, 592, 595, 598 | **In-Depth Resources:** **Unit 5:** 22, 25, 37 **Access for Students Acquiring English** 194-195, 196, 199, 288 **TAKS Spiraled Content Review** 81-82 | **Electronic Library of Primary Sources** Chapter 17 **Critical Thinking Transparencies** CT24, 27 **TAKS Practice Transparencies** TT94 |
| **(E) describe the dynamic relationship between U.S. international trade policies and the U.S. free enterprise system.** | 799, 872, 873, 894, 895 | 872, 873, 890, 894, 895 | **In-Depth Resources:** **Unit 7:** 55-56 **Access for Students Acquiring English** 279-280, 282, 286-287, 296-298 **TAKS Spiraled Content Review** 83-84 | **Critical Thinking Transparencies** CT40 **TAKS Practice Transparencies** TT122 |
| **(US21) Culture. The student understands how people from various groups, including racial, ethnic, and religious groups, adapt to life in the United States and contribute to our national identity. The student is expected to:** | | | | |
| **(A) explain actions taken by people from racial, ethnic, and religious groups to expand economic opportunities and political rights in American society; and** | 24-28, 145-147, 186-188, 204-206, 245, 246, 256-258, 286, 287, 313, 324, 325, 335-337, 355, 392-395, 452-454, 505-509, 592, 593, 662, 663, 710, 711, 714-719, 722, 723, 768-771, 843-845 | 24, 42, 146, 187, 188, 190, 204, 258, 259, 287, 288, 300, 301, 336, 337, 359, 393, 395, 454, 505-507, 509, 522, 523, 593, 663, 664, 711, 714-716, 723, 726, 768-771, 843, 845, 856, 857 | **In-Depth Resources:** **Unit 1:** 34, 57, 81, 104, 109, 118, 133-135, 136, 137 **Unit 2:** 1, 12, 18, 75 **Unit 4:** 18, 23 **Unit 6:** 20, 21, 22, 28-29, 30, 31, 32, 33, 34-36, 37, 38, 74, 75, 81 **Access for Students Acquiring English** 66, 70, 79, 81, 94, 101, 157, 161, 173-174, 177, 215, 231-232, 233, 234, 235, 237-238, 251-252, 253, 254, 257-258 **TAKS Spiraled Content Review** 85-86 | **Electronic Library of Primary Sources** Chapters 3, 4, 18, 19, 21 **American Stories Videos** War Outside My Window, Teacher of a Freed People, A Walk in Two Worlds, From China to Chinatown, Jump at the Sun, Justice in Montgomery **Critical Thinking Transparencies** CT4, 12, 63 **TAKS Practice Transparencies** TT87, 117 |

# Correlation to Texas Assessment of Knowledge and Skills (TAKS)

**TAKS**

| | Pupil's Edition and Teacher's Edition INSTRUCTION | Pupil's Edition and Teacher's Edition APPLICATION | Print Ancillaries | Technology and Transparencies |
|---|---|---|---|---|
| **(US21) Culture. The student understands how people from various groups, including racial, ethnic, and religious groups, adapt to life in the United States and contribute to our national identity. The student is expected to:** *(continued)* | | | | |
| **(D) identify the political, social, and economic contributions of women to American society.** | 32, 34, 56, 61, 64, 65, 147–149, 158–160, 173, 174, 216–219, 248, 249, 266, 286, 306–309, 313, 314, 332, 334, 335, 372, 388, 392, 395, 440–443, 474–477, 489, 495–498, 504–506, 562–567, 591, 644, 645, 700–702, 704, 705, 722, 744, 776–780, 820, 821, 836, 842, 843, 874, 875 | 32, 56, 61, 64, 65, 147, 148, 158, 165, 172, 174, 190, 249, 250, 307, 314, 335, 394, 441, 443, 460, 476, 477, 497, 498, 509, 522, 562, 565, 595, 645, 649, 707, 716, 744, 776–780, 788, 821, 842, 843, 874, 875 | **In-Depth Resources:** **Unit 1:** 81, 100, 136, 138 **Unit 2:** 13, 19, 54, 59, 76 **Unit 3:** 2, 13–14, 15, 17, 18, 23, 66 **Unit 4:** 21, 39, 61, 84 **Unit 5:** 22, 43, 65 **Unit 6:** 19, 30, 37 **Unit 7:** 21, 43, 64, 73 **Access for Students Acquiring English** 67, 78, 84, 94, 101, 118, 121, 156, 159, 161, 194, 196, 231, 233, 234, 251–252, 254, 271, 281 **TAKS Spiraled Content Review** 87–88 | **Electronic Library of Primary Sources** Chapters 3–9, 15, 17, 19, 26 **American Stories Videos** War Outside My Window, A Walk in Two Worlds, A Child on Strike, Jump at the Sun, Justice in Montgomery, Poisoned Playground **Critical Thinking Transparencies** CT8, 31, 65 **Humanities Transparencies** HT10 **TAKS Practice Transparencies** TT31, 118, 129 |
| **(US22) Science, technology, and society. The student understands the impact of science and technology on the economic development of the United States. The student is expected to:** | | | | |
| **(A) explain the effects of scientific discoveries and technological innovations such as electric power, the telegraph and telephone, petroleum-based products, medical vaccinations, and computers on the development of the United States; and** | 34, 35, 121, 140, 141, 211, 214, 215, 217, 230–233, 264, 276–281, 299, 306–309, 310–312, 314, 372–380, 384, 385, 422–425, 429, 438, 439, 441–443, 446–451, 480, 482, 510–512, 520, 521, 588, 589, 618, 619, 622, 623, 626, 627, 644, 646, 647, 652–655, 679–681, 808, 809, 811–813, 822–825, 876–881 | 35, 39, 121, 140, 152, 211, 215, 217, 231, 233, 250, 277–281, 299, 300, 309, 311, 376, 387, 406, 423–425, 427, 429, 430, 439, 442, 448, 449, 451, 460, 482, 511, 521, 522, 588, 589, 618, 623, 626, 646, 649, 652–654, 657, 664, 681, 683, 809, 811, 813, 817, 825–827, 877–881, 891 | **In-Depth Resources:** **Unit 1:** 29, 80, 138 **Unit 2:** 3, 20, 30, 48–49, 61 **Unit 3:** 34–35, 41 **Unit 4:** 3, 9–10, 30–31 **Unit 5:** 39 **Unit 7:** 48, 52 **Access for Students Acquiring English** 89–90, 91, 92, 93, 149, 152, 157, 160, 163–164, 194, 214–215, 217, 266–267, 280, 282, 283, 286–287 **TAKS Spiraled Content Review** 89–90 | **Electronic Library of Primary Sources** Chapters 8, 17 **American Stories Videos** Gusher!, From China to Chinatown, A Child on Strike, Ace of Aces **Critical Thinking Transparencies** CT7, 8, 13, 35, 60 **Humanities Transparencies** HT18, 24, 41, 42 **Geography Transparencies** GT13, 14, 16, 17, 22, 27 **TAKS Practice Transparencies** TT33, 80 |
| **(C) analyze the impact of technological innovations on the nature of work, the American labor movement, and businesses.** | 12, 121, 142, 143, 233, 279–281, 308, 309, 313, 314, 392–395, 422–426, 441–443, 510–512, 520, 521, 618, 619, 641–643, 646, 648, 649, 814, 869–871, 876–878 | 12, 121, 142, 143, 152, 233, 281, 309, 314, 394, 424, 425, 430, 442, 443, 511, 521, 522, 641–643, 649, 664, 814, 873, 877, 878, 890 | **In-Depth Resources:** **Unit 1:** 80 **Unit 2:** 3, 20, 48–49, 61 **Unit 4:** 19 **Unit 7:** 48, 52 **Access for Students Acquiring English** 89–90, 91, 93, 94 **TAKS Spiraled Content Review** 91–92 | **American Stories Videos** A Child on Strike **Critical Thinking Transparencies** CT5, 8 **TAKS Practice Transparencies** TT130 |

# Correlation to Texas Assessment of Knowledge and Skills (TAKS)

| | Pupil's Edition and Teacher's Edition INSTRUCTION | Pupil's Edition and Teacher's Edition APPLICATION | Print Ancillaries | Technology and Transparencies |
|---|---|---|---|---|
| **(US23) Science, technology, and society. The student understands the influence of scientific discoveries and technological innovations on daily life in the United States. The student is expected to:** | | | | |
| **(A)** analyze how scientific discoveries and technological innovations, including those in transportation and communication, have changed the standard of living in the United States. | 120, 121, 139-141, 208-210, 214, 215, 232, 233, 236-238, 264, 276-281, 359, 361, 366, 367, 425-427, 435, 447, 448, 465, 510-512, 626, 627, 646, 647, 650-655, 869-873, 876-881 | 121, 140, 141, 152, 209, 211, 215, 218, 233, 237, 240, 250, 266, 277-279, 281, 300, 367, 425, 427, 430, 435, 448, 465, 511, 522, 626, 646, 651, 653, 654, 664, 870, 871, 873, 878, 880, 881, 890 | **In-Depth Resources:**<br>**Unit 1:** 80<br>**Unit 2:** 3, 20, 48-49, 61<br>**Unit 4:** 9-10, 30-31<br>**Unit 7:** 48, 52<br>**Access for Students Acquiring English** 89-90, 91, 92, 93, 280, 282, 283, 286-287<br>**TAKS Spiraled Content Review** 93-94 | **American Stories Videos**<br>Gusher!, From China to Chinatown<br>**Critical Thinking Transparencies**<br>CT5, 13<br>**Humanities Transparencies**<br>HT42<br>**TAKS Practice Transparencies**<br>TT104, 105 |
| **(WG5) Geography. The student understands how political, economic, and social processes shape cultural patterns and characteristics in various places and regions. The student is expected to:** | | | | |
| **(B)** analyze political, economic, social, and demographic data to determine the level of development and standard of living in nations. | 5-13, 15, 16, 23, 24, 26-4, 40, 41, 66-109, 113, 119-129, 131, 133, 140, 142, 143, 145-149, 152, 202, 203, 206-210, 214-218, 230-232, 242-244, 254-261, 263, 267-271, 282-284, 286-291, 343, 344, 440-443, 564-567, 592-595, 641-649, 660-663, 684, 685, 689-691, 701, 702, 710, 711, 718, 719, 742-744, 768, 769, 771, 772, 776-780, 834-836, 839-845, 869-873, 882-889 | 6, 7, 10, 11, 13, 15, 16, 24, 26-33, 39, 41, 42, 65, 67, 69-71, 73, 76, 79, 83-109, 113, 117, 119, 121, 122, 124, 125, 129, 131-133, 140, 142, 143, 146-149, 152, 211, 215, 218, 226, 233, 242-244, 250, 255, 257-259, 261, 263, 268-273, 283-285, 288-291, 300, 301, 344, 441-443, 460, 564, 593-595, 598, 643-646, 648, 649, 663, 664, 685, 689-691, 696, 697, 701, 711, 716, 723, 726, 764, 773, 777, 778, 780, 788, 835, 836, 841-843, 845, 856, 857, 870-873, 882-887, 889, 890 | **In-Depth Resources:**<br>**Unit 1:** 17, 19, 20, 21-22, 25, 28, 37, 38, 59-68, 77-81, 94-95, 118-119<br>**Unit 2:** 1, 2, 3, 22, 39, 44, 48-49, 50-51, 59, 61, 62, 63<br>**Unit 3:** 1, 2, 13-14, 24, 26, 40, 49<br>**Unit 4:** 3, 19, 20, 21, 22, 41, 63<br>**Unit 5:** 67, 70, 76-77, 79, 80<br>**Unit 6:** 3, 20-33, 37, 41, 42, 64, 65, 72-73, 76,<br>**Unit 7:** 23, 32-33, 36, 38, 46, 48, 55-56<br>**Access for Students Acquiring English** 13-15, 20-21, 34-41, 51, 54, 55, 67, 79-80, 82-83, 89-93, 98-103, 109-110, 114, 118-119, 126-127, 128-129, 156-160, 214-219, 221-222, 224, 227, 231-233, 243, 251-255, 268-269, 279-280, 282, 284<br>**TAKS Spiraled Content Review** 95-96 | **Electronic Library of Primary Sources**<br>Chapters 1-5, 7, 12, 15, 17-19, 21, 23, 25, 26<br>**American Stories Videos**<br>Teacher of a Freed People, A Walk in Two Worlds, Gusher!, From China to Chinatown, A Child on Strike, A Song for His People, Justice in Montgomery<br>**Critical Thinking Transparencies**<br>CT2, 5, 7, 9, 13, 14, 15, 16, 18, 21, 26, 27, 28, 29, 31, 33, 37, 39, 43, 44, 46, 47, 48, 49, 50, 54, 55, 61, 65, 67, 69, 70, 71<br>**Humanities Transparencies**<br>HT7, 12, 15, 27, 35, 39<br>**Geography Transparencies**<br>GT3, 7, 8, 9, 13, 14, 31<br>**TAKS Practice Transparencies**<br>TT59 |

# Correlation to Texas Assessment of Knowledge and Skills (TAKS)

TAKS

| | Pupil's Edition and Teacher's Edition INSTRUCTION | Pupil's Edition and Teacher's Edition APPLICATION | Print Ancillaries | Technology and Transparencies |
|---|---|---|---|---|
| **(WG10) Economics. The student understands the distribution and characteristics of economic systems throughout the world. The student is expected to:** | | | | |
| (C) compare the ways people satisfy their basic needs through the production of goods and services such as subsistence agriculture versus market-oriented agriculture or cottage industries versus commercial industries. | 5, 6, 7, 10, 15, 23, 29, 31-34, 120-122, 140-142, 208-210, 214-218, 230-232, 241, 242, 343, 648, 649, 869-873 | 7, 13, 15, 29, 33, 39, 42, 121, 140, 143, 211, 215, 218, 226, 231, 233, 242, 250, 648, 649, 664, 870-873, 890 | **In-Depth Resources:** **Unit 1:** 75 **Unit 2:** 2, 3, 22 **Unit 4:** 3, 13, 15-16 **Unit 5:** 68 **Unit 7:** 23, 36, 46, 55-56 **Access for Students Acquiring English** 20-21, 55, 79-80, 82-83, 89-93, 105, 271, 279-280, 282 **TAKS Spiraled Content Review** 97-98 | **Electronic Library of Primary Sources** Chapters 25, 26 **American Stories Videos** Gusher! **Critical Thinking Transparencies** CT7, 14, 27, 41, 46, 48, 54, 67 **Geography Transparencies** GT3, 14 **TAKS Practice Transparencies** TT11, 32, 37 |
| **(4) The student will demonstrate an understanding of political influences on historical issues and events.** | | | | |
| **(8.3) History. The student understands the foundations of representative government in the United States. The student is expected to:** | | | | |
| (A) explain the reasons for the growth of representative government and institutions during the colonial period. | 24, 27, 28, 30, 35, 36, 46, 47, 49, 52, 53, 63 | 30, 35, 36, 39, 42, 53, 63 | **In-Depth Resources:** **Unit 1:** 20, 36, 37, 53, 59-62 **Access for Students Acquiring English** 26 **TAKS Spiraled Content Review** 99-100 | **Electronic Library of Primary Sources** Chapter 2 **TAKS Practice Transparencies** TT10 |
| **(8.16) Government. The student understands the American beliefs and principles reflected in the U.S. Constitution and other important historic documents. The student is expected to:** | | | | |
| (A) identify the influence of ideas from historic documents including the Magna Carta, the English Bill of Rights, [the Mayflower Compact,] the Declaration of Independence, the Federalist Papers, [and selected anti-federalist writings] on the U.S. system of government; and | 52-57, 70, 86, 97 | 53, 55, 70, 80 | **In-Depth Resources:** **Unit 1:** 32, 34 **Access for Students Acquiring English** 26, 28 **TAKS Spiraled Content Review** 101-102 | **Electronic Library of Primary Sources** Chapter 2 **TAKS Practice Transparencies** TT20 |
| (D) analyze how the U.S. Constitution reflects the principles of limited government, repubiicanism, checks and balances, federalism, separation of powers, popular sovereignty, and individual rights. | 68-71, 82, 83, 87, 89, 90, 93, 94, 95-103-105 | 69-71, 84, 87, 89, 90, 95-103, 105 | **In-Depth Resources:** **Unit 1:** 59-70, 108, 109 **Access for Students Acquiring English** 35-41 **TAKS Spiraled Content Review** 103-104 | **Critical Thinking Transparencies** CT5, 39 **TAKS Practice Transparencies** TT19 |

# Correlation to Texas Assessment of Knowledge and Skills (TAKS)

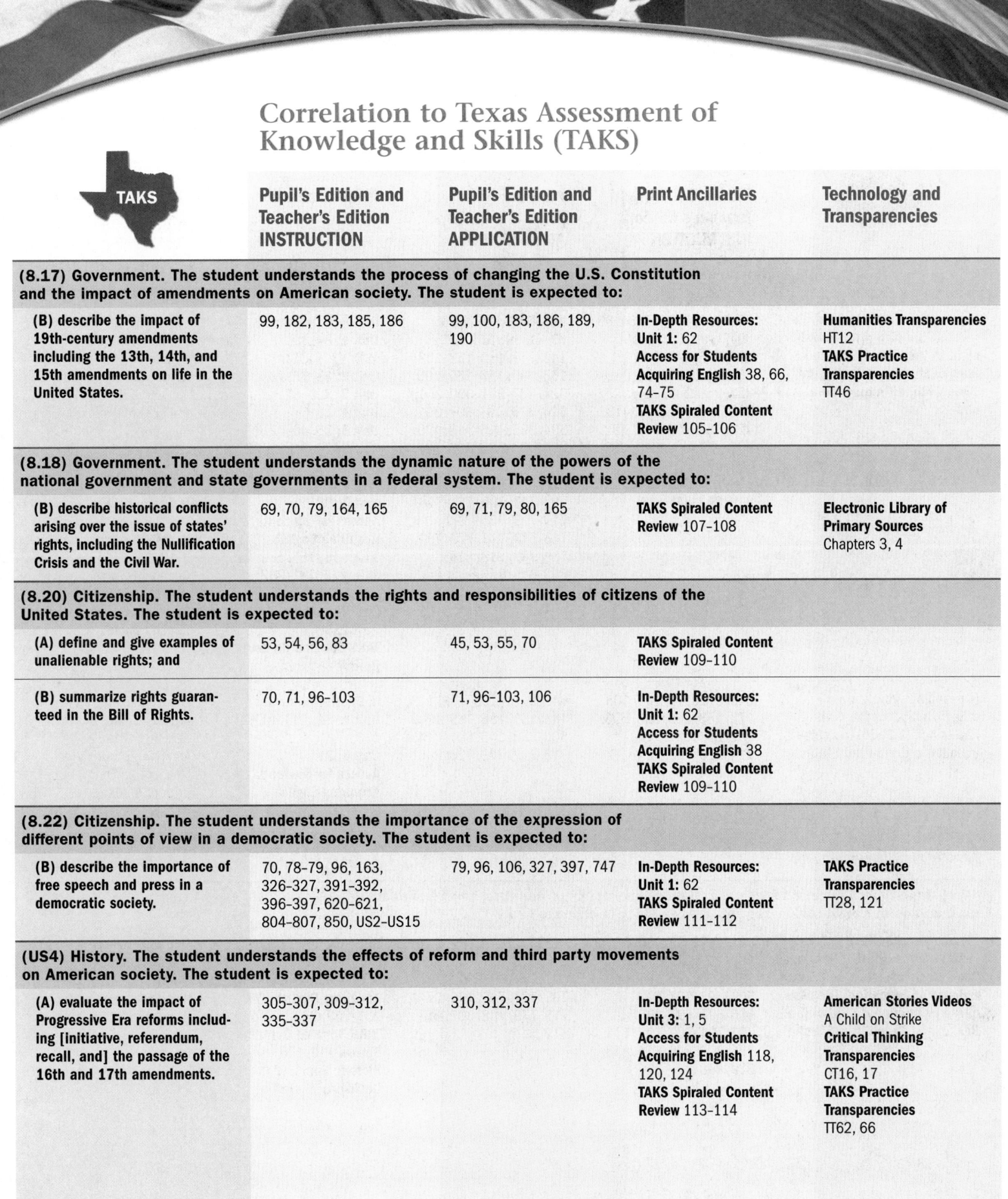

| TAKS | Pupil's Edition and Teacher's Edition INSTRUCTION | Pupil's Edition and Teacher's Edition APPLICATION | Print Ancillaries | Technology and Transparencies |
|---|---|---|---|---|
| **(8.17) Government. The student understands the process of changing the U.S. Constitution and the impact of amendments on American society. The student is expected to:** | | | | |
| **(B) describe the impact of 19th-century amendments including the 13th, 14th, and 15th amendments on life in the United States.** | 99, 182, 183, 185, 186 | 99, 100, 183, 186, 189, 190 | In-Depth Resources: Unit 1: 62 Access for Students Acquiring English 38, 66, 74–75 TAKS Spiraled Content Review 105–106 | Humanities Transparencies HT12 TAKS Practice Transparencies TT46 |
| **(8.18) Government. The student understands the dynamic nature of the powers of the national government and state governments in a federal system. The student is expected to:** | | | | |
| **(B) describe historical conflicts arising over the issue of states' rights, including the Nullification Crisis and the Civil War.** | 69, 70, 79, 164, 165 | 69, 71, 79, 80, 165 | TAKS Spiraled Content Review 107–108 | Electronic Library of Primary Sources Chapters 3, 4 |
| **(8.20) Citizenship. The student understands the rights and responsibilities of citizens of the United States. The student is expected to:** | | | | |
| **(A) define and give examples of unalienable rights; and** | 53, 54, 56, 83 | 45, 53, 55, 70 | TAKS Spiraled Content Review 109–110 | |
| **(B) summarize rights guaranteed in the Bill of Rights.** | 70, 71, 96–103 | 71, 96–103, 106 | In-Depth Resources: Unit 1: 62 Access for Students Acquiring English 38 TAKS Spiraled Content Review 109–110 | |
| **(8.22) Citizenship. The student understands the importance of the expression of different points of view in a democratic society. The student is expected to:** | | | | |
| **(B) describe the importance of free speech and press in a democratic society.** | 70, 78–79, 96, 163, 326–327, 391–392, 396–397, 620–621, 804–807, 850, US2–US15 | 79, 96, 106, 327, 397, 747 | In-Depth Resources: Unit 1: 62 TAKS Spiraled Content Review 111–112 | TAKS Practice Transparencies TT28, 121 |
| **(US4) History. The student understands the effects of reform and third party movements on American society. The student is expected to:** | | | | |
| **(A) evaluate the impact of Progressive Era reforms including [initiative, referendum, recall, and] the passage of the 16th and 17th amendments.** | 305–307, 309–312, 335–337 | 310, 312, 337 | In-Depth Resources: Unit 3: 1, 5 Access for Students Acquiring English 118, 120, 124 TAKS Spiraled Content Review 113–114 | American Stories Videos A Child on Strike Critical Thinking Transparencies CT16, 17 TAKS Practice Transparencies TT62, 66 |

# Correlation to Texas Assessment of Knowledge and Skills (TAKS)

TAKS

| | Pupil's Edition and Teacher's Edition INSTRUCTION | Pupil's Edition and Teacher's Edition APPLICATION | Print Ancillaries | Technology and Transparencies |
|---|---|---|---|---|
| **(US7) History. The student understands the impact of the American civil rights movement. The student is expected to:** | | | | |
| **(A)** trace the historical development of the civil rights movement in the 18th, 19th, and 20th centuries, including the 13th, 14th, 15th amendments; and | 33, 36, 39, 46, 47, 64, 65, 69–71, 82, 85, 98–100, 104, 105, 145–149, 158–165, 183, 185, 186, 221, 286–291, 324, 325, 335–337, 391–395, 413, 429, 453, 454, 566, 592, 593, 637, 638, 640, 662, 663, 671, 682, 690–695, 698–725, 768–780, 818, 819, 842–845 | 33, 36, 39, 42, 47, 65, 69–71, 99, 100, 105, 146–149, 152, 158, 159, 165, 185, 186, 189, 190, 221, 287–291, 300, 301, 324, 336, 337, 391, 392, 394, 395, 406, 413, 429, 454, 592, 593, 595, 637, 638, 640, 662, 663, 682, 691, 693, 695, 696, 701–707, 709, 711–716, 719–723, 725–727, 768–773, 777, 778, 780, 788, 789, 818, 819, 842–845, 856 | **In-Depth Resources:** **Unit 1:** 34, 49, 72, 81, 100, 137, 138 **Unit 2:** 63, 75, 76 **Unit 3:** 3, 5, 62 **Unit 4:** 18 **Unit 5:** 25, 40–42, 69 **Unit 6:** 20, 21, 22, 28–29, 30, 31, 32, 33, 34–36, 37, 38 **Unit 7:** 38 **Access for Students Acquiring English** 38, 110, 112, 113, 157, 161, 215, 219, 227, 231–232, 233, 234, 235, 237–238, 251–252, 253, 254, 255, 257–258 **TAKS Spiraled Content Review** 115–116 | **Electronic Library of Primary Sources** Chapters 1–4, 18–21, 23 **American Stories Videos** Teacher of a Freed People, A Walk in Two Worlds, Jump at the Sun, A Song for His People, Justice in Montgomery **Critical Thinking Transparencies** CT4, 11, 12, 29 **Humanities Transparencies** HT10, 11, 12, 27 **Geography Transparencies** GT29 **TAKS Practice Transparencies** TT111 |
| **(C)** evaluate government efforts, including the Civil Rights Act of 1964, to achieve equality in the United States. | 64, 65, 70, 71, 104, 105, 172, 183, 185, 186, 506, 637, 638, 691, 711, 714–716, 722, 723, 772, 773, 844 | 64, 65, 71, 105, 172, 173, 183, 185, 186, 189, 190, 506, 638, 640, 691, 714, 716, 722, 723, 726, 845 | **In-Depth Resources:** **Unit 1:** 62, 106, 107, 121, 138 **Unit 6:** 21 **Access for Students Acquiring English** 231–232, 234 **TAKS Spiraled Content Review** 117–118 | **Electronic Library of Primary Sources** Chapters 4, 19, 20 **American Stories Videos** Teacher of a Freed People **Critical Thinking Transparencies** CT12, 29, 45 **Humanities Transparencies** HT11, 12 |
| **(US17) Government. The student understands the impact of constitutional issues on American society in the 20th century. The student is expected to:** | | | | |
| **(A)** analyze the effects of 20th-century landmark U.S. Supreme Court decisions such as *Brown v. Board of Education,* [*Regents of the University of California v. Bakke,* and *Reynolds v. Sims*]. | 83, 97, 93, 99, 286, 287, 290, 291, 310–312, 334, 335, 353, 396, 397, 502, 503, 596, 597, 640, 690–693, 695, 696, 702–704, 708, 709, 774, 775, 779, 806, 814, 818, 819, 898 | 99, 290, 291, 397, 502, 503, 596, 597, 640, 691–693, 695, 696, 702, 703, 707, 709, 726, 774, 775, 779, 788, 807, 818, 819 | **In-Depth Resources:** **Unit 6:** 3, 20, 28–29 **Access for Students Acquiring English** 227, 231–232, 233, 237–238 **TAKS Spiraled Content Review** 119–120 **Historic Supreme Court Decisions** 73–78 | **Electronic Library of Primary Sources** Chapters 9, 21 **Humanities Transparencies** HT27 **TAKS Practice Transparencies** TT109 |

# Correlation to Texas Assessment of Knowledge and Skills (TAKS)

| | Pupil's Edition and Teacher's Edition INSTRUCTION | Pupil's Edition and Teacher's Edition APPLICATION | Print Ancillaries | Technology and Transparencies |
|---|---|---|---|---|
| **(US18) Citizenship. The student understands efforts to expand the democratic process. The student is expected to:** | | | | |
| **(B) evaluate various means of achieving equality of political rights, including the 19th, 24th, and 26th amendments.** | 98, 100-105, 182, 183, 186, 314-316, 334, 335, 395, 429, 504-506, 705-707, 710-716, 725, 769-774, 776-780, 798 | 101-105, 183, 316, 335, 429, 505, 506, 509, 705-707, 711, 713-716, 725, 726, 770-774, 777, 780, 788, 826 | **In-Depth Resources:** **Unit 1:** 62, 100, 104, 107, 108, 109, 121, 137, 138 **Unit 3:** 2, 5, 13-14 **Unit 6:** 21, 22, 28-29, 31, 32, 33, 37, 38, 74, 75, 81 **Access for Students Acquiring English** 35-41, 66, 231-232, 233, 234, 235, 237-238, 251-252, 253, 254, 257-258 **TAKS Spiraled Content Review** 121-122 | **Electronic Library of Primary Sources** Chapter 4 **American Stories Videos** Teacher of a Freed People, A Walk in Two Worlds, Justice in Montgomery **Critical Thinking Transparencies** CT12 **TAKS Practice Transparencies** TT73, 119 |
| **(5) The student will use critical thinking skills to analyze social studies information.** | | | | |
| **(US24) Social studies skills. The student applies critical-thinking skills to organize and use information acquired from a variety of sources including electronic technology. The student is expected to:** | | | | |
| **(A) [locate and] use primary and secondary sources [such as computer software, databases, media and news services, biographies, interviews, and artifacts] to acquire information about the United States;** | 3, 4, 14, 18, 21, 30, 31, 36, 39, 40, 45, 46, 52, 54-58, 60, 64, 66, 70, 72, 74, 79, 82-109, 111, 112, 117, 118, 120, 124, 128, 130, 139, 142, 144, 149, 156, 160, 165, 166, 168, 172, 175, 177, 184, 187, 201, 202, 206, 208, 212, 214, 216, 219, 223, 224, 229, 230, 234, 236, 241, 244, 245, 247, 253, 254, 256, 257, 260, 262, 265, 267, 268, 275-279, 282, 283, 286, 288, 290, 292, 298, 305, 306, 308, 313, 315, 317, 325-328, 331, 332, 337, 341, 342, 346, 352, 355, 358, 359, 364, 366, 371, 372, 374, 380, 381, 383, 385, 387, 388, 391, 392, 394, 396, 398, 404, 411-415, 419, 420, 422, 427, 428, 433-435, 437, 439, 440, 443, 444, 446, 449, 450, 452-454, 456-459, 463, 464, 469, 470, 472, 473, 476, 478, 479, 483, 487, 488, 490, 492, 494-497, 499, 502, | 2, 3, 4, 8, 11, 14, 16, 17, 21, 22, 24, 25, 27, 31, 32, 40, 42, 44-46, 48, 50, 54, 58, 64-66, 71-73, 78, 80, 107, 108, 110, 111, 113, 119, 121, 126, 129, 132, 134, 137, 140, 141, 145, 147, 154, 155, 157-159, 161, 164, 166-170, 173-175, 177-182, 184, 187-189, 201, 202, 210, 213, 220, 225, 229, 230, 235, 240, 250, 253, 261, 269, 275, 278, 280, 283, 291, 295, 299, 311, 319, 325, 327, 341, 354, 387, 397, 402, 405, 407, 411, 433, 435, 436, 443, 445, 459-461, 463, 467, 468, 481, 486, 489, 490, 492, 493, 497-501, 505, 508, 511, 513, 517, 520, 523, 526, 529, 543, 544, 546, 552, 554, 555, 557, 559, 561, 566, 568, 577, 582, 589, 597, 600, 601, 603, 607, 608, 610, 611, 613, 616-618, 620, 621, 625, 626, 629, 631-633, 637, 638, 644, 645, 647, 649, | **In-Depth Resources:** **Unit 1:** 15, 16, 25, 26-27, 28, 29, 30-32, 49-50, 51, 52, 53, 54-56, 59-63, 96-97, 98, 99, 100, 101-103, 121, 122, 123, 126-127, 130, 133-135 **Unit 2:** 12, 13, 14, 15-17, 30, 31, 32, 33, 34-36, 43, 53, 54, 55, 56-58, 73, 74, 75, 76, 77-79 **Unit 3:** 15, 16, 17, 18, 19-21, 22, 23, 38, 39, 40, 41, 42-44, 45, 46, 59, 60, 61, 62, 63-65, 66, 67 Unit 4: 11-12, 13, 14, 15-16, 17, 32, 33, 34, 35, 36-38, 51, 52, 53, 54, 55-57, 76, 77, 78, 79, 80-82 **Unit 5:** 13, 14-15, 16, 17-19, 20, 21, 36, 37, 38, 39, 40-42, 43, 44, 57, 58, 59, 60, 61-63, 64, 65, 78, 79, 80, 81, 82-83, 84, 85, 86 **Unit 6:** 11-12, 13, 14, 15-17, 18, 19, 30, 31, 32, 33, 34-36, 37, 38, 55, 56, 57, 58, 59-61, 74, 75, 76, | **Electronic Library of Primary Sources** Chapters 5-26 **American Stories Videos** War Outside My Window, Teacher of a Freed People, A Walk in Two Worlds, Gusher!, From China to Chinatown, A Child on Strike, Ace of Aces, Jump at the Sun, Broke but Not Broken, A Song for His People, Escaping the Final Solution, The Cold War Comes Home, Justice in Montgomery, Matters of Conscience, Poisoned Playground **TAKS Practice Transparencies** TT8, 124, 127 |

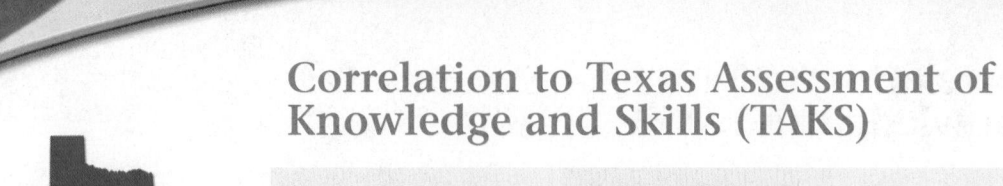

# Correlation to Texas Assessment of Knowledge and Skills (TAKS)

| TAKS | Pupil's Edition and Teacher's Edition INSTRUCTION | Pupil's Edition and Teacher's Edition APPLICATION | Print Ancillaries | Technology and Transparencies |
|---|---|---|---|---|
| **(US24) Social studies skills. The student applies critical-thinking skills to organize and use information acquired from a variety of sources including electronic technology. The student is expected to:** *(continued)* | | | | |
| **(A) [locate and] use primary and secondary sources [such as computer software, databases, media and news services, biographies, interviews, and artifacts] to acquire information about the United States;** *(continued)* | 504, 506, 508, 510, 513, 515, 516, 527, 528, 535, 536, 538, 541, 542, 544, 548–550, 554, 555, 560–563, 565, 566, 569, 570, 572, 576–578, 581, 582, 584, 586, 588, 590, 593, 595, 596, 601, 602, 605, 609, 616, 619, 620, 622, 627–629, 633, 634, 636, 639, 641, 642, 644, 649, 650, 652, 654–658, 660, 661, 669, 670, 672, 673, 676, 679, 681, 684, 687, 689, 699, 700, 705, 708, 710, 712, 714, 715, 717, 719–721, 724, 729, 730, 736, 737, 739, 740, 742, 743, 745–748, 751, 752, 754, 755, 759, 762–763, 767, 768, 772, 774, 776–779, 781, 783, 786, 787, 793, 794, 797, 800, 802, 804, 808, 810, 812, 818, 820, 821, 824, 829, 830, 832, 834, 835, 839, 842, 843, 846, 848, 853, 856, 860, 862, 864, 867, 869, 870, 876, 879, 882 | 651, 653–656, 659, 664, 665, 668, 669, 675, 677, 678, 680, 681, 688, 689, 691, 693, 695, 697, 699, 700, 702, 703, 706, 709, 711–716, 718, 719, 723, 728, 729, 731–734, 738, 739, 743, 745–747, 749, 750, 752, 758, 759, 763, 766, 767, 770, 773, 775, 783, 784, 787–789, 792, 793, 795, 798, 800, 805, 806, 809, 811, 813, 816, 819, 820, 824–829, 836, 838, 844, 849, 851, 852, 854, 857–859, 862–868, 871, 872, 875, 877–880, 883, 885, 886, 890, 895 | 77, 78–90<br>**Unit 7:** 13, 14, 15, 16, 17–19, 20, 21, 36, 37, 38, 39, 40–41, 42, 43, 44, 46, 47, 48, 49, 50–51, 52, 53 | |

# Correlation to Texas Assessment of Knowledge and Skills (TAKS)

| TAKS | Pupil's Edition and Teacher's Edition INSTRUCTION | Pupil's Edition and Teacher's Edition APPLICATION | Print Ancillaries | Technology and Transparencies |
|---|---|---|---|---|

**(US24) Social studies skills. The student applies critical-thinking skills to organize and use information acquired from a variety of sources including electronic technology. The student is expected to:** *(continued)*

| | | | | |
|---|---|---|---|---|
| **(B) analyze information by sequencing, categorizing, identifying cause-and-effect relationships, comparing, contrasting, finding the main idea, summarizing, making generalizations [and predictions], and drawing inferences and conclusions;** | | 2-18, 20, 22-28, 30, 32, 33, 35-39, 41, 42, 45, 47-53, 59-63, 65, 67-71, 73, 75-80, 82-104, 106, 107, 110, 111, 113-125, 127, 128, 131, 132, 134-143, 145-148, 152, 155-167, 169-171, 173-183, 185-190, 201, 203-206, 208-211, 213, 215, 217, 218, 220-223, 225, 226, 229, 231-233, 235, 237-241, 243-247, 249, 250, 253, 255-257, 259, 261, 263, 264, 266, 268-270, 272, 273, 277-279, 281, 283-285, 287-289, 291, 293-297, 299-301, 307, 308, 310, 312, 315, 316, 319, 322-325, 327, 329, 331, 333-337, 341, 343-345, 347-351, 353-358, 360, 361, 363, 365, 373, 374, 377, 379, 380, 382-384, 386, 387, 389-395, 397, 399, 400, 403, 405, 406, 415, 418, 420, 424-427, 429, 430, 433, 435-437, 439, 441-443, 445, 448-451, 453, 457, 459, 460, 463, 465-471, 473-477, 482-484, 486, 487, 489-494, 496, 497, 499, 501, 505-509, 511-514, 516, 518, 519, 521, 522, 526-538, 540-544, 546, 547, 550-558, 561, 564-581, 585-598, 600, 601, 603-608, 610-615, 617, 618, 620, 621, 623-630, 632-636, 638-649, 651-664, 668, 669, 671-675, 677, 678, 680-685, 687-693, 695, 696, 698, 699, 701-704, 706, 707, 709, 711-721, 723, 725-747, 749-761, | **In-Depth Resources:** **Unit 1:** 1, 2, 3, 4, 5, 6, 7, 8, 9, 10, 11, 12, 13, 22, 23, 25, 27, 28, 29, 32, 33, 34, 35, 36, 37, 38, 40, 41, 42, 48, 50, 51, 52, 53, 56, 57, 58, 64, 70, 71, 72, 73, 74, 76, 75, 77, 78, 79, 80, 81, 82, 83, 84, 85, 86, 93, 94, 97, 98, 99, 100, 103, 104, 105, 106, 107, 108, 109, 112, 113, 119, 121, 122, 123, 124, 127, 130, 135, 136, 137, 138<br>**Unit 2:** 2, 3, 5, 6, 11, 12, 13, 14, 17, 18, 19, 20, 21, 22, 24, 29, 30, 31, 32, 33, 36, 37, 38, 39, 40, 41, 43, 44, 46, 48, 49, 50, 53, 54, 55, 58, 59, 60, 61, 62, 63, 64, 66, 71, 72, 73, 74, 75, 76, 79, 80, 81<br>**Unit 3:** 1, 2, 3, 4, 5, 7, 14, 15, 16, 17, 18, 21, 22, 23, 24, 25, 26, 27, 29, 35, 36, 37, 38, 39, 40, 41, 44, 45, 46, 47, 48, 49, 50, 52, 58, 59, 60, 61, 62, 65, 66, 67<br>**Unit 4:** 1, 3, 5, 10, 12, 14, 17, 18, 19, 20, 21, 22, 25, 31, 32, 33, 34, 35, 38, 39, 40, 41, 42, 43, 45, 50, 52, 53, 54, 58, 59, 60, 61, 62, 64, 66, 73, 74, 77, 82, 83, 84<br>**Unit 5:** 1, 2, 3, 4, 6, 12, 13, 15, 16, 19, 20, 21, 27, 32, 33, 34-35, 36, 37, 38, 39, 42, 43, 44, 45, 46, 47, 48, 50, 56, 57, 59, 60, 63, 64, 65, 66, 67, 68, 69, 71, 77, 78, 79, 80, 81, 83, 84, 85, 86<br>**Unit 6:** 1, 2, 3, 5, 10, 12, 13, 14, 17, 18, 19, 20, 21, 22, 24, 29, 30, 31, 32, 33, 36, 37, 38, 39, 40, 41, 42, 43, 45, 52, 54, 55, 56, 57, 58, 61, 68, 69, 64, 65, 66, | **American Stories Videos**<br>War Outside My Window, Teacher of a Freed People, A Walk in Two Worlds, Gusher!, From China to Chinatown, A Child on Strike, Ace of Aces, Jump at the Sun, Broke but Not Broken, A Song for His People, Escaping the Final Solution, The Cold War Comes Home , Justice in Montgomery, Matters of Conscience, Poisoned Playground<br>**Critical Thinking Transparencies**<br>CT38, 39, 40, 41, 42, 43, 44, 45, 46, 47, 49, 50, 51, 52, 53, 54, 55, 56, 57, 62, 63, 65, 66, 68, 69, 70, 71<br>**TAKS Practice Transparencies**<br>TT3, 21, 22, 24, 29, 35, 36, 43, 44, 48, 49, 86, 108, 114, 128 |

# Correlation to Texas Assessment of Knowledge and Skills (TAKS)

| TAKS | Pupil's Edition and Teacher's Edition INSTRUCTION | Pupil's Edition and Teacher's Edition APPLICATION | Print Ancillaries | Technology and Transparencies |
|---|---|---|---|---|
| **(US24) Social studies skills. The student applies critical-thinking skills to organize and use information acquired from a variety of sources including electronic technology. The student is expected to:** *(continued)* | | | | |
| **(B) analyze information by sequencing, categorizing, identifying cause-and-effect relationships, comparing, contrasting, finding the main idea, summarizing, making generalizations [and predictions], and drawing inferences and conclusions;** *(continued)* | | 763, 764, 766–775, 777–785, 787, 792, 793, 795–801, 803–807, 809, 811–817, 820–826, 828, 829, 831–833, 835–838, 840–845, 847, 849–855, 857–859, 861, 862, 864–873, 877, 879–881, 883–890 | 68, 73, 74, 75, 76, 77, 80, 81, 82 **Unit 7:** 1, 2, 3, 4, 6, 12, 13, 14, 15, 16, 19, 20, 21, 22, 23, 24, 25, 32, 33, 34, 35, 36, 37, 38, 39, 41, 42, 43, 44, 45, 46, 47, 48, 56, 46, 47, 48, 49, 51, 52, 53, 58, 59, 60, 61, 62, 63, 64, 65, 66, 67, 68 **Access for Students Acquiring English** 15, 16, 19, 30, 32, 54, 58, 59, 72, 80–86, 88, 90–95, 97, 99, 100, 101–103, 106, 107, 110–115, 117, 119–125, 127, 129–133, 136, 137, 141–145, 147, 149–153, 155, 157–162, 164, 166–170, 172, 174–180, 182, 183, 186–191, 193, 195–200, 202, 203, 206–211, 213, 224–228, 230, 232–236, 238, 240–246, 248, 249, 252–257, 260–265, 267, 269–274, 276, 277, 280–285, 287–298 | |

# Correlation to Texas Assessment of Knowledge and Skills (TAKS)

| TAKS | Pupil's Edition and Teacher's Edition INSTRUCTION | Pupil's Edition and Teacher's Edition APPLICATION | Print Ancillaries | Technology and Transparencies |
|---|---|---|---|---|

**(US24) Social studies skills. The student applies critical-thinking skills to organize and use information acquired from a variety of sources including electronic technology. The student is expected to:** *(continued)*

| | | | | |
|---|---|---|---|---|
| **(C) explain and apply different methods that historians use to interpret the past, including the use of primary and secondary sources, points of view, frames of reference, and historical context; and** | 410, 411, 413, 432, 433, 435, 436, 438, 439, 452, 565-567, 570, 572-576, 581, 583-585, 587, 588, 593-597, 601, 602, 609, 616, 622, 628, 642, 644, 645, 649, 653-658, 661, 662, 793, 794, 802, 808, 810, 818, 820, 829, 830, 832, 834, 839, 846, 848, 859, 860, 869, 882, 888 | 2, 3, 8, 9, 11, 14-16, 19, 21, 22, 24, 26, 27, 31, 33-36, 40-42, 44-50, 52, 55-62, 64, 65, 67, 71-73, 75, 77, 78, 80-113, 115-121, 123-134, 136-145, 147-149, 154, 155, 157-159, 161-167, 169-190, 201, 202, 210, 215, 216, 220, 225, 226, 229, 236-238, 240, 241, 250, 253, 254, 261, 266, 275, 278, 280, 282, 283, 286, 291, 295, 297, 299, 312, 319, 324, 325, 327, 331, 336, 337, 354, 361, 387, 392, 403, 406, 411, 421, 433, 435-437, 439, 443, 445, 459, 463, 477, 481, 482, 486, 487, 489, 490, 492, 493, 497, 498, 500, 502, 503, 505, 506, 508, 511, 513, 517, 519, 520, 523, 526, 529, 531-535, 537-541, 543, 544, 546, 548, 549, 554, 555, 557, 560, 561, 563, 568-570, 577, 582-584, 586, 589-593, 596, 597, 600, 601, 603, 604, 607, 608, 610, 611, 613-615, 617, 618, 620, 621, 625, 626, 629, 631, 632, 635, 637, 638, 640, 644, 645, 647, 649, 651, 653-657, 659, 660, 664, 669, 670, 672, 679, 682, 684, 687, 688, 693, 699, 700, 708, 710, 712, 717, 724, 729, 730, 735, 736, 742, 747, 748, 753, 754, 762-764, 773, 775, 780, 787, 792-798, 800, 802, 803, 805-809, 811-816, 819-822, 824-829, 831-833, 836, 838, 840-844, 849-853, 857, 858, 860-875, 877-880, 882-886, 888, 889 | **In-Depth Resources:**<br>**Unit 1:** 10, 11, 12, 15, 16, 25, 26-27, 28, 29, 30-32, 33, 34, 42, 49-50, 51, 52, 53, 54-56, 57, 58, 59-63, 74, 78, 79, 83, 85, 96-97, 98, 99, 100, 101-103, 104, 106, 121, 122, 123, 126-127, 130, 133-135, 136, 137, 138<br>**Unit 2:** 12, 13, 14, 15-17, 18, 19, 30, 31, 32, 33, 34-36, 37, 38, 39, 40, 43, 46, 53, 54, 55, 56-58, 63, 64, 73, 74, 75, 76, 77-79<br>**Unit 3:** 2, 13, 15, 16, 17, 18, 19-21, 22, 23, 34-35, 36, 38, 39, 40, 41, 42-44, 45, 46, 47, 48, 57-58, 59, 60, 61, 62, 63-65, 66, 67<br>**Unit 4:** 2, 12, 13, 14, 15-16, 17, 18, 19, 21, 23, 30-31, 32, 33, 34, 35, 36-38, 39, 40, 42, 51, 52, 53, 54, 55-57, 58, 76, 77, 78, 79, 80-82, 83, 84<br>**Unit 5:** 1, 2, 3, 4, 6, 12, 13, 14-15, 16, 17-19, 20, 21, 23, 24, 33, 36, 37, 38, 39, 40-42, 43, 44, 47, 48, 50, 55-56, 57, 58, 59, 60, 61-63, 64, 65, 68, 69, 71, 76-77, 78, 79, 80, 81, 82-83, 84, 85, 86<br>**Unit 6:** 1, 3, 9-10, 11-12, 13, 14, 15-17, 18, 19, 20, 21, 22, 30, 31, 32, 33, 34-36, 37, 38, 39, 41, 42, 51-52, 55, 56, 57, 58, 58-61, 64, 65, 66, 68, 74, 75, 76, 77, 78-90<br>**Unit 7:** 2, 3, 4, 6, 11-12, 13, 14, 15, 16, 17-19, 20, 21, 23, 36, 37, 38, 39, 40-41, 42, 43, 44, 46, 47, 48, 49, 50-51, 52, 53<br>**Access for Students Acquiring English** 13, 14, 15, 18, 20, 22, 24-25, 26, 27, 35-38, 40-41, 45, 47, 49, 50-51, 52, 53, 54, 55, 56, 63-64, 65-66 | **Electronic Library of Primary Sources**<br>Chapters 5-26<br>**American Stories Videos**<br>War Outside My Window, Teacher of a Freed People, A Walk in Two Worlds, Gusher!, From China to Chinatown, A Child on Strike, Ace of Aces , Jump at the Sun, Broke but Not Broken, A Song for His People, Escaping the Final Solution, The Cold War Comes Home , Justice in Montgomery, Matters of Conscience, Poisoned Playground<br>**TAKS Practice Transparencies**<br>TT26, 30, 38, 41, 42, 57, 61, 90, 112 |

# Correlation to Texas Assessment of Knowledge and Skills (TAKS)

**TAKS**

| | Pupil's Edition and Teacher's Edition **INSTRUCTION** | Pupil's Edition and Teacher's Edition **APPLICATION** | Print Ancillaries | Technology and Transparencies |
|---|---|---|---|---|
| **(US24) Social studies skills. The student applies critical-thinking skills to organize and use information acquired from a variety of sources including electronic technology. The student is expected to:** *(continued)* | | | | |
| **(F) identify bias in written, [oral,] and visual material.** | 11, 48, 78, 127, 187, 189, 240, 250, 290, 426 | 11, 48, 50, 78, 126, 131, 161, 187, 189, 240, 250, 291, 312, 319, 351, 354, 361, 362, 371, 387, 395, 405–407, 426, 467, 534, 551, 564, 582, 585, 593, 655, 712, 732, 737, 795, 806, 825 | **In-Depth Resources:** **Unit 1:** 28, 51, 85, 99, 122, 123, 130, 133–135 **Unit 2:** 12, 18, 19, 30, 31, 32, 37, 38, 53, 54, 55, 56–58, 59, 74, 75, 76, 80 **Unit 4:** 14, 32, 52, 53, 58, 77 **Unit 5:** 27 **Unit 6:** 45 Unit 7: 6 | **American Stories Videos** War Outside My Window, Teacher of a Freed People, A Walk in Two Worlds, Gusher!, From China to Chinatown, A Child on Strike, Ace of Aces, Jump at the Sun, Broke but Not Broken, A Song for His People, Escaping the Final Solution, The Cold War Comes Home , Justice in Montgomery, Matters of Conscience, Poisoned Playground **TAKS Practice Transparencies** TT85, 115 |
| **(WG8) Geography. The student understands how people, places, and environments are connected and interdependent. The student is expected to:** | | | | |
| **(B) compare ways that humans depend on, adapt to, and modify the physical environment using [local,] state, national, and international human activities in a variety of cultural and technological contexts.** | 5, 7, 22, 29, 72, 137, 138, 214–217, 231, 234–237, 239, 276–279, 323, 324, 360, 361, 366, 367, 480, 491, 517, 520, 521, 646, 739, 822, US2–US15 | 7, 22, 29, 215, 231, 234, 235, 239, 250, 277, 278, 281, 300, 323, 360, 361, 367, 483, 491, 517, 521, 522, 646, 739, 741, 822 | **In-Depth Resources:** **Unit 1:** 7 **Unit 2:** 2, 3, 71–72 **Unit 3:** 3, 25–26, 32 **Unit 4:** 3, 30, 31, 74–75 **Unit 7:** 4, 15 **Access for Students Acquiring English** 54, 82, 83, 89, 92, 93, 116–117, 122, 128–129, 135–136, 163–164, 166, 183–184, 260, 263 | **American Stories Video** Poisoned Playground **Critical Thinking Transparencies** CT47 **Geography Transparencies** GT3, 14, 17, 27 **TAKS Practice Transparencies** TT2, 7, 64, 113, 123 |

# Correlation to Texas Assessment of Knowledge and Skills (TAKS)

| | Pupil's Edition and Teacher's Edition INSTRUCTION | Pupil's Edition and Teacher's Edition APPLICATION | Print Ancillaries | Technology and Transparencies |
|---|---|---|---|---|
| **(WG21) Social studies skills. The student applies critical-thinking skills to organize and use information acquired from a variety of sources including electronic technology. The student is expected to:** | | | | |
| **(C) [construct and] interpret maps to answer geographic questions, infer geographic relationships, and analyze geographic change.** | 416, 423, 474, 520, 521, 816, 846, 847, 866, 885, US2–US15, R25–R26 | 17, 22, 25, 29, 32, 38, 42, 59, 62, 73, 100, 164, 170, 235, 400, 406, 407, 416, 423, 474, 484, 521, 530, 532, 538, 556, 572, 575, 580, 591, 594, 605, 613, 624, 675, 685, 701, 733, 749, 775, 816, 847, 866, 885, 890 | **In-Depth Resources:** **Unit 1:** 9, 10, 11, 12, 19, 35, 36, 37, 38, 40, 41, 42, 52, 77, 78, 79, 80, 86, 92, 106, 107, 108, 109, 138 **Unit 2:** 11, 29, 49, 72 **Unit 3:** 14, 35, 36, 58 **Unit 4:** 31, 50, 73, 74 **Unit 5:** 12, 33 **Unit 6:** 10, 29, 51, 73 **Unit 7:** 33, 34, 56 **Access for Students Acquiring English** 13–16, 19, 26–32, 39, 47, 52–56, 60, 67–72, 77, 85, 88, 97, 127, 136, 137, 147, 155, 164, 172, 182, 193, 201, 203, 213, 229, 238, 248, 249, 258, 276, 277, 287 | **American Stories Videos** Teacher of a Freed People **Geography Transparencies** GeoQuest CD-ROM **TAKS Practice Transparencies** TT23, 126 |

# Correlation to Texas Assessment of Knowledge and Skills (TAKS)

**TAKS**

| | Pupil's Edition and Teacher's Edition **INSTRUCTION** | Pupil's Edition and Teacher's Edition **APPLICATION** | Print Ancillaries | Technology and Transparencies |
|---|---|---|---|---|
| **(WH26) Social studies skills. The student communicates in written, oral, and visual forms. The student is expected to:** | | | | |
| **(C) interpret [and create databases, research outlines, bibliographies, and] visuals including graphs, charts, timelines, and maps.** | 226, 255, 809, 813, 814, 827, 847, 857, R23–R28 | 10, 12, 13, 20, 26, 30, 32, 34, 36, 37, 42, 91, 96, 100, 122, 133, 135, 138, 159–162, 165, 170–174, 176, 179, 183, 189, 190, 210, 215, 218, 226, 232, 233, 240, 242, 244, 245, 248, 249, 255, 266, 272, 281, 351, 365, 380, 387, 395, 400, 403, 406, 407, 416–418, 421, 424, 427, 435, 439, 443, 453, 454, 457, 460, 471, 477, 483, 484, 491, 494, 501, 509, 514, 519, 522, 529, 531, 535, 541, 557, 558, 565, 567, 568, 577, 587, 595, 598, 608, 615, 621, 627, 636, 640, 649, 657, 663, 664, 678, 683, 685, 693, 696, 707, 726, 733, 735, 738, 741, 743, 747, 751, 759, 761, 764, 770, 773, 780, 784, 785, 788, 800, 801, 804, 809, 813, 814, 817, 823–827, 833, 835, 838, 844, 847, 849, 851, 852, 855–857, 865, 868, 872, 873, 881, 887, 890 | **In-Depth Resources:** **Unit 1:** 15, 16, 25, 26–27, 28, 29, 30-32, 49–50, 51, 52, 53, 54–56, 59–63, 96–97, 98, 99, 100, 101–103, 121, 122, 123, 126–127, 133–135 **Unit 2:** 12, 13, 14, 15–17, 30, 31, 32, 33, 34–36, 43, 53, 54, 55, 56–58, 73, 74, 75, 76, 77–79 **Unit 3:** 15, 16, 17, 18, 19–21, 22, 23, 38, 39, 40, 41, 42–44, 45, 46, 59, 60, 61, 62, 63–65, 66, 67 **Unit 4:** 11–12, 13, 14, 15–16, 17, 32, 33, 34, 35, 36–38, 51, 52, 53, 54, 55–57, 76, 77, 78, 79, 80–82 **Unit 5:** 13, 14–15, 16, 17–19, 20, 21, 36, 37, 38, 39, 40–42, 43, 44, 57, 58, 59, 60, 61–63, 64, 65, 78, 79, 80, 81, 82–83, 84, 85, 86 **Unit 6:** 11–12, 13, 14, 15–17, 18, 19, 30, 31, 32, 33, 34–36, 37, 38, 55, 56, 57, 58, 59–61, 74, 75, 76, 77, 78–90 **Unit 7:** 13, 14, 15, 16, 17–19, 20, 21, 36, 37, 38, 39, 40–41, 42, 43, 44, 46, 47, 48, 49, 50–51, 52, 53 **Access for Students Acquiring English** 35–38 | **Electronic Library of Primary Sources** Chapters 5–26 **American Stories Videos** War Outside My Window, Teacher of a Freed People, A Walk in Two Worlds, Gusher!, From China to Chinatown, A Child on Strike, Ace of Aces, Jump at the Sun, Broke but Not Broken, A Song for His People, Poisoned Playground **TAKS Practice Transparencies** TT9, 14, 17, 45, 72 |

# Table of Contents

# History Comes Alive

*The Americans: Reconstruction to the 21st Century* makes history more meaningful for students by presenting historical events through the eyes of the people who experienced them.

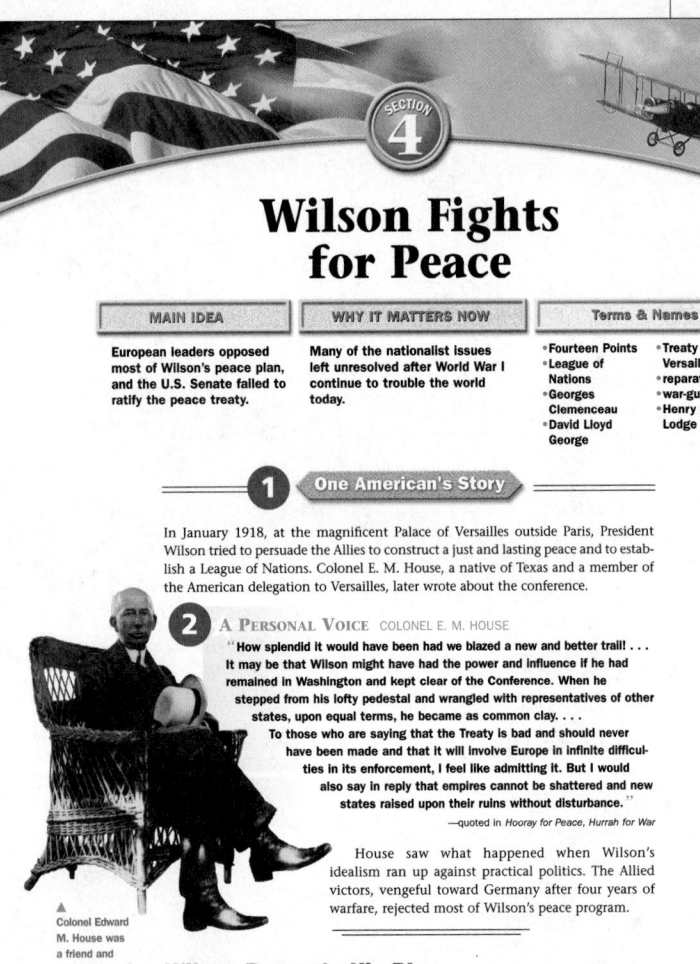

## SECTION 4

# Wilson Fights for Peace

| MAIN IDEA | WHY IT MATTERS NOW | Terms & Names |
|---|---|---|
| European leaders opposed most of Wilson's peace plan, and the U.S. Senate failed to ratify the peace treaty. | Many of the nationalist issues left unresolved after World War I continue to trouble the world today. | •Fourteen Points •League of Nations •Georges Clemenceau •David Lloyd George / •Treaty of Versailles •reparations •war-guilt clause •Henry Cabot Lodge |

### 1 One American's Story

In January 1918, at the magnificent Palace of Versailles outside Paris, President Wilson tried to persuade the Allies to construct a just and lasting peace and to establish a League of Nations. Colonel E. M. House, a native of Texas and a member of the American delegation to Versailles, later wrote about the conference.

### 2 A PERSONAL VOICE COLONEL E. M. HOUSE

" How splendid it would have been had we blazed a new and better trail! . . . It may be that Wilson might have had the power and influence if he had remained in Washington and kept clear of the Conference. When he stepped from his lofty pedestal and wrangled with representatives of other states, upon equal terms, he became as common clay. . . .
To those who are saying that the Treaty is bad and should never have been made and that it will involve Europe in infinite difficulties in its enforcement, I feel like admitting it. But I would also say in reply that empires cannot be shattered and new states raised upon their ruins without disturbance. "

—quoted in *Hooray for Peace, Hurrah for War*

House saw what happened when Wilson's idealism ran up against practical politics. The Allied victors, vengeful toward Germany after four years of warfare, rejected most of Wilson's peace program.

▲ Colonel Edward M. House was a friend and advisor to President Woodrow Wilson.

## Wilson Presents His Plan

Rejection was probably the last thing Wilson expected when he arrived in Europe. Everywhere he went, people gave him a hero's welcome. Italians displayed his picture in their windows; Parisians strewed the street with flowers. Representatives of one group after another, including Armenians, Jews, Ukrainians, and Poles, appealed to him for help in setting up independent nations for themselves.

**FOURTEEN POINTS** Even before the war was over, Wilson presented his plan for world peace. On January 18, 1918, he delivered his now famous **Fourteen Points** speech before Congress. The points were divided into three groups. The first five points were issues that Wilson believed had to be addressed to prevent another war:

1. There should be no secret treaties among nations.
2. Freedom of the seas should be maintained for all.
3. Tariffs and other economic barriers among nations should be lowered or abolished in order to foster free trade.
4. Arms should be reduced "to the lowest point consistent with domestic safety, thus lessening the possibility of military responses" during diplomatic crises.
5. Colonial policies should consider the interests of the colonial peoples as well as the interests of the imperialist powers.

The next eight points dealt with boundary changes. Wilson based these provisions on the principle of self-determination "along historically established lines of nationality." In other words, groups that claimed distinct ethnic identities were to form their own nation-states or decide for themselves to what nations they would belong.

The fourteenth point called for the creation of an international organization to address diplomatic crises like those that had sparked the war. This **League of Nations** would provide a forum for nations to discuss and settle their grievances without having to resort to war.

**THE ALLIES REJECT WILSON'S PLAN** Wilson's naiveté about the political aspects of securing a peace treaty showed itself in his failure to grasp the anger felt by the Allied leaders. The French premier, **Georges Clemenceau** (klĕm′ən-sō′), had lived through two German invasions of France and was determined to prevent future invasions. **David Lloyd George,** the British prime minister, had just won reelection on the slogan "Make Germany Pay." The Italian prime minister, Vittorio Orlando, wanted control of Austrian-held territory. Ⓐ

Contrary to custom, the peace conference did not include the defeated Central Powers. Nor did it include Russia, which was now under the control of a Communist government, or the smaller Allied nations. Instead, the "Big Four"—Wilson, Clemenceau, Lloyd George, and Orlando—worked out the treaty's details among themselves. Wilson conceded on most of his Fourteen Points in return for the establishment of the League of Nations.

*(left to right)* David Lloyd George, Georges Clemenceau, and Woodrow Wilson in Paris in 1919. ▷

### 3 KEY PLAYER

**WOODROW WILSON**
**1856–1924**

At the end of the war, President Wilson wanted the United States to become more involved in international affairs. He believed the nation had a moral obligation to help maintain peace in the world. Wilson's sense of moral purpose had a lasting influence on American foreign policy.

*The First World War* **399**

---

**① INTRODUCE STUDENTS TO HISTORY THROUGH PEOPLE**
**One American's Story** begins every section of a chapter with a true story of an American touched by the events discussed in that part of the text.

**② BRING HISTORY ALIVE THROUGH PRIMARY SOURCES**
**A Personal Voice** presents primary sources throughout the narrative.

**③ FOCUS ON KEY FIGURES**
**Key Player** features short biographies of significant historical figures at key points in the text.

## SECTION 2

# American Power Tips the Balance

| MAIN IDEA | WHY IT MATTERS NOW | Terms & Names |
|---|---|---|
| The United States mobilized a large army and navy to help the Allies achieve victory. | During World War I, the United States military evolved into the powerful fighting force that it remains today. | •Eddie Rickenbacker •Selective Service Act •convoy system •American Expeditionary Force •General John J. Pershing •Alvin York •conscientious objector •armistice |

### One American's Story

**Eddie Rickenbacker,** famous fighter pilot of World War I, was well known as a racecar driver before the war. He went to France as a driver but transferred to the aviation division. He learned to fly on his own time and eventually joined the U.S. Army Air Service. Rickenbacker repeatedly fought the dreaded Flying Circus—a German air squadron led by the "Red Baron," Manfred von Richthofen.

**A PERSONAL VOICE** EDDIE RICKENBACKER

"I put in six or seven hours of flying time each day. . . . My narrowest escape came at a time when I was fretting over the lack of action. . . . Guns began barking behind me, and sizzling tracers zipped by my head. . . . At least two planes were on my tail. . . .

They would expect me to dive. Instead I twisted upward in a corkscrew path called a 'chandelle.' I guessed right. As I went up, my two attackers came down, near enough for me to see their faces. I also saw the red noses on those Fokkers [German planes]. I was up against the Flying Circus again."

—*Rickenbacker: An Autobiography*

After engaging in 134 air battles and downing 26 enemy aircraft, Rickenbacker won fame as the Allied pilot with the most victories—"American ace of aces."

**VIDEO**
**ACE OF ACES**
Eddie Rickenbacker and the First World War

## America Mobilizes

The United States was not prepared for war. Only 200,000 men were in service when war was declared, and few officers had combat experience. Drastic measures were needed to build an army large and modern enough to make an impact in Europe.

*There is a peculiar gratification in receiving congratulations from one's squadron for a victory in the air. It is worth more to a pilot than the applause of the whole outside world. It means that one has won the confidence of men who share the misgivings, the aspirations, the trials and the dangers of airplane fighting.*

—*Eddie Rickenbacker*

4

*Ace of Aces: Eddie Rickenbacker and the First World War* introduces viewers to the exciting life of Eddie Rickenbacker, one of the greatest fighter pilots in U.S. history.

④ **PRESENT AMERICAN STORIES THROUGH VIDEOS**

**The *American Stories* Video Series** is integrated with the One American's Story feature in the textbook. These fascinating documentaries of 17 Americans are based on primary sources and are often narrated by direct descendants of the person featured.

# History Becomes Relevant

*The Americans: Reconstruction to the 21st Century* helps students understand the relevance of history by showing them how people and events of the past connect to the present.

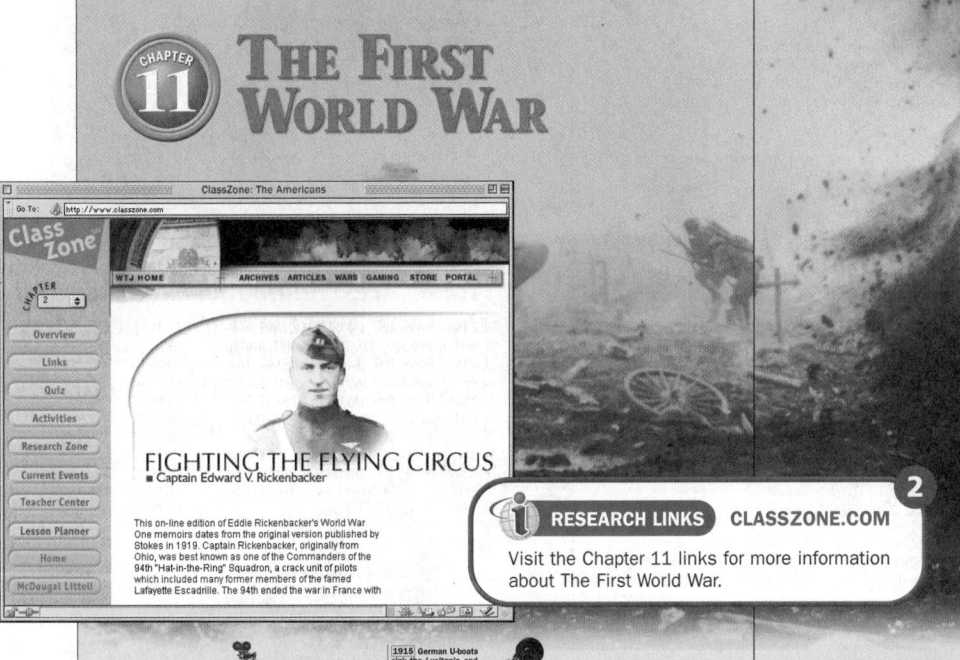

## CHAPTER 11 THE FIRST WORLD WAR

**ClassZone: The Americans**

Go To: http://www.classzone.com

**Class Zone**

CHAPTER 2

- Overview
- Links
- Quiz
- Activities
- Research Zone
- Current Events
- Teacher Center
- Lesson Planner
- Home
- McDougal Littell

WTJ HOME    ARCHIVES  ARTICLES  WARS  GAMING  STORE  PORTAL

## FIGHTING THE FLYING CIRCUS
■ Captain Edward V. Rickenbacker

This on-line edition of Eddie Rickenbacker's World War One memoirs dates from the original version published by Stokes in 1919. Captain Rickenbacker, originally from Ohio, was best known as one of the Commanders of the 94th "Hat-in-the-Ring" Squadron, a crack unit of pilots which included many former members of the famed Lafayette Escadrille. The 94th ended the war in France with

**2** ℹ RESEARCH LINKS  CLASSZONE.COM
Visit the Chapter 11 links for more information about The First World War.

**1** I N T E R A C T
**WITH HISTORY**

The year is 1917. A bitter war is raging in Europe—a war that has been called a threat to civilization. At home many people are urging America to wake up and get involved, while others are calling for the country to isolate itself and avoid the fight.

### Do you think America should enter the war?

**Examine the Issues**

- Is it right for America to intervene in foreign conflicts?
- When American lives are threatened, how should the government respond?
- Should America go to war to make the world "safe for democracy"?

### Timeline

**USA**

1914 Hollywood, California, becomes the center of movie production in the U.S.

1915 German U-boats sink the *Lusitania*, and 1,198 people die.
1915 Alexander Graham Bell makes first transcontinental telephone call.

1916 Woodrow Wilson is reelected president.

1917 The Selective Service Act sets up the draft.
1917 The United States declares war on Germany.

1918 Congress passes the Sedition Act.
1918 President Wilson proposes the League of Nations.

1919 Congress approves the Nineteenth Amendment, granting women the vote.

**USA / WORLD**

| 1914 | 1915 | 1916 | 1917 | 1918 | 1919 |

**WORLD**

1914 Archduke Franz Ferdinand and his wife are assassinated.
1914 Germany declares war on Russia and France. Great Britain declares war on Germany and Austria-Hungary.

1915 Albert Einstein proposes his general theory of relativity.

1916 The battles of Verdun and the Somme claim millions of lives.

1917 Russia withdraws from the war.

1918 The Bolsheviks establish a Communist regime in Russia.
1918 The First World War ends.

INFLUENZA PNEUMONIA

1918 A worldwide influenza epidemic kills over 30 million.

---

**1 GET STUDENTS INVOLVED WITH HISTORY**

**Interact with History** presents students with the opportunity to research, role-play, and actively question the information presented.

**2 EXTEND LEARNING BY USING THE INTERNET**

**ClassZone.com,** the companion Web site of *The Americans,* features activities, quizzes, background information, and links correlated to the textbook.

## MAIN IDEA ③ WHY IT MATTERS NOW

As World War I intensified, the United States was forced to abandon its neutrality.

The United States remains involved in European and world affairs.

---

### SECTION 1

# World War I Begins

| MAIN IDEA | WHY IT MATTERS NOW | Terms & Names |
|---|---|---|
| As World War I intensified, the United States was forced to abandon its neutrality. | The United States remains involved in European and world affairs. | •nationalism<br>•militarism<br>•Allies<br>•Central Powers<br>•Archduke Franz Ferdinand | •no man's land<br>•trench warfare<br>•*Lusitania*<br>•Zimmermann note |

#### One American's Story

It was about 1:00 A.M. on April 6, 1917, and the members of the U.S. House of Representatives were tired. For the past 15 hours they had been debating President Wilson's request for a declaration of war against Germany. There was a breathless hush as Jeannette Rankin of Montana, the first woman elected to Congress, stood up. Rankin declared, "I want to stand by my country but I cannot vote for war. I vote no." Later she reflected on her action.

**A PERSONAL VOICE** JEANNETTE RANKIN

" I believe that the first vote I cast was the most significant vote and a most significant act on the part of women, because women are going to have to stop war. I felt at the time that the first woman [in Congress] should take the first stand, that the first time the first woman had a chance to say no to war she should say it. "

—quoted in *Jeannette Rankin: First Lady in Congress*

▲ Jeannette Rankin was the only member of the House to vote against the U.S. entering both World War I and World War II.

After much debate as to whether the United States should join the fight, Congress voted in favor of U.S. entry into World War I. With this decision, the government abandoned the neutrality that America had maintained for three years. What made the United States change its policy in 1917?

#### Causes of World War I

Although many Americans wanted to stay out of the war, several factors made American neutrality difficult to maintain. As an industrial and imperial power, the United States felt many of the same pressures that had led the nations of Europe into devastating warfare. Historians generally cite four long-term causes of the First World War: nationalism, imperialism, militarism, and the formation of a system of alliances.

---

### History Through Film ④

#### ECHOES OF THE GREAT WAR

In the 1920s and 30s, a number of Hollywood horror films were influenced by memories of the Great War. *The Hunchback of Notre Dame* and *The Phantom of the Opera* featured men who, like many veterans, were forced to live with shameful disfigurements.

Other films recalled the war's bleak landscapes. In fact, parts of the movie *Frankenstein* were filmed on the same sets as *All Quiet on the Western Front*, the famous war film. James Whale, who directed *Frankenstein*, was a veteran of the war. Like many of his generation, he remained profoundly disturbed by the horrors the war had unleashed.

Chaney in *The Hunchback* ▲ of Notre Dame (1923)

◀ Lon Chaney in *The Phantom of the Opera* (1925)

(top) *All Quiet on the Western* (bottom) *Frankenstein* (1931)

#### SKILLBUILDER In

1. Why might the the powerful to the le
2. How do horror fil anxieties of the

SEE SKILLBU

WILSON REFUSES TO COMPROMISE Wilson unwisely ignored the Republican majority in the Senate when he chose the members of the American delegation. If he had been more willing to accept a compromise on the League, it would have been more likely that the Senate would have approved the treaty. Wilson, however, was exhausted from his efforts at Versailles.

Despite ill health, Wilson set out in September 1919 on an 8,000-mile tour. He delivered 34 speeches in about 3 weeks, explaining why the United States should join the League of Nations. On October 2, Wilson suffered a stroke (a ruptured blood vessel to the brain) and lay partially paralyzed for more than two months, unable to even meet with his cabinet. His once-powerful voice was no more than a thick whisper.

When the treaty came up for a vote in the Senate in November 1919, Senator Lodge introduced a number of amendments, the most important of which qualified the terms under which the United States would enter the League of Nations. It was feared that U.S. membership in the League would force the United States to form its foreign policy in accord with the League. Although the Senate rejected the amendments, it also failed to ratify the treaty.

Wilson refused to compromise. "I will not play for position," he proclaimed. "This is not a time for tactics. It is a time to stand square. I can stand defeat; I cannot stand retreat from conscientious duty." The treaty again came up for a vote in March 1920. The Senate again rejected the Lodge amendments—and again failed to muster enough votes for ratification.

The United States finally signed a separate treaty with Germany in 1921, after Wilson was no longer president. The United States never joined the League of Nations, but it maintained an unofficial observer at League meetings. ☺

MAIN IDEA

Making Inferences
☺ Why were some people afraid of the treaty's influence over American foreign policy?

---

### ③ SHOW STUDENTS WHY HISTORY MATTERS

**Main Idea** and **Why It Matters Now** at the beginning of every section build critical reading skills by telling students why the information they are about to read is important.

### ④ MAKE CONNECTIONS TO OTHER DISCIPLINES

**History through Film** helps students understand and evaluate how historical events have influenced the content of motion pictures. Other cross-discipline features are History through Art, History through Photographs, and History through Architecture.

# History Encourages Critical Thinking

*The Americans: Reconstruction to the 21st Century* promotes critical thinking and teaches students to become responsible and informed decision-makers.

In addition, for three years the Russians had fought on the side of the Allies, suffering higher casualties than any other nation. However, because Russia was excluded from the peace conference, it lost more territory than Germany did. The Union of Soviet Socialist Republics (or Soviet Union), as Russia was officially called after 1922, became determined to regain its former territory.

Finally, the treaty ignored claims of colonized people for self-determination, as in the case of Southeast Asia, where the Vietnamese people were beginning to demand the same political rights enjoyed by people in Western nations.

**OPPOSITION TO THE TREATY** When Wilson returned to the United States, he faced strong opposition to the treaty. Some people, including Herbert Hoover, believed it was too harsh. Hoover noted, "The economic consequences alone will pull down all Europe and thus injure the United States." Others considered the treaty a sell-out to imperialism because it simply exchanged one set of colonial rulers for another. Some ethnic groups objected to the treaty because the new national boundaries it established did not satisfy their particular demands for self-determination. For example, before the war many Poles had been under German rule. Now many Germans were under Polish rule.

**DEBATE OVER THE LEAGUE OF NATIONS** The main domestic opposition, however, centered on the issue of the League of Nations. A few opponents believed that the League threatened the U.S. foreign policy of isolationism. Conservative senators, headed by **Henry Cabot Lodge**, were suspicious of the provision for joint economic and military action against aggression, even though it was voluntary. They wanted the constitutional right of Congress to declare war included in the treaty.

## 1 POINT

**"The League of Nations was the world's best hope for lasting peace."**

President Wilson campaigned for the League of Nations as "necessary to meet the differing and unexpected contingencies" that could threaten world peace. Wilson believed that the League would create a forum where nations could talk through their disagreements. He also hoped it would provide collective security, in which nations would "respect and preserve as against external aggression the territorial integrity and existing political independence of all members of the League," and thereby prevent devastating warfare.

Critics complained that membership in the League would limit American independence in international affairs. However, Wilson argued that League membership included "a moral, not a legal, obligation" that would leave Congress free to decide its own course of action. Wilson tried to assure Congress as well as the general public that the League was "not a straightjacket, but a vehicle of life." It was also a definite guaranty . . . against the things that have just

## COUNTERPOINT

**"The League of Nations posed a threat to U.S. self-determination."**

Senator William Borah was one of the foremost critics of the Treaty of Versailles because he objected to U.S. membership in the League of Nations. Borah feared that membership in the League "would draw America away from her isolation and into the internal affairs and concerns of Europe" and involve the United States in foreign wars. "Once having surrendered and become a part of the European concerns," Borah wondered, "where, my friends, are you going to stop?"

Many opponents also feared that the League would nullify the Monroe Doctrine by limiting "the right of our people to govern themselves free from all restraint, legal or moral, of foreign powers."

Although Wilson argued that the League of Nations would have no such power of restraint, Borah was unconvinced. He responded to Wilson's argument by asking, "What will your League amount to if it does not contain powers that no one dreams of giving it?"

**THINKING CRITICALLY**

1. **CONNECT TO HISTORY** **Summarizing** Both supporters and opponents of the League hoped to preserve peace. How did each group propose to secure peace for the United States?

   **SEE SKILLBUILDER HANDBOOK, PAGE R4.**

## THINKING CRITICALLY 1

1. **CONNECT TO HISTORY** **Summarizing** Both supporters and opponents of the League hoped to preserve peace. How did each group propose to secure peace for the United States?

   **SEE SKILLBUILDER HANDBOOK, PAGE R4.**

2. **CONNECT TO TODAY** **Identifying Problems** What are some contemporary arguments against United States participation in international organizations such as the United Nations or the World Court?

---

## 2

**Vocabulary**
**segregated:** separated or isolated from others

**MAIN IDEA**

**Summarizing**
Ⓐ How did the United States raise an army for the war?

◀ Drafted men line up for service at Camp Travis in San Antonio, Texas, around 1917.

▲ James Montgomery Flagg's portrayal of Uncle Sam became the most famous recruiting poster in American history.

I WANT YOU FOR U.S. ARMY
NEAREST RECRUITING STATION

**RAISING AN ARMY** To meet the government's need for more fighting power, Congress passed the **Selective Service Act** in May 1917. The act required men to register with the government in order to be randomly selected for military service. By the end of 1918, 24 million men had registered under the act. Of this number, almost 3 million were called up. About 2 million troops reached Europe before the truce was signed, and three-fourths of them saw actual combat. Most of the inductees had not attended high school, and about one in five was foreign-born.

About 400,000 African Americans served in the armed forces. More than half of them served in France. African American soldiers served in segregated units and were excluded from the navy and marines. Most African Americans were assigned to noncombat duties, although there were exceptions. The all-black 369th Infantry Regiment saw more continuous duty on the front lines than any other American regiment. Two soldiers of the 369th, Henry Johnson and Needham Roberts, were the first Americans to receive France's highest military honor, the Croix de Guerre—the "cross of war."

The eight-month training period took place partly in the United States and partly in Europe. During this time the men put in 17-hour days on target practice, bayonet drill, kitchen duty, and cleaning up the grounds. Since real weapons were in short supply, soldiers often drilled with fake weapons—rocks instead of hand grenades, or wooden poles instead of rifles.

Although women were not allowed to enlist, the army reluctantly accepted women in the Army Corps of Nurses, but denied them army rank, pay, and benefits. Meanwhile, some 13,000 women accepted noncombat positions in the navy and marines, where they served as nurses, secretaries, and telephone operators, with full military rank. Ⓐ

**MASS PRODUCTION** In addition to the vast army that had to be created and trained, the United States had to find a way to transport men, food, and equipment over thousands of miles of ocean. It was an immense task, made more difficult by German submarine activity, which by early 1917 had sunk twice as much ship tonnage as the Allies had built. In order to expand its fleet, the U.S. government took four crucial steps.

**Vocabulary**
**segregated:** separated or isolated from others

**MAIN IDEA**

**Summarizing**
Ⓐ How did the United States raise an army for the war?

---

**1 ANALYZE OPPOSING VIEWPOINTS**
**Point/Counterpoint** encourages students to use critical thinking skills by comparing and evaluating opposing viewpoints on important issues.

**2 SUPPORT CRITICAL THINKING**
**Inner-column notes** provide Main Idea questions that ask students to think critically about their reading. **Vocabulary** notes give definitions of unfamiliar words at point of use. **Background** notes provide vital background information.

## HISTORIC DECISIONS OF THE SUPREME COURT

# SCHENCK v. UNITED STATES (1919)

**ORIGINS OF THE CASE** Charles Schenck, an official of the U.S. Socialist Party, distributed leaflets that called the draft a "deed against humanity" and compared conscription to slavery, urging conscripts to "assert your rights." Schenck was convicted of sedition and sentenced to prison, but he argued that the conviction, punishment, and even the law itself violated his right to free speech. The Supreme Court agreed to hear his appeal.

**THE RULING** A unanimous court upheld Schenck's conviction, stating that under wartime conditions, the words in the leaflets were not protected by the right to free speech.

### LEGAL REASONING

The Supreme Court's opinion in the *Schenck* case, written by Justice Oliver Wendell Holmes, Jr., has become famous as a guide for how the First Amendment defines the right of free speech. Holmes wrote:

> " The question in every case is whether the words used are used in such circumstances and are of such a nature as to create a clear and present danger that they will bring about the substantive evils that Congress has a right to prevent."

Justice Holmes noted that "in ordinary times" the First Amendment might have protected Schenck, but "[w]hen a nation is at war many things that might be said in time of peace . . . will not be endured."

The analogy that Holmes used to explain why Schenck could be punished for his words has become probably the best-known observation ever made about free speech:

> " Protection of free speech would not protect a man in falsely shouting 'Fire!' in a theatre and causing a panic."

Writing for the Court, Holmes implied that during wartime, Schenck's leaflet was just that dangerous.

Oliver Wendell Holmes, Jr.,
Supreme Court Justice
1902–1932 ▷

### LEGAL SOURCES

**LEGISLATION**

**U.S. CONSTITUTION, FIRST AMENDMENT (1791)**
"Congress shall make no law . . . abridging the freedom of speech, or of the press."

**THE SEDITION ACT (1918)**
"(W)hoever . . . shall willfully utter, print, write or publish any disloyal, profane, scurrilous, or abusive language about the form of government, . . . Constitution, . . . military or naval forces, . . . flag, . . . or the uniform of the Army or Navy . . . of the United States . . . shall be punished by a fine of not more than $10,000 or imprisonment for not more than twenty years, or both."

**RELATED CASES**

**DEBS v. UNITED STATES**
(MARCH, 1919)
The conviction against Eugene Debs for speaking against the war and the draft is upheld.

**FROHWERK v. UNITED STATES**
(MARCH, 1919)
The publisher of a newspaper that had criticized the war is sentenced with a fine and ten years in prison.

**ABRAMS v. UNITED STATES**
(NOV., 1919)
Leaflets criticizing the U.S. expeditionary force in Russia are found to be unprotected by the First Amendment. Holmes writes a dissenting opinion calling for the "free trade of ideas."

### WHY IT MATTERED

During the course of World War I, the federal government brought approximately 2,000 prosecutions for violations of the Espionage Act of 1917 or the Sedition Act of 1918, the same laws under which it convicted Schenck, Debs, and Frohwerk.

By the fall of 1919, however, Holmes had changed his mind. The case of *Abrams v. United States* concerned leaflets that criticized President Wilson's "capitalistic" government for sending troops to put down the Russian Revolution. Justice Holmes, joined by Justice Louis Brandeis, dissented from the majority of the Court which upheld the conviction. In his dissent, Holmes emphasized the importance of a free exchange of ideas so that truth will win out in the intellectual marketplace. His reasoning won him acclaim as a protector of free speech.

The belief that truth will eventually win out in the marketplace of ideas has become important legal justification for promoting freedom of speech.

▲ Eugene Debs was arrested for antiwar speeches like the one he gave at this 1916 presidential campaign stop.

### HISTORICAL IMPACT

Disagreements about what kinds of speech are "free" under the First Amendment continue. During the 1950s, when people were jailed for supporting Communism, and during the Vietnam War, when war protestors supported draft resistance, these issues again reached the Supreme Court.

The Court has also been asked to decide if young people in schools have the same First Amendment rights as adults. In *Tinker v. Des Moines School District* (1969), the Court ordered a school to readmit students who had been suspended for wearing black arm bands in protest of the war in Vietnam.

This so-called symbolic speech, such as wearing an armband or burning a draft card or a flag to express an opinion, has sparked heated debate. In *Texas v. Johnson* (1989), the Court, by a narrow five to four vote, invalidated a law under which a man who burned an American flag to protest Reagan administration policies had been convicted. The decision so outraged some people that members of Congress considered amending the Constitution to prohibit any "physical desecration" of the flag. The amendment did not pass. Our freedoms of expression continue to depend upon the words in the first article of the Bill of Rights, written more than 200 years ago.

◁ In 1965 Mary Beth Tinker and her brother, John, were suspended from school for wearing armbands that symbolically criticized the Vietnam War.

### THINKING CRITICALLY

**CONNECT TO HISTORY**

1. **Analyzing Primary Sources** Read Justice Holmes's dissent in *Abrams v. United States*. Compare it with the opinion he wrote in *Schenck v. United States*. Explain the major difference or similarity in the two opinions.

📖 SEE SKILLBUILDER HANDBOOK, PAGE R22.

**CONNECT TO TODAY**

2. 🖥 **INTERNET ACTIVITY** CLASSZONE.COM

Visit the links for Historic Decisions of the Supreme Court to research articles about free speech issues. Select several of these issues—such as whether hate groups have a right to march—to discuss with other students in your class. Choose one issue and, as a group, write down as many arguments as you can on both sides of the issue. Then present a debate to the class.

---

### ③ LEARN ABOUT SUPREME COURT DECISIONS

**Historic Decisions of the Supreme Court** helps students analyze, understand, and evaluate important Supreme Court decisions.

# Complete Instructional Support

*The Americans: Reconstruction to the 21st Century* offers a wide variety of resources to help you manage your clssroom and support students as they interact with history.

## TEACHER'S RESOURCE PACKAGE

### IN-DEPTH UNIT RESOURCES

Resources organized by unit, chapter, and section include

- Guided Reading
- Skillbuilder Practice
- Geography Applications
- Primary Sources
- Literature Selections
- American Lives (biographies)

### READING STUDY GUIDES
*with Answer Key*

Provide chapter summaries and reading comprehension questions written at the 6-7 grade level (English and Spanish)

### PLANNING FOR BLOCK SCHEDULES

Includes a pacing guide, chapter teaching models, organization charts, and suggestions for addressing multiple learning styles

### PRESIDENTIAL ELECTIONS HANDBOOK

Includes supplementary information on each presidential election through 2000

### HISTORIC SUPREME COURT CASES

Provides blackline masters for 27 cases that help students analyze, understand, and evaluate important Supreme Court decisions

## TELESCOPING THE TIMES: CHAPTER SUMMARIES

Offers teaching flexibility and opportunities for students to focus their reading and review key ideas from each chapter (English and Spanish)

### ACCESS FOR STUDENTS ACQUIRING ENGLISH: SPANISH TRANSLATIONS

Provides strategies for teaching ESL students and Spanish translations of selected In-Depth Resources

### FORMAL ASSESSMENT

Includes a variety of testing materials, including three levels of tests for each chapter, section quizzes, and rubrics for assessing writing

### INTEGRATED ASSESSMENT

Includes rubrics, portfolio assessment, cooperative learning, group discussion, and role-playing

### TAKS SPIRALED CONTENT REVIEW

This book reviews the social studies content covered on the Grade 11 Exit Level Social Studies Texas Assessment of Knowledge and Skills (TAKS).

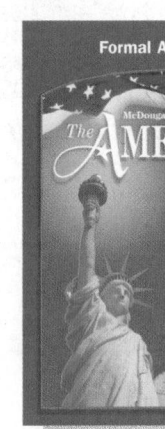

## TRANSPARENCIES

### HUMANITIES TRANSPARENCIES
Integrates political cartoons, fine art, photographs, and other historical artifacts into lessons

### GEOGRAPHY TRANSPARENCIES
Includes maps with overlays to provide additional information

### CRITICAL THINKING TRANSPARENCIES
Builds students' critical thinking skills through graphic organizers, cause-and-effect charts, and visual summaries

### TAKS PRACTICE TRANSPARENCIES
Includes one transparency for each section of the textbook that covers the preceding day's content and familiarizes students with a variety of testing items

## ADDITIONAL RESOURCES

### THE AMERICANS WORKBOOK
Features note-taking strategies and graphic organizers for enhancing reading comprehension

### WRITING FOR SOCIAL STUDIES
Offers support for writing research papers, historical narratives, essays, interviews, oral histories, book reviews, and short reports

# Comprehensive Assessment Support

Assessment materials in print, transparency, CD-ROM, and Internet formats offer students a variety of ways to prepare for tests.

## TEST GENERATOR CD-ROM

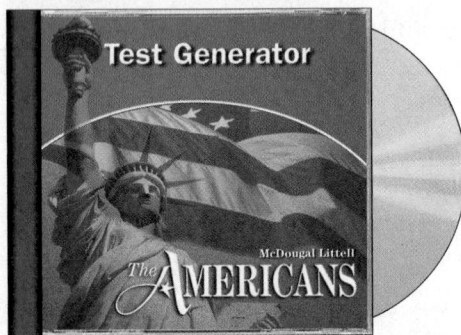

This CD-ROM contains a variety of pre-made tests and a test bank of items for creating customized tests. Questions are provided in three levels: basic, average, and advanced. Tools walk the user through the searching and editing steps and help you correlate tests to national and state standards.

## FORMAL ASSESSMENT

Includes section quizzes, three levels of tests for each chapter, and rubrics for assessing writing

## INTEGRATED ASSESSMENT

Includes rubrics, portfolio assessment, cooperative learning, group discussion, and role-playing activities

## TAKS PRACTICE TRANSPARENCIES

Includes one transparency for each section of the textbook that reviews content and familiarizes students with a variety of testing items

## TAKS SPIRALED CONTENT REVIEW

This book reviews the social studies contents covered on the Grade 11 Exit Level TAKS Test.

## TAKS PRACTICE TESTS

Contains tests to aid students in preparing for the TAKS test. Practice tests provide opportunities to experience a variety of test items.

## STRATEGIES FOR TAKING TAKS

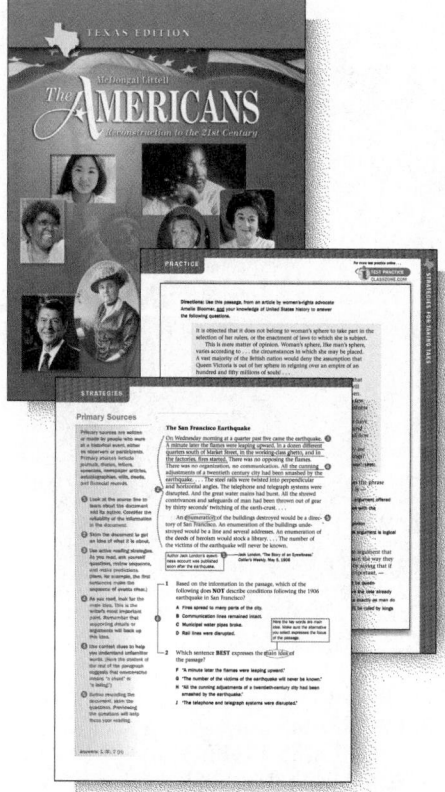

This innovative section of the Pupil's Edition offers students help and practice with the skills they need to study history and to prepare for TAKS tests. It includes strategies for multiple choice, constructed response, extended response, and document-based questions. It also includes strategies for analyzing primary and secondary sources and a variety of visual features. Each strategy is followed by a set of practice items.

## TAKS ONLINE TEST PRACTICE

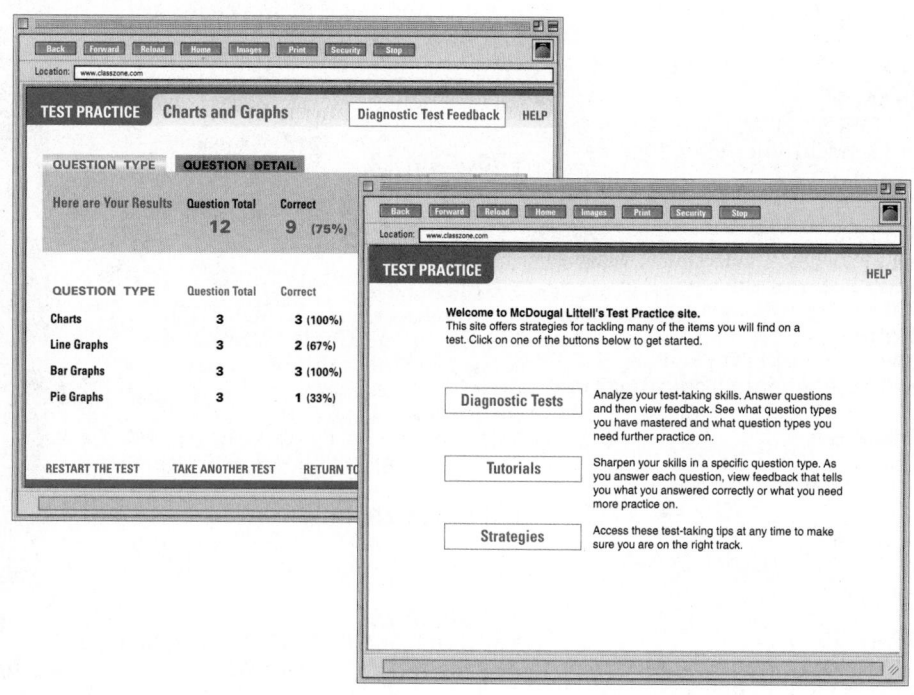

This online student test practice feature can be accessed through the *ClassZone* Web site. The test practice includes test-taking tips, diagnostic tests, skill-based tutorials, and skills and strategies help.

# *American Stories* Video Series

*American Stories* is a powerful video series integrated with the text of *The Americans*. Seventeen fascinating documentaries, each 8–10 minutes long, help you to introduce various sections of the text. In addition, an invaluable Teacher's Resource Book helps you to fully exploit the power of the videos with everything from teaching tips to lesson-extending information and activities.

**PROGRAM 1**
PATRIOT FATHER, LOYALIST SON: The Divided House of Benjamin and William Franklin

**PROGRAM 2**
RECRUITED BY LEWIS AND CLARK: Patrick Gass Chronicles the Journey West

**PROGRAM 3**
WAR OUTSIDE MY WINDOW: Mary Chesnut's Diary of the Civil War

**PROGRAM 4**
TEACHER OF A FREED PEOPLE: Robert Fitzgerald and Reconstruction

**PROGRAM 5**
A WALK IN TWO WORLDS: The Education of Zitkala-Ša, a Sioux

**PROGRAM 6**
FROM CHINA TO CHINATOWN: Fong See's American Dream

**PROGRAM 7**
GUSHER!: Pattilo Higgins and the Great Texas Oil Boom

**PROGRAM 8**
A CHILD ON STRIKE: The Testimony of Camella Teoli, Mill Girl

**PROGRAM 9**
ACE OF ACES: Eddie Rickenbacker and the First World War

**PROGRAM 10**
JUMP AT THE SUN: Zora Neale Hurston and the Harlem Renaissance

**PROGRAM 11**
BROKE BUT NOT BROKEN: Ann Marie Low Remembers the Dust Bowl

**PROGRAM 12**
A SONG FOR HIS PEOPLE: Pedro J. González and the Fight for Mexican-American Rights

**PROGRAM 13**
ESCAPING THE FINAL SOLUTION: Kurt Klein and Gerda Weissmann Klein Remember the Holocaust

**PROGRAM 14**
THE COLD WAR COMES HOME: Hollywood Blacklists the Kahn Family

**PROGRAM 15**
JUSTICE IN MONTGOMERY: Jo Ann Gibson Robinson and the Bus Boycott

**PROGRAM 16**
MATTERS OF CONSCIENCE: Stephan Gubar and the Vietnam War

**PROGRAM 17**
POISONED PLAYGROUND: Lois Gibbs and the Crisis at Love Canal

**VIDEOCASSETTES**

**VOLUME 1:** PROGRAMS 1–6
**VOLUME 2:** PROGRAMS 7–12
**VOLUME 3:** PROGRAMS 13–17
**VOLUME 4, 5, 6:** SPANISH VERSIONS

# Integrated Technology Resources

### THE AMERICANS: ELECTRONIC LIBRARY OF PRIMARY SOURCES

Support, enrich, and extend each chapter of the text with a compendium of carefully selected primary sources. Discover a wealth of documents that have shaped American history, along with personal accounts drawn from letters, diaries, and oral histories.

### THE AMERICANS: POWER PRESENTATIONS

These electronic presentations are a valuable tool for use in classroom instruction. Presentations contain outlines of each chapter, maps, and slides for key concepts and terms.

### ELECTRONIC TEACHER TOOLS

Access all of the resources from the Teacher's Resource Package on one CD-ROM. Search by chapter or browse by topic right from the computer.

# Internet Resources at classzone.com

McDougal Littell's companion Web site, **classzone.com**, is your classroom's online guide to *The Americans*. **ClassZone** will help you meet the challenges of teaching in today's classroom by providing access to a wide range of resources for you and activities for your students related to the chapters of *The Americans*. In **ClassZone** you will find the following resources:

- **Overviews** of each chapter
- **Self-scoring** quizzes for students to check understanding of each chapter
- Fun, **chapter-specific activities** such as online crossword puzzles and flip card games
- A weekly **current events quiz** of five questions
- **Internet links** correlated to the textbook for relevant Internet research and activities
- **Internet research tutorial** to help students conduct research on the web

Log on to **ClassZone** at **classzone.com**

Visit **ClassZone** frequently to see the latest additions and new features.

With the purchase of *The Americans*, you have immediate access to **ClassZone**.

**TEACHER KEY:** MCD359YAU76RT
**STUDENT KEY:** MCDLJCY3GMBEX

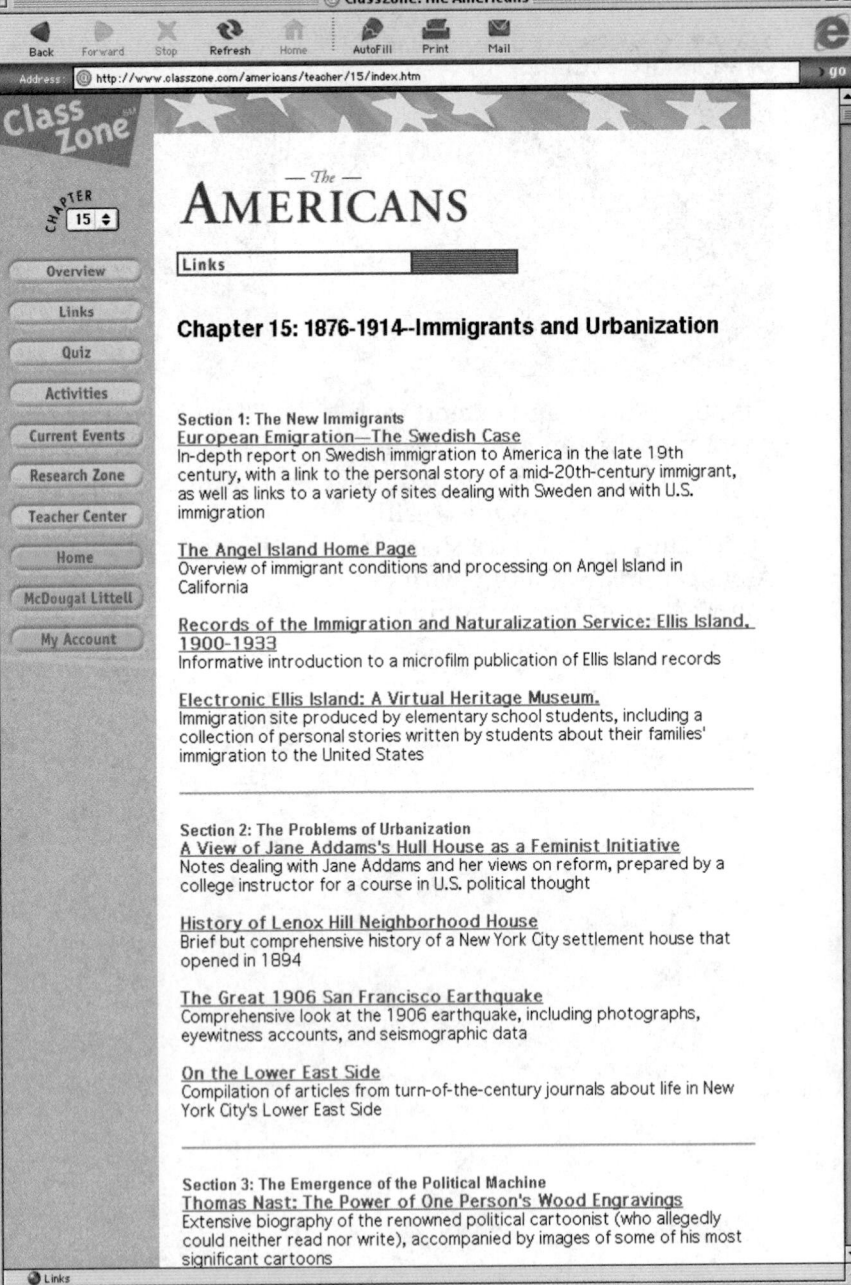

# *The Americans* Online Edition

On the Web at **classzone.com**, *The Americans* Online Edition includes features that enrich the learning experience for students while giving you the tools for teaching that save you time. With the full text of the book online . . .

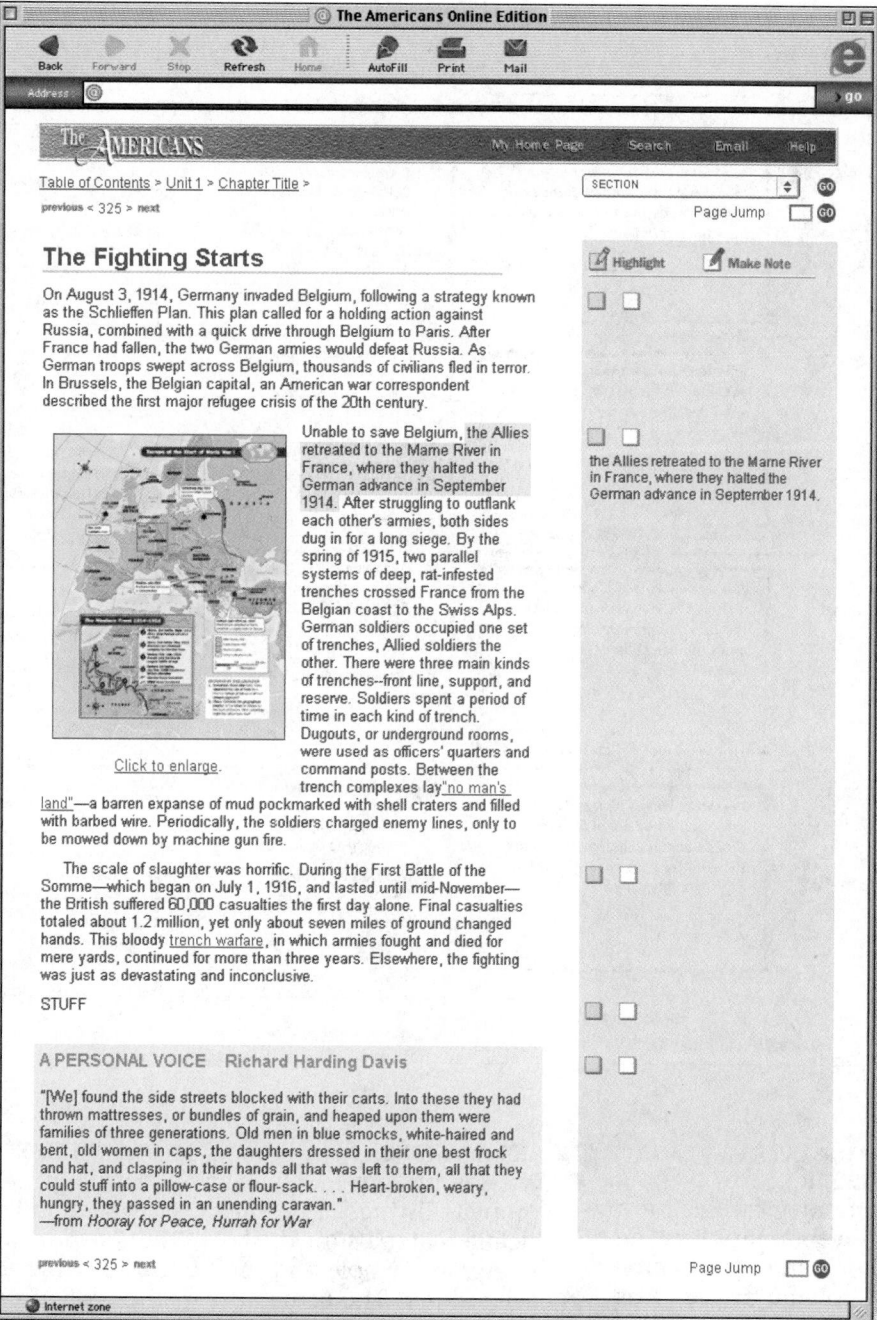

**STUDENTS CAN . . .**
- Learn about history through interactive maps and illustrations
- Look up glossary terms
- Highlight text
- Make notes in the margins

**STUDENTS CAN ALSO . . .**
- Take assessments online
- Read primary source documents at point of use
- Listen to section audio summaries
- Answer opinion poll questions

**YOU CAN . . .**
- Create margin notes to guide student reading activities
- Post homework assignments
- Place online worksheets at point of use
- Use animated maps and illustrations for presentations

Go to **www.mcdougallittell.com** for order information.

# Chapter Planning Guide

A convenient two-page Planning Guide can be found at the beginning of every chapter in the Teacher's Edition of *The Americans: Reconstruction to the 21st Century*. By giving an overview of the chapter's key ideas, copymasters, integrated technology, and assessment options, the Planning Guide can help you meet the diverse needs of the classroom.

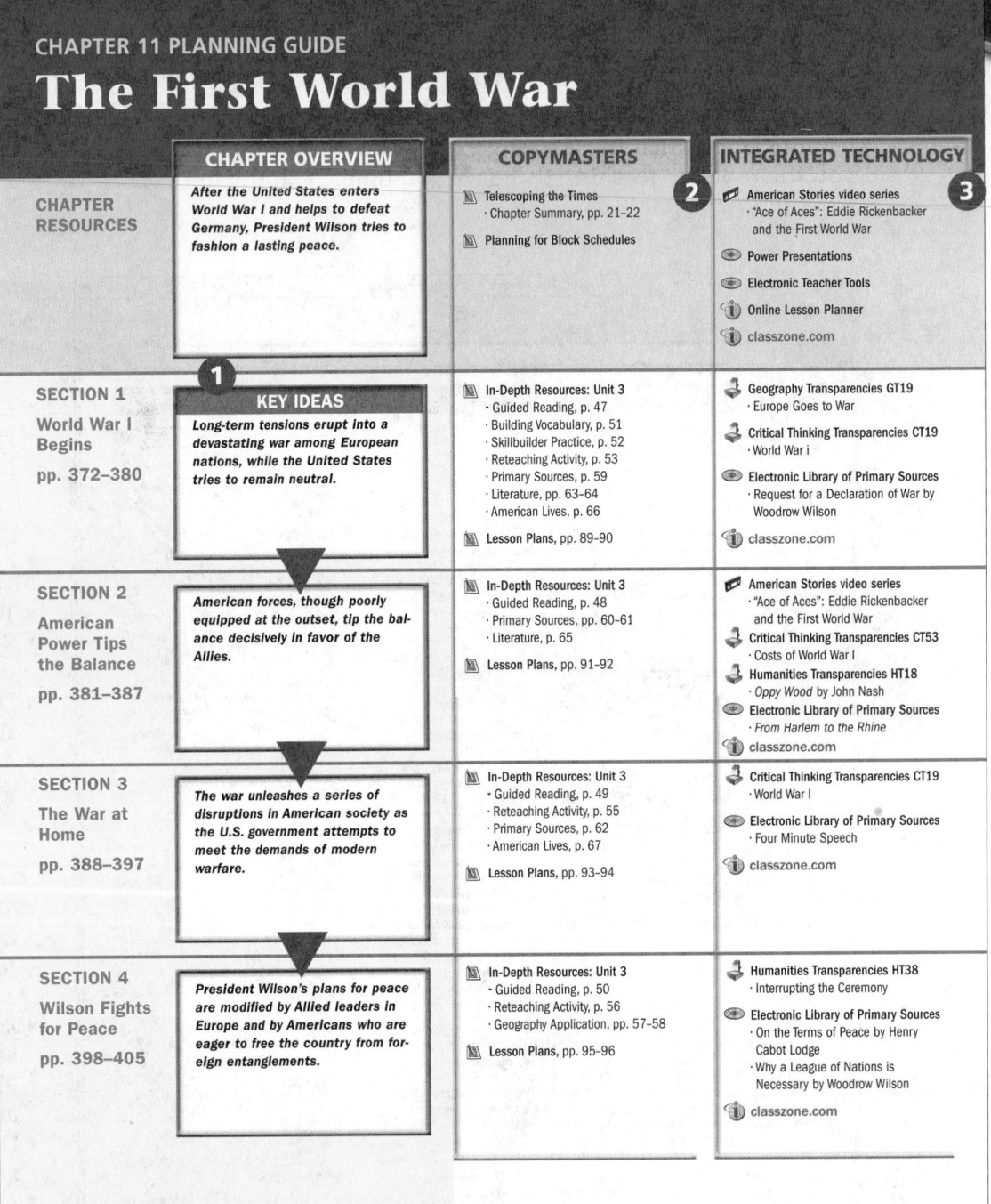

CHAPTER 11 PLANNING GUIDE

# The First World War

| | CHAPTER OVERVIEW | COPYMASTERS | INTEGRATED TECHNOLOGY |
|---|---|---|---|
| **CHAPTER RESOURCES** | After the United States enters World War I and helps to defeat Germany, President Wilson tries to fashion a lasting peace. | ▨ Telescoping the Times<br>· Chapter Summary, pp. 21–22<br><br>▨ Planning for Block Schedules | 🎞 American Stories video series<br>· "Ace of Aces": Eddie Rickenbacker and the First World War<br><br>👁 Power Presentations<br>👁 Electronic Teacher Tools<br>🖱 Online Lesson Planner<br>🖱 classzone.com |
| **SECTION 1**<br>World War I Begins<br>pp. 372–380 | **KEY IDEAS**<br>Long-term tensions erupt into a devastating war among European nations, while the United States tries to remain neutral. | ▨ In-Depth Resources: Unit 3<br>· Guided Reading, p. 47<br>· Building Vocabulary, p. 51<br>· Skillbuilder Practice, p. 52<br>· Reteaching Activity, p. 53<br>· Primary Sources, p. 59<br>· Literature, pp. 63–64<br>· American Lives, p. 66<br><br>▨ Lesson Plans, pp. 89–90 | 📊 Geography Transparencies GT19<br>· Europe Goes to War<br><br>📊 Critical Thinking Transparencies CT19<br>· World War i<br><br>👁 Electronic Library of Primary Sources<br>· Request for a Declaration of War by Woodrow Wilson<br><br>🖱 classzone.com |
| **SECTION 2**<br>American Power Tips the Balance<br>pp. 381–387 | American forces, though poorly equipped at the outset, tip the balance decisively in favor of the Allies. | ▨ In-Depth Resources: Unit 3<br>· Guided Reading, p. 48<br>· Primary Sources, pp. 60–61<br>· Literature, p. 65<br><br>▨ Lesson Plans, pp. 91–92 | 🎞 American Stories video series<br>· "Ace of Aces": Eddie Rickenbacker and the First World War<br>📊 Critical Thinking Transparencies CT53<br>· Costs of World War I<br>📊 Humanities Transparencies HT18<br>· Oppy Wood by John Nash<br>👁 Electronic Library of Primary Sources<br>· From Harlem to the Rhine<br>🖱 classzone.com |
| **SECTION 3**<br>The War at Home<br>pp. 388–397 | The war unleashes a series of disruptions in American society as the U.S. government attempts to meet the demands of modern warfare. | ▨ In-Depth Resources: Unit 3<br>· Guided Reading, p. 49<br>· Reteaching Activity, p. 55<br>· Primary Sources, p. 62<br>· American Lives, p. 67<br><br>▨ Lesson Plans, pp. 93–94 | 📊 Critical Thinking Transparencies CT19<br>· World War I<br><br>👁 Electronic Library of Primary Sources<br>· Four Minute Speech<br><br>🖱 classzone.com |
| **SECTION 4**<br>Wilson Fights for Peace<br>pp. 398–405 | President Wilson's plans for peace are modified by Allied leaders in Europe and by Americans who are eager to free the country from foreign entanglements. | ▨ In-Depth Resources: Unit 3<br>· Guided Reading, p. 50<br>· Reteaching Activity, p. 56<br>· Geography Application, pp. 57–58<br><br>▨ Lesson Plans, pp. 95–96 | 📊 Humanities Transparencies HT38<br>· Interrupting the Ceremony<br><br>👁 Electronic Library of Primary Sources<br>· On the Terms of Peace by Henry Cabot Lodge<br>· Why a League of Nations is Necessary by Woodrow Wilson<br><br>🖱 classzone.com |

**① CHAPTER OVERVIEW AND KEY IDEAS**
A chronological, section-by-section summary lists the key ideas in each chapter. Each column of key ideas connects to the main idea of the whole chapter.

**② COPYMASTERS**
This column gives complete listings of reproducible materials for the chapter as a whole and for each section. The listings reveal the depth of resource materials available.

**③ INTEGRATED TECHNOLOGY**
Technology is listed for each section and includes the *American Stories* videos, the Electronic Library of Primary Sources, audio resources, Internet ideas, and transparencies.

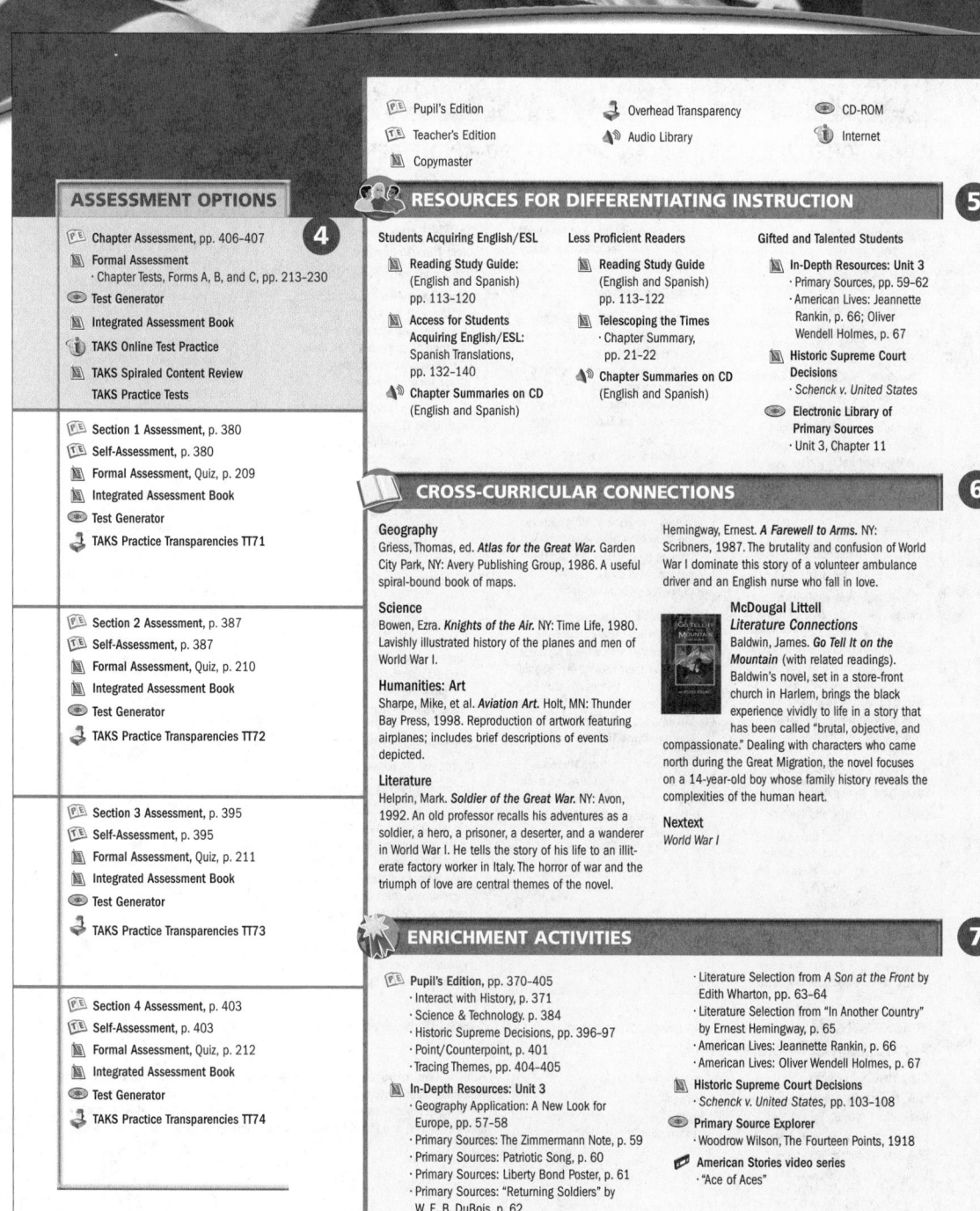

Legend:
- PE Pupil's Edition
- TE Teacher's Edition
- Copymaster
- Overhead Transparency
- Audio Library
- CD-ROM
- Internet

## ASSESSMENT OPTIONS

- PE Chapter Assessment, pp. 406–407 **4**
- Formal Assessment
  · Chapter Tests, Forms A, B, and C, pp. 213–230
- Test Generator
- Integrated Assessment Book
- TAKS Online Test Practice
- TAKS Spiraled Content Review
- TAKS Practice Tests

- PE Section 1 Assessment, p. 380
- TE Self-Assessment, p. 380
- Formal Assessment, Quiz, p. 209
- Integrated Assessment Book
- Test Generator
- TAKS Practice Transparencies TT71

- PE Section 2 Assessment, p. 387
- TE Self-Assessment, p. 387
- Formal Assessment, Quiz, p. 210
- Integrated Assessment Book
- Test Generator
- TAKS Practice Transparencies TT72

- PE Section 3 Assessment, p. 395
- TE Self-Assessment, p. 395
- Formal Assessment, Quiz, p. 211
- Integrated Assessment Book
- Test Generator
- TAKS Practice Transparencies TT73

- PE Section 4 Assessment, p. 403
- TE Self-Assessment, p. 403
- Formal Assessment, Quiz, p. 212
- Integrated Assessment Book
- Test Generator
- TAKS Practice Transparencies TT74

## RESOURCES FOR DIFFERENTIATING INSTRUCTION **5**

**Students Acquiring English/ESL**
- Reading Study Guide: (English and Spanish) pp. 113–120
- Access for Students Acquiring English/ESL: Spanish Translations, pp. 132–140
- Chapter Summaries on CD (English and Spanish)

**Less Proficient Readers**
- Reading Study Guide (English and Spanish) pp. 113–122
- Telescoping the Times · Chapter Summary, pp. 21–22
- Chapter Summaries on CD (English and Spanish)

**Gifted and Talented Students**
- In-Depth Resources: Unit 3 · Primary Sources, pp. 59–62 · American Lives: Jeannette Rankin, p. 66; Oliver Wendell Holmes, p. 67
- Historic Supreme Court Decisions · Schenck v. United States
- Electronic Library of Primary Sources · Unit 3, Chapter 11

## CROSS-CURRICULAR CONNECTIONS **6**

**Geography**
Griess, Thomas, ed. *Atlas for the Great War.* Garden City Park, NY: Avery Publishing Group, 1986. A useful spiral-bound book of maps.

**Science**
Bowen, Ezra. *Knights of the Air.* NY: Time Life, 1980. Lavishly illustrated history of the planes and men of World War I.

**Humanities: Art**
Sharpe, Mike, et al. *Aviation Art.* Holt, MN: Thunder Bay Press, 1998. Reproduction of artwork featuring airplanes; includes brief descriptions of events depicted.

**Literature**
Helprin, Mark. *Soldier of the Great War.* NY: Avon, 1992. An old professor recalls his adventures as a soldier, a hero, a prisoner, a deserter, and a wanderer in World War I. He tells the story of his life to an illiterate factory worker in Italy. The horror of war and the triumph of love are central themes of the novel.

Hemingway, Ernest. *A Farewell to Arms.* NY: Scribners, 1987. The brutality and confusion of World War I dominate this story of a volunteer ambulance driver and an English nurse who fall in love.

**McDougal Littell**
*Literature Connections*
Baldwin, James. *Go Tell It on the Mountain* (with related readings). Baldwin's novel, set in a store-front church in Harlem, brings the black experience vividly to life in a story that has been called "brutal, objective, and compassionate." Dealing with characters who came north during the Great Migration, the novel focuses on a 14-year-old boy whose family history reveals the complexities of the human heart.

**Nextext**
*World War I*

## ENRICHMENT ACTIVITIES **7**

- PE Pupil's Edition, pp. 370–405
  · Interact with History, p. 371
  · Science & Technology. p. 384
  · Historic Supreme Decisions, pp. 396–97
  · Point/Counterpoint, p. 401
  · Tracing Themes, pp. 404–405
- In-Depth Resources: Unit 3
  · Geography Application: A New Look for Europe, pp. 57–58
  · Primary Sources: The Zimmermann Note, p. 59
  · Primary Sources: Patriotic Song, p. 60
  · Primary Sources: Liberty Bond Poster, p. 61
  · Primary Sources: "Returning Soldiers" by W. E. B. DuBois, p. 62

- · Literature Selection from *A Son at the Front* by Edith Wharton, pp. 63–64
- · Literature Selection from "In Another Country" by Ernest Hemingway, p. 65
- · American Lives: Jeannette Rankin, p. 66
- · American Lives: Oliver Wendell Holmes, p. 67
- Historic Supreme Court Decisions · *Schenck v. United States*, pp. 103–108
- Primary Source Explorer · Woodrow Wilson, The Fourteen Points, 1918
- American Stories video series · "Ace of Aces"

---

**4 ASSESSMENT OPTIONS**
This column identifies appropriate pages in the Formal Assessment book, which contains section quizzes and chapter tests. TAKS resources include TAKS Spiraled Content Review, TAKS Practice Tests, TAKS PracticeTransparencies, and TAKS Online Test Practice. Also listed is the Integrated Assessment book.

**5 RESOURCES FOR DIFFERENTIATING INSTRUCTION**
Here are suggested resources for teaching students acquiring English, less proficient readers, and gifted and talented students. From worksheets and chapter summaries in Spanish to lists of primary-source materials, these suggestions offer practical help for diverse classroom needs.

**6 CROSS-CURRICULAR CONNECTIONS**
This section lists resources for connecting U.S. history to other subjects. Books are listed for geography, humanities, literature, science, and other subjects. Included are references to relevant books available from McDougal Littell.

**7 ENRICHMENT ACTIVITIES**
These are resources in *The Americans* that will help you to extend and enrich your teaching of the chapter.

# Block Scheduling and Teacher-Tested Activities

Block Scheduling Lesson Plan Options appear immediately after the Planning Guide for every chapter in the Teacher's Edition of *The Americans: Reconstruction to the 21st Century*. This easy-to-use guide is a valuable aid in planning lessons for block schedules.

## BLOCK SCHEDULE LESSON PLAN OPTIONS (90-MINUTE PERIOD)

### DAY 1

**CHAPTER 11 OPENER pp. 370–371**

**1** Class Time 30 minutes

**History from Visuals, p. 370**

**2** Class Time 20 minutes

*Options for Pacing and Variety*

· Time Saver Ask students to study the photograph on the pages 370–371. Refer to the TE for questions to assess previous knowledge. Ask students how they think the depicted battle differs from the way war is waged today. **Class Time 10 minutes**

**Interact with History, p. 371**

Class Time 20 minutes

*Options for Pacing and Variety*

**2** · Role-Playing Ask students to put themselves in the place of those in power. They must weigh the benefits and disadvantages of going to war. Was the United States' participation in war justified? How so, or why not? See TE page 371 for Interact with History questions. **Class Time 15 minutes**

**SECTION 1 pp. 372–380**

Class Time 30 minutes

*Options for Pacing and Variety*

· Internet Have students read the sidebar Crisis in the Balkans on page 374, and have them do the activity listed in the TE. **Class Time 30 minutes**

· Time Saver Have students study the map on page 375, and discuss the Geography Skillbuilder questions. As an extension, ask them

### DAY 1 continued

the Interpreting the Map questions in the TE, and the questions in the activity on the TE page. **Class Time 10 minutes**

· Peer Teaching Pair a less proficient reader with a more proficient reader for library research on Switzerland's neutrality. Follow the activity on page 376 of the TE. Collect the students' written answers. **Class Time 30 minutes**

**SECTION 2 pp. 381–387**

Class Time 30 minutes

*Options for Pacing and Variety*

· Time Saver Have students answer the Main Idea questions as they go through the section. Discuss the answers as a class. **Class Time 15 minutes**

· Peer Teaching Have each student choose one example from A Personal Voice. Pair them together based on their choice. They should make a list of questions inspired by reading the quote, and then find the answers in the library or on the Internet. **Class Time 20 minutes**

· Peer Evaluation Have students work on the Section 2 Assessment before pairing up to check each other's answers. **Class Time 15 minutes**

### DAY 2

**SECTION 3 pp. 388–397**

Class Time 30 minutes

*Options for Pacing and Variety*

· Time Saver After reading the subsection Anti-Immigrant Hysteria, have students study the Political Cartoon on page 391. Ask them the Skillbuilder questions. **Class Time 10 minutes**

· Role-Playing Have students do the activity on TE page 394, and write the journal over the week about the thoughts and feelings of the migrants. Have them look at the History Through Art example on page 393, to imagine some of the basic changes that migration entails. Have some students read from the journals before you collect them. **Class Time 15 minutes**

· Internet Ask students to read the featured Historic Decisions of The Supreme Court on pages 396–397. Have them do Option 1 under the Internet activity. Collect their written answers. **Class Time 20 minutes**

**SECTION 4 pp. 398–405**

Class Time 30 minutes

*Options for Pacing and Variety*

· Peer Competition Using Point / Counterpoint on page 401 for more information, have students complete question 2 of the Section Assessment on their own. Then recreate the chart on the board and have students give information to include on it. Hold a class discussion about the Critical Thinking questions and the Hypothesizing question. **Class Time 15 minutes**

### DAY 2 continued

· Internet Have students read the feature Schenck v. *United States* (1919) on pages 396–397. Then have them do the Internet activity. **Class Time 25 minutes**

· Time Saver Ask students to read America in World Affairs, the feature on pages 404–405. Discuss the Connect to History question. **Class Time 15 minutes**

**ASSESSMENT pp. 406–407**

Class Time 30 minutes

*Options for Pacing and Variety*

· Peer Evaluation Have students work in pairs and quiz each other on the terms and names of the chapter. **Class Time 15 minutes**

· History on Film View the American Stories video for Chapter 11, "Ace of Aces: Eddie Rickenbacker and the First World War." Discuss question 2 listed on page 407. **Class Time 30 minutes**

---

**3** **TEACHER-TESTED ACTIVITY**  Link Page, Broughton High School, Raleigh, North Carolina
**PRE-WORLD WAR I WORKSHEET**

**Class Time** 40 minutes

**Task** Developing a worksheet of pre-World War I events

**Purpose** To understand the sequence of events leading to World War I

**Supplies Needed**
· Textbook
· Paper
· Pens or pencils

**Activity** Have students work in pairs to develop a worksheet describing pre-World War I events in chronological order. Tell students to leave the names of countries blank, and to keep a separate answer sheet. (Example: [Blank] was angry at [blank] when it annexed [blank] and [blank].) Have students trade worksheets and fill them in.

---

**1** **ESTIMATED TIMES** The estimated time needed for each activity is provided to help you make efficient use of the block period.

**2** **NUMEROUS TEACHING OPTIONS** Numerous teaching options help to vary the pacing of the class and the types of activities in which students are engaged.

**3** **TEACHER-TESTED ACTIVITY** Beneath the Block Scheduling lesson plan options are activities written and used in the classroom by teachers of U.S. history.

# CHAPTER 11 CORRELATION

**①**

## CORRELATION TO THE TEXAS ESSENTIAL KNOWLEDGE AND SKILLS

Chapter 11 addresses the following standards of the Texas Essential Knowledge and Skills for U.S. History.

| TEKS | Instruction **②** | Student Question/Activity **③** |
|---|---|---|
| **(3B)** Identify the reasons for U.S. involvement in World War I. | **PE 378–380**—explanation of the events that prompted America to enter the war, including unrestricted submarine warfare by Germany | **TE 379**—Skillbuilder mini-lesson about evaluation America's decision to declare war |
| **(3C)** Analyze the impact of significant individuals including John J. Pershing, during World War I. | **PE 384**—examination of General John J. Pershing's life and the significant role he played in the war | **TE 384**—question about what made Pershing such an effective military leader |
| **(3D)** Analyze major issues raised by U.S. involvement in World War I, Wilson's Fourteen Points, and the Treaty of Versailles. | **PE 398–403**—analysis of the post-war peace efforts, including Wilson's Fourteen Points and the Treaty of Versailles | **PE 403**—Critical Thinking questions regarding various issues surrounding the Treaty of Versailles |
| **(9B)** Identify and explain reasons for changes in political boundaries such as international conflicts. | **PE 400**—dual map showing the dramatic change in political boundaries in Europe as a result of World War I | **PE 400**—questions that require students to interpret information about the map |
| **(10A)** Analyze the effects of changing demographic patterns resulting from migration within the United States. | **PE 393–394**—discussion of the causes and effects of the Great Migration, which brought thousands of Southern African Americans to the North | **TE 394**—writing activity examining the experiences of African Americans who migrated to the North |
| **(12E)** Describe the economic effects of international military conflicts on the United States. | **PE 389**—chart examining the ways in which the war impacted the U.S. economy | **PE 389**—questions that require students to interpret information about the chart |
| **(15B)** Explain the impact of significant international events such as World War I on changes in the role of the federal government. | **PE 388–392**—examination of how the federal government took a greater role in the economy and society during World War I | **PE 395**—Critical Thinking question about how the war affected the power of the federal government |
| **(21D)** Identify the political, social, and economic contributions of women to American society. | **PE 394**—discussion of the significant role American women played in the war effort | **PE 395**—question about efforts by women during the war |

**④**

## TAKS MINI-LESSONS

1. **Social Studies Skills: Objective 1 (US3.B):** Identify the reasons for U.S. involvement in World War I **Activity** Have students consider the significance of Germany's unrestricted submarine warfare in prompting the United States to enter the war.

2. **Social Studies Skills: Objective 1 (US3.C):** Analyze major issues raised by U.S. involvement in World War I **Activity** Have students summarize President Wilson's Fourteen Points as well as the debate in American over the Treaty of Versailles.

3. **Social Studies Skills: Objective 2 (US10.A):** Analyze the effects of changing demographic patterns resulting from migration within the United States **Activity** Have students complete the writing activity on TE page 394 regarding the Great Migration.

4. **English Language Arts Skills: Objective 1 (7.F):** Produce summaries of texts by identifying main ideas and their supporting details. **Activity** Have students summarize the weaknesses of the Treaty of Versailles.

5. **English Language Arts Skills: Objective 3 (19.B):** Analyze ideas as represented in various media **Activity** Have students answer the questions regarding the political cartoon on page 391.

# Technology in the Classroom

For every chapter in *The Americans: Reconstruction to the 21st Century*, the Teacher's Edition includes a page that provides an innovative strategy for using the Internet and other technologies in the classroom. These strategies will help you integrate technology into your teaching of *The Americans*.

**①** **TEKS CORRELATIONS**
The first chart on the page shows the TEKS objectives that are emphasized in the chapter.

**②** **INSTRUCTION IN TEKS OBJECTIVES**
This column lists specific pages that address TEKS objectives and explains how the objectives are met.

**③** **TEKS APPLICATIONS**
This column list questions and activities that help students master the knowledge and skills in the TEKS.

**④** **TAKS MINI-LESSONS**
For every chapter, five mini-lessons are recommended that are based on activities in the Pupil's Edition and Teacher's Edition. Three mini-lessons focus on social studies, while two focus on English language arts or reading.

# Teacher's Edition Lesson Support

*The Americans: Reconstruction to the 21st Century* Teacher's Edition provides you with a wealth of information and practical teaching suggestions at your fingertips. The side columns focus on core instruction. At the bottom of the pages, you will find optional suggestions and teaching activities—including those for block schedules.

## ❶ OBJECTIVES

1. Identify the long-term causes and the immediate circumstances that led to World War I.
2. Describe the first two years of the war.
3. Summarize U.S. public opinion about the war.
4. Explain why the United States entered the war.

### SKILLBUILDERS
· Geography Skillbuilder: location, place, p. 375
· Interpreting Graphs, p. 377

### CRITICAL THINKING
· Analyzing Causes, p. 373
· Analyzing Effects, pp. 374, 379
· Drawing Conclusions, p. 376
· Analyzing Motives, p. 377
· Making Inferences, p. 379
· Synthesizing, p. 380
· Summarizing, p. 380
· Analyzing Issues, p. 380

## ❷ Focus & Motivate

What do students do when someone insults their friends? Do they defend them? How?

## ❸ Instruct

### Instruct: Objective ❶

**Causes of World War I / An Assassination Leads to War**
TAKS SS11 1(US1.C)
· What caused World War I?
· What alliances divided Europe in 1914?
· What diplomatic crises sparked the war?

❹
📖 In-Depth Resources: Unit 3
· Guided Reading, p. 47
· America Lives: Jeannette Rankin, p. 66

💻 Electronic Library of Primary Sources
· Request for a Declaration of War, 1917

---

## SECTION 1

# World War I Begins

| MAIN IDEA | WHY IT MATTERS NOW | Terms & Names |
|---|---|---|
| As World War I intensified, the United States was forced to abandon its neutrality. | The United States remains involved in European and world affairs. | ▪nationalism ▪militarism ▪Allies ▪Central Powers ▪Archduke Franz Ferdinand · ▪no man's land ▪trench warfare ▪*Lusitania* ▪Zimmermann note |

**TEKS** U.S. History 1A, 1B, 1C, 3A, 3B, 24A, 24B, 25A, 25B, 25C, 25D

### One American's Story

It was about 1:00 A.M. on April 6, 1917, and the members of the U.S. House of Representatives were tired. For the past 15 hours they had been debating President Wilson's request for a declaration of war against Germany. There was a breathless hush as Jeannette Rankin of Montana, the first woman elected to Congress, stood up. Rankin declared, "I want to stand by my country but I cannot vote for war. I vote no." Later she reflected on her action.

**A PERSONAL VOICE** JEANNETTE RANKIN
"I believe that the first vote I cast was the most significant vote and a most significant act on the part of women, because women are going to have to stop war. I felt at the time that the first woman [in Congress] should take the first stand, that the first time the first woman had a chance to say no to war she should say it."
—quoted in *Jeannette Rankin: First Lady in Congress*

▲ Jeannette Rankin was the only member of the House to vote against the U.S. entering both World War I and World War II.

After much debate as to whether the United States should join the fight, Congress voted in favor of U.S. entry into World War I. With this decision, the government abandoned the neutrality that America had maintained for three years. What made the United States change its policy in 1917?

### ❶ Causes of World War I

Although many Americans wanted to stay out of the war, several factors made American neutrality difficult to maintain. As an industrial and imperial power, the United States felt many of the same pressures that had led the nations of Europe into devastating warfare. Historians generally cite four long-term causes of the First World War: nationalism, imperialism, militarism, and the formation of a system of alliances.

**372** CHAPTER 11

---

## ❶ OBJECTIVES
The objectives of the section are clearly spelled out. Each objective is number-coded to help you know when in the lesson you are teaching to that objective.

## ❷ FOCUS & MOTIVATE
A motivational question begins every section to help you focus student attention on the events covered in that section.

## ❸ INSTRUCT
An Instruct step appears in the Teacher's Edition for every blue head in the Pupil's Edition. Key questions are suggested to stimulate student discussion.

## ❹ REFERENCES TO RESOURCE MATERIALS
These references to specific program resources at point of use help you to use all of the program's resources effectively.

## ❺ PROGRAM RESOURCES
For your convenience, all of the program resources that are appropriate for teaching the section are listed at the bottom of that section.

**NATIONALISM** Throughout the 19th century, politics in the Western world were deeply influenced by the concept of **nationalism**—a devotion to the interests and culture of one's nation. Often, nationalism led to competitive and antagonistic rivalries among nations. In this atmosphere of competition, many feared Germany's growing power in Europe.

In addition, various ethnic groups resented domination by others and longed for their nations to become independent. Many ethnic groups looked to larger nations for protection. Russia regarded itself as the protector of Europe's Slavic peoples, no matter which government they lived under. Among these Slavic peoples were the Serbs. Serbia, located in the Balkans, was an independent nation, but millions of ethnic Serbs lived under the rule of Austria-Hungary. As a result, Russia and Austria-Hungary were rivals for influence over Serbia.

**IMPERIALISM** For many centuries, European nations had been building empires, slowly extending their economic and political control over various peoples of the world. Colonies supplied the European imperial powers with raw materials and provided markets for manufactured goods. As Germany industrialized, it competed with France and Britain in the contest for colonies. **A**

**MILITARISM** Empires were expensive to build and to defend. The growth of nationalism and imperialism led to increased military spending. Because each nation wanted stronger armed forces than those of any potential enemy, the imperial powers followed a policy of **militarism**—the development of armed forces and their use as a tool of diplomacy.

By 1890 the strongest nation on the European continent was Germany, which had set up an army reserve system that drafted and trained young men. Britain was not initially alarmed by Germany's military expansion. As an island nation, Britain had always relied on its navy for defense and protection of its shipping routes—and the British navy was the strongest in the world. However, in 1897, Wilhelm II, Germany's kaiser, or emperor, decided that his nation should also become a major sea power in order to compete more successfully against the British. Soon British and German shipyards competed to build the largest battleships and destroyers. France, Italy, Japan, and the United States quickly joined the naval arms race.

**ALLIANCE SYSTEM** By 1907 there were two major defense alliances in Europe. The Triple Entente, later known as the **Allies,** consisted of France, Britain, and Russia. The Triple Alliance consisted of Germany, Austria-Hungary, and Italy.

**MAIN IDEA**

**Analyzing Causes**
**A** How did nationalism and imperialism lead to conflict in Europe?

**A. Answer** Nationalism and imperialism encouraged each European nation to pursue its own interests and compete for power.

**Vocabulary**
**alliance:** a formal agreement or union between nations

◄ German Emperor Wilhelm II *(center)* marches with two of his generals, Hindenburg *(left)* and Ludendorff, during World War I.

**TEACHER'S EDITION NOTES ALSO INCLUDE:**
- Cooperative Learning Activities
- Activities for Students Acquiring English
- Activities for Less Proficient Readers
- Activities for Gifted and Talented Students
- Links to Other Subjects
- Skillbuilder Lessons
- Assessment Suggestions and Rubrics

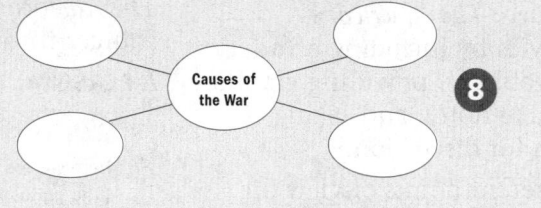
**6** **MORE ABOUT. . .**
These terrific nuggets of information occur often to supplement the text.

**7** **TRACING THEMES**
These boxes help you connect the Pupil's Edition narrative to the nine historical themes that are emphasized in *The Americans.*

**8** **DIFFERENTIATING INSTRUCTION**
Teaching options at the bottom of the Teacher's Edition pages offer a range of teaching choices. Many of these choices are for differentiating instruction for less proficient readers, students acquiring English, and gifted and talented students. Other activity options range from interdisciplinary links to cooperative learning activities.

# Helping Students Read History

**DONNA M. OGLE**

*Professor, Reading and Language*
*National-Louis University, Evanston, Illinois*
*President, International Reading Association*

Active, engaged readers make the best learners. Researchers have found that successful readers connect text information with what they already know. These readers build associations among ideas, create visual images of what they are reading, and continually refine their interpretations as they gather more information.

Encouraging active, engaged reading is difficult for teachers when they find that many students have learned to ignore their textbooks. This is often due to texts that are too difficult conceptually and are too dense in information. In contrast, many of the features in *The Americans* help students to gain access to the information that is presented

## SUPPORTING READERS

*The Americans* uses many strategies to help students become active and engaged readers.

**Various Learning Styles** We know that readers have different styles for learning. Some rely heavily on verbal input and discussion, some need visual supports, and some need to make notes and drawings or create graphic organizers as they learn. *The Americans* addresses various learning styles by including a variety of activity options, posing problems, providing graphic organizers to help students take notes, and asking thought-provoking questions for discussion.

In addition, presenting different points of view on issues stimulates deeper engagement and leads to more learning than does a simple exposition of factual information. The Point/Counterpoint feature in *The Americans* does just that.

| POINT | COUNTERPOINT |
|---|---|
| "The United States must occasionally intervene militarily in regional conflicts." | "The United States should not intervene militarily in regional conflicts." |

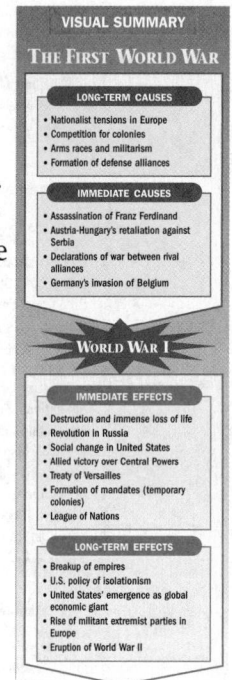

**VISUAL SUMMARY**

**THE FIRST WORLD WAR**

**LONG-TERM CAUSES**
- Nationalist tensions in Europe
- Competition for colonies
- Arms races and militarism
- Formation of defense alliances

**IMMEDIATE CAUSES**
- Assassination of Franz Ferdinand
- Austria-Hungary's retaliation against Serbia
- Declarations of war between rival alliances
- Germany's invasion of Belgium

**WORLD WAR I**

**IMMEDIATE EFFECTS**
- Destruction and immense loss of life
- Revolution in Russia
- Social change in United States
- Allied victory over Central Powers
- Treaty of Versailles
- Formation of mandates (temporary colonies)
- League of Nations

**LONG-TERM EFFECTS**
- Breakup of empires
- U.S. policy of isolationism
- United States' emergence as global economic giant
- Rise of militant extremist parties in Europe
- Eruption of World War II

**Visual Information** Many readers rely on visual information when reading unfamiliar material. Pictures in *The Americans* make abstractions of time and space more real. Photos and artifacts create a context for new ideas; maps help readers associate and compare ideas. In addition, charts of ideas and events in each chapter summarize and clarify information. A visual summary at the end of each chapter provides another way for remembering important ideas and events.

**Inner-Column Notes** Inner-column notes in *The Americans* help students read the text. Main Idea questions help students to think critically and synthesize information as they read. Vocabulary notes explain and define words and phrases. Background notes provide additional information about a person, idea, or event.

**Personal Connections** Personal stories and human connections can help to bring a subject such as history alive. Taking a personal point of view and thinking as if they are living the experiences can deepen students' learning. Studies on these techniques have generally shown significant increases in learning. *The Americans* uses personal stories and primary sources throughout to support student learning.

### A PERSONAL VOICE

**A PERSONAL VOICE** JOSEPH POLOWSKY

'Here we are, tremendously exhilarated, and there's a sea of dead. . . . [The platoon leader] was much moved. . . . He said, 'Joe, let's make a resolution with these Russians here and also the ones on the bank: this would be an important day in the lives of the two countries. . . .' It was a solemn moment. There were tears in the eyes of most of us. . . . We embraced. We swore never to forget."

—quoted in *The Good War*

**Students Acquiring English** Second-language learners, in particular, need to have information and ideas presented to them in multiple ways. Since many of these students are unfamiliar with the concepts and events of American history, being able to "see" history helps them make it real for themselves. Attending to illustrations of all kinds is essential for these students. *The*

*Americans* facilitates access to U.S. history for these students by clearly defining key terms; using a clearly organized head structure to outline each section for students; and integrating photograph, charts, and graphs to augment the text.

In addition, second-language learners have a greater variety of materials to read on the same topic, they will understand the language and concepts. Seeing the same concepts presented by different authors in different types of writing (first-person accounts, newspaper, official documents) and from different points of view helps these students build a better understanding of new ideas and terminology. The many primary sources in *The Americans* will help these students to read and comprehend the textbook narrative.

### EVOLVING FORMS OF READING

Students today need to be able to read in ways that earlier generations did not.

**Nonlinear Materials** Today's students must:

- gather ideas from multiple sources—resource books, magazines, computerized databases, CD-ROMs, the Internet
- find their way through nonlinear materials, such as by deciding which area of a computer screen contains the information they want.

Several components of *The Americans* will give students experience in accessing historical materials in these new formats. They include the Electronic Library of Primary Sources and *ClassZone*—the Web site for the program.

**GRAPHIC LAYOUTS** Today's readers must deal with informational materials that come in various formats.

- multiple columns of text with many pictures, graphs, and maps
- single-column texts with large marginal areas used for illustrations, highlighted information, and thought-provoking ideas
- combinations of layouts

*The Americans* familiarizes students with these multiple text formats, including single columns and double columns. The program teaches students strategies for effectively obtaining information from these various formats.

### STRATEGIES FOR TEACHERS

You can help your students become active, engaged, and confident readers of history. Here are some strategies you might try:

- Observe your students and ask them how they read.
- Do a "think aloud" as students begin to read a text. Ask them to tell you where they look on the page; when they look at the charts, maps, and pictures; and when they read the headings and titles.
- Introduce the text layout and features, and discuss students' options for reading.
- Have students experiment with reading the graphics first before reading the text on a page.
- Demonstrate how headings and subheadings can help readers find specific information.
- Use graphic organizers and reading guides to help students gain confidence.

Reading and discussing different types of written material and material expressing different points of view will help students learn to think critically about what they read. Help them learn to enjoy the search for information and ideas!

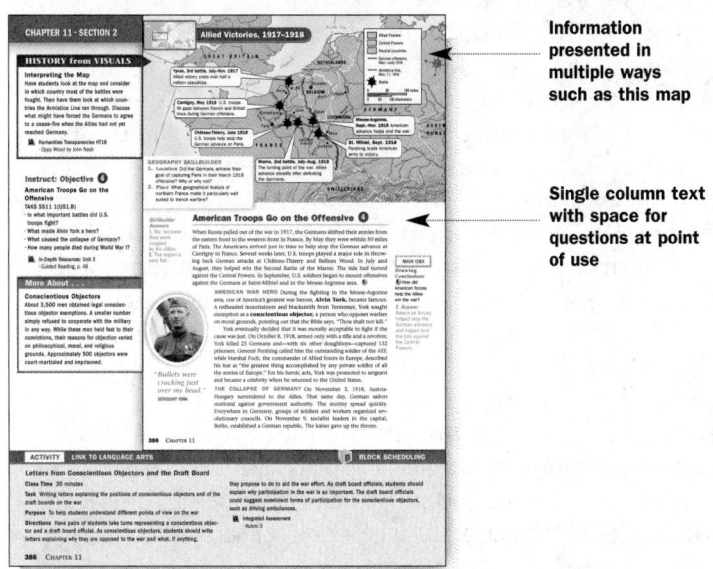

**Information presented in multiple ways such as this map**

**Single column text with space for questions at point of use**

# Teaching United States History Thematically

**MARY E. CONNOR**

*In the following article, Mary E. Connor, a U.S. history teacher at Westridge School in Pasadena, California, explains several advantages of thematic teaching and gives strategies for teaching themes successfully.*

How can today's educators convey the essentials of American history in a way that is engaging and memorable? One possible answer is a course organized around themes rather than chronological periods. The primary benefit of teaching the subject thematically is that it affords a better grasp of the principal developments in U.S. history by treating issues in depth.

A common problem in many high school U.S. history courses is the neglect of teaching about the recent past. It is not uncommon to hear of classes that never get to the Civil Rights movement or the Vietnam War, much less the events of more recent decades. The signal beauty of the thematic approach recommended here lies in the fact that in the first unit (mine is the American Character and American Belief System), students can be holding informed discussions of the views of our political leaders on current issues by mid-October. For example, a discussion of welfare reform can take place within a framework of knowledge about basic (and opposing) American values of self-reliance and social egalitarianism.

A thematic approach allows students to become involved, sometimes for weeks, with narratives and articles about one topic. Consider how a teacher might cover the traditional material in exploring the theme of **America in World Affairs.** The teacher outlines the causes and results of the American Revolution, the War of 1812, the Mexican War, the Spanish-American War, World War I, and the Korean War. Students study the Civil War, World War II, and Vietnam in depth. For World War II, students might read Studs Terkel's *The Good War* or *War Without Mercy* by John Dower. For Vietnam, differing interpretations of the Vietnam experience can be found in the movie *Coming Home* and in the book *A Rumor of War* by Philip Caputo. The cumulative effect of looking at the scope of American foreign affairs over a six-week period seizes the imagination.

> *"The signal beauty of the thematic approach lies in the fact that students can hold informed discussions about current issues by mid-October."*

In developing a theme, students could be offered different options for assignments. For example, for the theme **Immigration and Migration**, a student might research immigrants of the 19th century or interview a recent immigrant to America. One class that took my course interviewed immigrants from 30 countries on five continents. These interviews revealed that virtually no one felt discriminated against because of race or ethnicity, all believed they had achieved the American Dream, all preferred living in this country to anywhere else despite its problems, and the most difficult adjustment was learning the English language. This analysis of the immigrant experience took on added meaning as students discussed California Proposition 187.

In following a thematic approach, students journey from the past to the present more than ten times. The success of the method validates the venerable principle of repetition. There are frequent opportunities for discussing contemporary issues within an historical framework. For example, after studying the theme **Women and Political Power**, students discuss the challenges faced by women today and the debate over the current status of the women's movement. An examination of the theme **Economic Opportunity** ends with a discussion of the conflict over tariff regulation in today's global market economy.

Still another benefit of the thematic approach lies in the sheer power of the narrative. Sometimes the vitality of historical accounts can be lost using the traditional chronological approach, but thematic units have their own inner dynamic and can help students develop more far reaching perspectives on important issues in American history. For instance, the theme **Civil Rights** can include such topics as African-American history from slavery to the Million Man March and the recurrent debate over accepting newcomers into the country.

Moving through successive themes rather than chronological periods allows for greater creativity. The

text no longer determines how one does history, and each theme permits varied and absorbing activities. Students investigate their own family background to better understand their roots and to discover how their own histories are part of a larger history. Each student reports to the class on what has been discovered. Students may find ancestors on the *Mayflower* or at Jamestown, among freedmen or forty-niners. Ellis Island, the Great Depression, the D-Day invasion, and the 1960s student protests all may acquire a new luster when one's own or a friend's grandparent was there.

Examining themes in American history provides opportunities to view familiar materials in new ways. An example occurs in examining the theme **America in World Affairs.** When we study American history chronologically, our wars appear inevitable. But when students address conflict as a theme, they may more readily discern that there were opportunities for mediation and that had public opinion been shaped by different values or perspectives, different outcomes might have been possible.

A final element of importance in my thematic course is that of choice in student research. Preparation for the course begins during the summer, when incoming students receive a list of books organized under the themes used in the course. Students are encouraged to read two books, preferably on the same theme. This exposes them to some superb source materials and allows them to gain some in-depth knowledge before the academic year begins. The great majority will select a research topic related to their summer reading.

What are the particular difficulties of teaching American history thematically? Clearly, it will be easier for the seasoned teacher to move to a fully thematic course. However, one can develop a three-year plan to advance toward the ideal by expanding on themes encountered in the textbook currently used. Teaching thematically requires more time for planning, but the rewards for this approach are high: for the teacher, greater personal and professional satisfaction; for students, greater interest, performance, and retention. And, your students are likely to thank you.

*This essay is adapted from on article that appeared in the April/May 1997 issue of* Social Education.

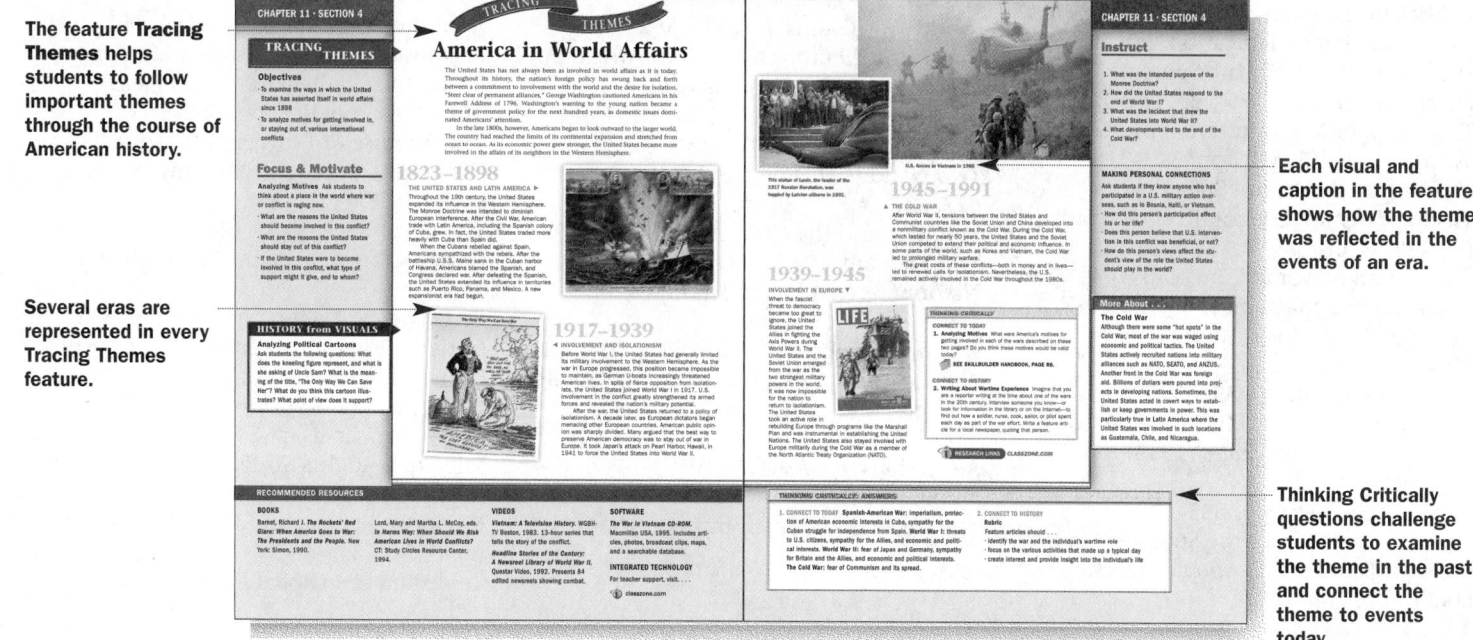

The feature **Tracing Themes** helps students to follow important themes through the course of American history.

Several eras are represented in every **Tracing Themes** feature.

Each visual and caption in the feature shows how the theme was reflected in the events of an era.

Thinking Critically questions challenge students to examine the theme in the past and connect the theme to events today.

# Teaching Themes in *The Americans: Reconstruction to the 21st Century*

For teachers and districts who wish to organize their modern U.S. history courses thematically, *The Americans: Reconstruction to the 21st Century* serves as a valuable resource. The lists below show how to organize the text around nine themes for a fully thematic course.

> ### Nine Themes in *The Americans: Reconstruction to the 21st Century*
> 1. **Diversity and the National Identity**
> 2. **America in World Affairs**
> 3. **Economic Opportunity**
> 4. **Science and Technology**
> 5. **Women and Political Power**
> 6. **Immigration and Migration**
> 7. **States' Rights**
> 8. **Voting Rights**
> 9. **Civil Rights**

## Diversity and the National Identity

Tracing Themes: Women and Political Power, pp. 64–65
Tracing Themes: Voting Rights, pp. 104–105
Cultures Clash on the Prairie, pp. 202–211
The New Immigrants, pp. 254–259
Tracing Themes: Diversity and the National Identity, pp. 260–261
The Challenges of Urbanization, pp. 262–266
Politics in the Gilded Age, pp. 267–271
Expanding Public Education, pp. 282–285
Historic Decisions of the Supreme Court: *Plessy* v. *Ferguson* (1896), pp. 290–291
The Dawn of Mass Culture, pp. 292–297
Women in Public Life, pp. 313–316
The War at Home, pp. 388–395
Tracing Themes: Economic Opportunity, pp. 428–429
The Twenties Woman, pp. 440–443
The Harlem Renaissance, pp. 452–457
The New Deal Affects Many Groups, pp. 504–507
The Home Front, pp. 590–595
Historic Decisions of the Supreme Court: *Korematsu* v. *United States* (1944), pp. 596–597
The Great Society, pp. 685–693
Historic Decisions of the Supreme Court: *Brown* v. *Board of Education of Topeka* (1954), pp. 708–709

The Triumph of a Crusade, pp. 710–716
Challenges and Changes in the Movement, pp. 717–716
Latinos and Native Americans Seek Equality, pp. 768–773
Women Fight for Equality, pp. 776–780
Geography Spotlight: The Movement of Migrant Workers, pp. 684–685
Culture and Counterculture, pp. 782–785
Social Concerns of the 80s, pp. 840–845
The Changing Face of America, pp. 882–887
American Literature: Women Writers Reflect American Diversity, pp. 864–865
Tracing Themes: Immigration and Migration, pp. 888–889

## America in World Affairs

America Claims an Empire, pp. 340–365
Geography Spotlight: The Panama Canal, pp. 366–367
The First World War, pp. 370—403
Tracing Themes: America in World Affairs, pp. 404–405
Postwar Trends, pp. 412–414
Harding Struggles for Peace, pp. 419–420
World War Looms, pp. 526–557
The War for Europe and North Africa, The War in the Pacific, pp. 569–589
The Origins of the Cold War, The Cold War Heats Up, pp. 602–615
Two Nations Live on the Edge, pp. 622–627
Kennedy and the Cold War, pp. 670–678
The Vietnam War Years, pp. 728–761
Nixon's Foreign Policy Triumphs, pp. 799–801
A Human Rights Foreign Policy, Triumph and Crisis in the Middle East, pp. 815–817
Foreign Policy After the Cold War, pp. 848–855
A Cautious Approach to Foreign Policy, pp. 863–864
The New Global Economy, pp. 869–873

## Economic Opportunity

Cattle Becomes Big Business, pp. 208–210
Daily Life: Gold Mining, pp. 212–213
Settling the Great Plains, pp. 214–218
Farmers and the Populist Movement, pp. 219–223
The Expansion of Industry, pp. 230–233
The Age of the Railroads, pp. 236–240
Big Business and Labor, pp. 241–249
Protecting American Business Interests, pp. 354–355
Foreign Influence in China, The Impact of U.S. Territorial Gains, pp. 356–358
A Time of Labor Unrest, pp. 417–418
The Business of America, pp. 422–427
Tracing Themes: Economic Opportunity, pp. 428–429
The Great Depression Begins, 462–483
A New Deal Fights the Depression, The Second New Deal Takes Hold, pp. 488–501
Historic Decisions of the Supreme Court: *NLRB* v. *Jones and Laughlin Steel Corp* (1937), pp. 502–503
The New Deal Affects Many Groups, pp. 504–509
A Production Miracle, pp. 564–567
Readjustment and Recovery, Meeting Economic Challenges, pp. 634–637
The Other America, pp. 660–663
The Promise of Progress, pp. 679–682
Geography Spotlight: Migrant Workers, pp. 684–685
The Great Society, pp. 686–693
Confronting a Stagnant Economy, pp. 798–799
Ford Tries to "Whip" Inflation, p. 811
Carter's Domestic Agenda, pp. 812–814
Conservative Policies Under Reagan and Bush, pp. 834–838
The Urban Crisis, p. 841
The Equal Rights Struggle, The Fight for Rights Continues pp. 842–845
Moderate Reform and Economic Boom, pp. 861–862
Trade and the Global Economy, p. 864

*"The Genius of America lies in its capacity to forge a single nation from peoples of remarkably diverse racial, religious, and ethnic origins. . . . The American identity will never be fixed and final: it will always be in the making."*

*Arthur M. Schlesinger, Jr.*

**MARTIN LUTHER KING, JR.,** *page 706*
Baptist minister and civil rights leader

**MAYA LIN,** *page 760*
Designer of the Vietnam Veterans Memorial

**BARBARA C. JORDAN**
*page 802*
United States representative
from Texas

**GERDA WEISSMANN KLEIN**
*page 542*
Holocaust survivor

**CÉSAR CHÁVEZ**
*page 770*
Political organizer

**RONALD W. REAGAN**
*page 832*
Fortieth president of
the United States

**JANE ADDAMS,** *page 266*
Social worker and peace
activist

**FRANKLIN D. ROOSEVELT**
*page 489*
Thirty-second president of
the United States

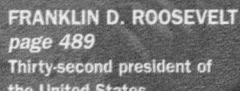

ii

# The AMERICANS

## Reconstruction to the 21st Century

Gerald A. Danzer

J. Jorge Klor de Alva

Larry S. Krieger

Louis E. Wilson

Nancy Woloch

**BEN NIGHTHORSE CAMPBELL,** *page 771*
United States senator from Colorado

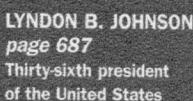

**QUEEN LILIUOKALANI,** *page 342*
Queen of Hawaii

**LYNDON B. JOHNSON**
*page 687*
Thirty-sixth president of the United States

**SANDRA DAY O'CONNOR**
*page 836*
United States Supreme Court justice

**PEDRO J. GONZÁLEZ**
*page 504*
Musician, radio personality, and civil rights activist

**McDougal Littell**
A HOUGHTON MIFFLIN COMPANY
Evanston, Illinois • Boston • Dallas

# Authors and Consultants

**Gerald A. Danzer, Ph.D.**
Gerald A. Danzer is Professor of History at the University of Illinois at Chicago. He served from 1992 to 1994 as Chair of the Council for Effective Teaching and Learning at UIC and was Director of the Chicago Neighborhood History Project. Dr. Danzer's area of specialization is historical geography, in which he has written *Discovering American History Through Maps and Views* and numerous other publications. Before entering university teaching, Dr. Danzer taught high school history in the Chicago area. Dr. Danzer received his Ph.D. in history from Northwestern University.

**J. Jorge Klor de Alva, J.D. and Ph.D.**
J. Jorge Klor de Alva is President of Apollo International, Inc., a global education provider. Formerly he was president of the University of Phoenix. Before that he was Class of 1940 Professor of Comparative Ethnic Studies and Anthropology at the University of California at Berkeley and former Professor of Anthropology at Princeton University. Dr. Klor de Alva's interests include interethnic relations, historical ethnography, and educational reform. His publications include *The Aztec Image of Self* and *Society and Interethnic Images: Discourse and Practice in the New World, 1492–1992*, as well as more than ten other books and more than seventy scholarly articles. Dr. Klor de Alva earned his J.D. from the University of California at Berkeley and his Ph.D. in history/anthropology from the University of California at Santa Cruz.

**Larry S. Krieger, B.A., M.A., M.A.T.**
Larry S. Krieger is the Social Studies Supervisor for Grades K–12 in Montgomery Township Public Schools in New Jersey. For 26 years he has been a world history teacher in public schools. He has also introduced many innovative in-service programs, such as "Putting the Story Back in History," and has co-authored several successful history textbooks. Mr. Krieger earned his B.A. and M.A.T. from the University of North Carolina and his M.A. from Wake Forest University.

**Louis E. Wilson, Ph.D.**
Louis E. Wilson is Associate Professor and from 1989 through 1998 was the Chair of the Afro-American and African Studies Department at Smith College. In 1999, Dr. Wilson was a Senior Fulbright History Professor at the University of Cape Town, South Africa. Previously Dr. Wilson was on the faculty at the University of Colorado, Boulder, and was a senior Fulbright Scholar at the University of Ghana, Legon. Dr. Wilson is the author of *The Krobo People of Ghana to 1892: A Political, Social, and Economic History* and *Genealogical and Militia Data on Blacks, Indians, and Mustees from Military American Revolutionary War Records*. He is also one of the authors of *Houghton Mifflin Social Studies*. Dr. Wilson is currently writing a book entitled *Forgotten Patriots: African Americans and Native Americans in the American Revolution from Rhode Island*. In 1991, Dr. Wilson received The Blackwell Fellowship and Prize as Outstanding Black New England Scholar. Dr. Wilson received his Ph.D. in history from the University of California at Los Angeles.

**Nancy Woloch, Ph.D.**
Nancy Woloch teaches history at Barnard College, where she has been on the faculty since 1988. Dr. Woloch's main scholarly interest is the history of women in the United States, and in this area she has published *Women and the American Experience* and *Early American Women: A Documentary History, 1600–1900*. She is also the author of *Muller v. Oregon* and the co-author of *The American Century*. Dr. Woloch was the recipient of two National Endowment for the Humanities Fellowships. She received her Ph.D. in history and American studies from Indiana University.

---

This book contains material written by **John S. Bowes** that originally appeared in *The Americans* © 1985 and © 1991.

**Constitution Consultant**
**Melvin Dubnick**
Professor of Political Science
Rutgers University, Trenton
Trenton, New Jersey

**Contributing Writer**
**Miriam Greenblatt**
Educational Writer and Consultant
Highland Park, Illinois

**Multicultural Advisory Board**
*The multicultural advisers reviewed the manuscript for appropriateness of content.*

**Pat A. Brown**
Director of the Indianapolis Public Schools Office of African-Centered Multicultural Education
Indianapolis Public Schools
Indianapolis, Indiana

**Ogle B. Duff**
Associate Professor of English
University of Pittsburgh
Pittsburgh, Pennsylvania

**Mary Ellen Maddox**
Black Education Commission
Director, Los Angeles
Unified School District
Los Angeles, California

**Jon Reyhner**
Associate Professor and Coordinator of the Bilingual Multicultural Ed. Program
Northern Arizona University
Flagstaff, Arizona

**Curtis L. Walker**
Executive Officer, Office of Equity and Compliance
Pittsburgh Public Schools
Pittsburgh, Pennsylvania

**Ruben Zepeda**
Compliance Advisor, Language Acquisition and Curriculum Development
Los Angeles, California

**Content Consultants**
*The content consultants reviewed the manuscript for historical depth and accuracy and for clarity of presentation.*

**Catherine Clinton**
Fellow of the W. E. B. Du Bois Institute
Harvard University
Cambridge, Massachusetts

**Theodore Karaminski**
Professor of History
Loyola University
Chicago, Illinois

**Joseph Kett**
Professor of History
University of Virginia
Charlottesville, Virginia

**Jack Rakove**
Professor of History
Stanford University
Stanford, California

**Harvard Sitkoff**
Professor of History
University of New Hampshire
Durham, New Hampshire

Copyright © 2003 by McDougal Littell Inc. All rights reserved.
Maps on pages A1-A21 © Rand McNally & Company. All rights reserved.
The USA TODAY®service mark has been licensed by USA TODAY®for use for certain purposes by McDougal Littell Inc. USA TODAY®charts, articles and photographs incorporated in these reading materials are displayed for informational and promotional purposes only. The USA TODAY® charts, articles and photographs incorporated herein are solely for private, personal and noncommercial use. Any other use of the USA TODAY®charts, articles and photographs incorporated herein, without prior express written permission of USA TODAY®, is strictly prohibited.
Warning: No part of this work may be reproduced or transmitted in any form or by any means, electronic or mechanical, including photocopying and recording, or by any information storage or retrieval system without prior written permission of McDougal Littell Inc. unless such copying is expressly permitted by federal copyright law. With the exception of not-for-profit transcription in Braille, McDougal Littell Inc. is not authorized to grant permission for further uses of copyrighted selections reprinted in this text without the permission of their owners. Permission must be obtained from the individual copyright owners as identified herein. Address inquiries to Manager, Rights and Permissions, McDougal Littell Inc., P.O. Box 1667, Evanston, IL 60204. Acknowledgments begin on page R108.
ISBN 0-618-18407-4
Printed in the United States of America.
1 2 3 4 5 6 7 8 9–DWO–07 06 05 04 03 02

## Teacher Consultants
*The following educators contributed ideas and activities for the program.*

**Edmund Austin**
William Tennant High School
Warminster, Pennsylvania

**William Brown**
Retired,
Northeast High School
Philadelphia, Pennsylvania

**Larry Bruno**
Denby High School
Detroit, Michigan

**Suzanne Cook**
Scarborough High School
Houston, Texas

**John Devine**
Elgin High School
Elgin, Illinois

**George Dyche**
West Aurora High School
Aurora, Illinois

**Steve Ellison**
Petaluma High School
Petaluma, California

**Betsy Fitzgerald**
Erskine Academy
South China, Maine

**Michael Fleming**
Jupiter High School
Jupiter, Florida

**Thomas J. Flynn**
Turner High School
Kansas City, Kansas

**Dominic Fruscello**
West Genesee High School
Camillus, New York

**Craig T. Grace**
Lanier High School
West Austin, Texas

**Cynthia M. Greene**
Ridley High School
Folsom, Pennsylvania

**Patti Harrold**
Edmond Memorial High School
Edmond, Oklahoma

**Korri Kinney**
Meridian High School
Meridian, Idaho

**Don A. Lee**
Mira Mesa High School
San Diego, California

**Dr. Carol D. McCree**
DeBakey Health Prof.
High School
Houston, Texas

**Harry McCown**
Hazelwood West High School
Hazelwood, Missouri

**Lou Morrison**
Lake Weir High School
Ocala, Florida

**Theresa C. Noonan**
West Irondequoit High School
Rochester, New York

**Gloria Remijio**
Del Valle High School
El Paso, Texas

**Diane M. Rodgers**
Crooksville High School
Crooksville, Ohio

**James Rosenberg**
Retired, Crystal Lake South
High School
Crystal Lake, Illinois

**John Seeley**
Westminster High School
Westminster, California

**Brenda G. Smith**
Instructional Supervisor,
Social Studies, Colorado
Springs District 11
Colorado Springs, Colorado

**Steve Smith**
Clayton High School
Clayton, North Carolina

**Ruby Thompson**
Athens Drive High School
Raleigh, North Carolina

**Linda Tillis**
South Oak Cliff High School
Dallas, Texas

**Mark A. Van Hecke**
Anchor Bay High School
New Baltimore, Michigan

**Joshua Weiner**
Benson High School
Portland, Oregon

## State-specific Reviewers
*The following educators reviewed state-specific materials for Texas.*

**James Boyce**
Performing and Visual Arts
High School
Houston, Texas

**Suzanne Cook**
Scarborough High School
Houston, Texas

**Pam Mayfield**
Pasadena High School
Houston, Texas

**Carol McCree**
DeBakey Health Prof.
High School
Houston, Texas

## Teacher Review Panels
*The following educators provided ongoing review during the development of prototypes, the table of contents, and key components of the program.*

### TEXAS TEACHER PANEL
**Patricia Brison**
Bellaire High School
Houston, Texas

**Brian Greeney**
Stratford High School
Spring Branch, Texas

**Jim Lee**
Lamar High School
Arlington, Texas

**Janie Maldonado**
Lanier High School
Austin, Texas

**Leonore Murray**
Lubbock High School
Lubbock, Texas

**Deborah Pennington**
The Woodlands High School
Conroe, Texas

**Gloria Remijio**
Dell Valley High School
Yselta, Texas

**H.V. Stafford**
MacArthur High School
Aldine, Texas

**Dawn Stapp**
Lee Freshman High School
Midland, Texas

### CALIFORNIA TEACHER PANEL
**Elaine Deatherage**
Hiram Johnson High School
Sacramento, California

**Steve Ellison**
Petaluma High School
Petaluma, California

**Judy Horrigan**
Moreno Valley High School
Moreno Valley, California

**Don Lee**
Mira Mesa High School
San Diego, California

**Russom Mesfun**
Fremont High School
Oakland, California

**Randy Sanford**
Hueneme High School
Oxnard, California

**John Seeley**
Westminster High School
Westminster, California

**Kathleen Torosian**
Herbert Hoover High School
Fresno, California

**Glenda Watanabe**
Banning High School
Los Angeles, California

### FLORIDA TEACHER PANEL
**David Debs**
Mandarin High School
Jacksonville, Florida

**Ronald Eckstein**
Hudson High School
Hudson, Florida

**Sharman Feliciani**
Land O'Lakes High School
Land O'Lakes, Florida

**Flossie Gautier**
Bay High School
Panama City, Florida

**Glenn Hallick**
Vanguard High School
Ocala, Florida

**Mary Kenney**
Astronaut High School
Titusville, Florida

**Lou Morrison**
Lake Weir High School
Ocala, Florida

**Brenda Sims Palmer**
Lehigh High School
Lehigh Acres, Florida

**Marsee Perkins**
Maynard Evans High School
Orlando, Florida

**Kent Rettig**
Pensacola High School
Pensacola, Florida

**Jim Sutton**
Edgewater High School
Orlando, Florida

### ILLINOIS TEACHER PANEL
**Rosemary Albright**
Conant High School
Hoffman Estates, Illinois

**Jeff Anhut**
Wheaton Warrenville South
High School
Wheaton, Illinois

**James Crider**
Downers Grove South
High School
Downers Grove, Illinois

**John Devine**
Elgin High School
Elgin, Illinois

**George Dyche**
West Aurora High School
Aurora, Illinois

**Diane Ring**
St. Charles High School
St. Charles, Illinois

**Jim Rosenberg**
Crystal Lake South
High School
Crystal Lake, Illinois

**Pam Zimmerman**
Stevenson High School
Lincolnshire, Illinois

## Manuscript Reviewers
*The following educators reviewed the prototype chapter and the manuscript of the entire book.*

**Arman Afshani**
North Tonawanda High School
North Tonawanda, New York

**Debra Brown**
Eisenhower High School
Houston, Texas

**Dianne Bumgarner**
Ashbrook High School
Mt. Holly, North Carolina

**Sherry Burgin**
Garland High School
Garland, Texas

**Maurice Bush**
South Point High School
Crouse, North Carolina

**Bruce Campbell**
Bemidji High School
Bemidji, Minnesota

*(continued on R118)*

## Student Board
*The following students reviewed prototype materials for the book.*

**John Afordakos**
Chantilly High School
Fairfax County, Virginia

**Marisha Cook**
Rockford East High School
Rockford, Illinois

**Matthew Cornejo**
New Bedford High School
New Bedford, Massachusetts

**Kevin Dodd**
Lanier High School
Austin, Texas

**Melissa Dugan**
Mount Lebanon High School
Mount Lebanon, Pennsylvania

*(continued on R118)*

# American Beginnings to 1877

Native Americans watch the arrival of a European ship, page 2.

The Battle of Lexington begins the American Revolution, p. 50.

The Supreme Court of the United States, page 93

**VIDEO**

*Patrick Gass Chronicles the Journey West,* page 112

An 1864 Mathew Brady photograph of Civil War soldiers, page 178

Immigrants arrive in New York Harbor, page 193.

 **CLASSZONE.COM** *Visit the links for Chapters 1–4.*

1877–1917

# Bridge to the 20th Century

A Sioux man and woman, page 203

The first light bulb, page 248

Coney Island amusement park, page 292

## UNIT 3

### 1890–1920

# Modern America Emerges

Teddy Roosevelt campaigns for president, page 318.

Uncle Sam rides upon two "hemispheres," page 351.

**CLASSZONE.COM**  *Visit the links for Chapters 5–11.*

VIDEO

*Eddie Rickenbacker and the First World War,* page 381

**UNIT 4**

**1919–1940**

# The 1920s and the Great Depression

"Big business" dances with Calvin Coolidge, page 426.

**VIDEO**

*Zora Neale Hurston and the Harlem Renaissance, page 452*

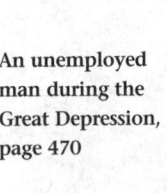

An unemployed man during the Great Depression, page 470

## UNIT 5

### 1931–1960
# World War II and Its Aftermath

VIDEO
*Kurt Klein and Gerda Weissmann Klein Remember the Holocaust,* page 542

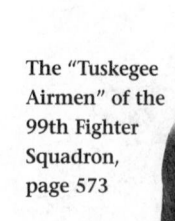

The "Tuskegee Airmen" of the 99th Fighter Squadron, page 573

The Cold War creates a climate of fear, page 628.

 CLASSZONE.COM  *Visit the links for Chapters 12–19.*

# UNIT 6

## 1954–1975
# Living with Great Turmoil

Kennedy and Johnson promise active leadership, page 670.

VIDEO

*Jo Ann Gibson Robinson and the Bus Boycott,* page 700

Farm workers protest, page 768.

## 1968–2001

# Passage to a New Century

Tape-recorded conversations ensnare the Nixon White House, page 806.

President George W. Bush (*second from left*) with other world leaders at an economic summit, page 895

CLASSZONE.COM *Visit the links for Chapters 20–26 and The War on Terrorism.*

# Special Features

## HISTORIC DECISIONS OF THE SUPREME COURT

## GEOGRAPHY SPOTLIGHT

## DAILY LIFE

## AMERICAN LITERATURE

## TRACING THEMES

# KEY PLAYER

# Special Features

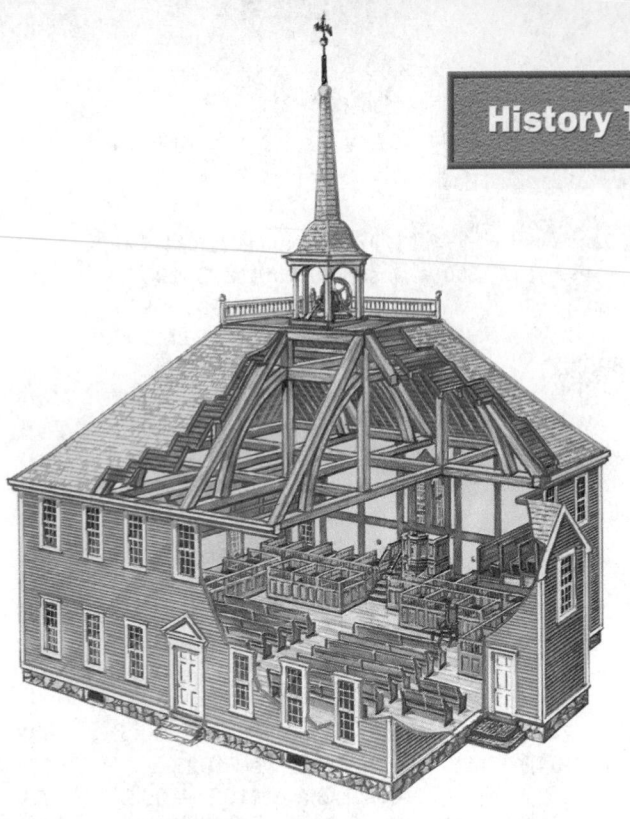

## History Through...

## HISTORICAL SPOTLIGHT

# Special Features

# Primary Sources and Personal Voices

## A PERSONAL VOICE
### SOJOURNER TRUTH

"Look at me! Look at my arm! I have ploughed, and planted, and gathered into barns, and no man could head me! And ain't I a woman?"

—quoted in *Narrative of Sojourner Truth*

# Primary Sources and Personal Voices

## A PERSONAL VOICE
### LUIS MUÑOZ RIVERA

" [G]ive us our independence and you will stand before humanity as . . . a great creator of new nationalities and a great liberator of oppressed peoples."

—quoted in *The Puerto Ricans*

## A PERSONAL VOICE
### DOROTHEA LANGE

" The people who are garrulous and wear their heart on their sleeve and tell you everything, that's one kind of person. But the fellow who's hiding behind a tree and hoping you don't see him, is the fellow that you'd better find out why."

—quoted in *Restless Spirit: The Life and Work of Dorothea Lange*

### A PERSONAL VOICE
FRANKLIN DELANO ROOSEVELT

"I have said not once, but many times, that I have seen war and I hate war. . . . As long as it is my power to prevent, there will be no blackout of peace in the U.S."

—radio speech, September 3, 1939

### A PERSONAL VOICE
MARTIN LUTHER KING, JR.

"We have been repeatedly faced with the cruel irony of watching Negro and white boys on TV screens as they kill and die together for a nation that has been unable to seat them together in the same schools."

—quoted in *America's Vietnam War: A Narrative History*

# Primary Sources and Personal Voices

## ★ A PERSONAL VOICE
### ALFRED S. BRADFORD

"I wanted to be part of that adventure and I believed that it was my duty as an American, both to serve my country and particularly not to stand by while someone else risked his life in my place."

—quoted in *Some Even Volunteered*

## ★ A PERSONAL VOICE   MAYA ANGELOU

"Lift up your faces, you have a piercing need
For this bright morning dawning for you.
History, despite its wrenching pain,
Cannot be unlived, but if faced
With courage, need not be lived again.

Lift up your eyes
Upon this day breaking for you.
Give birth again
To the dream."

—"On the Pulse of Morning"

## HISTORICAL AND POLITICAL MAPS

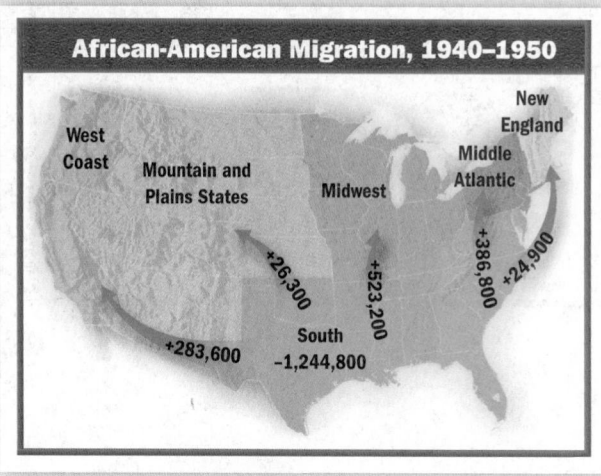

**African-American Migration, 1940–1950**

New England

West Coast

Mountain and Plains States

Midwest

Middle Atlantic

+26,300

+523,200

+386,800

+24,900

+283,600

South −1,244,800

# Graphs and Tables

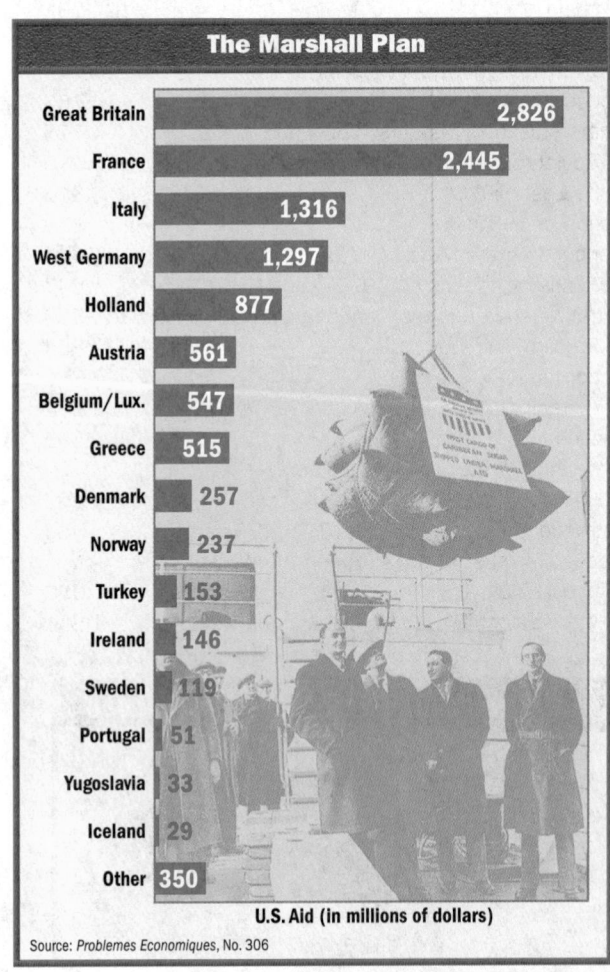

**The Marshall Plan**

| | |
|---|---|
| Great Britain | 2,826 |
| France | 2,445 |
| Italy | 1,316 |
| West Germany | 1,297 |
| Holland | 877 |
| Austria | 561 |
| Belgium/Lux. | 547 |
| Greece | 515 |
| Denmark | 257 |
| Norway | 237 |
| Turkey | 153 |
| Ireland | 146 |
| Sweden | 119 |
| Portugal | 51 |
| Yugoslavia | 33 |
| Iceland | 29 |
| Other | 350 |

**U.S. Aid (in millions of dollars)**

Source: *Problemes Economiques*, No. 306

## CHARTS

**Civilian Conservation Corps**

- The CCC provided almost 3 million men aged 18–25 with work and wages between 1933 and 1942.

- The men lived in work camps under a strict regime. The majority of the camps were racially segregated.

- By 1938, the CCC had an 11 percent African-American enrollment.

- Accomplishments of the CCC include planting over 3 billion trees, developing over 800 state parks, and building more than 46,000 bridges.

## TIME LINES

## The Technological Explosion, 1826–1903

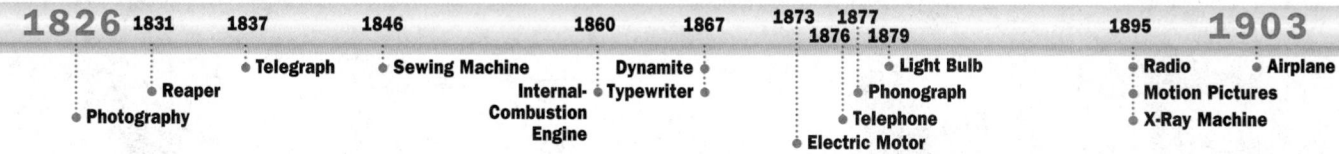

| 1826 | 1831 | 1837 | 1846 | 1860 | 1867 | 1873 | 1877 | 1876 | 1879 | 1895 | 1903 |
|---|---|---|---|---|---|---|---|---|---|---|---|

- Photography
- Reaper
- Telegraph
- Sewing Machine
- Internal-Combustion Engine
- Dynamite
- Typewriter
- Electric Motor
- Light Bulb
- Phonograph
- Telephone
- Radio
- Motion Pictures
- X-Ray Machine
- Airplane

# Infographics

## INFOGRAPHICS

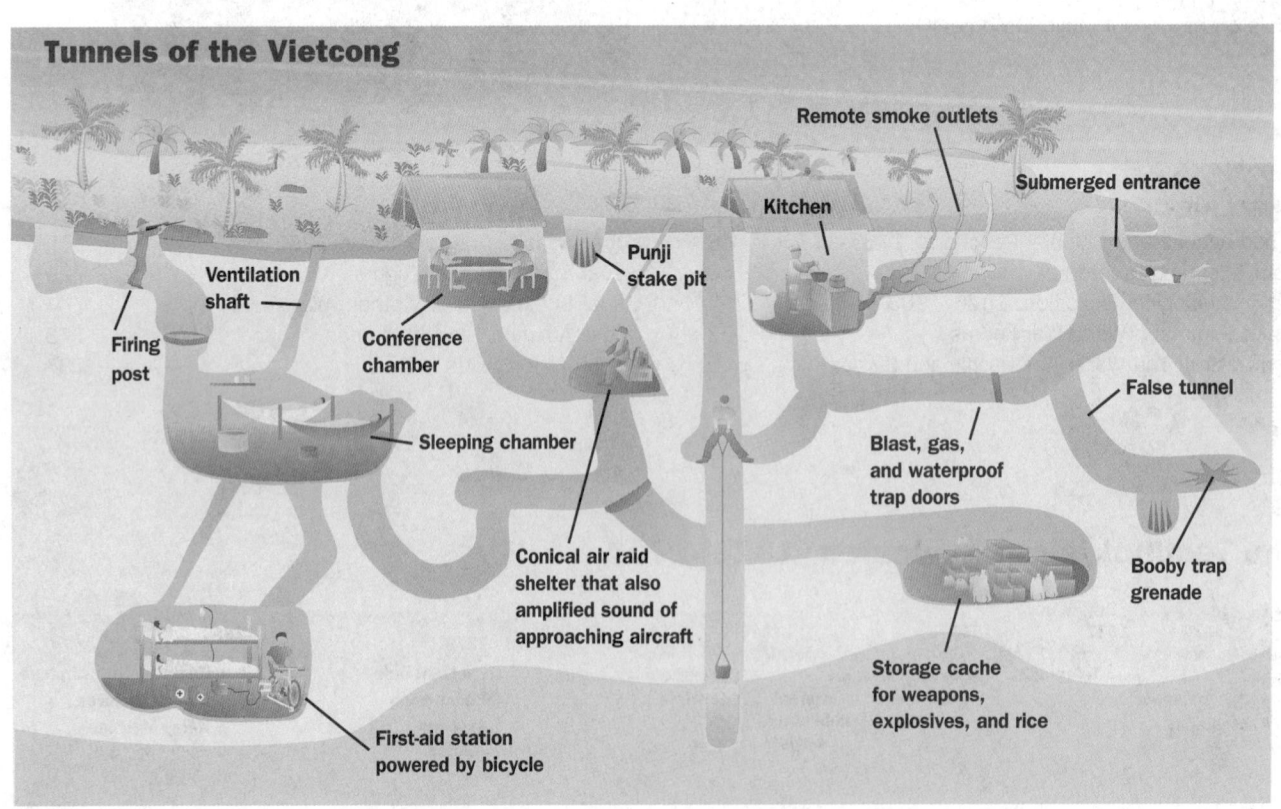

**Tunnels of the Vietcong**

Remote smoke outlets

Submerged entrance

Kitchen

Punji stake pit

Ventilation shaft

Firing post

Conference chamber

Sleeping chamber

False tunnel

Blast, gas, and waterproof trap doors

Conical air raid shelter that also amplified sound of approaching aircraft

Booby trap grenade

Storage cache for weapons, explosives, and rice

First-aid station powered by bicycle

# Skillbuilder Handbook / *American Stories* Videos

## SKILLBUILDER HANDBOOK

## *AMERICAN STORIES* VIDEO SERIES

*American Stories* is a powerful video series integrated with the text of *The Americans*. Seventeen fascinating documentaries, each ten to fifteen minutes long, help introduce various sections. Three volumes are available in English and Spanish.

### VOLUME 1

**PATRIOT FATHER, LOYALIST SON**  *The Divided House of Benjamin and William Franklin*—Chapter 2

**RECRUITED BY LEWIS AND CLARK**  *Patrick Gass Chronicles the Journey West*—Chapter 3

**WAR OUTSIDE MY WINDOW**  *Mary Chesnut's Diary of the Civil War*—Chapter 4

**TEACHER OF A FREED PEOPLE**  *Robert Fitzgerald and Reconstruction*—Chapter 4

**A WALK IN TWO WORLDS**  *The Education of Zitkala-Ša, a Sioux*—Chapter 5

**GUSHER!**  *Patillo Higgins and the Great Texas Oil Boom*—Chapter 6

### VOLUME 2

**FROM CHINA TO CHINATOWN**  *Fong See's American Dream*—Chapter 7

**A CHILD ON STRIKE**  *The Testimony Of Camella Teoli, Mill Girl*—Chapter 9

**ACE OF ACES**  *Eddie Rickenbacker and the First World War*—Chapter 11

**JUMP AT THE SUN**  *Zora Neale Hurston and the Harlem Renaissance*—Chapter 13

**BROKE BUT NOT BROKEN**  *Ann Marie Low Remembers the Dust Bowl*—Chapter 14

**A SONG FOR HIS PEOPLE**  *Pedro J. González and the Fight for Mexican-American Rights*—Chapter 15

### VOLUME 3

**ESCAPING THE FINAL SOLUTION**  *Kurt Klein and Gerda Weissmann Klein Remember the Holocaust*—Chapter 16

**THE COLD WAR COMES HOME**  *Hollywood Blacklists the Kahn Family*—Chapter 18

**JUSTICE IN MONTGOMERY**  *Jo Ann Gibson Robinson and the Bus Boycott*—Chapter 21

**MATTERS OF CONSCIENCE**  *Stephan Gubar and the Vietnam War*—Chapter 22

**POISONED PLAYGROUND**  *Lois Gibbs and the Crisis at Love Canal*—Chapter 24

# Themes in History

The Americans *focuses on nine themes, described on these pages. As you study U.S. history, you will encounter these and other themes again and again. The Thematic Review on pages 192–197 and the Tracing Themes features organize major events in United States history around these themes. What do you think are the important issues raised by each theme?*

## DIVERSITY AND THE NATIONAL IDENTITY

*E Pluribus Unum*—From the Many, One. Pick up a dollar bill and you'll find this Latin motto on the Great Seal of the United States. From the first settlement, this has been a land of many peoples, cultures, and faiths. This mixing of ethnic, racial, and religious groups has produced a rich and uniquely American culture. It has also led to competition and conflict. Today, the United States is more diverse than ever, yet the nation's motto remains *E Pluribus Unum*. (See **Tracing Themes** on page 260.)

**Critical Thinking** How do you think America today is enriched by its diversity?

## AMERICA IN WORLD AFFAIRS

From the earliest colonial times, the United States has been influenced by the events, people, and forms of government in other nations—and America has influenced world affairs. Today, relationships between the United States and other countries are more critical than ever, as modern communications and transportation have drawn the world closer together. As America continues to participate in world affairs, questions of trade, diplomacy, and regional conflict will grow in importance. (See **Tracing Themes** on page 404.)

**Critical Thinking** What do you think America's role in the world should be in the 21st century?

## ECONOMIC OPPORTUNITY

America has always been a land of economic opportunity. Blessed with fertile land and abundant resources, this has been a country where anyone who has worked hard has had a chance to prosper. Indeed, American history is full of heartening "rags-to-riches" success stories. Just as inspiring are the heroic struggles of women and minorities who fought to improve their economic prospects. As your generation enters the work force, you and your friends will have the opportunity to write your own success stories. (See **Tracing Themes** on page 428.)

**Critical Thinking** What do you think are the most exciting economic opportunities for Americans today?

## SCIENCE AND TECHNOLOGY

Americans have always had a deep respect for the power of science and technology to improve life. In the past two centuries, new inventions, new technologies, and scientific breakthroughs have transformed the United States—and continue to appear at a dizzying pace. Which ones will change your life? You can be sure that some will, and in ways that no one can yet predict. (See **Tracing Themes** on page 588.)

**Critical Thinking** How do you think science and technology will change American life in the 21st century?

## WOMEN AND POLITICAL POWER

More than half of all Americans are women, but only recently have their contributions and concerns found their way into history books. American women have helped shape the social and political history of every era. In their private roles as wives and mothers, they have strengthened families and raised America's children. In their more public roles as workers, reformers, and crusaders for equal rights, they have attacked the nation's worst social ills and challenged barriers to women's full participation in American life. (See **Tracing Themes** on page 64.)

**Critical Thinking** What do you think is the most important goal for American women today?

## IMMIGRATION AND MIGRATION

Seeking a better life seems to be part of the American character. This nation was first established by and has remained a magnet for immigrants. One out of every ten people living in the United States today was born in another country. Moreover, every year one out of every six Americans moves to a new address. (See **Tracing Themes** on page 888.)

| Critical Thinking | Why do you think people continue to have the dream of immigrating to the United States? |

## STATES' RIGHTS

The power struggle between states and the federal government has caused controversy since the country's beginning. In 1861 the conflict led to the Civil War, in which Southern states acted upon the belief that they had the right to nullfy acts of the federal government and even to leave the Union if they chose to do so. Throughout the history of this country, state and federal governments have squared off on this and other constitutional issues. (See **Tracing Themes** on page 128.)

| Critical Thinking | When do you think a state has the right to challenge a federal law? |

## VOTING RIGHTS

When Americans first began their experiment with democracy, only white men with property could vote or hold office. Over the past two centuries, women, African Americans, and other groups have fought for and won the right to vote and participate in government. Today the challenge is getting people to exercise the right to vote. In 2000, only 50.7 percent of eligible voters cast ballots in the presidential election. (See **Tracing Themes** on page 104.)

| Critical Thinking | What do you think can be done to bring more Americans into the democratic process? |

## CIVIL RIGHTS

The American system of government is based on a simple but revolutionary idea: Every citizen has certain rights and liberties. Among them are the right to participate in government and to exercise such liberties as freedom of speech and worship. Deciding who should have what rights, how these rights should be exercised, and how to protect a person's civil rights is anything but easy. Defining and protecting our civil rights is not likely to get any easier. (See **Tracing Themes** on page 724.)

| Critical Thinking | What issue of civil rights do you think is most critical in the United States today? |

# Themes in Geography

*The history of a nation is shaped as much by geography as by people and events. Paying attention to the following themes of geography can help you recognize when geographic forces are at work in the story of the United States.*

## LOCATION

Geographers speak of absolute location—the latitude and longitude of an area—and of relative location—where one area is in relation to another. In absolute terms, the city of San Francisco lies at 37°46' North latitude and 122°25' West longitude. This information allows you to pinpoint San Francisco on a map. In relative terms, San Francisco lies at the western edge of North America and looks out across the vast Pacific Ocean. This information helps explain San Francisco's history as a port city where people and ideas have come together.

**Critical Thinking** Locate your city or town on both a political and a physical map. How has location influenced the history of your city or town?

## REGION

Geographers use the idea of region to show what places in close proximity to one another have in common. As a part of the Pacific Coast region, San Francisco shares with Seattle, Washington, and Portland, Oregon, a mild, rainy climate and an economic interest in international shipping. As a part of California, San Francisco shares economic and environmental concerns of the state as a whole.

**Critical Thinking** To what region or regions does your area belong? How have the characteristics and concerns of your region changed over the last generation?

## HUMAN-ENVIRONMENT INTERACTION

Wherever people live, they affect the environment in the way they modify their natural surroundings. They build shelters and clear trees. They turn the earth inside out to extract its resources. People in the San Francisco Bay area have built bridges in order to move around more easily. People have also modified the bay itself, reducing its area by about one-third as they filled in tidelands for development.

**Critical Thinking** How have people in your area modified their surroundings? What consquences might these modifications have?

## PLACE

Place, in geography, refers to what an area looks like in physical and human terms. An area's landforms, soil, climate, and resources are aspects of place. So are the numbers and cultures of the population. San Francisco's natural harbor has made the city an international port. It is connected to the American River—where gold was discovered in 1848. Its position along a major fault line has subjected it to periodic earthquakes, the most disastrous in 1906. During its history, San Francisco has attracted people from North America, Europe, Asia, and various Pacific islands, making its population one of the most diverse in the United States.

**Critical Thinking** What is unique about the place where you live and the people who live there? What past events contributed to its uniqueness?

## MOVEMENT

One place or region can influence another through the movement of people, materials, and even ideas. San Francisco has been the site of many important movements of people and cultures. It has been a port of entry for immigrants, many of them Asian. It also lies along the path that Spanish missionaries trod in their quest to convert native peoples.

**Critical Thinking** When and by what groups was your area settled? What trends in movement today may shape the future of your area?

# STRATEGIES FOR TAKING TAKS

This section of the textbook helps you develop and practice the skills you need to study history and to take standardized tests. Part 1, **Strategies for Studying History,** takes you through the features of the textbook and offers suggestions on how to use these features to improve your reading and study skills.

Part 2, **TAKS Strategies and Practice,** offers specific strategies for tackling many of the items you'll find on the Texas Assessment of Knowledge and Skills. It gives tips for answering multiple-choice, constructed-response, extended-response, and document-based questions. In addition, it offers guidelines for analyzing primary and secondary sources, maps, political cartoons, charts, graphs, and time lines. Each strategy is followed by a set of questions you can use for practice.

## CONTENTS

# Part 1: Strategies for Studying History

Reading is the central skill in the effective study of history or any other subject. You can improve your reading skills by using helpful techniques and by practicing. The better your reading skills, the more you'll remember of what you read. Below you'll find several strategies that involve built-in features of *The Americans*. Careful use of these strategies will help you learn and understand history more effectively.

## Preview Chapters Before You Read

Each chapter begins with a two-page chapter opener. Study the chapter opener to help you get ready to read.

1. Read the chapter title. Look for clues that indicate what will be covered in the chapter.

2. Look at the chapter-opening visual. Try to identify the theme or themes of the chapter based on this illustration.

3. Preview the time line. Note the years that the chapter covers and identify the important events that took place in the United States and across the world during this time period.

4. Study the **Interact with History** feature. Examine the major issues discussed in the chapter by answering the questions.

# Preview Sections Before You Read

Each chapter consists of three, four, or five sections. These sections focus on shorter periods of time or on particular historical themes. Use the section openers to help you prepare to read.

**1** Study the sentences under the headings **Main Idea** and **Why It Matters Now.** These tell you what's important in the material that you're about to read.

**2** Preview the **Terms & Names** list. This will give you an idea of the issues and personalities you'll encounter in the section.

**3** Read **One American's Story** and **A Personal Voice** within it. These provide one individual's view of an important issue of the time.

**4** Notice the structure of the section. **Blue** heads label the major topics; **red** subheads signal smaller topics within a major topic. Together, these heads give you a quick outline of the section.

## Terms & Names

- nationalism
- militarism
- Allies
- Central Powers
- Archduke Franz Ferdinand
- no man's land
- trench warfare
- *Lusitania*
- Zimmermann note

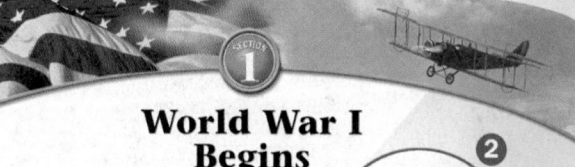

# World War I Begins

| MAIN IDEA | WHY IT MATTERS NOW | Terms & Names |
|---|---|---|
| As World War I intensified, the United States was forced to abandon its neutrality. | The United States remains involved in European and world affairs. | • nationalism  • no man's land<br>• militarism  • trench warfare<br>• Allies  • *Lusitania*<br>• Central Powers  • Zimmermann<br>• Archduke Franz  note<br>Ferdinand |

### One American's Story

It was about 1:00 A.M. on April 6, 1917, and the members of the U.S. House of Representatives were tired. For the past 15 hours they had been debating President Wilson's request for a declaration of war against Germany. There was a breathless hush as Jeannette Rankin of Montana, the first woman elected to Congress, stood up. Rankin declared, "I want to stand by my country but I cannot vote for war. I vote no." Later she reflected on her action.

#### A PERSONAL VOICE  JEANNETTE RANKIN

" I believe that the first vote I cast was the most significant vote and a most significant act on the part of women, because women are going to have to stop war. I felt at the time that the first woman [in Congress] should take the first stand, that the first time the first woman had a chance to say no to war she should say it. "

—quoted in *Jeannette Rankin: First Lady in Congress*

After much debate as to whether the United States should join the fight, Congress voted in favor of U.S. entry into World War I. With this decision, the government abandoned the neutrality that America had maintained for three years. What made the United States change its policy in 1917?

▲ Jeannette Rankin was the only member of the House to vote against the U.S. entering both World War I and World War II.

### Causes of World War I

Although many Americans wanted to stay out of the war, several factors made American neutrality difficult to maintain. As an industrial and imperial power, the United States felt many of the same pressures that had led the nations of Europe into devastating warfare. Historians generally cite four long-term causes of the First World War: nationalism, imperialism, militarism, and the formation of a system of alliances.

**NATIONALISM** Throughout the 19th century, politics in the Western world were deeply influenced by the concept of **nationalism**—a devotion to the interests and culture of one's nation. Often, nationalism led to competitive and antagonistic rivalries among nations. In this atmosphere of competition, many feared Germany's growing power in Europe.

In addition, various ethnic groups resented domination by others and longed for their nations to become independent. Many ethnic groups looked to larger nations for protection. Russia regarded itself as the protector of Europe's Slavic peoples, no matter which government they lived under. Among these Slavic peoples were the Serbs. Serbia, located in the Balkans, was an independent nation, but millions of ethnic Serbs lived under the rule of Austria-Hungary. As a result, Russia and Austria-Hungary were rivals for influence over Serbia.

**IMPERIALISM** For many centuries, European nations had been building empires, slowly extending their economic and political control over various peoples of the world. Colonies supplied the European imperial powers with raw materials and provided markets for manufactured goods. As Germany industrialized, it competed with France and Britain in the contest for colonies.

**MILITARISM** Empires were expensive to build and to defend. The growth of nationalism and imperialism led to increased military spending. Because each nation wanted stronger armed forces than those of any potential enemy, the imperial powers followed a policy of **militarism**—the development of armed forces and their use as a tool of diplomacy.

By 1890 the strongest nation on the European continent was Germany, which had set up an army reserve system that drafted and trained young men. Britain was not initially alarmed by Germany's military expansion. As an island nation, Britain had always relied on its navy for defense and protection of its shipping routes—and the British navy was the strongest in the world. However, in 1897, Wilhelm II, Germany's kaiser, or emperor, decided that his nation should also become a major sea power in order to compete more successfully against the British. Soon British and German shipyards competed to build the largest battleships and destroyers. France, Italy, Japan, and the United States quickly joined the naval arms race.

**ALLIANCE SYSTEM** By 1907 there were two major defense alliances in Europe. The Triple Entente, later known as the **Allies**, consisted of France, Britain, and Russia. The Triple Alliance consisted of Germany, Austria-Hungary, and Italy.

**MAIN IDEA**

Analyzing Causes

**A** How did nationalism and imperialism lead to conflict in Europe?

Vocabulary
**alliance:** a formal agreement or union between nations

◄ German Emperor Wilhelm II (center) marches with two of his generals, Hindenburg (left) and Ludendorff, during World War I.

# Use Active Reading Strategies As You Read

Now you're ready to read the chapter. Read one section at a time, from beginning to end.

**1** Try to visualize the people, places, and events you read about. Studying illustrated features, such as **Key Player,** and other visual materials, such as **Science & Technology,** will help you do this.

**2** Look for the story behind the events. Read **Background** notes for additional information on particular events.

**3** Skim the pages of the section to find key words. Use the **Vocabulary** notes in the margin to find the meaning of unfamiliar terms.

**4** Ask and answer questions as you read. Look for the **Main Idea** questions in the margin. Answering these will show whether you understand what you have just read.

---

MAIN IDEA

**Analyzing Effects**
**D** What were the physical and psychological effects of this new kind of warfare?

---

**1**

**KEY PLAYER**

GENERAL JOHN J. PERSHING
1860–1948

When General Pershing, the commander of the American Expeditionary Force (AEF), arrived in France, he found that the Allies intended to use American troops simply as reinforcements. Pershing, however, urged that the AEF operate as an independent fighting force, under American command.

Pershing believed in aggressive combat and felt that three years of trench warfare had made the Allies too defensive. Under Pershing, American forces helped to stop the German advance, capturing important enemy positions. After the war, Pershing was made General of the Armies of the United States—the highest rank given to an officer.

### Fighting "Over There"

The **American Expeditionary Force** (AEF), led by **General John J. Pershing,** included men from widely separated parts of the country. American infantrymen were nicknamed doughboys, possibly because of the white belts they wore, which they cleaned with pipe clay, or "dough." Most doughboys had never ventured far from the farms or small towns where they lived, and the sophisticated sights and sounds of Paris made a vivid impression. However, doughboys were also shocked by the unexpected horrors of the battlefield and astonished by the new weapons and tactics of modern warfare.

**NEW WEAPONS** The battlefields of World War I saw the first large-scale use of weapons that would become standard in modern war. Although some of these weapons were new, others, like the machine gun, had been so refined that they changed the nature of warfare. The two most innovative weapons were the tank and the airplane. Together, they heralded mechanized warfare, or warfare that relies on machines powered by gasoline and diesel engines. **C**

Tanks ran on caterpillar treads and were built of steel so that bullets bounced off. The British first used tanks during the 1916 Battle of the Somme, but not very effectively. By 1917, the British had learned how to drive large numbers of tanks through barbed wire defenses, clearing a path for the infantry.

The early airplanes were so flimsy that at first both sides limited their use to scouting. After a while, the two sides used tanks to fire at enemy planes that were gathering information. Early dogfights, or individual air combats, like the one described by Eddie Rickenbacker, resembled duels. Pilots sat in their open cockpits and shot at each other with pistols. Because it was hard to fly a plane and shoot a pistol at the same time, planes began carrying mounted machine guns. But the planes' propeller blades kept getting in the way of the bullets. Then the Germans introduced an interrupter gear that permitted the stream of bullets to avoid the whirring blades.

**3** Vocabulary
**tactics:** the science of using forces in combat

**2** Background
When the U.S. entered the war, its air power was weak. Then, in July 1917, Congress appropriated a hefty $675 million to build an air force.

Meanwhile, airplanes were built to travel faster and faster. By 1918 the British had built up a strategic bomber force of 22,000 planes with which to attack German weapons factories and army bases.

Observation balloons were used extensively by both sides in the war in Europe. Balloons were so important strategically that they were often protected by aircraft flying close by, and they became prime targets for Rickenbacker and other ace pilots.

### The War Introduces New Hazards

The new weapons and tactics of World War I led to horrific injuries and hazards. The fighting men were surrounded by filth, lice, rats, and polluted water that caused dysentery. They inhaled poison gas and smelled the stench of decaying bodies. They suffered from lack of sleep. Constant bombardments and other experiences often led to battle fatigue and "shell shock," a term coined during World War I to describe a complete emotional collapse from which many never recovered.

Physical problems included a disease called trench foot, caused by standing in cold wet trenches for long periods of time without changing into dry socks or boots. First the toes would turn red or blue, then they would become numb, and finally they would start to rot. The only solution was to amputate the toes, and in some cases the entire foot. A painful infection of the gums and throat, called trench mouth, was also common among the soldiers. **D**

Red Cross ambulances, often staffed by American volunteers, carried the wounded from the battlefield to the hospital. An American nurse named Florence Bullard recounted her experience in a hospital near the front in 1918.

**A PERSONAL VOICE** FLORENCE BULLARD

"The Army is only twelve miles away from us and only the wounded that are too severely injured to live to be carried a little farther are brought here. . . . Side by side I have Americans, English, Scotch, Irish, and French, and apart in the corners are Boche [Germans]. They have to watch each other die side by side. I am sent for everywhere—in the . . . operating-room, the dressing-room, and back again to the rows of men. . . . The cannon goes day and night and the shells are breaking over and around us. . . . I have had to write many sad letters to American mothers. I wonder if it will ever end."

—quoted in Over There: The Story of America's First Great Overseas Crusade

In fact, the end was near, as German forces mounted a final offensive.

**4** MAIN IDEA
Analyzing Effects
**D** What were the physical and psychological effects of this new kind of warfare?

---

**1** **Science** & **Technology**

**TECHNOLOGY AT WAR**
Both sides in World War I used new technology to attack more soldiers from greater distances than ever before. Aircraft and long-range guns were even used to fire on civilian targets—libraries, cathedrals, and city districts. The biggest guns could shell a city from 75 miles.

**Machine Guns**
Firepower increased to 600 rounds per minute.

**Airships and Airplanes**
One of the most famous WWI planes, the British Sopwith Camel, had a front-mounted machine gun for "dogfights." Planes were also loaded with bombs, as were the floating gas-filled "airships" called zeppelins.

Antiaircraft Gun

**Poison Gas**
A yellow-green chlorine fog sickened, suffocated, burned, and blinded its victims. Gas masks became standard issue.

**Tanks**
Tanks, like this French light tank, were used to "mow down" barbed wire and soldiers.

---

**Background**
When the U.S. entered the war, its air power was weak. Then, in July 1917, Congress appropriated a hefty $675 million to build an air force.

# Review and Summarize What You Have Read

When you finish reading a section, review and summarize what you've read. If necessary, go back and reread information that was not clear the first time through.

**1** Look again at the **blue** heads and **red** subheads for a quick summary of the major points covered in the section.

**2** Study any **maps** and **charts** in the section. These visual materials usually provide a condensed version of information in the section.

**3** Complete all the questions in the **Section Assessment.** This will help you think critically about the material you've just read.

### Domestic Consequences of World War I

- Accelerated America's emergence as the world's greatest industrial power

- Contributed to the movement of African Americans to Northern cities

- Intensified anti-immigrant and antiradical sentiments among mainstream Americans

- Brought millions of women into the work force

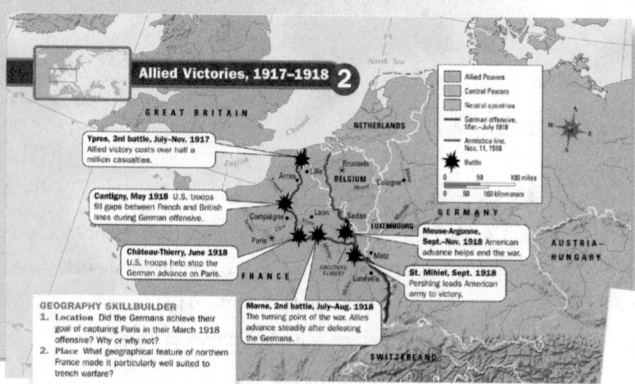

### Allied Victories, 1917–1918 **2**

Ypres, 3rd battle, July–Nov. 1917
Allied victory costs over half a million casualties.

Cantigny, May 1918 U.S. troops fill gaps between French and British lines during German offensive.

Château-Thierry, June 1918 U.S. troops help stop the German advance on Paris.

Meuse-Argonne, Sept.–Nov. 1918 American advance helps end the war.

St. Mihiel, Sept. 1918 Pershing leads American army to victory.

Marne, 2nd battle, July–Aug. 1918 The turning point of the war. Allies advance steadily after defeating the Germans.

**GEOGRAPHY SKILLBUILDER**
1. **Location** Did the Germans achieve their goal of capturing Paris in their March 1918 offensive? Why or why not?
2. **Place** What geographical feature of northern France made it particularly well suited to trench warfare?

## American Troops Go on the Offensive

**1**

When Russia pulled out of the war in 1917, the Germans shifted their armies from the eastern front to the western front in France. By May they were within 50 miles of Paris. The Americans arrived just in time to help stop the German advance at Cantigny in France. Several weeks later, U.S. troops played a major role in throwing back German attacks at Château-Thierry and Belleau Wood. In July and August, they helped win the Second Battle of the Marne. The tide had turned against the Central Powers. In September, U.S. soldiers began to mount offensives against the Germans at Saint-Mihiel and in the Meuse-Argonne area. **5**

**1**

"Bullets were cracking just over my head."
SERGEANT YORK

**MAIN IDEA**
Drawing Conclusions
**5** How did American forces help the Allies win the war?

**AMERICAN WAR HERO** During the fighting in the Meuse-Argonne area, one of America's greatest war heroes, **Alvin York,** became famous. A redheaded mountaineer and blacksmith from Tennessee, York sought exemption as a **conscientious objector,** a person who opposes warfare on moral grounds, pointing out that the Bible says, "Thou shalt not kill."

York eventually decided that it was morally acceptable to fight if the cause was just. On October 8, 1918, armed only with a rifle and a revolver, York killed 25 Germans and—with six other doughboys—captured 132 prisoners. General Pershing called him the outstanding soldier of the AEF, while Marshal Foch, the commander of Allied forces in Europe, described his feat as "the greatest thing accomplished by any private soldier of all the armies of Europe." For his heroic acts, York was promoted to sergeant and became a celebrity when he returned to the United States.

**THE COLLAPSE OF GERMANY** On November 3, 1918, Austria-Hungary surrendered to the Allies. That same day, German sailors mutinied against government authority. The mutiny spread quickly. Everywhere in Germany, groups of soldiers and workers organized revolutionary councils. On November 9, socialist leaders in the capital, Berlin, established a German republic. The kaiser gave up the throne.

## The Legacy of the War

When World War I ended, many Americans looked forward to a return of what Warren G. Harding called "normalcy." However, both the United States and the rest of the world had been utterly transformed by the war. At home, World War I had strengthened both the U.S. military and the power of government. It had also accelerated social change, especially for African Americans and women. In addition, the propaganda campaign had provoked powerful fears and antagonisms that were left unchallenged when the war finally came to an end.

In Europe the destruction and massive loss of life severely damaged social and political systems. In many countries the war created political instability and violence that persisted for decades. During the war years, the first Communist state was established in Russia, while after the war, the first fascist organizations seized control in Italy, Spain, and Germany.

Appalled by the scale of destruction, Americans began to call World War I "the war to end all wars," in the hope that humanity would never again be willing to fight such a war. However, unresolved issues in Europe would eventually drag America into an even wider war. The Treaty of Versailles had settled nothing. In fact, some Europeans longed to resume the fight. The ominous shape of things to come emerged in the writings of an Austrian named Adolf Hitler, an angry veteran of World War I: "It cannot be that two million [Germans] should have fallen in vain. . . . No, we do not pardon, we demand—vengeance!" Two decades after the end of the Great War, Adolf Hitler's desire for vengeance would plunge the world into an even greater war, in which the United States would play a leading role.

Vocabulary
**fascist:**
characteristic of or relating to fascism, a system of totalitarian government

### Domestic Consequences of World War I

- accelerated America's emergence as the world's greatest industrial power

- contributed to the movement of African Americans to Northern cities

- intensified anti-immigrant and anti-radical sentiments among mainstream Americans

- brought over one million women into the work force

**2**

**3** **4** **ASSESSMENT**

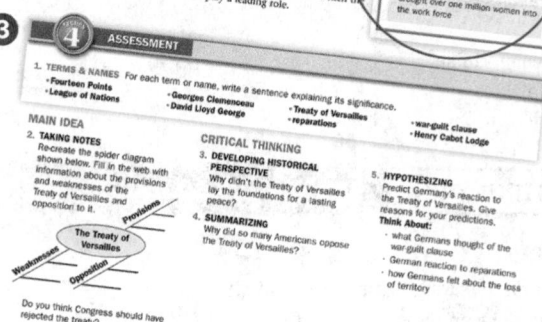

1. **TERMS & NAMES** For each term or name, write a sentence explaining its significance.
- Fourteen Points
- League of Nations
- Georges Clemenceau
- David Lloyd George
- Treaty of Versailles
- reparations
- war-guilt clause
- Henry Cabot Lodge

**MAIN IDEA**
2. **TAKING NOTES**
Recreate the spider diagram shown below. Fill in the web with information about the provisions and weaknesses of the Treaty of Versailles and opposition to it.

Provisions

The Treaty of Versailles

Weaknesses

Opposition

Do you think Congress should have rejected the treaty?

**CRITICAL THINKING**
3. **DEVELOPING HISTORICAL PERSPECTIVE**
Why didn't the Treaty of Versailles lay the foundations for a lasting peace?

4. **SUMMARIZING**
Why did so many Americans oppose the Treaty of Versailles?

5. **HYPOTHESIZING**
Predict Germany's reaction to the Treaty of Versailles. Give reasons for your predictions.
**Think About:**
- what Germans thought of the war guilt clause
- German reaction to reparations
- how Germans felt about the loss of territory

## USING STRATEGIES FOR . . .

**Multiple Choice**

Multiple-choice questions test the ability to choose the correct answer from several choices. The test taker reads each stem and decides which is the correct answer. Test takers are often asked to mark their answers on an answer sheet by filling in the circle or oval that has the same letter as the answer they have chosen.

Explain to students that they will do best on test questions by thinking them through carefully and by applying test-taking strategies, such as the following.

1. It is important to read the stem and evaluate each alternative to find the best answer. In question 1, (C) is the correct answer because the rest of the alternatives were part of the Allied forces.

2. Question 2 is an example of a question in which *All of the above* is incorrect. This is why you must make sure all of the alternatives are, indeed, correct. The correct answer is (H).

3. In question 3, look closely at (A) and (B). Since they directly contradict each other, it is likely that one of them is the correct answer. In this case, your knowledge of history tells you that (A) is correct.

4. In question 4, you can probably eliminate (H) and (J) because they use words that are absolutes, *alone* and *all*. Use your knowledge of history to eliminate (F), since Japan was not one of the Allies. The correct answer is (G).

**General Test-Taking Tips**

Share these tips with your students.

- The night before a test, make sure you get at least eight hours of sleep.
- Have a healthy breakfast or lunch before taking your test.
- Wear clothes that make you comfortable.
- Relax and enjoy the challenge!

# Part 2: TAKS Strategies and Practice

You can improve your test-taking skills by practicing the strategies discussed in this section. First, read the tips on the left-hand page. Then apply them to the practice items on the right-hand page.

## Multiple Choice

A multiple-choice question consists of a *stem* and a set of *alternatives*. The stem usually is in the form of a question or an incomplete sentence. One of the alternatives correctly answers the question or completes the sentence.

1. Read the stem carefully. Then read each alternative with the stem. Do not jump to conclusions about the correct answer until you have read all the alternatives.

2. Take care with questions that are stated negatively.

3. Look for key words or facts in a question.

4. Carefully read questions that include *All of the above* as an alternative.

5. If two alternatives directly contradict one another, one is likely to be the correct answer.

6. Eliminate alternatives you know are wrong.

7. Look for modifiers to help in selecting correct alternatives.

**stem**

**1** In 1942, the Allied forces included all of the following EXCEPT

**alternatives**

A the United States
B Great Britain
C Germany
D the Soviet Union

Take care with questions that contain words like *except* and *not*. Here, you are asked to identify the nation that was not a member of the Allies.

2 In June 1944, General Dwight D. Eisenhower oversaw the Allied invasion of —

F Africa
G Italy
H France
J All of the above

*1944* is key here. Eisenhower oversaw several Allied invasions, but only the invasion of France in 1944.

If you select *All of the above*, make sure all of the alternatives are, indeed, correct.

3 To win the fight against Japan in the Pacific, the Allies —

A focused on Japanese bases on certain islands
B ignored island bases and invaded Japan directly
C set a trap by inviting an attack on Australia
D concentrated on Japanese forces in China

4 After World War II ended, the Allies divided Germany into different zones controlled by —

F Great Britain, France, the United States, and Japan
G Great Britain, France, the United States, and the Soviet Union
H the United States alone
J all the countries of Europe

You can eliminate F if you remember that Japan was one of the Axis powers.

Absolute words like *all, alone, only, never,* and *always* frequently signal an incorrect answer.

answers: 1 (C), 2 (H), 3 (A), 4 (G)

---

## DIFFERENTIATING INSTRUCTION    STUDENTS ACQUIRING ENGLISH/ESL

### Understanding Vocabulary

Make sure students understand the following terms and concepts in the sample questions on these pages.

**Strategy Page**
Question 1 *forces:* armies
Question 3 *ignored:* skipped
  *concentrated:* focused; directed attention to

**Practice Page**
Question 1 *"Rough Riders":* a nickname for a famous American cavalry unit that fought under the leadership of Theodore Roosevelt
Question 2 *oil boom:* a huge increase in the production of oil
Question 3 *reforms:* changes
Question 4 *high tech industrial development:* industrial development based on electronic computation processes

**Directions:** Read each question carefully and choose the **BEST** answer from the four alternatives.

1   In which Texas city did Theodore Roosevelt's Rough Riders train before leaving for the Spanish-American War?

   **A** Austin

   **B** El Paso

   **C** Houston

   **D** San Antonio

2   The Texas oil boom began when Captain Anthony Lucas struck oil at —

   **F** Batson

   **G** Saratoga

   **H** Sour Lake

   **J** Spindletop Hill

3   Reforms supported by the Populists included —

   **A** government regulation of business

   **B** public ownership of railroads

   **C** free coinage of silver

   **D** All of the above

4   The high-tech industrial development in and around Austin is known as Silicon —

   **F** Alley

   **G** Hills

   **H** Plains

   **J** Valley

## PRACTICE QUESTIONS

### Thinking It Through

Share the following explanations with students as they discuss the strategies they used to answer the practice questions.

1. Use your knowledge of history to answer this question. The correct answer is (D).
2. Use your knowledge of history to choose the correct answer, (J).
3. This question is an example of an *All of the above* question. If you select (D), you must make sure that all of the choices are correct. In this question all of the choices were reforms supported by the Populists, so (D) is the correct answer.
4. Knowing that the area around Austin is hill country helps you choose the correct answer to this question, (G).

## TEKS and TAKS

| | Item Number | TEKS | TAKS |
|---|---|---|---|
| **STRATEGY** | 1. 2. 3. 4. | **(6)(B):** analyze major issues and events of World War II | **(US6)(B):** analyze major issues and events of World War II |
| | 2. | **(6)(C):** explain the roles played by significant military leaders of World War II | |
| **PRACTICE** | 1. | **(3)(A):** explain significant events of the Spanish-American War | |
| | 2. | **(1)(B):** apply chronology through the sequencing of significant events | **(US1)(B):** apply chronology through the sequencing of significant events |
| | 3. | **(2)(A):** analyze political issues in the U.S. from 1877 to 1898 <br> **(2)(B):** analyze economic issues in the U.S. from 1877 to 1898 | **(US2):** understand political changes in the U.S. from 1877 to 1898 <br> **(US2)(B):** analyze economic issues in the U.S. from 1877 to 1898 |
| | 4. | **(22)(A):** explain the effects of technological innovations on economic development in the U.S. | **(US22)(A):** explain the effects of technological innovations on economic development in the U.S. |

## USING STRATEGIES FOR . . .

### Primary Sources

Students can learn about the past by studying primary sources. As students read the primary source, have them try to answer the following questions: Who is it about? What is it about? Where did it happen? Why did it happen?

Explain to students that they will do best on test questions by thinking them through carefully and by applying test-taking strategies, such as the following.

1. Refer back to the primary source when answering the questions. Question 1 is an example of a question constructed in the negative. You should skim the passage to find the conditions that are described in the passage and eliminate these alternatives. The correct answer is (B), since it is not a condition described in the passage.

2. In question 2, the key words are *main idea.* You must choose the alternative that most closely expresses the author's main idea of the passage. Alternatives (F), (G), and (J) state specific details. The correct answer is (H) because this choice expresses the focus, or main idea, of the passage.

### General Test-Taking Tips

Share these tips with your students.

- Read the directions carefully before you begin to answer the questions.
- Plan the time you are given to take the test.
- Check your answers.
- Believe in yourself.

## Primary Sources

Primary sources are written or made by people who were at a historical event, either as observers or participants. Primary sources include journals, diaries, letters, speeches, newspaper articles, autobiographies, wills, deeds, and financial records.

**1** Look at the source line to learn about the document and its author. Consider the reliability of the information in the document.

**2** Skim the document to get an idea of what it is about.

**3** Use active reading strategies. As you read, ask yourself questions, review sequence, and make predictions. (Here, for example, the first sentences make the sequence of events clear.)

**4** As you read, look for the main idea. This is the writer's most important point. Remember that supporting details or arguments will back up this idea.

**5** Use context clues to help you understand unfamiliar words. (Here the content of the rest of the paragraph suggests that *enumeration* means "a count" or "a listing.")

**6** Before rereading the document, skim the questions. Previewing the questions will help focus your reading.

### The San Francisco Earthquake

On Wednesday morning at a quarter past five came the earthquake. **3** A minute later the flames were leaping upward. In a dozen different quarters south of Market Street, in the working-class ghetto, and in the factories, fires started. There was no opposing the flames. There was no organization, no communication. All the cunning **4** adjustments of a twentieth century city had been smashed by the earthquake. . . . The steel rails were twisted into perpendicular and horizontal angles. The telephone and telegraph systems were disrupted. And the great water mains had burst. All the shrewd contrivances and safeguards of man had been thrown out of gear by thirty seconds' twitching of the earth-crust. . . .

An enumeration of the buildings destroyed would be a directory of San Francisco. An enumeration of the buildings undestroyed would be a line and several addresses. An enumeration of the deeds of heroism would stock a library. . . . The number of the victims of the earthquake will never be known. **5**

Author Jack London's eyewitness account was published soon after the earthquake. **1**

—Jack London, "The Story of an Eyewitness." *Collier's Weekly,* May 5, 1906

**1** Based on the information in the passage, which of the following does **NOT** describe conditions following the 1906 earthquake in San Francisco?

A Fires spread to many parts of the city.

B Communication lines remained intact.

C Municipal water pipes broke.

D Rail lines were disrupted.

**6**

Here the key words are *main idea.* Make sure the alternative you select expresses the focus of the passage.

**2** Which sentence **BEST** expresses the main idea of the passage?

F "A minute later the flames were leaping upward."

G "The number of the victims of the earthquake will never be known."

H "All the cunning adjustments of a twentieth-century city had been smashed by the earthquake."

J "The telephone and telegraph systems were disrupted."

answers: 1 (B), 2 (H)

S8

### Understanding Vocabulary

Make sure students understand the following terms and concepts in the sample primary source and questions on these pages.

**Strategy Page**
**Primary Source**
*quarters:* sections of a city
*ghetto:* part of a city where a minority group lives
*cunning:* clever
*contrivances:* mechanical devices
Question 1 *municipal:* city-owned

**Practice Page**
**Primary Source**
*sphere:* the extent of a person's knowledge, interest, or social position
Question 1 *temperance:* not drinking alcohol
   *suffrage:* the right of voting
   *urban:* city
Question 2 *monarchs:* rulers

STRATEGIES FOR TAKING TAKS

**Directions:** Use this passage, from an article by women's-rights advocate Amelia Bloomer, <u>and</u> your knowledge of United States history to answer the following questions.

It is objected that it does not belong to woman's sphere to take part in the selection of her rulers, or the enactment of laws to which she is subject.

This is mere matter of opinion. Woman's sphere, like man's sphere, varies according to . . . the circumstances in which she may be placed. A vast majority of the British nation would deny the assumption that Queen Victoria is out of her sphere in reigning over an empire of an hundred and fifty millions of souls! . . .

But, again, one says votes would be unnecessarily multiplied, that women would vote just as the men do, therefore the man's vote will answer for both. Sound logic, truly! But let us apply this rule to men. Votes are unnecessarily multiplied now by so many men voting; a few could do it all, [rather than taking] the mass of men from their business and their families to vote. . . .

Again, another says, "It has always been as now; women never have had equal rights, and that is proof that they should not have." Sound logic again! . . . But whence did man derive this right [to vote], and how long has it been enjoyed? . . .

Must we continue to cling to old laws and customs because they are old? Why then did not [the American] people remain subject to kings?

—Amelia Bloomer, "Woman's Right to the Ballot" (1895)

**1** Bloomer's essay was part of the campaign to establish —

**A** temperance

**B** woman suffrage

**C** urban reform

**D** child labor laws

**2** Bloomer uses the example of Queen Victoria to show that —

**F** some countries accept that women can have a role in government

**G** the best monarchs are women

**H** a monarchy is preferable to democratic government

**J** people should follow traditional practices

**3** When Bloomer uses the phrase "sound logic," she is —

**A** agreeing with the argument offered

**B** pretending to agree with the argument offered

**C** stating her true opinion

**D** suggesting that the argument is logical

**4** Bloomer rejects the argument that things should remain the way they have always been by saying that if tradition were so important, —

**F** Victoria would not be queen

**G** women would have the vote already

**H** women would vote exactly as men do

**J** America would still be ruled by kings

## PRACTICE QUESTIONS

### Thinking It Through

Share the following explanations with students as they discuss the strategies they used to answer the practice questions.

1. You need to interpret the primary source to determine that it was part of the campaign to establish woman suffrage. The correct answer is (B).

2. Bloomer does not make the statements in (G) and (H) and argues against tradition, making (J) incorrect as well. (F) is correct; Bloomer is saying that women do have political roles in some places.

3. Bloomer does not agree with the "sound logic" or think it logical; so (A) and (D) are incorrect. (C) is incorrect because she is speaking ironically. She points out the weakness of this argument; therefore, (B) is the correct answer.

4. The passage does not support alternatives (F), (G), or (H). When Bloomer talks about tradition—"old laws and customs"—she asks why America is not still ruled by— "subject to"— kings, as in the correct answer, (J).

## ⭐ TEKS and TAKS

| | Item Number | TEKS | TAKS |
|---|---|---|---|
| **STRATEGY** | 1. 2. | **(9)(A):** analyze the effects of physical and human geographic factors on major events<br>**(24)(A):** use primary sources to acquire information | **(US9)(A):** analyze the effects of physical and human geographic factors on major events<br>**(US24)(A):** use primary sources to acquire information |
| **PRACTICE** | 1. 2. 3. 4. | **(4)(B):** evaluate the impact of reform leaders on American society<br>**(18)(A):** analyze the methods of expanding the right to participate in the democratic process<br>**(24)(A):** use primary sources to acquire information | **(US4)(B):** evaluate the impact of reform leaders on American society<br>**(US18)(B):** evaluate various means of achieving equality of political rights<br>**(US24)(A):** use primary sources to acquire information |

## STRATEGIES

# USING STRATEGIES FOR . . .

## Secondary Sources

Explain to students that they will do best on test questions by thinking them through carefully and by applying test-taking strategies, such as the following.

1. *First* is a key word in question 1. Reread the first sentence of the passage to find the correct answer. The reference in the sentence to the "ongoing conflict in Vietnam," should alert you that the correct answer is (B).

2. *Undesirable* and *domestic* are key words in question 2. This question is an example of an *All of the above* question. Read each alternative to make sure it is a correct answer. In this question, the only undesirable option from a *domestic* point of view was invading North Vietnam, since this option would increase antiwar sentiment at home. Therefore, (F) is the correct answer.

## General Test-Taking Tips

Share these tips with your students.

• Glance over the test to determine the types and numbers of questions.

• Estimate the amount of time you have to spend on each type of question.

# Secondary Sources

Secondary sources are written or made by people who were not at the original events. They often combine information from several primary sources. The most common types of written secondary sources are history books and biographies.

**1** Use the title to preview the content of the passage. (The title here signals that the passage is about the courses of action open to President Richard Nixon in Vietnam.)

**2** Look at the topic sentences of paragraphs. These, too, indicate what the content will be.

**3** Use context clues to help you understand unfamiliar words. (From the discussion of the options, you can tell that *flawed* means that each one had problems.)

**4** Read actively by asking yourself questions. (After learning Nixon's four options, you might ask yourself: "How did he overcome these problems?")

**5** Look for words like *because, since,* or *as a result* that indicate cause-effect relationships.

**6** Before rereading the passage, skim the questions to identify the information you need to find.

**1** **President Nixon's Options in Vietnam**

**2** When he became president, Richard Nixon had four options regarding the ongoing conflict in Vietnam, each of which was seriously **3** flawed. He could continue to fight an all-out war, but that effort was clearly not working. He could intensify the war by invading the north, but such a step would increase antiwar sentiment at home. He could withdraw American troops, but other countries might see that as a sign of weakness. He could try to negotiate a **4** peace, but North Vietnam was not willing to give up its claim to the south.

Nixon chose not one option but a combination. He announced that American troops would leave Vietnam. However, he made the pullout gradual and increased military aid to South **5** Vietnam. As a result, Nixon continued the war and avoided a show of weakness. He also pursued peace talks with North Vietnam. At the same time, though, he pressured the North to reach an agreement through an intensified bombing campaign and attacks on North Vietnamese bases in Cambodia.

**1** From the first sentence of the passage, it is clear that the —

A war in Vietnam was coming to an end

B war was being fought when Nixon took office

C United States was fighting South Vietnam

D United States was winning in Vietnam

Some questions focus on specific parts of the passage.

**2** Which of the following options was undesirable for domestic political reasons?

F Invading North Vietnam

G Negotiating a peace

H Pulling troops out of Vietnam

J All of the above

Here you are looking for an alternative that would cause Nixon political problems.

answers: 1 (B), 2 (F)

---

## DIFFERENTIATING INSTRUCTION    STUDENTS ACQUIRING ENGLISH/ESL

### Understanding Vocabulary

Make sure students understand the following terms and concepts in the sample secondary sources and questions on these pages.

**Strategy Page**
**Secondary Source**
*options:* choices
*intensify:* increase
*sentiment:* feelings
*negotiate:* arrange
Question 2 *domestic:* in one's own country

**Practice Page**
**Secondary Source**
*New Dealer:* supporter of New Deal legislative programs of President Roosevelt
*adversary:* opponent; competitor
*candor:* openness
*lobbyist:* person who tries to influence legislation
*junket:* a trip made by an official at public expense
*constituent:* a voter who has elected a public official
Question 4 *mentor:* a trusted counselor or guide

STRATEGIES FOR TAKING TAKS

**Directions:** Use the passage <u>and</u> your knowledge of United States history to answer the following questions.

## Mr. Sam Rayburn

Although a review of Sam Rayburn's legislative record reveals a pattern of broad consistency, his career is not easily reduced to categorization. Even though he sponsored or supported most of the New Deal legislation, he was regarded at the time as more of a "middle-of-the-roader" than a liberal or "New Dealer." Although he was viewed as a loyal "party man," he retained and exercised an independence of action that occasionally cut sharply across party aims, and though his complete mastery of political process made him a formidable congressional adversary, his fairness and candor within the process brought him respect from both sides of the aisle. Rayburn's personal integrity was legendary: he accepted no money from lobbyists, he went on only one congressional junket in forty-eight years (he paid his own way), and he even refused travel expenses on speaking tours. Within his Northeast Texas congressional district, Rayburn was known as a politician who kept in close touch with constituents. His informality allowed him to identify with the people of his largely rural district. He was known to be very effective in dealing with his constituents' individual problems, and he brought numerous projects to the district. . . .

—*The Handbook of Texas Online*

**1** Sam Rayburn represented a congressional district in —

**A** Northeast Texas

**B** Southeast Texas

**C** Southwest Texas

**D** Northwest Texas

**2** Even though he sponsored or supported most of the New Deal legislation, Sam Rayburn was regarded as a —

**F** New Dealer

**G** middle-of-the-roader

**H** liberal

**J** All of the above

**3** Sam Rayburn was known as a man of integrity because he —

**A** did not accept money from lobbyists

**B** only went on one political junket during his career

**C** would not accept travel expenses for speaking tours

**D** All of the above

**4** For which of the following Texas politicians did Sam Rayburn serve as a mentor?

**F** George W. Bush

**G** Phil Gramm

**H** Henry Gonzales

**J** Lyndon Johnson

cerpt from "Rayburn, Samuel Taliaferro," from *The Handbook of Texas Online*. http://www.tsha.utexas.edu/handbook/online/articles/view/
/fra49.html. Reprinted by permission of the Texas State Historical Association & The Center for Studies in Texas History.

**S11**

## PRACTICE QUESTIONS

### Thinking It Through
Share the following explanations with students as they discuss the strategies they used to answer the practice questions.

1. Skim the passage to find the answer to this question. The correct answer is (A).
2. Skim the question to identify information you need to find in the passage. Next, skim the passage to find information about how people regarded, or thought of, Sam Rayburn. The correct answer is (G).
3. This is an example of an *All of the above* question. Be sure that all of the choices are correct before you choose (D) as your answer. Since the passage states that (A), (B), and (C) are all true about Sam Rayburn, and since they indicate that he was a man of integrity, the correct answer is (D).
4. Use your knowledge of history to answer this question. The correct answer is (J).

## TEKS and TAKS

| | Item Number | TEKS | TAKS |
|---|---|---|---|
| **STRATEGY** | 1. 2. | **(6)(E):** analyze the conflict in Vietnam and describe its effects.<br>**(24)(A):** use secondary sources to acquire information about the United States | **(US6)(E):** analyze the conflict in Vietnam and describe its effects.<br>**(US24)(A):** use secondary sources to acquire information about the United States |
| **PRACTICE** | 1. 2. 3. 4. | **(19)(A):** Describe qualities of effective leadership<br>**(19)(B):** evaluate the contributions of significant political leaders in the United States<br>**(24)(A):** use secondary sources to acquire information about the United States | **(US24)(A):** use secondary sources to acquire information about the United States |

## USING STRATEGIES FOR . . .

### Political Cartoons

Political cartoons are one kind of primary source. Remind students to analyze the political cartoon before reading the questions. They should identify the subject, note important symbols and details, interpret the message, and analyze the point of view. Then they will read the question to identify the information they need to find.

Explain to students that they will do best on test questions by thinking them through carefully and by applying test-taking strategies, such as the following.

1. Question 1 asks you to interpret the cartoonist's message. Since the cartoonist shows each member pointing to the person next to him, the correct answer is (D). Each Tammany Ring member hopes to avoid being found guilty.
2. To answer question 2, look at how the cartoonist uses caricature in the cartoon. The cartoonist uses caricature to indicate that he is critical of the members of the Tammany Ring. However, the figures in the cartoon are not shown lying down, sleeping, or acting lazy in other ways. Also, the caption reads, "Who stole the people's money?" This caption hints at corruption rather than laziness. Therefore, (G) is the correct answer.

### General Test-Taking Tips

Share these tips with your students.
- Ask questions before the test begins.
- Know how to fill in the answer form.
- Read and listen to directions carefully.

## Political Cartoons

Political cartoons use a combination of words and images to express a point of view on political issues. They are a useful primary source, because they reflect the opinions of the time.

1. Identify the subject of the cartoon. The caption often gives an indication of the subject matter.

2. Try to identify the main characters in the cartoon. (The label in the foreground of the cartoon shows that they are members of the Tammany Ring, New York's Democratic political machine. "Boss" Tweed, the leader, is on the left.)

3. Identify any important symbols—ideas or images that stand for something else.

4. Review labels and any other written information in the cartoon.

5. Analyze the point of view. The use of caricature—the exaggeration of physical features—often signals the cartoonist's attitude.

6. Interpret the cartoonist's message.

The cartoonist uses a diamond stickpin to symbolize Tweed's excesses.

The labels identify other members of the Tweed Ring.

The Granger Collection, New York.

Tweed's physical appearance is exaggerated, making him look grossly overweight. This suggests that the cartoonist had a low opinion of Tweed and his followers.

1 Which sentence best summarizes the way members of the Tammany Ring would answer the question in the caption?

**A** They did not, and would not, steal the people's money.

**B** They accept responsibility for stealing the people's money.

**C** They do not know who stole the people's money.

**D** They each blame someone else for stealing the people's money.

2 Based on the cartoon, what word do you think the cartoonist might use to describe the Tammany Ring?

**F** Lazy

**G** Corrupt

**H** Honest

**J** Hard-working

Since you know that the cartoon is critical of the Tammany Ring, you can eliminate the two positive choices—**H** and **J**.

answers: 1 (D), 2 (G)

---

### DIFFERENTIATING INSTRUCTION    STUDENTS ACQUIRING ENGLISH/ESL

#### Understanding Vocabulary

Make sure students understand the following terms and concepts in the sample questions on these pages.

**Strategy Page**
Question 2 *corrupt:* dishonest

**Practice Page**
Question 3 *feminist:* a person who works on behalf of women's rights and interests
Question 4 *encounter:* come into contact with
  *"glass ceiling":* an invisible, artificial barrier to how high women can rise in job importance because of their gender

**Directions:** Use the political cartoon <u>and</u> your knowledge of United States history to answer the following questions.

MARLETTE ©1981 THE CHARLOTTE OBSERVER

FIRST DOLLAR

FIRST 59¢

**Doug Marlette, _Charlotte Observer_, 1981.**

**1** According to the cartoon, for every dollar that working men earned, working women earned —

A 49 cents

B 59 cents

C 69 cents

D 79 cents

**2** Which of the following **BEST** summarizes the point of the cartoon?

F Men are happier than women are.

G Working men have bigger offices than working women.

H Working women earn less than working men.

J Working women do the real work in an office.

**3** What phrase summarizes feminists' solution to the problem illustrated in the cartoon?

A "We Shall Overcome"

B "Equal Pay for Equal Work"

C "ERA Now"

D "Our Bodies, Ourselves"

**4** Today, women make up nearly 50 percent of the workforce. However, they still encounter problems in the workplace, including —

F the "glass ceiling"

G lack of quality child care

H sexual harassment

J All of the above

## PRACTICE QUESTIONS

### Thinking It Through

Share the following explanations with students as they discuss the strategies they used to answer the practice questions.

1. *Dollar* is a key word. After finding the framed dollar on the man's office wall, look at the woman's wall—she has framed 59 cents. The answer is (B).

2. *Best* is a key word. (F) could be correct because the man is smiling and the woman is not, but this is not the main idea of the cartoon. (G) cannot be correct because the two offices are about the same size. (J) is incorrect because the woman does not seem to be working more than the man is. The images and labeling on the walls make the point—working women are paid less than working men. The correct answer is (H).

3. The correct answer is (B), since the point of the cartoon is that working women are paid less than working men.

4. To answer this question, you need to use your knowledge of United States history. The "glass ceiling," the lack of quality child care, and sexual harassment all became more important issues as women entered the workplace, so (J) is the correct answer.

S13

## TEKS and TAKS

| | Item Number | TEKS | TAKS |
|---|---|---|---|
| STRATEGY | 1. 2. | **(2)(A):** analyze political issues such as the growth of political machines<br>**(24)(A):** use primary sources [political cartoons] to acquire information about the United States<br>**(24)(C):** apply methods that historians use to interpret points of view | **(US24)(A):** use political cartoons to acquire information about the United States<br>**(US24)(C):** apply methods that historians use to interpret points of view |
| PRACTICE | 1. 2. 3. 4. | **(24)(A):** use primary sources [political cartoons] to acquire information about the United States<br>**(24)(C):** apply methods that historians use to interpret points of view | **(US24)(A):** use political cartoons to acquire information about the United States<br>**(US24)(C):** apply methods that historians use to interpret points of view |

## USING STRATEGIES FOR . . .

### Charts

Explain to students that they will do best on test questions by thinking them through carefully and by applying test-taking strategies, such as the following.

1. Question 1 asks you to locate acts in the second column and read their descriptions in the third column to find the act that was not primarily aimed at promoting economic development. (A), (C), and (D) all are aimed to improve the economic development in certain areas. While improved education would help people get better jobs, economic improvement was not the *primary* goal of the Elementary and Secondary Education Act. The correct answer is (B).

2. Use the information in the chart to draw conclusions about which act focused on consumer protection. The Fair Packaging and Labeling Act set standards for labeling consumer goods, the focus was to protect the consumer. The correct answer is (H).

### General Test-Taking Tips

Share these tips with your students.

- Use practice tests, such as the one you are taking now, to learn about your test-taking habits and weaknesses.
- Use this information to practice strategies that will help you be a successful test-taker.

## Charts

Charts present information in a visual form. The chart most commonly found in standardized tests is the table. This organizes information in columns and rows for easy viewing.

**1** Read the title to see the topic and the time period covered by the chart.

**2** Examine the column and row headings and other labels to learn more information about the subject addressed in the chart. (Sometimes, terms used in headings are explained in footnotes.)

**3** Note how the information in the chart is organized. (This chart lists the Great Society legislation by year. Some charts might organize the legislation by the issue addressed.)

**4** Compare and contrast the information from column to column and row to row.

**5** Try to make generalizations on, and draw conclusions from, the information in the chart. (One generalization you might make here is that 1965 was the busiest year for Great Society legislation.)

**6** Read the questions and then study the chart again.

**1** Great Society Programs, 1964–1966

| Year | Act | Description |
|------|-----|-------------|
| 1964 | Economic Opportunity Act | Created programs to fight poverty |
|      | Civil Rights Act | Banned discrimination in public accommodations |
| 1965 | Medical Care Act | Created Medicare, Medicaid |
|      | Appalachian Regional Development Act | Provided economic aid to Appalachia |
|      | Omnibus Housing Act | Funded low-income housing |
|      | Elementary and Secondary Education Act | Gave local school systems money for educational needs |
|      | Voting Rights Act | Banned the literacy test for voting |
|      | Immigration Act | Ended national-origin immigration quotas |
|      | Water Quality Act | Required states to clean up rivers |
| 1966 | Clean Air Act Amendments | Set standards for auto emissions |
|      | Demonstration Cities and Metropolitan Area Redevelopment Act | Funded programs to rebuild inner cities |
|      | Fair Packaging and Labeling Act | Set standards for labeling of consumer goods |
|      | Highway Safety Act | Required states to develop highway safety programs |

**1** Which of the following acts was **NOT** primarily aimed at promoting economic development?

A Economic Opportunity Act

B Elementary and Secondary Education Act

C Appalachian Regional Development Act

D Demonstration Cities and Metropolitan Area Redevelopment Act

**2** Which of the following acts focused on consumer protection?

F Highway Safety Act

G Medical Care Act

H Fair Packaging and Labeling Act

J Water Quality Act

answers: 1 (B), 2 (H)

S14

---

## DIFFERENTIATING INSTRUCTION    STUDENTS ACQUIRING ENGLISH/ESL

### Understanding Vocabulary

Make sure students understand the following terms and concepts in the sample charts and questions on these pages.

**Strategy Page**

**Chart**

*Great Society:* legislation aimed at ending poverty

*Medicare and Medicaid:* government sponsored health insurance programs

*Appalachian:* related to the Appalachian Mountains

*omnibus:* containing many items

*metropolitan:* urban; large city

*banned:* prohibited; not allowed

*literacy test:* test of a person's ability to read and write

*immigration quotas:* a method of limiting the number of immigrants to the U.S.

*auto emissions:* discharge from cars

*consumer:* a person who buys a product

**Practice Page**

Question 1 *populous:* densely populated

Question 3 *exemplifies:* is an example of

   *trend:* tendency

For more test practice online . . .

**TEST PRACTICE**
CLASSZONE.COM

**Directions:** Use the chart <u>and</u> your knowledge of United States history to answer the following questions.

## Ten States with the Largest Population, 1900–2000

| 1900 | 1930 | 1960 | 2000 |
|------|------|------|------|
| 1. New York | 1. New York | 1. New York | 1. California |
| 2. Pennsylvania | 2. Pennsylvania | 2. California | 2. Texas |
| 3. Illinois | 3. Illinois | 3. Pennsylvania | 3. New York |
| 4. Ohio | 4. Ohio | 4. Illinois | 4. Florida |
| 5. Missouri | 5. Texas | 5. Ohio | 5. Illinois |
| 6. Texas | 6. California | 6. Texas | 6. Pennsylvania |
| 7. Massachusetts | 7. Michigan | 7. Michigan | 7. Ohio |
| 8. Indiana | 8. Massachusetts | 8. New Jersey | 8. Michigan |
| 9. Michigan | 9. New Jersey | 9. Massachusetts | 9. New Jersey |
| 10. Iowa | 10. Missouri | 10. Florida | 10. Georgia |

**Source:** U.S. Census Bureau

**1** In which regions were most of the ten most populous states in 1900?

**A** Northeast and Midwest

**B** Northeast and Southeast

**C** Northeast and Southwest

**D** Midwest and Southeast

**2** Which of the following statements describes a change in the top ten states listing between 1960 and 2000?

**F** Texas and Florida rose markedly in the standings.

**G** The Midwestern states fell in the standings.

**H** Massachusetts fell out of the top ten listing.

**J** All of the above

**3** This chart exemplifies what trend of the late twentieth century?

**A** The increase in the population of the Northeast

**B** The decrease in immigration to the United States

**C** The population shift from the Rustbelt to the Sunbelt

**D** The population shift from the Sunbelt to the Rustbelt

**4** What impact would population changes between 1960 and 2000 have on representation in Congress?

**F** California and Texas would gain representatives in the House.

**G** Florida and Georgia would lose representatives in the House.

**H** California and Georgia would lose members in the Senate.

**J** Texas and Florida would gain members in the Senate.

**S15**

## PRACTICE QUESTIONS

### Thinking It Through

Share the following explanations with students as they discuss the strategies they used to answer the practice questions.

1. The key word in this question is *1900*. Read the column headed "1900" to find the region of the country that had the largest populations. Only one state from the Southwest (Texas) and none from the Southeast are included in the top ten of 1900, so (B), (C), and (D) are incorrect. The correct answer is (A).

2. This item requires you to compare and contrast the columns headed "1960" and "2000." Since this item is an example of *All of the above*, you must study the chart and all the alternatives to find the correct answer. All of the alternatives are correct; therefore, the correct answer is (J).

3. Look for a trend by comparing and contrasting the information in the columns headed "1960" and "2000," since the question asks for a trend shown in the late twentieth century. The only two northeastern states shown had a decrease in population, so (A) is incorrect. The chart does not mention immigration, so you can eliminate (B). Population did not shift from the Sunbelt to the Rustbelt, but instead, shifted in the other direction, making (D) incorrect. The correct answer is (C).

4. You need to draw a conclusion from the information in the chart and your knowledge of United States history to answer this question. Since both Florida and Georgia would gain, not lose, (G) is incorrect. Population changes have no impact on the Senate, so (H) and (J) are incorrect. California and Texas both gained population, so the correct answer is (F).

## TEKS and TAKS

| | Item Number | TEKS | TAKS |
|---|---|---|---|
| STRATEGY | 1. 2. | **(1)(A):** identify and define the characteristics of major eras in U.S. history<br>**(19)(C):** identify contributions of Texans who have been President of the United States<br>**(24)(B):** analyze information by comparing and contrasting | **(US1)(A):** identify and define the characteristics of major eras in U.S. history<br>**(US24)(B):** analyze information by comparing and contrasting |
| PRACTICE | 1. 2. 3. 4. | **(8)(B):** answer questions about geographic distribution and patterns shown on charts<br>**(10)(A):** analyze the effects of migration within the U.S.<br>**(11)(A):** identify the effects of population growth [and distribution and predict future effects] | **(US8)(B):** answer questions about geographic distribution and patterns shown on charts<br>**(US10)(A):** analyze the effects of migration within the U.S.<br>**(US11)(A):** identify the effects of population growth |

## USING STRATEGIES FOR . . .

### Line and Bar Graphs

Remind students that the vertical axis goes up and down and is normally shown on the left side of the graph. The horizontal axis runs across the bottom of the graph.

Explain to students that they will do best on test questions by thinking them through carefully and by applying test-taking strategies, such as the following.

1. *Peak* is a key word in question 1. If you replace it with *lowest point,* the answer changes. Move your eyes up the vertical axis to find the highest unemployment rate. At this point, move your eyes down the grid line to the horizontal axis to find the date that the highest unemployment rate occurred. The correct answer is (B).
2. To answer question 2, you need to study the legend to learn which bars stand for 1990 and which bars stand for 2000. Using the information in the vertical axis, compare and contrast the population changes—the bar heights—from 1990 to 2000 in each city. On the horizontal line, find the city with the greatest gain in population between 1990 and 2000. The correct answer is (H).

### General Test-Taking Tips

Share these tips with your students.

- Do not spend too much time on one question.
- Skip a question you are having problems with. Go back to it later, if you have time.
- If you skip a question, be sure to skip the answer space for the same number on your answer sheet.

## Line and Bar Graphs

Graphs, like charts, display information in a visual form. Line graphs show changes and trends over time. Bar graphs allow for comparisons among numbers or sets of numbers.

**1** Read the title of the graph to learn what it is about.

**2** Study the labels on the vertical and horizontal axes to see the kinds of information presented in the graph. The vertical axis usually shows what is being graphed, while the horizontal axis indicates the time period covered. (On the bar graph below, the horizontal axis labels show the names of the cities being graphed.)

**3** Study the legend, if there is one. This, too, will provide information on what is being graphed.

**4** Review the information in the graph and note any trends or patterns. Look for explanations for these trends or patterns.

**5** Carefully read and answer the questions. Note if questions refer to a specific year or time period, or if they focus on trends or historical explanations for trends.

answers: 1 (B), 2 (H)

**S16**

**1** **Unemployment Rate, 1930–1960**

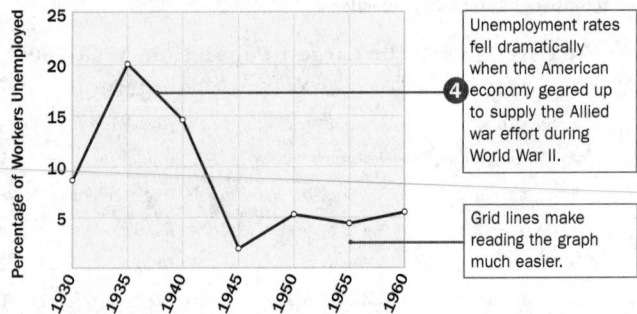

**4** Unemployment rates fell dramatically when the American economy geared up to supply the Allied war effort during World War II.

Grid lines make reading the graph much easier.

**Source:** *Statistical Abstract of the United States*

**5** **1** In which year did the unemployment rate hit its peak?

A 1930

B 1935

C 1945

D 1950

**1** **Texas Cities—1990 and 2000**

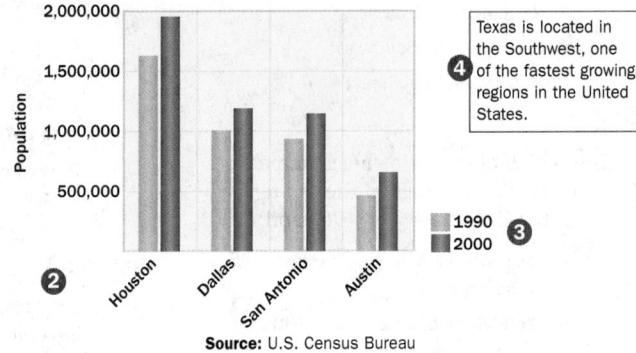

**4** Texas is located in the Southwest, one of the fastest growing regions in the United States.

**3** 1990 / 2000

**Source:** U.S. Census Bureau

**5** **2** Which of the cities shown on the graph made the greatest gain in population between 1990 and 2000?

F Austin

G Dallas

H Houston

J San Antonio

## DIFFERENTIATING INSTRUCTION
## STUDENTS ACQUIRING ENGLISH/ESL

### Understanding Vocabulary

Make sure students understand the following terms and concepts in the sample graphs and questions on these pages.

**Strategy Page**
**Line Graph**
*unemployment:* not having work
Question 1 *peak:* highest point

**Practice Page**
**Line Graph**
*media:* methods of communication, such as the telephone, television, and radio
Question 3 *elderly:* older
Question 4 *distribution:* spread

For more test practice online . . .

TEST PRACTICE
CLASSZONE.COM

STRATEGIES FOR TAKING TAKS

**Directions:** Use the graphs <u>and</u> your knowledge of United States history to answer the following questions.

### Percentage of Households with Selected Media, 1930–1998

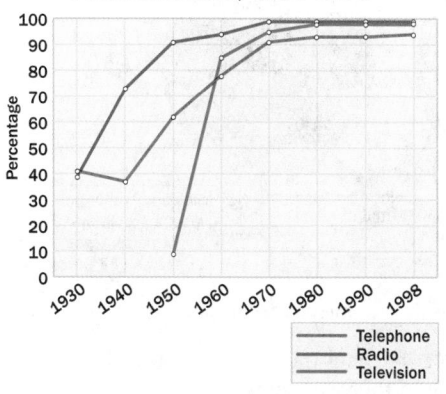

Telephone
Radio
Television

**Source:** *Statistical Abstract of the United States*

### Age Distribution of the Population, 1900–2000

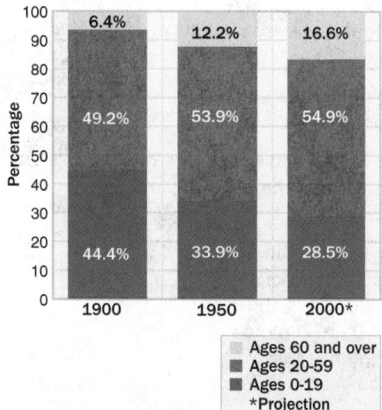

Ages 60 and over
Ages 20-59
Ages 0-19
*Projection

**Source:** *Historical Statistics of the United States; Statistical Abstract of the United States*

**1** The percentage of households with all three media first topped 90 percent in —

  A  1960

  B  1970

  C  1980

  D  1990

**2** What cultural trend resulted from the rapid spread of radios and televisions into nearly every American home?

  F  The rise of rock 'n' roll

  G  The growing influence of popular culture

  H  The decline in the power of the television networks

  J  The increase in popularity of newspapers and magazines

**3** How did the share of elderly people in the population change from 1900 to 2000?

  A  It decreased from 44.4 to 28.5 percent.

  B  It increased from 49.2 to 54.9 percent.

  C  It increased from 6.4 to 16.6 percent.

  D  It decreased from 33.9 to 12.2 percent.

**4** Which of the following describes changes in the age distribution of the population between 1900 and 2000?

  F  The percentage of people aged 60 or over grew.

  G  The percentage of people aged between 20 and 59 increased.

  H  The percentage of people aged 19 or younger fell.

  J  All of the above

S17

## THINKING IT THROUGH

Share the following explanations with students as they discuss the strategies they used to answer the practice questions.

1. *All* is a key word. You need to note the intervals between amounts and between dates. Since all three media first topped 90 percent in 1970, the correct answer is (B).

2. In this question, you need to use your knowledge of United States history to answer the question. Since radio came before rock 'n' roll, (F) is incorrect. Networks helped spread the use of radio and television for several decades, so (H) is incorrect. Newspapers have declined in circulation since the 1980s, so (J) is incorrect. The correct answer is (G).

3. You need to draw a conclusion based on the information in the bar graph. Use the legend to learn what the colors stand for in the bar graph. Then review the information for elderly people and note how the percentage of elderly people in the population changed from 1900 to 2000. Since (A) describes the trend for people 0-19 years old, and (B) describes the trend for those 20-59 years old, both are incorrect. Choice (D) is incorrect because it compares ages 0-19 years old with 60 and over during 1950. The correct answer is (C).

4. This is an example of an *All of the above* question. You must read each choice and find the information it describes on the graph to make sure it is correct. Since each choice describes changes on the graph correctly, the correct answer is (J) *All of the above*.

## TEKS and TAKS

| | Item Number | TEKS | TAKS |
|---|---|---|---|
| STRATEGY | 1. | **(8)(B):** answer questions about patterns shown on graphs<br>**(13)(C):** analyze the effects of the Great Depression | **(US8)(B):** answer questions about patterns shown on graphs<br>**(US13)(C):** analyze the effects of the Great Depression |
| STRATEGY | 2. | **(8)(B):** answer questions about geographic distribution shown on graphs<br>**(24)(B):** analyze information by comparing and contrasting | **(US8)(B):** answer questions about geographic distribution shown on graphs<br>**(US24)(B):** analyze information by comparing and contrasting |
| PRACTICE | 1. 2. | **(8)(B):** answer questions about geography patterns shown on graphs<br>**(20)(D):** analyze the relationship between culture and the economy<br>**(20)(E):** identify the impact of popular American culture<br>**(24)(B):** analyze information by comparing and contrasting | **(US8)(B):** answer questions about geography patterns shown on graphs<br><br><br>**(US24)(B):** analyze information by comparing and contrasting |
| PRACTICE | 3. 4. | **(8)(B):** answer questions about geography distribution and patterns shown on graphs<br>**(24)(B):** analyze information by comparing and contrasting | **(US8)(B):** answer questions about geography distribution shown on graphs<br>**(US24)(B):** analyze information by comparing and contrasting |

## USING STRATEGIES FOR . . .

### Pie Graphs

Remind students that a complete pie, or circle, graph represents a whole, or 100 percent. Each slice, or part, of a pie graph, stands for a percentage of the whole. The parts of each pie graph usually add up to exactly 100 percent. Note, however, that the parts of a pie graph might add up to slightly less than 100 percent because the numbers have been rounded.

Explain to students that they will do best on test questions by thinking them through carefully and by applying test-taking strategies, such as the following.

1. In question 1, you must study the data and make comparisons of both graphs. Be sure to look at the pie graph and legend to find the answer. (B), (C), and (D) all make inaccurate statements. The correct answer is (A).

2. In question 2 study and compare the data in both graphs. Make a generalization from your comparisons to choose the correct answer. As the strategies hint points out, (F), (H), and (J) are all inaccurate. Since the percentages of the United States, Europe, Japan, and Other all came closer together from 1950 to 1999, the correct answer is (G).

### General Test-Taking Tips

Share these tips with your students.

- Read the question and each answer choice before answering.
- Many items include choices that may seem right at first glance, but are actually wrong.

## Pie Graphs

A pie, or circle, graph is useful for showing relationships among the parts of a whole. These parts look like slices of a pie. The size of each slice is proportional to the percentage of the whole that it represents.

**1** Read the title of the graph to learn what it is about.

**2** Study the legend and note what each slice of the pie represents.

**3** Study the data on the graph and make comparisons among the slices of the pie. When there is more than one graph, make comparisons of the different graphs.

**4** Try to make generalizations and draw conclusions from your comparisons. (One generalization you might make is that today no one country or region dominates world motor vehicle production.)

**5** Read the questions carefully and use key words to reject incorrect alternatives.

**1 World Motor Vehicle Production, 1950 and 1999**

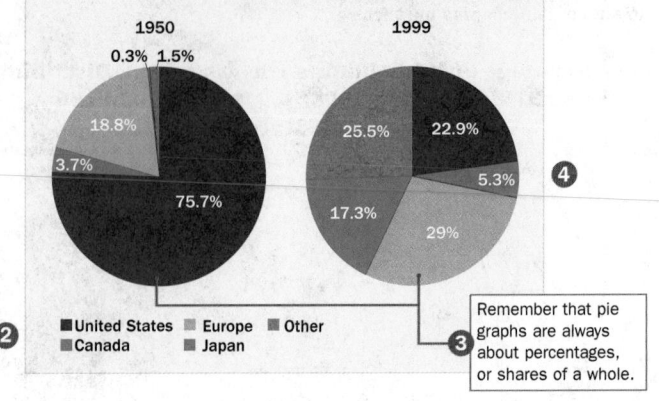

1950
0.3% 1.5%
18.8%
3.7%
75.7%

1999
25.5% 22.9%
5.3%
17.3%
29%

■ United States  ■ Europe  ■ Other
■ Canada  ■ Japan

**4**

**3** Remember that pie graphs are always about percentages, or shares of a whole.

**Source:** *World Almanac and Book of Facts* (2001)

**1** What phrase **BEST** describes the U.S. share of world motor vehicle production in the years shown?

A It fell dramatically from 1950 to 1999.

B It was less than 75 percent of the total in 1950.

C It was the same as Japan's share in 1999.

D It never exceeded Europe's share.

**2** What sentence **BEST** describes motor vehicle production over the years shown in the two graphs?

F Japan's share of motor vehicle production grew slightly.

G Motor vehicle production became more competitive around the world.

H The United States became the world's top producer of motor vehicles.

J Europe remained the dominant region for motor vehicle production.

**5** The key words *slightly*, *became*, and *remained* help you to eliminate alternatives **F**, **H**, and **J**. Japanese production grew markedly, not slightly. The United States fell from its position as the world's top producer of motor vehicles. Finally, Europe never dominated motor vehicle production.

answers: 1 (A), 2 (G)

S18

### Understanding Vocabulary

Make sure students understand the following terms and concepts in the sample pie graphs and questions.

**Strategy Page**
**Pie Graph**
*vehicle:* carrier
Question 1 *production:* output
  *dramatically:* greatly
  *exceeded:* went beyond

**Practice Page**
**Pie Graph**
*Race/Ethnicity:* ancestry
*Anglo:* a Caucasian living in the U.S. who is not of Latin-American descent

STRATEGIES FOR TAKING TAKS

**Directions:** Use the pie graphs <u>and</u> your knowledge of United States history to answer the following questions.

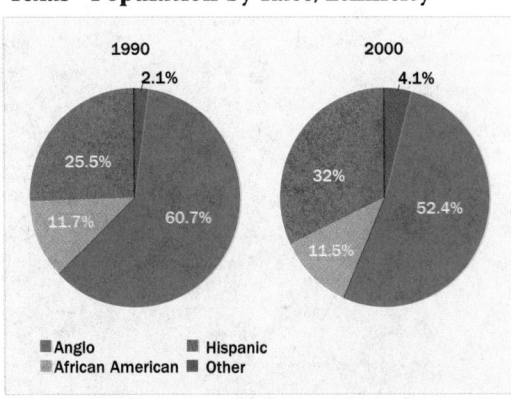

**Texas—Population by Race/Ethnicity**

1990

2000

Source: 1990—Texas State Data Center; 2000—U.S. Census Bureau

**1** Which is the largest ethnic/racial group in Texas?

A African American

B Anglo

C Hispanic

D Other

**2** Which category doubled its share of the total population between 1990 and 2000?

F African American

G Anglo

H Hispanic

J Other

**3** In 1990, Hispanics made up about one-fourth of the population of Texas. In 2000, they made up about —

A one-third

B one-half

C two-thirds

D three-quarters

**4** Which of the following statements about the African American population of Texas is true?

F In 1990, it was about one-fifth of the Anglo population.

G In 2000, it was slightly more than one-third of the Hispanic population.

H African Americans' share of the total population changed little between 1990 and 2000.

J All of the above

S19

## PRACTICE QUESTIONS

**Thinking It Through**
Share the following explanations with students as they discuss the strategies they used to answer the practice questions.

1. The key word in this question is *largest*. You should study and compare the data on the pie graphs to find the *largest* ethnic group in Texas. The correct answer is (B).
2. Compare the slices of the pies on both pie graphs. According to the graphs, the category "Other" doubled its share of the total population between 1990 and 2000.The correct answer is (J).
3. Use the legend to find the color used to stand for Hispanic on the pie graphs. Compare the slices of the pies on both pie graphs. The correct answer is (A).
4. To answer this question, read the question carefully and use key words to reject or verify each alternative. This is an example of an *All of the above* question. Be careful to check all choices. (F), (G), and (H) are all correct. The correct answer is (J).

## TEKS and TAKS

| | Item Number | TEKS | TAKS |
|---|---|---|---|
| **STRATEGY** | 1. 2. | **(8)(B):** answer questions about geographic distributions and patterns shown on graphs<br>**(24)(B):** analyze information by comparing and contrasting<br>**(24)(H):** use math skills to interpret social studies information on graphs | **(US8)(B):** answer questions about geographic distributions and patterns shown on graphs<br>**(US24)(B):** analyze information by comparing and contrasting |
| **PRACTICE** | 1. 2. 3. 4. | **(8)(B):** answer questions about geographic distributions and patterns shown on graphs<br>**(11)(A):** identify the effects of population growth and distribution<br>**(24)(B):** analyze information by comparing and contrasting<br>**(24)(H):** use math skills to interpret social studies information on graphs | **(US8)(B):** answer questions about geographic distributions and patterns shown on graphs<br>**(US11)(A):** identify the effects of population growth and distribution<br>**(US24)(B):** analyze information by comparing and contrasting |

## USING STRATEGIES FOR . . .

### Political Maps

Explain to students that they will do best on test questions by thinking them through carefully and by applying test-taking strategies, such as the following.

1. To answer question 1, use the compass rose to determine the directions on the map. Check each answer choice to see which country lies west of Alaska. The correct answer is (C).

2. To answer question 2, use the scale to estimate the distance from the Hawaiian Islands to the southwest coast of the United States. Use the compass rose to determine directions on the map. If you are allowed to use scratch paper during your test, place the paper next to the Hawaiian Islands (in the smaller box below the inset) and next to the southwest coast of the United States. Mark the length between these two places on your paper. Then use this length on the paper to measure the distance on the map scale. The correct answer is (G).

### General Test-Taking Tips

Share these tips with your students.

- Try to answer every question on the test.
- If you are not sure of an answer, make an educated guess.
- First eliminate the choices you are sure are not correct. Then choose from the choices that remain.

## Political Maps

Political maps show countries and the political divisions within them—states or provinces, for example. They also show the location of major cities. In addition, political maps often show physical features, such as mountains, oceans, seas, lakes, and rivers.

**1** Read the title of the map to identify the area shown and the time period covered.

**2** Read the labels on the map. This will reveal more information about the subject and purpose of the map.

**3** Note any special features of the map, such as insets.

**4** Study the legend to find the meaning of any symbols and colors used on the map.

**5** Look at the lines of longitude and latitude. This grid makes locating places much easier.

**6** Use the compass rose to determine directions on the map.

**7** Use the scale to estimate distances between places shown on the map.

**8** Read the questions and then carefully study the map to determine the answers.

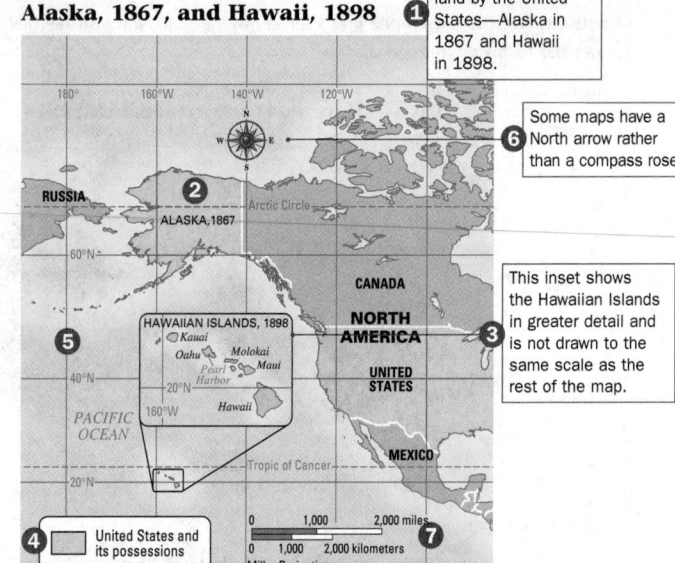

**Alaska, 1867, and Hawaii, 1898**

**1** This map deals with the acquisition of land by the United States—Alaska in 1867 and Hawaii in 1898.

**6** Some maps have a North arrow rather than a compass rose.

**3** This inset shows the Hawaiian Islands in greater detail and is not drawn to the same scale as the rest of the map.

**1** Which country lies to the west of Alaska?

A Canada
B Mexico
C Russia
D United States

**2** About how far are the Hawaiian Islands from the southwest coast of the United States?

F 1,000 miles
G 2,500 miles
H 4,000 miles
J 5,500 miles

answers: 1 (C), 2 (G)

## DIFFERENTIATING INSTRUCTION    STUDENTS ACQUIRING ENGLISH/ESL

### Understanding Vocabulary

Make sure students understand the following terms and concepts in the sample political maps and questions.

**Strategy Page**
**Political Map**
*acquisition:* purchase

**Practice Page**
Question 1 *international:* relating to a foreign country

STRATEGIES FOR TAKING TAKS

**Directions:** Use the map <u>and</u> your knowledge of United States history to answer the following questions.

**Texas—Political**

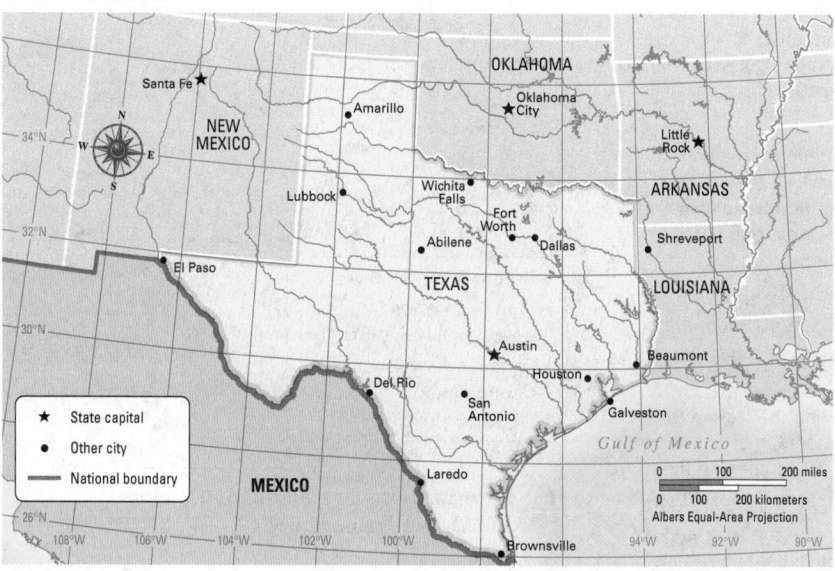

**1** Which of these cities is located on or close to an international border?

A Brownsville

B El Paso

C Laredo

D All of the above

**2** Which of the following cities is most likely to be threatened by hurricanes?

F Amarillo

G Del Rio

H Galveston

J Wichita Falls

**3** Which of the following is true about the location of Austin?

A It is located north of the 30°N line of latitude.

B It lies to the north of Fort Worth.

C It is more than 300 miles from Houston.

D All of the above

**4** If you took a trip from Houston to Lubbock, in which general direction would you be traveling?

F Northeast

G Southeast

H Southwest

J Northwest

**PRACTICE QUESTIONS**

**Thinking It Through**
Share the following explanations with students as they discuss the strategies they used to answer the practice questions.

1. *International* is a key word. You are looking for a city that is located close to the border of the U.S. and another country. This is an example of an *All of the above* question. Be sure that each choice is correct if you choose (D). Since all the cities are located close to the border of the U.S. and Mexico, the correct answer is (D).

2. Use your knowledge of U.S. history and the map to answer this question. Since most hurricanes occur near large bodies of water, and since Galveston is the only choice that is located near a body of water, the correct answer is (H).

3. Use the labels to find Austin on the map. Read each choice to find the true statement about the location of Austin. Use the lines of latitude, the compass rose, and the scale to decide if choices (A), (B), and (C) are true. This item is an example of *All of the above.* For the correct answer to be (D), all of the choices must be correct. Since (B) and (C) are incorrect, (D) cannot be the answer. (A) is the correct answer.

4. Use the compass rose and the labels on the map to answer this question. The correct answer is (J).

S21

**TEKS and TAKS**

| | Item Number | TEKS | TAKS |
|---|---|---|---|
| STRATEGY | 1. 2. | **(8)(B):** answer questions about geographic distributions and patterns shown on maps<br>**(9)(B):** identify reasons for changes in political boundaries<br>**(24)(H):** use math skills to interpret social studies information on maps | **(US8)(B):** answer questions about geographic distributions and patterns shown on maps |
| PRACTICE | 1. 2. 3. 4. | **(8)(B):** answer questions about geographic distributions and patterns shown on maps<br>**(24)(B):** analyze information by comparing and contrasting | **(US8)(B):** answer questions about geographic distributions and patterns shown on maps<br>**(US24)(B):** analyze information by comparing and contrasting |

## USING STRATEGIES FOR . . .

### Thematic Maps

Explain to students that they will do best on test questions by thinking them through carefully and by applying test-taking strategies, such as the following.

1. To answer question 1, use the legend and the labels on the map. Eliminate choices (A), (B), and (C) because they are all located on the Southern Pacific Railroad. The correct answer is (D).

2. To answer question 2, use the labels on the map and the legend to help you decide which railroad you would board to go from Forth Worth to Abilene. The correct answer is (J).

### General Test-Taking Tips

Share these tips with your students.
- Think positively.
- Tell yourself that you can do it!
- If you have studied for the test, you are prepared to succeed.

## Thematic Maps

A thematic map, or special-purpose map, focuses on a particular topic. Population density, election results, migration routes, a country's economic activities, international alliances, and major battles in a war are all topics you might see illustrated on a thematic map.

**1** Thematic maps show specialized information. Read the title to discover the subject and purpose of the map.

**2** Study the labels on the map to find more information about its subject and purpose.

**3** Examine the legend to find the meaning of any symbols and colors used on the map.

**4** Locate the symbols and colors on the map and try to make generalizations or draw conclusions about the information they convey.

**5** Read the questions and carefully study the map to determine the answers.

**1** Texas Railroads in the Late 1880s

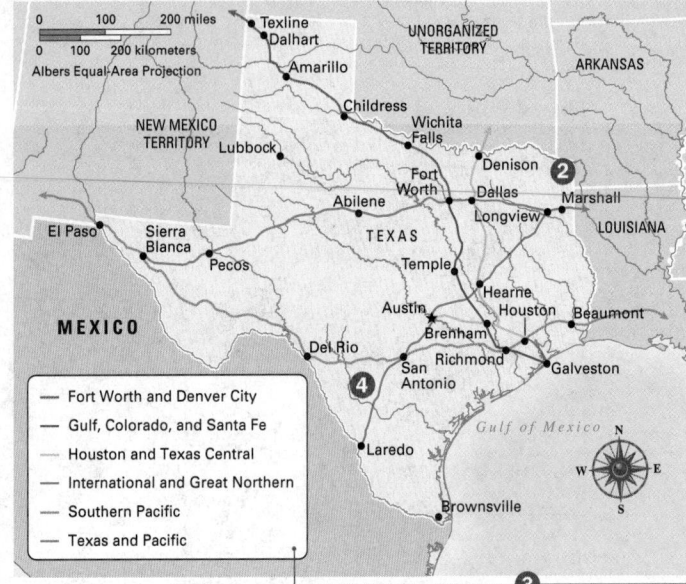

Legend:
— Fort Worth and Denver City
— Gulf, Colorado, and Santa Fe
⋯ Houston and Texas Central
— International and Great Northern
— Southern Pacific
— Texas and Pacific

**3** While a thematic map focuses on one topic, it often offers several kinds of information on that topic. So, the legend for a thematic map often is quite detailed.

**1** In which Texas city did the Gulf, Colorado, and Santa Fe railroad begin?

A  Beaumont

B  Del Rio

C  El Paso

D  Galveston

**2** If you traveled from Amarillo to Abilene by way of Fort Worth, which railroad would you board in Fort Worth to complete your journey?

F  Fort Worth and Denver City

G  International and Great Northern

H  Southern Pacific

J  Texas and Pacific

answers: 1 (D), 2 (J)

S22

---

DIFFERENTIATING INSTRUCTION    STUDENTS ACQUIRING ENGLISH/ESL

### Understanding Vocabulary

Make sure students understand the following terms and concepts on these pages.

**Strategy Page**
Question 2 *board:* get on; enter

**Practice Page**
**Thematic Map**
*ticket:* a list of candidates running for office

## PRACTICE QUESTIONS

**Directions:** Use the map and chart <u>and</u> your knowledge of United States history to answer the following questions.

### The 2000 Presidential Election

| Ticket | Popular Vote | Electoral Vote |
|---|---|---|
| Bush-Cheney | 50,456,062 | 271 |
| Gore-Lieberman | 50,996,582 | 264 |
| Nader-LaDuke | 2,858,843 | 0 |
| Buchanan-Foster | 438,760 | 0 |

**Source:** *Federal Register*

**1** The Gore-Lieberman ticket won all of the New England states **EXCEPT** —

A Maine
B Massachusetts
C New Hampshire
D Rhode Island

**2** The Gore-Lieberman ticket won most of the —

F Midwestern states
G Northeastern states
H Pacific-coast states
J All of the above

**3** Which areas did the Bush-Cheney ticket win?

A Most states in the Northeast and the West
B All of the South and the Midwest
C All of the South and most of the West
D Most states in the Northeast and the South

**4** Which of the following statements about the 2000 presidential election is true?

F The Bush-Cheney ticket won the electoral vote but not the popular vote.
G The Bush-Cheney ticket won all of the Deep South states.
H The Bush-Cheney ticket won more states than the Gore-Lieberman ticket.
J All of the above

### PRACTICE QUESTIONS

**Thinking It Through**
Share the following explanations with students as they discuss the strategies they used to answer the practice questions.

1. Take care with questions that have the word *except*. Use the legend to answer this question. The only New England state that Gore-Lieberman did not win was New Hampshire, so the correct answer is (C).
2. This is an *All of the above* question. Use the colors in the legend to answer this question too. You must check the map to see that each choice is correct. The correct answer is (J) *All of the above*.
3. Use the legend to answer this question. Check each answer choice against its color on the map. The correct answer is (C).
4. This question is another example of *All of the above*. Use the chart to answer this question. Check each answer choice against the chart. Since all of the answer choices are correct, the correct answer is (J).

S23

### TEKS and TAKS

| | Item Number | TEKS | TAKS |
|---|---|---|---|
| STRATEGY | 1. 2. | **(2)(B):** analyze the growth of railroads from 1877 to 1898<br>**(8)(B):** answer questions about geographic distributions and patterns | **(US2)(B):** analyze the growth of railroads from 1877 to 1898<br>**(US8)(B):** answer questions about geographic distributions and patterns |
| PRACTICE | 1. 2. 3. 4. | **(8)(B):** answer questions about geographic distributions and patterns<br>**(24)(B):** analyze information by comparing and contrasting | **(US8)(B):** answer questions about geographic distributions and patterns<br>**(US24)(B):** analyze information by comparing and contrasting |

## USING STRATEGIES FOR . . .

### Time Lines

Explain to students that they will do best on test questions by thinking them through carefully and by applying test-taking strategies, such as the following.

1. To answer question 1, locate each choice on the time line until you find the one that occurred first. The correct answer is (C).
2. To answer question 2, study the entire time line and use your knowledge of United States history. You can eliminate (F) and (G) as the strategy hint suggests. Read the question and then check each date against the time line. While federal courts and Congress played important roles, so did presidents. The correct answer is (J).

### General Test-Taking Tips

Share these tips with your students.
• Relax during the test.
• Several times during the test, take a few seconds to relax and breathe deeply.
• Occasional deep breaths will help relieve anxiety and keep you focused.

## Time Lines

A time line is a type of chart that lists historical events in the order in which they occurred. In other words, time lines are a visual method of showing what happened when.

❶ Read the title to discover the subject of the time line.

❷ Identify the period of history covered in the time line by noting the first and last dates shown.

❸ Read the events in chronological order. Notice the intervals between events.

❹ Note how events are related to one another. Look particularly for cause-effect relationships.

❺ Make generalizations about the information presented in the time line.

❻ Use the information you have gathered from the above strategies to answer the questions.

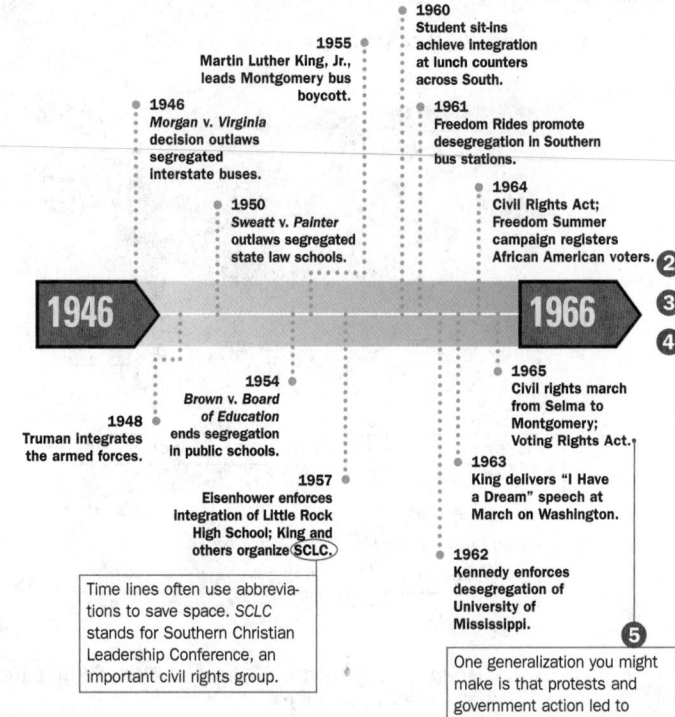

**❶ The Civil Rights Movement, 1940s–1960s**

**1946** *Morgan v. Virginia* decision outlaws segregated interstate buses.

**1948** Truman integrates the armed forces.

**1950** *Sweatt v. Painter* outlaws segregated state law schools.

**1954** *Brown v. Board of Education* ends segregation in public schools.

**1955** Martin Luther King, Jr., leads Montgomery bus boycott.

**1957** Eisenhower enforces integration of Little Rock High School; King and others organize SCLC.

**1960** Student sit-ins achieve integration at lunch counters across South.

**1961** Freedom Rides promote desegregation in Southern bus stations.

**1962** Kennedy enforces desegregation of University of Mississippi.

**1963** King delivers "I Have a Dream" speech at March on Washington.

**1964** Civil Rights Act; Freedom Summer campaign registers African American voters.

**1965** Civil rights march from Selma to Montgomery; Voting Rights Act.

**1946** → **1966**

Time lines often use abbreviations to save space. *SCLC* stands for Southern Christian Leadership Conference, an important civil rights group.

❺ One generalization you might make is that protests and government action led to advances in civil rights.

**1** Which was the first major civil rights activity in which Martin Luther King, Jr., was involved?

A "I Have a Dream" speech

B March from Selma to Montgomery

❻ C Montgomery bus boycott

D Organization of the SCLC

**2** The success of the civil rights movement resulted from organized protests by African Americans and actions by —

F state courts

G reformed state governments

H federal courts and Congress

J all three branches of the federal government

Recall that southern state governments often resisted civil rights in this period. Therefore, you can eliminate alternatives **F** and **G**.

answers: 1 (C), 2 (J)

S24

---

## DIFFERENTIATING INSTRUCTION    STUDENTS ACQUIRING ENGLISH/ESL

### Understanding Vocabulary

Make sure students understand the following terms and concepts in the sample time lines and questions.

**Strategy Page**
*civil rights:* the rights of citizens

**Practice Page**
**Time Line**
*assassinates:* murders
Question 4 *demilitarize:* to do away with the armed forces
*reparations:* compensation, or payment, for damage done during a war

For more test practice online . . .

**TEST PRACTICE**
CLASSZONE.COM

**Directions:** Use the time line <u>and</u> your knowledge of United States history to answer the following questions.

### World War I

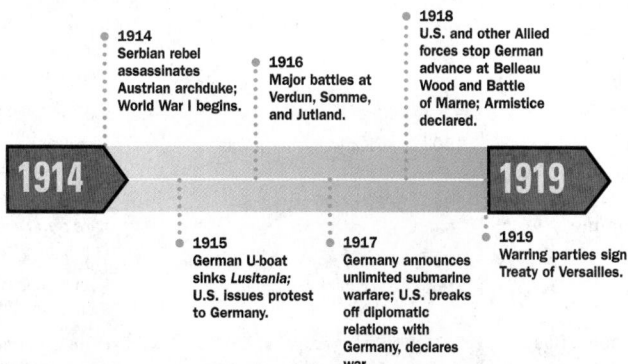

**1914**
Serbian rebel assassinates Austrian archduke; World War I begins.

**1916**
Major battles at Verdun, Somme, and Jutland.

**1918**
U.S. and other Allied forces stop German advance at Belleau Wood and Battle of Marne; Armistice declared.

**1914**

**1919**

**1915**
German U-boat sinks *Lusitania;* U.S. issues protest to Germany.

**1917**
Germany announces unlimited submarine warfare; U.S. breaks off diplomatic relations with Germany, declares war.

**1919**
Warring parties sign Treaty of Versailles.

**1** What event led the United States to protest German actions in 1915?

**A** Assassination of Austrian archduke

**B** Battle of Jutland

**C** Sinking of *Lusitania*

**D** Battle of Verdun

**2** Which of the following actions included U.S. troops?

**F** Jutland, 1916

**G** Verdun, 1916

**H** Somme, 1916

**J** Marne, 1918

**3** The Treaty of Versailles, which officially brought the war to an end, was signed in —

**A** 1917

**B** 1918

**C** 1919

**D** 1920

**4** The Treaty of Versailles called for Germany to —

**F** demilitarize

**G** pay war reparations

**H** admit sole responsibility for the war

**J** All of the above

**PRACTICE QUESTIONS**

**Thinking It Through**
Share the following explanations with students as they discuss the strategies they used to answer the practice questions.

1. The key word in this item is *1915*. Check the events that occurred on this date against the time line. The correct answer is (C).
2. Locate the events of the dates on the time line and use logical reasoning to answer the question. Answers (F), (G), and (H) are incorrect, because those battles happened before the U.S. entered the war. The correct answer is (J).
3. Locate each date on the time line to find the correct answer. The correct answer is (C).
4. Use your knowledge of United States history to answer the question. Since (F), (G), and (H) are all correct, the correct answer is (J).

**S25**

## TEKS and TAKS

| | Item Number | TEKS | TAKS |
|---|---|---|---|
| **STRATEGY** | 1. 2. | **(7)(A):** trace the historical development of the civil rights movement<br>**(7)(B):** identify significant leaders of the civil rights movement, including Martin Luther King, Jr.<br>**(7)(C):** evaluate government efforts to achieve equality in the U.S.<br>**(18)(B):** evaluate means of achieving equality of political rights<br>**(24)(B):** analyze information by sequencing and making generalizations | **(US7)(A):** trace the historical development of the civil rights movement<br>**(US7)(B):** identify significant leaders of the civil rights movement, including Martin Luther King, Jr.<br>**(US7)(C):** evaluate government efforts to achieve equality in the U.S.<br>**(US18)(B):** evaluate means of achieving equality of political rights<br>**(US24)(B):** analyze information by sequencing and making generalizations |
| **PRACTICE** | 1. 2. 3. 4. | **(1)(A):** identify major eras in U.S. history and describe their characteristics<br>**(1)(C):** explain the significance of 1914–1918<br>**(3)(B):** identify the reasons for U.S. involvement in World War I<br>**(24)(B):** analyze information by sequencing and summarizing | **(US1)(A):** identify major eras in U.S. history and describe their characteristics<br>**(US1)(C):** explain the significance of 1914–1918<br>**(US3)(B):** identify the reasons for U.S. involvement in World War I<br>**(US24)(B):** analyze information by sequencing and summarizing |

## USING STRATEGIES FOR . . .

### Constructed Response

Remind students of the following:

- In the constructed-response questions on this page, you need to use the document to answer the first two questions. In question 3, you need to use your knowledge of United States history to answer the question.

- Some constructed-response questions do not include a document. Instead, all the questions may require you to use your knowledge of United States history to answer the questions.

- Sometimes constructed-response questions start with short-answer questions and build up to a short essay. The short answers may help you write the short essay, so try to answer the questions in the order they are asked. Each part will be worth some points, but the short essay will probably be worth more than the short-answer questions.

- Useful information may be found in a title, a caption, or a source line as well as in the document itself.

### General Test-Taking Tips

Share these tips with your students.

- Be sure to answer all parts of constructed-response questions or as many parts as you can. Each part is worth points.

- As you answer each question, make sure that the number of the answer and the number of the question are the same.

## Constructed Response

Constructed-response questions focus on various kinds of documents. Each document is accompanied by one or more short-answer questions. For the most part, the answers to these questions can be found directly in the document. Some answers, however, require knowledge of the subject or time period addressed in the document.

**1** Read the title of the document to discover the subject addressed in the questions.

**2** Carefully study the document and take notes on what you see. (This document is a chart listing some of the important Supreme Court decisions of the 20th century.)

**3** Read the questions and then study the document again to locate the answers.

**4** Carefully write your answers. Unless the directions say otherwise, your answers need not be complete sentences.

**1** **Some Important 20th-Century Supreme Court Decisions**

**2**

| Year | Case | Impact |
|------|------|--------|
| 1950 | Sweatt v. Painter | Bans segregated state-run law school |
| 1954 | Brown v. Board of Education | Bans segregated public schools |
| 1961 | Mapp v. Ohio | Prohibits use of evidence obtained illegally |
| 1962 | Baker v. Carr | Requires states to draw legislative districts in which the number of people represented is more nearly equal |
| 1962 | Engel v. Vitale | Bans prayer in public schools |
| 1963 | Gideon v. Wainwright | Requires courts to provide free legal counsel to poor defendants |
| 1964 | Escobedo v. Illinois | Establishes right of suspects to have a lawyer present during police questioning |
| 1966 | Miranda v. Arizona | Requires police to warn suspects of their legal rights |
| 1971 | Swann v. Charlotte-Mecklenburg Board of Education | Permits busing to achieve school desegregation |
| 1978 | Regents of the University of California v. Bakke | Bans use of quotas for minority applicants as part of state-run school's affirmative action programs |
| 1979 | United Steelworkers of America v. Weber | Upholds quotas for affirmative action in hiring by private companies |

**3** **1** Which cases listed in the chart are concerned with criminal justice issues?

**4** *Mapp v. Ohio, Gideon v. Wainwright, Escobedo v. Illinois, and Miranda v. Arizona.*

**2** Which decision reflects the principle of "one person, one vote"? What issue does it address?

*Baker v. Carr; the drawing of legislative districts*

**3** How are the *Bakke* and *Weber* decisions related to the desegregation cases of the 1940s and 1950s?

*Bakke and Weber both address affirmative action, the name given programs created to try to overcome the lack of representation of minorities due to past discrimination, such as the segregation issues identified in the earlier cases.*

---

## DIFFERENTIATING INSTRUCTION    STUDENTS ACQUIRING ENGLISH/ESL

### Understanding Vocabulary

Make sure students understand the following terms and concepts in the sample documents and questions.

**Strategy Page**
**Document**
*Supreme Court:* the highest court in the U.S.
*legal counsel:* a person who helps interpret laws and defend a person accused of a crime
*defendant:* a person who is on trial
*suspect:* a person who is accused of a crime
*quotas:* share; percentage
*affirmative action:* methods used to help fix the effects of existing and past discrimination

**Practice Page**
**Document**
*patent:* official document giving an inventor the sole rights to make, use, or sell an invention

For more test practice online . . .

**TEST PRACTICE**
CLASSZONE.COM

**Directions:** Use the illustration <u>and</u> your knowledge of United States history to answer the questions that follow. Your answers need not be complete sentences.

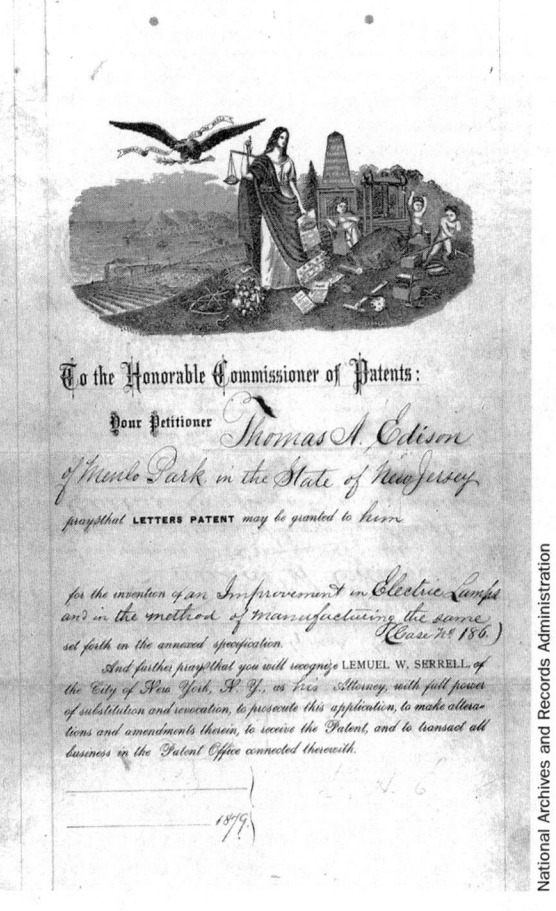

To the Honorable Commissioner of Patents:

Your Petitioner *Thomas A. Edison*

*of Menlo Park in the State of New Jersey*

*prays that* LETTERS PATENT *may be granted to him*

*for the invention of an Improvement in Electric Lamps and in the method of manufacturing the same* (Case No 186.)
*set forth in the annexed specification.*

*And further prays that you will recognize* LEMUEL W. SERRELL *of the City of New York, N. Y., as his Attorney, with full power of substitution and revocation, to prosecute this application, to make alterations and amendments therein, to receive the Patent, and to transact all business in the Patent Office connected therewith.*

*1879*

National Archives and Records Administration

**1** Which inventor applied for this patent? What invention is this patent for?

**2** When did the inventor apply for this patent?

**3** Identify two other developments or inventions for which this inventor is known.

## PRACTICE QUESTIONS

### Thinking It Through
Share the following explanations with students as they discuss the strategies they used to answer the practice questions.

1. Study and analyze the document. Next, read the question and then refer back to the document again to locate the answer. Be sure to read any title, caption, or text large enough to read within the document. The document says that the inventor who applied for this patent was Thomas A. Edison. The patent was for an improvement in electric lamps and in the method of manufacturing electric lamps.

2. Read the question and then refer back to the document to locate the answer. The answer is 1879.

3. You need to use your knowledge of United States history to answer this question. Edison's inventions are too numerous to list but include a system for producing and distributing electrical power, phonograph, kinetoscope, telephone transmitter, storage battery, electric pen, mimeograph, improvements in the telegraph, and stock ticker.

### Scoring Constructed-Response Questions
Constructed-response questions usually are scored using a rubric, or scoring guide. The questions on this page might be scored by giving one point for each question—a total score of 3 points. Another way of scoring these questions might be to give 1 point for each correct answer for questions 1 and 2, and 2 points for question 3 (1 point each for naming two other developments or inventions by Edison, such as the system for producing and distributing electrical power, phonograph, kinetoscope, telephone transmitter, storage battery, electric pen, mimeograph, improvements in the telegraph, and stock ticker)—a total score of 4 points.

## TEKS and TAKS

| | Item Number | TEKS | TAKS |
|---|---|---|---|
| STRATEGY | 1. 2. 3. | **(7)(A):** trace the historical development of the civil rights movement<br>**(7)(C):** evaluate government efforts to achieve equality in the U.S.<br>**(17)(A):** analyze the effects of 20th-century landmark U.S. Supreme Court decisions<br>**(18)(A):** analyze methods of expanding the right to participate in the democratic process<br>**(24)(B):** analyze information by identifying cause-and-effect relationships | **(US7)(A):** trace the historical development of the civil rights movement<br>**(US7)(C):** evaluate government efforts to achieve equality in the U.S.<br>**(US17)(A):** analyze the effects of 20th-century landmark U.S. Supreme Court decisions<br><br>**(US24)(B):** analyze information by identifying cause-and-effect relationships |
| PRACTICE | 1. 2. 3. | **(22)(A):** identify the effects of scientific discoveries and technological innovations<br>**(24)(A):** use primary sources to acquire information<br>**(24)(C):** apply different methods historians use to interpret the past | **(US22)(A):** identify the effects of scientific discoveries and technological innovations<br>**(US24)(A):** use primary sources to acquire information<br>**(US24)(C):** apply different methods historians use to interpret the past |

## USING STRATEGIES FOR . . .

### Extended Response
Remind students of the following:

- Read all the extended-response questions that go with one document before beginning to answer any questions. Look for words that tell you how to organize your answers.
- In question 1, you are to complete the chart by outlining the results of the Cold War events listed in the left-hand column. Use your knowledge of United States history to help you complete the chart.
- In question 2, you need to apply your knowledge to information in the document. Key words are *impact* and *international relations*. Jot down your ideas and create an outline on a separate piece of paper. Use this outline to write a short essay to answer the question. Support your main ideas with details and examples.

### General Test-Taking Tips
Share these tips with your students.

- Write in complete sentences whenever appropriate. Extended-response essays require complete sentences.
- Use correct grammar, punctuation, and spelling to help the scorer understand your answer.
- Remember, neatness counts! If the scorer cannot read your answer, you will not get credit for it.

## Extended Response

Extended-response questions, like constructed-response questions, usually focus on a document of some kind. However, they are more complex and require more time to complete than short-answer constructed-response questions. Some extended-response questions ask you to present the information in the document in a different form. Others require you to complete a chart, graph, or diagram. Still others ask you to write an essay, a report, or some other extended piece of writing. In most standardized tests, documents have only one extended-response question.

**①** Read the title of the document to get an idea of the subject.

**②** Carefully read the extended-response questions. (Question 1 asks you to complete a chart. Question 2 assumes that the chart is complete and asks you to write a brief essay based on information in the chart.)

**③** Study and analyze the document.

**④** Sometimes the question gives you a partial answer. Analyze that answer to determine what kind of information your answers should contain.

**⑤** If the question requires an essay or other piece of writing, jot down ideas in outline form. Use this outline to write your answer.

**④** Your answers should follow the pattern of this sample entry.

**①** Some Major Events in the Cold War

**③**

| Event | Result |
|---|---|
| The Hiss, Fuchs, and Rosenberg spy cases give rise to fears of Communist infiltration in the U.S. | Senator Joseph McCarthy rises to prominence by launching an anti-Communist crusade. |
| John Foster Dulles proposes the policy of brinkmanship—a policy heavily dependent on nuclear weapons and the airplanes that deliver them. | *The U.S. invests heavily in nuclear weapons and increases the size of its air force.* |
| The Soviet Union threatens to back Egypt's fight to gain control of the Suez Canal. | *The U.S. warns that it will defend the Middle East against any Communist attack* |
| The Soviet Union launches the satellite *Sputnik*. | *The U.S. and the Soviet Union begin a space race for control of outer space.* |
| The Soviet Union shoots down a U.S. spy plane flying over Soviet territory. | *U.S.-Soviet relations worsen.* |
| About 3 million Germans flee Communist East Germany for West Berlin. | *The Soviets and East Germans build a wall across Berlin to stem the flow of refugees to the West.* |
| The Soviet Union installs nuclear missiles in Cuba. | *Soviets remove missiles in exchange for U.S. pledge not to invade Cuba.* |

**1** In the right-hand column, briefly outline the result of the Cold War event listed in the left-hand column. The first entry has been completed for you.

**2** What impact did the Cold War have on international relations?

**⑤** **Essay Rubric:** The best essays will point out that the Cold War led to a division of Europe and much of the rest of the world between countries that sided with the United States and those that allied with the Soviet Union. Increased military spending related to the nuclear arms race made this division potentially very dangerous.

**S28**

## DIFFERENTIATING INSTRUCTION · STUDENTS ACQUIRING ENGLISH/ESL

### Understanding Vocabulary

Make sure students understand the following terms and concepts in the sample extended-response documents and questions.

**Strategy Page**
**Document**
*Cold War:* a conflict carried on without military action
*infiltration:* the act of getting into
*crusade:* campaign
*satellite:* an object orbiting in space

**Practice Page**
**Document**
*Reconstruction:* the reorganization and rebuilding of the former Confederate states after the Civil War
*ratified:* agreed to
*impeached:* charged with a crime
*vetoes:* prevents bill from becoming law
*overrides:* defeats or rejects
*amnesty:* the granting of forgiveness
Question 1 *significance:* importance

**Directions:** Use the time line <u>and</u> your knowledge of United States history to answer the questions that follow.

## The Period of Reconstruction

**1865**
**1865**
Andrew Johnson becomes president after Lincoln's assassination; Thirteenth Amendment is ratified.

**1867**
Reconstruction Act of 1867 is passed, beginning Radical Reconstruction.

**1866**
Johnson vetoes Civil Rights Act and Freedmen's Bureau Act; Congress overrides his veto.

**1868**
Fourteenth Amendment is ratified; Johnson is impeached; U.S. Grant wins presidency with Southern African-American votes; Ku Klux Klan, established in 1866, now has branches in every Southern state.

**1869**
Redemption begins as Democrats start to recapture Southern state governments.

**1870**
Fifteenth Amendment is ratified.

**1872**
Congress passes Amnesty Act.

**1873**
Financial panic and corruption in Grant administration weaken Republicans.

**1877**
Rutherford B. Hayes elected president in disputed election; Reconstruction ends.

**1877**

**1**  On a separate sheet of paper make a chart similar to the one below. Then complete the chart by listing the major events of Reconstruction and their significance.

| Year | Event | Significance |
|------|-------|--------------|
|      |       |              |
|      |       |              |

**2**  Identify the major turning points of the period of Reconstruction shown on the time line. Write a short essay explaining the impact these events had on the Reconstruction process.

S29

## PRACTICE QUESTIONS

### Thinking It Through
Share the following explanations with students as they discuss the strategies they used to answer the practice questions.

- Read the time line and the extended response questions. Question 1 asks you to organize information in the form of a chart. Use information from the time line and your knowledge of United States history to complete the chart.

- To answer question 2, use the information in your chart to write a short essay.

The chart and the essay should cover the following:
1865; Johnson president; continued Lincoln's policies, angering Radicals
1865; Amendment 13; slavery abolished
1866; Johnson vetoes Civil Rights and Freedmen's Bureau acts, Congress overrides veto; ended presidential Reconstruction and began congressional Reconstruction
1866; Ku Klux Klan; took away African Americans' political rights
1867; Reconstruction Act of 1867; abolished Confederate state governments
1868; Amendment 14; former slaves citizens
1868; Johnson impeached; Radical leaders tried to remove him from office
1868; Grant president; power of African-American vote
1869; Redemption; Reconstruction ending
1870; Amendment 15; former slaves vote
1872; Amnesty Act; forgave former Confederates
1873; Corruption in Grant administration; weakened the Republicans
1877; Hayes President; election ended Reconstruction

### Scoring Extended-Response Questions
Extended-response questions usually are scored using a rubric, or scoring guide. The questions on this page might be scored 0 through 4 or 5. Only the most complete answers receive the top score.

## TEKS and TAKS

| | Item Number | TEKS | TAKS |
|---|---|---|---|
| **STRATEGY** | 1. 2. 3. | **(1)(A):** identify a major era in U.S. history and its defining characteristics<br>**(6)(D):** describe U.S. response to Soviet aggression after World War II<br>**(6)(F):** describe the impact of McCarthyism and Sputnik I<br>**(24)(B):** analyze information by identifying cause-and-effect relationships | **(US1)(A):** identify a major era in U.S. history and its defining characteristics<br>**(US6)(D):** describe U.S. response to Soviet aggression after World War II<br>**(US6)(F):** describe the impact of McCarthyism and Sputnik I<br>**(24)(B):** analyze information by identifying cause-and-effect relationships |
| **PRACTICE** | 1. 2. 3. | **(1)(A):** identify a major era in U.S. history and its defining characteristics<br>**(21)(A):** explain actions taken by people to expand economic opportunities and political rights in U.S. society<br>**(24)(B):** analyze information by identifying cause-and-effect relationships<br>**(24)(C):** apply different methods historians use to interpret the past | **(US1)(A):** identify a major era in U.S. history and its defining characteristics<br>**(US21)(A):** explain actions taken by people to expand economic opportunities and political rights in U.S. society<br>**(US24)(B):** analyze information by identifying cause-and-effect relationships<br>**(US24)(C):** apply different methods historians use to interpret the past |

## USING STRATEGIES FOR . . .

### Document-Based Questions

Remind students of the following:

- Document-based questions are designed to help you work like a historian. You are given several documents from a variety of sources that you must analyze, evaluate, and synthesize in order to write an essay, much the same way a historian would proceed.
- Use the information in the "Introduction" to help you organize your essay. The "Historical Context" gives you the focus of the document-based question. The document-based question shown here focuses on environmental awareness in the United States after 1962.
- Use the information in the "Task" section to help you make a graphic organizer, such as an outline, a chart, or a concept web to organize the information for your essay. This "Task" section explains that the essay must discuss two things: (1) the progress on the environment made in the United States since the 1960s, and (2) the environmental challenges still facing the country today. Make a chart with two columns on a piece of scratch paper. In the first column write the heading "Progress on the Environment." In the second column write the heading "Environmental Challenges."
- As you answer the "Part 1: Short Answer" questions, also complete the chart.
- To answer the "Part 2: Essay" question, use the documents, the answers to the short-answer questions, the notes in your graphic organizer, and your knowledge of history to help you write the essay.

### General Test-Taking Tips

Share these tips with your students.

- Write legibly.
- Sometimes answer sheets are scanned for scoring purposes. If you do not write dark enough, they will not be readable.

## Document-Based Questions

A document-based question focuses on several documents—both visual and written. These documents often are accompanied by short-answer questions. Students use their answers to these questions and information from the documents to write an essay on a specified subject.

**1** Carefully read the "Historical Context" section to get an indication of the issue addressed in the question.

**2** Note the action words used in the "Task" section. These words will tell you exactly what the essay question requires.

**3** Study and analyze each document. Think about how the documents are connected to the essay question. Take notes on your ideas.

**4** Read and answer each of the document-specific questions.

### Introduction

**1** **Historical Context:** Rachel Carson's book *Silent Spring* (1962) awakened Americans to the issue of environmental pollution. Since that time, efforts have been made to protect the environment.

**2** **Task:** Trace the progress on the environment made in the United States since the 1960s and consider the environmental challenges still facing the country today.

### Part 1: Short Answer

Study each document carefully and answer the questions that follow.

**3** **Document 1: Recycling in the United States, 1970–1997**

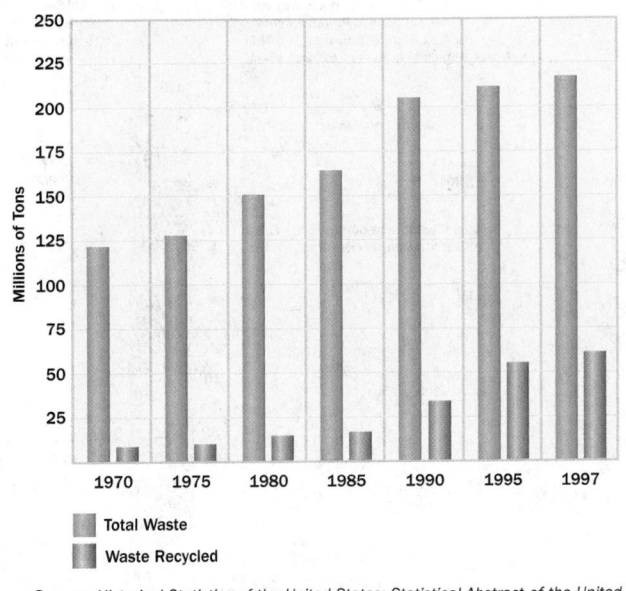

**Source:** *Historical Statistics of the United States; Statistical Abstract of the United States*

**4** **What positive and negative trends does this graph show?**

*The amount of waste recycled is increasing, but so, too, is total waste produced.*

---

## DIFFERENTIATING INSTRUCTION    STUDENTS ACQUIRING ENGLISH/ESL

### Understanding Vocabulary

Make sure students understand the following terms and concepts in the sample documents.

**Strategy Pages**
**Document 1**
*recycling:* reusing
**Document 2**
*alternative:* outside the usual or traditional
*alternatives:* choices
**Document 3**
*integrity:* soundness
*enactment:* act of making into law

*standards:* level of requirement
*recovery:* act of getting better
*diverse:* different

## Document 2: Solar Collectors in the Mojave Desert

**What alternative energy source is shown in the photograph? Why has the United States sought alternatives to such traditional energy sources as oil and coal?**

*solar energy; because supply of fossil fuels is limited and because oil, coal, and nuclear energy all carry a pollution risk*

## Document 3: Clean Water

With the enactment of the Clean Water Act in 1972, the nation . . . made a new commitment to restore and maintain the chemical, physical, and biological integrity of [its] waters.

America has honored its commitment to clean water. Since enactment of the Clean Water Act, the number of waters that are safe for fishing and swimming has doubled. National clean water standards stop billions of pounds of industrial pollution from flowing into waters each year. . . . Today, . . . many . . . water bodies that were once severely polluted are well on the way to recovery. . . .

Despite impressive progress, many of the nation's rivers, lakes, and coastal waters do not meet water quality goals. [And] many waters that are now clean face [a] threat . . . from diverse pollution sources.

—Clean Water Action Plan (EPA)

**What impact has the Clean Water Act had on America's waterways?**

*Many bodies of water that once were polluted are clean or well on their way to recovery.*

## Part 2: Essay

Using information from the documents, your answers to the questions in Part 1, and your knowledge of American history, write an essay tracing the progress on the environment made in the United States since the 1960s and considering the environmental challenges that still face the country today. ⑥

⑤ Carefully read the essay question. Then, write an outline for your essay.

⑥ Write your essay. Be sure that it has an introductory paragraph that introduces your argument, main body paragraphs that explain it, and a concluding paragraph that restates your position. In your essay, include extracts or details from specific documents to support your ideas. Add other supporting facts or details that you know from your study of American history.

**Essay Rubric** The best essays will note such progress as cleaner water (Document 3), increased recycling (Document 1), and the search for energy alternatives that neither deplete the country's natural resources nor threaten the environment (Document 2). Essays should refer to such challenges as the increasing amount of waste produced (Document 1) and lingering pollution threats to the water (Document 3).

## RUBRICS FOR DBQ ESSAYS

The following is a sample rubric that might be used to score a DBQ essay.

**To score a 5, the DBQ essay:**
- thoroughly answers all parts of Task.
- uses data from all the documents.
- is supported with relevant facts.
- has outside knowledge.
- is well developed and organized.
- has a strong intro and conclusion.

**To score a 4, the DBQ essay:**
- answers all parts of Task.
- uses data from most of the documents.
- is supported with relevant facts.
- has outside knowledge.
- is well developed and organized.
- has a good intro and conclusion.

**To score a 3, the DBQ essay:**
- answers most parts of Task.
- uses data from some documents.
- is supported with some relevant facts.
- has little outside knowledge.
- is satisfactorily developed and organized.
- restates the essay theme.

**To score a 2, the DBQ essay:**
- answers some parts of the Task or all parts in a limited way.
- uses limited data from the documents.
- uses few facts to support the essay.
- has little or no outside knowledge.
- is poorly organized.
- has limited or missing intro or conclusion.

**To score a 1, the DBQ essay:**
- shows limited understanding of the Task.
- uses limited data from the documents.
- uses few or no facts to support essay.
- has no outside knowledge.
- is poorly organized.
- has limited or missing intro or conclusion.

**To score a 0, the DBQ essay:**
- does not answer the Task.
- is illegible.
- is blank or missing.

## TEKS and TAKS

| | Item Number | TEKS | TAKS |
|---|---|---|---|
| **STRATEGY** | **Document 1** **Document 2** **Document 3** | **(11)(A):** identify the effects of population growth <br> **(11)(B):** trace the development of the conservation of natural resources <br> **(24)(A):** use secondary sources to acquire information <br> **(24)(B):** analyze information by drawing conclusions | **(US11)(A):** identify the effects of population growth <br> **(US24)(A):** use secondary sources to acquire information <br><br> **(US24)(B):** analyze information by drawing conclusions |
| | **Part 2: Essay** | **(11)(A):** identify the effects of population growth <br> **(11)(B):** trace the development of the conservation of natural resources <br> **(24)(A):** use secondary sources to acquire information <br> **(24)(B):** analyze information by drawing conclusions <br> **(24)(C):** apply methods historians use to interpret the past <br> **(24)(G):** support a point of view on a social studies issue or event <br> **(25)(D):** create written presentations of social studies information | **(US11)(A):** identify the effects of population growth <br><br> **(US24)(A):** use secondary sources to acquire information <br> **(US24)(B):** analyze information by drawing conclusions <br> **(US24)(C):** apply methods historians use to interpret the past |

## Thinking It Through

Share the following explanations with students as they discuss the strategies they used to answer the practice questions.

**Part 1: Short Answer**

**Document 1.** Analyze the line graph and use your knowledge of United States history to answer the question. The overall trend in federal spending in the New Deal years was upward.

**Document 2.** Analyze the political cartoon to answer the question. The answer is that the New Deal provided work for unemployed men who built roads, bridges, and parks, while the Old Deal provided only a handout.

**Document 3.** Use your knowledge of United States history to help you answer this question. Look for cause-and-effect relationships for the following answer. The National Labor Relations Act allowed workers to form unions to bargain collectively, in keeping with the second goal outlined in the document. The Fair Labor Standards Act set a federal minimum wage and maximum work week, in keeping with the first goal outlined in the document.

**Part 2: Essay** Share the sample rubric on page S31 with students so they know the criteria they must meet to earn the maximum amount of points for this essay. Tell the students the following.

- Use the information in the "Introduction" to help you organize your essay. Jot down things you know about the time period or theme of the question. Use the information in "Task" to help you make a graphic organizer. You might make an outline with two parts: I. Changes in the Role of the Federal Government and II. How the Changes Affect Life Today. As you answer the short-answer questions, also complete this outline.

- Use the documents, the answers to the short-answer questions, the notes in your graphic organizer, and your knowledge of history to help you write the essay.

## Introduction

**Directions:** Read the documents in Part 1 and answer the questions that follow each document. Then, read the directions for Part 2 and write your essay.

**Historical Context:** From 1929 to 1940, the United States suffered from a severe economic depression. Facing a damaged economy and a shaken public, President Franklin D. Roosevelt took action, creating a new role for the federal government.

**Task:** Describe how the role of the federal government changed during the Depression and discuss how that change continues to impact life in the United States today.

## Part 1: Short Answer

Study each document carefully and answer the questions that follow.

### Document 1: Federal Spending, 1925–1940

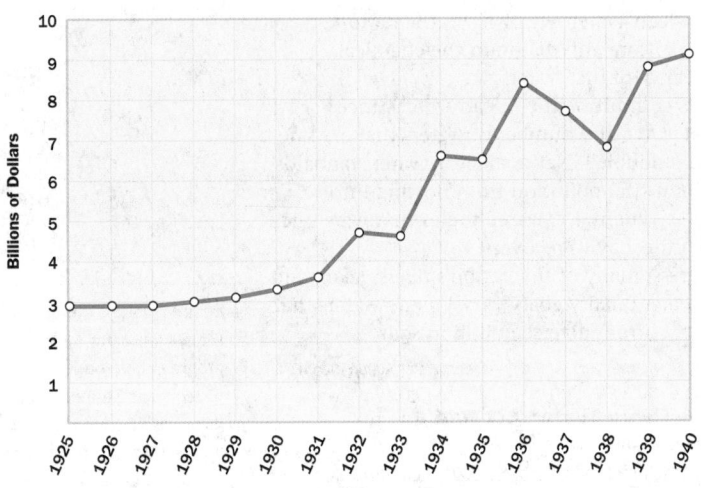

**Source:** *Historical Statistics of the United States*

**President Franklin D. Roosevelt began introducing New Deal policies soon after taking office in 1933. What was the overall trend in federal spending in the New Deal years?**

S32

## Understanding Vocabulary

Make sure students understand the following terms and concepts in the sample documents.

**Practice Pages**

**Document 1**

*trend:* general direction in which something moves

**Document 2**

*civilian:* ordinary; not military

*corps:* people working under common direction

**Document 3**

*competition:* rivalry

*controversies:* disagreements

*strikes:* work stoppages

*secure:* get

*equitable:* fair

## Document 2: The Civilian Conservation Corps

*The New York Daily News.*

How does the "Old Deal" differ from the "New Deal?"

## Document 3: A New Labor Policy (1936)

Among the first items in this growing labor policy of the American government are the following:

1. That the government ought to do everything in its power to establish minimum basic standards for labor, below which competition should not be permitted to force standards of health, wages, or hours.

2. That the government ought to use its influence to bring about arrangements which will make possible peaceful settlements of controversies and relieve labor of the necessity of resorting to strikes to secure equitable conditions and the right to be heard.

—Secretary of Labor Frances Perkins, "A National Labor Policy"

How did the National Labor Relations Act (1935) and the Fair Labor Standards Act (1938) put the New Deal labor policy into practice?

## Part 2: Essay

Using information from the documents, your answers to the questions in Part 1, and your knowledge of American history, write an essay in which you describe how the role of the federal government changed during the Depression and discuss how that change continues to impact life in the United States today.

Excerpt from "A National Labor Policy" by Frances Perkins. The American Academy of Political and Social Sciences, 1936. Reprinted by permission.

**S33**

## RUBRIC FOR ESSAY

The best essays will address both parts of the question: 1) how the role of the federal government changed during the Depression and 2) how that change continues to affect life in the United States today.

**How the role of the federal government changed during the Depression**

- regulation of banks and the stock market (outside knowledge)
- laws about labor standards and conditions of employment (Document 3)
- greater role in relief and public works projects, such as the CCC, causing increase in federal spending (Documents 1, 2, outside knowledge)
- funding of the TVA (outside knowledge)
- creation of the Social Security system (outside knowledge)

**How that change continues to affect life in the United States today**

- federal labor and minimum wage laws: keep employers from exploiting workers (outside knowledge)
- TVA: continues to control flooding and create electric power, among other activities (outside knowledge)
- Social Security: millions collect it and depend on it to supplement their income (outside knowledge)

---

## TEKS and TAKS

| | Item Number | TEKS | TAKS |
|---|---|---|---|
| **PRACTICE** | Parts 1 and 2 | **(13)(C):** analyze the effects of the Great Depression<br>**(15)(A):** evaluate impact of New Deal legislation on government roles.<br>**(24)(A):** use secondary and primary sources to acquire information<br>**(24)(B):** analyze information by drawing conclusions | **(US13)(C):** analyze the effects of the Great Depression<br>**(US15)(A):** evaluate impact of New Deal legislation on government roles.<br>**(US24)(A):** use secondary and primary sources to acquire information<br>**(US24)(B):** analyze information by drawing conclusions |
| | Part 2: Essay | **(13)(E):** analyze how New Deal agencies and programs continue to affect the lives of U.S. citizens<br>**(24)(C):** apply methods historians use to interpret the past<br>**(24)(G):** support a point of view on a social studies issue or event<br>**(25)(D):** create written presentations of social studies information | **(US13)(E):** analyze how New Deal agencies and programs continue to affect the lives of U.S. citizens<br>**(US24)(C):** apply methods historians use to interpret the past |

## Previewing the Unit

Unit 1 is a review unit covering United States history from its earliest beginnings through Reconstruction. The exploration and colonization of the land is the result of the contributions of many cultures. The colonists declare independence and establish a new nation rooted in one of the greatest governmental documents of all time—The Constitution of the United States. The nation eagerly expands to the west and regional ways of life develop. Failure to resolve the issues of slavery and regional differences leads to a civil war. Following the war, the nation slowly restores order and an American way of life.

UNIT PROJECT

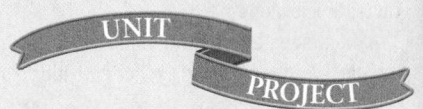

**HISTORICAL INQUIRY: LETTER TO THE EDITOR**

Use this project to teach students to support a point of view based on research.

**Supporting a Point of View**
Explain that supporting a point of view means presenting good reasons for what you believe. Discuss what makes a reason a good reason. *(logically supports the main point; true and based on best, most complete facts)*

One approach to supporting a point of view can be to argue against opposing views. For example, to support the view that people need liberty, one might describe how denying people liberty harms them.

*(continued on next page)*

REVIEW UNIT

1

# American Beginnings to 1877



UNIT PROJECT

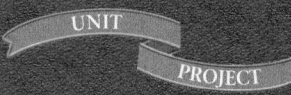

***Letter to the Editor***

This unit covers the War for Independence and the Civil War. Choose an issue in this unit for which you would be willing to fight. Explain your views in a letter to the editor.

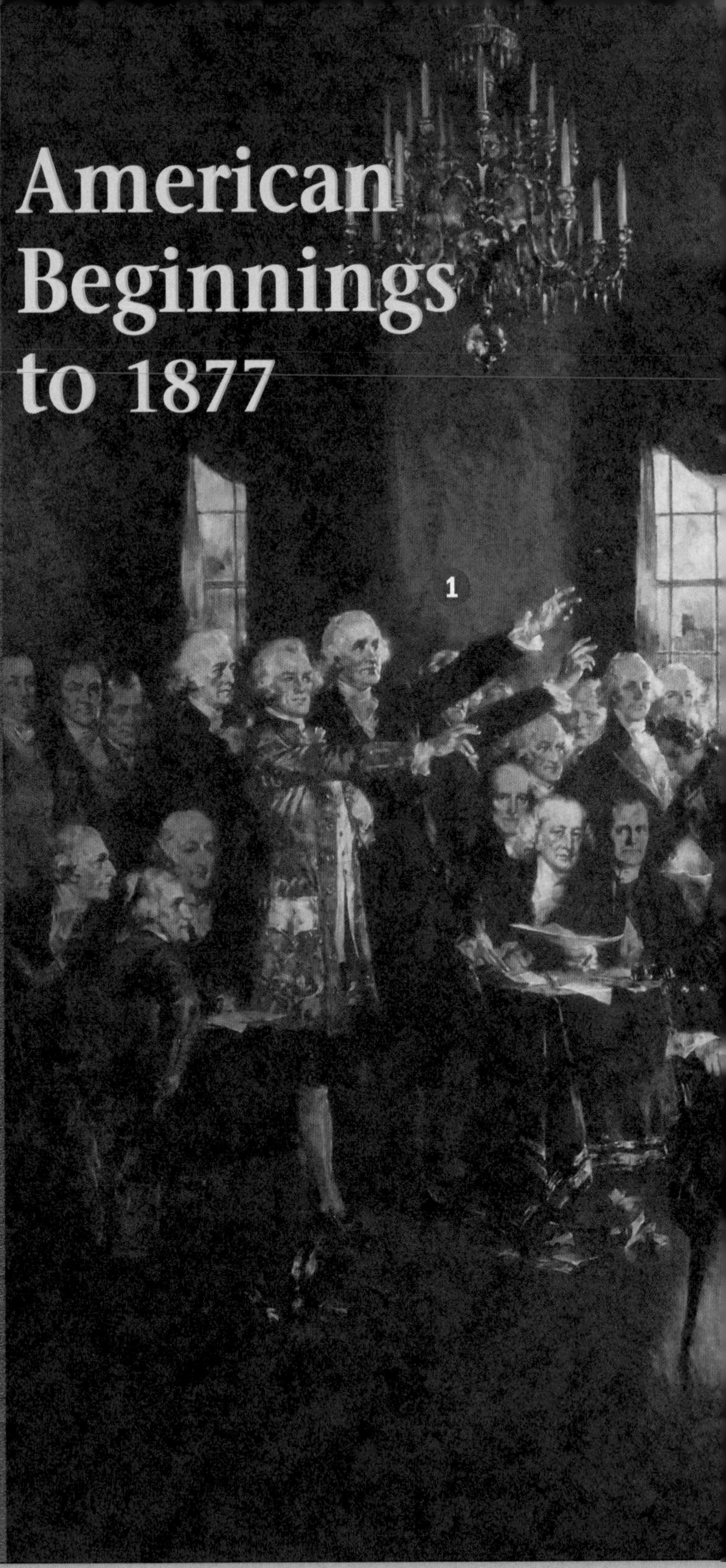


*Signing of the Constitution by Howard*

## More About the Image

Missing from the painting is Thomas Jefferson. He was in France as a diplomatic representative of the United States. James Madison, a fellow Virginian, sent him a draft of the proposed constitution. Although Jefferson approved of the reorganization of the government, he strongly objected to the lack of a Bill of Rights.

**1 The Delegates**

Many of the signers went on to become senators and representatives; several served in the Supreme Court; and two—Washington and Madison—were elected president.

**2 Alexander Hamilton—deputy from New York**

Hamilton was an advocate of a strong central government that would dominate the states. His plan had little impact on the delegates. Later, Hamilton wrote about two-thirds of the essays in *The Federalist*, a book supporting the Constitution.

### Researching to Support a Point of View

· Remind students that their research should include the varied points of view on the issue.

· Students should identify their most important reasons and then look for facts, events, and statistics to support them.

### Tips on Letters

· Remind students that their purpose is persuasive and that using standard grammar, spelling, sentence structure, and punctuation will help them achieve this purpose.

### Rubrics

A Letter to the Editor should . . .

· present a cogent justification of the writer's position on an issue raised in the Unit

· include relevant, historically accurate supporting details

· use standard grammar, spelling, sentence structure, and punctuation

## HISTORY from VISUALS

### Interpreting the Painting

George Washington is the main figure in this painting. Notice how the uplifted arms of the delegates at the back of the room (the left side of the painting) draw the eye to Washington. Washington's presence is enhanced by placing him standing on a dais. He seems to balance the presence of all of the rest of the delegates. Christy deliberately based his 1940 painting on Trumbull's 1891 "Signing of the Independence in Congress." Christy's painting hangs in the House wing of the United States Capitol.

Ask students to describe how the makeup of leadership in the nation would be shown today. *(More persons of color and women would be included.)*

**Extension** Ask students: How did the Constitution itself make it possible for equal rights to become available to more people?

**3** **Benjamin Franklin—deputy from Pennsylvania**

The elder statesman at the convention, Franklin believed the nation should be led by an executive committee and have a unicameral legislature. Although both notions failed, Franklin was a strong backer of the new constitution.

**4** **James Madison—deputy from Virginia**

Because of his plan and his brilliant political leadership at the Constitutional Convention, Madison is known as the Father of the Constitution. Madison kept a record of the proceedings that gives insight into the activities of the delegates.

**5** **George Washington—deputy from Virginia**

Confidence in Washington's judgment and the assumption that he would be the first president helped ease concerns about the power of the new federal government.

# Exploration and the Colonial Era

| | **CHAPTER OVERVIEW** | **COPYMASTERS** | **INTEGRATED TECHNOLOGY** |
|---|---|---|---|
| **CHAPTER RESOURCES** | Native Americans develop complex societies. Starting in 1492, Europeans and then Africans bring their cultures to the New World. British colonies thrive, and Britain dominates North America after defeating France at war. | 📄 Telescoping the Times<br>· Chapter Summary, pp. 1–2<br><br>📄 Planning for Block Schedules | 🔊 America's Music CD<br>👁 Power Presentations<br>👁 Electronic Teacher Tools<br>ℹ Online Lesson Planner<br>ℹ classzone.com |
| **SECTION 1**<br><br>The Americas, West Africa, and Europe<br><br>pp. 4–13 | **KEY IDEAS**<br><br>Long before the founding of the United States, the ancestors of its early inhabitants live in diverse societies in North America, Africa, and Europe. | 📄 In-Depth Resources: Unit 1<br>· Guided Reading, p. 9<br>· Building Vocabulary, p. 13<br>· Skillbuilder Practice, p. 14<br>· Reteaching Activity, p. 17<br>· Primary Sources, p. 25<br><br>📄 Lesson Plans, pp. 1–2 | 🔧 Critical Thinking Transparencies CT35<br>· Inventions, 1190–1500<br>🔧 Humanities Transparencies HT2<br>· Ritual Cache Figures<br>👁 Electronic Library of Primary Sources<br>· "Portuguese-African Slave Trade"<br>ℹ classzone.com |
| **SECTION 2**<br><br>Spanish North America<br><br>pp. 14–20 | Following Columbus's voyage in 1492, Europeans explore North, Central, and South America, and Spanish conquistadors claim an empire for Spain. | 📄 In-Depth Resources: Unit 1<br>· Guided Reading, p. 10<br>· Skillbuilder Practice, p. 15<br>· Reteaching Activity, p. 18<br>· Outline Map, pp. 23–24<br>· Primary Sources, pp. 26–27<br>· Literature, pp. 30–32<br><br>📄 Lesson Plans, pp. 3–4 | 🔧 Geography Transparencies GT1<br>· Discovery and Exploration<br>🔧 Critical Thinking Transparencies CT1<br>· Exploration of the Americas<br>🔧 Humanities Transparencies HT1, HT3<br>· Map of North America<br>· Indians Giving Cortés a Necklace<br>👁 Electronic Library of Primary Sources<br>ℹ classzone.com |
| **SECTION 3**<br><br>Early British Colonies<br><br>pp. 21–30 | English settlers overcome hardship to found colonies in North America where they can survive economically and express their religious and moral ideas. | 📄 In-Depth Resources: Unit 1<br>· Guided Reading, p. 11<br>· Reteaching Activity, p. 19<br>· Primary Sources, p. 28<br>· American Lives, p. 33<br><br>📄 Lesson Plans, pp. 5–6 | 🔧 Geography Transparencies GT2, GT35<br>· The European Colonies, 1650<br>· Original Thirteen Colonies<br>🔧 Critical Thinking Transparencies CT2, CT36<br>· Puritan Migration<br>· American Colonies<br>🔧 Humanities Transparencies HT4<br>· Women Working in an Onion Field<br>👁 Electronic Library of Primary Sources<br>· "The First Supply," by John Smith<br>· from The Book of General Laws<br>ℹ classzone.com |
| **SECTION 4**<br><br>The Colonies Come of Age<br><br>pp. 31–41 | A thriving agricultural economy in the South and a commercial economy in the North help England and its colonies prosper, although colonists begin to question British authority. Britain defeats France for dominance in the New World. | 📄 In-Depth Resources: Unit 1<br>· Guided Reading, p. 12<br>· Skillbuilder Practice, p. 16<br>· Reteaching Activity, p. 20<br>· Geography Application, pp. 21–22<br>· Primary Sources, p. 29<br>· American Lives, p. 34<br><br>📄 Lesson Plans, pp. 7–8 | 🔧 Critical Thinking Transparencies CT3, CT37<br>· French and Indian War<br>· Africans in the Colonies<br>👁 Electronic Library of Primary Sources<br>· from Olaudah Equiano<br>· "Relations with the Indians"<br>· from "How Our Cities Looked"<br>ℹ classzone.com |

## Legend

| | | | | | | |
|---|---|---|---|---|---|---|
| PE Pupil's Edition | | Overhead Transparency | | CD-ROM | | |
| TE Teacher's Edition | | Audio Library | | Internet | | |
| Copymaster | | | | | | |

## ASSESSMENT OPTIONS

- PE **Chapter Assessment**, pp. 42–43
- **Formal Assessment**
  · Chapter Tests, Forms A, B, and C, pp. 9–20
- **Test Generator**
- **Integrated Assessment Book**
- **TAKS Online Test Practice**
- **TAKS Spiraled Content Review**
- **TAKS Practice Tests**

- PE **Section 1 Assessment**, p. 13
- TE **Self-Assessment**, p. 13
- **Formal Assessment**, Quiz, p. 5
- **Integrated Assessment Book**
- **Test Generator**
- **TAKS Practice Transparencies TT1–3**

- PE **Section 2 Assessment**, p. 20
- TE **Self-Assessment**, p. 20
- **Formal Assessment**, Quiz, p. 6
- **Integrated Assessment Book**
- **Test Generator**
- **TAKS Practice Transparencies TT4–6**

- PE **Section 3 Assessment**, p. 30
- TE **Self-Assessment**, p. 30
- **Formal Assessment**, Quiz, p. 7
- **Integrated Assessment Book**
- **Test Generator**
- **TAKS Practice Transparencies TT7–9**

- PE **Section 4 Assessment**, p. 39
- TE **Self-Assessment**, p. 39
- **Formal Assessment**, Quiz, p. 8
- **Integrated Assessment Book**
- **Test Generator**
- **TAKS Practice Transparencies TT10–13**

## RESOURCES FOR DIFFERENTIATING INSTRUCTION

### Students Acquiring English/ESL

- **Reading Study Guide:** (English and Spanish) pp. 5–12
- **Access for Students Acquiring English/ESL:** Spanish Translations, pp. 11–23
- **Chapter Summaries on CD** (English and Spanish)

### Less Proficient Readers

- **Reading Study Guide** (English and Spanish) pp. 5–12
- **Telescoping the Times** · Chapter Summary, pp. 1–2
- **Chapter Summaries on CD** (English and Spanish)

### Gifted and Talented Students

- **In-Depth Resources: Unit 1** · Primary Sources, pp. 25–29 · American Lives: John Winthrop, p. 33; Olaudah Equiano, p. 34
- **Electronic Library of Primary Sources** · Unit 1, Chapter 1

## CROSS-CURRICULAR CONNECTIONS

### World Cultures
Fritz, Jean, et al. *The World in 1492.* NY: Holt, 1995. A survey of world regions—Europe, Asia, Africa, Oceania, and the Americas—on the eve of the great voyages of discovery.

### Popular Culture
Hale, Anna W. *The Mayflower People: Triumphs and Tragedies.* Niwot, CO: Holt, 1995. A colorful coverage of the ocean voyage filled with human detail; useful bibliography.

### Health
Terkel, Susan N. *Colonial American Medicine.* NY: Franklin Watts, 1993. From the Colonial America series, this book looks at the "cures"—from herbs to leeches—with which doctors in the 1600s and 1700s treated the diseases and epidemics of their day.

### Literature
Dorris, Michael. *The Crown of Columbus.* NY: HarperCollins, 1991. In this novel, an anthropologist finds a lost diary of Christopher Columbus and embarks on a quest for the truth about the great explorer.

West, Jessamyn. *Massacre at Fall Creek.* NY: Harcourt, 1975. In the early 1800s, five men are charged with murdering several Native Americans. This novel follows their trials.

### McDougal Littell *Literature Connections*

Achebe, Chinua. *Things Fall Apart (with related readings).* Contact with outside forces brings deep changes to a traditional community.

## ENRICHMENT ACTIVITIES

- PE **Pupil's Edition**, pp. 2–43
  Interact with History, pp. 2–3
  Science & Technology, p. 12
  Daily Life, pp. 40–41

- **In-Depth Resources: Unit 1**
  · Geography Application: The Triangular Trade, pp. 21–22
  · Outline Map, pp. 23–24
  · Primary Source: *from* The Iroquois Constitution, p. 25
  · Primary Source: from *Journals of Christopher Columbus*, p. 26–27
  · Primary Source: from *Travels and Works of Captain John Smith*, p. 28

- · Primary Source: from *The Autobiography* by Benjamin Franklin, p. 29
- · Literature Selection from *Memoirs of Christopher Columbus* by Stephen Marlowe, pp. 30–32
- · American Lives: John Winthrop p. 33
- · American Lives: Olaudah Equiano, p. 34

- **Primary Source Explorer**
  · Iroquois Great Law of Peace
  · The Mayflower Compact
  · The Fundamental Orders of Connecticut

- **America's Music CD**

- **Electronic Library of Primary Sources**
  · Unit 1, Chapter 1

## BLOCK SCHEDULE LESSON PLAN OPTIONS (90-MINUTE PERIOD)

### DAY 1

**CHAPTER 1 OPENER**
pp. 2–3
**Class Time** 30 minutes

**History from Visuals, p. 2**
**Class Time** 15 minutes

*Options for Pacing and Variety*

· **Time Saver** Ask students to study the painting and explain what they believe is occurring and how they think the Native Americans in the painting feel about what they are experiencing.
**Class Time** 10 minutes

**Interact with History, p. 3**
**Class Time** 15 minutes

*Options for Pacing and Variety*

· **Role-Playing** Ask students to read the questions next to the painting and discuss, as a class or in small groups, the different perspectives with which cultures can be viewed.
**Class Time** 15 minutes

**SECTION 1, pp. 4–13**
**Class Time** 30 minutes

*Options for Pacing and Variety*

· **Peer Teaching** Assign small groups to investigate each one of the Native American groups shown on the map on page 7. Have students research the physical environment of each group as well as its culture. Then develop visual displays illustrating the culture.
**Class Time** 45 minutes

### DAY 1 continued

· **Internet** Have students go to **classzone.com** or other Internet sites to choose one of the topic areas to visit on a virtual field trip. Among the possibilities might be Columbus, the Maya, or the Aztecs. Have students create a list of relevant Web sites to visit.
**Class Time** 30 minutes

· **Time Saver** Read to students the sidebar on "The Power of Dreams" on TE page 8. Discuss related beliefs in our own culture, such as the meaning of dreams in Freudian analysis, visions in childhood literature, such as *Alice in Wonderland*, or people's increasing interest in the beliefs of traditional societies, such as animal spirits, etc.
**Class Time** 10 minutes

**SECTION 2, pp. 14–20**
**Class Time** 30 minutes

*Options for Pacing and Variety*

· **Peer Teaching** Divide students into groups of three. Have each group summarize for the others one of the three subheadings of the section. Then have them ask the other two groups the Main Ideas questions in their subheading.
**Class Time** 20 minutes

· **Peer Evaluation** Have students work in small groups and quiz each other on the Terms & Names of the section. Then have them work together to complete the Section 2 Assessment.
**Class Time** 20 minutes

### DAY 2

**SECTION 3, pp. 21–30**
**Class Time** 30 minutes

*Options for Pacing and Variety*

· **Internet** Have students read page 22, "Rediscovering Fort James," and answer the Skillbuilder questions. Then have them search the Internet for more information on archaeological finds at Jamestown. Ask students to write up a summary of their findings.
**Class Time** 25 minutes

· **Role-Playing** Have students create a mock trial, according to Differentiating Instruction on TE page 23. They can work in groups on the different perspectives, and each choose one person for each relevant part in the proceedings.
**Class Time** 45 minutes

· **Time Saver** Have students read the feature on page 27, "History Through Architecture," and discuss the Skillbuilder questions on the page. **Class Time** 10 minutes

**SECTION 4, pp. 31–41**
**Class Time** 30 minutes

*Options for Pacing and Variety*

· **Time Saver** While discussing the objectives and main points of Section 4, ask students if they think it is possible to be wealthy without relying on the work of poorer people. Discuss in what ways this work is employed. **Class Time** 10 minutes

### DAY 2 continued

· **Peer Teaching** Have students choose and read one of the four accounts included in *The Classic Slave Narratives*, edited by Henry Louis Gates. Then discuss them.
**Class Time** 30 minutes

· **Peer Teaching** Have students look at the map on page 38 and discuss as a class the Geography Skillbuilder questions. Then have students work in small groups to make a chart comparing the French and English colonies, like the one specified on TE page 37.
**Class Time** 20 minutes

· **History on Film** Have students read the feature on pages 40–41, "Daily Life: Colonial Courtship." Then view the video, *The Marriage of Pocahontas*, which looks at that famous marriage and its effects.
**Class Time** 30 minutes

**ASSESSMENT**
pp. 42–43
**Class Time** 30 minutes

*Options for Pacing and Variety*

· **Peer Evaluation** Have students work in groups to review the Main Ideas questions and quiz each other on them. **Class Time** 20 minutes

· **Time Saver** Assign the Critical Thinking questions on page 42 for homework. Discuss the answers as a class. **Class Time** 10 minutes

---

**TEACHER-TESTED ACTIVITY**

**NEWS BROADCAST**

**CYNTHIA M. GREENE, RIDLEY HIGH SCHOOL, FOLSOM, PENNSYLVANIA**

**Class Time** 90 minutes

**Task** Presenting a news broadcast about the colonial regions

**Purpose** To recognize the social, political, and economic differences between northern colonies and southern colonies

**Supplies Needed**
· Textbook
· Library research materials or Internet access

**Activity** Divide the class into three groups: northern colonies, southern colonies, and news media. Students in the regional groups should do research in order to explain their region's social, political, and economic characteristics. News media members should develop a list of probing questions to ask the colonists. After the interview, have a media member summarize regional differences.

# CHAPTER 1 CORRELATION

## CORRELATION TO THE TEXAS ESSENTIAL KNOWLEDGE AND SKILLS

Chapter 1 addresses the following standards of the Texas Essential Knowledge and Skills for U.S. History.

| TEKS | Instruction | Student Question/Activity |
|---|---|---|
| **(8B)** Pose and answer questions about geographic distributions and patterns shown on maps, graphs, charts, models, and databases. | **PE 7** map depicting the location of various Native American cultures during the 1400s | **PE 7** questions that require students to interpret the map |
| **(18A)** Identify and analyze methods of expanding the right to participate in the democratic process. | **PE 23** discussion of the creation of the early forms of representative government in the colonies, including the House of Burgesses, the Mayflower Compact, and the Fundamental Orders of Connecticut | **TE 23** question about comparisons to the House of Burgesses and the modern-day U.S. Congress |
| **(20D)** Analyze the relationship between culture and the economy. | **PE 31–34** discussion of how the South's agricultural economy helped to create a culture centered around large plantations and slavery | **TE 32** Taking Notes activity in which students provide details about the different cultural groups in the South |
| **(21A)** Explain actions taken by people from racial, ethnic, and religious groups to expand political rights in American society. | **PE 24–25** examination of the efforts by Puritan dissenters to exercise greater religious freedom | **TE 24** Civics Activity in which students analyze the debate over different religious beliefs in Puritan society |
| **(22A)** Explain the effects of scientific discoveries on the development of the United States. | **PE 34–35** discussion of the effects of the Enlightenment on the American colonies | **TE 35** activity in which the students analyze the impact of the Enlightenment |
| **(22B)** Explain how scientific discoveries and technological innovations resulted from specific needs. | **PE 12–13** discussion of the many sailing inventions and innovations that resulted from Europeans interest in overseas exploration | **PE 13** question about the inventions and innovations that gave Europeans an advantage over Africans and Native Americans during the war |

## TAKS MINI-LESSONS

1. **Social Studies Skills: Objective 1 (8.1.C):** Explain the significance of the date 1607 **Activity** Have students trace the establishment of the colony at Jamestown.

2. **Social Studies Skills: Objective 2 (WG1.B):** Trace the spatial diffusion of a phenomenon and describe its effects on regions of contact **Activity** Have students discuss what they feel were the two most significant Columbian Exchange items shown on the map on page 15.

3. **Social Studies Skills: Objective 4 (8.3.A):** Explain the reasons for the growth of representative government and institutions during the colonial period **Activity** Have students summarize the powers of the colonial governments.

4. **English Language Arts Skills: Objective 1 (7.F):** Produce summaries of texts by identifying main ideas and their supporting details **Activity** Have students summarize the factors that led to the age of European exploration.

5. **English Language Arts Skills: Objective 5 (2.C):** Proofread writing for appropriateness of organization, content, and style **Activity** Have students work in pairs and proofread each other's answers to the Section 2 Critical Thinking questions on page 20.

# REVIEW CHAPTER 1

# EXPLORATION AND THE COLONIAL ERA

## HISTORY from VISUALS

### Interpreting the Painting

Ask students to study the painting and explain what they believe is occurring. Then ask them to suggest what thoughts the Native Americans in the painting might be experiencing. (*A group of Native Americans is beholding for the first time a European ship far out at sea. Students might say the Native Americans experienced a sense of wonder and excitement at seeing such a curious sight and also a sense of fear at witnessing something so strange and out of place.*)

**Extension** Ask students to write a brief dialogue that they imagine might have taken place among the Native Americans observing the ship.

## Time Line Discussion

Explain to students that this time line covers thousands of years of prehistory and early history.

· Ask students to identify the world culture that predated the Aztecs. (*Rome*)

· Ask students how long after the English defeated the Spanish Armada did they found the colony at Jamestown. (*19 years*)

· Ask students why 1763 was a significant year for the British. (*They greatly enlarged their empire with North America.*)

Native Americans observe the arrival of a European ship.

| AMERICAS WORLD | **B.C.*** | | **A.D.*** | | | |
|---|---|---|---|---|---|---|
| | 20,000 | 1000 | 1000 | 1100 | 1200 | 1300 |

**c. 20,000 B.C.** Asian peoples migrate to America.

**753 B.C.** Rome is founded.

**A.D. 1096** The Crusades begin.

**c. 1200** The Aztec settle the valley of Mexico.

**Early 1300s** Timbuktu becomes a center of Islamic learning.

\* B.C. corresponds to B.C.E., or "before the common era"
 A.D. corresponds to C.E., or "common era"

**2** CHAPTER 1 *Exploration and the Colonial Era*

## THEMES IN CHAPTER 1

### IMMIGRATION AND MIGRATION

Everyone in the United States has ancestors who originally came from somewhere else. All eras in U.S. history have been shaped by the movement of peoples across America in search of opportunity.

**See Teacher's Edition notes, pp. 5, 15.**

### DIVERSITY AND NATIONAL IDENTITY

European exploration led to the meeting of many cultures in the Americas. Drawn to North America from many countries, for many reasons, settlers carved out diverse colonies. An influx of immigrants and slaves made the colonies a cultural mosaic.

**See Teacher's Edition notes, pp. 6, 9, 18, 34.**

### SCIENCE AND TECHNOLOGY

New war technology gave European monarchs the tools to forge powerful nations. New maritime technology propelled these nations to sea. Later, the Enlightenment spread from Europe to the Americas, bringing with it a belief in reason and science that prompted many inventions and discoveries.

**See Teacher's Edition note, p. 36.**

### VOTING RIGHTS

English settlers had brought their political traditions and ideals with them, including the belief in self-government. Dissenters such as Roger Williams and Anne Hutchinson and dreamers such as William Penn dared to introduce such freedoms as religious tolerance and expanded suffrage.

**See Teacher's Edition note, p. 25.**

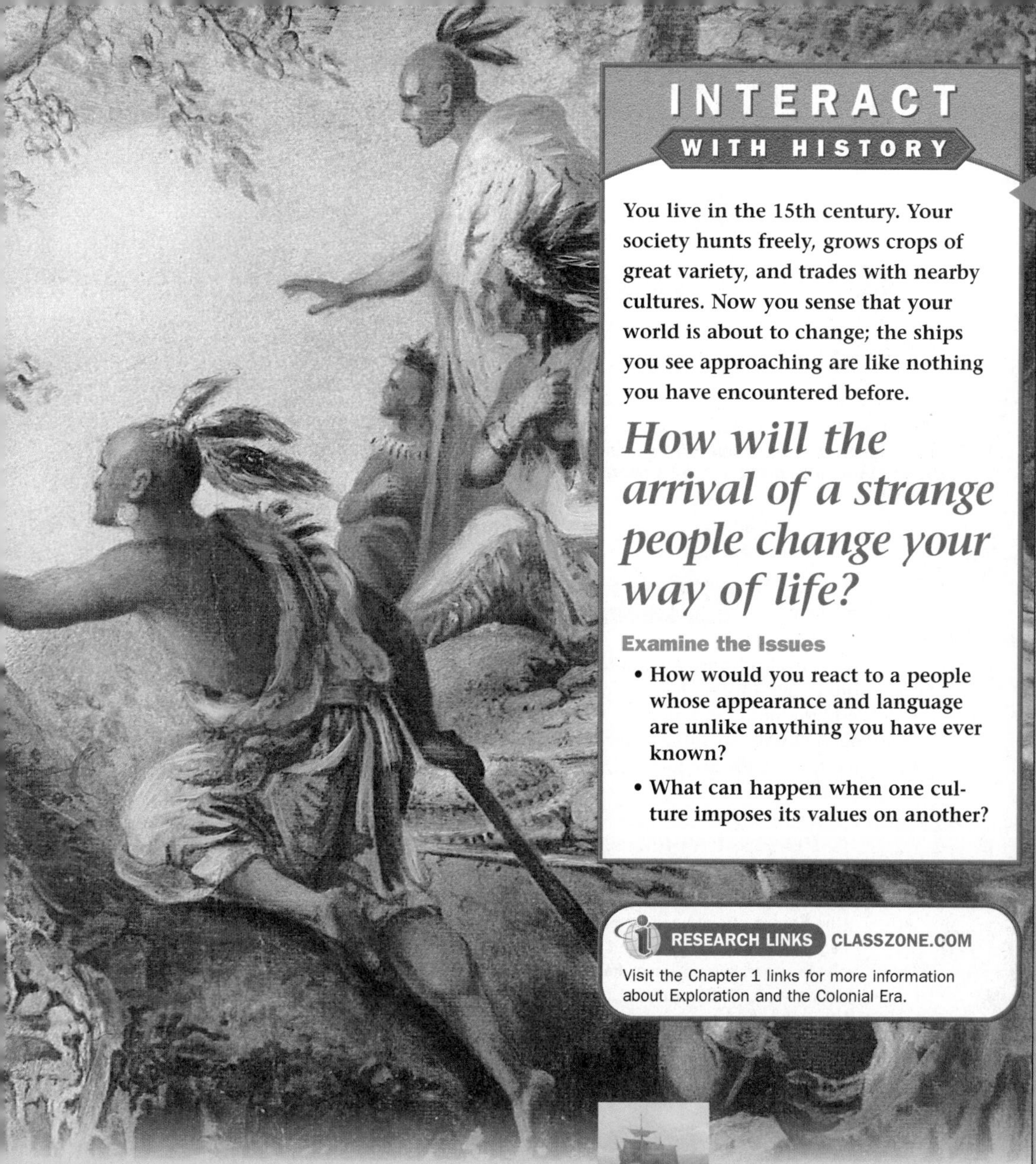

# INTERACT
## WITH HISTORY

You live in the 15th century. Your society hunts freely, grows crops of great variety, and trades with nearby cultures. Now you sense that your world is about to change; the ships you see approaching are like nothing you have encountered before.

## How will the arrival of a strange people change your way of life?

### Examine the Issues

- How would you react to a people whose appearance and language are unlike anything you have ever known?
- What can happen when one culture imposes its values on another?

---

**RESEARCH LINKS** CLASSZONE.COM

Visit the Chapter 1 links for more information about Exploration and the Colonial Era.

---

**1492** Columbus first reaches North America.

**1521** The Spanish destroy the Aztec empire.

**1607** Jamestown is founded.

**1620** "Pilgrims" settle in Plymouth.

**1681** William Penn founds Pennsylvania.

**1754** French and Indian War begins.

**1400**      **1500**      **1600**      **1700**

**1440** Johann Gutenberg develops his printing press.

**1543** The Reformation begins in England with the Act of Supremacy.

**1588** England defeats Spanish Armada.

**1642** English Civil War begins between royalist forces and parliamentary forces led by Oliver Cromwell.

**1763** With the Treaty of Paris, Britain acquires a vast North American empire.

REVIEW UNIT 3

---

# INTERACT
## WITH HISTORY

### Objectives

· To motivate students to learn more about the meeting of the Native American and European cultures
· To help students understand the consequences that arise when two or more cultures converge

### Examine the Issues

1. Have students consider how persons or groups normally react when encountering something strange and unknown.
2. Ask students whether they think one type of culture should be considered better than another.
3. Have students consider times when the United States tried to impose its will on another nation or people and discuss the consequences of such action.

---

## RECOMMENDED RESOURCES

### BOOKS FOR THE TEACHER

Davidson, Basil. *The Lost Cities of Africa.* Boston: Little, 1988.

Tuchman, Barbara. *A Distant Mirror.* New York: Ballantine, 1996. Riveting account of medieval Europe.

Jennings, Francis. *The Founders of America.* New York: Norton, 1993.

Weber, David J. *The Spanish Frontier in North America.* New Haven: Yale, 1992.

Wilson, James. *The Earth Shall Weep: A History of Native America.* Grove Press, 2000. Compelling narrative of Native American tribes and their histories.

### BOOKS FOR THE STUDENT

Champagne, Duane. *Native America.* Detroit: Visible Ink, 1994. Many tribes.

*The First Americans.* Alexandria, Va.: Time-Life, 1994.

### VIDEOS

*500 Nations.* Warner Home Video, 1995. An 8-part documentary series on the Indians of North America. Also available in CD-ROM.

*Colonial Economy.* CRM Films, 800-421-0833. Analyzes colonial economy.

### SOFTWARE

*Columbus: Day by Day.* CD-ROM. Educational Software Institute, 800-955-5570.

*History and Culture of Africa.* CD-ROM. Educational Software Institute.

### INTEGRATED TECHNOLOGY

For teacher support, visit . . .

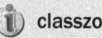 classzone.com

*Exploration and the Colonial Era* **3**

# OBJECTIVES

1. Describe the ancient cultures in the Americas.
2. Identify the diverse Native American groups in North America.
3. Describe West African societies of the 1400s.
4. Understand European societies of the 1400s and the forces that led them to undertake exploration.

## SKILLBUILDERS

· Geography Skillbuilder: region, location, p. 7
· Interpreting Visual Sources, p. 11

## CRITICAL THINKING

· Analyzing Effects, pp. 5, 13
· Summarizing, pp. 6, 13
· Making Inferences, pp. 8, 10, 13
· Comparing, p. 9
· Analyzing Causes, pp. 11, 13
· Developing Historical Perspective, p. 12

# Focus & Motivate

Have students read One American's Story on page 4 to learn how one woman helped preserve the knowledge and customs of her Native American culture. Ask students to describe traditions, memories, or family stories they would like to preserve for future generations.

# Instruct

## Instruct: Objective 1

### Ancient Cultures in the Americas
TAKS SS11 2(WG1.A)

· When did the first people come to the Americas?
· How did ancient American cultures change with the introduction of agriculture?

In-Depth Resources: Unit 1
· Guided Reading, p. 9

---

# The Americas, West Africa, and Europe

| MAIN IDEA | WHY IT MATTERS NOW | Terms & Names |
|---|---|---|
| On the eve of their interaction, Native American, West African, and European peoples lived in complex societies. | The interaction of these cultures helped create the present-day culture of the United States. | • nomadic    • Kongo<br>• Aztec    • Islam<br>• Anasazi    • Christianity<br>• Pueblo    • Reformation<br>• Iroquois    • Renaissance<br>• Benin |

U.S. History
8A, 8B, 20B, 21C, 22B, 22C, 24A, 24B, 24C, 24D, 24F, 24G, 25A, 25B, 25C, 25D

## One American's Story

Essie Parrish, a Native American spiritual leader and healer, kept alive stories from a time when her people, the Kashaya Pomo, flourished along the northern California coast. One day in 1958, she invited Robert Oswalt, an anthropologist at the University of California, to time travel with her to the 1540s. As Parrish spoke, the centuries rolled back.

**A PERSONAL VOICE** ESSIE PARRISH

"In the old days, before the white people came up here, there was a boat sailing on the ocean from the south. Because before that . . . [the Kashaya Pomo] had never seen a boat, they said, "Our world must be coming to an end. Couldn't we do something? This big bird floating on the ocean is from somewhere, probably from up high. . . ." [T]hey promised Our Father [a feast,] saying that destruction was upon them. When they had done so, they watched [the ship] sail way up north and disappear. . . . They were saying that nothing had happened to them —the big bird person had sailed northward without doing anything— because of the promise of a feast. . . . Consequently they held a feast and a big dance."

—quoted in *Kashaya Texts*

In this chapter, you will learn about three complex societies that met in North America in the late 1400s: the European, the West African, and the Native American. However, it is with the ancient peoples of the Americas that American history actually begins.

▲ Dressed for a ceremony in the 1950s, spiritual leader Essie Parrish wears a feathered headdress and holds two bead-covered staffs.

## 1 Ancient Cultures in the Americas

No one knows for sure when the first Americans arrived, but it may have been as long as 22,000 years ago. At that time, the glaciers of the last Ice Age had frozen

---

# PROGRAM RESOURCES

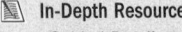 **In-Depth Resources: Unit 1**
· Guided Reading, p. 9
· Building Vocabulary, p. 13
· Skillbuilder Practice: Interpreting Maps, p. 14
· Reteaching Activity, p. 17
· Primary Sources: The Iroquois Constitution, p. 25

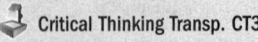 **Reading Study Guide** (English and Spanish), pp. 5–6

**Access for Students Acquiring English/ESL**
· Guided Reading, p. 13
· Skillbuilder Practice: Interpreting Maps, p. 17

**Formal Assessment**
· Section Quiz, p. 5

**Integrated Assessment**
· Rubrics

## INTEGRATED TECHNOLOGY

 **Critical Thinking Transp. CT35**
· Inventions, 1190–1500

 **Humanities Transp. HT2**
· Mimbres cache of ritual figures

 **classzone.com**

## TEXAS RESOURCES

 TAKS Spiraled Content Review

TAKS Practice Tests

TAKS Practice Transparencies TT1–3

TAKS Online Test Practice

vast quantities of the earth's water, lowering sea levels and possibly creating a land bridge between Asia and Alaska across what is now the Bering Strait. Ancient hunters may have trekked across the frozen land, known as Beringia, into North America.

**HUNTING AND GATHERING** Archaeologists believe that the earliest Americans lived as big-game hunters. That way of life changed around 12,000 to 10,000 years ago when temperatures warmed, glaciers melted, and sea levels rose once again. The land bridge disappeared under the Bering Sea, bringing to an end land travel between the Asian and North American continents. As the climate grew warmer, the large animals no longer thrived. People gradually switched to hunting smaller game and fish and gathering nuts and berries.

**AGRICULTURE DEVELOPS** While many ancient groups settled in North America, others continued south into what is now Mexico and South America. Between 10,000 and 5,000 years ago, an agricultural revolution quietly took place in what is now central Mexico. There, people began to plant crops. Eventually, agricultural techniques spread throughout the Americas.

The introduction of agriculture made it possible for people to settle in one place and to store surplus food. From this agricultural base developed larger communities. However, some Native American cultures never adopted agriculture and remained **nomadic,** moving from place to place in search of food and water. Other tribes mixed nomadic and non-nomadic lifestyles. Ⓐ

**MAYA, AZTEC, AND INCA SOCIETIES FLOURISH** The first empire of the Americas emerged as early as 1200 B.C. in what is now southern Mexico, where the Olmec people created a thriving civilization. In the wake of the Olmec's mysterious collapse, around 400 B.C., the Maya built a dynamic culture in Guatemala and the Yucatán Peninsula between A.D. 250 and 900. Later, the **Aztec** settled the Valley of Mexico in the 1200s and developed a sophisticated civilization.

In South America, the most prominent empire builders were the Inca. Around A.D. 1400, the Inca created a glittering empire that stretched nearly 2,500 miles along the mountainous western coast of South America.

**COMPLEX SOCIETIES ARISE IN NORTH AMERICA** In time, several North American groups, including the Hohokam and the **Anasazi** (ä′nə-sä′zē), introduced crops into the arid deserts of the Southwest. Later, between 300 B.C. and A.D. 1400, each group had established its own culture.

**MAIN IDEA**

**Analyzing Effects**

Ⓐ What were the effects of agriculture on the hunting and gathering people of the Americas?

*A. Answer* Agriculture made it possible for people to stay in one place and store surplus food.

▲ Hunters roaming over 10,000 years ago in what is now southern Arizona may have used this spear point to kill large prey.

Artist's rendering of Tenochtitlán, the Aztec capital in the middle of Lake Texcoco.
▼

**More About . . .**

**Essie Parrish**
Born in 1902, Essie Parrish learned her love of tradition from her grandmother and other elders. "I used to like to be around the old people," she recalled. "They used to talk of the old ways." Parrish, who served as spiritual leader of the Kashaya Pomo from 1943 until her death in 1979, worked with anthropologists to ensure that these ways would be recorded. She participated in more than two dozen films and helped compile a Kashaya dictionary and a collection of tribal songs and legends. By the time Parrish died, the Kashaya Pomo numbered less than 100.

**Tracing Themes**
**IMMIGRATION AND MIGRATION**

**Push-Pull Factors**
Immigration is the act of moving to a region of which one is not a native. Migration is the act of moving from one area or region to another. A number of "push-pull" factors have always compelled people to immigrate and migrate. These factors include the need for food, the need for adventure, the wish to escape from or be united with family members, and the need for economic and employment opportunities. While some immigrants sought religious and political freedom, others suffered the complete loss of freedom through enslavement.

REVIEW UNIT **5**

---

**DIFFERENTIATING INSTRUCTION** **LESS PROFICIENT READERS**

**Clarifying Ideas**

Before reading Section 1, have less proficient readers apply the five steps of the SQ3R study method:

**Survey** Skim paragraphs and topic headings and look over the two maps and the time lines.

**Question** Jot down any questions about the early peoples of the Americas and how they lived.

**Read** Read pages 4–13, looking for answers to the questions.

**Recite** Discuss and record the answers found.

**Review** Review the information, checking for answers to any questions that remain.

📄 Integrated Assessment
· Rubric 2

To the east and west of the Mississippi River, another series of complex societies developed—the Adena, the Hopewell, and the Mississippian. These societies excelled at trade and at building massive earthen mounds as tombs and as platforms for temples and other buildings. **B**

These early peoples were the ancestors of the many Native American groups that inhabited North America on the eve of its encounter with the European world.

## ❷ Native American Societies of the 1400s

The varied regions of the North American continent provided for many different ways of life. The native groups that populated the continent's coasts, deserts, and forests 500 years ago were as diverse as their surroundings.

**DIVERSE PEOPLES** The inhabitants of California adapted to the region's varied environments. The Kashaya Pomo lived in marshlands along the central coast, hunting waterfowl with slingshots and nets. To the north of them, the Yurok and Hupa searched the forests for acorns and trapped fish in mountain streams.

The waterways and forests of the Northwest Coast sustained large communities year-round. On a coastline that stretched from what is now southern Alaska to northern California, groups such as the Kwakiutl, Nootka, and Haida collected shellfish from the beaches and hunted the ocean for whales, sea otters, and seals.

In the dry Southwest, the **Pueblo** and Pima tribes, descendants of the Anasazi and Hohokam, lived in multistory houses made of stone or adobe, a sun-dried brick of clay and straw, and grew maize (corn), beans, melons, and squash.

Beneath the forest canopy of the Northeast, members of the **Iroquois** (ĭr′ə-kwoi′) nation hunted fish and game, such as wild turkeys, deer, and bear. In the Northeast, where winters could be long and harsh, Northeast peoples relied heavily on wild animals for clothing and food. In the warmer Southeast, groups lived mainly off the land, growing such crops as maize, squash, and beans.

A Northwest pow wow, or multitribal gathering, in Cashmere, Washington state, 1989. Gatherings like these preserve a 500-year cultural tradition. ▼

6    CHAPTER 1 *Exploration and the Colonial Era*

# North American Cultures in the 1400s

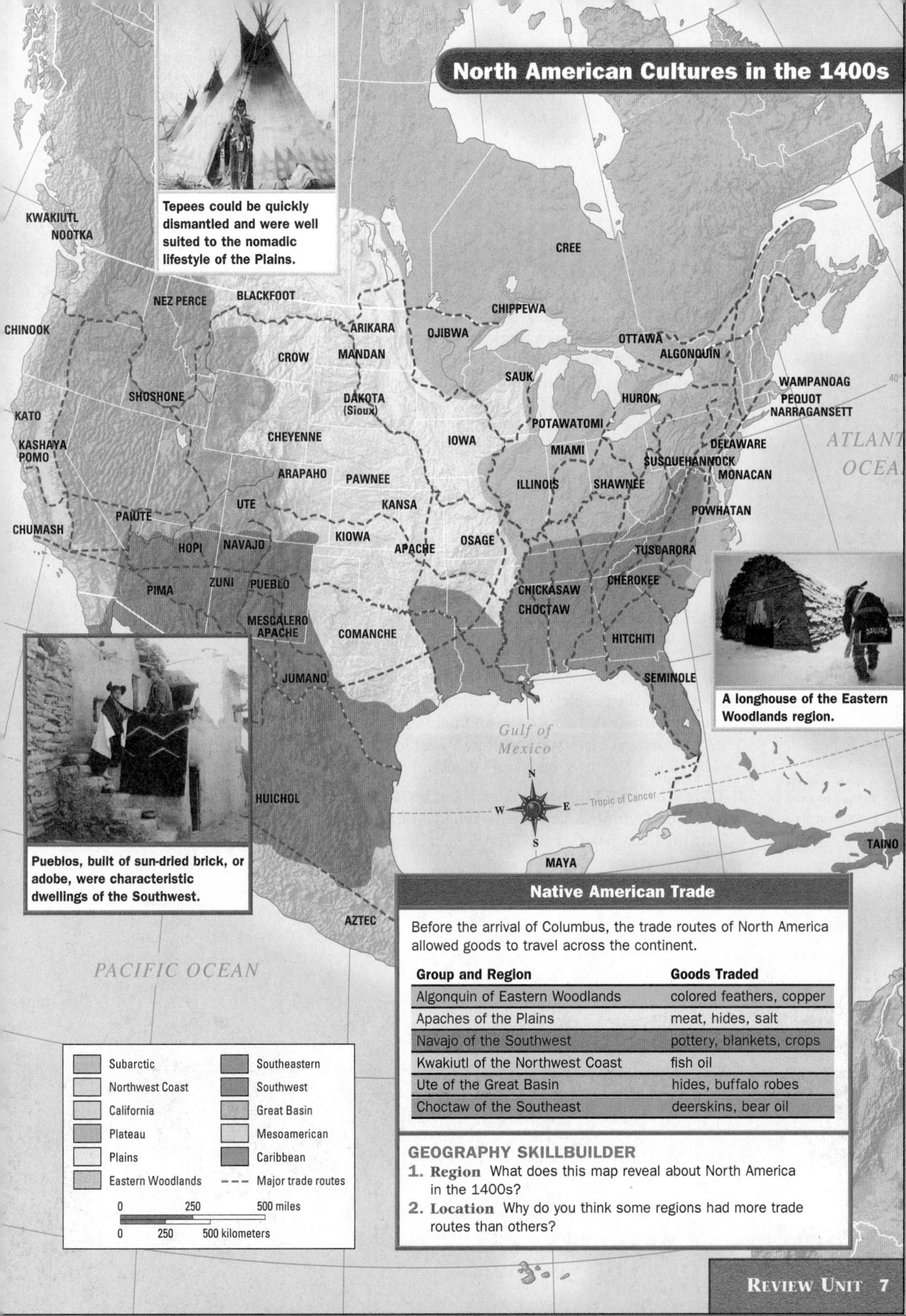

Tepees could be quickly dismantled and were well suited to the nomadic lifestyle of the Plains.

KWAKIUTL
NOOTKA
CHINOOK
NEZ PERCE   BLACKFOOT
CREE
CHIPPEWA
ARIKARA   OJIBWA   OTTAWA
CROW   MANDAN   ALGONQUIN
SHOSHONE   SAUK
DAKOTA   HURON   WAMPANOAG
(Sioux)   PEQUOT
KATO   CHEYENNE   POTAWATOMI   NARRAGANSETT
KASHAYA   IOWA   MIAMI   DELAWARE
POMO   ARAPAHO   PAWNEE   SUSQUEHANNOCK
ILLINOIS   SHAWNEE   MONACAN
UTE   KANSA   POWHATAN
PAIUTE
CHUMASH   KIOWA   OSAGE   TUSCARORA
HOPI   NAVAJO   APACHE
PIMA   ZUNI   PUEBLO   CHICKASAW   CHEROKEE
MESCALERO   CHOCTAW
APACHE   COMANCHE   HITCHITI
JUMANO   SEMINOLE
HUICHOL
ATLANT
OCEA
Pueblos, built of sun-dried brick, or adobe, were characteristic dwellings of the Southwest.
AZTEC
PACIFIC OCEAN
Gulf of Mexico
N
W   E
S
Tropic of Cancer
MAYA
TAINO

A longhouse of the Eastern Woodlands region.

### Legend
| | |
|---|---|
| Subarctic | Southeastern |
| Northwest Coast | Southwest |
| California | Great Basin |
| Plateau | Mesoamerican |
| Plains | Caribbean |
| Eastern Woodlands | – – – Major trade routes |

0   250   500 miles
0   250   500 kilometers

## Native American Trade

Before the arrival of Columbus, the trade routes of North America allowed goods to travel across the continent.

| Group and Region | Goods Traded |
|---|---|
| Algonquin of Eastern Woodlands | colored feathers, copper |
| Apaches of the Plains | meat, hides, salt |
| Navajo of the Southwest | pottery, blankets, crops |
| Kwakiutl of the Northwest Coast | fish oil |
| Ute of the Great Basin | hides, buffalo robes |
| Choctaw of the Southeast | deerskins, bear oil |

### GEOGRAPHY SKILLBUILDER
1. **Region**  What does this map reveal about North America in the 1400s?
2. **Location**  Why do you think some regions had more trade routes than others?

## HISTORY from VISUALS

### Interpreting the Map
Explain to students that this map is a special-purpose map. Point out that a special-purpose map shows information about a topic, such as rainfall, temperatures, or population distribution. Ask: What is the special topic of this map? *(Native American trade routes)*

## Connections Across Time
**1400S AND TODAY**

### Native American Business
Native Americans have found ways to thrive in today's business world. Since 1971, for instance, the Blackfeet Indian Writing Company, on the Blackfeet Indian Reservation in Montana, has been producing writing instruments, stationaries, and coasters for office supply dealers throughout the country. More recently, the descendants of the Oglala Lakota Sioux chief, Red Cloud, have created a successful business selling tipis. On a more individual level, some Native Americans have moved higher and higher up the corporate ladder in recent years. One such climber is Tom Smith, a Cherokee and CEO of a $23 million plastic-molding firm in Ohio.

---

**ACTIVITY**   SKILLBUILDER LESSON    BLOCK SCHEDULING

### Interpreting Maps

**Explaining the Skill**  Tools for understanding maps include:
· The *legend* shows at a glance what each color or symbol represents.
· The *compass rose* shows the map's orientation by pointing to the north.
· The *scale* indicates how much actual distance is represented on the map.

**Applying the Skill**  Ask students to point out the legend and scale on the map above. Then ask the following questions: What cultural region is northernmost on this map? *(Cree)* In which region did trade cross bodies of water? *(Eastern Woodlands)* About how far, in miles, were the Ojibwa people from the Hopi? *(About 1,250 miles)*

In-Depth Resources: Unit 1
· Skillbuilder Practice: Interpreting Maps, p. 14

## More About . . .

### The Power of Dreams

Native Americans throughout the Americas believed that spirits spoke to them in dreams and visions. One widespread vision preserved in the oral histories of Native Americans across the continents involved the coming of light-skinned strangers. A few, such as the Aztec, believe the strangers were gods. Many others saw them as destroyers. Recalled one Lassik woman, "My grandpa, before white people came, had a dream. . . . My grandpa say: 'White Rabbit'—he mean white people—'gonta devour our grass, our seed, our living. We won't have nothing.'"

## Instruct: Objective ❸

### West African Societies of the 1400s

TAKS SS11 5(US24.B)

· What were the three major kingdoms of West Africa?

· How did these kingdoms organize trade?

 In-Depth Resources: Unit 1
· Guided Reading, p. 9

---

**COMMON CHARACTERISTICS** Many of the Native American cultures had in common certain patterns of trade, attitudes toward land use, religious beliefs, and social values. As in other parts of the world, trade helped the spread of customs and beliefs. Tribes traded among each other both locally and over long distances. So extensive was the network of forest trails and river roads that an English sailor named David Ingram claimed in 1568 to have walked along Native American trade routes all the way from the Gulf of Mexico to Nova Scotia.

Native Americans traded many things, but land was not one of them. Land was regarded as the source of life, not as a commodity to be sold. "We cannot sell the lives of men and animals," said one Blackfoot chief in the 1800s, "therefore we cannot sell this land." **C**

Nearly all Native Americans thought of the natural world as filled with spirits. Every object—both living and nonliving—possessed a voice that might be heard if one listened closely. Some cultures worshiped one supreme being, variously called "Great Spirit," "Great Mystery," or "the Creative Power."

The basic unit of organization among all Native American groups was the family, which included aunts, uncles, cousins, and other relatives. Some tribes further organized the families into clans, or groups of families descended from a common ancestor.

In the late 1400s, on the eve of the first encounter with Europeans, the rhythms of Native American family life were highly developed. All phases of a person's life—birth, marriage, and death—were guided by traditions that often went back hundreds or perhaps thousands of years. On the other side of the Atlantic, in West Africa, customs equally ancient guided another diverse group of people.

## ❸ West African Societies of the 1400s

Like North America, West Africa in the 1400s was home to a variety of long-established, sophisticated societies. From this region, especially from the coasts, originated most of the people who were enslaved and brought to the Americas in the centuries that followed. Their African traditions and beliefs played a major role in forming American history and culture. Notable among West African societies in the late 1400s were three powerful kingdoms: Songhai, Benin, and Kongo.

**THE KINGDOM OF SONGHAI** From about 600 to 1600, a succession of empires—first Ghana, then Mali, and finally Songhai—gained power and wealth by controlling the trans-Sahara trade. The rulers of these empires grew rich by taxing the

A desert caravan approaches the fabled Songhai city of Timbuktu. ▼

**MAIN IDEA**

*Making Inferences*
**C** Why would Native American attitudes toward land ownership lead to conflict with Europeans?

*C Answer*
Europeans, who believed in private property, would try to privatize land and stop Native Americans from using it.

---

| DIFFERENTIATING INSTRUCTION | GIFTED AND TALENTED | ⓘ classzone.com |

### A Virtual Field Trip

Have students familiar with the Internet go to classzone.com or other Internet sites to choose one of the topic areas to visit on a virtual field trip. Among the possibilities might be Columbus, the Maya, or the Aztecs. Have students create a plan for a Web site that would take students on a virtual field trip involving the topic they choose.

To share their prospective Web sites with their classmates, students can create a poster or storyboard that shows navigational paths for the site, pictures that might be included, and possible maps, graphs, or charts. Suggest that students circulate around the room making notes on the Web sites they find most informative.

goods that passed through their realms. In 1067 an Arab geographer in Spain, named Al Bakri, described the duties (import and export taxes) levied in Ghana.

### A PERSONAL VOICE AL BAKRI

" For every donkey loaded with salt that enters the country, the king takes a duty of one golden dinar [about one-eighth ounce of gold], and two dinars from every one that leaves. From a load of copper the duty due to the king is five mithquals [also about one-eighth ounce of gold], and from a load of merchandise ten mithquals. . . . The [gold] nuggets found in all the mines . . . are reserved for the king, only gold dust being left for the people. "

—quoted in *Africa in the Days of Exploration*

With such wealth, the rulers who controlled the north-south trade routes could raise large armies and conquer new territory. They could also build cities, administer laws, and support the arts and education.

**KINGDOMS OF BENIN AND KONGO** At its height in the 1500s, Songhai's power extended across much of West Africa. However, it did not control the forest kingdoms along the southern coast. In the 1400s, one of these kingdoms, **Benin,** dominated a large region around the Niger Delta. Leading the expansion was a powerful oba, or ruler, named Ewuare, who developed Benin City.

Within another stretch of rain forest, in West Central Africa, the powerful kingdom of **Kongo** arose on the lower Congo (Zaire) River. In the late 1400s, Kongo consisted of a series of small kingdoms ruled by a single leader called the *manikongo*, who lived in what is today Angola.

**WEST AFRICAN CULTURE** Most West Africans lived in small villages, where life revolved around family, the community, and tradition. Bonds of kinship—that is, family ties—formed the basis of most aspects of life.

Political leaders claimed authority on the basis of religion. Although West Africans might worship a variety of gods and ancestral spirits, most believed in a single creator.

Throughout West Africa, people supported themselves by farming, herding, hunting, fishing, and by mining and trading. Almost all groups believed in collective ownership of land. Individuals farmed the land, but it reverted to family or village ownership when not in use. **D**

**TRADING PATTERNS WITH THE WIDER WORLD** By the 1400s, West Africa had long been connected to the wider world through trade. The city of Timbuktu was the hub of a well-established trading network that connected most of West Africa to the ports of North Africa, and through these ports to markets in Europe and Asia. Along trade routes across the Sahara Desert, merchants carried goods from Mediterranean cities and salt from Saharan mines to exchange for gold, ivory, and dyed cotton cloth.

Along with goods, traders from North Africa also brought across the Sahara the Islamic faith, which increasingly influenced West African cultures. **Islam** is a monotheistic religion—that is, one based on the belief in a single god. The religion of Islam was founded in Arabia in 622 by the prophet Muhammad and spread quickly across the Middle East and North Africa.

---

**MAIN IDEA**

Comparing
**D** What did the kingdoms of West Africa have in common?

*D Answer*
Songhai, Benin, and Kongo all had strong governments and powerful rulers; the ordinary people lived in rural villages, where their lives centered on family and tradition.

---

### HISTORICAL SPOTLIGHT

#### ISLAM

Islam was founded by the prophet Muhammad (about A.D. 570–632), who worked as a merchant in Mecca, a trading city on the Arabian peninsula. When he was about 40, he believed the angel Gabriel appeared to him and told him to preach a new religion to the Arabs. This religion became known as Islam, which in Arabic means "surrender [to Allah]." (*Allah* is the Arabic word for God.) The followers of Islam are called Muslims, "those who submit to God's will."

The words that Muhammad received from the angel were recorded by his followers in the Qur'an, the holy book of Islam. The Qur'an teaches that "there is no God but Allah, and Muhammad is His Prophet." The Qur'an also sets forth certain duties for righteous Muslims, including a series of daily prayers, the giving of charity, and a pilgrimage to the holy city of Mecca.

---

### Tracing Themes
**DIVERSITY AND NATIONAL IDENTITY**

#### Three African Kingdoms
The West African kingdoms were diverse in a number of ways, including the varied physical environments and the cultures that developed there. The savanna kingdom of Songhai was heir to a long tradition of trade with North Africa, including the legendary gold-salt trade. It had a strong Muslim influence. The rain forest kingdoms of Benin and Kongo were more compact. Each arose along a major river—Benin on the Niger and Kongo on the Congo River. All three kingdoms dominated tribes in the region and molded them into a larger political unit.

### More About . . .

#### West African Society
In West Africa, the task of preserving people's history belonged to the *griots*—a class of professional storytellers. Traditionally assigned to important families or rulers, griots spent years learning and memorizing all the important facts about a people. In addition, they served as advisers, masters of ceremony, and official spokespersons. The first enslaved Africans to arrive in the Americas carried this tradition of storytelling with them and used it as a way to keep alive their connections with the ancestral homeland.

### HISTORICAL SPOTLIGHT

#### Islam
Ask students to begin a chart comparing three of the world's monotheistic religions: Christianity, Islam, and Judaism. Suggest that they use the following headings to organize their research: Name of Supreme Being, Holy Book, Duties or Beliefs, Key Prophets or Founders, Holy Cities or Other Sites.

**REVIEW UNIT** 9

---

**ACTIVITY** | **COOPERATIVE LEARNING**  **BLOCK SCHEDULING**

### Planning an Itinerary

**Class Time** One class period

**Task** Planning an itinerary for a merchant traveling from Tripoli to Timbuktu in about the year 1500

**Purpose** To help students understand the economic exchanges that fueled the growth of West African empires

**Directions** Assign groups of students to plan a trading expedition from North Africa to Timbuktu. Students should determine a route map, trade items carried to Timbuktu, trade items sought in Timbuktu, numbers of camels, estimated travel time, and so on. (Arabian camels can carry an average of about 330 pounds, travel about 3 miles per hour, and typically cover up to 25 miles a day.)

📖 Integrated Assessment
· Rubric 5

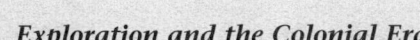

## Instruct: Objective ④

**European Societies of the 1400s**
TAKS SS11 2(WH23.A)

· How was society organized in medieval Europe?

· What was the center of daily life in medieval Europe?

· What factors prompted Europe to enter an age of exploration?

 In-Depth Resources: Unit 1
· Guided Reading, p. 9

### KEY PLAYER

**"King Isabella"**
Tell students that Isabella was an extraordinary woman in many ways. Once, when she was well into her fourth pregnancy, she insisted on joining her husband away at a battle. When someone tried to discourage her from going, the queen replied, "Glory is not won without danger." She was an early advocate of the rights of Native Americans. When Christopher Columbus first returned from the Americas—carrying a number of Native Americans to be used as slaves—the queen ordered that some of them be released. Discuss with students why Isabella's traits might have made her such an impressive leader.

**THE PORTUGUESE** Mariners from Portugal made trading contacts along the West African coast starting in the 1440s. These early contacts with Portuguese traders had two significant consequences for West Africa and the Americas. First, direct trade between the Portuguese and the coastal people of West Africa bypassed the routes across the Sahara and pulled the coastal region into a closer relationship with Europe. Second, the Portuguese began the European trade in enslaved West Africans.

## ④ European Societies of the 1400s

In the late 1400s, most Europeans, like most Native Americans and most Africans, lived in small villages, bound to the land and to rhythms of life that had been in place for centuries. For the majority of Europeans, change came slowly.

**THE SOCIAL HIERARCHY** European communities were based on social hierarchy, that is, they were organized according to rank. At the top of the hierarchy were monarchs and the aristocracy, the landowning elite, who held most of the wealth and power. Members of the clergy also ranked high in the social order. At the bottom were agricultural laborers, or peasants.

Few individuals rose above the social position of their birth. One group that did achieve mobility was the growing number of artisans and merchants, the people who created and traded goods for money. There were relatively few members of this group in the 1400s. However, the profit they earned from trade would eventually make them a valuable source of tax revenue to monarchs seeking to finance costly overseas exploration and expansion. **E**

**CHRISTIANITY SHAPES THE EUROPEAN OUTLOOK** The dominant religion in Western Europe was **Christianity,** a religion based on the life and teachings of Jesus. The leader of the church—the pope—and his bishops held great political as well as spiritual authority.

As the influence of Christianity and Islam spread, the two religions came into conflict. In 1096, Christian armies from all over Western Europe responded to the church's call to force the Muslims out of the Holy Land around Jerusalem. Over the next two centuries, Europeans launched the Crusades, a series of military expeditions to the Middle East in the name of Christianity.

In the end, these bloody Crusades failed to "rescue" the Holy Land, but they resulted in two consequences that encouraged European exploration and expansion. First, the Crusades opened up Asian trade routes, supplying Europeans with luxuries from the east, especially spices such as cinnamon, cloves, nutmeg, and pepper. Second, the Crusades weakened the power of European nobles, many of whom lost their lives or fortunes in the wars. Monarchs eventually took advantage of the nobles' weakened ranks to consolidate their own power.

By the early 1500s, many church leaders and ordinary people were eager for reforms. This desire for change led to a movement called the **Reformation,** which criticized church practices and challenged the authority of the pope.

Mini-Lesson 4:
SS11 2(US10.A)

**"KING" ISABELLA**
**1451–1504**
Queen Isabella, who played a central role in European exploration by sponsoring Christopher Columbus's voyages to the Americas, made her mark on the Old World as well. As co-ruler of Spain, Isabella actively participated in her country's religious and military affairs.

In championing Spain's Catholicism, the queen often fought openly with the pope to make sure that her candidates were appointed to positions in the Spanish church. In addition, Isabella had tasted battle far more than most rulers, either male or female. The queen rode among her troops in full armor, personally commanding them in Ferdinand's absence. Whenever Isabella appeared on a horse, her troops shouted, "Castile, Castile, for our King Isabella!"

**MAIN IDEA**

**Making Inferences**
**E** Why were merchants able to achieve social mobility?

*E Answer*
Their growing wealth made them powerful members of society.

**Background**
Spices were important in the Middle Ages when European farmers preserved meat by packing it between layers of salt. Spices helped disguise the bad taste of the meat.

**10** CHAPTER 1 *Exploration and the Colonial Era*

---

**DIFFERENTIATING INSTRUCTION** | **LESS PROFICIENT READERS**

**Cause-and-Effect Chart**

Make sure students understand the meaning of cause and effect. Then use the graphic organizer shown to help students identify the causes and effects of the Crusades and the Reformation. Direct them to the section headed "Christianity Shapes the European Outlook," and ask *why* the Europeans went on the Crusades. Write the answer in the "Effect" box.

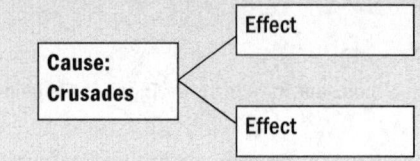

### History Through *Art*

**JUNE, *FROM* LES TRES RICHES HEURES DU DUC DE BERRY**

This miniature painting, representing the month of June, is a page from a prayer book calendar begun by the Limbourg brothers around the year 1416. The book was made for a younger son of the French king, and tells us a great deal about the aristocratic view of the European social order.

In the background, the walls of the city of Paris protect a palace and the royal chapel, buildings that represent the two most powerful institutions in medieval European society: church and aristocracy.

In the foreground, peasants mow the fields, in an orderly world of peace and tranquility. However, the image is a fantasy, an idealized vision painted to please the aristocracy. There is no hint of the peasants' grinding poverty or of the violence of the Hundred Years' War that was at that moment devastating northern France.

**SKILLBUILDER** Interpreting Visual Sources
1. What does the painting tell you about the importance of gender in the division of labor during the 1400s?
2. Why might images of poverty have displeased the aristocracy?

**SEE SKILLBUILDER HANDBOOK, PAGE R23.**

### History Through *Art*

Tell students that there were three Limbourg brothers, Paul, Hermann, and Jehanequin (Jean). The brothers' famous prayer book calendar includes 12 paintings—one representing each month. The most famous piece from the calendar is often thought to be September, which depicts peasants harvesting grapes and carrying them into a beautifully detailed chalet. Not long after they completed the calendar book, all three brothers died, apparently from an epidemic.

**SKILLBUILDER ANSWERS**
1. Both are doing heavy manual labor.
2. The aristocracy may not have wanted to be reminded of the poverty suffered by peasants on their land.

---

**MAIN IDEA**

**Analyzing Causes**

**F** How did religious events in Europe help spur exploration and settlement of new lands?

**Vocabulary**
**medieval:** of or during the Middle Ages, often dated from A.D. 476 to 1453

The Reformation led to a religious schism, or split, throughout Europe: those who supported the Reformation became known as Protestants because of their opposition to the established Catholic church. This split deepened the rivalries among European nations during the period of North American colonization a century later and sent some Protestants and some Catholics across the Atlantic to seek religious freedom. **F**

**EUROPEAN NATIONS TAKE SHAPE** During the 1400s, four major nations were taking shape in Europe: Portugal, Spain, France, and England. Ambitious monarchs extended their reach by collecting new taxes, raising professional armies, and forming stronger governments. Among their new allies were the merchants, who paid taxes in exchange for the protection and expansion of trade.

**THE RENAISSANCE** The 1400s also saw a cultural awakening in Europe, known as the **Renaissance** (rĕn′ĭ-säns′)—a term meaning "rebirth" of the kind of interest in the physical world that had characterized ancient Greece and Rome. In the arts, this meant rejecting the flat, two-dimensional images of medieval painting in favor of the deep perspectives and fully rounded forms of ancient sculpture and painting. Starting in Italy, a region stimulated by commercial contact with Asia and Africa, the Renaissance soon spread throughout Europe. Renaissance artists created works of lasting influence, while European scholars reexamined the texts of ancient philosophers, mathematicians, geographers, and scientists.

Although their themes were still often religious in nature, Renaissance artists portrayed their subjects more realistically than had medieval artists, using new

*F Answer* The Reformation created opposing groups of Christians, some of whom sought religious freedom in North America.

### More About . . .

**The Renaissance**
The name *Renaissance* originated from a French term meaning "rebirth." The event that played perhaps the most significant role in the spread of Renaissance ideas and styles was the invasion of Italy in 1494 by France, which had long claimed sovereignty over the kingdom of Naples. While French forces scored several early victories, an alliance of Italian powers eventually forced them to retreat. French troops returned home with stories of the splendors of Italy and soon word had spread of the extraordinary events taking place on the Italian peninsula.

---

**DIFFERENTIATING INSTRUCTION**     **GIFTED AND TALENTED**

### Researching the Crusades

Have interested students research the Crusades and compose reports and displays to present to the rest of the class. Suggest that students work together to decide who will focus on topics such as Christianity and Islam, knighthood, or trade, during this period.

 Integrated Assessment
· Rubric 4

## HISTORY from VISUALS

### Interpreting Infographics

Be sure students know the meaning of words such as *lateen*, *sternpost*, and *rudder* as they read the diagram.

**Extension** Have students write a short essay explaining how the caravel proved the old adage, "Bigger is not always better."

 Critical Thinking Transparencies CT35
· Inventions, 1190–1500

## Science & Technology

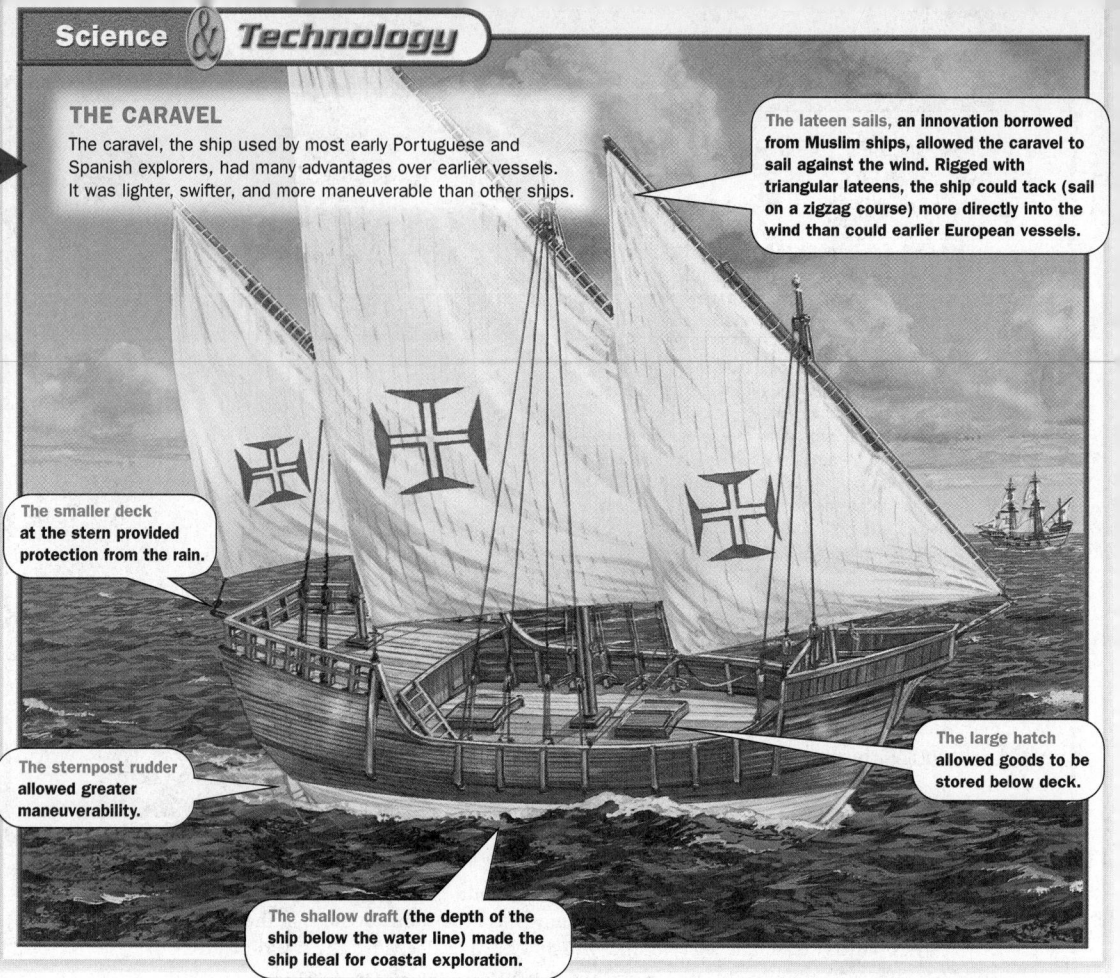

### THE CARAVEL

The caravel, the ship used by most early Portuguese and Spanish explorers, had many advantages over earlier vessels. It was lighter, swifter, and more maneuverable than other ships.

**The lateen sails, an innovation borrowed from Muslim ships, allowed the caravel to sail against the wind. Rigged with triangular lateens, the ship could tack (sail on a zigzag course) more directly into the wind than could earlier European vessels.**

**The smaller deck at the stern provided protection from the rain.**

**The sternpost rudder allowed greater maneuverability.**

**The large hatch allowed goods to be stored below deck.**

**The shallow draft (the depth of the ship below the water line) made the ship ideal for coastal exploration.**

techniques such as perspective. Leonardo da Vinci, investigating how things worked, kept notebooks in which he made detailed drawings of human anatomy and of his inventions, including a flying machine. This energetic spirit of inquiry infused the early explorers and adventurers who, like Christopher Columbus, grew up during the Renaissance.

The spread of the Renaissance was advanced by Johann Gutenberg's introduction of printing from movable type in the 1450s. This development made books easier and cheaper to produce, which aided the spread of ideas.

The Renaissance encouraged people to think of themselves as individuals, to have confidence in their capabilities, and to look forward to the fame their achievements might bring. This attitude prompted many to seek glory through adventure, discovery, and conquest. **G**

**EUROPE ENTERS A NEW AGE OF EXPANSION** The European interest in overseas expansion probably began in the 1200s with the journey of Marco Polo to China. Later, the publication in 1477 of the first printed edition of Polo's vivid —and sometimes exaggerated—account caused renewed interest in the East. Like other merchants, Polo traveled to Asia by land. The expense and peril involved in such journeys led Europeans to seek alternative routes. In the 1400s, Europeans used the work of Ptolomy, a second-century scholar, along with the work of Arab and

*G Answer* The Renaissance renewed interest in the physical world and prompted many to seek glory through exploration and conquest.

**MAIN IDEA**

**Developing Historical Perspective**
**G** How did Renaissance attitudes encourage the European age of exploration?

**12** CHAPTER 1 *Exploration and the Colonial Era*

---

**DIFFERENTIATING INSTRUCTION** | **LESS PROFICIENT READERS**

### Summarizing

In order to help students keep track of the various factors that contributed to the beginnings of European exploration, have them create and complete a chart such as the one shown here.

| Factors Influencing Exploration | |
|---|---|
| Factor | Result |
|  |  |
|  |  |
|  |  |
|  |  |

Jewish scholars, to revive the art of cartography, or mapmaking. Although imperfect, the new maps inspired Europeans to start exploring for water routes to Asia.

European monarchs had powerful motives to finance the search for new lands and trading routes: they needed money to maintain their growing armies and administrative bureaucracies. By the mid-1400s, Europe's gold and silver mines were running low. So the monarchs of Portugal, Spain, France, and England began looking overseas for wealth.

Beginning in the 1300s, monarchs invested some of their tax revenues in new weapons—such as longbows and cannons—which they used to limit the power of the independent nobles. These new weapons, along with the hand-held firearms that were developed in the 1400s, also gave them military advantages over the Africans and Native Americans whom they later encountered.

**SAILING TECHNOLOGY IMPROVES** European ship captains in the 1400s experimented with new sailing vessels such as the caravel and navigating tools such as the compass and the astrolabe, which helped sailors plot direction at sea. They also took advantage of sailing innovations, like those that allowed caravels to sail against the wind.

One leader in developing and employing these innovations was Prince Henry the Navigator of Portugal, who gathered mariners, geographers, and navigators to his court. According to a contemporary chronicler, Gomes Eanes de Zurara, the prince's driving motivation was the need to know.

For almost 40 years, Prince Henry sent his captains sailing south along the west coast of Africa. Exploration continued after the prince's death. In 1488, Portuguese sailor Bartolomeu Dias rounded the southern tip of Africa; fellow Portuguese explorer Vasco da Gama reached India ten years later. By sailing around Africa to eastern Asia via the Indian Ocean, Portuguese traders were able to cut their costs and increase their profits.

As cartographers redrew their maps to show this eastern route to Asia, an Italian sea captain named Christopher Columbus believed there was an even shorter route—one that headed west across the Atlantic.

**Vocabulary**
**bureaucracies**: government departments staffed with nonelected officials

**MAIN IDEA**

**Summarizing**
**H** What military advantages did Europeans have over Africans and Native Americans?

*H Answer*
Europeans had more sophisti-catefd weapons

*"The best ships that sailed the seas . . ."*
ALVISE DA CADAMOSTO, OF THE CARAVEL

**More About . . .**

**Prince Henry the Navigator**
Prince Henry may have been nicknamed the Navigator, but he rarely went exploring himself; instead, he planned and financed explorations. His own biggest adventure came at age 19, when he and his two brothers, hoping to prove themselves worthy of knighthood, led an armada and captured Ceuta, a Muslim stronghold on the African coast opposite Gibraltar.

## Assess & Reteach

**SECTION 1 ASSESSMENT**
Have students work together to answer the questions. Tell them to note the locations of the answers in the text.

Formal Assessment
· Section Quiz, p. 5

**SELF-ASSESSMENT**
Have students complete these two sentences:

Before reading this section, I thought the history of our nation began with _____.
Now I think it should begin with _____ because _____.

**RETEACH**
Use the Guided Reading Worksheet for Section 1 to help review the main ideas of the section.

In-Depth Resources: Unit 1
· Reteaching Activity, p. 17

---

## SECTION 1 ASSESSMENT

**1. TERMS & NAMES** For each term or name, write a sentence explaining its significance.

- nomadic
- Aztec
- Anasazi
- Pueblo
- Iroquois
- Benin
- Kongo
- Islam
- Christianity
- Reformation
- Renaissance

**MAIN IDEA**

**2. TAKING NOTES**
For each region and time period shown, write 2 or 3 sentences to describe how it was affected by trade and commerce.

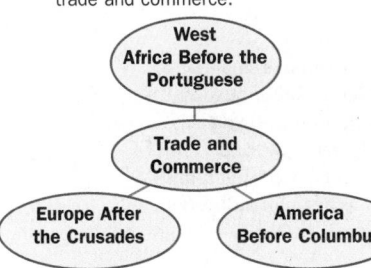

West Africa Before the Portuguese

Trade and Commerce

Europe After the Crusades

America Before Columbus

**CRITICAL THINKING**

**3. MAKING INFERENCES**
Why do you think other European nations lagged behind Portugal in overseas exploration? Support your reasons with details from the text.
**Think About:**
• the geography of Portugal
• the power of monarchs in the 1400s
• the economic and political situation of European nations during this time

**4. ANALYZING CAUSES**
What factors do you think contributed to the thriving trade system that flourished in West Africa? Use evidence from the text to support your response.

**5. ANALYZING EFFECTS**
What effects did Portuguese trade have on West Africa?

---

**1. TERMS & NAMES**
nomadic, p. 5
Aztec, p. 5
Anasazi, p. 5
Pueblo, p. 6
Iroquois, p. 6
Benin, p. 9
Kongo, p. 9
Islam, p. 9
Christianity, p. 10
Reformation, p. 11
Renaissance, p. 11

**2. TAKING NOTES**
**West Africa** The trans-Sahara trade brought wealth, power, and the Islamic faith.
**Europe** The Crusades opened up Asian trade routes, bringing luxuries from the east.
**America** A complex system of trade routes allowed goods to be transported across the continent.

**3. MAKING INFERENCES**
Portugal was relatively close to North Africa. In addition, new sailing vessels like the caravel helped in exploration.

**4. ANALYZING CAUSES**
The trading network connected most of West Africa to the ports of North Africa, and through these ports to markets in Europe and Asia.

**5. ANALYZING EFFECTS**
The Portuguese began the European trade in enslaved West Africans.

## OBJECTIVES

**1** Describe the Spanish exploration of the Americas and its effects on Native Americans, Africans, and Europeans.

**2** Describe the pattern of conquest used by the Spanish.

**3** Summarize the goals of Spanish explorers and settlers and to understand why Native Americans resisted.

### SKILLBUILDERS

· Geography Skillbuilder: human-environment interaction, p. 15; movement, place, p. 17

### CRITICAL THINKING

· Analyzing Events, p. 15
· Summarizing, p. 16
· Analyzing Motives, p. 18
· Analyzing Effects, p. 20
· Drawing Conclusions, p. 20

## Focus & Motivate

Ask students how it would feel to venture into the unknown, where there are no accounts from someone who has gone before, no maps, and no assurance of ever coming back. Point out that Christopher Columbus did just that.

## Instruct

### Instruct: Objective **1**

**Columbus Crosses the Atlantic**
TAKS SS11 2(WG1.B)
· What did Columbus encounter when he reached the Americas?
· What impact did Columbus's voyages have on Native Americans, Africans, and Europeans?
· What was the Columbian Exchange?

📄 **In-Depth Resources: Unit 1**
· Guided Reading, p. 10

👁 **Electronic Library of Primary Sources**
· *from* A letter to the Treasurer of Spain, 1493 by C. Columbus

---

# Spanish North America

| MAIN IDEA | WHY IT MATTERS NOW | Terms & Names |
|---|---|---|
| Beginning with the voyage of Christopher Columbus, the Spanish built a vast colonial empire in the Americas. | The Spanish left an impact on the cultures of North and South America that helped to shape present-day America. | • Christopher Columbus • Taino • Treaty of Tordesillas • Columbian Exchange    • conquistador • Hernándo Cortés • Montezuma • *mestizo* • *encomienda* • New Spain • New Mexico |

🔷 **U.S. History**
8A, 8B, 24B, 25A, 25B, 25C, 25D

### One European's Story

On August 3, 1492, the Genoese mariner **Christopher Columbus** set out on a bold expedition: to find a route to Asia by sailing west across the Atlantic Ocean. It was a journey destined to change the course of world history. A seeker of fame and fortune, Columbus began his travel journal by restating the deal he had struck with the Spanish rulers financing his voyage.

**A PERSONAL VOICE** CHRISTOPHER COLUMBUS

" Based on the information that I had given Your Highnesses about the land of India and about a Prince who is called the Great Khan [of China] . . . Your Highnesses decided to send me . . . to the regions of India, to see . . . the peoples and the lands, and to learn of . . . the measures which could be taken for their conversion to our Holy Faith. . . . I was to go by way of the west, whence until today we do not know with certainty that anyone has gone. "

—*The Log of Christopher Columbus*

Columbus never reached Asia. He landed on an island he thought was off the coast of Asia but was actually in the Caribbean Sea. Instead of finding the Great Khan, Columbus set in motion a process that brought together the American, European, and African worlds.

▲ Christopher Columbus from a painting done in 1519.

## **1** Columbus Crosses the Atlantic

In October 1492, roughly two months after leaving Spain, Columbus's small fleet of ships, the *Niña*, the *Pinta*, and the *Santa María*, reached land. Columbus went ashore, where he encountered a group of people who would become known as the **Taino** (tī′nō), from their word for "noble ones." He planted Spanish banners and renamed their island San Salvador ("Holy Savior"), claiming it for Spain. Columbus spent 96 days exploring four coral islands in the Bahamas and the coastlines of two larger Caribbean islands, known today as Cuba and Hispaniola.

---

## PROGRAM RESOURCES

📄 **In-Depth Resources: Unit 1**
· Guided Reading, p. 10
· Skillbuilder Practice: Using the Internet, p. 15
· Reteaching Activity, p. 18
· Outline Map: Spain Explores North America, pp. 23–24
· Primary Sources: Journals of Christopher Columbus, pp. 26–27
· Literature: from *Memoirs of Christopher Columbus*, pp. 30–31

📄 **Reading Study Guide**
(English and Spanish), pp. 7–8

📄 **Access for Students Acquiring English/ESL**
· Guided Reading, p. 14
· Skillbuilder Practice, p. 18
· Outline Map, pp. 22–23

📄 **Formal Assessment**
· Section Quiz, p. 6

📄 **Integrated Assessment**
· Rubrics

**INTEGRATED TECHNOLOGY**

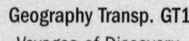 **Geography Transp. GT1**
· Voyages of Discovery

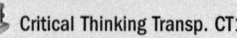 **Critical Thinking Transp. CT1**
· Exploration of the Americas

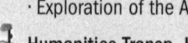 **Humanities Transp. HT3**
· Indians giving Cortés a necklace

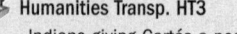 **Electronic Library of Primary Sources**

 **classzone.com**

**TEXAS RESOURCES**

 **TAKS Spiraled Content Review**

 **TAKS Practice Tests**

 **TAKS Practice Transparencies TT4–5**

 **TAKS Online Test Practice**

Convinced that he had landed on islands off Asia, known to Europeans as the Indies, Columbus called the people he met *los indios*. Thus the name *Indian* came to be mistakenly applied to all the diverse peoples of the Americas. The Spanish monarchs were thrilled with Columbus's discoveries and funded three more of his voyages—this time to colonize the lands he had claimed.

**Vocabulary**
**colonize:** to establish settlements under the control of a parent country

**THE IMPACT ON NATIVE AMERICANS** By the time Columbus set sail for his return to Hispaniola in 1493, Europeans had already developed a pattern for colonization. They had glimpsed the profitability of the plantation system, realized the economic benefits of using native or local peoples for forced labor, and learned to use European weapons to dominate native peoples. These tactics would be used in the Americas.

The arrival of the Europeans devastated Native Americans by another means: disease. The Taino, for example, had not developed any natural immunity to measles, mumps, chickenpox, smallpox, typhus, or other diseases Europeans had unknowingly brought with them. Consequently, the Taino died by the thousands once they were exposed.

**THE IMPACT ON AFRICANS** With the decline of the native work force the European settlers of the Americas eventually turned to Africa for slaves. The Atlantic slave trade devastated many African societies, particularly in West Africa. Starting in the 1500s, African cultures lost many of their young and more able members. Before the Atlantic slave trade ended in the 1800s, it had drained Africa of at least 10 million people.

**THE IMPACT ON EUROPEANS** Columbus's voyages had profound effects on Europeans as well. In search of new lives, Europeans began to cross the Atlantic by the thousands in what would become one of the biggest voluntary migrations in world history. Overseas expansion inflamed national rivalries in Europe. In 1494, Spain and Portugal signed the **Treaty of Tordesillas** (tôr´də-sē´əs), in which they agreed to divide the Western Hemisphere between them. **A**

**MAIN IDEA**

**Analyzing Events**
**A** What did Spain and Portugal agree to do in the Treaty of Tordesillas?

**THE COLUMBIAN EXCHANGE** The voyages of Columbus and those after him led to the discovery of plants and animals in the Americas that were new to Europeans and Africans. Ships took items such as corn, potatoes, and tobacco from the Americas to Europe and to Africa. From these countries, they brought back livestock, grains, fruit, and coffee. This global transfer of living things, called the **Columbian Exchange,** began with Columbus's first voyage and continues today.

*A Answer* They agreed to divide the Western Hemisphere between them.

*Skillbuilder Possible Answer* It has added variety to the foods people eat and their sources of nutrition.

**More About . . .**

**Christopher Columbus**
Even death did not stop Columbus's journeys across the Atlantic. After he died in 1506, his remains rested for several decades in Seville, Spain. But it was decided that his body should rest on the other side of the Atlantic. With great ceremony, he was laid to rest in Santo Domingo, in what is now the Dominican Republic. Some historians believe officials moved his remains to Cuba when Spain ceded the island to France. Other historians believe the remains—or alleged remains—were returned to Spain when the United States seized Cuba from Spain after the Spanish–American War in 1898. Finally, many believe his bones are still in Santo Domingo.

📖 In-Depth Resources: Unit 1
· Primary Sources: Journals of Christopher Columbus, pp. 23-24

**Tracing Themes**
**IMMIGRATION AND MIGRATION**

**African Americans**
Even today, with thousands of immigrants flooding into the United States from Asia and Latin America, the makeup of the U.S. population still reflects the deep impact of the arrival of Africans in the colonies. According to the 2000 census, for example, there were 34.7 million African Americans, which represented about 12 percent of the total U.S. population.

**HISTORY from VISUALS**

**Interpreting the Infographic**
Point out the number of continents involved in the exchange. *(Four)* Ask students why this back-and-forth flow of goods has been called an "ecological revolution."

## The Columbian Exchange

NORTH AMERICA

**AMERICAS TO EUROPE, AFRICA, AND ASIA**

Sweet Potato · Corn · Avocado · Cassava · Peanut · Potato · Tomato · Tobacco
Quinine · Pineapple · Vanilla · Beans · Cacao Bean
Squash · Peppers · Turkey · Pumpkin

EUROPE · ASIA

ATLANTIC OCEAN

Disease
· Smallpox
· Influenza
· Typhus
· Measles
· Malaria
· Diphtheria
· Whooping Cough

Livestock
· Cattle
· Sheep
· Pig
· Horse

Grains
· Wheat
· Rice
· Barley
· Oats

Sugar Cane

Honeybee

Peach & Pear

**EUROPE, AFRICA, AND ASIA TO AMERICAS**

Coffee Bean · Onion · Olive · Citrus Fruits · Banana · Grape · Turnip

AFRICA

**GEOGRAPHY SKILLBUILDER**
**Human-environment interaction** How do you think the Columbian Exchange has enriched each hemisphere?

 Mini-Lesson 2: SS11 2(WG1.B)

**REVIEW UNIT 15**

**ACTIVITY** | **COOPERATIVE LEARNING**

**Designing Storyboards**

**Class Time** One class period

**Task** Creating storyboards showing Spanish colonization of Hispaniola from the Native American perspective

**Purpose** To illustrate the effects of the arrival of the Spaniards on such peoples as the Taino

 **BLOCK SCHEDULING**

**Directions** Have groups of students create storyboards that present a visual history of the Spanish conquest of the Taino. Suggest that students use the art on this page as a model. A helpful hint might be to tell students to think of storyboards as frames in a filmstrip or a comic book.

📖 In-Depth Resources: Unit 1
· Outline Map: Spain Explores North America, pp. 23-24

## ❷ The Spanish Claim a New Empire

In the wake of Columbus's voyages, Spanish explorers took to the seas to claim new colonies for Spain. These explorers were lured by the prospect of vast lands filled with gold and silver. Known as ***conquistadors*** (kŏng-kē′stə-dôrz′) (conquerors), they conquered much of the Americas.

**CORTÉS SUBDUES THE AZTEC** Soon after landing in Mexico in 1519, **Hernándo Cortés** learned of the vast and wealthy Aztec empire in the region's interior. With a force of 508 men, 16 horses, 10 cannons, and numerous dogs, the conquistador marched inland.

The Spaniards marveled at Tenochtitlán, the Aztec capital, with its towering temples and elaborate engineering works—including a system that brought fresh water into the city. "We were amazed," one of Cortés's soldiers said of his first glimpse of Tenochtitlán. "Some of our soldiers even asked whether the things we saw were not a dream." While the Aztec city astonished the Spaniards, the capital's glittering gold stock seemed to hypnotize them. "They picked up the gold and fingered it like monkeys," one native witness recalled. "They hungered like pigs for that gold."

The Aztec emperor, **Montezuma,** convinced at first that Cortés was an armor-clad god, agreed to give the Spanish explorer a share of the empire's existing gold supply. The conquistador was not satisfied. Cortés eventually forced the Aztec to mine more gold and silver. In the spring of 1520, the Aztec rebelled against the Spaniards' intrusion. Regarding Montezuma as a traitor, the Aztec are believed to have stoned their ruler to death before driving out Cortés's forces.

While they had successfully repelled the Spanish invaders, the Aztec were falling victim to the diseases that the Spanish had brought with them. By the time Cortés launched a counterattack in 1521, the Spanish and their native allies overran an Aztec force that had been greatly reduced by smallpox and measles. After several months of fighting, the invaders sacked and burned Tenochtitlán, and the Aztec surrendered. **B**

**THE SPANISH PATTERN OF CONQUEST**
In building their American empire, the Spaniards lived among the native people and sought to impose their own culture upon them. The settlers, mostly men, tended to intermarry with native women. This practice eventually created a large ***mestizo*** (mĕs-tē′zō)—or mixed Spanish and Native American—population in the Spanish colonies. Nonetheless, the Spanish also oppressed the people among whom they lived. In their effort to exploit the land for its resources, they forced Native American workers to labor in an ***encomienda*** (ĕng-kô-myĕn′dä) system. Under that system, natives farmed, ranched, or mined for Spanish landlords, who received the rights to their labor from Spanish authorities.

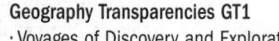

## KEY PLAYER

### HERNÁNDO CORTÉS 1485–1547

Cortés made himself the enemy of thousands of Native Americans, but the daring conquistador did not have many friends among Spaniards. Spanish authorities on Cuba, where Cortés owned land, accused the conquistador of murdering his wife, Catalina Juárez. "There were ugly accusations, but none proved," wrote Juárez's biographer.

In addition, the Cuban governor, Diego Velázquez, who resented Cortés's arrogance, relieved him of the command of a gold-seeking expedition to the mainland. Cortés left Cuba anyway. As he fought his way through Mexico, Cortés had to battle not only the Native Americans but also the Spanish forces that Velázquez sent to arrest him.

**16** CHAPTER 1 *Exploration and the Colonial Era*

---

· How were the Spaniards able to conquer Native American peoples?
· How did American wealth help enrich Spain?

  **In-Depth Resources: Unit 1**
· Guided Reading, p. 10

 **Geography Transparencies GT1**
· Voyages of Discovery and Exploration, 1271–1580

### More About . . .

**The Conquistadors**
Records show that a variety of men were attracted to the ranks of the conquistadors. Some were wealthy, and some were seeking to improve their modest holdings. Some were second sons who by Spanish law could not inherit family fortunes. Many were commoners seeking wealth and adventure. Gonzalo Fernandez de Oviedo reports there were Italians, Germans, Scots, Englishmen, Hungarians, Poles, Greeks, Portuguese, and men "from all the other nations of Asia, Africa and Europe."

### KEY PLAYER

**Hernándo Cortés**
Cortés was as ruthless in his dealings with his Spanish enemies as he was with his Native American opponents. In the midst of battling the Aztecs, Cortés learned of an assassination plot against him. He quickly apprehended the chief conspirator, Antonio de Villafaña, an associate of Diego Velázquez, and had him hanged from a nearby window. Discuss with students why a conquistador might have to be ruthless and strong willed in order to succeed.

  **Humanities Transparencies   HT3**
· Indians Giving Cortés a Necklace

---

**MAIN IDEA**

**Summarizing**
**B** What factors enabled the Spanish to conquer the Aztec?

*B Answers*
Montezuma believed at first that Cortes was a god; the Aztec fell victim to the diseases brought by the Spanish.

*Skillbuilder Answers*
1. 4
2. **English:** 1610 and 1497: northeastern Canada. **French:** 1524 and 1534: eastern coast; 1672 and 1679: Great Lakes and Mississippi River.

---

**ACTIVITY    SKILLBUILDER LESSON**

 **BLOCK SCHEDULING**

### Using the Internet

**Explaining the Skill** Show students where to type **Classzone.com** and explain how to use the buttons labeled "back," "forward," and "home." Encourage students to explore various pages by clicking on all the labels on the web page. Tell them to pursue each page until they are satisfied that they know where it leads them.

**Applying the Skill** Give students an assignment to find specific information on the Internet, letting them explore as necessary in order to find it. Some possible topics include: Aztec and Inca cultures, Hernándo Cortés, conquistadores, and exploration of the Americas.

  **In-Depth Resources: Unit 1**
· Skillbuilder Practice, p. 15

## European Exploration of the Americas, 1492–1682

GREENLAND

ICELAND

Arctic Circle

Hudson 1610

Hudson 1609

Cabot 1497

ENGLAND

*Hudson Bay*

NORTH AMERICA

Cartier 1534–35

EUROPE

La Salle 1679–1682

FRANCE

Joliet and Marquette 1672–73

PORTUGAL

SPAIN

DeSoto 1539–42

Coronado 1540–42

Santa Fe

Ponce de Léon 1512–13

*ATLANTIC OCEAN*

*Azores*

Cabrillo 1542–43

*Madeira*

*PACIFIC OCEAN*

of Cancer

*Gulf of Mexico*

*Hispaniola*

*Canary Islands*

Cortés 1519

CUBA

Verrazzano 1524

AFRICA

Cabeza de Vaca 1528–36

Veracruz

Santo Domingo

Columbus 1492

Columbus 1493–95

Tenochtitlán (Mexico City)

*Caribbean Sea*

Columbus 1502–03

Vespucci 1499

Equator

Balboa 1510–13

Columbus 1498

Pizarro 1530–33

SOUTH AMERICA

120°W    100°W    20°W

N E S

Spanish
Columbus
French
English
Dutch

0    1,000    2,000 miles
0    1,000    2,000 kilometers

Juan de la Cosa, pilot-navigator on Columbus's ship *Niña*, drew the known world on this oxhide map in 1500. Europeans' shaky understanding of the geography of the Americas at this time is revealed in the coastline of North and South America (*shown in green*).

### GEOGRAPHY SKILLBUILDER

1. **Movement** How many voyages to the Americas did Columbus make?
2. **Place** In what years did the English and French sail to the Americas and which regions did they explore?

---

## HISTORY from VISUALS

### Interpreting the Map

Explain that the arrows show more than the routes followed by each explorer. They also connect European nations with the lands they later sought to claim. Which explorer laid the basis for Spanish claims to California? (*Cabrillo*) Which explorer laid the basis for French claims to Canada? (*Cartier*)

**Extension** Divide the class into small groups and have each group research and write a brief biography of an explorer whose travels are shown on the map. Have an individual from each team report the team's findings to the class.

## More About . . .

### European Explorers

Giovanni da Verrazano, an Italian navigator and explorer sailing for France, was one of the earliest explorers of North America. Sailing up the East Coast, he discovered New York and Narragansett bays. However, it was after another earlier Italian explorer that the American continents were named. During the early 1500s, Amerigo Vespucci made several voyages to the Americas and determined that they were not part of Asia—as everyone then believed—but a separate land. In 1507, a German cartographer published a map of Vespucci's travels and named this "new" land America.

Critical Thinking Transparencies CT1
· Exploration of the Americas

---

## DIFFERENTIATING INSTRUCTION    GIFTED AND TALENTED

classzone.com

### Researching the Explorers

Have interested students use the Internet and library resources to write a travel journal of an explorer. They should describe the explorer's journey in detail. Encourage students to use as many quotes and primary sources as possible. Include a map showing the route taken by the explorer. All reports should include a bibliography, including Web sites consulted.

Ask for volunteers who would be willing to do an oral reading of a travel journal. Encourage them to immerse themselves in the role—even adding props, costumes, and sound effects, if they'd like.

Remind student performers to stick to the narrative in the journal and to give attributions for direct quotations cited. If the activity is successful, other interested students can photograph, audio record, or videotape the readings.

 In-Depth Resources: Unit 1
· Literature: from *Memoirs of Christopher Columbus*, pp. 30–31

## Instruct: Objective ❸

**Spain Explores the Southwest and West**

· Why did the Spanish begin to explore the lands north of Mexico?

· What did the Spanish explorers find in these lands?

📄 In-Depth Resources: Unit 1
· Guided Reading, p. 10

👁 Electronic Library of Primary Sources
· from *La Relación*, 1530s by Cabeza de Vaca

### Tracing Themes
**DIVERSITY AND NATIONAL IDENTITY**

**Spanish Influence in the United States**

The Spanish search for more golden empires to conquer led the conquistadores northward into what is now the United States. The missionaries and settlers who followed in their footsteps established a chain of scattered outposts that eventually would reach from Florida through the Southwest and into California. The addition of these lands to the United States centuries later would increase the diversity of an already diverse nation.

---

A number of Spanish priests demanded an end to the harsh encomienda system. In 1511, Fray Antonio de Montesinos delivered a fiery sermon in which he attacked the use of the native population for slave labor.

**A PERSONAL VOICE** FRAY ANTONIO DE MONTESINOS

"Tell me, by what right or justice do you hold these Indians in such a cruel and horrible servitude? . . . Why do you keep them so oppressed and exhausted, without giving them enough to eat or curing them of the sicknesses they incur from the excessive labor you give them? . . . Are you not bound to love them as you love yourselves? Don't you understand this? Don't you feel this?"

—quoted in *Reflections, Writing for Columbus*

In 1542, the Spanish monarchy abolished the encomienda system, and to meet their labor needs, the Spaniards began to use enslaved Africans. **C**

**SPAIN ENJOYS A GOLDEN AGE** In 1532, Francisco Pizarro plundered the wealthy Inca empire on the western coast of South America. With this conquest and others, the Spanish built a vast empire, which included **New Spain** (Mexico, and part of what is now Guatemala), as well as lands in Central and South America and the Caribbean. Spanish explorers also undertook expeditions into what is now the southern United States. There, they established a string of outposts to protect their holdings and to spread their culture and religion to the Native Americans. Beginning with the efforts of Ponce de León in 1513, the Spanish settled in what is now Florida. In 1565 they established the outpost of St. Augustine on the Florida coast. The settlement has survived to become the oldest European-founded city in the United States.

## ❸ Spain Explores the Southwest and West

Throughout the mid-1500s, the Spanish also explored and settled in what are now the southwest and west regions of the United States. In 1540, Francisco Vásquez de Coronado led a most ambitious venture, as he traveled throughout much of what is now Texas, Oklahoma, Arizona, New Mexico, and Kansas in search of another wealthy empire to conquer. Failing to find gold and other treasures, the dejected conquistador returned home. After wandering for two years, the only precious metal Coronado carried home was his own battered gold-plated armor.

**THE SPANISH FOUND NEW MEXICO** Some 50 years later, the Spanish returned to the modern-day Southwest—in search not of riches but of Christian converts. In its Royal Orders of New Discoveries of 1573, Spain outlined the duties of these new explorers who now included Roman Catholic priests. When converting the Native Americans, priests were ordered to provide them with "the many . . . essentials of life—bread, silk, linen, horses, cattle, tools, and weapons, and all the rest that Spain has had." Numerous Spanish priests had arrived in the Americas to spread Roman Catholicism. The barren land north of New Spain may have held little gold, but it was home to many Native American souls to convert. In the winter of 1609–1610, Pedro de Peralta, governor of Spain's northern holdings, called **New Mexico,** led settlers to a tributary of the upper Rio Grande. Together they built a capital called Santa Fe, or "Holy Faith." The hooves of pack mules wore down an 1,800-mile trail known as El Camino Real or "the Royal Road," as they carried goods back and forth between Santa Fe and Mexico City. In the next two decades, a string of Catholic missions arose among the Pueblos in the area. **D**

**THE SPANISH OPEN MISSIONS IN TEXAS** As early as 1519, Alonso Álvarez de Piñeda of Spain had mapped the coast of what is today Texas. Soon afterward, in 1528, the first Europeans had begun to settle in the interior. Over the next two

MAIN IDEA

Analyzing Motives
**C** Why did some Spanish priests demand an end to the encomienda system?

**C Answer** They felt that it was a cruel system.

**D Answer** At first they came for gold; later they came in order to convert Native Americans to Christianity.

MAIN IDEA

Analyzing Motives
**D** What attracted the Spanish to what is now the Southwest?

---

**DIFFERENTIATING INSTRUCTION** | **LESS PROFICIENT READERS**

### Taking Notes

Distribute three-by-five-inch index cards to students. Have them turn each subhead under "Spain Explores the Southwest and West" into a question. One example might be, "How did the Spanish come to found New Mexico?" Instruct students to write each question on the front of one of the index cards. Tell students to find the answer and write it on the back of the card as they read the section. Repeat this process with the rest of the section. Students can exchange their "flashcards" to quiz each other or to review for the section quiz.

*How did the Spanish come to found New Mexico?*

hundred years, using the San Antonio area as their administrative center, the Spanish sent more than 30 expeditions inland to explore and to settle. The land was already sparsely inhabited by Native Americans, including members of the large and diverse Apache group, whom Spanish missionaries sought to convert to Christianity. The first two Spanish missions in Texas were founded in 1682 near what is now El Paso.

Beginning in 1718, a number of missions opened along the San Antonio River. Founded in 1720, Mission San José y San Miguel de Aguayo in San Antonio was by many accounts the most beautiful and successful Texas mission. Its compound included buildings for living, worshipping, storing grain, spinning and weaving cotton and wool, carpentry, iron working, and tailoring.

**A STRING OF MISSIONS SPANS CALIFORNIA** In 1542 the navigator Juan Rodriguez Cabrillo, exploring the west coast of North America, discovered the harbor that was later named San Diego. In 1769, the Spanish missionary Father Junípero Serra founded the first California mission at San Diego.

By 1823, Spanish Franciscan priests, followers of Saint Francis of Assisi, had founded a string of 21 missions, each one day's walk (about 30 miles) from the next. Many of the missions were protected by forts, called presidios, built nearby. A presidio and a mission founded in 1776 in San Francisco preceded the development of that city. The aims of the missionaries in California, as in Texas, were to convert the Native Americans to Christianity, to educate them in European ways and skills, and to secure the area for Spanish settlement. Many Spanish mis-

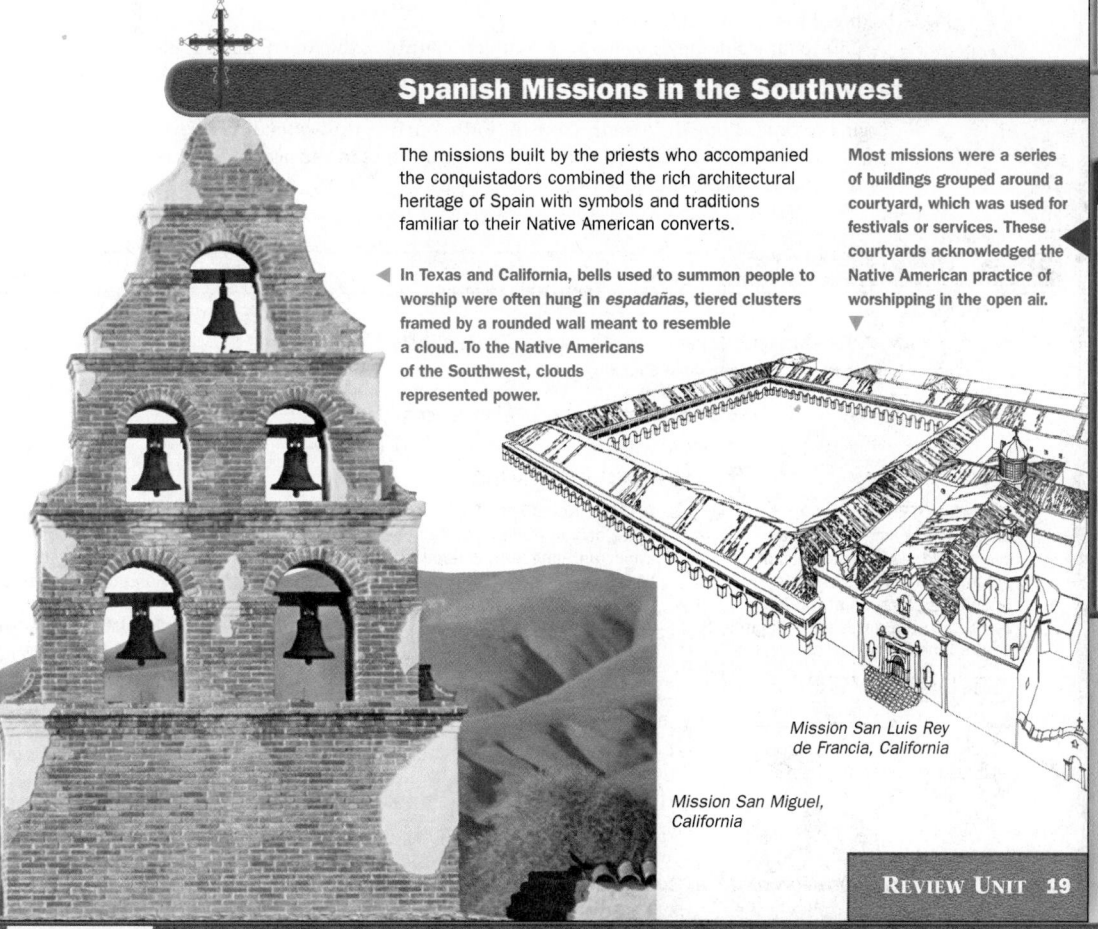

## Spanish Missions in the Southwest

The missions built by the priests who accompanied the conquistadors combined the rich architectural heritage of Spain with symbols and traditions familiar to their Native American converts.

◀ In Texas and California, bells used to summon people to worship were often hung in *espadañas*, tiered clusters framed by a rounded wall meant to resemble a cloud. To the Native Americans of the Southwest, clouds represented power.

Most missions were a series of buildings grouped around a courtyard, which was used for festivals or services. These courtyards acknowledged the Native American practice of worshipping in the open air. ▼

*Mission San Luis Rey de Francia, California*

*Mission San Miguel, California*

REVIEW UNIT  19

# Assess & Reteach

### SECTION 2 ASSESSMENT

Ask students to work in pairs to answer the questions. As they write their answers, have them note passages that support their answers.

 Formal Assessment
· Section Quiz, p. 6

### SELF-ASSESSMENT

Have students explore their own understanding of the clash between the Spanish and American cultures by making a list of the Spanish expectations and the Native American responses.

### RETEACH

Use the map on page 15 (the Columbian Exchange) to help review the main ideas of the section.

 In-Depth Resources: Unit 1
· Reteaching Activity, p. 18

---

sions are still standing and some are still in use. They remain as lasting memorials to the great cultures reflected in their architecture.

**RESISTANCE TO THE SPANISH** The impact of the Spanish missions on Native American cultures has been a subject of much historical controversy. Recent historians assert that the mission system negatively affected many Native American communities in several ways. The Spanish required Native Americans who converted to Christianity to live inside the missions, separating them from their families and cultures. Native Americans who tried to leave were punished. The Spanish also forced Native Americans to provide labor for farming and construction, give up their self-government, and adopt European dress, diet, and living arrangements. During the 1670s, priests and soldiers around Santa Fe began forcing Native Americans to help support the missions by paying a tribute, an offering of either goods or services. The tribute was usually a bushel of maize or a deer hide, but the Spanish also forced Native Americans to work for them and sometimes abused them physically. Native Americans who practiced their native religion or refused to pay a tribute were beaten.

*"The heathen have concealed a mortal hatred for our holy faith and enmity for the Spanish nation."*

**SPANISH OFFICER, WRITING OF POPÉ'S REBELLION**

Spanish priests punished the Pueblo religious leader Popé for his worship practices, which they interpreted as witchcraft. In 1680, the angered leader led a well-organized uprising against the Spanish that involved some 17,000 warriors from villages all over New Mexico. The triumphant fighters destroyed Catholic churches, executed priests and settlers, and drove the Spaniards back into New Spain. For the next 12 years—until the Spanish regained control of the area—the southwest region of the future United States once again belonged to its original inhabitants.

But Spain would never again have complete control of the Americas. In 1588, England had defeated the Spanish Armada, a naval fleet assembled to invade England, ending Spain's naval dominance in the Atlantic. In time, England began forging colonies along the eastern shore of North America, thus extending its own empire in the New World. But Spain's influence continues in the people and customs of the Southeast and Southwest.

 **ASSESSMENT**

**1. TERMS & NAMES** For each term or name, write a sentence explaining its significance.
- Christopher Columbus
- Taino
- Treaty of Tordesillas
- Columbian Exchange
- conquistador
- Hernándo Cortés
- Montezuma
- *mestizo*
- *encomienda*
- New Spain
- New Mexico

## MAIN IDEA

**2. TAKING NOTES**
Create a time line of the major events and significant dates of Columbus's voyages and the Spanish exploration of the New World. Use the dates already plotted on the time line below as a guide.

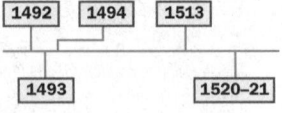

## CRITICAL THINKING

**3. ANALYZING EFFECTS**
What do you think were the most important long-term consequences of Columbus's encounters in the Americas? **Think About:**
- conquering and claiming land
- forced labor of Native Americans and Africans
- the impact on Africa, Europe, and the Americas

**4. DRAWING CONCLUSIONS**
State three conclusions about Spanish exploration and settlement north of Mexico and the Spaniards' interaction with Native Americans there. Why did the Native Americans of New Mexico revolt against the Spanish settlers?

**20** CHAPTER 1 *Exploration and the Colonial Era*

---

 **ASSESSMENT** **Answers**

 Mini-Lesson 4: SS 5(2.C)

### 1. TERMS & NAMES
Christopher Columbus, p. 14
Taino, p. 14
Treaty of Tordesillas, p. 15
Columbian Exchange, p. 15
conquistador, p. 16
Hernándo Cortés, p. 16
Montezuma, p. 16
Mestizo, p. 16

encomienda, p. 16
New Spain, p. 18
New Mexico, p. 18

### 2. TAKING NOTES
**1492** Columbus's first voyage to the Americas, **1493** Columbus's return trip, **1494** The Treaty of Tordesillas, **1513** Ponce de León explored La Florida, **1520-21** Aztecs rebelled and Cortés retook Tenochtitlán

### 3. ANALYZING EFFECTS
The pattern of violating human rights in conquering new lands; the African slave trade; the emergence of various nations in North and South America; the permanent alteration of global environments and societies as a result of the Columbian Exchange; the multicultural character of the Americas.

### 4. DRAWING CONCLUSIONS
Failure to find gold or silver north of Mexico limited settlement to missions and defensive outposts; missionaries provided Native Americans with material goods, but suppressed their culture; some Native Americans converted to Christianity, but others resisted.

# Early British Colonies

| MAIN IDEA | WHY IT MATTERS NOW | Terms & Names |
|---|---|---|
| Beginning in the early 1600s, the English established colonies along the eastern shore of North America. | The original 13 English colonies in North America formed the foundation of what would become the United States of America. | • John Smith   • John Winthrop<br>• Jamestown   • King Philip's War<br>• joint-stock   • William Penn<br>  companies   • Quaker<br>• indentured   • mercantilism<br>  servant   • Navigation Acts<br>• Puritan |

**TEKS** U.S. History 8A, 8B, 18A, 21A, 22B, 24A, 24B, 24D, 24G, 25A, 25B, 25C, 25D, 26A

### One European's Story

**John Smith** craved adventure. Smith's father had urged him to be a merchant, but the restless Englishman wanted to see the world. In 1606, he offered his services as a colonist to the Virginia Company, a group of merchants charged with starting an English colony in North America. He later recalled his vision of the opportunities that awaited those who settled the Americas.

**A PERSONAL VOICE** JOHN SMITH

❝What man who is poor or who has only his merit to advance his fortunes can desire more contentment than to walk over and plant the land he has obtained by risking his life? . . . Here nature and liberty . . . give us freely that which we lack or have to pay dearly for in England. . . . What pleasure can be greater than to grow tired from . . . planting vines, fruits, or vegetables? . . .❞

—*The General History of Virginia*

John Smith, seen here in a 19th century painting based on a 1616 engraving, was a self-proclaimed soldier of fortune, sea captain, and poet.

Smith would need all of his abilities to steer the new colony, Jamestown, through what turned out to be a disastrous beginning. In time, however, the colony survived to become England's first permanent settlement in North America.

## The English Settle at Jamestown ①

In April of 1607, nearly four months after the Virginia Company's three ships had left England, they reached the North American shore. Sailing part way up a broad river leading into Chesapeake Bay, the colonists selected a small, defensible peninsula and built Fort James to protect the settlement of **Jamestown,** named for their king.

**A DISASTROUS START** Unlike Spanish colonies, which were funded by Spanish rulers, the English colonies were originally funded by **joint-stock companies.** Stock companies allowed several investors to pool their wealth in support of a colony that would, they hoped, yield a profit. Investors in the Jamestown colony demanded a quick return on their investment, and the colonists hoped to find gold to satisfy them. Consequently, they neglected farming and soon

**TAKS** Mini-Lesson 4: SS11 1(8.1C)

---

## OBJECTIVES

① Describe the English settlement at Jamestown.

② Identify the motives that led Puritans to New England and the colonies they founded.

③ Explain the pattern of life at New Netherland and Pennsylvania.

④ Understand the economic relationship between England and its North American colonies.

### SKILLBUILDERS
· Geography Skillbuilder: location, region, p. 25; region, p. 29
· Interpreting Visual Sources, p. 27

### CRITICAL THINKING
· Analyzing Causes, p. 23
· Analyzing Issues, pp. 23, 24, 25
· Forming Generalizations, p. 24
· Predicting Effects, pp. 26, 30
· Analyzing Events, p. 26
· Contrasting, p. 28
· Analyzing Effects, pp. 28, 30
· Evaluating, p. 30

## Focus & Motivate

If students were to create an ideal community, what features would it have? How would students handle dissenters?

## Instruct

### Instruct: Objective ①
**The English Settle at Jamestown**
TAKS SS11 1(8.1C)
· Who paid to establish Jamestown?
· What difficulties did the English face?
· How did the growing of tobacco affect the Jamestown colony?
· Why did the colonists and Native Americans clash?

📖 In-Depth Resources: Unit 1
· Guided Reading, p. 11
· Primary Sources, p. 28

---

## PROGRAM RESOURCES

 **In-Depth Resources: Unit 1**
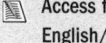· Guided Reading, p. 11
· Reteaching Activity, p. 19
· Primary Sources: Travel and Works of Captain John Smith, p. 28
· American Lives: John Winthrop, p. 33

📖 **Reading Study Guide** (English and Spanish), pp. 9–10

📖 **Access for Students Acquiring English/ESL**
· Guided Reading (Spanish), p. 15

📖 **Formal Assessment**
· Section Quiz, p. 7

📖 **Integrated Assessment**
· Rubrics

### INTEGRATED TECHNOLOGY

 **Geography Transp. GT2, GT3**
· The European Colonies, 1650

 **Critical Thinking Transp. CT2, CT36**
· Puritan Migration; American Colonies

 **Humanities Transp. HT1, HT4**
· Map of North America

👁 **Electronic Library of Primary Sources**

ⓘ **classzone.com**

### TEXAS RESOURCES
📖 TAKS Spiraled Content Review
📖 TAKS Practice Tests
📖 TAKS Practice Transparencies TT7–9
ⓘ TAKS Online Test Practice

## Rediscovering Fort James

Erosion turned the Jamestown Peninsula into an island and, for many years, the site of the original Fort James was assumed to be under water. However, in 1996, archaeologists from the Association for the Preservation of Virginia Antiquities discovered artifacts on what they concluded was the original site of the fort.

Since then, archaeologists have discovered armor, weapons, even games used by the first colonists. Archaeologists and historians are constantly learning more and more about this long buried treasure of American history.

16th-century helmet and breastplate. ▶

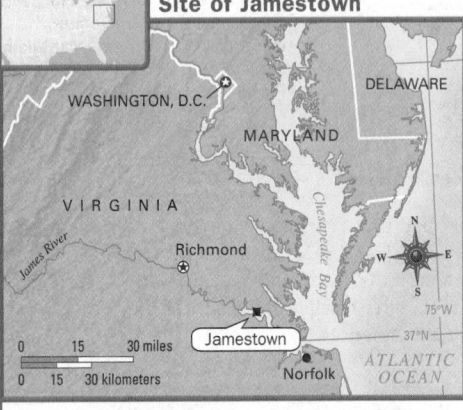

### Site of Jamestown

DELAWARE

WASHINGTON, D.C.

MARYLAND

VIRGINIA

Chesapeake Bay

James River

Richmond

Jamestown

Norfolk

ATLANTIC OCEAN

0    15    30 miles
0    15    30 kilometers

75°W

37°N

An archaeologist kneels beside holes left from the original palisade fence of Fort James. Note that the palisades were less than one foot in width.

Rounded bulwarks, or watch towers, mounted with cannon were located at each corner of the fort. The range of each cannon was approximately one mile.

The walls of the triangular-shaped fort measured 420 feet on the river side and 300 feet on the other two sides.

A barracks or "bawn" stood along the wall.

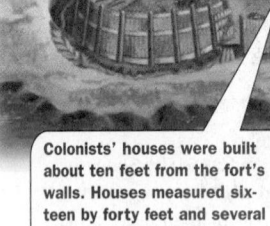

Colonists' houses were built about ten feet from the fort's walls. Houses measured sixteen by forty feet and several colonists lived in each.

The main gate, located on the long side, faced the James river.

This illustration recreates what historians and archaeologists now believe Fort James looked like early in its history.

**22** CHAPTER 1 *Exploration and the Colonial Era*

 classzone.com

suffered the consequences. Disease from contaminated river water struck them first, followed soon by hunger. After several months, one settler described the terrifying predicament: "Thus we lived for the space of five months in this miserable distress, . . . our men night and day groaning in every corner of the fort, most pitiful to hear." **A**

Smith held the colony together by forcing the colonists to farm and by securing food and support from the native Powhatan peoples. Then Smith was injured and returned to England. Without Smith's leadership, the colony eventually deteriorated to the point of famine. The settlement was saved, however, by the arrival of new colonists and by the development of a highly profitable crop, tobacco.

**TOBACCO REQUIRES A SUPPLY OF LABOR** In order to grow tobacco, the Virginia Company needed field laborers. Immigration jumped in 1618, when the company introduced the headright system, offering 50 acres of land to "adventurers" who would pay their own or anothers' transportation from England. Many of those who arrived in Virginia, however, came as **indentured servants.** In exchange for passage to North America and food and shelter upon arrival, an indentured servant agreed to a limited term of servitude—usually four to seven years. Indentured servants were mainly from the lower classes of English society and therefore had little to lose by leaving for a new world.

The first enslaved Africans arrived in Virginia aboard a Dutch merchant ship in 1619. After a few years, most of them received land and freedom. It would be several decades before the English colonists in North America began the systematic use of enslaved Africans as laborers.

**COLONISTS CLASH WITH NATIVE AMERICANS** The colonists' desire for more land—to accommodate their growing population and the demand for more crop space—led to warfare with the original inhabitants of Virginia. Unlike the Spanish, the English followed a pattern of driving away the people they defeated. Their conquest over the native peoples was total and complete, which is one reason a large mestizo-like population never developed in the United States.

**ECONOMIC DIFFERENCES SPLIT VIRGINIA** The English colonists who migrated to North America in increasing numbers battled not only Native Americans but sometimes each other. By the 1670s, one-quarter of the free white men in Virginia were poor former indentured servants who lived mainly on the western frontier of Virginia, where they constantly fought with Native Americans for land.

Although Virginia's governor, William Berkeley, proposed building forts to protect the settlers, the settlers refused to pay taxes to maintain these forts. The colonists, under the leadership of a young planter named Nathaniel Bacon, marched on Jamestown in September of 1676. Bacon confronted colonial leaders with a number of grievances, including the frontier's lack of representation in Virginia's colonial legislature, or law-making body, the House of Burgesses. Although Bacon's Rebellion ultimately failed, it exposed the restlessness of the colony's former indentured servants. **B**

---

**MAIN IDEA**

**Analyzing Causes**

**A** Why was the early settlement at Jamestown a near disaster?

*A Answer*
The Colonists neglected farming and suffered from hunger.

---

*B Answer*
They did not want to pay taxes to pay for their defense; they felt that they were not being represented in the legislature.

**MAIN IDEA**

**Analyzing Issues**

**B** Why were Virginia's frontier settlers frustrated with their government?

---

**HISTORICAL**
## SPOTLIGHT

**EARLY REPRESENTATIVE GOVERNMENT**

As the English settlers colonized North America, they sowed the seeds of the representative style of government that would become the foundation of American democracy.

Virginia's House of Burgesses served as the first representative body in colonial America. The House first met in Jamestown in 1619 and included two citizens, or burgesses, from each of Virginia's eleven districts. The body claimed the authority to raise taxes and pass legislation—subject to veto by the English governor.

The Mayflower Compact, which the Pilgrims crafted as they sailed to North America in 1620, created a civil government and pledged loyalty to the king. It stated that the purpose of their government in America would be to frame "just and equal laws . . . for the general good of the colony."

Created in 1639, the Fundamental Orders of Connecticut extended voting rights to a greater number of white males in that colony. It also declared that the colonial legislature could assemble without a call by the governor.

---

### Connections Across Time

**1600s AND TODAY**

**Indentured Labor**
Indentured servitude still exists in some parts of the developing world. In India and Pakistan, for example, poverty-stricken parents will bond their children to shops where they receive food and clothes in exchange for their labor. Adults sometimes bond themselves, too, so that they can pay off old debts or gain the use of land.

---

### More About . . .

**The First Africans in Virginia**
The first Africans to arrive in Virginia came as the result of a deal with a Dutch ship captain who traded them for food. The Africans had Spanish-sounding names—Pedro, Angelo, Antoney, and Isabella—so the colonists suspected the Dutch had stolen them from a Spanish slave ship. The Spaniards often baptized and renamed enslaved Africans.

---

### HISTORICAL SPOTLIGHT

**Early Representative Government**
Have students consider features shared by the House of Burgesses and the U.S. Congress and features that separate them. *(Shared features—power to raise taxes and make legislation, subject to veto by executive; distinguishing features—unicameral vs. bicameral structure, constituency of white landowners vs. constituency of all U.S. citizens age 18 and over.)*

---

**DIFFERENTIATING INSTRUCTION** | **GIFTED AND TALENTED**

### Conducting a Mock Trial

Have students imagine that Nathaniel Bacon had not died—that Governor Berkeley had captured him instead. Ask students to create a mock trial in which the governor charges Bacon with treason. Remind students that Bacon had the right to a jury trial, but members of the jury would have been drawn from the same land-owning class that exercised the franchise. Encourage students to do outside research to ensure historical authenticity.

Some suggested steps for students to follow are:

· Write up Governor Berkeley's formal accusation of Bacon.
· Assign roles of prosecutor and defense attorney.
· Draft the "case" for and against Bacon.
· Choose a judge.
· Conduct the trial, with each side presenting its argument.
· Have the class act as jury, and take a vote after the presentation of the case.

◀ Puritans cherished their Bibles, passing them down as family treasures from one generation to the next. This Bible belonged to Governor William Bradford of the Plymouth Colony.

## Instruct: Objective ❷

**Puritans Create a "New England"**
TAKS SS11 3(US21.A)

· Why did the Puritans come to America?
· What was life like in Puritan New England?
· How did Puritans treat people with religious beliefs different from their own?
· How did religion and the use of the land cause conflict between Native Americans and New England colonists?

 **In-Depth Resources: Unit 1**
· Guided Reading, p. 11
· American Lives: John Winthrop, p. 33

 **Electronic Library of Primary Sources**
· *The Journal of the Ship May-flower*, 1620, by T. Jones
· *The Book of General Laws*, 1685, by the Inhabitants of New Plymouth

### Connections Across Time

**1621 AND TODAY**

#### Thanksgiving

Americans link Thanksgiving to a 1621 feast held by Pilgrims. Despite all the traditions, very little is known about the event except a brief description provided in a letter by Edward Winslow. Said Winslow: "Our harvest being gotten in, our governor sent four men on fowling, that we might, after a special manner, rejoice together after we had gathered the fruit of our labors. . . . At which time . . . many Indians coming amongst us . . . [including] Massasoit, with some 90 men, whom for three days we entertained and feasted, and they went and killed five deer, which they . . . bestowed on our governor."

 **Critical Thinking Transparencies CT2**
· Puritan Migration

## ❷ Puritans Create a "New England"

After King Henry VIII (1491–1547) broke with Roman Catholicism in the 1530s, the Church of England was formed. Although the new church was free of Catholic control, one religious group, the **Puritans,** felt that the church had kept too much Catholic ritual. They wanted to "purify," or reform, the church by eliminating all traces of Catholicism. Some Puritans, called Separatists, wanted to separate from the English Church. They often met in secret to avoid the punishment inflicted upon those who did not follow the Anglican form of worship. **C**

One congregation of Separatists, known today as the Pilgrims, eventually migrated to America. There, in 1620, this small group of families founded the Plymouth Colony, the second permanent English colony in North America. Their Mayflower Compact, named for the ship on which they sailed to North America, became an important landmark in the development of American democracy.

**THE MASSACHUSETTS BAY COLONY** Other Puritans who were not Separatists turned their thoughts toward New England in the 1620s. They felt the burden of increasing religious persecution, political repression, and dismal economic conditions. In 1630, a group of Puritans established the Massachusetts Bay Colony along the upper coast of North America. The port town of Boston soon became the colony's thriving capital. Settlers established other towns nearby and eventually incorporated the Plymouth Colony into the Massachusetts Bay Colony.

The Puritans believed they had a special covenant, or agreement, with God. To fulfill their part, they were to create a moral society that would serve as a beacon for others to follow. Puritan leader **John Winthrop** expressed the sense of mission that bound the Puritans together, in a sermon delivered aboard the flagship *Arbella*: "We [in New England] shall be as a City upon a Hill; the eyes of all people are on us."

Although Puritans made no effort to create a democracy, the Massachusetts Bay Company extended the right to vote to all adult male members of the Puritan church—40 percent of the colony's men. As their system of self-government evolved, so did the close relationship between the government and the Puritan church. The Puritan view dominated Massachusetts society: taxes supported the Puritan church, and laws required church attendance. **D**

**DISSENT IN THE PURITAN COMMUNITY** The Puritans came to America to follow their own form of worship, and they were intolerant of people who had dissenting religious beliefs. One such dissenter was Roger Williams, an extreme Separatist, who expressed two controversial views. First, he declared that the English settlers had no rightful claim to the land unless they purchased it from Native Americans. Second, he argued that every person should be free to worship according to his or her conscience.

**C Answer**
They felt that the Church of England retained too much Catholic ritual.

**MAIN IDEA**

**Analyzing Issues**
**C** Why were the Puritans unhappy with the Church of England?

**Vocabulary**
**repression:** the act of putting down by force

**MAIN IDEA**

**Forming Generalizations**
**D** What type of society did the Puritans want to create?

**D Answer**
They wanted to create a society dominated by Puritan religious views.

---

**ACTIVITY** | **LINK TO CIVICS** | **BLOCK SCHEDULING**

## Challenges to Puritan Leaders

**Class Time** 30 minutes

**Task** Writing a statement describing challenges to Puritan authority or responding to such a statement

**Purpose** To analyze the conflict that placed the Puritan leaders of Massachusetts on opposing sides from dissenters Roger Williams and Anne Hutchinson

**Directions** Divide the class into pairs. Direct each pair to research the conflicts that arose between the Puritan leaders of Massachusetts and either Roger Williams or Anne Hutchinson. One of the pair writes a speech stating the reasons Puritan leaders might have given for banishing Williams or Hutchinson. The second member writes a reply that the person banished might have given. Have volunteers read their speeches in front of the class. Ask for class reactions as to which speeches were most convincing.

MAIN IDEA
**Analyzing Issues**
**E** In what principles did the government of Providence differ from that of Massachusetts?

**E Answer** Separation of church and state and religious freedom.

When officials tried to deport Williams back to England, he fled Massachusetts and traveled south. He negotiated with a local Native American group for a plot of land and set up a new colony, which he called Providence. In Providence, later the capital of Rhode Island, Williams guaranteed religious freedom and separation of church and state. **E**

Another dissenter, Anne Hutchinson, taught that worshippers did not need the church or its ministers to interpret the Bible for them. Banished from the colony, Hutchinson, with her family and a band of followers, fled first to Rhode Island and, after her husband died, to New Netherland—which later became part of New York—where she died in a war with Native Americans.

**NATIVE AMERICANS RESIST COLONIAL EXPANSION** While Williams and his followers were settling Rhode Island, thousands of other white settlers fanned out to western Massachusetts and to new colonies in New Hampshire and Connecticut. From the beginning, Native Americans had helped the colonists, providing them with land and giving them agricultural advice. Soon, however, disputes between the Puritans and Native Americans arose over land and religion. As Native Americans saw their lands taken over by settlers, they feared an end to their way of life. In addition, Native Americans resented the Puritans' efforts to convert them and bristled under Puritan laws such as the prohibition of hunting and fishing on Sunday.

**KING PHILIP'S WAR** Great tension continued between Native Americans and settlers for nearly 40 years. Eventually, the Wampanoag chief Metacom, whom the English called King Philip, organized his tribe and several others into an alliance to wipe out the invaders. The eruption of **King Philip's War** in the spring of 1675 startled the Puritans with its intensity. Native Americans attacked

*Skillbuilder Answers*
1. Plymouth
2. Delaware River

**Tracing Themes**
VOTING RIGHTS

**Puritan Dissenters**
Although most Puritans believed in the concept of government by consent, they did not uphold the idea of religious freedom. Majority rule in Massachusetts Bay had little room for individual dissenters, such as Roger Williams and Anne Hutchinson. Protection of the rights of religious minorities was established in Rhode Island, where Williams formulated the principles of separation of church and state and religious tolerance.

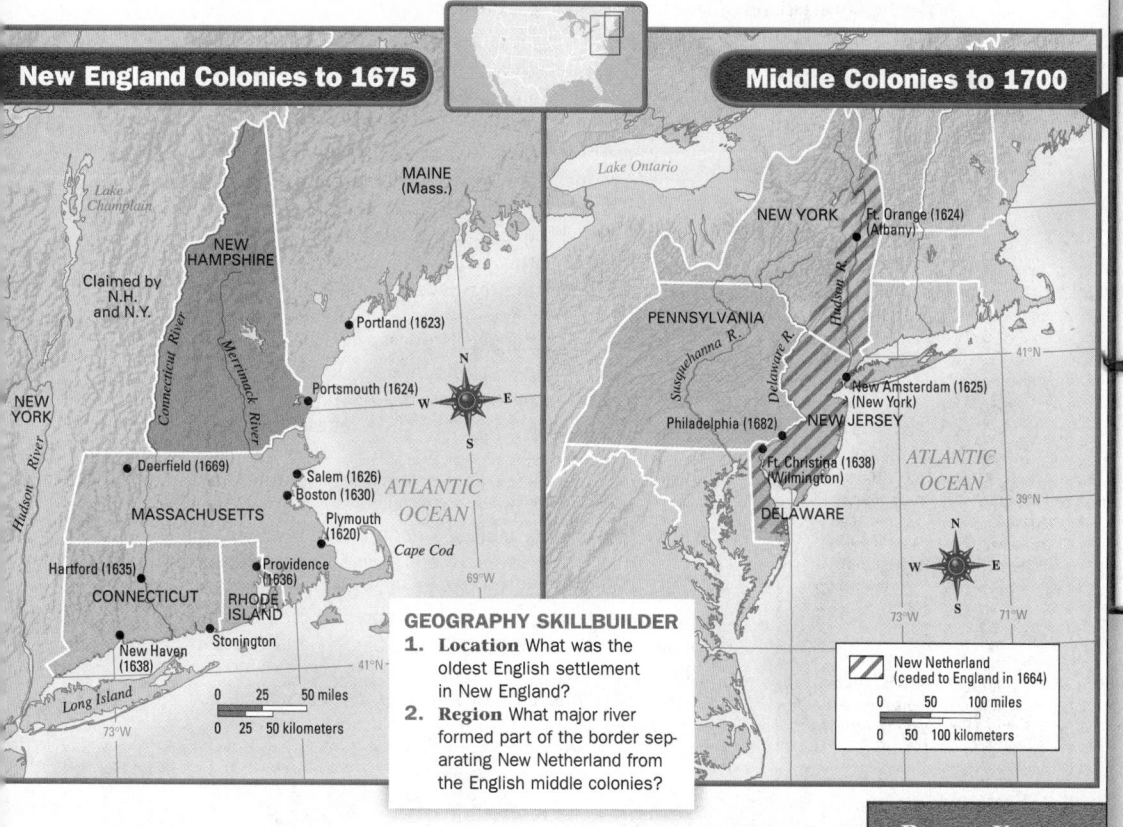

**New England Colonies to 1675**

**Middle Colonies to 1700**

**GEOGRAPHY SKILLBUILDER**
1. **Location** What was the oldest English settlement in New England?
2. **Region** What major river formed part of the border separating New Netherland from the English middle colonies?

New Netherland (ceded to England in 1664)

**HISTORY from VISUALS**

**Interpreting the Maps**
Explain to students that the New England colonies grew into a distinct region. Refer them to the map and ask: What colonies made up this region? How would you describe the geographic location of these colonies? Based on the Middle Colonies map, why might the English have called New Netherland "the Dutch wedge"?

**Extension** Ask students how they would describe the physical location of these colonies. What inferences could they make about the ways the people of these regions could earn their living? (*Parts are near the sea, which could provide employment in fishing, shipbuilding, and sea trade.*)

**DIFFERENTIATING INSTRUCTION**    **GIFTED AND TALENTED**

## Metacom

Have interested students do additional research on King Philip (also called Metacom) and the events of King Philip's War. The focus should be on the action and reactions of the Native Americans, the colonists, and the British government. Then they can create a documentary style presentation for the class. If possible, videotape the presentation.

Suggest that students begin by developing a step-by-step plan, either working individually or in pairs. The plan should cover the tasks involved, how they will be completed, and by whom. They might use an outline form similar to the one at right.

**Metacom**
I. Research background on his life by using the Internet.
II. Summarize King Phillip's War.
  A. Native American reactions
  B. Reactions of colonists and British government
III. Plan scenes to be covered in documentary.

## Instruct: Objective ③

### Settlement of the Middle Colonies
TAKS SS11 5(US24.B)

· Who founded New Netherland and why?
· Which European nation took control of New Netherland from its founders? Why?
· How was Pennsylvania founded?

📄 In-Depth Resources: Unit 1
· Guided Reading, p. 11

and burned outlying settlements throughout New England. Within months they were striking the outskirts of Boston. The alarmed and angered colonists responded by killing as many Native Americans as they could, even some from friendly tribes. For over a year, the two sides waged a war of mutual brutality and destruction. Finally, food shortages, disease, and heavy casualties wore down the Native Americans' resistance, and they gradually surrendered or fled. **F**

## ③ Settlement of the Middle Colonies

While English Puritans were establishing colonies in New England, the Dutch were founding one to the south. As early as 1609, Henry Hudson—an Englishman employed by the Dutch—had sailed up the river that now bears his name. The Dutch soon established a fur trade with the Iroquois and built trading posts on the Hudson River.

**THE DUTCH FOUND NEW NETHERLAND** In 1621, the Dutch government granted the newly formed Dutch West India Company permission to colonize New Netherland and expand the thriving fur trade. New Amsterdam (now New York City), founded in 1625, became the capital of the colony (see map on page 25). In 1655, the Dutch extended their claims by taking over New Sweden, a tiny colony of Swedish and Finnish settlers that had established a rival fur trade along the Delaware River. To encourage settlers to come and stay, the colony opened its doors to a variety of ethnic and religious groups. **G**

In 1664, the English took over the colony without a fight. The duke of York, the new proprietor, or owner, of the colony, renamed it New York. The duke later gave a portion of this land to two of his friends, naming this territory New Jersey for the British island of Jersey.

### WORLD STAGE

#### THE ENGLISH CIVIL WAR AND RESTORATION

From 1642 to 1651, England was torn apart by great wars between loyalist supporters of King Charles I, and those who supported Parliament, many of whom were Puritans. The parliamentary armies were victorious, and Charles I was tried for treason and executed in 1649. For a decade, England became a commonwealth, or republic, headed first by Oliver Cromwell, a Puritan, and then by his son Richard.

However, the English grew weary of the rather grim and sober Puritan rule, and in 1660 the monarchy was restored under Charles II. The Restoration would have a profound effect on America, leading to the creation of new colonies and to more direct involvement by the Crown in colonial affairs.

**THE QUAKERS SETTLE PENNSYLVANIA** The acquisition of New Netherland was one step in England's quest to extend its American empire after 1660, when the English monarchy was restored after a period of civil war and Puritan rule. The new king, Charles II, owed a debt to the father of a young man named **William Penn.** As payment, Charles gave the younger Penn a large property that the king insisted be called Pennsylvania, or "Penn's Woods," after the father. Following this, in 1682, Penn acquired more land from the duke of York, the three counties that became Delaware.

William Penn belonged to the Society of Friends, or **Quakers,** a Protestant sect that held services without formal ministers, allowing any person to speak as the spirit moved him or her. They dressed plainly, refused to defer to persons of rank, opposed war, and refused to serve in the military. For their radical views, they were scorned and harassed by Anglicans and Puritans alike.

Penn wanted to establish a good and fair society in keeping with Quaker ideals of equality, cooperation, and religious toleration. Penn guaranteed every adult male settler 50 acres of land and the right to vote. His plan for government called for a representative assembly and freedom of religion. Like Roger Williams before him, Penn believed that the land belonged to the Native Americans, and he saw to it that they were paid for it.

26   CHAPTER 1 *Exploration and the Colonial Era*

### MAIN IDEA

**Predicting Effects**
**F** What long-term effects would you predict followed King Philip's War?

*F Answer*
Students might suggest lasting bitterness between Native Americans and Europeans and the colonists' continual encroachment on Native American lands.

### MAIN IDEA

**Analyzing Events**
**G** How did the Dutch create an ethnically diverse colony?

*G Answer*
They welcomed a variety of ethnic and religious groups.

---

## DIFFERENTIATING INSTRUCTION    STUDENTS ACQUIRING ENGLISH

### Using Proper Nouns

To help students expand their use of proper nouns in relation to country of origin, pair proficient English speakers with students who are acquiring English. Have student pairs recreate the chart shown on the right. Have the students complete the chart for the groups who settled in the Middle Colonies. They might then use their charts to record details on the various groups.

| Country/Continent of Origin | Name of Group |
|---|---|
| Sweden | Swedes |
| Netherlands | Dutch |
| England | English |
| Germany | Germans |
| Africa | Africans |

 Integrated Assessment
· Rubric 2

## COLONIAL MEETINGHOUSES

The Puritans of the Northeast, the Quakers of Pennsylvania, and the Anglicans of the Southern colonies held profound but often different convictions about community, social responsibility, and individual freedom. These convictions were expressed in the religious services of each group and in the architecture of the places of worship where these services were held.

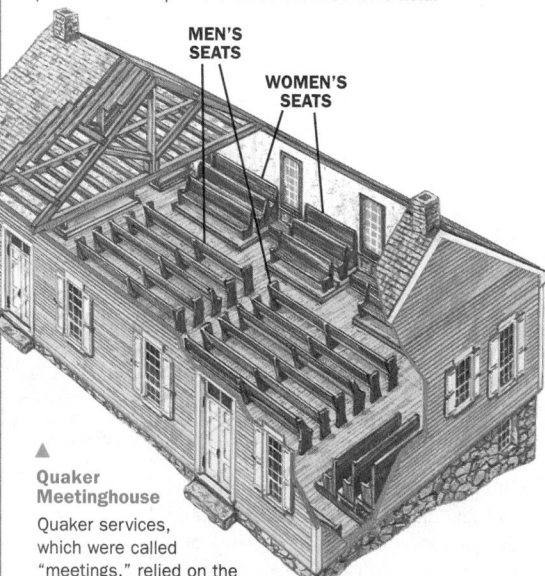

**MEN'S SEATS**

**WOMEN'S SEATS**

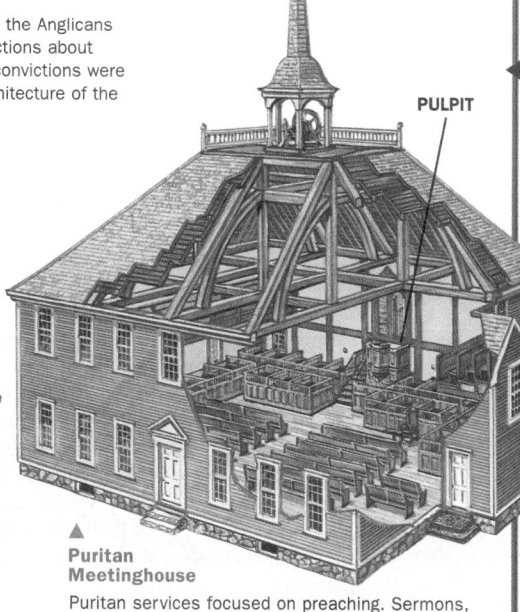

**PULPIT**

▲ **Puritan Meetinghouse**

Puritan services focused on preaching. Sermons, which sometimes lasted for hours, instructed the individual conscience to be mindful of the common good.

The pulpit was the focal point of the meetinghouse. A plain interior reflected a value for austerity and simplicity. Meetinghouses were also used for town meetings.

▲ **Quaker Meetinghouse**

Quaker services, which were called "meetings," relied on the inspiration of the "inner light." Meetings reflected a respect for conscience and freedom of speech.

Men and women entered by separate doors and sat on opposite sides, facing each other. In some meetinghouses, women sat in slightly elevated seats. Both men and women could speak during the meeting.

### More About . . .

**Quaker Services**

As the openness of their meeting houses suggests, the Quakers were more welcoming of input from women than other colonial groups. Female members of society were allowed to speak freely at Quaker religious services. It was, noted one observer, "among the Quakers that the spiritual rights of women attained their apogee." As one Quaker leader remarked, "The Lamb of God, the Son of God, is but one in all His males and females, sons and daughters, and they all are one in Christ, and Christ one in them all."

**PULPIT     ALTAR**

◄ **Anglican Church**

The head of the Anglican church was the British monarch. Anglican services valued ritual. Their churches stressed the importance of authority and status.

Anglican churches emphasized the altar through ornamentation and elaborate windows. A screen separated the altar from the congregation. Elaborate pews were reserved for wealthy church members.

**SKILLBUILDER** Interpreting Visual Sources

1. In what ways do the Puritan and Quaker meetinghouses resemble each other? In what ways are they different?
2. How does the interior of the Anglican church show respect for hierarchy?

 **SEE SKILLBUILDER HANDBOOK, PAGE R23.**

**REVIEW UNIT   27**

**ACTIVITY    COOPERATIVE LEARNING**

**BLOCK SCHEDULING**

## Investigating Puritan Life

**Class Time** Two class periods

**Task** Investigating the Puritans and creating a visual display on their customs

**Purpose** To understand the customs, traditions, family life, and community life of the Puritans in Massachusetts

**Directions** Divide the class into small groups. Have them select from the following topics: food, clothing, religious practices, social customs, laws and traditions, work and income, education, and entertainment. After researching their topics, have students create visual displays as well as written descriptions of their findings and present them to the class. Other history classes might be invited to sit in on the presentations.

## Instruct: Objective ④

**England and Its Colonies Prosper**

TAKS SS11 4(8.3A)

· How did mercantilism work?

· What was the general structure of colonial government?

 **In-Depth Resources: Unit 1**
· Guided Reading, p.11

**Critical Thinking Transparencies CT36**
· American Colonies

---

### More About . . .

**Mercantilism**

Colonies under mercantilism were supposed to supply materials that the mother country lacked. The manufacturing of these colonial goods competed with English producers: wool in 1699; hats in 1732; and wrought iron and steel in 1750. On the eve of the American Revolution, the colonies continued to serve as a major market for British goods. Remarked the *London* magazine in 1766, "The American is apparelled from head to foot in our manufactures . . . he scarcely drinks, sits, moves, labours or recreates himself, without contributing to the emolument of the mother country."

---

Penn himself spent only about four years in Pennsylvania. Meanwhile, his idealistic vision had faded but did not disappear. The Quakers became a minority in a colony thickly populated by people from all over western Europe. Slavery was introduced, and, in fact, many prominent Quakers in Pennsylvania owned slaves. However, the principles of equality, cooperation, and religious tolerance on which he had founded his vision would eventually become fundamental values of the new American nation. **Ⓗ**

## ④ England and Its Colonies Prosper

**THIRTEEN COLONIES** Throughout the 1600s and 1700s, more British colonies in North America were founded, each for very different reasons. In 1632, King Charles I granted land north of Chesapeake Bay to George Calvert, the first Lord Baltimore. Calvert's son Cecil, the second Lord Baltimore, named the colony Maryland, after Queen Henrietta Maria, Charles's wife. In 1663, King Charles II awarded a group of key supporters the land between Virginia and Spanish Florida, a territory that soon became North and South Carolina.

In 1732, an English philanthropist named James Oglethorpe, along with several associates, received a charter for a colony they hoped could be a haven for those imprisoned for debt. Oglethorpe named the colony Georgia, after King George II. Few debtors actually came to Georgia, and the British Crown assumed direct control of the colony in 1752. By that time, the Crown had begun to exercise more and more control over colonial economies and governments.

The thirteen British colonies existed primarily for the benefit of England. The colonies exported to England a rich variety of raw materials, such as lumber and furs, and in return they imported the manufactured goods that England produced. The thirteen colonies that became the original United States were founded over a period of 125 years. Together, the colonies represented a wide variety of people, skills, motives, industries, resources, and agricultural products.

**MERCANTILISM AND THE NAVIGATION ACTS** Beginning in the 16th century, the nations of Europe competed for wealth and power through a new economic system called **mercantilism** (mûr´kən-tē-lĭz´əm), in which the colonies played a critical role. According to the theory of mercantilism, a nation could increase its wealth and power in two ways: by obtaining as much gold and silver as possible, and by establishing a favorable balance of trade, in which it sold more goods than it bought. A nation's ultimate goal was to become self-sufficient so that it did not have to depend on other countries for goods.

The key to this process was the establishment of colonies. Colonies provided products, especially raw materials, that could not be found in the home country.

In 1651, England's Parliament, the country's legislative body, moved to tighten control of colonial trade by passing a series of measures known as the **Navigation Acts.** These acts enforced the following rules:

- No country could trade with the colonies unless the goods were shipped in either colonial or English ships.
- All vessels had to be operated by crews that were at least three-quarters English or colonial.
- The colonies could export certain products, including tobacco and sugar—and later rice, molasses, and furs—only to England.
- Almost all goods traded between the colonies and Europe first had to pass through an English port.

The system created by the Navigation Acts obviously benefited England. It proved to be good for most colonists as well. By restricting trade to English or colonial

**28** CHAPTER 1 *Exploration and the Colonial Era*

---

### MAIN IDEA

**Contrasting**
**Ⓗ** How did Penn's actions toward Native Americans differ from those of the Puritans in Massachusetts?

*H Answer*
**Penn:** Sought their respect and friendship and paid them for their land; **Puritans:** Sought to push them off the land once attempts to convert them had failed.

**Vocabulary**
**charter:** A document issued by a monarch or other authority creating a public or private corporation

*Skillbuilder Answer*
Massachusetts, New Hampshire, Connecticut, New York, and Pennsylvania: The New England and Middle Colonies

---

## ACTIVITY   LINK TO ART/LANGUAGE ARTS

**Advertising the Colonies**

**Class Time** One class period

**Task** Creating a recruiting brochure

**Purpose** To summarize attractions of the colonies for new settlers

**Directions** Assign groups of students either a Middle Colony, Jamestown, or Massachusetts Bay. Have the groups create an advertising brochure to attract new settlers to the colony. Tell students to identify their target audience, attractive features of the area, the message, and the action they want their readers to take before beginning to work on their brochures. Have them draw or photocopy pictures and maps for their brochures.

 **Integrated Assessment**
· Rubric 4

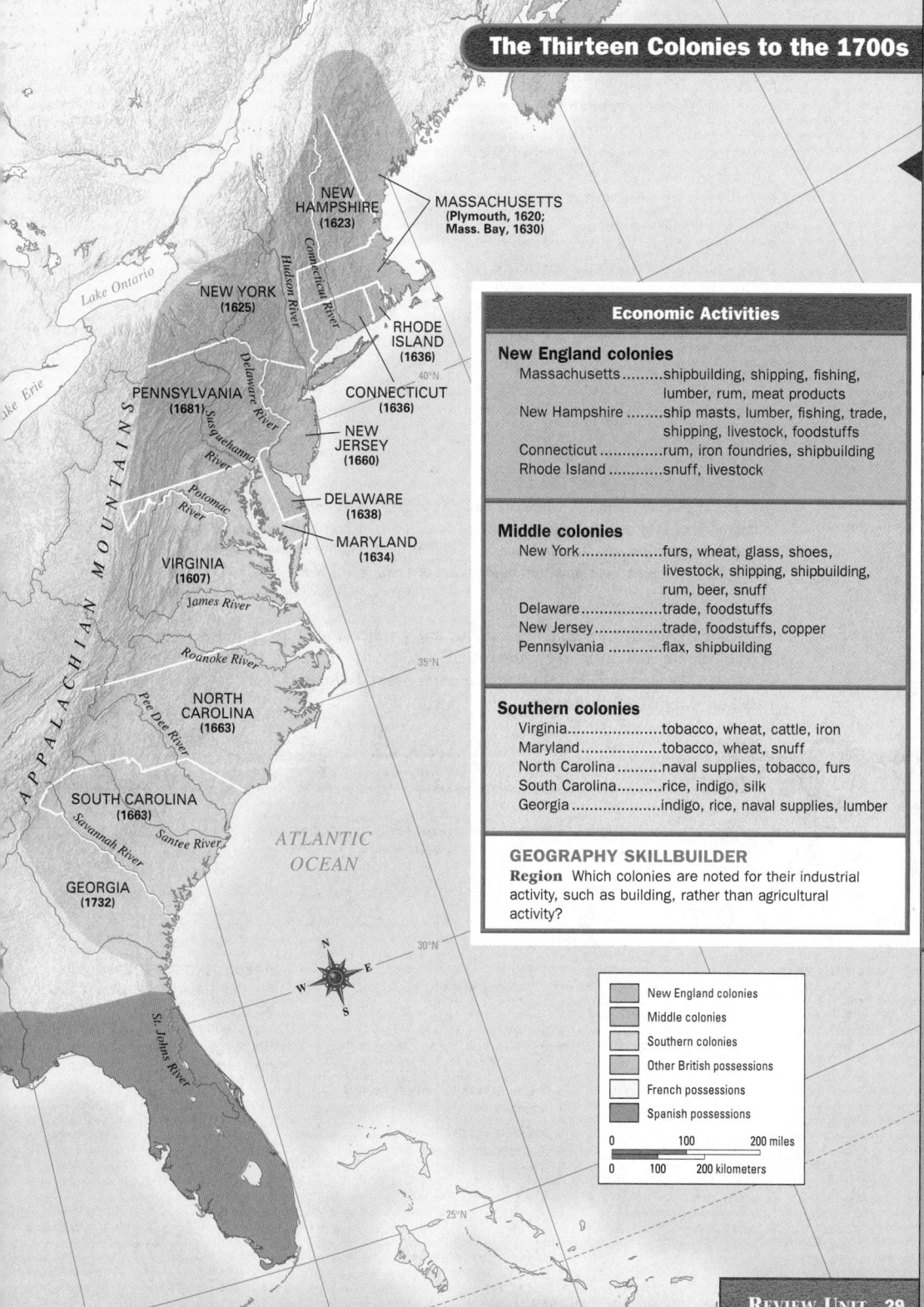

### Economic Activities

**New England colonies**

| | |
|---|---|
| Massachusetts | shipbuilding, shipping, fishing, lumber, rum, meat products |
| New Hampshire | ship masts, lumber, fishing, trade, shipping, livestock, foodstuffs |
| Connecticut | rum, iron foundries, shipbuilding |
| Rhode Island | snuff, livestock |

**Middle colonies**

| | |
|---|---|
| New York | furs, wheat, glass, shoes, livestock, shipping, shipbuilding, rum, beer, snuff |
| Delaware | trade, foodstuffs |
| New Jersey | trade, foodstuffs, copper |
| Pennsylvania | flax, shipbuilding |

**Southern colonies**

| | |
|---|---|
| Virginia | tobacco, wheat, cattle, iron |
| Maryland | tobacco, wheat, snuff |
| North Carolina | naval supplies, tobacco, furs |
| South Carolina | rice, indigo, silk |
| Georgia | indigo, rice, naval supplies, lumber |

### GEOGRAPHY SKILLBUILDER
**Region** Which colonies are noted for their industrial activity, such as building, rather than agricultural activity?

Map legend:
- New England colonies
- Middle colonies
- Southern colonies
- Other British possessions
- French possessions
- Spanish possessions

0   100   200 miles
0   100   200 kilometers

## HISTORY from VISUALS

### Interpreting the Map
Tell students that this map provides many different types of information. Have them identify some of these categories: physical topography east of the Mississippi, political boundaries of the colonies, economic activities of the colonies, European holdings east of the Mississippi River, and so on.

## More About . . .

### Shipbuilding
Shipbuilding was one of the more viable economic activities in the colonies. The main reason was the abundant supply of oak and timber growing along the eastern seaboard. As one observer put it, "practically the whole coast was clothed with timber." With so much wood available, the colonies could build a ship for England at a fraction of what it would cost the mother country to build one itself—since there was little wood in England and importing it from other nations was costly. Ironically, by the American Revolution, a third of all British vessels were American built.

Geography Transparencies GT3
· The Colonial Economies

---

## ACTIVITY    COOPERATIVE LEARNING

### Mapping Colonial Economic Activities

**Class Time** One class period

**Task** Creating a pictorial map that shows the economic activities of the 13 English colonies

**Purpose** To illustrate the economic diversity of the colonies

**Directions** Request volunteers to draw wall-size outlines of the 13 colonies. Tell them to show only the political boundaries on the map. Then assign groups of students one or more of the colonies, and have them think of various symbols to show the ways in which people earned a living in these colonies at this time. Students can refer to an atlas for ideas of symbols, or to a natural resources map in an encyclopedia.

*Exploration and the Colonial Era* **29**

## More About . . .

### Self-Determination

Nehemiah Grew wasn't the only one troubled by the colonies' growing desire for self-determination. Governor George Clinton of New York expressed his displeasure with the autonomous tendencies of the colonial assemblies. In a report back home, he complained of the "Incroachments the Assemblys of this Province have from time to time made on His Majesty's Perogitive and Authority" and suggested that British officials do more to "put a stop to these usurpations."

Mini-Lesson 3:
SS11 4(8.3A)

## Assess & Reteach

### SECTION 3 ASSESSMENT

Have students edit each other's answers, indicating whether or not answers match directions, such as "Evaluating."

 Formal Assessment
· Section Quiz, p. 7

### SELF-ASSESSMENT

Have students create a before-and-after chart showing what they knew about the early histories of the English colonies prior to reading Section 3 and what they learned as a result of their reading.

### RETEACH

Use the Guided Reading worksheet for Section 3 to help review the main ideas of this section.

 In-Depth Resources: Unit 1
· Reteaching Activity, p. 19

---

ships, the acts spurred a boom in the colonial shipbuilding industry and helped support the development of numerous other colonial industries. ⬇

**COLONIAL GOVERNMENTS** Whatever their form of charter, by the mid 1700s, most colonies were similar in the structure of their governments. In nearly every colony, a governor appointed by the Crown served as the highest authority. The governor presided over an advisory council, usually appointed by the governor, and a local assembly elected by landowning white males. The governor had the authority to appoint and dismiss judges and oversee colonial trade.

In addition to raising money through taxes, the colonial assembly initiated and passed laws. The governor could veto any law but did so at a risk—because in most colonies the colonial assembly, not the Crown, paid the governor's salary. Using this power of the purse liberally, the colonists influenced the governor in a variety of ways, from the approval of laws to the appointment of judges.

**GROWING SPIRIT OF SELF–DETERMINATION** The colonies were developing a taste for self-government that would ultimately create the conditions for rebellion. Nehemiah Grew, a British mercantilist, voiced one of the few early concerns when he warned his compatriots about the colonies' growing self-determination in 1707.

### A PERSONAL VOICE NEHEMIAH GREW

" The time may come . . . when the colonies may become populous and with the increase of arts and sciences strong and politic, forgetting their relation to the mother countries, will then confederate and consider nothing further than the means to support their ambition of standing on their [own] legs."

—quoted in *The Colonial Period of American History*

Aside from a desire for more economic and political breathing room, however, the colonies had little in common that would unite them against Britain. In particular, the Northern and Southern colonies were developing distinct societies, based on sharply contrasting economic systems.

---

### SECTION 3 ASSESSMENT

1. **TERMS & NAMES** For each term or name, write a sentence explaining its significance.

- John Smith
- Jamestown
- joint-stock companies
- indentured servant
- Puritan
- John Winthrop
- King Philip's War
- William Penn
- Quaker
- mercantilism
- Navigation Acts

#### MAIN IDEA

2. **TAKING NOTES**
Identify the effects of each of the causes listed in the chart below.

| Cause | Effect |
|---|---|
| Virginia colonists need labor to grow tobacco | |
| Puritans are persecuted in England | |
| William Penn acquires Pennsylvania | |
| Parliament passes the Navigation Acts | |

#### CRITICAL THINKING

3. **EVALUATING**
In your judgment, what were the benefits and drawbacks of using indentured servants for labor in Virginia? Support your judgment with references to the text. **Think About:**

- the labor demands of growing tobacco
- the characteristics and cost of indentured servants
- the causes and consequences of Bacon's Rebellion

4. **PREDICTING EFFECTS**
Reread Nehemiah Grew's prediction for the colonies in the Personal Voice above. How do you think the British government would respond to his prediction? What issues do you see arising as potential sources of tension between the colonies and Great Britain?

---

**MAIN IDEA**
Analyzing Effects
⬇ What effects did the Navigation Acts have on both Britain and its colonies?
*I Answer* They benefited England by channeling trade through English ports; they also spurred a boom in the colonial shipbuilding industry.

---

### SECTION 3 ASSESSMENT Answers

**1. TERMS & NAMES**
John Smith, p. 21
Jamestown, p. 21
joint-stock company, p. 21
indentured servant, p. 23
Puritan, p. 24
John Winthrop, p. 24
King Philip's War, p. 25

William Penn, p. 26
Quaker, p. 26
mercantilism, p. 28
Navigation Acts, p. 28

**2. TAKING NOTES**
Cause: Virginia colonists—Effect: Enslaved Africans are brought to the English colonies. Cause: Persecution—Effect: Puritan migration to New England. Cause: William Penn—Effect: Colony is established on Quaker principles. Cause: Navigation Acts—Effect: They spurred a boom in the colonial shipbuilding industry.

**3. EVALUATING**
**Benefits** indentured servants were available, willing, and economical labor. **Drawbacks** terms of service relatively short; since they earned little or no money during service, former servants were unable to buy land; they remained poor and had few rights.

**4. PREDICTING EFFECTS**
The British government would not want to see this happen. Issues of trade and taxation may become a source of tension.

# The Colonies Come of Age

**OBJECTIVES**

1. Characterize the plantation economy in the South.

2. Recognize the varied economy in the North.

3. Summarize the impact of Enlightenment thinking and the influence of the Great Awakening on people in the colonies.

4. Understand the French and Indian War.

**SKILLBUILDERS**

· Geography Skillbuilder: region, place, p. 38

**CRITICAL THINKING**

· Summarizing, pp. 32, 39
· Making Inferences, pp. 33, 39
· Drawing Conclusions, p. 33
· Analyzing Effects, pp. 35, 36
· Contrasting, p. 37
· Analyzing Causes, p. 39
· Analyzing Primary Sources, p. 39
· Analyzing Issues, p. 39

| MAIN IDEA | WHY IT MATTERS NOW | Terms & Names |
|---|---|---|
| Even though both Northern and Southern colonies prospered, many colonists began to question British authority. | Regional differences between Northern and Southern colonies have survived in the culture and politics of the modern United States. | • triangular trade • middle passage • Enlightenment • Benjamin Franklin • Great Awakening • Jonathan Edwards • French and Indian War • William Pitt • Pontiac • Proclamation of 1763 |

U.S. History
7A, 8B, 9A, 9B, 10B, 18A, 19A, 20D, 21C, 21D, 22A, 24A, 24B, 24D, 25A, 25B, 25C, 25D

### One American's Story

In 1773, Philip Vickers Fithian left his home in Princeton, New Jersey, for the unfamiliar world of Virginia. Fithian, a theology student, had agreed to tutor the children of Robert Carter III and his wife at their magnificent brick manor house. In Fithian's journal of his one-year stay there, he recalled an evening walk along the property.

**A PERSONAL VOICE** PHILIP VICKERS FITHIAN

"We stroll'd down the Pasture quite to the River, admiring the Pleasantness of the evening, & the delightsome Prospect of the River, Hills, Huts on the Summits, low Bottoms, Trees of various Kinds, and Sizes, Cattle & Sheep feeding some near us, & others at a great distance on the green sides of the Hills."

—Journal & Letters of Philip Vickers Fithian

Plantations, or large farms, like the Carters' played a dominant role in the South's economy, which had come to rely heavily on agriculture. The development of this plantation economy led to a largely rural society, in which enslaved Africans played an unwilling yet important role.

▲ The Shirley plantation house in Virginia is representative of many old Southern mansions. Built in 1723, it was the birthplace of Ann Hill Carter, the mother of Civil War general Robert E. Lee.

## ① A Plantation Economy Arises in the South

While there were cities in the South, on the whole the region developed as a rural society of self-sufficient plantations. Plantations sprang up along the rivers, making it possible for planters to ship their goods directly to the Northern colonies and Europe without the need for public dock facilities. Because plantation owners produced much of what they needed on their property, they did not often need shops, bakeries, and markets.

## Focus & Motivate

Ask students if they think it is possible to be wealthy without relying on the work of poorer people.

## Instruct

### Instruct: Objective ①

**A Plantation Economy Arises in the South**
TAKS SS11 5(US24.A)

· On what was the South's economy based?
· In what ways was Southern society diverse?
· What was the Middle Passage?
· How did enslaved Africans cope in their new world?

 In-Depth Resources: Unit 1
· Guided Reading, p. 12

**PROGRAM RESOURCES**

 **In-Depth Resources: Unit 1**
· Guided Reading, p. 12
· Skillbuilder Practice: Visual, Audio, Multimedia Sources, p. 16
· Reteaching Activity, p. 20
· Geography Application: The Triangular Trade, pp. 21–22
· Primary Sources: *The Autobiography* by Benjamin Franklin, p. 29
· American Lives: Olaudah Equiano, p. 34

 **Reading Study Guide** (English and Spanish), pp. 11–12

 **Access for Students Acquiring English/ESL**
· Guided Reading (Spanish), p. 16
· Skillbuilder Practice, p. 19
· Geography Application: The Triangular Trade, pp. 20–21

 **Formal Assessment**
· Section Quiz, p. 8

 **Integrated Assessment**
· Rubrics

**INTEGRATED TECHNOLOGY**

🖥 **Critical Thinking Transp. CT37**
· Africans in the Colonies

💿 **Electronic Library of Primary Sources**

ⓘ **classzone.com**

**TEXAS RESOURCES**

 TAKS Spiraled Content Review

 TAKS Practice Tests

 TAKS Practice Transparencies TT10–13

ⓘ TAKS Online Test Practice

## More About . . .

### The Middle Passage

The highest rate of deaths aboard slave ships occurred during the 16th century, when a voyage across the Atlantic took anywhere from 12 to 20 weeks—plenty of time for diseases to emerge and spread. With the construction of faster boats in the 18th and 19th centuries, a transatlantic trip took only between 5 and 8 weeks. Thus, the death rate aboard the ships dropped slightly.

## More About . . .

### Slavery in the Americas

The transatlantic slave trade spanned roughly 400 years, from the 15th to the 19th centuries, and drained Africa of an estimated 25–30 million people. A majority of those enslaved men and women transported to the Americas went to the sugar plantations in the Caribbean and Latin America. The 18th century was the busiest era of the Atlantic slave trade, as more than 6 million Africans came over—and about half of them went to the Caribbean. By the end of the 1700s, slaves made up more than 80 percent of the population of many Caribbean colonies.

 Critical Thinking Transparencies CT37
· Africans in the Colonies

 In-Depth Resources: Unit 1
· Geography Application: The Triangular Trade, pp. 21–22

Plantations specialized in raising a single cash crop—one grown primarily for sale rather than for livestock feed. In Maryland, Virginia, and North Carolina, planters grew tobacco. Planters in South Carolina and Georgia harvested rice and later indigo (for blue dye) as cash crops.

**LIFE IN A DIVERSE SOUTHERN SOCIETY** In addition to English settlers, thousands of German immigrants as well as Scots and Scots-Irish settled in the South. Women in Southern society, as in the North, endured second-class citizenship. For the most part they could not vote, preach, or own property.

While small farmers made up the majority of the Southern population, prosperous plantation owners controlled much of the South's economy as well as its political and social institutions.

At the bottom of Southern society were enslaved Africans. In the 18th century, Southerners turned increasingly to slavery to fill the labor needs of their agricultural economy. By 1690, about 13,000 slaves were working in the Southern colonies. By 1750, the number of slaves had increased to more than 200,000. **A**

**THE MIDDLE PASSAGE** During the 17th century, Africans had become part of a transatlantic trading network described as the **triangular trade.** This term refers to a trading process in which goods and enslaved people were exchanged across the Atlantic Ocean. For example, merchants carrying rum and other goods from the New England colonies exchanged their merchandise for enslaved Africans. Africans were then transported to the West Indies where they were sold for sugar and molasses. These goods were then sold to rum producers in New England and the cycle began again.

The voyage that brought Africans to the West Indies and later to North America was known as the **middle passage**, after the middle leg of the transatlantic trade triangle. Extreme cruelty characterized this journey. In the ports of West Africa, European traders branded Africans for identification and packed them into the dark holds of large ships. On board a slave ship, Africans were beaten into submission and often fell victim to diseases that spread rapidly. Some committed suicide by jumping overboard. Nearly 13 percent of the Africans aboard each slave ship perished during the

**MAIN IDEA**

**Summarizing**
**A** Describe the social structure of Southern society.

*A Answer*
Enslaved Africans at the bottom of society; above them small farmers; at the very top, prosperous plantation owners.

This plan and section of the British slave ship *Brookes* was published in London around 1790 by a leading British antislavery advocate named Thomas Clarkson. The image effectively conveys the degradation and inhumanity of the slave trade, which reduced human beings to the level of merchandise.

32   CHAPTER 1 *Exploration and the Colonial Era*

---

**ACTIVITY**  **LINK TO LANGUAGE ARTS**

## Describing Southern Social Groups

**Class Time** One–two class periods

**Task** Writing character sketches of the different social groups in the Southern colonies

**Purpose** To illustrate the similarities and differences among the social groups

**Directions** Divide the class into four groups, assigning each group to one of these social groups in the South: planters, small farmers, women, or slaves. Ask students to research and discuss the details that make their group similar to or different from the others. Then have them choose a fictional character representing their social group, and write a character sketch of that person and his or her life in the South. Collect the sketches into a classroom portfolio.

brutal trip to the New World. One enslaved African, Olaudah Equiano, recalled the inhumane conditions on his trip from West Africa to the West Indies in 1762 when he was 12 years old.

**Olaudah Equiano**

### MAIN IDEA

**Making Inferences**
**B** If 13 percent of the enslaved Africans died on the journey to America, why did the merchants treat them so badly?

*B Possible Answers* It was cheaper to replace the slaves than to keep them alive and healthy; racist merchants did not think the slaves deserved humane treatment.

**A PERSONAL VOICE** OLAUDAH EQUIANO

" The closeness of the place and the heat of the climate, added to the number in the ship, which was so crowded that each had scarcely room to turn himself, almost suffocated us. This produced copious perspirations, so that the air soon became unfit for respiration from a variety of loathsome smells, and brought on a sickness among the slaves, of which many died. . . ."

—*The Interesting Narrative of the Life of Olaudah Equiano*

**AFRICANS COPE IN THEIR NEW WORLD** Africans who survived the ocean voyage entered an extremely difficult life of bondage in North America. Probably 80 to 90 percent worked in the fields. The other 10 to 20 percent worked as domestic slaves or as artisans. Domestic slaves worked in the houses of their masters, cooking, cleaning, and helping to raise the master's children. Artisans developed skills as carpenters, blacksmiths, and bricklayers and were sometimes loaned out to the master's neighbors.

In the midst of the horrors of slavery, Africans developed a way of life based on their cultural heritage. They kept alive their musical, dance, and storytelling traditions. When a slave owner sold a parent to another plantation, other slaves stepped in to raise the children left behind.

Slaves also resisted their position of subservience. Throughout the colonies, planters reported slaves faking illness, breaking tools, and staging work slowdowns. A number of slaves tried to run away, even though escape attempts brought severe punishment. **C**

Some slaves even pushed their resistance to open revolt. One uprising, the Stono Rebellion, began on a September Sunday in 1739. That morning, about 20 slaves gathered at the Stono River just south of Charles Town (later Charleston), South Carolina. Wielding guns and other weapons, they killed several planter families and marched south, beating drums and inviting other slaves to join them in their plan to flee to Spanish-held Florida. Many slaves died in the fighting that followed. Those captured were executed. Despite the rebellion's failure, it sent a chill through many Southern colonists and led to the tightening of harsh slave laws already in place.

### MAIN IDEA

**Drawing Conclusions**
**C** How did enslaved Africans maintain their sense of self esteem?

*C Answer* Enslaved Africans kept alive their musical, dance, and storytelling traditions.

## ❷ Commerce Grows in the North

The development of thriving commercial cities and diverse economic activities gradually made the North radically different from the South. Grinding wheat, harvesting fish, and sawing lumber became thriving industries. By the 1770s, the colonists had built one-third of all British ships and were producing more iron than England did. Many colonists prospered. In particular, the number of merchants grew. By the mid-1700s, merchants were one of the most powerful groups in the North. In contrast to the South, where Charles Town was the only major port, the North boasted Boston, New York, and Philadelphia.

**COLONIAL CITIES AND TRADE** The expansion of trade caused port cities to grow. Philadelphia became the second largest port in the British empire, after London. Toward the end of the 1700s, Yankee traders were sailing around Cape Horn at the tip of South America to trade with Spanish missionaries as far away as California. There they exchanged manufactured goods for hides, tallow, wine, olive oil, and grain raised with the help of the Native American labor on the missions.

**Vocabulary**
**tallow:** fat from livestock used to make candles and soap

---

### More About . . .

**Olaudah Equiano**

Also known as Gustavus Vassa, Equiano was enslaved and sold in the West Indies in about 1755. Eventually he bought his freedom for 40 pounds. He became an active abolitionist in England and helped lead the way for the establishment of Freetown, Sierra Leone, as an African sanctuary for freed slaves. In 1789 Equiano published *The Interesting Narrative of the Life of Olaudah Equiano, or Gustavus Vassa, the African.* The book was a best seller, which Equiano later followed with his *Miscellaneous Verses.*

🖥 Electronic Library of Primary Sources
· *The Interesting Narrative of the Life of Olaudah Equiano*

📖 In-Depth Resources: Unit 1
· American Lives: Olaudah Equiano, p. 34

### Connections Across Time
**COLONIAL TIMES AND TODAY**

**Gullah**
One legacy of African slaves is the quick-paced words of Gullah, a combination of English colonial speech and the language from several West African societies. Nearly 6,000 African words have been identified as Gullah, for example, *peanut* and *juke* (as in *jukebox*). Gullah speakers, the American descendants of slaves, live on the Sea Islands of South Carolina and Georgia and on the mainland nearby.

### Instruct: Objective ❷
**Commerce Grows in the North**
TAKS SS11 2(WG6.A)
· What type of economy characterized the Northern colonies?
· What different ethnic groups lived in the North?

📖 In-Depth Resources: Unit 1
· Guided Reading, p. 12

---

## DIFFERENTIATING INSTRUCTION · GIFTED AND TALENTED

**Wealthy British and Southern Landowners**

Ask students to research the lives of wealthy landowners in Britain and compare and contrast them with the lives of plantation owners in the Southern colonies. Students' reports might take the form of fictional letters between a planter and an English aristocrat or a short piece of historical fiction in which the child of a wealthy Southern planter goes to England to be educated.

Post a large map of the Southern colonies in the classroom. As students present their work, mark the map to show the fictional locations of the landowners and plantation owners described. Have students add brief captions at these locations on the map to indicate the circumstances of each person's life in the South. You might use this map to add other useful sites, dates, and events pertaining to the Southern colonies.

📖 Integrated Assessment
· Rubric 1

## Daily Urban Life in Colonial Times

By the mid-18th century, colonial cities were prosperous and growing. Brick rowhouses were replacing the wooden structures of the 17th century, while large mansions and churches, built of brick or stone, were rising everywhere.

English colonists had brought with them a preference for houses (as opposed to apartments, which were the norm in the cities of other European countries). As in Britain, the size of the house indicated the social position of its occupant.

▲ In contemporary Philadelphia, Elfreth's Alley preserves the scale and appearance of a mid-18th century city street. Narrow rowhouses like these were occupied by artisans and shopkeepers. A neighborhood like this could have commercial and residential uses. Many people lived above the shops where they worked.

◄ The house known as Cliveden, also in Philadelphia, was completed in 1767. In contrast to the artisan or lower-middle-class housing of Elfreth's Alley, this large freestanding mansion shows the kind of building that the rich could afford.

The Northern colonies attracted a variety of immigrants. During the 18th century, about 463,000 Europeans migrated to America. Before 1700, most immigrants came as indentured servants from England, but by 1755, over one-half of all European immigrants were from other countries. They included large numbers of Germans and Scots-Irish. Other ethnic groups included the Dutch in New York, Scandinavians in Delaware, and Jews in such cities as Newport and Philadelphia.

**FARMING IN THE NORTH** Unlike Southern plantations, a farm in New England and the middle colonies typically produced several cash crops rather than a single one. Because growing wheat and corn did not require as much labor as did growing tobacco and rice, Northerners had less need to rely on slave labor. However, slavery did exist in New England and was extensive throughout the middle colonies, as was racial prejudice against blacks—free or enslaved. As in the South, women in the North had extensive work responsibilities but few legal or social rights.

### ❸ The Enlightenment

During the 1700s, the Enlightenment, an intellectual movement that began in Europe, and the Great Awakening, a colonial religious movement, influenced people's thinking throughout the thirteen colonies.

**EUROPEAN IDEAS INSPIRE THE COLONISTS** During the Renaissance in Europe, scientists had begun looking beyond religious beliefs and traditional assumptions for answers about how the world worked. Careful observation and reason, or rational thought, led to the discovery of some of the natural laws and principles governing the world and human behavior. The work of Nicolaus Copernicus, Galileo Galilei, and Sir Isaac Newton established that the earth

**34** CHAPTER 1 *Exploration and the Colonial Era*

revolved around the sun and not vice versa. This observation, which challenged the traditional assumption that the earth was the center of the universe, was at first fiercely resisted. It was thought to contradict the Bible and other religious teachings. The early scientists also concluded that the world is governed by fixed mathematical laws rather than solely by the will of God. These ideas about nature led to a movement called the **Enlightenment,** in which philosophers valued reason and scientific methods.

Enlightenment ideas spread from Europe to the colonies, where people such as **Benjamin Franklin** embraced the notion of obtaining truth through experimentation and reason. For example, Franklin's most famous experiment—flying a kite in a thunderstorm—demonstrated that lightning is a form of electrical power.

Enlightenment ideas spread quickly through the colonies by means of books and pamphlets. Literacy was particularly high in New England because the Puritans had long supported public education, partly to make it possible for everyone to read the Bible. However, Enlightenment views were disturbing to some people. The Enlightenment suggested that people could use science and logic—rather than the pronouncements of church authorities—to arrive at truths. As the English poet John Donne had written, "[The] new philosophy calls all in doubt."

The Enlightenment also had a profound effect on political thought in the colonies. Colonial leaders such as Thomas Jefferson reasoned that human beings are born with natural rights that governments must respect. Enlightenment principles eventually would lead many colonists to question the authority of the British monarchy. **D**

## The Great Awakening ❸

By the early 1700s, the Puritans had lost some of their influence. Under the new Massachusetts charter of 1691, Puritans were required to practice religious tolerance and could no longer limit voting privileges to members of their own church. Furthermore, as Puritan merchants prospered, they developed a taste for fine houses, stylish clothes, and good food and wine. As a result, their interest in maintaining the strict Puritan code declined. A series of religious revivals aimed at restoring the intensity and dedication of the early Puritan church swept through the colonies. These came to be known collectively as the **Great Awakening.**

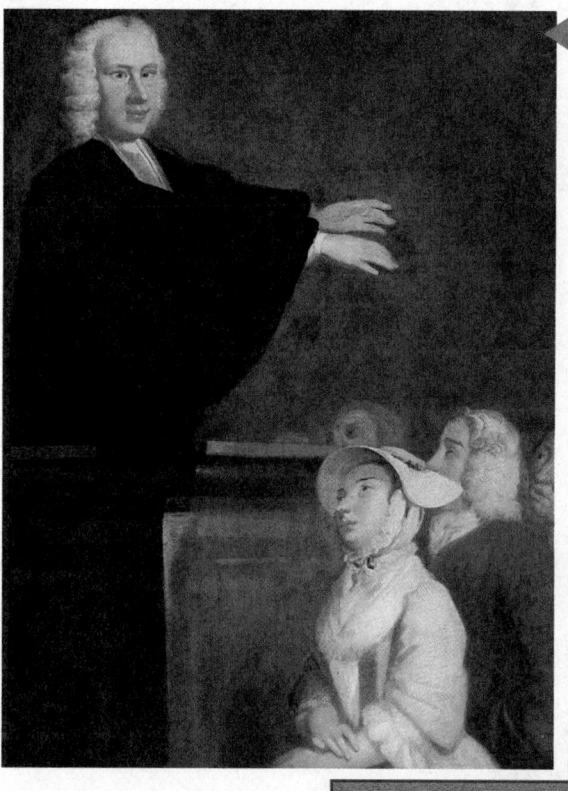

The British minister George Whitefield was a major force behind the Great Awakening. In his seven journeys to the American colonies between 1738 and 1769, Whitefield preached dramatic sermons that brought many listeners to tears.

**MAIN IDEA**

**Analyzing Effects**
**D** What effects did the Enlightenment have on political thought in the colonies?

*D Answer*
Colonists reasoned that individuals have natural rights, which the government must respect; colonists also began questioning the authority of the British monarchy.

**Vocabulary**
**revival:** a time of reawakened interest in religion

**More About . . .**

**The Enlightenment**
A major idea from the Enlightenment was John Locke's assertion that a social contract existed between a government and those who were governed. This meant that those who were governed gave their consent to be governed in return for certain benefits. They also had the right to change a government that did not meet its side of the contract. This idea was embraced by Virginia's Thomas Jefferson, a noted Enlightenment thinker and chief author of the Declaration of Independence.

**More About . . .**

**George Whitefield**
Whitefield's tremendous success as a preacher can be attributed in part to his acting ability. In his sermons he would first play the role of God and then switch to the role of the devil. "What a spell he casts over an audience," said Jonathan Edwards's wife, "by proclaiming the simplest truths of the Bible. I have seen upwards of a thousand people hang on his words with breathless silence, broken only by an occasional half-suppressed sob."

---

**DIFFERENTIATING INSTRUCTION**   **LESS PROFICIENT READERS**

### Clarifying Concepts

Help students understand the impact of the Enlightenment and the Great Awakening by reviewing the effects of the movements. First review the meaning of the terms. Next ask the students to read each paragraph under the headings and write out one sentence from each paragraph that illustrates an effect of the Enlightenment or the Great Awakening. When they have completed the sentences have them write a summary sentence beginning, "The effects of the Enlightenment/Great Awakening were . . ."

To get started, students might use a web graphic to organize information as shown at right.

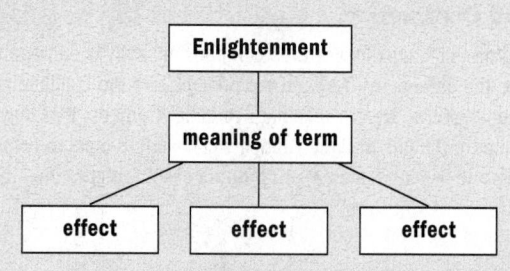

*Exploration and the Colonial Era* **35**

## KEY PLAYERS

### Franklin and Edwards

Have students compare and contrast Franklin's and Edwards's ideas, particularly the two men's views of the individual and of destiny. A Venn diagram may be helpful in making this comparison.

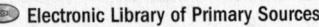

Franklin's Ideas

Shared Ideas

Edwards's Ideas

◉ Electronic Library of Primary Sources
· *Sinners in the Hands of an Angry God*, 1741, by J. Edwards

📖 In-Depth Resources: Unit 1
· Primary Sources: *The Autobiography* by Benjamin Franklin, p. 29

## Tracing Themes

### SCIENCE AND TECHNOLOGY

#### New Ways of Thinking

The Enlightenment that spread from Europe to the Americas brought with it an optimistic belief in science and reason that prompted a general spirit of inquiry and invention as well as an openness to new ideas. Electricity, for example, was still a new and mysterious idea when Ben Franklin conducted his famed experiments, which duplicated and expanded the work being done in France and England at the time. Franklin himself coined or popularized several of the terms used in the study of electricity—*conductor, battery, positive,* and *negative.*

## KEY PLAYERS

**BENJAMIN FRANKLIN**
**1706–1790**

A true student of the Enlightenment, Benjamin Franklin devised an orderly method to develop moral perfection in himself. In his autobiography, he records how he decided on a list of virtues he thought he should have. Then, every night, he reviewed whether his behavior lived up to those standards and recorded his faults in a notebook.

Originally, he concentrated on only 12 virtues until a Quaker friend told him he was too proud. Franklin promptly added a 13th virtue to the list—the virtue of humility, which he felt he never quite achieved.

Franklin took great pleasure in seeing his character improve. He wrote: "I was surpris'd to find myself so much fuller of faults than I had imagined; but I had the satisfaction of seeing them diminish."

**JONATHAN EDWARDS**
**1703–1758**

Unlike Benjamin Franklin, Jonathan Edwards did not believe that humans had the power to perfect themselves. Descended from a long line of Puritan ministers, he believed that "however you may have reformed your life in many things," all were sinners who were destined for hell unless they had a "great change of heart."

Edwards was a brilliant thinker who entered Yale College when he was only 13. His preaching was one of the driving forces of the Great Awakening. Ironically, when the religious revival died down, Edwards's own congregation rejected him for being too strict about doctrine. Edwards moved to Stockbridge, Massachusetts, in 1751, where he lived most of his remaining years as a missionary to a Native American settlement.

**RELIGIOUS REVIVALS** Among those clergy who sought to revive the fervor of the original Puritan vision was **Jonathan Edwards,** of Northampton, Massachusetts. One of the most learned religious scholars of his time, Edwards preached that it was not enough for people simply to come to church. In order to be saved, they must feel their sinfulness and feel God's love for them. In his most famous sermon, delivered in 1741, Edwards vividly described God's mercy toward sinners.

### A PERSONAL VOICE
JONATHAN EDWARDS

"**The God that holds you over the pit of Hell, much as one holds a spider, or some loathsome insect over the fire, abhors [hates] you, and is dreadfully provoked: His wrath towards you burns like fire; He looks upon you as worthy of nothing else but to be cast into the fire . . . and yet it is nothing but His hand that holds you from falling into the fire every moment.**"
—"Sinners in the Hands of an Angry God"

While the Great Awakening, which lasted throughout the 1730s and 1750s, restored many colonists' Christian religious faith, the movement also challenged the authority of established churches. Preachers traveled from village to village, attracting thousands to outdoor revival meetings, giving impassioned sermons, and stirring people to rededicate themselves to God. Some colonists abandoned their old Puritan or Anglican congregations, while independent denominations, such as the Baptists and Methodists, gained new members.

**EFFECTS OF THE GREAT AWAKENING AND ENLIGHTENMENT** Although the Great Awakening emphasized emotionalism and the Enlightenment emphasized reason, the two movements had similar consequences. Both caused people to question traditional authority. Moreover, both stressed the importance of the individual: the Enlightenment by emphasizing human reason, and the Great Awakening by de-emphasizing the role of church authority. Because these movements helped lead the colonists to question Britain's authority over their lives, they were important in creating the intellectual and social atmosphere that eventually led to the American Revolution. **Ⓔ**

36   CHAPTER 1 *Exploration and the Colonial Era*

*E Answer* It caused people to question traditional authority and led them to question Britain's authority over their lives.

**MAIN IDEA**

**Analyzing Effects**
**Ⓔ** What effects did the Great Awakening have on organized religion in the colonies?

## ACTIVITY   COOPERATIVE LEARNING

### Comparing and Contrasting

Students can build on the "Franklin/Edwards comparison" activity on page 36 by going on to explore the differences between the principles of the Enlightenment and the religious principles of the Great Awakening. You might suggest that they set up a simple chart similar to the one at right. Students can work in pairs to complete this activity, or record their remarks as a group on an easel tablet in the classroom.

| Differences Between | |
| --- | --- |
| **Enlightenment**   and | **Great Awakening** |
| 1. | 1. |
| | |
| 2. | 2. |

## ❹ The French and Indian War

**Background**
Hats made from beaver skin were popular in Europe beginning in the late 16th century. Because of the demand for beaver, the fur trade was enormously successful.

**MAIN IDEA**

**Contrasting**
Ⓕ How was the French colony in North America unlike the British colonies?

*F Answer*
France focused on developing the fur trade rather than on creating permanent settlements; enjoyed better relations with Native Americans; sent missionaries to convert Native Americans to Catholicism.

As the French empire in North America expanded, it collided with the growing British empire. During the late 17th and first half of the 18th centuries, France and Great Britain had fought three inconclusive wars. Each war had begun in Europe but spread to their overseas colonies. In 1754, after six relatively peaceful years, the French–British conflict reignited. This conflict is known as the **French and Indian War.**

**RIVALS FOR AN EMPIRE** From the start the French colony in North America, called New France, differed from the British colonies. Typical French colonists were young, single men who engaged in the fur trade and Catholic priests who sought to convert Native Americans. The French were more interested in exploiting their territories than in settling them. However, they usually enjoyed better relations with Native Americans, in part because they needed the local people as partners in the fur trade. In fact, several military alliances developed out of the French–Native American trade relationship. Ⓕ

**WAR ERUPTS** One major area of contention between France and Great Britain was the rich Ohio River valley just west of Pennsylvania and Virginia. In 1754, the French built Fort Duquesne in the region despite the fact that the Virginia government had already granted 200,000 acres of land in the Ohio country to a group of wealthy planters. In response, the Virginia governor sent militia, a group of ordinary citizens who performed military duties, to evict the French. This was the opening of the French and Indian War, the fourth war between Great Britain and France for control of North America.

In the first battle of the war, the French delivered a crushing defeat to the outnumbered Virginians and their leader, an ambitious 22-year-old officer named George Washington.

A year after his defeat, Washington again headed into battle, this time as an aide to the British general Edward Braddock. Braddock's first task was to relaunch an attack on Fort Duquesne. As Braddock and nearly 1,500 soldiers neared the fort, French soldiers and their Native American allies ambushed them. The startled British soldiers turned and fled.

In this scene from the French and Indian War, the British general Edward Braddock meets defeat and death on his march to Fort Duquesne in July of 1755.
▼

---

**CHAPTER 1 · SECTION 4**

**Instruct: Objective** ❹
**The French and Indian War**
TAKS SS11 5(WH26.C)
· For what reason did war break out between Britain and France in North America?
· What were consequences of the war for the French and British?

📄 In-Depth Resources: Unit 1
· Guided Reading, p. 12

**More About . . .**

**The Fur Trade**
Fashionable top hats made from beaver skins were extremely popular in Europe beginning in the late 16th century. Because of this demand for beaver, the fur trade proved enormously successful for all involved. Eventually the fur supply began to decrease, and silk hats replaced beaver hats as the fashion in Europe.

**More About . . .**

**George Washington**
George Washington's military career nearly ended shortly after it began. In 1754, as the British prepared to wage war on France in North America, Washington eagerly awaited a position with the regular British army. In reassembling an army to become part of a British regiment, the commander of the Virginia militia offered Washington the rank of captain—a demotion from his position as colonel. Washington angrily rejected the offer. He later swallowed his pride for the good of the British and colonial cause and relaunched his military career as an aide to General Braddock.

---

**DIFFERENTIATING INSTRUCTION**     **LESS PROFICIENT READERS**

**Comparing Colonies**

In order to help students to better understand the differences between the French and English colonies in North America, have them create and complete a comparison chart such as the one shown here. Charts should include the headings, "Type of Settlers," "Economic Activities," and "Relations with Native Americans." Ask students to be as specific as possible as they record details about each category. Have them exchange charts and compare them.

|  | English colonies | French colonies |
|---|---|---|
| Type of settlers |  |  |
| Economic Activities |  |  |
| Relations with Native Americans |  |  |

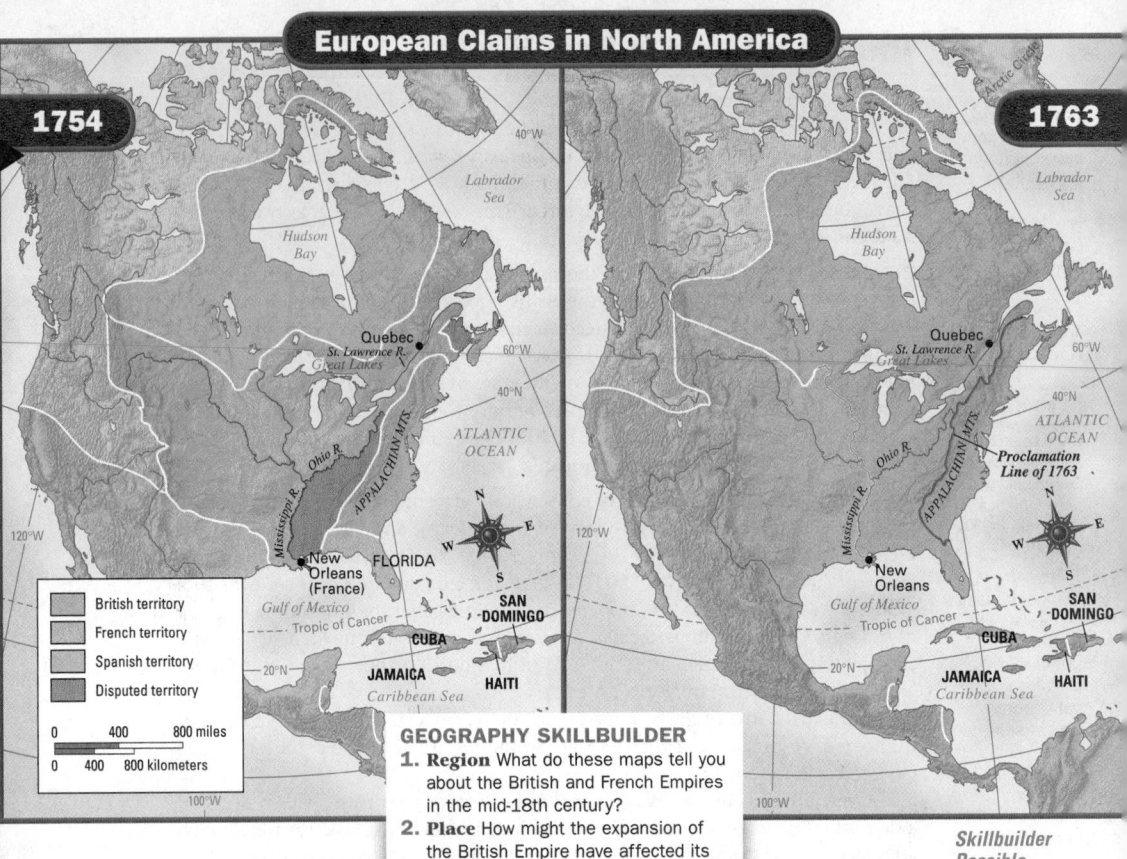

## European Claims in North America

**1754**

**1763**

Legend:
- British territory
- French territory
- Spanish territory
- Disputed territory

0       400       800 miles
0   400   800 kilometers

**GEOGRAPHY SKILLBUILDER**
1. **Region** What do these maps tell you about the British and French Empires in the mid-18th century?
2. **Place** How might the expansion of the British Empire have affected its relationship with the colonies?

## HISTORY from VISUALS

**Interpreting the Map**
Ask whether the British acquired all of present-day Canada in 1763. *(No.)*

**Extension** Have students use a map or atlas to identify the present-day U.S. states that Britain acquired as a result of the French and Indian War.

## More About . . .

### William Pitt
William Pitt (1708–1778) was the statesman often credited with securing, through victory in the French and Indian War, Britain's leading position as a colonial power. Pitt insisted on huge government expenditures as well as young, new generals to fortify his army. Pitt's brilliant military strategy assured victory for the British even though his first battle, an attack on Fort Ticonderoga, was a disaster.

---

The weakness of the British army surprised Washington, who showed great courage. As Washington tried to rally the troops, two horses were shot from under him and four bullets pierced his coat—yet he escaped unharmed. Many other colonists began to question the competence of the British army, which suffered defeat after defeat during 1755 and 1756.

**BRITAIN DEFEATS AN OLD ENEMY** Angered by French victories, Britain's King George II selected new leaders to run his government in 1757. One of these was **William Pitt** the elder, an energetic, self-confident politician. Under Pitt, the British and colonial troops finally began winning battles. These successes earned Britain the support of the powerful Iroquois, giving Britain some Native American allies to counterbalance those of France.

In September 1759, the war took a dramatic and decisive turn on the Plains of Abraham just outside Quebec. Under cover of night, British troops scaled the high cliffs that protected the city and defeated the French in a surprise attack. The British triumph at Quebec brought them victory in the war.

The war officially ended in 1763 with the signing of the Treaty of Paris. Great Britain claimed Canada and virtually all of North America east of the Mississippi River. Britain also took Florida from Spain, which had allied itself with France. The treaty permitted Spain to keep possession of its lands west of the Mississippi and the city of New Orleans, which it had gained from France in 1762. France retained control of only a few islands and small colonies near Newfoundland, in the West Indies, and elsewhere.

**38** CHAPTER 1 *Exploration and the Colonial Era*

---

### Annotated Maps

**Class Time** One class period

**Task** Creating annotated maps of the battles and territorial gains of the French and Indian War

**Purpose** To understand the sequence of events and the geographical results of the French and Indian War

**Directions** To illustrate the battles of the French and Indian War, students should create two or three maps, a single map with overlays, or a set of computer graphics. They may include labels with critical information about battles (such as number of people involved, dates, and results), brief descriptions of events, boundaries, and geographic features. Have them refer to the textbook, atlases, and other resource books if they need help.

 Integrated Assessment
· Rubric 4

**CHANGES FOR NATIVE AMERICANS** Others who lost ground in the war were the Native Americans, who found the victorious British harder to bargain with than the French had been. Native Americans resented the growing number of British settlers crossing the Appalachian Mountains and feared the settlers would soon drive away the game they depended on for survival. In the spring of 1763, the Ottawa leader Pontiac recognized that the French loss was a loss for Native Americans. **G**

**MAIN IDEA**

**Making Inferences**
**G** How did Great Britain's victory over France affect Native Americans?

**G Answer**
Native Americans found the British harder to deal with than the French had been. They resented the growing number of British settlers crossing the Appalachian Mountains.

### A PERSONAL VOICE PONTIAC

"When I go to see the English commander and say to him that some of our comrades are dead, instead of bewailing their death, as our French brothers do, he laughs at me and at you. If I ask for anything for our sick, he refuses with the reply that he has no use for us. For all this you can well see that they are seeking our ruin. Therefore, my brothers, we must all swear their destruction and wait no longer."

—quoted in *Red and White*

Led by **Pontiac,** Native Americans captured eight British forts in the Ohio Valley and the Great Lakes area and laid siege to another. In response, British officers deliberately presented blankets contaminated with smallpox to two Delaware chiefs during peace negotiations, and the virus spread rapidly among the Native Americans. Weakened by disease and tired of fighting, most Native American groups negotiated treaties with the British by the summer of 1766.

To avoid further costly conflicts with Native Americans, the British government prohibited colonists from settling west of the Appalachian Mountains. The **Proclamation of 1763** established a Proclamation Line along the Appalachians, which the colonists were not allowed to cross. However, the colonists, eager to expand westward from the increasingly crowded Atlantic seaboard, ignored the proclamation and continued to stream onto Native American lands.

---

## More About . . .

### Pontiac
Pontiac became tribal chief of the Ottawa in 1755, and in 1762 he organized the alliance of the Great Lakes tribes that fought in Pontiac's War. A shrewd military strategist, Pontiac arranged surprise attacks on several British forts and is especially admired for his capture of Detroit. In 1769, three years after concluding a peace treaty with the British, Pontiac was killed by a member of the Peoria tribe, an incident that sparked a bitter inter-tribal war.

## Assess & Reteach

### SECTION 4 ASSESSMENT
Have a student volunteer direct the class in a group review of the questions and responses.

Formal Assessment
· Section Quiz, p. 8

### SELF-ASSESSMENT
Have students write their own questions, exchange them with a partner, and answer their partner's questions. Partners can then review the section together to find information for any incorrect answers.

### RETEACH
Use the Personal Voices, inner column questions, and Key Players to review the main ideas of this section.

In-Depth Resources: Unit 1
· Reteaching Activity, p. 20

---

### 4 · ASSESSMENT

**1. TERMS & NAMES** For each term or name write a sentence explaining its signficance.
- triangular trade
- middle passage
- Enlightenment
- Benjamin Franklin
- Great Awakening
- Jonathan Edwards
- French and Indian War
- William Pitt
- Pontiac
- Proclamation of 1763

**MAIN IDEA**

**2. TAKING NOTES**
Recreate the tree diagram below. Fill in the diagram to show developments that took place in the colonies during the 18th century.

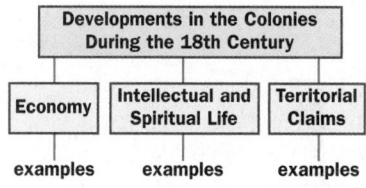

Which events or developments helped prepare the colonies for independence?

**CRITICAL THINKING**

**3. ANALYZING CAUSES**
Why did the plantation system come to play such an important role in the Southern economy?

**4. SUMMARIZING**
How did the Enlightenment affect the colonies?

**5. ANALYZING PRIMARY SOURCES**
Read the following quotation, written in 1774 by the African-American poet, Phillis Wheatley. How does the quotation express both religious belief and Enlightenment thought?

"For in every human breast God has implanted a principle, which we call love of freedom."

**6. ANALYZING ISSUES**
In what ways was slavery a brutal system? Support your statement with examples from the text.
**Think About:**
- how people were taken from Africa
- the working conditions of enslaved people
- the attitudes toward enslaved people

---

**Answers** ASSESSMENT **4**

**1. TERMS & NAMES**
triangular trade, p. 32
middle passage, p. 32
Enlightenment, p. 35
Benjamin Franklin, p. 35
Great Awakening, p. 35
Jonathan Edwards, p. 36
French and Indian War, p. 37
William Pitt, p. 38
Pontiac, p. 39
Proclamation of 1763, p. 39

**2. TAKING NOTES**
**Economy** Plantation economy based on slave labor; commerce grows in the North.
**Intellectual and Spiritual Life** Enlightenment ideas spread; the Great Awakening revives religious life.
**Territorial Claims** After the French and Indian War

**3. ANALYZING CAUSES**
The South developed a rural economy based on the plantation system.

**4. SUMMARIZING**
Both movements stressed the importance of the individual and were important in creating the intellectual and social atmosphere that led to the American Revolution.

**5. ANALYZING PRIMARY SOURCES**
The Enlightenment idea that all humans are born with a love of freedom is combined with the religious idea that God has planted this desire for freedom.

**6. ANALYZING ISSUES**
Free people were enslaved on the basis of race alone and treated like merchandise; neither slaves nor their children could free themselves; slaves were transported and lived under inhumane conditions; work was grueling; families were often torn apart; slaves' lives were completely controlled.

## Objectives

· Compare and contrast the courtship customs of different colonial groups.

· Summarize marriage statistics among different colonial groups.

## Focus & Motivate

Have students imagine they are reporting current-day American social customs to foreign readers. What would they say about the age at which typical Americans begin dating? About the age at which they marry? What specific courtship or dating customs would they mention?

## More About . . .

### The Puritans

In contrast to Church of New England teachings, the Puritans felt marriage should be a civil contract, claiming that nowhere in the Bible was it tied to ministry. Performed by Governor Bradford, the first Pilgrim marriage was between recent widow Susanna Fuller White and widower Edward Winslow, who went on to become the colony's governor and in that capacity performed marriages himself.

---

**DAILY LIFE** **1630–1763**

# Colonial Courtship

The concept of dating among teenagers was nonexistent in colonial times. Young people were considered either children or adults, and as important as marriage was in the colonies, sweethearts were older than one might suspect. The practices of courtship and marriage varied among the different communities.

▼ **FRONTIER OR BACKCOUNTRY PEOPLE**

Andrew Jackson, depicted with his wife in the painting below, "stole" his wife (she was willing) from her family. Jackson was following a custom of the backcountry people, who lived along the western edge of the colonies.

These colonists, mostly Scots-Irish, based their marriages on the old custom of "abduction"—stealing the bride—often with her consent. Even regular marriages began with the groom and his friends coming to "steal" the bride. Much drinking and dancing accompanied these wild and hilarious weddings.

**PURITANS**

For Puritans, marriage was a civil contract, not a religious or sacred union. Although adults strictly supervised a couple's courting, parents allowed two unusual practices. One was the use of a courting stick, a long tube into which the couple could whisper while the family was in another room. The other was the practice of "bundling": a young man spent the night in the same bed as his sweetheart, with a large bundling board (shown below) between them.

Before marrying, the couple had to allow for Puritan leaders to voice any objections to the marriage at the meeting house. Passing that, the couple would marry in a very simple civil ceremony and share a quiet dinner.

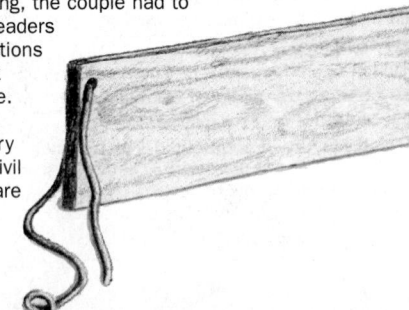

**40** CHAPTER 1 *Exploration and the Colonial Era*

---

## RECOMMENDED RESOURCES

### BOOKS

Blackburn, Joyce. *Phoebe's Secret Diary: Daily Life & First Romance of a Colonial Girl*, 1742. Fort Frederica Association, 1993.

Duncan, Emrich. *The Folklore of Weddings and Marriage.* New York: American Heritage, 1970. An illustrated study of marriage and the marriage ceremony.

Lemay, J. A. Leo. *Robert Boiling Woos Anne Miller.* Charlottesville: UP of Virginia, 1990. Love and courtship in colonial Virginia in 1760.

Longfellow, Henry W. "The Courtship of Miles Standish" in *Evangeline and Selected Tales and Poems.* New York: New American Library, 1964.

A Romantic-era narrative poem about a famous colonial-era courtship.

Rothman, Ellen K. *Hands and Hearts.* New York: Basic, 1984. A history of courtship in America.

### VIDEOS

*Colonial America, 1500–1600.* Master Vision, 1982. Colonial customs and traditions.

*The Colonial Way of Life.* CRM Films. Diverse American colonists create a unified culture.

*The Marriage of Pocahantas.* Dir. Emma De'ath. Ambrose Video, 1995. A look at the famous marriage and its historical effects.

**THE SOUTH ▲**

Many African slaves married in a "jumping the broomstick" ceremony, in which the bride and groom jumped over a broomstick to seal their union. Although there is disagreement among African-American scholars, some suggest that the above painting depicts a slave wedding on a South Carolina plantation in the late 1700s.

**◄ QUAKERS**

Quaker couples intent on marrying needed the consent not only of the parents but also of the whole Quaker community. Quakers who wanted to marry had to go through a 16-step courtship phase before they could wed. Quaker women, however, were known to reject men at the last minute.

**VIRGINIA ▶**

In Virginia, marriage was a sacred union. Since the marriage often involved a union of properties, and love was not necessary, parents were heavily involved in the negotiations. In this illustration from a dance manual (right), a young upper-class couple work to improve their social graces by practicing an elaborate dance step.

# DATA FILE

**WHO MARRIED?**

**Puritans:**
- 98% of males and 94% of females married
- Grooms were usually a few years older than brides
- Discouraged marriages between first cousins

**Virginians:**
- 25% of males never married; most females married
- Grooms nearly 10 years older than brides
- Allowed first-cousin marriages

**Quakers:**
- 16% of women single at age 50
- forbade first-cousin marriages

**Frontier People:**
- Almost all women and most men married
- Ages of bride and groom about the same
- Youngest group to marry

**Average Age at Marriage**

| Group | Males | Females |
|---|---|---|
| Puritan | 26 | 23 |
| Virginians | 26 | 19 |
| Quakers | | |
| in Delaware | 31 | 29 |
| in Penn. & N.J. | 26 | 22 |
| Philadelphians | 26 | 23 |
| Frontier People | 21 | 19 |
| Modern Americans | 25 | 24 |

**Who Could Divorce?**

| | |
|---|---|
| **Puritans:** | Yes |
| **Virginians:** | No |
| **Quakers:** | No |

*Source:* David Hackett Fischer, *Albion's Seed*

**THINKING CRITICALLY**

**CONNECT TO HISTORY**

1. **Interpreting Data** What was a common characteristic of courtship among Puritans, Quakers, and Virginians?

   📁 **SEE SKILLBUILDER HANDBOOK, PAGE R22**

**CONNECT TO TODAY**

2. **Synthesizing** Research modern courtship practices by interviewing your parents or relatives. Write a brief paper comparing and contrasting modern-day and colonial courtship practices.

🔵 **RESEARCH LINKS** CLASSZONE.COM

## Instruct

· What common courtship practice of today was nonexistent during the colonial period?

· How did courtship customs vary among different colonial groups?

· Why might the courtship process among Quakers be considered the most difficult?

**MAKING PERSONAL CONNECTIONS**

Have students discuss the notion of courtship today. Which colonial courtship practice most resembles those of today? What do students think is the best way to court a member of the opposite sex?

### More About . . .

**Colonial Courtship**

During the early colonial period, men greatly outnumbered women—and thus the courtship game proved much easier for the female population. By 1666, South Carolina was so lacking in women that colonial leaders publicized this advertisement in England: "If any maid or single woman have a desire to go over, they will think themselves in the golden age, when men paid a dowry for their wives; for if they be but civil, and under fifty years of age, some honest man or other, will purchase them for their wives."

**THINKING CRITICALLY: ANSWERS**

1. **CONNECT TO HISTORY** The family and/or community had a say in whether or not couples could wed; courting couples were allowed to spend some time together; most people were past 20 when they married; most courtships led to marriage.

2. **CONNECT TO TODAY**

**Rubric**

The paper should . . .

· clearly state the student's purpose and conclusion, and provide necessary facts and examples to support the conclusion

· present similarities and differences between modern-day and colonial courtship practices

· include a list of the questions used in the interview along with the names of the interviewees

*Exploration and the Colonial Era* **41**

## TERMS & NAMES

1. nomadic, p. 5
2. Reformation, p. 11
3. Christopher Columbus, p. 14
4. Columbian Exchange, p. 15
5. indentured servant, p. 23
6. Puritan, p. 24
7. Navigation Acts, p. 28
8. triangular trade, p. 32
9. Enlightenment, p. 35
10. French and Indian War, p. 37

## MAIN IDEAS

1. The trade routes pulled the people of West Africa into closer contact with Europe and prepared the way for Portuguese involvement in the slave trade.

2. The Renaissance led to a greater interest in the physical world; it also prompted many to seek glory through adventure and conquest.

3. The Columbian Exchange improved nutrition but also helped spread disease among Native Americans.

4. At first the Spanish wanted a faster route to the Orient; later the Spanish were searching for gold and for converts to Christianity.

5. The Jamestown colonists wanted to get rich quick; the Puritans came to establish a community based on religious principles.

6. The Navigation Acts were passed to tighten control of colonial trade; they spurred a boom in the colonial shipbuilding industry.

7. Immigration introduced large numbers of Germans and Scots-Irish.

8. The Southern colonies developed with largely rural economies based on the plantation system. The Northern colonies developed a commercial economy.

---

# REVIEW CHAPTER 1 ASSESSMENT

## TERMS & NAMES

For each term or name write a sentence explaining its connection to exploration and the colonial era.

1. nomadic
2. Reformation
3. Christopher Columbus
4. Columbian Exchange
5. indentured servant
6. Puritan
7. Navigation Acts
8. triangular trade
9. Enlightenment
10. French and Indian War

## MAIN IDEAS

Use your notes and the information in the chapter to answer the following questions.

**The Americas, West Africa, and Europe** (pages 4–13)

1. What effects did Portuguese trade routes have on West Africa?
2. In what ways did Renaissance ideas and attitudes inspire and motivate European explorers?

**Spanish North America** (pages 14–20)

3. What impact did the Columbian Exchange have on people's lives throughout the world?
4. Why did the Spanish want to colonize the Americas?

**Early British Colonies** (pages 21–30)

5. How did the goals of the Jamestown colonists differ from those of the Puritan colonists in Massachusetts?
6. Why did the English Parliament pass the Navigation Acts? What effects did they have?

**The Colonies Come of Age** (pages 31–39)

7. How did immigration contribute to the ethnic diversity of the American colonies after 1700?
8. How did the differences between the Northern and Southern economies lead to the development of two distinct cultural regions?

## CRITICAL THINKING

1. **USING YOUR NOTES** In a chart like the one shown, compare and contrast Spanish and British colonial policies toward Native Americans.

| Colonial Policies Toward Native Americans | |
|---|---|
| Spanish | British |
|  |  |

2. **DEVELOPING HISTORICAL PERSPECTIVE** What were some of the cultural characteristics of the ancient civilizations that flourished in the Americas?

3. **INTERPRETING MAPS** Look at the map on page 33. Compare the economic activities of the three regions of British colonies in the Americas—New England, Middle, and Southern.

---

## VISUAL SUMMARY  EXPLORATION AND THE COLONIAL ERA

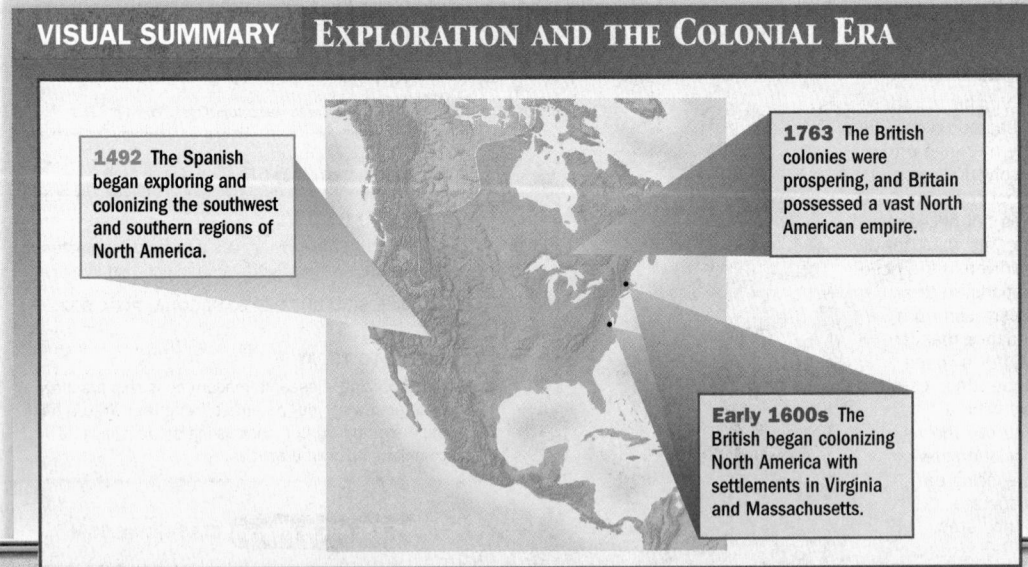

**1492** The Spanish began exploring and colonizing the southwest and southern regions of North America.

**1763** The British colonies were prospering, and Britain possessed a vast North American empire.

**Early 1600s** The British began colonizing North America with settlements in Virginia and Massachusetts.

---

## CRITICAL THINKING

1. **Using Your Notes** Spanish: The Spanish converted and often enslaved Native Americans. British: The British followed a pattern of driving away the people they defeated.

2. **Developing Historical Perspective** Native Americans did not believe that land could be bought and sold; Europeans believed in private property. This would lead to friction as Europeans gradually extended private ownership over what had once been public lands.

3. **Interpreting Maps** The countries of northern Europe tended to explore and colonize areas in the northern hemisphere, while southern European countries tended to explore and colonize southern regions of the Americas.

## Standardized Test Practice

Use the cartoon below and your knowledge of U.S. history to answer question 1.

JOIN, or DIE.

1. Benjamin Franklin drew and published this cartoon in 1754, soon after the start of the French and Indian War. The cartoon depicts a snake divided into eight parts representing the eight colonies at the time. What message did Franklin intend?

   A The colonies have been broken apart by the war.

   B The colonies should unite to protect themselves from the French and the Native Americans.

   C The colonies should join with the French to protect themselves from the Native Americans.

   D The colonies should unite to declare independence from Britain.

2. Anne Hutchinson was banished from Massachusetts because she taught that —

   F colonists should remain loyal to the English king.

   G individuals could interpret the Bible for themselves.

   H the colonists should not trade with local Native Americans.

   J the Puritans should break away from the Church of England.

3. In the 1700s an intellectual movement known as the Enlightenment developed in Europe and spread to the colonies. Benjamin Franklin and Thomas Jefferson were among those colonists heavily influenced by Enlightenment ideas. In which of the following ways did the Enlightenment affect the colonists?

   A Enlightenment ideas led people to expand the trade in enslaved persons.

   B Enlightenment ideas stirred people to rededicate themselves to God.

   C Enlightenment ideas persuaded people to establish colonies in order to generate a favorable balance of trade.

   D Enlightenment ideas convinced people of the importance of civil rights.

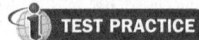

ADDITIONAL TEST PRACTICE, pages S1–S33.

 TEST PRACTICE CLASSZONE.COM

## ALTERNATIVE ASSESSMENT

1. **INTERACT WITH HISTORY**  Recall your discussion of the question on page 3:

   *How will the arrival of a strange people change your way of life?*

   Now that you know how Native Americans' way of life was changed by the arrival of the Europeans, discuss the following question: Would you have resisted or helped the Europeans if you had been a Native American during the days of European colonization?

2. **LEARNING THROUGH MEDIA**  How did lawyers defend their clients against some of the colonists' very strict laws?

   Using legal documents from colonial days, find out the legal punishments for infractions of certain laws in specific colonies. Use the CD-ROM *Electronic Library of Primary Sources* and other reference materials to research a specific law and punishment in 17th-century America.

   **Cooperative Learning Activity** With a group of students, enact a colonial trial. The rest of the class, acting as a colonial jury, must decide the verdict and punishment. Then, have a class discussion about the value of the law and its punishment.

REVIEW UNIT 43

---

## Standardized Test Practice

1. The correct letter is **B**.

   Letter A is incorrect because the colonies have not been broken apart. The letter C is incorrect because the colonies had no interest in joining the French or Native Americans. The letter D is incorrect because in 1754 the colonies were not considering independence.

2. The correct answer is letter **G**.

   Hutchinson was banished over religious issues so letters F and H are incorrect. Hutchinson did not advocate breaking away from the Church of England.

3. The correct answer is letter **D**.

   Letter A is incorrect because the Enlightenment did not advocate slavery. Letter B is incorrect because it refers to the Great Awakening. Letter C is incorrect because it refers to mercantilism.

UNIT PROJECT

### LETTER TO THE EDITOR

**Tips for Teaching**

· Students will need to select the war they wish to write about.

· Remind students who have selected the Revolutionary War to begin to look for reasons why colonists may desire independence.

Formal Assessment
· Chapter Test, Forms A, B, and C, pp. 9–20

---

## ALTERNATIVE ASSESSMENT

### 1. INTERACT WITH HISTORY
**Rubric**

The discussion should . . .

· enumerate reasons for resistance to European colonization

· identify positive reasons for accepting European colonization

· reflect an understanding of the validity of both positions

### 2. LEARNING THROUGH MEDIA
**Rubric**

The jury trial should . . .

· reflect research into colonial law and traditions

· present testimony that reflects the experiences of colonists

· exhibit creativity in the presentation of the trial

# Revolution and the Early Republic

| | CHAPTER OVERVIEW | COPYMASTERS | INTEGRATED TECHNOLOGY |
|---|---|---|---|
| **CHAPTER RESOURCES** | *Colonists declare their independence and win a war to gain the right to govern themselves. Leaders meet to write the Constitution. George Washington guides the new nation, as two major political parties emerge. The country also faces conflict with European nations.* | Telescoping the Times<br>· Chapter Summary, pp. 3–4<br><br>Planning for Block Schedules | American Stories video series<br>· "Patriot Father, Loyalist Son"<br>Power Presentations<br>Electronic Teacher Tools<br>Online Lesson Planner<br>classzone.com |
| **SECTION 1**<br>Colonial Resistance and Rebellion<br>pp. 46–57 | **KEY IDEAS**<br>*Ideas about freedom and self-determination spur the colonies to unite in their resistance to Britain and declare independence.* | In-Depth Resources: Unit 1<br>· Guided Reading, p. 35<br>· Building Vocabulary, p. 39<br>· Reteaching Activity, p. 43<br>· Primary Sources, pp. 49–50<br><br>Lesson Plans, pp. 9–10 | Critical Thinking Transparencies CT4<br>· The War for Independence<br>Humanities Transparencies HT5, HT31<br>Battle of Bunker Hill; Political Cartoon<br>Electronic Library of Primary Sources<br>· Unit 1, Chapter 2<br>Primary Source Explorer<br>classzone.com |
| **SECTION 2**<br>The War for Independence<br>pp. 58–65 | *With the help of European allies, the colonists defeat the mighty British army and establish a new nation.* | In-Depth Resources: Unit 1<br>· Guided Reading, p. 36<br>· Skillbuilder Practice, p. 40<br>· Reteaching Activity, p. 44<br>· Geography Application, pp. 47–48<br>· Primary Sources, pp. 51–52<br>· American Lives, p. 57<br>Lesson Plans, pp. 11–12 | Geography Transparencies GT4<br>· North America 1783<br>Critical Thinking Transparencies CT4<br>· The War for Independence<br>Humanities Transparencies HT6, HT32<br>· Signing the Treaty of Paris, 1783<br>· Mrs. General Washington<br>classzone.com |
| **SECTION 3**<br>Confederation and the Constitution<br>pp. 66–73 | *The delegates to the 1787 Philadelphia convention create a new Constitution to replace the Articles of Confederation. After the Bill of Rights is added, the Constitution is finally ratified.* | In-Depth Resources: Unit 1<br>· Guided Reading, p. 37<br>· Skillbuilder Practices, p. 41<br>· Reteaching Activity, p. 45<br>· Primary Sources, p. 53<br>· Literature, pp. 54–56<br>· American Lives, p. 58<br>Lesson Plans, pp. 13–14 | Geography Transparencies GT4<br>· Land Ceded by States: 1782–1802<br>Critical Thinking Transparencies CT4<br>· The Constitutional Convention<br>Electronic Library of Primary Sources<br>· Unit 1, Chapter 2<br>classzone.com |
| **SECTION 4**<br>Launching the Nation<br>pp. 74–79 | *The new nation begins to take shape both governmentally and physically. Conflicts with European powers outside its borders and with Native Americans within its borders test the spirit of the nation.* | In-Depth Resources: Unit 1<br>· Guided Reading, p. 38<br>· Skillbuilder Practice, p. 42<br>· Reteaching Activity, p. 46<br><br>Lesson Plans, pp. 15–16 | Humanities Transparencies HT7<br>· The Republican Court<br>Electronic Library of Primary Sources<br>· Unit 1, Chapter 2<br>classzone.com |
| **The Living Constitution**<br>pp. 82–105 | *The full text of the U.S. Constitution, including explanatory notes and critical thinking questions.* | In-Depth Resources: Unit 1<br>· Guided Reading, pp. 59–62<br>· Building Vocabulary, p. 63<br>· Skillbuilder Practice, p. 64<br>· Reteaching Pages. pp. 65–68<br>· Geography Application. pp. 69–70<br>· American Lives pp. 71–72<br><br>Lesson Plans, pp. 17–24 | Primary Source Explorer<br>· The Constitution of the United States<br>classzone.com |

## ASSESSMENT OPTIONS

PE **Chapter Assessment,** pp. 80–81

**Formal Assessment**
· Chapter Tests, Forms A, B, and C, pp. 25–42

**Test Generator**

**Integrated Assessment Book**

**TAKS Online Test Practice**

**TAKS Spiraled Content Review**

**TAKS Practice Tests**

---

PE **Section 1 Assessment,** p. 53

TE **Self-Assessment,** p. 53

**Formal Assessment,** Quiz, p. 21

**Integrated Assessment Book**

**Test Generator**

**TAKS Practice Transparencies TT14, TT15**

---

PE **Section 2 Assessment,** p. 63

TE **Self-Assessment,** p. 63

**Formal Assessment,** Quiz, p. 22

**Integrated Assessment Book**

**Test Generator**

**TAKS Practice Transparencies TT16, TT17**

---

PE **Section 3 Assessment,** p. 71

TE **Self-Assessment,** p. 71

**Formal Assessment,** Quiz, p. 23

**Integrated Assessment Book**

**Test Generator**

**TAKS Practice Transparencies TT18–20**

---

PE **Section 4 Assessment,** p. 79

TE **Self-Assessment,** p. 79

**Formal Assessment,** Quiz, p. 24

**Integrated Assessment Book**

**Test Generator**

**TAKS Practice Transparencies TT21, TT22**

---

PE **Living Constitution Assessment,** pp. 106–107

**Formal Assessment,** Quiz, p. 410
· Quizzes, pp. 43–46
· Living Constitution Test, pp. 47–55

## RESOURCES FOR DIFFERENTIATING INSTRUCTION

### Students Acquiring English/ESL

**Reading Study Guide**
(English and Spanish)
pp. 15–34

**Access for Students Acquiring English/ESL:**
Spanish Translations,
pp. 24–45

**Chapter Summaries on CD**
(English and Spanish)

### Less Proficient Readers

**Reading Study Guide**
(English and Spanish)
pp. 15–34

**Telescoping the Times**
· Chapter Summary,
pp. 3–4

**Chapter Summaries on CD**
(English and Spanish)

### Gifted and Talented Students

**In-Depth Resources: Unit 6**
· Primary Sources, pp. 49–53
· Literature, pp. 54–56
· American Lives: Haym Salomon, p. 57; Patrick Henry, p. 58

**Electronic Library of Primary Sources**
· Unit 1, Chapter 2

**Primary Source Explorer**
· The Declaration of Independence
· The Constitution of the United States

## CROSS-CURRICULAR CONNECTIONS

### Primary Sources
Meltzer, Milton, ed. *The American Revolution: A History in Their Own Words 1750–1800.* NY: Harper Trophy, 1993. Chronological collection of first-person accounts.

Webster, Mary E. *The Federalist Papers : In Modern Language.* Bellevue,Washington: Merril Press, 1999. The Federalist papers indexed to today's political issues.

### Humanities: Music
Brand, Oscar. *Songs of '76: A Folksinger's History of the Revolution.* Philadelphia: Evans, 1988. A collection of songs from old manuscripts, newspapers, and personal accounts.

### Geography
Barner, Bob. *Which Way to the Revolution?* NY: Holiday House Press, 1998. Text and maps describe the route traveled by Paul Revere.

### Culture
Cox, Clinton. *Come All You Brave Soldiers: Blacks in the Revolutionary War.* NY: Cartwheel Books. A factual, easy-to-read account of African-American contributions to the Revolution

### Literature
Roberts, Kenneth. *Oliver Wiswell.* NY: Doubleday, 1940. This historically accurate story of the American Revolution is told from the viewpoint of a Tory.

Irving, Washington. *Rip Van Winkle and the Legend of Sleepy Hollow.* Tarrytown, NY: Sleepy Hollow Press, 1980. These much-loved ghost stories are set in colonial America.

### McDougall Littell
**Nextext**
*Founding a Nation*

**The Language of Literature**
*American Literature*
Unit 2, Part 2

## ENRICHMENT ACTIVITIES

PE **Pupil's Edition,** pp. 44–81/82–105
Interact with History, pp. 44–45
The Declaration of Independence, pp. 54–57
Tracing Themes, p. 64
Geography Spotlight, p. 72
Projects for Citizenship, pp. 108–109

**In-Depth Resources: Unit 1**
· Geography Application: The Siege of Yorktown, pp. 47–48
· Primary Source: The Boston Tea Party, pp. 49–50
· Primary Source: Political Cartoon, p. 51
· Primary Source: Valley Forge Diary, p. 52

· Primary Source: U.S. Constitution First Draft, p. 53
· Literature: from *Legacy,* pp. 54–56
· American Lives: Haym Salomon, p. 57
· American Lives: Patrick Henry, p. 58

**Electronic Library of Primary Sources**
· Unit 1, Chapter 2

**Primary Source Explorer**
· The Declaration of Independence
· The Constitution of the United States

 **American Stories video series**
· "Patriot Father, Loyalist Son"

## BLOCK SCHEDULE LESSON PLAN OPTIONS (90-MINUTE PERIOD)

### DAY 1

**CHAPTER OPENER pp. 44–45**

**Class Time** 30 minutes

**History from Visuals, p. 44**

**Class Time** 15 minutes

*Options for Pacing and Variety*

- **Time Saver** Have students study the map and ask them to notice the different classes of colonists basically working together. Have them speculate on the reasons the rebellion reached the height that it did and keep those reasons in mind as they read the chapter. **Class Time** 15 minutes

**Interact with History, p. 45**

**Class Time** 15 minutes

*Options for Pacing and Variety*

- **Role-Playing** Have students read the questions and discuss them as a class, paying close attention to the Examine the Issues questions. Discuss the strengths and weaknesses of a strong national government. **Class Time** 15 minutes

**SECTION 1, pp. 46–57**

**Class Time** 30 minutes

*Options for Pacing and Variety*

- **Internet** Have students read the sidebar on page 47, on Proposition 13. Then have them use the Internet to examine the effects of Proposition 13 on California. They should list the Web sites they

### DAY 1 continued

found and whether or not the sites were helpful. **Class Time** 25 minutes

- **Peer Teaching** Ask students to read The Declaration of Independence on pages 54–55. Then have them do the activity Paraphrasing the Declaration on page 55, working in pairs, and share their passages with the class. **Class Time** 10 minutes

- **Time Saver** Have students read the feature on pages 56–57. Discuss Abigail Adams's statement that "all Men would be tyrants if they could." **Class Time** 10 minutes

**SECTION 2, pp. 58–65**

**Class Time** 45 minutes

*Options for Pacing and Variety*

- **History on Film** View the video *Patriot Father, Loyalist Son: The Divided House of Benjamin* and *William Franklin.* **Class Time** 20 minutes

- **Geography Transparencies** Have students do the activity on TE page 61, using Geography Transparency 4 to help them create their own maps. They can work in pairs. **Class Time** 25 minutes

### DAY 2

**SECTION 3, pp. 66–73**

**Class Time** 45 minutes

*Options for Pacing and Variety*

- **Peer Evaluation** Let students work in pairs to turn subheads of this section into questions and then find the answers within the subsection. Start with the section "Ratifying the Constitution" on page 69. **Class Time** 20 minutes

- **Time Saver** Have students read pages 72–73 on the Land Ordinance of 1785 and discuss it, using the questions on both pages of the PE and TE. **Class Time** 5 minutes

**THE LIVING CONSTITUTION pp. 82–105**

**Class Time** 45 minutes

*Options for Pacing and Variety*

- **Peer Teaching** Divide the class into groups of four. Assign each group a section of the Constitution. Each group should create a graphic illustrating the assigned section. Then have each group explain their graphic to the class. **Class Time** 15 minutes

- **Internet** Have students begin the working on "Researching a Constitutional Question" as explained on p. 45. Pair students with similar interests. Have them begin to search the Internet for sources to answer their questions. **Class Time** 30 minutes

### DAY 3

**SECTION 4, pp. 74–79**

**Class Time** 45 minutes

*Options for Pacing and Variety*

- **Time Saver** Have students read the sidebar on page 75 and the chart on page 76 on Jefferson and Hamilton and answer the Skillbuilder questions on page 76. **Class Time** 20 minutes

- **Peer Competition** Divide groups of eight to ten students into two teams. Have one team represent the interests of the United States and the other, the interests of Native American peoples. Students should negotiate a land treaty that makes fair concessions to both sides. Students should also discuss how to ensure compliance. **Class Time** 45 minutes

**ASSESSMENT pp. 80–81**

**Class Time** 45 minutes

*Options for Pacing and Variety*

- **Role-Playing** Review the questions raised at the beginning of the chapter on the amount of power the federal government should have. Use the points in question 1 of Alternative Assessment on page 81. **Class Time** 15 minutes

- **Peer Teaching** Have students work in pairs to answer the Critical Thinking questions on page 80. **Class Time** 15 minutes

---

**TEACHER-TESTED ACTIVITY**

**REVOLUTIONARY WAR GAME**

Korri Kinney, Meridian High School, Meridian, Idaho

**Class Time** 30 minutes

**Task** Creating a game about the Revolutionary War

**Purpose** To help students determine and retain important facts about the Revolutionary War

Supplies Needed

- Textbook
- Index cards

**Activity** Tell students that they will create a game about the Revolutionary War. Help students come up with a set of game rules. Divide students into groups and have every group write at least six questions about each section of the chapter. Have the groups write the questions on index cards, with the question on one side and the answer on the opposite side. Have groups exchange games, and then play the game, with one student acting as the host and the other members acting as the contestants.

# CHAPTER 2 CORRELATION

## CORRELATION TO THE TEXAS ESSENTIAL KNOWLEDGE AND SKILLS

Chapter 2 addresses the following standards of the Texas Essential Knowledge and Skills for U.S. History.

| TEKS | Instruction | Student Question/Activity |
|------|-------------|---------------------------|
| **(16B)** Evaluate the impact of events on relationships among the legislative, executive, and judicial branches of government. | **PE 74–75** examination of the shaping of the three branches of the federal government | **PE 79** Critical Thinking questions about Washington's actions in shaping the federal government |
| **(18A)** Identify and analyze methods of expanding the right to participate in the democratic process. | **PE 64–65** feature on the growth of women's political power in America | **PE 65** Critical Thinking questions about political advances by women highlighted in the feature |
| **(19B)** Evaluate the contributions of significant political leaders in the United States. | **PE 52–53** analysis of Thomas Jefferson's significant contributions to the forging of an independent America | **PE 53** Critical Thinking question about Jefferson's writing of the Declaration of Independence |
| **(20A)** Describe how the characteristics and issues of various eras in U.S. history have been reflected in literature. | **PE 52** discussion of *Common Sense* and the impact it had on the independence movement | **TE 52** activity calling on students to create their own political pamphlet about the cause of independence |
| **(21D)** Identify the political, social, and economic contributions of women to American society. | **PE 61** examination of the role of women in helping the colonists win the American Revolution | **PE 61** question asking students to summarize the contributions women made to the war effort |
| **(24A)** Locate and use primary and secondary sources to acquire information about the United States. | **PE 54–57** presentation of the Declaration of Independence along with annotations to help students better understand the document | **TE 55** activity in which students rewrite the major themes of the Declaration in their own words |

## TAKS MINI-LESSONS

1. **Social Studies Skills: Objective 1 (8.4.B):** Explain the roles played by significant individuals during the American Revolution **Activity** Have students summarize the achievements of the following: Samuel Adams, Thomas Paine, Thomas Jefferson, and George Washington.

2. **Social Studies Skills: Objective 1 (8.4.C):** Explain the significant issues surrounding the American Revolution **Activity** Have students complete the TE writing activity regarding the Declaration of Independence on page 55.

3. **Social Studies Skills: Objective 4 (8.3.A):** Analyze how the U.S. Constitution reflects the principles of limited government **Activity** Have students write a paragraph describing the Constitution using the following words: *separation of powers*, *checks and balances*, and *Bill of Rights*.

4. **English Language Arts Skills: Objective 2 (11.C):** Identify conflicts and how they are addressed and resolved **Activity** Have students identify the conflicts at the Constitutional Convention and how each was resolved.

5. **English Language Arts Skills: Objective 3 (7.E):** Analyze text structures such as compare and contrast **Activity** Have students summarize the differences between the Loyalists and Patriots.

CHAPTER 2 · OBJECTIVE

To analyze the causes of the American Revolution and understand the important events of the war, and to trace the development of the American republic

# REVIEW CHAPTER 2

# REVOLUTION AND THE EARLY REPUBLIC

## HISTORY from VISUALS

### Interpreting the Painting

Have students study the painting and ask them what words they would use to describe the colonists depicted. In toppling the statue of King George, what message are the colonists sending? What does the fire along the left side of the painting indicate? *(angry, excited, determined; they no longer respect the authority of the king or British rule; the colonists may be destroying other signs of British rule)*

**Extension** Have half of the class write brief descriptions of this scene from a colonist's point of view and the other half from the point of view of a British soldier stationed in the colonies.

### Time Line Discussion

Explain to students that the time line covers roughly the last three decades of the 18th century, during much of which the colonists spent achieving their independence and forging a new nation.

· Ask students how long after the British surrendered did the colonists ratify the Constitution of the United States. *(7 years)*

· Ask students which events indicate that there were political troubles in the early republic. *(1786, Shays's Rebellion; 1794, Whiskey Rebellion)*

The Sons of Liberty pull down a statue of George III on the Bowling Green, New York, July 9, 1776.

**1765** British Parliament passes the Stamp Act.

**1773** Colonists stage the Boston Tea Party.

**1774** Parliament passes the Intolerable Acts. First Continental Congress convenes.

**1775** Second Continental Congress convenes.

**1776** Colonies declare independence.

USA
WORLD

**1765**

**1775**

**1760** George III becomes king of Great Britain.

**1774** Reign of Louis XVI begins in France.

**1776** Adam Smith's *The Wealth of Nations* is published.

**44** CHAPTER 2 *Revolution and the Early Republic*

## THEMES IN CHAPTER 2

### ECONOMIC OPPORTUNITY

Britain's economic policies toward the colonies were a major cause of the Revolution. The new nation's economy was largely based on agricultural products, which the government used to develop a profitable trade with Europe.

**See Teacher's Edition notes, pp. 47, 75.**

### WOMEN AND POLITICAL POWER

During the Revolution, women managed farms and businesses while the men were off fighting. They also performed tasks such as making supplies for the troops. Those women who traveled with their soldier husbands usually remained in the army camps.

**See Teacher's Edition note, p. 61.**

### CIVIL RIGHTS

One of the greatest problems faced by the new confederation was unequal representation of citizens within states, which led to rebellion against unfair taxation. Eventually, a bill of rights created a government in which the needs of the nation were balanced with the rights of the individual.

**See Teacher's Edition note, p. 70.**

### IMMIGRATION AND MIGRATION

Soon after the new government was launched, the United States began extending its borders. Many courageous people were willing to brave hardships and dangers to pioneer the country's westward expansion.

**See Teacher's Edition note, p. 77.**

# INTERACT
## WITH HISTORY

The year is 1787. You have recently helped your fellow patriots overthrow decades of oppressive British rule. However, it is easier to destroy an old system of government than to create a new one. In a world of kings and tyrants, your new republic struggles to find its place.

## How much power should the national government have?

### Examine the Issues

- Which should have more power, the states or the national government?
- How can the new nation avoid a return to tyranny?
- How can the rights of all people be protected?

🛈 **RESEARCH LINKS** CLASSZONE.COM

Visit the Chapter 2 links for more information about Revolution and the Early Republic.

# INTERACT
## WITH HISTORY

### Objectives

· To help students recognize the numerous issues involved in creating a new nation
· To help students understand how Americans constructed their new government

### Examine the Issues

1. Have students consider what conflicts might arise between the national and state governments.
2. Ask students why the colonists feared that a strong national government eventually could lead to tyranny.
3. Have students consider the various ways in which the United States affords all its citizens equal rights.

---

**1781** The British surrender at Yorktown.

**1786** Daniel Shays leads a rebellion against higher taxes.

**1788** The Constitution is ratified.

**1789** George Washington is elected president.

**1792** George Washington is reelected.

## 1785          1795

**1781** Joseph II allows religious toleration in Austria.

**1785** British preacher Edmund Cartwright invents the first power loom.

**1787** Sierra Leone in Africa is made a haven for freed American slaves.

**1789** The French Revolution starts.

**1793** French king Louis XVI is executed.

**REVIEW UNIT 45**

---

## RECOMMENDED RESOURCES

### BOOKS FOR THE TEACHER

Draper, Theodore. *A Struggle for Power.* New York: Times, 1996. Study of the British and colonists.

Madison, James. *Notes of Debates in the Federal Convention of 1787.* New York: Norton, 1987.

Sugden, John. *Tecumseh's Last Stand.* Norman: U of Oklahoma P, 1985.

### BOOKS FOR THE STUDENT

Bailyn, Bernard. *Faces of Revolution.* New York: Vintage, 1992. Profiles of a wide variety of subjects.

Rutland, Robert. *James Madison and the Search for Nationhood.* Washington, D.C.: Library of Congress, 1981. Illustrated sketch of Madison's life and work; full of letters.

### VIDEOS

*The American Revolution.* History Channel home video. Six-tape documentary.

*Bill of Rights in Action.* Encyclopaedia Britannica, 800-554-9862. Connection of Bill of Rights to current issues.

### SOFTWARE

*U.S. Government—Part 1.* CD-ROM Educational Software Institute, 800-955-5570.

### INTEGRATED TECHNOLOGY

For teacher support, visit . . .
🛈 classzone.com

## OBJECTIVES

1 Summarize colonial resistance to British taxation.

2 Trace the mounting tension in Massachusetts.

3 Examine efforts made to avoid war between the colonies and the British.

4 Summarize the historical background of the Declaration of Independence.

### SKILLBUILDERS

· Interpreting Visual Sources, p. 48
· Interpreting Charts, p. 49

### CRITICAL THINKING

· Analyzing Issues, p. 47
· Summarizing, pp. 47, 53
· Analyzing Motives, p. 49
· Evaluating, pp. 50, 53
· Developing Historical Perspective, p. 51
· Making Inferences, p. 52
· Analyzing Effects, p. 53

## Focus & Motivate

Ask students how small quarrels between people mushroom into larger fights.

## Instruct

### Instruct: Objective 1

**The Colonies Organize to Resist Britain**
TAKS SS11 1(8.4.B)

· How did the British seek to pay off the huge debt from the French and Indian War?

· What was the Stamp Act and why did so many colonists oppose it?

 In-Depth Resources: Unit 1
· Guided Reading, p. 35

# Colonial Resistance and Rebellion

| MAIN IDEA | WHY IT MATTERS NOW | Terms & Names |
|---|---|---|
| Conflicts between Great Britain and the American colonies escalated, until the colonists finally declared their independence. | The ideas put forth by the colonists in the Declaration of Independence remain the guiding principles of the United States today. | • King George III · John Locke<br>• Sugar Act · *Common Sense*<br>• Stamp Act · Thomas Jefferson<br>• Samuel Adams · Declaration of<br>• Boston Massacre Independence<br>• Boston Tea Party |

 U.S. History 7A, 19A, 19B, 20A, 20B, 20C, 24A, 24B, 24C, 24D, 24F, 25A, 25B, 25C, 25D

### One American's Story

Crispus Attucks was a sailor of African and Native-American ancestry. On the night of March 5, 1770, he was part of a large and angry crowd that had gathered at the Boston Customs House to harass the British soldiers stationed there. More soldiers soon arrived, and the mob began hurling stones and snowballs at them. Attucks then stepped forward.

**A PERSONAL VOICE** JOHN ADAMS

" This Attucks . . . appears to have undertaken to be the hero of the night; and to lead this army with banners . . . up to King street with their clubs . . . . This man with his party cried, 'Do not be afraid of them,' . . . He had hardiness enough to fall in upon them, and with one hand took hold of a bayonet, and with the other knocked the man down. "

—quoted in *The Black Presence in the Era of the American Revolution*

▲ Crispus Attucks

Attucks's action ignited the troops. Ignoring orders not to shoot civilians, one soldier and then others fired on the crowd. Five people were killed; several were wounded. Crispus Attucks was, according to a newspaper account, the first to die.

## 1 The Colonies Organize to Resist Britain

Because the Proclamation of 1763 sought to halt expansion by the colonists west of the Appalachian Mountains, it convinced the colonists that the British government did not care about their needs. A second result of the French and Indian War—Britain's financial crisis—brought about new laws that reinforced the colonists' opinion.

**THE SUGAR ACT** Great Britain had borrowed so much money during the war that it nearly doubled its national debt. **King George III,** who had succeeded his grandfather in 1760, hoped to lower that debt. To do so, in 1763 the king chose a financial expert, George Grenville, to serve as prime minister.

---

## PROGRAM RESOURCES

 **In-Depth Resources: Unit 1**
· Guided Reading, p. 35
· Building Vocabulary, p. 39
· Reteaching Activity, p. 43
· Primary Sources: The Boston Tea Party, pp. 49–50

 **Reading Study Guide** (English and Spanish), pp. 15–16

 **Access for Students Acquiring English/ESL**
· Guided Reading (Spanish), p. 26

 **Formal Assessment**
· Section Quiz, p. 21

 **Integrated Assessment**
· Rubrics

### INTEGRATED TECHNOLOGY

 **Critical Thinking Transp. CT4**
· War for Independence

 **Humanities Transp. HT5, HT31**
· The Battle of Bunker Hill
· Bunker's Hill or America's Head Dress

 **Electronic Library of Primary Sources**

 **classzone.com**

### TEXAS RESOURCES

**TAKS Spiraled Content Review**

**TAKS Practice Tests**

**TAKS Practice Transparencies TT14, TT15**

**TAKS Online Test Practice**

By the time Grenville took over, tensions between Britain and one colony, Massachusetts, were on the rise. During the French and Indian War, the British had cracked down on colonial smuggling to ensure that merchants were not doing business in any French-held territories. In 1761, the royal governor of Massachusetts authorized the use of the writs of assistance, a general search warrant that allowed British customs officials to search any colonial ship or building they believed to be holding smuggled goods. Because many merchants worked out of their residences, the writs enabled British officials to enter and search colonial homes whether there was evidence of smuggling or not. The merchants of Boston were outraged.

Grenville's actions, however, soon angered merchants throughout the colonies. The new prime minister noticed that the American customs service, which collected duties, or taxes on imports, was losing money. Grenville concluded that the colonists were smuggling goods into the country without paying duties. In 1764 he prompted Parliament to enact a law known as the Sugar Act.

The **Sugar Act** did three things. It halved the duty on foreign-made molasses in the hopes that colonists would pay a lower tax rather than risk arrest by smuggling. It placed duties on certain imports that had not been taxed before. Most important, it provided that colonists accused of violating the act would be tried in a vice-admiralty court rather than a colonial court. There, each case would be decided by a single judge rather than by a jury of sympathetic colonists.

Colonial merchants complained that the Sugar Act would reduce their profits. Merchants and traders further claimed that Parliament had no right to tax the colonists because the colonists had not elected representatives to the body. The new regulations, however, had little effect on colonists besides merchants and traders. **A**

**THE STAMP ACT** In March 1765 Parliament passed the **Stamp Act**. This act imposed a tax on documents and printed items such as wills, newspapers, and playing cards. A stamp would be placed on the items to prove that the tax had been paid. It was the first tax that affected colonists directly because it was levied on goods and services. Previous taxes had been indirect, involving duties on imports.

In May of 1765, the colonists united to defy the law. Boston shopkeepers, artisans, and laborers organized a secret resistance group called the Sons of Liberty to protest the law. Meanwhile, the colonial assemblies declared that Parliament lacked the power to impose taxes on the colonies because the colonists were not represented in Parliament. In October 1765, merchants in New York, Boston, and Philadelphia agreed to a boycott of British goods until the Stamp Act was repealed. The widespread boycott worked, and in March 1766 Parliament repealed the law.

But on the same day that it repealed the Stamp Act, Parliament passed the Declaratory Act, which asserted Parliament's full right "to bind the colonies and people of America in all cases whatsoever." Then, in 1767, Parliament passed the Townshend Acts, named after Charles Townshend, the leading government minister. The Townshend Acts taxed goods that were imported into the colony from Britain, such as lead, glass, paint, and paper. The Acts also imposed a tax on tea, the most popular drink in the colonies. Led by men such as **Samuel Adams,** one of the founders of the Sons of Liberty, the colonists again boycotted British goods. **B**

*A. Answer*
The colonists believed that the Sugar Act would reduce their profits and that these taxes violated their rights because they were not represented in Parliament.

**MAIN IDEA**

**Analyzing Issues**
**A** How did the Sugar Act cause tension between the colonists and Britain?

*B. Answer*
Colonists protested, adopted resolutions denouncing adopted resolutions denouncing the Stamp Act, and boycotted British goods.

**MAIN IDEA**

**Summarizing**
**B** How did the colonists respond to the Stamp Act and the Townshend Acts?

**NOW & THEN**

**PROPOSITION 13**

A more recent tax revolt occured in California on June 6, 1978, when residents voted in a tax reform law known as Proposition 13. By the late 1970s, taxes in California were among the highest in the nation. The property tax alone was fifty-two percent above the national norm.

Proposition 13, initiated by ordinary citizens, limited the tax on real property to one percent of its assessed value in 1975–1976. It passed with sixty-five percent of the vote.

Because of the resulting loss of revenue, many state agencies were scaled down or cut. In 1984, California voters approved a state lottery that provides supplemental funds for education. But Proposition 13 still remains a topic of heated debate, as Californians—like other Americans across the country—struggle with conflicting desires: more government services vs. less taxes.

**TAKS**

Mini-Lesson 1:
SS11 1(8.4.B)

**NOW & THEN**

**Proposition 13**
**Analyzing Effects** Have students use the Internet or library resources to examine the effects of Proposition 13 on California. Have students look for how the proposition impacted the state's tax base and tax-related services as well as its real estate market. Have students share their findings with the class.

**Tracing Themes**
**ECONOMIC OPPORTUNITY**

**Taxation**
Economic factors played a key role in causing the American Revolution. Direct and indirect taxes especially outraged the colonists, whose rallying cry became "No taxation without representation." The colonists had no representation in the taxing body, the British Parliament. A direct tax is a tax paid by the individual, such as income or property tax. An indirect tax is a duty paid by a producer or importer that is passed along to consumers via a price increase. An example would be sales tax.

In the years leading up to the war, Britain imposed new taxes on the colonists, and also followed policies that squelched the colonies' economic development and their expansion into the newly acquired territories.

📀 **Electronic Library of Primary Sources**
· Resolutions for American Duties, 1764 by Members of British Parliament

**DIFFERENTIATING INSTRUCTION    LESS PROFICIENT READERS**

**Guided Reading**

Suggest that students focus their reading by turning each heading and subheading into a question and then reading the material below it to find the answer. For example, the main section heading on page 46 could be turned into this question: How did the colonies organize to resist Britain? The subheadings in this section could be turned into these questions: What was the Sugar Act? Why did colonists object to it? What was the Stamp Act? Who protested the Stamp Act and how did they protest?

| Heading | Question |
| --- | --- |
| The Colonies Organize to Resist Britain | How did the colonize organize to resist Britain? |
|  |  |

## Instruct: Objective ❷

**Tension Mounts in Massachusetts**
TAKS SS11 1(8.4.B)

· What colonial resistance and British countermeasures prompted the Boston Massacre and Boston Tea Party?

· What were the Intolerable Acts and how did the colonists respond to them?

 **In-Depth Resources: Unit 1**
· Guided Reading, p. 35
· Primary Sources: The Boston Tea Party, pp. 49–50

 **Electronic Library of Primary Sources**
· "An Account of a Late Military Massacre," 1770 by P. Revere

---

### History Through *Art*

Paul Revere's engraving contains several historical inaccuracies. While his work depicts the British soldiers standing in formation and firing on the helpless colonists, both sides actually were engaged in belligerent and riotous behavior when the shooting started. Revere's engraving shows a blue daytime sky with only the moon hinting at the actual time of the event—after nine o'clock in the evening. Evidence indicates that Revere copied engraver Henry Pelham's rough drawing of the Massacre and then quickly produced his work before Pelham could finish his.

**SKILLBUILDER ANSWERS**

1. The British soldiers are armed and organized. The artist may possibly be trying to suggest that the colonists should be armed and organized themselves.

2. The smoke is spreading over the city, even as violence seems to be spreading throughout the colonies.

---

## British Actions and Colonial Reactions, 1765–1775

### 1765 STAMP ACT

**British Action**
Britain passes the Stamp Act, a tax law requiring colonists to purchase special stamped paper for printed items.

**Colonial Reaction**
Colonists harass stamp distributors, boycott British goods, and prepare a Declaration of Rights and Grievances.

### 1767 TOWNSHEND ACTS

**British Action**
Britain taxes certain colonial imports and stations troops at major colonial ports to protect customs officers.

**Colonial Reaction**
Colonists protest "taxation without representation" and organize a new boycott of imported goods.

### 1770 BOSTON MASSACRE

**British Action**
Taunted by an angry mob, British troops fire into the crowd, killing five colonists.

**Colonial Reaction**
Colonial agitators label the conflict a massacre and publish a dramatic engraving depicting the violence.

▲ This colonial engraving was meant to warn of the effects of the Stamp Act.

## Tension Mounts in Massachusetts ❷

As hostilities between the colonists and the British mounted, the atmosphere in Boston grew increasingly tense. The city soon erupted in bloody clashes and later in a daring tax protest, all of which pushed the colonists and Britain closer to war.

**VIOLENCE ERUPTS IN BOSTON** On March 5, 1770, a mob gathered in front of the Boston Custom House and taunted the British soldiers standing guard there. Shots were fired and five colonists, including Crispus Attucks, were killed or mortally wounded. Colonial leaders quickly labeled the confrontation the **Boston Massacre**.

Despite strong feelings on both sides, the political atmosphere relaxed somewhat during the next three years. Lord Frederick North, who later followed Grenville as the prime minister, realized that the Townshend Acts were costing more to enforce than they would ever bring in: in their first year, for example, the taxes raised only 295 pounds, while the cost of sending British troops to Boston

**Background**
Pounds are the basic monetary unit of British currency.

---

### History Through *Art*

**THE BOSTON MASSACRE (1770)**

Paul Revere was not only a patriot, but a silversmith and an engraver as well. One of the best known of his engravings, depicting the Boston Massacre, is a masterful piece of anti-British propaganda. Widely circulated, Revere's engraving played a key role in rallying revolutionary fervor.

• The sign above the soldiers reads "Butcher's Hall."
• The British commander, Captain Preston (standing at the far right of the engraving) appears to be inciting the troops to fire. In fact, he tried to calm the situation.
• At the center foreground is a small dog, a detail that gave credence to the rumor that, following the shootings, dogs licked the blood of the victims from the street.

**SKILLBUILDER Interpreting Visual Sources**
1. According to the details of the engraving, what advantages do the soldiers have that the colonists do not? What point does the artist make through this contrast?
2. What do you think is the intended message behind the artist's use of smoke spreading out from the soldiers' rifles?

 **SEE SKILLBUILDER HANDBOOK, PAGE R23.**

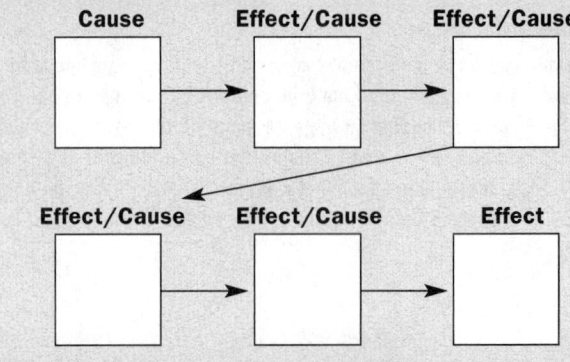
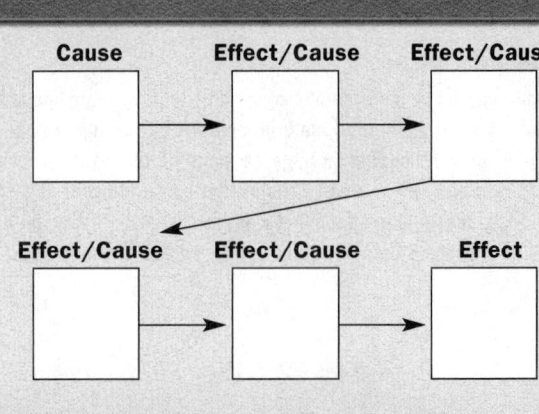

**48** CHAPTER 2 *Revolution and the Early Republic*

---

**DIFFERENTIATING INSTRUCTION**   **LESS PROFICIENT READERS**

### Analyzing Cause and Effect

To help students understand the chain of events that led to the start of the Revolution, fill in a diagram to reflect the causes and effects of the events shown on the top of pages 48–49. Ask for volunteers to add to the diagram and to explain their additions to the class. Remind students that sometimes one effect actually becomes the cause of the next event.

| Cause | Effect/Cause | Effect/Cause |
|---|---|---|
| | | |

| Effect/Cause | Effect/Cause | Effect |
|---|---|---|
| | | |

## 1773 TEA ACT

**British Action**
Britain gives the East India Company special concessions in the colonial tea business and shuts out colonial tea merchants.

**Colonial Reaction**
Colonists in Boston rebel, dumping 18,000 pounds of East India Company tea into Boston harbor.

## 1774 INTOLERABLE ACTS

**British Action**
King George III tightens control over Massachusetts by closing Boston Harbor and quartering troops.

**Colonial Reaction**
Colonial leaders form the First Continental Congress and draw up a declaration of colonial rights.

## 1775 LEXINGTON AND CONCORD

**British Action**
General Gage orders troops to march to Concord, Massachusetts, and seize colonial weapons.

**Colonial Reaction**
Minutemen intercept the British and engage in battle—first at Lexington, and then at Concord.

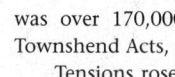

This bottle contains tea that colonists threw into Boston harbor during the Boston Tea Party.

**SKILLBUILDER** Interpreting Charts
In what ways did colonial reaction to British rule intensify between 1765 and 1775?

was over 170,000 pounds. North persuaded Parliament to repeal the Townshend Acts, except for the tax on tea.

Tensions rose again in 1772 when a group of Rhode Island colonists attacked a British customs schooner that patrolled the coast for smugglers. The colonists boarded the vessel, which had accidentally run aground near Providence, and burned it to the waterline. In response, King George named a special commission to seek out the suspects and bring them to England for trial.

The plan to haul Americans to England for trial ignited widespread alarm. The assemblies of Massachusetts and Virginia set up committees of correspondence to communicate with other colonies about this and other threats to American liberties. By 1774, such committees formed a buzzing communication network linking leaders in nearly all the colonies.

**THE BOSTON TEA PARTY** In 1773, Lord North devised the Tea Act in order to save the nearly bankrupt British East India Company. The act granted the company the right to sell tea to the colonies free of the taxes that colonial tea sellers had to pay. This action would have cut colonial merchants out of the tea trade by enabling the East India Company to sell its tea directly to consumers for less. North hoped the American colonists would simply buy the cheaper tea; instead, they protested dramatically.

On the moonlit evening of December 16, 1773, a large group of Boston rebels disguised themselves as Native Americans and proceeded to take action against three British tea ships anchored in the harbor. In this incident, later known as the **Boston Tea Party**, the "Indians" dumped 18,000 pounds of the East India Company's tea into the waters of Boston harbor.

**THE INTOLERABLE ACTS** An infuriated King George III pressed Parliament to act. In 1774, Parliament responded by passing a series of measures that colonists called the Intolerable Acts. One law shut down Boston harbor. Another, the Quartering Act, authorized British commanders to house soldiers in vacant private homes and other buildings. In addition to these measures, General Thomas Gage, commander-in-chief of British forces in North America, was appointed the new governor of Massachusetts. To keep the peace, he placed Boston under martial law, or rule imposed by military forces. **C**

In response to Britain's actions, the committees of correspondence assembled the First Continental Congress. In September 1774, 56 delegates met in Philadelphia and drew up a declaration of colonial rights. They defended the colonies' right to run their own affairs and stated that, if the British used force against the colonies, the colonies should fight back.

**C. Answer** He wanted to isolate and punish Massachusetts in the hope it would become more obedient and in order to keep the conflict from spreading.

**MAIN IDEA**

Analyzing Motives
**C** What do you think King George set out to achieve when he disciplined Massachusetts?

**ACTIVITY** COOPERATIVE LEARNING

**BLOCK SCHEDULING**

## Letters from Committees of Correspondence

**Class Time** 45 minutes

**Task** Writing letters as a member of a committee of correspondence in 1774

**Purpose** To understand the colonists' reactions to British actions

**Directions** Divide the class into small groups and assign each a colony to represent. Ask each group to write a letter to a committee of correspondence in another colony. Students might supplement historical details from their texts with information that they research in library books or other references. Ask a volunteer from each group to read the letters to the class. Discuss pertinent points that students raise in their letters.

 Integrated Assessment
· Rubric 5

## Instruct: Objective ❸

**The Road to Revolution**

TAKS SS11 1(8.4.C)

· What were the causes and outcomes of the battles at Lexington and Concord?

· What were the consequences of the Battle of Bunker Hill?

 In-Depth Resources: Unit 1
· Guided Reading, p. 35

 Humanities Transparencies HT5, HT31
· The Battle of Bunker Hill
· Bunker's Hill or America's Head Dress

### More About . . .

**Lexington and Concord**

The last person believed to have died in the battles of Lexington and Concord was neither a Minuteman nor a redcoat—but a teenage boy. As the British fought their way back from Concord to Boston, they passed through Charlestown, home of 14-year-old Edward Barber. Barber rushed to the window of his home to watch the regulars (soldiers) pass. By this time, British troops had endured numerous hit-and-run attacks from colonists. As a result, they considered anyone moving in a house to be a possible sniper. A British soldier aimed his musket at the Barber home and killed young Edward with one shot.

▲ The Battle of Lexington, as depicted in a mid-nineteenth-century painting.

## ❸ The Road to Revolution

After the First Continental Congress met, colonists in many eastern New England towns stepped up military preparations. Minutemen—civilian soldiers who pledged to be ready to fight against the British on a minute's notice—quietly stockpiled firearms and gunpowder. General Thomas Gage soon learned about these activities. In the spring of 1775, he ordered troops to march from Boston to nearby Concord, Massachusetts, and to seize illegal weapons. ⓓ

**FIGHTING AT LEXINGTON AND CONCORD** Colonists in Boston were watching, and on the night of April 18, 1775, Paul Revere, William Dawes, and Samuel Prescott rode out to spread word that 700 British troops were headed for Concord. The darkened countryside rang with church bells and gunshots—prearranged signals, sent from town to town, that the British were coming.

The king's troops, known as "redcoats" because of their uniforms, reached Lexington, Massachusetts, five miles short of Concord, on the cold, windy dawn of April 19. As they neared the town, they saw 70 minutemen drawn up in lines on the village green. The British commander ordered the minutemen to lay down their arms and leave, and the colonists began to move out without laying down their muskets. Then someone fired, and the British soldiers sent a volley of shots into the departing militia. Eight minutemen were killed and ten more were wounded, but only one British soldier was injured. The Battle of Lexington, the first battle of the Revolutionary War, lasted only 15 minutes.

The British marched on to Concord, where they found an empty arsenal. After a brief skirmish with minutemen, the British soldiers lined up to march back to Boston, but the march quickly became a slaughter. Between 3,000 and 4,000 minutemen had assembled by now, and they fired on the marching troops from behind stone walls and trees. British soldiers fell by the dozen. Bloodied and humiliated, the remaining British soldiers made their way back to Boston that night. Colonists had become enemies of Britain and now held Boston and its encampment of British troops under siege.

**MAIN IDEA**

**Evaluating**

ⓓ Do you think the British underestimated the colonists in 1770–1775?

**D. Possible Answers**
**Yes:** they failed to notice how angry and unified the colonists were. **No:** the British believed that taxing the colonies was justified, because the colonies existed to benefit the British empire, and they expected continued loyalty from the colonists.

**50** CHAPTER 2 *Revolution and the Early Republic*

---

**DIFFERENTIATING INSTRUCTION**    **GIFTED AND TALENTED**

### Create a Political Cartoon

Ask students to create a political cartoon based on an event described in the subsection "The Road to Revolution." For example, students might make a cartoon depicting the attack on the British at Concord, or the meeting of delegates at the Second Continental Congress. Point out to students that the cartoon should exaggerate events, use recognizable symbols that are relevant to the event, appeal to a particular audience, and make some sort of statement or comment on the event.

Make sure students understand that humor is often an element of political cartoons; however, some topics may be too serious to warrant a humorous treatment. Post the cartoons around the classroom, and ask students to circulate to view them. Ask: Which cartoons make their points most effectively? Which ones make the best use of humor? What statement about the event does each cartoon seem to make?

 Integrated Assessment
· Rubric 4

**THE SECOND CONTINENTAL CONGRESS** In May of 1775, colonial leaders called the Second Continental Congress in Philadelphia to debate their next move. The loyalties that divided colonists sparked endless debates at the Second Continental Congress. Some delegates called for independence, while others argued for reconciliation with Great Britain. Despite such differences, the Congress agreed to recognize the colonial militia as the Continental Army and appointed George Washington as its commander.

**THE BATTLE OF BUNKER HILL** Cooped up in Boston, British general Thomas Gage decided to strike at militiamen on Breed's Hill, north of the city and near Bunker Hill. On June 17, 1775, Gage sent 2,400 British soldiers up the hill. The colonists held their fire until the last minute and then began to mow down the advancing redcoats before finally retreating. By the time the smoke cleared, the colonists had lost 450 men, while the British had suffered over 1,000 casualties. The misnamed Battle of Bunker Hill would prove to be the deadliest battle of the war.

By July, the Second Continental Congress was readying the colonies for war though still hoping for peace. Most of the delegates, like most colonists, felt deep loyalty to George III and blamed the bloodshed on the king's ministers. On July 8, Congress sent the king the so-called Olive Branch Petition, urging a return to "the former harmony" between Britain and the colonies. **E**

King George flatly rejected the petition. Furthermore, he issued a proclamation stating that the colonies were in rebellion and urged Parliament to order a naval blockade to isolate a line of ships meant for the American coast.

**Vocabulary**
**reconciliation:** the restoration of a former state of harmony or friendship

---

**MAIN IDEA**

**Developing Historical Perspective**
**E** Do you think that the Olive Branch Petition was too little too late?

*E. Possible Answers*
**Yes:** because King George had only responded to the colonists with punishments and by sending troops. **No:** because a war would be costly, both financially and in terms of fatalities.

---

**More About . . .**

**General Washington**
George Washington did not become commander of the Continental Army without some reservations. Colonial leaders from New England, for example, voiced concerns about handing the army over to a Southerner—Washington was from Virginia. On some occasions Washington himself questioned his own abilities. He ultimately accepted the post, but declared, "I feel great distress from a consciousness that my abilities and military experience may not be equal to the extensive and important trust."

---

**More About . . .**

**Bunker Hill**
Questionable tactics and overconfidence may have played a role in Britain's difficulties in taking Breed's Hill. British troops moved in tight formation, wearing over 100 pounds of gear each. Positioned so close together and slowed by their added weight, the redcoats made easy targets for the colonials shooting at them from above. When the bloody battle had ended, one British officer stated, "From an absurd and destructive confidence, carelessness, or ignorance, we have lost a thousand of our best men and officers."

**Humanities Transparencies**
· Battle of Bunker Hill HT5
· Bunker's Hill or America's Head Dress HT31

This painting shows "Bunker's Hill" before the battle, as shells from Boston set nearby Charlestown ablaze. At the battle, the British employed a formation they used throughout the war. They massed together, were visible for miles, and failed to take advantage of ground cover.

---

## Social Studies Vocabulary

To help students understand the many social studies concept vocabulary words in this section, have them write down the following terms:

| | |
|---|---|
| militia | continental |
| musket | congress |
| intolerable | delegate |
| committees | boycott |
| correspondence | repeal |

Have students look up these words in a dictionary. Help them understand each word by discussing its meaning and use. Then have students write a definition of the term in their own words, and finally, write a sentence using the term in the appropriate context. Discuss any terms that appear to be particularly difficult for students, and work together in the large group to write sentences for those words.

## Instruct: Objective ❹

### The Patriots Declare Independence
TAKS SS11 1(8.4.C)

· How did Paine's *Common Sense* seek to persuade colonists to support the cause of independence?

· For what reasons did the colonists declare their independence from Great Britain?

 In-Depth Resources: Unit 1
· Guided Reading, p. 35

---

### More About . . .

#### Thomas Paine
Thomas Paine came to Philadelphia in 1774 on the advice of Ben Franklin, whom Paine had met in London. Two years later, Paine published *Common Sense*. He kept prices low so that his editions could be widely circulated. He later returned to England, where his defense of the French Revolution, *The Rights of Man*, prompted an indictment for treason. Returning to France, Paine became caught up in the Reign of Terror and was imprisoned. While in prison, he published part one of *The Age of Reason*, an attack on organized religion that earned him many enemies.

👁 Electronic Library of Primary Sources
· *Common Sense*, 1776 by T. Paine

---

## ❹ The Patriots Declare Independence

Despite the growing crisis, many colonists were uncertain about the idea of independence. However, in the months following the Olive Branch Petition, public opinion began to shift.

**THE IDEAS BEHIND THE REVOLUTION** This shift in public opinion occurred in large part because of the Enlightenment ideas that had spread throughout the colonies in the 1760s and 1770s. One of the key Enlightenment thinkers was English philosopher **John Locke.** Locke maintained that people have natural rights to life, liberty, and property. Furthermore, he contended, every society is based on a social contract—an agreement in which the people consent to choose and obey a government so long as it safeguards their natural rights. If the government violates that social contract by taking away or interfering with those rights, people have the right to resist and even overthrow the government. **Ⓕ**

Other influences on colonial leaders who favored independence were religious traditions that supported the cause of liberty. One preacher of the time, Jonathan Mayhew, wrote that he had learned from the holy scriptures that wise, brave, and virtuous men were always friends of liberty. Some ministers even spoke from their pulpits in favor of liberty.

Yet the ideas of limited government and civil rights had been basic to English law since even before A.D. 1215, when the English nobility had forced King John to sign Magna Carta, or the Great Charter. Magna Carta acknowledged certain specific rights of the barons against the king, including some rights to due process, a speedy trial, and trial by a jury of one's peers. Its main significance, though, was to recognize that the sovereign did not have absolute authority, but was subject like all men and women to the rule of law. This principle was reaffirmed by the English Bill of Rights, accepted by King William and Queen Mary in 1689.

**THOMAS PAINE'S *COMMON SENSE*** Just as important were the ideas of Thomas Paine. In a widely read 50-page pamphlet titled ***Common Sense,*** Paine attacked King George and the monarchy. Paine, a recent immigrant, argued that responsibility for British tyranny lay with "the royal brute of Britain." Paine explained that his own revolt against the king had begun with Lexington and Concord.

Thomas Paine's pamphlet *Common Sense* helped to overcome many colonists' doubts about separating from Britain.

### A PERSONAL VOICE   THOMAS PAINE
"No man was a warmer wisher for a reconciliation than myself, before the fatal nineteenth of April, 1775, but the moment the event of that day was made known, I rejected the hardened, sullen tempered Pharaoh of England for ever . . . the wretch, that with the pretended title of Father of his people can unfeelingly hear of their slaughter, and composedly sleep with their blood upon his soul."
—*Common Sense*

Paine declared that independence would allow America to trade more freely. He also stated that independence would give American colonists the chance to create a better society—one free from tyranny, with equal social and economic opportunities for all. *Common Sense* sold some 150,000 copies in 1776 and was widely applauded. In April 1776, George Washington wrote, "I find *Common Sense* is working a powerful change in the minds of many men."

**52** CHAPTER 2 *Revolution and the Early Republic*

---

**MAIN IDEA**

**Making Inferences**
Ⓕ Why might the ideals of the Enlightenment appeal to the colonists?
*F. Answer* American colonists seeking independence found support for their views in Locke's assertion that people have a right to resist and overthrow an unfair government.

---

| ACTIVITY | COOPERATIVE LEARNING | | Ⓑ BLOCK SCHEDULING |

### Creating a Political Pamphlet

**Class Time** 30 minutes

**Task** Creating political pamphlets that support or oppose independence

**Purpose** To understand the colonists' feelings about the war

**Directions** Assign groups of three or four students to work together to design folded pamphlets to persuade colonists to support or oppose independence. Tell students to imagine that the pamphlet will be printed and circulated soon after a particular episode or event—the Battle of Bunker Hill, for example, or the signing of the Declaration of Independence.

 Integrated Assessment
· Rubric 4

**DECLARING INDEPENDENCE** By the early summer of 1776, the wavering Continental Congress finally decided to urge each colony to form its own government. On June 7, Virginia delegate Richard Henry Lee moved that "these United Colonies are, and of a right ought to be, free and independent States."

While talks on this fateful motion were under way, the Congress appointed a committee to prepare a formal **Declaration of Independence**. Virginia lawyer **Thomas Jefferson** was chosen to prepare the final draft.

Drawing on Locke's ideas of natural rights, Jefferson's document declared the rights of "Life, Liberty, and the pursuit of Happiness" to be "unalienable" rights—ones that can never be taken away. Jefferson then asserted that a government's legitimate power can only come from the consent of the governed, and that when a government denies their unalienable rights, the people have the right to "alter or abolish" that government. Jefferson provided a long list of violations committed by the king and Parliament against the colonists' unalienable rights. On that basis, the American colonies declared their independence from Britain.

The Declaration states flatly that "all men are created equal." When this phrase was written, it expressed the common belief that free citizens were political equals. It did not claim that all people had the same ability or ought to have equal wealth. It was not meant to embrace women, Native Americans, or African-American slaves—a large number of Americans. However, Jefferson's words presented ideals that would later help these groups challenge traditional attitudes. In his first draft, Jefferson included an eloquent attack on the cruelty and injustice of the slave trade. However, South Carolina and Georgia, the two colonies most dependent on slavery, objected. In order to gain the votes of those two states, Jefferson dropped the offending passage.

On July 2, 1776, the delegates voted unanimously that the American colonies were free, and on July 4, 1776, they adopted the Declaration of Independence. The colonists had declared their freedom from Britain. They would now have to fight for it.

---

**MAIN IDEA**

**Summarizing**
**G** What reasons did Jefferson give to justify revolt by the colonies?

**G. Answer** When a government fails to protect people's unalienable rights, these people have a right to rebel and form a government that will protect their rights.

---

**CHAPTER 2 · SECTION 1**

## Connections Across Time

**1776 AND TODAY**

### Independence Day

As most students know, Americans celebrate the signing of the Declaration of Independence each year on July 4. Independence Day was first celebrated in Philadelphia on July 4, 1777, the one-year anniversary of the adoption of the Declaration of Independence. Flag Day, June 14, commemorates the 1777 adoption of the Stars and Stripes as the U.S. flag by the Continental Congress. Flag Day is a legal holiday only in Pennsylvania.

## Assess & Reteach

### SECTION 1 ASSESSMENT
Students might work in pairs to respond to the questions.

📄 Formal Assessment
· Section Quiz, p. 21

### SELF-ASSESSMENT
To assess what they have learned, students might write their own questions, exchange them with a partner, and try to answer their partner's questions.

### RETEACH
Use the Guided Reading worksheet for Section 1 to help in reviewing the main idea of this section.

📄 In-Depth Resources: Unit 1
· Reteaching Activity, p. 43

---

## ① SECTION ASSESSMENT

**1. TERMS & NAMES** For each term or name, write a sentence explaining its significance.

- King George III
- Sugar Act
- Stamp Act
- Samuel Adams
- Boston Massacre
- Boston Tea Party
- John Locke
- *Common Sense*
- Thomas Jefferson
- Declaration of Independence

**MAIN IDEA**

**2. TAKING NOTES**
Create a cluster diagram like the one shown and fill it with events that demonstrate the conflict between Great Britain and the American colonies.

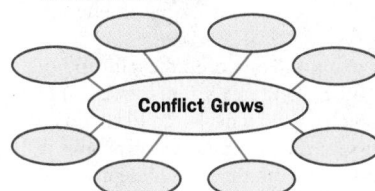

Choose one event to further explain in a paragraph.

**CRITICAL THINKING**

**3. EVALUATING**
Explain whether you think the British government acted wisely in its dealings with the colonies between 1765 and 1775. Support your explanation with examples from the text. **Think About:**
- the reasons for British action
- the reactions of colonists
- the results of British actions

**4. ANALYZING EFFECTS**
While Jefferson borrowed John Locke's ideas, he changed Locke's definition of the rights of men from "life, liberty, and property" to "life, liberty, and the pursuit of happiness." How do you think Jefferson's rewording of Locke's words has affected American life?
**Think About:**
- the experience of immigrants seeking new lives
- the experience of African Americans and Native Americans
- the socioeconomic groups living in America

**REVIEW UNIT 53**

---

Answers **ASSESSMENT** ①

**1. TERMS & NAMES**
King George III, p. 46
Sugar Act, p. 47
Stamp Act, p. 47
Samuel Adams, p. 47
Boston Massacre, p. 48
Boston Tea Party, p. 49
John Locke, p. 52
*Common Sense*, p. 52
Thomas Jefferson, p. 53
Declaration of Independence, p. 53

**2. TAKING NOTES**
Forming Sons of Liberty; protesting Stamp Act; seizure of *Liberty;* Boston Massacre; Boston Tea Party; closing Boston Harbor; Quartering Act; placing Boston under martial law; stockpiling arms; stationing British troops at Concord; Battle of Lexington; colonists' retaliation at Concord

**3. EVALUATING**
Some may argue that Parliament only clamped down when colonists became too rebellious. Others may say that taxing tea to save the East India Company was politically naive. And others may note that Parliament should have avoided confrontational tactics such as the Intolerable Acts.

**4. ANALYZING EFFECTS**
While the "pursuit of happiness" has meant for some making fortunes and accumulating property, for others it has meant happiness rooted in the freedom from oppression and the ability to pursue education and a place in society. Still, as in the case of African Americans and Native Americans, those freedoms were not available to everyone.

*Revolution and the Early Republic* **53**

# The Declaration of Independence

## The Declaration of Independence

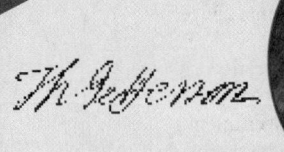

Thomas Jefferson's Declaration of Independence is one of the most important and influential legal documents of modern times. Although the text frequently refers to eighteenth-century events, its Enlightenment philosophy and politics have continuing relevance today. For more than 200 years the Declaration of Independence has inspired leaders of other independence movements and has remained a crucial document in the struggle for civil rights and human rights.

### More About . . .

**The Declaration of Independence**

The Declaration is divided into four parts: a preamble that announces the reason for the document; a section that explains the political principles underlying the rights of people; a list of the unfair acts of the British king; and the actual declaration of independence from Britain.

### Connections Across Time

**1776 AND TODAY**

**Charters of Freedom**

Known as the Charters of Freedom, the Declaration of Independence, the U.S. Constitution, and the Bill of Rights are on display at the National Archives in Washington, D.C. The documents are moved to a bombproof vault every day at closing time. Over time, the outside elements have invaded the glass cases that contain them. As a result, the documents are beginning to show slight signs of decay. A team of scientists, engineers, designers, and archivists is working to create an advanced, airtight encasement for the documents by 2003.

Jefferson begins the Declaration by attempting to legally and philosophically justify the revolution that was already underway. Here Jefferson is saying that, now that the colonists have begun to separate themselves from British rule, it is time to explain why the colonists have taken this course of action.

These passages reveal the influence of the English philosopher John Locke. In *Two Treatises of Government* (1690), Locke argued that if a government does not allow its citizens to enjoy certain rights and freedoms, the people have a right to replace that government.

Here begins the section in which Jefferson condemns the behavior of King George, listing the king's many tyrannical actions that have forced his American subjects to rebel.

## In Congress, July 4, 1776.

A Declaration by the Representatives of the United States of America, in General Congress assembled.

When in the Course of human events, it becomes necessary for one people to dissolve the political bands which have connected them with another, and to assume among the powers of the earth, the separate and equal station to which the Laws of Nature and of Nature's God entitle them, a decent respect to the opinions of mankind requires that they should declare the causes which impel them to the separation.

We hold these truths to be self-evident, that all men are created equal, that they are endowed by their Creator with certain unalienable Rights, that among these are Life, Liberty and the pursuit of Happiness; that, to secure these rights, Governments are instituted among Men, deriving their just powers from the consent of the governed; that whenever any Form of Government becomes destructive of these ends, it is the Right of the People to alter or to abolish it, and to institute new Government, laying its foundation on such principles and organizing its powers in such form, as to them shall seem most likely to effect their Safety and Happiness. Prudence, indeed, will dictate that Governments long established should not be changed for light and transient causes; and accordingly all experience hath shewn that mankind are more disposed to suffer, while evils are sufferable, than to right themselves by abolishing the forms to which they are accustomed. But when a long train of abuses and usurpations, pursuing invariably the same Object, evinces a design to reduce them under absolute Despotism, it is their right, it is their duty, to throw off such Government, and to provide new Guards for their future security.

Such has been the patient sufferance of these Colonies; and such is now the necessity which constrains them to alter their former Systems of Government. The history of the present King of Great Britain is a history of repeated injuries and usurpations, all having in direct object the establishment of an absolute Tyranny over these States. To prove this, let facts be submitted to a candid world.

He has refused his Assent to Laws, the most wholesome and necessary for the public good.

He has forbidden his Governors to pass Laws of immediate and pressing importance, unless suspended in their operation till his assent should be obtained; and, when so suspended, he has utterly neglected to attend to them.

He has refused to pass other Laws for the accommodation of large districts of people, unless those people would relinquish the right of Representation in the Legislature, a right inestimable to them, and formidable to tyrants only.

---

## RECOMMENDED RESOURCES

### BOOKS FOR THE TEACHER

Fleming, Thomas. *1776: Year of Illusions.* New York: Norton, 1975. Provides context of events surrounding the Declaration.

Maier, Pauline. *American Scripture: Making the Declaration of Independence.* New York: Vintage, 1998. Account of the forging of the document.

Wills, Gary. *Inventing America.* NY: Buccaneer Books, 1994. The Declaration in American thought.

### BOOKS FOR THE STUDENT

Fehrenbach, T.R. *Greatness to Spare: The Heroic Sacrifices of the Men Who Signed the Declaration of Independence.* Replica Books, 2000. Lives of the Declaration signers.

### VIDEOS

*The Adams Chronicles, 1976.* Films, Inc., 800-323-4222. Early debate.

*The Declaration of Independence by the Colonies.* Encyclopaedia Britannica, 800-554-9862.

### SOFTWARE

*The American Revolution.* CD-ROM. Educational Software Institute, 800-955-5570.

*The Pennsylvania Gazette, Folio III 1766-1783: The American Revolution.* CD-ROM. Accessible Archives, 697 Sugartown Road, Malvern, PA, 19355.

### INTEGRATED TECHNOLOGY

For teacher support, visit . . .

 classzone.com

He has called together legislative bodies at places unusual, uncomfortable, and distant from the depository of their public Records, for the sole purpose of fatiguing them into compliance with his measures.

He has dissolved Representative Houses repeatedly, for opposing with manly firmness his invasions on the rights of the people.

He has refused for a long time, after such dissolutions, to cause others to be elected; whereby the Legislative powers, incapable of Annihilation, have returned to the people at large for their exercise; the State remaining in the mean time exposed to all the dangers of invasions from without, and convulsions within.

He has endeavoured to prevent the population of these States; for that purpose obstructing the Laws for Naturalization of Foreigners; refusing to pass others to encourage their migration hither, and raising the conditions of new Appropriations of Lands.

He has obstructed the Administration of Justice, by refusing his Assent to Laws for establishing Judiciary powers.

He has made Judges dependent on his Will alone, for the tenure of their offices, and the amount and payment of their salaries.

He has erected a multitude of New Offices, and sent hither swarms of Officers to harass our people and eat out their substance.

He has kept among us, in times of peace, Standing Armies, without the Consent of our legislatures.

He has affected to render the Military independent of and superior to the Civil power.

He has combined with others to subject us to a jurisdiction foreign to our constitution and unacknowledged by our laws; giving his Assent to their Acts of pretended Legislation:

For quartering large bodies of armed troops among us;

For protecting them, by a mock Trial, from punishment for any Murders which they should commit on the Inhabitants of these States;

For cutting off our Trade with all parts of the world;

For imposing Taxes on us without our Consent;

For depriving us, in many cases, of the benefits of Trial by Jury;

For transporting us beyond Seas to be tried for pretended offenses;

For abolishing the free System of English Laws in a neighboring Province, establishing therein an Arbitrary government, and enlarging its Boundaries so as to render it at once an example and fit instrument for introducing the same absolute rule into these Colonies;

For taking away our Charters, abolishing our most valuable laws, and altering fundamentally the Forms of our Governments;

For suspending our own Legislatures, and declaring themselves invested with power to legislate for us in all cases whatsoever.

## HISTORICAL SPOTLIGHT

### INDEPENDENCE AND SLAVERY

The Declaration of Independence went through many revisions before the final draft. Jefferson, a slaveholder himself, regretted having to eliminate one passage in particular—a condemnation of slavery and the slave trade. However, in the face of opposition of delegates from Southern states, the anti-slavery passage was deleted.

This is a reference to the 10,000 troops that the British government stationed in North America after the French and Indian War. Although the British government saw the troops as protection for the colonists, the colonists themselves viewed the troops as a standing army that threatened their freedom.

Here Jefferson condemns both the king and Parliament for passing the Intolerable Acts. Most of these laws were intended to punish the people of Massachusetts for the Boston Tea Party. For example, the Quartering Act of 1765 forced colonists to provide lodging for British troops. Another act allowed British soldiers accused of murder to be sent back to England for trial. The Boston Port Act closed the port of Boston, "cutting off our trade with all parts of the world."

Here Jefferson refers to the Quebec Act, which extended the boundaries of the province. He then refers to another act that changed the charter of Massachusetts and restricted town meetings.

## HISTORICAL SPOTLIGHT

### Independence and Slavery

Ask students to consider why Jefferson would compromise on the slavery issue. Remind students that Jefferson was a Southerner and in fact owned slaves as well. *(He may have felt it was the only way to achieve the goal of Independence, and that the issue of slavery could be dealt with later.)* Next ask students how this compromise made in 1776 still has implications in the United States in the 21st century. *(Answers will vary.)*

## More About . . .

### Further Grievances Against the King

Later in this section of the grievances against the king, the Declaration refers to actions by the British military against the colonists. Falmouth (now Portland), Maine, was burned in 1775, and the coast of Virginia was attacked in the same year. These actions reinforced the colonists' belief that Britain would not resolve differences with the colonies. Furthermore, Virginia's Governor Dunmore was inciting Ohio Valley Indians on the frontiers of Virginia. Rumors were flying about the hiring of mercenaries to attack the colonies.

---

### Paraphrasing the Declaration

**Class Time** 30 minutes

**Task** Paraphrasing and explaining in modern language the four parts of the Declaration

**Purpose** To read closely one of the greatest documents in U.S. history

**Mini-Lesson 2: SS11 1(8.4.C)**

**Directions** Assign each group one of the four sections of the Declaration: (1) Preamble, (2) Declaration of Rights, (3) List of Grievances (Several groups should work on selected portions of the List of Grievances.), (4) Statement of Independence. Students will rewrite the section in modern English, using words everyone in the group understands and agrees to use. Each group should also include information on the background and the meaning of the passage(s).

## ANOTHER PERSPECTIVE

Abigail Adams, wife of John Adams, was a gifted letter writer, and her writings are considered unsurpassed by those of any other American woman of her time in volume and literary quality. Ask students to discuss why they agree or disagree with her statement that "all Men would be tyrants if they could."

# PERSPECTIVE

### "ALL MEN WOULD BE TYRANTS IF THEY COULD."

Although the Declaration dealt with issues of equality, justice, and independence, it did not address conditions of inequality within the colonies themselves. Husbands dominated their wives, for example, and slaves lived under complete control of their owners. Speaking on behalf of women, Abigail Adams (above) had this to say to her husband John, who served in the Continental Congress:

> "Remember the Ladies, and be more generous and favourable to them than your ancestors. Do not put such limited power into the hands of the Husbands. Remember all Men would be tyrants if they could. If particular care . . . is not paid to the Ladies, we are determined to foment a Rebellion."

Here Jefferson turns his attention away from the king and toward the British people. Calling the British the "common kindred" of the colonists, Jefferson reminds them how often the Americans have appealed to their sense of justice. Reluctantly the colonists are now forced to break their political connections with their British kin.

In this passage, the delegates declare independence.

## More About . . .

### The Statement of Independence

In declaring their independence, the colonists made sure to clearly express that they were not merely rebels, but a free people with all the powers of an independent nation. The main reason for such a purposeful and deliberate statement was to secure foreign aid. The colonies desperately desired an alliance with France. Aid to the colonists, however, would constitute entry into Britain's internal affairs and thus violate international law—unless the colonies made it clear to the world community that they were a viable and free state.

He has abdicated Government here, by declaring us out of his Protection and waging War against us.

He has plundered our seas, ravaged our Coasts, burnt our towns, and destroyed the lives of our people.

He is at this time transporting large Armies of foreign Mercenaries to compleat the works of death, desolation, and tyranny, already begun with circumstances of Cruelty & perfidy scarcely paralleled in the most barbarous ages, and totally unworthy the Head of a civilized nation.

He has constrained our fellow Citizens, taken Captive on the high Seas, to bear Arms against their Country, to become the executioners of their friends and Brethren, or to fall themselves by their Hands.

He has excited domestic insurrections amongst us, and has endeavoured to bring on the inhabitants of our frontiers the merciless Indian Savages, whose known rule of warfare is an undistinguished destruction of all ages, sexes and conditions.

In every stage of these Oppressions We have Petitioned for Redress in the most humble terms; Our repeated Petitions have been answered only by repeated injury. A Prince, whose character is thus marked by every act which may define a Tyrant, is unfit to be the ruler of a free people.

Nor have We been wanting in attentions to our British brethren. We have warned them from time to time of attempts by their legislature to extend an unwarrantable jurisdiction over us. We have reminded them of the circumstances of our emigration and settlement here. We have appealed to their native justice and magnanimity, and we have conjured them by the ties of our common kindred, to disavow these usurpations, which would inevitably interrupt our connections and correspondence. They too have been deaf to the voice of justice and of consanguinity. We must, therefore, acquiesce in the necessity, which denounces our Separation, and hold them, as we hold the rest of mankind, Enemies in War, in Peace Friends.

We, therefore, the Representatives of the United States of America, in General Congress, Assembled, appealing to the Supreme Judge of the world for the rectitude of our intentions, do, in the name, and by the Authority of the good People of these Colonies solemnly publish and declare, That these United Colonies are, and of Right ought to be, Free and Independent States, that they are Absolved from all Allegiance to the British Crown, and that all political connection between them and the State of Great Britain is, and ought to be, totally dissolved; and that as Free and Independent States, they have full Power to levy War, conclude Peace, contract Alliances, establish Commerce, and do all other Acts and Things which Independent States may of right do.

---

**DIFFERENTIATING INSTRUCTION**      **LESS PROFICIENT READERS**

### The Colonists' Responses

Remind students that the tension between the colonies and Britain was caused by the action of both. Use a graphic like this one to help students review the responses of the colonists to the actions of the king. For example, imposing taxes without consent was met by the Stamp Act Congress and the boycott and protests by the colonists. Ask the students to think of other action-reaction situations.

| British Action | Colonial Response |
|---|---|
| Imposing taxes without consent | Stamp Act Congress; boycotts; protest |
| | |

 Integrated Assessment
· Rubric 2

And for the support of this Declaration, with a firm reliance on the protection of divine Providence, we mutually pledge to each other our Lives, our Fortunes, and our sacred Honor.

*[Signed by]*

*John Hancock* **[President of the Continental Congress]**

**[Georgia]**
*Button Gwinnett*
*Lyman Hall*
*George Walton*

**[Rhode Island]**
*Stephen Hopkins*
*William Ellery*

**[Connecticut]**
*Roger Sherman*
*Samuel Huntington*
*William Williams*
*Oliver Wolcott*

**[North Carolina]**
*William Hooper*
*Joseph Hewes*
*John Penn*

**[South Carolina]**
*Edward Rutledge*
*Thomas Heyward, Jr.*
*Thomas Lynch, Jr.*
*Arthur Middleton*

**[Maryland]**
*Samuel Chase*
*William Paca*
*Thomas Stone*
*Charles Carroll*

**[Virginia]**
*George Wythe*
*Richard Henry Lee*
*Thomas Jefferson*
*Benjamin Harrison*
*Thomas Nelson, Jr.*
*Francis Lightfoot Lee*
*Carter Braxton*

**[Pennsylvania]**
*Robert Morris*
*Benjamin Rush*
*Benjamin Franklin*
*John Morton*
*George Clymer*
*James Smith*
*George Taylor*
*James Wilson*
*George Ross*

**[Delaware]**
*Caesar Rodney*
*George Read*
*Thomas McKean*

**[New York]**
*William Floyd*
*Philip Livingston*
*Francis Lewis*
*Lewis Morris*

**[New Jersey]**
*Richard Stockton*
*John Witherspoon*
*Francis Hopkinson*
*John Hart*
*Abraham Clark*

**[New Hampshire]**
*Josiah Bartlett*
*William Whipple*
*Matthew Thornton*

**[Massachusetts]**
*Samuel Adams*
*John Adams*
*Robert Treat Paine*
*Elbridge Gerry*

The Declaration ends with the delegates' pledge, or pact. The delegates at the Second Continental Congress knew that, in declaring their independence from Great Britain, they were committing treason—a crime punishable by death. "We must all hang together," Benjamin Franklin reportedly said, as the delegates prepared to sign the Declaration, "or most assuredly we shall all hang separately."

## KEY PLAYER

**JOHN HANCOCK**
**1737–1793**

Born in Braintree, Massachusetts, and raised by a wealthy uncle, John Hancock became one of the richest men in the colonies. He traveled around Boston in a luxurious carriage and dressed only in the finest clothing. "He looked every inch an aristocrat," noted one acquaintance, "from his dress and powdered wig to his smart pumps of grained leather."
Beneath Hancock's refined appearance, however, burned the heart of a patriot. He was only too glad to lead the Second Continental Congress. When the time came to sign the Declaration of Independence, Hancock scrawled his name in big, bold letters. "There," he reportedly said, "I guess King George will be able to read that."

## KEY PLAYER

**John Hancock**
John Hancock's real ambition was to lead the Continental Army. Throughout the early stages of the Revolutionary War, Hancock pleaded with Washington to let him command a regiment. Each time, Washington diplomatically declined his requests. Hancock finally got his command in 1778 when the legislature of Massachusetts put him in charge of the campaign to free Rhode Island from British occupation. The campaign failed, and Hancock's military career ended before it even began. Have students discuss what they think makes a successful military leader.

## More About . . .

**Lesser-Known Signers**
Elbridge Gerry (Mass.) served as vice-president under James Madison. Richard Stockton (N.J.) was captured by the British and treated so harshly that he became an invalid. Thomas Lynch, Jr. (S.C.), signed the Declaration but did little else in the Revolution. He disappeared at sea with his wife. Button Gwinnett (Ga.) was killed in a duel during the Revolutionary War. Charles Carroll (Md.) was the only Roman Catholic to sign the Declaration and the last signer to die, living until 1832.

---

**DIFFERENTIATING INSTRUCTION**     **GIFTED AND TALENTED**

### Researching a Signer

In addition to the more prominent colonial leaders who signed the Declaration of Independence, a number of lesser-known colonists inked their name to the famous document. Have interested students choose one of the little-known signers and write a brief biography of that person. Tell students to examine the person's life before and after the signing of the Declaration as well as what drove him to become so involved in the creation of this document.

Students volunteers can either read their biographies aloud, or turn them into monologues to present to the class. If students are interested, they might put together a group dramatization of these signers' lives, using props, costumes, and sound effects.

 Integrated Assessment
· Rubric 1

## OBJECTIVES

**1** Trace the war through the winter at Valley Forge.

**2** Examine civilian life during the Revolution.

**3** Trace the war in the South through the siege of Yorktown.

**4** Recognize the symbolic value of the Revolution.

### SKILLBUILDERS

· Geography Skillbuilder: location, place, p. 59; place, movement, p. 62

### CRITICAL THINKING

· Forming Generalizations, p. 59
· Developing HIstorical Perspective, p. 60
· Summarizing, p. 61
· Evaluating, pp. 62, 63
· Analyzing Effects, p. 63

## Focus & Motivate

Ask students what the American Revolution means to them.

## Instruct

### Instruct: Objective **1**

**The War for Independence / The War Begins**

TAKS SS11 1(8.4.B)
· Why did some Americans become Loyalists, while others became Patriots?
· What was the significance of the colonists' victory at Saratoga?

 In-Depth Resources: Unit 1
· Guided Reading, p. 36
· Primary Source: Political Cartoon, p. 51

 Critical Thinking Transparency CT4
· The War for Independence

 Humanities Transparency HT32

# The War for Independence

| MAIN IDEA | WHY IT MATTERS NOW | Terms & Names |
|---|---|---|
| Key American victories reversed British advances during the American Revolutionary War. | The American Revolution is today a national, even international, symbol of the fight for freedom. | • Loyalists • Charles<br>• Patriots Cornwallis<br>• Saratoga • Yorktown<br>• Valley Forge • Treaty of Paris<br>• inflation • egalitarianism<br>• Marquis de<br>Lafayette |

**TEKS** U.S. History 8B, 9A, 9B, 19A, 19B, 21D, 24A, 24B, 24C, 25A, 25B, 25C, 25D

### One American's Story

Benjamin Franklin, the famous American writer, scientist, statesman, and diplomat, represented the colonies in London throughout the growing feud with Britain. As resistance in the colonies turned to bloodshed, however, Franklin fled London in 1775 and sailed home to Philadelphia.

Ironically, the issue of loyalty versus independence that was dividing the American colonies from their mother country was also dividing Franklin's own family. Franklin's son William, the royal governor of New Jersey, was stubbornly loyal to King George and opposed the rebellious atmosphere in the colonies. In one of his many letters to British authorities regarding the conflict in the colonies, William stated his position and that of others who resisted revolutionary views.

**A PERSONAL VOICE** WILLIAM FRANKLIN

" There is indeed a dread in the minds of many here that some of the leaders of the people are aiming to establish a republic. Rather than submit . . . we have thousands who will risk the loss of their lives in defense of the old Constitution. [They] are ready to declare themselves whenever they see a chance of its being of any avail. "

—quoted in *A Little Revenge: Benjamin Franklin and His Son*

**William Franklin**

Because of William's stand on colonial issues, communication between him and his father virtually ceased. The break between Benjamin Franklin and his son mirrored the chasm that now divided the colonies from Britain. The notion of fighting Britain frightened and horrified some colonists even as it inspired others. Both sides believed that they were fighting for their country and being loyal to what was best for America.

**VIDEO**
*PATRIOT FATHER, LOYALIST SON*
**The Divided House of Benjamin and William Franklin**

**58** CHAPTER 2 *Revolution and the Early Republic*

---

## PROGRAM RESOURCES

 **In-Depth Resources: Unit 1**
· Guided Reading, p. 36
· Skillbuilder Practice: Analyzing Causes & Effects, p. 40
· Reteaching Activity, p. 44
· Geography Application: The Siege of Yorktown, pp. 47–48
· Primary Sources, pp. 51–52
· American Lives: Haym Salomon, p. 57

 **Reading Study Guide** (English and Spanish), pp. 17–18

 **Access for Students Acquiring English/ESL**
· Guided Reading (Spanish), p. 27
· Skillbuilder Practice, p. 30
· Geography Application, pp. 33–34

 **Formal Assessment**
· Section Quiz, p. 22

 **Integrated Assessment**
· Rubrics

### INTEGRATED TECHNOLOGY

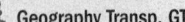 **Geography Transp. GT4**
· North America, 1783

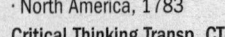 **Critical Thinking Transp. CT4**
· The War for Independence

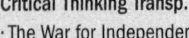 **Humanities Transp. HT6, HT32**
· Signing the Treaty of Paris
· Mrs. General Washington bestowing Stripes on Britannia

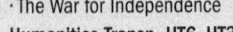 classzone.com

### TEXAS RESOURCES

 TAKS Spiraled Content Review

 TAKS Practice Tests

 TAKS Practice Transparencies TT16, TT17

 TAKS Online Test Practice

**58** CHAPTER 2

# 1 The War Begins

Mini-Lesson 5: SS11 3(7.E)

As they took on the mighty British Empire, the colonists suffered initial losses in the Middle States, which served as the Revolutionary War's early battleground. In time, however, the colonists would battle their way back.

**LOYALISTS AND PATRIOTS** As the war began, Americans found themselves on different sides of the conflict. **Loyalists**—those who opposed independence and remained loyal to the British king—included judges and governors, as well as people of more modest means. Many Loyalists thought that the British were going to win and wanted to avoid punishment as rebels. Still others thought that the Crown would protect their rights more effectively than the new colonial governments would.

**Patriots**—the supporters of independence—drew their numbers from people who saw political and economic opportunity in an independent America. Many Americans remained neutral. **Ⓐ**

The conflict presented dilemmas for other groups as well. Many African Americans fought on the side of the Patriots, but others joined the Loyalists because the British promised freedom to slaves who would fight for the Crown. Most Native Americans supported the British because they viewed colonial settlers as a greater threat to their lands.

**EARLY VICTORIES AND DEFEATS** As part of a plan to stop the rebellion by isolating New England, the British quickly attempted to seize New York City. The British sailed into New York harbor in the summer of 1776 with a force of about 32,000 soldiers. They included thousands of German mercenaries, or hired soldiers, known as Hessians because many of them came from the German region of Hesse.

---

**MAIN IDEA**

**Forming Generalizations**
**Ⓐ** How did the thinking of Loyalists differ from that of Patriots?
**A. Answer Loyalists:** maintained respect for the king and preferred British rule. **Patriots:** agreed with Paine and wanted to be free of tyrannical laws imposed by Britain.

---

## Revolutionary War, 1775–1778

CANADA (British)

Québec, 1775
MAINE (MASS.)
Montréal
Colonel Arnold
St. Lawrence R.
Lake Champlain
General Burgoyne
Fort Ticonderoga, 1775, 1777
Saratoga, 1777
N.H.
Lexington, 1775
Concord, 1775
Bunker Hill, 1775
General Gates
Albany
MASS. Boston
Lake Ontario
N.Y.
CONN.
R.I.
Hudson R.
General Washington
APPALACHIAN MOUNTAINS
Delaware R.
PENN.
New York
Admiral Howe
Lake Erie
Valley Forge
Long Island, 1776
Trenton, 1776
Philadelphia
N.J.
ATLANTIC OCEAN
40°N
Brandywine, 1777
MD.
DEL.
Lake Huron

American campaign
British campaign
American victory
British victory

100      200 miles
100   200 kilometers

VIRGINIA

NORTH CAROLINA
35°N
75°W      70°W      65°W

### GEOGRAPHY SKILLBUILDER
1. **Location** From which city did General Burgoyne march his troops to Saratoga?
2. **Place** What characteristic did many of the battle sites have in common? Why do you think this was so?

---

## Military Strengths and Weaknesses

### UNITED STATES

| Strengths | Weaknesses |
|---|---|
| • familiarity of home ground<br>• leadership of George Washington and other officers<br>• inspiring cause—independence | • most soldiers untrained and undisciplined<br>• shortage of food and ammunition<br>• inferior navy<br>• no central government to enforce wartime policies |

### GREAT BRITAIN

| Strengths | Weaknesses |
|---|---|
| • strong, well-trained army and navy<br>• strong central government with available funds<br>• support of colonial Loyalists and Native Americans | • large distance separating Britain from battlefields<br>• troops unfamiliar with terrain<br>• weak military leaders<br>• sympathy of certain British politicans for the American cause |

REVIEW UNIT  **59**

---

### More About . . .

**The Opposing Armies**
The Continental Army was officially formed by the Second Continental Congress in June 1775 from the standing militias that all colonies except Pennsylvania possessed. The Congress also voted to raise ten new companies of riflemen and put George Washington in charge of the entire army. The British, meanwhile, hired German mercenaries, most of them Hessians (from Hesse-Kassel in what is now central Germany), to supplement their forces.

---

## HISTORY from VISUALS

**Reading the Map**
Have students follow the American campaign on the map.
**Extension** Have students name the site at which Burgoyne's troops scored a victory on the way to Saratoga. *(Fort Ticonderoga)*

**SKILLBUILDER ANSWERS**
1. Location: Montreal
2. They were near waterways. Waterways allowed an easier transport of troops.

---

In-Depth Resources: Unit 1
· Primary Source: Valley Forge Diary, p. 52

---

**ACTIVITY**   **COOPERATIVE LEARNING**

**BLOCK SCHEDULING**

### Reporting on the Revolution

**Class Time** 45 minutes

**Task** Creating front pages of a newspaper that covers different Revolutionary battles

**Purpose** To understand the military, psychological, and historical effects of different Revolutionary battles

**Directions** Each group should choose an audience for the report (Loyalists, Patriots, or both, or the British). Students should focus on one battle and do further research. The front page might include straight news, interviews, background pieces, or a human-interest feature about soldiers or civilians affected by the war. Students might serve as researchers, writers, editors, and page layout designers.

 Integrated Assessment
· Rubrics 1, 5

Although the Continental Army attempted to defend New York in late August, the untrained and poorly equipped colonial troops soon retreated. By late fall, the British had pushed Washington's army across the Delaware River into Pennsylvania.

Desperate for an early victory, Washington risked everything on one bold stroke set for Christmas night, 1776. In the face of a fierce storm, he led 2,400 men in small rowboats across the ice-choked Delaware River. They then marched to their objective—Trenton, New Jersey—and defeated a garrison of Hessians in a surprise attack. The British soon regrouped, however, and in the September of 1777, they captured the American capital at Philadelphia.

**SARATOGA AND VALLEY FORGE** In the meantime, one British general was marching straight into the jaws of disaster. In a complex scheme, General John Burgoyne planned to lead an army down a route of lakes from Canada to Albany, where he would meet British troops as they arrived from New York City. The two regiments would then join forces to isolate New England from the rest of the colonies.

As Burgoyne traveled through forested wilderness, militiamen and soldiers from the Continental Army gathered from all over New York and New England. While he was fighting off the colonial troops, Burgoyne didn't realize that his fellow British officers were preoccupied with holding Philadelphia and weren't coming to meet him. American troops finally surrounded Burgoyne at **Saratoga**, where he surrendered on October 17, 1777.

The surrender at Saratoga turned out to be one of the most important events of the war. Although the French had secretly aided the Patriots since early 1776, the Saratoga victory bolstered France's belief that the Americans could win the war. As a result, the French signed an alliance with the Americans in February 1778 and openly joined them in their fight. **B**

While this hopeful turn of events took place in Paris, Washington and his Continental Army—desperately low on food and supplies—fought to stay alive at winter camp in **Valley Forge**, Pennsylvania. More than 2,000 soldiers died, yet the survivors didn't desert. Their endurance and suffering filled Washington's letters to the Congress and his friends.

**A PERSONAL VOICE** GEORGE WASHINGTON

"It may be said that no history . . . can furnish an instance of an Army's suffering uncommon hardships as ours have done. . . . To see the men without clothes to cover their nakedness, without blankets to lie upon, without shoes, . . . and submitting without a murmur, is a proof of patience and obedience which in my opinion can scarcely be paralleled."

—quoted in *Ordeal at Valley Forge*

## Life During the Revolution **2**

One huge problem that the Continental Congress faced was paying the troops. When the Congress ran out of hard currency—silver and gold—it printed paper money called (like the Revolutionary soldiers) Continentals. As Congress printed more and more money, its value plunged, causing rising prices, or **inflation.** The Congress also struggled against great odds to equip the beleaguered army.

### MAIN IDEA

**Developing Historical Perspective**

**B** Why were these early victories so important to the Continental Army?

**B. Answer** These victories restored the soldiers' confidence after numerous losses.

**Background** See *inflation* on page R42 in the Economics Handbook.

---

## KEY PLAYER

### George Washington

There was one thing Washington would not tolerate from anyone in his ranks—cowardice. Washington wrote a letter of warning to all officers regarding cowardice. Cowardice, he declared, was a "Crime of all others, the most infamous in a Soldier, the most injurious to an Army, and the last to be forgiven. . . . [E]very Officer . . . who shall betray his Country, dishonour the Army and his General, by basely keeping back and shrinking from his duty in any engagement; shall be held up as an infamous Coward and punish'd as such, with the utmost martial severity." Ask students why Washington might have taken such a harsh view of cowardice.

---

**Instruct: Objective** **2**

**Life During the Revolution**
TAKS SS11 5(US24.B)
· What hardships did the colonial population face during the Revolution?
· In what ways did women and African Americans help in the war effort?

 In-Depth Resources: Unit 1
 · Guided Reading, p. 36
 · American Lives: Haym Salomon, p. 57

---

## KEY PLAYER

### GEORGE WASHINGTON
### 1732–1799

During the Revolutionary War, Commander in Chief George Washington became a national hero. An imposing man, Washington stood six feet two inches tall. He was broad-shouldered, calm, and dignified, and he was an expert horseman. But it was Washington's character that won hearts and, ultimately, the war.

Washington persistently roused dispirited men into a fighting force. At Princeton, he galloped on his white horse into the line of fire, shouting and encouraging his men. At Valley Forge, he bore the same cold and privation as every suffering soldier. Time and again, Washington's tactics saved his smaller, weaker force to fight another day. By the end of the war, the entire nation idolized General Washington, and adoring soldiers crowded near him just to touch his boots when he rode by.

---

| ACTIVITY | SKILLBUILDER LESSON |

 **BLOCK SCHEDULING**

### Analyzing Causes and Effects

**Explaining the Skill** History often involves more than a simple string of causes and effects, with one following after another. For example, a cause can have more than one effect, and an effect can become the cause of something else.

**Applying the Skill** Have students examine the text on pages 59 and 60 and chart the causes and effects of the events leading up to the colonists' victory at Saratoga. Students' charts might look like the graphic at the right:

| *cause:* British strategy is to isolate New England from rest of colonies. | → | *effect:* Gen. Burgoyne leads his army from Canada toward Albany. |
|---|---|---|
| *cause/effect:* American troops gather and battle Burgoyne's troops. | → | *effect:* Burgoyne finds himself surrounded and without reinforcements at Saratoga. |
| *cause/effect:* American troops defeat British at Saratoga. | → | *effect:* French sign alliance with colonists. |

 In-Depth Resources: Unit 1
 · Skillbuilder Practice: Analyzing Causes and Effects, p. 40

◀ Molly Pitcher was the heroine of the Battle of Monmouth in New Jersey, which was fought in 1778. Afterward, General Washington appointed her as a noncommissioned officer to honor her brave deeds.

In 1781, the Congress appointed a rich Philadelphia merchant named Robert Morris as superintendent of finance. His associate was Haym Salomon, a Jewish political refugee from Poland. Morris and Salomon begged and borrowed on their personal credit to raise money to provide salaries for the Continental army. They raised funds from Philadelphia's Quakers and Jews. On September 8, 1781, a Continental major wrote in his diary, "This day will be famous in the Annals of History for being the first on which the Troops of the United States received one Month's Pay in Specie [coin]."

The demands of war also affected civilians. When men marched off to fight, many wives stepped into their husbands' shoes, managing farms and businesses as well as households and families. Hundreds of women also followed their husbands to the battlefield, where they washed and cooked for the troops—while some, including Molly Pitcher, even risked their lives in combat. **C**

The war opened some doors for African Americans. Thousands of slaves escaped to freedom in the chaos of war. About 5,000 African Americans served in the Continental Army, where their courage, loyalty, and talent impressed white Americans. Native Americans, however, remained on the fringes of the Revolution, preferring to remain independent and true to their own cultures.

## Winning the War ❸

In February 1778, in the midst of the frozen winter at Valley Forge, American troops began an amazing transformation. Friedrich von Steuben, a Prussian captain and talented drillmaster, helped to train the Continental Army. Other foreign military leaders, such as the **Marquis de Lafayette** (mär-kē′ də lăf′ē-ĕt′), also arrived to offer their help. Lafayette lobbied France for French reinforcements in 1779, and led a command in Virginia in the last years of the war. With the help of such European military leaders, the raw Continental Army became an effective fighting force.

---

**MAIN IDEA**

**Summarizing**
**C** What important contributions did women make in the Revolutionary War?

**C. Answer**
Women managed farms and businesses as well as households and families. Some women washed and cooked for the troops in the battlefield. A few women risked their lives in combat.

---

### HISTORICAL SPOTLIGHT

#### JOHN PAUL JONES

As the Revolutionary War raged on land, Britain and the colonies also engaged each other at sea. The newly formed Continental navy was no match for the mighty British fleet. It was only after France and Spain joined the colonists' cause that Britain lost its maritime supremacy.

Nonetheless, the colonists scored several morale-boosting victories over the British navy, due in large part to the heroics of American naval commander John Paul Jones. The Scottish-born Jones captured a number of British vessels, including the *Serapis* in 1779. It was during his epic battle against this ship that Jones rejected the British demand that he surrender by uttering the famous line, "I have not yet begun to fight."

---

### Tracing Themes
**WOMEN AND POLITICAL POWER**

#### Women's War Efforts
During the Revolutionary War, women managed farms and businesses while the men were off fighting. Women also supported the Patriot cause by making ammunition, clothing, and other supplies for the troops and by helping to feed and house soldiers in their area. Women who traveled with their soldier husbands usually remained in the army camps, doing cooking, washing, and sewing. In addition to such ordinary tasks, they tended to wounds and illnesses when necessary and occasionally took arms themselves.

---

### HISTORICAL SPOTLIGHT

#### John Paul Jones
Discuss with students why control of the Atlantic Ocean would be a major goal of both sides in the war. *(The British needed control of the Atlantic in order to continuously supply their armed forces, while the colonists wanted control of the seas in order to impede the British.)*

#### Instruct: Objective ❸
**Winning the War**
TAKS SS11 1(8.4.C)
· How did the Battle of Yorktown end?
· What was the result of the Treaty of Paris?

📄 In-Depth Resources: Unit 1
· Guided Reading, p. 36
· Geography Application: The Siege of Yorktown, pp. 47–48

---

### Learning Visually

Visual learners may find it easier to absorb information about Revolutionary battles if they map out the details themselves. Encourage students to expand on the maps in this section of their text, creating a single map with all the important battle sites. You may want to give students copies of Geography Transparency GT4 to help them create their own maps. Each visual learner might work with a more verbal partner who supplies appropriate details from the text or from additional research about the Revolution.

Post the maps in the classroom as part of a display on the American Revolution. Allow students to revise or add to their maps as they study the time period.

📄 Integrated Assessment
· Rubric 4

## HISTORY from VISUALS

**Interpreting the Map**
After students have read the section on the Yorktown surrender, ask them what the blue arrow in the Atlantic Ocean represents on the map. *(The French naval force blockading the entrance to Chesapeake Bay)*
**Extension** Ask students what conclusions they might draw, based on the map, about the Spanish strategy. *(Spain took advantage of the British forces' occupation elsewhere to make inroads in the Southeast.)*

### SKILLBUILDER ANSWERS
1. Place: Virginia and the South
2. Yorktown bordered the sea, leaving Cornwallis vulnerable to being isolated.

### More About . . .

**The Treaty of Paris**
Concluding the peace treaty took almost two years—and a lot of talking. At one point, Franklin told the British representative a tale from ancient Rome. A small state, defeated by the mighty Romans, asked the Roman senate how long the peace would last. The country's ambassador replied that the duration of the peace would depend on the conditions Rome set: "If conditions were reasonable, the peace would last long; if not, it would be short."

🎞 Humanities Transparency HT6
· *Signing of the Treaty of Paris*

### Revolutionary War, 1778–1781

*Map legend:*
- American/French campaign
- British campaign
- American/French victory
- British victory
- Thirteen Colonies
- Other British territory

0    100    200 miles
0    100    200 kilometers

**GEOGRAPHY SKILLBUILDER**
1. **Place** Where were most of the later Revolutionary War battles fought?
2. **Movement** Why might General Cornwallis's choice of Yorktown as a base have left him at a military disadvantage?

**THE BRITISH MOVE SOUTH** After their devastating defeat at Saratoga, the British began to shift their operations to the South. At the end of 1778, a British expedition easily took Savannah, Georgia. In their greatest victory of the war, the British under Generals Henry Clinton and **Charles Cornwallis** captured Charles Town, South Carolina, in May 1780. Clinton then left for New York, while Cornwallis continued to conquer land throughout the South.

In early 1781, despite several defeats, the colonists finally turned back Cornwallis—foiling his efforts to take the Carolinas. The British general then chose to move the fight to Virginia. He led his army of 7,500 onto the peninsula between the James and York rivers and camped at **Yorktown.** Cornwallis planned to fortify Yorktown, take Virginia, and then move north to join Clinton's forces.

**Vocabulary**
**peninsula:** a piece of land that projects into a body of water

**THE BRITISH SURRENDER AT YORKTOWN** Shortly after learning of Corwallis's actions, the armies of Lafayette and Washington moved south toward Yorktown. Meanwhile, a French naval force defeated a British fleet and then blocked the entrance to the Chesapeake Bay, thereby obstructing British sea routes to the bay. By mid-September, about 17,000 French and American troops surrounded the British on the Yorktown peninsula and began bombarding them day and night. A month later, on October 19, 1781, Cornwallis finally surrendered. The Americans had shocked the world and defeated the British.

*D. Possible Answers:* How the government would unify the colonies; how the government would remain answerable to the people; how the government would maintain respect of European allies.

Peace talks began in Paris in 1782. The American negotiating team included John Adams, John Jay of New York, and Benjamin Franklin. In September 1783, the delegates signed the **Treaty of Paris,** which confirmed U.S. independence and set the boundaries of the new nation. The United States now stretched from the Atlantic Ocean to the Mississippi River and from Canada to the Florida border. **D**

**MAIN IDEA**

**Evaluating**
**D** What was the most important challenge that faced the new United States?

**62** CHAPTER 2 *Revolution and the Early Republic*

---

**ACTIVITY**   **LINK TO GEOGRAPHY**

 **BLOCK SCHEDULING**

### Displaying Claims to North America

**Class Time** 20 minutes

**Task** Creating a map of claims to North America after the Revolutionary War

**Purpose** To identify claims of European nations and Americans to the lands of North America

**Directions** Have students either create a map of North America or use an outline map of the continent. Using a historical atlas, they should find out which European nations claimed parts of the North American continent in 1781. Remind students to be sure to include Mexico, Alaska, and Canada. They should indicate these claims on the map. The map should include a legend.

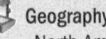 **Geography Transparency GT4**
· *North America, 1783*

## 4 The War Becomes a Symbol of Liberty

Revolutionary ideals set a new course for American society. During the war, social distinctions had begun to blur as the wealthy wore homespun clothing and as military leaders showed respect for all of their soldiers. Changes like these stimulated the rise of **egalitarianism** (ĭ-găl′ĭ-târ′ē-ə-nĭz′əm)—a belief in the equality of all people. This belief fostered a new attitude: the idea that ability, effort, and virtue, not wealth or family background, defined one's worth.

The egalitarianism of the 1780s, however, applied only to white males. It did not bring any new political rights to women. A few states made it possible for women to divorce, but common law still dictated that a married woman's property belonged to her husband.

Moreover, most African Americans were still enslaved, and even those who were free usually faced discrimination and poverty. However by 1804, many New England and Middle states had taken steps to outlaw slavery.

For Native Americans, the Revolution brought uncertainty. During both the French and Indian War and the Revolution, many Native American communities had been either destroyed or displaced, and the Native American population living east of the Mississippi had declined by about 50 percent. Postwar developments further threatened Native American interests, as settlers began taking tribal lands left unprotected by the Treaty of Paris.

In the closing days of the Revolution, the Continental Congress had chosen a quotation from the works of the Roman poet Virgil as a motto for the reverse side of the Great Seal of the United States. The motto, *Novus Ordo Seclorum,* means "a new order of the ages." Establishing a government and resolving internal problems in that new order would be a tremendous challenge for citizens of the newborn United States.

*E. Answer*
The Revolution brought destruction and uncertainty in that colonists saw economic opportunities in lands occupied by Native Americans and gradually began to take that land from them.

**MAIN IDEA**

**Analyzing Effects**
**E** How had the American Revolution affected the lives of Native Americans?

English potter Josiah Wedgwood designed this anti-slavery cameo and sent copies of it to Benjamin Franklin.

---

 **ASSESSMENT**

1. **TERMS & NAMES** For each term or name, write a sentence explaining its significance.
   - Loyalists
   - Patriots
   - Saratoga
   - Valley Forge
   - inflation
   - Marquis de Lafayette
   - Charles Cornwallis
   - Yorktown
   - Treaty of Paris
   - egalitarianism

**MAIN IDEA**

2. **TAKING NOTES**
On a chart like the one below, list five significant events of the Revolutionary War in the column on the left. Note the significance of each event towards the American cause in the column on the right.

| Event | Significance |
|-------|--------------|
|       |              |
|       |              |

**CRITICAL THINKING**

3. **EVALUATING**
Do you think the colonists could have won their independence without aid from foreigners? Explain.
**Think About:**
- the military needs of the Americans and the strengths of the French
- the colonists' military efforts in the South
- the Americans' belief in their fight for independence

4. **ANALYZING EFFECTS**
What were the effects of the Revolutionary War on the American colonists? **Think About:**
- political effects
- economic effects
- social effects

---

**1. TERMS & NAMES**
Loyalists, p. 59
Patriots, p. 59
Saratoga, p. 60
Valley Forge, p. 60
inflation, p. 60
Marquis de Lafayette, p. 61
Charles Cornwallis, p. 62
Yorktown, p. 62
Treaty of Paris, p. 62
egalitarianism, p. 63

**2. TAKING NOTES**
Victories at Trenton and Saratoga helped to boost morale in the Continental Army; civilians aid the war effort with money, food, clothing, and participation in the fighting; Von Steuben and Lafayette lead Europeans in aiding the American colonists; victory at Yorktown resulted in British surrender; Treaty of Paris confirms U.S. independence and establishes its borders.

**3. EVALUATING**
**No** The colonists needed the French fleet to block sea routes to win the battle at Yorktown; American troops needed Von Steuben's training. **Yes** The determination of the American Patriots would have carried them to victory; American troops were weakening the British and winning in the Carolinas; once isolated at Yorktown, the British might still have been defeated.

**4. ANALYZING EFFECTS**
Politically, the colonists gained a great deal of stature, as they became leaders of a large, independent country. Economically, the war forced many colonists to confront inflation. Socially, the war sparked a growing sense of egalitarianism.

---

**Instruct: Objective 4**

**The War Becomes a Symbol of Liberty**
TAKS SS11 1(8.4.C)
· How did the war promote egalitarianism?
· In what ways did the Revolution fail to change the lives of women and minorities?

📖 In-Depth Resources: Unit 1
· Guided Reading, p. 36

## Assess & Reteach

**SECTION 2 ASSESSMENT**
Have small groups of students complete the chart for question 2. Groups should exchange their charts and compare the information. The groups should discuss discrepancies between charts.

📖 Formal Assessment
· Section Quiz, p. 22

**SELF-ASSESSMENT**
Have students write a paragraph describing the viewpoints of a Patriot and a Loyalist regarding the Revolution.

**RETEACH**
Use the Main Idea questions to help in reviewing this section.

📖 In-Depth Resources: Unit 1
· Reteaching Activity, p. 44

### Objectives

· Explain women's contributions to the American Revolution.

· Summarize the struggle for political power by American women over the centuries.

## Focus & Motivate

Have students consider their own definitions of the term "women's rights." Ask them: Which aspects of the definition relate to political power? In their opinion, what is the state of women's rights in America today?

## More About . . .

### Women in Political Power

In addition to holding more elected offices than ever before, American women in the late 20th century broke the "glass ceiling" in appointed political offices. In 1981 President Reagan appointed the first woman to the Supreme Court, Sandra Day O'Connor. A decade later, President Clinton appointed Janet Reno to be the first woman attorney general in the United States. After his re-election in 1996, Clinton appointed the first woman, Madeleine K. Albright (who had been serving as UN ambassador), to the top Cabinet position of U.S. secretary of state.

## TRACING THEMES

# Women and Political Power

In their families and in the workplace, in speeches and in print, countless American women have worked for justice for all citizens. Throughout the history of the United States, women have played whatever roles they felt were necessary to better this country. They also fought to expand their own political power, a power that throughout much of American history has been denied them.

## 1770s

**PROTEST AGAINST BRITAIN** ▶

In the tense years leading up to the Revolution, American women found ways to participate in the protests against the British. Homemakers boycotted tea and British-made clothing. In the painting at right, Sarah Morris Mifflin, shown with her husband Thomas, spins her own thread rather than use British thread. Some business women, such as printer Mary Goddard, who produced the official copies of the Declaration of Independence, took more active roles.

## 1848

### A WOMAN'S DECLARATION

ELIZABETH CAD\
the cruel and unju\
the office of her f\
child, to find a way\
to the abolitionist\
ly into the curren\
foundation for the\
for woman's right\
inspiring leader. T\
executed the first\
Falls, New York, J\

**SENECA FALLS** ▶

As America grew, women became acutely aware of their unequal status in society, particularly their lack of suffrage, or the right to vote.

In 1848, two women—Elizabeth Cady Stanton, shown above, and Lucretia Mott—launched the first woman suffrage movement in the United States at the Seneca Falls Convention in Seneca Falls, N.Y. During the convention, Stanton introduced her Declaration of Sentiments, in which she demanded greater rights for women, including the right to vote.

## 1920

**THE RIGHT TO VOTE** ▶

More than a half-century after organizing for the right to vote, women finally won their struggle. In 1920, the United States adopted the Nineteenth Amendment, which granted women the right to vote.

Pictured to the right is one of the many suffrage demonstrations of the early 1900s that helped garner public support for the amendment.

## RECOMMENDED RESOURCES

### BOOKS

Flexner, Eleanor. ***Century of Struggle: The Woman's Rights Movement in the United States.*** Boston: Belknap Press, 1996. Extensive examination of women's struggles.

Gurko, Miriam. ***The Ladies of Seneca Falls.*** New York: Schocken, 1987. America's woman suffrage movement.

Hoffert, Sylvia. ***When Hens Crow.*** Bloomington: Indiana UP, 1995. Women's rights in pre-Civil War America.

Schneir, Miriam, ed. ***Feminism: The Essential Historical Writings.*** New York: Random, 1972. Includes the Seneca Falls declaration, Sojourner Truth's speeches, Virginia Woolf's writings, and much more.

### VIDEOS

***One Woman, One Vote.*** PBS Video, 1995. TV documentary about the woman suffrage movement.

***Sojourner Truth: Ain't I Woman?*** Coronet/MTI, 1989. Focus on Truth's famous speeches.

***Women in American Life.*** National Women's History Project, 1988. From the Civil War to the late 1970s.

### SOFTWARE

***Women in America.*** CD-ROM. Woodbridge, CT: Research Publications, 1994.

### INTEGRATED TECHNOLOGY

For teacher support, visit . . .

 classzone.com

# 1972–1982

ERA YES

**THE EQUAL RIGHTS AMENDMENT MOVEMENT ▶**

During the mid-1900s, as more women entered the workforce, many women recognized their continuing unequal status, including the lack of equal pay for equal work. By passing an Equal Rights Amendment, some women hoped to obtain the same social and economic rights as men.

Although millions supported the amendment, many men and women feared the measure would prompt unwanted change. The ERA ultimately failed to be ratified for the Constitution.

## 2001

**WOMEN IN CONGRESS ▲**

In spite of the failure of the ERA, many women have achieved strong positions for themselves—politically as well as socially and economically.

In the 107th Congress, sixty women served in the House and thirteen served in the Senate. Shown above are Washington's senators Patty Murray (left) and Maria Cantwell in 2000.

## Instruct

1. How did women help in the colonial protests against Britain?

2. What did women demand in the Declaration of Sentiments?

3. What was the significance of the Nineteenth Amendment?

**MAKING PERSONAL CONNECTIONS**

Ask students to consider the status of women today. In what areas do they think women have gained equal rights? Why? Then have them discuss those areas in which they feel women have yet to gain equal status to men.

---

### More About . . .

**Women in Congress**

In November 2000, Hillary Rodham Clinton, wife of then President Bill Clinton, became the first sitting first lady to win elected office when she won the race for a vacant U.S. Senate seat from New York. At a victory celebration on election night, Clinton thanked supporters for her historic win. "You taught me, you tested me, and you shared with me your challenges and your concerns," she said. Asked about her achievement, her husband remarked, "I'm the first president in history with a wife in the Senate, and I like it."

---

**THINKING CRITICALLY**

**CONNECT TO HISTORY**

1. **Synthesizing** How did women's political status change from 1770 to 2001?

   SEE SKILLBUILDER HANDBOOK, PAGE R19.

**CONNECT TO TODAY**

2. **Researching and Reporting** Think of a woman who has played an important role in your community. What kinds of things did this woman do? What support did she receive in the community? What problems did she run into? Report your findings to the class.

**RESEARCH LINKS** CLASSZONE.COM

---

**THINKING CRITICALLY: ANSWERS**

1. **CONNECT TO HISTORY** Women in the 1770s boycotted British products. In the 1840s, women began demanding the right to vote, which was finally granted in 1920. In the 1970s and 1980s, many supported an Equal Rights Amendment to the Constitution, which failed to be ratified. By 2001, 60 women served in the House of Representatives and 13 in the Senate.

2. **CONNECT TO TODAY**
   **Rubric**
   Reports should . . .
   · stress the achievements of a community leader, past or present
   · clearly express the significance of the woman's role in the community
   · examine community support that she received and problems that she encountered, if any
   · support general statements with factual details

*Revolution and the Early Republic* **65**

SECTION **3**

# Confederation and the Constitution

| MAIN IDEA | WHY IT MATTERS NOW | Terms & Names |
|---|---|---|
| American leaders created the Constitution as a blueprint of government for the United States. | More than 200 years after its creation, the Constitution remains the nation's guiding document for a working government. | • republic<br>• Articles of Confederation<br>• Northwest Ordinance of 1787<br>• Shays's Rebellion<br>• James Madison<br>• federalism<br>• checks and balances<br>• ratification<br>• Federalists<br>• Antifederalists<br>• Bill of Rights |

**TEKS** U.S. History 7A, 7C, 7D, 8B, 9B, 19A, 19B, 24A, 24B, 24C, 24D, 24G, 25A, 25B, 25C, 25D, 26A, 26B

### One American's Story

John Dickinson understood, perhaps better than other delegates to the Continental Congress, the value of compromise. In 1776 Dickinson hoped for reconciliation with Britain and refused to sign the Declaration of Independence. Yet, eight days after the Declaration was adopted, Dickinson presented Congress with the first draft of a plan for setting up a workable government for the new states.

**A PERSONAL VOICE** JOHN DICKINSON

" Two rules I have laid down for myself throughout this contest . . . first, on all occasions where I am called upon, as a trustee for my countrymen, to deliberate on questions important to their happiness, disdaining all personal advantages to be derived from a suppression of my real sentiments . . . openly to avow [declare] them; and, secondly, . . . whenever the public resolutions are taken, to regard them though opposite to my opinion, as sacred . . . and to join in supporting them as earnestly as if my voice had been given for them. "

—quoted in *The Life and Times of John Dickinson, 1732–1808*

John Dickinson

Dickinson's two rules became guiding principles for the leaders who faced the formidable task of forming a new nation.

## **1** Experimenting with Confederation

As citizens of a new and independent nation, Americans had to create their own political system. Fighting the Revolutionary War gave the states a common goal, but they remained reluctant to unite under a strong central government.

**66** CHAPTER 2 *Revolution and the Early Republic*

After the Revolution, many Americans favored a **republic**—a government in which citizens rule through their elected representatives. However, many also feared that a democracy—government directly by the people—placed power in the hands of the uneducated masses. These fears and concerns deeply affected the planning of the new government.

**THE ARTICLES OF CONFEDERATION** The Second Continental Congress set up a new plan of government in a set of laws called the **Articles of Confederation.** The plan established a form of government called a confederation, or alliance, among the thirteen states.

The Articles set up a Congress in which each state would have one vote regardless of population. Powers were divided between the states and the national government. The national government had the power to declare war, make peace, and sign treaties. It could borrow money, set standards for coins and for weights and measures, and establish a postal service. After approval by all thirteen states, the Articles of Confederation went into effect in March 1781.

One of the first issues the Confederation faced had to do with the the Northwest Territory, lands west of the Appalachians, where many people settled after the Revolutionary War. To help govern these lands, Congress passed the Land Ordinance of 1785, which established a plan for surveying the land. (See Geography Spotlight on page 72.) In the **Northwest Ordinance of 1787,** Congress provided a procedure for dividing the land into no fewer than three and no more than five states. The ordinance also set requirements for the admission of new states, which, however, overlooked Native American land claims. **A**

The Land Ordinance of 1785 and the Northwest Ordinance of 1787 became the Confederation's most significant achievements. Overshadowing such successes, however, were the Confederation's many problems. The most serious problem was that each state functioned independently by pursuing its own interests rather than considering those of the nation as a whole. The government had no means of raising money or enforcing its laws. Moreover, there was no national court system to settle legal disputes. The Articles of Confederation created a weak central government and little unity among the states.

**SHAYS'S REBELLION** The need for a stronger central government became obvious in 1786 when many farmers in western Massachusetts rose up in protest over increased state taxes. The farmers' discontent boiled over into mob action in January of 1787 when Daniel Shays, a fellow farmer, led an army of 1,200 farmers toward the arsenal at Springfield, Massachusetts. State officials hurriedly called out the militia to head off the army of farmers, killing four of the rebels and scattering the rest.

**Shays's Rebellion,** as the farmers' protest came to be called, caused panic and dismay throughout the nation. It was clearly time to talk about a stronger national government. Because the states had placed such severe limits on the government to prevent abuse of power, the government was unable to solve many of the nation's problems. News of the rebellion spread throughout the states. The revolt persuaded twelve states to send delegates to a convention called by Congress in Philadelphia in May of 1787. **B**

---

*A. Answer* Land Ordinance: established a plan for surveying the land,. **Northwest Ordinance:** provided for dividing the land into territories and established the requirements for admission of new states.

**MAIN IDEA**

**Contrasting**
**A** What was the difference between the Land Ordinance of 1785 and the Northwest Ordinance of 1787?

**MAIN IDEA**

**Making Inferences**
**B** Why do you think news of Shays's Rebellion made states eager to participate in the Philadelphia convention?

*B. Answer* They may have feared the possibility of other uprisings. Shays's rebellion showed the weaknesses of the new national government in dealing with economic problems.

---

**Weaknesses of the Articles of Confederation**

- Congress could not enact and collect taxes.
- Each state had only one vote in Congress, regardless of population.
- Nine out of thirteen states needed to agree to pass any law.
- Articles could be amended only if all states approved.
- There was no executive branch to enforce laws of Congress.
- There was no national court system to settle legal disputes.
- There were thirteen separate states that lacked national unity.

---

**HISTORY from VISUALS**

**Interpreting the Chart**
Have students identify at least one consequence of each weakness listed in the chart. **Extension** Have students create an illustrated chart of the weaknesses and consequences of the Articles of Confederation.

**More About . . .**

**Western Land Claims**
Western land claims originated in vaguely worded colonial charters that gave some colonies control of territory reaching from the Atlantic to the Pacific oceans. After the Revolution, new states scrambled to claim as much territory as they could.

Geography Transparency GT5
· Land ceded by states to the Federal Government, 1782–1802

**More About . . .**

**Daniel Shays**
Although the farmers' revolt of 1786–1787 bears his name, Daniel Shays was only one of several leaders of the rebellion. Shays held political office at Pelham, Massachusetts, and he became sympathetic to the farmers' plight. After the state militia defeated the rebels at Petersham Shays escaped to Vermont. The government placed a death penalty on his head but later pardoned him.

---

---

**ACTIVITY**  **COOPERATIVE LEARNING**

**BLOCK SCHEDULING**

**Letters to the Editor**

**Class Time** 20 minutes

**Task** Writing letters to the editor, expressing the viewpoint of a citizen regarding the problems of the Confederation

**Purpose** To understand how weaknesses of the Confederation affected citizens

**Directions** Assign groups of three to five students to investigate and discuss problems the Confederation encountered. Then have group members assume the roles of a farmer, a merchant, or another citizen and have each write a letter to the editor of a newspaper, stating how these problems affect them.

 Integrated Assessment
· Rubric 5

**Instruct: Objective ②**

**Creating a New Government**
TAKS SS11 4(8.16.D)

· What were the key conflicts at the Constitutional Convention and how were they solved?

· What were the three branches of government under the Constitution and what were their roles?

 In-Depth Resources: Unit 1
· Guided Reading, p. 37

 Critical Thinking Transparency CT5
· The Constitutional Convention

 In-Depth Resources: Unit 1
· Primary Sources, p. 53
· American Lives: Patrick Henry, p. 58

---

**KEY PLAYER**

**James Madison**

Madison himself wrote to an admirer that he could not take credit as "Father of the Constitution." Modestly, he said that the Constitution "ought to be regarded as the work of many heads and many hands." Discuss with students whether Madison was too modest in his appraisal of his role in creating the Constitution.

---

Mini-Lesson 4:
SS11 2(11.C)

## ② Creating a New Government

Most of the delegates at the Constitutional Convention recognized the need to strengthen the central government. Within the first five days of the meeting, they gave up the idea of fixing the Articles of Confederation and decided to form an entirely new government that would replace the one created by the Articles.

**CONFLICT AND COMPROMISE** One major issue that the delegates faced was giving fair representation to both large and small states. **James Madison** proposed the Virginia Plan, which called for a bicameral, or two-house, legislature, with membership based on each state's population. Delegates from the small states vigorously objected to the Virginia Plan because it gave more power to states with large populations. Small states supported William Paterson's New Jersey Plan, which proposed a single-house congress in which each state had an equal vote.

The debate became deadlocked and dragged on through the hot and humid summer days. Eventually, Roger Sherman suggested the Great Compromise, which offered a two-house Congress to satisfy both small and big states. Each state would have equal representation in the Senate, or upper house. The size of the population of each state would determine its representation in the House of Representatives, or lower house. Voters of each state would choose members of the House. The state legislatures would choose members of the Senate.

The Great Compromise settled one major issue but led to conflict over another. Southern delegates, whose states had large numbers of slaves, wanted slaves included in the population count that determined the number of representatives in the House. Northern delegates, whose states had few slaves, disagreed. Not counting them would give the northern states more representatives than the Southern states in the House of Representatives. The delegates eventually agreed to the Three-Fifths Compromise, which called for three-fifths of a state's slaves to be counted as part of the population. **C**

**DIVISION OF POWERS** After the delegates reached agreement on the difficult questions of slavery and representation, they dealt with other issues somewhat more easily. They divided power between the states and the national government, and they separated the national government's power into three branches. Thus, they created an entirely new government.

The new system of government that the delegates were building was a form of **federalism,** in which power is divided between a national government and several state governments. The powers granted to the national government by the Constitution are known as delegated powers, or enumerated powers. These include such powers as the control of foreign affairs and regulation of trade between the states. Powers not specifically granted to the national government but kept by the states are called reserved powers. These include powers such as providing for and supervising education. Some powers, such as the right to tax and establish courts, were shared by both the national and the state governments.

**KEY PLAYER**

**JAMES MADISON**
**1751–1836**

The oldest of 12 children, James Madison grew up in Virginia. He was a sickly child who suffered all his life from physical ailments. Because of a weak speaking voice, he decided not to become a minister and thus entered politics.

Madison's Virginia Plan resulted from extensive research that he had done on political systems before the convention. He asked Edmund Randolph, a fellow delegate from Virginia, to present the plan because his own voice was too weak to be heard throughout the assembly.

Besides providing brilliant political leadership, Madison kept a record of the debates that took place at the convention. Because of his plan and his leadership, Madison is known as the Father of the Constitution.

---

**MAIN IDEA**

**Analyzing Issues**
**C** In what ways did the Great Compromise resolve certain problems even as it created new ones?

**C. Answer** It resolved the problem of the potentially unequal representation of states in Congress, but it created the problem of how to count slaves as part of a state's population.

---

**68** CHAPTER 2 *Revolution and the Early Republic*

---

**DIFFERENTIATING INSTRUCTION** | **GIFTED AND TALENTED** |  classzone.com

**Analyzing a Primary Source Document**

Tell students to log on to classzone.com and explore the Internet resources for Chapter 2 of *The Americans*. They will find resources about the Constitutional Convention. After exploring, they should choose one resource to examine in depth and write a description and review to share with the class.

 Integrated Assessment
· Rubrics 1, 2, 5

## Key Conflicts in the Constitutional Convention

### STRONG CENTRAL GOVERNMENT vs. STRONG STATES

| | |
|---|---|
| • Authority derives from the people. <br> • In a new plan of government, the central government should be stronger than the states. | • Authority derives from the states. <br> • Under a modified Articles of Confederation, the states should remain stronger than the central government. |

### LARGE STATES vs. SMALL STATES

| | |
|---|---|
| • Congress should be composed of two houses. <br> • The number of delegates to both houses of Congress should be assigned according to population. | • A Congress of one house should be preserved. <br> • Each state should have one vote. |

### NORTH vs. SOUTH

| | |
|---|---|
| • Slaves should not be counted when deciding the number of congressional delegates. <br> • Slaves should be counted when levying taxes. | • Slaves should be counted when determining congressional representation. <br> • Slaves should not be counted when levying taxes. |

**SKILLBUILDER  Interpreting Charts**
1. Why do you think the Southern states wanted slaves counted for determining the number of representatives in the House of Representatives?
2. Why did the small states object to delegates being assigned according to population?

Mini-Lesson 4: SS11 2(8.3.A)

**MAIN IDEA**

**Making Inferences**
**D** Why did the delegates fear that one branch of the government would gain too much power?

**SEPARATION OF POWERS** The delegates also limited the authority of the national government. First, they created three branches of government:
- a legislative branch to make laws
- an executive branch to carry out laws
- a judicial branch to interpret the laws and settle disputes

Then the delegates established a system of **checks and balances** to prevent any one branch from dominating the other two. The procedure the delegates established for electing the president reflected their fear of placing too much power in the hands of the people. Instead of choosing the president directly, each state would choose a number of electors equal to the number of senators and representatives that the state had in Congress. This group of electors chosen by the states, known as the electoral college, would then cast ballots for the presidential candidates. **D**

**CHANGING THE CONSTITUTION** The delegates also provided a means of changing the Constitution through the amendment process. After four months of debate and compromise, the delegates succeeded in creating a Constitution that was an enduring document. In other words, by making the Constitution flexible, the delegates enabled it to pass the test of time.

### ③ Ratifying the Constitution

George Washington adjourned the Constitutional Convention on September 17, 1787. The Convention's work was over, but the new government could not become a reality until at least nine states ratified, or approved, the Constitution. Thus, the battle over **ratification** began.

**FEDERALISTS AND ANTIFEDERALISTS** Supporters of the Constitution called themselves **Federalists,** because they favored the new Constitution's balance of power between the states and the national government. Their opponents became known as **Antifederalists** because they opposed having such a strong central government and thus were against the Constitution.

### HISTORY from VISUALS

**Interpreting the Chart**
Have pairs of students read aloud the contrasting sides of each conflict. Have students explain how the Great Compromise and the Three-Fifths Compromise resolved conflicts.

**SKILLBUILDER ANSWERS**
1. It would give the Southern States greater representation
2. Smaller states wanted equal representation with larger states so their views would be considered

### More About . . .

**The Constitutional Convention**
Legend has it that to preserve the secrecy of the convention, delegates appointed chaperones to accompany Ben Franklin to dinner parties. They felt that the talkative and aging Franklin might disclose details of the meetings. No official journal of the proceedings was kept, and delegates' private notes were not published until the 19th century. James Madison's journal provided the most complete record of the convention.

 Electronic Library of Primary Sources
- "Notes on Slavery at the Federal Convention," by J. Madison
- "On the Constitution" by B. Franklin

**Instruct: Objective ③**

**Ratifying the Constitution**
TAKS SS11 4(8.16.A)
- What opposing views did the Federalists and Antifederalists hold?
- What was the purpose of the Bill of Rights?

 In-Depth Resources: Unit 1
- Guided Reading, p. 37

 Electronic Library of Primary Sources
- *Federalist 51,* 1788

---

**ACTIVITY      SKILLBUILDER LESSON**

**BLOCK SCHEDULING**

### Interpreting Charts

**Explaining the Skill** A chart is a visual presentation of information that is organized in a way that makes the material easy to understand. To interpret the chart, first determine what the topic is. Look at how the chart is divided or laid out. Think about whether comparisons of information are presented or if the information is for reference.

**Applying the Skill** Have pairs of students create charts from information on one of the following: the causes and results of Shays's Rebellion; The Great Compromise and the two plans: the Virginia Plan and the New Jersey Plan; the division of powers in the Constitution. Then have groups trade charts and interpret the information on each other's charts.

 In-Depth Resources: Unit 1
- Skillbuilder Practice: Interpreting Charts, p. 41

## The Bill of Rights

Throughout history, governments have reflected the ideas and values of the time, which is why the Bill of Rights did not apply to Native Americans, women, or slaves. During the nation's early years these groups were considered second-class citizens undeserving of equal rights. The civil rights movement and the women's movement brought about the inclusion and equal protection under law of excluded groups. By organizing, petitioning the government, and raising public awareness, excluded groups gained access to those rights previously withheld from them.

## The English Bill of Rights

In 1689 the English Parliament passed a number of acts that became known as the English Bill of Rights. The Bill of Rights stated that the king or queen could not cancel laws or impose taxes unless Parliament agreed. It also required that free elections be held and that Parliament meet frequently, and it gave the "power of the purse" to the House of Commons. Many of the amendments in the English Bill of Rights served as the basis for the first ten amendments to the Constitution, including bans on excessive fines or cruel punishments and the right to bring complaints before the king or queen in Parliament. Perhaps most important, the English Bill of Rights established a principle that would greatly influence both the American Bill of Rights and the concept of American democracy: government would be based on laws and the rights of its citizens, not on the authority of a single ruler.

Both sides waged a war of words in the public debate over ratification. *The Federalist*, a series of 85 essays defending the Constitution, appeared in New York newspapers. These were essays written by three influential supporters of ratification: Alexander Hamilton, James Madison, and John Jay.

All three writers felt that there were defects in the new Constitution, but they also felt that its stronger central government was superior to the weak congress provided by the Articles of Confederation. Using the pen name "Publius," the authors addressed those who argued that ratification should be delayed until a more perfect document could be written. In the following excerpt from one of the essays (now known to be written by Madison), the author asks his readers to compare the admittedly flawed Constitution with its predecessor, the Articles.

James Madison

### A PERSONAL VOICE JAMES MADISON

" It is a matter both of wonder and regret that those who raise so many objections against the new Constitution should never call to mind the defects of that which is to be exchanged for it [The Articles]. It is not necessary that the former should be perfect; it is sufficient that the latter is more imperfect. "
—*The Federalist*, Number 38, 1788

The Antifederalists' main opposition to the new Constitution was that it contained no guarantee that the government would protect the rights of the people or of the states. Antifederalists included such notable figures as Patrick Henry, George Mason, and Richard Henry Lee. *Letters from the Federal Farmer*, most likely written by Lee, was the most widely read Antifederalist publication. Lee listed the rights that Antifederalists believed should be protected, such as freedom of the press and of religion, guarantees against unreasonable searches of people and their homes, and the right to a trial by jury.

The Antifederalists' demand for a bill of rights—a formal summary of citizens' rights and freedoms—stemmed from their fear of a strong central government. All state constitutions guaranteed individual rights, and seven of them included a bill of rights. The states believed they would serve as protectors of the people. Yet in the end, the Federalists yielded to people's overwhelming desire and promised to add a bill of rights if the states would ratify the Constitution. In June 1788, New Hampshire became the ninth state to approve the Constitution, making it the law of the land. **E**

**ADOPTION OF A BILL OF RIGHTS** By December 1791, the states also had ratified ten amendments to the Constitution, which became known as the **Bill of Rights.** The first eight amendments spell out the personal liberties the states had requested. The First Amendment guarantees citizens' rights to freedom of religion, speech, the press, and political activity. According to the Second and Third Amendments, the government cannot deny citizens the right to bear arms as members of a militia of citizen-soldiers, nor can the government house troops in private homes in peacetime. The Fourth Amendment prevents the search of citizens' homes without proper warrants. The Fifth through Eighth Amendments guarantee fair treatment for individuals accused of crimes. The Ninth and Tenth Amendments impose general limits on the powers of the federal government.

*E. Answer* The Antifederalists argued that, because the Constitution granted significant powers to the national government, the Constitution must have specific safeguards to to prevent the government from abusing those powers.

MAIN IDEA

**Summarizing**
**E** Why did the Antifederalists insist that the Constitution must have a bill of rights?

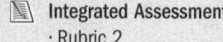

The protection of rights and freedoms did not apply to all Americans at the time the Bill of Rights was adopted. Native Americans and slaves were excluded. Women were not mentioned in the Constitution. The growing number of free blacks did not receive adequate protection from the Constitution. Although many states permitted free blacks to vote, the Bill of Rights offered them no protection against whites' discrimination and hostility.

## ④ Continuing Relevance of the Constitution

The United States Constitution is the oldest written national constitution still in use. It is a "living" document, capable of meeting the changing needs of Americans. One reason for this capability lies in Article I, Section 8, which gives Congress the power "To make all laws which shall be necessary and proper for carrying into execution" the powers that the Constitution enumerates. This clause is referred to as the "elastic clause" because it stretches the power of the government. The framers of the Constitution included these implied powers in order to allow the authority of the government to expand to meet unforeseen circumstances.

The Constitution also can be formally changed when necessary through amendments. The Constitution provides ways for amendments to be proposed and to be ratified. However, the writers made the amendment process difficult in order to avoid arbitrary changes. Through the ratification process, the writers of the Constitution have also ensured that any amendment has the overwhelming support of the people.

In more than 200 years, only 27 amendments have been added to the Constitution. These amendments have helped the government meet the challenges of a changing world, while still preserving the rights of the American people. **F**

**F. Answer** It showed that the Constitution could be changed to meet the fundamental rights and protection of the people.

**MAIN IDEA**

**Drawing Conclusions**
**F** How did the adoption of the Bill of Rights show the flexibility of the Constitution?

---

### SECTION 3 ASSESSMENT

**1. TERMS & NAMES** For each term or name, write a sentence explaining its significance.
- republic
- Articles of Confederation
- Northwest Ordinance
- Shays's Rebellion
- James Madison
- federalism
- checks and balances
- ratification
- Federalists
- Antifederalists
- Bill of Rights

**MAIN IDEA**

**2. TAKING NOTES**
Re-create the web below on your paper, and fill it in with specific issues that were debated at the Constitutional Convention.

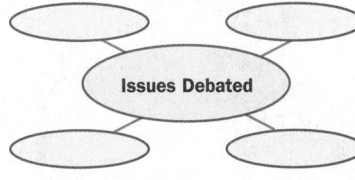

Choose one issue and explain how the delegates resolved that issue.

**CRITICAL THINKING**

**3. EVALUATING**
Do you think the Federalists or the Antifederalists had the more valid arguments? Support your opinion with examples from the text. **Think About:**
- Americans' experience with the Articles of Confederation
- Americans' experience with Great Britain

**4. ANALYZING ISSUES**
Several states ratified the Constitution only after being assured that a bill of rights would be added to it. In your opinion, what is the most important value of the Bill of Rights? Why?

**5. ANALYZING VISUAL SOURCES**
The cartoon above shows a parade held in New York to celebrate the new constitution. Why is Hamilton's name displayed under the "Ship of State" float?

---

## Instruct

### Instruct: Objective ④
**Continuing Relevance of the Constitution**
TAKS SS11 4(8.16.D)
· What is the elastic clause and how does it help the Constitution remain relevant?
· How are changes made to the Constitution?

📖 In-Depth Resources: Unit 1
· Guided Reading, p. 37
· Literature: from *Legacy*, pp. 54–56

## Assess & Reteach

### SECTION 3 ASSESSMENT
Divide students into groups and assign one of the assessment questions to each group. After groups have answered the questions, form new groups consisting of one member from each of the original groups. Have students share the answers to the questions.

📖 Formal Assessment
· Section Quiz, p. 23

### SELF-ASSESSMENT
Ask each student to write a paragraph explaining why a federal government was necessary for the new nation.

### RETEACH
Have students work in groups to outline the section. Instruct them to use the boldfaced headings as main ideas. Then have them fill in the supporting details from the text.

📖 In-Depth Resources: Unit 1
· Reteaching Activity, p. 45

---

**Answers** ASSESSMENT ③

**1. TERMS & NAMES**
republic, p. 67
Articles of Confederation, p. 67
Northwest Ordinance, p. 67
Shays's Rebellion, p. 67
James Madison, p. 68
federalism, p. 68
checks and balances, p. 69
ratification, p. 69
Federalists, p. 69
Antifederalists, p. 69
Bill of Rights, p. 70

**2. TAKING NOTES**
Fair representation of big states and small states in Congress; how to divide power between the states and the central government

**3. EVALUATING**
**For Federalists** The strength of a government with central authority and the protections coming from the division of power and the system of checks and balances. **For Antifederalists** Centralized authority could lead to abuses of power; the country was too large to be managed by one government.

**4. ANALYZING ISSUES**
Guaranteeing individual freedoms and protecting people against the government

**5. ANALYZING VISUAL SOURCES**
Because of Hamilton's significant role in shaping public opinion in favor of ratification

*Revolution and the Early Republic* **71**

## GEOGRAPHY SPOTLIGHT

### Objectives

· Describe how the Land Ordinance of 1785 promoted settlement of the Old Northwest.

· Explain how the Land Ordinance of 1785 and the Northwest Ordinance of 1787 established patterns for all future expansion.

## Focus & Motivate

Have students imagine they are state planners in charge of developing a large rural or suburban parcel of land. What goals would they have in developing the land? What services would they provide or practices would they encourage to ensure that those settling on the land become productive citizens?

## More About . . .

### The Northwest Ordinance

The Northwest Ordinance was a landmark law in the history of the republic. In an unusual move, the ordinance stipulated that the territories of the Old Northwest would not be colonies of the states but instead would be able to join the Union on an equal footing with older states. Left out of the equation, of course, were the Native Americans who already inhabited the area and were already in conflict with incoming settlers.

# The Land Ordinance of 1785

▲ Aerial photograph showing how the Land Ordinance transformed the landscape into a patchwork of farms.

When states ceded, or gave up, their western lands to the United States, the new nation became "land rich" even though it was "money poor." Government leaders searched for a way to use the land to fund such services as public education.

The fastest and easiest way to raise money would have been to sell the land in huge parcels. However, only the rich would have been able to purchase land. The Land Ordinance of 1785 made the parcels small and affordable.

The Land Ordinance established a plan for dividing the land. The government would first survey the land, dividing it into townships of 36 square miles, as shown on the map below. Then each township would be divided into 36 sections of 1 square mile, or about 640 acres, each. An individual or a family could purchase a section and divide it into farms or smaller units. A typical farm of the period was equal to one-quarter section, or 160 acres. The minimum price per acre was one dollar.

Government leaders hoped the buyers would develop farms and establish communities. In this way settlements would spread across the western territories in an orderly way. Government surveyors repeated the process thousands of times, imposing frontier geometry on the land.

In 1787, the Congress further provided for the orderly development of the Northwest Territory by passing the Northwest Ordinance, which established how states would be created out of the territory.

▼ The map below shows how an eastern section of Ohio has been subdivided according to the Land Ordinance of 1785.

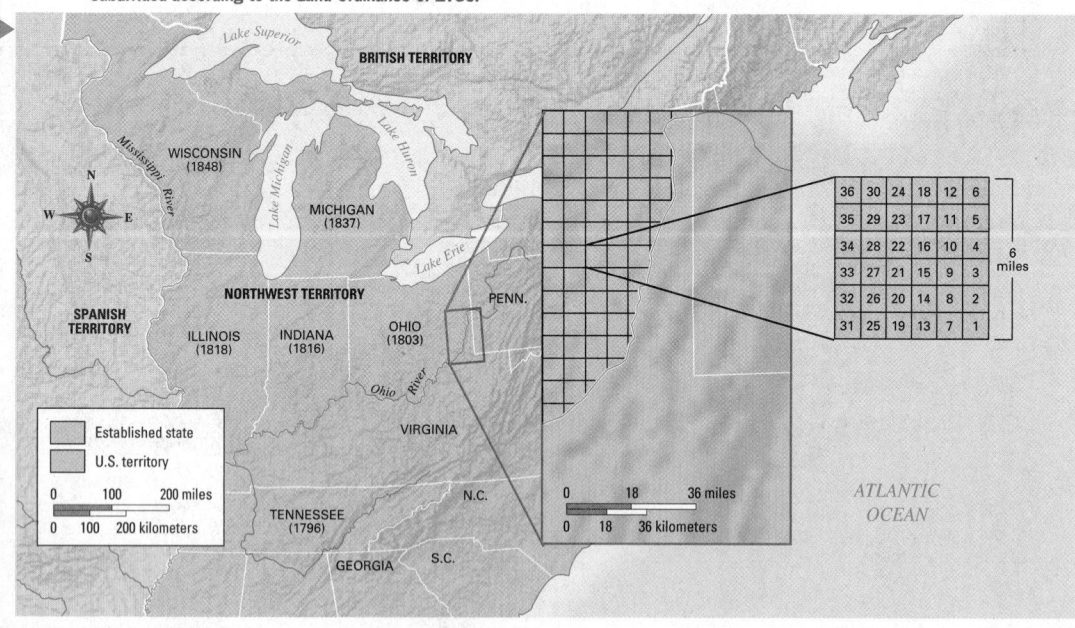

## RECOMMENDED RESOURCES

### BOOKS

Eckert, Allan W. *Gateway to Empire.* Boston: Little, 1983. A history of the Old Northwest.

Hunter, Lloyd A. *Pathways to the Old Northwest.* Indianapolis: Indiana Historical Society, 1988. Eight lectures on the Northwest Ordinance.

Hurt, R. Douglas *The Ohio Frontier: Crucible of the Old Northwest, 1720-1830.* Bloomington: Indiana UP, 1998. Ohio from territory to province.

Onuf, Peter S. *Statehood and Union: A History of the Northwest Ordinance.* Bloomington: Indiana UP, 1992.

Williams, Frederick D., ed. *The Northwest Ordinance.* East Lansing: Michigan State UP, 1989. A collection of essays.

### VIDEOS

*Settling the Old Northwest.* Encyclopaedia Britannica 1990. A dynamic account of conflicts between Native Americans and early settlers.

*The Northwest Territory.* Coronet/MTI, 1989. A history of the Old Northwest from Native American days to the growth of Chicago in the late 19th century.

### INTEGRATED TECHNOLOGY

For teacher support, visit . . .

 classzone.com

This map shows how a township, ▶ now in Meigs County, Ohio, was divided in 1787 into parcels of full square-mile sections and smaller, more affordable plots. The names of the original buyers are written on the full sections.

Ⓐ **RELIGION** To encourage the growth of religion within the township, the surveyors set aside a full section of land. Most of the land within the section was sold to provide funds for a church and a minister's salary. This practice was dropped after a few years because of concern about the separation of church and state.

Ⓑ **EDUCATION** The ordinance encouraged public education by setting aside section 16 of every township for school buildings. Local people used the money raised by the sale of land within this section to build a school and hire a teacher. This section was centrally located so that students could reach it without traveling too far.

Ⓒ **REVENUE** Congress reserved two or three sections of each township for sale at a later date. Congress planned to sell the sections then at a tidy profit. The government soon abandoned this practice because of criticism that it should not be involved in land speculation.

Ⓓ **WATER** Rivers and streams were very important to early settlers, who used them for transportation. Of most interest, however, was a meandering stream, which indicated flat bottomland that was highly prized for its fertility.

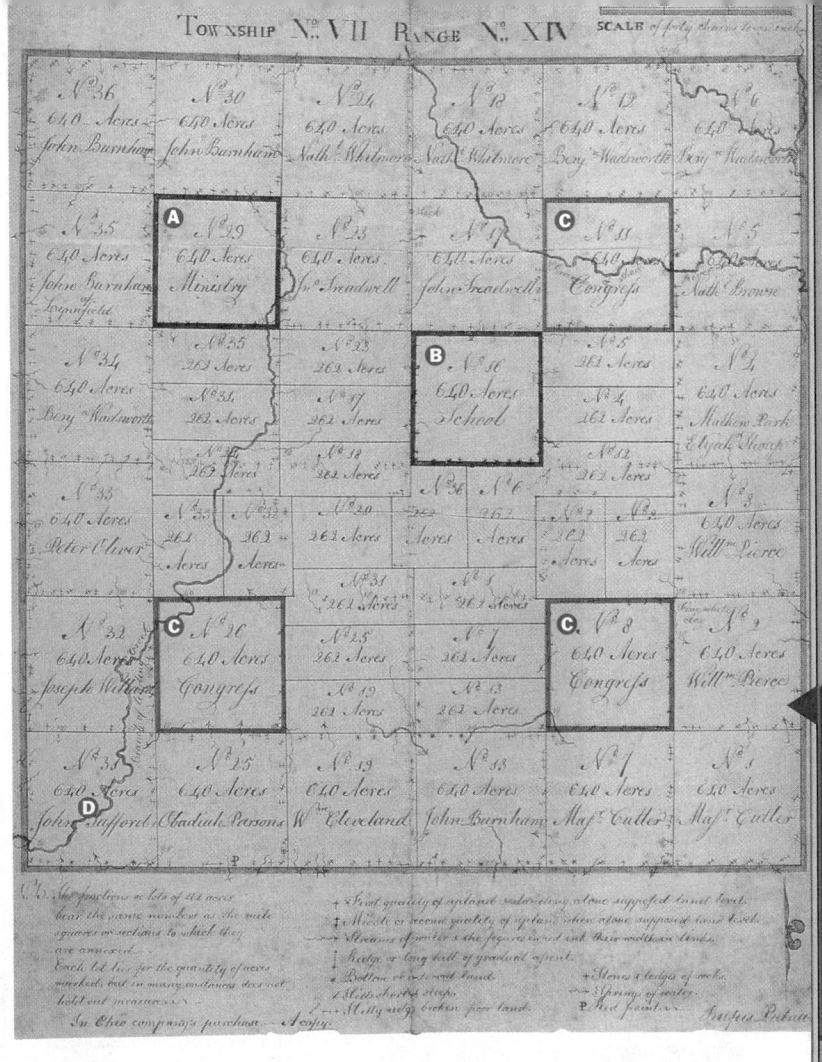

# Instruct

1. How did the Land Ordinance of 1785 encourage small landowners to settle in the Northwest Territories?

2. How did the ordinance encourage religion and public education?

3. What present-day states made up the Northwest Territory?

**MAKING PERSONAL CONNECTIONS**

Have students discuss the way in which their community is organized, from neighborhoods to streets to addresses. Have them discuss the possible reasons for such organization.

## HISTORY from VISUALS

**Interpreting the Images**
Have students study and compare the different maps and insets. In what sense was the area in question the "Northwest"? *(It was the northwesternmost land possessed by the new nation at the time.)* What bodies of water essentially define the boundaries of the Old Northwest Territory? *(The Great Lakes, the Ohio River, and the Mississippi River)*

---

**THINKING CRITICALLY**

1. **Analyzing Distributions** How did the Land Ordinance of 1785 provide for the orderly development of the Northwest Territory? How did it make land affordable?

    **SEE SKILLBUILDER HANDBOOK, PAGE R30.**

2. **Creating a Chart** Create a table that organizes and summarizes the information in the map above. To help you organize your thoughts, pose questions that the map suggests and that a table could help answer.

**ⓘ RESEARCH LINKS** CLASSZONE.COM

**THINKING CRITICALLY: ANSWERS**

1. ANALYZING DISTRIBUTIONS It surveyed the land and established a plan for parceling it out. Instead of dividing the land into huge parcels that only the rich could afford, it allowed families or individuals to purchase smaller parcels and to subdivide them further if necessary.

2. CREATING A CHART Important advantages to consider are fertile soil, reasonably flat passable terrain; distance from Native Americans; and proximity to a church, to a school, to one or more streams, to friends or loved ones also settling in the area, and/or to the more built-up "civilization" in Pennsylvania and Virginia in the east.

# Launching the New Nation

| MAIN IDEA | WHY IT MATTERS NOW | Terms & Names |
|---|---|---|
| With George Washington as its first president, the United States began creating a working government for its new nation. | The country's early leaders established precedents for organizing government that the United States still follows. | • Judiciary Act of 1789<br>• Alexander Hamilton<br>• cabinet<br>• two-party system | • Democratic-Republican<br>• protective tariff<br>• XYZ Affair<br>• Alien and Sedition Acts<br>• nullification |

 U.S. History
10A, 16A, 16B, 19A, 19B, 24A, 24B, 24C, 24D, 24F, 25A, 25B, 25C, 25D

### One American's Story

As the hero of the Revolution, George Washington was the unanimous choice in the nation's first presidential election. When the news reached him on April 14, 1789, Washington accepted the call to duty—despite his uncertainty about how to lead the new country. Two days later he set out for New York City to take the oath of office.

**A PERSONAL VOICE** GEORGE WASHINGTON

"About ten o'clock I bade adieu [farewell] to Mount Vernon, to private life, and to domestic felicity [happiness]; and with a mind oppressed with more anxious and painful sensations than I have words to express, set out for New York . . . with the best dispositions [intentions] to render service to my country in obedience to its call, but with less hope of answering its expectations."

—The Diaries of George Washington

George Washington

When Washington took office as the first president of the United States under the Constitution, he and Congress faced a daunting task to create an entirely new government. The momentous decisions that these early leaders made have resounded through American history.

## 1 Washington Heads the New Government

Although the Constitution provided a strong foundation, it was not a detailed blueprint for governing. To create a working government, Washington and Congress had to make many practical decisions. Perhaps James Madison put it best: "We are in a wilderness without a single footstep to guide us."

**JUDICIARY ACT OF 1789** One of the first tasks Washington and Congress faced was the creation of a judicial system. The **Judiciary Act of 1789** provided for a Supreme Court and federal circuit and district courts. The Judiciary Act allowed state court decisions to be appealed to a federal court when constitutional issues

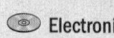

were raised. It also guaranteed that federal laws would remain "the supreme law of the land."

**WASHINGTON SHAPES THE EXECUTIVE BRANCH** The nation's leaders also faced the task of building an executive branch. To help the president govern, Congress created three executive departments: the Department of State, to deal with foreign affairs; the Department of War, to handle military matters; and the Department of the Treasury, to manage finances.

To head these departments, Washington chose capable leaders—Thomas Jefferson as secretary of state, **Alexander Hamilton** as secretary of the treasury, Henry Knox as secretary of war. These department heads soon became the president's chief advisers, or **cabinet**.

**HAMILTON AND JEFFERSON: TWO CONFLICTING VISIONS** Hamilton and Jefferson held very different political ideas. Hamilton believed in a strong central government led by a prosperous, educated elite of upper-class citizens. Jefferson distrusted a strong central government and the rich. He favored strong state and local governments rooted in popular participation. Hamilton believed that commerce and industry were the keys to a strong nation; Jefferson favored a society of farmer-citizens. **Ⓐ**

| MAIN IDEA |
| --- |
| **Contrasting**<br>**Ⓐ** How did Jefferson's and Hamilton's views of government differ? |

**HAMILTON'S ECONOMIC PLAN** As secretary of the treasury, Hamilton's job was to put the nation's economy on a firm footing. To do this, he called on the nation to pay off its debts, a large amount of which was incurred during the Revolution. He also proposed the establishment of a national bank that would be funded by both the federal government and wealthy private investors. This bank would issue paper money and handle taxes and other government funds.

Opponents of a national bank, such as James Madison, argued that since the Constitution made no provision for such an institution, Congress had no right to authorize it. This argument began the debate between those, like Hamilton, who favored a loose interpretation of the Constitution and those, like Madison, who favored a strict interpretation—a vital debate that has continued throughout U.S. history.

**KEY PLAYERS**

**Hamilton and Jefferson**
In addition to holding different political ideas, Hamilton and Jefferson disliked each other personally. Jefferson accused the secretary of the treasury of meddling in virtually every aspect of government and trying to "swallow up the whole executive powers." Jefferson encouraged a writer friend, Philip Freneau, to start a Republican newspaper attacking Hamilton and his policies. Hamilton responded to the attacks by calling Jefferson "the promoter of national disunion, national insignificance, public disorder and discredit." The feud between the two men became so heated that President Washington had to step in, pleading with Hamilton for "mutual forbearances and temporising yieldings on all sides."

**Tracing Themes**
**ECONOMIC OPPORTUNITY**

**The U.S. Economy**
The U.S. economy has changed significantly over the past 200 years. Early on, the nation's economy relied on agriculture, a system favored by Jefferson. After the Industrial Revolution in the 1800s, the economy relied more on manufacturing, a system favored by Hamilton. If both men were to observe America's economy today, Jefferson might be saddened by the decline of family-owned farms and of working-class wages. Hamilton probably would approve of the growth of industry but be shocked at the national debt.

---

**Activating Prior Knowledge**

Before students begin reading page 75, initiate a brief discussion about debts and banks. Ask the following questions:

· Where do people turn to when they don't have enough money to pay for something?

· How do banks make a profit?

· What happens when people have trouble paying off their debts to a bank?

Have students keep the answers to these questions in mind as they read about Hamilton's economic plan.

 Integrated Assessment
· Rubric 2

## HISTORY from VISUALS

### Interpreting the Chart

Remind students that Hamilton's views of the powers of the federal government were considered "loose" and Jefferson's were "strict." Encourage students to explain what is meant by a "loose" and a "strict" interpretation of the Constitution by using examples from the chart.

### SKILLBUILDER ANSWERS

1. Wealthy people would more likely support Hamilton's plan because they often earned a living from shipping and manufacturing.
2. Jefferson had more faith in "plain people" then did Hamilton. He was much more in favor of power sharing in government.

### More About . . .

### The Whiskey Rebellion

The Whiskey Rebellion was fairly widespread, affecting more than 20 counties in Pennsylvania, Maryland, Virginia, Kentucky, Ohio, and North Carolina. When the armed rebels gathered in Pittsburgh in 1794, they were not only angry about the whiskey tax but about their under-representation in state legislatures.

 Electronic Library of Primary Sources
· Proclamation Regarding the Whiskey Rebellion, 1794 by G. Washington

### Instruct: Objective ❷

**Challenges at Home and Abroad**
TAKS SS11 2(WG1.A)
· Why did the United States develop a neutral stance regarding the French Revolution?
· Why did Jay's Treaty provoke anger among some Americans?

📄 In-Depth Resources: Unit 1
· Guided Reading, p. 38

---

### Contrasting Views of the Federal Government

| HAMILTON | JEFFERSON |
|---|---|
| • Concentrating power in federal government | • Sharing power with state and local governments; limited national government |
| • Fear of mob rule | • Fear of absolute power or ruler |
| • Republic led by a well-educated elite | • Democracy of virtuous farmers and tradespeople |
| • Loose interpretation of the Constitution | • Strict interpretation of the Constitution |
| • National bank constitutional (loose interpretation) | • National bank unconstitutional (strict interpretation) |
| • Economy based on shipping and manufacturing | • Economy based on farming |
| • Payment of national and state debts (favoring creditors) | • Payment of only the national debt (favoring debtors) |
| • Supporters: merchants, manufacturers, landowners, investors, lawyers, clergy | • Supporters: the "plain people" (farmers, tradespeople) |

**SKILLBUILDER  Interpreting Charts**
1. Whose view of the federal government was a wealthy person more likely to favor? Why?
2. How do you think Jefferson differed from Hamilton in his view of people and human nature?

**THE FIRST POLITICAL PARTIES** The differences within Washington's cabinet intensified and soon helped to give rise to a **two-party system.** Those who shared Hamilton's vision of a strong central government (mostly Northerners) called themselves Federalists. Those who supported Jefferson's vision of strong state governments (mostly Southerners) called themselves **Democratic-Republicans.**

**THE WHISKEY REBELLION** During Washington's second term, an incident occurred that reflected the tension between federal and regional interests. Previously, Congress had passed a **protective tariff,** an import tax on goods produced abroad meant to encourage American production. To generate even more revenue, Secretary Hamilton pushed through an excise tax—a tax on a product's manufacture, sale, or distribution—to be levied on the manufacture of whiskey.

In 1794, furious whiskey producers in western Pennsylvania refused to pay the tax and attacked the tax collectors. The federal government responded by sending some 13,000 militiamen to end the conflict. The Whiskey Rebellion, as it came to be known, marked the first use of armed force to assert federal authority.

**Background**
In addition to promoting American goods, the tariff of 1789, as well as tariffs that followed, provided the majority of the federal government's revenue until the twentieth century.

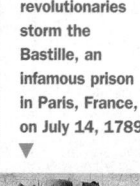

French revolutionaries storm the Bastille, an infamous prison in Paris, France, on July 14, 1789. ▼

## Challenges at Home ❷ and Abroad

At the same time, the new government faced critical problems and challenges overseas as well as at home along the western frontier.

**ADDRESSING FOREIGN AFFAIRS** In 1789 a stunning revolution in France ended the French monarchy and brought hope for a government based on the will of the people. By 1793, France was engaged in war with Great Britain as well as with other European countries.

In the United States, reaction to the conflict tended to split along party lines. Democratic-Republicans supported France.

---

**ACTIVITY** **SKILLBUILDER LESSON**  **BLOCK SCHEDULING**

### Comparing and Contrasting

**Explaining the Skill** Finding the differences between ideas, institutions, behaviors, or events helps students understand historical events more clearly. Often, one concept is easier to grasp if its features can be contrasted with similar features of something else. For example, understanding the rules of rugby might be made easier by contrasting them with the rules of soccer or football.

**Applying the Skill** To contrast the differences between the Federalists and Democratic-Republicans, students need to identify the issues about which the two parties disagreed (the role of the central government, governmental leadership, national bank, and the economy). Have students study the chart on this page and identify how the two points of view differ over these issues.

 In-Depth Resources: Unit 1
· Skillbuilder Practice: Comparing and Contrasting, p. 42

Federalists wanted to back the British. President Washington took a middle position. He issued a declaration of neutrality, a statement that the United States would support neither side in the conflict. Washington remained wary of foreign involvement throughout his tenure in office. In his farewell address in 1796, he warned the nation to "steer clear of permanent Alliances with any portion of the foreign World."

In another significant foreign matter, Thomas Pinckney negotiated a treaty with Spain in 1795. According to Pinckney's Treaty, Spain agreed to give up all claims to land east of the Mississippi (except Florida) and recognized the 31st parallel as the northern boundary of Florida. Spain also agreed to open the Mississippi River to American traffic and allow traders to use the port of New Orleans. The treaty was important because it helped pave the way for U.S. expansion west of the Appalachians. **B**

**CHALLENGES IN THE NORTHWEST** Meanwhile, Americans faced trouble along their western border, where the British still maintained forts and Native Americans continued to resist white settlers. In 1794, after numerous skirmishes, the U.S. military led by General Anthony Wayne defeated a confederacy of Native Americans at the Battle of Fallen Timbers, near present-day Toledo, Ohio. The victory helped to establish the settlers' supremacy in the region.

**JAY'S TREATY** At the time of the Battle of Fallen Timbers, John Jay, the chief justice of the Supreme Court, was in London to negotiate a treaty with Great Britain. One of the disputed issues was which nation would control territories west of the Appalachian Mountains. When news of Wayne's victory at Fallen Timbers arrived, the British agreed to evacuate their posts in the Northwest Territory because they did not wish to fight both the United States and the French, with whom they were in conflict, at the same time.

Although Jay's Treaty, signed on November 19, 1794, was a diplomatic victory, the treaty provoked outrage at home. For one thing, it allowed the British to continue their fur trade on the American side of the U.S.-Canadian border. This angered western settlers. Also, the treaty did not resolve a dispute over neutral American trade in the Caribbean. Americans believed that their ships had the right to free passage there. The British, however, had seized a number of these ships, confiscating their crews and cargo. Despite serious opposition, the treaty managed to pass the Senate.

The bitter political fight over Jay's Treaty, along with the growing division between the Federalists and Democratic-Republicans, convinced Washington not to seek a third term.

## ③ Adams Provokes Criticism

In the election of 1796, the United States faced a new situation: a contest between opposing parties. The Federalists nominated Vice President John Adams for president, while the Democratic-Republicans chose Thomas Jefferson.

In the election, Adams received 71 electoral votes, while Jefferson received 68. Because the Constitution stated that the runner-up should become vice-president, the country found itself with a Federalist president and a Democratic-Republican vice-president.

The election also underscored the growing danger of sectionalism—placing the interests of one region over those of the nation as a whole. Almost all the electors from the Southern states voted for Jefferson, while all the electors from the Northern states voted for Adams.

**MAIN IDEA**

Developing Historical Perspective
**B** Why did the United States want access to the Mississippi River?

*B. Answer*
Travel and trade were difficult on the frontier, and the Mississippi offered the easiest means of transport for frontier farmers and merchants.

▲ Portrait of a young John Adams by Joseph Badger

### Tracing Themes
**IMMIGRATION AND MIGRATION**

#### The Western Territories
Americans continuously moved inland, seeking rich farmland and greater opportunity in the West. They were willing to endure numerous hardships and fight Native Americans to settle this land. Americans continue to migrate throughout the country for numerous reasons. Today, a great number of people settle in the West, the Southwest, and the Southeast, due largely to these regions' comfortable weather and appealing economies.

### More About . . .

#### The Battle of Fallen Timbers
The leader of the U.S. troops was General "Mad Anthony" Wayne, known for his reckless courage. Wayne's troops were greatly outnumbered by nearly 2,000 Shawnee, Ottawa, and Chippewa. Wayne sent an advance party to draw the Native American warriors out of hiding. The warriors chased the American soldiers, who led them to Wayne's troops. Forced out into the open to fight a conventional battle, the Native Americans were surrounded on all sides. The battle was over within 40 minutes.

### Instruct: Objective ③

**Adams Provokes Criticism**
TAKS SS11 4(8.18.B)
· What was the XYZ Affair and how did it nearly lead the United States and France into war?
· What were the Alien and Sedition Acts?
· What did the Virginia and Kentucky resolutions state?

 In-Depth Resources: Unit 1
· Guided Reading, p. 38

---

**BLOCK SCHEDULING**

### Negotiating a Treaty

**Class Time** 45 minutes

**Task** Drafting a treaty that deals fairly with the Native Americans

**Purpose** To help students understand that the Native Americans were frequently cheated in their dealings with the U.S. government

**Directions** Divide groups of eight to ten students into two teams. Have one team represent the interests of the United States. Have the other team represent the interests of the Native American people. Students should negotiate a treaty about land holdings that makes fair concessions to both sides.

 Integrated Assessment
· Rubric 3

## More About . . .

### John Adams

Unlike George Washington, John Adams did not achieve great popularity during his political career. Because he was frequently blunt and impatient, people perceived him as a cold man. However, those who knew Adams well had great fondness for him. Even Jefferson, his political opponent, wrote to a friend that Adams was "so amiable, that I pronounce you will love him if ever you become acquainted with him." Relations between the two men became strained after 1790. However, after Adams and Jefferson retired from public life, they renewed their friendship. Remarkably, both men died on July 4, 1826. Adams's last words were "Thomas Jefferson still lives."

◉ **Electronic Library of Primary Sources**
· Inaugural Address, 1792 by J. Adams

**ADAMS TRIES TO AVOID WAR** Soon after taking office, President Adams faced his first crisis: a looming war with France. The French government regarded the U.S.-British agreement over the Northwest Territory a violation of the French-American alliance. In retaliation they began to seize American ships bound for Britain. Adams sent a three-man team to Paris to negotiate a solution. **C**

This team, which included future Chief Justice John Marshall, planned to meet with the French foreign minister, Talleyrand. Instead, the French sent three low-level officials, whom Adams in his report to Congress called "X, Y, and Z." The French officials demanded a $250,000 bribe as payment for seeing Talleyrand. News of this insult, which became known as the **XYZ Affair**, provoked a wave of anti-French feeling at home. "Millions for defense, but not one cent for tribute" became the slogan of the day. In 1798, Congress created a navy department and authorized American ships to seize French vessels. For the next two years, an undeclared naval war raged between France and the United States.

The Federalists called for a full-scale war against France, but Adams refused to take that step. Through diplomacy, the two countries eventually smoothed over their differences. Adams damaged his standing among the Federalists, but he kept the United States out of war.

**THE ALIEN AND SEDITION ACTS** Although Democratic-Republicans cheered Adams for avoiding war with France, they criticized him mercilessly on many other issues. Tensions between Federalists and Democratic-Republicans rose to a fever pitch. Adams regarded Democratic-Republican ideas as dangerous to the welfare of the nation. He and other Federalists accused the Democratic-Republicans of favoring foreign powers.

Many immigrants were active in the Democratic-Republican party. Some of the most vocal critics of the Adams administration were foreign-born. They included French and British radicals as well as recent Irish immigrants who lashed out at anyone who was even faintly pro-British, including the Federalist Adams.

To counter what they saw as a growing threat against the government, the Federalists pushed through Congress in 1798 four measures that became known as the **Alien and Sedition Acts.** Three of these measures, the Alien Acts, raised the residence requirement for American citizenship from 5 years to 14 years and allowed the president to deport or jail any alien considered undesirable.

**MAIN IDEA**

**Analyzing Motives**
**C** Why did the French begin to seize U.S. ships?
**C. Answer** In retaliation for the U.S.-British agreement over the Northwest territory, which they regarded as a violation of the U.S. alliance of 1778.

**Vocabulary**
**alien:** belonging to or coming from another country; foreign
**sedition:** rebellion against one's country; treason

## Analyzing *Political Cartoons*

### SKILLBUILDER ANSWERS

1. The Americans appear normal and well dressed compared to the French, who are portrayed as monsters. The Americans are standing up to the monster.

2. There is a guillotine in the background reminiscent of the Reign of Terror. Others are playing cards—perhaps gambling.

## Analyzing   *Political Cartoons*

### "THE PARIS MONSTER"

"*Cinque-tetes*, or the Paris Monster" is the title of this political cartoon satirizing the XYZ Affair. On the right, the five members of the French Directory, or ruling executive body, are depicted as a five-headed monster demanding money. The three American representatives, Elbridge Gerry, Charles Pinckney, and John Marshall, are on the left, exclaiming "Cease bawling, monster! We will not give you six-pence!"

**SKILLBUILDER** Analyzing Political Cartoons
1. How would you contrast the cartoon's depiction of the U.S. representatives with its depiction of the French Directory?
2. What other details in the cartoon show the cartoonist's attitude toward the French?

 **SEE SKILLBUILDER HANDBOOK, PAGE R24.**

**78** CHAPTER 2 *Revolution and the Early Republic*

---

**DIFFERENTIATING INSTRUCTION** | **LESS PROFICIENT READERS**

### Making Connections

Help students to connect to the emotion in the XYZ Affair and the Alien and Sedition Acts by asking: How would you feel if the clerk at a grocery store gave you the wrong change but would not talk with you about it? Instead, the clerk makes you explain the problem to a bagger at the counter? (*probably insulted and angry*)

Say: Now put yourself in the place of a delegate to a foreign country. How might John Marshall and the other American delegates have felt when the French foreign minister sent underlings to see them? (*insulted and angry*)

Ask: Why might a new government react to criticism more harshly than a well-established government? (*A new government may not be sure of its authority and may be more likely to become defensive.*)

The fourth measure, the Sedition Act, set fines and jail terms for anyone trying to hinder the operation of the government or expressing "false, scandalous, and malicious statements" against the government. Under the terms of this act, the federal government prosecuted and jailed a number of Democratic-Republican editors, publishers, and politicians. Outraged Democratic-Republicans called the laws a violation of freedom of speech guaranteed by the First Amendment.

**VIRGINIA AND KENTUCKY RESOLUTIONS** The two main Democratic-Republican leaders, Thomas Jefferson and James Madison, saw the Alien and Sedition Acts as a serious misuse of power on the part of the federal government. They decided to organize opposition to the Alien and Sedition Acts by appealing to the states. Madison drew up a set of resolutions that were adopted by the Virginia Legislature, while Jefferson wrote resolutions that were approved in Kentucky. The resolutions warned of the dangers that the Alien and Sedition Acts posed to a government of checks and balances guaranteed by the Constitution.

*D. Answer* It asserted the principal of nullification which held that, if a state considered an act of Congress to be unconstitutional, it had the right to declare that action null and void.

## A PERSONAL VOICE

"Let the honest advocate of confidence [in government] read the alien and sedition acts, and say if the Constitution has not been wise in fixing limits to the government it created, and whether we should be wise in destroying those limits."

—*8th Resolution*, The Virginia and Kentucky Resolutions

The Kentucky Resolutions in particular asserted the principle of **nullification:** the states had the right to nullify, or consider void, any act of Congress that they deemed unconstitutional. Virginia and Kentucky viewed the Alien and Sedition Acts as unconstitutional violations of the First Amendment that deprived citizens of their rights.

The resolutions also called for other states to adopt similar declarations. No other state did so, however, and the issue died out by the next presidential election. Nevertheless, the resolutions showed that the balance of power between the states and the federal government remained a controversial issue. In fact, the election of 1800 between Federalist John Adams and Democratic-Republican Thomas Jefferson would center on this critical debate.

**MAIN IDEA**

**Analyzing Issues**
**D** How did the Kentucky Resolutions challenge the authority of the federal government?

### 4 ASSESSMENT

**1. TERMS & NAMES** For each term or name, write a sentence explaining its significance.
- **Judiciary Act of 1789**
- **Alexander Hamilton**
- **cabinet**
- **Democratic-Republican**
- **two-party system**
- **protective tariff**
- **XYZ Affair**
- **Alien and Sedition Acts**
- **nullification**

**MAIN IDEA**

**2. TAKING NOTES**
In a chart, list the leaders, beliefs, and goals of the country's first political parties.

| Federalists | Democratic-Republicans |
|---|---|
| | |
| | |

If you had lived in that time, which party would you have favored? Why?

**CRITICAL THINKING**

**3. EVALUATING LEADERSHIP**
How would you judge the leadership qualities of President Washington in his decision to put two such opposed thinkers as Hamilton and Jefferson in his cabinet? Who do you think was the more significant member of the cabinet?

**4. ANALYZING EVENTS**
Do you agree with the Democratic-Republicans that the Alien and Sedition Acts were a violation of the First Amendment? Were they necessary? Support your opinion with evidence from the text.
**Think About:**
- the intent of the First Amendment
- what was happening in Europe
- what was happening in the United States

### Connections Across Time
**1798 AND 1832**

**The Principle of Nullification**
Some 30 years after the Virginia and Kentucky resolutions asserted the principle of nullification, another state, South Carolina, put forth the same argument. In 1832, Congress passed a tax law that South Carolinians criticized as oppressive. They declared the tax, along with a previous one, "null, void, and no law," and threatened to withdraw from the Union if the government tried to enforce the laws. Compromise legislation that gradually lowered the tax ended the standoff.

## Assess & Reteach

**SECTION 4 ASSESSMENT**
Encourage students to work in small groups to answer the questions.

📄 Formal Assessment
· Section Quiz, p. 24

**SELF-ASSESSMENT**
To explore their understanding of Section 4, have students create a web identifying three of the four issues that divided Federalists and Democratic-Republicans. Then have them mark those issues that seem relevant today.

**RETEACH**
Ask students to create a time line to map events discussed in Section 4.

📄 In-Depth Resources: Unit 1
· Reteaching Activity, p. 46

Answers **ASSESSMENT**

**1. TERMS & NAMES**
Judiciary Act of 1789, p. 74
Alexander Hamilton, p. 75
cabinet, p. 75
Democratic-Republican, p. 76
two-party system, p. 76
protective tariff, p. 76
XYZ Affair, p. 78
Alien and Sedition Acts, p. 78
nullification, p. 79

**2. TAKING NOTES**
**Federalists** Hamilton; led by educated, upper class; favored commerce, strong government, loose interpretation of the Constitution, and national bank.
**Democratic-Republicans** Jefferson; supported common people; favored agriculture, weak central government, strict interpretation of Constitution; opposed national bank.

**3. EVALUATING LEADERSHIP**
Many students may think that Washington was a strong leader who listened to both sides of an issue and was secure enough not to be threatened by surrounding himself with brilliant people who would give him the best advice. Others may think he should have chosen cabinet members whose views did not conflict so sharply.

**4. ANALYZING EVENTS**
Those who agree with the Federalists will say that the country needed to control the vocal members of the Democratic-Republican Party from seeming to threaten the stability of the young government. Those who agree with the Democratic-Republicans will see these measures as a violation of freedom of speech.

## TERMS & NAMES

1. Stamp Act, p. 47
2. Thomas Jefferson, p. 53
3. Declaration of Independence, p. 53
4. Valley Forge, p. 60
5. Treaty of Paris, p. 62
6. Articles of Confederation, p. 67
7. checks and balances, p. 69
8. Antifederalist, p. 69
9. cabinet, p. 75
10. Democratic-Republicans, p. 76

## MAIN IDEAS

1. They drew up a Declaration of Rights that defended the colonies' right to run their own affairs and suggested that, if Britain continued to use force, the colonies had the right to fight back.

2. The criticism was deleted so as to secure the votes of Georgia and South Carolina and adopt the Declaration.

3. Some remained loyal to Britain because of jobs they held, such as judges or governors. Others believed that Britain would win and they feared punishment. Still others believed that the British crown would protect their rights more than new and inexperienced colonial governments would.

4. Victory boosted morale and impressed the French, who signed an alliance with the Americans in February 1778.

5. Congress could not enact and collect taxes; each state had only one vote in Congress, 9 out of 13 states needed for a law to pass; Articles could only be amended if all states approved; no national court system; 13 separate states lacked national unity.

6. The Great Compromise offered a two-house congress that resolved the problem of big-state, small state representation.

7. The Judiciary Act of 1789, Whiskey Rebellion of 1794, XYZ Affair

8. Questions about governmental sharing of power, interpretation of the constitution, payment of national debt.

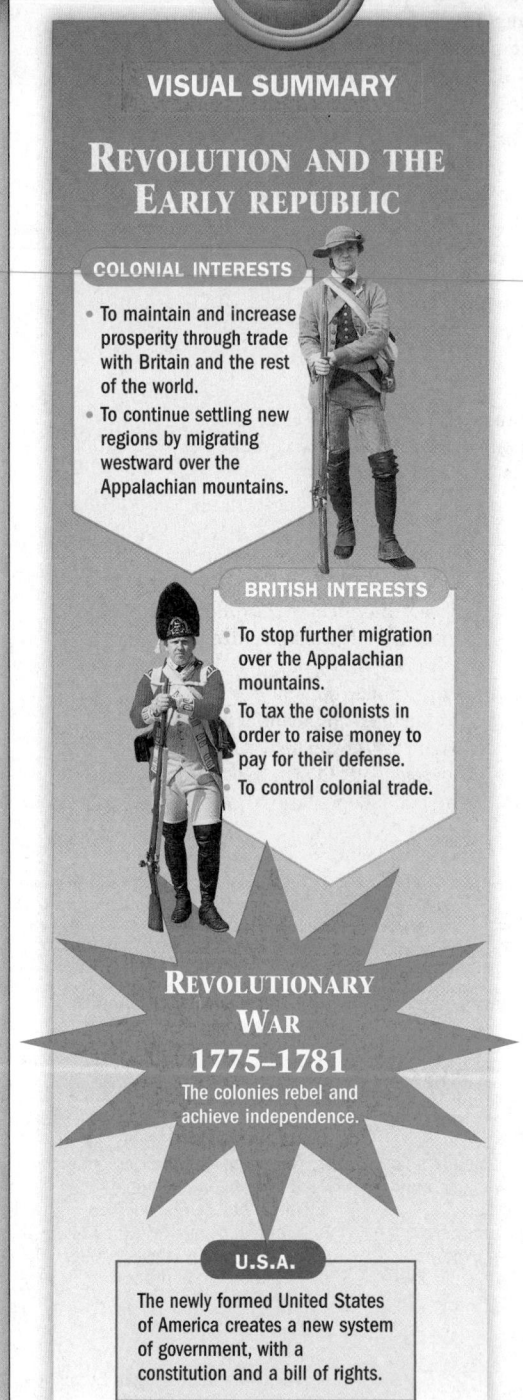

## REVIEW CHAPTER 2 ASSESSMENT

### VISUAL SUMMARY

### REVOLUTION AND THE EARLY REPUBLIC

**COLONIAL INTERESTS**

- To maintain and increase prosperity through trade with Britain and the rest of the world.
- To continue settling new regions by migrating westward over the Appalachian mountains.

**BRITISH INTERESTS**

- To stop further migration over the Appalachian mountains.
- To tax the colonists in order to raise money to pay for their defense.
- To control colonial trade.

### REVOLUTIONARY WAR 1775–1781

The colonies rebel and achieve independence.

**U.S.A.**

The newly formed United States of America creates a new system of government, with a constitution and a bill of rights.

## TERMS & NAMES

For each term or name below, write a sentence explaining its significance.

1. Stamp Act
2. Thomas Jefferson
3. Declaration of Independence
4. Valley Forge
5. Treaty of Paris
6. Articles of Confederation
7. checks and balances
8. Antifederalists
9. cabinet
10. Democratic-Republican

## MAIN IDEAS

Use your notes and the information in the chapter to answer the following questions.

**Colonial Resistance and Rebellion** (pages 46–53)

1. How did the first Continental Congress prepare the way for an armed uprising against Britain?
2. Why did Jefferson eliminate criticism of the slave trade from the Declaration of Independence?

**The War for Independence** (pages 58–63)

3. Why did so many colonists remain loyal to Britain during the Revolutionary War?
4. How did the American victory at Saratoga affect the course of the war?

**Confederation and the Constitution** (pages 66–71)

5. What were some of the problems with the kind of government set up by the Articles of Confederation?
6. What was the Great Compromise?

**Launching the New Nation** (pages 74–79)

7. What events after 1789 helped to unify the nation?
8. What issues led to the development of a two-party system?

## CRITICAL THINKING

1. **USING YOUR NOTES** In a chart like the one below, show the ideological differences between the two political groups.

| Federalists | Antifederalists |
|---|---|
|  |  |

2. **DEVELOPING HISTORICAL PERSPECTIVE** In what ways did regional interests assert themselves after the creation of the United States?

3. **EVALUATING** In your view, which compromise during the Constitutional Convention was more important, the Great Compromise or the Three-Fifths Compromise? Explain your choice.

## CRITICAL THINKING

1. **Using Your Notes Federalists:** Led by Hamilton; favored educated, upper class; favored commerce, strong government, loose interpretation of the Constitution; favored national bank. **Democratic-Republicans:** Led by Jefferson; supported common people; favored agriculture, weak central government, strict interpretation of the Constitution; opposed national bank.

2. **Developing Historical Perspective** Following the Revolution, many New England and Middle states took steps to outlaw slavery, while Southern states did not.

3. **Evaluating Great Compromise:** Brought a sense of equity to the states, created a balance of power in government. Three-fifths Compromise: Did not solve the slavery issue and as such was a factor in the Civil War.

## Standardized Test Practice

Use the cartoon and your knowledge of U.S. history to answer question 1.

1. This British cartoon was published during the winter of 1775–1776. In it, King George III and his ministers are shown killing the goose that laid the golden egg. The cartoon is criticizing —

   A the killing of British soldiers at Concord and Bunker Hill.

   B British response to the Olive Branch Petition.

   C John Locke's theory of natural rights.

   D Thomas Paine's *Common Sense*.

2. Both Shays's Rebellion and the Boston Tea Party were the result of anger over —

   F religious intolerance.

   G the Boston Massacre.

   H taxes.

   J slavery.

Use the information in the box and your knowledge of U.S. history to answer question 3.

> • Declaration of Independence
> • Battles of Lexington and Concord
> • Second Continental Congress

3. Which of the following lists the events in chronological order from first to last?

   A Declaration of Independence, Battles of Lexington and Concord, Second Continental Congress

   B Battles of Lexington and Concord, Second Continental Congress, Declaration of Independence

   C Second Continental Congress, Battles of Lexington and Concord, Declaration of Independence

   D Second Continental Congress, Declaration of Independence, Battles of Lexington and Concord

ADDITIONAL TEST PRACTICE, pages S1–S33.

 **TEST PRACTICE** CLASSZONE.COM

## ALTERNATIVE ASSESSMENT

1.  Recall your discussion of the question on page 45:

### *How much power should the national government have?*

Imagine that it is 1787. You have been present at a gathering of your friends who have discussed at length their ideas, concerns, and hopes for the new constitution being written in Philadelphia. Write a journal entry in which you try to record what you heard. Mention some of the conflicts being discussed at the Continental Congress, noting the criticisms as well as the support for the federal government proposed by the Constitution.

2. **VIDEO** **LEARNING FROM MEDIA** View the *American Stories* video, "Patriot Father, Loyalist Son." Discuss the following questions in a small group; then do the activity.

   • What political views and concerns did Benjamin Franklin originally share with his son William?

   • How did certain events in the American colonies' struggle for independence contribute to the conflict between Benjamin and William Franklin?

**Cooperative Learning Activity** Both Benjamin and William Franklin had strong opinions about loyalty and patriotism. In your opinion, what makes someone a patriot? Using books, magazines, and newspapers, make a list of people you consider to be patriots. List their names as well as the reasons why you chose them on a chart in your classroom.

---

## Standardized Test Practice

1. The correct answer is **B.** The cartoonist viewed the American Colonies as a great source of revenue for the king. The Olive Branch Petition was an effort to reduce tension. By rejecting it the king was killing the "golden goose."

   Letter A is not correct because the British soldiers cannot be considered an example of a "golden goose."

   Letters C, D are not correct because they deal with political writings that would not generate money for the king.

2. The correct answer is **H.** Both actions were started by colonists unhappy about taxes.

   Letter F is not correct because few activities protesting religious intolerance took place in the time period in which these actions took place.

   Letter G is not correct because Shays's Rebellion took place long after the Boston Massacre and thus would not be considered a cause for the rebellion.

   Letter J is not correct because both take place in Massachusetts where slavery was not an issue.

3. The correct answer is **B.** Lexington and Concord took place in April of 1775, the Second Continental Congress in June of 1775, Declaration of Independence in July of 1776.

### LETTER TO THE EDITOR

**Tips for Teaching**

· Advise students who chose the Revolutionary War to carefully study this chapter to identify reasons and facts that support their position.

· Model a letter to the editor or look at examples from a newspaper or magazine.

📖 Formal Assessment
· Chapter Test, Forms A, B, and C, pp. 25–42

---

## ALTERNATIVE ASSESSMENT

### 1. INTERACT WITH HISTORY
**Rubric**

Journal entry should . . .

· identify the conflicts over issues of power for the government

· summarize arguments supporting and opposing a federal government

· evaluate the positions to form a personal opinion

### 2. LEARNING FROM MEDIA
**Rubric**

The list should . . .

· include a method of evaluation to determine the qualities of a patriot

· include specific names of patriots

· show how each of the patriots included in the list embodies the qualities of a patriot

To analyze the principles of the U.S. Constitution, and summarize the purposes for and the processes of changing the U.S. Constitution

# The Living Constitution

U.S. History
8.16A, 8.16C, 8.16D, 8.18, 8.20A, 8.20B, 8.22B

## Focus & Motivate

To help students gain insight into the structure of the Constitution, ask them to answer the following questions: What are the five purposes of the Constitution, as stated in the Preamble? How many articles and amendments does the Constitution have? Then have students read the opening quotation on this page. Ask students what comparison President Wilson draws. Ask them what they think the comparison might suggest about the purpose of the Constitution.

*"The Constitution was not made to fit us like a straightjacket. In its elasticity lies its chief greatness."*
*President Woodrow Wilson*

## PURPOSES OF THE CONSTITUTION

The official charge to the delegates who met in Philadelphia in 1787 was to amend the Articles of Confederation. They soon made a fateful decision, however, to ignore the Articles and to write an entirely new constitution. These delegates—the "framers"—set themselves five purposes to fulfill in their effort to create an effective constitution.

### 1. ESTABLISH LEGITIMACY

First, the framers of the Constitution had to establish the new government's legitimacy—its right to rule. The patriots' theory of government was set out in the Declaration of Independence, which explained why British rule over the colonies was illegitimate. Now the framers had to demonstrate that their new government met the standards of legitimacy referred to in the Declaration.

For the framers of the Constitution, legitimacy had to be based on a compact or contract among those who are to be ruled. This is why the Constitution starts with the words "We the people of the United States . . . do ordain and establish this Constitution."

### 2. CREATE APPROPRIATE STRUCTURES

The framers' second purpose was to create appropriate structures for the new government. The framers were committed to the principles of representative democracy. They also believed that any new government must include an important role for state governments and ensure that the states retained some legitimacy to rule within their borders.

To achieve their goals, the framers created the Congress, the presidency, and the judiciary to share the powers of the national government. They also created a system of division of powers between the national government and the state governments.

The original manuscript of the Constitution is now kept in the National Archives in Washington, D.C. ▶

We the People of the United States, in order to form a more perfect Union, establish Justice, insure domestic Tranquility, provide for the common defense, promote the general Welfare, and secure the Blessings of Liberty to ourselves and our Posterity, do ordain and establish this Constitution for the United States of America.

Article I.

## THEMES IN THE LIVING CONSTITUTION

### IMMIGRATION AND MIGRATION

The United States is often called a nation of immigrants. Through naturalization, hundreds of thousands of immigrants become U.S. citizens each year. The Constitution gives Congress the power to establish a uniform rule of naturalization.

**See Teacher's Edition note, p. 88.**

### CIVIL RIGHTS

The Fourteenth Amendment guarantees equal protection of the law for all citizens. Subsequent civil rights legislation provides for equal opportunity as well. The broadening of equality through affirmative action policies has sometimes led to conflict.

**See Teacher's Edition note, p. 99.**

### WOMEN AND POLITICAL POWER

Ratification of the Nineteenth Amendment was the culmination of years of struggle by women's movements in the United States. Beginning in 1878, a woman suffrage amendment was introduced annually in Congress for 40 years.

**See Teacher's Edition note, p. 101.**

### VOTING RIGHTS

Throughout the nation's history, the right to vote has been fought for by many groups. Over the years, limits on suffrage have been lifted so that more Americans are able to cast votes to choose representatives for their government and to influence public policy.

**See Teacher's Edition note, p. 104.**

## 3. DESCRIBE AND DISTRIBUTE POWER

The framers had as their third purpose to describe governmental powers and to distribute them among the structures they created. The powers of the legislative branch, which are those of Congress, are listed in Article 1, Section 8, of the Constitution. Many of the executive powers belonging to the president are listed in Article 2, Sections 2 and 3. The courts are given judicial powers in Article 3. The words of Article 4 imply that the states retain authority over many public matters.

## 4. LIMIT GOVERNMENT POWERS

The fourth purpose of the framers was to limit the powers of the structures they created. Limits on the Congress's powers are found in Article 1, Section 9. Some of the limits on the powers of state governments are found in Article 1, Section 10. There the framers enumerate functions that are delegated to the national government and so cannot be directed by the states.

## 5. ALLOW FOR CHANGE

The framers' fifth purpose was to include some means for changing the Constitution. Here they faced a dilemma: they wanted to make certain that the government endured by changing with the times, but they did not want to expose the basic rules of government to so many changes that the system would be unstable. So in Article 5 they created a difficult but not impossible means for amending the Constitution.

**RESEARCH LINKS** CLASSZONE.COM
Visit the Constitution links for more information.

---

### CONSTITUTION PROJECT

### RESEARCHING A CONSTITUTIONAL QUESTION

As you study the Constitution, think about a constitutional question that interests you. Here are some possible questions:

- How much, if at all, can the federal government or a state government restrict the sale of firearms?

- Under what conditions does the president have the power to order American troops into battle without congressional approval?

- Under what conditions may a police officer conduct a search of the inside of an automobile?

Once you have chosen a constitutional question, research that question in articles and books on the Constitution. Also check the indexes of well-known newspapers, such as the *New York Times*, for articles that are relevant.

### HOW TO READ THE CONSTITUTION

The Constitution, which appears on pages 84–103, is printed on a beige background, while the explanatory notes next to each article, section, or clause are printed on blue. Each article is divided into sections, and the sections are subdivided into clauses. Headings have been added and the spelling and punctuation modernized for easier reading. Portions of the Constitution no longer in use have been crossed out. The Constitutional Insight questions and answers will help you understand significant issues related to the Constitution.

---

# INTERACT
## WITH HISTORY

### RESEARCHING A CONSTITUTIONAL QUESTION

Discuss the ways of conducting the research.

- To help guide the research and investigate the constitutional issue in depth, write questions using the words *who, what, where, when, why,* and *how.*

- Explore a variety of sources. Refer to the *Readers' Guide to Periodical Literature* and the *Social Science Index.* Also, check the Internet.

- Examine Supreme Court cases pertaining to a constitutional issue. For example, *United States* v. *Miller,* 1939, relates to the sale of firearms. *Horton* v. *California,* 1990, to police searches with a warrant.

- Skim your sources, looking for information that answers your research questions.

- Take notes, using one or more of the following techniques: quoting the source directly, paraphrasing, and summarizing.

---

## RECOMMENDED RESOURCES

### BOOKS FOR THE TEACHER

Garraty, John. *Quarrels That Have Shaped the Constitution.* New York: Harper, 1987. Landmark cases.

Levy, Leonard Williams. *Origins of the Bill of Rights.* New Haven: Yale UP, 1999. In-depth examination of first ten amendments.

Lyons, Owen, and others. *Exiled in the Land of the Free.* Santa Fe, N.M.: Clear Light, 1992. Argues that Native American political organizations influenced the Constitution.

### BOOKS FOR THE STUDENT

Currie, David P. *The Constitution of the United States: A Primer for the People.* Chicago: U of Chicago P, 2000.

Extensive look at the Constitution and the federal government.

Ketcham, Ralph, ed. *The Anti-Federalist Papers and the Constitutional Convention Debates.* New York: Mentor, 1986. Leading tracts against the Constitution.

Morris, Richard B. *Witnesses at the Creation.* New York: Holt, 1985. Lives of Madison, Hamilton, and Jay.

### SOFTWARE

*U.S. Constitution Tutor.* Diskette. Educational Software Institute, 800-955-5570.

### INTEGRATED TECHNOLOGY

For teacher support, go to . . .
 classzone.com

## OBJECTIVES

 **1** Explain the purpose for establishing the Constitution

**2** Identify the powers of the legislature

### SKILLBUILDER
· Interpreting Charts, p. 87

## Focus & Motivate

Ask students what they prize most about living in a democracy.

## Instruct

### Instruct: Objective **1**

**Preamble**

TAKS SS11 1(8.16C)

· What did the Framers of the Constitution state as the main goals for government?

 In-Depth Resources: Unit 1
· Guided Reading, p. 59

 Critical Thinking Transparencies CT39
· The Federal System

### More About . . .

**A Dream for All**

In 1963, Dr. Martin Luther King Jr.'s "I Have a Dream" speech echoed the vision of America reflected in the Preamble: "When the architects of our republic wrote the magnificent words of the Constitution and the Declaration of Independence, they were signing a promissory note to which every American was to fall heir. This note was the promise that all men, yes, black men as well as white men, would be guaranteed the unalienable rights of life, liberty, and the pursuit of happiness."

---

### PREAMBLE

***Constitutional Insight** Preamble*
*Why does the Preamble say "We the people of the United States . . . ordain and establish" the new government?* The Articles of Confederation was an agreement among the states. But the framers of the Constitution wanted to be sure its legitimacy came from the American people, not from the states, which might decide to withdraw their support at any time. This is a basic principle of the Constitution.

### ARTICLE 1

***Constitutional Insight** Section 1*
*Why does the first article of the Constitution focus on Congress rather than on the presidency or the courts?* The framers were intent on stressing the central role of the legislative branch in the new government because it is the branch that most directly represents the people and is most responsive to them.

**A CRITICAL THINKING**
Do you think Congress is still the branch of the federal government that is most directly responsible to the people? Why or why not?

***Constitutional Insight** Section 2.1*
*Why are members of the House of Representatives elected every two years?* The House of Representatives was designed to be a truly representative body, with members who reflect the concerns and sentiments of their constituents as closely as possible. The framers achieved this timely representation by establishing two years as a reasonable term for members of the House to serve.

**B CRITICAL THINKING**
Do you think electing members of the House of Representatives every two years is a good idea? Why or why not?

**Requirements for Holding Federal Office**

| POSITION | MINIMUM AGE | RESIDENCY | CITIZENSHIP |
|---|---|---|---|
| Representative | 25 | state in which elected | 7 years |
| Senator | 30 | state in which elected | 9 years |
| President | 35 | 14 years in the United States | natural-born |
| Supreme Court Justice | none | none | none |

---

# The Constitution

## PREAMBLE. *Purpose of the Constitution*

We the people of the United States, in order to form a more perfect Union, establish justice, insure domestic tranquility, provide for the common defense, promote the general welfare, and secure the blessings of liberty to ourselves and our posterity, do ordain and establish this Constitution for the United States of America.

## ARTICLE 1. *The Legislature* **2**

**SECTION 1. CONGRESS** All legislative powers herein granted shall be vested in a Congress of the United States, which shall consist of a Senate and House of Representatives.

**SECTION 2. THE HOUSE OF REPRESENTATIVES**

1. **ELECTIONS** The House of Representatives shall be composed of members chosen every second year by the people of the several states, and the electors in each state shall have the qualifications requisite for electors of the most numerous branch of the state legislature.

2. **QUALIFICATIONS** No person shall be a Representative who shall not have attained to the age of twenty-five years, and been seven years a citizen of the United States, and who shall not, when elected, be an inhabitant of that state in which he shall be chosen.

3. **NUMBER OF REPRESENTATIVES** Representatives ~~and direct taxes~~ shall be apportioned among the several states which may be included within this Union, according to their respective numbers, ~~which shall be determined by adding to the whole number of free persons, including those bound to service for a term of years, and excluding Indians not taxed, three fifths of all other persons.~~ The actual enumeration shall be made within three years after the first meeting of the Congress of the United States, and within every subsequent term of ten years, in such manner as they shall by law direct. The number of Representatives shall not exceed one for every thirty thousand, but each state shall have at least one Representative; ~~and until such enumeration shall be made, the state of New Hampshire shall be entitled to choose three, Massachusetts eight, Rhode Island and Providence Plantations one, Connecticut five, New York six, New Jersey four, Pennsylvania eight, Delaware one, Maryland six, Virginia ten, North Carolina five, South Carolina five, and Georgia three.~~

4. **VACANCIES** When vacancies happen in the representation from any state, the executive authority thereof shall issue writs of election to fill such vacancies.

5. **OFFICERS AND IMPEACHMENT** The House of Representatives shall choose their Speaker and other officers; and shall have the sole power of impeachment.

---

 **In-Depth Resources: Unit 1**
· Guided Reading, pp. 59–62
· Building Vocabulary, p. 63
· Skillbuilder Practice, p. 64
· Reteaching Activity, pp. 65–68
· Geography Application: The Electoral College, pp. 69–70
· American Lives: James Madison, p. 71; Thurgood Marshall, p. 72
· Projects for Citizenship, pp. 73–76

 **Reading Study Guide** (English and Spanish), pp. 25–32

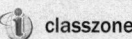 **Access for Students Acquiring English/ESL**
· Guided Reading (Spanish), pp. 35–39
· Skillbuilder, p. 39
· Geography Application: The Electoral College, pp. 40–41
· Projects for Citizenship, pp. 42–45

 **Formal Assessment**
· Section Quizzes, pp. 43–46
· Living Constitution, pp. 47–55

 **Integrated Assessment**
· Rubrics

**INTEGRATED TECHNOLOGY**

 **Critical Thinking Transparencies CT39**
· The Federal System

 classzone.com

**TEXAS RESOURCES**

TAKS Spiraled Content Review

TAKS Practice Tests

TAKS Practice Transparencies TT14, TT15

TAKS Online Test Practice

## SECTION 3. THE SENATE

**1. NUMBERS** The Senate of the United States shall be composed of two Senators from each state, ~~chosen by the legislature thereof,~~ for six years; and each Senator shall have one vote.

**2. CLASSIFYING TERMS** Immediately after they shall be assembled in consequence of the first election, they shall be divided as equally as may be into three classes. The seats of the Senators of the first class shall be vacated at the expiration of the second year, of the second class at the expiration of the fourth year, and of the third class at the expiration of the sixth year, so that one third may be chosen every second year; ~~and if vacancies happen by resignation, or otherwise, during the recess of the legislature of any state, the executive thereof may make temporary appointments until the next meeting of the legislature, which shall then fill such vacancies.~~

**3. Qualifications** No person shall be a Senator who shall not have attained to the age of thirty years, and been nine years a citizen of the United States, and who shall not, when elected, be an inhabitant of that state for which he shall be chosen.

**4. ROLE OF VICE-PRESIDENT** The Vice-President of the United States shall be President of the Senate, but shall have no vote, unless they be equally divided.

**5. OFFICERS** The Senate shall choose their other officers, and also a President pro tempore, in the absence of the Vice-President, or when he shall exercise the office of President of the United States.

**6. IMPEACHMENT TRIALS** The Senate shall have the sole power to try all impeachments. When sitting for that purpose, they shall be on oath or affirmation. When the President of the United States is tried, the Chief Justice shall preside: and no person shall be convicted without the concurrence of two thirds of the members present.

**7. PUNISHMENT FOR IMPEACHMENT** Judgment in cases of impeachment shall not extend further than to removal from office, and disqualification to hold and enjoy any office of honor, trust or profit under the United States; but the party convicted shall nevertheless be liable and subject to indictment, trial, judgment and punishment, according to law.

## SECTION 4. CONGRESSIONAL ELECTIONS

**1. REGULATIONS** The times, places and manner of holding elections for Senators and Representatives shall be prescribed in each state by the legislature thereof; but the Congress may at any time by law make or alter such regulations, except as to the places of choosing Senators.

**2. SESSIONS** The Congress shall assemble at least once in every year, ~~and such meeting shall be on the first Monday in December, unless they shall by law appoint a different day.~~

---

*Constitutional Insight* Section 3.1
*Why are members of the Senate elected every six years?* The framers feared the possibility of instability in the government. So they decided that senators should have six-year terms and be elected by the state legislatures rather than directly by the people. The Seventeenth Amendment, as you will see later, changed this. The framers also staggered the terms of the senators so that only one-third of them are replaced at any one time. This stabilizes the Senate still further.

 **CRITICAL THINKING**
Do you think it is important today for the Senate to have more stability than the House of Representatives? If so, why?

*Constitutional Insight* Sections 3.6 and 3.7 *Must an impeached president step down from office?* Not necessarily. An impeachment is the equivalent of a formal accusation. By impeaching the president, the U.S. House of Representatives is officially accusing the nation's chief executive of one or more wrongdoings that warrant possible removal from office. It is then the responsibility of the Senate to conduct a trial to determine whether the president is guilty or not guilty of the charges—and thus whether or not the president must step down. Conviction requires a two-thirds vote of the Senate.

**D** **CRITICAL THINKING**
Do you think a president should be put on trial for a crime while he or she is still in office? Explain.

---

## Instruct: Objective ❷

### The Legislature
TAKS SS11 4(8.16D)
· What is the main role of the legislative branch?
· How do the qualifications and terms of office differ for senators and representatives?
· How does the Constitution limit the power of Congress?

📖 In-Depth Resources: Unit 1
· Guided Reading, p. 59
· Reteaching Activity, p. 65

## Critical Thinking

### Answers
A. Yes—Citizens vote directly for representatives and voice their views to them. No—The president is more effective.

B. Yes—keeps them more accountable. No—limits their ability to carry out their agendas.

C. Yes—House membership can change every two years. No—History has proved both houses to be fairly stable.

D. Yes—Presidents should stand trial during office because they are not above the law. No—Trials should occur after their terms of office to maintain national stability.

---

---

**DIFFERENTIATING INSTRUCTION**    **LESS PROFICIENT READERS**

### Finding Main Ideas

Tell students that finding main ideas involves finding words, phrases, or sentences that sum up what selections are about. To find a main idea, identify the topic of a passage. Then look for details that support the general idea of the topic. Think about how the details are related to each other.

Look at the paragraph labeled *4. Role of Vice-President* on this page. What details support the general idea of the role of the vice-president? *(President of Senate, no vote except in a tie)* These details support the main idea of the job and power of the vice-president. Use other headings on this page to find the main idea. Remember to look for connections between the details.

## More About . . .

### Congressional Record

The *Congressional Record*, begun in 1873, is published daily while Congress is in session. It prints everything spoken in Congress except secret matters, such as those involving national security. Members of Congress receive a copy of the *Record* for the previous day's session. They may make changes in their speeches before the speeches appear in the *Record*.

## More About . . .

### Congressional Salaries

In 1790, senators and representatives earned six dollars a day for each day they met. By 1950, they earned a little over $10,000 per year. In 1978, their salaries had risen to about $60,000 per year. The salary reached $141,300 in the year 2000. In the same period, by comparison, salaries and compensation for business leaders rose even more rapidly; hourly wages rose less sharply.

## Critical Thinking

### Answers

E. The chairman controls which legislation reaches the floor for consideration.

F. Yes—to curb presidential power. No—to curb congressional power over the president's decisions on legislation.

---

*Constitutional Insight* Section 5.2

*What kinds of rules does Congress make for itself?* The Constitution gives each house control over most of its rules of procedure and membership. Rules are important, for they help shape the kinds of laws and policies that pass each body. Senate rules allow a filibuster, whereby a senator holds the floor as long as he or she likes in order to block consideration of a bill he or she dislikes. In recent years, a "cloture" rule has been used to end debate if 60 or more members vote to do so.

In contrast, the House of Representatives has rules to limit debate. A rules committee has the primary task of determining how long a bill on the floor of the House may be discussed and whether any amendments can be offered to the bill. In recent years, the power of the Rules Committee has been limited, but being able to shape the rules remains a powerful tool of members of Congress.

**Ⓔ CRITICAL THINKING**

Why do you think the chair of the Rules Committee is in a powerful position?

*Constitutional Insight* Section 7.1

*Why must all bills to raise revenue originate in the House?* Because its members all stand for election every two years, the House was expected to be more directly responsive to the people. The tradition of restricting the powers of taxation to the people's representatives dates prior to the English Bill of Rights (1689), which granted to Parliament and withheld from the king the right to raise taxes. When colonists protesting the Stamp Act and the Intolerable Acts protested "no taxation without representation," they were appealing to a longstanding right codified in the English Bill of Rights.

*Constitutional Insight* Section 7.2

*How often do presidents use the veto, and how often is that action overridden?* The use of the veto, which is the refusal to approve a bill, depends on many factors, especially the political conditions of the time. Until 1865, only nine presidents exercised the veto for 36 pieces of legislation, including Andrew Jackson who used it 12 times. Since 1865, every president has used the veto power, some on relatively few occasions, others as frequently as over a hundred times. Usually, Congress is unable to produce the votes (those of two-thirds of the members present in each house) needed to override presidential vetoes.

**Ⓕ CRITICAL THINKING**

Do you think it should be easier for Congress to override a president's veto? Why or why not?

---

### SECTION 5. RULES AND PROCEDURES

1. **QUORUM** Each house shall be the judge of the elections, returns and qualifications of its own members, and a majority of each shall constitute a quorum to do business; but a smaller number may adjourn from day to day, and may be authorized to compel the attendance of absent members, in such manner, and under such penalties, as each house may provide.

2. **RULES AND CONDUCT** Each house may determine the rules of its proceedings, punish its members for disorderly behavior, and, with the concurrence of two thirds, expel a member.

3. **CONGRESSIONAL RECORDS** Each house shall keep a journal of its proceedings, and from time to time publish the same, excepting such parts as may in their judgment require secrecy; and the yeas and nays of the members of either house on any question shall, at the desire of one fifth of those present, be entered on the journal.

4. **ADJOURNMENT** Neither house, during the session of Congress, shall, without the consent of the other, adjourn for more than three days, nor to any other place than that in which the two houses shall be sitting.

### SECTION 6. PAYMENT AND PRIVILEGES

1. **SALARY** The Senators and Representatives shall receive a compensation for their services, to be ascertained by law, and paid out of the treasury of the United States. They shall in all cases, except treason, felony and breach of the peace, be privileged from arrest during their attendance at the session of their respective houses, and in going to and returning from the same; and for any speech or debate in either house, they shall not be questioned in any other place.

2. **RESTRICTIONS** No Senator or Representative shall, during the time for which he was elected, be appointed to any civil office under the authority of the United States, which shall have been created, or the emoluments whereof shall have been increased, during such time; and no person holding any office under the United States shall be a member of either house during his continuance in office.

### SECTION 7. HOW A BILL BECOMES A LAW

1. **TAX BILLS** All bills for raising revenue shall originate in the House of Representatives; but the Senate may propose or concur with amendments as on other bills.

2. **LAWMAKING PROCESS** Every bill which shall have passed the House of Representatives and the Senate shall, before it become a law, be presented to the President of the United States; if he approves he shall sign it, but if not he shall return it with his objections to that house in which it shall have originated, who shall enter the objections at large on their journal, and proceed to reconsider it. If after such reconsideration two thirds of that house shall agree to pass the bill, it shall be sent, together with the objections, to the other house, by which it shall likewise be reconsidered, and if approved by two thirds of that house, it shall become a law. But in all such

---

### Studying Vocabulary

Have students point out words with which they are unfamiliar. Ask them to read the words aloud and pronounce them correctly. Next, discuss the definitions. For example, call their attention to the word *indictment* on the previous page (Section 3, paragraph 7). Be sure to explain that a grand jury is not a trial jury. A grand jury's purpose is to seek information to decide if a crime has been committed. If it concludes that there has been a crime and there is reason to suspect a particular person, the grand jury can issue an indictment against the person. Next, point to the word *quorum* on this page (Section 5, paragraph 1). Tell the students that a quorum usually consists of half the total number of the group, plus one. Thus, the 100-member Senate has a quorum when 51 senators are present.

cases the votes of both houses shall be determined by yeas and nays, and the names of the persons voting for and against the bill shall be entered on the journal of each house respectively. If any bill shall not be returned by the President within ten days (Sundays excepted) after it shall have been presented to him, the same shall be a law, in like manner as if he had signed it, unless the Congress by their adjournment prevent its return, in which case it shall not be a law.

3. **ROLE OF THE PRESIDENT** Every order, resolution, or vote to which the concurrence of the Senate and House of Representatives may be necessary (except on a question of adjournment) shall be presented to the President of the United States; and before the same shall take effect, shall be approved by him, or being disapproved by him, shall be repassed by two thirds of the Senate and House of Representatives, according to the rules and limitations prescribed in the case of a bill.

*Skillbuilder*
*Answer*
Both the House and the Senate must pass a common version of a bill which the president may accept or reject (veto). If the president rejects a bill, it still becomes a law with a two-thirds vote in each house. So, the House and Senate can check each other and the president, while the president can check the Congress.

## How a Bill in Congress Becomes a Law

**1** A bill is introduced in the House or the Senate and referred to a standing committee for consideration.

**2** A bill may be reported out of committee with or without changes—or it may be shelved.

**3** Either house of Congress debates the bill and may make revisions. If passed, the bill is sent to the other house.

**4** If the House and the Senate pass different versions of a bill, both versions go to a conference committee to work out the differences.

**5** The conference committee submits a single version of the bill to the House and the Senate.

**6** If both houses accept the compromise version, the bill is sent to the president to be signed.

**7** If the president signs the bill, it becomes law.

**8** If the president vetoes the bill, the House and the Senate may override the veto by a vote of two thirds of the members present in each house, and then the bill becomes law.

**SKILLBUILDER** Interpreting Charts
How is the constitutional principle of checks and balances reflected in the process of a bill's becoming a law?

**REVIEW UNIT 87**

## Tracing Themes
### IMMIGRATION AND MIGRATION

### Becoming a U.S. Citizen
Legal immigrants may become naturalized citizens by following a procedure established by Congress. Applicants must be at least 18 years old and must have been a permanent resident for at least the previous five years. They must prove that they are of good moral character and are loyal to American principles of government. Applicants must pass an examination that tests their knowledge of U.S. history and government. A final hearing takes place in court, where the applicant takes a loyalty oath in front of a judge.

## NOW & THEN

### Modern Money
**Predicting** Ask students if the newly designed bills will most likely reduce the counterfeiting of U.S. currency. *(The security thread, fine-line printing patterns, and watermark seem to make counterfeiting more difficult.)*

## More About . . .

### The Elastic Clause
The elastic clause has proved to be one of the most farsighted measures in the Constitution. Broadly interpreted, the clause gave Congress authority to do much more than the simple list of duties in clauses 1 through 17 of Section 8. And in the 1819 Supreme Court case *McCulloch* v. *Maryland*, Chief Justice John Marshall ruled that Congress could use "all means which are appropriate. . . which are not prohibited" to fulfill legitimate ends.

---

***Constitutional Insight*** **Section 8** The powers given to Congress are in Section 8 of Article 1. The first 17 clauses of Section 8 are often called the enumerated powers because they name individually Congress's specific powers. These powers deal with issues ranging from taxation and the national debt to calling out the armed forces of the various states to governing the nation's capital district (Washington, D.C.).

The 18th and final clause is different. It gives Congress the power to do what is "necessary and proper" to carry out the enumerated powers. Thus, the enumerated powers of Congress "to lay and collect taxes," "to borrow money," "to regulate commerce," and "to coin money" imply the power to create a bank in order to execute these powers. Early in the country's history, this Elastic Clause, as it has been called, was used by Congress to establish the controversial Bank of the United States in 1791 and the Second Bank of the United States in 1816.

**G** **CRITICAL THINKING**
Why do you think the Elastic Clause is still important today?

### NOW & THEN

**MODERN MONEY**
Because of frequent counterfeiting of U.S. currency, a new design was released for the $100 and $50 bills in 1996. To make these bills more difficult to counterfeit, the new design included enlarged, off-center portraits of Benjamin Franklin and Ulysses S. Grant, a security thread, fine-line printing patterns, color-shifting ink, and a watermark to the right of each portrait. Since then, a $20 bill was introduced in 1998, and a $10 and $5 bill were introduced in 2000.

---

### SECTION 8. POWERS GRANTED TO CONGRESS

1. **TAXATION** The Congress shall have power to lay and collect taxes, duties, imposts and excises, to pay the debts and provide for the common defense and general welfare of the United States; but all duties, imposts and excises shall be uniform throughout the United States;

2. **CREDIT** To borrow money on the credit of the United States;

3. **COMMERCE** To regulate commerce with foreign nations, and among the several states, and with the Indian tribes;

4. **NATURALIZATION, BANKRUPTCY** To establish a uniform rule of naturalization, and uniform laws on the subject of bankruptcies throughout the United States;

5. **MONEY** To coin money, regulate the value thereof, and of foreign coin, and fix the standard of weights and measures;

6. **COUNTERFEITING** To provide for the punishment of counterfeiting the securities and current coin of the United States;

7. **POST OFFICE** To establish post offices and post roads;

8. **PATENTS, COPYRIGHTS** To promote the progress of science and useful arts, by securing for limited times to authors and inventors the exclusive right to their respective writings and discoveries;

9. **FEDERAL COURTS** To constitute tribunals inferior to the Supreme Court;

10. **INTERNATIONAL LAW** To define and punish piracies and felonies committed on the high seas, and offenses against the law of nations;

11. **WAR** To declare war, grant letters of marque and reprisal, and make rules concerning captures on land and water;

12. **ARMY** To raise and support armies, but no appropriation of money to that use shall be for a longer term than two years;

13. **NAVY** To provide and maintain a navy;

14. **REGULATION OF ARMED FORCES** To make rules for the government and regulation of the land and naval forces;

15. **MILITIA** To provide for calling forth the militia to execute the laws of the Union, suppress insurrections and repel invasions;

16. **REGULATIONS FOR MILITIA** To provide for organizing, arming, and disciplining the militia, and for governing such part of them as may be employed in the service of the United States, reserving to the states respectively the appointment of the officers, and the authority of training the militia according to the discipline prescribed by Congress;

17. **DISTRICT OF COLUMBIA** To exercise exclusive legislation in all cases whatsoever, over such district (not exceeding ten miles square) as may, by cession of particular states, and the acceptance of Congress, become the seat of the government of the United States, and to exercise like authority over all places purchased by the consent of the legislature of the state in which the same shall be, for the erection of forts, magazines, arsenals, dockyards, and other needful buildings;—and

18. **ELASTIC CLAUSE** To make all laws which shall be necessary and proper for carrying into execution the foregoing powers, and all other powers vested by this Constitution in the government of the United States, or in any department or officer thereof.

---

**ACTIVITY** | **LINK TO GOVERNMENT**  **classzone.com**

### Images on Money

**Class Time** 30 minutes

**Task** Investigating the images placed on denominations of U.S. currency

**Purpose** To identify American symbols and individuals on U.S. currency and to hypothesize about the use of those images

**Directions** Divide the class into small groups. The groups should research the images that appear on the following U.S. currencies: $1, 2, 5, 10, 20, 50, 100. They should also research the reasons why the images were selected for that particular denomination. They should create an illustrated chart showing each bill—front and back—and include identification of the elements on each side. Finally, they should write one sentence or hypothesis about why the images were chosen for a specific denomination.

## SECTION 9. POWERS DENIED CONGRESS

1. ~~Slave Trade~~ ~~The migration or importation of such persons as any of the states now existing shall think proper to admit, shall not be prohibited by the Congress prior to the year one thousand eight hundred and eight, but a tax or duty may be imposed on such importation, not exceeding ten dollars for each person.~~

2. **HABEAS CORPUS** The privilege of the writ of habeas corpus shall not be suspended, unless when in cases of rebellion or invasion the public safety may require it.

3. **ILLEGAL PUNISHMENT** No bill of attainder or ex post facto law shall be passed.

4. **DIRECT TAXES** No capitation, ~~or other direct, tax~~ shall be laid, ~~unless in proportion to the census or enumeration herein before directed to be taken.~~

5. **EXPORT TAXES** No tax or duty shall be laid on articles exported from any state.

6. **NO FAVORITES** No preference shall be given by any regulation of commerce or revenue to the ports of one state over those of another: nor shall vessels bound to, or from, one state be obliged to enter, clear, or pay duties in another.

7. **PUBLIC MONEY** No money shall be drawn from the treasury, but in consequence of appropriations made by law; and a regular statement and account of the receipts and expenditures of all public money shall be published from time to time.

8. **TITLES OF NOBILITY** No title of nobility shall be granted by the United States: and no person holding any office of profit or trust under them shall, without the consent of the Congress, accept of any present, emolument, office, or title, of any kind whatever, from any king, prince, or foreign state.

## SECTION 10. POWERS DENIED THE STATES

1. **RESTRICTIONS** No state shall enter into any treaty, alliance, or confederation; grant letters of marque and reprisal; coin money; emit bills of credit; make anything but gold and silver coin a tender in payment of debts; pass any bill of attainder, ex post facto law, or law impairing the obligation of contracts, or grant any title of nobility.

2. **IMPORT AND EXPORT TAXES** No state shall, without the consent of the Congress, lay any imposts or duties on imports or exports, except what may be absolutely necessary for executing its inspection laws; and the net produce of all duties and imposts, laid by any state on imports or exports, shall be for the use of the treasury of the United States; and all such laws shall be subject to the revision and control of the Congress.

---

### Constitutional Insight  Section 9

*Why didn't the framers include a bill of rights in the original Constitution?* Actually, they did. Article 1, Section 9, defines limits on the powers of Congress, just as the first ten amendments (which we call the Bill of Rights) do. While some of the provisions focus on such issues as slavery and taxation, there are three explicit prohibitions dealing with citizens' rights:

- *Writ of habeas corpus.* Section 9, Clause 2 says that, except in time of rebellion or invasion, Congress cannot suspend people's right to a writ of habeas corpus. This means that people cannot be held in prison or jail without being formally charged with a crime.

- *Bill of attainder.* Clause 3 prohibits the passage of any law that convicts or punishes a person directly and without a trial. Any legislative action that would punish someone without recourse to a court of law is called a bill of attainder.

- *Ex post facto law.* The same clause prohibits ex post facto laws. Such a law would punish a person for an act that was legal when it was performed.

The fact that these particular rights were protected by the original document issued by the framers reflects both the framers' experiences during the Revolution and their fear of excessive government power.

**Ⓗ  CRITICAL THINKING**
Why are American citizens today so intent on having protections against government violations of their rights?

---

### More About . . .

### Habeas Corpus

During the Civil War, President Lincoln suspended the writ of habeas corpus to suppress disloyalty and dissent. Consequently, more than 13,000 suspected Confederate sympathizers in the Union were arrested without trial, although most were soon released.

### Critical Thinking

#### Answers

G. It provides needed flexibility.

H. Americans still prize personal freedom and fear government's potential to abuse power.

### More About . . .

### Bills of Attainder

The individual rights protected by the bill of attainder clause (Section 9, clause 3) are among the few cited in the Constitution before the Bill of Rights. The issue was first tested in court after the Civil War. Southerners who wanted to practice law were required to take an oath that they had not participated in the Confederate rebellion. But the courts struck down that requirement as being a bill of attainder; the would-be lawyers were being deprived of their livelihood without being convicted of any crime. In 1965, on the same basis, the Supreme Court stuck down a law barring a member of the Communist Party from holding office in a labor union.

📄 Formal Assessment
· Living Constitution, Section Quiz, Preamble and Article 1, p. 43

---

## DIFFERENTIATING INSTRUCTION     LESS PROFICIENT READERS

### Understanding Economic Terms

In order to help students understand the various economic terms on this page, have students work in pairs to pick out the economics-related words with which they are unfamiliar. The words include *duty, export, import, appropriations, receipts,* and *expenditures.* The students should work together to write out a definition of each word and use the word in a sentence.

**OBJECTIVE**

**1** Explain the powers and duties of the president

## Focus & Motivate

What traits do students think a president needs to lead the country? Why?

## Instruct

### Instruct: Objective **1**

**The Executive**

TAKS SS11 4(8.16D)

· What is the main role of the executive branch?

· How does the Constitution limit the power of the president?

 In-Depth Resources: Unit 1
· Guided Reading, p. 60
· Reteaching Activity, p. 66

### More About . . .

**The Electoral College**

The Framers set up the electoral college as a way to get informed votes on the presidency. The Framers assumed that state electors would know which candidate could best serve the people of their state.

By the 20th century, many people had come to believe that the electoral system was outdated and unfair. The principle of "winner takes all" means that a candidate gets 100 percent of a state's electoral votes, even if he or she gets only 50.1 percent of the popular vote. The election of 2000 brought public discussion about the electoral college into sharp focus after candidate Al Gore lost the electoral votes of Florida to George W. Bush in a tightly contested and controversial election.

 **ARTICLE 2**

***Constitutional Insight* Section 1.1**
*What exactly is "executive power"?* We know the president has it, but nowhere is it explicitly defined. It is most often defined as the power to carry out the laws of the land, but of course no one person can handle such a chore alone. A more appropriate definition is found in Section 3 of this article, which empowers the president to "take care that the laws be faithfully executed." In this sense, the president is the chief administrator.

**🄘 CRITICAL THINKING**
Why is it important to have an executive who is the chief administrator?

3. **PEACETIME AND WAR RESTRAINTS** No state shall, without the consent of Congress, lay any duty of tonnage, keep troops or ships of war in time of peace, enter into any agreement or compact with another state, or with a foreign power, or engage in war, unless actually invaded, or in such imminent danger as will not admit of delay.

**1** **ARTICLE 2.** *The Executive*

**SECTION 1. THE PRESIDENCY**

1. **TERMS OF OFFICE** The executive power shall be vested in a President of the United States of America. He shall hold his office during the term of four years and, together with the Vice-President, chosen for the same term, be elected as follows:

2. **ELECTORAL COLLEGE** Each state shall appoint, in such manner as the legislature thereof may direct, a number of electors, equal to the whole number of Senators and Representatives to which the state may be entitled in the Congress; but no Senator or Representative, or person holding an office of trust or profit under the United States, shall be appointed an elector.

3. ~~**Former Method of Electing President**~~ ~~The electors shall meet in their respective states, and vote by ballot for two persons, of whom one at least shall not be an inhabitant of the same state with themselves. And they shall make a list of all the persons voted for, and of the number of votes for each; which list they shall sign and certify, and transmit sealed to the seat of the government of the United States, directed to the President of the Senate. The President of the Senate shall, in the presence of the Senate and House of Representatives, open all the certificates, and the votes shall then be counted. The person having the greatest number of votes shall be the President, if such number be a majority of the whole number of electors appointed; and if there be more than one who have such majority, and have an equal number of votes, then the House of Representatives shall immediately choose by ballot one of them for President; and if no person have a majority, then from the five highest on the list the said house shall in like manner choose the President. But in choosing the President, the votes shall be taken by states, the representation from each state having one vote; a quorum for this purpose shall consist of a member or members from two thirds of the states, and a majority of all the states shall be necessary to a choice. In every case, after the choice of the President, the person having the greatest number of votes of the electors shall be the Vice-President. But if there should remain two or more who have equal votes, the Senate shall choose from them by ballot the Vice-President.~~

4. **ELECTION DAY** The Congress may determine the time of choosing the electors, and the day on which they shall give their votes; which day shall be the same throughout the United States.

---

### The Electoral College

**Class Time** 45 minutes

**Task** Creating a table to illustrate the link between popular and electoral votes

**Purpose** To analyze problems with the electoral college

**Directions** Ask students to calculate the number of electoral votes necessary to win the presidency. In pairs or small groups, have students create a chart showing the total popular vote and electoral vote for each state from the most recent

presidential election. Ask students to scan the chart for states where the popular vote was close. How many votes would it have taken to change the result in those states? Would such a change have altered the outcome of the national election? Could a candidate have lost the popular vote but won the election?

 In-Depth Resources: Unit 1
· Geography Application: The Electoral College, pp. 69–70

**5. QUALIFICATIONS** No person except a natural-born citizen, ~~or a citizen of the United States at the time of the adoption of this Constitution,~~ shall be eligible to the office of President; neither shall any person be eligible to that office who shall not have attained to the age of thirty-five years, and been fourteen years a resident within the United States.

**6. SUCCESSION** In case of the removal of the President from office, or of his death, resignation, or inability to discharge the powers and duties of the said office, the same shall devolve on the Vice-President, and the Congress may by law provide for the case of removal, death, resignation, or inability, both of the President and Vice-President, declaring what officer shall then act as President, and such officer shall act accordingly, until the disability be removed, or a President shall be elected.

**7. SALARY** The President shall, at stated times, receive for his services a compensation, which shall neither be increased nor diminished during the period for which he shall have been elected, and he shall not receive within that period any other emolument from the United States, or any of them.

**8. OATH OF OFFICE** Before he enter on the execution of his office, he shall take the following oath or affirmation:—"I do solemnly swear (or affirm) that I will faithfully execute the office of President of the United States, and will to the best of my ability, preserve, protect and defend the Constitution of the United States."

**SECTION 2. POWERS OF THE PRESIDENT**

**1. MILITARY POWERS** The President shall be commander in chief of the army and navy of the United States, and of the militia of the several states, when called into the actual service of the United States; he may require the opinion, in writing, of the principal officer in each of the executive departments, upon any subject relating to the duties of their respective offices, and he shall have power to grant reprieves and pardons for offenses against the United States, except in cases of impeachment.

**2. TREATIES, APPOINTMENTS** He shall have power, by and with the advice and consent of the Senate, to make treaties, provided two thirds of the Senators present concur; and he shall nominate, and by and with the advice and consent of the Senate, shall appoint ambassadors, other public ministers and consuls, judges of the Supreme Court, and all other officers of the United States, whose appointments are not herein otherwise provided for, and which shall be established by law; but the Congress may by law vest the appointment of such inferior officers, as they think proper, in the President alone, in the courts of law, or in the heads of departments.

**3. VACANCIES** The President shall have power to fill up all vacancies that may happen during the recess of the Senate, by granting commissions which shall expire at the end of their next session.

---

***Constitutional Insight*** Section 1.6
*What happens when the vice-president succeeds a dead or incapacitated president?* Section 1.6 provides that the vice-president shall assume the powers and duties of the presidential office. But until the Twenty-fifth Amendment was added to the Constitution in 1967, there was no explicit statement in the document that the vice-president is to become president. That procedure owes its origin to John Tyler, the tenth president of the United States, who in 1841 succeeded William Henry Harrison—the first president to die in office. Tyler decided to take the oath of office and assume the title of president of the United States. Congress voted to go along with his decision, and the practice was repeated after Lincoln was assassinated. It would take another century for the written provisions of the Constitution to catch up with the practice.

**J** CRITICAL THINKING
Why is it important to know the order of succession if a president dies in office?

***Constitutional Insight*** Section 2.1
*Just how much authority does the president have as "commander in chief" of the armed forces?* The president has the power to give orders to American military forces. There have been several instances in U.S. history when presidents have used that authority in spite of congressional wishes.

President Harry Truman involved the armed forces of the United States in the Korean War from 1950 to 1953 without a congressional declaration of war.

Reacting to criticism of the Vietnam War, Congress in 1973 enacted the War Powers Resolution, making the president more accountable to Congress for any military actions he or she might take. Every president since Richard Nixon has called the resolution unconstitutional. Nevertheless, every president has reported to Congress within 48 hours of sending troops into an international crisis, as is required by the War Powers Resolution.

**K** CRITICAL THINKING
Why is it important that the commander in chief of the armed forces of the United States be a civilian (the president) rather than a military general?

---

## Critical Thinking

**Answers**

I. To make sure laws are faithfully executed.

J. To ensure smooth and orderly transfer of leadership.

K. To safeguard the nation from becoming a military dictatorship; to make military decisions from a broader perspective.

### More About . . .

**The Power of the President**
Most scholars agree that the power of the president increased dramatically during the Civil War, when Abraham Lincoln took extraordinary measures to meet the crisis. However, the greatest expansion of presidential powers occurred during the presidency of Franklin D. Roosevelt. Confronted with both the Great Depression and World War II, Roosevelt took unprecedented steps to save the country. Many of these steps strengthened the executive branch of the government. Since World War II, the emergence of the United States as a world power also increased the power of the American president as a foreign-policy leader.

---

**DIFFERENTIATING INSTRUCTION    LESS PROFICIENT READERS**

### Organizing Information

To help students keep track of the president's powers, put this organizational tree on the chalkboard and help them fill in the missing examples.

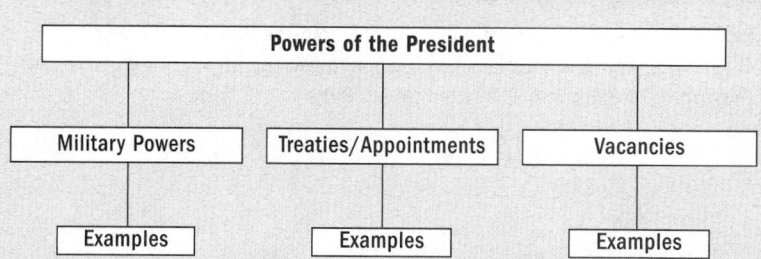

| Powers of the President |
| Military Powers | Treaties/Appointments | Vacancies |
| Examples | Examples | Examples |

### More About . . .

**Presidential Duties**

The Constitution does not specifically call for the president to assemble and consult a cabinet of presidential advisers. But it does mention executive departments. The heads of the executive departments have become part of the president's advisory board—the cabinet. George Washington's cabinet consisted of four members—the secretaries of state, the treasury, and war, plus the attorney general. Today's cabinet includes the heads of 14 departments. The president may also give cabinet rank to other high-level officials whose advice on issues could prove valuable.

### OBJECTIVE

**1** Explain how judicial review expands the power of the judiciary.

## Focus & Motivate

Have students think about the courtroom scenes that they have seen on television or in movies. How would they describe the role that the judges play in the proceedings?

## Instruct

### Instruct: Objective **1**

**The Judiciary**

TAKS SS11 4(8.16D)

· What is the main role of the judicial branch?

· What is the power of judicial review?

📄 **In-Depth Resources: Unit 1**
· Guided Reading, p. 60
· Reteaching, p. 66

---

**Constitutional Insight** Section 3

*Is it necessary for the president to deliver a State of the Union address before a joint session of Congress at the start of each legislative year?* The Constitution requires only that the president report to Congress on the state of the Union from time to time, and nowhere does it call for an annual address. In 1913, President Woodrow Wilson wanted to influence Congress to take action without delay on some legislation that he thought was important. Wilson revived the tradition—which had been discontinued by Jefferson—of delivering the State of the Union address in person.

**L** **CRITICAL THINKING**
How does the president use the State of the Union address today?

**Constitutional Insight** Section 4

*Have high-level public officials ever been impeached?* In all of American history, the House has impeached two presidents, and neither had to leave office. In 1868, the Senate found President Andrew Johnson not guilty by one vote after the House impeached him, charging him with violating a Congressional Act. In 1999, Senators acquitted President Bill Clinton after the House impeached him with charges of lying under oath and obstructing justice in the attempted cover-up of a White House scandal.

The only other president to come close to impeachment was Richard Nixon. In 1974, the House Judiciary Committee, in what is the first step of the impeachment process, recommended three articles of impeachment against Nixon for his role in the infamous Watergate scandal. Before the full House could vote for or against the articles of impeachment, however, Nixon resigned from office.

**M** **CRITICAL THINKING**
Why do you think the framers of the Constitution created such an elaborate and seemingly difficult procedure for removing a sitting president?

---

**SECTION 3. PRESIDENTIAL DUTIES** He shall from time to time give to the Congress information of the state of the Union, and recommend to their consideration such measures as he shall judge necessary and expedient; he may, on extraordinary occasions, convene both houses, or either of them, and in case of disagreement between them, with respect to the time of adjournment, he may adjourn them to such time as he shall think proper; he shall receive ambassadors and other public ministers; he shall take care that the laws be faithfully executed, and shall commission all the officers of the United States.

**SECTION 4. IMPEACHMENT** The President, Vice-President and all civil officers of the United States shall be removed from office on impeachment for, and conviction of, treason, bribery, or other high crimes and misdemeanors.

*(above)* Rep. Henry Hyde, chairman of the House Judiciary Committee, swears in Independent Counsel Kenneth Starr during the Committee's hearings on impeachment charges against President Bill Clinton in 1998; *(right)* President Andrew Johnson is handed the articles of impeachment before his trial in 1868.

**1** **ARTICLE 3.** *The Judiciary*

**SECTION 1. FEDERAL COURTS AND JUDGES** The judicial power of the United States shall be vested in one Supreme Court, and in such inferior courts as the Congress may from time to time ordain and establish. The judges, both of the Supreme and inferior courts, shall hold their offices during good behavior, and shall, at stated times, receive for their services a compensation, which shall not be diminished during their continuance in office.

---

**Researching Nixon's Offenses**

Read aloud the following front-page headline from *The New York Times* of August 8, 1974: "Nixon Resigns," on the front page. "He Urges a Time of 'Healing'; Ford Will Take Office Today," was the subheading.

Explain that the House Judiciary Committee's articles of impeachment against President Richard Nixon for high crimes and misdemeanors spurred his resignation. Have students research Nixon's alleged violations of the Constitution and report their findings to the class.

## SECTION 2. THE COURTS' AUTHORITY

**1. GENERAL AUTHORITY** The judicial power shall extend to all cases, in law and equity, arising under this Constitution, the laws of the United States, and treaties made, or which shall be made, under their authority;—to all cases affecting ambassadors, other public ministers and consuls;—to all cases of admiralty and maritime jurisdiction;—to controversies to which the United States shall be a party;—to controversies between two or more states;—between a state and citizens of another state;—between citizens of different states;—between citizens of the same state claiming lands under grants of different states, and between a state, or the citizens thereof, and foreign states, citizens or subjects.

**2. SUPREME COURT** In all cases affecting ambassadors, other public ministers and consuls, and those in which a state shall be party, the Supreme Court shall have original jurisdiction. In all the other cases before mentioned, the Supreme Court shall have appellate jurisdiction, both as to law and fact, with such exceptions, and under such regulations, as the Congress shall make.

**3. TRIAL BY JURY** The trial of all crimes, except in cases of impeachment, shall be by jury; and such trial shall be held in the state where the said crimes shall have been committed; but when not committed within any state, the trial shall be at such place or places as the Congress may by law have directed.

## SECTION 3. TREASON

**1. DEFINITION** Treason against the United States shall consist only in levying war against them, or in adhering to their enemies, giving them aid and comfort. No person shall be convicted of treason unless on the testimony of two witnesses to the same overt act, or on confession in open court.

**2. PUNISHMENT** The Congress shall have power to declare the punishment of treason, but no attainder of treason shall work corruption of blood, or forfeiture except during the life of the person attainted.

## ARTICLE 3

***Constitutional Insight*** Section 2.1
*What is judicial review? Is it the same as judicial power?* Actually, they are not the same. Judicial power is the authority to hear cases involving disputes over the law or the behavior of people. Judicial review, in contrast, is a court's passing judgment on the constitutionality of a law or government action that is being disputed. Interestingly, nowhere does the Constitution mention judicial review. There are places where it is implied (for example, in Section 2 of Article 6), but the only explicit description of the responsibility of the courts is the reference to judicial power in Section 1 of Article 3. The Supreme Court's power to review laws passed by Congress was explicitly affirmed by the Court itself in *Marbury* v. *Madison.* (See page 118.)

 **CRITICAL THINKING**
Why is judicial review, although not mentioned in the Constitution, an important activity of the Supreme Court?

The Supreme Court of the United States in 1994. In the front row (*left to right*) are Associate Justices Antonin Scalia and John Paul Stevens, Chief Justice William H. Rehnquist, and Associate Justices Sandra Day O'Connor and Anthony Kennedy. In the back row are Associate Justices Ruth Bader Ginsburg, David Souter, Clarence Thomas, and Stephen Breyer.

## ARTICLE 3

### More About . . .

**Federal Courts**
The Constitution actually creates only one court—the U.S. Supreme Court. It gives Congress the ability to set up "inferior" courts. Today the federal court system consists of three tiers. At the lowest level are 94 U.S. district courts. These are courts where federal trials take place. The second level in the court system includes 12 U.S. Courts of Appeal. These courts hear cases "on appeal." At the third level is the highest court of appeal, the U.S. Supreme Court.

### Critical Thinking

**Answers**
L. To outline key policies the president will address in the coming year.

M. To make certain that a president could not be removed for reasons of partisan politics, thus endangering the stability of the presidency.

N. To ensure that laws and government action do not violate the Constitution.

### More About . . .

**Treason**
The Constitution sets a high standard of proof for treason. The framers knew from examples in English history that charges of treason were often politically motivated. Thus, the Constitution requires open acts of treason—not merely disloyal thoughts or words—before a person can be convicted. Aaron Burr, a former vice-president, was tried for treason under this law in 1807. Burr was suspected of trying to establish a Western empire by taking over part of the United States. But the evidence against him did not meet the high constitutional standard, and he was acquitted.

Formal Assessment
· Living Constitution, Section Quiz, Articles 2 and 3, p. 44

---

**DIFFERENTIATING INSTRUCTION**  |  **GIFTED AND TALENTED STUDENTS**  |  classzone.com

## Examining Treason

Have interested students use the Internet and other sources to research a recent case of alleged treason against the United States. Have students write a brief report detailing the episode, including the alleged treasonous act, the motive supposedly behind it, as well as how the matter was resolved. If the matter is ongoing, describe its current status. Have students read their report aloud and then have the class discuss various points of the case, such as whether the punishment was just.

Integrated Assessment
· Rubrics 1, 5

## OBJECTIVES

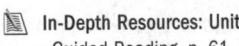

**1** Describe how the states are interdependent and subject to the federal government

**2** Cite ways of proposing and ratifying amendments

# Focus & Motivate

Ask students what would happen if criminals could escape punishment by fleeing to another state.

# Instruct

## Instruct: Objective **1**

### Relations Among States
TAKS SS11 4(8.18)

· How does the policy of extradition work?
· How does the federal government have ultimate authority over the states?

📖 In-Depth Resources: Unit 1
· Guided Reading, p. 61

## More About . . .

### "Domestic Violence"
In addition to disasters such as the World Trade Center bombings in 2001, floods, droughts, hurricanes, earthquakes, and tornadoes can also be classified as incidents of "domestic violence." In Article 4, Section 4, the federal government guarantees that it will protect the states in the event of such disasters. The Federal Emergency Management Agency (FEMA) responds to these kinds of emergencies and paves the way for supplying federal funds and aid to victims.

## Instruct: Objective **2**

### Amending the Constitution
TAKS SS11 4(8.17)

· How is the Constitution amended?

📖 In-Depth Resources: Unit 1
· Guided Reading, p. 61

---

## ARTICLE 4

**Constitutional Insight** Section 2.1
*Why do college students attending public universities outside their state of residence have to pay higher tuition fees?*
The Supreme Court has interpreted the "privileges and immunities" clause to allow higher tuition fees (and fees for hunting permits, etc.) for nonresidents when a state can give a "substantial reason" for the difference. Since state colleges and universities receive some financial support from the states' taxpayers, the difference is regarded as justified in most states. If a student establishes residency in the state, he or she can pay in-state tuition after one year.

**O** CRITICAL THINKING
Do you think it is fair that a nonresident must pay higher tuition fees at a state college than a resident of the state must pay? Explain.

**Constitutional Insight** Section 3.1
*Should there be a West Virginia?* The Constitution states that "no new state shall be formed or erected within the jurisdiction of any other state" without the permission of the legislature of the state involved and of the Congress. Vermont, Kentucky, Tennessee, and Maine were created from territory taken from existing states, with the approval of the sitting legislatures.
West Virginia, however, is a different story. During the Civil War, the residents of the westernmost counties of Virginia were angry with their state's decision to secede from the Union. They petitioned Congress to have their counties declared a distinct state. Congress agreed, and so the state of West Virginia was created. After the Civil War, the legislature of Virginia gave its formal approval, perhaps because it was in no position to dispute the matter.

**P** CRITICAL THINKING
Suppose a section of Texas should decide to become a new state today. Could it do this? Why or why not?

**94** THE LIVING CONSTITUTION

---

**1** ## ARTICLE 4. *Relations Among States*

**SECTION 1. STATE ACTS AND RECORDS** Full faith and credit shall be given in each state to the public acts, records, and judicial proceedings of every other state. And the Congress may by general laws prescribe the manner in which such acts, records, and proceedings shall be proved, and the effect thereof.

**SECTION 2. RIGHTS OF CITIZENS**

1. **CITIZENSHIP** The citizens of each state shall be entitled to all privileges and immunities of citizens in the several states.

2. **EXTRADITION** A person charged in any state with treason, felony, or other crime, who shall flee from justice, and be found in another state, shall on demand of the executive authority of the state from which he fled, be delivered up, to be removed to the state having jurisdiction of the crime.

3. ~~**Fugitive Slaves** No person held to service or labor in one state, under the laws thereof, escaping into another, shall, in consequence of any law or regulation therein, be discharged from such service or labor, but shall be delivered up on claim of the party to whom such service or labor may be due.~~

**SECTION 3. NEW STATES**

1. **ADMISSION** New states may be admitted by the Congress into this Union; but no new state shall be formed or erected within the jurisdiction of any other state; nor any state be formed by the junction of two or more states, or parts of states, without the consent of the legislatures of the states concerned as well as of the Congress.

2. **CONGRESSIONAL AUTHORITY** The Congress shall have power to dispose of and make all needful rules and regulations respecting the territory or other property belonging to the United States; and nothing in this Constitution shall be so construed as to prejudice any claims of the United States, or of any particular state.

**SECTION 4. GUARANTEES TO THE STATES** The United States shall guarantee to every state in this Union a republican form of government, and shall protect each of them against invasion; and on application of the legislature, or of the executive (when the legislature cannot be convened), against domestic violence.

**2** ## ARTICLE 5. *Amending the Constitution*

The Congress, whenever two thirds of both houses shall deem it necessary, shall propose amendments to this Constitution, or, on the application of the legislatures of two thirds of the several states, shall call a convention for proposing amendments, which, in either case, shall be valid to all intents and purposes, as part of this Constitution, when ratified by the legislatures of three fourths of the several states, or by conventions in three fourths thereof, as the one or the other mode of ratification may be proposed by the Congress; ~~provided that no amendment which may be made prior to the year one thousand eight hundred and eight shall in any manner affect the first and fourth clauses in the ninth section of the first article;~~ and that no state, without its consent, shall be deprived of its equal suffrage in the Senate.

---

## ACTIVITY   COOPERATIVE LEARNING

## BLOCK SCHEDULING

### Proposing and Ratifying Amendments

**Class Time** 45 minutes

**Task** Proposing an amendment by a two-thirds majority of the group and ratifying the amendment by a three-fourths majority of the class

**Purpose** To gain understanding of the amendment process

**Directions** Divide students into groups of six. Each group will propose an amendment by a two-thirds majority of its members. Each group will then present its amendment to the class for ratification. A three-fourths majority vote is required. Conclude with a class discussion of the following questions:

· Which was more difficult to achieve—the two-thirds majority to propose the amendment or the three-fourths majority to ratify it?

· Do you think the procedure for amending the Constitution provides enough flexibility for the document to change with the times? Why or why not?

## ARTICLE 6. *Supremacy of the National Government*

**SECTION 1. VALID DEBTS** All debts contracted and engagements entered into, before the adoption of this Constitution, shall be as valid against the United States under this Constitution, as under the Confederation.

**SECTION 2. SUPREME LAW** This Constitution, and the laws of the United States which shall be made in pursuance thereof; and all treaties made, or which shall be made, under the authority of the United States, shall be the supreme law of the land; and the judges in every state shall be bound thereby, anything in the constitution or laws of any state to the contrary notwithstanding.

**SECTION 3. LOYALTY TO CONSTITUTION** The Senators and Representatives before mentioned, and the members of the several state legislatures, and all executive and judicial officers, both of the United States and of the several states, shall be bound by oath or affirmation to support this Constitution; but no religious test shall ever be required as a qualification to any office or public trust under the United States.

## ARTICLE 7. *Ratification*

The ratification of the conventions of nine states shall be sufficient for the establishment of this Constitution between the states so ratifying the same. Done in convention by the unanimous consent of the states present, the seventeenth day of September in the year of our Lord one thousand seven hundred and eighty-seven and of the independence of the United States of America the twelfth. In witness whereof we have hereunto subscribed our names.

*George Washington—President and deputy from Virginia*

**Delaware:** *George Read, Gunning Bedford, Jr., John Dickinson, Richard Bassett, Jacob Broom*

**Maryland:** *James McHenry, Dan of St. Thomas Jenifer, Daniel Carroll*

**Virginia:** *John Blair, James Madison, Jr.*

**North Carolina:** *William Blount, Richard Dobbs Spaight, Hugh Williamson*

**South Carolina:** *John Rutledge, Charles Cotesworth Pinckney, Charles Pinckney, Pierce Butler*

**Georgia:** *William Few, Abraham Baldwin*

**New Hampshire:** *John Langdon, Nicholas Gilman*

**Massachusetts:** *Nathaniel Gorham, Rufus King*

**Connecticut:** *William Samuel Johnson, Roger Sherman*

**New York:** *Alexander Hamilton*

**New Jersey:** *William Livingston, David Brearley, William Paterson, Jonathan Dayton*

**Pennsylvania:** *Benjamin Franklin, Thomas Mifflin, Robert Morris, George Clymer, Thomas FitzSimons, Jared Ingersoll, James Wilson, Gouverneur Morris*

Critical Thinking Answers

Q. National disunity might result if U.S. citizens were subject to conflicting laws.

R. Yes—All states would recognize the Constitution's value and flexibility.
No—Unresolved differences over states' sovereignty and rights might emerge.

### ARTICLE 6

*Constitutional Insight* **Section 2** *Just how "supreme" is the "law of the land"?* The Constitution and all federal laws and treaties are the highest law of the land. All state constitutions and laws and all local laws rank below national law and cannot be enforced if they contradict national law. For example, if the United States enters into a treaty protecting migratory Canadian birds, the states must change their laws to fit the provisions of that agreement. That was the decision of the Supreme Court in the case of *Missouri* v. *Holland* (1920). The state of Missouri argued that the national government could not interfere with its power to regulate hunting within its borders, but the Supreme Court concluded that the treaty was a valid exercise of national power and therefore took priority over state and local laws. The states had to adjust their rules and regulations accordingly.

**Q CRITICAL THINKING**
What would happen if the national law were not supreme?

### ARTICLE 7

*Constitutional Insight* *Why was ratification by only 9 states sufficient to put the Constitution into effect?* In taking such a momentous step as replacing one constitution (the Articles of Confederation) with another, the framers might have been expected to require the agreement of all 13 states. But the framers were political realists. They knew that they would have a difficult time winning approval from all 13 states. But they also knew that they had a good chance of getting 9 or 10 of the states "on board" and that once that happened, the rest would follow. Their strategy worked, but just barely. Although they had the approval of 9 states by the end of June 1788, 2 of the most important states—Virginia and New York—had not yet decided to ratify. Without the approval of these influential states, the new government would have had a difficult time surviving. Finally, by the end of July, both had given their blessing to the new constitution, but not without intense debate.

And then there was the last holdout—Rhode Island. Not only had Rhode Island refused to send delegates to the Constitutional Convention in 1787, but it turned down ratification several times before finally giving its approval in 1790 under a cloud of economic and even military threats from neighboring states.

**R CRITICAL THINKING**
Do you think all 50 states would ratify the Constitution today? Why or why not?

## OBJECTIVES

 Explain the authority of federal law

Describe how the Constitution was ratified

## Focus & Motivate

Ask students who belong to school clubs if all members approve of their club's rules.

## Instruct

### Instruct: Objective ❶

**Supremacy of the National Government**
TAKS SS11 4(8.16D)

· In what ways is the national government supreme?

📖 In-Depth Resources: Unit 1
· Guided Reading, p. 61

### Instruct: Objective

**Ratification**
TAKS SS11 4(8.16D)

· What was the process for ratifying the Constitution?

· Who were some of the more prominent signers of the Constitution?

📖 In-Depth Resources: Unit 1
· American Lives: James Madison, p. 71

### More About . . .

**The Signers**
Of the 39 signers, only Roger Sherman signed all four of the most important documents in the history of the new nation. He signed the Articles of Association (1774), the Declaration of Independence (1776), the Articles of Confederation (1781), and the Constitution (1787). Many of the signers went on to become senators and representatives, several served on the Supreme Court, and two—Washington and Madison—were elected president.

---

**ACTIVITY   COOPERATIVE LEARNING**

**B BLOCK SCHEDULING**

### Examining the Flexibility of the Constitution

**Class Time** 30 minutes

**Task** Examining various views about the Constitution

**Purpose** To evaluate the document's flexibility

**Directions** Have students work in small groups to compare the following views of the Constitution. Then, discuss what each says about the document's durability and flexibility.

· "A Constitution is framed for ages to come, and is designed to approach immortality as nearly as human institutions can approach it. . . . The people made the Constitution, and the people can unmake it. It is the creature of their will, and lives only by their will." John Marshall, *Cohens* v. *Virginia*, 1821

· "When the Constitution was first framed, I predicted that it would last fifty years. I was mistaken. . . . But I was mistaken only in point of time. The crash will come, but not so quick as I thought." Aaron Burr, 1835

· "Amendments to the Constitution ought not to be too frequently made; . . . [if] continually tinkered with it would lose all its prestige and dignity, and the old instrument would be lost sight of altogether in a short time." President Andrew Johnson, 1866

*The Living Constitution* **95**

## OBJECTIVE

**1** Identify basic freedoms guaranteed by the first ten amendments.

**SKILLBUILDER**

· Analyzing Political Cartoons, p. 97

## Focus & Motivate

Ask students to name their rights as U.S. citizens. Then have them create a chart comparing the rights they cited with the Bill of Rights.

## Instruct

### Instruct: Objective **1**

**The Bill of Rights**
TAKS SS11 4(8.20B)

· What rights do the first ten amendments guarantee?
· How does the Bill of Rights limit the power of the federal government?

 In-Depth Resources: Unit 1
· Guided Reading, p. 62
· Reteaching Activity, p. 68

### Analyzing *Political Cartoons*

**SKILLBUILDER ANSWERS**

1. They are represented by pillars neatly aligned and joined at the top.
2. They are represented by pillars that are toppling (North Carolina) or crumbling (Rhode Island). These two states may have difficulties surviving apart from the other 11 United States.

---

### BILL OF RIGHTS

***Constitutional Insight*** Amendment 1
*Do Americans have an absolute right to free speech?* The right to free speech is not without limits. In the case of *Schenck* v. *United States* (1919), Justice Oliver Wendell Holmes wrote that this right does "not protect a man in falsely shouting fire in a theatre and causing a panic." Thus, there are some forms of speech that are not protected by the First Amendment, and Congress is allowed to make laws regarding certain types of expression. (See *Schenck* v. *United States* on page 396.)

**A** CRITICAL THINKING
Why is there controversy over freedom of speech today?

***Constitutional Insight*** Amendment 4
*Can the police search your car without a court-issued search warrant when they stop you for speeding?* The answer, according to Supreme Court decisions, depends on whether they have good reasons—called "probable cause"—for doing so. If a state trooper notices bloody clothing on the back seat of a vehicle she stops for a traffic violation, there might be probable cause for her to insist on searching the vehicle. There is probably not sufficient reason for a search if the trooper is merely suspicious of the driver because of the way he is acting. In such cases, the trooper may make a casual request, such as "Do you mind if I look inside your vehicle?" If the answer is no, then according to the Court, the driver has waived his or her constitutional right against unreasonable searches.

**B** CRITICAL THINKING
Why do you think the right against unreasonable searches and seizures is highly important to most people?

***Constitutional Insight*** Amendment 5
*Can you be tried twice for the same offense?* The prohibition against "double jeopardy" protects you from having the same charge twice brought against you for the same offense, but you can be tried on different charges related to that offense.

**C** CRITICAL THINKING
What do you think could happen if a person could be tried twice for the same offense?

---

# The Bill of Rights
## and Amendments 11–27

### *Amendments 1–10* **1**

Proposed by Congress September 25, 1789. Ratified December 15, 1791.

**AMENDMENT 1. RELIGIOUS AND POLITICAL FREEDOM (1791)** Congress shall make no law respecting an establishment of religion, or prohibiting the free exercise thereof; or abridging the freedom of speech, or of the press; or the right of the people peaceably to assemble, and to petition the government for a redress of grievances.

**AMENDMENT 2. RIGHT TO BEAR ARMS (1791)** A well-regulated militia being necessary to the security of a free state, the right of the people to keep and bear arms shall not be infringed.

**AMENDMENT 3. QUARTERING TROOPS (1791)** No soldier shall, in time of peace, be quartered in any house without the consent of the owner, nor in time of war, but in a manner to be prescribed by law.

**AMENDMENT 4. SEARCH AND SEIZURE (1791)** The right of the people to be secure in their persons, houses, papers, and effects, against unreasonable searches and seizures, shall not be violated, and no warrants shall issue, but upon probable cause, supported by oath or affirmation, and particularly describing the place to be searched, and the persons or things to be seized.

**AMENDMENT 5. RIGHTS OF ACCUSED PERSONS (1791)** No person shall be held to answer for a capital or otherwise infamous crime, unless on a presentment or indictment of a grand jury, except in cases arising in the land or naval forces, or in the militia, when in actual service in time of war or public danger; nor shall any person be subject for the same offense to be twice put in jeopardy of life or limb; nor shall be compelled in any criminal case to be a witness against himself, nor be deprived of life, liberty, or property, without due process of law; nor shall private property be taken for public use, without just compensation.

### Analyzing *Political Cartoons*

**"THE FEDERAL EDIFICE"**
This 1778 cartoon celebrated the ratification of the Constitution by New York, the 11th state to ratify it. This left only North Carolina and Rhode Island to complete all 13 pillars of the federal structure.

**SKILLBUILDER** Analyzing Political Cartoons
1. What details in the cartoon convey the unity of the states who have voted for ratification?
2. How does the cartoonist contrast the states who have voted for ratification with those who have not? What message does this convey?

 SEE SKILLBUILDER HANDBOOK, PAGE R24.

---

**ACTIVITY    SKILLBUILDER LESSON**

### Clarifying

**Explaining the Skill** Clarifying, or confirming one's understanding of what someone else has said, is a basic skill. Clarifying readings from primary sources, such as the Constitution, should involve defining unfamiliar words and working through complicated sentence structures to restate the ideas more simply.

**Applying the Skill** To help students understand the Constitution, ask them to read the First Amendment, and then answer the following questions:

1. What does *respecting* mean? *(about)*
2. What word does *thereof* refer to? *(religion)*
3. What does *abridging* mean? *(curtailing or diminishing)*
4. What is a redress of grievances? *(righting wrongs)*

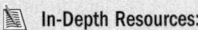 In-Depth Resources: Unit 1
· Skillbuilder Practice: Clarifying, p. 64

**AMENDMENT 6. RIGHT TO A SPEEDY, PUBLIC TRIAL (1791)** In all criminal prosecutions, the accused shall enjoy the right to a speedy and public trial, by an impartial jury of the state and district wherein the crime shall have been committed, which district shall have been previously ascertained by law, and to be informed of the nature and cause of the accusation; to be confronted with the witnesses against him; to have compulsory process for obtaining witnesses in his favor, and to have the assistance of counsel for his defense.

**AMENDMENT 7. TRIAL BY JURY IN CIVIL CASES (1791)** In suits at common law, where the value in controversy shall exceed twenty dollars, the right of trial by jury shall be preserved, and no fact tried by a jury shall be otherwise reexamined in any court of the United States, than according to the rules of the common law.

**AMENDMENT 8. LIMITS OF FINES AND PUNISHMENTS (1791)** Excessive bail shall not be required, nor excessive fines imposed, nor cruel and unusual punishments inflicted.

**AMENDMENT 9. RIGHTS OF PEOPLE (1791)** The enumeration in the Constitution, of certain rights, shall not be construed to deny or disparage others retained by the people.

**AMENDMENT 10. POWERS OF STATES AND PEOPLE (1791)** The powers not delegated to the United States by the Constitution, nor prohibited by it to the states, are reserved to the states respectively, or to the people.

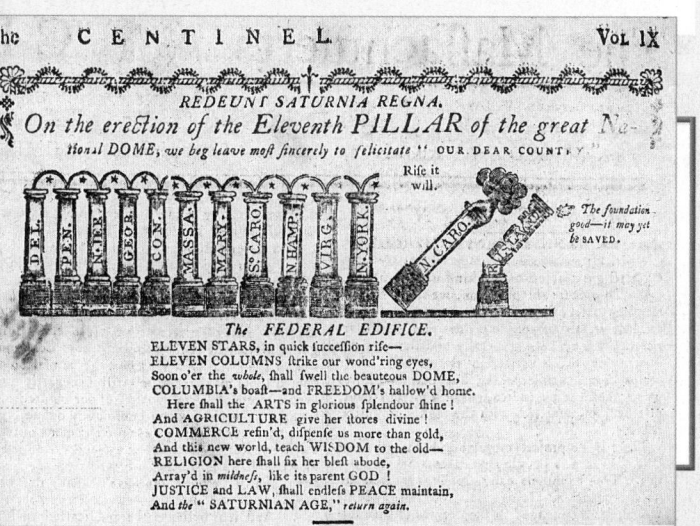

*Constitutional Insight* **Amendment 6**
*What are the Miranda rights?* The term comes from the Supreme Court's decision in *Miranda* v. *Arizona* (1966), in which the justices established basic rules that the police must follow when questioning a suspect. If suspected of a crime, you must be told that you have a right to remain silent and that anything you say "can and will" be used against you. You also need to be informed that you have a right to an attorney and that the attorney may be present during questioning. (See *Miranda* v. *Arizona* on page 694.)

**D CRITICAL THINKING**
How do the Miranda rights protect you?

*Constitutional Insight* **Amendment 7**
*What are the "rules of the common law"?* The common law is the body of legal practices and decrees developed in England and English-speaking America from A.D. 1066 through the present. It includes Magna Carta (1215), which acknowledges versions of rights affirmed in the Fifth, Sixth, and Seventh Amendments, as well as the English Bill of Rights (1689), which codified rights asserted in the First, Second, Seventh, and Eighth Amendments. The common law also includes the decisions and published opinions of state and federal appeals courts, including the U.S. Supreme Court.

*Constitutional Insight* **Amendment 9**
*Do you have a right to privacy?* Until 1965, no such right had ever been explicitly stated by the courts. That year, in the case of *Griswold* v. *Connecticut*, the Court said there is an implied right of American citizens to make certain personal choices without interference from the government; this case concerned the right to use birth control. Years later, in *Roe* v. *Wade* (1973), the same logic was used to declare unconstitutional a Texas law restricting a woman's right to an abortion in the first stages of pregnancy. Since that decision, both the right to privacy and abortion rights have become the focus of major political controversies.

**E CRITICAL THINKING**
How do you define the right to privacy?

**The *Miranda* Case**
The Supreme Court case *Miranda* v. *Arizona* involved a man named Ernesto Miranda, who was charged with kidnapping and rape. After being questioned by police, he confessed and signed a written statement. However, he had never been told that he had a right to say nothing or to have a lawyer. A jury convicted him, based on his written confession.

**Cruel and Unusual Punishment**
In 1972, the Supreme Court ruled that the death penalty itself was not "cruel and unusual" punishment. However, the Court said that the way the death penalty was being administered did violate the Constitution, because death penalties were arbitrary and unpredictable. States quickly revised their laws to meet the Court's objections. In 1976, the Court allowed the death penalty under one of these new laws.

### Critical Thinking

**Answers**

A. One person's freedom of speech may infringe on another's personal freedom.

B. Most oppose invasion of privacy and want protection against arbitrary police searches.

C. The first trial verdict would have no enduring validity.

D. They protect citizens from being forced into divulging information that might be used to convict them of a crime.

E. The guarantee that government will not intrude in people's personal lives and dictate their decisions.

### Restating the Bill of Rights

To help students understand their rights and the impact of the Bill of Rights on their lives, have them select one of the following amendments: 1, 2, 4, 5, 6, or 8. Have students work in pairs to use the headings to gain the main idea of the amendment. Next, have them look for details about the main idea. Finally, have them write out the selected amendment in their own words. Have them list one or more ways this amendment affects people's lives today.

## OBJECTIVE

 Summarize Amendments 11-27.

# Focus & Motivate

Ask students to think about how parents change the standards for their children's behavior as time passes. Why do parents drop some old rules and create new ones?

# Instruct

## Instruct: Objective

### Amendments 11-27

TAKS SS11 4(US7.A)

· How do Amendments 11-27 reflect the ways the Constitution has developed to meet the changing needs of society?

· What amendments ensure voting rights for specific groups in society?

📖 In-Depth Resources: Unit 1
· Guided Reading, p. 68

## NOW & THEN

### Election Reform

**Forming and Supporting Opinions** Which of the proposed election reforms discussed here do you think would help the most? Explain why. *(Answers will vary; accept all reasonable responses.)*

## Critical Thinking

### Answers

F. It reflected the growing role of political parties in nominating presidential and vice-presidential candidates.

G. Agree—If separate facilities that vary widely in quality are vehicles for fostering discrimination. Disagree—if separate facilities are uniform in quality.

---

**Constitutional Insight** Amendment 12
*How did the election of 1800 lead to the Twelfth Amendment?* The election ended in a tie vote between the Republican running mates. The election was decided in Jefferson's favor on the House's 36th ballot. Almost immediately Alexander Hamilton and others designed an amendment that established that the presidential electors would vote for both a presidential and a vice-presidential candidate. This amendment prevents a repeat of the problem experienced in the 1800 election.

 **CRITICAL THINKING**
Why is the Twelfth Amendment important?

### NOW & THEN

**ELECTION REFORM**

A new wave of electoral reform efforts was triggered by the controversial presidential election of 2000, in which George W. Bush's narrow victory over Al Gore left many Americans questioning the system in which a candidate can lose the popular vote but win the election.

Eliminating or reworking the Electoral College has been historically the most frequently proposed constitutional amendment. Other reform proposals have included improving access to polling places by allowing voting on weekend hours or making Election Day a national holiday. Still other proposals would modernize inaccurate polling and counting machines or replace them with computer stations or online voting.

---

##  *Amendments 11–27*

**AMENDMENT 11. LAWSUITS AGAINST STATES (1795)** Passed by Congress March 4, 1794. Ratified February 7, 1795.
*Note: Article 3, Section 2, of the Constitution was modified by the Eleventh Amendment.*

The Judicial power of the United States shall not be construed to extend to any suit in law or equity, commenced or prosecuted against one of the United States by citizens of another state, or by citizens or subjects of any foreign state.

**AMENDMENT 12. ELECTION OF EXECUTIVES (1804)** Passed by Congress December 9, 1803. Ratified June 15, 1804.
*Note: A portion of Article 2, Section 1, of the Constitution was superseded by the Twelfth Amendment.*

The electors shall meet in their respective states and vote by ballot for President and Vice-President, one of whom, at least, shall not be an inhabitant of the same state with themselves; they shall name in their ballots the person voted for as President, and in distinct ballots the person voted for as Vice-President, and they shall make distinct lists of all persons voted for as President, and of all persons voted for as Vice-President, and of the number of votes for each, which lists they shall sign and certify, and transmit sealed to the seat of the government of the United States, directed to the President of the Senate;—the President of the Senate shall, in the presence of the Senate and House of Representatives, open all the certificates and the votes shall then be counted;—the person having the greatest number of votes for President shall be the President, if such number be a majority of the whole number of electors appointed; and if no person have such majority, then from the persons having the highest numbers not exceeding three on the list of those voted for as President, the House of Representatives shall choose immediately, by ballot, the President. But in choosing the President, the votes shall be taken by states, the representation from each state having one vote; a quorum for this purpose shall consist of a member or members from two thirds of the states, and a majority of all the states shall be necessary to a choice. And if the House of Representatives shall not choose a President whenever the right of choice shall devolve upon them, ~~before the fourth day of March next following,~~ then the Vice-President shall act as President, as in the case of the death or other constitutional disability of the President. The person having the greatest number of votes as Vice-President shall be the Vice-President, if such number be a majority of the whole number of electors appointed, and if no person have a majority, then from the two highest numbers on the list, the Senate shall choose the Vice-President; a quorum for the purpose shall consist of two thirds of the whole number of Senators, and a majority of the whole number shall be necessary to a choice. But no person constitutionally ineligible to the office of President shall be eligible to that of Vice-President of the United States.

**AMENDMENT 13. SLAVERY ABOLISHED (1865)** Passed by Congress January 31, 1865. Ratified December 6, 1865.
*Note: A portion of Article 4, Section 2, of the Constitution was superseded by the Thirteenth Amendment.*

---

**DIFFERENTIATING INSTRUCTION** | **LESS PROFICIENT READERS**

## Summarizing Main Ideas

Pair less proficient readers with more proficient ones to summarize key points of Amendments 11–27. Have student pairs follow these steps:

· Skim pages 98–103, noting the boldfaced titles of the amendments and sections.

· Read each amendment, along with any accompanying Constitutional Insight.

· Rewrite the amendment title as a main-idea sentence, highlighting the most important concept.

To help students get started, you may wish to write these examples on the chalkboard as models:

Amendment 12: Presidential electors will cast votes for president and vice-president on separate ballots.

Amendment 13: Slavery must end in the United States and its territories.

**SECTION 1** Neither slavery nor involuntary servitude, except as a punishment for crime whereof the party shall have been duly convicted, shall exist within the United States, or any place subject to their jurisdiction.

**SECTION 2** Congress shall have power to enforce this article by appropriate legislation.

**AMENDMENT 14. CIVIL RIGHTS (1868)** Passed by Congress June 13, 1866. Ratified July 9, 1868.

*Note: Article 1, Section 2, of the Constitution was modified by Section 2 of the Fourteenth Amendment.*

**SECTION 1** All persons born or naturalized in the United States, and subject to the jurisdiction thereof, are citizens of the United States and of the state wherein they reside. No state shall make or enforce any law which shall abridge the privileges or immunities of citizens of the United States; nor shall any state deprive any person of life, liberty, or property, without due process of law; nor deny to any person within its jurisdiction the equal protection of the laws.

**SECTION 2** Representatives shall be apportioned among the several states according to their respective numbers, counting the whole number of persons in each state, excluding Indians not taxed. But when the right to vote at any election for the choice of electors for President and Vice-President of the United States, Representatives in Congress, the executive and judicial officers of a state, or the members of the legislature thereof, is denied to any of the male inhabitants of such state, being twenty-one years of age, and citizens of the United States, or in any way abridged, except for participation in rebellion, or other crime, the basis of representation therein shall be reduced in the proportion which the number of such male citizens shall bear to the whole number of male citizens twenty-one years of age in such state.

**SECTION 3** No person shall be a Senator or Representative in Congress, or elector of President and Vice-President, or hold any office, civil or military, under the United States, or under any state, who, having previously taken an oath, as a member of Congress, or as an officer of the United States, or as a member of any state legislature, or as an executive or judicial officer of any state, to support the Constitution of the United States, shall have engaged in insurrection or rebellion against the same, or given aid or comfort to the enemies thereof. But Congress may, by a vote of two thirds of each house, remove such disability.

**SECTION 4** The validity of the public debt of the United States, authorized by law, including debts incurred for payment of pensions and bounties for services in suppressing insurrection or rebellion, shall not be questioned. But neither the United States nor any state shall assume or pay any debt or obligation incurred in aid of insurrection or rebellion against the United States, or any claim for the loss or emancipation of any slave; but all such debts, obligations and claims shall be held illegal and void.

**SECTION 5** The Congress shall have power to enforce, by appropriate legislation, the provisions of this article.

*Constitutional Insight* Amendment 14, Section 1 *Which personal status takes priority—that of U.S. citizen or that of state citizen?* The Fourteenth Amendment firmly notes that Americans are citizens of both the nation and the states but that no state can "abridge the privileges or immunities" of U.S. citizens, deprive them "of life, liberty, or property, without due process of law," or deny them "equal protection of the laws."
*What does it mean to have "equal protection of the laws"?* Equal protection means that the laws are to be applied to all persons in the same way. The legal system may discriminate between persons—treat them differently, or unequally—if there are relevant reasons to do so. For example, a person's income and number of dependants are relevant for how much income tax the person should pay; a person's gender is not. The Supreme Court's 1954 decision in *Brown v. Board of Education of Topeka* (see page 708), which declared segregated public schools unconstitutional, was based on an Equal Protection claim; a child's race is not a relevant reason for the state to assign that child to a particular school.

**G CRITICAL THINKING**
Do you agree or disagree with the Supreme Court's decision that separate educational facilities are unequal? Explain your position.

The lawyers who successfully challenged segregation in the *Brown v. Board of Education* case in 1954 included (*left to right*) George E. C. Hayes, Thurgood Marshall, and James M. Nabrit, Jr.

## Tracing Themes
### CIVIL RIGHTS

### Affirmative Action
In the 1960s, the government began promoting affirmative action to help African Americans, women, and other minorities gain education and jobs. Affirmative-action programs involve making special efforts to hire or enroll groups that have suffered from discrimination in the past. In the late 1970s, some people began to criticize these programs as "reverse discrimination," claiming the programs that set hiring or enrollment quotas deprived whites of opportunities. Affirmative action continues to be an issue of debate today.

## More About . . .

### Thurgood Marshall (1908–1993)
Recalling his reaction to the *Brown* v. *Board of Education* ruling, Thurgood Marshall declared, "I was so happy, I was numb." The outcome of the case—Marshall's most stunning victory up to that time—heralded his brilliant legal career to come. In 1967, he became the first African American to serve as a Supreme Court justice. He dedicated his life to championing civil rights and battling racial injustice.

In-Depth Resources: Unit 1
· American Lives: Thurgood Marshall, p. 72

---

**ACTIVITY  LINK TO ART**

### Creating a Mural

**Class Time** 45 minutes

**Task** Creating a design for a mural

**Purpose** To identify the impact on American society of the Thirteenth, Fourteenth, and Fifteenth Amendments

**Directions** Divide the class into small groups, and have each group design an outdoor mural—using drawing paper and art supplies—to show how the Thirteenth, Fourteenth, and Fifteenth amendments have changed life in the United States. Post all the designs and create a final design by combining ideas from all the plans. The class may wish to paint the design on a large roll of paper.

Integrated Assessment
· Rubric 4

## More About . . .

### Income Tax

A pay-as-you-go tax plan began in 1943. It provided for employers to withhold tax from employees' paychecks and send the money directly to the Internal Revenue Service. On April 15 of each year, taxpayers file a tax return stating how much taxable income they received the previous year. If the amount withheld is less than they are required to pay according to a tax rate schedule, they must pay additional taxes. If it is more than they are required to pay, they receive a refund.

## More About . . .

### Prohibition and Bootlegging

One effect of the Prohibition amendment was to create an illegal trade in alcohol. That trade was run by "bootleggers." The term comes from the practice of hiding flasks of liquor in a boot top. Bootleggers developed an entire chain of distribution from distillers or brewers to bars. Those bars often were called "speakeasies," because of the need for patrons to speak quietly to avoid attracting police attention.

---

***Constitutional Insight*** Amendment 15
*Can you be denied the right to vote?* The Fifteenth Amendment prohibits the United States or any state from keeping citizens from voting because of race or color or because they were once slaves. However, a person convicted of a crime can be denied the right to vote, as can someone found to be mentally incompetent.

**H** CRITICAL THINKING
Why do you think so many people do not exercise the right to vote?

***Constitutional Insight*** Amendment 16
*How has the ability of Congress to impose taxes been amended?* The Sixteenth Amendment permits a federal income tax and in so doing changes Article 1, Section 9, Clause 4, by stating that Congress has the power to levy an income tax—which is a direct tax—without apportioning such a tax among the states according to their populations.

**I** CRITICAL THINKING
Do you think Congress should have the power to impose an income tax on the people of the nation? Explain your answer.

***Constitutional Insight*** Amendment 17
*How has the way senators are elected been changed?* The Seventeenth Amendment changes Article 1, Section 3, Clause 1, by stating that senators shall be elected by the people of each state rather than by the state legislatures.

**J** CRITICAL THINKING
Why is the direct election of senators by the people of each state important?

Federal agents enforcing the Eighteenth Amendment prepare to smash containers of illegal whiskey.

**100** THE LIVING CONSTITUTION

---

**AMENDMENT 15. RIGHT TO VOTE (1870)** Passed by Congress February 26, 1869. Ratified February 3, 1870.

**SECTION 1** The right of citizens of the United States to vote shall not be denied or abridged by the United States or by any state on account of race, color, or previous condition of servitude.

**SECTION 2** The Congress shall have power to enforce this article by appropriate legislation.

**AMENDMENT 16. INCOME TAX (1913)** Passed by Congress July 12, 1909. Ratified February 3, 1913.
*Note: Article 1, Section 9, of the Constitution was modified by the Sixteenth Amendment.*

The Congress shall have power to lay and collect taxes on incomes, from whatever source derived, without apportionment among the several states, and without regard to any census or enumeration.

**AMENDMENT 17. DIRECT ELECTION OF SENATORS (1913)** Passed by Congress May 13, 1912. Ratified April 8, 1913.
*Note: Article 1, Section 3, of the Constitution was modified by the Seventeenth Amendment.*

**CLAUSE 1** The Senate of the United States shall be composed of two Senators from each state, elected by the people thereof, for six years; and each Senator shall have one vote. The electors in each state shall have the qualifications requisite for electors of the most numerous branch of the state legislatures.

**CLAUSE 2** When vacancies happen in the representation of any state in the Senate, the executive authority of such state shall issue writs of election to fill such vacancies: Provided, that the legislature of any state may empower the executive thereof to make temporary appointments until the people fill the vacancies by election as the legislature may direct.

**CLAUSE 3** This amendment shall not be so construed as to affect the election or term of any Senator chosen before it becomes valid as part of the Constitution.

**AMENDMENT 18. PROHIBITION (1919)** Passed by Congress December 18, 1917. Ratified January 16, 1919. Repealed by Amendment 21.

**SECTION 1** After one year from the ratification of this article the manufacture, sale, or transportation of intoxicating liquors within, the importation thereof into, or the exportation thereof from the United States and all territory subject to the jurisdiction thereof for beverage purposes is hereby prohibited.

**SECTION 2** The Congress and the several states shall have concurrent power to enforce this article by appropriate legislation.

**SECTION 3** This article shall be inoperative unless it shall have been ratified as an amendment to the Constitution by the legislatures of the several states, as provided in the Constitution, within seven years from the date of the submission hereof to the states by the Congress.

---

| ACTIVITY | LINK TO WORLD HISTORY |  classzone.com |

### Researching Suffrage Movements

**Class Time** 45 minutes

**Task** Tracing woman suffrage movements in other parts of the world

**Purpose** To identify the links between the American suffrage movement and similar movements in other countries

**Directions** Divide students into small groups. They should use library or Internet resources to research suffrage movements both in the United States and in other countries. Tell them to look for connections or comparisons among the various movements. Next, each group should create a graphic to illustrate the information that they have found. The graphic could be a time line, a world map, a sequence chart, or another visual means of showing the information.

Integrated Assessment
· Rubrics 1, 2, 4

**AMENDMENT 19. WOMAN SUFFRAGE (1920)** Passed by Congress June 4, 1919. Ratified August 18, 1920.

**CLAUSE 1** The right of citizens of the United States to vote shall not be denied or abridged by the United States or by any state on account of sex.

**CLAUSE 2** Congress shall have power to enforce this article by appropriate legislation.

**AMENDMENT 20. "LAME DUCK" SESSIONS (1933)** Passed by Congress March 2, 1932. Ratified January 23, 1933.

*Note: Article 1, Section 4, of the Constitution was modified by Section 2 of this amendment. In addition, a portion of the Twelfth Amendment was superseded by Section 3.*

**SECTION 1** The terms of the President and Vice-President shall end at noon on the 20th day of January, and the terms of Senators and Representatives at noon on the 3rd day of January, of the years in which such terms would have ended if this article had not been ratified; and the terms of their successors shall then begin.

**SECTION 2** The Congress shall assemble at least once in every year, and such meeting shall begin at noon on the 3rd day of January, unless they shall by law appoint a different day.

**SECTION 3** If, at the time fixed for the beginning of the term of the President, the President elect shall have died, the Vice-President elect shall become President. If a President shall not have been chosen before the time fixed for the beginning of his term, or if the President elect shall have failed to qualify, then the Vice-President elect shall act as President until a President shall have qualified; and the Congress may by law provide for the case wherein neither a President elect nor a Vice-President elect shall have qualified, declaring who shall then act as President, or the manner in which one who is to act shall be selected, and such person shall act accordingly until a President or Vice-President shall have qualified.

**SECTION 4** The Congress may by law provide for the case of the death of any of the persons from whom the House of Representatives may choose a President whenever the right of choice shall have devolved upon them, and for the case of the death of any of the persons from whom the Senate may choose a Vice-President whenever the right of choice shall have devolved upon them.

**SECTION 5** Sections 1 and 2 shall take effect on the 15th day of October following the ratification of this article.

**SECTION 6** This article shall be inoperative unless it shall have been ratified as an amendment to the Constitution by the legislatures of three fourths of the several states within seven years from the date of its submission.

**AMENDMENT 21. REPEAL OF PROHIBITION (1933)** Passed by Congress February 20, 1933. Ratified December 5, 1933.

**SECTION 1** The eighteenth article of amendment to the Constitution of the United States is hereby repealed.

**SECTION 2** The transportation or importation into any state, territory, or possession of the United States for delivery or use therein of intoxicating liquors, in violation of the laws thereof, is hereby prohibited.

---

*Constitutional Insight* Amendment 19
*When did women first get the right to vote in the United States?* Women had the right to vote in the state of New Jersey between 1776 and 1807. In the late 19th century, some states and territories began to extend full or limited suffrage to women. Then, in 1920, the Nineteenth Amendment prohibited the United States or any state from denying women the right to vote.

**Ⓚ CRITICAL THINKING**
How does the right of women to vote affect politics today?

*Constitutional Insight* Amendment 20
*Why is the Twentieth Amendment usually called the "Lame Duck" amendment?* A lame duck is a person who continues to hold office after his or her replacement has been elected. Such a person is called a lame duck because he or she no longer has any strong political influence. The Twentieth Amendment reduces the time between the election of a new president and vice-president in November and their assumption of the offices, which it sets at January 20 instead of March 4. It also reduces the time new members of Congress must wait to take their seats from 4 months to about 2 months. They are now seated on January 3 following the November election. As a result, the lame duck period is now quite short.

**Ⓛ CRITICAL THINKING**
Why may the framers have specified a longer lame duck period?

*Constitutional Insight* Amendment 21
*What is unique about the Twenty-first Amendment?* Besides being the only amendment that explicitly repeals another, it was the first, and is so far the only one, to have been ratified by the state convention method outlined in Article 5. Congress, probably fearing that state legislatures would not deal swiftly with the issue of repeal, chose to have each state call a special convention to consider the amendment. The strategy worked well, for the elected delegates to the conventions represented public opinion on the issue and ratified the amendment without delay.

**Ⓜ CRITICAL THINKING**
Why is it necessary to pass another amendment to revoke or remove an existing amendment?

---

## Tracing Themes
### WOMEN AND POLITICAL POWER

### Woman Suffrage
By 1920, women had full voting rights in 15 states. Twelve other states granted them the right to vote in presidential elections. The Nineteenth Amendment had strong support in the House of Representatives in 1918. One representative left his wife's deathbed, at her request, to vote for the amendment. Another representative was brought in on a stretcher. The amendment passed the House but was defeated in the Senate until 1919.

## Critical Thinking

### Answers
H. Voter apathy may lead to lack of awareness of candidates and issues.

I. Yes—Americans demand services from the federal government that must be paid for. No—The burden of an income tax falls most heavily on the poor and middle class.

J. The senators are more directly responsible to the voters.

K. Higher voter turnout, more women candidates and office holders, and greater focus on women's issues.

L. In the late 1700s, representatives spent a much longer time traveling from their home states to the nation's capital.

M. To ensure an orderly legal procedure.

---

**ACTIVITY COOPERATIVE LEARNING**     **BLOCK SCHEDULING**

### Preparing Voting Requirements

**Class Time** 45 minutes

**Task** Discussing voting requirements that students would like enacted for the next election

**Purpose** To gain insight into the decision-making process for establishing voting rights

**Directions** Divide students into groups of six. Each group will address the following questions:

· Should the voting age be amended?
· Who do you think should be eligible to vote?

· Should anyone's voting rights be denied? If so, whose?
· Do you think that voting should be limited to people who are able to read and write?
· Should an elementary school diploma be a voting requirement? What about a high school diploma?
· Should military or community service be a requirement?

Groups should discuss their voting requirements with the class.

*The Living Constitution* **101**

## NOW & THEN

### Congressional Term Limits

**Forming Opinions** The issue of restricting the term of office for senators and representatives still sparks debate. Those who serve for several terms compile a wealth of legislative experience and contribute to the stability of Congress. Do you think forcing experienced leaders to leave Congress because of term limits would disrupt this stability? Why or why not?

## More About . . .

### Roosevelt's Four Terms

When Franklin Roosevelt accepted the nomination for a third term, even some of his strongest supporters objected. His previous vice-president, John Nance Garner, was among those who disagreed. With war raging in Europe and economic depression still a threat in the United States, Roosevelt ran in 1944 on the idea that the country shouldn't "switch horses in the middle of the stream." As World War II continued, Roosevelt won a fourth term. Fearing an "imperial presidency," Congress took steps to institutionalize the custom of a two-term presidency. The Twenty-Second Amendment guaranteed that no future president would match FDR's record.

### NOW & THEN

#### CONGRESSIONAL TERM LIMITS

In 1995, the Supreme Court struck down all state laws limiting congressional terms, stating that they were unconstitutional. The Court ruled that only a constitutional amendment—such as the Twenty-second, which limits the president to two terms—could impose term limits on members of Congress.

Proposed constitutional amendments for Congressional term limits were defeated in Congress in 1995 and in 1997.

*Constitutional Insight* **Amendment 23**
*Why were residents of the District of Columbia without a vote in presidential elections?* First, the district was merely an idea at the time the Constitution was written. Second, no one expected the district to include many residents. Third, the framers designed the electoral college on a state framework. By 1960, however, the fact that nearly 800,000 Americans living in the nation's capital could not vote in presidential elections was an embarrassment. The Twenty-third Amendment gives Washington, D.C., residents the right to vote in presidential elections by assigning them electoral votes.

**Ⓝ CRITICAL THINKING**
Do you think the District of Columbia should be made a separate state?

*Constitutional Insight* **Amendment 24**
*Why was the poll tax an issue important enough to require an amendment?* The poll tax was used in some places to prevent African-American voters—at least the many who were too poor to pay the tax—from participating in elections. As the civil rights movement gained momentum, the abuse of the poll tax became a major issue, but the national government found it difficult to change the situation because the constitutional provisions in Article 1, Section 4, leave the qualifications of voters in the hands of the states. The Twenty-fourth Amendment changed this by prohibiting the United States or any state from including payment of any tax as a requirement for voting.

**Ⓞ CRITICAL THINKING**
What impact do you think the Twenty-fourth Amendment has had on elections?

**SECTION 3** This article shall be inoperative unless it shall have been ratified as an amendment to the Constitution by conventions in the several states, as provided in the Constitution, within seven years from the date of the submission hereof to the states by the Congress.

**AMENDMENT 22. LIMIT ON PRESIDENTIAL TERMS (1951)** Passed by Congress March 21, 1947. Ratified February 27, 1951.

**SECTION 1** No person shall be elected to the office of the President more than twice, and no person who has held the office of President, or acted as President, for more than two years of a term to which some other person was elected President shall be elected to the office of the President more than once. ~~But this article shall not apply to any person holding the office of President when this article was proposed by the Congress, and shall not prevent any person who may be holding the office of President, or acting as President, during the term within which this article becomes operative from holding the office of President or acting as President during the remainder of such term.~~

**SECTION 2** This article shall be inoperative unless it shall have been ratified as an amendment to the Constitution by the legislatures of three fourths of the several states within seven years from the date of its submission to the states by the Congress.

**AMENDMENT 23. VOTING IN DISTRICT OF COLUMBIA (1961)** Passed by Congress June 17, 1960. Ratified March 29, 1961.

**SECTION 1** The district constituting the seat of government of the United States shall appoint in such manner as Congress may direct:

A number of electors of President and Vice-President equal to the whole number of Senators and Representatives in Congress to which the district would be entitled if it were a state, but in no event more than the least populous state; they shall be in addition to those appointed by the states, but they shall be considered, for the purposes of the election of President and Vice-President, to be electors appointed by a state; and they shall meet in the district and perform such duties as provided by the twelfth article of amendment.

**SECTION 2** The Congress shall have power to enforce this article by appropriate legislation.

**AMENDMENT 24. ABOLITION OF POLL TAXES (1964)** Passed by Congress August 27, 1962. Ratified January 23, 1964.

**SECTION 1** The right of citizens of the United States to vote in any primary or other election for President or Vice-President, for electors for President or Vice-President, or for Senator or Representative in Congress, shall not be denied or abridged by the United States or any state by reason of failure to pay any poll tax or other tax.

**SECTION 2** The Congress shall have power to enforce this article by appropriate legislation.

**AMENDMENT 25. PRESIDENTIAL DISABILITY, SUCCESSION (1967)** Passed by Congress July 6, 1965. Ratified February 10, 1967.
*Note: Article 2, Section 1, of the Constitution was affected by the Twenty-fifth Amendment.*

---

**ACTIVITY** **COOPERATIVE LEARNING**

 **classzone.com**

### Debating Term Limits

**Class Time** Two class periods

**Task** Debating the idea of term limits

**Purpose** To pose and answer questions about the proposal to limit the number of terms that a person can serve in Congress

**Directions** Divide the class into two sections. Direct one group to present arguments in favor of term limits and the other, arguments against limits. Have students research their side and write out a minimum of three questions and answers supporting their position. Next, divide the class into sets of four—two students from the pro side with two students from the con side. Let the students conduct their debates within these small-group settings, using the questions and answers that they generated.

**SECTION 1.** In case of the removal of the President from office or of his death or resignation, the Vice-President shall become President.

**SECTION 2** Whenever there is a vacancy in the office of the Vice-President, the President shall nominate a Vice-President who shall take office upon confirmation by a majority vote of both houses of Congress.

**SECTION 3** Whenever the President transmits to the President pro tempore of the Senate and the Speaker of the House of Representatives his written declaration that he is unable to discharge the powers and duties of his office, and until he transmits to them a written declaration to the contrary, such powers and duties shall be discharged by the Vice-President as Acting President.

**SECTION 4** Whenever the Vice-President and a majority of either the principal officers of the executive departments or of such other body as Congress may by law provide, transmit to the President pro tempore of the Senate and the Speaker of the House of Representatives their written declaration that the President is unable to discharge the powers and duties of his office, the Vice-President shall immediately assume the powers and duties of the office as Acting President.

Thereafter, when the President transmits to the President pro tempore of the Senate and the Speaker of the House of Representatives his written declaration that no inability exists, he shall resume the powers and duties of his office unless the Vice-President and a majority of either the principal officers of the executive department[s] or of such other body as Congress may by law provide, transmit within four days to the President pro tempore of the Senate and the Speaker of the House of Representatives their written declaration that the President is unable to discharge the powers and duties of his office. Thereupon Congress shall decide the issue, assembling within forty-eight hours for that purpose if not in session. If the Congress, within twenty-one days after receipt of the latter written declaration, or, if Congress is not in session, within twenty-one days after Congress is required to assemble, determines by two thirds vote of both houses that the President is unable to discharge the powers and duties of his office, the Vice-President shall continue to discharge the same as Acting President; otherwise, the President shall resume the powers and duties of his office.

**AMENDMENT 26. 18-YEAR-OLD VOTE (1971)** Proposed by Congress March 23, 1971. Ratified July 1, 1971.

> Note: Amendment 14, Section 2, of the Constitution was modified by Section 1 of the Twenty-sixth Amendment.

**SECTION 1** The right of citizens of the United States, who are eighteen years of age or older, to vote shall not be denied or abridged by the United States or by any state on account of age.

**SECTION 2** The Congress shall have power to enforce this article by appropriate legislation.

**AMENDMENT 27. CONGRESSIONAL PAY (1992)** Passed by Congress September 25, 1789. Ratified May 7, 1992.

No law, varying the compensation for the services of the Senators and Representatives, shall take effect, until an election of Representatives shall have intervened.

---

***Constitutional Insight*** Amendment 26
*Why was the Twenty-sixth Amendment passed?* Granting 18-year-olds the right to vote became an issue in the 1960s, during the Vietnam War, when people questioned the justice of requiring 18-year-old men to submit to the military draft but refusing them the right to vote. In 1970, Congress passed a voting rights act giving 18-year-olds the right to vote in elections. When the constitutionality of this act was challenged, the Supreme Court decided that states had to honor the 18-year-old vote for congressional and presidential elections but could retain higher age requirements for state and local elections. To avoid confusion at the polls, the Twenty-sixth Amendment was passed. It guarantees 18-year-olds the right to vote in national and state elections.

**P  CRITICAL THINKING**
Do you think 18-year-olds should have the right to vote? Why or why not?

*(above)* President Richard M. Nixon signs the Twenty-sixth Amendment to the Constitution, adopted in 1971.

***Constitutional Insight*** Amendment 27
*How long did it take to ratify this amendment?* Although the Twenty-seventh Amendment was one of the 12 amendments proposed in 1789 as part of the Bill of Rights, it was not ratified until 1992. This amendment, which deals with congressional compensation, allows the members of Congress to increase Congressional pay, but delays the increase until after a new Congress is seated.

**Q  CRITICAL THINKING**
Do you think members of Congress should be able to vote themselves a pay increase? Explain your answer.

---

### More About . . .

**The Twenty-Fifth Amendment**
In 1973, Vice-President Spiro Agnew resigned from office. Under the provisions of the Twenty-Fifth Amendment, Congress approved President Nixon's appointment of Gerald Ford to fill the vacancy. When Nixon resigned the following year, Ford became president. President Ford then nominated Nelson Rockefeller as vice-president. Congress approved Rockefeller's appointment. That was the only time in the nation's history when neither the sitting president nor the vice-president had been elected to office.

### Critical Thinking

**Answers**

N. Yes—Washington, D.C., residents should have the same privileges as other citizens. No—The capital's size and population are not comparable to those of the other fifty states.

O. The poll tax can no longer be used to keep African Americans from voting; more African-American candidates have won elections.

P. Yes—18-year-olds are capable of learning about candidates and issues, and of making informed decisions. No—they need more life experience to make informed decisions.

Q. Yes—If members abused this privilege, they could be voted out of office. No—As public servants, they should not be granted this privilege.

 **Formal Assessment**
· Living Constitution, Section Quiz, The Amendments, p. 46

---

**ACTIVITY  COOPERATIVE LEARNING**

**BLOCK SCHEDULING**

### Reviewing the Constitution

**Class Time** 45 minutes

**Task** Reviewing the Constitution

**Purpose** To summarize the Constitution in contemporary language

**Directions** Assign groups of four students two articles or sections of the document to summarize in contemporary language. (The number of articles or sections assigned may depend on class size.) All groups will present their summaries, in effect teaching one another the document. Suggest that students create bulleted lists of key points as a study aid.

*The Living Constitution* **103**

TRACING THEMES

## Objectives

· To summarize the expansion of voting rights in America

· To identify constitutional amendments passed to expand voting rights and the year in which each was ratified

## Focus & Motivate

Ask students why they think so many people, especially among those aged 18 to 21, fail to vote. How might people's attitudes toward voting change if the privilege were suddenly denied?

## Tracing Themes

### VOTING RIGHTS

#### The Voting Rights Act of 1965

A landmark of the civil rights movement, the Voting Rights Act of 1965 had several important provisions. One did away with devices such as literacy tests, used in many Southern states to prevent African Americans from voting. Another gave the U.S. attorney general authority to register voters in areas where groups such as African Americans were clearly not voting in reasonable numbers.

# Voting Rights

When the American colonists declared their independence from Great Britain in 1776, their struggle to create a representative government was just beginning. The state constitutions that were drafted at that time established voting rights, but only for certain citizens. Voting rights established by the Articles of Confederation were similarly restricted.

Even the new Constitution that replaced the Articles in 1788 did not extend voting rights to many groups of people living in the new United States. As the Constitution has been amended over the years however, things changed. The right to vote was gradually extended to more and more citizens, enabling them to participate in local and national government.

## 1789

### MALE PROPERTY OWNERS ▶

In the early years of the United States, property qualifications were relaxed in some states (Pennsylvania, Delaware, North Carolina, Georgia, and Vermont) to include all male taxpayers. With few exceptions, women were not allowed to vote. Most state constitutions also required that a voting male be at least 21 years of age.

Those who qualified to vote were generally white, although some states allowed free African Americans to vote.

## 1870

### ◀ AFRICAN-AMERICAN MALES

The Fifteenth Amendment to the Constitution attempted to guarantee African-American males the right to vote by stating that the right of U.S. citizens "to vote shall not be denied or abridged [limited] by the United States or by any state on account of race, color, or previous condition of servitude." The picture to the left shows African-American males voting in a state election in 1867. African-American males, however, were often kept from voting through the use of poll taxes, which were finally abolished by the Twenty-fourth Amendment in 1964, and literacy tests, which were suspended by the Voting Rights Act of 1965.

**104** THE LIVING CONSTITUTION

## RECOMMENDED RESOURCES

### BOOKS

Bott, Alexander J. *Handbook of United States Election Laws and Practices.* Westport, CT: Greenwood, 1991. An in-depth look at ten political rights.

Cultice, Wendell W. *Youth's Battle for the Ballot.* Westport, CT: Greenwood, 1992. Historical changes in America's voting age.

Frost, Elizabeth, and Kathryn Cullen-DuPont. *Women's Suffrage in America.* New York: Facts on File, 1992. Primary sources in the struggle for woman suffrage.

Johnson, Thomas J., et al. *Engaging the Public.* Lanham, MD: Rowman and Littlefield, 1998. Essays examining voter disinterest and possible solutions.

Lusane, Clarence. *No Easy Victories.* Danbury, CT: Franklin, 1996. The African-American struggle for the vote.

### VIDEOS

*One Woman, One Vote.* PBS Video, 1995. TV documentary about the woman suffrage movement.

*United States Elections: How We Vote.* Encyclopaedia Britannica. A walk through the election process.

### SOFTWARE

*U.S. Constitution Tutor.* World Associates, dist. ESI. Tutorial and test on the Constitution.

## 1920

◀ **WOMAN SUFFRAGE**

In 1920, the Nineteenth Amendment, granting voting rights to women, was finally ratified. Elizabeth Cady Stanton, Susan B. Anthony, and many other women, such as those shown at left marching in a woman suffrage parade in 1919, worked tirelessly for women's voting rights.

Four years after ratification of the Nineteenth Amendment, in 1924, citizenship—including the right to vote—was extended to Native Americans.

## 1971

▼ **EIGHTEEN-YEAR-OLD VOTE**

The Twenty-sixth Amendment, ratified in 1971, granted the right to vote to citizens "eighteen years of age or older." Voting rights for young people had become an issue in the 1960s during the Vietnam War. Many people questioned drafting 18-year-olds to fight but refusing them the right to vote. The picture below shows a young woman exercising her new right to vote.

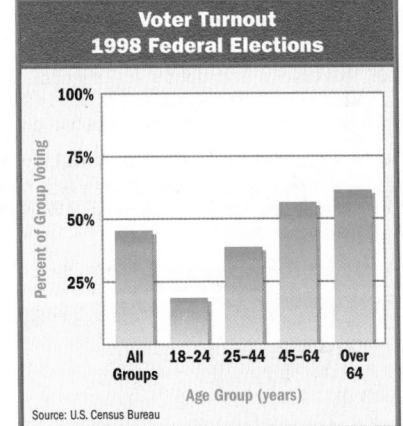

**Voter Turnout 1998 Federal Elections**

Percent of Group Voting

100% / 75% / 50% / 25%

Age Group (years): All Groups, 18–24, 25–44, 45–64, Over 64

Source: U.S. Census Bureau

---

### THINKING CRITICALLY

**CONNECT TO HISTORY**

1. **Forming Generalizations** What does the information on these pages demonstrate about how voting rights in the United States have changed? How did the Constitution help bring about the changes?
   **SEE SKILLBUILDER HANDBOOK, PAGE R21.**

**CONNECT TO TODAY**

2. **Interpreting Data** Research voter turnout statistics from a recent election. What age group scored highest? Which scored lowest?

 **RESEARCH LINKS** CLASSZONE.COM

## MAIN IDEAS

1. House members are elected from congressional districts and Senate members from each state. The legislature makes laws.

2. The number of representatives is based on population, while each state has two senators only.

3. To tax, borrow money, regulate commerce, coin money, establish post offices, create federal courts, declare war, raise armed forces, make laws

4. **Congress may not:** suspend habeas corpus, illegally punish people, levy direct taxes, levy export taxes on goods from any state, show preference among states, take money illegally from the treasury, or confer titles of nobility. **States may not:** use any powers listed in Article 1, Section 10, for example, enter treaties on their own, coin money, illegally imprison people, levy import/export taxes, or engage in war on their own.

5. To carry out the laws made by Congress

6. The electoral college, by vote of the states' electors

7. If convicted of a crime before election time

8. The president nominates them; the Senate approves them.

9. Those appealed from lower courts; not to hear a case means that the lower court ruling stands with no further appeal.

10. It exemplifies cooperation among the states.

11. Three-fourths of the states, or 38 states. Answers about why may vary but should reflect the gravity of the amendment process.

12. It makes the Constitution the supreme law of the land. All laws at every level of government are bound to uphold the Constitution.

13. No, there are limits. For example, you may not yell, "Fire!" in a crowded theater, causing a riot.

14. The Twenty-seventh Amendment. It prevents members of Congress from using taxpayer's money for their own gain.

# THE LIVING CONSTITUTION ASSESSMENT

## MAIN IDEAS

### Article 1. The Legislature

1. Why does the legislative branch of the government represent the people most directly? What is the principal job of this branch?
2. Why are there more members of the House of Representatives than of the Senate?
3. Name four powers Congress has.
4. What powers are denied to Congress? to the states?

### Article 2. The Executive

5. What is the main function of the executive branch?
6. Who officially elects the president of the United States? Explain.
7. How can the president lose his or her job before election time?

### Article 3. The Judiciary

8. How are Supreme Court justices appointed?
9. What kinds of cases go before the Supreme Court? Why is the Court's decision whether to hear a case important?

### Article 4. Relations Among States

10. To extradite is to send a fugitive back to the state in which he or she is accused of committing a crime. How is this an example of relations among states?

### Article 5. Amending the Constitution

11. How many states must ratify an amendment for it to become part of the Constitution? Why do you think it takes that many?

### Article 6. Supremacy of the National Government

12. How does Article 6 establish the supremacy of the Constitution?

### The Amendments

13. Does the First Amendment allow complete freedom of speech—the right to say anything you want at any time, anywhere? Explain your answer.
14. What is the newest amendment? What protection does that amendment give to the American people?

## THINKING CRITICALLY

1. **TAKING NOTES** The powers of the federal government are separated among the three branches. Create a chart like the one below that shows how the Constitution's framers used checks and balances to ensure that no one branch of the government could become too much stronger than the others.

| Executive | Legislative | Judicial |
|-----------|-------------|----------|
|           |             |          |
|           |             |          |

2. **MAKING INFERENCES** How does the Constitution reflect the fear of too strong a central government?

3. **EVALUATING** The Bill of Rights guarantees a defendant a speedy, public trial. Do you think it is being observed today? Explain.

4. **ANALYZING MOTIVES** Why did the framers make it so difficult to amend the Constitution? Do you agree or disagree with their philosophy? Explain.

5. **DEVELOPING HISTORICAL PERSPECTIVE** The Fifteenth, Nineteenth, and Twenty-sixth amendments give voting rights to specific groups. Why was it necessary for Congress to spell out these groups' rights in amendments?

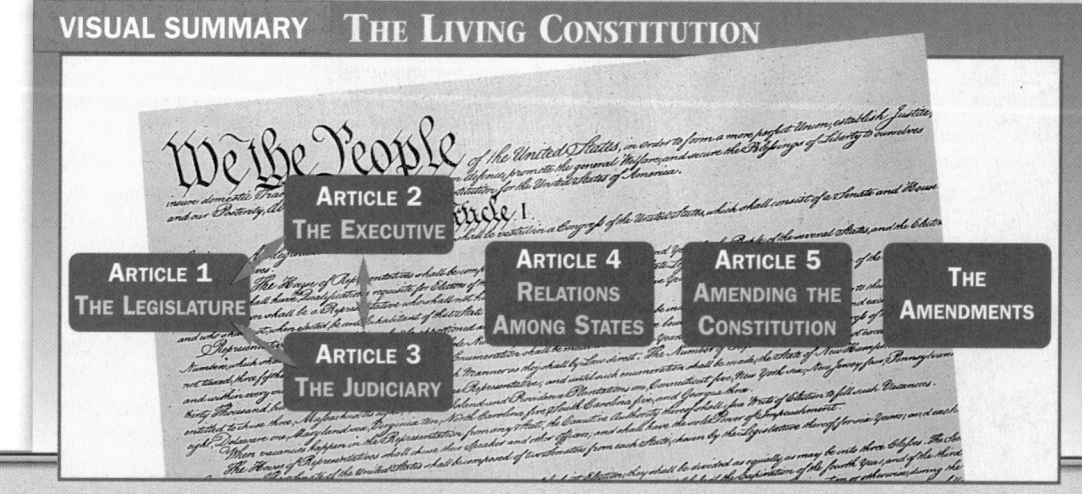

**VISUAL SUMMARY** THE LIVING CONSTITUTION

ARTICLE 1 THE LEGISLATURE · ARTICLE 2 THE EXECUTIVE · ARTICLE 3 THE JUDICIARY · ARTICLE 4 RELATIONS AMONG STATES · ARTICLE 5 AMENDING THE CONSTITUTION · THE AMENDMENTS

## CRITICAL THINKING

1. **Executive:** Checks legislative with vetoes; checks judicial with appointments and reprieves or pardons. **Legislative:** checks executive with controls on spending, veto override, impeachment; checks judicial with lower courts and impeachment. **Judicial:** checks executive and legislative by declaring their acts unconstitutional.

2. The Constitution divides powers among three branches and provides checks by each branch on the others.

3. It is observed today in principle, but the process of honoring a defendant's rights does slow down legal procedures.

4. They did not want the opinion of the times to prompt changes in the law of the land without a great deal of thought.

5. Original voters were white, male property owners. Each of the groups not franchised had to fight for its rights.

## Standardized Test Practice

Use the cartoon and your knowledge of U.S. history to answer question 1.

"It's awful the way they're trying to influence Congress. Why don't they serve cocktails and make campaign contributions like we do?"

1. In the Constitutional Convention, the framers adopted certain principles to be embodied in the Constitution. Which of the following Constitutional principles does the cartoon support?

   A The federal government's power should be divided into separate branches.

   B The federal government should be stronger than the state governments.

   C The federal legislature should be responsive to the will of the people.

   D The legislature and the president should check each other's power.

Use the quotation and your knowledge of U.S. history to answer question 2.

" [The president] shall have power, by and with the advice and consent of the Senate, to make treaties, provided two thirds of the Senators present concur; and he shall nominate, and by and with the advice and consent of the Senate, shall appoint ambassadors, other public ministers and consuls, judges of the Supreme Court, and all other officers of the United States . . ."

—U.S. Constitution, Art. 2, Sec. 2, part 2

2. The passage describes checks on the power of—

   F the president.

   G the Senate.

   H the judiciary.

   J the states.

3. Which of the following must ratify Constitutional amendments?

   A Congress

   B the people

   C the states

   D the president

ADDITIONAL TEST PRACTICE, pages S1–S33.

 **TEST PRACTICE** CLASSZONE.COM

## Standardized Test Practice

1. The correct answer is letter **C**.
   The people are asking Congress for help. Letters A, B, and D are incorrect because the cartoon has nothing to do with the relationship between branches of government.

2. The correct answer is letter **F**.
   The Senate checks the power of the president to make appointments. The letters G, H, and J are incorrect because the passage does not refer to a check on their power.

3. The correct answer is **C**.
   Amendments are ratified by state legislatures. The letters A, B, and D are incorrect because neither Congress, the president, nor the people are involved directly in the ratification process.

### RESEARCHING A CONSTITUTIONAL QUESTION

**Project Presentation Rubrics**

The constitutional question research should . . .

· clearly state the constitutional issue chosen for study

· identify questions researched

· include citations from Supreme Court cases about the issue

· present a bibliography of sources consulted

Formal Assessment
· Living Constitution, Test Forms A, B, and C, pp. 47–55

## ALTERNATIVE ASSESSMENT

1. **Journal Entry** Imagine that it is 1787, and you are a citizen of one of the original thirteen states. Your vote is necessary to ratify the new Constitution that has been approved by the convention in Philadelphia. You have studied the seven articles and listened to spirited discussions about how you and your state will be affected. Write a journal entry in which you express your views about this document that is so important for the new United States. Make sure you include references to what you have read and heard about the Constitution.

2. **INTERNET ACTIVITY** CLASSZONE.COM

   Visit the links for Chapter Assessment to learn more about how bills become law. Because of the process by which bills become laws, problems may occur when the president and a majority of members of Congress are from different political parties. Using the Internet, research bills that were proposed by the president but became stalled in Congress because of party differences. Then divide into groups and do the activity.

   **Cooperative Learning Activity** Have each group research a different bill. Try to follow the debate and see how party differences affected the discussion. Did the bill pass and become law? Present your findings to the class.

## ALTERNATIVE ASSESSMENT

### JOURNAL ENTRY
**Rubric**

The journal entry should. . .

· reflect the student's understanding of basic concepts

· include references to what the student has read and heard about the Constitution

· clearly state the student's views on the Constitution

### INTERNET ACTIVITY
**Rubric**

The report should. . .

· reflect a basic understanding of how the lawmaking process worked regarding the specific bill researched

· present information in a logical, interesting sequence

· discuss the fate of the bill

PROJECTS FOR CITIZENSHIP

# Applying the Constitution

The United States Constitution is admired the world over. But a healthy democracy depends on the continuing participation of its citizens—including you. Here are four projects that will help you learn the rewards and challenges of responsible citizenship.

 **RESEARCH LINKS** CLASSZONE.COM Visit the links for the Constitution for more information that will help you with these Projects for Citizenship.

## OBJECTIVES

**PROJECT 1**
- Learn about candidates currently campaigning for office.
- Evaluate the accuracy and completeness of campaign information.
- Use a range of sources to write an endorsement.

**PROJECT 2**
- Express an opinion on an issue by writing a letter to the editor.
- Explore an issue fully by reading about it and then by developing and supporting an argument about it.

---

## PROJECT 1

### Becoming an Educated Voter
**TIPS FOR TEACHING**

- If students have access to the Internet, they may be able to complete this project in three to five days. Without access, a time line of two weeks is more reasonable.
- If a local campaign is under way, you might invite the candidates to address the class, to send representatives, or to send information.
- Help students sort out fallacies in political advertising, such as either-or thinking, false analogies, and begging the question.

**STANDARDS FOR EVALUATION**

The endorsement should meet the following criteria:
- Includes the candidate's stand on several major issues.
- Incorporates endorsements from news media and interest groups, as well as information from the candidate's party and nonpartisan voting groups.
- Is clearly written and well-supported.
- Is sent to an appropriate media outlet.

📝 In-Depth Resources: Unit 1
 · Projects for Citizenship, p. 73

## PROJECT 2

### Expressing Political Opinions
**TIPS FOR TEACHING**

- Explain that students may choose an international, national, state, or local issue.
- Urge students to identify the most convincing arguments in the letters they gather and analyze why the arguments are effective.

---

## PROJECT 1

### BECOMING AN EDUCATED VOTER

**ENDORSING A CANDIDATE**

Choose a campaign for elective office  and learn about the issues and the candidates in the campaign. After doing your research, write an endorsement, or a statement in favor, of one of the candidates.

**LEARNING ABOUT THE CANDIDATES**

✔ **Examine news media and news services.** During campaigns, some services and publications offer endorsements that explain why particular candidates are worthy of support.

✔ **Get information from political parties.** They provide information on the candidates, but their perspective is biased toward their own candidates. The major parties have Internet sites, as do many local groups and individual candidates.

✔ **Contact interest groups,** such as the Sierra Club and the National Association of Manufacturers. They often list candidates' positions on issues and support candidates who share their beliefs.

✔ **Look at databases and voters' guides** published by nonpartisan organizations such as the League of Women Voters and Project Vote Smart.

As you use each source, try to identify any bias. Think about the following questions.

- What does the author of this source stand to gain from supporting a particular candidate?
- Is the information in the source complete and accurate?
- Does the author use loaded or inflammatory language?

**PRESENTING YOUR PROJECT**

After you have written your endorsement, you might send it to a media outlet, such as a newspaper or a television station, or post it on the Internet. Or you might send it to your local or school newspaper.

- Point out notices in newspapers and magazines that give requirements for letters and where they should be sent.
- Emphasize that persuasive letters maintain an even, reasoned tone.

**STANDARDS FOR EVALUATION**
- The letter to the editor should meet the following criteria:
- Focuses on a single issue.
- Explains the writer's point of view and includes reasons and facts to support it.

---

## PROJECT 2

### EXPRESSING POLITICAL OPINIONS

**WRITING A LETTER TO THE EDITOR**

Identify an issue that concerns you. Then write a letter or send an e-mail message about that issue to the editor of a newspaper or magazine.

**WRITING A PERSUASIVE LETTER**

✔ **Find an issue** that has been in the news lately and about which you feel strongly.

✔ **Read recent articles,** editorials, and cartoons in newspapers or magazines. Notice how they have addressed this issue.

✔ **Compose a letter** that clearly and concisely explains your views about the issue you have chosen. Your letter should also include reasons and facts that support your opinion on the issue. It might also advocate some specific action to be taken to address the issue.

✔ **Identify the person** to whom you should send your letter, and note any requirements the newspaper or magazine has for writing letters to the editor.

✔ **Edit your letter carefully.** Be sure to use standard grammar, spelling, sentence structure, and punctuation.

**PRESENTING YOUR PROJECT**

Present the letter you wrote to the rest of the class. When you do, explain why you chose to write about this issue.

A student expresses her political opinions as she addresses an audience.

- Reflects knowledge of opposing viewpoints and others' approach to the issue.
- Is clearly and concisely written and reflects the standards for submission set by the intended place of publication.

📝 In-Depth Resources: Unit 1
 · Projects for Citizenship, p. 74

## PROJECT 3

### UNDERSTANDING HOW TO LOBBY

#### PLANNING A LOBBYING CAMPAIGN

Form a committee with other students to organize a lobbying campaign—a campaign to influence legislation or public policy. Create a plan for the campaign that includes materials to be presented to government officials. In creating your plan, keep the following points in mind.

#### CREATING A LOBBYING PLAN

✔ **Establish a clear goal** of what you want to achieve. Make sure all members of the group understand and agree with the established goal.

✔ **Identify the appropriate people to lobby**—the people who can best help you to achieve your goal. For example, if your group is planning to lobby to have a bill passed, you would lobby the legislators who will vote on the bill. However, if your group wants to lobby for a local improvement—such as cleaning up an abandoned factory site—you should lobby the local officials who make those decisions.

✔ **Gather statistics** and other information that support your case. Explore a variety of resources, including the library, the Internet, and news services. Conduct interviews with appropriate state or local officials. Use the information you gather to develop a brief written report that can be given to the officials you intend to lobby.

✔ **Organize public opinion** in favor of your case. Gather signatures on petitions or conduct a letter-writing campaign to encourage people who support your goal to contact government officials. You can also create fliers calling attention to your cause.

✔ **Present your case** to government officials firmly but politely. Practice your presentation several times before you actually appear before them.

#### PRESENTING YOUR PROJECT

Share your lobbying plan with the rest of the class in the form of a written proposal that includes materials, such as petition forms, that you will use in your lobbying effort. If you implement your lobbying plan, describe to the class what response you received from the officials you lobbied.

## PROJECT 4

### VOLUNTEERING IN YOUR COMMUNITY

#### MAKING AN ORAL REPORT

Identify a local community organization that you might want to help. Find out what kinds of volunteer activities the organization has, such as answering phones in the office, serving food to the homeless, or cleaning vacant lots. Then volunteer to participate in one of those activities. Prepare an oral report to present to the rest of the class about your experiences as a volunteer. Keep the following points in mind as you choose which organization to help.

A group of young volunteers in the Summer of Service project discusses plans with carpenters.

#### SUGGESTIONS FOR VOLUNTEERING

✔ **Decide what kinds of public service projects might interest you.** You might talk to your parents, a teacher, friends, a local church, or a local political organization to learn what kinds of volunteer services are needed in your community.

✔ **Call local community organizations** to find out what kinds of volunteer opportunities they offer and decide whether you would like to volunteer for those projects.

✔ **Decide what cause you want to support** and identify an organization that addresses that cause.

✔ **Decide what type of work you want to do** and work with that organization.

#### PRESENTING YOUR PROJECT

Deliver an oral report to your class about your experiences as a volunteer. Explain why you chose the specific volunteer activity that you did. Describe the activity you performed. Then explain what effect your volunteering had as well as whether you felt the experience was a good one.

*The Living Constitution* **109**

# The Growth of a Young Nation

| | CHAPTER OVERVIEW | COPYMASTERS | INTEGRATED TECHNOLOGY |
|---|---|---|---|
| **CHAPTER RESOURCES** | In the first half of the 1800s, the United States grows—adding land and people. The economy grows throughout the nation, but the different regions develop varied ways of life and attitudes. | 📄 **Telescoping the Times** · Chapter Summary, pp. 5–6  <br> 📄 **Planning for Block Schedules** | 📹 **American Stories** · "Recruited by Lewis and Clark"  <br> 👁 **Power Presentations**  <br> 👁 **Electronic Teacher Tools**  <br> 🔱 **Online Lesson Planner**  <br> 🔱 **classzone.com** |
| **SECTION 1** <br> The Jeffersonian Era <br> pp. 112–119 | **KEY IDEAS** <br> Thomas Jefferson leads the growing country into the 19th century as it confirms its status as a free and independent nation. | 📄 **In-Depth Resources: Unit 1** · Guided Reading, p. 77 · Building Vocabulary, p. 82 · Skillbuilder Practice, pp. 83, 84 · Reteaching Activity, p. 87 · American Lives, p. 104 <br> 📄 **Lesson Plans,** pp. 25–26 | 🔱 **Critical Thinking Transparencies CT6** · War of 1812 <br> 👁 **Electronic Library of Primary Sources** · Unit 1, Chapter 3 <br> 🔱 **classzone.com** |
| **SECTION 2** <br> The Age of Jackson <br> pp. 120–129 | Sectionalism causes tensions, but a strong national spirit—represented by Andrew Jackson—holds the nation together. | 📄 **In-Depth Resources: Unit 1** · Guided Reading, p. 78 · Reteaching Activity, p. 88 · Outline Map, pp. 94–95 · Primary Sources, pp. 96–97 · American Lives, p. 105 <br> 📄 **Lesson Plans,** pp. 27–28 | 🔱 **Critical Thinking Transparencies CT7, CT41** · Industrial Revolution · Cotton Production and Exports, 1800–1860 <br> 🔱 **Humanities Transparencies HT33** · General Jackson slaying the many headed monster <br> 👁 **Electronic Library of Primary Sources** <br> 🔱 **classzone.com** |
| **SECTION 3** <br> Manifest Destiny <br> pp. 130–138 | Americans continue to move westward toward the Pacific Ocean, and the United States claims new territories—sometimes as the result of war. | 📄 **In-Depth Resources: Unit 1** · Guided Reading, p. 79 · Skillbuilder Practice, p. 85 · Reteaching Activity, p. 89 · Geography Application, pp. 92–93 · Primary Sources, p. 98 · Literature, pp. 101–103 <br> 📄 **Lesson Plans,** pp. 29–30 | 🔱 **Critical Thinking Transparencies CT9, CT43** · Westward movement · Growth of U.S. Population and Area 1790–1850 <br> 🔱 **Humanities Transparencies HT9** · General Winfield Scott <br> 🔱 **classzone.com** |
| **SECTION 4** <br> The Market Revolution <br> pp. 139–143 | The Industrial Revolution comes to America, creating new opportunities for some and new problems for others. | 📄 **In-Depth Resources: Unit 1** · Guided Reading, p. 80 · Reteaching Activity, p. 90 <br> 📄 **Lesson Plans,** pp. 31–32 | 🔱 **Geography Transparencies GT9** · American Cities, 1820 and 1860 <br> 👁 **Electronic Library of Primary Sources** · Unit 1, Chapter 3 <br> 🔱 **classzone.com** |
| **SECTION 5** <br> Reforming American Society <br> pp. 144–151 | As the country's economy and political systems change, a new spiritual awakening and a series of social reform movements sweep the nation. | 📄 **In-Depth Resources: Unit 1** · Guided Reading, p. 81 · Skillbuilder Practice, p. 86 · Reteaching Activity, p. 91 · Primary Sources, pp. 99, 100 <br> 📄 **Lesson Plans,** pp. 33–34 | 🔱 **Geography Transparencies GT8** · Distribution of Slaves <br> 🔱 **Critical Thinking Transparencies CT8** · Reform Movement <br> 🔱 **Humanities Transparencies HT8** · Religious Camp Meeting <br> 👁 **Electronic Library of Primary Sources** <br> 🔱 **classzone.com** |

## ASSESSMENT OPTIONS

- PE Chapter Assessment, pp. 152–153
- Formal Assessment
  · Chapter Tests, Forms A, B, and C, pp. 61–78
- Test Generator
- Integrated Assessment Book
- TAKS Online Test Practice
- TAKS Spiraled Content Review
  TAKS Practice Tests

- PE Section 1 Assessment, p. 117
- TE Self-Assessment, p. 117
- Formal Assessment, Quiz, p. 56
- Integrated Assessment Book
- Test Generator
- TAKS Practice Transparencies TT23, TT24

- PE Section 2 Assessment, p. 127
- TE Self-Assessment, p. 127
- Formal Assessment, Quiz, p. 57
- Integrated Assessment Book
- Test Generator
- TAKS Practice Transparencies TT25–28

- PE Section 3 Assessment, p. 138
- TE Self-Assessment, p. 138
- Formal Assessment, Quiz, p. 58
- Integrated Assessment Book
- Test Generator
- TAKS Practice Transparencies TT34, TT35

- PE Section 4 Assessment, p. 143
- TE Self-Assessment, p. 143
- Formal Assessment, Quiz, p. 59
- Integrated Assessment Book
- Test Generator
- TAKS Practice Transparencies TT33

- PE Section 5 Assessment, p. 149
- TE Self-Assessment, p. 79
- Formal Assessment, Quiz, p. 24
- Integrated Assessment Book
- Test Generator
- TAKS Practice Transparencies TT29–32

## RESOURCES FOR DIFFERENTIATING INSTRUCTION

**Students Acquiring English/ESL**

- **Reading Study Guide**
  (English and Spanish)
  pp. 35–46
- **Access for Students Acquiring English/ESL:**
  Spanish Translations,
  pp. 46–60
- **Chapter Summaries on CD**
  (English and Spanish)

**Less Proficient Readers**

- **Reading Study Guide**
  (English and Spanish)
  pp. 35–46
- **Telescoping the Times**
  · Chapter Summary,
    pp. 5–6
- **Chapter Summaries on CD**
  (English and Spanish)

**Gifted and Talented Students**

- **In-Depth Resources: Unit 1**
  · Primary Sources,
    pp. 96–100
  · Literature, pp. 101–103
  · American Lives: Tecumseh,
    p. 104; Henry Clay, p. 105
- **Electronic Library of Primary Sources**
  · Unit 1, Chapter 3

## CROSS-CURRICULAR CONNECTIONS

**Geography**
Lourie, Peter. *In the Path of Lewis and Clark: Traveling the Missouri.* Englewood Cliffs, NJ: Silver Burdett Press, Inc., 1997. Lourie travels with writer William Least Heat-Moon to retrace the steps of the explorers.

**Culture**
Hilton, Suzanne. *A Capital City, 1790–1814.* NY: Atheneum, 1992. An engaging account of the first 25 years of Washington, D.C.

**Science**
Weitzman, David. *Old Ironsides: Americans Build a Fighting Ship.* Boston: Houghton Mifflin, 1997. Illustrated with detailed charts and drawings.

**Literature**
Bohner, Charles. *Bold Journey: West with Lewis and Clark.* Boston: Houghton Mifflin, 1990. Private Hugh McNeal tells of his travels with Lewis and Clark.

Kingsolver, Barbara. *Pigs in Heaven.* NY: Harper & Rowe, 1994. In this modern novel, a Native American

child is the center of a complex situation involving family and heritage.

Michener, James. *Texas.* NY: Fawcett Books, 1994 . Spanning four and a half centuries, this saga of Texas begins in the early 1500s. Paths of the characters and the descendants cross and recross as the narrative develops.

**McDougal Littell**
*Literature Connections*

Twain, Mark. *The Adventures of Huckleberry Finn (with related readings).* Through a remarkable river journey with two unforgettable characters, Twain captures the essence of mid-19th-century America.

*The Language of Literature*
American Literature: Unit 3, Part 1

## ENRICHMENT ACTIVITIES

- PE **Pupil's Edition, pp. 110–151**
  Interact with History, pp. 110–111
  Historic Supreme Court Decisions, pp. 118–119
  Science and Technology, p. 121
  Tracing Themes, pp. 128–129
  Geography Spotlight, pp. 150–151

- **In-Depth Resources: Unit 1**
  - Geography Application: Mexico Cedes Land to the U.S., pp. 92–93
  · Outline Map: Indian Removal Act, pp. 94–95
  · Primary Sources: from *The Webster-Hayne Debates*, pp. 96–97
  · Primary Sources: from *Polk's Speech on War with Mexico*, p. 98
  · Primary Sources: Propaganda Images, p. 99

  · Primary Sources: from The Seneca Falls "Declaration of Sentiments," p. 100
  · Literature: from *Roughing It*, pp. 101–103
  · American Lives: Tecumseh, p. 104
  · American Lives: Henry Clay, p. 105

- **Electronic Library of Primary Sources**
  · Unit 1, Chapter 3

- **Historic Supreme Court Decisions**
  · *Marbury* v. *Madison* pp. 1–6

- **American Stories**
  · "Recruited by Lewis and Clark"

- **Primary Source Explorer**
  · The Monroe Doctrine, 1823

## BLOCK SCHEDULE LESSON PLAN OPTIONS (90-MINUTE PERIOD)

### DAY 1

**CHAPTER 3 OPENER, pp. 110–111**

**Class Time** 30 minutes

**History from Visuals, p. 110**

**Class Time** 10 minutes

*Options for Pacing and Variety*

· Time Saver Have students look at the picture and the time line on the pages and discuss the questions in the TE. **Class Time** 10 minutes

**Interact with History, p. 111**

**Class Time** 20 minutes

*Options for Pacing and Variety*

· Role-Playing Ask students to read the situation given on the page. Discuss the Examine the Issues questions in the PE and the TE. **Class Time** 15 minutes

**SECTION 1, pp. 112–119**

**Class Time** 60 minutes

*Options for Pacing and Variety*

· Internet Have students read the feature on page 115 on the Lewis and Clark expedition. Then have them use the Internet or library to find a primary source on the journey that details its difficulties. Students should paraphrase the story or anecdote they find and share it with the class. **Class Time** 35 minutes

· Internet Have students read the feature on pages 118–119, "Historic Decisions of The Supreme Court: Marbury v. Madison (1803)," and then answer question 2 to learn more about important cases. **Class Time** 25 minutes

### DAY 2

**SECTION 2, pp. 120–129**

**Class Time** 45 minutes

*Options for Pacing and Variety*

· Time Saver Have students read the quote on the Cherokees in "A Personal Voice" on page 124 and look at the chart on page 125. Ask them to write a paragraph explaining the knowledge they gained from the two different sources. **Class Time** 20 minutes

· Peer Teaching Have students look at the political cartoon on page 126 and discuss the Skillbuilder questions with a partner. **Class Time** 10 minutes

· Peer Competition Ask students to read the feature on pages 128–129, "Tracing Themes: States' Rights." Then have students work on question 2, listing arguments that would help them debate the issues. Write arguments for both sides on the board to help students understand the different perspectives. **Class Time** 30 minutes

**SECTION 3, pp. 130–138**

**Class Time** 45 minutes

*Options for pacing and variety*

· Peer Teaching Have students complete the essay discussing the different points of view on the war with Mexico on TE page 136. Allow them to share their opinions with the class. **Class Time** 30 minutes

· Peer Evaluation Have students individually work on the Section Assessment. Discuss their responses for questions 2 and 3. **Class Time** 25 minutes

### DAY 3

**SECTION 4, pp. 139–143**

**Class Time** 30 minutes

*Options for Pacing and Variety*

· Internet Ask students to read the paragraphs about inventions on pages 142–143. Have students choose one of the inventions to research on the Internet. Students should share their findings with the class. **Class Time** 30 minutes

· Peer Teaching Have students work together to create lists of the mill workers' demands. Refer to TE page 142 for the activity. **Class Time** 20 minutes

· Time Saver Assign the Section Assessment for homework, and then discuss the responses to question 5. **Class Time** 10 minutes

**SECTION 5, pp. 144–151**

**Class Time** 30 minutes

*Options for Pacing and Variety*

· Peer Teaching Have students find a passage from one of the books of fiction or non-fiction mentioned in this section. Have them write a paragraph about the passage that explains why they chose the passage and what is the significance of the passage. Ask a few students to read their passages to the class and have each explain why they chose it. **Class Time** 20 minutes

· Peer Evaluation Have students work in pairs to quiz each other on the terms and names from the section. **Class Time** 10 minutes

### DAY 3 continued

**ASSESSMENT pp. 152–153**

**Class Time** 30 minutes

*Options for Pacing and Variety*

· Internet Give students 20 minutes to complete as much of the Standardized Test Practice as possible. This activity will help them become familiar with working under pressure. Go to **classzone.com** for more test practice. **Class Time** 20 minutes

· Peer Evaluation Ask students to complete the Critical Thinking questions for homework. In class, have them exchange papers and correct errors or add important facts that were missed. **Class Time** 20 minutes

---

**TEACHER-TESTED ACTIVITY**
**AMERICAN PROFILES**

**Dr. Carol D. McCree, DeBakey High School for Health Professionals, Houston, Texas**

**Class Time** 45 minutes

**Task** Profiling Americans during westward expansion

**Purpose** To understand which Americans were the most likely to settle the West

**Supplies Needed**

· Textbooks and library resources
· Poster board
· Markers

**Activity** Have students use poster board to create profiles of typical Americans of the era of westward expansion, such as bankers, missionaries, and traders. Each description should include name (fictitious), age, gender, economic status, ethnicity, job, living conditions, marital status, and so on. Display the profiles and discuss with the class whether or not these characters would have moved west.

## CORRELATION TO THE TEXAS ESSENTIAL KNOWLEDGE AND SKILLS

Chapter 3 addresses the following standards of the Texas Essential Knowledge and Skills for U.S. History.

| TEKS | Instruction | Student Question/Activity |
|---|---|---|
| **(7A)** Trace the historical development of the civil rights movement in the 19th century. | **PE 145–147** discussion of the rise of the abolition movement in America | **TE 146** activity in which students write their own article for the abolition newspaper *The Liberator* |
| **(9B)** Identify and explain reasons for changes in political boundaries. | **PE 116** examination of how the United States gained Florida and the Oregon Territory and established its northern boundary line | **PE 116** map with Skillbuilder questions about the country's boundary settlements |
| **(16B)** Evaluate the impact of events on relations between the legislative, executive, and judicial branches. | **PE 118–119** analysis of the *Marbury* v. *Madison* case, in which the Supreme Court established its right to declare laws unconstitutional | **PE 119** Critical Thinking questions about the landmark court case |
| **(18A)** Identify and analyze the methods of expanding the right to participate in the democratic process. | **PE 123** discussion of the expansion of voting rights during the 1820s, as well as the efforts by Andrew Jackson to promote greater citizen participation in government | **PE 127** writing activity requiring students to demonstrate their knowledge of the term *Jacksonian Democracy* |
| **(19B)** Evaluate the contributions of significant political leaders in the United States. | **PE 112–114** examination of the accomplishments of President Thomas Jefferson | **PE 117** Critical Thinking question about Jefferson's goals as president |
| **(21D)** Identify the political, social, and economic contributions of women to American society. | **PE 147–149** examination of the significant role women played in the nation's various reform movements | **TE 147** Cooperative Activity in which students explore more deeply women's role in the reform movement |
| **(23A)** Analyze how scientific discoveries and technological innovations, including those in transportation and communication, have changed the standard of living in the United States. | **PE 140–141** discussion of the impact of the telegraph on communication as well as the effect of various transportation innovations, including the steamboat and railroads and canals | **PE 143** Primary Sources question about the effect of the inventions and innovations of the time |

## TAKS MINI-LESSONS

1. **Social Studies Skills: Objective 2 (US11.A):** Identify the effects of population growth on the physical environment **Activity** Have students summarize the reason for the wave of western resettlement during the mid-1800s.

2. **Social Studies Skills: Objective 3 (WG10.C):** Compare the ways people satisfy their basic needs through the production of goods and services, such as cottage industries versus commercial industries **Activity** Have students define the market revolution and explain how it changed the nation's economic activity.

3. **Social Studies Skills: Objective 4 (8.18.B):** Describe historical conflicts arising over the issue of states' rights, including the Nullification Crisis **Activity** Have students complete the cooperative activity on TE page 124 regarding the issue of states' rights.

4. **English Language Arts Skills: Objective 3 (7.E):** Analyze text structures, such as cause-and-effect, for how they influence understanding **Activity** Have students create a chart summarizing the causes and effects of the War of 1812.

5. **English Language Arts Skills: Objective 3 (19.B):** Analyze ideas as represented in various media **Activity** Have students answer the questions regarding the political cartoon of Andrew Jackson on page 126.

To analyze the Jefferson Era, the Age of Jackson, manifest destiny, the market revolution, and various reform movements during the first half of the 19th century

REVIEW CHAPTER 3

# THE GROWTH OF A YOUNG NATION

## HISTORY from VISUALS

### Interpreting the Painting

Have students study the painting and suggest words to describe the United States in the early 1800s. *(industrious; prosperous)* Ask students what they think the painting reveals about American involvement in trade. *(America was actively involved in trade.)*

**Extension** Have each student suggest a title for this painting. Ask students to share their ideas with the class.

## Time Line Discussion

Explain to students that this time line spans the first half of the 19th century (1800–1850).

· Ask students approximately how long the War of 1812 lasted. *(two years)*

· Ask students what year and event marked an advance in communications. *(1844—Samuel Morse sends first telegraph message)*

· Ask students to identify British legislation that abolitionists would have supported. *(Britain outlawed slavery in 1833.)*

The port of New Orleans, Louisiana, was a major center for the cotton trade.

**1803** The United States purchases the Louisiana Territory from France.

**1814** The Treaty of Ghent is signed, ending the War of 1812.

**1820** Congress passes the Missouri Compromise.

| USA WORLD | **1800** | **1810** | **1820** |
|---|---|---|---|

**1802** Toussaint L'Ouverture defeats French forces sent to recapture Saint Domingue (Haiti).

**1810** Mexican War of Independence begins.

**1815** Napoleon is defeated at Waterloo.

**1821** Mexico wins its independence from Spain.

| PRESIDENTS | 1800: Thomas Jefferson | 1804: Thomas Jefferson | 1808: James Madison | 1812: James Madison | 1816: James Monroe | 1820: James Monroe | 1824: John Quincy Adams | 1828: Andrew Jackson |
|---|---|---|---|---|---|---|---|---|

**110** CHAPTER 3 *The Growth of a Young Nation*

## THEMES IN CHAPTER 3

### AMERICA IN WORLD AFFAIRS

The United States established a foreign policy—the Monroe Doctrine—to defend American commercial interests and to protect territorial interests.

**See Teacher's Edition Note, p. 114.**

### SCIENCE AND TECHNOLOGY

By the 1830s, new methods of manufacturing had revolutionized industry and transformed New England society.

**See Teacher's Edition Note, p. 121.**

### CIVIL RIGHTS

Although many Americans gained the right to vote, African Americans, Native Americans, and women faced continued discrimination.

**See Teacher's Edition Notes, p. 125, p. 146.**

### IMMIGRATION AND MIGRATION

Americans responded to the Mexican government's advertisement of inexpensive land in Texas and migrated in search of economic prosperity. Some settlers would later rebel against Mexican authority.

**See Teacher's Edition Note, p. 133.**

# INTERACT
## WITH HISTORY

The year is 1828. You are a senator from a Southern state. Congress has just passed a high tax on imported cloth and iron in order to protect Northern industry. The tax will raise the cost of these goods in the South and will cause Britain to buy less cotton. Southern states intend to ignore such federal laws that they consider unfair.

## *Would you support the federal or your state government?*

### Examine the Issues

- What might happen if some states enforce laws and others don't?
- How can Congress address the needs of different states?
- What does it mean to be a nation?

**RESEARCH LINKS** **CLASSZONE.COM**

Visit the Chapter 3 links for more information about The Growth of a Young Nation.

---

# INTERACT
## WITH HISTORY

### Objectives

- To motivate students to examine the growing regional divide in the United States
- To help students understand the different outlooks and ways of life in the various sections of the country

### Examine the Issues

1. Have students consider what America would be like if each state were an independent nation.
2. Ask students how representatives serve their constituents.
3. Ask students why disobeying federal laws might undermine national unity.

---

**1831** William Lloyd Garrison publishes *The Liberator.*

**1836** Texas establishes itself as a republic, with Sam Houston as its first president.

**1838–39** Native Americans are relocated in the Trail of Tears.

**1844** Samuel Morse sends first telegraph message.

**1846** The war with Mexico begins.

**1848** Woman's rights convention held at Seneca Falls, New York.

## 1830        1840        1850

**1833** Great Britain abolishes slavery in the empire.

**1837** Victoria becomes queen of England.

**1845** The Great Potato Famine begins in Ireland.

**1848** Karl Marx's *The Communist Manifesto* is published.

**1832:** Andrew Jackson | **1836:** Martin Van Buren | **1840:** William Henry Harrison | **1841:** John Tyler (William Henry Harrison dies) | **1844:** James K. Polk | **1848:** Zachary Taylor | **1850:** Millard Filmore (Zachary Taylor dies)

---

## RECOMMENDED RESOURCES

### BOOKS FOR THE TEACHER

Ellis, Joseph J. *American Sphinx: The Character of Thomas Jefferson.* New York: Knopf, 1997.

Walters, Ronald G. *American Reformers 1815-1860.* New York: Hill, 1997.

White, Richard. *It's Your Misfortune and None of My Own.* Norman: Oklahoma UP, 1993. A history of American expansion in the West.

### BOOKS FOR THE STUDENT

Douglass, Frederick. *A Narrative of the Life of Frederick Douglass.* Yale U Press: 2001.

Elting, John Robert. *Amateurs, to Arms! A Military History of the War of 1812.* New York: Da Capo Press, 1995.

Griffith, Elisabeth. *In Her Own Right.* New York: Oxford UP, 1992. Life of Elizabeth Cady Stanton.

### VIDEOS

*Canals and Steamboats.* Agency for Instructional Technology, 800-457-4509.

*A History of Slavery in America.* Schlessinger Video Productions, 1994, 800-843-3620.

### SOFTWARE

*The Industrial Revolution in America.* CD-ROM. Educational Software Institute, 800-955-5570.

*Social Reform Movements.* CD-ROM. Educational Software Institute, 800-955-5570.

### INTEGRATED TECHNOLOGY

For teacher support, visit . . .

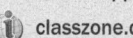 classzone.com

# The Jeffersonian Era

| MAIN IDEA | WHY IT MATTERS NOW | Terms & Names |
|---|---|---|
| During the presidencies of Thomas Jefferson, James Madison, and James Monroe, the country grew in both size and prestige. | Today's Democratic Party traces its roots to Jefferson and the Democratic-Republicans. | •Democratic-Republicans •Jeffersonian republicanism •*Marbury* v. *Madison* •John Marshall •judicial review •Louisiana Purchase •impressment •James Monroe •Monroe Doctrine |

 U.S. History 9B, 19B, 24B, 24H, 25A, 25B, 25C, 25D

### One American's Story

Patrick Gass was among those who took part in the famous Lewis and Clark expedition. Setting out in 1804, this expedition traveled overland from St. Louis, Missouri, to the Pacific. Along the way, Gass kept a journal in which he took notes on people, places, and the dramatic events he witnessed. Gass described one of those events in his journal entry for May 14, 1805.

**A PERSONAL VOICE** PATRICK GASS

" This forenoon we passed a large creek on the North side and a small river on the South. About 4 in the afternoon we passed another small river on the South side near the mouth of which some of the men discovered a large brown bear, and six of them went out to kill it. They fired at it; but having only wounded it, it made battle and was near seizing some of them, but they all fortunately escaped, and at length succeeded in dispatching it. These bears are very bold and ferocious; and very large and powerful. The natives say they have killed a number of their brave men. "

—*A Journal of the Voyages and Travels of a Corps of Discovery*

**VIDEO**

**RECRUITED BY LEWIS AND CLARK**
**Patrick Gass Chronicles the Journey West**

The journey Gass undertook with Lewis and Clark helped lay the foundations for expansion. The explorers brought back to the new government reports about the vast regions that lay to the west. Meanwhile, other Americans continued to shape the government in their growing nation.

## **1** Jefferson's Presidency

The election of 1800 pitted Thomas Jefferson, a leader of the **Democratic-Republicans** (sometimes shortened to "Republicans"), against President John Adams and his Federalist Party.

It was a hard-fought struggle. Each party hurled wild charges at the other.

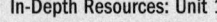
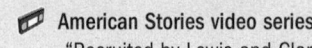

Democratic-Republicans called Adams a tool of the rich who wanted to turn the executive branch into a British-style monarchy. Federalists protested that Jefferson was a dangerous supporter of revolutionary France and an atheist.

**THE ELECTION OF 1800** In the balloting in the Electoral College, Jefferson defeated Adams by eight electoral votes. However, since Jefferson's running mate, Aaron Burr, received the same number of votes as Jefferson, the House of Representatives was called upon to break the tie and choose between the two running mates. For six feverish days, the House took one ballot after another— 35 ballots in all. Finally, Alexander Hamilton intervened. Although Hamilton opposed Jefferson's philosophy of government, he regarded Burr as unqualified for the presidency. Hamilton persuaded enough Federalists to cast blank votes that Jefferson received a majority of two votes. Burr then became vice-president.

The deadlock revealed a flaw in the electoral process established by the Constitution. As a result, Congress passed the Twelfth Amendment, which called for electors to cast separate ballots for president and vice-president. This system is still in effect today.

In his inaugural address, Jefferson extended the hand of peace to his opponents. "Every difference of opinion is not a difference of principle," he said. "We are all Republicans; we are all Federalists."

**SIMPLIFYING THE GOVERNMENT** Jefferson's theory of government, often called **Jeffersonian republicanism,** held that the people should control the government and that a simple government best suited the needs of the people. In accord with his belief in decentralized power, Jefferson tried to shrink the government and cut costs wherever possible. He reduced the size of the army, halted a planned expansion of the navy, and lowered expenses for government social functions. He also rolled back Hamilton's economic program by eliminating all internal taxes and reducing the influence of the Bank of the United States. Ⓐ

Jefferson was the first president to take office in the new federal capital, Washington, D.C. Though in appearance the city was a primitive place of dirt roads and few buildings, its location between Virginia and Maryland reflected the growing importance of the South in national politics. In fact, Jefferson and the two presidents who followed him— James Madison and James Monroe—all were from Virginia. This pattern of Southern dominance underscored the declining influence of both New England and the Federalists in national political life at that time.

**JOHN MARSHALL AND THE SUPREME COURT** Just before leaving office, President Adams had tried to influence future judicial decisions by filling federal judgeships with Federalists. But the signed documents authorizing some of the appointments had not been delivered by the time Adams left office. Jefferson argued that these appointments were invalid and ordered Madison, his secretary of state, not to deliver them.

This argument led to one of the most important Supreme Court decisions of all time in ***Marbury* v. *Madison*** (1803). (See page 118.) The Federalist chief justice **John Marshall** declared that part of Congress's Judiciary Act of 1789, which would have forced Madison to hand over the papers, was unconstitutional. The decision strengthened the Supreme Court by establishing the principle of **judicial review**—the ability of the Supreme Court to declare a law, in this case an act of Congress, unconstitutional. Ⓑ

▲ *John Marshall, Chief Justice of the United States (about 1832), by William James Hubard.*

**A. Answer** He cut taxes, reduced expenses, and simplified the government.

**MAIN IDEA**

**Making Inferences**
Ⓐ How did Jefferson's actions reflect his theory of government?

**B. Answer** It provided the Supreme Court with the right to review acts of Congress, thereby maintaining the checks and balances system created by the Constitution.

**MAIN IDEA**

**Evaluating Decisions**
Ⓑ Why was the principle of judicial review important for the future of the Supreme Court?

REVIEW UNIT 113

---

**Thomas Jefferson**
Jefferson brought an unprecedented informality to the office of president. Jefferson held no formal receptions. When he entertained dinner guests, he did not seat them according to rank. He would not even designate a guest of honor. Despite his casual style, Jefferson possessed a brilliant mind and revolutionary spirit. Among his many interests were farming, architecture, law, geography, botany, natural history, and culinary arts. Jefferson's personal library contained almost 6,500 books.

**Judicial Review**
The principle of judicial review is considered a cornerstone of modern American law and government. Many scholars agree that the Supreme Court's authority to determine the constitutionality of the law is vital to the preservation of democracy. Such power, granted to the Supreme Court and not to the president or Congress, means that the judicial branch of the federal government is responsible for upholding the Constitution.

---

**ACTIVITY** | **SKILLBUILDER LESSON**

## MAKING INFERENCES

**Explaining the Skill** Making inferences means drawing conclusions based on facts, examples, and the author's use of language instead of from explicit statements.

**Applying the Skill** Have students review the concept of Jeffersonian republicanism and Chief Justice John Marshall's decision in *Marbury* v. *Madison* on this page.

1. What is the central tenet of Jeffersonian republicanism? (*A simple government is best*)

2. What was the main effect of the Supreme Court decision in *Marbury*? (*It gave more power to the Supreme Court.*)

3. Infer from the above what Thomas Jefferson thought about Marshall's opinion in *Marbury*. (*Jefferson opposed it because it gave more power to the judicial branch*)

 In-Depth Resources: Unit 1
· Skillbuilder Practice: Making Inferences, p. 83

## Instruct: Objective 2

**Madison and the War of 1812**
TAKS SS11 2(US8.B)

· What factors led to the War of 1812?

· What were the major consequences of the war?

📄 **In-Depth Resources: Unit 1**
· Guided Reading, p. 77

⬇ **Critical Thinking Transparencies CT6**
· The War of 1812

### More About . . .

#### Impressment

Britain adopted the policy of impressment, or drafting men from another country's ships, to fill its great need for sailors in the Royal Navy. Although the Royal Navy was the largest in the world, few men chose to enlist. Many who did enlist deserted. For the most part, conditions on American ships were better than on British naval vessels. Many British subjects, including some deserters, preferred to work on American merchant ships.

### Tracing Themes

#### AMERICA IN WORLD AFFAIRS

#### The War of 1812

The War of 1812 was caused by American outrage over the British policy of impressment and the desire to protect national economic and territorial interests. President Madison was incensed by what he saw as British interference with American expansion. The Monroe Doctrine, set forth by President Monroe a decade later, focused on keeping European powers out of the affairs of the Western Hemisphere.

**THE LOUISIANA PURCHASE** In 1800, Napoleon Bonaparte of France had persuaded Spain to return to France the Louisiana Territory, the land spanning from the Mississippi River west to the Rocky Mountains. France had handed this territory over to Spain in 1762, after the French and Indian War, but Napoleon planned to use it as a "breadbasket" for the colonial empire that he hoped to build in the West Indies. Many Americans were alarmed when they heard of this transfer, as they feared that a strong French presence in North America would force the United States into an alliance with Britain.

However, by 1803, Napoleon had abandoned his ideas of an American empire and offered to sell the Louisiana Territory to the United States. Jefferson doubted whether the Constitution gave him the power to make such a purchase, but he decided to proceed. At a price of $15 million, the **Louisiana Purchase** more than doubled the size of the United States. Under the direction of President Jefferson, Meriwether Lewis and William Clark organized and led a group, including Patrick Gass, and set off in 1804 to explore the new territory. The explorers brought back valuable information about the West and showed that transcontinental travel was possible.

## 2 Madison and the War of 1812

Jefferson easily won reelection in 1804 but a crisis clouded his second administration. Renewed fighting between Britain and France threatened American shipping. The crisis continued into the administration of James Madison, who was elected president in 1808. Some four years later, Madison led the nation into the War of 1812 against Great Britain.

**THE CAUSES OF THE WAR** Although France and Britain both threatened U.S. ships between 1805 and 1814, Americans focused their anger on the British. One reason was the British policy of **impressment,** the practice of seizing Americans at sea and "impressing," or drafting, them into the British navy. Americans grew even angrier after learning that officials in British Canada were supplying arms to Native Americans in support of their ongoing battle against American settlers. A group of young congressmen from the South and the West, known as the war hawks, demanded war.

**THE COURSE OF THE WAR** By the spring of 1812, President Madison had decided to commit America to war against Britain, and Congress approved the war declaration in mid-June.

Republican funding cuts and a lack of popular support had left the American military with few volunteers and ill-prepared for war. Britain, however, was too preoccupied with Napoleon in Europe to pay much attention to the Americans. Nonetheless, the British scored a stunning victory in August of 1814, when they brushed aside American troops and sacked Washington, D.C. Madison and other federal officials fled the city as the British burned the Capitol, the Presidential Mansion, and other public buildings. The most impressive American victory occurred at the Battle of New Orleans. There, on January 8, 1815, U.S. troops led by General Andrew Jackson of Tennessee routed a British force. Ironically, British and American diplomats had already signed a peace agreement before the Battle of New Orleans, but news of the pact had not reached Jackson in time. The Treaty of Ghent, signed on Christmas Eve, 1814, declared an armistice, or end to the fighting.

**THE CONSEQUENCES OF THE WAR** The war had three important consequences. First, it led to the end of the Federalist Party, whose members generally opposed the war. Second, it encouraged the growth of American industries to manufacture products no longer available from Britain because of the war. Third, it confirmed the status of the United States as a free and independent nation. **C**

### Background

Napoleon Bonaparte seized control of the French government in 1799 and expanded French territory until his defeat at Waterloo in Belgium in 1815.

*Skillbuilder Answers*
**1.** About 3500.
**2.** About 5 miles per day.

*C. Answer*
It led to the end of the Federalist party; it encouraged U.S. production of goods formerly imported from Britain; it continued the status of the U.S. as an independent nation.

**MAIN IDEA**

**Summarizing**
**C** What were the principal consequences of the War of 1812?

---

**DIFFERENTIATING INSTRUCTION**  |  **LESS PROFICIENT READERS**

**Clarifying** To help students better understand the war of 1812, suggest that they read the headings on page 114 and formulate questions such as:

· What were the causes of the war?

· What were the main actions in the course of the war?

· What were the consequences of the war?

Have students look for the answers as they read.

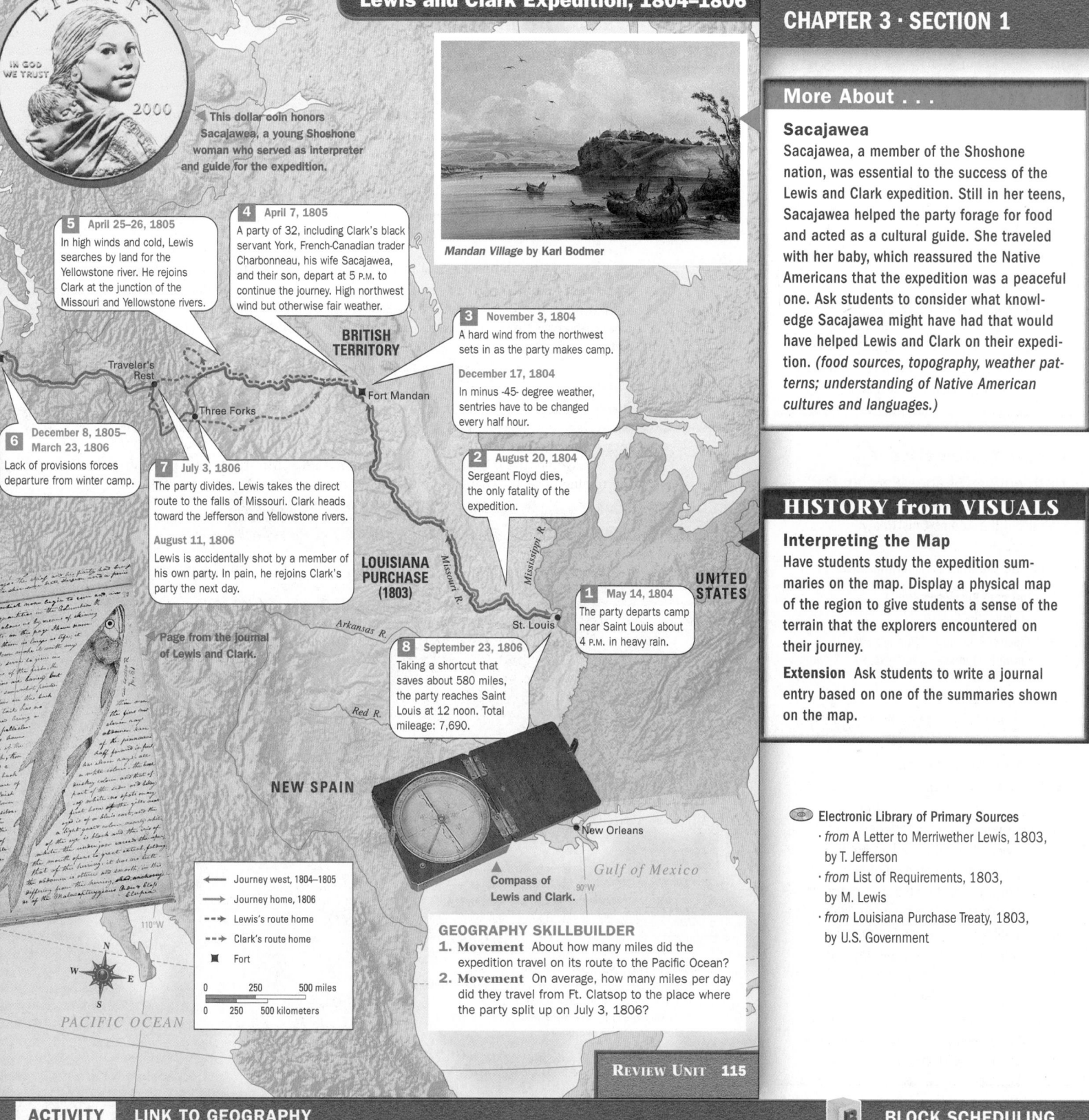

## Lewis and Clark Expedition, 1804–1806

**This dollar coin honors Sacajawea, a young Shoshone woman who served as interpreter and guide for the expedition.**

**Mandan Village by Karl Bodmer**

**5** **April 25–26, 1805**
In high winds and cold, Lewis searches by land for the Yellowstone river. He rejoins Clark at the junction of the Missouri and Yellowstone rivers.

**4** **April 7, 1805**
A party of 32, including Clark's black servant York, French-Canadian trader Charbonneau, his wife Sacajawea, and their son, depart at 5 P.M. to continue the journey. High northwest wind but otherwise fair weather.

**3** **November 3, 1804**
A hard wind from the northwest sets in as the party makes camp.

**December 17, 1804**
In minus -45- degree weather, sentries have to be changed every half hour.

**BRITISH TERRITORY**

Traveler's Rest

Three Forks

Fort Mandan

**6** **December 8, 1805– March 23, 1806**
Lack of provisions forces departure from winter camp.

**7** **July 3, 1806**
The party divides. Lewis takes the direct route to the falls of Missouri. Clark heads toward the Jefferson and Yellowstone rivers.

**August 11, 1806**
Lewis is accidentally shot by a member of his own party. In pain, he rejoins Clark's party the next day.

**LOUISIANA PURCHASE (1803)**

Missouri R.

Mississippi R.

Arkansas R.

**2** **August 20, 1804**
Sergeant Floyd dies, the only fatality of the expedition.

**UNITED STATES**

**1** **May 14, 1804**
The party departs camp near Saint Louis about 4 P.M. in heavy rain.

St. Louis

**Page from the journal of Lewis and Clark.**

**8** **September 23, 1806**
Taking a shortcut that saves about 580 miles, the party reaches Saint Louis at 12 noon. Total mileage: 7,690.

Red R.

**NEW SPAIN**

New Orleans

*Gulf of Mexico*

90°W

**Compass of Lewis and Clark.**

110°W

N
W E
S

Journey west, 1804–1805
Journey home, 1806
Lewis's route home
Clark's route home
Fort

0    250    500 miles
0    250    500 kilometers

*PACIFIC OCEAN*

### GEOGRAPHY SKILLBUILDER

1. **Movement** About how many miles did the expedition travel on its route to the Pacific Ocean?
2. **Movement** On average, how many miles per day did they travel from Ft. Clatsop to the place where the party split up on July 3, 1806?

### More About . . .

#### Sacajawea

Sacajawea, a member of the Shoshone nation, was essential to the success of the Lewis and Clark expedition. Still in her teens, Sacajawea helped the party forage for food and acted as a cultural guide. She traveled with her baby, which reassured the Native Americans that the expedition was a peaceful one. Ask students to consider what knowledge Sacajawea might have had that would have helped Lewis and Clark on their expedition. *(food sources, topography, weather patterns; understanding of Native American cultures and languages.)*

### HISTORY from VISUALS

#### Interpreting the Map

Have students study the expedition summaries on the map. Display a physical map of the region to give students a sense of the terrain that the explorers encountered on their journey.

**Extension** Ask students to write a journal entry based on one of the summaries shown on the map.

**Electronic Library of Primary Sources**
· from A Letter to Merriwether Lewis, 1803, by T. Jefferson
· from List of Requirements, 1803, by M. Lewis
· from Louisiana Purchase Treaty, 1803, by U.S. Government

---

**ACTIVITY** **LINK TO GEOGRAPHY**

**BLOCK SCHEDULING**

## Taking Part in an Expedition

**Class Time** Two class periods

**Task** Creating a plan for an expedition

**Purpose** To help students understand what is involved in organizing and carrying out an expedition

**Directions** Display a topographic map and have groups of students select an area they want to explore. They should study the area's terrain, climate, and possible inhabitants. Students should map out possible routes and prepare an equipment and supplies list. Have each group create a plan to complete their expedition based on their observations. Ask students to present their maps, lists, and plans to the class.

## Instruct: Objective

**Nationalism Shapes Foreign Policy**
TAKS SS11 5(US24.A)
· What did the Adams-Onís Treaty accomplish?
· What did the Monroe Doctrine declare?

 In-Depth Resources: Unit 1
· Guided Reading, p. 77

Electronic Library of Primary Sources
· *from* First Inaugural Address, by J. Monroe

## More About . . .

**The Monroe Doctrine**
Great Britain proposed a joint alliance with the United States in its effort to keep other European powers from interfering in the Western Hemisphere. President Monroe and former presidents Jefferson and Madison were all in favor of the idea. Secretary of State John Quincy Adams warned against such an alliance. He reasoned that the British were out to protect their own interests. Monroe decided to take Adams' advice and declined the British invitation to form an alliance. Instead, James Monroe created his own American policy, which came to be called the Monroe Doctrine.

# Nationalism Shapes Foreign Policy

As with James Madison, foreign affairs dominated the first term of President **James Monroe,** who was elected in 1816. His secretary of state, John Quincy Adams, established a foreign policy based on nationalism—a belief that national interests should be placed ahead of regional concerns, such as slavery in the South or tariffs in the Northeast.

**TERRITORY AND BOUNDARIES** High on Adams's list of national interests were the security of the nation and the expansion of its territory. To further these interests, Adams arranged the Convention of 1818, which fixed the U.S. border at the 49th parallel from Michigan west to the Rocky Mountains. Adams also reached a compromise with Britain to jointly occupy the Oregon Territory, the territory west of the Rockies, for ten years. He also convinced Don Luis de Onís, the Spanish minister to the United States, to transfer Florida to the United States. The Adams-Onís Treaty (1819) also established a western boundary for the United States that extended along the Sabine River from the Gulf of Mexico north to the Arkansas River to its source, and then north to the 42nd parallel, and west to the Pacific Ocean. **D**

**THE MONROE DOCTRINE** When Napoleon invaded Portugal and Spain in 1807, the two countries did not have the money or military force to both defend themselves and keep control of their overseas territories at the same time. But when Napoleon was defeated in 1815, Portugal and Spain wanted to reclaim their former colonies in Latin America.

Meanwhile, the Russians, who had been in Alaska since 1784, were establishing trading posts in what is now California. In 1821, Czar Alexander I of Russia

**Skillbuilder Answers**
1. British Territory, later known as Canada.
2. The area between the Mississippi River and the Rocky Mountains—the Great Plains; much of the Gulf Coast; and Florida.

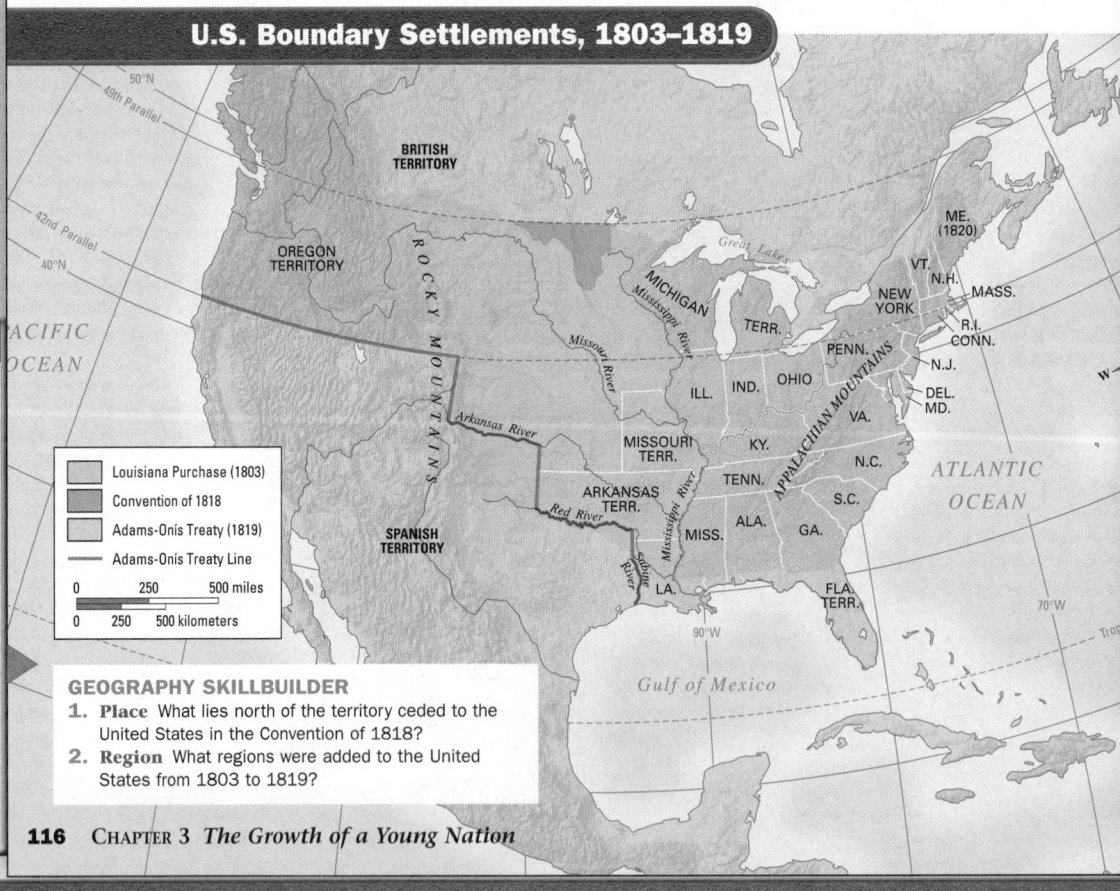

### U.S. Boundary Settlements, 1803–1819

Legend:
- Louisiana Purchase (1803)
- Convention of 1818
- Adams-Onís Treaty (1819)
- Adams-Onís Treaty Line

**GEOGRAPHY SKILLBUILDER**
1. **Place** What lies north of the territory ceded to the United States in the Convention of 1818?
2. **Region** What regions were added to the United States from 1803 to 1819?

**116** CHAPTER 3 *The Growth of a Young Nation*

---

**ACTIVITY**    **SKILLBUILDER LESSON**

## SYNTHESIZING

**Explaining the Skill** Synthesizing involves initially gathering information from various sources on a specific topic or event. The next step is taking this new information and putting it into context in order to arrive at a new understanding of the subject.

**Applying the Skill** To understand John Quincy Adams implementation of foreign policy based on nationalism, students will need to identify national interests. Using pages 116–117 and the map consider the following:

· U.S. territorial expansion throughout the acquisition of northern Mexico and Florida
· continuation of profitable trade with China
· national security

Now ask students how did the Monroe Doctrine continue the foreign policy of nationalism?

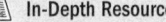 In-Depth Resources: Unit 1
· Skillbuilder Practice: Synthesizing, p. 84

claimed that Alaska's southern boundary was the 51st parallel, just north of Vancouver Island. He forbade foreign vessels from using the coast north of this line.

With Spain and Portugal trying to move back into their old colonial areas, and with Russia pushing in from the northwest, the United States knew that it had to do something. Many Americans were interested in acquiring northern Mexico and the Spanish colony of Cuba. Moreover, the Russian action posed a threat to American trade with China, which brought huge profits.

Accordingly, in his 1823 message to Congress, President Monroe warned all European powers not to interfere with affairs in the Western Hemisphere. They should not attempt to create new colonies, he said, or try to overthrow the newly independent republics in the hemisphere. The United States would consider such action "dangerous to our peace and safety." At the same time, the United States would not involve itself in European affairs or interfere with existing colonies in the Western Hemisphere.

### A PERSONAL VOICE  PRESIDENT JAMES MONROE

"**Our policy in regard to Europe . . . is not to interfere in the internal concerns of any of its powers. . . . But in regard to those continents [of the Western Hemisphere], circumstances are eminently and conspicuously different. It is impossible that the allied [European] powers should extend their political system to any portion of either continent without endangering our peace and happiness.**"

—Annual Message to Congress, December 2, 1823

**James Monroe**

These principles became known as the **Monroe Doctrine.** The doctrine became a foundation for future American policy and represented an important step onto the world stage by the assertive young nation. At home however, sectional differences soon challenged national unity, requiring strong patriotic sentiments and strong leaders like Andrew Jackson to hold the nation together.

*E. Possible Answers*
*It could be a source of peace if it prevented foreign nations from intruding upon U.S. territory. It could be a source of conflict if foreign nations ignored the Monroe doctrine and the U.S. were forced into armed conflict to defend its interests.*

**MAIN IDEA**

**Predicting Effects**
**E** Do you think that the Monroe Doctrine would be a source of peace or conflict for the United States? Why?

---

 **ASSESSMENT**

1. **TERMS & NAMES** For each term or name, write a sentence explaining its significance.
   - **Democratic-Republicans**
   - **Jeffersonian republicanism**
   - **Marbury v. Madison**
   - **John Marshall**
   - **judicial review**
   - **Louisiana Purchase**
   - **impressment**
   - **James Monroe**
   - **Monroe Doctrine**

**MAIN IDEA**

2. **TAKING NOTES**
   In a chart like the one below, list an event from the administration of each president and note its significance.

   | Thomas Jefferson |
   | --- |
   | Event |
   | Significance |

   | James Madison |
   | --- |
   | Event |
   | Significance |

   | James Monroe |
   | --- |
   | Event |
   | Significance |

**CRITICAL THINKING**

3. **EVALUATING LEADERSHIP**
   How successful was Thomas Jefferson as president in achieving his goal of simplifying the government? **Think About:**
   - the Louisiana Purchase
   - military spending
   - Jefferson's attitude toward the national bank

4. **EVALUATING**
   Why was the War of 1812 a turning point for the early United States?

5. **DRAWING CONCLUSIONS**
   How did the Monroe Doctrine assert American nationalism?

---

### The Monroe Doctrine

Several 19th century presidents followed the policy set forth in the Monroe Doctrine. In 1845, President James Polk cited the doctrine in advising Europe not to get involved in the conflict between the United States and Mexico. In 1895, President Grover Cleveland used the doctrine to justify his demand that Britain submit to arbitration regarding a boundary dispute in Latin America. Cleveland's Secretary of State Richard Olney declared, "The United States is practically sovereign on this continent."

## Assess & Reteach

**SECTION 1 ASSESSMENT**

Have students work with a partner to answer the Section Assessment questions.

📄 Formal Assessment
· Section Quiz, p. 56

**SELF-ASSESSMENT**

Ask students to make a two-column chart. In the first column, have them write down facts or topics that they were familiar with before reading this section. In the second column, have students list what they learned.

**RETEACH**

Use the section quiz to review the main ideas and themes covered in this section.

📄 In-Depth Resources: Unit 1
· Reteaching Activity, p. 87

---

 Answers  **ASSESSMENT**

**1. TERMS & NAMES**
Democratic-Republicans, p. 112
Jeffersonian republicanism, p. 113
*Marbury v. Madison*, p. 113
John Marshall, p. 113
judicial review, p. 113
Louisiana Purchase, p. 114
impressment, p. 114
James Monroe, p. 116
Monroe Doctrine, p. 117

**2. TAKING NOTES**
Thomas Jefferson: Event—Louisiana Purchase; Significance—territorial expansion
James Madison: Event—War of 1812; Significance—United States' sovereignty
James Monroe: Event—Monroe Doctrine; Significance—protected United States economic and territorial interests

**3. EVALUATING LEADERSHIP**
Jefferson: reduced size of military; decreased power of the Bank of the United States; authorized the Louisiana Purchase; failed to address the issue of British interference in American affairs

**4. EVALUATING**
The War of 1812: contributed to the demise of the Federalist Party;

encouraged American industrial independence from Britain; confirmed the independence of the United States

**5. DRAWING CONCLUSIONS**
The Monroe Doctrine allowed the United States to claim sovereignty in the Western Hemisphere.

*The Growth of a Young Nation*  **117**

## HISTORIC DECISIONS OF THE SUPREME COURT

### Objectives

· To examine the central issues in *Marbury v. Madison* and the significance of the Supreme Court's ruling

· To recognize the impact of judicial review on the American political system

## Focus & Motivate

**Evaluating** Ask students to describe the role of the Supreme Court in the United States government. Ask them why they think it might be important for the Supreme Court to have the authority to interpret the Constitution.

## More About . . .

### Marbury v. Madison

There were a number of critics of the Supreme Court's ruling in *Marbury v. Madison*. Thomas Jefferson did not believe that the Supreme Court had the right to declare Congressional acts unconstitutional. In 1804, while president, Jefferson wrote, "[The] opinion which gives to the judges the right to decide what laws are constitutional, and what not, not only for themselves in their own sphere of action, but for the legislature and executive also, in their spheres, would make the judiciary a despotic branch." In other words, Thomas Jefferson feared the Supreme Court, as just one branch of the government, would wield too much power.

📄 Historical Decisions of the Supreme Court
· *Marbury v. Madison*, pp. 1–6

## MARBURY v. MADISON (1803)

**ORIGINS OF THE CASE** A few days before Thomas Jefferson's inauguration, outgoing president John Adams appointed William Marbury to be a justice of the peace. But the commission was not delivered to Marbury. Later, Jefferson's new secretary of state, James Madison, refused to give Marbury the commission. Marbury asked the Supreme Court to force Madison to give him his commission.

**THE RULING** The Court declared that the law on which Marbury based his claim was unconstitutional, and therefore it refused to order Madison to give Marbury his commission.

### LEGAL REASONING

Writing for the Court, Chief Justice John Marshall decided that Marbury had a right to his commission, and he scolded Madison at length for refusing to deliver it.

However, he then considered Marbury's claim that, under the Judiciary Act of 1789, the Supreme Court should order Madison to deliver the commission. As Marshall pointed out, the powers of the Supreme Court are set by the Constitution, and Congress does not have the authority to alter them. The Judiciary Act attempted to do just that.

Marshall reasoned that, since the Constitution is the "supreme law of the land, no law that goes against the Constitution can be valid."

> " If . . . the courts are to regard the constitution, and the constitution is superior to any ordinary act of the legislature, the constitution, and not such ordinary act, must govern the case to which they both apply."

If an act of Congress violates the Constitution, then a judge must uphold the Constitution and declare the act void. In choosing to obey the Constitution, the Supreme Court did declare the Judiciary Act unconstitutional and void, and so refused to grant Marbury's request.

◀ **Chief Justice John Marshall**

### LEGAL SOURCES

#### U.S. CONSTITUTION

**U.S. CONSTITUTION, ARTICLE III, SECTION 1 (1789)**
"The judicial power shall extend to all cases . . . arising under this Constitution, the laws of the United States, and treaties made . . . under their authority."

**U.S. CONSTITUTION, ARTICLE VI, SECTION 2 (1789)**
"This Constitution, and the laws of the United States which shall be made in pursuance thereof . . . shall be the supreme law of the land; and the judges in every State shall be bound thereby."

#### RELATED CASES

**FLETCHER v. PECK (1810)**
The Court ruled a state law unconstitutional for the first time.

**COHENS v. VIRGINIA (1821)**
The Court overturned a state court decision for the first time.

**GIBBONS v. OGDEN (1824)**
The Court ruled that the federal Congress—not the states—had the power under the Constitution to regulate interstate commerce.

## RECOMMENDED RESOURCES

### BOOKS

Clinton, Robert Lowry. *Marbury v. Madison and Judicial Review.* Lawrence: U of Kansas P, 1991. In-depth study of the historic case.

Kahn, Paul. *The Reign of Law: Marbury v. Madison and the Construction of America.* New Haven: Yale University Press, 1997.

Nelson, William E. *Marbury v. Madison: The Origins and Legacy of Judicial Review.* Lawrence: University of Kansas Press, 2000. Student-friendly study of the impact of the landmark Supreme Court case.

Smith, Jean Edward. *John Marshall: Definer of a Nation.* New York: Henry Holt, 1998. Comprehensive biography of a Supreme Court Chief Justice.

### INTEGRATED TECHNOLOGY

For teacher support and more information about the Supreme Court including the full text of the Supreme Court decisions, visit . . .

 classzone.com

◄ William
Marbury

## WHY IT MATTERED

In 1803, interest in Marbury's commission was primarily about partisan politics. The fight was just one skirmish in the ongoing battle between Federalists, such as Adams, and Democratic-Republicans, led by Jefferson and Madison, which had intensified in the election of 1800.

When Jefferson won the election, Adams made a final effort to hinder Jefferson's promised reforms. Before leaving office, he tried to fill the government with Federalists, including the "midnight" justices such as Marbury. Madison's refusal to deliver Marbury's appointment was part of Jefferson's subsequent effort to rid his administration of Federalists.

Marshall's opinion in *Marbury* might seem like a victory for Jefferson because it denied Marbury his commission. However, by scolding Madison and extending the principle of judicial review—the power of courts to decide whether or not specific laws are valid—the Court sent a message to Jefferson and to the Congress that the judiciary had the power to affect legislation. The Marshall Court, however, never declared another act of Congress unconstitutional.

## HISTORICAL IMPACT

In striking down part of the Judiciary Act, an act of Congress, Marshall gave new force to the principle of judicial review. The legacy of John Marshall and of *Marbury* is that judicial review has become a cornerstone of American government. One scholar has called it "America's novel contribution to political theory and the practice of constitutional government." As Justice Marshall recognized, judicial review is an essential component of democratic government; by ensuring that Congress exercises only those powers granted by the Constitution, the courts protect the sovereignty of the people.

Perhaps more importantly, the principle of judicial review plays a vital role in our federal system of checks and balances. With *Marbury,* the judicial branch secured its place as one of three coequal branches of the federal government. The judiciary has no power to make laws or to carry them out. However, judges have an important role in deciding what the law is and how it is carried out.

In *City of Boerne* v. *Flores* (1997), for instance, the Supreme Court declared void the Religious Freedom Restoration Act of 1993. Members of Congress had passed the act in an attempt to change the way federal courts apply the First Amendment's Free Exercise Clause. The Supreme Court ruled that Congress does not have the authority to decide what the First Amendment means—in effect, to define its own powers. The Court, and not Congress, is the interpreter of the Constitution.

Through the 1999–2000 term, the Court had rendered 151 decisions striking down—in whole or part—acts of Congress. It had also voided or restricted the enforcement of state laws 1,130 times. That the entire country has with few exceptions obeyed these decisions, no matter how strongly they disagreed, proves Americans' faith in the Supreme Court as the protector of the rule of law.

1. What was the reasoning behind the Supreme Court's decision in *Marbury* v. *Madison?*
2. What is the principle of judicial review?
3. How did *City of Boerne* v. *Flores* exemplify the ongoing relevance of *Marbury* v. *Madison?*

### MAKING PERSONAL CONNECTIONS

Ask students whether they have a person, or persons, in their lives who have the final say on what they are allowed to do. How do they feel about such an arrangement?

### More About . . .

#### Judicial Review

The power of judicial review was demonstrated in the 1974 case, *United States* v. *Nixon.* During an investigation of the Watergate scandal, the Supreme Court ordered President Richard Nixon to turn over tape recordings of White House conversations to investigators. Many Americans saw the ruling as a democratic triumph. In the 2000 presidential election, the vote recount dispute ended up in the U.S. Supreme Court. The Supreme Court ruled that the Selectively-applied recount procedure violated the Equal Protection Clause of the Fourteenth Amendment. Some Americans felt that the Supreme Court had overstepped its authority by becoming involved in a process that decided the outcome of an election.

---

## THINKING CRITICALLY

### CONNECT TO HISTORY

1. **Comparing** Read encyclopedia articles about another Marshall Court decision, such as *Fletcher* v. *Peck*, *Cohens* v. *Virginia*, or *Gibbons* v. *Ogden*. Compare that decision with *Marbury* and consider what the two cases and opinions have in common. Write a paragraph explaining the major similarities between the cases.

 **SEE SKILLBUILDER HANDBOOK, PAGE R8.**

### CONNECT TO TODAY

2.  **INTERNET ACTIVITY** CLASSZONE.COM

Visit the links for Historic Decisions of the Supreme Court to research a recent Supreme Court decision involving judicial review of an act of Congress. Write a case summary in which you describe the law's purpose, the Court's ruling, and the potential impact of the decision.

---

## THINKING CRITICALLY: ANSWERS

### 1. CONNECT TO HISTORY
**Rubrics**

Student paragraphs should:

· document the similarities between selected cases

· explain the reasoning behind the comparison

· provide factual evidence and background information about the cases to support the opinion

### 2. CONNECT TO HISTORY
**Rubrics**

Student summaries should:

· briefly describe the background of each case

· present the crucial facts and court decisions

· include quotes and other research findings

 classzone.com

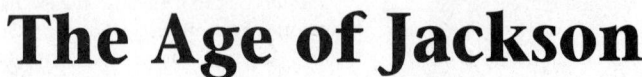

## OBJECTIVES

1. Describe the regional economic differences in the early United States.
2. Summarize tensions between national and sectional interests.
3. Examine the crucial issues and events of Andrew Jackson's presidency.
4. Identify the presidents that followed Jackson and the challenges they faced.

### SKILLBUILDERS

· Geography Skillbuilder: place, movement, p. 125
· Analyzing Political Cartoons, p. 126

### CRITICAL THINKING

· Analyzing Causes, pp. 121, 127
· Analyzing Motives, pp. 122, 126
· Summarizing, p. 122
· Analyzing Events, p. 124
· Making Predictions, p. 124
· Evaluating, p. 127

## Focus & Motivate

Ask students their opinion on voting. Do they plan to exercise their right to vote when they turn 18? Then ask them if they think a government has the right to displace the native peoples of the countries it conquers. Why or why not?

## Instruct

### Instruct: Objective 1

**Regional Economies Create Differences**

TAKS SS11 3(US22.C)

· How did the onset of the Industrial Revolution change American society in the North?
· Why did the South remain primarily agricultural?

 Critical Thinking Transparencies CT17, CT41
· Industrial Revolution
· Cotton Production and Exports, 1800–1860

# The Age of Jackson

| MAIN IDEA | WHY IT MATTERS NOW | Terms & Names |
|---|---|---|
| During a time of growing sectionalism, Andrew Jackson's election in 1828 ushered in a new era of popular democracy. | Jackson's use of presidential powers laid the foundation for the modern presidency. | • Henry Clay • American System • John C. Calhoun • Missouri Compromise • Andrew Jackson • John Quincy Adams • Jacksonian democracy • Trail of Tears • John Tyler |

U.S. History 8B, 10A, 19B, 22A, 22B, 22C, 23A, 24A, 24B, 24C, 24F, 25A, 25B, 25C, 25D

### One American's Story

Robert Fulton designed and built the first commercially successful steamboat. In 1807 his *Clermont* made the 150-mile trip up the Hudson River from New York City to Albany in 32 hours. Another one of Fulton's boats, the *Paragon*, was so luxurious that it had a paneled dining room and bedrooms. Fulton even posted regulations on his luxurious steamboats.

**A PERSONAL VOICE** ROBERT FULTON

" As the steamboat has been fitted up in an elegant style, order is necessary to keep it so; gentlemen will therefore please to observe cleanliness, and a reasonable attention not to injure the furniture; for this purpose no one must sit on a table under the penalty of half a dollar each time, and every breakage of tables, chairs, sofas, or windows, tearing of curtains, or injury of any kind must be paid for before leaving the boat. "

—quoted in *Steamboats Come True: American Inventors in Action*

Steamboats, like the one pictured here, could move against a river's current or a strong wind.

Steamboats like the one Fulton described did more than comfortably transport passengers. They also carried freight and played an important role in uniting the nation economically. Although tensions continued to arise between the different sections of the nation, a growing national spirit kept the country together. This spirit was ultimately personified by Andrew Jackson—a self-made man from the growing West who was both confident and dynamic.

## 1 Regional Economies Create Differences

In the early decades of the 19th century, the economies of the various regions of the United States developed differently. The Northeast began to industrialize while the South and West continued to be more agricultural.

---

## PROGRAM RESOURCES

 **In-Depth Resources: Unit 1**
· Guided Reading, p. 78
· Reteaching Activity, p. 88
· Outline Map: Indian Removal Act, pp. 94–95
· Primary Source: from *The Webster-Hayne Debates*, pp. 96–97
· American Lives: Henry Clay, p. 105

 **Reading Study Guide** (English and Spanish), pp. 37–38

 **Access for Students Acquiring English/ESL**
· Guided Reading (Spanish), p. 49
· Outline Map, pp. 59–60

 **Formal Assessment**
· Section Quiz, p. 57

 **Integrated Assessment**
· Rubrics

**INTEGRATED TECHNOLOGY**

 **Critical Thinking Transp. CT7, CT41**
· Industrial Revolution
· Cotton Production and Exports, 1800–1860

 **Humanities Transp. HT33**
· General Jackson slaying the many headed monster

 Electronic Library of Primary Sources

 classzone.com

### TEXAS RESOURCES

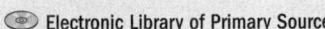 TAKS Spiraled Content Review

TAKS Practice Tests

TAKS Practice Transparencies TT25–28

TAKS Online Test Practice

**A. Answer**
Farmers produced livestock or specialized crops that they sold in urban markets and then purchased goods that had been manufactured in Northern factories.

**EARLY INDUSTRY IN THE UNITED STATES** The Industrial Revolution—large-scale production resulting in massive change in social and economic organization—began in Great Britain in the 18th century and gradually reached the United States.

Industry took off first in New England, whose economy depended on shipping and foreign trade. Agriculture there was not highly profitable, so New Englanders were more ready than other Americans to embrace new forms of manufacturing—and prime among these were mechanized textile, or fabric, mills.

Soon, farmers in the North began to specialize in one or two crops or types of livestock (such as corn and cattle), sell what they produced to urban markets, and then purchase with cash whatever else they needed from stores. Increasingly, these were items made in Northern factories. As a result, a market economy began to develop in which agriculture and manufacturing each supported the growth of the other. **A**

**THE SOUTH REMAINS AGRICULTURAL** Meanwhile, the South continued to grow as an agricultural power. Eli Whitney's invention of a cotton gin (short for "engine," or machine) in 1793 made it possible for Southern farmers to produce cotton more profitably. The emergence of a Cotton Kingdom in the South—and

**MAIN IDEA**

**Analyzing Causes**
**A** How did agriculture and industry support a market economy in the North?

## Science & Technology

### THE COTTON GIN

In 1794, Eli Whitney was granted a patent for a "new and useful improvement in the mode of Ginning Cotton." Workers who previously could clean only one pound of cotton by hand per day could now clean as much as fifty pounds per day. Because of Whitney's cotton gin, cotton production in the United States increased from three thousand bales in 1790 to more than two million bales in 1850.

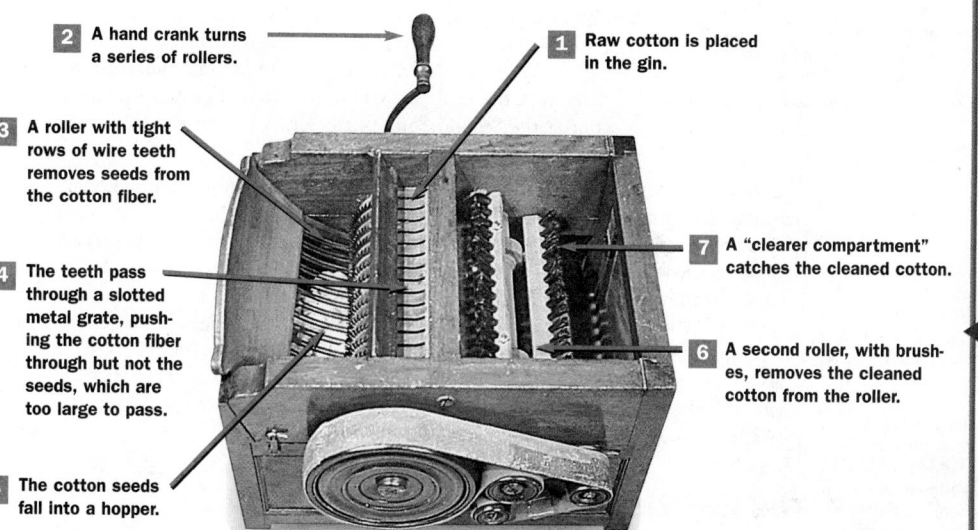

**2** A hand crank turns a series of rollers.

**1** Raw cotton is placed in the gin.

**3** A roller with tight rows of wire teeth removes seeds from the cotton fiber.

**4** The teeth pass through a slotted metal grate, pushing the cotton fiber through but not the seeds, which are too large to pass.

**5** The cotton seeds fall into a hopper.

**7** A "clearer compartment" catches the cleaned cotton.

**6** A second roller, with brushes, removes the cleaned cotton from the roller.

## Tracing Themes
**SCIENCE AND TECHNOLOGY**

### Impact of Industrialization on Society

New manufacturing methods, introduced in the early 1800s, transformed industry in the United States. Towns across New England grew and thrived, bolstered by the emergence of factories and an influx of workers. Many rural areas, however, began to decline. The industrial wave of change left traditional families in its wake. Sons and daughters moved from their parents' farms and headed off to find factory work.

## Science & Technology

### The Cotton Gin

Early gins, before Whitney's invention took the stage, were similar to washing machine clothes wringers. Friction from the grooved rollers could remove seeds from long-staple cotton, but not from shorter cotton fibers. As the shorter cotton was best suited to the southern climate and soil, a more adequate tool would be necessary to reap all the benefits from the crop.

## HISTORY from VISUALS

### Interpreting the Graphic

Have students study the graphic. Ask students to calculate how many pounds of cotton workers could clean in ten days—before and after the invention of the cotton gin. *(Before—10 pounds; after—500 pounds)*

**Extension** Ask students how they think the cotton gin impacted workers' lives.

---

**ACTIVITY** | **COOPERATIVE LEARNING**  classzone.com

## Debating the Merits of Progress

**Class Time** 45 minutes

**Task** Role-playing a debate between citizens in the 1800s

**Purpose** To analyze the effects of the Industrial Revolution on American society

**Directions** Have students work in groups to research the impact of a newly constructed textile mill on working- and middle-class citizens. Have students prepare for a class debate. Half of the students in each group will oppose the mill, and the other half will support it. Encourage students to bolster their arguments with specific details from their research.

Integrated Assessment
· Rubric 3

*The Growth of a Young Nation* **121**

## Instruct: Objective ❷

**Balancing Nationalism
and Sectionalism**

TAKS SS11 1(US1.A)

· What was the American System?

· How did the Missouri Compromise temporarily settle the debate over slavery?

 **In-Depth Resources: Unit 1**
· Guided Reading, p. 78
· American Lives: Henry Clay, p. 105

---

### HISTORICAL SPOTLIGHT

**The Supreme Court Boosts
National Power**

Ask students to discuss some of the functions of state and local governments. *(county—prosecuting criminals, passing local laws; state—issuing driver's licenses, running prisons)*

---

## Instruct: Objective ❸

**The Election of Andrew Jackson /
Jacksonian Democracy /
Nullification and the Bank War**

TAKS SS11 4(8.18.B)

· How did Jackson help to expand democracy and change politics?

· How did Jackson deal with Native Americans?

· What were the causes and consequences of the Nullification Crisis?

· Why did Jackson seek to bring down the National Bank?

 **In-Depth Resources: Unit 1**
· Guided Reading, p. 78

 **Humanities Transparencies HT33**
· General Jackson slaying the many headed monster

👁 **Electronic Library of Primary Sources**
· *from* Proclamation to the People of the United States, 1832, by A. Jackson

thus the need for more field labor—contributed to the expansion of slavery. Between 1790 and 1820, the enslaved population increased from less than 700,000 to over 1.5 million. In the North, things were different. By 1804, states north of Delaware had either abolished slavery or had enacted laws for gradual emancipation. Slavery declined in the North, but some slaves remained there for decades.

**Vocabulary
emancipation:** the act of freeing from bondage or slavery

## ❷ Balancing Nationalism and Sectionalism

These economic differences often created political tensions between the different sections of the nation. Throughout the first half of the 19th century, however, American leaders managed to keep the nation together.

**CLAY'S AMERICAN SYSTEM** As the North, South, and West developed different economies, President Madison developed a plan to move the United States toward economic independence from Britain and other European powers. In 1815 he presented his plan to Congress. It included three major points:

- establishing a protective tariff
- rechartering the national bank
- sponsoring the development of transportation systems and other internal improvements in order to make travel throughout the nation easier

House Speaker **Henry Clay** promoted the plan as the **"American System." B**

Madison and Clay supported tariffs on imports to protect U.S. industry from British competition. Most Northeasterners also welcomed protective tariffs. However, people in the South and West, whose livelihoods did not depend on manufacturing, were not as eager to tax European imports. Nevertheless, Clay, who was from the West (Kentucky), and **John C. Calhoun,** a Southerner (South Carolina), convinced congressmen from their regions to approve the Tariff of 1816. Also in 1816, Congress voted to charter the Second Bank of the United States for a 20-year period and to create a unified currency.

**THE MISSOURI COMPROMISE** In spite of these efforts to unify the national economy, sectional conflicts remained part of American politics. In 1818 settlers in Missouri requested admission to the Union. Northerners and Southerners disagreed, however, on whether Missouri should be admitted as a free state or a slave state.

Behind the leadership of Henry Clay, Congress passed a series of agreements in 1820–1821 known as the **Missouri Compromise.** Under these agreements, Maine was admitted as a free state and Missouri as a slave state. The rest of the Louisiana Territory was split into two parts. The dividing line was set at 36°30′ north latitude. South of the line, slavery was legal. North of the line—except in Missouri—slavery was banned. **C**

## The Election of Andrew Jackson ❸

Despite these sectional tensions, the story of America in the early 19th century was one of expansion—expanding economies, expanding territory, and expanding democracy. The man who embraced the spirit of that expansion and to many personified it was **Andrew Jackson,** who captured the presidency in 1828.

**C. Answer**
Maine was admitted as a free state and Missouri as a slave state. The rest of the Louisiana Territory was split into two parts at 36°30′ north latitude. South of the line, slavery was legal. North of the line—except for Missouri—slavery was banned.

**B. Answer**
The "American System" was supposed to unite the nation's economic interests and promote economic independence for the nation.

**MAIN IDEA**

**Analyzing Motives**
**B** What was the intention behind the "American System?"

**MAIN IDEA**

**Summarizing**
**C** What agreements comprised the Missouri Compromise?

---

### DIFFERENTIATING INSTRUCTION   LESS PROFICIENT READERS

**Clarifying**

To help students clarify the regional attitudes toward slavery and the Tariff of 1816, have them make a two-column chart, such as the one shown, and fill in the pertinent information.

| Regional Attitudes | |
| --- | --- |
| Tariff of 1816 | Slavery in the Territories |
| Northeasterners liked the tariff because it helped them sell their products | |
| Southerners . . . | |

**THE ELECTION OF 1824** In 1824, Andrew Jackson lost his bid for the presidency to **John Quincy Adams.** Jacksonians, or followers of Jackson, accused Adams and Jackson's political enemy, Henry Clay, of stealing the presidency. Then, because Adams appointed Clay secretary of state, the Jacksonians claimed Adams had struck a corrupt bargain. The split between Clay and Jackson tore apart the Democratic-Republican party. While Clay and his faction were called the National Republican Party, the Jacksonians became known as the Democratic Party.

**Vocabulary**
**corrupt:** marked by bribery

**EXPANDING DEMOCRACY CHANGES POLITICS** During John Quincy Adams's presidency, most states had eased property requirements for voting, thereby enlarging the voting population. In the election of 1824, approximately 350,000 white males voted for the presidency. In 1828, over three times that number voted. Many of these new voters were common people who viewed the rugged westerner Jackson as their champion. The support of this new voting bloc gave Jackson victory in the election of 1828.

## Jacksonian Democracy ❸

**THE SPOILS SYSTEM** Jackson's ideal of political power for all classes is often called **Jacksonian democracy.** As part of this philosophy, Jackson sought to give common people a chance to participate in government. He did this through the spoils system, in which new administrations hire their own supporters to replace supporters of the previous administration. Using the spoils system, Jackson gave away huge numbers of jobs to friends and also to political allies.

President-elect Andrew Jackson greets well-wishers on his way to Washington, D.C., to be inaugurated president in 1829.
▼

### KEY PLAYER

**ANDREW JACKSON
1767–1845**

Andrew Jackson thought of himself as a man of the people. He had been born in poverty in the Carolina backcountry, the son of Scots-Irish immigrants. He was the first president since George Washington without a college education.

At the time of his election at the age of 61, however, Jackson was hardly one of the common people. He had built a highly successful career in Tennessee in law, politics, land speculation, cotton planting, and soldiering. His home, the Hermitage, was a mansion, not a log cabin. Anyone who owned more than a hundred slaves, as Jackson did, was very wealthy.

### More About . . .

#### John Quincy Adams

During his campaign for reelection, Adams refused to respond to the harsh criticisms of Jackson and his supporters. Adams believed it was beneath the dignity of the presidency to take part in political mudslinging. Ultimately, Adams kept his dignity but not the presidency. Jackson won the election of 1828. Following his defeat, Massachusetts voters elected John Quincy Adams to the House of Representatives, where he would serve for 17 years. On winning election to the House, Adams said, "My election as President of the United States was not half so gratifying . . . "

### KEY PLAYER

#### Andrew Jackson

When he was only 13, Jackson fought in the Revolutionary War and was captured by British soldiers. As general during the War of 1812, Jackson proved his toughness. On the way to New Orleans in 1813, he received orders to disband his army but disobeyed them. After fighting in New Orleans, Jackson led his men back to Tennessee through 500 miles of wilderness. "He's tough," one soldier said of Jackson. "Tough as hickory," replied another. Thus, Jackson earned his nickname, "Old Hickory." Ask students how Jackson's background belied his "man of the people" image?

---

**ACTIVITY   LINK TO CIVICS**

 **BLOCK SCHEDULING**

### Creating a Political Advertisement

**Class Time** Parts of two class periods

**Task** Planning a political advertisement for Andrew Jackson's 1828 presidential campaign

**Purpose** To analyze how political ads affect voters' impressions of a candidate

**Directions** Divide the class into small groups. Ask each to create a three-minute TV ad on videotape. Explain that the ad should "sell" Jackson as a presidential candidate, stressing his political beliefs and views on issues and perhaps containing information on his life. Have students show the ads to the class. Then discuss whether ads are effective political tools.

 Integrated Assessment
· Rubric 6

## More About . . .

### Jackson and Native Americans

Controversy surrounds Andrew Jackson's treatment of Native Americans during his presidency. He was notorious for speaking about native peoples in hostile terms. Yet, Native American allies joined his troops at the Battle of Horseshoe Bend. After a battle in 1813, Jackson took a three-year-old Indian boy, whose parents had been killed by Jackson's own troops, under his protection. Jackson, an orphan himself, said he felt "an unusual bond of sympathy" for the child, whom he sent home to his wife Rachel to raise with their adopted son.

👁 Electronic Library of Primary Sources
· *from* A Message to Congress on Indian Policy, 1835 by A. Jackson

👁 Electronic Library of Primary Sources
· *from* Address to the People of the United States, 1832 by J. Calhoun

## More About . . .

### The Webster-Hayne debates

After Hayne's first speech of the debates, Congressman Edward Everett asked Webster whether he had taken notes. Webster held up a small piece of paper. "I have it all," he said. "That is his speech." The following day, Webster countered Hayne in his now-famous speech. A member of the House told Webster, "Mr. Webster, I think you had better die now and rest your fame on that speech." Overhearing the remark, Hayne said, "You ought not to die: a man who can make such speeches as that ought never to die."

📄 In-Depth Resources: Unit 1
· from The Webster-Hayne Debates, pp. 96–97

**THE INDIAN REMOVAL ACT** In 1830 Congress, with the support of Jackson, passed the Indian Removal Act. Under this law, the federal government provided funds to negotiate treaties that would force the Native Americans to move west.

Many of the tribes signed removal treaties. However, the Cherokee Nation refused and fought the government in the courts. In 1832, the Supreme Court ruled in *Worcester* v. *Georgia* that the state of Georgia could not regulate the Cherokee Nation by law or invade Cherokee lands. However, Jackson refused to abide by the Supreme Court decision, saying, "John Marshall has made his decision; now let him enforce it." **D**

**THE TRAIL OF TEARS** In the years following the Court's ruling, U.S. troops rounded up the Cherokee and drove them into camps to await the journey west. A Baptist missionary described the scene.

▲ *Trail of Tears,* a 1992 painting by Troy Anderson, a Cherokee artist

**A PERSONAL VOICE** EVAN JONES

"The Cherokees are nearly all prisoners. They had been dragged from their houses and encamped at the forts and military places, all over the nation. In Georgia especially, multitudes were allowed no time to take anything with them except the clothes they had on. Well-furnished houses were left as prey to plunderers."

—*Baptist Missionary Magazine*, June 16, 1838

Beginning in the fall of 1838, the Cherokee were sent off in groups of about 1,000 each on the 800-mile journey, mostly on foot. As winter came, more and more Cherokee died. The Cherokee buried more than a quarter of their people along the **Trail of Tears,** the forced marches the Cherokee followed from Georgia to the Indian Territory. (See map on page 125.)

## ③ Nullification and the Bank War

In 1824 and again in 1828, Congress increased the Tariff of 1816. Jackson's vice-president, John C. Calhoun of South Carolina, called the 1828 tariff a Tariff of Abominations because he blamed it for economic problems in the South.

The South's economy depended on cotton exports. Yet the high tariff on manufactured goods reduced British exports to the United States, and because of this, Britain bought less cotton. With the decline of British goods, the South was now forced to buy the more expensive Northern manufactured goods. From the South's point of view, the North was getting rich at the expense of the South.

**THE NULLIFICATION CRISIS** To try to free South Carolinians from the tariff, Calhoun developed a theory of nullification. Calhoun's theory held that the U.S. Constitution was based on a compact among the sovereign states. If the Constitution had been established by 13 sovereign states, he reasoned, then the states must still be sovereign, and each would have the right to determine whether acts of Congress were constitutional. If a state found an act to be unconstitutional, the state could declare the offending law nullified, or inoperative, within its borders. **E**

The Senate debated the tariff question (and the underlying states' rights issue). Senator Daniel Webster of Massachusetts opposed nullification and South Carolina Senator Robert Hayne aired Calhoun's views.

*Skillbuilder Answers*
1. Indian Territory.
2. Many sickened and died on the journey, and others completed the journey to find inferior land. These events probably demoralized many Native Americans.

**MAIN IDEA**

Analyzing Events
**D** How did the federal government initially try to enforce the Indian Removal Act?

*D. Answer* The government tried to negotiate treaties that would force the Native Americans to sell their lands and resettle in the West.

*E. Possible Answers* Some might argue that nullification would weaken federal authority and lead to disunion. Others might say that it would merely return proper authority to the states.

**MAIN IDEA**

Making Predictions
**E** What do you think might be the consequences of Calhoun's nullification theory for federal-state relations?

---

**ACTIVITY** **COOPERATIVE LEARNING**  **BLOCK SCHEDULING**

### Discussing States' Rights

**Class Time** One class period

**Task** Writing and performing a dialogue among Andrew Jackson, John Calhoun, and Henry Clay about the crisis in South Carolina

**Purpose** To help students clarify the positions taken during the crisis

TAKS Mini-Lesson 3: SS11 4(8.18.B)

**Directions** Have each student in a group play a specific role. Three students should play the parts of Jackson, Calhoun, and Clay. One student should direct the dialogue. All of the students in each group should work together to write the dialogue. Have students perform the dialogues in class.

## Effects of the Indian Removal Act, 1830s–1840s

Sequoyah, or George Guess, devised the Cherokee alphabet in 1821 to help preserve the culture of the Cherokee Nation against the growing threat of American expansion. ▶

Many Cherokees in the western territory, like the woman pictured here, taught their children at home in order to keep the Cherokee language and customs alive.

By 1840, about 15,000 Cherokee had been forcibly moved 800 miles west on routes afterward called the Trail of Tears. On the Trail of Tears they suffered from cold, hunger, and diseases such as pneumonia, tuberculosis, smallpox, and cholera. About one-fourth died.

Nearly 15,000 Creek, many in manacles and chains, were moved from Alabama and Georgia to the Candian River in Indian Territory in 1835.

By 1834, about 14,000 Choctaw had relocated along the Red River under the terms of the Indian Removal Act of 1830. About 7,000 remained in Mississippi.

Lake Superior

Lake Michigan

Lake Huron

Lake Erie

WISCONSIN TERRITORY

Mississippi River

MICHIGAN

Ottawa

Sauk and Fox

Potawatomi

Miami

Delaware

OHIO
Shawnee and Seneca

INDIANA

ILLINOIS

Arkansas River

Ohio River

MISSOURI

KENTUCKY

INDIAN TERRITORY

Canadian River

ARKANSAS

Tennessee River

Chickasaw

Cherokee

MISSISSIPPI
Choctaw

ALABAMA

GEORGIA

Red River

Creek

REPUBLIC OF TEXAS
(after 1836)

LOUISIANA

Seminole

90°W

Gulf of Mexico

MEXICO

VT.

PENNSYLVANIA

NEW JERSEY

DELAWARE

MARYLAND

VIRGINIA

NORTH CAROLINA

TENNESSEE

SOUTH CAROLINA

FLORIDA TERRITORY

30°N

80°W

ATLANTIC OCEAN

N W S E

| | |
|---|---|
| Cherokee | |
| Chickasaw | |
| Choctaw | |
| Creek | |
| Seminole | |
| Other tribes | |

0    100    200 miles
0    100    200 kilometers

Detail from *Trail of Tears*, a painting by Robert Lindeux

**GEOGRAPHY SKILLBUILDER**
1. **Place** Where were most of the tribes moved?
2. **Movement** What do you think were the effects of this removal on Native Americans?

## HISTORY from VISUALS

### Interpreting the Map
Ask students to study the Chickasaw and Choctaw routes out of Mississippi and the Delaware, Shawnee, and Seneca routes out of Ohio. Ask students what these trails had in common? *(Followed major rivers)*

**Extension** Remind students that the Cherokee made much of their journey on foot. Ask why so many Cherokee died along the Trail of Tears during the forced removal. *(More than 25 percent died of exhaustion and disease, and cold in winter.)*

📖 In-Depth Resources: Unit 1
· Outline Map: Indian Removal Act, pp. 93–94

## Tracing Themes
**CIVIL RIGHTS**

### Native American Rights
The Cherokee refused to abide by the Indian Removal Act and appealed to the courts for protection of their rights. "We wish to remain on the land of our fathers," stated a written appeal from the Cherokee Nation. "We have a perfect and original right to remain without interruption or molestation. The treaties with us, and laws of the United States made in pursuance of treaties, guaranty our residence, and our privileges, and secure us against intruders. Our only request is, that these treaties may be fulfilled, and these laws executed." The United States Supreme Court upheld the rights of the Cherokee Nation.

---

**ACTIVITY**  **LINK TO LANGUAGE ARTS**

**BLOCK SCHEDULING**

## Expressing a Point of View

**Class Time** 45 minutes

**Task** Writing a letter about a national issue

**Purpose** To evaluate the Indian Removal Act from various perspectives

**Directions** Explain to students that the Indian Removal Act affected sovereign Native American nations whose rights were protected under treaty. Ask students to write to President Jackson expressing the point of view of the Southeastern Native American nations. Remind students that the purpose of their letters is to influence the President. Read the finished letters in class.

📖 Integrated Assessment
· Rubric 5

*The Growth of a Young Nation*   **125**

In 1832 the issue of states' rights was put to a test when Congress raised tariffs again. South Carolinians declared the tariffs of 1828 and 1832 "null, void, and no law." Then they threatened to secede, or withdraw from the Union, if customs officials tried to collect duties.

In response, an outraged Jackson urged Congress to pass the Force Bill to allow the federal government to use the military if state authorities resisted paying proper duties. A bloody confrontation seemed likely until Henry Clay forged a compromise in 1833. Clay proposed a tariff bill that would gradually lower duties over a ten-year period. The compromise also included passage of the Force Bill. The tension between states' rights and federal authority subsided—temporarily.

**JACKSON'S BANK WAR** Although Jackson defended federal power in the nullification crisis, he tried to decrease federal power when it came to the Second Bank of the United States. Jackson believed that the national bank was an agent of the wealthy, and that its members cared nothing for the common people.

In 1832 Jackson won reelection despite the efforts of his critics to make a campaign issue out of Jackson's opposition to the bank. After his reelection, he tried to kill the bank by withdrawing all government deposits from the bank's branches and placing them in certain state banks called "pet banks" because of their loyalty to the Democratic Party. As a result, the Bank of the United States became just another bank. **F**

Jackson won the bank war, but his tactics and policies angered many people. Many accused him of acting more like a king than a president. In 1832, his opponents formed a new political party, which they later called the Whig Party.

*F. Answer*
He thought the national bank was a tool of the upper classes and a threat to democracy.

**MAIN IDEA**

**Analyzing Motives**
**F** What were some of Jackson's reasons for opposing the Second Bank of the United States?

## Analyzing *Political Cartoons*

### "KING ANDREW THE FIRST"

Andrew Jackson once justified his tendency to place personal prerogative above constitutional law or national policy by stating that "One man with courage makes a majority." His critics replied with accusations of tyranny. The *New York American* condemned Jackson as a "maniac," who would "trample the rights of our people under his feet." The Whig convention of 1834 declared, "Your president has become your MONARCH."

Both of those sentiments are reflected in this political cartoon that portrays Jackson as a king.

- Ancient portraits of kings often depicted them grinding their conquered enemies beneath their heel. Beneath Jackson's feet are the torn pages of the Constitution.

- In one hand, Jackson is holding a scepter, a symbol of kingly power, while in the other, he is holding the veto, a symbol of presidential power.

### SKILLBUILDER Analyzing Political Cartoons

1. What does this cartoon suggest about Jackson's attitude toward the Constitution?
2. How does this cartoon particularly comment on Jackson's use of presidential power?

BORN TO COMMAND.

OF VETO MEMORY.

HAD I BEEN CONSULTED.

KING ANDREW THE FIRST.

---

**DIFFERENTIATING INSTRUCTION**    **GIFTED AND TALENTED**

### Creating Political Cartoons

Have students work alone, or in groups, to create a political cartoon about an event or person described in Section 2. For example, students might draw a cartoon depicting Jackson's distrust of the national bank, or one illustrating some aspect of the Hayne and Webster debates.

**Rubrics**

A political cartoon should . . .

· be aimed at a specific audience
· use elements of exaggeration
· make use of recognizable symbols

 Integrated Assessment
· Rubric 4

## 4 Successors Deal with Jackson's Legacy

When Jackson announced that he would not run for a third term in 1836, the Democrats chose Vice-President Martin Van Buren as their candidate. The newly formed Whig Party ran three regional candidates against him. With Jackson's support, however, Van Buren easily won the election.

**THE PANIC OF 1837** Along with the presidency, however, Van Buren inherited the consequences of Jackson's bank war. Many of the pet banks that accepted federal deposits were wildcat banks that printed bank notes wildly in excess of the gold and silver they had on deposit. Such wildcat banks were doomed to fail when people tried to redeem their currency for gold or silver.

By May 1837, many banks stopped accepting paper currency. In the panic of 1837, bank closings and the collapse of the credit system cost many people their savings, bankrupted hundreds of businesses, and put more than a third of the population out of work.

**HARRISON AND TYLER** In 1840 Van Buren ran for reelection against Whig Party candidate William Henry Harrison, who was known as "Tippecanoe" for a battle he won against Native Americans in 1811. The Whigs blamed Van Buren for the weak economy and portrayed Harrison, the old war hero, as a man of the people and Van Buren as an aristocrat.

Harrison won the election, but died just a month after his inauguration. **John Tyler,** Harrison's vice-president, became president. A strong-minded Virginian and former Democrat, Tyler opposed many parts of the Whig program. He halted hopes for significant Whig reforms.

The Democrat and Whig parties went on to dominate national politics until the 1850s. The new politicians appealed more to passion than to reason. They courted popularity in a way that John Quincy Adams and his predecessors never would have. Thus, the style of politics in America had changed drastically since the 1790s. Political speeches became a form of mass entertainment, involving far more Americans in the political process. Also, the West was playing an increasing role in national politics. That trend would continue as more Americans moved to places like Texas and California.

**MAIN IDEA**

**Analyzing Causes**
**G** How did "wildcat banks" contribute to the panic of 1837?

**G. Answer**
"Wildcat banks" printed paper currency in excess of the gold and silver necessary to back it up. Eventually, other banks stopped accepting that currency and the nation's economy collapsed.

---

### SECTION 2 ASSESSMENT

**1. TERMS & NAMES** For each term or name, write a sentence explaining its significance.
- Henry Clay
- American System
- John C. Calhoun
- Missouri Compromise
- Andrew Jackson
- John Quincy Adams
- Jacksonian democracy
- Trail of Tears
- John Tyler

**MAIN IDEA**

**2. TAKING NOTES**
In a chart like the one shown, write newspaper headlines that tell the significance of each date.

| Dates | Headlines |
|-------|-----------|
| 1815  |           |
| 1820  |           |
| 1828  |           |
| 1832  |           |
| 1837  |           |
| 1838  |           |

**CRITICAL THINKING**

**3. EVALUATING**
In what ways do you think the Missouri Compromise and the nullification crisis of 1832 might be considered important milestones in American history? **Think About:**
- the expansion of slavery into the West
- Calhoun's nullification theory
- Jackson's reaction to South Carolina's actions

**4. ANALYZING CAUSES**
What factors set the stage for the Indian Removal Act of 1830 and the Trail of Tears? **Think About:**
- U.S. expansion to the west
- removal treaties
- Jackson's response to *Worcester* v. *Georgia*

---

## Instruct: Objective 4

**Successors Deal with Jackson's Legacy**
TAKS SS11 5(US24.B)

- What issues did Martin Van Buren face as president?
- What prompted the Panic of 1837?
- What factors helped William Henry Harrison win the presidency?

 In-Depth Resources: Unit 1
· Guided Reading, p. 78

### Connections Across Time

**1837 AND 1929**

**The Great Depression**
Like the Panic of 1837, the Great Depression in the 1930s resulted in bank closings, unemployment, and widespread suffering. To aid recovery, the U.S. government assumed greater control over banks and the stock market. The government increased monetary output to support new programs, a practice known as deficit spending, to help boost the economy.

## Assess & Reteach

**SECTION 2 ASSESSMENT**
Have students take turns quizzing each other on the questions.

 Formal Assessment
· Section Quiz, p. 57

**SELF-ASSESSMENT**
Have students create a three-column chart, on which they list Jackson's policies on Native Americans, states' rights, and the economy and note the impact of the policies.

**RETEACH**
Review the main ideas by writing the central point of each sub-head in the section.

 In-Depth Resources: Unit 1
· Reteaching Activity, p. 88

---

**Answers** ASSESSMENT 2

**1. TERMS & NAMES**

**2. TAKING NOTES**
1815—"Henry Clay Proposes American System"
1820—"Congress Compromises on Missouri Issue"
1828—"Jackson Wins Presidency"
1832—"South Carolina Nullifies Tariff"
1837—"Banks Says No More Paper, Panic Follows"
1838—"Trail of Tears"

**3. EVALUATING**
The Missouri Compromise and the nullification crisis opened debate on issues of nationalism and sectionalism. The Missouri Compromise marks the beginning of government action to retard the growth of slavery. The nullification crisis threatened to destroy the Union by raising the issue of states rights.

**4. ANALYZING CAUSES**
Factors—discrimination against Native Americans; U.S. territorial expansion; Jackson's rejection of *Worcester v. Georgia*

*The Growth of a Young Nation* **127**

TRACING **THEMES**

## Objectives

· To explain the significance of states' rights

· To summarize the conflicts between state and federal powers

## Focus & Motivate

**Making Decisions** Ask students to imagine a job with two bosses who give different orders. What are possible causes and effects of such a conflict? Ask students what they would do if faced with such a situation.

## More About . . .

### States' Rights

Clarify that the Supreme Court's 1996 decision sided with the states against the U.S. Justice Department, which to effect a recent expansion of the Voting Rights Act, had set up the districts to try to increase African-American representation. The Supreme Court decided that such redistricting was unconstitutional.

# TRACING THEMES

# States' Rights

The power struggle between states and the federal government has caused controversy since the country's beginning. At its worst, the conflict resulted in the Civil War. Today, state and federal governments continue to square off on jurisdictional issues.

- In 1996, the Supreme Court ruled that congressional districts in Texas and North Carolina that had been redrawn to increase minority representation were unconstitutional.
- In 2000, the Supreme Court agreed to hear another case in the ongoing—since 1979—dispute between the federal government and the state of Alaska over who has authority to lease offshore land for oil and gas drilling.

Constitutional conflicts between states' rights and federal jurisdiction are pictured here. As you read, see how each issue was resolved.

## 1787

▼ **CONSTITUTIONAL CONVENTION**

**ISSUE: The Constitution tried to resolve the original debate over states' rights versus federal authority.**

At the Constitutional Convention in Philadelphia, delegates wanted to create a federal government that was stronger than the one created by the Articles of Confederation. But delegates disagreed about whether the federal government should have more power than the states. They also disagreed about whether large states should have more power than small states in the national legislature. The convention compromised—the Constitution reserves certain powers for the states, delegates other powers to the federal government, divides some powers between state and federal governments, and tries to balance the differing needs of the states through two houses of Congress.

## 1832

**NULLIFICATION** ▲

**ISSUE: The state of South Carolina moved to nullify, or declare void, a tariff set by Congress.**

In the cartoon above, President Andrew Jackson, right, is playing a game called bragg. One of his opponents, Vice President John C. Calhoun, is hiding two cards, "Nullification" and "Anti-Tariff," behind him. Jackson is doing poorly in this game, but he eventually won the real nullification dispute. When Congress passed high tariffs on imports in 1832, politicians from South Carolina, led by Calhoun, tried to nullify the tariff law, or declare it void. Jackson threatened to enforce the law with federal troops. Congress reduced the tariff to avoid a confrontation, and Calhoun resigned the vice-presidency.

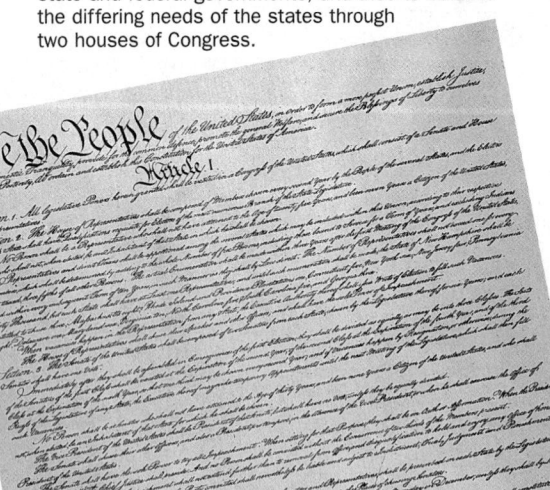

**128** CHAPTER 3 *The Growth of a Young Nation*

## RECOMMENDED RESOURCES

Ellis, Richard E. *The Union at Risk.* New York: Oxford UP, 1990. An exploration of Jacksonian democracy, states' rights, and the nullification crisis.

McDonald, Forrest. *States' Rights and the Union: Imperium in Imperio, 1776–1876.* Lawrence, Univ. of Kansas Press 2000. Struggle between federal and state governments.

Mason, Alpheus Thomas, ed. *The States' Rights Debate.* rev. ed. New York: Oxford UP, 1972. A collection of views on antifederalism and the Constitution.

Wilkinson, J. Havie. *From Brown to Bakke.* New York: Oxford UP, 1981. An account of 20th-century Supreme Court decisions regarding school integration.

**VIDEOS**

*Federalism.* MTI Film & Video, 1986. Focuses on federal vs. state and local government powers.

*Hamilton and Jefferson on Democracy.* Encyclopaedia Britannica, 1982. Bill of Rights in Action series.

**SOFTWARE**

*U.S. Government: The First 200 Years.* Clearvue, dist. ESL.

## 1860

◀ SOUTH CAROLINA'S SECESSION

**ISSUE: The conflict over a state's right to secede, or withdraw, from the Union led to the Civil War.**

In December 1860, Southern secessionists cheered "secession" enthusiastically in front of the Mills House (left), a hotel in Charleston, South Carolina. South Carolina seceded after the election of Abraham Lincoln, whom the South perceived as anti-states' rights and antislavery. Lincoln took the position that states did not have the right to secede from the Union. In 1861, he ordered that provisions be sent to the federal troops stationed at Fort Sumter in Charleston harbor. South Carolinians fired on the fort—and the Civil War was under way. The Union's victory in the war ended the most serious challenge to federal authority: states did not have the right to secede from the Union.

## 1957

LITTLE ROCK CENTRAL HIGH SCHOOL ▲

**ISSUE: Some Southern governors refused to obey federal desegregation mandates for schools.**

In 1957, President Eisenhower mobilized federal troops in Little Rock, Arkansas, to enforce the Supreme Court's 1954 ruling in the case of *Brown* v. *Board of Education of Topeka*. This ruling made segregation in public schools illegal. The Arkansas National Guard escorted nine African-American students into Little Rock Central High School against the wishes of Governor Orval Faubus, who had tried to prevent the students from entering the school. After this incident, Faubus closed the high schools in Little Rock in 1958 and 1959, thereby avoiding desegregation.

---

### THINKING CRITICALLY

**CONNECT TO HISTORY**

1. **Creating a Chart** For each incident pictured, create a chart that tells who was on each side of the issue, summarizes each position, and explains how the issue was resolved.

**CONNECT TO TODAY**

2. **Using Primary and Secondary Sources** Research one of the controversies in the bulleted list in the opening paragraph or another states' rights controversy of the 1990s or 2000s. Decide which side you support. Write a paragraph explaining your position on the issue.
**SEE SKILLBUILDER HANDBOOK, PAGE R22.**

  **RESEARCH LINKS** CLASSZONE.COM

## Instruct

1. What were the disagreements that emerged over federal and state power during the Constitutional Convention?

2. What was the nullification crisis?

3. Why were federal troops sent to Little Rock?

**MAKING PERSONAL CONNECTIONS**

Have students voice their opinions on federal vs. state power. What roles do they feel each should play as governing bodies?

Ask students to think of issues that involve a dispute between their local government and the state or the federal government.

---

### More About . . .

**Little Rock**
President Eisenhower insisted that his decision to send federal troops to maintain order in Little Rock—thus superseding Arkansas authority—was one he did not make lightly. "The running of our school system and the maintenance of peace and order in each of our states are strictly local affairs, and the federal government does not interfere except in very few special cases," he declared. He added, however, that the "very basis of our individual rights and freedoms rests upon the certainty that the President and the executive branch of government will support and insure the carrying out of the decisions by the federal courts, even, when necessary, with all the means at the President's command."

---

### THINKING CRITICALLY: ANSWERS

**1. CONNECT TO TODAY**

**Rubrics**

A chart should . . .
· identify the groups on either side of the issue and indicate leading figures in each group
· summarize each side's position
· explain how the issue was resolved
· include factual supporting evidence

**2. CONNECT TO HISTORY**

**Rubrics**

Student paragraphs should . . .
· include references to important primary and secondary sources on a states' rights controversy
· lend support to one side of the issue
· give a well-reasoned explanation for the position

# Manifest Destiny

| MAIN IDEA | WHY IT MATTERS NOW | Terms & Names |
|---|---|---|
| Through settlement and war, the United States greatly expanded its boundaries during the mid-1800s. | The actions Americans took during this period established the current borders of the 48 contiguous states. | • manifest destiny • Santa Fe Trail • Oregon Trail • Stephen F. Austin • Texas Revolution • the Alamo • Sam Houston • James K. Polk • Republic of California • Treaty of Guadalupe Hidalgo |

**TEKS** U.S. History 8A, 9A, 9B, 10A, 10B, 20A, 24B, 24G, 24H, 25A, 25B, 25C, 25D, 26B

### One American's Story

In 1821, Stephen F. Austin led the first of several groups of American settlers to a fertile area along the Brazos River. Drawn by the promise of inexpensive land and economic opportunity, Austin established a colony of American settlers in Tejas, or Texas, then the northernmost province of the Mexican state of Coahuila. However, Austin's plans didn't work out as well as he had hoped; 12 years later, he found himself in a Mexican prison and his new homeland in an uproar. After his release, Austin spoke about the impending crisis between Texas and Mexico.

⭐ **A PERSONAL VOICE** STEPHEN F. AUSTIN
" Texas needs peace, and a local government; its inhabitants are farmers, and they need a calm and quiet life. . . . [But] my efforts to serve Texas involved me in the labyrinth of Mexican politics. I was arrested, and have suffered a long persecution and imprisonment. . . . I fully hoped to have found Texas at peace and in tranquillity, but regret to find it in commotion; all disorganized, all in anarchy, and threatened with immediate hostilities. . . . Can this state of things exist without precipitating the country into a war? I think it cannot. "

—quoted in *Lone Star: A History of Texas and Texans*

**Stephen F. Austin**

Austin's prediction was correct. War did break out in Texas—twice. First, Texans rebelled against the Mexican government. Then, the United States went to war against Mexico over the boundaries of Texas. These conflicts were the climax of decades of competition over the western half of North America—a competition that involved the United States, Mexico, Native Americans, and various European nations. The end result of the competition would be U.S. control over a huge swath of the continent, from the Atlantic to the Pacific.

 Mini-Lesson 1: SS11 2(US11.A)

## **1** Settling the Frontier

As various presidents established policies in the early 19th century that expanded U.S. territory, American settlers pushed first into the Northwest Territory and then headed farther west.

---

## PROGRAM RESOURCES

**AMERICANS PURSUE MANIFEST DESTINY** For a quarter century after the War of 1812, only a few Americans explored the West. Then, in the 1840s, expansion fever gripped the country. Many Americans began to believe that their movement westward was predestined by God. The phrase **"manifest destiny"** expressed the belief that the United States was ordained to expand to the Pacific Ocean and into Mexican and Native American territory. Many Americans also believed that this destiny was manifest, or obvious and inevitable.

Most Americans had practical reasons for moving west. For settlers, the abundance of land was the greatest attraction. As the number of western settlers climbed, merchants and manufacturers followed, seeking new markets for their goods. Many Americans also trekked west because of personal economic problems in the East. The panic of 1837, for example, had disastrous consequences and convinced many Americans that they would be better off attempting a fresh start in the West. **A**

**TRAILS WEST** The settlers and traders who made the trek west used a series of old Native American trails as well as new routes. One of the busiest routes was the **Santa Fe Trail**, which stretched 780 miles from Independence, Missouri, to Santa Fe in the Mexican province of New Mexico. (See map on page 132.) Each spring from 1821 through the 1860s, American traders loaded their covered wagons with goods and set off toward Santa Fe.

For about the first 150 miles, traders traveled individually. After that, fearing attacks by Native Americans, traders banded into organized groups of up to 100 wagons. Cooperation, though, came to an abrupt end when Santa Fe came into view. Traders raced off on their own as each tried to be the first to arrive. After a few days of trading, they loaded their wagons with goods, restocked their animals, and headed back to Missouri.

The **Oregon Trail** stretched from Independence, Missouri, to Oregon City, Oregon. It was blazed in 1836 by two Methodist missionaries named Marcus and Narcissa Whitman. By driving their wagon as far as Fort Boise (near present-day Boise, Idaho), they proved that wagons could travel on the Oregon Trail.

Following the Whitmans' lead, many pioneers migrated west on the Oregon Trail. Some bought "prairie schooners," wooden-wheeled wagons covered with sailcloth and pulled by oxen. Most walked, however, pushing handcarts loaded with a few precious possessions, food, and other supplies. The trip took months, even if all went well.

**THE MORMON MIGRATION** One group migrated westward along the Oregon Trail to escape persecution. These people were the Mormons, a religious community that would play a major role in the development of the West. Founded by Joseph Smith in upstate New York in 1827, the Mormon community moved to Ohio and then Illinois to escape persecution. After an anti-Mormon mob murdered Smith, a leader named Brigham Young urged the Mormons to move farther west. Thousands of believers walked to Nebraska, across Wyoming to the Rockies, and then southwest. In 1847, the Mormons stopped at the edge of the desert near the Great Salt Lake, in what is now Utah. Young boldly

**MAIN IDEA**

**Predicting Effects**

**A** How might manifest destiny later affect U.S. relations with Native Americans?

**A. Possible Answer** Many settlers will feel entitled to the land currently occupied by Native Americans and will try to force them out, leading to tension and most likely violence.

**Background** The Mormon religion was controversial for its belief in polygamy, a practice that allowed a man to have more than one wife.

## More About . . .

### Traveling the Santa Fe Trail
Council Grove, in present-day Kansas, was the last rendezvous point for joining a caravan to Santa Fe. The two-to-three-month journey from Missouri to New Mexico covered approximately 780 miles. The return trip covered the same distance, but often in half the time due to lighter loads. The high point of the trip was the arrival in Santa Fe. Whole towns turned out to greet the wagoneers, who were dressed in their best clothes in honor of the occasion.

## HISTORICAL SPOTLIGHT

### JIM BECKWOURTH 1798–1867?
James Pierson Beckwourth (or Beckwirth) was the toughest kind of pioneer, a mountain man. The son of an African-American woman, he ventured westward with a fur-trading expedition in 1823 and found the place that would become his home for nearly the next quarter century—the Rocky Mountains. He greatly impressed the Crow, who gave him the name "Bloody Arm" because of his skill as a fighter.

Beckwourth served from 1837 until 1848 as an Army scout and trading-post operator. In 1848, he discovered a passage in the Sierra Nevada range that led to California's Sacramento Valley and decided to settle down near the pass and become a rancher. "In the spring of 1852 I established myself in Beckwourth Valley, and finally found myself transformed into a hotel-keeper and chief of a trading-post."

## HISTORICAL SPOTLIGHT

### Jim Beckwourth
Before they read about Jim Beckwourth, ask students to list some qualities of a successful pioneer. (*courage, independence, strength, adaptability, resourcefulness, patience*) Have students read about Beckwourth and make note of qualities that he possessed.

## More About . . .

### Life on the Oregon Trail
Settlers who were headed out West faced diseases such as cholera. There was no known treatment for cholera, and the victim often died within days. With no time for elaborate funerals, it was not uncommon for a wagon train to leave a dying person by the side of the road. Sometime the sufferer was left with a "watcher," whose job it was to dig the grave. Often the victim sat and watched. Historians suspect that occasionally, due to the haste of the watcher to catch up to the wagon train, the victim might have been buried while still alive.

---

**ACTIVITY** **SKILLBUILDER LESSON**

## Analyzing Assumptions

**Explaining the Skill** When using historical sources, historians look for assumptions, or bias, in the writer's presentation. For example, the statement "You would not understand; you are only ten" is based on the unstated assumption that a ten-year-old would not be capable of understanding. Some assumptions are based on factual evidence, while others are based only on opinion.

**Applying the Skill** Have students analyze the assumptions underlying the concept of "manifest destiny." Ask the following questions:

· What underlying beliefs are reflected in the concept of manifest destiny? (*God looks favorably on the United States, but not on Native Americans.*)

· What does it mean for something to be destined? (*meant to be; inevitable; fate*)

📄 In-Depth Resources: Unit 1
· Skillbuilder Practice: Analyzing Assumptions, p. 85

## HISTORY from VISUALS

### Interpreting the Map

Based on the topographic map, ask students what types of natural obstacles the settlers might have encountered on the trails. *(Mountain passes, rivers, danger, the elements)*

### Extension
Ask students to determine the length of the longest trail. *(The Butterfield Overland)*

## More About . . .

### The Westward Settlers

After one woman began her journey westward, she wrote in her diary: "Who is there that does not recollect their first night when started on a long journey, the well-known voices of our friends still ring in our ears." Many of the women who traveled westward described missing their friends. Men, on the other hand, seemed less concerned about losing old friends. As one man wrote in his diary about his wife, "She thought much of home—friends—prospects—& present condition. I tried to have her get above these things."

## American Trails West, 1860

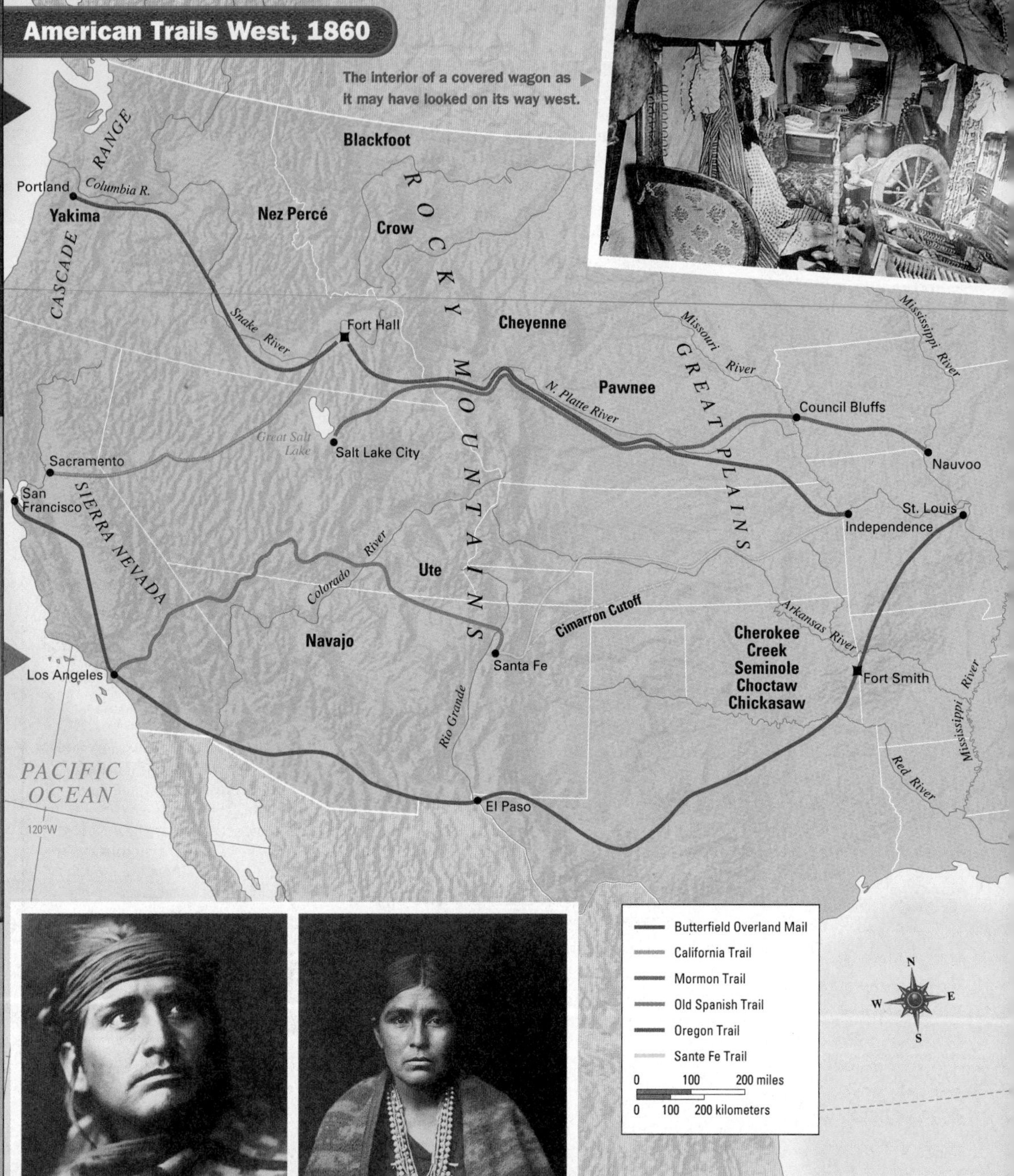

The interior of a covered wagon as it may have looked on its way west.

Blackfoot
Portland
Yakima
Nez Percé
Crow
ROCKY RANGE
CASCADE
Columbia R.
Snake River
Fort Hall
Cheyenne
MOUNTAINS
Missouri River
Mississippi River
N. Platte River
Pawnee
Council Bluffs
Great Salt Lake
Salt Lake City
GREAT PLAINS
Nauvoo
Sacramento
San Francisco
SIERRA NEVADA
Colorado River
Ute
St. Louis
Independence
Cimarron Cutoff
Arkansas River
Navajo
Santa Fe
Cherokee
Creek
Seminole
Choctaw
Chickasaw
Fort Smith
Los Angeles
Rio Grande
Mississippi River
Red River
PACIFIC OCEAN
120°W
El Paso

A Navajo man and woman in photographs taken by Edward S. Curtis.

**Legend:**
- Butterfield Overland Mail
- California Trail
- Mormon Trail
- Old Spanish Trail
- Oregon Trail
- Sante Fe Trail

0   100   200 miles
0   100   200 kilometers

### GEOGRAPHY SKILLBUILDER
1. **Region** Approximately how long was the trail from St. Louis to El Paso?
2. **Movement** At a wagon train speed of 15 miles a day, about how long would that trip take?

132   CHAPTER 3 *The Growth of a Young Nation*

### Interviewing Settlers

**Class Time** 45 minutes

**Task** Interviewing settlers on their westward journey

**Purpose** To explore what life was like on the westward trails

**Directions** Divide the class into groups. Have each group decide who will play the role of settlers and who will be the interviewer. Tell the interviewers that they are reporters assigned to write about life on the trails from the settlers' perspective. Each group should research its role in the library or on the Internet in preparation for the question and answer session. Have students tape their interviews. Play each tape for the class.

Integrated Assessment
· Rubric 3

**MAIN IDEA**

**Analyzing Motives**
**B** Why did the Mormons move farther west in their search for a new home?

**B. Answer**
The Mormons were persecuted for their religion. They moved to a bleak, unpopulated area where nobody would bother them.

declared, "This is the place." Soon they had coaxed settlements and farms from the bleak landscape by irrigating their fields. Salt Lake City blossomed out of the land the Mormons called Deseret. **B**

**SETTING BOUNDARIES** In the early 1840s, Great Britain still claimed areas near the Canadian border in parts of what are now Maine and Minnesota. The Webster-Ashburton Treaty of 1842 settled these territorial disputes in the East and the Midwest, but the two nations merely continued the "joint occupation" of the Oregon Territory that they had first established in 1818. In 1846 the two countries agreed to extend the mainland boundary along the 49th parallel westward from the Rocky Mountains to Puget Sound, establishing the current boundary between the United States and Canada. Unfortunately, establishing the boundary in the Southwest with Mexico would not be so peaceful.

# Texan Independence ❷

After 300 years of Spanish rule, only a few thousand Mexican settlers had migrated to what is now Texas. After 1820, that changed as Texas became an important region in Mexico and then an independent republic.

**MEXICAN INDEPENDENCE AND TEXAN LAND GRANTS** The mission system used by Spain declined after Mexico had won independence from Spain in 1821. After freeing the missions from Spanish control, the Mexican government offered the surrounding lands to government officials and ranchers. To make the land more secure and stable, the Mexican government also encouraged Americans to settle in Texas.

**MAIN IDEA**

**Developing Historical Perspective**
**C** Why did many Americans initially settle in Texas?

**C. Answer**
The Mexican government invited settlers there. Many Americans rushed at the chance to buy inexpensive land.

Many Americans rushed at the chance to buy inexpensive land in Texas. The population of Anglo, or English-speaking, settlers from the United States soon surpassed the population of Tejanos, or Mexican settlers, who lived in Texas. Among the more prominent leaders of these American settlers was **Stephen F. Austin.** **C**

Austin's father, Moses Austin, had received a land grant from Spain to establish a colony between the Brazos and Colorado rivers but died before he was able to carry out his plans. Stephen obtained permission, first from Spain and then from Mexico after it had won its independence, to carry out his father's project. In 1821 he established a colony where "no drunkard, no gambler, no profane swearer, and no idler" would be allowed.

The main settlement of the colony was named San Felipe de Austin, in Stephen's honor. By 1825, Austin had issued 297 land grants to the group that later became known as Texas's Old Three Hundred. Each family received either 177 very inexpensive acres of farmland, or 4,428 acres for stock grazing, as well as a 10-year exemption from paying taxes. "I am convinced," Austin said, "that I could take on fifteen hundred families as easily as three hundred if permitted to do so." By 1830, there were more than 20,000 Americans in Texas.

**THE TEXAS REVOLUTION** Despite peaceful cooperation between Anglos and Tejanos, differences over cultural issues intensified between Anglos and the Mexican government. The overwhelmingly Protestant Anglo settlers spoke English instead of Spanish. Furthermore, many of the settlers were Southerners, who had brought slaves with them to Texas. Mexico, which had abolished slavery in 1829, insisted in vain that the Texans free their slaves.

*Skillbuilder Answers*
1. About 1,100 miles.
2. Roughly 74 days.

Meanwhile, Mexican politics had become increasingly unstable. Austin had traveled to Mexico City late in 1833 to present petitions to Mexican president Antonio López de Santa Anna for greater self-government for Texas. While Austin was on his way home, Santa Anna had Austin imprisoned for inciting revolution. After Santa Anna suspended local powers in Texas and other

**Connections Across Time**
**1840S AND TODAY**

**The Mormons**
Today, the Mormons make up about 70 percent of the population of Utah. The Mormon Church maintains an extensive educational system that includes Brigham Young University in Provo, Utah. Mormons also promote the arts and music. The Mormon Tabernacle Choir in Salt Lake City is famous throughout the world for its concert tours.

**Instruct: Objective ❷**
**Texas Independence**
TAKS SS11 5(US24.A)
· How did Mexicans encourage American settlement in Texas?
· What were the causes of the Texas Revolution?
· What was the significance of the battle at the Alamo?

📖 In-Depth Resources: Unit 1
· Guided Reading, p. 79

**Tracing Themes**
**IMMIGRATION AND MIGRATION**

**Migration to Texas**
Many American settlers moved to Texas because of the availability of cheap land. Others migrated to escape the congestion of life in the East. While there were stretches of harsh and unforgiving terrain, the region boasted many miles of lush and tranquil landscapes. "I should be driven to extremities in attempting to spread before you the singularly picturesque appearance of most of the upper country," said one settler in north Texas.

---

**DIFFERENTIATING INSTRUCTION**    **LESS PROFICIENT READERS**

**Clarifying**

To help students understand the impact of Mexican independence, have them create a cause-and-effect chart like the one in the column to the right and fill in the missing information.

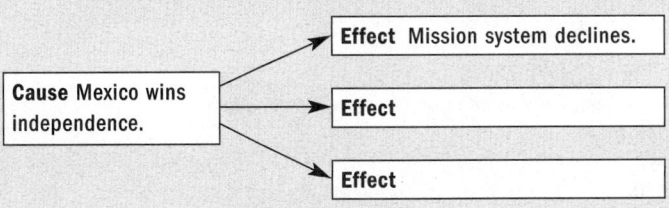

**Cause** Mexico wins independence.

**Effect** Mission system declines.

**Effect**

**Effect**

*The Growth of a Young Nation*  **133**

## More About . . .

### Davy Crockett at the Alamo

A Mexican soldier who fought at the Alamo witnessed Crockett's valor during the siege. The soldier wrote: "Of the many soldiers who took deliberate aim at him and fired, not one ever hit him. On the contrary, he never missed a shot. He killed at least eight of our men, besides wounding several others. This being observed by a lieutenant who had come in over the wall, he sprang at him and dealt him a deadly blow with his sword, just over the right eye, which felled him to the ground, and in an instant he was pierced by not less than 20 bayonets."

## HISTORY from VISUALS

### Interpreting the Map

Point out that the star-shaped symbols on the map are color-coded to represent either Texan victories or Mexican victories. Have students make a two-column chart showing the Texans' win-loss record, based on information in the map. (*Texan wins—San Antonio and San Jacinto; Texan losses—Alamo, Goliad, and Refugio*)

**Extension** Ask students what the names of the Texan cities suggest about early Spanish and British involvement in the region. (*Cities are named in both Spanish and English; Washington-on-the-Brazos reflects a combination of both cultures.*)

---

Mexican states, several rebellions broke out, including one that would be known as the **Texas Revolution**.

When Austin returned to Texas in 1835, he was convinced that war was its "only resource." Determined to force Texas to obey Mexican law, Santa Anna marched his army toward San Antonio. At the same time, Austin and his followers issued a call for Texans to arm themselves. **D**

**"REMEMBER THE ALAMO!"** In San Antonio, the commander of the Anglo troops, Lieutenant Colonel William Travis, moved his men into **the Alamo**, a mission and fort in what is now San Antonio. Travis believed that maintaining control of the Alamo would prevent Santa Anna's movement farther north.

From February 23, 1836, Santa Anna and his troops attacked the rebels holed up in the Alamo. On March 2, 1836, as the battle for the Alamo raged, Texans declared their independence from Mexico and quickly ratified a constitution based on that of the United States. The 13-day siege finally ended on March 6, 1836, when Mexican troops scaled the Alamo's walls. All 187 U.S. defenders and hundreds of Mexicans died.

Later in March, Santa Anna's troops executed 300 rebels at Goliad. The Alamo and the Goliad executions whipped the Texan rebels into a fury. Six weeks after the defeat at the Alamo, the rebels' commander in chief, **Sam Houston,** and 900

*Skillbuilder Answers*
1. The Red River.
2. Control of the land west of the Republic of Texas up to the Rio Grande.

### MAIN IDEA

**Analyzing Issues**
**D** What disagreement led to the Texas Revolution?

**D. Answer** Texans wanted more self-government; Mexico wanted Texans to obey Mexican laws.

## War for Texas Independence, 1835–1836

Henry Arthur McArdle conveys the brutality of the fighting in *Dawn at the Alamo*, painted between 1876 and 1883.

Legend:
- Texan forces
- Mexican forces
- ✦ Texan victory
- ✦ Mexican victory

0    75    150 miles
0    75    150 kilometers

Land disputed by Texas and Mexico

UNITED STATES

REPUBLIC OF TEXAS

Red River
Sabine River
Nacogdoches
Trinity River
Neches River
Brazos River
Colorado River
Pecos River
Rio Grande

Waterloo (Austin)
ALAMO, Feb. 23–Mar. 6, 1836
SAN ANTONIO, Dec. 10, 1835
Washington-on-the-Brazos
SAN JACINTO, Apr. 21, 1836
Santa Anna
Houston
Galveston
GOLIAD, Mar. 20, 1836
Nueces River
Matagorda
Gulf of Mexico
REFUGIO, Mar. 12–15, 1836
Laredo
Corpus Christi
MEXICO
Matamoros

95°W    91°W

### GEOGRAPHY SKILLBUILDER

1. **Place** What geographical feature marked the northern border of the Republic of Texas?
2. **Region** What does the map show as a major disagreement left unresolved by the war?

**134** CHAPTER 3 *The Growth of a Young Nation*

---

### Creating a Pictorial Essay of the Alamo

**Class Time** 45 minutes

**Task** Creating a pictorial essay

**Purpose** To examine the events that took place at the Alamo

**Directions** Have students work in groups to find pictures or descriptions of the battle at the Alamo. Remind students that they can draw pictures, make photocopies, or print material from the Internet. Ask students to include a current picture of the Alamo. Students should arrange the pictures, write captions, and present their pictorial essays to the class.

📄 Integrated Assessment
· Rubric 4

**SAM HOUSTON**
**1793–1863**

Sam Houston ran away from home in Tennessee at about age 15 and lived for three years with the Cherokee. He later fought in the U.S. Army, studied law, was elected to Congress, and became governor of Tennessee.

In his memoirs Houston told of listening in vain for the signal guns indicating that the Alamo still stood. "I listened with an acuteness of sense which no man can understand whose hearing has not been sharpened by the teachings of the dwellers of the forest."

The Republic of Texas chose Houston to be its first president. When Texas became a state, he was elected to the U.S. Senate.

**SANTA ANNA**
**1785–1876**

Antonio López de Santa Anna reportedly once said, "If I were God, I would wish to be more." Santa Anna began his career fighting for Spain in the war over Mexican independence. Later, he switched sides to fight for Mexico.

Declaring himself the "Napoleon of the West," Santa Anna took control of the government after Mexico won independence in 1821. He spent the next 35 years alternately serving as president, leading troops into battle, and living in exile. Santa Anna served as president of Mexico 11 times.

Santa Anna was a complex man with much charm. He sacrificed his considerable wealth to return again and again to the battlefield and died in poverty, almost forgotten.

**KEY PLAYERS**

**Sam Houston and Santa Anna**
Sam Houston developed an unusual combat strategy. He ordered his soldiers to retreat, hoping to lure the Mexican army deeper into Texas. He would wait until the Mexicans were overextended and then attack. Initially, Houston's officers doubted he would take the offensive and engage in battle. But the victory at the Battle of San Jacinto proved there was merit to his strategy.

**More About . . .**

**The Election of 1844**
James Polk was not even expected to run for president, much less win. Many were certain the race would be between Henry Clay for the Whigs and Martin Van Buren for the Democrats. Van Buren and Clay went so far as to meet before any official nomination and agreed to sidestep the most controversial issue of the day—the annexation of Texas. Clay won the Whig nomination, but Van Buren was not nominated. Democratic leaders, in favor of annexation, nominated Polk, who wanted to make Texas a state. Polk won a razor-thin victory over Clay.

soldiers surprised a group of Mexicans near the San Jacinto River. With shouts of "Remember the Alamo!" the Texans killed 630 of Santa Anna's soldiers in 18 minutes and captured Santa Anna himself, who allegedly attempted to escape by dressing in a private's uniform. The victorious Texans set Santa Anna free only after he signed the Treaty of Velasco, which granted independence to Texas. In September 1836, Sam Houston was elected president of the new Republic of Texas.

**TEXAS MOVES TOWARD THE UNION** Most Texans hoped that the United States would annex their republic, but U.S. opinion divided along sectional lines. Southerners wanted Texas in order to extend slavery, which already had been established there. Northerners feared that the annexation of more slave territory would tip the uneasy balance in the Senate in favor of slave states—and prompt war with Mexico.

The 1844 U.S. presidential campaign focused on westward expansion. The winner, **James K. Polk,** a slaveholder, firmly favored the annexation of Texas.

---

**MAIN IDEA**

**Contrasting**
 How would you contrast the Northern and Southern positions on the annexation of Texas?

**E. Answers**
**North:** opposed the admission of Texas as a slave state because this would tip the balance in the Senate in favor of slave-holding states. **South:** believed that Texas should be admitted to the Union as a slave state.

---

## The War with Mexico

In March 1845, angered by U.S.-Texas negotiation on annexation, the Mexican government recalled its ambassador from Washington. On December 29, 1845, Texas entered the Union. Events moved quickly toward war.

**POLK URGES WAR** President Polk believed that war with Mexico would bring not only Texas into the Union, but also New Mexico and California. Hence, the president supported Texan claims in disputes with Mexico over the Texas–Mexico border. While Texas insisted that its southern border extended to the Rio Grande, Mexico maintained that Texas's border stopped at the Nueces River, 100–150 miles northeast of the Rio Grande.

Despite the fact that Mexico had ceased formal diplomatic relations with the U.S., Polk hoped to negotiate secretly the boundary dispute, as well as the sale of California and New Mexico. He dispatched John Slidell, a congressman from Louisiana, to negotiate both matters. The Mexican government refused to receive Slidell. When Polk heard this news, he ordered U.S. troops into Mexican territory.

**Instruct: Objective**

**The War with Mexico**
TAKS SS11 5(WH26.C)
· What events precipitated the war with Mexico?
· What was the result of the Treaty of Guadalupe Hidalgo?

In-Depth Resources: Unit 1
· Primary Source: from *Polk's Speech on War with Mexico*, p. 98

Humanities Transparencies HT9
· General Winfield Scott

---

**DIFFERENTIATING INSTRUCTION** **LESS PROFICIENT READERS**

**Summarizing**
Some students might be unclear about the events leading up to Texan Independence. Have students make a time line and highlight the significant events that led up to the formation of the Republic of Texas.

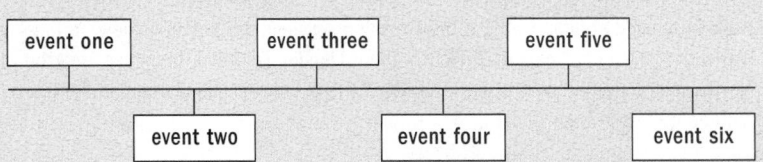

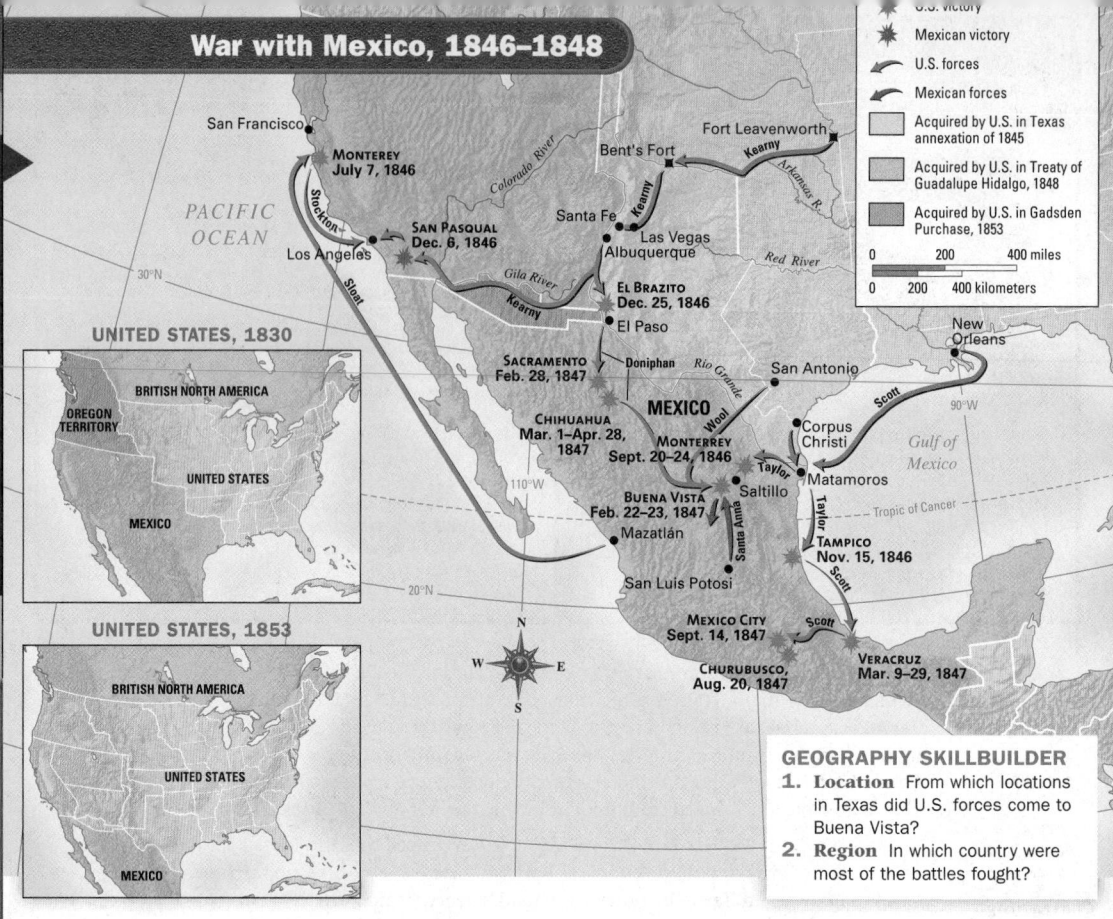

## War with Mexico, 1846–1848

**GEOGRAPHY SKILLBUILDER**
1. **Location** From which locations in Texas did U.S. forces come to Buena Vista?
2. **Region** In which country were most of the battles fought?

## HISTORY from VISUALS

### Interpreting the Map
Ask students to study the two maps: United States, 1830; United States, 1853. Ask them to estimate how much Mexican territory became part of the United States as a result of the war. *(about half)*

**Extension** Ask students how this redistribution of territory might have affected Mexico and the United States. *(Mexico lost farmland and natural resources; the United States gained valuable resources and expanded its borders.)*

## More About . . .

### Stephen Kearny
Stephen Kearny and John C. Frémont both led forces in California during the Mexican American War. When Frémont refused to obey Kearny's authority as the commander in charge of all western armies, Kearny had him arrested. Frémont was later court-martialed, found guilty of insubordination, and resigned from the army. U.S. Senator Thomas Benton, whose daughter, Jessie, was married to Frémont, was among Kearny's critics. When Kearny's nomination for a major general's commission was submitted to the Senate, Benton fought it for two weeks before finally backing down. Kearny himself regretted his role in the episode. On his deathbed, in 1848, he asked to see Mrs. Frémont. She refused his request.

*Skillbuilder Answers*
1. San Antonio, Corpus Christi, and El Paso.
2. Mexico

**THE WAR BEGINS** In 1845, John C. Frémont led an American military exploration party into California, violating Mexico's territorial rights. In response, Mexican troops crossed the Rio Grande. In a skirmish near Matamoros, Mexican soldiers killed 11 U.S. soldiers. Polk immediately called for war and Congress approved. **F**

In 1846, Polk ordered Colonel Stephen Kearny and his troops to march from Fort Leavenworth, Kansas, to Santa Fe, New Mexico. They were met there by a New Mexican contingent that included upper-class Mexicans who wanted to join the United States. New Mexico fell to the United States without a shot.

**THE REPUBLIC OF CALIFORNIA** In California, a group of American settlers seized the town of Sonoma in June 1846. Hoisting a flag that featured a grizzly bear, the rebels proudly declared their independence from Mexico and proclaimed the nation of the **Republic of California.** Kearny arrived from New Mexico and joined forces with Frémont and an American naval expedition. The Mexican troops quickly gave way, leaving U.S. forces in control of California.

**AMERICA WINS THE WAR** Meanwhile, American troops in Mexico, led by U.S. generals Zachary Taylor and Winfield Scott, scored one military victory after another. After about a year of fighting, Mexico conceded defeat. On February 2, 1848, the United States and Mexico signed the **Treaty of Guadalupe Hidalgo.** Mexico agreed to the Rio Grande as the border between Texas and Mexico and ceded the New Mexico and California territories to the United States. The United

**MAIN IDEA**

**Analyzing Issues**
**F** What border dispute affected the war with Mexico?

*F. Answer*
The dispute was over the Texas-Mexico border. Texans believed that Texas extended to the Rio Grande; Mexico contended that the Texas border was the Nueces River.

**136** CHAPTER 3 *The Growth of a Young Nation*

---

## DIFFERENTIATING INSTRUCTION · GIFTED AND TALENTED

### Exploring Different Viewpoints

Have interested students write a brief essay discussing the points of view on the war with Mexico of: President Polk; Abraham Lincoln, Frederick Douglass, and the Northeasterners; Santa Anna and the Mexican government. Encourage students to include quotes in their papers.

The essay should . . .
· present the points of view of all parties on the war
· included at least two quotations
· be clear, focused, and logical

 Integrated Assessment
· Rubric 5

States agreed to pay $15 million for the Mexican cession, which included present-day California, Nevada, New Mexico, Utah, most of Arizona, and parts of Colorado and Wyoming.

Five years later, in 1853, President Franklin Pierce authorized James Gadsden to pay Mexico an additional $10 million for another piece of territory south of the Gila River in order to secure a southern railroad route to the Pacific Ocean. Along with the settlement of the Oregon boundary and the Treaty of Guadalupe Hidalgo, the Gadsden Purchase established the current borders of the contiguous 48 states.

## The California Gold Rush **④**

The United States quickly benefited from its new territories when gold was discovered at Sutter's Mill in the California Sierra Nevada mountains.

**THE FORTY-NINERS** On the cold clear morning of January 24, 1848, a carpenter named James Marshall discovered a few shiny particles lying near John Sutter's sawmill. Marshall took what he had found to Sutter, who confirmed the carpenter's suspicions: the particles were gold. Soon, more gold was found by other workers at Sutter's mill, and news of the chance discovery began to spread with lightning speed.

When the news reached San Francisco, virtually the whole town hustled to the Sacramento Valley to pan for gold. On June 6, 1848, Monterey's mayor, Walter Colton, sent a scout to report on what was happening. The scout returned on June 14 with news of gold, and the mayor described the scene that followed as news traveled along the town's main street.

▲ Goldminers at Spanish Flat, California, 1852

**A PERSONAL VOICE** WALTER COLTON

" The blacksmith dropped his hammer, the carpenter his plane, the mason his trowel, the farmer his sickle, the baker his loaf, and the tapster [bartender] his bottle. All were off for the mines. . . . I have only a community of women left, and a gang of prisoners, with here and there a soldier who will give his captain the slip at first chance. I don't blame the fellow a whit; seven dollars a month, while others [prospectors] are making two or three hundred a day! "

—quoted in *California: A Bicentennial History*

As gold fever traveled eastward, overland migration to California rose from 400 in 1848 to 44,000 in 1850. By the end of 1849, California's population exceeded 100,000, including Mexicans, free African-American miners, and slaves.

The rest of the world caught the fever as well. Among the so-called forty-niners—the prospectors who flocked to California in 1849 in the California gold rush—were people from Asia, South America, and Europe. In time, the names of

### Instruct: Objective **④**

**The California Gold Rush**

TAKS SS11 5(US24.B)
· Who were the Forty-Niners?
· What was the impact of the gold rush on California?

In-Depth Resources: Unit 1
· Guided Reading, p. 79
· Literature: from *Roughing It*, by Mark Twain

### More About . . .

**Foreign Miners**

Excitement about the prospect of finding gold and getting rich spread to Europe. In France, lotteries were held to win tickets to California. French miners remained together in the gold fields because of the language barrier. Other miners sometimes called them "Keskydees"—a nickname derived from the French expression "Qu'est-ce qu'il dit?," or "What is he saying?" Many Mexicans made the journey north to mine for gold. Mexican miners used a special pan made out of wood to sift gravel for gold. They shared this method with American miners.

---

**ACTIVITY** | **COOPERATIVE LEARNING**

 classzone.com

**Creating a Newspaper about the Gold Rush**

**Class Time** Two class periods

**Task** Creating a newspaper

**Purpose** To explore the causes and effects of the California gold rush

**Directions** Divide the class into groups. Some students might write background articles about the gold rush; others might do features on the miners. Students should include editorials and relevant advertisements. Remind them to include pictures, photos, and other graphics along with the articles and ads. If possible, students should design and print the newspaper using desktop publishing software.

Integrated Assessment
· Rubrics 1, 2, 5, 6

## More About . . .

### San Francisco in the Gold Rush Days

In the early 1850s, the ratio of men to women in San Francisco was 10 to 1. Diverse ethnic, racial, and religious groups populated the city. Lawlessness and violence were common. In 1851, a young clergyman wrote, "Most of our citizens, if not all, go armed." He carried a cane, which, he revealed, "was found to contain a sword two-and-a-half feet long."

## Assess & Reteach

### SECTION 3 ASSESSMENT

Have a student volunteer direct the class in a group review session.

 Formal Assessment
· Section Quiz, p. 58

### SELF-ASSESSMENT

To document what they have learned, ask students to list the key people introduced in Section 3. Have them make note of the historical role each person played.

### RETEACH

Use the quiz for Section 3 to help students review the main ideas.

 In-Depth Resources: Unit 1
· Reteaching Activity, p. 89

▲ Crowded buildings and a forest of masts stand out in this 1850 photograph of San Francisco.

**H. Answer**
Gold financed the development of farming, manufacturing, shipping, and banking.

the mining camps that sprung up in California reflected the diversity of its growing population: French Corral, Irish Creek, Chinese Camp. **G**

**THE GOLDEN ECONOMY** The discovery of gold revolutionized California's economy. Gold financed the development of farming, manufacturing, shipping, and banking. By 1855, more newspapers were published in San Francisco than in London, more books were published than in all the rest of the United States west of the Mississippi. Because of its location as a supply center, San Francisco became "a pandemonium of a city." Ships linked California markets to the expanding markets of the rest of the United States.

Mining continued in California throughout the 1850s, but the peak of the gold rush was over by 1853. While most individual efforts yielded little or no profit, those who were able to use more sophisticated methods made fortunes. By 1857, ten years after James Marshall's discovery of a few shiny flakes, the total value of gold production in California approached two billion dollars. **H**

**"GO WEST, YOUNG MAN!"** Horace Greeley, editor of the *New York Tribune*, had declared in his paper prior to the gold rush that anyone who made the dangerous journey west was a fool. But when he heard of the discovery in the Sierra Nevadas his curiosity was aroused. Before long, he made the journey west himself and declared California to be "the new El Dorado." "Go west, young man!" Greeley advised. In the spirit of manifest destiny, countless settlers heeded his words in the decades that followed.

**MAIN IDEA**

Analyzing Effects
**G** In what ways did the gold rush change the population of California?

**G. Answer**
The population increased to over 100,000 in 1849. This population included Mexicans, free African Americans, and slaves, as well as immigrants from Europe and Asia.

**MAIN IDEA**

Analyzing Effects
**H** How did the discovery of gold affect California's economy?

### SECTION 3 ASSESSMENT

1. **TERMS & NAMES** For each term or name, write a sentence explaining its significance.
   - manifest destiny
   - Santa Fe Trail
   - Oregon Trail
   - Stephen F. Austin
   - Texas Revolution
   - the Alamo
   - Sam Houston
   - James K. Polk
   - Republic of California
   - Treaty of Guadalupe Hidalgo

**MAIN IDEA**

2. **TAKING NOTES**
   Draw a chart like the one below to show how the boundaries of the U.S. mainland were formed from the 1840s to 1853.

   | Year | Boundary Change |
   | --- | --- |
   | 1845 | Texas annexed |
   | | |
   | | |
   | | |

**CRITICAL THINKING**

3. **ANALYZING ISSUES**
   What were the benefits and drawbacks of believing in manifest destiny? Use specific references to the section to support your response.
   **Think About:**
   - the growth of new cities and towns
   - the impact on Native Americans
   - the impact on the nation as a whole

4. **EVALUATING**
   Would you have supported the war with Mexico? Why or why not? Explain your answer, including details from the chapter.

5. **DEVELOPING HISTORICAL PERSPECTIVE**
   How did the California gold rush transform the West in the American imagination?

**138** CHAPTER 3 *The Growth of a Young Nation*

---

 SECTION 3 ASSESSMENT Answers

**1. TERMS & NAMES**
manifest destiny, p. 131
Santa Fe Trail, p. 131
Oregon Trail, p. 131
Stephen F. Austin, p. 133
Texas Revolution, p. 134
The Alamo, p. 134
Sam Houston, p. 134
James K. Polk, p. 135
Republic of California, p. 136
Treaty of Guadalupe Hidalgo, p. 136

**2. TAKING NOTES**
1845—Texas annexed; 1846—northwest set boundary at 49th parallel; 1848—Treaty of Guadalupe Hidalgo; 1853—Gadsden Purchase

**3. ANALYZING ISSUES**
Manifest destiny encouraged westward expansion. The disregard for the territorial rights of Native Americans and Mexicans was a negative aspect.

**4. EVALUATING**
Students should recognize that proslavery forces supported the war, and antislavery forces opposed it. Students may also note that from the Mexican perspective, the war was an unjust attempt by the United States to take Mexican territory.

**5. DEVELOPING HISTORICAL PERSPECTIVE**
Students may respond that before the gold rush people thought of the West as a dangerous place, but after, as a place of adventure and limitless possibility.

# The Market Revolution

| MAIN IDEA | WHY IT MATTERS NOW | Terms & Names |
|---|---|---|
| Inventions and economic developments in the early 19th century helped transform American society. | The market revolution and free enterprise system that took hold during this period still drive the nation's economy today. | •market revolution •strike<br>•free enterprise •immigration<br>•entrepreneurs •National Trades'<br>•Samuel F. B. Union<br>Morse •*Commonwealth*<br>•Lowell textile v. *Hunt*<br>mills |

**TEKS** U.S. History 22A, 22C, 23A, 24B, 24G, 25A, 25B, 25C, 25D

### One American's Story

At sunrise on July 4, 1817, a cannon blast from the United States arsenal in Rome, New York, announced the groundbreaking for the Erie Canal. With visiting dignitaries and local residents in attendance, Samuel Young opened the ceremony.

**A PERSONAL VOICE** SAMUEL YOUNG

" We have assembled to commence the excavation of the Erie Canal. This work when accomplished will connect our western inland seas with the Atlantic Ocean. . . . By this great highway, unborn millions will easily transport their surplus productions to the shores of the Atlantic, procure their supplies, and hold a useful and profitable intercourse with all the maritime nations of the earth. . . . Let us proceed then to the work, animated by the prospect of its speedy accomplishment, and cheered with the anticipated benedictions of a grateful posterity. "

—quoted in *Erie Water West*

A lock on the Erie Canal in Lockport, New York, shown here in an 1838 engraving, was one of 83 that helped link the Great Lakes with the Northeast.

When the canal was completed, it stretched 363 miles from Albany, New York, to Lake Erie. The human-made waterway ushered in a new era, in which technology and improved transportation sent new products to markets across the United States.

## The Market Revolution ❶

Changes like those brought by the Erie Canal contributed to vast economic changes in the first half of the 19th century in the United States. In this period, known as the **market revolution**, people increasingly bought and sold goods rather than make them for themselves.

Mini-Lesson 2:
SS11 3(WG10.C)

---

## OBJECTIVES

**1** Describe the impact of new markets, entrepreneurs, and inventions on the 19th-century American economy.

**2** Explain the ways in which workplaces changed during the market revolution.

**3** Summarize the efforts of workers to improve their economic security.

### CRITICAL THINKING
Synthesizing, p. 140
Summarizing, pp. 141, 142
Making Inferences, p. 142
Analyzing Issues, p. 143
Analyzing Primary Sources, p. 143

## Focus & Motivate

Ask students what inventions or new technologies have improved their lives. Discuss how such technologies have affected the American economy.

## Instruct

### Instruct: Objective ❶
**The Market Revolution**
TAKS SS11 3(WG10.C)
· What was the market revolution?
· What inventions and improvements emerged in the mid-1800s?
· How did the market revolution transform the nation?

📖 In-Depth Resources: Unit 1
· Guided Reading, p. 80

---

## PROGRAM RESOURCES

📖 **In-Depth Resources: Unit 1**
· Guided Reading, p. 80
· Reteaching Activity, p. 90

📖 **Reading Study Guide** (English and Spanish), pp. 41–42

📖 **Access for Students Acquiring English/ESL**
· Guided Reading (Spanish), p. 51

📖 **Formal Assessment**
· Section Quiz, p. 59

📖 **Integrated Assessment**
· Rubrics

### INTEGRATED TECHNOLOGY

🖥 **Geography Transp. GT9**
· American Cities, 1820 and 1860

👁 **Electronic Library of Primary Sources**

ⓘ **classzone.com**

### TEXAS RESOURCES

📖 TAKS Spiraled Content Review

📖 TAKS Practice Tests

📖 TAKS Practice Transparencies TT33

ⓘ TAKS Online Test Practice

## More About . . .

### Samuel F. B. Morse

While Samuel Morse was a student at Yale University, he learned about the new science of electricity and constructed batteries in a chemistry class. More interested in art than science, however, Morse embarked on a distinguished career in painting. Realizing the difficulty of supporting himself as an artist, Morse later concentrated on scientific work.

## More About . . .

### Robert Fulton

Early in life, Robert Fulton demonstrated a knack for inventing. In 1778, at the age of 13, he is said to have invented a skyrocket. During the American Revolution, Lancaster was a central location for gun production. The craft greatly appealed to young Fulton. He became an expert gunsmith and supplied the established gun makers in the town with drawings for different types of new guns.

## NOW & THEN

### From Telegraph to Internet
**Predicting Effects** Have students think about futuristic inventions for communicating that have been featured in science fiction movies or stories. Ask students to describe the look and function of these devices. How would such inventions revolutionize people's lives?

---

**U.S. MARKETS EXPAND** Over a few decades, buying and selling multiplied while incomes rose. In the 1840s alone, the national economy grew more than it had in the first 40 years of the century. The quickening pace of U.S. economic growth coincided with the growth of **free enterprise**—the freedom of private businesses to operate competitively for profit with little government regulation.

In their pursuit of profit, businessmen called **entrepreneurs**, from a French word that means "to undertake," invested their own money in new industries. In doing this, entrepreneurs risked losing their investment if a venture failed, but they also stood to earn huge profits if it succeeded. **A**

**INVENTIONS AND IMPROVEMENTS** Inventor-entrepreneurs began to develop goods to make life more comfortable for more people. While some inventions simply made life more enjoyable, others fueled the economic revolution and transformed manufacturing, transportation, and communication.

New communication links began to put people into instant contact with one another. In 1837, **Samuel F. B. Morse,** a New England artist, patented the telegraph, which sent messages in code over a wire in a matter of seconds. Businesses used the new communication device to transmit orders and relay up-to-date information on prices and sales. The new railroads employed the telegraph to keep trains moving regularly and to warn engineers of safety hazards. By 1854, 23,000 miles of telegraph wire crossed the country.

Meanwhile, better transportation systems improved the movement of people and goods. In 1807, Pennsylvanian Robert Fulton had ushered in the steamboat era when his boat, the *Clermont*, made the 150-mile trip up the Hudson River from New York City to Albany in 32 hours, a remarkable speed for that era. By 1830, 200 steamboats traveled the nation's western rivers that flowed into the Mississippi River. Steamboats slashed freight rates as well as voyage times.

Water transport was particularly important in moving raw materials such as lead, copper, and heavy

**MAIN IDEA**

**Synthesizing**
**A** How did entrepreneurs contribute to the market revolution?

*A. Answer*
Entrepreneurs created new businesses and new products to be bought and sold.

### NOW & THEN

**FROM TELEGRAPH TO INTERNET**

What do the telegraph and the Internet have in common? They are both tools for instant communication. While the telegraph relied on a network of wires that spanned the country, the Internet—an international network of smaller computer networks—allows any computer user to communicate instantly with any other computer user in the world.

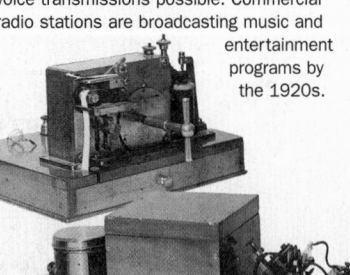

**MORSE CODE** In 1837 Samuel Morse patents the telegraph, the first instant electronic communicator. Morse taps on a key to send bursts of electricity down a wire to the receiver, where an operator "translates" the coded bursts into understandable language within seconds.

**TELEPHONE** In 1876 Alexander Graham Bell invents the telephone, which relies on a steady stream of electricity, rather than electrical bursts, to transmit sounds. By 1900, there are over one million telephones in the United States.

**MARCONI RADIO** In 1895, Guglielmo Marconi, an Italian inventor, sends telegraph code through the air as electromagnetic waves. By the early 1900s, "the wireless" makes voice transmissions possible. Commercial radio stations are broadcasting music and entertainment programs by the 1920s.

1837          1876          1895

**140** CHAPTER 3 *The Growth of a Young Nation*

---

**ACTIVITY** | **COOPERATIVE LEARNING**

 classzone.com

### Researching the Electronics Revolution

**Class Time** 45 minutes

**Task** Researching and writing reports on electronic communication

**Purpose** To explore the impact of modern technology on society

**Directions** Divide students into small groups. Each student in the group will report on a modern form of electronic communication, such as computers, fax machines, e-mail, or the Internet. Have students conduct Internet or library research. Suggest that they include illustrations or computer graphics in their reports. Group members should get together to discuss their findings and compile their reports.

📄 Integrated Assessment
· Rubrics 1, 4, 5, 6

machinery. Where waterways didn't exist, Americans made them by building canals. By the 1840s, America boasted more than 3,300 miles of canals.

Canals, however, soon gave way to railroads, which offered the important advantage of speed as well as winter travel. Developed in England in the early 1800s, steam-powered locomotives began operating in the United States in the 1830s. By 1850, over 9,000 miles of track had been laid across the United States.

**THE MARKET REVOLUTION TRANSFORMS THE NATION** Although most Americans during the early 1800s still lived in rural areas and only 14 percent of workers had manufacturing jobs, these workers produced more and better goods at lower prices than ever before. Many of these goods became affordable for ordinary Americans, and improvements in transportation allowed people to purchase items manufactured in distant places.

By the 1840s, improved transportation and communication also made America's regions more interdependent. Steamboats went up as well as down the Mississippi, linking North to South. The Erie Canal, and eventually railroads and telegraph wires, soon linked the East and the West.

Heavy investment in canals and railroads transformed the Northeast into the center of American commerce. As the Northeast began to industrialize, many people then moved away to farm the fertile soil of the Midwest. They employed new machines, such as the John Deere steel plow, for cultivating the tough prairie sod, and Cyrus McCormick's reaper, for harvesting grain. Meanwhile, most of the South remained agricultural and relied on such crops as cotton, tobacco, and rice.

## Changing Workplaces ❷

The new market economy in the United States did not only affect what people bought and sold; it also changed the ways Americans worked. Moving production from the home to the factory split families, created new communities, and transformed relationships between employers and employees.

By the mid-nineteenth century, new machines allowed unskilled workers to perform tasks that once had taken the effort of trained artisans. To do this work, though, workers needed factories.

**TELEVISION** In the late 1800s, scientists begin to experiment with transmitting pictures as well as words through the air. In 1923 Vladimir Zworykin, a Russian-born American scientist, files a patent for the iconoscope, the first television camera tube suitable for broadcasting, and in 1924 for the kinescope, the picture tube used in receiving television signals. In 1929, Zworykin demonstrated the first all-electronic television.

**COMPUTERS** Scientists develop electronically powered computers during the 1940s. In 1951, UNIVAC I (UNIVersal Advanced Computer) becomes the first commercially available computer. In 1964, IBM initiates System/360, a family of mutually compatible computers that allow several terminals to be attached to one computer system.

**INTERNET** Today, on the Internet, through e-mail (electronic mail) or online conversation, any two people can have instant dialogue. The Internet becomes the modern tool for instant global communication not only of words, but images, too. And it is just as amazing now as the telegraph was in its time.

1929          1964          2000

### More About . . .

**The Erie Canal**
One man's initiative and determination led to the construction of the Erie Canal. In 1812, Clinton De Witt, a New York politician, petitioned the federal government for funds to build the canal. His request was denied. Undaunted, De Witt convinced the state of New York to pay for the project. Construction got underway in 1817, the same year that De Witt became governor of New York. The canal construction took eight years and cost about $7 million. Critics mockingly referred to the waterway as "Clinton's Ditch." When the canal opened in 1825, however, few could deny its merits. The Erie Canal cut transportation costs, stimulated the growth of cities, and opened up new trade routes.

### Instruct: Objective ❷
**Changing Workplaces**
TAKS SS11 5(US24.B)
· How did the new market economy affect the way people worked?
· What were working conditions like in the Lowell textile mills?

📄 **In-Depth Resources: Unit 1**
· Guided Reading, p. 80

💿 **Electronic Library of Primary Sources**
· *from* The Pleasures of Factory Life, 1840, by S. Bagley

**B. Answer**
Technology influenced the North and Midwest by improving means of transportation and communication. Inventions such as the steel plow and the reaper also improved farming in the Midwest.

**MAIN IDEA**

**Summarizing**
**B** How did technology influence both the North and the Midwest in the 1840s?

---

 **classzone.com**

### Researching an Inventor

Have interested students research the life of one of the inventors mentioned on pages 140 and 141. Using library materials as well as the Internet have them write a brief biography of the inventor. Students should focus on how their subject became an inventor and on the subject's most successful inventions.

**Rubrics**

The biography should . . .
· accurately convey information about the inventor's life
· include mention of the inventor's most successful inventions
· be logically organized

📄 **Integrated Assessment**
· Rubrics 1, 5

*The Growth of a Young Nation*   **141**

### More About . . .

**Factory Life**

By the late 1820s, conditions in the boarding houses where the factory workers lived had begun to worsen. Six to eight women often had to share one crowded room. After working 13 or more hours a day, the women were usually fed only bread and gravy for supper. In 1828, mill women in Dover, New Hampshire, went on strike. It was the first mill workers' strike organized entirely by women. The community was shocked at the sight of several hundred women parading down the street, carrying banners and setting off gunpowder. It was an impressive but short-lived spectacle. The women returned to work when mill owners threatened to hire new workers.

**Instruct: Objective ③**

**Workers Seek Better Conditions**

TAKS SS11 3(US2.B)

· What were the reasons that the Lowell workers went on strike?

· Why did many immigrants face discrimination in the United States?

· What gains and setbacks did unions experience?

 In-Depth Resources: Unit 1
· Guided Reading, p. 80

### Tracing Themes

**ECONOMIC OPPORTUNITY**

**Economic Inequities**

In the mid-1800s, many business owners prospered, but many workers did not. One reason was that companies paid low wages to keep costs down. In time, the federal government established a minimum wage, an ever-changing amount below which a company could not pay a worker.

---

**THE LOWELL TEXTILE MILLS** In the 1820s, a group of entrepreneurs built several large textile mills in Lowell, Massachusetts. The **Lowell textile mills** soon became booming enterprises. Thousands of people, mostly women, left family farms to find work in Lowell.

Mill owners sought female employees because women provided an abundant source of labor and owners could pay lower wages to women than men. To the girls in the mills, though, textile work offered better pay than their main alternatives: teaching, sewing, and domestic work. In some 1846 letters to her father in New Hampshire, 16-year-old Mary Paul expressed her satisfaction with her situation at Lowell.

**C. Answer**
Most factory owners regarded their workers in the same way that they regarded their machinery. They were to be maintained to provide maximum production and discarded when no longer of any use.

★ **A PERSONAL VOICE** MARY PAUL

"I have a very good boarding place, have enough to eat. . . . The girls are all kind and obliging. . . . I think that the factory is the best place for me and if any girl wants employment, I advise them to come to Lowell."

—quoted in *Women and the American Experience*

Before long, however, work conditions deteriorated. The workday at Lowell was more than 12 hours long. In addition, mills often were dark, hot, and cramped. Factory owners often showed little sympathy for the plight of workers. In the mid-1840s one mill manager said, "I regard my workpeople just as I regard my machinery. So long as they can do my work for what I choose to pay them, I keep them, getting out of them all I can." **C**

### ③ Workers Seek Better Conditions

As industry grew, strikes began to break out when workers protested poor working conditions and low wages.

**WORKERS STRIKE** In 1834, when the Lowell mills announced a 15 percent wage cut, 800 mill girls organized a **strike,** a work stoppage to force an employer to respond to demands. Criticized by the Lowell press and clergy, most of the strikers agreed to return to work at reduced wages. The mill owners fired the strike leader. In 1836, Lowell mill workers struck again, but as in 1834, the company won, and most of the strikers returned to their jobs.

Although only 1 or 2 percent of workers in the United States were organized, the 1830s and 1840s saw dozens of strikes—many for higher wages, but some for shorter hours. Employers defeated most of these strikes because they could easily replace unskilled workers with people recently arrived from Europe who desperately needed jobs. **D**

**IMMIGRATION INCREASES** European **immigration,** leaving one country and settling in another, rose dramatically in the United States between 1830 and 1860. In the decade 1845–1854 alone, nearly 3 million immigrants were added to the population. More than 1 million were Irish immigrants, who fled their homeland after a disease on potatoes caused the Great Potato Famine and led to mass starvation.

Irish immigrants faced prejudice, both because they were Roman Catholic and because they were poor. Frightened by allegations of a Catholic conspiracy to take over the country, Protestant mobs in big cities constantly harassed them. Other workers resented the Irish for their willingness to work as cheap labor, a willingness which made them more desirable to employers.

**142** CHAPTER 3 *The Growth of a Young Nation*

---

▲ A young mill girl from around 1840. Her swollen hands suggest that she worked as a warper, someone who straightened the strands of cotton or wool as they entered the loom.

**MAIN IDEA**

**Making Inferences**
**C** What was the attitude of many factory owners toward their workers?

**D. Answer**
Workers were not well organized, they had little public support, and strikers could be easily replaced.

**MAIN IDEA**

**Summarizing**
**D** Why were most labor strikes of the 1880s and 1840s ineffective?

**Background**
During the Great Potato Famine of 1845–1847, about 750,000 Irish died of starvation and disease.

---

**ACTIVITY**  **COOPERATIVE LEARNING**  ⓑ **BLOCK SCHEDULING**

**Writing a List of Demands**

**Class Time** 45 minutes

**Task** Writing a list of mill workers' demands

**Purpose** To help students understand the working conditions in the mills

**Directions** Have students get together in groups to discuss working conditions in the mills. They should agree on a list of specific demands to be presented to the mill owners. Remind students to write their lists from the point of view of women mill workers in the 1830s. The demands should be reasonable and written in a professional tone. Ask each group to read its list to the class. Create a master list from the group lists.

European immigrants arriving in New York City (from a colored engraving made in 1858)

### More About . . .

**Irish Immigrants**
More than half of the Irish immigrants who fled to the United States were women. Many of them became maids or textile workers. By the 1840s, in fact, Irish women were replacing native-born American women in the Lowell mills. The poorest Irish men often dug canals and cellars or served wealthy families. To secure this work, the Irish competed directly with poor, free blacks. Irish men who could secure skilled jobs competed with native-born white workers. As a result, according to one immigrant, there was "no love for [the Irish worker]—no protection of life—[he] can be shot down, run through, kicked, cuffed, spat upon. . . ."

**NATIONAL TRADES' UNION** Amidst the growing labor unrest in the 1830s, the trade unions in different towns began to join together to expand their power. Journeymen's organizations from several industries united in 1834 to form the **National Trades' Union.** The national trade union movement faced fierce opposition from bankers and owners. In addition, workers' efforts to organize were at first hampered by court decisions declaring strikes illegal. In 1842, however, the Massachusetts Supreme Court supported the workers' right to strike in the case of *Commonwealth v. Hunt.*

The workplace was not the only area of American life that experienced unrest in the mid-19th century. Indeed, a series of religious and social reform movements went hand in hand with these economic changes.

### 4 ASSESSMENT

1. **TERMS & NAMES** For each term or name, write a sentence explaining its significance.
   - **market revolution**
   - **free enterprise**
   - **entrepreneurs**
   - **Samuel F. B. Morse**
   - **Lowell textile mills**
   - **strike**
   - **immigration**
   - **National Trades' Union**
   - *Commonwealth* v. *Hunt*

**MAIN IDEA**

2. **TAKING NOTES**
   Create a time line like the one below on which you label and date important developments in manufacturing during the early 19th century.

   **1807**

   Write a paragraph explaining which development was most important and why.

**CRITICAL THINKING**

3. **ANALYZING ISSUES**
   Do you think the positive effects of mechanizing the manufacturing process outweighed the negative effects? Why or why not?
   **Think About:**
   - changes in job opportunities for unskilled laborers
   - changes in employer-employee relationships
   - working conditions in factories
   - the cost of manufactured goods

4. **ANALYZING PRIMARY SOURCES**
   A 20th-century historian said of the 1820s: "It was the miraculous machinery of the times . . . which made it obvious that things were getting better all the time." How do you think the people you have read about in this chapter would have responded to that statement?

## Assess & Reteach

### SECTION 4 ASSESSMENT
Have students work on the questions individually, then compare their answers with a partner.

 Formal Assessment
· Section Quiz, p. 59

### SELF-ASSESSMENT
Have students write up to three questions about specific themes or events that they did not completely understand. Have students skim the sections to look for the answers.

### RETEACH
Have students compile a bulleted list of main points under each of the section's three main headings.

 In-Depth Resources: Unit 1
· Reteaching Activity, p. 90

---

Answers **ASSESSMENT**

**1. TERMS & NAMES**
market revolution, p. 139
free enterprise, p. 140
entrepreneurs, p. 140
Samuel F. B. Morse, p. 140
Lowell textile mills, p. 142
strike, p. 142
immigration, p. 142
National Trades' Union, p. 143
*Commonwealth* v. *Hunt*, p. 143

**2. TAKING NOTES**
1807—*Clermont* trip begins steamboat era; 1817—Ground breaking for Erie Canal; 1837—Morse patents the telegraph; 1834—Strike in Lowell textile mills, National Trades' Union formed; 1842—*Commonwealth* v. *Hunt*

**3. ANALYZING ISSUES**
Some students may refer to the reduced cost of manufactured items and to expanding opportunities for women. Other students may mention the break-up of traditional families.

**4. ANALYZING PRIMARY SOURCES**
Students may suggest that inventors, such as Samuel Morse, would have marveled at the progress of technology. Farmers may have been grateful for new machinery. Laborers and factory workers might have pointed out how machinery made their lives more difficult with poor working conditions.

*The Growth of a Young Nation* **143**

# Reforming American Society

| MAIN IDEA | WHY IT MATTERS NOW | Terms & Names |
|---|---|---|
| Throughout the mid-19th century, men and women embarked on a widespread effort to solve problems in American society. | A number of achievements from this period, including laws enacted and institutions established, still exist today. | • abolition<br>• Unitarians<br>• Ralph Waldo Emerson<br>• transcendentalism<br>• William Lloyd Garrison<br>• Frederick Douglass<br>• Nat Turner<br>• Elizabeth Cady Stanton<br>• Seneca Falls convention<br>• Sojourner Truth |

 U.S. History 7A, 7B, 8B, 18A, 19A, 21A, 21D, 24A, 24B, 24C, 24H, 25A, 25B, 25C, 25D

### One American's Story

James Forten's great-grandfather had been brought from Africa to the American colonies in chains, but James was born free. By the 1830s Forten had become a wealthy sailmaker. A leader of Philadelphia's free black community, Forten took an active role in a variety of political causes. When some people argued that free blacks should return to Africa, Forten disagreed and responded with sarcasm.

**A PERSONAL VOICE** JAMES FORTEN

"Here I have dwelt until I am nearly sixty years of age, and have brought up and educated a family. . . . Yet some ingenious gentlemen have recently discovered that I am still an African; that a continent three thousand miles, and more, from the place where I was born, is my native country. And I am advised to go home. . . . Perhaps if I should only be set on the shore of that distant land, I should recognize all I might see there, and run at once to the old hut where my forefathers lived a hundred years ago."

—quoted in *Forging Freedom: The Formation of Philadelphia's Black Community 1720–1840*

James Forten

Forten's unwavering belief that he was an American not only led him to oppose colonization—the effort to resettle free blacks in Africa—but also pushed him fervently to oppose slavery. Forten was joined in his opposition to slavery by a growing number of Americans in the 19th century. **Abolition,** the movement to abolish slavery, became the most important of a series of reform movements in America.

## **1** A Spiritual Awakening Inspires Reform

Many of these movements had their roots in a spiritual awakening that swept the nation after 1790. People involved in these movements began to emphasize individual responsibility for seeking salvation and insisted that people could improve themselves and society. These religious attitudes were closely linked to

---

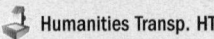
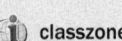

the ideas of Jacksonian democracy that stressed the importance and power of the common person.

**THE SECOND GREAT AWAKENING** The Second Great Awakening was a widespread Christian movement to awaken religious sentiments that lasted from the 1790s to the 1840s. The primary forum for the movement was the revival meeting, where participants attempted to revive religious faith through impassioned preaching. Revival meetings might last for days as participants studied the Bible, reflected on their lives, and heard emotional sermons. Revivalism had a strong impact on the American public. According to one estimate, in 1800 just 1 in 15 Americans belonged to a church, but by 1850 1 in 6 was a member.

**UNITARIANS AND TRANSCENDENTALISTS** Another growing religious group was the **Unitarians,** who shared with revivalism a faith in the individual. But instead of appealing to emotions, Unitarians emphasized reason as the path to perfection.

As the Second Great Awakening reached its maturity in the 1830s, another kind of awakening led by a writer, philosopher, and former Unitarian minister named **Ralph Waldo Emerson** began in New England. In 1831, Emerson traveled to England, where he discovered romanticism, an artistic and intellectual movement that emphasized nature, human emotions, and the imagination. From these romantic ideals, Emerson, along with other thinkers, developed a philosophy called **transcendentalism,** which emphasized that truth could be discovered intuitively by observing nature and relating it to one's own emotional and spiritual experience.

**THE AFRICAN–AMERICAN CHURCH** The urge to reform was growing among African Americans, too. Slaves in the rural South heard the same sermons and sang the same hymns as did their owners, but they often interpreted the stories they heard, especially those describing the Exodus from Egypt, as a promise of freedom.

In the North, however, free African Americans were able to form their own churches. These churches often became political, cultural, and social centers for African Americans by providing schools and other services that whites denied free blacks. **A**

## Slavery and Abolition ❷

By the 1820s, abolition—the movement to free African Americans from slavery—had taken hold. More than 100 antislavery societies were advocating that African Americans be resettled in Africa. In 1817, the American Colonization Society had been founded to encourage black emigration. Other abolitionists, however, demanded that African Americans remain in the United States as free citizens.

**WILLIAM LLOYD GARRISON** The most radical white abolitionist was a young editor named **William Lloyd Garrison.** Active in religious reform movements in Massachusetts, Garrison became the editor of an antislavery paper in 1828. Three years later he established his own paper, *The Liberator*, to deliver an uncompromising demand: immediate emancipation.

| |
|---|
| **MAIN IDEA** |

**Evaluating**
**A** How did the existence of separate black churches benefit the African-American community?

*A. Answer*
These churches enabled African Americans in the North to have political, educational, and social centers in places where, while technically free, they were still subject to prejudice and discrimination.

◀ William Lloyd Garrison's *The Liberator* was published from 1831 to 1865. Its circulation never grew beyond 3,000.

### More About . . .

**Ralph Waldo Emerson**
Emerson stood at the center of one of the most vibrant literary communities in American history, which flourished in New England from the 1830s to the 1850s. His friends included fellow transcendentalist Henry David Thoreau, essayist Margaret Fuller, and the famous novelists Nathaniel Hawthorne and Herman Melville. These writers produced an impressive selection of American literature.

### More About . . .

**The African-American Church**
The church was an integral part of life for many free and enslaved African Americans. Religious worship built community and fostered hope. Noted one theologian, "Black religion has always concerned itself with the fascination of an incorrigibly religious people with the mystery of God, but it has been equally concerned with the yearning of a . . . subjugated people with freedom of man— freedom from the religious, economic, social, and political domination which white men have exercised over Black men since the beginning of the African slave trade."

### Instruct: Objective ❷
**Slavery and Abolition**
TAKS SS11 3(US21.A)
· What contributions did William Lloyd Garrison and Frederick Douglass make to the abolition movement?
· What was life like for an enslaved person?
· Why were slave owners opposed to abolition?

 In-Depth Resources: Unit 1
· Guided Reading, p. 81

---

**DIFFERENTIATING INSTRUCTION** | **GIFTED AND TALENTED**

 **classzone.com**

### Researching the African Methodist Episcopal Church

By the early 1990s, the African Methodist Episcopal Church had become the eighth largest religious body in the United States. Have interested students use the Internet and library resources to write a brief research paper about the church, highlighting significant historical events and modern-day teachings and philosophies.

**Rubrics**
The research paper should . . .
· show evidence of research into a variety of sources
· include significant historical events
· clearly state the teachings of the church

 Integrated Assessment
· Rubrics 1, 5

*The Growth of a Young Nation* **145**

**Tracing Themes**

CIVIL RIGHTS

### Abolitionism

Remind students that white and black abolitionists worked together to rid the nation of the institution of slavery. While race did not divide the abolitionists, strategy sometimes did. Some abolitionists advocated emancipation by any means necessary, while others were committed to nonviolent tactics. Proponents of nonviolence believed that their methods were more likely to win people's sympathy and support. Other abolitionists were ready to go to any lengths to put an immediate end to slavery.

### More About . . .

### Frederick Douglass

When Douglass arrived in New England, he discovered prejudice prevented him from finding suitable work. He was forced to do odd jobs for three years to support himself. "There was no work too hard—none too dirty," he once said. In 1841, Douglass became a lecturer in the anti-slavery movement. In the early 1840s, Douglass protested segregated seating on trains by sitting in whites-only cars. Once, when he refused to leave the car, a group of white men tried to force him out of his seat. Douglass resisted. The men pulled the seat out of the floor of the car—with Douglass still hanging on to the seat.

Electronic Library of Primary Sources
· *from* a Lecture on the Anti-Slavery Movement, 1855, by F. Douglass

Before Garrison's call for the immediate emancipation of slaves, support for that position had been limited. In the 1830s, however, that position gained support. Whites who opposed abolition hated Garrison. In 1835 a Boston mob paraded him through town at the end of a rope. Nevertheless, Garrison enjoyed widespread black support; three out of four early subscribers to *The Liberator* were African Americans.

*"I consider it settled that the black and white people of America ought to share common destiny."*
FREDERICK DOUGLASS, 1851

**FREDERICK DOUGLASS** One of those eager readers was **Frederick Douglass,** who escaped from bondage to become an eloquent and outspoken critic of slavery. Garrison heard him speak and was so impressed that he sponsored Douglass to speak for various anti-slavery organizations. Hoping that abolition could be achieved without violence, Douglass broke with Garrison, who believed that abolition justified whatever means were necessary to achieve it. In 1847, Douglass began his own antislavery newspaper. He named it *The North Star*, after the star that guided runaway slaves to freedom.

**LIFE UNDER SLAVERY** In the 18th century, most slaves were male, had recently arrived from the Caribbean or Africa, and spoke one of several languages other than English. By 1830, however, the numbers of male and female slaves had become more equal. The majority had been born in America and spoke English. However, two things remained constant in the lives of slaves—hard work and oppression.

The number of slaves owned by individual masters varied widely across the South. Most slaves worked as house servants, farm hands, or in the fields. Some states allowed masters to free their slaves and even allowed slaves to purchase their freedom over time. But these "manumitted" or freed slaves were very few. The vast majority of African Americans in the South were enslaved and endured lives of suffering and constant degradation. (See "Southern Plantations" on page 147.) **B**

**TURNER'S REBELLION** Some slaves rebelled against their condition of bondage. One of the most prominent rebellions was led by Virginia slave **Nat Turner.** In August 1831, Turner and more than 50 followers attacked four plantations and killed about 60 whites. Whites eventually captured and executed many members of the group, including Turner.

**SLAVE OWNERS OPPOSE ABOLITION** The Turner rebellion frightened and outraged slaveholders. In some states, people argued that the only way to prevent slave revolts was through emancipation. Others, however, chose to tighten restrictions on all African Americans to prevent them from plotting insurrections. Some proslavery advocates began to argue that slavery was a benevolent institution. They used the Bible to defend slavery and cited passages that counseled servants to obey their masters.

MAIN IDEA

**Making Inferences**
**B** How would you describe the lives of enslaved African Americans in the 1830s?

*B. Answer*
Enslaved African Americans experienced poor living conditions, hard work, and harsh treatment from their masters.

---

**DIFFERENTIATING INSTRUCTION**    **GIFTED AND TALENTED**     classzone.com

### Writing an Article for *The Liberator*

Ask interested students to use the Internet and library resources to find excerpts from *The Liberator*. Have them write their own article for the paper. The article should:

· address an injustice in the world today
· advocate a course of action
· be written in the tone and style of Garrison's anti-slavery paper

Encourage students to compile their articles in an "anti-injustice" paper that the rest of the class can read.

 Integrated Assessment
· Rubrics 1, 5

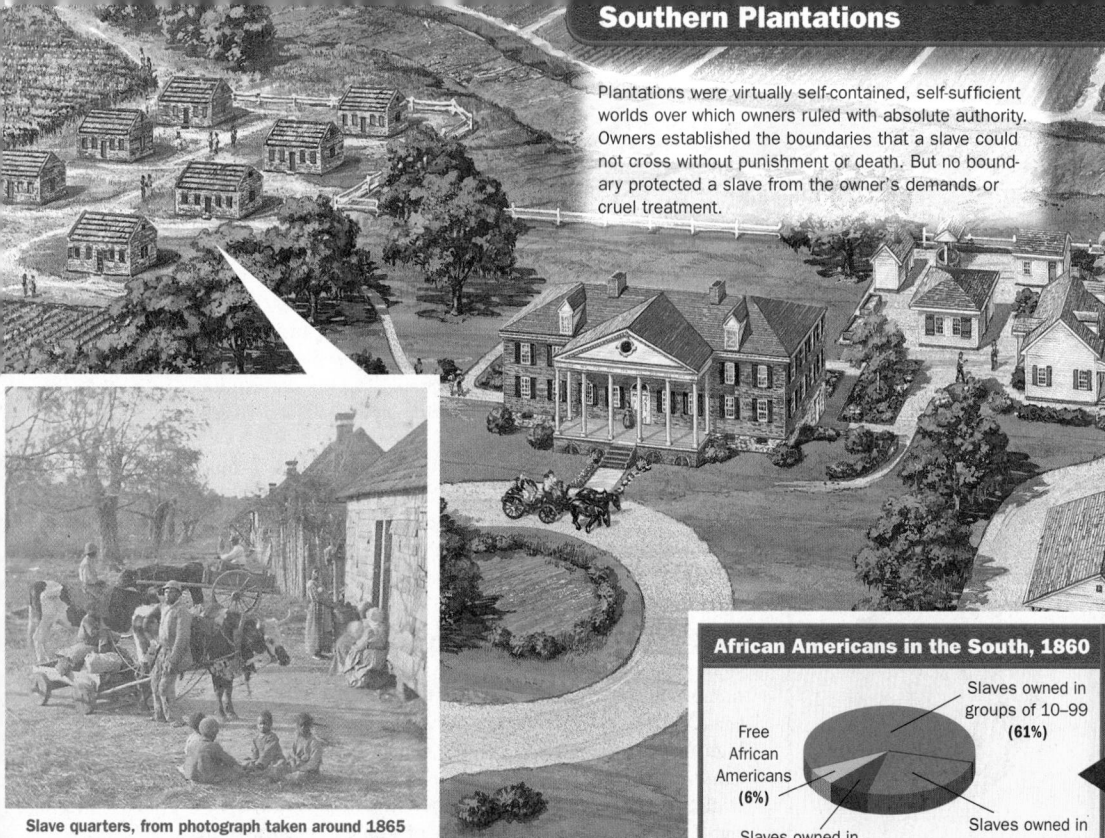

## Southern Plantations

Plantations were virtually self-contained, self-sufficient worlds over which owners ruled with absolute authority. Owners established the boundaries that a slave could not cross without punishment or death. But no boundary protected a slave from the owner's demands or cruel treatment.

Slave quarters, from photograph taken around 1865

### African Americans in the South, 1860

- Slaves owned in groups of 10–99 **(61%)**
- Free African Americans **(6%)**
- Slaves owned in groups of 100 or more **(8%)**
- Slaves owned in groups of 1–9 **(25%)**

Sources: 1860 figures from *Eighth Census of the United States;* Lewis C. Gray, *History of Agriculture in the Southern United States.*

**SKILLBUILDER Interpreting Graphs**
According to the pie graph, what was the smallest group of African Americans living in the American South in 1860?

Nevertheless, opposition to slavery refused to disappear. Much of the strength of the abolition movement came from the efforts of women—many of whom contributed to other reform movements, including a women's rights movement.

## Women and Reform ③

In the early 19th century, women faced limited options. Prevailing customs encouraged women to restrict their activities after marriage to the home and family. As a result, they were denied full participation in the larger community.

**WOMEN MOBILIZE FOR REFORM** Despite such pressures, women actively participated in all the important reform movements of the 19th century. For many, their efforts to improve society had been inspired by the optimistic message of the Second Great Awakening. From abolition to education, women worked for reform despite the cold reception they got from many men.

Perhaps the most important reform effort that women participated in was abolition. Women abolitionists raised money, distributed literature, and collected signatures for antislavery petitions to Congress.

Women also played key roles in the temperance movement, the effort to prohibit the drinking of alcohol. Some women, most notably Dorothea Dix, fought to improve treatment for the mentally disabled. Dix also joined others in the effort to reform the nation's harsh and often inhumane prison system.

*C. Answer*
Abolition, temperance, improving conditions for the mentally disabled, and prison reform.

**MAIN IDEA**

**Analyzing Issues**
Ⓒ What were some of the areas of society that women worked to reform?

**REVIEW UNIT** 147

---

 CHAPTER 3 · SECTION 5

### Instruct: Objective ③
**Women and Reform**
TAKS SS11 3(US21.D)
· In what reform movements did women participate?
· How did women improve their educational opportunities?
· What factors led to the emergence of the women's rights movement?

🛠 **Critical Thinking Transparencies CT43**
· Increasing School Enrollment

💿 **Electronic Library of Primary Sources**
· Disappointment Is the Lot of Women, 1855, by L. Stone

## HISTORY from VISUALS

**Interpreting the Graph**
Discuss with students the fact that free African Americans were no longer owned as slaves. Have students compare the percentages of free African Americans and slaves in the South.

📖 **In-Depth Resources: Unit 1**
· Primary Sources: Propaganda Images, p. 99

🛠 **Geography Transparencies GT 8**
· Distribution of Slaves

*Skillbuilder Answer*
Free African Americans.

## More About . . .

**Women Abolitionists**
Sarah and Angelina Grimké were two prominent female abolitionists. The sisters grew up on a wealthy plantation in Charleston, South Carolina. Each Grimké child had his or her own "companion," a slave child to cater to every need. Early on, Sarah expressed her discomfort with the arrangement. She considered her "companion" her equal. Later, Sarah taught a slave woman to read and write—a violation of South Carolina law. "The light was put out," she recalled, "the keyhole screened, and flat on our stomachs, before the fire, with the spelling-book under our eyes, we defied the laws of South Carolina."

---

**ACTIVITY** | **COOPERATIVE LEARNING**                    🌐 **classzone.com**

### Interviewing Women Reformers

**Class Time** 45 minutes

**Task** Interviewing women reformers

**Purpose** To better understand the women in the reform movement

**Directions** Have students work in pairs to research the life and accomplishments of a woman reformer. Students should then prepare a question-and-answer interview script using their research material. Finally, each pair should make a class presentation, with one student acting as the interviewer, the other as the reformer.

📖 Integrated Assessment
· Rubrics 1, 3

### More About . . .

#### Elizabeth Blackwell

Blackwell applied to 29 medical schools before she was accepted at Geneva College in 1847. Later, Blackwell discovered that the administration had given the students the final say on her admission. In jest, they accepted her. Blackwell faced continued discrimination at Geneva College. Instructors would not let women attend operations or anatomy classes. When Blackwell finally did observe an operation, she wrote in her journal, "That dissection was just as much as I could bear. Some of the students blushed, some were hysterical, not one could keep in a smile . . . I sat in grave indifference, though the effort made my heart palpitate [beat] most painfully."

### KEY PLAYER

#### Elizabeth Cady Stanton

Stanton was an exceptional student. She studied law with her father, a judge, but was refused admission to the bar because she was a woman. Stanton went on to become a prominent activist for women's rights as well as the mother of seven children.

Have students contrast Stanton with the image of an ideal woman in the 19th century. How did her actions and attitudes differ from those expected of women at that time? *(Stanton was strong willed and outspoken and took part in the world outside of her home.)*

 In-Depth Resources: Unit 1
· Primary Source: from the Seneca Falls "Declaration of Sentiments," p. 100

**EDUCATION FOR WOMEN** Work for abolition and temperance accompanied gains in education for women. Until the 1820s, American girls had few educational opportunities beyond elementary school. As Sarah Grimké complained in *Letters on the Equality of the Sexes and the Condition of Woman* (1838), a woman who knew "chemistry enough to keep the pot boiling, and geography enough to know the location of the different rooms in her house" was considered learned enough. Grimké believed that increased education for women was a better alternative.

Still, throughout the 1800s, more and more educational institutions for women began to appear. In 1821 Emma Willard opened one of the nation's first academically-oriented schools for girls in Troy, New York. In addition to classes in domestic sciences, the Troy Female Seminary offered classes in math, history, geography, languages, art, music, writing, and literature. The Troy Female Seminary became the model for a new type of women's school. Despite tremendous ridicule—people mocked that "they will be educating cows next"—Willard's school prospered.

In 1833, the first class of Ohio's Oberlin College included four women, thus becoming the nation's first fully coeducational college. In 1837, Mary Lyon surmounted heated resistance to found another important institution of higher learning for women, Mount Holyoke Female Seminary (later Mount Holyoke College) in South Hadley, Massachusetts. **D**

**EDUCATION AND WOMEN'S HEALTH** Improvement in women's education began to improve women's lives, most notably in health reform. Elizabeth Blackwell, who in 1849 became the first woman to graduate from medical college, later opened the New York Infirmary for Women and Children. In the 1850s, Catharine Beecher, sister of novelist Harriet Beecher Stowe, and a respected educator in her own right, undertook a national survey of women's health. To her dismay, Beecher found three sick women for every healthy one. It was no wonder: women rarely bathed or exercised, and the fashionable women's clothing of the day included corsets so restrictive that breathing sometimes was difficult.

Unfortunately, black women enjoyed even fewer educational opportunities than their white counterparts. In 1831 Prudence Crandall, a white Quaker, opened a school for girls in Canterbury, Connecticut. Two years later she admitted an African-American girl named Sarah Harris. The townspeople protested so vigorously that Crandall decided to enroll only African Americans. This aroused even more opposition, and in 1834 Crandall was forced to close the school and leave town. Only after the Civil War would the severely limited educational opportunities for black women slowly begin to expand.

**WOMEN'S RIGHTS MOVEMENT EMERGES** The reform movements of the mid-19th century fed the growth of the women's movement by providing women with increased opportunities to act outside the home. **Elizabeth Cady Stanton** and Lucretia Mott had been ardent abolitionists. Male abolitionists discriminated against them at the World's Anti-Slavery Convention in 1840, so the pair resolved to hold a women's rights convention. In 1848, more than 300 women convened in Seneca Falls, New York. Before the convention started, Stanton and Mott composed an agenda and a detailed statement of grievances.

### KEY PLAYER

#### ELIZABETH CADY STANTON 1815–1902

Stanton was an ardent abolitionist, and she timed her marriage in 1840 so that she and her new husband could travel together to London for the World's Anti-Slavery Convention.

She also believed that women deserved the same rights as men and even persuaded the minister to omit the word "obey" from her vow in the marriage ceremony because she felt no need to "obey one with whom I supposed I was entering into an equal relation."

At the antislavery convention, Stanton and the other women delegates were barred from participation in the convention and were forced to sit and listen from a curtained gallery. There she met Lucretia Mott. Stanton and Mott vowed "to hold a convention as soon as we returned home, and form a society to advocate the rights of women." Eight years later, the Seneca Falls convention fulfilled that vow.

**Background**
Sarah Grimké and her sister Angelina were leading voices in the abolition and women's rights movements.

**MAIN IDEA**

**Summarizing**
**D** What improvements in women's education occurred in the 1820s and '30s?

*D. Answer*
More and more schools opened just for women and schools that formerly admitted only men now began to admit women.

---

## ACTIVITY    SKILLBUILDER LESSON

### Identifying Problems

**Explaining the Skill** Identifying historical problems includes researching and summarizing the difficulties faced by individuals or groups during a specific time period. In reading history, students will find that some problems may be stated directly, while others might be implied by the ways people act. For example, gang violence in a community probably indicates problems exist in other areas of community life, such as economic activities and family structure.

**Applying the Skill** Help students identify some of the problems that were the focus of the women's reform movement in the early 1800s. *(slavery; lack of education and equality for women)* After identifying a general problem area, such as equality for women, have students determine if there are other problems in society that contribute to the overall problem. For example, within equality for women, the problem of lower pay could be addressed.

 In-Depth Resources: Unit 1
· Skillbuilder Practice: Identifying Problems, p. 86

The participants at the **Seneca Falls convention** approved all parts of the declaration, including a resolution calling for women to have the right to vote. In spite of all the political activity among middle-class white women, African-American women found it difficult to gain recognition of their problems. A former slave named **Sojourner Truth** did not let that stop her, however. At a women's rights convention in 1851, Truth, an outspoken abolitionist, refuted the arguments that because she was a woman she was weak, and because she was black, she was not feminine.

### A PERSONAL VOICE  SOJOURNER TRUTH

" **Look at me! Look at my arm! I have ploughed, and planted, and gathered into barns, and no man could head me! And ain't I a woman? I could work as much and eat as much as a man—when I could get it—and bear the lash as well! And ain't I a woman? I have borne thirteen children, and seen most all sold off to slavery, and when I cried out with my mother's grief, none but Jesus heard me! And ain't I a woman?** "

—quoted in *Narrative of Sojourner Truth*

▲ With her dignified bearing and powerful voice, Sojourner Truth made audiences snap to attention. Truth fought for women's rights, abolition, prison reform, and temperance.

*E. Answer*
Sojourner Truth had done back-breaking work, been beaten severely, and seen most of her thirteen children sold into slavery.

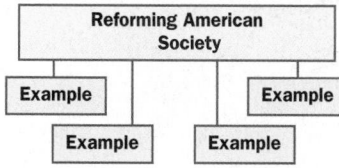

**MAIN IDEA**

Analyzing Issues
**E** How did Sojourner Truth describe her life as an African-American woman?

As Truth showed, hard work was a fact of life for most women. But she also pointed to the problem of slavery that continued to vex the nation. As abolitionists intensified their attacks, proslavery advocates strengthened their defenses. Before long the issue of slavery threatened to destroy the Union. **E**

## Assess & Reteach

**SECTION 5 ASSESSMENT**
Have students work in pairs to answer the questions.

📄 Formal Assessment
· Section Quiz, p. 60

**SELF-ASSESSMENT**
To document what students have learned, have them list the insights they gained into the abolition movement and the changing status of women in the mid-1800s.

**RETEACH**
Ask students to skim the section and make note of women reformers and their causes. Have students create a list to keep track of this information.

📄 In-Depth Resources: Unit 1
· Reteaching Activity, p. 91

---

### SECTION 5 ASSESSMENT

**1. TERMS & NAMES** For each term or name, write a sentence explaining its significance.

- abolition
- Unitarians
- Ralph Waldo Emerson
- transcendentalism
- William Lloyd Garrison
- Frederick Douglass
- Nat Turner
- Elizabeth Cady Stanton
- Seneca Falls convention
- Sojourner Truth

**MAIN IDEA**

**2. TAKING NOTES**
In a diagram similar to the one shown, fill in historical events or key figures related to reforming American society in the 19th century.

Reforming American Society
- Example
- Example
- Example
- Example

Write a paragraph about one of the examples you chose, explaining its significance.

**CRITICAL THINKING**

**3. EVALUATING**
Which do you think was a more effective strategy—violence or nonviolence—for eliminating slavery? Why? **Think About:**
- Frederick Douglas
- Nat Turner
- William Lloyd Garrison
- Sojourner Truth

**4. MAKING INFERENCES**
Consider the philosophical and religious ideas expressed during the Second Great Awakening. How did they influence the activities of 19th-century reformers? **Think About:**
- concepts of individualism and Jacksonian democracy
- the views of Emerson
- the activities of Garrison, Douglass, Stanton, and Truth

---

Answers  **ASSESSMENT**

**1. TERMS & NAMES**
abolition, p. 144
Unitarians, p. 145
Ralph Waldo Emerson, p. 145
transcendentalism, p. 145
William Lloyd Garrison, p. 145
Frederick Douglass, p. 146
Nat Turner, p. 146
Elizabeth Cady Stanton, p. 148
Seneca Falls convention, p. 149
Sojourner Truth, p. 149

**2. TAKING NOTES**
William Lloyd Garrison—*The Liberator;* Frederick Douglass—*North Star;* Sarah Grimké—*Letters on the Equality of the Sexes . . .;* Catharine Beecher; Elizabeth Blackwell's Infirmary; Elizabeth Cady Stanton; Lucretia Mott; Seneca Falls convention; Sojourner Truth

**3. EVALUATING**
Some students may suggest that violence may have been necessary to emancipate the slaves; others may point out that Nat Turner's violent rebellion inspired an equally violent counterattack from slaveholders.

**4. MAKING INFERENCES**
Must students may note that reformers shared a strong belief in the power of the individual to change conditions in society. The efforts of many reformers were aimed at expanding individual freedoms and achieving equality for all.

*The Growth of a Young Nation*  **149**

# GEOGRAPHY SPOTLIGHT

## GEOGRAPHICAL SPOTLIGHT

### Objectives

· To explain Preuss's map of the Oregon Trail

· To describe the hardships that settlers faced in traversing the trail

## Focus & Motivate

**Making Inferences** Have students try to imagine traveling to a place they had never visited before. Ask them why a map would be useful. Ask them also what troubles a person would encounter in creating the first accurate map of the area?

## More About . . .

### The Oregon Trail

About 2,000 miles long, the Oregon Trail was the longest-used overland route to the West. Fur traders and missionaries used the trail years before Frémont's mapping expedition. In 1843, a year after Frémont's first expedition, the missionaries Marcus and Narcissa Whitman led 1,000 settlers along the trail. All told, about 12,000 pioneers traversed the trail to Oregon, their wagon wheels cutting so deep that the tracks are still visible today along some parts of the trail. After railroads made wagon trains obsolete, the trail was used to drive cattle and sheep east to market.

# Mapping the Oregon Trail

In 1841, Congress appropriated $30,000 for a survey of the Oregon Trail and named John C. Frémont to head the expeditions. Frémont earned his nickname "the Pathfinder" by leading three expeditions—which included artists, scientists, and cartographers, among them the German-born cartographer Charles Preuss—to explore the American West between 1842 and 1848. When Frémont submitted the report of his first expedition, Congress immediately ordered the printing of 10,000 copies, which were widely distributed.

The "Topographical Map of the Road from Missouri to Oregon," drawn by Preuss, appeared in seven sheets. Though settlers first used this route in 1836, it was not until 1846 that Preuss published his map to guide them. The long, narrow map shown here is called a "strip" map, a map that shows a thin strip of the earth's surface—in this case, the last stretch of the trail before reaching Fort Wallah-Wallah.

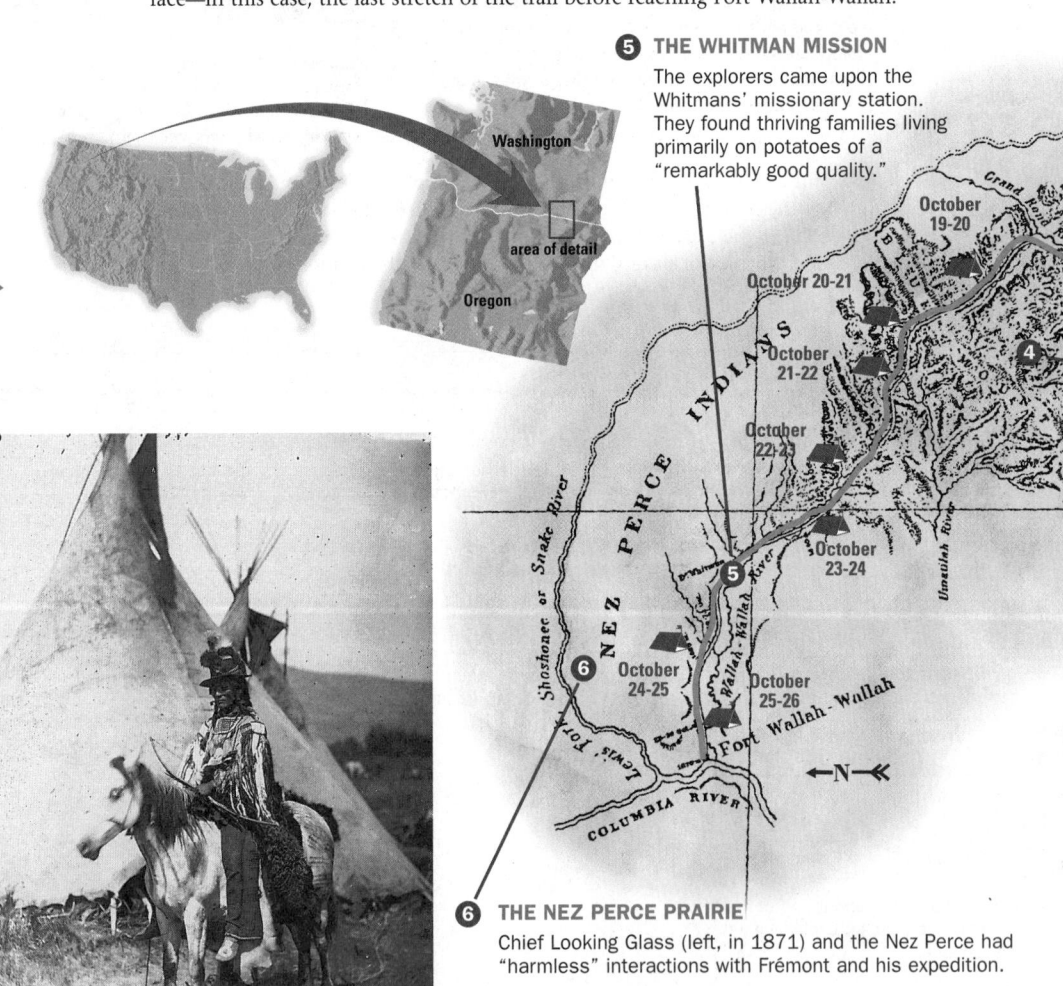

**5 THE WHITMAN MISSION**
The explorers came upon the Whitmans' missionary station. They found thriving families living primarily on potatoes of a "remarkably good quality."

**6 THE NEZ PERCE PRAIRIE**
Chief Looking Glass (left, in 1871) and the Nez Perce had "harmless" interactions with Frémont and his expedition.

150

## RECOMMENDED RESOURCES

### BOOKS

Egan, Ferol. *Frémont, Explorer for a Restless Nation.* Garden City, NY: Doubleday, 1977.

Guthrie, A. B. *The Way West.* Boston: Houghton, 1949. A Pulitzer Prize-winning novel about the Oregon Trail.

Parkman, Francis. *The Oregon Trail.* New York: Viking, 1989. Reprint of the famous 1849 chronicle of Parkman's 1,700-mile journey from Missouri to Wyoming and back.

### VIDEOS

*As the Wind Rocks the Cradle.* APL Educational Video, 1991. A pioneer woman describes her experiences on the trail west.

*The Real West.* Filmic Archives. The Oregon Trail and the people of the American West, narrated by actor Gary Cooper.

*Settling the Oregon Territory.* Encyclopedia Britannica. How a belief in manifest destiny brought settlers to Oregon.

*The West.* PBS Video, 1996, Ken Burn's nine-part look at the American West

includes Episode 2, "Empire upon the Trails."

### SOFTWARE

*Oregon Trail I and II.* MECC. Puts users in the shoes of pioneers travelling the Oregon Trail.

**150** CHAPTER 3

## ① FORT BOISÉE (BOISE)

This post became an important stopping point for settlers along the trail. Though salmon were plentiful in summer, Frémont noted that in the winter Native Americans often were forced to eat "every creeping thing, however loathsome and repulsive," to stay alive.

# Instruct

1. Why did Congress appropriate money for a survey of the Oregon Trail?
2. What types of human-environment interaction took place on the journey?
3. What was the importance of mapping trails to the settlement of the West?

### MAKING PERSONAL CONNECTIONS

Ask students to consider how long it took to the cross this portion of the Oregon Trail.

Have students suggest what supplies they might need to take in order to explore that terrain at that time of the year.

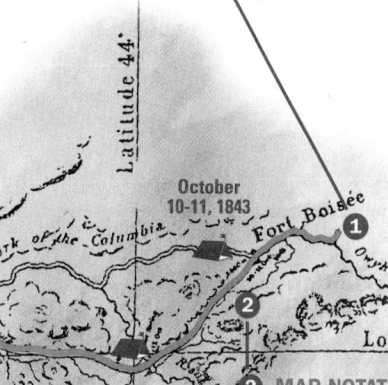

## ② MAP NOTATION

Preuss recorded dates, distances, temperatures, and geographical features as the expedition progressed along the trail.

## ③ RECORDING NATURAL RESOURCES

On October 13, Frémont traveled through a desolate valley of the Columbia River to a region of "arable mountains," where he observed "nutritious grasses" and good soil that would support future flocks and herds.

## ④ CROSSING THE MOUNTAINS

Pioneers on the trail cut paths through the Blue Mountains, a wooded range that Frémont believed had been formed by "violent and extensive igneous [volcanic] action."

### HISTORY from VISUALS

**Interpreting the Map**

Have students examine the strip map and its labels. Then ask them which way is north and the strip map and how would they determine the direction. *(Left is north; the latitude lines are vertical instead of horizontal and the line for 45 degrees is left of the line for 44 degrees.)*

**Extension** On the basis of the photos, write three or four sentences about what the explorers would have encountered along the trail. *(The explorers would have found some forts along the trail, where they might have gotten supplies. They would have had to cross mountains and through waters and forests. They also would have encountered Native Americans.)*

---

### THINKING CRITICALLY

1. **Analyzing Patterns** Use the map to identify natural obstacles that settlers faced on the Oregon Trail.

2. **Creating a Thematic Map** Do research to find out more about early mapping efforts for other western trails. Then create a settler's map of a small section of one trail. To help you decide what information you should show, pose some questions that a settler might have and that your map will answer. Then, sketch and label your map.

**SEE SKILLBUILDER HANDBOOK, PAGE R32.**

**RESEARCH LINKS** CLASSZONE.COM

---

### THINKING CRITICALLY: ANSWERS

#### 1. ANALYZING PATTERNS

Students' responses should include references to the rivers, desolate valleys, mountains, and forests. Some might also mention wildlife.

#### 2. CREATING A THEMATIC MAP

**Rubric**

Thematic maps should . . .

· be drawn roughly to scale

· accurately reflect one portion of a western trail

· include accurate geographic labels and notes highlighting areas of interest

## TERMS & NAMES

1. Jeffersonian republicanism, p. 113
2. Monroe Doctrine, p. 117
3. Missouri Compromise, p. 122
4. Jacksonian democracy, p. 123
5. Trail of Tears, p. 124
6. Stephen F. Austin, p. 133
7. market revolution, p. 139
8. Lowell textile mills, p. 142
9. Frederick Douglass, p. 146
10. Elizabeth Cady Stanton, p. 148

## MAIN IDEAS

1. It doubled the size of the nation. Jefferson expanded the power of the presidency.
2. It brought an end to the War of 1812.
3. Easing of voting requirements increased the number of voters; more than three times as many white males voted in 1828 as in 1824, and they helped elect Andrew Jackson.
4. He regarded it as insensitive to the needs of common people and believed its financial strength and power threatened American democracy.
5. Many Americans were eager to control the Western lands, and they believed it was a destiny ordained by God.
6. A Mexican army killed 187 defenders of the Alamo, while hundreds of Mexicans also died. Fury over the massacre spurred the Texans to win their independence.
7. Transportation systems strengthened Northern industry and commerce. The steel plow and the reaper improved Midwest agriculture. Steamboats allowed the South to ship agricultural products north.
8. Workers organized unions and went on strike when their working conditions deteriorated and their wages fell. They organized to try to regain control over their workplaces.
9. Belief in the individual's ability to improve himself or herself and society and belief in a democratic God who would offer salvation to all. Ideas like these could be found in the Second Great Awakening.
10. To gain support for women's rights and declare women's equality with men

## TERMS & NAMES

For each term or name below, write a sentence explaining its connection to the nation's growth during the early and mid-1800s.

1. Jeffersonian republicanism
2. Monroe Doctrine
3. Missouri Compromise
4. Jacksonian democracy
5. Trail of Tears
6. Stephen F. Austin
7. market revolution
8. Lowell textile mills
9. Frederick Douglass
10. Elizabeth Cady Stanton

## MAIN IDEAS

Use your notes and the information in the chapter to answer the following questions.

### The Jeffersonian Era (pages 112–117)

1. How did the Louisiana Purchase affect the United States?
2. What did the Treaty of Ghent accomplish?

### The Age of Jackson (pages 120–127)

3. What changes occurred in the voting population and in voting patterns between the presidential elections of 1824 and 1828?
4. Why did Jackson oppose the Bank of the United States?

### Manifest Destiny (pages 130–138)

5. Why was the concept of manifest destiny such an appealing one to Americans in the 1840s?
6. Describe the battle of the Alamo and explain why it is an important symbol in U.S. history.

### The Market Revolution (pages 139–143)

7. How did the inventions and innovations of the mid-19th century help fuel the nation's economy?
8. Why did workers go on strike and begin to form trade unions in the 1830s?

### Reforming American Society (pages 144–149)

9. What new religious ideas set the stage for the reform movements of the mid-19th century?
10. What was the purpose of the Seneca Falls convention?

## CRITICAL THINKING

1. **USING YOUR NOTES** What were America's goals and ideals during this period of expansion and economic change? Draw a chart in which you list goals from the period, how they were achieved, and in what ways their effects were positive or negative.

| Goal | How Achieved | Positive/Negative Effects |
|---|---|---|
|  |  |  |

2. **EVALUATING IMPACT** In what ways did the reform movement of the mid-19th century affect the lives of women—both white and black, both free and enslaved? Support your answers with examples from the text.

3. **FORMING GENERALIZATIONS** Westward expansion helped shape the personal identity of Americans in the early 19th century. What values and traits characterized many Western settlers of this era? Think about Jim Beckwourth's life (See the Historical Spotlight on page 131) and the rise of the common person during the Age of Jackson.

---

**VISUAL SUMMARY** **THE GROWTH OF A YOUNG NATION**

**TERRITORIES AND EXPLORATION**
- National boundaries are extended in the North, West, and South.
- Lewis and Clark expand knowledge of the Louisiana Territory.
- The Oregon and Santa Fe trails extend exploration of and settlement in the Northwest and Southwest.
- The California Gold Rush creates an influx of settlers in the West.

**SOCIAL REFORMS**
- Voting rights are expanded in many states, although for males only.
- National Trades' Unions call for improved working conditions.
- Women's institutions of higher education are founded.
- Abolitionists call for the end of slavery.

**TECHNOLOGY AND COMMERCE**
- The telegraph expands the possibilities of communication.
- Textile mills increase manufacturing in the North.
- The cotton gin allows for greater agricultural profits in the South.
- Canals and railroads improve transportation throughout the country.

## CRITICAL THINKING

1. **Using Your Notes** Goals: find new markets; increase economic opportunities; territorial expansion. How achieved: westward expansion and trade; new inventions; war and treaties to acquire new land. Positive effects: expanded U.S. political sovereignty; more technologically advanced. Negative effects: Native Americans displaced; expanded slavery; lost lives in warfare.

2. **Evaluating Impact** The women's reform movement improved women's education and health care. Improvements in education were limited to white women who were able to afford it. The efforts of black women reformers, such as Sojourner Truth, raised national consciousness about slavery and became an inspiration for women's participation in the abolition movement.

3. **Forming Generalizations** Many showed optimism, resourcefulness, versatility, and rugged individualism. They also believed in social mobility and individual freedom.

## Standardized Test Practice

Use the image below and your knowledge of U.S history to answer question 1.

1. This print by Robert Cruikshank, entitled *The President's Levee* [reception], or *All Creation Going to the White House*, was issued in 1829. It is satirizing —

   A the Louisiana Purchase.
   B the California gold rush.
   C Jacksonian democracy.
   D the Indian Removal Act.

2. The Supreme Court decision *Marbury* v. *Madison* is important for affirming which of the following principles?

   F impressment
   G the "American System"
   H popular sovereignty
   J judicial review

3. The main effect of the Missouri Compromise was to —

   A admit Missouri as a state.
   B resolve disputes over slavery in the territories.
   C change the balance of free and slave states.
   D incline Southerners toward secession.

4. Between 1830 and 1850, the geographic area of the United States increased by about one third. Most of this land was acquired by —

   F war.
   G purchase.
   H exchange.
   J inciting rebellion.

---

ADDITIONAL TEST PRACTICE, pages S1–S33.

 **TEST PRACTICE** CLASSZONE.COM

---

## ALTERNATIVE ASSESSMENT

1. **INTERACT WITH HISTORY** Recall your discussion of the question on page 111:

   *Would you support the federal or your state government?*

   Imagine that you are a visitor to the United States Senate in 1828, listening to senators express their views on a strong federal government versus states' rights. Write a letter to a friend describing what you saw and heard. Include events and issues from U.S. history that senators from the North and South might have used in making their arguments.

2. **VIDEO** **LEARNING FROM MEDIA** View the *American Stories* video, "Recruited by Lewis and Clark: Patrick Gass Chronicles the Journey West." Discuss the following questions in a small group; then do the activity.

   • What were some of the roles played by Native Americans in the journey of Lewis and Clark? Provide examples that stand out for you.

   • What aspect of the journey do you think that Patrick Gass found most difficult? Why?

   **Cooperative Learning Activity** An explorer can be anyone who discovers important things about living in the world. Who are the explorers of our own day? Using examples you may have read about in books, magazines, or newspapers or seen on television, choose someone you consider to be an important explorer. Prepare a report and present it to the class.

REVIEW UNIT **153**

---

## Standardized Test Practice

1. The correct answer is **C**. It shows a large group of Jackson's supporters in a festive mood on the White House lawn.

2. The correct answer is **J**. *Marbury* v. *Madison* affirmed judicial review. Letter F is not correct because impressment was the British practice of drafting sailors. Letter G is not correct because the "American System" refers to President Madison's national plan. Letter H is not correct because the case did not concern popular sovereignty.

3. The correct answer is **B**. The Missouri Compromise divided the Louisiana Purchase territory into free and slave territories. Letter A is not correct because Missouri's state status was not in dispute. Letter C is not correct because it did not effect the balance of slavery and free states. Letter D is not correct because it did not make Southerners want to succeed.

4. The correct answer is **F**. The United States acquired western and southwestern territories in the war with Mexico. Letter G is not correct because the United States purchased little land in this time period. Letter H is not correct because the United States did not exchange territories. Letter J is not correct because no rebellion was incited in order to acquire the land.

### LETTER TO THE EDITOR

**Tips for Teaching**

· Remind students to make sure they have clearly stated and supported their points of view.

· Tell students they have a week to complete the final draft.

 Formal Assessment
 · Chapter Test, Forms A, B, and C, pp. 61–78

---

## ALTERNATIVE ASSESSMENT

### 1. INTERACT WITH HISTORY
**Rubrics**

Student letters should . . .

· be informal accounts of the states' rights debates

· offer opinions about the events, speeches, and senators' standpoints on issues

· draw conclusions and give insights about what life is like in the United States

### 2. LEARNING FROM MEDIA
**Rubrics**

Student reports should . . .

· focus on the life and expeditions of a specific explorer

· describe the explorer's major accomplishments, discoveries, or adventures

· use examples, quotes, and supporting evidence

# The Union in Peril

| | CHAPTER OVERVIEW | COPYMASTERS | INTEGRATED TECHNOLOGY |
|---|---|---|---|
| **CHAPTER RESOURCES** | *Slavery divides the nation. North and South enter a long and destructive civil war that ends slavery. African Americans briefly enjoy full civil rights, but new laws discriminate against them.* | Telescoping the Times<br>· Chapter Summary, pp. 7–8<br><br>Planning for Block Schedules | American Stories video series<br>· "War Outside My Window"<br>· "Teacher of a Freed People"<br>Power Presentations<br>Electronic Teacher Tools<br>Online Lesson Planner<br>classzone.com |
| **SECTION 1**<br>The Divisive Politics of Slavery<br>pp. 156–167 | **KEY IDEAS**<br>*The issue of slavery leads to increased tension and violence between the North and the South and finally brings the nation to the brink of war.* | In-Depth Resources: Unit 1<br>· Guided Reading, p. 106<br>· Building Vocabulary, p. 110<br>· Skillbuilder Practice, p. 111<br>· Reteaching Activity, p. 114<br>· Primary Sources, pp. 122–123<br>· American Lives, p. 136<br>Lesson Plans, pp. 35–36 | Geography Transparencies GT10<br>· Presidential Elections; 1856, 1960<br>Critical Thinking Transparencies CT10, CT44<br>· Compromise of 1859<br>· Population Growth: 1820–1860<br>Humanities Transparencies HT10<br>· No 10 Harriet Tubman series<br>Electronic Library of Primary Sources<br>classzone.com |
| **SECTION 2**<br>The Civil War Begins<br>pp. 168–174 | *The Civil War becomes a more prolonged, deadly conflict than anyone had predicted and has a significant impact on civilians, soldiers, and African Americans.* | In-Depth Resources: Unit 1<br>· Guided Reading, p. 107<br>· Skillbuilder Practice, p. 112<br>· Reteaching Activity, p. 115<br>· Outline Map, pp. 120–121<br>· Primary Sources, p. 124<br>Lesson Plans, pp. 36–37 | Geography Transparencies GT11, GT37<br>· Union and Confederacy: 1861<br>· Slavery and the Civil War<br>Critical Thinking Transparencies CT11, CT45<br>· The Civil War<br>· North vs. South<br>Electronic Library of Primary Sources<br>classzone.com |
| **SECTION 3**<br>The North Takes Charge<br>pp. 175–183 | *The South surrenders to the North. However, the war has an enduring effect on the nation and on American lives.* | In-Depth Resources: Unit 1<br>· Guided Reading, p. 108<br>· Reteaching Activity, p. 116<br>· Primary Sources, p. 125<br>Historic Supreme Court Decisions,<br>· *Dred Scott* v. *Sanford*, pp. 61–66<br>Lesson Plans, pp. 38–39 | Humanities Transparencies HT11<br>· Abraham Lincoln<br>Critical Thinking Transparencies CT11<br>· The Civil War<br>Electronic Library of Primary Sources<br>classzone.com |
| **SECTION 4**<br>Reconstruction and Its Effects<br>pp. 184–189 | *Reconstruction results in many political, social, and economic changes in the South before being ended in 1877.* | In-Depth Resources: Unit 1<br>· Guided Reading , p. 109<br>· Skillbuilder Practice, p. 113<br>· Reteaching Activity, p. 117<br>· Geography Application, pp. 118–119<br>· Primary Sources, p. 126<br>· American Lives, p. 137<br>Lesson Plans, pp. 40–41 | Geography Transparencies GT12<br>· The Barrow Plantation<br>Critical Thinking Transparencies CT12<br>· Reconstruction<br>Humanities Transparencies HT12, HT34<br>· The Fifteenth Amendment<br>· A. Johnson, Tailor<br>Electronic Library of Primary Sources<br> classzone.com |

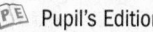

| | | |
|---|---|---|
| PE Pupil's Edition | Overhead Transparency | CD-ROM |
| TE Teacher's Edition | Audio Library | Internet |
| Copymaster | | |

# ASSESSMENT OPTIONS

- PE Chapter Assessment, pp. 190–191
- Formal Assessment
  · Chapter Tests, Forms A, B, and C, pp. 83–102
- Test Generator
- Integrated Assessment Book
- TAKS Online Test Practice
- TAKS Spiraled Content Review
- TAKS Practice Tests

---

- PE Section 1 Assessment, p. 165
- TE Self-Assessment, p. 165
- Formal Assessment, Quiz, p. 79
- Integrated Assessment Book
- Test Generator
- TAKS Practice Transparencies TT37–TT40

---

- PE Section 2 Assessment, p. 174
- TE Self-Assessment, p. 174
- Formal Assessment, Quiz, p. 80
- Integrated Assessment Book
- Test Generator
- TAKS Practice Transparencies TT41, TT42

---

- PE Section 3 Assessment, p. 183
- TE Self-Assessment, p. 183
- Formal Assessment, Quiz, p. 81
- Integrated Assessment Book
- Test Generator
- TAKS Practice Transparencies TT43–TT45

---

- PE Section 4 Assessment, p. 189
- TE Self-Assessment, p. 189
- Formal Assessment, Quiz, p. 82
- Integrated Assessment Book
- Test Generator
- TAKS Practice Transparencies TT46–TT48

# RESOURCES FOR DIFFERENTIATING INSTRUCTION

**Students Acquiring English/ESL**

- Reading Study Guide:
  (English and Spanish)
  pp. 47–56
- Access for Students
  Acquiring English/ESL:
  Spanish Translations,
  pp. 61–74
- Chapter Summaries on CD
  (English and Spanish)

**Less Proficient Readers**

- Reading Study Guide
  (English and Spanish)
  pp. 47–56
- Telescoping the Times
  · Chapter Summary,
  pp. 7–8
- Chapter Summaries on CD
  (English and Spanish)

**Gifted and Talented Students**

- In-Depth Resources: Unit 1
  · Primary Sources,
  pp. 122–126
  · American Lives: Harriet
  Tubman, p. 136; Thaddeus
  Stevens, p. 137
- Historic Supreme Court
  Decisions
  · *Dred Scott* v. *Sanford*,
  pp. 61–66
- Electronic Library of
  Primary Sources
  · Unit 1, Chapter 4

# CROSS-CURRICULAR CONNECTIONS

## Primary Sources

Time-Life Books Editors. *Soldier Life.* NY: Time-Life, 1996. Compilation of reminiscences of common soldiers and their families, accompanied by photos.

Lincoln, Abraham. *Abraham Lincoln: Speeches and Writing 1859-1865.* Don E. Gehernbacher, ed. NY: Literary Classics of United States, 1989. Excellent for browsing or for research.

## Geography

The Conservation Fund, Frances H. Kennedy, ed. *The Civil War Battlefield Guide.* Boston: Houghton Mifflin, 1998. New edition of a guide to 384 battles and battlefields with 83 maps.

## Humanities: Art

McPherson, James M. *Images of the Civil War: The Paintings of Mort Kunstler.* NY: Gramercy, 1992. Color paintings of Civil War scenes so detailed that Civil War buffs refer to them for details.

## Literature

Crane, Stephen. *The Red Badge of Courage.* NY: Ballantine, 1985. This classic novel of the Civil War tells of a young soldier's battle experiences.

Vidal, Gore. *Lincoln.* NY: Ballantine, 1985. This novel reveals the political and personal struggles of President Lincoln as he guides the nation through the Civil War.

## McDougal Littell Nextext

*Slavery in America; The Civil War*

## Literature Connections

Gaines, Ernest. *The Autobiography of Miss Jane Pittman* (with related readings). In this novel, a black woman who has lived for 110 years tells her memorable story both as a slave and as a witness to the civil rights movement of the 1960s.

# ENRICHMENT ACTIVITIES

- PE Pupil's Edition, pp. 154–189
  Interact with History, pp. 154–155
  Supreme Court, p. 166
- In-Depth Resources: Unit 1
  · Geography Application: Slave Populations in
  the U.S., pp. 118–119
  · Outline Map: The States Choose Sides,
  pp. 120–121
  · Primary Source: Lincoln-Douglas Debates,
  pp. 122–123
  · Primary Source: Emancipation Proclamation,
  p. 124
  · Primary Source: On the Burning of South
  Carolina, p. 125

- · Primary Source: An Inquiry on the Condition
  of the South, p. 126
- · American Lives: Harriet Tubman, p. 136
- · American Lives: Thaddeus Stevens, p. 137
- Historic Supreme Court Decisions
  *Dred Scott* v. *Sanford*, pp. 61–66
- Electronic Library of Primary Sources
  · Unit 1, Chapter 4
- Primary Source Explorer
- American Stories video series
  · "War Outside My Window"
  · "Teacher of a Freed People"

## BLOCK SCHEDULE LESSON PLAN OPTIONS (90-MINUTE PERIOD)

### DAY 1

**CHAPTER OPENER**
pp. 154–155

**Class Time** 20 minutes

**History from Visuals, p. 154**

**Class Time** 10 minutes

*Options for Pacing and Variety*

· Time Saver Ask students questions related to the time line on the page. **Class Time** 5 minutes

**Interact with History, p. 155**

**Class Time** 20 minutes

*Options for Pacing and Variety:*

· Role-Playing Ask students to write notes as if preparing for a debate on the issue of slavery. Have them decide the ultimate goals of those in favor of slavery and those opposed to slavery, and ask them to consider if there is a compromise that would satisfy both parties. Students should think about slavery in terms of how it affected people both personally and economically. **Class Time** 20 minutes

**SECTION 1, pp. 156–167**

**Class Time** 30 minutes

*Options for Pacing and Variety*

· Time Saver Ask students to look at the map of the Underground Railroad on page 159 and answer the Skillbuilder questions. **Class Time** 15 minutes

### DAY 1 continued

· Peer Teaching Have students work in groups and ask each other the Main Idea questions in the section. Then have them work together to create a time line of the significant events that led to the Civil War. **Class Time** 30 minutes

· Internet Have students read the feature, "Historic Decision of The Supreme Court: *Dred Scott* v. *Sanford*," on pages 166-167 and answer the questions using the Internet. **Class Time** 30 minutes

**SECTION 2, pp. 168–174**

**Class Time** 30 minutes

*Options for Pacing and Variety*

· Peer Teaching Have students study the map on page 170 and work in small groups to create a map showing a specific strategy of the Union. Students should use the library and Internet resources to complete the map. **Class Time** 30 minutes

· Time Saver Assign the Section Assessment for homework and review the answers as a class. **Class Time** 10 minutes

### DAY 2

**SECTION 3, pp. 175–183**

**Class Time** 30 minutes

*Options for Pacing and Variety*

· History on Film View the video "War Outside My Window: Mary Chesnut's Diary of the Civil War." Do the Learning from Media activity on page 191. **Class Time** 30 minutes

· Peer Teaching Read aloud The Gettysburg Address. Then discuss the ideas expressed in the speech and the explicit and implicit requests made to the public. Also, have students write down phrases or words that are difficult to understand and then work together to define them. **Class Time** 30 minutes

· Internet Have students read the feature "History Through: Photojournalism" and discuss the questions as a class. Students should look in library resources or on the Internet to find photographs from later wars. Then discuss the differences and similarities of the impact and subject matter of the photographs. Ask students if they have seen video footage of a war and how the impact of video differs from photographs. **Class Time** 30 minutes

### DAY 2 continued

**SECTION 4, pp. 184–189**

**Class Time** 30 minutes

*Options for Pacing and Variety*

· Time Saver Ask students to look at the political cartoon on page 187. Discuss the Skillbuilder questions. **Class Time** 10 minutes

· Peer Evaluation Have students work in groups to quiz each other on the Terms & Names of the section. Discuss the completed the Section Assessment as a class. **Class Time** 30 minutes

**ASSESSMENT**
pp. 190–191

**Class Time** 30 minutes

*Options for Pacing and Variety*

· Peer Evaluation Have students work in pairs to quiz each other on the Main Ideas questions of the chapter. Have them record each other's answers. **Class Time** 20 minutes

· Time Saver Assign the Critical Thinking questions for homework. Discuss the answers in class. **Class Time** 10 minutes

---

**TEACHER-TESTED ACTIVITY**
**CIVIL WAR ORAL HISTORIES**

**Class Time** Two class periods

**Task** Giving an oral presentation as a person who lived during the Civil War

**Purpose** To gain an understanding of the challenges people faced during the Civil War era

**Craig T. Grace, Lanier High School, West Austin, Texas**

**Supplies Needed**

· List from the textbook of significant people during the Civil Era (prepared by the teacher)

· Textbook and research materials

· Audio or video recorder

· Costumes and appropriate props (optional)

**Activity** Have students choose a name from your list. Tell them to gather information about their subject that is relevant to their lives and their roles in the Civil War. Students will pretend to be that person and will introduce themselves as such to the class. For example: "My name is Ulysses S. Grant. I was a former army officer living in Galena when the Civil War began. . . ." If possible, record the presentations.

# CHAPTER 4 CORRELATION

## CORRELATION TO THE TEXAS ESSENTIAL KNOWLEDGE AND SKILLS

Chapter 4 addresses the following standards of the Texas Essential Knowledge and Skills for U.S. History.

| TEKS | Instruction | Student Question/Activity |
|------|-------------|---------------------------|
| **(4C)** Evaluate the impact of third parties and their candidates. | **PE 164** discussion of the 1860 presidential election and how the presence of candidates from four parties allowed Lincoln to win with less than half the popular vote | **TE 164** government activity in which students research more deeply the election of 1860 to produce a map of the election results |
| **(7A)** Trace the historical development of the civil rights movement in the 19th century, including the 13th, 14th, and 15th amendments. | **PE 182, 185–186** examination of the impact of the 13th, 14th, and 15th amendments on the attempts by African Americans to improve their lives | **PE 189** writing activity that tests students' understanding of the 14th and 15th amendments |
| **(8B)** Pose and answer questions about geographic distributions and patterns shown on maps, graphs, charts, models, and databases. | **PE 169** graph depicting Northern and Southern human resources at the start of the Civil War | **PE 169** Skillbuilder questions requiring students to interpret the graph |
| **(19B)** Evaluate the contributions of significant political leaders and social leaders in the United States. | **PE 168–183** examination of the Civil War, including the prominent role that President Abraham Lincoln played in the conflict | **TE 172** question about the characteristics that made Lincoln a successful leader |
| **(20A)** Describe how the characteristics and issues of various eras in U.S. history have been reflected in works of art, music, and literature. | **PE 178** examination of the Civil War photography of Matthew Brady | **PE 178** Skillbuilder questions requiring students to interpret Brady's photography |
| **(21A)** Explain the actions taken by people from racial, ethnic, and religious groups to expand economic opportunities and political rights in American society. | **PE 187–188** discussion of the efforts—both political and economic—by former slaves to improve their lives during Reconstruction | **PE 188** Main Idea question about how African Americans responded to their new status as free persons |
| **(24A)** Locate and use primary and secondary sources to acquire information about the United States. | **PE 177** presentation of Abraham Lincoln's Gettysburg Address | **TE 177** civics activity in which students conduct in-depth analysis of the famous speech |

## TAKS MINI-LESSONS

1. **Social Studies Skills: Objective 1 (8.1.C):** Explain the significance of the following dates: 1861–1865 **Activity** Have students create a time line of significant events of the Civil War.

2. **Social Studies Skills: Objective 4 (8.17.B):** Describe the impact of the 19th-century amendments including the 13th, 14th, and 15th amendments on life in the United States **Activity** Have students create a chart defining the 13th, 14th, and 15th amendments and what impact they had on the life of African Americans.

3. **Social Studies Skills: Objective 5 (US24.A):** Locate and use primary and secondary sources to acquire information about the United States **Activity** Have students complete the activity tracing the roots of the Emancipation Proclamation on TE page 172.

4. **English Language Arts Skills: Objective 1 (8.B):** Read in a varied sources such as diaries, journals, textbooks, maps, newspapers, letters, speeches, and memoranda **Activity** Have students discuss the feelings and emotions expressed in the excerpt from Mary Chestnut's diary on page 175.

5. **English Language Arts Skills: Objective 6 (2.C):** Proofread writing for appropriateness of organization, content, style, and conventions **Activity** Have pairs of students proofread each other's answers to the Critical Thinking questions in the Section 4 Assessment.

# CHAPTER 4 · OBJECTIVE

To understand the events that led to the Civil War, the course and outcome of the war, and the establishment and eventual failure of Reconstruction.

## HISTORY from VISUALS

### Interpreting the Painting

There is no mistaking the intensity of feelings depicted in the painting of a debate in the U.S. Senate on the question of slavery. Ask students for their general reactions to the painting and why they think that slavery became the dominant political issue of the time. (*Students' responses will vary.*)

## Time Line Discussion

Explain to students that the time line covers events in the United States and the world from the period just before the Civil War, through the war (1861–1865), to the end of Reconstruction in 1877. Ask students the following questions:

· Ask students what world event occurred that mirrored an event of the Civil War? (*the emancipation of the serfs in Russia by Czar Alexander II*)

· Ask students when did the Civil War start and end? (*1861-1865*)

· Ask students how Andrew Johnson became President? (*He took the place of the assassinated Lincoln.*)

· Ask students what event followed election of Hayes as President? (*The end of Reconstruction*)

## REVIEW CHAPTER 4

# THE UNION IN PERIL

Union soldiers arrest abolitionist John Brown and his followers at the federal arsenal at Harpers Ferry, Virginia (now West Virginia), 1859. Brown had hoped to steal weapons and use them to instigate a nationwide slave rebellion.

| USA | 1850 | | 1860 |
|---|---|---|---|
| WORLD | | | |

**1852** Franklin Pierce is elected president.

**1852** *Uncle Tom's Cabin* published.

**1856** James Buchanan is elected president.

**1857** The Supreme Court rules against Dred Scott.

**1860** Abraham Lincoln wins presidential election.

**1860** South Carolina secedes.

**1861** The Confederacy is formed. Civil War begins.

**1851** The Great Exhibition opens in London.

**1854** Charles Dickens's *Hard Times* is published.

**1861** Russian serfs emancipated by Czar Alexander II.

## THEMES IN CHAPTER 4

### ECONOMIC OPPORTUNITY

The era of the 1840s and 1850s saw a few women, including Harriet Tubman and Harriet Beecher Stowe, attain prominence, but many women led harsh lives, struggling to eke out an existence for themselves and their families.

**See Teacher's Edition note, p. 158.**

### STATES' RIGHTS

By the 1860s, the issue of slavery had so divided the nation that South Carolina challenged the Constitution and seceded from the Union. Ten other states followed.

**See Teacher's Edition note, p. 169.**

### CIVIL RIGHTS

The Fourteenth Amendment laid the groundwork for future civil rights legislation. However, the Ku Klux Klan used violence and terror to take away the civil rights of African Americans.

**See Teacher's Edition note, p. 185.**

### VOTING RIGHTS

After the war, fundamental rights, such as the right to vote were intensely defeated. The Fifteenth Amendment secured voting rights for males and forbid discrimination against voters based on race, color, or previous condition of servitude.

**See Teacher's Edition note, p. 186.**

# INTERACT
## WITH HISTORY

The year is 1850. Across the United States a debate is raging, dividing North from South: Is slavery a property right or is it a violation of liberty and human dignity? The future of the Union depends on compromise—but for many people on both sides, compromise is unacceptable.

## How can the Union be saved?

### Examine the Issues

- Is it possible to compromise on an ethical issue such as slavery?
- What are the obstacles to altering an institution, such as slavery, that is fundamental to a region's economy and way of life?

**RESEARCH LINKS** · **CLASSZONE.COM**

Visit the Chapter 4 links for more information about The Union in Peril.

# INTERACT
## WITH HISTORY

### Objectives

- To identify the constitutional issues surrounding slavery
- To describe the significance of the debate over slavery to the future of the United States

### Examine the Issues

1. Have students consider the concept that there are issues, such as slavery, upon which it is morally difficult to compromise.
2. Ask students to consider how impossible it was for white Southerners to envision life without slavery, which was integral to their economy and culture.

**1863** Battles of Gettysburg and Vicksburg

**1865** Civil War ends.

**1865** Lincoln is assassinated; Andrew Johnson becomes president.

**1868** Ulysses S. Grant is elected president.

**1876** Rutherford B. Hayes is elected president.

**1877** Reconstruction ends.

**1870**

**1877**

**1864** Maximilian of Austria becomes emperor of Mexico.

**1868** Cubans revolt against Spain.

**1876** Japan forces Korea to open ports to trade.

REVIEW UNIT  155

## Recommended Resources

### BOOKS FOR THE TEACHER

Foner, Eric. *Free Soil, Free Labor, Free Men.* New York: Oxford UP, 1970. Early years of Republican Party.

Foote, Shelby. *The Civil War.* 3 vols. New York: Random House, 1958–74. Highly readable history.

Franklin, John Hope. *Reconstruction After the Civil War,* 2nd ed. Chicago: U of Chicago P, 1994. By a noted African-American historian.

### BOOKS FOR THE STUDENT

Catton, Bruce. *A Stillness at Appomattox.* Franklin Center, Pa: Franklin Library, 1977. Civil war classic.

Botkin, B. A., ed. *Lay My Burden Down.* U of Georgia P, 1989. Remembrances of slavery.

Foner, Eric, *A Short History of Reconstruction.* New York: Oxford UP, 1991.

Smith, George Winston, and Charles Judah, eds. *Life in the North During the Civil War.* Albuquerque: U of N.M. P, 1966.

### VIDEOS

*Roots of Resistance.* PBS Home Video, 1989. 800-424-7963. Story of Underground Railroad.

### SOFTWARE

*African American History: Slavery to Civil rights.* CD-ROM. Queue, 1995. Educational Software Institute, 800-955-5570.

### INTEGRATED TECHNOLOGY

For teacher support, visit . . .

 classzone.com

## OBJECTIVES

**1** Identify differences between the North and the South.

**2** Describe the operation of the Underground Railroad and other forms of protest against slavery.

**3** Explain the political conditions that gave rise to the Republican Party and divided the Whigs.

**4** Describe the conflicts that led to secession.

### SKILLBUILDERS

· Geography Skillbuilder: movement, place, location, p. 159; place, region, p. 160

· Interpreting Visual Sources, p. 164

### CRITICAL THINKING

· Developing Historical Perspective, pp. 157, 165

· Summarizing, pp. 158, 164

· Analyzing Events, p. 160

· Analyzing Effects, p. 161

· Contrasting, p. 162

· Comparing, p. 163

· Evaluating Decisions, p. 163

· Summarizing, p. 164

· Hypothesizing, p. 165

· Evaluating Leadership, p. 165

## Focus & Motivate

Ask students to think of some issues on which they could never compromise. Ask what happens when people discuss these issues.

# The Divisive Politics of Slavery

| MAIN IDEA | WHY IT MATTERS NOW | Terms & Names |
|---|---|---|
| Disagreements over slavery heightened regional tensions and led to the breakup of the Union. | The modern Democratic and Republican parties emerged from the political tensions of the mid-19th century. | • secession<br>• popular sovereignty<br>• Underground Railroad<br>• Harriet Tubman<br>• Harriet Beecher Stowe<br>• Franklin Pierce<br>• Dred Scott<br>• Stephen Douglas<br>• Abraham Lincoln<br>• Confederacy<br>• Jefferson Davis |

**TEKS** U.S. History 4B, 4C, 7A, 8A, 8B, 9B, 10A, 19A, 19B, 20A, 21D, 24A, 24B, 24C, 25A, 25B, 25C, 25D, 26B

### One American's Story

Senator John C. Calhoun was a sick man, too sick to deliver his speech to the Senate. On March 4, 1850, Calhoun asked Senator James M. Mason of Virginia to read his speech for him.

**A PERSONAL VOICE** JOHN C. CALHOUN

"I have, Senators, believed from the first that the agitation of the subject of slavery would, if not prevented by some timely and effective measure, end in disunion. . . . The agitation has been permitted to proceed . . . until it has reached a period when it can no longer be disguised or denied that the Union is in danger. You have thus had forced upon you the greatest and the gravest question that can ever come under your consideration: How can the Union be preserved?"

—quoted in *The Compromise of 1850*

John C. Calhoun

As Senator Calhoun and other Southern legislators demanded the expansion of slavery, Northerners just as vehemently called for its abolition. Once again, the issue of slavery was deepening the gulf between the North and the South.

## **1** Differences Between North and South

Over the centuries, the Northern and Southern sections of the United States had developed into two very different cultural and economic regions. The distinction between North and South had its roots in the early 17th century, when British colonists began settling Virginia in the South and Massachusetts in the North. Along with differences in geography and climate, the two regions were noticeably dissimilar in their religious and cultural traditions. However, it was the Southern dependence on the "peculiar institution" of slavery that increased tensions between the regions and that eventually brought them into conflict.

**156** CHAPTER 4 *The Union in Peril*

---

## PROGRAM RESOURCES

 **In-Depth Resources: Unit 1**
· Guided Reading, p. 106
· Building Vocabulary, p. 110
· Skillbuilder Practice: Creating Databases, p. 111
· Reteaching Activity, p. 114
· Primary Sources: Lincoln-Douglas Debates, pp. 122–123
· American Lives: Harriet Tubman, p. 136

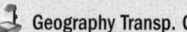 **Reading Study Guide** (English and Spanish), pp. 47–48

**Access for Students Acquiring English/ESL**
· Guided Reading (Spanish), p. 63
· Skillbuilder Practice, p. 67

**Formal Assessment**
· Section Quiz, p. 79

**Integrated Assessment**
· Rubrics

### INTEGRATED TECHNOLOGY

**Geography Transp. GT10**
· Presidential Elections 1856, 1860

**Critical Thinking Transp. CT10**
· The Compromise of 1850

**Humanities Transp. HT10**
· No. 10 Harriet Tubman series

**Electronic Library of Primary Sources**

**classzone.com**

 **TEXAS RESOURCES**

 TAKS Spiraled Content Review

 TAKS Practice Tests

 TAKS Practice Transparencies
TT37–TT40

 TAKS Online Test Practice

The South, with its plantation economy, had come to rely on an enslaved labor force. The North, with its diversified industries, was less dependent on slavery. As the North industrialized, Northern opposition to slavery grew more intense. The controversy over slavery only worsened as new territories and states were admitted to the union. Supporters of slavery saw an opportunity to create more slave states, while opponents remained equally determined that slavery should not spread. **A)**

## Slavery in the Territories ❶

The issue of slavery in California and in the western territories led to heated debates in the halls of Congress, and eventually to a fragile compromise.

**STATEHOOD FOR CALIFORNIA** Due in large part to the gold rush, California had grown quickly and applied for statehood in December 1849. California's new constitution forbade slavery, a fact that alarmed and angered many Southerners. They had assumed that because most of California lay south of the Missouri Compromise line of 36°30′, the state would be open to slavery. Southerners wanted the 1820 compromise to apply to territories west of the Louisiana Purchase, thus ensuring that California would become a slave state.

**THE COMPROMISE OF 1850** As the 31st Congress opened in December 1849, the question of statehood for California topped the agenda. Of equal concern was the border dispute in which the slave state of Texas claimed the eastern half of the New Mexico Territory, where the issue of slavery had not yet been settled. As passions mounted, threats of Southern **secession,** the formal withdrawal of a state from the Union, became more frequent.

Once again, Henry Clay worked to shape a compromise that both the North and the South could accept. After obtaining support of the powerful Massachusetts senator Daniel Webster, Clay presented to the Senate a series of resolutions later called the Compromise of 1850.

Clay's compromise contained provisions to appease Northerners as well as Southerners. To please the North, the compromise provided that California be

**1** Daniel Webster strongly supported Clay's compromise. He left the Senate before Stephen Douglas could engineer passage of all the bill's provisions.

**2** Henry Clay offered his compromise to the Senate in January 1850. In his efforts to save the Union, Clay earned for himself the name the Great Compromiser.

**3** John C. Calhoun opposed the compromise. He died two months after Clay proposed it.

## Instruct: Objective ❷

### Protest, Resistance, and Violence
TAKS SS11 2(US8.B)

· What were the organization and functions of the Underground Railroad?

· Who were Harriet Tubman and Harriet Beecher Stowe?

· What violence erupted in Kansas over slavery and in Congress between Senator Charles Sumner and Representative Preston S. Brooks?

 In-Depth Resources: Unit 1
· Guided Reading, p. 106
· American Lives: Harriet Tubman, p. 136

 Humanities Transparencies HT10
· No. 10 Harriet Tubman Series

---

### More About . . .

**The Underground Railroad**
Because the Underground Railroad was not a formal organization, no records were kept. So, historians have had to estimate the number of slaves who successfully made their way to freedom. Estimates range from 40,000 to 100,000.

---

### Tracing Themes
#### ECONOMIC OPPORTUNITY

Harriet Tubman and Harriet Beecher Stowe achieved prominence in the 1850s. But for many women in the North, the 1850s were hard years. Bad economic times made it difficult for poor families to get by on meager earnings. Unmarried women toiled at jobs as servants or in factories. Many worked in the sewing trades. The introduction of Elias Howe's sewing machine in 1846 enabled one woman to do the work of six, drastically reducing the demand for a woman's labor.

---

Harriet Tubman was called "Moses" by those she helped escape on the Underground Railroad. In her later years, Tubman opened a home for elderly, orphaned, and needy African Americans. ▼

---

admitted to the Union as a free state. To please the South, the compromise proposed a new and more effective fugitive slave law. To placate both sides, a provision allowed **popular sovereignty,** the right to vote for or against slavery, for residents of the New Mexico and Utah territories.

Despite the efforts of Clay and Webster, the Senate rejected the proposed compromise in July. Tired, ill, and discouraged, Clay withdrew from the fight and left Washington. Senator Stephen A. Douglas of Illinois picked up the pro-compromise reins. Douglas unbundled the package of resolutions and reintroduced them one at a time, hoping to obtain a majority vote for each measure individually. The death of President Taylor aided Douglas's efforts. Taylor's successor, Millard Fillmore, quickly made it clear that he supported the compromise.

At last, in September, after eight months of effort, the Compromise of 1850 became law. For the moment, the crisis over slavery in the territories had passed. However, relief was short-lived. Another crisis loomed on the horizon—enforcement of the new fugitive slave law. **B**

## ❷ Protest, Resistance, and Violence

The harsh terms of the Fugitive Slave Act surprised many people. Under the law, alleged fugitive slaves were not entitled to a trial by jury. In addition, anyone convicted of helping a fugitive was liable for a fine of $1,000 and imprisonment for up to six months. Infuriated by the Fugitive Slave Act, some Northerners resisted it by organizing "vigilance committees" to send endangered African Americans to safety in Canada. Others resorted to violence to rescue fugitive slaves. Still others worked to help slaves escape from slavery.

**THE UNDERGROUND RAILROAD** Attempting to escape from slavery was a dangerous process. It meant traveling on foot at night without any sense of distance or direction, except for the North Star and other natural signs. It meant avoiding patrols of armed men on horseback and struggling through forests and across rivers. Often it meant going without food for days at a time.

As time went on, free African Americans and white abolitionists developed a secret network of people who would, at great risk to themselves, hide fugitive slaves. The system of escape routes they used became known as the **Underground Railroad**. "Conductors" on the routes hid fugitives in secret tunnels and false cupboards, provided them with food and clothing, and escorted or directed them to the next "station." Once fugitives reached the North, many chose to remain there. Others journeyed to Canada to be completely out of reach of their "owners". **C**

One of the most famous conductors was **Harriet Tubman,** born a slave in Maryland in 1820 or 1821. In 1849, after Tubman's owner died, she heard rumors that she was about to be sold. Fearing this possibility, Tubman decided to make a break for freedom and succeeded in reaching Philadelphia. Shortly after passage of the Fugitive Slave Act, Tubman resolved to become a conductor on the Underground Railroad. In all, she made 19 trips back to the South and is said to have helped 300 slaves—including her own parents—flee to freedom.

**UNCLE TOM'S CABIN** Meanwhile, another woman brought the horrors of slavery into the homes of a great many Americans. In 1852, **Harriet Beecher Stowe** published her novel *Uncle Tom's Cabin*, which stressed that slavery was not just a political contest, but also a great moral struggle. As a young girl, Stowe had watched boats filled with people on their way to be sold at slave markets. *Uncle Tom's Cabin* expressed her lifetime hatred of slavery. The book stirred Northern abolitionists to increase their protests against the Fugitive Slave Act, while

---

**Vocabulary**
**fugitive:** running away or fleeing

---

**MAIN IDEA**

**Summarizing**
**B** What was the compromise that allowed California to be admitted to the Union?

**B. Answer** The Compromise of 1850 provided that California be admitted to the Union as a free state and created a new and more effective fugitive slave law.

---

**MAIN IDEA**

**Summarizing**
**C** How did the Underground Railroad operate?

**C. Answer** "Conductors" would hide fugitive slaves and help them work their way North from one "station" to the next.

---

**ACTIVITY    COOPERATIVE LEARNING**                                     **BLOCK SCHEDULING**

**Responding to *Uncle Tom's Cabin***

**Class Time** 45 minutes

**Task** Writing letters to the editor in praise or criticism of *Uncle Tom's Cabin*

**Purpose** To help students use historical perspective to examine the influence of the book on the events of the 1850s

**Directions** Have students read selections from *Uncle Tom's Cabin* and critical essays that describe its impact on both North and South in the 1850s. Then, have students write a letter the perspective of from either a Northerner converted to the cause of abolition by the book, or a Southerner who takes the position that most slave owners treat their slaves well and the book is dishonest in its portrayal of plantation life.

📄 Integrated Assessment
· Rubric 5

---

## The Underground Railroad, 1850–1860

CANADA (British)

Montreal

MAINE

Lake Superior

VT.

N.H.

ORGANIZED TERRITORY

WISCONSIN

NEW YORK

Boston
MASS.
CONN.
R.I.

MINNESOTA
(Statehood in 1858)

MICHIGAN

Lake Ontario

Niagara Falls

Detroit

Lake Erie

Erie

New York City

NEBRASKA TERRITORY

IOWA

Chicago

Sandusky

PENNSYLVANIA

NEW JERSEY

ILLINOIS

INDIANA

OHIO

Cincinnati
Ripley

Baltimore
MD.

Washington, D.C.

DEL.

KANSAS TERRITORY

St. Louis

Evansville

Ohio River

VIRGINIA

Petersburg

ATLANTIC OCEAN

MISSOURI

Cairo

KENTUCKY

NORTH CAROLINA

INDIAN TERRITORY

Fort Smith

Mississippi River

ARKANSAS

TENNESSEE

SOUTH CAROLINA

TEXAS

MISSISSIPPI

ALABAMA

GEORGIA

N W E S

LOUISIANA

New Orleans

FLORIDA

80°W

Gulf of Mexico

90°W

### Legend

| | |
|---|---|
| | Free states |
| | Slave states |
| | Areas with slave population of 50% or more in 1860 |
| ⌒ | Routes of the Underground Railroad |
| ● | Station on Underground Railroad |

0    100    200 miles
0    100    200 kilometers

▲ Runaway slaves arriving at Leon Coffin's farm in Indiana, along the Underground Railroad.

**GEOGRAPHY SKILLBUILDER**
1. **Movement** What does this map tell you about the routes of the Underground Railroad?
2. **Place** Name three cities that were destinations on the Underground Railroad.
3. **Location** Why do you think these cities were destinations?

## HISTORY from VISUALS

### Interpreting the Map

Tell students that this is a flow-line map. The arrows show the movement of slaves to free states. Ask students the following questions:

· Why do the arrows continue into Canada? (*Slaves fled all the way to Canada.*)

· Which slave state had no area where the slave population was 50 percent or more? (*Missouri*)

· Why do you think the route from Chicago to Detroit was over water rather than land? (*Students should infer that there would be less likelihood of capture on the water than over on land.*)

· What does the concentration of slaves along the Mississippi River tell you about the economy of the lower Mississippi Valley? (*Slaves worked on plantations, and many of these plantations were concentrated along the Mississippi because the land was richer and it was easier to transport goods to market.*)

**Extension** Ask students to visit the web site of the National Underground Railroad Freedom Center and report on some aspect of their findings.

⊙ **Electronic Library of Primary Sources**
· "On Slavery" by Harriet Tubman *from* The Fugitive Slave Act

🛈 classzone.com

## Experiencing the Underground Railroad

**Class Time** 45 minutes

**Task** Preparing and delivering oral reports that describe specific people and events that were part of the Underground Railroad

**Purpose** To examine in depth the motivation of individuals who participated in the Underground Railroad

**Directions** Have students work in small groups to research the Underground Railroad. Direct them to both historical and fictional accounts to explore the feelings of escaped slaves, the dangers of the journey, and personalities of the people who took risks to help. Suggested sources include books by Alex Haley and Virginia Hamilton; the autobiography of John Parker, a conductor on the Underground Railroad; and books about the most famous conductor, Harriet Tubman. Have them prepare an oral report that describes the people and events they researched.

## HISTORY from VISUALS

### Interpreting the Map
Point out that the maps should be studied individually and as a group. Have students consider the changing political balance over the years and ask them to note the reasons for the change.

**Extension** Have students list free states and slave states in 1854, using these maps and an Atlas of the United States. *(Free: 16 states—Maine, Vermont, New Hampshire, Massachusetts, Rhode Island, Connecticut, New York, New Jersey, Pennsylvania, Ohio, Indiana, Illinois, Michigan, Wisconsin, Iowa, California. Slave: 15 states—Delaware, Maryland, Virginia, North Carolina, South Carolina, Georgia, Florida, Alabama, Mississippi, Louisiana, Texas, Arkansas, Tennessee, Kentucky, Missouri)*

## Free and Slave States and Territories, 1820–1854

### The Missouri Compromise, 1820–1821

### The Compromise of 1850

- Free states
- Territory closed to slavery
- Slave states
- Territory open to slavery

### The Kansas-Nebraska Act of 1854

### GEOGRAPHY SKILLBUILDER
1. **Place** How did the number of slave states change between 1821 and 1854?
2. **Region** How did the Kansas-Nebraska Act affect the amount of land that was open to slavery?

*Skillbuilder Answers*
1. Slave states increased by three.
2. The Act increased the land that was open to slavery.

Southerners criticized the book as an attack on the South. The furor over *Uncle Tom's Cabin* had barely begun to settle when the issue of slavery in the territories surfaced once again.

### TENSION IN KANSAS AND NEBRASKA
The Compromise of 1850 had provided for popular sovereignty in New Mexico and Utah. To Senator Stephen Douglas, popular sovereignty seemed like an excellent way to decide whether slavery would be allowed in the Nebraska Territory.

### A PERSONAL VOICE
STEPHEN A. DOUGLAS

" If the people of Kansas want a slaveholding state, let them have it, and if they want a free state they have a right to it, and it is not for the people of Illinois, or Missouri, or New York, or Kentucky, to complain, whatever the decision of Kansas may be. "
—quoted in *The Civil War* by Geoffrey C. Ward

The only difficulty was that, unlike New Mexico and Utah, the Kansas and Nebraska territory lay north of the Missouri Compromise line of 36°30′ and therefore was legally closed to slavery. Douglas introduced a bill in Congress on January 23, 1854, that would divide the area into two territories: Nebraska in the north and Kansas in the south. If passed, the bill would repeal the Missouri Compromise and establish popular sovereignty for both territories. Congressional debate was bitter. Some Northern congressmen saw the bill as part of a plot to turn the territories into slave states. Southerners strongly defended the proposed legislation. After months of struggle, the Kansas-Nebraska Act became law in 1854. **D**

**"BLEEDING KANSAS"** The race for Kansas was on. Both supporters and opponents of slavery attempted to populate Kansas in order to win the vote on slavery in the territory. By March 1855 Kansas had enough settlers to hold an election for a territorial legislature. However, thousands of "border ruffians" from the slave state of Missouri crossed into Kansas, voted illegally, and won a fraudulent majority for the proslavery candidates. A government was set up at Lecompton and promptly issued a series of proslavery acts. Furious over these events, abolitionists organized a rival government in Topeka in the fall of 1855. It wasn't long before bloody violence surfaced in the struggle for Kansas, earning the territory the name "Bleeding Kansas."

**VIOLENCE IN THE SENATE** Violence was not restricted to Kansas. In May, Senator Charles Sumner of Massachusetts delivered an impassioned speech in the Senate, entitled "The Crime Against Kansas." For two days he verbally attacked

### MAIN IDEA

**Analyzing Events**
**D** Why was the debate over the Kansas-Nebraska Act so bitter?

*D. Answer* The bill would repeal the Missouri Compromise and establish popular sovereignty for Kansas and Nebraska.

## More About . . .

### Border Ruffians
Violence was nothing new for the "border ruffians." Fifteen years before the struggle over Kansas, these ruffians had persecuted and burned the Mormons out of Missouri. When Senator David Atchison wrote to Jefferson Davis about his plans for Kansas, he said: "We will be compelled to shoot, burn & hang, but the thing will soon be over. We intend to 'Mormonize' the Abolitionists."

---

### Considering Slavery and Democracy

**Class Time** 45 minutes

**Task** Analyzing and writing a response to Senator Stephen Douglas's position on popular sovereignty and slavery in Kansas and Nebraska

**Purpose** To explore conflicting political ideas

**Directions** Have students read the quotation from Stephen A. Douglas in "A Personal Voice" on this page. Ask them to consider the implications of the Senator's views. If the majority of the people vote for slavery, is slavery right? Is the majority always right? What are the limits of democracy? Have students explore these issues and write a response to Douglas's position either supporting it or against it, giving consideration to ethical and moral problems.

 Integrated Assessment
· Rubric 5

SOUTHERN CHIVALRY — ARGUMENT versus CLUB'S.

**Interpreting the Political Cartoon**
Ask students to identify the two most important characters in this cartoon. What side does each character represent? Ask for opinions on the meaning of the caption.

**Extension** Have students review the main events of this section and then create a cartoon based on one of the most important personalities or events.

the South and slavery, singling out Senator Andrew P. Butler of South Carolina for his proslavery beliefs.

Soon after, Butler's nephew, Congressman Preston S. Brooks, walked into the Senate chamber and struck Sumner on the head repeatedly with a cane until the cane broke. Sumner suffered brain damage and did not return to his Senate seat for more than three years.

The widening gulf between the North and the South had far-reaching implications for party politics as well. As the two regions grew further apart, the old national parties ruptured, and new political parties emerged, including a party for antislavery Northerners.

This 1856 cartoon, with its ironic caption, gives the Northern view of Preston Brooks's beating of Charles Sumner.

## New Political Parties Emerge ❸

By the end of 1856, the nation's political landscape had a very different appearance than it had exhibited in 1848. The Whig Party had split over the issue of slavery and had lost support in both the North and the South. The Democratic Party, which had survived numerous crises in its history, was still alive, though scarred. A new Republican Party had formed and was moving within striking distance of the presidency. **E**

**SLAVERY DIVIDES WHIGS** In 1852 the Whig vote in the South fell dramatically, which helped produce a victory for the Democratic candidate, **Franklin Pierce**. In 1854 the Kansas-Nebraska Act completed the demise of the Whigs. Unable to agree on a national platform, the Southern faction splintered as its members looked for a proslavery, pro-Union party to join. At the same time, Whigs in the North sought a political alternative of their own.

One alternative that appeared was the American Party, which soon became known as the Know-Nothing Party, because members were instructed to answer questions about their activities by saying, "I know nothing." The Know-Nothings supported nativism, the favoring of native-born people over immigrants. However, like the Whigs, the Know-Nothings split over the issue of slavery in the territories. Southern Know-Nothings looked for another alternative to the Democrats. Meanwhile, Northern Know-Nothings began to edge toward the Republican Party.

**MAIN IDEA**

**Analyzing Effects**

**E** What impact did the slavery issue have on the Democratic and Whig parties?

*E. Answer* The slavery issue had caused a split in the Whig Party and weakened the Democratic Party.

### More About . . .

**Charles Sumner and Preston Brooks**
Sumner served as a senator from Massachusetts from 1852 to 1874. He was a passionate foe of slavery, attacking both the Fugitive Slave Law and the Kansas-Nebraska Act. He returned to the Senate after his recuperation and served as chairman of the Foreign Relations Committee from 1861 to 1871 and was a Republican leader in the Senate. Sumner also was one of the Radical Republicans who opposed President Johnson's Reconstruction program. As for Brooks, he resigned from Congress following the incident but was reelected by his constituents. He died the next year.

**Instruct: Objective ❸**

**New Political Parties Emerge**
TAKS SS11 5(US24.B)
· How did slavery affect the Whig and Know-Nothing parties?
· What issue united the Republican Party?

 In-Depth Resources: Unit 1
· Guided Reading, p. 106

 Geography Transparencies GT10
· Presidential Elections 1856, 1860

---

**ACTIVITY** | **SKILLBUILDER LESSON**

### Creating Databases

**Explaining the Skill** A database is information arranged in a way that makes it easy to manipulate and to retrieve. For example, telephone numbers of resident in a city are data. Arranging the numbers in alphabetical order by the resident's name makes the numbers a useful database; it allows the numbers to be easily retrieved by name. The way the data is organized can also be changed. For example, the numbers could be arranged according to three-digit prefixes instead of names.

**Applying the Skill** Have students make a database of the political parties of the era. Students might include the Whig, Democratic, Republican, and Know-Nothing parties. In addition to party name, the database might include founding dates, leaders, philosophy, and positions on major issues.

 In-Depth Resources: Unit 1
· Skillbuilder Practice: Creating Databases, p. 111

## More About . . .

### The Formation of the Republican Party

A group of antislavery Whigs, Democrats, and Free-Soilers held an informal meeting in a Ripon, Wisconsin schoolhouse on February 28, 1854 and again on March 20, 1854. They vowed to form a new political party if the Kansas-Nebraska bill was enacted. The name "Republican" was chosen because of its connection with Jeffersonian Republicanism, which placed national interest above sectional interest and States' rights. After the Kansas-Nebraska Act passed, the Republican Party held its first convention in Jackson, Michigan, on July 6th. The party achieved rapid success, because it united northern antislavery sentiment. The party's slogan in the 1856 presidential campaign was "Free soil, free labor, free speech, free men, Frémont."

## Instruct: Objective ④

### Conflicts Lead to Secession
TAKS SS11 4(8.18.B)

· What was the *Dred Scott* decision and why was it so important in the slavery conflict?
· What was the disagreement between Lincoln and Douglas?
· What happened at Harpers Ferry?
· How did Lincoln's election cause in secession?

📄 In-Depth Resources: Unit 1
· Guided Reading, p. 106

## More About . . .

### Dred Scott

Dred Scott's owner was a New Yorker named John F. Sanford (the Court misspelled the name as *Sandford*). When the case was over, Scott, his wife, and two daughters were returned to a former owner, the Blow family, who gave them their freedom in May 1857. Scott worked as a porter until his death in 1858 of tuberculosis.

---

Two antislavery parties had also emerged during the 1840s. The Liberty Party was formed for the purpose of pursuing the cause of abolition by passing new laws, but received only a small percentage of votes in the 1848 presidential election. In that same election, the Free-Soil Party, which opposed the extension of slavery into the territories, received ten percent of the popular vote in the presidential election. From this strong showing, it was clear that many Northerners opposed the extension of slavery in the territories.

**THE FREE-SOILERS' VOICE** Northern opposition to slavery in the territories was not necessarily based on positive feelings toward African Americans. It was not unusual for Northerners to be Free-Soilers without being abolitionists. Unlike abolitionists, a number of Northern Free-Soilers supported racist laws prohibiting settlement by blacks in their communities and denying them the right to vote.

What Free-Soilers primarily objected to was slavery's competition with free white workers, or a wage-based labor force, upon which the North depended. They feared that such competition would drive down wages. Free-Soilers detected a dangerous pattern in such events as the passage of the Fugitive Slave Act and the repeal of the Missouri Compromise. They were convinced that a conspiracy existed on the part of the "diabolical slave power" to spread slavery throughout the United States. **F**

**THE NEW REPUBLICAN PARTY** In 1854 opponents of slavery in the territories formed a new political party, the Republican Party. The Republicans were united in opposing the Kansas-Nebraska Act and in keeping slavery out of the territories. Apart from these issues, however, the Repulican party embraced a wide range of opinions. As the party grew, it took in Free-Soilers, antislavery Whigs and Democrats, and nativists, mostly from the North. The conservative faction hoped to resurrect the Missouri Compromise. At the opposite extreme were some radical abolitionists.

During the election of 1856 the Republicans chose as their candidate John C. Frémont. The Democrats nominated James Buchanan of Pennsylvania. If Frémont had won, the South might have seceded then and there. However, Buchanan won, and the threat of secession was temporarily averted.

Dred Scott's lawsuit in 1857 set off even more controversy over slavery. ▼

## Conflicts Lead to Secession ④

Political conflicts only intensified after the election of President Buchanan. The first slavery-related controversy arose on March 6, 1857, just two days after he took office.

**THE DRED SCOTT DECISION** A major Supreme Court decision was brought about by **Dred Scott,** a slave whose owner took him from the slave state of Missouri to free territory in Illinois and Wisconsin and back to Missouri. Scott appealed to the Supreme Court for his freedom on the grounds that living in a free state—Illinois—and a free territory—Wisconsin—had made him a free man.

The case was in court for years. Finally, on March 6, 1857, the Supreme Court ruled against Dred Scott. According to the ruling, Scott lacked any legal standing to sue in federal court because he was not, and never could be, a citizen. Moreover, the Court ruled that being in free territory did not make a slave free. The Fifth Amendment protected property, including slaves. For territories to exclude slavery would be to deprive slaveholders of their property.

**MAIN IDEA**

**Contrasting**
**F** How did Free-Soilers differ from abolitionists?

*F. Answer*
**Abolitionists:** wished to abolish slavery because they considered it immoral.
**Freesoilers:** objected to slavery only because it reduced employment opportunities for free white workers.

**Background**
The *Dred Scott* case was only the second one in American history in which the Supreme Court reversed a federal legislative act.

---

**DIFFERENTIATING INSTRUCTION**     **LESS PROFICIENT READERS**

### Identifying Cause and Effect

Help students understand the five events covered in this section (pages 162–165) that contributed to the outbreak of the Civil War. Have students list each subhead of the section on a piece of paper and then as they read jot down at least one way that the event helped lead to division between the North and the South.

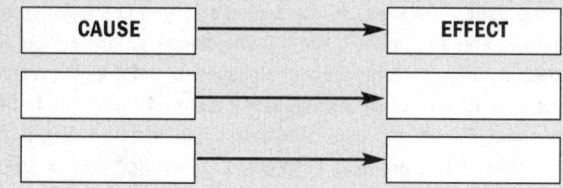

Sectional passions exploded immediately. Many Northerners showered a torrent of abuse upon the Supreme Court, in part because a majority of its justices were Southerners. Warnings about the slave states' influence on the national government spread. Southern slaveholders, on the other hand, were jubilant. In their interpretation, the *Dred Scott* decision not only permitted the extension of slavery but actually guaranteed it. (See *Dred Scott* v. *Sandford* on page 166.)

**LINCOLN–DOUGLAS DEBATES** Several months after the *Dred Scott* decision, one of Illinois's greatest political contests got underway: the 1858 race for the U.S. Senate between Democratic incumbent **Stephen Douglas** and Republican challenger Congressman **Abraham Lincoln.** To many outsiders it must have seemed like an uneven match. Douglas was a well-known two-term senator with an outstanding record and a large campaign chest, while Lincoln was a self-educated man who had been elected to one term in Congress in 1846. To counteract Douglas, Lincoln challenged the man known as the "Little Giant" to a series of debates on the issue of slavery in the territories. Douglas accepted the challenge, and the stage was set for some of the most celebrated debates in U.S. history.

The two men's positions were simple and consistent. Neither wanted slavery in the territories, but they disagreed on how to keep it out. Douglas believed deeply in popular sovereignty. Lincoln, on the other hand, believed that slavery was immoral. However, he did not expect individuals to give up slavery unless Congress abolished slavery with an amendment.

In their second debate, Lincoln asked his opponent a crucial question: Could the settlers of a territory vote to exclude slavery before the territory became a state? Everyone knew that the *Dred Scott* decision said no—that territories could not exclude slavery. Popular sovereignty, Lincoln implied, was thus an empty phrase.

Douglas replied that, if the people of a territory were Free-Soilers, then all they had to do was elect representatives who would not enforce slave property laws in that territory. In other words, people could get around *Dred Scott*.

Douglas won the Senate seat, but his response had widened the split in the Democratic Party. As for Lincoln, his attacks on the "vast moral evil" of slavery drew national attention, and some Republicans began thinking of him as an excellent candidate for the presidency in 1860. **G**

**HARPERS FERRY** While politicians debated the slavery issue, the abolitionist John Brown was studying the slave uprisings that had occurred in ancient Rome and, more recently, on the French island of Haiti. He believed that the time was ripe for similar uprisings in the United States. Brown secretly obtained financial backing from several prominent Northern abolitionists. On the night of October 16, 1859, he led a band of 21 men, black and white, into Harpers Ferry, Virginia (now West Virginia). His aim was to seize the federal arsenal there and start a general slave uprising.

*(left)* A Mathew Brady Studio photo of Stephen Douglas from 1860.
*(right)* A photograph of Abraham Lincoln, also from 1860. ▼

*G. Answer* Both were against slavery. However, Lincoln thought the federal government should keep slavery out of the territories, while Douglas thought residents of each territory should decide.

**MAIN IDEA**

**Comparing**
**G** Compare and contrast Lincoln's and Douglas's views on slavery.

**More About . . .**

**The Lincoln-Douglas Debates**
During the debates, Lincoln made a striking physical contrast to his opponent, over whom he towered. While Douglas was stocky and energetic, Lincoln was thin and gangling. While Douglas dressed smartly, Lincoln's clothes were plain and rumpled. The pair also had very different speaking styles. Douglas exuded self-confidence, using his fists to pound home his points. Lincoln, on the other hand, used plain language to deliver his comments.

📄 In-Depth Resources: Unit 1
· Primary Sources: Lincoln-Douglas Debates, pp. 126–127

**More About . . .**

**Reporting on Political Events**
At the time of the Lincoln-Douglas debates, newspapers seldom reported political events objectively because the papers depended on political organizations for their survival. Affiliating with a political party guaranteed a paper a certain number of subscribers, as well as legal and political advertising. Partisan reporting appeared not just in editorials but in news articles as well. As a result, people reading the "text" of the Lincoln-Douglas debates were not reading exact transcripts of what the two men said, but rather what partisan editors reported that their candidates said. Since papers more accurately quoted the candidate they opposed, the best way to find out what either man *really* said was to read the paper that opposed him.

---

 **ACTIVITY** | **COOPERATIVE LEARNING**

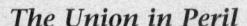 **BLOCK SCHEDULING**

**Writing a Newspaper Account**

**Class Time** 45 minutes

**Task** Writing a newspaper account of one of the Lincoln-Douglas debates

**Purpose** To evaluate the issues dividing Lincoln and douglas

**Directions** Divide the class into groups of four. Within each group designate one pair of students to work on Lincoln's views and one to work on Douglas's views. Have students research one of the Lincoln-Douglas debates. Each pair should prepare an article describing the viewpoint of their man and how his views are different from the other man. After the articles are written the pairs should exchange articles and make comments about the accurate of the views.

📄 Integrated Assessment
· Rubric 5

## HISTORY from VISUALS

### Interpreting the Painting

Horace Pippin (1888–1946) was an African-American folk painter who favored themes about African-American life and about war. Pippin often painted from experience. He was a World War I veteran, who received a combat wound that left his right arm partially disabled. For years, Pippin painted in obscurity in his hometown of West Chester, Pennsylvania. He was discovered in 1937 and hailed as the foremost African-American painter of his time.

### SKILLBUILDER ANSWERS

1. She is looking away from the scene because she admires John Brown and cannot stand to see him punished. Her expression is both anguished and angry.

2. Hopelessness is expressed through the bareness of the trees, the starkness of the colors, and the rigidity of the figures.

### More About . . .

#### John Brown's Execution

Among those standing at attention as John Brown mounted the gallows steps were three men who were to play major roles in the drama of the Civil War. One was an actor from Richmond named John Wilkes Booth, who would assassinate President Lincoln in 1865. Another was Thomas J. Jackson, later known as "Stonewall" Jackson for his stand on the battlefield of Bull Run in 1862. The third was Edmund Ruffin, who is believed to have fired one of the first shot at the battle of Fort Sumter in 1861.

---

### History Through  Art

#### JOHN BROWN GOING TO HIS HANGING

This painting by the African-American artist Horace Pippin shows John Brown being transported by wagon to his execution. The artist has focused our attention on the cruelty of Brown's fate. The abolitionist is shown tied with the rope that will be used to hang him, sitting on the coffin that will receive his body after death. Brown's dark shape is silhouetted by the large white building behind him, a structure that combines the features of both courthouse and prison.

#### SKILLBUILDER  Interpreting Visual Sources

1. Why do you think the African-American woman in the right-hand corner is looking away from the scene? How would you describe her expression?
2. How has the artist expressed the hopelessness of the situation?

📁 **SEE SKILLBUILDER HANDBOOK, PAGE R23.**

---

No such uprising occurred, however. Instead, troops put down the rebellion. Later, authorities tried Brown and put him to death. Public reaction to Brown's execution was immediate and intense in both sections of the country. In the North, bells tolled, guns fired salutes, and huge crowds gathered to hear fiery speakers denounce the South. The response was equally extreme in the South, where mobs assaulted whites who were suspected of holding antislavery views.

**LINCOLN IS ELECTED PRESIDENT** As the 1860 presidential election approached, the Republicans nominated Abraham Lincoln. Lincoln appeared to be moderate in his views. Although he pledged to halt the further spread of slavery, he also tried to reassure Southerners that a Republican administration would not "interfere with their slaves, or with them, about their slaves." Nonetheless, many Southerners viewed him as an enemy.

As the campaign developed, three major candidates besides Lincoln vied for office. The Democratic Party finally split over slavery. Northern Democrats rallied behind Douglas and his doctrine of popular sovereignty. Southern Democrats, who supported the *Dred Scott* decision, lined up behind Vice President John C. Breckinridge of Kentucky. Former Know-Nothings and Whigs from the South organized the Constitutional Union Party and nominated John Bell of Tennessee as their candidate. Lincoln emerged as the winner with less than half the popular vote and with no electoral votes from the South. He did not even appear on the ballot in most of the slave states because of Southern hostility toward him. The outlook for the Union was grim. **H**

**SOUTHERN SECESSION** Lincoln's victory convinced Southerners—who had viewed the struggle over slavery partly as a conflict between the states' right of self-determination and federal government control—that they had lost their political voice in the national government. Some Southern states decided to act. South Carolina led the way, seceding from the Union on December 20, 1860. When the news reached Northern-born William Tecumseh Sherman, superintendent of the Louisiana State Seminary of Learning and Military Academy

*H. Answer* The Democratic Party split over slavery.

**MAIN IDEA**

**Summarizing**
**H** What happened to the Democratic Party as the 1860 presidential election approached?

---

 classzone.com

### The Election of 1860

**Class Time** 30 minutes

**Task** Analyzing the election of 1860, identifying each candidate and his stand on the issue of slavery, and then drawing a map that displays the electoral results

**Purpose** To better understand the issues and results of a pivotal election in American history

**Directions** Have students research the election of 1860 in library sources or on the Internet. Ask then to identify four candidates and their positions on slavery. Then, have students use an outline map of the United States to draw an electoral map that shows the results of the election.

 Integrated Assessment
· Rubrics 1, 2, 4

(now Louisiana State University), he poured out his fears for the South.

### A PERSONAL VOICE WILLIAM TECUMSEH SHERMAN

"This country will be drenched in blood. . . . [T]he people of the North . . . are not going to let this country be destroyed without a mighty effort to save it. . . . Besides, where are your men and appliances of war to contend against them? . . . You are rushing into war with one of the most powerful, ingeniously mechanical and determined people on earth—right at your doors. . . . Only in spirit and determination are you prepared for war. In all else you are totally unprepared."

—quoted in *None Died in Vain*

Mississippi soon followed South Carolina's lead, as did Florida, Alabama, Georgia, Louisiana, and Texas. In February 1861, delegates from the secessionist states met in Montgomery, Alabama, where they formed the Confederate States of America, or **Confederacy.** They also drew up a constitution that closely resembled that of the United States, but with a few notable differences. The most important difference was that it "protected and recognized" slavery in new territories.

The Confederates then unanimously elected former senator **Jefferson Davis** of Mississippi as president. The North had heard threats of secession before. When it finally happened, no one was shocked. But one key question remained in everyone's mind: Would the North allow the South to leave the Union without a fight?

---

**HISTORICAL SPOTLIGHT**

### SECESSION AND THE BORDER STATES

Four slave states—Maryland, Kentucky, Missouri, and Delaware—were undecided about secession. Lincoln believed that these states would be essential to the success of the Union if war broke out. They had large populations, numerous factories, and strategic access to the Ohio River. Moreover, Maryland nearly surrounded Washington, D.C., the seat of government.

Lincoln faced a choice: free the slaves and make abolitionists happy, or ignore slavery for the moment to keep from alienating the border states. He chose the latter, but that did not prevent violent conflicts between secessionists and Unionists in Maryland, Kentucky, and Missouri. With the intervention of the militia, and some political maneuvering in those states' legislatures, Lincoln kept the four border states in the Union.

---

### HISTORICAL SPOTLIGHT

**Secession and the Border States**

Have students refer back to the map on page 159 and offer an explanation of why the border states did not secede from the Union and join the Confederacy. *(Their geographic location, close to the Union states, acted as a restraint. Students should also note the lesser population of slaves in these states, as shown on the map.)*

## Assess & Reteach

### SECTION 1 ASSESSMENT

Have students work in pairs to help each other answer the questions.

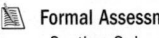 **Formal Assessment**
· Section Quiz, p. 79

### SELF-ASSESSMENT

Have students use question 3 to gauge their knowledge of the issues covered in the section. Instruct them to write down any of the issues that they are still unsure about and write a question for each issue.

### RETEACH

Use the Guided Reading Worksheet for Section 1 to help review the main ideas of the section.

 **In-Depth Resources: Unit 1**
· Reteaching Activity, p. 114

---

### ⓵ ASSESSMENT

**1. TERMS & NAMES** For each term or name, write a sentence explaining its significance.

- secession
- popular sovereignty
- Underground Railroad
- Harriet Tubman
- Harriet Beecher Stowe
- Franklin Pierce
- Dred Scott
- Stephen Douglas
- Abraham Lincoln
- Confederacy
- Jefferson Davis

#### MAIN IDEA

**2. TAKING NOTES**
Create a time line like the one below, showing the events that heightened the tensions between the North and the South.

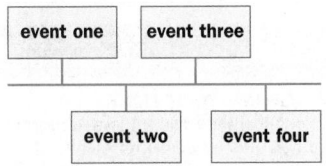

Select one event and explain its significance.

#### CRITICAL THINKING

**3. HYPOTHESIZING**
Review issues and events in this section that reflect the growing conflict between the North and the South. Do you think there were any points at which civil war might have been averted? **Think About:**

- the Compromise of 1850, the Fugitive Slave Act, and the Kansas-Nebraska Act
- the new political parties
- the Supreme Court's ruling in the *Dred Scott* decision
- the election of Abraham Lincoln as president in 1860

**4. EVALUATING LEADERSHIP**
John Brown, Harriet Tubman, Harriet Beecher Stowe, and Stephen Douglas all opposed slavery. Who do you think had the greatest impact on American history and why?

**5. DEVELOPING HISTORICAL PERSPECTIVE**
How did the tension between states' rights and national government authority manifest itself in the events leading up to the Civil War?

---

Answers **ASSESSMENT** ⓵

**1. TERMS & NAMES**
secession, p. 157
popular sovereignty, p. 157
Underground Railroad, p. 159
Harriet Tubman, p. 159
Harriet Beecher Stowe, p. 159
Franklin Pierce, p. 161
Dred Scott, p. 162
Stephen Douglas, p. 163
Abraham Lincoln, p. 163
Confederacy, p. 165
Jefferson Davis, p. 165

**2. TAKING NOTES**
Event one—The Compromise of 1850—includes a new fugitive slave law; event two—1852, *Uncle Tom's Cabin*—book on slavery stirs strong reactions; event three—1857, the *Dred Scott Decision*—Supreme Court case causes sectional passions to explode; event four—1859, John Brown attacks Harpers Ferry—attempt to start a slave uprising intensifies sectional feeling in the country.

**3. HYPOTHESIZING**
Some students may say that the Supreme Court made a major blunder in the Dred Scott decision. Others may think that the conflict was inevitable.

**4. EVALUATING LEADERSHIP**
Student responses should reflect understanding of the strengths and weaknesses of each individual and an awareness of their contributions.

**5. DEVELOPING HISTORICAL PERSPECTIVE**
Popular sovereignty reinforced states' rights. The Dred Scott decision convinced many Northerners that the slave states were influencing the national government. Lincoln's election frightened supporters of states' rights, because he believed that Congress could abolish slavery.

### Objectives

· To analyze the legal reasoning of the Supreme Court in the *Dred Scott* case

· To explain the impact of the decision on the politics of the struggle over slavery

## Focus & Motivate

**Drawing Conclusions** Have students consider why the Supreme Court's decision that Congress had no power to regulate slavery in the territories made it more difficult for the North and the South to negotiate a compromise over slavery.

## More About . . .

### Roger B. Taney

Taney (1777–1864), a protégé of Andrew Jackson, had a long and distinguished career in politics and on the Supreme Court. He served as attorney general in the first Jackson administration and played a key role in killing the Bank of the United States. In retribution, Jackson's opponents blocked Taney's appointment as secretary of the treasury. The incident marked the first time that Congress had failed to approve a presidential cabinet appointment. In 1835, after the death of Chief Justice John Marshall, Jackson appointed Taney to the post. Despite opposition from Henry Clay, Daniel Webster, John C. Calhoun, and other senators, Taney was confirmed and served until his death in 1864 at the age of 87.

## HISTORIC DECISIONS OF THE SUPREME COURT

# DRED SCOTT v. SANDFORD (1857)

**ORIGINS OF THE CASE** Dred Scott's slave master had brought him from the slave state of Missouri to live for a time in free territory and in the free state of Illinois. Eventually they returned to Missouri. Scott believed that because he had lived in free territory, he should be free. In 1854 he sued in federal court for his freedom. The court ruled against him, and he appealed to the Supreme Court.

**THE RULING** The Supreme Court ruled that African Americans were not and could never be citizens. Thus, Dred Scott had no right even to file a lawsuit and remained enslaved.

### LEGAL REASONING

The Court's decision, conceived and written by Chief Justice Roger Taney, made two key findings. First, it held that because Scott was a slave, he was not a citizen and had no right to sue in a United States court.

> "We think they [slaves] . . . are not included, and were not intended to be included, under the word 'citizens' in the Constitution, and can therefore claim none of the rights and privileges which that instrument provides for and secures to citizens of the United States."

This could have been the end of the matter, but Taney went further. He said that by banning slavery, Congress was, in effect, taking away property. Such an action, he wrote, violated the Fifth Amendment, which guarantees the right not to be deprived of property without due process of law (such as a hearing). Thus, all congressional efforts to ban slavery in the territories were prohibited.

Justices John McLean and Benjamin Curtis strongly dissented on both points. They showed that the U.S. Constitution, state constitutions, and other laws had recognized African Americans as citizens. They also pointed to the clause in the Constitution giving Congress the power to "make all needful Rules and Regulations" to govern U.S. territories. In their view, this clause gave Congress the power to prohibit slavery in the territories.

◀ Chief Justice Roger Taney

### LEGAL SOURCES

#### U.S. CONSTITUTION

**U.S. CONSTITUTION, ARTICLE 4, SECTION 2 (1789)**
"No person held to service or labor in one state, . . . escaping into another, shall, in consequence of any law or regulation therein, be discharged from such service or labor. . . ."

**U.S. CONSTITUTION, ARTICLE 4, SECTION 3 (1789)**
"The Congress shall have Power to dispose of and make all needful Rules and Regulations respecting the Territory or other Property belonging to the United States. . . ."

**U.S. CONSTITUTION, FIFTH AMENDMENT (1791)**
"No person shall be . . . deprived of life, liberty, or property, without due process of law. . . ."

#### RELATED CASES

**ABLEMAN v. BOOTH (1858)**
The Court decided that the Fugitive Slave Act was constitutional and that laws passed in Northern states that prohibited the return of fugitive slaves were unconstitutional.

**166** CHAPTER 4 *The Union in Peril*

## RECOMMENDED RESOURCES

### BOOKS

Fehrenbacher, Don E. *The Dred Scott Case: Its Significance in Law and Politics.* New York: Oxford UP, 2001.

Finkelman, Paul. *Dred Scott v. Sandford: A Brief History with Documents.* New York: St. Martin's Press, 1997.

Freedman, Suzanne. *Roger Taney: The Dred Scott Legacy.* Springfield, NJ: Enslow Press, 1995.

Steiner, Bernard C. *Life of Roger Brooke Taney: Chief Justice of the United States.* Holmes Beach, FL: Gaunt, Inc., 1997.

### INTEGRATED TECHNOLOGY

For teacher support and more information about the Supreme Court including the full text of the Supreme Court decisions, visit. . . .

 classzone.com

## WHY IT MATTERED

Taney's opinion in *Dred Scott* had far reaching consequences. Legally, the opinion greatly expanded the reach of slavery. Politically, it heightened the sectional tensions that would lead to the Civil War.

Before the Court decided *Dred Scott*, Americans widely accepted the idea that Congress and the states could limit slavery. As the dissenters argued, many previous acts of Congress had limited slavery—for example, the Northwest Ordinance had banned slavery in the Northwest Territory—and no one had claimed that those acts violated property rights.

Taney's opinion in *Dred Scott*, however, was a major change. This expansion of slaveholders' rights cast doubt on whether free states could prevent slave owners from bringing or even selling slaves into free areas.

As a result, *Dred Scott* intensified the slavery debate as no single event had before. In going beyond what was needed to settle the case before him, Taney's ruling became a political act, and threw into question the legitimacy of the Court. Further, Taney's opinion took the extreme proslavery position and installed it as the national law. It not only negated all the compromises made to date by pro- and anti-slavery forces, but it seemed to preclude any possible future compromises.

## HISTORICAL IMPACT

It took five years of bitter civil war to find out if Taney's opinion would stand as the law of the land. It would not. Immediately after the Civil War, the federal government moved to abolish slavery with the Thirteenth Amendment (1865) and then to extend state and national citizenship with the Fourteenth Amendment (1868) to "[a]ll persons born or naturalized in the United States." The wording of these amend-

▲
Contemporary newspaper article describing the *Dred Scott* case.

ments was expressly intended to nullify *Dred Scott*.

These amendments meant that *Dred Scott* would no longer be used as a precedent—an earlier ruling that can be used to justify a current one. Instead, it is now pointed to as an important lesson on the limits of the Supreme Court's power, as a key step on the road to the Civil War, and as one of the worst decisions ever made by the Supreme Court.

---

### THINKING CRITICALLY

**CONNECT TO HISTORY**

1. **Developing Historical Perspective** Use the library to find commentaries on *Dred Scott* written at the time the decision was made. Read two of these commentaries and identify which section—North or South—the writer or speaker came from. Explain how each person's region shaped his or her views.

 **SEE SKILLBUILDER HANDBOOK, PAGE R11.**

**CONNECT TO TODAY**

2.  **INTERNET ACTIVITY** CLASSZONE.COM

Visit the links for Historic Decisions of the Supreme Court to research what it means to be a citizen of the United States and what rights that citizenship extends. Research which constitutional amendments, U.S. laws, and Supreme Court decisions guarantee the rights of citizens. Prepare an oral presentation or annotated display to summarize your findings.

---

1. What did the Court rule about Dred Scott?
2. How did the Court go beyond the fate of Scott in its opinion?
3. What reasoning did Taney use to support his decision?
4. How did the Dred Scott decision influence American history?

📖 Historic Supreme Court Cases
· Dred Scott v. Sanford, pp. 61–66

### MAKING PERSONAL CONNECTIONS

Have students brainstorm about issues that really matter to them, such as students' rights, regulation of the Internet, and censorship of music and other art forms.

Ask students to consider how they would feel and what they would do if a Court ruling on one of these issues seemed to limit their freedom.

### More About . . .

**Justice John McLean's Dissent**
McLean was also a Jackson appointee to the Court. In his dissenting opinion, McLean disagreed sharply with Taney. McLean pointed out that having elector status was not necessary to sue in federal court, since both women and minors were permitted to sue yet lacked elector (suffrage) status. He went on to point out that being a Negro did not prevent Scott from claiming citizenship.

---

### THINKING CRITICALLY: ANSWERS

**1. CONNECT TO HISTORY**
**Rubric**
The explanation should:
· provide a bibliography of the commentaries
· identify the section of the nation from which the writer comes
· reflect ways in which the culture of the section shaped the writers views

**2. CONNECT TO TODAY**
**Rubric**
The oral presentation should:
· state the specific citizenship issue that was researched
· identify specific constitutional amendments, U.S. laws, and Supreme Court decisions that deal with the selected citizenship issue
· clearly analyze the impact of the identified material on an aspect of citizenship

# The Civil War Begins

## OBJECTIVES

1. Analyze the strengths strategies of both sides at the beginning of the Civil War.
2. Identify the key political issues that affected the conduct of the war.
3. Describe aspects of military and civilian life during wartime.

### SKILLBUILDERS

· Interpreting Graphs, p. 169
· Geography Skillbuilder: region, place, p. 170

### CRITICAL THINKING

· Making Inferences, pp. 169, 170
· Drawing Conclusions, p. 171
· Analyzing Motives, p. 173
· Analyzing Effects, p. 174
· Contrasting, p. 174
· Analyzing Primary Sources, p. 174

## Focus & Motivate

Ask students to describe memories of their thoughts right before a difficult challenge and have them compare those memories with memories of the actual experience.

## Instruct

### Instruct: Objective 1

**Union and Confederate Forces Clash**

TAKS SS11 1(8.1.C)

· Where were the first battles of the war fought?
· What were the relative strengths and weaknesses of each side?
· What strategy did each side follow early in the war?
· Why did Lincoln remove McClellan from command?

 **In-Depth Resources: Unit 1**
· Guided Reading, p. 107

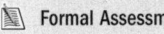 **Critical Thinking Transparencies CT45**
· North vs. South

| MAIN IDEA | WHY IT MATTERS NOW | Terms & Names |
|---|---|---|
| Shortly after the nation's Southern states seceded from the Union, war began between the North and South. | The nation's identity was forged in part by the Civil War. Sectional divisions remain very strong today. | • Fort Sumter<br>• Bull Run<br>• Stonewall Jackson<br>• Ulysses S. Grant<br>• Robert E. Lee<br>• Antietam<br>• Emancipation Proclamation<br>• conscription<br>• Clara Barton<br>• income tax |

**U.S. History**
TEKS 7B, 7C, 8A, 8B, 9A, 19B, 21A, 24A, 24B, 24C, 24H, 25A, 25B, 25C, 25D

### One American's Story

On April 18, 1861, Major Robert Anderson was traveling by ship from Charleston, South Carolina, to New York City. That day, Anderson wrote a report to the secretary of war in which he described his most recent command.

▲ Major Robert Anderson observes the firing at Fort Sumter in 1861.

**A PERSONAL VOICE** ROBERT ANDERSON

" Having defended Fort Sumter for thirty-four hours, until the quarters were entirely burned, the main gates destroyed by fire, . . . the magazine surrounded by flames, . . . four barrels and three cartridges of powder only being available, and no provisions but pork remaining, I accepted terms of evacuation . . . and marched out of the fort . . . with colors flying and drums beating . . . and saluting my flag with fifty guns. "

—quoted in *Fifty Basic Civil War Documents*

Months earlier, as soon as the Confederacy was formed, Confederate soldiers in each secessionist state began seizing federal installations—especially forts. By the time of Lincoln's inauguration on March 4, 1861, only four Southern forts remained in Union hands. The most important was **Fort Sumter,** on an island in Charleston harbor.

Lincoln decided to neither abandon Fort Sumter nor reinforce it. He would merely send in "food for hungry men." At 4:30 A.M. on April 12, Confederate batteries began thundering away to the cheers of Charleston's citizens. The deadly struggle between North and South was under way.

### 1 Union and Confederate Forces Clash

News of Fort Sumter's fall united the North. When Lincoln called for volunteers, the response throughout the Northern states was overwhelming. However, Lincoln's call for troops provoked a very different reaction in the states of the

Mini-Lesson 1: SS11 1(8.1.C)

## PROGRAM RESOURCES

 **In-Depth Resources: Unit 1**
· Guided Reading, p. 107
· Skillbuilder Practice: Following Chronological Order, p. 112
· Reteaching Activity, p. 115
· Primary Sources: Emancipation Proclamation, p. 128
· Outline Map: The States Choose Sides, pp. 124–125

 **Reading Study Guide** (English and Spanish), pp. 49–50

 **Access for Students Acquiring English/ESL**
· Guided Reading (Spanish), p. 64
· Skillbuilder Practice, p. 68
· Outline Map, pp. 72–73

 **Formal Assessment**
· Section Quiz, p. 80

**Integrated Assessment**
· Rubrics

### INTEGRATED TECHNOLOGY

 **Geography Transp. GT11**
· Union and Confederacy, 1861

 **Critical Thinking Transp. CT11, CT45**
· The Civil War
· North vs. South

 **Electronic Library of Primary Sources**

 **classzone.com**

### TEXAS RESOURCES

TAKS Spiraled Content Review

TAKS Practice Tests

TAKS Practice Transparencies TT41, TT42

TAKS Online Test Practice

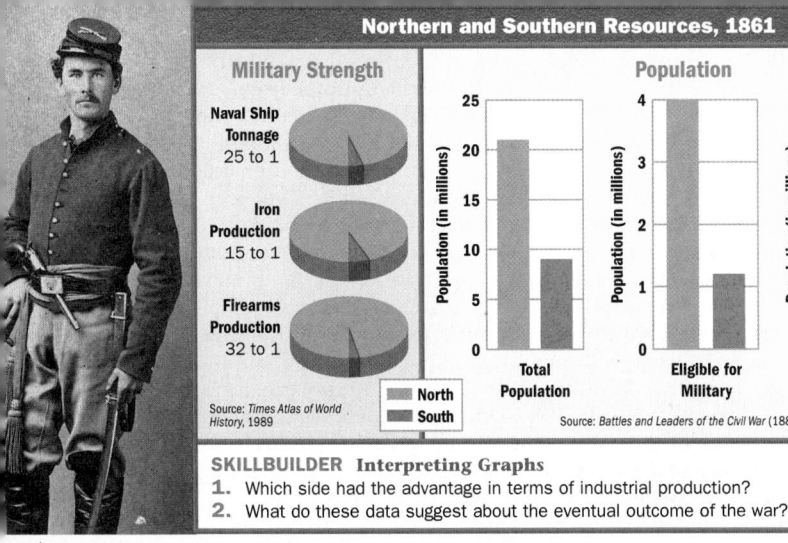

**Northern and Southern Resources, 1861**

**Military Strength**

Naval Ship
Tonnage
25 to 1

Iron
Production
15 to 1

Firearms
Production
32 to 1

Source: *Times Atlas of World History*, 1989

**Population**

Population (in millions)

Total Population

Eligible for Military

Industrial Workers

■ North
■ South

Source: *Battles and Leaders of the Civil War* (1884–1888; reprinted ed., 1956)

**SKILLBUILDER Interpreting Graphs**
1. Which side had the advantage in terms of industrial production?
2. What do these data suggest about the eventual outcome of the war?

**HISTORY from VISUALS**

**Interpreting the Graphs**
Ask students to infer from the graphs which side had the advantage in a long war and which side might have had an advantage in a short war. *(The North's greater population and other strengths would give it an advantage in a long war, as resources became depleted. In a shorter war, neither side might have had a decided advantage in resources.)*

---

▲
**Most Union troops saw the war as a struggle to preserve the Union.**

▲
**Most Confederate soldiers fought to protect the South from Northern aggression.**

*Skillbuilder Answers*
1. The North.
2. Based on the data, it appears that the North might win an easy victory.

**Tracing Themes**

**STATES' RIGHTS**

Opposing constitutional interpretations of the issue of states' rights versus national supremacy reached a dramatic climax in the Civil War. The outbreak of war spurred four more states—Virginia, Arkansas, North Carolina and Tennessee—to secede from the Union and join the seven states that earlier had formed the Confederate States of America. Echoing John C. Calhoun's view of states' rights, the constitution of the Confederacy began, "We the People of the Confederate States, each state acting in its sovereign independent character . . ."

---

upper South. In April and May, Virginia, Arkansas, North Carolina, and Tennessee seceded, bringing the number of Confederate states to eleven. The western counties of Virginia opposed slavery, so they seceded from Virginia and were admitted into the Union as West Virginia in 1863. The four remaining slave states—Maryland, Delaware, Kentucky, and Missouri—remained in the Union.

**STRENGTHS AND STRATEGIES** The Union and the Confederacy were unevenly matched. The Union enjoyed enormous advantages in resources over the South—more people, more factories, greater food production, and a more extensive railroad system. The Confederacy's advantages included "King Cotton," first-rate generals, and highly motivated soldiers. **A**

Both sides adopted military strategies suited to their objectives and resources. The Union, which had to conquer the South to win, devised a three-part plan:

- The navy would blockade Southern ports, so they could neither export cotton nor import much-needed manufactured goods.
- Union riverboats and armies would move down the Mississippi River and split the Confederacy in two.
- Union armies would capture the Confederate capital at Richmond, Virginia.

The Confederacy's strategy was mostly defensive, although Southern leaders encouraged their generals to attack the North if the opportunity arose.

**BULL RUN** The first bloodshed on the battlefield occurred about three months after Fort Sumter fell, near the little creek of **Bull Run**, just 25 miles from Washington, D.C. The battle was a seesaw affair. In the morning the Union army gained the upper hand, but the Confederates held firm, inspired by General Thomas J. Jackson. "There stands Jackson like a stone wall!" another general shouted, coining the nickname **Stonewall Jackson.** In the afternoon Confederate reinforcements helped win the first Southern victory. Fortunately for the Union, the Confederates were too exhausted to follow up their victory with an attack on Washington. Still, Confederate morale soared. Many Confederate soldiers, confident that the war was over, left the army and went home.

**UNION ARMIES IN THE WEST** Lincoln responded to the defeat at Bull Run by stepping up enlistments. He also appointed General George McClellan to lead the Union forces encamped near Washington. While McClellan drilled his troops, the Union forces in the west began the fight for control of the Mississippi River.

**MAIN IDEA**

**Making Inferences**
**A** Why were Northern factories and railroads so advantageous to the Union's war effort?

*A. Answer*
Factories could produce the firearms needed for the conflict; railroads could convey troops and supplies quickly to different locations.

---

**ACTIVITY**   **COOPERATIVE LEARNING**

 **classzone.com**

**Designing a Military Strategy**

**Class Time** Two class periods

**Task** Analyzing the economic, political, and military advantages and disadvantages of the Union and Confederate forces and designing a winning strategy for each side

**Purpose** To better understand the role of political and economic forces in designing a successful military strategy

**Directions** Have small groups of students research the positions of the Union and the Confederacy at the beginning of the war, taking political, economic, and military issues into consideration. Have student groups choose to design a strategy for either the Union or the Confederacy. Then, ask each group to present its strategy to the class and have the class analyze each plan's strengths and weaknesses.

 Integrated Assessment
· Rubric 2

## More About . . .

### Military Strategy of the Confederacy

The South, in fighting a defensive war, had a very different strategy from the Union's. The goal of the Confederacy was to persevere until political support for the North weakened and Union leaders would be forced to sue for peace. This way, the South would not have to win battles, only wear down Union morale. The problem for Lee and other Confederate generals was that Grant's strategy of a war of attrition depleted Confederate forces. The Confederacy simply did not have the resources to prevail in a war of attrition. Grant had recognized the Southern strategy and countered it effectively.

## HISTORY from VISUALS

### Interpreting the Maps

Explain to students how the maps depict the Union strategy of cutting the South in half by gaining control of the lower Mississippi.

**Extension** Students might do further research on the battles shown on the map to fill in details, including commanders, strategy, numbers of troops involved, and numbers of casualties.

In February 1862 a Union army invaded western Tennessee. (See the Battles of the West map below.) At its head was General **Ulysses S. Grant**, a brave and decisive military commander. In just eleven days, Grant's forces captured two Confederate forts, Fort Henry on the Tennessee River and Fort Donelson on the Cumberland River. Two months later, Grant narrowly escaped disaster near Shiloh, a small church in Tennessee close to the Mississippi border. After Grant failed to have his troops dig trenches or set out adequate guards and patrols, thousands of Confederate soldiers carried out a surprise attack. Grant averted disaster by reorganizing his troops and driving the Confederate forces away the next day. However, Shiloh demonstrated what a bloody slaughter the war was becoming. Nearly one-fourth of the 100,000 men who fought there were killed, wounded, or captured.

As Grant pushed toward the Mississippi River, David G. Farragut, commanding a Union fleet of about 40 ships, seized New Orleans, the Confederacy's largest city and busiest port. (See the Fall of New Orleans map below.) By June, Farragut had taken control of much of the lower Mississippi. Between Grant and Farragut, the Union had nearly achieved its goal of cutting the Confederacy in two. Only Port Hudson, Louisiana, and Vicksburg, Mississippi, still stood in the way. **B**

**THE WAR FOR THE CAPITALS** In the spring of 1862, while McClellan was leading his army toward Richmond, he met a Confederate army commanded by General Joseph E. Johnston. (See the Battles of the East map on page 171.) After a series of battles, Johnston was wounded, and command of the army passed on to **Robert E. Lee**. Lee was very different from McClellan—modest rather than vain, and willing to go beyond military textbooks in his tactics. Determined to save the Confederate capital, Lee drove McClellan away from Richmond.

*B. Answer*
Control of the Mississippi would allow the Union to split the Confederacy in two.

**MAIN IDEA**

**Making Inferences**
**B** Why was control of the Mississippi River so important to the Union?

*Skillbuilder Answers*
1. The West.
2. Maryland and Pennsylvania.

### Civil War, 1861–1862

Area controlled by Union
Area won by Union, 1861–1862
Area controlled by Confederacy
Union troop movements
Confederate troop movements
Union victory
Confederate victory
Fort
Capital

0        200        400 miles
0     200     400 kilometers

### Battles of the West

ILLINOIS
IND.
Ohio R.
Mississippi R.
Curtis
MISSOURI
Grant & Foote
KY.
Pope
FT. HENRY Feb. 1862
PEA RIDGE Mar. 1862
FT. DONELSON Feb. 1862
Grant
Buell
TENN.
ARK.
Corinth
Johnston
SHILOH Apr. 1862
MISS.
ALA.

0    50    100 miles
0   50   100 kilometers

40°N

30°N

130°W

#### GEOGRAPHY SKILLBUILDER
1. **Region** In which region of the country did Northern forces have the most success?
2. **Place** In which states did Confederate troops attempt invasions of the North?

### Fall of New Orleans

Vicksburg
LOUISIANA
MISS.
ALA.
Mississippi R.
Farragut
NEW ORLEANS April 1862
Gulf of Mexico

0    50    100 miles
0   50   100 kilometers

**170** CHAPTER 4 *The Union in Peril*

---

### Following Chronological Order

**Explaining the Skill** Understanding the relationships between events aids in understanding causes and effects. Using dates provided in the text and clue words about a time, students can place events they read about in correct chronological order and begin to see relationships between events.

**Applying the Skill** Help students put the events described on this page in chronological order on a time line. Start by having students identify dates and clue words about time: (*In February 1862, In just eleven days, Two months later, By June, In the spring of 1862*)

In-Depth Resources: Unit 1
· Skillbuilder Practice: Following Chronological Order, p. 112

**C. Answer**
Britain had a strong navy and industrial power. Neither the North nor the South wanted Britain to support the other.

**Vocabulary**
**casualties:** those who are injured, killed, captured, or missing in action

Now it was Lee's turn to move against Washington. In September his troops crossed the Potomac into the Union state of Maryland. At this point McClellan had an incredible stroke of luck. A Union corporal found a copy of Lee's orders wrapped around some cigars! The plan revealed that Lee's and Stonewall Jackson's armies were separated for the moment.

McClellan ordered his men to pursue Lee, and the two sides fought on September 17 near a creek called the **Antietam** (ăn-tē′təm). The clash proved to be the bloodiest single-day battle in American history, with casualties totaling more than 26,000. The next day, instead of pursuing the battered Confederate army into Virginia and possibly ending the war, McClellan did nothing. As a result, Lincoln removed him from command.

## The Politics of War ②

**MAIN IDEA**
**Drawing Conclusions**
**C** Why did both the Union and Confederacy care about British neutrality?

After secession occurred, many Southerners believed that dependence on Southern cotton would force Great Britain to formally recognize the Confederacy as an independent nation. Unfortunately for the South, Britain had accumulated a huge cotton inventory just before the outbreak of war. Instead of importing Southern cotton, the British now needed Northern wheat and corn. Britain decided that neutrality was the best policy. **C**

**HISTORICAL SPOTLIGHT**

**BOYS IN WAR**

Both the Union and Confederate armies had soldiers who were under 18 years of age. Examination of some Confederate recruiting lists for 1861–1862 reveals that approximately 5 percent were 17 or younger—with some as young as 13. The percentage of boys in the Union army was lower, perhaps 1.5 percent. These figures, however, do not count the great number of boys who ran away to follow each army without officially enlisting.

### HISTORICAL SPOTLIGHT

**Boys in War**
Ask students what they think should be the minimum age at which a person is allowed to enlist in the armed forces. Have students give reasons for their answer. *(Answers will vary. Students might say 18, because it is the age of legal majority today.)*

### Instruct: Objective ②

**The Politics of War**
TAKS SS11 5(US24.A)
· Why did the South expect British help?
· What reasoning did Lincoln use to support the Emancipation Proclamation?
· How did Lincoln deal with dissent?

📖 In-Depth Resources: Unit 1
· Guided Reading, p. 107

### HISTORY from VISUALS

**Interpreting the Maps**
Students should note that if Lee's forces had won the battle, the Confederates could have had access to Washington, D.C.

**Extension** Have students list the battles on both maps in chronological order indicate the victor.

### Battles of the East

PENNSYLVANIA
N.J.
Sharpsburg
**ANTIETAM**
**Sept. 17, 1862** McClellan
MARYLAND
Harpers Ferry
Lee
Pope
Washington, D.C.
DEL.
**BULL RUN**
**July 1861 and**
**Aug. 1862**
Manassas Jct.
**FREDERICKSBURG**
**Dec. 1862**
Lee
Rappahannock R.
VIRGINIA
Richmond
McClellan
James R.
**SEVEN DAYS'**
**June–July 1862**
**MONITOR vs. MERRIMACK**
**Mar. 1862**
0  25  50 miles
0  25  50 kilometers

MAINE
L. Superior
VT.
N.H.
WISCONSIN
L. Huron
NEW YORK
MASS.
L. Ontario
CONN. R.I.
MICHIGAN
L. Erie
PENNSYLVANIA
N.J.
IOWA
OHIO
MD.
DEL.
Washington, D.C.
ILLINOIS
INDIANA
Ohio R.
Richmond
VIRGINIA
MISSOURI
KENTUCKY
NORTH CAROLINA
Ft. Henry
Ft. Donelson
TENN.
SOUTH CAROLINA
ARKANSAS
Corinth
Charleston
Union Blockade
GEORGIA
ALABAMA
Fort Sumter
MISSISSIPPI
ATLANTIC OCEAN
LOUISIANA
New Orleans
FLORIDA
Gulf of Mexico
Tropic of Cancer
90°W   80°W   70°W   80°W

 **classzone.com**

### Naval Blockade

**Class Time** 45 minutes

**Task** Researching the effect of the Union blockade of Confederate ports

**Purpose** To better understand the effect of the Union blockade of Confederate ports

**Directions** Have students work in small groups to research the effect of the Naval blockade on Confederate ports. Assign groups of students to study the Atlantic ports and other groups to study the Gulf ports. Students could assemble a chart of affected items, such as cotton exports and the embargoed imports of food, arms, and manufactured goods. Have students share their charts with the rest of the class.

## KEY PLAYERS

### Lincoln and Davis

The North had many advantages in the Civil War, and executive leadership was one. Lincoln, who was consistently underestimated by his rivals both Republican and Democratic, rose to the occasion. He demonstrated leadership skills that made him one of the great presidents. Davis, however, proved unsuited to lead in the crisis of wartime. He did not delegate authority well and his military judgement was considered questionable at times. Ask students what they think made Lincoln such a great leader. *(Lincoln had courage, steadfastness, and patience.)*

### More About . . .

### Slavery and Lincoln's Policy

Though slavery was one of the root causes of the Civil War, many Northerners and Southerners were unwilling to admit that truth. Lincoln held that the federal government had no power over slavery in the slave states and insisted that his main goal was preserving the Union. Gradually, however, the more radical members of Congress passed laws intended to free the slaves. Lincoln thought such laws were not constitutional and refused to enforce them. But by the end of 1862, Lincoln recognized the need for action. He used his powers as commander in chief to authorize the Union army to free the slaves, just as he authorized Union soldiers to seize Confederate supplies. The culmination of these measures was the Emancipation Proclamation of January 1, 1863.

## KEY PLAYERS

### ABRAHAM LINCOLN
### 1809–1865

People question why Lincoln believed so passionately in the Union. A possible answer lies in his life story. He was born into poverty, the son of illiterate parents. Lincoln once said that in his boyhood there was "absolutely nothing to excite ambition for education," yet he hungered for knowledge.

Apart from a year's worth of school, Lincoln educated himself and, after working as rail-splitter, flatboatman, storekeeper, and surveyor, he taught himself to be a lawyer. This led to careers in politics and law—and eventually to the White House. Perhaps because of this upward mobility, Lincoln fought passionately to preserve the democracy he described as "the last best hope of earth."

### JEFFERSON DAVIS
### 1808–1889

Davis, who was named after Thomas Jefferson, was born in Kentucky but grew up in Mississippi. After graduating from West Point, he served in the military, then settled down as a planter, before going into politics. He served terms in the U.S. Senate.

His election as president of the Confederacy dismayed him. As his wife Varina wrote, "I thought his genius was military, but as a party manager he would not succeed. He did not know the arts of the politician . . ." Varina was right. Davis fought frequently with other Confederate leaders and was blamed for the refusal of many Southern states to put the Confederacy's welfare above their own.

**PROCLAIMING EMANCIPATION** As Jefferson Davis's Confederacy struggled in vain to gain foreign recognition, abolitionist feeling grew in the North. Although Lincoln disliked slavery, he did not believe that the federal government had the power to abolish it where it already existed.

As the war progressed, however, Lincoln did find a way to use his constitutional war powers to end slavery. The Confederacy used the labor of slaves to build fortifications and grow food. Lincoln's powers as commander-in-chief allowed him to order his troops to seize enemy resources. Therefore, he decided that, just as he could order the Union army to take Confederate supplies, he could also authorize the army to emancipate slaves. Emancipation was not just a moral issue; it became a weapon of war.

On January 1, 1863, Lincoln issued his **Emancipation Proclamation.** The following portion captured national attention.

*from* THE EMANCIPATION PROCLAMATION  ABRAHAM LINCOLN

"I do order and declare that all persons held as slaves within these said designated States and parts of States are, and henceforward shall be free; and that the Executive Government of the United States, including the military and naval authorities thereof, will recognize and maintain the freedom of said persons.

And I hereby enjoin upon the people so declared to be free to abstain from all violence, unless in necessary self-defense; and I recommend to them, that in all cases, when allowed, they labor faithfully for reasonable wages.

And I further declare and make known that such persons of suitable condition will be received into the armed service of the United States to garrison forts, positions, stations, and other places, and to man vessels of all sorts in said service.

And, upon this, sincerely believed to be an act of justice, warranted by the Constitution, upon military necessity, I invoke the considerate judgment of mankind and the gracious favor of Almighty God."

—from The Emancipation Proclamation, January 1, 1863

**172**  CHAPTER 4 *The Union in Peril*

---

### Tracing the Roots of the Emancipation Proclamation

**Class Time** 45 minutes

**Task** Creating a graphic organizer showing phases of the Union's policy for freeing the slaves

**Purpose** To help students better understand how federal policies are shaped over time

 Mini-Lesson 3: SS11 5(US24.A)

**Directions** Have students research federal policy toward slaves, including the Confiscation Acts of 1861 and 1862 and the Emancipation Proclamation of 1863. Then, ask students to organize their research into a flow chart, organization tree, time line, or other graphic organizer to show the evolution of federal policy. Ask students to include explanatory notes with their graphic organizer.

 In-Depth Resources: Unit 1
· Primary Sources: Emancipation Proclamation, p. 128

**MAIN IDEA**

**Analyzing Motives**

 In what way was the Emancipation Proclamation a part of Lincoln's military strategy?

The proclamation did not free any slaves immediately because it applied only to areas behind Confederate lines, outside Union control. Nevertheless, for many, the proclamation gave the war a moral purpose by turning the struggle into a fight to free the slaves. It also ensured that compromise was no longer possible. **D**

**BOTH SIDES FACE POLITICAL DISSENT** Neither side in the Civil War was completely unified. The North harbored thousands of Confederate sympathizers, while the South had thousands of Union sympathizers.

Lincoln dealt forcefully with disloyalty and dissent. He suspended the writ of *habeas corpus,* which prevents the government from holding citizens without formally charging them with crimes. Jefferson Davis also adopted this practice.

## Life During Wartime ❸

**Vocabulary**
**desertion:** the act of abandoning an assigned post or duty

*D. Answer* It gave the war a moral purpose by turning the struggle into a fight to free the slaves. It may also have encouraged enslaved people in the South to resist their enslavement and sabotage the plantations.

The war led to social upheaval and political unrest in both the North and the South. As the fighting intensified, heavy casualties and widespread desertions led each side to impose **conscription,** a draft that forced men to serve in the army. In the North, conscription led to draft riots, the most violent of which took place in New York City. Sweeping changes occurred in the wartime economies of both sides as well as in the roles played by African Americans and women.

**AFRICAN AMERICANS FIGHT FOR FREEDOM** Although African Americans made up only 1 percent of the North's population, by war's end about 180,000 African Americans had fought for the Union—about 10 percent of the Northern army. In spite of their dedication, African-American soldiers in the Union army suffered discrimination. They served in separate regiments commanded by white officers and earned lower pay for most of the war.

**SOLDIERS SUFFER ON BOTH SIDES** Both Union and Confederate soldiers had marched off to war thinking it would be a glorious affair. They were soon disillusioned, not just by heavy battlefield casualties but also by such unhealthy conditions as filthy surroundings, a limited diet, and inadequate medical care. In the 1860s, the technology of killing had outrun the technology of medical care.

Except when fighting or marching, most soldiers lived amid heaps of rubbish and open latrines. As a result, body lice, dysentery, and diarrhea were common.

If conditions in the army camps were bad, those in war prisons were atrocious. The Confederate camps were especially overcrowded and unsanitary. The South's lack of food and tent canvas also contributed to the appalling conditions. Prison camps in the North were only slightly better. Northern prisons provided

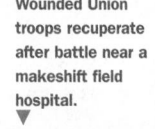

Wounded Union troops recuperate after battle near a makeshift field hospital. ▼

REVIEW UNIT **173**

**More About . . .**

**Lincoln and Dissent**
When a Baltimore mob attacked a Union regiment on its way to Washington, Lincoln sent in federal troops and declared martial law. More than 13,000 dissenters were imprisoned in the North. Most were released quickly, but throughout the war Lincoln and federal commanders had suspected Confederate sympathizers and draft resisters arrested and tried in military, not civilian courts. Lincoln ignored Chief Justice Roger B. Taney's order that Lincoln's suspension of habeas corpus was unconstitutional. It is important to note that censorship was not imposed and that despite the suspension of habeas corpus, generally there was more freedom for dissenters in the Civil War than in either World War I or II.

## Instruct: Objective ❸

**Life During Wartime**
TAKS SS11 3(US21.B)
· How did African Americans assist in the fight for their freedom?
· How did the war affect regional economies?
· What additional suffering aside from combat, did soldiers face?
· How did women help improve conditions for soldiers?

 In-Depth Resources: Unit 1
· Guided Reading, p. 107

 Electronic Library of Primary Sources
· from *Letters to Eliza from a Union Soldier* by G. Fowle
· from *Diary of a Confederate Soldier* by J.S. Jackman

 classzone.com

---

**ACTIVITY**    **LINK TO SCIENCE**

### Civil War Medicine and Health

**Class Time** 45 minutes

**Task** Researching medical and sanitary practices of Civil War field hospitals

**Purpose** To better understand the conditions faced by soldiers and the scientific beliefs and medical practices of the period

**Directions** Have students work in small groups to use library and Internet resources to research medical and sanitary practices of Civil War hospitals, including the role played by Union nurses such as Clara Barton. Students should identify statistics for both deaths caused by wounds and deaths caused by disease. Have students create charts or graphs to illustrate their findings.

Integrated Assessment
· Rubrics 1, 4

## More About . . .

### Clara Barton

Before the war, Barton (1821–1912) was one of the few women employed by the federal government. She worked at the U.S. Patent Office. During the war, she displayed great initiative and organizational skill as a battlefield nurse. In June 1864 she was appointed Superintendent of Nurses for the Army of the James. In 1865, Lincoln appointed her to head a government agency to aid in the search for missing men. After the war, Barton went to Europe. She became involved with relief work during the Franco-Prussian War and later with the International Red Cross. She organized the American Red Cross in 1881 and served as its president until 1904.

# Assess & Reteach

### SECTION 2 ASSESSMENT

Have student pairs give feedback on each other's responses and then revise their final answers.

 Formal Assessment
· Section Quiz, p. 80

### SELF-ASSESSMENT

Have student pairs write and exchange questionnaires about this section. Then, have them meet to evaluate each other's answers.

### RETEACH

Use the maps and graphs to review the key ideas of the section.

 In-Depth Resources: Unit 1
· Reteaching Activity, p. 115

---

more space and adequate amounts of food. However, thousands of Confederate prisoners, housed in quarters with little or no heat, contracted pneumonia and died. Historians estimate that 15 percent of Union prisoners in Southern prisons died, while 12 percent of Confederate prisoners died in Northern prisons.

**WOMEN WORK TO IMPROVE CONDITIONS** Although women did not fight, thousands contributed to the war effort. Some 3,000 women served as Union army nurses. One dedicated Union nurse was **Clara Barton,** who went on to found the American Red Cross after the war. Barton cared for the sick and wounded, often at the front lines of battle. Thousands of Southern women also volunteered for nursing duty. Sally Tompkins, for example, performed so heroically in her hospital duties that she eventually was commissioned as a captain.

Both sides benefited because women devoted so much time and energy to nursing. Women's help was desperately needed as a series of battles in the Mississippi Valley and in the East soon sent casualties flooding into Northern and Southern hospitals alike.

▲ Union nurses, such as Clara Barton *(above)* and Louisa May Alcott, faced the hazards of disease in field hospitals.

**THE WAR AFFECTS REGIONAL ECONOMIES** In general, the war expanded the North's economy and shattered the South's. The Confederacy soon faced a food shortage due to the drain of manpower into the army, the Union occupation of food-growing areas, and the loss of enslaved field workers. Food prices skyrocketed, and the inflation rate rose 7,000 percent.

Overall, the war's effect on the economy of the North was much more positive. The army's need for supplies supported woolen mills, steel foundries, and many other industries. The economic boom had a dark side, however. Wages did not keep up with prices, and many people's standard of living declined. When white male workers went out on strike, employees hired free blacks, immigrants, and women to replace them for lower wages. As the Northern economy grew, Congress decided to help pay for the war by collecting the nation's first **income tax,** a tax that takes a specified percentage of an individual's income.

## 2 · ASSESSMENT

1. **TERMS & NAMES** For each term or name, write a sentence explaining its significance.

- Fort Sumter
- Bull Run
- Stonewall Jackson
- Ulysses S. Grant
- Robert E. Lee
- Antietam
- Emancipation Proclamation
- conscription
- income tax
- Clara Barton

### MAIN IDEA

2. **TAKING NOTES**
Create a chart like the one shown, listing the military actions and social and economic changes of the first two years of the Civil War.

| Military Actions | Social & Economic Changes |
|---|---|
| 1. | 1. |
| 2. | 2. |

What changes brought about by the war had the most effect on civilians in both the South and the North?

### CRITICAL THINKING

3. **ANALYZING EFFECTS**
What effects did the Civil War have on women and African Americans?
**Think About:**
- the impact of the Emancipation Proclamation
- women's role in the war effort

4. **CONTRASTING**
What advantages did the Union have over the South?

5. **ANALYZING PRIMARY SOURCES**
This medical kit was used during the Civil War. What difficulties would caregivers and patients have faced during this time?

---

## 2 ASSESSMENT   Answers

### 1. TERMS & NAMES
Fort Sumter, p. 168
Bull Run, p. 169
Stonewall Jackson, p. 169
Ulysses S. Grant, p. 170
Robert E. Lee, p. 170
Antietam, p. 171
Emancipation Proclamation, p. 172
conscription, p. 173
income tax, p. 174
Clara Barton, p. 174

### 2. TAKING NOTES
**Military Actions:** Bull Run, Shiloh, Antietam
**Social and Economic Changes:** African Americans join Union army, food shortages in South, battlefield medicine, first income tax
Student answers will vary on the changes that most affected civilians but should clearly present persuasive reasons for the choices.

### 3. ANALYZING EFFECTS
Opportunities expanded for both groups. For example, the Emancipation Proclamation allowed African Americans to fight for the Union, and new jobs, such as nursing, opened to women.

### 4. CONTRASTING
The Union had greater human resources, more factories, greater food production, and a more extensive railroad system.

### 5. ANALYZING PRIMARY SOURCES
Surgery without anesthetics would have been very painful. Also, there was great risk of infection during operations.

# The North Takes Charge

| MAIN IDEA | WHY IT MATTERS NOW | Terms & Names |
|---|---|---|
| After four years of bloody fighting, the Union wore down the Confederacy and won the war. | The Union victory confirmed the authority of the federal government over the states. | • Gettysburg<br>• Gettysburg Address<br>• Vicksburg<br>• William Tecumseh Sherman<br>• Appomattox Court House<br>• Thirteenth Amendment<br>• John Wilkes Booth |

 U.S. History 7A, 7B, 7C, 8A, 8B, 9A, 18A, 18B, 19B, 20A, 22B, 24A, 24B, 24C, 24G, 24H, 25A, 25C, 25D, 26A, 26B

### One American's Story

Mary Chesnut was the daughter of a South Carolina governor and the wife of a U.S. senator who resigned his office to serve in the Confederate government. During the war, she recorded her observations and thoughts in a diary. In 1864, Chesnut went to hear Benjamin H. Palmer, a minister and professor, speak about the war. In her diary, she described how Palmer's pessimistic words filled her with foreboding about the future of the Confederacy.

**A PERSONAL VOICE** MARY CHESNUT

"September 21st . . . I did not know before how utterly hopeless was our situation. This man is so eloquent. It was hard to listen and not give way. Despair was his word—and martyrdom. He offered us nothing more in this world than the martyr's crown. . . . He spoke of these times of our agony. And then came the cry: 'Help us, oh God. Vain is the help of man.' And so we came away—shaken to the depths."

—quoted in *Mary Chesnut's Civil War*

**VIDEO**
*WAR OUTSIDE MY WINDOW*
**Mary Chesnut's Diary of the Civil War**

By September 1864, the Northern armies had won several decisive battles. Mary Chesnut must already have had some idea of the threat posed to her way of life, however. In 1863 she wrote that the South, "the only world we cared for," had been "literally kicked to pieces."

## The Tide Turns ❶

The year 1863 actually had begun well for the South. In December 1862, Lee's army had defeated the Union Army of the Potomac at Fredericksburg, Virginia. Then, in May, the South defeated the North again at Chancellorsville, Virginia.

**OBJECTIVES**

❶ Explain how decisive battles, such as Gettysburg and Vicksburg, changed the tide of the war.

❷ Describe instances of total war waged by Grant and Sherman.

❸ Explain how the war changed the nation and people's lives.

**SKILLBUILDERS**

· Geography Skillbuilder: movement, location, pp. 176, 179
· Analyzing Visual Sources, p. 178
· Interpreting Graphs, p. 182

**CRITICAL THINKING**

· Analyzing Motives, pp. 176, 180
· Analyzing Effects, pp. 177, 182
· Forming Generalizations, p. 177
· Making Inferences, p. 179
· Evaluating, p. 181
· Developing Historical Perspective, p. 183
· Analyzing Issues, p. 183
· Summarizing, p. 183
· Drawing Conclusions, p. 183

## Focus & Motivate

Ask students to think of an effort in which they were involved such as mastering a skill or recovering from an injury or illness. Can they identify a pivotal moment in the effort? If so, did they recognize at the time that it *was* pivotal and the tide had turned?

## Instruct

### Instruct: Objective ❶

**The Tide Turns**
TAKS SS11 5(US24.A)
· What were the decisive events at the Battle of Gettysburg?
· How did the Gettysburg Address change America?
· Why was the Battle of Vicksburg so important?

 In-Depth Resources: Unit 1
· Guided Reading, p. 108

**PROGRAM RESOURCES**

 In-Depth Resources: Unit 1
· Guided Reading, p. 108
· Reteaching Activity, p. 116
· Primary Sources: On the Burning of South Carolina, p. 122

 Reading Study Guide (English and Spanish), pp. 51-52

 Access for Students Acquiring English/ESL
· Guided Reading (Spanish), p. 65

 Formal Assessment
· Section Quiz, p. 81

 Integrated Assessment
· Rubrics

**INTEGRATED TECHNOLOGY**

 Humanities Transp. HT11
· Abraham Lincoln riding into Richmond, Virginia

Critical Thinking Transp. CT11
· The Civil War

Electronic Library of Primary Sources

classzone.com

**TEXAS RESOURCES**

 TAKS Spiraled Content Review

 TAKS Practice Tests

TAKS Practice Transparencies TT43, TT44, TT45

 TAKS Online Test Practice

## More About . . .

### Stonewall Jackson

Thomas Jonathan Jackson earned his famous nickname at the first Battle of Bull Run. He and his troops withstood a Union charge, and a fellow officer remarked, "Look, there stands Jackson like a stone wall." Jackson was the most talented Confederate general next to Lee. He excelled at quick maneuvers, in which he used speed and surprise to defeat larger forces. At Chancellorsville, Jackson had executed just such a maneuver on Hooker's right flank to turn the tide of battle to the Confederates.

## HISTORY from VISUALS

### Interpreting the Map

Review the color coding on the map key representing Union and Confederate positions for each day of the battle. Have students reread the portions of the text describing the military maneuvers that occurred on July 1–3 to help them visualize how map symbols illustrate the daily progression of the battle.

**Extension** Have students research the geography of the battlefield and report on how geographic location gave one side the advantage.

---

The North's only consolation after Chancellorsville came as the result of an accident. As General Stonewall Jackson returned from a patrol on May 2, Confederate guards accidentally shot him in the left arm. A surgeon amputated his arm the following day. When Lee heard the news, he exclaimed, "He has lost his left arm but I have lost my right." The true loss was still to come; Jackson caught pneumonia and died on May 10.

Despite Jackson's death, Lee decided to press his military advantage and invade the North. He needed supplies and he thought that a major Confederate victory on Northern soil might tip the balance of public opinion in the Union to the pro-slavery politicians. Accordingly, he crossed the Potomac into Maryland and then pushed on into Pennsylvania. **A**

**THE BATTLE OF GETTYSBURG** Near the sleepy town of **Gettysburg**, in southern Pennsylvania, the most decisive battle of the war was fought. The Battle of Gettysburg began on July 1 when Confederate soldiers led by A. P. Hill encountered several brigades of Union cavalry under the command of John Buford, an experienced officer from Illinois.

Buford ordered his men to take defensive positions on the hills and ridges surrounding the town. When Hill's troops marched toward the town from the west, Buford's men were waiting. The shooting attracted more troops and both sides called for reinforcements. By the end of the first day of fighting, 90,000 Union troops under the command of General George Meade had taken the field against 75,000 Confederates, led by General Lee.

> **MAIN IDEA**
>
> Analyzing Motives
> **A** What did Lee hope to gain by invading the North?
>
> **A. Answer** Lee needed supplies and thought that a major Confederate victory on Northern soil might tip the balance of public opinion in the Union to the pro-slavery politicians.

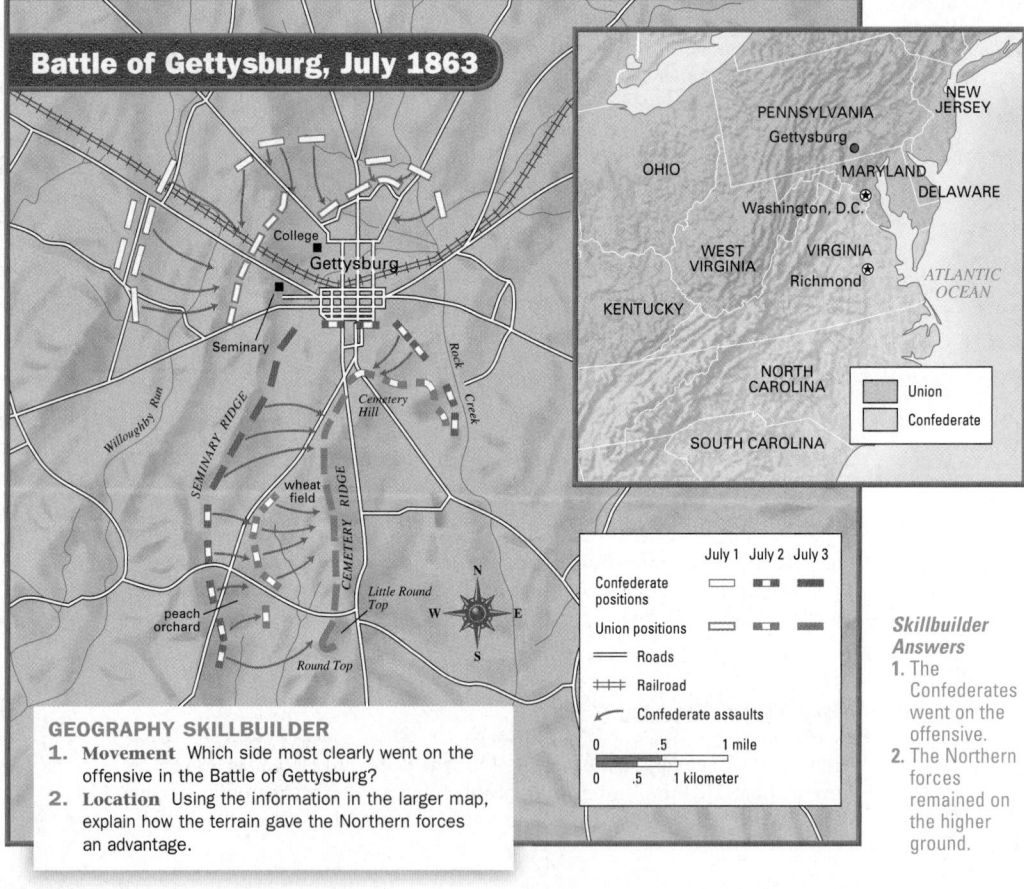

**Battle of Gettysburg, July 1863**

|  | July 1 | July 2 | July 3 |
|---|---|---|---|
| Confederate positions | | | |
| Union positions | | | |

Roads
Railroad
Confederate assaults

0    .5    1 mile
0    .5    1 kilometer

### GEOGRAPHY SKILLBUILDER
1. **Movement** Which side most clearly went on the offensive in the Battle of Gettysburg?
2. **Location** Using the information in the larger map, explain how the terrain gave the Northern forces an advantage.

*Skillbuilder Answers*
1. The Confederates went on the offensive.
2. The Northern forces remained on the higher ground.

**176** CHAPTER 4 *The Union in Peril*

---

**DIFFERENTIATING INSTRUCTION**     **LESS PROFICIENT READERS**

### Tracking Sequence

To help less proficient readers trace the sequence of military actions during the Battle of Gettysburg, put the following set of three flow charts on the board. Then have students fill in the boxes with key events in chronological order as they read pages 176–177.

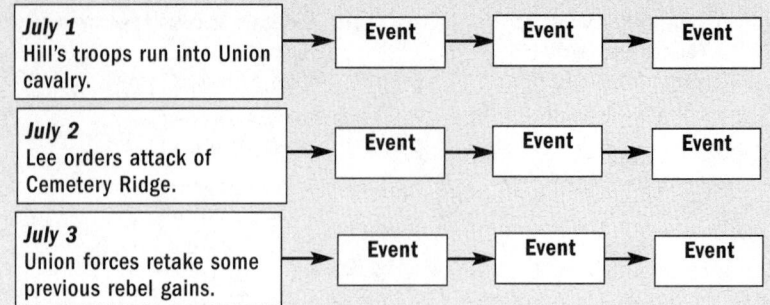

*July 1* Hill's troops run into Union cavalry. → Event → Event → Event

*July 2* Lee orders attack of Cemetery Ridge. → Event → Event → Event

*July 3* Union forces retake some previous rebel gains. → Event → Event → Event

By the second day of battle, the Confederates had driven the Union troops from Gettysburg and had taken control of the town. However, the North still held positions on Cemetery Ridge, the high ground south of Gettysburg. On July 2, Lee ordered General James Longstreet to attack Cemetery Ridge. At about 4:00 P.M., Longstreet's troops advanced from Seminary Ridge, where they were positioned in a peach orchard and wheat field that stood between them and most of the Union army on Cemetery Ridge. The Confederates repeatedly attacked the Union lines. Although the Union troops were forced to concede some territory, their lines withheld the withering Confederate onslaught.

On July 3, Lee ordered an artillery barrage on the center of the Union lines on Cemetery Ridge. For two hours, the two armies fired at one another in a vicious exchange that could be heard in Pittsburgh. Believing they had silenced the Union guns, the Confederates then charged the lines. Confederate forces marched across the farmland between their position and the Union high ground. Suddenly, Northern artillery renewed its barrage, and the infantry fired on the rebels as well. Devastated, the Confederates staggered back to their lines. After the battle, Lee gave up any hopes of invading the North and led his army back to Virginia.

The three-day battle produced staggering losses: 23,000 Union men and 28,000 Confederates were killed or wounded. Total casualties were more than 30 percent. Despite the devastation, Northerners were enthusiastic about breaking "the charm of Robert Lee's invincibility." **B**

**THE GETTYSBURG ADDRESS**  In November 1863, a ceremony was held to dedicate a cemetery in Gettysburg. There, President Lincoln spoke for a little more than two minutes. According to some contemporary historians, Lincoln's **Gettysburg Address** "remade America." Before Lincoln's speech, people said, "The United States are . . ." Afterward, they said, "The United States is . . ." In other words, the speech helped the country to realize that it was not just a collection of individual states; it was one unified nation.

---

### THE GETTYSBURG ADDRESS  ABRAHAM LINCOLN

Four score and seven years ago our fathers brought forth on this continent a new nation, conceived in Liberty and dedicated to the proposition that all men are created equal.

Now we are engaged in a great civil war, testing whether that nation, or any nation so conceived and so dedicated, can long endure. We are met on a great battle-field of that war. We have come to dedicate a portion of that field, as a final resting-place for those who here gave their lives that that nation might live. It is altogether fitting and proper that we should do this.

But, in a larger sense, we can not dedicate—we can not consecrate—we can not hallow—this ground. The brave men, living and dead, who struggled here, have consecrated it, far above our poor power to add or detract. The world will little note, nor long remember what we say here, but it can never forget what they did here. It is for us the living, rather, to be dedicated here to the unfinished work which they who fought here have thus far so nobly advanced. It is rather for us to be here dedicated to the great task remaining before us—that from these honored dead we take increased devotion to that cause for which they gave the last full measure of devotion—that we here highly resolve that these dead shall not have died in vain—that this nation, under God, shall have a new birth of freedom—and that government of the people, by the people, for the people, shall not perish from the earth.  **C**

—"The Gettysburg Address," November 19, 1863

---

### Sidebar notes

**MAIN IDEA**

**Analyzing Effects**
**B** Why was the Battle of Gettysburg a disaster for the South?

**B. Answer** It cost a huge number of casualties and demoralized the Confederates.

**C. Answer** That it is one nation rather than just a collection of states, that it was worth dying for, and that it should not be destroyed.

**MAIN IDEA**

**Forming Generalizations**
**C** What ideas about the United States did Lincoln express in the Gettysburg Address?

---

### More About . . .

**Little Round Top**
Gettysburg was not a planned battle. The action ensued over three days from decisions made by Union and Confederate commanders. The Union defense of a hill known as Little Round Top on Day Two was probably the decisive action in the battle. Confederate troops from Alabama assaulted the Union troops from Maine commanded by Colonel Joshua Chamberlain, a language professor in civilian life. Chamberlain's troops suffered such heavy casualties that they would not be available to contain another Confederate attack. In a bold move, he ordered his troops to fix bayonets and attack the Confederates, who were massing for another assault. The surprised and exhausted Confederate troops, who had marched 25 miles the day before, surrendered. Loss of Little Round Top would have exposed the rest of the Union lines to Confederate artillery and probably given Lee the victory at Gettysburg.

### More About . . .

**The Gettysburg Address**
The featured speaker at the Gettysburg ceremony was the noted orator Edward Everett, not Lincoln. Everett's speech lasted more than two hours. At the time, reporters lauded Everett's speech and mocked Lincoln's. But Everett knew the truth. He wrote to Lincoln, "I should be glad if I could flatter myself that I came as near to the central idea of the occasion, in two hours, as you did in two minutes."

---

**ACTIVITY**  LINK TO CIVICS                                             **BLOCK SCHEDULING**

### "Government of the People, by the People, for the People"

**Class Time**  45 minutes

**Task**  Analyzing the Gettysburg Address and providing examples for Lincoln's words

**Purpose**  To understand and give examples of democratic government

**Directions**  Have students take turns doing an oral reading of the Gettysburg Address. Then ask them to work in pairs to analyze the meaning of and provide examples for Lincoln's closing words "government of the people, by the people, for the people."

Integrated Assessment
· Rubrics 2, 3

*The Union in Peril*  **177**

## History Through *Photojournalism*

### Interpreting the Photographs

Some of the power of Brady's work lies in its brutal realism. Ask students to compare the photographs on this page with the painting of Lee and Grant on page 181. Ask students which images they find more immediate and "real." *(Students will probably find greater reality in the Brady photographs, but they might mention that the painting shows attention to realistic detail.)*

### SKILLBUILDER ANSWERS

1. The soldiers seem posed. The deserted camp looks realistic.

2. The photographs show soldiers in ordinary situations. There are none of the heroic gestures that are often associated with traditional history paintings.

### More About . . .

#### Matthew Brady

Brady (1823–1896) was the first great war photographer. He learned how to make daguerreotypes from Samuel F. B. Morse and opened studios in New York and Washington. At the outset of the Civil War, Brady hired a group of photographers to help him document the war. He took many of the pictures himself, including photos of Lincoln and the battlefields at Bull Run, Antietam, and Gettysburg. Brady had expected that the federal government to buy his photographs at the end of the war, but it did not. He died impoverished and forgotten.

## History Through *Photojournalism*

### MATHEW BRADY'S PHOTOGRAPHS

The Civil War marked the first time in United States history that photography, a resource since 1839, played a major role in a military conflict. Hundreds of photographers traveled with the troops, working both privately and for the military. The most famous Civil War photographer was Mathew Brady, who employed about 20 photographers to meet the public demand for pictures from the battlefront. This was the beginning of American news photography, or photojournalism.

Many of Brady's photographs are a mix of realism and artificiality. Due to the primitive level of photographic technology, subjects had to be carefully posed and remain still during the long exposure times.

In this 1864 photograph Brady posed a kneeling soldier, offering a canteen of water, beside a wounded soldier with his arm in a sling. Images like this, showing the wounded or the dead, brought home the harsh reality of war to the civilian population. ▼

▲ "Encampment of the Army of the Potomac" (May 1862). Few photographs of the Civil War are as convincing in their naturalism as this view over a Union encampment. Simply by positioning the camera behind the soldiers, the photographer draws the viewer into the composition. Although we cannot see the soldiers' faces, we are compelled to see through their eyes.

**SKILLBUILDER** Interpreting Visual Sources

1. What elements in the smaller photograph seem posed or contrived? What elements are more realistic?

2. How do these photographs compare with more heroic imagery of traditional history painting?

 SEE SKILLBUILDER HANDBOOK, PAGE R23.

**178** CHAPTER 4 *The Union in Peril*

---

classzone.com

### Examining the Images of War

**Class Time** 45 minutes

**Task** Examining the war photographs of Matthew Brady and commenting on the power of the images, on the world they portray, and on the reality of war

**Purpose** To deepen student understanding of the Civil War and its place in American memory

**Directions** Have students use the library or Internet to find additional Brady war photographs. Ask students to examine the photographs and to discuss their reactions with other students. Then, have students respond to the photographs through prose, poetry, art, or another expressive means and share their work with the rest of the class.

**GRANT WINS AT VICKSBURG** While Meade's Army of the Potomac was destroying Confederate hopes in Gettysburg, Union general Ulysses S. Grant fought to take **Vicksburg**, one of the two remaining Confederate strongholds on the Mississippi River. Vicksburg itself was particularly important because it rested on bluffs above the river from which guns could control all water traffic. In the winter of 1862–1863, Grant tried several schemes to reach Vicksburg and take it from the Confederates. Nothing seemed to work—until the spring of 1863.

Grant began by weakening the Confederate defenses that protected Vicksburg. He sent Benjamin Grierson to lead his cavalry brigade through the heart of Mississippi. Grierson succeeded in destroying rail lines and distracting Confederate forces from Union infantry working its way toward Vicksburg. Grant was able to land his troops south of Vicksburg on April 30 and immediately sent his men in search of Confederate troops in Mississippi. In 18 days, Union forces had sacked Jackson, the capital of the state.

Their confidence growing with every victory, Grant and his troops rushed to Vicksburg, hoping to take the city while the rebels were reeling from their losses. Grant ordered two frontal attacks on Vicksburg, neither of which succeeded. So, in the last week of May 1863, Grant settled in for a siege. He set up a steady barrage of artillery, shelling the city from both the river and the land for several hours a day, forcing the city's residents into caves that they dug out of the yellow clay hillsides.

After food supplies ran so low that people were reduced to eating dogs and mules, the Confederate command of Vicksburg asked Grant for terms of surrender. The city fell on July 4. Five days later Port Hudson, Louisiana, the last Confederate holdout on the Mississippi, also fell. The Union had achieved another of its major military objectives, and the Confederacy was cut in two. **D**

*D. Answer*
Control of the Mississippi allowed the Union to split the Confederacy in two.

**MAIN IDEA**

**Making Inferences**
**D** Why was the Union so intent on gaining control of the Mississippi River?

---

**More About . . .**

**The Naval Hero of Vicksburg**
Commander David Porter was the naval officer who made the successful siege of Vicksburg possible. The key to Grant's final campaign was his ability to recross the Mississippi south of Vicksburg. Porter had sailed his fleet past the Confederate batteries at Vicksburg to meet Grant at Bruinsburg and bring Grant's army across the river. For his heroics, Porter was promoted to rear admiral by a grateful Congress.

*Skillbuilder Answers*
1. 5 days.
2. Control of Vicksburg allowed Union forces to control the Mississippi River.

---

## Vicksburg Campaign, April–July 1863

**Legend:**
- Union forces
- Union positions
- Confederate forces
- Confederate positions
- Union victory
- Railroad

0    10    20 miles
0    10    20 kilometers

MISSISSIPPI

Milliken's Bend
Yazoo River
Duckport Canal
Sherman
Big Black River, May 17
Bridgeport
Bolton Depot
Johnston
Clinton
Grant
Williams-Grant Canal
Mississippi River
Siege of Vicksburg begins May 19. City surrenders July 4.
Champion Hill, May 16
Sherman and McPherson
Jackson, May 14
Raymond, May 12
McClernand and Sherman
New Carthage
Grant
Big Black River
LOUISIANA
Hard Times
Rocky Springs
Big Bayou Pierre
Bruinsburg
Port Gibson, May 1

**April 20**
Grant moves main body of Union forces south.

**April 30**
Grant's army crosses Mississippi unopposed.

N W E S

**GEOGRAPHY SKILLBUILDER**
1. **Movement** How many days did it take Union forces to reach Vicksburg after the victory at Jackson?
2. **Location** Why was it important for the Union to control Vicksburg?

---

**HISTORY from VISUALS**

**Interpreting the Map**
Point out to students the topography of the Vicksburg area, noting the hills and the configuration of the rivers. Remind students of the strategic location of Vicksburg in the context of the North's military strategy of dividing the Confederacy at the Mississippi River.

**Extension** Ask students to discuss how landforms made the capture of Vicksburg so difficult. *(The city is set on a high bluff that overlooks the river. Union troops had to travel far south by water to bypass the bluff.)*

---

---

**ACTIVITY    COOPERATIVE LEARNING**

 **classzone.com**

### Researching the Battles of Vicksburg and Gettysburg

**Class Time** 45 minutes

**Task** Researching aspects of either the Battle of Gettysburg or the Battle of Vicksburg

**Purpose** To discover how these battles helped determine the outcome of the war

**Directions** Have students work in small groups, with each group choosing either Gettysburg or Vicksburg as its research subject. Ask students to use the text, library and Internet resources to research some aspect of the campaign that they have chosen. Help students to define the subject of their research and to choose a method of illustrating their findings. This might be a written or oral report, a graphic organizer, or some other visual display.

📄 Integrated Assessment
· Rubrics 1, 2, 4, 5

## ❷ The Confederacy Wears Down

The twin defeats at Gettysburg and Vicksburg cost the South much of its limited manpower. The Confederacy was already low on food, shoes, uniforms, guns, and ammunition. No longer able to attack, it could hope only to hang on long enough to destroy Northern morale and work toward an armistice.

**Vocabulary**
**armistice:** truce

That plan proved increasingly unrealistic, however, in part because Southern morale was weakening. Many Confederate soliders had deserted, while newspapers, state legislatures, and individuals throughout the South began to call openly for peace. Worse yet for the Confederacy, Lincoln finally found not just one but two generals who would fight.

**TOTAL WAR** In March 1864, President Lincoln appointed Ulysses S. Grant commander of all Union armies. Grant in turn appointed **William Tecumseh Sherman** as commander of the military division of the Mississippi. These two appointments would change the course of the war.

Old friends and comrades in arms, both men believed in waging total war. They reasoned that it was the strength of the people's will that was keeping the war going. If the Union could destroy the Southern population's will to fight, the Confederacy would collapse.

Grant's overall strategy was to decimate Lee's army in Virginia while Sherman raided Georgia. Even if his casualties ran twice as high as those of Lee—and they did—the North could afford it; the South could not. ❶

**SHERMAN'S MARCH** In the spring of 1864, Sherman began his march southeast through Georgia to the sea, creating a wide path of destruction. His army burned almost every house in its path and destroyed livestock and railroads. Sherman was determined to make Southerners

---

### Instruct: Objective ❷

**The Confederacy Wears Down**

TAKS SS11 1(8.1.C)

· What was total war?
· How did Sherman help defeat the South?
· What aided Lincoln's reelection in 1864?
· What terms of surrender did Grant give Lee?

 **In-Depth Resources: Unit 1**
· Guided Reading, p. 108
· Primary Sources: On the Burning of South Carolina, p. 122

---

### KEY PLAYERS

**Ulysses S. Grant and Robert E. Lee**

The Civil War produced two enduring military heroes. Both are highly regarded as honorable men, respected by the troops that served under them. Lee is generally given higher marks as a tactician, but Grant's plan to fight a war of attrition was the strategy that brought a Union victory.

---

### More About . . .

**William Tecumseh Sherman**

Sherman's first Civil War experience was the Union disaster at Bull Run. His performance there and in subsequent battles caused him to lose confidence. A victory at Shiloh, plus the respect of President Lincoln and his good friend Grant, restored his confidence. When Grant became commanding general of all Union forces, Sherman succeeded him as commander of the military division of the Mississippi. He then began his famous "March to the Sea" through Georgia. In 1869, President Grant promoted Sherman to Grant's old post as commanding general of the army which he held until 1884.

 **Electronic Library of Primary Sources**
· from A Letter to General Hood by General Sherman

---

## KEY PLAYERS

**ULYSSES S. GRANT**
**1822–1885**

Born Hiram Ulysses Grant, the future president did not correct a clerk at West Point who recorded his name as Ulysses Simpson Grant. Thereafter, he went by the name U. S. Grant.

Grant once said of himself, "A military life had no charms for me." Yet a military man was what he was destined to be. He fought in the war with Mexico—even though he termed it "wicked"—because he believed his duty was to serve his country. His next post was in the West, where Grant grew so lonely for his family that he resigned.

When the Civil War broke out, the Illinois governor made Grant a colonel of volunteers because George McClellan had been too busy to see him! However, once Grant began fighting in Tennessee, Lincoln was quick to recognize his special strength. When newspapers demanded Grant's dismissal after Shiloh, Lincoln replied firmly, "I can't spare this man. He fights."

**ROBERT E. LEE**
**1807–1870**

Lee was an aristocrat, related to some of Virginia's leading families. In fact, his father had been one of George Washington's favorite lieutenants, and his wife, Mary Ann Randolph Custis, was the great-granddaughter of Martha Washington. His sense of family honor may have contributed to his allegiance to his state. As a man who believed slavery was evil, Lee fought for the Confederacy only because of his loyalty to his beloved Virginia. "I did only what my duty demanded. I could have taken no other course without dishonor," he said.

As a general, Lee was tactically brilliant, but he seldom challenged Confederate civilian leaders about their failure to provide his army with adequate food, clothing, or weapons. On the other hand, his soldiers almost worshiped him because he never abused them and always insisted on sharing their hardships. His men called him "Uncle Robert," just as the Union troops called Grant Uncle Sam.

---

**MAIN IDEA**

**Analyzing Motives**

**E** Why did Sherman and Grant want to wage "total war"?

*E. Answer* They believed that only total war would break the Southern people's will to fight.

---

**ACTIVITY** COOPERATIVE LEARNING

 **classzone.com**

### Evaluating the Ethics of Total War

**Class Time** 45 minutes

**Task** Debating the ethics and morality of total war

**Purpose** To evaluate the impact of warfare on civilians and the ethics of total warfare

**Directions** Have students work in small groups use library or Internet resources to research the theory of total war as practiced by Grant and Sherman. Give students the option of debating the ethics of total war or of writing editorials in favor of or in opposition to it. Have students share what they learned from the exercise with the rest of the class.

 **Integrated Assessment**
· Rubrics 1, 3, 5

**MAIN IDEA**

**Evaluating**

**F** Do you think that Sherman's destructive march to the sea was necessary? Why or why not?

*F. Possible Answers*
**Yes:** It was necessary to end the war quickly.
**No:** Nothing can justify Sherman's assault on the civilian population.

"so sick of war that generations would pass away before they would again appeal to it." By mid-November he had burned most of Atlanta. After reaching the ocean, Sherman's forces—followed by 25,000 former slaves—turned north to help Grant "wipe out Lee." **F**

**THE ELECTION OF 1864** Despite the war, politics in the Union went on as usual. As the 1864 presidential election approached, Lincoln faced heavy opposition from the Democrats and from a faction within his own party. A number of Northerners were dismayed at the war's length and its high casualty rates.

Lincoln was pessimistic about his chances. "I am going to be beaten," he said in August, "and unless some great change takes place, badly beaten." However, some great change did take place. News of General Sherman's victories inspired the North and helped Lincoln win re-election.

**THE SURRENDER AT APPOMATTOX** On April 3, 1865, Union troops conquered Richmond, the Confederate capital. Southerners had abandoned the city the day before, setting it afire to keep the Northerners from taking it. On April 9, 1865, in a Virginia town called **Appomattox** (ăp′ə-măt′əks) **Court House,** Lee and Grant met at a private home to arrange a Confederate surrender. At Lincoln's request, the terms were generous. Grant paroled Lee's soldiers and sent them home with their possessions and three days' worth of rations. Officers were permitted to keep their side arms. Within a month all remaining Confederate resistance collapsed. After four long years, the Civil War was over.

## The War Changes the Nation ❸

The Civil War caused tremendous political, economic, technological, and social change in the United States. It also exacted a high price in terms of human life. Approximately 360,000 Union soldiers and 260,000 Confederates died, nearly as many American combat deaths as in all other American wars combined.

*Thomas Lovell's Surrender at Appomattox is a modern rendering of Lee's surrender to Grant. This is Lovell's version of the scene—no photographs of the event exist.*
▼

**More About . . .**

**The Election of 1864**
Lincoln faced opposition on two fronts in 1864. War fatigue had grown in the North, and Lincoln looked beatable. The Democrats nominated George McClellan, who attracted the support of Copperheads. McClellan, still angry at being dismissed by Lincoln, was eager for the race. Radical Republicans, tired of Lincoln's political moderation, recruited John C. Frémont to run. Lincoln was saved by events. On August 5, Admiral David Farragut took Mobile, the last remaining Confederate port. Sherman captured Atlanta in September. A month later, General Philip Sheridan succeeded in driving Confederate troops out of the Shenandoah Valley. The news of the victories changed the political tide in the North and resulted in Lincoln's victory.

**Instruct: Objective** ❸

**The War Changes the Nation /
The War Changes Lives**
TAKS SS11 4(8.17.B)
· What political and economic changes were caused by the war?
· How was the Civil War the first modern war?
· How did the Thirteenth Amendment affect the lives of slaves?
· Why was Lincoln assassinated?

In-Depth Resources: Unit 1
· Guided Reading, p. 108

**DIFFERENTIATING INSTRUCTION**    **GIFTED AND TALENTED**    classzone.com

### Researching the Election of 1864

Ask students to investigate the election of 1864. Students should identify the candidates, the political parties that they represented, the events that influenced the election, and the final outcome. The research should include the final figures for the popular and electoral votes. Encourage students to use charts and graphs to report their findings. For example, they may wish to create bar graphs to show the number of electoral and popular votes each candidate received and circle graphs to show the percentages of electoral and popular votes. Finally a one paragraph analysis of the findings should be included.

**Rubric**
Election charts or graphs should:
· clearly identify and label candidates and their parties
· present the visual information in a style that will enhance viewer understanding
· use a compare and contrast method for evaluation

Integrated Assessment
· Rubric 2

## HISTORY from VISUALS

### Interpreting Graphs

The title of a graph is an important indicator of what to look for in the visual. In this case, "costs" involve both money and lives.

**Extension** Have students expand the bar graph to show the number of American casualties in the following 20th century wars:

| | |
|---|---|
| World War I: | 320,710 |
| World War II: | 1,078,162 |
| Korean War: | 157,530 |
| Vietnam War: | 211,324 |

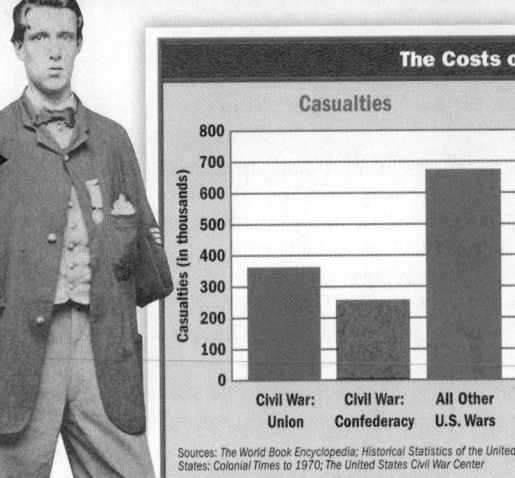

Though many Union and Confederate soldiers were lucky to escape the war with their lives, thousands—like this young amputee—faced an uncertain future.

### More About . . .

### Wartime Economics

The war was an economic disaster for the South, and it was a burden for millions of Northerners. But it also accelerated economic development. Huge wartime demand launched the careers of some great business tycoons such as meatpacker Philip Armour, oil mogul John D. Rockefeller, and steel czar Andrew Carnegie. The war began an age of industrialism that favored concentrations of capital and large economic entities, such as the corporation.

---

### The Costs of the Civil War

#### Casualties

Casualties (in thousands) — y-axis: 0, 100, 200, 300, 400, 500, 600, 700, 800

- Civil War: Union
- Civil War: Confederacy
- All Other U.S. Wars

Sources: *The World Book Encyclopedia; Historical Statistics of the United States: Colonial Times to 1970; The United States Civil War Center*

#### Economic Costs

- Union war costs totaled $2.3 billion.
- Confederate war costs ran to $1 billion.
- Union war costs increased the national debt from $65 million in 1860 to $2.7 billion in 1865.
- Confederate debt ran over $1.8 billion in 1864.
- Union inflation peaked at 182% in 1864.
- Confederate inflation rose to 7,000%.

**SKILLBUILDER Interpreting Graphs**
1. Based on the bar graph, how did the combined Union and Confederate losses compare with those of other wars?
2. Which side suffered greater inflation?

**POLITICAL AND ECONOMIC CHANGES** The Civil War greatly increased the federal government's power and authority. During the war, the federal government passed laws, including income tax and conscription laws, that gave it much more control over individual citizens. And after the war, no state ever threatened secession again.

Economically, the Civil War dramatically widened the gap between North and South. During the war, the economy of the Northern states boomed. The Southern economy, on the other hand, was devastated. The war not only marked the end of slavery as a labor system but also wrecked most of the region's industry and farmland. The economic gulf between the regions would not diminish until the 20th century.

**A REVOLUTION IN WARFARE** Because of developments in technology, the Civil War has been called the last old-fashioned war, or the first modern war. The two deadliest technological improvements were the rifle and the minié ball, a soft lead bullet that was more destructive than earlier bullets. Two other weapons that became more lethal were hand grenades and land mines.

Another technological improvement was the ironclad ship, which could splinter wooden ships by ramming them, withstand cannon fire, and resist burning. On March 9, 1862, every wooden warship in the world became obsolete after the North's ironclad *Monitor* exchanged fire with the South's ironclad *Merrimack*. **G**

## The War Changes Lives

The war not only revolutionized weaponry but also changed people's lives. Perhaps the biggest change came for African Americans.

**THE THIRTEENTH AMENDMENT** The Emancipation Proclamation freed only those slaves who lived in states that were behind Confederate lines, and not yet under Union control. The government had to decide what to do about the border states, where slavery still existed. The president believed that the only solution was a constitutional amendment abolishing slavery.

**Background**
Many tycoons of the late 19th century launched their careers during the war. War profiteering helped men like John D. Rockefeller become rich.

**MAIN IDEA**

**Analyzing Effects**
**G** How did technology affect the Civil War?

**G. Answer** Deadlier weapons caused greater destruction. Ironclad ships made wooden ones obsolete.

182 CHAPTER 4 *The Union in Peril*

---

DIFFERENTIATING INSTRUCTION    STUDENTS ACQUIRING ENGLISH/ESL

### Rereading Phrases

The phrases below are taken from the first two subsections on page 182. Review them with students, rephrasing the italicized words to ensure comprehension.

- "the United States *underwent* great political change." *(went through)*
- "including income tax and *conscription* laws." *(laws for drafting into the military)*
- "The Civil War *dramatically widened the economic gap*." *(made the difference between rich and poor even greater)*

- "The economy of the Northern states *boomed*." *(grew rapidly)*
- "The *economic gulf* between the regions." *(difference in wealth)*
- "*withstand* cannon fire" *(survive)*

After some political maneuvering, the **Thirteenth Amendment** was ratified at the end of 1865. The U.S. Constitution now stated, "Neither slavery nor involuntary servitude, except as a punishment for crime whereof the party shall have been duly convicted, shall exist within the United States."

**LINCOLN IS ASSASSINATED** Whatever further plans Lincoln had to reunify the nation after the war, he never got to implement them. On April 14, 1865, five days after Lee surrendered to Grant at Appomattox, Lincoln and his wife went to Ford's Theatre in Washington to see a British comedy, *Our American Cousin*. During its third act, a man crept up behind Lincoln and shot the president in the back of his head.

Lincoln, who never regained consciousness, died on April 15. It was the first time a president of the United States had been assassinated. After the shooting, the assassin, **John Wilkes Booth**—a 26-year-old actor and Southern sympathizer— then leaped down from the presidential box to the stage and escaped. Twelve days later, Union cavalry trapped him in a Virginia tobacco shed and shot him dead.

The funeral train that carried Lincoln's body from Washington to his hometown of Springfield, Illinois, took 14 days for its journey. Approximately 7 million Americans, or almost one-third of the entire Union population, turned out to mourn publicly their martyred leader.

The Civil War had ended. Slavery and secession were no more. Now the country faced two new problems: how to restore the Southern states to the Union and how to integrate approximately 4 million newly freed African Americans into national life.

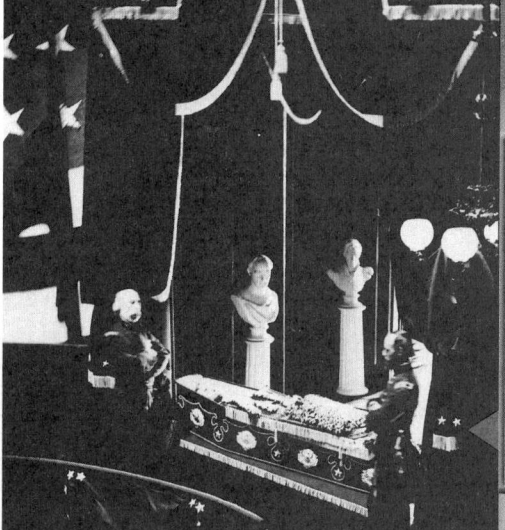

▲ Lincoln's body lies in state in 1865.

*H. Possible Answers*
*Yes: They would want to punish the South for rebelling.*
*No: They would want to reunify peacefully and quickly.*

**MAIN IDEA**

**Developing Historical Perspective**
**H** Do you think that the Union would take revenge on the Southern states after the war is over?

# Assess & Reteach

**SECTION 3 ASSESSMENT**
Have students work individually to answer questions. Then, have them share the multiple effects chart that they created for Taking Notes with the class.

📄 Formal Assessment
· Section Quiz, p. 81

**SELF-ASSESSMENT**
Have students create a time line of events covered by the section.

**RETEACH**
Review the battle maps of Gettysburg and Vicksburg with students, reinforcing the pivotal role the battles played in turning the tide of the war.

📄 In-Depth Resources: Unit 1
· Reteaching Activity, p. 116

---

## SECTION 3 ASSESSMENT

**1. TERMS & NAMES** For each term or name, write a sentence explaining its significance.

- Gettysburg
- Gettysburg Address
- Vicksburg
- William Tecumseh Sherman
- Appomattox Court House
- Thirteenth Amendment
- John Wilkes Booth

### MAIN IDEA

**2. TAKING NOTES**
Copy the multiple-effects chart below on your paper and fill it in with consequences of the Civil War.

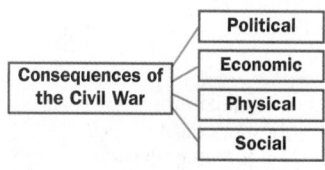

Which consequence of the Civil War do you think has had the most impact on modern life?

### CRITICAL THINKING

**3. ANALYZING ISSUES**
Grant and Sherman used the strategy of total war. Do you think the end justifies the means? That is, did defeating the Confederacy justify harming civilians? Explain.
**Think About:**
- their reasons for targeting the civilian population
- Sherman's remark about Georgia quoted on page 181
- Sherman's march through Georgia

**4. SUMMARIZING**
How did Lincoln abolish slavery in all states?

**5. DRAWING CONCLUSIONS**
Why did the Union's victory strengthen the power of the national government?

---

Answers ASSESSMENT

**1. TERMS & NAMES**
Gettysburg, p. 176
Gettysburg Address, p. 177
Vicksburg, p. 179
William Tecumseh Sherman, p. 180
Appomattox Court House, p. 181
Thirteenth Amendment, p. 183
John Wilkes Booth, p. 183

**2. TAKING NOTES**
Political: Freed enslaved people; prevented disintegration of Union. Economic: Stimulated economic growth of the North and contributed to economic decline of the South. Physical: Widespread destruction of houses, livestock, and railroads in the South; increased industrialization in the North. Social: Family life in both North and South disrupted by departure of millions of men to fight in the war and the high casualty rate. Answers will vary.

**3. ANALYZING ISSUES**
Students might say that saving the Union and abolishing slavery were worth the cost of civilian lives. Students who disagree might claim that killing defenseless citizens is immoral under any circumstances.

**4. SUMMARIZING**
Lincoln thought that a constitutional amendment would be necessary to abolish slavery, and the Thirteenth Amendment was passed at the end of 1865.

**5. DRAWING CONCLUSIONS**
It ensured that states would never again threaten secession.

# Reconstruction and Its Effects

| MAIN IDEA | WHY IT MATTERS NOW | Terms & Names |
|---|---|---|
| After the Civil War, the nation embarked on a period known as Reconstruction, during which attempts were made to readmit the South to the Union. | The Fourteenth and Fifteenth Amendments, passed as part of Reconstruction, gave civil rights to Americans of all races. | • Freedmen's Bureau  • Fifteenth Amendment<br>• Reconstruction  • scalawag<br>• Radical Republicans  • carpetbagger<br>• Andrew Johnson  • Hiram Revels<br>• Fourteenth Amendment  • sharecropping<br>  • Ku Klux Klan (KKK) |

**U.S. History**
7A, 7C, 7D, 8A, 15C, 16A, 18A, 19B, 21A, 24A, 24B, 24C, 24F, 24G, 25A, 25B, 25C, 25D, 26A

## One American's Story

Robert G. Fitzgerald was born a free African American in Delaware in 1840. During the Civil War, he served in both the U.S. Army and the U.S. Navy. In 1866, he taught former slaves in a small Virginia town. A year after his arrival in Virginia, Fitzgerald looked back on what he had accomplished.

**A PERSONAL VOICE** ROBERT G. FITZGERALD

"I came to Virginia one year ago on the 22nd of this month. Erected a school, organized and named the Freedman's Chapel School. Now (June 29th) have about 60 who have been for several months engaged in the study of arithmetic, writing, etc. etc. This morning sent in my report accompanied with compositions from about 12 of my advanced writers instructed from the Alphabet up to their [present] condition, their progress has been surprisingly rapid."

—quoted in *Proud Shoes*

Fitzgerald was working for the **Freedmen's Bureau,** which had been established by Congress to provide food, clothing, hospitals, legal protection, and education for former slaves and poor whites in the South in 1865.

**VIDEO**
TEACHER OF A FREED PEOPLE
Robert Fitzgerald and Reconstruction

## 1 The Politics of Reconstruction

The need to help former slaves was just one of many issues the nation confronted after the war. In addition, the government, led by Andrew Johnson, Lincoln's vice president and eventual successor, had to determine how to bring the Confederate states back into the Union. **Reconstruction,** the period during which the United States began to rebuild after the Civil War, lasted from 1865 to 1877. The term also refers to the process the federal government used to readmit

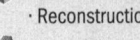
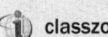

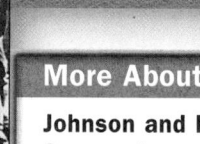
the defeated Confederate states to the Union. Complicating the process was the fact that Abraham Lincoln, Andrew Johnson, and the members of Congress all had different ideas about how Reconstruction should be handled.

**LINCOLN'S PLAN** Lincoln made it clear that he favored a lenient Reconstruction policy. In December 1863, Lincoln announced his Proclamation of Amnesty and Reconstruction, also known as the Ten-Percent Plan. Under this plan, the government would pardon all Confederates—except high-ranking officials and those accused of crimes against prisoners of war—who would swear allegiance to the Union. As soon as ten percent of those who had voted in 1860 took this oath of allegiance, a Confederate state could form a new state government and send representatives and senators to Congress. Under Lincoln's terms, three states—Arkansas, Louisiana, and Tennessee—moved toward readmission to the Union.

However, Lincoln's Reconstruction plan angered a minority of Republicans in Congress, known as **Radical Republicans.** The Radicals, led by Senator Charles Sumner of Massachusetts and Representative Thaddeus Stevens of Pennsylvania, wanted to destroy the political power of former slaveholders. Most of all, they wanted African Americans to be given full citizenship and the right to vote.

**JOHNSON'S PLAN FOR RECONSTRUCTION** Lincoln was assassinated before he could fully implement his Reconstruction plan. In May 1865, his successor, **Andrew Johnson,** announced his own plan. Johnson's plan differed little from Lincoln's. The major difference was that Johnson tried to break the planters' power by excluding high-ranking Confederates and wealthy Southern landowners from taking the oath needed for voting privileges. However, Johnson also pardoned more than 13,000 former Confederates because he believed that "white men alone must manage the South." Ⓐ

The seven remaining ex-Confederate states quickly agreed to Johnson's terms. In the following months, these states set up new state governments and elected representatives to Congress. In December 1865, the newly elected Southern legislators arrived in Washington to take their seats. Congress, however, refused to admit the new Southern legislators. At the same time, moderate Republicans pushed for new laws to remedy weaknesses they saw in Johnson's plan. In 1866, Congress voted to enlarge the Freedmen's Bureau and passed the Civil Rights Act of 1866. That law gave African Americans citizenship and forbade states from passing discriminatory laws—black codes—that severely restricted African Americans' lives.

Johnson shocked everyone when he vetoed both the Freedmen's Bureau Act and the Civil Rights Act. Congress, Johnson contended, had gone far beyond "anything contemplated by the authors of the Constitution."

**CONGRESSIONAL RECONSTRUCTION** Angered by Johnson's actions, radical and moderate Republican factions decided to work together to shift the control of the Reconstruction process from the executive branch to the legislature. In mid-1866, they overrode the president's vetoes of the Civil Rights Act and Freedmen's Bureau Act. In addition, Congress drafted the **Fourteenth Amendment,** which prevented states from denying rights and privileges to any U.S. citizen, now defined as "all persons born or naturalized in the United States." This definition was expressly intended to overrule and nullify the *Dred Scott* decision.

**Vocabulary**
**amnesty:** a general pardon by a government, usually for political offenses

*A. Answer*
**Lincoln and Johnson:** favored a lenient approach to Southerners. **Radicals:** wanted to punish the South severely and wanted to grant African Americans civil rights, including voting rights.

**MAIN IDEA**

**Contrasting**
Ⓐ How did the views of Presidents Lincoln and Johnson on Reconstruction differ from the views of the Radical Republicans?

Mini-Lesson 2:
SS11 4(8.17.B)

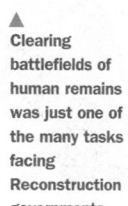

▲
**Clearing battlefields of human remains was just one of the many tasks facing Reconstruction governments.**

**More About . . .**

**Johnson and Presidential Succession**
Andrew Johnson, a Tennessee Democrat and a states' rights advocate, was selected to be Lincoln's running mate in the 1864 election as a way to broaden the base of the Republican Party. Less than six weeks after his inauguration as vice president, Johnson succeeded to the presidency. His tenure was marked by constant conflict with Radical Republicans in Congress, whose views on the treatment of the defeated South differed sharply from his. After leaving office, he again served in the U.S. Senate.

**Tracing Themes**
**CIVIL RIGHTS**

Despite the constitutional guarantees of the Fourteenth Amendment, African Americans were denied their civil rights for almost a century. It required new civil rights legislation in the 1960s and 1970s and Supreme Court decisions such as the ruling in *Brown* v. *Board of Education* in 1954, to guarantee full civil rights to African Americans. Though its guarantees were delayed the Fourteenth Amendment did serve as the legal basis for civil rights legislation and the Supreme Court decisions.

---

**ACTIVITY** | **LINK TO GOVERNMENT**

 **BLOCK SCHEDULING**

**Comparing Reconstruction Plans**

**Class Time** 30 minutes

**Task** Comparing and contrasting the Reconstruction plans of Lincoln, Johnson, and Congress

**Purpose** To understand the different approaches to reconstruction of the South after the Civil War

**Directions** Ask students to study the three Reconstruction plans. Have them keep in mind that each plan offered a vision of how the South would be reintegrated into the Union. Have students use a graphic organizer of their choice to compare and contrast the plans.

📄 Integrated Assessment
· Rubric 2

## More About . . .

### The Impeachment of President Johnson

Johnson's trial before the Senate began in March 1868 and lasted until May 26, 1868. Until the final moment, no one could predict the outcome. When the last senator declared, "Not guilty," the vote was 35 to 19, one short of the two-thirds majority needed to convict the president. The last not-guilty vote was cast by a young first-term Kansas Republican, Edmund Ross. Ross may have preserved constitutional government by his vote, but he was shunned by his party and eventually forced out of politics.

## Tracing Themes

### VOTING RIGHTS

The Fifteenth Amendment was aimed not only at the South. African-American men could not vote in 16 states. One Radical Republican wrote, "We have no moral right to impose an obligation on one part of the land which the rest will not accept." Despite the passage of the Amendment it was poorly enforced and it wasn't until the 1965 Voting Rights Act that some of the intentions of the Amendment were actually realized.

 Humanities Transparencies HT12
· The Fifteenth Amendment

## Instruct: Objective ❷

### Reconstructing Society

TAKS SS11 3(US21.A)
· What groups were in conflict in the South?
· How did former slaves improve their lives?
· What role did African Americans play in Reconstruction?
· How did sharecropping limit the prospects of African Americans?

 In-Depth Resources: Unit 1
· Guided Reading, p. 109

In the 1866 elections, moderate and radical Republicans gained control of Congress. They joined together to pass the Reconstruction Act of 1867, which did not recognize state governments formed under the Lincoln and Johnson plans.

The act divided the former Confederate states into five military districts. The states were required to grant African-American men the vote and to ratify the Fourteenth Amendment in order to reenter the Union. When Johnson vetoed the Reconstruction legislation, Congress promptly overrode the veto. **B**

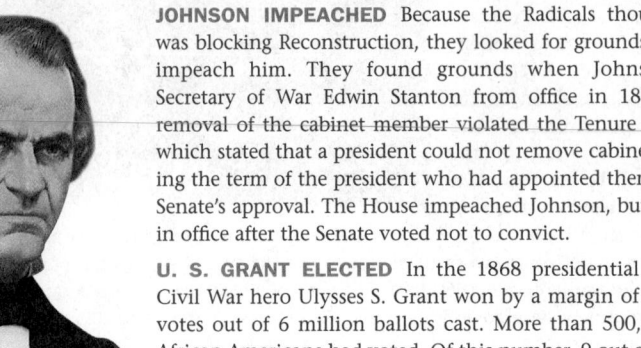

*"I say, as to the leaders, punishment."*

**ANDREW JOHNSON**

**JOHNSON IMPEACHED** Because the Radicals thought Johnson was blocking Reconstruction, they looked for grounds on which to impeach him. They found grounds when Johnson removed Secretary of War Edwin Stanton from office in 1868. Johnson's removal of the cabinet member violated the Tenure of Office Act, which stated that a president could not remove cabinet officers during the term of the president who had appointed them without the Senate's approval. The House impeached Johnson, but he remained in office after the Senate voted not to convict.

**U. S. GRANT ELECTED** In the 1868 presidential election, the Civil War hero Ulysses S. Grant won by a margin of only 300,000 votes out of 6 million ballots cast. More than 500,000 Southern African Americans had voted. Of this number, 9 out of 10 voted for Grant. The importance of the African-American vote to the Republican Party was obvious.

After the election, the Radicals introduced the **Fifteenth Amendment**, which states that no one can be kept from voting because of "race, color, or previous condition of servitude." The Fifteenth Amendment, which was ratified by the states in 1870, was an important victory for the Radicals. **C**

## ❷ Reconstructing Society

Under the congressional Reconstruction program, state constitutional conventions met and Southern voters elected new, Republican-dominated governments. By 1870, all of the former Confederate states had completed the process. However, even after all the states were back in the Union, the Republicans did not end the process of Reconstruction because they wanted to make economic changes in the South.

**CONDITIONS IN THE POSTWAR SOUTH** The war had devastated the South economically. Southern planters returned home to find that the value of their property had plummeted. Throughout the South, many small farms were ruined. The region's population was also devastated. Hundreds of thousands of Southern men had died in the war. The Republican governments began public works programs to repair the physical damage and to provide social services.

**POLITICS IN THE POSTWAR SOUTH** Another difficulty facing the new Republican governments was that the three groups that constituted the Republican Party in the South—scalawags, carpetbaggers, and African Americans—often had conflicting goals.

**Scalawags** were white Southerners who joined the Republican Party. Many were small farmers who wanted to improve their economic position and did not want the former wealthy planters to regain power. **Carpetbaggers** were Northerners who moved to the South after the war. This negative name came from the misconception that they arrived with so few belongings that they carried everything in small traveling bags made of carpeting.

**MAIN IDEA**

Analyzing Effects

**B** How did the election of 1866 affect the process of Reconstruction?

**B. Answer** Republicans gained control of Congress; they passed the Reconstruction Act of 1867, which required the states to grant the vote to African-American men.

**MAIN IDEA**

Making Inferences

**C** Why was the African-American vote so important to the Republicans?

**C. Answer** Republicans needed the African-American vote in order to have a voice in the South.

**186** CHAPTER 4 *The Union in Peril*

## ACTIVITY  SKILLBUILDER LESSON

### Making Generalizations

**Explaining the Skill** To make generalizations means to make broad judgments based on information. Generalizations are based on several pieces of information that support a statement that incorporates all the ideas.

**Applying the Skill** Sudy the information under the heading **Reconstructing Society**. Think about what aspects of society were changed or reconstructed. Use the topic sentences and the subheads to help you. (governments, Southern economy, lives of former slaves) Now create a sentence that covers the ideas you noted, for example: Reconstruction involved changes in the government, the economy, and the lives of the people of the South.

 In-Depth Resources: Unit 1
· Skillbuilder Practice: Forming Generalizations, p. 113

## Analyzing *Political Cartoons*

### UNWELCOME GUEST

Of all the political cartoonists of the 19th century, Thomas Nast (1840–1902) had the greatest and most long-lasting influence. Nast created or popularized symbols that have become part of America's visual heritage, symbols that include the Democratic donkey, the Republican elephant, Uncle Sam, and Santa Claus.

This cartoon from a Southern Democratic newspaper depicts Carl Schurz, a liberal Republican who advocated legal equality for African Americans. Schurz is shown as a carpetbagger trudging down a dusty Southern road as a crowd of people watch his arrival.

**SKILLBUILDER** Analyzing Political Cartoons

1. Is Schurz shown in a positive or negative light? How can you tell?
2. Why do you think the cartoonist chose to place the crowd of onlookers at such a great distance from Schurz?

📁 **SEE SKILLBUILDER HANDBOOK, PAGE R24.**

a carpet bag

## Analyzing *Political Cartoons*

**SKILLBUILDER ANSWERS**

1. Schurz is shown in a negative light; he is depicted as a grim and intense intruder. His clenched fist may express greed.
2. The people of the South stand together, unable to prevent the carpetbagger's arrival.

## More About . . .

### Suffrage, African Americans, and Reconstruction

The key to the success of Reconstruction was guaranteeing suffrage to African Americans. Only through suffrage would they have a voice in society after federal troops left the South. The collapse of Reconstruction was the result of governments in Southern states being able to deny to African Americans suffrage and equal social standing before the law.

The third and largest group of Southern Republicans—African Americans—gained voting rights as a result of the Fifteenth Amendment. During Reconstruction, African-American men registered to vote for the first time; nine out of ten of them supported the Republican Party. Although many former slaves could neither read nor write and were politically inexperienced, they were eager to exercise their voting rights.

**A PERSONAL VOICE** WILLIAM BEVERLY NASH

"We are not prepared for this suffrage. But we can learn. Give a man tools and let him commence to use them and in time he will earn a trade. So it is with voting. We may not understand it at the start, but in time we shall learn to do our duty."

—quoted in *The Trouble They Seen: Black People Tell the Story of Reconstruction*

The differing goals of scalawags, carpetbaggers, and African Americans led to a lack of unity in the Republican Party. In particular, few scalawags shared the Republican commitment to civil rights for African Americans.

The new status of African Americans required fundamental changes in the attitudes of most Southern whites. However, many white Southerners refused to accept blacks' new status and resisted the idea of equal rights. **D**

**FORMER SLAVES IMPROVE THEIR LIVES** Before the Civil War, African Americans had been denied full membership in many churches. During Reconstruction African Americans founded their own churches, which often became the center of the African American community, and the only institutions that African Americans fully controlled. Many African American ministers emerged as influential community leaders who also played an important role in the broader political life of the country.

With 95% of former slaves illiterate, former slaves required education to become economically self-sufficient. In most of the Southern states, the first public school systems were established by the Reconstruction governments. The new African American churches, aided by missionaries from Northern churches and by $6 million from the Freedmen's Bureau, worked to create and run these and other

**D. Answer**
Scalawags: wanted to prevent wealthy planters from regaining power. Carpetbaggers: saw an opportunity to gain power; supported equal rights. African Americans: wanted civil rights.

**MAIN IDEA**

**Contrasting**
**D** Why did scalawags, carpetbaggers, and African Americans support the Radicals?

## More About . . .

### The Freedmen's Bureau

The Freedmen's Bureau was the agency charged with supervising all relief and improvement efforts for freed slaves. It was run by the War Department in Washington, D.C., and staffed with military officers. Because of its centralized records, it has proved to be a treasure trove for historians attempting to put a human face on life in the South after the war.

👁 Electronic Library of Primary Sources
· *from* An Interview with a Former Slave by Annie Ruth Davis

---

### Researching African-American Colleges

**Class Time** 45 minutes

**Task** Researching the origins and history of African-American colleges and universities

**Purpose** To better understand the educational efforts of Reconstruction and the history of African Americans

**Directions** Have small groups of students use library or Internet resources to research the history of such African-American colleges and universities as Alcorn State University, Fisk University, Howard University, and Hampton Institute. Most were founded during Reconstruction. Ask students to compile relevant information, such as founding date, location, size, the origin of its name, and educational programs offered today. Have students create a classroom display of the information.

## KEY PLAYER

### Hiram Revels

Revels spent his two years in the Senate trying to maintain a balance between the interests of African Americans and white Southerners. He then left politics and was appointed president of Alcorn University, near Lorman, Mississippi.

## More About . . .

### African Americans in Reconstruction

During Reconstruction African-American churches played an important role in helping former slaves expand their economic opportunities. With support from Reconstruction governments, churches throughout the South not only helped to establish and run new schools, they also served as schools for their communities, using their influence to promote education and to provide a safe location in which teaching and learning could take place. Due in large part to the efforts of churches and religious organizations, African Americans would eventually gain access to the education they would need to pursue employment as teachers, civil servants, law enforcement officials, lawyers, and doctors—careers that had usually been well beyond their reach in the decades following the Civil War.

## Instruct: Objective ❸

### The Collapse of Reconstruction
TAKS SS11 5(US24.B)

· Why was the Ku Klux Klan opposed to Reconstruction?
· How did the Panic of 1873 affect Reconstruction?
· How did the election of 1876 affect Reconstruction?

 In-Depth Resources: Unit 1
· Guided Reading, p. 109
· Primary Source: An Inquiry on the Condition of the South, p. 123

### KEY PLAYER

THE FIRST COLORED SENATOR AND REPRESENTATIVES.

**HIRAM REVELS**
**1822–1901**

Hiram Revels of Mississippi, pictured above on the far left, was born of free parents in Fayetteville, North Carolina. Because he could not obtain an education in the South, he attended Knox College in Illinois. As an African Methodist Episcopal minister, he recruited African Americans to fight for the Union during the Civil War and also served as an army chaplain.

In 1865, Revels settled in Mississippi, where he helped organize African-American schools and churches. He served on the Natchez city council and then was elected to Mississippi's state senate in 1869. In 1870, Revels became the first African American elected to the U.S. Senate. Ironically, he held the seat that had once belonged to Jefferson Davis, the former president of the Confederacy.

schools. Atlanta, Fisk, and Howard Universities, for instance, were all founded by religious groups such as the American Missionary Association.

Thousands of African Americans also took advantage of their new freedom by migrating to reunite with family members or to find jobs in Southern towns and cities.

**AFRICAN AMERICANS IN RECONSTRUCTION** After the war, African Americans took an active role in the political process. Not only did they vote, but for the first time they held office in local, state, and federal government.

Nevertheless, even though there were more black citizens than white citizens in the South, African-American officeholders remained in the minority. Out of 125 Southerners elected to the U.S. Congress during congressional Reconstruction, only 16 were African Americans. Among these was **Hiram Revels**, the first African-American senator. African Americans also served in political offices on the state and local levels. **E**

In January 1865, General Sherman had promised the former slaves who followed his army 40 acres per family and the use of army mules. For the most part, however, former slaves received no land. Most Republicans considered private property a basic American right, and thus refused to help redistribute it. As a result, many plantation owners in the South retained their land.

**SHARECROPPING AND TENANT FARMING** Without their own land, freed African Americans could not grow crops to sell or to use to feed their families. Therefore, economic necessity forced many former slaves to become sharecroppers. In the system of **sharecropping**, landowners divided their land and assigned each head of household a few acres, along with seed and tools. Sharecroppers kept a small share of their crops and gave the rest to the landowners. In reality, the sharecropping system differed little from the slave plantation. ❸

## The Collapse of Reconstruction

Most white Southerners swallowed whatever resentment they felt over African-American suffrage and participation in government. Some whites expressed their feelings by refusing to register to vote. Others, however, were frustrated by their loss of political power and by the South's economic stagnation. These were the people who formed vigilante groups and used violence to intimidate African Americans.

**OPPOSITION TO RECONSTRUCTION** The most notorious and widespread of the Southern vigilante groups was the **Ku Klux Klan (KKK).** The Klan's goals were to destroy the Republican Party, to throw out the Reconstruction governments, to aid the planter class, and to prevent African Americans from exercising their political rights. To achieve these goals, the Klan and other groups killed perhaps 20,000 men, women, and children. In addition to violence, some white Southerners refused to hire or do business with African Americans who voted Republican.

To curtail Klan violence and Democratic intimidation, Congress passed a series of Enforcement Acts in 1870 and 1871. One act provided for the federal

**188** CHAPTER 4 *The Union in Peril*

### MAIN IDEA

**Forming Generalizations**
**E** How did Southern African Americans respond to their new status?

*E. Answer* African Americans took an active role in the political process, voting and holding office in local, state, and federal government.

**Vocabulary**
**vigilante:** one who takes law enforcement into one's own hands

---

 **ACTIVITY**   **LINK TO ECONOMICS**                                **classzone.com**

### Analyzing Sharecropping and Tenant Farming

**Class Time** 45 minutes

**Task** Analyzing the practice and economics of sharecropping and tenant farming

**Purpose** To understand how sharecropping and tenant farming kept African Americans in poverty

**Directions** Have students use library and Internet resources to research the practice and economics of sharecropping and tenant farming. Ask students to analyze how these farming practices kept African Americans from escaping the cycle of poverty. Have students suggest what possible reforms could have been enacted under Reconstruction that would have helped African Americans economically.

supervision of elections in Southern states. Another act gave the president the power to use federal troops in areas where the Klan was active.

Although Congress seemed to shore up Republican power with the Enforcement Acts, it soon passed legislation that severely weakened the power of the Republican Party in the South. In May 1872, Congress passed the Amnesty Act, which returned the right to vote and the right to hold federal and state offices to about 150,000 former Confederates. In the same year Congress allowed the Freedmen's Bureau to expire. These actions allowed Southern Democrats to regain political power. **F**

**SUPPORT FOR RECONSTRUCTION FADES** Eventually, support for Reconstruction weakened. The breakdown of Republican unity made it even harder for the Radicals to continue to impose their Reconstruction plan on the South. In addition, a series of bank failures known as the panic of 1873 triggered a five-year depression, which diverted attention in the North away from the South's problems. The Supreme Court also began to undo some of the social and political changes that the Radicals had made. Although political violence continued in the South and African Americans were denied civil and political rights, Republicans slowly retreated from the policies of Reconstruction.

**DEMOCRATS "REDEEM" THE SOUTH** As the Republicans' hold on the South loosened, Southern Democrats began to regain control of the region. As a result of "redemption"—as the Democrats called their return to power—and a political deal made during the national election of 1876, congressional Reconstruction came to an end.

In the election of 1876, Democratic candidate Samuel J. Tilden won the popular vote, but was one vote short of the electoral victory. Southern Democrats in Congress agreed to accept Hayes if federal troops were withdrawn from the South. After Republican leaders agreed to the demands, Hayes was elected, and Reconstruction ended in the South.

Reconstruction ended without much real progress in the battle against discrimination. However, the Thirteenth, Fourteenth, and Fifteenth Amendments remained part of the Constitution. In the 20th century, these amendments provided the necessary constitutional foundation for important civil rights legislation.

### Sidebar (left margin)

**MAIN IDEA**

**Summarizing**
**F** How did Southern Democrats regain political power?

*F. Answer* In 1872, Congress passed the Amnesty Act, which returned the right to vote and the right to hold federal and state offices to former Confederates.

**Background**
The Twelfth Amendment (1804) gives the House of Representatives the power to elect the president if no candidate has a majority of electoral votes.

### Sidebar (right)

**Disputed Elections**
The disputed election of 2000 brought the election of 1876 back into the historical spotlight. In 1876, Tilden had won 184 electoral votes, lacking only one for a majority and a victory in the election. But three Southern states and Oregon reported two different sets of results. Congress appointed a 15-member electoral commission to award the votes. The commission—8 Republicans and 7 Democrats—voted along party lines, giving all the votes to Hayes

## Assess & Reteach

**SECTION 4 ASSESSMENT**
Have students answer the questions. Then have them discuss and compare their answers with the class.

 Formal Assessment
· Section Quiz, p. 82

**SELF-ASSESSMENT**
To document what they have learned, ask students to list insights that they have gained regarding the changes in the South after the Civil War.

**RETEACH**
Have students review the Reconstruction plans of Lincoln, Johnson, and Congress.

 In-Depth Resources: Unit 1
· Reteaching Activity, p.117

---

 **ASSESSMENT**

**1. TERMS & NAMES** For each term or name, write a sentence explaining its significance.

- Freedmen's Bureau
- Reconstruction
- Radical Republicans
- Andrew Johnson
- Fourteenth Amendment
- Fifteenth Amendment
- scalawag
- carpetbagger
- Hiram Revels
- sharecropping
- Ku Klux Klan (KKK)

**MAIN IDEA**

**2. TAKING NOTES**
Use a table like the one below to list five problems facing the South after the Civil War. Then describe the solution that was attempted for each problem.

| Problem | Attempted Solution |
|---------|-------------------|
| 1. | |
| 2. | |
| 3. | |
| 4. | |
| 5. | |

**CRITICAL THINKING**

**3. DRAWING CONCLUSIONS**
Do you think that Reconstruction had positive effects on Southern society? Why or why not?
**Think About:**
- the formation of the Ku Klux Klan
- the establishment of African American churches and schools
- why so many African Americans turned to sharecropping

**4. SUMMARIZING**
How did the Radical Republicans hope to reconstruct the South?

**5. ANALYZING PRIMARY SOURCES**
This humorous ticket was printed around the time of the Hayes-Tilden presidential election. What does it tell you about popular attitudes toward the candidates?

TILDEN. HAYES.
OF THE TWO EVILS
CHOOSE THE LEAST.

---

Answers **ASSESSMENT**

**1. TERMS & NAMES**
Freedmen's Bureau, p. 184
Reconstruction, p. 184
Radicals, p. 185
Andrew Johnson, p. 185
Fourteenth Amendment, p. 185
Fifteenth Amendment, p. 186
scalawag, p. 186
carpetbagger, p. 186
Hiram Revels, p. 188
sharecropping, p. 188
Ku Klux Klan, p. 188

**2. TAKING NOTES**
1. Reuniting North and South—congressional Reconstruction.
2. Physical devastation of the South—public works programs.  3. Former slaves need assistance—Freedmen's Bureau established.  4. Former slaves need land—40 acres and a mule plan.
5. Vigilante groups arise—Enforcement Acts.

**3. DRAWING CONCLUSIONS**
Some students may say that Reconstruction had positive effects because it led to the establishment of African-American churches and schools, which in turn led to greater economic opportunity. Other students may say that Reconstruction had negative effects because it led to the rise of the Ku Klux Klan and forced African Americans to become sharecroppers.

**4. SUMMARIZING**
The Radical Republicans wanted to destroy the political power of former slaveholders. They also wanted African Americans to be given full citizenship, including the right to vote.

**5. ANALYZING PRIMARY SOURCES**
People did not think that the candidates were very different from each other and did not like either one.

## TERMS & NAMES

## MAIN IDEAS

1. The Compromise of 1850 allowed California to be admitted to the Union as a free state and also proposed a new and more effective fugitive-slave law.

2. Free-Soilers, antislavery Whigs and Democrats, nativists, and some radical abolitionists

3. North—blockade Southern ports; split the Confederacy; capture Richmond. South—prevent a Union invasion

4. African Americans fought for the Union; women served as nurses on both sides.

5. The Union strategy of total war, as shown in Sherman's March to the Sea, helped destroy morale.

6. The economy of the Northern states boomed; the Southern economy was devastated.

7. The Radicals thought that Johnson was obstructing their Reconstruction efforts.

8. They traveled to find jobs; organized schools, colleges, and churches; and participated in the political process.

9. Some regained power through coercion and terror, others through the compromise over the election of 1876.

REVIEW
# CHAPTER 4 ASSESSMENT

## VISUAL SUMMARY

## THE UNION IN PERIL

### 1840s AND 1850s

Tensions between Northern and Southern states intensify over the issues of slavery and Congressional representation. Violence erupts in new territories and states.

### 1861–1865 CIVIL WAR

Civil War leads to the deaths of hundreds of thousands, the destruction of towns and cities, and the collapse of the Southern economy.

### 1865–1877

During Reconstruction, the victorious North forces Southern states back into the Union. Congress attempts to rebuild the South and extend civil rights to African Americans. However, Southern Democrats regain control in the South and bring about an end to Reconstruction.

## TERMS & NAMES

For each term or name below, write a sentence explaining its significance to the Civil War and Reconstruction.

1. Underground Railroad
2. Harriet Beecher Stowe
3. Dred Scott
4. Bull Run
5. Emancipation Proclamation
6. Clara Barton
7. Gettysburg
8. William Tecumseh Sherman
9. Fifteenth Amendment
10. Ku Klux Klan

## MAIN IDEAS

Use your notes and the information in the chapter to answer the following questions.

**The Divisive Politics of Slavery** (pages 156–165)
1. What was the Compromise of 1850?
2. Who supported the Republican Party that was formed in 1854?

**The Civil War Begins** (pages 168–174)
3. What were the military strategies of the North and the South at the onset of the Civil War?
4. What role did African Americans and women play in the Civil War?

**The North Takes Charge** (pages 175–183)
5. Which Northern tactic helped destroy morale in the South after the defeats at Gettysburg and Vicksburg?
6. What effect did the war have on the economies of the North and the South?

**Reconstruction and Its Effects** (pages 184–189)
7. Why did the Radicals want to impeach Andrew Johnson?
8. In what ways did emancipated slaves exercise their freedom?
9. How did Southern whites regain political power during Reconstruction?

## CRITICAL THINKING

1. **USING YOUR NOTES** In a chart like the one shown, list the results and the significance of the national elections of 1856, 1860, 1866, 1868, and 1876.

| Election Year | Results | Significance |
|---|---|---|
| 1856 | | |
| 1860 | | |
| 1866 | | |
| 1868 | | |
| 1876 | | |

2. **DEVELOPING HISTORICAL PERSPECTIVE** How close did African Americans come to gaining full civil rights during Reconstruction? Explain your answer.

3. **INTERPRETING MAPS** Look at the maps on pages 170–171. What was the most important river in the Union's tactic of splitting the Confederacy in two? What city became essential to this goal after the fall of New Orleans?

## CRITICAL THINKING

1. **USING YOUR NOTES** 1856—Buchanan wins; Buchanan's victory averts the threat of secession. 1860—Lincoln wins; Lincoln's victory provokes Southern states to secede from the Union. 1866—Republicans win large majority; Congress able to override presidential vetoes. 1868—Grant wins; shows importance of African-American votes. 1876—Hayes wins; leads to the end of Reconstruction in the South

2. **DEVELOPING HISTORICAL PERSPECTIVE** During Reconstruction, African-American men voted and held office in local, state, and federal government. However, Ku Klux Klan violence and political intimidation denied African Americans their civil and political rights.

3. **INTERPRETING MAPS** The Mississippi River; Vicksburg

## Standardized Test Practice

Use the information in the passage and your knowledge of U.S. history to answer questions 1 and 2.

> "In these days, men have learned the art of sinning expertly and genteely, so as not to shock the eyes and sense of respectable society. Human property is high in the market; and is, therefore, well fed, well cleaned, tended, and looked after, that it may come to sale sleek, strong, and shining."
>
> —Harriet Beecher Stowe, *Uncle Tom's Cabin*

1. In the mid-19th century, Harriet Beecher Stowe was a leader in the struggle for —

   A abolition.
   B women's rights.
   C better working conditions.
   D tax-supported public schools.

2. *Uncle Tom's Cabin* was written in response to —

   F the raid on Harpers Ferry.
   G the Lincoln-Douglas debates.
   H the Fugitive Slave Act.
   J the *Dred Scott* decision.

3. Grant's siege of Vicksburg was part of the Union's strategy to —

   A destroy Southern morale.
   B blockade Southern ports.
   C split the Confederacy in two.
   D capture the Confederate capital.

4. In the Reconstruction Act of 1867, Congress set requirements for readmission of former Confederate states into the Union. Which of the following problems did the act address?

   F Southern states did not allow African Americans to vote.
   G Southern states had little money to pay for public works projects.
   H Former slaves needed education.
   J Confederate bonds and money were worthless.

**ADDITIONAL TEST PRACTICE, pages S1–S33.**

 **TEST PRACTICE CLASSZONE.COM**

## Standardized Test Practice

1. The correct answer is letter **A.**
   Letters B, C, and D are not correct because Harriet Beecher Stowe confined her protest efforts to abolition.
2. The correct answer is letter **H.**
   Letters F, G, and J are incorrect because these events happened after the book was published in 1852—Dred Scott decision (1857), Lincoln-Douglas debates (1858), Harpers Ferry raid (1859).
3. The correct answer is letter **C.**
   Letters A, B, and D are incorrect, even though all three were also goals of Union forces.
4. The correct answer is letter **F.**
   Letters G, H, and J are incorrect, because the act was limited only to African-American male suffrage.

## LETTER TO THE EDITOR
**Tips for Teaching**
· Suggest students print out a copy of their letter to the editor
· Have students exchange letters for peer feedback

**Rubrics**
The letter to the editor should . . .
· clearly express a point of view on an issue significant to either side in the War for Independence or the Civil War
· include supporting details and facts that shed light on writer's argument
· conclude with a concise recap to end the letter

## ALTERNATIVE ASSESSMENT

1. **INTERACT WITH HISTORY** Recall your discussion of the question on page 155:

   ### How can the Union be saved?

   Suppose you are a British tourist traveling through the United States in 1860. Write a letter to your friends at home describing the political climate in America. Give your opinion about the possibility of saving the Union.

2. **VIDEO LEARNING FROM MEDIA** View the *American Stories* videos "War Outside My Window" and "Teacher of a Freed People." Discuss the following questions in a group; then do the activity.

   • What is your overall impression of Mary Chesnut?
   • What, if anything, surprised you about her diary entries?
   • Which experiences in Fitzgerald's life helped foster his passion for learning and teaching?
   • How did Fitzgerald respond to the difficulties he faced?

   **Cooperative Learning Activity** Imagine that Mary Chesnut and Robert Fitzgerald met to discuss their beliefs. As a group, write a dialogue that might have taken place between the two. Take turns role-playing the pair to establish their personalities and clarify their ideas.

**REVIEW UNIT 191**

## ALTERNATIVE ASSESSMENT

### 1. INTERACT WITH HISTORY
**Rubric**
The letter should . . .
· Clearly describe the political climate in the United States in 1860
· State an opinion about the possibility of saving the Union
· Follows the rules of spelling, punctuation, and grammar along with proper paragraph usage

### 2. LEARNING FROM MEDIA
**Rubric**
The dialogue should . . .
· Accurately portray each personality and ideas they may hold
· Reflect the differences in the attitudes of the defeated Southerner and the newly freed African American
· Capture the audience's attention with an interesting and lively presentation

## OBJECTIVES

**1** Analyze the impact of diverse cultures on American life.

**2** Explain how migration and immigration shaped the early United States.

**3** Describe changing U.S. roles in world affairs between 1792 and 1877.

**4** Summarize the expansion of voting rights to include more members of society.

**5** Trace the conflict over the relative power of state and national governments.

**6** Identify the changes in women's roles between 1792 and 1877.

**7** Determine how science and technology affected American life in the 1800s.

**8** Analyze the civil rights issues that emerged during the Civil War and Reconstruction.

**9** Describe the changes in the American economy in the 19th century.

### CRITICAL THINKING

· Drawing Conclusions, pp. 192, 194
· Forming Generalizations, p. 193
· Developing Historical Perspective, p. 194
· Identifying Problems, p. 195
· Comparing and Contrasting, p. 195
· Analyzing Effects, pp. 196, 197
· Analyzing Issues, p. 196

## Focus & Motivate

After reviewing the themes on pp. 192–197, ask students which of these themes they think played the most important role in American history up to 1877. Then ask which of the themes they think might play the most important role in the 20th century.

# The Changing American Dream:
## *Beginnings Through Reconstruction*

$\mathscr{F}$or two centuries, the American Dream has been the hope that helped America become a great nation. It was the Puritans' desire to find religious freedom and tolerance. It was the patriots' wish to found a new republic that guaranteed the rights of its citizens. It was the reformers' goal of a just society. And it was the guiding beacon for all those who have struggled to make a better life for their families and their compatriots.

To help you make sense of the formative years of the American republic and of the developing American Dream, the next six pages provide a review that is organized around the nine historical themes that are woven into *The Americans*. This Thematic Review will help you focus on the major issues that had emerged in American history by the end of Reconstruction in 1877.

The mission system played a vital role in the development of the Southwest.

### DIVERSITY AND THE NATIONAL IDENTITY   **1**

The United States developed a diverse population, but through continual contact, the diverse groups developed many commonalities. For centuries, Native American groups had followed many different ways of life, each suited to a particular environment. While adopting some aspects of European culture, they passed on parts of their own culture. English settlers did not respect Native American culture, but adopted many native terms and agricultural practices. In the Spanish colonies, settlers and native peoples interacted closely.

As settlers brought different cultures to different regions, continued contact led to the blending of cultures. Nevertheless, the diversity of the populations and the unequal status of the different cultures caused tension. Dutch New Amsterdam and Quaker Pennsylvania showed more tolerance of religious differences than Puritan New England did. German and Scots-Irish immigrants settled from New Netherlands to as far south as the Carolinas. The Southwest and California reflected the culture of the Spanish settlers and the cowboy.

Over time, the Northern and Southern regions of the United States developed distinct cultures. A key feature of Southern culture was slavery. While forced to adapt to slave status in Southern culture, African Americans maintained as best they could their traditions of family relations, dance, music, and crafts. These in turn helped shape Southern culture as Southerners adopted the ways of their captives.

| MAIN IDEA |
|---|

**Drawing Conclusions**

**A** What impact did the different cultures in North America have on the United States?

---

## THEMATIC REVIEW RESOURCES

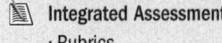 In-Depth Resources: Unit 1
· Thematic Review of Unit 1, p. 138

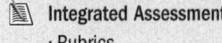 Access for Students Acquiring English/ESL
· Thematic Review of Unit 1, p. 74

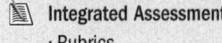 Formal Assessment
· Thematic Review of Unit 1, pp. 101–102

 Integrated Assessment
· Rubrics

**INTEGRATED TECHNOLOGY**

(i) classzone.com

Immigrants arrive in New York harbor in the mid-1800s.

## IMMIGRATION AND MIGRATION

The movement of people has played an important role in shaping American history. Most anthropologists believe that humans began migrating to the Americas about 40,000 years ago, crossing a land bridge that connected Asia to Alaska. Over the centuries, these people spread throughout North and South America.

In 1492, Columbus completed his first voyage to this New World. People from several countries soon started colonies there. The English settled along the Atlantic Coast, in Jamestown (1607), Plymouth Colony (1620), and Massachusetts Bay Colony (1630). The Dutch settled in New Amsterdam (now New York) in 1625. The French established a settlement to the north, in Quebec City.

The Spanish built a fort at St. Augustine, on the Florida coast, and established a capital in the Southwest at Santa Fe, New Mexico. A number of Spanish missions arose in New Mexico and in California.

After centuries of isolation, Native Americans had no defenses against European diseases. They died by the thousands, making it more difficult for them to resist European expansion. Another group that suffered terribly from immigration were the millions of Africans who were forcibly brought to the colonies as enslaved people.

After the colonies won their independence from England, the United States continued to attract new immigrants. Groups already settled in the United States did not always welcome newcomers. But the stream of immigrants—primarily Irish and Germans—continued. By the 1840s, many of these immigrants joined native-born Americans moving west. They drove their long wagon trains as far as the Pacific Coast, where they met thousands of Chinese immigrants who had come to California to work on railroads and in the mines. Americans had spread from coast to coast.

### MAIN IDEA
**Forming Generalizations**

**B** In what ways did immigration and migration shape the early United States?

---

## Instruct

### Instruct: Objective
**Diversity and the National Identity**
TAKS SS11 3(US21.A)
· Which groups arrived in North America to settle and work the land?
· Why were Native American cultures and societies displaced?
· Why did different regions within the United States develop different cultures?

### Main Idea

**Answer**
A. Native Americans—adaptations to various environments; Europeans—law, customs, tolerance of religious differences, Spanish language and customs; Africans—dance, music, crafts

### Instruct: Objective
**Immigration and Migration**
TAKS SS11 2(US10)
· When did people begin arriving on the North American continent?
· In which geographic regions did the immigrants settle?
· What changes took place with the arrival of European settlers?

### Main Idea

**Answer**
B. Immigration and migration settled the country, led to cultural diversity, and the growth of large cities.

---

**ACTIVITY**  **COOPERATIVE LEARNING**                              classzone.com

### Exhibiting Immigrant Experiences

**Class Time** Two class periods

**Task** Preparing a multimedia exhibit on immigrant experiences in America

**Purpose** To analyze immigrant experiences in their new home

**Directions** Divide students into small groups. Have each group select an immigrant group or a theme, such as the voyage to America or finding a home there. Then students should search the Internet or other research materials to locate information on their group or theme topic. The report should include, photos, diary entries, government documents, or artifacts. The information should be organized into a multimedia presentation. Have each group present their work to the class.

 Integrated Assessment
· Rubrics 1, 6

*Thematic Review*  **193**

## Instruct

### Instruct: Objective

**America in World Affairs**
TAKS SS11 1(US3)
· Which European nations competed for territory in North America?
· What is the meaning of the concept of "manifest destiny?"
· How did the United States establish itself on the world stage?

### Main Idea

**Answer**
C. the country's growing confidence and assertiveness on the world stage

### Instruct: Objective

**Voting Rights**
TAKS SS11 1(US3)
· Which groups of individuals won the right to vote between the founding of the country and 1877?
· Which groups failed to gain voting rights or had them taken away?

### Main Idea

**Answer**
D. The Constitution established democratic institutions that protected citizens rights, and voting rights were expanded.

The French Revolution was partly inspired by the colonists' revolt against the British in North America.

## AMERICA IN WORLD AFFAIRS

The European settlement of North America began as part of a contest for empire. The British pushed the Dutch out of what is now New York. Then, in 1763, they drove the French from North America. Just 15 years later, though, the British colonies rebelled. The French and Spanish helped them win their independence by supplying money, soldiers, and ships.

England, France, and Spain still held much of the continent, but that changed in the next few decades. First, France sold the United States the Louisiana Territory, doubling the nation's size. Soon, though, conflict with Native Americans and anger over British actions led to the War of 1812, which brought no clear victory but did produce a surge of nationalist feeling. Treaties with Britain and Spain added additional territories.

More confident, the United States began to flex its muscles. With the Monroe Doctrine, the United States warned European powers to stay out of the Western Hemisphere.

After the United States began to act on the idea of "manifest destiny," or the belief that the country should expand to the Pacific coast, Americans in Texas proclaimed a new republic, removing that region from Mexican control. Soon the United States annexed Texas, which led to the War with Mexico. After a swift victory by U.S. forces, the Treaty of Guadalupe Hidalgo gave California and the Southwest to the United States.

In summary, international relations in the nation's early years were marked by two major achievements: establishment of the United States on the world stage and expansion of its territory.

**MAIN IDEA**

**Drawing Conclusions**

**C** What was the most important change in the United States' involvement in foreign affairs from 1789 to 1877?

## VOTING RIGHTS ④

The years up to 1877 were critical to the establishment of a stable constitutional democracy in the United States. The Constitution and the Bill of Rights were ratified. The important democratic institutions—Congress, the Presidency, the Supreme Court, and political parties—were firmly established.

During the 1800s, the right to vote was gradually broadened to include more members of society. In the 1820s, state governments enlarged the voter base by easing voter requirements, such as property qualifications. These new voters were critical to the election of Andrew Jackson in 1828 and 1832.

While growing numbers of white males had won the right to vote, women were still denied that right. Elizabeth Cady Stanton led other women to push for this right and other reforms to give women equal status with men. Their efforts were often met with scorn.

Democratic rights were extended to African Americans after the Civil War, when the Fifteenth Amendment gave them the right to vote. Within a few years, though, Southern states instituted harsh new laws against blacks, called black codes. When courts upheld these laws, African Americans lost their rights. Northerners, tired of decades of conflict over slavery and its aftermath, turned their attention away from the status of former slaves and toward other matters.

**MAIN IDEA**

**Developing Historical Perspective**

**D** In the period from 1789 until 1877, what were the signs that the United States had developed a stable constitutional democracy?

---

**DIFFERENTIATING INSTRUCTION**  **GIFTED AND TALENTED STUDENTS**

### Monroe Doctrine

**Class Time** 45 minutes

**Task** Preparing a report on success of the Monroe Doctrine

**Purpose** To evaluate the impact of the Monroe Doctrine on the role of America in world affairs

**Directions** Have small groups of students prepare a written report evaluating the role of the Monroe Doctrine in placing the United States on the world stage. They should determine why the doctrine was issued and then find out when the principles of the doctrine were applied to justify actions of the United States, especially in the Western Hemisphere. Encourage students to trace the use of the doctrine's principles through the 20th century.

 Integrated Assessment
· Rubrics 1, 5

## STATES' RIGHTS 5

By the 1770s, the feeling had grown that the colonists' rights would not be secure so long as they remained subject to Great Britain. They fought the Revolutionary War to win their independence.

When the nation's leaders set out to construct a framework for the new government, their first attempt, the Articles of Confederation, leaned too heavily toward protecting states' independence. When a new Constitution was proposed, several leaders expressed alarm at the strong central government that would be created. Only with the promise of passing several amendments that guaranteed individual freedoms—the Bill of Rights—did the framers win approval of the Constitution.

Questions about the relative power of state and national governments still remained. South Carolina threatened to nullify, or disallow, a federal law in the 1830s, but the crisis was defused. The issue of slavery, though, threatened to tear the Union apart. The Civil War was the greatest constitutional crisis the country faced. The war settled the matter of secession, but the balance between states' rights and federal power continued to be an important constitutional issue.

Major Robert Anderson observes the defense of Fort Sumter. South Carolina asserted its right to secede by firing on Fort Sumter, starting the Civil War.

**MAIN IDEA**

**Identifying Problems**

**E** What difficulties arose from assertions of states' rights against the United States between 1789 and 1877? How were these issues resolved?

## WOMEN AND POLITICAL POWER 6

Beginning in colonial times, women in America confronted many limits, including lack of suffrage. Laws in some colonies prohibited them from owning property. Laws in others said that only single women or widows could run their own businesses.

During the American Revolution, women expanded their roles by filling in for their husbands on the farms and in the shops and, occasionally, taking up arms. In the new nation, however, the concept of republican motherhood emphasized the role of women in preparing the next generation of citizens.

In the early 1800s, many women became more socially active. Reformers such as Elizabeth Cady Stanton and Lucretia Mott pushed for women's rights. Others, like Harriet Beecher Stowe and Sojourner Truth, spoke out against slavery. Women worked to advance the temperance movement against alcohol and to improve health and education.

Women endured much during the Civil War, whether they lived in the North or the South. Many gained strength by meeting new demands placed on them. With hundreds of thousands of men serving in armies and out of the work force, women filled the void by serving as laborers in farms and factories.

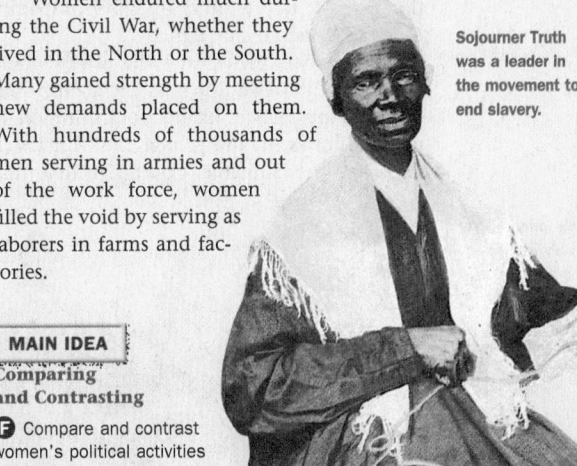

Sojourner Truth was a leader in the movement to end slavery.

**MAIN IDEA**

**Comparing and Contrasting**

**F** Compare and contrast women's political activities in the United States in the mid-19th century with those in the Colonial era.

REVIEW UNIT **195**

### Instruct: Objective 5

**States' Rights**

TAKS SS11 4(8.18.B)

· Why did the U.S. Constitution replace the Articles of Confederation?

· How did the issue of slavery produce a debate over the power of the federal government versus state governments that culminated in the Civil War?

**Main Idea**

**Answer**

E. Questions about the right of nullification and about slavery arose and were resolved by the Civil War.

### Instruct: Objective 6

**Women and Political Power**

TAKS SS11 3(US21.D)

· Why did women face limits as early as colonial times?

· Why did women become active in social reform movements in the 1800s?

· How did women meet the new demands placed on them during the Civil War?

**Main Idea**

**Answer**

F. In the 1800s, women expanded their roles by being active in many reform movements. But women still had no official political role because they did not have the vote.

### Slavery and States Rights

**Task** Debating the issue of states rights

**Purpose** To evaluate the positions for and against strong states rights

**Directions** Divide the class into small groups. Within each group, divide into two sides. One side will represent those who view states' rights as more important than federal rights. The other will argue for federal power over the states. Next have them do research to determine the best arguments for and against strong states' rights. After preparing a case, combine several groups and have them debate the issue.

## Instruct: Objective ⑦

### Science and Technology

TAKS SS11 3(US23)

· What were the effects of improved transportation and communication?

· How did the new inventions of the 1800s produce wide-ranging economic and social effects?

## Main Idea

### Answer

G. Sewing machine—made clothing cheaper, but also of good quality; cotton gin—increased importance of slavery; railroads—improved mobility, boosted factories.

## Instruct: Objective ⑧

### Civil Rights

TAKS SS11 4(US7.A)

· Why did the Southern states maintain and expand the institution of slavery?

· How important was the Supreme Court's ruling in the Dred Scott case that slaves were property?

· Why did the legal rights granted by the Civil War amendments not give African Americans complete equality?

## Main Idea

### Answer

H. The 13th, 14th, and 15th Amendments banned slavery and extended citizenship and voting rights. However, Reconstruction was unable to prevent a return to power of those in the South who would undermine legal protections.

"OUR FIELD IS THE WORLD."

LIGHT DRAFT. SUPERIOR DESIGN.
CLEAN AND RAPID CUTTER.

McCormick Harvesting Machine Co., Chicago.
ESTABLISHED 1831.

Inventions such as McCormick's reaper increased the productivity of laborers.

## SCIENCE AND TECHNOLOGY ⑦

During the 1800s, the United States established itself as highly innovative and quick to find commercial applications for technological advances. For instance, the cotton gin—invented by a Northerner, Eli Whitney—speeded up the processing of cotton and spurred a cotton boom. The boom in cotton led, in turn, to the renewed growth of slavery.

The cotton was shipped to the North, where in the mid-19th century entrepreneurs built new factories that turned it into cloth. New shoemaking and sewing machines sped up clothing manufacture. These changes affected Northern society. Skilled artisans gave way to factory workers skilled in the techniques of mass production. Feeling powerless compared with the factory owners, workers tried to organize labor unions.

As the nation expanded, inventors created new technologies that improved transportation and communication. Pioneers traveled over roads and trails to reach the frontier. The Erie Canal brought food from the Midwest to the ports of the east, helping to make New York City a major commercial center. Steamboats sped up and down rivers, increasing trade. Railroads linked cities. With the completion of the transcontinental railroad in 1869, rails stretched from sea to sea. Telegraph lines allowed people to send messages instantly over vast distances.

**MAIN IDEA**
Analyzing Effects

G What was one innovation that affected how Americans worked and lived? What were the effects of this innovation?

## CIVIL RIGHTS ⑧

Racism, labor shortages, and the establishment of plantation agriculture had led to the entrenchment of slavery in the South during the early 19th century. As slaves, African-Americans had no civil rights.

Southerners feared that the North would increase its power in Congress and abolish slavery. They pushed to extend the institution to new territories. In the pivotal 1857 *Dred Scott* decision, the Supreme Court declared that slaves were not people, but property, and thus had no rights. Less than ten years later, the North and South fought a bloody civil war.

The Civil War amendments ended slavery (Thirteenth Amendment), recognized African Americans as citizens (Fourteenth Amendment), and banned the denial of voting rights on the basis of race or color (Fifteenth Amendment). African Americans briefly enjoyed full civil rights, but the Supreme Court undermined legal protections. After Southern Democrats regained political power and enacted black codes, Reconstruction ended, leaving African Americans again without civil rights. In the 1950s and the 1960s, however, the Civil War amendments would become powerful tools in the quest for equal rights.

This former slave family welcomed the passage of the Thirteenth Amendment, which abolished slavery.

**MAIN IDEA**
Analyzing Issues

H What were the successes and failures of the Civil War and Reconstruction in extending civil rights to African Americans?

196  THEMATIC REVIEW

## DIFFERENTIATING INSTRUCTION    LESS PROFICIENT READERS

### Organizing Information

Some students may have difficulty understanding the effects of an invention such as the cotton gin. Draw the following organizer on the board and help students fill in the missing information.

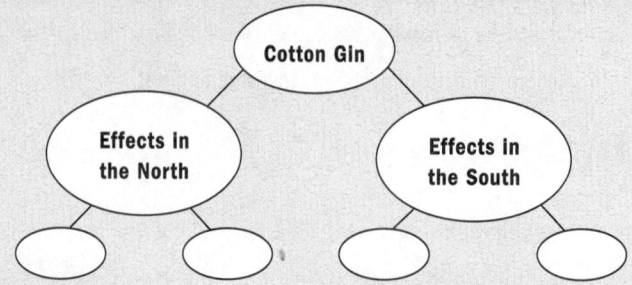

Cotton Gin

Effects in the North

Effects in the South

During the California gold rush of 1849, tens of thousands of people gave up their old lives to go west in hopes of striking it rich.

## ECONOMIC OPPORTUNITY

Europeans were first attracted to the New World by the promise of wealth. Seeing the vast riches that the Spanish had won in conquering native empires, other European nations scrambled to begin their own colonies. Early settlements were created by companies of investors hoping to strike it rich in the new land. The lure of the land and the hope of economic success continued to fuel immigration to the United States—and the movement of people within the country.

Regional differences developed in the American economy during the colonial period. The North focused on farming and some industry. New transportation routes, such as the Erie Canal, brought increased trade among Northern states. As the Industrial Revolution took hold in the early 1800s, factories sprung up throughout the Northern states and farming declined. After this, the rich farmlands of the Midwest became the breadbasket of the nation. The Civil War accelerated economic growth in the North and Midwest. Industry boomed. Farm output grew as well.

A plantation economy geared to raising cash crops for export arose early in the South. At first, planters grew tobacco, rice, and indigo. Beginning in the 1800s, the main crop was cotton. Cotton was called "king," and a small group of large landowners dominated the Southern economy and society. They became wealthy and powerful by exploiting the labor of masses of enslaved African Americans.

With the end of the Civil War, enslaved persons gained their freedom and finally had a chance for economic opportunity. The Congress decided not to redistribute the land, however. Though legally free, many blacks became economically controlled by landowners—mostly whites—through tenant farming or sharecropping.

**MAIN IDEA**
Analyzing Effects

 What was one important economic development in the United States between the colonial period and 1877? How did this development affect the everyday lives of Americans?

---

## Instruct: Objective  9
### Economic Opportunity
TAKS SS11 3(US22.C)
· How did the lure of economic success help fuel immigration and migration?
· Why did the Civil War accelerate industrial growth in the North and not the South?
· Why did many freed African Americans remain economically dependent as a result of the sharecropping system?

### Main Idea
**Answer**
I. Industrial Revolution—movement from farms to factories; movement to Midwest—wealthier farms; growth of cotton—increased use of slave labor; emancipation of slaves—rise of sharecropping

## Assess & Reteach

### THEMATIC REVIEW ASSESSMENT
Have students form small groups to discuss the Main Idea questions.

 Formal Assessment
· Thematic Review of Unit 1, pp. 101–102

### SELF-ASSESSMENT
Ask students to choose a theme and create an essay question about it. Then have students trade questions with a partner and write responses.

### RETEACH
Use the Thematic Review activities to explore the nine themes of American history to 1877.

In-Depth Resources: Unit 1
· Thematic Review, p. 138

 classzone.com

---

**ACTIVITY**  **LINK TO ECONOMICS**

### Understanding Taxes

**Task** Creating a chart to illustrate the differences and effects of various types of taxes

**Purpose** To compare the effects of different types of taxes on the consumer

**Directions** Explain to students that the issue of taxes was a integral part of the early history of the United States. Have students determine the difference between direct and indirect taxes and how they affect the consumer. Next have them find out the differences between sales tax, income tax, and property tax. Finally, they should create an illustrated chart or poster to explain information they have researched.

## Previewing the Unit

Unit 2 describes how the United States transforms itself from a mostly rural, agricultural society to an urban, industrial one. Farmers, miners, and ranchers settle all regions of the West, costing Native Americans their land. Large businesses begin to dominate the economy. Providing much of the labor for these huge new concerns are millions of immigrants who stream to the major cities of the North and East. New manufacturing and selling techniques begin to create mass consumer markets for goods and services.

**UNIT PROJECT**

### HISTORICAL INQUIRY: ORAL REPORT

Use this project to teach students how to research, interpret, and use multiple sources.

#### Researching Multiple Sources

Tell students that historians need to use multiple sources of information to ensure that their information is complete and reliable. Ask what types of materials might provide historical information. *(history books and periodicals, historical [old] books and periodicals, government documents, personal letters, artifacts, and others) Ask where they might find historical sources. (school library, public library, Internet, museum)*

#### Interpreting Multiple Sources

Ask students why they ought not to believe everything they read. *(Most writers do not know the truth, or the whole truth; some have an interest in distorting the truth.)*

*(continued on next page)*

---

## UNIT 2

# Bridge to the 20th Century 1877–1917

**UNIT PROJECT**

### Oral Report

This unit describes how the United States transformed itself from a rural, agricultural society to an urban, industrial one. Prepare an oral report that summarizes one or more of the factors that caused this change. Create visuals to accompany your report.

*Champions of the Mississippi* by Currier and Ives

---

## More About the Image

**1** Paddlewheel boats worked best in water that was not subject to storms or high waves. They moved along large and small rivers, canals, and a few moved in coastal waters. They were the most successful where there were few roads or railways.

**2** Sidewheelers had the engine placed in the center of the boat. Sternwheelers had the engines at the rear or stern of the boat. Most were built with two or three decks to carry passengers or freight.

**3** Paddlewheel boats were a transition between early craft and metal ships that would be used later. The hull was between three and eight feet deep with a squared off stern and a pointed bow. There were no watertight bulkheads to protect the boat. If the hull was damaged, the ship sank.

Review with students the lessons in the Skillbuilder Handbook on pages R2–R29. Remind students to use these reading and critical thinking skills as they review their sources.

### Using Multiple Sources

Instruct students to review their notes and prepare an outline of the ideas they wish to use in their reports. This will help them to focus their topics and to determine which information to include. They should organize their information topically, not according to its source.

### Rubrics

An Oral Report should . . .
· have a clear focus and organization
· include and synthesize information from several sources
· include important and interesting details about the selected topic

## HISTORY from VISUALS

### Interpreting the Painting

Currier and Ives prints allowed Americans to see color images of life in many parts of America. The prints allowed people to learn about their country and the people and activities in it. Ask students what might be learned about American life from this print. *(Huge sidewheel paddleboats moved people on the Mississippi.)* Ask students why it was important to move goods and people on the Mississippi. *(The movement allowed growth and settlement of the interior of the country)*

**Extension** The heyday of steamboats in the United States was between 1820 and 1880. Have students do research to find out how much cargo and how many passengers moved along the Mississippi on steamboats during that time period.

**4** Notice the piles of wood stacked on the main deck. Because of the heat from the engines the main deck was very hot and only people who could not afford full fare would ride there.

**5** The *Queen of the West* was actually the name of a sidewheeler out of Cincinnati. It was, however, not like the one pictured here. It was a side-wheel towboat that was converted to a ram in 1862 by Union forces. She was used in the Battle of Memphis in 1862 and even engaged an ironclad—the CSS *Arkansas*. The *Queen of the West* captured four Confederate steamers and eventually was captured herself by Confederate forces. She was repaired and served as a Confederate warship before being sunk by Union forces.

# Changes on the Western Frontier

| | CHAPTER OVERVIEW | COPYMASTERS | INTEGRATED TECHNOLOGY |
|---|---|---|---|
| **CHAPTER RESOURCES** | *In the late 1800s, growing numbers of white settlers move to the West, and Native Americans lose their lands. Railroads cross the nation, and both the cattle kingdom and Populism rise and fall* | Telescoping the Times · Chapter Summary, pp. 9–10  Planning for Block Schedules | American Stories · A Walk in Two Worlds  Power Presentations  Electronic Teacher Tools  Online Lesson Planner  classzone.com |
| **SECTION 1** Cultures Clash on the Prairie pp. 202–213 | **KEY IDEAS** *Pursuit of economic opportunity leads settlers to push westward. Settlers confront established Native American cultures. With the help of cowboys, the cattle industry thrives as the Native American culture of Great Plains declines. About 1890 the frontier is closed.* | In-Depth Resources: Unit 2 · Guided Reading, p. 1 · Building Vocabulary, p. 4 · Skillbuilder Practice, p. 6 · Reteaching Activity, p. 7 · Primary Source, p. 12 · American Lives, p. 18  Lesson Plans, pp. 45–46 | Humanities Transparencies HT13 · Sierra Nevada Mountains  Electronic Library of Primary Sources · On the Use of English in Indian Schools · from *The Log of a Cowboy*  classzone.com |
| **SECTION 2** Settling on the Great Plains pp. 214–218 | *The promise of cheap, fertile land draws thousands of settlers westward to seek their fortunes as farmers. Settlers face extreme hardships in taming the land.* | In-Depth Resources: Unit 2 · Guided Reading, p. 2 · Reteaching Activity, p. 8 · Geography Application, pp. 10–11 · Primary Sources, p. 13 · Literature, pp. 15–17  Lesson Plans, pp. 47–48 | Geography Transparencies GT13 · Railroad Land Grants, 1871  Critical Thinking Transparencies CT13, CT47 · Transcontinental Railroad · Population Changes in the West, 1850–1900  Electronic Library of Primary Sources · *Letters of a Homesteader*  classzone.com |
| **SECTION 3** Farmers and the Populist Movement pp. 219–223 | *Farmers band together to address their economic problems giving rise to the Populist movement. Economic troubles lead to clashes over silver or gold as the basis of the monetary system.* | In-Depth Resources: Unit 2 · Guided Reading, p. 3 · Skillbuilder Practice, p. 5 · Reteaching Activity, p. 9 · Primary Sources, p. 14 · American Lives, p. 19  Lesson Plans, pp. 49–50 | classzone.com |

| | | | |
|---|---|---|---|
| PE | Pupil's Edition | | |

**Legend (top):**
- PE Pupil's Edition
- TE Teacher's Edition
- Copymaster
- Overhead Transparency
- Audio Library
- CD-ROM
- Internet

## ASSESSMENT OPTIONS

- PE Chapter Assessment, pp. 226–227
- Formal Assessment
  · Chapter Tests, Forms A, B, and C, pp. 106–117
- Test Generator
- Integrated Assessment Book
- TAKS Online Test Practice
- TAKS Spiraled Content Review
- TAKS Practice Tests

- PE Section 1 Assessment, p. 211
- TE Self-Assessment, p. 211
- Formal Assessment, Quiz, p. 103
- Integrated Assessment Book
- Test Generator
- TAKS Practice Transparencies TT49

- PE Section 2 Assessment, p. 218
- TE Self-Assessment, p. 218
- Formal Assessment, Quiz, p. 104
- Integrated Assessment Book
- Test Generator
- TAKS Practice Transparencies TT50

- PE Section 3 Assessment, p. 223
- TE Self-Assessment, p. 223
- Formal Assessment, Quiz, p. 105
- Integrated Assessment Book
- Test Generator
- TAKS Practice Transparencies TT51

## RESOURCES FOR DIFFERENTIATING INSTRUCTION

### Students Acquiring English/ESL

- **Reading Study Guide** (English and Spanish) pp. 57–64
- **Access for Students Acquiring English/ESL:** Spanish Translations, pp. 75–83
- **Chapter Summaries on CD** (English and Spanish)

### Less Proficient Readers

- **Reading Study Guide** (English and Spanish) pp. 57–64
- **Telescoping the Times** · Chapter Summary, pp. 9–10
- **Chapter Summaries on CD** (English and Spanish)

### Gifted and Talented Students

- **In-Depth Resources: Unit 2** · Primary Sources, pp. 12–14 · American Lives: Chief Joseph, p. 18; Mary Elizabeth Lease, p. 19
- **Electronic Library of Primary Sources** · Unit 2, Chapter 5

## CROSS-CURRICULAR CONNECTIONS

### Economics
Harvey, Brett. *Farmers and Ranchers.* NY: Holt, 1995. Part of a well-documented series describing how people worked in the West.

### Primary Sources
Brown, Dee. *Bury My Heart at Wounded Knee: An Indian History of the American West.* NY: Holt, 1993. A poignant and illuminating collection of original documents.

### Popular Culture
Wilson, R.L. with Greg Martin. *Buffalo Bill's Wild West: An American Legend.* NY: Random House, 1998. Illustrated with photographs and posters.

### Literature
Cather, Willa. *O Pioneers!* NY: Penguin, 1994. Story of the hardships and suffering of a daughter of Swedish immigrants on the prairie.

Rolvaag, Ole Edvart. *Giants in the Earth.* NY: HarperCollins, 1991. Heroic tales of Norwegian settlers in the plains of South Dakota.

### McDougal Littell *The Language of Literature* American Literature
· Black Elk, told through John G. Neihardt, " High Horse's Courting," from *Black Elks Speaks*
· Chief Joseph, "I Will Fight No More Forever"
· Elinore Pruitt Steart, from *Letters of a Woman Homesteader*

### McDougal Littell *Literature Connections*

Willa Cather
*My Antonia*
A novel about a woman on the Nebraska prairie. Cather writes about the land and characters she remembers from her childhood.

## ENRICHMENT ACTIVITIES

- PE **Pupil's Edition,** pp. 200–227
  Interact With History, pp. 200–201
  Daily Life, pp. 212–213
  Science & Technology, pp. 217–218
  American Literature, pp. 224–225
- **In-Depth Resources: Unit 2**
  · Geography Application: The Regions of the West, pp. 10–11
  · Primary Source: The Battle of Little Bighorn, p. 12

· Primary Source: Letter from a Woman Homesteader, p. 13
· Primary Source: Cross of Gold Speech, p. 14
· Literature Selection from *My Antonia* by Willa Cather, pp. 15–17
· American Lives: Chief Joseph, p. 18
· American Lives: Mary Elizabeth Lease, p. 19
- **Electronic Library of Primary Sources**
  · Unit 2, Chapter 5

## BLOCK SCHEDULE LESSON PLAN OPTIONS (90-MINUTE PERIOD)

### DAY 1

**CHAPTER 5 OPENER**
pp. 200–201

**Class Time** 15 minutes

*Options for Pacing and Variety*

- **History from Visuals**, p. 200
  **Class Time** 15 minutes

- **Humanities Transparencies** Have students look at the picture on page 200 and Humanities Transparency 13: *Among the Sierra Nevada Mountains* for an idea of the beauty and richness of the West. Contrast how white settlers and Native Americans might view this environment.
  **Class Time** 15 minutes

**Interact with History**, p. 201

**Class Time** 15 minutes

*Options for Pacing and Variety*

- **Role-Playing** Have each student write a first-person paragraph or two on what he or she would expect to find on settling in the West, taking into account the Examine the Issues questions.
  **Class Time** 15 minutes

**SECTION 1**, pp. 202–213

**Class Time** 30 minutes

*Options for Pacing and Variety*

- **Geography Transparencies** See page 205 and the Geography Skillbuilder questions in the TE. Also, use Geography Transparency 38 with its two overlays for a visual demonstration of the land lost by Native Americans.
  **Class Time** 15 minutes

### DAY 1 continued

- **Time Saver** Ask students to read the spread features on gold mining, pp. 212–213, and discuss the questions on PE and TE page 213.
  **Class Time** 15 minutes

**SECTION 2**, pp. 214–218

**Class Time** 30 minutes

*Options for Pacing and Variety*

- **Time Saver** Have students make a bubble chart like the one on TE page 215, detailing the land offered by the government and the use people made of it.
  **Class Time** 10 minutes

- **Peer Teaching** Have students work in pairs and read A Personal Voice on page 216 about the role of the West in shaping the national character of America. Ask them to discuss and write down whether they feel this is a correct statement, or if they think the point is overemphasized. They can refute the argument by giving examples of the way other regions and forces had a lasting affect on American character, such as New England, Pennsylvania, and the southern colonies. As a class discuss their arguments.
  **Class Time** 20 minutes

### DAY 2

**SECTION 3**, pp. 219–225

**Class Time** 50 minutes

*Options for Pacing and Variety*

- **Time Saver** Ask students to look at the political cartoon on page 220, and read the sidebar included. Discuss the Skillbuilder questions.
  **Class Time** 10 minutes

- **Peer Teaching** Have students work in groups to complete the Section 3 assessment. Discuss the answers with the groups.
  **Class Time** 20 minutes

- **Internet** Have students read pp. 224–225 on Literature of the West. Then have them use the Internet to find contemporary reactions to Chief Satanta's speech, which was published in many newspapers at the time. Have them search for newspaper editorials on the speech and the situation it discusses, as well as the different reactions across the country. If they cannot find information on this topic, have them search for information on the Medicine Lodge Treaty.
  **Class Time** 25 minutes

### DAY 2 continued

**ASSESSMENT**
pp. 226–227

**Class Time** 40 minutes

*Options for Pacing and Variety*

- **History on Film** View the video *A Walk in Two Worlds: The Education of Zitkala*. Discuss question 2 in the alternative assessment on page 227.
  **Class Time** 25 minutes

- **Peer Evaluation** Have students work in groups and quiz each other on the terms and names in the chapter, and then have them work together on the Critical Thinking questions on page 226.
  **Class Time** 15 minutes

---

**TEACHER-TESTED ACTIVITY**
**COAT OF ARMS**

**Class Time** 30 minutes

**Task** Designing a coat of arms

**Purpose** To create an interpretive symbol of a person or a group associated with the Western frontier

Diane M. Rodgers, Crooksville High School, Crooksville, Ohio

**Supplies Needed**

- Textbook
- Coat-of-arms facsimile
- Construction paper
- Markers
- Ruler

**Activity** Show students an example of a coat of arms or group insignia. Explain that its design is symbolic of the actions and characteristics of the person or group using it. Have students design a coat of arms for an individual, family, or other group discussed in Chapter 5. Tell them that the visual elements in their coat of arms should enable others to identify what the person or group stands for.

## CORRELATION TO THE TEXAS ESSENTIAL KNOWLEDGE AND SKILLS

Chapter 5 addresses the following standards of the Texas Essential Knowledge and Skills for U.S. History.

| TEKS | Instruction | Student Question/Activity |
|---|---|---|
| **(2A)** Analyze political issues such as Indian policies. | **PE 204–208** analysis of nation's Indian policies and the clashes it led to in the West | **TE 204** cooperative activity in which students debate the issue of western settlement from the viewpoints of white settlers and Native Americans |
| **(2B)** Analyze economic issues such as the growth of railroads. | **PE 214–215** examination of how the growth of the railroads helped to promote settlement of the West | **PE 205** question about how railroads helped open the West |
| **(4C)** Evaluate the impact of third parties and their candidates. | **PE 221–223** explanation of the rise and fall of Populism | **TE 221** activity in which students research and report on the outcomes of the Populist Party reforms |
| **(9A)** Analyze the effects of physical geographic factors on major events. | **PE 216–217** discussion of the innovations that helped farmers overcome the physical obstacles of western settlement | **TE 216** research activity in which students find out more about one of the inventions used to help tame the West |
| **(10A)** Analyze the effects of changing demographic patterns resulting from migration within the United States. | **PE 214–216** examination of what groups settled the West and for what reasons | **PE 218** Taking Notes activity about the events that shaped the settling of the West |
| **(20A)** Describe how the characteristics and issues of various eras in U.S. history have been reflected in works of art. | **PE 210** presentation of painting by Frederic Remington, best known for his depictions of western life | **PE 210** question that requires students to interpret the painting |
| **(21A)** Analyze the how contributions of people of various ethnic groups have helped to shape the national identity. | **PE 208–209** explanation of how the American cowboy was influenced by early Spanish ranchers in Mexicos | **PE 209** question about what the cowboy tradition owes to the Mexican vaquero |

## TAKS MINI-LESSONS

1. **Social Studies Skills: Objective 2 (US8.B):** Answer questions about geographic distributions and patterns shown on maps **Activity** Have students answer the Geography Skillbuilder questions regarding the map on page 205.

2. **Social Studies Skills: Objective 2 (US10.A):** Analyze the effects of changing demographic patterns resulting from the migration within the United States **Activity** Have students create a cause-and-effect chart of the settlement of the West.

3. **Social Studies Skills: Objective 2 (WH23.A):** Give examples of technological innovations that occurred in different periods in history and described the changes produced by these innovations **Activity** Have students complete the research activity on TE page 216 regarding the inventions that aided settlement of the West.

4. **English Language Arts Skills: Objective 3 (10.B):** Use elements of text to defend interpretations **Activity** Have students write several paragraphs explaining why the real life a cowboy was less glamorous than their life as portrayed in popular media.

5. **English Language Arts Skills: Objective 3 (19.B):** Analyze ideas as represented in various media **Activity** Have students answer the skillbuilder questions regarding the political cartoon about the plight of farmers (page 220).

# CHAPTER 5

# CHANGES ON THE WESTERN FRONTIER

## HISTORY from VISUALS

**Interpreting the Photograph**
Ask students to study the photograph and to describe the scene in their own words. Then ask why *owning* this land would be so attractive to so many people. *(Owning one's own land offered an opportunity for greater economic freedom and a new start in life.)*

## Time Line Discussion

Explain to students that the time line covers key U.S. and world events during the last 40 years of the 19th century.

· Ask students what year Congress passed the Homestead Act. *(1862)*

· Ask students what position Chester Arthur held before becoming president, based on information in the time line. *(vice president)*

· Ask students to cite an incident on the time line that shows how western expansion affected the Native Americans. *(Western expansion was disastrous for the Native Americans, as evidenced by the massacre at Wounded Knee.)*

Until the 1860s, the migratory Indians of Montana—including the Blackfeet shown here—followed the buffalo herds and traded peacefully with whites in the region.

**1870** Red Cloud, chief of the Oglala Sioux, states his people's case in Washington, D.C.

**1880** James Garfield is elected president.

**1881** Garfield is assassinated. Chester Arthur becomes president.

**1884** Grover Cleveland is elected president.

USA
WORLD

**1870**

**1880**

**1869** Suez Canal is opened.

**1872** Secret ballot is adopted in Britain.

**1881** French occupy Tunisia.

**200** CHAPTER 5

## THEMES IN CHAPTER 5

### DIVERSITY AND NATIONAL IDENTITY

The dreams of Native Americans, white settlers, and immigrants conflicted, and violent confrontation often resulted. Much of this conflict dealt with the use of land. Settlers believed in private property rights, but Native Americans had a different view of land.
**See Teacher's Edition note, p. 203.**

Cowboys were a melting pot of diverse cultures—whites, African Americans, Mexicans, and Native Americans. These diverse groups lived and worked together harmoniously, despite cultural clashes in the society at large.
**See Teacher's Edition note, p. 210.**

### ECONOMIC OPPORTUNITY

A major lure of the frontier was economic opportunity. The government contributed to economic development by financing the building of railroads and making land available to settlers at little or no cost. Economic opportunity was influenced by currency issues and economic panic.
**See Teacher's Edition note, p. 209.**

# INTERACT
## WITH HISTORY

It is the late 1890s. The American West is the last frontier. Ranchers, cowboys, and miners have changed forever the lives of the Native Americans who hunted on the Western plains. Now westward fever intensifies as "boomers" rush to grab "free" farm land with the government's blessing.

## What do you expect to find on settling in the West?

### Examine the Issues

- What might be some ways to make a living on the Western frontier?
- If native peoples already live in your intended home, how will you co-exist?
- How might settlers and Native Americans differ regarding use of the land?

# INTERACT
## WITH HISTORY

### Objectives

· To interest students in the events encompassing the settling of the West
· To help students understand the reasons for settling the frontier and how such settlement affected Native Americans

### Examine the Issues

1. Have students consider what are some of the most important jobs that would accompany the settlement of a wild and unsettled frontier region.
2. Have students think about those aspects of their culture that might keep the Native Americans and white settlers from living together peacefully.
3. Ask students to consider the notion of private property rights and how that concept differs from the view of land held by Native Americans.

 RESEARCH LINKS CLASSZONE.COM

Visit the Chapter 5 links for more information about Changes on the Western Frontier.

---

1889 Oklahoma opened for settlement; the land rush begins.

1890 Sioux are massacred at Wounded Knee.

1893 Diminished U.S. gold reserve triggers the panic of 1893.

1896 William McKinley is elected president.

1896 William Jennings Bryan runs for president.

## 1890

## 1900

1893 France takes over Indochina.

1899 Berlin Conference divides Africa among European nations.

1900 Boxer Rebellion takes place in China.

*Changes on the Western Frontier* **201**

---

## RECOMMENDED RESOURCES

### BOOKS FOR THE TEACHER

Brown, Dee. *Bury My Heart at Wounded Knee.* New York: Holt, 2001. A Native American view of the West.

McMath, Robert C., et al., eds. *American Populism: A Social History, 1877-1898.* Hill-Warp, 1992. In-depth look at the great protest movement that swept rural America.

Ward, Geoffrey C. *The West: An Illustrated History.* New York: Little, 1996.

### BOOKS FOR THE STUDENT

Freeman, Russell. *Cowboys of the Wild West.* Boston: Houghton, 2000.

Peavy, Linda and Ursula Smith. *Pioneer Women: The Lives of Women on the Frontier.* Norman: Oklahoma, 1998.

### VIDEOS

*How the West Was Lost* (3 tapes), *How the West Was Lost II* (4 tapes). Discovery Channel Home Video.

*The West.* 9-part series. Produced by Stephen Ives and Ken Burns. Time-Life Video, 1996.

### SOFTWARE

*500 Nations.* CD-ROM. Microsoft, 800-555-4512.

*The Wild West.* CD-ROM. Educational Software Institute, 800-955-5570.

### INTEGRATED TECHNOLOGY

For teacher support, visit . . .

 classzone.com

# OBJECTIVES

**1** Contrast the cultures of Native Americans and white settlers and explain why white settlers moved west.

**2** Identify restrictions imposed by the government on Native Americans and describe the consequences.

**3** Identify the government's policy of assimilation as well as continuing conflicts between Native Americans and settlers.

**4** Trace the development of the cattle industry.

**5** Describe both the myth and the reality of the American cowboy and explain the end of the open range.

## SKILLBUILDERS

· Geography Skillbuilder: location, movement, p. 205; region, place, p. 209
· Analyzing Visuals, p. 207

## CRITICAL THINKING

· Summarizing, pp. 203, 209
· Analyzing Issues, p. 204
· Analyzing Effects, p. 206
· Analyzing Causes, pp. 208, 211
· Drawing Conclusions, pp. 209, 211
· Comparing, p. 211
· Making Inferences, p. 211

## Focus & Motivate

Have students answer the following questions and save their answers to reexamine after reading the section. What are students' images of cowboys? How have movies and novels influenced those images? How true do students think those images are to the reality of life on the open range?

**SECTION 1**

# Cultures Clash on the Prairie

| MAIN IDEA | WHY IT MATTERS NOW | Terms & Names |
|---|---|---|
| The cattle industry boomed in the late 1800s, as the culture of the Plains Indians declined. | Today, ranchers and Plains Indians work to preserve their cultural traditions. | • Great Plains  • Treaty of Fort Laramie  • Sitting Bull  • George A. Custer  • assimilation |
| | | • Dawes Act  • Battle of Wounded Knee  • longhorn  • Chisholm Trail  • long drive |

**TEKS** U.S. History 2A, 2B, 8A, 8B, 9A, 10A, 11A, 20A, 20B, 20C, 20E, 21A, 21B, 21C, 22A, 22B, 23A, 24A, 24B, 24C, 24D, 24H, 25A, 25B, 25C, 25D

### One American's Story

Zitkala-Ša was born a Sioux in 1876. As she grew up on the Great Plains, she learned the ways of her people. When Zitkala-Ša was eight years old she was sent to a Quaker school in Indiana. Though her mother warned her of the "white men's lies," Zitkala-Ša was not prepared for the loss of dignity and identity she experienced, which was symbolized by the cutting of her hair.

**A PERSONAL VOICE** ZITKALA-ŠA

" I cried aloud . . . and heard them gnaw off one of my thick braids. Then I lost my spirit. Since the day I was taken from my mother I had suffered extreme indignities. . . . And now my long hair was shingled like a coward's! In my anguish I moaned for my mother, but no one came. . . . Now I was only one of many little animals driven by a herder. "

—*The School Days of an Indian Girl*

Zitkala-Ša experienced firsthand the clash of two very different cultures that occurred as ever-growing numbers of white settlers moved onto the Great Plains. In the resulting struggle, the Native American way of life was changed forever.

## 1 The Culture of the Plains Indians

Zitkala-Ša knew very little about the world east of the Mississippi River. Most Easterners knew equally little about the West, picturing a vast desert occupied by savage tribes. That view could not have been more inaccurate. In fact, distinctive and highly developed Native American ways of life existed on the **Great Plains**, the grassland extending through the west-central portion of the United States. (See map on page 205.)

**VIDEO**
*A WALK IN TWO WORLDS*
The Education of Zitkala-Ša, a Sioux

202 CHAPTER 5

---

## PROGRAM RESOURCES

In-Depth Resources: Unit 2
· Guided Reading, p. 1
· Building Vocabulary, p. 4
· Skillbuilder Practice: Creating Models, p. 6
· Reteaching Activity, p. 7
· Primary Sources: The Battle of Little Bighorn, p. 12
· American Lives: Chief Joseph, p. 18

Reading Study Guide (English and Spanish), pp. 57–58

Access for Students Acquiring English/ESL
· Guided Reading (Spanish), p. 77
· Skillbuilder Practice, p. 81

Formal Assessment
· Section Quiz, p. 103

Integrated Assessment
· Rubrics

### INTEGRATED TECHNOLOGY

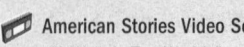American Stories Video Series
· "A Walk in Two Worlds"

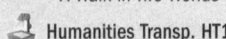Humanities Transp. HT13

Electronic Library of Primary Sources

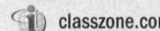classzone.com

### TEXAS RESOURCES

TAKS Spiraled Content Review

TAKS Practice Tests

TAKS Practice Transparencies TT49

TAKS Online Test Practice

**202** CHAPTER 5

To the east, near the lower Missouri River, tribes such as the Osage and Iowa had, for more than a century, hunted and planted crops and settled in small villages. Farther west, nomadic tribes such as the Sioux and Cheyenne gathered wild foods and hunted buffalo. Peoples of the Plains, abiding by tribal law, traded and produced beautifully crafted tools and clothing.

**THE HORSE AND THE BUFFALO** After the Spanish brought horses to New Mexico in 1598, the Native American way of life began to change. As the native peoples acquired horses—and then guns—they were able to travel farther and hunt more efficiently. By the mid-1700s, almost all the tribes on the Great Plains had left their farms to roam the plains and hunt buffalo.

Their increased mobility often led to war when hunters in one tribe trespassed on other tribe's hunting grounds. For the young men of a tribe, taking part in war parties and raids was a way to win prestige. But a Plains warrior gained more honor by "counting coup" than by killing enemies. This practice involved touching a live enemy with a coup stick and escaping unharmed. And sometimes warring tribes would call a truce so that they could trade goods, share news, or enjoy harvest festivals. Native Americans made tepees from buffalo hides and also used the skins for clothing, shoes, and blankets. Buffalo meat was dried into jerky or mixed with berries and fat to make a staple food called pemmican. While the horse gave Native Americans speed and mobility, the buffalo provided many of their basic needs and was central to life on the Plains. (See chart on page 207.) **A**

**FAMILY LIFE** Native Americans on the plains usually lived in small extended family groups with ties to other bands that spoke the same language. Young men trained to become hunters and warriors. The women helped butcher the game and prepared the hides that the men brought back to the camp; young women sometimes chose their own husbands.

The Plains Indian tribes believed that powerful spirits controlled events in the natural world. Men or women who showed particular sensitivity to the spirits became medicine men or women, or shamans. Children learned proper behavior and culture through stories and myths, games, and good examples. Despite their communal way of life, however, no individual was allowed to dominate the group. The leaders of a tribe ruled by counsel rather than by force, and land was held in common for the use of the whole tribe.

### ① Settlers Push Westward

The culture of the white settlers differed in many ways from that of the Native Americans on the plains. Unlike Native Americans, who believed that land could not be owned, the settlers believed that owning land, making a mining claim, or starting a business would give them a stake in the country. They argued that the Native Americans had forfeited their rights to the land because they hadn't settled down to "improve" it. Concluding that the plains were "unsettled," migrants streamed westward along railroad and wagon trails to claim the land.

**Vocabulary**
**coup:** a feat of bravery performed in battle

---

**MAIN IDEA**

**Summarizing**
**A** How did the horse influence Native American life on the Great Plains?

*A. Answer*
The horse gave them increased mobility, extending their hunting territory. But the horse also sometimes promoted greater communication, and sometimes clashes, with other tribes.

---

▲
A portrait of a Sioux man and woman in the late 19th century.

This Yankton Sioux coup stick was used by warriors.
▼

---

## Instruct

### Instruct: Objective ①

**The Culture of the Plains Indians / Settlers Push Westward**
TAKS SS11 2(US10.A)

· What were the characteristics of the Plains Indians culture?
· How did the culture of white settlers differ from that of the Plains Indians?
· Why did settlers continue to push westward?

📖 In-Depth Resources: Unit 2
· Guided Reading, p. 1

---

### Tracing Themes
**DIVERSITY AND NATIONAL IDENTITY**

**Conflicting Dreams**
The dreams of white settlers and immigrants conflicted with those of Native Americans. Both groups wanted to use Western land and its resources, but while Native Americans believed that the land belonged to no one, the settlers advocated private property rights. A possible compromise might have been to set aside lands and resources for Native Americans so they could pursue their way of life. However, when it came to the issue of land, the two groups would choose confrontation and bloodshed over compromise.

**203**

---

**Main Ideas and Supporting Details**

On the board, write the main ideas for subsections "The Horse and the Buffalo" and "Family Life." Have students work in pairs to identify the main ideas of the section and the details that support them. Then compare lists and agree on one statement of main ideas and supporting details.

**The Horse and the Buffalo**

**Main Idea:** Horses changed how Native Americans hunted.

**Detail:** Horses made most Native Americans into buffalo hunters.

**Family Life**

**Main Idea:** Native Americans on the Plains had a strong family life.

**Detail:** Children learned culture and behavior through myths.

## Instruct: Objective ❷

### The Government Restricts Native Americans / Bloody Battles Continue

TAKS SS11 2(US8.B)

· How did the government attempt to deal with the growing conflict between Native Americans and white settlers?

· Why did the Black Hills become a contested territory between Native Americans and whites?

· What were the consequences of the defeat of General Custer's forces?

 In-Depth Resources: Unit 2
· Guided Reading, p. 1
· Primary Sources: The Battle of Little Bighorn, p. 12

### KEY PLAYER

#### Sitting Bull

Eager to shed his childhood nickname—Slow—Sitting Bull proved his quickness and courage by killing a buffalo at age 10. Over the years, he became a much loved and respected leader of his people. Remarked one U.S. military official, "Since the days of Pontiac, Tecumseh, and Red Jacket, no Indian has had the power of drawing to himself so large a following . . . and molding it and wielding it against the authority of the United States." Ask students to describe the attributes suggested by the name Sitting Bull. How might those character traits be useful to a warrior, a tribal leader, and a representative of his people?

---

**THE LURE OF SILVER AND GOLD** The prospect of striking it rich was one powerful attraction of the West. The discovery of gold in Colorado in 1858 drew tens of thousands of miners to the region.

Most mining camps and tiny frontier towns had filthy, ramshackle living quarters. Rows of tents and shacks with dirt "streets" and wooden sidewalks had replaced unspoiled picturesque landscapes. Fortune seekers of every description —including Irish, German, Polish, Chinese, and African-American men—crowded the camps and boomtowns. A few hardy, business-minded women tried their luck too, working as laundresses, freight haulers, or miners. Cities such as Virginia City, Nevada, and Helena, Montana, originated as mining camps on Native American land.

## ❷ The Government Restricts Native Americans

While allowing more settlers to move westward, the arrival of the railroads also influenced the government's policy toward the Native Americans who lived on the plains. In 1834, the federal government had passed an act that designated the entire Great Plains as one enormous reservation, or land set aside for Native American tribes. In the 1850s, however, the government changed its policy and created treaties that defined specific boundaries for each tribe. Most Native Americans spurned the government treaties and continued to hunt on their traditional lands, clashing with settlers and miners—with tragic results. **B**

**MASSACRE AT SAND CREEK** One of the most tragic events occurred in 1864. Most of the Cheyenne, assuming they were under the protection of the U.S. government, had peacefully returned to Colorado's Sand Creek Reserve for the winter. Yet General S. R. Curtis, U.S. Army commander in the West, sent a telegram to militia colonel John Chivington that read, "I want no peace till the Indians suffer more." In response, Chivington and his troops descended on the Cheyenne and Arapaho—about 200 warriors and 500 women and children—camped at Sand Creek. The attack at dawn on November 29, 1864 killed over 150 inhabitants, mostly women and children.

**DEATH ON THE BOZEMAN TRAIL** The Bozeman Trail ran directly through Sioux hunting grounds in the Bighorn Mountains. The Sioux chief, Red Cloud (Mahpiua Luta), had unsuccessfully appealed to the government to end white settlement on the trail. In December 1866, the warrior Crazy Horse ambushed Captain William J. Fetterman and his company at Lodge Trail Ridge. Over 80 soldiers were killed. Native Americans called this fight the Battle of the Hundred Slain. Whites called it the Fetterman Massacre.

Skirmishes continued until the government agreed to close the Bozeman Trail. In return, the **Treaty of Fort Laramie,** in which the Sioux agreed to live on a reservation along the Missouri River, was forced on the leaders of the Sioux in 1868. **Sitting Bull** (Tatanka Iyotanka), leader of the Hunkpapa Sioux, had never signed it. Although the Ogala and Brule Sioux did sign the treaty, they expected to continue using their traditional hunting grounds.

---

### KEY PLAYER

#### SITTING BULL
1831–1890

As a child, Sitting Bull was known as Hunkesni, or Slow; he earned the name Tatanka Iyotanka (Sitting Bull) after a fight with the Crow, a traditional enemy of the Sioux.

Sitting Bull led his people by the strength of his character and purpose. He was a warrior, spiritual leader, and medicine man, and he was determined that whites should leave Sioux territory. His most famous fight was at the Little Bighorn River. About his opponent, George Armstrong Custer, he said, "They tell me I murdered Custer. It is a lie. . . . He was a fool and rode to his death."

After Sitting Bull's surrender to the federal government in 1881, his dislike of whites did not change. He was killed by Native American police at Standing Rock Reservation in December 1890.

---

**MAIN IDEA**

**Analyzing Issues**
**B** What was the government's policy toward Native American land?

**B. Answer** The government wanted to restrict all Native Americans to designated areas.

**Skillbuilder Answers**
1. Little Bighorn, Wounded Knee.
2. 1894—about 90%; 2000—less than 1%.

---

**ACTIVITY** | COOPERATIVE LEARNING  **BLOCK SCHEDULING**

### Cross-Cultural Debate

**Class Time** 30 minutes

**Task** Staging a debate between a white settler and a Native American about settlement of the West

**Purpose** To help students understand the clashes of beliefs and aims that occurred during the settlement of the West

**Directions** Assign small groups of students to represent either the Native Americans' or the settlers' point of view. Groups will prepare statements of their beliefs about settlement, addressing the meaning of the land itself and the methods used in settling it. The groups should present their statements in the form of a debate. Be sure students understand that they are exploring ideas more than they are trying to decide which group is on the right or wrong side of the argument.

 Integrated Assessment
· Rubric 3

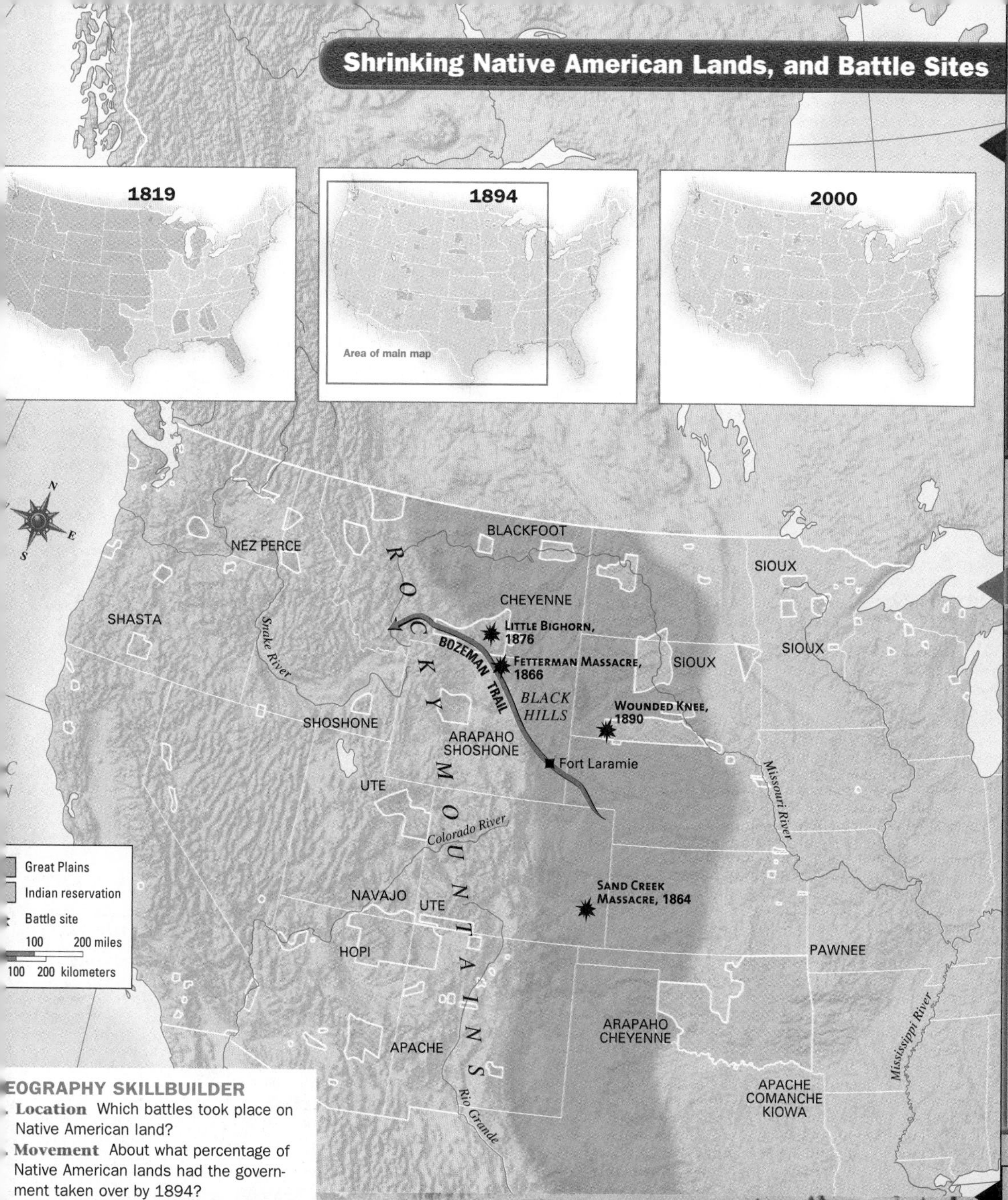

### 1819

### 1894

Area of main map

### 2000

NEZ PERCE

BLACKFOOT

SIOUX

SHASTA

CHEYENNE

R O C K Y

Little Bighorn, 1876

Fetterman Massacre, 1866

SIOUX

SIOUX

*Snake River*

BOZEMAN TRAIL

*BLACK HILLS*

WOUNDED KNEE, 1890

SHOSHONE

ARAPAHO SHOSHONE

● Fort Laramie

*Missouri River*

UTE

M O U N T A I N S

*Colorado River*

Great Plains

Indian reservation

Battle site

100        200 miles

100   200 kilometers

NAVAJO    UTE

SAND CREEK MASSACRE, 1864

HOPI

PAWNEE

APACHE

ARAPAHO CHEYENNE

*Rio Grande*

*Mississippi River*

APACHE COMANCHE KIOWA

### GEOGRAPHY SKILLBUILDER
. **Location** Which battles took place on Native American land?
. **Movement** About what percentage of Native American lands had the government taken over by 1894?

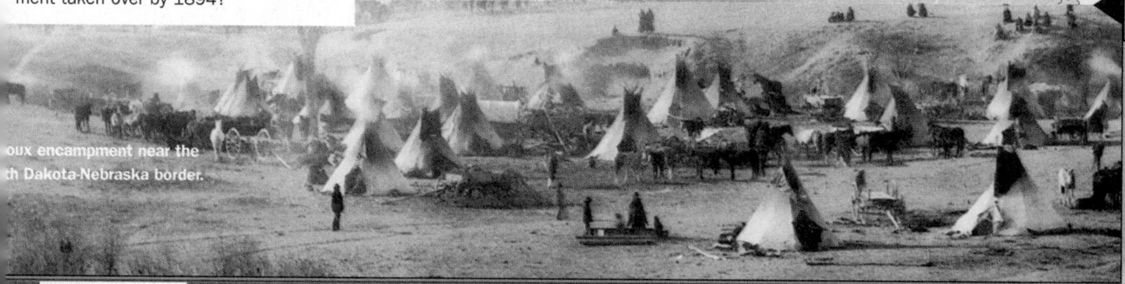

*Sioux encampment near the South Dakota-Nebraska border.*

**George Armstrong Custer**
Lt. Col. Custer (1839-1876) went to the West after a distinguished career in the Civil War. Although he was last in his class at West Point, he became, at age 23, the youngest general in the Union Army. (He was later demoted.)

**The Battle of Little Bighorn**
At Sitting Bull's camp in the valley of the Little Bighorn, about 2,000 Indians had gathered. A Cheyenne woman later said, "There were more Indians . . . than I ever saw anywhere together." Custer's scouts were Crow. The scouts tried to warn Custer of the size of the Indian encampment, but Custer replied, "I guess we'll get through them in one day." When Custer finally saw the size of the Indian village, he told his scouts they could leave.

 In-Depth Resources: Unit 2
· Primary Sources: The Battle of Little Bighorn, p. 12

**Instruct: Objective**

**The Government Supports Assimilation / The Battle of Wounded Knee**
TAKS SS11 5(WH26.C)

· What was the Dawes Act and what goal did it seek to achieve?

· Why was the destruction of the buffalo so detrimental to the Native American way of life?

· What were the causes and consequences of the Battle of Wounded Knee?

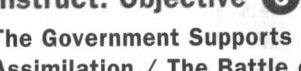 American Stories video series
· "A Walk in Two Worlds"

In-Depth Resources: Electronic Library of Primary Sources
· On the use of English in Indian Schools, 1887

## ② Bloody Battles Continue

The Treaty of Fort Laramie provided only a temporary halt to warfare. The conflict between the two cultures continued as settlers moved westward and Native American nations resisted the restrictions imposed upon them. A Sioux warrior explained why.

### A PERSONAL VOICE GALL, A HUNKPAPA SIOUX

" [We] have been taught to hunt and live on the game. You tell us that we must learn to farm, live in one house, and take on your ways. Suppose the people living beyond the great sea should come and tell you that you must stop farming, and kill your cattle, and take your houses and lands, what would you do? Would you not fight them?"

—quoted in *Bury My Heart at Wounded Knee*

**RED RIVER WAR** In late 1868, war broke out yet again as the Kiowa and Comanche began a six-year raiding spree that finally led to the Red River War of 1874–1875. The U.S. Army responded by herding the people of friendly tribes onto reservations while opening fire on all others. General Philip Sheridan, a Union Army veteran, gave orders "to destroy their villages and ponies, to kill and hang all warriors, and to bring back all women and children." With such tactics, the army crushed resistance on the southern plains.

**GOLD RUSH** Within four years of the Treaty of Fort Laramie, miners began searching the Black Hills for gold. The Sioux, Cheyenne, and Arapaho protested to no avail. In 1874, when Colonel **George A. Custer** reported that the Black Hills had gold "from the grass roots down," a gold rush was on. Red Cloud and Spotted Tail, another Sioux chief, vainly appealed again to government officials in Washington.

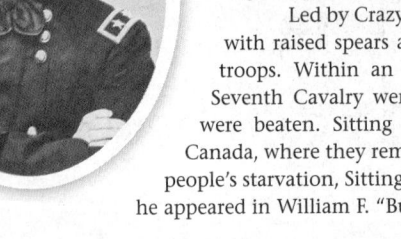

Colonel George Armstrong Custer, 1865
▼

**CUSTER'S LAST STAND** In early June 1876, the Sioux and Cheyenne held a sun dance, during which Sitting Bull had a vision of soldiers and some Native Americans falling from their horses. When Colonel Custer and his troops reached the Little Bighorn River, the Native Americans were ready for them.

Led by Crazy Horse, Gall, and Sitting Bull, the warriors—with raised spears and rifles—outflanked and crushed Custer's troops. Within an hour, Custer and all of the men of the Seventh Cavalry were dead. By late 1876, however, the Sioux were beaten. Sitting Bull and a few followers took refuge in Canada, where they remained until 1881. Eventually, to prevent his people's starvation, Sitting Bull was forced to surrender. Later, in 1885, he appeared in William F. "Buffalo Bill" Cody's Wild West Show. Ⓒ

## ③ The Government Supports Assimilation

The Native Americans still had supporters in the United States, and debate over the treatment of Native Americans continued. The well-known writer Helen Hunt Jackson, for example, exposed the government's many broken promises in her 1881 book *A Century of Dishonor*. At the same time many sympathizers supported **assimilation,** a plan under which Native Americans would give up their beliefs and way of life and become part of the white culture.

**THE DAWES ACT** In 1887, Congress passed the **Dawes Act** aiming to "Americanize" the Native Americans. The Act broke up the reservations and gave some of the reservation land to individual Native Americans—160 acres to each

**MAIN IDEA**

Analyzing Effects
Ⓒ What were the results of Custer's last stand?

*C. Answer* Death of Custer and all his soldiers, continued raids on Native American camps, eventual defeat of the Sioux.

The Winchester '76 rifle used by government troops, and a Sioux war bow.

---

**DIFFERENTIATING INSTRUCTION**  **LESS PROFICIENT READERS**

**Identifying Supporting Details**

Help students choose supporting details as answers to questions. First ask them to rewrite each head and subhead as a question:

**The Government Supports Assimilation:** *How did the government support assimilation?*

**The Dawes Act:** *What was the Dawes Act?*

**The Destruction of the Buffalo:** *How were the buffalo destroyed?* or *Why were the buffalo destroyed?* or *How did the destruction of the buffalo affect assimilation?*

Point out that finding answers to the question will provide them with details that support the main idea.

head of household and 80 acres to each unmarried adult. The government would sell the remainder of the reservations to settlers, and the resulting income would be used by Native Americans to buy farm implements. By 1932, whites had taken about two-thirds of the territory that had been set aside for Native Americans. In the end, the Native Americans received no money from the sale of these lands.

**THE DESTRUCTION OF THE BUFFALO** Perhaps the most significant blow to tribal life on the plains was the destruction of the buffalo. Tourists and fur traders shot buffalo for sport. U.S. General Sheridan noted with approval that buffalo hunters were destroying the Plains Indians' main source of food, clothing, shelter, and fuel. In 1800, approximately 65 million buffalo roamed the plains; by 1890, fewer than 1000 remained. In 1900, the United States sheltered, in Yellowstone National Park, a single wild herd of buffalo.

## ❸ The Battle of Wounded Knee

The Sioux continued to suffer poverty and disease. In desperation, they turned to a Paiute prophet who promised that if the Sioux performed a ritual called the Ghost Dance, Native American lands and way of life would be restored.

The Ghost Dance movement spread rapidly among the 25,000 Sioux on the Dakota reservation. Alarmed military leaders ordered the arrest of Sitting Bull. In December 1890, about 40 Native American police were sent to arrest him. Sitting Bull's friend and bodyguard, Catch-the-Bear, shot one of them. The police then killed Sitting Bull. In the aftermath, Chief Big Foot led the fearful Sioux away.

**WOUNDED KNEE** On December 29, 1890, the Seventh Cavalry—Custer's old regiment—rounded up about 350 starving and freezing Sioux and took them to a camp at Wounded Knee Creek in South Dakota. The soldiers demanded that the Native Americans give up all their weapons. A shot was fired; from which side, it was not clear. The soldiers opened fire with deadly cannon.

### Connections Across Time
**1890 AND 1973**

**Wounded Knee**

In February of 1973, members of the American Indian Movement (AIM), a protest organization that sought greater rights for Native Americans, led a takeover of the town of Wounded Knee. The seizure was prompted in part by anger over the recent stabbing death of young Native American by a white man who was charged only with second-degree manslaughter. AIM members also demanded a review of all Native American treaties and a U.S. Senate investigation into the plight of Native Americans. During the roughly two-month standoff, several shootouts left two Native Americans dead and one federal marshal seriously wounded. Eventually, the protesters surrendered in exchange for a promise of an investigation into Indian grievances.

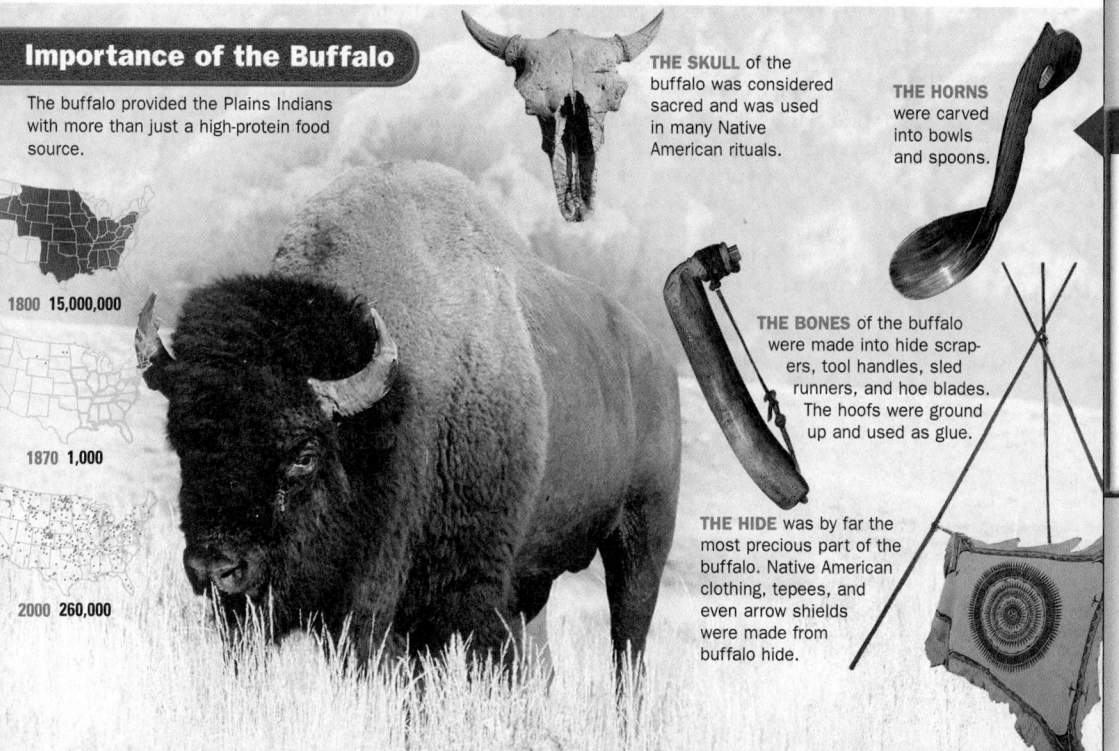

## Importance of the Buffalo

The buffalo provided the Plains Indians with more than just a high-protein food source.

1800 **15,000,000**

1870 **1,000**

2000 **260,000**

**THE SKULL** of the buffalo was considered sacred and was used in many Native American rituals.

**THE HORNS** were carved into bowls and spoons.

**THE BONES** of the buffalo were made into hide scrapers, tool handles, sled runners, and hoe blades. The hoofs were ground up and used as glue.

**THE HIDE** was by far the most precious part of the buffalo. Native American clothing, tepees, and even arrow shields were made from buffalo hide.

### HISTORY from VISUALS

**Reading the Infographic**
Make sure students understand that, in addition to the uses of the buffalo listed at the right, the meat was a major source of food. Also, bring to their attention the similarities between the sequence of the three maps here and the one on page 205.

**Extension** Have students research the policies and programs that enabled the buffalo population to increase between 1865 and 1996.

---

**DIFFERENTIATING INSTRUCTION** GIFTED AND TALENTED

### Creating a Storyboard

Have students choose from Sitting Bull, Red Cloud, or another Native American leader mentioned in this section, and research his life, his efforts to resist white settlement or removal to a reservation, and his treatment by the government. Using this information, have students create a storyboard for a television presentation on the leader. Have students include quotes from and about the leader. A sample storyboard is shown at right.

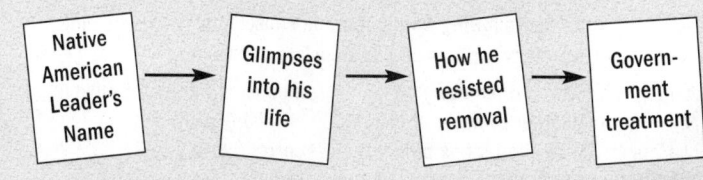

In-Depth Resources: Unit 2
· American Lives: Chief Joseph, p. 18

## NOW & THEN

### Nez Perce in Oregon

**Predicting Outcomes** Have students discuss how the return of the Nez Perce might benefit both the Nez Perce and Wallowa County.

### Instruct: Objective

**Cattle Becomes Big Business**

TAKS SS11 5(WH26.B)

· What influence did Spanish ranchers have on the American cowboy?

· How did the growth of railroads and cities impact the cattle business?

· Where did the Chisholm Trail run?

 In-Depth Resources: Unit 2
· Guided Reading, p. 1

### More About . . .

#### The Cowboy Hat

A cowboy could tell a lot about another cowboy by looking at his hat. If the hat had a wide brim and a high crown, the wearer was from the Southwest, where he needed extra protection from the sun. If the hat had a narrow brim and a low crown, the hat's owner was probably from the northern plains, where it was very windy. A hat did more than cover a cowboy's head, though. It served as a pillow, a bucket to carry water, a fan to start a fire, and a paddle to slap a steer and control a stampede.

---

## NOW & THEN

**NEZ PERCE IN OREGON**

Forced off their tribal lands in Wallowa County, Oregon, in 1877, the Nez Perce are returning almost 120 years later. 1999 figures put the number of Nez Perce in the Oregon area at around 3,000.

In 1997, Wallowa community leaders obtained a grant to develop the Wallowa Band Nez Perce Trail Interpretive Center—a cultural center that hosts powwows and other activities to draw tourists.

"I never thought I'd see the day," said Earl (Taz) Conner, a direct descendant of Chief Joseph, the best known of the Nez Perce. And, in the words of Soy Redthunder, another tribe member, "[We] look at it as homecoming."

---

Within minutes, the Seventh Cavalry slaughtered 300 unarmed Native Americans, including several children. The soldiers left the corpses to freeze on the ground. This event, the **Battle of Wounded Knee,** brought the Indian wars—and an entire era—to a bitter end.

### A PERSONAL VOICE  BLACK ELK

"I did not know then how much was ended. When I look back . . . I can still see the butchered women and children lying heaped and scattered all along the crooked gulch. . . . And I can see that something else died there in the bloody mud, and was buried in the blizzard. A people's dream died there. It was a beautiful dream."

—*Black Elk Speaks*

## Cattle Becomes Big Business ④

As the great herds of buffalo disappeared, and Native Americans were forced onto smaller and less desirable reservations, horses and cattle flourished on the plains. As cattle ranchers opened up the Great Plains to big business, ranching from Texas to Kansas became a profitable investment.

**VAQUEROS AND COWBOYS** American settlers had never managed large herds on the open range, and they learned from their Mexican neighbors how to round up, rope, brand, and care for the animals. The animals themselves, the Texas **longhorns,** were sturdy, short-tempered breeds accustomed to the dry grasslands of southern Spain. Spanish settlers raised longhorns for food and brought horses to use as work animals and for transportation.

As American as the cowboy seems today, his way of life stemmed directly from that of those first Spanish ranchers in Mexico. The cowboy's clothes, food, and vocabulary were heavily influenced by the Mexican *vaquero*, who was the first to wear spurs, which he attached with straps to his bare feet and used to control his horse. His *chaparreras*, or leather overalls, became known as chaps. He ate *charqui*, or "jerky"—dried strips of meat. The Spanish *bronco caballo*, or "rough horse" that ran wild, became known as a bronco or bronc. The strays, or *mesteños*, were the same mustangs that the American cowboy tamed and prized. The Mexican *rancho* became the American ranch. Finally, the English words *corral* and

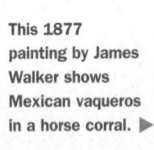

This 1877 painting by James Walker shows Mexican vaqueros in a horse corral. ▶

---

**Analyzing Causes**

D What events led to the Battle of Wounded Knee?

*D. Answer* Spread of the Ghost Dance movement, killing of Sitting Bull.

*Skillbuilder Answers*
1. Abilene, Kansas; Ellsworth, Kansas; Sedalia, Missouri; Kansas City, Missouri; Ogallala, Nebraska; Cheyenne, Wyoming.
2. Cheyenne, Wyoming; Denver, Colorado; Pueblo, Colorado; Albuquerque, New Mexico.

**208**

---

**DIFFERENTIATING INSTRUCTION**  **STUDENTS ACQUIRING ENGLISH**

### Spanish Words, English Translations

On the board, write the following words from the subsection "Vaqueros and Cowboys." Ask students to pronounce and translate each word.

*vaquero* (buckaroo, or cowboy)
*chaparreras* (leather overalls, or chaps)
*charqui* (jerky, or dried strips of meat)
*caballo bronco* ("rough horse," or bronc)

*mesteños* (strays, or mustangs)
*rancho* (ranch)
*corral* (corral)
*rodeo* (rodeo)

Students might turn these words and their English translations into a set of flashcards for the section. Spanish-speaking students might pronounce these Spanish terms for their non-Spanish-speaking classmates.

**MAIN IDEA**

**Drawing Conclusions**

**E** What does the American cowboy tradition owe to the Mexican vaquero?

**E. Answer** Mexicans taught American cowboys how to rope and ride. They greatly influenced cowboys' language, clothes, food, and daily life.

**MAIN IDEA**

**Summarizing**

**F** What developments led to the rapid growth of the cattle industry?

**F. Answer** Expanded rail lines and increased demand for beef after the Civil War.

*rodeo* were borrowed from Spanish. In his skills, dress, and speech, the Mexican vaquero was the true forerunner of the American "buckaroo" or cowboy. **E**

Despite the plentiful herds of Western cattle, cowboys were not in great demand until the railroads reached the Great Plains. Before the Civil War, ranchers for the most part didn't stray far from their homesteads with their cattle. There were, of course, some exceptions. During the California gold rush in 1849, some hardy cattlemen on horseback braved a long trek, or drive, through Apache territory and across the desert to collect $25 to $125 a head for their cattle. In 1854, two ranchers drove their cattle 700 miles to Muncie, Indiana, where they put them on stock cars bound for New York City. When the cattle were unloaded in New York, the stampede that followed caused a panic on Third Avenue. Parts of the country were not ready for the mass transportation of animals.

**GROWING DEMAND FOR BEEF** After the Civil War, the demand for beef skyrocketed, partly due to the rapidly growing cities. The Chicago Union Stock Yards opened in 1865, and by spring 1866, the railroads were running regularly through Sedalia, Missouri. From Sedalia, Texas ranchers could ship their cattle to Chicago and markets throughout the East. They found, however, that the route to Sedalia presented several obstacles: including thunderstorms and rain-swollen rivers. Also, in 1866, farmers angry about trampled crops blockaded cattle in Baxter Springs, Kansas, preventing them from reaching Sedalia. Some herds then had to be sold at cut-rate prices, others died of starvation. **F**

**THE COW TOWN** The next year, cattlemen found a more convenient route. Illinois cattle dealer Joseph McCoy approached several Western towns with plans to create a shipping yard where the trails and rail lines came together. The tiny Kansas town of Abilene enthusiastically agreed to the plan. McCoy built cattle pens, a three-story hotel, and helped survey the **Chisholm Trail**—the major cattle route from San Antonio, Texas, through Oklahoma to Kansas. Thirty-five thousand head of cattle were shipped out of the yard in Abilene during its first

**Tracing Themes**

**ECONOMIC OPPORTUNITY**

**Growth of the Meat Industry**
The railroads directly influenced major meat-packing centers such as Chicago and Omaha, as well as shipping centers, such as Abilene and Sedalia. The growth of cattle ranching—which spurred Americans to settle greater amounts of western land—occurred at the expense of Native Americans. When land disputes arose between the two groups, the government tended to be more sympathetic to the needs of ranchers and meat producers because it benefited the economy.

**HISTORY from VISUALS**

**Interpreting the Map**
Have students locate the beginnings of the cattle trails and follow the arrows to their termination at railroad junctions.

**Extension** Have students work in pairs to plot three possible routes from ranch to meatpacking center. Ask them to use the map scale to measure the distances the cattle traveled on foot and by train.

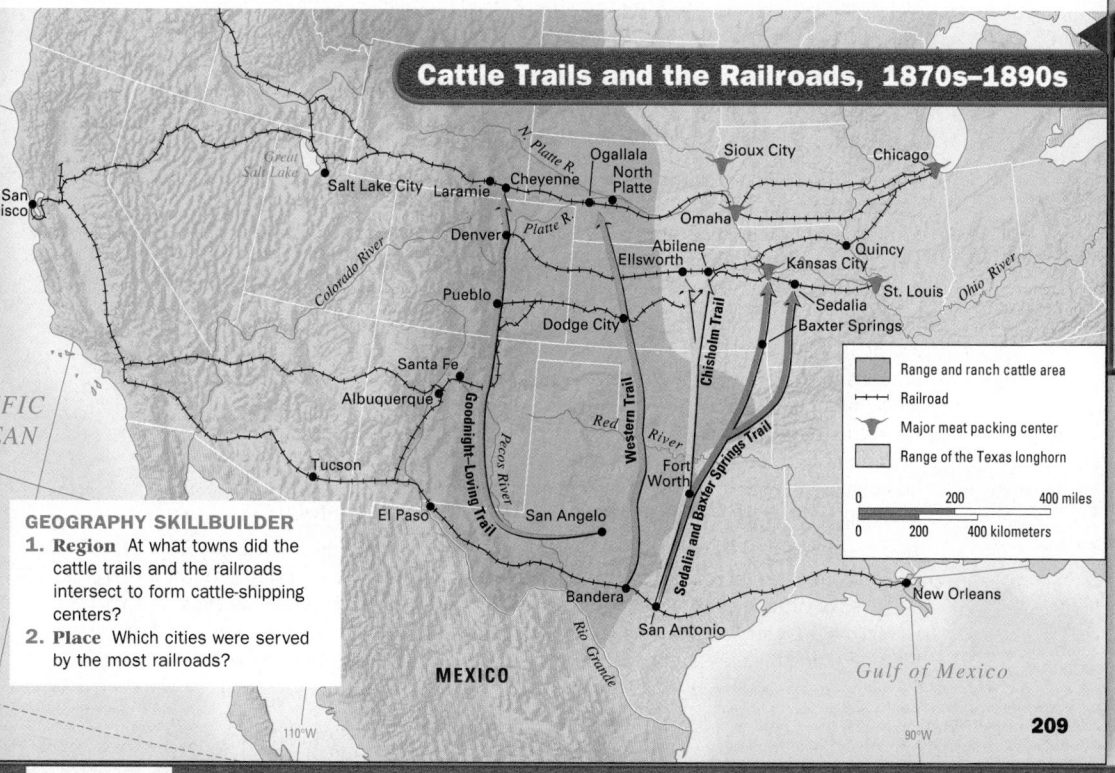

**Cattle Trails and the Railroads, 1870s–1890s**

Legend:
- Range and ranch cattle area
- Railroad
- Major meat packing center
- Range of the Texas longhorn

0 — 200 — 400 miles
0 — 200 — 400 kilometers

**GEOGRAPHY SKILLBUILDER**
1. **Region** At what towns did the cattle trails and the railroads intersect to form cattle-shipping centers?
2. **Place** Which cities were served by the most railroads?

209

**ACTIVITY** | **COOPERATIVE LEARNING**

**Researching Cowboy Music**

**Class Time** 45 minutes

**Task** Analyzing cowboy music for a class presentation

**Purpose** To explore the importance of music and its message about the cowboy's life

**BLOCK SCHEDULING**

**Directions** Students should research how cowboys used music as entertainment and as a means of communication. They should select one song and prepare a written report that includes the song lyrics and an analysis of how it reflects cowboy life. Then they might play a recording or perform the song and explain it to the class.

### History Through *Art*

Frederic Remington left Yale University after a year and a half and headed to the frontier. He worked as a rancher, a military scout, a hunter and trapper, and a reporter. Later, he devoted much of his painting and sculpting career to capturing the spirit of the untamed West. Remington's paintings and sculptures portray both the realism and fantasy of the West in a single work.

### History Through *Art*

**STAMPEDED BY LIGHTNING (1908)**

Painter and sculptor Frederic Remington is best known for his romantic and spirited depictions of the Western frontier. Remington liked to paint in a single dominant color. Native Americans, cowboys at work, and other familiar Western scenes were all subjects of Remington's work. **What do you learn about the work of the cowboy in this painting?**

## Instruct: Objective 5

**A Day in the Life of a Cowboy / The End of the Open Range**
TAKS SS11 5(US24.B)
· How did the ordinary cowboy's life differ from the popular conception of it?
· What was the long drive?
· What factors helped bring an end to the open range?

 Electronic Library of Primary Sources
· The Log of a Cowboy, 1903 by A. Adams

## Tracing Themes
### DIVERSITY AND NATIONAL IDENTITY

**Cowboys**
A diverse group of men worked as cowboys. A few women even rode the range. Despite their different backgrounds, these people lived and worked together in harmony and cooperation for the most part. One reason for this may have been the fact that a cowboy's worth was measured not by the color of his skin, but by his skill at riding and roping.

year in operation. The following year, business more than doubled, to 75,000 head. Soon ranchers were hiring cowboys to drive their cattle to Abilene. Within a few years, the Chisholm Trail had worn wide and deep.

## 5 A Day in the Life of a Cowboy

The meeting of the Chisholm Trail and the railroad in Abilene ushered in the heyday of the cowboy. As many as 55,000 worked the plains between 1866 and 1885. Although folklore and postcards depicted the cowboy as Anglo-American, about 25 percent of them were African American, and at least 12 percent were Mexican. The romanticized American cowboy of myth rode the open range, herding cattle and fighting villains. Meanwhile, the real-life cowboy was doing nonstop work.

**A DAY'S WORK** A cowboy worked 10 to 14 hours a day on a ranch and 14 or more on the trail, alert at all times for dangers that might harm or upset the herds. Some cowboys were as young as 15; most were broken-down by the time they were 40. A cowboy might own his saddle, but his trail horse usually belonged to his boss. He was an expert rider and roper. His gun might be used to protect the herd from wild or diseased animals rather than to hurt or chase outlaws.

**ROUNDUP** The cowboy's season began with a spring roundup, in which he and other hands from the ranch herded all the longhorns they could find on the open range into a large corral. They kept the herd penned there for several days, until the cattle were so hungry that they preferred grazing to running away. Then the cowboys sorted through the herd, claiming the cattle that were marked with the brand of their ranch and calves that still needed to be branded. After the herd was gathered and branded, the trail boss chose a crew for the long drive.

**THE LONG DRIVE** This overland transport, or **long drive,** of the animals often lasted about three months. A typical drive included one cowboy for every 250 to 300 head of cattle; a cook who also drove the chuck wagon and set up camp; and a wrangler who cared for the extra horses. A trail boss earned $100 or more a month for supervising the drive and negotiating with settlers and Native Americans.

**210** CHAPTER 5

---

**B    BLOCK SCHEDULING**

### Separating Fact from Fiction

**Class Time** 30 minutes

**Task** Separating facts from myths regarding the lives of cowboys

**Purpose** To understand the real life of a cowboy

**Directions** Working in small groups, students should create a chart listing various myths about cowboys along with the truths about their lives discussed in the text.

 **Mini-Lesson 4: SS11 3(WH10.B)**

Student charts might look like this:

| Myth | Truth |
|------|-------|
| Good guys wore white hats. | Cowboys wore hats of different colors. |
| | |
| | |

During the long drive, the cowboy was in the saddle from dawn to dusk. He slept on the ground and bathed in rivers. He risked death and loss every day of the drive, especially at river crossings, where cattle often hesitated and were swept away. Because lightning was a constant danger, cowboys piled their spurs, buckles, and other metal objects at the edge of their camp to avoid attracting lightning bolts. Thunder, or even a sneeze, could cause a stampede. **G**

**LEGENDS OF THE WEST** Legendary figures like James Butler "Wild Bill" Hickok and Martha Jane Burke (Calamity Jane) actually never dealt with cows. Hickok served as a scout and a spy during the Civil War and, later, as a marshal in Abilene, Kansas. He was a violent man who was shot and killed while holding a pair of aces and a pair of eights in a poker game, a hand still known as the "dead man's hand." Calamity Jane was an expert sharpshooter who dressed as a man. She may have been a scout for Colonel George Custer.

**MAIN IDEA**

**Comparing**
**G** How did the cowboy's life differ from the myth about it?

**G. Answer**
The cowboy's life was hard, boring, and unromantic, unlike the romanticized myth of dangerous encounters and adventure.

### ❺ The End of the Open Range

Almost as quickly as cattle herds multiplied and ranching became big business, the cattle frontier met its end. Overgrazing of the land, extended bad weather, and the invention of barbed wire were largely responsible.

Between 1883 and 1887 alternating patterns of dry summers and harsh winters wiped out whole herds. Most ranchers then turned to smaller herds of high-grade stock that would yield more meat per animal. Ranchers fenced the land with barbed wire, invented by Illinois farmer Joseph F. Glidden. It was cheap and easy to use and helped to turn the open plains into a series of fenced-in ranches. The era of the wide-open West was over.

---

**HISTORICAL SPOTLIGHT**

**THE WILD WEST SHOW**
In the 1880s, William F. Cody toured the country with a show called Buffalo Bill's Wild West. The show featured trick riding and roping exhibitions. It thrilled audiences with mock battles between cowboys and Indians.

Wild Bill Hickok, Annie Oakley, Calamity Jane (shown here), and even Sitting Bull toured in Wild West shows. Their performances helped make Western life a part of American mythology.

---

**HISTORICAL SPOTLIGHT**

**The Wild West Show**
Discuss with students how the Wild West show might have helped perpetuate the myths about cowboys and Native Americans.

## Assess & Reteach

**SECTION 1 ASSESSMENT**
Assign pairs of students to ask each other the questions and find supporting evidence in the text.

📝 Formal Assessment
· Section Quiz, p. 103

**SELF-ASSESSMENT**
Have students look back at the questions they answered about cowboys at the beginning of the section. Ask them to note new information they learned from their reading and discuss how their ideas have changed.

**RETEACH**
Use the maps in this section to help students review the main ideas about the clashes between white settlers and Native Americans, as well as the growth of the cattle industry.

📝 In-Depth Resources: Unit 2
· Reteaching Activity, p. 7

---

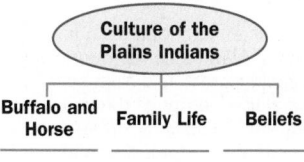

**SECTION 1 ASSESSMENT**

**1. TERMS & NAMES** For each term or name, write a sentence explaining its significance.
- Great Plains
- Treaty of Fort Laramie
- Sitting Bull
- George A. Custer
- assimilation
- Dawes Act
- Battle of Wounded Knee
- longhorn
- Chisholm Trail
- long drive

**MAIN IDEA**

**2. TAKING NOTES**
Fill in supporting details about the culture of the Plains Indians.

```
        Culture of the
        Plains Indians

Buffalo and    Family Life    Beliefs
Horse
_____         _____         _____
_____         _____         _____
_____         _____         _____
```

**CRITICAL THINKING**

**3. MAKING INFERENCES**
Why do you think the assimilation policy of the Dawes Act failed? Support your opinion with information from the text.
**Think About:**
- the experience of Native Americans such as Zitkala-Ša
- the attitudes of many white leaders toward Native Americans
- the merits of owning property
- the importance of cultural heritage

**4. ANALYZING CAUSES**
What economic opportunities drew large numbers of people to the Great Plains beginning in the mid-1800s?

**5. DRAWING CONCLUSIONS**
Identify the reasons for the rise and the decline of the cattle industry.

*Changes on the Western Frontier* **211**

---

Answers **ASSESSMENT** **1**

**1. TERMS & NAMES**
Great Plains, p. 202
Treaty of Fort Laramie, p. 204
Sitting Bull, p. 204
George A. Custer, p. 206
assimilation, p. 206
Dawes Act, p. 206
Battle of Wounded Knee, p. 208
longhorn, p. 208

Chisholm Trail, p. 209
long drive, p. 210

**2. TAKING NOTES**
**Buffalo and Horse:** source of food, clothes, shelter, and transportation;
**Family Life:** communal property and government, individualism valued;
**Beliefs:** focus on the present, world inhabited by spirits

**3. MAKING INFERENCES**
Lack of support by the government, abuses of the act by white opportunists, and Native Americans' lack of interest in private property.

**4. ANALYZING CAUSES**
Growth of the railroads, the burgeoning cattle industry, and government support of "free land."

**5. DRAWING CONCLUSIONS**
**Rise:** the seizure of Native American lands; the adaptation of the longhorn to the Plains; the growing demand for beef; **Decline:** overgrazing; bad weather; barbed wire and end of the open plains.

## DAILY LIFE

### Objectives

· Summarize the role of gold in luring people to the American West.

· Describe people's experiences in their often fruitless efforts to find gold.

## Focus & Motivate

Students might be interested to know that the phrase *strike it rich* originated during the American gold rush of 1849. The term was later generalized to include other sources of quick wealth. Discuss with students natural resources other than gold that figure in the modern American striking it rich. Students might mention oil and precious stones, such as diamonds.

## More About . . .

### Placer Mining

The word *placer* comes not from the English word *place*, but from the Spanish word *placer*, which means "sandbar," one of the places that placer deposits are found. Placer deposits are created when gold-bearing rock is eroded and the particles are washed downstream. Because gold is heavier than other minerals, it is deposited more quickly, often in places like sandbars, where the current of the stream slows down.

 Humanities Transparencies HT13
· *Among the Sierra Nevada Mountains* (1868) by Albert Bierstadt

---

# Gold Mining

GOLD! Some struck it rich—some struck out. Between the Civil War and the turn of the century, deposits of the precious yellow metal were discovered in scattered sites from the Black Hills of South Dakota and Cripple Creek, Colorado, to Nome, Alaska. The dream of riches lured hundreds of thousands of prospectors into territories that were previously inhabited only by native peoples. The fortune seekers came from all walks: grizzled veterans from the California gold rush of 1849, youths seeking adventure, middle-class professionals, and even some families.

**PANNING FOR GOLD ▶**

At the start of a gold rush, prospectors usually looked for easily available gold—particles eroded from rocks and washed downstream. Panning for it was easy—even children could do it. They scooped up mud and water from the streambed in a flat pan and swirled it. The circular motion of the water caused the sand to wash over the side and the remaining minerals to form layers according to weight. Gold, which is heavier than most other minerals, sank to the bottom.

**◀SLUICES AND ROCKERS**

In 1898, prospectors like this mother and son in Fairbanks, Alaska, found sluicing to be more efficient than panning, since it could extract gold from soil. They would shovel soil into a sluice—a trough through which water flowed—and the water would carry off lightweight materials. The gold sank to the bottom, where it was caught in wooden ridges called cleats. A rocker was a portable sluice that combined the mobility of panning with the efficiency of sluicing.

---

## RECOMMENDED RESOURCES

### BOOKS

London, Jack. *Novels and Stories.* New York: Viking, 1982. "The Call of the Wild," "White Fang," "Klondike," "To Build a Fire," and other tales.

Marks, Paula Mitchell. *Precious Dust.* New York: William Morrow, 1994. Mining and prospecting in the gold rush.

Seeyle, John, ed. *Stories of the Old West.* New York: Penguin, 1994. Tales of mining and cattle ranches.

Twain, Mark. *Roughing It.* Berkeley: U of California P, 1996. Twain's witty 1872 account of his experiences in the mining camps and towns of the West after the Civil War.

Ward, Geoffrey. *The West: An Illustrated History.* Boston: Little,

1996. Companion volume to the 1996 PBS series.

### VIDEOS

*Had You Lived Then: Life in a Gold Mining Camp.* AIMS.

*The Way West.* PBS Video, 1994. A 6-hour miniseries from the California gold rush to the Battle of Wounded Knee.

### SOFTWARE

*America Goes West.* Queue. Mountain men, placer gold, ranch life, and other aspects of the American West.

### INTEGRATED TECHNOLOGY

For teacher support, visit . . .

 classzone.com

## ▼ IN THE BOWELS OF THE EARTH

Although surface gold could be extracted by panning and sluicing, most gold was located in veins in underground rock. Mining these deposits involved digging tunnels along the veins of gold and breaking up tons of ore—hard and dangerous work. Tunnels often collapsed, and miners who weren't killed were trapped in utter darkness for days.

Heat was a problem, too. As miners descended into the earth, the temperature inside the mine soared. At a depth of about 2,000 feet, the temperature of the water that invariably flooded the bottom of a mine could be 160°F.

Cave-ins and hot water weren't the only dangers that miners faced. The pressure in the underground rock sometimes became so intense that it caused deadly explosions.

## A FAMILY AFFAIR ▲

This early placer, or surface, mine at Cripple Creek attracted many women and children. It grew out of the vision of a young rancher, Bob Womack. He had found gold particles washed down from higher land and was convinced that the Cripple Creek area was literally a gold mine.

Because Womack was generally disliked, the community ignored him. When a German count struck gold there, however, business boomed. Womack died penniless—but the mines produced a $400 million bonanza.

## DATA FILE

### BOOM TO BUST

This old signpost from Gleeson, Nevada, illustrates how a gold-rush town that had mushroomed overnight could die just as quickly when the gold ran out.

### LONG ODDS

These statistics for the Klondike gold rush, from 1896 to 1899, show the incredible odds against striking it rich.

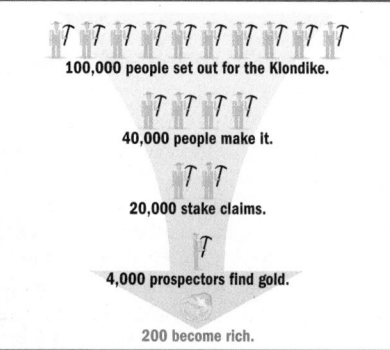

100,000 people set out for the Klondike.

40,000 people make it.

20,000 stake claims.

4,000 prospectors find gold.

200 become rich.

### DEADLY DIGGING

An estimated 7,500 people died while digging for gold and silver during the Western gold rushes. That was more than the total number of people who died in the Indian wars.

---

### THINKING CRITICALLY

**CONNECT TO HISTORY**

1. **Creating Graphs** Use the Data File to create a bar graph that shows the percentage of people who set out for the Klondike who did not get there, got there, staked claims, found gold, and became rich.

   📕 **SEE SKILLBUILDER HANDBOOK, PAGE R30.**

**CONNECT TO TODAY**

2. **Researching Ghost Towns** Research the history of a ghost town from boom to bust. Present a short report on life in the town and its attempts to survive beyond the gold rush.

 **RESEARCH LINKS** CLASSZONE.COM

*Changes on the Western Frontier* **213**

---

## Instruct

1. What precious mineral drew many miners to the West during the late 1800s?
2. What problems did prospectors face in underground mines?
3. How did "panning" work?

**MAKING PERSONAL CONNECTIONS**
Ask if any students have been in a mine. What was the experience like? How would they tolerate the dangers, heat, poor air, and cramped quarters?

### More About . . .

**Mining Hazards**
In very deep mines, the pressure within the rock sometimes caused it to explode, killing miners with flying debris. Miners also were careless with the copper blasting caps they used. When children found the caps, they sometimes accidentally set off an explosion. In some mining camps, an average of one boy a week lost fingers in such mishaps.

**THINKING CRITICALLY**

**CONNECT TO HISTORY**
1. **Rubric**
   Graphs should . . .
   · make appropriate use of the data on the Klondike Gold Rush
   · accurately show the percentages of people in each category
   · be clearly labeled

**CONNECT TO TODAY**
2. **Rubric**
   Reports should . . .
   · focus on a single town
   · trace the town's experience in time order
   · explain how discovery of gold established or expanded the town
   · discuss the town's attempts to survive beyond the gold rush

---

**ACTIVITY** | **SKILLBUILDER LESSON** | **BLOCK SCHEDULING**

## Creating Models

**Explaining the Skill** A model is a three-dimensional representation of information. To create a model, first determine what information is to be portrayed. Next determine the method to portray it, such as a diorama, a three-dimensional mock-up, or a stylized version of the information. Sketch out a plan for the model. Finally, determine the materials you need to complete the task.

**Applying the Skill** Have students choose which type of gold mining they would do if they were mining for gold. Then have them create a model showing how their chosen method works. Have students explain and demonstrate how their models work.

📄 In-Depth Resources: Unit 2
· Skillbuilder Practice: Creating Models, p. 6

214 CHAPTER 5

## OBJECTIVES

1 Explain the rapid settlement of the Great Plains due to homesteading.

2 Describe how early settlers survived on the plains and transformed them into profitable farm land.

### CRITICAL THINKING

· Analyzing Causes, p. 215
· Analyzing Effects, p. 215
· Summarizing, pp. 216, 217
· Evaluating, p. 218
· Drawing Conclusions, p. 218
· Identifying Problems, p. 218

## Focus & Motivate

Ask students to think about the students who set the trends in their school and what they have in common.

## Instruct

### Instruct: Objective 1

**Settlers Move Westward to Farm**
TAKS SS11 2(US10.A)

· How did the transcontinental railroad open up the West for settlement?

· How did the federal government encourage western settlement?

· What steps did the government take to preserve the nation's dwindling open land space?

 In-Depth Resources: Unit 2
· Guided Reading, p. 2
· Geography Application: The Regions of the West, p. 10

 Critical Thinking Transparencies CT13, CT47
· Transcontinental Railroad
· Populations Changes in the West, 1850-1900

 Geography Transparencies GT13
· Railroad Land Grants, 1871

---

**TAKS** Mini-Lesson 4:
SS11 2(US10.A)

# Settling on the Great Plains

SECTION 2

| MAIN IDEA | WHY IT MATTERS NOW | Terms & Names |
|---|---|---|
| Settlers on the Great Plains transformed the land despite great hardships. | The Great Plains region remains the bread basket of the United States. | •Homestead Act  •Morrill Act  •exoduster  •bonanza farm  •soddy |

**TEKS** U.S. History 1B, 2B, 8A, 9A, 10A, 12A, 21D, 22A, 22B, 23A, 24B, 24C, 25A, 25B, 25C, 25D

### One American's Story

When Esther Clark Hill was a girl on the Kansas prairie in the 1800s, her father often left the family to go on hunting or trading expeditions. His trips left Esther's mother, Allena Clark, alone on the farm.

Esther remembered her mother holding on to the reins of a runaway mule team, "her black hair tumbling out of its pins and over her shoulders, her face set and white, while one small girl clung with chattering teeth to the sides of the rocking wagon." The men in the settlement spoke admiringly about "Leny's nerve," and Esther thought that daily life presented a challenge even greater than driving a runaway team.

**A PERSONAL VOICE** ESTHER CLARK HILL

" I think, as much courage as it took to hang onto the reins that day, it took more to live twenty-four hours at a time, month in and out, on the lonely and lovely prairie, without giving up to the loneliness. "

—quoted in *Pioneer Women*

▲ Plains settlers, like this woman depicted in Harvey Dunn's painting *Pioneer Woman*, had to be strong and self-reliant.

As the railroads penetrated the frontier and the days of the free-ranging cowboy ended, hundreds of thousands of families migrated west, lured by vast tracts of cheap, fertile land. In their effort to establish a new life, they endured extreme hardships and loneliness.

### 1 Settlers Move Westward to Farm

It took over 250 years—from the first settlement at Jamestown until 1870—to turn 400 million acres of forests and prairies into flourishing farms. Settling the second 400 million acres took only 30 years, from 1870 to 1900. Federal land policy and the completion of transcontinental railroad lines made this rapid settlement possible.

**RAILROADS OPEN THE WEST** From 1850 to 1871, the federal government made huge land grants to the railroads—170 million acres, worth half a billion

*B. Answer*
By making land available cheaply through various land grants.

---

## PROGRAM RESOURCES

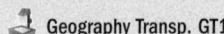 In-Depth Resources: Unit 2
· Guided Reading, p. 2
· Reteaching Activity, p. 8
· Geography Application: The Regions of the West, p. 10
· Primary Sources: Letter from a Woman Homesteader, p. 13
· Literature: from *My Antonia*, pp. 15–17

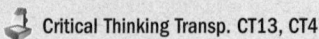 Reading Study Guide (English and Spanish), pp. 59–60

Access for Students Acquiring English/ESL
· Guided Reading (Spanish), p. 78
· Geography Application: The Regions of the West, p. 82

Formal Assessment
· Section Quiz, p. 104

Integrated Assessment
· Rubrics

### INTEGRATED TECHNOLOGY

 Geography Transp. GT13

 Critical Thinking Transp. CT13, CT47

 Electronic Library of Primary Sources

 classzone.com

### TEXAS RESOURCES

TAKS Spiraled Content Review

TAKS Practice Tests

TAKS Practice Transparencies TT50

TAKS Online Test Practice

dollars—for laying track in the West. In one grant, both the Union Pacific and the Central Pacific received 10 square miles of public land for every mile of track laid in a state and 20 square miles of land for every mile of track laid in a territory.

In the 1860s, the two companies began a race to lay track. The Central Pacific moved eastward from Sacramento, and the Union Pacific moved westward from Omaha. Civil War veterans, Irish and Chinese immigrants, African Americans, and Mexican Americans did most of the grueling labor. In late 1868, workers for the Union Pacific cut their way through the solid rock of the mountains, laying up to eight miles of track a day. Both companies had reached Utah by the spring of 1869. Fifteen years later, the country boasted five transcontinental railroads. The rails to the East and West Coasts were forever linked.

The railroad companies sold some of their land to farmers for two to ten dollars an acre. Some companies successfully sent agents to Europe to recruit buyers. By 1880, 44 percent of the settlers in Nebraska and more than 70 percent of those in Minnesota and Wisconsin were immigrants. **A**

**GOVERNMENT SUPPORT FOR SETTLEMENT** Another powerful attraction of the West was the land itself. In 1862, Congress passed the **Homestead Act**, offering 160 acres of land free to any citizen or intended citizen who was head of the household. From 1862 to 1900, up to 600,000 families took advantage of the government's offer. Several thousand settlers were **exodusters**—African Americans who moved from the post-Reconstruction South to Kansas.

Despite the massive response by homesteaders, or settlers on this free land, private speculators and railroad and state government agents sometimes used the law for their own gain. Cattlemen fenced open lands, while miners and woodcutters claimed national resources. Only about 10 percent of the land was actually settled by the families for whom it was intended. In addition, not all plots of land were of equal value. Although 160 acres could provide a decent living in the fertile soil of Iowa or Minnesota, settlers on drier Western land required larger plots to make farming worthwhile.

Eventually, the government strengthened the Homestead Act and passed more legislation to encourage settlers. In 1889, a major land giveaway in what is now Oklahoma attracted thousands of people. In less than a day, land-hungry settlers claimed 2 million acres in a massive land rush. Some took possession of the land before the government officially declared it open. Because these settlers claimed land sooner than they were supposed to, Oklahoma came to be known as the Sooner State. **B**

*A. Answer*
They made it possible for people to travel quickly and also recruited settlers.

MAIN IDEA
**Analyzing Causes**
**A** How did the railroads help open the West?

**Vocabulary**
**speculator:** a person who buys or sells something that involves a risk on the chance of making a profit

MAIN IDEA
**Analyzing Effects**
**B** In what ways did government policies encourage settlement of the West?

Posters like the one shown here drew hundreds of thousands of settlers to the West. Among the settlers were thousands of exodusters—freed slaves who had left the South. ▼

## More About . . .

### Building the Railroads
On the Central Pacific line, more than 90 percent of the labor force, about 12,000 people, were Chinese. They labored under extremely difficult conditions—including avalanches and 40-foot snow drifts—for as little as $30–$35 a month. White workers often received about the same pay but got board and lodging.

## More About . . .

### The Exodusters
To reach Kansas, many former slaves took riverboats as far as St. Louis, but others walked the entire way to Kansas. In 1877, former slaves from Kentucky started a settlement in northwest Kansas that they named Nicodemus. To survive their first winter before they could harvest a crop, some of the new Kansans worked for the Kansas Pacific Railroad, while others earned money by selling buffalo bones. By 1887, Nicodemus was a thriving town with churches, a store, and two newspapers.

Ho for Kansas!
Brethren, Friends, & Fellow Citizens:
I feel thankful to inform you that the
REAL ESTATE
AND
Homestead Association,
Will Leave Here the
15th of April, 1878

---

**DIFFERENTIATING INSTRUCTION** | **LESS PROFICIENT READERS**

### Previewing and Visualizing
Preview the text on page 215 under "Government Support for Settlement." Point out that the free land in the Homestead Act was intended only for the homesteaders; the government encouraged settlers to use their private property rights and farm this land. However, only 10 percent of the land was actually homesteaded. Others also took advantage of the offer. Have students read the text on page 215 and fill in information in a concept web, such as the one shown on the right.

Settled by homesteaders

Fenced in by cattle ranchers

Free land offered by the government

Grabbed by spectators, miners, woodcutters

Held by railroad companies

## More About . . .

### Yellowstone National Park

Fueled by General Washburn's enthusiasm for the natural wonders near the Yellowstone River, Congress created the first national park there in 1872. Four more national parks were created in the 1890s—Yosemite, Sequoia, and General Grant (now Kings Canyon) in California and Mount Rainier in Washington. The Army controlled Yellowstone National Park from 1886 until 1916, when the National Park Service was established.

## Instruct: Objective ❷

### Settlers Meet the Challenges of the Plains

TAKS SS11 2(WH23.A)

· What forms of shelter did the plains settlers develop?

· What technology did settlers rely on to help them tame the prairie?

· What hardships did farmers face in the late 1800s?

 In-Depth Resources: Unit 2
· Guided Reading, p. 2
· Literature: from My Antonia, pp. 15–17

**THE CLOSING OF THE FRONTIER** As settlers gobbled up Western land, Henry D. Washburn and fellow explorer Nathaniel P. Langford asked Congress to help protect the wilderness from settlement. In 1870, Washburn, who was surveying land in northwestern Wyoming, described the area's geysers and bubbling springs as: "objects new in experience . . . possessing unlimited grandeur and beauty."

In 1872, the government created Yellowstone National Park. Seven years later, the Department of the Interior forced railroads to give up their claim to Western landholdings that were equal in area to New York, New Jersey, Pennsylvania, Delaware, Maryland, and Virginia combined. Even so, by 1880, individuals had bought more than 19 million acres of government-owned land. Ten years later, the Census Bureau declared that the country no longer had a continuous frontier line—the frontier no longer existed. To many, the frontier was what had made America unique. In an 1893 essay entitled "The Significance of the Frontier in American History," the historian Frederick Jackson Turner agreed.

**A PERSONAL VOICE** FREDERICK JACKSON TURNER

" American social development has been continually beginning over again on the frontier. This perennial rebirth, this fluidity of American life, this expansion westward with its new opportunities, its continuous touch with the simplicity of primitive society, furnish the forces dominating American character. "

—"The Significance of the Frontier in American History"

Today many historians question Turner's view. They think he gave too much importance to the frontier in the nation's development and in shaping a special American character. **ⓒ**

## ❷ Settlers Meet the Challenges of the Plains

The frontier settlers faced extreme hardships—droughts, floods, fires, blizzards, locust plagues, and occasional raids by outlaws and Native Americans. Yet the number of people living west of the Mississippi River grew from 1 percent of the nation's population in 1850 to almost 30 percent by the turn of the century.

**DUGOUTS AND SODDIES** Since trees were scarce, most settlers built their homes from the land itself. Many pioneers dug their homes into the sides of ravines or small hills. A stovepipe jutting from the ground was often the only clear sign of such a dugout home.

Those who moved to the broad, flat plains often made freestanding houses by stacking blocks of prairie turf. Like a dugout, a sod home, or **soddy**, was warm in

**Background**
The U.S. Census Bureau is the permanent collector of timely, relevant data about the people and economy of the United States.

*C. Answer*
That it shaped the American character.

**MAIN IDEA**

**Summarizing**
ⓒ What was Turner's view of the role of the American frontier in 1893?

**Vocabulary**
**locust:** any of numerous grasshoppers that travel in large swarms, often doing great damage to crops

A pioneer family stands in front of their soddy near Coburg, Nebraska, in 1887. ▶

216

---

## Exploring and Invention

Have interested students research the origins of one of the inventions listed in the Science & Technology feature on page 217. Tell students to use library sources and the Internet to write a brief report about how the invention came about, including the person or persons involved in the invention and the process it followed from idea to reality. Have students use their report to create a visual on their invention to display in the classroom. Trifold posterboards work well, as shown at right.

 Integrated Assessment
· Rubric 3

**TAKS** Mini-Lesson 3: SS11 2(WH23.A)

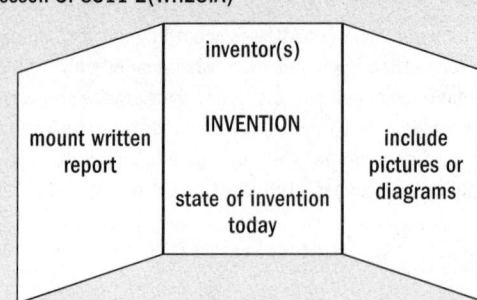

inventor(s)

mount written report

INVENTION

state of invention today

include pictures or diagrams

winter and cool in summer. Soddies were small, however, and offered little light or air. They were havens for snakes, insects, and other pests. Although they were fireproof, they leaked continuously when it rained.

**WOMEN'S WORK** Virtually alone on the flat, endless prairie, homesteaders had to be almost superhumanly self-sufficient. Women often worked beside the men in the fields, plowing the land and planting and harvesting the predominant crop, wheat. They sheared the sheep and carded wool to make clothes for their families. They hauled water from wells that they had helped to dig, and made soap and candles from tallow. At harvest time, they canned fruits and vegetables. They were skilled in doctoring—from snakebites to crushed limbs. Women also sponsored schools and churches in an effort to build strong communities.

**D. Answer**
Inventions such as barbed wire, the steel plow, and the reaper, helped farmers increase production and led to the development of bonanza farms.

**MAIN IDEA**

**Summarizing**
**D** How did new inventions change farming in the West?

**TECHNICAL SUPPORT FOR FARMERS** Establishing a homestead was challenging. Once accomplished, it was farming the prairie, year in and year out, that became an overwhelming task. In 1837, John Deere had invented a steel plow that could slice through heavy soil. In 1847, Cyrus McCormick began to mass-produce a reaping machine. But a mass market for these devices didn't fully develop until the late 1800s with the migration of farmers onto the plains.

Other new and improved devices made farm work speedier—the spring-tooth harrow to prepare the soil (1869), the grain drill to plant the seed (1841), barbed wire to fence the land (1874), and the corn binder (1878). Then came a reaper that could cut and thresh wheat in one pass. By 1890, there were more than 900 manufacturers of farm equipment. In 1830, producing a bushel of grain took about 183 minutes. By 1900, with the use of these machines, it took only 10 minutes. These inventions made more grain available for a wider market. **D**

**AGRICULTURAL EDUCATION** The federal government supported farmers by financing agricultural education. The **Morrill Act** of 1862 and 1890 gave federal land to the states to help finance agricultural colleges, and the Hatch Act of 1887 established agricultural experiment stations to inform farmers of new developments. Agricultural researchers developed grains for arid soil and techniques for dry farming, which helped the land to retain moisture. These innovations enabled the dry eastern plains to flourish and become "the breadbasket of the nation."

## Science & Technology

**INVENTIONS THAT TAMED THE PRAIRIE**
On the Great Plains, treeless expanses, root-filled soil, and unpredictable weather presented challenges to farming.

**STEEL PLOW** The steel plow made planting more efficient in root-filled soil.

**BARBED WIRE** Barbed wire prevented animals from trampling crops and wandering off.

**REAPER** By speeding up harvesting, the reaper saved crops from inclement weather.

**STEEL WINDMILL** In regions of unpredictable rainfall, the steel windmill prevented crop dehydration by bringing up underground water for irrigation.

*Changes on the Western Frontier* **217**

## More About . . .

### Bonanza Farms

The labor needed to plow and harvest the bonanza farms was seasonal. A farm that required only a few hands most of the year might need 150 men for the April plowing and 400 men for the fall harvesting. Harvesting crews moved from one farm to another, from south to north, during the summer. According to the writer Hamlin Garland, "They reached our neighborhood in July, arriving like a flight of unclean birds, and vanished into the north as mysteriously as they had appeared."

Bonanza farms like this one required the labor of hundreds of farm hands and horses.

## Assess & Reteach

### SECTION 2 ASSESSMENT

Have pairs of students split questions 2–5. Each student should present the answers for his or her two questions to the other for discussion and modification, if necessary.

📄 Formal Assessment
· Section Quiz, p. 104

### SELF-ASSESSMENT

Have students review the questions they could not answer. Ask them to find the answer in the text and then to write an additional question to test their understanding of the problematic concept.

### RETEACH

Use the Science & Technology feature on page 217 to review the problems that settlers faced on the plains.

📄 In-Depth Resources: Unit 2
· Reteaching Activity, p. 8

**FARMERS IN DEBT** Elaborate machinery was expensive, and farmers often had to borrow money to buy it. When prices for wheat were higher, farmers could usually repay their loans. When wheat prices fell, however, farmers needed to raise more crops to make ends meet. This situation gave rise to a new type of farming in the late 1870s. Railroad companies and investors created **bonanza farms**, enormous single-crop spreads of 15,000–50,000 acres. The Cass-Cheney-Dalrymple farm near Cassleton, North Dakota, for example, covered 24 square miles. By 1900, the average farmer had nearly 150 acres under cultivation. Some farmers mortgaged their land to buy more property, and as farms grew bigger, so did farmers' debts. Between 1885 and 1890, much of the plains experienced drought, and the large single-crop operations couldn't compete with smaller farms, which could be more flexible in the crops they grew. The bonanza farms slowly folded into bankruptcy.

Farmers also felt pressure from the rising cost of shipping grain. Railroads charged Western farmers a higher fee than they did farmers in the East. Also, the railroads sometimes charged more for short hauls, for which there was no competing transportation, than for long hauls. The railroads claimed that they were merely doing business, but farmers resented being taken advantage of. "No other system of taxation has borne as heavily on the people as those extortions and inequalities of railroad charges" wrote Henry Demarest Lloyd in an article in the March 1881 edition of *Atlantic Monthly*.

Many farmers found themselves growing as much grain as they could grow, on as much land as they could acquire, which resulted in going further into debt. But they were not defeated by these conditions. Instead, these challenging conditions drew farmers together in a common cause.

**Vocabulary**
**mortgage:** to legally pledge property to a creditor as security for the payment of a loan or debt

**Vocabulary**
**extortion:** illegal use of one's official position or powers to obtain property or funds

---

### SECTION 2 ASSESSMENT

**1. TERMS & NAMES** For each term or name, write a sentence explaining its significance.
- Homestead Act
- soddy
- bonanza farm
- exoduster
- Morrill Act

#### MAIN IDEA

**2. TAKING NOTES**
Create a time line of four events that shaped the settling of the Great Plains.

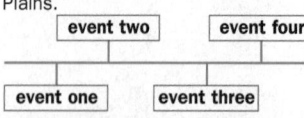

How might history be different if one of these events hadn't happened?

#### CRITICAL THINKING

**3. EVALUATING**
How successful were government efforts to promote settlement of the Great Plains? Give examples to support your answer. **Think About:**
- the growth in population on the Great Plains
- the role of railroads in the economy
- the Homestead Act

**4. DRAWING CONCLUSIONS**
Review the changes in technology that influenced the life of settlers on the Great Plains in the late 1800s. Explain how you think settlement of the plains would have been different without these inventions.

**5. IDENTIFYING PROBLEMS**
How did the railroads take advantage of farmers?

**218** CHAPTER 5

---

### 2 ASSESSMENT  Answers

**1. TERMS & NAMES**
Homestead Act, p. 215
exoduster, p. 215
soddy, p. 216
Morrill Act, p. 217
bonanza farm, p. 218

**2. TAKING NOTES**
1862: Homestead Act
1869: Completion of the first transcontinental railroad
1874: Development of barbed wire
1889: Oklahoma land rush

**3. EVALUATING**
**Success:** Increased miles of railroad track and population helped settle the plains.
**Failure:** Despite the private property rights of homesteaders, only about 10 percent of the land was actually settled by the families for whom it was intended; the railroads subsidized by the government became overly powerful.

**4. DRAWING CONCLUSIONS**
Without technology there would have been more crop dehydration; wandering animals and trampled crops; and crops ruined by inclement weather.

**5. IDENTIFYING PROBLEMS**
Railroads charged plains farmers a higher fee than they did farmers in the east; they charged more for short hauls and forced the farmers deeper into debt.

# Farmers and the Populist Movement

| MAIN IDEA | WHY IT MATTERS NOW | Terms & Names |
|---|---|---|
| Farmers united to address their economic problems, giving rise to the Populist movement. | Many of the Populist reform issues, such as income tax and legally protected rights of workers, are now taken for granted. | • Oliver Hudson Kelley • Grange • Farmers' Alliances • Populism |  • bimetallism • gold standard • William McKinley • William Jennings Bryan |

 U.S. History 2A, 2B, 4B, 4C, 5B, 7A, 19B, 21D, 24A, 24B, 24C, 24D, 25A, 25B, 25C, 25D

## One American's Story

As a young adult in the early 1870s, Mary Elizabeth Lease left home to teach school on the Kansas plains. After marrying farmer Charles Lease, she joined the growing Farmers' Alliance movement and began speaking on issues of concern to farmers. Lease joked that her tongue was "loose at both ends and hung on a swivel," but her golden voice and deep blue eyes hypnotized her listeners.

A PERSONAL VOICE MARY ELIZABETH LEASE

" What you farmers need to do is to raise less corn and more Hell! We want the accursed foreclosure system wiped out. . . . We will stand by our homes and stay by our firesides by force if necessary, and we will not pay our debts to the loan-shark companies until the Government pays its debts to us. "

—quoted in "The Populist Uprising"

Farmers had endured great hardships in helping to transform the plains from the "Great American Desert" into the "breadbasket of the nation," yet every year they reaped less and less of the bounty they had sowed with their sweat.

 Mary Elizabeth Lease, the daughter of Irish immigrants, was a leader of the Populist Party.

## 1 Farmers Unite to Address Common Problems

In the late 1800s, many farmers were trapped in a vicious economic cycle. Prices for crops were falling, and farmers often mortgaged their farms so that they could buy more land and produce more crops. Good farming land was becoming scarce, though, and banks were foreclosing on the mortgages of increasing numbers of farmers who couldn't make payments on their loans. Moreover, the railroads were taking advantage of farmers by charging excessive prices for shipping and storage.

*Changes on the Western Frontier* **219**

---

## OBJECTIVES

1 Identify the problems farmers faced and their cooperative efforts to solve them.
2 Explain the rise and fall of the Populist Party.

### SKILLBUILDERS
· Analyzing Political Cartoons, pp. 220, 222

### CRITICAL THINKING
· Analyzing Issues, pp. 220, 223
· Analyzing Causes, pp. 220, 222
· Summarizing, p. 221
· Evaluating, p. 223
· Making Inferences, p. 223
· Comparing and Contrasting, p. 223

## Focus & Motivate

Have students read the One American's Story of Mary Elizabeth Lease and discuss how she might have come to be such a vocal promoter of the cause of farmers.

## Instruct

### Instruct: Objective 1

**Farmers Unite to Address Common Problems**
TAKS SS11 5(US24.A)
· What economic problems did many farmers face during the late 1800s?
· Why did farmers favor "cheap money"?
· How did farmers try to address their problems and grievances?

 In-Depth Resources: Unit 2
· Guided Reading, p. 3
· American Lives: Mary Elizabeth Lease, p. 19

---

## PROGRAM RESOURCES

 **In-Depth Resources: Unit 2**
· Guided Reading, p. 3
· Skillbuilder Practice: Creating Written Presentations, p. 5
· Reteaching Activity, p. 9
· Primary Sources: Cross of Gold Speech, p. 14
· American Lives: Mary Elizabeth Lease, p. 19

 **Reading Study Guide** (English and Spanish), pp. 61-62

**Access for Students Acquiring English/ESL**
· Guided Reading (Spanish), p. 79
· Skillbuilder Practice: Creating Written Presentations, p. 80

**Formal Assessment**
· Section Quiz, p. 105

**Integrated Assessment**
· Rubrics

### INTEGRATED TECHNOLOGY
Electronic Library of Primary Sources

classzone.com

### TEXAS RESOURCES

 TAKS Spiraled Content Review

 TAKS Practice Tests

 TAKS Practice Transparencies TT51

 TAKS Online Test Practice

## More About . . .

### U.S. Currency

The U.S. monetary system was established by the Coinage Act of 1792. It was a bimetallic system in which both gold and silver were used as legal tender. The government began issuing paper currency during the Revolutionary War, but it printed so much that the money became almost worthless. It was not until the 1860s that the government again issued paper money, "greenbacks," that could not be exchanged for gold or silver. Paper currency is no longer backed by any metal.

## More About . . .

### Richard Parks Bland

It was little surprise that Congressman Richard Parks Bland was a co-sponsor of the Bland-Allison Act. Known for his undying support of the bimetallic standard of currency or "Free Silver," Bland very much identified with the groups who supported such a standard the most—frontier farmers and laborers. Born in Kentucky, Bland spent 10 years as a miner, prospector, and school teacher in California, Colorado, and Nevada. What's more, the rural Missouri district that he represented was made up mostly of miners, farmers, and others who would benefit from "cheap money."

## Analyzing *Political Cartoons*

### THE PLIGHT OF THE FARMERS

Farmers were particularly hard hit in the decades leading to the financial panic of 1893. They regarded big business interests as insurmountable enemies who were bringing them to their knees and leaving them with debts at every turn. This cartoon is a warning of the dangers confronting not only the farmers but the entire nation.

### SKILLBUILDER Analyzing Political Cartoons

1. How does this cartoon depict the plight of the farmers?
2. Who does the cartoonist suggest is responsible for the farmers' plight?

 SEE SKILLBUILDER HANDBOOK, PAGE R24.

**ECONOMIC DISTRESS** The troubles of the farmers were part of a larger economic problem affecting the entire nation. During the Civil War, the United States had issued almost $500 million in paper money, called greenbacks. Greenbacks could not be exchanged for silver or gold money. They were worth less than hard money of the same face value. Hard money included both coins and paper money printed in yellow ink that could be exchanged for gold. After the war, the government began to take the greenbacks out of circulation.

Retiring the greenbacks caused some discontent. It increased the value of the money that stayed in circulation. It meant that farmers who had borrowed money had to pay back their loans in dollars that were worth more than the dollars they had borrowed. At the same time they were receiving less money for their crops. Between 1867 and 1887, for example, the price of a bushel of wheat fell from $2.00 to 68 cents. In effect, farmers lost money at every turn. **A**

Throughout the 1870s, the farmers and other debtors pushed the government to issue more money into circulation. Those tactics failed—although the Bland-Allison Act of 1878 required the government to buy and coin at least $2 million to $4 million worth of silver each month. It wasn't enough to support the increase in the money supply that the farmers wanted.

**PROBLEMS WITH THE RAILROADS** Meanwhile, farmers paid outrageously high prices to transport grain. Lack of competition among the railroads meant that it might cost more to ship grain from the Dakotas to Minneapolis by rail than from Chicago to England by boat. Also, railroads made secret agreements with middlemen—grain brokers and merchants—that allowed the railroads to control grain storage prices and to influence the market price of crops.

Many farmers mortgaged their farms for credit with which to buy seed and supplies. Suppliers charged high rates of interest, sometimes charging more for items bought on credit than they did for cash purchases. Farmers got caught in a cycle of credit that meant longer hours and more debt every year. It was time for reform. **B**

**B. Answer** Deflation, high railroad rates, cycle of mortgage and debt.

**THE FARMERS' ALLIANCES** To push effectively for reforms, however, farmers needed to organize. In 1867, **Oliver Hudson Kelley** started the Patrons of

**MAIN IDEA**

**Analyzing Issues**
**A** Why did farmers think that an increased money supply would help solve their economic problems?
**A. Answer** It would increase prices for their products.

**MAIN IDEA**

**Analyzing Causes**
**B** What were some of the causes of farmers' economic problems?

---

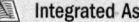

Husbandry, an organization for farmers that became popularly known as the **Grange**. Its original purpose was to provide a social outlet and an educational forum for isolated farm families. By the 1870s, however, Grange members spent most of their time and energy fighting the railroads. The Grange's battle plan included teaching its members how to organize, how to set up farmers' cooperatives, and how to sponsor state legislation to regulate railroads.

The Grange gave rise to other organizations, such as **Farmers' Alliances.** These groups included many others who sympathized with farmers. Alliances sent lecturers from town to town to educate people about topics such as lower interest rates on loans and government control over railroads and banks. Spellbinding speakers such as Mary Elizabeth Lease helped get the message across.

Membership grew to more than 4 million—mostly in the South and the West. The Southern Alliance, including white Southern farmers, was the largest. About 250,000 African Americans belonged to the Colored Farmers' National Alliance. Some alliance members promoted cooperation between black and white alliances, but most members accepted the separation of the organizations.

**Vocabulary**
**regulate:** to control or direct according to a rule or law

**Background**
See *interest rate* on page R42 of the Economics Handbook.

## HISTORICAL SPOTLIGHT

### THE COLORED FARMERS' NATIONAL ALLIANCE

A white Baptist missionary, R. M. Humphrey, organized the Colored Farmers' National Alliance in 1886 in Houston, Texas. Like their counterparts in the white alliances, members of the local colored farmers' alliances promoted cooperative buying and selling. Unlike white organizations, however, the black alliances had to work mostly in secret to avoid racially motivated violence at the hands of angry landowners and suppliers.

## ❷ The Rise and Fall of Populism

Leaders of the alliance movement realized that to make far-reaching changes, they would need to build a base of political power. **Populism**—the movement of the people—was born with the founding of the Populist, or People's, Party, in 1892. On July 2, 1892, a Populist Party convention in Omaha, Nebraska, demanded reforms to lift the burden of debt from farmers and other workers and to give the people a greater voice in their government.

**THE POPULIST PARTY PLATFORM** The economic reforms proposed by the Populists included an increase in the money supply, which would produce a rise in prices received for goods and services; a graduated income tax; and a federal loan program. The proposed governmental reforms included the election of U.S. senators by popular vote, single terms for the president and the vice-president, and a secret ballot to end vote fraud. Finally, the Populists called for an eight-hour workday and restrictions on immigration.

The proposed changes were so attractive to struggling farmers and desperate laborers that in 1892 the Populist presidential candidate won almost 10 percent of the total vote. In the West, the People's Party elected five senators, three governors, and about 1,500 state legislators. The Populists' programs eventually became the platform of the Democratic Party and kept alive the concept that the government is responsible for reforming social injustices. **C**

**THE PANIC OF 1893** Then, in 1893, political issues were overtaken by economic concerns. During the 1880s, farmers were overextended with debts and loans. Railroad construction had expanded faster than markets. In February 1893, the Philadelphia and Reading Railroad went bankrupt, followed by the Erie, the Northern Pacific, the Union Pacific, and the Santa Fe. The government's gold reserves had worn thin, mainly due to its obligation to purchase silver. People panicked and traded paper money for gold. As a result, the stock market crashed. The price of silver then plunged, causing silver mines to close. By the end of the year, over 15,000 businesses and 500 banks had collapsed.

*C. Answer*
increase in the money supply; graduated income tax; federal loan program; election to U.S. senate by popular vote; single terms for president and vice president; secret ballot; eight-hour workday; immigration restrictions.

**MAIN IDEA**
**Summarizing**
**C** What was the Populist Party platform?

*Changes on the Western Frontier* **221**

---

 classzone.com

**ACTIVITY** **COOPERATIVE LEARNING**

**Researching Populist Reforms**

**Class Time** 45 minutes

**Task** Writing a report on the outcome of the reforms promoted by the Populist Party

**Purpose** To help students understand the Populist platform and to recognize that minor political parties can have far-reaching effects

**Directions** Using history texts, encyclopedias, or the Internet, student groups will research one of the platform planks of the Populist Party mentioned on page 221. They should determine if the reform has subsequently been enacted, if the issue is still being debated, or if it has now been forgotten. Finally, they will write a report on the issue to be shared with the class.

## KEY PLAYER

### William Jennings Bryan

William Jennings Bryan was known as the "silver-tongued orator from Nebraska." His powerful voice and his strong beliefs in the "common people" won him two terms in Congress and a presidential nomination at age 36. He made and lost two more bids for president in 1900 and 1908. Although he never again held elective office, Bryan remained influential in the Democratic Party. He was appointed Secretary of State by Woodrow Wilson in 1912. Many reforms that he fought for, such as an eight-hour workday and woman suffrage, later became law. Ask students how they think Bryan was able to influence reform without being elected president.

 **In-Depth Resources: Unit 2**
· Primary Sources: Cross of Gold Speech, p. 14

## KEY PLAYER

**WILLIAM JENNINGS BRYAN**
**1860–1925**

William Jennings Bryan might be considered a patron saint of lost causes, largely because he let beliefs, not politics, guide his actions. He resigned his position as secretary of state (1913–1915) under Woodrow Wilson, for example, to protest the president's movement away from neutrality regarding the war in Europe.

Near the end of his life, he went to Tennessee to assist the prosecution in the Scopes "monkey trial," contesting the teaching of evolution in public schools. He is perhaps best characterized by a quote from his own "Cross of Gold" speech: "The humblest citizen in all the land, when clad in the armor of a righteous cause, is stronger than all the hosts of error."

Investments declined, and consumer purchases, wages, and prices also fell. Panic deepened into depression as 3 million people lost their jobs. By December 1894, a fifth of the work force was unemployed. Many farm families suffered both hunger and unemployment. **D**

**SILVER OR GOLD** Populists watched as the two major political parties became deeply divided in a struggle between different regions and economic interests. Business owners and bankers of the industrialized Northeast were Republicans; the farmers and laborers of the agrarian South and West were Democrats.

The central issue of the campaign was which metal would be the basis of the nation's monetary system. On one side were the "silverites," who favored **bimetallism**, a monetary system in which the government would give citizens either gold or silver in exchange for paper currency or checks. On the other side were President Cleveland and the "gold bugs," who favored the **gold standard**—backing dollars solely with gold.

The backing of currency was an important campaign issue because people regarded paper money as worthless if it could not be turned in for gold or silver. Because silver was more plentiful than gold, backing currency with both metals, as the silverites advocated, would make more currency (with less value per dollar) available. Supporters of bimetallism hoped that this measure would stimulate the stagnant economy. Retaining the gold standard would provide a more stable, but expensive, currency.

**BRYAN AND THE "CROSS OF GOLD"** Stepping into the debate, the Populist Party called for bimetallism and free coinage of silver. Yet their strategy was undecided: should they join forces with sympathetic candidates in the major parties and risk losing their political identity, or should they nominate their own candidates and risk losing the election?

As the 1896 campaign progressed, the Republican Party stated its firm commitment to the gold standard and nominated Ohioan **William McKinley** for president. After much debate, the Democratic Party came out in favor of a combined gold and silver standard, including unlimited coinage of silver. At the Democratic convention, former Nebraska congressman **William Jennings Bryan**, editor of the *Omaha World-Herald*, delivered an impassioned address to the assembled

**MAIN IDEA**

**Analyzing Causes**
**D** What caused the panic of 1893?

**D. Answer** Overexpansion of key industries, especially the railroads, and a shrinking federal gold reserve.

## HISTORY from VISUALS

### Reading the Chart

Suggest to students that they first read the chart vertically to understand how the Gold Bug and Silverite positions may lead respectively to deflation and inflation. Then have them read it horizontally to recognize contrasts in the characteristics of the two positions.

**Extension** Ask students what information for each side would be placed in a category labeled **Harm**.

| Gold Bugs and Silverites | | |
|---|---|---|
| | **Gold Bugs** | **Silverites** |
| **Who They Were** | bankers and businessmen | farmers and laborers |
| **What They Wanted** | gold standard<br>less money in circulation | bimetallism<br>more money in circulation |
| **Why** | Loans would be repaid in stable money. | Products would be sold at higher prices. |
| **Effects** | DEFLATION<br>• Prices fall.<br>• Value of money increases.<br>• Fewer people have money. | INFLATION<br>• Prices rise.<br>• Value of money decreases.<br>• More people have money. |

 **BLOCK SCHEDULING**

### Creating Written Presentations

**Explaining the Skill** The first step in planning a written presentation is to determine the purpose of the presentation and its audience. Next, the main points and supporting details should be identified. Then the material can be written in the appropriate form, such as letters, journal entries, speeches, radio scripts, position papers, or reports.

**Applying the Skill** Have each student write a letter to the editor of a newspaper on behalf of the party of his or her choice, either the Republicans (McKinley) or the Democrats (Bryan). If writing for the Republicans, the letter should tell why the gold standard is important; a letter for the Democrats should extol the virtues of having both gold- and silver-backed money.

 **In-Depth Resources: Unit 2**
· Skillbuilder Practice: Creating Written Presentations, p. 5

delegates. An excerpt of what has become known as the "Cross of Gold" speech follows.

### A PERSONAL VOICE WILLIAM JENNINGS BRYAN

"Having behind us the producing masses of this nation and the world, supported by the commercial interests, the laboring interests, and the toilers everywhere, we will answer their demand for a gold standard by saying to them: You shall not press down upon the brow of labor this crown of thorns, you shall not crucify mankind upon a cross of gold."

—Democratic convention speech, Chicago, July 8, 1896

▲ William Jennings Bryan's "Cross of Gold" speech inspired many cartoonists.

Bryan won the Democratic nomination. When the Populist convention met two weeks later, the delegates were both pleased and frustrated. They liked Bryan and the Democratic platform, but they detested the Democratic vice-presidential candidate, Maine banker Arthur Sewall. Nor did they like giving up their identity as a party. They compromised by endorsing Bryan, nominating their own candidate, Thomas Watson of Georgia, for vice-president, and keeping their party organization intact. **E**

**THE END OF POPULISM** Bryan faced a difficult campaign. His free-silver stand had led gold bug Democrats to nominate their own candidate. It also weakened his support in cities, where consumers feared inflation because it would make goods more expensive. In addition, Bryan's meager funds could not match the millions backing McKinley. Bryan tried to make up for lack of funds by campaigning in 27 states and sometimes making 20 speeches a day. McKinley, on the other hand, campaigned from his front porch, while thousands of well-known people toured the country speaking on his behalf.

McKinley got approximately 7 million votes and Bryan about 6.5 million. As expected, McKinley carried the East, while Bryan carried the South and the farm vote of the Middle West. The voters of the industrial Middle West, with their fear of inflation, brought McKinley into office.

With McKinley's election, Populism collapsed, burying the hopes of the farmers. The movement left two powerful legacies, however: a message that the downtrodden could organize and have political impact, and an agenda of reforms, many of which would be enacted in the 20th century.

---

**MAIN IDEA**

**Analyzing Issues**
**E** Why was the metal that backed paper currency such an important issue in the 1896 presidential campaign?

*E. Answer*
Because people thought that paper currency had value only if it could be turned in for precious metals, such as gold or silver.

---

## Assess & Reteach

**SECTION 3 ASSESSMENT**
Have students answer the questions, then exchange papers to assess their answers.

📄 Formal Assessment
· Section Quiz, p. 105

**SELF-ASSESSMENT**
Have students identify two incorrect or weak answers they had given and discuss those questions with their classmates. Then ask them to revise their answers.

**RETEACH**
Make a problem-solution chart on the board and ask students to fill it in with the problems that farmers faced and the solutions they proposed to solve them. Then discuss how effective those solutions were.

📄 In-Depth Resources: Unit 2
· Reteaching Activity, p. 9

---

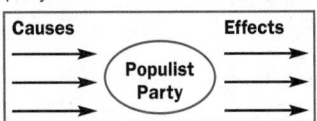

## 3 ASSESSMENT

1. **TERMS & NAMES** For each term or name, write a sentence explaining its significance.
   - **Oliver Hudson Kelley**
   - **Grange**
   - **Farmers' Alliances**
   - **Populism**
   - **bimetallism**
   - **gold standard**
   - **William McKinley**
   - **William Jennings Bryan**

**MAIN IDEA**

2. **TAKING NOTES**
Identify the causes of the rise of the Populist Party and the effects the party had.

| Causes | | Effects |
|---|---|---|
| → | Populist Party | → |

Which effect has the most impact today? Explain.

**CRITICAL THINKING**

3. **EVALUATING**
What do you think were the most significant factors in bringing an end to the Populist Party? **Think about:**
   - monetary policy
   - third-party status
   - source of popular support
   - popular participation policy

4. **MAKING INFERENCES**
How did the Grange and the Farmers' Alliances pave the way for the Populist Party?

*Changes on the Western Frontier* **223**

---

### Objectives

· Learn how the literature of the West reflected its diverse population.

· Learn views of the American frontier expressed in the works of literature.

## Focus & Motivate

Have students comment on what roles they think stories, tales, yarns, songs, and ballads served in the changing West. Then have students brainstorm a list of the types of heroes, plain folk, and problems depicted in the literature of the West.

### More About . . .

**The Diverse Literature of the West**
The years following the Civil War brought an explosion of life, movement, and progress. In the West, the novel and short story continued to develop. Native Americans produced not only oratory but a long tradition of myths, tales, and poetry. Among settlers, a wave of poetry, song, and folk tales burst forth, recreating the lives and tales of lumberjacks, miners, railroad workers, cowboys, and outlaws. Songs like "The Old Chisolm Trail" and "Git Along, Little Dogies" as well as tall tales about Paul Bunyan are all expressions of the West.

# Literature of the West

**1850–1900** After gold was discovered in California, Americans came to view the West as a region of unlimited possibility. Those who could not venture there in person enjoyed reading about the West in colorful tales by writers such as Mark Twain (Samuel Clemens) and Bret Harte. Dime novels, cheaply bound adventure stories that sold for a dime, were also enormously popular in the second half of the 19th century.

Since much of the West was Spanish-dominated for centuries, Western literature includes legends and songs of Hispanic heroes and villains. It also includes the haunting words of Native Americans whose lands were taken and cultures threatened as white pioneers moved west.

▲ Mark Twain

**THE CELEBRATED JUMPING FROG OF CALAVERAS COUNTY**

The American humorist Samuel Clemens—better known as Mark Twain—was a would-be gold and silver miner who penned tales of frontier life. "The Celebrated Jumping Frog of Calaveras County" is set in a California mining camp. Most of the tale is told by Simon Wheeler, an old-timer given to exaggeration.

"Well, Smiley kep' the beast in a little lattice box, and he used to fetch him downtown sometimes and lay for a bet. One day a feller—a stranger in the camp, he was—come acrost him with his box, and says:

"'What might it be that you've got in the box?'

"And Smiley says, sorter indifferent-like, 'It might be a parrot, or it might be a canary, maybe, but it ain't—it's only just a frog.'

"And the feller took it, and looked at it careful, and turned it round this way and that, and says, 'H'm—so 'tis. Well, what's *he* good for?'

"'Well,' Smiley says, easy and careless, 'he's good enough for *one* thing, I should judge—he can outjump any frog in Calaveras County.'

"The feller took the box again, and took another long, particular look, and give it back to Smiley, and says, very deliberate, 'Well,' he says, 'I don't see no p'ints about that frog that's any better'n any other frog.'

"'Maybe you don't,' Smiley says. 'Maybe you understand frogs and maybe you don't understand 'em; maybe you've had experience, and maybe you ain't only a amature, as it were. Anyways, I've got my opinion, and I'll resk forty dollars that he can outjump any frog in Calaveras County.'"

—Mark Twain, "The Celebrated Jumping Frog of Calaveras County"
(1865)

## RECOMMENDED RESOURCES

### BOOKS

Bierhorst, John, ed. *In the Trail of the Wind: American Indian Poems and Ritual Orations.* New York: Farrar, Strauss, and Giroux, 1998.

Cather, Willa. *O Pioneers!* New York: Eighteen Hundred Seventy Three Press, 2000. Cather's first farm novel depicts pioneer life in Nebraska.

Muir, John. *The Mountains of California.* San Francisco: Sierra Club Books, 1989. Early travel and description by America's premier naturalist explorer.

Norris, Frank. *McTeague: A Story of San Francisco.* Oxford U. P., 2000. Characters struggle with the American dream of success.

Velie, Alan R., ed. *American Indian Literature.* Norman: U of Oklahoma, 1991. Anthology that includes songs, tales, memoirs, oratory, poetry, and fiction.

### SOUND RECORDINGS

*Black Elk Speaks.* Berkeley, Ca: Audio Literature, 1991. Recording of Black Elk as told to John G. Neihardt, abridged from the book of the same title.

### VIDEOS

*Call of the Wild.* Carlsbad, Ca: Bridgestone Multimedia, 1994. Motion picture drama based on Jack London's tale of wilderness survival in Alaska.

### INTEGRATED TECHNOLOGY

For teacher support, visit . . .

 classzone.com

## THE BALLAD OF GREGORIO CORTEZ

In the border ballads, or *corridos*, of the American Southwest, few figures are as famous as the Mexican vaquero, Gregorio Cortez. This excerpt from a ballad about Cortez deals with a confrontation between Cortez and a group of Texas lawmen. Although he is hotly pursued, Cortez has an amazingly long run before being captured.

. . . And in the county of Kiansis
They cornered him after all;
Though they were more than
    three hundred
He leaped out of their corral.

Then the Major Sheriff said,
As if he was going to cry,
"Cortez, hand over your weapons;
We want to take you alive."

Then said Gregorio Cortez,
And his voice was like a bell,
"You will never get my
    weapons
Till you put me in a cell."

Then said Gregorio Cortez,
With his pistol in his hand,
"Ah, so many mounted Rangers
Just to take one Mexican!"

—Anonymous, "The Ballad of Gregorio Cortez," translated by Américo Paredes

*Vaquero* (modeled 1980/cast 1990), *Luis Jiménez*. National Museum of American Art/Art Resource, New York.

▲ Chief Satanta

## CHIEF SATANTA'S SPEECH AT THE MEDICINE LODGE CREEK COUNCIL

Known as the Orator of the Plains, Chief Satanta represented the Kiowa people in the 1867 Medicine Lodge Creek negotiations with the U.S. government. The speech from which this excerpt is taken was delivered by Satanta in Spanish but was translated into English and widely published in leading newspapers of the day.

All the land south of the Arkansas belongs to the Kiowas and Comanches, and I don't want to give away any of it. I love the land and the buffalo and will not part with it. I want you to understand well what I say. Write it on paper. Let the Great Father [U.S. president] see it, and let me hear what he has to say. I want you to understand also, that the Kiowas and Comanches don't want to fight, and have not been fighting since we made the treaty. I hear a great deal of good talk from the gentlemen whom the Great Father sends us, but they never do what they say. I don't want any of the medicine lodges [schools and churches] within the country. I want the children raised as I was. When I make peace, it is a long and lasting one—there is no end to it. . . . A long time ago this land belonged to our fathers; but when I go up to the river I see camps of soldiers on its banks. These soldiers cut down my timber; they kill my buffalo; and when I see that, my heart feels like bursting; I feel sorry. I have spoken.

—Chief Satanta, speech at the Medicine Lodge Creek Council (1867)

### THINKING CRITICALLY

1. **Comparing and Contrasting** Compare and contrast the views these selections give of the American frontier in the second half of the 19th century. Use details from the selections to help explain your answer.

    **SEE SKILLBUILDER HANDBOOK, PAGE R8.**

2.  **INTERNET ACTIVITY** CLASSZONE.COM

   From the gauchos of the Argentine pampas to the workers on Australian sheep stations, many nations have had their own versions of the cowboys of the American West. Use the links for American Literature to research one such nation. Prepare a bulletin-board display that shows the similarities and differences between Western cowboys and their counterparts in that country.

*Changes on the Western Frontier* **225**

**CHAPTER 5 ASSESSMENT**

## TERMS & NAMES

## MAIN IDEAS

1. Native Americans—hunters and gatherers; settlers—farmers. Native Americans—communal property; settlers—personal property. Native Americans—migratory; settlers—stationary.

2. It was a failure.

3. With the growth of cities, the market for beef increased. The development of railways provided a link between the cattle frontier and the cities.

4. Over one third of cowboys were non-whites, mostly African Americans and Mexican descended.

5. The Homestead Act and the Morrill Land Grants.

6. They built houses in the sides of hills or out of sod. They worked extremely long hours. Every member of a family contributed.

7. High railroad shipping rates; crop failures; increasing loans and changing currency values.

8. Using silver for coinage and backing the dollar with both gold and silver would put more money in circulation. This would raise prices for farmed goods and help farmers to repay their debts.

---

## TERMS & NAMES

**For each term or name below, write a sentence explaining its connection to changes on the Great Plains.**

1. Homestead Act
2. Sitting Bull
3. assimilation
4. Morrill Act
5. Exoduster
6. George A. Custer
7. William Jennings Bryan
8. William McKinley
9. Populism
10. Grange

## MAIN IDEAS

**Use your notes and the information in the chapter to answer the following questions.**

### Cultures Clash on the Prairie (pages 202–211)

1. Identify three differences between the culture of the Native Americans and the culture of the white settlers on the Great Plains.
2. How effective was the Dawes Act in promoting the assimilation of Native Americans into white culture?
3. Why did the cattle industry become a big business in the late 1800s?
4. How did cowboy culture reflect the ethnic diversity of the United States?

### Settling on the Great Plains (pages 214–218)

5. What measures did the government take to support settlement of the frontier?
6. How did settlers overcome the challenges of living on the Great Plains?

### Farmers and the Populist Movement (pages 219–223)

7. What economic problems confronted American farmers in the 1890s?
8. According to farmers and other supporters of free silver, how would bimetallism help the economy?

## CRITICAL THINKING

1. **USING YOUR NOTES** Create a cause/effect diagram identifying the reasons that agricultural output from the Great Plains increased during the late 1800s.

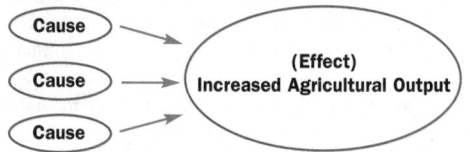

2. **ANALYZING MOTIVES** In 1877, Nez Perce Chief Joseph said, "My people have always been the friends of white men. Why are you in such a hurry?" Why do you think white people hurried to settle the West, with so little regard for Native Americans? Give evidence from the chapter to support your position.

3. **INTERPRETING CHARTS** Look at the chart of Gold Bugs and Silverites on page 222. What would be the result of the policies favored by the gold bugs? By the silverites?

---

**VISUAL SUMMARY** **CHANGES ON THE WESTERN FRONTIER**

**NATIVE AMERICANS**
Native Americans of the plains hunted, farmed, and traded in traditional ways. Plains peoples relied on the buffalo for a variety of survival needs.

**MINERS**
Discoveries of gold and other precious metals led to the growth of mining camps and boomtowns in the Rocky Mountains and to the west.

**CLASH OF CULTURES ON THE FRONTIER**

**RANCHERS AND COWHANDS**
Ranchers and cowboys ushered in the era of the long drive and the roundup. Texas longhorn cattle took the place of the buffalo as the dominant animal on the Great Plains.

**FARMERS AND THE POPULIST MOVEMENT**
New settlement, barbed wire, and bad weather ended the cattle boom. Farmers across the South, Midwest, and West organized to address their common economic problems.

**HOMESTEADERS**
Hundreds of thousands of homesteaders settled on the plains, claiming land grants from the U.S. government.

---

## CRITICAL THINKING

1. **Using Your Notes Causes:** Increased land available for agriculture, due to Homestead Act and Morrill Land Grants, population growth, new mechanical farming technologies, new crops and farming methods.

2. **Analyzing Motives** Answers will vary, but students should mention the plight of farmers, immigrants, and former slaves before the rush westward; the use of private property rights to claim ownership of land previously occupied by Native Americans; the entrepreneurial spirit of America in the 1800s; and a disregard for Native Americans due to bias and prejudice.

3. **Interpreting Charts Goldbugs:** Policies would help city dwellers by keeping prices low for consumer goods; ensure a more stable dollar value; bankers and those with reserves of paper money would also benefit, as their dollars would be worth more. **Silverites:** Policies would help those in debt who could pay back loans with devalued currency; help farmers attain higher prices for their crops and livestock.

## Standardized Test Practice

**Use the flowchart and your knowledge of U.S. history to answer question 1.**

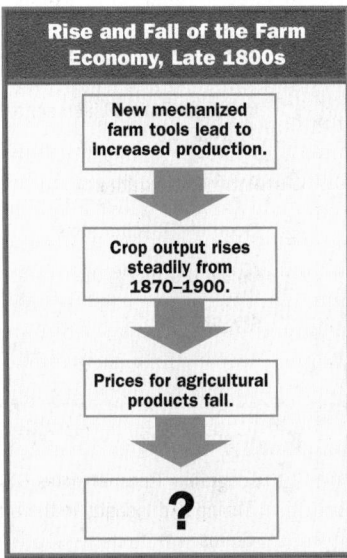

**Rise and Fall of the Farm Economy, Late 1800s**

New mechanized farm tools lead to increased production.

↓

Crop output rises steadily from 1870–1900.

↓

Prices for agricultural products fall.

↓

**?**

1. Which effect accurately completes the flowchart?

   **A** Farmers have less money to repay loans, and many lose their farms.

   **B** Small farmers live off the land, so are not affected by the economy.

   **C** Wealthy farmers hoard gold, rather than depend on paper money.

   **D** The government subsidizes farmers to help them pay their bills.

**Use the quotation and your knowledge of U.S. history to answer question 2.**

"[We] have been taught to hunt and live on the game. You tell us that we must learn to farm, live in one house, and take on your ways. Suppose the people living beyond the great sea should come and tell you that you must stop farming, and kill your cattle, and take your houses and lands, what would you do? Would you not fight them?"

—Gall, a Hunkpapa Sioux, quoted in *Bury My Heart at Wounded Knee*

2. What was Gall's view of future relations between the Plains Indians and the settlers?

   **F** peaceful coexistence

   **G** further conflict

   **H** mutual respect

   **J** equality before the law

3. How did the invention of barbed wire in 1874 change the look of the western frontier?

   **A** It endangered wildlife.

   **B** It ended the cattle frontier.

   **C** It increased cattle stocks.

   **D** It enriched the cow towns.

ADDITIONAL TEST PRACTICE, pages S1–S33.

 **TEST PRACTICE**   CLASSZONE.COM

## Standardized Test Practice

1. The correct answer is letter **A**.
   Letter B is not correct because all farmers are affected by the economy. Letter C is not correct because the flow chart does not address gold or paper money. Letter D is not correct because government subsidies are not addressed.

2. The correct answer is letter **G**.
   Letter F is not correct because Gall speaks of fighting, not being peaceful. Letter H is not correct because Gall does not seem to believe the lifestyle of Native Americans is being respected. Letter J is not correct because Native Americans did not receive equality before the law.

3. The correct answer is letter **B**.
   Letter A is not correct because wildlife was not endangered. Letter C is not correct because the question asked about the look of the frontier, not about changes in herd size. Letter D is not correct because grazing lands were enclosed, not cow towns.

### ORAL REPORT

**Tips for Teaching**

· Point out to students that this chapter provides many opportunities to create artifacts. They may want to create a model as suggested on page 213.

· This chapter has several infographics that would aid students in creating charts or posters.

📄 Formal Assessment
· Chapter Test, Forms A, B, and C, pp. 106–117

## ALTERNATIVE ASSESSMENT

1. **INTERACT WITH HISTORY** Recall your discussion of the question on page 201:

*What do you expect to find on settling in the West?*

Suppose you are a frontier settler. Write a letter to the family members you left behind describing your journey west and how you are living now. Perhaps, for example, you and your companions have built a soddy. Use information from Chapter 5 to provide some vivid impressions of life on the frontier.

2.  **VIDEO** **LEARNING FROM MEDIA** View the American Stories video, "A Walk in Two Worlds." Discuss the following questions in small groups.

   • How did Zitkala-Ša react to life in the boarding school?

   • What lessons about clashes of cultures did you learn from Zitkala-Ša's experience?

   • How might people make interactions with other cultures a positive, rather than a negative, experience?

   Stage a panel discussion for the class.

*Changes on the Western Frontier* **227**

## ALTERNATIVE ASSESSMENT

### 1. INTERACT WITH HISTORY
**Rubric**

Letters should . . .

· include a description of the method of transportation and journey to the West

· include specific reference to living arrangements

· provide a colorful description of aspects of life on the frontier

### 2. LEARNING FROM MEDIA
**Rubric**

Panel discussions should . . .

· represent a range of viewpoints on the issue

· result in a list of suggestions for positive cultural interactions

· use details from Zitkala-Sa's story to explain lessons learned about cultural clashes

# A New Industrial Age

| | CHAPTER OVERVIEW | COPYMASTERS | INTEGRATED TECHNOLOGY |
|---|---|---|---|
| **CHAPTER RESOURCES** | *Technological innovations and the growth of the railroad industry help fuel an industrial boom. Some business leaders follow corrupt practices, and workers, suffering harsh working conditions, try to organize.* | 📄 Telescoping the Times · Chapter Summary, pp. 11–12<br><br>📄 Planning for Block Schedules | 📹 American Stories video series · Gusher!<br><br>💿 Power Presentations<br><br>💿 Electronic Teacher Tools<br><br>🖥 Online Lesson Planner<br><br>🖥 classzone.com |
| **SECTION 1**<br>**The Expansion of Industry**<br>pp. 230–235 | **KEY IDEAS**<br>*Industry booms as natural resources, creative ideas, and growing markets fuel technological development.* | 📄 In-Depth Resources: Unit 2 · Guided Reading, p. 20 · Building Vocabulary, p. 23 · Skillbuilder Practice, p. 24 · Reteaching Activity, p. 25 · Primary Sources, p. 30<br><br>📄 Lesson Plans, pp. 51-52 | 📹 American Stories video series<br><br>🗺 Geography Transparencies GT14 · Mining and Industry in the United States<br><br>🗺 Critical Thinking Transparencies CT14 · Industrial Growth<br><br>🗺 Humanities Transparencies HT14 · The Gun Foundry<br><br>🖥 classzone.com |
| **SECTION 2**<br>**The Age of Railroads**<br>pp. 236–240 | *The growth and consolidation of the railroads benefit the nation but lead to corruption and regulation.* | 📄 In-Depth Resources: Unit 2 · Guided Reading, p. 21 · Reteaching Activity, p. 26 · Literature, from *The Bride Comes to Yellow Sky*, pp. 34–36<br><br>📄 Lesson Plans, pp. 53-54 | 💿 Electronic Library of Primary Sources · How Women are Treated by the Pullman Company<br><br>🖥 classzone.com |
| **SECTION 3**<br>**Big Business and Labor**<br>pp. 241–249 | *The expansion of industry in the North results in the growth of big business and in the formation of unions by laborers seeking to better their working conditions and pay.* | 📄 In-Depth Resources: Unit 2 · Guided Reading, p. 22 · Skillbuilder Practice, p. 24 · Reteaching Activity, p. 27 · Geography Application, pp. 28–29 · Primary Sources, pp. 31–33 · American Lives, pp. 37–38<br><br>📄 Lesson Plans, pp. 55-56 | 🗺 Critical Thinking Transparencies CT48 · Horizontal Consolidation and Vertical Integration<br><br>🗺 Humanities Transparencies HT35 · The Bosses of the Senate<br><br>💿 Electronic Library of Primary Sources · The Two Acre Lot · On the Goals of Trade Unions · 141 Die in Factory Fire<br><br>🖥 classzone.com |

## Key to Resource Icons

| | | | | | |
|---|---|---|---|---|---|
| PE | Pupil's Edition | | Overhead Transparency | | CD-ROM |
| TE | Teacher's Edition | | Audio Library |  | Internet |
| | Copymaster | | | | |

# ASSESSMENT OPTIONS

- PE **Chapter Assessment**, pp. 250–251
- **Formal Assessment**
  · Chapter Tests, Forms A, B, and C, pp. 121–132
- **Test Generator**
- **Integrated Assessment Book**
- **TAKS Online Test Practice**
- **TAKS Spiraled Content Review**
- **TAKS Practice Tests**

---

- PE **Section 1 Assessment**, p. 233
- TE **Self-Assessment**, p. 233
- **Formal Assessment**, Quiz, p. 118
- **Integrated Assessment Book**
- **Test Generator**
- **TAKS Practice Transparencies TT52**

---

- PE **Section 2 Assessment**, p. 240
- TE **Self-Assessment**, p. 240
- **Formal Assessment**, Quiz, p. 119
- **Integrated Assessment Book**
- **Test Generator**
- **TAKS Practice Transparencies TT53**

---

- PE **Section 3 Assessment**, p. 249
- TE **Self-Assessment**, p. 249
- **Formal Assessment**, Quiz, p. 120
- **Integrated Assessment Book**
- **Test Generator**
- **TAKS Practice Transparencies TT54**

# RESOURCES FOR DIFFERENTIATING INSTRUCTION

### Students Acquiring English/ESL

- **Reading Study Guide** (English and Spanish) pp. 84–85
- **Access for Students Acquiring English/ESL:** Spanish Translations, pp. 65–72
- **Chapter Summaries on CD** (English and Spanish)

### Less Proficient Readers

- **Reading Study Guide** (English and Spanish) pp. 84–85
- **Telescoping the Times** · Chapter Summary, pp. 11–12
- **Chapter Summaries on CD** (English and Spanish)

### Gifted and Talented Students

- **In-Depth Resources: Unit 2** · Primary Sources, pp. 30–33
  · American Lives: Andrew Carnegie, p. 37; Mary Harris, "Mother" Jones, p. 38
- **Electronic Library of Primary Sources** · Unit 2, Chapter 6

# CROSS-CURRICULAR CONNECTIONS

### Literature

Brown, Dee. *Hear That Lonesome Whistle Blow.* NY: Simon and Schuster, 1994. By the end of the 19th century, the Iron Horse had conquered the West, and railroads linked the two coasts of the United States. Dee Brown tells the story of this extraordinary undertaking.

Goble, Paul. *Death of the Iron Horse.* NY: Aladdin Books, 1993. A group of Cheyenne derail and raid a freight train in 1867 as an act of defiance against the encroachment of whites on their land.

### Geography

Murphy, Jim. *Across America on an Emigrant Train.* NY: Clarion, 1993. In 1879, writer Robert Louis Stevenson traveled to California by train. His journal vividly describes his adventure and forms the basis for the author's account of the development of the transcontinental railroads.

### Economics

Gourley, Catherine. *Good Girl Work: Factories, Sweatshops, and How Women Changed Their Role in the American Workforce.* Brookfield, CT: Millbrook Press, 1999. The detailed personal histories of girls and women who labored long hours for little money and of the women who ultimately protested against these conditions.

### Science

Amram, Fred M., et al. *African-American Inventors: Lonnie Johnson, Frederick McKinley Jones, Marjorie Steward Joyner, Elijah McCoy, Garrett Augustus Morgan.* Mankato, MN: Capstone Press, 1996. Short and informative survey about inventors.

Israel, Paul. *Edison: A Life of Invention.* NY: John Wiley & Sons, 1998. A complete biography covering both his life and his inventions, with a look at Edison's lesser-known inventions.

# ENRICHMENT ACTIVITIES

- PE **Pupil's Edition**, pp. 228–249
  Interact with History, p. 229
  Geography Spotlight, pp. 234–235
- **In-Depth Resources: Unit 2**
  · Geography Application: The Changing Labor Force, pp. 28–29
  · Primary Source: Birth of the Telephone, p. 30
  · Primary Source: "Wealth and Its Uses," p. 31
  · Primary Source: *The History of the Standard Oil Company*, p. 32
  · Primary Source: Labor Poster, p. 33

- · Literature Selection from "The Bride Comes to Yellow Sky" by Stephen Crane, pp. 34–36
- · American Lives: Andrew Carnegie, p. 37
- · American Lives: Mary Harris, "Mother" Jones, p. 38
- **Primary Source Explorer** · Unit 2, Chapter 6
- **American Stories video series** · Gusher!

## BLOCK SCHEDULE LESSON PLAN OPTIONS (90-MINUTE PERIOD)

### DAY 1

**CHAPTER 6 OPENER**
pp. 230–235
**Class Time** 30 minutes

**History from Visuals, p. 228**
**Class Time** 10 minutes
*Options for Pacing and Variety*

- Time Saver Ask students to read the time line on pages 228–229, and then discuss the questions in the TE.
**Class Time** 10 minutes

**Interact with History, p. 229**
**Class Time** 20 minutes
*Options for Pacing and Variety*

- Role-Playing Ask students to think about the issues raised in the questions. Ask them what their primary concerns would be if they were assigned the story and who they would interview to obtain varying opinions.
**Class Time** 15 minutes

**SECTION 1** pp. 230–235
**Class Time** 30 minutes
*Options for Pacing and Variety*

- Peer Teaching Have students work together on the section assessment. Collect their answers.
**Class Time** 20 minutes

- Time Saver Follow the activity on TE page 232, using a chronological chart to organize information about inventions and their dates of origin.
**Class Time** 10 minutes

- Internet Ask students to read the feature on pp. 234–235, Geography Spotlight: Industry

### DAY 1 continued

Changes the Environment. Discuss the questions, using the Internet to research question 2.
**Class Time** 25 minutes

**SECTION 2** pp. 236–240
**Class Time** 30 minutes
*Options for Pacing and Variety*

- Role-Playing Stage a debate about company towns, using the activity on page 238. Divide students into several groups, with each group supporting a different position.
**Class Time** 30 minutes

- Peer Evaluation Have students complete the Section Assessment for homework, and then switch papers in class and correct them before collecting them.
**Class Time** 10 minutes

### DAY 2

**SECTION 3** pp. 241–249
**Class Time** 45 minutes
*Options for Pacing and Variety*

- Time Saver After reading the rags-to-riches story of Andrew Carnegie, ask students to give examples of why Social Darwinism was a popular theory in relation to the American dream.
**Class Time** 10 minutes

- Role-Playing Have students choose a union to join, using the activity on TE p. 245, Differentiating Instruction: Summarizing.
**Class Time** 20 minutes

- Peer Teaching Have students work in groups to complete the Section Assessment. Students should write their own answers and turn them in at the end of the group session.
**Class Time** 20 minutes

**CHAPTER 6 ASSESSMENT**
pp. 250–251
**Class Time** 40 minutes
Options for Pacing and Variety

- History on Film View the *American Stories* video, "Gusher! Pattillo Higgins and the Great Texas Oil Boom." Discuss the questions under 2 on p. 251.
**Class Time** 20 minutes

- Time Saver Ask students to complete the Standardized Test Practice Questions. Go over the answers and discuss the view expressed in Critical Thinking question 2 on p. 250. Ask students to reflect back on their reading and thinking on Social Darwinism.
**Class Time** 15 minutes

---

**TEACHER-TESTED ACTIVITY**
**LATE 19TH–CENTURY LETTER**

**Class Time** 20 minutes, plus homework assignment

**Task** Writing a letter from the perspective of a teenager from the North or South

**Purpose** To understand living conditions in the Industrial Age (1876–1900)

**Thomas J. Flynn, Turner High School, Kansas City, Kansas**

**Supplies Needed**
- Textbook
- Paper
- Pen

**Activity** Give students, as homework, an assignment to research jobs and working conditions during the Industrial Age. Then, in class, have each student write a letter from the point of view of a teenager from either the North or the South during the Industrial Age. Students should describe their jobs and the town they live in. Tell them to write about available products, prices, and what they would be able to afford. They also should describe the sights, sounds, and smells that are familiar to them.

# CHAPTER 6 CORRELATION

## CORRELATION TO THE TEXAS ESSENTIAL KNOWLEDGE AND SKILLS

Chapter 6 addresses the following standards of the Texas Essential Knowledge and Skills for U.S. History.

| TEKS | Instruction | Student Question/Activity |
|---|---|---|
| **(2B)** Analyze economic issues, such as the growth of labor unions. | **PE 244–246** discussion of the emergence of labor unions in America | **TE 245** activity in which students examine the characteristics of several prominent labor unions |
| **(8B)** Answer questions about geographic distributions and patterns shown on maps. | **PE 231** map depicting the emergence of major industrial cities during the late 1800s | **PE 231** questions that require students to interpret the map |
| **(12B)** Compare the purpose of the Interstate Commerce Commission with its performance over time. | **PE 239–240** discussion of the factors that led to the creation of the Interstate Commerce Commission as well as the difficulties it faced in its task | **PE 240** question about the role of government in regulating the railroads |
| **(12C)** Describe the impact of the Sherman Antitrust Act on business. | **PE 244** examination of the Sherman Antitrust Act and its impact on the business community | **PE 249** activity requiring students to display their knowledge of the Sherman Antitrust Act by using it in a sentence |
| **(19B)** Evaluate the contributions of significant political and social leaders such as Andrew Carnegie. | **PE 241–242** discussion of Andrew Carnegie and his role in the rise of big business | **TE 242** activity examining the business techniques that helped Andrew Carnegie create a steel empire |
| **(21D)** Identify the political, social, and economic contributions of women to American society. | **PE 248–249** examination of the role women played in the nation's emerging labor movement | **TE 248** math activity in which students compare wages of men and women |
| **(22A)** Explain the effects of scientific discoveries and technological innovations on the development of the United States. | **PE 230–233** discussion of major innovations and inventions that helped prompt the rapid industrialization of America | **PE 233** Critical Thinking questions about which invention had the greatest impact on industrialization |

## TAKS MINI-LESSONS

1. **Social Studies Skills: Objective 3 (US2.B):** Analyze economic issues such as industrialization and the growth of railroads **Activity** Have students complete the research activity on TE page 239 regarding the growth of railroads.

2. **Social Studies Skills: Objective 3 (US22.A):** Explain the effects of scientific discoveries and technological innovations on the development of the United States **Activity** Have students complete the writing activity on TE page 232 regarding significant inventions of the 1800s.

3. **Social Studies Skills: Objective 3 (US22.A):** Analyze the impact of technological innovations on the nature of work and the American labor movement **Activity** Have students summarize the condition of workers during the Industrial age.

4. **English Language Arts Skills: Objective 1 (6.E):** Use reference material to determine precise meaning and usage **Activity** Have students use the dictionary to define any unfamiliar economic terms, including *stock, production, wages, and dividends.*

5. **English Language Arts Skills: Objective 2 (11.D):** Analyze the melodies of literary language, including the use of evocative words and rhythms **Activity** Have students discuss what words help the writer create a strong visual image in the Personal Voice on page 247.

# CHAPTER 6 · OBJECTIVE

To analyze the effects of various scientific discoveries and manufacturing innovations on the nature of work, the American labor movement, and businesses

# A NEW INDUSTRIAL AGE

CHAPTER 6

## HISTORY from VISUALS

### Interpreting the Photograph

Ask students to examine the photograph and suggest words they would use to describe the work of constructing railroads. Ask them why building tracks through the mountains might be so difficult. *(dangerous, exciting, back-breaking, monotonous; workers have to blast and dig their way through the mountains before they can lay track.)*

**Extension** Have students write a list of questions they might ask the people in this photograph and then pair up with another student to try to answer each other's inquiries.

## Time Line Discussion

Explain to students that the time line covers key dates in America's rise to an industrial power in the late 1800s.

· Ask students what year Alexander Graham Bell invented the telephone. *(1876)*

· Ask students which event made communication and trade among different parts of the country easier. *(1869—Transcontinental Railroad completed)*

· Ask students which events show that labor unions were gaining members. *(1875—British unions win right to strike; Great Strike of 1877; 1886—Haymarket riot; 1894—Pullman strike)*

Laborers blasted tunnels and constructed bridges to send the railroad through the rugged Sierra Nevada mountains.

**1869** Central Pacific and Union Pacific complete the transcontinental railroad.

**1876** Alexander Graham Bell invents the telephone.

**1877** *Munn v. Illinois* establishes government regulation of railroads.

Mother Jones supports the Great Strike of 1877.

**1879** Thomas A. Edison invents a workable light bulb.

**1884** Grover Cleveland is elected president.

USA
WORLD

**1870**

**1880**

**1870** Franco-Prussian War breaks out.

**1875** British labor unions win right to strike.

**1882** United States restricts Chinese immigration.

**1883** Germany becomes the first nation to provide national health insurance.

**228** CHAPTER 6

## THEMES IN CHAPTER 6

### SCIENCE AND TECHNOLOGY

The rapid expansion of the railroads and the development of new inventions and improved technologies ushered in a new age for Americans. Where people lived, how they worked, what they ate, and how they spent their leisure time were changed forever.

**See Teacher's Edition notes, p. 236.**

### ECONOMIC OPPORTUNITY

Newcomers to this country and settlers who crowded the frontier pursued the American dream to create a good life for themselves and their families. For some, however—men, women, and children who toiled long hours for low pay—the dream remained out of reach.

**See Teacher's Edition notes, p. 243.**

### WOMEN AND POLITICAL POWER

Industrialization enabled women to enter the labor force in great numbers. They played a significant role in the labor movement and worked tirelessly to improve working conditions for themselves and their children. They wanted recognition for their contributions, however, and "Equal pay for equal work" became their rallying cry.

**See Teacher's Edition notes, p. 248.**

# INTERACT
## WITH HISTORY

The year is 1863 and railroad construction is booming. In six years, the U.S. will be linked by rail from coast to coast. Central Pacific Railroad employs mainly Chinese immigrants to blast tunnels, lay track, and drive spikes, all for low wages. You are a journalist assigned to describe this monumental construction project for your readers.

## What are the pros and cons of railroad expansion?

### Examine the Issues

- What dangers do the railroad workers encounter?
- How will businesses and the general public benefit from the transcontinental railroad?
- How might railroad construction affect the environment?

 **RESEARCH LINKS** CLASSZONE.COM

Visit the Chapter 6 links for more information about A New Industrial Age.

**1886** Haymarket riot turns public sentiment against unions.

**1890** Congress passes the Sherman Antitrust Act.

**1894** President Cleveland sends federal troops to Illinois to end the Pullman strike.

**1894** William McKinley is elected president.

**1900** William McKinley is reelected.

## 1890

## 1900

**1890** Colonization of sub-Saharan Africa peaks.

**1893** Women in New Zealand gain voting rights.

**1896** First modern Olympic Games are held in Athens, Greece.

*A New Industrial Age* **229**

---

## INTERACT
### WITH HISTORY

### Objectives

- To help students understand the consequences, both good and bad, of railroad expansion
- To help students recognize the different ways in which growth and progress impact the United States

### Examine the Issues

1. Have students consider the possible dangers of work that involves digging and blasting through rock and working in snowy, mountainous terrain.
2. Ask students to consider how a transcontinental railroad might facilitate trade and communication.
3. Ask students to consider how the environment is affected by the building of a railroad and all that follows it, such as the creation and growth of towns near the railroad.

---

## RECOMMENDED RESOURCES

### BOOKS FOR THE TEACHER

Chernow, Ron. *Titan: The Life of John D. Rockefeller, Sr.* New York: Random House, 1998. In-depth portrait of the nation's oil giant.

Dulles, Foster Rhea. *Labor in America: A History.* New York: Knopf, 1999.

Foner, Philip Sheldon. *Women and the American Labor Movement.* New York: Free Press, 1979.

Josephson, Matthew. *The Robber Barons.* San Diego: Harcourt, 1995.

### BOOKS FOR THE STUDENT

Alger, Horatio, Jr. *Struggling Upward and Other Works.* New York: Crown, 1945.

Carnegie, Andrew. *Autobiography of Andrew Carnegie.* Boston: Northeastern, 1986.

### VIDEOS

*American History: The Game of Monopoly.* MasterVision, 969 Park Avenue, New York, NY 10028.

*Andrew Carnegie: The Original Man of Steel.* Video (VHS) or Laserdisc available from Aims Multimedia 800-367-2467.

### SOFTWARE

*Industrial Revolution in America.* CD-ROM. Educational Software Institute, 800-955-5570.

### INTEGRATED TECHNOLOGY

For teacher support, visit . . .

 classzone.com

*A New Industrial Age* **229**

# The Expansion of Industry

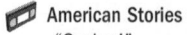
---

| MAIN IDEA | WHY IT MATTERS NOW | Terms & Names |
|---|---|---|
| At the end of the 19th century, natural resources, creative ideas, and growing markets fueled an industrial boom. | Technological developments of the late 19th century paved the way for the continued growth of American industry. | • Edwin L. Drake<br>• Bessemer process<br>• Thomas Alva Edison<br>• Christopher Sholes<br>• Alexander Graham Bell |

**TEKS** U.S. History 1B, 2B, 8A, 8B, 22A, 22B, 22C, 23A, 24A, 24B, 24C, 25A, 25B, 25C, 25D

### One American's Story

One day, Pattillo Higgins noticed bubbles in the springs around Spindletop, a hill near Beaumont in eastern Texas. This and other signs convinced him that oil was underground. If Higgins found oil, it could serve as a fuel source around which a vibrant industrial city would develop.

Higgins, who had been a mechanic and a lumber merchant, couldn't convince geologists or investors that oil was present, but he didn't give up. A magazine ad seeking investors got one response—from Captain Anthony F. Lucas, an experienced prospector who also believed that there was oil at Spindletop. When other investors were slow to send money, Higgins kept his faith, not only in Spindletop, but in Lucas.

**A PERSONAL VOICE** PATTILLO HIGGINS

" Captain Lucas, . . . these experts come and tell you this or that can't happen because it has never happened before. You believe there is oil here, . . . and I think you are right. I know there is oil here in greater quantities than man has ever found before. "

—quoted in *Spindletop*

**VIDEO**
*GUSHER!*
Pattillo Higgins and the Great Texas Oil Boom

In 1900, the two men found investors, and they began to drill that autumn. After months of difficult, frustrating work, on the morning of January 10, 1901, oil gushed from their well. The Texas oil boom had begun.

## **1** Natural Resources Fuel Industrialization

After the Civil War, the United States was still largely an agricultural nation. By the 1920s—a mere 60 years later—it had become the leading industrial power in the world. This immense industrial boom was due to three major factors: a wealth of natural resources, government support for business, and a growing urban population that provided both cheap labor and markets for new products.

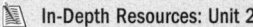
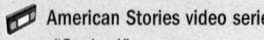

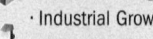

**BLACK GOLD** Though eastern Native American tribes had made fuel and medicine from crude oil long before Europeans arrived on the continent, early American settlers had little use for oil. In the 1840s, Americans began using kerosene to light lamps after the Canadian geologist Abraham Gesner discovered how to distill the fuel from oil or coal.

It wasn't until 1859, however, when **Edwin L. Drake** successfully used a steam engine to drill for oil near Titusville, Pennsylvania, that removing oil from beneath the earth's surface became practical. This breakthrough started an oil boom that spread to Kentucky, Ohio, Illinois, Indiana, and, later, Texas. Petroleum-refining industries arose in Cleveland and Pittsburgh as entrepreneurs rushed to transform the oil into kerosene. Gasoline, a byproduct of the refining process, originally was thrown away. But after the automobile became popular, gasoline became the most important form of oil.

**BESSEMER STEEL PROCESS** Oil was not the only natural resource that was plentiful in the United States. There were also abundant deposits of coal and iron. In 1887, prospectors discovered iron ore deposits more than 100 miles long and up to 3 miles wide in the Mesabi Range of Minnesota. At the same time, coal production skyrocketed—from 33 million tons in 1870 to more than 250 million tons in 1900.

Iron is a dense metal, but it is soft and tends to break and rust. It also usually contains other elements, such as carbon. Removing the carbon from iron produces a lighter, more flexible, and rust-resistant metal—steel. The raw materials needed to make steel were readily available; all that was needed was a cheap and efficient manufacturing process. The **Bessemer process,** developed independently by the British manufacturer Henry Bessemer and American ironmaker William Kelly around 1850, soon became widely used. This technique involved injecting air into molten iron to remove the carbon and other impurities. By 1880, American manufacturers were using the new method to produce more than 90 percent of the nation's steel. In this age of rapid change and innovation, even

**Vocabulary**
**entrepreneur:** a person who organizes, operates, and assumes the risk for a business venture

*Skillbuilder Answers*
1. Pennsylvania
2. An abundance of coal and iron ore, plus access to a major river, contributed to Pittsburgh's high levels of steel production.

## More About . . .

### Petroleum-Based Products
The development of petroleum-based products revolutionized everyday life in the United States and played a key role in how the nation developed. One example is the production of oil, which helped to fuel the automobile industry in the United States. Another is asphalt, a petroleum-based product that played a major role in the construction of the national highway system. Today, oil provides about 40 percent of the energy Americans consume and 97 percent of our transportation fuels. Products made from petroleum include heart valves, tires, eyeglasses, crayons, golf balls, and compact discs.

Ask, What effect did petroleum-based products have on the development of the United States? *(A petroleum-based product—oil—enabled the development of the automobile industry, asphalt played a role in the construction of roads and highways throughout the nation, and petroleum-based products led to the creation of important new products.)*

Humanities Transparencies HT14
· The Gun Foundry

## Natural Resources and the Birth of a Steel Town, 1886–1906

MESABI RANGE
L. Superior
Minneapolis
Milwaukee
Detroit
Chicago
Cleveland
Pittsburgh
Titusville
Buffalo
Wilkes-Barre
40°N
New York
Philadelphia
Baltimore
Boston
Omaha
Indianapolis
Cincinnati
St. Louis
APPALACHIAN MOUNTAINS
Atlanta
ATLANTIC OCEAN
New Orleans
90°W
80°W
70°W

**Pittsburgh**
Ohio River
Allegheny River
Pittsburgh
City Limits
City Limits
Monongahela R.

○ Steel mills, 1886
● Steel mills, 1906

Map legend:
▣ Major industrial city
• Other cities
▦ Coal mining
▤ Iron ore mining
⚒ Oil
⚒ Steel production
0   150   300 miles
0   150   300 kilometers

### GEOGRAPHY SKILLBUILDER
1. **Region** Which state had the most steel-producing areas?
2. **Human-Environment Interaction** What connection can you draw between natural resources (including water) and steel production in Pittsburgh?

## HISTORY from VISUALS

### Interpreting the Maps
Remind students that the map of Pittsburgh is projected out from the United States map. Ask students why there were more steel mills in 1906 than in 1886. (*Demand for the steel probably increased, making it profitable to open a steel mill.*)

**Extension** Have students choose a city other than Pittsburgh and identify the nearest coal and iron deposits and waterways.

Geography Transparencies GT14
· Mining and Industry in the United States, 1850–1900

231

---

**ACTIVITY**  **COOPERATIVE LEARNING**                                  **B** **BLOCK SCHEDULING**

## Tracking the Growth of Steel

**Class Time** 45 minutes

**Task** Organizing information about the production and uses of steel into a class museum display

**Purpose** To recognize the importance of steel and the interrelatedness of science, technology, and daily life

**Directions** Working in small groups, students will research a topic related to the production or uses of steel, such as the Bessemer process. Each group will provide

illustrations and text for their topic, and one group will design, coordinate, and produce a class museum display. The museum display might include:

· a basic description of the topic, with all terms clearly defined and explained
· diagrams of any processes involved
· photographs of the process and the workers involved in it
· sketch map showing major U.S. centers for this work

Integrated Assessment
· Rubric 4

## The Technological Explosion, 1826–1903

| 1826 | 1831 | 1837 | 1846 | 1860 | 1867 | 1873 | 1877 | 1879 | 1895 | 1903 |
|------|------|------|------|------|------|------|------|------|------|------|
| | | | | | | | 1876 | | | |

- Photography
- Reaper
- Telegraph
- Sewing Machine
- Internal-Combustion Engine
- Dynamite
- Typewriter
- Electric Motor
- Light Bulb
- Phonograph
- Telephone
- Radio
- Motion Pictures
- X-Ray Machine
- Airplane

## HISTORY from VISUALS

### Interpreting a Time Line

Ask students the following questions. How much time elapsed between the telegraph and the telephone? *(39 years)* How much time elapsed between the internal-combustion engine and the airplane? *(43 years)* In which decade were the most new inventions created? *(the 1870s)*

## HISTORICAL SPOTLIGHT

### Illuminating the Light Bulb

Share with students Thomas Edison's definition of genius: "One percent inspiration and 99 percent perspiration." Ask them to discuss how his search for the perfect lamp filament illustrates this definition.

### Instruct: Objective ❷

**Inventions Promote Change**

TAKS SS11 3(US22.A)

- How did the harnessing of electricity transform American business?
- How did new inventions and products affect people at home and at work?

📓 In-Depth Resources: Unit 2
- Guided Reading, p. 20
- Primary Sources: Birth of the Telephone, p. 30

### HISTORICAL SPOTLIGHT

#### ILLUMINATING THE LIGHT BULB

Shortly after moving into a long wooden shed at Menlo Park, Thomas Alva Edison and his associates set to work to develop the perfect incandescent bulb. Arc lamps already lit some city streets and shops, using an electric current passing between two sticks of carbon, but they were glaring and inefficient.

Edison hoped to create a long-lasting lamp with a soft glow, and began searching for a filament that would burn slowly and stay lit. Edison tried wires, sticks, blades of grass, and even hairs from his assistants' beards. Finally, a piece of carbonized bamboo from Japan did the trick. Edison's company used bamboo filaments until 1911, when it began using tungsten filaments, which are still used today.

the successful Bessemer process was bettered by the 1860. It was eventually replaced by the open-hearth process, enabling manufacturers to produce quality steel from scrap metal as well as from raw materials. **A**

**NEW USES FOR STEEL** The railroads, with thousands of miles of track, became the biggest customers for steel, but inventors soon found additional uses for it. Joseph Glidden's barbed wire and McCormick's and Deere's farm machines helped transform the plains into the food producer of the nation.

Steel changed the face of the nation as well, as it made innovative construction possible. One of the most remarkable structures was the Brooklyn Bridge. Completed in 1883, it spanned 1,595 feet of the East River in New York City. Its steel cables were supported by towers higher than any man-made and weight-bearing structure except the pyramids of Egypt. Like those ancient marvels, the completed bridge was called a wonder of the world.

Around this time, setting the stage for a new era of expansion upward as well as outward, William Le Baron Jenney designed the first skyscraper with a steel frame—the Home Insurance Building in Chicago. Before Jenney had his pioneering idea, the weight of large buildings was supported entirely by their walls or by iron frames, which limited the buildings' height. With a steel frame to support the weight, however, architects could build as high as they wanted. As structures soared into the air, not even the sky seemed to limit what Americans could achieve.

### ❷ Inventions Promote Change

By capitalizing on natural resources and their own ingenuity, inventors changed more than the landscape. Their inventions affected the very way people lived and worked.

**THE POWER OF ELECTRICITY** In 1876, **Thomas Alva Edison** became a pioneer on the new industrial frontier when he established the world's first research laboratory in Menlo Park, New Jersey. There Edison perfected the incandescent light bulb—patented in 1880—and later invented an entire system for producing and distributing electrical power. Another inventor, George Westinghouse, along with Edison, added innovations that made electricity safer and less expensive.

The harnessing of electricity completely changed the nature of business in America. By 1890, electric power ran numerous machines, from fans to printing presses. This inexpensive, convenient source of energy soon became available in homes and spurred the invention of time-saving appliances. Electric streetcars made urban travel cheap and efficient and also promoted the outward spread of cities.

More important, electricity allowed manufacturers to locate their plants

**MAIN IDEA**

**Summarizing**
**A** What natural resources were most important for industrialization?

**A. Answer**
oil, coal, iron ore, water

**Vocabulary**
**incandescent:** giving off visible light as a result of being heated

## DIFFERENTIATING INSTRUCTION — LESS PROFICIENT READERS

### Using a Chronological Chart

Draw a chart on the board like the one at the right, using only the dates. Encourage students to find dates in the text between pages 232–233 and fill in the inventions and their inventors.

 Mini-Lesson 2: SS11 3(US22.A)

| Date | Inventor | Invention |
|------|----------|-----------|
| 1867 | Christopher Sholes | Typewriter |
| 1876 | Alexander Graham Bell and Thomas Watson | Telephone |
| 1880 | Thomas Alva Edison | Incandescent light bulb |

MAIN IDEA

Analyzing
Effects
 How did
electricity change
American life?

*B. Answer*
*It changed the
nature of busi-
ness, made pos-
sible the inven-
tion of new
appliances, and
helped cities
and industries
grow.*

wherever they wanted—not just near sources of power, such as rivers. This enabled industry to grow as never before. Huge operations, such as the Armour and Swift meatpacking plants, and the efficient processes that they used became the models for new consumer industries.

**INVENTIONS CHANGE LIFESTYLES** Edison's light bulb was only one of several revolutionary inventions. **Christopher Sholes** invented the typewriter in 1867 and changed the world of work. Next to the light bulb, however, perhaps the most dramatic invention was the telephone, unveiled by **Alexander Graham Bell** and Thomas Watson in 1876. It opened the way for a worldwide communications network.

The typewriter and the telephone particu-larly affected office work and created new jobs for women. Although women made up less than 5 percent of all office workers in 1870, by 1910 they accounted for nearly 40 percent of the clerical work force. New inventions also had a tremendous impact on factory work, as well as on jobs that traditionally had been done at home. For example, women had previously sewn clothing by hand for their families. With industrialization, clothing could be mass-pro-duced in factories, creating a need for garment workers, many of whom were women.

Industrialization freed some factory work-ers from backbreaking labor and helped improve workers' standard of living. By 1890, the average workweek had been reduced by about ten hours. However, many laborers felt that the mechanization of so many tasks reduced human workers' worth. As consumers, though, workers regained some of their lost power in the marketplace. The country's expanding urban population provided a vast potential market for the new inventions and products of the late 1800s.

▲ The typewriter
shown here dates
from around
1890.

## Assess & Reteach

**SECTION 1 ASSESSMENT**
Have students create questions on the mate-rial in the section, separate into teams, and then test each other in a game-show format.

Formal Assessment
· Section Quiz, p. 118

**SELF-ASSESSMENT**
Have students mark the questions on the Section 1 Assessment that they could not answer. Ask them to find the answers in the text.

**RETEACH**
Use the video *Gusher!* to review the main ideas of this section.

In-Depth Resources: Unit 2
· Reteaching Activity, p. 25

---

## SECTION 1 ASSESSMENT

**1. TERMS & NAMES** For each term or name, write a sentence explaining its significance.
- Edwin L. Drake
- Bessemer process
- Thomas Alva Edison
- Christopher Sholes
- Alexander Graham Bell

**MAIN IDEA**

**2. TAKING NOTES**
In a chart like the one below, list resources, ideas, and markets that affected the industrial boom of the 19th century. In the second column, note how each item contributed to industrialization.

| Resources, Ideas, Markets | Impact |
|---|---|
| | |
| | |

**CRITICAL THINKING**

**3. MAKING INFERENCES**
Do you think that consumers gained power as industry expanded in the late 19th century? Why or why not?

**4. HYPOTHESIZING**
If the U.S. had been poor in natural resources, how would industrialization have been affected?

**5. ANALYZING EFFECTS**
Which invention or development described in this section had the greatest impact on society? Justify your choice. **Think About:**
- the applications of inventions
- the impact of inventions on people's daily lives
- the effect of inventions on the workplace

*A New Industrial Age* **233**

---

Answers **ASSESSMENT** 1

**1. TERMS & NAMES**
Edwin L. Drake, p. 231
Bessemer process, p. 231
Thomas Alva Edison, p. 232
Christopher Sholes, p. 233
Alexander Graham Bell, p. 233

**2. TAKING NOTES**
**oil drill:** oil boom, wealth; **Bessemer process:** bridge construc-tion, more railroads; **steel:** frame buildings; **electrical power:** artificial light widely available; **telephone:** faster communications

**3. MAKING INFERENCES**
**Yes:** Availability of products; more leisure time **No:** low wages; less skill and craft

**4. HYPOTHESIZING**
Less wealth; less industry; slower growth

**5. ANALYZING EFFECTS**
**Electricity:** changed business and home environments; **Telephone:** sped up communication, faster service, faster growth; **Bessemer process:** steel used for buildings, machines, fac-tories, bridges, railroads

GEOGRAPHY SPOTLIGHT

# Industry Changes the Environment

By the mid-1870s, new ideas and technology were well on the way to changing almost every aspect of American life. The location of Cleveland, Ohio, on the shores of Lake Erie, gave the city access to raw materials and made it ripe for industrialization. What no one foresaw were the undesirable side effects of rapid development and technological progress.

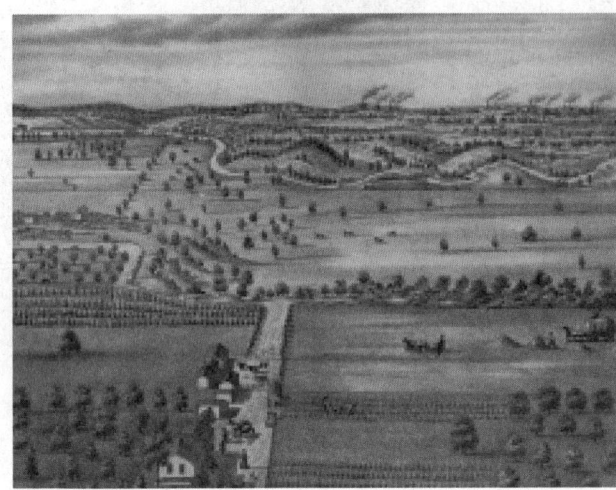

**❶ FROM HAYSTACKS TO SMOKESTACKS**

In 1874, parts of Cleveland were still rural, with farms like the one pictured dotting the landscape. The smokestacks of the Standard Oil refinery in the distance, however, indicate that industrialization had begun.

**❷ REFINING THE LANDSCAPE**

Industries like the Standard Oil refinery shown in this 1889 photo soon became a source of prosperity for both Cleveland and the entire country. The pollution they belched into the atmosphere, however, was the beginning of an ongoing problem: how to balance industrial production and environmental concerns.

**234** CHAPTER 6

## RECOMMENDED RESOURCES

### BOOKS

Burns, Noel M. *Erie: The Lake That Survived.* Totowa, NJ: Rowman & Littlefield, 1985. How cleanup efforts helped Lake Erie recover from pollution.

Campbell, Thomas F., and Edward M. Miggins. *The Birth of Modern Cleveland.* Cleveland: Western Reserve Historical Society, 1988.

Schuyler, David. *The New Urban Landscape.* Baltimore: Johns Hopkins UP, 1988. Environmental aspects of the growth of cities in the 19th century.

Tarbell, Ida M. *The History of the Standard Oil Company.* Temecula, CA: Reprint Services Corp., 1993.

### VIDEOS

*Great Lakes, Fragile Seas.* National Geographic and WQED, 1991. Past pollution and present efforts to correct it.

*The Rise of the American City.* Encyclopaedia Britannica, 1969. The growth of cities and the consequent problems.

*U.S. Cities 1984.* Encyclopaedia Britannica. Focus on industrial development.

### SOFTWARE

*Balance of the Planet.* CD-ROM. Broderbund. Students must try to sustain industry and the environment.

*Planetary Manager.* Videodisc. National Geographic. Impact of fossil fuels, solid-waste management, and water pollution.

### INTEGRATED TECHNOLOGY

For teacher support, visit . . .

 classzone.com

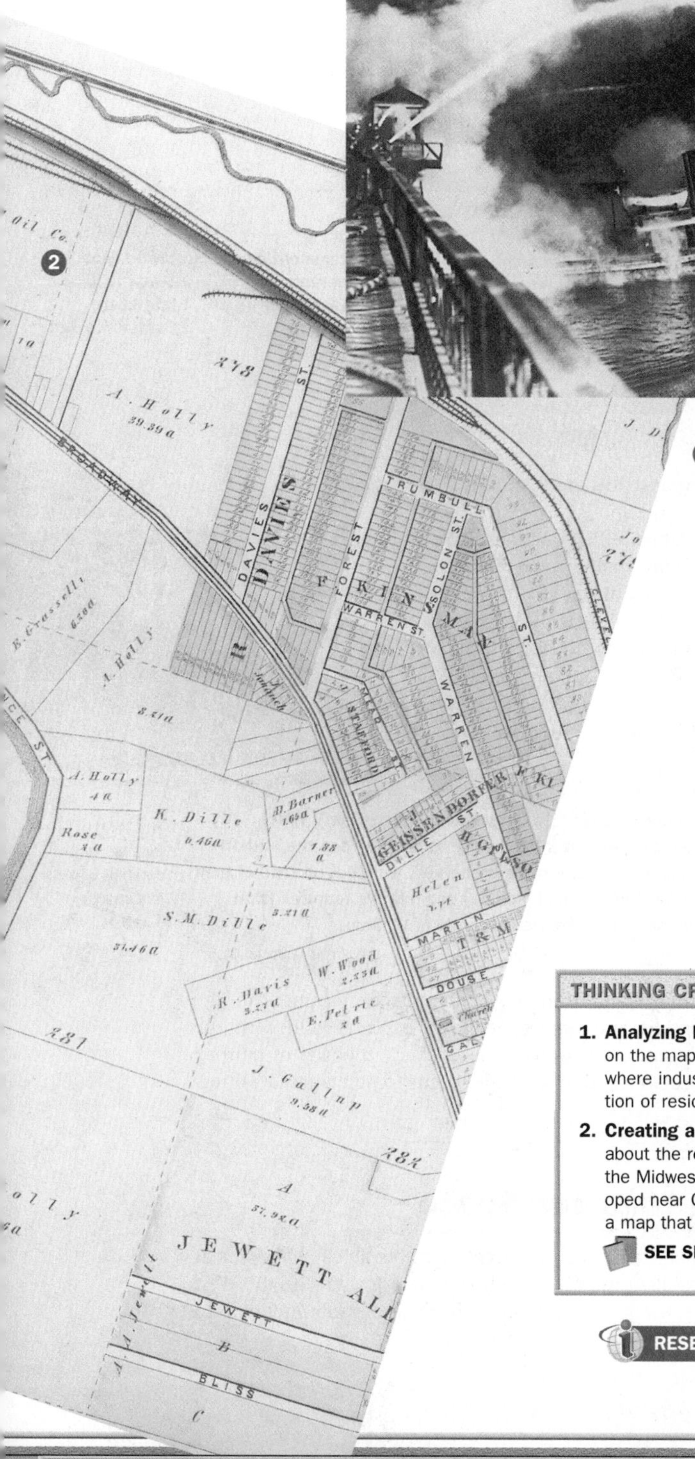

## Instruct

1. Why was Cleveland considered an ideal town to undergo an industrial boom?
2. In what ways did industrialization improve life for the residents of Cleveland?
3. How did the industrialization of Cleveland affect the city's Cuyahoga River?

**MAKING PERSONAL CONNECTIONS**
Have students consider environmental problems affecting their city or region. What are the causes of the problems? What is being done, or should be done, to correct them?

**❸ A RIVER OF FIRE**

Industrial pollution would affect not only the air but also the water. Refineries and steel mills discharged so much oil into the Cuyahoga River that major fires broke out on the water in 1936, 1952, and 1969. The 1952 blaze, pictured above, destroyed three tugboats, three buildings, and the ship-repair yards. In the decade following the 1969 fire, changes in the way industrial plants operated, along with the construction of wastewater treatment plants, helped restore the quality of the water.

## HISTORY from VISUALS

**Interpreting the Images**
Why might John D. Rockefeller have chosen the location he did for his Standard Oil company? *(the accessibility of both railroad lines and water transportation in the form of the Cuyahoga River and canals)* Discuss with students the irony of a river on fire and the incredible quantities of oil that must have accumulated to cause the Cuyahoga to go up in flames three times.

**THINKING CRITICALLY**

1. **Analyzing Patterns** Locate the Standard Oil Company on the map of Cleveland. What can you conclude about where industry was located as compared with the location of residential neighborhoods?
2. **Creating a Thematic Map** Pose a historical question about the relationship between industry and areas of the Midwest. For example, what types of industry developed near Chicago and why? Then research and create a map that answers your question.
   **SEE SKILLBUILDER HANDBOOK, PAGE R32.**

**RESEARCH LINKS** CLASSZONE.COM

*A New Industrial Age* **235**

**THINKING CRITICALLY: ANSWERS**

1. **ANALYZING PATTERNS** The industry is located along the river and away from residential neighborhoods. It probably wasn't a very pleasant place to live near.

2. **CREATING A THEMATIC MAP**

   **Rubric**
   A thematic map should . . .
   · demonstrate in-depth research on the selected area
   · fully demonstrate analysis and evaluation of the information
   · clearly present selected information in an acceptable spatial configuration

## OBJECTIVES

1. Identify the role of the railroads in unifying the country.

2. List positive and negative effects of railroads on the nation's economy.

3. Summarize reasons for, and outcomes of, the demand for railroad reform.

### SKILLBUILDERS

· Geography Skillbuilder, human-environment interaction, movement, p. 239
· Analyzing Political Cartoons, p. 240

### CRITICAL THINKING

· Analyzing Effects, p. 237
· Summarizing, p. 238
· Analyzing Issues, p. 239
· Making Inferences, p. 240
· Synthesizing, p. 240
· Analyzing Motives, p. 240

## Focus & Motivate

What name might students give the present age? ("The Age of the Car" or "The Age of the Computer") In formulating their answers, have them consider the technology that exerts the most influence on all aspects of American life. Do they think the railroads played a similar role in American life in the late 19th century? Why or why not?

## Instruct

### Instruct: Objective 1

**Railroads Span Time and Space**
TAKS SS11 2(US2.03)

· How did the government facilitate the expansion of the railroads?
· What were the positive and negative aspects of railroad expansion?
· How did railroad time work?

 **In-Depth Resources: Unit 2**
· Guided Reading, p. 21
· Literature: from *The Bride Comes to Yellow Sky*, pp. 34–36

 SECTION 2

# The Age of the Railroads

| MAIN IDEA | WHY IT MATTERS NOW | Terms & Names |
|---|---|---|
| The growth and consolidation of railroads benefited the nation but also led to corruption and required government regulation. | Railroads made possible the expansion of industry across the United States. | • transcontinental railroad • George M. Pullman • Crédit Mobilier • *Munn* v. *Illinois* • Interstate Commerce Act |

 **U.S. History**
**TEKS** 2A, 2B, 2C, 8A, 8B, 9A, 10A, 12B, 23A, 24A, 24B, 24C, 24D, 24F, 25A, 25B, 25C, 25D

### One American's Story

In October 1884, the economist Richard Ely visited the town of Pullman, Illinois, to write about it for *Harper's* magazine. At first, Ely was impressed with the atmosphere of order, planning, and well-being in the town George M. Pullman had designed for the employees of his railroad-car factory. But after talking at length with a dissatisfied company officer, Ely concluded the town had a fatal flaw: it too greatly restricted its residents. Pullman employees were compelled to obey rules in which they had no say. Ely concluded that "the idea of Pullman is un-American."

**A PERSONAL VOICE** RICHARD T. ELY

" It is benevolent, well-wishing feudalism [a medieval social system], which desires the happiness of the people, but in such way as shall please the authorities. . . . If free American institutions are to be preserved, we want no race of men reared as underlings. . . . [The town should include] cooperative features [that would] awaken in the residents an interest and a pride in Pullman."

—"Pullman: A Social Study"

▲ The town of Pullman was carefully laid out and strictly controlled.

As the railroads grew, they came to influence many facets of American life. They caused the standard time and time zones to be set and influenced the growth of towns and communities. However, the unchecked power of railroad companies led to widespread abuses that spurred citizens to demand federal regulation of the industry.

## 1 Railroads Span Time and Space

Rails made local transit reliable and westward expansion possible for business as well as for people. Realizing how important railroads were for settling the West and developing the country, the government made huge land grants and loans to the railroad companies.

**236** CHAPTER 6

---

## PROGRAM RESOURCES

 **In-Depth Resources: Unit 2**
· Guided Reading, p. 21
· Reteaching Activity, p. 26
· Literature: from *The Bride Comes to Yellow Sky*, pp. 34–36
 **Reading Study Guide** (English and Spanish), pp. 67–68

 **Access for Students Acquiring English/ESL**
· Guided Reading (Spanish), p. 87
**Formal Assessment**
· Section Quiz, p. 119
**Integrated Assessment**
· Rubrics

**INTEGRATED TECHNOLOGY**

 **Electronic Library of Primary Sources**

**classzone.com**

**TEXAS RESOURCES**

 TAKS Spiraled Content Review

 TAKS Practice Tests

 TAKS Practice Transparencies TT53

 TAKS Online Test Practice

**A NATIONAL NETWORK** By 1856, the railroads extended west to the Mississippi River, and three years later, they crossed the Missouri. Just over a decade later, crowds across the United States cheered as the Central Pacific and Union Pacific Railroads met at Promontory, Utah, on May 10, 1869. A golden spike marked the spanning of the nation by the first **transcontinental railroad**. Other transcontinental lines followed, and regional lines multiplied as well. At the start of the Civil War, the nation had had about 30,000 miles of track. By 1890, that figure was nearly six times greater.

**ROMANCE AND REALITY** The railroads brought the dreams of available land, adventure, and a fresh start within the grasp of many Americans. This romance was made possible, however, only by the harsh lives of railroad workers.

The Central Pacific Railroad employed thousands of Chinese immigrants. The Union Pacific hired Irish immigrants and desperate, out-of-work Civil War veterans to lay track across treacherous terrain while enduring attacks by Native Americans. Accidents and diseases disabled and killed thousands of men each year. In 1888, when the first railroad statistics were published, the casualties totaled more than 2,000 employees killed and 20,000 injured.

**RAILROAD TIME** In spite of these difficult working conditions, the railroad laborers helped to transform the diverse regions of the country into a united nation. Though linked in space, each community still operated on its own time, with noon when the sun was directly overhead. Noon in Boston, for example, was almost 12 minutes later than noon in New York. Travelers riding from Maine to California might reset their watches 20 times.

In 1869, to remedy this problem, Professor C. F. Dowd proposed that the earth's surface be divided into 24 time zones, one for each hour of the day. Under his plan, the United States would contain four zones: the Eastern, Central, Mountain, and Pacific time zones. The railroad companies endorsed Dowd's plan enthusiastically, and many towns followed suit.

Finally, on November 18, 1883, railroad crews and towns across the country synchronized their watches. In 1884, an international conference set worldwide time zones that incorporated railroad time. The U.S. Congress, however, didn't officially adopt railroad time as the standard for the nation until 1918. As strong a unifying force as the railroads were, however, they also opened the way for abuses that led to social and economic unrest. Ⓐ

### Opportunities and Opportunists ❷

The growth of the railroads influenced the industries and businesses in which Americans worked. Iron, coal, steel, lumber, and glass industries grew rapidly as they tried to keep pace with the railroads' demand for materials and parts. The rapid spread of railroad lines also fostered the growth of towns, helped establish new markets, and offered rich opportunities for both visionaries and profiteers.

---

**MAIN IDEA**

**Analyzing Effects**
Ⓐ What were the effects of railroad expansion?

*A. Answer*
The growth of industries that could ship to new markets; hazardous jobs for railroad workers; an increase of immigration and migration to the West.

---

HISTORICAL SPOTLIGHT

**CHINESE IMMIGRANTS AND THE RAILROADS**

Although the railroads paid all their employees poorly, Asians usually earned less than whites. The average pay for whites working a ten-hour day was $40 to $60 a month plus free meals. Chinese immigrants hired by the Central Pacific performed similar tasks from dawn to dusk for about $35 a month—and they had to supply their own food.

The immigrants' working conditions were miserable, as depicted by artist Jake Lee below. In 1866, for example, the railroad hired them to dig a tunnel through a granite mountain. For five months of that year, the Chinese lived and worked in camps surrounded by banks of snow. The total snowfall reached over 40 feet. Hundreds of the men were buried in avalanches or later found frozen, still clutching their shovels or picks.

---

**HISTORICAL SPOTLIGHT**

**Chinese Immigrants and the Railroads**
Have students discuss why they think that many Chinese immigrants were willing to engage in such harsh and dangerous work. *(They were in search of a better life in America but were unable to find good jobs, possibly due to prejudice.)*

**More About . . .**

**Railroad Time**
Railroad engineers were very flexible about their schedules. An engineer on the Old Colony Railroad in Massachusetts stopped to collect eggs from an elderly woman every day. Once she persuaded him to wait until her hen laid an egg to make a full dozen. The Delaware, Lackawanna, and Western Railroad (the D.L. & W.) was nicknamed the "Delay, Linger, and Wait"; the Newburgh, Dutchess, and Connecticut (the N.D. & C.) became the "Never Did and Couldn't."

**Instruct: Objective ❷**

**Opportunities and Opportunists**
TAKS SS11 2(US2.03)
· How did the growth of railroad lines promote the growth of cities and trade?
· What was the Crédit Mobilier scandal?

📄 In-Depth Resources: Unit 2
· Guided Reading, p. 21

👁 Electronic Library of Primary Sources
· How Women Are Treated by the Pullman Company, 1894, by J. Curtiss

*A New Industrial Age* **237**

---

**DIFFERENTIATING INSTRUCTION** | **LESS PROFICIENT READERS**

**Using a Problem Solving Process**

Ask students how individual communities might determine when it was noon. *(when the sun was directly overhead)* Then perform this experiment. Place a tall drinking glass on a large sheet of paper on the ground at exactly noon. Draw a line around the shadow of the glass every 10 minutes until you get a series of outlines. The series of shadow outlines shows that the earth is constantly moving to a different position under the sun.

Help students see how calculating local time by the sun could differ by several minutes in different parts of one state. Then have them consider the advantages and disadvantages of reckoning time using a local system versus using a standardized time system. *(Local time in sync with nature; standardized time zones are in sync with the rest of the world.)*

## Tracing Themes
### SCIENCE AND TECHNOLOGY

**New Technology**
The new technology that contributed to the rapid growth had negative as well as positive effects on society. The impact on different groups of people, such as farmers, ranchers, Native Americans, settlers, and business owners, highlights the fact that new technology brings not only opportunity but opportunists.

## Instruct: Objective ❸

**The Grange and the Railroads**
TAKS SS11 5(WH26.C)

· For what reasons were farmers angry at railroad companies?
· How did the Granger laws help farmers?
· What was the Interstate Commerce Act?

 In-Depth Resources: Unit 2
· Guided Reading, p. 21

---

**Pullman cars brought luxury to the rails, as shown in this advertisement from around 1890.** ▼

---

**NEW TOWNS AND MARKETS** By linking previously isolated cities, towns, and settlements, the railroads promoted trade and interdependence. As part of a nationwide network of suppliers and markets, individual towns began to specialize in particular products. Chicago soon became known for its stockyards and Minneapolis for its grain industries. These cities prospered by selling large quantities of their products to the entire country. New towns and communities also grew up along the railroad lines. Cities as diverse as Abilene, Kansas; Flagstaff, Arizona; Denver, Colorado; and Seattle, Washington, owed their prosperity, if not their very existence, to the railroads. **B**

**PULLMAN** The railroads helped cities not only grow up but branch out. In 1880, for example, **George M. Pullman** built a factory for manufacturing sleepers and other railroad cars on the Illinois prairie. The nearby town that Pullman built for his employees followed in part the models of earlier industrial experiments in Europe. Whereas New England textile manufacturers had traditionally provided housing for their workers, the town of Pullman provided for almost all of workers' basic needs. Pullman residents lived in clean, well-constructed brick houses and apartment buildings with at least one window in every room—a luxury for city dwellers. In addition, the town offered services and facilities such as doctors' offices, shops, and an athletic field.

As Richard Ely observed, however, the town of Pullman remained firmly under company control. Residents were not allowed to loiter on their front steps or to drink alcohol. Pullman hoped that his tightly controlled environment would ensure a stable work force. However, Pullman's refusal to lower rents after cutting his employees' pay led to a violent strike in 1894.

**CRÉDIT MOBILIER** Pullman created his company town out of the desire for control and profit. In some other railroad magnates, or powerful and influential industrialists, these desires turned into self-serving corruption. In one of the most infamous schemes, stockholders in the Union Pacific Railroad formed, in 1864, a construction company called **Crédit Mobilier** (krĕd'ĭt mō-bēl'yər). The stockholders gave this company a contract to lay track at two to three times the actual cost—and pocketed the profits. They donated shares of stock to about 20 representatives in Congress in 1867.

A congressional investigation of the company, spurred by reports in the *New York Sun*, eventually found that the officers of the Union Pacific had taken up to $23 million in stocks, bonds, and cash. Testimony implicated such well-known and respected federal officials as Vice President Schuyler Colfax and Congressman James Garfield, who later became president. Although these public figures kept their profits and received little more than a slap on the wrist, the reputation of the Republican Party was tarnished. **C**

## The Grange and the Railroads ❸

Farmers were especially affected by corruption in the railroads. The Grangers—members of the Grange, a farmers' organization founded in 1867—began demanding governmental control over the railroad industry.

**MAIN IDEA**

**Summarizing**
**B** How did the railroads affect cities?

*B. Answer*
Railroads led to a growth of cities in the Northeast and the Midwest and led to the development of new cities in the West.

**MAIN IDEA**

**Summarizing**
**C** How did railroad owners use Crédit Mobilier to make huge, undeserved profits?

*C. Answer*
By charging too much for railroad construction and paying off government officials.

---

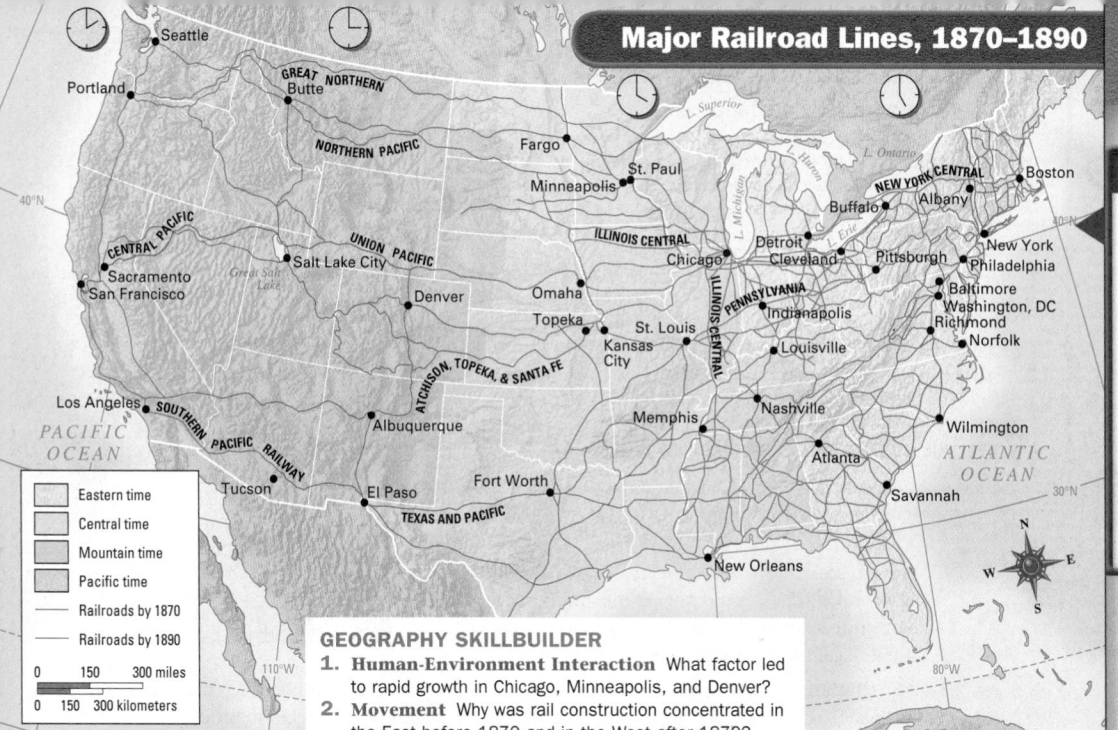

## Major Railroad Lines, 1870–1890

Eastern time
Central time
Mountain time
Pacific time
— Railroads by 1870
— Railroads by 1890

0    150    300 miles
0    150    300 kilometers

**GEOGRAPHY SKILLBUILDER**
1. **Human-Environment Interaction** What factor led to rapid growth in Chicago, Minneapolis, and Denver?
2. **Movement** Why was rail construction concentrated in the East before 1870 and in the West after 1870?

### HISTORY from VISUALS

**Interpreting the Map**
Have students study the distribution of railroads throughout the country and the land forms associated with various regions. What connections can they draw? *(The greatest concentration of railroads is in the relatively flat Midwest.)*

**Extension** Have students trace possible railroad routes from Boston to Sacramento, from Cleveland to Los Angeles, or from Seattle to Omaha.

---

**Background**
Price fixing occurs when companies within an industry all agree to charge the same price for a given service, rather than competing to offer the lowest price.

**RAILROAD ABUSES** Farmers were angry with railroad companies for a host of reasons. They were upset by misuse of government land grants, which the railroads sold to other businesses rather than to settlers, as the government intended. The railroads also entered into formal agreements to fix prices, which helped keep farmers in their debt. In addition, they charged different customers different rates, often demanding more for short hauls—for which there was no alternative carrier—than they did for long hauls.

**GRANGER LAWS** In response to these abuses by the railroads, the Grangers took political action. They sponsored state and local political candidates, elected legislators, and successfully pressed for laws to protect their interests. In 1871 Illinois authorized a commission "to establish maximum freight and passenger rates and prohibit discrimination." Grangers throughout the West, Midwest, and Southeast convinced state legislators to pass similar laws, called Granger laws.

The railroads fought back, challenging the constitutionality of the regulatory laws. In 1877, however, in the case of **Munn v. Illinois,** the Supreme Court upheld the Granger laws by a vote of seven to two. The states thus won the right to regulate the railroads for the benefit of farmers and consumers. The Grangers also helped establish an important principle—the federal government's right to regulate private industry to serve the public interest. **D**

**INTERSTATE COMMERCE ACT** The Grangers' triumph was short-lived, however. In 1886, the Supreme Court ruled that a state could not set rates on interstate commerce—railroad traffic that either came from or was going to another state. In response to public outrage, Congress passed the **Interstate Commerce Act** in 1887. This act reestablished the right of the federal government to supervise railroad activities and established a five-member Interstate Commerce Commission (ICC) for that purpose. The ICC had difficulty regulating railroad rates because of a long legal process and resistance from the railroads. The final

**MAIN IDEA**

**Analyzing Issues**
**D** How did the Grangers, who were largely poor farmers, do battle with the giant railroad companies?

*Skillbuilder Answers*
1. Their location as railroad hubs.
2. In 1869, the transcontinental railroad was complete, which spurred the need for new, smaller rail lines across the West.

*D. Answer*
The farmers took political action in one united front. They pressed legislators to pass laws to protect them.

### More About . . .

**Interstate Commerce Commission (ICC)**
The ICC was the first independent federal regulatory agency, with the specific purpose of restraining the monopolistic railroad companies and ensuring just and reasonable railroad freight rates. Its history is largely one of attempts by Congress to respond as the railroad companies discovered and exploited new ways to evade compliance.

The creation of the ICC temporarily mollified the public, even though the new agency had no power to regulate rates or practices, only to investigate. In 1903, the ICC's power was significantly strengthened by the Elkins Act, which banned some types of collusion that railroads had used to escape federal controls. The Hepburn Act (1906) finally gave the ICC the authority to set rates and made its orders legally binding, and it outlawed numerous monopolistic practices.

*A New Industrial Age* **239**

---

**DIFFERENTIATING INSTRUCTION**   **GIFTED AND TALENTED**

### Exploring the Railroad Lines

Have interested students choose one of the railroad lines depicted on the map on this page, and create a museum display exploring the history of the line. Students should trace the line from its origin through its heyday and decline, and examine its current status. Displays might include:

· copies of photographs of the railroad from various points in its history
· accounts from people who rode the line
· enlarged U.S. map showing the line's route and noting any famous accidents or other interesting information

 Mini-Lesson 1: SS11 3(US2.B)

Students might also include a time line that covers the history of the line. Have them start with the basic time line frame below and add dates and captions as appropriate:

date of inception                    status today

## Analyzing *Political Cartoons*

### SKILLBUILDER ANSWERS

1. A criticism. The colossus is supposed to be terrifying, controlling everything, a threat to freedom and fairness.

2. Controlling the tracks and the station implies that Vanderbilt has total control of the whole operation. He can make it do what he wants.

# Assess & Reteach

### SECTION 2 ASSESSMENT

Have students work in small groups to answer the questions. Have them indicate the portion of the text that best substantiates each answer.

 Formal Assessment
· Section Quiz, p. 119

### SELF-ASSESSMENT

Have students write a paragraph about the most surprising thing they learned in this section.

### RETEACH

Have a small group of students volunteer to present a summary of the main ideas of the section to the class.

 In-Depth Resources: Unit 2
· Reteaching Activity, p. 26

## Analyzing *Political Cartoons*

**"THE MODERN COLOSSUS OF (RAIL) ROADS"**
Joseph Keppler drew this cartoon in 1879, featuring the railroad "giants" William Vanderbilt (top), Jay Gould (bottom right), and Cyrus W. Fields (bottom left). The three magnates formed a railroad trust out of their Union Pacific, New York Central, and Lake Shore & Dependence lines.

**SKILLBUILDER Analyzing Political Cartoons**

1. The title of this cartoon is a pun on the Colossus of Rhodes, a statue erected in 282 B.C. on an island near Greece. According to legend, the 100-foot-tall statue straddled Rhodes's harbor entrance. Do you think the artist means the comparison as a compliment or a criticism? Why?

2. The reins held by the railroad magnates attach not only to the trains but also to the tracks and the railroad station. What does this convey about the magnates' control of the railroads?

 **SEE SKILLBUILDER HANDBOOK, PAGE R24.**

*Skillbuilder Answers*
1. Criticism. The Colossus of Rhodes protected the harbor; the magnates controlled the railroads for their own gain.
2. Controlling the tracks and the station implies that Vanderbilt has total control of the whole operation.

blow to the commission came in 1897, when the Supreme Court ruled that it could not set maximum railroad rates. Not until 1906, under President Theodore Roosevelt, did the ICC gain the power it needed to be effective.

**PANIC AND CONSOLIDATION** Although the ICC presented few problems for the railroads, corporate abuses, mismanagement, overbuilding, and competition pushed many railroads to the brink of bankruptcy. Their financial problems played a major role in a nationwide economic collapse. The panic of 1893 was the worst depression up to that time: by the end of 1893, around 600 banks and 15,000 businesses had failed, and by 1895, 4 million people had lost their jobs. By the middle of 1894, a quarter of the nation's railroads had been taken over by financial companies. Large investment firms such as J. P. Morgan & Company reorganized the railroads. As the 20th century dawned, seven powerful companies held sway over two-thirds of the nation's railroad tracks.

**Vocabulary**
**consolidation:** the act of uniting or combining

 **ASSESSMENT**

1. **TERMS & NAMES** For each term or name, write a sentence explaining its significance.
   - **transcontinental railroad**
   - **George M. Pullman**
   - **Crédit Mobilier**
   - ***Munn* v. *Illinois***
   - **Interstate Commerce Act**

### MAIN IDEA

2. **TAKING NOTES**
In a chart like the one below, fill in effects of the rapid growth of railroads.

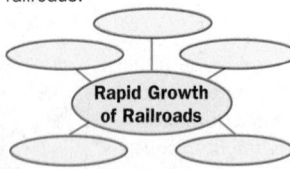
Rapid Growth of Railroads

How did the growth of railroads affect people's everyday lives? How did it affect farmers?

### CRITICAL THINKING

3. **MAKING INFERENCES**
Do you think the government and private citizens could have done more to curb the corruption and power of the railroads? Give examples to support your opinion.
**Think About:**
- why the railroads had power
- the rights of railroad customers and workers
- the scope of government regulations

4. **SYNTHESIZING**
The federal government gave land and made loans to the railroad companies. Why was the government so eager to promote the growth of railroads?

5. **ANALYZING MOTIVES**
Reread "Another Perspective" on railroads (page 238). Why do you think that some Americans disliked this new means of transportation?

**240** CHAPTER 6

 **ASSESSMENT** Answers

**1. TERMS & NAMES**
transcontinental railroad, p. 237
George M. Pullman, p. 238
Crédit Mobilier, p. 238
*Munn* v. *Illinois*, p. 239
Interstate Commerce Act, p. 239

**2. TAKING NOTES**
Regulation of industry; growth of towns and cities; creation of nationwide market; corruption; consolidation of railroads.

**3. MAKING INFERENCES**
**Yes:** Consumer boycotts; more regulation; better prosecution of corrupt officials.
**No:** *Munn* v. *Illinois* broke new ground for regulation; more regulation would have slowed industrial growth.

**4. SYNTHESIZING**
Railroads increased U.S. settlement and built up U.S. commerce.

**5. ANALYZING MOTIVES**
Pollution and social changes brought on by railroads impeded freedoms. Some feared change because of unknown consequences.

# Big Business and Labor

| MAIN IDEA | WHY IT MATTERS NOW | Terms & Names |
|---|---|---|
| The expansion of industry resulted in the growth of big business and prompted laborers to form unions to better their lives. | Many of the strategies used today in industry and in the labor movement, such as consolidation and the strike, have their origins in the late 19th century. | • Andrew Carnegie • vertical and horizontal integration • Social Darwinism • John D. Rockefeller • Sherman Antitrust Act • Samuel Gompers • American Federation of Labor (AFL) • Eugene V. Debs • Industrial Workers of the World (IWW) • Mary Harris Jones |

 **U.S. History** 1B, 2B, 2C, 4C, 8A, 12C, 19B, 21A, 21D, 24B, 24C, 24H, 25A, 25B, 25C, 25D

### One American's Story

Born in Scotland to penniless parents, **Andrew Carnegie** came to this country in 1848, at age 12. Two years later, he worked his way up to become private secretary to the local superintendent of the Pennsylvania Railroad. One morning, Carnegie single-handedly relayed messages that unsnarled a tangle of freight and passenger trains. His boss, Thomas A. Scott, rewarded Carnegie by giving him a chance to buy stock. Carnegie's mother mortgaged the family home to make the purchase possible. Soon Carnegie received his first dividend.

**A PERSONAL VOICE** ANDREW CARNEGIE

" One morning a white envelope was lying upon my desk, addressed in a big John Hancock hand, to 'Andrew Carnegie, Esquire.' . . . All it contained was a check for ten dollars upon the Gold Exchange Bank of New York. I shall remember that check as long as I live. . . . It gave me the first penny of revenue from capital—something that I had not worked for with the sweat of my brow. 'Eureka!' I cried. 'Here's the goose that lays the golden eggs.' "

—*Autobiography of Andrew Carnegie*

Andrew Carnegie was one of the first industrial moguls to make his own fortune. His rise from rags to riches, along with his passion for supporting charities, made him a model of the American success story.

▲ Nineteenth century industrialist Andrew Carnegie gave money to build public libraries, hoping to help others write their own rags-to-riches story.

## ① Carnegie's Innovations

By 1865, Carnegie was so busy managing the money he had earned in dividends that he happily left his job at the Pennsylvania Railroad. He entered the steel business in 1873 after touring a British steel mill and witnessing the awesome spectacle of the Bessemer process in action. By 1899, the Carnegie Steel Company

---

## OBJECTIVES

1 Identify management and business strategies that contributed to the success of business tycoons such as Andrew Carnegie.

2 Explain Social Darwinism and its effects on society.

3 Summarize the emergence and growth of unions.

4 Explain the violent reactions of industry and government to union strikes.

### SKILLBUILDERS
· Interpreting Graphs, p. 247

### CRITICAL THINKING
· Summarizing, pp. 242, 243, 249
· Evaluating, p. 244
· Synthesizing, p. 244
· Analyzing Issues, p. 245
· Contrasting, p. 246
· Analyzing Causes, p. 247
· Evaluating Leadership, p. 249
· Drawing Conclusions, p. 249
· Hypothesizing, p. 249

## Focus & Motivate

Ask students what personal qualities they think a person would need to become a billionaire in today's world.

## Instruct

### Instruct: Objective ①
**Carnegie's Innovations**
TAKS SS11 3(US22.C)
· What business did Andrew Carnegie dominate?
· What was the difference between vertical integration and horizontal integration?

 In-Depth Resources: Unit 2
· Guided Reading, p. 22

---

## PROGRAM RESOURCES

In-Depth Resources: Unit 2
· Guided Reading, p. 22
· Skillbuilder Practice: Creating Oral Presentations, p. 24
· Reteaching Activity, p. 27
· Geography Application: The Changing Labor Force, pp. 28–29
· Primary Sources, pp. 31–33
· American Lives: Andrew Carnegie, p. 37; Mary Harris "Mother" Jones, p. 38

 Reading Study Guide (English and Spanish), pp. 69–70
 Access for Students Acquiring English/ESL
· Guided Reading (Spanish), p. 88
· Skillbuilder Practice, p. 89
· Geography Application, pp. 90–91
 Formal Assessment
· Section Quiz, p. 120
 Integrated Assessment
· Rubrics

### INTEGRATED TECHNOLOGY

Critical Thinking Transp. CT48
· Horizontal Consolidation and Vertical Integration

Humanities Transp. HT35
·The Bosses of the Senate

Electronic Library of Primary Sources

classzone.com

### TEXAS RESOURCES

 TAKS Spiraled Content Review
 TAKS Practice Tests
 TAKS Practice Transparencies TT54
 TAKS Online Test Practice

### Vertical and Horizontal Integration

RESOURCES
Raw materials, fields, forests, and farms

MANUFACTURING
Production and processing

DISTRIBUTION
Shipping and transportation, delivery to customers

manufactured more steel than all the factories in Great Britain.

**NEW BUSINESS STRATEGIES**
Carnegie's success was due in part to management practices that he initiated and that soon became widespread. First, he continually searched for ways to make better products more cheaply. He incorporated new machinery and techniques, such as accounting systems that enabled him to track precise costs. Second, he attracted talented people by offering them stock in the company, and he encouraged competition among his assistants.

In addition to improving his own manufacturing operation, Carnegie attempted to control as much of the steel industry as he could. He did this mainly by **vertical integration,** a process in which he bought out his suppliers—coal fields and iron mines, ore freighters, and railroad lines—in order to control the raw materials and transportation systems. Carnegie also attempted to buy out competing steel producers. In this process, known as **horizontal integration,** companies producing similar products merge. Having gained control over his suppliers and having limited his competition, Carnegie owned almost the entire steel industry. By the time he sold his business in 1901, Carnegie's companies produced by far the largest portion of the nation's steel. Ⓐ

## Social Darwinism and Business ❷

Andrew Carnegie explained his extraordinary success by pointing to his hard work, shrewd investments, and innovative business practices. Late-19th-century social philosophers, thought that Carnegie's achievement could be explained scientifically by a new theory—Social Darwinism.

**PRINCIPLES OF SOCIAL DARWINISM** The philosophy called **Social Darwinism** grew out of the English naturalist Charles Darwin's theory of biological evolution. In his book *On the Origin of Species*, published in 1859, Darwin described his observations that some individuals of a species flourish and pass their traits along to the next generation, while others do not. He explained that a process of "natural selection" weeded out less-suited individuals and enabled the best-adapted to survive.

The English philosopher Herbert Spencer used Darwin's biological theories to explain the evolution of human society. Soon, economists found in Social Darwinism a way to justify the doctrine of laissez faire (a French term meaning "allow to do"). According to this doctrine, the marketplace should not be regulated. William G. Sumner, a social science professor at Yale University, promoted the theory that success and failure in business were governed by natural law and that no one had the right to intervene.

**A NEW DEFINITION OF SUCCESS** The premise of the survival and success of the most capable naturally made sense to the 4,000 millionaires who had emerged since the Civil War. Because the theory supported the notion of individual responsibility and blame, it also appealed to the Protestant work ethic of

Popular literature promoted the possibility of rags-to-riches success for anyone who was virtuous and hard-working. ▼

RISEN *from the* RANKS

HORATIO ALGER JR.

---

many Americans. According to Social Darwinism, riches were a sign of God's favor, and therefore the poor must be lazy or inferior people who deserved their lot in life.

## ② Fewer Control More

Although some business owners endorsed the "natural law" in theory, in practice most entrepreneurs did everything they could to control the competition that threatened the growth of their business empires.

**GROWTH AND CONSOLIDATION** Many industrialists took the approach "If you can't beat 'em, join 'em." They often pursued horizontal integration in the form of mergers. A merger usually occurred when one corporation bought out the stock of another. A firm that bought out all its competitors could achieve a monopoly, or complete control over its industry's production, wages, and prices.

One way to create a monopoly was to set up a holding company, a corporation that did nothing but buy out the stock of other companies. Headed by banker J. P. Morgan, United States Steel was one of the most successful holding companies. In 1901, when it bought the largest manufacturer, Carnegie Steel, it became the world's largest business.

Corporations such as the Standard Oil Company, established by **John D. Rockefeller,** took a different approach to mergers: they joined with competing companies in trust agreements. Participants in a trust turned their stock over to a group of trustees—people who ran the separate companies as one large corporation. In return, the companies were entitled to dividends on profits earned by the trust. Trusts were not legal mergers, however. Rockefeller used a trust to gain total control of the oil industry in America. **B**

**ROCKEFELLER AND THE "ROBBER BARONS"** In 1870, Rockefeller's Standard Oil Company of Ohio processed two or three percent of the country's crude oil. Within a decade, it controlled 90 percent of the refining business. Rockefeller reaped huge profits by paying his employees extremely low wages and driving his competitors out of business by selling his oil at a lower price than it cost to produce it. Then, when he controlled the market, he hiked prices far above original levels.

Alarmed at the tactics of industrialists, critics began to call them robber barons. But industrialists were also philanthropists. Although Rockefeller kept most of his assets, he still gave away over $500 million, establishing the Rockefeller Foundation, providing funds to found the University of Chicago, and creating a medical institute that helped find a cure for yellow fever.

---

**Background**
See *monopoly* on page R43 in the Economics Handbook.

**TAKS**
Mini-Lesson 4: SS11 1(6.E)

**MAIN IDEA**
**Summarizing**
**B** What strategies enabled big businesses to eliminate competition?

**B. Answer**
Big businesses formed partnerships to create monopolies. They merged small companies into large corporations. They aimed for total control of an industry, so that they could fix prices and wages to their advantage.

---

# KEY PLAYER

**JOHN D. ROCKEFELLER**
**1839–1937**

At the height of John Davison Rockefeller's power, an associate noted that he "always sees a little farther than the rest of us—and then he sees around the corner."

Rockefeller's father was a flashy peddler of phony cancer cures with a unique approach to raising children. "I cheat my boys every chance I get. . . . I want to make 'em sharp," he boasted.

It seems that this approach succeeded with the oldest son, John D., who was sharp enough to land a job as an assistant bookkeeper at the age of 16. Rockefeller was very proud of his own son, who succeeded him in the family business. At the end of his life, Rockefeller referred not to his millions but to John D., Jr., as "my greatest fortune."

---

This 1900 cartoon, captioned "What a funny little government!" is a commentary on the power of the Standard Oil empire. John D. Rockefeller holds the White House in his hand.

---

## KEY PLAYER

**John D. Rockefeller**
Tell students that Rockefeller's mother started her son on his first business enterprise when he was just seven years old: raising turkeys. Later, he hoed potatoes for 37 cents a day. He lent his savings back to the farmer and quickly found that "it was a good thing to let money be my slave and not make myself a slave to money." Have students compare the attitudes of Rockefeller and his father toward their children.

 **In-Depth Resources: Unit 2**
· Primary Source: *The History of Standard Oil Company*, p. 32

 **Humanities Transparencies HT35**
· The Bosses of the Senate

---

## Tracing Themes
**ECONOMIC OPPORTUNITY**

### Social Darwinism
In the late 19th century, the theory of Social Darwinism maintained that those most able to survive will demonstrate their fitness by accumulating property, wealth, and social status. The prevailing climate of optimism suggested that with perseverance, hard work, and intelligence, anyone might rise from humble beginnings to good fortune.

👁 **Electronic Library of Primary Sources**
· "The Two Acre Lot" by Horatio Alger

---

*A New Industrial Age* **243**

---

## Creating Oral Presentations

**Explaining the Skill** To create an oral presentation, first determine the topic to be presented. Then gather and organize the information. Think about the audience that will hear the presentation and determine what information will be most interesting to the audience. Organize that information in a clear and orderly way. Practice your speech before presenting it.

**Applying the Skill** Have pairs of students tape record an interview of a famous business person from history, such as Alger, Rockefeller, Morgan, or Carnegie. The team should decide what the person would say about how to make money. One student will be the business person and the other a reporter. Then make a tape of the interview. Present the oral presentations to the class.

📖 **In-Depth Resources: Unit 2**
· Skillbuilder Practice: Creating Oral Presentations, p. 24

## Connections Across Time

**1890 AND 1999**

### The Antitrust Case Against Microsoft

In November 1999, a federal judge declared that Microsoft, a leading computer technology company, had violated the Sherman Antitrust Act by gaining a monopoly hold over the computer industry and using its power to unfairly crush competition.

The judge sanctioned the U.S. government's proposal to break Microsoft in two—one company that would sell its Windows operating system and one that would sell everything else. Microsoft, which has claimed from the beginning that it has acted competitively but not unfairly, vowed to fight on in the courts.

In June 2001, another federal judge rejected the breakup of Microsoft, stating that the original judge who decided the antitrust case had shown partiality by holding secret interviews with members of the media. The case remains unsettled.

**C. Answer**
Agree: Everyone is dependent on the millionaires to run businesses efficiently and to provide for the needs of the surrounding communities. or, Disagree: If the millionaires control everything, they will always make people work unfairly and pay unfair prices.

In this photograph, taken by Lewis Hine in 1912, a young sweatshop laborer in New York City carries piecework home.
▼

**244** CHAPTER 6

---

### Instruct: Objective ❸

**Labor Unions Emerge / Union Movements Diverge**
TAKS SS11 3(US2.B)
· What conditions did many factory workers face in the late 19th century?
· What did labor unions advocate?
· What different types of unions emerged during the nation's industrial boom?

 In-Depth Resources: Unit 2
· Guided Reading, p. 22
· Geography Application: The Changing Labor Force, pp. 28–29

Electronic Library of Primary Sources
· On the Goals of Trade Unions by Samuel Gompers

---

Andrew Carnegie donated about 90 percent of the wealth he accumulated during his lifetime; his fortune still supports the arts and learning today. "It will be a great mistake for the community to shoot the millionaires," he said, "for they are the bees that make the most honey, and contribute most to the hive even after they have gorged themselves full." **C**

**SHERMAN ANTITRUST ACT** Despite Carnegie's defense of millionaires, the government was concerned that expanding corporations would stifle free competition. In 1890, the **Sherman Antitrust Act** made it illegal to form a trust that interfered with free trade between states or with other countries.

Prosecuting companies under the Sherman act was not easy, however, because the act didn't clearly define terms such as *trust*. In addition, if firms such as Standard Oil felt pressure from the government, they simply reorganized into single corporations. The Supreme Court threw out seven of the eight cases the federal government brought against trusts. Eventually, the government stopped trying to enforce the Sherman act, and the consolidation of businesses continued.

**BUSINESS BOOM BYPASSES THE SOUTH** Industrial growth concentrated in the North, where natural and urban resources were plentiful. The South was still trying to recover from the Civil War, hindered by a lack of capital—money for investment. After the war, people were unwilling to invest in risky ventures. Northern businesses already owned 90 percent of the stock in the most profitable Southern enterprise, the railroads, thereby keeping the South in a stranglehold. The South remained mostly agricultural, with farmers at the mercy of railroad rates. Entrepreneurs suffered not only from excessive transportation costs, but also from high tariffs on raw materials and imported goods, and from a lack of skilled workers. The post-Reconstruction South seemed to have no way out of economic stagnation. However, growth in forestry and mining, and in the tobacco, furniture, and textile industries, offered hope. **D**

### ❸ Labor Unions Emerge

As business leaders merged and consolidated their forces, it seemed necessary for workers to do the same. Although Northern wages were generally higher than Southern wages, exploitation and unsafe working conditions drew workers together across regions in a nationwide labor movement. Laborers—skilled and unskilled, female and male, black and white—joined together in unions to try to improve their lot.

**LONG HOURS AND DANGER** One of the largest employers, the steel mills, often demanded a seven-day workweek. Seamstresses, like factory workers in most industries, worked 12 or more hours a day, six days a week. Employees were not entitled to vacation, sick leave, unemployment compensation, or reimbursement for injuries suffered on the job.

Yet injuries were common. In dirty, poorly ventilated factories, workers had to perform repetitive, mind-dulling tasks, sometimes with dangerous or faulty equipment. In 1882, an average of 675 laborers were killed in work-related accidents each week. In addition, wages were so low that most families could not survive unless everyone held a job. Between 1890 and 1910, for example, the number of women working for wages

**MAIN IDEA**

**Evaluating**
**C** Do you agree with Carnegie's defense of millionaires? Why or why not?

**MAIN IDEA**

**Synthesizing**
**D** How did economic factors limit industrialization in the South?

**D. Answer**
The South had a devastated economy from the Civil War. It was at the mercy of Northern railroad companies for transporting goods to markets. It also paid added costs for raw materials due to high tariffs.

---

**DIFFERENTIATING INSTRUCTION**   **GIFTED AND TALENTED**    **classzone.com**

### Researching Working Conditions

Have students research working conditions in the late 1800s, using books and Internet sites. Direct students to find at least three quotations from workers in different industries that describe some aspect of their workdays. Students should copy the quotes, not to exceed one or two paragraphs, and document their sources with the title, author, and date of the book or the full Web site address and its supporting organization.

**TAKS** Mini-Lesson 3: SS11 3(US22C)

Allow students to read their quotations to the class.

For particularly vivid quotes, interested students might consider using costumes or props to dramatize their reading. A number of students could develop a "Reader's Theatre" production based on dramatic readings of their quotations.

Integrated Assessment
· Rubric 3

doubled, from 4 million to more than 8 million. Twenty percent of the boys and 10 percent of the girls under age 15—some as young as five years old—also held full-time jobs. With little time or energy left for school, child laborers forfeited their futures to help their families make ends meet.

In sweatshops, or workshops in tenements rather than in factories, workers had little choice but to put up with the conditions. Sweatshop employment, which was tedious and required few skills, was often the only avenue open to women and children. Jacob Riis described the conditions faced by "sweaters."

### A Personal Voice JACOB RIIS

"The bulk of the sweater's work is done in the tenements, which the law that regulates factory labor does not reach. . . . In [them] the child works unchallenged from the day he is old enough to pull a thread. There is no such thing as a dinner hour; men and women eat while they work, and the 'day' is lengthened at both ends far into the night."

—How the Other Half Lives

Not surprisingly, sweatshop jobs paid the lowest wages—often as little as 27 cents for a child's 14-hour day. In 1899, women earned an average of $267 a year, nearly half of men's average pay of $498. The very next year Andrew Carnegie made $23 million—with no income tax.

**EARLY LABOR ORGANIZING** Skilled workers had formed small, local unions since the late 1700s. The first large-scale national organization of laborers, the National Labor Union (NLU), was formed in 1866 by ironworker William H. Sylvis. The refusal of some NLU local chapters to admit African Americans led to the creation of the Colored National Labor Union (CNLU). Nevertheless, NLU membership grew to 640,000. In 1868, the NLU persuaded Congress to legalize an eight-hour day for government workers. **E**

NLU organizers concentrated on linking existing local unions. In 1869, Uriah Stephens focused his attention on individual workers and organized the Noble Order of the Knights of Labor. Its motto was "An injury to one is the concern of all." Membership in the Knights of Labor was officially open to all workers, regardless of race, gender, or degree of skill. Like the NLU, the Knights supported an eight-hour workday and advocated "equal pay for equal work" by men and women. They saw strikes, or refusals to work, as a last resort and instead advocated arbitration. At its height in 1886, the Knights of Labor had about 700,000 members. Although the Knights declined after the failure of a series of strikes, other unions continued to organize.

### ③ Union Movements Diverge

As labor activism spread, it diversified. Two major types of unions made great gains under forceful leaders.

**CRAFT UNIONISM** One approach to the organization of labor was craft unionism, which included skilled workers from one or more trades. **Samuel Gompers** led the Cigar Makers' International Union to join with other craft unions in 1886. The **American Federation of Labor (AFL),**

---

**E. Answer**
Poor working conditions and low wages forced workers to organize into unions to demand fair treatment.

**MAIN IDEA**

**Analyzing Issues**
**E** How did industrial working conditions contribute to the growth of the labor movement?

**Vocabulary**
**arbitration**: a method of settling disputes in which both sides submit their differences to a mutually approved judge

---

### HISTORICAL SPOTLIGHT

#### AFRICAN AMERICANS AND THE LABOR MOVEMENT

Angered by their exclusion from the NLU, African American laborers formed the Colored National Labor Union (CNLU) in 1869. Led by Isaac Meyers, a caulker from Baltimore, the CNLU emphasized cooperation between management and labor and the importance of political reform.

The CNLU disbanded in the early 1870s, but many African-American laborers found a home in the Knights of Labor, the first union to welcome blacks and whites alike. The Great Strike of 1877 brought whites and African Americans together, but the labor movement remained largely divided along racial lines.

Management often hired African Americans as strikebreakers, which intensified white unions' resistance to accepting blacks. African Americans continued to organize on their own, but discrimination and their small numbers relative to white unions hurt black unions' effectiveness.

---

### More About . . .

#### Women and Children at Work

The number of women and children in the work force doubled between 1870 and 1890 to 4 million women workers and 1.5 million child workers (ages 10 to 15). The death rate for female workers was twice that of other workers. Women were the first to be laid off, and often endured abuse from male coworkers and bosses. Children often earned only pennies, but at best they received about half the pay of a male adult worker.

### HISTORICAL SPOTLIGHT

#### African Americans and the Labor Environment

Discuss with students why the CNLU might have preferred to negotiate rather than strike. (*Because its membership was small, strikes might not have been effective.*)

### More About . . .

#### Samuel Gompers

With the exception of 1895, Samuel Gompers (1850–1924) remained president of the AFL until his death. He became the first registered member of the Cigar Makers' International Union at age 14, and continued to work in cigar shops for 20 years, even after he became active in union activities.

👁 Electronic Library of Primary Sources
· On the Goals of Trade Unions, 1883, by S. Gompers

---

*A New Industrial Age* **245**

---

**DIFFERENTIATING INSTRUCTION** | **LESS PROFICIENT READERS**

### Summarizing

On the board, draw the simple chart shown here. Tell students their task is to choose a union to join. As they read about unions on pages 244–246, ask them to take turns filling in the name and membership of each union. When they decide to join a union, they may add their own name to the chart. Ask students to explain why their chosen union will help them.

| Union | Characteristics | Student Members |
|---|---|---|
| NLU | | |
| CNLU | | |
| Knights of Labor | | |
| AFL | | |
| ARU | | |
| IWW | | |

▲ In New York City's Union Square in 1914, IWW members protest violence against striking coal miners in Colorado.

*" The strike is the weapon of the oppressed. "*
EUGENE V. DEBS

with Gompers as its president, focused on collective bargaining, or negotiation between representatives of labor and management, to reach written agreements on wages, hours, and working conditions. Unlike the Knights of Labor, the AFL used strikes as a major tactic. Successful strikes helped the AFL win higher wages and shorter workweeks. Between 1890 and 1915, the average weekly wages in unionized industries rose from $17.50 to $24, and the average workweek fell from almost 54.5 hours to just under 49 hours.

**INDUSTRIAL UNIONISM** Some labor leaders felt that unions should include all laborers—skilled and unskilled—in a specific industry. This concept captured the imagination of **Eugene V. Debs,** who made the first major attempt to form such an industrial union—the American Railway Union (ARU). Most of the new union's members were unskilled and semiskilled laborers, but skilled engineers and firemen joined too. In 1894, the new union won a strike for higher wages. Within two months, its membership climbed to 150,000, dwarfing the 90,000 enrolled in the four skilled railroad brotherhoods. Though the ARU, like the Knights of Labor, never recovered after the failure of a major strike, it added to the momentum of union organizing. **F**

**SOCIALISM AND THE IWW** In an attempt to solve the problems faced by workers, Eugene Debs and some other labor activists eventually turned to socialism, an economic and political system based on government control of business and property and equal distribution of wealth. Socialism, carried to its extreme form—communism, as advocated by the German philosopher Karl Marx—would result in the overthrow of the capitalist system. Most socialists in late-19th-century America drew back from this goal, however, and worked within the labor movement to achieve better conditions for workers. In 1905, a group of radical unionists and socialists in Chicago organized the **Industrial Workers of the World (IWW),** or the Wobblies. Headed by William "Big Bill" Haywood, the Wobblies included miners, lumberers, and cannery and dock workers. Unlike the ARU, the IWW welcomed African Americans, but membership never topped 100,000. Its only major strike victory occurred in 1912. Yet the Wobblies, like other industrial unions, gave dignity and a sense of solidarity to unskilled workers.

**OTHER LABOR ACTIVISM IN THE WEST** In April 1903, about 1,000 Japanese and Mexican workers organized a successful strike in the sugar-beet fields of Ventura County, California. They formed the Sugar Beet and Farm Laborers' Union of Oxnard. In Wyoming, the State Federation of Labor supported a union of Chinese and Japanese miners who sought the same wages and treatment as other union miners. These small, independent unions increased both the overall strength of the labor movement and the tension between labor and management.

---

## ④ Strikes Turn Violent

Industry and government responded forcefully to union activity, which they saw as a threat to the entire capitalist system.

**THE GREAT STRIKE OF 1877** In July 1877, workers for the Baltimore and Ohio Railroad (B&O) struck to protest their second wage cut in two months. The work stoppage spread to other lines. Most freight and even some passenger traffic, covering over 50,000 miles, was stopped for more than a week. After several state governors asked President Rutherford B. Hayes to intervene, saying that the strikers were impeding interstate commerce, federal troops ended the strike.

**THE HAYMARKET AFFAIR** Encouraged by the impact of the 1877 strike, labor leaders continued to press for change. On the evening of May 4, 1886, 3,000 people gathered at Chicago's Haymarket Square to protest police brutality—six strikers had been killed or wounded at the McCormick Harvester plant the day before. Rain began to fall at about 10 o'clock, and the crowd was dispersing when police arrived. Then someone tossed a bomb into the police line. Police fired on the workers; seven police officers and several workers died in the chaos that followed. No one ever learned who threw the bomb, but the three speakers at the demonstration and five other radicals were charged with inciting a riot. All eight were convicted; four were hanged and one committed suicide in prison. After Haymarket, the public began to turn against the labor movement. **G**

**THE HOMESTEAD STRIKE** Despite the violence and rising public anger, workers continued to strike. The writer Hamlin Garland described conditions at the Carnegie Steel Company's Homestead plant in Pennsylvania.

---

**A PERSONAL VOICE** HAMLIN GARLAND

" Everywhere . . . groups of pale, lean men slouched in faded garments, grimy with the soot and grease of the mills. . . . The mill itself was hell: A roar as of a hundred lions, a thunder as of cannons, . . . jarring clang of falling iron! "

—quoted in *McClure's Magazine*

---

The steelworkers finally called a strike on June 29, 1892, after the company president, Henry Clay Frick, announced his plan to cut wages. Frick hired armed

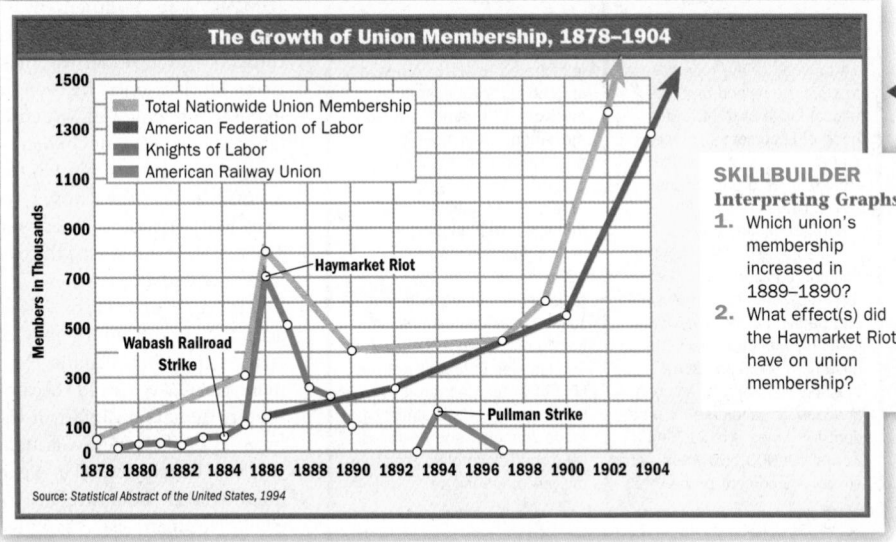

**The Growth of Union Membership, 1878–1904**

- Total Nationwide Union Membership
- American Federation of Labor
- Knights of Labor
- American Railway Union

*Members in Thousands* (1500, 1300, 1100, 900, 700, 500, 300, 100, 0)

Haymarket Riot

Wabash Railroad Strike

Pullman Strike

1878 1880 1882 1884 1886 1888 1890 1892 1894 1896 1898 1900 1902 1904

Source: *Statistical Abstract of the United States, 1994*

**SKILLBUILDER**
**Interpreting Graphs**
1. Which union's membership increased in 1889–1890?
2. What effect(s) did the Haymarket Riot have on union membership?

---

### Sidebar (left margin)

**MAIN IDEA**

**Analyzing Causes**
**G** How did the 1877 strike and Haymarket cause the public to resent the labor movement?

*G. Answer*
The public began to associate labor activists with violence and danger.

*Skillbuilder Answers*
1. The American Federation of Labor
2. Membership in the Knights of Labor declined sharply.

**TAKS**

Mini-Lesson 5: SS11 2(11.A)

---

### Sidebar (right)

**Instruct: Objective ④**

**Strikes Turn Violent**
TAKS SS11 3(US21.D)
· What were the reasons for the various strikes during the late 19th century?
· What role did women play in the labor movement?
· How did management and the government react to union activity?

In-Depth Resources: Unit 2
· Guided Reading, p. 22

**More About . . .**

**The Haymarket Affair**
The three surviving men of the eight convicted of the Haymarket bombings were pardoned by the governor of Illinois, John Peter Altgeld. He justified the pardon because he believed that the accused had not received a fair trial. Altgeld was a staunch supporter of labor, and in 1894, he opposed President Grover Cleveland's decision to send federal troops into Pullman to stop striking railroad workers.

**HISTORY from VISUALS**

**Interpreting the Graph**
Have students trace the lines showing the development of each union. Ask them when AFL membership and total union membership in the nation were essentially the same. *(about 1897)*

**Extension** Have students research the membership of the AFL today—now known as the AFL-CIO. *(About 13 million as of 2001)* You might also ask them to identify other influential unions, such as the Teamsters Union.

---

---

**ACTIVITY** | **COOPERATIVE LEARNING**

**BLOCK SCHEDULING**

**Reporting on Union Goals**

**Class Time** 45 minutes

**Task** Creating an oral presentation about the history and goals of a specific union

**Purpose** To help students understand the causes and effects of union activity

**Directions** Each group of students should research the history of a particular union, for example: electrical workers, plumbers, building trades, steel workers, mine workers, and agricultural workers. Groups should identify the founder, reason for founding, the main goals established by the union, and which goals were met and when. They should then create a presentation for the class accompanied by visual aids, such as time lines or charts.

 Integrated Assessment
· Rubric 3

### Tracing Themes
**WOMEN AND POLITICAL POWER**

#### Women in the Labor Movement

Women from all backgrounds lent their hands to the nation's labor movement of the late 19th and early 20th centuries. Mary Elisabeth Dreier headed the Women's Trade Union League from 1906 to 1914. It was a coalition of women workers and middle-to-upper-class women reformers who sought to organize working women and educate the public about labor conditions. Women labor reformers also hailed from the lower ranks of society. Mary Anderson, for example, immigrated to the United States from Sweden, where she worked as a dishwasher and stitcher at a shoe factory before becoming a prominent activist.

### KEY PLAYERS

#### Eugene Debs and Mother Jones

Ask students to consider what might have driven Jones to become the "Mother" of union activism. Have them also write a paragraph describing the relationship between Debs's labor activism and his belief in socialism.

 In-Depth Resources: Unit 2
· American Lives: Mary Harris "Mother" Jones, p. 38

---

guards from the Pinkerton Detective Agency to protect the plant so that he could hire scabs, or strikebreakers, to keep it operating. In a pitched battle that left at least three detectives and nine workers dead, the steelworkers forced out the Pinkertons and kept the plant closed until the Pennsylvania National Guard arrived on July 12. The strike continued until November, but by then the union had lost much of its support and gave in to the company. It would take 45 years for steelworkers to mobilize once again.

**THE PULLMAN COMPANY STRIKE** Strikes continued in other industries, however. During the panic of 1893 and the economic depression that followed, the Pullman company laid off more than 3,000 of its 5,800 employees and cut the wages of the rest by 25 to 50 percent, without cutting the cost of its employee housing. After paying their rent, most workers took home less than $6 a week. A strike was called in the spring of 1894, when the economy improved and the Pullman company failed to restore wages or decrease rents. Eugene Debs asked for arbitration, but Pullman refused to negotiate with the strikers. So the ARU began boycotting Pullman trains.

After Pullman hired strikebreakers, the strike turned violent, and President Grover Cleveland sent in federal troops. In the bitter aftermath, Debs was jailed. Pullman fired most of the strikers, and the railroads blacklisted many others, so they could never again get railroad jobs.

**WOMEN ORGANIZE** Although women were barred from many unions, they united behind powerful leaders to demand better working conditions, equal pay for equal work, and an end to child labor. Perhaps the most prominent organizer in the women's labor movement was **Mary Harris Jones.** Jones supported the Great Strike of 1877 and later organized for the United Mine Workers of America (UMW). She endured death threats and jail with the coal miners, who gave her the nickname Mother Jones. In 1903, to expose the cruelties of child labor, she led 80 mill children—many with hideous injuries—on a march to the home of President Theodore Roosevelt. Their crusade influenced the passage of child labor laws.

Other organizers also achieved significant gains for women. In 1909, Pauline Newman, just 16 years old, became the first female organizer of the International Ladies' Garment Workers' Union (ILGWU). A garment worker from the age of eight, Newman also supported

### KEY PLAYERS

**EUGENE V. DEBS**
**1855–1926**

Born in Indiana, Eugene V. Debs left home at the age of 14 to work for the railroads. In 1875 he helped organize a local lodge of the Brotherhood of Locomotive Firemen, and after attempts to unite the local railroad brotherhoods failed, Debs organized the American Railway Union.

While in prison following the Pullman strike in 1894, Debs read the works of Karl Marx and became increasingly disillusioned with capitalism. He became a spokesperson for the Socialist Party of America and was its candidate for president five times. In 1912, he won about 900,000 votes—an amazing 6 percent of the total.

**MOTHER JONES**
**1830–1930**

Mary Harris "Mother" Jones was a native of Ireland who immigrated to North America as a child. She became involved in the American labor movement after receiving assistance from the Knights of Labor. According to a reporter who followed "the mother of the laboring class" on her children's march in 1903, "She fights their battles with a Mother's Love." Jones continued fighting until her death at age 100.

Jones was definitely not the kind of woman admired by industrialists. "God almighty made women," she declared, "and the Rockefeller gang of thieves made ladies."

---

### Comparing Men's and Women's Pay

**Class Time** 30 minutes

**Task** Charting the annual earnings for men and women for various years

**Purpose** To recognize the disparity in pay between men and women

**Directions** Have students make a bar graph showing the relative annual earnings of men and women. Have them use the figures at the right and research and add others, if desired.

· 1899: women $267; men $498
· 1904: women $289; men $540
· 1909: women $339; men $631

Students' bar graphs might look like this:

$600
$400
$200

| Women Men | Women Men | Women Men |
|---|---|---|
| 1889 | 1904 | 1909 |

the "Uprising of the 20,000," a 1909 seamstresses' strike that won labor agreements and improved working conditions for some strikers.

The public could no longer ignore conditions in garment factories after a fire broke out at the Triangle Shirtwaist Factory in New York City on March 25, 1911. The fire spread swiftly through the oil-soaked machines and piles of cloth, engulfing the eighth, ninth, and tenth floors. As workers attempted to flee, they discovered that the company had locked all but one of the exit doors to prevent theft. The unlocked door was blocked by fire. The factory had no sprinkler system, and the single fire escape collapsed almost immediately. In all, 146 women died; some were found huddled with their faces raised to a small window. Public outrage flared after a jury acquitted the factory owners of manslaughter. In response, the state of New York set up a task force to study factory working conditions. **H**

---

**MAIN IDEA**

**Summarizing**
**H** What factors made the Triangle Shirtwaist fire so lethal?

**H. Answer**
The factory had only one fire escape and no sprinklers. The factory was full of cloth and oil.

---

### MANAGEMENT AND GOVERNMENT PRESSURE UNIONS

The more powerful the unions became, the more employers came to fear them. Management refused to recognize unions as representatives of the workers. Many employers forbade union meetings, fired union members, and forced new employees to sign "yellow-dog contracts," swearing that they would not join a union.

Finally, industrial leaders, with the help of the courts, turned the Sherman Antitrust Act against labor. All a company had to do was say that a strike, picket line, or boycott would hurt interstate trade, and the state or federal government would issue an injunction against the labor action. Legal limitations made it more and more difficult for unions to be effective. Despite these pressures, workers—especially those in skilled jobs—continued to view unions as a powerful tool. By 1904, the AFL had about 1,700,000 members in its affiliated unions; by the eve of World War I, AFL membership would climb to about 2 million.

The fire department's ladders reached only to the sixth floor, two floors below the burning Triangle Shirtwaist Company.

**More About . . .**

**The Triangle Fire**
The cause of the fire was unknown; it may have been a lit cigarette or match dropped into flammable waste. More than 50 of the dead were killed jumping from the windows to the street. The rest were either burned or trampled to death. Public outrage over the fire led to sweeping reforms in building and factory laws, especially with regard to fire safety.

👁 Electronic Library of Primary Sources
· from "141 Die in Factory Fire"

## Assess & Reteach

**SECTION 3 ASSESSMENT**
Ask students to discuss questions 3 and 4 and answer them as a group.

📄 Formal Assessment
· Section Quiz, p. 120

**SELF-ASSESSMENT**
Have students list three new facts that they learned and one misconception that was corrected as they read this section.

**RETEACH**
Draw a time line on the board and have students fill in major events in labor activism.

📄 In-Depth Resources: Unit 2
· Reteaching Activity, p. 27

---

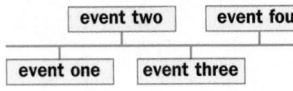

**ASSESSMENT**

1. **TERMS & NAMES** For each term or name, write a sentence explaining its significance.
   - Andrew Carnegie
   - vertical and horizontal integration
   - Social Darwinism
   - John D. Rockefeller
   - Sherman Antitrust Act
   - Samuel Gompers
   - American Federation of Labor (AFL)
   - Eugene V. Debs
   - Industrial Workers of the World (IWW)
   - Mary Harris Jones

**MAIN IDEA**

2. **TAKING NOTES**
Make a time line of the notable achievements and setbacks of the labor movement between 1876 and 1911.

| event two | | event four |
|---|---|---|

| event one | event three | |
|---|---|---|

In what ways did strikes threaten industry?

**CRITICAL THINKING**

3. **EVALUATING LEADERSHIP**
Do you think that the tycoons of the late 19th century are best described as ruthless robber barons or as effective captains of industry?
**Think About:**
   - their management tactics and business strategies
   - their contributions to the economy
   - their attitude toward competition

4. **DRAWING CONCLUSIONS**
Does the life of Andrew Carnegie support or counter the philosophy of Social Darwinism? Explain.

5. **HYPOTHESIZING**
If the government had supported unions instead of management in the late 19th century, how might the lives of workers have been different?

*A New Industrial Age* **249**

---

**1. TERMS & NAMES**
Andrew Carnegie, p. 241
vertical and horizontal integration, p. 242
Social Darwinism, p. 242
John D. Rockefeller, p. 243
Sherman Antitrust Act, p. 244
Samuel Gompers, p. 245
AFL, p. 245
Eugene V. Debs, p. 246
IWW, p. 246
Mary Harris Jones, p. 248

**2. TAKING NOTES**
**1866** NLU organized; **1868** KOL organized; **1869** CNLU organized; **1877** The Great Strike; **1886** The Haymarket Affair; **1886** AFL organized; **1892** steel strike; **1894** Pullman Strike; **1905** IWW organized; **1911** Triangle fire

**3. EVALUATING LEADERSHIP**
**"Barons"**—exploitation of workers; greed; personal gain
**"Captains"**—philanthropy; national commerce; jobs

**4. DRAWING CONCLUSIONS**
**Support**—Carnegie well-suited to his society; caused his success
**Counter**—advantages beyond Carnegie's personal qualities

**5. HYPOTHESIZING**
Labor relations more peaceful; larger unions; higher wages, safer working conditions; lower profits

*A New Industrial Age* **249**

## TERMS & NAMES

1. Thomas Alva Edison, p. 232
2. Alexander Graham Bell, p. 233
3. George M. Pullman, p. 238
4. transcontinental railroad, p. 237
5. Interstate Commerce Act, p. 239
6. Andrew Carnegie, p. 241
7. Sherman Antitrust Act, p. 244
8. Samuel Gompers, p. 245
9. AFL, p. 245
10. Mary Harris Jones, p. 248

## MAIN IDEAS

1. Steel created demand for coal and iron ore; it was used extensively in the railroad, agriculture, food, and construction industries.
2. They opened up new jobs for women, drew people to the cities, and made jobs less backbreaking.
3. Railroad companies were very powerful and often corrupt.
4. Railroads had a great deal of political power and fought legal battles against regulation.
5. They used ruthless tactics to amass great wealth.
6. The Southern economy and terrain had been devastated by the Civil War and had to be rebuilt. The South had less capital for investment.
7. Workers realized that they needed to unite to protect themselves and to increase wages, shorten work hours, and improve working conditions.
8. Government support of management; the use of violence and scabs to break strikes.

# CHAPTER 6 ASSESSMENT

CHAPTER 6 ASSESSMENT

## VISUAL SUMMARY

### A NEW INDUSTRIAL AGE

**LONG-TERM CAUSES**

- abundant natural resources
- harnessing of early power sources such as water and coal
- invention of the steam engine
- construction of roads, canals, and railroads in early 1800s

**IMMEDIATE CAUSES**

- expansion of railroads in late 1800s
- cheap labor supply provided by increasing immigration
- burst of technological innovation
- new management techniques and business strategies
- investment capital

### BIG BUSINESS BOOMS

### 1880–1914

**IMMEDIATE EFFECTS**

- growth of large corporations
- new and plentiful manufactured goods
- poor working conditions in factories and sweatshops
- increased labor activism

**LONG-TERM EFFECTS**

- regional economies are linked
- labor movement wins shorter workweek

## TERMS & NAMES

For each term or name below, write a sentence explaining its connection to the industrialization of the late 19th century.

1. Thomas Alva Edison
2. Alexander Graham Bell
3. George M. Pullman
4. transcontinental railroad
5. Interstate Commerce Act
6. Andrew Carnegie
7. Sherman Antitrust Act
8. Samuel Gompers
9. American Federation of Labor (AFL)
10. Mary Harris Jones

## MAIN IDEAS

Use your notes and the information in the chapter to answer the following questions.

**The Expansion of Industry** (pages 230–233)

1. How did the growth of the steel industry influence the development of other industries?
2. How did inventions and developments in the late 19th century change the way people worked?

**The Age of the Railroads** (pages 236–240)

3. Why did people, particularly farmers, demand regulation of the railroads in the late 19th century?
4. Why were attempts at railroad regulation often unsuccessful?

**Big Business and Labor** (pages 241–249)

5. Why were business leaders such as John D. Rockefeller called robber barons?
6. Why did the South industrialize more slowly than the North did?
7. Why did workers form unions in the late 19th century?
8. What factors limited the success of unions?

## CRITICAL THINKING

1. **USING YOUR NOTES** In a chart like the one shown, list what you see as the overall costs and benefits of industrialization.

| INDUSTRIALIZATION | |
|---|---|
| Costs | Benefits |
| | |

2. **RECOGNIZING BIAS** In 1902 George Baehr, head of the Philadelphia and Reading Railway Company, said, "The rights and interests of the labor man will be protected and cared for not by the labor agitators but by the Christian men to whom God in his infinite wisdom has given the control of the property interests of the country." What bias does this statement reveal? How does Baehr's view reflect Social Darwinism?

3. **IDENTIFYING PROBLEMS** Consider the problems that late-19th-century workers faced and the problems that workers face today. How important do you think unions are for present-day workers? Support your answer.

## CRITICAL THINKING

1. **Using Your Notes Costs:** Increased power of big business; corruption; labor-management conflicts; dangerous jobs; loss of creativity and skill in manual labor; Social Darwinism leads to discrimination. **Benefits:** Better transportation; faster communications; less isolation; economic opportunities for women; advances in construction.

2. **Recognizing Bias** Baehr's statement reveals a bias that favors wealthy people and successful entrepreneurs. His view is typical of Social Darwinism, the belief that the wealthy and successful people are naturally better suited to have positions of power in society.

3. **Identifying Problems** Some students may say that unions are less important today because job safety is better regulated and protected by government and industry. Others may support the need for modern unions to resolve ongoing conflicts between labor and management, to protect workers from layoffs, and from excessive hours.

## Standardized Test Practice

Use the quotation below and your knowledge of U.S. history to answer question 1.

> "No man, however benevolent, liberal, and wise, can use a large fortune so that it will do half as much good in the world as it would if it were divided into moderate sums and in the hands of workmen who had earned it by industry and frugality."
>
> —Rutherford B. Hayes, from *Diary and Letters of Rutherford Birchard Hayes*

1. Which of the following people could best be described by Rutherford B. Hayes's words *benevolent*, *liberal*, and *a large fortune*?

   A Thomas Edison

   B Eugene V. Debs

   C Charles Darwin

   D Andrew Carnegie

2. The American Federation of Labor (AFL) differed from the Knights of Labor in that the AFL focused on —

   F collective bargaining and aggressive use of strikes.

   G organizing both skilled and unskilled workers.

   H arbitration and use of strikes as a last resort.

   J winning a shorter workweek.

3. How did the railroads both benefit from and contribute to the industrialization of the United States?

   A The railroads needed government protection, and their development helped government grow.

   B The railroads used new inventions and brought people to see the inventions.

   C The railroads used steel and coal and delivered both to new markets.

   D The railroads needed passengers, and passengers needed to get to new industries.

4. In the 19th century, government attempts to regulate industry in the United States included the Interstate Commerce Act (1887) and the Sherman Antitrust Act (1890). What posed the biggest obstacle to enforcement of these laws?

   F the business tactics of industrialists

   G the use of vertical integration

   H the rulings of the Supreme Court

   J the theory of Social Darwinism

ADDITIONAL TEST PRACTICE, pages S1–S33.

 **TEST PRACTICE** CLASSZONE.COM

## Standardized Test Practice

1. The correct answer is letter **D**.
   Letter A is not correct because Edison was not known for being benevolent. Letter B is not correct because Debs did not have a large fortune. Letter C is not correct because Darwin was a philosopher and not characterized by the traits listed here.

2. The correct answer is letter **H**.
   Letter F is not correct because the Knights of Labor did not support the aggressive use of strike. Letter G is not correct because the AFL only organized skilled workers. Letter J is not correct because both groups wanted a shorter workweek.

3. The correct answer is letter **C**.
   Letter A is not correct because growth of government does not contribute to industrialization. Letters B and D are not correct because the activities listed do not contribute to industrialization.

4. The correct answer is letter **H**.
   Letters F, G, J are not correct because only the Supreme Court could block enforcement of the laws.

## ORAL REPORT

**Tips for Teaching**

· Remind students that oral presentations should not be spontaneous. They should be well planned and practiced in advance of actual presentation.

· Suggest to students that this chapter has many individuals whose work changed American life. They may want to profile them for the presentation.

📄 Formal Assessment
· Chapter Test, Forms A, B, and C, pp. 121–132

## ALTERNATIVE ASSESSMENT

1.  Recall your answer to the question on page 229:

   *What are the pros and cons of railroad expansion?*

   Consider how your answer might be different based on what you now know about the effects of railroad expansion and business consolidation. Then write a newspaper editorial about the Great Strike of 1877 (see page 247), supporting the position of either the railroad owners or the striking workers.

2. **VIDEO** **LEARNING FROM MEDIA** View the *American Stories* video, "Gusher! Pattillo Higgins and the Great Texas Oil Boom." Discuss the following questions with a small group; then do the activity.

   • What were the effects of the discovery of oil at Spindletop?

   • What lessons can people learn from Pattillo Higgins?

   **Cooperative Learning Activity** Make a poster describing Pattillo Higgins's personal qualities and how they helped him to achieve his dream. What present-day figures share Higgins's traits? Add images of these people, with captions, to the poster and display it in your classroom.

*A New Industrial Age* 251

## ALTERNATIVE ASSESSMENT

### 1. INTERACT WITH HISTORY
**Rubric**
The editorial should . . .
· demonstrate the ability to evaluate both sides and form an opinion
· clearly state a position with either the owners or the workers
· present a set of supporting arguments for the position

### 2. LEARNING FROM MEDIA
**Rubric**
The poster should . . .
· identify Higgins' personal qualities
· convey Higgins' personal qualities in a visual manner
· exhibit grade level artistic skill and presentation

# Immigrants and Urbanization

| | CHAPTER OVERVIEW | COPYMASTERS | INTEGRATED TECHNOLOGY |
|---|---|---|---|
| **CHAPTER RESOURCES** | *The population rises as immigrants supply a willing workforce for urban industrialization and a political base for many urban politicians. Abuses in local and national government prompt calls for reform.* | 📓 Telescoping the Times · Chapter Summary, pp. 13–14 <br><br> 📓 Planning for Block Schedules | 🎞 American Stories · From China to Chinatown <br><br> 💿 Power Presentations <br><br> 💿 Electronic Teacher Tools <br><br> 🛈 Online Lesson Planner <br><br> 🛈 classzone.com |

|  | KEY IDEAS | | |
|---|---|---|---|
| **SECTION 1** <br> **The New Immigrants** <br> pp. 254–261 | *New immigrants from southern and eastern Europe, Asia, the Caribbean, and Mexico face culture shock and prejudice—as well as the opportunity for a better life— in the United States.* | 📓 In-Depth Resources: Unit 2 · Guided Reading, p. 39 · Building Vocabulary, p. 42 · Skillbuilder Practice, p. 43 · Reteaching Activity, p. 45 · Geography Application, pp. 48–49 · Primary Sources, p. 52 · Literature, pp. 56–58 <br><br> 📓 Lesson Plans, pp. 57–58 | 🎞 American Stories · From China to Chinatown <br><br> 📊 Geography Transparencies GT15 · Where Foreign-Born Lived 1900 <br><br> 💿 Electronic Library of Primary Sources · from *The Days of Our Years* · *from* The Chinese Exclusion Act of 1882 <br><br> 🛈 classzone.com |
| **SECTION 2** <br> **The Challenges of Urbanization** <br> pp. 262–266 | *The rapid growth of cities creates many challenges: how to provide adequate housing, transportation, water, and sanitation and how to fight fire and crime. The search for solutions begins.* | 📓 In-Depth Resources: Unit 2 · Guided Reading, p. 40 · Skillbuilder Practice, p. 44 · Reteaching Activity, p. 46 · Outline Map, pp. 50–51 · Primary Sources, pp. 53, 54 · American Lives, p. 59 <br><br> 📓 Lesson Plans, pp. 59–60 | 📊 Geography Transparencies GT15 · Where Foreign-Born Lived 1900 <br><br> 📊 Critical Thinking Transparencies CT15, CT49 · Urban Growth · From Country to City, 1870–1920 <br><br> 📊 Humanities Transparencies HT15 · Cliff Dwellers <br><br> 🛈 classzone.com |
| **SECTION 3** <br> **Politics in the Gilded Age** <br> pp. 267–271 | *The political machine emerges as cities attempt to deal with the problems of rapid urbanization. Local and national political corruption during the Gilded Age leads to a call for reform.* | 📓 In-Depth Resources: Unit 2 · Guided Reading, p. 41 Reteaching Activity, p. 47 · Primary Sources, p. 55 · American Lives, p. 60 <br><br> 📓 Lesson Plans, pp. 61–62 | 📊 Critical Thinking Transparencies CT15 · Urban Growth <br><br> 🛈 classzone.com |

| | |
|---|---|
| PE Pupil's Edition | Overhead Transparency | CD-ROM |
| TE Teacher's Edition | Audio Library | Internet |
| Copymaster | | |

## ASSESSMENT OPTIONS

- PE **Chapter Assessment**, pp. 272–273
- **Formal Assessment**
  · Chapter Tests, Forms A, B, and C, pp. 136–147
- **Test Generator**
- **Integrated Assessment Book**
- TAKS Online Test Practice
- TAKS Spiraled Content Review
- TAKS Practice Tests

- PE **Section 1 Assessment**, p. 259
- TE **Self-Assessment**, p. 259
- **Formal Assessment**, Quiz, p. 133
- **Integrated Assessment Book**
- **Test Generator**
- **TAKS Practice Transparencies TT55**

- PE **Section 2 Assessment**, p. 266
- TE **Self-Assessment**, p. 266
- **Formal Assessment**, Quiz, p. 134
- **Integrated Assessment Book**
- **Test Generator**
- **TAKS Practice Transparencies TT56**

- PE **Section 3 Assessment**, p. 271
- TE **Self-Assessment**, p. 271
- **Formal Assessment**, Quiz, p. 135
- **Integrated Assessment Book**
- **Test Generator**
- **TAKS Practice Transparencies TT57**

## RESOURCES FOR DIFFERENTIATING INSTRUCTION

### Students Acquiring English/ESL

- **Reading Study Guide:**
  (English and Spanish)
  pp. 73–80
- **Access for Students Acquiring English/ESL:**
  Spanish Translations,
  pp. 92–101
- **Chapter Summaries on CD**
  (English and Spanish)

### Less Proficient Readers

- **Reading Study Guide**
  (English and Spanish)
  pp. 73–80
- **Telescoping the Times**
  · Chapter Summary,
  pp. 13–14
- **Chapter Summaries on CD**
  (English and Spanish)

### Gifted and Talented Students

- **In-Depth Resources: Unit 2**
  · Primary Sources,
  pp. 52–55
  Literature, pp. 56–58
  · American Lives: Jane
  Addams, p. 59; William
  Marcy Tweed, p. 59
- **Electronic Library of Primary Sources**
  · Unit 2, Chapter 7

## CROSS-CURRICULAR CONNECTIONS

### Economics
Bundles, A'Leilia Perry. *Madam C.J. Walker.* Broomall, PA: Chelsea House, 1991. A biography of the entrepreneur, millionaire, and philanthropist by her great-great-great granddaughter.

### Geography
Samuelson, Time et al. Above *Chicago: A New Collection of Original Aerial Photographs of Chicago.* San Francisco: Cameron & Co., 1992. The layout of the great city through aerial photographs.

### Culture
Hoobler, Dorothy and Hoobler, Thomas. *The Chinese American Family Album.* NY: Oxford University Press, 1998. The immigrant experience through intimate portraits. Features vintage photographs and an introduction by Bette Bao Lord.

### Literature
Dreiser, Theodore. *Sister Carrie.* NY: Bantam, 1993. Dreiser transforms the conventional "fallen woman" story into a study of the persistent idealism and the grasping and seductive materialism of the American culture.

Yezierska, Anzia. *Bread Givers.* NY: Persea Books, 1975. This touching tale tells the story of Jewish immigrants trying to find their way in the United States and the conflict between a father of the old world and a daughter of the new world.

**McDougal Littell**
*Literature Connections*
Uchida, Yoshiko. *Picture Bride (with related readings).* This novel follows the experiences of a Japanese woman who comes to the United States in 1917 to marry a man she has never met. The story ends in a Japanese internment camp in Utah in 1943.

***The Language of Literature***
American Literature: Unit 5, Part 2

**Nextext**
*The Immigrants*

## ENRICHMENT ACTIVITIES

- PE **Pupil's Edition**, pp. 252–271
  Interact with History, pp. 252–253
  Tracing Themes, pp. 260–261
- **In-Depth Resources: Unit 2**
  · Geography Application: Industry and Urban
  Growth, pp. 48–49
  · Outline Map: The Urbanization of America,
  pp. 50–51
  · Primary Source: Artifacts from Ellis Island,
  p. 52
  · Primary Source: from *How the Other Half Lives*, p. 53

- · Primary Source: from *Twenty Years at Hull House*, p. 54
- · Primary Source: from The *Shame of the Cities*, p. 55
- · Literature: from *Call It Sleep*, pp. 56–58
- · American Lives: Jane Addams, p. 59
- · American Lives: William Marcy Tweed, p. 60
- **Electronic Library of Primary Sources**
  · Unit 2, Chapter 7
- **American Stories video series**
  · From China to Chinatown

## BLOCK SCHEDULE LESSON PLAN OPTIONS (90-MINUTE PERIOD)

### DAY 1

**CHAPTER 7 OPENER**
pp. 252–253

**Class Time** 30 minutes

**History from Visuals,** p. 252

**Class Time** 10 minutes

*Options for Pacing and Variety*

· Time Saver Have students look at the photograph on page 252 and describe the scene, asking them questions from the TE page. **Class Time** 10 minutes

**Interact with History,** p. 253

**Class Time** 20 minutes

*Options for Pacing and Variety*

· Role-Playing Ask students to read the situation depicted on page 253, and discuss as a class the issues raised in the questions. **Class Time** 15 minutes

**SECTION 1,** pp. 254–261

**Class Time** 60 minutes

*Options for Pacing and Variety*

· Peer Teaching Have students work in groups and choose one of the quotations from "A Personal Voice" appearing throughout the section. Have them research in the library or on the Internet the subject of the quotation, for example, early Chinese immigrants or immigration tests. A representative from the group should summarize the facts they found. **Class Time** 30 minutes

· Internet Have students compare the immigration controversy that occurred during 1870–1920 to

### DAY 1 continued

the current-day immigration controversy, using the Internet and library resources to investigate the issues. Also, have them evaluate the information they found on the Internet and determine the accuracy of the sites they visited. **Class Time** 40 minutes

· Internet Ask students to read the feature "Tracing Themes: Diversity and the National Identity" and answer the questions, using the Internet to do research for question 2. **Class Time** 20 minutes

### DAY 2

**SECTION 2,** pp. 262–266

**Class Time** 30 minutes

*Options for Pacing and Variety*

· Peer Teaching Have students read excerpts from books about the lives of poorer city residents in the late 19th and early 20th centuries, using the activity on TE page 264, Differentiating Instruction: Clarifying Ideas. Take turns doing dramatic readings for the class. **Class Time** 30 minutes

· Time Saver Ask students to choose one of the urban problems discussed in this section and write a one-paragraph solution for homework. Have some students share their responses in class. **Class Time** 15 minutes

**SECTION 3,** pp. 267–271

**Class Time** 30 minutes

*Options for Pacing and Variety*

· Time Saver Ask students to look at the political cartoon on page 269, on Boss Tweed. Discuss the questions, and ask them to speculate on the power of pictures over a written condemnation. Read them the additional information in the TE on Tweed's attempts to bribe the *New York Times* and Thomas Nast, and ask them what might have happened had the bribe been accepted. **Class Time** 15 minutes

· Peer Teaching Have students complete the Section Assessment on their own, then share their graphics for question 2. **Class Time** 25 minutes

### DAY 2 continued

**ASSESSMENT**
pp. 272–273

**Class Time** 30 minutes

*Options for Pacing and Variety*

· Peer Teaching Have students work in small groups to complete the Critical Thinking questions. Discuss the answers with the class. **Class Time** 20 minutes

· History on Film View the *American Stories* video "From China to Chinatown: Fong See's American Dream," and have students discuss the questions in small groups. Then have them complete the Assessment activity on page 273. **Class Time** 30 minutes

---

**TEACHER-TESTED ACTIVITY**
**POLITICAL CARTOON**

Lou Morrison, Lake Weir High School, Ocala, Florida

**Class Time** 45 minutes

**Task** Creating a political cartoon

**Purpose** To recognize myths and misconceptions about immigration to America

**Supplies Needed**

· Drawing paper

· Markers

· Standard reference materials or Internet access

**Activity** Have students analyze political cartoons of the era that stereotype or show discrimination against immigrants to America. Then tell students to create a political cartoon depicting the immigrant experience in the United States or Americans' reaction to immigration. Have students create cartoons that are not stereotypical or discriminatory. Display the cartoons for discussion.

# CHAPTER 7 CORRELATION

 ## CORRELATION TO THE TEXAS ESSENTIAL KNOWLEDGE AND SKILLS

Chapter 7 addresses the following standards of the Texas Essential Knowledge and Skills for U.S. History.

| TEKS | Instruction | Student Question/Activity |
|---|---|---|
| **(2A)** Analyze political issues such as Indian policies, the growth of political machines, and civil service reform. | **PE 267–268** examination of the emergence of political machines | **PE 271** Critical Thinking question about the actions of political machines |
| **(2C)** Analyze social issues such as the treatment of minorities, child labor, growth of cities, and problems of immigrants. | **PE 258–259** discussion of the various problems that immigrants to the United States faced | **PE 259** Critical Thinking questions about the challenges posed to the nation's new immigrants |
| **(4B)** Evaluate the impact of reform leaders. | **PE 266** discussion of the significant reform efforts of Jane Addams | **TE 266** Key Player question about Addams and her accomplishments |
| **(10A)** Analyze the effects of changing demographic patterns resulting from immigration to the United States. | **PE 255** map depicting the settlement patterns immigrants in the United States | **PE 255** Skillbuilder questions that require students to interpret the map |
| **(11A)** Identify the effects of population growth on the physical environment. | **PE 264–265** examination of the problems associated with the explosive growth of the nation's cities | **PE 266** Critical Thinking questions about the problems that accompanied massive urban growth |
| **(21B)** Explain efforts of the Americanization movement to assimilate immigrants into American culture. | **PE 263** discussion of the efforts of the Americanization movement | **PE 263** side column question about the Americanization movement |
| **(21C)** Analyze how the contributions of people of various racial, ethnic, and religious groups have helped to shape the national identity. | **PE 260–261** feature about how the country's cultural diversity has shaped its national identity | **PE 261** Critical Thinking questions about the information in the feature |

## TAKS MINI-LESSONS

1. **Social Studies Skills: Objective 2 (US10.B):** Analyze the effects of the changing demographic pattern resulting from immigration to the United States **Activity** Have students answer the Geography Skillbuilder questions regarding U.S. immigration patterns on page 255.

2. **Social Studies Skills: Objective 2 (WG6.A):** Observe patterns in the size and distribution of cities using maps **Activity** Have students answer the Geographic Skillbuilder questions regarding the immigrant distribution in New York at the turn of the 20th century on page 263.

3. **Social Studies Skills: Objective 3 (US2.C):** Analyze social issues such as the growth of cities and the problems of immigrants **Activity** Have students create a chart listing the challenges associated with the rapid growth of cities.

4. **English Language Arts Skills: Objective 1 (7.F):** Produce summaries of texts by identifying main ideas and their supporting details **Activity** Have students identify the main idea and supporting details of the text below the heading "Immigrant Restrictions" on pages 258–259.

5. **English Language Arts Skills: Objective 6 (2.C):** Proofread writing for appropriateness of organization, content, style, and conventions **Activity** Have pairs of students proofread each other's answers to the Critical Thinking questions.

## CHAPTER 7 · IMMIGRANTS AND URBANIZATION

The intersection of Orchard and Hester Streets on New York City's Lower East Side, 1905.

### HISTORY from VISUALS

**Interpreting the Photograph**
Have students study the photograph and suggest words to describe the scene. (*busy, crowded, lively*) Ask students to comment on favorable and unfavorable aspects of city life depicted in this photograph. (*favorable—friendly people, sense of community, availability of food and goods; unfavorable—lack of privacy, crowded conditions*)

**Extension** Imagine you are an immigrant stepping onto the streets of New York City for the first time. Write a letter to your family and friends back home and describe the scene.

### Time Line Discussion

Explain to students that this time line spans from the end of the 19th century through the beginning of the 20th century. Ask students to answer questions based on the time line:

· What year would be considered a milestone in aviation history. Why? (*1903; the Wright Brothers took the first successful airplane flight*)

· How and when did the nation expand geographically? (*U.S. annexed Hawaii in 1898*)

· What international event had a profound impact on the United States? (*Panama Canal opened*)

**USA WORLD**

**1876** Rutherford B. Hayes is elected president.

**1880** James A. Garfield is elected president.

**1881** Chester A. Arthur succeeds Garfield after Garfield's assassination.

**1884** Grover Cleveland is elected president.

**1888** Benjamin Harrison is elected president.

**1892** Grover Cleveland is elected to a second term.

**1876** Porfirio Díaz seizes power in Mexico.

**1884** Berlin Conference meets to divide Africa among European nations.

**1885** Indian National Congress forms.

**1893** France establishes Indochina.

**1880**

**1890**

**252** CHAPTER 7

---

### THEMES IN CHAPTER 7

**AMERICA IN WORLD AFFAIRS**

At the turn of the century, many countries experienced a marked increase in immigration. Immigrants came in search of economic opportunity, freedom from persecution, and a chance to improve their lives.

See Teacher's Edition note, p. 256.

**IMMIGRATION AND MIGRATION**

The settlers' quest for rich farmland, the California gold rush, the Homestead Act, the transcontinental railroad, and the Great Depression all contributed to migration within the United States.

See Teacher's Edition note, p. 257.

Access to education has long been a part of the American dream. Education enabled many immigrants to adjust to their new world. In school, children learned about democracy and civic responsibility.

See Teacher's Edition note, p. 263.

**DIVERSITY AND NATIONAL IDENTITY**

Immigrants brought their religious beliefs, languages, and social customs with them to the United States. Many immigrants also took advantage of the opportunities to learn about American culture by going to museums, theaters, and concerts.

See Teacher's Edition note, p. 265.

# INTERACT
## WITH HISTORY

The year is 1880. New York City's swelling population has created a housing crisis. Immigrant families crowd into apartments that lack light, ventilation, and sanitary facilities. Children have nowhere to play except in the streets and are often kept out of school to work and help support their families. You are a reformer who wishes to help immigrants improve their lives.

## What would you do to improve conditions?

### Examine the Issues

- How can immigrants gain access to the services they need?
- What skills do newcomers need?
- How might immigrants respond to help from an outsider?

**RESEARCH LINKS** CLASSZONE.COM

Visit the Chapter 7 links for more information about Immigrants and Urbanization.

# INTERACT
## WITH HISTORY

## Objectives

- To motivate students to consider the problems brought on by rapid urbanization
- To help students understand how reformers endeavored to find solutions and improve city life

### Examine the Issues

1. What types of services would immigrants need?
2. Where might immigrants find work and what skills would they need to do the job?
3. Why might immigrants feel uncertain about accepting outside help?

**1896** William McKinley is elected president.

**1898** Hawaii is annexed by the United States.

**1900** McKinley is reelected.

**1903** The Wright Brothers achieve the first successful airplane flight.

**1910** The appearance of Halley's Comet causes widespread panic.

**1912** Woodrow Wilson is elected president.

**1900**

**1910**

**1901** The Commonwealth of Australia is founded.

**1905** Workers revolt in St. Petersburg, Russia.

**1908** Oil is discovered in Persia.

**1912** Qing Dynasty in China is overthrown.

**1914** Panama Canal opens.

*Immigrants and Urbanization* **253**

---

## RECOMMENDED RESOURCES

### BOOKS FOR THE TEACHER

Daniels, Roger. *Coming to America: A History of Immigration and Ethnicity in American Life.* Harperperennial Library, 1991. Comprehensive examination of immigration.

Higham, John. *Strangers in the Land.* New York: Rutgers U Press, 1988. Immigrants and nativists.

Patterson, Jerry. *First Four Hundred: New York in the Gilded Age.* Rizzoli, 2000. Life in the opulent age.

### BOOKS FOR THE STUDENT

Coan, Peter Morton. *Ellis Island Interviews.* Checkmark Books, 1998. Immigrants in their own words.

Kessler-Harris, Alice. *Out of Work.* New York: Oxford UP, 1983. Women in the industrialized workplace.

### VIDEOS

*The Great San Francisco Earthquake.* PBS Home Video, 1988. 877-PBS-SHOP. Documentary.

*Journey to America.* PBS Home Video, 1988. 877-PBS-SHOP.

*Ragtime.* Dir. Milos Forman. 1981. Critics Choice Video.

### SOFTWARE

*Who Built America?* CD-ROM. Voyager, 800-446-2001.

### INTEGRATED TECHNOLOGY

For teacher support, visit . . .

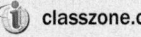 classzone.com

# The New Immigrants

| MAIN IDEA | WHY IT MATTERS NOW | Terms & Names |
|---|---|---|
| Immigration from Europe, Asia, the Caribbean, and Mexico reached a new high in the late 19th and early 20th centuries. | This wave of immigration helped make the United States the diverse society it is today. | • Ellis Island  • Chinese Exclusion Act<br>• Angel Island<br>• melting pot  • Gentlemen's Agreement<br>• nativism |

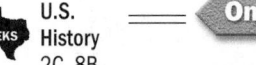

**TEKS** U.S. History 2C, 8B, 10B, 21A, 21C, 24A, 24B, 24C, 24D, 24H, 25A, 25B, 25C, 25D, 26B

**One American's Story**

In 1871, 14-year-old Fong See came from China to "Gold Mountain"—the United States. Fong See stayed, worked at menial jobs, and saved enough money to buy a business. Despite widespread restrictions against the Chinese, he became a very successful importer and was able to sponsor many other Chinese who wanted to enter the United States. Fong See had achieved the American dream. However, as his great-granddaughter Lisa See recalls, he was not satisfied.

**A PERSONAL VOICE** LISA SEE

"He had been trying to achieve success ever since he had first set foot on the Gold Mountain. His dream was very 'American.' He wanted to make money, have influence, be respected, have a wife and children who loved him. In 1919, when he traveled to China, he could look at his life and say he had achieved his dream. But once in China, he suddenly saw his life in a different context. In America, was he really rich? Could he live where he wanted? . . . Did *Americans* care what he thought? . . . The answers played in his head—no, no, no."

—*On Gold Mountain*

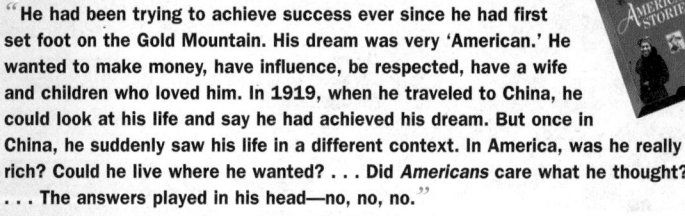

**VIDEO**
*FROM CHINA TO CHINATOWN*
Fong See's American Dream

Despite Fong See's success, he could not, upon his death in 1957, be buried next to his Caucasian wife because California cemeteries were still segregated.

## **1** Through the "Golden Door"

Millions of immigrants like Fong See entered the United States in the late 19th and early 20th centuries, lured by the promise of a better life. Some of these immigrants sought to escape difficult conditions—such as famine, land shortages, or religious or political persecution. Others, known as "birds of passage," intended to immigrate temporarily to earn money, and then return to their homelands.

**EUROPEANS** Between 1870 and 1920, approximately 20 million Europeans arrived in the United States. Before 1890, most immigrants came from countries in western and northern Europe. Beginning in the 1890s, however, increasing numbers came from southern and eastern Europe. In 1907 alone, about a million people arrived from Italy, Austria-Hungary, and Russia.

Why did so many leave their homelands? Many of these new immigrants left to escape religious persecution. Whole villages of Jews were driven out of Russia by pogroms, organized attacks often encouraged by local authorities. Other Europeans left because of rising population. Between 1800 and 1900, the population in Europe doubled to nearly 400 million, resulting in a scarcity of land for farming. Farmers competed with laborers for too few industrial jobs. In the United States, jobs were supposedly plentiful. In addition, a spirit of reform and revolt had spread across Europe in the 19th century. Influenced by political movements at home, many young European men and women sought independent lives in America.

**CHINESE AND JAPANESE** While waves of Europeans arrived on the shores of the East Coast, Chinese immigrants came to the West Coast in smaller numbers. Between 1851 and 1883, about 300,000 Chinese arrived. Many came to seek their fortunes after the discovery of gold in 1848 sparked the California gold rush. Chinese immigrants helped build the nation's railroads, including the first transcontinental line. When the railroads were completed, they turned to farming, mining, and domestic service. Some, like Fong See, started businesses. However, Chinese immigration was sharply limited by a congressional act in 1882.

In 1884, the Japanese government allowed Hawaiian planters to recruit Japanese workers, and a Japanese emigration boom began. The United States annexation of Hawaii in 1898 increased Japanese immigration to the West Coast. It continued to increase as word of comparatively high American wages spread. The wave peaked in 1907, when 30,000 left Japan for the United States. By 1920, more than 200,000 Japanese lived on the West Coast.

**Background**
From 1815 to 1848, a wave of revolutions—mostly sparked by a desire for constitutional governments—shook Europe. In 1830, for example, the Polish people rose up against their Russian rulers.

*Skillbuilder Answers*
1. New York
2. Japan

## More About . . .

### Chinese Railroad Labor
In 1865, the Central Pacific Railroad hired approximately 50 Chinese workers to lay tracks for the transcontinental line leading east from Sacramento. Within two years, 12,000 Chinese were employed on the project—about 90 percent of the work force. The work ethic and the ability of the Chinese immigrants impressed company officials. Company superintendent Charles Crocker said, "We are training them to do all kinds of labor: blasting, driving horses, handling rock as well as pick and shovel."

## U.S. Immigration Patterns, as of 1900

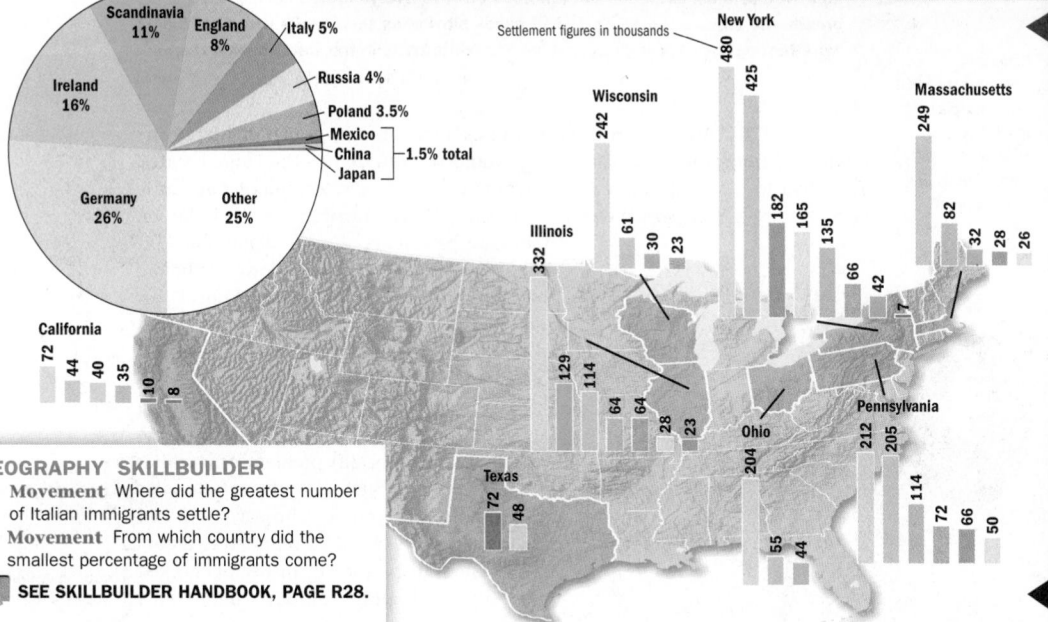

Settlement figures in thousands

### GEOGRAPHY SKILLBUILDER
1. **Movement** Where did the greatest number of Italian immigrants settle?
2. **Movement** From which country did the smallest percentage of immigrants come?

**SEE SKILLBUILDER HANDBOOK, PAGE R28.**

## HISTORY from VISUALS

**Interpreting the Infographic**
Show students that the map, bar graph, and pie chart present essentially the same information in different ways. For example, green represents Irish immigrants on the pie chart and on the bar graphs.

**Extension** Ask students to use a world almanac to find the latest U.S. immigration figures. Have students create a bar graph to show immigration percentages to the United States by continent.

Geography Transparencies GT15
· Where Foreign-Born Lived, 1900

 Mini-Lesson 1: SS11 2(US10.B)

*Immigrants and Urbanization* **255**

---

### Audio Multimedia Sources

**Explaining the Skill** Historians use audio sources, such as recorded speeches, interviews, and radio programs, to build on the tradition of oral history.

**Applying the Skill** Ask students to choose an audio source and prepare an oral history about immigrant experiences. Suggest that students go to the library and check out records or tapes. They might also record interviews with family or friends who have stories to tell about immigrating. Have students present their oral histories to the class.

📄 In-Depth Resources: Unit 2
· Skillbuilder Practice: Audio Multimedia Sources, p. 44

### Immigration Around the World

Immigration increased around the world during the late 1800s and early 1900s. Between 1850 and 1930, about 6.5 million people immigrated to Canada from Great Britain and the United States. In the late 1800s, some Chinese immigrants moved to Canada to work on railroad construction. Between 1850 and 1930, Italian, Spanish, and Portuguese immigrants settled in Latin America.

## Instruct: Objective ❷

### Life in the New Land
TAKS SS11 5(US24.A)

· What difficulties did immigrants face on their journey to the United States?
· What were the differences and similarities between the two U.S. immigration centers?
· How did many immigrants cope after arriving in America?

 In-Depth Resources: Unit 2
· Guided Reading, p. 39

## More About . . .

### The Transatlantic Journey

In the late 1800s, the price of a steerage ticket across the Atlantic was $15, which was considerably less than it had been in the early 1800s. Toward the end of the 19th century, the United States was exporting raw materials such as cotton, timber, tobacco, and wheat to Europe. On the return trip, the ships carried less bulky items, such as china, linens, and wine. There was plenty of room for passengers if they were willing to ride in the cargo holds.

---

**THE WEST INDIES AND MEXICO** Between 1880 and 1920, about 260,000 immigrants arrived in the eastern and southeastern United States from the West Indies. They came from Jamaica, Cuba, Puerto Rico, and other islands. Many West Indians left their homelands because jobs were scarce and the industrial boom in the United States seemed to promise work for everyone.

Mexicans, too, immigrated to the United States to find work, as well as to flee political turmoil. The 1902 National Reclamation Act, which encouraged the irrigation of arid land, created new farmland in Western states and drew Mexican farm workers northward. After 1910, political and social upheavals in Mexico prompted even more immigration. About 700,000 people—7 percent of the population of Mexico at the time—came to the U.S. over the next 20 years. **Ⓐ**

## ❷ Life in the New Land

No matter what part of the globe immigrants came from, they faced many adjustments to an alien—and often unfriendly—culture.

**A DIFFICULT JOURNEY** By the 1870s, almost all immigrants traveled by steamship. The trip across the Atlantic Ocean from Europe took approximately one week, while the Pacific crossing from Asia took nearly three weeks.

Many immigrants traveled in steerage, the cheapest accommodations in a ship's cargo holds. Rarely allowed on deck, immigrants were crowded together in the gloom, unable to exercise or catch a breath of fresh air. They often had to sleep in louse-infested bunks and share toilets with many other passengers. Under these conditions, disease spread quickly, and some immigrants died before they reached their destination. For those who survived, the first glimpse of America could be breathtaking.

### A PERSONAL VOICE ROSA CAVALLERI

" **America!** . . . We were so near it seemed too much to believe. Everyone stood silent—like in prayer. . . . Then we were entering the harbor. The land came so near we could almost reach out and touch it. . . . Everyone was holding their breath. Me too. . . . Some boats had bands playing on their decks and all of them were tooting their horns to us and leaving white trails in the water behind them. "

—quoted in *Rosa: The Life of an Italian Immigrant*

**ELLIS ISLAND** After initial moments of excitement, the immigrants faced the anxiety of not knowing whether they would be admitted to the United States. They had to pass inspection at immigration stations, such as the one at Castle Garden in New York, which was later moved to **Ellis Island** in New York Harbor. About 20 percent of the immigrants at Ellis Island were detained for a day or more before being inspected. However, only about 2 percent of those were denied entry.

The processing of immigrants on Ellis Island was an ordeal that might take five hours or more. First, they had to pass a physical examination by a doctor. Anyone with a serious health problem or a contagious disease, such as tuberculosis, was promptly sent home. Those who passed the medical exam then reported to a government inspector. The inspector checked documents and questioned immigrants

European governments used passports to control the number of professionals and young men of military age who left the country. ▼

## MAIN IDEA

**Analyzing Causes**
**Ⓐ** What reasons did people from other parts of the world have for immigrating to the United States?

*A. Answer*
The desire to escape conditions such as land shortages, famine, and political or religious persecution; the prospect of land, jobs, or higher wages.

**Vocabulary**
**tuberculosis:** a bacterial infection, characterized by fever and coughing, that spreads easily

---

### Clarifying Ideas

Reading a passage twice can help clarify meaning. This is especially true when the material is packed with information. Choose a detailed page or passage, such as Ellis Island on pages 256–257, and apply this technique.

After students read this section, have them select a difficult passage or page to read a second time. Point out that people who read highly technical material often read and reread sections in order to understand them. Ask students if and why they think this method might be useful for them.

Many immigrants, like these arriving at Ellis Island, were subjected to tests such as the one below. To prove their mental competence, they had to identify the four faces looking left in 14 seconds. Can you do it?

TESTS FOR DETECTION OF DEFECT

## More About . . .

### Ellis Island
The buildings on Ellis Island were restored during the 1980s, and the Ellis Island Immigration Museum opened in 1990. One exhibit is a display of belongings that immigrants brought over from their home countries. Steerage passengers were allowed to bring only a hundred pounds of goods. Immigrants had to leave many of their possessions behind. The museum display includes musical instruments, fine lace, tools, books, religious objects, family pictures, and handmade quilts.

📄 In-Depth Resources: Unit 2
· Primary Sources: Artifacts from Ellis Island, p. 52
· Literature: *Call It Sleep*, pp. 56–58

**Vocabulary**
**felony:** any one of the most serious crimes under the law, including murder, rape, and burglary

to determine whether they met the legal requirements for entering the United States. The requirements included proving they had never been convicted of a felony, demonstrating that they were able to work, and showing that they had some money (at least $25 after 1909). One inspector, Edward Ferro, an Italian immigrant himself, gave this glimpse of the process.

### A PERSONAL VOICE EDWARD FERRO
"The language was a problem of course, but it was overcome by the use of interpreters. . . . It would happen sometimes that these interpreters—some of them—were really softhearted people and hated to see people being deported, and they would, at times, help the aliens by interpreting in such a manner as to benefit the alien and not the government."
—quoted in *I Was Dreaming to Come to America*

**B. Answer**
Medical and administrative inspections and, on Angel Island, harsh questioning and detention.

From 1892 to 1924, Ellis Island was the chief immigration station in the United States. An estimated 17 million immigrants passed through its noisy, bustling facilities.

**ANGEL ISLAND** While European immigrants arriving on the East Coast passed through Ellis Island, Asians—primarily Chinese—arriving on the West Coast gained admission at **Angel Island** in San Francisco Bay. Between 1910 and 1940, about 50,000 Chinese immigrants entered the United States through Angel Island. Processing at Angel Island stood in contrast to the procedure at Ellis Island. Immigrants endured harsh questioning and a long detention in filthy, ramshackle buildings while they waited to find out whether they would be admitted or rejected. **B**

**MAIN IDEA**

**Identifying Problems**
**B** What difficulties did immigrants face in gaining admission to the United States?

**COOPERATION FOR SURVIVAL** Once admitted to the country, immigrants faced the challenges of finding a place to live, getting a job, and getting along in daily life while trying to understand an alien language and culture. Many immigrants sought out people who shared their cultural values, practiced their religion,

### Tracing Themes
#### IMMIGRATION AND MIGRATION

### Migration Within America
American settlers have been on the move since the nation was founded. Many early settlers stayed along the east coast, but others moved westward in search of farmland. Some southerners moved west to Kentucky and Tennessee when their land began to erode. The California gold rush and the Homestead Act of 1862 spurred even more westward migration. African Americans migrated north during the "Great Migration" to escape Southern persecution. The Great Depression and drought of the 1930s put Americans on the move again.

*Immigrants and Urbanization* **257**

---

ACTIVITY     LINK TO LANGUAGE ARTS

### Writing Letters or Poems About Immigrant Experiences

**Class Time** 45 minutes

**Task** Writing letters or poems based on an imagined immigrant experience

**Purpose** To sensitize students to the difficulties faced by newcomers to a foreign culture

**Directions** Ask each student to imagine what it would have been like to be an immigrant. Have students create a letter or a poem about their imagined experience. Ask students to describe their feelings and observations and the challenges of being a newcomer. Ask students to share their creative writing with the class.

📄 Integrated Assessment
· Rubric 5

and spoke their native language. The ethnic communities were life rafts for immigrants. People pooled their money to build churches or synagogues. They formed social clubs and aid societies. They founded orphanages and old people's homes, and established cemeteries. They even published newspapers in their own languages.

Committed to their own cultures but also trying hard to grow into their new identities, many immigrants came to think of themselves as "hyphenated" Americans. As hard as they tried to fit in, these new Polish- and Italian- and Chinese-Americans felt increasing friction as they rubbed shoulders with people born and raised in the United States. Native-born people often disliked the immigrants' unfamiliar customs and languages, and viewed them as a threat to the American way of life. **ⓒ**

## ③ Immigration Restrictions

Many native-born Americans thought of their country as a **melting pot,** a mixture of people of different cultures and races who blended together by abandoning their native languages and customs. Many new immigrants, however, did not wish to give up their cultural identities. As immigration increased, strong anti-immigrant feelings emerged.

**THE RISE OF NATIVISM** One response to the growth in immigration was **nativism,** or overt favoritism toward native-born Americans. Nativism gave rise to anti-immigrant groups and led to a demand for immigration restrictions.

Many nativists believed that Anglo-Saxons—the Germanic ancestors of the English—were superior to other ethnic groups. These nativists did not object to immigrants from the "right" countries. Prescott F. Hall, a founder in 1894 of the Immigration Restriction League, identified desirable immigrants as "British, German, and Scandinavian stock, historically free, energetic, progressive." Nativists thought that problems were caused by immigrants from the "wrong" countries— "Slav, Latin, and Asiatic races, historically down-trodden . . . and stagnant."

Nativists sometimes objected more to immigrants' religious beliefs than to their ethnic backgrounds. Many native-born Americans were Protestants and thought that Roman Catholic and Jewish immigrants would undermine the democratic institutions established by the country's Protestant founders. The American Protective Association, a nativist group founded in 1887, launched vicious anti-Catholic attacks, and many colleges, businesses, and social clubs refused to admit Jews.

In 1896, Congress—influenced by the Immigration Restriction League—passed a bill requiring a literacy test for immigrants. Those who could not read 40 words in English or their native language would be refused entry. Although President Cleveland vetoed the bill, it was a powerful statement of public sentiment. In 1917, a similar bill would be passed into law in spite of President Woodrow Wilson's veto.

**ANTI-ASIAN SENTIMENT** Nativism also found a foothold in the labor movement, particularly in the West, where native-born workers feared that jobs would go to Chinese

Chinese immigrants wait outside the hospital on Angel Island in San Francisco Bay, 1910. ▼

immigrants, who would accept lower wages. The depression of 1873 intensified anti-Chinese sentiment in California. Work was scarce, and labor groups exerted political pressure on the government to restrict Asian immigration. The founder of the Workingmen's Party, Denis Kearney, headed the anti-Chinese movement in California. He made hundreds of speeches throughout the state, each ending with the message, "The Chinese must go!"

In 1882, Congress slammed the door on Chinese immigration for ten years by passing the **Chinese Exclusion Act.** This act banned entry to all Chinese except students, teachers, merchants, tourists, and government officials. In 1892, Congress extended the law for another ten years. In 1902, Chinese immigration was restricted indefinitely; the law was not repealed until 1943.

**THE GENTLEMEN'S AGREEMENT** The fears that had led to anti-Chinese agitation were extended to Japanese and other Asian people in the early 1900s. In 1906, the local board of education in San Francisco segregated Japanese children by putting them in separate schools. When Japan raised an angry protest at this treatment of its emigrants, President Theodore Roosevelt worked out a deal. Under the **Gentlemen's Agreement** of 1907–1908, Japan's government agreed to limit immigration of unskilled workers to the United States in exchange for the repeal of the San Francisco segregation order.

Although doorways for immigrants had been all but closed to Asians on the West Coast, cities in the East and the Midwest teemed with European immigrants—and with urban opportunities and challenges.

▲ Fear and resentment of Chinese immigrants sometimes resulted in mob attacks, like the one shown here.

## Assess & Reteach

**SECTION 1 ASSESSMENT**
Have groups of students divide up the questions and work together to find the answers.

📄 Formal Assessment
· Section Quiz, p. 133

**SELF-ASSESSMENT**
Have students compare the immigration controversy that occurred between 1870 and 1920 and present day immigration controversy.

**RETEACH**
Show the video "From China to Chinatown" again and discuss the immigration issues raised in the film.

📄 In-Depth Resources: Unit 2
· Reteaching Activity, p. 45

 **ASSESSMENT**

**1. TERMS & NAMES** For each term or name, write a sentence explaining its significance.
- Ellis Island
- Angel Island
- melting pot
- nativism
- Chinese Exclusion Act
- Gentlemen's Agreement

### MAIN IDEA

**2. TAKING NOTES**
Create a diagram such as the one below. List two or more causes of each effect.

| Causes ———→ | Effects |
|---|---|
| 1.<br>2.<br>3. | Immigrants leave their home countries. |
| 1.<br>2.<br>3. | Immigrants face hardships in the United States. |
| 1.<br>2.<br>3. | Some nativists want to restrict immigration. |

### CRITICAL THINKING

**3. IDENTIFYING PROBLEMS**
Which group of immigrants do you think faced the greatest challenges in the United States? Why?

**4. ANALYZING EFFECTS**
What were the effects of the massive influx of immigrants to the U.S. in the late 1800s?

**5. EVALUATING**
What arguments can you make against nativism and anti-immigrant feeling? **Think About:**
- the personal qualities of immigrants
- the reasons for anti-immigrant feeling
- the contributions of immigrants to the United States

*Immigrants and Urbanization* **259**

**1. TERMS & NAMES**
Ellis Island, p. 256
Angel Island, p. 257
melting pot, p. 258
nativism, p. 258
Chinese Exclusion Act, p. 259
Gentlemen's Agreement, p. 259

**2. TAKING NOTES**
Leaving home countries: poverty, religious persecution, shortage of land, lack of jobs.
Hardships: foreign culture, interrogation, detention, discrimination, urban life.
Nativist opposition: intolerance, prejudice, economic depression.

**3. IDENTIFYING PROBLEMS**
The Chinese were subjected to interrogation and detention on Angel Island. Nativists pushed for immigration restriction. The Chinese Exclusion Act of 1882 made it extremely difficult for the Chinese to enter the United States.

**4. ANALYZING EFFECTS**
Rapid urban growth; formation of ethnic

communities, rise of nativism and anti-immigrant sentiments, competition for jobs.

**5. EVALUATING**
Immigrants were brave and willing to work hard; there is value in being exposed to many ways of life; nativists themselves were descendants of immigrants.

## OBJECTIVES

· Describe the growth of diversity in the United States.

· Recognize the contributions that immigrants have made to the United States.

## Focus & Motivate

Ask students to discuss the meaning of the motto on the presidential seal, "E pluribus unum," or "out of many, one."

## More About . . .

### The Statue of Liberty

The Statue of Liberty rises 151 feet above the entrance to New York's harbor. Broken shackles lie at her feet. She holds a tablet in her hand that bears the inscription, "July 4, 1776," the date of the Declaration of Independence. The French gave the statue to the United States to commemorate 100 years of American independence from Great Britain. The Statue of Liberty was built in Paris, disassembled, shipped to New York, and put back together. President Grover Cleveland officially dedicated it on October 28, 1886.

# Diversity and the National Identity

Before the first Europeans arrived, a variety of cultural groups—coastal fishing societies, desert farmers, plains and woodland hunters—inhabited North America. With the arrival of Europeans and Africans, the cultural mix grew more complex. Although this diversity has often produced tension, it has also been beneficial. As different groups learned from one another about agriculture, technology, and social customs, American culture became a rich blend of cultures from around the world.

## 1610s–1870s

◄ **SPANISH NORTH AMERICA**

Spanish missionaries in the Southwest tried to impose their culture upon Native Americans. However, many Native Americans retained aspects of their original cultures even as they took on Spanish ways. For example, today many Pueblo Indians of New Mexico perform ancient ceremonies, such as the Corn Dance, in addition to celebrating the feast days of Catholic saints. Later, the first cowboys—descendants of the Spanish—would introduce to white Americans cattle-ranching techniques developed in Mexico.

## 1776

**THE DECLARATION OF INDEPENDENCE** ▶

The signers of the Declaration of Independence were descendants of immigrants. The founders' ancestors had come to North America in search of economic opportunity and freedom of religious expression. When the Second Continental Congress declared a "United States" in 1776, they acknowledged that the country would contain diverse regions and interests. Thus the founders placed on the presidential seal the motto *E Pluribus Unum*—"out of many, one."

## 1862–1863

**THE EMANCIPATION PROCLAMATION** ▲

At the midpoint of the Civil War, President Abraham Lincoln issued the Emancipation Proclamation, freeing all slaves in areas of the Union that were in rebellion. Although the Proclamation could not be enforced immediately, it was a strong statement of opposition to slavery, and it paved the way for African Americans' citizenship.

---

## RECOMMENDED RESOURCES

### BOOKS

Guarneri, Carl and John Higham, eds. *Hanging Together: Unity and Diversity in American Culture.* New Haven: Yale UP, 2001. Essays about the multicultural identity of America.

Kammen, Michael G. *Contested Values: Democracy and Diversity in American Culture.* New York: Bedford/St. Martin's, 1994.

Naylor, Larry L., ed. *Cultural Diversity in the United States.* Greenwood, 1997.

Shinagawa, Larry Hajime, and Michael Jang. *Atlas of American Diversity.* Altamira Press, 1998. In-depth look at America's major cultural groups. Includes more than 200 graphics.

Susser, Ida, and Thomas Carl Patterson, eds. **Cultural Diversity in the United States: A Critical Reader.** Williston: Blackwell Publishers, 2001. Collection of contemporary writings on the issue of diversity in America.

### VIDEOS

**America Becoming.** Dir. Charles Burnett. USA, 1991. Documents the experience of American newcomers in six cities across the United States

*America's Multi-Cultural Heritage.* Educational Video Network. 1996. A historical look at the mixing of different cultures in the United States.

### INTEGRATED TECHNOLOGY

For teacher support, visit . . .

 classzone.com

# 1886

**THE STATUE OF LIBERTY ▶**

Poet Emma Lazarus wrote the famous lines inscribed at the foot of the Statue of Liberty, "Give me your tired, your poor,/Your huddled masses yearning to breathe free, . . ." The statue's dedication took place during the most extensive wave of immigration the United States has ever known.

   Many native-born Americans felt that the newcomers should fully immerse themselves in their new culture. However, most immigrants combined American language and customs with their traditional ways. As immigrants celebrated Independence Day and Thanksgiving, they introduced into American culture new celebrations, such as Chinese New Year and Cinco de Mayo.

# 2000

 **21ST-CENTURY DIVERSITY**

In 1998, three countries (Mexico, China, and India) contributed a third of the total number of immigrants to the United States. The rest of 1998's immigrants came from countries as diverse as Vietnam, Sudan, and Bosnia.

   American athletes at the 2000 Olympic Games in Sydney, Australia, reflected the increasing diversity of the U.S., pointing toward a future in which there may no longer be a majority racial or ethnic group.

---

**THINKING CRITICALLY**

**CONNECT TO HISTORY**

1. **Analyzing Motives** Why do you think some groups have tried to suppress the culture of others over the course of history? Why have many groups persisted in retaining their cultural heritage?

   📁 **SEE SKILLBUILDER HANDBOOK, PAGE R6.**

**CONNECT TO TODAY**

2. **Predicting Effects** Research current U.S. policy on immigration. How might this policy affect cultural diversity? Write a short editorial from one of the following viewpoints:
   • U.S. immigration policy needs to change.
   • U.S. immigration policy should be maintained.

🔍 **RESEARCH LINKS** CLASSZONE.COM

*Immigrants and Urbanization* **261**

## Instruct

1. In what ways have Native Americans kept their cultural traditions alive?
2. What is the significance of the Emancipation Proclamation?
3. What immigrant contributions to United States culture are discussed in this section?

**MAKING PERSONAL CONNECTIONS**
Ask students to discuss the cultural diversity they observe and experience on a daily basis at school and in the community.

### More About . . .

**21st Century Diversity**
According to the 2000 census, the United States population is 71 percent Caucasian, 12 percent African American, 12 percent Hispanic, 4 percent Asian, and around 1 percent Native American. In 2050, observers predict that Caucasians will comprise approximately 53 percent of the population, African Americans about 13 percent, Asians close to 9 percent, and Native Americans 1 percent. The greatest increase is expected for Hispanics, who will account for almost 25 percent of the U.S. population by the middle of the century.

---

**THINKING CRITICALLY: ANSWERS**

1. **CONNECT TO HISTORY** Attempts to suppress: racist beliefs, religious prejudice, economic competition, fear of political or social takeover by newcomers, fear of difference.
Cultural traditions: Formed close communities, valued heritage, passed down beliefs to next generation.

2. **CONNECT TO TODAY**
   **Rubrics**
   An editorial should . . .
   · show evidence of research on current U.S. immigration policy
   · present an organized and supported argument for one of the viewpoints

## OBJECTIVES

**1** Describe the movement of immigrants to cities and the opportunities they found there.

**2** Explain how cities dealt with housing, transportation, sanitation, and safety issues.

**3** Describe some of the organizations and people who offered help to urban immigrants.

### SKILLBUILDERS

· Geography Skillbuilder: place, movement, p. 263

### CRITICAL THINKING

· Analyzing Motives, pp. 263, 266
· Identifying Problems, p. 264
· Analyzing Effects, pp. 265, 266
· Evaluating, p. 266

## Focus & Motivate

Discuss with students what it would be like for them to adjust to school in a foreign country. Ask students to suggest ways they might help a foreign student adjust to school in the United States.

## Instruct

### Instruct: Objective **1**

**Urban Opportunities**
TAKS SS11 3(US2.C)

· Why did many immigrants settle in the nation's cities?

· What was the goal of the Americanization movement?

· For what reasons did a number of Americans move from the country to the cities?

 Critical Thinking Transparencies CT15
· Urban Growth

---

**SECTION 2**

# The Challenges of Urbanization

| MAIN IDEA | WHY IT MATTERS NOW | Terms & Names |
|---|---|---|
| The rapid growth of cities forced people to contend with problems of housing, transportation, water, and sanitation. | Consequently, residents of U.S. cities today enjoy vastly improved living conditions. | • urbanization  • Social Gospel • Americanization   movement  movement  • settlement house • tenement  • Jane Addams • mass transit |

**TEKS** U.S. History 2C, 4B, 8A, 8B, 10A, 11A, 19B, 21B, 21D, 22A, 23A, 24B, 24C, 24D, 25A, 25B, 25C, 25D, 26A

**One American's Story**

In 1870, at age 21, Jacob Riis left his native Denmark for the United States. Riis found work as a police reporter, a job that took him into some of New York City's worst slums, where he was shocked at the conditions in the overcrowded, airless, filthy tenements. Riis used his talents to expose the hardships of New York City's poor.

**A PERSONAL VOICE** JACOB RIIS

" Be a little careful, please! The hall is dark and you might stumble over the children pitching pennies back there. Not that it would hurt them; kicks and cuffs are their daily diet. They have little else. . . . Close [stuffy]? Yes! What would you have? All the fresh air that ever enters these stairs comes from the hall-door that is forever slamming. . . . Listen! That short hacking cough, that tiny, helpless wail—what do they mean? . . . The child is dying with measles. With half a chance it might have lived; but it had none. That dark bedroom killed it. "

—*How the Other Half Lives*

▲ As many as 12 people slept in rooms such as this one in New York City, photographed by Jacob Riis around 1889.

Making a living in the late 19th and early 20th centuries was not easy. Natural and economic disasters had hit farmers hard in Europe and in the United States, and the promise of industrial jobs drew millions of people to American cities. The urban population exploded from 10 million to 54 million between 1870 and 1920. This growth revitalized the cities but also created serious problems that, as Riis observed, had a powerful impact on the new urban poor.

## **1** Urban Opportunities

The technological boom in the 19th century contributed to the growing industrial strength of the United States. The result was rapid **urbanization**, or growth of cities, mostly in the regions of the Northeast and Midwest.

**262** CHAPTER 7

---

## PROGRAM RESOURCES

 **In-Depth Resources: Unit 2**
· Guided Reading, p. 40
· Skillbuilder Practice, p. 43
· Reteaching Activity, p. 46
· Geography Application, pp. 48–49
· Outline Map, pp. 50–51
· Primary Sources: *How the Other Half Lives*, p. 53; from *Twenty Years at Hall House*, p. 54
· American Lives: Jane Addams, p. 59

 **Reading Study Guide** (English and Spanish), pp. 75–76

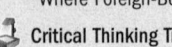 **Access for Students Acquiring English/ESL**
· Guided Reading (Spanish), p. 95
· Geography Application, pp. 98–99
· Outline Map, pp. 100–101

 **Formal Assessment**
· Section Quiz, p. 134

 **Integrated Assessment**
· Rubrics

### INTEGRATED TECHNOLOGY

 **Geography Transp. GT15**
· Where Foreign-Born Lived, 1900

 **Critical Thinking Transp. CT15, CT49**
· Urban Growth
· From County to City, 1870–1920

 **Humanities Transp. HT15**
· Cliff Dwellers

 **Electronic Library of Primary Sources**

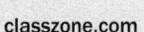 classzone.com

### TEXAS RESOURCES

 TAKS Spiraled Content Review

 TAKS Practice Tests

 TAKS Practice Transparencies TT56

 TAKS Online Test Practice

## IMMIGRANTS SETTLE IN CITIES

Most of the immigrants who streamed into the United States in the late 19th century became city dwellers because cities were the cheapest and most convenient places to live. Cities also offered unskilled laborers steady jobs in mills and factories. By 1890, there were twice as many Irish residents in New York City as in Dublin, Ireland. By 1910, immigrant families made up more than half the total population of 18 major American cities.

The **Americanization movement** was designed to assimilate people of wide-ranging cultures into the dominant culture. This social campaign was sponsored by the government and by concerned citizens. Schools and voluntary associations provided programs to teach immigrants skills needed for citizenship, such as English literacy and American history and government. Subjects such as cooking and social etiquette were included in the curriculum to help the newcomers learn the ways of native-born Americans. **A**

Despite these efforts, many immigrants did not wish to abandon their traditions. Ethnic communities provided the social support of other immigrants from the same country. This enabled them to speak their own language and practice their customs and religion. However, these neighborhoods soon became overcrowded, a problem that was intensified by the arrival of new transplants from America's rural areas.

**MIGRATION FROM COUNTRY TO CITY** Rapid improvements in farming technology during the second half of the 19th century were good news for some farmers but bad news for others. Inventions such as the McCormick reaper and the steel plow made farming more efficient but meant that fewer laborers were needed to work the land. As more and more farms merged, many rural people moved to cities to find whatever work they could.

Many of the Southern farmers who lost their livelihoods were African Americans. Between 1890 and 1910, about 200,000 African Americans moved north and west, to cities such as Chicago and Detroit, in an effort to escape racial violence, economic hardship, and political oppression. Many found conditions only somewhat better than those they had left behind. Segregation and discrimination were often the reality in Northern cities. Job competition between blacks and white immigrants caused further racial tension.

---

**MAIN IDEA**

**Analyzing Motives**
**A** Why did native-born Americans start the Americanization movement?

**A. Answer**
To encourage newcomers to assimilate into the dominant culture.

---

**New York City, 1910**

Ethnic enclaves of at least 20% of population:
- Austro-Hungarian
- German
- Irish
- Italian
- Russian
- Scandinavian
- Nonresidential
- Boundary between Brooklyn and Queens

BRONX

MANHATTAN

QUEENS

BROOKLYN

**GEOGRAPHY SKILLBUILDER**
1. **Place** What general pattern of settlement do you notice?
2. **Movement** Which ethnic group settled in the largest area of New York City?

*Skillbuilder Answers*
1. Immigrants often settled near others of similar backgrounds.
2. Germans

**TAKS**

Mini-Lesson 2:
SS11 2(WG6.A)

---

## HISTORY from VISUALS

### Interpreting the Map
Point out that each ethnic group is represented by a different color on the map. Ask students to look at the map and answer the following question: Which of the four areas of New York City appears to have the most diverse population and why might that diversity have occurred there? *(Brooklyn: possibly the location of jobs and inexpensive housing. Manhattan: some students may suggest that many immigrants settled in this urban area of New York City)*

## Tracing Themes
**IMMIGRATION AND MIGRATION**

### Educational Opportunities
To many new immigrants, free education seemed a miracle. One immigrant recalled her father had "brought his children to school as if it were an act of consecration." In school, children learned about American history and government and gained proficiency in English. Many immigrant parents worked during the day and went to school at night. They also had the opportunity to learn English, American history, and the fundamentals of democratic government.

📖 In-Depth Resources: Unit 2
· Geography Application, pp. 48–49
· Outline Map, pp. 50–51

🗒 Critical Thinking Transparencies CT49
· From County to City, 1870–1920

---

*Immigrants and Urbanization* 263

---

**ACTIVITY** | **SKILLBUILDER LESSON**

## Creating Maps

**Explaining the Skill** Maps are visual representations of information about geographic areas. When creating a map, students might find it helpful to use another map as a guide.

**Applying the Skill** Ask students to make a map of the United States showing major areas of immigrant settlement. *(New York, Chicago, Los Angeles, German settlements in North Dakota, Norwegian settlements in Minnesota, Japanese in California, or Latin Americans in Texas or Florida.)* You may want to use your community or state for this activity.

📖 In-Depth Resources: Unit 2
· Skillbuilder Practice: Creating Maps, p. 43

## 2 Urban Problems

As the urban population skyrocketed, city governments faced the problems of how to provide residents with needed services and safe living conditions.

Mini-Lesson 3: SS11 3(US2.C)

**HOUSING** When the industrial age began, working-class families in cities had two housing options. They could either buy a house on the outskirts of town, where they would face transportation problems, or rent cramped rooms in a boardinghouse in the central city. As the urban population increased, however, new types of housing were designed. For example, row houses—single-family dwellings that shared side walls with other similar houses—packed many single-family residences onto a single block.

After working-class families left the central city, immigrants often took over their old housing, sometimes with two or three families occupying a one-family residence. As Jacob Riis pointed out, these multifamily urban dwellings, called **tenements,** were overcrowded and unsanitary.

In 1879, to improve such slum conditions, New York City passed a law that set minimum standards for plumbing and ventilation in apartments. Landlords began building tenements with air shafts that provided an outside window for each room. Since garbage was picked up infrequently, people sometimes dumped it into the air shafts, where it attracted vermin. To keep out the stench, residents nailed windows shut. Though established with good intent, these new tenements soon became even worse places to live than the converted single-family residences. **B**

**TRANSPORTATION** Innovations in **mass transit,** transportation systems designed to move large numbers of people along fixed routes, enabled workers to go to and from jobs more easily. Street cars were introduced in San Francisco in 1873 and electric subways in Boston in 1897. By the early 20th century, mass-transit networks in many urban areas linked city neighborhoods to one another and to outlying communities. Cities struggled to repair old transit systems and to build new ones to meet the demand of expanding populations.

**WATER** Cities also faced the problem of supplying safe drinking water. As the urban population grew in the 1840s and 1850s, cities such as New York and Cleveland built public waterworks to handle the increasing demand. As late as the 1860s, however, the residents of many cities had grossly inadequate piped water—or none at all. Even in large cities like New York, homes seldom had indoor plumbing, and residents had to collect water in pails from faucets on the street and heat it for bathing. The necessity of improving water quality to control diseases such as cholera and typhoid fever was obvious. To make city water safer, filtration was introduced in the 1870s and chlorination in 1908. However, in the early 20th century, many city dwellers still had no access to safe water.

**SANITATION** As the cities grew, so did the challenge of keeping them clean. Horse manure piled up on the streets, sewage flowed through open gutters, and factories spewed foul smoke into the air. Without dependable trash collection, people dumped their garbage on the streets. Although private contractors called scavengers were hired to sweep the streets, collect garbage, and clean outhouses, they

**MAIN IDEA**
Identifying Problems
**B** What housing problems did urban working-class families face?

*B. Answer* Transportation difficulties, overcrowding, and unsanitary conditions.

**Vocabulary**
**chlorination:** a method of purifying water by mixing it with the chemical chlorine

### Instruct: Objective 2
**Urban Problems**
TAKS SS11 3(US2.C)
· What were the housing problems that many poor city dwellers faced?
· What other difficulties did immigrants and poor residents encounter?

 In-Depth Resources: Unit 2
· Guided Reading, p. 40

Humanities Transparencies HT15
· Cliff Dwellers

### Connections Across Time
**1910 AND TODAY**
**Immigrants and Cities**
Today, immigrants to urban areas in the United States often find that jobs are scarce. Many work in fast-food restaurants, laundries, car washes, dry cleaners, or as domestics. Some immigrants receive a government subsidy until they become fully self supporting. Government welfare was not available to immigrants in the early 20th century, although charitable organizations offered some assistance.

### More About . . .
**Transportation**
In the 1800s, the streets of most American cities were not paved. Roads were dusty in summer and muddy in winter. Improvements were slow, and there was controversy over paving materials. Asphalt was smooth, long lasting, and easy to clean, but expensive. Engineers finally developed a cheaper way to produce asphalt, and it became widely used in paving city streets.

Sanitation problems in big cities were overwhelming. It was not unusual to see a dead horse in the street. ▼

**264** CHAPTER 7

**DIFFERENTIATING INSTRUCTION** | **LESS PROFICIENT READERS**

**Clarifying Ideas**
One way to show students what big cities were like in the late 19th and early 20th centuries is to take them to a local historical society or museum. If an outing is not an option, read first-person accounts of life at that time. Read selected portions from factual or fictional accounts aloud. Have students take turns doing dramatic readings. At right is a list of suggested reading.

*All for the Better: A Story of El Barrio* by Nicholasa Mohr
*David Copperfield* by Charles Dickens
*How the Other Half Lives* by Jacob A. Riis
"Thank You, M'am" by Langston Hughes
*The Lost Garden* by Lawrence Yep

**MAIN IDEA**

Analyzing
Effects

**C** How did
conditions in cities
affect people's
health?

*C. Answer*
Lack of clean
water and
inadequate san-
itation spread
disease.

often did not do the jobs properly. By 1900, many cities had developed sewer lines and created sanitation departments. However, the task of providing hygienic living conditions was an ongoing challenge for urban leaders. **C**

**CRIME** As the populations of cities increased, pickpockets and thieves flourished. Although New York City organized the first full-time, salaried police force in 1844, it and most other city law enforcement units were too small to have much impact on crime.

**FIRE** The limited water supply in many cities contributed to another menace: the spread of fires. Major fires occurred in almost every large American city during the 1870s and 1880s. In addition to lacking water with which to combat blazes, most cities were packed with wooden dwellings, which were like kindling waiting to be ignited. The use of candles and kerosene heaters also posed a fire hazard. In San Francisco, deadly fires often broke out during earthquakes. Jack London described the fires that raged after the San Francisco earthquake of 1906.

### A PERSONAL VOICE JACK LONDON

" On Wednesday morning at a quarter past five came the earthquake. A minute later the flames were leaping upward. In a dozen different quarters south of Market Street, in the working-class ghetto, and in the factories, fires started. There was no opposing the flames. . . . And the great water-mains had burst. All the shrewd contrivances and safeguards of man had been thrown out of gear by thirty seconds' twitching of the earth-crust. "

—"The Story of an Eye-witness"

At first, most city firefighters were volunteers and not always available when they were needed. Cincinnati, Ohio, tackled this problem when it established the nation's first paid fire department in 1853. By 1900, most cities had full-time professional fire departments. The introduction of a practical automatic fire sprinkler in 1874 and the replacement of wood as a building material with brick, stone, or concrete also made cities safer.

### Tracing Themes
#### DIVERSITY AND NATIONAL IDENTITY

**The City's Offerings**

In 1900, many American city-dwellers lived just within their means. Although they could not afford expensive outings, there were many culturally enriching activities available in the city that were not costly. Jane Addams Hull House in Chicago and the Henry Street Settlement House in New York offered classes in art, music, and drama. Museums had free days, and cultural groups, such as Yiddish theater in New York, offered reasonably priced entertainment.

---

| FIRE: Enemy of the City | |
|---|---|
| **The Great Chicago Fire** October 8–10, 1871 | **The San Francisco Earthquake** April 18, 1906 |
| • The fire burned for 29 hours. | • The quake lasted 28 seconds; fires burned for 4 days. |
| • An estimated 300 people died. | • An estimated 1,000 people died. |
| • 100,000 were left homeless. | • 250,000 were left homeless. |
| • More than 3 square miles of the city center was destroyed. | • Fire swept through 5 square miles of the city. |
| • Property loss was estimated at $200 million. | • Property loss was estimated at $500 million. |
| • 17,500 buildings were destroyed. | • 28,000 buildings were destroyed. |

### HISTORY from VISUALS

**Interpreting the Graphic**
Point out to students that this graphic makes comparisons. They could make charts of their own with the following headings: Length of the event, Number of deaths, Number left homeless, Square miles destroyed, Estimated property loss, Number of buildings destroyed.

**Extension** Ask students what measures experts might use today to prevent or contain damage from fires and earthquakes. *(They now design earthquake proof buildings. Experts know how to fire-proof buildings and use asbestos for fire-fighting gear.)*

*Immigrants and Urbanization* **265**

---

| **ACTIVITY** | **COOPERATIVE LEARNING** |
|---|---|

 **classzone.com**

### Researching Catastrophes

**Class Time** Two class periods

**Task** Researching the San Francisco earthquake of 1906 and the Great Chicago Fire and writing short reports comparing the two disasters

**Purpose** To compare the impact of both catastrophes

**Directions** Form teams of three or four students and ask groups to choose one of the following topics to research:

· What role did city government have in the recovery efforts?
· Which of the two cities recovered more quickly? Why?
· What effects did each disaster have on long-range city planning?
· What are some of the important differences between the San Francisco earthquake of 1906 and the Great Chicago Fire?

The answers to the questions should be placed in a written report.

## KEY PLAYER

**Jane Addams (1860-1935)**

Addams said she founded Hull House as an "effort to aid in the solution of the social and industrial problems which are [caused] by the modern conditions of life in a great city." Have students discuss on what basis they think Addams qualified for the Nobel Peace Prize. *(She was a peace advocate, an anti-war activist, and a fighter for racial justice.)*

## Instruct: Objective ❸

**Reformers Mobilize**

TAKS SS11 5(US24.A)
· What was the Social Gospel movement?
· What was the purpose of settlement houses?
· Who was Jane Addams?

 **In-Depth Resources: Unit 2**
· Guided Reading, p. 40
· Primary Sources: *Twenty Years at Hull House*, p. 54
· American Lives: Jane Addams, p. 59

# Assess & Reteach

## SECTION 2 ASSESSMENT

Have students answer the questions and then note the pages on which the answers can be found.

 **Formal Assessment**
· Section Quiz, p. 134

## SELF-ASSESSMENT

Ask students to choose one of the urban problems discussed in this section and write a one-paragraph solution to the problem.

## RETEACH

Survey students to find out what part of this section was difficult for them. Use the graphic on page 263 as a discussion starter.

 **In-Depth Resources: Unit 2**
· Reteaching Activity, p. 46

---

## KEY PLAYER

**JANE ADDAMS
1860–1935**

During a trip to England, Jane Addams visited Toynbee Hall, the first settlement house. Addams believed that settlement houses could be effective because there, workers would "learn from life itself" how to address urban problems. She cofounded Chicago's Hull House in 1889.

Addams was also an antiwar activist, a spokesperson for racial justice, and an advocate for quality-of-life issues, from infant mortality to better care for the aged. In 1931, she was a co-winner of the Nobel Peace Prize.

Until the end of her life, Addams insisted that she was just a "very simple person." But many familiar with her accomplishments consider her a source of inspiration.

---

## Reformers Mobilize ❸

As problems in cities mounted, concerned Americans worked to find solutions. Social welfare reformers targeted their efforts at relieving urban poverty.

**THE SETTLEMENT HOUSE MOVEMENT** An early reform program, the **Social Gospel movement**, preached salvation through service to the poor. Inspired by the message of the Social Gospel movement, many 19th-century reformers responded to the call to help the urban poor. In the late 1800s, a few reformers established **settlement houses,** community centers in slum neighborhoods that provided assistance to people in the area, especially immigrants. Many settlement workers lived at the houses so that they could learn firsthand about the problems caused by urbanization and help create solutions.

Run largely by middle-class, college-educated women, settlement houses provided educational, cultural, and social services. They provided classes in such subjects as English, health, and painting, and offered college extension courses. Settlement houses also sent visiting nurses into the homes of the sick and provided whatever aid was needed to secure "support for deserted women, insurance for bewildered widows, damages for injured operators, furniture from the clutches of the installment store."

Settlement houses in the United States were founded by Charles Stover and Stanton Coit in New York City in 1886. **Jane Addams**—one of the most influential members of the movement—and Ellen Gates Starr founded Chicago's Hull House in 1889. In 1890, Janie Porter Barrett founded Locust Street Social Settlement in Hampton, Virginia—the first settlement house for African Americans. By 1910, about 400 settlement houses were operating in cities across the country. The settlement houses helped cultivate social responsibility toward the urban poor.

---

## ❷ ASSESSMENT

**1. TERMS & NAMES** For each term or name, write a sentence explaining its significance.
· **urbanization**          · **tenement**          · **Social Gospel movement**          · **Jane Addams**
· **Americanization movement**          · **mass transit**          · **settlement house**

### MAIN IDEA

**2. TAKING NOTES**
Re-create the spider map below on your paper. List urban problems on the vertical lines. Fill in details about attempts that were made to solve each problem.

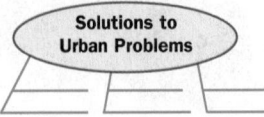
**Solutions to Urban Problems**

### CRITICAL THINKING

**3. ANALYZING MOTIVES**
Why did immigrants tend to group together in cities?

**4. EVALUATING**
Which solution (or attempted solution) to an urban problem discussed in this section do you think had the most impact? Why?

**5. ANALYZING EFFECTS**
What effects did the migration from rural areas to the cities in the late 19th century have on urban society?
**Think About:**
• why people moved to cities
• the problems caused by rapid urban growth
• the differences in the experiences of whites and blacks

**266** CHAPTER 7

---

 ## ❷ ASSESSMENT Answers

**1. TERMS & NAMES**
urbanization, p. 262
Americanization movement, p. 263
tenement, p. 264
mass transit, p. 264
Social Gospel movement, p. 266
settlement house, p. 266
Jane Addams, p. 266

**2. TAKING NOTES**
Students should choose three problems. Housing—dumbbell tenements, row houses; transportation—new streetcar lines, subways; unsafe water—public waterworks, chlorination, filtration; sanitation—sewer lines, sanitation departments; fire—full-time fire departments, wood replaced with brick, stone, concrete.

**3. ANALYZING MOTIVES**
For mutual support and access to jobs

**4. EVALUATING**
Settlement houses because they established the need and ways to address the problems of the urban poor. Chlorination because it made drinking water safe and improved people's health.

**5. ANALYZING EFFECTS**
Competition for jobs; overcrowded housing; water and sanitation problems; increased crime; segregation and discrimination

# Politics in the Gilded Age

| MAIN IDEA | WHY IT MATTERS NOW | Terms & Names |
|---|---|---|
| Local and national political corruption in the 19th century led to calls for reform. | Political reforms paved the way for a more honest and efficient government in the 20th century and beyond. | • political machine • graft • Boss Tweed • patronage • civil service • Rutherford B. Hayes · James A. Garfield · Chester A. Arthur · Pendleton Civil Service Act · Grover Cleveland · Benjamin Harrison |

**U.S. History 2A, 24A, 24B, 24D, 24F, 25A, 25B, 25C, 25D**

## One American's Story

Mark Twain described the excesses of the late 19th century in a satirical novel, *The Gilded Age*, a collaboration with the writer Charles Dudley Warner. The title of the book has since come to represent the period from the 1870s to the 1890s. Twain mocks the greed and self-indulgence of his characters, including Philip Sterling.

### A PERSONAL VOICE
MARK TWAIN AND CHARLES DUDLEY WARNER

" There are many young men like him [Philip Sterling] in American society, of his age, opportunities, education and abilities, who have really been educated for nothing and have let themselves drift, in the hope that they will find somehow, and by some sudden turn of good luck, the golden road to fortune. . . . He saw people, all around him, poor yesterday, rich to-day, who had come into sudden opulence by some means which they could not have classified among any of the regular occupations of life. "

—*The Gilded Age*

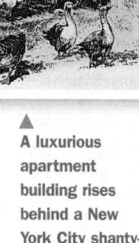

▲ A luxurious apartment building rises behind a New York City shantytown in 1889.

Twain's characters find that getting rich quick is more difficult than they had thought it would be. Investments turn out to be worthless; politicians' bribes eat up their savings. The glittering exterior of the age turns out to hide a corrupt political core and a growing gap between the few rich and the many poor.

## 1 The Emergence of Political Machines

In the late 19th century, cities experienced rapid growth under inefficient government. In a climate influenced by dog-eat-dog Social Darwinism, cities were receptive to a new power structure, the political machine, and a new politician, the city boss.

*Immigrants and Urbanization* **267**

## More About . . .

### Political Machines

Despite the tendency of political machines for corruption and graft, some scholars insist they also served a worthwhile purpose. Political observer Frank Sorauf remarked, "In its fabled heyday the urban machine in America offered the new arrivals to the cities a range of services that made it, in contemporary terms, a combination of employment agency, legal aid society, social worker, domestic relations counselor, and community social center. And in the new style, urban 'club' parties in the American cities and suburbs, the parties cater to the social and intellectual needs of a mobile, educated, ideological, often isolated upper middle class."

## More About . . .

### The Pendergast Family

After his wife's death in 1905, "Big Jim" Pendergast lost interest in politics. In 1910, he gave his younger brother, Tom, control of the Democratic Party. Under Tom's leadership, the Kansas City political machine reached its height of power and corruption. Alcohol flowed despite Prohibition, gambling flourished, and elections were rigged. Tom was strong as a leader but weak when it came to gambling. In 1939, he was charged with failing to pay taxes on bribe money he had used to pay off gambling debts. Tom Pendergast served 15 months in prison, after which he lived out the rest of his life quietly at his home.

**THE POLITICAL MACHINE** An organized group that controlled the activities of a political party in a city, the **political machine** also offered services to voters and businesses in exchange for political or financial support. In the decades after the Civil War, political machines gained control of local government in Baltimore, New York, San Francisco, and other major cities.

The machine was organized like a pyramid. At the pyramid's base were local precinct workers and captains, who tried to gain voters' support on a city block or in a neighborhood and who reported to a ward boss. At election time, the ward boss worked to secure the vote in all the precincts in the ward, or electoral district. Ward bosses helped the poor and gained their votes by doing favors or providing services. As Martin Lomasney, elected ward boss of Boston's West End in 1885, explained, "There's got to be in every ward a guy that any bloke can come to . . . and get help. Help, you understand; none of your law and your justice, but help." At the top of the pyramid was the city boss, who controlled the activities of the political party throughout the city. Precinct captains, ward bosses, and the city boss worked together to elect their candidates and guarantee the success of the machine. **A**

**THE ROLE OF THE POLITICAL BOSS** Whether or not the boss officially served as mayor, he controlled access to municipal jobs and business licenses, and influenced the courts and other municipal agencies. Bosses like Roscoe Conkling in New York used their power to build parks, sewer systems, and waterworks, and gave money to schools, hospitals, and orphanages. Bosses could also provide government support for new businesses, a service for which they were often paid extremely well.

It was not only money that motivated city bosses. By solving urban problems, bosses could reinforce voters' loyalty, win additional political support, and extend their influence.

**IMMIGRANTS AND THE MACHINE** Many precinct captains and political bosses were first-generation or second-generation immigrants. Few were educated beyond grammar school. They entered politics early and worked their way up from the bottom. They could speak to immigrants in their own language and understood the challenges that newcomers faced. More important, the bosses were able to provide solutions. The machines helped immigrants with naturalization (attaining full citizenship), housing, and jobs—the newcomers' most pressing needs. In return, the immigrants provided what the political bosses needed—votes. **B**

"Big Jim" Pendergast, an Irish-American saloonkeeper, worked his way up from precinct captain to Democratic city boss in Kansas City by aiding Italian, African-American, and Irish voters in his ward. By 1900, he controlled Missouri state politics as well.

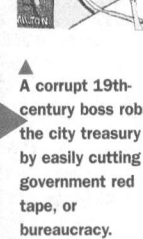
▲ A corrupt 19th-century boss robs the city treasury by easily cutting government red tape, or bureaucracy.

**A PERSONAL VOICE** JAMES PENDERGAST

" I've been called a boss. All there is to it is having friends, doing things for people, and then later on they'll do things for you. . . . You can't coerce people into doing things for you—you can't make them vote for you. I never coerced anybody in my life. Wherever you see a man bulldozing anybody he don't last long. "

—quoted in *The Pendergast Machine*

**268** CHAPTER 7

---

 **MAIN IDEA**

**Summarizing**

**A** In what way did the structure of the political machine resemble a pyramid?

*A. Answer*
Many local precinct workers and captains formed the base of the organization. In the middle were a few ward bosses. At the top was one city boss.

**MAIN IDEA**

**Analyzing Motives**

**B** Why did immigrants support political machines?

*B. Answer*
Because the machines could provide solutions to the immigrants' most pressing problems.

---

**DIFFERENTIATING INSTRUCTION**   **GIFTED AND TALENTED STUDENTS**    classzone.com

### Writing a Biography

Have interested students research and write a biographical sketch about one of the people mentioned on pages 268 and 269. Students should use the Internet and other resource materials. Encourage students to include quotes in their sketches.

📝 Integrated Assessment
· Rubrics 1, 5

## ❷ Municipal Graft and Scandal

While the well-oiled political machines provided city dwellers with services, many political bosses fell victim to corruption as their influence grew.

**ELECTION FRAUD AND GRAFT** When the loyalty of voters was not enough to carry an election, some political machines turned to fraud. Using fake names, party faithfuls cast as many votes as were needed to win.

Once a political machine got its candidates into office, it could take advantage of numerous opportunities for **graft,** the illegal use of political influence for personal gain. For example, by helping a person find work on a construction project for the city, a political machine could ask the worker to bill the city for more than the actual cost of materials and labor. The worker then "kicked back" a portion of the earnings to the machine. Taking these kickbacks, or illegal payments for their services, enriched the political machines—and individual politicians.

Political machines also granted favors to businesses in return for cash and accepted bribes to allow illegal activities, such as gambling, to flourish. Politicians were able to get away with shady dealings because the police rarely interfered. Until about 1890, police forces were hired and fired by political bosses.

**THE TWEED RING SCANDAL** William M. Tweed, known as **Boss Tweed,** became head of Tammany Hall, New York City's powerful Democratic political machine, in 1868. Between 1869 and 1871, Boss Tweed led the Tweed Ring, a group of corrupt politicians, in defrauding the city.

One scheme, the construction of the New York County Courthouse, involved extravagant graft. The project cost taxpayers $13 million, while the actual construction cost was $3 million. The difference went into the pockets of Tweed and his followers.

Thomas Nast, a political cartoonist, helped arouse public outrage against Tammany Hall's graft, and the Tweed Ring was finally broken in 1871. Tweed was indicted on 120 counts of fraud and extortion and was sentenced to 12 years in jail. His sentence was reduced to one year, but after leaving jail, Tweed was quickly arrested on another charge. While serving a second sentence, Tweed escaped. He was captured in Spain when officials identified him from a Thomas Nast cartoon. By that time, political corruption had become a national issue.

**Vocabulary**
**extortion:** illegal use of one's official position to obtain property or funds

▲ Boss Tweed, head of Tammany Hall.

**Instruct: Objective ❷**

**Municipal Graft and Scandal**
TAKS SS11 5(WH26.C)
· What means did many political machines use to maintain power?
· For what reasons was the Tweed Ring so notorious?

 In-Depth Resources: Unit 2
 · Guided Reading, p. 41
 · Primary Sources: The Shame of Cities, p. 55
 · American Lives: William Marcy Tweed, p. 59

### More About . . .

**Boss Tweed**

Tweed's downfall began in 1871 when several disgruntled machine officials turned over evidence of Tammany Hall's corruption to the *New York Times.* Upon learning of the damaging information held by the *Times,* Tweed offered the owner of the newspaper $5 million not to publish the material. He also offered Thomas Nast $500,000 to cease his cartoon attacks. Both offers were refused. Estimates of the total amount that his machine stole from New York City range from $30 million to $200 million.

---

## Analyzing *Political Cartoons*

**"THE TAMMANY TIGER LOOSE"**

Political cartoonist Thomas Nast ridiculed Boss Tweed and his machine in the pages of *Harper's Weekly.* Nast's work threatened Tweed, who reportedly said, "I don't care so much what the papers write about me—my constituents can't read; but . . . they can see pictures!"

**SKILLBUILDER** Analyzing Political Cartoons
1. Under the Tammany tiger's victim is a torn paper that reads "LAW." What is its significance?
2. Boss Tweed and his cronies, portrayed as noblemen, watch from the stands on the left. The cartoon's caption reads "What are you going to do about it?" What effect do you think Nast wanted to have on his audience?

 **SEE SKILLBUILDER HANDBOOK, PAGE R24.**

### Analyzing *Political Cartoons*

**SKILLBUILDER ANSWERS**
1. The torn paper represents the way Tammany Hall has broken the law.
2. Nast wanted his audience to be outraged by it and take action against Tammany Hall.

*Immigrants and Urbanization* **269**

---

| ACTIVITY | COOPERATIVE LEARNING |

**Creating Political Cartoons**

**Class Time** 45 minutes

**Task** Creating one or more political cartoons or graphics reflecting the urban political scene in the late 1800s

**Purpose** To understand the way cartoonists use pictures to make political commentary

**Directions** Have students work in pairs or on their own to create one or more political cartoons. Suggest a few ideas:

· How a political machine uses graft
· How political bosses provide services to immigrants in exchange for their votes
· How a political machine affects taxpayers

 Integrated Assessment
 · Rubrics 2, 4

## Instruct: Objective ③

**Civil Service Replaces Patronage**
TAKS SS11 5(US24.A)

· What were the consequences of the patronage system?

· What political reform efforts did Hayes, Garfield, and Arthur undertake?

· What was the Pendleton Civil Service Act?

 **In-Depth Resources: Unit 2**
· Guided Reading, p. 41

---

### More About . . .

#### Chester A. Arthur

Before moving into the White House, President Arthur had it completely cleaned out and refurnished. He managed to fill 24 wagons with items that had accumulated over the years, including a hat that had belonged to John Quincy Adams and a pair of trousers worn by Abraham Lincoln. These and other items were sold at auction. Rumors circulated that a sideboard that the Women's Christian Temperance Union had presented to Mrs. Rutherford Hayes, nicknamed "Lemonade Lucy," because she had refused to serve liquor in the White House, was bought by a Washington saloon keeper, who installed it in his barroom. Ultimately, the story proved to be false.

---

**RUTHERFORD B. HAYES (1877–1881)**

*"Nobody ever left the presidency with less regret . . . than I do."*

**JAMES A. GARFIELD (1881)**

*"Assassination can be no more guarded against than death by lightning."*

**CHESTER A. ARTHUR (1881–1885)**

*"There doesn't seem to be anything else for an ex-president to do but . . . raise big pumpkins."*

---

## ③ Civil Service Replaces Patronage

The desire for power and money that made local politics corrupt in the industrial age also infected national politics.

**PATRONAGE SPURS REFORM** Since the beginning of the 19th century, presidents had complained about the problem of **patronage,** or the giving of government jobs to people who had helped a candidate get elected. In Andrew Jackson's administration, this policy was known as the spoils system. People from cabinet members to workers who scrubbed the steps of the Capitol owed their jobs to political connections. As might be expected, some government employees were not qualified for the positions they filled. Moreover, political appointees, whether qualified or not, sometimes used their positions for personal gain.

Reformers began to press for the elimination of patronage and the adoption of a merit system of hiring. Jobs in **civil service**—government administration—should go to the most qualified persons, reformers believed. It should not matter what political views they held or who recommended them. **C**

**REFORM UNDER HAYES, GARFIELD, AND ARTHUR** Civil service reform made gradual progress under Presidents Hayes, Garfield, and Arthur. Republican president **Rutherford B. Hayes,** elected in 1876, could not convince Congress to support reform, so he used other means. Hayes named Independents to his cabinet. He also set up a commission to investigate the nation's customhouses, which were notoriously corrupt. On the basis of the commission's report, Hayes fired two of the top officials of New York City's customhouse, where jobs were controlled by the Republican Party. These firings enraged the Republican New York senator and political boss Roscoe Conkling and his supporters, the Stalwarts.

When Hayes decided not to run for reelection in 1880, a free-for-all broke out at the Republican convention, between the Stalwarts—who opposed changes in the spoils system—and reformers. Since neither Stalwarts nor reformers could win a majority of delegates, the convention settled on an independent presidential candidate, Ohio congressman **James A. Garfield.** To balance out Garfield's ties to reformers, the Republicans nominated for vice president **Chester A. Arthur,** one of Conkling's supporters. Despite Arthur's inclusion on the ticket, Garfield angered the Stalwarts by giving reformers most of his patronage jobs once he was elected.

On July 2, 1881, as President Garfield walked through the Washington, D.C., train station, he was shot two times by a mentally unbalanced lawyer named Charles Guiteau, whom Garfield had turned down for a job. The would-be assassin announced, "I did it and I will go to jail for it. I am a Stalwart and Arthur is now president." Garfield finally died from his wounds on September 19. Despite his ties to the Stalwarts, Chester Arthur turned reformer when he became president. His first message to Congress urged legislators to pass a civil service law.

The resulting **Pendleton Civil Service Act** of 1883 authorized a bipartisan civil service commission to make

---

**MAIN IDEA**

**Analyzing Causes**

**C** How did patronage contribute to government incompetence and fraud?

*C. Answer*
By allowing people to be hired for government jobs on the basis of political beliefs rather than ability, and by providing opportunities for misuse of influence.

---

### Clarifying

Demonstrate the effect of a tariff on prices with a scale, or homemade teeter-totter. Balance a ruler on top of a book standing on end. Label the two ends of the ruler "Cost to Importer" and "Cost to Consumer" respectively. Make weights by wrapping chalk or erasers in rubber bands. Hang equal weights at both ends of the ruler. Label and additional weight "tariff."

Ask the class what will happen when you add this "tariff" to the importer's cost. *("Cost to Consumer" will go up)* Demonstrate and discuss why adding a cost at one end causes the cost at the other end to rise.

---

appointments to federal jobs through a merit system based on candidates' performance on an examination. By 1901, more than 40 percent of all federal jobs had been classified as civil service positions, but the Pendleton Act had mixed consequences. On the one hand, public administration became more honest and efficient. On the other hand, because officials could no longer pressure employees for campaign contributions, politicians turned to other sources for donations.

## Business Buys Influence

**MAIN IDEA**

**Analyzing Effects**
**D** What were the positive and the negative effects of the Pendleton Civil Service Act?

**D. Answer**
**Positive:** More competent and honest federal workers.
**Negative:** Closer ties between government and big business.

With employees no longer a source of campaign contributions, politicians turned to wealthy business owners. Therefore, the alliance between government and big business became stronger than ever. **D**

**HARRISON, CLEVELAND, AND HIGH TARIFFS** Big business hoped the government would preserve, or even raise, the tariffs that protected domestic industries from foreign competition. The Democratic Party, however, opposed high tariffs because they increased prices. In 1884, the Democratic Party won a presidential election for the first time in 28 years with candidate **Grover Cleveland.** As president, Cleveland tried to lower tariff rates, but Congress refused to support him.

In 1888, Cleveland ran for reelection on a low-tariff platform against the former Indiana senator **Benjamin Harrison,** the grandson of President William Henry Harrison. Harrison's campaign was financed by large contributions from companies that wanted tariffs even higher than they were. Although Cleveland won about 100,000 more popular votes than Harrison, Harrison took a majority of the electoral votes and the presidency. Once in office, he won passage of the McKinley Tariff Act of 1890, which raised tariffs to their highest level yet.

In 1892, Cleveland was elected again—the only president to serve two nonconsecutive terms. He supported a bill for lowering the McKinley Tariff but refused to sign it because it also provided for a federal income tax. The Wilson-Gorman Tariff became law in 1894 without the president's signature. In 1897, William McKinley was inaugurated president and raised tariffs once again.

The attempt to reduce the tariff had failed, but the spirit of reform was not dead. New developments in areas ranging from technology to mass culture would help redefine American society as the United States moved into the 20th century.

### SECTION 3 ASSESSMENT

**1. TERMS & NAMES** For each term or name, write a sentence explaining its significance.
- political machine
- graft
- Boss Tweed
- patronage
- civil service
- Rutherford B. Hayes
- James A. Garfield
- Chester A. Arthur
- Pendleton Civil Service Act
- Grover Cleveland
- Benjamin Harrison

**MAIN IDEA**

**2. TAKING NOTES**
In a chart like the one shown, list examples of corruption in 19th-century politics.

**CRITICAL THINKING**

**3. EVALUATING LEADERSHIP**
Reread the quotation from James Pendergast on page 268. Explain whether you agree or disagree that machine politicians did not coerce people.

**4. ANALYZING CAUSES**
Why do you think tariff reform failed? Support your response with evidence from the chapter.

**5. HYPOTHESIZING**
How do you think politics in the United States would have been different if the Pendleton Civil Service Act had not been passed?
**Think About:**
- the act's impact on federal workers
- the act's impact on political fundraising
- Republican Party conflicts

*Immigrants and Urbanization* **271**

**Instruct: Objective**  **4**
**Business Buys Influence**
TAKS SS11 5(US24.B)
· Where did Cleveland and Harrison stand on the tariff issue?
· What was the McKinley Tariff Act of 1890?
· What happened to tariffs when Cleveland was reelected, and how did things change when McKinley took office?

📖 **In-Depth Resources: Unit 2**
· Guided Reading, p. 41

### More About . . .

**Tariffs**
A tariff is a tax imposed by a government on imported or exported goods. Throughout American history, manufacturing interests have tended to support tariffs on imports because they keep prices for imported goods high. Consumers, on the other hand, have tended to oppose tariffs because they add to the cost of imported goods.

## Assess & Reteach

**SECTION 3 ASSESSMENT**
Have students work individually to answer the questions; then have them share with the class the graphics they created for item 2.

📖 **Formal Assessment**
· Section Quiz, p. 135

**SELF-ASSESSMENT**
Ask students to review what they wrote for item 4.

**RETEACH**
Survey students to find out what material in the section was most difficult for them. Then review that material with students.

📖 **In-Depth Resources: Unit 2**
· Reteaching Activity, p. 47

---

**Answers** **ASSESSMENT**

**1. TERMS & NAMES**
political machine, p. 268
graft, p. 269
Boss Tweed, p. 269
patronage, p. 270
civil service, p. 270
Rutherford B. Hayes, p. 270
James A. Garfield, p. 270
Chester A. Arthur, p. 270
Pendleton Civil Service Act, p. 270
Grover Cleveland, p. 271
Benjamin Harrison, p. 271

**2. TAKING NOTES**
election fraud, kickbacks, bribery, graft, patronage

**3. EVALUATING LEADERSHIP**
Agree: Immigrants chose to support the machines because the machines could help them with everyday problems.
Disagree: Immigrants were coerced into supporting the machines. If they didn't, no politicians would help them.

**4. ANALYZING CAUSES**
Because the companies that benefited from the tariff donated money to Harrison, the pro-tariff presidential candidate

**5. HYPOTHESIZING**
Federal employment would have continued to be dominated by politics, politicians would have been less dependent on big business for campaign funds, a key issue would have continued to divide the Republicans.

*Immigrants and Urbanization* **271**

## TERMS & NAMES

1. Ellis Island, p. 256
2. Gentlemen's Agreement, p. 259
3. Americanization movement, p. 263
4. Jane Addams, p. 266
5. political machine, p. 268
6. graft, p. 269
7. Boss Tweed, p. 269
8. patronage, p. 270
9. Rutherford B. Hayes, p. 270
10. Pendleton Civil Service Act, p. 270

## MAIN IDEAS

1. Poverty, famine, shortage of land, lack of jobs, religious or political persecution, and a spirit of rebellion
2. Coping with an unfamiliar culture, the effects of nativism, and the struggle to make a living
3. Industrialization, new technology, and an influx of workers
4. The need to provide adequate housing, transportation, water, and sanitation, and to fight fire and crime
5. Educational, cultural, and social services offered in poor, urban neighborhoods
6. The growing need for city services and the large number of immigrants required a new power structure
7. Inefficiency, fraud, and incompetence
8. Cleveland wanted to reduce tariffs; Harrison wanted to keep them high.

## TERMS & NAMES

For each term or name below, write a sentence explaining its connection to immigration and urbanization.

1. Ellis Island
2. Gentlemen's Agreement
3. Americanization movement
4. Jane Addams
5. political machine
6. graft
7. Boss Tweed
8. patronage
9. Rutherford B. Hayes
10. Pendleton Civil Service Act

## MAIN IDEAS

Use your notes and the information in the chapter to answer the following questions.

### The New Immigrants (pages 254–259)

1. What trends or events in other countries prompted people to move to the United States in the late 19th and early 20th centuries?
2. What difficulties did many of these new immigrants face?

### The Challenges of Urbanization
(pages 262–266)

3. Why did cities in the United States grow rapidly in the decades following the Civil War?
4. What problems did this rapid growth pose for cities?
5. What solutions to urban problems did the settlement-house movement propose?

### Politics in the Gilded Age (pages 267–271)

6. Why did machine politics become common in big cities in the late 19th century?
7. What government problems arose as a result of patronage?
8. Summarize the views of Grover Cleveland and Benjamin Harrison on tariffs.

## CRITICAL THINKING

1. **USING YOUR NOTES** In a diagram like the one below, show one result of and one reaction against (a) the increase in immigration and (b) the increase in machine politics.

| | Result | Reaction |
|---|---|---|
| Increased Immigration | → ____ → | ____ |
| Increased Machine Politics | → ____ → | ____ |

2. **EVALUATING** In the 1860s, Horace Greeley—editor of the *New York Tribune*—remarked, "We cannot all live in the cities, yet nearly all seem determined to do so." Why do you think this was true at the end of the 19th century? Do you think it is still true? Why or why not?

3. **COMPARING** How were politicians like Boss Tweed similar to industrial magnates like Carnegie and Rockefeller?

## VISUAL SUMMARY IMMIGRANTS AND URBANIZATION

### IMMIGRATION AND MIGRATION

- Poverty and persecution cause millions of people to leave Europe, China, Japan, the Caribbean, and Mexico for the United States.
- Immigrants are forced to adapt to a new language and culture.
- Changes in agriculture cause people to migrate from the rural U.S. to the cities in search of work.
- Many immigrants and migrants face discrimination in their efforts to find jobs and housing.

### URBANIZATION

- The influx of immigrants and migrants causes a population boom in cities.
- City services, such as housing, transportation, water, and sanitation, are stretched to the limit.
- Reformers try to fix urban problems through education, training, charity, and political action.

### POLITICS

- Political machines develop to take advantage of the needs of immigrants and the urban poor.
- City politicians use fraud and graft to maintain political power.
- Corruption in national politics results in the call for civil service jobs to be awarded on the basis of merit.
- Big business's growing influence on politics defeats tariff reform that would aid wage-earners.

## CRITICAL THINKING

1. **Using Your Notes** Increased immigration
   Result: growth of urban populations
   Reaction: growth of nativism
   Increase in machine politics
   Result: widespread corruption
   Reaction: support for civil service reform

2. **Evaluating** At the end of the 19th century, cities offered jobs and other economic opportunities. Regarding the present-day situation, students might mention the movement from the cities to the suburbs or cities as centers of business and industry.

3. **Comparing** Both amassed huge fortunes—not always legally—but also did some social good.

## Standardized Test Practice

Use the quotation and your knowledge of U.S. history to answer question 1.

> "The Chinese . . . ask for fair treatment. . . . Since the first restriction law was passed the United States has received as immigrants more than two million Austro-Hungarians, two million Italians and a million and a half Russians and Finns. Each of these totals is from five to seven times the whole amount of Chinese immigration of all classes during thirty years of free immigration. . . . The question is not now of the admission of laborers, but whether other Chinese who are entitled to come under both law and treaty shall receive the same courtesies as people of other nations, and shall be relieved from many harassing regulations. They must no longer be detained, photographed and examined as if they were suspected of crime."
>
> —Ng Poon Chew, from *The Treatment of the Exempt Classes of Chinese in the United States*

1. The information in the passage supports which *one* of the following points of view?

   A European immigration should be restricted.

   B Chinese laborers should be allowed to immigrate.

   C All immigrants are treated like criminals.

   D Chinese immigrants and European immigrants should be treated the same.

Use the cartoon and your knowledge of U.S. history to answer question 2.

2. The cartoon suggests that Boss Tweed (the large figure at left) —

   F was solely responsible for stealing the people's money.

   G did not steal the people's money.

   H had help from his associates in stealing the people's money.

   J was loyal to his associates.

ADDITIONAL TEST PRACTICE, pages S1–S33.

 TEST PRACTICE  CLASSZONE.COM

## ALTERNATIVE ASSESSMENT

1. **INTERACT WITH HISTORY**  Recall your discussion of the question on page 253:

   *What would you do to improve conditions?*

   With what you have learned about the challenges faced by immigrants in the 19th century, consider how you would revise your answer. Discuss the following issue:

   • What were the best solutions attempted by government and reformers in the 1800s?

   Create a pamphlet promoting the reform, improvement, or government solution you chose.

2. **VIDEO**  **LEARNING FROM MEDIA**  View the *American Stories* video, "From China to Chinatown: Fong See's American Dream." Discuss the following questions with a small group; then do the activity.

   • How did Fong See overcome the difficulties facing Asian immigrants in America during his lifetime?

   • What did Lisa See learn about living in a diverse society from her great-grandfather's experience?

   **Cooperative Learning Activity**  Share stories of immigration or the experiences of recent immigrants to the U.S. that you have heard or read about. With the group, create a multimedia presentation of these stories. Use pictures, text, and sound to represent the stories.

*Immigrants and Urbanization* **273**

---

## Standardized Test Practice

1. The correct answer is letter **D**. The quote urges that the Chinese receive the same treatment as the Europeans. Letter A is not correct because restricting European immigration is not mentioned. Letter B is not correct because the immigration of Chinese laborers is not in question. Letter C is not correct because the passage only refers to the Chinese being treated like criminals.

2. The correct answer is letter **H**. Boss Tweed was head of a corruption ring. Letter F is not correct because Boss Tweed did not work alone. Letter G is not correct because Boss Tweed and his gang cheated taxpayers out of millions. Letter J is not correct because Boss Tweed was interested in his own personal gain and was not loyal to his associates.

### UNIT PROJECT

**ORAL REPORT**

**Tips for Teaching**

· Remind students that the report should include visuals or artifacts which they should be creating.

· Review the student's outlines of their presentations.

Formal Assessment
· Chapter Test, Forms A, B, and C, pp. 136–147

---

## ALTERNATIVE ASSESSMENT

### 1. INTERACT WITH HISTORY
**Rubrics**

A pamphlet should . . .

· be concise and compelling

· promote the solution through visuals, slogans, important facts

· advocate a position based on an understanding of the government and reform movements of the 1800s

### 2. LEARNING FROM MEDIA
**Rubrics**

A multimedia presentation should . . .

· Use more than one type of media

· Offer insight into the immigrant experience

· Conclude with a summary of main points

# Life at the Turn of the 20th Century

| | CHAPTER OVERVIEW | COPYMASTERS | INTEGRATED TECHNOLOGY |
|---|---|---|---|
| **CHAPTER RESOURCES** | As the 20th century begins, American culture changes due to new technological advances, cultural forms, and mass media. Some Americans, though, protest discrimination that denies them rights. | 📄 Telescoping the Times<br>· Chapter Summary, pp. 15–16<br><br>📄 Planning for Block Schedules | 💿 America's Music CD<br>💿 Power Presentations<br>💿 Electronic Teacher Tools<br>👤 Online Lesson Planner<br>👤 classzone.com |
| **SECTION 1**<br>**Science and Urban Life**<br>pp. 276–281 | **KEY IDEAS**<br>Advances in science and technology address urban problems, including lack of space and inadequate systems of transportation and communication. | 📄 In-Depth Resources: Unit 2<br>· Guided Reading, p. 61<br>· Building Vocabulary, p. 65<br>· Reteaching Activity, p. 67<br>· Geography Application, pp. 71–72<br>· Primary Sources, pp. 73–74<br><br>📄 Lesson Plans, pp. 63-64 | 🗺️ Geography Transparencies GT16<br>· Telephone Long Distances lines: 1890–1917<br>💿 Electronic Library of Primary Sources<br>· from "Automobiles: The Other Side of the Shield"<br>· from A Visit to the World's Columbian Exposition<br>👤 classzone.com |
| **SECTION 2**<br>**Expanding Public Education**<br>pp. 282–285 | The impulses of moral uplift and economic necessity spur changes in education, a rise in national literacy, and the promotion of high culture. | 📄 In-Depth Resources: Unit 2<br>· Guided Reading, p. 62<br>· Reteaching Activity, p. 68<br>· Primary Sources, p. 75<br>· American Lives, p. 80<br><br>📄 Lesson Plans, pp. 65-66 | 🗺️ Critical Thinking Transparencies CT16, CT50<br>· Expansion of Education<br>· Increasing School Enrollment 1870–1920<br>👤 classzone.com |
| **SECTION 3**<br>**Segregation and Discrimination**<br>pp. 286–291 | African Americans lead the fight against institutionalized racism in the form of voting restrictions and Jim Crow laws. | 📄 In-Depth Resources: Unit 2<br>· Guided Reading, p. 63<br>· Skillbuilder Practice, p. 66<br>· Reteaching Activity, p. 69<br>· Primary Sources, p. 76<br><br>📄 Lesson Plans, pp. 67-68 | 💿 Electronic Library of Primary Sources<br>· from The Autobiography of Ida B. Wells<br>👤 classzone.com |
| **SECTION 4**<br>**The Dawn of Mass Culture**<br>pp. 292–299 | Americans have more time for leisure activities and a modern mass culture emerges, especially through newspapers and retail advertising. | 📄 In-Depth Resources: Unit 2<br>· Guided Reading, p. 64<br>· Reteaching Activity, p. 70<br>· Primary Sources, p. 74<br>· Literature, pp. 77–79<br>· American Lives, p. 81<br><br>📄 Lesson Plans, pp. 69-70 | 🗺️ Humanities Transparencies HT16<br>· Washington Square North<br>💿 Electronic Library of Primary Sources<br>· from "The Base-Ball Season"<br>👤 classzone.com |

## Legend

**PE** Pupil's Edition  
**TE** Teacher's Edition  
**(copymaster icon)** Copymaster  
**(overhead icon)** Overhead Transparency  
**(audio icon)** Audio Library  
**(CD-ROM icon)** CD-ROM  
**(internet icon)** Internet

---

## ASSESSMENT OPTIONS

**PE** Chapter Assessment, pp. 300–301  
**(copymaster)** Formal Assessment  
· Chapter Tests, Forms A, B, and C, pp. 152–169  
**(CD-ROM)** Test Generator  
**(copymaster)** Integrated Assessment Book  
**(internet)** TAKS Online Test Practice  
**(copymaster)** TAKS Spiraled Content Review  
TAKS Practice Tests

**PE** Section 1 Assessment, p. 281  
**TE** Self-Assessment, p. 281  
**(copymaster)** Formal Assessment, Quiz, p. 148  
**(copymaster)** Integrated Assessment Book  
**(CD-ROM)** Test Generator  
**(overhead)** TAKS Practice Transparencies TT58

**PE** Section 2 Assessment, p. 285  
**TE** Self-Assessment, p. 285  
**(copymaster)** Formal Assessment, Quiz, p. 149  
**(copymaster)** Integrated Assessment Book  
**(CD-ROM)** Test Generator  
**(overhead)** TAKS Practice Transparencies TT59

**PE** Section 3 Assessment, p. 289  
**TE** Self-Assessment, p. 289  
**(copymaster)** Formal Assessment, Quiz, p. 150  
**(copymaster)** Integrated Assessment Book  
**(CD-ROM)** Test Generator  
**(overhead)** TAKS Practice Transparencies TT60

**PE** Section 4 Assessment, p. 189  
**TE** Self-Assessment, p. 189  
**(copymaster)** Formal Assessment, Quiz, p. 82  
**(copymaster)** Integrated Assessment Book  
**(CD-ROM)** Test Generator  
**(overhead)** TAKS Practice Transparencies TT61

---

## RESOURCES FOR DIFFERENTIATING INSTRUCTION

### Students Acquiring English/ESL
**(copymaster)** Reading Study Guide: (English and Spanish) pp. 81–90  
**(copymaster)** Access for Students Acquiring English/ESL: Spanish Translations, pp. 102–110  
**(audio)** Chapter Summaries on CD (English and Spanish)

### Less Proficient Readers
**(copymaster)** Reading Study Guide (English and Spanish) pp. 81–90  
**(copymaster)** Telescoping the Times · Chapter Summary, pp. 15–16  
**(audio)** Chapter Summaries on CD (English and Spanish)

### Gifted and Talented Students
**(copymaster)** In-Depth Resources: Unit 2  
· Primary Sources, pp. 73–76  
· Literature, pp. 77–79  
· American Lives, pp. 80–81  
**(copymaster)** Historic Supreme Court Decisions  
· *Plessy v. Ferguson,* pp. 67–72  
**(CD-ROM)** Electronic Library of Primary Sources  
· Unit 2, Chapter 8

---

## CROSS-CURRICULAR CONNECTIONS

### Science: Technology
Jakob, Peter L. and Crouch, Tom D. *Visions of a Flying Machine: The Wright Brothers and the Process of Invention.* Washington, D.C.: Smithsonian Institute Press, 1997. A fascinating description of the trials and tribulations that lead up to the Wright brothers' first airplane flight.

### Humanities: Art
Sewell, Darrel (editor) et al. *Thomas Eakins.* New Haven, CT: Yale University Press, 2001. Known for realism in his art, Thomas Eakins's vibrant artwork is thoroughly displayed in this beautiful book.

### Humanities: Music
Jasen, David A. and Jones, Gene. *Black Bottom Stomp: Eight Masters of Ragtime and Early Jazz.* NY: Routledge, 2001. This book focuses on nine of the most important musicians in American history, including Jelly Roll Morton, Louis Armstrong, and Scott Joplin.

### Literature
Anderson, Sherwood. *Winesburg, Ohio.* NY: Penguin, 1996. In this modern classic, Anderson mixes his memories of his childhood in Clyde, Ohio, with his observations of life in turn-of-the-20th-century Chicago. In the book, the inhabitants of Winesburg confide their disappointed dreams and dashed hopes to a young reporter. This deeply honest portrait of life in small-town America was a shock to many readers at the time.

Erdrich, Louise. *Tracks.* NY: Harper Collins, 1989. This novel, third in a cycle, tells the story of the Chippewa's struggle to preserve their land and culture in a world dominated by white people.

### McDougal Littell *Literature Connections*

Du Bois, W. E. B. *The Souls of Black Folk (with related readings).* In this collection of essays, Du Bois considers the condition of African Americans in the early 1900s. Among the ideas discussed in the book is Du Bois's famous assertion: "The problem in the 20th Century is the problem of the color line."

---

## ENRICHMENT ACTIVITIES

**PE** Pupil's Edition, pp. 274–299  
Interact with History, p. 274–275  
Science and Technology, p. 280  
Supreme Court, pp. 290–291  
Daily Life, pp. 298–299  

**(copymaster)** In-Depth Resources: Unit 2  
· Geography Application: New York's Central Park, pp. 71–72  
· Primary Source: from *Orville Wright's Diary,* p. 73  
· Primary Source: Advertisement, p. 74  
· Primary Source: "The Talented Tenth," p. 75  
· Primary Source: "Lynching and the Excuse for It," p. 76  
· Literature: from *Ragtime,* pp. 77–79  
· American Lives: W. E. B. Du Bois, p. 80  
· American Lives: Lillian Gish, p. 81  

**(CD-ROM)** Electronic Library of Primary Sources  
· Unit 2, Chapter 8  

**(copymaster)** Historic Supreme Court Decisions  
· *Plessy v. Fergusen,* pp. 67–72  

**(CD-ROM)** America's Music CD

## BLOCK SCHEDULE LESSON PLAN OPTIONS (90-MINUTE PERIOD)

### DAY 1

**CHAPTER 8 OPENER**
pp. 274–275

**Class Time** 30 minutes

**History from Visuals,** p. 274

**Class Time** 10 minutes

*Options for Pacing and Variety*

- **Time Saver** Have students read the time line. Ask them the questions in the TE. **Class Time** 10 minutes

**Interact with History,** p. 275

**Class Time** 20 minutes

*Options for Pacing and Variety*

- **Role-Playing** Discuss as a class the issues of new technology. Help students put themselves in the mindset of the time of these new recreations and time-saving inventions. Ask them what they would think of the new inventions and how these inventions would change their lives. **Class Time** 20 minutes

**SECTION 1,** pp. 276–281

**Class Time** 30 minutes

*Options for Pacing and Variety*

- **Internet** Have students read the feature on page 278, "History Through: Architecture," and answer the questions. Then have them read "Science and Technology" on page 280 and use the Internet for more information. **Class Time** 20 minutes

- **Peer Teaching** Have students work in small groups to answer the questions. Have the groups share their answers. **Class Time** 15 minutes

### DAY 1 continued

**SECTION 2,** pp. 282–285

**Class Time** 30 minutes

*Options for Pacing and Variety*

- **Internet** Ask students to look at the chart on page 283. Have them research the Internet to find current school-age population and illiteracy rates. Refer to TE page 283. **Class Time** 20 minutes

- **Peer Teaching** Have students work in groups to generate ideas to reform the turn of the century school system. Refer to TE page 284 for activity. **Class Time** 30 minutes

- **Peer Evaluation** Have students write questions about the material in section 2 and then exchange lists with another student. **Class Time** 15 minutes

### DAY 2

**SECTION 3,** pp. 286–291

**Class Time** 30 minutes

*Options for Pacing and Variety*

- **Time Saver** Ask students the questions under Focus & Motivate on page 286, as well as the Objective questions, to start them thinking about the concepts in the section. **Class Time** 10 minutes

- **Peer Teaching** Have students work in pairs to create a chart comparing the nature of discrimination in the South, North, and West. Discuss their completed charts as a class. **Class Time** 15 minutes

- **Peer Teaching** Ask students to read the feature "Historic Decisions of the Supreme Court: *Plessy* v. *Ferguson* (1896)" on pages 290–291. Have students work in pairs to answer question 1. **Class Time** 15 minutes

**SECTION 4,** pp. 292–299

**Class Time** 30 minutes

*Options for Pacing and Variety*

- **Time Saver** Have students complete the Clarifying activity on TE page 293 to practice taking notes and studying. **Class Time** 10 minutes

- **Internet** Ask students to read the feature "Daily Life, 1877–1917: Going to the Show" on pages 298–299 and look at the chart detailing the changing hours per week that people worked. Then ask them to use the Internet to research the number of hours the average person worked in 1960, 1980, and 2000. **Class Time** 25 minutes

### DAY 2 continued

**ASSESSMENT**
pp. 300–301

**Class Time** 30 minutes

Options for Pacing and Variety

- **Peer Evaluation** Have students complete the Critical Thinking questions on page 300 and then exchange papers with another student to correct his or her responses. **Class Time** 20 minutes

- **Time Saver** Have students complete the Standardized Test Practice on page 301 and discuss the answers as a class. **Class Time** 10 minutes

---

**TEACHER-TESTED ACTIVITY**
**PRIMARY SOURCE ANALYSIS**

Edmund Austin, William Tenant High School, Warminster, Pennsylvania

**Class Time** 45 minutes

**Task** Analyzing a primary source

**Purpose** To develop a strategy for analyzing primary source material while learning more about the Triangle Fire

**Supplies Needed**

- Primary sources on the Triangle Fire from the textbook or Internet

**Activity** Have students analyze a primary source about the Triangle Shirtwaist Fire tragedy in 1911. Tell them to use the SOAPS strategy. SOAPS stands for subject, occasion, audience, purpose, and speaker. As they read the source material have them identify each of the items in the strategy for each primary source. Then have students share their findings in a class discussion.

# CHAPTER 8 CORRELATION

## CORRELATION TO THE TEXAS ESSENTIAL KNOWLEDGE AND SKILLS

Chapter 8 addresses the following standards of the Texas Essential Knowledge and Skills for U.S. History.

| TEKS | Instruction | Student Question/Activity |
|---|---|---|
| **(2C)** Analyze social issues such as the treatment of minorities. | **PE 286–289** examination of the widespread discrimination and prejudice against African Americans and other minorities | **PE 289** Critical Thinking questions about the nation's racial discrimination at the turn of the 20th century |
| **(4B)** Evaluate the impact of reform leaders such as W. E. B. Du Bois. | **PE 285** discussion of the civil rights efforts by W. E. B. Du Bois | **PE 285** Critical Thinking question comparing the strategies of Du Bois and Booker T. Washington |
| **(17A)** Analyze the effects of 20th century landmark cases. | **PE 290–291** examination of Supreme Court case *Plessy* v. *Ferguson,* which established the policy of "separate but equal" | **PE 291** Critical Thinking questions about the landmark court case |
| **(20A)** Describe how the characteristics and issues of various eras in U.S. history have been reflected in works of art, music, and literature. | **PE 294–296** discussion of new forms of art and literature that gained popularity during the turn of the 20th century | **PE 296** inner column question about the growth in popularity of dime novels |
| **(20D)** Analyze the relationship between culture and the economy. | **PE 296–297** examination of the growth of department stores, advertising, and catalogues | **TE 296** activity asking students to outline the information about the nation's new selling techniques |
| **(22A)** Explain the effects of scientific discoveries and technological innovations on the development of the United States. | **PE 276–281** discussion of the science of urban planning as well as advances in printing, aviation, and photography | **PE 281** Critical Thinking questions about the impact of the era's various inventions and innovations |

## TAKS MINI-LESSONS

1. **Social Studies Skills: Objective 3 (US23.A):** Analyze how scientific discoveries and technological innovations have changed the standard of living in the United States **Activity** Have students discuss their answers to the Critical Thinking questions of the Section 1 Assessment on page 281.

2. **Social Studies Skills: Objective 4 (US7.A):** Trace the historical development of the civil rights movement in the 18th, 19th, and 20th centuries **Activity** Have students summarize the differing views of Booker T. Washington and W. E. B. DuBois regarding the struggle for racial equality.

3. **Social Studies Skills: Objective 5 (WH26.C):** Interpret visuals including graphs, charts, timelines, and maps **Activity** Have students answer the Interpreting Graphs questions regarding the expansion of education on page 283.

4. **English Language Arts Skills: Objective 3 (7.E):** Analyze text structures such as cause and effect for how they influence understanding **Activity** Have students list the causes and effects of the various discriminatory acts taken against African Americans around the turn of the 20th century.

5. **English Language Arts Skills: Objective 3 (19.B):** Analyze ideas as represented in various media **Activity** Have students answer the questions regarding the political cartoon in the Section 4 Assessment on page 297.

CHAPTER 8 · OBJECTIVE

To analyze significant turn-of-the-20th-century trends in such areas as technology, education, race relations, and mass culture.

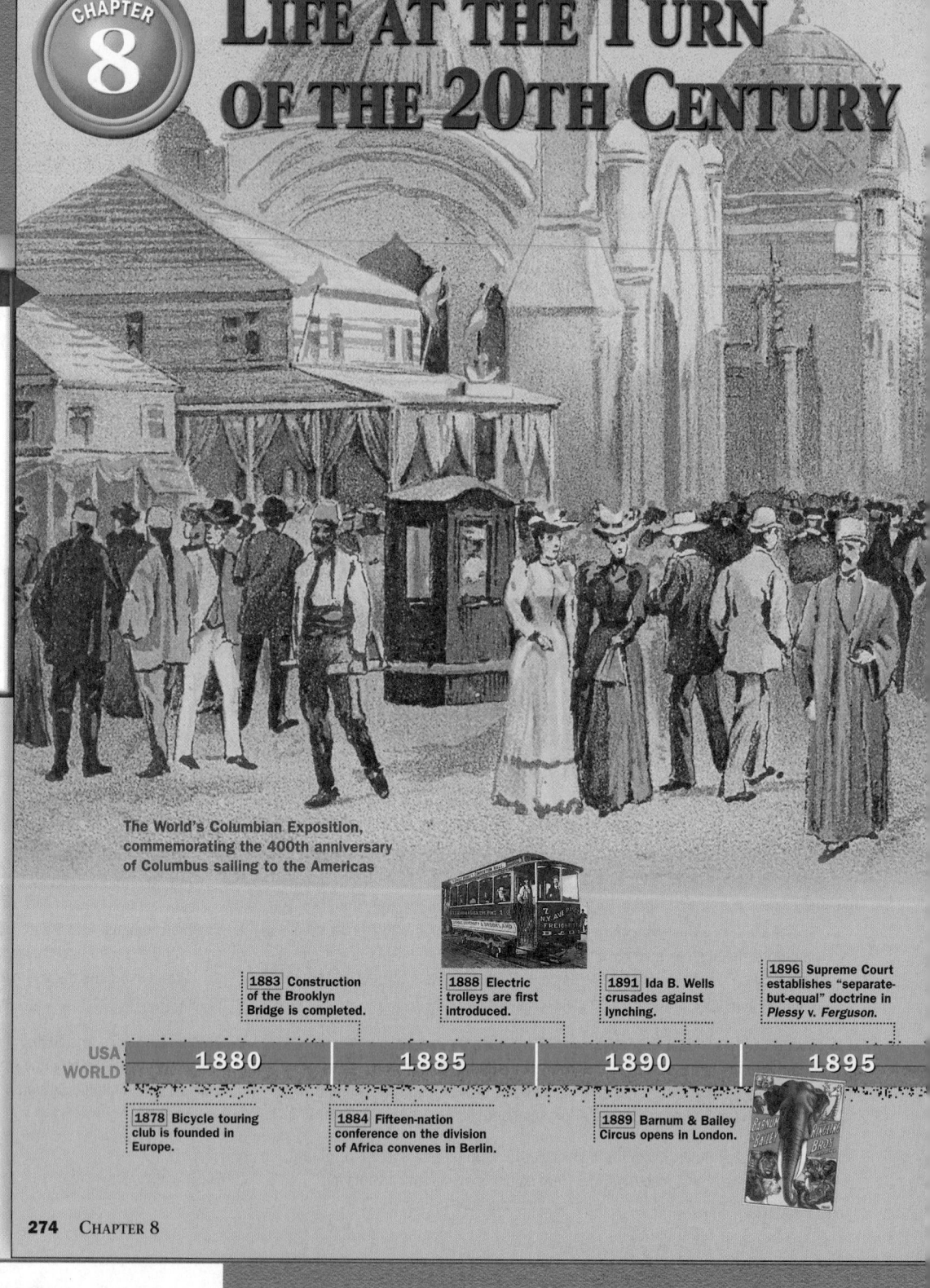

# CHAPTER 8

# LIFE AT THE TURN OF THE 20TH CENTURY

## HISTORY from VISUALS

**Interpreting the Painting**
Have students study the painting and suggest words to describe the atmosphere at the World's Columbian Exposition in Chicago. *(lively, crowded, relaxed)* Ask students if they notice anything reminiscent of modern times. *(Ferris wheel)* Ask them why a camel and building with Arabian-style architecture might be featured at an exposition commemorating Columbus's voyage to the Americas. *(the meeting of the Eastern and Western worlds)*

**Extension** Write an advertisement for the Columbian Exposition based on your observations of the painting.

## Time Line Discussion

Explain to students that this time line includes some of the significant events that took place in the United States in the late 1800s and early 1900s.

· Ask students how many years after the invention of the electric trolley was the Model T. Ford introduced. *(20 years)*

· Ask students in what year Theodore Roosevelt was elected president in his own right. *(1904)*

· Ask students in what year was segregation made legal. *(1896—Plessy v. Ferguson)*

The World's Columbian Exposition, commemorating the 400th anniversary of Columbus sailing to the Americas

**1883** Construction of the Brooklyn Bridge is completed.

**1888** Electric trolleys are first introduced.

**1891** Ida B. Wells crusades against lynching.

**1896** Supreme Court establishes "separate-but-equal" doctrine in *Plessy v. Ferguson.*

USA
WORLD

**1880** **1885** **1890** **1895**

**1878** Bicycle touring club is founded in Europe.

**1884** Fifteen-nation conference on the division of Africa convenes in Berlin.

**1889** Barnum & Bailey Circus opens in London.

**274** CHAPTER 8

## THEMES IN CHAPTER 8

### SCIENCE AND TECHNOLOGY

Technology helped cities grow upward with skyscrapers and outward with better roads, bridges, subways, and streetcars to accommodate the influx of immigrants and rural migrants to urban areas.

**See Teacher's Edition Note,** p. 277.

### IMMIGRATION AND MIGRATION

Education was vitally important for millions of immigrants who came to America. Besides schools, employers, labor unions, and political organizations helped immigrants to assimilate.

**See Teacher's Edition Note,** p. 284.

### CIVIL RIGHTS

Booker T. Washington and W. E. B. Du Bois were leaders in the struggle for racial equality. Washington advocated a gradual approach that would engender economic independence for African Americans. Du Bois sought a more immediate end to inequality.

**See Teacher's Edition Note,** p. 287.

# INTERACT
## WITH HISTORY

It is the summer of 1893. In Chicago, the World's Columbian Exposition is in full swing. Besides Thomas Edison's kinetograph—a camera that records motion, attractions include a towering "Ferris wheel" that lifts trolley cars into the sky and the first hamburgers in America. More than 21 million people will attend the exposition. You will be one of them.

## How will the latest technology change your life?

### Examine the Issues

- How can technology contribute to new forms of recreation?
- What types of inventions transform communications?
- Why would mass media emerge at this time?

**RESEARCH LINKS** CLASSZONE.COM

Visit the Chapter 8 links for more information about Life at the Turn of the 20th Century.

# INTERACT
## WITH HISTORY

## Objectives

- To motivate students to consider turn-of-the-20th-century technological advances
- To help students understand the impact of new technology on American life

### Examine the Issues

1. Have students consider how technology changed the typical American workday.
2. Ask students to think of the impact of more rapid communication.
3. Ask students how technology brought Americans together and helped create a mass culture.

---

**1901** McKinley is assassinated.

**1900** William McKinley is reelected.

**1901** Theodore Roosevelt becomes president.

**1904** Theodore Roosevelt is elected president.

**1908** Henry Ford introduces the Model T.

**1908** William H. Taft is elected president.

**1912** Woodrow Wilson is elected president.

**1916** Woodrow Wilson is reelected.

**1900**     **1905**     **1910**     **1915**

**1899** German psychoanalyst Sigmund Freud publishes *The Interpretation of Dreams.*

**1910** Mexican Revolution begins.

**1914** World War I begins in Europe.

*Life at the Turn of the 20th Century* **275**

---

## RECOMMENDED RESOURCES

### BOOKS FOR THE TEACHER

Ayers, Edward L. *The Promise of the New South: Life after Reconstruction.* New York: Oxford UP, 1993.

McMurry, Linda O. *To Keep the Waters Troubled: The Life of Ida B. Wells.* New York: Oxford UP, 2000.

Schlereth, Thomas J. *Victorian America: Transformations in Everyday Life, 1876-1915.* New York: Harper, 1992.

### BOOKS FOR THE STUDENT

Bryson, Bill. *Made in America.* New York: Morrow, 1996.

Du Bois, W. E. B. *The Souls of Black Folk.* Chicago: Lushena Books, 2000.

McCullough, David. *The Great Bridge.* New York: Simon, 2001. Account of the building of the Brooklyn Bridge.

### VIDEOS

*Baseball.* Dir. Ken Burns. PBS Home Video, 1994. "Inning 1" discusses the origins of professional baseball.

*Booker T. Washington's Tuskegee America.* AIMS Multimedia, 1983.

*Coney Island.* Direct Cinema, 1991, 800-525-0000.

*Hollywood.* Dir. David Gill and Kevin Brownlow. HBO Video, 1990.

*Mr. Sears's Catalogue.* PBS Home Video, 800-424-7963.

### INTEGRATED TECHNOLOGY

For teacher support, visit . . .

 classzone.com

# Science and Urban Life

| MAIN IDEA | WHY IT MATTERS NOW | Terms & Names |
|---|---|---|
| Advances in science and technology helped solve urban problems, including overcrowding. | American cities continue to depend on the results of scientific and technological research. | • Louis Sullivan  • Daniel Burnham  • Frederick Law Olmsted  • Orville and Wilbur Wright  • George Eastman |

 U.S. History 8A, 10A, 11A, 22A, 22B, 22C, 23A, 24A, 24B, 24C, 24D, 25A, 25B, 25C, 25D, 26A

### One American's Story

The Brooklyn Bridge, connecting Brooklyn to the island of Manhattan in New York City, opened in 1883. It took 14 years to build. Each day, laborers descended to work in a caisson, or water-tight chamber, that took them deep beneath the East River. E. F. Farrington, a mechanic who worked on the bridge, described the working conditions.

**A PERSONAL VOICE** E. F. FARRINGTON

" Inside the caisson everything wore an unreal, weird appearance. There was a confused sensation in the head . . . What with the flaming lights, the deep shadows, the confusing noise of hammers, drills, and chains, the half-naked forms flitting about . . . one might, if of a poetic temperament, get a realizing sense of Dante's Inferno. "

—quoted in *The Great Bridge*

Four years later, trains ran across the bridge 24 hours a day and carried more than 30 million travelers each year.

▲ In 1883, New Yorkers celebrated the opening of the world's longest suspension bridge, the 1,595-foot-long Brooklyn Bridge.

## **1** Technology and City Life

Engineering innovations, such as the Brooklyn Bridge, laid the groundwork for modern American life. Cities in every industrial area of the country expanded both outward and upward. In 1870, only 25 American cities had populations of 50,000; by 1890, 58 cities could make that claim. By the turn of the 20th century, due to the increasing number of industrial jobs, four out of ten Americans made their homes in cities.

In response to these changes, technological advances began to meet the nation's needs for communication, transportation, and space. One remedy for more urban space was to build toward the sky.

**276** CHAPTER 8

**SKYSCRAPERS** Architects were able to design taller buildings because of two factors: the invention of elevators and the development of internal steel skeletons to bear the weight of buildings. In 1890-1891, architect **Louis Sullivan** designed the ten-story Wainwright Building in St. Louis. He called the new breed of skyscraper a "proud and soaring thing." The tall building's appearance was graceful because its steel framework supported both floors and walls.

The skyscraper became America's greatest contribution to architecture, "a new thing under the sun" according to the architect Frank Lloyd Wright, who studied under Sullivan. Skyscrapers solved the practical problem of how to make the best use of limited and expensive space. The unusual form of another skyscraper, the Flatiron Building, seemed perfect for its location at one of New York's busiest intersections. **Daniel Burnham** designed this slender 285-foot tower in 1902. The Flatiron Building and other new buildings served as a symbol of a rich and optimistic society. **A**

**ELECTRIC TRANSIT** As skyscrapers expanded upward, changes in transportation allowed cities to spread outward. Before the Civil War, horses had drawn the earliest streetcars over iron rails embedded in city streets. In some cities during the 1870s and 1880s, underground moving cables powered streetcar lines. Electricity, however, transformed urban transportation.

In 1888 Richmond, Virginia, became the first American city to electrify its urban transit. Other cities followed. By the turn of the twentieth century, intricate networks of electric streetcars—also called trolley cars—ran from outlying neighborhoods to downtown offices and department stores.

New railroad lines also fed the growth of suburbs, allowing residents to commute to downtown jobs. New York's northern suburbs alone supplied 100,000 commuters each day to the central business district.

A few large cities moved their streetcars far above street level, creating elevated or "el" trains. Other cities, like New York, built subways by moving their rail lines underground. These streetcars, elevated trains, and subways enabled cities to annex suburban developments that mushroomed along the advancing transportation routes. **B**

**ENGINEERING AND URBAN PLANNING** Steel-cable suspension bridges, like the Brooklyn Bridge, also brought cities' sections closer together. Sometimes these bridges provided recreational opportunities. In his design for the Brooklyn Bridge, for example, John Augustus Roebling provided an elevated promenade whose "principal use will be to allow people of leisure, and old and young invalids, to promenade over the bridge on fine days." This need for open spaces in the midst of crowded commercial cities inspired the emerging science of urban planning.

City planners sought to restore a measure of serenity to the environment by designing recreational areas. Landscape architect **Frederick Law Olmsted** spearheaded the movement for planned urban parks.

In 1857 Olmsted, along with English-born architect Calvert Vaux, helped draw up a plan for "Greensward," which was selected to become Central Park, in New York. Olmsted envisioned the park as a rustic haven in the center of the busy city. The finished park featured boating and

---

**MAIN IDEA**

**Analyzing Causes**

**A** How did new technologies make the building of skyscrapers practical?

*A. Answer* The elevator made tall buildings usable; steel frames could bear the weight of tall buildings.

*B. Answer* It led to growth of subways; made commuting easier.

**MAIN IDEA**

**Summarizing**

**B** How did electric transit impact urban life?

**Vocabulary**
**promenade:** a public place for walking

---

The Flatiron Building, shown here under construction, stands at the intersection of Fifth Avenue and 23rd Street in New York City. ▼

---

---

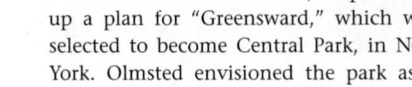
**DIFFERENTIATING INSTRUCTION    GIFTED AND TALENTED**

**Writing a Biography**

Have interested students use the Internet and library resources to do research on an architect or urban planner mentioned on page 277. Have students write short biographies that focus, chronologically, on significant events and major accomplishments in their subjects' lives. Encourage them to include quotes both about and by their subject.

The biographical sketches should . . .

· show the importance of the architect or urban planner
· provide concrete details about the person's life
· exhibit evidence of research from a variety of sources

---

## More About . . .

### Central Park

In 1844, William Cullen Bryant, a poet and editor, called for the preservation of a large section of park land in Manhattan. Andrew Jackson Dowling, an eminent landscape designer, echoed Bryant's sentiment. The park preservation campaign took 12 years. In 1856, the city spent $5 million in state funds to purchase the majority of the 840 acres of park land. The park officially opened in 1876.

 **In-Depth Resources: Unit 2**
· Geography Application: Central Park, pp. 71–72

### History Through *Architecture*

#### SKILLBUILDER ANSWERS

1. Chicago had a lakefront location, good harbors for shipping, and available park land.

2. Burnham moved the harbor system away from the business district.

---

tennis facilities, a zoo, and bicycle paths. Olmsted hoped that the park's beauty would soothe the city's inhabitants and let them enjoy a "natural" setting.

**A PERSONAL VOICE** FREDERICK LAW OLMSTED

"The main object and justification [of the park] is simply to produce a certain influence in the minds of people and through this to make life in the city healthier and happier. The character of this influence . . . is to be produced by means of scenes, through observation of which the mind may be more or less lifted out of moods and habits."

—quoted in *Frederick Law Olmsted's New York*

In the 1870s, Olmsted planned landscaping for Washington, D.C., and St. Louis. He also drew the initial designs for "the Emerald Necklace," Boston's parks system. Boston's Back Bay area, originally a 450-acre swamp, was drained and developed by urban planners into an area of elegant streets and cultural attractions, including Olmstead's parks.

**CITY PLANNING** By contrast, Chicago, with its explosive growth from 30,000 people in 1850 to 300,000 in 1870, represented a nightmare of unregulated expansion. Fortunately for the city, a local architect, Daniel Burnham, was intrigued

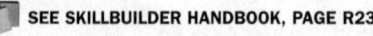

## History Through *Architecture*

### THE CHICAGO PLAN

This map from Daniel Burnham's original plan of Chicago looks deceptively like an ordinary map today. But at the time, it was almost revolutionary in its vision, and it inspired city planners all over the country.

**1** **Chicago's Lakefront** First, Burnham designed the "White City" to host the 1893 World's Columbian Exposition. His greatest legacy to Chicago may have been his idea for a lakefront park system, complete with beaches, playing fields, and playgrounds.

**2** **Neighborhood Parks** Though not all cities could claim a lakefront vista for recreation, most cities sprinkled neighborhood parks where their residents needed them. Urban planners provided for local parks—such as Lincoln Park in Chicago—so that "the sweet breath of plant life" would be available to everyone.

**3** **Harbors For Cities** On the Great Lakes, the shipping business depended on accessible harbors. Burnham saw the advantage of harbors for recreation and commercial purposes, but he advocated moving the harbors away from the central business districts to free space for public use.

**4** **The Civic Center** Burnham redesigned the street pattern to create a group of long streets that would converge on a grand plaza, a practice reflected in other American cities. The convergence of major thoroughfares at a city's center helped create a unified city from a host of neighborhoods.

#### SKILLBUILDER Interpreting Visual Sources

1. Why did Chicago's location make it a good choice for urban planning?
2. How was Chicago's importance as a shipping center maintained?

**SEE SKILLBUILDER HANDBOOK, PAGE R23.**

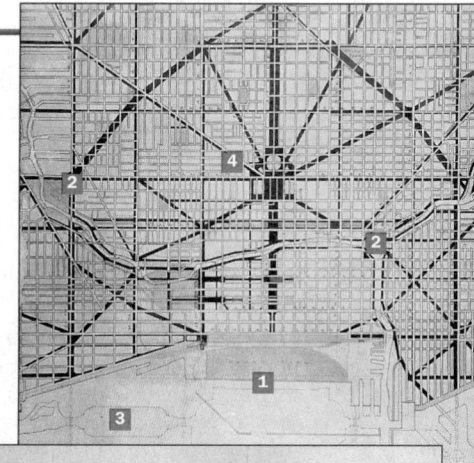

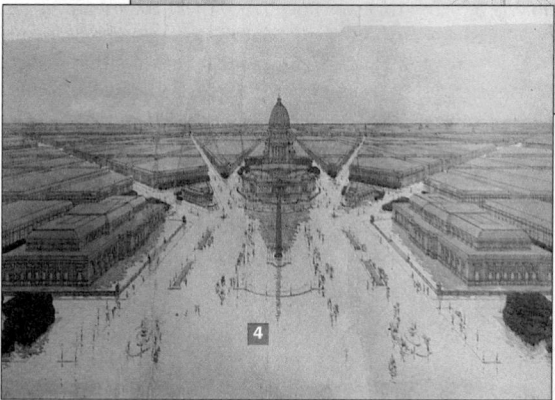

▲ Unity was the goal of the architect of Chicago's city center.

---

**ACTIVITY** **COOPERATIVE LEARNING**

**B** **BLOCK SCHEDULING**

### Planning Ideal Cities

**Class Time** Two class periods

**Task** Creating ideal city plans for current and future urban settings

**Purpose** To understand the achievements of turn-of-the-20th-century urban planners

**Directions** Divide the class into groups. Ask students to imagine they are urban planners and have been assigned to brainstorm solutions to urban challenges, such as housing, transportation, economic development, and recreation. Have each group design comprehensive city plans. Encourage students to use visual aids, such as sketches or blueprints.

 **Integrated Assessment**
· Rubric 4

by the prospect of remaking the city. His motto was "Make no little plans. They have no magic to stir men's blood." He oversaw the transformation of a swampy area near Lake Michigan into a glistening White City for Chicago's 1893 World's Columbian Exposition. Majestic exhibition halls, statues, the first Ferris wheel, and a lagoon greeted more than 21 million visitors who came to the city.

Many urban planners saw in Burnham's White City glorious visions of future cities. Burnham, however, left Chicago an even more important legacy: an overall plan for the city, crowned by elegant parks strung along Lake Michigan. As a result, Chicago's lakefront today features curving banks of grass and sandy beaches instead of a jumbled mass of piers and warehouses. **C**

## New Technologies ❷

New developments in communication brought the nation closer together. In addition to a railroad network that now spanned the nation, advances in printing, aviation, and photography helped to speed the transfer of information.

**A REVOLUTION IN PRINTING** By 1890, the literacy rate in the United States had risen to nearly 90 percent. Publishers turned out ever-increasing numbers of books, magazines, and newspapers to meet the growing demand of the reading public. A series of technological advances in printing aided their efforts.

American mills began to produce huge quantities of cheap paper from wood pulp. The new paper proved durable enough to withstand high-speed presses. The electrically powered web-perfecting press, for example, printed on both sides of a continuous paper roll, rather than on just one side. It then cut, folded, and counted the pages as they came down the line. Faster production and lower costs made newspapers and magazines more affordable. People could now buy newspapers for a penny a copy.

**AIRPLANES** In the early 20th century, brothers Orville and Wilbur Wright, bicycle manufacturers from Dayton, Ohio, experimented with new engines powerful enough to keep "heavier-than-air" craft aloft. First the Wright brothers built a glider. Then they commissioned a four-cylinder internal combustion engine, chose a propeller, and designed a biplane with a 40∏4© wingspan. Their first successful flight—on December 17, 1903, at Kitty Hawk, North Carolina—covered 120 feet and lasted 12 seconds. Orville later described the take-off.

**A PERSONAL VOICE** ORVILLE WRIGHT

" After running the motor a few minutes to heat it up, I released the wire that held the machine to the track, and the machine started forward into the wind. Wilbur ran at the side of the machine to balance it. . . . Unlike the start on the 14th, made in a calm, the machine, facing a 27-mile wind, started very slowly. . . . One of the life-saving men snapped the camera for us, taking a picture just as the machine had reached the end of the track and had risen to a height of about two feet. "

—quoted in *Frontiers of Flight*

### MAIN IDEA

**Summarizing**
**C** List three major changes in cities near the turn of the century. What effect did each have?

**C. Answer**
Skyscrapers conserved space by allowing cites to grow upward; new transportation systems and bridges drew neighborhoods closer together; urban planning put parks into cities.

**Vocabulary**
**internal combustion engine:** an engine in which fuel is burned within the engine rather than in an external furnace

Orville (*right*) and Wilbur Wright at home in Dayton, Ohio in 1909. ▼

---

**THE GARDEN CITY**

Urban planning in the United States had European counterparts. In *Tomorrow: A Peaceful Path to Social Reform* (1898), for example, the British city planner Ebenezer Howard wrote of a planned residential community called a garden city.

Howard wanted to combine the benefits of urban life with easy access to nature. His city plan was based on concentric circles—with a town at the center and a wide circle of rural land on the perimeter. The town center included a garden, concert hall, museum, theater, library, and hospital.

The circle around the town center included a park, a shopping center, a conservatory, a residential area, and industry. Six wide avenues radiated out from the town center. In 1903, Letchworth, England served as the model for Howard's garden city.

---

**The Garden City**
**Comparing** Ask students to consider why nature and wildlife might be important to city life. Ask students to identify a city, town, or neighborhood that exemplifies aspects of Howard's garden city plan.

**More About . . .**

**The Columbian Exposition**
Cities across the nation competed to host the World's Columbian Exposition to celebrate the 400th anniversary of Columbus's arrival in the Americas. With the help of Daniel Burnham's architectural innovation, Chicago was chosen to host the celebration. The "White City," so called for its white buildings, became the majestic location for the World's Columbian Exposition in 1893. President Grover Cleveland opened the fair by flicking a switch in Washington, D.C., to turn on the lights in Chicago.

 Electronic Library of Primary Sources
· *from* A visit to the World's Columbian Exposition, 1886 by C. Bolton

**Instruct: Objective ❷**

**New Technologies**
TAKS SS11 3(US23.A)
· What effect did advances in paper, printing, and photography have on publishing and journalism?
· How did airplanes revolutionize communication as well as transportation?

 In-Depth Resources: Unit 2
· Guided Reading, p. 61

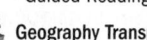 Geography Transparencies GT16
· Telephone Long Distance Lines, 1890 and 1917

*Life at the Turn of the 20th Century* **279**

---

**Visual Learners**

Many students grasp concepts more readily when the information is presented visually. Such students might benefit from drawing a two-column chart that lists turn-of-the-20th-century technological improvements and their uses.

| Technological Improvements | Uses |
| --- | --- |
| electricity | streetcars, elevated trains and subways |
| steel construction | suspension bridges, skyscrapers |
| internal combustion engines | automobiles, airplanes |

## HISTORY from VISUALS

### Interpreting the Infographic

Point out to students that the chart shows the decrease in weight of airplane engines from the late 1800s through the mid-1900s.

**Extension** Ask students between what years the greatest decrease in airplane engine weight occurred. *(Between the 1880s and 1903)*

## More About . . .

### The Wright Brothers

Orville Wright's inaugural flight lasted 12 seconds and covered 120 feet. It was the first successful flight in a powered aircraft ever taken. After several more attempts that same day, a gust of wind flipped the airplane, and it was severely damaged. Orville and his brother Wilbur kept trying. Undaunted by the skepticism of family and friends, the brothers built another plane and continued their flight experiments. In October of 1905, on an airfield near Dayton, Ohio, the Wright brothers made a circular flight of about 24 miles.

## Science & *Technology*

### Air Travel

In the years since the flight at Kitty Hawk, tremendous technological advances have been made. On October 14, 1947, Chuck Yeager, an air force pilot, flew the first plane to break the sound barrier—reaching a velocity of 700 miles per hour at 43,000 feet. In 1976, the Concorde—a commercial airplane that travels more than twice the speed of sound—was introduced. With its bent nose and sleek design, it can carry up to 100 passengers and make the trip from Paris to New York in about four hours—about half the time it takes the average passenger plane.

---

## Science & *Technology*

### AVIATION PIONEERS

In 1892, Orville and Wilbur Wright opened a bicycle shop in Dayton, Ohio. They used the profits to fund experiments in aeronautics, the construction of aircraft. In 1903, the Wright brothers took a gasoline-powered airplane that they had designed to a sandy hill outside Kitty Hawk, North Carolina.

▶ The airplane was powered by a 4-cylinder 12-horse-power piston engine, designed and constructed by the bicycle shop's mechanic, Charles Taylor. The piston—a solid cylinder fit snugly into a hollow cylinder that moves back and forth under pressure—was standard until jet-propelled aircraft came into service in the 1940s.

▶ The engine is the heaviest component in airplane construction. The design of lighter engines was the most important development in early aviation history.

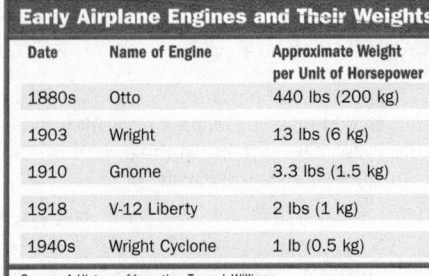

### Early Airplane Engines and Their Weights

| Date | Name of Engine | Approximate Weight per Unit of Horsepower |
|------|----------------|-------------------------------------------|
| 1880s | Otto | 440 lbs (200 kg) |
| 1903 | Wright | 13 lbs (6 kg) |
| 1910 | Gnome | 3.3 lbs (1.5 kg) |
| 1918 | V-12 Liberty | 2 lbs (1 kg) |
| 1940s | Wright Cyclone | 1 lb (0.5 kg) |

Source: *A History of Invention*, Trevor I. Williams

◀ On December 17, Orville Wright made the first successful flight of a powered aircraft in history. The public paid little attention. But within two years, the brothers were making 30-minute flights. By 1908, the pioneer aviators had signed a contract for production of the Wright airplane with the U.S. Army.

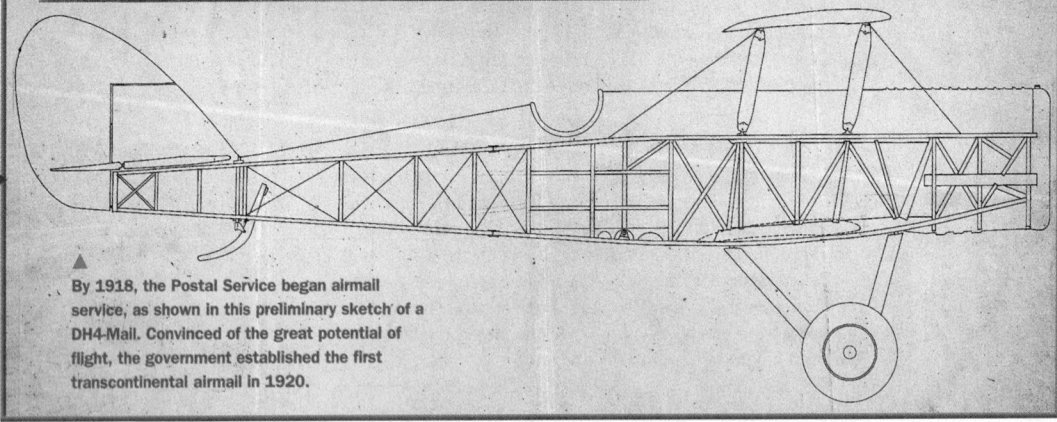

By 1918, the Postal Service began airmail service, as shown in this preliminary sketch of a DH4-Mail. Convinced of the great potential of flight, the government established the first transcontinental airmail in 1920.

---

**ACTIVITY  LINK TO SCIENCE**

 classzone.com

### The Wright Brothers' Flight

**Class Time** Two class periods

**Task** Examining the principles of flight and creating a multimedia presentation

**Purpose** To better understand airplane innovation

**Directions** Have students work in small groups to create a multimedia presentation. Have them research the Wright Brothers' experiments with the principles of aerodynamics, such as lift and drag that led to their first successful flight. Groups might use illustrations, computer graphics, or other visual medium to augment their presentations.

📄 Integrated Assessment
· Rubrics 4, 6

Within two years, the Wright brothers had increased their flights to 24 miles. By 1920, convinced of the great potential of flight, the U.S. government had established the first transcontinental airmail service.

**PHOTOGRAPHY EXPLOSION** Before the 1880s, photography was a professional activity. Because of the time required to take a picture and the weight of the equipment, a photographer could not shoot a moving object. In addition, photographers had to develop their shots immediately.

New techniques eliminated the need to develop pictures right away. **George Eastman** developed a series of more convenient alternatives to the heavy glass plates previously used. Now, instead of carrying their darkrooms around with them, photographers could use flexible film, coated with gelatin emulsions, and could send their film to a studio for processing. When professional photographers were slow to begin using the new film, Eastman decided to aim his product at the masses.

In 1888, Eastman introduced his Kodak camera. The purchase price of $25 included a 100-picture roll of film. After taking the pictures, the photographer would send the camera back to Eastman's Rochester, New York, factory. For $10, the pictures were developed and returned with the camera reloaded. Easily held and operated, the Kodak prompted millions of Americans to become amateur photographers. The camera also helped to create the field of photojournalism. Reporters could now photograph events as they occurred. When the Wright brothers first flew their simple airplane at Kitty Hawk, an amateur photographer captured the first successful flight on film.

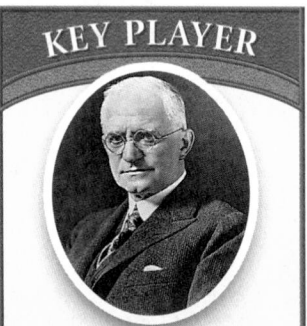

## KEY PLAYER

**GEORGE EASTMAN
1854–1932**

In 1877, when George Eastman took up photography as a hobby, he had to lug more than 100 pounds of equipment for one day's outing. To lighten his load, he replaced heavy glass plates with film that could be rolled onto a spool.

In 1888, Eastman sold his first roll-film camera. Eastman called his new camera (shown at left) the Kodak, because the made-up name was short and memorable. It was popularized by the slogan "You Press the Button, We Do the Rest."

## KEY PLAYER

**George Eastman**
Eastman was a longtime proponent of education. He made his first donation to the cause of higher learning in 1887—a $50 gift to the Mechanics Institute, since renamed the Rochester Institute of Technology. In time, he would give away more than $75 million to educational institutions. Ask students why Eastman's slogan and other sales methods were so effective. *(Quality products; slogan stressed ease of use; simple operating instructions; sending new film back added value)*

## Assess & Reteach

**SECTION 1 ASSESSMENT**
Have students work in small groups to answer the questions.

📝 Formal Assessment
· Section Quiz, p. 148

**SELF-ASSESSMENT**
Ask students to write a short essay about the impact of a specific technology that they found surprising.

**RETEACH**
Have students make a list of major technological advances presented in this section. Discuss with students the impact of such advances on Americans' lives at the turn of the 20th century.

📝 In-Depth Resources: Unit 2
· Reteaching Activity, p. 67

---

## SECTION 1 ASSESSMENT

**1. TERMS & NAMES** For each term or name, write a sentence explaining its significance.

- Louis Sullivan
- Frederick Law Olmsted
- George Eastman
- Daniel Burnham
- Orville and Wilbur Wright

### MAIN IDEA

**2. TAKING NOTES**
Using a three-column chart, such as the one below, list three important changes in city design, communication, and transportation.

| City Design | Communication | Transportation |
|---|---|---|
| 1. | 1. | 1. |
| 2. | 2. | 2. |
| 3. | 3. | 3. |

Which change had the greatest impact on urban life? Why?

### CRITICAL THINKING

**3. HYPOTHESIZING**
If you had been an urban planner at the turn of the century, what new ideas would you have included in your plan for the ideal city?
**Think About:**
- Olmsted's plans for Central Park
- Burnham's ideas for Chicago
- the concept of the garden city

Mini-Lesson 1:
SS11 3(US23.A)

**4. EVALUATING**
Which scientific or technological development described in this section had the greatest impact on American culture? Use details from the text to justify your choice.

**5. SUMMARIZING**
How did bridge building contribute to the growth of cities?

---

Answers **ASSESSMENT** 1

**1. TERMS & NAMES**
Louis Sullivan, p. 277
Daniel Burnham, p. 277
Frederick Law Olmsted, p. 277
Orville and Wilbur Wright, p. 279
George Eastman, p. 281

**2. TAKING NOTES**
City design: bridges; skyscrapers; urban planning; parks
Communication: high-speed printing presses; Linotype machine; photography
Transportation: Electric streetcars; trains; subways; airplanes

**3. HYPOTHESIZING**
Students might mention additional recreational facilities or increased numbers of parks.

**4. EVALUATING**
Students should cite reasons, such as the long-term impact of air travel or the widespread influence of low-cost printing, to support their answers. air travel; low-cost printing; urban planning.

**5. SUMMARIZING**
outward expansion of cities; increased travel to and from cities; encouraged technological advance in other areas; catalyst for upward growth; skyscrapers

# OBJECTIVES

1 Analyze the expansion of public education at the turn-of-the-20th-century.

2 Describe the growth of higher education.

## SKILLBUILDERS
· Interpreting Graphs, p. 283

## CRITICAL THINKING
· Drawing Conclusions, p. 283
· Summarizing, p. 284
· Synthesizing, p. 285
· Hypothesizing, p. 285
· Comparing, p. 285

## Focus & Motivate

Ask students how an educational system might help a nation meet its social needs.

## Instruct

### Instruct: Objective 1

**Expanding Public Education**
TAKS SS11 5(WH26.C)
· What were the main reasons for the expansion and improvement of public education?
· What factors contributed to the growth of high schools?
· How did educational experiences differ for African Americans and immigrants?

 In-Depth Resources: Unit 2
· Guided Reading, p. 62

 Critical Thinking Transparencies CT16
· Expanding Education

# Expanding Public Education

| MAIN IDEA | WHY IT MATTERS NOW | Terms & Names |
|---|---|---|
| Reforms in public education led to a rise in national literacy and the promotion of public education. | The public education system is the foundation of the democratic ideals of American society. | • Booker T. Washington • Tuskegee Normal and Industrial Institute • W. E. B. Du Bois • Niagara Movement |

TEKS U.S. History 2C, 4B, 10B, 19B, 21B, 24A, 24B, 24C, 24D, 24H, 25A, 25B, 25C, 25D

 One American's Story

William Torrey Harris was an educational reformer who saw the public schools as a great instrument "to lift all classes of people into . . . civilized life." As U.S. commissioner of education from 1889 to 1906, Harris promoted the ideas of great educators like Horace Mann and John Dewey—particularly the belief that schools exist for the children and not the teachers. Schools, according to Harris, should properly prepare students for full participation in community life.

**A PERSONAL VOICE** WILLIAM TORREY HARRIS

" Every [educational] method must . . . be looked at from two points of view: first, its capacity to secure the development of rationality or of the true adjustment of the individual to the social whole; and, second, its capacity to strengthen the individuality of the pupil and avoid the danger of obliterating the personality of the child by securing blind obedience in place of intelligent cooperation, and by mechanical memorizing in place of rational insight. "

—quoted in *Public Schools and Moral Education*

Many other middle-class reformers agreed with Harris and viewed the public schools as training grounds for employment and citizenship. People believed that economic development depended on scientific and technological knowledge. As a result, they viewed education as a key to greater security and social status. Others saw the public schools as the best opportunity to assimilate the millions of immigrants entering American society. Most people also believed that public education was necessary for a stable and prosperous democratic nation.

▲ Compulsory attendance laws, though slow to be enforced, helped fill classrooms at the turn of the 20th century.

## 1 Expanding Public Education

Although most states had established public schools by the Civil War, many school-age children still received no formal schooling. The majority of students who went to school left within four years, and few went to high school.

---

## PROGRAM RESOURCES

 **In-Depth Resources: Unit 2**
· Guided Reading, p. 62
· Reteaching Activity, p. 68
· Primary Source: "The Talented Tenth," p. 75
· American Lives: W. E. B. Du Bois, p. 80

 **Reading Study Guide** (English and Spanish), pp. 83–84

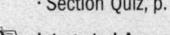 **Access for Students Acquiring English/ESL**
· Guided Reading (Spanish), p. 105

Formal Assessment
· Section Quiz, p. 149

Integrated Assessment
· Rubrics

### INTEGRATED TECHNOLOGY

 Critical Thinking Transp. CT16, CT50
· Expanding Education
· Increasing School Enrollment, 1870-1920

 classzone.com

### TEXAS RESOURCES

 TAKS Spiraled Content Review

 TAKS Practice Tests

 TAKS Practice Transparencies TT59

 TAKS Online Test Practice

**SCHOOLS FOR CHILDREN** Between 1865 and 1895, states passed laws requiring 12 to 16 weeks annually of school attendance by students between the ages of 8 and 14. The curriculum emphasized reading, writing, and arithmetic. However, the emphasis on rote memorization and the uneven quality of teachers drew criticism. Strict rules and physical punishment made many students miserable.

One 13-year-old boy explained to a Chicago school inspector why he hid in a warehouse basement instead of going to school.

### A PERSONAL VOICE

"They hits ye if yer don't learn, and they hits ye if ye whisper, and they hits ye if ye have string in yer pocket, and they hits ye if yer seat squeaks, and they hits ye if ye don't stan' up in time, and they hits ye if yer late, and they hits ye if ye fer-get the page."

—anonymous schoolboy quoted in *The One Best System*

In spite of such problems, children began attending school at a younger age. Kindergartens, which had been created outside the public school system to offer childcare for employed mothers, became increasingly popular. The number of kindergartens surged from 200 in 1880 to 3,000 in 1900, and, under the guidance of William Torrey Harris, public school systems began to add kindergartens to their programs. **A**

Although the pattern in public education in this era was one of growth, opportunities differed sharply for white and black students. In 1880, about 62 percent of white children attended elementary school, compared to about 34 percent of African-American children. Not until the 1940s would public school education become available to the majority of black children living in the South.

**THE GROWTH OF HIGH SCHOOLS** In the new industrial age, the economy demanded advanced technical and managerial skills. Moreover, business leaders like Andrew Carnegie pointed out that keeping workers loyal to capitalism required society to "provide ladders upon which the aspiring can rise."

By early 1900, more than half a million students attended high school. The curriculum expanded to include courses in science, civics, and social studies. And new vocational courses prepared male graduates for industrial jobs in drafting, carpentry, and mechanics, and female graduates for office work.

#### MAIN IDEA

**Drawing Conclusions**
**A** Why did American children begin attending school at a younger age?

**A. Answer** Kindergartens became popular and were supported by the public school system.

Mini-Lesson 3: SS11 5(WH26.C)

### Expanding Education/Increasing Literacy

| Year | School-Age Population (5 to 18 Years of Age) | Illiteracy (% of Total Population) |
|------|----------------------------------------------|-----------------------------------|
| 1870 | 👤👤👤👤👤👤 12,000,000 | 20.0% |
| 1880 | 👤👤👤👤👤👤👤 15,065,767 | 17.0% |
| 1890 | 👤👤👤👤👤👤👤👤 18,543,201 | 13.0% |
| 1900 | 👤👤👤👤👤👤👤👤👤 21,404,322 | 10.7% |
| 1910 | 👤👤👤👤👤👤👤👤👤👤 24,360,888 | 7.7% |
| 1920 | 👤👤👤👤👤👤👤👤👤👤👤👤 27,728,788 | 6.9% |

👤 = 2,000,000 students

Sources: *Statistical Abstract of the United States, 1921; Historical Statistics of the United States.*

**SKILLBUILDER**
**Interpreting Graphs**
1. By how much did the illiteracy rate drop from 1870 to 1920?
2. Does the number of immigrants during this period make the reduction more or less impressive? Why?

*Skillbuilder Answers*
1. about 13%.
2. *Possible Answer:* More impressive, because millions of immigrants could not read English when they arrived in America.

**Connections Across Time**

1900 AND TODAY

#### Public Education
At the turn-of-the-20th-century, public school education usually consisted of eight years of grade school and four years of high school. Some educators believed middle-grade students would better learn and socialize in a different setting. And so, junior high school was born. Recent educational trends include block scheduling, the use of video and computer technologies, and preschool training.

### HISTORY from VISUALS

**Interpreting the Graph**
Remind students that each figure on the graph is equal to 2 million students. So, the six figures in the top row (1870) represent 12 million students.

**Extension** Have students do research on the Internet to discover the school-age population (5 to 18 Years of Age) and the illiteracy rate for the current year.

🖐 Critical Thinking Transparencies CT50
· Increasing School Enrollment, 1870–1920

*Life at the Turn of the 20th Century* **283**

---

### DIFFERENTIATING INSTRUCTION     LESS PROFICIENT READERS

#### Guided Reading

Suggest that students focus their reading by turning headings and subheadings into questions. Have students read the material and look for the answers. For example, the headings and subheadings on pages 283 and 284 could be turned into the following questions:

· What was the state of public education at the turn of the century?
· Why did high schools grow?
· What group faced discrimination and in what ways?
· What education was available for immigrants?

### Immigrant Education
Education was a vital resource for millions of immigrants who came to America from 1880 to 1920. Immigrant children attended school by day. Parents had the opportunity to take adult education courses at night or to participate in Americanization programs at work. Immigrants were also indirectly assimilated into American culture through their experiences in labor unions and political organizations. Encourage students to offer their own definitions of Americanization and to discuss its historical importance.

## NOW & THEN

### Technology and Schools
**Evaluating** Have students discuss the role of computers in the classroom. Do they think computers are overrated? How might computers be educational tools? Are computers an essential part of the classroom?

### Instruct: Objective ❷

**Expanding Higher Education**
TAKS SS11 3(US21.A)
· What changes did many universities make in their curriculum and why?
· How did African Americans work to gain a higher education?

 In-Depth Resources: Unit 2
· Guided Reading, p. 62

---

**RACIAL DISCRIMINATION** African Americans were mostly excluded from public secondary education. In 1890, fewer than 1 percent of black teenagers attended high school. More than two-thirds of these students went to private schools, which received no government financial support. By 1910, about 3 percent of African Americans between the ages of 15 and 19 attended high school, but a majority of these students still attended private schools.

**EDUCATION FOR IMMIGRANTS** Unlike African Americans, immigrants were encouraged to go to school. Of the nearly 10 million European immigrants settled in the United States between 1860 and 1890, many were Jewish people fleeing poverty and systematic oppression in eastern Europe. Most immigrants sent their children to America's free public schools, where they quickly became "Americanized." Years after she became a citizen, the Russian Jewish immigrant Mary Antin recalled the large numbers of non-English-speaking immigrant children. By the end of the school year, they could recite "patriotic verses in honor of George Washington and Abraham Lincoln . . . with plenty of enthusiasm."

Some people resented the suppression of their native languages in favor of English. Catholics were especially concerned because many public school systems had mandatory readings from the (Protestant) King James Version of the Bible. Catholic communities often set up parochial schools to give their children a Catholic education.

Thousands of adult immigrants attended night school to learn English and to qualify for American citizenship. Employers often offered daytime programs to Americanize their workers. At his Model T plant in Highland Park, Michigan, Henry Ford established a "Sociology Department," because "men of many nations must be taught American ways, the English language, and the right way to live." Ford's ideas were not universally accepted. Labor activists often protested that Ford's educational goals were aimed at weakening the trade union movement by teaching workers not to confront management. ❷

## Expanding Higher Education ❷

Although the number of students attending high school had increased by the turn of the century, only a minority of Americans had high school diplomas. At the same time, an even smaller minority—only 2.3 percent—of America's young people attended colleges and universities.

**CHANGES IN UNIVERSITIES** Between 1880 and 1920, college enrollments more than quadrupled. And colleges instituted major changes in curricula and admission policies. Industrial development changed the nation's educational needs. The research university emerged—offering courses in modern languages, the physical sciences, and the new disciplines of psychology and sociology. Professional schools in law and medicine were established. Private colleges and universities required entrance exams, but some state universities began to admit students by using the high school diploma as the entrance requirement.

**HIGHER EDUCATION FOR AFRICAN AMERICANS** After the Civil War, thousands of freed African Americans pursued higher education, despite their exclusion from white institutions. With the help of the Freedmen's Bureau and other groups, blacks founded Howard, Atlanta, and Fisk Universities, all of which opened

---

**TECHNOLOGY AND SCHOOLS**

In 1922, Thomas Alva Edison wrote, "I believe that the motion picture is destined to revolutionize our educational system and that in a few years it will supplant . . . the use of textbooks." Today's high schools show that the brilliant inventor was mistaken.

Recently, some people have predicted that computers will replace traditional classrooms and texts.

Computers allow video course-sharing, in which students in many schools view the same instructors. Students also use computers to access up-to-the-minute scientific data, such as weather information.

---

**Vocabulary**
**parochial school:** a school supported by a church parish

---

**MAIN IDEA**

**Summarizing**
Ⓑ What institutions encouraged European immigrants to become assimilated?

*B. Answer*
Public schools; night schools; large companies like Ford Motor Co.

---

### Reforming Public Education

**Class Time** 45 minutes

**Task** Creating a plan to reform turn of the 20th century public schools

**Purpose** To understand the methods and goals of educational reformers at the turn of the 20th century

**Directions** Have students work in groups of five or six. Each group should act as a school board at the turn of the 20th century. They are to devise a plan to reform their school district. Student plans should account for factors such as the recent influx of immigrant children, increasing school age populations, and new industrial jobs available in their area.

 Integrated Assessment
· Rubrics 2, 5

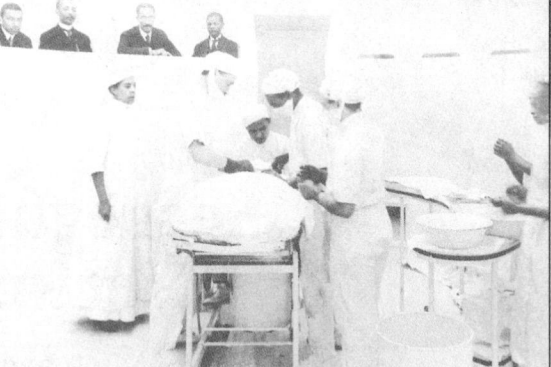

between 1865 and 1868. Private donors could not, however, financially support or educate a sufficient number of black college graduates to meet the needs of the segregated communities. By 1900, out of about 9 million African Americans, only 3,880 were in attendance at colleges or professional schools. **C**

The prominent African American educator, **Booker T. Washington,** believed that racism would end once blacks acquired useful labor skills and proved their economic value to society. Washington, who was born enslaved, graduated from Virginia's Hampton Institute. By 1881, he headed the **Tuskegee Normal and Industrial Institute,** now called Tuskegee University, in Alabama. Tuskegee aimed to equip African Americans with teaching diplomas and useful skills in agricultural, domestic, or mechanical work."No race," Washington said, "can prosper till it learns that there is as much dignity in tilling a field as in writing a poem."

By contrast, **W. E. B. Du Bois,** the first African American to receive a doctorate from Harvard (in 1895), strongly disagreed with Washington's gradual approach. In 1905, Dubois founded the **Niagara Movement,** which insisted that blacks should seek a liberal arts education so that the African American community would have well-educated leaders.

Du Bois proposed that a group of educated blacks, the most "talented tenth" of the community, attempt to achieve immediate inclusion into mainstream American life. "We are Americans, not only by birth and by citizenship," Du Bois argued, "but by our political ideals. . . . And the greatest of those ideals is that ALL MEN ARE CREATED EQUAL."

By the turn of the 20th century, millions of people received the education they needed to cope with a rapidly changing world. At the same time, however, racial discrimination remained a thorn in the flesh of American society.

---

**MAIN IDEA**

**Synthesizing**

**C** Describe the state of higher education for African Americans at the turn of the century.

**C. Answer**
All-black colleges and universities opened, but only a tiny percentage of African Americans received a college education.

**TAKS**

Mini-Lesson 2: SS11 4(US7.A)

▲ Medical students and their professors work in the operating theater of the Moorland-Spingarn Research Center at Howard University.

---

**W. E. B. Du Bois**

In his third book, *The Souls of Black Folk* (1903), Du Bois characterized the African-American experience as such, "One ever feels his twoness,—an American, a Negro; two souls, two thoughts, two unreconciled strivings. . . . He simply wishes to make it possible for a man to be both a Negro and an American, without being cursed and spit upon by his fellows, without having the doors of Opportunity closed roughly in his face."

📄 In-Depth Resources: Unit 2
  · Primary Source: "The Talented Tenth," p. 75
  · American Lives: W. E. B. Du Bois, p. 80

---

## Assess & Reteach

**SECTION 2 ASSESSMENT**
Students might work in pairs to respond to the questions.

📄 Formal Assessment
  · Section Quiz, p. 149

**SELF-ASSESSMENT**
Have students write questions about the material in section 2 and then exchange lists with another student.

**RETEACH**
Ask students to consider the three most important educational changes at the turn of the 20th century and discuss the reasons such changes occurred.

📄 In-Depth Resources: Unit 2
  · Reteaching Activity, p. 68

---

## ② ASSESSMENT

1. **TERMS & NAMES** For each term or name, write a sentence explaining its significance.
   - Booker T. Washington
   - Tuskegee Normal and Industrial Institute
   - W. E. B. Du Bois
   - Niagara Movement

**MAIN IDEA**

2. **TAKING NOTES**
In a chart like the one below, list at least three developments in education at the turn of the 20th century and their major results.

| Development | Result |
|---|---|
| 1. | |
| 2. | |
| 3. | |

Which educational development do you think was most important? Explain your choice.

**CRITICAL THINKING**

3. **HYPOTHESIZING**
How might the economy and culture of the United States have been different without the expansion of public schools? **Think About:**
   - the goals of public schools and whether those goals have been met
   - why people supported expanding public education
   - the impact of public schools on the development of private schools

4. **COMPARING**
Compare and contrast the views of Booker T. Washington and W. E. B. Du Bois on the subject of the education of African Americans.

---

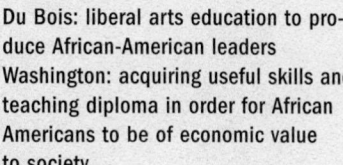

Answers ASSESSMENT ②

**1. TERMS & NAMES**
Booker T. Washington, p. 285
Tuskegee Normal and Industrial Institute, p. 285
W. E .B. Du Bois, p. 285
Niagara Movement, p. 285

**2. TAKING NOTES**
Compulsory education: Literacy increased.
Growth of high schools: College enrollments increased.
Racial discrimination: All-black colleges founded.

**3. HYPOTHESIZING**
less economic growth, immigrants slower to adapt to American life, decrease in college enrollment

**4. COMPARING**
Du Bois: liberal arts education to produce African-American leaders
Washington: acquiring useful skills and teaching diploma in order for African Americans to be of economic value to society

# OBJECTIVES

**1** Trace the historical underpinnings of legalized segregation and the African-American struggle against racism in the United States.

**2** Summarize turn-of-the-20th-century race relations in the North and the South.

**3** Identify discrimination against minorities in the American West.

## CRITICAL THINKING

· Analyzing Effects, p. 287
· Summarizing, p. 288
· Contrasting, pp. 288, 289
· Identifying Problems, p. 289
· Comparing, p. 289

## Focus & Motivate

Ask students whether they have ever felt discriminated against. Discuss various forms of prejudice and discrimination. Consider discrimination based on factors such as race, gender, and age.

## Instruct

### Instruct: Objective **1**

**African Americans Fight Legal Discrimination**

TAKS SS11 3(US21.A)

· What post-Reconstruction voting restrictions were imposed on African Americans in the South?
· What were Jim Crow laws?
· What was the significance of the Supreme Court ruling in *Plessy v. Ferguson*?

📄 In-Depth Resources: Unit 2
· Guided Reading, p. 63

👁 Electronic Library of Primary Sources
· *from* The Autobiography of Ida B. Wells, 1892 by I.B. Wells

---

# Segregation and Discrimination

| MAIN IDEA | WHY IT MATTERS NOW | Terms & Names |
|---|---|---|
| African Americans led the fight against voting restrictions and Jim Crow laws. | Today, African Americans have the legacy of a century-long battle for civil rights. | • Ida B. Wells • poll tax • grandfather clause • segregation • Jim Crow laws • *Plessy* v. *Ferguson* • debt peonage |

U.S. History
1B, 2C, 4B, 7A, 7B, 10A, 11B, 17A, 21A, 24B, 24C, 25A, 25B, 25C, 25D, 26A

### One American's Story

Born into slavery shortly before emancipation, **Ida B. Wells** moved to Memphis in the early 1880s to work as a teacher. She later became an editor of a local paper. Racial justice was a persistent theme in Wells's reporting. The March 9 events of 1892 turned that theme into a crusade. Three African-American businessmen, friends of Wells, were lynched—illegally executed without trial. Wells saw lynching for what it was.

**A PERSONAL VOICE** IDA B. WELLS

" Thomas Moss, Calvin McDowell, and Lee Stewart had been lynched in Memphis . . . [where] no lynching had taken place before. . . . This is what opened my eyes to what lynching really was. An excuse to get rid of Negroes who were acquiring wealth and property and thus keep the race terrorized. "

—quoted in *Crusade for Justice*

▲ Ida B. Wells moved North to continue her fight against lynching by writing, lecturing, and organizing for civil rights.

African Americans were not the only group to experience violence and racial discrimination. Native Americans, Mexican residents, and Chinese immigrants also encountered bitter forms of oppression, particularly in the American West.

## **1** African Americans Fight Legal Discrimination

As African Americans exercised their newly won political and social rights during Reconstruction, they faced hostile and often violent opposition from whites. African Americans eventually fell victim to laws restricting their civil rights but never stopped fighting for equality. For at least ten years after the end of Reconstruction in 1877, African Americans in the South continued to vote and occasionally to hold political office. By the turn of the 20th century, however, Southern states had adopted a broad system of legal policies of racial discrimination and devised methods to weaken African-American political power.

---

**VOTING RESTRICTIONS** All Southern states imposed new voting restrictions and denied legal equality to African Americans. Some states, for example, limited the vote to people who could read, and required registration officials to administer a literacy test to test reading. Blacks trying to vote were often asked more difficult questions than whites, or given a test in a foreign language. Officials could pass or fail applicants as they wished.

Another requirement was the **poll tax**, an annual tax that had to be paid before qualifying to vote. Black as well as white sharecroppers were often too poor to pay the poll tax. To reinstate white voters who may have failed the literacy test or could not pay the poll tax, several Southern states added the **grandfather clause** to their constitutions. The clause stated that even if a man failed the literacy test or could not afford the poll tax, he was still entitled to vote if he, his father, or his grandfather had been eligible to vote before January 1, 1867. The date is important because before that time freed slaves did not have the right to vote. The grandfather clause therefore did not allow them to vote.

**JIM CROW LAWS** During the 1870s and 1880s, the Supreme Court failed to overturn the poll tax or the grandfather clause, even though the laws undermined all federal protections for African Americans' civil rights. At the same time that blacks lost voting rights, Southern states passed racial **segregation** laws to separate white and black people in public and private facilities. These laws came to be known as **Jim Crow laws** after a popular old minstrel song that ended in the words "Jump, Jim Crow." Racial segregation was put into effect in schools, hospitals, parks, and transportation systems throughout the South.

**PLESSY v. FERGUSON** Eventually a legal case reached the U.S. Supreme Court to test the constitutionality of segregation. In 1896, in **Plessy v. Ferguson**, the Supreme Court ruled that the separation of races in public accommodations was legal and did not violate the Fourteenth Amendment. The decision established the doctrine of "separate but equal," which allowed states to maintain segregated facilities for blacks and whites as long as they provided equal service. The decision permitted legalized racial segregation for almost 60 years. (See *Plessy v. Ferguson*, page 290.) **Ⓐ**

## Turn-of-the-Century Race Relations ❷

African Americans faced not only formal discrimination but also informal rules and customs, called racial etiquette, that regulated relationships between whites and blacks. Usually, these customs belittled and humiliated African Americans, enforcing their second-class status. For example, blacks and whites never shook hands, since shaking hands would have implied equality. Blacks also had to yield the sidewalk to white pedestrians, and black men always had to remove their hats for whites.

▲ This theater in Leland, Mississippi, was segregated under the Jim Crow laws.

**Vocabulary**
**minstrel:** one of a troupe of entertainers in blackface presenting a comic variety show

---

**MAIN IDEA**

**Analyzing Effects**
**Ⓐ** How did the *Plessy* v. *Ferguson* ruling affect the civil rights of African Americans?

**A. Answer** The Supreme Court decision opened the door for the legal segregation of almost all public facilities.

*Life at the Turn of the 20th Century*  **287**

---

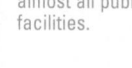

*Life at the Turn of the 20th Century*  **287**

## HISTORICAL SPOTLIGHT

### Washington vs. Du Bois

Have students discuss each scholar's approach to the struggle for racial equality. What were the differences and the similarities between their views on the politics of race in America? *(Both were leaders in the struggle to end racial discrimination. Both favored higher education for African Americans. But Washington advocated a gradual approach to change while Du Bois called for a more immediate end to racial injustice.)*

## More About . . .

### Segregated Neighborhoods

Harlem, in New York City, would become a famous African-American neighborhood in the early 20th century. Even before the city's first subway line opened in 1904, real-estate speculators began building apartments there, hoping to appeal to middle class whites. When the middle class did not arrive, Philip A. Payton, an African-American developer, stepped in and promised high rents to landlords who would allow African-American tenants. Soon, despite the higher rents, African Americans began moving to Harlem. For many, Harlem was to be a cultural mecca and a home.

## Instruct: Objective ③

### Discrimination in the West

TAKS SS11 3(US21.A)

· What were the difficulties that Mexicans encountered in the United States?
· How were Chinese immigrants treated?

 In-Depth Resources: Unit 2
· Guided Reading, p. 63

---

## HISTORICAL SPOTLIGHT

### WASHINGTON *VS.* DU BOIS

Booker T. Washington argued for a gradual approach to racial equality—suggesting that "it is at the bottom of life we must begin, and not at the top."

Ten years later, W. E. B. Du Bois denounced this view of gradual equality. Du Bois demanded full social and economic equality for African Americans, declaring that "persistent manly agitation is the way to liberty."

In 1909 the Niagara Movement, founded by Du Bois in 1905, became the National Association for the Advancement of Colored People (NAACP), with Du Bois as the editor of its journal, *The Crisis*. He wrote, "We refuse to surrender . . . leadership . . . to cowards and trucklers. We are men; we will be treated as men." The NAACP continues the fight for racial equality today.

---

Some moderate reformers, like Booker T. Washington, earned support from whites. Washington suggested that whites and blacks work together for social progress.

**A PERSONAL VOICE** BOOKER T. WASHINGTON

" To those of the white race . . . I would repeat what I say to my own race. . . . Cast down your bucket among these people who have, without strikes and labour wars, tilled your fields, cleared your forests, builded your railroads and cities, and brought forth treasures from the bowels of the earth. . . . In all things that are purely social we can be as separate as the fingers, yet one as the hand in all things essential to mutual progress."

—Atlanta Exposition address, 1895

Washington hoped that improving the economic skills of African Americans would pave the way for long-term gains. People like Ida B. Wells and W. E. B. Du Bois, however, thought that the problems of inequality were too urgent to postpone. **B**

**VIOLENCE** African Americans and others who did not follow the racial etiquette could face severe punishment or death. All too often, blacks who were accused of violating the etiquette were lynched. Between 1882 and 1892, more than 1,400 African-American men and women were shot, burned, or hanged without trial in the South. Lynching peaked in the 1880s and 1890s but continued well into the 20th century.

**DISCRIMINATION IN THE NORTH** Most African Americans lived in the segregated South, but by 1900, a number of blacks had moved to Northern cities. Many blacks migrated to Northern cities in search of better-paying jobs and social equality. But after their arrival, African Americans found that there was racial discrimination in the North as well. African Americans found themselves forced into segregated neighborhoods. They also faced discrimination in the workplace. Labor unions often discouraged black membership, and employers hired African-American labor only as a last resort and fired blacks before white employees.

Sometimes the competition between African Americans and working-class whites became violent, as in the New York City race riot of 1900. Violence erupted after a young black man, believing that his wife was being mistreated by a white policeman, killed the policeman. Word of the killing spread, and whites retaliated by attacking blacks. Northern blacks, however, were not alone in facing discrimination. Non-whites in the West also faced oppression. **C**

## ③ Discrimination in the West

Western communities were home to people of many backgrounds working and living side by side. Native Americans still lived in the Western territories claimed by the United States. Asian immigrants went to America's Pacific Coast in search of wealth and work. Mexicans continued to inhabit the American Southwest. African Americans were also present, especially in former slave-holding areas, such as Texas. Still, racial tensions often made life difficult.

**MEXICAN WORKERS** In the late 1800s, the railroads hired more Mexicans than members of any other ethnic group to construct rail lines in the Southwest.

**MAIN IDEA**

**Summarizing**
**B** What were Booker T. Washington's views about establishing racial equality?

**B. Answer**
He believed it was best not to emphasize legal equality but to concentrate on creating economic opportunities for African Americans.

**MAIN IDEA**

**Contrasting**
**C** How did conditions for African Americans in the North differ from their circumstances in the South?

**C. Answer**
Discrimination existed in both the North and the South, but the rules of segregation were more strict and pervasive in the South.

---

## ACTIVITY   COOPERATIVE LEARNING

### Debating Discrimination

**Class Time** 45 minutes

**Task** Investigating racism in the early 20th century

**Purpose** To understand the role of racism in American society in the early 20th century

**Directions** Groups of four or five students should conduct research about such topics as racial discrimination against African Americans, African-American leaders, or segregation in the early 20th century. (Examples—*Plessy v Ferguson*, Jim Crow laws, debt peonage, W. E. B. Du Bois, Ida B. Wells, Booker T. Washington). A representative from each group should present the group's findings as a lead-in to class discussion on the role of racism in American society in the early 20th century.

Mexican track workers for the Southern Pacific railroad posed for this group photo taken sometime between 1910 and 1915.

Mexicans were accustomed to the region's hot, dry climate. But the work was grueling, and the railroads made them work for less money than other ethnic groups.

Mexicans were also vital to the development of mining and agriculture in the Southwest. When the 1902 National Reclamation Act gave government assistance for irrigation projects, many southwest desert areas bloomed. Mexican workers became the major labor force in the agricultural industries of the region.

Some Mexicans, however, as well as African Americans in the Southwest, were forced into **debt peonage,** a system that bound laborers into slavery in order to work off a debt to the employer. Not until 1911 did the Supreme Court declare involuntary peonage a violation of the Thirteenth Amendment.

**Vocabulary**
**peon:** a worker bound in servitude to a landlord creditor

**EXCLUDING THE CHINESE** By 1880, more than 100,000 Chinese immigrants lived in the United States. White fear of job competition with the Chinese immigrants often pushed the Chinese into segregated schools and neighborhoods. Strong opposition to Chinese immigration developed, and not only in the West. (See Chinese Exclusion Act, page 259.)

Racial discrimination posed terrible legal and economic problems for non-whites throughout the United States at the turn of the century. More people however, whites in particular, had leisure time for new recreational activities, as well as money to spend on a growing arrray of consumer products.

## More About . . .

### Chinese Exclusion
In 1882, Congress passed the Chinese Exclusion Act, which prohibited virtually any more Chinese immigrants from entering the United States and suspended naturalization for those already in the country. In 1892, legislators extended the law for another ten years. In 1902, it was extended indefinitely. Congress finally repealed the Chinese Exclusion Act in 1943.

# Assess & Reteach

### SECTION 3 ASSESSMENT
Have students volunteer to lead a class discussion on questions 4 and 5.

Formal Assessment
· Section Quiz, p. 150

### SELF-ASSESSMENT
Have students make a two-column chart on the topic of segregation and racial discrimination at the turn of the 20th century. In the left column, have students list what they already knew; in the right column, what they learned in the section.

### RETEACH
Review regional variations of race relations, discrimination, and segregation. Refer to each section for specific examples.

In-Depth Resources: Unit 2
· Reteaching Activity, p. 69

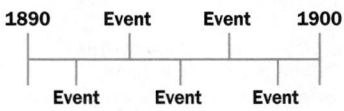
**ASSESSMENT**

**1. TERMS & NAMES** For each term or name, write a sentence explaining its significance.
- **Ida B. Wells**
- **poll tax**
- **grandfather clause**
- **segregation**
- **Jim Crow laws**
- *Plessy* v. *Ferguson*
- **debt peonage**

### MAIN IDEA

**2. TAKING NOTES**
Review the section, and find five key events to place on a time line as shown.

1890  Event  Event  1900

Event  Event  Event

Which of these events do you think was most important? Why?

### CRITICAL THINKING

**3. IDENTIFYING PROBLEMS**
How did segregation and discrimination affect the lives of African Americans at the turn of the 20th century?

**4. COMPARING**
What did some African-American leaders do to fight discrimination?

**5. CONTRASTING**
How did the challenges and opportunities for Mexicans in the United States differ from those for African Americans? **Think About:**
- the types of work available to each group
- the effects of government policies on each group
- the effect of the legal system on each group

---

**Answers**  **ASSESSMENT**

**1. TERMS & NAMES**
Ida B. Wells, p. 286
poll tax, p. 287
grandfather clause, p. 287
segregation, p. 287
Jim Crow laws, p. 287
*Plessy* v. *Ferguson*, p. 287
debt peonage, p. 289

**2. TAKING NOTES**
1890s: Ida B. Wells' anti-lynching campaign; Booker T. Washington and W. E. B. Du Bois emerge as leaders.
1896: *Plessy* v. *Ferguson*
1900: New York City race riot.
early 1900s: Mexicans settle in Southwest.

**3. IDENTIFYING PROBLEMS**
African Americans were victimized by voting restrictions, Jim Crow laws, and the "separate but equal" doctrine established by *Plessy* v. *Ferguson*.

**4. COMPARING**
Ida B. Wells fought lynching; Homer Plessy took his case to the Supreme Court; Booker T. Washington advocated a gradual approach to racial equality; W. E. B. Du Bois founded the NAACP.

**5. CONTRASTING**
Answers will vary but should indicate that Mexicans in the United States faced discrimination but it was not legalized, and that there were job opportunities but they were low-paying.

## HISTORIC DECISIONS OF THE SUPREME COURT

### Objectives

· To examine the reasoning behind the *Plessy* v. *Ferguson* decision

· To understand the impact of *Plessy* v. *Ferguson* on African Americans and American society as a whole

## Focus & Motivate

**Evaluating** Ask students what they think of when they hear the phrase, "separate by equal." Discuss with students why this could be considered a contradictory statement.

## More About . . .

### Justice John Marshall Harlan

John Marshall Harlan was born in Kentucky, in 1833, the son of a slave owner. He began his legal career at the age of 20 and served a short term as a county judge. From 1863 to 1867, he served as Kentucky attorney general. President Hayes appointed Harlan to the Supreme Court in 1877. He soon gained a reputation for often disagreeing with the court majority. Justice Harlan wrote the only dissenting opinion in the *Plessy* v. *Ferguson* case. In his dissent he wrote, "I am of opinion that the statute . . . is inconsistent with the personal liberty of citizens, white and black . . . and hostile to both the spirit and the letter of the Constitution of the United States."

# PLESSY v. FERGUSON (1896)

**ORIGINS OF THE CASE** In 1892, Homer Plessy took a seat in the "Whites Only" car of a train and refused to move. He was arrested, tried, and convicted in the District Court of New Orleans for breaking Louisiana's segregation law. Plessy appealed, claiming that he had been denied equal protection under the law. The Supreme Court handed down its decision on May 18, 1896.

**THE RULING** The Court ruled that separate-but-equal facilities for blacks and whites did not violate the Constitution.

## LEGAL REASONING

Plessy claimed that segregation violated his right to equal protection under the law. Moreover he claimed that, being "of mixed descent," he was entitled to "every recognition, right, privilege and immunity secured to the citizens of the United States of the white race."

Justice Henry B. Brown, writing for the majority, ruled:

> "The object of the [Fourteenth] amendment was . . . undoubtedly to enforce the absolute equality of the two races before the law, but . . . it could not have been intended to abolish distinctions based upon color, or to enforce social, as distinguished from political equality, or a commingling of the two races upon terms unsatisfactory to either. Laws permitting, and even requiring, their separation in places where they are liable to be brought into contact do not necessarily imply the inferiority of either race to the other."

In truth, segregation laws did perpetrate an unequal and inferior status for African Americans. Justice John Marshall Harlan understood this fact and dissented from the majority opinion. He wrote, "In respect of civil rights, all citizens are equal before the law." He condemned the majority for letting "the seeds of race hate . . . be planted under the sanction of law." He also warned that "The thin disguise of 'equal' accommodations . . . will not mislead any one, nor atone for the wrong this day done."

**Justice John Marshall Harlan**

### LEGAL SOURCES

#### LEGISLATION

**U.S. CONSTITUTION, FOURTEENTH AMENDMENT (1868)**
"No state shall . . . deny to any person within its jurisdiction the equal protection of the laws."

**LOUISIANA ACTS 1890, NO. 111**
". . . that all railway companies carrying passengers in their coaches in this State, shall provide equal but separate accommodations for the white, and colored races."

#### RELATED CASES

**CIVIL RIGHTS CASES (1883)**
The Court ruled that the Fourteenth Amendment could not be used to prevent private citizens from discriminating against others on the basis of race.

**WILLIAMS v. MISSISSIPPI (1898)**
The Court upheld a state literacy requirement for voting that, in effect, kept African Americans from the polls.

**CUMMING v. BOARD OF EDUCATION OF RICHMOND COUNTY (1899)**
The Court ruled that the federal government cannot prevent segregation in local school facilities because education is a local, not federal, issue.

## RECOMMENDED RESOURCES

### BOOKS

Beth, Loren P. *John Marshall Harlan: The Last Whig Justice.* Lexington: U of Kentucky Press, 1992. Biography of the outspoken justice known for his liberal dissents on a conservative court.

Brinkley, Douglas. *Rosa Parks.* New York: Viking Press, 2000. A look at the life of the woman who helped spark the civil rights movement.

Fremon, David K. *The Jim Crow Laws and Racism in American History.* Berkeley, New Jersey: Enslow Publishers, 2000.

Haskins, James. *Separate but Not Equal: The Dream and the Struggle.* New York: Scholastic Trade, 1997. Concise history of the African-American struggle for equal rights to education.

Thomas, Brook, ed. *Plessy v Ferguson: A Brief History With Documents.* Boston: Bedford Books, 1997. In-depth examination of the landmark court decision.

### IINTEGRATED TECHNOLOGY

For teacher support and more information about the Supreme Court including the full text of the Supreme Court decisions, visit. . . .

 classzone.com

▲ One result of Jim Crow laws was separate drinking fountains for whites and African Americans.

## WHY IT MATTERED

In the decades following the Civil War [1861–1865], Southern state legislatures passed laws that aimed to limit civil rights for African Americans. The Black Codes of the 1860s, and later Jim Crow laws, were intended to deprive African Americans of their newly won political and social rights granted during Reconstruction.

*Plessy* was one of several Supreme Court cases brought by African Americans to protect their rights against segregation. In these cases, the Court regularly ignored the Fourteenth Amendment and upheld state laws that denied blacks their rights. *Plessy* was the most important of these cases because the Court used it to establish the separate-but-equal doctrine.

As a result, city and state governments across the South—and in some other states—maintained their segregation laws for more than half of the 20th century. These laws limited African Americans' access to most public facilities, including restaurants, schools, and hospitals. Without exception, the facilities reserved for whites were superior to those reserved for nonwhites. Signs reading "Colored Only" and "Whites Only" served as constant reminders that facilities in segregated societies were separate but not equal.

## HISTORICAL IMPACT

It took many decades to abolish legal segregation. During the first half of the 20th century, the National Association for the Advancement of Colored People (NAACP) led the legal fight to overturn *Plessy*. Although they won a few cases over the years, it was not until 1954 in *Brown* v. *Board of Education* that the Court overturned any part of *Plessy*. In that case, the Supreme Court said that separate-but-equal was unconstitutional in public education, but it did not completely overturn the separate-but-equal doctrine.

In later years, the Court did overturn the separate-but-equal doctrine, and it used the *Brown* decision to do so. For example, in 1955, Rosa Parks was convicted for violating a Montgomery, Alabama, law for segregated seating on buses. A federal court overturned the conviction, finding such segregation unconstitutional. The case was appealed to the Supreme Court, which upheld without comment the lower court's decision. In doing so in this and similar cases, the Court signaled that the reasoning behind *Plessy* no longer applied.

▲ As secretary of the Montgomery chapter of the NAACP, Rosa Parks had protested segregation through everyday acts long before Sepember 1955.

### THINKING CRITICALLY

#### CONNECT TO TODAY

1. **Analyzing Primary Sources** Read the part of the Fourteenth Amendment reprinted in this feature. Write a paragraph explaining what you think "equal protection of the laws" means. Use evidence to support your ideas.

 **SEE SKILLBUILDER HANDBOOK, PAGE R22.**

#### CONNECT TO HISTORY

2.  **INTERNET ACTIVITY** CLASSZONE.COM

Visit the links for Historic Decisions of the Supreme Court to research and read Justice Harlan's entire dissent in *Plessy* v. *Ferguson*. Based on his position, what view might Harlan have taken toward laws that denied African Americans the right to vote? Write a paragraph or two expressing what Harlan would say about those laws.

*Life at the Turn of the 20th Century* **291**

## CHAPTER 8 · SECTION 3

## Instruct

1. What was the Supreme Court's ruling in *Plessy v. Ferguson*?
2. How did the Supreme Court's ruling affect Southern states?
3. How and when was the *Plessy* decision overturned?

📄 Historic Supreme Court Decisions
· *Plessy v. Ferguson*, pp. 67–72

## MAKING PERSONAL CONNECTIONS

Ask students how they might feel if they were prohibited from attending certain restaurants or other public places because of their skin color. How would it make them feel? How would they react?

### More About. . .

#### Rosa Parks

In 1999, Rosa Parks received the Congressional Gold Medal—the nation's highest civil honor. President Bill Clinton presented the medal to Parks for her pivotal contribution to the Civil Rights movement. "Forty-three years ago, in Alabama, Rosa Parks boarded a public bus, took a seat, and began a remarkable journey. Her action that December day was, in itself, a simple one; but it required uncommon courage. . . . Rosa Parks' short bus trip, and all the distance she has traveled in the years since, have brought the American people ever closer to the promised land we know it can truly be."

### THINKING CRITICALLY: ANSWERS

#### 1. CONNECT TO TODAY

**Rubric**

Student paragraphs should:

· Begin with a topic sentence that summarizes the main idea
· Demonstrate an understanding of the Fourteenth Amendment and explain the phrase "equal protection of the laws"
· Present accurate, historical evidence
· Conclusion by restating the central argument

#### 2. CONNECT TO HISTORY

**Rubric**

Student paragraphs should:

· Begin with a statement about the implications of Harlan's *Plessy* dissent
· Demonstrate a clear understanding of the opinion
· Present evidence to support a position on Harlan's present attitude toward African-American voting rights
· Conclude by restating the main idea

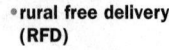

## OBJECTIVES

1. Give examples of turn-of-the-20th-century leisure activities and popular sports.

2. Analyze the spread of mass culture in the United States at the turn of the 20th century.

3. Describe turn-of-the-20th-century innovations in marketing and advertising.

### CRITICAL THINKING

· Making Inferences, p. 293
· Drawing Conclusions, pp. 294, 295
· Analyzing Causes, p. 296
· Summarizing, p. 297
· Analyzing Visual Sources, p. 297

## FOCUS & MOTIVATE

Ask students what they enjoy doing in their free time. Then ask them to consider the impact of particular leisure activities on American culture.

## Instruct

### Instruct: Objective 1

**American Leisure**
TAKS SS11 5(US24.A)
· What leisure activities became popular with Americans at the turn of the 20th century?
· What spectator sports did many Americans enjoy?

 In-Depth Resources: Unit 2
· Guided Reading, p. 64

---

# Dawn of Mass Culture

| MAIN IDEA | WHY IT MATTERS NOW | Terms & Names |
|---|---|---|
| As Americans had more time for leisure activities, a modern mass culture emerged. | Today, the United States has a worldwide impact on mass culture. | • Joseph Pulitzer<br>• William Randolph Hearst<br>• Ashcan school<br>• Mark Twain<br>• rural free delivery (RFD) |

 U.S. History
20A, 20B, 20D, 24A, 24B, 24C, 24D, 25A, 25B, 25C, 25D

### One American's Story

Along the Brooklyn seashore, on a narrow sandbar just nine miles from busy Manhattan, rose the most famous urban amusement center, Coney Island. In 1886, its main developer, George Tilyou, bragged, "If Paris is France, then Coney Island . . . is the world." Indeed, tens of thousands of visitors mobbed Coney Island after work each evening and on Sundays and holidays. When Luna Park, a spectacular amusement park on Coney Island, opened in May 1903, a reporter described the scene.

**A PERSONAL VOICE** BRUCE BLEN

" [Inside the park was] an enchanted, storybook land of trellises, columns, domes, minarets, lagoons, and lofty aerial flights. And everywhere was life—a pageant of happy people; and everywhere was color—a wide harmony of orange and white and gold. . . . It was a world removed—shut away from the sordid clatter and turmoil of the streets. "

—quoted in *Amusing the Million*

Coney Island offered Americans a few hours of escape from the hard work week. A schoolteacher who walked fully dressed into the ocean explained her unusual behavior by saying, "It has been a hard year at school, and when I saw the big crowd here, everyone with the brakes off, the spirit of the place got the better of me." The end of the 19th century saw the rise of a "mass culture" in the United States.

▲ The sprawling amusement center at Coney Island became a model for urban amusement parks.

## 1 American Leisure

Middle-class Americans from all over the country shared experiences as new leisure activities, nationwide advertising campaigns, and the rise of a consumer culture began to level regional differences. As the 19th century drew to a close, many Americans fought off city congestion and dull industrial work by enjoying amusement parks, bicycling, new forms of theater, and spectator sports.

---

## PROGRAM RESOURCES

 **In-Depth Resources: Unit 2**
· Guided Reading, p. 64
· Reteaching Activity, p. 70
· Primary Sources: Advertisement, p. 74
· Literature: from *Ragtime*, pp. 77–79
· American Lives: Lillian Gish, p. 81

 **Reading Study Guide** (English and Spanish), pp. 87–88

 **Access for Students Acquiring English/ESL**
· Guided Reading (Spanish), p. 107

 **Formal Assessment**
· Section Quiz, p. 151

**Integrated Assessment**
· Rubrics

### INTEGRATED TECHNOLOGY

 **Humanities Transp. HT16**
· *Washington Square North, New York City*

 **Electronic Library of Primary Sources**

 **classzone.com**

### TEXAS RESOURCES

 TAKS Spiraled Content Review

TAKS Practice Tests

TAKS Practice Transparencies TT61

TAKS Online Test Practice

**AMUSEMENT PARKS** To meet the recreational needs of city dwellers, Chicago, New York City, and other cities began setting aside precious green space for outdoor enjoyment. Many cities built small playgrounds and playing fields throughout their neighborhoods for their citizens' enjoyment.

Some amusement parks were constructed on the outskirts of cities. Often built by trolley-car companies that sought more passengers, these parks boasted picnic grounds and a variety of rides. The roller coaster drew daredevil customers to Coney Island in 1884, and the first Ferris wheel drew enthusiastic crowds to the World's Columbian Exhibition in Chicago in 1893. Clearly, many Americans were ready for new and innovative forms of entertainment—and a whole panorama of recreational activities soon became available.

**BICYCLING AND TENNIS** With their huge front wheels and solid rubber tires, the first American bicycles challenged their riders. Because a bump might toss the cyclist over the handlebars, bicycling began as a male-only sport. However, the 1885 manufacture of the first commercially successful "safety bicycle," with its smaller wheels and air-filled tires, made the activity more popular. And the Victor safety bicycle, with a dropped frame and no crossbar, held special appeal to women.

Abandoning their tight corsets, women bicyclists donned shirtwaists (tailored blouses) and "split" skirts in order to cycle more comfortably. This attire soon became popular for daily wear. The bicycle also freed women from the scrutiny of the ever-present chaperone. The suffragist Susan B. Anthony declared, "I think [bicycling] has done more to emancipate women than anything else in the world. . . . It gives women a feeling of freedom and self-reliance." Fifty thousand men and women had taken to cycles by 1888. Two years later 312 American firms turned out 10 million bikes in one year. **A**

Americans took up the sport of tennis as enthusiastically as they had taken up cycling. The modern version of this sport originated in North Wales in 1873. A year later, the United States saw its first tennis match. The socialite Florence Harriman recalled that in the 1880s her father returned from England with one of New York's first tennis sets. At first, neighbors thought the elder Harriman had installed the nets to catch birds.

Hungry or thirsty after tennis or cycling? Turn-of-the-century enthusiasts turned to new snacks with recognizable brand names. They could munch on a Hershey chocolate bar, first sold in 1900, and wash down the chocolate with a Coca-Cola®. An Atlanta pharmacist originally formulated the drink as a cure for headaches in 1886. The ingredients included extracts from Peruvian cocoa leaves as well as African cola nuts.

*"Eight hours for work, eight hours for rest, eight hours for what we will"*
THE CARPENTERS' UNION,
WORCESTER, MASSACHUSETTS

---

**MAIN IDEA**

**Making Inferences**
**A** How did the mass production of bicycles change women's lives?

---

## More About . . .

### Bicycling
The development of the bicycle was an international affair. As early as 1818, people began creating models for the bicycle. Pierre Michaux and his son Ernest introduced the modern bicycle in France in the 1860s. Pierre Lallement, the Michaux mechanic, emigrated to America in 1866. He joined forces with James Carroll from Ansonia, Connecticut to patent the first bicycle in the United States. European designers made later modifications. John Boyd Dunlop, a Northern Irish veterinarian, introduced the pneumatic tire.

## More About . . .

### Women and Bicycling
At the turn of the 20th century in the United States, the "Gibson girl"—as drawn by *Life* magazine artist Charles Dana Gibson—represented the ideal of female beauty. However, this glamorous woman with the corseted, hourglass figure, was not dressed to ride a bicycle. She would have to abandon the corset. Bicycle riding was an activity that represented new freedom and opportunity for women.

Bicycling and other new sports became fads in the late 1800s.
▼

---

**DIFFERENTIATING INSTRUCTION**    **LESS PROFICIENT READERS**

### Clarifying

In reading pages 292–297, less proficient readers might use the SQ3R study method, as follows:

· Survey the pages by skimming for headings and topic sentences.

· Question the information by jotting down questions about turn-of-the-20th-century mass culture and leisure activities.

· Read the pages, looking for answers to these questions.

· Recite or record any answers that are found.

· Review the information to answer any questions that remain.

*Life at the Turn of the 20th Century*    **293**

The Negro ▶
Leagues were
first formed in
1920.

**SPECTATOR SPORTS** Americans not only participated in new sports, but became avid fans of spectator sports, especially boxing and baseball. Though these two sports had begun as popular informal activities, by the turn of the 20th century they had become profitable businesses. Fans who couldn't attend an important boxing match jammed barber shops and hotel lobbies to listen to telegraphed transmissions of the contest's highlights.

**BASEBALL** New rules transformed baseball into a professional sport. In 1845, Alexander J. Cartwright, an amateur player, organized a club in New York City and set down regulations that used aspects of an English sport called rounders. Five years later, fifty baseball clubs had sprung up in the United States, and New York alone boasted 12 clubs in the mid-1860s.

In 1869, a professional team named the Cincinnati Red Stockings toured the country. Other clubs soon took to the road, which led to the formation of the National League in 1876 and the American League in 1900. In the first World Series, held in 1903, the Boston Pilgrims beat the Pittsburgh Pirates. African-American baseball players, who were excluded from both leagues because of racial discrimination, formed their own clubs and two leagues—the Negro National League and the Negro American League.

The novelist Mark Twain called baseball "the very symbol . . . and visible expression of the drive and push and rush and struggle of the raging, tearing, booming nineteenth century." By the 1890s, baseball had a published game schedule, official rules, and a standard-sized diamond. **B**

## ❷ The Spread of Mass Culture

As increasing numbers of Americans attended school and learned to read, the cultural vistas of ordinary Americans expanded. Art galleries, libraries, books, and museums brought new cultural opportunities to more people. Other advances fostered mass entertainment. New media technology led to the release of hundreds of motion pictures. Mass-production printing techniques gave birth to thousands of books, magazines, and newspapers.

**MASS CIRCULATION NEWSPAPERS** Looking for ways to captivate readers' attention, American newspapers began using sensational headlines. For example, to introduce its story about the horrors of the Johnstown, Pennsylvania flood of 1889, in which more than 2,000 people died, one newspaper used the headline "THE VALLEY OF DEATH."

**Joseph Pulitzer**, a Hungarian immigrant who had bought the *New York World* in 1883, pioneered popular innovations, such as a large Sunday edition,

---

comics, sports coverage, and women's news. Pulitzer's paper emphasized "sin, sex, and sensation" in an attempt to surpass his main competitor, the wealthy **William Randolph Hearst**, who had purchased the New York *Morning Journal* in 1895. Hearst, who already owned the San Francisco *Examiner*, sought to outdo Pulitzer by filling the *Journal* with exaggerated tales of personal scandals, cruelty, hypnotism, and even an imaginary conquest of Mars. **C**

The escalation of their circulation war drove both papers to even more sensational news coverage. By 1898, the circulation of each paper had reached more than one million copies a day.

**PROMOTING FINE ARTS** By 1900, at least one art gallery graced every large city. Some American artists, including Philadelphian Thomas Eakins, began to embrace realism, an artistic school that attempted to portray life as it is really lived. Eakins had studied anatomy with medical students and used painstaking geometric perspective in his work. By the 1880s, Eakins was also using photography to make realistic studies of people and animals.

In the early 20th century, the **Ashcan School** of American art, led by Eakins's student Robert Henri, painted urban life and working people with gritty realism and no frills. Both Eakins and the Ashcan school, however, soon were challenged by the European development known as abstract art, a direction that most people found difficult to understand.

In many cities, inhabitants could walk from a new art gallery to a new public library, sometimes called "the poor man's university." By 1900, free circulating libraries in America numbered in the thousands.

**MAIN IDEA**

Drawing
Conclusions
**C** How did the
*World* and the
*Journal* attract
readers?

## History Through *Art*

THE CHAMPION SINGLE
SCULLS (MAX SCHMITT IN
A SINGLE SCULL)
(1871)

This painting by Thomas Eakins is an example of the realist movement—an artistic school that aimed at portraying people and environments as they really are.

**What realistic details do you see portrayed in this painting?**

*Life at the Turn of the 20th Century* **295**

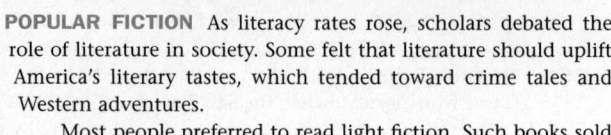

## More About . . .

### Mark Twain
Samuel Clemens grew up in the Mississippi River town of Hannibal, Missouri. His pen name came from the riverboat pilot's cry, "mark twain," which indicated the water was two fathoms deep and safe for boat crossing. Twain's pioneer work of fiction, *The Adventures of Huckleberry Finn*, is usually cited as his masterpiece. "All modern American literature," Ernest Hemingway once observed, "comes from one book by Mark Twain called *Huckleberry Finn*."

## Instruct: Objective ③

### New Ways to Sell Goods
TAKS SS11 3(US22.C)
· How did the growth of cities change the way in which goods were sold?
· How did mail-order catalogs and advertising contribute to the growth of mass culture?

 In-Depth Resources: Unit 2
· Guided Reading, p. 64
· Primary Source: Advertisement, p. 74

---

**POPULAR FICTION** As literacy rates rose, scholars debated the role of literature in society. Some felt that literature should uplift America's literary tastes, which tended toward crime tales and Western adventures.

Most people preferred to read light fiction. Such books sold for a mere ten cents, hence their name, "dime novels." Dime novels typically told glorified adventure tales of the West and featured heroes like Edward Wheeler's *Deadwood Dick*. Wheeler published his first Deadwood Dick novel in 1877 and in less than a decade produced over 30 more. **D**

Some readers wanted a more realistic portrayal of American life. Successful writers of the era included Sarah Orne Jewett, Theodore Dreiser, Stephen Crane, Jack London, and Willa Cather. Most portrayed characters less polished than the upper-class men and women of Henry James's and Edith Wharton's novels. Samuel Langhorne Clemens, the novelist and humorist better known as **Mark Twain,** inspired a host of other young authors when he declared his independence of "literature and all that bosh." Yet, some of his books have become classics of American literature. *The Adventures of Huckleberry Finn*, for example, remains famed for its rendering of life along the Mississippi River.

Although art galleries and libraries attempted to raise cultural standards, many Americans had scant interest in high culture—and others did not have access to it. African Americans, for example, were excluded from visiting many museums and other white-controlled cultural institutions.

 Highly popular dime novels often featured adventure stories.

MAIN IDEA

**Analyzing Causes**
**D** What factors contributed to the popularity of dime novels?

## ③ New Ways to Sell Goods

Along with enjoying new leisure activities, Americans also changed the way they shopped. Americans at the turn of the 20th century witnessed the beginnings of the shopping center, the development of department and chain stores, and the birth of modern advertising.

**URBAN SHOPPING** Growing city populations made promising targets for enterprising merchants. The nation's earliest form of a shopping center opened in Cleveland, Ohio, in 1890. The glass-topped arcade contained four levels of jewelry, leather goods, and stationery shops. The arcade also provided band music on Sundays so that Cleveland residents could spend their Sunday afternoons strolling through the elegant environment and gazing at the window displays.

Retail shopping districts formed where public transportation could easily bring shoppers from outlying areas. To anchor these retail shopping districts, ambitious merchants started something quite new, the modern department store.

**THE DEPARTMENT STORE** Marshall Field of Chicago first brought the department store concept to America. While working as a store clerk, Field found that paying close attention to women customers could increase sales considerably. In 1865, Field opened his own store, featuring several floors of specialized departments. Field's motto was "Give the lady what she wants." Field also pioneered the bargain basement, selling bargain goods that were "less expensive but reliable."

**THE CHAIN STORE** Department stores prided themselves on offering a variety of personal services. New chain stores—retail stores offering the same merchandise under the same ownership—sold goods for less by buying in quantity and limiting personal service. In the 1870s, F. W. Woolworth found that if he offered an item at a very low price, "the consumer would purchase it on the spur of the

**Vocabulary**
**consumer:** a person who purchases goods or services for direct use or ownership

---

### Outlining

In order to help less proficient readers gain insight into the reading on pages 296 and 297, have them make an outline of the section "New Ways to Sell Goods." Suggest that students list the subheadings and bullet point the main ideas under each subheading. See the example at the right.

New Ways to Sell Goods
I  Urban Shopping
· arcade
· retail shopping districts
II  The Department Store
· several floors of specialized departments
III  The Chain Store
· retail stores—same merchandise different location
IV  Advertising
· newspapers, magazine
· billboards
V  Catalogs and RFD
· merchandise to farms and small towns

moment" because "it was only a nickel." By 1911, the Woolworth chain boasted 596 stores and sold more than a million dollars in goods a week.

**ADVERTISING** An explosion in advertising also heralded modern consumerism. Expenditures for advertising were under $10 million a year in 1865 but increased tenfold, to $95 million, by 1900. Patent medicines grabbed the largest number of advertising lines, followed by soaps and baking powders. In addition to newspapers and magazines, advertisers used ingenious methods to push products. Passengers riding the train between New York and Philadelphia in the 1870s might see signs for Dr. Drake's Plantation Bitters on barns, houses, billboards, and even rocks.

**CATALOGS AND RFD** Montgomery Ward and Sears Roebuck brought retail merchandise to small towns. Ward's catalog, launched in 1872, grew from a single sheet the first year to a booklet with ordering instructions in ten languages. Richard Sears started his company in 1886. Early Sears catalogs stated that the company received "hundreds of orders every day from young and old who never [before] sent away for goods." By 1910, about 10 million Americans shopped by mail. The United States Post Office boosted mail-order businesses. In 1896 the Post Office introduced a **rural free delivery (RFD)** system that brought packages directly to every home.

The turn of the 20th century saw prosperity that caused big changes in Americans' daily lives. At the same time, the nation's growing industrial sector faced problems that called for reform.

**CATALOG SHOPPING**

Catalogs were a novelty when Sears and Montgomery Ward arrived on the scene. However, by the mid-1990s, more than 13 billion catalogs filled the mail boxes of Americans.

Today, the world of mail-order business is changing. After over 100 years of operation, Montgomery Ward filed for bankruptcy on December 28, 2000.

Online shopping threatens to dominate mail-order commerce today. Online retail sales have grown from $500 million in 1995 to $7.8 billion in 1998. What do catalog shoppers order? Clothing ranks first, electronics second. Online book sales also lead—in 1998, book sales had risen over 300% to total $650 million.

**SECTION 4 ASSESSMENT**

**1. TERMS & NAMES** For each term or name, write a sentence explaining its significance.
- Joseph Pulitzer
- Ashcan School
- rural free delivery (RFD)
- William Randolph Hearst
- Mark Twain

**MAIN IDEA**

**2. TAKING NOTES**
Re-create the spider diagram below. Add examples to each category.

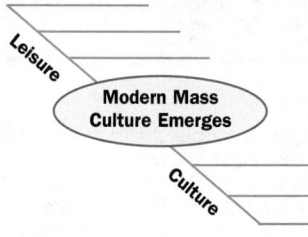

Why is mass culture often described as a democratic phenomenon?

**CRITICAL THINKING**

**3. SUMMARIZING**
How did American methods of selling goods change at the turn of the 20th century?
**Think About:**
- how city people did their shopping
- how rural residents bought goods
- how merchants advertised their products

**4. ANALYZING VISUAL SOURCES**
This cartoon shows the masters of the "new journalism." According to the cartoonist, where were Pulitzer and Hearst leading American journalism?

*Life at the Turn of the 20th Century* **297**

DAILY LIFE

## Objectives

· To identify types of entertainment that were popular with Americans during the turn of the 20th century

· To understand what the popularity of such entertainment demonstrates about the social values of Americans at this time

## Focus & Motivate

While most students are probably familiar with circuses and movies, ask them what they might know about vaudeville theater and ragtime music.

## More About . . .

### Minstrel Shows

African Americans participated in minstrel shows because, for a time, it was one of the only ways to break into the entertainment business. Even so, it did not prove easy for African Americans to move beyond the minstrel stage. The African-American entertainer Sam Lucas, a minstrel star by the mid-1870s, had difficulty finding other work in the theater. After years of persistence, Lucas did star in several serious plays, including a production of *Uncle Tom's Cabin.* Unfortunately, steady work in theater was hard to come by, especially for African Americans, and the wages were low. Sam Lucas had to return to minstrel shows in order to make a living.

DAILY LIFE 1877–1917

# Going to the Show

As Americans moved from rural areas to cities, they looked for new ways to spend their weekend and evening leisure time. Live theatrical performances brought pleasure to cities and small towns alike. Stars, popular performers who could attract large audiences, compensated for the less-talented supporting actors. Audiences could choose from a wide range of music, drama, circus, and the latest in entertainment—moving pictures.

◄ VAUDEVILLE THEATER

Performances that included song, dance, juggling, slapstick comedy, and sometimes chorus lines of female performers were characteristic of vaudeville. Promoters sought large audiences with varied backgrounds. Writing in *Scribner's Magazine* in October 1899, actor Edwin Milton Royle hailed vaudeville theater as "an American invention" that offered something to attract nearly everyone.

Until the 1890s, African-American performers filled roles mainly in minstrel shows that featured exaggerated imitations of African-American music and dance and reinforced racist stereotypes of blacks. By the turn of the century, however, minstrel shows had largely been replaced by more sophisticated musicals, and many black performers entertained in vaudeville.

Bill "Bojangles" Robinson was a popular tap dancer.

▲ THE CIRCUS

The biggest spectacle of all was often the annual visit of the Barnum & Bailey Circus, which its founders, P. T. Barnum and Anthony Bailey, touted as "The Greatest Show on Earth." Established in 1871, the circus arrived by railroad and staged a parade through town to advertise the show.

298 CHAPTER 8

## RECOMMENDED RESOURCES

### BOOKS

Berlin, Edward A. *King of Ragtime: Scott Joplin and His Era.* New York: Oxford University Press, 1996. A biography of the famous ragtime entertainer.

Bowers, Q. David. *Nickelodeon Theatres and Their Music.* Lanham, Maryland: Scarecrow Press, 1999. History of the early years of the motion picture business.

Jasen, David and Gene Jones. *That American Rag: The Story of Ragtime from Coast to Coast.* New York: Schirmer Books, 2000. History of ragtime music.

Slide, Anthony. *The Encyclopedia of Vaudeville.* Westport, Connecticut: Greenwood Publishing Group, 1994. Extensive facts and highlights of the popular turn-of-the-century form of entertainment.

Warrick, Karen Clemens. *P.T. Barnum: Genius of the Three-Ring Circus.* Berkeley Heights, New Jersey: Enslow Publishers, 2001.

## ▲ THE SILVER SCREEN

The first films, one-reel 10-minute sequences, consisted mostly of vaudeville skits or faked newsreels. In 1903 the first modern film—an 8-minute silent feature called *The Great Train Robbery*—debuted in five-cent theaters called nickelodeons. By showing a film as often as 16 times a day, entrepeneurs could generate greater profits than by a costly stage production. By 1907, an estimated 3,000 nickelodeons dotted the country.

## ◄ RAGTIME MUSIC

A blend of African-American spirituals and European musical forms, ragtime originated in the 1880s in the saloons of the South. African-American pianist and composer Scott Joplin's ragtime compositions made him famous in the first decade of the 1900s. Ragtime led later to jazz, rhythm and blues, and rock 'n' roll. These forms of popular American culture spread worldwide, creating new dances and fashions that emulated the image of "loud, loose, American rebel."

---

# DATA FILE

## A LOOK AT THE FACTS

A shorter workweek allowed many Americans more time for leisure activities, and they certainly took advantage of it.

- In 1890, an average of 60,000 fans attended professional baseball games daily.

- In 1893, a crowd of 50,000 attended the Princeton-Yale football game.

- *A Trip to Chinatown,* one of the popular new musical comedies, ran for an amazing 650 performances in the 1890s.

- In 1900, 3 million phonograph records of Broadway-produced musical comedies were sold.

- The love of the popular musicals contributed to the sale of $42 million worth of musical instruments in 1900.

- By 1900, almost 500 men's social clubs existed. Nine hundred college fraternity and sorority chapters had over 150,000 members.

| Changes in the U.S. Workweek | |
|---|---|
| Year | Hours per week |
| 1860 | 66 |
| 1890 | 60 |
| 1920 | 50 |

Source: *Historical Statistics of the United States*

---

## THINKING CRITICALLY

### CONNECT TO HISTORY

1. **Interpreting Data** Study the statistics in the Data File. What summary statements about the culture and attitudes of this time period can you make? Is this a time in history when you would like to have lived? Why or why not?

   **SEE SKILLBUILDER HANDBOOK, PAGE R27.**

### CONNECT TO TODAY

2. **Chronological Order** Trace the development and impact on the rest of the world of one area—music, theater, or film—of popular American culture. Use a time line from the turn of the 20th to the 21st century with "United States developments" on one side and "world impacts" on the other.

**RESEARCH LINKS** CLASSZONE.COM

*Life at the Turn of the 20th Century* **299**

---

# Instruct

1. How was vaudeville theater different from earlier minstrel shows?
2. How did the first motion pictures differ from today's films?
3. What musical forms were blended to form ragtime?

📖 **In-Depth Resources: Unit 2**
· American Lives: Lillian Gish

💿 **Electronic Library of Primary Sources**
· *from* The Movies and Me, Mr. Griffith, and Me, 1914 by L. Gish

## MAKING PERSONAL CONNECTIONS

Ask students to discuss their favorite type of entertainment and what makes it so popular with them.

---

## More About . . .

### Scott Joplin

Scott Joplin, "King of Ragtime," studied piano as a child in Texas. Later, he traveled throughout the Midwest and performed at a variety of venues, including the Chicago Columbian Exposition in 1893. After continuing his musical training at George R. Smith College for Negroes in Missouri, Joplin began composing. He became famous for original works such as "Maple Leaf Rag" and "The Entertainer." Scott Joplin spent his final years in New York City, working mainly on a three-act opera called *Treemonisha*.

---

## THINKING CRITICALLY: ANSWERS

1. **CONNECT TO HISTORY** New technologies allowed for more leisure time. Leisure activities gained popularity. Theater and entertainment industries drew large audiences. Participation in spectator sports grew. Enrollment in colleges and universities rose.

2. **CONNECT TO TODAY**
   **Rubric**
   A time line should . . .
   · be presented in chronological order
   · be clearly labeled and detail key achievements, events, and persons related to their subject
   · demonstrate students' understanding of the developments in music, theater, film, or sports in the late 1800s and early 1900s

## TERMS AND NAMES

1. Louis Sullivan, p. 277
2. Orville and Wilbur Wright, p. 279
3. Booker T. Washington, p. 285
4. W. E. B. Du Bois, p. 285
5. Niagara Movement, p. 285
6. Ida B. Wells, p. 286
7. Jim Crow laws, p. 287
8. *Plessy* v. *Ferguson*, p. 287
9. debt peonage, p. 289
10. rural free delivery, p. 297

## MAIN IDEAS

1. Bridges and trains helped cities to grow outward; skyscrapers helped cities grow upward.
2. Printing and paper became less expensive; photography became widespread; airplanes carried people and mail across the nation.
3. The population of school-age children increased; immigrant children enrolled in school; and reformers focused on educational programs.
4. Some did not want their children Americanized; others had religious objections.
5. The Supreme Court legalized segregation in *Plessy* v. *Ferguson;* Congress enacted the Chinese Exclusion Act; Debt peonage was allowed.
6. Mexicans worked in mining, agriculture, railroad construction, and irrigation projects—helping to make the desert "bloom."
7. Popular leisure activities included bicycling, spectator sports, amusement parks, theatre, the circus, and reading fiction.
8. Advertising, shopping centers, department stores, and mail-order catalogs changed the way Americans shopped.

### TERMS & NAMES

For each term or name, write a sentence explaining its connection to late 19th-century American life.

1. Louis Sullivan
2. Orville and Wilbur Wright
3. Booker T. Washington
4. W. E. B. DuBois
5. Niagara Movement
6. Ida B. Wells
7. Jim Crow laws
8. *Plessy* v. *Ferguson*
9. debt peonage
10. rural free delivery

### MAIN IDEAS

Use your notes and the information in the chapter to answer the following questions.

**Science and Urban Life** *(pages 276–281)*

1. How did new technology promote urban growth around the turn of the century?
2. In what ways did methods of communication improve in the late 19th and early 20th centuries?

**Expansion of Public Education**
*(pages 282–285)*

3. How did late 19th century public schools change?
4. Why did some immigrants oppose sending their children to public schools?

**Segregation and Discrimination**
*(pages 286–289)*

5. In what ways was racial discrimination reinforced by the federal government's actions and policies?
6. How did Mexicans help make the Southwest prosperous in the late 19th century?

**Dawn of Mass Culture** *(pages 292–297)*

7. What leisure activities flourished at the turn of the 20th century?
8. What innovations in retail methods changed the way Americans shopped during this time period?

### CRITICAL THINKING

1. **USING YOUR NOTES** Create a table similar to the one shown, listing at least six important trends at the turn of the century, along with a major impact of each.

| Trend | Impact |
|---|---|
| 1. | |
| 2. | |
| 3. | |
| 4. | |
| 5. | |
| 6. | |

2. **DRAWING CONCLUSIONS** How had changes in technology affected urban life by the turn of the 20th century?

3. **INTERPRETING GRAPHS** Look at the graph of Expanding Education/Increasing Literacy on page 283. Which year reported the greatest gain in the literacy rate? What do you think were the implications on society of a more literate population?

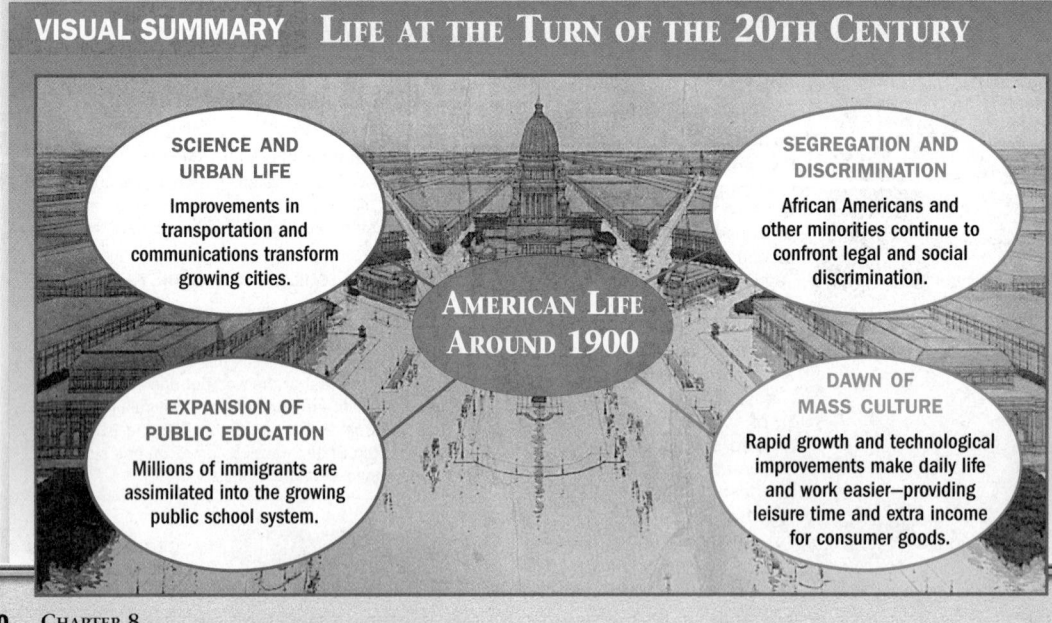

**VISUAL SUMMARY** LIFE AT THE TURN OF THE 20TH CENTURY

**SCIENCE AND URBAN LIFE**
Improvements in transportation and communications transform growing cities.

**SEGREGATION AND DISCRIMINATION**
African Americans and other minorities continue to confront legal and social discrimination.

AMERICAN LIFE AROUND 1900

**EXPANSION OF PUBLIC EDUCATION**
Millions of immigrants are assimilated into the growing public school system.

**DAWN OF MASS CULTURE**
Rapid growth and technological improvements make daily life and work easier—providing leisure time and extra income for consumer goods.

### CRITICAL THINKING

1. **Using Your Notes**
   **Trends and Impacts:** Engineering innovation—urban expansion
   New technology—increased leisure time and activities
   Public education—literacy; reforms
   Jim Crow—segregation; restricted freedom and civil rights of African Americans
   *Plessy* v. *Ferguson*—legalized segregation

   Printing, paper, photography—mass culture

2. **Drawing Conclusions** New technologies made urban expansion possible. Leisure time increased, as did the popularity of leisure activities. Improved printing, paper, and photography led to the widespread availability of newspapers, catalogs, and print advertisements. A mass culture was born.

3. **Interpreting Graphs** Greatest gain in literacy rate was in 1890. Literacy gave more American citizens the tools to participate in the social, political, and cultural aspects of American society.

## Standardized Test Practice

Use the quotation below and your knowledge of U.S. history to answer question 1.

> "We boast of the freedom enjoyed by our people above all other peoples. But it is difficult to reconcile that boast with a state of the law which, practically, puts the brand of servitude and degradation upon a large class of our fellow-citizens, our equals before the law."
>
> —Justice John Marshall Harlan in the dissenting opinion in *Plessy* v. *Ferguson*

1. Justice Harlan used this reasoning for what purpose?

   A to celebrate American democracy

   B to justify segregation

   C to denounce the "separate-but-equal" argument

   D to demonstrate that equality before the law is not practical

2. Which of the following was *not* an outcome of expanding public education in the early 20th century?

   F the establishment of public high schools and colleges

   G the growth of equal education for all

   H a rise in the literacy rate

   J the founding of kindergartens

3. The turn of the 20th century brought shorter work hours and more leisure time to many urban Americans. Which of the following bar graphs correctly reflects these factors?

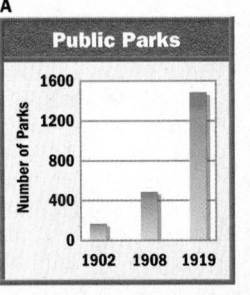
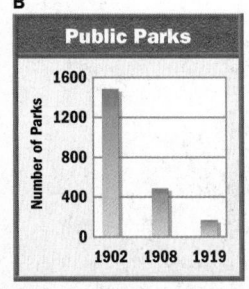
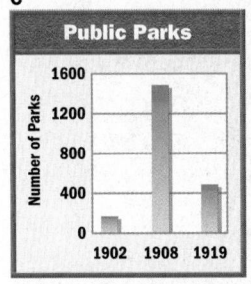
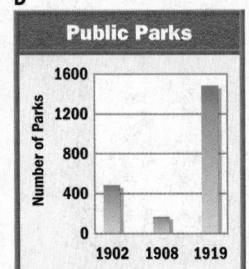

ADDITIONAL TEST PRACTICE, pages S1–S33.

 TEST PRACTICE  CLASSZONE.COM

## Standardized Test Practice

1. The correct answer is letter **C**.
   Harlan disagreed with the decision to uphold segregation.
   Letter A is not correct because Harlan was not celebrating democracy. Letter B is not correct because Harlan was not in favor of segregation. Letter D is not correct because Harlan believed in equality before the law.

2. The correct answer is letter **G**.
   African Americans often not have access to educational opportunities. Letters F, H, and J all occurred.

3. The correct answer is letter **A**.
   The graph shows an increase in the number of public parks from 1902 to 1919. Letters B, C, D do not show a steady increase in public parks.

### ORAL REPORT

**Tips for Teaching**
· Allow class time for students to rehearse.
· Remind students that if they need special equipment for their presentations they should make arrangements for it.

**Project Presentation Rubric**
An oral report should . . .
· Have a clear organization and contain a conclusion that summarizes the main points of the presentation
· Capture the audience's attention with interesting introduction and information
· Include visuals or artifacts from the time period

 Formal Assessment
· Chapter Test, Forms A, B, and C, pp. 152–169

---

## ALTERNATIVE ASSESSMENT

1. **INTERACT WITH HISTORY**  Recall your discussion of the question of page 275:

   *How will the latest technology change your life?*

   Now that you know more about the role of technology in people's lives, would you change any of your responses? Discuss your ideas with a small group. Then make a cause-and-effect chart about one technological innovation of the era and its lasting impacts on society.

2. **INTERNET ACTIVITY**  CLASSZONE.COM

   Visit the links for Chapter Assessment to find out more about the World's Columbian Exposition held in Chicago in 1893.

   In a small group, make a list of the "famous firsts," such as the first elevated railway, introduced at the exposition. Illustrate your list, adding pictures and informative captions, on a colorful poster for display in the classroom.

*Life at the Turn of the 20th Century*  **301**

---

## ALTERNATIVE ASSESSMENT

### 1. INTERACT WITH HISTORY
**Rubrics**

A cause-and-effect chart should . . .
· be a two-column chart with appropriate headings and labels
· list significant technological innovations from the turn of the 20th century
· accurately define and list the impact of each innovation

### 2. INTERNET ACTIVITY
**Rubrics**

A poster should . . .
· include pictures, illustrations, headlines, cartoons, or other visual aids
· highlight the theme of "famous firsts" at the 1893 Exposition
· reflect the contributions and research of the whole group

## Previewing the Unit

Unit 3 describes how the modern United States begins taking shape in the first two decades of the 20th century. Americans embrace the progressive movement, which leads to greater government involvement in many aspects of life. Starting with the move to gain colonies overseas and ending with participation in World War I, America also plays a greater role in world affairs than ever before.

### HISTORICAL INQUIRY: NEWS STORY

Use this project to teach students to explain and apply the use of point of view in historical inquiry.

**Explaining Point of View**

Explain that a person's point of view is his or her manner of understanding or interpreting things; it includes the person's versions of stories and events and the person's interests, attitudes, and opinions on issues. Tell students that historians try to understand the points of view of different people involved in historical events. Ask why students think this might be. *(Understanding a person's point of view helps one explain why that person acted as he or she did; understanding historical events or issues from several points of view gives one a fuller understanding of the times.)*

*(continued on next page)*

---

# UNIT 3

### CHAPTER 9
**The Progressive Era**
1890–1920

### CHAPTER 10
**America Claims an Empire**
1890–1920

### CHAPTER 11
**The First World War**
1914–1920

*News Story*

As you read Unit 3, identify a person, issue, or event that interests you. Plan and write an illustrated news story about the subject you have chosen. Use your text as well as information that you research in the library and on the Internet.

*The Statue of Liberty* by Francis Hopkinson Smith

---

# Modern America Emerges 1890–1920

---

## More About the Image

### Statue of Liberty Facts

· The statue was commissioned in 1875 and was intended to be a gift for the centennial anniversary of the United States. It was ten years late in arriving.

· President Grover Cleveland accepted the statue on behalf of the American people on October 28, 1886. At the ceremony he said, "We will not forget that liberty here made her home; nor shall her chosen altar be neglected."

· The sculptor was Frederic Auguste Bartholdi. The interior structure which supported the copper skin of the statue was designed by Alexandre Gustave Eiffel, the designer of the Eiffel Tower in Paris.

· The statue was completed in France in July 1884 and shipped in pieces to New York. The Statue was deconstructed into 350 individual pieces and delivered in 214 crates.

· The statue is 305'1" from the ground to the tip of the torch. The statue itself is 151'1" from the base to the tip of the torch.

## Applying Point of View

Tell students that their news stories should show the points of view of more than one historical figure. They should also describe the points of view in order to compare and/or contrast them. Tell students to gather as much information about the figures as they can, even though they will not include it all in their stories. Explain that the more one knows about a person's life and experiences, the better one can understand his or her point of view.

## Rubric

A News Story should . . .

· have a clear focus and organization
· present a clear narrative of a chain of events
· both display and describe the points of view of more than one historical character

## HISTORY from VISUALS

### Interpreting the Painting

Tell the students that the picture was painted by Francis Hopkinson Smith, an engineer and artist who worked with the firm that built the pedestal for the Statue of Liberty. The official dedication of the statue took place on October 28, 1886. Notice that one of the ships flies the French flag. The statue was a gift to the people of the United States from the people of France in recognition of the friendship established between the countries during the American Revolution.

Ask students what significance the American Revolution had to the history of France. *(The American Revolution was an inspiration to the French who began their own revolution.)* What symbolism might the artist be using in the painting? *(The statue is seen emerging out of the fog. Perhaps the artist believed America was emerging into the view of many countries.)*

**Extension** Ask students what role images of the Statue of Liberty played in the days following the World Trade Center bombing.

· The statue weighs in at 62,000 (31 tons) of copper and 250,000 pounds (125 tons) of steel. The copper sheeting is $\frac{3}{32}$ inches thick.

· The statue's crown has seven rays representing the seven continents and seven seas of the earth. There are 25 windows in her crown symbolizing gemstones found on earth.

· The tablet which the statue holds in the left hand has an inscription which reads, "July 4, 1776" in Roman numerals.

For additional information on the Statue of Liberty check the Web site of the Statue of Liberty National Monument and Ellis Island.

# The Progressive Era

| | CHAPTER OVERVIEW | COPYMASTERS | INTEGRATED TECHNOLOGY |
| --- | --- | --- | --- |
| **CHAPTER RESOURCES** | ***In the first two decades of the 1900s, Americans embrace the progressive movement and many of its reforms.*** | **Telescoping the Times**<br>· Chapter Summary, pp. 17–18<br>**Planning for Block Schedules** | **American Stories video series**<br>· "A Child on Strike"<br>**Power Presentations**<br>**Electronic Teacher Tools**<br>**Online Lesson Planner**<br>**classzone.com** |
| **SECTION 1**<br>**The Origins of Progressivism**<br>**pp. 306–312** | **KEY IDEAS**<br>***Social and economic changes during the late 19th century create broad reform movements in American society.*** | **In-Depth Resources: Unit 3**<br>· Guided Reading, p. 1<br>· Building Vocabulary, p. 6<br>· Skillbuilder Practice, p. 7<br>· Reteaching Activity, p. 8<br>· Primary Sources, pp. 15–16<br>· American Lives, p. 22<br>**Lesson Plans,** pp. 71–72 | **Geography Transparencies GT17**<br>· Continental United States in 1900<br>**Critical Thinking Transparencies CT17, CT52**<br>· The Progressive Movement<br>· U.S. Trade with Central America<br>**Electronic Library of Primary Sources**<br>· The Taylor System, 1912<br>**classzone.com** |
| **SECTION 2**<br>**Women in Public Life**<br>**pp. 313–316** | ***Many of the social and economic changes giving rise to progressivism lead women into public life as reformers and workers.*** | **In-Depth Resources: Unit 3**<br>· Guided Reading, p. 2<br>· Reteaching Activity, p. 9<br>· Primary Sources, pp. 17–18<br>**Lesson Plans,** pp. 73–74 | **Electronic Library of Primary Sources**<br>· from *The United States of America* v. *Susan B. Anthony*, 1873<br>**classzone.com** |
| **SECTION 3**<br>**Teddy Roosevelt's Square Deal**<br>**pp. 317–327** | ***Theodore Roosevelt pursues a reform agenda known as the Square Deal. His energetic style contributes to the emergence of the modern presidency.*** | **In-Depth Resources: Unit 3**<br>· Guided Reading, p. 3<br>· Reteaching Activity, p. 10<br>· Literature, pp. 19-21<br>**Lesson Plans,** pp. 75–76 | **Electronic Library of Primary Sources**<br>· from *Whatever Is, Is Wrong*, 1900s<br>**classzone.com** |
| **SECTION 4**<br>**Progressivism Under Taft**<br>**pp. 328–331** | ***William H. Taft pursues a more cautious progressive program during his one term as president.*** | **In-Depth Resources: Unit 3**<br>· Guided Reading, p. 4<br>· Reteaching Activity, p. 11<br>**Lesson Plans,** pp. 77–78 | **Humanities Transparencies HT36**<br>· from "Goodness Gracious, I Must Have Been Dozing"<br>**Electronic Library of Primary Sources**<br>**classzone.com** |
| **SECTION 5**<br>**Wilson's New Freedom**<br>**pp. 332–337** | ***Woodrow Wilson claims the presidency as a progressive leader and establishes a strong reform agenda.*** | **In-Depth Resources: Unit 3**<br>· Guided Reading, p. 5<br>· Reteaching Activity, p. 12<br>· Geography Application, pp. 13–14<br>· American Lives: p. 23<br>**Lesson Plans,** pp. 79-80 | **classzone.com** |

**Key**

- PE Pupil's Edition
- TE Teacher's Edition
- Copymaster
- Overhead Transparency
- Audio Library
- CD-ROM
- Internet

## ASSESSMENT OPTIONS

- PE Chapter Assessment, pp. 338–339
- Formal Assessment
  · Chapter Tests, Forms A, B, and C, pp. 175–192
- Test Generator
- Integrated Assessment Book
- TAKS Online Test Practice
- TAKS Spiraled Content Review
- TAKS Practice Tests

- PE Section 1 Assessment, p. 312
- TE Self-Assessment, p. 312
- Formal Assessment, Quiz, p. 170
- Integrated Assessment Book
- Test Generator
- TAKS Practice Transparencies TT62

- PE Section 2 Assessment, p. 316
- TE Self-Assessment, p. 316
- Formal Assessment, Quiz, p. 171
- Integrated Assessment Book
- Test Generator
- TAKS Practice Transparencies TT63

- PE Section 3 Assessment, p. 325
- TE Self-Assessment, p. 325
- Formal Assessment, Quiz, p. 172
- Integrated Assessment Book
- Test Generator
- TAKS Practice Transparencies TT64

- PE Section 4 Assessment, p. 331
- TE Self-Assessment, p. 331
- Formal Assessment, Quiz, p. 173
- Integrated Assessment Book
- Test Generator
- TAKS Practice Transparencies TT65

- PE Section 5 Assessment, p. 337
- TE Self-Assessment, p. 337
- Formal Assessment, Quiz, p. 174
- Integrated Assessment Book
- Test Generator
- TAKS Practice Transparencies TT66

## RESOURCES FOR DIFFERENTIATING INSTRUCTION

**Students Acquiring English/ESL**

- Reading Study Guide (English and Spanish) pp. 91–100
- Access for Students Acquiring English/ESL: Spanish Translations, pp. 113–120
- Chapter Summaries on CD (English and Spanish)

**Less Proficient Readers**

- Reading Study Guide (English and Spanish) pp. 91–100
- Telescoping the Times
  · Chapter Summary, pp. 17–18
- Chapter Summaries on CD (English and Spanish)

**Gifted and Talented Students**

- In-Depth Resources: Unit 3
  · Primary Sources, pp. 15–18
  · Literature, pp. 19–21
  · American Lives: Robert M. La Follette, p. 22
  · American Lives: Carrie Chapman Catt, p. 23
- Electronic Library of Primary Sources
  · Unit 3, Chapter 9

## CROSS-CURRICULAR CONNECTIONS

**Primary Sources**

Muir, John and Gifford, Terry (editor). *John Muir: His Life and Letters and Other Writings.* Seattle: Mountaineers Books, 1996. A collection of Muir's vivid writing, including parts of his autobiography and other less famous selections.

**Culture**

Freedman, Russell and Hine, Lewis (photographer). *Kids at Work: Lewis Hine and the Crusade Against Child Labor.* NY: Clarion Books, 1998. Moving photographs by the great reformer, with informative, well-written text.

**Civics**

Sullivan, George. *The Day the Women Got the Vote: A Photo History of the Women's Rights Movement.* NY: Scholastic, 1994. A photographic record of the fight for the vote.

**Geography**

Pyne, Stephen J. *How the Canyon Became Grand: A Short History.* NY: Viking, 1998. The author knows the canyon from the point of view of a rafter and a hiker, as well as a historian.

**Literature**

Perez, N. A. *Breaker.* Boston: Houghton Mifflin, 1988. After his father's death, 14-year-old Pat is forced to work in the coal mines in his Pennsylvania town. He becomes involved in the mine workers' strike of 1902.

Sandburg, Carl. *Chicago Poems.* NY: Dover, 1994. This is Sandburg's first book of poetry. These free-verse poems celebrate the voices of the people and are concerned with themes of injustice and the effects of industrialization on humanity.

## ENRICHMENT ACTIVITIES

- PE Pupil's Edition, pp. 304–337
  Interact with History, pp. 304–305
  American Literature, pp. 326–327
- In-Depth Resources: Unit 3
  · Geography Application: The Movement Toward Woman Suffrage, pp. 13–14
  · Primary Source: Declaration of the WCTU, p. 15
  · Primary Source: Child Labor in the Coal Mines, p. 16
  · Primary Source: Political Poster, p. 17

- · Primary Source: from "The Status of Woman" by Susan B. Anthony, p. 18
- · Literature: from *The Jungle* by Upton Sinclair, pp. 19–21
- · American Lives: Robert M. La Follette, p. 22
- · American Lives: Carrie Chapman Catt, p. 23
- Electronic Library of Primary Sources
  · Unit 3 Chapter 9
- American Stories video series
  · "A Child on Strike"

## BLOCK SCHEDULE LESSON PLAN OPTIONS (90-MINUTE PERIOD)

### DAY 1

**CHAPTER 9 OPENER**
pp. 304–305

**Class Time** 30 minutes

**History from Visuals, p. 304**

**Class Time** 15 minutes

*Options for Pacing and Variety*

· Time Saver Have students study the photograph and the time line. Ask them to explain what event is occurring, who the participants are, and why they are dressed that way. **Class Time** 10 minutes

**Interact with History, p. 305**

**Class Time** 20 minutes

*Options for Pacing and Variety*

· Internet Ask students to read the sidebar on page 305 and visit classzone.com for more information about reform movements of the Progressive Era. Have them write a few paragraphs on the main question. **Class Time** 15 minutes

**SECTION 1, pp. 306–312**

**Class Time** 30 minutes

*Options for Pacing and Variety*

· History on Film View the video *A Child on Strike*.
**Class Time** 30 minutes

· Peer Teaching Have student groups research the influence of muckrakers on politics. Have each group share their work with the class.
**Class Time** 60 minutes

### DAY 1 continued

· Time Saver Have students read the sidebar on page 311, "History Through Photojournalism," and discuss the PE and the TE questions. **Class Time** 10 minutes

**SECTION 2, pp. 313–316**

**Class Time** 30 minutes

*Options for Pacing and Variety*

· Time Saver For homework, have students complete the Main Idea questions in the section as they read. Discuss and collect their answers. **Class Time** 10 minutes

· Peer Teaching Have students work in small groups to complete the Section 2 Assessment. Discuss the answers with each group.
**Class Time** 15 minutes

### DAY 2

**SECTION 3, pp. 317–327**

**Class Time** 45 minutes

*Options for Pacing and Variety*

· Time Saver Ask students the questions on Understanding Presidential Succession on TE page 318.
**Class Time** 10 minutes

· Internet Have students read the subheading "Roosevelt and Civil Rights" on page 324. Then have groups do research online or at the library on W.E.B. Du Bois and Booker T. Washington and their different and sometimes antagonistic ideas. Students should summarize their findings or choose one modern example of the legacy of either man to share with the class.
**Class Time** 30 minutes

**SECTION 4, pp. 328–331**

**Class Time** 45 minutes

*Options for Pacing and Variety*

· Peer Evaluation Have students complete the Section 4 Assessment with a partner, and then have partners switch papers with another set of partners and correct the answers as the class discusses them.
**Class Time** 25 minutes

· Role-Playing Have students write a letter to the editor according to the instructions on TE page 329, and have them share their letters either individually with other students or with the class.
**Class Time** 25 minutes

### DAY 3

**SECTION 5, pp. 332–337**

**Class Time** 45 minutes

*Options for Pacing and Variety*

· Time Saver For homework, have students answer the Main Idea questions as they read the section. Discuss the answers in class.
**Class Time** 10 minutes

· Time Saver Have students read the sidebar "History Through Architecture" on page 336 and conduct a discussion of the Skillbuilder questions. **Class Time** 10 minutes

· Internet Have students read the feature on pages 336–337, "American Literature: The Muckrakers." Have them begin research for the article specified in question 2.
**Class Time** 30 minutes

**ASSESSMENT**
pp. 338–339

**Class Time** 45 minutes

*Options for Pacing and Variety*

· Peer Teaching Have students work in pairs on the Critical Thinking questions on page 338. Go through the Venn diagram for question 1 with the class. **Class Time** 15 minutes

· Peer Evaluation Have pairs of students quiz each other on the terms and names and Main Ideas questions for the chapter.
**Class Time** 20 minutes

---

**TEACHER-TESTED ACTIVITY**   George Dyche, West Aurora High School, Aurora, Illinois
### SELF-QUIZ ON WOMEN OF THE ERA

**Class Time** 45 minutes

**Task** Creating a self-quiz on notable women

**Purpose** To understand the achievements of women from this era

**Supplies Needed**
· Paper
· Pen or pencil

**Activity** Ask students to draw a vertical line to separate the page, leaving one-third of the paper's width on the left. In this third, have them list all of the women included in the chapter. On the right, have them write at least one accomplishment for each woman. Then have students fold their papers on the line so that only one column shows. Have them use either list to quiz themselves.

# CHAPTER 9 CORRELATION

## CORRELATION TO THE TEXAS ESSENTIAL KNOWLEDGE AND SKILLS

Chapter 9 addresses the following standards of the Texas Essential Knowledge and Skills for U.S. History.

| TEKS | Instruction | Student Question/Activity |
|---|---|---|
| **(2A)** Analyze political issues such as civil service reform. | **PE 309–310** discussion of civil service reforms including activities of reform mayors during the Progressive Era | **PE 310** question about changes in city government during the Progressive Era |
| **(2C)** Analyze social issues such as child labor. | **PE 310–311** examination of efforts to reduce the use of child labor | **TE 311** activity formulating and writing briefs on child labor issues |
| **(4A)** Evaluate the impact of Progressive Era reforms including initiative, referendum, recall, and the passage of the 16th and 17th amendments. | **PE 312** examination of election reforms, including the initiative, referendum, and recall, as well as passage of the 17th amendment | **PE 312** Critical Thinking question about various election reforms |
| **(4B)** Evaluate the impact of reform leaders such as W. E. B. Du Bois. | **PE 324–325** discussion of the life and reform efforts of W. E. B. Du Bois | **PE 325** question about the views of W. E. B. Du Bois |
| **(11B)** Trace the development of the conservation of natural resources, including the establishment of the National Park System. | **PE 323** map denoting the establishment of federal conservation lands between 1872 and 1996 | **PE 323** questions that require students to interpret information about the map |
| **(12C)** Describe the impact of the Sherman Antitrust Act on businesses. | **PE 319** discussion of the causes and impact of the Sherman Antitrust Act | **PE 319** questions about a political cartoon dealing with the Sherman Antitrust Act |
| **(18A)** Identify and analyze methods of expanding the right to participate in the democratic process. | **PE 334–335** examination of women's successful effort to win the right to vote | **PE 335** question about the women's suffrage movement |
| **(21D)** Identify the political, social, and economic contributions of women to American society. | **PE 307–308; 314–316** analysis of women's contributions to the Progressive Era reform movements | **PE 316** Critical Thinking questions about the role of women in reform movements |

## TAKS MINI-LESSONS

1. **Social Studies Skills: Objective 4 (US4.A):** Evaluate the impact of Progressive Era reforms **Activity** Have students create a chart highlighting significant political reforms during the Progressive Era.

2. **Social Studies Skills: Objective 3 (US4.B):** Evaluate reform leaders such as Susan B. Anthony, W.E.B. Du Bois, and Robert La Follette **Activity** Have students conduct research and write a brief biography of one of these reformers.

3. **Social Studies Skills: Objective 3 (US21.D):** Identify the political, social, and economic contributions of women to American society **Activity** Have students complete the writing activity on TE page 314 regarding the woman suffrage movement.

4. **English Language Arts Skills: Objective 3 (10.B):** Use elements of text to defend, clarify, and negotiate interpretations **Activity** Have students interpret both Roosevelt's and Wilson's stance on civil rights and support their interpretations with details from the text.

5. **English Language Arts Skills: Objective 3 (7.G):** Draw inferences such as conclusions, generalizations, and predictions, and support them with text evidence **Activity** Have students make a generalization about the goals of progressivism and support it with details from the text.

To explain how the progressive movement managed to increase the power of government to regulate business and to protect society from the injustices fostered by big business

# THE PROGRESSIVE ERA

**CHAPTER 9**

## HISTORY from VISUALS

### Interpreting the Photograph

Ask students to study the photograph. Ask them to explain what event is occurring, who the participants are, and why they are dressed the way they are. *(Students should be able to identify it as a parade or a protest march advocating votes for women and should mention that the women were trying to make the march appear patriotic.)*

**Extension** Ask students to write a lead paragraph for a news story about this march.

## Time Line Discussion

Explain to students that the time line covers key events in the United States and the world from the end of the 19th century through the first two decades of the 20th century.

· Ask students to identify W. E. B. Du Bois. *(He cofounded the National Association for the Advancement of Colored People, NAACP.)*

· Ask students what the Nineteenth Amendment did and the year in which it became law. *(It gave women the right to vote; 1920.)*

· Ask students under what circumstances Theodore Roosevelt became president. *(President McKinley was assassinated.)*

A 1916 suffrage parade.

**1896** William McKinley is elected president.

**1900** William McKinley is reelected.

**1901** McKinley is assassinated; Theodore Roosevelt becomes president.

**1904** Theodore Roosevelt is elected president.

USA
WORLD

**1890**

**1900**

**1889** Eiffel Tower opens for visitors.

**1898** Marie Curie discovers radium.

**1899** Boer War in South Africa begins.

**1901** Commonwealth of Australia is created.

**304** CHAPTER 9

## THEMES IN CHAPTER 9

### ECONOMIC OPPORTUNITY

The progressive movement responded to a growing public demand for government to become involved in curbing abuse of workers, especially children. Reformers also wanted changes in business practices that harmed the public.

**See Teacher's Edition note**, p. 307.

### WOMEN AND POLITICAL POWER

Women entered the work force in increasing numbers. Though usually paid less than their male counterparts, women's increasing visibility in the public arena at the beginning of World War I helped spur the movement seeking woman suffrage. Ratification of the Nineteenth Amendment took place in 1920.

**See Teacher's Edition note**, p. 315.

### STATES' RIGHTS

Theodore Roosevelt changed the role of the president by using the White House as a bully pulpit to influence public policy and expanding the responsibilities of the office. His actions shaped what would become the modern presidency.

**See Teacher's Edition note**, p. 319.

# INTERACT
## WITH HISTORY

It is the dawn of the 20th century, and the reform movement is growing. Moral reformers are trying to ban alcoholic beverages. Political reformers work toward fair government and business practices. Women fight for equal wages and the right to vote. Throughout society, social and economic issues take center stage.

## What kinds of actions can bring about social change?

### Examine the Issues

- What types of actions might pressure big business to change?
- How can individuals bring about change in their government?
- How might reformers recruit others?

**RESEARCH LINKS** CLASSZONE.COM

Visit the Chapter 9 links for more information about The Progressive Era.

# INTERACT
## WITH HISTORY

## Objectives

· To help students understand the scope of reform movements in early 20th century America
· To motivate students to connect political and moral reform movements with the expansion of democracy

### Examine the Issues

1. Ask students which of the following they think is more effective in changing the actions of business—governmental action, fines, or public protests.
2. Have students consider what options citizens have to get government officials to change a policy.
3. Ask students to discuss why it is important to have grassroots support for reforms.

---

**1908** William H. Taft is elected president.

**1909** W. E. B. Du Bois helps found the National Association for the Advancement of Colored People (NAACP).

**1912** Woodrow Wilson is elected president.

**1916** Woodrow Wilson is reelected.

**1918** Eighteenth Amendment outlaws alcoholic beverages.

**1920** Nineteenth Amendment grants women the right to vote.

VOTES for WOMEN

## 1910

## 1920

**1910** Mexican revolution begins.

**1913** China's Qin Dynasty topples.

**1914** World War I begins in Europe.

**1918** Mohandas Gandhi becomes leader of the independence movement in India.

*The Progressive Era* **305**

---

## RECOMMENDED RESOURCES

### BOOKS FOR THE TEACHER

Schlereth, Thomas J. *Victorian America: Transformations in Everyday Life, 1876–1915.* New York: Harper Collins, 1991. A useful overview of the period.

Woloch, Nancy. *Women and the American Experience, second edition.* New York: McGraw-Hill, Inc., 1994. An introduction to the history of American women.

### BOOKS FOR THE STUDENT

Addams, Jane. *Twenty Years at Hull House.* Urbana: U of Illinois P, 1990. Addams' story of the settlement house; originally published in 1910.

Wilson, Dorothy Clarke. *Bright Eyes: The Story of Susette La Flesche, an Omaha Indian.* New York: McGraw, 1974. A readable account.

### VIDEOS

*One Woman, One Vote.* Prod. Ruth Pollak. PBS Home Video, 1995. Final drive for woman suffrage.

*Theodore Roosevelt: Roughrider to Rushmore.* Prod. Arthur Drooker. A&E Home Video, 1996. Life of an energetic president.

### SOFTWARE

*Her Heritage.* **CD-ROM.** Pilgrim New Media, 1994. From the database of Robert McHenry, editor-in-chief, Encyclopedia Britannica.

### INTEGRATED TECHNOLOGY

For teacher support, visit . . .

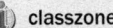 classzone.com

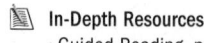
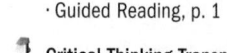
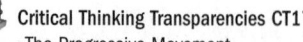
# SECTION 1

# The Origins of Progressivism

| MAIN IDEA | WHY IT MATTERS NOW | Terms & Names |
|---|---|---|
| Political, economic, and social change in late 19th century America led to broad progressive reforms. | Progressive reforms such as labor and voting rights have helped to make life in America what it is today. | •progressive movement •Florence Kelley •prohibition •muckraker •scientific management — •Robert M. La Follette •initiative •referendum •recall •Seventeenth Amendment |

**U.S. History**
2B, 2C, 4B, 10A, 18A, 18B, 21A, 21D, 22A, 22C, 24B, 25A, 25B, 25D

### One American's Story

Camella Teoli was just 12 years old when she began working in a Lawrence, Massachusetts, textile mill to help support her family. Soon after she started, a machine used for twisting cotton into thread tore off part of her scalp. The young Italian immigrant spent seven months in the hospital and was scarred for life.

Three years later, when 20,000 Lawrence mill workers went on strike for higher wages, Camella was selected to testify before a congressional committee investigating labor conditions such as workplace safety and underage workers. When asked why she had gone on strike, Camella answered simply, "Because I didn't get enough to eat at home." She explained how she had gone to work before reaching the legal age of 14.

**A PERSONAL VOICE** CAMELLA TEOLI

" I used to go to school, and then a man came up to my house and asked my father why I didn't go to work, so my father says I don't know whether she is 13 or 14 years old. So, the man say 'You give me $4 and I will make the papers come from the old country [Italy] saying that you are 14.' So my father gave him the $4, and in one month came the papers that I was 14. I went to work, and about two weeks later got hurt in my head. "
—at congressional hearings, March 1912

After nine weeks of striking, the mill workers won the sympathy of the nation as well as 5 to 10 percent pay raises. Stories like Camella's set off a national investigation of labor conditions, and reformers across the country organized to address the problems of industrialization.

▲ Mill workers on strike in 1912 in Lawrence, Massachusetts

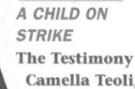 **VIDEO**
A CHILD ON STRIKE
The Testimony of Camella Teoli, Mill Girl

**Mini-Lesson 5: SS11 3(US7.G)**

## 1 Four Goals of Progressivism

At the dawn of the new century, middle-class reformers addressed many of the problems that had contributed to the social upheavals of the 1890s. Journalists and writers exposed the unsafe conditions often faced by factory workers, including

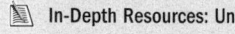

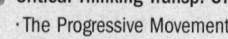
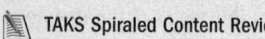
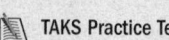
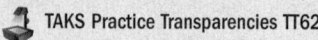
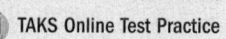

women and children. Intellectuals questioned the dominant role of large corporations in American society. Political reformers struggled to make government more responsive to the people. Together, these reform efforts formed the **progressive movement,** which aimed to return control of the government to the people, restore economic opportunities, and correct injustices in American life.

Even though reformers never completely agreed on the problems or the solutions, each of their progressive efforts shared at least one of the following goals:

- protecting social welfare
- promoting moral improvement
- creating economic reform
- fostering efficiency

**PROTECTING SOCIAL WELFARE** Many social welfare reformers worked to soften some of the harsh conditions of industrialization. The Social Gospel and settlement house movements of the late 1800s, which aimed to help the poor through community centers, churches, and social services, continued during the Progressive Era and inspired even more reform activities.

The Young Men's Christian Association (YMCA), for example, opened libraries, sponsored classes, and built swimming pools and handball courts. The Salvation Army fed poor people in soup kitchens, cared for children in nurseries, and sent "slum brigades" to instruct poor immigrants in middle-class values of hard work and temperance.

**Vocabulary**
**temperance:** refraining from alcohol consumption

In addition, many women were inspired by the settlement houses to take action. **Florence Kelley** became an advocate for improving the lives of women and children. She was appointed chief inspector of factories for Illinois after she had helped to win passage of the Illinois Factory Act in 1893. The act, which prohibited child labor and limited women's working hours, soon became a model for other states.

**PROMOTING MORAL IMPROVEMENT** Other reformers felt that morality, not the workplace, held the key to improving the lives of poor people. These reformers wanted immigrants and poor city dwellers to uplift themselves by improving their personal behavior. **Prohibition,** the banning of alcoholic beverages, was one such program.

**A. Possible Answer** Many women believed this was an area in which they could make a difference in society.

Prohibitionist groups feared that alcohol was undermining American morals. Founded in Cleveland in 1874, the Woman's Christian Temperance Union (WCTU) spearheaded the crusade for prohibition. Members advanced their cause by entering saloons, singing, praying, and urging saloonkeepers to stop selling alcohol. As momentum grew, the Union was transformed by Frances Willard from a small midwestern religious group in 1879 to a national organization. Boasting 245,000 members by 1911, the WCTU became the largest women's group in the nation's history. **A**

**MAIN IDEA**

**Analyzing Motives**
**A** Why did the prohibition movement appeal to so many women?

WCTU members followed Willard's "do everything" slogan and began opening kindergartens for immigrants, visiting

◄ In the 1890s, Carry Nation worked for prohibition by walking into saloons, scolding the customers, and using her hatchet to destroy bottles of liquor.

FLORENCE KELLEY
1859–1932

The daughter of an antislavery Republican congressman from Pennsylvania, Florence Kelley became a social reformer whose sympathies lay with the powerless, especially working women and children. During a long career, Kelley pushed the government to solve America's social problems.

In 1899, Kelley became general secretary of the National Consumers' League, where she lobbied to improve factory conditions. "Why," Kelley pointedly asked while campaigning for a federal child-labor law, "are seals, bears, reindeer, fish, wild game in the national parks, buffalo, [and] migratory birds all found suitable for federal protection, but not children?"

**KEY PLAYER**

**Florence Kelley**
After working at Hull House, Kelley moved to New York and took up residence at the Henry Street Settlement on the Lower East Side. There, she worked closely with its founder, Lillian Wald. Kelley wrote numerous articles and books about child labor and other reform issues. Kelley was instrumental in supporting the landmark labor case *Muller* v. *Oregon*, which concerned the welfare of women in the workplace. Ask students what they think motivated Kelley to spend her life working for such reform. *(Students should infer that Kelley cared deeply about people and was upset by injustices she witnessed.)*

👁 Electronic Library of Primary Sources
· On the Need for Child Labor Laws, 1905, by F. Kelley

**Tracing Themes**
**ECONOMIC OPPORTUNITY**

**Progressivism**
Progressivism was not a single movement. Behind the four goals of progressivism can be seen an effort to redress imbalances, or curb excesses, that had arisen in the period of industrial growth and national expansion following the Civil War. A key to the success of progressive reform was the growth of a national media. Publications such as *McClure's Magazine*, and the growth and expansion of newspapers in major cities, allowed for the dissemination of ideas and debate on a national level.

📄 In-Depth Resources: Unit 3
· Primary Source: Declaration of the WCTU, p. 15

307

**Differentiating Goals**

Some students might have difficulty understanding and differentiating the four goals of progressivism. Have these students create a chart in which they list examples of each goal, write a brief sentence that defines or explains the goal, and write one or two examples from the text. Encourage students to refer to the list during class discussion of the section.

| Goal | Meaning | Example |
|------|---------|---------|
|      |         |         |
|      |         |         |
|      |         |         |
|      |         |         |
|      |         |         |

📄 Integrated Assessment
· Rubric 2

## HISTORICAL SPOTLIGHT

### Anti-Saloon League

Help students understand the feminist background to Prohibition by placing the issue in the context of families in which women did not work. In such circumstances, men could put the security of the entire family in jeopardy by abusing alcohol. Ask students the following question: **What specific reasons did the league have for advocating a ban on alcohol?** *(Among the reasons were religious convictions as well as problem behaviors induced by drinking, including violence, abuse, and job loss.)*

👁 Electronic Library of Primary Sources
· On Prohibition and Liberty, 1914, by P. Andreac

## More About . . .

### Eugene V. Debs

Debs was a union organizer who led the Pullman strike of 1894. He was jailed for his actions in the strike. Debs was convicted of contempt of court for violating an injunction under the Sherman Anti-Trust Act. Debs was among the early founders of the Socialist Party of America. He ran for president five times: in 1900, 1904, 1908, 1912, and 1920. Debs ran his 1920 campaign from prison and received nearly one million votes.

👁 Electronic Library of Primary Sources
· The Taylor System, 1912, by F. Taylor

---

### HISTORICAL SPOTLIGHT

#### ANTI–SALOON LEAGUE

Quietly founded by progressive women in 1895, the Anti-Saloon League called itself "the Church in action against the saloon." Whereas early temperance efforts had asked individuals to change their ways, the Anti-Saloon League worked to pass laws to force people to change and to punish those who drank.

The Anti-Saloon League endorsed politicians who opposed "Demon Rum," no matter which party they belonged to or where they stood on other issues. It also organized statewide referendums to ban alcohol. Between 1900 and 1917, voters in nearly half of the states—mostly in the South and the West—prohibited the sale, production, and use of alcohol. Individual towns, city wards, and rural areas also voted themselves "dry."

---

inmates in prisons and asylums, and working for suffrage. The WCTU reform activities, like those of the settlement-house movement, provided women with expanded public roles, which they used to justify giving women voting rights.

Sometimes efforts at prohibition led to trouble with immigrant groups. Such was the case with the Anti-Saloon League, founded in 1895. As members sought to close saloons to cure society's problems, tension arose between them and many immigrants, whose customs often included the consumption of alcohol. Additionally, saloons filled a number of roles within the immigrant community such as cashing paychecks and serving meals.

**CREATING ECONOMIC REFORM** As moral reformers sought to change individual behavior, a severe economic panic in 1893 prompted some Americans to question the capitalist economic system. As a result, some Americans, especially workers, embraced socialism. Labor leader Eugene V. Debs, who helped organize the American Socialist Party in 1901, commented on the uneven balance among big business, government, and ordinary people under the free-market system of capitalism.

**Background**
See *capitalism* and *socialism* on pages R38 and R44 in the Economics Handbook.

**A PERSONAL VOICE** EUGENE V. DEBS

"Competition was natural enough at one time, but do you think you are competing today? Many of you think you are competing. Against whom? Against [oil magnate John D.] Rockefeller? About as I would if I had a wheelbarrow and competed with the Santa Fe [railroad] from here to Kansas City."

—*Debs: His Life, Writings and Speeches*

Though most progressives distanced themselves from socialism, they saw the truth of many of Debs's criticisms. Big business often received favorable treatment from government officials and politicians and could use its economic power to limit competition.

Journalists who wrote about the corrupt side of business and public life in mass circulation magazines during the early 20th century became known as **muckrakers** (mŭk′rāk′r). (The term refers to John Bunyan's "Pilgrim's Progress," in which a character is so busy using a rake to clean up the muck of this world that he does not raise his eyes to heaven.) In her "History of the Standard Oil Company," a monthly serial in *McClure's Magazine*, the writer Ida M. Tarbell described the company's cutthroat methods of eliminating competition. "Mr. Rockefeller has systematically played with loaded dice," Tarbell charged, "and it is doubtful if there has been a time since 1872 when he has run a race with a competitor and started fair." **B**

**FOSTERING EFFICIENCY** Many progressive leaders put their faith in experts and scientific principles to make society and the workplace more efficient. In defending an Oregon law that limited women factory and laundry workers to a ten-hour day, lawyer Louis D. Brandeis paid little attention to legal argument. Instead, he focused on data produced by social scientists documenting the high costs of long working hours for both the individual and society. This type of argument—the "Brandeis brief"—would become a model for later reform litigation.

Within industry, Frederick Winslow Taylor began using time and motion studies to improve efficiency by breaking manufacturing tasks into simpler parts. "Taylorism" became a management fad, as industry reformers applied these **scientific management** studies to see just how quickly each task could be performed.

**MAIN IDEA**

**Evaluating**
**B** What contribution did muckrakers make to the reform movement?

*B. Answer* Muckrakers exposed the dangers and corruption of industrial life to the public.

---

**ACTIVITY**  **LINK TO LITERATURE**   **classzone.com**

### Writers as Muckrakers

**Class Time** Two class periods

**Task** Researching the activities of muckrakers and their ability to bring about change

**Purpose** To deepen understanding of the influence of muckrakers on politics and public policy

**Directions** Have small groups choose one of the following writers: Lincoln Steffens, Ida Tarbell, Upton Sinclair, or Ray Stannard Baker. Using library and Internet resources, they should find titles of significant books and articles the authors wrote, abuses they attacked, and reforms that resulted from their writing. Have students compile their findings in a chart and share their work with the rest of the class. Interested students might present passages from some of these works to the class.

◄ Workers at the Ford flywheel factory cope with the demanding pace of the assembly line to earn five dollars a day—a good wage in 1914.

However, not all workers could work at the same rate, and although the introduction of the assembly lines did speed up production, the system required people to work like machines. This caused a high worker turnover, often due to injuries suffered by fatigued workers. To keep automobile workers happy and to prevent strikes, Henry Ford reduced the workday to eight hours and paid workers five dollars a day. This incentive attracted thousands of workers, but they exhausted themselves. As one homemaker complained in a letter to Henry Ford in 1914, "That $5 is a blessing—a bigger one than you know but oh they earn it."

Such efforts at improving efficiency, an important part of progressivism, targeted not only industry, but government as well. **C**

---

**MAIN IDEA**

**Contrasting**
**C** Contrast the goals of scientific management with other progressive reforms.

*C. Answer*
Scientific management reformers worked to improve efficiency and productivity, while other reformers aimed at improving behavior or addressing economic inequality.

---

*" Everybody will be able to afford [a car], and about everyone will have one."*
**HENRY FORD, 1909**

## Cleaning Up Local Government ❷

Cities faced some of the most obvious social problems of the new industrial age. In many large cities, political bosses rewarded their supporters with jobs and kickbacks and openly bought votes with favors and bribes. Efforts to reform city politics stemmed in part from the desire to make government more efficient and more responsive to its constituents. But those efforts also grew from distrust of immigrants' participation in politics.

**REFORMING LOCAL GOVERNMENT** Natural disasters sometimes played an important role in prompting reform of city governments. In 1900, a hurricane and tidal wave almost demolished Galveston, Texas. The politicians on the city council botched the huge relief and rebuilding job so badly that the Texas legislature appointed a five-member commission of experts to take over. Each expert took charge of a different city department, and soon Galveston was rebuilt. This success prompted the city to adopt the commission idea as a form of government, and by 1917, 500 cities had followed Galveston's example.

Another natural disaster—a flood in Dayton, Ohio, in 1913—led to the widespread adoption of the council-manager form of government. Staunton, Virginia, had already pioneered this system, in which people elected a city council to make laws. The council in turn appointed a manager, typically a person with training and experience in public administration, to run the city's departments. By 1925, managers were administering nearly 250 cities.

*The Progressive Era* **309**

---

## Instruct: Objective ❸

### Reform at the State Level
TAKS SS11 3(US4.B)

· How did reforms protect children?
· How did reforms change working conditions?
· What kinds of political reforms took place at the state level?

 In-Depth Resources: Unit 3
  · Guided Reading, p. 1
  · Primary Sources: Child Labor in the Coal Mines, p. 16

 Critical Thinking Transparencies CT51
  · Child Labor, 1890–1930

---

## HISTORICAL SPOTLIGHT

### James S. Hogg

Hogg saw his job as making war on the unscrupulous businesses that plagued Texas. A popular governor who accomplished a great deal in his first two-year term, Hogg was reelected to office in 1892. Hogg served a total of four years as governor of Texas. Ask students why they think Hogg was a staunch supporter of anti-trust legislation and was influential in the establishment of a railroad commission in Texas.

---

## More About . . .

### Robert M. La Follette

La Follette was one of the giants of the progressive movement. As a governor, he instituted a policy called the "Wisconsin Idea." He used University of Wisconsin professors as experts in drafting legislation and running governmental commissions. Later, as a U.S. senator, he tackled the power of the big banks. In 1924, he ran for president as the candidate of the Progressive Party.

 In-Depth Resources: Unit 3
  · American Lives: Robert M. La Follette, p. 22

---

**REFORM MAYORS** In some cities, mayors such as Hazen Pingree of Detroit, Michigan (1890–1897), and Tom Johnson of Cleveland, Ohio (1901–1909), introduced progressive reforms without changing how government was organized.

Concentrating on economics, Pingree instituted a fairer tax structure, lowered fares for public transportation, rooted out corruption, and set up a system of work relief for the unemployed. Detroit city workers built schools, parks, and a municipal lighting plant.

Johnson was only one of 19 socialist mayors who worked to institute progressive reforms in America's cities. In general, these mayors focused on dismissing corrupt and greedy private owners of utilities—such as gasworks, waterworks, and transit lines—and converting the utilities to publicly owned enterprises. Johnson believed that citizens should play a more active role in city government. He held meetings in a large circus tent and invited them to question officials about how the city was managed. **D**

## ❸ Reform at the State Level

 Mini-Lesson 1: SS11 4(US4.A)

Local reforms coincided with progressive efforts at the state level. Spurred by progressive governors, many states passed laws to regulate railroads, mines, mills, telephone companies, and other large businesses.

**REFORM GOVERNORS** Under the progressive Republican leadership of **Robert M. La Follette,** Wisconsin led the way in regulating big business. "Fighting Bob" La Follette served three terms as governor before he entered the U.S. Senate in 1906. He explained that, as governor, he did not mean to "smash corporations, but merely to drive them out of politics, and then to treat them exactly the same as other people are treated."

La Follette's major target was the railroad industry. He taxed railroad property at the same rate as other business property, set up a commission to regulate rates, and forbade railroads to issue free passes to state officials. Other reform governors who attacked big business interests included Charles B. Aycock of North Carolina and James S. Hogg of Texas.

**PROTECTING WORKING CHILDREN** As the number of child workers rose dramatically, reformers worked to protect workers and to end child labor. Businesses hired children because they performed unskilled jobs for lower wages and because children's small hands made them more adept at handling small parts and tools. Immigrants and rural migrants often sent their children to work because they viewed their children as part of the family economy. Often wages were so low for adults that every family member needed to work to pull the family out of poverty.

In industrial settings, however, children were more prone to accidents caused by fatigue. Many developed serious health problems and suffered from stunted growth. **E**

Formed in 1904, the National Child Labor Committee sent investigators to gather evidence of children working in harsh conditions. They then organized exhibitions with photographs and statistics to dramatize the children's plight. They were joined by labor union members who argued that child labor lowered wages for all workers. These groups pressured

**HISTORICAL SPOTLIGHT**

**JAMES S. HOGG, TEXAS GOVERNOR (1891–1895)**
Among the most colorful of the reform governors was James S. Hogg of Texas. Hogg helped to drive illegal insurance companies from the state and championed antitrust legislation. His chief interest, however, was in regulating the railroads. He pointed out abuses in rates—noting, for example, that it cost more to ship lumber from East Texas to Dallas than to ship it all the way to Nebraska. A railroad commission, established largely as a result of his efforts, helped increase milling and manufacturing in Texas by lowering freight rates.

**MAIN IDEA**

**Summarizing**
**D** How did city government change during the Progressive Era?

*D. Answer* The commission system and council-manager system were introduced; some reform mayors made citizens more active in managing cities.

*E. Answer* Businesses exploited children, paying them low wages and forcing them to work long hours in dangerous conditions.

**MAIN IDEA**

**Analyzing Causes**
**E** Why did reformers seek to end child labor?

---

**ACTIVITY    SKILLBUILDER LESSON**

 **BLOCK SCHEDULING**

### Formulating Historical Questions

**Explaining the Skill** Asking questions about events and issues helps historians focus their research to find meaningful information and to reach new insights. In examining historical issues, a historian might also ask about the source of the information, the possible causes of the event, and what influence the issue or event had on the future.

**Applying the Skill** Review the progressive efforts to end child labor. Ask students why employers used child labor, why families allowed children to work, and why reformers opposed child labor. *(Children worked for lower wages and could work in small places with small tools. Children's income was needed for the family. Child labor was harmful to children and kept wages low for adults.)*

 In-Depth Resources: Unit 3
  · Skillbuilder Practice, p. 7

## History Through *Photojournalism*

### IMAGES OF CHILD LABOR

In 1908, Lewis Hine quit his teaching job to document child labor practices. Hine's photographs and descriptions of young laborers—some only three years old—were widely distributed and displayed in exhibits. His compelling images of exploitation helped to convince the public of the need for child labor regulations.

Hine devised a host of clever tactics to gain access to his subjects, such as learning shop managers' schedules and arriving during their lunch breaks. While talking casually with the children, he secretly scribbled notes on paper hidden in his pocket.

Because of their small size, spindle boys and girls *(top)* were forced to climb atop moving machinery to replace parts. For four-year-old Mary *(left)*, shucking two pots of oysters was a typical day's work.

**SKILLBUILDER** Interpreting Visual Sources
1. Lewis Hine believed in the power of photography to move people to action. What elements of these photographs do you find most striking?
2. Why do you think Hine was a successful photographer?

SEE SKILLBUILDER HANDBOOK, PAGE R23.

### Interpreting a Photograph

Ask students what they find unusual about the photograph. *(Students should find the sight of children working with factory machinery unusual. They should notice the age of the boys and their bare feet.)* Ask what dangers they think the children faced. *(Students should realize that the machinery could be dangerous to hands and feet, and that such factories could be dangerous places for children.)*

### SKILLBUILDER ANSWERS

1. Answers will vary. Most students may refer to the young age of the children pictured and the poor conditions they endured.
2. Students may suggest that Hine's ability to capture candid scenes at close range made his photographs realistic portrayals of daily life.

### More About . . .

### Louis D. Brandeis

Brandeis was the son of Czech Jews who immigrated to America in 1849. He was born and raised in Louisville, Kentucky, and later graduated first in his class at Harvard Law School. Known as the "people's attorney," he defended the constitutionality of several state laws prescribing maximum work hours and minimum wages. He also promoted federal antitrust laws in his 1914 book, *Other People's Money, and How the Bankers Use It,* about the control that investment bankers exercised over American industry. In 1916, President Woodrow Wilson appointed Brandeis to the U.S. Supreme Court. He was the first Jewish person to be so honored. In 1948, seven years after his death, Brandeis University was founded and named in his honor.

---

national politicians to pass the Keating-Owen Act in 1916. The act prohibited the transportation across state lines of goods produced with child labor.

Two years later the Supreme Court declared the act unconstitutional due to interference with states' rights to regulate labor. Reformers did, however, succeed in nearly every state by effecting legislation that banned child labor and set maximum hours.

**EFFORTS TO LIMIT WORKING HOURS** The Supreme Court sometimes took a more sympathetic view of the plight of workers. In the 1908 case of *Muller* v. *Oregon,* Louis D. Brandeis—assisted by Florence Kelley and Josephine Goldmark—persuasively argued that poor working women were much more economically insecure than large corporations. Asserting that women required the state's protection against powerful employers, Brandeis convinced the Court to uphold an Oregon law limiting women to a ten-hour workday. Other states responded by enacting or strengthening laws to reduce women's hours of work. A similar Brandeis brief in *Bunting* v. *Oregon* in 1917 persuaded the Court to uphold a ten-hour workday for men.

Progressives also succeeded in winning workers' compensation to aid the families of workers who were hurt or killed on the job. Beginning with Maryland in 1902, one state after another passed legislation requiring employers to pay benefits in death cases.

*The Progressive Era* **311**

---

**ACTIVITY**   **COOPERATIVE LEARNING**

### Child Labor Briefs

**Class Time** Two class periods

**Task** Formulating and writing briefs on child labor issues

**Purpose** To critically evaluate and compare and contrast different issues teenagers need to know about work situations

**Directions** Divide the class into small groups. Have each group discuss the needs and concerns of people under 18 years old who work or who want to work. Have one group use the Internet to find out what the child labor laws in your state are.

Then have each group compare their ideas with the laws on the books. What would they change? What arguments can they create to support the changes? Ask for students who have a part-time job to share their work experiences with the class. Ask them to comment on whether they receive special treatment because of their ages, and whether they feel they are treated fairly.

**More About . . .**

**Reforming Elections**
Tell students that before the reforms, many members of the city, county, and sometimes state legislature owed their jobs to their party boss. These local parties were run by political bosses who selected almost all candidates for office. So, when the legislature "voted" on the boss' candidate for office, that candidate was sure to win. Today, candidates often have to run in a primary. They must gain approval from a majority of voters.

## Assess & Reteach

### SECTION 1 ASSESSMENT
Have the students work in small groups to answer the questions. Have each group share their answer to question 3 with the class.

 Formal Assessment
· Section Quiz, p. 170

### SELF-ASSESSMENT
Ask students to write two paragraphs—one summarizing what they learned about reform movements, and a second stating which reforms they found most important.

### RETEACH
Have students work in groups to outline one of the three subsections of Section 1. They should use the boldface headings as main ideas and fill in supporting details.

 In-Depth Resources: Unit 3
· Reteaching Activity, p. 8

---

**REFORMING ELECTIONS** In some cases, ordinary citizens won state reforms. William S. U'Ren prompted his state of Oregon to adopt the secret ballot (also called the Australian ballot), the initiative, the referendum, and the recall. The initiative and referendum gave citizens the power to create laws. Citizens could petition to place an **initiative**—a bill originated by the people rather than lawmakers—on the ballot. Then voters, instead of the legislature, accepted or rejected the initiative by **referendum,** a vote on the initiative. The **recall** enabled voters to remove public officials from elected positions by forcing them to face another election before the end of their term if enough voters asked for it. By 1920, 20 states had adopted at least one of these procedures. **F**

In 1899, Minnesota passed the first mandatory statewide primary system. This enabled voters, instead of political machines, to choose candidates for public office through a special popular election. About two-thirds of the states had adopted some form of direct primary by 1915.

**DIRECT ELECTION OF SENATORS** It was the success of the direct primary that paved the way for the Seventeenth Amendment to the Constitution. Before 1913, each state's legislature had chosen its own United States senators, which put even more power in the hands of party bosses and wealthy corporation heads. To force senators to be more responsive to the public, progressives pushed for the popular election of senators. At first, the Senate refused to go along with the idea, but gradually more and more states began allowing voters to nominate senatorial candidates in direct primaries. As a result, Congress approved the **Seventeenth Amendment** in 1912. Its ratification in 1913 made direct election of senators the law of the land.

Government reform—including efforts to give Americans more of a voice in electing their legislators and creating laws—drew increased numbers of women into public life. It also focused renewed attention on the issue of woman suffrage.

> **MAIN IDEA**
> **Summarizing**
> **F** Summarize the impact of the direct election of senators.
>
> *F. Answer*
> Members of the Senate were no longer appointed by state legislatures, over whom special interests had influence. Instead senators were elected by popular vote.

## 1 ASSESSMENT

**1. TERMS & NAMES** For each term or name, write a sentence explaining its significance.

- progressive movement
- Florence Kelley
- prohibition
- muckraker
- scientific management
- Robert M. La Follette
- initiative
- referendum
- recall
- Seventeenth Amendment

### MAIN IDEA

**2. TAKING NOTES**
Copy the web below on your paper. Fill it in with examples of organizations that worked for reform in the areas named.

Which group was most successful and why?

### CRITICAL THINKING

**3. FORMING GENERALIZATIONS**
In what ways might Illinois, Wisconsin, and Oregon all be considered trailblazers in progressive reform? Support your answers. **Think About:**
- legislative and electoral reforms at the state level
- the leadership of William U'Ren and Robert La Follette
- Florence Kelley's appointment as chief inspector of factories for Illinois

**4. INTERPRETING VISUAL SOURCES**
This cartoon shows Carry Nation inside a saloon that she has attacked. Do you think the cartoonist had a favorable or unfavorable opinion of this prohibitionist? Explain.

---

 **ASSESSMENT** Answers

**1. TERMS & NAMES**
progressive movement, p. 307
Florence Kelley, p. 307
prohibition, p. 307
muckraker, p. 308
scientific management, p. 308
Robert M. La Follette, p. 310
initiative, p. 312
referendum, p. 312
recall, p. 312
Seventeenth Amendment, p. 312

**2. TAKING NOTES**
**Social Welfare**—YMCA; Salvation Army
**Moral**—WCTU; Anti-Saloon League
**Economic**—American Socialist Party; muckrakers
**Political**—National Child Labor Committee
Students should give reasons for their choice of the most successful group.

**3. FORMING GENERALIZATIONS**
Reforms first instituted in Illinois, Wisconsin, and Oregon soon spread to other states: Illinois—prohibition of child labor and limit of women's working hours; Wisconsin—regulation of big business and adoption of the direct primary; Oregon—adoption of the secret ballot, the initiative, the referendum, and the recall.

**4. INTERPRETING VISUAL SOURCES**
The cartoonist portrays Carry Nation as a tough and destructive character. She has demolished the inside of the bar and frightened the bartender.

# Women in Public Life

| MAIN IDEA | WHY IT MATTERS NOW | Terms & Names |
|---|---|---|
| As a result of social and economic change, many women entered public life as workers and reformers. | Women won new opportunities in labor and education that are enjoyed today. | •NACW  •Susan B. Anthony  •suffrage  •NAWSA |

**U.S. History**
TEKS
2B, 2C, 4B, 10A, 18A, 18B, 21A, 21D, 22A, 22C, 24B, 25A, 25B, 25D

### One American's Story

In 1879, Susette La Flesche, a young Omaha woman, traveled east to translate into English the sad words of Chief Standing Bear, whose Ponca people had been forcibly removed from their homeland in Nebraska. Later, she was invited with Chief Standing Bear to go on a lecture tour to draw attention to the Ponca's situation.

#### A PERSONAL VOICE  SUSETTE LA FLESCHE

" We are thinking men and women. . . . We have a right to be heard in whatever concerns us. Your government has driven us hither and thither like cattle. . . . Your government has no right to say to us, Go here, or Go there, and if we show any reluctance, to force us to do its will at the point of the bayonet. . . . Do you wonder that the Indian feels outraged by such treatment and retaliates, although it will end in death to himself? "

—quoted in *Bright Eyes*

▲ Susette La Flesche

La Flesche testified before congressional committees and helped win passage of the Dawes Act of 1887, which allowed individual Native Americans to claim reservation land and citizenship rights. Her activism was an example of a new role for American women, who were expanding their participation in public life.

## ① Women in the Work Force

Before the Civil War, married middle-class women were generally expected to devote their time to the care of their homes and families. By the late 19th century, however, only middle-class and upper-class women could afford to do so. Poorer women usually had no choice but to work for wages outside the home.

**FARM WOMEN**  On farms in the South and the Midwest, women's roles had not changed substantially since the previous century. In addition to household tasks such as cooking, making clothes, and laundering, farm women handled a host of other chores such as raising livestock. Often the women had to help plow and plant the fields and harvest the crops.

**WOMEN IN INDUSTRY**  As better-paying opportunities became available in towns, and especially cities, women had new options for finding jobs, even though men's labor unions excluded them from membership. At the turn of the century,

*The Progressive Era*  **313**

---

### OBJECTIVES

1 Describe the growing presence of women in the workforce at the turn of the 20th century.

2 Identify leaders of the woman suffrage movement.

3 Explain how woman suffrage was achieved.

### CRITICAL THINKING

Analyzing Causes, p. 314
Analyzing Effects, p. 315
Making Inferences, p. 316
Synthesizing, p. 316
Analyzing Issues, p. 316

## Focus & Motivate

Ask students whether they think boys and girls have the same opportunities. Do they think men and women should have equal rights in public life? Would they vote for a woman for president?

## Instruct

### Instruct: Objective ①

**Women in the Work Force**
TAKS SS11 3(US21.D)
· What kind of work was available to American women before the Civil War?
· How did women's pay compare with men's pay in factories?
· Why did women take white-collar jobs?

📄 In-Depth Resources: Unit 3
· Guided Reading, p. 2

---

## PROGRAM RESOURCES

 **In-Depth Resources: Unit 3**
· Guided Reading, p. 2
· Reteaching Activity, p. 9
· Primary Sources: Political Poster, p. 17; *from* "The Status of Woman" by Susan B. Anthony, p. 18

 **Reading Study Guide** (English and Spanish), pp. 93–94

 **Access for Students Acquiring English/ESL**
· Guided Reading (Spanish), p. 114

 **Formal Assessment**
· Section Quiz, p. 171

**Integrated Assessment**
· Rubrics

### INTEGRATED TECHNOLOGY

👁 Electronic Library of Primary Sources

ⓘ classzone.com

### TEXAS RESOURCES

 TAKS Spiraled Content Review

 TAKS Practice Tests

 TAKS Practice Transparencies TT63

 TAKS Online Test Practice

◀ Telephone operators manually connect phone calls in 1915.

## Instruct: Objective ❷

### Women Lead Reform

**TAKS SS11 3(US24.B)**
· How did the opening of women's colleges help create new opportunities for women?
· Why were there women leaders in the movements to reform social welfare, public morals, and race relations?
· How did Susan B. Anthony help the cause of women?

 **In-Depth Resources: Unit 3**
· Guided Reading p. 2
· Primary Sources: Political Poster, p. 17; *from* "The Status of Woman" by Susan B. Anthony, p. 18

**NOW & THEN**

**TELEPHONE OPERATORS**
Today, when Americans use the telephone, an automated voice often greets them with instructions about which buttons to press. In the 19th century, every telephone call had to be handled by a telephone operator, a person who connected wires through a switchboard.

Young men, the first telephone operators, proved unsatisfactory. Patrons complained that the male operators used profane language and talked back to callers. Women soon largely replaced men as telephone operators, and were willing to accept the ten-dollar weekly wage.

Department stores advertised shopping by telephone as a convenience. One ad in the Chicago telephone book of 1904 declared, "Every [telephone] order, inquiry, or request will be quickly and intelligently cared for." The ad pictured a line of female telephone operators.

one out of five American women held jobs; 25 percent of them worked in manufacturing.

The garment trade claimed about half of all women industrial workers. They typically held the least skilled positions, however, and received only about half as much money as their male counterparts or less. Many of these women were single and were assumed to be supporting only themselves, while men were assumed to be supporting families.

Women also began to fill new jobs in offices, stores, and classrooms. These jobs required a high school education, and by 1890, women high school graduates outnumbered men. Moreover, new business schools were preparing bookkeepers and stenographers, as well as training female typists to operate the new machines. **Ⓐ**

**DOMESTIC WORKERS** Many women without formal education or industrial skills contributed to the economic survival of their families by doing domestic work, such as cleaning for other families. After almost 2 million African-American women were freed from slavery, poverty quickly drove nearly half of them into the work force. They worked on farms and as domestic workers, and migrated by the thousands to big cities for jobs as cooks, laundresses, scrubwomen, and maids. Altogether, roughly 70 percent of women employed in 1870 were servants.

Unmarried immigrant women also did domestic labor, especially when they first arrived in the United States. Many married immigrant women contributed to the family income by taking in piecework or caring for boarders at home.

## ❷ Women Lead Reform

Dangerous conditions, low wages, and long hours led many female industrial workers to push for reforms. Their ranks grew after 146 workers, mostly young women, died in a 1911 fire in the Triangle Shirtwaist Factory in New York City. Middle- and upper-class women also entered the public sphere. By 1910, women's clubs, at which these women discussed art or literature, were nearly half a million strong. These clubs sometimes grew into reform groups that addressed issues such as temperance or child labor.

**WOMEN IN HIGHER EDUCATION** Many of the women who became active in public life in the late 19th century had attended the new women's colleges. Vassar

**314** CHAPTER 9

---

College—with a faculty of 8 men and 22 women—accepted its first students in 1865. Smith and Wellesley Colleges followed in 1875. Though Columbia, Brown, and Harvard Colleges refused to admit women, each university established a separate college for women.

Although women were still expected to fulfill traditional domestic roles, women's colleges sought to grant women an excellent education. In her will, Smith College's founder, Sophia Smith, made her goals clear.

**A PERSONAL VOICE** SOPHIA SMITH

" [It is my desire] to furnish for my own sex means and facilities for education equal to those which are afforded now in our College to young men. . . . It is not my design to render my sex any the less feminine, but to develop as fully as may be the powers of womanhood & furnish women with means of usefulness, happiness, & honor now withheld from them. "

—quoted in *Alma Mater*

---

**MAIN IDEA**

**Analyzing Effects**

**B** What social and economic effects did higher education have on women?

**B. Answer**
Women who attended college no longer relied on marriage as their only option; some pursued professional careers, while others did volunteer reform work.

---

By the late 19th century, marriage was no longer a woman's only alternative. Many women entered the work force or sought higher education. In fact, almost half of college-educated women in the late 19th century never married, retaining their own independence. Many of these educated women began to apply their skills to needed social reforms. **B**

**WOMEN AND REFORM** Uneducated laborers started efforts to reform workplace health and safety. The participation of educated women often strengthened existing reform groups and provided leadership for new ones. Because women were not allowed to vote or run for office, women reformers strove to improve conditions at work and home. Their "social housekeeping" targeted workplace reform, housing reform, educational improvement, and food and drug laws.

In 1896, African-American women founded the National Association of Colored Women, or **NACW**, by merging two earlier organizations. Josephine Ruffin identified the mission of the African-American women's club movement as "the moral education of the race with which we are identified." The NACW managed nurseries, reading rooms, and kindergartens.

After the Seneca Falls convention of 1848, women split over the Fourteenth and Fifteenth Amendments, which granted equal rights including the right to vote to African American men, but excluded women. **Susan B. Anthony,** a leading proponent of woman **suffrage,** the right to vote, said "[I] would sooner cut off my right hand than ask the ballot for the black man and not for women." In 1869 Anthony and Elizabeth Cady Stanton had founded the National Women Suffrage Association (NWSA), which united with another group in 1890 to

Suffragists recruit supporters for a march.
▼

**HISTORY from VISUALS**

**Interpreting the Photograph**
Remind students that one of the First Amendment freedoms is the freedom of assembly. Peaceful demonstration is one way to bring people's attention to a cause in order to recruit supporters and initiate debate. Help students pay close attention to the details: the matching dresses, the coordinated umbrellas, and the "rain or shine" theme.

**ACTIVITY** | **COOPERATIVE LEARNING**

**BLOCK SCHEDULING**

## Creating Political Placards

**Class Time** 45 minutes

**Task** Creating placards or signs that demonstrators in favor of woman suffrage might carry

**Purpose** To understand the history and goals of the woman suffrage movement

**Directions** Have groups of students make a list of slogans. Then, have each group make one or two placards that can be displayed at a rally for woman suffrage. They can use the text and other resources, including the Internet, for additional information. Bring the class together for a review of the placards and discussion. Students could also vote on the most effective slogan.

 Integrated Assessment
· Rubric 4

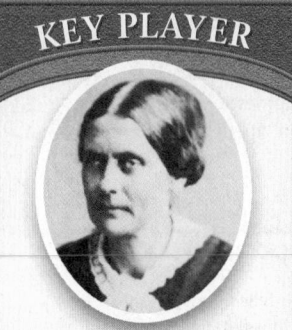

**KEY PLAYER**

**Susan B. Anthony**

Anthony was reviled and scorned in her early years as a leader of the woman suffrage movement. By the 1890s, she had become a national heroine, welcomed at the World Columbian Exposition in Chicago in 1893 and various other national and international meetings. Ask students how they think Susan B. Anthony felt being treated as a national heroine after years of hostile receptions. *(Students might infer that while cheers are more welcome than boos, Anthony might have still have been frustrated since woman suffrage had not yet been enacted.)*

👁 Electronic Library of Primary Sources
· from *The United States of America* v. *Susan B. Anthony*, 1873

## Assess & Reteach

### SECTION 2 ASSESSMENT

Have gifted students work with less proficient readers to answer the questions in the Section Assessment.

📄 Formal Assessment
· Section Quiz, p. 171

### SELF-ASSESSMENT

Have pairs of students use the Main Idea questions to review the main ideas in this section. Students should locate the portion of the text that helps answer each question.

### RETEACH

Use the Section Quiz to help students understand the section's key concepts.

📖 In-Depth Resources: Unit 3
· Reteaching Activity, p. 9

---

**KEY PLAYER**

**SUSAN B. ANTHONY**
**1820–1906**

Born to a strict Quaker family, Susan B. Anthony was not allowed to enjoy typical childhood entertainment such as music, games, and toys. Her father insisted on self-discipline, education, and a strong belief system for all of his eight children. At an early age, Anthony developed a positive view of womanhood from a teacher named Mary Perkins who educated the children in their home.

After voting illegally in the presidential election of 1872, Anthony was fined $100 at her trial. "Not a penny shall go to this unjust claim," she defiantly declared. She never paid the fine.

---

become the National American Woman Suffrage Association, or **NAWSA.** Other prominent leaders included Lucy Stone and Julia Ward Howe, the author of "The Battle Hymn of the Republic."

Woman suffrage faced constant opposition. The liquor industry feared that women would vote in support of prohibition, while the textile industry worried that women would vote for restrictions on child labor. Many men simply feared the changing role of women in society.

**A THREE-PART STRATEGY FOR SUFFRAGE** Suffragist leaders tried three approaches to achieve their objective. First, they tried to convince state legislatures to grant women the right to vote. They achieved a victory in the territory of Wyoming in 1869, and by the 1890s Utah, Colorado, and Idaho had also granted voting rights to women. After 1896, efforts in other states failed.

Second, women pursued court cases to test the Fourteenth Amendment, which declared that states denying their male citizens the right to vote would lose congressional representation. Weren't women citizens, too? In 1871 and 1872, Susan B. Anthony and other women tested that question by attempting to vote at least 150 times in ten states and the District of Columbia. The Supreme Court ruled in 1875 that women were indeed citizens—but then denied that citizenship automatically conferred the right to vote.

Third, women pushed for a national constitutional amendment to grant women the vote. Stanton succeeded in having the amendment introduced in California, but it was killed later. For the next 41 years, women lobbied to have it reintroduced, only to see it continually voted down. **C**

Before the turn of the century, the campaign for suffrage achieved only modest success. Later, however, women's reform efforts paid off in improvements in the treatment of workers and in safer food and drug products—all of which President Theodore Roosevelt supported, along with his own plans for reforming business, labor, and the environment.

*C. Answer* The leaders hoped that by pursuing several strategies they were more likely to achieve their goal.

**MAIN IDEA**

**Making Inferences**
**C** Why did suffragist leaders employ a three-part strategy for gaining the right to vote?

---

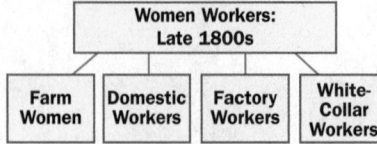

**SECTION 2 ASSESSMENT**

**1. TERMS & NAMES** For each term or name, write a sentence explaining its significance.
• NACW          • suffrage          • Susan B. Anthony          • NAWSA

**MAIN IDEA**

**2. TAKING NOTES**
In a chart like the one below, fill in details about working women in the late 1800s.

> **Women Workers: Late 1800s**
> Farm Women | Domestic Workers | Factory Workers | White-Collar Workers

What generalizations can you make about women workers at this time?

**CRITICAL THINKING**

**3. SYNTHESIZING**
What women and movements during the Progressive Era helped dispel the stereotype that women were submissive and nonpolitical?

**4. MAKING INFERENCES**
Why do you think some colleges refused to accept women in the late 19th century?

**5. ANALYZING ISSUES**
Imagine you are a woman during the Progressive Era. Explain how you might recruit other women to support the following causes: improving education, housing reform, food and drug laws, the right to vote. **Think About:**
• the problems that each movement was trying to remedy
• how women benefited from each cause

**316** CHAPTER 9

---

 **ASSESSMENT** Answers

**1. TERMS & NAMES**
NACW, p. 315
suffrage, p. 315
Susan B. Anthony, p. 315
NAWSA, p. 316

**2. TAKING NOTES**
**Farm Women**—domestic work and farm labor
**Domestic Workers**—servants, cooks, laundresses, maids; often African Americans or immigrants
**Factory Workers**—manufacturing, garment trades; often single women
**White-collar Workers**—stenographers, typists, bookkeepers, teachers; required high school or business degree

**3. SYNTHESIZING**
Women speaking out on reform subjects, including Susan B. Anthony, Elizabeth Cady Stanton, Lucy Stone, and Julia Ward Howe, and organizations such as NAWSA and the NACW.

**4. MAKING INFERENCES**
Many people believed that a woman's place was in the home and that higher education should be reserved for men.

**5. ANALYZING ISSUES**
Public demonstrations, soliciting with flyers and information, and public speaking were ways to inform other women and gain their support. Students may refer to how winning the right to vote would give women a voice in governing or how higher education would allow women to secure better jobs.

# Teddy Roosevelt's Square Deal

| MAIN IDEA | WHY IT MATTERS NOW | Terms & Names |
|---|---|---|
| As president, Theodore Roosevelt worked to give citizens a Square Deal through progressive reforms. | As part of his Square Deal, Roosevelt's conservation efforts made a permanent impact on environmental resources. | •Upton Sinclair •*The Jungle* •Theodore Roosevelt •Square Deal • •Meat Inspection Act •Pure Food and Drug Act •conservation •NAACP |

U.S. History 2A, 2BB, 2C, 4B, 7A, 8A, 11, 12B, 12C, 19A, 19B, 21A, 24A, 24B, 24C, 24D, 24F, 24G, 25A, 25B, 25C, 25D

### One American's Story

When muckraking journalist **Upton Sinclair** began research for a novel in 1904, his focus was the human condition in the stockyards of Chicago. Sinclair intended his novel to reveal "the breaking of human hearts by a system [that] exploits the labor of men and women for profits." What most shocked readers in Sinclair's book *The Jungle* (1906), however, was the sickening conditions of the meatpacking industry.

**A PERSONAL VOICE** UPTON SINCLAIR

" There would be meat that had tumbled out on the floor, in the dirt and sawdust, where the workers had tramped and spit uncounted billions of consumption [tuberculosis] germs. There would be meat stored in great piles in rooms; . . . and thousands of rats would race about on it. . . . A man could run his hand over these piles of meat and sweep off handfuls of the dried dung of rats. These rats were nuisances, and the packers would put poisoned bread out for them; they would die, and then rats, bread, and meat would go into the hoppers together. "

—*The Jungle*

President **Theodore Roosevelt,** like many other readers, was nauseated by Sinclair's account. The president invited the author to visit him at the White House, where Roosevelt promised that "the specific evils you point out shall, if their existence be proved, and if I have the power, be eradicated."

▲ Upton Sinclair poses with his son at the time of the writing of *The Jungle.*

## ❶ A Rough-Riding President

Theodore Roosevelt was not supposed to be president. In 1900, the young governor from New York was urged to run as McKinley's vice-president by the state's political bosses, who found Roosevelt impossible to control. The plot to nominate Roosevelt worked, taking him out of state office. However, as vice-president,

*The Progressive Era* **317**

---

---

When the president spared a bear cub on a hunting expedition, a toymaker marketed a popular new product, the teddy bear.

Roosevelt stood a heartbeat away from becoming president. Indeed, President McKinley had served barely six months of his second term before he was assassinated, making Roosevelt the most powerful person in the government.

**ROOSEVELT'S RISE** Theodore Roosevelt was born into a wealthy New York family in 1858. An asthma sufferer during his childhood, young Teddy drove himself to accomplish demanding physical feats. As a teenager, he mastered marksmanship and horseback riding. At Harvard College, Roosevelt boxed and wrestled.

At an early age, the ambitious Roosevelt became a leader in New York politics. After serving three terms in the New York State Assembly, he became New York City's police commissioner and then assistant secretary of the U.S. Navy. The aspiring politician grabbed national attention, advocating war against Spain in 1898. His volunteer cavalry brigade, the Rough Riders, won public acclaim for its role in the battle at San Juan Hill in Cuba. Roosevelt returned a hero and was soon elected governor of New York and then later the vice-presidency.

**THE MODERN PRESIDENCY** When Roosevelt was thrust into the presidency in 1901, he became the youngest president ever at 42 years old. Unlike previous presidents, Roosevelt soon dominated the news with his many exploits. While in office, Roosevelt enjoyed boxing, although one of his opponents blinded him in the left eye. On another day, he galloped 100 miles on horseback, merely to prove the feat possible.

In politics, as in sports, Roosevelt acted boldly, using his personality and popularity to advance his programs. His leadership and publicity campaigns helped create the modern presidency, making him a model by which all future presidents would be measured. Citing federal responsibility for the national welfare, Roosevelt thought the government should assume control whenever states proved incapable of dealing with problems. He explained, "It is the duty of the president to act upon the theory that he is the steward of the people, and . . . to assume that he has the legal right to do whatever the needs of the people demand, unless the Constitution or the laws explicitly forbid him to do it."

Teddy Roosevelt enjoyed an active lifestyle, as this 1902 photo reveals. ▶

**318**

MAIN IDEA

**Synthesizing**
**A** What actions and characteristics of Teddy Roosevelt contributed to his reputation as the first modern president?

Roosevelt saw the presidency as a "bully pulpit," from which he could influence the news media and shape legislation. If big business victimized workers, then President Roosevelt would see to it that the common people received what he called a **Square Deal.** This term was used to describe the various progressive reforms sponsored by the Roosevelt administration. **A**

## Using Federal Power **2**

Roosevelt's study of history—he published the first of his 42 books at the age of 24—convinced him that modern America required a powerful federal government. "A simple and poor society can exist as a democracy on the basis of sheer individualism," Roosevelt declared, "but a rich and complex industrial society cannot so exist." The young president soon met several challenges to his assertion of federal power.

**Background**
See *trust* on page R47 in the Economics Handbook.

TRUSTBUSTING  By 1900, trusts—legal bodies created to hold stock in many companies—controlled about four-fifths of the industries in the United States. Some trusts, like Standard Oil, had earned poor reputations with the public by the use of unfair business practices. Many trusts lowered their prices to drive competitors out of the market and then took advantage of the lack of competition to jack prices up even higher. Although Congress had passed the Sherman Antitrust Act in 1890, the act's vague language made enforcement difficult. As a result, nearly all the suits filed against the trusts under the Sherman Act were ineffective.

President Roosevelt did not believe that all trusts were harmful, but he sought to curb the actions of those that hurt the public interest. The president concentrated his efforts on filing suits under the Sherman Antitrust Act. In 1902, Roosevelt made newspaper headlines as a trustbuster when he ordered the Justice Department to sue the Northern Securities Company, which had established a monopoly over northwestern railroads. In 1904, the Supreme Court dissolved the company. Although the Roosevelt administration filed 44 antitrust suits, winning a number of them and breaking up some of the trusts, it was unable to slow the merger movement in business.

A. Answer
Roosevelt was an active, forceful, and energetic executive; he used his position to shape legislation and influence the media.

**Instruct: Objective 2**
**Using Federal Power**
TAKS SS11 4(US4.A)
· How did Roosevelt's intervention in a coal strike set a precedent for federal arbitration?
· What did Roosevelt do to the trusts and railroads?

📄 In-Depth Resources: Unit 3
· Guided Reading, p. 3

### Tracing Themes
STATES' RIGHTS

**Roosevelt and the Square Deal**
The significance of the progressive era is not just the reforms that came into being but the precedent for an activist presidency. Roosevelt took office and, unlike past presidents, set the national agenda. There was little precedent for intervention by federal authorities in domestic affairs. Roosevelt expanded the responsibilities of the presidency as described in the Constitution. For example, Roosevelt established a federal role in arbitrating labor disputes and regulating business.

### Analyzing *Political Cartoons*

"THE LION-TAMER"
As part of his Square Deal, President Roosevelt aggressively used the Sherman Antitrust Act of 1890 to attack big businesses engaging in unfair practices. His victory over his first target, the Northern Securities Company, earned him a reputation as a hard-hitting trustbuster committed to protecting the public interest. This cartoon shows Roosevelt trying to tame the wild lions that symbolize the great and powerful companies of 1904.

SKILLBUILDER  Analyzing Political Cartoons
1. What do the lions stand for?
2. Why are all the lions coming out of a door labeled "Wall St."?
3. What do you think the cartoonist thinks about trustbusting? Cite details from the cartoon that support your interpretation.

📁 SEE SKILLBUILDER HANDBOOK, PAGE R24.

THE LION-TAMER

### Analyzing *Political Cartoons*

SKILLBUILDER ANSWERS
1. The lions represent the powerful businessmen who run the trusts.
2. Wall Street stands for the location of the New York Stock Exchange and the power of big corporations.
3. The positive image of Roosevelt suggests that the cartoonist admires Roosevelt's efforts at trustbusting. Roosevelt is not afraid. He welcomes the chance to bring over and curb the power of big business.

*The Progressive Era*   **319**

ACTIVITY   COOPERATIVE LEARNING

 classzone.com

**Creating Political Cartoons**

**Class Time**  45 minutes

**Task**  Creating a page containing four or five political cartoons on a single subject

**Purpose**  To discover how humor and exaggeration can effectively convey political ideas

**Directions**  Divide students into small groups. Have each group select a national political or cultural issue. Tell students to use online resources to find political cartoons on the topic. Each student should download several cartoons. As a whole, the group should select four or five cartoons to mount on posterboard and write a sentence explaining the political idea each one conveys.

**More About . . .**

**1902 Coal Strike**
Federal Intervention suppressed the Pullman Strike of 1894. In the 1902 coal strike, the coal mine operators were astonished when Roosevelt refused to do their bidding.

**More About . . .**

**The ICC and the Hepburn Act**
After 1906 the ICC used its new powers to set and successfully enforce freight rates. Over time, its authority increased to include railroad worker wages and working conditions, water freight rates, and trucking freight rates.

Ask students to compare the ICC's purpose with its performance over time. (Initially, the ICC had no real power and failed at its purpose of setting fair railroad rates. After the Elkins Act (1903) and the Hepburn Act (1906) it became much more successful.)

**NOW & THEN**

**Meat Inspection**
Predicting Effects The outbreak of mad cow disease in Great Britain was reported in 1996. A subsequent outbreak that swept across Europe (France, Spain, Germany) in 2000 brought new attention and concern to the issue of meat inspection.

**Instruct: Objective ❸**

**Health and the Environment**
TAKS SS11 4(US4.A)
· What legislation passed during Roosevelt's presidency protected citizens?
· What did Roosevelt do to protect the environment?

 In-Depth Resources: Unit 3
· Guided Reading, p. 3
· Literature: from *The Jungle* by U. Sinclair, pp. 19–21

**1902 COAL STRIKE** When 140,000 coal miners in Pennsylvania went on strike and demanded a 20 percent raise, a nine-hour workday, and the right to organize a union, the mine operators refused to bargain. Five months into the strike, coal reserves ran low. Roosevelt, seeing the need to intervene, called both sides to the White House to talk, and eventually settled the strike. Irked by the "extraordinary stupidity and bad temper" of the mine operators, he later confessed that only the dignity of the presidency had kept him from taking one owner "by the seat of the breeches" and tossing him out of the window.

Faced with Roosevelt's threat to take over the mines, the opposing sides finally agreed to submit their differences to an arbitration commission—a third party that would work with both sides to mediate the dispute. In 1903, the commission issued its compromise settlement. The miners won a 10 percent pay hike and a shorter, nine-hour workday. With this, however, they had to give up their demand for a closed shop—in which all workers must belong to the union—and their right to strike during the next three years.

*"In life, as in a football game, the principle . . . is: Hit the line hard."*
**THEODORE ROOSEVELT**

President Roosevelt's actions had demonstrated a new principle. From then on, when a strike threatened the public welfare, the federal government was expected to intervene. In addition, Roosevelt's actions reflected the progressive belief that disputes could be settled in an orderly way with the help of experts, such as those on the arbitration commission. **B**

**RAILROAD REGULATION** Roosevelt's real goal was federal regulation. In 1887, Congress had passed the Interstate Commerce Act, which prohibited wealthy railroad owners from colluding to fix high prices by dividing the business in a given area. The Interstate Commerce Commission (ICC) was set up to enforce the new law but had little power. With Roosevelt's urging, Congress passed the Elkins Act in 1903, which made it illegal for railroad officials to give, and shippers to receive, rebates for using particular railroads. The act also specified that railroads could not change set rates without notifying the public.

The Hepburn Act of 1906 strictly limited the distribution of free railroad passes, a common form of bribery. It also gave the ICC power to set maximum railroad rates. Although Roosevelt had to compromise with conservative senators who opposed the act, its passage boosted the government's power to regulate the railroads.

# Health and the Environment

President Roosevelt's enthusiasm and his considerable skill at compromise led to laws and policies that benefited both public health and the environment. He wrote, "We recognize and are bound to war against the evils of today. The remedies are partly economic and partly spiritual, partly to be obtained by laws, and in greater part to be obtained by individual and associated effort."

**REGULATING FOODS AND DRUGS** After reading *The Jungle* by Upton Sinclair, Roosevelt responded to the public's clamor for action. He appointed a commission of experts to investigate the meatpacking industry. The commission issued a scathing report backing up Sinclair's account of the disgusting conditions in the industry. True to his word, in 1906 Roosevelt pushed for passage of the **Meat Inspection Act,**

**NOW & THEN**

**MEAT INSPECTION**
During the Progressive Era, people worried about the kinds of things that might fall—or walk—into a batch of meat being processed. Today, Americans worry more about contamination by unseen dangers, such as E. coli bacteria, mad cow disease, and antibiotics or other chemicals that may pose long-range health risks to people.

In July 1996, Congress passed the most extensive changes in standards for meat inspection since the Meat Inspection Act of 1906. The costs of the new, more scientific inspections amount to about a tenth of a penny per pound of meat. The FDA has also adopted restrictions on importation of feed and livestock from other countries to prevent the spread of disease.

**B. Answer** From that point on, the federal government was expected to play a more active role in settling labor disputes.

**MAIN IDEA**

**Analyzing Effects**
**B** What was significant about the way the 1902 coal strike was settled?

**Vocabulary**
**collude:** to act together secretly to achieve an illegal or deceitful purpose

---

**DIFFERENTIATING INSTRUCTION** | **GIFTED AND TALENTED STUDENTS**

**Books and Public Policy**

Have students do research to find out what impact one of the following books had on public opinion and legislation during the Progressive Era: *Looking Backward* by Edward Bellamy, *The Octopus* by Frank Norris, *The Shame of the Cities* by Lincoln Steffens, *The Jungle* by Upton Sinclair, or *The History of the Standard Oil Company* by Ida Tarbell. Then they should write a summary outlining the impact of the book.

After students have finished their summaries, use a chart similar to the one below to record the impact of each book.

| BOOK | IMPACT |
|---|---|
| Looking Backward | |
| | |
| | |
| | |
| | |

## Coal Mining in the Early 1900s

Coal played a key role in America's industrial boom around the turn of the century, providing the United States with about 90 percent of its energy. Miners often had to dig for coal hundreds of feet below the earth's surface. The work in these mines was among the hardest and most dangerous in the world. Progressive Era reforms helped improve conditions for miners, as many won wage increases and shorter work hours.

The coal mines employed thousands of children, like this boy pictured in 1909. In 1916, progressives helped secure passage of a child labor law that forbade interstate commerce of goods produced by children under the age of 14. ▶

Most underground mines had two shafts—an elevator shaft (shown here) for transporting workers and coal, and an air shaft for ventilation.

◀ Like these men working in 1908, miners typically spent their days in dark, cramped spaces underground.

The miners' main tool was the pick. Many also used drilling machines.

Donkeys or mules pulled the coal cars to the elevators, which transported the coal to the surface.

pillars   air shaft   room   elevator shaft

room

Most mines used a room-and-pillar method for extracting coal. This entailed digging out "rooms" of coal off a series of tunnels, leaving enough coal behind to form a pillar that prevented the room from collapsing.

*The Progressive Era* **321**

### HISTORY from VISUALS

#### Analyzing Diagrams

Coal mining was dirty, dangerous work. Men and boys were underground, breathing coal dust and bad air, for 10 to 12 hours a day. During the winter months, miners went to work and returned home in darkness. Ask students to use the diagram to find out how mines used both old and new technology. (*Students should understand that the use of rail tracks was new technology, and the donkey pulling the cart was old technology.*)

### More About . . .

#### Dangers of Coal Mining

While collapse was a danger for miners, the most feared danger was explosion. Following a fire or explosion, miners would descend into the mines. They carried a canary in a cage down the mineshaft with them. A dead bird meant that the gases were accumulating and it was time to get out.

---

**ACTIVITY** | **LINK TO SCIENCE**

 **BLOCK SCHEDULING**

### Health Hazards of Mining

**Class Time** One class period

**Task** Researching the dangers of coal mining

**Purpose** To understand the dangers faced by coal miners at the start of the 20th century

**Directions** Have students work in groups to research the causes and symptoms of black lung disease, mine explosions and collapses, and other disasters. Students should assemble three or four basic facts about their topic. Then they should illustrate their information, place it in a chart, and report back to the rest of the class.

 Integrated Assessment
· Rubric 1

Government workers inspect meat as it moves through the packinghouse. ▶

which dictated strict cleanliness requirements for meatpackers and created the program of federal meat inspection that was in use until it was replaced by more sophisticated techniques in the 1990s.

The compromise that won the act's passage, however, left the government paying for the inspections and did not require companies to label their canned goods with date-of-processing information. The compromise also granted meatpackers the right to appeal negative decisions in court.

**PURE FOOD AND DRUG ACT** Before any federal regulations were established for advertising food and drugs, manufacturers had claimed that their products accomplished everything from curing cancer to growing hair. In addition, popular children's medicines often contained opium, cocaine, or alcohol. In a series of lectures across the country, Dr. Harvey Washington Wiley, chief chemist at the Department of Agriculture, criticized manufacturers for adding harmful preservatives to food and brought needed attention to this issue.

In 1906, Congress passed the **Pure Food and Drug Act,** which halted the sale of contaminated foods and medicines and called for truth in labeling. Although this act did not ban harmful products outright, its requirement of truthful labels reflected the progressive belief that given accurate information, people would act wisely. **C**

**CONSERVATION AND NATURAL RESOURCES** Before Roosevelt's presidency, the federal government had paid very little attention to the nation's natural resources. Despite the establishment of the U.S. Forest Bureau in 1887 and the subsequent withdrawal from public sale of 45 million acres of timberlands for a national forest reserve, the government stood by while private interests gobbled up the shrinking wilderness.

A typical late-19th-century product advertisement.
▼

HALL'S HAIR RENEWER VEGETABLE SICILIAN

THICKENS THE GROWTH OF THE HAIR, PREVENTS BALDNESS, CURES DANDRUFF, AND RESTORES GRAY HAIR TO ITS ORIGINAL COLOR AND BEAUTY.

R. P. HALL & CO. PROPRIETORS, NASHUA, N.H.

---

**MAIN IDEA**

**Comparing**
**C** What similarities did the Meat Inspection Act and Pure Food and Drug Act share?

*C. Answer* Both acts created regulations that protected consumers' health.

**322** CHAPTER 9

---

In the late 19th century Americans had shortsightedly exploited their natural environment. Pioneer farmers leveled the forests and plowed up the prairies. Ranchers allowed their cattle to overgraze the Great Plains. Coal companies cluttered the land with refuse from mines. Lumber companies ignored the effect of their logging operations on flood control and neglected to plant trees to replace those they had cut down. Cities dumped untreated sewage and industrial wastes into rivers, poisoning the streams and creating health hazards.

**CONSERVATION MEASURES** Roosevelt condemned the view that America's resources were endless and made conservation a primary concern. John Muir, a naturalist and writer with whom Roosevelt camped in California's Yosemite National Park in 1903, persuaded the president to set aside 148 million acres of forest reserves. Roosevelt also set aside 1.5 million acres of water-power sites and another 80 million acres of land that experts from the U.S. Geological Survey would explore for mineral and water resources. Roosevelt also established more than 50 wildlife sanctuaries and several national parks.

True to the Progressive belief in using experts, in 1905 the president named Gifford Pinchot as head of the U.S. Forest Service. A professional conservationist, Pinchot had administrative skill as well as the latest scientific and technical information. He advised Roosevelt to conserve forest and grazing lands by keeping large tracts of federal land exempt from private sale.

Conservationists like Roosevelt and Pinchot, however, did not share the views of Muir, who advocated complete preservation of the wilderness. Instead, **conservation** to them meant that some wilderness areas would be preserved while others would be developed for the common good. Indeed, Roosevelt's federal water projects transformed some dry wilderness areas to make agriculture possible. Under the National Reclamation Act of 1902, known as the Newlands

*Skillbuilder Answers*
1. The West.
2. Roosevelt helped establish a strong conservative movement in the United States.

**HISTORY from VISUALS**

**Interpreting the Map**
Ask students to study the map to determine in which time period the greatest share of lands were acquired. Ask students why they think the lands were added at that time.

## Federal Conservation Lands, 1872–1996

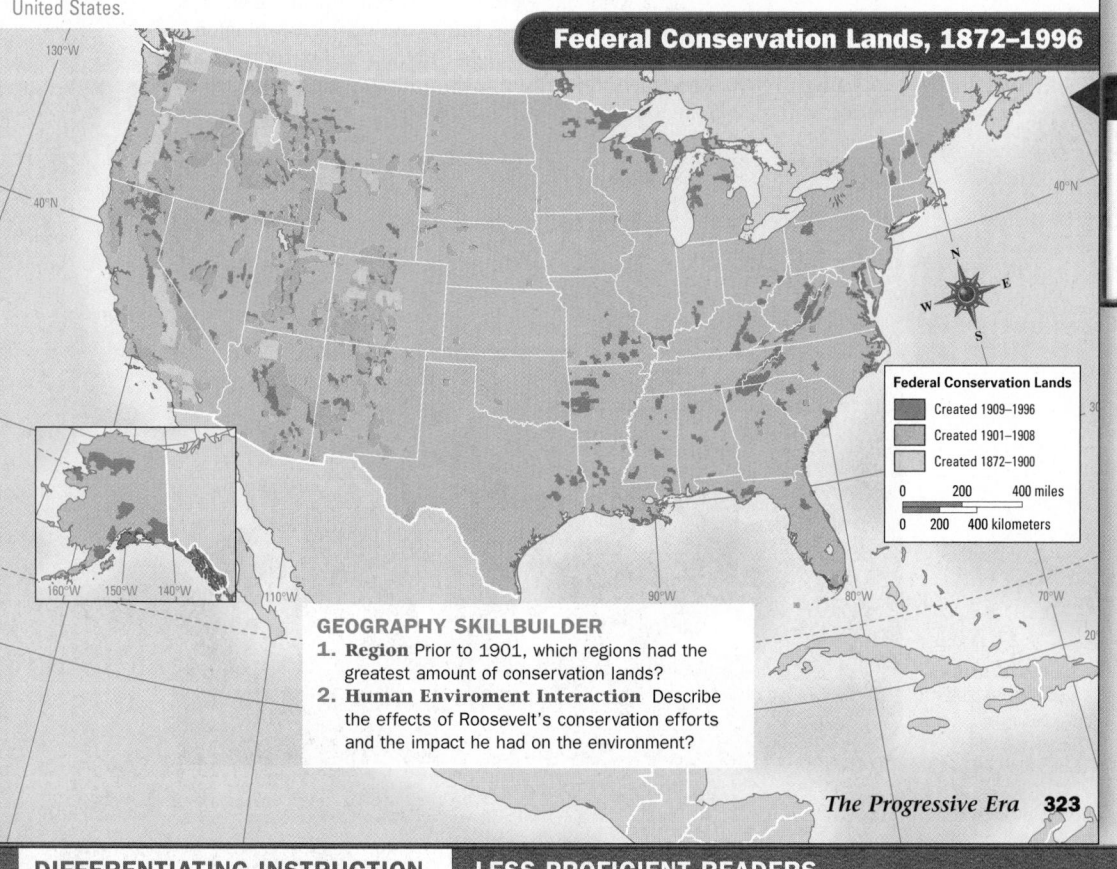

**Federal Conservation Lands**
- Created 1909–1996
- Created 1901–1908
- Created 1872–1900

0    200    400 miles
0    200    400 kilometers

**GEOGRAPHY SKILLBUILDER**
1. **Region** Prior to 1901, which regions had the greatest amount of conservation lands?
2. **Human Enviroment Interaction** Describe the effects of Roosevelt's conservation efforts and the impact he had on the environment?

*The Progressive Era* **323**

---

**DIFFERENTIATING INSTRUCTION**    **LESS PROFICIENT READERS**

### Clarifying Ideas

To help students compare the differing positions of Muir, Roosevelt and Pinchot, and the business interests, have them make a chart similar to the one at right. Label the top line *Land Policy*. Down the left side, list three entries: *John Muir, Roosevelt & Pinchot,* and *Business.* Have students fill in the positions held by the three entries as they read the sections "Conservation and Natural Resources" and "Conservation Measures."

|  | **Land Policy** |
| --- | --- |
| John Muir |  |
| Roosevelt & Pinchot |  |
| Business |  |

## HISTORICAL SPOTLIGHT

### Yosemite National Park

The Yosemite Valley was originally home to the southern Miwok Indians. Yosemite was designated a World Heritage Site by the United Nations Educational, Scientific and Cultural Organization in 1984. Tell students that in the midst of the natural splendor of the Yosemite Valley there are traffic jams into and out of the park in the summer months. Ask them what they think about traffic jams in the wilderness. *(Students should note the irony of so many people wanting to see Yosemite's natural beauty that they cause traffic jams in a wilderness area. )*

### Instruct: Objective ❹

**Roosevelt and Civil Rights**

TAKS SS11 3(US4.B)

· Who was Booker T. Washington?

· Who was W. E. B. Du Bois, and what famous civil rights organization did he help found?

 In-Depth Resources: Unit 3
· Guided Reading, p. 3

## More About . . .

### Booker T. Washington

Washington (1856–1915) was born in Virginia, the son of a slave. He grew up to become a successful educator and spokesman for African Americans. Washington advocated self-improvement. In 1895, he gave a speech in which he urged African Americans to accept their status under Jim Crow laws and to work to improve themselves through vocational training and economic self-reliance. The speech made Washington popular among whites, but Du Bois and other black leaders disagreed with Washington's apparent acceptance of segregation.

**HISTORICAL SPOTLIGHT**

**YOSEMITE NATIONAL PARK**

The naturalist John Muir visited the Yosemite region of central California in 1868 and made it his home base for a period of six years while he traveled throughout the West.

Muir was the first to suggest that Yosemite's spectacular land formations had been shaped by glaciers. Today the park's impressive cliffs, waterfalls, lakes, and meadows draw sports enthusiasts and tourists in all seasons.

Act, money from the sale of public lands in the West funded large-scale irrigation projects, such as the Roosevelt Dam in Arizona and the Shoshone Dam in Wyoming. The Newlands Act established the precedent that the federal government would manage the precious water resources of the West.

## Roosevelt and Civil Rights ❹

Roosevelt's care for the land and its inhabitants was not matched in the area of civil rights. Though Roosevelt's father had supported the North, his mother, Martha, may well have been the model for the Southern belle Scarlet O'Hara in Margaret Mitchell's famous novel, *Gone with the Wind*. In almost two terms as president, Roosevelt—like most other progressives—failed to support civil rights for African Americans. He did, however, support a few individual African Americans.

Despite opposition from whites, Roosevelt appointed an African American as head of the Charleston, South Carolina, customhouse. In another instance, when some whites in Mississippi refused to accept the black postmistress he had appointed, he chose to close the station rather than give in. In 1906, however, Roosevelt angered many African Americans when he dismissed without question an entire regiment of African-American soldiers accused of conspiracy in protecting others charged with murder in Brownsville, Texas.

As a symbolic gesture, Roosevelt invited Booker T. Washington to dinner at the White House. Washington—head of the Tuskegee Normal and Industrial Institute, an all-black training school—was then the African American leader most respected by powerful whites. Washington faced opposition, however, from other African

Civil rights leaders gather at the 1905 Niagara Falls conference. ▶

**MAIN IDEA**

**Summarizing**
ⓓ Summarize Roosevelt's approach to environmental problems.

*D. Answer* Roosevelt worked for conservation, preserving some resources but allowing some to be used, too.

Mini-Lesson 4: SS11 3(US10.B)

---

**DIFFERENTIATING INSTRUCTION** | **GIFTED AND TALENTED STUDENTS**

### Judging the Past with Contemporary Values

Historians and students of history are faced with the challenge of determining cultural context. Particular past events may not adhere to our current value system. Examining race relations in the United States often presents such a dilemma. An action that may have been progressive for its time (for example, Washington's invitation to the White House) may seem regressive by contemporary standards. Ask students to work in groups to consider this dilemma and to propose some standards for viewing the history of race relations in the United States.

Americans, such as W. E. B. Du Bois, for his accommodation of segregationists and for blaming black poverty on blacks and urging them to accept discrimination.

Persistent in his criticism of Washington's ideas, Du Bois renewed his demands for immediate social and economic equality for African Americans. In his 1903 book *The Souls of Black Folk*, Du Bois wrote of his opposition to Washington's position.

Mini-Lesson 2:
SS11 3(US24.B)

### A PERSONAL VOICE · W. E. B. DU BOIS

" So far as Mr. Washington preaches Thrift, Patience, and Industrial Training for the masses, we must hold up his hands and strive with him. . . . But so far as Mr. Washington apologizes for injustice, North or South, does not rightly value the privilege and duty of voting, belittles the emasculating effects of caste distinctions, and opposes the higher training and ambition of our brighter minds,—so far as he, the South, or the Nation, does this,—we must unceasingly and firmly oppose them. "

—*The Souls of Black Folk*

**Background**
The Niagara
Movement was
comprised of 29
black intellectuals.
They met secretly
in 1905 to
compose a civil
rights manifesto.

Du Bois and other advocates of equality for African Americans were deeply upset by the apparent progressive indifference to racial injustice. In 1905 they held a civil rights conference in Niagara Falls, and in 1909 a number of African Americans joined with prominent white reformers in New York to found the **NAACP**—the National Association for the Advancement of Colored People. The NAACP, which had over 6,000 members by 1914, aimed for nothing less than full equality among the races. That goal, however, found little support in the Progressive Movement, which focused on the needs of middle-class whites. The two presidents who followed Roosevelt also did little to advance the goal of racial equality.

**KEY PLAYER**

**W. E. B. DU BOIS**
**1868–1963**

In 1909, W. E. B. Du Bois helped to establish the NAACP and entered into the forefront of the early U.S. civil rights movement. However, in the 1920s, he faced a power struggle with the NAACP's executive secretary, Walter White.

Ironically, Du Bois had retreated to a position others saw as dangerously close to that of Booker T. Washington. Arguing for a separate economy for African Americans, Du Bois made a distinction, which White rejected, between enforced and voluntary segregation. By mid-century, Du Bois was outside the mainstream of the civil rights movement. His work remained largely ignored until after his death in 1963.

### ASSESSMENT 3

1. **TERMS & NAMES** For each term or name, write a sentence explaining its significance.
   - **Upton Sinclair**
   - *The Jungle*
   - **Theodore Roosevelt**
   - **Square Deal**
   - **Meat Inspection Act**
   - **Pure Food and Drug Act**
   - **conservation**
   - **NAACP**

#### MAIN IDEA

2. **TAKING NOTES**
   Create five problem-solution diagrams like the one below to show how the following problems were addressed during Roosevelt's presidency:
   (a) 1902 coal strike, (b) Northern Securities Company monopoly, (c) unsafe meat processing, (d) exploitation of the environment, and (e) racial injustice.

   | Problems | → | Solutions |

   Write headlines announcing the solutions.

#### CRITICAL THINKING

3. **FORMING GENERALIZATIONS**
   In what ways do you think the progressive belief in using experts played a role in shaping Roosevelt's reforms? Refer to details from the text. **Think About:**
   - Roosevelt's use of experts to help him tackle political, economic, and environmental problems
   - how experts' findings affected legislative actions

4. **EVALUATING**
   Research the coal strike of 1902. Do you think Roosevelt's intervention was in favor of the strikers or of the mine operators? Why?

5. **ANALYZING ISSUES**
   Why did W. E. B. Du Bois oppose Booker T. Washington's views on racial discrimination?

---

**1. TERMS & NAMES**
Upton Sinclair, p. 317
*The Jungle*, p. 317
Theodore Roosevelt, p. 317
Square Deal, p. 319
Meat Inspection Act, p. 320
Pure Food and Drug Act, p. 322
conservation, p. 323
NAACP, p. 325

**2. TAKING NOTES**
(a) federal arbitration, (b) Supreme Court's dissolution of the Northern Securities Company, (c) passage of the Meat Inspection Act, (d) legislation passed to protect the environment. Students' headlines will vary.

**3. FORMING GENERALIZATIONS**
Roosevelt used an arbitration commission to mediate the 1902 coal strike and appointed experts to investigate the meatpacking industry. Dr. Wiley, chief chemist at the Department of Agriculture, helped get the Pure Food and Drug Act passed. Gifford Pinchot, a professional conservationist, headed the U.S. Forest Service.

**4. EVALUATING**
Responses will vary but should include adequate support from students' research on the 1902 coal strike.

**5. ANALYZING ISSUES**
Du Bois viewed Washington as too accommodating of segregationists. Du Bois wanted immediate equality.

## AMERICAN LITERATURE

### OBJECTIVES

· To examine examples of historical primary sources of the Progressive Era

· To compare the way each writer uses detail to make a point

## Focus & Motivate

**Evaluating** Ask students to think of an issue they have read about, or one they would like to see investigated. Discuss how private organizations, businesses, and government agencies have an interest in maintaining a positive public image. Then, discuss how one of the roles of journalists is to investigate and report on what is happening behind the scenes.

## More About . . .

### Ida M. Tarbell

Tarbell was a pioneering investigative journalist. Investigative reporting was not an occupation women were encouraged to pursue at the turn of the 19th century. But Tarbell, always an independent-minded person, went to the Sorbonne in Paris after graduating from Allegheny College. She began writing for *McClure's Magazine.* Tarbell's articles, which later became a book about John D. Rockefeller's unscrupulous tactics, blew away the smokescreen of respectability from the trusts and changed public opinion. In much the same way, decades later, Bob Woodward and Carl Bernstein would help bring down President Richard Nixon. This was reporting that had immediate and significant historical impact.

# The Muckrakers

**1890–1920** The tradition of the investigative reporter uncovering corruption was established early in the 20th century by the writers known as muckrakers. Coined by President Theodore Roosevelt, the term *muckraker* alludes to the English author John Bunyan's famous 17th-century religious allegory *The Pilgrim's Progress*, which features a character too busy raking up the muck to see a heavenly crown held over him. The originally negative term soon was applied to many writers whose reform efforts Roosevelt himself supported. The muckraking movement spilled over from journalism as writers such as Upton Sinclair made use of the greater dramatic effects of fiction.

◄ **IDA M. TARBELL**

Ida M. Tarbell's "The History of the Standard Oil Company" exposed the ruthlessness with which John D. Rockefeller had turned his oil business into an all-powerful monopoly. Her writing added force to the trustbusting reforms of the early 20th century. Here Tarbell describes how Standard Oil used lower transportation rates to drive out smaller refineries, such as Hanna, Baslington and Company.

> Mr. Hanna had been refining since July, 1869. . . . Some time in February, 1872, the Standard Oil Company asked [for] an interview with him and his associates. They wanted to buy his works, they said. "But we don't want to sell," objected Mr. Hanna. "You can never make any more money, in my judgment," said Mr. Rockefeller. "You can't compete with the Standard. We have all the large refineries now. If you refuse to sell, it will end in your being crushed." Hanna and Baslington were not satisfied. They went to see . . . General Devereux, manager of the Lake Shore road. They were told that the Standard had special rates; that it was useless to try to compete with them. General Devereux explained to the gentlemen that the privileges granted the Standard were the legitimate and necessary advantage of the larger shipper over the smaller. . . . General Devereux says they "recognised the propriety" of his excuse. They certainly recognised its authority. They say that they were satisfied they could no longer get rates to and from Cleveland which would enable them to live, and "reluctantly" sold out. It must have been reluctantly, for they had paid $75,000 for their works, and had made thirty per cent. a year on an average on their investment, and the Standard appraiser allowed them $45,000.

—Ida M. Tarbell, "The History of the Standard Oil Company" (1904)

## RECOMMENDED RESOURCES

### BOOKS

Brady, Kathleen. *Ida Tarbell: Portrait of a Muckraker.* Pittsburgh, Penn.: U of Pittsburgh P, 1989.

Miraldi, Robert, ed., *The Muckrakers: Evangelical Crusaders.* Westport, Conn.: Praeger Publishers, 2000. An anthology of articles by historians and social critics.

Kaplan, Justin. *Lincoln Steffens: A Biography.* New York: Simon and Schuster, 1974.

Steffens, Lincoln. *The Autobiography of Lincoln Steffens.* New York: Harcourt, Brace and Company, 1931.

Weinberg, Arthur and Lila Shaffer, eds. *The Muckrakers.* U of Illinois P, 2001. An anthology of muckraker writings, including Tarbell, Steffens, and Sinclair.

### VIDEOS

*Ida Tarbell: All in the Day's Work.* Lisa and Rich Gensheimer, WQLN Pubic Television of Northwestern Pennsylvania.

**LINCOLN STEFFENS** ▶

Lincoln Steffens is usually named as a leading figure of the muckraking movement. He published exposés of business and government corruption in *McClure's Magazine* and other magazines. These articles were then collected in two books: *The Shame of the Cities* and *The Struggle for Self-Government*. Below is a section from an article Steffens wrote to expose voter fraud in Philadelphia.

> The police are forbidden by law to stand within thirty feet of the polls, but they are at the box and they are there to see that the [Republican political] machine's orders are obeyed and that repeaters whom they help to furnish are permitted to vote without "intimidation" on the names they, the police, have supplied. The editor of an anti-machine paper who was looking about for himself once told me that a ward leader who knew him well asked him into a polling place. "I'll show you how it's done," he said, and he had the repeaters go round and round voting again and again on the names handed them on slips. . . . The business proceeds with very few hitches; there is more jesting than fighting. Violence in the past has had its effect; and is not often necessary nowadays, but if it is needed the police are there to apply it.

—Lincoln Steffens, *The Shame of the Cities* (1904)

**UPTON SINCLAIR**

Upton Sinclair's chief aim in writing *The Jungle* was to expose the shocking conditions that immigrant workers endured. The public, however, reacted even more strongly to the novel's revelations of unsanitary conditions in the meatpacking industry. Serialized in 1905 and published in book form one year later, *The Jungle* prompted a federal investigation that resulted in passage of the Meat Inspection Act in 1906.

> Jonas had told them how the meat that was taken out of pickle would often be found sour, and how they would rub it up with [baking] soda to take away the smell, and sell it to be eaten on free-lunch counters; also of all the miracles of chemistry which they performed, giving to any sort of meat, fresh or salted, whole or chopped, any color and any flavor and any odor they chose. . . .
>
> It was only when the whole ham was spoiled that it came into the department of Elzbieta. Cut up by the two-thousand-revolutions-a-minute flyers, and mixed with half a ton of other meat, no odor that ever was in a ham could make any difference. There was never the least attention paid to what was cut up for sausage; there would come all the way back from Europe old sausage that had been rejected, and that was moldy and white—it would be dosed with borax and glycerine, and dumped into the hoppers, and made over again for home consumption.

—Upton Sinclair, *The Jungle* (1906)

**THINKING CRITICALLY**

1. **Comparing and Contrasting** State the main idea of each of these selections. What role do details play in making the passages convincing?

    **SEE SKILLBUILDER HANDBOOK, PAGE R8.**

2.  **INTERNET ACTIVITY** CLASSZONE.COM

   Visit the links for American Literature: The Muckrakers to learn more about the muckrakers. What topics did they investigate? How did they affect public opinion? What legal changes did they help to bring about? Write a summary of the muckrakers' impact on society.

**Instruct**

1. How extensive was corruption in the second half of the 19th century?
2. Why did individuals seem to get lost in the expansion of the country, government, and business?
3. Who were the muckrakers, and why was their work so valuable?

**MAKING PERSONAL CONNECTIONS**

· Have students talk about investigative reporting, such as the type that uncovered governmental scandals in the late 20th century.

· Ask students if they think that investigative reporters are as needed now as they were in the 19th century.

**More About . . .**

**Lincoln Steffens**

Steffens (1866–1936) was considered a muckraker journalist. He became managing editor of *McClure's Magazine* in 1901. Ida Tarbell, one of the "pioneer muckrakers," wrote for the magazine from 1894–1906. Steffens gradually moved from reform to more radical views. In 1919, he traveled to Russia and returned to pen the famous quote, "I have seen the future; and it works." He then championed many radical causes. The publication of his autobiography in 1931 coincided with a leftist turn in the country and brought him additional popular acclaim.

**THINKING CRITICALLY: ANSWERS**

1. **COMPARING AND CONTRASTING** *The History of the Standard Oil Company:* Although Hanna and Baslington did not want to sell their business, they sold out to Standard Oil Company at a huge loss. They would have been crushed if they had not. Details about the sale price helped to convince readers that they had no choice. *The Shame of the Cities:* At the polls, the police actually assist "repeaters," or people who vote more than one time. Details about the ward leader demonstrating the process of illegal voting help to make the idea of political corruption convincing.

   *The Jungle:* Even meat that had gone bad was treated chemically or processed so that it could be sold. Details about the ham and sausage, as well as descriptive words such as *moldy,* make the process of treating bad meat more revolting to the reader.

2. **INTERNET ACTIVITY** The summary should clearly state the impact of muckrackers and give supporting reasons.

# Progressivism Under Taft

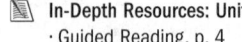

| MAIN IDEA | WHY IT MATTERS NOW | Terms & Names |
|---|---|---|
| Taft's ambivalent approach to progressive reform led to a split in the Republican Party and the loss of the presidency to the Democrats. | Third-party candidates continue to wrestle with how to become viable candidates. | •Gifford Pinchot •William Howard Taft •Payne-Aldrich Tariff •Bull Moose Party •Woodrow Wilson |

### One American's Story

U.S. History
2A, 2B, 4C, 11B, 24B, 24C, 24G, 25A, 25B, 25D, 26A, 26B

Early in the 20th century, Americans' interest in the preservation of the country's wilderness areas intensified. Writers proclaimed the beauty of the landscape and new groups like the Girl Scouts gave city children the chance to escape from their environment. The desire for preservation clashed with business interests that favored unrestricted development. **Gifford Pinchot** (pĭn'shō'), head of the U.S. Forest Service under President Roosevelt, took a middle ground. He believed that wilderness areas could be scientifically managed to yield public enjoyment while allowing private development.

▲ Gifford Pinchot

**A PERSONAL VOICE** GIFFORD PINCHOT

" The American people have evidently made up their minds that our natural resources must be conserved. That is good. But it settles only half the question. For whose benefit shall they be conserved for the benefit of the many, or for the use and profit of the few? . . . There is no other question before us that begins to be so important, or that will be so difficult to straddle, as the great question between special interest and equal opportunity, between the privileges of the few and the rights of the many, between government by men for human welfare and government by money for profit. "

—The Fight for Conservation

President Roosevelt, a fellow conservationist, favored Pinchot's multi-use land program. However, when he left office in 1909, this approach came under increasing pressure from business people who favored unrestricted commercial development.

### 1 Taft Becomes President

After winning the election in 1904, Roosevelt pledged not to run for reelection in 1908. He handpicked his secretary of war, **William Howard Taft,** to run against William Jennings Bryan, who had been nominated by the Democrats for the third time. Under the slogan "Vote for Taft this time, You can vote for Bryan any time," Taft and the Republicans won an easy victory.

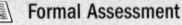
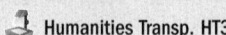
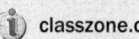

**TAFT STUMBLES** As president, Taft pursued a cautiously progressive agenda, seeking to consolidate rather than to expand Roosevelt's reforms. He received little credit for his accomplishments, however. His legal victories, such as busting 90 trusts in a four-year term, did not bolster his popularity. Indeed, the new president confessed in a letter to Roosevelt that he never felt like the president. "When I am addressed as 'Mr. President,'" Taft wrote, "I turn to see whether you are not at my elbow."

The cautious Taft hesitated to use the presidential bully pulpit to arouse public opinion. Nor could he subdue troublesome members of his own party. Tariffs and conservation posed his first problems.

**Background**
See *tariff* on page R46 in the Economics Handbook.

**THE PAYNE–ALDRICH TARIFF** Taft had campaigned on a platform of lowering tariffs, a staple of the progressive agenda. When the House passed the Payne Bill, which lowered rates on imported manufactured goods, the Senate proposed an alternative bill, the Aldrich Bill, which made fewer cuts and increased many rates. Amid cries of betrayal from the progressive wing of his party, Taft signed the **Payne-Aldrich Tariff,** a compromise that only moderated the high rates of the Aldrich Bill. This angered progressives who believed Taft had abandoned progressivism. The president made his difficulties worse by clumsily attempting to defend the tariff, calling it "the best [tariff] bill the Republican party ever passed."

**DISPUTING PUBLIC LANDS** Next, Taft angered conservationists with his conservation efforts. Taft appointed as his secretary of the interior Richard A. Ballinger, a wealthy lawyer from Seattle. Ballinger, who disapproved of conservationist controls on western lands, removed 1 million acres of forest and mining lands from the reserved list and returned it to the public domain.

When a Department of the Interior official was fired for protesting Ballinger's actions, the fired worker published a muckraking article against Ballinger in *Collier's Weekly* magazine. Pinchot added his voice. In congressional testimony he accused Ballinger of letting commercial interests exploit the natural resources that rightfully belonged to the public. President Taft sided with Ballinger and fired Pinchot from the U.S. Forest Service. **(A)**

**MAIN IDEA**

**Analyzing Issues**
**(A)** How did Taft's appointee Richard Ballinger anger conservationists?

*A. Answer*
Ballinger didn't approve of conserving western lands; he permitted the sale of reserved lands to business interests.

## The Republican Party Splits ❷

Taft's cautious nature made it impossible for him to hold together the two wings of the Republican Party: progressives who sought change and conservatives who did not. The Republican Party began to fragment.

**PROBLEMS WITHIN THE PARTY** Republican conservatives and progressives split over Taft's support of the political boss Joseph Cannon, House Speaker from Illinois. A rough-talking, tobacco-chewing politician, "Uncle Joe" often disregarded seniority in filling committee slots. As chairman of the House Rules Committee, which decides what bills Congress considers, Cannon often weakened or ignored progressive bills.

Reform-minded Republicans decided that their only alternative was to strip Cannon of his power. With the help of Democrats, they succeeded in March 1910 with a resolution that called for the entire House to elect the Committee on Rules and that excluded the speaker from membership in the committee.

**William Howard Taft**

*The Progressive Era* **329**

---

### DIFFICULT DECISIONS

**CONTROLLING RESOURCES**

Historically, conservationists such as Gifford Pinchot have stood for the balanced use of natural resources, preserving some and using others for private industry. Free-market advocates like Richard Ballinger pressed for the private development of wilderness areas. Preservationists such as John Muir advocated preserving all remaining wilderness.

1. Examine the pros and cons of each position. With which do you agree? What factors do you think should influence decisions about America's wilderness areas?

2. If you'd been asked in 1902 to decide whether to develop or preserve America's wilderness areas, what would you have decided? Why?

### DIFFICULT DECISIONS

Review with students these steps in a decision-making process: (1) identify a situation that requires a decision, (2) gather information, (3) identify options, (4) predict consequences, and (5) take action to implement the decision.

**Controlling Resources**

1. Factors may include job loss, health concerns, unknown results affecting the balance of nature, and the threat of extinction to certain species.

2. Some students will indicate that the wilderness should be preserved at all costs. Others may suggest that, in 1902, the need to develop the West may have seemed vital—and, at the time, the resources of the West may have seemed inexhaustible.

### Instruct: Objective ❷

**The Republican Party Splits**
TAKS SS11 5(US24.A)

· How did Taft's support of Joe Cannon alienate progressive Republicans?
· How did Roosevelt come to oppose Taft for the presidency in 1912?

📄 In-Depth Resources: Unit 3
· Guided Reading, p. 4

---

**Writing a Letter to the Editor**

**Class Time** 20 minutes

**Task** Writing a letter expressing an opinion

**Purpose** To express opinions on issues concerning the environment and development

**Directions** Tell students to put themselves in the role of citizens during the Taft administration. Ask them to write a letter to the editor of a newspaper expressing their opinion on the controversy regarding Secretary of the Interior Richard Ballinger's removal of land from the reserved list and subsequent firing of Gifford Pinchot when he protested. Students could share their letters.

📄 Integrated Assessment
· Rubric 5

## KEY PLAYER

**William Howard Taft**

Taft had a significant career after serving as president. He taught constitutional law at Yale, chaired the National War Labor Board during World War I, and was an outspoken supporter of the League of Nations after the war. In 1921, Taft became Chief Justice of the U.S. Supreme Court. Ask students to think how the job requirements of being president or chief justice differ. *(A president needs to be one of the people, to embody people's hopes and dreams, and to be a strong leader. A chief justice needs to have a judicious and analytical mind.)*

## Instruct: Objective ③

**Democrats Win in 1912**

TAKS SS11 5(WH26.C)

· Who were the candidates in the 1912 election?

· What event helped Wilson win the election of 1912?

 In-Depth Resources: Unit 3
· Guided Reading, p. 4

## KEY PLAYER

**WILLIAM HOWARD TAFT 1857–1930**

William Howard Taft never wanted to be president. After serving one term, Taft left the White House, which he called "the lonesomest place in the world," and taught constitutional law at Yale for eight years.

In 1921, President Harding named Taft chief justice of the Supreme Court. The man whose family had nicknamed him "Big Lub" called this appointment the highest honor he had ever received. As chief justice, Taft wrote that "in my present life I don't remember that I ever was President."

However, Americans remember Taft for, among many other things, initiating in 1910 the popular presidential custom of throwing out the first ball of the major league baseball season.

By the midterm elections of 1910, however, the Republican Party was in shambles, with the progressives on one side and the "old guard" on the other. Voters voiced concern over the rising cost of living, which they blamed on the Payne-Aldrich Tariff. They also believed Taft to be against conservation. When the Republicans lost the election, the Democrats gained control of the House of Representatives for the first time in 18 years.

**THE BULL MOOSE PARTY** After leaving office, Roosevelt headed to Africa to shoot big game. He returned in 1910 to a hero's welcome, and responded with a rousing speech proposing a "New Nationalism," under which the federal government would exert its power for "the welfare of the people."

By 1912, Roosevelt had decided to run for a third term as president. The primary elections showed that Republicans wanted Roosevelt, but Taft had the advantage of being the incumbent—that is, the holder of the office. At the Republican convention in June 1912, Taft supporters maneuvered to replace Roosevelt delegates with Taft delegates in a number of delegations. Republican progressives refused to vote and formed a new third party, the Progressive Party. They nominated Roosevelt for president.

The Progressive Party became known as the **Bull Moose Party**, after Roosevelt's boast that he was "as strong as a bull moose." The party's platform called for the direct election of senators and the adoption in all states of the initiative, referendum, and recall. It also advocated woman suffrage, workmen's compensation, an eight-hour workday, a minimum wage for women, a federal law against child labor, and a federal trade commission to regulate business. **B**

The split in the Republican ranks handed the Democrats their first real chance at the White House since the election of Grover Cleveland in 1892. In the 1912 presidential election, they put forward as their candidate a reform governor of New Jersey named **Woodrow Wilson**.

### ③ Democrats Win in 1912

Under Governor Woodrow Wilson's leadership, the previously conservative New Jersey legislature had passed a host of reform measures. Now, as the Democratic presidential nominee, Wilson endorsed a progressive platform called the New Freedom. It demanded even stronger antitrust legislation, banking reform, and reduced tariffs.

The split between Taft and Roosevelt, former Republican allies, turned nasty during the fall campaign. Taft labeled Roosevelt a "dangerous egotist," while Roosevelt branded Taft a "fathead" with the brain of a "guinea pig." Wilson distanced himself, quietly gloating, "Don't interfere when your enemy is destroying himself."

The election offered voters several choices: Wilson's New Freedom, Taft's conservatism, Roosevelt's progressivism, or the Socialist Party policies of Eugene V. Debs. Both Roosevelt and Wilson supported a stronger government role in economic affairs but differed over strategies. Roosevelt supported government action to supervise big business but did not oppose all business monopolies, while Debs

**Vocabulary**
**"old guard":** conservative members of a group

---

**MAIN IDEA**

**Contrasting**
**B** What were the differences between Taft's and Roosevelt's campaign platforms?

*B. Answer*
Roosevelt's campaign platform was much more progressive. He advocated for change using the government's power.

---

**ACTIVITY** | **LINK TO GOVERNMENT**  **classzone.com**

**Researching Third Parties**

**Class Time** One class period

**Task** Researching the influence of third parties in presidential elections

**Purpose** To determine the effect of third parties in presidential elections

**Directions** Divide students into small groups to research the elections of 1992 and 2000. Have students who study the 1992 election focus on the platform and influence of Ross Perot. Have students who study the 2000 election focus on Green Party candidate Ralph Nader and his influence on the outcome of the election. Then conduct a class discussion on the role of third parties in presidential elections.

 Integrated Assessment
· Rubric 1

called for an end to capitalism. Wilson supported small business and free-market competition and characterized all business monopolies as evil. In a speech, Wilson explained why he felt that all business monopolies were a threat.

### A PERSONAL VOICE
WOODROW WILSON

" If the government is to tell big business men how to run their business, then don't you see that big business men have to get closer to the government even than they are now? Don't you see that they must capture the government, in order not to be restrained too much by it? . . . I don't care how benevolent the master is going to be, I will not live under a master. That is not what America was created for. America was created in order that every man should have the same chance as every other man to exercise mastery over his own fortunes."

—quoted in *The New Freedom*

*C. Answer*
Wilson might concentrate on the relationship between business and government.

Although Wilson captured only 42 percent of the popular vote, he won an overwhelming electoral victory and a Democratic majority in Congress. As a third-party candidate, Roosevelt defeated Taft in both popular and electoral votes. But reform claimed the real victory, with more than 75 percent of the vote going to the reform candidates—Wilson, Roosevelt, and Debs. In victory, Wilson could claim a mandate to break up trusts and to expand the government's role in social reform. **C**

| Election of 1912 | | | |
|---|---|---|---|
| Party | Candidate | Electoral votes | Popular vote |
| Democratic | Woodrow Wilson | 435 | 6,296,547 |
| Progressive | Theodore Roosevelt | 88 | 4,118,571 |
| Republican | William H. Taft | 8 | 3,486,720 |
| Socialist | Eugene V. Debs | 0 | 900,672 |

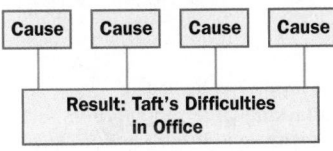

## HISTORY from VISUALS

### Interpreting a Map
Point out that electoral votes in most states are assigned on a winner-take-all basis. Taft and Roosevelt split the Republican vote, so Wilson did not need to win 50 percent of the popular votes. Wilson won the electoral votes of 40 states. The 1912 election was the first presidential election for the new states of New Mexico (47th) and Arizona (48th). Ask students to look at the popular vote totals. Would Wilson have been able to win if the Republicans had not split? *(Yes, even though he might not have won the popular vote, he would have had the electoral votes to be elected.)*

## Assess & Reteach

### SECTION 4 ASSESSMENT
Have students work individually to answer the questions. Then have them hold an informal debate on negative campaign tactics based on their answers to item 4.

Formal Assessment
· Section Quiz, p. 173

### SELF-ASSESSMENT
Have students identify specific passages that helped them answer each assessment question.

### RETEACH
Have students trace Taft's action that led to the split in the Republican Party.

In-Depth Resources: Unit 3
· Reteaching Activity, p. 11

## SECTION 4 ASSESSMENT

**1. TERMS & NAMES** For each term or name, write a sentence explaining its significance.
- Gifford Pinchot
- Payne-Aldrich Tariff
- Woodrow Wilson
- William Howard Taft
- Bull Moose Party

### MAIN IDEA

**2. TAKING NOTES**
Re-create the chart below on your paper. Then fill in the causes Taft supported that made people question his leadership.

| Cause | Cause | Cause | Cause |
|---|---|---|---|

| Result: Taft's Difficulties in Office |
|---|

Which causes do you think would upset most people today? Explain.

### CRITICAL THINKING

**3. HYPOTHESIZING**
What if Roosevelt had won another term in office in 1912? Speculate on how this might have affected the future of progressive reforms. Support your answer. **Think About:**
- Roosevelt's policies that Taft did not support
- the power struggles within the Republican Party
- Roosevelt's perception of what is required of a president

**4. EVALUATING**
Both Roosevelt and Taft resorted to mudslinging during the 1912 presidential campaign. Do you approve or disapprove of negative campaign tactics? Support your opinion.

*The Progressive Era* **331**

## OBJECTIVES

**1** Describe Woodrow Wilson's background and the progressive reforms of his presidency.

**2** List the steps leading to woman suffrage.

**3** Explain the limits of Wilson's progressivism.

### SKILLBUILDERS

· Interpreting Graphs, p. 334
· Interpreting Visual Sources, p. 336

### CRITICAL THINKING

· Summarizing, p. 333
· Evaluating, p. 334
· Analyzing Events, p. 335
· Analyzing Effects, p. 337
· Analyzing Primary Sources, p. 337
· Analyzing Motives, p. 337

## Focus & Motivate

Ask students if it is an advantage, when it comes to politics, to have "the courage of your convictions," or it if is it better to be flexible and able to compromise. Tell students they are going to read about a president whose strength was the courage of his convictions, but who lacked the ability to compromise.

## Instruct

### Instruct: Objective **1**

**Wilson Wins Financial Reforms**
TAKS SS11 4(US4.A)

· What legislation did Wilson use to attack trusts and monopolies?
· How were the lowering of the tariff and the introduction of the income tax related?
· How did Wilson reform banking?

 In-Depth Resources: Unit 3
· Guided Reading, p. 5
· Geography Application, pp. 13–14
· American Lives: Carrie Chapman Catt, p. 23

# Wilson's New Freedom

**MAIN IDEA**

Woodrow Wilson established a strong reform agenda as a progressive leader.

**WHY IT MATTERS NOW**

The passage of the Nineteenth Amendment during Wilson's administration granted women the right to vote.

**Terms & Names**

· Carrie Chapman Catt
· Clayton Antitrust Act
· Federal Trade Commission (FTC)
· Federal Reserve System
· Nineteenth Amendment

**TEKS** U.S. History 1B, 2A, 2B, 2C, 4A, 4B, 7A, 7B, 16B, 17A, 17B, 18A, 18B, 19A, 19B, 21A, 21D, 24A, 24B, 24C, 24D, 24H, 25A, 25C, 25D

### One American's Story

On March 3, 1913, the day of Woodrow Wilson's inauguration, 5,000 woman suffragists marched through hostile crowds in Washington, D.C. Alice Paul and Lucy Burns, the parade's organizers, were members of the National American Woman Suffrage Association (NAWSA). As police failed to restrain the rowdy gathering and congressmen demanded an investigation, Paul and Burns could see the momentum building for suffrage.

By the time Wilson began his campaign for a second term in 1916, the NAWSA's president, **Carrie Chapman Catt**, saw victory on the horizon. Catt expressed her optimism in a letter to her friend Maud Wood Park.

**A PERSONAL VOICE** CARRIE CHAPMAN CATT

" I do feel keenly that the turn of the road has come. . . . I really believe that we might pull off a campaign which would mean the vote within the next six years if we could secure a Board of officers who would have sufficient momentum, confidence and working power in them. . . . Come! My dear Mrs. Park, gird on your armor once more. "

—letter to Maud Wood Park

▲ Carrie Chapman Catt

Catt called an emergency suffrage convention in September 1916, and invited President Wilson, who cautiously supported suffrage. He told the convention, "There has been a force behind you that will . . . be triumphant and for which you can afford. . . . to wait." They did have to wait, but within four years, the passage of the suffrage amendment became the capstone of the progressive movement.

## **1** Wilson Wins Financial Reforms

Like Theodore Roosevelt, Woodrow Wilson claimed progressive ideals, but he had a different idea for the federal government. He believed in attacking large concentrations of power to give greater freedom to average citizens. The prejudices of his Southern background, however, prevented him from using federal power to fight off attacks directed at the civil rights of African Americans.

---

## PROGRAM RESOURCES

 In-Depth Resources: Unit 3
· Guided Reading, p. 5
· Reteaching Activity, p. 12
· Geography Application: The Movement Toward Woman Suffrage, pp. 13–14
· American Lives: Carrie Chapman Catt, p. 23

 Reading Study Guide (English and Spanish), pp. 99–100
 Access for Students Acquiring English/ESL
· Guided Reading (Spanish), p. 117
· Geography Application, p. 119
 Formal Assessment
· Section Quiz, p. 174
 Integrated Assessment
· Rubrics

**INTEGRATED TECHNOLOGY**

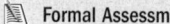 classzone.com

**TEXAS RESOURCES**

 TAKS Spiraled Content Review

 TAKS Practice Tests

 TAKS Practice Transparencies TT66

 TAKS Online Test Practice

**WILSON'S BACKGROUND** Wilson spent his youth in the South during the Civil War and Reconstruction. The son, grandson, and nephew of Presbyterian ministers, he received a strict upbringing. Before entering the political arena, Wilson spent time as a lawyer and president of Princeton University. In 1910, Wilson became the governor of New Jersey. As governor, he supported progressive legislation programs such as a direct primary, worker's compensation, and the regulation of public utilities and railroads.

As America's newly elected president, Wilson moved to enact his program, the "New Freedom," and planned his attack on what he called the triple wall of privilege: the trusts, tariffs, and high finance.

**TWO KEY ANTITRUST MEASURES** "Without the watchful . . . resolute interference of the government," Wilson said, "there can be no fair play between individuals and such powerful institutions as the trusts. Freedom today is something more than being let alone." During Wilson's administration, Congress enacted two key antitrust measures. The first, the **Clayton Antitrust Act** of 1914, sought to strengthen the Sherman Antitrust Act of 1890. The Clayton Act prohibited corporations from acquiring the stock of another if doing so would create a monopoly; if a company violated the law, its officers could be prosecuted.

The Clayton Act also specified that labor unions and farm organizations not only had a right to exist but also would no longer be subject to antitrust laws. Therefore, strikes, peaceful picketing, boycotts, and the collection of strike benefits became legal. In addition, injunctions against strikers were prohibited unless the strikers threatened damage that could not be remedied. Samuel Gompers, president of the American Federation of Labor (AFL), saw great value to workers in the Clayton Act. He called it a Magna Carta for labor, referring to the English document, signed in 1215, in which the English king recognized that he was bound by the law and that the law granted rights to his subjects.

**Vocabulary**
**injunction:** a court order prohibiting a party from a specific course of action

The second major antitrust measure, the Federal Trade Commission Act of 1914, set up the **Federal Trade Commission (FTC).** This "watchdog" agency was given the power to investigate possible violations of regulatory statutes, to require periodic reports from corporations, and to put an end to a number of unfair business practices. Under Wilson, the FTC administered almost 400 cease-and-desist orders to companies engaged in illegal activity. Ⓐ

**A NEW TAX SYSTEM** In an effort to curb the power of big business, Wilson worked to lower tariff rates, knowing that supporters of big business hadn't allowed such a reduction under Taft.

Wilson lobbied hard in 1913 for the Underwood Act, which would substantially reduce tariff rates for the first time since the Civil War. He summoned Congress to a special session to plead his case, and established a precedent of delivering the State of the Union message in person. Businesses lobbied too, looking to block tariff reductions. When manufacturing lobbyists—people hired by manufacturers to present their case to government officials—descended on the capital to urge senators to vote no, passage seemed unlikely. Wilson denounced the lobbyists and urged voters to monitor their senators' votes. Because of the new president's use of the bully pulpit, the Senate voted to cut tariff rates even more deeply than the House had done.

**MAIN IDEA**

**Summarizing**
Ⓐ What was the impact of the two antitrust measures?

**A. Answer** Wilson placed greater government regulations on businesses.

---

**More About . . .**

**Carrie Chapman Catt**
Catt succeeded Susan B. Anthony as president of the National American Woman Suffrage Association in 1900 and helped lead the suffrage movement to the successful passage of the Nineteenth Amendment in 1920. She then became a founding member of the League of Women Voters and was a leader of the peace movement during the 1920s and 1930s.

📄 In-Depth Resources: Unit 3
· American Lives: Carrie Chapman Catt, p. 23

---

**NOW & THEN**

**DEREGULATION**

In recent years the railroad, airline, and telecommunications industries have all been deregulated, or permitted to compete without government control. It is hoped that this will improve their efficiency and lower prices.

During the Progressive Era, reformers viewed regulation as a necessary role of government to ensure safety and fairness for consumers as well as industrial competitors. Opponents of regulation, however, believed that government regulation caused inefficiency and high prices.

Modern critics of deregulation argue that deregulated businesses may skimp on safety. They may also neglect hard-to-serve populations, such as elderly, poor, or disabled people, while competing for more profitable customers.

---

**NOW & THEN**

**Deregulation**
**Analyzing Effects** Discuss the impact of deregulation on consumers today. Emphasize to students that deregulation can affect consumers through price changes for services such as airline flights and cable television. What happens when large companies in an industry are allowed to merge or purchase their competitors? Have students investigate how prices have been impacted by major corporation mergers in industries such as airlines, telecommunications, or automobiles.

*The Progressive Era* **333**

---

**DIFFERENTIATING INSTRUCTION** | **LESS PROFICIENT READERS**

**Clarifying Ideas**

Help students clarify Wilson's antitrust measures. List the following concepts on the board, and have the students give an example of each.

· Monopolies: (Review *monopoly* on page 259.) A business cannot buy another business if that purchase results in exclusive control over a commercial activity. *Example: There cannot be only one telephone company.*

· Unions: Unions have a right to exist and are not subject to antitrust laws. *Example: Union members can strike, boycott, picket, and collect strike benefits.*

· FTC: The FTC is a federally created agency that has the power to investigate business practices. *Example: The Federal Trade Commission can force companies to stop misleading labeling.*

 Integrated Assessment
· Rubric 2

## HISTORY from VISUALS

### Interpreting a Graph

Ask students to look at the graph and compare the period 1915–1955 with the period 1955–1995. Ask students to use their knowledge of history and current events to contrast the two periods. *(Students might infer that during the period 1915–1955 low tax revenues resulted in relatively low federal spending. In contrast, during the period 1955–1995, tax revenues increased dramatically, as did federal spending.)* Students may ask why taxes did not rise rapidly during World War II. Tell students that the war was largely financed by bonds rather than tax revenues.

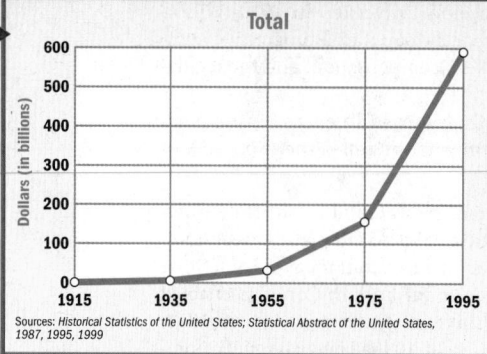

**Revenue from Individual Federal Income Tax, 1915–1995**

Total

Dollars (in billions): 600, 500, 400, 300, 200, 100, 0

1915  1935  1955  1975  1995

Sources: *Historical Statistics of the United States; Statistical Abstract of the United States,* 1987, 1995, 1999

**SKILLBUILDER** Interpreting Graphs
1. About what year did income tax revenues first begin to rise sharply?
2. About how much revenue did the income tax bring in 1995?

*Skillbuilder Answers*
1. About 1955.
2. Just under $600 billion.

### Instruct: Objective ❷

**Women Win Suffrage**

TAKS SS11 4(US18.B)

· How did women finally win the vote?
· What was the Nineteenth Amendment?

📖 In-Depth Resources: Unit 3
· Geography Application: The Movement Toward Woman Suffrage, pp. 13–14

**FEDERAL INCOME TAX** With lower tariff rates, the federal government had to replace the revenue that tariffs had previously supplied. Ratified in 1913, the Sixteenth Amendment legalized a graduated federal income tax, which provided revenue by taxing individual earnings and corporate profits.

Under this graduated tax, larger incomes were taxed at higher rates than smaller incomes. The tax began with a modest tax on family incomes over $4,000, and ranged from 1 percent to a maximum of 6 percent on incomes over $500,000. Initially, few congressmen realized the potential of the income tax, but by 1917, the government was receiving more money on the income tax than it had ever gained from tariffs. Today, income taxes on corporations and individuals represent the federal government's main source of revenue.

**Background**
See *taxation* on page R46 in the Economics Handbook.

**FEDERAL RESERVE SYSTEM** Next, Wilson turned his attention to financial reform. The nation needed a way to strengthen the ways in which banks were run, as well as a way to quickly adjust the amount of money in circulation. Both credit availability and money supply had to keep pace with the economy.

Wilson's solution was to establish a decentralized private banking system under federal control. The Federal Reserve Act of 1913 divided the nation into 12 districts and established a regional central bank in each district. These "banker's banks" then served the other banks within the district.

The federal reserve banks could issue new paper currency in emergency situations, and member banks could use the new currency to make loans to their customers. Federal reserve banks could transfer funds to member banks in trouble, saving the banks from closing and protecting customers' savings. By 1923, roughly 70 percent of the nation's banking resources were part of the **Federal Reserve System**. One of Wilson's most enduring achievements, this system still serves as the basis of the nation's banking system. **B**

### ❷ Women Win Suffrage

While Wilson pushed hard for reform of trusts, tariffs, and banking, determined women intensified their push for the vote. The educated, native-born, middle-class women who had been active in progressive movements had grown increasingly impatient about not being allowed to vote. As of 1910, women had federal voting rights only in Wyoming, Utah, Colorado, Washington, and Idaho.

Determined suffragists pushed on, however. They finally saw success come within reach as a result of three developments: the increased activism of local groups, the use of bold new strategies to build enthusiasm for the movement, and the rebirth of the national movement under Carrie Chapman Catt.

**LOCAL SUFFRAGE BATTLES** The suffrage movement was given new strength by growing numbers of college-educated women. Two Massachusetts organizations, the Boston Equal Suffrage Association for Good Government and the College Equal Suffrage League, used door-to-door campaigns to reach potential

**MAIN IDEA**

**Evaluating**
**B** Why were tariff reform and the Federal Reserve System important?

*B. Answer*
Wilson's tariff reform cut tariffs and reduced the power of monopolies. The Federal Reserve System made the money supply responsive to the state of the economy.

**334** CHAPTER 9

---

### Researching the Federal Reserve Board

In the post–Cold War world where economic rather than ideological issues have become paramount, some say that the chairman of the Federal Reserve Board (the Fed), rather than the president, is the most powerful person in the country. Have students use library and Internet resources to explore the structure and role of the Fed and how it influences both the American economy and American politics. Then prepare a multimedia presentation for the class.

supporters. Founded by Radcliffe graduate Maud Wood Park, the Boston group spread the message of suffrage to poor and working-class women. Members also took trolley tours where, at each stop, crowds would gather to watch the unusual sight of a woman speaking in public.

Many wealthy young women who visited Europe as part of their education became involved in the suffrage movement in Britain. Led by Emmeline Pankhurst, British suffragists used increasingly bold tactics, such as heckling government officials, to advance their cause. Inspired by their activism, American women returned to the United States armed with similar approaches in their own campaigns for suffrage.

**CATT AND THE NATIONAL MOVEMENT** Susan B. Anthony's successor as president of NAWSA was Carrie Chapman Catt, who served from 1900 to 1904 and resumed the presidency in 1915. When Catt returned to NAWSA after organizing New York's Women Suffrage Party, she concentrated on five tactics: (1) painstaking organization; (2) close ties between local, state, and national workers; (3) establishing a wide base of support; (4) cautious lobbying; and (5) gracious, ladylike behavior.

Although suffragists saw victories, the greater number of failures led some suffragists to try more radical tactics. Lucy Burns and Alice Paul formed their own more radical organization, the Congressional Union, and its successor, the National Woman's Party. They pressured the federal government to pass a suffrage amendment, and by 1917 Paul had organized her followers to mount a round-the-clock picket line around the White House. Some of the picketers were arrested, jailed, and even force-fed when they attempted a hunger strike.

These efforts, and America's involvement in World War I, finally made suffrage inevitable. Patriotic American women who headed committees, knitted socks for soldiers, and sold liberty bonds now claimed their overdue reward for supporting the war effort. In 1919, Congress passed the **Nineteenth Amendment,** granting women the right to vote. The amendment won final ratification in August 1920—72 years after women had first convened and demanded the vote at the Seneca Falls convention in 1848.

*C. Possible Answer* A combination of factors, including women's growing experience in the public realm, their economic and social power, and their importance in the war effort.

**MAIN IDEA**

**Analyzing Events**
**C** Why do you think women won the right to vote in 1920, after earlier efforts had failed?

**Vocabulary**
**appease:** pacify by granting concessions

**WORLD STAGE**

**EMMELINE PANKHURST**
American women struggling for suffrage received valuable tutoring from their English counterparts, whose bold maneuvers had captured media coverage.

The noted British suffragist Emmeline Pankhurst, who helped found the National Women's Social and Political Union, often engaged in radical tactics. Pankhurst and other suffragists staged parades, organized protest meetings, endured hunger strikes, heckled candidates for Parliament, and spat on policemen who tried to quiet them. They were often imprisoned for their activities, before Parliament granted them the right to vote in 1928.

## The Limits of Progressivism ③

Despite Wilson's economic and political reforms, he disappointed Progressives who favored social reform. In particular, on racial matters Wilson appeased conservative Southern Democratic voters but disappointed his Northern white and black supporters. He placed segregationists in charge of federal agencies, thereby expanding racial segregation in the federal government, the military, and Washington, D.C.

**WILSON AND CIVIL RIGHTS** Like Roosevelt and Taft, Wilson retreated on civil rights once in office. During the presidential campaign of 1912, he won the support of the NAACP's black intellectuals and white liberals by promising to treat blacks equally and to speak out against lynching.

*The Progressive Era* **335**

---

**Frank Lloyd Wright**

Frank Lloyd Wright was a prolific American architect. The clean lines of Wright's designs, and his championing of native materials and buildings that grew naturally from their surroundings, set him apart as an architect. Another Wright principle was continuous space, where rooms flowed into each other. Perhaps this principle is best exemplified by the spiral structure of the Guggenheim Museum (1956–1959) in New York City.

**SKILLBUILDER ANSWERS**

1. Answers will vary. Many students may note that Robie House is built much more horizontally than the Victorian house. Students may point to the sleek lines of Wright's house as contrasting with the spires and detailed ornateness of the Victorian.

2. Answers will vary, though many students may indicate that in general Wright's building is designed to fit in with its natural environment. Robie House is part of its landscape.

### History Through *Architecture*

**FROM SPLENDOR TO SIMPLICITY**

The progressive movement, which influenced numerous aspects of society, also impacted the world of American architecture. One of the most prominent architects of the time was Frank Lloyd Wright, who studied under the renowned designer Louis Sullivan. In the spirit of progressivism, Wright sought to design buildings that were orderly, efficient, and in harmony with the world around them.

 Architecture of the Gilded Age featured ornate decoration and detail, as seen here in this Victorian-style house built between 1884 and 1886. Wright rejected these showy and decorative styles in favor of more simplistic designs.

 Wright's "prairie style" design features a low, horizontal, and well-defined structure made predominantly of wood, concrete, brick, and other simple materials. Shown here is the Robie House (1909), one of Wright's most famous prairie-style structures, which incorporates these architectural qualities.

**SKILLBUILDER** Interpreting Visual Sources
1. What are the most striking differences between the two houses? Cite examples that contrast the two buildings.
2. How does Wright's style reflect the progressive spirit?

**SEE SKILLBUILDER HANDBOOK, PAGE R23.**

As president, however, Wilson opposed federal antilynching legislation, arguing that these crimes fell under state jurisdiction. In addition, the Capitol and the federal offices in Washington, D.C., which had been desegregated during Reconstruction, resumed the practice of segregation shortly after Wilson's election.

Wilson appointed to his cabinet fellow white Southerners who extended segregation. Secretary of the Navy Josephus Daniels, for example, proposed at a cabinet meeting to do away with common drinking fountains and towels in his department. According to an entry in Daniel's diary, President Wilson agreed because he had "made no promises in particular to negroes, except to do them justice." Segregated facilities, in the president's mind, were just.

African Americans and their liberal white supporters in the NAACP felt betrayed. Oswald Garrison Villard, a grandson of the abolitionist William Lloyd Garrison, wrote to Wilson in dismay, "The colored men who voted and worked for you in the belief that their status as American citizens was safe in your hands are deeply cast down." Wilson's response—that he had acted "in the interest of the negroes" and "with the approval of some of the most influential negroes I know"—only widened the rift between the president and some of his former supporters.

**ACTIVITY** | **LINK TO HUMANITIES** | classzone.com

**Creating a Biographical Sketch**

**Class Time** One class period

**Task** Researching the work of great architects who have worked in the United States

**Purpose** To identify and gain an appreciation of the work of great architects

**Directions** Have students choose one of the following architects to be the subject of a brief biographical essay: Louis Sullivan, Frank Lloyd Wright, Ludwig Mies Van Der Rohe, Philip Johnson, I. M. Pei, Louis Kahn, Michael Graves, or Frank Gehry. Have students download images of the architect and the architect's works from the Internet to accompany the essay.

 Integrated Assessment
· Rubric 1

On November 12, 1914, the president's reception of an African-American delegation brought the confrontation to a bitter climax. William Monroe Trotter, editor-in-chief of the *Guardian*, an African-American Boston newspaper, led the delegation. Trotter complained that African Americans from 38 states had asked the president to reverse the segregation of government employees, but that segregation had since increased. Trotter then commented on Wilson's inaction.

**MAIN IDEA**

**Analyzing Effects**
**D** What actions of Wilson disappointed civil rights advocates?

### A PERSONAL VOICE WILLIAM MONROE TROTTER

" Only two years ago you were heralded as perhaps the second Lincoln, and now the Afro-American leaders who supported you are hounded as false leaders and traitors to their race. . . . As equal citizens and by virtue of your public promises we are entitled at your hands to freedom from discrimination, restriction, imputation, and insult in government employ. Have you a 'new freedom' for white Americans and a new slavery for your 'Afro-American fellow citizens'? God forbid! "
—address to President Wilson, November 12, 1914

Wilson found Trotter's tone infuriating. After an angry Trotter shook his finger at the president to emphasize a point, the furious Wilson demanded that the delegation leave. Wilson's refusal to extend civil rights to African Americans pointed to the limits of progressivism under his administration. America's involvement in the war raging in Europe would soon reveal other weaknesses. **D**

**THE TWILIGHT OF PROGRESSIVISM** After taking office in 1913, Wilson had said, "There's no chance of progress and reform in an administration in which war plays the principal part." Yet he found that the outbreak of World War I in Europe in 1914 demanded America's involvement. Meanwhile, distracted Americans and their legislators allowed reform efforts to stall. As the pacifist and reformer Jane Addams mournfully reflected, "The spirit of fighting burns away all those impulses . . . which foster the will to justice."

International conflict was destined to be part of Wilson's presidency. During the early years of his administration, Wilson had dealt with issues of imperialism that had roots in the late 19th century. However, World War I dominated most of his second term as president. The Progressive Era had come to an end.

**More About . . .**

**William Monroe Trotter**
Like W. E. B. Du Bois, Trotter was a Harvard graduate who worked with the Niagara movement to found the NAACP. Trotter later criticized the NAACP's policy of racial accommodation and reliance on financial support from whites. He established another organization, the National Equal Rights League, to protest discrimination. Trotter led several nonviolent protests and demonstrations to address the issues of racial and social justice.

## Assess & Reteach

**SECTION 5 ASSESSMENT**
Have students create a two-column chart on which they compare their own responses to the section assessment (column 1) with the portions of the text that best answer each question (column 2).

📝 Formal Assessment
· Section Quiz, p. 174

**SELF-ASSESSMENT**
Using a two-column chart, students should list the reforms outlined in this chapter. Then, students should prepare a second list explaining how these reforms affect their lives today.

**RETEACH**
Use the Critical Thinking Transparency on the Progressive Era to review concepts.

📝 In-Depth Resources: Unit 3
· Reteaching Activity, p. 12

---

## SECTION 5 ASSESSMENT

**1. TERMS & NAMES** For each term or name, write a sentence explaining its significance.
- Carrie Chapman Catt
- Clayton Antitrust Act
- Federal Trade Commission (FTC)
- Federal Reserve System
- Nineteenth Amendment

**MAIN IDEA**

**2. TAKING NOTES**
Create a time line of key events relating to Progressivism during Wilson's first term. Use the dates already plotted on the time line below as a guide.

```
1913   1914   1915   1916
```

Write a paragraph explaining which event you think best demonstrates progressive reform.

**CRITICAL THINKING**

**3. ANALYZING PRIMARY SOURCES**
Wilson said, "Without the watchful . . . resolute interference of the government, there can be no fair play between individuals and . . . the trusts." How does this statement reflect Wilson's approach to reform? Support your answer. **Think About:**
- the government's responsibility to the public
- the passage of two key antitrust measures

**4. ANALYZING MOTIVES**
Why do you think Wilson failed to push for equality for African Americans, despite his progressive reforms? **Think About:**
- progressive presidents before Wilson
- Wilson's background
- the primary group of people progressive reforms targeted

*The Progressive Era* **337**

**1. TERMS & NAMES**
Carrie Chapman Catt, p. 332
Clayton Antitrust Act, p. 333
Federal Trade Commission, p. 333
Federal Reserve System, p. 334
Nineteenth Amendment, p. 335

**2. TAKING NOTES**
**1913**—NAWSA protests on Wilson's inauguration day.; Federal Reserve Act passed.
**1914**—Federal Trade Act establishes Federal Trade Commission; Clayton Antitrust Act strengthens the Sherman Antitrust Act; African-American delegation confronts Wilson on his segregation policies.
**1916**—Suffragists picket the Democratic Party convention.

**3. ANALYZING PRIMARY SOURCES**
Wilson believed the exploitative practices of big businesses threatened the freedom of consumers and workers. He thought that the government had the responsibility to safeguard public welfare. Students' paragraphs will vary.

**4. ANALYZING MOTIVES**
Wilson, like Roosevelt and Taft, pushed aggressively for economic and political reforms but retreated on civil rights issues. Swayed by his southern upbringing and the support of northern whites, Wilson refused to expand the civil rights of African Americans.

## TERMS & NAMES

1. progressive movement, p. 307
2. muckraker, p. 308
3. suffrage, p. 315
4. Susan B. Anthony, p. 315
5. Theodore Roosevelt, p. 317
6. NAACP, p. 325
7. Gifford Pinchot, p. 328
8. Woodrow Wilson, p. 330
9. Clayton Antitrust Act, p. 333
10. Federal Reserve System, p. 334

## MAIN IDEAS

1. Protecting social welfare, promoting moral reform, creating economic reform, and fostering efficiency.
2. Laws setting minimum age, limiting work hours, and providing workers' compensation.
3. Government became more responsive to the people, elections were reformed, Senators directly elected and the public had more voice in law-making. Democracy was expanded.
4. Women who lacked education or skills worked as domestic workers.
5. The NACW promoted the moral education of African Americans. The NAWSA was committed to winning women's right to vote.
6. Sinclair's descriptions of the meat-packing industry's corrupt practices disgusted both the public and Roosevelt, who pushed Congress to pass the Meat Inspection Act.
7. Roosevelt filed suits under the Sherman Antitrust Act, thus breaking up some of the trusts. He also ordered the Justice Department to sue the Northern Securities Company which, until the Supreme Court dissolved the company, held a monopoly over northwestern railroads.
8. Taft was a more cautious progressive than Roosevelt but did break up more trusts than Roosevelt had.
9. Taft was unable to appease both the reform-minded progressives and the conservatives within his party.
10. It recognized the legality of labor unions, strikes, peaceful picketing, boycotts, and strike benefits; it limited the use of injunctions in court disputes.
11. Child labor laws, because he felt they were unconstitutional; federal antilynching laws, because he believed such crimes fell under state jurisdictions.

### TERMS & NAMES

**For each term or name below, write a sentence explaining its connection to the Progressive Era.**

1. progressive movement
2. muckraker
3. suffrage
4. Susan B. Anthony
5. Theodore Roosevelt
6. NAACP
7. Gifford Pinchot
8. Woodrow Wilson
9. Clayton Antitrust Act
10. Federal Reserve System

### MAIN IDEAS

**Use your notes and the information in the chapter to answer the following questions.**

#### The Origins of Progressivism (pages 306–312)

1. What were the four goals that various progressive reform movements struggled to achieve?
2. What kind of state labor laws resulted from progressives' lobbying to protect workers?
3. How did government change during the Progressive Era? How were these changes important?

#### Women in Public Life (pages 313–316)

4. In the late 1890s, what job opportunities were available to uneducated women without industrial skills?
5. Give two examples of national women's organizations committed to social activism. Briefly describe their progressive missions.

#### Teddy Roosevelt's Square Deal (pages 317–325)

6. What scandalous practices did Upton Sinclair expose in his novel *The Jungle*? How did the American public, Roosevelt, and Congress respond?
7. How did Roosevelt earn his reputation as a trust-buster?

#### Progressivism Under Taft (pages 328–331)

8. As a progressive, how did Taft compare with Roosevelt?
9. Why did the Republican Party split during Taft's administration?

#### Wilson's New Freedom (pages 332–337)

10. How did the Clayton Antitrust Act benefit labor?
11. Cite two examples of social welfare legislation that Wilson opposed during his presidency and the arguments he used to defend his position.

### CRITICAL THINKING

1. **USING YOUR NOTES** Create a Venn diagram to show some of the similarities and differences between Roosevelt's Square Deal and Wilson's New Freedom.

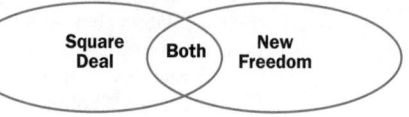

Square Deal — Both — New Freedom

2. **DEVELOPING HISTORICAL PERSPECTIVE** What social, political, and economic trends in American life do you think caused the reform impulse during the Progressive Era? Support your answer with details from the text.

---

## VISUAL SUMMARY  THE PROGRESSIVE ERA

### ECONOMIC
- Roosevelt establishes a Square Deal
- new tax system is instituted
- Roosevelt breaks up trusts

### POLITICAL
- elections are reformed
- citizens given greater voice in government: recall, initiative, referendum

**PROGRESSIVISM**

### SOCIAL & MORAL
- women fight for the right to vote
- Eighteenth Amendment bans alcoholic beverages
- Social services for women, children, and the poor

### INDUSTRY
- National Child Labor Committee organizes to end child labor
- reformers improve workplace conditions and set maximum working hours

### HEALTH & ENVIRONMENT
- conservationists establish wilderness conservation areas and preserve natural resources
- Pure Food and Drug Act protects consumers

---

## CRITICAL THINKING

1. **USING YOUR NOTES Similarities:** promoted a strong executive branch; progressive ideals; tackled the problems of trusts; excluded the cause of civil rights for African Americans **Differences:** Roosevelt favored regulating trusts, thought the federal government should get bigger; Wilson favored breaking trusts up; smaller government

2. **DEVELOPING HISTORICAL PERSPECTIVE** Urbanization and its related poverty and industrialization; Social Gospel; increase in the number of college-educated women; exploitative business practices; rise of socialism; popularity of muckraking magazines; corruption in politics.

## Standardized Test Practice

Use the quotation and your knowledge of U.S. history to answer question 1.

> " Labor began to organize itself in Trade Unions and to confront the industrialists with a stiff bargaining power. These developments were to lead to a period of protest and reform in the early twentieth century. The gains conferred by large-scale industry were great and lasting, but the wrongs that had accompanied their making were only gradually righted. "
>
> —Winston Churchill, *The Great Republic: A History of America*

1. In the passage, Winston Churchill attempts to explain what prompted Progressive Era reformers. The passage explains the actions of which of the following labor reform leaders?

   A Maria Mitchell
   B Carry Nation
   C Susan B. Anthony
   D Florence Kelley

2. The muckrakers served Progressivism by —

   F informing people about abuses so that they could protest.
   G enacting legislation to prevent political corruption.
   H cleaning up unhealthy meat processing plants.
   J filing and prosecuting antitrust lawsuits.

3. In the presidential election of 1912, three candidates attempted to win the liberal, progressive vote. Which candidate for president in 1912 ran on a conservative platform?

   A Woodrow Wilson
   B William Taft
   C Theodore Roosevelt
   D Eugene Debs

ADDITIONAL TEST PRACTICE, pages S1–S33.

 TEST PRACTICE CLASSZONE.COM

## Standardized Test Practice

1. The correct answer is letter **D.**
   Letters A, B, C are not correct because only Florence Kelly worked with the labor movement.
2. The correct answer is letter **F.**
   Letters G, H, J are not correct because muckrakers as journalists only informed the public with regard to abuses. Others had to act to correct those abuses.
3. The correct answer is letter **B.**
   Letter A is not correct because Wilson was categorized as a reform candidate. Letter C is not correct because Roosevelt was considered a progressive. Letter D is not correct because Debs was a socialist.

**NEWS STORY**

**Tips for Teaching**

· Remind students that they have about two weeks in which to complete the unit project.
· Give students suggested Internet links or key words to find information.

## ALTERNATIVE ASSESSMENT

1. **INTERACT WITH HISTORY** Recall your discussion of the question on page 305:

   ### What kinds of actions can bring about social change?

   Now that you have read chapter 9, use your knowledge of the Progressive Era to answer these questions:
   - How did Progressive Era reformers recruit others?
   - How did progressive reformers bring about changes in government?
   - What did progressives do to bring about changes in business?
   - What else might Progressive Era reformers have done to be more effective?

   Explain your answers with examples.

2. **VIDEO** **LEARNING FROM MEDIA** View the *American Stories* video, "A Child on Strike." Discuss the following questions in a group; then do the activity.

   - What was your reaction to Camella Teoli's accident?
   - What labor practices are taken for granted today that were not afforded to people living in 1910?

   **Cooperative Learning Activity** In your group, imagine you are reporters covering the congressional hearing. Write two articles—one that objectively reports on the findings of the hearings, and one that has bias in favor of the mill. Share the articles with the class and analyze how language can affect the reporting of information.

*The Progressive Era* **339**

Formal Assessment
· Chapter Test, Forms A, B, and C, pp. 175–192

## ALTERNATIVE ASSESSMENT

### 1. INTERACT WITH HISTORY
· Education and public demonstrations to recruit others.
· Helped reform elections and the direct election of senators.
· Laws to regulate railroads, mines, mills, and big businesses; laws to protect working children.
· Responses will vary.

### 2. LEARNING FROM MEDIA
**Rubric**
Effective articles should . . .
· include fictional details from the hearing
· accurately reflect the result of the hearing
· use language to make the article either objective or biased

# America Claims an Empire

| | CHAPTER OVERVIEW | COPYMASTERS | INTEGRATED TECHNOLOGY |
|---|---|---|---|
| **CHAPTER RESOURCES** | *To compete with other powers, America gains colonies overseas, although some Americans object.* | 📄 Telescoping the Times<br>· Chapter Summary, pp. 19–20<br><br>📄 Planning for Block Schedules | 💿 Power Presentations<br>💿 Electronic Teacher Tools<br>ⓘ Online Lesson Planner<br>⚓ classzone.com |

| | **KEY IDEAS** | | |
|---|---|---|---|
| **SECTION 1**<br><br>Imperialism and America<br><br>pp. 342–345 | *Economic and cultural factors convince U.S. policymakers to join the competition for new markets in territories overseas, including Hawaii.* | 📄 In-Depth Resources: Unit 3<br>· Guided Reading, p. 24<br>· Building Vocabulary, p. 28<br>· Reteaching Activity, p. 30<br>· Literature, pp. 42–44<br><br>📄 Lesson Plans, pp. 81–82 | ⚒ Critical Thinking Transparencies CT18<br>· U.S. Policies for Overseas Expansion<br>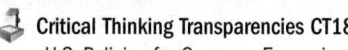<br>ⓘ classzone.com · |
| **SECTION 2**<br><br>The Spanish-American War<br><br>pp. 346–351 | *The United States goes to war with Spain over Cuban independence and emerges with colonies in Guam, Puerto Rico, and the Philippine Islands.* | 📄 In-Depth Resources: Unit 3<br>· Guided Reading, p. 25<br>· Skillbuilder Practice, p. 29<br>· Reteaching Activity, p. 31<br>· Primary Sources, pp. 38–40<br>· American Lives, pp. 45–46<br><br>📄 Lesson Plans, pp. 83–84 | 💿 Electronic Library of Primary Sources<br>· from *The "Maine": An Account of Her Destruction,* 1898, Capt. C.D. Sigsbee<br><br>ⓘ classzone.com |
| **SECTION 3**<br><br>Acquiring New Lands<br><br>pp. 352–358 | *The United States encounters continuing conflict in Puerto Rico, Cuba, and Philippines as well as in its attempt to expand trade with China.* | 📄 In-Depth Resources: Unit 3<br>· Guided Reading, p. 26<br>· Reteaching Activity, p. 32<br><br>📄 Lesson Plans, pp. 85–86 | ⚒ Humanities Transparencies HT17, HT37<br>· *Athletic Contest*<br>· Declined With Thanks<br><br>💿 Electronic Library of Primary Sources<br>· On the War in the Philippines, 1900, by A. Beveridge<br><br>ⓘ classzone.com |
| **SECTION 4**<br><br>America as a World Power<br><br>pp. 359–367 | *Presidents Theodore Roosevelt and Woodrow Wilson continue to use American military power in territories around the world, including Panama and Mexico.* | 📄 In-Depth Resources: Unit 3<br>· Guided Reading, p. 27<br>· Reteaching Activity, p. 33<br>· Geography Application, pp. 34–35<br>· Outline Map, pp. 36–37<br>· Primary Sources, p. 41<br><br>📄 Historic Supreme Court Decisions, *Schenck v. United States,* p. 103<br><br>📄 Lesson Plans, pp. 87–88 | ⚒ Geography Transparencies GT18<br>· United States Intervenes in Latin America, 1890–1920<br><br>⚒ Critical Thinking Transparencies CT52<br>· U.S. Trade with Central America, 1913–1920<br><br>💿 Electronic Library of Primary Sources<br><br>ⓘ classzone.com |

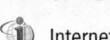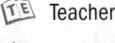
## ASSESSMENT OPTIONS

- **Chapter Assessment**, pp. 368–369
- **Formal Assessment**
  · Chapter Tests, Forms A, B, and C, pp. 197–208
- **Test Generator**
- **Integrated Assessment Book**
- **TAKS Online Test Practice**
- **TAKS Spiraled Content Review**
- **TAKS Practice Tests**

---

- **Section 1 Assessment**, p. 345
- **Self-Assessment**, p. 345
- **Formal Assessment**, Quiz, p. 193
- **Integrated Assessment Book**
- **Test Generator**
- **TAKS Practice Transparencies TT67**

---

- **Section 2 Assessment**, p. 351
- **Self-Assessment**, p. 351
- **Formal Assessment**, Quiz, p. 194
- **Integrated Assessment Book**
- **Test Generator**
- **TAKS Practice Transparencies TT68**

---

- **Section 3 Assessment**, p. 358
- **Self-Assessment**, p. 358
- **Formal Assessment**, Quiz, p. 195
- **Integrated Assessment Book**
- **Test Generator**
- **TAKS Practice Transparencies TT69**

---

- **Section 4 Assessment**, p. 365
- **Self-Assessment**, p. 365
- **Formal Assessment**, Quiz, p. 196
- **Integrated Assessment Book**
- **Test Generator**
- **TAKS Practice Transparencies TT70**

## RESOURCES FOR DIFFERENTIATING INSTRUCTION

**Students Acquiring English/ESL**

- **Reading Study Guide:**
  (English and Spanish)
  pp. 103–110
- **Access for Students
  Acquiring English/ESL:**
  Spanish Translations,
  pp. 123–131
- **Chapter Summaries on CD**
  (English and Spanish)

**Less Proficient Readers**

- **Reading Study Guide**
  (English and Spanish)
  pp. 103–110
- **Telescoping the Times**
  · Chapter Summary,
  pp. 19–20
- **Chapter Summaries on CD**
  (English and Spanish)

**Gifted and Talented Students**

- **In-Depth Resources: Unit 3**
  · Primary Sources,
  pp. 38–41
  · Literature, pp. 42–44
  · American Lives, pp. 45–46
- **Electronic Library of
  Primary Resources**
  Unit 3, Chapter 10

## CROSS-CURRICULAR CONNECTIONS

### Humanities: Art

Cruz, Barbara C. *Jose Clemente Orzoco: Mexican Artist (Hispanic Biographies).* Berkeley Heights, NJ: Enslow Publishers, 1998. This biography of one of Mexico's greatest muralists not only tells the interesting story of his life and work but places it within the context of Mexican history in the 19th century.

### Government

Abodaher, David J. *Puerto Rico: America's 51st State?* NY: Watts, 1993. A history of the island, with a lengthy section on the leadership of the Munoz family (Luis Munoz Rivera and his son Luis Munoz Marin).

### Culture

Blumberg, Rhoda. *Commodore Perry in the Land of the Shogun.* NY: Lothrop, 1985. The story of Perry's remarkable voyage to Japan, addressing both economic and cultural issues.

### Science: Technology

Keller, Ulrich (editor). *The Building of the Panama Canal in Historic Photographs.* Mineola, NY: Dover Publications, 1984. A fascinating story of technological feats; the photographs bring the long years of building to life.

### Literature

Ferre, Rosario. *The House on the Lagoon.* NY: Farrar, 1995. Nominated for a National Book Award, this novel is about the history of a Puerto Rican family whose secrets and conflicts add up to the larger story of Puerto Rico itself.

Iida, Deborah. *Middle Son.* Chapel Hill, NC: Algonquin Books, 1996. The narrator of this novel tells the story of his Japanese-American family who were sugar-cane cutters in Hawaii working for the huge corporations that controlled the business. The richness and tragedy of their family life and the narrator's final communion with his mother make this novel memorable.

## ENRICHMENT ACTIVITIES

- **Pupil's Edition**, pp. 340–367
  Interact with History, pp. 340–341
  Science & Technology, p. 361
  Geography Spotlight, pp. 366–367
- **In-Depth Resources: Unit 3**
  · Geography Application: Geography of the
  Panama Canal, pp. 34-35
  · Outline Map: America Becomes a World
  Power, pp. 36–37
  · Primary Sources: Newspaper Front Page,
  p. 38

· Primary Sources: from *The Rough Riders,* by
Theodore Roosevelt, p. 39
· Primary Sources: In Favor of Imperialism,
p. 40
· Primary Sources: Building the Panama Canal,
p. 41
· Literature: from *Hawaii,* pp. 42–44
· American Lives: José Martí, p. 45
· American Lives: William Randolph Hearst, p. 46

- **Electronic Library of Primary Sources**
  · Unit 3, Chapter 10

## BLOCK SCHEDULE LESSON PLAN OPTIONS (90-MINUTE PERIOD)

### DAY 1

**CHAPTER 10 OPENER**
pp. 340–341

**Class Time** 30 minutes

**History from Visuals, p. 340**

**Class Time** 15 minutes

*Options for Pacing and Variety*

· Time Saver Have students look at the painting on the spread and ask them the Interpreting the Painting questions in the TE. Also have them study the time line and ask them the questions that correspond in the TE.
**Class Time** 10 minutes

**Interact with History, p. 341**

**Class Time** 20 minutes

*Options for Pacing and Variety*

· Role-Playing Have students read the paragraph and discuss the Examine the Issues questions. For more questions to keep the discussion going, use the Examine the Issues on TE page 341.
**Class Time** 15 minutes

**SECTION 1 pp. 342–345**

**Class Time** 30 minutes

*Options for Pacing and Variety*

· Role-Playing Assign the following roles to small groups of students: American planters, native Hawaiians, contract laborers, Queen Liliuokalani, U.S. ambassador John L. Stevens, President Cleveland, and President McKinley. Use a loose debate structure and ask a general question on whether the annexation of Hawaii is good for the United States, Hawaii, or both.
**Class Time** 25 minutes

### DAY 1 continued

· Peer Teaching Have students work in pairs to complete the Section 1 Assessment. Discuss the answers as a class.
**Class Time** 15 minutes

**SECTION 2 pp. 346–351**

**Class Time** 30 minutes

*Options for Pacing and Variety*

· Internet Read for the class the "Tracing Themes: Yellow Journalism" information panel in the TE. Have students search the Internet for more about the tactics of yellow journalism. They might start by searching the examples given in the text—William Randolph Hearst or Joseph Pulitzer—together with the term "yellow journalism." Have them look for other examples, which could be modern examples or examples related to Cuba, and try to trace some effects of exaggeration by the media.
**Class Time** 30 minutes

· Time Saver Ask students to study the maps on page 349 and answer the Geography Skillbuilder questions. Have students discuss the possible effects of a naval blockade on a blockaded country.
**Class Time** 10 minutes

### DAY 2

**SECTION 3 pp. 352–358**

**Class Time** 30 minutes

*Options for Pacing and Variety*

· Time Saver As the class discusses the section, ask students the Instruct questions on TE pages 352, 355, 356, and 358 to help them understand the main points of the section.
**Class Time** 15 minutes

· Peer Teaching Have students work in pairs to complete questions 2, 3, and 4 of the Section 3 Assessment. Discuss the answers as a class.
**Class Time** 15 minutes

· Internet Have students work in pairs. Ask them to read "A Personal Voice: Mark Twain" on page 358 and contrast the main motives for U.S. imperialism with other views of those motives. Have them search the Internet, beginning with Mark Twain, for objections to imperialism at the time. Have students summarize the arguments they find and make a chart for the contrasting opinions of what ideas fuel imperialism. **Class Time** 40 minutes

**SECTION 4 pp. 359–369**

**Class Time** 30 minutes

*Options for Pacing and Variety*

· Team Teaching Have students look at the painting Orozco's *Zapatistas* on page 364. Read the information on the painting in the TE. If there is an art teacher in the school who knows about the Mexican Renaissance, ask him or her to talk to the class about the artistic

### DAY 2 continued

movement and its close ties with revolutionary ideas. Find more examples of paintings from that movement on the Internet.
**Class Time** 30 minutes

· Peer Teaching Have students work in pairs to complete the Section 4 Assessment. Have them add to their answers as they discuss them with another group.
**Class Time** 20 minutes

· History on Film Have students read the Geography Spotlight on "The Panama Canal" on pages 366–367. View part or all of the video *Panama Canal* listed in resources on TE page 366.
**Class Time** 40 minutes

**ASSESSMENT**
pp. 368–369

**Class Time** 30 minutes

*Options for Pacing and Variety*

· Peer Teaching Have students work in small groups to complete the Critical Thinking questions. Discuss the answers as class.
**Class Time** 20 minutes

· Peer Evaluation Have students work in pairs and quiz each other on the terms and names and Main Ideas questions. They should look in the book to correct each other.
**Class Time** 15 minutes

---

**TEACHER-TESTED ACTIVITY**       Brenda G. Smith, Instructional Supervisor, Social Studies, District 11, Colorado Springs, Colorado

**COMPUTER SLIDE SHOW: BUILDING THE PANAMA CANAL**

**Class Time** 90 minutes

**Task** Creating a a computer slideshow

**Purpose** To learn about a specific aspect of the building of the Panama Canal

**Supplies Needed**

· Textbook
· Internet access

**Activity** Have students work in pairs. Tell them to choose a specific aspect—such as engineering or politics—of the building of the Panama Canal. Have them download images from the National Archives Web site to create a computer slideshow. Each image should have an explanatory caption. Then give students time to view the work of their classmates.

# CHAPTER 10 CORRELATION

## CORRELATION TO THE TEXAS ESSENTIAL KNOWLEDGE AND SKILLS

Chapter 10 addresses the following standards of the Texas Essential Knowledge and Skills for U.S. History.

| TEKS | Instruction | Student Question/Activity |
|---|---|---|
| **(1C)** Explain the significance of dates in U.S. history, including 1898. | **PE 348–351**—discussion of the outbreak and progression of the Spanish-American War in 1898 | **PE 351**—questions regarding the war with Spain |
| **(3A)** Explain why significant events and individuals, including Alfred Thayer Mahan, moved the United States into the position of a world power. | **PE 343**—examination of Alfred Thayer Mahan's life and impact on America's growth as a world power | **PE 345**—activity writing a sentence explaining Mahan's significance |
| **(9B)** Identify and explain reasons for changes in political boundaries such as those resulting from statehood. | **PE 344–345**—discussion of events leading up to the annexation of Hawaii as the 50th state in the Union | **TE 344**—writing activity to help students recognize the different viewpoints regarding the annexation of Hawaii |
| **(12D)** Analyze the effects of economic policies including the Open Door Policy. | **PE 356-357**—examination of the establishment of the Open Door Policy in China | **PE 358**—Critical Thinking question about the formation of the Open Door Policy |
| **(17A)** Analyze the effects of 20th-century landmark Supreme Court cases. | **PE 353**—discussion of the Insular Cases, which addressed questions about U.S. citizenship in the nation's acquired territories | **TE 353**—research activity to learn more about the Insular Cases |
| **(19B)** Evaluate the contributions of significant political leaders in the United States. | **PE 359-363**—Examination of how Theodore Roosevelt helped to build the United States into a world power | **PE 365**—questions about Roosevelt's foreign policies |
| **(23A)** Analyze how scientific discoveries and technological innovations have changed the standard of living in the United States. | **PE 361**—Science and Technology feature on workings of the Panama Canal | **PE 367**—questions about the impact of the Panama Canal on U.S. trade routes |

## TAKS MINI-LESSONS

1. **Social Studies Skills: Objective 1 (US3.A):** Explain why significant events and individuals moved the United States into the position of a world power **Activity** Have students create a time line of significant events of the Spanish-American War.

2. **Social Studies Skills: Objective 2 (US9.A):** Analyze the effects of physical and human geographic factors on major events including the building of the Panama Canal **Activity** Have students complete the geography activity about the two possible canal routes through Central America on TE page 360.

3. **Social Studies Skills: Objective 5 (US24.F):** Identify bias in written materials **Activity** Have students complete the skillbuilder mini-lesson on identifying bias on TE page 348.

4. **English Language Arts Skills: Objective 2 (11.F):** Understand literary forms and terms **Activity** Have students summarize the excerpt from Mark Twain's satirical piece condemning imperialism.

5. **English Language Arts Skills: Objective 3 (20.B):** Deconstruct media to get the main idea of the message's content **Activity** Have students answer the Skillbuilder questions regarding the political cartoon on U.S. imperialism on page 354.

# CHAPTER 10 · AMERICA CLAIMS AN EMPIRE

This lithograph of Roosevelt leading the Rough Riders at San Juan Hill shows the men on horseback, although they actually fought on foot.

## HISTORY from VISUALS

### Interpreting the Painting

Ask students to examine the painting and suggest words they would use to describe the scene. Ask them how the painting depicts Theodore Roosevelt, the leader of the Rough Riders at the Battle of San Juan Hill. How does such a depiction differ from the way in which most soldiers probably act during battle? (Scene—chaotic, frightening, exciting; Roosevelt—heroic, fearless, and calm under fire; soldiers—frightened and anxious)

**Extension** Ask students to write the lead paragraph of a news story about the charge up San Juan Hill based on this painting.

## Time Line Discussion

Explain to students that the time line covers key U.S. and world events just before and after the turn of the 20th century.

· Ask students what year the Spanish-American war began. (1898)

· Ask students who became president of the United States in 1901, and what was unique about the way in which he attained the presidency. (Theodore Roosevelt; he became president after William McKinley was assassinated)

· Ask students how long after Panama declared its independence from Colombia the United States opened the Panama Canal. (11 years)

**1893** Sugar planters, aided by U.S. marines, over-throw Hawaii's Queen Liliuokalani.

**1898** U.S.S. Maine explodes and sinks. The Spanish-American War begins.

**1901** Theodore Roosevelt becomes president after McKinley is assassinated.

USA
WORLD

**1890**

**1900**

**1895** Guglielmo Marconi invents the radio.

**1898** Marie Curie discovers radium.

**1900** In China, the Boxers rebel.

**1903** Panama declares its independence from Colombia.

**340** CHAPTER 10

## THEMES IN CHAPTER 10

### SCIENCE AND TECHNOLOGY

Technological advances fueled U.S. imperialism at the turn of the 20th century. Improved equipment increased farm and factory output. Increased output led to a surplus of goods and prompted the need for overseas markets.

**See Teacher's Edition note,** p. 343.

### AMERICA IN WORLD AFFAIRS

The late 1800s are often referred to as the "Age of Imperialism." During this time, several European nations took control of much of Africa and parts of Asia and the Pacific. The United States joined in the pursuit of colonies.

**See Teacher's Edition note,** p. 350.

### CIVIL RIGHTS

As the United States acquired new territory, questions were raised about the civil rights of the people in these newly acquired lands.

**See Teacher's Edition note,** p. 353.

### DIVERSITY AND NATIONAL IDENTITY

African Americans serving in the military in the Philippines struggled with questions of national identity and the task of putting down an independence movement.

**See Teacher's Edition note,** p. 355.

# INTERACT
## WITH HISTORY

In the late 1890s, American newspapers are running sensational stories about Spain's harsh rule of Cuba. Such articles anger Americans. Among those willing to fight for Cuba's freedom are a group of volunteers, the Rough Riders. Led by future president Theodore Roosevelt, the Rough Riders become a model for others to follow.

## *Does the U.S. have a duty to fight for freedom in neighboring countries?*

### Examine the Issues

- When should the U.S. intervene in the affairs of another country?
- In what ways do dramatic headlines influence American opinion?

 **RESEARCH LINKS** CLASSZONE.COM

Visit the Chapter 10 links for more information related to America Claims an Empire.

# INTERACT
## WITH HISTORY

### Objectives

· To help students understand the media's potential to sway public opinion and even to dictate events
· To help students recognize some of the main reasons why the United States declared war on Spain

### Examine the Issues

1. Have students consider what circumstances might prompt the United States to fight on behalf of a neighboring country.
2. Ask students to discuss the importance of a free press in a democratic society, as well as whether or not the media have any duties or responsibilities in such a society.

---

**1909** William Howard Taft is elected president.

**1912** Woodrow Wilson is elected president.

**1914** The Panama Canal opens.

**1917** Puerto Ricans become U.S. citizens.

**1917** The United States enters World War I.

**1910**

**1920**

**1910** The Mexican Revolution begins.

**1914** World War I begins in Europe.

**1917** Mexico revises and adopts its constitution.

*America Claims an Empire* **341**

---

## RECOMMENDED RESOURCES

### BOOKS FOR THE TEACHER

Marks, George P., ed. *The Black Press Views American Imperialism.* New York: Arno Press, 1971. Unusual perspective on imperialism.

Musicant, Ivan. *Empire by Default: The Spanish-American War & the Dawn of the American Century.* New York: Henry Holt & Company, Inc., 1998. Comprehensive telling of the war.

### BOOKS FOR THE STUDENT

McCullough, David G. *The Path Between the Seas: The Creation of the Panama Canal, 1870–1914.* New York: Simon and Schuster, 1977.

Rydell, Robert W. *All the World's a Fair: Visions of Empire at American International Expositions: 1876–1916.* Chicago: U of Chicago Press, 1984.

### VIDEOS

*The Big Stick.* 1991. RMI Media, 800-745-5480. U.S. foreign policy in Latin America.

*The Hunt for Pancho Villa.* PBS Home Video, 1993. 800-424-7963.

*The 1890s.* 1994. Video Knowledge, 516-367-4250. U.S. Imperialism.

### SOFTWARE

*American History: Becoming a World Power.* World Associates, 3226 Robincrest Drive, Northbrook, IL 60062.

### INTEGRATED TECHNOLOGY

For teacher support, visit . . .

 classzone.com

*America Claims an Empire* **341**

# Imperialism and America

| MAIN IDEA | WHY IT MATTERS NOW | Terms & Names |
|---|---|---|
| Beginning in 1867 and continuing through the century, global competition caused the United States to expand. | During this time period, the United States acquired Hawaii and Alaska, both of which became states in 1959. | • Queen Liliuokalani  • imperialism  • Alfred T. Mahan   • William Seward  • Pearl Harbor  • Sanford B. Dole |

 **U.S. History** 3A, 8A, 8B, 9B, 10B, 19A, 24B, 24G, 25A, 25B, 25C, 25D, 26B

### One American's Story

In 1893 **Queen Liliuokalani** (lə-lē′ə-ō-kə-lä′nē) realized that her reign in Hawaii had come to an end. More than 160 U.S. sailors and marines stood ready to aid the *haoles* (white foreigners) who planned to overthrow the Hawaiian monarchy. In an eloquent statement of protest, the proud monarch surrendered to the superior force of the United States.

**A PERSONAL VOICE** QUEEN LILIUOKALANI

" I, Liliuokalani, . . . do hereby solemnly protest against any and all acts done against myself and the constitutional government of the Hawaiian Kingdom. . . . Now, to avoid any collision of armed forces and perhaps the loss of life, I do under this protest . . . yield my authority until such time as the Government of the United States shall . . . undo the action of its representatives and reinstate me in the authority which I claim as the constitutional sovereign of the Hawaiian Islands. "

—quoted in *Those Kings and Queens of Old Hawaii*

▲ Hawaii's "Queen Lil" announced that if restored to power, she would behead those who had conspired to depose her.

U.S. ambassador to Hawaii John L. Stevens informed the State Department, "The Hawaiian pear is now fully ripe, and this is the golden hour for the United States to pluck it." The annexation of Hawaii was only one of the goals of America's empire builders in the late 19th century.

## **1** American Expansionism

Americans had always sought to expand the size of their nation, and throughout the 19th century they extended their control toward the Pacific Ocean. However, by the 1880s, many American leaders had become convinced that the United States should join the imperialist powers of Europe and establish colonies overseas. **Imperialism**—the policy in which stronger nations extend their economic, political, or military control over weaker territories—was already a trend around the world.

**Analyzing Effects**

**A** How did European imperialism affect Africa?

*A. Answer* Only two African nations remained independent; the rest of the continent was divided up among European nations.

**GLOBAL COMPETITION** European nations had been establishing colonies for centuries. In the late 19th century Africa had emerged as a prime target of European expansionism. By the early 20th century, only two countries in all of Africa—Ethiopia and Liberia—remained independent. **A**

Imperialists also competed for territory in Asia, especially in China. In its late-19th-century reform era, Japan replaced its old feudal order with a strong central government. Hoping that military strength would bolster industrialization, Japan joined European nations in competition for China in the 1890s.

Most Americans gradually warmed to the idea of expansion overseas. With a belief in manifest destiny, they already had pushed the U.S. border to the Pacific Ocean. Three factors fueled the new American imperialism:

- desire for military strength
- thirst for new markets
- belief in cultural superiority

**DESIRE FOR MILITARY STRENGTH** Seeing that other nations were establishing a global military presence, American leaders advised that the United States build up its own military strength. One such leader was Admiral **Alfred T. Mahan** of the U.S. Navy. Mahan urged government officials to build up American naval power in order to compete with other powerful nations. As a result of the urging of Mahan and others, the United States built nine steel-hulled cruisers between 1883 and 1890. The construction of modern battleships such as the *Maine* and the *Oregon* transformed the country into the world's third largest naval power.

**Background** In the late 1800s, new farm machinery greatly improved grain production. For example, plows, harrows, threshing machines, and reapers increased corn production by 264 percent and the wheat harvest by 252 percent.

**THIRST FOR NEW MARKETS** In the late 19th century, advances in technology enabled American farms and factories to produce far more than American citizens could consume. Now the United States needed raw materials for its factories and new markets for its agricultural and manufactured goods. Imperialists viewed foreign trade as the solution to American overproduction and the related problems of unemployment and economic depression.

**KEY PLAYER**

**ADMIRAL ALFRED T. MAHAN 1840–1914**

Alfred T. Mahan joined the U.S. Navy in the late 1850s and served for nearly forty years. In 1886, he became president of the newly established Naval War College in Newport, Rhode Island.

Throughout his lifetime, Mahan was one of the most outspoken advocates of American military expansion. In his book *The Influence of Sea Power upon History, 1660–1783* (published in 1890), Mahan called for the United States to develop a modern fleet capable of protecting American business and shipping interests around the world. He also urged the United States to establish naval bases in the Caribbean, to construct a canal across the Isthmus of Panama, and to acquire Hawaii and other Pacific islands.

**KEY PLAYER**

**Admiral Alfred T. Mahan**
One of the early admirers of Mahan's work was Theodore Roosevelt, then the U.S. civil service commissioner. "I can say with perfect sincerity that I think it very much the clearest and most instructive general work of the kind with which I am acquainted," Roosevelt wrote Mahan after reading *The Influence of Sea Power in History* in the summer of 1890. "It is a very good book—admirable; and I am greatly in error if it does not become a naval classic." Discuss with students what Roosevelt's comments might suggest about the actions he would take as president.

**Tracing Themes**

**SCIENCE AND TECHNOLOGY**

**Advances in Food Production**
From 1870 to 1900, new and improved farm machinery greatly increased grain production in the United States. For example, plows, harrows, grain drills, reapers, and threshing machines boosted the nation's corn harvest by 147 percent and the wheat harvest by 134 percent. Faced with such a surplus of farm products, the United States increased its foreign trade as it sought new markets for these goods.

In the early 1900s, the Navy's Great White Fleet, so named because its ships were painted white, was a sign of America's growing military power. ▶

**DIFFERENTIATING INSTRUCTION**   **LESS PROFICIENT READERS**

**Understanding Main Causes**

Help students understand why the United States embraced imperialism.

- List the three major factors on the board, as shown at right.
- Ask students to tell what each factor means in their own words.
- Then have students find an example of each cause on text pages 343 and 344.

Have students copy the list and examples to use during class discussion of the section.

| Factor | Meaning | Example |
|---|---|---|
| 1. Desire for Military Strength | | |
| 2. Thirst for new markets | | |
| 3. Belief in Cultural Superiority | | |

## Instruct: Objective ❷

**The United States Acquires Alaska /
The United States Takes Hawaii**

TAKS SS11 1(US3.A)

· Why was the purchase of Alaska significant?

· What groups were interested in increasing America's presence in Hawaii? Why?

· How did Hawaii eventually come under the control of the United States?

 In-Depth Resources: Unit 3
· Guided Reading, p. 24
· Literature: from *Hawaii*, pp. 42–44

---

**BELIEF IN CULTURAL SUPERIORITY** Cultural factors also were used to justify imperialism. Some Americans combined the philosophy of Social Darwinism—a belief that free-market competition would lead to the survival of the fittest—with a belief in the racial superiority of Anglo-Saxons. They argued that the United States had a responsibility to spread Christianity and "civilization" to the world's "inferior peoples." This viewpoint narrowly defined "civilization" according to the standards of only one culture.

## The United States Acquires Alaska ❷

An early supporter of American expansion was **William Seward,** Secretary of State under presidents Abraham Lincoln and Andrew Johnson. In 1867, Seward arranged for the U.S. to buy Alaska from the Russians for $7.2 million. Seward had some trouble persuading the House of Representatives to approve the treaty. Some people thought it was silly to buy what they called "Seward's Icebox" or "Seward's folly." Time showed how wrong they were. In 1959, Alaska became a state. For about two cents an acre, the United States had acquired a land rich in timber, minerals, and, as it turned out, oil. **Ⓑ**

## The United States Takes Hawaii ❷

In 1867, the same year in which Alaska was purchased, the United States took over the Midway Islands, which lie in the Pacific Ocean about 1300 miles north of Hawaii. No one lived on the islands, so the event did not attract much attention.

Hawaii was another question. The Hawaiian Islands had been economically important to the United States for nearly a century. Since the 1790s, American merchants had stopped there on their way to China and East India. In the 1820s, Yankee missionaries founded Christian schools and churches on the islands. Their children and grandchildren became sugar planters who sold most of their crop to the United States.

**THE CRY FOR ANNEXATION** In the mid-19th century, American-owned sugar plantations accounted for about three-quarters of the islands' wealth. Plantation owners imported thousands of laborers from Japan, Portugal, and China. By 1900, foreigners and immigrant laborers outnumbered native Hawaiians about three to one.

White planters profited from close ties with the United States. In 1875, the United States agreed to import Hawaiian sugar duty-free. Over the next 15 years, Hawaiian sugar production increased nine times. Then the McKinley Tariff of 1890 provoked a crisis by eliminating the duty-free status of Hawaiian sugar. As a result, Hawaiian sugar growers faced competition in the American market. American planters in Hawaii called for the United States to annex the islands so they wouldn't have to pay the duty.

U.S. military and economic leaders already understood the value of the islands. In 1887, they pressured Hawaii to allow the United States to build a naval base at **Pearl Harbor,** the kingdom's best port. The base became a refueling station for American ships.

---

### MAIN IDEA

**Developing Historical Perspective**
**Ⓑ** How did time prove that the purchase of Alaska was not an act of folly?

**B. Answer**
Alaska is rich in timber, minerals, and oil.

---

**Vocabulary**
**annex:** to incorporate territory into an existing country or state

---

**Skillbuilder Answers**
1. The percentage of native Hawaiians declined from about 98% in 1853 to about 16% in 1920. The percentage of other populations (mostly Asian) increased from about 1% in 1853 to about 62% in 1920.
2. These changes may have led to tensions between native Hawaiians and newcomers.

---

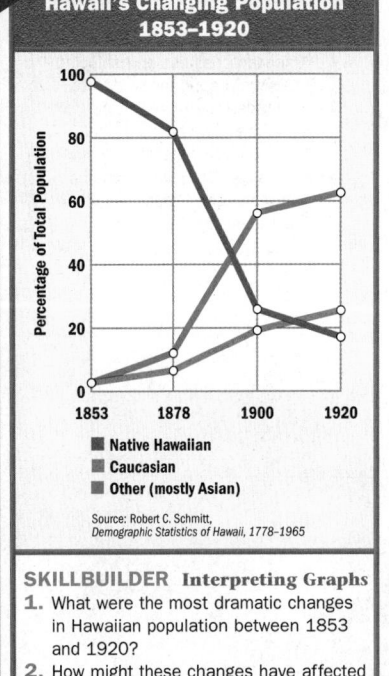

**Hawaii's Changing Population 1853–1920**

Percentage of Total Population

■ Native Hawaiian
■ Caucasian
■ Other (mostly Asian)

Source: Robert C. Schmitt,
*Demographic Statistics of Hawaii, 1778–1965*

**SKILLBUILDER** Interpreting Graphs
1. What were the most dramatic changes in Hawaiian population between 1853 and 1920?
2. How might these changes have affected the political climate there?

---

**THE END OF A MONARCHY** Also in that year, Hawaii's King Kalakaua had been strong-armed by white business leaders. They forced him to amend Hawaii's constitution to grant voting rights only to wealthy land owners. But when Kalakaua died in 1891, his sister Queen Liliuokalani came to power with a "Hawaii for Hawaiians" agenda. She proposed removing the property-owning qualifications for voting. To prevent this from happening, business groups—encouraged by Ambassador John L. Stevens—organized a revolution. With the help of marines, they overthrew the queen and set up a government headed by **Sanford B. Dole.**

President Cleveland directed that the queen be restored to her throne. When Dole refused to surrender power, Cleveland formally recognized the Republic of Hawaii. But he refused to consider annexation unless a majority of Hawaiians favored it.

In 1897, William McKinley, who favored annexation, succeeded Cleveland as president. On August 12, 1898, Congress proclaimed Hawaii an American territory, although Hawaiians had never had the chance to vote. In 1959, Hawaii became the 50th state of the United States. **C**

**MAIN IDEA**

**Analyzing Events**
**C** What factors led to the annexation of Hawaii in 1898?

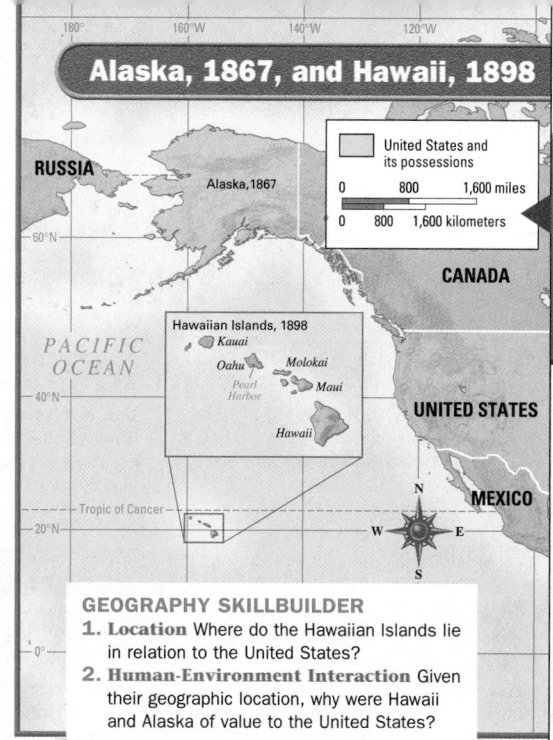

**Alaska, 1867, and Hawaii, 1898**

United States and its possessions

Alaska, 1867

0   800   1,600 miles
0   800   1,600 kilometers

RUSSIA

CANADA

PACIFIC OCEAN

Hawaiian Islands, 1898
Kauai
Oahu · Molokai
Pearl Harbor · Maui
Hawaii

UNITED STATES

MEXICO

Tropic of Cancer

**GEOGRAPHY SKILLBUILDER**
1. **Location** Where do the Hawaiian Islands lie in relation to the United States?
2. **Human-Environment Interaction** Given their geographic location, why were Hawaii and Alaska of value to the United States?

---

## SECTION 1 ASSESSMENT

**1. TERMS & NAMES** For each term or name, write a sentence explaining its significance.
- **Queen Liliuokalani**
- **imperialism**
- **Alfred T. Mahan**
- **William Seward**
- **Pearl Harbor**
- **Sanford B. Dole**

**MAIN IDEA**

**2. TAKING NOTES**
Copy this web on your paper and fill it in with events and concepts that illustrate the roots of imperialism.

Political
Roots of U.S. Imperialism
Economic
Cultural

Choose one event to explain further in a paragraph.

**CRITICAL THINKING**

**3. DRAWING CONCLUSIONS**
Manifest destiny greatly influenced American policy during the first half of the 19th century. How do you think manifest destiny set the stage for American imperialism at the end of the century?

**4. EVALUATING**
In your opinion, did Sanford B. Dole and other American planters have the right to stage a revolt in Hawaii in 1893? **Think About:**
- American business interests in Hawaii
- the rights of native Hawaiians

**5. ANALYZING PRIMARY SOURCES**
In the following passage, how does Indiana Senator Albert J. Beveridge explain the need for the U.S. to acquire new territories?

"Fate has written our policy for us; the trade of the world must and shall be ours. . . . We will establish trading points throughout the world as distributing points for American products. . . Great colonies governing themselves, flying our flag and trading with us, will grow about our posts of trade."

—quoted in *Beveridge and the Progressive Era*

# The Spanish-American War

| MAIN IDEA | WHY IT MATTERS NOW | Terms & Names |
|---|---|---|
| In 1898, the United States went to war to help Cuba win its independence from Spain. | U.S. involvement in Latin America and Asia increased greatly as a result of the war and continues today. | • José Martí  • George Dewey<br>• Valeriano Weyler  • Rough Riders<br>• yellow journalism  • San Juan Hill<br>• *U.S.S. Maine*  • Treaty of Paris |

 U.S. History 1C, 2A, 3A, 8A, 9B, 12E, 19A, 24B, 24C, 24F, 24G, 24H, 25A, 25B, 25C, 25D

**One American's Story**

Early in 1896, James Creelman traveled to Cuba as a *New York World* reporter, covering the second Cuban war for independence from Spain. While in Havana, he wrote columns about his observations of the war. His descriptions of Spanish atrocities aroused American sympathy for Cubans.

**A PERSONAL VOICE** JAMES CREELMAN

" No man's life, no man's property is safe [in Cuba]. American citizens are imprisoned or slain without cause. American property is destroyed on all sides. . . . Wounded soldiers can be found begging in the streets of Havana. . . . The horrors of a barbarous struggle for the extermination of the native population are witnessed in all parts of the country. Blood on the roadsides, blood in the fields, blood on the doorsteps, blood, blood, blood! . . . Is there no nation wise enough, brave enough to aid this blood-smitten land? "

—*New York World*, May 17, 1896

Newspapers during that period often exaggerated stories like Creelman's to boost their sales as well as to provoke American intervention in Cuba.

 Mini-Lesson 1: SS11 1(US3.A)

## **1** Cubans Rebel Against Spain

By the end of the 19th century, Spain—once the most powerful colonial nation on earth—had lost most of its colonies. It retained only the Philippines and the island of Guam in the Pacific, a few outposts in Africa, and the Caribbean islands of Cuba and Puerto Rico in the Americas.

**AMERICAN INTEREST IN CUBA** The United States had long held an interest in Cuba, which lies only 90 miles south of Florida. In 1854, diplomats recommended to President Franklin Pierce that the United States buy Cuba from Spain. The Spanish responded by saying that they would rather see Cuba sunk in the ocean.

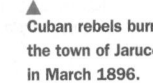
Cuban rebels burn the town of Jaruco in March 1896.

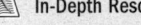

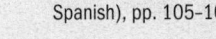

But American interest in Cuba continued. When the Cubans rebelled against Spain between 1868 and 1878, American sympathies went out to the Cuban people.

The Cuban revolt against Spain was not successful, but in 1886 the Cuban people did force Spain to abolish slavery. After the emancipation of Cuba's slaves, American capitalists began investing millions of dollars in large sugar cane plantations on the island.

**THE SECOND WAR FOR INDEPENDENCE** Anti-Spanish sentiment in Cuba soon erupted into a second war for independence. **José Martí,** a Cuban poet and journalist in exile in New York, launched a revolution in 1895. Martí organized Cuban resistance against Spain, using an active guerrilla campaign and deliberately destroying property, especially American-owned sugar mills and plantations. Martí counted on provoking U.S. intervention to help the rebels achieve *Cuba Libre!*—a free Cuba.

**Vocabulary**
**guerrilla:** a member of a military force that harasses the enemy

Public opinion in the United States was split. Many business people wanted the government to support Spain in order to protect their investments. Other Americans, however, were enthusiastic about the rebel cause. The cry "Cuba Libre!" was, after all, similar in sentiment to Patrick Henry's "Give me liberty or give me death!" (A)

MAIN IDEA
**Analyzing Motives**
(A) Why did José Martí encourage Cuban rebels to destroy sugar mills and plantations?

*A. Answer*
Martí hoped to provoke the United States into helping Cuba win independence from Spain.

## War Fever Escalates 2

In 1896, Spain responded to the Cuban revolt by sending General **Valeriano Weyler** to Cuba to restore order. Weyler tried to crush the rebellion by herding the entire rural population of central and western Cuba into barbed-wire concentration camps. Here civilians could not give aid to rebels. An estimated 300,000 Cubans filled these camps, where thousands died from hunger and disease.

**HEADLINE WARS** Weyler's actions fueled a war over newspaper circulation that had developed between the American newspaper tycoons William Randolph Hearst and Joseph Pulitzer. To lure readers, Hearst's *New York Journal* and Pulitzer's *New York World* printed exaggerated accounts—by reporters such as James Creelman—of "Butcher" Weyler's brutality. Stories of poisoned wells and of children being thrown to the sharks deepened American sympathy for the rebels. This sensational style of writing, which exaggerates the news to lure and enrage readers, became known as **yellow journalism.**

TAKS
Mini-Lesson 3:
SS11 5(US24.F)

Hearst and Pulitzer fanned war fever. When Hearst sent the gifted artist Frederic Remington to Cuba to draw sketches of reporters' stories, Remington informed the publisher that a war between the United States and Spain seemed very unlikely. Hearst reportedly replied, "You furnish the pictures and I'll furnish the war."

**THE DE LÔME LETTER** American sympathy for "Cuba Libre!" grew with each day's headlines. When President William McKinley took office in 1897, demands for American intervention in Cuba were on the rise. Preferring to avoid war with Spain, McKinley tried diplomatic means to resolve the crisis. At first, his efforts appeared to succeed. Spain recalled General Weyler, modified the policy regarding concentration camps, and offered Cuba limited self-government.

### KEY PLAYER

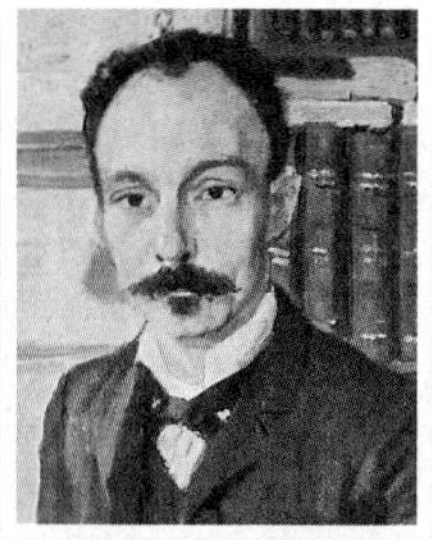

**JOSÉ MARTÍ**
**1853–1895**

The Cuban political activist José Martí dedicated his life to achieving independence for Cuba. Expelled from Cuba at the age of 16 because of his revolutionary activities, Martí earned a master's degree and a law degree. He eventually settled in the United States.

Wary of the U.S. role in the Cuban struggle against the Spanish, Martí warned, "I know the Monster, because I have lived in its lair." His fears of U.S. imperialism turned out to have been well-founded. U.S. troops occupied Cuba on and off from 1906 until 1922.

Martí died fighting for Cuban independence in 1895. He is revered today in Cuba as a hero and martyr.



### KEY PLAYER

**José Martí**
Martí admired one aspect of America—its promotion of personal freedom and individual rights. "One is able to breathe freely, to possess here freedom, [which is] the basis, emblem, and essence of life. Here one can feel proud of one's species." Ask students to discuss other aspects of the United States that foreigners might view favorably.

In-Depth Resources: Unit 3
- American Lives: José Martí, p. 45

## Instruct: Objective 2

**War Fever Escalates**
**TAKS SS11 5(US24.F)**
- How did the Spanish react to the uprising in Cuba?
- What factors helped to arouse American feelings of animosity toward Spain?

In-Depth Resources: Unit 3
- Guided Reading, p. 25
- American Lives: William Randolph Hearst, p. 46

### More About . . .

**Yellow Journalism**
One of Hearst's gimmicks to boost newspaper sales was a color comic strip. The term *yellow journalism* comes from the comic strip's main character, "The Yellow Kid." Hearst's and Pulitzer's role in sensationalizing events such as the sinking of the *Maine* prompted this response from the editor of the New York *Evening Post:* "Nothing so disgraceful . . . has been known in the history of American journalism."

**DIFFERENTIATING INSTRUCTION** | **LESS PROFICIENT READERS**

### Analyzing the Increasing Hostility Toward Spain

Some students might have difficulty understanding the factors that brought the United States and Spain to the brink of war. Have students create a web diagram, such as the one shown here, explaining the factors mentioned on pages 347 and 348. In the diagram, the students should:

- Label the three ovals: Yellow Journalism, The De Lôme letter, Explosion of U.S.S. *Maine.*
- Within each of the three ovals explain each factor in their own words.

Encourage students to use the diagram during class discussion of the section

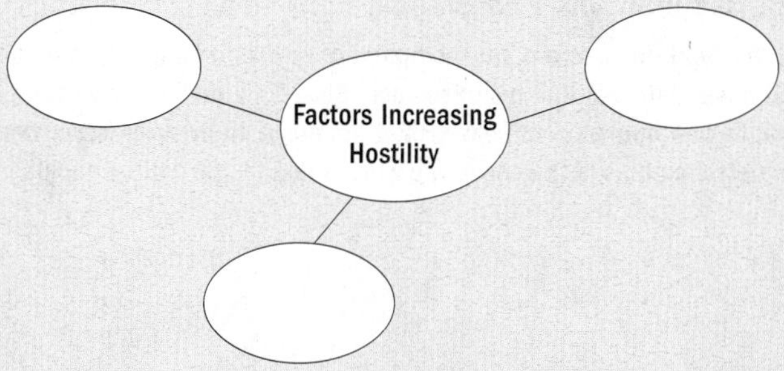

#### The Mystery of the *Maine*

Two different theories have emerged about what caused the mysterious explosion onboard the *Maine*. In 1911, the U.S. Army Corps of Engineers examined the *Maine* on the ocean floor. Based on the discovery of a piece of the ship's hull that was dented from the outside and bent inward, it was determined that a small mine had rocked the vessel.

In 1976, navy researchers examined the piece of bent hull and the photographs taken during the 1911 probe. They concluded that a massive internal explosion had caused the ship's damage. The most likely cause of the explosion was a spontaneous fire in a coal bunker that ignited a nearby supply of weapons.

### Instruct: Objective ❸

#### War with Spain Erupts
**TAKS SS11 1(US3.A)**

· Where was the Spanish-American War fought?

· What were the consequences of the war for Spain and the United States?

· Why did the Treaty of Paris cause such debate among Americans?

📖 **In-Depth Resources: Unit 3**
· Guided Reading, p. 25
· Primary Source: Newspaper Front Page, p. 38

👁 **Electronic Library of Primary Sources**
· from *The "Maine": An Account of Her Destruction*, 1898, Capt. C. D. Sigsbee

In February 1898, however, the *New York Journal* published a private letter written by Enrique Dupuy de Lôme, the Spanish minister to the United States. A Cuban rebel had stolen the letter from a Havana post office and leaked it to the newspaper, which was thirsty for scandal. The de Lôme letter criticized President McKinley, calling him "weak" and "a bidder for the admiration of the crowd." The embarrassed Spanish government apologized, and the minister resigned. Still, Americans were angry over the insult to their president.

**THE *U.S.S. MAINE* EXPLODES** Only a few days after the publication of the de Lôme letter, American resentment toward Spain turned to outrage. Early in 1898, President McKinley had ordered the ***U.S.S. Maine*** to Cuba to bring home American citizens in danger from the fighting and to protect American property. On February 15, 1898, the ship blew up in the harbor of Havana. More than 260 men were killed.

To this day, no one really knows why the ship exploded. In 1898, however, American newspapers claimed the Spanish had blown up the ship. The *Journal*'s headline read "The warship *Maine* was split in two by an enemy's secret infernal machine." Hearst's paper offered a reward of $50,000 for the capture of the Spaniards who supposedly had committed the outrage. **B**

### ❸ War with Spain Erupts

Now there was no holding back the forces that wanted war. "Remember the *Maine!*" became the rallying cry for U.S. intervention in Cuba. It made no difference that the Spanish government agreed, on April 9, to almost everything the United States demanded, including a six-month cease-fire.

▲ When the *U.S.S. Maine* exploded in the harbor of Havana, newspapers like the *New York Journal* were quick to place the blame on Spain.

---

#### Analyzing Assumptions and Biases

**Explaining the Skill** Bias, or a prejudiced point of view, often appears in primary sources and other materials that historians use. Biased material usually favors a special point of view and may not convey the truth about an event or issue. One strategy for detecting bias is to analyze the writer's reasons for writing about the topic.

**Applying the Skill** On the chalkboard write the *New York Journal*'s headline, "THE WARSHIP MAINE WAS SPLIT IN TWO BY AN ENEMY'S SECRET INFERNAL MACHINE." What were the views of William Randolph Hearst, publisher of the *Journal*, concerning Cuba? *(He wanted the United States to go to war with Spain over Cuba. Stories about Cuba were selling subscriptions to the paper.)*

📖 **In-Depth Resources: Unit 3**
· Skillbuilder Practice: Analyzing Assumptions and Biases, p. 29

## The Spanish-American War, 1898

### War in the Caribbean

FLORIDA
Tampa
ATLANTIC
OCEAN
BAHAMAS
(Br.)
Shafter June 22–July 1, 1898
Havana
CUBA
Schley
Santiago
Sampson
HAITI
DOMINICAN
REPUBLIC
JAMAICA
(Br.)
Miles July 25–Aug. 13, 1898
PUERTO
RICO
Cervera May 1898
Caribbean Sea
Tropic of Cancer
15°N

U.S. Forces
U.S. Naval Blockade
Spanish Forces
Battle

0   100   300 miles
0   100   300 kilometers

### War in the Philippines

Hong Kong
20°N
Dewey Apr. 25–May 1, 1898
PACIFIC
OCEAN
Luzon
Manila
Philippine
Islands
Mindoro
Samar
Panay
South
China
Sea
10°N
Negros
Palawan
Mindanao

U.S. Forces
Battle

0   100   200 miles
0   100   200 kilometers

**GEOGRAPHY SKILLBUILDER**
1. **Location** Where does Cuba lie in relation to the United States?
2. **Location** Look at the location of the Philippines. How does the map help explain why Spain was surprised by the American attack in the Philippines?

*Skillbuilder Answer*
1. Cuba lies close to the United States, to the south of Florida.
2. The Philippines lie in the Pacific, hundreds of miles away from the United States. Spain would not be expecting U.S. forces to come from Hong Kong.

---

**MAIN IDEA**

**Analyzing Events**
**C** How did the Spanish try to avoid war with the United States?

*C. Answer* The Spanish agreed to all of the demands of the United States, including a six month cease fire.

Despite the Spanish concessions, public opinion favored war. On April 11, McKinley asked Congress for authority to use force against Spain. After a week of debate, Congress agreed, and on April 20 the United States declared war. **C**

**THE WAR IN THE PHILIPPINES** The Spanish thought the Americans would invade Cuba. But the first battle of the war took place in a Spanish colony on the other side of the world—the Philippine Islands.

On April 30, the American fleet in the Pacific steamed to the Philippines. The next morning, Commodore **George Dewey** gave the command to open fire on the Spanish fleet at Manila, the Philippine capital. In seven hours, Dewey's men had captured or destroyed every Spanish ship there. Dewey's victory allowed U.S. troops to land in the Philippines.

Dewey had the support of the Filipinos who, like the Cubans, also wanted freedom from Spain. Over the next two months, 11,000 Americans joined forces with Filipino rebels led by Emilio Aguinaldo. In August, Spanish troops in Manila surrendered to the United States.

**THE WAR IN THE CARIBBEAN** In the Caribbean, hostilities began with a naval blockade of Cuba. Admiral William T. Sampson effectively sealed up the Spanish fleet in the harbor of Santiago de Cuba.

Dewey's victory at Manila had demonstrated the superiority of United States naval forces. In contrast, the army maintained only a small professional force, supplemented by a larger inexperienced and ill-prepared volunteer force. About

*America Claims an Empire* **349**

---

### HISTORY from VISUALS

**Interpreting the Map**
Point out to students that the row of small triangles in the map on the left indicates the extent of the U.S. naval blockade. Have students consult a globe to help them understand the location of the Philippines shown in the map on the right in relation to the United States.

**Extension** Remind students of Alfred T. Mahan's argument for a strong U.S. navy in his book, *The Influence of Sea Power upon History 1660–1783* (see page 343). Have students discuss the possible effects of a naval blockade on a country.

### More About . . .

**Commodore George Dewey**
Commodore Dewey's success in the Philippines made him a hero in the United States. With his popularity so high, Dewey ran for the presidency in 1900. He soon discovered, however, that running for high office is difficult, even for war heroes. After a series of campaign blunders, including an admission that he never voted, Dewey soon gave up his run for the White House.

---

**ACTIVITY** LINK TO WORLD HISTORY

 classzone.com

### Examining the History of the Philippines

**Class Time** 45 minutes

**Task** Creating a short history of the Philippines

**Purpose** To provide background for learning about U.S. involvement in the Philippines

**Directions** Divide students into small groups. Each group should be responsible for researching and writing about a particular period or aspect of Philippine history up to 1920 (social, economic, or political). Students should provide a list of the Internet and library sources that they used. Have each group choose one student to present the group's findings to the class.

 Integrated Assessment
· Rubric 5

**More About . . .**

## Battle of San Juan Hill

Twenty years after the battle, Roosevelt stated, "San Juan was the great day of my life." He believed that he deserved the Congressional Medal of Honor for his part in the war, but the award was denied him.

 **In-Depth Resources: Unit 3**
· Primary Sources: from *The Rough Riders*, by Theodore Roosevelt, p. 39

**Tracing Themes**

**AMERICA IN WORLD AFFAIRS**

## U.S. Imperialism

The United States wanted to take over the Philippines for a number of reasons. The U.S. government wanted to forestall Germany and other imperialist countries. Many people believed that an independent Philippine Republic would lead to a scramble for territory by several European countries. The United States also needed new markets for its exports and believed that China, with its vast population, would be a promising choice. The Philippines would provide a commercial base in that part of the world.

**In-Depth Resources: Unit 3**
· Primary Source: In Favor of Imperialism, p. 40

---

125,000 Americans had volunteered to fight. The new soldiers were sent to training camps that lacked adequate supplies and effective leaders. Moreover, there were not enough modern guns to go around, and the troops were outfitted with heavy woolen uniforms unsuitable for Cuba's tropical climate. In addition, the officers—most of whom were Civil War veterans—had a tendency to spend their time recalling their war experiences rather than training the volunteers.

**ROUGH RIDERS** Despite these handicaps, American forces landed in Cuba in June 1898 and began to converge on the port city of Santiago. The army of 17,000 included four African-American regiments of the regular army and the **Rough Riders,** a volunteer cavalry under the command of Leonard Wood and Theodore Roosevelt. Roosevelt, a young New Yorker, had given up his job as Assistant Secretary of the Navy to lead the group of volunteers. He would later become president of the United States.

The most famous land battle in Cuba took place near Santiago on July 1. The first part of the battle, on nearby Kettle Hill, featured a dramatic uphill charge by the Rough Riders and two African-American regiments, the Ninth and Tenth

▲
These African-American troops prepare for battle during the Spanish-American War.

Cavalries. Their victory cleared the way for an infantry attack on the strategically important **San Juan Hill.** Although Roosevelt and his units played only a minor role in the second victory, U.S. newspapers declared him the hero of San Juan Hill.

Two days later, the Spanish fleet tried to escape the American blockade of the harbor at Santiago. The naval battle that followed, along the Cuban coast, ended in the destruction of the Spanish fleet. On the heels of this victory, American troops invaded Puerto Rico on July 25.

**TREATY OF PARIS** The United States and Spain signed an armistice, a cease-fire agreement, on August 12, ending what Secretary of State John Hay called "a splendid little war." The actual fighting in the war had lasted only 16 weeks.

On December 10, 1898, the United States and Spain met in Paris to agree on a treaty. At the peace talks, Spain freed Cuba and turned over the islands of Guam in the Pacific and Puerto Rico in the West Indies to the United States. Spain also sold the Philippines to the United States for $20 million. **D**

**DEBATE OVER THE TREATY** The **Treaty of Paris** touched off a great debate in the United States. Arguments centered on whether or not the United States had the right to annex the Philippines, but imperialism was the real issue. President McKinley told a group of Methodist ministers that he had prayed for guidance on Philippine annexation and had concluded "that there was nothing left for us to do but to take them all [the Philippine Islands], and to educate the Filipinos, and uplift and Christianize them." McKinley's need to justify imperialism may

**Background**
The Rough Riders trained as cavalry but fought on foot because their horses didn't reach Cuba in time.

*D. Answer*
Spain freed Cuba and turned over the islands of Guam and Puerto Rico to the United States. Spain also sold the Philippines to the United States for $20 million.

**MAIN IDEA**

**Summarizing**
**D** What were the terms of the Treaty of Paris?

---

**ACTIVITY** | **COOPERATIVE LEARNING** |  **BLOCK SCHEDULING**

## Covering the Rough Riders

**Class Time** 45 minutes

**Task** Role-playing as reporters and members of the Rough Riders to create a TV news broadcast about the key battles of the war in Cuba

**Purpose** To help students better understand the major battles of the Spanish-American War and the reasons why the United States won

**Directions** Have student pairs do further research on the Rough Riders as well as the battles of Kettle Hill and San Juan Hill. One student will play a reporter, while the other plays members of the Rough Riders. The students should write a script for the news broadcast. The reporter will interview the Rough Rider about his experiences in the war for the class.

**Integrated Assessment**
· Rubric 3

have clouded his memory—most Filipinos had been Christian for centuries.

Other prominent Americans presented a variety of arguments—political, moral, and economic—against annexation. Some felt that the treaty violated the Declaration of Independence by denying self-government to the newly acquired territories. The African-American educator Booker T. Washington argued that the United States should settle race-related issues at home before taking on social problems elsewhere. The labor leader Samuel Gompers feared that Filipino immigrants would compete for American jobs.

On February 6, 1899, the annexation question was settled with the Senate's approval of the Treaty of Paris. The United States now had an empire that included Cuba, Guam, Puerto Rico, and the Philippines. The next question Americans faced was how and when the United States would add to its dominion.

COASTING.

▲ This lithograph criticizes American foreign policy in 1898. In the cartoon, Uncle Sam is riding a bicycle with wheels labeled "western hemisphere" and "eastern hemisphere." He has abandoned his horse, on whose saddle appears "Monroe Doctrine," because the horse is too slow.

## HISTORY from VISUALS

**Interpreting the Lithograph**
Remind students that by issuing the Monroe Doctrine in 1823, the United States warned European nations to stay out of the Western Hemisphere while promising not to intervene in the affairs of the European nations. By becoming an imperial power, however, the United States seemed to be ignoring that pledge.

## Assess & Reteach

### SECTION 2 ASSESSMENT
Have the students work in small groups to answer the questions in the section assessment.

📄 Formal Assessment
· Section Quiz, p. 194

### SELF-ASSESSMENT
Have pairs of students use the Main Idea questions to review the main ideas in this section. Students should locate the portion of the text that helps answer each question.

### RETEACH
Have groups of students work together to outline the main points of each boldfaced heading in this section. Groups should share their outlines with the class.

📄 In-Depth Resources: Unit 3
· Reteaching Activity, p. 31

---

 **ASSESSMENT**

**1. TERMS & NAMES** For each term or name, write a sentence explaining its significance.

- José Martí
- Valeriano Weyler
- yellow journalism
- *U.S.S. Maine*
- George Dewey
- Rough Riders
- San Juan Hill
- Treaty of Paris

### MAIN IDEA

**2. TAKING NOTES**
In 1898, a debate raged in the United States over whether the U.S. had the right to annex the Philippines. Use a graphic organizer like the one below to summarize the pros and cons of this debate.

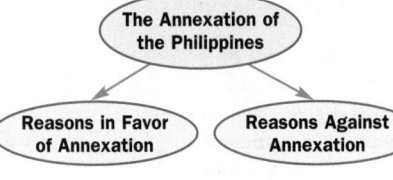

Which side do you support? Why?

### CRITICAL THINKING

**3. MAKING INFERENCES**
What do you think were the unstated editorial policies of yellow journalism? Support your answer with evidence from the text.
**Think About:**
- James Creelman's account of Spanish atrocities against Cubans (page 346)
- Hearst's remark to Remington
- the *Journal* headline about the explosion of the battleship *Maine*

**4. ANALYZING EFFECTS**
Many anti-imperialists worried that imperialism might threaten the American democratic system. How might this happen?

**5. DRAWING CONCLUSIONS**
In 1898 Theodore Roosevelt resigned his post as Assistant Secretary of the Navy to organize the Rough Riders. Why do you think Roosevelt was willing to take this risk? How do you think this decision affected his political career?

*America Claims an Empire* **351**

---

**Answers** ASSESSMENT

**1. TERMS & NAMES**
José Martí, p. 347
Valeriano Weyler, p. 347
yellow journalism, p. 347
U.S.S. *Maine*, p. 348
George Dewey, p. 349
Rough Riders, p. 350
San Juan Hill, p. 350
Treaty of Paris, p. 350

**2. TAKING NOTES**
**In favor:** to educate the people and make them Christians
**Against:** Annexation would be a violation of self-government, which is guaranteed by the Constitution.

**3. MAKING INFERENCES**
To create news rather than to document it; to sensationalize events by distorting the truth; to exploit the public's

fears; to manipulate the public's perceptions of events; to write articles that sell newspapers; to advance the newspaper publisher's political views

**4. ANALYZING EFFECTS**
Imperialism does not consider the rights of native peoples. It violates basic rights granted to Americans by the Declaration of Independence and the U.S. Constitution.

**5. DRAWING CONCLUSIONS**
Roosevelt loved adventure and the idea of helping the weak defeat the strong. The publicity that he got as a result of his participation probably added to his appeal as a political candidate.

*America Claims an Empire* **351**

# OBJECTIVES

**1** Describe U.S. involvement in Puerto Rico and in Cuba

**2** Identify causes and effects of the Philippine-American War.

**3** Explain the purpose of the Open Door Policy in China.

**4** Summarize the views regarding U.S. imperialism.

## SKILLBUILDERS

· Analyzing Political Cartoons, p. 354
· Geography Skillbuilder: location, human-environment interaction, p. 356

## CRITICAL THINKING

· Analyzing Issues, pp. 353, 358
· Contrasting, p. 355
· Analyzing Causes, p. 356
· Evaluating, p. 358
· Comparing, p. 358

## Focus & Motivate

Ask students how they try to convince their parents to give them greater independence. Then ask them how colonial populations might convince the United States to grant them greater freedom and self-government.

## Instruct

### Instruct: Objective **1**

**Ruling Puerto Rico / Cuba and the United States**

TAKS SS11 1(US3.A)
· What was the significance of the Foraker Act?
· What did the Platt Amendment state?
· Why did the United States wish to attain a strong influence in Cuba?

 In-Depth Resources: Unit 3
· Guided Reading, p. 26

# Acquiring New Lands

| MAIN IDEA | WHY IT MATTERS NOW | Terms & Names |
|---|---|---|
| In the early 1900s, the United States engaged in conflicts in Puerto Rico, Cuba, and the Philippines. | Today, the United States maintains a strong military and political presence in strategic worldwide locations. | • Foraker Act • John Hay<br>• Platt Amendment • Open Door notes<br>• protectorate • Boxer Rebellion<br>• Emilio Aguinaldo |

**U.S. History** 1B, 2B, 3A, 8A, 8B, 9B, 12D, 12E, 17A, 19A, 21A, 24A, 24B, 24C, 24F, 25A, 25B, 25C, 25D

### One American's Story

When Puerto Rico became part of the United States after the Spanish-American War, many Puerto Ricans feared that the United States would not give them the measure of self-rule that they had gained under the Spanish. Puerto Rican statesman and publisher Luis Muñoz Rivera was one of the most vocal advocates of Puerto Rican self-rule. Between 1900 and 1916, he lived primarily in the United States and continually worked for the independence of his homeland. Finally, in 1916, the U.S. Congress, facing possible war in Europe and wishing to settle the issue of Puerto Rico, invited Muñoz Rivera to speak. On May 5, 1916, Muñoz Rivera stood before the U.S. House of Representatives to discuss the future of Puerto Rico.

▲ Luis Muñoz Rivera

**A PERSONAL VOICE** LUIS MUÑOZ RIVERA

" You, citizens of a free fatherland, with its own laws, its own institutions, and its own flag, can appreciate the unhappiness of the small and solitary people that must await its laws from your authority. . . . when you acquire the certainty that you can found in Puerto Rico a republic like that founded in Cuba and Panama . . . give us our independence and you will stand before humanity as . . . a great creator of new nationalities and a great liberator of oppressed peoples. "

—quoted in *The Puerto Ricans*

Muñoz Rivera returned to Puerto Rico where he died in November 1916. Three months later, the United States made Puerto Ricans U.S. citizens.

## **1** Ruling Puerto Rico

Not all Puerto Ricans wanted independence, as Muñoz Rivera did. Some wanted statehood, while still others hoped for some measure of local self-government as an American territory. As a result, the United States gave Puerto Ricans no promises regarding independence after the Spanish-American War.

---

## PROGRAM RESOURCES

 In-Depth Resources: Unit 3
· Guided Reading, p. 26
· Reteaching Activity, p. 32

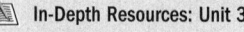 Reading Study Guide (English and Spanish), pp. 107–108

Access for Students Acquiring English/ESL
· Guided Reading (Spanish), p. 125

 Formal Assessment
· Section Quiz, p. 195

 Integrated Assessment
· Rubrics

## INTEGRATED TECHNOLOGY

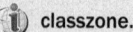 Humanities Transp. HT17, HT37
· Athletic Contest
· Declined with Thanks

Electronic Library of Primary Sources

classzone.com

## TEXAS RESOURCES

 TAKS Spiraled Content Review

 TAKS Practice Tests

 TAKS Practice Transparencies TT69

 TAKS Online Test Practice

**MILITARY RULE** During the Spanish-American War, United States forces, under General Nelson A. Miles, occupied the island. As his soldiers took control, General Miles issued a statement assuring Puerto Ricans that the Americans were there to "bring you protection, not only to yourselves but to your property, to promote your prosperity, and to bestow upon you the immunities and blessings of the liberal institutions of our government." For the time being, Puerto Rico would be controlled by the military until Congress decided otherwise.

**RETURN TO CIVIL GOVERNMENT** Although many Puerto Ricans had dreams of independence or statehood, the United States had different plans for the island's future. Puerto Rico was strategically important to the United States, both for maintaining a U.S. presence in the Caribbean and for protecting a future canal that American leaders wanted to build across the Isthmus of Panama. In 1900, Congress passed the **Foraker Act,** which ended military rule and set up a civil government. The act gave the president of the United States the power to appoint Puerto Rico's governor and members of the upper house of its legislature. Puerto Ricans could elect only the members of the legislature's lower house. **Ⓐ**

In 1901, in the Insular Cases, the U.S. Supreme Court ruled that the Constitution did not automatically apply to people in acquired territories. Congress, however, retained the right to extend U.S. citizenship, and it granted that right to Puerto Ricans in 1917. It also gave them the right to elect both houses of their legislature.

## ❶ Cuba and the United States

When the United States declared war against Spain in 1898, it recognized Cuba's independence from Spain. It also passed the Teller Amendment, which stated that the United States had no intention of taking over any part of Cuba. The Treaty of Paris, which ended the war, further guaranteed Cuba the independence that its nationalist leaders had been demanding for years.

**AMERICAN SOLDIERS** Though officially independent, Cuba was occupied by American troops when the war ended. José Martí, the Cuban patriot who had led the movement for independence from Spain, had feared that the United States would merely replace Spain and dominate Cuban politics. In some ways, Martí's prediction came true. Under American occupation, the same officials who had served Spain remained in office. Cubans who protested this policy were imprisoned or exiled.

On the other hand, the American military government provided food and clothing for thousands of families, helped farmers put land back into cultivation, and organized elementary schools. Through improvement of sanitation and medical research, the military government helped eliminate yellow fever, a disease that had killed hundreds of Cubans each year.

---

**MAIN IDEA**

**Analyzing Issues**
**Ⓐ** Why was Puerto Rico important to the United States?

**Background**
Yellow fever damages many body parts, especially the liver. Dr. Carlos Finlay discovered that the disease is carried by mosquitoes. Clearing out the mosquitos' breeding places helped eliminate the disease in Cuba.

---

**NOW & THEN**

**PUERTO RICO**

Ever since their transfer under the Treaty of Paris from Spain to the United States, Puerto Ricans have debated their status, as shown above. In 1967, 1993, and 1998, Puerto Ricans rejected both statehood and independence in favor of commonwealth, a status given the island in 1952.

As members of a commonwealth, Puerto Ricans are U.S. citizens. They can move freely between the island and the mainland and are subjected to the military draft but cannot vote in U.S. presidential elections. A majority of Puerto Ricans have rejected statehood because they fear it would mean giving up their Latino culture.

---

**NOW & THEN**

**Puerto Rico**

**Analyzing Issues** Have groups of students research Puerto Rico's latest vote to choose statehood, independence, or commonwealth status. The students should divide into three smaller groups, with one group presenting the arguments for statehood, one group presenting the arguments of those favoring independence, and a third presenting arguments for remaining a commonwealth. Have the three groups discuss their findings with each other.

**Tracing Themes**

**CIVIL RIGHTS**

**Constitutional Protections for Territories**
The U.S. Constitution does not explicitly address the rights of people in acquired territories. The U.S. Supreme Court ultimately ruled that the Constitution does not automatically apply to residents of acquired territories. Some justices disagreed with this view, including Justice John Marshall Harlan. He wrote that, in essence, the Constitution should follow the flag.

*America Claims an Empire* **353**

---

**DIFFERENTIATING INSTRUCTION** **GIFTED AND TALENTED**

 **classzone.com**

**Researching the Insular Cases**

The Insular Cases were some 14 U.S. Supreme Court decisions from 1901 to 1904 that addressed the application of the U.S. Constitution to overseas territories. Have interested students research one of the cases using the Internet and library resources, and write a report on the decision. In writing their report, students should address the questions at the right, among others.

· What legal arguments did each side put forth in the case?
· Why did the Court rule the way it did?
· If the Court's ruling was not unanimous, what view did the dissenting justices take?

 Integrated Assessment
· Rubric 1, 5

TAKS

Mini-Lesson 5:
SS11 3(20.B)

## More About . . .

### The Platt Amendment

The Platt Amendment was named after Senator Orville Platt of Connecticut, chairman of the Senate Committee on Cuban Relations. Much of the document was crafted by Secretary of War Elihu Root, who made no secret of his opinion that the Cuban people lacked the ability to govern themselves. Not surprisingly, the Platt Amendment met with great opposition from the Cuban people. Juan Gualberto Gómez, a leader in the fight against Spain, angrily declared that the amendment had "reduced the independence and sovereignty of the Cuban republic to a myth."

**PLATT AMENDMENT** In 1900 the newly formed Cuban government wrote a constitution for an independent Cuba. The constitution, however, did not specify the relationship between Cuba and the United States. Consequently, in 1901, the United States insisted that Cuba add to its constitution several provisions, known as the **Platt Amendment,** stating that

- Cuba could not make treaties that might limit its independence or permit a foreign power to control any part of its territory
- the United States reserved the right to intervene in Cuba
- Cuba was not to go into debt
- the United States could buy or lease land on the island for naval stations and refueling stations

The United States made it clear that its army would not withdraw until Cuba adopted the Platt Amendment. In response, a torchlight procession marched on the residence of Governor-General Leonard Wood in protest. Some protestors even called for a return to arms to defend their national honor against this American insult. The U.S. government stood firm, though, and Cubans reluctantly ratified the new constitution. In 1903, the Platt Amendment became part of a treaty between the two nations, and it remained in effect for 31 years. Under the terms of the treaty, Cuba became a U.S. **protectorate,** a country whose affairs are partially controlled by a stronger power.

**Vocabulary**
**ratify:** to make valid by approving

**PROTECTING AMERICAN BUSINESS INTERESTS** The most important reason for the United States to maintain a strong political presence in Cuba was to protect American businesses that had invested in the island's sugar, tobacco, and mining industries, as well as in its railroads and public utilities.

## Analyzing *Political Cartoons*

### SKILLBUILDER ANSWERS

1. Bill of fare: Cuba Steak, Porto Rico pig, Philippine Floating Islands, Sandwich Islands
2. The waiter portrays President William McKinley, who was a staunch imperialist.
3. Uncle Sam's attitude seems to be that he can have the pick of anything on the menu.

### Analyzing 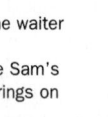 *Political Cartoons*

#### "WELL, I HARDLY KNOW WHICH TO TAKE FIRST!"

Throughout the early 1900s, the United States intervened in the affairs of its Latin American neighbors several times. American troops withdrew from Cuba in 1902 but later returned three times to quell popular uprisings against conservative leaders. The U.S. also intervened in Nicaragua and Haiti. Not surprisingly, few Latin Americans welcomed United States intervention. As the cartoon shows, the United States had a different point of view.

#### SKILLBUILDER
**Analyzing Political Cartoons**
1. What is on the bill of fare, or menu, in this restaurant?
2. Which president does the waiter portray?
3. What seems to be Uncle Sam's attitude toward the offerings on the menu?

SEE SKILLBUILDER HANDBOOK, PAGE R24.

WELL, I HARDLY KNOW WHICH TO TAKE FIRST!

**354** CHAPTER 10

---

**DIFFERENTIATING INSTRUCTION**    **LESS PROFICIENT READERS**

### Analyzing the Platt Amendment

Help students understand why the United States insisted on the Platt Amendment in Cuba's constitution. List each provision on the board as shown at the right. Ask students to think of a reason why each provision would be advantageous to the United States. *(Example: Provision 4, the United States could buy or lease land—then the United States could carry on business.)* To help students get ideas, have them reread the text under "Protecting American Business Interests" on pages 354–355.

| Provisions | Advantages for the United States |
|---|---|
| 1. Cuba could not make treaties that might limit its independence. | |
| 2. The United States reserved the right to intervene in Cuba. | |
| 3. Cuba was not to go into debt. | |
| 4. The United States could buy or lease land. | |

Although many businesspeople were convinced that annexing and imposing colonial rule on new territories was necessary to protect American business interests, some were concerned about colonial entanglements. The industrialist Andrew Carnegie argued against the taking of nations as colonies.

**A PERSONAL VOICE** ANDREW CARNEGIE

" The exports of the United States this year [1898] are greater than those of any other nation in the world. Even Britain's exports are less, yet Britain 'possesses' . . . a hundred 'colonies' . . . scattered all over the world. The fact that the United States has none does not prevent her products and manufactures from invading . . . all parts of the world in competition with those of Britain. "

—quoted in *Distant Possessions*

Despite such concerns, the U.S. state department continued to push for control of its Latin American neighbors. In the years to come, the United States would intervene time and again in the affairs of other nations in the Western Hemisphere.

## ② Filipinos Rebel

In the Philippines, Filipinos reacted with outrage to the Treaty of Paris, which called for American annexation of the Philippines. The rebel leader **Emilio Aguinaldo** (ĕ-mēl′yō ä′gē-näl′dō) believed that the United States had promised independence. When he and his followers learned the terms of the treaty, they vowed to fight for freedom.

**PHILIPPINE–AMERICAN WAR** In February 1899, the Filipinos, led by Aguinaldo, rose in revolt. The United States assumed almost the same role that Spain had played, imposing its authority on a colony that was fighting for freedom. When Aguinaldo turned to guerrilla tactics, the United States forced Filipinos to live in designated zones, where poor sanitation, starvation, and disease killed thousands. This was the very same practice that Americans had condemned Spain for using in Cuba.

During the occupation, white American soldiers looked on the Filipinos as inferiors. However, many of the 70,000 U.S. troops sent to the Philippines were African Americans. When African-American newspapers questioned why blacks were helping to spread racial prejudice to the Philippines, some African-American soldiers deserted to the Filipino side and developed bonds of friendship with the Filipinos.

It took the Americans nearly three years to put down the rebellion. About 20,000 Filipino rebels died fighting for independence. The war claimed 4,000 American lives and cost $400 million—20 times the price the United States had paid to purchase the islands. **B**

**AFTERMATH OF THE WAR** After suppressing the rebellion, the United States set up a government similar to the one it had established for Puerto Rico. The U.S. president would appoint a governor, who would then appoint the upper house of the legislature. Filipinos would elect the lower house. Under American rule, the Philippines moved gradually toward independence and finally became an independent republic on July 4, 1946.

▲ U.S. military action in the Philippines resulted in suffering for Filipino civilians. About 200,000 people died as a result of malnutrition, disease, and such guerrilla tactics as the burning of villages.

**MAIN IDEA**

**Contrasting**
**B** What were the aims of the Filipinos? of the Americans?

**B. Answer**
Filipinos wanted independence. The U.S. wanted to govern the islands.

*America Claims an Empire* **355**

**Instruct: Objective ②**

**Filipinos Rebel**
TAKS SS11 5(US8.B)
· Why did many Filipinos feel betrayed by the United States?
· How was the Philippine-American War a costly one for both the Philippines and the United States?

In-Depth Resources: Unit 3
· Guided Reading, p. 26

Electronic Library of Primary Sources
· On the War in the Phillipines, 1900, by A. Beveridge

**Tracing Themes**
**DIVERSITY AND NATIONAL IDENTITY**

**African Americans in the Philippines**
Filipino rebel leader Emilio Aguinaldo recognized the irony of African Americans fighting to put down the independence movement of another oppressed people of color. He signed a proclamation that was delivered to the 24th U.S. Infantry, an African-American regiment. It read in part: "Your masters have thrown you into the . . . fight with double purpose—to make you the instrument of their ambition and also your hard work will soon make the extinction of your race." While some African Americans did put down their weapons and abandon the American cause, many others refused to do so. African-American soldiers protested that they were "just as loyal to the old flag as white Americans."

---

## Vocabulary

Help students understand these terms from the text in order to comprehend the types of rule that the United States established for Puerto Rico, Cuba, and the Philippines:

**Puerto Rico:** independence, statehood, intervention, strategically important, protecting, elect, houses of legislature

**Cuba:** protectorate, occupation, constitution, provisions, amendment, economic interests, intervene

**Philippines:** rebel, rebellion, annexation, independent republic

## U.S. Imperialism, 1867–1906

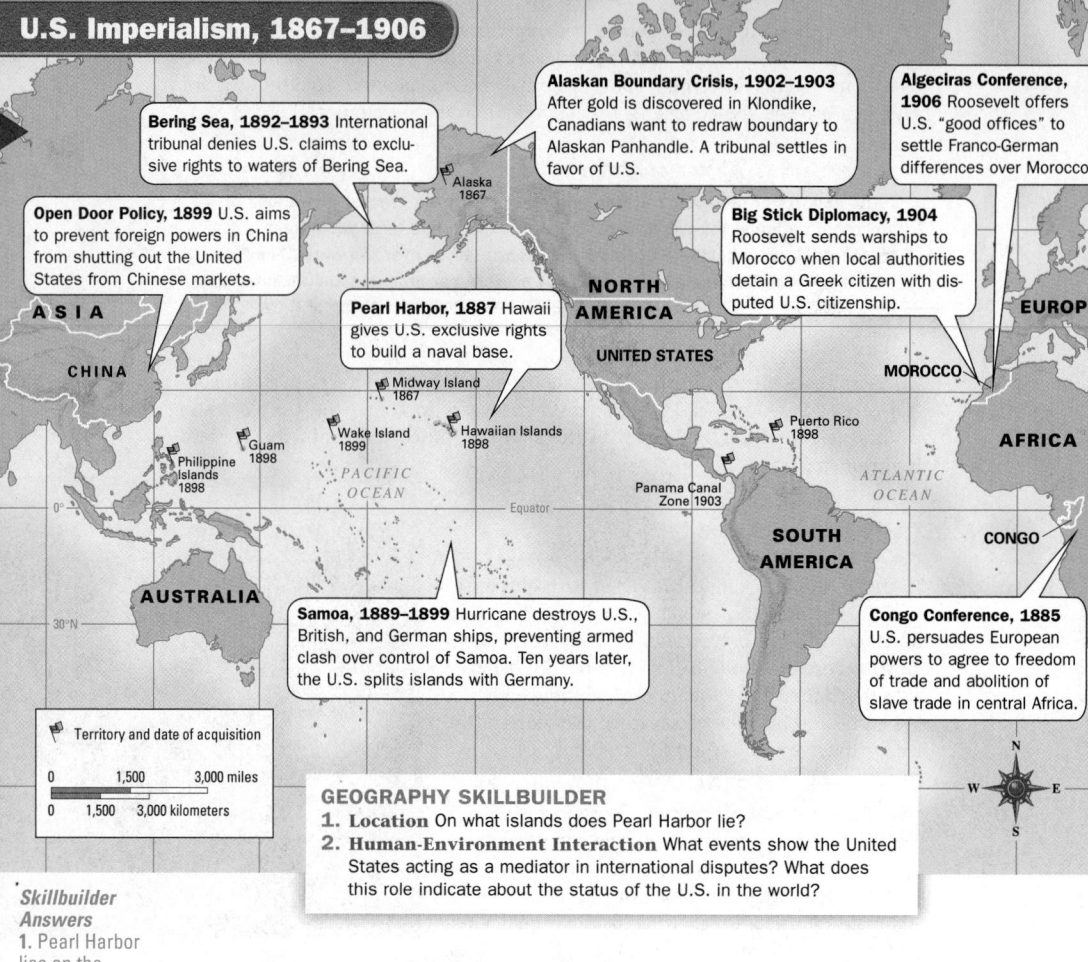

**Bering Sea, 1892–1893** International tribunal denies U.S. claims to exclusive rights to waters of Bering Sea.

**Alaskan Boundary Crisis, 1902–1903** After gold is discovered in Klondike, Canadians want to redraw boundary to Alaskan Panhandle. A tribunal settles in favor of U.S.

**Algeciras Conference, 1906** Roosevelt offers U.S. "good offices" to settle Franco-German differences over Morocco.

**Open Door Policy, 1899** U.S. aims to prevent foreign powers in China from shutting out the United States from Chinese markets.

**Big Stick Diplomacy, 1904** Roosevelt sends warships to Morocco when local authorities detain a Greek citizen with disputed U.S. citizenship.

**Pearl Harbor, 1887** Hawaii gives U.S. exclusive rights to build a naval base.

Alaska 1867

Midway Island 1867

Wake Island 1899

Guam 1898

Philippine Islands 1898

Hawaiian Islands 1898

Puerto Rico 1898

Panama Canal Zone 1903

**Samoa, 1889–1899** Hurricane destroys U.S., British, and German ships, preventing armed clash over control of Samoa. Ten years later, the U.S. splits islands with Germany.

**Congo Conference, 1885** U.S. persuades European powers to agree to freedom of trade and abolition of slave trade in central Africa.

ASIA · CHINA · AUSTRALIA · NORTH AMERICA · UNITED STATES · MOROCCO · EUROPE · AFRICA · CONGO · SOUTH AMERICA · PACIFIC OCEAN · ATLANTIC OCEAN · Equator

Territory and date of acquisition

0 — 1,500 — 3,000 miles
0 — 1,500 — 3,000 kilometers

### GEOGRAPHY SKILLBUILDER
1. **Location** On what islands does Pearl Harbor lie?
2. **Human-Environment Interaction** What events show the United States acting as a mediator in international disputes? What does this role indicate about the status of the U.S. in the world?

*Skillbuilder Answers*
1. Pearl Harbor lies on the Hawaiian Islands.
2. *Mediator:* The Algeciras and Congo conferences. *Status:* It shows the growing power and prestige of the United States, because other powerful nations chose the U.S. to help settle their disputes.

## ❸ Foreign Influence in China

U.S. imperialists saw the Philippines as a gateway to the rest of Asia, particularly to China. China was seen as a vast potential market for American products. It also presented American investors with new opportunities for large-scale railroad construction.

Weakened by war and foreign intervention, China had become known as the "sick man of Asia." France, Germany, Britain, Japan, and Russia had established prosperous settlements along the coast of China. They also had carved out spheres of influence, areas where each nation claimed special rights and economic privileges.

**JOHN HAY'S OPEN DOOR NOTES** The United States began to fear that China would be carved into colonies and American traders would be shut out. To protect American interests, U.S. Secretary of State **John Hay** issued, in 1899, a series of policy statements called the **Open Door notes.** The notes were letters addressed to the leaders of imperialist nations proposing that the nations share their trading rights with the United States, thus creating an open door. This meant that no single nation would have a monopoly on trade with any part of China. The other imperialist powers reluctantly accepted this policy. **ⓒ**

*C. Answer*
To protect American access to Chinese markets and to help maintain the independence of China.

**MAIN IDEA**

Analyzing Causes
**ⓒ** Why did Secretary of State John Hay issue the policy statements known as the Open Door notes?

---

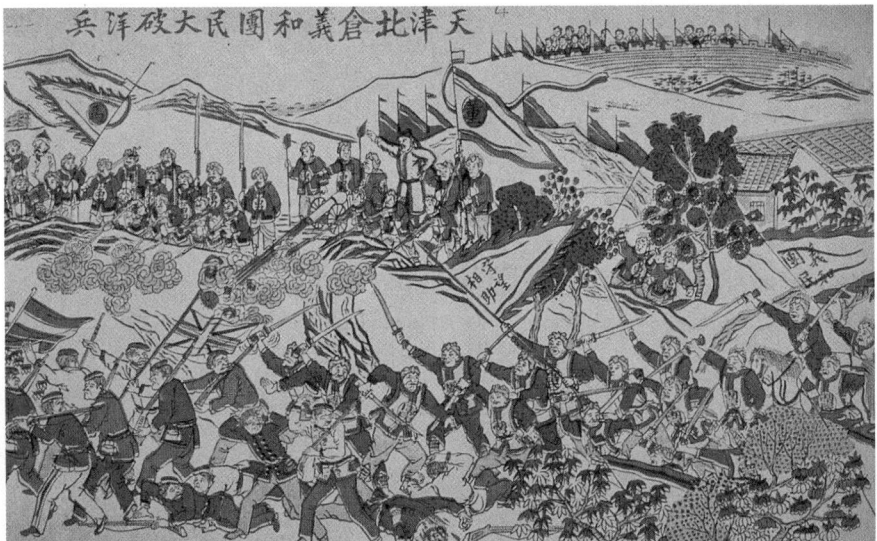

During the Boxer Rebellion, shown here in this Chinese print, Chinese patriots demanded that all foreigners be expelled from the country. The Boxers surrounded the European section of Beijing and kept it under siege for several months.

**THE BOXER REBELLION IN CHINA** Although China kept its freedom, Europeans dominated most of China's large cities. Resentment simmered beneath the surface as some Chinese formed secret societies pledged to rid the country of "foreign devils." The most famous of these secret groups were the Boxers, so named by Westerners because members practiced martial arts.

The Boxers killed hundreds of missionaries and other foreigners, as well as Chinese converts to Christianity. In August 1900, troops from Britain, France, Germany, and Japan joined about 2,500 American soldiers and marched on the Chinese capital. Within two months, the international forces put down the **Boxer Rebellion.** Thousands of Chinese people died during the fighting.

**PROTECTING AMERICAN RIGHTS** After the Boxer Rebellion, the United States feared that European nations would use their victory to take even greater control of China. To prevent this, John Hay issued a second series of Open Door notes, announcing that the United States would "safeguard for the world the principle of equal and impartial trade with all parts of the Chinese Empire." This policy paved the way for greater American influence in Asia.

The Open Door policy reflected three deeply held American beliefs about the United States industrial capitalist economy. First, Americans believed that the growth of the U.S. economy depended on exports. Second, they felt the United States had a right to intervene abroad to keep foreign markets open. Third, they feared that the closing of an area to American products, citizens, or ideas threatened U.S. survival. These beliefs became the bedrock of American foreign policy.

**Vocabulary**
**martial arts:** combat or self defense arts that originated in East Asia, such as judo or karate

## WORLD STAGE

### THE BOXER PROTOCOL

On September 7, 1901, China and 11 other nations signed the Boxer Protocol—a final settlement of the Boxer Rebellion.

The Qing government agreed to execute some Chinese officials, to punish others, and to pay about $332 million in damages. The United States was awarded a settlement of $24.5 million. It used about $4 million to pay American citizens for actual losses incurred during the rebellion. In 1908, the U.S. government returned the rest of the money to China to be used for the purpose of educating Chinese students in their own country and in the United States.

### More About . . .

#### The Boxers
The Boxers are believed to have formed around the beginning of the 19th century. The group's real name was Tho ch'üan, or "Righteous and Harmonious Fists," from which the term "Boxers" came. The Boxers opposed Christianity, the Chinese power structure, and foreigners. Most of its members were young peasant men, and those who joined the group had to follow strict lifestyle guidelines.

### ON THE WORLD STAGE

#### The Boxer Protocol
**Analyzing Motives** Ask students why they think the United States chose to return to China some of the money it received from the Boxer Protocol settlement. *(U.S. officials hoped that by returning the money they might improve relations with China and reduce some of the resentment the Chinese might have felt about American intervention in their country.)*

 **Humanities Transparencies HT17**
· *Athletic Contest* by Max Weber

---

**DIFFERENTIATING INSTRUCTION** | **GIFTED AND TALENTED** |  **classzone.com**

### Investigating the Life and Rule of Empress Cixi

Empress Cixi (also spelled Tzu Hsi), who ruled China during the Boxer Rebellion, was one of the most powerful women in the history of China. Like the Boxers, Cixi detested foreign influence in China. "The foreigners are like fish in the stewpan," she said. "For forty years have I . . . eaten bitterness because of them."

Have interested students research and report on Empress Cixi's reign and her role in the Boxer Rebellion. Students should consider the following questions:

· Why did she endorse and then eventually condemn the rebellion?
· How did she maintain power after Western nations put down the uprising?

📋 **Integrated Assessment**
· Rubric 1, 5

**The Impact of U.S. Territorial Gains**

TAKS SS11 5(US24.A)

· What did the reelection of William McKinley seem to indicate about the American public's view of imperialism?

· What view of imperialism did supporters of the Anti-Imperialism League take?

 In-Depth Resources: Unit 3
· Guided Reading, p. 26

## Assess & Reteach

### SECTION 3 ASSESSMENT

Have students work in small groups to answer the questions. Have one student from each group read the group's answer to question 3 before the class. (If the group formed two opinions, have two students read.)

 Formal Assessment
· Section Quiz, p. 195

### SELF-ASSESSMENT

Have students work in study groups to form answers to the inner column questions.

### RETEACH

Divide the class into five groups and have each group prepare a summary of the information under one of the section's boldfaced headings. Have each group present its summary to the class.

In-Depth Resources: Unit 3
· Reteaching Activity, p. 32

---

## 4 The Impact of U.S. Territorial Gains

In 1900, Republican William McKinley, a reluctant but confirmed imperialist, was elected to a second term against Democrat William Jennings Bryan, who staunchly opposed imperialism. McKinley's reelection confirmed that a majority of Americans favored his policies. Under McKinley, the United States had gained an empire.

Yet even before McKinley was reelected, an Anti-Imperialist League had sprung into being. The league included some of the most prominent people in America, such as former president Grover Cleveland, industrial leader Andrew Carnegie, the social worker Jane Addams, and many leading writers. Anti-imperialists had different and sometimes conflicting reasons for their opposition, but all agreed that it was wrong for the United States to rule other people without their consent. The novelist Mark Twain questioned the motives for imperialism in a satirical piece written in 1901.

**TAKS**

Mini-Lesson 4:
SS11 2(11.F)

**A PERSONAL VOICE** MARK TWAIN

"Shall we go on conferring our Civilization upon the peoples that sit in darkness, or shall we give those poor things a rest? . . . Extending the Blessings of Civilization to our Brother who Sits in Darkness has been a good trade and has paid well, on the whole; and there is money in it yet . . . but not enough, in my judgment, to make any considerable risk advisable."

—quoted in *To the Person Sitting in Darkness*

As a novelist, Twain had great influence on American culture but little influence on foreign policy. In the early 20th century, the United States under President Theodore Roosevelt and President Woodrow Wilson would continue to exert its power around the globe.

▲ Mark Twain

---

## SECTION 3 ASSESSMENT

**1. TERMS & NAMES** For each term or name, write a sentence explaining its significance.

- Foraker Act
- Platt Amendment
- protectorate
- Emilio Aguinaldo
- John Hay
- Open Door notes
- Boxer Rebellion

### MAIN IDEA

**2. TAKING NOTES**

Create a time line of key events relating to U.S. relations with Cuba, Puerto Rico, and the Philippines. Use the dates already plotted on the time line below as a guide.

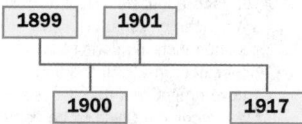

Which event do you think was most significant? Why?

### CRITICAL THINKING

**3. EVALUATING**

How did American rule of Puerto Rico harm Puerto Ricans? How did it help Puerto Ricans? Do you think the benefits outweighed the harmful effects? Why or why not?

**4. COMPARING**

How was U.S. policy toward China different from U.S. policy toward the Philippines? To what can you attribute the difference?

**5. ANALYZING ISSUES**

How did U.S. foreign policy at the turn of the century affect actions taken by the United States toward China? **Think About:**

- why the United States wanted access to China's markets
- the purpose of the Open Door notes
- the U.S. response to the Boxer Rebellion

358 CHAPTER 10

---

## SECTION 3 ASSESSMENT Answers

### 1. TERMS & NAMES

Foraker Act, p. 353
Platt Amendment, p. 354
protectorate, p. 354
Emilio Aguinaldo, p. 355
John Hay, p. 356
Open Door notes, p. 356
Boxer Rebellion, p. 357

### 2. TAKING NOTES

1899—Aguinaldo's armed revolt sparks Philippine-American War. **1900**—Foraker Act denies citizenship to Puerto Ricans and gives the U.S. president partial control of the Puerto Rican government; McKinley is reelected as president. **1901**—Platt Amendment authorizes U.S. intervention in Cuba. **1917**—Congress grants U.S. citizenship to Puerto Ricans.

### 3. EVALUATING

**Harm**—The people of the island were unable to choose their own government. **Help**—The island fell under the protection of the U.S. government. **Yes**—because the United States protected Puerto Rico from the rule of harsh dictators. **No**—because the people of Puerto Rico were not granted self-government.

### 4. COMPARING

The United States annexed the Philippines but only established spheres of influence in China. The U.S. goal in China was to get the same rights as other trading nations. The annexation of China was never a goal.

### 5. ANALYZING ISSUES

The U.S. government believed it had the right to intervene to keep foreign markets open to the United States. The Open Door notes were a nonmilitary attempt to get trading rights in China.

# America as a World Power

**OBJECTIVES**

1 Explain how Theodore Roosevelt's foreign policy promoted American power around the world.

2 Describe how Woodrow Wilson's missionary diplomacy ensured U.S. dominance in Latin America.

**SKILLBUILDERS**

· Analyzing Political Cartoons, p. 362

**CRITICAL THINKING**

· Analyzing Effects, p. 360
· Identifying Problems, p. 361
· Analyzing Motives, p. 363
· Comparing and Contrasting, p. 365
· Evaluating Decisions, p. 365

| MAIN IDEA | WHY IT MATTERS NOW | Terms & Names |
|---|---|---|
| The Russo-Japanese War, the Panama Canal, and the Mexican Revolution added to America's military and economic power. | American involvement in conflicts around 1900 led to involvement in World War I and later to a peacekeeper role in today's world. | •Panama Canal  •Roosevelt Corollary  •dollar diplomacy  •Francisco "Pancho" Villa  •Emiliano Zapata  •John J. Pershing |

**TEKS** U.S. History 3A, 8A, 9A, 19A, 19B, 20A, 22B, 23A, 24B, 24C, 24F, 24G, 25A, 25B, 25C, 25D, 26A, 26B

### One American's Story

Joseph Bucklin Bishop, a policy adviser to the canal's chief engineer, played an important role in the building of the Panama Canal. As editor of the *Canal Record*, a weekly newspaper that provided Americans with updates on the project, Bishop described a frustrating problem that the workers encountered.

**A PERSONAL VOICE** JOSEPH BUCKLIN BISHOP

" The Canal Zone was a land of the fantastic and the unexpected. No one could say when the sun went down what the condition of the Cut would be when [the sun] rose. For the work of months or even years might be blotted out by an avalanche of earth or the toppling over of a mountain of rock. It was a task to try men's souls; but it was also one to kindle in them a joy of combat . . . and a faith in ultimate victory which no disaster could shake. "

—quoted in *The Impossible Dream: The Building of the Panama Canal*

▲ Workers digging the Panama Canal faced hazardous landslides and death from disease.

The building of the Panama Canal reflected America's new role as a world power. As a technological accomplishment, the canal represented a confident nation's refusal to let any physical obstacle stand in its way.

## Teddy Roosevelt and the World 1

The assassination of William McKinley in 1901 thrust Vice-President Theodore Roosevelt into the role of a world leader. Roosevelt was unwilling to allow the imperial powers of Europe to control the world's political and economic destiny. In 1905, building on the Open Door notes to increase American influence in East Asia, Roosevelt mediated a settlement in a war between Russia and Japan.

## Focus & Motivate

Ask students how they would resolve a conflict between two friends. Then ask them how the United States might try to resolve a conflict between two countries.

## Instruct

### Instruct: Objective 1

**Teddy Roosevelt and the World**
TAKS SS11 2(US9.A)
· What role did President Roosevelt play in ending the Russo-Japanese War?
· What events led to the building of the Panama Canal?
· What did the Roosevelt Corollary state?
· What was dollar diplomacy?

📄 In-Depth Resources: Unit 3
· Guided Reading, p. 27
· Outline Map: America Becomes a World Power, pp. 36–37
· Primary Source: Building the Panama Canal, p. 41

**PROGRAM RESOURCES**

 **In-Depth Resources: Unit 3**
· Guided Reading, p. 27
· Reteaching Activity, p. 33
· Geography Application: Geography of the Panama Canal, pp. 34–35
· Outline Map: America Becomes a World Power, pp. 36–37
· Primary Source: Building the Panama Canal, p. 41

 **Reading Study Guide** (English and Spanish), pp. 109–110

 **Access for Students Acquiring English/ESL**
· Guided Reading (Spanish), p. 126
· Geography Application, pp. 128–129
· Outline Map, pp. 130–131

 **Formal Assessment**
· Section Quiz, p. 196

 **Integrated Assessment**
· Rubrics

**INTEGRATED TECHNOLOGY**

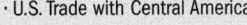 **Geography Transp. GT18**
· United States Intervenes in Latin America

**Critical Thinking Transp. CT52**
· U.S. Trade with Central America

 **Electronic Library of Primary Sources**

 **classzone.com**

**TEXAS RESOURCES**

 TAKS Spiraled Content Review

 TAKS Practice Tests

 TAKS Practice Transparencies TT70

 TAKS Online Test Practice

**ROOSEVELT THE PEACEMAKER** In 1904, Tsar Nicholas II of Russia declared war on Japan, Russia's neighbor in East Asia. Russia and Japan were both imperialist powers, and they were competing for control of Korea. The Japanese took the first action in the war with a surprise attack on the Russian Pacific fleet. To everyone's surprise, Japan destroyed it. Japan then proceeded to destroy a second fleet sent as reinforcement. Japan also won a series of land battles, securing Korea and Manchuria.

As a result of these battles, Japan began to run out of men and money, a fact that it did not want to reveal to Russia. Instead, Japanese officials approached President Roosevelt in secret and asked him to mediate peace negotiations. Roosevelt agreed, and in 1905, Russian and Japanese delegates convened in Portsmouth, New Hampshire.

The first meeting took place on the presidential yacht. Roosevelt had a charming way of greeting people with a grasp of the hand, a broad grin, and a hearty "Dee-lighted." Soon the opposing delegates began to relax and cordially shook hands.

The Japanese wanted Sakhalin Island, off the coast of Siberia, and a large sum of money from Russia. Russia refused. Roosevelt persuaded Japan to accept half the island and forgo the cash payment. In exchange, Russia agreed to let Japan take over Russian interests in Manchuria and Korea. The successful efforts in negotiating the Treaty of Portsmouth won Roosevelt the 1906 Nobel Peace Prize.

As U.S. and Japanese interests expanded in East Asia, the two nations continued diplomatic talks. In later agreements, they pledged to respect each other's possessions and interests in East Asia and the Pacific. Ⓐ

**PANAMA CANAL** By the time Roosevelt became president, many Americans, including Roosevelt, felt that the United States needed a canal cutting across Central America. Such a canal would greatly reduce travel time for commercial and military ships by providing a shortcut between the Atlantic and Pacific oceans. (See Geography Spotlight, page 366.) As early as 1850, the United States and Britain had agreed to share the rights to such a canal. In the Hay-Pauncefote Treaty of 1901, however, Britain gave the United States exclusive rights to build and control a canal through Central America.

Engineers identified two possible routes for the proposed canal. One, through Nicaragua, posed fewer obstacles because much of it crossed a large lake. The other route crossed through Panama (then a province of Colombia) and was shorter and filled with mountains and swamps. In the late 1800s, a French company had tried to build a canal in Panama. After ten years, the company gave up. It sent an agent, Philippe Bunau-Varilla, to Washington to convince the United States to buy its claim. In 1903, the president and Congress decided to use the Panama route and agreed to buy the French company's route for $40 million.

Before beginning work on the **Panama Canal,** the United States had to get permission from Colombia, which then ruled Panama. When these negotiations broke down, Bunau-Varilla helped organize a Panamanian rebellion against Colombia. On November 3, 1903, nearly a dozen U.S. warships were present as Panama declared its independence. Fifteen days later, Panama and the United

## KEY PLAYER

### Theodore Roosevelt

Theodore Roosevelt tried to promote the United States as a strong but respectful leader in international affairs. "In foreign affairs the principle from which we never deviated was to have the Nation behave toward other nations precisely as a strong, honorable, and upright man behaves in dealing with his fellow-men," he wrote. "It is folly of the criminal type for the Nation not to keep up its navy, not to fortify its vital strategic points, and not to provide an adequate army for its needs. On the other hand, it is wicked for the Nation to fail in either justice, courtesy, or consideration when dealing with any other power, big or little."

## KEY PLAYER

**THEODORE ROOSEVELT**
**1858–1919**

Rimless glasses, a bushy mustache, and prominent teeth made Roosevelt easy for cartoonists to caricature. His great enthusiasm for physical activity—boxing, tennis, swimming, horseback riding, and hunting—provided cartoonists with additional material. Some cartoons portrayed Roosevelt with the toy teddy bear that he inspired.

Roosevelt had six children, who became notorious for their rowdy antics. Their father once sent a message through the War Department, ordering them to call off their "attack" on the White House. Roosevelt thrived on the challenges of the presidency. He wrote, "I do not believe that anyone else has ever enjoyed the White House as much as I have."

## More About . . .

### Roosevelt and the Canal

Roosevelt considered the Panama Canal the greatest accomplishment of his presidency. While he denied any role in planning the revolution that freed Panama from Colombia, he gave it covert support. He later said, "I took the canal zone and let Congress debate, and while the debate goes on the canal does also."

---

### Examining the Canal Routes

**Class Time** 30 minutes

**Task** Examining the two possible canal routes to determine their geographic advantages and disadvantages

**Purpose** To help students better understand how geography plays a role in decisions and events in history

**Directions** Have students work in pairs to analyze the proposed routes for a canal. They should research each region and examine a physical map of Central America.

TAKS Mini-Lesson 4: SS11 2(US9.A)

Have students make a chart like the one below that lists the advantages and disadvantages of each route.

| Possible Canal Route | Advantages | Disadvantages |
|---|---|---|
| Nicaragua | | |
| Panama | | |

## Science & Technology

### THE PANAMA CANAL

Locks are used to raise and lower ships a total of 170 feet during the 51-mile trip through the Panama Canal. For example, ships from the Atlantic Ocean are lifted by the Gatun Locks to the level of Gatun Lake. The ships cross the human-made lake, then move through another waterway, the Galliard Cut. The Pedro Miguel and Miraflores locks then lower the ships to the level of the Pacific Ocean.

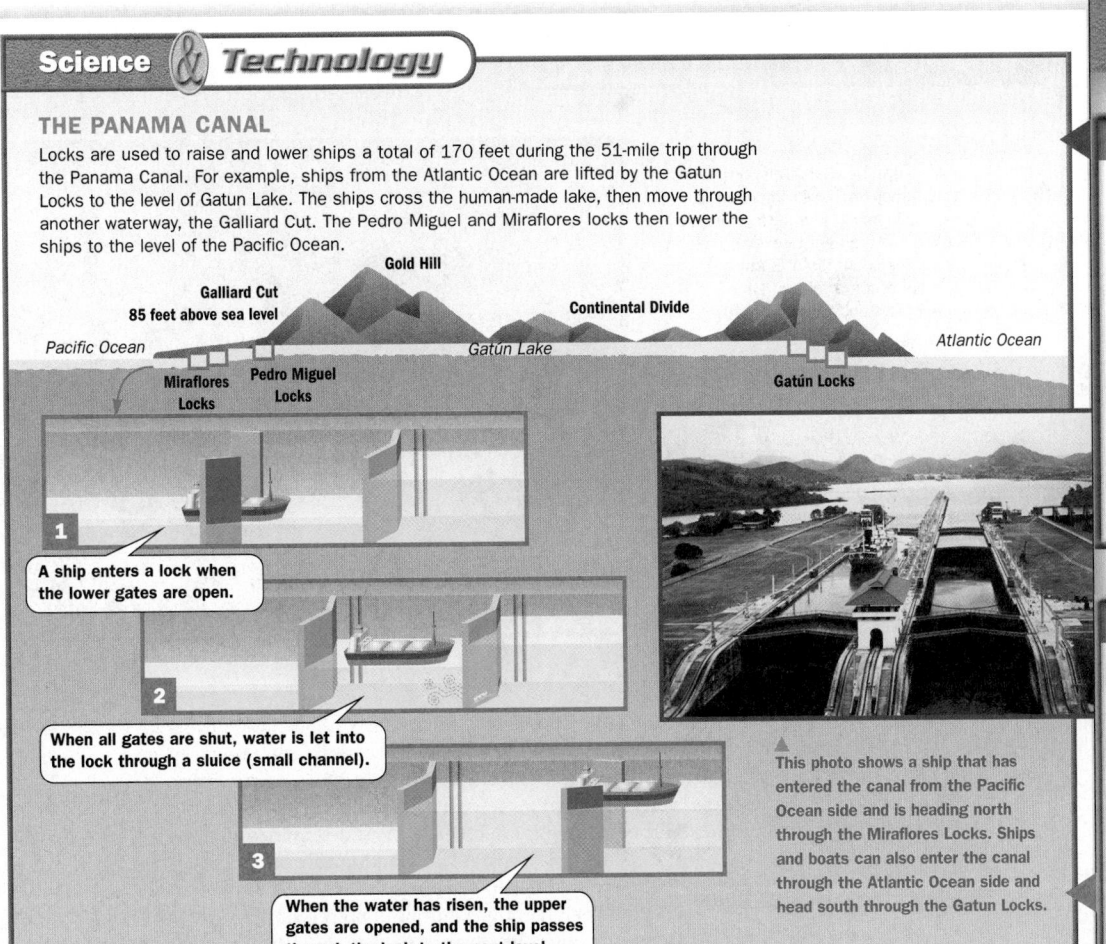

A ship enters a lock when the lower gates are open.

When all gates are shut, water is let into the lock through a sluice (small channel).

When the water has risen, the upper gates are opened, and the ship passes through the lock to the next level.

This photo shows a ship that has entered the canal from the Pacific Ocean side and is heading north through the Miraflores Locks. Ships and boats can also enter the canal through the Atlantic Ocean side and head south through the Gatun Locks.

## Science & Technology

Point out to students that the Atlantic Ocean and Pacific Ocean are not at the same level, making the locks necessary. The lock chambers are 1,000 feet long, 110 feet wide, and 41 feet deep. Many of today's large oceangoing ships are too large for the locks. Ask students if they think the canal has outlived its usefulness. *(Students may respond that there are still many vessels that use the canal.)*

In-Depth Resources: Unit 3
· Geography Application, pp. 34–35

## More About

### Constructing the Panama Canal

Human geographic factors greatly influenced the building of the Panama Canal. With tens of thousands of workers involved in the construction of the canal, organizers were faced with problems of feeding and housing the huge work force. At first living conditions were appalling; disease was rampant, and 3 out of 4 American workers abandoned the site and returned home. However, with the replacement of the chief engineer, the situation improved dramatically. John Stevens, the new chief engineer, had built the Great Northern Railroad across the Pacific Northwest. He understood that the key to success was the creation of a healthy and well-cared for work force. Under Stevens's supervision, the mosquito-infested swamps were drained and roads were laid through the jungle. New towns were built to provide workers with not only housing but schools, religious buildings, and social halls. Ask, How did human geographic factors influence the building of the Panama Canal? *(Construction workers had to drain mosquito-infested swamps and overcome the challenges of the physical environment in order to build the canal.)*

**B. Answer**
Builders fought diseases and the difficult removal of soft volcanic soil. They also had to clear brush and drain swamps.

**MAIN IDEA**

**Identifying Problems**
**B** What problems did canal workers encounter in constructing the canal?

States signed a treaty in which the United States agreed to pay Panama $10 million plus an annual rent of $250,000 for an area of land across Panama, called the Canal Zone. The payments were to begin in 1913.

**CONSTRUCTING THE CANAL** Construction of the Panama Canal ranks as one of the world's greatest engineering feats. Builders fought diseases, such as yellow fever and malaria, and soft volcanic soil that proved difficult to remove from where it lay. Work began in 1904 with the clearing of brush and draining of swamps. By 1913, the height of the construction, more than 43,400 workers were employed. Some had come from Italy and Spain; three-quarters were blacks from the British West Indies. More than 5,600 workers on the canal died from accidents or disease. The total cost to the United States was about $380 million. **B**

On August 15, 1914, the canal opened for business, and more than 1,000 merchant ships passed through during its first year. U.S.-Latin American relations, however, had been damaged by American support of the rebellion in Panama. The resulting ill will lasted for decades, despite Congress's paying Colombia $25 million in 1921 to compensate the country for its lost territory.

*America Claims an Empire* **361**

 classzone.com

---

### Tropical Diseases

**Class Time** 45 minutes

**Task** Researching the efforts to eliminate malaria and yellow fever in the Canal Zone

**Purpose** To explain one of the many challenges the United States faced in constructing the Panama Canal

**Directions** Divide the class into small groups. Have one half of the groups research the efforts to end yellow fever in the Canal Zone and the other half research the efforts to end malaria there. Students should create posters showing the cause of the diseases, how they are spread, the number of workers who died from them, and how they are prevented.

 Integrated Assessment
· Rubrics 1, 4

## Analyzing *Political Cartoons*

### SKILLBUILDER ANSWERS

1. Roosevelt is portrayed as a giant carrying a gigantic stick. The contrast between his size and the size of the other people suggests his exaggerated power.

2. "The World Constable" is a good title because Roosevelt is acting as a policeman, separating Europe and Latin America.

Geography Transparencies GT18
· United States Intervenes in Latin America

Critical Thinking Transparencies CT52
· U.S. Trade with Central America

---

## Analyzing *Political Cartoons*

### "THE WORLD'S CONSTABLE"

This cartoon, drawn by Louis Dalrymple in 1905, shows Teddy Roosevelt implementing his new world diplomacy. The cartoon implies that Roosevelt has the right to execute police power to keep the countries of Europe (shown on the right) out of the affairs of Latin American countries (shown on the left).

### SKILLBUILDER
**Analyzing Political Cartoons**

1. How does the cartoonist portray President Roosevelt?
2. Why is "The World's Constable" a good title for this cartoon?

**SEE SKILLBUILDER HANDBOOK, PAGE R24.**

---

## Connections Across Time

### 1911 AND 1986

### The Iran-Contra Affair

The Iran-Contra Affair was a scandal that involved the covert sale of arms to Iran for the possible release of American hostages being held in Lebanon. It also involved the use of the profits from the $48 million in arms sales to aid the Nicaraguan non-Communist rebels, known as the Contras, in their fight against the Marxist Sandinista government. Both actions were in direct violation of U.S. laws. Months of legal and congressional investigations into the matter led to the prosecution of several top officials in the Reagan administration.

---

**THE ROOSEVELT COROLLARY** Financial factors drew the United States further into Latin American affairs. In the late 19th century, many Latin American nations had borrowed huge sums from European banks to build railroads and develop industries. Roosevelt feared that if these nations defaulted on their loans, Europeans might intervene. He was determined to make the United States the predominant power in the Caribbean and Central America.

Roosevelt reminded European powers of the Monroe Doctrine, which had been issued in 1823 by President James Monroe. The Monroe Doctrine demanded that European countries stay out of the affairs of Latin American nations. Roosevelt based his Latin America policy on a West African proverb that said, "Speak softly and carry a big stick." In his December 1904 message to Congress, Roosevelt added the **Roosevelt Corollary** to the Monroe Doctrine. He warned that disorder in Latin America might "force the United States . . . to the exercise of an international police power." In effect, the corollary said that the United States would now use force to protect its economic interests in Latin America.

**Vocabulary**
**corollary:** an additional statement that follows logically from the first one

*"Speak softly and carry a big stick; you will go far."*
**THEODORE ROOSEVELT**

**DOLLAR DIPLOMACY** During the next decade, the United States exercised its police power on several occasions. For example, when a 1911 rebellion in Nicaragua left the nation near bankruptcy, President William H. Taft, Roosevelt's successor, arranged for American bankers to loan Nicaragua enough money to pay its debts. In return, the bankers were given the right to recover their money by collecting Nicaragua's customs duties. The U.S. bankers also gained control of Nicaragua's state-owned railroad system and its national bank. When Nicaraguan citizens heard about this deal, they revolted against President Adolfo Díaz. To prop up

---

**ACTIVITY** | **LINK TO GOVERNMENT/CIVICS**

 classzone.com

### Intervention Abroad

**Class Time** Two class periods

**Task** Describing U.S. intervention and its effects

**Purpose** To understand the intended goal and the effects of U.S. intervention in Latin America

**Directions** Have students choose one of the following countries: the Dominican Republic, Haiti, Cuba, Nicaragua, Mexico. They should research the reasons for U.S. intervention in the country they selected, the dates of the interventions, the form of the intervention, and its effects. Students should present their findings in a brief written report.

Integrated Assessment
· Rubrics 1, 5

Díaz's government, some 2,000 marines were sent to Nicaragua. The revolt was put down, but some marine detachments remained in the country until 1933.

The Taft administration followed the policy of using the U.S. government to guarantee loans made to foreign countries by American businesspeople. This policy was called **dollar diplomacy** by its critics and was often used to justify keeping European powers out of the Caribbean.

## Woodrow Wilson's Missionary Diplomacy

The Monroe Doctrine, issued by President James Monroe in 1823, had warned other nations against expanding their influence in Latin America. The Roosevelt Corollary asserted, in 1904, that the United States had a right to exercise international police power in the Western Hemisphere. In 1913, President Woodrow Wilson gave the Monroe Doctrine a moral tone.

According to Wilson's "missionary diplomacy," the United States had a moral responsibility to deny recognition to any Latin American government it viewed as oppressive, undemocratic, or hostile to U.S. interests. Prior to this policy, the United States recognized any government that controlled a nation, regardless of that nation's policies or how it had come to power. Wilson's policy pressured nations in the Western Hemisphere to establish democratic governments. Almost immediately, the Mexican Revolution put Wilson's policy to the test.

**THE MEXICAN REVOLUTION** Mexico had been ruled for more than three decades by a military dictator, Porfirio Díaz. A friend of the United States, Díaz had long encouraged foreign investments in his country. As a result, foreigners, mostly Americans, owned a large share of Mexican oil wells, mines, railroads, and ranches. While foreign investors and some Mexican landowners and politicians had grown rich, the common people of the country were desperately poor.

In 1911, Mexican peasants and workers led by Francisco Madero overthrew Díaz. Madero promised democratic reforms, but he proved unable to satisfy the conflicting demands of landowners, peasants, factory workers, and the urban middle class. After two years, General Victoriano Huerta took over the government and executed Madero. Wilson refused to recognize the government that Huerta formed. He called it "a government of butchers." **C**

**INTERVENTION IN MEXICO** Wilson adopted a plan of "watchful waiting," looking for an opportunity to act against Huerta. The opportunity came in April 1914, when one of Huerta's officers arrested a small group of American sailors in Tampico, on Mexico's eastern shore. The Mexicans quickly released them and apologized, but Wilson used the incident as an excuse to intervene in Mexico and ordered U.S. marines to occupy Veracruz, an important Mexican port. Eighteen Americans and at least 200 Mexicans died during the invasion.

The incident brought the United States and Mexico close to war. Argentina, Brazil, and Chile stepped in to mediate the conflict. They proposed that Huerta step down and that U.S. troops withdraw without paying Mexico for damages. Mexico rejected the plan, and Wilson refused to recognize a government that had come to power as a result of violence. The Huerta regime soon collapsed, however, and Venustiano Carranza, a nationalist leader, became president in 1915. Wilson withdrew the troops and formally recognized the Carranza government.

### MAIN IDEA

**Analyzing Motives**
**C** Why did President Wilson refuse to recognize Huerta's government?

**C. Answer** Wilson was following his policy of missionary diplomacy. He considered Huerta a murderer because Huerta had ordered rebel leader Francisco Madero executed.

---

### ANOTHER PERSPECTIVE

**INTERVENTION IN MEXICO**

Most U.S. citizens supported American intervention in Mexico. Edith O'Shaughnessy, wife of an American diplomat in Mexico City, had another perspective. After touring Veracruz, O'Shaughnessy wrote to her mother:

"I think we have done a great wrong to these people; instead of cutting out the sores with a clean, strong knife of war, . . . we have only put our fingers in each festering wound and inflamed it further."

---

**Instruct: Objective 2**

**Woodrow Wilson's Missionary Diplomacy**

TAKS SS11 1(US3.A)

· What was Woodrow Wilson's "missionary diplomacy"?
· Why did the United States become involved in the affairs of Mexico?

📄 **In-Depth Resources: Unit 3**
· Guided Reading, p. 27

---

### ANOTHER PERSPECTIVE

**Intervention in Mexico**

Edith O'Shaughnessy wrote numerous letters from Mexico, which eventually were published in two books, *A Diplomat's Wife in Mexico* (1916) and *Diplomatic Days* (1917). She went on to publish other books, including two works of fiction. One of them, *Viennese Medley* (1924), about life in Vienna after World War I, was made into a movie.

**Evaluating** Why do you think Edith O'Shaughnessy's opinion might be more valid than that of others? (*Because she was an eyewitness to the effects of U.S. intervention in Mexico*)

*America Claims an Empire* **363**

---

**Debating Wilson's Missionary Diplomacy**

**Class Time** 45 minutes

**Task** Debating whether the United States is within its right to try to impose its morals and beliefs on other nations and cultures

**Purpose** To discuss what role morality and human rights play in foreign affairs

**Directions** Divide the class into pairs. Assign one half of the class to develop arguments for "missionary diplomacy" and the other half to develop arguments against the philosophy. Students can research Wilson's involvement in Mexico or investigate more recent situations. When students have developed their arguments, match pairs with opposite views to debate their positions.

📄 **Integrated Assessment**
· Rubric 3

*America Claims an Empire* **363**

## History Through *Art*

José Orozco started to paint after losing his left hand in a laboratory accident. His early efforts included political cartoons and a series on the slums of Mexico City. Orozco fled Mexico in 1917 and returned in 1920. Orozco decorated some of Mexico's public buildings with murals that highlighted patriotic and revolutionary themes. During the 1930s, Orozco worked with fellow muralist Diego Rivera and others to bring about a period of artistic achievement in Mexico known as the Mexican Renaissance.

*(The painter shows unity by compressing many bodies, all with the same outline, shape, and body direction—moving forward,— into the painting. The bold landscape and striking colors show strength.)*

## History Through *Art*

### ZAPATISTAS (1931)

José Orozco, one of Mexico's foremost artists, painted these Zapatistas (followers of Zapata), to honor the peasant men and women who fought in the Mexican revolution. Orozco did many paintings in support of the revolution.
**What aspects of the image does the artist use to convey strength and unity?**

## Connections Across Time

**1910 AND TODAY**

### Zapatista National Liberation Army
A rebel group bearing the name of Emiliano Zapata—and espousing his doctrine of land reform and greater rights for the poor—announced its presence on New Year's Day 1994. It seized several towns in Mexico's poverty-stricken state of Chiapas and demanded social and economic reforms for the country's native peoples. A two-week clash with authorities followed, and nearly 150 people were killed. Since then, the government and rebels have tried to reach an agreement acceptable to both sides.

**REBELLION IN MEXICO** Carranza was in charge, but like others before him, he did not have the support of all Mexicans. Rebels under the leadership of **Francisco "Pancho" Villa** (vē′ə) and **Emiliano Zapata** (ĕ-mēl-yä′nō zə-pä′tə) opposed Carranza's provisional government. Zapata—son of a mestizo peasant—was dedicated to land reform. "It is better to die on your feet than live on your knees," Zapata told the peasants who joined him. Villa, a fierce nationalist, had frequently courted the support and aid of the United States.

### A PERSONAL VOICE PANCHO VILLA
" [A]s long as I have anything to do with the affairs in Mexico there will be no further friction between my country and my friends of the North . . . To President Wilson, the greatest American, I stand pledged to do what I can to keep the faith he has in my people, and if there is anything he may wish I will gladly do it, for I know it will be for the good of my country."

—*New York Times*, January 11, 1915

Despite Villa's talk of friendship, when President Wilson recognized Carranza's government, Villa threatened reprisals against the United States. In January 1916, Carranza invited American engineers to operate mines in northern Mexico. Before they reached the mines, however, Villa's men took the Americans off a train and shot them. Two months later, some of Villa's followers raided Columbus, New Mexico, and killed 17 Americans. Americans held Villa responsible.

**CHASING VILLA** With the American public demanding revenge, President Wilson ordered Brigadier General **John J. Pershing** and an expeditionary force of about 15,000 soldiers into Mexico to capture Villa dead or alive. For almost a year, Villa eluded Pershing's forces. Wilson then called out 150,000 National Guardsmen and stationed them along the Mexican border. In the meantime,

**364** CHAPTER 10

### Creating a Time Line

Help students keep track of the events related to the Mexican Revolution and United States intervention in Mexico by creating a time line like the one shown here. Begin with the date 1911 and end with 1917. Under each date, list the key events that happened that year. Have students compare their time lines with those of their classmates.

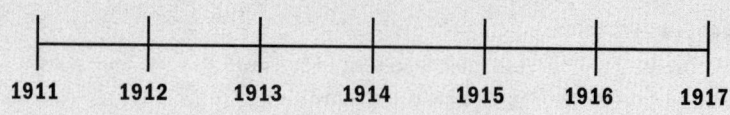

1911   1912   1913   1914   1915   1916   1917

Mexicans grew angrier over the U.S. invasion of their land. In June 1916, U.S. troops clashed with Carranza's army, resulting in deaths on both sides.

Carranza demanded the withdrawal of U.S. troops, but Wilson refused. War seemed imminent. However, in the end, both sides backed down. The United States, facing war in Europe, needed peace on its southern border. In February 1917, Wilson ordered Pershing to return home. Later that year, Mexico adopted a constitution that gave the government control of the nation's oil and mineral resources and placed strict regulations on foreign investors.

▲ Pancho Villa directs a column of his troops through northern Mexico in 1914.

Although Carranza had called for the constitution of 1917, he failed to carry out its measures. Instead, he ruled oppressively until 1920 when a moderate named Alvaro Obregón came to power. Obregón's presidency marked the end of civil war and the beginning of reform.

U.S. intervention in Mexican affairs provided a clear model of American imperialist attitudes in the early years of the 20th century. Americans believed in the superiority of free-enterprise democracy, and the American government attempted to extend the reach of this economic and political system, even through armed intervention.

The United States pursued and achieved several foreign policy goals in the early 20th century. First, it expanded its access to foreign markets in order to ensure the continued growth of the domestic economy. Second, the United States built a modern navy to protect its interests abroad. Third, the United States exercised its international police power to ensure dominance in Latin America.

## SECTION 4 · ASSESSMENT

1. **TERMS & NAMES** For each term or name below, write a sentence explaining its significance.
   - **Panama Canal**
   - **Roosevelt Corollary**
   - **dollar diplomacy**
   - **Francisco "Pancho" Villa**
   - **Emiliano Zapata**
   - **John J. Pershing**

### SUMMARIZING

2. **TAKING NOTES**
   In a two-column chart, list ways Teddy Roosevelt and Woodrow Wilson used American power around the world during their presidencies.

   | Using American Power | |
   |---|---|
   | **Roosevelt** | **Wilson** |
   | | |

   Choose one example and discuss its impact with your classmates.

### CRITICAL THINKING

3. **COMPARING AND CONTRASTING**
   What do you think were the similarities and differences between Roosevelt's Big Stick policy and Wilson's missionary diplomacy? Use evidence from the text to support your response. **Think About:**
   - the goal of each of these foreign policies
   - how the policies defined the role of U.S. intervention in international affairs
   - how the policies were applied

4. **EVALUATING DECISIONS**
   In your opinion, should the United States have become involved in the affairs of Colombia, Nicaragua, and Mexico during the early 1900s? Support your answer with details. **Think About:**
   - the effect of the Roosevelt Corollary
   - the results of dollar diplomacy
   - the implication of Wilson's missionary diplomacy

*America Claims an Empire* **365**

---

**1. TERMS & NAMES**
Panama Canal, p. 360
Roosevelt Corollary, p. 362
dollar diplomacy, p. 363
Francisco "Pancho" Villa, p. 364
Emiliano Zapata, p. 364
John J. Pershing, p. 364

**2. TAKING NOTES**
**Roosevelt:** helped mediate the settlement in Russo-Japanese War; launched construction of Panama Canal; formulated the Roosevelt Corollary to the Monroe Doctrine
**Wilson:** formulated "missionary diplomacy"; ordered U.S. military occupation of Veracruz; sent General Pershing and expeditionary forces to pursue Pancho Villa in Mexico

**3. COMPARING AND CONTRASTING**
Both were foreign policies that broadened the Monroe Doctrine and addressed potentially dangerous situations in Latin America. "Big stick" policy cast the United States in the role of international police officer and had an economic focus. "Missionary diplomacy" cast the United States in the role of judge and had a moral tone.

**4. EVALUATING DECISIONS**
Yes—The Roosevelt Corollary justified intervention; the United States needed to protect its various economic interests in Latin America; and the United States felt morally bound to protect democracy in Latin America. No—The U.S. belief in its own superiority led to the use of excessive military forces against those countries. They had the right to choose their own governments.

## GEOGRAPHY SPOTLIGHT

# The Panama Canal: Funnel for Trade

### Objectives

· To summarize the development of the Panama Canal

· To identify the benefits of building the canal

## Focus & Motivate

**Developing Historical Perspective** Have students imagine that they are workers on the Panama Canal and discuss what personal qualities they would need to possess to see them through the job. *(Patience, physical strength, the ability to work as part of a team)*

## More About . . .

### The Panama Canal

In 1882, the French tried to carve out a canal through Panama. Heading up the project was Ferdinand Marie De Lesseps. He had directed the construction of Egypt's Suez Canal—which opened in 1869. The Panama endeavor quickly ran into problems. A group of dishonest politicians, who supported De Lesseps, stole large amounts of money from the canal company. Also, French engineers lacked the proper tools to complete the huge digging project. In addition, scientists did not yet know how to combat the region's deadly viruses. De Lessep's company went bankrupt in 1889 and shortly thereafter abandoned the canal project.

By the late 19th century, the U.S. position in global trade was firmly established. A glance at a world map during that time revealed the trade advantages of cutting through the world's great landmasses at two strategic points. The first cut, through the Isthmus of Suez in Egypt, was completed in 1869 and was a spectacular success. A second cut, this one through Panama, in Central America, would be especially advantageous to the United States. Such a cut, or canal, would substantially reduce the sailing time between the nation's Atlantic and Pacific ports.

It took the United States ten years, from 1904 to 1914, to build the Panama Canal. By 1999, more than 700,000 vessels, flying the flags of about 70 nations, had passed through its locks. In the year 2000, Panama assumed full control of the canal.

**INTERCOASTAL TRADE ▲**
The first boat through the canal heralded the arrival of increased trade between the Atlantic and Pacific ports of the United States.

**NUMBERS TELL THE STORY ▶**
A ship sailing from New York to San Francisco by going around South America travels 13,000 miles; the canal shortens the journey to 5,200 miles.

San Francisco

to Asia

San Francisco    New York

■ 13,000 mi.
■ 5,200 mi.

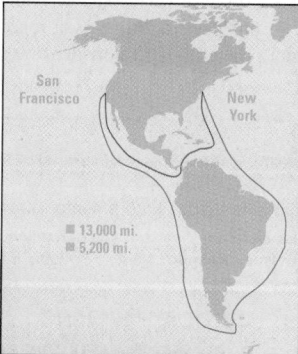

**◀ OCEANGOING VESSELS**
Ships, like this one, must be of a certain dimension in order to fit through the canal's locks. These container ships must be no more than 106 feet across and 965 feet in length, with a draft (the depth of the vessel below the water line when fully loaded) of no more than 39.5 feet. Each ship pays a toll based on its size, its cargo, and the number of passengers it carries.

## RECOMMENDED RESOURCES

### BOOKS

Chidsey, Donald Barr. *The Panama Canal*. New York: Crown, 1970. An informal history.

Fast, Howard. *Goethals and the Panama Canal*. New York: Julian Messner, 1942. A popular account of George Washington Goethals, the canal's builder.

McCullough, David G. *The Path Between the Seas*. New York: Simon, 1977. A well-known account of the creation of the canal.

Snapp. Jeremy S. *Destiny by Design: The Construction of the Panama Canal*. Pacific Heritage Press, 2000. Photo essay and narrative of the building of the canal.

### VIDEOS

*A Man, A Plan, A Canal: Panama.* Coronet, 1988. A history of the canal and its construction, produced with Boston PBS channel WGBH.

*Americans Build the Panama Canal.* Agency for Instructional Technology (AIT), 1991. Construction of the canal from 1901 to 1914.

*Panama Canal.* A&E Home Video, 1994. A historical documentary in the Modern Marvels series.

### SOFTWARE

*Who Built America?* Voyager. Teddy Roosevelt digging the Panama Canal is among the ample historical video, audio, images, and documents in this program for grades 10–12.

◀ **NEW YORK CITY**
New York City and other U.S. Atlantic ports accounted for about 60 percent of the traffic using the Panama Canal in the early decades of its existence.

**NEW ORLEANS** ▲
Since its founding in 1718, New Orleans has served as a major port for the products of the areas along the Mississippi River. In 1914, the Panama Canal brought Pacific markets into its orbit.

New York
to Europe
to Africa

ew
eans

Panama Canal

to South America

Panama is a narrow stretch of land—or isthmus —that connects North and South America. In building the canal, engineers took advantage of natural waterways. Moving ships through the mountains of the Continental Divide required the use of massive locks. Locks allow a section of the canal to be closed off so that the water level can be raised or lowered.

## Instruct

1. How long did it take to complete construction of the Panama Canal?
2. What are the dimension restrictions on ships passing through the canal?
3. How did the Panama Canal enhance world trade and America's role in it?

**MAKING PERSONAL CONNECTIONS**
Ask students to think about what types of goods would be shipped through the canal. (bulky items, oil, grain, and cargo containers) Ask what would happen to the price of these goods if it took longer to ship them to the part of the country where the students live. (Prices would increase.)

## HISTORY from VISUALS

**Interpreting the Images**
Have students examine the main map and then briefly identify routes from other continents that could probably have been included. (A route from Europe or Africa through the canal to the west coast of North America and vice versa; a route from Europe or Africa through the canal to Asia and vice versa; a route from the east coast of South America through the canal to the west coast of North America or Asia and vice versa)

### THINKING CRITICALLY

1. **Analyzing Patterns** On a world map, identify the route that ships took to get from New York City to San Francisco before the Panama Canal opened. How did this route change after the opening of the canal?

2. **Creating a Model** Use clay to shape a model of a cross-section of the Panama Canal as shown in the Science and Technology feature on page 361. For the locks, use styrofoam blocks or pieces of wood which you have glued together. Paint the model, and then label each part of the canal.

**SEE SKILLBUILDER HANDBOOK, PAGE R31.**

**RESEARCH LINKS** CLASSZONE.COM

*America Claims an Empire* 367

---

### THINKING CRITICALLY: ANSWERS

#### 1. ANALYZING PATTERNS

Ships leaving New York City would have to make the roughly 13,000-mile-trip around the continents of South America in order to reach San Francisco. The route was considerably shortened by passage through the canal.

#### 2. CREATING A MODEL

**Rubric**
A model should . . .
· demonstrate in-depth understanding of the mechanics of a lock system
· clearly represent the concepts of a lock system in a three-dimensional manner
· exhibit grade level artistic skill

## TERMS & NAMES

1. Queen Liliuokalani, p. 342
2. imperialism, p. 342
3. José Martí, p. 347
4. yellow journalism, p. 347
5. U.S.S. *Maine*, p. 348
6. protectorate, p. 354
7. Open Door notes, p. 356
8. Boxer Rebellion, p. 357
9. Panama Canal, p. 360
10. Roosevelt Corollary, p. 362

## MAIN IDEAS

1. Economic competition; political and military competition; a belief in the racial and cultural superiority of Anglo-Saxons
2. She wanted to preserve Hawaii for Hawaiians, while American imperialists wanted to annex the islands.
3. U.S. businessmen sided with Spain because they wanted to protect their investments. The Americans, however, sympathized with the Cuban demand for independence.
4. Cuba's independence; Spain's relinquishing of Puerto Rico and Guam to the United States; U.S. payment of $20 million for the Philippines
5. Puerto Rico was strategically important to the United States as a way to assert its presence in the Caribbean and as a base for protecting a possible canal through the Isthmus of Panama.
6. The Boxers staged a revolt to expel foreigners from China. In August 1900, troops from Britain, France, Germany, Japan, and the United States marched on the Chinese capital. The international force put an end to the rebellion.
7. U.S. economy's dependence on exports to ensure growth; U.S. right to intervene abroad to keep foreign markets open; closing an area to American products threatened U.S. survival
8. A dispute over Korea
9. To construct the canal, workers fought diseases, such as yellow fever and bubonic plague. They also fought soft volcanic soil that was difficult to remove. Thousands died in clearing brush and draining swamps.
10. Teddy Roosevelt's "big stick" diplomacy demanded that European countries stay out of the affairs of Latin American nations. Wilson's "missionary diplomacy" demanded that countries in Latin America set up democracies.

## VISUAL SUMMARY

### AMERICA CLAIMS AN EMPIRE

**CAUSES**

- Economic competition among industrial nations
- Political and military competition, including the creation of a strong naval force
- A belief in Anglo-Saxon superiority

**AMERICAN IMPERIALISM**

**EFFECTS**

- The U.S. purchased Alaska in 1867.
- The U.S. annexed Hawaii in 1898.

- In 1898, the U.S. helped Cuba win independence from Spain.
- In the Treaty of Paris, the U.S. gained Puerto Rico, Guam, and the Philippine Islands.

- Following the Spanish-American War, the U.S.
  —reorganized the government of Puerto Rico
  —established a protectorate over Cuba
  —crushed a revolt in Philippines
- In 1899, the Open Door policy established U.S. trading rights in China.

- In the early 1900s, President Roosevelt initiated plans for the Panama Canal and asserted the right of the U.S. to exercise police power in the Western Hemisphere.
- President Wilson pressured Mexico and other countries in the Western Hemisphere to establish democratic governments.

## TERMS & NAMES

For each term or name below, write a sentence explaining its significance to U.S. foreign policy between 1890 and 1920.

1. Queen Liliuokalani
2. imperialism
3. José Martí
4. yellow journalism
5. *U.S.S. Maine*
6. protectorate
7. Open Door notes
8. Boxer Rebellion
9. Panama Canal
10. Roosevelt Corollary

## MAIN IDEAS

Use your notes and the information in the chapter to answer the following questions.

**Imperialism and America** (pages 342–345)
1. What three factors spurred American imperialism?
2. How did Queen Liliuokalani's main goal conflict with American imperialists' goals?

**The Spanish-American War** (pages 346–351)
3. Why was American opinion about Cuban independence divided?
4. Briefly describe the terms of the Treaty of Paris of 1898.

**Acquiring New Lands** (pages 352–358)
5. Why was the U.S. interested in events in Puerto Rico?
6. What sparked the Boxer Rebellion in 1900, and how was it crushed?
7. What three key beliefs about America's industrial capitalist economy were reflected in the Open Door policy?

**America as a World Power** (pages 359–365)
8. What conflict triggered the war between Russia and Japan?
9. Why is the construction of the Panama Canal considered or of the world's greatest engineering feats?
10. Explain the key difference between Woodrow Wilson's mora diplomacy and Teddy Roosevelt's "big stick" diplomacy.

## CRITICAL THINKING

1. **USING YOUR NOTES** Create a Venn diagram like the one below to show the similarities and differences between José Martí of Cuba and Emilio Aguinaldo of the Philippines.

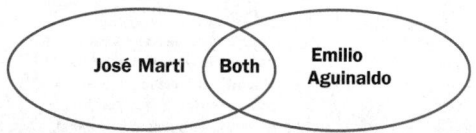

2. **HYPOTHESIZING** Would Cuba have won its independence in the late 19th century if the United States had not intervened there? Support your opinion with details from the text.

3. **INTERPRETING MAPS** Look carefully at the Caribbean map c page 349 and the world map on page 356. Why do you think American naval bases in the Caribbean and the Pacific were beneficial to the United States?

## CRITICAL THINKING

1. **Using Your Notes** Martí—Cuba; lived in exile in New York; worked as journalist and poet; died fighting for Cuban independence in 1895; revered today as a hero **Both**—Born in former Spanish colony; feared American domination; political activist and rebel leader; fought for independence and used guerrilla tactics

**Aguinaldo**—Philippines; proclaimed the Philippines an independent republic; drafted a constitution; February 1899, led a Filipino armed revolt; captured by American forces in 1901

2. **Hypothesizing** Spain might have kept Cuba from achieving independence at first, but since Cuba had a history of rebellion, it probably would have won independence eventually.

3. **Interpreting Maps** The nearness of Cuba to Florida meant that the United States could better defend its coast; bases on Pacific islands would afford the United States strategic defensive and offensive military positions, could provide stops for trading ships, and would spread U.S.influence.

## Standardized Test Practice

**Use the cartoon and your knowledge of U.S. history to answer question 1.**

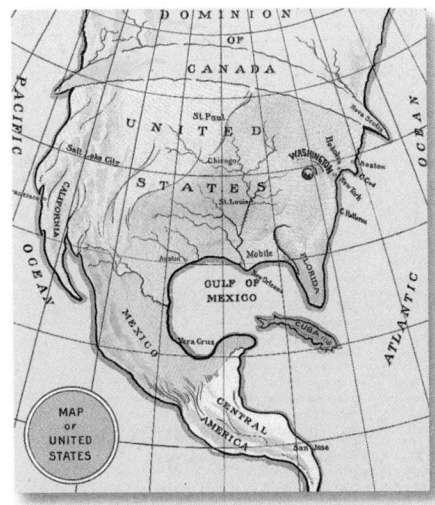

1. What is the cartoonist's point of view concerning the relationship between the United States and Cuba?

   A The United States wishes to be friends with Cuba.
   B The United States will devour Cuba.
   C The United States is wasting its time fighting over such a small area.
   D The United States has no interest in Cuba.

**Use the map and your knowledge of U.S. history to answer question 2.**

2. How did the building of the Panama Canal support United States efforts to become a world power?

   F It gave the United States a colony in Central America.
   G It prevented Japan and China from attacking Hawaii.
   H It opened up a new avenue for trade with China.
   J By providing a short cut between the Atlantic Ocean and Pacific Ocean, it opened up new trading opportunities.

**ADDITIONAL TEST PRACTICE, pages S1–S33.**

TEST PRACTICE  CLASSZONE.COM

## ALTERNATIVE ASSESSMENT

1. **INTERACT WITH HISTORY**   Recall your discussion of the question on page 341:

   *Does the U.S. have a duty to fight for freedom in neighboring countries?*

   Suppose your are a journalist at the end of the Spanish-American War. You work for William Randolph Hearst's the *New York Journal*. Write a newspaper editorial that presents your point of view about whether or not the Senate should ratify the Treaty of Paris, thus annexing the Philippines.

2.  **LEARNING FROM MEDIA** Use the CD-ROM *Electronic Library of Primary Sources* and other resources to research opinions on imperialism between 1895 and 1920.

   • Choose a document, incident, or piece of writing about imperialism. Decide if you support it or disagree with it.
   • Write a speech that presents your point of view. Decide how you will make your arguments clear and convincing while also addressing opposing concerns.
   • Practice your speech aloud and then present it to the class.

## Standardized Test Practice

1. The correct answer is letter **B.**
   Point out to students that the cartoonist has portrayed the United States as the head of Uncle Sam. The expression is menacing. None of the other answers involve a menacing attitude.

2. The correct answer is letter **J.**
   Building the canal allowed the United States more access to trade with Asia. The letter **F** is not correct because the Canal Zone technically was not considered a colony. The letter **G** is not correct because the canal would not have an impact on the ability of China or Japan to attack Hawaii. The letter **H** is not correct because trade included more than just China.

### UNIT PROJECT

**NEWS STORY**

**Tips for Teaching**
· Have students submit their headlines and a one paragraph summary of their articles.
· Provide a checklist for the students to monitor their work. For example: Have I checked my spelling, punctuation, grammar, and paragraph construction?

Formal Assessment
· Chapter Test, Forms A, B, and C, pp. 197–208

## ALTERNATIVE ASSESSMENT

### 1. INTERACT WITH HISTORY
**Rubric**
The editorial should . . .
· clearly state a position on the annexation of the Philippines
· present both sides of the issue and then strategically refute the counterargument with facts
· demonstrate in-depth understanding of the issues surrounding the annexation of the Philippines

### 2. LEARNING FROM MEDIA
**Rubric**
The speech should . . .
· identify the document, incident, or piece of writing and its connection to imperialism
· clearly state a position and give information to support the position taken
· contain a conclusion that summarizes the main points and restates the speaker's position
· capture the attention of the audience with an interesting presentation

# The First World War

| | CHAPTER OVERVIEW | COPYMASTERS | INTEGRATED TECHNOLOG |
|---|---|---|---|
| **CHAPTER RESOURCES** | *After the United States enters World War I and helps to defeat Germany, President Wilson tries to fashion a lasting peace.* | 📄 Telescoping the Times<br>· Chapter Summary, pp. 21–22<br><br>📄 Planning for Block Schedules | 📼 American Stories video series<br>· "Ace of Aces": Eddie Rickenbacker and the First World War<br><br>💿 Power Presentations<br><br>👁 Electronic Teacher Tools<br><br>👆 Online Lesson Planner<br><br>💧 classzone.com |
| **SECTION 1**<br>World War I Begins<br>pp. 372–380 | **KEY IDEAS**<br>*Long-term tensions erupt into a devastating war among European nations, while the United States tries to remain neutral.* | 📄 In-Depth Resources: Unit 3<br>- Guided Reading, p. 47<br>· Building Vocabulary, p. 51<br>· Skillbuilder Practice, p. 52<br>· Reteaching Activity, p. 53<br>· Primary Sources, p. 59<br>· Literature, pp. 63–64<br>· American Lives, p. 66<br><br>📄 Lesson Plans, pp. 89–90 | ⛏ Geography Transparencies GT19<br>· Europe Goes to War<br><br>⛏ Critical Thinking Transparencies CT19<br>· World War i<br><br>👁 Electronic Library of Primary Sources<br>· Request for a Declaration of War by Woodrow Wilson<br><br>💧 classzone.com |
| **SECTION 2**<br>American Power Tips the Balance<br>pp. 381–387 | *American forces, though poorly equipped at the outset, tip the balance decisively in favor of the Allies.* | 📄 In-Depth Resources: Unit 3<br>· Guided Reading, p. 48<br>· Primary Sources, pp. 60–61<br>· Literature, p. 65<br><br>📄 Lesson Plans, pp. 91–92 | 📼 American Stories video series<br>· "Ace of Aces": Eddie Rickenbacker and the First World War<br>⛏ Critical Thinking Transparencies CT53<br>· Costs of World War I<br>⛏ Humanities Transparencies HT18<br>· *Oppy Wood* by John Nash<br>👁 Electronic Library of Primary Sources<br>· *From Harlem to the Rhine*<br>💧 classzone.com |
| **SECTION 3**<br>The War at Home<br>pp. 388–397 | *The war unleashes a series of disruptions in American society as the U.S. government attempts to meet the demands of modern warfare.* | 📄 In-Depth Resources: Unit 3<br>- Guided Reading, p. 49<br>· Reteaching Activity, p. 55<br>· Primary Sources, p. 62<br>· American Lives, p. 67<br><br>📄 Lesson Plans, pp. 93–94 | ⛏ Critical Thinking Transparencies CT19<br>· World War I<br><br>👁 Electronic Library of Primary Sources<br>· Four Minute Speech<br><br>💧 classzone.com |
| **SECTION 4**<br>Wilson Fights for Peace<br>pp. 398–405 | *President Wilson's plans for peace are modified by Allied leaders in Europe and by Americans who are eager to free the country from foreign entanglements.* | 📄 In-Depth Resources: Unit 3<br>- Guided Reading, p. 50<br>· Reteaching Activity, p. 56<br>· Geography Application, pp. 57–58<br><br>📄 Lesson Plans, pp. 95–96 | ⛏ Humanities Transparencies HT38<br>· Interrupting the Ceremony<br><br>👁 Electronic Library of Primary Sources<br>· On the Terms of Peace by Henry Cabot Lodge<br>· Why a League of Nations is Necessary by Woodrow Wilson<br><br>💧 classzone.com |

## ASSESSMENT OPTIONS

PE Chapter Assessment, pp. 406–407

Formal Assessment
· Chapter Tests, Forms A, B, and C, pp. 213–230

Test Generator

Integrated Assessment Book

TAKS Online Test Practice

TAKS Spiraled Content Review

TAKS Practice Tests

---

PE Section 1 Assessment, p. 380

TE Self-Assessment, p. 380

Formal Assessment, Quiz, p. 209

Integrated Assessment Book

Test Generator

TAKS Practice Transparencies TT71

---

PE Section 2 Assessment, p. 387

TE Self-Assessment, p. 387

Formal Assessment, Quiz, p. 210

Integrated Assessment Book

Test Generator

TAKS Practice Transparencies TT72

---

PE Section 3 Assessment, p. 395

TE Self-Assessment, p. 395

Formal Assessment, Quiz, p. 211

Integrated Assessment Book

Test Generator

TAKS Practice Transparencies TT73

---

PE Section 4 Assessment, p. 403

TE Self-Assessment, p. 403

Formal Assessment, Quiz, p. 212

Integrated Assessment Book

Test Generator

TAKS Practice Transparencies TT74

## RESOURCES FOR DIFFERENTIATING INSTRUCTION

### Students Acquiring English/ESL

Reading Study Guide:
(English and Spanish)
pp. 113–120

Access for Students
Acquiring English/ESL:
Spanish Translations,
pp. 132–140

Chapter Summaries on CD
(English and Spanish)

### Less Proficient Readers

Reading Study Guide
(English and Spanish)
pp. 113–122

Telescoping the Times
· Chapter Summary,
pp. 21–22

Chapter Summaries on CD
(English and Spanish)

### Gifted and Talented Students

In-Depth Resources: Unit 3
· Primary Sources, pp. 59–62
· American Lives: Jeannette
Rankin, p. 66; Oliver
Wendell Holmes, p. 67

Historic Supreme Court
Decisions
· Schenck v. United States

Electronic Library of
Primary Sources
· Unit 3, Chapter 11

## CROSS-CURRICULAR CONNECTIONS

### Geography
Griess, Thomas, ed. *Atlas for the Great War.* Garden City Park, NY: Avery Publishing Group, 1986. A useful spiral-bound book of maps.

### Science
Bowen, Ezra. *Knights of the Air.* NY: Time Life, 1980. Lavishly illustrated history of the planes and men of World War I.

### Humanities: Art
Sharpe, Mike, et al. *Aviation Art.* Holt, MN: Thunder Bay Press, 1998. Reproduction of artwork featuring airplanes; includes brief descriptions of events depicted.

### Literature
Helprin, Mark. *Soldier of the Great War.* NY: Avon, 1992. An old professor recalls his adventures as a soldier, a hero, a prisoner, a deserter, and a wanderer in World War I. He tells the story of his life to an illiterate factory worker in Italy. The horror of war and the triumph of love are central themes of the novel.

Hemingway, Ernest. *A Farewell to Arms.* NY: Scribners, 1987. The brutality and confusion of World War I dominate this story of a volunteer ambulance driver and an English nurse who fall in love.

### McDougal Littell
### *Literature Connections*
Baldwin, James. *Go Tell It on the Mountain* (with related readings). Baldwin's novel, set in a store-front church in Harlem, brings the black experience vividly to life in a story that has been called "brutal, objective, and compassionate." Dealing with characters who came north during the Great Migration, the novel focuses on a 14-year-old boy whose family history reveals the complexities of the human heart.

### Nextext
*World War I*

## ENRICHMENT ACTIVITIES

PE Pupil's Edition, pp. 370–405
· Interact with History, p. 371
· Science & Technology. p. 384
· Historic Supreme Decisions, pp. 396–97
· Point/Counterpoint, p. 401
· Tracing Themes, pp. 404–405

In-Depth Resources: Unit 3
· Geography Application: A New Look for
  Europe, pp. 57–58
· Primary Sources: The Zimmermann Note, p. 59
· Primary Sources: Patriotic Song, p. 60
· Primary Sources: Liberty Bond Poster, p. 61
· Primary Sources: "Returning Soldiers" by
  W. E. B. DuBois, p. 62

· Literature Selection from *A Son at the Front* by
  Edith Wharton, pp. 63–64
· Literature Selection from "In Another Country"
  by Ernest Hemingway, p. 65
· American Lives: Jeannette Rankin, p. 66
· American Lives: Oliver Wendell Holmes, p. 67

Historic Supreme Court Decisions
· Schenck v. United States, pp. 103–108

Primary Source Explorer
· Woodrow Wilson, The Fourteen Points, 1918

American Stories video series
· "Ace of Aces"

## BLOCK SCHEDULE LESSON PLAN OPTIONS (90-MINUTE PERIOD)

### DAY 1

**CHAPTER 11 OPENER**
pp. 370–371

**Class Time** 30 minutes

**History from Visuals, p. 370**

**Class Time** 30 minutes

*Options for Pacing and Variety*

· **Time Saver** Ask students to study the photograph on the pages 370–371. Refer to the TE for questions to assess previous knowledge. Ask students how they think the depicted battle differs from the way war is waged today. **Class Time** 10 minutes

**Interact with History, p. 371**

**Class Time** 20 minutes

*Options for Pacing and Variety*

· **Role-Playing** Ask students to put themselves in the place of those in power. They must weigh the benefits and disadvantages of going to war. Was the United States' participation in war justified? How so, or why not? See TE page 371 for Interact with History questions. **Class Time** 15 minutes

**SECTION 1 pp. 372–380**

**Class Time** 30 minutes

*Options for Pacing and Variety*

· **Internet** Have students read the sidebar Crisis in the Balkans on page 374, and have them do the activity listed in the TE. **Class Time** 30 minutes

· **Time Saver** Have students study the map on page 375, and discuss the Geography Skillbuilder questions. As an extension, ask them

### DAY 1 continued

the Interpreting the Map questions in the TE, and the questions in the activity on the TE page.

**Class Time** 10 minutes

· **Peer Teaching** Pair a less proficient reader with a more proficient reader for library research on Switzerland's neutrality. Follow the activity on page 376 of the TE. Collect the students' written answers. **Class Time** 30 minutes

**SECTION 2 pp. 381–387**

**Class Time** 30 minutes

*Options for Pacing and Variety*

· **Time Saver** Have students answer the Main Idea questions as they go through the section. Discuss the answers as a class. **Class Time** 15 minutes

· **Peer Teaching** Have each student choose one example from A Personal Voice. Pair them together based on their choice. They should make a list of questions inspired by reading the quote, and then find the answers in the library or on the Internet. **Class Time** 20 minutes

· **Peer Evaluation** Have students work on the Section 2 Assessment before pairing up to check each other's answers. **Class Time** 15 minutes

### DAY 2

**SECTION 3 pp. 388–397**

**Class Time** 30 minutes

*Options for Pacing and Variety*

· **Time Saver** After reading the subsection Anti-Immigrant Hysteria, have students study the Political Cartoon on page 391. Ask them the Skillbuilder questions. **Class Time** 10 minutes

· **Role-Playing** Have students do the activity on TE page 394, and write the journal over the week about the thoughts and feelings of the migrants. Have them look at the History Through Art example on page 393, to imagine some of the basic changes that migration entails. Have some students read from the journals before you collect them. **Class Time** 15 minutes

· **Internet** Ask students to read the featured Historic Decisions of The Supreme Court on pages 396-397. Have them do Option 1 under the Internet activity. Collect their written answers. **Class Time** 20 minutes

**SECTION 4 pp. 398–405**

**Class Time** 30 minutes

*Options for Pacing and Variety*

· **Peer Competition** Using Point / Counterpoint on page 401 for more information, have students complete question 2 of the Section Assessment on their own. Then recreate the chart on the board and have students give information to include on it. Hold a class discussion about the Critical Thinking questions and the Hypothesizing question. **Class Time** 15 minutes

### DAY 2 continued

· **Internet** Have students read the feature *Schenck* v. *United States* (1919) on pages 396–397. Then have them do the Internet activity. **Class Time** 25 minutes

· **Time Saver** Ask students to read America in World Affairs, the feature on pages 404–405. Discuss the Connect to History question. **Class Time** 15 minutes

**ASSESSMENT**
pp. 406–407

**Class Time** 30 minutes

*Options for Pacing and Variety*

· **Peer Evaluation** Have students work in pairs and quiz each other on the terms and names of the chapter. **Class Time** 15 minutes

· **History on Film** View the American Stories video for Chapter 11, "Ace of Aces: Eddie Rickenbacker and the First World War." Discuss question 2 listed on page 407. **Class Time** 30 minutes

---

**TEACHER-TESTED ACTIVITY**      Link Page, Broughton High School, Raleigh, North Carolina

**PRE-WORLD WAR I WORKSHEET**

**Class Time** 40 minutes

**Task** Developing a worksheet of pre-World War I events

**Purpose** To understand the sequence of events leading to World War I

**Supplies Needed**

· Textbook
· Paper
· Pens or pencils

**Activity** Have students work in pairs to develop a worksheet describing pre-World War I events in chronological order. Tell students to leave the names of countries blank, and to keep a separate answer sheet. (Example: [Blank] was angry at [blank] when it annexed [blank] and [blank].) Have students trade worksheets and fill them in.

# CHAPTER 11 CORRELATION

 **CORRELATION TO THE TEXAS ESSENTIAL KNOWLEDGE AND SKILLS**

Chapter 11 addresses the following standards of the Texas Essential Knowledge and Skills for U.S. History.

| TEKS | Instruction | Student Question/Activity |
|---|---|---|
| **(3B)** Identify the reasons for U.S. involvement in World War I. | **PE 378–380**—explanation of the events that prompted America to enter the war, including unrestricted submarine warfare by Germany | **TE 379**—Skillbuilder mini-lesson about evaluation America's decision to declare war |
| **(3C)** Analyze the impact of significant individuals including John J. Pershing, during World War I. | **PE 384**—examination of General John J. Pershing's life and the significant role he played in the war | **TE 384**—question about what made Pershing such an effective military leader |
| **(3D)** Analyze major issues raised by U.S. involvement in World War I, Wilson's Fourteen Points, and the Treaty of Versailles. | **PE 398–403**—analysis of the post-war peace efforts, including Wilson's Fourteen Points and the Treaty of Versailles | **PE 403**—Critical Thinking questions regarding various issues surrounding the Treaty of Versailles |
| **(9B)** Identify and explain reasons for changes in political boundaries such as international conflicts. | **PE 400**—dual map showing the dramatic change in political boundaries in Europe as a result of World War I | **PE 400**—questions that require students to interpret information about the map |
| **(10A)** Analyze the effects of changing demographic patterns resulting from migration within the United States. | **PE 393–394**—discussion of the causes and effects of the Great Migration, which brought thousands of Southern African Americans to the North | **TE 394**—writing activity examining the experiences of African Americans who migrated to the North |
| **(12E)** Describe the economic effects of international military conflicts on the United States. | **PE 389**—chart examining the ways in which the war impacted the U.S. economy | **PE 389**—questions that require students to interpret information about the chart |
| **(15B)** Explain the impact of significant international events such as World War I on changes in the role of the federal government. | **PE 388–392**—examination of how the federal government took a greater role in the economy and society during World War I | **PE 395**—Critical Thinking question about how the war affected the power of the federal government |
| **(21D)** Identify the political, social, and economic contributions of women to American society. | **PE 394**—discussion of the significant role American women played in the war effort | **PE 395**—question about efforts by women during the war |

## TAKS MINI-LESSONS

1. **Social Studies Skills: Objective 1 (US3.B):** Identify the reasons for U.S. involvement in World War I **Activity** Have students consider the significance of Germany's unrestricted submarine warfare in prompting the United States to enter the war.

2. **Social Studies Skills: Objective 1 (US3.C):** Analyze major issues raised by U.S. involvement in World War I **Activity** Have students summarize President Wilson's Fourteen Points as well as the debate in American over the Treaty of Versailles.

3. **Social Studies Skills: Objective 2 (US10.A):** Analyze the effects of changing demographic patterns resulting from migration within the United States **Activity** Have students complete the writing activity on TE page 394 regarding the Great Migration.

4. **English Language Arts Skills: Objective 1 (7.F):** Produce summaries of texts by identifying main ideas and their supporting details. **Activity** Have students summarize the weaknesses of the Treaty of Versailles.

5. **English Language Arts Skills: Objective 3 (19.B):** Analyze ideas as represented in various media **Activity** Have students answer the questions regarding the political cartoon on page 391.

**CHAPTER 11 · OBJECTIVE**
To understand the causes of World War I, the reasons the United States entered the war in 1917, and the consequences of the war

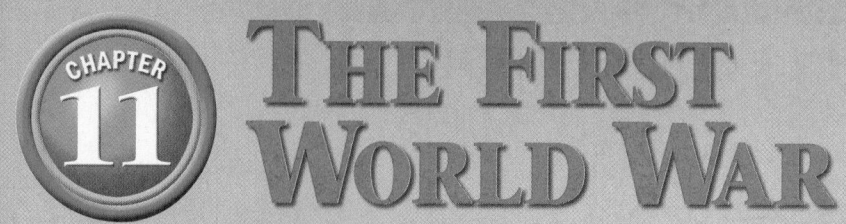

# CHAPTER 11 THE FIRST WORLD WAR

## HISTORY from VISUALS

### Interpreting the Photograph

Ask students to study the photograph and suggest adjectives that could be used to describe the battlefield. Also ask what the soldiers are doing. *(The students might describe the battlefield as destroyed, torn apart, or desolate. The soldiers running across the field, carrying their rifles, might be attacking or retreating. Aside from the rifles, there are tanks in the photograph and an explosion—evidence of artillery, mines, or bombs.)*

**Extension** Ask students to write a paragraph discussing how the battle scene in the photograph is similar to or different from the way war is waged today.

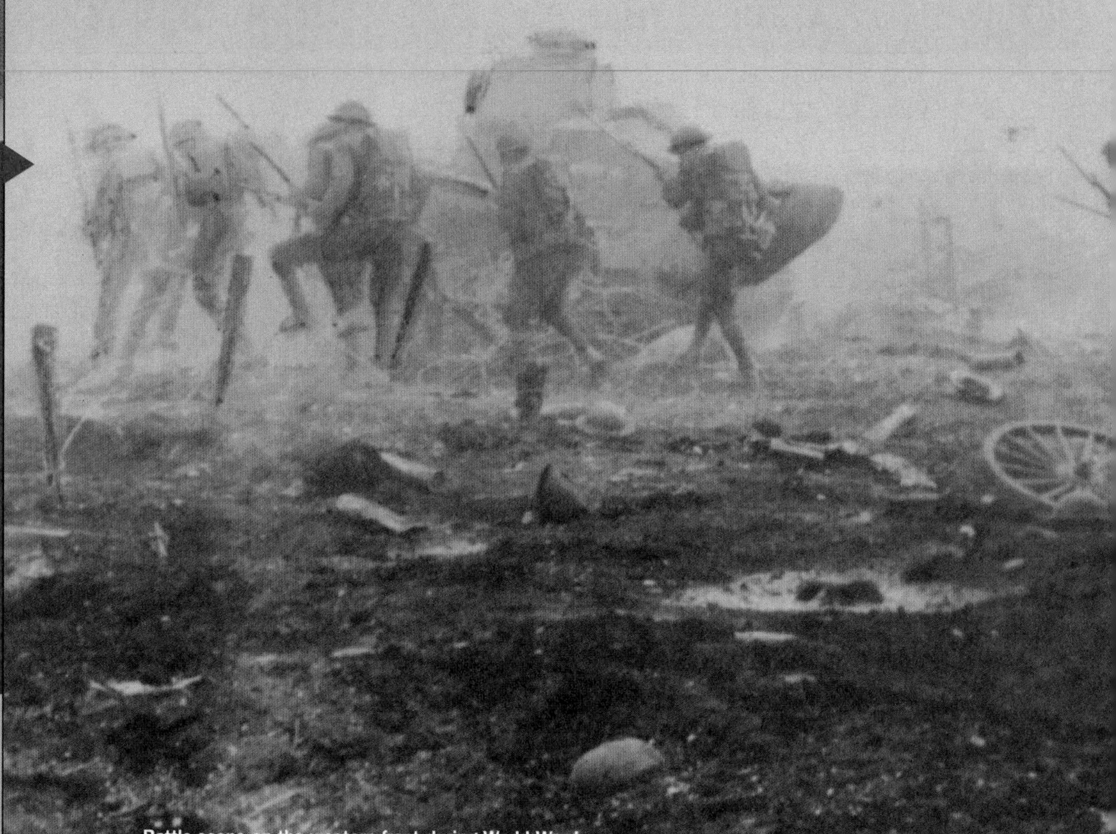

Battle scene on the western front during World War I.

### Time Line Discussion

Explain to students that this time line covers the years during which World War I was fought.

- Ask students what year war broke out in Europe. *(1914)*
- Ask students which nation withdrew from the war in the same year the United States entered it. *(Russia)*
- Ask students what event in 1918 suggests a move to reduce world conflict. *(Wilson proposed the League of Nations.)*

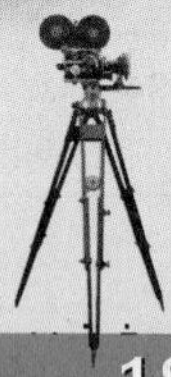

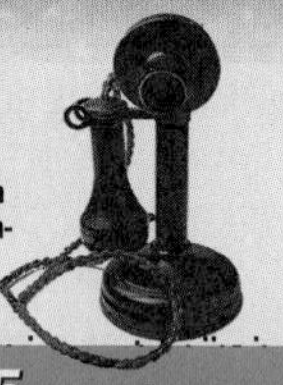

USA

- 1914 Hollywood, California, becomes the center of movie production in the U.S.
- 1915 German U-boats sink the *Lusitania*, and 1,198 people die.
- 1915 Alexander Graham Bell makes first transcontinental telephone call.
- 1916 Woodrow Wilson is reelected president.

1914 | 1915 | 1916

WORLD

- 1914 Archduke Franz Ferdinand and his wife are assassinated.
- 1914 Germany declares war on Russia and France. Great Britain declares war on Germany and Austria-Hungary.
- 1915 Albert Einstein proposes his general theory of relativity.
- 1916 The battles of Verdun and the Somme claim millions of lives.

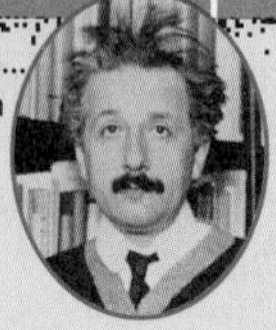



## THEMES IN CHAPTER 11

### SCIENCE AND TECHNOLOGY

When thinking about war and technology, people usually focus on new weapons. However, the First World War also led to new developments in medicine, including plastic surgery.

**See Teacher's Edition note,** p. 385.

### IMMIGRATION AND MIGRATION

During the war years, many African Americans moved to cities and to the North in search of jobs, equal treatment, and greater opportunities.

**See Teacher's Edition note,** p. 393.

### AMERICA IN WORLD AFFAIRS

Imperialism was one of the major causes of World War I. In the 19th and early 20th centuries, the United States and other nations competed for colonies. This competition led to conflict among nations.

**See Teacher's Edition note,** p. 373.

At the war's end, Wilson wanted to use the peace conference to help spread peace and democracy around the world. The Treaty of Versailles, however, did not do this.

**See Teacher's Edition note,** p. 399.

# INTERACT
## WITH HISTORY

The year is 1917. A bitter war is raging in Europe—a war that has been called a threat to civilization. At home many people are urging America to wake up and get involved, while others are calling for the country to isolate itself and avoid the fight.

# Do you think America should enter the war?

### Examine the Issues

- Is it right for America to intervene in foreign conflicts?
- When American lives are threatened, how should the government respond?
- Should America go to war to make the world "safe for democracy"?

**RESEARCH LINKS** CLASSZONE.COM

Visit the Chapter 11 links for more information about The First World War.

# INTERACT
## WITH HISTORY

### Objectives

- To motivate students to study the causes and consequences of World War I
- To help students understand the reasons the United States entered the First World War

### Examine the Issues

1. Have students consider the factors that pushed the United States into war before 1917, including the War of 1812 and the Spanish–American War.
2. Ask students to consider the different options the government might have to protect American lives.
3. Have students discuss the importance of defending democracy as a cause of U.S. intervention in the First World War. Ask students to think of examples in which the United States refused to fight even when democracy was threatened.

---

**1917** The Selective Service Act sets up the draft.

**1917** The United States declares war on Germany.

**1918** Congress passes the Sedition Act.

**1918** President Wilson proposes the League of Nations.

**1919** Congress approves the Nineteenth Amendment, granting women the vote.

## 1917    1918    1919

**1917** Russia withdraws from the war.

**1918** The Bolsheviks establish a Communist regime in Russia.

**1918** The First World War ends.

**1919** A worldwide influenza epidemic kills over 30 million.

INFLUENZA
FREQUENTLY COMPLICATED WITH
PNEUMONIA
IS PREVALENT AT THIS TIME THROUGHOUT AMERICA.
THIS THEATRE IS COOPERATING WITH THE DEPARTMENT OF HEALTH.
YOU MUST DO THE SAME
IF YOU HAVE A COLD AND ARE COUGHING AND SNEEZING DO NOT ENTER THIS THEATRE
GO HOME AND GO TO BED UNTIL YOU ARE WELL

HELP US TO KEEP CHICAGO THE
HEALTHIEST CITY

*The First World War* **371**

---

## RECOMMENDED RESOURCES

### BOOKS FOR THE TEACHER

Haythornthwaite, Philip J. *The World War I Sourcebook.* Collingdale, PA: DIANE Publishing Company, 2000. Encyclopedia covers all aspects of the war.

Tuchman, Barbara. *The Guns of August.* New York: Ballantine, 1992. Dramatic account of the early months of the war.

### BOOKS FOR THE STUDENT

Ellis, Edward Robb. *Echoes of Distant Thunder: Life in the United States, 1914–1918.* New York: Kodansha America, 1996. Describes U.S. society from 1914 to 1918.

Winter, J. M. *The Experience of World War I.* New York: Oxford, 1989.

### VIDEOS

*The Great War and the Shaping of the 20th Century.* PBS Home Video, 1996.

*Sergeant York.* Dir. Howard Hawks. 1941. Twentieth Century Fox Video, 1982. Illustrated description of military and home life.

### SOFTWARE

*World War I.* CD-ROM. First Electronic Publishing, 211 Congress Street, Boston, MA 02110, 617-338-6820.

### INTEGRATED TECHNOLOGY

For teacher support, visit . . .

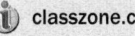 classzone.com

# World War I Begins

| MAIN IDEA | WHY IT MATTERS NOW | Terms & Names |
|---|---|---|
| As World War I intensified, the United States was forced to abandon its neutrality. | The United States remains involved in European and world affairs. | • nationalism • militarism • Allies • Central Powers • Archduke Franz Ferdinand • no man's land • trench warfare • *Lusitania* • Zimmermann note |

**TEKS** U.S. History 1A, 1B, 1C, 3A, 3B, 24A, 24B, 25A, 25B, 25C, 25D

### One American's Story

It was about 1:00 A.M. on April 6, 1917, and the members of the U.S. House of Representatives were tired. For the past 15 hours they had been debating President Wilson's request for a declaration of war against Germany. There was a breathless hush as Jeannette Rankin of Montana, the first woman elected to Congress, stood up. Rankin declared, "I want to stand by my country but I cannot vote for war. I vote no." Later she reflected on her action.

**A PERSONAL VOICE** JEANNETTE RANKIN

"I believe that the first vote I cast was the most significant vote and a most significant act on the part of women, because women are going to have to stop war. I felt at the time that the first woman [in Congress] should take the first stand, that the first time the first woman had a chance to say no to war she should say it."

—quoted in *Jeannette Rankin: First Lady in Congress*

▲ Jeannette Rankin was the only member of the House to vote against the U.S. entering both World War I and World War II.

After much debate as to whether the United States should join the fight, Congress voted in favor of U.S. entry into World War I. With this decision, the government abandoned the neutrality that America had maintained for three years. What made the United States change its policy in 1917?

## **1** Causes of World War I

Although many Americans wanted to stay out of the war, several factors made American neutrality difficult to maintain. As an industrial and imperial power, the United States felt many of the same pressures that had led the nations of Europe into devastating warfare. Historians generally cite four long-term causes of the First World War: nationalism, imperialism, militarism, and the formation of a system of alliances.

**NATIONALISM** Throughout the 19th century, politics in the Western world were deeply influenced by the concept of **nationalism**—a devotion to the interests and culture of one's nation. Often, nationalism led to competitive and antagonistic rivalries among nations. In this atmosphere of competition, many feared Germany's growing power in Europe.

In addition, various ethnic groups resented domination by others and longed for their nations to become independent. Many ethnic groups looked to larger nations for protection. Russia regarded itself as the protector of Europe's Slavic peoples, no matter which government they lived under. Among these Slavic peoples were the Serbs. Serbia, located in the Balkans, was an independent nation, but millions of ethnic Serbs lived under the rule of Austria-Hungary. As a result, Russia and Austria-Hungary were rivals for influence over Serbia.

**IMPERIALISM** For many centuries, European nations had been building empires, slowly extending their economic and political control over various peoples of the world. Colonies supplied the European imperial powers with raw materials and provided markets for manufactured goods. As Germany industrialized, it competed with France and Britain in the contest for colonies.

**MILITARISM** Empires were expensive to build and to defend. The growth of nationalism and imperialism led to increased military spending. Because each nation wanted stronger armed forces than those of any potential enemy, the imperial powers followed a policy of **militarism**—the development of armed forces and their use as a tool of diplomacy.

By 1890 the strongest nation on the European continent was Germany, which had set up an army reserve system that drafted and trained young men. Britain was not initially alarmed by Germany's military expansion. As an island nation, Britain had always relied on its navy for defense and protection of its shipping routes—and the British navy was the strongest in the world. However, in 1897, Wilhelm II, Germany's kaiser, or emperor, decided that his nation should also become a major sea power in order to compete more successfully against the British. Soon British and German shipyards competed to build the largest battleships and destroyers. France, Italy, Japan, and the United States quickly joined the naval arms race.

**ALLIANCE SYSTEM** By 1907 there were two major defense alliances in Europe. The Triple Entente, later known as the **Allies,** consisted of France, Britain, and Russia. The Triple Alliance consisted of Germany, Austria-Hungary, and Italy.

**MAIN IDEA**

**Analyzing Causes**
Ⓐ How did nationalism and imperialism lead to conflict in Europe?

*A. Answer* Nationalism and imperialism encouraged each European nation to pursue its own interests and compete for power.

**Vocabulary**
**alliance:** a formal agreement or union between nations

◄ German Emperor Wilhelm II *(center)* marches with two of his generals, Hindenburg *(left)* and Ludendorff, during World War I.

373

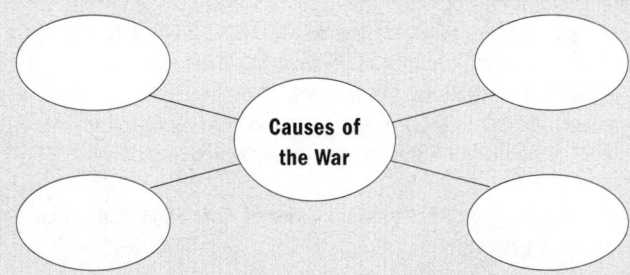

Causes of the War

Germany and Austria-Hungary, together with the Ottoman Empire—an empire of mostly Middle Eastern lands controlled by the Turks—were later known as the **Central Powers.** The alliances provided a measure of international security because nations were reluctant to disturb the balance of power. As it turned out, a spark set off a major conflict.

## ① An Assassination Leads to War

That spark flared in the Balkan Peninsula, which was known as "the powder keg of Europe." In addition to the ethnic rivalries among the Balkan peoples, Europe's leading powers had interests there. Russia wanted access to the Mediterranean Sea. Germany wanted a rail link to the Ottoman Empire. Austria-Hungary, which had taken control of Bosnia in 1878, accused Serbia of subverting its rule over Bosnia. The "powder keg" was ready to explode.

In June 1914, **Archduke Franz Ferdinand,** heir to the Austrian throne, visited the Bosnian capital Sarajevo. As the royal entourage drove through the city, Serbian nationalist Gavrilo Princip stepped from the crowd and shot the Archduke and his wife Sophie. Princip was a member of the Black Hand, an organization promoting Serbian nationalism. The assassinations touched off a diplomatic crisis. On July 28, Austria-Hungary declared what was expected to be a short war against Serbia.

The alliance system pulled one nation after another into the conflict. On August 1, Germany, obligated by treaty to support Austria-Hungary, declared war on Russia. On August 3, Germany declared war on Russia's ally France. After Germany invaded Belgium, Britain declared war on Germany and Austria-Hungary. The Great War had begun. **B**

## The Fighting Starts ②

On August 3, 1914, Germany invaded Belgium, following a strategy known as the Schlieffen Plan. This plan called for a holding action against Russia, combined with a quick drive through Belgium to Paris; after France had fallen, the two German armies would defeat Russia. As German troops swept across Belgium, thousands of civilians fled in terror. In Brussels, the Belgian capital, an American war correspondent described the first major refugee crisis of the 20th century.

> **A PERSONAL VOICE** RICHARD HARDING DAVIS
>
> "[We] found the side streets blocked with their carts. Into these they had thrown mattresses, or bundles of grain, and heaped upon them were families of three generations. Old men in blue smocks, white-haired and bent, old women in caps, the daughters dressed in their one best frock and hat, and clasping in their hands all that was left to them, all that they could stuff into a pillow-case or flour-sack. . . . Heart-broken, weary, hungry, they passed in an unending caravan."
>
> —from *Hooray for Peace, Hurrah for War*

---

**MAIN IDEA**

**Analyzing Effects**
**B** Why were so many European nations pulled into the conflict?

**B. Answer**
The alliance system pulled one nation after another into the conflict.

**Vocabulary**
**refugee:** a person who flees in search of protection or shelter, as in times of war or religious persecution

**Skillbuilder Answers**
1. About 10 miles.
2. The Allies surrounded the Central Powers; because of this, Germany had to fight on two fronts.

---

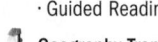

**NOW & THEN**

**Crisis in the Balkans**
**Forming Opinions** Have groups of students use the Internet or periodicals available in the local library to research the current situation in the Balkans. Ask each group to concentrate on the point of view of one specific ethnic group. Have students discuss their findings in class. Ask them whether they think the Balkan Peninsula is still a powder keg.

**Instruct: Objective ②**

**The Fighting Starts**
TAKS SS11 2(US9.A)
· What was Germany's Schlieffen Plan?
· What characteristics describe trench warfare during World War I?

📄 In-Depth Resources: Unit 3
· Guided Reading, p. 47

🗺 Geography Transparencies GT19
· Europe Goes to War

---

**NOW & THEN**

**CRISIS IN THE BALKANS**
After World War I, Bosnia became part of a country that eventually became known as Yugoslavia. Although Yugoslavia included various religious and ethnic groups, the government was dominated by Serbs.

In 1991, Yugoslavia broke apart, and Bosnia declared independence in 1992. However, Serbs wanted Bosnia to remain part of Serbian-controlled Yugoslavia.

A bloody civil war broke out. This war became notorious for the mass murder and deportation of Bosnian Muslims, a process known as "ethnic cleansing." In 1995, the United States helped negotiate a cease-fire.

But peace in the Balkans did not last. In the late 1990s, Albanians in the province of Kosovo also tried to break away from Serbia. Serbia's violent response, which included the "ethnic cleansing" of Albanians, prompted NATO to intervene. Today, peacekeepers in the Balkans struggle to control the continuing ethnic violence.

**374** CHAPTER 11

---

**Researching Diplomacy and War**

Explain to students that from the assassination of Franz Ferdinand in June through the beginning of the war in August, European governments made numerous attempts to find a diplomatic resolution to the crisis. All of these efforts failed, however. Have students use the Internet or encyclopedias to research the reasons that diplomacy failed. Have them use the following questions to focus their research:

· How did Austria-Hungary respond to the assassination of Franz Ferdinand? What demands did it make of Serbia?

· How did Serbia respond to the demands of Austria-Hungary?
· What role did the alliance system play in preventing Austria-Hungary and Serbia from coming to a compromise settlement?
· How did the European people—as opposed to their governments—respond to the crisis? Did they clamor for war, or did they want a peaceful settlement?

📄 Integrated Assessment
· Rubric 5

**NORWAY**

**SWEDEN**

British Blockade

Petrograd (St. Petersburg)

*North Sea*

**Tannenberg, Aug. 1914**
Germans stop Russian advance.

*ATLANTIC*

**IRELAND** (Br.)

**DENMARK**

• Moscow

**R U S S I A**

*Baltic Sea*

**Tannenberg**

*OCEAN*

**GREAT BRITAIN**

**NETHERLANDS**

London ⊗

Brussels ⊗
**BELGIUM**

⊗ Paris **LUXEMBOURG**

**GERMANY**

Berlin •

Eastern Front Oct. 1917

**May 1915**
*Lusitania* sunk.

*Bay of Biscay*

**FRANCE**

**SWITZERLAND**

Vienna •

**AUSTRIA-HUNGARY**

**ROMANIA**

*Adriatic Sea*

Sarajevo •

**SERBIA**

*Black Sea*

**PORTUGAL**

**SPAIN**

**ITALY**

**MONTENEGRO**

Rome •

**B A L K A N**
**P E N I N S U L A**

**BULGARIA**

**Sarajevo, June 1914**
Archduke Franz Ferdinand is assassinated.

**ALBANIA**

⊗ Constantinople (Istanbul)

*Mediterranean Sea*

**GREECE**

*Aegean Sea*

**GALLIPOLI**

**O T T O M A N**
**E M P I R E**

0°

20°E

**Gallipoli, April 1915–Jan. 1916**
Allied forces defeated in bid to establish a supply route to Russia.

---

## The Western Front 1914–1916

**NETHERLANDS**

*English Channel*

⊗ Brussels
**BELGIUM**

Meuse

**LUXEMBOURG**

Somme

Front on July 1, 1916

Oise

Aisne

Paris ⊗

Marne

Seine

**Farthest German advance, Sept. 5, 1914**

Metz •

Lunéville •

Rhine

**G E R M A N Y**

Meuse

Moselle

**F R A N C E**

**SWITZERLAND**

**A** **MARNE, 1st battle, Sept. 1914**
Allies stop German advance on Paris.

**B** **YPRES, 2nd battle, May 1915**
Germans use chemical weapons for the first time.

**C** **VERDUN, Feb.–July 1916**
French hold the line in longest battle of the war.

**D** **SOMME, 1st battle, July–Nov. 1916**
Disastrous British offensive.

→ German troop movement

→ Allied troop movement

0     50     100 miles
0     50     100 kilometers

**Legend**

☐ Allied Powers, 1916
☐ Central Powers, 1916
☐ Neutral countries
▨ German submarine activity
✷ Battle

0     250     500 miles
0     250     500 kilometers

### GEOGRAPHY SKILLBUILDER

1. **Location** About how many miles separated the city of Paris from German forces at the point of their closest approach?
2. **Place** Consider the geographical location of the Allies in relation to the Central Powers. What advantage might the Allies have had?

---

## HISTORY from VISUALS

### Interpreting the Map

Ask students to examine the borders of the European countries on the large map and to explain why France and Russia might have felt threatened by the nations known as the Central Powers. *(France and Russia shared borders with the Central Powers.)* Ask students to explain how the boxed area on the smaller map corresponds to the larger map. *(It shows the Western Front in relation to the rest of Europe.)*

## Connections Across Time

**1915 AND 1980**

### Poison Gas Warfare

The Germans used poison gas as a weapon at Ypres in April 1915. In retaliation, the Allies used poison gas, too.

In 1925, many nations signed an agreement, known as the Geneva Protocol, banning the use of toxic and biological weapons during the war. Though gas was not used during World War II, toxic gases have been used by some countries since then. For example, Iraq used poison gas during its war with Iran in the 1980s.

---

**ACTIVITY** | **LINK TO GEOGRAPHY**

**BLOCK SCHEDULING**

## Interpreting Maps

**Class Time** 10 minutes

**Task** Identifying geographic features of World War I battlegrounds

**Purpose** To draw conclusions about some of the challenges involved in invading and defending territory

**Directions** Have students work in pairs to examine the map and answer the following questions:

· For what geographical reasons did the Germans march through Belgium to get to France?

· Why did the Germans not take the alternate route of attacking through Switzerland?

## More About . . .

### Life in the Trenches

Life in the trenches was bleak and uncomfortable. Trenches were only wide enough for two people to pass and provided little shelter from the elements. This is how one soldier described the trenches: "Nothing to see but bare mud walls, nowhere to sit but on a wet muddy ledge; no shelter of any kind against the weather except the clothes you are wearing; no exercise you can take in order to warm yourself."

The close conditions in the trenches were more than unpleasant. Disease often affected the soldiers. One of the most common was trench fever. The fever was caused by the bite of a body louse. The site of the bite would ulcerate and even become gangrenous. The victim would run a high fever and develop a rash. If not treated, death due to the high fever was a possibility. Many of the soldiers had lice, so the potential for getting the fever was high.

## HISTORY from VISUALS

### Interpreting the Infographic

Ask students to think about what it would be like to be a soldier in the trenches. How much space would there be? What would it be like in the trenches in different weather conditions? What protection did the soldiers have from enemy artillery or machine gun fire? How far away were the soldiers from opposing armies? *(There was little to protect the soldiers from the elements. Staying in the trench would protect soldiers from machine guns but not from artillery. With the opposing armies within yards of each other, they could sometimes converse when there were lulls in the fighting.)*

Unable to save Belgium, the Allies retreated to the Marne River in France, where they halted the German advance in September 1914. After struggling to outflank each other's armies, both sides dug in for a long siege. By the spring of 1915, two parallel systems of deep, rat-infested trenches crossed France from the Belgian coast to the Swiss Alps. German soldiers occupied one set of trenches, Allied soldiers the other. There were three main kinds of trenches—front line, support, and reserve. Soldiers spent a period of time in each kind of trench. Dugouts, or underground rooms, were used as officers' quarters and command posts. Between the trench complexes lay **"no man's land"**—a barren expanse of mud pockmarked with shell craters and filled with barbed wire. Periodically, the soldiers charged enemy lines, only to be mowed down by machine gun fire. **C**

The scale of slaughter was horrific. During the First Battle of the Somme—which began on July 1, 1916, and lasted until mid-November—the British suffered 60,000 casualties the first day alone. Final casualties totaled about 1.2 million, yet only about seven miles of ground changed hands. This bloody **trench warfare**, in which armies fought for mere yards of ground, continued for over three years. Elsewhere, the fighting was just as devastating and inconclusive.

**C. Possible Answer**
To maintain their morale by changing their surroundings periodically.

**MAIN IDEA**

**Drawing Conclusions**
**C** Why do you think soldiers were rotated in the trenches?

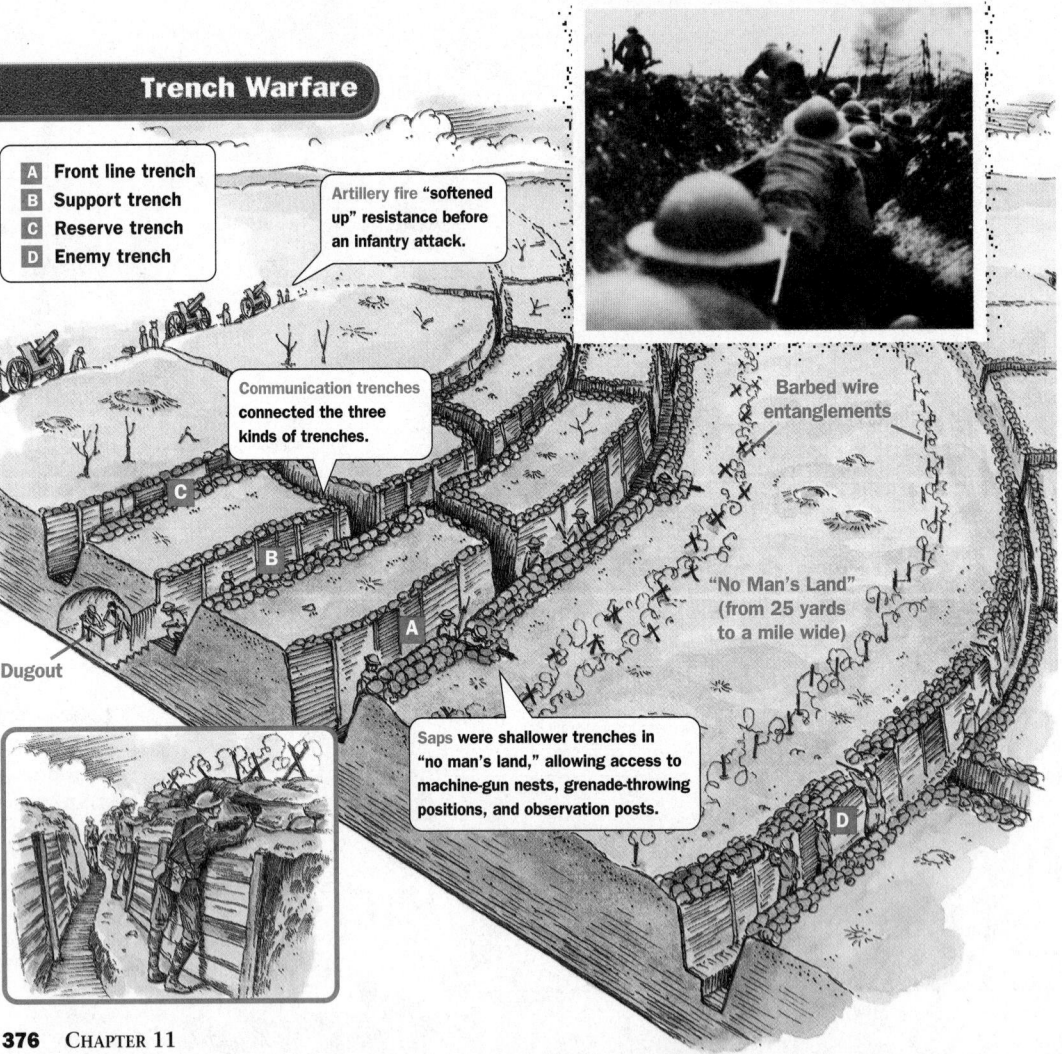

**Trench Warfare**

| A | Front line trench |
| B | Support trench |
| C | Reserve trench |
| D | Enemy trench |

Artillery fire **"softened up" resistance before an infantry attack.**

Communication trenches **connected the three kinds of trenches.**

Barbed wire entanglements

"No Man's Land" (from 25 yards to a mile wide)

Dugout

Saps **were shallower trenches in "no man's land," allowing access to machine-gun nests, grenade-throwing positions, and observation posts.**

**376** CHAPTER 11

---

**DIFFERENTIATING INSTRUCTION** | **GIFTED AND TALENTED** |  classzone.com

### Analyzing Switzerland's Neutrality

Tell students that unlike the United States, Switzerland remained neutral throughout World War I. In fact, Switzerland has managed to maintain an armed neutrality since 1815. Have students use the Internet or encyclopedia sources in the library to research Swiss neutrality by answering these questions:

· How has Switzerland managed to remain the only European country to preserve its neutrality through two world wars?
· What role, if any, did Switzerland play in the two wars?
· How did the people of other European countries benefit from Switzerland's neutrality?
· Why has Switzerland decided to remain neutral?

# Americans Question Neutrality ③

In 1914, most Americans saw no reason to join a struggle 3,000 miles away. The war did not threaten American lives or property. This does not mean, however, that individual Americans were indifferent to who would win the war. Public opinion was strong—but divided.

**DIVIDED LOYALTIES** Socialists criticized the war as a capitalist and imperialist struggle between Germany and England to control markets and colonies in China, Africa, and the Middle East. Pacifists, such as lawyer and politician William Jennings Bryan, believed that war was evil and that the United States should set an example of peace to the world.

Many Americans simply did not want their sons to experience the horrors of warfare, as a hit song of 1915 conveyed.

"I didn't raise my boy to be a soldier,
I brought him up to be my pride and joy.
Who dares to place a musket on his shoulder,
To shoot some other mother's darling boy?"

**Vocabulary**
**emigrate:** to leave one's country or region to settle in another; to move

Millions of naturalized U.S. citizens followed the war closely because they still had ties to the nations from which they had emigrated. For example, many Americans of German descent sympathized with Germany. Americans of Irish descent remembered the centuries of British oppression in Ireland and saw the war as a chance for Ireland to gain its independence.

On the other hand, many Americans felt close to Britain because of a common ancestry and language as well as similar democratic institutions and legal systems. Germany's aggressive sweep through Belgium increased American sympathy for the Allies. The Germans attacked civilians, destroying villages, cathedrals, libraries, and even hospitals. Some atrocity stories—spread by British propaganda—later proved to be false, but enough proved true that one American magazine referred to Germany as "the bully of Europe."

**D. Answer**
The U.S. favored Britain and France because it traded extensively with them and because Germany was the aggressor.

More important, America's economic ties with the Allies were far stronger than its ties with the Central Powers. Before the war, American trade with Britain and France was more than double its trade with Germany. During the first two years of the war, America's transatlantic trade became even more lopsided, as the Allies flooded American manufacturers with orders for all sorts of war supplies, including dynamite, cannon powder, submarines, copper wire and tubing, and armored cars. The United States shipped millions of dollars of war supplies to the Allies, but requests kept coming. By 1915, the United States was experiencing a labor shortage. **D**

**MAIN IDEA**

**Analyzing Motives**
**D** Why did the United States begin to favor Britain and France?

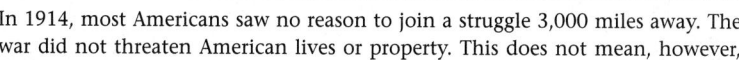

**ECONOMIC BACKGROUND**

**TRADE ALLIANCES**

Maintaining neutrality proved difficult for American businesses. Trade with Germany became increasingly risky. Shipments were often stopped by the British blockade. In addition, President Wilson and others spoke out against German atrocities and warned of the threat that the German Empire posed to democracy.

From 1912 to 1917, U.S. trade relationships with European countries shifted dramatically. From 1914 on, trade with the Allies quadrupled, while trade with Germany fell to near zero.

Also, by 1917, American banks had loaned $2.3 billion to the Allies, but only $27 million to the Central Powers. Many U.S. leaders, including Treasury Secretary William McAdoo, felt that American prosperity depended upon an Allied victory. (See *trade* on page R47 in the Economics Handbook.)

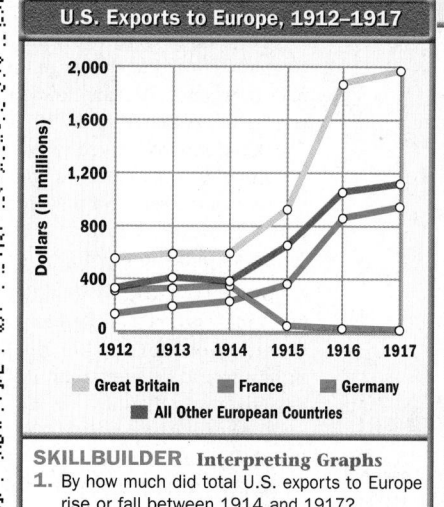

**U.S. Exports to Europe, 1912–1917**

Dollars (in millions): 2,000 / 1,600 / 1,200 / 800 / 400 / 0

1912 1913 1914 1915 1916 1917

- Great Britain
- France
- Germany
- All Other European Countries

**SKILLBUILDER Interpreting Graphs**
1. By how much did total U.S. exports to Europe rise or fall between 1914 and 1917?
2. What trends does the graph show before the start of the war, and during the war?

*The First World War* **377**

**Instruct: Objective ③**

**Americans Question Neutrality/ The War Hits Home**
TAKS SS11 1(US3.B)

· What motivated those who opposed entering the war?
· What motivated those who favored it?
· What factors increased American sympathy for the Allies?

📖 In-Depth Resources: Unit 3
· Guided Reading, p. 47

**ECONOMIC BACKGROUND**

**Trade Alliances**
Discuss the economic motivation for U.S. entry into the war. Ask students whether they think the United States would have joined forces with the Central Powers if the United States had been financially backing those countries instead of Britain and France. Would the United States have entered the war if U.S. banks had not lent money to either side?

**HISTORY from VISUALS**

**Interpreting the Graph**
Ask students to use the graph to determine which country received the most U.S. exports in 1915 and which country received the fewest. *(Great Britain received the most, and Austria-Hungary received the fewest.)*

---

**Analyzing Points of View on the War**

**Class Time** 30 minutes

**Task** Researching different American points of view on World War I. The groups shall then report on how different people viewed the war and how the United States should respond to the war.

**Purpose** To help students understand different points of view on the war from 1914 to 1917

 **BLOCK SCHEDULING**

**Directions** Divide students into four groups. Give each group one of the following questions to discuss. They should then report on their group's findings.

· How did German and Irish immigrants view the war in Europe?
· Which groups of Americans were most likely to want to support the Allies?
· What were the main arguments people gave to support neutrality?
· How did trade affect the U.S. attitude about the war?

## HISTORY from VISUALS

### Interpreting the Illustration

Ask the students to discuss how the artist portrays the sinking of the *Lusitania*. *(Students may notice that there are a lot of women on the lifeboats, the two hands coming out of the water in center foreground, and a man climbing onto the raft. Some students may say the ad would have kept them from sailing for fear of being attacked.)*

## More About . . .

### Blockade vs. Submarines

The British naval blockade of Germany was a far more effective weapon than Germany's submarine warfare. The naval blockade of Germany reduced shipping into Germany to almost nothing. By contrast, German subs were only capable of preventing a small percentage of ships bound for Britain from reaching their destination. For example, in March 1915, roughly 6,000 ships sailed for Britain. The Germans sank only 21 of them. Meanwhile, German submarines were constantly harassed by new anti-submarine measures. For instance, the British invented depth charges, which were canisters dropped from ships. These charges exploded under water in the vicinity of a sub. The shock waves usually damaged the subs, forcing them to the surface where a British ship's guns would fire on the sub.

▲ This image of a U-boat crew machine-gunning helpless survivors of the *Lusitania* was clearly meant as propaganda. In fact, U-boats seldom lingered after an attack.

**TAKS**

Mini-Lesson 1:
SS11 1(US3.B)

# The War Hits Home ③

Although the majority of Americans favored victory for the Allies rather than the Central Powers, they did not want to join the Allies' fight. By 1917, however, America had mobilized for war against the Central Powers for two reasons: to ensure Allied repayment of debts to the United States and to prevent the Germans from threatening U.S. shipping.

**THE BRITISH BLOCKADE** As fighting on land continued, Britain began to make more use of its naval strength. It blockaded the German coast to prevent weapons and other military supplies from getting through. However, the British expanded the definition of contraband to include food. They also extended the blockade to neutral ports and mined the entire North Sea.

The results were two fold. First, American ships carrying goods for Germany refused to challenge the blockade and seldom reached their destination. Second, Germany found it increasingly difficult to import foodstuffs and fertilizers for crops. By 1917, famine stalked the country. An estimated 750,000 Germans starved to death as a result of the British blockade.

Americans had been angry at Britain's blockade, which threatened freedom of the seas and prevented American goods from reaching German ports. However, Germany's response to the blockade soon outraged American public opinion.

**GERMAN U–BOAT RESPONSE** Germany responded to the British blockade with a counterblockade by U-boats (from *Unterseeboot*, the German word for a submarine). Any ship found in the waters around Britain would be sunk—and it would not always be possible to warn crews and passengers of an attack.

One of the worst disasters occurred on May 7, 1915, when a U-boat sank the British liner **Lusitania** (lo͞oˈsĭ-tāˈnē-ə) off the southern coast of Ireland. Of the 1,198 persons lost, 128 were Americans. The Germans defended their action on the grounds that the liner carried ammunition. Despite Germany's explanation, Americans became outraged with Germany because of the loss of life. American public opinion turned against Germany and the Central Powers.

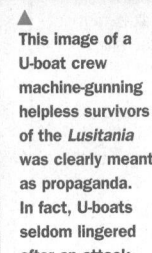

OCEAN STEAMSHIPS.

**CUNARD**

EUROPE VIA LIVERPOOL

**LUSITANIA**

Fastest and Largest Steamer now in Atlantic Service Sails SATURDAY, MAY 1, 10 A. M.
Transylvania, Fri., May 7, 10 A
Orduna, · · Tues., May 18, 10 A
Tuscania, · · Fri., May 21, 10 A
LUSITANIA, Sat., May 29, 10 A
Transylvania, Fri., June 4, 5 P

Gibraltar–Genoa–Naples–Piraeus
S.S. Carpathia, Thur., May 13, No
ROUND THE WORLD TOURS
Through bookings to all principal P
of the World
Company's office, 21-24 State St., N

## NOTICE!

TRAVELLERS intending embark on the Atlantic voyage are reminded that a state war exists between Germany and her allies and Great Britain and her allies; that the zone war includes the waters adjacent to the British Isles; that in accordance with formal notice given by the Imperial German Government, vessels flying the flag of Great Britain, or any of her allies, are liable to destruction in those waters and that travellers sailing in the war zone on ships of Great Britain or her allies do so at their own risk.

IMPERIAL GERMAN EMBASSY
WASHINGTON, D. C., APRIL 22, 1915

▲ A newspaper ad for the *Lusitania* included a warning from the German Embassy.

---

**DIFFERENTIATING INSTRUCTION** | **STUDENTS ACQUIRING ENGLISH/ESL**

### Understanding Main Ideas

Write the heading "The War Hits Home" on the board. Explain to students that this phrase refers to the fact that even though the war was being fought in distant countries, it still had an impact on the people in the United States. Ask students to create a list of the ways the war affected life in the United States. Read the section "The War Hits Home" with students. Then ask them to point out the statements in the text that support the heading.

Some of the statements they might write include:

· "American ships carrying goods for Germany refused to challenge the blockade and seldom reached their destination."

· "Of the 1,198 persons lost, 128 were Americans."

· "Americans became outraged with Germany because of the loss of life."

 Integrated Assessment
· Rubric 2

Despite this provocation, President Wilson ruled out a military response in favor of a sharp protest to Germany. Three months later, in July 1915, a U-boat sank another British liner, the *Arabic*, drowning two Americans. Again the United States protested, and this time Germany agreed not to sink any more passenger ships. But in March 1916 Germany broke its promise and torpedoed an unarmed French passenger steamer, the *Sussex*. The *Sussex* sank, and about 80 passengers, including Americans, were killed or injured. Once again the United States warned that it would break off diplomatic relations unless Germany changed its tactics. Again Germany agreed, but there was a condition: if the United States could not persuade Britain to lift its blockade against food and fertilizers, Germany would consider renewing unrestricted submarine warfare. (E)

MAIN IDEA

**Analyzing Effects**

(E) How did the German U-boat campaign affect U.S. public opinion?

*E. Answer* Because the U-boat campaign killed Americans and destroyed American property, it turned American public opinion against Germany.

**THE 1916 ELECTION** In November 1916 came the U.S. presidential election. The Democrats renominated Wilson, and the Republicans nominated Supreme Court Justice Charles Evans Hughes. Wilson campaigned on the slogan "He Kept Us Out of War." Hughes pledged to uphold America's right to freedom of the seas but also promised not to be too severe on Germany.

The election returns shifted from hour to hour. In fact, Hughes went to bed believing he had been elected. When a reporter tried to reach him with the news of Wilson's victory, an aide said, "The president can't be disturbed." "Well," replied the reporter, "when he wakes up, tell him he's no longer president."

THE MAN OF THE HOUR
WOODROW WILSON

▲ Wilson campaign button

### More About . . .

**Hughes and the 1916 Election**

During the campaign, Hughes took part in various political activities designed to bolster his reputation. Hughes was rumored to have attended a rodeo to meet the cowboys and ventured down into a copper mine to talk with the miners. Despite his efforts, Hughes lost the election by a narrow margin of 23 electoral votes.

## 4 The United States Declares War

After the election, Wilson tried to mediate between the warring alliances. The attempt failed. In a speech before the Senate in January 1917, the president called for "a peace without victory. . . . a peace between equals," in which neither side would impose harsh terms on the other. Wilson hoped that all nations would join in a "league for peace" that would work to extend democracy, maintain freedom of the seas, and reduce armaments.

**GERMAN PROVOCATION** The Germans ignored Wilson's calls for peace. Germany's leaders hoped to defeat Britain by resuming unrestricted submarine warfare. On January 31 the kaiser announced that U-boats would sink all ships in British waters—hostile or neutral—on sight. Wilson was stunned. The German decision meant that the United States would have to go to war. However, the president held back, saying that he would wait for "actual overt acts" before declaring war.

The overt acts came. First was the **Zimmermann note,** a telegram from the German foreign minister to the German ambassador in Mexico that was intercepted by British agents. The telegram proposed an alliance between Mexico and Germany and promised that if war with the United States broke out, Germany would support Mexico in recovering "lost territory in Texas, New Mexico, and Arizona." Next came the sinking of four unarmed American merchant ships, with a loss of 36 lives. (F)

*F. Answer* It raised the possibility of the war spreading to the Americas.

MAIN IDEA

**Making Inferences**

(F) Why did the Zimmermann note alarm the U.S. government?

Finally, events in Russia removed the last significant obstacle to direct U.S. involvement in the war. In March, the oppressive Russian monarchy was

**Alliances During WWI**

| Allies | | Central Powers |
|---|---|---|
| Australia | India | Austria-Hungary |
| Belgium | Italy | Bulgaria |
| British Colonies | Japan | Germany |
| Canada & Newfoundland | Montenegro | Ottoman Empire |
| France | New Zealand | |
| French North Africa & French Colonies | Portugal | |
| | Romania | |
| | Russia | |
| | Serbia | |
| Great Britain | South Africa | |
| Greece | United States | |

**Although not all of the countries listed above sent troops into the war, they all joined the war on the Allied side at various times.**

### Instruct: Objective 4

**The United States Declares War**

TAKS SS11 1(US3.B)

- Why did the German threat to sink all ships in British waters push the United States to declare war?
- What did the Zimmermann note reveal about Germany's plans?

In-Depth Resources: Unit 3
- Guided Reading, p. 47
- Primary Source: The Zimmermann Note, p. 59
- Literature: from *A Son at the Front*, pp. 63–64



ACTIVITY | SKILLBUILDER LESSON | BLOCK SCHEDULING

### Evaluating Decisions and Courses of Action

**Explaining the Skill** In order to understand historical decisions, historians will often look at a situation or event from various angles. Evaluating historical decisions involves analyzing the pros and cons of a particular course of action, and examining the conditions, expectations, and values of the times.

**Applying the Skill** Have students review the events leading up to the U.S. entrance into World War I. Ask students to consider various ways President Wilson could have responded to Germany's counterblockade and how effective each alternative might have been. *(Wilson could have insisted on staying out of the war entirely, but the German counterblockade by U-boats raised American calls for war. Wilson could have kept the United States from shipping supplies to the Allies and thus prevented German submarine attacks on U.S. ships. However, businessmen probably would have opposed such restrictions on trade. Or, Wilson could have argued that the United States should enter the war on the side of the Allies.)*

In-Depth Resources: Unit 3
- Skillbuilder Practice, p. 52

## WORLD STAGE

### Revolution in Russia

**Analyzing Motives** Ask students why the Russian people were unwilling to fight against the Central Powers for the czar or for the Kerensky government. *(The people felt no allegiance to either the czarist regime or the new government.)*

# Assess & Reteach

 **SECTION 1 ASSESSMENT**

Have pairs of students work together to answer the questions in the Section Assessment.

📄 Formal Assessment
· Section Quiz, p. 209

**SELF-ASSESSMENT**

Have students jot down what they found most interesting, most surprising, and most challenging in the section.

**RETEACH**

Use the map on page 375 to review the progress of the fighting during the early years of the war.

 In-Depth Resources: Unit 3
· Reteaching Activity, p. 53

---

## WORLD STAGE

### REVOLUTION IN RUSSIA

At first, the Russians surprised the Germans by mobilizing rapidly. Russian troops advanced quickly into German territory but were turned back at the Battle of Tannenberg in August 1914.

Throughout 1915, the Russians endured defeats and continued to retreat. By the end of 1915 they had suffered about 2.5 million casualties. The war also caused massive bread shortages in Russia.

Revolutionaries ousted the czar in March 1917 and established a provisional government. In November, the Bolsheviks, led by Lenin and Trotsky, overthrew the provisional government. They set up a Communist state and sought peace with the Central Powers.

---

replaced with a representative government. Now supporters of American entry into the war could claim that this was a war of democracies against brutal monarchies.

**AMERICA ACTS** A light drizzle fell on Washington on April 2, 1917, as senators, representatives, ambassadors, members of the Supreme Court, and other guests crowded into the Capitol building to hear President Wilson deliver his war resolution.

### A PERSONAL VOICE WOODROW WILSON

" **Property can be paid for; the lives of peaceful and innocent people cannot be. The present German submarine warfare against commerce is a warfare against mankind. . . . We are glad . . . to fight . . . for the ultimate peace of the world and for the liberation of its peoples. . . . The world must be made safe for democracy. . . . We have no selfish ends to serve. We desire no conquest, no dominion. We seek no indemnities. . . . It is a fearful thing to lead this great peaceful people into war. . . . But the right is more precious than peace.** "

—quoted in *American Voices*

Congress passed the resolution a few days later. With the hope of neutrality finally shattered, U.S. troops would follow the stream of American money and munitions that had been heading to the Allies throughout the war. But Wilson's plea to make the world "safe for democracy" wasn't just political posturing. Indeed, Wilson and many Americans truly believed that the United States had to join the war to pave the way for a future order of peace and freedom. A resolved but anxious nation held its breath as the United States prepared for war.

---

 **ASSESSMENT**

1. **TERMS & NAMES** For each term or name, write a sentence explaining its significance.

- nationalism
- militarism
- Allies
- Central Powers
- Archduke Franz Ferdinand
- no man's land
- trench warfare
- *Lusitania*
- Zimmermann note

**MAIN IDEA**

2. **TAKING NOTES**
In a chart like the one shown, list the causes for the outbreak of World War I.

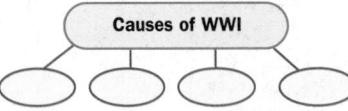

Causes of WWI

Which was the most significant cause? Explain your answer.

**CRITICAL THINKING**

3. **SYNTHESIZING**
Describe some ways in which World War I threatened the lives of civilians on both sides of the Atlantic.

4. **SUMMARIZING**
Why were America's ties with the Allies stronger than its ties with the Central Powers?

4. **ANALYZING ISSUES**
Why do you think Germany escalated its U-boat attacks in 1917? **Think About:**

- Germany's military buildup
- the effects of the British blockade
- Germany's reason for using submarine warfare

---

 **ASSESSMENT** Answers

**1. TERMS & NAMES**
nationalism, p. 373
militarism, p. 373
Allies, p. 373
Central Powers, p. 374
Archduke Franz Ferdinand, p. 374
no man's land, p. 376
trench warfare, p. 376
*Lusitania*, p. 378
Zimmermann note, p. 379

**2. MAIN IDEA**
nationalism; imperialism, militarism; alliance system
Answers will vary. Some students may say that the alliance system was the most significant cause.

**3. SYNTHESIZING**
German U-boats threatened transatlantic ships carrying civilians.

**4. SUMMARIZING**
Americans felt close ties to Britain because of a common ancestry and language, as well as similar political and legal institutions. Before the war, American trade with Britain and France was more than double that with Germany. During the war, trade with the Allies increased.

**5. ANALYZING ISSUES**
Germany was finding it increasingly difficult to import foodstuffs and fertilizers. Famine spread throughout the country. Perhaps, Germany saw the U.S. refusal to challenge the blockade as an expression of allegiance to the Allies. Germany sent out U-boats prepared to sink any ship found in British waters.

# SECTION 2

# American Power Tips the Balance

| MAIN IDEA | WHY IT MATTERS NOW | Terms & Names |
|---|---|---|
| The United States mobilized a large army and navy to help the Allies achieve victory. | During World War I, the United States military evolved into the powerful fighting force that it remains today. | • Eddie Rickenbacker<br>• Selective Service Act<br>• convoy system<br>• American Expeditionary Force<br>• General John J. Pershing<br>• Alvin York<br>• conscientious objector<br>• armistice |

**TEKS** U.S. History 1A, 1B, 1C, 3C, 3D, 24A, 24B, 24C, 25A, 25B, 25D

### One American's Story

**Eddie Rickenbacker,** famous fighter pilot of World War I, was well known as a racecar driver before the war. He went to France as a driver but transferred to the aviation division. He learned to fly on his own time and eventually joined the U.S. Army Air Service. Rickenbacker repeatedly fought the dreaded Flying Circus—a German air squadron led by the "Red Baron," Manfred von Richthofen.

**A PERSONAL VOICE** EDDIE RICKENBACKER

" I put in six or seven hours of flying time each day. . . . My narrowest escape came at a time when I was fretting over the lack of action. . . . Guns began barking behind me, and sizzling tracers zipped by my head. . . . At least two planes were on my tail. . . .
They would expect me to dive. Instead I twisted upward in a corkscrew path called a 'chandelle.' I guessed right. As I went up, my two attackers came down, near enough for me to see their faces. I also saw the red noses on those Fokkers [German planes]. I was up against the Flying Circus again."

—*Rickenbacker: An Autobiography*

**VIDEO**
***ACE OF ACES***
**Eddie Rickenbacker and the First World War**

After engaging in 134 air battles and downing 26 enemy aircraft, Rickenbacker won fame as the Allied pilot with the most victories—"American ace of aces."

## America Mobilizes ❶

The United States was not prepared for war. Only 200,000 men were in service when war was declared, and few officers had combat experience. Drastic measures were needed to build an army large and modern enough to make an impact in Europe.

---

## OBJECTIVES

❶ Describe how the United States mobilized for war.

❷ Summarize U.S. battlefield successes.

❸ Identify the new weapons and the medical problems faced in World War I.

❹ Describe U.S. offensives and the end of the war.

### SKILLBUILDERS

· Geography Skillbuilder: location, place, p. 386

### CRITICAL THINKING

· Summarizing, pp. 382, 383
· Analyzing Effects, p. 385
· Forming Generalizations, p. 384
· Drawing Conclusions, pp. 386, 387
· Analyzing Visual Sources, p. 387

## Focus & Motivate

How would students react if their nation went to war? Would they volunteer to serve? Would they refuse to go, or would they protest the nation's involvement in the conflict?

## Instruct

### Instruct: Objective ❶

**America Mobilizes**
TAKS SS11 1(US3.D)
· How did the United States raise an army during World War I?
· How did the United States increase ship production?

 In-Depth Resources: Unit 3
· Guided Reading, p. 48
· Literature: from *In Another Country*, p. 65

---

## PROGRAM RESOURCES

 **In-Depth Resources: Unit 3**
· Guided Reading, p. 48
· Reteaching Activity, p. 54
· Primary Source: Patriotic Song, p. 60
· Primary Source: Liberty Bond Poster, p. 61
· Literature: from *In Another Country*, p. 65

 **Reading Study Guide** (English and Spanish), pp. 115–116

 **Access for Students Acquiring English/ESL**
· Guided Reading (Spanish), p. 135

 **Formal Assessment**
· Section Quiz, p. 210

 **Integrated Assessment**
· Rubrics

### INTEGRATED TECHNOLOGY

 **American Stories, video series**
· Eddie Rickenbacker and the First World War

 **Critical Thinking Trans. CT53**
· The Human and Financial Costs of World War I

 **Humanities Transp. HT18**
· *Oppy Wood* by John Nash

 **Electronic Library of Primary Sources**

classzone.com

### TEXAS RESOURCES

TAKS Spiraled Content Review

TAKS Practice Tests

TAKS Practice Transparencies TT72

TAKS Online Test Practice

▼ Drafted men line up for service at Camp Travis in San Antonio, Texas, around 1917.

I WANT YOU FOR U.S. ARMY
NEAREST RECRUITING STATION

▲ James Montgomery Flagg's portrayal of Uncle Sam became the most famous recruiting poster in American history.

**RAISING AN ARMY** To meet the government's need for more fighting power, Congress passed the **Selective Service Act** in May 1917. The act required men to register with the government in order to be randomly selected for military service. By the end of 1918, 24 million men had registered under the act. Of this number, almost 3 million were called up. About 2 million troops reached Europe before the truce was signed, and three-fourths of them saw actual combat. Most of the inductees had not attended high school, and about one in five was foreign-born.

About 400,000 African Americans served in the armed forces. More than half of them served in France. African American soldiers served in segregated units and were excluded from the navy and marines. Most African Americans were assigned to noncombat duties, although there were exceptions. The all-black 369th Infantry Regiment saw more continuous duty on the front lines than any other American regiment. Two soldiers of the 369th, Henry Johnson and Needham Roberts, were the first Americans to receive France's highest military honor, the Croix de Guerre—the "cross of war."

The eight-month training period took place partly in the United States and partly in Europe. During this time the men put in 17-hour days on target practice, bayonet drill, kitchen duty, and cleaning up the grounds. Since real weapons were in short supply, soldiers often drilled with fake weapons—rocks instead of hand grenades, or wooden poles instead of rifles.

Although women were not allowed to enlist, the army reluctantly accepted women in the Army Corps of Nurses, but denied them army rank, pay, and benefits. Meanwhile, some 13,000 women accepted noncombat positions in the navy and marines, where they served as nurses, secretaries, and telephone operators, with full military rank. **A**

**MASS PRODUCTION** In addition to the vast army that had to be created and trained, the United States had to find a way to transport men, food, and equipment over thousands of miles of ocean. It was an immense task, made more difficult by German submarine activity, which by early 1917 had sunk twice as much ship tonnage as the Allies had built. In order to expand its fleet, the U.S. government took four crucial steps.

**Vocabulary**
**segregated:** separated or isolated from others

**A. Answer** Congress passed the Selective Service Act, which required 24 million men to register for the draft.

**MAIN IDEA**

**Summarizing**
**A** How did the United States raise an army for the war?

382 CHAPTER 11

First, the government exempted many shipyard workers from the draft and gave others a "deferred" classification, delaying their participation in the draft. Second, the U.S. Chamber of Commerce joined in a public relations campaign to emphasize the importance of shipyard work. They distributed service flags to families of shipyard workers, just like the flags given to families of soldiers and sailors. They also urged automobile owners to give shipyard employees rides to and from work, since streetcars were so crowded. Third, shipyards used prefabrication techniques. Instead of building an entire ship in the yard, standardized parts were built elsewhere and then assembled at the yard. This method reduced construction time substantially. As a result, on just one day—July 4, 1918—the United States launched 95 ships. Fourth, the government took over commercial and private ships and converted them for transatlantic war use. **B**

---

> **MAIN IDEA**
>
> **Summarizing**
> **B** How did the United States expand its navy so quickly?
>
> **B. Answer**
> It exempted shipyard workers from the draft, used a public relations campaign to stress the importance of shipbuilding, used prefabrication construction techniques, and took control of private ships for transatlantic duty.

## America Turns the Tide **2**

German U-boat attacks on merchant ships in the Atlantic were a serious threat to the Allied war effort. American Vice Admiral William S. Sims convinced the British to try the **convoy system,** in which a heavy guard of destroyers escorted merchant ships back and forth across the Atlantic in groups. By fall of 1917, shipping losses had been cut in half.

The U.S. Navy also helped lay a 230-mile barrier of mines across the North Sea from Scotland to Norway. The barrier was designed to bottle up the U-boats that sailed from German ports and keep them out of the Atlantic Ocean.

By early 1918 the Germans found it increasingly difficult to replace their losses and to staff their fleet with trained submariners. Of the almost 2 million Americans who sailed to Europe during the war, only 637 were lost to U-boat attacks.

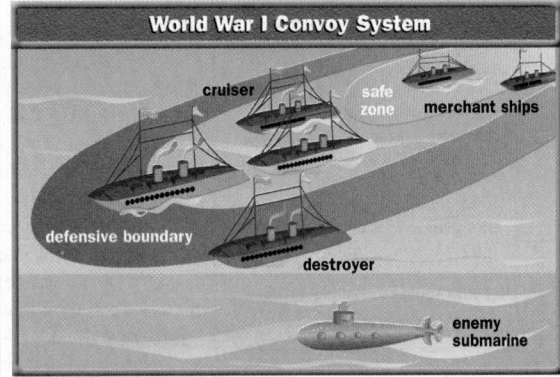

**World War I Convoy System**

cruiser — safe zone — merchant ships — defensive boundary — destroyer — enemy submarine

**FIGHTING IN EUROPE** After two and a half years of fighting, the Allied forces were exhausted and demoralized. One of the main contributions that American troops made to the Allied war effort, apart from their numbers, was their freshness and enthusiasm. They were determined to hit the Germans hard. Twenty-two-year-old Joseph Douglas Lawrence, a U.S. Army lieutenant, remarked on the importance of American enthusiasm when he described his first impression of the trenches.

**A PERSONAL VOICE** JOSEPH DOUGLAS LAWRENCE

" I have never seen or heard of such an elaborate, complete line of defense as the British had built at this point. There was a trench with dugouts every three hundred yards from the front line in Ypres back four miles to and including Dirty Bucket. Everything was fronted with barbed wire and other entanglements. Artillery was concealed everywhere. Railroad tracks, narrow and standard gauge, reached from the trenches back into the zone of supply. Nothing had been neglected to hold this line, save only one important thing, enthusiasm among the troops, and that was the purpose of our presence."

—*Fighting Soldier: The AEF in 1918*

Lieutenant Joseph D. Lawrence

*The First World War* **383**

---

### Instruct: Objective **2**

**America Turns the Tide**
TAKS SS11 5(W68.B)

· What was the significance of the convoy system?

· How did the arrival of new American troops affect the spirit of Allied troops?

In-Depth Resources: Unit 3
· Guided Reading, p. 48

### More About . . .

**Joseph D. Lawrence**

Joseph Douglas Lawrence was born in Roanoke, Virginia, in 1895. He enlisted in the army in 1917, after finishing high school in South Carolina. He survived the war and returned home to study mining engineering at the University of Virginia. The postwar depression forced him to leave school, and he headed west looking for work. He worked many jobs in many places and "hoboed" on trains to get from place to place. He eventually returned to South Carolina and built a career in banking. After he retired, Lawrence worked on international economic development programs.

---

**ACTIVITY**    **LINK TO GEOGRAPHY**        **B** **BLOCK SCHEDULING**

### Interpreting a Map of the War at Sea

**Class Time** 20 minutes

**Task** Interpreting maps of the naval battle between the Allies and the Central Powers

**Purpose** To understand the naval conflict between the Allies and the Germans

**Directions** Have students use a map of Europe and the information in the textbook to find the following: the English Channel, Gibraltar, and the areas where the Allies laid mines in the North Sea.

· Ask students to find the most direct water routes from North America to Germany.

· Ask students which nations existed on each shore of the English Channel, and point out to them that the British controlled Gibraltar.

· Ask them what advantages the Allies had by controlling these sea lanes.

· Have one or two students use an encyclopedia to find where the Battle of Jutland occurred and the result of that battle, and have them brief the class on it.

· Have the students discuss what options the Germans had to defeat the Allies at sea.

## Instruct: Objective ③

**Fighting "Over There"/ The War Introduces New Hazards**
TAKS SS11 2(WH23.A)

· Who led the American troops in Europe?

· What new weapons were used during World War I?

· How did medical services respond to the physical and emotional wounds suffered by the soldiers?

 In-Depth Resources: Unit 3
· Guided Reading, p. 48

### KEY PLAYER

**General John J. Pershing**
One general referred to Pershing as "the coolest man under fire that I ever saw." Discuss with students why such a trait would help make him a successful military leader.

### Connections Across Time

**1777 AND 1917**

**Pershing and Lafayette**
Tell students that after the American troops joined the Allies in France, the saying "Lafayette, we are here!" became popular. The comment is usually attributed to General Pershing. In fact, it was delivered at an address at the grave of Lafayette in Paris on July 4, 1917, by Colonel C. E. Stanton. The statement reminded Americans that French troops under the Marquis de Lafayette had aided Washington and the cause of the American Revolution. The landing of American soldiers in France in World War I represented America's repayment of its debt to France.

**KEY PLAYER**

**GENERAL JOHN J. PERSHING**
**1860–1948**

When General Pershing, the commander of the American Expeditionary Force (AEF), arrived in France, he found that the Allies intended to use American troops simply as reinforcements. Pershing, however, urged that the AEF operate as an independent fighting force, under American command.

Pershing believed in aggressive combat and felt that three years of trench warfare had made the Allies too defensive. Under Pershing, American forces helped to stop the German advance, capturing important enemy positions. After the war, Pershing was made General of the Armies of the United States—the highest rank given to an officer.

## Fighting "Over There" ③

The **American Expeditionary Force** (AEF), led by **General John J. Pershing**, included men from widely separated parts of the country. American infantrymen were nicknamed doughboys, possibly because of the white belts they wore, which they cleaned with pipe clay, or "dough." Most doughboys had never ventured far from the farms or small towns where they lived, and the sophisticated sights and sounds of Paris made a vivid impression. However, doughboys were also shocked by the unexpected horrors of the battlefield and astonished by the new weapons and tactics of modern warfare.

**NEW WEAPONS** The battlefields of World War I saw the first large-scale use of weapons that would become standard in modern war. Although some of these weapons were new, others, like the machine gun, had been so refined that they changed the nature of warfare. The two most innovative weapons were the tank and the airplane. Together, they heralded mechanized warfare, or warfare that relies on machines powered by gasoline and diesel engines. **C**

Tanks ran on caterpillar treads and were built of steel so that bullets bounced off. The British first used tanks during the 1916 Battle of the Somme, but not very effectively. By 1917, the British had learned how to drive large numbers of tanks through barbed wire defenses, clearing a path for the infantry.

The early airplanes were so flimsy that at first both sides limited their use to scouting. After a while, the two sides used tanks to fire at enemy planes that were gathering information. Early dogfights, or individual air combats, like the one described by Eddie Rickenbacker, resembled duels. Pilots sat in their open cockpits and shot at each other with pistols. Because it was hard to fly a plane and shoot a pistol at the same time, planes began carrying mounted machine guns. But the planes' propeller blades kept getting in the way of the bullets. Then the Germans introduced an interrupter gear that permitted the stream of bullets to avoid the whirring blades.

**C. Answer**
World War I introduced new weapons and refined existing weapons; tanks and airplanes helped introduce mechanized warfare.

**MAIN IDEA**

**Forming Generalizations**
**C** How did World War I change the nature of warfare?

**Background**
When the U.S. entered the war, its air power was weak. Then, in July 1917, Congress appropriated a hefty $675 million to build an air force.

## Science & Technology

**TECHNOLOGY AT WAR**

Both sides in World War I used new technology to attack more soldiers from greater distances than ever before. Aircraft and long-range guns were even used to fire on civilian targets—libraries, cathedrals, and city districts. The biggest guns could shell a city from 75 miles.

**Machine Guns**
Firepower increased to 600 rounds per minute.

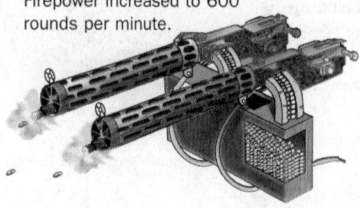

**Airships and Airplanes**
One of the most famous WWI planes, the British Sopwith Camel, had a front-mounted machine gun for "dogfights." Planes were also loaded with bombs, as were the floating gas-filled "airships" called zeppelins.

**384** CHAPTER 11

---

**DIFFERENTIATING INSTRUCTION**　　**LESS PROFICIENT READERS**

### Summarizing the Effects of Technology

To help students organize the information about the new weapons used during World War I, have students create a chart to take notes on these new weapons and their uses. A sample chart is shown at right.

| New Weapon | Notes |
|---|---|
| Machine gun | · Increased firepower to 600 rounds per minute |
| | · Easily mowed down charging enemy infantry |
| Airplane | |
| Anti-aircraft gun | |
| Poison gas | |
| Tank | |

Meanwhile, airplanes were built to travel faster and carry heavy bomb loads. By 1918 the British had built up a strategic bomber force of 22,000 planes with which to attack German weapons factories and army bases.

Observation balloons were used extensively by both sides in the war in Europe. Balloons were so important strategically that they were often protected by aircraft flying close by, and they became prime targets for Rickenbacker and other ace pilots.

## ③ The War Introduces New Hazards

The new weapons and tactics of World War I led to horrific injuries and hazards. The fighting men were surrounded by filth, lice, rats, and polluted water that caused dysentery. They inhaled poison gas and smelled the stench of decaying bodies. They suffered from lack of sleep. Constant bombardments and other experiences often led to battle fatigue and "shell shock," a term coined during World War I to describe a complete emotional collapse from which many never recovered.

Physical problems included a disease called trench foot, caused by standing in cold wet trenches for long periods of time without changing into dry socks or boots. First the toes would turn red or blue, then they would become numb, and finally they would start to rot. The only solution was to amputate the toes, and in some cases the entire foot. A painful infection of the gums and throat, called trench mouth, was also common among the soldiers. **D**

Red Cross ambulances, often staffed by American volunteers, carried the wounded from the battlefield to the hospital. An American nurse named Florence Bullard recounted her experience in a hospital near the front in 1918.

---

**MAIN IDEA**

**Analyzing Effects**

**D** What were the physical and psychological effects of this new kind of warfare?

**D. Answer**
The new warfare caused physical ailments such as trench foot and psychological ailments such as shell shock.

---

### A PERSONAL VOICE   FLORENCE BULLARD

"**The Army is only twelve miles away from us and only the wounded that are too severely injured to live to be carried a little farther are brought here. . . . Side by side I have Americans, English, Scotch, Irish, and French, and apart in the corners are Boche [Germans]. They have to watch each other die side by side. I am sent for everywhere—in the . . . operating-room, the dressing-room, and back again to the rows of men. . . . The cannon goes day and night and the shells are breaking over and around us. . . . I have had to write many sad letters to American mothers. I wonder if it will ever end.**"

—quoted in *Over There: The Story of America's First Great Overseas Crusade*

In fact, the end was near, as German forces mounted a final offensive.

---

### More About . . .

**Shell Shock**
Military doctors recognized that thousands of their patients were suffering from the same mental illness. Doctors called the illness war neurosis, but almost everyone else called it shell shock. Many of the soldiers' nervous systems had been shattered by noisy shelling. Today, this is recognized as Post Traumatic Stress Disorder.

### Tracing Themes

**SCIENCE AND TECHNOLOGY**

**World War I and Surgery**
As new weapons and trench warfare devastated soldiers' bodies, medical doctors learned more than ever before about how to treat wounds and injuries. Because wounded soldiers were stuck in filthy conditions, doctors needed to improve methods of fighting infection. Doctors also learned that rehabilitation was necessary to completely heal a wound after surgery. In addition, soldiers with gunshot wounds to the face were helped by a French army surgeon, who used new skin-graft techniques to help heal wounds. His work helped found the field of plastic surgery.

---

**Antiaircraft Gun**

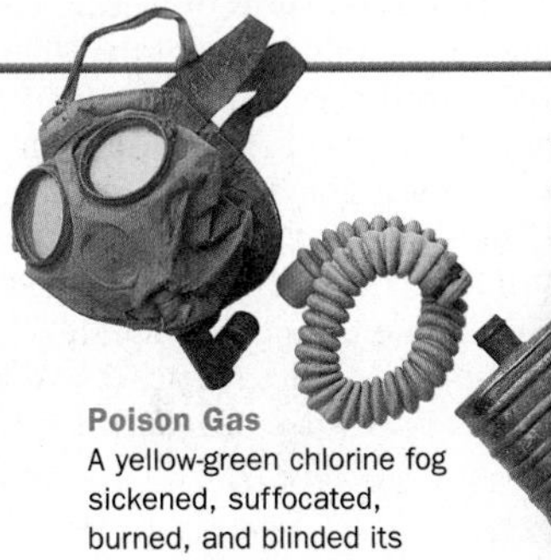

**Poison Gas**
A yellow-green chlorine fog sickened, suffocated, burned, and blinded its victims. Gas masks became standard issue.

**Tanks**
Tanks, like this French light tank, were used to "mow down" barbed wire and soldiers.

*The First World War* **385**

---

**DIFFERENTIATING INSTRUCTION**   **GIFTED AND TALENTED**   classzone.com

### Researching New Weapons

Explain to students that military technology, weapons, and tactics, have changed throughout history. Have students choose one weapon or military tactic used during World War I and research its history. Have students create a presentation on that weapon or tactic, including pictures or diagrams, if possible. As the students research their topic, they can complete a web diagram similar to the one shown at right.

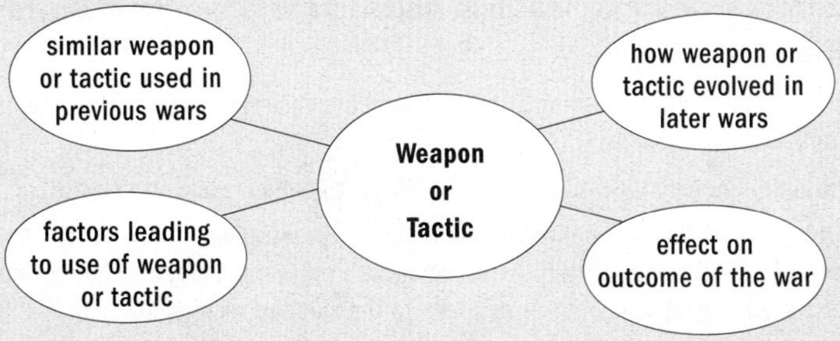

similar weapon or tactic used in previous wars

how weapon or tactic evolved in later wars

Weapon or Tactic

factors leading to use of weapon or tactic

effect on outcome of the war

## HISTORY from VISUALS

### Interpreting the Map

Have students look at the map and consider in which country most of the battles were fought. Then have them look at which countries the Armistice Line ran through. Discuss what might have forced the Germans to agree to a cease-fire when the Allies had not yet reached Germany.

📖 Humanities Transparencies HT18
· *Oppy Wood* by John Nash

### Instruct: Objective ④

**American Troops Go on the Offensive**

TAKS SS11 1(US1.B)

· In what important battles did U.S. troops fight?
· What made Alvin York a hero?
· What caused the collapse of Germany?
· How many people died during World War I?

📖 In-Depth Resources: Unit 3
· Guided Reading, p. 48

### More About . . .

**Conscientious Objectors**

About 3,500 men obtained legal conscientious objector exemptions. A smaller number simply refused to cooperate with the military in any way. While these men held fast to their convictions, their reasons for objection varied on philosophical, moral, and religious grounds. Approximately 500 objectors were court-martialed and imprisoned.

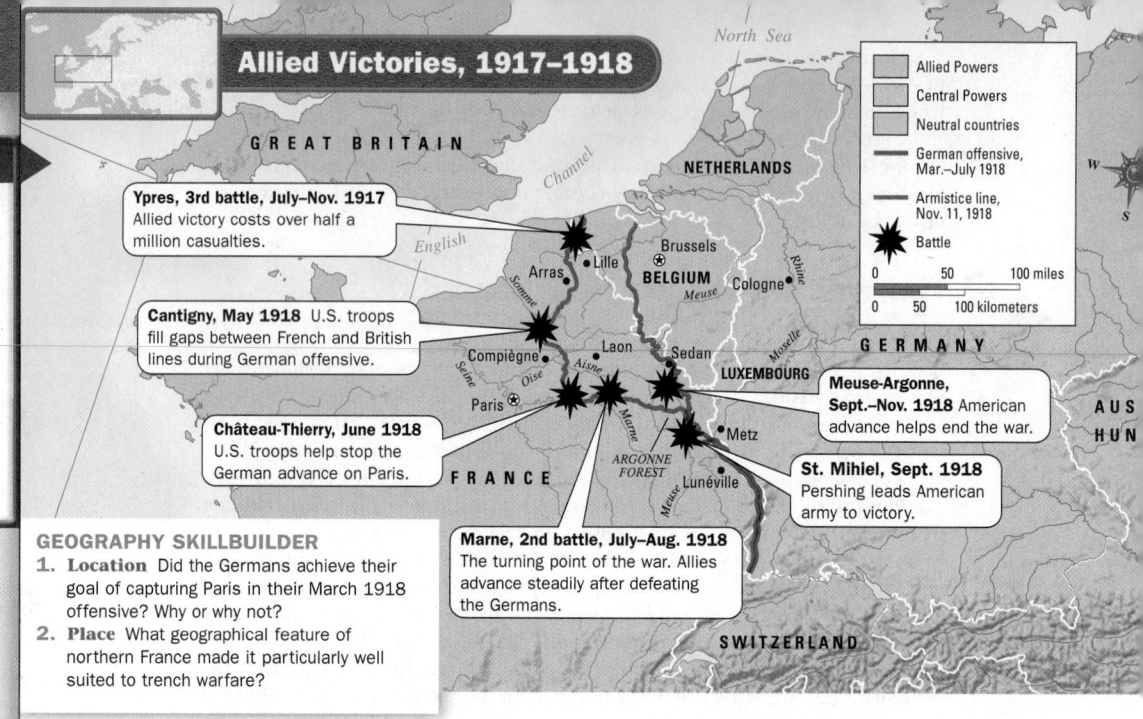

## Allied Victories, 1917–1918

Ypres, 3rd battle, July–Nov. 1917 Allied victory costs over half a million casualties.

Cantigny, May 1918 U.S. troops fill gaps between French and British lines during German offensive.

Château-Thierry, June 1918 U.S. troops help stop the German advance on Paris.

Meuse-Argonne, Sept.–Nov. 1918 American advance helps end the war.

St. Mihiel, Sept. 1918 Pershing leads American army to victory.

Marne, 2nd battle, July–Aug. 1918 The turning point of the war. Allies advance steadily after defeating the Germans.

**Allied Powers**
**Central Powers**
**Neutral countries**
— German offensive, Mar.–July 1918
— Armistice line, Nov. 11, 1918
✴ Battle

### GEOGRAPHY SKILLBUILDER

1. **Location** Did the Germans achieve their goal of capturing Paris in their March 1918 offensive? Why or why not?
2. **Place** What geographical feature of northern France made it particularly well suited to trench warfare?

*Skillbuilder Answers*
1. No, because they were stopped by the Allies.
2. The region is very flat.

## American Troops Go on the Offensive ④

When Russia pulled out of the war in 1917, the Germans shifted their armies from the eastern front to the western front in France. By May they were within 50 miles of Paris. The Americans arrived just in time to help stop the German advance at Cantigny in France. Several weeks later, U.S. troops played a major role in throwing back German attacks at Château-Thierry and Belleau Wood. In July and August, they helped win the Second Battle of the Marne. The tide had turned against the Central Powers. In September, U.S. soldiers began to mount offensives against the Germans at Saint-Mihiel and in the Meuse-Argonne area. Ⓔ

*"Bullets were cracking just over my head."*
**SERGEANT YORK**

**AMERICAN WAR HERO** During the fighting in the Meuse-Argonne area, one of America's greatest war heroes, **Alvin York,** became famous. A redheaded mountaineer and blacksmith from Tennessee, York sought exemption as a **conscientious objector,** a person who opposes warfare on moral grounds, pointing out that the Bible says, "Thou shalt not kill."

York eventually decided that it was morally acceptable to fight if the cause was just. On October 8, 1918, armed only with a rifle and a revolver, York killed 25 Germans and—with six other doughboys—captured 132 prisoners. General Pershing called him the outstanding soldier of the AEF, while Marshal Foch, the commander of Allied forces in Europe, described his feat as "the greatest thing accomplished by any private soldier of all the armies of Europe." For his heroic acts, York was promoted to sergeant and became a celebrity when he returned to the United States.

**THE COLLAPSE OF GERMANY** On November 3, 1918, Austria-Hungary surrendered to the Allies. That same day, German sailors mutinied against government authority. The mutiny spread quickly. Everywhere in Germany, groups of soldiers and workers organized revolutionary councils. On November 9, socialist leaders in the capital, Berlin, established a German republic. The kaiser gave up the throne.

**MAIN IDEA**

**Drawing Conclusions**
Ⓔ How did American forces help the Allies win the war?

*E. Answer*
American forces helped stop the German advance and helped turn the tide against the Central Powers.

---

Ⓑ **BLOCK SCHEDULING**

### Letters from Conscientious Objectors and the Draft Board

**Class Time** 30 minutes

**Task** Writing letters explaining the positions of conscientious objectors and of the draft boards on the war

**Purpose** To help students understand different points of view on the war

**Directions** Have pairs of students take turns representing a conscientious objector and a draft board official. As conscientious objectors, students should write letters explaining why they are opposed to the war and what, if anything,

they propose to do to aid the war effort. As draft board officials, students should explain why participation in the war is so important. The draft board officials could suggest nonviolent forms of participation for the conscientious objectors, such as driving ambulances.

📖 Integrated Assessment
· Rubric 5

Although there were no Allied soldiers on German territory and no truly decisive battle had been fought, the Germans were too exhausted to continue fighting. So at the eleventh hour, on the eleventh day, in the eleventh month of 1918, Germany agreed to a cease-fire and signed the **armistice,** or truce, that ended the war.

**THE FINAL TOLL** World War I was the bloodiest war in history up to that time. Deaths numbered about 22 million, more than half of them civilians. In addition, 20 million people were wounded, and 10 million more became refugees. The direct economic costs of the war may have been about $338 billion. The United States lost 48,000 men in battle, with another 62,000 dying of disease. More than 200,000 Americans were wounded.

For the Allies, news of the armistice brought great relief. Private John Barkley described the reaction to the news.

### A PERSONAL VOICE JOHN L. BARKLEY

" About 9 o'clock in the evening we heard wild commotion in the little town. The French people, old and young, were running through the streets. Old men and women we'd seen sitting around their houses too feeble to move, were out in the streets yelling, 'Vive la France! Vive la France! Vive l'America!'. . . .

Down the street came a soldier. He was telling everybody the armistice had been signed. I said, 'What's an armistice?' It sounded like some kind of machine to me. The other boys around there didn't know what it meant either.

When the official word came through that it meant peace, we couldn't believe it. Finally Jesse said, 'Well kid, I guess it really does mean the war is over.'

I said, 'I just can't believe it's true.'

But it was."

—*No Hard Feelings*

Across the Atlantic, Americans also rejoiced at the news. Many now expected life to return to normal. However, people found their lives at home changed almost as much as the lives of those who had fought in Europe.

## SECTION 2 ASSESSMENT

**1. TERMS & NAMES** For each term or name, write a sentence explaining its significance.

- •Eddie Rickenbacker
- •Selective Service Act
- •convoy system
- •American Expeditionary Force
- •General John J. Pershing
- •Alvin York
- •conscientious objector
- •armistice

### MAIN IDEA

**2. TAKING NOTES**
Fill in a web like the one below to show how Americans responded to the war.

American Responses to World War I

Why was the entire population affected by America's entry into World War I?

### CRITICAL THINKING

**3. DRAWING CONCLUSIONS**
In what ways did WWI represent a frightening new kind of warfare? **Think About:**
- the casualty figures
- new military technology
- shell shock

**4. ANALYZING VISUAL SOURCES**
This World War I poster shows the role of non-combatants overseas. What is the message in this propaganda poster?

**Back our girls over there**
United War Work Campaign
Y.W.C.A.

*The First World War* **387**

Critical Thinking Transparencies CT53
· The Human and Financial Costs of World War I

# Assess & Reteach

## SECTION 2 ASSESSMENT
Have gifted students work with less proficient readers to answer the questions in the Section Assessment.

Formal Assessment
· Section Quiz, p. 210

## SELF-ASSESSMENT
Have students use a chart to explore how their understanding of World War I has developed. In the first column, students should list what they knew about the war before reading Section 2. In the second column, they should list what they have learned.

## RETEACH
Review the section by creating a time line of events, beginning with American mobilization and ending with the armistice.

In-Depth Resources: Unit 3
· Reteaching Activity, p. 54

---

Answers **ASSESSMENT**

**1. TERMS & NAMES**
Eddie Rickenbacker, p. 381
Selective Service Act, p. 382
convoy system, p. 383
American Expeditionary Force, p. 384
General John J. Pershing, p. 384
Alvin York, p. 386
conscientious objector, p. 386
armistice, p. 387

**2. TAKING NOTES**
The government quickly raised an army and navy; the government encouraged people to work in the shipyards; American troops were enthusiastic participants in the conflict; American troops helped turn the tide against the Central Powers.
The war effort required participation by every citizen.

**3. DRAWING CONCLUSIONS**
World War I introduced mechanized warfare. This new technology meant that more soldiers could be attacked from a greater distance than ever before. Fire power increased and casualty rates skyrocketed. The horrific conditions on the battlefront led many to suffer from shell shock.

**4. ANALYZING VISUAL SOURCES**
The message is that women should train themselves and get jobs in American industry in order to support the military.

## OBJECTIVES

**1** Explain how business and government cooperated during the war.

**2** Show how the government promoted the war.

**3** Describe the attacks on civil liberties that occurred.

**4** Summarize the social changes that affected African Americans and women.

### SKILLBUILDERS
· Interpreting Graphs, p. 389
· Analyzing Political Cartoons, p. 391

### CRITICAL THINKING
· Making Inferences, pp. 389, 393, 395
· Summarizing, p. 390
· Developing Historical Perspective, p. 391
· Analyzing Effects, pp. 392, 394
· Drawing Conclusions, p. 395
· Evaluating, p. 395
· Analyzing Primary Sources, p. 397

## Focus & Motivate

Ask students whether they believe it is disloyal or unpatriotic to voice opposition to government policies during wartime.

## Instruct

### Instruct: Objective **1**

**Congress Gives Power to Wilson**
TAKS SS11 3(US21.A)
· Why was the WIB established?
· How did the war affect the U.S. economy?
· How did U.S. civilians respond to the war?

 In-Depth Resources: Unit 3
· Guided Reading, p. 49

 Critical Thinking Transparencies CT19
· World War I

# The War at Home

| MAIN IDEA | WHY IT MATTERS NOW | Terms & Names |
|---|---|---|
| World War I spurred social, political, and economic change in the United States. | Such changes increased government powers and expanded economic opportunities. | •War Industries Board<br>•Bernard M. Baruch<br>•propaganda<br>•George Creel<br>•Espionage and Sedition Acts<br>•Great Migration |

**TEKS** U.S. History 10A, 15B, 21A, 21B, 22B, 24A, 24B, 25A, 25B, 25D

### One American's Story

The suffragist Harriot Stanton Blatch visited a munitions plant in New Jersey during World War I and proudly described women at work.

**A PERSONAL VOICE** HARRIOT STANTON BLATCH

"The day I visited the place, in one of the largest shops women had only just been put on the work, but it was expected that in less than a month they would be found handling all of the twelve hundred machines under that one roof alone. The skill of the women staggers one. After a week or two they master the operations on the 'turret,' gauging and routing machines. The best worker on the 'facing' machine is a woman. She is a piece worker, as many of the women are. . . . This woman earned, the day I saw her, five dollars and forty cents. She tossed about the fuse parts, and played with that machine, as I would with a baby."

—quoted in *We, the American Women*

▲ Harriot Stanton Blatch followed in the footsteps of her famous mother, Elizabeth Cady Stanton.

Before World War I, women had been excluded from many jobs. However, the wartime need for labor brought over a million more women into the work force. For women, as for the rest of society, World War I brought about far-reaching changes.

## **1** Congress Gives Power to Wilson

Winning the war was not a job for American soldiers alone. As Secretary of War Newton Baker said, "War is no longer Samson with his shield and spear and sword, and David with his sling. It is the conflict of smokestacks now, the combat of the driving wheel and the engine." Because World War I was such an immense conflict, the entire economy had to be refocused on the war effort. The shift from producing consumer goods to producing war supplies was too complicated and important a job for private industry to handle on its own, so business and government collaborated in the effort. In the process, the power of government was greatly expanded. Congress gave President Wilson direct control over much of the economy, including the power to fix prices and to regulate—even to nationalize—certain war-related industries.

---

## PROGRAM RESOURCES

 In-Depth Resources: Unit 3
· Guided Reading, p. 49
· Reteaching Activity, p. 55
· Primary Source: "Returning Soldiers" by W. E. B. DuBois, p. 62
· American Lives: Oliver Wendell Holmes, p. 67

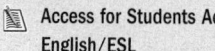 Reading Study Guide (English and Spanish), pp. 117–118

 Access for Students Acquiring English/ESL
· Guided Reading (Spanish), p. 136

 Formal Assessment
· Section Quiz, p. 211

Integrated Assessment
· Rubrics

**INTEGRATED TECHNOLOGY**

 Critical Thinking Transp. CT19
· World War I

 Electronic Library of Primary Sources

 classzone.com

**TEXAS RESOURCES**

 TAKS Spiraled Content Review

TAKS Practice Tests

TAKS Practice Transparencies TT73

TAKS Online Test Practice

**WAR INDUSTRIES BOARD** The main regulatory body was the **War Industries Board** (WIB). It was established in 1917 and reorganized in 1918 under the leadership of **Bernard M. Baruch** (bə-rōōk´), a prosperous business-man. The board encouraged companies to use mass-production techniques to increase efficiency. It also urged them to eliminate waste by standardizing products—for instance, by making only 5 colors of typewriter ribbons instead of 150. The WIB set production quotas and allocated raw materials.

Under the WIB, industrial production in the United States increased by about 20 percent. However, the WIB applied price controls only at the wholesale level. As a result, retail prices soared, and in 1918 they were almost double what they had been before the war. Corporate profits soared as well, especially in such industries as chemicals, meatpacking, oil, and steel.

The WIB was not the only federal agency to regulate the economy during the war. The Railroad Administration controlled the railroads, and the Fuel Administration monitored coal supplies and rationed gasoline and heating oil. In addition, many people adopted "gasless Sundays" and "lightless nights" to conserve fuel. In March 1918, the Fuel Administration introduced another conservation measure: daylight-saving time, which had first been proposed by Benjamin Franklin in the 1770s as a way to take advantage of the longer days of summer.

**WAR ECONOMY** Wages in most industries rose during the war years. Hourly wages for blue-collar workers—those in the metal trades, shipbuilding, and meatpacking, for example—rose by about 20 percent. A household's income, however, was largely undercut by rising food prices and housing costs.

By contrast, stockholders in large corporations saw enormous profits. One industrial manufacturer, the DuPont Company, saw its stock multiply in value 1,600 percent between 1914 and 1918. By that time the company was earning a $68-million yearly profit. As a result of the uneven pay between labor and management, increasing work hours, child labor, and dangerously "sped-up" conditions, unions boomed. Union membership climbed from about 2.5 million in 1916 to more than 4 million in 1919. More than 6,000 strikes broke out during the war months.

To deal with disputes between management and labor, President Wilson established the National War Labor Board in 1918. Workers who refused to obey board decisions could lose their draft exemptions. "Work or fight," the board told them. However, the board also worked to improve factory conditions. It pushed for an eight-hour workday, promoted safety inspections, and enforced the child labor ban. **A**

**FOOD ADMINISTRATION** To help produce and conserve food, Wilson set up the Food Administration under Herbert Hoover. Instead of rationing food, he called on people to follow the "gospel of the clean plate." He declared one day a week "meatless," another "sweetless," two days "wheatless," and two other days "porkless." Restaurants removed sugar bowls from the table and served bread only after the first course.

---

**Background**
In 1913 Henry Ford speeded up factory production with a constantly moving assembly line. Wartime production spread this technique throughout the country.

**A. Answer**
Labor disputes would slow down production and jeopardize the American war effort.

**MAIN IDEA**

**Making Inferences**
**A** Why would labor disputes affect the war effort?

**Skillbuilder Answers**
1. The prices doubled, while income more than doubled.
2. A working family would have benefited from the increase in buying power.

---

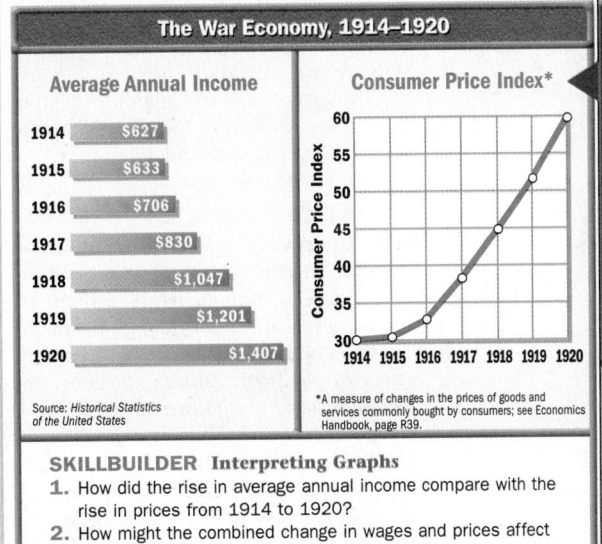

**The War Economy, 1914–1920**

**Average Annual Income**

| Year | Income |
|------|--------|
| 1914 | $627 |
| 1915 | $633 |
| 1916 | $706 |
| 1917 | $830 |
| 1918 | $1,047 |
| 1919 | $1,201 |
| 1920 | $1,407 |

Source: *Historical Statistics of the United States*

**Consumer Price Index\***

*A measure of changes in the prices of goods and services commonly bought by consumers; see Economics Handbook, page R39.

**SKILLBUILDER Interpreting Graphs**
1. How did the rise in average annual income compare with the rise in prices from 1914 to 1920?
2. How might the combined change in wages and prices affect a working family?

---

**More About . . .**

**Bernard Baruch**
Baruch had trouble dealing with the steel industry, led by U.S. Steel board chairman Elbert Gary. U.S. Steel made enormous wartime profits. In September 1917, Baruch threatened to take over U.S. Steel unless the company agreed to lower its prices. When Gary responded that the government wasn't capable of running the company, Baruch replied that he would get a second lieutenant to do the job. And he added, "If those mill towns find out why we've taken over, they'll present you with your mills brick by brick." Gary lowered his prices.

**HISTORY from VISUALS**

**Interpreting the Graph**
Have students compare the graph of average income with that showing the consumer price index. Ask them to observe what happened to prices and income. *(Both increased.)*

**Extension** Ask students why they think income and prices continued to rise after the war. *(Possible Response: It took the economy a while to adjust after the war.)*

---

**ACTIVITY** **LINK TO ECONOMICS**

classzone.com

**Researching Inflation**

**Class Time** 30 minutes

**Task** Researching U.S. inflation from 1913 to the present

**Purpose** To understand the effect of the war on prices in the United States

**Direction** Have students use the Internet to research the history of inflation in the United States. The Bureau of Labor Statistics offers inflation (Consumer Price Index) data from 1913 to the present. To focus their research, have students think about the following questions:

· What was the U.S. inflation rate during the years World War I was fought? *(1914=1.0%; 1915=1.0%; 1916=7.9%; 1917=17.4%; 1918=18.0%)*
· Since 1913, has inflation ever been as high as it was during World War I? Explain. *(No. It was never as high as during 1917 and 1918, although 1919, 1920, 1947, and 1980 were close.)*

 **Integrated Assessment**
· Rubric 1

A Japanese-American family tends a victory garden in New York City in 1917.

Food *is* Ammunition— *Don't waste it.*

▲ A wartime poster encourages Americans to conserve resources.

Homeowners planted "victory gardens" in their yards. Schoolchildren spent their after-school hours growing tomatoes and cucumbers in public parks. As a result of these and similar efforts, American food shipments to the Allies tripled. Hoover also set a high government price on wheat and other staples. Farmers responded by putting an additional 40 million acres into production. In the process, they increased their income by almost 30 percent.

## ② Selling the War

Once the government had extended its control over the economy, it was faced with two major tasks: raising money and convincing the public to support the war.

**WAR FINANCING** The United States spent about $35.5 billion on the war effort. The government raised about one-third of this amount through taxes, including a progressive income tax (which taxed high incomes at a higher rate than low incomes), a war-profits tax, and higher excise taxes on tobacco, liquor, and luxury goods. It raised the rest through public borrowing by selling "Liberty Loan" and "Victory Loan" bonds.

The government sold bonds through tens of thousands of volunteers. Movie stars spoke at rallies in factories, in schools, and on street corners. As Treasury Secretary William G. McAdoo put it, only "a friend of Germany" would refuse to buy war bonds. **B**

**COMMITTEE ON PUBLIC INFORMATION** To popularize the war, the government set up the nation's first **propaganda** agency, the Committee on Public Information (CPI). Propaganda is a kind of biased communication designed to influence people's thoughts and actions. The head of the CPI was a former muckraking journalist named **George Creel.**

Creel persuaded the nation's artists and advertising agencies to create thousands of paintings, posters, cartoons, and sculptures promoting the war. He recruited some 75,000 men to serve as "Four-Minute Men," who spoke about everything relating to the war: the draft, rationing, bond drives, victory gardens, and topics such as "Why We Are Fighting" and "The Meaning of America."

Nor did Creel neglect the written word. He ordered a printing of almost 25 million copies of "How the War Came to America"—which included Wilson's war message—in English and other languages. He distributed some 75 million pamphlets, booklets, and leaflets, many with the enthusiastic help of the Boy

**390** CHAPTER 11

---

Scouts. Creel's propaganda campaign was highly effective. However, while the campaign promoted patriotism, it also inflamed hatred and violations of the civil liberties of certain ethnic groups and opponents of the war.

## 3 Attacks on Civil Liberties Increase

Early in 1917, President Wilson expressed his fears about the consequences of war hysteria.

### A PERSONAL VOICE WOODROW WILSON

"Once lead this people into war and they'll forget there ever was such a thing as tolerance. To fight you must be brutal and ruthless, and the spirit of ruthless brutality will enter into the very fiber of our national life, infecting Congress, the courts, the policeman on the beat, the man in the street. Conformity would be the only virtue, and every man who refused to conform would have to pay the penalty."

—quoted in *Cobb of "The World"*

The president's prediction came true. As soon as war was declared, conformity indeed became the order of the day. Attacks on civil liberties, both unofficial and official, erupted.

**ANTI-IMMIGRANT HYSTERIA** The main targets of these attacks were Americans who had emigrated from other nations, especially those from Germany and Austria-Hungary. The most bitter attacks were directed against the nearly 2 million Americans who had been born in Germany, but other foreign-born persons and Americans of German descent suffered as well. **C**

Many Americans with German names lost their jobs. Orchestras refused to play the music of Mozart, Bach, Beethoven, and Brahms. Some towns with German names changed them. Schools stopped teaching the German language, and librarians removed books by German authors from the shelves. People even resorted to violence against German Americans, flogging them or smearing them

*C. Answer*
Recent immigrants suffered persecution; German immigrants and those of German descent suffered the most bitter attacks.

**MAIN IDEA**

**Developing Historical Perspective**
**C** What effect did the war have on the lives of recent immigrants?

---

### Analyzing *Political Cartoons*

**THE ENEMY WITHIN**

After the United States entered the war, government propaganda helped inflame prejudice against recent immigrants. In the suspicious atmosphere of the time, conspiracy theories flourished, and foreign spies were believed to be everywhere. This cartoon reveals the hysteria that gripped the country in 1917.

**SKILLBUILDER** Analyzing Political Cartoons
1. What is happening in this cartoon?
2. What does the cartoonist suggest will happen to "enemy aliens"?

 **SEE SKILLBUILDER HANDBOOK, PAGE R24.**

Stripped!    By J. H. Cassel

*The First World War* **391**

with tar and feathers. A mob in Collinsville, Illinois, wrapped a German flag around a German-born miner named Robert Prager and lynched him. A jury cleared the mob's leader.

Finally, in a burst of anti-German fervor, Americans changed the name of German measles to "liberty measles." Hamburger—named after the German city of Hamburg—became "Salisbury steak" or "liberty sandwich," depending on whether you were buying it in a store or eating it in a restaurant. Sauerkraut was renamed "liberty cabbage," and dachshunds turned into "liberty pups."

**ESPIONAGE AND SEDITION ACTS** In June 1917 Congress passed the Espionage Act, and in May 1918 it passed the Sedition Act. Under the **Espionage and Sedition Acts** a person could be fined up to $10,000 and sentenced to 20 years in jail for interfering with the war effort or for saying anything disloyal, profane, or abusive about the government or the war effort.

Like the Alien and Sedition Acts of 1798, these laws clearly violated the spirit of the First Amendment. Their passage led to over 2,000 prosecutions for loosely defined antiwar activities; of these, over half resulted in convictions. Newspapers and magazines that opposed the war or criticized any of the Allies lost their mailing privileges. The House of Representatives refused to seat Victor Berger, a socialist congressman from Wisconsin, because of his antiwar views. Columbia University fired a distinguished psychologist because he opposed the war. A colleague who supported the war thereupon resigned in protest, saying, "If we have to suppress everything we don't like to hear, this country is resting on a pretty wobbly basis."

The Espionage and Sedition Acts targeted socialists and labor leaders. Eugene V. Debs was handed a ten-year prison sentence for speaking out against the war and the draft. The anarchist Emma Goldman received a two-year prison sentence and a $10,000 fine for organizing the No Conscription League. When she left jail, the authorities deported her to Russia. "Big Bill" Haywood and other leaders of the Industrial Workers of the World (IWW) were accused of sabotaging the war effort because they urged workers to strike for better conditions and higher pay. Haywood was sentenced to 30 years in prison. Under such federal pressure, the IWW faded away. **D**

▲
This Industrial Workers of the World (IWW) sticker encourages workers to join the union.

**Vocabulary**
**sedition:** rebellion against one's government; treason

**MAIN IDEA**

**Analyzing Effects**
**D** What impact did the Espionage and Sedition Acts have on free speech?

*D. Answer*
The Acts led to thousands of prosecutions; people were fired from their jobs; antiwar newspapers and magazines lost their mailing privileges.

## The War Encourages Social Change 4

Wars often unleash powerful social forces. The period of World War I was no exception; important changes transformed the lives of African Americans and women.

**AFRICAN AMERICANS AND THE WAR** Black public opinion about the war was divided. On one side were people like W. E. B. Du Bois, who believed that blacks should support the war effort.

**A PERSONAL VOICE** W. E. B. DU BOIS
" That which the German power represents today spells death to the aspirations of Negroes and all darker races for equality, freedom and democracy. . . . Let us, while this war lasts, forget our special grievances and close our ranks shoulder to shoulder with our own white fellow citizens and the allied nations that are fighting for democracy."
—"Close Ranks"

W. E. B. Du Bois ▶

Du Bois believed that African-American support for the war would strengthen calls for racial justice. In contrast, William Monroe Trotter, founder of the *Boston Guardian*, believed that victims of racism should not support a racist government. Trotter condemned Du Bois's accommodationist approach and favored protest instead. Nevertheless, despite grievances over continued racial inequality in the United States, most African Americans backed the war.

**THE GREAT MIGRATION** In concrete terms, the greatest effect of the First World War on African Americans' lives was that it accelerated the **Great Migration,** the large-scale movement of hundreds of thousands of Southern blacks to cities in the North. This great population shift had already begun before the war in the late 19th century, when African Americans trickled northward to escape the Jim Crow South—but after the turn of the century, the trickle became a tidal wave.

Several factors contributed to the tremendous increase in black migration. First, many African Americans sought to escape racial discrimination in the South, which made it hard to make a living and often threatened their lives. Also, a boll weevil infestation, aided by floods and droughts, had ruined much of the South's cotton fields. In the North, there were more job opportunities. For example, Henry Ford opened his automobile assembly line to black workers in 1914. The outbreak of World War I and the drop in European immigration increased job opportunities for African Americans in steel mills, munitions plants, and stockyards. Northern manufacturers sent recruiting agents to distribute free railroad passes through the South. In addition, the publisher of the black-owned newspaper *Chicago Defender* bombarded Southern blacks with articles contrasting Dixieland lynchings with the prosperity of African Americans in the North. **E**

*E. Answer*
World War I increased job opportunities for African Americans in steel mills, munitions plants, and stockyards.

**MAIN IDEA**

**Making Inferences**
**E** How did the war open opportunities for African Americans?

### History Through *Art*

**THE MIGRATION OF THE NEGRO, PANEL NO. 1 (1940–41)**
This painting by Jacob Lawrence shows three of the most common destinations for African Americans leaving the South. **Why do you think the artist has not shown any individual facial features?**

### Tracing Themes
**IMMIGRATION AND MIGRATION**

**The Great Migration**
Although migrants faced many challenges, employment in the North did offer an escape from sharecropping, boll weevil infestations, floods, lynchings, and political disenfranchisement in the South. One man wrote to a friend back in Mississippi: "I just begin to feel like a man. . . . I don't have to humble to no one. I have registered. Will vote in the next election."

### History Through *Art*

Jacob Lawrence's parents were part of the Great Migration. His father moved north from South Carolina, and his mother migrated from Virginia. They met during their journey north, and in 1917, Lawrence was born in Atlantic City, New Jersey. As he grew up, he began to see how the story of his life fit into the history of African Americans. In 1940, he began a series of paintings on the Great Migration. The series is intended to show the "triumph over adversity" of African Americans who "left the South on a quest for freedom, justice, and dignity."

*(The artist wanted to represent not individuals but an entire people on the move.)*

*The First World War* **393**

---

### Finding Main Ideas

As a way to focus students' attention and set a purpose for reading, write the headings from this section on the board and identify them as Main Ideas (MI). As you read the section together, have students identify the important details (D) that support each main idea. Write them in an outline format, such as the example that follows.

**MI:** The war encourages social change, especially for African Americans and women.

D. Most African Americans backed the war.

D. The war accelerated the movement of African Americans to the North, called the Great Migration.

D. Women moved into jobs that had been held exclusively by men.

D. The service of women helped bolster public support for woman suffrage, leading to the ratification of the 19th Amendment.

D. An international flu epidemic affected about one-fourth of the U.S. population, killing about 500,000 Americans during 1918–1919.

## HISTORICAL SPOTLIGHT

### Race Riots

Discuss current race relations and racial prejudice in the United States. Ask students to think about the race riots of 1917 and 1919. How do these events relate to race relations in the United States today? *(Some students may say that race relations have gotten much better since 1919 and may point to civil rights laws as evidence. Others may say that racism continues to exist.)*

## More About . . .

### Women in the War

Men went off to war, and women went to work in their place. The army did not allow women to enlist as soldiers, but did allow them to serve in noncombat roles such as nurses and ambulance drivers. At home, the industrial war effort created an enormous demand for labor. Women volunteered and were recruited to work in industry, agriculture, wherever they were needed. As the role of women in the workplace began to shift, a parallel shift in their social status occurred.

## HISTORICAL SPOTLIGHT

### RACE RIOTS

Racial prejudice against African Americans in the North sometimes took violent forms. In July 1917, a race riot exploded in East St. Louis, Illinois. White workers, furious over the hiring of African Americans as strikebreakers at a munitions plant, rampaged through the streets. Forty blacks and nine whites died.

Another riot erupted in July 1919 in Chicago when a 17-year-old African American swam from the water off a "black beach" to the water off a "white beach." There, white bathers threw rocks at him until he drowned.

African Americans retaliated, and several riots broke out in the city. Order was restored after several days of violence that involved about 10,000 people.

However, racial prejudice against African Americans also existed in the North. The press of new migrants to Northern cities caused overcrowding and intensified racial tensions.

Nevertheless, between 1910 and 1930, hundreds of thousands of African Americans migrated to such cities as Chicago, New York, and Philadelphia. Author Richard Wright described the great exodus.

### A PERSONAL VOICE RICHARD WRIGHT

" We are bitter no more; we are leaving! We are leaving our homes, pulling up stakes to move on. We look up at the high southern sky and remember all the sunshine and all the rain and we feel a sense of loss, but we are leaving. We look out at the wide green fields which our eyes saw when we first came into the world and we feel full of regret, but we are leaving. We scan the kind black faces we have looked upon since we first saw the light of day, and, though pain is in our hearts, we are leaving. We take one last furtive look over our shoulders to the Big House— high upon a hill beyond the railroad tracks—where the Lord of the Land lives, and we feel glad, for we are leaving. "

—quoted in *12 Million Black Voices*

**WOMEN IN THE WAR** While African Americans began new lives, women moved into jobs that had been held exclusively by men. They became railroad workers, cooks, dockworkers, and bricklayers. They mined coal and took part in shipbuilding. At the same time, women continued to fill more traditional jobs as nurses, clerks, and teachers. Many women worked as volunteers, serving at Red Cross facilities and encouraging the sale of bonds and the planting of victory gardens. Other women, such as Jane Addams, were active in the peace movement. Addams helped found the Women's Peace Party in 1915 and remained a pacifist even after the United States entered the war. **F**

President Wilson acknowledged, "The services of women during the supreme crisis have been of the most signal usefulness and distinction; it is high time that part of our debt should be acknowledged." While acknowledgment of that debt did not include equal pay for equal work, it did help bolster public support for woman suffrage. In 1919, Congress finally passed the Nineteenth Amendment, granting women the right to vote. In 1920 the amendment was ratified by the states.

### MAIN IDEA

**Analyzing Effects**
**F** What effect did the war have on women's lives?

*F. Answer*
Women moved into jobs that had been held exclusively by men.

◀ Women worked in a variety of jobs during the war. Here, women assemble an aircraft wing.

394

---

**ACTIVITY** **LINK TO LANGUAGE ARTS**

**BLOCK SCHEDULING**

### Writing a Journal

**Class Time** 30 minutes

**Task** Creating a journal entry from a historical perspective

**Purpose** To describe the experiences of African Americans who migrated north during the war

**Directions** Pose the following scenario: In an old trunk at a flea market students have found the journal of an African American who participated in the Great Migration. Ask them to consider the thoughts and feelings such migrants might have had at the time—why they left the South, what they were looking for in the North, and what they found when they got there. Then have the students write entries that the migrant's journal might have contained, describing daily life. Use the journal entries to frame a discussion about the Great Migration.

 Integrated Assessment
· Rubric 5

**THE FLU EPIDEMIC** In the fall of 1918, the United States suffered a home-front crisis when an international flu epidemic affected about one-quarter of the U.S. population. The effect of the epidemic on the economy was devastating. Mines shut down, telephone service was cut in half, and factories and offices staggered working hours to avoid contagion. Cities ran short of coffins, and the corpses of poor people lay unburied for as long as a week. The mysterious illness seemed to strike people who were otherwise in the best of health, and death could come in a matter of days. Doctors did not know what to do, other than to recommend cleanliness and quarantine. One epidemic survivor recalled that "so many people died from the flu they just rang the bells; they didn't dare take [corpses] into the church."

In the army, where living conditions allowed contagious illnesses to spread rapidly, more than a quarter of the soldiers caught the disease. In some AEF units, one-third of the troops died. Germans fell victim in even larger numbers than the Allies. Possibly spread around the world by soldiers, the epidemic killed about 500,000 Americans before it disappeared in 1919. Historians believe that the influenza virus killed as many as 30 million people worldwide.

World War I brought death and disease to millions but, like the flu epidemic, the war also came to a sudden end. After four years of slaughter and destruction, the time had come to forge a peace settlement. Americans hoped that this "war to end all wars" would do just that. Leaders of the victorious nations gathered at Versailles outside Paris to work out the terms of peace, and President Wilson traveled to Europe to ensure it.

New York City street cleaners wore masks to avoid catching influenza.
▼

---

**MAIN IDEA**

**Making Inferences**
**G** How did wartime conditions help spread the flu?

*G. Answer*
In the army, living conditions allowed contagious illnesses to spread rapidly.

---

**More About . . .**

**The Flu Epidemic**
The flu epidemic was one of the worst plagues in history, second only to the Bubonic Plague of 1347–1351, which killed one out of every three Europeans. Americans came up with all sorts of ways to treat the flu. Some people recommended snuff, while others suggested chewing tobacco. Even some doctors proposed far-fetched treatments, including removing the flu patients' tonsils, extracting all their teeth, and sprinkling sulfur in their shoes.

---

## Assess & Reteach

**SECTION 3 ASSESSMENT**
Have students work in small groups to answer the questions in the Section Assessment.

📄 Formal Assessment
· Section Quiz, p. 211

**SELF-ASSESSMENT**
To document what students have learned in Section 3, have them make a list of the economic and social changes brought about in the United States by the First World War.

**RETEACH**
Use the Section Quiz to help students understand the section's key concepts.

📄 In-Depth Resources: Unit 3
· Reteaching Activity, p. 55

📄 Formal Assessment
· Chapter Test, Forms A, B, and C, pp. 213–230

---

### SECTION 3 ASSESSMENT

1. **TERMS & NAMES** For each term or name, write a sentence explaining its significance.

- War Industries Board
- Bernard M. Baruch
- propaganda
- Espionage and Sedition Acts
- George Creel
- Great Migration

**MAIN IDEA**

2. **TAKING NOTES**
In a chart like the one shown, list some of the changes that the war brought about for each group.

| Changes Brought About by the War | |
|---|---|
| African Americans | |
| Women | |
| Immigrants | |

Explain how each group benefited from or was disadvantaged by these changes.

**CRITICAL THINKING**

3. **DRAWING CONCLUSIONS**
How did the war affect government power? **Think About:**
- how private business worked with government
- how much control the president gained over the economy
- the Espionage and Sedition Acts

4. **MAKING INFERENCES**
Why do you think the flu spread so quickly among the troops?

5. **EVALUATING**
Do you think that the war had a positive or a negative effect on American society? **Think About:**
- how the propaganda campaign influenced people's behavior
- the new job opportunities for African Americans and women
- how the government controlled industry

*The First World War* **395**

---

Answers **ASSESSMENT** 3

**1. TERMS & NAMES**
War Industries Board, p. 389
Bernard M. Baruch, p. 389
propaganda, p. 390
George Creel, p. 390
Espionage and Sedition Acts, p. 392
Great Migration, p. 393

**2. TAKING NOTES**
The war accelerated the Great Migration and expanded job opportunities for African Americans; women got jobs once exclusively held by men; immigrants encountered suspicion and persecution.

**3. DRAWING CONCLUSIONS**
The war expanded government power over private business and the economy and interfered with civil liberties and free speech.

**4. MAKING INFERENCES**
The flu spread so quickly among the troops because of the cramped living conditions.

**5. EVALUATING**
Positive effects of the war: expanded opportunities for African Americans and women; Negative effects of the war: increased government control and eroded personal liberties; encouraged persecution of ethnic groups.

## HISTORIC DECISIONS OF THE SUPREME COURT

### HISTORIC DECISIONS OF THE SUPREME COURT

### Objectives

· To analyze the Supreme Court case of *Schenck* v. *United States* (1919) in its historical context

· To study the legal reasoning behind the Supreme Court's opinion and the historical significance of this case for freedom of speech

## Focus & Motivate

**Making Predictions** Have students think about the meaning of the term "freedom of speech" and what factors restrict people from saying anything they want any time they want. Then, have them predict what issues might lead to conflicts over freedom of speech.

## More About . . .

### Oliver Wendell Holmes, Jr.

Oliver Wendell Holmes, Jr., was one of the most influential Supreme Court justices in U.S. history. Born to a prominent family in Boston, Massachusetts, he attended Harvard Law School after serving in the Civil War. In 1881, he wrote *The Common Law,* a landmark work in legal theory. In that book, he wrote one of the most famous statements ever made about the law: "The life of the law has not been logic: it has been experience." By that he meant that the law is shaped more by the demands of the time than by the application of formal legal principles. In other words, the law changes with history. That view helped to transform U.S. legal thought early in the 20th century. In 1902, President Theodore Roosevelt appointed Holmes to the U.S. Supreme Court.

 **In-Depth Resources: Unit 3**
· American Lives: Oliver Wendell Holmes Jr., p. 67

# SCHENCK v. UNITED STATES (1919)

**ORIGINS OF THE CASE** Charles Schenck, an official of the U.S. Socialist Party, distributed leaflets that called the draft a "deed against humanity" and compared conscription to slavery, urging conscripts to "assert your rights." Schenck was convicted of sedition and sentenced to prison, but he argued that the conviction, punishment, and even the law itself violated his right to free speech. The Supreme Court agreed to hear his appeal.

**THE RULING** A unanimous court upheld Schenck's conviction, stating that under wartime conditions, the words in the leaflets were not protected by the right to free speech.

### LEGAL REASONING

The Supreme Court's opinion in the *Schenck* case, written by Justice Oliver Wendell Holmes, Jr., has become famous as a guide for how the First Amendment defines the right of free speech. Holmes wrote:

> " The question in every case is whether the words used are used in such circumstances and are of such a nature as to create a clear and present danger that they will bring about the substantive evils that Congress has a right to prevent."

Justice Holmes noted that "in ordinary times" the First Amendment might have protected Schenck, but "[w]hen a nation is at war many things that might be said in time of peace . . . will not be endured."

The analogy that Holmes used to explain why Schenck could be punished for his words has become probably the best-known observation ever made about free speech:

> " Protection of free speech would not protect a man in falsely shouting 'Fire!' in a theatre and causing a panic."

Writing for the Court, Holmes implied that during wartime, Schenck's leaflet was just that dangerous.

Oliver Wendell Holmes, Jr., Supreme Court Justice 1902–1932 ▶

### LEGAL SOURCES

#### LEGISLATION

**U.S. CONSTITUTION, FIRST AMENDMENT (1791)**
"Congress shall make no law . . . abridging the freedom of speech, or of the press."

**THE SEDITION ACT (1918)**
"(W)hoever . . . shall willfully utter, print, write or publish any disloyal, profane, scurrilous, or abusive language about the form of government, . . . Constitution, . . . military or naval forces, . . . flag, . . . or the uniform of the Army or Navy . . . of the United States . . . shall be punished by a fine of not more than $10,000 or imprisonment for not more than twenty years, or both."

#### RELATED CASES

**DEBS v. UNITED STATES (MARCH, 1919)**
The conviction against Eugene Debs for speaking against the war and the draft is upheld.

**FROHWERK v. UNITED STATES (MARCH, 1919)**
The publisher of a newspaper that had criticized the war is sentenced with a fine and ten years in prison.

**ABRAMS v. UNITED STATES (NOV., 1919)**
Leaflets criticizing the U.S. expeditionary force in Russia are found to be unprotected by the First Amendment. Holmes writes a dissenting opinion calling for the "free trade of ideas."

**396** CHAPTER 11

## RECOMMENDED RESOURCES

### BOOKS

Burton, Steven J. ed. *The Path of the Law and Its Influence: The Legacy of Oliver Wendell Holmes.* New York: Cambridge University Press, 2000.

Polenberg, Richard. *Fighting Faiths: The Abrams Case, the Supreme Court, and Free Speech.* Ithaca: NY: Cornell UP, 1999.

Shriver, Harry Clair. *What Gusto: Stories and Anecdotes about Justice Oliver Wendell Holmes.* Potomac, Md.: Fox Hills Press, 1970.

Strum, Philippa. *When the Nazis Came to Skokie: Freedom for Speech We Hate.* Lawrence: UP of Kansas, 1999.

White, G. Edward. *Justice Oliver Wendell Holmes: Law and the Inner Self.* Oxford: Oxford UP, 1995.

### INTEGRATED TECHNOLOGY

For teacher support and more information about the Supreme Court, including the full text of the Supreme Court opinions, visit. . . .

 classzone.com

## WHY IT MATTERED

During the course of World War I, the federal government brought approximately 2,000 prosecutions for violations of the Espionage Act of 1917 or the Sedition Act of 1918, the same laws under which it convicted Schenck, Debs, and Frohwerk.

By the fall of 1919, however, Holmes had changed his mind. The case of *Abrams* v. *United States* concerned leaflets that criticized President Wilson's "capitalistic" government for sending troops to put down the Russian Revolution. Justice Holmes, joined by Justice Louis Brandeis, dissented from the majority of the Court which upheld the conviction. In his dissent, Holmes emphasized the importance of a free exchange of ideas so that truth will win out in the intellectual marketplace. His reasoning won him acclaim as a protector of free speech.

The belief that truth will eventually win out in the marketplace of ideas has become important legal justification for promoting freedom of speech.

Eugene Debs was arrested for antiwar speeches like the one he gave at this 1916 presidential campaign stop.

## HISTORICAL IMPACT

Disagreements about what kinds of speech are "free" under the First Amendment continue. During the 1950s, when people were jailed for supporting Communism, and during the Vietnam War, when war protestors supported draft resistance, these issues again reached the Supreme Court.

The Court has also been asked to decide if young people in schools have the same First Amendment rights as adults. In *Tinker* v. *Des Moines School District* (1969), the Court ordered a school to readmit students who had been suspended for wearing black arm bands in protest of the war in Vietnam.

This so-called symbolic speech, such as wearing an armband or burning a draft card or a flag to express an opinion, has sparked heated debate. In *Texas* v. *Johnson* (1989), the Court, by a narrow five to four vote, invalidated a law under which a man who burned an American flag to protest Reagan administration policies had been convicted. The decision so outraged some people that members of Congress considered amending the Constitution to prohibit any "physical desecration" of the flag. The amendment did not pass. Our freedoms of expression continue to depend upon the words in the first article of the Bill of Rights, written more than 200 years ago.

◀ In 1965 Mary Beth Tinker and her brother, John, were suspended from school for wearing armbands that symbolically criticized the Vietnam War.

### THINKING CRITICALLY

**CONNECT TO HISTORY**
1. **Analyzing Primary Sources** Read Justice Holmes's dissent in *Abrams* v. *United States*. Compare it with the opinion he wrote in *Schenck* v. *United States*. Explain the major difference or similarity in the two opinions.

📁 SEE SKILLBUILDER HANDBOOK, PAGE R22.

**CONNECT TO TODAY**
2. **INTERNET ACTIVITY** CLASSZONE.COM

Visit the links for Historic Decisions of the Supreme Court to research articles about free speech issues. Select several of these issues—such as whether hate groups have a right to march—to discuss with other students in your class. Choose one issue and, as a group, write down as many arguments as you can on both sides of the issue. Then present a debate to the class.

1. What does the First Amendment say about the freedom of speech? How do you think the First Amendment affects state and local laws that restrict speech?
2. Do you think some limits on the freedom of speech are necessary? Explain.
3. What was Justice Holmes' main argument in the Court's opinion in *Schenck*? Do you agree with the Court's opinion?

**MAKING PERSONAL CONNECTIONS**

· Ask students if they believe there are any factors that prevent them from fully exercising their right to free speech? If so, have them explain whether they think those factors are fair or not.

· Have the class try to arrive at a consensus of what would be reasonable limits to the right to free speech.

## More About . . .

**University Speech Codes**
In the 1960s and 1970s, the number of women and racial and ethnic minorities in U.S. colleges increased. Some of these students faced sexual or racial discrimination. As a preventative measure, many universities instituted speech codes, which gave the school the power to discipline students for discriminatory or harassing speech. Before long, critics went to the courts to challenge these codes as a violation of the freedom of speech. On this basis, federal courts have struck down speech codes at a number of schools, including the University of Michigan, as being too restrictive. Universities have continued to look for ways to prevent discriminatory speech without violating the First Amendment.

### THINKING CRITICALLY: ANSWERS

1. **CONNECT TO HISTORY** Students' responses should include specific references to the opinions in both *Schenck* and *Abrams*. They should also discuss the differences and similarities between the two opinions.

2. **CONNECT TO TODAY**
**Rubric**
Student debates should . . .
· include references to important primary and secondary sources on freedom of speech and hate groups
· include arguments based on evidence
· demonstrate a fair and reasoned approach to all sides of the issue

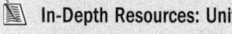
# Wilson Fights for Peace

| MAIN IDEA | WHY IT MATTERS NOW | Terms & Names |
|---|---|---|
| European leaders opposed most of Wilson's peace plan, and the U.S. Senate failed to ratify the peace treaty. | Many of the nationalist issues left unresolved after World War I continue to trouble the world today. | •Fourteen Points<br>•League of Nations<br>•Georges Clemenceau<br>•David Lloyd George<br>•Treaty of Versailles<br>•reparations<br>•war-guilt clause<br>•Henry Cabot Lodge |

**TEKS U.S. History**

3D, 24A, 24B, 25A, 25B, 25D

### One American's Story

In January 1918, at the magnificent Palace of Versailles outside Paris, President Wilson tried to persuade the Allies to construct a just and lasting peace and to establish a League of Nations. Colonel E. M. House, a native of Texas and a member of the American delegation to Versailles, later wrote about the conference.

**A PERSONAL VOICE** COLONEL E. M. HOUSE

" How splendid it would have been had we blazed a new and better trail! . . . It may be that Wilson might have had the power and influence if he had remained in Washington and kept clear of the Conference. When he stepped from his lofty pedestal and wrangled with representatives of other states, upon equal terms, he became as common clay. . . . To those who are saying that the Treaty is bad and should never have been made and that it will involve Europe in infinite difficulties in its enforcement, I feel like admitting it. But I would also say in reply that empires cannot be shattered and new states raised upon their ruins without disturbance."

—quoted in *Hooray for Peace, Hurrah for War*

House saw what happened when Wilson's idealism ran up against practical politics. The Allied victors, vengeful toward Germany after four years of warfare, rejected most of Wilson's peace program.

▲ Colonel Edward M. House was a friend and advisor to President Woodrow Wilson.

## Wilson Presents His Plan 1

Rejection was probably the last thing Wilson expected when he arrived in Europe. Everywhere he went, people gave him a hero's welcome. Italians displayed his picture in their windows; Parisians strewed the street with flowers. Representatives of one group after another, including Armenians, Jews, Ukrainians, and Poles, appealed to him for help in setting up independent nations for themselves.

**398** CHAPTER 11

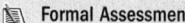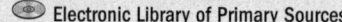

**FOURTEEN POINTS** Even before the war was over, Wilson presented his plan for world peace. On January 18, 1918, he delivered his now famous **Fourteen Points** speech before Congress. The points were divided into three groups. The first five points were issues that Wilson believed had to be addressed to prevent another war:

1. There should be no secret treaties among nations.
2. Freedom of the seas should be maintained for all.
3. Tariffs and other economic barriers among nations should be lowered or abolished in order to foster free trade.
4. Arms should be reduced "to the lowest point consistent with domestic safety, thus lessening the possibility of military responses" during diplomatic crises.
5. Colonial policies should consider the interests of the colonial peoples as well as the interests of the imperialist powers.

The next eight points dealt with boundary changes. Wilson based these provisions on the principle of self-determination "along historically established lines of nationality." In other words, groups that claimed distinct ethnic identities were to form their own nation-states or decide for themselves to what nations they would belong.

The fourteenth point called for the creation of an international organization to address diplomatic crises like those that had sparked the war. This **League of Nations** would provide a forum for nations to discuss and settle their grievances without having to resort to war.

**THE ALLIES REJECT WILSON'S PLAN** Wilson's naiveté about the political aspects of securing a peace treaty showed itself in his failure to grasp the anger felt by the Allied leaders. The French premier, **Georges Clemenceau** (klĕm′ən-sō′), had lived through two German invasions of France and was determined to prevent future invasions. **David Lloyd George**, the British prime minister, had just won reelection on the slogan "Make Germany Pay." The Italian prime minister, Vittorio Orlando, wanted control of Austrian-held territory. **A**

Contrary to custom, the peace conference did not include the defeated Central Powers. Nor did it include Russia, which was now under the control of a Communist government, or the smaller Allied nations. Instead, the "Big Four"—Wilson, Clemenceau, Lloyd George, and Orlando—worked out the treaty's details among themselves. Wilson conceded on most of his Fourteen Points in return for the establishment of the League of Nations.

**(left to right) David Lloyd George, Georges Clemenceau, and Woodrow Wilson in Paris in 1919.**

**Vocabulary**
**free trade:** the buying and selling of goods without tariffs, or fees

---

**MAIN IDEA**

**Developing Historical Perspective**
**A** Why did the Allies reject Wilson's plan?

*A. Answer* Clemenceau was determined to prevent another German invasion of France; the Allied leaders were all angry with Germany.

---

**KEY PLAYER**

KEY PLAYER

**WOODROW WILSON**
**1856–1924**

At the end of the war, President Wilson wanted the United States to become more involved in international affairs. He believed the nation had a moral obligation to help maintain peace in the world. Wilson's sense of moral purpose had a lasting influence on American foreign policy.

**Woodrow Wilson**
Tell students that Woodrow Wilson was a renowned scholar before becoming president. When he ran for the presidency in 1912, he campaigned on a progressive domestic agenda. "It would be the irony of fate," he said before taking office, "if my administration had to deal chiefly with foreign affairs."

**Extension** Ask students if they think Wilson was more effective in domestic or foreign affairs. *(Those who say he was more effective in domestic affairs may point to his trustbusting. They might also mention his failure to win ratification of the Treaty of Versailles. Those who say he was more effective in foreign affairs may point to his role in winning the war.)*

**Tracing Themes**
**AMERICA IN WORLD AFFAIRS**

**Fourteen Points**
Discuss Wilson's Fourteen Points, especially the one that led to the creation of the League of Nations. Tell students that Wilson hoped to create a new world order through democratic reform. Ask students whether they believe Wilson's plan was practical. Then point out that today the United Nations (UN) serves much the same purpose as Wilson's proposed League of Nations. Would Wilson have been satisfied with the organization? Has the UN been successful in providing a forum for nations and in preventing war?

*The First World War* **399**

---

**ACTIVITY** **COOPERATIVE LEARNING**

**B** **BLOCK SCHEDULING**

**Conducting a Model Peace Conference**

**Class Time** 40 Minutes

**Task** Conducting a model peace conference and producing a model peace treaty to end World War I

**Purpose** To understand the issues that the delegates faced in creating a treaty

**Directions** Divide students into small groups and assign each group a particular nation. (You can allow them to take the roles of Russia and Germany even though defeated nations did not have a say in shaping the Treaty of Versailles.) Have each group consider the position of its assigned nation at the beginning of the peace conference at Versailles. Have the groups conduct a model peace conference and develop a treaty that all are willing to accept.

**400** CHAPTER 11

### HISTORY from VISUALS

**Interpreting the Map**
Have students compare the maps of Europe before and after World War I with a map of modern Europe. Discuss any changes students notice in the national boundaries since the Treaty of Versailles.

### Instruct: Objective ②

**Debating the Treaty of Versailles**
TAKS SS11 1(US3.D)

· What were the main provisions of the Treaty of Versailles?
· What were some weaknesses of the Treaty?
· How did Americans react to the Treaty?
· Why did Americans disagree about the League of Nations?

 In-Depth Resources: Unit 3
· Geography Application: A New Look for Europe, p. 57

### More About . . .

**The Hall of Mirrors at Versailles**
In 1871, the Kaiser's grandfather was proclaimed head of the new German Empire, also known as the Second Reich, in the Hall of Mirrors in the Palace of Versailles. The French felt the hall was an appropriate place to sign a treaty marking Germany's defeat in World War I and the end of the Second Reich.

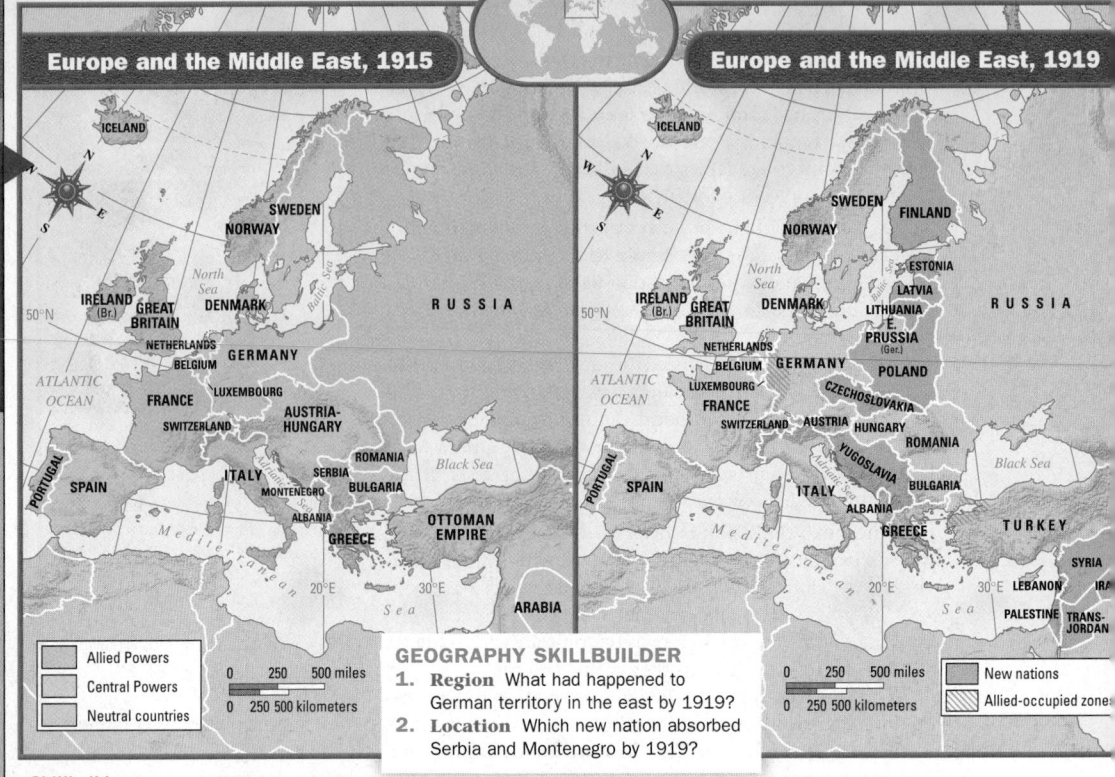

**Europe and the Middle East, 1915**

**Europe and the Middle East, 1919**

Allied Powers
Central Powers
Neutral countries

New nations
Allied-occupied zone

**GEOGRAPHY SKILLBUILDER**
1. **Region** What had happened to German territory in the east by 1919?
2. **Location** Which new nation absorbed Serbia and Montenegro by 1919?

*Skillbuilder Answers*
1. Poland had been formed out of parts of German territory in the east.
2. Yugoslavia had absorbed Serbia and Montenegro.

## Debating the Treaty of Versailles ②

On June 28, 1919, the Big Four and the leaders of the defeated nations gathered in the Hall of Mirrors of the Palace of Versailles to sign the peace treaty. After four years of devastating warfare, everyone hoped that the treaty would create stability for a rebuilt Europe. Instead, anger held sway.

**PROVISIONS OF THE TREATY** The **Treaty of Versailles** (vər-sī′) established nine new nations—including Poland, Czechoslovakia, and Yugoslavia—and shifted the boundaries of other nations. It carved five areas out of the Ottoman Empire and gave them to France and Great Britain as mandates, or temporary colonies. Those two Allies were to administer their respective mandates until the areas were ready for self-rule and then independence.

The treaty barred Germany from maintaining an army. It also required Germany to return the region of Alsace-Lorraine to France and to pay **reparations,** or war damages, amounting to $33 billion to the Allies.

**THE TREATY'S WEAKNESSES** This treatment of Germany weakened the ability of the Treaty of Versailles to provide a lasting peace in Europe. Several basic flaws in the treaty sowed the seeds of postwar international problems that eventually would lead to the Second World War.

First, the treaty humiliated Germany. It contained a **war-guilt clause** forcing Germany to admit sole responsibility for starting World War I. Although German militarism had played a major role in igniting the war, other European nations had been guilty of provoking diplomatic crises before the war. Furthermore, there was no way Germany could pay the huge financial reparations. Germany was stripped of its colonial possessions in the Pacific, which might have helped it pay its reparations bill. **B**

*B. Answer*
The treaty forced Germany to assume sole responsibility for starting World War I; it forced the nation to pay huge war reparations and stripped it of its colonial possessions in the Pacific.

**MAIN IDEA**

**Summarizing**
**B** How did the Treaty of Versailles affect Germany?

---

**ACTIVITY** | **LINK TO GEOGRAPHY**

 **BLOCK SCHEDULING**

### Creating a Map

**Class Time** 30 minutes

**Task** Creating a pair of maps that show territory gained and lost during the war

**Purpose** To understand the boundary changes that resulted from World War I

**Directions** Have students choose one nation that gained or lost territory as a result of World War I. Then have them draw two maps of that nation. The first map should show the nation's boundaries before the war, or, if the nation was not in existence, the first map should show which nations controlled the territories that would be included in the new nation after the war. The second map should show the nation's boundaries after the war. The maps should include national populations, cultures, and resources gained or lost as a result of the war.

In addition, for three years the Russians had fought on the side of the Allies, suffering higher casualties than any other nation. However, because Russia was excluded from the peace conference, it lost more territory than Germany did. The Union of Soviet Socialist Republics (or Soviet Union), as Russia was officially called after 1922, became determined to regain its former territory.

Finally, the treaty ignored claims of colonized people for self-determination, as in the case of Southeast Asia, where the Vietnamese people were beginning to demand the same political rights enjoyed by people in Western nations.

**OPPOSITION TO THE TREATY** When Wilson returned to the United States, he faced strong opposition to the treaty. Some people, including Herbert Hoover, believed it was too harsh. Hoover noted, "The economic consequences alone will pull down all Europe and thus injure the United States." Others considered the treaty a sell-out to imperialism because it simply exchanged one set of colonial rulers for another. Some ethnic groups objected to the treaty because the new national boundaries it established did not satisfy their particular demands for self-determination. For example, before the war many Poles had been under German rule. Now many Germans were under Polish rule.

**DEBATE OVER THE LEAGUE OF NATIONS** The main domestic opposition, however, centered on the issue of the League of Nations. A few opponents believed that the League threatened the U.S. foreign policy of isolationism. Conservative senators, headed by **Henry Cabot Lodge,** were suspicious of the provision for joint economic and military action against aggression, even though it was voluntary. They wanted the constitutional right of Congress to declare war included in the treaty.

### Connections Across Time

**1919 AND 1945**

### Provisions of the World War II Treaty

Tell students that at the end of World War II, at the Yalta Conference in 1945, the Allied leaders met to discuss the problems of postwar Europe. Among other points, the leaders agreed to establish a world peacekeeping organization—which would become the United Nations. They also agreed to help the defeated countries create democratic governments.

## POINT    COUNTERPOINT

**"The League of Nations was the world's best hope for lasting peace."**

President Wilson campaigned for the League of Nations as "necessary to meet the differing and unexpected contingencies" that could threaten world peace. Wilson believed that the League would create a forum where nations could talk through their disagreements. He also hoped it would provide collective security, in which nations would "respect and preserve as against external aggression the territorial integrity and existing political independence of all members of the League," and thereby prevent devastating warfare.

Critics complained that membership in the League would limit American independence in international affairs. However, Wilson argued that League membership included "a moral, not a legal, obligation" that would leave Congress free to decide its own course of action. Wilson tried to assure Congress as well as the general public that the League was "not a straightjacket, but a vehicle of life." It was also a definite guaranty . . . against the things that have just come near bringing the whole structure of civilization into ruin."

**"The League of Nations posed a threat to U.S. self-determination."**

Senator William Borah was one of the foremost critics of the Treaty of Versailles because he objected to U.S. membership in the League of Nations. Borah feared that membership in the League "would draw America away from her isolation and into the internal affairs and concerns of Europe" and involve the United States in foreign wars. "Once having surrendered and become a part of the European concerns," Borah wondered, "where, my friends, are you going to stop?"

Many opponents also feared that the League would nullify the Monroe Doctrine by limiting "the right of our people to govern themselves free from all restraint, legal or moral, of foreign powers."

Although Wilson argued that the League of Nations would have no such power of restraint, Borah was unconvinced. He responded to Wilson's argument by asking, "What will your League amount to if it does not contain powers that no one dreams of giving it?"

### THINKING CRITICALLY

1. **CONNECT TO HISTORY Summarizing** Both supporters and opponents of the League hoped to preserve peace. How did each group propose to secure peace for the United States?

    **SEE SKILLBUILDER HANDBOOK, PAGE R4.**

2. **CONNECT TO TODAY Identifying Problems** What are some contemporary arguments against United States participation in international organizations such as the United Nations or the World Court?

### POINT COUNTERPOINT

### Objective

To understand American support for and opposition to ratification of the Treaty of Versailles

· Why did Wilson support the League of Nations?

· What were the main objections to U.S. participation in the League?

· Which side made the strongest argument for or against joining the League?

Electronic Library of Primary Sources
· Why a League of Nations Is Necessary, by W. Wilson
· On the Terms of Peace, by H. Cabot Lodge

*The First World War* **401**

### THINKING CRITICALLY: ANSWERS

1. **CONNECT TO HISTORY** American supporters believed that members of the League of Nations would respect and preserve each other's territory and political independence and would work together to secure peace.

2. **CONNECT TO TODAY** Before students make suggestions for a new treaty, encourage them to do the following:
   · Pinpoint the weaknesses of the old treaty.
   · Make a list of the goals of both sides.
   · Make a list of the objections raised by opponents of the treaty.
   · Address each objection and decide what compromises could be made.

### History Through *Film*

**History Through** *Film*

**SKILLBUILDER ANSWERS**

1. In the years after World War I, disfigured veterans were a common sight.
2. Answers will vary. Some students may note that many modern horror films include a great deal of violence against individuals, which may reflect fears of increasing violent crime rates.

#### ECHOES OF THE GREAT WAR

In the 1920s and 30s, a number of Hollywood horror films were influenced by memories of the Great War. *The Hunchback of Notre Dame* and *The Phantom of the Opera* featured men who, like many veterans, were forced to live with shameful disfigurements.

Other films recalled the war's bleak landscapes. In fact, parts of the movie *Frankenstein* were filmed on the same sets as *All Quiet on the Western Front*, the famous war film. James Whale, who directed *Frankenstein*, was a veteran of the war. Like many of his generation, he remained profoundly disturbed by the horrors the war had unleashed.

◀ Lon Chaney in *The Phantom of the Opera* (1925)

Chaney in *The Hunchback of Notre Dame* (1923) ▲

(top) *All Quiet on the Western Front* (1930) ▲
(bottom) *Frankenstein* (1931)

**SKILLBUILDER  Interpreting Visual Sources**

1. Why might the theme of human disfigurement be especially powerful to the generation that lived through World War I?
2. How do horror films of your time reflect specific fears and anxieties of the current generation?

**SEE SKILLBUILDER HANDBOOK, PAGE R23.**

**More About . . .**

#### Henry Cabot Lodge

Henry Cabot Lodge served as a member of the House of Representatives for three terms before being elected to the Senate in 1892, where he remained until 1924. Lodge intensely disliked Wilson and was an outspoken opponent of the League of Nations.

 Electronic Library of Primary Sources
· On the Terms of Peace by Henry Cabot Lodge

**WILSON REFUSES TO COMPROMISE** Wilson unwisely ignored the Republican majority in the Senate when he chose the members of the American delegation. If he had been more willing to accept a compromise on the League, it would have been more likely that the Senate would have approved the treaty. Wilson, however, was exhausted from his efforts at Versailles.

Despite ill health, Wilson set out in September 1919 on an 8,000-mile tour. He delivered 34 speeches in about 3 weeks, explaining why the United States should join the League of Nations. On October 2, Wilson suffered a stroke (a ruptured blood vessel to the brain) and lay partially paralyzed for more than two months, unable to even meet with his cabinet. His once-powerful voice was no more than a thick whisper.

When the treaty came up for a vote in the Senate in November 1919, Senator Lodge introduced a number of amendments, the most important of which qualified the terms under which the United States would enter the League of Nations. It was feared that U.S. membership in the League would force the United States to form its foreign policy in accord with the League. Although the Senate rejected the amendments, it also failed to ratify the treaty.

Wilson refused to compromise. "I will not play for position," he proclaimed. "This is not a time for tactics. It is a time to stand square. I can stand defeat; I cannot stand retreat from conscientious duty." The treaty again came up for a vote in March 1920. The Senate again rejected the Lodge amendments—and again failed to muster enough votes for ratification.

The United States finally signed a separate treaty with Germany in 1921, after Wilson was no longer president. The United States never joined the League of Nations, but it maintained an unofficial observer at League meetings. **C**

*C. Answer* It was feared that U.S. membership in the League would force the United States to shape its foreign policy in accord with the League.

**MAIN IDEA**

**Making Inferences**
**C** Why were some people afraid of the treaty's influence over American foreign policy?

---

**ACTIVITY**  **COOPERATIVE LEARNING**                    **B BLOCK SCHEDULING**

#### Debating the League of Nations

**Class Time** 40 minutes

**Task** Debating whether the U.S. Senate should ratify the Treaty of Versailles

**Purpose** To understand the arguments of both supporters and opponents of the Treaty of Versailles

**Directions** Divide the class into an even number of small groups. After choosing a position through a lottery, students should research the arguments for and against ratification of the treaty. They can take notes on the arguments used to defend their own position. They should also list the arguments offered by the opposing side and decide which ones they should concede and which ones they can challenge with counterarguments. After students have prepared their arguments, pair opposing groups and have them conduct their debate.

## ❸ The Legacy of the War

When World War I ended, many Americans looked forward to a return of what Warren G. Harding called "normalcy." However, both the United States and the rest of the world had been utterly transformed by the war. At home, World War I had strengthened both the U.S. military and the power of government. It had also accelerated social change, especially for African Americans and women. In addition, the propaganda campaign had provoked powerful fears and antagonisms that were left unchanneled when the war finally came to an end.

In Europe the destruction and massive loss of life severely damaged social and political systems. In many countries the war created political instability and violence that persisted for decades. During the war years, the first Communist state was established in Russia, while after the war, militant fascist organizations seized control in Italy, Spain, and Germany.

**Vocabulary**
**fascist:**
characteristic of or relating to fascism, a system of totalitarian government

Appalled by the scale of destruction, Americans began to call World War I "the war to end all wars," in the hope that humanity would never again be willing to fight such a war. However, unresolved issues in Europe would eventually drag America into an even wider war. The Treaty of Versailles had settled nothing. In fact, some Europeans longed to resume the fight. The ominous shape of things to come emerged in the writings of an Austrian named Adolf Hitler, an angry veteran of World War I: "It cannot be that two million [Germans] should have fallen in vain. . . . No, we do not pardon, we demand—vengeance!" Two decades after the end of the Great War, Adolf Hitler's desire for vengeance would plunge the world into an even greater war, in which the United States would play a leading role.

**Domestic Consequences of World War I**

• accelerated America's emergence as the world's greatest industrial power

• contributed to the movement of African Americans to Northern cities

• intensified anti-immigrant and anti-radical sentiments among mainstream Americans

• brought over one million women into the work force

### Instruct: Objective ❸

**The Legacy of the War**
TAKS SS11 5(WH26.C)
· Why did Germany object to the Treaty of Versailles?
· How did the war affect Germany?
· How did the war affect U.S. power and prestige in the world?

📖 In-Depth Resources: Unit 3
· Guided Reading, p. 50

## Assess & Reteach

### SECTION 4 ASSESSMENT
Have students discuss the Section Assessment questions in class.

📖 Formal Assessment
· Section Quiz, p. 212

### SELF-ASSESSMENT
Have students make a two-column chart. In the first column, students should list what they knew about the Treaty of Versailles, the League of Nations, and the legacy of World War I before they read the section. In the second column, students should list what they have learned.

### RETEACH
Use the Point/Counterpoint feature on page 401 to review the debate over the League of Nations.

📖 In-Depth Resources: Unit 3
· Reteaching Activity, p. 56

**ASSESSMENT**

1. **TERMS & NAMES** For each term or name, write a sentence explaining its significance.
   - •Fourteen Points
   - •League of Nations
   - •Georges Clemenceau
   - •David Lloyd George
   - •Treaty of Versailles
   - •reparations
   - •war-guilt clause
   - •Henry Cabot Lodge

**MAIN IDEA**

2. **TAKING NOTES**
Re-create the spider diagram shown below. Fill in the web with information about the provisions and weaknesses of the Treaty of Versailles and opposition to it.

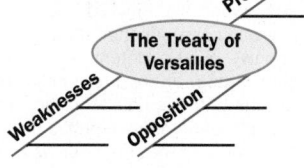

Do you think Congress should have rejected the treaty?

**CRITICAL THINKING**

3. **DEVELOPING HISTORICAL PERSPECTIVE**
Why didn't the Treaty of Versailles lay the foundations for a lasting peace?

4. **SUMMARIZING**
Why did so many Americans oppose the Treaty of Versailles?

5. **HYPOTHESIZING**
Predict Germany's reaction to the Treaty of Versailles. Give reasons for your predictions.
**Think About:**
   • what Germans thought of the war-guilt clause
   • German reaction to reparations
   • how Germans felt about the loss of territory

*The First World War* **403**

**1. TERMS & NAMES**
Fourteen Points, p. 399
League of Nations, p. 399
Georges Clemenceau, p. 399
David Lloyd George, p. 399
Treaty of Versailles, p. 400
reparations, p. 400
war-guilt clause, p. 400
Henry Cabot Lodge, p. 401

**2. TAKING NOTES**
Provisions: 9 new nations; France and Britain temporarily gain 4 areas of the Ottoman Empire; Germany has no army and forced to pay war costs.
Weaknesses: The severe treatment of Germany fails to provide a lasting peace.
Opposition: too harsh with dire economic consequences; did not end colonialism; treaty did not satisfy self-determination demands of ethnic groups.

**3. DEVELOPING HISTORICAL PERSPECTIVE**
The Treaty of Versailles created resentment among the German citizens and their government officials.

**4. SUMMARIZING**
Many Americans believed the economic consequences would ruin Europe and the United States.

**5. HYPOTHESIZING**
Student responses should identify the thoughts of Germans about the war-guilt clause, reparations, and the loss of territory.

### Objectives

· To examine the ways in which the United States has asserted itself in world affairs since 1898

· To analyze motives for getting involved in, or staying out of, various international conflicts

## Focus & Motivate

**Analyzing Motives** Ask students to think about a place in the world where war or conflict is raging now.

· What are the reasons the United States should become involved in this conflict?

· What are the reasons the United States should stay out of this conflict?

· If the United States were to become involved in this conflict, what type of support might it give, and to whom?

## HISTORY from VISUALS

**Analyzing Political Cartoons**
Ask students the following questions: What does the kneeling figure represent, and what is she asking of Uncle Sam? What is the meaning of the title, "The Only Way We Can Save Her"? What do you think this cartoon illustrates? What point of view does it support?

# America in World Affairs

The United States has not always been as involved in world affairs as it is today. Throughout its history, the nation's foreign policy has swung back and forth between a commitment to involvement with the world and the desire for isolation. "Steer clear of permanent alliances," George Washington cautioned Americans in his Farewell Address of 1796. Washington's warning to the young nation became a theme of government policy for the next hundred years, as domestic issues dominated Americans' attention.

In the late 1800s, however, Americans began to look outward to the larger world. The country had reached the limits of its continental expansion and stretched from ocean to ocean. As its economic power grew stronger, the United States became more involved in the affairs of its neighbors in the Western Hemisphere.

## 1823–1898

**THE UNITED STATES AND LATIN AMERICA ▶**

Throughout the 19th century, the United States expanded its influence in the Western Hemisphere. The Monroe Doctrine was intended to diminish European interference. After the Civil War, American trade with Latin America, including the Spanish colony of Cuba, grew. In fact, the United States traded more heavily with Cuba than Spain did.

When the Cubans rebelled against Spain, Americans sympathized with the rebels. After the battleship U.S.S. *Maine* sank in the Cuban harbor of Havana, Americans blamed the Spanish, and Congress declared war. After defeating the Spanish, the United States extended its influence in territories such as Puerto Rico, Panama, and Mexico. A new expansionist era had begun.

DESTRUCTION OF THE U.S. BATTLESHIP MAINE

The Only Way We Can Save Her

"STAY OUT! STAY OUT FOR MY SAKE, AS WELL AS YOUR OWN!"

DEMOCRACY

AMERICA THE LAST REFUGE OF DEMOCRACY

## 1917–1939

**◄ INVOLVEMENT AND ISOLATIONISM**

Before World War I, the United States had generally limited its military involvement to the Western Hemisphere. As the war in Europe progressed, this position became impossible to maintain, as German U-boats increasingly threatened American lives. In spite of fierce opposition from isolationists, the United States joined World War I in 1917. U.S. involvement in the conflict greatly strengthened its armed forces and revealed the nation's military potential.

After the war, the United States returned to a policy of isolationism. A decade later, as European dictators began menacing other European countries, American public opinion was sharply divided. Many argued that the best way to preserve American democracy was to stay out of war in Europe. It took Japan's attack on Pearl Harbor, Hawaii, in 1941 to force the United States into World War II.

**404** CHAPTER 11

## RECOMMENDED RESOURCES

### BOOKS

Barnet, Richard J. *The Rockets' Red Glare: When America Goes to War: The Presidents and the People.* New York: Simon, 1990.

Lord, Mary and Martha L. McCoy, eds. *In Harms Way: When Should We Risk American Lives in World Conflicts?* CT: Study Circles Resource Center, 1994.

### VIDEOS

*Vietnam: A Television History.* WGBH-TV Boston, 1983. 13-hour series that tells the story of the conflict.

*Headline Stories of the Century: A Newsreel Library of World War II.* Questar Video, 1992. Presents 84 edited newsreels showing combat.

### SOFTWARE

*The War in Vietnam CD-ROM.* Macmillan USA, 1995. Includes articles, photos, broadcast clips, maps, and a searchable database.

### INTEGRATED TECHNOLOGY

For teacher support, visit. . . .

 classzone.com

U.S. forces in Vietnam in 1968

This statue of Lenin, the leader of the 1917 Russian Revolution, was toppled by Latvian citizens in 1991.

## 1945–1991

### ▲ THE COLD WAR

After World War II, tensions between the United States and Communist countries like the Soviet Union and China developed into a nonmilitary conflict known as the Cold War. During the Cold War, which lasted for nearly 50 years, the United States and the Soviet Union competed to extend their political and economic influence. In some parts of the world, such as Korea and Vietnam, the Cold War led to prolonged military warfare.

The great costs of these conflicts—both in money and in lives—led to renewed calls for isolationism. Nevertheless, the U.S. remained actively involved in the Cold War throughout the 1980s.

## 1939–1945

### INVOLVEMENT IN EUROPE ▼

When the fascist threat to democracy became too great to ignore, the United States joined the Allies in fighting the Axis Powers during World War II. The United States and the Soviet Union emerged from the war as the two strongest military powers in the world. It was now impossible for the nation to return to isolationism. The United States took an active role in rebuilding Europe through programs like the Marshall Plan and was instrumental in establishing the United Nations. The United States also stayed involved with Europe militarily during the Cold War as a member of the North Atlantic Treaty Organization (NATO).

---

### THINKING CRITICALLY

#### CONNECT TO TODAY

1. **Analyzing Motives** What were America's motives for getting involved in each of the wars described on these two pages? Do you think these motives would be valid today?

   **SEE SKILLBUILDER HANDBOOK, PAGE R6.**

#### CONNECT TO HISTORY

2. **Writing About Wartime Experience** Imagine that you are a reporter writing at the time about one of the wars in the 20th century. Interview someone you know—or look for information in the library or on the Internet—to find out how a soldier, nurse, cook, sailor, or pilot spent each day as part of the war effort. Write a feature article for a local newspaper, quoting that person.

 **RESEARCH LINKS** CLASSZONE.COM

---

---

## Instruct

1. What was the intended purpose of the Monroe Doctrine?
2. How did the United States respond to the end of World War I?
3. What was the incident that drew the United States into World War II?
4. What developments led to the end of the Cold War?

### MAKING PERSONAL CONNECTIONS

Ask students if they know anyone who has participated in a U.S. military action overseas, such as in Bosnia, Haiti, or Vietnam.

· How did this person's participation affect his or her life?

· Does this person believe that U.S. intervention in this conflict was beneficial, or not?

· How do this person's views affect the student's view of the role the United States should play in the world?

### More About . . .

#### The Cold War

Although there were some "hot spots" in the Cold War, most of the war was waged using economic and political tactics. The United States actively recruited nations into military alliances such as NATO, SEATO, and ANZUS. Another front in the Cold War was foreign aid. Billions of dollars were poured into projects in developing nations. Sometimes, the United States acted in covert ways to establish or keep governments in power. This was particularly true in Latin America where the United States was involved in such locations as Guatemala, Chile, and Nicaragua.

---

### THINKING CRITICALLY: ANSWERS

1. **CONNECT TO TODAY** **Spanish-American War:** imperialism, protection of American economic interests in Cuba, sympathy for the Cuban struggle for independence from Spain. **World War I:** threats to U.S. citizens, sympathy for the Allies, and economic and political interests. **World War II:** fear of Japan and Germany, sympathy for Britain and the Allies, and economic and political interests. **The Cold War:** fear of Communism and its spread.

2. **CONNECT TO HISTORY**
   **Rubric**
   Feature articles should . . .
   · identify the war and the individual's wartime role
   · focus on the various activities that made up a typical day
   · create interest and provide insight into the individual's life

## TERMS & NAMES

1. nationalism, p. 373
2. trench warfare, p. 376
3. Zimmermann Note, p. 379
4. Selective Service Act, p. 382
5. General John J. Pershing, p. 384
6. armistice, p. 387
7. Espionage and Sedition Acts, p. 392
8. Great Migration, p. 393
9. Fourteen Points, p. 399
10. Treaty of Versailles, p. 400

## MAIN IDEAS

1. U.S. economic ties with the Allies were stronger than its ties with the Central powers; Germany's counterblockade by U-boats outraged many Americans; the Zimmermann Note raised suspicions of a German alliance with Mexico.

2. Germany invaded Belgium, creating a refugee crisis.

3. The Selective Service Act allowed the government to randomly select up to 3 million men for military service.

4. Machine guns increased firepower; long-range guns shelled civilian and military targets; poison gas sickened and blinded its victims; submarine attacks led to civilian deaths.

5. The government advertised and sold war bonds; the Committee on Public Information popularized the war through a massive propaganda campaign.

6. The establishment of a propaganda agency led to a campaign that encouraged hatred and violations of civil liberties. The Espionage and Sedition Acts also violated civil liberties—anti-war publications lost their mailing privileges and people lost their jobs.

7. The Treaty of Versailles created international problems that would eventually lead to World War II, humiliated Germany, provoked Russia's determination to regain former Russian territory, and ignored the claims of colonized people for self-determination.

8. Many senators objected to the provision calling for the League, yet Wilson was unwilling to compromise on it.

---

## VISUAL SUMMARY

## THE FIRST WORLD WAR

### LONG-TERM CAUSES

- Nationalist tensions in Europe
- Competition for colonies
- Arms races and militarism
- Formation of defense alliances

### IMMEDIATE CAUSES

- Assassination of Franz Ferdinand
- Austria-Hungary's retaliation against Serbia
- Declarations of war between rival alliances
- Germany's invasion of Belgium

## WORLD WAR I

### IMMEDIATE EFFECTS

- Destruction and immense loss of life
- Revolution in Russia
- Social change in United States
- Allied victory over Central Powers
- Treaty of Versailles
- Formation of mandates (temporary colonies)
- League of Nations

### LONG-TERM EFFECTS

- Breakup of empires
- U.S. policy of isolationism
- United States' emergence as global economic giant
- Rise of militant extremist parties in Europe
- Eruption of World War II

---

## TERMS & NAMES

For each term or name below, write a sentence explaining its connection to World War I.

1. nationalism
2. trench warfare
3. Zimmermann note
4. Selective Service Act
5. General John J. Pershing
6. armistice
7. Espionage and Sedition Acts
8. Great Migration
9. Fourteen Points
10. Treaty of Versailles

## MAIN IDEAS

Use your notes and the information in the chapter to answer the following questions.

**World War I Begins** (pages 372–380)

1. What were the main reasons for U.S. involvement in the war?
2. Where did Germany begin its war offensive, and what happened there?

**American Power Tips the Balance** (pages 381–387)

3. How did the United States mobilize a strong military during World War I?
4. What new weapons made fighting in World War I deadlier than fighting in previous wars?

**The War at Home** (pages 388–395)

5. What methods did the U.S. government use to sell the war to the nation?
6. What events during the war undermined civil liberties?

**Wilson Fights for Peace** (pages 398–403)

7. What were the major effects of the Treaty of Versailles?
8. How did Wilson's support for the League of Nations stand in the way of Senate support for the Treaty of Versailles?

## CRITICAL THINKING

1. **USING YOUR NOTES** In a chart like the one shown, provide causes for the listed effects of World War I.

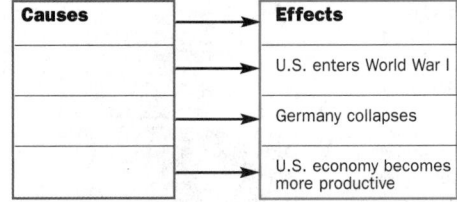

| Causes | | Effects |
|---|---|---|
| | → | U.S. enters World War I |
| | → | Germany collapses |
| | → | U.S. economy becomes more productive |

2. **DEVELOPING HISTORICAL PERSPECTIVE** Between 1914 and 1920, Americans debated the role their country should have in world affairs. From the events of World War I, what might Americans have learned about intervention in the affairs of other nations?

3. **INTERPRETING MAPS** Look at the maps of Europe before and after World War I (page 400). Describe the changes in national boundaries after the Versailles peace settlement.

---

## CRITICAL THINKING

1. **USING YOUR NOTES** U.S. enters WWI: Germany resumes submarine warfare; Zimmermann Note intercepted; Americans killed when U-boats sink ships. Germany collapses: German war machine and war economy too exhausted to keep fighting; German sailors mutiny. U.S. economy becomes more productive: wages rise dramatically.

2. **DEVELOPING HISTORICAL PERSPECTIVE** Paying attention to international situations that could lead to crises, such as extreme nationalism or militarism; the importance of nations helping one another in global affairs; the importance of diplomacy in drawing up treaties so as not to punish offending nations; the importance of listening to and helping smaller nations.

3. **INTERPRETING MAPS** New nations were established: Finland, Estonia, Latvia, Lithuania, Poland, Czechoslovakia, Yugoslavia, Syria, Iraq, Lebanon, Palestine, and Trans-Jordan. The territory of Austria-Hungary was greatly reduced. Austria-Hungary itself was divided into two nations: Austria and Hungary.

## Standardized Test Practice

Use the map and your knowledge of United States history to answer question 1.

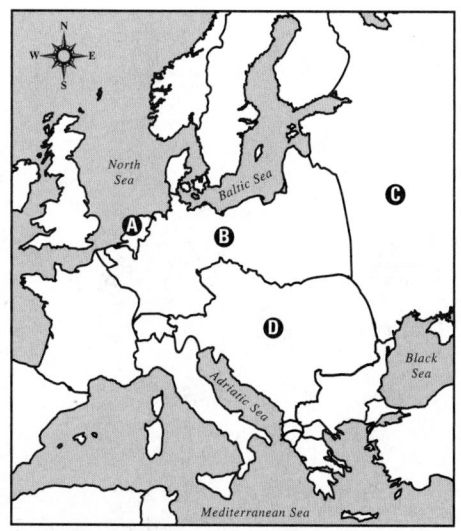

Use the graph and your knowledge of United States history to answer question 2.

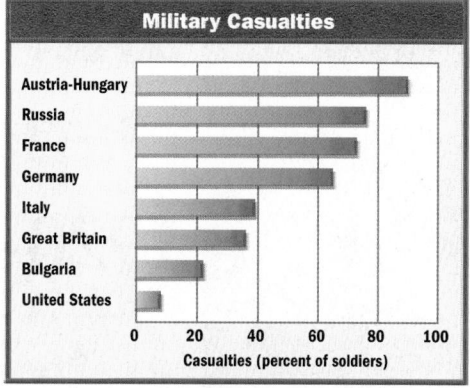

**Military Casualties**

Casualties (percent of soldiers)

1. Which country was an ally of the United States during World War I?

   A country A
   B country B
   C country C
   D country D

2. The countries with the greatest percentage of military casualties were all —

   F members of the Allied Powers.
   G members of the Central Powers.
   H located far from the battlefront.
   J bordering one of the war's two fronts.

**ADDITIONAL TEST PRACTICE, pages S1–S33.**

 **TEST PRACTICE** CLASSZONE.COM

## Standardized Test Practice

1. The correct answer is letter **C**.
   Remind students that in answering the question they need to know that the United States was fighting on the side of the Allies. Letters B (Germany) and D (Austro-Hungarian Empire) are not correct because they are part of the Central Powers. Letter A (the Netherlands) is not correct because it remained neutral during the war.

2. The correct answer is letter **J**.
   Battles along the eastern front had very high casualties. The letters F and G are not correct because one of the top two nations is a member of the Allied Powers and one is a member of the Central Powers. Letter H is not correct because distance from the battlefront usually means less casualties.

**NEWS ARTICLE**

**Tips for Teaching**

· Remind students to copy, print out, or create illustrations for their article.
· Have students exchange articles to proof-read and do a peer evaluation.

**Project Presentation Rubric**

The article should . . .

· have a headline and present or portray the person, event, or issue accurately
· have an introduction that clearly states the topic and purpose and a conclusion to end the piece
· engage the reader in a manner that educates about the selected topic

📰 Formal Assessment
   · Chapter Test, Forms A, B, and C, pp. 213–230

---

## ALTERNATIVE ASSESSMENT

1. **INTERACT WITH HISTORY** Recall your discussion of the question on page 371:

   *Do you think America should enter the war?*

   Write a speech, arguing for or against American involvement in World War I. Use information from the chapter to support your argument. Give your speech to the class.

2. **VIDEO** **LEARNING FROM MEDIA** View the *American Stories* video "Ace of Aces: Eddie Rickenbacker and the First World War." Discuss the following questions in a group; then do the activity.

   • What is your impression of Eddie Rickenbacker?
   • How did Rickenbacker adapt his skills and talents to wartime?

   **Cooperative Learning Activity** Rickenbacker's bravery and aviation skills made him a hero. What qualities make people heroes? Using stories and images from magazines and newspapers, make a list of current heroes on a chart for display in your classroom.

*The First World War* **407**

## ALTERNATIVE ASSESSMENT

### 1. INTERACT WITH HISTORY
**Rubric**
The student's speech should. . .
· present a clear position including points to support the position on American involvement
· reflect a deep understanding of the tenor of the times
· capture the audience's attention with a lively and interesting presentation

### 2. LEARNING FROM MEDIA
**Rubric**
Charts and displays should . . .
· demonstrate a definition of a hero
· present the concept clearly through positioning of pictures or words
· persuade the viewer of the correctness of the choices presented

# UNIT 4

# The 1920s and the Great Depression 1920–1940

**1**

## Previewing the Unit

Unit 4 covers the changes in the United States from 1920 to 1940, as people feel a clash between the values of a traditional rural society and those of a growing urban culture. Underlying economic problems are obscured by apparent prosperity until a long deep economic slowdown causes widespread suffering. In response, President Franklin Roosevelt experiments with various approaches to rebuild the economy.

### HISTORICAL INQUIRY: MULTI-MEDIA PRESENTATION

Use this project to teach students to explain and apply the use of frame of reference in historical inquiry.

**Explaining Frame of Reference**
Explain that a person's frame of reference is the events and circumstances that influence his or her point of view. Tell students that any historical understanding includes knowledge of the frame of reference of the historical figures. Ask why this must be. *(Understanding a person's frame of reference is necessary to understand that person's point of view; understanding frame of reference allows historians to place actions and events in historical context.)*

**Applying Frame of Reference**
Explain that differently situated people have different frames of reference; thus, students' presentations should include sources reflect-

*(continued on next page)*

**CHAPTER 12**
## Politics of the Roaring Twenties
**1920–1929**

**CHAPTER 13**
## The Roaring Life of the 1920s
**1920–1929**

**CHAPTER 14**
## The Great Depression Begins
**1929–1933**

**CHAPTER 15**
## The New Deal
**1933–1940**

UNIT PROJECT

### Multi-Media Presentation

Create a multi-media presentation that reflects popular culture in the 1920s. Gather a wide variety of sources including excerpts from vintage radio broadcasts and selections of literature. Use sound, visuals, and text in your presentation.

*Drouth Stricken Area by Alexandre Hogue*

408

**2**

**3**

## More About the Image

**1** **Shapes and colors**

Hogue's use of strong lines and vivid colors echoes techniques associated with folk art. Many regionalist artists of the 1930s used such techniques. Here, the shapes and colors also help stress the harshness of the landscape.

**2** **Lonely house**

The starkness of the scene is emphasized by the absence of people. The vast distance between this farmhouse and the one in the background emphasizes the loneliness of life on the Great Plains.

**3** **Starving cow**

The devastation of the Dust Bowl is evident in the skeletal cow. Underscoring the misery of the scene, it looks forlornly at the water tank that has no water.

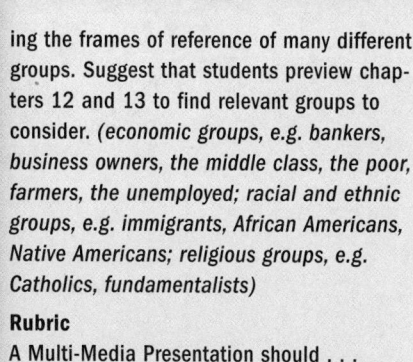

ing the frames of reference of many different groups. Suggest that students preview chapters 12 and 13 to find relevant groups to consider. *(economic groups, e.g. bankers, business owners, the middle class, the poor, farmers, the unemployed; racial and ethnic groups, e.g. immigrants, African Americans, Native Americans; religious groups, e.g. Catholics, fundamentalists)*

**Rubric**

A Multi-Media Presentation should . . .

· include a wide variety of visual, textual, and audio sources
· reflect a wide variety of popular pursuits and popular culture of the 1920s, such as the arts, sports, movies, popular music, radio, hobbies, fashions, politics, and working life
· provide information on the frames of reference of a wide variety of groups
· provide a context for understanding issues and events of the 1920s leading up to the Great Depression

## HISTORY from VISUALS

### Interpreting the Painting

Alexandre Hogue grew up in West Texas and became a part of a regionalist movement of artists who attempted to create a unique style of American art. He came to believe that plowing the land broke a sacred bond owed to it. He felt that the farmers deserved some of the blame for the Dust Bowl because of their farming methods.

Ask students to think of adjectives to describe the feeling of the painting. Then have them look at the photograph on page 474 and have them describe this image. Ask students how the images are similar and different. Which image conveys the impact of the Dust Bowl more convincingly?

**Extension** Using Internet sources or other research materials, find other paintings or photographs of the Dust Bowl to compare.

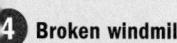 **Broken windmill**

The useless windmill shows the power of nature in two ways. The blades have been broken by the Plains' wind and are not repaired. The well has not produced any water and the water tank is filled with death-bringing dust.

 **Dunes**

The destruction is evident in the mount of dust that has partially engulfed the house.

**6 Vulture**

To remove any doubt about the fate of the cow—and of the way of life on the plains—Hogue includes the waiting vulture.

**7 No relief**

The scene contains no sign of relief. The dust-filled sky contains one cloud that seems unlikely to bring rain. The other birds in the sky may be circling vultures.

# Politics of the Roaring Twenties

| | CHAPTER OVERVIEW | COPYMASTERS | INTEGRATED TECHNOLOGY |
|---|---|---|---|
| **CHAPTER RESOURCES** | *Americans lash out at those who are different while they enjoy prosperity and new conveniences produced by American businesses.* | ▦ Telescoping the Times<br>· Chapter Summary, pp. 23–24<br><br>▦ Planning for Block Schedules | ◉ Power Presentations<br>◉ Electronic Teacher Tools<br>▥ Online Lesson Planner<br>▥ classzone.com |
| **SECTION 1**<br><br>**America Struggles with Postwar Issues**<br><br>pp. 412–418 | **KEY IDEAS**<br>*The Russian Revolution brings a Communist government to power. Many Americans fear that a similar revolution will occur in the United States. Political radicals and labor activists meet with increasing opposition.* | ▦ In-Depth Resources: Unit 4<br>· Guided Reading, p. 1<br>· Building Vocabulary, p. 4<br>· Reteaching Activity, p. 6<br>· Primary Sources, pp. 11–13<br>· Literature, pp. 15–17<br>· American Lives, p. 18<br><br>▦ Lesson Plans, pp. 97–98 | ⚒ Geography Transparencies GT20<br>⚒ Critical Thinking Transparencies CT20<br>◉ Electronic Library of Primary Sources<br>· Instructions Regarding Conduct on Raids, 1920 by U.S. Dept. of Justice<br>· From A Letter Regarding Immigration, 1924 by L. Marshall<br>▥ classzone.com |
| **SECTION 2**<br><br>**The Harding Presidency**<br><br>pp. 419–421 | *The Republicans return to isolationism and the kind of policies that had characterized the period before the reforms of the Progressive Era.* | ▦ In-Depth Resources: Unit 4<br>· Guided Reading, p. 2<br>· Building Vocabulary, p. 4<br>· Skillbuilder Practice, p. 5<br>· Reteaching Activity, p. 7<br><br>▦ Lesson Plans, pp. 99–100 | ⚒ Humanities Transparencies HT39<br>· *Looking Backward*<br>◉ Electronic Library of Primary Sources<br>· Senate Demands Information on Teapot Dome<br>▥ classzone.com |
| **SECTION 3**<br><br>**The Business of America**<br><br>pp. 422–429 | *During the prosperous 1920s, the automobile industry and other industries flourish. Americans' standard of living rises to new heights.* | ▦ In-Depth Resources: Unit 4<br>· Guided Reading, p. 3<br>· Reteaching Activity, p. 8<br>· Geography Application, pp. 9–10<br>· Primary Sources, p. 14<br>· American Lives, p. 19<br><br>▦ Lesson Plans, pp. 101–102 | ⚒ Critical Thinking Transparencies CT54<br>· Consumer Spending Power, 1920–1929<br>▥ classzone.com |

## ASSESSMENT OPTIONS

PE Chapter Assessment, pp. 430–431

📋 Formal Assessment
 · Chapter Tests, Forms A, B, and C, pp. 231–245

👁 Test Generator

📋 Integrated Assessment Book

🏆 TAKS Online Test Practice

📋 TAKS Spiraled Content Review

 TAKS Practice Tests

---

PE Section 1 Assessment, p. 418

TE Self-Assessment, p. 418

📋 Formal Assessment, Quiz, p. 231

📋 Integrated Assessment Book

👁 Test Generator

🔧 TAKS Practice Transparencies TT75

---

PE Section 2 Assessment, p. 421

TE Self-Assessment, p. 421

📋 Formal Assessment, Quiz, p. 232

📋 Integrated Assessment Book

👁 Test Generator

🔧 TAKS Practice Transparencies TT76

---

PE Section 3 Assessment, p. 427

TE Self-Assessment, p. 427

📋 Formal Assessment, Quiz, p. 233

📋 Integrated Assessment Book

👁 Test Generator

🔧 TAKS Practice Transparencies TT77

## RESOURCES FOR DIFFERENTIATING INSTRUCTION

**Students Acquiring English/ESL**

📋 Reading Study Guide:
 (English and Spanish)
 pp. 123–130

📋 Access for Students
 Acquiring English/ESL:
 Spanish Translations,
 pp. 141–148

🔊 Chapter Summaries on CD
 (English and Spanish)

**Less Proficient Readers**

📋 Reading Study Guide
 (English and Spanish)
 pp. 123–130

📋 Telescoping the Times
 · Chapter Summary,
 pp. 23–24

🔊 Chapter Summaries on CD
 (English and Spanish)

**Gifted and Talented Students**

📋 In-Depth Resources: Unit 4
 · Primary Sources,
 pp. 11–14
 · American Lives: Ernesto
 Galarza p. 18, Henry Ford,
 p. 19
 · Literature, pp. 15–17

👁 Electronic Library of
 Primary Sources
 · Unit 4, Chapter 12

## CROSS-CURRICULAR CONNECTIONS

**Primary Sources**
Rogers, Will. *The Wit and Wisdom of Will Rogers.* Ed.
Alex Ayers. NY: Meridien Books, 1993. Over 2,000
quotes by this well-known cowboy philosopher.

**Humanities: Art**
Chevlowe, Susan, et. al. *Common Man, Mythic
Vision: The Paintings of Ben Shahn.* Princeton, NJ:
Princeton University Press, 1998. This book about a
Lithuanian emigrant artist focuses on his Socialist
realist paintings of Depression-era America.

**Pop Culture**
Miller, Ray and Glen Embree. *Henry's Lady: An
Illustrated History of the Model A Ford (Ford Road
Series).* Denver: Evergreen Press, 1972. This book
contains excellent photos and covers all the various
styles of the Model A in great detail.

**Literature**
Hammett, Dashiell. *Red Harvest.* NY: Vintage, 1989.
This superb crime novel depicts gang war and labor
organization. It is a classic exploration of corruption
and violence in 1920s America.

Lewis, Sinclair. *Main Street.* NY: Bantam, 1996. A
small Midwestern prairie town in the 1920s is the
setting of this famous novel. The story is about a city
girl who marries the town doctor and attempts to
bring culture to the village. Her efforts are met with
gossip, greed, and bigotry, resulting in a horrifying
picture of small-town life.

## ENRICHMENT ACTIVITIES

PE **Pupil's Edition,** pp. 410–429
 Interact with History, pp. 410–411
 Tracing Themes, pp. 428–429

📋 **In-Depth Resources: Unit 4**
 · Geography Application: The Automobile
 Industry, pp. 9–10
 · Primary Sources: Speech to the Jury,
 pp. 11–12
 · Primary Sources: Report on the Steel Strike
 of 1919, p. 13

 · Primary Sources: Advertisement, p. 14
 · Literature Selection from *The Big Money* by
 John Dos Passos, pp. 15–16
 · Literature Selection "Justice Denied in
 Massachusetts," p. 17
 · American Lives: Ernesto Galarza, p. 18
 · American Lives: Henry Ford, p. 19

👁 **Electronic Library of Primary Sources**
 · Unit 4, Chapter 12

# CHAPTER 12: PACING GUIDE

## BLOCK SCHEDULE LESSON PLAN OPTIONS (90-MINUTE PERIOD)

### DAY 1

**CHAPTER 12 OPENER**
pp. 410–411

**Class Time** 30 minutes

**History from Visuals, p. 410**

**Class Time** 15 minutes

*Options for Pacing and Variety*

· Time Saver Ask students to examine the photograph and describe what is happening. Ask them the questions on the TE page. Also have them look at the time line and ask them the relevant questions in the TE under Time Line Discussion. **Class Time** 10 minutes

**Interact With History, p. 411**

**Class Time** 15 minutes

*Options for Pacing and Variety*

· Role-Playing Have students read the paragraph on the page and discuss what decisions they might make and on what they would base their decisions. What dangers are involved in each option: to participate in the strike or not to participate? **Class Time** 15 minutes

**SECTION 1, pp. 412–418**

**Class Time** 30 minutes

*Options for Pacing and Variety*

· Internet Have students work in groups researching the roots of the Red Scare. See TE page 413 for more details. **Class Time** 20 minutes

### DAY 1 continued

· Time Saver Ask students to look at the map and graph on page 416 and discuss the Geography Skillbuilder questions. **Class Time** 10 minutes

· Peer Teaching Have students work in pairs to answer questions 2 and 3 of the Section 1 Assessment, and then, as a class, discuss questions 4 and 5. **Class Time** 20 minutes

**SECTION 2, pp. 419–421**

**Class Time** 30 minutes

*Options for Pacing and Variety*

· Peer Teaching Ask students to read A Personal Voice on page 419. Have them write a few paragraphs on the implications of such a view: whether it was right in terms of what people wanted and what was good for the country. Give them a few questions, and then let them discuss the issues with a partner before writing. **Class Time** 25 minutes

· Peer Evaluation Have students quiz each other on the Terms Names. Then have pairs of students complete the Section 2 Assessment and check their answers with another pair. **Class Time** 20 minutes

### DAY 2

**SECTION 3, pp. 422–429**

**Class Time** 45 minutes

*Options for Pacing and Variety*

· Peer Teaching Have students work in small groups on the activity on TE page 425 and present their ad to the class. They should look at what age, social, or economic group the ad is aimed—and how that group is targeted. What do the ads say about priorities and important issues for these groups? **Class Time** One period

· Time Saver Discuss A Personal Voice on page 427 with students. Ask them how such plans encourage people to overextend themselves financially and what other payment options work similarly **Class Time** 10 minutes

**ASSESSMENT**
pp. 430–431

**Class Time** 45 minutes

· Peer Evaluation Have students answer the Main Idea questions. Then ask them to switch papers with a partner and correct the answers as much as they can. **Class Time** 15 minutes

*Options for Pacing and Variety*

· Peer Teaching Ask students to work in pairs to complete the Critical Thinking questions on page 430. **Class Time** 15 minutes

### DAY 2 continued

· Peer Evaluation Have students work in pairs to make up questions that have the terms and names of the chapter as answers. Then have students give the questions to another group to answer. **Class Time** 20 minutes

---

**TEACHER-TESTED ACTIVITY**
**RATING PRESIDENT HARDING**

James Rosenberg, Crystal Lake South High School, Crystal Lake, Illinois

**Class Time** 50 minutes

**Task** Developing a transparency summarizing and rating the Harding administration

**Purpose** To think critically about presidential actions

**Supplies Needed**

· Transparencies
· Markers

**Activity** Have students list the qualities of a great president. Then have small groups each create a transparency listing the positive and negative events of Harding's administration. Groups should use their lists to evaluate and rate Harding's presidency, with 1 being the lowest rating and 6 the highest. Have groups justify their ratings.

# CHAPTER 12 CORRELATION

## CORRELATION TO THE TEXAS ESSENTIAL KNOWLEDGE AND SKILLS

Chapter 12 addresses the following standards of the Texas Essential Knowledge and Skills for U.S. History.

| TEKS | Instruction | Student Question/Activity |
|---|---|---|
| **(5A)** Analyze causes and effects of significant issues such as the Red Scare. | **PE 413–414** discussion of the causes and effects of the Red Scare in America | **TE 413** research activity about the roots of the Red Scare |
| **(5B)** Analyze the impact of significant individuals such as Henry Ford. | **PE 423–424** examination of the impact of the automobile on American society | **PE 427** question that requires students to interpret a graph showing the rise in automobile registrations |
| **(8B)** Answer questions about geographic distributions and patterns shown on maps and graphs. | **PE 416** map and graph analyzing the wave of European immigration to the United States during the 1920s | **PE 416** questions that require students to interpret information about the graph |
| **(10A)** Analyze the effects of changing demographic patterns resulting from migration within the United States. | **PE 423–424** examination of changing demographic patterns brought on by the rise of the automobile | **PE 423** questions that require students to interpret a map showing the impact of the automobile on the population of the West |
| **(12A)** Analyze the relationship between private property rights and the settlement of the Great Plains. | **PE 428** feature examining, in part, how the Homestead Act helped to increase settlement of the Great Plains | **PE 429** question about the obstacles homesteaders faced |
| **(13A)** Analyze the causes of economic growth and prosperity in the 1920s. | **PE 422–423; 425–427** examination of the causes and effects of the nation's economic boom during the 1920s | **PE 427** questions about economic growth in the 1920s |
| **(15C)** Evaluate the effects of political incidents such as Teapot Dome. | **PE 420–421** examination of the scandals that plagued the Harding administration, including the Teapot Dome scandal | **PE 421** question about the effect of the Harding scandals on the country |

## TAKS MINI-LESSONS

1. **Social Studies Skills: Objective 1 (US5.A):** Analyze causes and effects of significant issues such as immigration and the Red Scare **Activity** Have students complete the research activity about the roots of the Red Scare on page 413.

2. **Social Studies Skills: Objective 3 (US13.A):** Analyze causes of economic growth and prosperity in the 1920s **Activity** Have students create a chart summarizing the factors that helped create an economic boom in the 1920s.

3. **Social Studies Skills: Objective 3 (US23.A):** Analyze how scientific discoveries and technological innovations have changed the standard of living in the United States **Activity** Have students write a paragraph summarizing how the significant innovations during the 1920s helped to improve Americans' standard of living.

4. **English Language Arts Skills: Objective 3 (7.G):** Draw inferences, such as conclusions, and support them with text evidence **Activity** Have students explain in a paragraph the meaning of the heading "A Superficial Prosperity" on page 426.

5. **English Language Arts Skills: Objective 4 (5.A):** Evaluate writing for both mechanics and content **Activity** Have students work with a partner to evaluate each other's answers to the Critical Thinking questions for Section 2 on page 421.

# CHAPTER 12 · POLITICS OF THE ROARING TWENTIES

## HISTORY from VISUALS

### Interpreting the Photograph

Ask students to examine the photograph and describe what is happening. *(A riot is in progress. Students may guess that the workers have spontaneously revolted. Some will notice the woman holding the child and the injured people on the ground.)*

## Time Line Discussion

Explain to students that the time line covers key events in the United States and the world during the years from 1919 to 1929.

· What happened in 1927? *(Henry Ford introduced the Model A.)*

· How and when did Calvin Coolidge become President? *(He succeeded to the presidency on the death of Harding in 1923.)*

· Examine the time lines for both U.S. and world events. What do the events listed suggest about working conditions? *(There are many strikes, which suggests conflicts regarding fair pay and better working conditions.)*

Angry mill workers riot after walking off the job during a strike of Tennessee textile plants.

**1919–1920** Palmer Raids

**1920** Warren G. Harding is elected president.

**1921** Sacco and Vanzetti are convicted.

**1921** Federal-Aid Road Act funds a national highway system.

**1923** President Harding dies and Calvin Coolidge becomes president.

USA
WORLD

1919   1921   1923

**1921** Chinese Communist Party is founded in Shanghai.

**1922** Benito Mussolini is appointed prime minister of Italy.

**1923** German economic crisis.

**410**   CHAPTER 12

### ECONOMIC OPPORTUNITY

During World War I, workers were not allowed to strike because the government wouldn't let anything interfere with the war effort. After the war, union membership increased, as did strikes for higher wages and better working conditions.

**See Teacher's Edition notes, p. 417.**

During the Harding administration, the United States raised taxes on imported goods. The Fordney-McCumber Tariff had far-reaching effects.

**See Teacher's Edition notes, p. 420.**

### ECONOMIC OPPORTUNITY

In the 1920s the pursuit of the American dream was paramount. Americans were buying more products and living better lives than they had been before.

**See Teacher's Edition notes, p. 425.**

### SCIENCE AND TECHNOLOGY

In the 1920s many Americans were able to buy cars. The automobile industry had a profound impact on American lives and the American landscape.

**See Teacher's Edition notes, p. 424.**

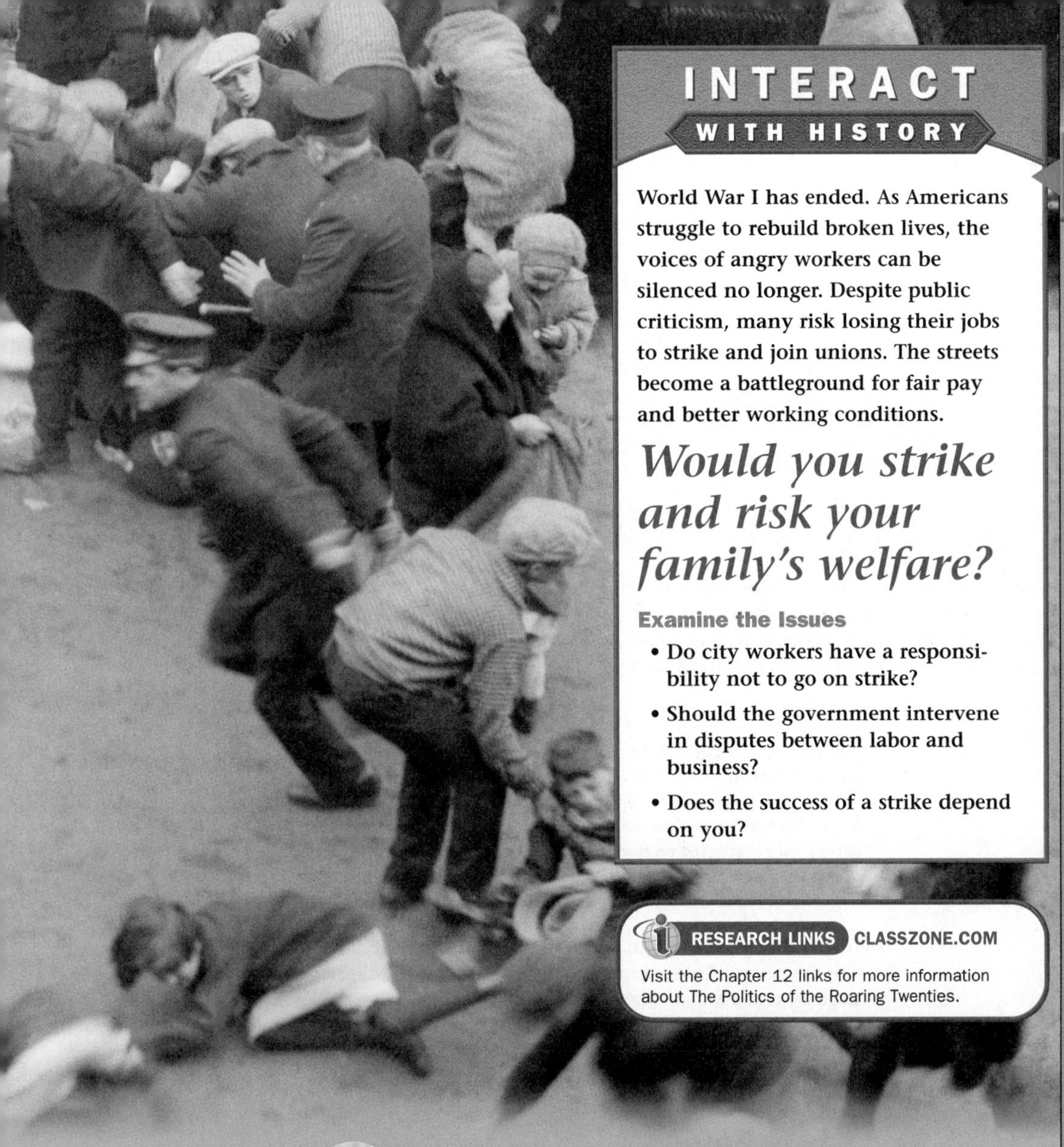

# INTERACT
## WITH HISTORY

World War I has ended. As Americans struggle to rebuild broken lives, the voices of angry workers can be silenced no longer. Despite public criticism, many risk losing their jobs to strike and join unions. The streets become a battleground for fair pay and better working conditions.

## Would you strike and risk your family's welfare?

### Examine the Issues

- Do city workers have a responsibility not to go on strike?
- Should the government intervene in disputes between labor and business?
- Does the success of a strike depend on you?

**RESEARCH LINKS** CLASSZONE.COM

Visit the Chapter 12 links for more information about The Politics of the Roaring Twenties.

# INTERACT
## WITH HISTORY

### Objectives

- To motivate students to examine the labor issues of the 1920s
- To help students understand the effects of labor organizing and strikes on the participants and the economy

### Examine the Issues

1. Have students consider the rights of workers versus the needs of all citizens for essential services like transit, police and fire protection, and sanitation.
2. Ask students to consider the possible conflict of interest involved in government intervention in a municipal workers' strike. Point out that the government is the employer.
3. Discuss with students what happens when individual workers choose not to participate in a strike.

**1924** Calvin Coolidge is elected president.

**1925** A. Philip Randolph organizes the Brotherhood of Sleeping Car Porters.

**1927** Henry Ford introduces the Model A.

**1928** Herbert Hoover is elected president.

**1925**　**1927**　**1929**

**1924** Vladimir Ilich Lenin, founder of the Soviet Union, dies.

**1926** British laborers declare a general strike.

**1926** Hirohito becomes emperor of Japan.

**1928** Joseph Stalin launches the first of his Five-Year-Plans in the USSR.

**1929** National Revolutionary Party is organized in Mexico.

*Politics of the Roaring Twenties* **411**

---

## BOOKS FOR THE TEACHER

Boyer, Richard O., and Herbert M. Morais. *Labor's Untold Story.* New York: United Electrical, Radio and Machine Workers of America, 1955.

Daniels, Roger. *Coming to America: A History of Immigration and Ethnicity in American Life.* New York: Harper, 1990.

## BOOKS FOR THE STUDENT

Allen, Frederick Lewis. *Only Yesterday: An Informal History of the 1920's.* Harperperennial Library, 2000.

Parrish, Michael. *Anxious Decades: America in Prosperity and Depression 1920-1941.* New York: Norton, 1992.

## VIDEOS

*Los Mineros.* PBS Home Video. 1990. Documentary of Mexican-American miners.

## SOFTWARE

*Between the Wars (1918-1939).* CD-ROM. AIMS Multimedia.

## INTEGRATED TECHNOLOGY

For teacher support, visit . . .

 classzone.com

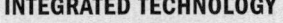

# Americans Struggle with Postwar Issues

| MAIN IDEA | WHY IT MATTERS NOW | Terms & Names |
|---|---|---|
| A desire for normality after the war and a fear of communism and "foreigners" led to postwar isolationism. | Americans today continue to debate political isolationism and immigration policy. | •nativism  •isolationism  •communism  •anarchists  •Sacco and Vanzetti  •quota system  •John L. Lewis |

 U.S. History 5A, 5B, 7A, 8A, 8B, 9A, 10B, 19A, 19B, 20A, 24B, 24C, 24G, 24H, 25A, 25B, 25C, 25D, 26A, 26B

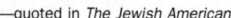 One American's Story

During the 1920s and 1930s, Irving Fajans, a department store sales clerk in New York City, tried to persuade fellow workers to join the Department Store Employees Union. He described some of the techniques union organizers used.

**A PERSONAL VOICE** IRVING FAJANS

" If you were caught distributing . . . union literature around the job you were instantly fired. We thought up ways of passing leaflets without the boss being able to pin anybody down. . . . We . . . swiped the key to the toilet paper dispensers in the washroom, took out the paper, and substituted printed slips of just the right size! We got a lot of new members that way—It appealed to their sense of humor. "

—quoted in *The Jewish Americans*

During the war, workers' rights had been suppressed. In 1919, workers began to cry out for fair pay and better working conditions. Tensions arose between labor and management, and a rash of labor strikes broke out across the country. The public, however, was not supportive of striking workers. Many citizens longed to get back to normal, peaceful living—they felt resentful of anyone who caused unrest.

▲ Irving Fajans organized department store workers in their efforts to gain better pay and working conditions during the 1920s.

## 1 Postwar Trends

World War I had left much of the American public exhausted. The debate over the League of Nations had deeply divided America. Further, the Progressive Era had caused numerous wrenching changes in American life. The economy, too, was in a difficult state of adjustment. Returning soldiers faced unemployment or took their old jobs away from women and minorities. Also, the cost of living had doubled. Farmers and factory workers suffered as wartime orders diminished.

Many Americans responded to the stressful conditions by becoming fearful of outsiders. A wave of **nativism**, or prejudice against foreign-born people, swept the nation. So, too, did a belief in **isolationism**, a policy of pulling away from involvement in world affairs.

412 CHAPTER 12

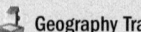
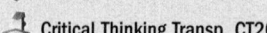
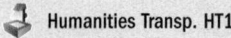

# 1 Fear of Communism

One perceived threat to American life was the spread of **communism**, an economic and political system based on a single-party government ruled by a dictatorship. In order to equalize wealth and power, Communists would put an end to private property, substituting government ownership of factories, railroads, and other businesses.

**THE RED SCARE** The panic in the United States began in 1919, after revolutionaries in Russia overthrew the czarist regime. Vladimir I. Lenin and his followers, or Bolsheviks ("the majority"), established a new Communist state. Waving their symbolic red flag, Communists, or "Reds," cried out for a worldwide revolution that would abolish capitalism everywhere.

A Communist Party formed in the United States. Seventy-thousand radicals joined, including some from the Industrial Workers of the World (IWW). When several dozen bombs were mailed to government and business leaders, the public grew fearful that the Communists were taking over. U.S. Attorney General A. Mitchell Palmer took action to combat this "Red Scare."

## A PERSONAL VOICE A. MITCHELL PALMER

" The blaze of revolution was sweeping over every American institution of law and order . . . . eating its way into the homes of the American workman, its sharp tongues of revolutionary heat . . . licking the altars of the churches, leaping into the belfry of the school bell, crawling into the sacred corners of American homes, . . . burning up the foundations of society. "

—"The Case Against the Reds"

**THE PALMER RAIDS** In August 1919, Palmer appointed J. Edgar Hoover as his special assistant. Palmer, Hoover, and their agents hunted down suspected Communists, socialists, and **anarchists**—people who opposed any form of government. They trampled people's civil rights, invading private homes and offices and jailing suspects without allowing them legal counsel. Hundreds of foreign-born radicals were deported without trials.

But Palmer's raids failed to turn up evidence of a revolutionary conspiracy— or even explosives. Many thought Palmer was just looking for a campaign issue to gain support for his presidential aspirations. Soon, the public decided that Palmer didn't know what he was talking about. **A**

**SACCO AND VANZETTI** Although short-lived, the Red Scare fed people's suspicions of foreigners and immigrants. This nativist attitude led to ruined reputations and wrecked lives. The two most famous victims of this attitude were Nicola Sacco and Bartolomeo Vanzetti, a shoemaker and a fish peddler. Both were Italian immigrants and anarchists; both had evaded the draft during World War I.

In May 1920, **Sacco and Vanzetti** were arrested and charged with the robbery and murder of a factory paymaster and his guard in South Braintree, Massachusetts. Witnesses had said the criminals appeared to be Italians. The accused asserted their innocence and provided alibis; the evidence against them was circumstantial; and the presiding judge made prejudicial remarks. Nevertheless, the jury still found them guilty and sentenced them to death.

---

*A. Answer* He believed that a Communist revolution was imminent in the United States, and he needed an issue on which to campaign for the 1920 Democratic presidential nomination.

**MAIN IDEA**

**Analyzing Motives**
**A** Why did Attorney General A. Mitchell Palmer launch a series of raids against suspected Communists?

---

### ECONOMIC BACKGROUND

#### ROOTS OF COMMUNISM

The first Communist government in Russia was based on the teachings of Karl Marx and Friedrich Engels. In 1848, these two had published *The Communist Manifesto*, which outlined a theory of class struggle. It said that a class that had economic power also had social and political power.

It also said that two classes, the "haves" and the "have-nots," have struggled for control throughout history. During the Industrial Revolution, Communists believed, the struggle was between the capitalists, who owned capital—land, money, and machinery— and workers, who owned only their labor. Marx and Engels urged workers to seize political power and the means of production. Ultimately, they believed, laborers would overthrow capitalism in all industrialized nations.

---

### ECONOMIC BACKGROUND

#### Roots of Communism

The American Communist Party firmly believed in the possibility of revolution in the United States. Ambitious politicians used the perceived threat of communist revolt as justification for their attacks on radicals and labor activists. Such attacks, which created a climate of fear and repression, served to maintain the status quo.

### More About . . .

#### The Palmer Raids

The Palmer Raids occurred between 1919 and 1920. After Palmer's house was bombed on June 2, 1919, the raids intensified. Union offices and headquarters of communist and socialist organizations were the targets. Attorney General Palmer also focused on aliens, since they had fewer rights. The most famous raid took place in December 1919, when 249 resident aliens were rounded up and placed on board the ship *Buford*, headed for the Soviet Union.

Electronic Library of Primary Resources
· Instructions Regarding Conduct on Raids, 1920 by U.S. Dept. of Justice.

---

*Politics of the Roaring Twenties* **413**

---

#### Researching the Roots of the Red Scare

Have students use Internet and library resources to research one of the following topics found in the section:
· Communism in America      · media coverage of significant events
· postwar labor conditions     · the Palmer raids

Once they have gathered information on their chosen topic, have them pursue a chosen angle or form a hypothesis. For instance, students might wish to trace the development of the FBI out of the antiradical division of the Justice Department under J. Edgar Hoover.

Have students narrow their topic by answering questions like those at the right.

 Mini-Lesson 1: SS11 1(US5.A)

#### Questions to narrow the topic:

1. What do I find most interesting about my topic?
2. What do I find mysterious or confusing about my topic?
3. If I had been alive at the time, what position would I have taken on my topic?

Have students write a newspaper column or editorial on their topic, taking a position they might have held.

## History Through *Art*

### Sacco and Vanzetti

The Sacco and Vanzetti case aroused protests all over the world. After the announcement of the guilty verdict, violent protests broke out. In Paris, a bomb exploded at the house of the American ambassador. In Rome, a mob threatened the American embassy. Some protests were peaceful. In Uruguay, citizens mounted a general strike and a boycott of American goods. *(Shahn depicts Governor Fuller as a smaller figure to show his disrespect for the governor and, by contrast, his respect for Sacco and Vanzetti.)*

 Humanities Transparencies HT19
· *The Passion of Sacco and Vanzetti* by Ben Shahn

---

## More About . . .

### Ben Shahn

Ben Shahn (1898–1969) was outraged at the brazen injustice of the Sacco and Vanzetti case. Shahn created a series of 23 protest paintings. His works helped galvanize support for Sacco and Vanzetti and made the artist famous. Ben Shahn went on to have a distinguished career as a painter and graphic artist.

---

## Instruct: Objective ❷

### Limiting Immigration

TAKS SS11 1(US5.A)

· Why did the United States limit immigration?
· How did the anti-immigration sentiment strengthen the Ku Klux Klan's attack on ethnic and religious minorities?
· How did the Ku Klux Klan regard foreign-born Americans?
· What was the quota system?

 In-Depth Resources: Unit 4
· Guided Reading, p. 1

 Electronic Library of Primary Sources
· from A Letter Regarding Immigration, 1924 by L. Marshall

---

## History Through Art

### SACCO AND VANZETTI (1932)

The painting by Ben Shahn shows (*right to left*) Nicola Sacco, Bartolomeo Vanzetti, a miniature Governor Fuller, and a group of Sacco and Vanzetti supporters. **Why do you think Shahn depicts Sacco and Vanzetti as so much larger than Governor Fuller?**

---

Protests rang out in the United States, Europe, and Latin America. Many people thought Sacco and Vanzetti were mistreated because of their radical beliefs; others asserted it was because they were immigrants. The poet Edna St. Vincent Millay donated proceeds from her poem "Justice Denied in Massachusetts" to their defense. She personally appealed to Governor Fuller of Massachusetts for their lives. However, after reviewing the case and interviewing Vanzetti, the governor decided to let the executions go forward. The two men died in the electric chair on August 23, 1927. Before he was executed, Vanzetti made a statement.

### A PERSONAL VOICE BARTOLOMEO VANZETTI

"In all my life I have never stole, never killed, never spilled blood. . . . We were tried during a time . . . when there was hysteria of resentment and hate against the people of our principles, against the foreigner. . . . I am suffering because I am a radical and indeed I am a radical; I have suffered because I was an Italian and indeed I am an Italian. . . . If you could execute me two times, and if I could be reborn two other times, I would live again to do what I have done already." **B**

—quoted in *The National Experience*

In 1961, new ballistics tests showed that the pistol found on Sacco was in fact the one used to murder the guard. However, there was no proof that Sacco had actually pulled the trigger.

## ❷ Limiting Immigration

During the wave of nativist sentiment, "Keep America for Americans" became the prevailing attitude. Anti-immigrant attitudes had been growing in the United States ever since the 1880s, when new immigrants began arriving from southern and eastern Europe. Many of these immigrants were willing to work for low wages in industries such as coal mining, steel production, and textiles. But after World War I, the need for unskilled labor in the United States decreased. Nativists believed that because the United States now had fewer unskilled jobs available, fewer immigrants should be let into the country. Nativist feelings were fueled by

**B. Answer**
Because he was a political radical and a foreigner

**MAIN IDEA**

**Analyzing Events**
**B** According to Vanzetti, what were the reasons for his imprisonment?

**Background**
On August 23, 1977, exactly 50 years after the executions, Massachusetts governor Michael Dukakis declared that Sacco and Vanzetti had not been given a fair trial.

**414** CHAPTER 12

---

**B** BLOCK SCHEDULING

### Staging a Retrial for Sacco and Vanzetti

**Class Time** Two class periods

**Task** Researching the Sacco and Vanzetti case and staging a trial for the accused

**Purpose** To study the historical record of the Sacco and Vanzetti case and develop a feeling for the issues involved

**Directions** During the first day, and as homework, have students research the case and take notes on the evidence presented at the trial.

During the second class period, assign groups to the prosecution and defense teams, and appoint a judge and jury.

Stage a retrial of the accused. Allow both teams to present their evidence. Encourage the judge to make sure all arguments are heard. Once the jury has heard all the evidence, have them render their verdict.

Conduct a post-trial discussion in which all participants explain what the experience was like for them.

 Integrated Assessment
· Rubric 3

the fact that some of the people involved in postwar labor disputes were immigrant anarchists and socialists, who many Americans believed were actually Communists. Racist ideas like those expressed by Madison Grant, an anthropologist at the American Museum of Natural History in New York City, fed people's attitudes.

### A PERSONAL VOICE MADISON GRANT

" The result of unlimited immigration is showing plainly in the rapid decline in the birth rate of native Americans . . . [who] will not bring children into the world to compete in the labor market with the Slovak, the Italian, the Syrian and the Jew. The native American is too proud to mix socially with them. "

—quoted in *United States History: Ideas in Conflict*

**Vocabulary**
**bigot:** a person who is intolerant of any creed, race, religion, or political belief that differs from his own

**THE KLAN RISES AGAIN** As a result of the Red Scare and anti-immigrant feelings, different groups of bigots used anti-communism as an excuse to harass any group unlike themselves. One such group was the Ku Klux Klan (KKK). The KKK was devoted to "100 percent Americanism." By 1924, KKK membership reached 4.5 million "white male persons, native-born gentile citizens." The Klan also believed in keeping blacks "in their place," destroying saloons, opposing unions, and driving Roman Catholics, Jews, and foreign-born people out of the country. KKK members were paid to recruit new members into their world of secret rituals and racial violence. Though the Klan dominated state politics in many states, by the end of the decade its criminal activity led to a decrease in power. **C**

▲ In 1925, nearly 60,000 Ku Klux Klan members marched along Pennsylvania Avenue in Washington, D.C.

**MAIN IDEA**

**Analyzing Issues**
**C** What were the main goals of the Ku Klux Klan at this time?

*C. Possible Answer* To keep America under the control of white, native-born males; to get rid of other groups, including Roman Catholics, Jews, and foreign-born people, and radicals; to oppose union organizers; to help enforce prohibition.

**THE QUOTA SYSTEM** From 1919 to 1921, the number of immigrants had grown almost 600 percent—from 141,000 to 805,000 people. Congress, in response to nativist pressure, decided to limit immigration from certain countries, namely those in southern and eastern Europe.

The Emergency Quota Act of 1921 set up a **quota system**. This system established the maximum number of people who could enter the United States from each foreign country. The goal of the quota system was to cut sharply European immigration to the United States. As the charts on page 416 show, the system achieved that goal.

As amended in 1924, the law limited immigration from each European nation to 2 percent of the number of its nationals living in the United States in 1890. This provision discriminated against people from eastern and southern Europe—mostly Roman Catholics and Jews—who had not started coming to the United States in large numbers until after 1890. Later, the base year was shifted to 1920. However, the law also reduced the total number of persons to be admitted in any one year to 150,000.

In addition, the law prohibited Japanese immigration, causing much ill will between the two nations. Japan—which had faithfully kept the Gentlemen's Agreement to limit emigration to the United States, negotiated by Theodore Roosevelt in 1907—expressed anger over the insult.

*Politics of the Roaring Twenties* **415**

**More About . . .**

**The Ku Klux Klan**
The leader of the Ku Klux Klan was known as the Imperial Wizard. The chief organizer was the Imperial Kleagle. Kleagles kept four dollars of the ten-dollar initiation fee they collected from new recruits. Local factions were called Domains and were run by Grand Goblins. Several Domains made up a Realm, which was led by a King Kleagle.

**History from Visuals**

**Interpreting a Photograph**
Remind students that the First Amendment protects the rights of groups to assemble freely. The Ku Klux Klan, in the 1920s, had an estimated four to five million members. It controlled politics in many areas of the country. Ask students why groups demonstrate or march in Washington, D.C. (*To make their presence and power known to political leaders; to promote their political agendas.*)

---

**DIFFERENTIATING INSTRUCTION** | **STUDENTS ACQUIRING ENGLISH/ESL**

## Understanding Main Ideas and Details

Pair students who are native English speakers with students who are non-native speakers. Ask each pair to outline one paragraph in the section, "Limiting Immigration." Show students how to label the main idea with a Roman numeral and how to list supporting details with capital letters under the main idea.

An example is shown at the right.

**Outline Format**
I. Keep America for Americans
  A. Anti-immigrant attitudes
    1. growing since the 1880s
    2. resulting from the arrival of new immigrants

## History from Visuals

### Reading the Graph
The bar graph drastically illustrates the sharp reduction in European immigration between 1921 and 1929. Ask students how the reduction in immigration affected political life in the countries shown on the map. *(It might have increased political and economic tension in those countries, since people who wanted to immigrate to the United States were not able to.)*

## More About . . .

### Quota System
It is interesting to compare the economic and political climates of the 1920s and 1950s. Immigration restrictions were enacted during both decades. The Emergency Quota Act of 1921 created the quota system. In the 1950s, the McCarran-Walter Act of 1952 reinforced restrictions on immigration and established a system for screening out communists and deporting suspected subversives. Labor conflicts and anti-communist sentiments influenced the political climate in both the Twenties and the Fifties.

 Critical Thinking Transparency CT20
· Isolationist Policy of the 1920s

 Electronic Library of Primary Sources
· A Letter Regarding Immigration, 1924 by L. Marshall

Geography Transparency GT20
· European Immigration, 1820–1920

## U.S. Patterns of Immigration, 1921–1929

The map and graph below show the change in immigration patterns resulting from the Emergency Quota Act, among other factors. Hundreds of thousands of people were affected. For example, while the number of immigrants from Mexico rose from 30,758 in 1921 to 40,154 in 1929, the number of Italian immigrants dropped drastically from 222,260 in 1921 to 18,008 in 1929.

Ellis Island in Upper New York Bay was the port of entry for most European immigrants.

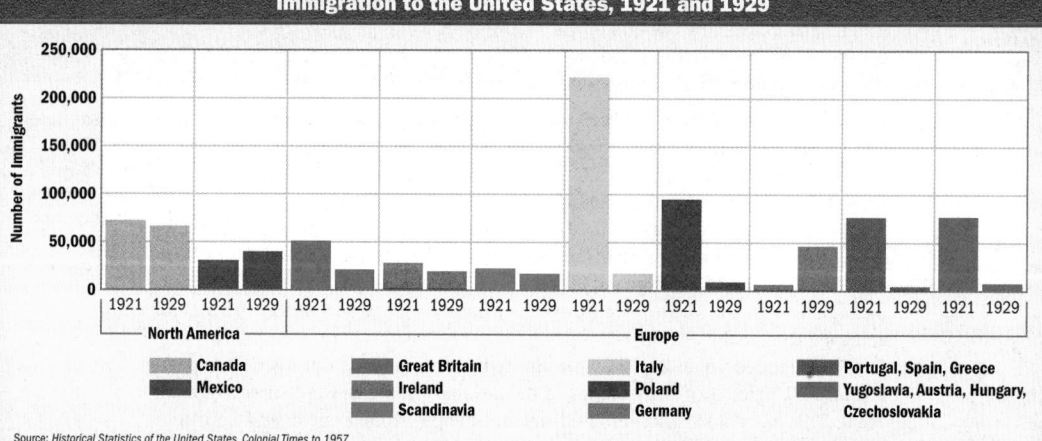

**Immigration to the United States, 1921 and 1929**

Source: *Historical Statistics of the United States, Colonial Times to 1957*

Legend:
- Canada
- Mexico
- Great Britain
- Ireland
- Scandinavia
- Italy
- Poland
- Germany
- Portugal, Spain, Greece
- Yugoslavia, Austria, Hungary, Czechoslovakia

**SKILLBUILDER** Interpreting Graphs
1. Which geographical areas show the sharpest decline in immigration to the U.S. between 1921 and 1929? What are the only areas to register an increase in immigration to the U.S.?
2. How did the quota system affect where immigrants came from?

 **SEE SKILLBUILDER HANDBOOK, PAGE R28.**

---

### Family Mobility

**Class Time** 45 minutes

**Task** Creating a chart showing American states and foreign countries in which students' families originally lived

**Purpose** To describe the mobility of Americans and the diversity of the American population

**Directions** As homework, ask students to find out where their ancestors originally came from. Encourage students to explore American and overseas connections.

In class, have students list the states and/or countries in which their ancestors lived, and create a visual presentation of the results. They could use the form of a family tree, a web, or another diagram of their own design. Display the results, and have students who wish to do so discuss their diagrams.

**Developing Historical Perspective**
**D** Why did Congress make changes in immigration laws during the 1920s?

**D. Answer**
The number of immigrants increased sharply, and many Americans did not want people from foreign countries entering the nation, since some of them were anarchists and socialists and some were believed to be Communists.

*Skillbuilder Answers*
**1. Decline:** Southern and central Europe; **Increase:** Mexico and Germany.
**2.** Fewer immigrants came from southern and central Europe, except immigration from Germany increased.

**E. Answer**
Neither strike was successful: The police lost their jobs, and the steel workers won nothing.

**Comparing**
**E** Compare the results of the Boston police strike and the steel strike.

The national origins quota system did not apply to immigrants from the Western Hemisphere, however. During the 1920s, about a million Canadians and almost 500,000 Mexicans crossed the nation's borders. **D**

## A Time of Labor Unrest ③

Another severe postwar conflict formed between labor and management. During the war, the government wouldn't allow workers to strike because nothing could interfere with the war effort. The American Federation of Labor (AFL) pledged to avoid strikes.

However, 1919 saw more than 3,000 strikes during which some 4 million workers walked off the job. Employers didn't want to give raises, nor did they want employees to join unions. Some employers, either out of a sincere belief or because they saw a way to keep wages down, attempted to show that union members were planning a revolution. Employers labeled striking workers as Communists. Newspapers screamed, "Plots to Establish Communism." Three strikes in particular grabbed public attention.

**THE BOSTON POLICE STRIKE** The Boston police had not been given a raise since the beginning of World War I. Among their many grievances was that they had been denied the right to unionize. When representatives asked for a raise and were fired, the remaining policemen decided to strike. Massachusetts governor Calvin Coolidge called out the National Guard. He said, "There is no right to strike against the public safety by anybody, anywhere, any time." The strike ended but members weren't allowed to return to work; new policemen were hired instead. People praised Coolidge for saving Boston, if not the nation, from communism and anarchy. In the 1920 election he became Warren G. Harding's vice-presidential running mate.

**THE STEEL MILL STRIKE** Workers in the steel mills wanted the right to negotiate for shorter working hours and a living wage. They also wanted union recognition and collective bargaining rights. In September 1919, the U.S. Steel Corporation refused to meet with union representatives. In response, over 300,000 workers walked off their jobs. Steel companies hired strikebreakers—employees who agreed to work during the strike—and used force. Striking workers were beaten by police, federal troops, and state militias. Then the companies instituted a propaganda campaign, linking the strikers to Communists. In October 1919, negotiations between labor and management produced a deadlock. President Woodrow Wilson made a written plea to the combative "negotiators."

▲ Strikers included working women tailors who fought for improved working conditions.

**A PERSONAL VOICE** WOODROW WILSON

" At a time when the nations of the world are endeavoring to find a way of avoiding international war, are we to confess that there is no method to be found for carrying on industry except . . . the very method of war? . . . Are our industrial leaders and our industrial workers to live together without faith in each other? "

—quoted in *Labor in Crisis*

The steel strike ended in January 1920. In 1923, a report on the harsh working conditions in steel mills shocked the public. The steel companies agreed to an eight-hour day, but the steelworkers remained without a union. **E**

---

### Instruct: Objective ③

**A Time of Labor Unrest**
TAKS SS11 3(US2.B)
· Why did conflict between labor and management increase after the war?
· Why did the public turn against strikers?
· Why did labor union membership decline in the 1920s?

📖 **In-Depth Resources: Unit 4**
· Primary Sources: *from* Report on Steel Strike of 1919, p. 13
· American Lives: Ernesto Galarza, p. 18

#### More About . . .

**The Boston Police Strike**
The Boston Police strike had immediate consequences in terms of robberies and civil unrest. At first Governor Calvin Coolidge refused to intervene. It was Boston Mayor, Andrew J. Peters who called in Boston companies of the militia. Only later, once the situation was under control, did Coolidge act and send in the National Guard. Coolidge, with his defiant statement denying the right of public safety workers to strike, received publicity that propelled him into the White House.

#### Tracing Themes
**ECONOMIC OPPORTUNITY**

Discuss the factors that fostered labor unrest after the war. Ask students why workers had not been allowed to strike during the war. *(Because nothing was allowed to interfere with the war effort.)* Why did so many strikes occur after the war? *(Because wages had not kept pace with rising prices.)* Ask students whether they think labor unions harmed or helped the workers' cause. Ask them to evaluate the U.S. government's role during the 1919 strikes.

*Politics of the Roaring Twenties* **417**

---

**DIFFERENTIATING INSTRUCTION**    **LESS PROFICIENT READERS**

### Cause and Effect

Help students identify the causes and effects of labor unrest after World War I.

1. Label a two-column chart Causes and Effects.
2. List the causes of labor unrest from pages 417 and 418. Examples: low wages, long hours, unsafe working conditions.
3. List the effects. Examples: strikes, decline in union membership.

| Causes | Effects |
|---|---|
| low wages | strikes |
| long hours | |
| unsafe working conditions | |

KEY PLAYER

**JOHN LLEWELLYN LEWIS
1880–1969**

John L. Lewis was born in the lit-tle mining town of Lucas, Iowa. His family had traditionally been concerned with labor rights and benefits.

Lewis grew up with a fierce determination to fight for what he believed companies owed their employees: decent working condi-tions and a fair salary. As he said years later,

"I have pleaded your case not in the tones of a feeble mendicant [beggar] asking alms but in the thundering voice of the captain of a mighty host, demanding the rights to which free men are entitled."

---

## KEY PLAYER

### John Llewellyn Lewis

Lewis's greatest accomplishment was organizing the Congress of Industrial Organizations (CIO) for workers in mass-pro-duction industries such as the automobile, electrical, rubber, and other industries. The CIO soon had more members than the AFL, which was dedicated to its strategy of only organizing craft unions.

Why do you think Lewis needed to speak in a "thundering" voice? *(Management had a long history of treating workers unfairly. Once workers organized, they had the power of a thundering voice.)*

## Assess & Reteach

### SECTION 1 ASSESSMENT

Have students work in small groups to answer the questions in the Section Assessment. Have each group share their answer to question 3 with the class.

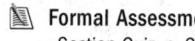 Formal Assessment
· Section Quiz, p. 231

### SELF-ASSESSMENT

Have students make a list of three or four of the key people discussed in Section 1 and the roles they played in dealing with such issues as the Red Scare, immigration, and labor unrest.

### RETEACH

Use the Guided Reading worksheet to review the section.

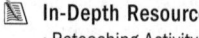 In-Depth Resources: Unit 4
· Reteaching Activity, p. 6

---

**THE COAL MINERS' STRIKE** Unionism was more success-ful in America's coalfields. In 1919, the United Mine Workers of America, organized since 1890, got a new leader—**John L. Lewis**. In protest of low wages and long workdays, Lewis called his union's members out on strike on November 1, 1919. Attorney General Palmer obtained a court order send-ing the miners back to work. Lewis then declared it over, but he quietly gave the word for it to continue. In defiance of the court order, the mines stayed closed another month. Then President Wilson appointed an arbitrator, or judge, to put an end to the dispute. The coal miners received a 27 percent wage increase, and John L. Lewis became a national hero. The miners, however, did not achieve a shorter workday and a five-day workweek until the 1930s.

**LABOR MOVEMENT LOSES APPEAL** In spite of limited gains, the 1920s hurt the labor movement badly. Over the decade, union membership dropped from more than 5 million to around 3.5 million. Membership declined for several reasons:

- much of the work force consisted of immigrants will-ing to work in poor conditions,
- since immigrants spoke a multitude of languages, unions had difficulty organizing them,
- farmers who had migrated to cities to find factory jobs were used to relying on themselves, and
- most unions excluded African Americans.

By 1929, about 82,000 African Americans—or less than 1 percent of their population—held union memberships. By contrast, just over 3 percent of all whites were union mem-bers. However, African Americans joined some unions like the mine workers', longshoremen's, and railroad porters' unions. In 1925, A. Philip Randolph founded the Brotherhood of Sleeping Car Porters to help African Americans gain a fair wage.

While America's attitude toward unions was changing, so, too, was its faith in the presidency.

---

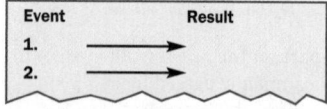 **ASSESSMENT**

**1. TERMS & NAMES**  For each term or name, write a sentence explaining its significance.

- nativism
- isolationism
- communism
- anarchists
- Sacco and Vanzetti
- quota system
- John L. Lewis

### MAIN IDEA

**2. TAKING NOTES**
In a cause-and-effect chart like the one shown, list examples of the aftereffects of World War I.

| Event | Result |
|-------|--------|
| 1. | |
| 2. | |

What event do you think was the most significant? Explain your choice.

### CRITICAL THINKING

**3. EVALUATING**
Do you think Americans were justified in their fear of radicals and foreigners in the decade following World War I? Explain your answer.
**Think About:**
- the goals of the leaders of the Russian Revolution
- the challenges facing the United States

**4. ANALYZING ISSUES**
In the various fights between management and union members, what did each side believe?

**5. DRAWING CONCLUSIONS**
What do you think the Sacco and Vanzetti case shows about America in the 1920s?

---

 **ASSESSMENT**  **Answers**

**1. TERMS & NAMES**
nativism, p.412
isolationism, p. 412
communism, p. 413
anarchists, p. 413
Sacco and Vanzetti, p. 413
quota system, p. 415
John L. Lewis, p. 418

**2. MAIN IDEA**
Answers will vary. Nativism led to the Red Scare and new immigration laws; labor strife led to strikes.

**3. EVALUATING**
**Yes:** Radicals and immigrants threatened American traditions. The Communists' desire to overthrow the capitalist system posed a threat to the American way of life. **No:** Radical movements in this coun-try were small, membership in the Communist Party was minimal, and the country had enough resources to accom-modate immigrants.

**4. ANALYZING ISSUES**
Workers believed they deserved better wages and shorter workdays. Management believed that workers had no right to strike, unions caused unrest, and cheap immigrant labor was readily available.

**5. DRAWING CONCLUSIONS**
Those years were ones of suspicion, persecution, and fear.

# The Harding Presidency

| MAIN IDEA | WHY IT MATTERS NOW | Terms & Names |
|---|---|---|
| The Harding administration appealed to America's desire for calm and peace after the war, but resulted in scandal. | The government must guard against scandal and corruption to merit public trust. | • **Warren G. Harding** • **Charles Evans Hughes** • **Fordney-McCumber Tariff** • **Ohio gang** • **Teapot Dome scandal** • **Albert B. Fall** |

**U.S. History**
5A, 5B,
8A, 15C, 19B,
24B, 24C, 24D,
24G, 25A, 25B,
25D, 26A, 26B

### One American's Story

**Warren G. Harding** was described as a good-natured man who "looked like a president ought to look." When the silver-haired Ohio senator assumed the presidency in 1921, the public yearned for what Harding described as "normalcy," or the simpler days before the Progressive Era and the Great War. His words of peace and calm comforted the healing nation.

**A PERSONAL VOICE** WARREN G. HARDING

" America's present need is not heroics, but healing; not nostrums, but normalcy; not revolution, but restoration; not agitation, but adjustment; not surgery, but serenity; not the dramatic, but the dispassionate; . . . not submergence in internationality, but sustainment in triumphant nationality."

—quoted in *The Rise of Warren Gamaliel Harding*

Despite Harding's soothing speeches, his judgment turned out to be poor. The discord among the major world powers and the conduct within his own cabinet would test his politics and his character.

▲ Warren G. Harding, shown here in 1923, looked presidential, but he is considered one of the least successful presidents.

## ① Harding Struggles for Peace

After World War I, problems surfaced relating to arms control, war debts, and the reconstruction of war-torn countries. In 1921, President Harding invited several major powers to the Washington Naval Conference. Russia was left out because of its Communist government. At the conference, Secretary of State **Charles Evans Hughes** urged that no more warships be built for ten years. He suggested that the five major naval powers—the United States, Great Britain, Japan, France, and Italy—scrap many of their battleships, cruisers, and aircraft carriers.

Conference delegates cheered, wept, and threw their hats into the air. For the first time in history, powerful nations agreed to disarm. Eventually, in 1928, fifteen

---

**OBJECTIVES**

① Contrast Harding's policy of "normalcy" with progressive era reforms.

② Identify scandals that plagued the Harding administration.

**CRITICAL THINKING**
· Summarizing, p. 420
· Evaluating Leadership, p. 420
· Making Inferences, p. 421
· Evaluating, p. 421
· Analyzing Effects, p. 421

## Focus & Motivate

Ask students how they feel after getting back from a vacation. Are they glad to get back to their normal routines? Discuss how excitement and change can be fun but can also be exhausting.

## Instruct

### Instruct: Objective ①

**Harding Struggles for Peace**
TAKS SS11 5(US24.B)
· What was Harding's attitude towards the reforms of the Progressive Era?
· Why was the Kellogg-Briand Pact ineffective?
· How did Harding's tax policy on imports affect Britain and France and the war debt issue?

In-Depth Resources: Unit 4
· Guided Reading, p. 2

Humanities Transparencies HT39

---

**PROGRAM RESOURCES**

 In-Depth Resources: Unit 4
· Guided Reading, p. 2
· Building Vocabulary, p. 4
· Skillbuilder Practice, p. 5
· Reteaching Activity, p. 7

 Reading Study Guide (English and Spanish), pp. 125–126

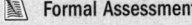 Access for Students Acquiring English/ESL
· Guided Reading (Spanish), p. 144
· Skillbuilder Practice, p. 146

 Formal Assessment
· Section Quiz, p. 232

 Integrated Assessment
· Rubrics

**INTEGRATED TECHNOLOGY**

 Humanities Transp. HT39
· *Looking Backward*

Electronic Library of Primary Sources

classzone.com

**TEXAS RESOURCES**

 TAKS Spiraled Content Review

 TAKS Practice Tests

 TAKS Practice Transparencies TT76

 TAKS Online Test Practice

### History from Visuals

**Interpreting the Photograph**

Ask students to consider the impact of sky-rocketing inflation that hit Germany in 1923. Inflation was so high that it was as if $10 and $20 bills were only nickels and dimes. Ask students how they think rich and poor people were affected by such economic conditions. *(The rich found themselves with a lot less money. The poor were left with even less. Ironically, inflation made it easier for both groups to pay off their debts.)*

### Instruct: Objective ②

**Scandal Hits Harding's Administration**

TAKS SS11 5(US24.B)

· How did Harding's friends damage his administration?

· How did the corruption scandals contribute to Harding's death?

 In-Depth Resources: Unit 4
· Guided Reading, p. 2

 Electronic Library of Primary Sources
· Senate Demands Information on Teapot Dome

### Tracing Themes

**ECONOMIC OPPORTUNITY**

Discuss the Harding administration's decision to raise taxes on imports. Ask students why the government chose to adopt the Fordney-McCumber Tariff. *(To protect American businesses from foreign competition.)*

In 1923, a German man papers his walls with money made nearly worthless by high inflation following World War I.

countries signed the Kellogg-Briand Pact, which renounced war as a national policy. However, the pact was futile, as it provided no means of enforcement.

**HIGH TARIFFS AND REPARATIONS** New conflicts arose when it came time for Britain and France to pay back the $10 billion they had borrowed from America. They could do this in two ways: by selling goods to the United States or by collecting reparations from Germany. However, in 1922, America adopted the **Fordney-McCumber Tariff**, which raised taxes on U.S. imports to 60 percent—the highest level ever. The tax protected U.S. businesses—especially in the chemical and metals industries—from foreign competition, but made it impossible for Britain and France to sell enough goods in the U.S. to repay debts. **Ⓐ**

The two countries looked to Germany, which was experiencing terrible inflation. When Germany defaulted on (failed to make) payment, French troops marched in. To avoid another war, American banker Charles G. Dawes was sent to negotiate loans. Through what came to be known as the Dawes Plan, American investors loaned Germany $2.5 billion to pay back Britain and France with annual payments on a fixed scale. Those countries then paid the United States. Thus, the United States arranged to be repaid with its own money.

The solution caused resentment all around. Britain and France considered the United States a miser for not paying a fair share of the costs of World War I. Further, the U.S. had benefited from the defeat of Germany, while Europeans had paid for the victory with millions of lives. At the same time, the United States considered Britian and France financially irresponsible.

### ② Scandal Hits Harding's Administration

On domestic issues, Harding favored a limited role for government in business affairs and in social reform. Still, he did set up the Bureau of the Budget to help run the government more efficiently, and he urged U.S. Steel to abandon the 12-hour day.

**HARDING'S CABINET** Harding appointed Charles Evans Hughes as secretary of state. Hughes later went on to become chief justice of the Supreme Court. The president made Herbert Hoover the secretary of commerce. Hoover had done a masterful job of handling food distribution and refugee problems during World War I. Andrew Mellon, one of the country's wealthiest men, became secretary of the treasury and set about drastically cutting taxes and reducing the national debt. However, the cabinet also included the so-called **Ohio gang**, the president's poker-playing cronies, who would soon cause a great deal of embarrassment. **Ⓑ**

**SCANDAL PLAGUES HARDING** The president's main problem was that he didn't understand many of the issues. He admitted as much to a secretary.

> ★ **A PERSONAL VOICE** WARREN G. HARDING
>
> "John, I can't make a . . . thing out of this tax problem. I listen to one side and they seem right, and then . . . I talk to the other side and they seem just as right. . . . I know somewhere there is an economist who knows the truth, but I don't know where to find him and haven't the sense to know him and trust him when I find him. . . . What a job!"
>
> —quoted in *Only Yesterday*

**Vocabulary**
**reparations:** payments demanded from a defeated enemy

**MAIN IDEA**

**Summarizing**
**Ⓐ** What were the reasons European countries were not paying their war debts?

*A. Possible Answers* Their economies had been weakened in the war; they were unable to raise money because U.S. exports were limited by high tariffs; Germany failed to pay them expected reparations.

*B. Possible Answers* That although he made some good appointments, his appointment of cronies from his home state showed poor judgement.

**MAIN IDEA**

**Evaluating Leadership**
**Ⓑ** What do Harding's appointments indicate about his judgment?

---

**Clarifying; Summarizing**

**Explaining the Skill** To summarize means to present a condensed version of a passage by stating the main ideas of the original version in one's own words.

**Applying the Skill** Have students read about high tariffs and reparations, identify the main points, and write a summary. The main points include the following:

Britain and France owed the United States money. They could repay the debt by selling goods or collecting reparations. Tariffs made it impossible for Britain and France to pay their debts. The Germans defaulted on war reparations. To avoid war, the United States lent Germany the money.

 In-Depth Resources: Unit 4
· Skillbuilder Practice: Clarifying; Summarizing, p. 5

Mini-Lesson 5:
S11 4(5.A)

Harding's administration began to unravel as his corrupt friends used their offices to become wealthy through graft. Charles R. Forbes, the head of the Veterans Bureau, was caught illegally selling government and hospital supplies to private companies. Colonel Thomas W. Miller, the head of the Office of Alien Property, was caught taking a bribe.

**THE TEAPOT DOME SCANDAL** The most spectacular example of corruption was the **Teapot Dome scandal.** The government had set aside oil-rich public lands at Teapot Dome, Wyoming, and Elk Hills, California, for use by the U.S. Navy. Secretary of the Interior **Albert B. Fall,** a close friend of various oil executives, managed to get the oil reserves transferred from the navy to the Interior Department. Then, Fall secretly leased the land to two private oil companies, including Henry Sinclair's Mammoth Oil Company at Teapot Dome. Although Fall claimed that these contracts were in the government's interest, he suddenly received more than $400,000 in "loans, bonds, and cash." He was later found guilty of bribery and became the first American to be convicted of a felony while holding a cabinet post. **C**

In the summer of 1923, Harding declared, "I have no trouble with my enemies. . . . But my friends . . . they're the ones that keep me walking the floor nights!" Shortly thereafter, on August 2, 1923, he died suddenly, probably from a heart attack or stroke.

Americans sincerely mourned their good-natured president. The crimes of the Harding administration were coming to light just as Vice-President Calvin Coolidge assumed the Presidency. Coolidge, a respected man of integrity, helped to restore people's faith in their government and in the Republican Party. The next year, Coolidge was elected President.

*C. Answer* The government lost revenue when veterans' hospitals overcharged it; in the Teapot Dome scandal, public oil reserves were leased for private gain.

**MAIN IDEA**

**Making Inferences**
**C** How did the scandals of the Harding administration hurt the country economically?

▲
The elephant, shaped like a teapot here, is the symbol of the Republican Party (Grand Old Party). The cartoonist implies that Republicans were responsible for the Teapot Dome scandal.

---

**SECTION 2 ASSESSMENT**

1. **TERMS & NAMES** For each term or name, write a sentence explaining its significance.
   - Warren G. Harding
   - Charles Evans Hughes
   - Fordney-McCumber Tariff
   - Ohio gang
   - Teapot Dome scandal
   - Albert B. Fall

**MAIN IDEA**

2. **TAKING NOTES**
List five significant events from this section and their effects, using a table like the one shown.

| Event | Effects |
|-------|---------|
| 1. | |
| 2. | |

Which event benefited the country the most? Why?

**CRITICAL THINKING**

3. **MAKING INFERENCES**
How do you think the Harding administration viewed the role of America in world affairs? Support your response with examples from the text.

4. **EVALUATING**
How successful was Harding in fulfilling his campaign pledge of returning the country to "normalcy"? Support your opinion with specific examples.

5. **ANALYZING EFFECTS**
How do you think the post-war feelings in America influenced the election of 1920? **Think About:**
   • the desire for normalcy
   • Harding's image
   • the issues Americans wanted to focus on

*Politics of the Roaring Twenties* **421**

---

Answers **ASSESSMENT**

**1. TERMS & NAMES**
Warren G. Harding, p.419
Charles Evans Hughes, p. 419
Fordney-McCumber Tariff, p.420
Ohio gang, p. 420
Teapot Dome scandal, p.421
Albert B. Fall, p. 421

**2. MAIN IDEA**
Events: Kellogg-Briand Pact, Fordney-McCumber Tariff, Dawes Plan, Quota Act, Teapot Dome scandal.
Effects: Kellogg-Briand Pact: naval disarmament, Fordney-McCumber Tariff: raised tariffs to highest level, Dawes Plan: U.S. loans to Germany repay reparations, Quota Act: immigration restricted, Teapot Dome scandal: government corruption

**3. MAKING INFERENCES**
Isolationist: high tariffs, Quota Act and failure to enforce international agreements, limited United States involvement with other nations. Peacemaker: urging international disarmament.

**4. EVALUATING**
Harding had some success at restoring normalcy with the Kellogg-Briand Pact. High tariffs, immigration restrictions, and government corruption created an atmosphere of distrust that was not normal.

**5. ANALYZING EFFECTS**
Perhaps Harding's call for peace and normalcy swayed public opinion.

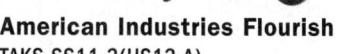

# SECTION 3

# The Business of America

| MAIN IDEA | WHY IT MATTERS NOW | Terms & Names |
|---|---|---|
| Consumer goods fueled the business boom of the 1920s as America's standard of living soared. | Business, technological, and social developments of the 1920s launched the era of modern consumerism. | • Calvin Coolidge  • urban sprawl  • installment plan |

### One American's Story

In 1927, the last Model T Ford—number 15,077,033—rolled off the assembly line. On December 2, some 1 million New Yorkers mobbed show rooms to view the new Model A. One striking difference between the two models was that customers could order the Model A in such colors as "Arabian sand" and "Niagara blue"; the old Model T had come only in black. A Ford spokesman explained some additional advantages of the new automobile.

 TAKS
Mini-Lesson 2:
SS11 3(US13.A)

▲ The Model A was a more luxurious car than the Model T. It was introduced at $495. Model T's were selling for $290.

### A PERSONAL VOICE

❝ Good-looking as that car is, its performance is better than its appearance. We don't brag about it, but it has done seventy-one miles an hour. It will ride along a railroad track without bouncing. . . . It's the smoothest thing you ever rode in. ❞

—a Ford salesman quoted in *Flappers, Bootleggers, "Typhoid Mary," and the Bomb*

The automobile became the backbone of the American economy in the 1920s (and remained such until the 1970s). It profoundly altered the American landscape and American society, but it was only one of several factors in the country's business boom of the 1920s.

## **1** American Industries Flourish

 U.S. History
5B, 8A, 8B, 9A, 10A, 13A, 19A, 19B, 20D, 22A, 22C, 23A, 23B, 24B, 24H, 25A, 25B, 25C, 25D, 26A, 26B

The new president, **Calvin Coolidge**, fit into the pro-business spirit of the 1920s very well. It was he who said, "The chief business of the American people is business. . . . The man who builds a factory builds a temple—the man who works there worships there." Both Coolidge and his Republican successor, Herbert Hoover, favored government policies that would keep taxes down and business profits up, and give businesses more available credit in order to expand. Their goal was to keep government interference in business to a minimum and to allow private enterprise to flourish. For most of the 1920s, this approach seemed to work. Coolidge's administration continued to place high tariffs on foreign imports,

*Skillbuilder Answers*
**1.** Possible Answers: With a Southwestern route, engineers did not have to build a road across the Rocky Mountains. Also, Route 66 would help open up the sparsely populated Southwest to the rest of the country and thus spur population growth and economic development. **2.** Cities along the route grew as traffic brought more business to the area.

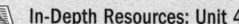
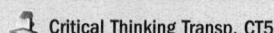

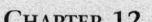

which helped American manufacturers. Reducing income taxes meant that people had more money in their pockets. Wages were rising because of new technology and so was productivity.

**THE IMPACT OF THE AUTOMOBILE** The automobile literally changed the American landscape. Its most visible effect was the construction of paved roads suitable for driving in all weather. One such road was the legendary Route 66, which provided a route for people trekking west from Chicago to California. Many, however, settled in towns along the route. In addition to the changing landscape, architectural styles also changed, as new houses typically came equipped with a garage or carport and a driveway—and a smaller lawn as a result. The automobile also launched the rapid construction of gasoline stations, repair shops, public garages, motels, tourist camps, and shopping centers. The first automatic traffic signals began blinking in Detroit in the early 1920s. The Holland Tunnel, the first underwater tunnel designed specifically for motor vehicles, opened in 1927 to connect New York City and Jersey City, New Jersey. The Woodbridge Cloverleaf, the first cloverleaf intersection, was built in New Jersey in 1929. **A**

The automobile liberated the isolated rural family, who could now travel to the city for shopping and entertainment. It also gave families the opportunity to vacation in new and faraway places. It allowed both women and young people to become more independent through increased mobility. It allowed workers to live

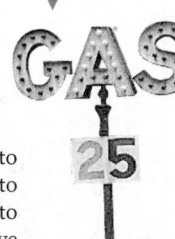

Gas for cars was cheap and plentiful. Gas stations sprung up on Rt. 66 charging 25¢ per gallon.

*A. Possible Answers* Roads were paved, and shopping centers and other services for cars were built; people commuted to work, and urban sprawl developed; regional differences diminished.

**MAIN IDEA**

**Analyzing Effects**

**A** What was the impact of the automobile?

**More About . . .**

**Impact of the Automobile**
Prior to the advent of the automobile, men and women had few places for private meetings. Young people enjoyed new freedom with access to automobiles. A variety of courting customs became popular, such as taking long drives, going out on the town, or "parking" in a secluded location.

**Route 66**

Commissioned on the cusp of the Depression, Route 66 symbolized the road to opportunity. Also known as "the Mother Road," it became the subject of countless songs, films, books and legends.
**1916** Federal-Aid Road Act sets up highway program with the federal government paying half the cost of states' highway construction.
**1921** Highway construction in 11 western states begins under administration of Bureau of Public Roads.
**1926** U.S. Highway 66, which would run 2,448 miles from Chicago to Los Angeles, California, is established.

Roadside stands offering food, drink, and other items appeared in increasing numbers.

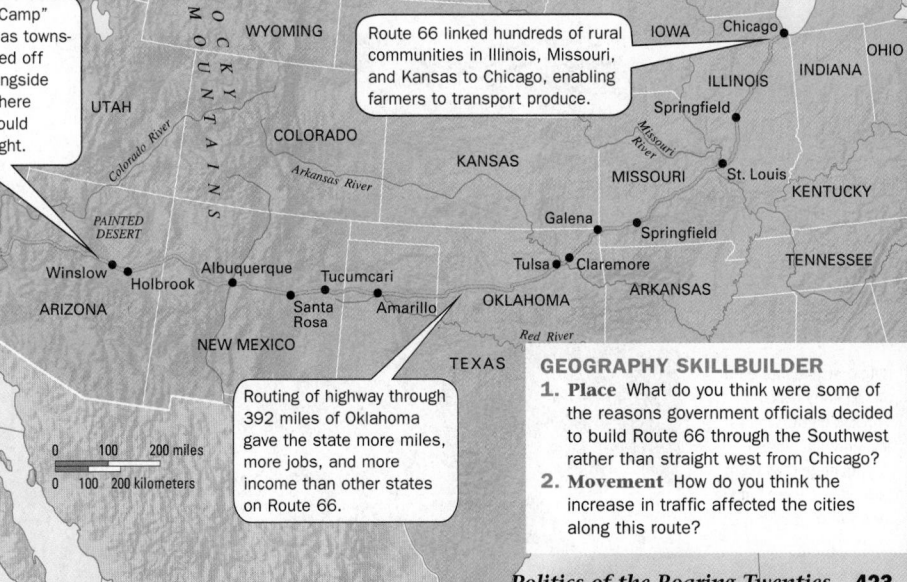

The "Auto Camp" developed as townspeople roped off spaces alongside the road where travelers could sleep at night.

Route 66 linked hundreds of rural communities in Illinois, Missouri, and Kansas to Chicago, enabling farmers to transport produce.

Routing of highway through 392 miles of Oklahoma gave the state more miles, more jobs, and more income than other states on Route 66.

**GEOGRAPHY SKILLBUILDER**
1. **Place** What do you think were some of the reasons government officials decided to build Route 66 through the Southwest rather than straight west from Chicago?
2. **Movement** How do you think the increase in traffic affected the cities along this route?

**HISTORY from VISUALS**

**Interpreting Infographics**
Ask students in which direction they think most traffic flowed on Route 66.
*(People looking for a new start were likely to travel from east to west.)*

**Extension** Have students plan a road trip following Route 66. They should include a list of sites to visit along the way.

**DIFFERENTIATING INSTRUCTION** **GIFTED & TALENTED STUDENTS**  classzone.com

**Early Car Companies**

Have students use the Internet to research car companies that thrived in the 1920s, but have since gone out of business. Some examples: Pierce-Arrow, Packard, and Hudson. Have students choose a car and put together a multimedia profile that includes a picture of the car and information on why the company was not successful in the long run.

**Rubrics**
The multimedia profile should . . .
· Provide an in-depth view of the car company
· Utilize two or more media
· Include an analysis of the reasons for the failure of the company

 Integrated Assessment
· Rubric 6

**KEY PLAYER**

**CALVIN COOLIDGE**
**1872–1933**

Stepping into office in 1923, the tightlipped Vermonter was respected for his solemnity and wisdom. Coolidge supported American business and favored what he called "a constructive economy."

Known for his strength of character, Coolidge forced the resignation of Attorney General Daugherty and other high officials who had created scandal in office.

Shortly after Coolidge was elected, his son died of blood poisoning. Coolidge later wrote, "The power and the glory of the presidency went with him." When he decided not to seek reelection in 1928, Coolidge stumped the nation. Keeping in character, he said, "Goodby, I have had a very enjoyable time in Washington."

miles from their jobs, resulting in **urban sprawl** as cities spread in all directions. The automobile industry also provided an economic base for such cities as Akron in Ohio, and Detroit, Dearborn, Flint, and Pontiac in Michigan. The industry drew people to such oil-producing states as California and Texas. The automobile even became a status symbol—both for individual families and to the rest of the world. In their work *Middletown*, the social scientists Robert and Helen Lynd noted one woman's comment: "I'll go without food before I'll see us give up the car."

The auto industry symbolized the success of the free enterprise system and the Coolidge era. Nowhere else in the world could people with little money own their own automobile. By the late 1920s, around 80 percent of all registered motor vehicles in the world were in the United States—about one automobile for every five people. The humorist Will Rogers remarked to Henry Ford, "It will take a hundred years to tell whether you helped us or hurt us, but you certainly didn't leave us where you found us." **B**

**THE YOUNG AIRPLANE INDUSTRY** Automobiles weren't the only form of transportation taking off. The airplane industry began as a mail carrying service for the U.S. Post Office. Although the first flight in 1918 was a disaster, a number of successful flights soon established the airplane as a peacetime means of transportation. With the development of weather forecasting, planes began carrying radios and navigational instruments. Henry Ford made a trimotor airplane in 1926. Transatlantic flights by Charles Lindbergh and Amelia Earhart helped to promote cargo and commercial airlines. In 1927, the Lockheed Company produced a single-engine plane, the Vega. These were two of the most popular transport airplanes of the late 1920s. Founded in 1927, Pan American Airways inaugurated the first transatlantic passenger flights.

Flight attendants train for an early United Airlines flight. When commercial airline flights began, all flight attendants were female and white. ▶

**424** CHAPTER 12

## ② America's Standard of Living Soars

The years from 1920 to 1929 were prosperous ones for the United States. Americans owned around 40 percent of the world's wealth, and that wealth changed the way most Americans lived. The average annual income rose more than 35 percent during the period—from $522 to $705. People found it easy to spend all that extra income and then some.

**ELECTRICAL CONVENIENCES** Gasoline powered much of the economic boom of the 1920s, but the use of electricity also transformed the nation. American factories used electricity to run their machines. Also, the development of an alternating electrical current made it possible to distribute electric power efficiently over longer distances. Now electricity was no longer restricted to central cities but could be transmitted to suburbs. The number of electrified households grew, although most farms still lacked power.

By the end of the 1920s, more and more homes had electric irons, while well-to-do families used electric refrigerators, cooking ranges, and toasters. Eunice Fuller Barnard listed prices for electrical appliances in a 1928 magazine article:

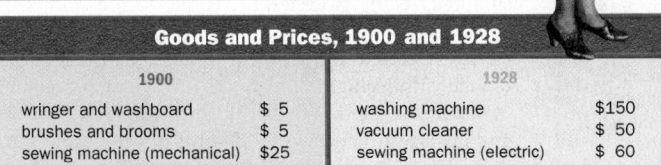

| Goods and Prices, 1900 and 1928 | | | |
|---|---|---|---|
| **1900** | | **1928** | |
| wringer and washboard | $ 5 | washing machine | $150 |
| brushes and brooms | $ 5 | vacuum cleaner | $ 50 |
| sewing machine (mechanical) | $25 | sewing machine (electric) | $ 60 |

▲
American consumers in the 1920s could purchase the latest household electrical appliances, such as a refrigerator, for as little as a dollar down and a dollar a week.

These electrical appliances made the lives of housewives easier, freed them for other community and leisure activities, and coincided with a growing trend of women working outside the home. **©**

**THE DAWN OF MODERN ADVERTISING** With new goods flooding the market, advertising agencies no longer just informed the public about products and prices. Now they hired psychologists to study how to appeal to people's desire for youthfulness, beauty, health, and wealth. Results were impressive. The slogan "Say it with flowers" doubled florists' business between 1912 and 1924. "Reach for a Lucky instead of a sweet" lured weight-conscious Americans to cigarettes and away from candy. Brand names became familiar from coast to coast, and luxury items now seemed like necessities.

One of those "necessities" was mouthwash. A 1923 Listerine advertisement aimed to convince readers that without Listerine a person ran the risk of having halitosis—bad breath—and that the results could be a disaster.

### A PERSONAL VOICE

"She was a beautiful girl and talented too. She had the advantages of education and better clothes than most girls of her set. She possessed that culture and poise that travel brings. Yet in the one pursuit that stands foremost in the mind of every girl and woman—marriage—she was a failure."

—Listerine Advertisement

Businesspeople applied the power of advertising to other areas of American life. Across the land, they met for lunch with fellow members of such service organizations as Rotary, Kiwanis, and the Lions. As one observer noted, they sang

*Politics of the Roaring Twenties* **425**

---

**Instruct: Objective ②**

**America's Standard of Living Soars**
TAKS SS11 1(US23.D)

· What role did credit play in the American economy in the 1920s?
· What role did mass advertising play in the American economy in the 1920s?

📖 In-Depth Resources: Unit 4
· Guided Reading, p. 3

🖨 Critical Thinking Transparency CT54
· Consumer Spending Power

---

**Tracing Themes**

**ECONOMIC OPPORTUNITY**

During the prosperous years of the 1920s, many Americans believed they were living a better life than their ancestors. Electricity and appliances made life easier and more pleasant. The introduction of the installment plan made access to goods once reserved for the rich a possibility for many not-so-wealthy Americans.

---

TAKS
Mini-Lesson 3:
S11 3(US23.A)

**MAIN IDEA**

**Forming Generalizations**
**©** How did the use of electricity affect Americans' lifestyle?

**C. Possible Answers**
**Advantages:** People could buy many goods over a period of time with little money down at low interest.
**Disadvantages:** People easily went too far into debt without really thinking about it.

---

**ACTIVITY** **LINK TO POPULAR CULTURE**

ⓑ **BLOCK SCHEDULING**

## Advertising Messages

**Class Time** One class period

**Task** Analyzing advertisements to determine the underlying messages

**Purpose** To understand how advertisements appeal to people's emotions

**Directions** Have students work in small groups to review advertisements found in print media or on television. Have students pay attention to how the product is displayed, the people and/or setting, colors, and any other noticeable features. Have them place stick-on notes next to each element that they identify and explain its purpose.

📖 Integrated Assessment
· Rubric 2

*The Business of America* **425**

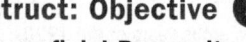

### ANOTHER PERSPECTIVE

**THE NEEDY**

While income rose for many Americans in the 1920s, it did not rise for everyone. Industries such as textile and steel manufacturing made very little profit. Mining and farming actually suffered losses. Farmers were deeply in debt because they had borrowed money to buy land and machinery so that they could produce more crops during World War I. When European agriculture bounced back after the war, the demand for U.S. crops fell, as did prices. Before long there were U.S. farm surpluses.

Many American farmers could not make their loan and mortgage payments. They lost their purchasing power, their equipment, and their farms. As one South Dakota state senator remarked, "There's a saying: 'Depressions are farm led and farm fed.'"

songs, raised money for charities, and boosted the image of the businessman "as a builder, a doer of great things, yes, and a dreamer whose imagination was ever seeking out new ways of serving humanity." Many Americans idolized business during these prosperous times.

## A Superficial Prosperity ❸

During the 1920s, most Americans believed prosperity would go on forever—the average factory worker was producing 50 percent more at the end of the decade than at its start. Hadn't national income grown from $64 billion in 1921 to $87 billion in 1929? Weren't most major corporations making fortunes? Wasn't the stock market reaching new heights?

**PRODUCING GREAT QUANTITIES OF GOODS** As productivity increased, businesses expanded. There were numerous mergers of companies that manufactured automobiles, steel, and electrical equipment, as well as mergers of companies that provided public utilities. Chain stores sprouted, selling groceries, drugs, shoes, and clothes. Five-and-dime stores like Woolworth's also spread rapidly. Congress passed a law which allowed national banks to branch within cities of their main office. But as the number of businesses grew, so did the income gap between workers and managers. There were a number of other clouds in the blue sky of prosperity. The iron and railroad industries, among others, weren't very prosperous, and farms nationwide suffered losses—with new machinery, they were producing more food than was needed and this drove down food prices.

**BUYING GOODS ON CREDIT** In addition to advertising, industry provided another solution to the problem of luring consumers to purchase the mountain of goods produced each year: easy credit, or "a dollar down and a dollar forever." The **installment plan**, as it was then called, enabled people to buy goods over

**Background**
See *productivity* on page R44 in the Economics Handbook.

### Analyzing *Political Cartoons*

**"YES, SIR, HE'S MY BABY"**
This cartoon depicts Calvin Coolidge playing a saxophone labeled "Praise" while a woman representing "Big Business" dances up a storm.

**SKILLBUILDER** Analyzing Political Cartoons
1. The dancing woman is a 1920s "flapper"—independent, confident, and assertive. In what ways was big business in the 1920s comparable to the flappers?
2. What do you think the cartoonist suggests about Coolidge's relationship with big business?

 SEE SKILLBUILDER HANDBOOK, PAGE R24.

426   CHAPTER 12

---

an extended period, without having to put down much money at the time of purchase. Banks provided the money at low interest rates. Advertisers pushed the "installment plan" idea with such slogans as "You furnish the girl, we'll furnish the home" and "Enjoy while you pay."

Some economists and business owners worried that installment buying might be getting out of hand and that it was really a sign that fundamental weaknesses underlie the superficial economic prosperity. One business owner even wrote to President Coolidge and related a conversation he had overheard on a train. **D**

### A PERSONAL VOICE

"Have you an automobile yet?"

"No, I talked it over with John and he felt we could not afford one."

"Mr. Budge who lives in your town has one and they are not as well off as you are."

"Yes, I know. Their second installment came due, and they had no money to pay it."

"What did they do? Lose the car?"

"No, they got the money and paid the installment."

"How did they get the money?"

"They sold the cook-stove."

"How could they get along without a cook-stove?"

"They didn't. They bought another on the installment plan."

—a business owner quoted in *The Time of Silent Cal*

Still, most Americans focused their attention on the present, with little concern for the future. What could possibly go wrong with the nation's economy? The decade of the 1920s had brought about many technological and economic changes. And yet the Coolidge era was built on paradox—the president stood for economy and a frugal way of life, but he was favored by a public who had thrown all care to the wind. Life definitely seemed easier and more enjoyable for hundreds of thousands of Americans. From the look of things, there was little warning of what was to come. **E**

**MAIN IDEA**

**Analyzing Issues**

**D** What were the main advantage and disadvantage of buying on credit?

*D. Answer*
**Advantage:** People could buy goods they could not otherwise afford.
**Disadvantage:** People could go far into debt without realizing it.

**MAIN IDEA**

**Predicting Effects**

**E** How do you think the changes in spending will affect the economy?

*E. Possible Answer*
The economy may falter when consumers are unable to meet their credit obligations.

---

**3 ASSESSMENT**

1. **TERMS & NAMES** For each term or name, write a sentence explaining its significance.
   • Calvin Coolidge          • urban sprawl          • installment plan

**MAIN IDEA**

2. **TAKING NOTES**
Re-create the web below on your paper and fill it in with events that illustrate the central idea.

Technology & Business Changes of the 1920s

Choose one event from the web and explain its significance in the 1920s.

**CRITICAL THINKING**

3. **EVALUATING**
Do you agree with President Coolidge's statement "The man who builds a factory builds a temple—the man who works there worships there"? Explain your answer. **Think About:**
   • the goals of business and of religion
   • the American idolization of business
   • the difference between workers and management

**Automobile Registration 1910–1930**

Source: *Historical Statistics of the United States.*

4. **INTERPRETING GRAPHS**
What trend does the graph show between 1920 and 1930? What were some of the reasons for this trend?

---

**Assess & Reteach**

**SECTION 3 ASSESSMENT**
After the students have answered the questions, discuss question 3 in class.

📄 Formal Assessment
· Section Quiz, p. 233

**SELF-ASSESSMENT**
Have students create a cluster diagram listing five characteristics of American business in the 1920s.

**RETEACH**
Use the cartoon on page 426 to review the role of business and consumer goods in the 1920s.

📄 In-Depth Resources: Unit 4
· Reteaching Activity, p. 8

---

**More About . . .**

**Easy Credit**
Credit financing played a pivotal role in the Twenties economy. Advertisers needed a mass market for automobiles, electrical appliances, and "big ticket" items. The installment plan seemed the ideal solution. Consumers bought goods with abandon and, for the most part, ignored their accumulating debts. The Twenties economy began to resemble a financial house of cards. It was precarious, at best, when disaster hit the stock market in 1929.

---

**Answers** **ASSESSMENT** **3**

**1. TERMS & NAMES**
Calvin Coolidge, p. 422
urban sprawl, p. 424
installment plan, p. 426

**2. MAIN IDEA**
Development of the automobile industry; expansion of the airline industry; invention of new electrical appliances; spread of modern advertising; use of the installment plan.

**3. EVALUATING**
**Agree:** A business and a religion both serve important needs. The workers must put their faith in the management of the factory where they work.
**Disagree:** A business is organized for financial gain. A religious institution serves the spiritual needs of its members.

**4. INTERPRETING GRAPHS**
Registration increased between 1920 and 1930. Reasons: automobile production, more roads, advertising, and automobile purchases made on the installment plan.

TRACING THEMES

## OBJECTIVES

· Examine examples of the adventurous economic spirit of Americans throughout American history.

· Explain how providing equal opportunity for all Americans remains a national challenge.

## Focus & Motivate

Ask students what risks they have taken. Have they been successful? Does failure discourage them from taking another risk?

### More About . . .

**Success and Failure**

American history is full of examples of triumph, failure, and perseverance. Thousands of families failed at homesteading in the Great Plains. Thousands of immigrants came to the United States, and some did not stay. Recently, Internet start-ups produced young millionaires, but many of these companies went out of business.

TRACING THEMES

# Economic Opportunity

The courage to take risks, the confidence to rely on one's self, the strength to stand in the face of despair, and the resourcefulness to make the most of opportunity—these are all qualities often considered distinctly American. Freedom requires individuals to discover or create opportunities for themselves. However, the government has also played a key role in distributing and creating economic opportunities.

CARAVAN OF EMIGRANTS FOR CALIFORNIA.
(Crossing the Great American Desert in Nebraska.)

## 1830s–1860s

◄ HOMESTEADING

Even before 1763, Americans looked toward the untamed west in search of greater wealth and freedom. In the 1830s, the Mormons went west to escape religious as well as economic persecution. The government helped to expand economic opportunities for whites by first clearing the land of its native inhabitants, relocating them to reservations or killing them.

As the nation claimed ownership of the land, it also gave it away. The Homestead Act of 1862 provided free of charge 160 acres of public land to anyone over the age of 21 or the head of a family who would inhabit the land for five years and improve it. This provided Americans a chance to be independent and self-sufficient if they would work hard. From 1862 until 1900, between 400,000 and 600,000 families were provided homesteads.

## 1900s

IMMIGRATION ►

While many people have come to the U.S. seeking political and religious freedom, economic opportunity has also been a key reason for immigration. In 1905, for instance, almost half a million people from Southern and Eastern Europe migrated to the United States in search of economic freedom and opportunity, as well as to escape religious persecution. Many found work at menial jobs for low pay but still were able to save enough money to eventually open their own businesses.

**428** CHAPTER 12

RECOMMENDED RESOURCES

**BOOKS**

Carter, Stephen L. *Reflections of an Affirmative Action Baby.* New York: Basic Books, 1991.

Daniels, Roger. *Coming to America: A History of Immigration and Ethnicity in American Life.* New York: Harper Collins, 1990.

Levy, Steven. *Hackers: Heroes of the Computer Revolution.* New York: Penguin Books, 2001.

Wollaston, Percy. *Homesteading: A Montana Family Album.* New York: Penguin Putnam, Inc., 1999. A family memoir.

Raban, Jonathan. *Bad Land: An American Romance.* New York: Pantheon, 1996. The story of east Montana homesteaders challenged by drought.

**VIDEOS**

*The West.* PBS Home Video, 1996. Dir. Stephen Ives. An eight-part series produced by Ken Burns.

**INTEGRATED TECHNOLOGY**

For teacher support and more information about economic opportunity in U.S. history, visit . . .

 classzone.com

# 1960s–1970s

**EQUALITY OF OPPORTUNITY AND AFFIRMATIVE ACTION ▶**

In the 1960s and 1970s, groups pressed for changes in the law to remove barriers to economic opportunity. A religious-based group, the Southern Christian Leadership Conference, was at the forefront of this movement. Laws such as the Civil Rights Act of 1964 were passed to prevent discrimination against women and racial and ethnic minorities in order to provide equity in educational and business opportunities.

Later, affirmative action programs—a term first used by Lyndon B. Johnson in 1965—opened work and educational opportunities to members of historically disadvantaged groups. Some have labeled affirmative action "reverse discrimination," while others view it as a means to counterbalance continued discrimination that the law has been unable to prevent.

# 2000s

**▼ COMPUTERS AND INTERNET STARTUPS**

In recent years, many of the brightest college students have chosen to study computer science in hopes of landing a high-paying job. Alternatively, independent-minded computer experts might become entrepreneurs—people who start and run their own businesses. For an initial period of several months to several years, an entrepreneur may work upwards of 70 or 80 hours each week, yet the business will have no income.

Since the late 1990s, both groups have increasingly looked to the Internet for opportunities. Entrepreneurs seek money-making opportunities as they develop ways to expand the capabilities of this new technology. In turn, the growth of Internet-based businesses creates jobs for people who have specialized computer skills.

---

**THINKING CRITICALLY**

**CONNECT TO HISTORY**

1. **Identifying Problems** What were some obstacles to achieving equal opportunity in each of the cases described on these two pages? Choose one of the time periods discussed and write a paragraph describing how these obstacles were overcome.

 **SEE SKILLBUILDER HANDBOOK, PAGE R5.**

**CONNECT TO TODAY**

2. **Evaluating a Business Opportunity** What economic opportunities available to you seem most promising? Discuss with your family and teachers or guidance counselor what jobs and business opportunities they think you might be suited for, then choose one and investigate it. Summarize your research by making a chart listing the pros and cons of the opportunity.

 **RESEARCH LINKS** CLASSZONE.COM

*Politics of the Roaring Twenties* **429**

## Instruct

1. How did land figure in Americans' pursuit of wealth?
2. What economic factors brought immigrants to the United States?
3. What are the goals of affirmative action?
4. How did the Internet provide new economic opportunities?

**MAKING PERSONAL CONNECTIONS**

Discuss with students the role of supply and demand in determining economic opportunity in the labor market. Ask them why they think people with computer skills are currently in demand, while those with other skills may find it harder to get a job.

---

**More About . . .**

**Internet Start-Ups and Downs**

Following a meteoric rise in "dot.coms"—businesses on the Internet—in the 1990s, the early years of new century brought the "dot.bombs"—business failures. Venture capital, which is needed to establish businesses, dried up when stocks of dot.com companies began to drop in value. Thousands of companies went bankrupt, and thousands of their employees lost their jobs.

---

**THINKING CRITICALLY: ANSWERS**

1. **CONNECT TO HISTORY** Homesteading: physical ability, need for capital to get to the Great Plains; Immigrants: physical ability and health; capital for transportation; Internet: education and knowledge; capital.

2. **CONNECT TO TODAY** Be sure students find out the educational requirements and skills needed for each job they research. Emphasize to students that since business can change so rapidly, it might be hard to train for a specific job. Employers often look for candidates with fundamental knowledge and skills who are adaptable and able to learn.

## TERMS & NAMES

1. communism, p. 413
2. Sacco and Vanzetti, p. 413
3. Calvin Coolidge, p.422
4. John L. Lewis, p. 418
5. Warren G. Harding, p. 419
6. Fordney-McCumber Tariff, p. 420
7. isolationism, p. 412
8. quota system, p. 415
9. Teapot Dome scandal, p. 421
10. installment plan, p. 426

## MAIN IDEAS

1. All three events reflected fear of immigrants and radical movements.
2. The goal of the quota system was to reduce European immigration to the United States.
3. Harding wanted to get America back to the simpler days before the Progressive Era reforms.
4. The scandal was about corruption in the leasing of government oil reserves to private companies; one cabinet member received bonds, cash, and ranches in exchange for oil contracts.
5. The automobile prompted the building of new roads, gave people more mobility, and created jobs; airplanes improved transportation and communication; electrical appliances freed up time for other activities.
6. The income gap between workers and managers was growing; some industries were stagnant or losing money; people were increasing their debt.

## TERMS & NAMES

**For each term or name below, write a sentence explaining its connection to the decade following World War I.**

1. communism
2. Sacco and Vanzetti
3. Calvin Coolidge
4. John L. Lewis
5. Warren G. Harding
6. Fordney-McCumber Tariff
7. isolationism
8. quota system
9. Teapot Dome scandal
10. installment plan

## MAIN IDEAS

**Use your notes and the information in the chapter to answer the following questions.**

### Americans Struggle with Postwar Issues
*(pages 412–418)*

1. Explain how the Red Scare, the Sacco and Vanzetti case, and the rise of the Ku Klux Klan reflected concerns held by many Americans.
2. Describe the primary goal of the immigration quota system established in 1921.

### The Harding Presidency *(pages 419–421)*

3. What did Harding want to do to return America to "normalcy"?
4. Summarize the Teapot Dome scandal.

### The Business of America *(pages 422–427)*

5. How did changes in technology in the 1920s influence American life?
6. What evidence suggests that the prosperity of the 1920s was not on a firm foundation?

## CRITICAL THINKING

1. **USING YOUR NOTES** Create a cause-and-effect web, similar to the one shown, in which you give several causes for the declining power of labor unions in the 1920s and give examples of the unions' decline.

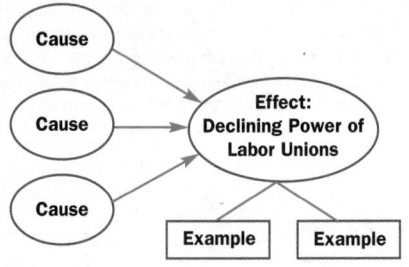

2. **HISTORICAL PERSPECTIVE** Calvin Coolidge said, "After all, the chief business of the American people is business." What events and trends of the 1920s support Coolidge's statement?

3. **INTERPRETING MAPS** Look at the path of Route 66 in the map on page 423. What factors may have influenced where and why the highway was built? Explain your answer.

---

**VISUAL SUMMARY** **POLITICS OF THE ROARING TWENTIES**

**LIFE IN POSTWAR AMERICA**

**ECONOMIC**
- a superficial prosperity ensued
- increased production of consumer goods
- buying on credit
- increased standard of living and consumer spending

**GOVERNMENTAL**
- election of probusiness presidents Harding and Coolidge
- isolationist philosophy
- immigration quotas
- tariffs on imports to discourage foreign business competition
- corruption in Harding's administration

**SOCIETAL/SOCIAL**
- a perceived threat of communism
- fear and distrust of immigrants
- fear of the labor movement and faith in business
- strikes and worker unrest

**TECHNOLOGY/INDUSTRY**
- growth of automobile industry
- introduction of airlines as transportation
- widespread use of electricity
- advertising gains popularity

## CRITICAL THINKING

1. **Using Your Notes**
   **Causes:** Association of unions with radicalism; difficulty recruiting immigrants. **Effects:** New membership declines; strikers fired in Boston; troops prevent picketing; negative public perception of unions.

2. **Historical Perspective**
   American's standard of living went up during the 1920s; 80 percent of all registered motor vehicles were in the United States; the number of electrical appliances increased; growth of advertising; credit increased demand for goods.

3. **Interpreting Maps**
   The road was built through the Southwest to bypass the Rocky Mountains; the road was meant to promote vacation, travel, and regional growth.

## Standardized Test Practice

Use the cartoon and your knowledge of United States history to answer question 1.

WHAT A FRIEND WE HAVE IN COOLIDGE!

THE CASH REGISTER CHORUS.

1. The cartoon criticizes President Coolidge by suggesting that —

   **A** Coolidge's policies benefited wealthy business owners.

   **B** Coolidge was known as "Silent Cal" because he had no economic policy.

   **C** Coolidge provided cash assistance to struggling industries.

   **D** Coolidge had supported the Immigration Act.

2. After World War I ended, workers in many industries went on strike for wage increases and better working conditions. But in the decade that followed, public support of labor unions declined, as did union membership. Which of the following helps to explain this decline in labor union popularity?

   **F** Wages and working conditions in most industries had already improved before the mid-1920s.

   **G** Most labor unions actively opposed isolationist policies.

   **H** Most labor unions had large immigrant memberships.

   **J** Few labor unions would allow unskilled veterans returning from the war to join.

3. Which of the following beliefs did *not* result from America's desire for "normalcy" after World War I?

   **A** isolationism

   **B** conservatism

   **C** nativism

   **D** anarchism

ADDITIONAL TEST PRACTICE, pages S1–S33.

 **TEST PRACTICE** CLASSZONE.COM

## ALTERNATIVE ASSESSMENT

1. **INTERACT WITH HISTORY** Recall your discussion of the question on page 411:

### Would you strike and risk your family's welfare?

Suppose you are a reporter covering the Boston police strike. Write a column for your newspaper that explains why people acted as they did. Also describe the mood and tension created by the strike. Invent realistic quotations from workers, union members, strikebreakers, and management.

2.  **INTERNET ACTIVITY** CLASSZONE.COM

Visit the links for Chapter Assessment to research incomes, prices, employment levels, divorce rates, or other statistics that show how people were affected by the events of the 1920s.

- Decide the main purpose of your graph. What statistics will you show?
- Choose the type of graph that would best show your data. Consider using a pie chart, bar or line graph, or circle graph.
- Clearly label the parts of the graph.
- Share your graph with the class.

*Politics of the Roaring Twenties* **431**

## Standardized Test Practice

1. The correct answer is letter **A.**
   Coolidge supported the free enterprise system and big business.
   Letter B is not correct because Coolidge did have an economic policy. Letter C is not correct because struggling industries did not receive government aid. Letter D is not correct because the Immigration Act was not an economic policy.

2. The correct answer is letter **F.**
   With some improvement in wages and working conditions by the mid-1920s, fewer workers felt the need to unionize. Letter G is not correct because unions were not particularly opposed to isolationist policies. Letter H is not correct because unions had very few immigrant members. Letter J is not correct because labor unions did allow war veterans to join.

3. The correct answer is letter **D.**
   America's desire for "normalcy" did not promote opposition to all forms of government. Letter A is not correct because the United States did pull away from world affairs in an attempt to restore "normalcy." Letter B is not correct because the call for "normalcy" gave rise to conservatism. Letter C is not correct because many Americans feared that foreign-born people were a threat to "normalcy."

UNIT PROJECT

**MULTIMEDIA PRESENTATION**
**Tips for Teaching**

· Suggest students read an overview of the topic they will use to provide a framework for organizing the project.
· Give students suggested key words, Internet links, or library resources to find information.

📄 Formal Assessment
· Chapter Test, Forms A, B, and C, pp. 234–245

## ALTERNATIVE ASSESSMENT

### 1. INTERACT WITH HISTORY
**Rubric**
A newspaper article should . . .
· Describe the events of the Boston police strike in an organized and detailed manner
· Support editorial opinion with factual evidence and appropriate quotes
· Give insight into the economic, social, and political conditions surrounding the events of the strike

### 2. INTERNET ACTIVITY
**Rubric**
A graph should . . .
· Present historical statistics in a logical, readable format
· Highlight pertinent information with labels, colors, or other visual aids
· Present a quantitative analysis of how people were affected by the events of the 1920s

# The Roaring Life of the 1920s

| | CHAPTER OVERVIEW | COPYMASTERS | INTEGRATED TECHNOLOGY |
|---|---|---|---|
| **CHAPTER RESOURCES** | *During the 1920s, rural America clashes with a faster-paced urban culture. Women's attitudes and roles change, influenced in part by the mass media. Many African Americans join in the new urban culture.* | 📄 **Telescoping the Times** · Chapter Summary, pp. 25–26   📄 **Planning for Block Schedules** | 📼 **American Stories video series** · "Jump at the Sun"   👁 **America's Music CD**   👁 **Power Presentations**   💿 **Electronic Teacher Tools**   ⓘ **Online Lesson Planner**   ⓘ **classzone.com** |
| **SECTION 1** **Changing Ways of Life** pp. 434–439 | **KEY IDEAS** *Americans experience cultural conflicts as customs and values change in the United States during the 1920s.* | 📄 **In-Depth Resources: Unit 4** · Guided Reading, p. 20 · Building Vocabulary, p. 24 · Reteaching Activity, p. 26 · Primary Sources, p. 32–33 · Literature, p. 36–38   📄 **Lesson Plans,** pp. 103–104 | 🗺 **Geography Transparencies GT21** · Prohibition: 1890 and 1915   🗺 **Critical Thinking Transparencies CT21** · Prohibition   👁 **Electronic Library of Primary Sources** · from "My Bootlegger" by Samuel Hopkins Adams   ⓘ **classzone.com** |
| **SECTION 2** **The Twenties Woman** pp. 440–445 | *American women of the 1920s pursue new lifestyles and assume new jobs and different roles in society.* | 📄 **In-Depth Resources: Unit 4** · Guided Reading, p. 21 · Reteaching Activity, p. 27   📄 **Lesson Plans,** pp. 105–106 | 👁 **Electronic Library of Primary Sources** · from "Flapper Jane" by Bruce Bliven   ⓘ **classzone.com** |
| **SECTION 3** **Education and Popular Culture** pp. 446–451 | *The mass media, movies, and spectator sports play important roles in the popular culture of the 1920s.* | 📄 **In-Depth Resources: Unit 4** · Guided Reading, p. 22 · Skillbuilder Practice, p. 25 · Reteaching Activity, p. 28 · Geography Application, pp. 30–31 · Primary Sources, p. 34 · American Lives, p. 39   📄 **Lesson Plans,** pp. 107–108 | 🗺 **Humanities Transparencies GT20** · *Automat* by Edward Hopper   👁 **Electronic Library of Primary Sources** · "The Sultan of Swat Steals a World Series Show" by Heywood Broun   ⓘ **classzone.com** |
| **SECTION 4** **The Harlem Renaissance** pp. 452–459 | *African-American ideas, politics, art, literature, and music flourish in Harlem and elsewhere in the United States.* | 📄 **In-Depth Resources: Unit 4** · Guided Reading, p. 23 · Reteaching Activity, p. 29 · Primary Sources, p. 35 · American Lives, p. 40   📄 **Lesson Plans,** pp. 109–110 | 📼 **American Stories video series** · "Jump at the Sun"   🗺 **Critical Thinking Transparencies CT55** · African-American Migration   👁 **America's Music CD**   ⓘ **classzone.com** |

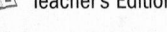 Pupil's Edition

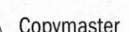 Teacher's Edition

Copymaster

Overhead Transparency

Audio Library

CD-ROM

Internet

# ASSESSMENT OPTIONS

Chapter Assessment, pp. 460–461

Formal Assessment
· Chapter Tests, Forms A, B, and C, pp. 250–261

Test Generator

Integrated Assessment Book

TAKS Online Test Practice

TAKS Spiraled Content Review

TAKS Practice Tests

---

Section 1 Assessment, p. 439

Self-Assessment, p. 439

Formal Assessment, Quiz, p. 246

Integrated Assessment Book

Test Generator

TAKS Practice Transparencies TT78

---

Section 2 Assessment, p. 443

Self-Assessment, p. 443

Formal Assessment, Quiz, p. 247

Integrated Assessment Book

Test Generator

TAKS Practice Transparencies TT79

---

Section 3 Assessment, p. 451

Self-Assessment, p. 451

Formal Assessment, Quiz, p. 248

Integrated Assessment Book

Test Generator

TAKS Practice Transparencies TT80

---

Section 4 Assessment, p. 457

Self-Assessment, p. 457

Formal Assessment, Quiz, p. 249

Integrated Assessment Book

Test Generator

TAKS Practice Transparencies TT81

# RESOURCES FOR DIFFERENTIATING INSTRUCTION

### Students Acquiring English/ESL

Reading Study Guide:
(English and Spanish)
pp. 131–140

Access for Students
Acquiring English/ESL:
Spanish Translations,
pp. 151–157

Chapter Summaries on CD
(English and Spanish)

### Less Proficient Readers

Reading Study Guide
(English and Spanish)
pp. 131–140

Telescoping the Times
· Chapter Summary,
pp. 25–26

Chapter Summaries on CD
(English and Spanish)

### Gifted and Talented Students

In-Depth Resources: Unit 4
· Primary Sources, pp. 32–35
· Literature, pp. 36–38
· American Lives: Georgia
O'Keefe; p. 39, Louis
Armstrong, p. 40

Electronic Library of
Primary Sources
· Unit 4, Chapter 13

# CROSS-CURRICULAR CONNECTIONS

### Pop Culture
McKissak, Patricia. *Black Diamond: The Story of the Negro Baseball Leagues.* Madison, WI: Demco, 1995. Richly detailed, enjoyable history of the players, the teams, and their game.

### Science
Szabo, Corinne. *Sky Pioneer: A Photography of Amelia Earhart.* Washington: National Geographic, 1997. Brief, heavily illustrated biography of the famous flier.

### Drama and Poetry
Bloom, Harold (designer). *Black American Poets and Dramatists of the Harlem Renaissance.* Broomall, PA: Chelsea House, 1994. Anthology with biographical information about some of the great writers of the United States.

### Literature
Levine, Gail Carson. *Dave at Night.* NY: Harper Collins, 1999. When young Dave runs away from the Hebrew Home for Boys, he becomes a part of the world of the Harlem Renaissance.

Lindbergh, Charles. *The Spirit of St. Louis.* NY: Scribner, 1998. Pulitzer-Prize winning memoir written in 1953.

Lindbergh, Reeve. *Under a Wing: A Memoir.* NY: Simon & Schuster, 1998. A funny, lyrical, and observant memoir by the youngest daughter of Charles and Anne Morrow Lindbergh.

### McDougal Littell
### Nextext

*The Harlem Renaissance*

### Language of Literature
Unit 6, Part 1 and 2

# ENRICHMENT ACTIVITIES

Pupil's Edition, pp. pp. 432–459
Interact with History, pp. 432–433
Daily Life, pp. 444–445
American Literature, pp. 458–459

In-Depth Resources: Unit 4
· Geography Application, From Coast to Coast
by Train or Plane, pp. 30–31
· Primary Source: Political Cartoon, p. 32
· Primary Source: The Scopes Trial, p. 33
· Primary Source: Interview with Charles
Lindbergh, p. 34
· Primary Source: "When the Negro Was in
Vogue," p. 35

· Literature: from *Inherit the Wind,* pp. 36–38
· American Lives: Georgia O'Keefe, p. 39
· American Lives: Louis Armstrong, p. 40

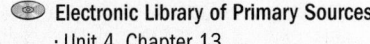 American Stories video series
· "Jump at the Sun"

Electronic Library of Primary Sources
· Unit 4, Chapter 13

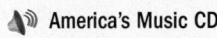 America's Music CD

# CHAPTER 13: PACING GUIDE

## BLOCK SCHEDULE LESSON PLAN OPTIONS (90-MINUTE PERIOD)

### DAY 1

**CHAPTER 13 OPENER**
**pp. 432–433**

**Class Time** 25 minutes

**History from Visuals, p. 432**

**Class Time** 10 minutes

*Options for Pacing and Variety*

· Time Saver Ask students to look at the photograph on page 432 and suggest how it symbolizes the Roaring Twenties and African-American culture during this period. Then have them look over the time line on the spread for an overview of the period in the world and the United States.
**Class Time** 15 minutes

**Interact with History, p. 433**

**Class Time** 15 minutes

*Options for Pacing and Variety*

· Role-Playing Ask students to think about changes that would occur in their lives if they found themselves suddenly prosperous after a time of hardship. Discuss the issues raised in the questions.
**Class Time** 15 minutes

**SECTION 1, pp. 434–439**

**Class Time** 35 minutes

*Options for Pacing and Variety*

· Time Saver Have students read "History Through Art" on page 435 and discuss the questions.
**Class Time** 10 minutes

· Peer Teaching Have students work in pairs, and choose one of the quotations from "A Voice From the

### DAY 1 continued

Past" in the section. Then have them summarize the main points of the quote and identify the speaker, the tone of the quote, and the implications of the statement.
**Class Time** 15 minutes

· Peer Teaching Assign pairs of students to answer alternate questions in the Section Assessment. Then have them share their answers. **Class Time** 15 minutes

**Section 2, pp. 440–445**

**Class Time** 30 minutes

*Options for Pacing and Variety:*

· Peer Evaluation Assign the section assessment for homework, and then have students switch their papers in class and correct the answers as the class discusses them. **Class Time** 15 minutes

· Internet Ask students to read the feature "Daily Life, 1920–1929: Youth in the Roaring Twenties," on pages 444–445, and choose one topic to further research on the Internet at classzone.com.
**Class Time** 25 minutes

### DAY 2

**SECTION 3, pp. 446–451**

**Class Time** 30 minutes

*Options for Pacing and Variety*

· Peer Teaching Have groups of students do the activity on art on TE page 450, and make a short presentation to the class.
**Class Time** 30 minutes

· Time Saver Assign the Section Assessment for homework and collect the answers.
**Class Time** 5 minutes

**SECTION 4, pp. 452–459**

**Class Time** 30 minutes

*Options for Pacing and Variety*

· History on Film Watch the video *Jump at the Sun* to learn about Zora Neale Hurston and the Harlem Renaissance. Using the Teacher's Resource Book as a guide, explore Hurston's background in Florida. Then discuss her participation in the Harlem Renaissance and engage in extension activities using key primary sources.
**Class Time** 30 minutes

· Peer Teaching Have students work together to complete the Section Assessment. Then discuss question 4 as a class.
**Class Time** 20 minutes

· Internet Ask students to read the feature "American Literature: Literature in the Jazz Age," on pages 456–457, and then do the Internet Activity, question 2, on page 457. **Class Time** 20 minutes

### DAY 2 continued

**ASSESSMENT**
**pp. 460–461**

**Class Time** 30 minutes

*Options for Pacing and Variety*

· Peer Evaluation Assign pairs of students to quiz each other on the Terms & Names of the chapter and the Main Ideas questions.
**Class Time** 20 minutes

· Time Saver Assign for homework the Critical Thinking questions and discuss the answers as a class.
**Class Time** 15 minutes

---

**TEACHER-TESTED ACTIVITY**     Patti Harrold, Edmond Memorial High School, Edmond, Oklahoma

## SCRIPTS ABOUT FAMOUS AMERICANS

**Class Time** Two class periods

**Task** Creating scripts about Americans in the 1920s

**Purpose** To learn more about Americans who were famous during the 1920s

**Supplies Needed**

· Textbooks
· Library and Internet resources

**Activity** Assign a hero, writer, performer, or other notable person of the 1920s to pairs or small groups of students. Tell them to research the person's life to determine for what he or she is famous. Students should write a brief "living history" script, focusing on one or more highlights of their subject's life. Have students take turns reading their scripts aloud.

# CHAPTER 13 CORRELATION

## CORRELATION TO THE TEXAS ESSENTIAL KNOWLEDGE AND SKILLS

Chapter 13 addresses the following standards of the Texas Essential Knowledge and Skills for U.S. History.

| TEKS | Instruction | Student Question/Activity |
|---|---|---|
| **(5A)** Analyze causes and effects of significant issues such as the changing role of women. | **PE 440–443** examination of the dramatic changes women's lives underwent during the 1920s | **PE 443** Critical Thinking questions about women's changing roles |
| **(5B)** Analyze the impact of significant individuals, such as Clarence Darrow and William Jennings Bryan. | **PE 438–439** discussion of Darrow's and Bryan's role in the Scopes trial | **PE 439** Critical Thinking question about the Scopes trial |
| **(10A)** Analyze the effects of changing demographic patterns resulting from migration within the United States. | **PE 452–453** discussion of the Great Migration that brought millions of African Americans from the South to the North | **PE 453** question about how the influx of so many African Americans changed Northern cities |
| **(17B)** Analyze reasons for the adoption of 20th-century constitutional amendments. | **PE 436–437** analysis of the causes and effects of the Eighteenth Amendment's banning the sale and consumption of alcohol | **PE 439** Critical Thinking questions about Prohibition |
| **(20A)** Describe how the characteristics and issues of various eras in U.S. history have been reflected in works of literature. | **PE 450–451** examination of the prominent writers of the 1920s and the messages they sought to convey | **TE 450** Cooperative Activity in which groups of students research the work of a famous artist or writer |
| **(20B)** Describe the impact of significant examples of cultural movements in art, music, and literature, including the Harlem Renaissance. | **PE 452–457** examination of the emergence of the Harlem Renaissance and of the cultural contributions it provided | **TE 454** activity in which students explore the various themes expressed by the prominent figures of the Harlem Renaissance |
| **(22A)** Explain the effects of scientific discoveries and technological innovations on the development of the United States. | **PE 447–448** discussion of the development of the radio and its impact on American society | **PE 448** questions about the reason for radio's popularity |

## TAKS MINI-LESSONS

1. **Social Studies Skills: Objective 1 (US5.A):** Analyze causes and effects of significant issues such as the changing role of women **Activity** Have students write a paragraph summarizing the ways in which women's lives changed during the 1920s.

2. **Social Studies Skills: Objective 1 (US5.B):** Analyze the impact of significant individuals, such as Charles Lindbergh **Activity** Have groups of students research Lindbergh's flight and present several interesting details about the event to the class.

3. **Social Studies Skills: Objective 3 (US21.A):** Explain actions taken by people from racial, ethnic, and religious groups to expand their opportunities **Activity** Have students make a list of four or five prominent figures of the Harlem Renaissance and what notable contribution each made.

4. **English Language Arts Skills: Objective 2 (11.D):** Analyze literary language, including its use of evocative words and rhythms **Activity** Have students discuss the ways in which the excerpt from *Babbitt* on page 450 ridicules the conformity and materialism of American life.

5. **English Language Arts Skills: Objective 4 (1.C):** Organize ideas in writing to ensure coherence, logical progression, and support for ideas **Activity** Have students answer the Critical Thinking questions in the Section 1 Assessment with the above goals in mind (page 439).

To understand such issues as Prohibition, the changing role of women, and the influence of the Harlem Renaissance

# THE ROARING LIFE OF THE 1920s

## HISTORY from VISUALS

### Interpreting the Photograph

Ask students to study the photograph and suggest how it symbolizes the Roaring Twenties. Then ask what the photo demonstrates about African-American culture during this period. *(It depicts an exciting and carefree scene; African-American culture blossomed during this period and became more popular with mainstream America.)*

**Extension** Ask students to imagine that they are reporters covering this competition and have them write a short news story about the event based on what they see in the photograph.

## Time Line Discussion

Explain to students that the time line covers the decade of the 1920s.

· Ask students why women might consider the year 1920 so significant. *(The Nineteenth Amendment was ratified.)*

· Ask students what year the Scopes Trial took place. *(1925)*

· Ask students what contrasting events took place in the United States and the world in 1928. *(A president was elected in the United States, and a president was assassinated in Mexico.)*

Blues singer Gertrude "Ma" Rainey performs with her Georgia Jazz Band in Chicago, Illinois, 1923.

**1920** Nineteenth Amendment gives women the right to vote.

**1922** Louis Armstrong plays for King Oliver's Creole Jazz Band in Chicago.

**1923** *Time* magazine begins publication.

**1924** Calvin Coolidge is elected president.

USA
WORLD

**1920**  **1922**  **1924**

**1921** China's Communist Party is founded.

**1922** King Tut's tomb is discovered in Egypt.

**1923** Mustafa Kemal becomes first president of new Republic of Turkey.

**432** CHAPTER 13

## THEMES IN CHAPTER 13

### WOMEN AND POLITICAL POWER

Women's role in society changed significantly in the 1920s. Young women, especially, became more assertive in their quest for equality. The U.S. Dept. of Labor created the Women's Bureau to represent women workers.

**See Teacher's Edition note, p. 443.**

### SCIENCE AND TECHNOLOGY

The first radio broadcast to the home took place in 1920. By the end of the decade, more than 10 million American families had radios in their homes. The mass media revolutionized communication and created a shared national experience.

**See Teacher's Edition note, p. 447.**

### IMMIGRATION AND MIGRATION

By the end of the 1920s, more than one-third of all African Americans lived in cities. This migration to urban areas marked the beginning of a new era in African-American history. It also sparked a wave of violence in many northern cities.

**See Teacher's Edition note, p. 453.**

## INTERACT
### WITH HISTORY

The year is 1920. The World War has just ended. Boosted by the growth of the wartime industry, the U.S. economy is flourishing. Americans live life to the fullest as new social and cultural trends sweep the nation.

## How might the new prosperity affect your everyday life?

### Examine the Issues

- As Americans leave farms and small towns to take jobs in the cities, how might their lives change?
- How will economic prosperity affect married and unmarried women?
- How might rural and urban areas change as more and more families acquire automobiles?

🌐 **RESEARCH LINKS** **CLASSZONE.COM**

Visit the Chapter 13 links for more information about The Roaring Life of the 1920s.

## INTERACT
### WITH HISTORY

### Objectives

- To motivate students to learn more about American society during the 1920s
- To help students understand the effects of prosperity on different groups in the United States

### Examine the Issues

1. Have students consider how life in cities differs from life on farms and in small towns.
2. Ask students to analyze the impact of a strong economy on American society.
3. Have students think about how acquiring an automobile changed American's lives.

---

**1925** The Scopes trial takes place in Tennessee.

**1927** Charles Lindbergh makes the first nonstop solo transatlantic flight.

**1928** Herbert Hoover is elected president.

## 1926     1928     1930

**1926** Hirohito becomes emperor of Japan.

**1928** President Álvaro Obregón of Mexico is assassinated.

*The Roaring Life of the 1920s* **433**

---

## RECOMMENDED RESOURCES

### BOOKS FOR THE TEACHER

Anderson, Jervis. *This Was Harlem: A Cultural Portrait, 1900–1950.* New York: Farrar, 1982.

Lewis, Thomas. *Empire of the Air.* New York: Burlingame, 1991. Story of the men responsible for the creation of radio.

### BOOKS FOR THE STUDENT

Torrence, Bruce. *Hollywood: the First Hundred Years.* New York: New York Zoetrope, 1982. Rise of the movie industry.

Wall, Cheryl. *Women of the Harlem Renaissance.* Bloomington: Indiana UP, 1995. Look at notable women of the period, including Zora Neale Hurston and Bessie Smith.

### VIDEOS

*The Age of Ballyhoo.* Dir. David Shepard. Republic Pictures Home Video, 1975. Society and culture.

*Amelia Earhart.* Dir. Nancy Porter. PBS Video, 1993. Documentary.

*Lindbergh.* Dir. Stephen Ives. PBS Video, 1990. Documentary about aviator's triumph and subsequent difficulties.

### SOFTWARE

*Cultural Contributions of Black Americans.* CD-ROM. Available from Educational Software Institute, 800-955-5570.

*The Instrumental History of Jazz.* CD-ROM. CLEARVUE/eav, 800-253-2788.

### INTEGRATED TECHNOLOGY

For teacher support, visit . . .

 classzone.com

# Changing Ways of Life

| MAIN IDEA | WHY IT MATTERS NOW | Terms & Names |
|---|---|---|
| Americans experienced cultural conflicts as customs and values changed in the 1920s. | The way in which different groups react to change often causes conflict today. | •Prohibition •fundamentalism<br>•speakeasy •Clarence Darrow<br>•bootlegger •Scopes trial |

 U.S. History
1B, 5A, 5B, 6H, 8A, 10A, 11A, 17B, 20A, 21C, 22A, 23A, 24A, 24B, 24C, 24D, 24G, 25A, 25B, 25C, 25D, 26A, 26B

**One American's Story**

As the 1920s dawned, social reformers who hoped to ban alcohol—and the evils associated with it—rejoiced. The Eighteenth Amendment to the Constitution, banning the manufacture, sale, and transportation of alcohol, took effect in January of 1920. Billy Sunday, an evangelist who preached against the evils of drinking, predicted a new age of virtue and religion.

**A PERSONAL VOICE** BILLY SUNDAY

" The reign of tears is over! The slums will soon be only a memory. We will turn our prisons into factories and our jails into storehouses and corncribs. Men will walk upright now, women will smile and the children will laugh. Hell will be forever for rent! "

—quoted in *How Dry We Were: Prohibition Revisited*

Sunday's dream was not to be realized in the 1920s, as the law proved unenforceable. The failure of Prohibition was a sign of cultural conflicts most evident in the nation's cities. Lured by jobs and by the challenge and freedom that the city represented, millions of people rode excitedly out of America's rural past and into its urban future.

## **1** Rural and Urban Differences

▲ 1920s evangelist Billy Sunday

America changed dramatically in the years before 1920, as was revealed in the 1920 census. According to figures that year, 51.2 percent of Americans lived in communities with populations of 2,500 to more than 1 million. Between 1922 and 1929, migration to the cities accelerated, with nearly 2 million people leaving farms and towns each year. "Cities were the place to be, not to get away from," said one historian. The agricultural world that millions of Americans left behind was largely unchanged from the 19th century—that world was one of small towns and farms bound together by conservative moral values and close social relationships. Yet small-town attitudes began to lose their hold on the American mind as the city rose to prominence.

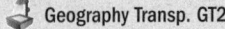
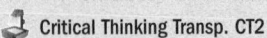
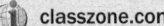
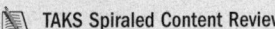
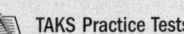

**THE NEW URBAN SCENE** At the beginning of the 1920s, New York, with a population of 5.6 million people, topped the list of big cities. Next came Chicago, with nearly 3 million, and Philadelphia, with nearly 2 million. Another 65 cities claimed populations of 100,000 or more, and they grew more crowded by the day. Life in these booming cities was far different from the slow-paced, intimate life in America's small towns. Chicago, for instance, was an industrial powerhouse, home to native-born whites and African Americans, immigrant Poles, Irish, Russians, Italians, Swedes, Arabs, French, and Chinese. Each day, an estimated 300,000 workers, 150,000 cars and buses, and 20,000 trolleys filled the pulsing downtown. At night people crowded into ornate movie theaters and vaudeville houses offering live variety shows.

*"How ya gonna keep 'em down on the farm, after they've seen Paree?"*

**POPULAR SONG OF THE 1920s**

For small-town migrants, adapting to the urban environment demanded changes in thinking as well as in everyday living. The city was a world of competition and change. City dwellers read and argued about current scientific and social ideas. They judged one another by accomplishment more often than by background. City dwellers also tolerated drinking, gambling, and casual dating—worldly behaviors considered shocking and sinful in small towns. **A**

For all its color and challenge, though, the city could be impersonal and frightening. Streets were filled with strangers, not friends and neighbors. Life was fast-paced, not leisurely. The city demanded endurance, as a foreign visitor to Chicago observed.

**MAIN IDEA**

**Contrasting**
**A** How did small-town life and city life differ?

*A. Answer* Small towns were bound by traditional morals and close ties of family, friends, and religion. Cities offered varied perspectives and options because of their large, mixed populations; cultural variety; and greater tolerance of values and ideas.

**A PERSONAL VOICE** WALTER L. GEORGE

" It is not for nothing that the predominating color of Chicago is orange. It is as if the city, in its taxicabs, in its shop fronts, in the wrappings of its parcels, chose the color of flame that goes with the smoky black of its factories. It is not for nothing that it has repelled the geometric street arrangement of New York and substituted . . . great ways with names that a stranger must learn if he can. . . . He is in a [crowded] city, and if he has business there, he tells himself, 'If I weaken I shan't last long.'"

—*Hail Columbia!*

*Skillbuilder Answers*
1. *Possible Answer:* The person in the center with the saxophone is the focal point.
2. *Possible Answer:* The figure on the right is running toward the big city buildings.
3. *Possible Answer:* The figure in the center appears to be joyous as he raises his arms upwards.

### History Through *Art*

**SONG OF THE TOWERS**

This mural by Aaron Douglas is part of a series he painted inside the 135th Street Branch of the New York Public Library to symbolize different aspects of African-American life during the 1920s. In this panel, *Song of the Towers*, he depicts figures before a city backdrop. As seen here, much of Douglas's style was influenced by jazz music and geometric shapes.

**SKILLBUILDER** Analyzing Visual Sources
1. What is the focal point of this panel?
2. What parts of this painting might be symbolic of African Americans' move north?
3. How does Douglas represent new freedoms in this mural? Support your answer with examples.

 **SEE SKILLBUILDER HANDBOOK, PAGE R23.**

### History Through *Art*

Aaron Douglas was born in Kansas in 1898. He received a degree in art from the University of Nebraska. After graduation, he taught drawing at a high school in Kansas City for a year, before making his way to Harlem in 1924. There, he began studying art with German artist, Winold Reiss. Encouraged by Reiss, Douglas began to incorporate aspects of African art—namely geometric shapes and designs—into his works. Many of Douglas' paintings depict African Americans in their daily lives. "I refuse to compromise and see blacks as anything less than a proud and majestic people," Douglas said.

---

**DIFFERENTIATING INSTRUCTION**    **LESS PROFICIENT READERS**

## Contrasting

To help students comprehend the differences between urban and rural life in the 1920s, have them create a comparison chart like the one shown here. Have them fill it in with examples of the differences between life in the cities and in smaller communities as described in the text.

| Urban life | Rural life |
|---|---|
|  |  |
|  |  |
|  |  |
|  |  |

## DIFFICULT DECISIONS

Review the decision-making steps described in the Difficult Decisions lesson on TE page 329.

1. Favor prohibition: because of the devastating impact of alcohol on human lives. Oppose prohibition: because such a restriction would limit individual freedom.

2. For prohibition: Such an amendment would improve society; Against prohibition: Unnecessary and difficult to enforce.

3. Some may suggest the government is too intrusive in personal decisions. Others may believe a better society will be created.

## More About . . .

### The Eighteenth Amendment
Public officials continued to debate the merits of the Eighteenth Amendment throughout the 1920s. The 1928 Republican presidential candidate, Herbert Hoover, supported Prohibition. The Democratic candidate, Alfred Smith, opposed it. For Hoover, Prohibition was part of the U.S. Constitution and, thus, had to be fully enforced. He challenged his critics to target Prohibition by the "methods provided in the Constitution itself." Eventually, that is just what they did. In 1933, the nation ratified the Twenty-first Amendment to the Constitution, which repealed the Eighteenth Amendment.

 Geography Transparencies GT21
· Prohibition: 1890 and 1915

 Critical Thinking Transparencies CT21
· Prohibition

### DIFFICULT DECISIONS

#### TO PROHIBIT ALCOHOL OR NOT?
The question of whether to outlaw alcohol divided Americans. Many believed the government should make alcohol illegal to protect the public, while others believed it was a personal decision, and not morally wrong.

1. Examine the pros and cons of each position. Which do you agree with? What other factors, if any, do you think would influence your position?

2. If you had been a legislator asked to vote for the Eighteenth Amendment, what would you have said? Explain.

3. What happens when the government legislates moral values? Give contemporary examples to support your answer.

In the city, lonely migrants from the country often ached for home. Throughout the 1920s, Americans found themselves caught between rural and urban cultures—a tug that pitted what seemed to be a safe, small-town world of close ties, hard work, and strict morals against a big-city world of anonymous crowds, moneymakers, and pleasure seekers.

**THE PROHIBITION EXPERIMENT** One vigorous clash between small-town and big-city Americans began in earnest in January 1920, when the Eighteenth Amendment went into effect. This amendment launched the era known as **Prohibition,** during which the manufacture, sale, and transportation of alcoholic beverages were legally prohibited.

Reformers had long considered liquor a prime cause of corruption. They thought that too much drinking led to crime, wife and child abuse, accidents on the job, and other serious social problems. Support for Prohibition came largely from the rural South and West, areas with large populations of native-born Protestants. The church-affiliated Anti-Saloon League had led the drive to pass the Prohibition amendment. The Woman's Christian Temperance Union, which considered drinking a sin, had helped push the measure through.

At first, saloons closed their doors, and arrests for drunkenness declined. But in the aftermath of World War I, many Americans were tired of making sacrifices; they wanted to enjoy life. Most immigrant groups did not consider drinking a sin but a natural part of socializing, and they resented government meddling.

Eventually, Prohibition's fate was sealed by the government, which failed to budget enough money to enforce the law. The Volstead Act established a Prohibition Bureau in the Treasury Department in 1919, but the agency was underfunded. The job of enforcement involved patrolling 18,700 miles of coastline as well as inland borders, tracking down illegal stills (equipment for distilling liquor), monitoring highways for truckloads of illegal alcohol, and overseeing all the industries that legally used alcohol to be sure none was siphoned off for illegal purposes. The task fell to approximately 1,500 poorly paid federal agents and local police—clearly an impossible job.

**SPEAKEASIES AND BOOTLEGGERS** To obtain liquor illegally, drinkers went underground to hidden saloons and nightclubs known as **speakeasies**—so called because when inside, one spoke quietly, or "easily," to avoid detection. Speakeasies could be found everywhere—in penthouses, cellars, office buildings, rooming houses, tenements, hardware stores, and tearooms. To be admitted to a speakeasy, one had to present a card or use a password. Inside, one would find a mix of fashionable middle-class and upper-middle-class men and women.

Before long, people grew bolder in getting around the law. They learned to distill alcohol and built their own stills. Since alcohol was allowed for medicinal and religious purposes, prescriptions

 A young woman demonstrates one of the means used to conceal alcohol—hiding it in containers strapped to one's legs. ▶

---

## DIFFERENTIATING INSTRUCTION — LESS PROFICIENT READERS

### Recognizing Cause and Effect

Help students use the following methods to recognize cause-effect relationships:

· Use a cause and effect graphic organizer like the one at the right.

· Look for statements that indicate a list of causes or effects will follow. (Example on p. 437: "Prohibition not only generated disrespect for the law but also contributed to organized crime.")

· Look for key words, such as, *because, therefore,* and *as a result.* (Example on page 438: "They believed that the Bible was inspired by God, and therefore its stories in all their details were true.")

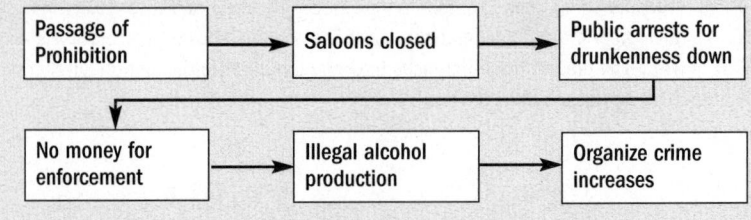

| Passage of Prohibition | → | Saloons closed | → | Public arrests for drunkenness down |
| No money for enforcement | → | Illegal alcohol production | → | Organize crime increases |

for alcohol and sales of sacramental wine (intended for church services) skyrocketed. People also bought liquor from **bootleggers** (named for a smuggler's practice of carrying liquor in the legs of boots), who smuggled it in from Canada, Cuba, and the West Indies. "The business of evading [the law] and making a mock of it has ceased to wear any aspects of crime and has become a sort of national sport," wrote the journalist H. L. Mencken. **B**

ORGANIZED CRIME Prohibition not only generated disrespect for the law, but also contributed to organized crime in nearly every major city. Chicago became notorious as the home of Al Capone, a gangster whose bootlegging empire netted over $60 million a year. Capone took control of the Chicago liquor business by killing off his competition. During the 1920s, headlines reported 522 bloody gang killings and made the image of flashy Al Capone part of the folklore of the period. In 1940, the writer Herbert Asbury recalled the Capone era in Chicago.

### A Personal Voice HERBERT ASBURY

" The famous seven-ton armored car, with the pudgy gangster lolling on silken cushions in its darkened recesses, a big cigar in his fat face, and a $50,000 diamond ring blazing from his left hand, was one of the sights of the city; the average tourist felt that his trip to Chicago was a failure unless it included a view of Capone out for a spin. The mere whisper: 'Here comes Al,' was sufficient to stop traffic and to set thousands of curious citizens craning their necks along the curbing. "

—*Gem of the Prairie*

By the mid-1920s, only 19 percent of Americans supported Prohibition. The rest, who wanted the amendment changed or repealed, believed that Prohibition caused worse effects than the initial problem. Rural Protestant Americans, however, defended a law that they felt strengthened moral values. The Eighteenth Amendment remained in force until 1933, when it was repealed by the Twenty-first Amendment. **C**

---

**MAIN IDEA**

**Developing Historical Perspective**

**B** Why do you think the Eighteenth Amendment failed to eliminate alcohol consumption?

*B. Possible Answers* The consumption of alcohol was a traditional part of many cultures; the government failed to provide sufficient staff and resources to enforce the law; the means of manufacturing, selling, and transporting liquor were many and could easily be concealed.

---

**MAIN IDEA**

**Analyzing Effects**

**C** How did criminals take advantage of prohibition?

*C. Answer* Criminals broke the law by smuggling, as well as by making alcohol and selling it for profit.

---

**HISTORICAL SPOTLIGHT**

**AL CAPONE**

By age 26, Al Capone headed a criminal empire in Chicago, which he controlled through the use of bribes and violence. From 1925 to 1931, Capone bootlegged whiskey from Canada, operated illegal breweries in Chicago, and ran a network of 10,000 speakeasies. In 1927, the "Big Fellow," as he liked to be called, was worth an estimated $100 million.

The end came quickly for Capone, though. In 1931, the gangster chief was arrested for tax evasion and went to jail. That was the only crime of which the authorities were ever able to convict him. Capone was later released from jail, but he died several years later at age 48.

---

**HISTORICAL SPOTLIGHT**

**Al Capone**

Discuss with students why many people remain fascinated with Al Capone. (*notorious figure, media attention, movies and TV shows*) Have students write newspaper editorials in response to the following question: Should America continue to promote fascination with Capone through museums, memorabilia, and tours of gangland sites?

⊕ Electronic Library of Primary Sources
· from "My Bootlegger" by Samuel Hopkins Adams

---

| Prohibition, 1920–1933 | |
|---|---|
| **Causes** | **Effects** |
| • Various religious groups thought drinking alcohol was sinful. | • Consumption of alcohol declined. |
| • Reformers believed that the government should protect the public's health. | • Disrespect for the law developed. |
| • Reformers believed that alcohol led to crime, wife and child abuse, and accidents on the job. | • An increase in lawlessness, such as smuggling and bootlegging, was evident. |
| • During World War I, native-born Americans developed a hostility to German-American brewers and toward other immigrant groups that used alcohol. | • Criminals found a new source of income. |
| | • Organized crime grew. |

---

**HISTORY from VISUALS**

**Interpreting a Chart**

This chart lists some important causes and effects of Prohibition. Ask students to study the chart and to consider the relationship between causes and effects

**Extension** Have each student create a cause-and-effect chart based on the information in the subheadings: "Speakeasies and Bootleggers" and "Organized Crime."

---

*The Roaring Life of the 1920s* **437**

---

**ACTIVITY**  **COOPERATIVE LEARNING**

**BLOCK SCHEDULING**

### Creating a Dictionary of 1920s Slang

**Class Time** 30 minutes

**Task** Illustrating 1920s slang terms for a dictionary

**Purpose** To examine how popular culture affects language

**Directions** Assign the following 1920s slang terms to groups of students: *bee's knees, bootlegger, cement overshoes, cheaters, flapper, gatecrasher, heebie-jeebies, jake, jalopy, lounge lizard,* and *main drag.* Instruct students to find the meanings of the terms, write definitions in a dictionary format, and draw illustrations to accompany the definitions. Groups should combine their work to create a classroom dictionary of 1920s slang.

## Instruct

### Instruct: Objective ②

**Science and Religion Clash**

TAKS SS11 1(US5.B)

· What did fundamentalists believe about the biblical account of creation?
· How did this differ from the view of many liberal thinkers?
· What main issue did the Scopes trial address?

 **In-Depth Resources: Unit 4**
· Guided Reading, p. 20
· Primary Sources: The Scopes Trial, p.33
· Literature: from *Inherit the Wind*, pp. 36–38

---

### NOW & THEN

**Evolution, Creationism, and Education**

**Summarizing** Have students research an example of the ongoing debate over the teaching of evolution. Students should summarize the information they found in a paragraph or two.

---

### More About . . .

**The Scopes Trial**

Despite the fact that a stubborn heat wave drove temperatures in the courtroom above 100 degrees, spectators jammed inside each day. At one point, the presiding judge decided to move the court proceedings onto the courthouse lawn. The crowds inside—with all their clapping and stomping in the intense heat—had weakened the floor. Court was held that day in front of 5,000 spectators.

---

## ② Science and Religion Clash

Another bitter controversy highlighted the growing rift between traditional and modern ideas during the 1920s. This battle raged between fundamentalist religious groups and secular thinkers over the truths of science.

**AMERICAN FUNDAMENTALISM** The Protestant movement grounded in a literal, or nonsymbolic, interpretation of the Bible was known as **fundamentalism**. Fundamentalists were skeptical of scientific knowledge; they argued that all important knowledge could be found in the Bible. They believed that the Bible was inspired by God, and that therefore its stories in all their details were true.

Their beliefs led fundamentalists to reject the theory of evolution advanced by Charles Darwin in the 19th century—a theory stating that plant and animal species had developed and changed over millions of years. The claim they found most unbelievable was that humans had evolved from apes. They pointed instead to the Bible's account of creation, in which God made the world and all its life forms, including humans, in six days.

Fundamentalism expressed itself in several ways. In the South and West, preachers led religious revivals based on the authority of the Scriptures. One of the most powerful revivalists was Billy Sunday, a baseball player turned preacher who staged emotional meetings across the South. In Los Angeles, Aimee Semple McPherson, a theatrical woman who dressed in flowing white satin robes, used Hollywood showmanship to preach the word to homesick Midwestern migrants and devoted followers of her radio broadcasts. In the 1920s, fundamentalism gained followers who began to call for laws prohibiting the teaching of evolution. **D**

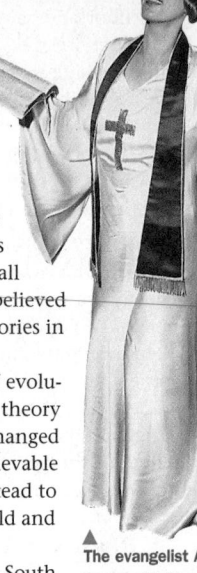

▲ The evangelist Aimee Semple McPherson in 1922

**MAIN IDEA**

**Summarizing**
**D** Summarize the beliefs of fundamentalism.

**THE SCOPES TRIAL** In March 1925, Tennessee passed the nation's first law that made it a crime to teach evolution. Immediately, the American Civil Liberties Union (ACLU) promised to defend any teacher who would challenge the law. John T. Scopes, a young biology teacher in Dayton, Tennessee, accepted the challenge. In his biology class, Scopes read this passage from *Civic Biology:* "We have now learned that animal forms may be arranged so as to begin with the simple one-celled forms and culminate with a group which includes man himself." Scopes was promptly arrested, and his trial was set for July.

The ACLU hired **Clarence Darrow,** the most famous trial lawyer of the day, to defend Scopes. William Jennings Bryan, three-time Democratic candidate for president and a devout fundamentalist, served as a special prosecutor. There was no real question of guilt or innocence: Scopes was honest about his action. The **Scopes trial** was a fight over evolution and the role of science and religion in public schools and in American society.

The trial opened on July 10, 1925, and almost overnight became a national sensation. Darrow called Bryan as an expert on the Bible—the contest that everyone had been waiting for. To handle the throngs of Bryan supporters, Judge Raulston moved the court outside, to a platform built under the maple trees. There, before a crowd of several

**Vocabulary**
**culminate:** to come to completion; end

**D. Answer** Fundamentalists believed that all important knowledge could be found in the Bible and that what was in the Bible was true. They rejected Darwin's theory of evolution.

---

### NOW & THEN

**EVOLUTION, CREATIONISM, AND EDUCATION**

There is still great controversy today over the teaching of evolution in the public schools. Some people believe that creation theory should be taught as a theory of the origin of life, along with evolution. As recently as 1999, the Kansas State School Board voted to eliminate the teaching of evolution from the curriculum.

The issue of what should be taught about the origin of life—and who should decide this issue—continues to stir up debate. Some have suggested that science and religion are not necessarily incompatible. They believe that a theory of the origin of life can accommodate both the scientific theory of evolution and religious beliefs.

---

**DIFFERENTIATING INSTRUCTION** | **GIFTED AND TALENTED**  **classzone.com**

### Interpreting Points of View

Have interested students work in pairs to present dramatic readings of the courtroom exchanges between Darrow and Bryan. Suggest that they locate a transcript of the trial or portions of the trial (such as those provided in Leslie H. Allen's *Bryan and Darrow at Dayton* and in *Six Days or Forever?*). If students have trouble finding a transcript of the trial, they might obtain a copy of *Inherit the Wind* from the library. Then have them look for passages in the play to present to the class in their dramatic readings. Ask the class to summarize Darrow and Bryan's points of view.

**Rubric**

The dramatic readings should . . .

· have an introduction explaining the circumstances of the debate
· include main points of Bryan and Darrow
· capture the attention and interests of the audience

📄 **Integrated Assessment**
· Rubric 3

thousand, Darrow relentlessly questioned Bryan about his beliefs. Bryan stood firm, a smile on his face.

### A PERSONAL VOICE
CLARENCE DARROW AND WILLIAM JENNINGS BRYAN

**Mr. Darrow—** " You claim that everything in the Bible should be literally interpreted? "

**Mr. Bryan—** " I believe everything in the Bible should be accepted as it is given there. Some of the Bible is given illustratively. For instance: 'Ye are the salt of the earth.' I would not insist that man was actually salt, or that he had flesh of salt, but it is used in the sense of salt as saving God's people. "

—quoted in *Bryan and Darrow at Dayton*

*E. Answer*
*Fundamentalists believed that God created the world in six days, whereas evolutionists argued that modern species developed from earlier forms of life over millions of years.*

**MAIN IDEA**

**Analyzing Issues**
**E** What was the conflict between fundamentalists and those who accepted evolution?

Darrow asked Bryan if he agreed with Bishop James Ussher's calculation that, according to the Bible, Creation happened in 4004 B.C. Had every living thing on earth appeared since that time? Did Bryan know that ancient civilizations had thrived before 4004 B.C.? Did he know the age of the earth? Bryan grew edgy but stuck to his guns. Finally, Darrow asked Bryan, "Do you think the earth was made in six days?" Bryan answered, "Not six days of 24 hours." People sitting on the lawn gasped. **E**

With this answer, Bryan admitted that the Bible might be interpreted in different ways. But in spite of this admission, Scopes was found guilty and fined $100. The Tennessee Supreme Court later changed the verdict on a technicality, but the law outlawing the teaching of evolution remained in effect.

This clash over evolution, the prohibition experiment, and the emerging urban scene all were evidence of the changes and conflicts occurring during the 1920s. During that period, women also experienced conflict as they redefined their roles and pursued new lifestyles.

*"When Shall We Three Meet Again?"*

▲
A 1925 newspaper cartoon portrays Bryan (*left*) and Darrow (*right*) at the close of the Scopes "monkey" trial on the teaching of evolution, so-called because of a theory of evolution that man evolved from apes.

---

### More About . . .

**Clarence Darrow**
The most noted American lawyer in the early 1900s, Clarence Darrow gained his fame as a defender of labor interests. Darrow was nearly 70 years old when he tried his most famous criminal cases. In 1924, he defended Nathan Leopold and Richard Loeb, two young men who admitted kidnapping and killing a 14-year-old boy. To prevent them from receiving the death penalty, Darrow successfully argued that they were mentally ill when they committed the murder.

---

## Assess & Reteach

**SECTION 1 ASSESSMENT**
Assign pairs of students to answer alternate questions. Then have them share their answers.

📄 Formal Assessment
· Section Quiz, p. 246

**SELF-ASSESSMENT**
Have each student use the Main Idea questions to review the key ideas of this section. Students should verify their answers in the text.

**RETEACH**
Use the Guided Reading worksheet for Section 1 to reinforce understanding.

📄 In-Depth Resources: Unit 4
· Reteaching Activity, p. 26

---

## ASSESSMENT

**1. TERMS & NAMES**  For each term or name, write a sentence explaining its significance.
- **Prohibition**
- **speakeasy**
- **bootlegger**
- **fundamentalism**
- **Clarence Darrow**
- **Scopes trial**

TAKS  Mini-Lesson 2: SS11 4(1.C)

### MAIN IDEA

**2. TAKING NOTES**
Create two diagrams like the one below. Show how government attempted to deal with (a) problems thought to stem from alcohol use and (b) the teaching of evolution.

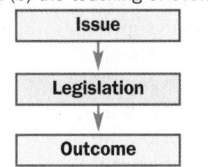

**Issue**
↓
**Legislation**
↓
**Outcome**

Was the legislation effective? Explain.

### CRITICAL THINKING

**3. ANALYZING ISSUES**
How might the overall atmosphere of the 1920s have contributed to the failure of Prohibition?

**4. ANALYZING CAUSES**
Why do you think organized crime spread so quickly through the cities during the 1920s? Explain your answer.

**5. EVALUATING**
Do you think the passage of the Volstead Act and the ruling in the Scopes trial represented genuine triumphs for traditional values?
**Think About:**
- changes in urban life in the 1920s
- the effects of Prohibition
- the legacy of the Scopes trial

*The Roaring Life of the 1920s*  **439**

---

Answers  **ASSESSMENT**  1

**1. TERMS & NAMES**
Prohibition, p. 436
speakeasy, p. 436
bootlegger, p. 437
fundamentalism, p. 438
Clarence Darrow, p. 438
Scopes trial, p. 438

**2. TAKING NOTES**
**Issue:** Prohibition
**Legislation:** The Eighteenth Amendment banned the manufacture, sale, and transportation of alcohol.
**Outcome:** Many Americans broke the law.
**Issue:** teaching evolution
**Legislation:** A Tennessee state law made it a crime to teach evolution.
**Outcome:** Biology teacher John Scopes broke the law, was arrested, and was convicted.

**3. ANALYZING ISSUES**
People living in cities felt freer and less bound by traditional values; immigrants brought their own cultures, habits, and religious values.

**4. ANALYZING CAUSES**
Organized crime grew as people sought illegal means by which to manufacture and transport alcohol during Prohibition.

**5. EVALUATING**
**Yes:** These events raised people's awareness and have had a lasting influence. The teaching of evolution still provokes legal controversy. **No:** The Volstead Act not only did not stop people from drinking alcohol but caused the growth of organized crime. The conviction of John Scopes failed to discredit the theory of evolution.

# The Twenties Woman

| MAIN IDEA | WHY IT MATTERS NOW | Terms & Names |
|---|---|---|
| American women pursued new lifestyles and assumed new jobs and different roles in society during the 1920s. | Workplace opportunities and trends in family life are still major issues for women today. | •flapper    •double standard |

 **U.S. History** 5A, 5B, 8A, 13A, 21D, 22A, 22C, 23B, 24A, 24B, 24C, 24D, 25A, 25B, 25C, 25D, 26A, 26B

### One American's Story

When Zelda Sayre broke off her engagement with would-be writer F. Scott Fitzgerald in 1925, she told him that he would have to become successful on his own. Later, she wrote about how a woman can achieve greatness.

**A PERSONAL VOICE** ZELDA SAYRE FITZGERALD

" Rouge means that women want to choose their man—not take what lives in the next house. . . . Look back over the pages of history and see how the loveliness of women has always stirred men—and nations—on to great achievement! There have been women who were not pretty, who have swayed hearts and empires, but these women . . . did not disdain that thing for which paint and powder stands. They wanted to choose their destinies—to be successful competitors in the great game of life. "

—"Paint and Powder," *The Smart Set*, May 1929

**Zelda Sayre Fitzgerald**

Zelda Sayre and F. Scott Fitzgerald married one week after Scott published his first novel, and Zelda continued to be the model for Scott's independent, unconventional, ambitious female characters. He even copied from her letters and other writings. Ironically, Zelda's devotion to her marriage and to motherhood stifled her career ambitions. Nevertheless, she became a model for a generation of young American women who wanted to break away from traditions and forget the hardships of the war years.

**Mini-Lesson 1: SS11 3(US5.A)**

## **1** Young Women Change the Rules

By the 1920s, the experiences of World War I, the pull of cities, and changing attitudes had opened up a new world for many young Americans. These "wild young people," wrote John F. Carter, Jr., in a 1920 issue of *Atlantic Monthly*, were experiencing a world unknown to their parents: "We have seen man at his lowest, woman at her lightest, in the terrible moral chaos of Europe. We have been forced to question, and in many cases to discard, the religion of our fathers. . . .We have been forced to live in an atmosphere of 'tomorrow we die,' and so, naturally, we drank and were merry." In the rebellious, pleasure-loving atmosphere of the twenties, many women began to assert their independence, reject the values of the 19th century, and demand the same freedoms as men.

**440** CHAPTER 13

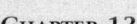

**More About . . .**

**The Twenties Woman**
During the 1920s, many women were shedding traditional submissive roles—and the nation was noticing. The "new" woman, declared one contemporary writer, "occupies herself, passionately, with everything, except the things that used to occupy the minds of girls." Women of the Twenties, added another observer, were "demanding recognition as individuals first, and as wives and mothers second."

**THE FLAPPER** During the twenties, a new ideal emerged for some women: the **flapper**, an emancipated young woman who embraced the new fashions and urban attitudes of the day. Close-fitting felt hats, bright waistless dresses an inch above the knees, skin-toned silk stockings, sleek pumps, and strings of beads replaced the dark and prim ankle-length dresses, whalebone corsets, and petticoats of Victorian days. Young women clipped their long hair into boyish bobs and dyed it jet black.

Many young women became more assertive. In their bid for equal status with men, some began smoking cigarettes, drinking in public, and talking openly about sex—actions that would have ruined their reputations not many years before. They danced the fox trot, camel walk, tango, Charleston, and shimmy with abandon.

Attitudes toward marriage changed as well. Many middle-class men and women began to view marriage as more of an equal partnership, although both agreed that housework and child-rearing remained a woman's job. **(A)**

**THE DOUBLE STANDARD** Magazines, newspapers, and advertisements promoted the image of the flapper, and young people openly discussed courtship and relationships in ways that scandalized their elders. Although many young women donned the new outfits and flouted tradition, the flapper was more of an image of rebellious youth than a widespread reality; it did not reflect the attitudes and values of many young people. During the 1920s, morals loosened only so far. Traditionalists in churches and schools protested the new casual dances and women's acceptance of smoking and drinking.

In the years before World War I, when men "courted" women, they pursued only women they intended to marry. In the 1920s, however, casual dating became increasingly accepted. Even so, a **double standard**—a set of principles granting greater sexual freedom to men than to women—required women to observe stricter standards of behavior than men did. As a result, many women were pulled back and forth between the old standards and the new.

**MAIN IDEA**

**Evaluating**
**(A)** How was the flapper like and unlike women of today?

**A. Possible Answer**
**Like:** Flappers used clothing, hairstyles, and behavior to claim a new freedom.
**Unlike:** Today's women have more freedoms.

> **▲**
> Female flappers compete in a Charleston dance competition in 1926.

**Instruct**

**Instruct: Objective ❷**

**Women Shed Old Roles at Home and at Work**
TAKS SS11 1(US5.A)
· How did the nation's booming economy provide greater work opportunities for women?
· What forms of inequality and discrimination did women face in the professional world?
· How did family life change during the 1920s?

📄 **In-Depth Resources: Unit 4**
· Guided Reading, p. 21
👁 **Electronic Library of Primary Sources**
· *from* "Flapper Jane" by Bruce Bliven

## ❷ Women Shed Old Roles at Home and at Work

The fast-changing world of the 1920s produced new roles for women in the workplace and new trends in family life. A booming industrial economy opened new work opportunities for women in offices, factories, stores, and professions. The same economy churned out time-saving appliances and products that reshaped the roles of housewives and mothers.

---

**DIFFERENTIATING INSTRUCTION**   **LESS PROFICIENT READERS**

**Understanding Cause and Effect**
Help students understand the reasons for, and consequences of, the changing status of women during the 1920s. Have them create a flow chart that lists the causes and effects of women's changing roles.

| Causes |
| :---: |
| ↓ |
| Changing Roles |
| ↓ |
| Effects |

A young woman works as a typesetter in a publishing house in 1920.

**NEW WORK OPPORTUNITIES** Although women had worked successfully during the war, afterwards employers who believed that men had the responsibility to support their families financially often replaced female workers with men. Women continued to seek paid employment, but their opportunities changed. Many female college graduates turned to "women's professions" and became teachers, nurses, and librarians. Big businesses required extensive correspondence and record keeping, creating a huge demand for clerical workers such as typists, filing clerks, secretaries, stenographers, and office-machine operators. Others became clerks in stores or held jobs on assembly lines. A handful of women broke the old stereotypes by doing work once reserved for men, such as flying airplanes, driving taxis, and drilling oil wells. **B**

By 1930, 10 million women were earning wages; however, few rose to managerial jobs, and wherever they worked, women earned less than men. Fearing competition for jobs, men argued that women were just temporary workers whose real job was at home. Between 1900 and 1930, the patterns of discrimination and inequality for women in the business world were established.

**THE CHANGING FAMILY** Widespread social and economic changes reshaped the family. The birthrate had been declining for several decades, and it dropped at a slightly faster rate in the 1920s. This decline was due in part to the wider availability of birth-control information. Margaret Sanger, who had opened the first birth-control clinic in the United States in 1916, founded the American Birth Control League in 1921 and fought for the legal rights of physicians to give birth-control information to their patients.

At the same time, social and technological innovations simplified household labor and family life. Stores overflowed with ready-made clothes, sliced bread, and canned foods. Public agencies provided services for the elderly, public health clinics served the sick, and workers' compensation assisted those who could no longer work. These innovations and institutions had the effect of freeing homemakers from some of their traditional family responsibilities. Many middle-class housewives, the main shoppers and money managers, focused their attention on their homes, husbands, children, and pastimes. "I consider time for reading clubs and my children more important than . . . careful housework and I just don't do it," said an Indiana woman in the 1920s.

**MAIN IDEA**

*Analyzing Effects*
**B** How did the growth of business and industry affect women?

*B. Answer*
Big business and industry produced time-saving appliances that freed women from some household chores, and business growth also created jobs for millions of women, but most women were confined to traditional jobs.

---

**HISTORY from VISUALS**

**Interpreting the Graph**
Have students note the time span of the pie charts. To provide background, the first chart deals with a year (1910) before the time period of this chapter.

**Extension** Ask students to check an almanac or a statistical abstract to find the percentages of women employed in these ways today.

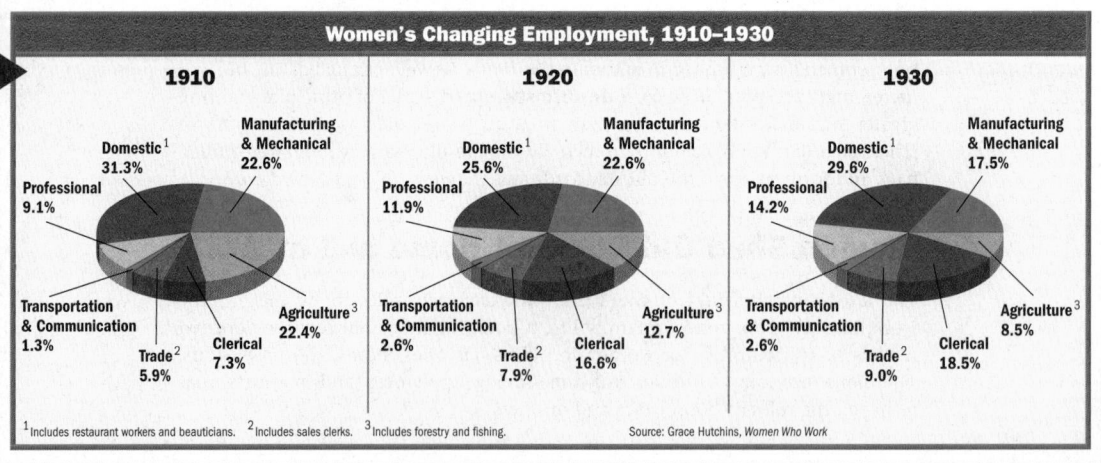

**Women's Changing Employment, 1910–1930**

**1910**
- Domestic[1] 31.3%
- Manufacturing & Mechanical 22.6%
- Professional 9.1%
- Transportation & Communication 1.3%
- Trade[2] 5.9%
- Clerical 7.3%
- Agriculture[3] 22.4%

**1920**
- Domestic[1] 25.6%
- Manufacturing & Mechanical 22.6%
- Professional 11.9%
- Transportation & Communication 2.6%
- Trade[2] 7.9%
- Clerical 16.6%
- Agriculture[3] 12.7%

**1930**
- Domestic[1] 29.6%
- Manufacturing & Mechanical 17.5%
- Professional 14.2%
- Transportation & Communication 2.6%
- Trade[2] 9.0%
- Clerical 18.5%
- Agriculture[3] 8.5%

[1] Includes restaurant workers and beauticians.  [2] Includes sales clerks.  [3] Includes forestry and fishing.    Source: Grace Hutchins, *Women Who Work*

**442** CHAPTER 13

---

As women's spheres of activity and influence expanded, they experienced greater equality in marriage. Marriages were based increasingly on romantic love and companionship. Children, no longer thrown together with adults in factory work, farm labor, and apprenticeships, spent most of their days at school and in organized activities with others their own age. At the same time, parents began to rely more heavily on manuals of child care and the advice of experts.

Working-class and college-educated women quickly discovered the pressure of juggling work and family, but the strain on working-class women was more severe. Helen Wright, who worked for the Women's Bureau in Chicago, recorded the struggle of an Irish mother of two.

### A PERSONAL VOICE HELEN WRIGHT

" She worked in one of the meat-packing companies, pasting labels from 7 a.m. to 3:30 p.m. She had entered the eldest child at school but sent her to the nursery for lunch and after school. The youngest was in the nursery all day. She kept her house 'immaculately clean and in perfect order,' but to do so worked until eleven o'clock every night in the week and on Saturday night she worked until five o'clock in the morning. She described her schedule as follows: on Tuesday, Wednesday, Thursday, and Friday she cleaned one room each night; Saturday afternoon she finished the cleaning and put the house in order; Saturday night she washed; Sunday she baked; Monday night she ironed. "

—quoted in *Wage-Earning Women*

As women adjusted to changing roles, some also struggled with rebellious adolescents, who put an unprecedented strain on families. Teens in the 1920s studied and socialized with other teens and spent less time with their families. As peer pressure intensified, some adolescents resisted parental control, much as the flappers resisted societal control.

This theme of adolescent rebelliousness can be seen in much of the popular culture of the 1920s. Education and entertainment reflected the conflict between traditional attitudes and modern ways of thinking.

*C. Answer*
The birthrate dropped; household labor was simplified by technology; children spent their days in school; adolescent rebelliousness increased.

**MAIN IDEA**

**Summarizing**
 What changes affected families in the 1920s?

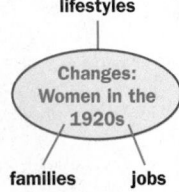

## ASSESSMENT

1. **TERMS & NAMES** For each term or name, write a sentence explaining its significance.
   • flapper
   • double standard

**MAIN IDEA**

2. **TAKING NOTES**
   Copy the concept web shown below and add to it examples that illustrate how women's lives changed in the 1920s.

   lifestyles

   Changes: Women in the 1920s

   families    jobs

   Write a paragraph explaining how you think women's lives changed most dramatically in the 1920s.

**CRITICAL THINKING**

3. **EVALUATING**
   During the 1920s, a double standard required women to observe stricter codes of behavior than men. Do you think that some women of this decade made real progress towards equality? Support your answer with examples. **Think About:**
   • the flapper's style and image
   • changing views of marriage

4. **ANALYZING PRIMARY SOURCES**
   In 1920, veteran suffragist Anna Howard Shaw stated that equality in the workplace would be harder for women to achieve than the vote.

   " You younger women will have a harder task than ours. You will want equality in business, and it will be even harder to get than the vote. "

   —Anna Howard Shaw

   Why do you think Shaw held this belief? Support your answer with evidence from the text.

### The Women's Bureau

The U.S. Department of Labor Women's Bureau was established by Congress in 1920 to work specifically on behalf of wage-earning women. Its first director was Mary Anderson, who served from 1920 to 1944. Alexis Herman, who served as its director from 1977 to 1981, went on to become the first African-American U.S. Secretary of Labor, holding that post from 1997 to 2001.

# Assess & Reteach

### SECTION 2 ASSESSMENT

Assign the questions as homework or as a class activity.

Formal Assessment
· Section Quiz, p. 247

### SELF-ASSESSMENT

Ask students to consider whether women today face any of the barriers and prejudices that women endured in the 1920s. If so, which ones?

### RETEACH

Have students write a set of questions based on the main topics in this section. Then, have them answer the questions on a separate sheet of paper. Have pairs of students answer each other's questions and work together to verify the answers.

In-Depth Resources: Unit 4
· Reteaching Activity, p. 27

---

**Answers** ASSESSMENT

**1. TERMS & NAMES**
flapper, p. 441
double standard, p. 441

**2. TAKING NOTES**
**Lifestyles**–wearing new clothing styles, dancing, cutting their hair; **families**–decline in birthrate, more leisure time for housewives because of labor-saving devices, more pressure on working-class women, rebellious adolescents; **jobs**–teachers, nurses, librarians, clerical workers, store clerks, factory workers.

**3. EVALUATING**
**Yes:** women laid the foundation for equality when they became more open and assertive in communicating with men their age, dated casually, dressed nontraditionally, and viewed marriage as an equal partnership. **No:** the new ways of dressing and casual dating were superficial changes.

**4. ANALYZING PRIMARY SOURCES**
Shaw may have believed that voting equality could be achieved by passing a law. Equality in the workplace, however, would be more dependent on people's attitudes and acceptance, which could only be earned over time.

**DAILY LIFE**
**1920–1929**

### Objectives

· To describe the popular culture of the 1920s

· To explain why the youth-dominated decade came to be called the Roaring Twenties

## Focus & Motivate

**Evaluating** Have students think of some of the hallmarks of contemporary American popular culture. What are some of the fads and fashions of today's pop culture? What impact do fads and fashions have on the young?

## More About . . .

### Popular Figures of the 1920s

In the 1920s, Americans loved contests of all sorts. Some of their biggest heroes were sports figures, such as baseball's Babe Ruth, who hit a record-breaking 60 home runs in 1927, and Gertrude Ederle, the 19-year-old American who was the first woman to swim the English Channel. Other sports stars of the 1920s included football's Red Grange and Knute Rockne, the heavyweight boxers Jack Dempsey and Gene Tunney, the golfer Bobby Jones, the tennis champ Bill Tilden, and the thoroughbred racehorse Man O'War, who won all his starts but the one that he lost to a horse named Upset.

# Youth in the Roaring Twenties

The decade known as the Roaring Twenties was a celebration of youth and its culture. Crazy and frenetic dances, silly songs, and radically new styles of clothing captured the public's fancy.

During this period of relative prosperity, many people questioned the values of the past and were willing to experiment with new values and behavior as well as with new fashions. This was an especially liberating period for women, who received the right to vote in 1920. Many women also opted for a liberating change of fashion—short skirts and short hair—as well as the freedom to smoke and drink in public.

▼ **FLAGPOLE SITTING**

One of the more bizarre fads of the 1920s began in 1924 as a publicity stunt to attract viewers to movie theaters. The most famous flagpole sitter was "Shipwreck" Kelly (right, waving from high above a movie theater in Union City, New Jersey). In 1929, for a total of 145 days, Kelly took up residence atop various flagpoles throughout the country. Imitators, of course, followed. At one point that year, Baltimore had at least 17 boys and 3 girls sitting atop 18-foot hickory poles, with their friends and families cheering them on.

**BESSIE SMITH** ▶

Bessie Smith was "Empress of the Blues." In 1923, she sold a million recordings of "Down Hearted Blues."

**444** CHAPTER 13

---

## RECOMMENDED RESOURCES

### BOOKS

Andrist, Ralph K., ed. *The American Heritage History of the '20s & '30s.* New York: American Heritage, 1970. An illustrated account.

Kay, Jackie. *Bessie Smith.* Absolute Press, 1997. Detailed look at the blues legend.

Stevenson, Elizabeth. *Babbitts and Bohemians: From the Great War to the Great Depression.* Transactions Publishers, 1997. America in the Roaring Twenties.

*The Jazz Age: The 20s.* Alexandria, VA: Time-Life, Inc., 1998. A fascinating pictorial history.

### VIDEOS

*The Jazz Age.* Ambrose Video Publishing, 1990. Newsreels and vintage photos capture the 1920s; part of the series *America: A Look Back.*

*Lowell Thomas Remembers: The Roaring Twenties.* Republic Pictures Home Video, 1986. Two videocassettes covering the Roaring Twenties.

*The Twenties.* PBS Video, 1989. Part of the acclaimed PBS series *A Walk Through the 20th Century* with Bill Moyers.

*The Twenties: From Illusion to Disillusion.* Films for the Humanities and Sciences.

**◄ BOBBED HAIR**

In keeping with the liberating influence of their new clothing, women bobbed their hair—that is, they had it cut much shorter—freeing themselves of the long tresses that had been fashionable for years. The woman shown is having her hair cut at a barber shop.

**◄ DANCE FADS**

The Charleston was the dance craze of the 1920s. An energetic dance that involved wild, flailing movements of the arms and legs, it demanded an appropriate costume for the woman dancer—a short, straight dress without a waistline.

Another craze was the dance marathon, a contest in which couples would dance continuously for days—taking a 15-minute break every hour—with each alternately holding up the other as he or she slept. Needless to say, dancers dropped from exhaustion.

**▼ GENTLEMEN'S FASHIONS**

Gentlemen enjoyed some outrageous fashions of their own. This young man, with the aid of two flappers, displays the latest fashion in trousers, sometimes called Oxford bags. He also sports "patent-leather hair," parted on the side or in the middle and slicked down close to the head.

# DATA FILE

## SCHOOL DAYS, SCHOOL DAYS

During the 1920s, children studied reading, writing, and arithmetic in elementary school. In high school, students also studied history and literature and had vocational training. Girls learned cooking and sewing, and boys learned woodworking.

| Slang Expressions | |
|---|---|
| crush | an infatuation |
| gatecrasher | someone who attends an event uninvited or without paying |
| keen | attractive or appealing |
| ritzy | elegant |
| scram | to leave in a hurry |
| screwy | crazy |
| bee's knees | a superb person or thing |

### RADIO

- KDKA, Pittsburgh, the first commercial radio station, went on the air on November 2, 1920. It was owned by Westinghouse.
- In 1922, 500 radio stations were in operation in the United States.
- In 1924, over 3 million radios were in use throughout the United States. By the end of the 1920s, over 10 million radios were in use. Popular radio shows included *Amos 'n' Andy* and *Jones and Hare.*

### SONG TITLES

"Baby Face"
"Barney Google"
"Blue Skies"
"Bye Bye Blackbird"
"Charleston"
"Crazy Rhythm"

"I Want to Be Happy"
"Let A Smile Be Your Umbrella"
"Makin' Whoopie"
"My Blue Heaven"
"My Heart Stood Still"
"Singin' in the Rain"

## THINKING CRITICALLY

### CONNECT TO TODAY

1. **Comparing** With a small group, listen to several of the songs listed above or to others from the period. Discuss their lyrics and melodies, and compare them with those of popular songs today. What commonalities can you find? How does the music from each period reflect its times? Report your findings to the class.

 **SEE SKILLBUILDER HANDBOOK, PAGE R8.**

### CONNECT TO HISTORY

2. **Researching Clothing Styles** Find out more about the clothing styles just before the flapper era. How severe were the changes in fashion in the 1920s? How do you think parents of flappers reacted to these changes? If you had lived at this time, would you have chosen to wear the new styles? Why or why not?

 **RESEARCH LINKS** CLASSZONE.COM

*The Roaring Life of the 1920s* **445**

## Instruct

1. Why were so many young people willing to experiment with new values, behaviors, and fashions during the 1920s?
2. Why were so many women involved in exploring such new ways of living?
3. What are some examples of what were considered young people's rebellious activities?

### MAKING PERSONAL CONNECTIONS

Ask students to consider how their fashions and leisure activities set them apart from the older generation. What beliefs and values are different from their parent's generation?

### More About . . .

**Bessie Smith**

Smith began singing for money on street corners in Chattanooga, Tennessee, and eventually broke into the world of entertainment as a dancer. From there, her career as a blues vocalist quickly took off. "Bessie Smith was a fabulous deal to watch," recalled guitarist Danny Barker. "She could bring about mass hypnotism." Smith and a companion died in an automobile accident on September 26, 1937, near Clarksdale, Mississippi. For years after the incident, it was rumored that Smith bled to death because the local white hospital refused to admit her. Such rumors eventually turned out to be false.

### THINKING CRITICALLY: ANSWERS

1. **CONNECT TO TODAY** If possible, provide recordings for students, or suggest that they borrow from libraries, relatives, or friends. Point out that they can look for collections of 1920s songs or hunt for songs individually. For example, "Stardust" and "Blue Skies" appear on the Willie Nelson CD *Stardust.* If necessary, students might use music-store, online music catalogs, or library music references to locate CDs or cassettes.

2. **CONNECT TO HISTORY** Students might examine books containing photographs of the 1900–1920 period for more on clothing just before the Roaring Twenties. After comparing the more conservative clothing of earlier years, they may say that parents of flappers were shocked or outraged by their children's dress. Descriptions of what students would have chosen to wear will vary, but they should offer reasons for their choices.

## OBJECTIVES

**1** Describe the popular culture of the 1920s.

**2** Explain why the youth-dominated decade came to be called the Roaring Twenties.

### SKILLBUILDERS

· Interpreting Graphs, p. 447

### CRITICAL THINKING

· Summarizing, pp. 447, 451
· Analyzing Effects, p. 448
· Making Inferences, p. 450
· Analyzing Causes, p. 451
· Synthesizing, p. 451
· Evaluating, p. 451

## Focus & Motivate

Ask students to name three well-known Americans who they consider heroes—people worthy of respect. List their suggestions on the chalkboard and ask them to identify the field in which each is famous. Then ask students why they admire these people.

## Instruct

### Instruct: Objective **1**

**Schools and the Mass Media Shape Culture**

TAKS SS11 5(WH26.C)

· How did public high schools play a role in preparing students for the future?
· How did various forms of media help to shape American culture in the 1920s?

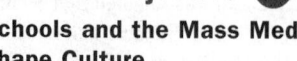 In-Depth Resources: Unit 4
· Guided Reading, p. 22

# Education and Popular Culture

| MAIN IDEA | WHY IT MATTERS NOW | Terms & Names |
|---|---|---|
| The mass media, movies, and spectator sports played important roles in creating the popular culture of the 1920s—a culture that many artists and writers criticized. | Much of today's popular culture can trace its roots to the popular culture of the 1920s. | •Charles A. Lindbergh •George Gershwin •Georgia O'Keeffe •Sinclair Lewis • •F. Scott Fitzgerald •Edna St. Vincent Millay •Ernest Hemingway |

 **U.S. History**
1B, 5B, 9A, 10B, 20A, 20B, 20C, 20D, 21B, 22A, 22, 23A, 23, 24B, 25A, 25B, 25C, 25D, 26A, 26B

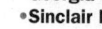 **One American's Story**

On September 22, 1927, approximately 50 million Americans sat listening to their radios as Graham McNamee, radio's most popular announcer, breathlessly called the boxing match between the former heavyweight champ Jack Dempsey and the current titleholder, Gene Tunney.

★ **A PERSONAL VOICE** GRAHAM MCNAMEE

"**Good evening, Ladies & Gentlemen of the Radio Audience. This is a big night. Three million dollars' worth of boxing bugs are gathering around a ring at Soldiers' Field, Chicago. . . .**

**Here comes Jack Dempsey, climbing through the ropes . . . white flannels, long bathrobe . . . Here comes Tunney . . . The announcer shouting in the ring . . . trying to quiet 150,000 people. . . . Robes are off.**"

—*Time* magazine, October 3, 1927

▲ Gene Tunney, down for the "long count," went on to defeat Jack Dempsey in their epic 1927 battle.

After punches flew for seven rounds, Tunney defeated the legendary Dempsey. So suspenseful was the brutal match that a number of radio listeners died of heart failure. The "fight of the century" was just one of a host of spectacles and events that transformed American popular culture in the 1920s.

## **1** Schools and the Mass Media Shape Culture

During the 1920s, developments in education and mass media had a powerful impact on the nation.

**SCHOOL ENROLLMENTS** In 1914, approximately 1 million American students attended high school. By 1926, that number had risen to nearly 4 million, an increase sparked by prosperous times and higher educational standards for industry jobs.

Prior to the 1920s, high schools had catered to college-bound students. In contrast, high schools of the 1920s began offering a broad range of courses such as vocational training for those interested in industrial jobs.

---

## PROGRAM RESOURCES

 In-Depth Resources: Unit 4
· Guided Reading, p. 22
· Skillbuilder Practice: Drawing Conclusions, p. 25
· Reteaching Activity, p. 28
· Geography Application, pp. 30–31
· Primary Sources: Interview with Charles Lindbergh, p. 34
· American Lives: Georgia O'Keefe, p. 39

Reading Study Guide (English and Spanish), pp. 135–136

Access for Students Acquiring English/ESL
· Guided Reading (Spanish), p. 153
· Skillbuilder Practice: Drawing Conclusions, p. 155
· Geography Application, pp. 156–157

Formal Assessment
· Section Quiz, p. 248

Integrated Assessment
· Rubrics

**INTEGRATED TECHNOLOGY**

Humanities Transp. HT20
· Automat

Electronic Library of Primary Sources

classzone.com

**TEXAS RESOURCES**

 TAKS Spiraled Content Review

 TAKS Practice Tests

 TAKS Practice Transparencies TT80

 TAKS Online Test Practice

The public schools met another challenge in the 1920s—teaching the children of new immigrant families. The years before World War I had seen the largest stream of immigrants in the nation's history—close to 1 million a year. Unlike the earlier English and Irish immigrants, many of the new immigrants spoke no English. By the 1920s their children filled city classrooms. Determined teachers met the challenge and created a large pool of literate Americans. **A**

Taxes to finance the schools increased as well. School costs doubled between 1913 and 1920, then doubled again by 1926. The total cost of American education in the mid-1920s amounted to $2.7 billion a year.

---

**MAIN IDEA**

**Summarizing**
**A** How did schools change during the 1920s?

**A. Answer**
More students were able to attend school during this prosperous time; schools had to adapt to teaching students of new immigrant families; schools offered a broad range of courses for students to train for industrial jobs.

---

### High School Enrollment, 1910–1940

Source: *Historical Statistics of the United States*

**SKILLBUILDER** Interpreting Graphs
What was the approximate increase in the number of high school students between 1920 and 1930?

---

**EXPANDING NEWS COVERAGE** Widespread education increased literacy in America, but it was the growing mass media that shaped a mass culture. Newspaper circulation rose as writers and editors learned how to hook readers by imitating the sensational stories in the tabloids. By 1914, about 600 local papers had shut down and 230 had been swallowed up by huge national chains, giving readers more expansive coverage from the big cities. Mass-circulation magazines also flourished during the 1920s. Many of these magazines summarized the week's news, both foreign and domestic. By the end of the 1920s, ten American Magazines—including *Reader's Digest* (founded in 1921) and *Time* (founded in 1923)—boasted a circulation of over 2 million each.

**RADIO COMES OF AGE** Although major magazines and newspapers reached big audiences, radio was the most powerful communications medium to emerge in the 1920s. Americans added terms such as "airwaves," "radio audience," and "tune in" to their everyday speech. By the end of the

---

### Radio Broadcasts of the 1920s

Radio dance parties were common in the 1920s.

Prior to the 1920s, radio broadcasts were used primarily for transmitting important messages and speeches regarding World War I. After the first commercial radio station—KDKA Pittsburgh—made its debut on the airwaves in 1920, the radio industry changed forever. Listeners tuned in for news, entertainment, and advertisements.

By 1930, 40 percent of U.S. households had radios, like this 1927 Cosser three-valve Melody Maker.

In the 1920s, radio was a formal affair. Announcers and musicians dressed in their finest attire, even without a live audience.

**447**

---

**DIFFERENTIATING INSTRUCTION** | **GIFTED AND TALENTED**

### Radio Broadcasts of the 1920s

Have interested students work in groups to present radio broadcasts similar to those of the 1920s. They may choose to report on sports events, political events, or news, or to present entertainment shows. Encourage them to make the broadcasts as authentic as possible by copying the styles of the times. As part of their research, they can listen to recordings of old radio shows in order to gain a sense of what such broadcasts were like.

Students can present the radio broadcasts "live," or record them to be played for the class. They may want to include advertisements for products sold in the 1920s.

 Integrated Assessment
· Rubric 3

## Instruct: Objective ②

**America Chases New Heroes and Old Dreams**

TAKS SS11 1(US5.B)

· Which heroes and events inspired Americans during the 1920s?

· What new styles did writers, artists, and composers experiment with in the decade?

· How did the literature of the time express a clash of values within society?

📖 **In-Depth Resources: Unit 4**
· Guided Reading, p. 22

👁 **Electronic Library of Primary Sources**
· "The Sultan of Swat Steals a World Series Show" by Heywood Broun

---

### More About . . .

#### Helen Wills

Helen Wills was a doctor's daughter from San Francisco. She joined a tennis club when she was 14 and played every day. However, she said that she improved her technique by watching better players. "Children are great imitators," she remarked. "I watched the seniors play, and the visiting Australian champions." Before hanging up her tennis racket, she won 31 major tennis titles and an Olympic gold medal. Her professional name was Helen Wills Moody after she married in 1929.

---

decade, the radio networks had created something new in the United States—the shared national experience of hearing the news as it happened. The wider world had opened up to Americans, who could hear the voice of their president or listen to the World Series live. **B**

## ② America Chases New Heroes and Old Dreams

During the 1920s, many people had money and the leisure time to enjoy it. In 1929, Americans spent $4.5 billion on entertainment, much of it on ever-changing fads. Early in the decade, Americans engaged in new leisure pastimes such as working crossword puzzles and playing mahjong, a Chinese game whose playing pieces resemble dominoes. In 1922, after explorers opened the dazzling tomb of the Egyptian pharaoh Tutankhamen, consumers mobbed stores for pharaoh-inspired accessories, jewelry, and furniture. In the mid-1920s, people turned to flagpole sitting and dance marathons. They also flooded athletic stadiums to see sports stars, who were glorified as super-heroes by the mass media.

### Sports Heroes of the 1920s

Although the media glorified sports heroes, the Golden Age of Sports reflected common aspirations. Athletes set new records, inspiring to ordinary Americans. When poor, unknown athletes rose to national fame and fortune, they restored Americans' belief in the power of the individual to improve his or her life.

**Gertude Ederle ▶**
In 1926, at the age of 19, Gertrude Ederle became the first woman to swim the English Channel. Here, an assistant applies heavy grease to help ward off the effects of the cold Channel waters.

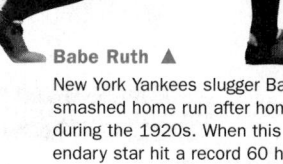

**Babe Ruth ▲**
New York Yankees slugger Babe Ruth smashed home run after home run during the 1920s. When this legendary star hit a record 60 home runs in 1927, Americans went wild.

**◀ Andrew "Rube" Foster**
A celebrated pitcher and team manager, Andrew "Rube" Foster made his greatest contribution to black baseball in 1920 when he founded the Negro National League. Although previous attempts to establish a league for black players had failed, Foster led the league to success, earning him the title "The Father of Black Baseball."

**Helen Wills ▶**
Helen Wills dominated women's tennis, winning the singles title at the U.S. Open seven times and the Wimbledon title eight times. Her nickname was Little Miss Poker Face.

**MAIN IDEA**

Analyzing Effects

**B** Why did radio become so popular?

*B. Answer*
For the first time, Americans could hear news as it happened.

---

### DIFFERENTIATING INSTRUCTION · LESS PROFICIENT READERS

#### Finding Main Ideas

Demonstrate the following technique for identifying main ideas in text:

Read the heading on page 448: "America Chases New Heroes and Old Dreams." Then restate the heading as a question or series of questions:

· Who were the new heroes of the 1920s?

· What were the dreams of the age?

· How does America "chase" heroes and dreams?

Skim the text under the heading to find the answers to the questions. The answers generally state the main ideas. Have students practice the technique with other headings.

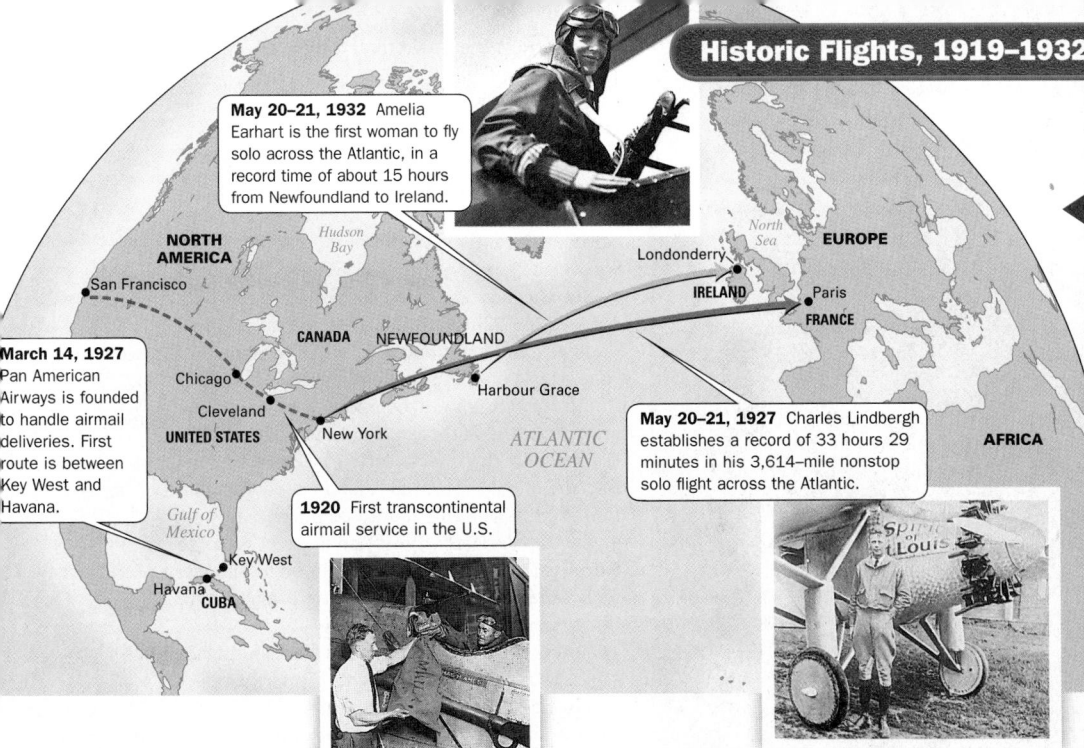

**May 20–21, 1932** Amelia Earhart is the first woman to fly solo across the Atlantic, in a record time of about 15 hours from Newfoundland to Ireland.

**NORTH AMERICA**

Hudson Bay

San Francisco

North Sea

**EUROPE**

Londonderry

**IRELAND**

Paris

**FRANCE**

**CANADA** NEWFOUNDLAND

Chicago

Cleveland

**UNITED STATES** New York

Harbour Grace

**ATLANTIC OCEAN**

**AFRICA**

**March 14, 1927** Pan American Airways is founded to handle airmail deliveries. First route is between Key West and Havana.

**May 20–21, 1927** Charles Lindbergh establishes a record of 33 hours 29 minutes in his 3,614–mile nonstop solo flight across the Atlantic.

Gulf of Mexico

Key West

Havana **CUBA**

**1920** First transcontinental airmail service in the U.S.

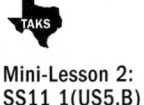

**TAKS**

**Mini-Lesson 2: SS11 1(US5.B)**

**Interpreting the Map**

Have students list the flights mentioned on the map in chronological order.

**Extension** Students might do some research in order to add dates of other historic flights during this period (1919-1932), or they might add dates of later historic flights.

**More About . . .**

**Charles A. Lindbergh**

A few years after his heroic flight, Lindbergh's life took a tragic turn. The first of his six children, Charles A. Lindbergh, Jr., born in 1930, and was kidnapped and murdered in 1932. To escape the relentless publicity generated by the case, Lindbergh and his family moved to England in 1935. The famous aviator returned to the United States in 1939, where he experienced more dark days. A vocal opponent of the United States entering World War II, Lindbergh delivered a speech in 1941 that many considered anti-Semitic. He faced much public criticism for his views. After American entry into the war, he supported the war effort and flew combat missions in the Pacific.

📄 **In-Depth Resources: Unit 4**
· Primary Sources: Interview with Charles Lindbergh, p. 34
· Geography application: From Coast to Coast by Train or Plane, pp. 30–31

**LINDBERGH'S FLIGHT** America's most beloved hero of the time wasn't an athlete but a small-town pilot named **Charles A. Lindbergh,** who made the first nonstop solo flight across the Atlantic. A handsome, modest Minnesotan, Lindbergh decided to go after a $25,000 prize offered for the first nonstop solo trans-atlantic flight. On May 20, 1927, he took off near New York City in the *Spirit of St. Louis,* flew up the coast to Newfoundland, and headed over the Atlantic. The weather was so bad, Lindbergh recalled, that "the average altitude for the whole . . . second 1,000 miles of the [Atlantic] flight was less than 100 feet." After 33 hours and 29 minutes, Lindbergh set down at Le Bourget airfield outside of Paris, France, amid beacons, searchlights, and mobs of enthusiastic people.

Paris threw a huge party. On his return to the U.S., New York showered Lindbergh with ticker tape, the president received him at the White House, and America made him its idol. In an age of sensationalism, excess, and crime, Lindbergh stood for the honesty and bravery the nation seemed to have lost. The novelist F. Scott Fitzgerald, a fellow Minnesotan, caught the essence of Lindbergh's fame.

**A PERSONAL VOICE** F. SCOTT FITZGERALD

"In the spring of 1927, something bright and alien flashed across the sky. A young Minnesotan who seemed to have nothing to do with his generation did a heroic thing, and for a moment people set down their glasses in country clubs and speakeasies and thought of their old best dreams."

—quoted in *The Lawless Decade*

Lindbergh's accomplishment paved the way for others. In the next decade, Amelia Earhart was to undertake many brave aerial exploits, inspired by Lindbergh's example.

*The Roaring Life of the 1920s* **449**

**ACTIVITY** **SKILLBUILDER LESSON**

**Drawing Conclusions**

**Explaining the Skill** Drawing conclusions about a historical event or condition means forming an opinion or making an inference based on facts and available evidence. In the process of drawing conclusions, historians also consider evidence in light of what they know to be true from past experience.

**Applying the Skill** Have students read about Lindbergh's flight. Then direct their attention to the quotation from F. Scott Fitzgerald. Ask students to draw conclusions about Fitzgerald's opinion of the flight and of the lifestyles of the 1920s. Have students support their conclusions with specific evidence from the text.

 **In-Depth Resources: Unit 4**
· Skillbuilder Practice, p. 25

In *Radiator Building—Night, New York* (1927), Georgia O'Keeffe showed the dark buildings of New York City thrusting into the night sky.

Mini-Lesson 4: SS11 2(11.D)

## More About . . .

### Georgia O'Keeffe

The changes in American lifestyle around the turn of the 20th century revolutionized its art, as well as its music and other forms of artistic expression. In her paintings, Georgia O'Keefe often made one object—a flower, for example—the sole inhabitant, or focus, of the picture space. Deliberately, she created tension between the persistent presence of the object and the opportunity for free expression. In this way, O'Keefe pointed to a contrast like that between the dependence on the machine and the fear of its dehumanizing possibilities. Ask, How does O'Keefe's work reflect the issues of her time? *(The stark quality of many of her paintings pointed to what was not there—leaving much to the imagination in a time of many social changes and future uncertainties.)*

 In-Depth Resources: Unit 4
· American Lives: Georgia O'Keefe, p. 39

## More About . . .

### Writers of the 1920s

Dorothy Parker, Robert Benchley, and Robert Sherwood worked together as writers and editors at *Vanity Fair* and *The New Yorker*, which were popular magazines of the period. Their famous "Algonquin Round Table" lunches attracted some of the most brilliant writers and artists of the time. The members called themselves the "Vicious Circle" because of their practice of insulting others and enjoying laughs at the expense of others.

**ENTERTAINMENT AND THE ARTS** Despite the feats of real-life heroes, America's thirst for entertainment in the arts and on the screen and stage seemed unquenchable in the 1920s.

Even before the introduction of sound, movies became a national pastime, offering viewers a means of escape through romance and comedy. The first major movie with sound, *The Jazz Singer*, was released in 1927. Walt Disney's *Steamboat Willie*, the first animated film with sound, was released in 1928. By 1930, the new "talkies" had doubled movie attendance, with millions of Americans going to the movies every week. **C**

Both playwrights and composers of music broke away from the European traditions of the 1920s. Eugene O'Neill's plays, such as *The Hairy Ape*, forced Americans to reflect upon modern isolation, confusion, and family conflict. Fame was given to concert music composer **George Gershwin** when he merged traditional elements with American jazz, thus creating a new sound that was identifiably American.

Painters appealed to Americans by recording an America of realities and dreams. Edward Hopper caught the loneliness of American life in his canvases of empty streets and solitary people, while **Georgia O'Keeffe** produced intensely colored canvases that captured the grandeur of New York.

**WRITERS OF THE 1920s** The twenties also brought an outpouring of fresh and insightful writing, making it one of the richest eras in the country's literary history.

**Sinclair Lewis,** the first American to win a Nobel Prize in literature, was among the era's most outspoken critics. In his novel *Babbitt*, Lewis used the main character of George F. Babbitt to ridicule Americans for their conformity and materialism.

### A PERSONAL VOICE SINCLAIR LEWIS

" **A sensational event was changing from the brown suit to the gray the contents of his pockets. He was earnest about these objects. They were of eternal importance, like baseball or the Republican Party. They included a fountain pen and a silver pencil . . . which belonged in the righthand upper vest pocket. Without them he would have felt naked. On his watch-chain were a gold penknife, silver cigar-cutter, seven keys . . . and incidentally a good watch. . . . Last, he stuck in his lapel the Boosters' Club button. With the conciseness of great art the button displayed two words: 'Boosters—Pep!'** "

—*Babbitt*

It was **F. Scott Fitzgerald** who coined the term "Jazz Age" to describe the 1920s. In *This Side of Paradise* and *The Great Gatsby*, he revealed the negative side of the period's gaiety and freedom, portraying wealthy and attractive people leading imperiled lives in gilded surroundings. In New York City, a brilliant group of writers routinely lunched together at the Algonquin Hotel's "Round Table." Among the best known of them was Dorothy Parker, a short story writer, poet, and essayist. Parker was famous for her wisecracking wit, expressed in such lines as "I was the toast of two continents—Greenland and Australia."

MAIN IDEA

**Making Inferences**
**C** Why were Americans so delighted by movies in the 1920s?

**C. Answer**
Movies provided excitement and romance through a medium that was new and changing; they offered adventure to people whose lives were taken up mostly with earning a living.

---

**ACTIVITY** COOPERATIVE LEARNING  BLOCK SCHEDULING

## Presenting Art

**Class Time** 45 minutes

**Task** Presenting the work of famous artists of the period

**Purpose** To understand the variety of artistic achievement in the 1920s

**Directions** Instruct each group of three or four students to choose a particular artist discussed in this chapter, do research on the artist's work, and then present their findings about the artist to the class. A group's presentation might include examples of the artist's writings, music, or paintings, as well as the artist's own statements about what he or she was trying to achieve.

 Integrated Assessment
· Rubrics 3, 4

Many writers also met important issues head on. In *The Age of Innocence*, Edith Wharton dramatized the clash between traditional and modern values that had undermined high society 50 years earlier. Willa Cather celebrated the simple, dignified lives of people such as the immigrant farmers of Nebraska in *My Ántonia*, while **Edna St. Vincent Millay** wrote poems celebrating youth and a life of independence and freedom from traditional constraints.

Some writers such as Fitzgerald, Ernest Hemingway, and John Dos Passos were so soured by American culture that they chose to settle in Europe, mainly in Paris. Socializing in the city's cafes, they formed a group that the writer Gertrude Stein called the Lost Generation. They joined other American writers already in Europe such as the poets Ezra Pound and T. S. Eliot, whose poem *The Waste Land* presented an agonized view of a society that seemed stripped of humanity. **D**

Several writers saw action in World War I, and their early books denounced war. Dos Passos's novel *Three Soldiers* attacked war as a machine designed to crush human freedom. Later, he turned to social and political themes, using modern techniques to capture the mood of city life and the losses that came with success. **Ernest Hemingway,** wounded in World War I, became the best-known expatriate author. In his novels *The Sun Also Rises* and *A Farewell to Arms*, he criticized the glorification of war. He also introduced a tough, simplified style of writing that set a new literary standard, using sentences a *Time* reporter compared to "round stones polished by rain and wind."

During this rich literary era, vital developments were also taking place in African-American society. Black Americans of the 1920s began to voice pride in their heritage, and black artists and writers revealed the richness of African-American culture.

**D. Answer**
Many American writers found American culture shallow and materialistic; they believed society lacked any unified ideals.

**MAIN IDEA**

**Analyzing Causes**
**D** Why did some writers reject American culture and values?

**Vocabulary**
expatriate: a person who has taken up residence in a foreign country

**KEY PLAYER**

**F. SCOTT FITZGERALD**
**1900–1940**

F. Scott Fitzgerald married vivacious Zelda Sayre in 1920 after his novel *This Side of Paradise* became an instant hit. He said of this time in his life:

"Riding in a taxi one afternoon between very tall buildings under a mauve and rosy sky, I began to bawl because I had everything I wanted and knew I would never be so happy again."

Flush with money, the couple plunged into a wild social whirl and outspent their incomes. The years following were difficult. Zelda suffered from repeated mental breakdowns, and Scott's battle with alcoholism took its toll.

**KEY PLAYER**

**F. Scott Fitzgerald**
Fitzgerald was distantly related to Francis Scott Key, the composer of "The Star Spangled Banner," for whom he was named. After more than a decade of fast living, Fitzgerald suffered a nervous collapse in 1935—an episode that he chronicled in series of 1945 essays entitled "The Crack-Up." By that time, Zelda's mental illness had begun to require hospitalization, and the couple spent more and more time apart. Fitzgerald ended his career in Hollywood, where he struggled to stay afloat as a screenwriter. Discuss with students how Fitzgerald and his wife epitomized the Jazz Age.

## Assess & Reteach

**SECTION 3 ASSESSMENT**
Assign students to study groups and have them work together to answer the questions.

Formal Assessment
· Section Quiz, p. 248

**SELF-ASSESSMENT**
Have each student create a six-column chart in which he or she lists important figures of this period in the fields of sports, movies, theater, music, painting, and literature.

**RETEACH**
Use the Guided Reading worksheet for Section 1 to reinforce understanding.

In-Depth Resources: Unit 4
· Reteaching Activity, p. 28

---

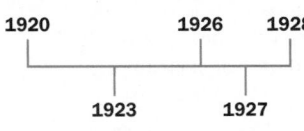 **ASSESSMENT**

1. **TERMS & NAMES** For each of the following names, write a sentence explaining his or her significance.
- **Charles A. Lindbergh**
- **George Gershwin**
- **Georgia O'Keeffe**
- **Sinclair Lewis**
- **F. Scott Fitzgerald**
- **Edna St. Vincent Millay**
- **Ernest Hemingway**

**MAIN IDEA**

**2. TAKING NOTES**
Create a time line of key events relating to 1920s popular culture. Use the dates below as a guide.

| 1920 | | 1926 | 1928 |
|---|---|---|---|
| | 1923 | 1927 | |

In a sentence or two, explain which of these events interests you the most and why.

**CRITICAL THINKING**

**3. SYNTHESIZING**
In what ways do you think the mass media and mass culture helped Americans create a sense of national community in the 1920s? Support your answer with details from the text. **Think About:**
- the content and readership of newspapers and magazines
- attendance at sports events and movie theaters
- the scope of radio broadcasts

**4. EVALUATING**
Do you think the popular heroes of the 1920s were heroes in a real sense? Why or why not?

**5. SUMMARIZING**
In two or three sentences, summarize the effects of education and mass media on society in the 1920s.

*The Roaring Life of the 1920s* **451**

---

Answers **ASSESSMENT** 3

**1. TERMS & NAMES**
Charles A. Lindbergh, p. 449
George Gershwin, p. 450
Georgia O'Keeffe, p. 450
Sinclair Lewis, p. 450
F. Scott Fitzgerald, p. 450
Edna St. Vincent Millay, p. 451
Ernest Hemingway, p. 451

**2. TAKING NOTES**
1920–first commercial radio broadcast, Negro National League (baseball) founded;
1923–founding of *Time*; 1926–Gertrude Ederle swims the English Channel;
1927–Tunney-Dempsey boxing match; Lindbergh's solo flight to Paris; *The Jazz Singer*, Babe Ruth's record-breaking 60 home runs; 1928–*Steamboat Willie*, the first animated film with sound

**3. SYNTHESIZING**
Radio and the news media enabled people nationwide to experience the same entertainment, sports, and information.

**4. EVALUATING**
**Yes:** They were examples of good virtues and exceptional talent. **No:** Their accomplishments were not enduring changes to American life.

**5. SUMMARIZING**
Paragraphs should mention the creation of a literate population and a national identity as a result of mass media.

**452** CHAPTER 13

## OBJECTIVES

**1** Identify the causes and results of the migration of African Americans to Northern cities in the early 1900s.

**2** Describe the prolific African-American artistic activity that became known as the Harlem Renaissance.

### CRITICAL THINKING
· Analyzing Effects, p. 453
· Summarizing, pp. 454, 457
· Synthesizing, p. 456
· Analyzing Causes, p. 457
· Forming Generalizations, p. 457
· Drawing Conclusions, p. 457

## Focus & Motivate

Watch the video "Jump at the Sun" to find out about Zora Neale Hurston and the Harlem Renaissance. Using the *Teacher's Resource Book* as a guide, explore the background of Hurston in Florida. Then, discuss her participation in the Harlem Renaissance and engage in extension activities, using key primary sources.

## Instruct

### Instruct: Objective **1**

**African-American Voices in the 1920s**

TAKS SS11 3(US21.A)
· What factors prompted many African Americans to move to Northern cities?
· What ways did African-American leaders propose to combat discrimination and violence?

 In-Depth Resources: Unit 4
· Guided Reading, p. 23
· Primary Sources: "When the Negro Was in Vogue," p. 35

---

**SECTION 4**

# The Harlem Renaissance

| MAIN IDEA | WHY IT MATTERS NOW | Terms & Names |
|---|---|---|
| African-American ideas, politics, art, literature, and music flourished in Harlem and elsewhere in the United States. | The Harlem Renaissance provided a foundation of African-American intellectualism to which African-American writers, artists, and musicians contribute today. | • Zora Neale Hurston • James Weldon Johnson • Marcus Garvey • Harlem Renaissance • Claude McKay • Langston Hughes • Paul Robeson • Louis Armstrong • Duke Ellington • Bessie Smith |

**TEKS** U.S. History 4B, 5B, 7A, 8A, 11A, 19A, 19B, 20A, 20B, 20C, 21A, 21C, 24A, 24B, 25A, 25B, 25C, 25D, 26A, 26B

**TAKS**

Mini-Lesson 3: SS11 3(US21.A)

### One American's Story

When the spirited **Zora Neale Hurston** was a girl in Eatonville, Florida, in the early 1900s, she loved to read adventure stories and myths. The powerful tales struck a chord with the young, talented Hurston and made her yearn for a wider world.

**A PERSONAL VOICE** ZORA NEALE HURSTON

" My soul was with the gods and my body in the village. People just would not act like gods. . . . Raking back yards and carrying out chamber-pots, were not the tasks of Thor. I wanted to be away from drabness and to stretch my limbs in some mighty struggle. "

—quoted in *The African American Encyclopedia*

After spending time with a traveling theater company and attending Howard University, Hurston ended up in New York where she struggled to the top of African-American literary society by hard work, flamboyance, and, above all, grit. "I have seen that the world is to the strong regardless of a little pigmentation more or less," Hurston wrote later. "I do not weep at [being Negro]—I am too busy sharpening my oyster knife." Hurston was on the move, like millions of others. And, like them, she went after the pearl in the oyster—the good life in America.

**VIDEO**
*JUMP AT THE SUN:*
**Zora Neale Hurston and the Harlem Renaissance**

### **1** African-American Voices in the 1920s

During the 1920s, African Americans set new goals for themselves as they moved north to the nation's cities. Their migration was an expression of their changing attitude toward themselves—an attitude perhaps best captured in a phrase first used around this time, "Black is beautiful."

**THE MOVE NORTH** Between 1910 and 1920, in a movement known as the Great Migration, hundreds of thousands of African Americans had uprooted

---

## PROGRAM RESOURCES

 **In-Depth Resources: Unit 4**
· Guided Reading, p. 23
· Reteaching Activity, p. 29
· Primary Sources: "When the Negro was in Vogue," p. 35
· American Lives: Louis Armstrong, p. 40
 **Reading Study Guide** (English and Spanish), pp. 137–138

 **Access for Students Acquiring English/ESL**
· Guided Reading (Spanish), p. 154
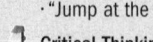 **Formal Assessment**
· Section Quiz, p. 249
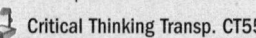 **Integrated Assessment**
· Rubrics

**INTEGRATED TECHNOLOGY**

 American Stories video series
· "Jump at the Sun"
Critical Thinking Transp. CT55
· African-American Migration from the South
Electronic Library of Primary Sources

classzone.com

**TEXAS RESOURCES**

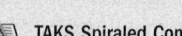 TAKS Spiraled Content Review
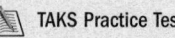 TAKS Practice Tests
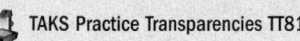 TAKS Practice Transparencies TT81
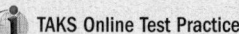 TAKS Online Test Practice

themselves from their homes in the South and moved north to the big cities in search of jobs. By the end of the decade, 5.2 million of the nation's 12 million African Americans—over 40 percent—lived in cities. Zora Neale Hurston documented the departure of some of these African Americans.

**A PERSONAL VOICE** ZORA NEALE HURSTON

"Some said goodbye cheerfully . . . others fearfully, with terrors of known dangers in their mouths . . . others in their eagerness for distance said nothing. The daybreak found them gone. The wind said North."

—quoted in *Sorrow's Kitchen: The Life and Folklore of Zora Neale Hurston*

---

**MAIN IDEA**

**Analyzing Effects**

**A** How did the influx of African Americans change Northern cities?

**A. Answer** The movement of millions of African Americans to Northern cities greatly increased their black populations, and heightened racial tensions that sometimes resulted in discrimination and violence.

---

However, Northern cities in general had not welcomed the massive influx of African Americans. Tensions had escalated in the years prior to 1920, culminating, in the summer of 1919, in approximately 25 urban race riots. **A**

**AFRICAN-AMERICAN GOALS** Founded in 1909, The National Association for the Advancement of Colored People (NAACP) urged African Americans to protest racial violence. W. E. B. Du Bois, a founding member of the NAACP, led a parade of 10,000 African-American men in New York to protest such violence. Du Bois also used the NAACP's magazine, *The Crisis*, as a platform for leading a struggle for civil rights.

Under the leadership of **James Weldon Johnson**—poet, lawyer, and NAACP executive secretary—the organization fought for legislation to protect African-American rights. It made anti-lynching laws one of its main priorities. In 1919, three anti-lynching bills were introduced in Congress, although none was passed. The NAACP continued its campaign through anti-lynching organizations that had been established in 1892 by Ida B. Wells. Gradually, the number of lynchings dropped. The NAACP represented the new, more militant voice of African Americans.

**MARCUS GARVEY AND THE UNIA** Although many African Americans found their voice in the NAACP, they still faced daily threats and discrimination. **Marcus Garvey,** an immigrant from Jamaica, believed that African Americans should build a separate society. His different, more radical message of black pride aroused the hopes of many.

In 1914, Garvey founded the Universal Negro Improvement Association (UNIA). In 1918, he moved the UNIA to New York City and opened offices in urban ghettos in order to recruit followers. By the mid-1920s, Garvey claimed he had a million followers. He appealed to African Americans with a combination of spellbinding oratory, mass meetings, parades, and a message of pride.

**Vocabulary**

**oratory:** the art of public speaking

**A PERSONAL VOICE** MARCUS GARVEY

"In view of the fact that the black man of Africa has contributed as much to the world as the white man of Europe, and the brown man and yellow man of Asia, we of the Universal Negro Improvement Association demand that the white, yellow, and brown races give to the black man his place in the civilization of the world. We ask for nothing more than the rights of 400 million Negroes."

—speech at Liberty Hall, New York City, 1922

---

**KEY PLAYER**

**JAMES WELDON JOHNSON 1871–1938**

James Weldon Johnson worked as a school principal, newspaper editor, and lawyer in Florida. In 1900, he wrote the lyrics for "Lift Every Voice and Sing," the song that became known as the black national anthem. The first stanza begins as follows:

"Lift every voice and sing
Till earth and heaven ring,
Ring with the harmonies of
  Liberty;
Let our rejoicing rise
High as the listening skies,
Let it resound loud as the
  rolling sea."

In the 1920s, Johnson straddled the worlds of politics and art. He served as executive secretary of the NAACP, spearheading the fight against lynching. In addition, he wrote well-known works, such as *God's Trombones*, a series of sermon-like poems, and *Black Manhattan*, a look at black cultural life in New York during the Roaring Twenties.

---

**Tracing Themes**

**IMMIGRATION AND MIGRATION**

**The Great Migration**

A number of push-and-pull factors led to the Great Migration: **push**—racial violence, economic discrimination, and natural disasters in the South; **pull**—job opportunities and better pay in the North. Life in Northern cities, however, remained a struggle for many African Americans. There, they continued to encounter discrimination, violence, and poverty. Many also were forced to live in overcrowded and slum conditions.

Critical Thinking Transparencies CT19
· African-American Migration from the South

---

**KEY PLAYER**

**James Weldon Johnson**

A true "Renaissance man," Johnson worked much of his adult life to lift the status of African Americans. "Johnson was not the man to throw down the gauntlet to America," stated writer Jean Wagner. "He preferred to appeal to its reason and to persuade it that, since blacks and whites are irrevocably destined to live in association, the welfare of one group can only be maintained through assuring the welfare of another." Discuss with students how Johnson's success as a writer made him a successful leader in the fight to protect African-American rights.

---

*The Roaring Life of the 1920s* **453**

---

**DIFFERENTIATING INSTRUCTION** | **LESS PROFICIENT READERS**

**Identifying Important Details**

Some students may have difficulty identifying details that support the main ideas of this section. To help these students organize the information, have them create a chart similar to the one at the right. As they read, have them identify important details and record them in the chart. A completed version of the chart can be used to review the section.

| Changes in Society | |
| --- | --- |
| **Group** | **Changes** |
| Youth | rebelled against values of the past<br>wanted fun and freedom<br>stayed in school longer |
| Women | |
| African Americans | |

# Instruct

## Instruct: Objective ❷

**The Harlem Renaissance Flowers in New York**

TAKS SS11 3(US21.A)

· What ideals did the Harlem Renaissance writers promote?

· How did African-American performers and musicians popularize black culture?

 In-Depth Resources: Unit 4
· Guided Reading, p. 23

---

### More About . . .

#### The Harlem Renaissance

The Harlem Renaissance created a distinctive African-American culture in the United States. The writers and artists of the Harlem Renaissance celebrated their culture, and few of them addressed the problems that most African Americans faced in the 1920s. The Harlem Renaissance was brief, but it remains a lasting tribute to the artistic creativity of African Americans.

---

Garvey also lured followers with practical plans, especially his program to promote African-American businesses. Further, Garvey encouraged his followers to return to Africa, help native people there throw off white colonial oppressors, and build a mighty nation. His idea struck a chord in many African Americans, as well as in blacks in the Caribbean and Africa. Despite the appeal of Garvey's movement, support for it declined in the mid-1920s, when he was convicted of mail fraud and jailed. Although the movement dwindled, Garvey left behind a powerful legacy of newly awakened black pride, economic independence, and reverence for Africa. **B**

▲ Marcus Garvey designed this uniform of purple and gold, complete with feathered hat, for his role as "Provisional President of Africa."

## The Harlem Renaissance ❷ Flowers in New York

Many African Americans who migrated north moved to Harlem, a neighborhood on the Upper West Side of New York's Manhattan Island. In the 1920s, Harlem became the world's largest black urban community, with residents from the South, the West Indies, Cuba, Puerto Rico, and Haiti. James Weldon Johnson described Harlem as the capital of black America.

⭐ **A PERSONAL VOICE** JAMES WELDON JOHNSON

"Harlem is not merely a Negro colony or community, it is a city within a city, the greatest Negro city in the world. It is not a slum or a fringe, it is located in the heart of Manhattan and occupies one of the most beautiful . . . sections of the city. . . . It has its own churches, social and civic centers, shops, theaters, and other places of amusement. And it contains more Negroes to the square mile than any other spot on earth."

—"Harlem: The Culture Capital"

Like many other urban neighborhoods, Harlem suffered from overcrowding, unemployment, and poverty. But its problems in the 1920s were eclipsed by a flowering of creativity called the **Harlem Renaissance,** a literary and artistic movement celebrating African-American culture.

**AFRICAN–AMERICAN WRITERS** Above all, the Harlem Renaissance was a literary movement led by well-educated, middle-class African Americans who expressed a new pride in the African-American experience. They celebrated their heritage and wrote with defiance and poignancy about the trials of being black in a white world. W. E. B. Du Bois and James Weldon Johnson helped these young talents along, as did the Harvard-educated former Rhodes scholar Alain Locke. In 1925, Locke published *The New Negro*, a landmark collection of literary works by many promising young African-American writers.

**Claude McKay,** a novelist, poet, and Jamaican immigrant, was a major figure whose militant verses urged African Americans to resist prejudice and discrimination. His poems also expressed the pain of life in the black ghettos and the strain of being black in a world dominated by whites. Another gifted writer of the time was Jean Toomer. His experimental book *Cane*—a mix of poems and sketches about blacks in the North and the South—was among the first full-length literary publications of the Harlem Renaissance.

Missouri-born **Langston Hughes** was the movement's best-known poet. Many of Hughes's 1920s poems described the difficult lives of working-class African Americans. Some of his poems moved to the tempo of jazz and the blues. (See Literature in the Jazz Age on page 458.)

**454** CHAPTER 13

---

---

**DIFFERENTIATING INSTRUCTION**     **LESS PROFICIENT READERS**

### Exploring Themes

The major Harlem Renaissance writers expressed a variety of different ideas. To help students keep track of the different themes these artists expressed in their writings, have students create a chart like the one shown at the right and fill it in as they read.

| Themes | |
|---|---|
| McKay | pain of life in black ghettos |
| Toomer | |
| Hughes | |
| Hurston | |
| West | |

## Harlem in the 1920s

At the turn of the century, New York's Harlem neighborhood was overbuilt with new apartment houses. Enterprising African-American realtors began buying and leasing property to other African Americans who were eager to move into the prosperous neighborhood. As the number of blacks in Harlem increased, many whites began moving out. Harlem quickly grew to become the center of black America and the birthplace of the political, social, and cultural movement known as the Harlem Renaissance.

The Fletcher Henderson Orchestra became one of the most influential jazz bands during the Harlem Renaissance. Here, Henderson, the band's founder, sits at the piano, with Louis Armstrong on trumpet (rear, center).

**New York City**

predominantly black neighborhoods

0 ____ 1 mile
0 ____ 1 kilometer

145th St.
Cotton Club
140th St.
Savoy Theatre
James Weldon Johnson home
135th St.
Library
Lafayette Theatre
130th St.
Marcus Garvey home
125th St.
Apollo Theatre

Harlem River
North
River

In the mid 1920s, the Cotton Club was one of a number of fashionable entertainment clubs in Harlem. Although many venues like the Cotton Club were segregated, white audiences packed the clubs to hear the new music styles of black performers such as Duke Ellington and Bessie Smith.

In 1927, Harlem was a bustling neighborhood.

### More About . . .

**African-American Artists**

The visual arts were also an important part of the Harlem Renaissance. African-American artists often used Africa and African-American life as themes for their paintings. Among these artists were Lois Mailou Jones, William H. Johnson, Palmer Hayden, Archibald Motley, Jr., Aaron Douglas, and Jacob Lawrence. Douglas's *Song of the Towers* is shown on page 435.

### Connections Across Time

**1920s AND TODAY**

**Another Harlem Renaissance**

Harlem fell on hard times for much of the mid and late 20th century, due mainly to overcrowding, high unemployment, and deteriorating buildings. It has experienced a rebirth of sorts in recent years. Harlem's 125th Street, popularly known as the "Main Stem," has witnessed an economic boom, luring retailers and new construction. The neighborhood's prestige received a further boost when former President Bill Clinton made Harlem the site of his post-presidential office.

*The Roaring Life of the 1920s* **455**

---

**ACTIVITY    COOPERATIVE LEARNING**

 **BLOCK SCHEDULING**

### Celebrating African-American Culture

**Class Time** 45 minutes

**Task** Developing presentations honoring writers, performers, and musicians of the Harlem Renaissance

**Purpose** To recognize the impact of the Harlem Renaissance on American culture

**Directions** Divide students into three groups representing writers, performers, and musicians. Each group should develop a presentation celebrating the work of the African-American artists they represent. Presentations might include recordings of music, posters advertising performances, book reviews, dramatic readings, and role-playing. Provide time for the groups to share their presentations with the class.

 Integrated Assessment
· Rubric 3, 4

### More About . . .

**Paul Robeson**
Robeson excelled at nearly everything he did. An academic standout at Rutgers College, he also became the school's first All-American in football. He went on to earn a law degree from Columbia University. Encouraged to explore the theater, Robeson soon won wide acclaim for his acting abilities. "The stage," wrote one critic, "was an arena where his race, far from impeding his career, actually enabled him to capitalize on his talents much more quickly than would ordinarily have been the case." Because of his support of the Communist Party, he was blacklisted. As a result, he had difficulty finding work and his yearly income fell from a high of more than $100,000 to $2,000.

### More About . . .

**Louis Armstrong**
At the age of 12, Louis Armstrong was arrested for firing a gun on New Year's Eve and sent to a home for boys in New Orleans. In that institution, Armstrong first learned to play the cornet. He continued to develop the talent that eventually made him one of the most influential jazz musicians of all time and an internationally known performer. Once, when asked to define jazz, Armstrong replied, "Man, if you gotta ask, you'll never know."

 In-Depth Resources: Unit 4
· American Lives: Louis Armstrong, p.40

In many of her novels, short stories, poems, and books of folklore, Zora Neale Hurston portrayed the lives of poor, unschooled Southern blacks—in her words, "the greatest cultural wealth of the continent." Much of her work celebrated what she called the common person's art form—the simple folkways and values of people who had survived slavery through their ingenuity and strength. **C**

**AFRICAN–AMERICAN PERFORMERS** The spirit and talent of the Harlem Renaissance reached far beyond the world of African-American writers and intellectuals. Some observers, including Langston Hughes, thought the movement was launched with *Shuffle Along*, a black musical comedy popular in 1921. "It gave just the proper push to that negro vogue of the '20s," he wrote. Several songs in *Shuffle Along*, including "Love Will Find a Way," won popularity among white audiences. The show also spotlighted the talents of several black performers, including the singers Florence Mills, Josephine Baker, and Mabel Mercer.

During the 1920s, African Americans in the performing arts won large followings. The tenor Roland Hayes rose to stardom as a concert singer, and the singer and actress Ethel Waters debuted on Broadway in the musical *Africana*. **Paul Robeson,** the son of a one-time slave, became a major dramatic actor. His performance in Shakespeare's *Othello*, first in London and later in New York City, was widely acclaimed. Subsequently, Robeson struggled with the racism he experienced in the United States and the indignities inflicted upon him because of his support of the Soviet Union and the Communist Party. He took up residence abroad, living for a time in England and the Soviet Union.

The Hot Five included (*from left*) Louis Armstrong, Johnny St. Cyr, Johnny Dodds, Kid Ory, and Lil Hardin Armstrong.

**AFRICAN AMERICANS AND JAZZ** Jazz was born in the early 20th century in New Orleans, where musicians blended instrumental ragtime and vocal blues into an exuberant new sound. In 1918, Joe "King" Oliver and his Creole Jazz Band traveled north to Chicago, carrying jazz with them. In 1922, a young trumpet player named **Louis Armstrong** joined Oliver's group, which became known as the Creole Jazz Band. His talent rocketed him to stardom in the jazz world.

Famous for his astounding sense of rhythm and his ability to improvise, Armstrong made personal expression a key part of jazz. After two years in Chicago, in 1924 he joined Fletcher Henderson's band, then the most important big jazz band in New York City. Armstrong went on to become perhaps the most important and influential musician in the history of jazz. He often talked about his anticipated funeral.

**A PERSONAL VOICE** LOUIS ARMSTRONG

" They're going to blow over me. Cats will be coming from everywhere to play. I had a beautiful life. When I get to the Pearly Gates I'll play a duet with Gabriel. We'll play 'Sleepy Time Down South.' He wants to be remembered for his music just like I do. "

—quoted in *The Negro Almanac*

Jazz quickly spread to such cities as Kansas City, Memphis, and New York City, and it became the most popular music for dancing. During the 1920s, Harlem pulsed to the sounds of jazz, which lured throngs of whites to the showy, exotic nightclubs there, including the famed Cotton Club. In the late 1920s, **Edward Kennedy "Duke" Ellington,** a jazz pianist and composer, led his

MAIN IDEA

**Synthesizing**
**C** In what ways did writers of the Harlem Renaissance celebrate a "rebirth"?

*C. Answer*
They expressed their pride in African-American experience; they celebrated their heritage and folklore.

**Background**
See Historical Spotlight on page 617.

---

ACTIVITY    LINK TO MUSIC                                        BLOCK SCHEDULING

**All That Jazz**

**Class Time** 45 minutes

**Task** Defining jazz music

**Purpose** To listen to and identify characteristics of an American musical form

**Directions** Remind students that jazz is a distinctively American form of music, combining blues, ragtime, and African rhythms. Play an example of each type of music so that students can listen for those elements in jazz. Play cuts by a variety of jazz musicians of the period. Ask students to take notes about the characteristics of the music they hear. Compile their ideas and create a class definition of jazz.

ten-piece orchestra at the Cotton Club. In a 1925 essay titled "The Negro Spirituals," Alain Locke seemed almost to predict the career of the talented Ellington.

### A PERSONAL VOICE ALAIN LOCKE

"Up to the present, the resources of Negro music have been tentatively exploited in only one direction at a time—melodically here, rhythmically there, harmonically in a third direction. A genius that would organize its distinctive elements in a formal way would be the musical giant of his age."

—quoted in *Afro-American Writing: An Anthology of Prose and Poetry*

Through the 1920s and 1930s, Ellington won renown as one of America's greatest composers, with pieces such as "Mood Indigo" and "Sophisticated Lady."

Cab Calloway, a talented drummer, saxophonist, and singer, formed another important jazz orchestra, which played at Harlem's Savoy Ballroom and the Cotton Club, alternating with Duke Ellington. Along with Louis Armstrong, Calloway popularized "scat," or improvised jazz singing using sounds instead of words.

**Bessie Smith,** a female blues singer, was perhaps the outstanding vocalist of the decade. She recorded on black-oriented labels produced by the major record companies. She achieved enormous popularity and in 1927 became the highest-paid black artist in the world. **D**

The Harlem Renaissance represented a portion of the great social and cultural changes that swept America in the 1920s. The period was characterized by economic prosperity, new ideas, changing values, and personal freedom, as well as important developments in art, literature, and music. Most of the social changes were lasting. The economic boom, however, was short-lived.

**D. Answer**
African Americans were outstanding in the performing arts.

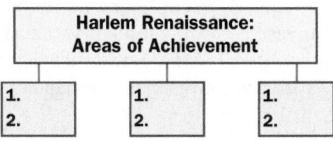

**Summarizing**
**D** Besides literary accomplishments, in what areas did African Americans achieve remarkable results?

---

### KEY PLAYER

**DUKE ELLINGTON**
**1899–1974**
Edward Kennedy "Duke" Ellington, one of the greatest composers of the 20th century, was largely a self-taught musician. He developed his skills by playing at family socials. He wrote his first song, "Soda Fountain Rag," at age 15 and started his first band at 22.

During the five years Ellington played at Harlem's glittering Cotton Club, he set a new standard, playing mainly his own stylish compositions. Through radio and the film short *Black and Tan*, the Duke Ellington Orchestra was able to reach nationwide audiences. Billy Strayhorn, Ellington's long-time arranger and collaborator, said, "Ellington plays the piano, but his real instrument is his band."

---

### KEY PLAYER

**Duke Ellington**
Many critics say that Ellington's orchestra reached its peak between the mid-1930s and the 1940s, when it premiered his suite "Black, Brown, and Beige," a musical history of African Americans. Ellington continued composing, playing, and touring until the 1970s. Have students consider what type of memorial they would make to commemorate Ellington's contributions to American culture. Possible kinds of memorials are postage stamps, plaques, statues, poems, songs, and pictures.

## Assess & Reteach

### SECTION 4 ASSESSMENT
Use the Section 4 Assessment as an oral pretest for the section quiz. Ask volunteers to answer the questions in class, and have other students take note of any questions they could not answer.

📄 Formal Assessment
· Section Quiz, p. 249

### SELF-ASSESSMENT
As a homework assignment, students should write answers to the questions that they could not answer in the oral pretest.

### RETEACH
Repeat the video "Jump at the Sun" and discuss the African-American experience, with particular reference to the Harlem Renaissance.

📄 In-Depth Resources: Unit 4
· Reteaching Activity, p. 29

---

## 4 ASSESSMENT

**1. TERMS & NAMES** For each term or name, write a sentence explaining its significance.

- Zora Neale Hurston
- Harlem Renaissance
- Paul Robeson
- Duke Ellington
- James Weldon Johnson
- Claude McKay
- Louis Armstrong
- Bessie Smith
- Marcus Garvey
- Langston Hughes

### MAIN IDEA

**2. TAKING NOTES**
In a tree diagram, identify three areas of artistic achievement in the Harlem Renaissance. For each, name two outstanding African Americans.

```
Harlem Renaissance:
Areas of Achievement

1.      1.      1.
2.      2.      2.
```

Write a paragraph explaining the impact of these achievements.

### CRITICAL THINKING

**3. ANALYZING CAUSES**
Speculate on why an African-American renaissance flowered during the 1920s. Support your answer. **Think About:**
- racial discrimination in the South
- campaigns for equality in the North
- Harlem's diverse cultures
- the changing culture of all Americans

**4. FORMING GENERALIZATIONS**
How did popular culture in America change as a result of the Great Migration?

**5. DRAWING CONCLUSIONS**
What did the Harlem Renaissance contribute to both black and general American history?

*The Roaring Life of the 1920s* **457**

---

Answers ASSESSMENT **4**

**1. TERMS & NAMES**
Zora Neale Hurston, p. 452
James Weldon Johnson, p. 453
Marcus Garvey, p. 453
Harlem Renaissance, p. 454
Claude McKay, p. 454
Langston Hughes, p. 454
Paul Robeson, p. 456
Louis Armstrong, p. 456
Duke Ellington, p. 456
Bessie Smith, p. 457

**2. TAKING NOTES**
**Writing:** Langston Hughes, Zora Neale Hurston
**Performing:** Paul Robeson, Ethel Waters
**Music:** Bessie Smith, Louis Armstrong

**3. ANALYZING CAUSES**
African Americans migrated north in large numbers and found more equality and a community that supported the arts. Mingling with Caribbean people and Northerners created a unique cultural exchange and served as inspiration for the arts.

**4. FORMING GENERALIZATIONS**
African-American performers had many fans. Jazz quickly spread across the country and became popular dance music.

**5. DRAWING CONCLUSIONS**
The Harlem Renaissance nurtured African-American pride, and contributed great literature, drama, and music to American culture.

AMERICAN
LITERATURE

## Objectives

· To describe the role of American literature in the 1920s

· To recognize three 1920s literary icons and give examples of their works

## Focus & Motivate

**Evaluating** Have students think about celebrated Americans today. Which of these people do students think best captures the spirit of the time? Who would students name as America's greatest writer today? Students should cite achievements to support their opinions.

### More About . . .

**Edna St. Vincent Millay**
Millay was raised by a mother who encouraged her children to explore artistic pursuits. At her mother's insistence, Millay, about 20 years old, entered her poem "Renascence" in a poetry contest. It won fourth place and helped earn her a scholarship to Vassar College.

AMERICAN LITERATURE

# Literature in the Jazz Age

**1920–1929** After World War I, American literature—like American jazz—moved to the vanguard of the international artistic scene. Many American writers remained in Europe after the war, some settling in London but many more joining the expatriate community on the Left Bank of the Seine River in Paris, where they could live cheaply.

Back in the United States, such cities as Chicago and New York were magnets for America's young artistic talents. New York City gave birth to the Harlem Renaissance, a blossoming of African-American culture named for the New York City neighborhood where many African-American writers and artists settled. Further downtown, the artistic community of Greenwich Village drew literary talents such as the poets Edna St. Vincent Millay and E. E. Cummings and the playwright Eugene O'Neill.

### F. SCOTT FITZGERALD

The foremost chronicler of the Jazz Age was the Minnesota-born writer F. Scott Fitzgerald, who in Paris, New York, and later Hollywood rubbed elbows with other leading American writers of the day. In the following passage from Fitzgerald's novel *The Great Gatsby*, the narrator describes a fashionable 1920s party thrown by the title character at his Long Island estate.

By seven o'clock the orchestra has arrived, no thin five-piece affair, but a whole pitful of oboes and trombones and saxophones and viols and cornets and piccolos, and low and high drums. The last swimmers have come in from the beach now and are dressing up-stairs; the cars from New York are parked five deep in the drive, and already the halls and salons and verandas are gaudy with primary colors, and hair shorn in strange new ways, and shawls beyond the dreams of Castile. The bar is in full swing, and floating rounds of cocktails permeate the garden outside, until the air is alive with chatter and laughter, and casual innuendo and introductions forgotten on the spot, and enthusiastic meetings between women who never knew each other's names.

The lights grow brighter as the earth lurches away from the sun, and now the orchestra is playing yellow cocktail music, and the opera of voices pitches a key higher. Laughter is easier minute by minute, spilled with prodigality, tipped out at a cheerful word. The groups change more swiftly, swell with new arrivals, dissolve and form in the same breath; already there are wanderers, confident girls who weave here and there among the stouter and more stable, become for a sharp, joyous moment the center of a group, and then, excited with triumph, glide on through the sea-change of faces and voices and color under the constantly changing light.

Suddenly one of these gypsies, in trembling opal, seizes a cocktail out of the air, dumps it down for courage and, moving her hands like Frisco, dances out alone on the canvas platform. A momentary hush; the orchestra leader varies his rhythm obligingly for her, and there is a burst of chatter as the erroneous news goes around that she is Gilda Gray's understudy from the Follies. The party has begun.

—F. Scott Fitzgerald, *The Great Gatsby* (1925)

## RECOMMENDED RESOURCES

**BOOKS**

Cheney, Anne. *Millay in Greenwich Village.* U of Alabama P. 1975. A biography of the young Millay.

Cowley, Malcolm. *Exile's Return.* New ed. New York: Viking, 1994. A famous literary history of the 1920s.

Fitzgerald, F. Scott. *The Great Gatsby.* New York: Penguin, 2000. Fitzgerald's masterpiece.

Lewis, David L. *When Harlem Was in Vogue.* New York: Viking Penguin, 1997. A well-known account of the Harlem Renaissance.

Millay, Edna St. Vincent. *Collected Poems.* New York: Harper, 1981. All the famous poems and sonnets.

Walker, Alice. *Langston Hughes, American Poet.* New York: Harper, 2002. Illustrated biography of the famous Harlem poet.

**VIDEOS**

*Against the Odds.* PBS Video, 1994. Describes artists of the Harlem Renaissance.

*The Great Gatsby.* Dir. Jack Clayton. Paramount, 1974. Fitzgerald's novel on screen.

*Langston Hughes: Poet.* Dir. Rhonda Fabian and Jerry Baber. Schlessinger Video Productions, 1994. Part of the Black Americans of Achievement Video Collection.

*Langston Hughes: The Poet in Our Hearts.* Chip Taylor Communications, 1994. Readings of several of Hughes's poems.

◄ **EDNA ST. VINCENT MILLAY**

In the 1920s, Edna St. Vincent Millay was the quintessential modern young woman, a celebrated poet living a bohemian life in New York's Greenwich Village. The following quatrain memorably proclaims the exuberant philosophy of the young and fashionable in the Roaring Twenties.

> My candle burns at both ends;
>     It will not last the night;
> But ah, my foes, and oh, my friends—
>     It gives a lovely light!

—Edna St. Vincent Millay, "First Fig,"
from *A Few Figs from Thistles* (1920)

## Instruct

1. Why might the nation's large cities have been a magnet for many writers of the time?
2. How does the scene that Fitzgerald describes capture the essence of the Roaring Twenties?
3. What double meanings are conveyed in the language of the poems of Millay and Hughes?

### MAKING PERSONAL CONNECTIONS

Have students discuss literature, music, movies, or other forms of entertainment that they have encountered that depict American society today. What do students think that this particular artistic piece is saying about modern culture?

**LANGSTON HUGHES ▶**

A towering figure of the Harlem Renaissance, Langston Hughes often imbued his poetry with the rhythms of jazz and blues. In the poem "Dream Variations," for example, the two stanzas resemble improvised passages played and varied by a jazz musician. The dream of freedom and equality is a recurring symbol in Hughes's verse and has appeared frequently in African-American literature since the 1920s, when Hughes penned this famous poem.

> To fling my arms wide
> In some place of the sun,
> To whirl and to dance
> Till the white day is done.
> Then rest at cool evening
> Beneath a tall tree
>     Dark like me—
> That is my dream!
>
> To fling my arms wide
> In the face of the sun,
> Dance! Whirl! Whirl!
> Till the quick day is done.
> Rest at pale evening . . .
> A tall, slim tree . . .
> Night coming tenderly
>     Black like me.

—Langston Hughes, "Dream Variations,"
from *The Weary Blues* (1926)

### More About . . .

**Langston Hughes**

Hughes was an unknown writer employed as a busboy when the eminent poet Vachel Lindsay came into the Washington, D.C., restaurant where Hughes worked. Hoping for recognition, Hughes left some of his poems beside Lindsay's plate. Later that day, Lindsay read them and was so impressed that he praised them to reporters. Hughes's name appeared in the newspapers the next day. Not long afterward, Alfred A. Knopf published Hughes's first poetry collection, *The Weary Blues* (1926).

---

**THINKING CRITICALLY**

1. **Comparing** What connections can you make between the literary and music scenes during the jazz age?

 **SEE SKILLBUILDER HANDBOOK, PAGE R8.**

2.  **INTERNET ACTIVITY** **CLASSZONE.COM**

Visit the links for American Literature to research writers of the Jazz Age. Then, create a short report on one writer's life. Include titles of published works and an example of his or her writing style.

*The Roaring Life of the 1920s* **459**

---

**THINKING CRITICALLY: ANSWERS**

1. **COMPARING** Some of the literature of the Jazz Age reflected elements of jazz music, such as Langston Hughes's rhythmic poetry. Many writers and musicians of this time expressed exuberance and unconventional emotions in their works. Both music and literature were marked by the new styles and attitudes that society reflected. The music and literature of the Jazz Age gained great popularity because of their fresh and expressive perspectives.

2. **INTERNET ACTIVITY** Reports will vary, but should demonstrate thorough research on one writer of the Jazz Age. Students should include biographical information, a list of published works, and a sample of the author's writing that exemplifies his or her style.

## TERMS & NAMES

1. bootlegger, p. 437
2. fundamentalism, p. 438
3. flapper, p. 441
4. Charles A. Lindbergh, p. 449
5. George Gershwin, p. 450
6. F. Scott Fitzgerald, p. 450
7. Zora Neale Hurston, p. 452
8. Harlem Renaissance, p. 454
9. Langston Hughes, p. 454
10. Paul Robeson, p. 456

## MAIN IDEAS

1. Government had to patrol coastlines and inland borders for alcohol smugglers, monitor highways for trucks carrying illegal alcohol, and oversee industries that used alcohol.
2. Scopes broke a Tennessee law that made teaching evolution a crime. He was found guilty, but a higher court later set aside the verdict.
3. Flappers sported boyish haircuts and wore short, waistless dresses. Many drank or smoked in public and dated casually.
4. The birthrate declined, more married women worked, and labor-saving devices provided more leisure time.
5. High schools broadened their curricula to meet the needs of a wide range of students, offered vocational training and home economics, and taught English to immigrants.
6. Conformity; materialism; shallowness of middle-class values; glorification of war
7. They showed the desire of African Americans to escape inequality and poverty, fight injustice, and improve their lives.
8. Pride; racial justice; equality; richness of folklore

---

### VISUAL SUMMARY

## THE ROARING LIFE OF THE 1920s

#### NEW FORMS OF ENTERTAINMENT

- Movies become a national pastime.
- Radio is a prime source of news and entertainment.
- Americans celebrate sports heroes.

#### NEW MOVEMENTS IN THE ARTS

- Composers create distinctly American music.
- Writers explore new topics.
- Artists depict life in the 1920s.
- Harlem Renaissance flourishes.

#### PROBLEMS OF URBANIZATION

- Industrialization leads to growth of big cities.
- African Americans continue to move North.
- Cities struggle with prohibition and organized crime.

#### NEW ATTITUDES AND FASHION

- Changing attitudes toward women allow them greater freedoms.
- Americans adopt radical new fashions and style.
- Traditional and modern ideals collide.

---

## TERMS & NAMES

For each term or name below, write a sentence explaining its historical significance or contribution to the 1920s.

1. bootlegger
2. fundamentalism
3. flapper
4. double standard
5. Charles A. Lindbergh
6. George Gershwin
7. F. Scott Fitzgerald
8. Zora Neale Hurston
9. Harlem Renaissance
10. Paul Robeson

## MAIN IDEAS

Use your notes and the information in the chapter to answer the following questions.

**Changing Ways of Life** *(pages 434–439)*
1. Why was heavy funding needed to enforce the Volstead Act?
2. Explain the circumstances and outcome of the trial of the biology teacher John Scopes.

**The Twenties Woman** *(pages 440–443)*
3. In what ways did flappers rebel against the earlier styles and attitudes of the Victorian age?
4. What key social, economic, and technological changes of the 1920s affected women's marriages and family life?

**Education and Popular Culture** *(pages 446–451)*
5. How did high schools change in the 1920s?
6. Cite examples of the flaws of American society that some famous 1920s authors attacked in their writing.

**The Harlem Renaissance** *(pages 452–457)*
7. What do the Great Migration and the growth of the NAACP and UNIA reveal about the African-American experience in this period?
8. What were some of the important themes treated by African-American writers in the Harlem Renaissance?

## CRITICAL THINKING

1. **USING YOUR NOTES** Create a concept web like the one below and fill it in with trends in popular culture that emerged in the 1920s and continue to influence American society today.

Enduring Cultural Trends of the Roaring Twenties

2. **EVALUATING** In "Literature in the Jazz Age," on pages 458–459, you read excerpts from works written in the 1920s by F. Scott Fitzgerald, Edna St. Vincent Millay, and Langston Hughes. How might a phrase current at the time—"flaming youth"—be an appropriate and accurate phrase to describe the young people and voices in these excerpts?

---

## CRITICAL THINKING

1. **Using Your Notes** Media hyping of sensational trials; public fascination with stories in tabloids; hero worship of sports celebrities; popularity of spectator sports and movies; popularity of African-American music; novels and social protest; poetry with political messages; fashion as a statement of rebellion.

2. **Evaluating** The images of bright lights, parties, dancing, whirling, and candles all seem to belong to a world of fast living and a brief but luminous existence that suggests youthful excitement.

## Standardized Test Practice

## Standardized Test Practice

Use the visual below and your knowledge of United States history to answer question 1.

1. The woman shown on this magazine cover represents a lifestyle championed by which of the following 1920s figures?

   A Zelda Sayre Fitzgerald
   B Edna St. Vincent Millay
   C Anna Howard Shaw
   D Aimee Semple McPherson

2. The great flowering of African-American artistic activity in the 1920s is known as —

   F the Jazz Age
   G the speakeasy
   H the Harlem Renaissance
   J American fundamentalism

Use the quotation and your knowledge of U.S. history to answer question 3.

" No more fear, no more cringing, no more sycophantic begging and pleading; but the Negro must strike straight from the shoulder for manhood rights and for full liberty. Africa calls now more than ever."

3. The quotation supports the "Back to Africa" movement. One important leader of this movement in the 1920s was —

   A Marcus Garvey
   B James Weldon Johnson
   C Zora Neale Hurston
   D Paul Robeson

**ADDITIONAL TEST PRACTICE, pages S1–S33.**

TEST PRACTICE  CLASSZONE.COM

---

1. The correct answer is letter **A.**
   Zelda Sayre Fitzgerald was a model for the young women of the 1920s who wanted to break away from traditions. The letter C is not correct because Anna Howard Shaw was interested in woman suffrage, and not in the flapper lifestyle. The letter D is not correct because Aimee Semple McPherson's interest was in religion.

2. The correct answer is letter **H.**
   The great flowering of African-American artistic activity centered around Harlem, a section of New York City. The letter F is incorrect because the Jazz Age refers to an era of the 1920s itself. The letter G is incorrect because a speakeasy is a building. The letter J is incorrect because it refers to a religious movement of the time.

3. The correct answer is **A.**
   Marcus Garvey founded an organization that promoted "Back to Africa" among African Americans. The letters B and C are incorrect because James Weldon Johnson and Zora Neale Hurston both sought a better life for African Americans in the United States. The letter D is incorrect because Paul Robeson's Communist beliefs led him to live abroad in Europe rather than Africa.

## UNIT PROJECT

**MULTI-MEDIA PRESENTATION**
**Tips for Teaching**
· Remind students to copy or print out pictures or other information for their presentation.
· Find partners for students who may be having difficulty getting started on the project.

---

## ALTERNATIVE ASSESSMENT

1. **INTERACT WITH HISTORY**  Recall your discussion of the question on page 433:

   ### How might the new prosperity affect your everyday life?

   Now that you have read about life in the 1920s, what do you think was the most significant cultural development during this time? Write a paragraph describing how this change impacted society and how it evolved. Share your paragraph with your class.

2. **VIDEO**  **LEARNING FROM MEDIA**  View the *American Stories* video "Jump at the Sun." Discuss the following questions in a group; then do the activity.
   • What effect did World War I have on the attitudes of African Americans?
   • What effect might growing up in Eatonville, Florida, have had on Zora Neale Hurston?
   • How did Hurston connect the study of anthropology with the world of her youth?

   **Cooperative Learning Activity**  With your group, think of visuals that represent Zora Neale Hurston's dramatic life. Search through books, magazines, and encyclopedias for pictures that seem to capture her spirit and life experiences. Make copies of the pictures and assemble them in a collage.

*The Roaring Life of the 1920s* **461**

 Formal Assessment
· Chapter Test, Forms A, B, and C, pp. 250–261

---

## ALTERNATIVE ASSESSMENT

### 1. INTERACT WITH HISTORY
**Rubric**
The paragraph should. . .
· begin with a clear statement of the cultural development chosen
· reflect the student's understanding of how the cultural change affected American life in the 1920s
· present necessary facts and examples to support the student's viewpoint

### 2. LEARNING FROM MEDIA
**Rubric**
A collage should . . .
· demonstrate an understanding of Zora Neale Hurston's life
· clearly present the spirit and life of Zora Neale Hurston through juxtapositions of words and pictures
· exhibit grade level artistic skill

# The Great Depression Begins

| | CHAPTER OVERVIEW | COPYMASTERS | INTEGRATED TECHNOLOGY |
|---|---|---|---|
| **CHAPTER RESOURCES** | *The economic boom of the 1920s collapses in 1929 as the United States enters a deep economic depression. Millions of Americans lose their jobs, and President Hoover is unable to end the downslide.* | 📘 Telescoping the Times <br> · Chapter Summary, pp. 27–28 <br><br> 📘 Planning for Block Schedules | 📹 American Stories video series <br> · "Broke but not Broken" <br><br> 💿 Power Presentations <br><br> 💿 Electronic Teacher Tools <br><br> 💿 America's Music CD <br><br> 🔘 Online Lesson Planner <br><br> 🔘 classzone.com |
| **SECTION 1** <br><br> The Nation's Sick Economy <br><br> pp. 464–471 | **KEY IDEAS** <br><br> *Economic problems affecting industries, farmers, and consumers lead to the Great Depression.* | 📘 In-Depth Resources: Unit 4 <br> · Guided Reading, p. 41 <br> · Building Vocabulary, p. 44 <br> · Skillbuilder Practice, p. 45 <br> · Reteaching Activity, p. 46 <br> · Primary Sources, pp. 51–52 <br> · American Lives, pp. 58–59 <br><br> 📘 Lesson Plans, pp. 111–112 | 🗺 Geography Transparencies GT22 <br> · Growth and Electricity, 1918 and 1933 <br><br> 🗺 Critical Thinking Transparencies CT22 <br> · The Great Depression <br><br> 💿 Electronic Library of Primary Sources <br> · "On Minding your Own Business" <br><br> 🔘 classzone.com |
| **SECTION 2** <br><br> Hardship and Suffering During the Depression <br><br> pp. 472–477 | *The Great Depression brings suffering of many kinds and degrees to people from all walks of life.* | 📘 In-Depth Resources: Unit 4 <br> · Guided Reading, p. 42 <br> · Skillbuilder Practice, p. 45 <br> · Reteaching Activity, p. 47 <br> · Geography Application, pp. 49–50 <br> · Primary Sources, p. 53 <br> · Literature, pp. 55–57 <br><br> 📘 Lesson Plans, pp. 113–114 | 📹 American Stories video series <br> · "Broke but not Broken" <br><br> 🗺 Humanities Transparencies HT21 <br> · Dust storm <br><br> 💿 Electronic Library of Primary Sources <br> · "Beans, Bacon, and Gravy" <br> · "Childhood During the Depression" <br><br> 🔘 classzone.com |
| **SECTION 3** <br><br> Hoover Struggles with the Depression <br><br> pp. 478–483 | *President Hoover tries to restore confidence and halt the Depression, but his actions are ineffective.* | 📘 In-Depth Resources: Unit 4 <br> · Guided Reading, p. 43 <br> · Reteaching Activity, p. 48 <br> · Primary Sources, p. 54 <br><br> 📘 Lesson Plans, pp. 115–116 | 💿 Electronic Library of Primary Sources <br> · from A *Report on the Employment of Federal Troops* <br><br> · from *B.E.F. The Whole Story of the Bonus Army* <br><br> 🔘 classzone.com |

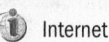
## ASSESSMENT OPTIONS

PE Chapter Assessment, pp. 484–485

📄 Formal Assessment
· Chapter Tests, Forms A, B, and C, pp. 265–282

◉ Test Generator

📄 Integrated Assessment Book

ⓘ TAKS Online Test Practice

📄 TAKS Spiraled Content Review

TAKS Practice Tests

---

PE Section 1 Assessment, p. 471

TE Self-Assessment, p. 471

📄 Formal Assessment, Quiz, p. 262

📄 Integrated Assessment Book

◉ Test Generator

↧ TAKS Practice Transparencies TT82

---

PE Section 2 Assessment, p. 477

TE Self-Assessment, p. 477

📄 Formal Assessment, Quiz, p. 263

📄 Integrated Assessment Book

◉ Test Generator

↧ TAKS Practice Transparencies TT83

---

PE Section 3 Assessment, p. 483

TE Self-Assessment, p. 483

📄 Formal Assessment, Quiz, p. 264

📄 Integrated Assessment Book

◉ Test Generator

↧ TAKS Practice Transparencies TT84

## RESOURCES FOR DIFFERENTIATING INSTRUCTION

### Students Acquiring English/ESL

📄 **Reading Study Guide:**
(English and Spanish)
pp. 141–148

📄 **Access for Students Acquiring English/ESL:**
Spanish Translations,
pp. 158–165

◀)) **Chapter Summaries on CD**
(English and Spanish)

### Less Proficient Readers

📄 **Reading Study Guide**
(English and Spanish)
pp. 141–148

📄 **Telescoping the Times**
· Chapter Summary,
pp. 27–28

◀)) **Chapter Summaries on CD**
(English and Spanish)

### Gifted and Talented Students

📄 **In-Depth Resources: Unit 4**
· Primary Sources,
pp. 51–54
· Literature, pp. 55–57
· American Lives: Gordon
Parks, p. 58; Alfred E.
Smith, p. 59

◉ **Electronic Library of Primary Sources**
· Unit 4, Chapter 14

## CROSS-CURRICULAR CONNECTIONS

### Humanities: Art
Partridge, Elizabeth. *Restless Spirit: The Life and Work of Dorothea Lange.* NY: Viking, 1998. Illustrated with more than 60 images by the famous chronicler of the Depression.

### Culture
Uys, Errol Lincoln. *Riding the Rails: Teenagers on the Move During the Great Depression.* NY: TV Books, 1999. Fascinating information about the lives, adventures, and misadventures of the more than 250,000 young people who rode freight trains across the nation.

### Economics
Morris, Scott Edward (ed.) and De Blij, Harm J. (designer). *The Economy of the World.* Broomall, PA: Chelsea House, 1995. Information about economics presented visually.

### Literature
Hurston, Zora Neale. *Their Eyes Were Watching God.* NY: Harper & Row, 1990. First published in 1937, this novel focuses on a proud, independent African-

American woman's search for identity. In a journey that takes her through three marriages and back to her roots, this story powerfully affirms and celebrates African-American culture.

Steinbeck, John. *Of Mice and Men.* NY: Penguin Books, 1994. In Depression-era California, two migrant workers dream of better days until an act of unintentional violence leads to tragedy.

### McDougal Littell Nextext
*The Great Depression*

### Literature Connections

Foote, Horton. *To Kill a Mockingbird (the screenplay) (with related readings).* Adapted from the Pulitzer Prize–winning novel by Harper Lee, this screenplay is a series of episodes concerning the trial of an unjustly accused African-American man. It examines the consequences of ignorance, prejudice, and hate, and the values of courage, honor, and decency.

## ENRICHMENT ACTIVITIES

PE **Pupil's Edition,** pp. 462–483
Interact with History, pp. 462–463

📄 **In-Depth Resources: Unit 4**
· Geography Application: The Great Depression
Takes Its Toll, pp. 49–50
· Primary Source: The Stock Market
Crash, p. 51
· Primary Source: Political Cartoon, p. 52
· Primary Source: Letter from a Dust Bowl
Survivor, p. 53
· Primary Source: Attack on the Bonus Army, p. 54
· Literature: from *"In the Beginning,"* pp. 55–57

· American Lives: Gordon Parks, p. 58
· American Lives: Alfred E. Smith, p. 59

◉ **Electronic Library of Primary Sources**
· Unit 4, Chapter 14

📹 **American Stories video series**
· "Broke but not Broken"

◉ **America's Music CD**

## BLOCK SCHEDULE LESSON PLAN OPTIONS (90-MINUTE PERIOD)

### DAY 1

**CHAPTER 14 OPENER**
**pp. 462–463**

**Class Time** 30 minutes

**History from Visuals, p. 462**

**Class Time** 10 minutes

*Options for Pacing and Variety*

- Time Saver Have students read the time line on the spread, and ask them the TE questions included. **Class Time** 10 minutes

**Interact with History, p. 463**

**Class Time** 20 minutes

*Options for Pacing and Variety*

- Role-Playing Ask students to read the Interact, and discuss the issues presented in the questions. Use the TE for further questions. **Class Time** 15 minutes

**SECTION 1, pp. 464–471**

**Class Time** 60 minutes

*Options for Pacing and Variety*

- Peer Teaching Assign student pairs to do the activity Analyzing Causes and Effects on TE page 465. **Class Time** 15 minutes

- Time Saver Ask students to read the feature "Depression Indicators" on page 470, and discuss the Skillbuilder questions. **Class Time** 20 minutes

- Peer Teaching Have students work in small groups to answer the Section 1 Assessment questions. Have each group share its answer to question 4 with the class. **Class Time** 20 minutes

### DAY 2

**SECTION 2, pp. 472–477**

**Class Time** 30 minutes

*Options for Pacing and Variety*

- Team Teaching Have students read excerpts from some of the literature mentioned in this section. Ask an English literature teacher to discuss with your class the parallels between the hardships of the times and the subject matter and the use of symbols and setting in literature of the time. **Class Time** 30 minutes

- Peer Teaching Have students work in pairs and choose a quote from "A Voice From the Past," occurring throughout the chapter. Have them write a paragraph analyzing the tone, subject, focus on generalities or more specific events, and implications of the quote. Have one of the pairs share their responses with the class. **Class Time** 25 minutes

- Peer Teaching Have students work in pairs to answer the Section 2 Assessment questions. Draw the chart for question 2 on the board, and work as a class to fill in the possible answers. **Class Time** 20 minutes

**SECTION 3, pp. 478–483**

**Class Time** 30 minutes

*Options for Pacing and Variety*

- Time Saver Ask students to evaluate President Hoover's decisions. Use the sidebar on page 482 for some preliminary questions, and have students support their answers with evidence from the text. **Class Time** 15 minutes

### DAY 2 continued

- Peer Teaching Have students work in small groups to answer the Section 3 Assessment questions. Have each group share its answer to question 3 with the class. **Class Time** 15 minutes

**ASSESSMENT**
**pp. 484–485**

**Class Time** 30 minutes

*Options for Pacing and Variety*

- History on Film Watch the American Stories video *Broke but Not Broken,* and discuss the questions in the Alternative Assessment question 2 in groups or as a class. **Class Time** 30 minutes

- Time Saver Ask students to look at the cartoon on page 485 and answer the Standardized Test Practice questions. **Class Time** 15 minutes

---

**TEACHER-TESTED ACTIVITY**
**ECONOMIC INDICATOR GRAPHS**

Harry McCown, Hazelwood West High School, Hazelwood, Missouri

**Class Time** 45 minutes

**Task** Graphing economic indicators

**Purpose** To compare the economies of Germany and the United States in the 1920s and 1930s

**Supplies Needed**

- Textbooks
- Library and Internet resources

**Activity** Have students work in small groups to create line graphs comparing the economies of the United States and Germany during the 1920s and 1930s. Groups should research and graph one of the following for both countries: GNP (Gross National Product), rate of unemployment, or rate of inflation. Display the graphs. Have students compare them, and discuss the role of economics in later events.

# CHAPTER 14 CORRELATION

 **CORRELATION TO THE TEXAS ESSENTIAL KNOWLEDGE AND SKILLS**

Chapter 14 addresses the following standards of the Texas Essential Knowledge and Skills for U.S. History.

| TEKS | Instruction | Student Question/Activity |
|---|---|---|
| **(1C)** Explain the significance of the date 1929. | **PE 467–468** discussion of the impact of the stock market crash of 1929 | **TE 467** activity in which students create their own political cartoon illustrating the impact of the stock market crash |
| **(8B)** Answer questions about geographic distributions and patterns shown on maps. | **PE 474** map depicting the spread of the Dust Bowl | **PE 474** questions that require students to interpret the map |
| **(13B)** Analyze the causes of the Great Depression. | **PE 464–471** examination of the long-term and short-term causes of the Great Depression | **PE 471** Critical Thinking questions about the causes of the Great Depression |
| **(13C)** Analyze the effects of the Great Depression on the U.S. economy and government. | **PE 472–477; 478–483** analysis of how the Great Depression affected the nation's economy and government | **TE 479** activity in which students write a letter to President Herbert Hoover explaining their concern over economic issues |
| **(18A)** Identify and analyze methods of expanding the right to participate in the democratic process. | **PE 482–483** discussion of the protest by the Bonus Army in an effort to obtain their World War I bonuses | **TE 482** activity in which students debate the government's treatment of the Bonus Army |
| **(19B)** Evaluate the contributions of significant political leaders in the United States. | **PE 478–483** examination of the steps Herbert Hoover took to address the Great Depression | **PE 483** Critical Thinking questions about Hoover's response to the Depression |
| **(21D)** Identify the economic contributions of women to American society. | **PE 475–476** discussion of how women coped during the Great Depression | **PE 476** question about how the Great Depression affected women |

## TAKS MINI-LESSONS

1. **Social Studies Skills: Objective 1 (US1.C):** Explain the significance of the year 1929 **Activity** Have students answer the questions about the political cartoon regarding the stock market crash of 1929.

2. **Social Studies Skills: Objective 3 (US13.B):** Analyze the causes of the Great Depression **Activity** Have students provide an example from the text of each cause of the Great Depression mentioned on page 471.

3. **Social Studies Skills: Objective 3 (US13.C):** Analyze the effects of the Great Depression **Activity** Have students complete the cooperative activity on TE page 473 about how the Great Depression affected people's lives.

4. **English Language Arts Skills: Objective 1 (7.F):** Produce summaries of texts by identifying main ideas and their supporting details **Activity** Have students summarize President Hoover's philosophy about the federal government's role in combating the Great Depression.

5. **English Language Arts Skills: Objective 5 (2.C):** Proofread writing for appropriateness or organization, content, and style **Activity** Have students work in pairs to proofread each other's answers to the Section 2 Critical Thinking questions.

To understand the causes and consequences of the Great Depression and the futility of Hoover's actions to limit the damage

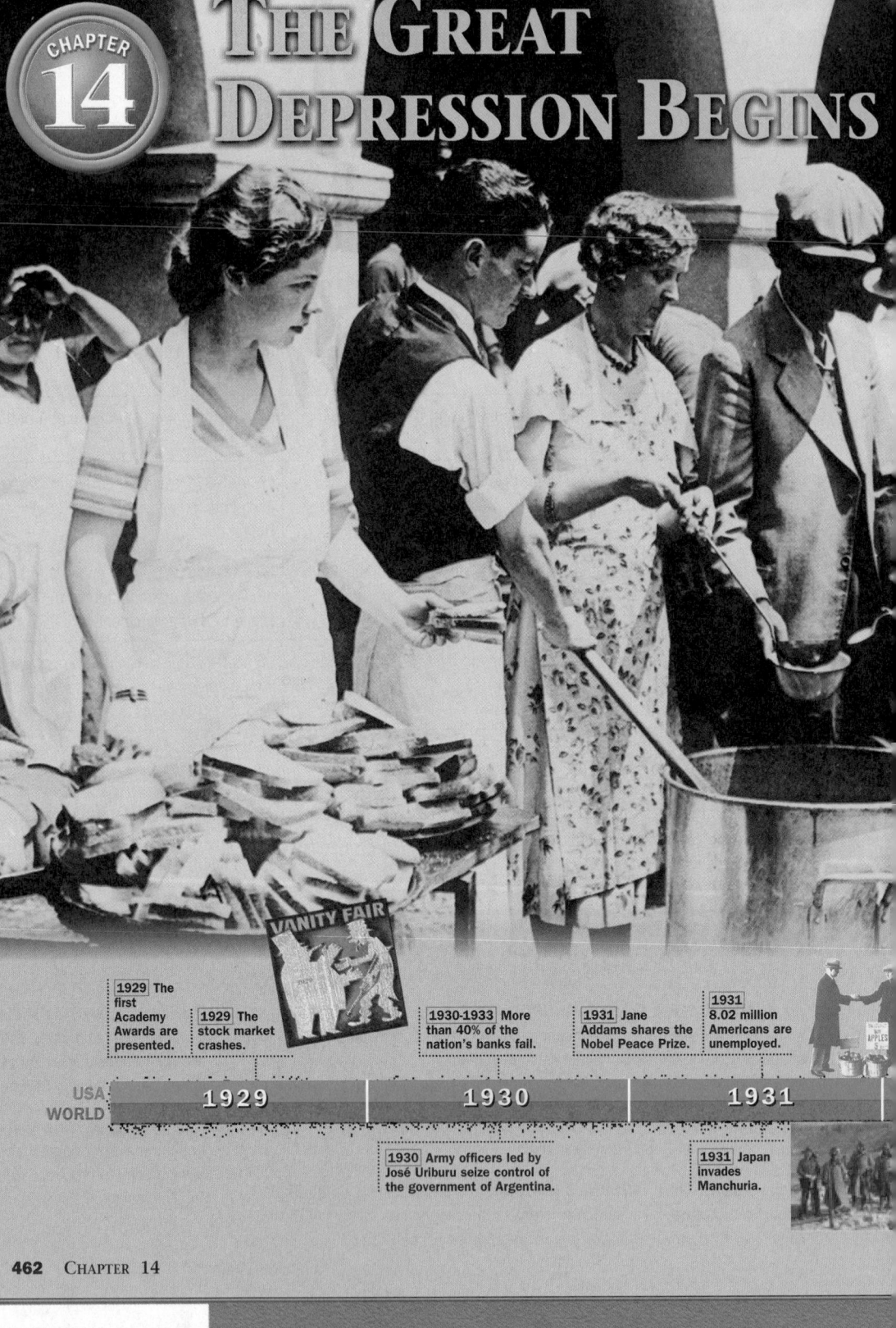

# THE GREAT DEPRESSION BEGINS

**CHAPTER 14**

## HISTORY from VISUALS

### Interpreting the Photograph

Ask students to examine the photograph and identify details of the photo that tell what is going on. (*People are lining up for free soup and bread, served by women.*) Ask students how they think the people in the photograph might have felt at the moment the picture was taken. (*The people in line might have been relieved or happy they were going to get something to eat as well as discouraged, ashamed, or angry that they needed a handout to feed themselves. The women serving might have been pleased to be helping others.*)

## Time Line Discussion

Explain to students that the time line covers key U.S. and world events from 1929–1934.

· Ask students what year the Japanese invaded Manchuria. (*1931*)

· Ask students how long after the Stock Market crash large numbers of banks failed. (*1-4 years*)

· Ask students how many more people were unemployed in 1933 than in 1931. (*about 5 million*)

**1929** The first Academy Awards are presented.

**1929** The stock market crashes.

**1930-1933** More than 40% of the nation's banks fail.

**1931** Jane Addams shares the Nobel Peace Prize.

**1931** 8.02 million Americans are unemployed.

USA
WORLD
**1929**       **1930**       **1931**

**1930** Army officers led by José Uriburu seize control of the government of Argentina.

**1931** Japan invades Manchuria.

---

## THEMES IN CHAPTER 14

### ECONOMIC OPPORTUNITY

The dominant theme of the Great depression was the lack of economic opportunity. In the years immediately prior to and during the Great Depression, many Americans called on the government to create more economic opportunity for citizens. The Republican presidents Coolidge and Hoover stuck to their economic beliefs and did not intervene.

**See Teacher's Edition notes, pp. 465, 481.**

### IMMIGRATION AND MIGRATION

The effects of the Great Depression and dust storms forced farm families to leave their land. Their mass migration to urban areas and California helped further the U.S. transformation into an urban society and caused disruption and hardship throughout the country.

**See Teacher's Edition note, p. 474.**

### DIVERSITY AND NATIONAL IDENTITY

The Great Depression undermined the notion of the American Dream as millions of people endured hardship and despair. The hard times caused some Americans to doubt the ideas of capitalism and democracy, part of the national identity.

**See Teacher's Edition note, pp. 477, 479.**

## INTERACT
### WITH HISTORY

The year is 1929. The U.S. economy has collapsed. Farms, businesses, and banks nationwide are failing, causing massive unemployment and poverty. You are out of work with little prospect of finding a job.

## What would you do to feed your family?

### Examine the Issues

• What groups of people will be most hurt by the economic crash?

• What can you do to find a paying job?

• What can unemployed and impoverished people do to help each other?

**RESEARCH LINKS** CLASSZONE.COM

Visit the Chapter 14 links for more information related to The Great Depression Begins.

Women serve soup and slices of bread to unemployed men in an outdoor breadline in Los Angeles, California during the Great Depression.

---

## INTERACT
### WITH HISTORY

### Objectives

· To motivate students to understand the dimensions of hardship endured by Americans during the Great Depression

· To help students empathize with the suffering of the Great Depression

### Examine the Issues

1. Have students consider which types of jobs might be "depression proof."

2. Ask students to think of what other things they might do for money if they can't get a job with an established company.

3. Ask students to contrast their knowledge of social services available today with what was available to unemployed people in 1929.

---

**1932** The Bonus Army arrives in Washington, D.C.

**1932** Franklin Delano Roosevelt is elected president.

**1933** "Century of Progress Exposition" begins.

**1933** The Twenty-first Amendment ends Prohibition.

**1933** More than 13 million Americans are unemployed.

### 1932　　1933　　1934

**1932** Ibn Sa'ud becomes king of newly-united Saudi Arabia.

**1932** From prison, Mohandas K. Gandhi leads a protest against British policies in India.

**1933** Adolf Hitler takes power in Germany.

**1933** Japan withdraws from the League of Nations.

*The Great Depression Begins* **463**

---

## RECOMMENDED RESOURCES

### BOOKS FOR THE TEACHER

Bendiner, Robert. *Just Around the Corner.* New York: Dutton, 1968. Amusing "selective history" of life in the 1930s.

McIllvaine, Robert S. *The Great Depression.* New York: Times Books, 1993. Overview of the Depression.

### BOOKS FOR THE STUDENT

Graubert, Judah, and Alice Graubert, eds. *Decade of Destiny.* Chicago: Contemporary, 1978. Reminiscences of the Depression.

Terkel, Studs, *Hard Times.* New York: Pantheon, 1970. Oral history of the Depression by a master of the genre.

### VIDEOS

*Sounder.* Dir. Martin Ritt. Paramount Pictures, 1972. The struggles of an African-American sharecropper family.

*The Great Depression.* WGBH-TV, 1993. Videocassette series.

### SOFTWARE

*U.S. History: The Great Depression.* CD-ROM. Clearview. Educational Software Institute, 800-955-5570.

### INTEGRATED TECHNOLOGY

For teacher support, visit. . . .

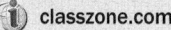 classzone.com

# The Nation's Sick Economy

| MAIN IDEA | WHY IT MATTERS NOW | Terms & Names |
|---|---|---|
| As the prosperity of the 1920s ended, severe economic problems gripped the nation. | The Great Depression has had lasting effects on how Americans view themselves and their government. | • price support<br>• credit<br>• Alfred E. Smith<br>• Dow Jones Industrial Average<br>• speculation<br>• Great Depression<br>• buying on margin<br>• Black Tuesday<br>• Hawley-Smoot Tariff Act |

**TEKS** U.S. History 1C, 8A, 13A, 13B, 13C, 19A, 19B, 20A, 23A, 24A, 24B, 24D, 24F, 24H, 25A, 25B, 25C, 25D, 26A, 26B

### One American's Story

Gordon Parks, now a well-known photographer, author, and filmmaker, was a 16-year-old high school student in the fall of 1929. He supported himself as a busboy at the exclusive Minnesota Club, where prosperous club members spoke confidently about the economy. Parks, too, looked forward to a bright future. Then came the stock market crash of October 1929. In his autobiography, Parks recalled his feelings at the time.

**A PERSONAL VOICE** GORDON PARKS

" I couldn't imagine such financial disaster touching my small world; it surely concerned only the rich. But by the first week of November . . . I was without a job. All that next week I searched for any kind of work that would prevent my leaving school. Again it was, 'We're firing, not hiring.'. . . I went to school and cleaned out my locker, knowing it was impossible to stay on. A piercing chill was in the air as I walked back to the rooming house. "

—*A Choice of Weapons*

▲ Gordon Parks, shown here in 1968 discussing the movie version of his autobiographical novel, *The Learning Tree.*

The crash of 1929, and the depression that followed, dealt a crushing blow to the hopes and dreams of millions of Americans. The high-flying prosperity of the 1920s was over. Hard times had begun.

## **1** Economic Troubles on the Horizon

As the 1920s advanced, serious problems threatened economic prosperity. Though some Americans became wealthy, many more could not earn a decent living. Important industries struggled, and farmers grew more crops and raised more livestock than they could sell at a profit. Both consumers and farmers were steadily going deeper into debt. As the decade drew to a close, these slippages in the economy signaled the end of an era.

**INDUSTRIES IN TROUBLE** The superficial prosperity of the late 1920s shrouded weaknesses that would signal the onset of the Great Depression. Key basic industries, such as railroads, textiles, and steel had barely made a profit. Railroads lost business to new forms of transportation (trucks, buses, and private automobiles, for instance).

Mining and lumbering, which had expanded during wartime, were no longer in high demand. Coal mining was especially hard-hit, in part due to stiff competition from new forms of energy, including hydroelectric power, fuel oil, and natural gas. By the early 1930s, these sources supplied more than half the energy that had once come from coal. Even the boom industries of the 1920s—automobiles, construction, and consumer goods—weakened. One important economic indicator that declined during this time was housing starts—the number of new dwellings being built. When housing starts fall, so do jobs in many related industries, such as furniture manufacturing and lumbering. **A**

**MAIN IDEA**

**Identifying Problems**

**A** What industrial weakness signaled a declining economy in the 1920s?

**A. Answer** The older industries such as textiles, steel, and railroads, which were basic to the fundamental well-being of the economy, were barely profitable.

**FARMERS NEED A LIFT** Perhaps agriculture suffered the most. During World War I, prices rose and international demand for crops such as wheat and corn soared. Farmers had planted more and taken out loans for land and equipment. However, demand fell after the war, and crop prices declined by 40 percent or more.

Farmers boosted production in the hopes of selling more crops, but this only depressed prices further. Between 1919 and 1921 annual farm income declined from $10 billion to just over $4 billion. Farmers who had gone into debt had difficulty in paying off their loans. Many lost their farms when banks foreclosed and seized the property as payment for the debt. As farmers began to default on their loans, many rural banks began to fail. Auctions were held to recoup some of the banks' losses.

Congress tried to help out farmers with a piece of legislation called the McNary-Haugen bill. This called for federal **price-supports** for key products such as wheat, corn, cotton, and tobacco. The government would buy surplus crops at guaranteed prices and sell them on the world market.

President Coolidge vetoed the bill twice. He commented, "Farmers have never made money. I don't believe we can do much about it."

**CONSUMERS HAVE LESS MONEY TO SPEND** As farmers' incomes fell, they bought fewer goods and services, but the problem was larger. By the late 1920s,

Farm equipment is auctioned off in Hastings, Nebraska. ▼

**CHAPTER 14 · SECTION 1**

**More About . . .**

**Gordon Parks**

Parks grew up in rural Kansas and began his career as a photographer with the Farm Security Administration during the Great Depression. He later worked for *Life* magazine and became known as one of the great photographers in the world. Parks wrote several books, directed popular movies, wrote film scores and other music and was a prominent worker for civil rights in the 1950s and 1960s.

In-Depth Resources: Unit 4
· American Lives: Gordon Parks, p. 58

**Tracing Themes**

**ECONOMIC OPPORTUNITY**

**Federal Price Supports**

To a free market man like Coolidge, price supports were intolerable. But farmers were lost without them. Economists credit a full blown agricultural depression in the 1920s as one of the causal factors of the Great Depression that followed the stock market crash.

**HISTORY from VISUALS**

**Interpreting the Photograph**

Explain to students that farmers typically operate in debt, borrowing against future crops. In the 1920s, the collapse of farm prices meant that farmers could not make enough money to make their payments. Banks were quick to foreclose on mortgaged farms, selling off equipment and other assets. Ask students what they imagine the spirit of a farm auction was in the 1920s and '30s.

(*The tragedy of a family losing everything it had worked for and the economic fact of neighbors looking for bargains.*)

**DIFFERENTIATING INSTRUCTION**    **LESS PROFICIENT READERS**

**Analyzing Causes and Effects**

Have students find the answers to these "Why did?" questions to help them understand why the U.S. economy weakened in the 1920s. Direct students to look under the following subheads:

**Industries in Trouble**

1. Why did key basic industries lose business?

2. Why did the coal mining industry suffer?

3. Why did businesses fail after housing fell off?

**Farmers Need a Lift**

4. Why did the farming industry grow weak?

**Living on Credit**

5. Why did more Americans start living on credit?

**Uneven Distribution of Income**

6. Why did the uneven distribution of income affect producers of goods?

 Integrated Assessment
· Rubric 2

## ECONOMIC BACKGROUND

The fabled prosperity of the 1920s was illusory for most Americans, as the pie chart shows. What the chart does not show is that the impact of mass production of goods, advertising, and mass media created a pressure for people to consume. The creation of shaky credit policy that was based on a perpetually rising economy gave people the means to purchase what they couldn't afford and helped create the house of cards that came crashing down with the stock market.

Ask students what percentage of Americans had incomes under $5000. *(94 percent)*

### More About . . .

#### Alfred E. Smith

Smith was governor of New York. Nicknamed the "Happy Warrior" by Franklin D. Roosevelt, Smith was a self-made man from the Lower East Side immigrant neighborhood of New York City. Smith got his start in politics with the Irish Tammany Hall Machine. Smith was the first Roman Catholic to run for president.

In the 1928 campaign, the Ku Klux Klan and other nativist groups attacked Smith as a tool of the Pope. One ad showed the Holland Tunnel under construction, claiming it was a secret passageway to Rome for the Pope to come rule the United States.

In-Depth Resources: Unit 4
American Lives: Alfred E. Smith, p. 59

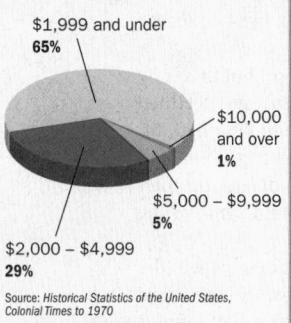

### ECONOMIC BACKGROUND

#### UNEVEN INCOME DISTRIBUTION, 1929

The 1920s were an era that favored big business. Life was good for the rich. They made up just 0.1 percent of the population and had yearly incomes of more than $100,000. Conversely, much of the population had to scrape to get by. Many earned so little that everyone in the family, including children, had to work. Nearly 80 percent of all families had no savings.

$1,999 and under
**65%**

$10,000 and over
**1%**

$5,000 – $9,999
**5%**

$2,000 – $4,999
**29%**

Source: *Historical Statistics of the United States, Colonial Times to 1970*

*"We in America are nearer to the final triumph over poverty than ever before."*

**HERBERT HOOVER**

Americans were buying less—mainly because of rising prices, stagnant wages, unbalanced distribution of income, and overbuying on credit in the preceding years. Production had also expanded much faster than wages, resulting in an ever-widening gap between the rich and the poor.

**LIVING ON CREDIT** Although many Americans appeared to be prosperous during the 1920s, in fact they were living beyond their means. They often bought goods on **credit**— an arrangement in which consumers agreed to buy now and pay later for purchases. This was often in the form of an installment plan (usually in monthly payments) that included interest charges.

By making credit easily available, businesses encouraged Americans to pile up a large consumer debt. Many people then had trouble paying off their growing debts. Faced with debt, consumers cut back on spending.

**UNEVEN DISTRIBUTION OF INCOME** During the 1920s, the rich got richer, and the poor got poorer. Between 1920 and 1929, the income of the wealthiest 1 percent of the population rose by 75 percent, compared with a 9 percent increase for Americans as a whole.

More than 70 percent of the nation's families earned less than $2,500 per year, then considered the minimum amount needed for a decent standard of living. Even families earning twice that much could not afford many of the household products that manufacturers produced. Economists estimate that the average man or woman bought a new outfit of clothes only once a year. Scarcely half the homes in many cities had electric lights or a furnace for heat. Only one city home in ten had an electric refrigerator. This unequal distribution of income meant that most Americans could not participate fully in the economic advances of the 1920s. Many people did not have the money to purchase the flood of goods that factories produced. The prosperity of the era rested on a fragile foundation. **B**

### ❶ Hoover Takes the Nation

Although economic disaster was around the corner, the election of 1928 took place in a mood of apparent national prosperity. This election pitted Republican candidate Herbert Hoover against Democrat **Alfred E. Smith.**

**THE ELECTION OF 1928** Hoover, the secretary of commerce under Harding and Coolidge, was a mining engineer from Iowa who had never run for public office. Smith was a career politician who had served four terms as governor of New York. He was personable and enjoyed being in the limelight, unlike the quiet and reserved Hoover. Still, Hoover had one major advantage: he could point to years of prosperity under Republican administrations since 1920. Many Americans believed him when he declared, "We in America are nearer to the final triumph over poverty than ever before."

It was an overwhelming victory for Hoover. The message was clear: most Americans were happy with Republican leadership.

**DREAMS OF RICHES IN THE STOCK MARKET** By 1929, some economists had warned of weaknesses in the economy, but most Americans

**MAIN IDEA**

**Forming Generalizations**
**B** What did the experience of farmers and consumers at this time suggest about the health of the economy?

**B. Answer**
Beneath the surface prosperity of the 1920s, the economy was in trouble.

**466** CHAPTER 14

---

**ACTIVITY**     **LINK TO ECONOMICS**                              **classzone.com**

#### Economic Recession or Depression

**Class Time** 45 minutes

**Task** Contrasting a contemporary recession with the Great Depression

**Purpose** To evaluate differences between recession and depression

**Directions** Tell students the definition of a recession is two consecutive quarters of negative growth in the GDP—the Gross Domestic Product—or the sum total of goods and services produced in the United States for one year. Divide the class into two groups. Using text, library, and Internet resources, assign one group to find out what happened in the recession of 1981-82. Have the other group

research data for the Great Depression. Then have the two groups create a Venn diagram like the one below to compare the data and duration of the events.

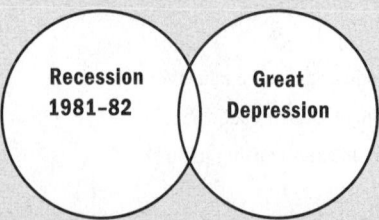

Recession 1981–82

Great Depression

**Vocabulary**
**stock:** a share of ownership in a company

maintained the utmost confidence in the nation's economic health. In increasing numbers, those who could afford to invested in the stock market. The stock market had become the most visible symbol of a prosperous American economy. Then, as now, the **Dow Jones Industrial Average** was the most widely used barometer of the stock market's health. The Dow is a measure based on the stock prices of 30 representative large firms trading on the New York Stock Exchange.

Through most of the 1920s, stock prices rose steadily. The Dow had reached a high of 381 points, nearly 300 points higher than it had been five years earlier. Eager to take advantage of this "bull market"—a period of rising stock prices—Americans rushed to buy stocks and bonds. One observer wrote, "It seemed as if all economic law had been suspended and a new era opened up in which success and prosperity could be had without knowledge or industry." By 1929, about 4 million Americans—or 3 percent of the nation's population—owned stocks. Many of these investors were already wealthy, but others were average Americans who hoped to strike it rich.

However, the seeds of trouble were taking root. People were engaging in **speculation**—that is, they bought stocks and bonds on the chance of a quick profit, while ignoring the risks. Many began **buying on margin**—paying a small percentage of a stock's price as a down payment and borrowing the rest. With easy money available to investors, the unrestrained buying and selling fueled the market's upward spiral. The government did little to discourage such buying or to regulate the market. In reality, these rising prices did not reflect companies' worth. Worse, if the value of stocks declined, people who had bought on margin had no way to pay off the loans. **C**

| **MAIN IDEA** |
| --- |

**Analyzing Events**
**C** How did speculation and margin buying cause stock prices to rise?

*C. Answer* They caused over investment as people ignored the risks and bought more than they could pay for.

## The Stock Market Crashes ❷

In early September 1929, stock prices peaked and then fell. Confidence in the market started to waver, and some investors quickly sold their stocks and pulled out. On October 24, the market took a plunge. Panicked investors unloaded their shares. But the worst was yet to come.

**More About . . .**

**Stock Market Booms Today**
The dot-com boom of the late 1990s provides a good example of boom psychology that says the market can only go up. When normally sober market commentators abandon restraint, the boom psychology takes over. Articles in respected publications and books talked of the Dow Jones average rising from the 10,000 range to 36,000 in a few years. By the second quarter of 2000, reality set in. The hugely overvalued dot-coms and other technology issues came way down, bringing the rest of the market with them.

**Instruct: Objective ❷**

**The Stock Market Crashes**
TAKS SS11 1(US1.C)
· What happened on October 29, 1929?
· How did the stock market crash help cause the Great Depression?

---

## Analyzing **Political Cartoons**

**DAY OF WRATH**

After the apparent prosperity of the 1920s, virtually few were prepared for the devastating effects of the stock market crash. This cartoon by James N. Rosenberg, which shows Wall Street crumbling on October 29, 1929, is titled *Dies Irae*, Latin for "day of wrath."

**SKILLBUILDER** Analyzing Political Cartoons
1. What does the cartoonist suggest will happen to individuals because of the crash?
2. How does the cartoonist convey the sense of fear and shock?
3. What do the looks on people's faces indicate about the impact of the crash?

 **SEE SKILLBUILDER HANDBOOK, PAGE R24.**

 Mini-Lesson 1:
SS11 (US1.C)

### Analyzing **Political Cartoons**

**SKILLBUILDER ANSWERS**
1. It appears as though individuals will be crushed.
2. crashing buildings, horrified faces, mob panic in the streets
3. Their faces show fear, shock, and horror. Many may feel that their lives are being ruined by this event.

 Electronic Library of Primary Sources
· "On Minding Your Own Business" from the *New York Times*

*The Great Depression Begins* **467**

---

**Creating a Political Cartoon**

Discuss with students the cartoon on this page. Then encourage interested students to create their own cartoon that illustrates some aspect of the stock market crash, such as: its effect on business, on business people, on farmers, or on consumers.

Cartoons should . . .

· illustrate the effects of the crash
· convey the sense of fear and shock inspired by the crash
· include a caption or title that captures the essential spirit of the illustration

Have students create a display of their political cartoons in the classroom. Make sure each cartoon includes its title and caption. Allow students time to circulate around the room to view the cartoons. Conduct a discussion of which cartoons are most effective.

Integrated Assessment
· Rubric 4

### More About . . .

**The Crash of 1929**

Most of the early losers on Wall Street were speculators, not ordinary citizens. By October, an average stock had lost almost one-fourth of its value. By mid-November, industrial stocks had lost half their value. Although the market seemed to stabilize by mid-1931, stock prices kept falling into the summer of 1932. From October 1929 until June 1932, General Motors fell from 73 points to 8, U.S. Steel from 262 points to 21, Montgomery Ward from 138 to 4, and RCA from 101 to 2.5.

 In-Depth Resources: Unit 4
· Primary Sources: The Stock Market Crash, p. 51

 Critical Thinking Transparencies CT56
· Investing in Stock

**BLACK TUESDAY** On October 29—now known as **Black Tuesday**—the bottom fell out of the market and the nation's confidence. Shareholders frantically tried to sell before prices plunged even lower. The number of shares dumped that day was a record 16.4 million. Additional millions of shares could not find buyers. People who had bought stocks on credit were stuck with huge debts as the prices plummeted, while others lost most of their savings.

## NOW & THEN

### NEW YORK STOCK EXCHANGE

In the twenty-first century, the New York Stock Exchange (NYSE) remains at its core what it has been since it opened its doors in 1792: the nation's premier marketplace for the buying and selling of stocks. There, stockbrokers known as "members" take orders from their customers to buy and sell shares of stock in any one of more than 2,900 companies.

To execute their customers' orders, the members offer and receive bids in what resembles a loud and fast-paced auction. In general, customers submit two types of orders. A limit order tells the broker to buy or sell only if the stock reaches a certain price. A market order tells the broker to execute a transaction immediately, no matter what the price.

Despite remaining close to its roots, the NYSE is today undergoing perhaps the most significant changes in its long history, in large part due to the growth of computers and the Internet.

**A Pen and Paper Operation**

In the 1920s, orders to buy or sell a stock arrived at brokers' telephone booths located around the edge of the trading floor. They were then carried by hand or sent by pneumatic tube to the trading post where that stock would be traded.

NYSE employees called reporters had to record every transaction. For each new sale, they wrote out a slip of paper containing the stock's abbreviation, the number of shares, and the price, and then transmitted it to the ticker room. Market information was typed into a keyboard which converted the keystrokes into electrical impulses that drove the clattering print wheels in ticker machines along the network. People would read the current display at the trading posts.

The trading floor in 1914. ▲

**Technological Changes**

While still centered around human interaction, the exchange has incorporated a number of computer technologies to keep up with the times. For example, members now receive stock bids and offers through an electronic delivery system known as SuperDot, which enables them to make a trade in less than 12 seconds. Electronic communications networks now allow individuals to buy and sell stocks themselves over the Internet at a fraction of what it would cost to use a specialist. Such innovation has prompted some to insist that all future trading will be done via computers and there no longer will be a need for physical exchanges such as the NYSE.

**SKILLBUILDER**

1. **Hypothesizing** What scenarios can you imagine that might prompt someone to submit a market order on a certain stock?
2. **Comparing** How has technology on the trading floor changed since the 1920s?

The trading floor in 2000. ▼

---

### Popular Music of the 1930s

**Class Time** 20 minutes

**Task** Listening to a popular song of the 1930s

**Purpose** To understand the hardship faced by people during the Great Depression

**Directions** Have students examine the lyrics of the song, "Brother, Can You Spare a Dime?" (A few lines are shown here.) Tell students that when the song was recorded, one in four Americans was out of work. Ask students to discuss the meaning and significance of the lyrics and to suggest contemporary songs they know that address social concerns.

"Once I built a railroad / I made it run / Made it race against time. / Once I built a railroad / Now it's done / Brother, can you spare a dime?"

"Brother, Can You Spare a Dime?" by E. Y. Harburg and J. Gorney, copyright Warner Bros. Inc.

Ask an interested student to bring in recordings of this song—there are several folk-style recordings widely available.

 Integrated Assessment
· Rubric 3

By mid-November, investors had lost about $30 billion, an amount equal to how much America spent in World War I. The stock market bubble had finally burst. One eyewitness to these events, Frederick Lewis Allen, described the resulting situation.

**A PERSONAL VOICE** FREDERICK LEWIS ALLEN

"**The Big Bull Market was dead. Billions of dollars' worth of profits—and paper profits—had disappeared. The grocer, the window cleaner, and the seamstress had lost their capital [savings]. In every town there were families which had suddenly dropped from showy affluence into debt. . . . With the Big Bull Market gone and prosperity going, Americans were soon to find themselves living in an altered world which called for new adjustments, new ideas, new habits of thought, and a new order of values.**"

—*Only Yesterday*

## 3 Financial Collapse

The stock market crash signaled the beginning of the **Great Depression**—the period from 1929 to 1940 in which the economy plummeted and unemployment skyrocketed. The crash alone did not cause the Great Depression, but it hastened the collapse of the economy and made the depression more severe.

**BANK AND BUSINESS FAILURES** After the crash, many people panicked and withdrew their money from banks. But some couldn't get their money because the banks had invested it in the stock market. In 1929, 600 banks closed. By 1933, 11,000 of the nation's 25,000 banks had failed. Because the government did not protect or insure bank accounts, millions of people lost their savings accounts.

The Great Depression hit other businesses, too. Between 1929 and 1932, the gross national product—the nation's total output of goods and services—was cut nearly in half, from $104 billion to $59 billion. Approximately 90,000 businesses went bankrupt. Among these failed enterprises were once-prosperous automobile and railroad companies.

As the economy plunged into a tailspin, millions of workers lost their jobs. Unemployment leaped from 3 percent (1.6 million workers) in 1929 to 25 percent (13 million workers) in 1933. One out of every four workers was out of a job. Those who kept their jobs faced pay cuts and reduced hours.

Not everyone fared so badly, of course. Before the crash, some speculators had sold off their stocks and made money. Joseph P. Kennedy, the father of future president John F. Kennedy, was one who did. Most, however, were not so lucky or shrewd. **D**

This British ▲ election poster shows that the Great Depression was a global event.

**WORLDWIDE SHOCK WAVES** The United States was not the only country gripped by the Great Depression. Much of Europe, for example, had suffered throughout the 1920s. European countries trying to recover from the ravages of World War I faced high war debts. In addition, Germany had to pay war reparations—payments to compensate the Allies for the damages Germany had caused. The Great Depression compounded these problems by limiting America's ability to import European goods. This made it difficult to sell American farm products and manufactured goods abroad.

**MAIN IDEA**

*Analyzing Effects*
**D** What happened to ordinary workers during the Great Depression?

*D. Answer*
Many were out of a job. Others experienced pay cuts and reduced hours.

*The Great Depression Begins* **469**

**Instruct: Objective 3**
**Financial Collapse**
TAKS SS11 3(US13.B)
· What happened to banks and businesses in the economic collapse?
· How did the Great Depression affect other countries?
· How did the decrease in world trade affect overall economic activity?

### HISTORY from VISUALS

**Interpreting the Poster**
Ask students to examine the poster as a piece of political propaganda. Note the featured mother and suffering children and the gaunt-looking workingmen in the background. Ask: How does the caption on top of the poster lead to the conclusion on the bottom? *(The British National Government Party is a solution for the problem posed by smokeless chimneys and anxious mothers.)*

📖 In-Depth Resources: Unit 4
· Primary Sources: Political Cartoon, p. 52

### More About . . .

**International Trade and the Great Depression**
Attracted by high interest rates and the demand for capital in a rebuilding Germany after WWI, American banks made loans to Germany. After the crash, American banks demanded full payment of the loans, and German creditors could not meet the demands. The economic crisis caused governments to pass protective tariffs, crippling international trade. The United States and Europe learned how mutually dependent they were on each other.

---

**ACTIVITY** **LINK TO ECONOMICS**                    **BLOCK SCHEDULING**

**Creating a TV Special**

**Class Time** Two class periods

**Task** Writing a script for a television program about the stock market crash of 1929

**Purpose** To explore in-depth aspects of the stock market crash

**Directions** Have student groups choose an aspect of the stock market crash to research. Suggested topics: Black Tuesday, the Crash's effects on banks and business, Hoover and the government's response to the crash, or profiles of individual investors. After researching their topic, have each group write a television script based on their research and then present it to the class.

📖 Integrated Assessment
· Rubric 5

## HISTORY from VISUALS

### Interpreting the Graphs

Make the connections between unemployment and consumer spending. When people are out of work, they buy less, which causes demand to drop, which in turn results in increased layoffs and business closings. Ask students what needed to happen to get the United States out of the Depression. *(An increase in demand from some place in the economy would spur employment and spending, further increasing demand.)*

## HISTORY from VISUALS

### Interpreting the Photographs

Ask students to react to the photographs. Make sure they understand one effect of the Depression was that people who had lost their jobs also lost their hard-earned savings when banks closed. Ask students: How would you feel if you lost your money in a bank closing? Do you feel a bank is a safe place for your money now? Why, or why not? *(It would feel terrible to lose money in a bank closing, because you trust institutions like a bank. Today the Federal Deposit Insurance Corporation (FDIC) insures bank deposits up to $100,000.)*

## Depression Indicators

Economic indicators are measures that signal trends in a nation's economy. During the Great Depression several trends were apparent. Those indicated at the right are linked—the conditions of one can affect another. For instance, when banks fail **1**, some businesses may have to close down **2**, which can cause unemployment to rise **3**. Thus, people have less money and spending declines **4**.

**SKILLBUILDER** Interpreting Graphs
1. In what year did the biggest jump in bank failures occur?
2. What measure on the graphs seems to indicate an improvement in the U.S. economy during the Depression? What might explain this?

*Skillbuilder Answers*
1. 1933
2. Business failures dropped in 1933. There were fewer businesses remaining.

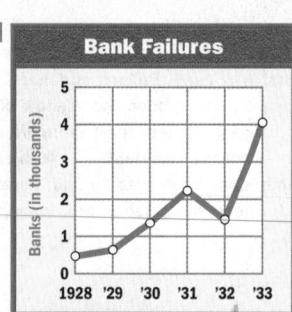

**Bank Failures**

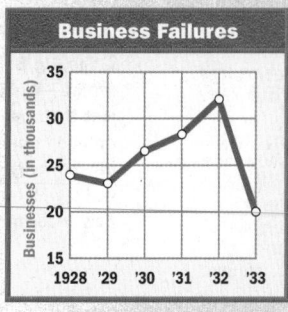

**Business Failures**

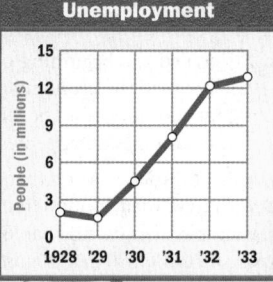

**Unemployment**

**Income and Spending**

Source: Historical Statistics of the United States

Distraught men try to withdraw their savings from a failing bank.

470 CHAPTER 14

---

**ACTIVITY** **SKILLBUILDER LESSON**  **BLOCK SCHEDULING**

### Interpreting Graphs

**Explaining the Skill** Tell students that a line graph similar to those shown on this page is a way to display data that changes over time. Often, a visual representation of data communicates information more clearly than a written description—and at a glance. Point out that students should make careful note of the graph's title and what its vertical and horizontal axes represent.

**Applying the Skill** Have students create a line graph using the following data:

**Wholesale Prices of Selected Commodities**
Annual Averages to the Nearest Half-Cent

|  | 1925 | 1929 | 1930 | 1931 |
|---|---|---|---|---|
| Wheat, bushel | $1.435 | $1.035 | $0.67 | $0.40 |
| Corn, bushel | 0.70 | 0.80 | 0.60 | 0.32 |
| Raw cotton, pound | 0.235 | 0.19 | 0.135 | 0.085 |
| Wool, pound | 1.40 | 0.985 | 0.765 | 0.62 |
| Tobacco, pound | 0.17 | 0.185 | 0.13 | 0.08 |

In-Depth Resources: Unit 4
· Skillbuilder Practice, p. 52

In 1930, Congress passed the **Hawley-Smoot Tariff Act,** which established the highest protective tariff in United States history. It was designed to protect American farmers and manufacturers from foreign competition. Yet it had the opposite effect. By reducing the flow of goods into the United States, the tariff prevented other countries from earning American currency to buy American goods. The tariff made unemployment worse in industries that could no longer export goods to Europe. Many countries retaliated by raising their own tariffs. Within a few years, world trade had fallen more than 40 percent. **E**

**CAUSES OF THE GREAT DEPRESSION** Although historians and economists differ on the main causes of the Great Depression, most cite a common set of factors, among them:

- tariffs and war debt policies that cut down the foreign market for American goods
- a crisis in the farm sector
- the availability of easy credit
- an unequal distribution of income

These factors led to falling demand for consumer goods, even as newly mechanized factories produced more products. The federal government contributed to the crisis by keeping interest rates low, thereby allowing companies and individuals to borrow easily and build up large debts. Some of this borrowed money was used to buy the stocks that later led to the crash.

At first people found it hard to believe that economic disaster had struck. In November 1929, President Hoover encouraged Americans to remain confident about the economy. Yet, the most severe depression in American history was well on its way.

Mini-Lesson 2:
SS11 3(US13.B)

---

### WORLD STAGE

**GLOBAL EFFECTS OF THE DEPRESSION**

As the American economy collapsed, so too did Europe's. The world's nations had become interdependent; international trade was important to most countries. However, when the U.S. economy failed, American investors withdrew their money from European mmarkets.

To keep U.S. dollars in America, the government raised tariffs on goods imported from other countries. World trade dropped. Unemployment rates around the world soared. Germany and Austria were particularly hard hit. In 1931 Austria's largest bank failed. In Asia, both farmers and urban workers suffered as the value of exports fell by half between 1929 and 1931. The crash was felt in Latin America as well. As U.S. and European demand for Latin American products like sugar, beef, and copper dropped, prices collapsed.

---

---

### SECTION 1 ASSESSMENT

**1. TERMS & NAMES** For each term or name, write a sentence explaining its significance.

- price support
- credit
- Alfred E. Smith
- Dow Jones Industrial Average
- speculation
- buying on margin
- Black Tuesday
- Great Depression
- Hawley-Smoot Tariff Act

**MAIN IDEA**

**2. TAKING NOTES**
In a diagram like this, record the causes of the 1929 stock market crash.

cause   cause
cause          cause

**Stock Market Crash**

Which do you see as the biggest cause? Why?

**CRITICAL THINKING**

**3. MAKING INFERENCES**
How did the economic trends of the 1920s help cause the Great Depression? **Think About:**
- what happened in industry
- what happened in agriculture
- what happened with consumers

**4. DRAWING CONCLUSIONS**
Judging from the events of the late 1920s and early 1930s, how important do you think public confidence is to the health of the economy? Explain. **Think About:**
- what happened when overconfidence in the stock market led people to speculate and buy on margin
- how confidence affects consumer borrowing

*The Great Depression Begins* **471**

---

**Answers** ASSESSMENT ①

**1. TERMS & NAMES**
price support, p. 465
credit, p. 466
Alfred E. Smith, p. 466
Dow Jones Industrial Average, p. 467
speculation, p. 467
buying on margin, p. 467
Black Tuesday, p. 468
Great Depression, p. 469
Hawley-Smoot Tariff Act, p. 471

**2. TAKING NOTES**
**Causes** speculation, buying on margin, falling stock prices, loss of confidence;
**Effects** loss of savings, bank failures, bankrupt businesses, high unemployment, worldwide depression

**3. MAKING INFERENCES**
**Industries** Less peacetime demand for their goods; **Agriculture** International demand for crops fell, farmers went bankrupt, and rural banks failed; **Consumers** Credit debt proved disastrous when the banks failed.

**4. DRAWING CONCLUSIONS**
Too much confidence can lead to making unwise decisions, such as taking on too much debt. Too little can lead to money being pulled out of the stock market and banks—triggering a panic.

## OBJECTIVES

**1** Describe how people struggled to survive during the Depression.

**2** Explain how the Depression affected men, women, and children.

### SKILLBUILDER

· Geography Skillbuilder: region, movement, p. 474

### CRITICAL THINKING

· Summarizing, p. 473
· Analyzing Causes, p. 475
· Analyzing Effects, pp. 476, 477
· Contrasting, p. 477
· Drawing Conclusions, p. 477

## Focus & Motivate

Ask students if they can imagine having no home to live in, no money to get food or clothing, and no government programs to assist them.

## Instruct

### Instruct: Objective **1**

**The Depression Devastates People's Lives**

TAKS SS11 3(US13.C)

· Why did people in cities live in shacks and wait in bread lines?
· How did competition for jobs impact race relations during the Great Depression?
· Why did many farm families leave their land during the Great Depression?

In-Depth Resources: Unit 4
· Guided Reading, p. 42
· Literature: *from* "In the Beginning," pp. 55-57

---

# Hardship and Suffering During the Depression

| MAIN IDEA | WHY IT MATTERS NOW | Terms & Names |
|---|---|---|
| During the Great Depression Americans did what they had to do to survive. | Since the Great Depression, many Americans have been more cautious about saving, investing, and borrowing. | • shantytown  • Dust Bowl<br>• soup kitchen  • direct relief<br>• bread line |

**TEKS U.S. History** 8A, 8B, 9A, 10A, 11B, 13C, 20D, 21D, 24B, 24C, 25A, 25B, 25C, 25D

### One American's Story

Ann Marie Low lived on her parents' North Dakota farm when the stock market crashed in 1929 and the Great Depression hit. Hard times were familiar to Ann's family. But the worst was yet to come. In the early 1930s, a ravenous drought hit the Great Plains destroying crops and leaving the earth dry and cracked. Then came the deadly dust storms. On April 25, 1934, Ann wrote an account in her diary.

**A PERSONAL VOICE** ANN MARIE LOW

" [T]he air is just full of dirt coming, literally, for hundreds of miles. It sifts into everything. After we wash the dishes and put them away, so much dust sifts into the cupboards we must wash them again before the next meal. . . . Newspapers say the deaths of many babies and old people are attributed to breathing in so much dirt. "

—*Dust Bowl Diary*

The drought and winds lasted for more than seven years. The dust storms in Kansas, Colorado, New Mexico, Nebraska, the Dakotas, Oklahoma, and Texas were a great hardship—but only one of many—that Americans faced during the Great Depression.

**VIDEO**

*BROKE, BUT NOT BROKEN*
**Ann Marie Low Remembers the Dust Bowl**

## **1** The Depression Devastates People's Lives

Statistics such as the unemployment rate tell only part of the story of the Great Depression. More important was the impact that it had on people's lives: the Depression brought hardship, homelessness, and hunger to millions.

**THE DEPRESSION IN THE CITIES** In cities across the country, people lost their jobs, were evicted from their homes and ended up in the streets. Some slept in parks or sewer pipes, wrapping themselves in newspapers to fend off the cold.

---

## PROGRAM RESOURCES

 **In-Depth Resources, Unit 4**
· Guided Reading, p. 42
· Skillbuilder Practice, p. 45
· Reteaching Activity, p. 47
· Geography Application, pp. 49-50
· Primary Sources: Letter from a Dust Bowl Survivor, p. 53
· Literature: *from* "In the Beginning," pp. 55-57

 **Reading Study Guide** (English and Spanish), pp. 143-144

 **Access for Students Acquiring English/ESL**
· Guided Reading (Spanish) p. 161
· Geography Application, pp. 164-165

 **Formal Assessment**
· Section Quiz, p. 263

 **Integrated Assessment**
· Rubrics

### INTEGRATED TECHNOLOGY

 **Humanities Transp. HT21**
· Dust Storm

 **Electronic Library of Primary Sources**

 **classzone.com**

### TEXAS RESOURCES

 TAKS Spiraled Content Review

 TAKS Practice Tests

 TAKS Practice Transparencies TT83

 TAKS Online Test Practice

Others built makeshift shacks out of scrap materials. Before long, numerous **shantytowns**—little towns consisting of shacks—sprang up. An observer recalled one such settlement in Oklahoma City: "Here were all these people living in old, rusted-out car bodies. . . . There were people living in shacks made of orange crates. One family with a whole lot of kids were living in a piano box. . . . People were living in whatever they could junk together."

Every day the poor dug through garbage cans or begged. **Soup kitchens** offering free or low-cost food and **bread lines,** or lines of people waiting to receive food provided by charitable organizations or public agencies, became a common sight. One man described a bread line in New York City.

**Background**
Relief programs largely discriminated against African Americans. However, some black organizations, like the National Urban League, were able to give private help.

▲ Unemployed people built shacks in a shantytown in New York City in 1932.

**A PERSONAL VOICE** HERMAN SHUMLIN

"Two or three blocks along Times Square, you'd see these men, silent, shuffling along in a line. Getting this handout of coffee and doughnuts, dealt out from great trucks. . . . I'd see that flat, opaque, expressionless look which spelled, for me, human disaster. Men . . . who had responsible positions. Who had lost their jobs, lost their homes, lost their families . . . They were destroyed men."
—quoted in *Hard Times*

Conditions for African Americans and Latinos were especially difficult. Their unemployment rates were higher, and they were the lowest paid. They also dealt with increasing racial violence from unemployed whites competing for the same jobs. Twenty-four African Americans died by lynching in 1933.

Latinos—mainly Mexicans and Mexican Americans living in the Southwest—were also targets. Whites demanded that Latinos be deported, or expelled from the country, even though many had been born in America. By the late 1930s, hundreds of thousands of people of Mexican descent relocated to Mexico. Some left voluntarily; others were deported by the federal government. **Ⓐ**

**THE DEPRESSION IN RURAL AREAS** Life in rural areas was hard, but it did have one advantage over city life: most farmers could grow food for their families. With falling prices and rising debt, though, thousands of farmers lost their land. Between 1929 and 1932, about 400,000 farms were lost through foreclosure—the process by which a mortgage holder takes back property if an occupant has not made payments. Many farmers turned to tenant farming and barely scraped out a living.

**MAIN IDEA**

**Summarizing**
**Ⓐ** How did the Great Depression affect minorities?

**A. Answer** African Americans and Latinos suffered from unemployment, low pay, and racial violence.

---

**ANOTHER**
**PERSPECTIVE**

**AN AFRICAN-AMERICAN VIEW OF THE DEPRESSION**
Although the suffering of the 1930s was severe for many people, it was especially grim for African Americans. Hard times were already a fact of life for many blacks, as one African-American man noted:

"The Negro was born in depression. It didn't mean too much to him, The Great American Depression. . . . The best he could be is a janitor or a porter or shoeshine boy. It only became official when it hit the white man."

Nonetheless, the African-American community was very hard hit by the Great Depression. In 1932, the unemployment rate among African Americans stood at over 50 percent, while the overall unemployment rate was approximately 25 percent.

---

**More About . . .**

**Mexican Americans and the Depression**
At the onset of the Great Depression, about 1.5 million Mexican Americans, or Chicanos, lived in the United States. The largest group, roughly 100,000, lived in Los Angeles. Between 1931 and 1934, as a result of racism and the struggle for scarce jobs, Los Angeles County officials deported nearly 13,000 Mexican Americans to Mexico. However, as journalist Carey McWilliams noted, many of the deportees eventually returned to Los Angeles after "having had a trip to Mexico at the expense of the county."

---

**ANOTHER PERSPECTIVE**

**An African-American View of the Depression**
Race relations suffered during the Depression. The Scottsboro Case in Alabama dominated the headlines for several years. In 1931, a group of African-American men, the youngest a boy of 12, were accused of raping two white women and sentenced to death in a trial in which numerous miscarriages of justice occurred. Twice the U.S. Supreme Court overturned the verdicts, but Alabama persisted even in the face of evidence that no crime had been committed. The Communist Party and other groups used the Scottsboro case to draw attention to racial injustice.

◉ **Electronic Library of Primary Sources**
· "Beans, Bacon, and Gravy",
Childhood During the Depression, by Cesar Chavez

*The Great Depression Begins* **473**

---

**ACTIVITY** | **SKILLBUILDER LESSON**

 **BLOCK SCHEDULING**

**Formulating Historical Questions**

**Explaining the Skill** Asking probing questions, such as who, what, when, where, why, and how, about information in primary sources helps historians learn more about historical events and conditions. Answers to these questions lead historians to a deeper understanding of the past.

**Applying the Skill** To better understand the conditions of the Great Depression have students read the two quotations and study the photograph on this page. Have the class create questions using What, When, Where, Why, and How. Sample questions: Why couldn't people find work? How were basic needs met?

📄 **In-Depth Resources: Unit 4**
· Skillbuilder Practice, p. 45

## The Dust Bowl, 1933–1936

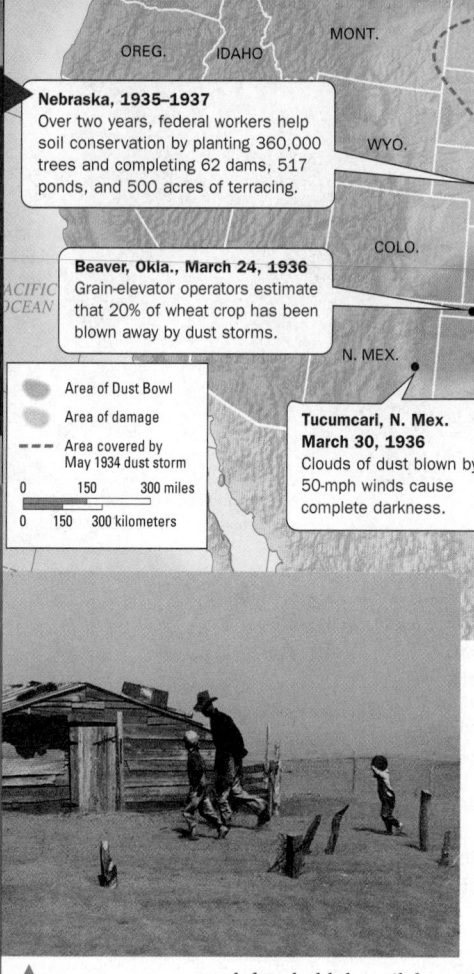

**Nebraska, 1935–1937**
Over two years, federal workers help soil conservation by planting 360,000 trees and completing 62 dams, 517 ponds, and 500 acres of terracing.

**Chicago, Nov. 1933**
Crowds at Chicago Exposition world's fair are caught in 50 mph gale of dust.

**Boston, May 1934**
Midwestern dust and bacteria is found on airplanes landing in Boston; collected on the planes at altitudes of up to 20,000 ft.

**Beaver, Okla., March 24, 1936**
Grain-elevator operators estimate that 20% of wheat crop has been blown away by dust storms.

**New York City, May 12, 1934**
Dust lowers humidity from normal 57% to 34%. Dust is reported on ships 500 miles out to sea.

**Tucumcari, N. Mex. March 30, 1936**
Clouds of dust blown by 50-mph winds cause complete darkness.

Area of Dust Bowl
Area of damage
- - - Area covered by May 1934 dust storm

0   150   300 miles
0   150   300 kilometers

### GEOGRAPHY SKILLBUILDER
1. **Region** Which states were in the region known as the Dust Bowl?
2. **Movement** Why might most of the migrants who left the Dust Bowl have traveled west?

▲
A farmer and his sons brave a dust storm in 1936.

**THE DUST BOWL** The drought that began in the early 1930s wreaked havoc on the Great Plains. During the previous decade, farmers from Texas to North Dakota had used tractors to break up the grasslands and plant millions of acres of new farmland. Plowing had removed the thick protective layer of prairie grasses. Farmers had then exhausted the land through overproduction of crops, and the grasslands became unsuitable for farming. When the drought and winds began in the early 1930s, little grass and few trees were left to hold the soil down. Wind scattered the topsoil, exposing sand and grit underneath. The dust traveled hundreds of miles. One windstorm in 1934 picked up millions of tons of dust from the plains and carried it to East Coast cities.

The region that was the hardest hit, including parts of Kansas, Oklahoma, Texas, New Mexico, and Colorado, came to be known as the **Dust Bowl.** Plagued by dust storms and evictions, thousands of farmers and sharecroppers left their land behind. They packed up their families and few belongings and headed west, following Route 66 to California. Some of these migrants—known as Okies (a term that originally referred to Oklahomans but came to be used negatively for all the migrants)—found work as farmhands. But others continued to wander in search of work. By the end of the 1930s, hundreds of thousands of farm families had migrated to California, and other Pacific Coast states.

### ❷ Effects on the American Family

In the face of the suffering caused by the Great Depression, the family stood as a source of strength for most Americans. Although some people feared that hard times would undermine moral values, those fears were largely unfounded. In gen-

---

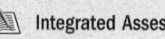

eral, Americans believed in traditional values and emphasized the importance of family unity. At a time when money was tight, many families entertained themselves by staying at home and playing board games, such as Monopoly (invented in 1933), and listening to the radio. Nevertheless, the economic difficulties of the Great Depression put severe pressure on family life. Making ends meet was a daily struggle, and, in some cases, families broke apart under the strain.

**MEN IN THE STREETS** Many men had difficulty coping with unemployment because they were accustomed to working and supporting their families. Every day, they would set out to walk the streets in search of jobs. As Frederick Lewis Allen noted in *Since Yesterday*, "Men who have been sturdy and self-respecting workers can take unemployment without flinching for a few weeks, a few months, even if they have to see their families suffer; but it is different after a year . . . two years . . . three years." Some men became so discouraged that they simply stopped trying. Some even abandoned their families.

During the Great Depression, as many as 300,000 transients—or "hoboes" as they were called—wandered the country, hitching rides on railroad boxcars and sleeping under bridges. These hoboes of the 1930s, mainly men, would occasionally turn up at homeless shelters in big cities. The novelist Thomas Wolfe described a group of these men in New York City. **B**

---

**MAIN IDEA**

**Analyzing Causes**

**B** Why did so many men leave their homes during the Depression?

*B. Answer* Many men were disheartened by their inability to support their families and so abandoned them. Others hoped to find work and send money home to their families.

---

**A PERSONAL VOICE** THOMAS WOLFE

"These were the wanderers from town to town, the riders of freight trains, the thumbers of rides on highways, the uprooted, unwanted male population of America. They . . . gathered in the big cities when winter came, hungry, defeated, empty, hopeless, restless . . . always on the move, looking everywhere for work, for the bare crumbs to support their miserable lives, and finding neither work nor crumbs."

—*You Can't Go Home Again*

During the early years of the Great Depression, there was no federal system of **direct relief**—cash payments or food provided by the government to the poor. Some cities and charity services did offer relief to those who needed it, but the benefits were meager. In New York City, for example, the weekly payment was just $2.39 per family. This was the most generous relief offered by any city, but it was still well below the amount needed to feed a family.

**WOMEN STRUGGLE TO SURVIVE** Women worked hard to help their families survive adversity during the Great Depression. Many women canned food and sewed clothes. They also carefully managed household budgets. Jeane Westin, the author of *Making Do: How Women Survived the '30s*, recalled, "Those days you did everything to save a penny. . . . My next door neighbor and I used to shop together. You could get two pounds of hamburger for a quarter, so we'd buy two pounds and split it—then one week she'd pay the extra penny and the next week I'd pay."

Many women also worked outside the home, though they usually received less money than men did. As the Depression wore on, however, working women became the targets of enormous resentment. Many people believed that women, especially married women, had no right to work when there were men who were unemployed.

*The Great Depression Begins* **475**

---

**HISTORICAL**
**SPOTLIGHT**

**HOBO SYMBOLS**

Hoboes shared a hidden language that helped them meet the challenges of the road. Over time a set of symbols developed for hoboes to alert each other as to where they could get food or work or a place to sleep, and what houses to avoid. They often marked the symbols, such as those shown below, on the sides of houses and fences near railroad yards.

 Sit down meal

 Only bread given here

 Good place for a handout

 Sleep in barn

 Good water

Danger

**HISTORICAL SPOTLIGHT**

**Hobo Symbols**

Ask students why they think hoboes, down on their luck and needing every bit of help they could get, would band together to help each other. *(People have a natural desire to help others. Those in need understand the value of help and would feel good about being able to help others.)*

**More About . . .**

**Women in the Depression**

While the Great Depression made victims of many women, it also moved others to action. In 1935, Margaret Bourke-White, a commercial photographer, photographed the Dust Bowl region for *Fortune* magazine. The experience changed her life. "I had never seen people caught helpless like this," she declared.

Bourke-White abandoned her glamorous lifestyle and began making photographic documentaries to promote social change. In the late 1930s, she helped produce the documentary, *You Have Seen Their Faces*, about sharecropping life in the South. After World War II broke out, she worked as a war photojournalist in Europe.

---

**DIFFERENTIATING INSTRUCTION** | **STUDENTS ACQUIRING ENGLISH/ESL**

**Understanding Syntax**

Students may have trouble with the style of the Thomas Wolfe quotation from *You Can't Go Home Again* in A Personal Voice. Tell them that Wolfe deliberately wrote in this abbreviated style to give his writing a forward motion. To help them read it, have them put *"They"* or *"They were"* after every comma. Let them read it aloud to each other in pairs to get a better understanding of the meaning.

📄 Integrated Assessment
· Rubric 2

In the early 1930s, some cities refused to hire married women as schoolteachers.

Many Americans assumed that women were having an easier time than men during the Great Depression because few were seen begging or standing in bread lines. As a matter of fact, many women were starving to death in cold attics and rooming houses. As one writer pointed out, women were often too ashamed to reveal their hardship.

## More About . . .

### Hardships of the Depression

In a still-lingering Victorian morality, there was sharp emphasis on class divisions, and on respectable and non-respectable behavior. People went to great efforts to keep up appearances despite abject poverty, as if pride were more important to staying alive than food.

### A PERSONAL VOICE MERIDEL LE SEUER

" I've lived in cities for many months, broke, without help, too timid to get in bread lines. I've known many women to live like this until they simply faint in the street. . . . A woman will shut herself up in a room until it is taken away from her, and eat a cracker a day and be as quiet as a mouse. . . . [She] will go for weeks verging on starvation, . . . going through the streets ashamed, sitting in libraries, parks, going for days without speaking to a living soul, shut up in the terror of her own misery. "

—*America in the Twenties*

**CHILDREN SUFFER HARDSHIPS** Children also suffered during the 1930s. Poor diets and a lack of money for health care led to serious health problems. Milk consumption declined across the country, and clinics and hospitals reported a dramatic rise in malnutrition and diet-related diseases, such as rickets. At the same time, child-welfare programs were slashed as cities and states cut their budgets in the face of dwindling resources.

Falling tax revenues also caused school boards to shorten the school year and even close schools. By 1933, some 2,600 schools across the nation had shut down, leaving more than 300,000 students out of school. Thousands of children went to work instead; they often labored in sweatshops under horrendous conditions. **C**

**Background**
Rickets is caused by a vitamin D deficiency and results in defective bone growth.

**MAIN IDEA**

**Analyzing Effects**
**C** How did the Great Depression affect women and children?

*C. Answers*
**Women:** Many women had to manage tight household budgets; women encountered opposition in holding jobs outside the home; **Children:** Many children suffered from poor diets and inadequate health care; many child welfare programs and even schools were shut down.

## More About . . .

### Health Problems Caused by the Depression

One true measure of the damage to public health caused by the Depression was found at the start of World War II. Millions of young and not-so-young men volunteered for the armed forces. Recruitment officials were stunned by the number of people they had to reject for ill health. The effects of malnutrition and stress caused by the Depression had a direct impact on manpower levels for the war effort.

*"If I leave my mother, it will mean one less mouth to feed."*
**EUGENE WILLIAMS, AGE 13**

Many teenagers looked for a way out of the suffering. Hundreds of thousands of teenage boys and some girls hopped aboard America's freight trains to zigzag the country in search of work, adventure, and an escape from poverty. These "wild boys" came from every section of the United States, from every corner of society. They were the sons of poor farmers, and out-of-work miners, and wealthy parents who had lost everything. "Hoover tourists," as they were called, were eager to tour America for free.

From the age of eleven until seventeen, George Phillips rode the rails, first catching local freights out of his home town of Princeton, Missouri.

"There is no feeling in the world like sitting in a side-door Pullman and watching the world go by, listening to the clickety-clack of the wheels, hearing that old steam whistle blowing for crossings and towns."

While exciting, the road could also be deadly. Many riders were beaten or jailed by "bulls"—armed freight yard patrolmen. Often riders had to sleep standing up in a constant deafening rumble. Some were accidentally locked in ice cars for days on end. Others fell prey to murderous criminals. From 1929 to 1939, 24,647 trespassers were killed and 27,171 injured on railroad property.

◀ Two young boys, ages 15 and 16, walk beside freight cars in the San Joaquin Valley.

---

**ACTIVITY**   **COOPERATIVE LEARNING**                                              **BLOCK SCHEDULING**

### Oral History

**Class Time** 45 minutes

**Task** Documenting the personal history of a "Hoover tourist"

**Purpose** To explore the impact of the Depression on teens in the 1930s.

**Directions** Have student pairs use the library and the Internet to research the lives of teenage hoboes ["Hoover tourists"] in the 1930s. Next, draft several basic questions about those events that will serve as the basis of an interview

Questions might include:
· Which events that you've listed were the most happy or exciting for you?
· Which were the scariest or most surprising?
· Which event or experience would you want to live through again, and why?
· Which experience did you learn the most from?

Have student pairs take turns interviewing other pairs, using their questions to generate a story of their lives. Have students share what they learned about each other from the interviewing process.

**SOCIAL AND PSYCHOLOGICAL EFFECTS** The hardships of the Great Depression had a tremendous social and psychological impact. Some people were so demoralized by hard times that they lost their will to survive. Between 1928 and 1932, the suicide rate rose more than 30 percent. Three times as many people were admitted to state mental hospitals as in normal times.

The economic problems forced many Americans to accept compromises and make sacrifices that affected them for the rest of their lives. Adults stopped going to the doctor or dentist because they couldn't afford it. Young people gave up their dreams of going to college. Others put off getting married, raising large families, or having children at all.

For many people, the stigma of poverty and of having to scrimp and save never disappeared completely. For some, achieving financial security became the primary focus in life. As one woman recalled, "Ever since I was twelve years old there was one major goal in my life . . . one thing . . . and that was to never be poor again."

During the Great Depression many people showed great kindness to strangers who were down on their luck. People often gave food, clothing, and a place to stay to the needy. Families helped other families and shared resources and strengthened the bonds within their communities. In addition, many people developed habits of saving and thriftiness—habits they would need to see themselves through the dark days ahead as the nation and President Hoover struggled with the Great Depression. These habits shaped a whole generation of Americans.

▲ This Ozark sharecropper family was photographed in Arkansas during the 1930s by the artist Ben Shahn.

### Tracing Themes
**DIVERSITY AND NATIONAL IDENTITY**

**The Legacy of the Depression**
The Great Depression shattered many people's dreams. But in terms of mental health there are two lessons to be drawn from the experience. It is clear that the suffering of the Great Depression became part of the national legacy. Fears of broken lives and ill health were handed down from parents to children. The other lesson is the resiliency of a people, who banded together to help each other, with millions of anonymous acts of kindness illuminating an otherwise bleak landscape.

## Assess & Reteach

### SECTION 2 ASSESSMENT
Have students work in pairs to answer the assessment questions. Draw the chart for question 2 on the board and work as a class to fill in the possible answers.

📄 Formal Assessment
· Section Quiz, p. 263

### SELF-ASSESSMENT
To demonstrate what students have learned, have them write four or five facts they learned about living conditions during the Depression.

### RETEACH
Review the map and section on the Dust Bowl with students.

📄 In-Depth Resources: Unit 4
· Reteaching Activity, p. 47

---

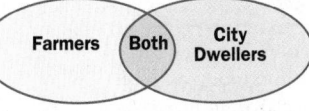

## 2 ASSESSMENT

1. **TERMS & NAMES** For each term or name, write a sentence explaining its significance.
   - shantytown
   - soup kitchen
   - bread line
   - Dust Bowl
   - direct relief

**MAIN IDEA**

2. **TAKING NOTES**
In a Venn diagram, list the effects that the Great Depression had on farmers and city dwellers. Find the differences and the similarities.

Farmers | Both | City Dwellers

Which group do you think suffered less?

**CRITICAL THINKING**

3. **CONTRASTING**
How was what happened to men during the Great Depression different from what happened to women? children? **Think About:**
   - each group's role in their families
   - the changes each group had to make
   - what help was available to them

4. **ANALYZING EFFECTS**
How did Dust Bowl conditions in the Great Plains affect the entire country?

5. **DRAWING CONCLUSIONS**
In what ways did the Great Depression affect people's outlook?

---

Answers **ASSESSMENT**

**1. TERMS & NAMES**
shantytown, p. 473
soup kitchen, p. 473
bread line, p. 473
Dust Bowl, p. 474
direct relief, p. 475

**2. TAKING NOTES**
**farmers:** lost land, grew their own food, turned to tenant farming; **city dwellers:** lost jobs, ended up in the streets, built shantytowns, took food from soup kitchens; **both:** lost their jobs and homes

**3. CONTRASTING**
**Men** Depressed over changes in their status and inability to provide for their families, wandered the country looking for work; **Women** Forced to take a more active role in the survival of their families by working outside the home; **Children** Stopped going to school, went to work, suffered from malnutrition and diet-related diseases.

**4. ANALYZING EFFECTS**
Eastern cities were covered with dirt blown from the plains. California's population swelled and increased unemployment there.

**5. DRAWING CONCLUSIONS**
The economic problems forced people to make compromises and sacrifices in their goal to be financially secure.

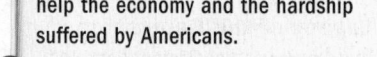
## OBJECTIVES

1 Explain Hoover's initial response to the Depression.

2 Summarize the actions Hoover took to help the economy and the hardship suffered by Americans.

3 Describe the Bonus Army and Hoover's actions toward it.

### CRITICAL THINKING

· Summarizing, pp. 479, 483
· Making Inferences, p. 481
· Evaluating Decisions, p. 481
· Analyzing Issues, p. 483
· Drawing Conclusions, p. 483

## Focus & Motivate

Ask students what objections there might be if the government helps people in need.

## Instruct

### Instruct: Objective 1

**Hoover Tries to Reassure the Nation**
TAKS SS11 5(US24.A)

· Why was Hoover reluctant to help people during the Depression?

· What types of action did Hoover take to remedy the effects of the Depression?

📰 In-Depth Resources: Unit 4
· Guided Reading, p. 43

---

# Hoover Struggles with the Depression

| MAIN IDEA | WHY IT MATTERS NOW | Terms & Names |
|---|---|---|
| President Hoover's conservative response to the Great Depression drew criticism from many Americans. | Worsening conditions in the country caused the government to become more involved in the health and wealth of the people. | • Herbert Hoover<br>• Boulder Dam<br>• Federal Home Loan Bank Act<br>• Reconstruction Finance Corporation<br>• Bonus Army |

 U.S. History 8A, 13C, 18A, 19A, 19B, 20A, 22A, 24A, 24B, 24C, 25A, 25B, 25C, 25D, 26A, 26B

### One American's Story

Oscar Ameringer was a newspaper editor in Oklahoma City during the Great Depression. In 1932, he traveled around the country collecting information on economic and social conditions. Testifying in unemployment hearings that same year, Ameringer described desperate people who were losing patience with the government. "Unless something is done for them and done soon you will have a revolution on hand." Ameringer told the following story.

**A PERSONAL VOICE** OSCAR AMERINGER

" The roads of the West and Southwest teem with hungry hitchhikers. . . . Between Clarksville and Russellville, Ark., I picked up a family. The woman was hugging a dead chicken under a ragged coat. When I asked her where she had procured the fowl, first she told me she had found it dead in the road, and then added in grim humor, 'They promised me a chicken in the pot, and now I got mine.' "

—quoted in *The American Spirit*

▲
A Depression-era family from Arkansas walks through Texas, looking for work in the cotton fields along the Rio Grande.

The woman was recalling President Hoover's empty 1928 campaign pledge: "A chicken in every pot and a car in every garage." Now many Americans were disillusioned. They demanded that the government help them.

## 1 Hoover Tries to Reassure the Nation

After the stock market crash of October 1929, President **Herbert Hoover** tried to reassure Americans that the nation's economy was on a sound footing. "Any lack of confidence in the economic future . . . is foolish," he declared. In his view, the important thing was for Americans to remain optimistic and to go about their business as usual. Americans believed depressions were a normal part of the business cycle. According to this theory, periods of rapid economic growth were naturally followed by periods of depression. The best course in a slump, many

**478** CHAPTER 14

---

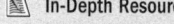

📰 In-Depth Resources: Unit 4
· Guided Reading, p. 43
· Reteaching Activity, p. 48
· Primary Sources: Attack on the Bonus Army, p. 54

📰 **Reading Study Guide** (English and Spanish), pp. 145–146

📰 Access for Students Acquiring English/ESL
· Guided Reading (Spanish), p. 162

📰 **Formal Assessment**
· Section Quiz, p. 264

📰 **Integrated Assessment**
· Rubrics

**INTEGRATED TECHNOLOGY**

👁 Electronic Library of Primary Sources

ℹ classzone.com

**TEXAS RESOURCES**

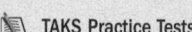

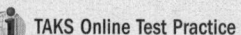

📰 TAKS Spiraled Content Review

📰 TAKS Practice Tests

⚡ TAKS Practice Transparencies TT84

ℹ TAKS Online Test Practice

experts believed, was to do nothing and let the economy fix itself. Hoover took a slightly different position. He felt that government could play a limited role in helping to solve problems.

**HOOVER'S PHILOSOPHY** Herbert Hoover had been an engineer, and he put great faith in the power of reason. He was also a humanitarian, as he made clear in one of his last speeches as president.

### A PERSONAL VOICE HERBERT HOOVER

"Our first objective must be to provide security from poverty and want. . . . We want to see a nation built of home owners and farm owners. We want to see their savings protected. We want to see them in steady jobs. We want to see more and more of them insured against death and accident, unemployment and old age. We want them all secure."

—"Challenge to Liberty," October 1936

Like many Americans of the time, Hoover believed that one of government's chief functions was to foster cooperation between competing groups and interests in society. If business and labor were in a conflict, for example, government should step in and help them find a solution that served their mutual interests. This cooperation must be voluntary rather than forced, he said. Government's role was to encourage and facilitate cooperation, not to control it.

On the other hand, Americans also valued "rugged individualism"—the idea that people should succeed through their own efforts. They should take care of themselves and their families, rather than depend on the government to bail them out. Thus, Hoover opposed any form of federal welfare, or direct relief to the needy. He believed that handouts would weaken people's self-respect and "moral fiber." His answer to the needy was that individuals, charities, and local organizations should pitch in to help care for the less fortunate. The federal government should direct relief measures, but not through a vast federal bureaucracy. Such a bureaucracy, he said, would be too expensive and would stifle individual liberties. **A**

However, when the Depression took hold, moral fiber wasn't what people were worried about. Hoover's response shocked and frustrated suffering Americans.

**HOOVER TAKES CAUTIOUS STEPS** Hoover's political philosophy caused him to take a cautious approach to the depression. Soon after the stock market crash, he called together key leaders in the fields of business, banking, and labor. He urged them to work together to find solutions to the nation's economic woes and to act in ways that would not make a bad situation worse. For example, he asked employers not to cut wages or lay off workers, and he asked labor leaders not to demand higher wages or go on strike. He also created a special organization to help private charities generate contributions for the poor.

None of these steps made much of a difference. A year after the crash, the economy was still shrinking, and unemployment was still rising. More companies went out of business, soup kitchens became a common sight, and general misery continued to grow. Shantytowns arose in every city, and hoboes continued to roam.

**MAIN IDEA**

**Summarizing**
**A** What were some of Hoover's key convictions about government?

*A. Answer*
Hoover believed that reason could solve problems, that government should foster cooperation between competing groups, and that individuals, charities, and private organizations should help care for the less fortunate.

---

### KEY PLAYER

**HERBERT HOOVER**
**1874–1964**

Born to a Quaker family in Iowa, Herbert Hoover was orphaned at an early age. His life was a rags-to-riches story. He worked his way through Stanford University and later made a fortune as a mining engineer and consultant in China, Australia, Europe, and Africa. During and after World War I, he coordinated U.S. relief efforts in Europe, earning a reputation for efficiency and humanitarian ideals.

As president, Hoover asserted,

"Every time we find solutions outside of government, we have not only strengthened character, but we have preserved our sense of real government."

---

*The Great Depression Begins* **479**

---

## Connections Across Time

**1930 AND 2000**

### Hoover Dam and the Nevada Economy

Construction on the Boulder Dam project began in 1930 and finished in 1936. An entire town—Boulder City—was built to house workers. Workers found few outdoor leisure activities there since much of Nevada has extreme summer temperatures and a harsh landscape. In 1931, the Nevada state legislature legalized gambling. Las Vegas, just 25 miles from the dam site, started to develop gambling and gaming establishments. Today, gaming provides employment for thousands in Nevada and taxes on gaming provide a substantial amount of the tax revenue of the state.

## More About . . .

### Hoovervilles

The shantytowns called Hoovervilles sprang up in almost every American city. People built shanties out of scrap wood and sheet metal, cardboard, and any other available material. Most Hoovervilles had some order to them, a "community chest" that shared donated goods and food. Hoovervilles sprang up in parks and on open land. In New York City, Riverside Park, on the Upper West Side, supported a large Hooverville.

LOOKING DOWNSTREAM, COLORADO RIVER

OAKES PHOTO

SHOWING THE IMMENSE CONCRETE FORMS OF BOULDER DAM

▲
This 1930s postcard, displaying a hand-colored photograph, shows the mammoth scale of Boulder Canyon and Boulder Dam.

**BOULDER DAM** One project that Hoover approved did make a difference. Years earlier, when Hoover served as secretary of commerce, one of his earliest proposed initiatives was the construction of a dam on the Colorado River. Aiming to minimize federal intervention, Hoover proposed to finance the dam's construction by using profits from sales of the electric power that the dam would generate. He also helped to arrange an agreement on water rights among the seven states of the Colorado River basin— Arizona, California, Colorado, Nevada, New Mexico, Utah, and Wyoming.

By the time the massive project won congressional approval in 1929, as part of a $700 million public works program, Hoover occupied the White House. In the fall of 1929, nearly two years into his presidency, Hoover was finally able to authorize construction of **Boulder Dam** (later called Hoover Dam). At 726 ft high and 1,244 ft long it would be the world's tallest dam and the second largest. In addition to providing electricity and flood control, the dam also provided a regular water supply, which enabled the growth of California's massive agricultural economy. Today, the dam also helps to provide water for cities such as Los Angeles and Las Vegas.

**DEMOCRATS WIN IN 1930 CONGRESSIONAL ELECTIONS** As the country's economic difficulties increased, the political tide turned against Hoover and the Republicans. In the 1930 congressional elections, the Democrats took advantage of anti-Hoover sentiments to win more seats in Congress. As a result of that election, the Republicans lost control of the House of Representatives and saw their majority in the Senate dwindle to one vote.

As Americans grew more and more frustrated by the depression, they expressed their anger in a number of ways. Farmers stung by low crop prices burned their corn and wheat and dumped their milk on highways rather than sell it at a loss. Some farmers even declared a "farm holiday" and refused to work their fields. A number blocked roads to prevent food from getting to market, hoping that food shortages would raise prices. Some farmers also used force to prevent authorities from foreclosing on farms.

By 1930, people were calling the shantytowns in American cities "Hoovervilles"—a direct slap at the president's policies. Homeless people called the newspapers they wrapped themselves in "Hoover blankets." Empty pockets turned inside out were "Hoover flags." Many Americans who had hailed Hoover as a great humanitarian a few years earlier now saw him as a cold and heartless leader.

---

**DIFFERENTIATING INSTRUCTION** **LESS PROFICIENT READERS**

### Clarifying

As students read pages 480-482, start a wall chart listing the actions Hoover took to combat the Depression. Encourage students to add to the list such actions as "public works projects," "Boulder Dam," and the like.

| Hoover's Actions to Combat the Depression ||
|---|---|
| **Action** | **Purpose** |
| 1. public works projects | |
| 2. Boulder Dam construction | |
| 3. Federal Farm Board | |
| 4. | |

Despite public criticism, Hoover continued to hold firm to his principles. He refused to support direct relief or other forms of federal welfare. Some Americans were going hungry, and many blamed Hoover for their plight. Criticism of the president and his policies continued to grow. An anonymous ditty of the time was widely repeated. (B)

> "Mellon pulled the whistle
> Hoover rang the bell
> Wall Street gave the signal
> And the country went to hell."

**MAIN IDEA**

**Making Inferences**

(B) Why do you think people blamed Hoover for the nation's difficulties?

*B. Possible Answer* Americans look to their leaders for results, and Hoover wasn't getting results.

In this cartoon, Americans point their fingers at a beleaguered President Hoover.

## Hoover Takes Action ❷

As time went on and the depression deepened, President Hoover gradually softened his position on government intervention in the economy and took a more activist approach to the nation's economic troubles.

**HOOVER BACKS COOPERATIVES** In Hoover's view, Boulder Dam was a model of how the federal government could encourage cooperation. His attempts to relieve the depression involved negotiating agreements among private entities, again reflecting his belief in small government. For example, he backed the creation of the Federal Farm Board, an organization of farm cooperatives. The Farm Board was intended to raise crop prices by helping members to buy crops and keep them off the market temporarily until prices rose.

In addition, Hoover tried to prop up the banking system by persuading the nation's largest banks to establish the National Credit Corporation. This organization loaned money to smaller banks, which helped them stave off bankruptcy.

**DIRECT INTERVENTION** By late 1931, however, many people could see that these measures had failed to turn the economy around. With a presidential election looming, Hoover appealed to Congress to pass a series of measures to reform banking, provide mortgage relief, and funnel more federal money into business investment. In 1932, Hoover signed into law the **Federal Home Loan Bank Act,** which lowered mortgage rates for homeowners and allowed farmers to refinance their farm loans and avoid foreclosure. It was not until Hoover's time in office was over that Congress passed the Glass-Steagall Banking Act, which separated investment from commercial banking and would, Congress hoped, prevent another crash.

**Vocabulary**

**refinance:** to provide new financing; to discharge a mortgage with a new mortgage obtained at a lower interest rate

Hoover's most ambitious economic measure, however, was the **Reconstruction Finance Corporation** (RFC), approved by Congress in January 1932. It authorized up to $2 billion for emergency financing for banks, life insurance companies, railroads, and other large businesses. Hoover believed that the money would trickle down to the average citizen through job growth and higher wages. Many critics questioned this approach; they argued that the program would benefit only corporations and that the poor still needed direct relief. Hungry people could not wait for the benefits to trickle down to their tables.

In its first five months of operation, the RFC loaned more than $805 million to large corporations, but business failures continued. The RFC was an unprecedented example of federal involvement in a peacetime economy, but in the end it was too little, too late. (C)

**MAIN IDEA**

**Evaluating Decisions**

(C) What were some of the projects proposed by Hoover, and how effective were they?

*C. Answers* Federal Farm Board; National Credit Corporation; Federal Home Loan Bank Act; Reconstruction Finance Corporation. These projects and measures were not able to turn the economy around.



### HISTORY from VISUALS

**Interpreting the Political Cartoon**

Help students see the cartoonist's real message: people from every class and walk of life are pictured in the cartoon. People who normally have nothing in common are united in one thing, blaming Hoover. Ask: How did Hoover unite the country? *(He united people in hating him.)*

### Instruct: Objective ❷

**Hoover Takes Action**

TAKS SS11 3(US13.B)

- What measures did Hoover take and what results did he achieve to help the economy?
- Why did Hoover use force against World War I veterans?

### Tracing Themes

ECONOMIC OPPORTUNITY

**Trickle-Down Economics**

Hoover was limited in his ability to respond to the crisis by the belief he had in lasséz faire economics. When he finally turned to the idea of some economic stimulus, it was limited to aiding business. Hoover believed in trickle-down economics: that is, if business had adequate capital it would expand, hire more workers, and thus end the crisis. Economists now recognize the crucial role played by consumer spending in driving the economy; when consumers either have little money or are reluctant to spend it, the economy will stagnate.

DIFFERENTIATING INSTRUCTION | STUDENTS ACQUIRING ENGLISH/ESL

**Decoding Idioms**

Some idioms or phrases under "Hoover Takes Action" may be unfamiliar or difficult to understand. Assign partners to help each other read and understand these idioms as they find them in the text:

- softened his position
- government intervention
- activist approach
- jump-start the economy
- prop up the banking system
- stave off bankruptcy
- presidential election looming
- funnel more money
- pump new life
- fueling business expansion
- trickle down to their tables

*The Great Depression Begins* 481

## Instruct: Objective ③

### Gassing the Bonus Army

TAKS SS11 5(US24.B)

· What was the Patman Bill and what happened when it failed in the Senate?

· What happened to the Bonus Army?

· How did the treatment of the Bonus Army affect President Hoover?

### Difficult Decisions

#### Hoover and Federal Projects

1. **Yes:** Hoover's limited intervention was appropriate, for too much government control of people's lives would undermine democracy. **No:** The severity of the Depression demanded that the government do more to provide relief.

2. Some students might answer they would have acted as Hoover had, while others might say they would have increased the number of government work projects and instituted a federal welfare program.

📄 **In-Depth Resources: Unit 4**
· Primary Sources: Attack on the Bonus Army, p. 54

💿 **Electronic Library of Primary Sources**
· *from* A Report on the Employment of Federal Troops, 1932, by General Douglas MacArthur
· from *B.E.F.: The Whole Story of the Bonus Army*, 1932

---

### DIFFICULT DECISIONS

#### HOOVER AND FEDERAL PROJECTS

On the one hand, President Hoover opposed federal welfare and intervention in the economy. On the other, he felt that government had a duty to help solve problems and ease suffering. The question was, What kind of assistance would be proper and effective?

1. Consider the pros and cons of Hoover's actions during the Depression. Did he do enough to try to end the Depression? Why or why not?

2. If you had been president during the Great Depression, what policies would you have supported? Explain the approach you would have taken.

---

## Gassing the Bonus Army ③

In 1932, an incident further damaged Hoover's image and public morale. That spring, between 10,000 and 20,000 World War I veterans and their families arrived in Washington, D.C., from various parts of the country. They called themselves the Bonus Expeditionary Force, or the **Bonus Army**.

**THE PATMAN BILL DENIED** Led by Walter Waters, an unemployed cannery worker from Oregon, the Bonus Army came to the nation's capital to support a bill under debate in Congress. The Patman Bill authorized the government to pay a bonus to World War I veterans who had not been compensated adequately for their wartime service. This bonus, which Congress had approved in 1924, was supposed to be paid out in 1945 in the form of cash and a life insurance policy, but Congressman Wright Patman believed that the money—an average of $500 per soldier—should be paid immediately.

Hoover thought that the Bonus Marchers were "communists and persons with criminal records" rather than veterans. He opposed the legislation, but he respected the marchers' right to peaceful assembly. He even provided food and supplies so that they could erect a shantytown within sight of the Capitol. On June 17, however, the Senate voted down the Patman Bill. Hoover then called on

In 1932, these veterans from Muncie, Indiana, decided to remain in the capitol until their bonus was paid to them.
▼

---

### Debating the Bonus Army March

**Class Time** 45 minutes

**Task** Debating the treatment of the Bonus Army

**Purpose** To take an in-depth look at Bonus Army riots

**Directions** Divide the class in half to debate the decision to forcibly disband the Bonus Army. One group will be those who support forcible removal and one group those who oppose it. Each group should do further research to support its position. The two groups can then debate each other.

📄 Integrated Assessment
· Rubric 3

the Bonus Army marchers to leave. Most did, but approximately 2,000, still hoping to meet with the president, refused to budge. **D**

**HOOVER DISBANDS THE BONUS ARMY** Nervous that the angry group could become violent, President Hoover decided that the Bonus Army should be disbanded. On July 28, a force of 1,000 soldiers under the command of General Douglas MacArthur and his aide, Major Dwight D. Eisenhower, came to roust the veterans. A government official watching from a nearby office recalled what happened next.

**A PERSONAL VOICE** A. EVERETTE MCINTYRE

"The 12th infantry was in full battle dress. Each had a gas mask and his belt was full of tear gas bombs. . . . At orders, they brought their bayonets at thrust and moved in. The bayonets were used to jab people, to make them move. Soon, almost everybody disappeared from view, because tear gas bombs exploded. The entire block was covered by tear gas. Flames were coming up, where the soldiers had set fire to the buildings to drive these people out. . . . Through the whole afternoon, they took one camp after another."

—quoted in *Hard Times*

In the course of the operation, the infantry gassed more than 1,000 people, including an 11-month-old baby, who died, and an 8-year-old boy, who was partially blinded. Two people were shot and many were injured. Most Americans were stunned and outraged at the government's treatment of the veterans.

Once again, President Hoover's image suffered, and now an election was nearing. In November, Hoover would face a formidable opponent, the Democratic candidate Franklin Delano Roosevelt. When Roosevelt heard about the attack on the Bonus Army, he said to his friend Felix Frankfurter, "Well, Felix, this will elect me." The downturn in the economy and Hoover's inability to deal effectively with the Depression had sealed his political fate.

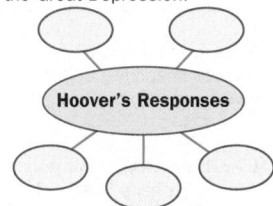

**ASSESSMENT**

**1. TERMS & NAMES** For each term or name, write a sentence explaining its significance.

- Herbert Hoover
- Boulder Dam
- Federal Home Loan Bank Act
- Reconstruction Finance Corporation
- Bonus Army

**MAIN IDEA**

**2. TAKING NOTES**
In a cluster diagram, record what Hoover said and did in response to the Great Depression.

**Hoover's Responses**

Which response was most helpful? Explain your choice.

**CRITICAL THINKING**

**3. ANALYZING ISSUES**
How did Hoover's belief in "rugged individualism" shape his policies during the Great Depression?
**Think About:**
- what his belief implies about his view of people
- how that translates into the role of government
- Hoover's policies

**4. DRAWING CONCLUSIONS**
When Franklin Delano Roosevelt heard about the attack on the Bonus Army, why was he so certain that he would defeat Hoover?
**Think About:**
- the American public's impression of Hoover
- Hoover's actions to alleviate the Great Depression
- how people judged Hoover after the attack

*The Great Depression Begins* **483**

**1. TERMS & NAMES**
Herbert Hoover, p. 478
Boulder Dam, p. 480
Federal Home Loan Bank Act, p. 481
Reconstruction Finance Corporation, p. 481
Bonus Army, p. 482

**2. TAKING NOTES**
"Any lack of confidence in the economic future . . . is foolish"; "rugged individualism"; public-works programs; Boulder Dam; Federal Farm Board; Federal Home Loan Bank Act; Reconstruction Finance Corporation; sending of troops against Bonus Army

**3. ANALYZING ISSUES**
Hoover's belief in "rugged individualism" implied limited government intervention and prompted him to take a cautious approach. Others may say that the public-works programs show that he stopped believing in rugged individualism.

**4. DRAWING CONCLUSIONS**
The public wanted a leader who would act to relieve its suffering. The attack made Hoover seem uncaring and cruel. Also, the public already blamed Hoover for its suffering, and the attack just confirmed that negative impression of him.

## TERMS & NAMES

## MAIN IDEAS

1. During the 1920s, farmers faced decreased demand for their products and lower crop prices. Those who were in debt could not repay loans, and rural banks failed. This pattern repeated itself in other sectors of the economy during the Depression.

2. The stock market crash triggered bank and business failures, high unemployment, and worldwide depression.

3. They were places where charitable organizations handed out food to the hungry.

4. Some unemployed whites were angered by job competition from minorities.

5. Unemployment, reduced household income, some families lost homes. Many adults lost the ability to provide for their families.

6. The harshness of the attack on the veterans and their families damaged Hoover's reputation.

7. He started public-works programs and backed the Federal Farm Board, Federal Home Loan Bank Act, and the RFC.

### VISUAL SUMMARY

## THE GREAT DEPRESSION BEGINS

**CAUSES**

- stock-based economy; superficial prosperity
- unequal distribution of income
- problems in industry and the farm sector
- increasing consumer debt
- stock market speculation and crash

**THE GREAT DEPRESSION**

**EFFECTS**

- people out of work
- rise of shantytowns
- banks fail and schools close
- world economy suffers
- Hoover employs more active governmental involvement

## TERMS & NAMES

For each term below, write a sentence explaining its connection to the period 1929–1933. For the person below, explain h role in the events of the period.

## MAIN IDEAS

Use your notes and the information in the chapter to answer the following questions.

### The Nation's Sick Economy (pages 464–471)

1. How did what happened to farmers during the 1920s foreshadow events of the Great Depression?
2. What were some of the effects of the stock market crash in October 1929?

### Hardship and Suffering During the Depression (pages 472–477)

3. How were shantytowns, soup kitchens, and bread lines a response to the Depression?
4. Why did minorities often experience an increase in discrimination during the Great Depression?
5. What pressures did the American family experience during the Depression?

### Hoover Struggles with the Depression (pages 478–483)

6. How did Hoover's treatment of the Bonus Army affect his standing with the public?
7. In what ways did Hoover try to use the government to relieve the Depression?

## CRITICAL THINKING

1. **USING YOUR NOTES** In a chart like the one shown below, show Hoover's responses to the Great Depression. Indicate how his philosophy changed and the reasons for that change.

**Herbert Hoover's Philosophy**

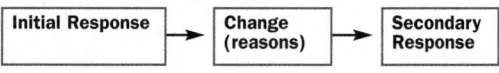

| Initial Response | → | Change (reasons) | → | Secondary Response |

2. **ECONOMIC OPPORTUNITY** Do you think it would have been difficult for individuals to recover financially during the Depression without the entire economy recovering? Why or why not?

3. **DEVELOPING HISTORICAL PERSPECTIVE** How do you think the Great Depression changed Americans' view of themselves Consider the roles of men, women, and children in society and in the family.

## CRITICAL THINKING

**1. Using Your Notes**
**Initial Response:** rugged individualism, little if no government assistance; **Change:** worsening conditions; **Secondary Response:** more government assistance, public works projects, Federal Home Loan Bank Act, RFC

**2. Economic Opportunity**
**Yes** Individuals can't recover financially if the banks, businesses, and people around them do not also recover. **No** Individuals can sell necessary goods or services that do not depend on outside agencies.

**3. Developing Historical Perspective**
Before the Depression people had faith in their ability to provide for themselves and their families. They found that honesty and hard work could not overcome the hard times. People began to look to the government for solutions.

### Standardized Test Practice

Use the cartoon and your knowledge of U.S. history to answer question 1.

**1.** The cartoon illustrates which event leading to the Great Depression?

A bank failures
B Black Tuesday
C Bonus March
D the election of Herbert Hoover

**2.** In the 1930s, some areas of the country suffered from especially harsh environmental conditions. Thousands of farmers and sharecroppers were forced to abandon their land and look for other work. In which of the following areas were these conditions worst?

F parts of Idaho, Wyoming, and Oregon
G parts of Missouri, Illinois, and Iowa
H parts of Florida, Alabama, and Georgia
J parts of Kansas, Texas, and Oklahoma

**3.** How did World War I contribute to causing the Great Depression?

A Soldiers returning from the war were unskilled and so had difficulty finding employment.
B Foreign countries had borrowed heavily to pay for the war and so could not afford to buy American goods.
C Americans had spent their money on war bonds and so had little savings.
D American industry was geared for producing weapons and could not retool to produce consumer goods.

**ADDITIONAL TEST PRACTICE, pages S1–S33.**

 **TEST PRACTICE** CLASSZONE.COM

## ALTERNATIVE ASSESSMENT

**1.** **INTERACT WITH HISTORY** Recall your discussion of the question on page 463:

### *What would you do to feed your family?*

Suppose the year is 1930 and you are the head of your household. Write a letter to a relative overseas in which you describe your family's situation and how you handled the crisis. Discuss the challenges created by the Great Depression and what you've learned as a result of enduring such hardships.

**2.** **VIDEO** **LEARNING FROM MEDIA** View the American Stories video *Broke but Not Broken*. Discuss the following questions in a small group:

- What choices did Ann Marie Low's family make during the Depression? Do you agree with their choices?
- What did you learn about the relationship between the government and the farmers?
- What did the older Ann Marie Low's comments add to your understanding of the Great Depression?
- Share your conclusions with the rest of the class.

*The Great Depression Begins* **485**

### Standardized Test Practice

1. The correct answer is letter **B.**
   The image shows a stock ticker and the date 1929. Letter A is not correct because banks are not shown in the image. Letter C is not correct because shantytowns are not shown. Letter D is not correct because Herbert Hoover was elected in 1928.
2. The correct answer is letter **J.**
   Letters F, G, H are not correct because those states were not in or little affected by the Dust Bowl conditions.
3. The correct answer is letter **B.**
   Letters A, C, D are not correct because the period after the war saw at least superficial prosperity for several years.

UNIT PROJECT

## MULTIMEDIA PRESENTATION

**Tips for Teaching**

· Remind students there are only two weeks until the presentation is due.
· Have each student or group of students working on a project submit a one paragraph summary of the project.

📖 Formal Assessment
· Chapter Test, Forms A, B, and C, pp. 265–282

## ALTERNATIVE ASSESSMENT

### 1. INTERACT WITH HISTORY
**Rubric**
The letter should. . .
· accurately reflect the thoughts and experiences of a family in the Depression Era
· clearly identify the challenges faced by the family
· present lessons learned from the hardships

### 2. LEARNING FROM MEDIA
**Rubric**
The group discussion should . . .
· include comments from all members of the group
· reflect the students' understanding of Ann Marie Low's experience
· discuss the relationship between government and farmers

# The New Deal

| | CHAPTER OVERVIEW | COPYMASTERS | INTEGRATED TECHNOLOGY |
|---|---|---|---|
| **CHAPTER RESOURCES** | *President Roosevelt launches a program aiming to end the Great Depression. The Depression and Roosevelt's New Deal have profound effects on the nation.* | 📄 **Telescoping the Times**<br>· Chapter Summary, pp. 29–30<br><br>📄 **Planning for Block Schedules** | 📼 **American Stories** video series<br>· "A Song for His People"<br>💿 **Power Presentations**<br>💿 **Electronic Teacher Tools**<br>ⓘ **Online Lesson Planner**<br>ⓘ **classzone.com** |
| **SECTION 1**<br>**A New Deal Fights The Depression**<br>pp. 488–494 | **KEY IDEAS**<br>*President Roosevelt takes many actions to combat the Depression.* | 📄 **In-Depth Resources: Unit 4**<br>· Guided Reading, p. 60<br>· Building Vocabulary, p. 65<br>· Skillbuilder Practice, p. 66<br>· Reteaching Activity, p. 67<br>· Primary Sources, p. 76<br>· American Lives, p. 83<br>📄 **Lesson Plans,** pp. 117–118 | 🗺 **Geography Transparencies G23**<br>· P. W. A. in Action<br>🗺 **Critical Thinking Transparencies CT23, CT57**<br>· The New Deal<br>· The U.S. Economic Indicators 1929–1939<br>🗺 **Humanities Transparencies HT40**<br>· Nine Old Men<br>💿 **Electronic Library of Primary Sources**<br>· Unit 4, Chapter 15<br>ⓘ **classzone.com** |
| **SECTION 2**<br>**The Second New Deal Takes Hold**<br>pp. 495–503 | *The Second New Deal institutes new programs to extend federal aid and stimulate the nation's economy.* | 📄 **In-Depth Resources: Unit 4**<br>· Guided Reading, p. 61<br>· Reteaching Activity, p. 68<br>📄 **Lesson Plans,** pp. 119–120 | 🗺 **Humanities Transparencies HT22**<br>· A relief center in Kentucky<br>🗺 **Critical Thinking Transparencies CT23**<br>· The New Deal<br>ⓘ **classzone.com** |
| **SECTION 3**<br>**The New Deal Affects Many Groups**<br>pp. 504–509 | *New Deal policies and actions affect Americans in all walks of life. The Democratic Party forms a new political coalition.* | 📄 **In-Depth Resources: Unit 4**<br>· Guided Reading, p. 62<br>· Reteaching Activity, p. 69<br>· Primary Sources, p. 77<br>· Literature, pp. 80–82<br>· American Lives, p. 84<br>📄 **Lesson Plans,** pp. 121–122 | 📼 **American Stories** video series<br>· "A Song for His People"<br>💿 **Electronic Library of Primary Sources**<br>· Unit 4, Chapter 15<br>ⓘ **classzone.com** |
| **SECTION 4**<br>**Society and Culture**<br>pp. 510–514 | *Motion pictures, radio, art, and literature all blossom during the period of the New Deal.* | 📄 **In-Depth Resources: Unit 4**<br>· Guided Reading, p. 63<br>· Reteaching Activity, p. 70<br>· Primary Sources, pp. 78–79<br>📄 **Lesson Plans,** pp. 123–124 | ⓘ **classzone.com** |
| **SECTION 5**<br>**The Impact Of The New Deal**<br>pp. 515–521 | *The New Deal affects American society not only in the 1930s but also in the decades that follow.* | 📄 **In-Depth Resources: Unit 4**<br>· Guided Reading, p. 64<br>· Reteaching Activity, p. 71<br>· Geography Application, pp. 72–73<br>· Outline Map, pp. 74–75<br>📄 **Lesson Plans,** pp. 125–125 | 🗺 **Critical Thinking Transparencies CT23, CT57**<br>· The New Deal<br>· The U.S. Economic Indicators 1929–1939<br>ⓘ **classzone.com** |

## ASSESSMENT OPTIONS

PE Chapter Assessment, pp. 522–523

Formal Assessment
· Chapter Tests, Forms A, B, and C, pp. 288–299

Test Generator

Integrated Assessment Book

TAKS Online Test Practice

TAKS Spiraled Content Review

TAKS Practice Tests

PE Section 1 Assessment, p. 494

TE Self-Assessment, p. 494

Formal Assessment, Quiz, p. 283

Integrated Assessment Book

Test Generator

TAKS Practice Transparencies TT85

PE Section 2 Assessment, p. 501

TE Self-Assessment, p. 501

Formal Assessment, Quiz, p. 284

Integrated Assessment Book

Test Generator

TAKS Practice Transparencies TT86

PE Section 3 Assessment, p. 509

TE Self-Assessment, p. 509

Formal Assessment, Quiz, p. 285

Integrated Assessment Book

Test Generator

TAKS Practice Transparencies TT87

PE Section 4 Assessment, p. 514

TE Self-Assessment, p. 514

Formal Assessment, Quiz, p. 286

Integrated Assessment Book

Test Generator

TAKS Practice Transparencies TT88

PE Section 5 Assessment, p. 519

TE Self-Assessment, p. 519

Formal Assessment, Quiz, p. 287

Integrated Assessment Book

Test Generator

TAKS Practice Transparencies TT89

## RESOURCES FOR DIFFERENTIATING INSTRUCTION

**Students Acquiring English/ESL**

Reading Study Guide (English and Spanish) pp. 149–160

Access for Students Acquiring English/ESL: Spanish Translations, pp. 166–177

Chapter Summaries on CD (English and Spanish)

**Less Proficient Readers**

Reading Study Guide (English and Spanish) pp. 149–160

Telescoping the Times
· Chapter Summary, pp. 29–30

Chapter Summaries on CD (English and Spanish)

**Gifted and Talented Students**

In-Depth Resources: Unit 4
· Geography Application, pp. 72–73
· Outline Map, pp. 74–75
· Primary Sources, pp. 76–79
· Literature, pp. 80–82
· American Lives: Huey Long, p. 83; Mary McLeod Bethune, p. 84

Electronic Library of Primary Sources
· Unit 4, Chapter 15

## CROSS-CURRICULAR CONNECTIONS

**Culture**

Allen, Franklin Lewis. *Since Yesterday: The 1930s in America, September 3, 1929–September 3, 1939.* NY: Harper Collins, 1986. Through information acquired by books, magazines, movies, and advertisements, Allen skillfully describes the 1930s in America and what it was like to live in the era.

Ulys, Errol Lincoln, *Riding the Rails: Teenagers on the Move During the Great Depression.* NY: TV Books, 1999. Fascinating information about the lives, adventures, and misadventures of the more the 250,000 young people who rode freight trains across the nation.

**Humanities: Art**

Bustard, Bruce I. *A New Deal for the Arts.* Seattle: University of Washington Press, 1997. A thorough look at the federal programs that were set up to benefit the arts during the Great Depression.

**Literature**

Farrell, James T. *Studs Lonigan.* NY: Vanguard Press, 1978. This novel about ordinary people expressing their opinions and struggling with issues of family and work is told with extraordinary honesty. The sad, funny, and ultimately tragic story brings the 1920s and 1930s vividly to life.

L Freedman, Russell. *Franklin Delano Roosevelt.* NY: Clarion, 1990. A photobiography showing the many sides of a remarkable man.

Warren, Robert Penn. *All the King's Men.* NY: Harcourt Brace, 1985. Winner of the Pulitzer Prize in 1947, this novel tells the story of Willie Stark, a southern politician whose character is based on Governor Huey Long of Louisiana. The mixture of good and evil in the novel adds up to a lyrical and painful story of idealism, politics, and personal history.

**McDougal Littell *Literature Connections***

 Rawls, Wilson. *Where the Red Fern Grows.* Set in the Depression on a farm in the Ozarks, this story tells of dreams, hard work, and the love of a boy for his hunting dogs.

## ENRICHMENT ACTIVITIES

PE Pupil's Edition, pp. 486–521
Interact with History, pp. 486–487
Supreme Court,p p. 502–503
Point/Counterpoint, p. 516
Geography Spotlight, pp. 520–521

In-Depth Resources: Unit 4
· Geography Application: Decade of Democrats, pp. 72–73
· Outline Map: Anatomy of the Tennessee Valley Authority, pp. 74–75
· Primary Source: Father Coughlin's Anti-New Deal, p. 76

· Primary Source: The Memorial Day Massacre, p. 77
· Primary Source: WPA Poster, p. 78
· Primary Source: *Let Us Now Praise Famous Men*, p. 79
· Literature: *Waiting for Lefty*, pp. 80–82
· American Lives: Huey Long, p. 83
· American Lives: Mary McLeod Bethune, p. 84

 **American Stories** video series
· "A Song for His People"

Electronic Library of Primary Sources
· Unit 4, Chapter 15

## BLOCK SCHEDULE LESSON PLAN OPTIONS (90-MINUTE PERIOD)

### DAY 1

**CHAPTER OPENER**
**pp. 486–487**

**Class Time** 20 minutes

**History from Visuals, p. 486**

**Class Time** 10 minutes

*Options for Pacing and Variety*

· Time Saver Have students read the time line and ask them the comprehension questions in the TE.
**Class Time** 5 minutes

**Interact with History, p. 487**

**Class Time** 10 minutes

· Internet Discuss the issues raised by the questions on page 487. Then have students visit **classzone.com** to learn more about the solutions that were proposed and adopted.
**Class Time** 10 minutes

**SECTION 1, pp. 488–494**

**Class Time** 35 minutes

*Options for Pacing and Variety*

· Peer Teaching Ask students to analyze the impact of Franklin D. Roosevelt's fireside chats, such as gaining the confidence of the people. Have students examine both the short- and long-term effects of this confidence. Record answers on the board. **Class Time** 20 minutes

· Peer Evaluation Ask students to work on the Section Assessment on their own and check their

### DAY 1 continued

answers with a partner. Then have students quiz each other on the Terms & Names in the chapter.
**Class Time** 20 minutes

· History on Film View one of the videos listed on TE page 487 on the New Deal or Eleanor Roosevelt.
**Class Time** 30 minutes

**SECTION 2, pp. 495–503**

**Class Time** 35 minutes

*Options for Pacing and Variety*

· Time Saver Ask students to study the photograph on page 497 and discuss the Skillbuilder questions.
**Class Time** 5 minutes

· Peer Competition Stage a debate on whether or not the Works Progress Administration (WPA) should have funded writers and artists during the Great Depression. Students should research the issue and understand why people were for or against this type of funding. Have the rest of the class come up with questions for both sides. The class should determine a winner of the debate.
**Class Time** 35 minutes

· Internet Ask students to read the feature on pages 502–503, "Historic Decisions of *The Supreme Court: NLRB v. Jones and Laughlin Steel Corp* (1937)," and answer the questions on the second page.
**Class Time** 20 minutes

### DAY 2

**SECTION 3, pp. 504–509**

**Class Time** 45 minutes

*Options for Pacing and Variety*

· Peer Teaching Have students work together in pairs to research the life of one of the following : Eleanor Roosevelt, Mary McLeod Bethune, Frances Perkins, or Marian Anderson. Students should write a short essay about this woman's life and accomplishments and share it with the class.
**Class Time** 35 minutes

· Internet Ask each student to choose one of the events or people from the section for further research. **Class Time** 40 minutes

**SECTION 4, pp. 510–514**

**Class Time** 45 minutes

*Options for Pacing and Variety*

· Time Saver Ask students to look at the picture of the mural on page 512 and read them the extra information provided in the TE. Then have them look at the picture of *American Gothic* (1930) and the quote on page 513. For homework, have students write a paragraph that draws conclusions and makes inferences from these various sources. **Class Time** 10 minutes

· Peer Teaching Have students work with a partner to answer the Section Assessment questions.
**Class Time** 20 minutes

### DAY 3

**SECTION 5, pp. 515–521**

**Class Time** 45 minutes

*Options for Pacing and Variety*

· Time Saver Have students read "Point/ Counterpoint" on page 516 and discuss the questions in the PE and TE.
**Class Time** 10 minutes

· Peer Evaluation Have students work in pairs to complete the Section Assessment, quizzing each other on the Terms & Names.
**Class Time** 20 minutes

· Time Saver Ask students to read the "Geography Spotlight: The Tennessee Valley Authority" on pages 520–521 and discuss question 1. Then ask students to consider how government programs impact the environment.
**Class Time** 20 minutes

**ASSESSMENT**
**pp. 522–523**

**Class Time** 45 minutes

*Options for Pacing and Variety*

· Time Saver Assign the Main Ideas questions for homework. In class, discuss the Thinking Critically questions. **Class Time** 20 minutes

· History on Film View the *American Stories* video "A Song for His People." Discuss the questions on page 523. **Class Time** 25 minutes

---

**TEACHER-TESTED ACTIVITY**      John Devine, Elgin High School, Elgin, Illinois

**A VOTE FOR HOOVER OR ROOSEVELT**

**Class Time** 40 minutes

**Task** Casting a hypothetical vote for Hoover or Roosevelt

**Purpose** To evaluate the effect of the economic crisis on the presidential election of 1932

**Supplies Needed**

· Textbooks

· Library resources or Internet access

· List of typical Americans in 1932, including autoworker with decreased hours, business executive with a declining company, business executive unaffected by the crisis, etc.

**Activity** Review Hoover's and Roosevelt's approaches to the economic crisis. Have students choose and assume the identity of an American from the list provided by the teacher. Then have them do some research to understand the economic conditions in various parts of the country in 1932. Have students take turns telling the class who they are, whom they voted for, and why they voted for that person. For example: "I'm a Georgia tenant farmer. I'm voting for [candidate] because . . ."

# CHAPTER 15 CORRELATION

## CORRELATION TO THE TEXAS ESSENTIAL KNOWLEDGE AND SKILLS

Chapter 15 addresses the following standards of the Texas Essential Knowledge and Skills for U.S. History.

| TEKS | Instruction | Student Question/Activity |
|---|---|---|
| **(6H)** Identify the origins of major domestic and foreign policy issues currently facing the United States. | **PE 515–519** discussion of New Deal programs, such as Social Security and the Federal Deposit Insurance Corporation, that remain part of the nation's domestic policies | **PE 519** Taking Notes activity in which students list the long-term effects of the New Deal |
| **(7D)** Discuss the participation of minorities in the political process. | **PE 505–506** examination of political activism by African Americans during the 1930s and its role in laying the groundwork for the future civil rights movement | **PE 505** Main Idea question about the importance of Roosevelt's "Black Cabinet" |
| **(8A)** Create thematic maps, graphs, charts, models, and databases representing various aspects of the United States. | **TPE 520–521** Geography Spotlight feature on the Tennessee Valley Authority | **PE 521** Activity asking students to create a 3-D model of a dam based on the information from the feature |
| **(13D)** Evaluate the effectiveness of New Deal measures in ending the Great Depression. | **PE 515–517** discussion of how effective the New Deal was in ending the Great Depression | **PE 516** Critical Thinking questions from Point/Counterpoint feature about the effectiveness of the New Deal |
| **(15A)** Evaluate the impact of New Deal legislation on the historical roles of state and federal governments. | **PE 502–503** in-depth feature on the Supreme Court case *NLRB* v. *Jones and Laughlin Steel Corp.,* which affirmed the power of Congress to regulate labor relations | **PE 503** Critical Thinking questions about the feature |
| **(16B)** Evaluate the impact of Franklin Roosevelt's attempt to increase the number of U.S. Supreme Court justices on the relationship among the legislative, judicial, and executive branches of government. | **PE 493** discussion of Roosevelt's attempt to increase the number of Supreme Court justices and the criticism it prompted | **PE 493** Skillbuilder questions related to a political cartoon about Roosevelt's battle with the Supreme Court |
| **(19B)** Evaluate the contributions of significant political leaders in the United States, such as Franklin D. Roosevelt. | **PE 488–519** discussion of Roosevelt's leadership throughout the New Deal era | **PE 519** Critical Thinking questions about Roosevelt's leadership and overall effectiveness. |
| **(20A)** Describe how characteristics and issues of various eras in U.S. history have been reflected in works of art. | **PE 512–514** examination of the arts during the Depression era, including a look at John Steinbeck's *The Grapes of Wrath* | **TE 513** cooperative activity in which students create a mural that reflects the Depression era |

## TAKS MINI-LESSONS

1. **Social Studies Skills: Objective 1 (US1.A):** Identify the major eras in U.S. history from 1877 to the present and describe their defining characteristics **Activity** Have students create a chart summarizing the significant aspects of the New Deal.

2. **Social Studies Skills: Objective 3 (US13.C):** Analyze the effects of the Great Depression on the U.S. economy and government **Activity** Have students discuss the ways in which the Roosevelt administration reacted to the Great Depression.

3. **Social Studies Skills: Objective 3 (US13.E):** Analyze how various New Deal agencies and programs continue to affect the lives of U.S. citizens **Activity** Have students do research and then write a paragraph explaining how the Federal Deposit Insurance Corporation and Social Security impact modern life.

4. **English Language Arts Skills: Objective 3 (8.D):** Interpret the possible influences of the historical context on literary works **Activity** Have students summarize how the turmoil and hardship of the Depression were captured in the literary works of the time.

5. **English Language Arts Skills: Objective 5 (5.A):** Evaluate writing for both mechanics and content **Activity** Have pairs of students evaluate each other's answers to the Critical Thinking questions of the Section 1 Assessment on page 494.

To understand the impetus for FDR's New Deal legislations and the impact these policies on the American nation

The Civilian Conservation Corps put unemployed young men to work during the Great Depression.

## HISTORY from VISUALS

### Interpreting the Photograph

Ask students to study the photograph and identify what type of work the men seem to be doing. *(Physical labor; construction)*

**Extension** Ask students why it might have been important for the government to address the problem of widespread unemployment during the Great Depression.

## Time Line Discussion

Explain to students that the time line covers the Great Depression years of 1933–1940.

· Ask students to identify the two leaders who took office in 1933. *(Hitler and Roosevelt)*

· Ask students when and why the SEC was created by Congress. *(1934; regulate the stock market)*

· Ask students to identify examples of global unrest. *(Italy invades Ethiopia; Germany invades Poland)*

# CHAPTER 15 · THE NEW DEAL

**1933** Franklin Delano Roosevelt is inaugurated.

**1934** Congress creates the SEC to regulate the stock market.

**1934** Indian Reorganization Act is passed.

**1935** Congress passes the Social Security Act.

**1936** President Roosevelt is reelected.

USA
WORLD

**1933**      **1934**      **1935**      **1936**

**1933** Hitler and the Nazi party come to power in Germany.

**1935** Mussolini leads Italian invasion of Ethiopia.

**1935** British Parliament passes the Government of India Act.

**1936** Civil war begins in Spain.

**486** CHAPTER 15

## THEMES IN CHAPTER 15

### ECONOMIC OPPORTUNITY

Roosevelt initiated his New Deal policies and programs to address the national crisis of the Great Depression. FDR created work programs to combat unemployment, and policies to support and regulate agriculture and industry.

See Teacher's Edition notes, pp. 491, 499.

### CULTURAL DIVERSITY

Although discrimination remained widespread in the 1930s, FDR's New Deal programs created new opportunities for women and minorities. The Indian Reorganization Act of 1934, for example, was aimed at helping Native Americans regain autonomy.

See Teacher's Edition note, p. 507.

### SCIENCE AND TECHNOLOGY

Motion pictures and radio programs were the entertainment of the day. Americans sought a pleasant escape from the harsh realities of the Great Depression.

See Teacher's Edition note, p. 511.

## INTERACT
### WITH HISTORY

It is 1933, the height of the Great Depression. Thousands of banks and businesses have failed, and a quarter of the adult population is out of work. Now a new president takes office, promising to bring relief to the ailing economy.

## How would you begin to revive the economy?

### Examine the Issues

- How can the government help failing industries?
- What can be done to ease unemployment?
- What would you do to restore public confidence and economic security?
- How would you get money to pay for your proposed recovery programs?

**RESEARCH LINKS** **CLASSZONE.COM**

Visit the Chapter 15 links for more information about The New Deal.

## INTERACT
### WITH HISTORY

### Objectives

- To motivate students to describe the economic challenges Roosevelt faced when he took office
- To help students identify business and consumer needs during the Depression

### Examine the Issues

Have students consider the effects of the Depression on economic supply and demand.

1. Help students evaluate the impact of New Deal work programs on business and the economy.
2. Ask students to analyze the causes and effects of decreased consumer spending.
3. Have students discuss why it might be important for the government to have the ability to borrow funds.

---

**1937** Labor unions begin using sit-down strikes.

**1938** Route 66 is completed, linking Chicago, Illinois, to Los Angeles, California.

**1939** *The Wizard of Oz* is released in movie theaters.

**1940** President Roosevelt is elected a third time.

| 1937 | 1938 | 1939 | 1940 |

**1937** Japan invades Northern China.

**1937** *Hindenburg* disaster

**1939** Germany invades Poland.

*The New Deal* **487**

---

## Recommended Resources

### BOOKS FOR THE TEACHER

Goodwin, Doris Kearns. *No Ordinary Time.* New York: Simon, 1997. Lives of Franklin and Eleanor Roosevelt.

Williams, T. Harry. *Huey Long.* New York: Knopf, 1969. Biography of Long.

### BOOKS FOR THE STUDENT

Aptheker, Herbert A., ed. *A Documentary History of the Negro People in the United States, Vol. 4.* New Jersey: Carol, 1992. From New Deal to World War II.

Banks, Ann, ed. *First Person America.* New York: Norton, 1991. Lives of 80 Americans, collected by Federal Writers Project.

### VIDEOS

*Eleanor Roosevelt: A Restless Spirit.* Dir. Harry Rasky. A& E Home Video, 1994.

*FDR.* PBS Video, 1994. Four hour documentary.

*The New Deal.* Republic Pictures Home Video, 1986. The TVA, the WPA, and other New Deal projects of the 1930s.

### SOFTWARE

*FDR.* CD-ROM. Corbis Publishing, 1996.

*U.S. History: The Great Depression.* CD-ROM. Clearvue. Educational Software Institute, 800-955-5570.

### INTEGRATED TECHNOLOGY

For teacher support, visit . . .

 classzone.com

# A New Deal Fights the Depression

| MAIN IDEA | WHY IT MATTERS NOW | Terms & Names |
|---|---|---|
| After becoming president, Franklin Delano Roosevelt used government programs to combat the Depression. | Americans still benefit from programs begun in the New Deal, such as bank and stock market regulations and the Tennessee Valley Authority. | • Franklin Delano Roosevelt • New Deal • Glass-Steagall Act • Federal Securities Act • Agricultural Adjustment Act (AAA) • Civilian Conservation Corps (CCC) • National Industrial Recovery Act (NIRA) • deficit spending • Huey Long |

**TEKS** U.S. History 8A, 11B, 13D, 13E, 15A, 16B, 19A, 19B, 21D, 24A, 24B, 24C, 24D, 25A, 25B, 25C, 25D

### One American's Story

Hank Oettinger was working as a printing press operator in a small town in Wisconsin when the Great Depression began. He lost his job in 1931 and was unemployed for the next two years. In 1933, however, President Roosevelt began creating work programs. Through one of these programs, the Civil Works Administration (CWA), Oettinger went back to work in 1933. As he later recalled, the CWA was cause for great celebration in his town.

**A PERSONAL VOICE** HANK OETTINGER

" I can remember the first week of the CWA checks. It was on a Friday. That night everybody had gotten his check. The first check a lot of them had in three years. . . . I never saw such a change of attitude. Instead of walking around feeling dreary and looking sorrowful, everybody was joyous. Like a feast day. They were toasting each other. They had money in their pockets for the first time. "

—quoted in *Hard Times*

▲ Civil Works Administration workers prepare for a parade for workers in San Francisco in 1934.

Programs like the CWA raised the hopes of the American people and sparked great enthusiasm for the new president. To many Americans, it appeared as if the country had turned a corner and was beginning to emerge from the nightmare of the Great Depression.

### **1** Americans Get a New Deal

**TAKS** Mini-Lesson 2: SS11 3(US13.C)

The 1932 presidential election showed that Americans were clearly ready for a change. Because of the depression, people were suffering from a lack of work, food, and hope.

**488** CHAPTER 15

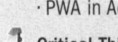
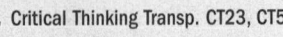
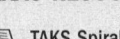

**ELECTING FRANKLIN DELANO ROOSEVELT** Although the Republicans renominated President Hoover as their candidate, they recognized he had little chance of winning. Too many Americans blamed Hoover for doing too little about the depression and wanted a new president. The Democrats pinned their hopes on **Franklin Delano Roosevelt,** known popularly as FDR, the two-term governor of New York and a distant cousin of former president Theodore Roosevelt.

As governor, FDR had proved to be an effective, reform-minded leader, working to combat the problems of unemployment and poverty. Unlike Hoover, Roosevelt possessed a "can-do" attitude and projected an air of friendliness and confidence that attracted voters.

Indeed, Roosevelt won an overwhelming victory, capturing nearly 23 million votes to Hoover's nearly 16 million. In the Senate, Democrats claimed a nearly two-thirds majority. In the House, they won almost three-fourths of the seats, their greatest victory since before the Civil War.

**WAITING FOR ROOSEVELT TO TAKE OVER** Four months would elapse between Roosevelt's victory in the November election and his inauguration as president in March 1933. The 20th Amendment, which moved presidential inaugurations to January, was not ratified until February 1933 and did not apply to the 1932 election.

FDR was not idle during this waiting period, however. He worked with his team of carefully picked advisers—a select group of professors, lawyers, and journalists that came to be known as the "Brain Trust." Roosevelt began to formulate a set of policies for his new administration. This program, designed to alleviate the problems of the Great Depression, became known as the **New Deal,** a phrase taken from a campaign speech in which Roosevelt had promised "a new deal for the American people." New Deal policies focused on three general goals: relief for the needy, economic recovery, and financial reform. Ⓐ

**THE HUNDRED DAYS** On taking office, the Roosevelt administration launched a period of intense activity known as the Hundred Days, lasting from March 9 to June 16, 1933. During this period, Congress passed more than 15 major pieces of New Deal legislation. These laws, and others that followed, significantly expanded the federal government's role in the nation's economy.

---

**MAIN IDEA**

**Summarizing**
Ⓐ What plans did Roosevelt make in the four months while he waited to take office?

**A. Answer** He began to formulate a set of policies to alleviate the problems of the Depression.

---

## KEY PLAYERS

**FRANKLIN D. ROOSEVELT**
**1882–1945**

Born into an old, wealthy New York family, Franklin Delano Roosevelt entered politics as a state senator in 1910 and later became assistant secretary of the navy. In 1921, he was stricken with polio and became partially paralyzed from the waist down. He struggled to regain the use of his legs, and he eventually learned to stand with the help of leg braces.

Roosevelt became governor of New York in 1928, and because he "would not allow bodily disability to defeat his will," he went on to the White House in 1933. Always interested in people, Roosevelt gained greater compassion for others as a result of his own physical disability.

**ELEANOR ROOSEVELT**
**1884–1962**

A niece of Theodore Roosevelt and a distant cousin of her husband, Franklin, Eleanor Roosevelt lost her parents at an early age. She was raised by a strict grandmother.

As first lady, she often urged the president to take stands on controversial issues. A popular public speaker, Eleanor was particularly interested in child welfare, housing reform, and equal rights for women and minorities. In presenting a booklet on human rights to the United Nations in 1958, she said, "Where, after all, do human rights begin? . . . [In] the world of the individual person: the neighborhood . . . the school . . . the factory, farm or office where he works."

*The New Deal* **489**

---

## More About . . .

### Election of 1932

During the presidential campaign, Hoover and the Republican Party made a concerted effort to paint Roosevelt in an unfavorable light. Hoover told the public that if Roosevelt were elected, things would go from bad to worse. However, the American people had lost faith in the Hoover administration. The Great Depression had taken its toll and many people were disappointed in Hoover's inability to rectify the situation. In 1932, Roosevelt won an overwhelming victory.

👁 Electronic Library of Primary Sources
· *from* Acceptance Speech, 1932, by
  F. D. Roosevelt
· *from* First Inaugural Address, 1933, by
  F. D. Roosevelt

## KEY PLAYERS

**Franklin and Eleanor Roosevelt**
Throughout his presidency, Roosevelt's actions were tempered by his wife. Eleanor Roosevelt reached out to African Americans, the poor, women, and children. Her dedication to humanitarian causes continued even after Franklin Roosevelt's death. Eleanor Roosevelt did pioneering work for human rights with the United Nations.

Ask students to consider whether Eleanor Roosevelt was a controversial figure. *(Her role as an activist challenged traditional gender roles.)*

---

| ACTIVITY | LINK TO GOVERNMENT |
| --- | --- |

 **classzone.com**

### The Role of the First Lady

**Class Time** 45 minutes

**Task** Analyzing the role of the first lady

**Purpose** To compare and contrast the accomplishments of past and present first ladies

**Directions** Have students research the histories of several first ladies from different periods of history. Be sure to include Eleanor Roosevelt and Hilary Clinton among those studied. Ask students to consider the similarities and differences between the two first ladies. Have the students create a chart or or other graphic comparing and contrasting the styles and impact of first ladies.

Some first ladies to consider:
Martha Washington
Abigail Adams
Dolley Madison
Mary Todd Lincoln
"Lemonade Lucy" Hayes
Edith Wilson
Eleanor Roosevelt
Jacqueline Kennedy
Claudia "Lady Bird" Johnson
Hillary Clinton

**More About . . .**

**FDR's Leadership**

Roosevelt was the first president to use the medium of live radio to address the nation regarding public policies. America needed a confident leader, and Roosevelt lent his voice to the cause. FDR's first fireside chat had a tremendous impact on national morale. When the banks reopened, the expected panic did not materialize. Roosevelt had been able to explain the situation in a manner that inspired hope for a brighter future.

**More About . . .**

**FDR's Disability**

FDR preferred not to be photographed in his wheelchair, and seldom made public reference to his physical infirmity. He made a point of standing, assisted by aides, and greeting the nation with an energetic wave. In March 1945, six weeks before his death, FDR made a rare reference to his disability: "I hope that you will pardon me for this unusual posture of sitting down . . . it makes it a lot easier for me not to have to carry about 10 pounds of steel around at the bottom of my legs."

**Extension** Ask students why FDR downplayed his disability. Discuss the 1930s standards of "normalcy."

Roosevelt's first step as president was to carry out reforms in banking and finance. By 1933, widespread bank failures had caused most Americans to lose faith in the banking system. On March 5, one day after taking office, Roosevelt declared a bank holiday and closed all banks to prevent further withdrawals. He persuaded Congress to pass the Emergency Banking Relief Act, which authorized the Treasury Department to inspect the country's banks. Those that were sound could reopen at once; those that were insolvent—unable to pay their debts—would remain closed. Those that needed help could receive loans. This measure revived public confidence in banks, since customers now had greater faith that the open banks were in good financial shape.

**AN IMPORTANT FIRESIDE CHAT** On March 12, the day before the first banks were to reopen, President Roosevelt gave the first of his many fireside chats—radio talks about issues of public concern, explaining in clear, simple language his New Deal measures. These informal talks made Americans feel as if the president were talking directly to them. In his first chat, President Roosevelt explained why the nation's welfare depended on public support of the government and the banking system. "We have provided the machinery to restore our financial system," he said, "and it is up to you to support and make it work." He explained the banking system to listeners.

> *" The only thing we have to fear is fear itself."*
> **FRANKLIN DELANO ROOSEVELT**

**A PERSONAL VOICE** FRANKLIN DELANO ROOSEVELT

" When you deposit money in a bank the bank does not put the money into a safe deposit vault. It invests your money. . . . A comparatively small part of the money that you put into the bank is kept in currency—an amount which in normal times is wholly sufficient to cover the cash needs of the average citizen. "

Franklin D. Roosevelt holds his dog Fala and talks to a young family friend.

The president then explained that when too many people demanded their savings in cash, banks would fail. This was not because banks were weak but because even strong banks could not meet such heavy demands. Over the next few weeks, many Americans returned their savings to banks. **B**

**REGULATING BANKING AND FINANCE** Congress took another step to reorganize the banking system by passing the **Glass-Steagall Act,** which established the Federal Deposit Insurance Corporation (FDIC). The FDIC provided federal insurance for individual bank accounts of up to $5,000, reassuring millions of bank customers that their money was safe. It also required banks to act cautiously with their customers' money.

Congress and the president also worked to regulate the stock market, in which people had lost faith because of the crash of 1929. The **Federal Securities Act,** passed in May 1933, required corporations to provide complete information on all stock offerings and made them liable for any misrepresentations. In June of 1934, Congress created the Securities and Exchange Commission (SEC) to regulate the stock market. One goal of this commission was to prevent people with inside information about companies from "rigging" the stock market for their own profit.

In addition, Roosevelt persuaded Congress to approve a bill allowing the manufacture and sale of some alcoholic beverages. The bill's main purpose was to raise government revenues by taxing alcohol. By the end of 1933, the passage of the 21st Amendment had repealed prohibition altogether.

**490** CHAPTER 15

**MAIN IDEA**

**Evaluating Leadership**
**B** How successful was FDR's fireside chat?

*B. Answer* It was very successful. Many Americans returned their savings to banks, showing increased confidence in the banking sysem.

---

**Delivering a Fireside Chat**

**Class Time** 45 minutes

**Task** Writing and recording a fireside chat

**Purpose** To analyze the impact of FDR's fireside chats

**Directions** Have students work in groups to prepare a fireside chat explaining a New Deal program. Ask students to research and analyze a New Deal program. Suggest they make note of the program's *purpose, benefits, drawbacks,* and *impact.* Have students write and record a fireside chat. Play the recordings in class.

**Rubrics**

The fireside chat should . . .
· clearly state a purpose for the selected New Deal program
· point out both benefits and drawbacks of the program
· project the impact of the program

 Integrated Assessment
· Rubrics 2, 3

While working on banking and financial matters, the Roosevelt administration also implemented programs to provide relief to farmers, perhaps the hardest hit by the depression. It also aided other workers and attempted to stimulate economic recovery.

**RURAL ASSISTANCE** The **Agricultural Adjustment Act (AAA)** sought to raise crop prices by lowering production, which the government achieved by paying farmers to leave a certain amount of every acre of land unseeded. The theory was that reduced supply would boost prices. In some cases, crops were too far advanced for the acreage reduction to take effect. As a result, the government paid cotton growers $200 million to plow under 10 million acres of their crop. It also paid hog farmers to slaughter 6 million pigs. This policy upset many Americans, who protested the destruction of food when many people were going hungry. It did, however, help raise farm prices and put more money in farmers' pockets.

An especially ambitious program of regional development was the Tennessee Valley Authority (TVA), established on May 18, 1933. (See Geography Spotlight on page 520.) Focusing on the badly depressed Tennessee River Valley, the TVA renovated five existing dams and constructed 20 new ones, created thousands of jobs, and provided flood control, hydroelectric power, and other benefits to an impoverished region.

**PROVIDING WORK PROJECTS** The administration also established programs to provide relief through work projects and cash payments. One important program, the **Civilian Conservation Corps (CCC),** put young men aged 18 to 25 to work building roads, developing parks, planting trees, and helping in soil-erosion and flood-control projects. By the time the program ended in 1942, almost 3 million young men had passed through the CCC. The CCC paid a small wage, $30 a month, of which $25 was automatically sent home to the worker's family. It also supplied free food and uniforms and lodging in work camps. Many of the camps were located on the Great Plains, where, within a period of eight years, the men of the CCC planted more than 200 million trees. This tremendous reforestation program was aimed at preventing another Dust Bowl.

The Public Works Administration (PWA), created in June 1933 as part of the **National Industrial Recovery Act (NIRA),** provided money to states to create jobs chiefly in the construction of schools and other community buildings. When these programs failed to make a sufficient dent in unemployment, President Roosevelt established the Civil Works Administration in November 1933. It provided 4 million immediate jobs during the winter of 1933–1934. Although some critics of the CWA claimed that the programs were "make-work" projects and a waste of money, the CWA built 40,000 schools and paid the salaries of more than 50,000 schoolteachers in America's rural areas. It also built more than half a million miles of roads. **C**

**Background**
See *supply and demand* on page R46 in the Economics Handbook.

**C. Answer** The TVA developed an impoverished area by providing flood control and power and by building dams. Members of the CCC planted trees to help prevent another Dust Bowl.

---

**MAIN IDEA**

**Analyzing Effects**
**C** How did New Deal programs affect various regions of the United States?

---

### Civilian Conservation Corps

- The CCC provided almost 3 million men aged 18–25 with work and wages between 1933 and 1942.

- The men lived in work camps under a strict regime. The majority of the camps were racially segregated.

- By 1938, the CCC had an 11 percent African-American enrollment.

- Accomplishments of the CCC include planting over 3 billion trees, developing over 800 state parks, and building more than 46,000 bridges.

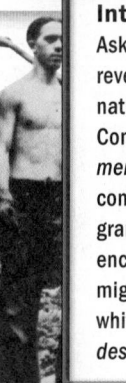

*The New Deal* **491**

---

---

**PROMOTING FAIR PRACTICES** The NIRA also sought to promote industrial growth by establishing codes of fair practice for individual industries. It created the National Recovery Administration (NRA), which set prices of many products to ensure fair competition and established standards for working hours and a ban on child labor. The aim of the NRA was to promote recovery by interrupting the trend of wage cuts, falling prices, and layoffs. The economist Gardiner C. Means attempted to justify the NRA by stating the goal of industrial planning.

> **A PERSONAL VOICE** GARDINER C. MEANS
>
> "The National Recovery Administration [was] created in response to an overwhelming demand from many quarters that certain elements in the making of industrial policy . . . should no longer be left to the market place and the price mechanism but should be placed in the hands of administrative bodies."
>
> —*The Making of Industrial Policy*

The codes of fair practice had been drafted in joint meetings of businesses and representatives of workers and consumers. These codes both limited production and established prices. Because businesses were given new concessions, workers made demands. Congress met their demands by passing a section of the NIRA guaranteeing workers' right to unionize and to bargain collectively. **D**

Many businesses and politicians were critical of the NRA. Charges arose that the codes served large business interests. There were also charges of increasing code violations.

**FOOD, CLOTHING, AND SHELTER** A number of New Deal programs concerned housing and home mortgage problems. The Home Owners Loan Corporation (HOLC) provided government loans to homeowners who faced foreclosure because they couldn't meet their loan payments. In addition, the 1934 National Housing Act created the Federal Housing Administration (FHA). This agency continues to furnish loans for home mortgages and repairs today.

Another program, the Federal Emergency Relief Administration (FERA), was funded with $500 million to provide direct relief for the needy. Half of the money was given to the states as direct grants-in-aid to help furnish food and clothing to the unemployed, the aged, and the ill. The rest was distributed to states to support work relief programs—for every $3 within the state program, FERA donated $1. Harry Hopkins, who headed this program, believed that, whereas money helped people buy food, it was meaningful work that enabled them to gain confidence and self-respect.

## The New Deal Comes Under Attack ❸

By the end of the Hundred Days, millions of Americans had benefitted from the New Deal programs. As well, the public's confidence in the nation's future had rebounded. Although President Roosevelt agreed to a policy of **deficit spending**—spending more money than the government receives in revenue—he did so with great reluctance. He regarded deficit spending as a necessary evil to be used only at a time of great economic crisis. Nevertheless, the New Deal did not end the depression, and opposition grew among some parts of the population.

---

### MAIN IDEA

**Evaluating**
**D** How did the New Deal support labor organizations?

*D. Answer* It guaranteed workers' right to unionize and to bargain collectively.

---

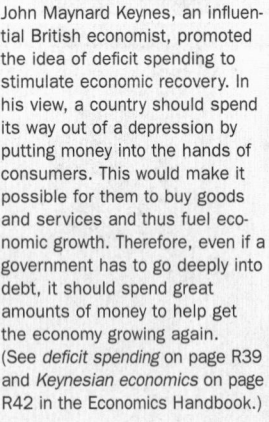

**ECONOMIC BACKGROUND**

**DEFICIT SPENDING**

John Maynard Keynes, an influential British economist, promoted the idea of deficit spending to stimulate economic recovery. In his view, a country should spend its way out of a depression by putting money into the hands of consumers. This would make it possible for them to buy goods and services and thus fuel economic growth. Therefore, even if a government has to go deeply into debt, it should spend great amounts of money to help get the economy growing again.
(See *deficit spending* on page R39 and *Keynesian economics* on page R42 in the Economics Handbook.)

---

## Analyzing *Political Cartoons*

### CHANGING COURSE

With hopes of lessening opposition to his programs, Roosevelt proposed a court reform bill that would essentially have allowed him to "pack" the Court with judges supportive of the New Deal. This cartoon shows Roosevelt as a sea captain ordering a shocked Congress to change course.

**SKILLBUILDER** Analyzing Political Cartoons
1. What "compass" did Roosevelt want to change? Explain.
2. How does the cartoonist portray FDR's attitude regarding his power as president?

**SEE SKILLBUILDER HANDBOOK, PAGE R24.**

THAT COMPASS DOESN'T POINT THE WAY I WANT TO GO. CHANGE IT. NOW!

## Analyzing *Political Cartoons*

Ask students to consider why the artist chose to portray Congress as a sailor and Roosevelt as a ship's captain. *(The use of captain and sailor reflect the political dynamic of the New Deal: Roosevelt led and Congress followed.)*

### SKILLBUILDER ANSWERS
1. Roosevelt wanted to change the compass of the Supreme Court. The Court had ruled two of his New Deal programs unconstitutional.
2. The cartoonist portrays Roosevelt as a president who believes he is entitled to exercise unlimited power.

Liberal critics argued that the New Deal did not go far enough to help the poor and to reform the nation's economic system. Conservative critics argued that Roosevelt spent too much on direct relief and used New Deal policies to control business and socialize the economy. Conservatives were particularly angered by laws such as the Agricultural Adjustment Act and the National Industrial Recovery Act, which they believed gave the federal government too much control over agriculture and industry. Many critics believed the New Deal interfered with the workings of a free-market economy. **E**

**THE SUPREME COURT REACTS** By the mid-1930s, conservative opposition to the New Deal had received a boost from two Supreme Court decisions. In 1935, the Court struck down the NIRA as unconstitutional. It declared that the law gave legislative powers to the executive branch and that the enforcement of industry codes within states went beyond the federal government's constitutional powers to regulate interstate commerce. The next year, the Supreme Court struck down the AAA on the grounds that agriculture is a local matter and should be regulated by the states rather than by the federal government.

Fearing that further Court decisions might dismantle the New Deal, President Roosevelt proposed in February 1937 that Congress enact a court-reform bill to reorganize the federal judiciary and allow him to appoint six new Supreme Court justices. This "Court-packing bill" aroused a storm of protest in Congress and the press. Many people believed that the president was violating principles of judicial independence and the separation of powers. As it turned out, the president got his way without reorganizing the judiciary. In 1937, an elderly justice retired, and Roosevelt appointed the liberal Hugo S. Black, shifting the balance of the Court. Rulings of the Court began to favor the New Deal. (See *NLRB* v. *Jones and Laughlin Steel Co.* on page 502.) Over the next four years, because of further resignations, Roosevelt was able to appoint seven new justices.

**THREE FIERY CRITICS** In 1934, some of the strongest conservative opponents of the New Deal banded together to form an organization called the American Liberty League. The American Liberty League opposed New Deal measures that it believed violated respect for the rights of individuals and property. Three of the toughest critics the president faced, however, were three men who expressed views that appealed to poor Americans: Charles Coughlin, Francis Townsend, and Huey Long.

**MAIN IDEA**

**Contrasting**
**E** How did liberal and conservative critics differ in their opposition to the New Deal?

*E. Answer*
**Liberals:** thought the New Deal did not go far enough in helping the poor and reforming the nation's economic system; **Conservatives:** believed the New Deal spent too much money on direct relief and was trying to control business and socialize the economy.

Father Charles Coughlin speaks to a radio audience in 1935. ▼

## More About . . .

### The Roles of State and Federal Government
The New Deal permanently altered the U.S. federal system. For instance, the CCC and the TVA transformed local reforestation, soil erosion, and flood control concerns into federal programs. The NLRA transferred power from the states to the federal government under the Commerce Clause. Block grants—federal money offered to states on condition that they take on specified tasks—enlarged both federal and state authority. Ask, How did the New Deal affect the role of state government? *(It increased the state role but also transferred some state roles to the federal government.)* Ask, How did the New Deal affect the role of the federal government? *(It vastly extended the federal role.)*

Humanities Transparencies HT40
· Nine Old Men

**ACTIVITY**   **SKILLBUILDER LESSON**

### Analyzing Issues

**Explaining the Skill** Historical issues might be economic, social, or political in nature. To analyze an issue students will need to ask a question with regard to the reason the issue is controversial. Analyzing such issues involves defining main ideas, identifying facts, examining points of view, and then drawing conclusions.

**Applying the Skill** To answer the questions about Roosevelt and the Supreme Court, students should consider the following aspects of the issue:

Ask the question: Why was Roosevelt's attempt to pack the court a problem?
· Important facts—What is important to know?
· Central problem—Why is this issue a problem?
· Points of view—What are the sides in the controversy saying?
Then students should draw conclusions about the information they found.

In-Depth Resources: Unit 4
· Skillbuilder Practice: Analyzing Issues, p. 66

## More About . . .

### Huey Long

A fiery and impassioned speaker, Long controlled Louisiana first as Governor then as a U.S. Senator. In both offices, he ruled with an iron fist, and setting up a family dynasty that lasted for 50 years. Long's program was to limit fortunes to $3-4 million and guarantee every American a $5,000 homestead, an income of $2,500, and a free college education. Though the financing for his plan was sketchy, Long's popularity was rising fast when he was killed. Had he lived, he likely would have been a factor in the election of 1936.

 In-Depth Resources: Unit 4
· American Lives: Huey Long, p. 83

## Assess & Reteach

### SECTION 1 ASSESSMENT

Have pairs of students work together to answer the questions in the Section Assessment.

 Formal Assessment
· Section Quiz, p. 283

### SELF-ASSESSMENT

Students can document what they learned by creating a cluster diagram and listing each New Deal program and its purpose.

### RETEACH

Use the Section Quiz to help students review main ideas and significant details.

 In-Depth Resources: Unit 4
· Reteaching Activity, p. 67

---

Every Sunday, Father Charles Coughlin, a Roman Catholic priest from a suburb of Detroit, broadcast radio sermons that combined economic, political, and religious ideas. Initially a supporter of the New Deal, Coughlin soon turned against Roosevelt. He favored a guaranteed annual income and the nationalization of banks. At the height of his popularity, Father Coughlin claimed a radio audience of as many as 40–45 million people, but his increasingly anti-Semitic (anti-Jewish) views eventually cost him support.

Another critic of New Deal policies was Dr. Francis Townsend, a physician and health officer in Long Beach, California. He believed that Roosevelt wasn't doing enough to help the poor and elderly, so he devised a pension plan that would provide monthly benefits to the aged. The plan found strong backing among the elderly, thus undermining their support for Roosevelt.

Perhaps the most serious challenge to the New Deal came from Senator **Huey Long** of Louisiana. Like Coughlin, Long was an early supporter of the New Deal, but he too turned against Roosevelt. Eager to win the presidency for himself, Long proposed a nationwide social program called Share-Our-Wealth. Under the banner "Every Man a King," he promised something for everyone.

**Vocabulary**
**nationalization:** conversion from private to governmental ownership

**Huey Long**

### A PERSONAL VOICE HUEY LONG

"We owe debts in America today, public and private, amounting to $252 billion. That means that every child is born with a $2,000 debt tied around his neck. . . . We propose that children shall be born in a land of opportunity, guaranteed a home, food, clothes, and the other things that make for living, including the right to education."

—*Record*, 74 Congress, Session 1

Long's program was so popular that by 1935 he boasted of having perhaps as many as 27,000 Share-Our-Wealth clubs and 7.5 million members. That same year, however, at the height of his popularity, Long was assassinated by a lone gunman.

As the initial impetus of the New Deal began to wane, President Roosevelt started to look ahead. He knew that much more needed to be done to help the people and to solve the nation's economic problems.

## ASSESSMENT

**1. TERMS & NAMES** For each of the terms and names below, write a sentence explaining its significance.

- •Franklin Delano Roosevelt
- •New Deal
- •Glass-Steagall Banking Act
- •Federal Securities Act
- •Agricultural Adjustment Act (AAA)
- •Civilian Conservation Corps (CCC)
- •National Industrial Recovery Act (NIRA)
- •deficit spending
- •Huey Long

### MAIN IDEA

**2. TAKING NOTES**
In a two-column chart, list problems that President Roosevelt confronted and how he tried to solve them.

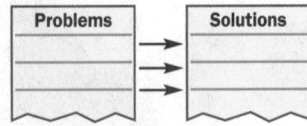

| Problems | Solutions |
|----------|-----------|
|          |           |
|          |           |
|          |           |

Write a paragraph telling which solution had the greatest impact, and why.

### CRITICAL THINKING

**3. EVALUATING**
Of the New Deal programs discussed in this section, which do you consider the most important? Explain your choice. **Think About:**
- the type of assistance offered by each program
- the scope of each program
- the impact of each program

**4. EVALUATING LEADERSHIP**
Do you think Roosevelt was wrong to try to "pack" the Supreme Court with those in favor of the New Deal? Explain your answer.

**5. DEVELOPING HISTORICAL PERSPECTIVE**
The New Deal has often been referred to as a turning point in American history. Cite examples to explain why.

**494** CHAPTER 15

---

 ASSESSMENT Answers

**1. TERMS & NAMES**
Franklin Delano Roosevelt, p. 489
New Deal, p. 489
Glass-Steagall Act, p. 490
Federal Securities Act, p. 490
Agricultural Adjustment Act, p. 491
Civilian Conservation Corps, p. 491
National Industrial Recovery Act, p. 491
deficit spending, p. 492
Huey Long, p. 494

**2. TAKING NOTES**
Problem: lack of confidence in banks. Solution: bank holiday, Treasury inspection, deposit insurance. Problem: low crop prices. Solution: paying farmers to slow crop production. Problem: massive unemployment. Solution: federal work programs.

**3. EVALUATING**
The FDIC: boosted confidence in banks; the CCC: provided aid for unemployment and helped the environment

**4. EVALUATING LEADERSHIP**
Students may suggest that, given the crisis of the Depression, it was necessary for FDR to restructure the Court. Others might say that FDR's proposed "Court-packing bill" was unfair.

**5. DEVELOPING HISTORICAL PERSPECTIVE**
The New Deal helped the failing banking system, restored people's hope in the future, provided assistance to farmers and those in need of housing, and provided people with jobs.

# The Second New Deal Takes Hold

| MAIN IDEA | WHY IT MATTERS NOW | Terms & Names |
|---|---|---|
| The Second New Deal included new programs to extend federal aid and stimulate the nation's economy. | Second New Deal programs continue to assist homebuyers, farmers, workers, and the elderly in the 2000s. | •Eleanor Roosevelt<br>•Works Progress Administration (WPA)<br>•National Youth Administration<br>•Wagner Act<br>•Social Security Act |

TEKS U.S. History
1B, 6H, 8A, 13E, 15A, 19A, 19B, 21D, 24A, 24B, 24C, 24D, 25A, 25B, 25C, 25D

### One American's Story

Dorothea Lange was a photographer who documented American life during the Great Depression and the era of the New Deal. Lange spent considerable time getting to know her subjects—destitute migrant workers—before she and her assistant set up their cameras.

**A PERSONAL VOICE** DOROTHEA LANGE

" So often it's just sticking around and remaining there, not swooping in and swooping out in a cloud of dust. . . . We found our way in . . . not too far away from the people we were working with. . . . The people who are garrulous and wear their heart on their sleeve and tell you everything, that's one kind of person. But the fellow who's hiding behind a tree and hoping you don't see him, is the fellow that you'd better find out why. "

—quoted in *Restless Spirit: The Life and Work of Dorothea Lange*

▲ Dorothea Lange taking photographs on the Texas plains in 1934.

Lange also believed that her distinct limp, the result of a childhood case of polio, worked to her advantage. Seeing that Lange, too, had suffered, people were kind to her and more at ease.

Much of Lange's work was funded by federal agencies, such as the Farm Security Administration, which was established to alleviate rural poverty. Her photographs of migrant workers helped draw attention to the desperate conditions in rural America and helped to underscore the need for direct relief.

## ① The Second Hundred Days

By 1935, the Roosevelt administration was seeking ways to build on the programs established during the Hundred Days. Although the economy had improved during FDR's first two years in office, the gains were not as great as he had expected. Unemployment remained high despite government work programs, and production still lagged behind the levels of the 1920s.

*The New Deal* **495**

---

### OBJECTIVES

1 Describe the purpose of the Second New Deal.

2 Summarize New Deal programs for farmers.

3 Identify the Second New Deal programs aimed at assisting young people and professionals.

4 Summarize labor and economic reforms carried out under the Second New Deal.

**SKILLBUILDER**
· Interpreting Visual Sources, p. 497

**CRITICAL THINKING**
· Summarizing, p. 496
· Evaluating, p. 499
· Analyzing Issues, p. 499
· Drawing Conclusions, p. 501
· Evaluating Decisions, p. 501
· Interpreting Visual Sources, p. 501

## Focus & Motivate

Ask students if they think the government should be involved in ensuring that people have opportunities for employment.

## Instruct

### Instruct: Objective ①
**The Second Hundred Days**
TAKS SS11 1(US13.C)
· What was the Second New Deal?
· Why was the Second New Deal so popular?
· What was significant about the election results of 1936?

📄 In-Depth Resources: Unit 4
· Guided Reading, p. 61

---

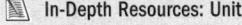

## Instruct: Objective ❷

### Helping Farmers

TAKS SS11 1(US13.C)

· Which legislation helped farmers?

· How did the government help sharecroppers and migrant workers?

📑 In-Depth Resources: Unit 4
· Guided Reading, p. 61

▲ Eleanor Roosevelt visits a children's hospital in 1937.

### More About . . .

#### The Grapes of Wrath

John Steinbeck's novel, *The Grapes of Wrath*, which focuses on the plight of migrant farm workers in the 1930s, is considered an American classic. The novel won the Pulitzer prize for fiction in 1940. In 1940, director John Ford made it into a classic movie starring Henry Fonda. Ford won the Oscar for Best Director. Steinbeck won the Nobel Prize for Literature in 1962.

Nevertheless, the New Deal enjoyed widespread popularity, and President Roosevelt launched a second burst of activity, often called the Second New Deal or the Second Hundred Days. During this phase, the president called on Congress to provide more extensive relief for both farmers and workers.

The president was prodded in this direction by his wife, **Eleanor Roosevelt,** a social reformer who combined her deep humanitarian impulses with great political skills. Eleanor Roosevelt traveled the country, observing social conditions and reminding the president about the suffering of the nation's people. She also urged him to appoint women to government positions. Ⓐ

**REELECTING FDR** The Second New Deal was under way by the time of the 1936 presidential election. The Republicans nominated Alfred Landon, the governor of Kansas, while the Democrats, of course, nominated President Roosevelt for a second term. The election resulted in an overwhelming victory for the Democrats, who won the presidency and large majorities in both houses. The election marked the first time that most African Americans had voted Democratic rather than Republican, and the first time that labor unions gave united support to a presidential candidate. The 1936 election was a vote of confidence in FDR and the New Deal.

### ❷ Helping Farmers

In the mid-1930s, two of every five farms in the United States were mortgaged, and thousands of small farmers lost their farms. The novelist John Steinbeck described the experience of one tenant farmer and his family.

▲ A poster promotes the movie adaption of John Steinbeck's novel *The Grapes of Wrath.*

**A PERSONAL VOICE** JOHN STEINBECK

" Across the dooryard the tractor cut, and the hard, foot-beaten ground was seeded field, and the tractor cut through again; the uncut space was ten feet wide. And back he came. The iron guard bit into the house-corner, crumbled the wall, and wrenched the little house from its foundation so that it fell sideways, crushed like a bug. . . . The tractor cut a straight line on, and the air and the ground vibrated with its thunder. The tenant man stared after it, his rifle in his hand. His wife was beside him, and the quiet children behind. And all of them stared after the tractor."

—*The Grapes of Wrath*

**FOCUSING ON FARMS** When the Supreme Court struck down the AAA early in 1936, Congress passed another law to replace it: the Soil Conservation and Domestic Allotment Act. This act paid farmers for cutting production of soil-depleting crops and rewarded farmers for practicing good soil conservation methods. Two years later, in 1938, Congress approved a second Agricultural Adjustment Act that brought back many features of the first AAA. The second AAA did not include a processing tax to pay for farm subsidies, a provision of the first AAA that the Supreme Court had declared unconstitutional.

**MAIN IDEA**

**Summarizing**
Ⓐ Why did Roosevelt launch the Second Hundred Days?

*A. Answer*
Roosevelt launched the Second Hundred Days based on the popularity of the first Hundred Days and the urging of his wife.

---

## DIFFERENTIATING INSTRUCTION   LESS PROFICIENT READERS

### Clarifying Ideas

To help students identify the Second New Deal programs initiated to aid farmers (pages 494–496), have them follow these steps:

· Read this section slowly, a paragraph at a time.

· Ask why the farmers needed help.

· Identify the programs set up to help.

· Note the purpose and impact of the programs.

Use a diagram like the one at the right to further clarify the programs for farmers, their purpose and impact.

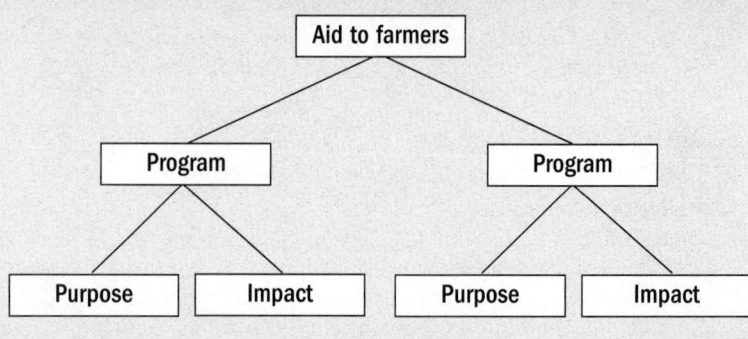

## History Through *Photojournalism*

### "MIGRANT MOTHER" (1936), DOROTHEA LANGE

In February 1936, Dorothea Lange visited a camp in Nipomo, California, where some 2,500 destitute pea pickers lived in tents or, like this mother of seven children, in lean-tos. Lange talked briefly to the woman and then took five pictures, successively moving closer to her subjects and directing more emphasis on the mother. The last photo, "Migrant Mother" (at right), was published in the *San Francisco News* March 10, 1936.

▶ "Migrant Mother" became one of the most recognizable symbols of the Depression and perhaps the strongest argument in support of New Deal relief programs. Roy Stryker, who hired Lange to document the harsh living conditions of the time, described the mother: "She has all the suffering of mankind in her, but all the perseverance too. A restraint and a strange courage."

◀ Lange reflected upon her assignment. "I saw and approached the hungry and desperate mother, as if drawn by a magnet. . . . She said that they had been living on frozen vegetables from the surrounding fields, and birds that the children killed. She had just sold the tires from her car to buy food."

**SKILLBUILDER** Interpreting Visual Sources
1. What might the woman be thinking about? Why do you think so?
2. Why do you think "Migrant Mother" was effective in persuading people to support FDR's relief programs?

📖 **SEE SKILLBUILDER HANDBOOK, PAGE R23.**

### More About . . .

#### Dorothea Lange (1895–1965)

Lange studied photography at Columbia University in New York City, and went on to become a documentary photographer. She captured moving images of the effects of the Depression on American life. The quality of her work landed her a job with the Farm Security Administration. Lange was assigned to document the sufferings of the rural poor. The body of her work includes photographs that have become historical and artistic documents of the era. In Lange's own words, "One should really use the camera as though tomorrow you'd be stricken blind."

### History Through *Photojournalism*

#### Interpreting the Photograph

Ask students to describe their reactions to Lange's photographs. Have them consider what the images reveal about the social and political conditions of the 1930s. Why do students think the Farm Security Administration would have wanted to hire Lange as a photographer? What elements of her style and subject matter made her work stand out? (*Lange documented human suffering in her photographs, but also captured the possibility of relief and recovery.*)

#### SKILLBUILDER ANSWERS

1. She may be thinking of how to feed, clothe, and shelter her children. She is surrounded by children.

2. The photograph clearly shows the suffering caused by the Great Depression.

---

**DIFFERENTIATING INSTRUCTION**    **GIFTED AND TALENTED STUDENTS**

### Essay on Photojournalism

Have interested students read *Let Us Now Praise Famous Men*. The collaborative work, published in 1941, features the writer, James Agee, and the photographer, Walker Evans. Have students who read the book write a brief essay describing their reactions. Ask students to select a favorite passage or photograph to share with the class.

**Rubric**

The essay should . . .
· have a topic sentence
· identify passages or photograph that were especially moving
· evaluate the impact of the book on their life

 Integrated Assessment
· Rubric 5

## Instruct: Objective ③

## Roosevelt Extends Relief

TAKS SS11 1(US13.C)

· What was the Works Progress Administration (WPA)?

· What was the National Youth Administration (NYA)?

 In-Depth Resources: Unit 4
· Guided Reading, p. 61

---

### More About . . .

#### The WPA

Some people objected to the WPA's giving assistance to writers and artists. Art, they claimed, was not real work. The program's critics probably didn't anticipate that the work produced then by many of the artists would be worth far more today than any wages the artists received from the WPA. One artist recalled the WPA's Federal Art Project: "The total cost of the Federal Art Project was $23 million. Many of these paintings, sculptures, and prints were given to museums, courthouses, public buildings . . . I think today those in museums alone are worth about $100 million."

 Humanities Transparencies HT22
· A relief center in Louisville, Kentucky

---

The Second New Deal also attempted to help sharecroppers, migrant workers, and many other poor farmers. The Resettlement Administration, created by executive order in 1935, provided monetary loans to small farmers to buy land. In 1937, the agency was replaced by the Farm Security Administration (FSA), which loaned more than $1 billion to help tenant farmers become landholders and established camps for migrant farm workers, who had traditionally lived in squalid housing.

The FSA hired photographers such as Dorothea Lange, Ben Shahn, Walker Evans, Arthur Rothstein, and Carl Mydans to take many pictures of rural towns and farms and their inhabitants. The agency used their photographs to create a pictorial record of the difficult situation in rural America.

## ③ Roosevelt Extends Relief

As part of the Second New Deal, the Roosevelt administration and Congress set up a series of programs to help youths, professionals, and other workers. One of the largest was the **Works Progress Administration (WPA),** headed by Harry Hopkins, the former chief of the Federal Emergency Relief Administration.

The WPA set out to create as many jobs as possible as quickly as possible. Between 1935 and 1943, it spent $11 billion to give jobs to more than 8 million workers, most of them unskilled. These workers built 850 airports throughout the country, constructed or repaired 651,000 miles of roads and streets, and put up more than 125,000 public buildings. Women workers in sewing groups made 300 million garments for the needy. Although criticized by some as a make-work project, the WPA produced public works of lasting value to the nation and gave working people a sense of hope and purpose. As one man recalled, "It was really great. You worked, you got a paycheck and you had some dignity. Even when a man raked leaves, he got paid, he had some dignity."

In addition, the WPA employed many professionals who wrote guides to cities, collected historical slave narratives, painted murals on the walls of schools

This photograph ▶ by Margaret Bourke-White shows people waiting for food in a Kentucky bread line in 1937.

---

 classzone.com

### The Legacy of the New Deal and WPA

**Class Time** One or two class periods

**Task** Identifying WPA buildings and public works

**Purpose** To analyze the historical impact of the New Deal and WPA

**Directions** Have students use the Internet and library sources to research WPA buildings and public works. Encourage students to locate WPA buildings in their community or state. If possible have students find photographs of the various sites. Have them work in groups to put together a visual presentation about the buildings and public works they researched.

**Rubric**

The visual presentation should . . .

· have sketches or pictures of the featured buildings
· include a map showing the location of the buildings
· be attractively displayed

Integrated Assessment
· Rubric 4

**MAIN IDEA**
**Evaluating**
**B** Do you think work programs like the WPA were a valid use of federal money? Why or why not?

*B. Possible Answers* Yes: they provided an income to people in need, while producing public works; No: private business, rather than the federal government, should provide jobs.

and other public buildings, and performed in theater troupes around the country. At the urging of Eleanor Roosevelt, the WPA made special efforts to help women, minorities, and young people. **B**

Another program, the **National Youth Administration** (NYA), was created specifically to provide education, jobs, counseling, and recreation for young people. The NYA provided student aid to high school, college, and graduate students. In exchange, students worked in part-time positions at their schools. One participant later described her experience.

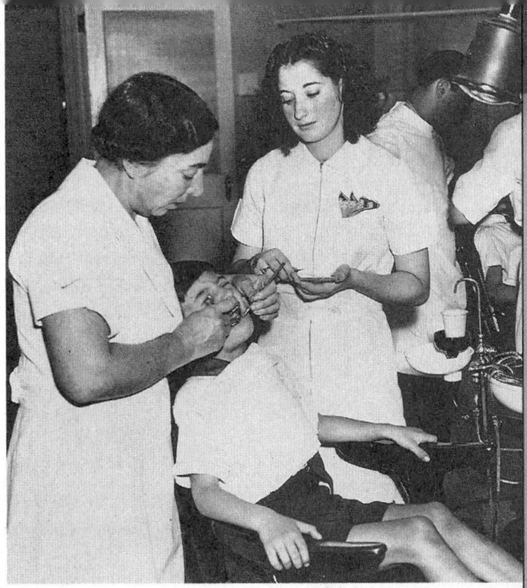

▲ The NYA helped young people, such as this dental assistant (*third from left*), receive training and job opportunities.

**A PERSONAL VOICE** HELEN FARMER

**"I lugged . . . drafts and reams of paper home, night after night. . . . Sometimes I typed almost all night and had to deliver it to school the next morning. . . . This was a good program. It got necessary work done. It gave teenagers a chance to work for pay. Mine bought me clothes and shoes, school supplies, some movies and mad money. Candy bars, and big pickles out of a barrel. It gave my mother relief from my necessary demands for money."**

—quoted in *The Great Depression*

For graduates unable to find jobs, or youth who had dropped out of school, the NYA provided part-time jobs, such as working on highways, parks, and the grounds of public buildings.

## Improving Labor and Other Reforms 4

In a speech to Congress in January 1935, the president declared, "When a man is convalescing from an illness, wisdom dictates not only cure of the symptoms but also removal of their cause." During the Second New Deal, Roosevelt, with the help of Congress, brought about important reforms in the areas of labor relations and economic security for retired workers. (See the chart on page 500.)

*C. Answer* The Wagner Act gave the federal government power to protect and aid workers.

**MAIN IDEA**
**Analyzing Issues**
**C** Why was the Wagner Act significant?

**IMPROVING LABOR CONDITIONS** In 1935, the Supreme Court declared the NIRA unconstitutional, citing that the federal government had violated legislative authority reserved for individual states. One of the first reforms of the Second New Deal was passage of the National Labor Relations Act. More commonly called the **Wagner Act,** after its sponsor, Senator Robert F. Wagner of New York, the act reestablished the NIRA provision of collective bargaining. The federal government again protected the right of workers to join unions and engage in collective bargaining with employers.

The Wagner Act also prohibited unfair labor practices such as threatening workers, firing union members, and interfering with union organizing. The act set up the National Labor Relations Board (NLRB) to hear testimony about unfair practices and to hold elections to find out if workers wanted union representation. **C**

In 1938, Congress passed the Fair Labor Standards Act, which set maximum hours at 44 hours per week, decreasing to 40 hours after two years. It also set minimum wages at 25 cents an hour, increasing to 40 cents an hour by 1945. In addition, the act set rules for the employment of workers under 16 and banned hazardous work for those under 18.



### Instruct: Objective 4

**Improving Labor and Other Reforms**

TAKS SS11 5(WH26.C)

- How did the New Deal help labor?
- What benefits did the Social Security system provide?
- How did the Second New Deal promote rural electrification?

In-Depth Resources: Unit 4
- Guided Reading, p. 61

### Tracing Themes

**ECONOMIC OPPORTUNITY**

The Wagner Act gave legal protection to labor union activities and negated the provisions of anti-trust legislation. Until the New Deal, business interests had managed to use legislative and judicial power to keep workers from organizing. While passage of the Wagner Act did not cause business interests to roll over, it certainly redressed the imbalance, giving rise to the greatest power of organized labor in American history in the years to come.

### More About . . .

**The Wagner Act**

There is no underestimating the importance of the Wagner Act to organized labor. From labor's point of view, it brought the authority of the federal government in to ensure that labor had the opportunity to organize workers without intimidation from management. Business-owners at the time did not see it that way and thought it gave labor an unfair advantage.

**ACTIVITY** LINK TO ECONOMICS — **B** BLOCK SCHEDULING

### The Wagner Act

**Class Time** 45 minutes

**Task** Interviewing a local labor leader, lawyer or historian about the significance of the Wagner Act to organized labor

**Purpose** To analyze a New Deal program with continuing impact

**Directions** Have students research the provisions of the Wagner Act and their current applications. Then invite a local labor leader, lawyer, or historian to class and have students prepare questions for the interview, which you could conduct like a press conference and videotape for a class historical archive.

Integrated Assessment
- Rubrics 4, 6

## HISTORY from VISUALS

### Interpreting a Chart

The chart categorizes the New Deal programs according to target area. Discuss with students how the New Deal expanded the scope of executive power. Point out that each of these agencies created by Congress became part of the executive branch of government.

**Extension** Have students reorganize the chart in chronological order. On the time line, help them identify which legislation was a product of the first Hundred Days, the first New Deal, and the Second New Deal.

## New Deal Programs

| EMPLOYMENT PROJECTS | | PURPOSE |
|---|---|---|
| 1933 | Civilian Conservation Corps (CCC) | Provided jobs for single males on conservation projects. |
| 1933 | Federal Emergency Relief Administration (FERA) | Helped states to provide aid for the unemployed. |
| 1933 | Public Works Administration (PWA) | Created jobs on government projects. |
| 1933 | Civil Works Administration (CWA) | Provided work in federal jobs. |
| 1935 | Works Progress Administration (WPA) | Quickly created as many jobs as possible—from construction jobs to positions in symphony orchestras. |
| 1935 | National Youth Administration (NYA) | Provided job training for unemployed young people and part-time jobs for needy students. |

| BUSINESS ASSISTANCE AND REFORM | | |
|---|---|---|
| 1933 | Emergency Banking Relief Act (EBRA) | Banks were inspected by Treasury Department and those stable could reopen. |
| 1933 | Federal Deposit Insurance Corporation (FDIC) | Protected bank deposits up to $5,000. (Today, accounts are protected up to $100,000.) |
| 1933 | National Recovery Administration (NRA) | Established codes of fair competition. |
| 1934 | Securities and Exchange Commission (SEC) | Supervised the stock market and eliminated dishonest practices. |
| 1935 | Banking Act of 1935 | Created seven-member board to regulate the nation's money supply and the interest rates on loans. |
| 1938 | Food, Drug and Cosmetic Act (FDC) | Required manufacturers to list ingredients in foods, drugs, and cosmetic products. |

| FARM RELIEF AND RURAL DEVELOPMENT | | |
|---|---|---|
| 1933 | Agricultural Adjustment Administration (AAA) | Aided farmers and regulated crop production. |
| 1933 | Tennessee Valley Authority (TVA) | Developed the resources of the Tennessee Valley. |
| 1935 | Rural Electrification Administration (REA) | Provided affordable electricity for isolated rural areas. |

| HOUSING | | |
|---|---|---|
| 1933 | Home Owners Loan Corporation (HOLC) | Loaned money at low interest to homeowners who could not meet mortgage payments. |
| 1934 | Federal Housing Administration (FHA) | Insured loans for building and repairing homes. |
| 1937 | United States Housing Authority (USHA) | Provided federal loans for low-cost public housing. |

| LABOR RELATIONS | | |
|---|---|---|
| 1935 | National Labor Relations Board (Wagner Act) | Defined unfair labor practices and established the National Labor Relations Board (NLRB) to settle disputes between employers and employees. |
| 1938 | Fair Labor Standards Act | Established a minimum hourly wage and a maximum number of hours in the workweek for the entire country. Set rules for the employment of workers under 16 and banned hazardous factory work for those under 18. |

| RETIREMENT | | |
|---|---|---|
| 1935 | Social Security Administration | Provided a pension for retired workers and their spouses and aided people with disabilities. |

---

**ACTIVITY** COOPERATIVE ACTIVITY

 BLOCK SCHEDULING

### Ongoing New Deal Agencies

**Class Time** 45 minutes

**Task** Researching the responsibilities and accomplishments of New Deal-era executive agencies

**Purpose** Develop a historical perspective of contemporary governmental agencies

**Directions** Divide the class into small groups and assign each group an agency from the chart such as the FDIC, TVA, FHA, NLRB, Social Security Administration. Have students research the original responsibilities of the agency, its accomplishments, and what it does now. Have each group report its findings to the class.

**Rubric**

The New Deal Agency report should . . .

· describe the original responsibilities of the agency
· list the accomplishments of the agency
· identify the agency's current programs

Integrated Assessment
· Rubric 3

**THE SOCIAL SECURITY ACT** One of the most important achievements of the New Deal was creating the Social Security system. The **Social Security Act,** passed in 1935, was created by a committee chaired by Secretary of Labor Frances Perkins. The act had three major parts:

- *Old-age insurance for retirees 65 or older and their spouses.* The insurance was a supplemental retirement plan. Half of the funds came from the worker and half from the employer. Although some groups were excluded from the system, it helped to make retirement comfortable for millions of people.

- *Unemployment compensation system.* The unemployment system was funded by a federal tax on employers. It was administered at the state level. The initial payments ranged from $15 to $18 per week.

- *Aid to families with dependent children and the disabled.* The aid was paid for by federal funds made available to the states.

Although the Social Security Act was not a total pension system or a complete welfare system, it did provide substantial benefits to millions of Americans. **D**

**EXPANDING AND REGULATING UTILITIES** The Second New Deal also included laws to promote rural electrification and to regulate public utilities. In 1935, only 12.6 percent of American farms had electricity. Roosevelt established under executive order the Rural Electrification Administration (REA), which financed and worked with electrical cooperatives to bring electricity to isolated areas. By 1945, 45 percent of America's farms and rural homes had electricity. That figure rose to 90 percent by 1949.

The Public Utility Holding Company Act of 1935 took aim at financial corruption in the public utility industry. It outlawed the ownership of utilities by multiple holding companies—a practice known as the pyramiding of holding companies. Lobbyists for the holding companies fought the law fiercely, and it proved extremely difficult to enforce.

As the New Deal struggled to help farmers and other workers overcome the Great Depression, it assisted many different groups in the nation, including women, African Americans, and Native Americans.

**MAIN IDEA**

**Drawing Conclusions**
**D** Whom did Social Security help?

*D. Answer* It helped retirees and their spouses, the unemployed, families with dependent children, and the disabled.

## SECTION 2 ASSESSMENT

**1. TERMS & NAMES** For each term or name, write a sentence explaining its significance.
- Eleanor Roosevelt
- Works Progress Administration (WPA)
- National Youth Administration
- Wagner Act
- Social Security Act

**MAIN IDEA**

**2. TAKING NOTES**
Create a chart similar to the one below to show how groups such as farmers, the unemployed, youth, and retirees were helped by Second New Deal programs.

| Second New Deal | |
|---|---|
| Group | How Helped |
| | |
| | |

Which group do you think benefited the most from the Second New Deal? Explain.

**CRITICAL THINKING**

**3. EVALUATING DECISIONS**
Why might the Social Security Act be considered the most important achievement of the New Deal?
**Think About:**
- the types of relief needed in the 1930s
- alternatives to government assistance to the elderly, the unemployed, and the disabled
- the scope of the act

**4. INTERPRETING VISUAL SOURCES**
Many WPA posters were created to promote New Deal programs—in this case the Rural Electrification Administration. How does this poster's simplistic design convey the program's goal?

**1. TERMS & NAMES**
Eleanor Roosevelt, p. 496
Works Progress Administration, p. 498
National Youth Administration, p. 499
Wagner Act, p. 499
Social Security Act, p. 501

**2. TAKING NOTES**
Farmers: second Agricultural Adjustment Act, Farm Security Administration, Rural Electrification Administration. Unemployed: Works Progress Administration, National Youth Administration, Social Security Administration, Works Progress Administration. Labor: Wagner Act, Fair Labor Standards Act. Retirees: Social Security Act.

**3. EVALUATING DECISIONS**
The Roosevelt administration aimed to eradicate the problems of the 1930s; provided immediate aid to the unemployed, the elderly, the disabled, and families with dependent children; New Deal program with the largest scope, affecting thousands of people, over many years.

**4. INTERPRETING VISUAL SOURCES**
The Rural Electrification Administration brought electricity to remote regions of the country. People in rural areas could finally enjoy the conveniences and life-changing benefits of electricity.

## HISTORIC DECISIONS OF THE SUPREME COURT

### Objectives

1. Analyze the Supreme Court case, *NLRB v. Jones and Laughlin Steel Corp.* (1937).

2. Explain the legal reasoning behind the Supreme Court decision in the Jones case.

## Focus & Motivate

**Making Predictions** Ask students to predict how the Supreme Court might rule in a case where a labor union used its authority to shut down a vital service such as police or bus and subway service in a city.

### More About . . .

#### Charles Evans Hughes

Hughes (1862-1948) had a remarkable career as jurist, statesman, and politician. A prominent New York lawyer, he was elected governor of New York in 1906. In 1910, President Taft appointed Hughes to the U.S. Supreme Court. He served six years before resigning, in 1916, to run for president on the Republican platform. Hughes lost the election to Woodrow Wilson by a narrow margin. In 1930, President Hoover appointed Hughes to the Supreme Court as Chief Justice.

# HISTORIC DECISIONS OF THE SUPREME COURT

# NLRB v. JONES AND LAUGHLIN STEEL CORP. (1937)

**ORIGINS OF THE CASE** In 1936, the Jones and Laughlin Steel Corporation was charged with intimidating union organizers and firing several union members. The National Labor Relations Board (NLRB) found the company guilty of "unfair labor practices" and ordered it to rehire the workers with back pay.

**THE RULING** The Supreme Court ruled that Congress had the power to regulate labor relations and confirmed the authority of the NLRB.

## LEGAL REASONING

In the 1935 National Labor Relations Act, or Wagner Act, which created the NLRB, Congress claimed that its authority to regulate labor relations came from the commerce clause of the Constitution. Jones and Laughlin Steel argued that its manufacturing business did not involve interstate commerce—it operated a plant and hired people locally.

The Court disagreed. Although production itself may occur within one state, it said, production is a part of the interstate "flow of commerce." If labor unrest at a steel mill would create "burdens and obstructions" to interstate commerce, then Congress has the power to prevent labor unrest at the steel mill.

The Court also explained that the act went "no further than to safeguard the right of employees to self-organization and to select representatives . . . for collective bargaining." Departing from earlier decisions, the Court affirmed that these are "fundamental" rights.

"Long ago we . . . said . . . that a single employee was helpless in dealing with an employer; that he was dependent . . . on his daily wage for the maintenance of himself and family; that, if the employer refused to pay him the wages that he thought fair, he was . . . unable to leave the employ and resist arbitrary and unfair treatment; that union was essential to give laborers opportunity to deal on an equality with their employer."

As a result, the Wagner Act was allowed to stand.

*Chief Justice Charles Evans Hughes*

### LEGAL SOURCES

#### LEGISLATION

**U.S. CONSTITUTION, ARTICLE 1, SECTION 8**
(COMMERCE CLAUSE)
"The Congress shall have Power . . . To regulate Commerce with foreign Nations and among the several States."

**NATIONAL LABOR RELATIONS ACT (1935)**
"The term 'affecting commerce' means . . . tending to lead to a labor dispute burdening or obstructing commerce or the free flow of commerce."

"It shall be an unfair labor practice for an employer . . . to interfere with, restrain, or coerce employees in the exercise of the rights [to organize unions]."

#### RELATED CASES

**SCHECHTER POULTRY CORP. v. UNITED STATES (1935)**
The Court struck down the National Industrial Recovery Act, a key piece of New Deal legislation.

**502** CHAPTER 15

## RECOMMENDED RESOURCES

### BOOKS

Hughes, Charles Evans. *The Autobiographical Notes of Charles Evans Hughes.* Cambridge: Harvard UP, 1973.

Hughes, Charles Evans. *The Supreme Court of the United States: Its Foundation, Methods and Achievements.* Washington, D.C.: Beard Books, 2000. A collection of Hughes' opinions and essays.

Perkins, Dexter, *Charles Evans Hughes and American Democratic Statesmanship.* Westport, CT: Greenwood Press, 1978. A biography by the noted American historian.

### INTEGRATED TECHNOLOGY

For teacher support and more information about the Supreme Court including the full text of the Supreme Court decisions, visit. . . .

 classzone.com

Choosing to work despite the strike, a storekeeper at the Jones and Laughlin Steel Corporation tries to pass through picket lines.

## WHY IT MATTERED

The 1935 Wagner Act was one of the most important pieces of New Deal legislation. Conservative justices on the Supreme Court, however, thought New Deal legislation increased the power of the federal government beyond what the Constitution allowed. By the time the Jones and Laughlin case reached the Court in 1937, the Court had already struck down numerous New Deal laws. It appeared to many as if the Wagner Act was doomed.

In February 1937, Roosevelt announced a plan to appoint enough justices to build a Court majority in favor of the New Deal. Critics immediately accused Roosevelt of trying to pack the Supreme Court, thus crippling the Constitution's system of checks and balances.

Two months later, the Court delivered its opinion in *Jones and Laughlin* and at about the same time upheld other New Deal legislation as well. Most historians agree that the Court's switch was not a response to Roosevelt's "Court-packing" plan, which already seemed destined for failure. Nevertheless, the decision resolved a potential crisis.

## HISTORICAL IMPACT

The protection that labor unions gained by the Wagner Act helped them to grow quickly. Union membership among non-farm workers grew from around 12 percent in 1930 to around 31 percent by 1950. This increase helped improve the economic standing of many working-class Americans in the years following World War II.

Most significantly, *Jones and Laughlin* greatly broadened Congress's power. Previously, neither the federal nor the state governments were thought to have sufficient power to control the large corporations and holding companies doing business in many states. Now, far beyond the power to regulate interstate commerce, Congress had the power to regulate anything "essential or appropriate" to that function. For example, federal laws barring discrimination in hotels and restaurants rest on the Court's allowing Congress to decide what is an "essential or appropriate" subject of regulation.

More recently, the Court has placed tighter limits on Congress's power to regulate interstate commerce. In *United States* v. *Lopez* (1995), the Court struck down a law that banned people from having handguns near a school. The Court said Congress was not justified in basing this law on its power to regulate interstate commerce.

## Instruct

1. Why was interstate commerce a central issue in the *Jones* case?

2. How did Chief Justice Hughes establish that Jones and Laughlin were engaged in interstate commerce?

3. What was Hughes' argument for the necessity of labor unions?

**MAKING PERSONAL CONNECTIONS**

Have students evaluate the role of unions today. Ask them to identify the pros and cons of organized labor.

## More About . . .

**Taft-Hartley Act**

The pro-union momentum of the 1930s was short lived. In 1947, Congress passed the Taft-Hartley Act, co-sponsored by Senator Robert Taft of Ohio. The law restricted some of the provisions of the Wagner Act. Specifically, it gave the president the power to intervene in any strike he thought might pose a potential threat to national health and safety. The Taft-Hartley Act also required union officers to take an oath stating that they were not communists.

---

### THINKING CRITICALLY

**CONNECT TO HISTORY**

1. **Developing Historical Perspective** Lawyers for Jones and Laughlin said that the Wagner Act violated the Tenth Amendment. Chief Justice Hughes said that since the act fell within the scope of the commerce clause, the Tenth Amendment did not apply. Read the Tenth Amendment and then write a paragraph defending Hughes's position.

 **SEE SKILLBUILDER HANDBOOK, PAGE R11.**

**CONNECT TO TODAY**

2.  **INTERNET ACTIVITY** CLASSZONE.COM

Visit the links for Historic Decisions of the Supreme Court and read the opening sections of *United States* v. *Lopez*. There, Chief Justice Rehnquist offers a summary of the Court's interpretation of the commerce clause over the years. Summarize in your own words Rehnquist's description of the current meaning of the commerce clause.

*The New Deal* **503**

---

### THINKING CRITICALLY: ANSWERS

**1. CONNECT TO HISTORY**

**Rubric**

Student paragraphs should . . .

· include a thorough and logical defense of Chief Justice Hughes' position on the commerce clause

· cite specific examples to support the ideas presented

· have a summary sentence

**2. CONNECT TO TODAY**

**Rubric**

Student summaries should . . .

· identify the main ideas in Rehnquist's description of the changing meaning of the commerce clause

· give a brief explanation of each main idea

· follow the rules of spelling, punctuation and grammar, along with proper paragraph usage

# The New Deal Affects Many Groups

| MAIN IDEA | WHY IT MATTERS NOW | Terms & Names |
|---|---|---|
| New Deal policies and actions affected various social and ethnic groups. | The New Deal made a lasting impact on increasing the government's role in the struggle for equal rights. | • Frances Perkins<br>• Mary McLeod Bethune<br>• John Collier<br>• New Deal coalition • Congress of Industrial Organizations (CIO) |

 U.S. History 1B, 7C, 7D, 8A, 10B, 13D, 13E, 15A, 18A, 18B, 19A, 19B, 21A, 21D, 24B, 25A, 25B, 25C, 25D

### One American's Story

Pedro J. González came to this country from Mexico in the early 1920s and later became a United States citizen. As the first Spanish-language disc jockey in Los Angeles, González used his radio program to condemn discrimination against Mexicans and Mexican Americans, who were often made scapegoats for social and economic problems during the Depression. For his efforts, González was arrested, jailed, and deported on trumped-up charges. Later in life, he reflected on his experiences.

**A PERSONAL VOICE** PEDRO J. GONZÁLEZ

" Seeing how badly they treated Mexicans back in the days of my youth I could have started a rebellion. But now there could be a cultural understanding so that without firing one bullet, we might understand each other. We [Mexicans] were here before they [Anglos] were, and we are not, as they still say, 'undesirables' or 'wetbacks.' They say we come to this land and it's not our home. Actually, it's the other way around."

—quoted in the *Los Angeles Times*, December 9, 1984

Pedro J. González became a hero to many Mexican Americans and a symbol of Mexican cultural pride. His life reflected some of the difficulties faced by Mexicans and other minority groups in the United States during the New Deal era.

 **VIDEO**

*A SONG FOR HIS PEOPLE*
Pedro J. Gonzáles and the Fight for Mexican-American Rights

## 1 The New Deal Brings New Opportunities

In some ways, the New Deal represented an important opportunity for minorities and women, but what these groups gained was limited. Long-standing patterns of prejudice and discrimination continued to plague them and to prevent their full and equal participation in national life.

**WOMEN MAKE THEIR MARK** One of the most notable changes during the New Deal was the naming of several women to important government positions. **Frances Perkins** became America's first female cabinet member. As secretary of labor, she played a major role in creating the Social Security system and super-

vised labor legislation. President Roosevelt, encouraged by his wife Eleanor and seeking the support of women voters, also appointed two female diplomats and a female federal judge.

However, women continued to face discrimination in the workplace from male workers who believed that working women took jobs away from men. A Gallup poll taken in 1936 reported that 82 percent of Americans said that a wife should not work if her husband had a job.

Additionally, New Deal laws yielded mixed results. The National Recovery Administration, for example, set wage codes, some of which set lower minimum wages for women. The Federal Emergency Relief Administration and the Civil Works Administration hired far fewer women than men, and the Civilian Conservation Corps hired only men.

In spite of these barriers, women continued their movement into the workplace. Although the overall percentage of women working for wages increased only slightly during the 1930s, the percentage of married women in the workplace grew from 11.7 percent in 1930 to 15.6 percent in 1940. In short, widespread criticism of working women did not halt the long-term trend of women working outside the home.

## African-American Activism

The 1930s experienced a growth of activism by African Americans. One notable figure was A. Philip Randolph, who organized the country's first all-black trade union, the Brotherhood of Sleeping Car Porters. His work and that of others laid the groundwork for what would become the civil rights movement.

**AFRICAN AMERICANS TAKE LEADERSHIP ROLES** During the New Deal, Roosevelt appointed more than 100 African Americans to key positions in the government. **Mary McLeod Bethune**—an educator who dedicated herself to promoting opportunities for young African Americans—was one such appointee. Hired by the president to head the Division of Negro Affairs of the National Youth Administration, Bethune worked to ensure that the NYA hired African-American administrators and provided job training and other benefits to minority students.

Bethune also helped organize a "Black Cabinet" of influential African Americans to advise the Roosevelt administration on racial issues. Among these figures were William H. Hastie and Robert C. Weaver, both appointees to Roosevelt's Department of Interior. Never before had so many African Americans had a voice in the White House.

Eleanor Roosevelt played a key role in opening doors for African Americans in government. She was also instrumental in bringing about one of the most dramatic cultural events of the

*A. Answer* It gave President Roosevelt valuable advice on racial issues and provided African Americans with a voice, for the first time, at the highest levels of government.

**MAIN IDEA**

**Synthesizing**
**A)** Why was the "Black Cabinet" important to the Roosevelt administration?

◀ Mary McLeod Bethune, a close friend of Eleanor Roosevelt, was a strong supporter of the New Deal.

**505**

**KEY PLAYER**

**FRANCES PERKINS 1882–1965**

As a student at Mount Holyoke College, Frances Perkins attended lectures that introduced her to social reform efforts. Her initial work in the settlement house movement sparked her interest in pursuing the emerging social service organizations. After witnessing the Triangle Shirtwaist Factory fire in 1911 (see Chapter 6, page 249), Perkins pledged to fight for labor reforms, especially those for women. A pioneer for labor and women's issues, she changed her name from Fannie to Frances, believing she would be taken more seriously in her work.

---

## More About . . .

**Marian Anderson (1897–1993)**
Conductor Arturo Toscanini said Marian Anderson had a voice "heard once in a hundred years." On tour in Europe, in the 1930s, Anderson received rave reviews. Back in the United States, Anderson was acclaimed for her performance at the Lincoln Memorial. In 1955, Marian Anderson would make history as the first African American to perform at the Metropolitan Opera in New York.

## Instruct: Objective ❸

**Mexican–American Fortunes / Native Americans Gain Support**
TAKS SS11 3(US21.A)
· Why did Mexican Americans support the New Deal?
· How did New Deal policies affect Native Americans?

📖 In-Depth Resources: Unit 4
· Guided Reading, p. 62

## HISTORICAL SPOTLIGHT

**Deportation of Mexican Americans**
Ask students why they think Mexican Americans were met with hostility during the Depression. *(Jobs were scarce; competition for employment was fierce.)* Ask students to consider why white workers accused ethnic minorities of taking their jobs. *(Employers hired minorities and paid them low wages; white workers felt they were entitled to those positions.)*

▲
Marian Anderson sang from the steps of the Lincoln Memorial on April 9, 1939.

period: a performance by the African-American singer Marian Anderson in 1939. When the Daughters of the American Revolution chose not to allow Anderson to perform in their concert hall in Washington, D.C., because of her race, Eleanor Roosevelt resigned from the organization. She then arranged for Anderson to perform at the Lincoln Memorial on Easter Sunday. At the concert, Walter White, an official of the NAACP, noticed one girl in the crowd.

**A PERSONAL VOICE** WALTER WHITE

" Her hands were particularly noticeable as she thrust them forward and upward, trying desperately . . . to touch the singer. They were hands which despite their youth had known only the dreary work of manual labor. Tears streamed down the girl's dark face. Her hat was askew, but in her eyes flamed hope bordering on ecstasy. . . . If Marian Anderson could do it, the girl's eyes seemed to say, then I can, too."

—*A Man Called White*

**THE PRESIDENT FAILS TO SUPPORT CIVIL RIGHTS** Despite efforts to promote racial equality, Roosevelt was never committed to full civil rights for African Americans. He was afraid of upsetting white Democratic voters in the South, an important segment of his supporters. He refused to approve a federal antilynching law and an end to the poll tax, two key goals of the civil rights movement. Further, a number of New Deal agencies clearly discriminated against African Americans, including the NRA, the CCC, and the TVA. These programs gave lower wages to African Americans and favored whites.

African Americans recognized the need to fight for their rights and to improve conditions in areas that the New Deal ignored. In 1934, they helped organize the Southern Tenant Farmers Union, which sought to protect the rights of tenant farmers and sharecroppers, both white and black. In the North, the union created tenants' groups and launched campaigns to increase job opportunities.

In general, however, African Americans supported the Roosevelt administration and the New Deal, generally seeing them as their best hope for the future. As one man recalled, "Roosevelt touched the temper of the black community. You did not look upon him as being white, black, blue or green. He was President Roosevelt." **B**

## Mexican-American Fortunes ❸

Mexican Americans also tended to support the New Deal, even though they received even fewer benefits than African Americans did. Large numbers of Mexican Americans had come to the United States during the 1920s, settling mainly in the Southwest. Most found work laboring on farms, an occupation that was essentially unprotected by state and federal laws. During the Depression, farm wages fell to as little as nine cents an hour. Farm workers who tried to unionize

### HISTORICAL SPOTLIGHT

**DEPORTATION OF MEXICAN AMERICANS**
Many Mexican Americans were long-time residents or citizens of the United States. Others came during the 1920s to work on farms in Texas, California, and Arizona. Valued for their low-cost labor during the good times, these migrant workers became the target of hostility during the Great Depression. Many returned to Mexico willingly, while others were deported by the United States government. During the 1930s, as many as 400,000 persons of Mexican descent, many of them U.S. citizens, were deported to Mexico.

**B. Possible Answer**
President Roosevelt was not committed to full civil rights for African Americans. He did not support a federal anti-lynching law and an end to poll taxes. Many African-American families benefited from work relief, but some New Deal programs discriminated against African Americans.

**MAIN IDEA**

**Evaluating**
**B** Evaluate the actions and policies of the Roosevelt administration on civil rights.

---

**DIFFERENTIATING INSTRUCTION** | **GIFTED AND TALENTED STUDENTS**

### Politics and Policy

FDR was not an active supporter of full civil rights for African Americans. His own political loyalties kept him on the fence. Roosevelt knew that the white southern vote would be his ticket to reelection. Have students identify a contemporary political issue and analyze the current president's position. Ask students to make inferences about the president's position and a possible bid for reelection. Then they should draw conclusions about politics and policy citing examples from Roosevelt's presidency and the current president. Students should present their findings in a brief report.

**Rubric**
The report should . . .
· present information regarding a policy of the current president
· include a set of conclusions regarding politics and policy
· identify examples to support the conclusions

often met with violence from employers and government authorities. Although the CCC and WPA helped some Mexican Americans, these agencies also discriminated against them by disqualifying from their programs migrant workers who had no permanent address. **C**

## Native Americans Gain Support ❸

Native Americans received strong government support from the New Deal. In 1924, Native Americans had received full citizenship by law. In 1933, President Roosevelt appointed **John Collier** as commissioner of Indian affairs. Collier helped create the Indian Reorganization Act of 1934. This act was an extreme change in government policy. It moved away from assimilation and toward Native American autonomy. It also helped to restore some reservation lands to tribal ownership. The act mandated changes in three areas:

- *economic*—Native American lands would belong to an entire tribe. This provision strengthened Native American land claims by prohibiting the government from taking over unclaimed reservation lands and selling them to people other than Native Americans.
- *cultural*—The number of boarding schools for Native American children was reduced, and children could attend school on the reservations.
- *political*—Tribes were given permission to elect tribal councils to govern their reservations.

Some Native Americans who valued their tribal traditions hailed the act as an important step forward. Others who had become more "Americanized" as individual landowners under the previous Dawes Act objected, because they were tired of white people telling them what was good for them. **D**

John Collier talks with Chief Richard, one of several Native American chiefs attending the Four Nation Celebration held at Niagara Falls, New York, in September 1934.

## FDR Creates the New Deal Coalition ❹

Although New Deal policies had mixed results for minorities, these groups generally backed President Roosevelt. In fact, one of FDR's great achievements was to create the **New Deal coalition**—an alignment of diverse groups dedicated to supporting the Democratic Party. The coalition included Southern whites, various urban groups, African Americans, and unionized industrial workers. As a result, Democrats dominated national politics throughout the 1930s and 1940s.

**LABOR UNIONS FLOURISH** As a result of the Wagner Act and other prolabor legislation passed during the New Deal, union members enjoyed better working conditions and increased bargaining power. In their eyes, President Roosevelt was a "friend of labor." Labor unions donated money to Roosevelt's reelection campaigns, and union workers pledged their votes to him.

Between 1933 and 1941, union membership grew from less than 3 million to more than 10 million. Unionization especially affected coal miners and workers in mass-production industries, such as the automobile, rubber, and electrical industries. It was in these industries, too, that a struggle for dominance within the labor movement began to develop.

*The New Deal* **507**

---

### Sidebar (left margin)

**MAIN IDEA**

**Identifying Problems**

**C** Why was life difficult for farm laborers during the Depression?

*C. Answer* Farm laborers were essentially unprotected by state and federal laws.

**MAIN IDEA**

**Summarizing**

**D** What changes occurred for Native Americans as a result of the New Deal?

*D. Answer* Native Americans received full citizenship by law; the Indian Reorganization Act turned Native American lands over to individual tribes, and allowed children to attend schools on the reservations and tribes to elect tribal councils to govern their reservations.

---

### Sidebar (right margin)

**Tracing Themes**

**CULTURAL DIVERSITY**

Minorities in America face the challenge of preserving their own cultural traditions, while at the same time living as Americans. Throughout much of the 20th century, there was tremendous pressure on ethnic minorities to assimilate. Many changed their names to sound more American. The Indian Reorganization Act challenged the push to assimilate. Native Americans affirmed their wish to maintain their own cultural traditions.

**Instruct: Objective ❹**

**FDR Creates the New Deal Coalition**

TAKS SS11 5(US24.A)

· Identify key components of the New Deal coalition.

· Why were urban voters likely to support FDR?

📖 In-Depth Resources: Unit 4
· Guided Reading, p. 62

**More About . . .**

**The New Deal Coalition**

Roosevelt's New Deal coalition was a cohesive element of the Democratic Party from the 1930s through the late 1960s. The Vietnam War years were marked by political divisions. In 1968, Southerners who had supported the coalition turned to the Republican party. With Ronald Reagan's election in 1980, the coalition was completely fragmented. In northern urban areas, African Americans and labor tend to support Democrats, but the decline in organized labor has reduced labor's influence on elections.

---

## The Growing Labor Movement, 1933–1940

**Robert F. Wagner**
A Democratic senator from New York (1927–1949), Robert F. Wagner was especially interested in workers' welfare. Wagner introduced the National Labor Relations Act in Congress in 1935.

**The Growth of Union Membership, 1930–1940**

Union Members (in millions)

9, 8, 7, 6, 5, 4, 3, 2, 1, 0

1930 1932 1934 1936 1938 1940

Source: *Historical Statistics of the United States*

◀ **Union membership soars**
A Ben Shahn poster from the late 1930s boasted of the rise in union membership.

**Sit-down strikes** ▶
Union workers—such as these CIO strikers at the Fisher automobile plant in Flint, Michigan, in 1937—found the sit-down strike an extremely effective method for getting their demands met.

*E. Answer* New Deal labor laws gave unions greater power to organize and negotiate with employers. As a result, unions grew in size and joined with other groups in the New Deal coalition.

The American Federation of Labor (AFL) had traditionally been restricted to the craft unions, such as carpenters and electricians. Most of the AFL leaders opposed industrywide unions that represented all the workers in a given industry, such as automobile manufacturing. **E**

Frustrated by this position, several key labor leaders, including John L. Lewis of the United Mine Workers of America and David Dubinsky of the International Ladies Garment Workers, formed the Committee for Industrial Organization to organize industrial unions. The committee rapidly signed up unskilled and semiskilled workers, and within two years it succeeded in gaining union recognition in the steel and automobile industries. In 1938, the Committee for Industrial Organization was expelled from the AFL and changed its name to the **Congress of Industrial Organizations (CIO).** This split lasted until 1955.

**LABOR DISPUTES** One of the main bargaining tactics of the labor movement in the 1930s was the sit-down strike. Instead of walking off their jobs, workers remained inside their plants, but they did not work. This prevented the factory owners from carrying on production with strikebreakers, or scabs. Some Americans disapproved of the sit-down strike, calling it a violation of private property. Nonetheless, it proved to be an effective bargaining tool.

Not all labor disputes in the 1930s were peaceful. Perhaps the most dramatic incident was the clash at the Republic Steel plant in Chicago on Memorial Day, 1937. Police attacked striking steelworkers outside the plant. One striker, an African-American man, recalled the experience.

**A PERSONAL VOICE** JESSE REESE
"I began to see people drop. There was a Mexican on my side, and he fell; and there was a black man on my side and he fell. Down I went. I crawled around in the grass and saw that people were getting beat. I'd never seen police beat women, not white women. I'd seen them beat black women, but this was the first time in my life I'd seen them beat white women—with sticks."
—quoted in *The Great Depression*

**MAIN IDEA**

**Analyzing Effects**
**E** How did New Deal policies affect organized labor?

**Background**
See *strike* on page R45 in the Economics Handbook.

**508** CHAPTER 15

Ten people were killed and 84 wounded in this incident, which became known as the Memorial Day Massacre. Shortly afterward, the National Labor Relations Board stepped in and required the head of Republic Steel, Tom Girdler, to negotiate with the union. This and other actions helped labor gain strength during the 1930s.

**FDR WINS IN 1936** Urban voters were another important component of the New Deal coalition. Support for the Democratic Party surged, especially in large Northern cities, such as New York, Boston, Philadelphia, and Chicago. These and other cities had powerful city political organizations that provided services, such as jobs, in exchange for votes. In the 1936 election, President Roosevelt carried the nation's 12 largest cities.

Support for President Roosevelt came from various religious and ethnic groups—Roman Catholics, Jews, Italians, Irish, and Polish and other Slavic peoples—as well as from African Americans. His appeal to these groups was based on New Deal labor laws and work-relief programs, which aided the urban poor. The president also made direct and persuasive appeals to urban voters at election time. To reinforce his support, he also appointed many officials of urban-immigrant backgrounds, particularly Roman Catholics and Jews, to important government positions.

▲ Chicago police attack strikers at what would become known as the Memorial Day Massacre (1937).

Women, African Americans, Mexican Americans, Native Americans, and workers from all walks of life were greatly affected by the New Deal. It also had a tremendous influence on American society and culture.

## More About . . .

### Election of 1936
Roosevelt's opponent in 1936 was Alf Landon, the governor of Kansas. The election was one of the greatest landslides in American history. Landon won only two states, Maine and Vermont. Roosevelt won the popular vote, 27 million to 17 million, and the electoral vote, 523-8.

## Assess and Reteach

### SECTION 3 ASSESSMENT
Have pairs of students work together to answer the questions in the Section Assessment.

📄 Formal Assessment
· Section Quiz, p. 285

### SELF-ASSESSMENT
Have students identify a quotation in this section that they think sums up important main ideas.

### RETEACH
Ask students which topics in this section were difficult for them. Review the material as a class.

📄 In-Depth Resources: Unit 4
· Reteaching Activity, p. 69

---

### ③ ASSESSMENT

**1. TERMS & NAMES** For each of the following terms and names, write a sentence explaining its significance.

- Frances Perkins
- Mary McLeod Bethune
- John Collier
- New Deal coalition
- Congress of Industrial Organizations (CIO)

#### MAIN IDEA

**2. TAKING NOTES**
Using a web diagram like the partial one shown here, note the effects of New Deal policies on American women, African Americans, Mexican Americans, Native Americans, unionized workers, and urban Americans.

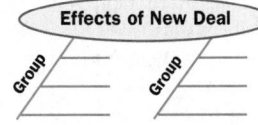

Effects of New Deal

Group          Group

Write a paragraph explaining the effects of the New Deal on one of the groups.

#### CRITICAL THINKING

**3. SUMMARIZING**
What steps did women make toward equality during the 1930s?
**Think About:**
- the role of women in government
- hiring practices in federal programs
- women's opportunities in business and industry

**4. EVALUATING**
In your opinion, did organized labor become too powerful in the 1930s? Explain your answer. **Think About:**
- why workers joined unions
- how unions organized workers
- the role of unions in politics

**5. ANALYZING MOTIVES**
Why did urban voters support President Roosevelt?

*The New Deal* 509

---

Answers **ASSESSMENT** ③

**1. TERMS & NAMES**
Frances Perkins, p. 504
Mary McLeod Bethune, p. 505
John Collier, p. 507
New Deal Coalition, p. 507
Congress of Industrial Organizations, p. 508

**2. TAKING NOTES**
**Women:** appointment of Frances Perkins; key government positions; **African Americans:** Mary McLeod Bethune and the "Black Cabinet;" **Mexican Americans:** Aided by New Deal programs; **Native Americans:** Indian Reorganization Act of 1934; **Unionized workers:** the Wagner Act.

**3. SUMMARIZING**
Women appointed to government positions; more women employed outside the home; expanding opportunities in the workplace; women activists and organizers.

**4. EVALUATING**
Students might argue that strikes interfered with business, or that labor disputes sometimes resulted in violence.

Other students might suggest that industrial workers were finally allowed to unionize, which resulted in better working conditions.

**5. ANALYZING MOTIVES**
New Deal labor and relief programs helped the urban poor. Roosevelt made direct appeals to urban voters during his campaign.

# Culture in the 1930s

| MAIN IDEA | WHY IT MATTERS NOW | Terms & Names |
|---|---|---|
| Motion pictures, radio, art, and literature blossomed during the New Deal. | The films, music, art, and literature of the 1930s still captivate today's public. | • *Gone With the Wind* • Orson Welles • Grant Wood  • Richard Wright • *The Grapes of Wrath* |

U.S. History 13D, 13E, 15A, 20A, 20B, 20C, 20D, 20E, 22A, 22C, 23A, 24A, 24B, 24C, 24D, 25A, 25B, 25C, 25D, 26A

### One American's Story

Don Congdon, editor of the book *The Thirties: A Time to Remember,* was a high school student when the New Deal began. While many writers and artists in the 1930s produced works that reflected the important issues of the day, it was the movies and radio that most clearly captured the public imagination. Congdon remembers the role movies played at the time.

**A PERSONAL VOICE** DON CONGDON

" Lots of us enjoyed our leisure at the movies. The experience of going was like an insidious [tempting] candy we could never get quite enough of; the visit to the dark theater was an escape from the drab realities of Depression living, and we were entranced by the never-ending variety of stories. Hollywood, like Scheherazade [the storyteller] in *The Thousand and One Nights,* supplied more the next night, and the next night after that."

—*The Thirties: A Time to Remember*

During the Great Depression, movies provided a window on a different, more exciting world. Despite economic hardship, many people gladly paid the 25 cents it cost to go to the movies. Along with radio, motion pictures became an increasingly dominant feature of American life.

People line up to get into a movie theater during the Great Depression.

## 1 The Lure of Motion Pictures and Radio

Although the 1930s were a difficult time for many Americans, it was a profitable and golden age for the motion-picture and radio industries. By late in the decade, approximately 65 percent of the population was attending the movies once a week. The nation boasted over 15,000 movie theaters, more than the number of banks and double the number of hotels. Sales of radios also greatly increased during the 1930s, from just over 13 million in 1930 to 28 million by 1940. Nearly 90 percent of American households owned a radio. Clearly, movies and radio had taken the country by storm.

**MOVIES ARE A HIT** Wacky comedies, lavish musicals, love stories, and gangster films all vied for the attention of the moviegoing public during the New Deal years. Following the end of silent films and the rise of "talking" pictures, new stars such as Clark Gable, Marlene Dietrich, and James Cagney rose from Hollywood, the center of the film industry. These stars helped launch a new era of glamour and sophistication in Hollywood.

Some films made during the 1930s offered pure escape from the hard realities of the Depression by presenting visions of wealth, romance, and good times. Perhaps the most famous film of the era, and one of the most popular of all time, was **Gone With the Wind** (1939). Another film, *Flying Down to Rio* (1933), was a light romantic comedy featuring Fred Astaire and Ginger Rogers, who went on to make many movies together, becoming America's favorite dance partners. Other notable movies made during the 1930s include *The Wizard of Oz* (1939) and *Snow White and the Seven Dwarfs* (1937), which showcased the dazzling animation of Walt Disney.

Comedies—such as *Monkey Business* (1931) and *Duck Soup* (1931), starring the zany Marx Brothers—became especially popular. So did films that combined escapist appeal with more realistic plots and settings. Americans flocked to see gangster films that presented images of the dark, gritty streets and looming skyscrapers of urban America. These movies featured hard-bitten characters struggling to succeed in a harsh environment where they faced difficulties that Depression-era audiences could easily understand. Notable films in this genre include *Little Caesar* (1930) and *The Public Enemy* (1931).

Several films, such as *Mr. Deeds Goes to Town* (1936) and *Mr. Smith Goes to Washington* (1939), by director Frank Capra, presented the social and political accomplishments of the New Deal in a positive light. These films portrayed honest, kindhearted people winning out over those with greedy special interests. In much the same way, the New Deal seemed to represent the interests of average Americans. **A**

**RADIO ENTERTAINS** Even more than movies, radio embodied the democratic spirit of the times. Families typically spent several hours a day gathered together, listening to their favorite programs. It was no accident that President Roosevelt chose radio as the medium for his "fireside chats." It was the most direct means of access to the American people.

Like movies, radio programs offered a range of entertainment. In the evening, radio networks offered excellent dramas and variety programs. **Orson Welles,** an actor, director, producer, and writer, created one of the most renowned radio broadcasts of all time, "The War of the Worlds." Later he directed movie classics such as *Citizen Kane* (1941) and *Touch of Evil* (1958). After making their reputation in

Clark Gable and Vivien Leigh starred in *Gone With the Wind*, a sweeping drama about life among Southern plantation owners during the Civil War.

## Tracing Themes
### SCIENCE AND TECHNOLOGY

Motion pictures and radio took center stage during the Depression. These new forms of entertainment provided a needed escape from the darker realities of the day. Talking pictures were still new in the 1930s, as were national radio shows. In both cases, technology offered a new form of recreation and bolstered the morale of the American people.

**MAIN IDEA**

**Developing Historical Perspective**

**A** Why do you think movies were so popular during the Depression?

*A. Answer* Movies provided realistic portrayals as well as escapist comedies and romances, all of which helped people to cope with Depression reality.

### HISTORICAL SPOTLIGHT

**WAR OF THE WORLDS**

On October 30, 1938, radio listeners were stunned by a special announcement: Martians had invaded Earth! Panic set in as many Americans became convinced that the world was coming to an end. Of course, the story wasn't true: it was a radio drama based on H. G. Wells's novel *The War of the Worlds*.

In his book, Wells describes the canisters of gas fired by the Martians as releasing "an enormous volume of heavy, inky vapour. . . . And the touch of that vapour, the inhaling of its pungent wisps, was death to all that breathes." The broadcast, narrated by Orson Welles (at left), revealed the power of radio at a time when Americans received fast-breaking news over the airwaves.

## HISTORICAL SPOTLIGHT

**War of the Worlds**
With Orson Welles' historic broadcast of *The War of the Worlds*, the power of mass media came crashing into living rooms across the nation. Some people ran out of their houses, with handkerchiefs over their mouths, to protect themselves from the impending Martian attack. When the electricity went out in a Washington town immediately following the broadcast, many residents were convinced it was the work of the Martians. Ask students why the broadcast caused such panic among listeners. *(People were accustomed to getting news by radio. The broadcast seemed real.)*

*The New Deal* **511**

---

**ACTIVITY**  **LINK TO HUMANITIES**

**BLOCK SCHEDULING**

## Realism and Escape

**Class Time** 45 minutes

**Task** Identifying radio programs and movies with realist and escapist themes

**Purpose** To analyze the role of the mass media during the Depression

**Directions** Have students work in small groups to identify popular Depression-era movies or radio shows that have either realist or escapist themes. Ask students to list three or four examples of each theme and give examples from the programs or movies that support the theme. Next ask students to hypothesize about why these movies or programs were popular. Finally lead a class discussion on the question: Which type of movie or radio program was more popular during the Depression and why?

## Instruct: Objective ❷

### The Arts in Depression America
TAKS SS11 5(US24.B)
· What was the Federal Art Project?
· Identify successful American writers of the Depression-era.

 In-Depth resources: Unit 4
· Guided Reading, p. 63
· Primary Sources: WPA Poster, p. 78; *Let Us Now Praise Famous Men*, p. 79

---

## More About . . .

### The Federal Art Project
The Federal Art Project was fueled by the vision of Holger Cahill, its first director. In 1936, Cahill commented, "The organization of the Project has proceeded on the principle that it is not the solitary genius but a sound general movement which maintains art as a vital, functioning part of any cultural scheme. Art is not a matter of rare, occasional masterpieces."

---

## More About . . .

### The Coit Tower Murals
Coit Tower, a San Francisco landmark, is home to some of the best-preserved works by WPA artists. The murals, created by some 25 artists, were painted in the style of social realism. Because of their realistic depiction of everyday life and working conditions during the Depression, the murals were shocking to some. There is an overwhelming sense of the dignity of work, however, visible in the WPA murals, which communicate the triumph of the human spirit in the face of adversity.

---

▲
The comedy couple George Burns and Gracie Allen delighted radio audiences for years, and their popularity continued on television.

radio, comedians Bob Hope, Jack Benny, and the duo Burns and Allen moved on to work in television and movies. Soap operas—so named because they were usually sponsored by soap companies—tended to play late morning to early afternoon for homemakers, while children's programs, such *The Lone Ranger*, generally aired later in the afternoon, when children were home from school.

One of the first worldwide radio broadcasts described for listeners the horrific crash of the *Hindenburg*, a German zeppelin (rigid airship), in New Jersey on May 6, 1937. Such immediate news coverage became a staple in society.

## The Arts in Depression America ❷

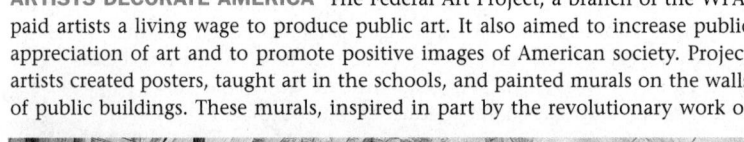

In contrast to many radio and movie productions of the 1930s, much of the art, music, and literature of the time was sober and serious. Despite grim artistic tones, however, much of this artistic work conveyed a more uplifting message about the strength of character and the democratic values of the American people. A number of artists and writers embraced the spirit of social and political change fostered by the New Deal. In fact, many received direct support through New Deal work programs from government officials who believed that art played an important role in national life. Also, as Harry Hopkins, the head of the WPA, put it, "They've got to eat just like other people." Ⓑ

**ARTISTS DECORATE AMERICA** The Federal Art Project, a branch of the WPA, paid artists a living wage to produce public art. It also aimed to increase public appreciation of art and to promote positive images of American society. Project artists created posters, taught art in the schools, and painted murals on the walls of public buildings. These murals, inspired in part by the revolutionary work of

**MAIN IDEA**

**Analyzing Causes**
Ⓑ Why did the New Deal fund art projects?

**B. Answer** New Deal officials believed that art played an important role in the life of the American people. They also believed that artists deserved work relief just as other unemployed Americans did.

This detail is from ▶ the mural *Industries of California*, painted in 1934 by Ralph Stackpole. It decorates San Francisco's Coit Tower, one of the best preserved sites of WPA mural projects.

---

### Create a Radio Show

**Class Time** One or two class periods

**Task** Creating a radio skit

**Purpose** To describe the most popular medium of the 1930s

**Directions** If possible, bring in a recording of a popular 1930s radio show. Have students create radio skits, in a similar style. Ask students to write, rehearse, and record their skits. Have students broadcast their skits for the class.

**Rubric**

The radio skit should . . .
· portray the historical era accurately
· use an interesting and creative style
· have a clear and logical organization

 Integrated Assessment
· Rubrics 3, 6

## History Through *Art*

### AMERICAN GOTHIC (1930)

Grant Wood's 1930 painting, *American Gothic,* became one of the most famous portrayals of life in the Midwest during the Great Depression. Painted in the style known as Regionalism, Wood painted familiar subjects in realistic ways. The house in the back-ground was discovered by Wood in Eldon, Iowa, while he was looking for subjects to paint. He returned home with a sketch and a photograph, and used his sister and his dentist as models for the farmer and daughter in the painting's foreground.

**SKILLBUILDER** *Interpreting Visual Sources*

1. What is the message Wood portrays in this painting? Explain your answer.
2. Do you think this painting is representative of the Great Depression? Why or why not?

 **SEE SKILLBUILDER HANDBOOK, PAGE R23.**

### History Through *Art*

**American Gothic (1930)**

Grant Wood's painting, *American Gothic,* is considered a classic work of American art. Each generation, individuals interpret the painting differently. To some, it represents the hardworking sensibility of the Great Plains settlers. To others, the painting reveals the repressed, judgmental sensibility of rural America. Ask students to study the painting and share their own reactions.

**SKILLBUILDER ANSWERS**

1. Wood wanted to portray the hardships Midwestern farm families endured during the Depression.

2. Yes: the painting does represent the hard-ships of the Great Depression in rural areas. No: it doesn't realistically depict the suffering of the urban poor.

Mexican muralists such as Diego Rivera, typically portrayed the dignity of ordi-nary Americans at work. One artist, Robert Gwathmey, recalled these efforts.

**A PERSONAL VOICE** ROBERT GWATHMEY

"The director of the Federal Arts Project was Edward Bruce. He was a friend of the Roosevelts—from a polite family—who was a painter. He was a man of real broad vision. He insisted there be no restrictions. You were a painter: Do your work. You were a sculptor: Do your work. . . . That was a very free and happy period."

—quoted in *Hard Times*

During the New Deal era, a number of American painters produced outstanding works of art, such as Edward Hopper, Thomas Hart Benton, and Iowa's **Grant Wood,** whose work includes the famous painting *American Gothic.*

The WPA's Federal Theater Project hired actors to perform plays and artists to provide stage sets and props for theater productions that played around the country. It subsidized the work of important American playwrights, including Clifford Odets, whose play *Waiting for Lefty* (1935) dramatized the labor struggles of the 1930s. **C**

**WOODY GUTHRIE SINGS OF AMERICA** Experiencing firsthand the tragedies of the Depression, singer and songwriter Woody Guthrie used music to capture the hardships of America. Along with thousands of people who were forced by the Dust Bowl to seek a better life, Guthrie traveled the country in search of brighter opportunities, and told of his troubles in his songs.

**MAIN IDEA**

**Summarizing**
**C** In what ways did the New Deal deliver art to the public?
*C. Answer* The Federal Art Project paid artists to pro-duce public art. It also promoted the teaching of art in schools and poster and mural painting. The Federal Theater Project assisted pro-ducing theater productions

**A PERSONAL VOICE** WOODY GUTHRIE

"Yes we ramble and we roam
And the highway, that's our home.
It's a never-ending highway
For a dust bowl refugee

Yes, we wander and we work
In your crops and in your fruit,
Like the whirlwinds on the desert,
That's the dust bowl refugees."

—"Dust Bowl Refugees"

*Copyright © Ludlow Music, Inc., New York, New York.*

**Woody Guthrie**

Guthrie wrote many songs about the plight of Americans during the Depression. His honest lyrics appealed to those who suffered similar hardships.

### More About . . .

**Woody Guthrie (1912-1967)**

Woody Guthrie was a folk singer who traveled the roads and rails in the 1930s. He did so in order to learn from experiences of hobos and the homeless. His songs about hard times and hope became popular around the country. Most notably, Guthrie's song, "This Land is Your Land," would become a classic American folk song. Woody Guthrie had a major influence on the course of American folk music.

*The New Deal* **513**

---

**ACTIVITY** **COOPERATIVE ACTIVITY**

## Class Mural

**Class Time** Two class periods for planning plus painting time

**Task** Creating a mural

**Purpose** To understand the use of art as social commentary

**Directions** Have students use the Internet and library resources to study murals from the 1930s. Then, divide students into groups to create their own mural designs that depict the 1930s. Next have the class select one of the designs for the entire class to create. Plan the painting process next. Finally have each group complete one portion of an entire class mural.

**Rubric**

The mural should . . .

· have an appropriate 1930s theme
· exhibit an understanding of art as a social commentary
· show evidence of participation by all groups

Integrated Assessment
· Rubric 4

## More About . . .

### Richard Wright

Wright was the first African-American writer to achieve mainstream recognition. His book, *Native Son*, became a best seller and was adapted to the stage by Orson Welles. After World War II, Wright moved to Paris and became an expatriate. He continued to write and to move generations of readers with his words.

## Assess & Reteach

### SECTION 4 ASSESSMENT

Have students answer the assessment questions and make note of the ones that give them the most trouble.

 Formal Assessment
· Section Quiz, p. 286

### SELF-ASSESSMENT

Have students list the insights they have gained on the impact of motion pictures, radio, art, and literature during the 1930s.

### RETEACH

Use the graphic in item 2 of the Section Assessment to review the material. Copy the graphic onto the chalkboard, and ask for students to volunteer names to fill in the chart.

 In-Depth Resources: Unit 4
· Reteaching Activity, p. 70

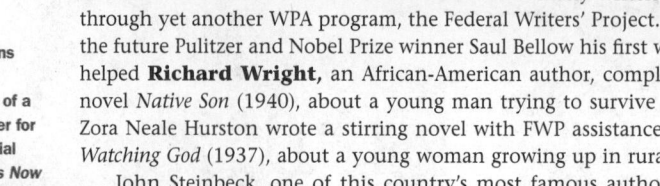

Walker Evans took this photograph of a sharecropper for the influential book *Let Us Now Praise Famous Men.*
▼

**DIVERSE WRITERS DEPICT AMERICAN LIFE**  Many writers received support through yet another WPA program, the Federal Writers' Project. This project gave the future Pulitzer and Nobel Prize winner Saul Bellow his first writing job. It also helped **Richard Wright**, an African-American author, complete his acclaimed novel *Native Son* (1940), about a young man trying to survive in a racist world. Zora Neale Hurston wrote a stirring novel with FWP assistance—*Their Eyes Were Watching God* (1937), about a young woman growing up in rural Florida.

John Steinbeck, one of this country's most famous authors, received assistance from the Federal Writers' Project. He was able to publish his epic novel *The Grapes of Wrath* (1939), which reveals the lives of Oklahomans who left the Dust Bowl and ended up in California, where their hardships continued. Before his success, however, Steinbeck had endured the difficulties of the Depression like most other writers. **D**

Other books and authors examined the difficulties of life during the 1930s. James T. Farrell's *Studs Lonigan* trilogy (1932–1935) provides a bleak picture of working-class life in an Irish neighborhood of Chicago, while Jack Conroy's novel *The Disinherited* (1933) portrays the violence and poverty of the Missouri coalfields, where Conroy's own father and brother died in a mine disaster.

Nevertheless, other writers found hope in the positive values of American culture. The writer James Agee and the photographer Walker Evans collaborated on a book about Alabama sharecroppers, *Let Us Now Praise Famous Men* (1941). Though it deals with the difficult lives of poor farmers, it portrays the dignity and strength of character in the people it presents. Thornton Wilder's play *Our Town* (1938) captures the beauty of small-town life in New England.

Although artists and writers recognized Americ's flaws, they contributed positively to the New Deal legacy. These intellectuals praised the virtues of American life and took pride in the country's traditions and accomplishments.

---

**MAIN IDEA**

**Analyzing Issues**
**D** How did the literature of the time reflect issues of the Depression?

**D. Answer**
Writers depicted the difficulties of the Depression Era, such as the Dust Bowl, working-class life, racism, and hardships in America.

---

 **4** **ASSESSMENT**

**1. TERMS & NAMES**  For each term or name below, write a sentence explaining its significance.

- *Gone With the Wind*
- *Grant Wood*
- *Richard Wright*
- *The Grapes of Wrath*
- *Orson Welles*

**MAIN IDEA**

**2. TAKING NOTES**
Create a web like the one below, filling in the names of those who contributed to each aspect of American culture in the 1930s.

**Cultural Figures of the 1930s**

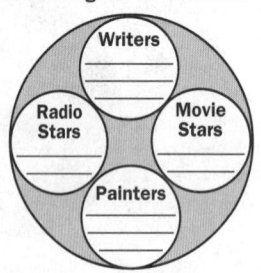

- Writers
- Radio Stars
- Movie Stars
- Painters

What contribution did each group make?

**CRITICAL THINKING**

**3. HYPOTHESIZING**
What type of movies do you think might have been produced if the government had supported moviemaking as part of the New Deal? Use evidence from the chapter to support your response.

**4. ANALYZING EFFECTS**
How did the entertainment industry affect the economy?

**5. DRAWING CONCLUSIONS**
In your opinion, what were the main benefits of government support for art and literature in the 1930s? Support your response with details from the text. **Think About:**
- the experiences of Americans in the Great Depression
- the writers who got their start through the FWP
- the subject matter of WPA murals and other New Deal-sponsored art

**514**  CHAPTER 15

---

 **4** **ASSESSMENT**  **Answers**

**1. TERMS & NAMES**
*Gone with the Wind,* p. 511
Orson Welles, p. 511
Grant Wood, p. 513
Richard Wright, p. 514
*The Grapes of Wrath,* p. 514

**2. TAKING NOTES**
Writers: Richard Wright, Zora Neale Hurston, James T. Farrell, John Steinbeck, Thorton Wilder. Movie Stars: Clark Gable, Marlene Dietrich, James Cagney, Vivien Leigh, Fred Astaire, Ginger Rogers. Painters: Edward Hopper, Thomas Hart Benton, Grant Wood.

**3. HYPOTHESIZING**
Movies that focused on social and political accomplishments, such as *Mr. Smith Goes to Washington;* documentaries about the Dust Bowl, the Depression; *(Answers will vary)*

**4. ANALYZING EFFECTS**
Entertainment, especially movies and radio, was a lucrative industry during the Depression. New movie theatres had regular patrons; nearly 90 percent of Americans owned radios by 1940.

**5. DRAWING CONCLUSIONS**
Writers produced literature about the hardships and daily struggle of the American people during the 1930s; a written and pictorial legacy of the Depression years; provided writers and artists the opportunity to create; the arts became more accessible to the public.

# The Impact of the New Deal

| MAIN IDEA | WHY IT MATTERS NOW | Terms & Names |
|---|---|---|
| The New Deal affected American society not only in the 1930s but also in the decades that followed. | Americans still debate over how large a role government should play in American life. | •Federal Deposit Insurance Corporation (FDIC) •Securities and Exchange Commission (SEC) •National Labor Relations Board (NLRB) •parity •Tennessee Valley Authority (TVA) |

**TEKS U.S. History**
1B, 6H, 8A, 11B, 13D, 13E, 15A, 19A, 19B, 24B, 24C, 24D, 24G, 25A, 25B, 25C, 25D, 26A

### One American's Story

George Dobbin, a 67-year-old cotton-mill worker, staunchly supported Franklin Delano Roosevelt and his New Deal policies. In an interview for a book entitled *These Are Our Lives,* compiled by the Federal Writers' Project, Dobbin explained his feelings about the president.

**A PERSONAL VOICE** GEORGE DOBBIN

" I do think that Roosevelt is the biggest-hearted man we ever had in the White House. . . . It's the first time in my recollection that a President ever got up and said, 'I'm interested in and aim to do somethin' for the workin' man.' Just knowin' that for once . . . [there] was a man to stand up and speak for him, a man that could make what he felt so plain nobody could doubt he meant it, has made a lot of us feel a sight [lot] better even when [there] wasn't much to eat in our homes. "

—quoted in *These Are Our Lives*

▲ A coal miner, Zeno Santinello, shakes hands with Franklin D. Roosevelt as he campaigns in Elm Grove, West Virginia, in 1932.

FDR was extremely popular among working-class Americans. Far more important than his personal popularity, however, was the impact of the policies he initiated. Even today, reforms begun under the New Deal continue to influence American politics and society.

## New Deal Reforms Endure ❶

During his second term in office, President Roosevelt hinted at plans to launch a Third New Deal. In his inaugural address, the president exclaimed, "I see millions of families trying to live on incomes so meager that the pall of family disaster hangs over them day by day. . . . I see one third of a nation ill-housed, ill-clad, ill-nourished."

However, FDR did not favor deficit spending. More importantly, by 1937 the economy had improved enough to convince many Americans that the Depression was finally ending. Although economic troubles still plagued the nation, President

*The New Deal* **515**

## OBJECTIVES

❶ Summarize opinions about the effectiveness of the New Deal.

❷ Describe the legacies of the New Deal.

**SKILLBUILDER**
· Interpreting Graphs, p. 517

**CRITICAL THINKING**
· Analyzing Issues, p. 516
· Comparing and Contrasting, p. 516
· Developing Historical Perspective, p. 518
· Recognizing Effects, p. 519
· Making Generalizations, p. 519
· Evaluating Leadership, p. 519
· Interpreting Visual Sources, p. 519

## Focus & Motivate

Ask students to consider how government policies and programs affect their lives.

## Instruct

### Instruct: Objective ❶

**New Deal Reforms Endure**
TAKS SS11 3(US13.E)
· How is the New Deal viewed today?
· What effect did New Deal policies have on labor, agriculture, banking, and finance?

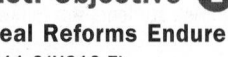 In-Depth Resources: Unit 4
· Guided Reading, p. 64

 Critical Thinking Transparencies CT23, CT57
· The New Deal
· U.S. Economic Indicators 1929–1939

## PROGRAM RESOURCES

 **In-Depth Resources: Unit 4**
· Guided Reading, p. 64
· Reteaching Activity, p. 71
· Geography Application: Decade of Democrats, pp. 72–73
· Outline Map: Anatomy of the Tennessee Valley Authority, pp. 74–75

 **Reading Study Guide,** (Spanish and English) pp. 157–158

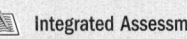 **Access for Students Acquiring English/ESL**
· Guided Reading (Spanish), p. 172
· Geography Application, pp. 174–175
· Outline Map, pp. 176–177

**Formal Assessment**
· Section Quiz, p. 287

**Integrated Assessment**
· Rubrics

**INTEGRATED TECHNOLOGY**

 Critical Thinking Transp. CT23, CT57
· The New Deal
· U.S. Economic Indicators

 classzone.com

**TEXAS RESOURCES**

 TAKS Spiraled Content Review

 TAKS Practice Tests

 TAKS Practice Transparencies TT89

 TAKS Online Test Practice

More About . . .

**FDR's Brain Trust**

Rexford Tugwell, Raymond Moley, and Adolph A. Berle, Jr. formed a group of advisors dubbed, "The Brain Trust." All three men were economists who taught at Columbia University in New York. Roosevelt's decision to have academic experts as advisors harkened back to La Follette's reliance on University of Wisconsin professors for advice during the Progressive era.

Roosevelt faced rising pressure from Congress to scale back New Deal programs, which he did. As a result, industrial production dropped again, and the number of unemployed increased from 7.7 million in 1937 to 10.4 million in 1938. By 1939, the New Deal was effectively over, and Roosevelt was increasingly concerned with events in Europe, particularly Hitler's rise to power in Germany. **A**

**SUPPORTERS AND CRITICS OF THE NEW DEAL** Over time, opinions about the New Deal have ranged from harsh criticism to high praise. Most conservatives think President Roosevelt's policies made the federal government too large and too powerful. They believe that the government stifled free enterprise and individual initiative. Liberal critics, in contrast, argue that President Roosevelt didn't do enough to socialize the economy and to eliminate social and economic inequalities. Supporters of the New Deal contend, however, that the president struck a reasonable balance between two extremes—unregulated capitalism and overregulated socialism—and helped the country recover from its economic difficulties. One of Roosevelt's top advisers made this assessment of the president's goals.

**MAIN IDEA**

**Analyzing Issues**
**A** Why did industrial production drop and unemployment go up again in 1938?

**A. Answer** Because, in response to pressure from Congress, FDR cut back on New Deal programs.

**A PERSONAL VOICE** REXFORD TUGWELL

"He had in mind a comprehensive welfare concept, infused with a stiff tincture of morality. . . . He wanted all Americans to grow up healthy and vigorous and to be practically educated. He wanted business men to work within a set of understood rules. Beyond this he wanted people free to vote, to worship, to behave as they wished so long as a moral code was respected; and he wanted officials to behave as though office were a public trust."

—quoted in *Redeeming the Time*

## POINT/COUNTERPOINT

### Objective

Analyze the fundamental disagreement among historians about the effectiveness of the New Deal. Ask students the following questions:

· Did the New Deal end the Depression?
· Did the New Deal provide enough relief to the suffering during the Depression?
· How did the New Deal impact the nation's economy in the long run?

### POINT

**"The New Deal transformed the way American government works."**

Supporters of the New Deal believe that it was successful. Many historians and journalists make this judgment by using the economic criterion of creating jobs. *The New Republic*, for example, argued that the shortcomings of the WPA "are insignificant beside the gigantic fact that it has given jobs and sustenance to a minimum of 1,400,000 and a maximum of 3,300,000 persons for five years."

Some historians stress that the New Deal was more than a temporary solution to a crisis. Professor A. A. Berle stated that, "human beings cannot indefinitely be sacrificed by millions to the operation of economic forces."

According to the historian William E. Luechtenburg, "It is hard to think of another period in the whole history of the republic that was so fruitful or of a crisis that was met with as much imagination."

To Pulitzer Prize-winning historian Allan Nevins, the New Deal was a turning point in which the U.S. government assumed a greater responsibility for the economic welfare of its citizens.

### COUNTERPOINT

**"Many more problems have been created than solved by the New Deal."**

Critics of the New Deal believe that it failed to reach its goals. The historian Barton J. Bernstein accepted the goals of the New Deal but declared that they were never met. To him, the New Deal "failed to raise the impoverished, it failed to redistribute income, [and] it failed to extend equality."

In Senator Robert A. Taft's opinion, "many more problems have been created than solved" by the New Deal. He maintained, "Whatever else has resulted from the great increase in government activity . . . it has certainly had the effect of checking private enterprise completely. This country was built up by the constant establishment of new business and the expansion of old businesses. . . . In the last six years this process has come to an end because of government regulation and the development of a tax system which penalizes hard work and success." Senator Taft claimed that "The government should gradually withdraw from the business of lending money and leave that function to private capital under proper regulation."

**THINKING CRITICALLY**

**CONNECT TO HISTORY**

1. **Comparing and Contrasting** How did the New Deal succeed? How did it fail? Write a paragraph that summarizes the main points.

 **SEE SKILLBUILDER HANDBOOK, PAGE R8.**

**CONNECT TO TODAY**

2. **Draft a Proposal** Research the programs of the WPA and draft a proposal for a WPA-type program that would benefit your community.

**THINKING CRITICALLY: ANSWERS**

**1. CONNECT TO HISTORY**

Success: *created jobs; gave government power to provide aid for social and economic problems; took steps to ensure economic prosperity.*
Failure: *created more problems than it solved; government too intrusive; did not redistribute wealth, reduce poverty, or extend equality.*

**2. CONNECT TO TODAY**

**Rubrics**

A proposal should . . .

· explain a specific program
· identify potential program benefits
· describe the various public works involved
· be well organized and clearly presented

**EXPANDING GOVERNMENT'S ROLE IN THE ECONOMY** The Roosevelt administration expanded the power of the federal government, giving it—and particularly the president—a more active role in shaping the economy. It did this by infusing the nation's economy with millions of dollars, by creating federal jobs, by attempting to regulate supply and demand, and by increasing the government's active participation in settling labor and management disputes. The federal government also established agencies, such as the **Federal Deposit Insurance Corporation (FDIC)** and the **Securities and Exchange Commission (SEC),** to regulate banking and investment activities. Although the New Deal did not end the Great Depression, it did help reduce the suffering of thousands of men, women, and children by providing them with jobs, food, and money. It also gave people hope and helped them to regain a sense of dignity.

The federal government had to go deeply into debt to provide jobs and aid to the American people. The federal deficit increased to $2.9 billion in fiscal year 1934. As a result of the cutbacks in federal spending made in 1937–1938, the deficit dropped to $100 million. But the next year it rose again, to $2.9 billion. What really ended the Depression, however, was the massive amount of spending by the federal government for guns, tanks, ships, airplanes, and all the other equipment and supplies the country needed for the World War II effort. During the war, the deficit reached a high of about $54.4 billion in 1944.

▲ Unemployed workers sit on a street in a 1936 photograph by Dorothea Lange.

## More About . . .

### FDIC and SEC
Established in response to the banking disasters that occurred in the 1930s, the FDIC insures depositors in member banks. Currently, a deposit is insured up to $100,000. The FDIC also monitors banking practices by sending regulators to inspect bank records.

After the collapse of the stock market in 1929, it was apparent that a regulatory commission was needed to monitor sales practices and watch for stock manipulation. The SEC performs that job along with registering securities and supervising the securities market and stock holders.

**TAKS**

Mini-Lesson 3: SS11 3(US13.E)

*Skillbuilder Answer*
1. 1943
2. Unemployment increases when there is less deficit spending and decreases when there is more deficit spending, perhaps because the deficit spending stimulates the creation of jobs.

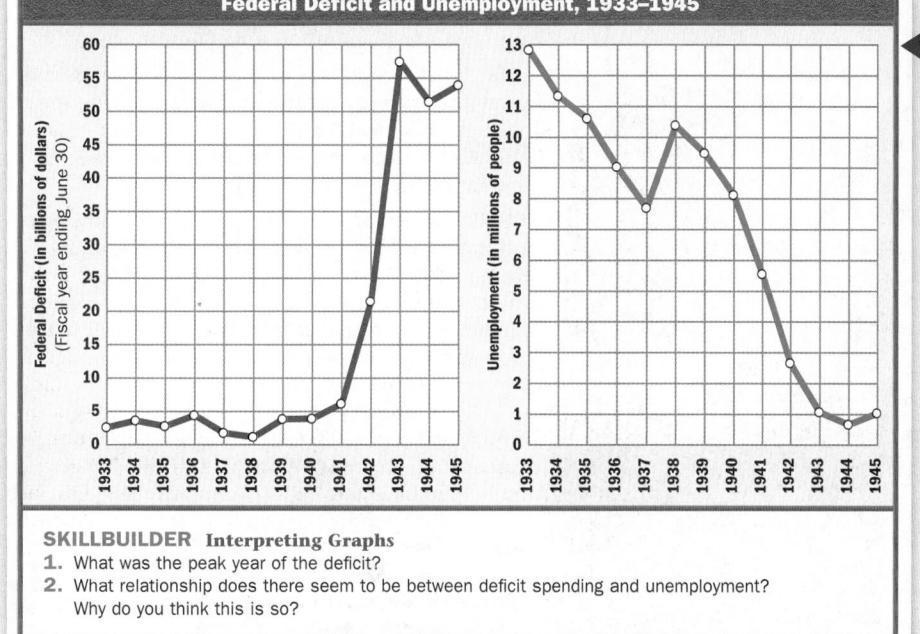

**Federal Deficit and Unemployment, 1933–1945**

*Federal Deficit (in billions of dollars) (Fiscal year ending June 30)*

*Unemployment (in millions of people)*

1933 1934 1935 1936 1937 1938 1939 1940 1941 1942 1943 1944 1945

**SKILLBUILDER** Interpreting Graphs
1. What was the peak year of the deficit?
2. What relationship does there seem to be between deficit spending and unemployment? Why do you think this is so?

## HISTORY from VISUALS

### Interpreting the Graphs
Help students to see the inverse relationship between deficit spending and unemployment. As deficit spending goes up, the unemployment rate goes down.

**Extension** Ask students to draw their own graphs of the relationship between deficit spending and unemployment. Have them use the same data and express the information in a different format. *(pie chart, bar graph)*

*The New Deal* **517**

---

**ACTIVITY** | **COOPERATIVE ACTIVITY**

 **BLOCK SCHEDULING**

### Debating The New Deal

**Class Time** One class period

**Task** Analyzing the New Deal through debate

**Purpose** To evaluate the New Deal's effectiveness

**Directions** Conduct a class debate on the topic: The New Deal failed to meet the needs of all citizens during the Depression. Have students work on their own, or in groups, to research the overall impact of the New Deal. Have students generate a list of pros and cons. Next, have them prepare an argument either criticizing or defending the New Deal. Students should use facts and examples to support their argument. Remind students they must prepare their arguments based on the debate topic. They also must be ready to answer the challenges of the opposing side.

## Instruct: Objective ❷

### Social and Environmental Effects

TAKS SS11 3(US13.E)

· What was unique about the New Deal's social policies?

· What did the New Deal do for the environment?

 In-Depth Resources: Unit 4
· Guided Reading, p. 64

### NOW & THEN

**Social Security**

**Predicting Effects** Ask students to predict what effects the trends mentioned in this featurette will have on social security benefits. *(More retirees demands and less income may mean reduced benefits.)*

**Extension** Have students do research to find articles on Social Security in the United States. Ask them to write a brief summary of their findings.

### Tracing Themes

#### ECONOMIC OPPORTUNITY

The continual rise and fall of business activity sometimes results in a recession. During a recession, consumer spending decreases and unemployment rises. The aim of New Deal programs, such as Social Security, the SEC, and the FDIC, was to regulate the market and provide some relief during hard times.

---

### NOW & THEN

#### SOCIAL SECURITY

Today the Social Security system continues to rely on mandatory contributions paid by workers—through payroll deductions—and by employers. The money is invested in a trust fund, from which retirement benefits are later paid. However, several problems have surfaced. For example, benefits have expanded, and Americans live longer than they did in 1935. Also, the ratio of workers to retirees is shrinking: fewer people are contributing to the system relative to the number who are eligible to receive benefits.

The long-range payment of benefits may be in jeopardy because of the large number of recipients. Continuing disagreement about how to address the costs has prevented legislative action.

◀ A Social Security poster proclaims the benefits of the system for those who are 65 or older.

---

**PROTECTING WORKERS' RIGHTS** One of the areas in which New Deal policies have had a lasting effect is the protection of workers' rights. New Deal legislation, such as the Wagner Act and the Fair Labor Standards Act, set standards for wages and hours, banned child labor, and ensured the right of workers to organize and to bargain collectively with employers. Today, the **National Labor Relations Board (NLRB),** created under the Wagner Act, continues to act as a mediator in labor disputes between unions and employers.

**BANKING AND FINANCE** New Deal programs established new policies in the area of banking and finance. The Securities and Exchange Commission (SEC), created in 1934, continues to monitor the stock market and enforce laws regarding the sale of stocks and bonds. The Federal Deposit Insurance Corporation (FDIC), created by the Glass-Steagall Act of 1933, has shored up the banking system by reassuring individual depositors that their savings are protected against loss in the event of a bank failure. Today, individual accounts in United States federal banks are insured by the Federal Deposit Insurance Corporation for up to $100,000.

## Social and Environmental Effects ❷

New Deal economic and financial reforms, including the creation of the FDIC, the SEC, and Social Security, have helped to stabilize the nation's finances and economy. Although the nation still experiences economic downturns, known as recessions, people's savings are insured, and they can receive unemployment compensation if they lose their jobs.

**SOCIAL SECURITY** One of the most important legacies of the New Deal has been that the federal government has assumed some responsibility for the social welfare of its citizens. Under President Roosevelt, the government undertook the creation of a Social Security system that would help a large number of needy Americans receive some assistance.

The Social Security Act provides an old-age insurance program, an unemployment compensation system, and aid to the disabled and families with dependent children. It has had a major impact on the lives of millions of Americans since its founding in 1935. **B**

**THE RURAL SCENE** New Deal policies also had a significant impact on the nation's agriculture. New Deal farm legislation set quotas on the production of crops such as wheat to control surpluses. Under the second Agricultural Adjustment Act, passed in 1938, loans were made to farmers by the Commodity Credit Corporation. The value of a loan was determined by the amount of a farmer's surplus crops and the **parity** price, a price intended to keep farmers' income steady. Establishing agricultural price supports set a precedent of federal aid to farmers that continued into the 2000s. Other government programs, such as rural electrification, helped to improve conditions in rural America.

> **MAIN IDEA**
>
> **Developing Historical Perspective**
> **B** Why was the establishment of the Social Security system such an important part of the New Deal?
> *B. Answer* The government began accepting responsibility for providing assistance to needy members of society.

---

#### Clarifying Ideas

To help less proficient readers interpret the main ideas in this section, suggest students follow these steps:

· Read pages 518–519.
· Make a list of ongoing New Deal programs.
· Create a graphic like the one shown at the right
· List each program and its benefits.

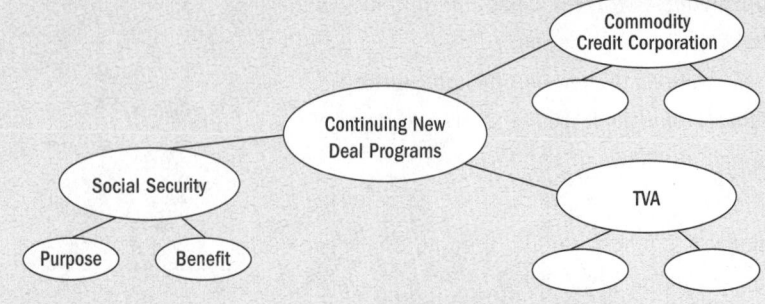

**THE ENVIRONMENT** Americans also continue to benefit from New Deal efforts to protect the environment. President Roosevelt was highly committed to conservation and promoted policies designed to protect the nation's natural resources. The Civilian Conservation Corps planted trees, created hiking trails, and built fire lookout towers. The Soil Conservation Service taught farmers how to conserve the soil through contour plowing, terracing, and crop rotation. Congress also passed the Taylor Grazing Act in 1934 to help reduce grazing on public lands. Such grazing had contributed to the erosion that brought about the dust storms of the 1930s.

The **Tennessee Valley Authority (TVA)** harnessed water power to generate electricity and to help prevent disastrous floods in the Tennessee Valley. The government also added to the national park system in the 1930s, established new wildlife refuges and set aside large wilderness areas. On the other hand, government-sponsored stripmining and coal burning caused air, land, and water pollution. **C**

The New Deal legacy has many dimensions. It brought hope and gratitude from some people for the benefits and protections they received. It also brought anger and criticism from those who believed that it took more of their money in taxes and curtailed their freedom through increased government regulations. The deficit spending necessary to fund New Deal programs grew immensely as the nation entered World War II.

*C Answer* They benefited the environment with new trees, hiking trails, fire lookouts, soil conservation, flood control, national parks, wildlife refuges, and wilderness areas. They harmed it with air, water, and land pollution.

**MAIN IDEA**

**Recognizing Effects**
**C** How did New Deal programs benefit and harm the environment?

 This 1933 cartoon depicts Roosevelt exhausting Congress with his many reform policies.

**More About . . .**

**Tennessee Valley Authority**
The Tennessee Valley Authority (TVA) has had a lasting effect on the southeastern United States. Since the construction of the dam system, flooding in the region has been minimal. River traffic greatly increased, and access to affordable electricity spurred industrial development. This formerly isolated rural region is now home to a large population.

# Assess & Reteach

**SECTION 5 ASSESSMENT**
Have students work together to answer the questions in the Section Assessment.

Formal Assessment
· Section Quiz, p. 287

**SELF-ASSESSMENT**
To document what they have learned, students should make a list of New Deal programs and their impact on American society.

**RETEACH**
Use the Point Counterpoint feature on page 516 to review the New Deal's effect on the role of government in public life.

In-Depth Resources: Unit 4
· Reteaching Activity, p. 71

---

 **ASSESSMENT**

1. **TERMS & NAMES** For each term or name, write a sentence explaining its significance.
   - Federal Deposit Insurance Corporation (FDIC)
   - Securities and Exchange Commission (SEC)
   - National Labor Relations Board (NLRB)
   - parity
   - Tennessee Valley Authority (TVA)

**MAIN IDEA**

2. **TAKING NOTES**
In a cluster diagram like the one below, show long-term effects of the New Deal.

New Deal's Long-Term Effects

Which long-term benefit do you think has had the most impact? Why?

**CRITICAL THINKING**

3. **MAKING GENERALIZATIONS**
Some critics have charged that the New Deal was antibusiness and anti–free enterprise. Explain why you agree or disagree with this charge.
**Think About:**
   - the expanded power of the federal government
   - the New Deal's effect on the economy
   - the New Deal's effect on the American people

4. **EVALUATING LEADERSHIP**
How successful do you think Franklin Roosevelt was as a president? Support your answer with details from the text.

5. **INTERPRETING VISUAL SOURCES**
Look at the political cartoon above. What does it suggest about Roosevelt's leadership and the role of Congress? Explain.

TAKS Mini-Lesson 1: SS11 1(US1.A)

*The New Deal* **519**

---

 **Answers** **ASSESSMENT** 5

**1. TERMS & NAMES**
Federal Deposit Insurance Corporation (FDIC), p. 517
Securities and Exchange Commission (SEC), p. 517
National Labor Relations Board, p. 518
parity, p. 518
Tennessee Valley Authority (TVA), p. 519

**2. TAKING NOTES**
National Labor Relations Board mediates labor disputes; Federal Deposit Insurance Corporation insures accounts up to $100,000; Securities and Exchange Commission monitors the stock market; Social Security provides assistance to eligible citizens.

**3. MAKING GENERALIZATIONS**
Agree: the New Deal weakened free enterprise business by increasing regulations, taxes, union membership, and wages. Disagree: increased government spending, improved economy, provided hope, aided free enterprise.
**4. EVALUATING LEADERSHIP**
Success: Roosevelt's New Deal programs addressed the crisis of the Depression. Failure: supporting civil rights for African Americans.
**5. INTERPRETING VISUAL SOURCES**
Roosevelt is leading Congress at a rapid rate. Congress is merely following him.

**GEOGRAPHY SPOTLIGHT**

## GEOGRAPHY SPOTLIGHT

### Objectives

· Analyze the federal government's role in establishing the Tennessee Valley Authority (TVA).

· Summarize the impact the TVA had on the Tennessee Valley region.

## Focus & Motivate

Have students consider what it would be like to live without electricity. Ask them to think of all the ways in which they rely on electricity every day.

### More About . . .

#### The Tennessee River

Before the creation of the TVA, the Tennessee River was subject to periodic flooding. The TVA project helped control flooding, which saved lives and crops. The dams curbed soil erosion and generated hydroelectricity, which was vital to industrial development. Damming the river also created the "Great Lakes of the South," which provided new recreational opportunities.

# The Tennessee Valley Authority

The Tennessee Valley Authority (TVA) is a federal agency that was established in 1933 to construct dams and power plants along the Tennessee River and its tributaries. The Tennessee River basin is one of the largest river basins in the United States, and people who live in this area have a number of common concerns. The TVA has helped the region in various ways: through flood and navigation control, the conservation of natural resources, and the generation of electric power, as well as through agricultural and industrial development.

The Tennessee Valley covers parts of seven states. Thus, the TVA became an enormous undertaking, eventually comprising dozens of major dams, each with associated power plants, recreational facilities, and navigation aids.

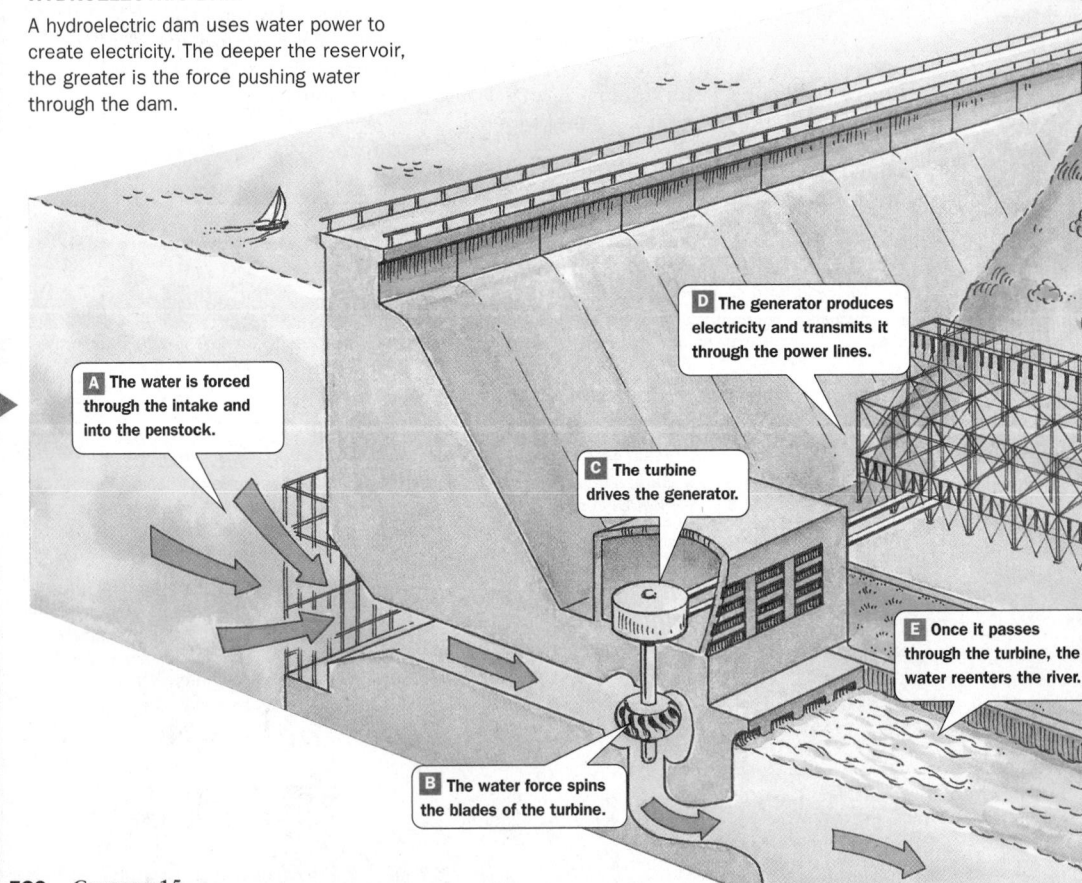

**HYDROELECTRIC DAM**

A hydroelectric dam uses water power to create electricity. The deeper the reservoir, the greater is the force pushing water through the dam.

**A** The water is forced through the intake and into the penstock.

**B** The water force spins the blades of the turbine.

**C** The turbine drives the generator.

**D** The generator produces electricity and transmits it through the power lines.

**E** Once it passes through the turbine, the water reenters the river.

**520** CHAPTER 15

---

### RECOMMENDED RESOURCES

#### BOOKS

Davidson, Donald. *The Tennessee.* New York: Rinehart, 1978. A two-volume history of the Tennessee River and valley and the TVA.

Duffus, R. L. *The Valley and Its People.* New York: Knopf, 1944. The story of the TVA, written not long after it was established.

*A History of the Tennessee Valley Authority.* Knoxville: TVA Information Office, 1982. A history written by the TVA.

Hubbard, Preston, J. *Origins of the TVA.* Norton: 1968. The TVA and the Muscle Shoals controversy that helped create it.

#### VIDEOS

*The Electric Valley.* Dir. Ross Spears. Agee Film, 1984. The 50-year history of the Tennessee Valley Authority.

*FDR.* Dir. Alan Kane. A&E Home Video, 1995.

**❶ KENTUCKY DAM**
Over a mile and a half long and
206 feet high, the Kentucky Dam
created the 184-mile-long Kentucky
Lake, a paradise for fishing.

**❷ THE CUMBERLAND RIVER**
A similar series of dams, operated
by the Corps of Engineers, is found
on the Cumberland River. This
system cooperates with the TVA.

# Instruct

1. What is the TVA?

2. Describe the benefits the TVA brought
   to the Tennessee Valley.

3. What should the government's role be in
   flood control, environmental protection,
   and disaster relief?

📖 In-Depth Resources: Unit 4
· Outline Map: Anatomy of the Tennessee
Valley Authority, pp. 74–75

## MAKING PERSONAL CONNECTIONS

Ask students to consider how government
programs impact the environment. Have them
research lakes that were formed as the result
of government dams. Ask students to consider recent disasters, such as storms, floods,
forest fires, or droughts. What role, if any, did
the Federal Emergency Management Agency
(FEMA) play in providing relief?

**❸ NORRIS DAM ▲**
Located on the
Clinch River, a
tributary of the
Tennessee River,
the Norris Dam is
named after
Senator George
W. Norris of
Nebraska. Norris
was a progres-
sive leader who
called for govern-
ment involvement
in the develop-
ment of the
power potential
of the Tennessee
River.

| | Tennessee River watershed |
| --- | --- |
| | Region served by TVA power |
| ⌒ | TVA Dam |

0    50    100 miles
0    50    100 kilometers

## HISTORY from VISUALS

**Viewing the Images**
Have students study the map and accompanying information.

List the seven states that the TVA served.
*(Alabama, Georgia, Kentucky, Mississippi,
North Carolina, Tennessee, Virginia)*

Identify two tributaries of the Tennessee
River. *(Cumberland River, Clinch River)*

▲
Before 1930, most homes in the area had no electricity.
Women wash clothes outside this homestead near
Andersonville, Tennessee, in 1933. Their estate was
submerged when the Norris Dam filled.

## THINKING CRITICALLY

1. **Analyzing Distributions** Locate the dams on this
   map. Why do you think they might have been placed in
   these particular areas?

2. **Creating a Model** Create a 3-D model of a dam.
   Before you begin, pose a historical question your
   model will answer. Think about environmental changes
   caused by the construction of a dam.

   **SEE SKILLBUILDER HANDBOOK, PAGE R31.**

🔵 **RESEARCH LINKS** CLASSZONE.COM

*The New Deal* **521**

## THINKING CRITICALLY: ANSWERS

**1. ANALYZING DISTRIBUTIONS**
flood prevention; control water flow through the river and tributaries; power generators; to aid the environment.

**2. CREATING A MODEL**
**Rubric**
Students' models should . . .

· represent a particular type of dam
· answer an historical question
· demonstrate an understanding of dam construction and purpose

# CHAPTER 15 ASSESSMENT

## TERMS & NAMES

1. Franklin Delano Roosevelt, p. 489
2. New Deal, p. 489
3. Eleanor Roosevelt, p. 496
4. Works Progress Administration, p. 498
5. Social Security Act, p. 501
6. Mary McLeod Bethune, p. 505
7. Congress of Industrial Organizations, p. 508
8. Orson Welles, p. 511
9. Richard Wright, p. 514
10. Tennessee Valley Authority, p. 519

## MAIN IDEAS

1. FDR expanded the role of the government through programs designed to restore public confidence and provide jobs.
2. Some said the New Deal gave government too much power. Others argued it didn't provide enough aid.
3. The New Deal offered aid through programs, such as the WPA, NYA, FSA, and Social Security. These programs offered jobs, loans, and aid to those in need.
4. The Wagner Act supported the right of workers to unionize.
5. FDR failed to support civil rights for African Americans. Mexican Americans worked for low wages. Native Americans benefited from the Indian Reorganization Act of 1934.
6. The Democrats supported labor legislation and programs that helped the urban poor.
7. Movie and radio gave Americans a pleasant escape from the reality of the Depression.
8. The programs funded artists and writers to produce works of art.
9. Federal Deposit Insurance Corporation, Securities and Exchange Commission, National Labor Relations Board, Social Security system, Tennessee Valley Authority
10. provided flood control, hydroelectric power, conservation, recreational facilities; coal burning caused environmental pollution

### VISUAL SUMMARY

## THE NEW DEAL

#### PROBLEMS

- Industries and farms failed.
- U.S. stock market crashed and banks closed.
- Bankrupt businesses
- Unemployment
- Homelessness

#### SOLUTIONS

- Work projects help the unemployed.
- Money given to farmers, sharecroppers, and migrant workers
- New opportunities for women and minorities
- Social Security Act allocates money to the elderly, the unemployed, and the disabled.
- NLRB protects workers' rights.
- SEC monitors stock market.
- FDIC protects individuals' deposits in banks.
- Fireside chats increase public confidence.

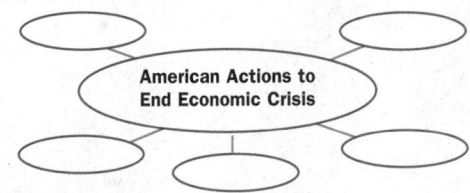

#### CONTINUING EFFECTS

- Banking and finance are reformed.
- Government takes a more active role in the economy.
- Workers benefit from labor standards.
- Social Security system continues to provide for the needy.
- Conservation efforts continue to preserve the environment.

## TERMS & NAMES

For each term or name below, write a sentence explaining its historical significance or contribution to the New Deal.

1. Franklin Delano Roosevelt
2. New Deal
3. Eleanor Roosevelt
4. Works Progress Administration (WPA)
5. Social Security Act
6. Mary McCloud Bethune
7. Congress of Industrial Organizations (CIO)
8. Orson Welles
9. Richard Wright
10. Tennessee Valley Authority (TVA)

## MAIN IDEAS

Use your notes and the information in the chapter to answer the following questions.

### A New Deal Fights the Depression (pages 488–494)

1. How did Franklin Roosevelt change the role of the federal government during his first Hundred Days?
2. Summarize the reasons why some people opposed the New Deal.

### The Second New Deal Takes Hold (pages 495–501)

3. In what ways did the New Deal programs extend federal aid?
4. How did the Wagner Act help working people?

### The New Deal Affects Many Groups (pages 504–509)

5. Summarize the impact the New Deal had on various ethnic groups.
6. Why did many urban voters support Roosevelt and the Democratic party?

### Culture in the 1930s (pages 510–514)

7. What purpose did movies and radio serve during the Great Depression?
8. Explain how the New Deal programs supported artists and writers in the 1930s.

### The Impact of the New Deal (pages 515–519)

9. List five New Deal agencies that are still in place today.
10. What benefits did the Tennessee Valley Authority provide? What negative impact did it have?

## THINKING CRITICALLY

1. **USING YOUR NOTES** Copy the web below and fill it in with actions that Americans took to end the economic crisis of the 1930s.

American Actions to End Economic Crisis

2. **DEVELOPING HISTORICAL PERSPECTIVE** What federal programs instituted in the 1930s and later discontinued might be of use to the nation today? Explain and support your opinion in a paragraph or two.

## CRITICAL THINKING

1. **Using Your Notes** FDR elected president; the federal government expanded role in the economy to aid banks, farmers, workers, and the unemployed.

2. **Developing Historical Perspective** A type of NYA program could help low-income students afford college; a type of WPA could be used for people who are unemployed; the government might reinstitute a CCC to help deal with environmental problems, to educate people about environmental concerns, and to employ young people.

## Standardized Test Practice

**Use the information on the time line and your knowledge of U.S. history to answer question 1.**

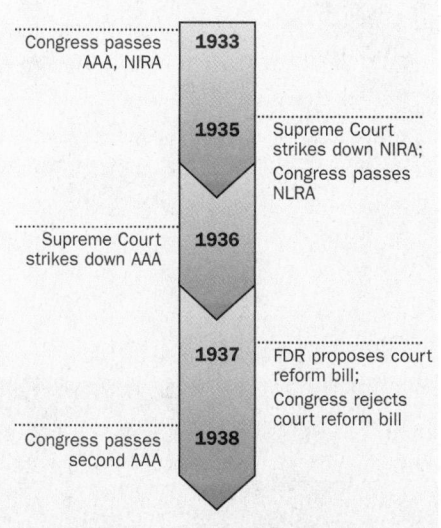

Congress passes AAA, NIRA — **1933**

**1935** — Supreme Court strikes down NIRA; Congress passes NLRA

Supreme Court strikes down AAA — **1936**

**1937** — FDR proposes court reform bill; Congress rejects court reform bill

Congress passes second AAA — **1938**

1. The Supreme Court killed several New Deal programs by declaring them unconstitutional. Which of the following resulted from those decisions?

   A FDR packed the Court with New Deal supporters.
   B Congress created replacement programs.
   C The New Deal lost popular support.
   D The power of the federal government was expanded.

2. What was the purpose of the Glass-Steagall Act?

   F to combat unemployment
   G to provide home mortgage loans
   H to assist farmers
   J to regulate the banking system

**Use the quotation and your knowledge of United States history to answer question 3.**

> "Little by little the American federation is transforming itself into a union, marked by the growth in importance of the role of the federal capital. In the beginning, the United States had only a small federal bureaucracy. Today the central administration is powerful and rich."
>
> — ANDRÉ MAUROIS, *This Was America*

3. Author André Maurois traveled through the United States in the 1930s and observed a growing unity in the American people. How did the New Deal help to bring Americans closer together?

   A The New Deal involved the federal government trying to fix a national problem.
   B New Deal jobs and public works programs gave people something to agree upon.
   C President Roosevelt, who designed the New Deal, was elected four times.
   D The New Deal encouraged the spread of popular culture through radio and the movies.

**ADDITIONAL TEST PRACTICE, pages S1–S33.**

 **TEST PRACTICE** CLASSZONE.COM

## Standardized Test Practice

1. The correct answer is letter **A**.
   FDR introduced the court-packing bill to counter opposition from the court. Letter B is not correct because Congress did create replacement programs. Letter C is not correct because the New Deal remained popular. Letter D is not correct because the power of the federal government was not expanded in response to the court.

2. The correct answer is letter **J**.
   The Glass-Steagall bill created the FDIC. Letters F, G, and H do not deal directly with banking issues.

3. The correct answer is letter **A**.
   The quote refers to the expansion of federal government. Letter B is not correct because not all Americans agreed on the New Deal. Letters C and D are not correct because the quote does not deal with elections or with culture.

**MULTIMEDIA PRESENTATION**

**Tips for Teaching**

· Provide students with some class time to work on the project.
· Give students a list of the rubrics you will use to evaluate the presentation.

**Rubrics**

A Multimedia Presentation should . . .

· engage the viewer by using an interesting and creative style
· clearly illustrate the theme of the "Roaring Twenties" through use of two or more media elements

Formal Assessment
· Chapter Test, Forms A, B, and C, pp. 288–299

## ALTERNATIVE ASSESSMENT

1. **INTERACT WITH HISTORY** Recall your discussion of the question on page 487:

   *How would you begin to revive the economy?*

   Now that you have read the chapter, do you think President Roosevelt adequately addressed the needs of the ailing economy? Do you think his New Deal policies extended far enough to restore public confidence? Support your opinions with examples.

2. **VIDEO** **LEARNING FROM MEDIA** View the *American Stories* video "A Song for His People." Discuss the following questions in a group, then do the activity.

   • Why were thousands of Mexican Americans sent back to Mexico in the 1930s?
   • Why did Pedro J. González become a hero to many Mexican Americans?

   **Cooperative Learning Activity** Write and present a short broadcast, such as González might have given, in which you comment on the New Deal's effects on immigrants and minorities.

## ALTERNATIVE ASSESSMENT

### 1. INTERACT WITH HISTORY

**Rubric**

Student responses should . . .

· answer the posed questions
· provide specific examples about the impact of FDR's New Deal on the economy

### 2. LEARNING FROM MEDIA

**Rubric**

Student broadcasts should . . .

· focus on the impact of the New Deal on minorities and immigrants
· express an opinion on the issue and back it up with historical facts
· conclude with a restatement of the main ideas

## Previewing the Unit

Unit 5 describes how militaristic dictators in Europe and Japan start a worldwide war that forces the United States to fight on two fronts. Victory leads to an uneasy peace with the Soviet Union, with the threat of nuclear war looming over the world. The economic expansion brought on by the war and the return to peace fuels a postwar economic boom and the spread of a suburb-based consumer culture.

### HISTORICAL INQUIRY: DEBATE

Use this project to teach students how to identify bias in oral presentations.

**Understanding Bias**
Tell students that a biased statement is one that reflects the personal viewpoints or prejudices of the author. Ask students why they should be on the watch for bias when they are reading or listening to historical accounts or arguments. *(Either might leave out important facts and give a one-sided view.)*

**Identifying Bias in Oral Sources**
Review with students the lesson on Analyzing Assumptions and Bias, Skillbuilder Handbook, page R15. Then discuss with students how detecting bias in an oral presentation compares and contrasts with detecting bias in written material. *(symptoms of bias would be the same but would be harder to detect because speech goes by quickly)*

*(continued on next page)*

# UNIT 5

## World War II and Its Aftermath 1931–1960

### Debate

As you read Unit 5, pay attention to arguments on either side of a political issue. Work with a group to stage a debate. Write a proposition, such as "Resolved: The U.S. has a responsibility to end its isolationism and enter World War II." Choose teams to argue either for or against the resolution.

*Dawn Patrol Launching* by Paul Sample

**524**

## More About the Image

**1** Carriers were used extensively in the Pacific Theatre of World War II. The first time an airplane took off from a ship was in November of 1910. Actually landing an airplane on the deck of a ship did not happen until January of 1911. The first true carrier was the British built HMS *Argus* developed during World War I.

**2** Battleship gun range was approximately 20 miles. Aircraft range was approximately 200 miles.

**3** Most of the airplanes abroad an aircraft carrier were single-seat fighters, dive-bombers, or torpedo planes.

Ask what students could do while listening to help them identify bias. *(take notes for later review)*

**Tips for Debating**

· Organize groups of two, four, or six students to choose a proposition and then divide into two teams, one arguing each side.
· Review with students the structure and rules for a formal debate.
· Remind students that they will be judged on their listening as well as on their research and presentation.
· Before each debate is presented, remind students in the audience to review the strategies for detecting bias.

**Rubrics**

Debaters should . . .

· present relevant facts and cogent arguments in support of the team's position
· respond logically to opposing arguments

Listeners should . . .

· identify the main arguments and supporting details presented by each team and
· identify biased arguments, misleading statements, and missing information

## HISTORY from VISUALS

### Interpreting the Painting

World War II is sometimes known as the age of the aircraft carrier. The attack on Pearl Harbor, carried out by carrier based planes, clearly demonstrated the value of this new style of warfare. Paul Sample's painting illustrates a series of planes ready for an early morning patrol assignment. The painting appeared in an issue of *Life* magazine. Ask students why *Life* magazine might have chosen to publish this painting. *(To show people what action on an aircraft carrier was like.)*

**Extension** Have student use library or Internet sources to investigate the development of airplanes that are found on aircraft carriers. They should put their findings in an illustrated chart.

**4** Folding wings enabled aircraft to be taken by elevator to below-deck hangers.

**5** The aircraft were fitted with retractable arrester hooks that caught wires across the deck, enabling them to brake to a stop.

**6** The superstructure on the side of the flight deck held the control tower. Aircraft used radio, radar, and visual signals from the deck.

# World War Looms

| CHAPTER OVERVIEW | COPYMASTERS | INTEGRATED TECHNOLOGY |
|---|---|---|
| **CHAPTER RESOURCES** | | |
| *An imperfect peace leads to the rise of brutal dictators who suppress opponents and innocent people at home and attack their neighbors. Soon the United States is plunged into worldwide war.* | 📄 Telescoping the Times <br> · Chapter Summary, pp. 31–32 <br><br> 📄 Planning for Block Schedules | 📹 American Stories video series <br> · "Escaping the Final Solution" <br><br> 👁 Power Presentations <br><br> 💿 Electronic Teacher Tools <br><br> 🖥 Online Lesson Planner <br><br> 🖥 classzone.com |

| **SECTION 1** <br><br> Dictators Threaten World Peace <br><br> pp. 528–535 | **KEY IDEAS** <br><br> *The United States remains isolated from world affairs as economic and political factors lead to the rise of nationalist leaders in the Soviet Union, Germany, and Italy.* | 📄 In-Depth Resources: Unit 5 <br> · Guided Reading, p. 1 <br> · Building Vocabulary, p. 5 <br> · Skillbuilder Practice, p. 6 <br> · Reteaching Activity, p. 7 <br> · Primary Sources, p. 13 <br><br> 📄 Lesson Plans, pp. 127–128 | 🖥 Humanities Transparencies HT23 <br> · German Nazi Party poster <br><br> 🖥 classzone.com |

| **SECTION 2** <br><br> War in Europe <br><br> pp. 536–541 | *A series of bold moves by Adolf Hitler—and weak countermoves by other leaders—triggers World War II in Europe.* | 📄 In-Depth Resources: Unit 5 <br> · Guided Reading, p. 2 <br> · Skillbuilder Activity, p. 6 <br> · Historical Perspective, p. 6 <br> · Reteaching Activity, p. 8 <br><br> 📄 Lesson Plans, pp. 129–130 | 🖥 Geography Transparencies GT24 <br> · Aggression in Europe, 1936-1939 <br><br> 👁 Electronic Library of Primary Sources <br> · Letter to Roosevelt by Winston Churchill <br><br> 🖥 classzone.com |

| **SECTION 3** <br><br> The Holocaust <br><br> pp. 542–549 | *Hitler's plans for conquering the world include the killing of Jews and other ethnic groups, which is carried out with frightening determination.* | 📄 In-Depth Resources: Unit 5 <br> · Guided Reading, p. 3 <br> · Reteaching Activity, p. 9 <br> · Literature, pp. 17–19 <br> · American Lives, p. 20 <br><br> 📄 Lesson Plans, pp. 131–132 | 📹 American Stories video series <br> · "Escaping the Final Solution" <br><br> 🖥 classzone.com |

| **SECTION 4** <br><br> America Moves Toward War <br><br> pp. 550–557 | *The United States provides aid to nations resisting Hitler and enters World War II after the bombing of Pearl Harbor.* | 📄 In-Depth Resources: Unit 5 <br> · Guided Reading, p. 4 <br> · Reteaching Activity, p. 10 <br> · Geography Application, p. 11–12 <br> · Primary Sources, pp. 14–16 <br> · American Lives, p. 21 <br><br> 📄 Lesson Plans, pp. 133–134 | 🖥 Critical Thinking Transparencies CT24, CT58 <br> · World War II Begins in Europe <br> · Time Line of Events Leading to World War II <br><br> 👁 Electronic Library of Primary Sources <br> · Unit 5, Chapter 16 <br><br> 🖥 classzone.com |

PE Pupil's Edition    Overhead Transparency    CD-ROM
TE Teacher's Edition    Audio Library    Internet
Copymaster

## ASSESSMENT OPTIONS

PE **Chapter Assessment**, pp. 558–559

**Formal Assessment**
· Chapter Tests, Forms A, B, and C, pp. 304–315

**Test Generator**

**Integrated Assessment Book**

**TAKS Online Test Practice**

**TAKS Spiraled Content Review**

**TAKS Practice Tests**

---

PE **Section 1 Assessment**, p. 535

TE **Self-Assessment**, p. 535

**Formal Assessment**, Quiz, p. 300

**Integrated Assessment Book**

**Test Generator**

**TAKS Practice Transparencies TT90**

---

PE **Section 2 Assessment**, p. 541

TE **Self-Assessment**, p. 541

**Formal Assessment**, Quiz, p. 301

**Integrated Assessment Book**

**Test Generator**

**TAKS Practice Transparencies TT91**

---

PE **Section 3 Assessment**, p. 549

TE **Self-Assessment**, p. 549

**Formal Assessment**, Quiz, p. 302

**Integrated Assessment Book**

**Test Generator**

**TAKS Practice Transparencies TT92**

---

PE **Section 4 Assessment**, p. 557

TE **Self-Assessment**, p. 557

**Formal Assessment**, Quiz, p. 303

**Integrated Assessment Book**

**Test Generator**

**TAKS Practice Transparencies TT93**

## RESOURCES FOR DIFFERENTIATING INSTRUCTION

**Students Acquiring English/ESL**

**Reading Study Guide:**
(English and Spanish)
pp. 161–162

**Access for Students Acquiring English/ESL:**
Spanish Translations,
p. 180

**Chapter Summaries on CD**
(English and Spanish)

**Less Proficient Readers**

**Reading Study Guide**
(English and Spanish)
pp. 161–162

**Telescoping the Times**
· Chapter Summary,
pp. 31–32

**Chapter Summaries on CD**
(English and Spanish)

**Gifted and Talented Students**

**In-Depth Resources: Unit 0**
· Primary Sources,
pp. 13–16
· American Lives: Elie
Wiesel, p. 20, Charles A.
Lindbergh, p. 21

**Electronic Library of
Primary Sources**
· Unit 5, Chapter 16

## CROSS-CURRICULAR CONNECTIONS

**World History**
Stalcup, Ann. *On the Home Front: Growing Up in
Wartime England.* Hamden, CT: Shoestring Press,
1998. A factual account that includes the author's
memories and historical information.

**Primary Sources**
Valavkova, Hana, ed. *I Never Saw Another Butterfly:
Children's Drawings and Poems from Terezin
Concentration Camp 1942–1944.* NY: Shocken Books,
1994. Over 15,000 children under the age of 15
passed through this camp and yet less than 100 survived. Through their words and pictures the reader can
only begin to understand their misery and tragic lives.

**Literature**
Hemingway, Ernest. *For Whom the Bell Tolls.* NY:
Scribner, 1996. Set on the eve of World War II, this
American classic tells the story of the impending
death of an American in the Spanish Civil War. A
deeply felt and timeless story of love and loss, of
courage and commitment, the novel reflects
Hemingway's passionate feelings about the nature of
war and the meaning of loyalty.

Uchida, Yoshiko. *Journey to Topaz.* NY: Scribner,
1971. After the attack on Pearl Harbor, an 11-year old
Japanese-American girl and her family are forced into
an internment camp called Topaz in the Utah desert.

Taylor, Theodore. *The Cay.* NY: Avon, 1991. Shipwrecked
and blinded during World War II, a young boy must rely
on Timothy, an old black man, for survival. The prejudiced boy learns to respect and love Timothy.

**McDougal Littell *Literature Connections***

Goodrich, Frances and Albert Hacket.
*The Diary of Anne Frank.* A play based
on the famous diary of the Jewish girl
who hid with her family from the Nazis.

**Nextext**

*The Holocaust* Features 24 source
documents and 22 photographs.

## ENRICHMENT ACTIVITIES

PE **Pupil's Edition**, pp. 526–557
Interact with History, pp. 526–527
Point/Counterpoint, p. 552
Science & Technology, p. 553

**In-Depth Resources: Unit 5**
· Geography Application: Japanese Aggression,
pp. 11–12
· Primary Source: Quarantine Speech, p. 13
· Primary Source: The Bombing of Pearl Harbor,
p. 14–15
· Primary Source: War Poster, p. 16

· Literature Selection from *Sophie's Choice* by
William Styron, pp. 17–19
· American Lives: Elie Wiesel, p. 20
· American Lives: Charles Lindbergh, p. 21

**Primary Source Explorer**
· Gerda Weissmann Klein, A Voice from the
Holocaust

**American Stories video series**
· "Escaping the Final Solution"

**America's Music CD**

## BLOCK SCHEDULE LESSON PLAN OPTIONS (90-MINUTE PERIOD)

### DAY 1

**CHAPTER 16 OPENER**
pp. 526–527

**Class Time** 30 minutes

**History from Visuals, p. 527**

**Class Time** 20 minutes

*Options for Pacing and Variety*

· Time Saver Ask students to examine the photograph and describe what is happening. Ask students the History from Visuals questions on the TE page.
**Class Time** 10 minutes

**Interact with History, p. 527**

**Class Time** 20 minutes

*Options for Pacing and Variety*

· Internet Have students read the paragraph and discuss the questions as a class. Have them visit the Chapter 16 links on **classzone.com** for more information about the beginning of World War II. Afterwards, discuss in more detail the Examine the Issues questions.
**Class Time** 20 minutes

**SECTION 1** pp. 528–535

**Class Time** 30 minutes

*Options for Pacing and Variety*

· Time Saver Ask students to study the map on page 530 and have them use the map to determine why democratic France might have felt threatened.
**Class Time** 10 minutes

· Peer Teaching Have students outline pages 532–533. Tell them to use the bold heads as roman

### DAY 1 continued

numerals and then find at least two supporting details for each bold head to include in their outline. When they are done, have students compare outlines and discuss what they have learned about Japanese and Italian aggression and the Spanish Civil War.
**Class Time** 20 minutes

· Peer Evaluation Have students work in groups to answer the Section 1 Assessment questions. For question 2, have each student fill in all the circles. Then they can compare answers and add to their own.
**Class Time** 20 minutes

**SECTION 2** pp. 536–541

**Class Time** 30 minutes

*Options for Pacing and Variety*

· Time Saver Explain to students the meaning of historical perspective. Using the application on TE page 537, have students discuss the issues that surrounded the creation of the Munich pact and why the pact evoked such different reactions as Churchill condemning the "appeasement" of Germany and Chamberlain proclaiming "peace with honor."
**Class Time** 10 minutes

· Peer Evaluation Have students answer the Section 2 Assessment questions individually, then compare answers with a partner.
**Class Time** 20 minutes

### DAY 2

**SECTION 3** pp. 542–549

**Class Time** 30 minutes

*Options for Pacing and Variety*

· History on Film View the video American Stories: "Escaping the Final Solution: Kurt Klein and Gerda Weissmann Klein Remember the Holocaust." See page 559 for discussion questions.
**Class Time** 20 minutes

· Time Saver Have students study the chart on page 545. Use the questions in the TE's History from Visuals and the activity on the bottom of TE page 545 as ways to help students comprehend the meaning of these figures.
**Class Time** 15 minutes

· Peer Teaching Use the activity on TE page 548, Exploring Holocaust Literature. Have students choose a first-hand account of the Holocaust. They should choose a short passage and write a two- or three-paragraph response on what the passage means to them and why they chose it. Have them meet in small groups to read the passage and then discuss their reactions.
**Class Time** 30 minutes

**SECTION 4** pp. 550–557

**Class Time** 30 minutes

*Options for Pacing and Variety*

· Time Saver Ask students to read Point Counterpoint on page 552. Have them make a web diagram emphasizing the main arguments for both isolationism and active defense. Then discuss as a class

### DAY 2 continued

how their claims have been justified or not in later years. See TE page 552 for discussion questions.
**Class Time** 15 minutes

· Team Teaching Have students do the activity Link to Science: Radar on TE page 553 as a class. A science teacher might be able to help explain the uses of radar and sonar and suggest Internet resources for further study.
**Class Time** 30 minutes

· Peer Evaluation Have students answer the questions for the Section 4 Assessment, then compare answers with a partner.
**Class Time** 20 minutes

**ASSESSMENT**
pp. 558–559

**Class Time** 30 minutes

*Options for Pacing and Variety*

· Peer Teaching Have students work together on the Main Ideas questions, quizzing each other and taking notes. Discuss the answers to a few questions as a class.
**Class Time** 20 minutes

· Internet Have students do the Standardized Test Practice on page 559. Have students either draw a political cartoon or find one on the Internet, or have them write an editorial about neutrality and isolationism in which they express their opinions on the theory and practice of neutrality.
**Class Time** 25 minutes

---

**TEACHER-TESTED ACTIVITY**     Theresa C. Noonan, West Irondequoit High School, Rochester, New York

**MAP OF HITLER'S AGGRESSION IN EUROPE**

**Class Time** 50 minutes

**Task** Mapping Hitler's aggression in Europe

**Purpose** To understand the geography of Europe and the role it played in Hitler's conquests prior to and at the beginning of World War II

**Supplies Needed**

· Textbook or historical atlas showing maps of Europe in the 1930s and 1940s

· Outline maps

· Markers

**Activity** Have groups of students create outline maps of the progression of Hitler's European conquests. Students should identify countries that fell, using arrows to indicate the sequence. Have them add a chart below the map naming the country, the date on which it fell, Hitler's military strategy, and any geographically significant issues. Students also should discuss the geographic difficulties posed by the United Kingdom and the USS to Hitler's military strategy.

# CHAPTER 16 CORRELATION

## CORRELATION TO THE TEXAS ESSENTIAL KNOWLEDGE AND SKILLS

Chapter 16 addresses the following standards of the Texas Essential Knowledge and Skills for U.S. History.

| TEKS | Instruction | Student Question/Activity |
|---|---|---|
| **(6A)** Identify reasons for U.S. involvement in World War II, including the growth of dictatorships and the attack on Pearl Harbor. | **PE 528–533; 554–557**—examination of events the led the United States into World War II, including the rise of dictatorships around the world and the attack on Pearl Harbor | **PE 557**—Critical Thinking questions about the attack on Pearl Harbor |
| **(6B)** Analyze major events of World War II, including the Holocaust. | **PE 542–549**—examination of the Holocaust | **PE 549**—Critical Thinking questions and writing activity about the Holocaust |
| **(9A)** Analyze the effects of physical geographic factors on major events. | **PE 528–533; 536–538**—discussion of the rise of dictatorships around the world and their desire to conquer neighboring lands | **PE 535**—writing activity focusing on the ambitions of the world's dictators |
| **(10B)** Analyze the effects of changing demographic patterns resulting from immigration to the United States. | **PE 543–544**—discussion of the immigration of Jews to the United States as a result of the Holocaust | **PE 549**—Critical Thinking question about the U.S. response to Jewish immigration |
| **(19B)** Evaluate the contributions of significant political leaders such as Franklin D. Roosevelt. | **PE 550–557**—Examination of Roosevelt's efforts to help the Allies and eventually move America into the war | **TE 551**—activity asking students to analyze the causes of Roosevelt's various policy decisions |
| **(24A)** Use primary sources to acquire information about the United States. | **PE 552**—Point/Counterpoint debate about U.S. neutrality drawing on quotes from contemporary figures | **PE 552**—questions that require students to accurately analyze each side of the debate |
| **(24H)** Use appropriate mathematical skills to interpret social studies information such as graphs. | **PE 545**—chart showing the death estimates of various ethnic groups during the Holocaust | **PE 545**—question about the chart that requires students to use mathematical skills |

## TAKS MINI-LESSONS

1. **Social Studies Skills: Objective 1 (US6.A):** Identify reasons for U.S. involvement in World War II, including the attack on Pearl Harbor **Activity** Have students complete the TE research activity regarding America's reaction to the attack on Pearl Harbor on TE page 555.

2. **Social Studies Skills: Objective 1 (US6.B):** Analyze major issues and events of World War II, such as the Holocaust **Activity** Have students create a cause-and-effect chart of the Holocaust.

3. **Social Studies Skills: Objective 3 (US14.A):** Describe the economic effects of World War II on the home front, including the end of the Great Depression **Activity** Have students answer the Economic Background question on TE page 557.

4. **English Language Arts Skills: Objective 1 (8.B):** Read in varied sources such as speeches **Activity** Have students analyze the excerpt from Franklin Roosevelt's radio speech on page 550.

5. **English Language Arts Skills: Objective 2 (11.F):** Understand literary forms and terms in selections being read **Activity** Have students discuss the literary forms, such as metaphors and analogies, used in Elie Wiesel's Personal Voice on page 549.

# CHAPTER 16

# WORLD WAR LOOMS

Flanked by storm troopers, Adolf Hitler arrives at a Nazi rally in September 1934.

## HISTORY from VISUALS

### Interpreting the Photograph

Ask students to examine the photograph and describe what is happening. Specifically, ask students the following questions:

· What do the swastikas and other Nazi paraphernalia mean to you?

· What do the details of the photo tell you about Hitler and the Nazis?

*(The swastikas suggest a sense of menace in the Nazi military pageantry. Students should also note the reverential look on the mustachioed officer's face as he looks up at Hitler from the left.)*

## Time Line Discussion

Explain to students that the time line covers key U.S. and world events from 1931–1941.

· Ask students what year Japan conquered Manchuria. *(1931)*

· Ask students which two leaders came to power in 1933. *(Hitler and Roosevelt, who was elected in 1932 and took office in 1933)*

· Ask students to generalize about what the events on the time line reveal about world affairs in the 1930s. *(Widespread political unrest)*

**USA WORLD**

**1931** The Empire State Building opens in New York City.

**1932** Franklin Delano Roosevelt is elected president.

**1933** Prohibition ends.

**1936** Jesse Owens wins four gold medals at Olympics in Berlin, Germany.

**1936** Roosevelt is reelected.

**1931** · **1933** · **1935**

**1931** Japan conquers Manchuria, in northern China.

**1933** Adolf Hitler is appointed German chancellor and sets up Dachau concentration camp.

**1934** Stalin begins great purge in USSR.

**1934** Chinese communists flee in the Long March.

**1936** Ethiopia's Halle Selassie asks League of Nations for help against Italian invasion.

**1936** General Francisco Franco leads a fascist rebellion in Spain.

**526**  CHAPTER 16

---

## THEMES IN CHAPTER 16

### AMERICA IN WORLD AFFAIRS

In the 1930s, the United States was very divided about its role in world affairs. Some people said the United States needed to function as a leader; others thought it should remain isolationist.

**See Teacher's Edition note, p. 534.**

### IMMIGRATION AND MIGRATION

During the 1930s, thousands of refugees from Nazi Germany and other totalitarian regimes came to the United States as immigrants. Their numbers, however, were limited by quotas imposed by the Immigration Act of 1924.

**See Teacher's Edition note, p. 543.**

### VOTING RIGHTS

Franklin D. Roosevelt's election to a third term in 1940 broke the unwritten rule that had limited previous presidents to a maximum of two terms. This led eventually to the 22nd Amendment, which imposed a constitutional limit of two terms for presidents.

**See Teacher's Edition note, p. 551.**

# INTERACT
## WITH HISTORY

In the summer of 1939, President Franklin Roosevelt addresses an anxious nation in response to atrocities in Europe committed by Hitler's Nazi Germany. Roosevelt declares in his broadcast that the United States "will remain a neutral nation." He acknowledges, however, that he "cannot ask that every American remain neutral in thought."

## Why might the United States try to remain neutral?

### Examine the Issues

- How might involvement in a large scale war influence the United States?
- How can neutral countries participate in the affairs of warring countries?

**RESEARCH LINKS** CLASSZONE.COM

Visit the Chapter 16 links for more information related to World War Looms.

# INTERACT
## WITH HISTORY

## Objectives

- To examine the conflict over strategic interests
- To explore the complexities of a policy of neutrality in wartime

### Examine the Issues

1. Ask students to consider what possible interests a country might have in avoiding a war fought by its friends and/or neighbors. How would geography influence such a decision?
2. Explore with students the option of providing arms and training while remaining technically neutral.

**1937** Amelia Earhart mysteriously disappears attempting solo round-the-world flight.

**1938** Orson Welles broadcasts *The War of the Worlds*, a fictional alien invasion.

**1940** Roosevelt is elected to a third term.

**1941** United States enters World War II.

**1937**

**1939**

**1941**

**1938** *Kristallnacht*— Nazis riot, destroying Jewish neighborhoods.

**1939** Germany invades Poland. Britain and France declare war.

**1941** Japan bombs Pearl Harbor.

*Evening Standard*

GERMANS INVADE AND BOMB POLAND
BRITAIN MOBILISES

*World War Looms* **527**

## RECOMMENDED RESOURCES

### BOOKS FOR THE TEACHER

Churchill, Winston. *The Gathering Storm.* Boston: Houghton Mifflin, 1986.

Dawidowicz, Lucy S. *The War Against the Jews, 1933–1945.* New York: Bantam Books, 1986.

Shirer, William. *The Rise and Fall of the Third Reich.* New York: Simon & Schuster, 1990.

### BOOKS FOR THE STUDENT

Time-Life Books. *World War II.* Englewood Cliffs, NJ: Prentice Hall, 1989.

Wiesel, Elie. *Night.* New York: Bantam, 1982. Survivor's moving account of Holocaust.

### VIDEOS

*Hitler: The Whole Story.* Dir. Christian Herrendoerfer. Discovery Communications, 1989.

*Shoah.* Dir. Claude Lanzmann. Aleph/Historia, 1985.

### SOFTWARE

*American Chronicle Series: Seeds of Discord (1936–39), Prelude to War (1935–1939), Finest Hour (1939–1941).* CD-ROM. AIMS Multimedia, 800-367-2467.

### INTEGRATED TECHNOLOGY

For teacher support, visit . . .

 classzone.com

# Dictators Threaten World Peace

| MAIN IDEA | WHY IT MATTERS NOW | Terms & Names |
|---|---|---|
| The rise of rulers with total power in Europe and Asia led to World War II. | Dictators of the 1930s and 1940s changed the course of history, making world leaders especially watchful for the actions of dictators today. | • Joseph Stalin • totalitarian • Benito Mussolini • fascism    • Adolf Hitler • Nazism • Francisco Franco • Neutrality Acts |

TEKS U.S. History 6A, 6C, 8A, 8B, 9A, 9B, 16A, 19A, 19B, 24B, 24C, 24D, 24F, 24H, 25A, 25B, 25C, 25D

### One American's Story

Martha Gellhorn arrived in Madrid in 1937 to cover the brutal civil war that had broken out in Spain the year before. Hired as a special correspondent for *Collier's Weekly*, she had come with very little money and no special protection. On assignment there, she met the writer Ernest Hemingway, whom she later married. To Gellhorn, a young American writer, the Spanish Civil War was a deadly struggle between tyranny and democracy. For the people of Madrid, it was also a daily struggle for survival.

**A PERSONAL VOICE** MARTHA GELLHORN

" You would be walking down a street, hearing only the city noises of streetcars and automobiles and people calling to one another, and suddenly, crushing it all out, would be the huge stony deep booming of a falling shell, at the corner. There was no place to run, because how did you know that the next shell would not be behind you, or ahead, or to the left or right? "

—*The Face of War*

Martha Gellhorn, one of the first women war correspondents, began her career during the Spanish Civil War.

Less than two decades after the end of World War I—"the war to end all wars"—fighting erupted again in Europe and in Asia. As Americans read about distant battles, they hoped the conflicts would remain on the other side of the world.

## **1** Nationalism Grips Europe and Asia

The seeds of new conflicts had been sown in World War I. For many nations, peace had brought not prosperity but revolution fueled by economic depression and struggle. The postwar years also brought the rise of powerful dictators driven by the belief in nationalism—loyalty to one's country above all else—and dreams of territorial expansion.

**528** CHAPTER 16

◀ Germany was expected to pay off huge debts while dealing with widespread poverty. By 1923, an inflating economy made a five-million German mark worth less than a penny. Here children build blocks with stacks of useless German marks.

## HISTORY from VISUALS

### Interpreting the Photograph
Tell students that Germany experienced hyperinflation in 1923. The economic demand of reparations payments, required by the Treaty of Versailles, was the prime cause of inflation. Ask students how they think Germans felt about their government and the Treaty of Versailles during that time. *(Germans felt betrayed by their government and angry with the victorious Allies for waging economic war on their country.)*

**FAILURES OF THE WORLD WAR I PEACE SETTLEMENT** Instead of securing a "just and secure peace," the Treaty of Versailles caused anger and resentment. Germans saw nothing fair in a treaty that blamed them for starting the war. Nor did they find security in a settlement that stripped them of their overseas colonies and border territories. These problems overwhelmed the Weimar Republic, the democratic government set up in Germany after World War I. Similarly, the Soviets resented the carving up of parts of Russia. (See map, Chapter 11, p. 400.)

The peace settlement had not fulfilled President Wilson's hope of a world "safe for democracy." New democratic governments that emerged in Europe after the war floundered. Without a democratic tradition, people turned to authoritarian leaders to solve their economic and social problems. The new democracies collapsed, and dictators were able to seize power. Some had great ambitions. **A**

**JOSEPH STALIN TRANSFORMS THE SOVIET UNION** In Russia, hopes for democracy gave way to civil war, resulting in the establishment of a communist state, officially called the Soviet Union, in 1922. After V. I. Lenin died in 1924, **Joseph Stalin,** whose last name means "man of steel," took control of the country. Stalin focused on creating a model communist state. In so doing, he made both agricultural and industrial growth the prime economic goals of the Soviet Union. Stalin abolished all privately owned farms and replaced them with collectives—large government-owned farms, each worked by hundreds of families.

Stalin moved to transform the Soviet Union from a backward rural nation into a great industrial power. In 1928, the Soviet dictator outlined the first of several "five-year plans," to direct the industrialization. All economic activity was placed under state management. By 1937, the Soviet Union had become the world's second-largest industrial power, surpassed in overall production only by the United States. The human costs of this transformation, however, were enormous.

In his drive to purge, or eliminate, anyone who threatened his power, Stalin did not spare even his most faithful supporters. While the final toll will never be known, historians estimate that Stalin was responsible for the deaths of 8 million to 13 million people. Millions more died in famines caused by the restructuring of Soviet society.

By 1939, Stalin had firmly established a **totalitarian** government that maintained complete control over its citizens. In a totalitarian state, individuals have no rights, and the government suppresses all opposition. **B**

### MAIN IDEA

**Identifying Problems**
**A** Why did the new democracies set up after World War I fail?

*A. Answer*
A lack of democratic tradition, failure of the Treaty of Versailles and economic devastation.

*B. Answer*
Complete control over citizens and ruthless suppression of opposition.

### MAIN IDEA

**Summarizing**
**B** What are the characteristics of a totalitarian state?

## More About . . .

### Stalin's Show Trials
In 1936, 1937, and on into 1938, Stalin eliminated challenges to his rule by attacking his closest allies and leaders of the revolution. The world watched the accused plead guilty to the state's outlandish charges of treason and counter-revolution, knowing full well that such confession would result in their execution. The show trials made a big impact on American Communists and sympathizers. Many saw the potential totalitarian underpinnings of Communism and deserted the movement.

*World War Looms* **529**

---

**DIFFERENTIATING INSTRUCTION** | **LESS PROFICIENT READERS**

### Organizing Information

As students read pages 528–533, have them use the following chart to organize information about Russia, Italy, Germany, and Japan. Tell students to record the name of each country's leader and at least two actions taken.

| | Russia | Italy | Germany | Japan |
|---|---|---|---|---|
| Type of Government | | | | |
| Leader | | | | |
| Actions Taken | | | | |

 Integrated Assessment
· Rubric 2

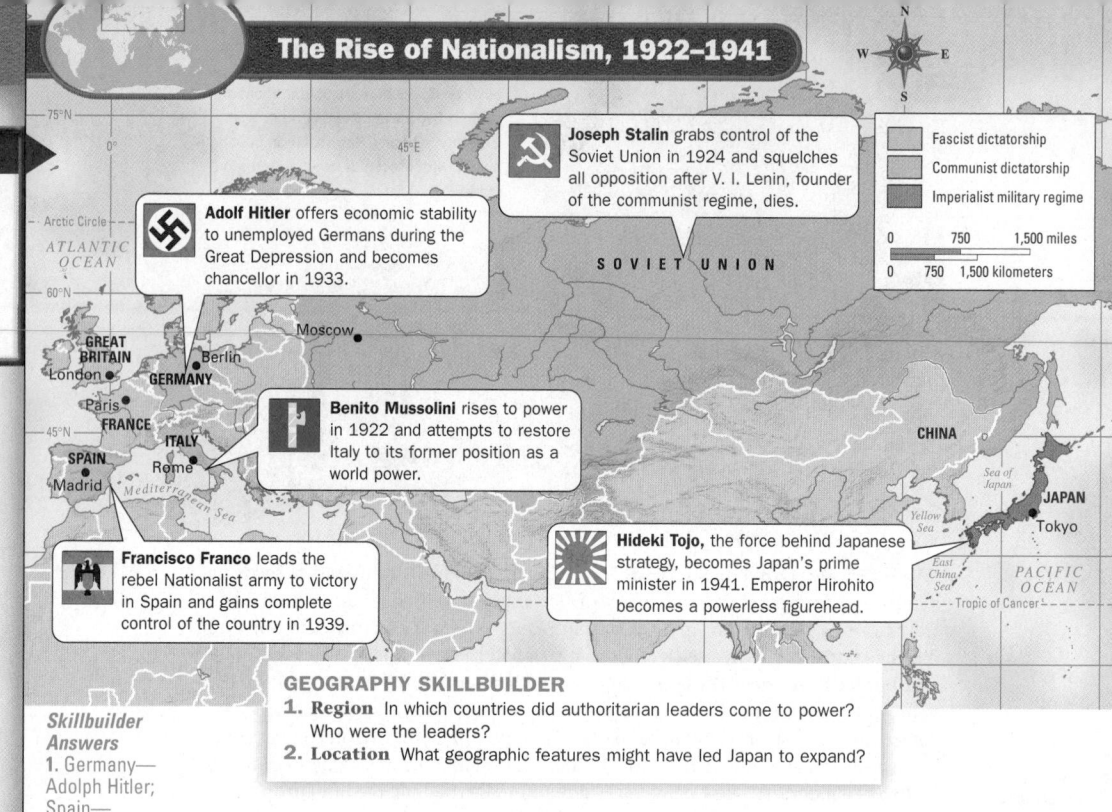

## The Rise of Nationalism, 1922–1941

**Joseph Stalin** grabs control of the Soviet Union in 1924 and squelches all opposition after V. I. Lenin, founder of the communist regime, dies.

**Adolf Hitler** offers economic stability to unemployed Germans during the Great Depression and becomes chancellor in 1933.

**Benito Mussolini** rises to power in 1922 and attempts to restore Italy to its former position as a world power.

**Francisco Franco** leads the rebel Nationalist army to victory in Spain and gains complete control of the country in 1939.

**Hideki Tojo,** the force behind Japanese strategy, becomes Japan's prime minister in 1941. Emperor Hirohito becomes a powerless figurehead.

- Fascist dictatorship
- Communist dictatorship
- Imperialist military regime

0    750    1,500 miles
0    750    1,500 kilometers

### GEOGRAPHY SKILLBUILDER
1. **Region** In which countries did authoritarian leaders come to power? Who were the leaders?
2. **Location** What geographic features might have led Japan to expand?

## HISTORY from VISUALS

### Interpreting a Map
Ask students to use the map to determine why democratic France might have felt threatened. *(It had authoritarian states on three of its borders: Germany, Italy, and Spain.)*

**Skillbuilder Answers**
1. Germany—Adolph Hitler; Spain—Francisco Franco; Italy—Benito Mussolini; Soviet Union—Joseph Stalin; Japan—Hideki Tojo.
2. Its status as island nation.

## More About . . .

### Benito Mussolini
Mussolini started his political career as a socialist rising through the ranks to become editor of the Socialist Party's newspaper, *Avanti!* Mussolini broke with his party over the issue of World War I. The Socialists opposed it. Mussolini, a nationalist at heart, favored it. In ideological terms, this offers some explanation for Mussolini's change in politics. One of the characteristics of Fascism is extreme patriotism.

**THE RISE OF FASCISM IN ITALY** While Stalin was consolidating his power in the Soviet Union, **Benito Mussolini** was establishing a totalitarian regime in Italy, where unemployment and inflation produced bitter strikes, some communist-led. Alarmed by these threats, the middle and upper classes demanded stronger leadership. Mussolini took advantage of this situation. A powerful speaker, Mussolini knew how to appeal to Italy's wounded national pride. He played on the fears of economic collapse and communism. In this way, he won the support of many discontented Italians.

> *" Italy wants peace, work, and calm. I will give these things with love if possible, with force if necessary."*
> **BENITO MUSSOLINI**

By 1921, Mussolini had established the Fascist Party. **Fascism** (făsh´ĭz´əm) stressed nationalism and placed the interests of the state above those of individuals. To strengthen the nation, Fascists argued, power must rest with a single strong leader and a small group of devoted party members. (The Latin *fasces*—a bundle of rods tied around an ax handle—had been a symbol of unity and authority in ancient Rome.)

In October 1922, Mussolini marched on Rome with thousands of his followers, whose black uniforms gave them the name "Black Shirts." When important government officials, the army, and the police sided with the Fascists, the Italian king appointed Mussolini head of the government.

Calling himself *Il Duce*, or "the leader," Mussolini gradually extended Fascist control to every aspect of Italian life. Tourists marveled that *Il Duce* had even "made the trains run on time." Mussolini achieved this efficiency, however, by crushing all opposition and by making Italy a totalitarian state. **C**

**C. Answer** Italians pride was hurt, rising inflation, unemployment, and social unrest.

**MAIN IDEA**

**Analyzing Causes**
**C** What factors led to the rise of Fascism in Italy?

---

**DIFFERENTIATING INSTRUCTION** | **STUDENTS ACQUIRING ENGLISH**

### Previewing Foreign Terms
Help students preview foreign terms they will encounter in the text, including those listed at right. First explain the meaning of the word. Then have them pronounce the term after you. Finally, have them find the sentence in the text where the term is used.

*Il Duce:* Italian for "leader," or "chief"

*Führer:* German for "leader" or "guide"

*Mein Kampf:* German for "my struggle" and the title of a book written by Adolf Hitler

*Nazi:* a shortened form of the German word for Nationalsozialist, or National Socialist

*Lebensraum:* German for "living space," or space for a growing population

*Reich:* German for *empire*

## The Faces of Totalitarianism

| Fascist Italy | Nazi Germany | Communist Soviet Union |
|---|---|---|
| • Extreme nationalism<br>• Militaristic expansionism<br>• Charismatic leader<br>• Private property with strong government controls<br>• Anticommunist | • Extreme nationalism and racism<br>• Militaristic expansionism<br>• Forceful leader<br>• Private property with strong government controls<br>• Anticommunist | • Create a sound communist state and wait for world revolution<br>• Revolution by workers<br>• Eventual rule by working class<br>• State ownership of property |

▲ Left to right:
Benito Mussolini,
Adolf Hitler,
Joseph Stalin

**THE NAZIS TAKE OVER GERMANY** In Germany, **Adolf Hitler** had followed a path to power similar to Mussolini's. At the end of World War I, Hitler had been a jobless soldier drifting around Germany. In 1919, he joined a struggling group called the National Socialist German Workers' Party, better known as the Nazi Party. Despite its name, this party had no ties to socialism.

Hitler proved to be such a powerful public speaker and organizer that he quickly became the party's leader. Calling himself *Der Führer*—"the Leader"—he promised to bring Germany out of chaos.

In his book *Mein Kampf* [My Struggle], Hitler set forth the basic beliefs of Nazism that became the plan of action for the Nazi Party. **Nazism** (nät′sĭz′əm), the German brand of fascism, was based on extreme nationalism. Hitler, who had been born in Austria, dreamed of uniting all German-speaking people in a great German empire.

Hitler also wanted to enforce racial "purification" at home. In his view, Germans—especially blue-eyed, blond-haired "Aryans"—formed a "master race" that was destined to rule the world. "Inferior races," such as Jews, Slavs, and all nonwhites, were deemed fit only to serve the Aryans.

A third element of Nazism was national expansion. Hitler believed that for Germany to thrive, it needed more *lebensraum*, or living space. One of the Nazis' aims, as Hitler wrote in *Mein Kampf*, was "to secure for the German people the land and soil to which they are entitled on this earth," even if this could be accomplished only by "the might of a victorious sword."  **D**

The Great Depression helped the Nazis come to power. Because of war debts and dependence on American loans and investments, Germany's economy was hit hard. By 1932, some 6 million Germans were unemployed. Many men who were out of work joined Hitler's private army, the *storm troopers* (or *Brown Shirts*). The German people were desperate and turned to Hitler as their last hope.

By mid 1932, the Nazis had become the strongest political party in Germany. In January 1933, Hitler was appointed chancellor (prime minister). Once in power, Hitler quickly dismantled Germany's democratic Weimar Republic. In its place he established the *Third Reich*, or Third German Empire. According to Hitler, the Third Reich would be a "Thousand-Year Reich"—it would last for a thousand years.

**D. Answer**
To reunite all Germans; Germans were a master race; other "races" were inferior; Germany needed more living space.

**MAIN IDEA**

**Summarizing**
**D** What were the key ideas and goals that Hitler presented in *Mein Kampf*?

**Background**
According to Hitler there were three German empires: the Holy Roman Empire; The German Empire of 1871–1918; and The Third Reich.

### More About . . .

#### The Election of Adolf Hitler
It is sometimes overlooked that Hitler was elected in a democratic election. It was the last such election of the Weimar Republic that governed Germany after World War I. Hitler and the Nazis accused the ruling Social Democrats of betraying Germany by signing the Treaty of Versailles, which resulted in the economic collapse. The election was marked by political infighting. Moderate and right wing party members made a disastrous mistake. They decided that Hitler was somebody they could "work with" and, thus, was preferable to the moderate left Social Democrats.

🖳 Humanities Transparencies HT23
· German Nazi Party poster

*World War Looms* **531**

---

**DIFFERENTIATING INSTRUCTION**   **GIFTED AND TALENTED**   ⓘ **classzone.com**

### Roosevelt and Hitler

Tell students that Roosevelt and Hitler both came to power in the same year, 1933. Both faced economic crisis. Ask students to use text, reference, and Internet resources to research the political and economic situations in Germany and the United States at that time. Have them create a chart or diagram that compares the economic situations and contrasts the political course that each leader took. Some students might use a web diagram similar to the one shown at right.

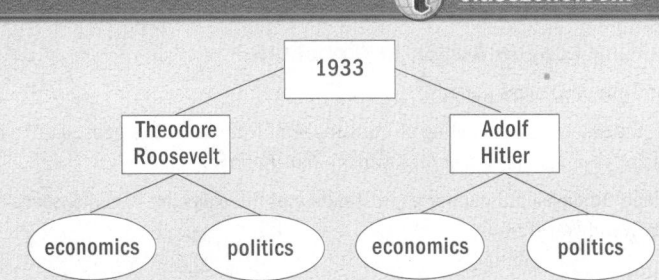

📝 Integrated Assessment
· Rubric 2

# HISTORY from VISUALS

## Interpreting the Map

Ask students to use the maps to answer the following question: Why would a strong navy and shipping fleet have been important for both Italy and Japan? *(They needed to send soldiers and supplies by ship to their invasion targets.)*

**Extension** Ask students to speculate about the effects the actions of Italy and Japan might have had on the United States. *(The locations of the countries and those they invaded were far away. It might not have directly affected the United States.)*

## More About . . .

### The League of Nations

The fatal flaw of the League of Nations was that it had no ability to enforce its edicts. By insisting on unanimity for action, it gave each country an effective veto over League judgments. By invading Manchuria, Japan was taking a calculated risk that there would be few repercussions from its aggression. Japanese leaders were proven right as Western nations rationalized that the fate of Manchuria had little strategic impact on their security. Unfortunately, Hitler and Mussolini were observing closely.

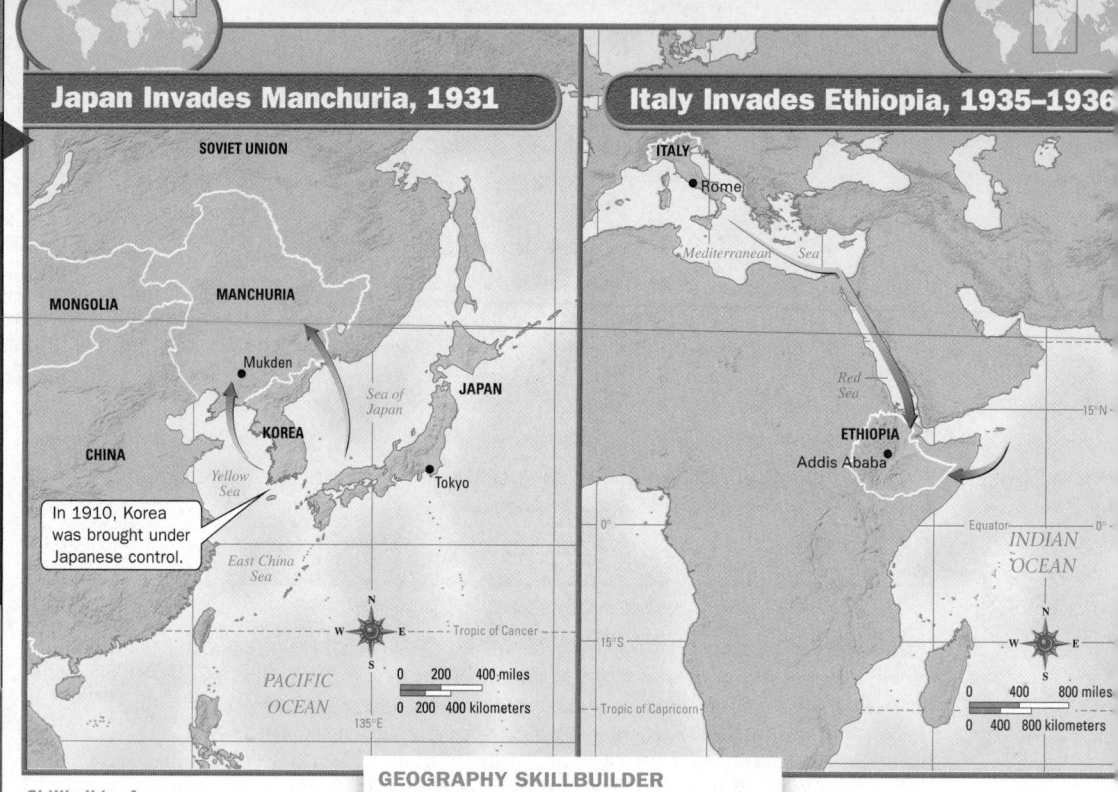

**Japan Invades Manchuria, 1931**

In 1910, Korea was brought under Japanese control.

**Italy Invades Ethiopia, 1935–1936**

*Skillbuilder Answers*
1. Italy, Germany, Japan
2. They were both small nations that invaded larger countries.

**GEOGRAPHY SKILLBUILDER**
1. **Location** What countries were aggressors during this period?
2. **Movement** Notice the size and location of Italy and of Japan with respect to the country each invaded. What similarities do you see?

**MILITARISTS GAIN CONTROL IN JAPAN** Halfway around the world, nationalistic military leaders were trying to take control of the imperial government of Japan. These leaders shared in common with Hitler a belief in the need for more living space for a growing population. Ignoring the protests of more moderate Japanese officials, the militarists launched a surprise attack and seized control of the Chinese province of Manchuria in 1931. Within several months, Japanese troops controlled the entire province, a large region about twice the size of Texas, that was rich in natural resources. **E**

The watchful League of Nations had been established after World War I to prevent just such aggressive acts. In this greatest test of the League's power, representatives were sent to Manchuria to investigate the situation. Their report condemned Japan, who in turn simply quit the League. Meanwhile, the success of the Manchurian invasion put the militarists firmly in control of Japan's government.

**AGGRESSION IN EUROPE AND AFRICA** The failure of the League of Nations to take action against Japan did not escape the notice of Europe's dictators. In 1933, Hitler pulled Germany out of the League. In 1935, he began a military buildup in violation of the Treaty of Versailles. A year later, he sent troops into the Rhineland, a German region bordering France and Belgium that was demilitarized as a result of the Treaty of Versailles. The League did nothing to stop Hitler.

*E. Answer* To gain "living space" and resources for people.

**MAIN IDEA**

**Analyzing Motives**
**E** Why did Japan invade Manchuria?

**Background**
Military government had centuries-old roots in Japan. The shogun lords of the Middle Ages had been military leaders.

**532** CHAPTER 16

---

**ACTIVITY** **COOPERATIVE LEARNING**

**BLOCK SCHEDULING**

## Debating League Action in Manchuria

**Class Time** Two class periods

**Task** Staging a policy meeting of the League of Nations on the question of what action to take against Japan for invading Manchuria

**Purpose** To develop a deeper understanding of the collective security issues that led to World War II

**Directions** Assign groups of students to be League of Nations delegates from the following nations: Great Britain, France, Italy, and Germany. The League of Nations will be meeting because Japan has resigned from the League. Have one student play the role of League Chairman. The issue is what action, if any, should be taken against Japan.

 Integrated Assessment
· Rubric 3

Meanwhile, Mussolini began building his new Roman Empire. His first target was Ethiopia, one of Africa's few remaining independent countries. By the fall of 1935, tens of thousands of Italian soldiers stood ready to advance on Ethiopia. The League of Nations reacted with brave talk of "collective resistance to all acts of unprovoked aggression."

When the invasion began, however, the League's response was an ineffective economic boycott—little more than a slap on Italy's wrist. By June 1936, Ethiopia had fallen. In desperation, Haile Selassie, the ousted Ethiopian emperor, appealed to the League for assistance. Nothing was done. "It is us today," he told them. "It will be you tomorrow."

**CIVIL WAR BREAKS OUT IN SPAIN** In 1936, a group of Spanish army officers led by General **Francisco Franco**, rebelled against the Spanish republic. Revolts broke out all over Spain, and the Spanish Civil War began. The war aroused passions not only in Spain but throughout the world. About 3,000 Americans formed the Abraham Lincoln Battalion and traveled to Spain to fight against Franco. "We knew, we just knew," recalled Martha Gellhorn, "that Spain was the place to stop fascism." Among the volunteers were African Americans still bitter about Mussolini's invasion of Ethiopia the year before.

Such limited aid was not sufficient to stop the spread of fascism, however. The Western democracies remained neutral. Although the Soviet Union sent equipment and advisers, Hitler and Mussolini backed Franco's forces with troops, weapons, tanks, and fighter planes. The war forged a close relationship between the German and Italian dictators, who signed a formal alliance known as the Rome-Berlin Axis. After a loss of almost 500,000 lives, Franco's victory in 1939 established him as Spain's fascist dictator. Once again a totalitarian government ruled in Europe. **F**

---

**MAIN IDEA**

**Summarizing**
**F** What foreign countries were involved in the Spanish Civil War?

**F. Answer**
Germany and Italy on the side of Franco; the Soviet Union in support of the Spanish government.

---

**HISTORICAL SPOTLIGHT**

**AFRICAN AMERICANS STAND BY ETHIOPIANS**

When Mussolini invaded Ethiopia, many Europeans and Americans—especially African Americans—were outraged. Almost overnight, African Americans organized to raise money for medical supplies, and a few went to fight in Ethiopia. Years later, the Ethiopian emperor Haile Selassie (shown above) said of these efforts,

"We can never forget the help Ethiopia received from Negro Americans during the terrible crisis. . . . It moved me to know that Americans of African descent did not abandon their embattled brothers, but stood by us."

---

**HISTORICAL SPOTLIGHT**

**African Americans Stand By Ethiopians**
In 1935, Ethiopia was one of Africa's few remaining independent nations. For many African Americans, Mussolini's invasion of Ethiopia symbolized another in a long line of historical atrocities committed against people of African descent. Ask students why they think African Americans supported Ethiopia. (*African Americans were aware and proud of Ethiopia's independence. The nation's independent status was especially significant because the majority of the African continent was still under European rule.*)

---

**More About . . .**

**Spanish Civil War**
Western democracies were guilty of looking the other way during the Spanish Civil War. The war was an insurrection against a legally constituted democratic, but left-leaning, government. The combination of the left-leaning Spanish republic and active support from the Soviet Union prompted Western democracies to maintain a neutral stance. Italy and Germany poured weapons and other assistance into Spain. The two countries used the Spanish Civil War as a testing ground for new weapons and tactics. The experience they gained would be put to good use in the first years of World War II.

---

◀ A French journalist escapes from Spain to France with a child he rescued from a street battle. Fighting would soon engulf not only France, but the rest of Europe and parts of Asia.

*World War Looms* **533**

---

**DIFFERENTIATING INSTRUCTION** | **LESS PROFICIENT READERS**

**Supporting Details**

Have students outline pages 532–533. Tell them to use the bold headings as roman numerals and find at least two supporting details for each heading to include in their outline. Have students compare outlines and discuss what they have learned about Japanese and Italian aggression and the Spanish Civil War. A basic outline form such as the one at right can be put on the board for students who need help getting started.

I. Militarists Gain Control in Japan
  A.
  B.
II. Aggression in Europe and Africa
  A.
  B.

III. Civil War Breaks Out in Spain
  A.
  B.

534 CHAPTER 16

## Instruct: Objective 2

### The United States Responds Cautiously

TAKS SS11 1(US6.A)

· What type of foreign policy did the United States adopt after World War I?

· What laws did Congress pass regarding foreign policy?

· Why did many Americans have difficulty with a policy of neutrality?

 **In-Depth Resources: Unit 5**
· Guided Reading, p. 1
· Primary Source: Roosevelt's Quarantine Speech, p. 13

## Tracing Themes

### AMERICA IN WORLD AFFAIRS

FDR's battle with the isolationists touches on a theme in American foreign policy that stretches back to George Washington's warning to avoid "entangling alliances." Many Americans had irrational fears of immigrants, Catholics, Jews, and all things foreign. Charles Lindbergh was a leading supporter of America First Committee, the vocal isolationist organization. Roosevelt, as an internationalist, had to maneuver carefully around the isolationists.

## Analyzing *Political Cartoons*

### SKILLBUILDER ANSWERS

1. Many Americans wanted to avoid being involved in Europe's problems.
2. isolationism
3. Americans were becoming aware that the Atlantic was not the protective buffer from foreign problems that they had once believed it to be.

---

## 2 The United States Responds Cautiously

Most Americans were alarmed by the international conflicts of the mid thirties but believed that the United States should not get involved. In 1928, the United States had signed the Kellogg-Briand Pact. The treaty was signed by 62 countries and declared war would not be used "as an instrument of national policy." Yet it did not include a plan to deal with countries that broke their pledge. The Pact was, therefore, only a small step toward peace.

**AMERICANS CLING TO ISOLATIONISM** In the early 1930s, a flood of books argued that the United States had been dragged into World War I by greedy bankers and arms dealers. Public outrage led to the creation of a congressional committee, chaired by North Dakota Senator Gerald Nye, that held hearings on these charges. The Nye committee fueled the controversy by documenting the large profits that banks and manufacturers made during the war. As the furor grew over these "merchants of death," Americans became more determined than ever to avoid war. Antiwar feeling was so strong that the Girl Scouts of America changed the color of its uniforms from khaki to green to appear less militaristic. **G**

Americans' growing isolationism eventually had an impact on President Roosevelt's foreign policy. When he had first taken office in 1933, Roosevelt felt comfortable reaching out to the world in several ways. He officially recognized the Soviet Union in 1933 and agreed to exchange ambassadors with Moscow. He continued the policy of nonintervention in Latin America—begun by Presidents Coolidge and Hoover—with his Good Neighbor Policy and withdrew armed forces stationed there. In 1934, Roosevelt pushed the Reciprocal Trade Agreement Act through Congress. This act lowered trade barriers by giving the president the power to make trade agreements with other nations and was aimed at reducing

**G. Answer** Evidence that large profits had been made by banks and arms industries during World War I; regret over having been involved in that war; hatred of militarism.

**MAIN IDEA**

**Analyzing Causes**
**G** What factors contributed to Americans' growing isolationism?

---

## Analyzing *Political Cartoons*

### "IT AIN'T WHAT IT USED TO BE"

During the late 1930s, Americans were divided about becoming involved in "Europe's quarrels." Some people felt that the United States should be more involved in the economic and political problems occurring across the Atlantic. Isolationists—people who believed the United States should stay completely out of other nations' affairs except in the defense of the United States—strictly opposed intervening. The idea that America and Europe were two separate worlds divided by an ocean that could guarantee safety was quickly eroding.

### SKILLBUILDER

**Analyzing Political Cartoons**
1. What does Uncle Sam's turning his back on Europe show about American attitudes in the late 1930s?
2. What U.S. policy does the cartoon imply?
3. Why might the Atlantic Ocean have appeared to shrink in the late 1930s?

 **SEE SKILLBUILDER HANDBOOK, PAGE R24.**

---

 **ACTIVITY** **COOPERATIVE LEARNING**                    **BLOCK SCHEDULING**

### Writing a Newspaper Editorial

**Class Time** One class period

**Task** Writing an editorial about President Roosevelt's foreign policy

**Purpose** To help students appreciate the difficulty Roosevelt faced in trying to promote world peace

**Directions** Divide the class into small groups. Tell each group that they are the editorial board of a newspaper. They have been assigned the job of writing editorials regarding President Roosevelt's foreign policy. Assign pro and con positions and have students research and write editorials. Have each group read the finished editorial to the class. Interested students can gather the editorials to post in the classroom, or use page-layout software to create a facsimile editorial page.

tariffs by as much as 50 percent. In an effort to keep the United States out of future wars, beginning in 1935, Congress passed a series of **Neutrality Acts**. The first two acts outlawed arms sales or loans to nations at war. The third act was passed in response to the fighting in Spain. This act extended the ban on arms sales and loans to nations engaged in civil wars.

**NEUTRALITY BREAKS DOWN** Despite congressional efforts to legislate neutrality, Roosevelt found it impossible to remain neutral. When Japan launched a new attack on China in July 1937, Roosevelt found a way around the Neutrality Acts. Because Japan had not formally declared war against China, the president claimed there was no need to enforce the Neutrality Acts. The United States continued sending arms and supplies to China. A few months later, Roosevelt spoke out strongly against isolationism in a speech delivered in Chicago. He called on peace-loving nations to "quarantine," or isolate, aggressor nations in order to stop the spread of war.

**A PERSONAL VOICE** FRANLKIN DELANO ROOSEVELT

"The peace, the freedom, and the security of 90 percent of the population of the world is being jeopardized by the remaining 10 percent who are threatening a breakdown of all international order and law. Surely the 90 percent who want to live in peace under law and in accordance with moral standards that have received almost universal acceptance through the centuries, can and must find some way . . . to preserve peace."

—"Quarantine Speech," October 5, 1937

At last Roosevelt seemed ready to take a stand against aggression—that is, until isolationist newspapers exploded in protest, accusing the president of leading the nation into war. Roosevelt backed off in the face of criticism, but his speech did begin to shift the debate. For the moment the conflicts remained "over there."

**More About . . .**

**Aggressor Nations**

In December 1937, two months after Roosevelt's Quarantine Speech, the *Panay* was attacked in China by Japanese planes. Two Americans were killed. Following an apology from Japan, FDR tried to take the offensive, but the isolationists resisted.

## Assess & Reteach

**SECTION 1 ASSESSMENT**

Have students work in groups of three to answer the questions. For question 2, have each student fill in the circle for a different dictator and discuss the question.

 Formal Assessment
· Section Quiz, p. 300

**SELF-ASSESSMENT**

Ask students to write a paragraph evaluating the neutrality position of the United States.

**RETEACH**

Have students work in pairs. They should use the diagram in question 2 to review the ambitions of the dictators discussed in this chapter.

 In-Depth Resources
· Reteaching Activity, p. 7

---

 **ASSESSMENT**

1. **TERMS & NAMES** For each term or name, write a sentence explaining its significance.

- •Joseph Stalin
- •totalitarian
- •Benito Mussolini
- •fascism
- •Adolf Hitler
- •Nazism
- •Francisco Franco
- •Neutrality Acts

**MAIN IDEA**

2. **TAKING NOTES**
Using a web diagram like the one below, fill it in with the main ambition of each dictator.

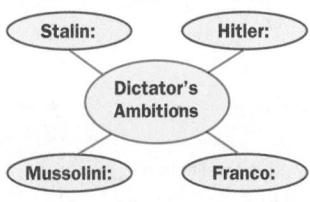

What ambitions did the dictators have in common?

**CRITICAL THINKING**

3. **ANALYZING CAUSES**
How did the Treaty of Versailles sow the seeds of instability in Europe?
**Think About:**
- effects of the treaty on Germany and the Soviet Union
- effects of the treaty on national pride
- the economic legacy of the war

4. **DRAWING CONCLUSIONS**
Why do you think Hitler found widespread support among the German people? Support your answer with details from the text.

5. **FORMING GENERALIZATIONS**
Would powerful nations or weak nations be more likely to follow an isolationist policy? Explain.

*World War Looms* **535**

---

Answers **ASSESSMENT**

**1. TERMS & NAMES**
Joseph Stalin, p. 529
totalitarian, p. 529
Benito Mussolini, p. 530
fascism, p. 530
Adolf Hitler, p. 531
Nazism, p. 531
Francisco Franco, p. 533
Neutrality Acts, p. 535

**2. TAKING NOTES**
**Stalin:** create a model Communist state and transform the Soviet Union into a great industrial power. **Mussolini:** make Italy a great world power. **Hitler:** unite the German "master race" into an empire destined to rule the world. **Franco:** become Spain's supreme military leader.

**3. ANALYZING CAUSES**
Germany and Russia's resentment of the treaty contributed to their renunciation of democratic values; the treaty did little to halt the rise of totalitarian governments.

**4. DRAWING CONCLUSIONS**
Germany was devastated by the effects of WWI. The nation suffered from severe economic depression. Hitler promoted the Nazi party as a way to restore national pride.

**5. FORMING GENERALIZATIONS**
Strong, self-sufficient nations can afford to adopt isolationist policies. Weaker nations are often too dependent on foreign powers.

## OBJECTIVES

**1** Explain Hitler's motives for expansion and how Britain and France responded.

**2** Describe the blitzkrieg tactics that Germany used against Poland.

**3** Summarize the first battles of World War II.

### SKILLBUILDERS

· Geography Skillbuilder:
region, location, p. 538

### CRITICAL THINKING

· Summarizing, p. 537
· Analyzing Motives, pp. 538, 540, 541
· Evaluating, p. 539
· Evaluating Decisions, p. 541
· Drawing Conclusions, p. 541

## Focus & Motivate

Ask students what they would do if someone demanded their money or coat. How would factors such as the size and strength of the opponent, place, and time influence their response?

## Instruct

### Instruct: Objective **1**

#### Austria and Czechoslovakia Fall

TAKS SS11 5(WG21.C)

· What foreign policy actions did Hitler take after he came to power?

· How did Britain and France respond to Germany's actions?

 In-Depth Resources: Unit 5
· Guided Reading, p. 2

# War in Europe

| MAIN IDEA | WHY IT MATTERS NOW | Terms & Names |
|---|---|---|
| Using the sudden mass attack called *blitzkrieg*, Germany invaded and quickly conquered many European countries. | Hitler's actions started World War II and still serve as a warning to be vigilant about totalitarian government. | • Neville Chamberlain • Winston Churchill • appeasement / • nonaggression pact • *blitzkrieg* • Charles de Gaulle |

 **TEKS** U.S. History 1B, 6B, 6C, 8A, 8B, 9A, 19A, 24B, 24C, 24D, 25A, 25B, 25C, 25D, 26B

### One American's Story

In 1940, CBS correspondent William Shirer stood in the forest near Compiègne, where 22 years earlier defeated German generals had signed the armistice ending World War I. Shirer was now waiting for Adolf Hitler to deliver his armistice terms to a defeated France. He watched as Hitler walked up to the monument and slowly read the inscription: "Here on the eleventh of November 1918 succumbed the criminal pride of the German empire . . . vanquished by the free peoples which it tried to enslave." Later that day, Shirer wrote a diary entry describing the führer's reaction.

**A PERSONAL VOICE** WILLIAM SHIRER

" I have seen that face many times at the great moments of his life. But today! It is afire with scorn, anger, hate, revenge, triumph. He steps off the monument and contrives to make even this gesture a masterpiece of contempt. . . . He glances slowly around the clearing, and now, as his eyes meet ours, you grasp the depth of his hatred. But there is triumph there too—revengeful, triumphant hate. "

—*Berlin Diary: The Journal of a Foreign Correspondent, 1934–1941*

▲ William Shirer, a journalist and historian, became well known for his radio broadcasts from Berlin at the beginning of World War II.

Again and again Shirer had heard Hitler proclaim that "Germany needs peace. . . . Germany wants peace." The hatred and vengefulness that drove the dictator's every action, however, drew Germany ever closer to war.

## **1** Austria and Czechoslovakia Fall

On November 5, 1937, Hitler met secretly with his top military advisers. He boldly declared that to grow and prosper Germany needed the land of its neighbors. His plan was to absorb Austria and Czechoslovakia into the Third Reich. When one of his advisors protested that annexing those countries could provoke war, Hitler replied, " 'The German Question' can be solved only by means of force, and this is never without risk."

**536** CHAPTER 16

---

## PROGRAM RESOURCES

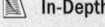 In-Depth Resources: Unit 3
· Guided Reading, p. 2
· Skillbuilder Practice: Developing Historical Perspective, p. 6
· Reteaching Activity, p. 8

 Reading Study Guide (English and Spanish), pp. 163–164

 Access for Students Acquiring English/ESL
· Guided Reading (Spanish), p. 181
· Skillbuilder Practice (Spanish), p. 184

 Formal Assessment
· Section Quiz, p. 301

Integrated Assessment
· Rubrics

### INTEGRATED TECHNOLOGY

 Geography Transp. GT24
· Aggression in Europe, 1936–1939

Electronic Library of Primary Sources

classzone.com

### TEXAS RESOURCES

 TAKS Spiraled Content Review

 TAKS Practice Tests

 TAKS Practice Transparencies TT91

 TAKS Online Test Practice

**KEY PLAYER**

**Adolf Hitler (1889–1945)**
Ask students to study the photographs and think about what emotions and attitudes Hitler was conveying to the audience with his gestures. Would such a communication style work well on television today? Why, or why not? *(Some students may suggest that such exaggerated gestures would seem melodramatic on television.)*

**UNION WITH AUSTRIA** Austria was Hitler's first target. The Paris Peace Conference following World War I had created the relatively small nation of Austria out of what was left of the Austro-Hungarian Empire. The majority of Austria's 6 million people were Germans who favored unification with Germany. On March 12, 1938, German troops marched into Austria unopposed. A day later, Germany announced that its *Anschluss*, or "union," with Austria was complete. The United States and the rest of the world did nothing.

**BARGAINING FOR THE SUDETENLAND** Hitler then turned to Czechoslovakia. About 3 million German-speaking people lived in the western border regions of Czechoslovakia called the Sudetenland. The mountainous region formed Czechoslovakia's main defense against German attack. (See map, p. 538.) Hitler wanted to annex Czechoslovakia in order to provide more living space for Germany as well as to control its important natural resources.

Hitler charged that the Czechs were abusing the Sudeten Germans, and he began massing troops on the Czech border. The U.S. correspondent William Shirer, then stationed in Berlin, wrote in his diary: "The Nazi press [is] full of hysterical headlines. All lies. Some examples: 'Women and Children Mowed Down by Czech Armored Cars,' or 'Bloody Regime—New Czech Murders of Germans.'"

Early in the crisis, both France and Great Britain promised to protect Czechoslovakia. Then, just when war seemed inevitable, Hitler invited French premier Édouard Daladier and British prime minister **Neville Chamberlain** to meet with him in Munich. When they arrived, the führer declared that the annexation of the Sudetenland would be his "last territorial demand." In their eagerness to avoid war, Daladier and Chamberlain chose to believe him. On September 30, 1938, they signed the Munich Agreement, which turned the Sudetenland, over to Germany without a single shot being fired. **A**

Chamberlain returned home and proclaimed: "My friends, there has come back from Germany peace with honor. I believe it is peace in our time."

**KEY PLAYER**

**ADOLF HITLER**
**1889–1945**

"All great world-shaking events have been brought about not by written matter, but by the spoken word!" declared Adolf Hitler. A shy and awkward speaker at first, Hitler rehearsed carefully. He even had photographs (shown above) taken of his favorite gestures so he could study them and make changes to produce exactly the desired effect.

Hitler's extraordinary power as a speaker, wrote Otto Strasser, stemmed from an intuitive ability to sense "the vibration of the human heart . . . telling it what it most wants to hear."

**Connections Across Time**

1938 AND 1968

**Munich and Vietnam**
Chamberlain and Daladier's decision to sign the Munich Agreement led to unforeseen disaster in Europe. Many historians agree that Hitler was unprepared for war and probably would have backed down if challenged. The memory of Munich continued to haunt the West after WWII. During the Vietnam War, the Munich decision was referred to in order to highlight the dangers of appeasement.

*A. Answer*
Annexation of Austria and the Sudetenland.

**MAIN IDEA**

**Summarizing**
**A** What moves did Germany make in its quest for *lebensraum*?

---

**ACTIVITY** | **SKILLBUILDER LESSON**

**BLOCK SCHEDULING**

**Developing Historical Perspective**

**Explaining the Skill** An historical perspective is a way of interpreting past events, conditions, decisions, and leaders in the context of their times.

**Applying the Skill** Point out that many historians argue that Chamberlain should not have bargained with Hitler and signed the Munich Agreement. Ask students why they think crowds cheered for Chamberlain when he returned from Munich and proclaimed "peace with honor." *(The people had lived through one terrible war and did not want another one.)*

In-Depth Resources: Unit 3
· Skillbuilder Practice: Developing Historical Perspective, p. 6

## German Advances, 1938–1941

Axis powers
Axis-controlled by Dec. 1941
Allied territory, Dec. 1941
Neutral countries
German troop movements
Maginot Line

0   200   400 miles
0   200   400 kilometers

---

## HISTORY from VISUALS

### Interpreting the Map

Point out to students that Central Europe has few natural barriers. Ask them to predict how Germany's geographic location might have been a military disadvantage. *(Germany was at a defensive disadvantage. The nation was vulnerable to invasion because of the lack of geographic barriers to slow down enemy attacks.)*

**Extension** Ask students what German advances meant to Great Britain by the end of 1941. *(Great Britain was essentially cut off form the rest of Europe.)*

 Geography Transparencies GT24
· Aggression in Europe, 1936–1939

---

## Instruct: Objective ❷

### The German Offensive Begins

TAKS SS11 1(US6.B)

· What action freed Hitler to invade Poland?
· What new tactics did Germany use in attacking Poland?
· What was the "phony war?"

 In-Depth Resources: Unit 5
· Guided Reading, p. 2

---

**Skillbuilder Answers**
1. Austria, Yugoslavia, Bulgaria, Greece, Romania, Slovakia, Hungary, Poland, Lithuania, Latvia, Estonia, Finland, Norway, France, Denmark, the Netherlands, Belgium, and the Soviet Union.
2. It was centrally located.

---

### GEOGRAPHY SKILLBUILDER

1. **Region** Which European countries did Germany invade?
2. **Location** How was Germany's geographic location an advantage?

---

Chamberlain's satisfaction was not shared by Winston Churchill, Chamberlain's political rival in Great Britain. In Churchill's view, by signing the Munich Agreement, Daladier and Chamberlain had adopted a shameful policy of **appeasement**—or giving up principles to pacify an aggressor. As Churchill bluntly put it, "Britain and France had to choose between war and dishonor. They chose dishonor. They will have war." Nonetheless, the House of Commons approved Chamberlain's policy toward Germany and Churchill responded with a warning.

**A PERSONAL VOICE**  WINSTON CHURCHILL

" [W]e have passed an awful milestone in our history. . . . And do not suppose that this is the end. . . . This is only the first sip, the first foretaste of a bitter cup which will be proffered to us year by year unless, by a supreme recovery of moral health and martial vigor, we arise again and take our stand for freedom as in the olden time." **B**

—speech to the House of Commons, quoted in *The Gathering Storm*

*B. Answer* An attempt to do whatever was necessary to pacify Hitler; Churchill saw it as an abandonment of moral principles that would lead to a war and national disaster.

**MAIN IDEA**

**Analyzing Motives**
**B** What was appeasement, and why did Churchill oppose it so strongly?

### ❷ The German Offensive Begins

As Hitler had warned, he was not finished expanding the Third Reich. As dawn broke on March 15, 1939, German troops poured into what remained of Czechoslovakia. At nightfall Hitler gloated, "Czechoslovakia has ceased to exist." After that, the German dictator turned his land-hungry gaze toward Germany's eastern neighbor, Poland.

**538**  CHAPTER 16

---

**DIFFERENTIATING INSTRUCTION**    **STUDENTS ACQUIRING ENGLISH/ESL**

### Decoding a Speech

Pair non-native speakers with students who are native English speakers. Ask students to decode the following phrases from Churchill's speech on page 538, using a chart similar to the one shown here. After they understand the meaning of each phrase, ask them to write a sentence summarizing the entire segment. The first phrase and decoding can be used as an example for students. Ask for volunteers to read their decodings and summary sentences to the class.

| PHRASE | DECODING |
|---|---|
| awful milestone | important or terrible step or stage |
| foretaste of a bitter cup | |
| which will be proffered | |
| martial vigor | |
| olden time | |
| SUMMARY SENTENCE: | |

**THE SOVIET UNION DECLARES NEUTRALITY** Like Czechoslovakia, Poland had a sizable German-speaking population. In the spring of 1939, Hitler began his familiar routine, charging that Germans in Poland were mistreated by the Poles and needed his protection. Some people thought that this time Hitler must be bluffing. After all, an attack on Poland might bring Germany into conflict with the Soviet Union, Poland's eastern neighbor. At the same time, such an attack would most likely provoke a declaration of war from France and Britain—both of whom had promised military aid to Poland. The result would be a two-front war. Fighting on two fronts had exhausted Germany in World War I. Surely, many thought, Hitler would not be foolish enough to repeat that mistake.

As tensions rose over Poland, Stalin surprised everyone by signing a **nonaggression pact** with Hitler. Once bitter enemies, on August 23, 1939 fascist Germany and communist Russia now committed never to attack each other. Germany and the Soviet Union also signed a second, secret pact, agreeing to divide Poland between them. With the danger of a two-front war eliminated, the fate of Poland was sealed.

**BLITZKRIEG IN POLAND** As day broke on September 1, 1939, the German *Luftwaffe*, or German air force, roared over Poland, raining bombs on military bases, airfields, railroads, and cities. At the same time, German tanks raced across the Polish countryside, spreading terror and confusion. This invasion was the first test of Germany's newest military strategy, the **blitzkrieg**, or lightning war. Blitzkrieg made use of advances in military technology—such as fast tanks and more powerful aircraft—to take the enemy by surprise and then quickly crush all opposition with overwhelming force. On September 3, two days following the terror in Poland, Britain and France declared war on Germany. **C**

The blitzkrieg tactics worked perfectly. Major fighting was over in three weeks, long before France, Britain, and their allies could mount a defense. In the last week of fighting, the Soviet Union attacked Poland from the east, grabbing some of its territory. The portion Germany annexed in western Poland contained almost two-thirds of Poland's population. By the end of the month, Poland had ceased to exist—and World War II had begun.

*C. Answer* The development of improved tanks and airplanes had made *blitzkrieg* tactics effective.

**Background** *Luftwaffe* in German means "air weapon."

**MAIN IDEA**

**Evaluating**
**C** How did German blitzkrieg tactics rely on new military technology?

**More About . . .**

**Stalin and the Non-Aggression Pact**
Stalin signed the German-Soviet Nonaggression Pact and shocked Communists and Soviet sympathizers. The agreement freed Hitler to attack Poland without fear of Soviet retaliation. It also freed Stalin to prepare his country for war without fear of German invasion. For two years the Soviets manufactured arms and trained soldiers. Many historians argue that without this preparation time, the Soviet Union would not have been able to withstand German aggression. When Germany attacked in 1941, the Soviets were surprised but not defeated.

**More About . . .**

**Blitzkrieg**
Blitzkrieg tactics consisted of new military technology adapted to the battlefields of Central Europe. The first stage featured the use of Stuka; a tactic designed to create shock and to immobilize the enemy. Tactical dive-bombers pounded enemy positions, disrupted communications, and compromised troops' mobility. Flanking infantry and motorized tank attacks followed. Skilled in ground combat and the use of tanks, the Germans could quickly outmaneuver and overpower the resistance.

German Junkers JU-87 dive-bombers, commonly known as Stukas, were a mainstay of Germany's blitzkrieg style of attack.

◄ A German tank unit in Western Poland in 1939.

**539**

---

**ACTIVITY** · **LINK TO GEOGRAPHY**  **BLOCK SCHEDULING**

### Blitzkrieg and Geography

**Class Time** One class period

**Task** Researching how blitzkrieg tactics were designed to work on the landscape of the battlefield

**Purpose** To reinforce the role geography plays in battlefield tactics

**Directions** Divide students into groups and have them draw a diagram of troop deployment in a blitzkrieg attack. Next, they should examine maps of the physical geography of Central Europe. Students should discuss why the tactics are so well suited to the geography of Central Europe and speculate on their effectiveness in mountainous terrain, or over long distances (like thousands of miles from Germany into Russia).

Integrated Assessment
· Rubric 4

## Instruct: Objective ③

### France and Britain Fight On
TAKS SS11 1(US6.B)
· What happened to France after the "phony war"?
· What was Britain's situation at the end of 1940?
· What was the result of the Battle of Britain?

📄 In-Depth Resources: Unit 5
· Guided Reading, p. 2

👁 Electronic Library of Primary Sources
· A Letter to Roosevelt, 1940, by Churchill

**THE PHONY WAR** For the next several months after the fall of Poland, French and British troops on the Maginot Line, a system of fortifications built along France's eastern border (see map on p. 538), sat staring into Germany, waiting for something to happen. On the Siegfried Line a few miles away German troops stared back. The blitzkrieg had given way to what the Germans called the *sitzkrieg* ("sitting war"), and what some newspapers referred to as the phony war.

After occupying eastern Poland, Stalin began annexing the Baltic states of Estonia, Latvia, and Lithuania. Late in 1939, Stalin sent his Soviet army into Finland. After three months of fighting, the outnumbered Finns surrendered.

Suddenly, on April 9, 1940, Hitler launched a surprise invasion of Denmark and Norway in order "to protect [those countries'] freedom and independence." But in truth, Hitler planned to build bases along the coasts to strike at Great Britain. Next, Hitler turned against the Netherlands, Belgium, and Luxembourg, which were overrun by the end of May. The phony war had ended. **D**

For months there was nothing much to defend against, as the war turned into a *sitzkrieg* endured by soldiers such as this French one on the Maginot Line.

## France and Britain Fight On ③

France's Maginot Line proved to be ineffective; the German army threatened to bypass the line during its invasion of Belgium. Hitler's generals sent their tanks through the Ardennes, a region of wooded ravines in northeast France, thereby avoiding British and French troops who thought the Ardennes were impassible. The Germans continued to march toward Paris.

**THE FALL OF FRANCE** The German offensive trapped almost 400,000 British and French soldiers as they fled to the beaches of Dunkirk on the French side of the English Channel. In less than a week, a makeshift fleet of fishing trawlers, tugboats, river barges, pleasure craft—more than 800 vessels in all—ferried about 330,000 British, French, and Belgian troops to safety across the Channel.

A few days later, Italy entered the war on the side of Germany and invaded France from the south as the Germans closed in on Paris from the north. On June 22, 1940, at Compiègne, as William Shirer and the rest of the world watched, Hitler handed French officers his terms of surrender. Germans would occupy the northern part of France, and a Nazi-controlled puppet government, headed by Marshal Philippe Pétain, would be set up at Vichy, in southern France.

After France fell, a French general named **Charles de Gaulle** fled to England, where he set up a government-in-exile. De Gaulle proclaimed defiantly, "France has lost a battle, but France has not lost the war."

**THE BATTLE OF BRITAIN** In the summer of 1940, the Germans began to assemble an invasion fleet along the French coast. Because its naval power could not compete with that of Britain, Germany also launched an air war at the same time. The Luftwaffe began making bombing

◀ Children watch with wonder and fear as the battling British and German air forces set the skies of London aflame.

runs over Britain. Its goal was to gain total control of the skies by destroying Britain's Royal Air Force (RAF). Hitler had 2,600 planes at his disposal. On a single day—August 15—1,000 of his planes ranged over Britain. Every night for two solid months, bombers pounded London.

The Battle of Britain raged on through the summer and fall. Night after night, German planes pounded British targets. At first the Luftwaffe concentrated on airfields and aircraft. Next it targeted cities. Londoner Len Jones was just 18 years old when bombs fell on his East End neighborhood.

### A PERSONAL VOICE LEN JONES

"After an explosion of a nearby bomb, you could actually feel your eyeballs being sucked out. I was holding my eyes to try and stop them going. And the suction was so vast, it ripped my shirt away, and ripped my trousers. Then I couldn't get my breath, the smoke was like acid and everything round me was black and yellow."

—quoted in *London at War*

The RAF fought back brilliantly. With the help of a new technological device called radar British pilots accurately plotted the flight paths of German planes, even in darkness. On September 15, 1940 the RAF shot down over 185 German planes; at the same time, they lost only 26 aircraft. Six weeks later, Hitler called off the invasion of Britain indefinitely. "Never in the field of human conflict," said Churchill in praise of the RAF pilots, "was so much owed by so many to so few."

Still, German bombers continued to pound Britain's cities trying to disrupt production and break civilian morale. British pilots also bombed German cities. Civilians in both countries unrelentingly carried on.

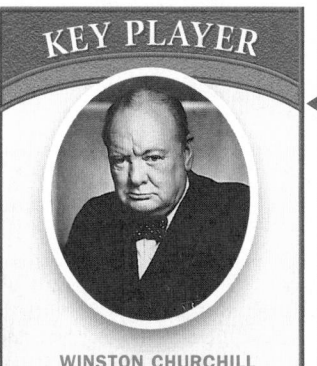

### KEY PLAYER

**WINSTON CHURCHILL 1874–1965**

Churchill was possibly Britain's greatest weapon as that nation faced the Nazis. A born fighter, Churchill became prime minister in May 1940 and used his gift as a speaker to arouse Britons and unite them:

"[W]e shall defend our island, whatever the cost may be, we shall fight on the beaches, we shall fight on the landing-grounds, we shall fight in the fields and in the streets, we shall fight in the hills; we shall never surrender."

### KEY PLAYER

**Winston Churchill (1874–1965)**
Tell students that rarely has a political leader played such an important role in keeping his country together as did Churchill during the dark days of World War II. Remind students that British cities were being bombarded every night—that Britain stood alone against Germany. Churchill made good use of the radio to communicate with his people. Ask students how they think Churchill was able to rally the British people. *(He rallied the British people by providing hope where none seemed to exist. He gave purpose to their hardship and told them that while times were hard, victory was achievable.)*

## Assess & Reteach

**SECTION 2 ASSESSMENT**
Have students answer the questions independently. Then have them compare answers with a partner and discuss any discrepancies.

 Formal Assessment
· Section Quiz, p. 301

**SELF-ASSESSMENT**
Have students review the events leading up to World War II. Ask them to identify the key steps in Hitler's plan to expand the German Reich between 1937 and 1940. Remind students to note any events they omit from their summaries.

**RETEACH**
Ask a volunteer to put his or her time line from question 2 on the board. Ask students to add events in order to create a complete class summary of events leading up to World War II.

 In-Depth Resources
· Reteaching Activity, p. 8

---

## 2 ASSESSMENT

**1. TERMS & NAMES** For each term or name, write a sentence explaining its significance.
- Neville Chamberlain
- Winston Churchill
- appeasement
- nonaggression pact
- *blitzkrieg*
- Charles de Gaulle

### MAIN IDEA

**2. TAKING NOTES**
Trace the movement of German expansion from 1937 to the end of 1940 by supplying events to follow the dates shown on the time line.

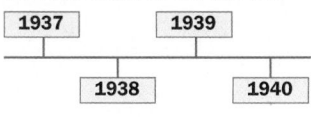

What event was the most significant? Why?

### CRITICAL THINKING

**3. ANALYZING MOTIVES**
To what extent do you think lies and deception played a role in Hitler's tactics? Support your answer with examples. **Think About:**
- William Shirer's diary entry about headlines in the Nazi newspapers
- Soviet-German relations
- Hitler's justifications for military aggression

**4. EVALUATING DECISIONS**
If you had been a member of the British House of Commons in 1938, would you have voted for or against the Munich Agreement? Support your decision.

**5. DRAWING CONCLUSIONS**
Review Germany's aggressive actions between 1938 and 1945. At what point do you think Hitler concluded that he could take any territory without being stopped? Why?

*World War Looms* **541**

---

Answers ASSESSMENT 2

**1. TERMS & NAMES**
Neville Chamberlain, p. 537
Winston Churchill, p. 538
appeasement, p. 538
nonaggression pact, p. 539
*blitzkrieg*, p. 539
Charles de Gaulle, p. 540

**2. TAKING NOTES**
(1937) Hitler plans expansion
(1938) Germany annexes Austria and Sudetenland
(1939) Germany invades Poland
(1940) Germany invades France; fights the Battle of Britain with England
(1939) World War II begins after Germany invades Poland.

**3. ANALYZING MOTIVES**
Hitler's deceptions included: charging the Czechs with abusing Sudeten Germans; claiming the Sudetenland was his last territorial demand; accusing Poles of brutalizing Germans; signing a secret pact with the Soviet Union dividing Poland; justifying the invasion of Denmark and Norway as necessary to safeguard his plans.

**4. EVALUATING DECISIONS**
**For:** Appeasement would help avert war; compromise is not a sign of weakness; **Against:** Appeasement would feed Hitler's military aggression; Great Britain should defend its honor and declare war.

**5. DRAWING CONCLUSIONS**
After taking Austria—France and Britain ignored pledge to protect Austria; after Munich Conference—Britain and France let Germany take Sudetenland.

# OBJECTIVES

**1** Explain the reasons behind the Nazi's persecution of the Jews and the problems facing Jewish refugees.

**2** Describe the Nazis's "final solution" to the Jewish problem and the horrors of the Holocaust.

**3** Identify and describe the profound and lasting effects of the Holocaust on survivors.

## SKILLBUILDERS

· Interpreting Charts, p. 545

## CRITICAL THINKING

· Analyzing Issues, p. 543
· Analyzing Effects, p. 544
· Summarizing, p. 547
· Evaluating Decisions, p. 549
· Developing Historical Perspective, p. 549
· Analyzing Motives, p. 549

# Focus & Motivate

Discuss with students what they already know about the Holocaust. Tell students that the term "holocaust" means great destruction or loss of life. Warn them that some of the material may be upsetting, but that it is historically accurate. The practice of genocide continues to take place around the world.

# Instruct

## Instruct: Objective **1**

**The Persecution Begins**
TAKS SS11 1(US6.B)
· What did the Nazis do to the Jews after taking power?
· Why was it almost impossible for Jews to escape from Germany?

 In-Depth Resources: Unit 5
· Guided Reading, p. 3

# The Holocaust

| MAIN IDEA | WHY IT MATTERS NOW | Terms & Names |
|---|---|---|
| During the Holocaust, the Nazis systematically executed 6 million Jews and 5 million other "non-Aryans." | After the atrocities of the Holocaust, agencies formed to publicize human rights. These agencies have remained a force in today's world. | • Holocaust · ghetto<br>• *Kristallnacht* · concentration<br>• genocide   camp |

**TEKS** U.S. History 6A, 6B, 8B, 10B, 24B, 24H, 25A, 25B, 25D

### One American's Story

Gerda Weissmann was a carefree girl of 15 when, in September 1939, invading German troops shattered her world. Because the Weissmanns were Jews, they were forced to give up their home to a German family. In 1942, Gerda, her parents, and most of Poland's 3,000,000 Jews were sent to labor camps. Gerda recalls when members of Hitler's elite *Schutzstaffel*, or "security squadron" (SS), came to round up the Jews.

**A PERSONAL VOICE** GERDA WEISSMANN KLEIN

" We had to form a line and an SS man stood there with a little stick. I was holding hands with my mother and . . . he looked at me and said, 'How old?' And I said, 'eighteen,' and he sort of pushed me to one side and my mother to the other side. . . . And shortly thereafter, some trucks arrived . . . and we were loaded onto the trucks. I heard my mother's voice from very far off ask, 'Where to?' and I shouted back, 'I don't know.' "
—quoted in the film *One Survivor Remembers*

**VIDEO**
**ESCAPING THE FINAL SOLUTION**
Kurt Klein and Gerda Weissmann Klein Remember the Holocaust

When the American lieutenant Kurt Klein, who would later become Gerda's husband, liberated her from the Nazis in 1945—just one day before her 21st birthday—she weighed 68 pounds and her hair had turned white. Even so, of all her family and friends, she alone had survived the Nazis' campaign to exterminate Europe's Jews.

 Mini-Lesson 2: SS11 2(US6.B)

## **1** The Persecution Begins

On April 7, 1933, shortly after Hitler took power in Germany, he ordered all "non-Aryans" to be removed from government jobs. This order was one of the first moves in a campaign for racial purity that eventually led to the **Holocaust**—the systematic murder of 11 million people across Europe, more than half of whom were Jews.

**542** CHAPTER 16

---

## PROGRAM RESOURCES

 In-Depth Resources: Unit 5
· Guided Reading, p. 3
· Reteaching Activity, p. 9
· Literature: from *Sophie's Choice*, pp. 17–19
· American Lives: Elie Wiesel, p. 20

**Reading Study Guide** (English and Spanish), pp. 165–166

 Access for Students Acquiring English/ESL
· Guided Reading (Spanish), p. 182

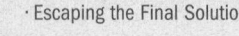 Formal Assessment
· Section Quiz, p. 302

 Integrated Assessment
· Rubrics

### INTEGRATED TECHNOLOGY

American Stories video series
· Escaping the Final Solution

Electronic Library of Primary Sources

classzone.com

### TEXAS RESOURCES

 TAKS Spiraled Content Review

 TAKS Practice Tests

 TAKS Practice Transparencies TT92

 TAKS Online Test Practice

◀ On November 17, 1938, two passersby examine the shattered window of a Jewish-owned store in the aftermath of *Kristallnacht*.

Jewish men holding a "star of David" ▶ are rounded up and marched through the streets on their way to a concentration camp.

**JEWS TARGETED** Although Jews were not the only victims of the Holocaust, they were the center of the Nazis' targets. Anti-Semitism, or hatred of the Jews, had a long history in many European countries. For decades many Germans looking for a scapegoat had blamed the Jews as the cause of their failures. Hitler found that a majority of Germans were willing to support his belief that Jews were responsible for Germany's economic problems and defeat in World War I.

As the Nazis tightened their hold on Germany, their persecution of the Jews increased. In 1935, the Nuremberg Laws stripped Jews of their German citizenship, jobs, and property. To make it easier for the Nazis to identify them, Jews had to wear a bright yellow Star of David attached to their clothing. Worse was yet to come.

**KRISTALLNACHT** November 9–10, 1938, became known as ***Kristallnacht*** (krĭs′täl′nächt′), or "Night of Broken Glass." Nazi storm troopers attacked Jewish homes, businesses, and synagogues across Germany. An American who witnessed the violence wrote, "Jewish shop windows by the hundreds were systematically and wantonly smashed. . . . The main streets of the city were a positive litter of shattered plate glass." Around 100 Jews were killed, and hundreds more were injured. Some 30,000 Jews were arrested and hundreds of synagogues were burned. Afterward, the Nazis blamed the Jews for the destruction. **A**

**A FLOOD OF JEWISH REFUGEES** Kristallnacht marked a step-up in the Nazi policy of Jewish persecution. Nazis tried to speed Jewish emigration but encountered difficulty. Jews fleeing Germany had trouble finding nations that would accept them. France already had 40,000 Jewish refugees and did not want more. The British worried about fueling anti-Semitism and refused to admit more than 80,000 Jewish refugees. They also controlled Palestine (later Israel) and allowed 30,000 refugees to settle there. Late in 1938, Germany's foreign minister, Joachim von Ribbentrop, observed, "We all want to get rid of our Jews. The difficulty is that no country wishes to receive them."

**Vocabulary**
**scapegoat:** someone who is made to bear the blame of others

*A. Answer*
Loss of employment and property; harrassment, humiliation, and physical harm; death threats and murder.

**MAIN IDEA**

**Analyzing Issues**
**A** What problems did German Jews face in Nazi Germany from 1935 to 1938?

*World War Looms* 543

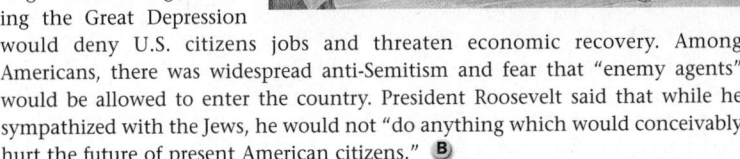

Muralist Ben Shahn depicts the 1933 emigration of Albert Einstein and thousands of other Jews to America to escape Nazi terrorism.

### Instruct: Objective ❷

**Hitler's "Final Solution"**

· What was the goal of the "final solution"?
· What did the Nazis do to the Jews?
· How did the Nazis industrialize the killing of Jews?

 In-Depth Resources: Unit 5
· Guided Reading, p. 3

Although the average Jew had little chance of reaching the United States, "persons of exceptional merit," including physicist Albert Einstein, author Thomas Mann, architect Walter Gropius, and the-ologian Paul Tillich were among 100,000 refugees the United States accepted. Many Americans wanted the door closed. Americans were concerned that let-ting in more refugees dur-ing the Great Depression would deny U.S. citizens jobs and threaten economic recovery. Among Americans, there was widespread anti-Semitism and fear that "enemy agents" would be allowed to enter the country. President Roosevelt said that while he sympathized with the Jews, he would not "do anything which would conceivably hurt the future of present American citizens." **B**

**THE PLIGHT OF THE *ST. LOUIS*** Official indifference to the plight of Germany's Jews was in evidence in the case of the ship *St. Louis*. This German ocean liner passed Miami in 1939. Although 740 of the liner's 943 passengers had U.S. immi-gration papers, the Coast Guard followed the ship to prevent anyone from dis-embarking in America. The ship was forced to return to Europe. "The cruise of the St. Louis," wrote the New York Times, "cries to high heaven of man's inhumani-ty to man." Passenger Liane Reif-Lehrer recalls her childhood experiences.

> **A PERSONAL VOICE** LIANE REIF-LEHRER
>
> "My mother and brother and I were among the passengers who survived. . . . We were sent back to Europe and given haven in France, only to find the Nazis on our doorstep again a few months later."
>
> —Liane Reif-Lehrer

More than half of the passengers were later killed in the Holocaust.

## ❷ Hitler's "Final Solution"

By 1939 only about a quarter million Jews remained in Germany. But other nations that Hitler occupied had millions more. Obsessed with a desire to rid Europe of its Jews, Hitler imposed what he called the "Final Solution"—a policy of **genocide,** the deliberate and systematic killing of an entire population.

**MAIN IDEA**

Analyzing Effects
**B** How did the United States respond to Jewish refugees?

*B. Answer* The United States refused to loosen immigra-tion restrictions to allow more Jews to immi-grate to the United States.

---

 **ACTIVITY** COOPERATIVE LEARNING                    **B** BLOCK SCHEDULING

**Debating Jewish Immigration**

**Class Time** One class period

**Task** Exploring the issues surrounding the restrictions on Jewish immigration

**Purpose** To examine underlying prejudices and unintended consequences of legislation

**Directions** Have students research American attitudes toward Jewish immigration in the 1930s. Have students debate the following topic: Does the United States have an obligation to aid victims of political oppression by allowing them into the country? Remind students of the economic circumstances in the United States in the 1930s and of the anti-Semitic actions of such groups as the Ku Klux Klan.

 Integrated Assessment
· Rubric 3

**Background**
The first person to use the term Final Solution was General George Custer. He was referring to the execution of Native Americans.

**THE CONDEMNED** Hitler's Final Solution rested on the belief that Aryans were a superior people and that the strength and purity of this "master race" must be preserved. To accomplish this, the Nazis condemned to slavery and death not only the Jews but other groups that they viewed as inferior or unworthy or as "enemies of the state."

After taking power in 1933, the Nazis had concentrated on silencing their political opponents—communists, socialists, liberals, and anyone else who spoke out against the government. Once the Nazis had eliminated these enemies, they turned against other groups in Germany. In addition to Jews, these groups included the following:

- *Gypsies*—whom the Nazis believed to be an "inferior race"
- *Freemasons*—whom the Nazis charged as supporters of the "Jewish conspiracy" to rule the world
- *Jehovah's Witnesses*—who refused to join the army or salute Hitler

The Nazis also targeted other Germans whom they found unfit to be part of the "master race." Such victims included homosexuals, the mentally deficient, the mentally ill, the physically disabled, and the incurably ill.

Hitler began implementing his Final Solution in Poland with special Nazi death squads. Hitler's elite Nazi "security squadrons" (or SS), rounded up Jews—men, women, children, and babies—and shot them on the spot.

**FORCED RELOCATION** Jews also were ordered into dismal, overcrowded **ghettos,** segregated Jewish areas in certain Polish cities. The Nazis sealed off the ghettos with barbed wire and stone walls.

Life inside the ghetto was miserable. The bodies of victims piled up in the streets faster than they could be removed. Factories were built alongside ghettos where people were forced to work for German industry. In spite of the impossible living conditions, the Jews hung on. While some formed resistance movements inside the ghettos, others resisted by other means. They published and distributed underground newspapers. Secret schools were set up to educate Jewish children. Even theater and music groups continued to operate.

*Skillbuilder Answer*
Over 65 percent

**ANOTHER PERSPECTIVE**

**DENMARK'S RESISTANCE**

King Christian X became an important symbol of Danish resistance in World War II. In 1942, he rejected the Nazis' demand to enforce the Nuremberg Laws against the Jews in occupied Denmark. In August 1943, the king spoke out against the German occupying forces, an act that led to his imprisonment for the remainder of the war.

### Estimated Jewish Losses

| | Pre-Holocaust Population | Number Killed | |
| --- | --- | --- | --- |
| | | Low Estimate | High Estimate |
| Austria | 191,000 | 50,000 | 65,500 |
| Belgium | 60,000 | 25,000 | 29,000 |
| Bohemia/Moravia | 92,000 | 77,000 | 78,300 |
| Denmark | 8,000 | 60 | 116 |
| Estonia | 4,600 | 1,500 | 2,000 |
| France | 260,000 | 75,000 | 77,000 |
| Germany | 566,000 | 135,000 | 142,000 |
| Greece | 73,000 | 59,000 | 67,000 |
| Hungary | 725,000 | 502,000 | 569,000 |
| Italy | 48,000 | 6,500 | 9,000 |
| Latvia | 95,000 | 70,000 | 72,000 |
| Lithuania | 155,000 | 130,000 | 143,000 |
| Luxembourg | 3,500 | 1,000 | 2,000 |
| Netherlands | 112,000 | 100,000 | 105,000 |
| Norway | 1,700 | 800 | 800 |
| Poland | 3,250,000 | 2,700,000 | 3,000,000 |
| Romania | 441,000 | 121,000 | 287,000 |
| Slovakia | 89,000 | 60,000 | 71,000 |
| USSR | 2,825,000 | 700,000 | 1,100,000 |
| Yugoslavia | 68,000 | 56,000 | 65,000 |
| **TOTALS** | 9,067,800 | 4,869,860 | 5,894,716 |

*Source: Columbia Guide to the Holocaust*

**SKILLBUILDER  Interpreting Charts**
Approximately what percentage of the total Jewish population in Europe was killed during the Holocaust?

**ANOTHER PERSPECTIVE**

**Denmark's Resistance**
Ask students to consider why the Danes resisted the Nuremberg Laws, while most Germans accepted those laws. *(Danes did not like Germans telling them anything, including how to treat the Jews.)*

**HISTORY from VISUALS**

**Interpreting Charts**
Use the chart to discuss how concrete facts can sometimes obscure, as well as illuminate, the meaning of events. How do we relate the numbers on the chart to the individuals who lost their lives? Ask students what impact the numbers on the chart would have if the individuals had died in a natural disaster. *(Students may say that the fact that these people were exterminated intensifies the tragedy of their deaths.)*

---

**ACTIVITY    LINK TO ART/LITERATURE**

**Creative Response**

**Class Time**  30 minutes

**Task**  Creating responses to the chart of Jewish losses on page 545

**Purpose**  To give human meaning to the numbers of victims of the Holocaust

**BLOCK SCHEDULING**

**Directions**  Ask students to contemplate the chart. While thinking about it, ask them to think of human beings—young and old, children and adult, men and women, boys and girls. Then ask them to use words, shapes, or color, to give creative expression to what the numbers mean to them. When they've finished, ask how many of them have visited the Museum of the Holocaust in Washington, D.C. Ask for a volunteer to describe some of the creative responses to the Holocaust that are on display in the museum.

## HISTORY from VISUALS

**Interpreting the Photographs**

Have students examine the image of the concentration camp inmates and the photo of the tray of hoarded wedding rings. Ask them to describe their emotional responses. If they find it difficult to respond, explain that there are no right answers; the horror of the Holocaust can defy logic and language. Ask: What would you say to a German administrator of a concentration camp? *(Answers will vary.)*

▲

On May 9, 1945, inmates at the Ebensee concentration camp in Austria were liberated by U.S. soldiers.

**CONCENTRATION CAMPS** Finally, Jews in communities not reached by the killing squads were dragged from their homes and herded onto trains or trucks for shipment to **concentration camps,** or labor camps. Families were often separated, sometimes—like the Weissmanns—forever.

Nazi concentration camps were originally set up to imprison political opponents and protesters. The camps were later turned over to the SS, who expanded the concentration camp and used it to warehouse other "undesirables." Life in the camps was a cycle of hunger, humiliation, and work that almost always ended in death.

The prisoners were crammed into crude wooden barracks that held up to a thousand people each. They shared their crowded quarters, as well as their meager meals, with hordes of rats and fleas. Hunger was so intense, recalled one survivor, "that if a bit of soup spilled over, prisoners would converge on the spot, dig their spoons into the mud and stuff the mess into their mouths."

Inmates in the camps worked from dawn to dusk, seven days a week, until they collapsed. Those too weak to work were killed. Some, like Rudolf Reder, endured. He was one of only two Jews to survive the camp at Belzec, Poland.

## More About . . .

**Rudolf Reder**

Rudolf Reder, a soap manufacturer from Lvov in the Soviet Union, was on one of the first trains carrying deportees to the concentration camp in Belzec on August 11, 1942. Reder managed to escape. He later described his experience in the camp: "I, together with all the others left over from the previous transports, began our work. We pulled out the corpses of those who were alive only a short time ago, we pulled them using leather belts to the huge mass graves while the camp orchestra played; played from morning 'till night."

▲

After stripping their victims of life and dignity, the Nazis hoarded whatever articles of value the victims had possessed, such as wedding rings and gold fillings from teeth.

**A PERSONAL VOICE** RUDOLF REDER

"The brute Schmidt was our guard; he beat and kicked us if he thought we were not working fast enough. He ordered his victims to lie down and gave them 25 lashes with a whip, ordering them to count out loud. If the victim made a mistake, he was given 50 lashes. . . . Thirty or 40 of us were shot every day. A doctor usually prepared a daily list of the weakest men. During the lunch break they were taken to a nearby grave and shot. They were replaced the following morning by new arrivals from the transport of the day. . . . It was a miracle if anyone survived for five or six months in Belzec."

—quoted in *The Holocaust*

**546** CHAPTER 16

DIFFERENTIATING INSTRUCTION    GIFTED AND TALENTED

**Investigative Report about the Warsaw Ghetto**

Not all Jews went passively to their deaths. In 1943, surviving Jews in the Warsaw Ghetto launched a doomed, but heroic, resistance to German troops. Have students research the Warsaw Ghetto insurrection and create an investigative report for either radio or television. Allow plenty of time for students to present their reports to the class. If the project goes well, you might invite another class to view the presentations.

Student reports might include:

· maps showing relevant places in Warsaw
· news clips, print or electronic, about conditions revealed after the war
· personal accounts of survivors from the Warsaw Ghetto
· photographs of actual camps or buildings
· audio or video footage from the 1940s with voice-over reporting

**Instruct: Objective** ③

**The Final Stage**

TAKS SS11 1(US6.B)

· What other brutalities took place in concentration camps?

· How have Holocaust survivors been affected by their experience?

 In-Depth Resources: Unit 5
· Guided Reading, p. 3
· Literature: from *Sophie's Choice* by William Styron, p. 17

---

**More About . . .**

**The Final Solution**

In a 1943 report on clearing out Jews from newly conquered territory, SS Chief Heinrich Himmler boasted, "This is a page of glory in our history, which has never been written and is never to be written, . . . Among ourselves it should be mentioned quite frankly, and yet we shall never speak of it publicly."

---

③ **The Final Stage**

The Final Solution reached its final stage in early 1942. At a meeting held in Wannsee, a lakeside suburb near Berlin, Hitler's top officials agreed to begin a new phase of the mass murder of Jews. To mass slaughter and starvation they would add a third method of killing—murder by poison gas. **C**

**MASS EXTERMINATIONS** As deadly as overwork, starvation, beatings, and bullets were, they did not kill fast enough to satisfy the Nazis. The Germans built six death camps in Poland including the one that had already been built, Chelmno. Each camp had several huge gas chambers in which as many as 12,000 people could be killed a day.

When prisoners arrived at Auschwitz, the largest of the death camps, they had to parade by several SS doctors. With a wave of the hand, the doctors separated those strong enough to work from those who would die that day. Both groups were told to leave all their belongings behind, with a promise that they would be returned later. Those destined to die were then led into a room outside the gas chamber and were told to undress for a shower. To complete the deception, the prisoners were even

---

**MAIN IDEA**

**Summarizing**
**C** What was the goal of the Nazis' Final Solution, and how was that goal nearly achieved?

*C. Answer*
Extermination of European Jews in death camps.

---

▲
Prisoners were required to wear color-coded triangles on their uniforms. The categories of prisoners include communists, socialists, criminals, emigrants, Jehovah's Witnesses, homosexuals, Germans "shy of work," and other nationalities "shy of work." The vertical categories show a variation. One for repeat offenders, one for prisoners assigned to punish other prisoners, and double triangles for Jews. Letters on top of a patch indicate nationality.

*World War Looms* **547**

---

**DIFFERENTIATING INSTRUCTION**   **LESS PROFICIENT READERS**

**Following Chronological Order**

To help less proficient readers understand the sequence of events perpetrated by the Nazis during the Holocaust, draw a time line that students can fill in as they read. Time lines might look like this:

Once a basic time line is in place, interested students can annotate the time line by adding drawings or copies of photographs, captions, sketch maps, and so on. The time line can continue to be embellished as students study the Holocaust and events surrounding it.

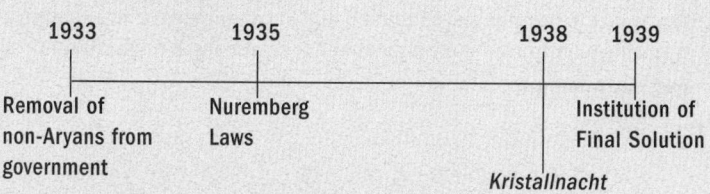

**Children taken ▶
from Eastern
Europe and
imprisoned in
Auschwitz
look out from
behind the
barbed-wire
fence in July
1944.**

## WORLD STAGE

### RIGHTEOUS PERSONS OF WORLD WAR II

In the midst of the world's overall indifference to the plight of
Jewish refugees, thousands of
non-Jews risked—and in many
cases lost—their own lives to
save Jews from the Nazis. In
recognition of such heroic
efforts, the Israeli Parliament,
the Knesset, bestowed on these
individuals the title of Righteous
Gentiles (or Righteous Persons).
As of the year 2000 more than
17,433 individuals were recognized for their courage and
morality.

Aristides de Sousa Mendes, a
Portuguese diplomat stationed in
France, defied his government's
orders and issued some 10,000
visas to Jews seeking entry to his
country. The Swedish diplomat
Raoul Wallenberg issued "protective passports" that allowed
thousands of Hungarian Jews to
escape the Nazi death camps.
Even citizens of Germany lent a
hand. And Sempo Sugihara,
Japanese consul in Lithuania,
helped over 2,000 Jews to
escape the Nazis' clutches, an
act that cost him his career.

given pieces of soap. Finally, they were led into the chamber and poisoned with cyanide gas that spewed from vents
in the walls. This orderly mass extermination was sometimes carried out to the accompaniment of cheerful music
played by an orchestra of camp inmates who had temporarily been spared execution.

At first the bodies were buried in huge pits. At Belzec,
Rudolf Reder was part of a 500-man death brigade that
labored all day, he said, "either at grave digging or empty-
ing the gas chambers." But the decaying corpses gave off a
stench that could be smelled for miles around. Worse yet,
mass graves left evidence of the mass murder. Lilli
Kopecky recalls her arrival at Auschwitz.

**A PERSONAL VOICE** LILLI KOPECKY

"When we came to Auschwitz, we smelt the sweet
smell. They said to us: 'There the people are gassed,
three kilometers over there.' We didn't believe it."
—quoted in *Never Again*

At some camps, to try to cover up the evidence of
their slaughter, the Nazis installed huge crematoriums, or
ovens, in which to burn the dead. At other camps, the
bodies were simply thrown into a pit and set on fire.

Gassing was not the only method of extermination
used in the camps. Prisoners were also shot, hanged, or
injected with poison.

Still others died as a result of horrible medical experiments carried out by camp doctors. Some of these victims
were injected with deadly germs in order to study the
effect of disease on different groups of people. Many more
were used to test methods of sterilization, a subject of
great interest to some Nazi doctors in their search for ways
to improve the "master race."

**548** CHAPTER 16

---

 **BLOCK SCHEDULING**

**THE SURVIVORS** An estimated six million Jews died in the death camps and in the Nazi massacres. But some miraculously escaped the worst of the Holocaust. Many had help from ordinary people who were appalled by the Nazis' treatment of Jews. Some Jews even survived the horrors of the concentration camps.

In Gerda Weissmann Klein's view, survival depended as much on one's spirit as on getting enough to eat. "I do believe that if you were blessed with imagination, you could work through it," she wrote. "If, unfortunately, you were a person that faced reality, I think you didn't have much of a chance." Those who did come out of the camps alive were forever changed by what they had witnessed. For survivor Elie Wiesel, who entered Auschwitz in 1944 at the age of 14, the sun had set forever.

*"Survival is both an exalted privilege and a painful burden."*
**GERTA WEISSMANN KLEIN**

### A PERSONAL VOICE ELIE WIESEL

" Never shall I forget that night, the first night in the camp, which has turned my life into one long night. . . . Never shall I forget the little faces of the children, whose bodies I saw turned into wreaths of smoke beneath a silent blue sky. Never shall I forget those flames which consumed my faith forever. Never shall I forget that nocturnal silence which deprived me, for all eternity, of the desire to live. Never shall I forget those moments which murdered my God and my soul and turned my dreams to dust. Never shall I forget these things, even if I am condemned to live as long as God Himself. Never. "

—*Night*

▲ Elie Wiesel, 1986

 Mini-Lesson 2:
SS11 2(11.F)

 **ASSESSMENT**

1. **TERMS & NAMES** For each term or name, write a sentence explaining its significance.
   - **Holocaust**
   - *Kristallnacht*
   - **genocide**
   - **ghetto**
   - **concentration camp**

### MAIN IDEA

2. **TAKING NOTES**
   List at least four events that led to the Holocaust.

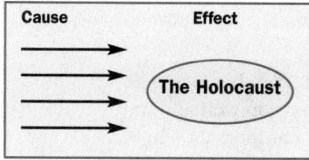

| Cause | Effect |
|---|---|
| → | |
| → | The Holocaust |
| → | |
| → | |

Write a paragraph summarizing one of the events that you listed.

### CRITICAL THINKING

3. **EVALUATING DECISIONS**
   Do you think that the United States was justified in not allowing more Jewish refugees to emigrate? Why or why not? **Think About:**
   - the views of isolationists in the United States
   - some Americans' prejudices and fears
   - the incident on the German luxury liner *St. Louis*

4. **DEVELOPING HISTORICAL PERSPECTIVE**
   Why do you think the Nazi system of systematic genocide was so brutally effective? Support your answer with details from the text.

5. **ANALYZING MOTIVES**
   How might concentration camp doctors and guards have justified to themselves the death and suffering they caused other human beings?

*World War Looms* **549**

---

Answers **ASSESSMENT**

**1. TERMS & NAMES**
Holocaust, p. 542
*Kristallnacht*, p. 543
genocide, p. 544
ghetto, p. 545
concentration camp, p. 546

**2. TAKING NOTES**
The removal of non-Aryans from government jobs; Nuremberg Laws; *Kristallnacht*, "final solution"
*(Paragraphs will vary.)*

**3. EVALUATING DECISIONS**
**Justified:** The United States had to protect the national security and the welfare of its citizens, including job security; **Not justified:** The United States was obligated to provide political asylum for victims of prejudice.

**4. DEVELOPING HISTORICAL PERSPECTIVE**
The Nazis lied about and covered up many of their activities.

**5. ANALYZING MOTIVES**
They believed that their prisoners were sub-human, thus they were not actually killing or torturing real human beings; they might claim that they were simply following orders and had no choice.

# America Moves Toward War

## OBJECTIVES

**1** Describe the U.S. response to the outbreak of war in Europe in 1939.

**2** Explain how Roosevelt assisted the Allies without declaring war.

**3** Summarize the events that brought the United States into armed conflict with Germany.

**4** Describe the American response to the Japanese attack on Pearl Harbor.

### SKILLBUILDERS

· Analyzing Political Cartoons, p. 551
· Geography Skillbuilder: region, movement, p. 556

### CRITICAL THINKING

· Analyzing Effects, p. 551
· Making Inferences, p. 552
· Drawing Conclusions, p. 553
· Analyzing Causes, p. 554
· Summarizing, p. 554
· Analyzing Issues, p. 555
· Evaluating Decisions, p. 557
· Predicting Effects, p. 557
· Analyzing Primary Sources, p. 557

| MAIN IDEA | WHY IT MATTERS NOW | Terms & Names |
|---|---|---|
| In response to the fighting in Europe, the United States provided economic and military aid to help the Allies achieve victory. | The military capability of the U. S. became a deciding factor in World War II and in world affairs ever since. | •Axis powers  •Allies<br>•Lend-Lease Act  •Hideki Tojo<br>•Atlantic Charter |

TAKS  U.S.
History
1B, 1C,
6A, 6B, 6C, 8A,
8B, 9A, 13D,
14A, 15B, 16A,
19A, 19B, 22B,
24A, 24B, 24C,
24E, 24F, 24G,
24H, 25A, 25B,
25C, 25D, 26A,
26B

## One American's Story

Two days after Hitler invaded Poland, President Roosevelt spoke reassuringly to Americans about the outbreak of war in Europe.

**A PERSONAL VOICE** FRANKLIN DELANO ROOSEVELT

" This nation will remain a neutral nation, but I cannot ask that every American remain neutral in thought as well. . . . Even a neutral cannot be asked to close his mind or his conscience. . . . I have said not once, but many times, that I have seen war and I hate war. . . . As long as it is my power to prevent, there will be no blackout of peace in the U.S. "

—radio speech, September 3, 1939

Although Roosevelt knew that Americans were still deeply committed to staying out of war, he also believed that there could be no peace in a world controlled by dictators.

▲ Franklin D. Roosevelt

## ① The United States Musters Its Forces

As German tanks thundered across Poland, Roosevelt issued an official proclamation of neutrality. At the same time, he began to prepare the nation for the struggle he feared lay just ahead.

**MOVING CAUTIOUSLY AWAY FROM NEUTRALITY** In September of 1939, Roosevelt persuaded Congress to pass a "cash-and-carry" provision that allowed warring nations to buy U.S. arms as long as they paid cash and transported them in their own ships. Providing the arms, Roosevelt argued, would help France and Britain defeat Hitler and keep the United States out of the war. Isolationists attacked Roosevelt for his actions. However, after six weeks of heated debate, Congress passed the Neutrality Act of 1939, and a cash-and-carry policy went into effect.

**550** CHAPTER 16

## Focus & Motivate

Ask students to consider under what circumstances the United States should enter a war.

## Instruct

### Instruct: Objective ①

**The United States Musters its Forces**
TAKS SS11 5(WH26.6)

· What did the United States do after World War II began in Europe?
· How did the formation of the Axis alliance affect the United States?

 In-Depth Resources: Unit 5
· Guided Reading, p. 4

---

## PROGRAM RESOURCES

 **In-Depth Resources: Unit 3**
· Guided Reading, p. 4
· Reteaching Activity, p. 10
· Geography Application: Japanese Aggression, pp. 11–12
· Primary Sources: The Bombing of Pearl Harbor, pp. 14–15; War poster, p. 16
· American Lives: Charles A. Lindbergh, p. 21

 **Reading Study Guide** (English and Spanish), pp. 167–168

 **Access for Students Acquiring English/ESL**
· Guided Reading (Spanish), p. 183
· Geography Application (Spanish), pp. 185–186

 **Formal Assessment**
· Section Quiz, p. 303

 **Integrated Assessment**
· Rubrics

### INTEGRATED TECHNOLOGY

 **Critical Thinking Transp. CT24, CT58**
· U.S. Joins the Allies in World War II
· Time Line of Events Leading to World War II

 **Electronic Library of Primary Sources**

 **classzone.com**

### TEXAS RESOURCES

 TAKS Spiraled Content Review

 TAKS Practice Tests

 TAKS Practice Transparencies TT93

 TAKS Online Test Practice

## Analyzing *Political Cartoons*

### CARVING IT UP

The three Axis nations—Germany, Italy, and Japan—were a threat to the entire world. They believed they were superior and more powerful than other nations, especially than the democracies. By signing a mutual defense pact, the Axis powers believed the United States would never risk involvement in a two-ocean war. This cartoon shows the Axis powers' obsession with global domination.

**SKILLBUILDER** Analyzing Political Cartoons
1. What are the Axis leaders—Hitler, Mussolini, and Tojo—greedily carving up?
2. What do you think the artist means by showing Hitler doing the carving?

**SEE SKILLBUILDER HANDBOOK, PAGE R24.**

### Analyzing *Political Cartoons*

**SKILLBUILDER ANSWERS**
1. They're carving up what appears to be the Earth, or perhaps a globe.
2. The artist is portraying Hitler as the mastermind.

**THE AXIS THREAT** The United States cash-and-carry policy began to look like too little, too late. By summer 1940, France had fallen and Britain was under siege. In September 1940, Americans were jolted by the news that Germany, Italy, and Japan had signed a mutual defense treaty, the Tripartite Pact. The three nations became known as the **Axis powers.**

The Tripartite Pact was aimed at keeping the United States out of the war. Under the treaty, each Axis nation agreed to come to the defense of the others in case of attack. This meant that if the United States were to declare war on any one of the Axis powers, it would face its worst military nightmare—a two-ocean war, with fighting in both the Atlantic and the Pacific.

Hoping to avoid this situation, Roosevelt scrambled to provide the British with "all aid short of war." By June 1940, he had sent Britain 500,000 rifles and 80,000 machine guns. In September, after the Tripartite Pact was signed, the United States traded 50 old destroyers for leases on British military bases in the Caribbean and Newfoundland. British prime minister Winston Churchill would later recall this move with affection as "a decidedly unneutral act."

**BUILDING U.S DEFENSES** Meanwhile, Roosevelt asked Congress to increase spending for national defense. In spite of years of isolationism, Nazi victories in 1940 changed U.S. thinking and Congress boosted defense spending. Congress also passed the nation's first peacetime military draft—the Selective Training and Service Act. Under this law 16 million men between the ages of 21 and 35 were registered. Of these, 1 million were to be drafted for one year but were only allowed to serve in the Western Hemisphere. Roosevelt himself drew the first draft numbers as he told a national radio audience, "This is a most solemn ceremony." **Ⓐ**

**ROOSEVELT RUNS FOR A THIRD TERM** That same year, Roosevelt decided to break the tradition of a two-term presidency, begun by George Washington, and run for reelection. To the great disappointment of isolationists, Roosevelt's Republican opponent, a public utilities executive named Wendell Willkie, supported Roosevelt's policy of aiding Britain. At the same time, both Willkie and Roosevelt promised to keep the nation out of war. Because there was so little difference between the candidates, the majority of voters chose the one they knew best. Roosevelt was reelected with nearly 55 percent of the votes cast.

*A. Answer*
Revision of the Neutrality Acts; dramatically increased defense spending; institution of the nation's first peacetime draft.

**MAIN IDEA**

Analyzing Effects
**Ⓐ** What impact did the outbreak of war in Europe have on U.S. foreign and defense policy?

### Tracing Themes
**VOTING RIGHTS**

#### The Election of 1940
By 1940, the wars in Europe and Asia made foreign affairs most important. Democrats used the international crisis as a reason to break tradition and have FDR run for a third term. Many Americans agreed that extraordinary times called for extraordinary measures. Not everyone agreed, however, as evidenced in the 1940 election returns. Roosevelt's opponent, Wendell Willkie, gave FDR a good contest.

In 1951, seven years after FDR had been elected to a *fourth term*, the 22nd Amendment was adopted. It states: "No person shall be elected to the office of President more than twice." Discuss with students whether this is a wise limitation.

*World War Looms* **551**

---

**DIFFERENTIATING INSTRUCTION**　　**LESS PROFICIENT READERS**

### Examining Causes and Effects

Work with students to identify the overarching cause of Roosevelt's policy decisions discussed in this section—the threat posed to the United States by Germany and Japan. Have students work in pairs to review the text and identify the actions that Roosevelt took to deal with this threat. See that they identify the following:

· cash-and-carry
· destroyers for base leases
· increased spending for national defense
· peacetime military draft
· run for third term

Students might fit these actions into a simple cause/effect chart similar to the one below:

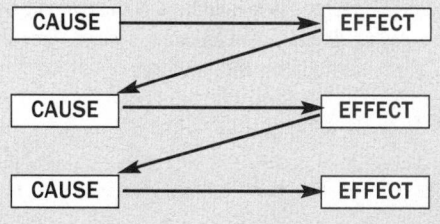

*World War Looms* **551**

## ② "The Great Arsenal of Democracy"

**"The Great Arsenal of Democracy"**
TAKS SS11 5(US24.B)
· How did Roosevelt help the Allies?
· Why were some Americans opposed to providing aid to the Soviet Union?
· What did the Germans do that threatened Roosevelt's lend-lease program?

 **In-Depth Resources: Unit 5**
· Guided Reading, p. 4

 **Electronic Library of Primary Sources**
· *from* "Are We Being Led into War?" by George A. Dondero
· *from* "Let Us Face the Truth," the *New York Times*

# POINT
# COUNTERPOINT

## Objective

· To analyze the argument in the 1930s about U.S. responsibilities in world affairs
· What did isolationists believe about America's role in the world?
· What was the interventionist position on America's world role?
· How did Charles Lindbergh risk his reputation?
· Why did FDR think the United States was threatened by what was happening in Europe?

 **In-Depth Resources: Unit 5**
· American Lives: Charles A. Lindbergh, p. 21

---

Not long after the election, President Roosevelt told his radio audience during a fireside chat that it would be impossible to negotiate a peace with Hitler. "No man can tame a tiger into a kitten by stroking it." He warned that if Britain fell, the Axis powers would be left unchallenged to conquer the world, at which point, he said, "all of us in all the Americas would be living at the point of a gun." To prevent such a situation, the United States had to help defeat the Axis threat by turning itself into what Roosevelt called "the great arsenal of democracy."

**THE LEND-LEASE PLAN** By late 1940, however, Britain had no more cash to spend in the arsenal of democracy. Roosevelt tried to help by suggesting a new plan that he called a lend-lease policy. Under this plan, the president would lend or lease arms and other supplies to "any country whose defense was vital to the United States."

Roosevelt compared his plan to lending a garden hose to a neighbor whose house was on fire. He asserted that this was the only sensible thing to do to prevent the fire from spreading to your own property. Isolationists argued bitterly against the plan, but most Americans favored it, and Congress passed the **Lend-Lease Act** in March 1941.

**Vocabulary**
**lease:** to grant use or occupation of under the terms of a contract

---

### P O I N T

**"The United States should not become involved in European wars."**

Still recovering from World War I and struggling with the Great Depression, many Americans believed their country should remain strictly neutral in the war in Europe.

Representative James F. O'Connor voiced the country's reservations when he asked, "Dare we set America up and commit her as the financial and military blood bank of the rest of the world." O'Connor maintained that the United States could not "right every wrong" or "police [the] world."

The widely admired aviator Charles Lindbergh risked his reputation by stating his hope that "the future of America . . . not be tied to these eternal wars in Europe." Lindbergh asserted that "Americans [should] fight anybody and everybody who attempts to interfere with our hemisphere." However, he went on to say, "Our safety does not lie in fighting European wars. It lies in our own internal strength, in the character of the American people and American institutions." Like many isolationists, Lindbergh believed that democracy would not be saved "by the forceful imposition of our ideals abroad, but by example of their successful operation at home."

### C O U N T E R P O I N T

**"The United States must protect democracies throughout the world."**

As the conflict in Europe deepened, interventionists embraced President Franklin D. Roosevelt's declaration that "when peace has been broken anywhere, peace of all countries everywhere is in danger." Roosevelt emphasized the global character of 20th-century commerce and communication by noting, "Every word that comes through the air, every ship that sails the sea, every battle that is fought does affect the American future."

Roosevelt and other political leaders also appealed to the nation's conscience. Secretary of State Cordell Hull noted that the world was "face to face . . . with an organized, ruthless, and implacable movement of steadily expanding conquest." In the same vein, Undersecretary of State Sumner Welles called Hitler "a sinister and pitiless conqueror [who] has reduced more than half of Europe to abject serfdom."

After the war expanded into the Atlantic, Roosevelt declared, "It is time for all Americans . . . to stop being deluded by the romantic notion that the Americas can go on living happily and peacefully in a Nazi-dominated world." He added, "Let us not ask ourselves whether the Americas should begin to defend themselves after the first attack . . . or the twentieth attack. The time for active defense is now."

#### THINKING CRITICALLY

1. **CONNECT TO TODAY  Making Inferences** After World War I, many Americans became isolationists. Do you recommend that the United States practice isolationism today? Why or why not?

2. **CONNECT TO HISTORY  Researching and Reporting** Do research to find out more about Charles Lindbergh's antiwar activities. Present yor findings in an editorial.

 **SEE SKILLBUILDER HANDBOOK, PAGE R34.**

---

## THINKING CRITICALLY: ANSWERS

**1. CONNECT TO TODAY** Many students will probably say that it would be impossible for the United States to be isolationist due to its political and economic strength. Students' responses should be well thought out and include specific references to today's political crises around the world. They should support their stands on U.S. isolationism with evidence.

**2. CONNECT TO HISTORY**
**Rubric**
An editorial should . . .
· advocate a position regarding isolationism in the United States
· support the opinion with factual evidence based on current or historical events
· give insight into the economic, political, and social factors influencing United States foreign policy

**SUPPORTING STALIN** Britain was not the only nation to receive lend-lease aid. In June 1941, Hitler broke the agreement he had made in 1939 with Stalin not to go to war and invaded the Soviet Union. Acting on the principle that "the enemy of my enemy is my friend," Roosevelt began sending lend-lease supplies to the Soviet Union. Some Americans opposed providing aid to Stalin, Roosevelt however, agreed with Winston Churchill, who had said "if Hitler invaded Hell," the British would be prepared to work with the devil himself. **B**

**GERMAN WOLF PACKS** Providing lend-lease aid was one thing, but to ensure the safe delivery of goods to Britain and to the Soviet Union, supply lines had to be kept open across the Atlantic Ocean. To prevent delivery of lend-lease shipments, Hitler deployed hundreds of German submarines—U-boats—to attack supply ships.

From the spring through the fall of 1941, individual surface attacks by individual U-boats gave way to what became known as the wolf pack attack. At night groups of up to 40 submarines patrolled areas in the North Atlantic where convoys could be expected. Wolf packs were successful in sinking as much as 350,000 tons of shipments in a single month. In June 1941, President Roosevelt granted the navy permission for U.S. warships to attack German U-boats in self-defense. By late 1943, the submarine menace was contained by electronic detection techniques (especially radar), and by airborne antisubmarine patrols operating from small escort aircraft carriers.

**MAIN IDEA**

**Drawing Conclusions**
**B** Why did Roosevelt take one "unneutral" step after another to assist Britain and the Soviet Union in 1941?

**B. Answer** Roosevelt believed that the best way to stop the Axis powers was to help their opponents—mainly Britain and the Soviet Union.

## More About . . .

### The U-Boats
After the fall of France in 1940, Hitler had a 3,000-mile coastline from which to launch submarine attacks on Allied ships. With the threat of invasion keeping British warships close to home, the U-Boats enjoyed excellent hunting. Between July 1940 and December 1941, a period referred to as "Happy Time," German U-Boats sank ship after ship. The U-Boats were so effective that Hitler refused, despite the urging of his naval commander, to push production of German submarines. Hitler's decision would turn out to be a crucial mistake.

## Science & Technology

### GERMAN WOLF PACKS
On October 17, 1940, near Rockall, west of Ireland, a British Convoy, SC-7 (shown below), was attacked by a German wolf pack. The convoy was outlined clearly against a moonlit sky, making the merchant ships easy prey.

▲ A tanker burns and sinks in the Atlantic Ocean after being torpedoed by a German U-boat.

At the start of the war, the British had too few war-ships to escort the convoys.

German aircraft could patrol 1,000 miles out to sea to scout for convoys.

The Germans used radios to summon U-boats into a fighting wolf pack.

U-boats used hydrophonic equipment to pick up the sound of convoy propellers up to 100 miles away.

Convoys pinned their hopes on finding U-boats using ASDIC—sonar apparatus that could detect submerged submarines. But the U-boats were attacking convoys on the surface.

## More About . . .

### U-Boat Combat
While science and technology clearly influenced the Battle of the Atlantic, in the end it was naval power that gave the Allies an advantage. The use of sonar, coupled with armed destroyers capable of attacking submarines, took a terrible toll on German U-Boats. The United States was in a de facto war with Germany by the summer of 1941 when Roosevelt gave U.S. ships the order to shoot any U-Boat on sight.

*World War Looms* **553**

---

**ACTIVITY**  **LINK TO SCIENCE**

## Radar

**Class Time** One class period

**Task** Investigating how radar/sonar works

**Purpose** To understand the scientific principles behind radar/sonar

**Directions** Divide students into small groups and have them use available text and Internet resources to find out how either radar or sonar works and how it got its name. Ask each group to create a poster that both shows and explains how radar works to identify objects. Direct students to identify nonmilitary uses for radar/sonar.

 classzone.com

### KEY PLAYER

**Hideki Tojo**

## ❸ FDR Plans for War

Although Roosevelt was popular, his foreign policy was under constant attack. American forces were seriously underarmed. Roosevelt's August 1941 proposal to extend the term of draftees passed in the House of Representatives by only one vote. With the army provided for, Roosevelt began planning for the war he was certain would come.

**THE ATLANTIC CHARTER** While Congress voted on the extension of the draft, Roosevelt and Churchill met secretly at a summit aboard the battleship the U.S.S. *Augusta.* Although Churchill hoped for a military commitment, he settled for a joint declaration of war aims, called the **Atlantic Charter.** Both countries pledged the following: collective security, disarmament, self-determination, economic cooperation, and freedom of the seas. Roosevelt disclosed to Churchill that he couldn't ask Congress for a declaration of war against Germany, but "he would wage war" and do "everything" to "force an incident."

The Atlantic Charter became the basis of a new document called "A Declaration of the United Nations." The term *United Nations* was suggested by Roosevelt to express the common purpose of the **Allies,** those nations that had fought the Axis powers. The declaration was signed by 26 nations, "four-fifths of the human race" observed Churchill. **Ⓒ**

**KEY PLAYER**

**HIDEKI TOJO
1884–1948**

U.S. newspapers described Hideki Tojo as "smart, hard-boiled, resourceful, [and] contemptuous of theories, sentiments, and negotiations."

The Nazi press in Germany praised Tojo as "a man charged with energy, thinking clearly and with a single purpose." To a British paper, Tojo was "the son of Satan" whose single purpose was "unleashing all hell on the Far East." In Japan, however, Tojo was looked up to as a man whose "decisive leadership was a signal for the nation to rise and administer a great shock to the anti-Axis powers."

**SHOOT ON SIGHT** After a German submarine fired on the U.S. destroyer *Greer* in the Atlantic on September 4, 1941, Roosevelt ordered navy commanders to respond. "When you see a rattlesnake poised to strike," the president explained, "you crush him." Roosevelt ordered the Navy to shoot the German submarines on sight.

Two weeks later, the *Pink Star,* an American merchant ship, was sunk off Greenland. In mid-October, a U-boat topedoed the U.S. destroyer *Kearny,* and 11 lives were lost.

Days later, German U-boats sank the U.S. destroyer *Reuben James,* killing more than 100 sailors. "America has been attacked," Roosevelt announced grimly. "The shooting has started. And history has recorded who fired the first shot." As the death toll mounted, the Senate finally repealed the ban against arming merchant ships. A formal declaration of a full-scale war seemed inevitable. **Ⓓ**

## ❹ Japan Attacks the United States

The United States was now involved in an undeclared naval war with Hitler. However, the attack that brought the United States into the war came from Japan.

**JAPAN'S AMBITIONS IN THE PACIFIC** Germany's European victories created new opportunities for Japanese expansionists. Japan was already in control of Manchuria. In July 1937, **Hideki Tojo** (hēʹd-kē tōʹjōʹ), chief of staff of Japan's Kwantung Army, launched the invasion into China. As French, Dutch, and British colonies lay unprotected in Asia, Japanese leaders leaped at the opportunity to unite East Asia under Japanese control by seizing the colonial lands. By 1941, the British were too busy fighting Hitler to block Japanese expansion. Only the U.S. and its Pacific islands remained in Japan's way.

---

The Japanese began their southward push in July 1941 by taking over French military bases in Indochina (now Vietnam, Cambodia, and Laos). The United States protested this new act of aggression by cutting off trade with Japan. The embargoed goods included one Japan could not live without—oil to fuel its war machine. Japanese military leaders warned that without oil, Japan could be defeated without its enemies ever striking a blow. The leaders declared that Japan must either persuade the United States to end its oil embargo or seize the oil fields in the Dutch East Indies. This would mean war. **E**

**MAIN IDEA**

**Analyzing Issues**

**E** How was oil a source of conflict between Japan and the United States?

**E. Answer**
Japan needed oil, and the United States had placed an embargo on it to protest Japanese aggression in Indochina.

**PEACE TALKS ARE QUESTIONED** Shortly after becoming the prime minister of Japan Hideki Tojo met with emperor Hirohito. Tojo promised the emperor that the Japanese government would attempt to preserve peace with the Americans. But on November 5, 1941, Tojo ordered the Japanese navy to prepare for an attack on the United States.

The U.S. military had broken Japan's secret communication codes and learned that Japan was preparing for a strike. What it didn't know was where the attack would come. Late in November, Roosevelt sent out a "war warning" to military commanders in Hawaii, Guam, and the Philippines. If war could not be avoided, the warning said, "the United States desires that Japan commit the first overt act." And the nation waited.

The peace talks went on for a month. Then on December 6, 1941, Roosevelt received a decoded message that instructed Japan's peace envoy to reject all American peace proposals. "This means war," Roosevelt declared.

**THE ATTACK ON PEARL HARBOR** Early the next morning, a Japanese dive-bomber swooped low over Pearl Harbor—the largest U.S. naval base in the Pacific. The bomber was followed by more than 180 Japanese warplanes launched from six aircraft carriers. As the first Japanese bombs found their targets, a radio operator flashed this message: "Air raid on Pearl Harbor. This is not a drill."

For an hour and a half, the Japanese planes were barely disturbed by U.S. antiaircraft guns and blasted target after target. By the time the last plane soared off around 9:30 A.M., the devastation was appalling. John Garcia, a pipe fitter's apprentice, was there.

▲ Newspaper headlines announce the surprise Japanese attack.

**A PERSONAL VOICE** JOHN GARCIA

" It was a mess. I was working on the U.S.S. *Shaw.* It was on a floating dry dock. It was in flames. I started to go down into the pipe fitter's shop to get my toolbox when another wave of Japanese came in. I got under a set of concrete steps at the dry dock where the battleship *Pennsylvania* was. An officer came by and asked me to go into the *Pennsylvania* and try to get the fires out. A bomb had penetrated the marine deck, and . . . three decks below. Under that was the magazines: ammunition, powder, shells. I said "There ain't no way I'm gonna go down there." It could blow up any minute. I was young and 16, not stupid. "

—quoted in *The Good War*

**HISTORY from VISUALS**

**Interpreting the Photograph**
Ask students to examine the photograph. What does the headline communicate? *(The headline, with its giant exclamation point, effectively communicates the horrifying news.)*

**Extension** Ask students to use what they have read in the previous pages to put themselves in the situation. How would they, as 16–18 year olds, have reacted to the news of war?

**More About . . .**

**John Garcia's War**
John Garcia lost a number of friends during the attack on Pearl Harbor, including his girlfriend, whose home was hit by an American shell. He tried to join the military, only to be refused because his work was considered essential to the war effort. A letter to President Roosevelt got Garcia into the military at age 17.

*World War Looms* **555**

---

**ACTIVITY** | **LINK TO WORLD HISTORY**

**Pearl Harbor**

**Class Time** One class period

**Task** Researching American reaction to attack on Pearl Harbor

**Purpose** To understand the impact of the Japanese attack on the United States

 **TAKS** Mini-Lesson 4: SS11 1(US6.A)

**Directions** Have students use available research materials to find out how newspapers and magazines responded to the Japanese attack. Direct students to use Internet searches to find newspapers and magazines from December 7–8, 1941. Have them prepare a collage of newspapers or magazine headlines.

 Integrated Assessment
· Rubric 4

**B** **BLOCK SCHEDULING**

## Japanese Aggression, 1931–1941

# HISTORY from VISUALS

### Interpreting the Map

Direct students' attention to the inset maps and ask what additional information the map conveys about the Japanese attack. *(The Japanese attacked in two waves. Japanese planes hit targets other than Pearl Harbor. They bombed planes at Wheeler Air Force Base and Kaneohe Naval Air Station.)* Ask students how Americans might have better defended themselves if the attack had not been a complete surprise. *(American planes could have attacked Japanese bombers; naval ships could have shot down attacking planes; ships could have been moved from their berths and spread out.)*

 In-Depth Resources
· Geography Application: Japanese Aggression, pp. 11–12

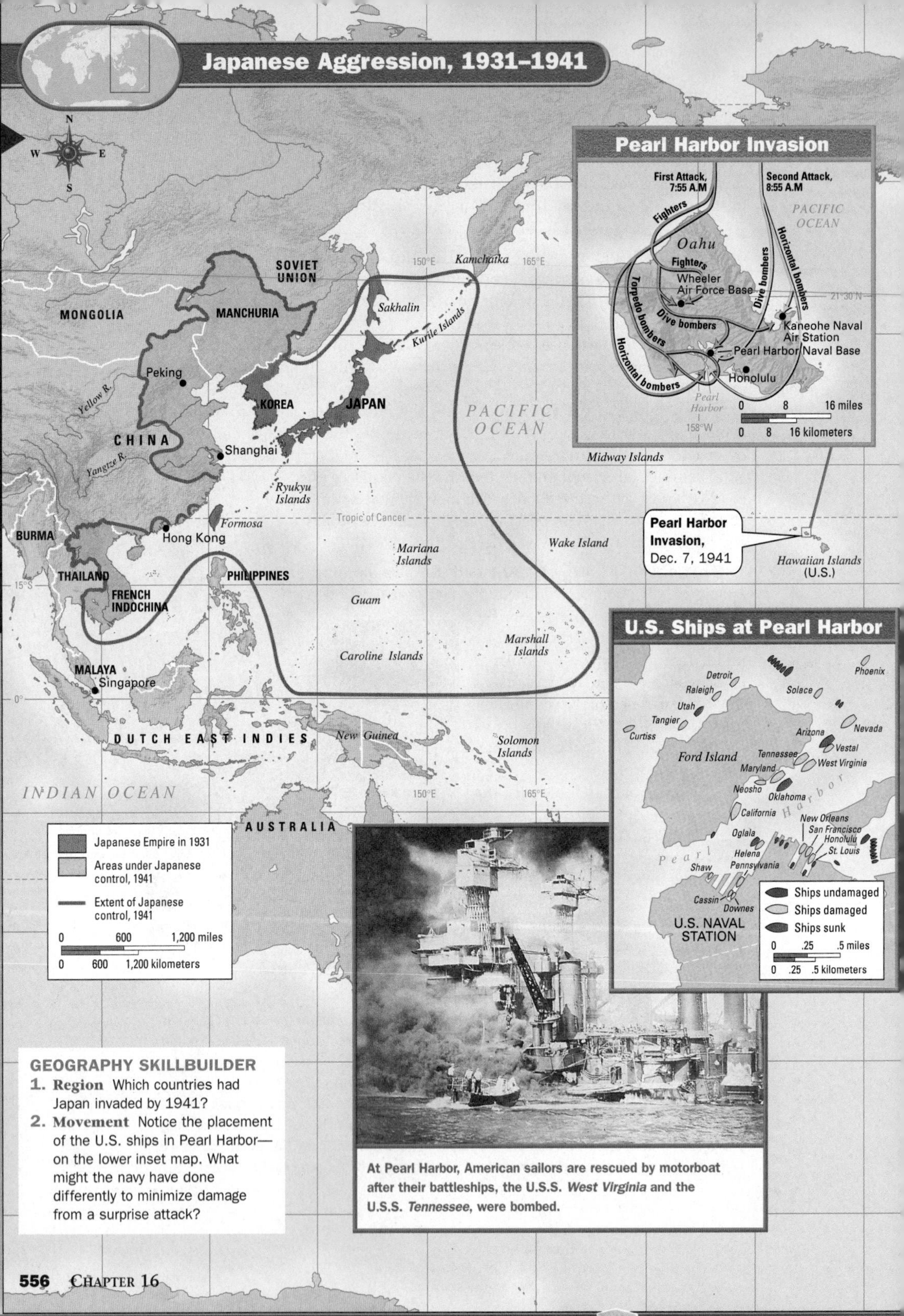

### Pearl Harbor Invasion

First Attack, 7:55 A.M
Second Attack, 8:55 A.M

PACIFIC OCEAN

*Oahu*

Fighters
Fighters
Wheeler Air Force Base
Horizontal bombers
Dive bombers
Torpedo bombers
Kaneohe Naval Air Station
Dive bombers
Pearl Harbor Naval Base
Horizontal bombers
Honolulu

21 30 N

*Pearl Harbor*

158°W

0    8    16 miles
0    8    16 kilometers

MONGOLIA
MANCHURIA
SOVIET UNION
Sakhalin
Kamchatka
150°E    165°E
Kurile Islands
Peking
Yellow R.
KOREA    JAPAN
CHINA
Shanghai
Yangtze R.
Ryukyu Islands
PACIFIC OCEAN
Midway Islands

Tropic of Cancer
Formosa
BURMA
Hong Kong
Mariana Islands
Wake Island
THAILAND
FRENCH INDOCHINA
PHILIPPINES
Guam
15°S
Caroline Islands
Marshall Islands
MALAYA
Singapore
0°

**Pearl Harbor Invasion, Dec. 7, 1941**

Hawaiian Islands (U.S.)

### U.S. Ships at Pearl Harbor

Detroit    Phoenix
Raleigh    Solace
Utah
Tangier    Nevada
Curtiss    Arizona
Ford Island    Tennessee    Vestal
Maryland    West Virginia
Neosho    Oklahoma
California    Harbor
New Orleans
Oglala    San Francisco
Honolulu    St. Louis
Helena    Pennsylvania
Pearl    Shaw
Cassin
Downes
U.S. NAVAL STATION

Ships undamaged
Ships damaged
Ships sunk

0    .25    .5 miles
0    .25    .5 kilometers

DUTCH EAST INDIES
New Guinea
Solomon Islands
INDIAN OCEAN
150°E    165°E
AUSTRALIA

Japanese Empire in 1931
Areas under Japanese control, 1941
Extent of Japanese control, 1941

0    600    1,200 miles
0    600    1,200 kilometers

At Pearl Harbor, American sailors are rescued by motorboat after their battleships, the U.S.S. *West Virginia* and the U.S.S. *Tennessee*, were bombed.

### GEOGRAPHY SKILLBUILDER

1. **Region** Which countries had Japan invaded by 1941?
2. **Movement** Notice the placement of the U.S. ships in Pearl Harbor— on the lower inset map. What might the navy have done differently to minimize damage from a surprise attack?

**556** CHAPTER 16

---

**ACTIVITY    LINK TO GEOGRAPHY**

**BLOCK SCHEDULING**

## Mapping Attack Sites

**Class Time** 30 minutes

**Task** Creating a map with dates and locations of Japanese aggression

**Purpose** To locate sites of Japanese aggression

**Directions** Have students do research to establish a series of dates and locations of Japanese attack between 1931 and 1941. Using a map of Asia and the western Pacific—or using the map on this page—ask students to label each location and the date it was taken.

As they complete their research, students may find photographs and news stories on these attacks. Interested students can mount the map on posterboard and add copies of the photos and captions with leader lines to the map. This will become an annotated, more informative map for students to refer to as they study the war.

Integrated Assessment
· Rubric 1

In less than two hours, the Japanese had killed 2,403 Americans and wounded 1,178 more. The surprise raid had sunk or damaged 21 ships, including 8 battleships—nearly the whole U.S. Pacific fleet. More than 300 aircraft were severely damaged or destroyed. These losses constituted greater damage than the U.S. Navy had suffered in all of World War I. By chance, three aircraft carriers at sea escaped the disaster. Their survival would prove crucial to the war's outcome.

**REACTION TO PEARL HARBOR** In Washington, the mood ranged from outrage to panic. At the White House, Eleanor Roosevelt watched closely as her husband absorbed the news from Hawaii, "each report more terrible than the last." Beneath the president's calm, Eleanor could see how worried he was. "I never wanted to have to fight this war on two fronts," Roosevelt told his wife. "We haven't the Navy to fight in both the Atlantic and the Pacific . . . so we will have to build up the Navy and the Air Force and that will mean that we will have to take a good many defeats before we can have a victory."

The next day, President Roosevelt addressed Congress. "Yesterday, December 7, 1941, a date which will live in infamy," he said, "[the Japanese launched] an unprovoked and dastardly attack." Congress quickly approved Roosevelt's request for a declaration of war against Japan. Three days later, Germany and Italy declared war on the United States.

For all the damage done at Pearl Harbor, perhaps the greatest was to the cause of isolationism. Many who had been former isolationists now supported an all-out American effort. After the surprise attack, isolationist senator Burton Wheeler proclaimed, "The only thing now to do is to lick the hell out of them."

**Vocabulary**
**infamy:** evil fame or reputation

**ECONOMIC BACKGROUND**

**WAR AND THE DEPRESSION**
The approach of war did what all the programs of the New Deal could not do—end the Great Depression. As defense spending skyrocketed in 1940, long-idle factories came back to life. A merry-go-round company began producing gun mounts; a stove factory made lifeboats; a famous New York toy maker made compasses; a pinball-machine company made armor-piercing shells.

With factories hiring again, the nation's unemployment rolls began shrinking rapidly—by 400,000 in August 1940 and by another 500,000 in September. By the time the Japanese attacked Pearl Harbor, America was heading back to work. (See *Keynesian Economics* on page R42 in the Economics Handbook.)

---

**ECONOMIC BACKGROUND**

**War and the Depression**
**Analyzing Issues** Discuss with students the long-debated question of whether war is "good for business." If so, does this mean that bankers and business leaders would promote wars for their own profit? Many Americans in the 1930s believed this to be true.

**Electronic Library of Primary Sources**
· "On the Declaration of War" by Franklin D. Roosevelt

**Critical Thinking Transparencies CT24, CT58**
· World War II Breaks out in Europe
· Time Line of Events Leading to World War II

**TAKS** Mini-Lesson 3: SS11 3(US14.A)

## Assess & Reteach

**SECTION 4 ASSESSMENT**
Have students answer the questions individually, then compare answers with a partner.

**Formal Assessment**
· Section Quiz, p. 303

**SELF-ASSESSMENT**
Have students note the questions they had trouble answering or answered incorrectly. Have them look for patterns that emerge in the types of questions they find difficult.

**RETEACH**
Stage a class debate on isolationism based on the material presented in the Point Counterpoint feature on page 550.

**In-Depth Resources: Unit 5**
· Reteaching Activity, p. 10

---

## SECTION 4 ASSESSMENT

**1. TERMS & NAMES** For each term or name, write a sentence explaining its significance.
- Axis powers
- Atlantic Charter
- Allies
- Lend-Lease Act
- Hideki Tojo

### MAIN IDEA

**2. TAKING NOTES**
Create a time line of key events leading to America's entry into World War II. Use the dates below as a guide.

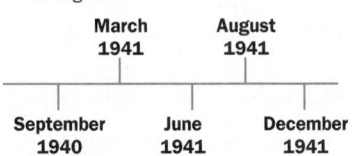

March 1941     August 1941

September 1940    June 1941    December 1941

Which of the events that you listed was most influential in bringing the United States into the war? Why?

### CRITICAL THINKING

**3. EVALUATING DECISIONS**
Do you think that the United States should have waited to be attacked before declaring war? **Think About:**
- the reputation of the United States
- the influence of isolationists
- the events at of Pearl Harbor

**4. PREDICTING EFFECTS**
What problem would the Japanese attack on Pearl Harbor solve for Roosevelt? What new problems would it create?

**5. ANALYZING PRIMARY SOURCES**
Although the U.S. Congress was still unwilling to declare war early in 1941, Churchill told his war cabinet,

> " We must have patience and trust to the tide which is flowing our way, and to events. "

What do you think Churchill meant by this remark? Support your answer.

---

**Answers** | **ASSESSMENT**

**1. TERMS & NAMES**
Axis powers, p. 551
Lend-Lease Act, p. 552
Atlantic Charter, p. 554
Hideki Tojo, p. 554
Allies, p. 554

**2. TAKING NOTES**
**Sept. 1940:** Japan, Germany, and Italy, sign the Tripartite Pact. **Mar. 1941:** Congress passes Lend-Lease Act. **June 1941:** Germany invades Soviet Union; Roosevelt orders U.S. Navy to protect lend-lease shipments, **Aug. 1941:** Roosevelt and Churchill draw up Atlantic Charter. **Dec. 1941:** Japan bombs Pearl Harbor.

**3. EVALUATING DECISIONS**
**Waited:** An attack by Japan would swing public opinion away from isolationism and allow Roosevelt to enter the war with the support of the American people. **Not waited:** An earlier declaration of war might have prevented the attack on Pearl Harbor.

**4. PREDICTING EFFECTS**
The attack would unify public support behind the war effort, but it would cripple the fleet needed to fight the war.

**5. ANALYZING PRIMARY SOURCES**
Churchill believed that the U.S. entry into World War II was inevitable; the United States was edging closer and closer to war.

## TERMS & NAMES

1. fascism, p. 530
2. Adolf Hitler, p. 531
3. Nazism, p. 531
4. Winston Churchill, p. 538
5. appeasement, p. 538
6. Charles de Gaulle, p. 540
7. Holocaust, p. 542
8. genocide p. 544
9. Axis powers, p. 551
10. Allies, p. 554

## MAIN IDEAS

1. To make the Soviet Union socialist by ending private enterprise; to transform it into a great industrial power by building state-owned factories and power plants.
2. Hitler and Mussolini's military support helped Franco take power in Spain.
3. It surprised the enemy and then crushed it with overwhelming force.
4. German occupation of northern France and the establishment of a Nazi-controlled puppet government in southern France; de Gaulle fled to England and set up a government-in-exile.
5. Jews, gypsies, homosexuals, people with mental or physical disabilities, Poles, Ukrainians, and Russians.
6. Some people risked death by hiding Jews in their homes or helping them to escape to neutral countries.
7. Increased defense spending, peacetime draft, Lend-Lease Act, and an end to the ban against arming merchant ships.
8. Because the Japanese bombed Pearl Harbor.

# CHAPTER 16 ASSESSMENT

## VISUAL SUMMARY
### WORLD WAR LOOMS

**1931**
1931 Japan invades Manchuria.

**1932**
1932 Nazi Party becomes the most powerful in Germany.

**1933**
Mar. 1933 First concentration camp opens at Oranienburg. Adolf Hitler becomes dictator of Germany.

**1934**

**1935**
Sept. 1935 Nuremberg Laws instituted against Jews in Germany.
Oct. 1935 Italian troops invade Ethiopia.

**1936**
Mar. 1936 Germany occupies Rhineland.
Jul. 1936 Spanish Civil War begins.
Oct. 1936 Germany and Italy form Axis.

**1937**
1937 Japan invades China.

**1938**
Nov. 1938 Kristallnacht, Night of Broken Glass, Nazis destroy property and arrest over 20,000 Jews.

**1939**
Mar. 1939 Germany invades the Sudetenland.
Sept. 1939 Germany invades Poland. Britain and France declare war on Germany and World War II begins.

**1940**
June 1940 France surrenders.
Sept. 1940 Japan signs tripartite pact with Germany and Italy.

**1941**
Mar. 1941 Roosevelt signs the Lend-Lease Act.
Jun. 1941 Nazis begin mass murder of the Jews.
Dec. 1941 Pearl Harbor is bombed. U.S. declares war.

## TERMS & NAMES

For each term or name below, write a sentence explaining its significance in U.S. foreign affairs between 1931 and 1941.

1. fascism
2. Adolf Hitler
3. Nazism
4. Winston Churchill
5. appeasement
6. Charles de Gaulle
7. Holocaust
8. genocide
9. Axis powers
10. Allies

## MAIN IDEAS

Use your notes and the information in the chapter to answer the following questions about the early years of World War II.

**Dictators Threaten World Peace** *(pages 528–535)*

1. What were Stalin's goals and what steps did he take to achieve them?
2. How did Germany's and Italy's involvement affect the outcome of the Spanish Civil War?

**War in Europe** *(pages 536–541)*

3. Why was the blitzkrieg effective?
4. What terms of surrender did Hitler demand of the French after the fall of France in 1940? What was General Charles de Gaulle's reaction?

**The Holocaust** *(pages 542–549)*

5. What groups did Nazis deem unfit to belong to the Aryan "master race?"
6. How did some Europeans show their resistance to Nazi persecution of the Jews?

**America Moves Toward War** *(pages 550–557)*

7. What congressional measures paved the way for the U.S. entry into World War II?
8. Why did the United States enter World War II?

## CRITICAL THINKING

1. **USING YOUR NOTES** In a chart like the one shown, identify the effects of each of these early events of World War II.

| Cause | Effect |
|-------|--------|
| First blitzkrieg | |
| Allies stranded at Dunkirk | |
| British radar detects German aircraft | |
| Lend-Lease Act | |

2. **COMPARING** Compare the ways in which Hitler, Churchill, and Roosevelt used their powers as gifted speakers to accomplish their political aims during World War II. Use details from the chapter text.

3. **INTERPRETING MAPS** Look at the map of German advances on page 538. How might Poland's location have influenced the secret pact that Germany and the Soviet Union signed on August 23, 1939?

## CRITICAL THINKING

1. **Using Your Notes** Blitzkrieg: the fall of Poland; Dunkirk: 338,000 soldiers saved. British forces leave Western Europe; Radar: the British able to hold off German occupation; Lend-Lease Act: U.S. supplied Allies with war goods, U.S. decision to favor the Allies.

2. **Comparing** All three motivated their audiences to embrace certain beliefs and fostered national unity. Hitler spread a message of hate and nationalism. Churchill aroused and united the British to defeat the Nazis. Roosevelt informed Americans about the policies and underscored his beliefs in democratic ideals.

3. **Interpreting Maps** After Hitler's troops invaded Poland from the west, the north, and the south, Stalin was afraid that the Soviet Union would soon become Hitler's next target.

## Standardized Test Practice

Use the cartoon and your knowledge of U.S. history to answer questions 1 and 2.

I HOPE YOU HAVE BETTER LUCK THAN I DID

WILSON

U.S. NEUTRALI

F.D.R.

1. All of the following are true of F.D.R.'s neutrality policy *except* —

   A Roosevelt found it hard to keep the United States neutral.

   B Roosevelt did not always enforce the Neutrality Acts.

   C Roosevelt promoted the Neutrality Policy of the United States throughout the war.

   D Roosevelt spoke out against isolationism.

2. President Wilson's image rises above President Roosevelt to wish him luck for —

   F helping to pass the bill he is signing.

   G keeping the United States out of a war.

   H winning the next presidential election.

   J gaining greater revenues from Europe.

Use the quotation and your knowledge of U.S. history to answer question 3.

" In the future days, which we seek to make secure, we look forward to a world founded upon four essential human freedoms. The first is freedom of speech and expression. —everywhere in the world. The second is freedom of every person to worship God in his own way. —everywhere in the world. The third is freedom from want. . . . The fourth is freedom from fear. "

—Franklin Roosevelt, Address to Congress, 1941

3. The "four freedoms" speech helped gain wide-spread support in the United States for —

   A increasing aid to the Allies.

   B decreasing immigration.

   C a military and arms buildup.

   D a presidential election.

---

**ADDITIONAL TEST PRACTICE, pages S1–S33.**

TEST PRACTICE   CLASSZONE.COM

## ALTERNATIVE ASSESSMENT

1. INTERACT WITH HISTORY   Recall your discussion of the question on page 527:

*Why might the United States try to remain neutral?*

As a political cartoonist for a major newspaper, your work is seen by millions of Americans. Draw a political cartoon that supports or opposes the policy of neutrality.

2.  VIDEO   **LEARNING FROM MEDIA**  View the *American Stories* video, "Escaping the Final Solution: Kurt Klein and Gerda Weissmann Klein Remember the Holocaust."

   • What conditions that Gerda faced would be most difficult for you to endure?

   **Cooperative Learning Activity**  It has been said, "Those who cannot remember the past are condemned to repeat it."

   As a group, collect quotations and historical data about the Holocaust. Then write a book introduction about the Holocaust that incorporates quotations and the importance of the first-person accounts of survivors, such as the Kleins.

---

## Standardized Test Practice

1. The correct answer is letter **C**.
   Following Japan's attack on Pearl Harbor, the United States declared war.
   Letter A is not correct because FDR did find it hard to keep U.S. neutrality. Letter B is not correct because FDR did not always enforce the Neutrality Acts. Letter D is not correct because FDR often publicly disagreed with the isolationists.

2. The correct answer is letter **G**.
   Wilson was president during WWI and is hoping FDR can keep the country out of another war.
   Letter F is not correct because Wilson did not try to pass a neutrality bill. Letter H is not correct because FDR is not running for reelection. Letter J is not correct because FDR is not attempting to gain revenues from Europe.

3. The correct answer is letter **C**.
   Roosevelt's address to Congress in 1941 was a call to declare war.
   Letter A is not correct because FDR was not seeking to send aid to the Allies. Letter B is not correct because immigration was not the issue of the day. Letter D is not correct because FDR was not preparing for an election.

UNIT PROJECT

**DEBATE**

**Tips for Teaching**

· Have students draft their proposition.

· Give students suggested Internet links or key words to find information on their issue.

📄 Formal Assessment
   · Chapter Test, Forms A, B, and C, pp. 304–315

---

## ALTERNATIVE ASSESSMENT

### 1. INTERACT WITH HISTORY

**Rubric**

A political cartoon should . . .

· clearly present a concept with the use of conventional images

· demonstrate an understanding of the policy of neutrality

· support or oppose neutrality

### 2. LEARNING FROM MEDIA

**Rubric**

A book introduction should . . .

· include the quote and background on the Kleins

· note the importance of first-person accounts as primary sources of information

· use an interesting style to engage the reader and to educate on the topic

# The United States in World War II

| | CHAPTER OVERVIEW | COPYMASTERS | INTEGRATED TECHNOLOGY |
|---|---|---|---|
| **CHAPTER RESOURCES** | *Soldiers abroad and Americans at home join in the effort to win World War II, which ends with victory for the Allies. But American society is transformed in the process.* | 📄 **Telescoping the Times**<br>· Chapter Summary, pp. 33–34<br><br>📄 **Planning for Block Schedules** | 👁 Power Presentations<br>👁 Electronic Teacher Tools<br>ⓘ Online Lesson Planner<br>ⓘ classzone.com |
| **SECTION 1**<br>**Mobilizing for Defense**<br>pp. 562–568 | **KEY IDEAS**<br>*The United States enters the war and mobilizes its citizens and resources to give its allies unprecedented military and industrial support.* | 📄 **In-Depth Resources: Unit 5**<br>· Guided Reading, p. 22<br>· Building Vocabulary, p. 26<br>· Skillbuilder Practice, p. 27<br>· Reteaching Activity, p. 28<br>· Primary Sources, p. 37<br>· American Lives, p. 43<br><br>📄 **Lesson Plans,** pp. 135–136 | 👁 Electronic Library of Primary Sources<br>· "What Can I Do?" by the Office of Civilian Defense<br>ⓘ classzone.com |
| **SECTION 2**<br>**The War for Europe and North Africa**<br>pp. 569–577 | *The United States, Great Britain, and the Soviet Union cooperate in the fight to defeat Germany and its allies.* | 📄 **In-Depth Resources: Unit 5**<br>· Guided Reading, p. 23<br>· Reteaching Activity, p. 29<br>· Geography Application, pp. 32–33<br>· Outline Map, pp. 34–35<br>· Primary Sources, p. 38<br>· American Lives, p. 44<br><br>📄 **Lesson Plans,** pp. 137–138 | 🕹 Critical Thinking Transparencies CT25<br>· U.S. Joins the Allies in World War II<br>🕹 Geography Transparencies GT25<br>· Battle of the Bulge<br>🕹 Humanities Transparencies HT24<br>· Flying Fortresses<br>👁 Electronic Library of Primary Sources<br>· *from* Instructions to the Third United States Army by George S. Patton<br>ⓘ classzone.com |
| **SECTION 3**<br>**The War in the Pacific**<br>pp. 578–589 | *America wages an aggressive military campaign against Japan in the Pacific islands and finally ends the war.* | 📄 **In-Depth Resources: Unit 5**<br>· Guided Reading, p. 24<br>· Reteaching Activity, p. 30<br>· Primary Sources, p. 39<br><br>📄 **Lesson Plans,** pp. 139–140 | 👁 Electronic Library of Primary Sources<br>· Statement on the Atomic Bomb by Harry S. Truman<br>ⓘ classzone.com |
| **SECTION 4**<br>**The Home Front**<br>pp. 590–597 | *Americans begin to adjust to new economic opportunities and continuing social problems after World War II.* | 📄 **In-Depth Resources: Unit 5**<br>· Guided Reading, p. 25<br>· Reteaching Activity, p. 31<br>· Primary Sources, p. 36<br>· Literature, pp. 40–42<br><br>📄 **Lesson Plans,** pp. 141–142 | 🕹 Critical Thinking Transparencies CT59<br>· Human Cost of World War II<br>👁 Electronic Library of Primary Sources<br>· Japanese-American Testimony from National Defense Migration Hearings<br>ⓘ classzone.com |

| | | | | | |
|---|---|---|---|---|---|
|  Pupil's Edition | | Overhead Transparency | | CD-ROM | |
| Teacher's Edition | | Audio Library | | Internet | |
| Copymaster | | | | | |

## ASSESSMENT OPTIONS

Chapter Assessment, pp. 598–599

Formal Assessment
· Chapter Tests, Forms A, B, and C, pp. 320–337

Test Generator

Integrated Assessment Book

TAKS Online Test Practice

TAKS Spiraled Content Review

TAKS Practice Tests

---

Section 1 Assessment, p. 568

Self-Assessment, p. 568

Formal Assessment, Quiz, p. 316

Integrated Assessment Book

Test Generator

TAKS Practice Transparencies TT94

---

Section 2 Assessment, p. 577

Self-Assessment, p. 577

Formal Assessment, Quiz, p. 317

Integrated Assessment Book

Test Generator

TAKS Practice Transparencies TT95

---

Section 3 Assessment, p. 587

Self-Assessment, p. 587

Formal Assessment, Quiz, p. 318

Integrated Assessment Book

Test Generator

TAKS Practice Transparencies TT96

---

Section 4 Assessment, p. 595

Self-Assessment, p. 595

Formal Assessment, Quiz, p. 319

Integrated Assessment Book

Test Generator

TAKS Practice Transparencies TT97

## RESOURCES FOR DIFFERENTIATING INSTRUCTION

**Students Acquiring English/ESL**

Reading Study Guide:
(English and Spanish)
pp. 171–178

Access for Students
Acquiring English/ESL:
Spanish Translations,
pp. 189–197

Chapter Summaries on CD
(English and Spanish)

**Less Proficient Readers**

Reading Study Guide
(English and Spanish)
pp. 171–178

Telescoping the Times
· Chapter Summary,
pp. 33–34

Chapter Summaries on CD
(English and Spanish)

**Gifted and Talented Students**

In-Depth Resources: Unit 5
· Primary Sources, pp. 36–39
· Literature, pp. 40–42
· American Lives, pp. 43–44

Historic Supreme Court
Decisions
· *Korematsu* v. *United
States*, pp. 157–163

Electronic Library of
Primary Sources
· Unit 5, Chapter 17

## CROSS-CURRICULAR CONNECTIONS

### Culture
Aaseng, Nathan. *Navajo Code Talkers.* NY: Walker, 1992. Fascinating story, not only of the science behind code making, but of Navajo life on the reservations and in the military.

### Science
Cohen, Daniel. *The Manhattan Project.* Brookfield, CT: 21st Century Books, 1999. Explains the science of the bomb and the history of its development.

### Economics
Colman, Penny and Gawain, Shakti (contributor). *Rosie the Riveter: Women Working on the Home Front in World War II*. NY: Knopf, 1995. A broad overview of women war workers, with photographs and quotes.

### Literature
Knowles, John. *A Separate Peace (with related readings)*. NY: Bantam Books, 1985. Consistently hailed as a modern classic, this story of two friends at an elite boarding school during the early years of World War II is a deeply moving novel of the confusions of adolescence.

Goodrich, Frances and Hacket, Albert. *The Diary of Anne Frank.* Boston: Houghton Mifflin College, 1996. A play based on the famous diary of the Jewish girl who hid with her family from the Nazis.

### McDougal Littell *Literature Connections*

Houston, Jeanne Wakatsukie and Houston, James D. *Farewell to Manzanar (with related readings).* The true story of a Japanese-American family's confinement in California's Manzanar internment camp.

## ENRICHMENT ACTIVITIES

Pupil's Edition, pp. 560–597
· Interact with History, pp. 560–561
· Point/Counterpoint, p. 585
· Tracing Themes, pp. 588–589
· Supreme Court, pp. 596–597

In-Depth Resources: Unit 5
· Geography Application: Thunderclap, pp. 32–33
· Outline Map: Crisis in Europe, pp. 34–35
· Primary Source: from *Farewell to Manzanar*, p. 36
· Primary Source: War Ration Stamps, p. 37
· Primary Source: War Dispatch from Ernie Pyle, p. 38
· Primary Source: Bombing of Nagasaki, p. 39

· Literature: from *Snow Falling on Cedars*, pp. 40–42
· American Lives: Oveta Culp Hobby, p. 43
· American Lives: George S. Patton, p. 44

Electronic Library of Primary Sources
· Unit 5, Chapter 17

Primary Source Explorer

Historic Supreme Court Decisions
· *Korematsu* v. *United States*, pp. 157–163

## BLOCK SCHEDULE LESSON PLAN OPTIONS (90-MINUTE PERIOD)

### DAY 1

**CHAPTER 17 OPENER**
**pp. 560–561**
**Class Time** 30 minutes

**History from Visuals, p. 560**
**Class Time** 10 minutes

*Options for Pacing and Variety*

· **Time Saver** Have students review the time line on the spread and ask them the questions in the TE to check comprehension. **Class Time** 10 minutes

**Interact With History, p. 561**
**Class Time** 20 minutes

*Options for Pacing and Variety*

· **Role-Playing** Ask students to read the situation and speculate on the way they would use their resources to the best advantage. **Class Time** 15 minutes

**SECTION 1 pp. 562–568**
**Class Time** 30 minutes

*Options for Pacing and Variety*

· **Time Saver** Have students complete the activity on TE page 564, Analyzing Bias. **Class Time** 20 minutes

· **History on Film** Show the film *The Great Dictator* by Charlie Chaplin, in part or in its entirety, to see a contemporary spoof of Adolf Hitler. Discuss students' reactions to the film. **Class Time** up to 90 minutes

· **Peer Teaching** Have students work in pairs to complete the Section Assessment. **Class Time** 20 minutes

### DAY 1 continued

**SECTION 2 pp. 569–577**
**Class Time** 30 minutes

*Options for Pacing and Variety*

· **Internet** Divide students into groups and have them use the Internet or the library to research and summarize the decoding of the Enigma Machine. Discuss interesting facts they discovered in their research. **Class Time** 30 minutes

· **Peer Teaching** Have students work in small groups to construct an annotated time line beginning with D-Day and ending with V-E Day. Use the activity on TE page 574. **Class Time** 20 minutes

### DAY 2

**SECTION 3 pp. 578–589**
**Class Time** 30 minutes

*Options for Pacing and Variety*

· **Peer Teaching** Have students work in groups to discuss the activity related to the atomic bomb and the responsibility of scientists for the practical results of their work. Read them the additional information in the TE about the first atomic bomb test. **Class Time** 20 minutes

· **Time Saver** Ask students to read "Point/Counterpoint" on page 585 and discuss the questions as a class. **Class Time** 15 minutes

· **Internet** Ask students to read the feature "Tracing Themes: Science and Technology" on pages 588–589 and discuss the Thinking Critically questions. Have students use the Internet to go into more depth with one of the questions. **Class Time** 25 minutes

**SECTION 4 pp. 590–597**
**Class Time** 30 minutes

*Options for Pacing and Variety*

· **Peer Teaching** Have students discuss the quotation from Maya Angelou in "A Personal Voice" on page 590 with a partner. Ask them what is left unstated in the quote. Discuss the man's and woman's reaction. **Class Time** 15 minutes

### DAY 2 continued

· **Time Saver** Have students discuss the attitudes towards women's roles in the 1940s and how those attitudes changed in a time of need. Use the activity on TE page 591. **Class Time** 15 minutes

· **Internet** Ask students to read the feature "Historic Decisions of The Supreme Court: *Korematsu* v. *United States* (1944)" on pages 596–597. Have some of them visit **classzone.com** to read the three dissenting opinions. Have other class members use the Internet to read original articles involving the Japanese population in California in 1941 and 1942. Have some students summarize some of their findings and conclusions for the class. **Class Time** 30 minutes

**ASSESSMENT**
**pp. 598–599**
**Class Time** 30 minutes

*Options for Pacing and Variety*

· **Peer Evaluation** Have students complete the Critical Thinking questions on page 598. Have them work with a partner to correct or add to their answers. **Class Time** 30 minutes

· **Peer Teaching** Have students quiz each other on the Terms & Names of the chapter and the Main Ideas questions. **Class Time** 20 minutes

---

**TEACHER-TESTED ACTIVITY**
**WOMEN-OF-TODAY POSTER**

Don A. Lee, Mira Mesa High School, San Diego, California

**Class Time** 45 minutes

**Task** Creating a poster representing today's working woman

**Purpose** To compare and contrast the working women of World War II with today's working women

**Supplies Needed**
· "We Can Do It" poster, (available from the National Archives and Records Administration at their web site)
· Poster board
· Markers

**Activity** Display the poster and discuss the following questions: What does the poster title mean? What does the bandanna signify? Why is a muscular woman shown? Where are her children? Was childcare available? How did women feel when they were no longer needed to work at the end of the war? Then have students work in small groups to create a poster reflecting today's working women. Have students create a slogan and an image of a working woman. Then discuss how the images and slogans are different and why they are different.

# CHAPTER 17 CORRELATION

## CORRELATION TO THE TEXAS ESSENTIAL KNOWLEDGE AND SKILLS

Chapter 17 addresses the following standards of the Texas Essential Knowledge and Skills for U.S. History.

| TEKS | Instruction | Student Question/Activity |
|---|---|---|
| **(1C)** Explain the significance of the dates 1941–1945. | **PE 560–595** examination of World War II and America's role in the conflict | **PE 598–599** questions about numerous aspects of World War II |
| **(6B)** Analyze major issues and events of World War II. | **PE 562–595** examination of the major events of the war | **PE 598–599** questions about the significant events of the war |
| **(6C)** Explain the roles played by significant military leaders during World War II. | **PE 572–574** discussion of Dwight Eisenhower and his role as commander of U.S. forces | **PE 573** activity in which students demonstrate their knowledge of Eisenhower by creating a multimedia presentation |
| **(6F)** Describe the impact of the GI Bill. | **PE 592** discussion of impact of the GI Bill of Rights | **PE 592** question about how the war affected families and personal lives |
| **(10A)** Analyze the effects of changing demographic patterns resulting from migration within the United States. | **PE 590–592** examination of the Great Migration, which brought millions of blacks from the South to the North | **PE 591** question about how the war caused the nation's population to shift |
| **(14A)** Describe the economic effects of World War II on the home front. | **PE 564–568** discussion of the war's impact on the home front, including women's employment and rationing | **TE 565** activity in which students examine the treatment of women in the labor force |
| **(15B)** Explain the impact of significant international events such as World War II on changes in the role of the federal government. | **PE 567–568** examination of how the government took greater control over the economy during the war effort | **TE 567** activity in which students examine how increased government regulations impacted Americans. |
| **(17A)** Analyze the effect of 20th-century landmark U.S. Supreme Court decisions. | **PE 596–597** analysis of the Supreme Court case *Korematsu* v. *United States*, which addressed the constitutionality of the internment of Japanese-Americans | **PE 597** Critical Thinking questions regarding the landmark case |

## TAKS MINI-LESSONS

1. **Social Studies Skills: Objective 1 (US6.B):** Analyze major issues and events of World War II **Activity** Have students complete the research activity on TE page 575 regarding the invasion of Normandy.

2. **Social Studies Skills: Objective 2 (US10.A):** Analyze the effects of changing demographic patterns resulting from migration within the United States **Activity** Have students complete Skillbuilder questions for the African-American migration map on page 591.

3. **Social Studies Skills: Objective 3 (US14.A):** Describe the economic effects of World War II on the home front **Activity** Have students discuss the ways in which Americans at home helped in the war effort.

4. **English Language Arts Skills: Objective 3 (12.A):** Analyze the characteristics of clearly written texts **Activity** Have students identify the main idea and supporting details of the text under the heading "Internment of Japanese Americans" on page 594.

5. **English Language Arts Skills: Objective 5 (3.A):** Produce legible work that shows accurate spelling and correct use of the conventions of punctuation and capitalization **Activity** Have students work in pairs to check the above the elements in each others answers to the Critical Thinking question.

# CHAPTER 17 · THE UNITED STATES IN WORLD WAR II

## HISTORY from VISUALS

### Interpreting the Photograph

Ask students to examine the photograph and describe the action. Ask them to supply adjectives that identify their reaction to it. *(Exciting, dramatic, fiery, scary)* Discuss the subject of perspective or point of view. Notice the painting's aerial point of view—above, yet still part of the action. Ask students to put themselves into different places in the painting: on each ship and plane pictured. How might their reaction or feeling change from being part of the action? *(It would be both terrifying and exciting.)*

### Time Line Discussion

Explain to students that the time line covers events during the war years, 1941–1945.

· What two significant military events occurred in 1941? *(Japanese bomb Pearl Harbor; Hitler invades Soviet Union.)*

· Identify what happened to Japanese Americans and in what year. *(Japanese Americans are sent to relocation centers in 1942.)*

· Who was president at the end of the war and how did he come to office? *(Harry S. Truman; his predecessor, Franklin D. Roosevelt, died in office.)*

The raid on Pearl Harbor disabled the bulk of the U.S. fleet, including *(left to right)* the *West Virginia, Tennessee,* and *Arizona.*

**1941** The Japanese bomb Pearl Harbor.

**1941** A. Philip Randolph demands that war industries hire African Americans.

**1942** Roosevelt creates the War Production Board to coordinate mobilization.

**1942** Japanese Americans are sent to relocation centers.

ARE YOU HELPING WITH SALVAGE

USA WORLD

**1941**

**1942**

**1941** Hitler invades the Soviet Union.

**1942** In the Pacific, the Battle of Midway turns the tide in favor of the Allies.

**1942** Nazis develop the "final solution" for exterminating Jews.

## THEMES IN CHAPTER 17

### WOMEN AND POLITICAL POWER

As Americans marched off to war, both the armed services and defense industries turned to women to meet their "manpower" needs. Women proved they could handle almost any job.

**See Teacher's Edition note, p. 563.**

### CIVIL RIGHTS

For America's minorities, the war meant a struggle for equal treatment in the workplace and in the military. The government violated the civil rights of Japanese Americans by sending them to internment camps.

**See Teacher's Edition note, p. 564.**

### IMMIGRATION AND MIGRATION

The war put unprecedented numbers of Americans on the move. Young men left home for military training and service overseas. As towns and cities with defense plants boomed to the bursting point, workers moved in to take jobs.

**See Teacher's Edition note, p. 591.**

### ECONOMIC OPPORTUNITY

The post-war period brought renewed opportunities for Americans to forge their dreams of the good life. The GI Bill of Rights promised to help returning veterans keep that dream alive.

**See Teacher's Edition note, p. 592.**

# INTERACT
## WITH HISTORY

It is December of 1941. After Japan's attack on Pearl Harbor, the U.S. has entered the war. As a citizen, you and millions like you must mobilize a depressed peacetime country for war. The United States must produce the workers, soldiers, weapons, and equipment that will help to win the war.

## How can the United States use its resources to achieve victory?

### Examine the Issues

- How can the government encourage businesses to convert to wartime production?
- What sacrifices will you and your family be willing to make?
- How can the military attract recruits?

**RESEARCH LINKS** CLASSZONE.COM

Visit the Chapter 17 links for more information about The United States in World War II.

# INTERACT
## WITH HISTORY

### Objectives

- To help students understand the challenges of mobilizing for war
- To describe the impact of the war in personal terms

### Examine the Issues

1. Have students consider the challenge in transforming car, appliance, and other heavy industry factories to accommodate the production of weapons and war material.
2. Have students consider the enormous courage it took for millions of men to go to war and the challenge and opportunities the war presented to Americans all over the country.
3. Discuss what media and advertising appeals the government would use to attract people to enlist in the military.

**1943** Zoot-suit riots rock Los Angeles.

**1944** GI Bill of Rights is passed.

**1944** President Roosevelt is elected to a fourth term.

**1945** U.S. marines take Iwo Jima.

**1945** Harry S. Truman becomes president when Roosevelt dies.

**1943**

**1944**

**1945**

**1943** Rommel's forces surrender in North Africa.

**1944** On June 6, the Allies launch D-Day, a massive invasion of Europe.

**1945** Nazi retreat begins after the Battle of the Bulge.

**1945** Japan surrenders after atomic bombing of Hiroshima and Nagasaki.

*The United States in World War II* **561**

## RECOMMENDED RESOURCES

### BOOKS FOR THE TEACHER

Goodwin, Doris K. *No Ordinary Time: Franklin & Eleanor Roosevelt: The Home Front in World War II.* New York: S&S Trade, 1994.

Leckie, Robert. *Delivered From Evil.* New York: Harper Trade, 1988. Narrative history of World War II.

### BOOKS FOR THE STUDENT

*Ernie's War: The Best of Ernie Pyle's World War II Dispatches.* David Nichols, ed. New York: Random, 1986.

Sulzberger, C. L. *The American Heritage Picture History of World War II.* New York: Wings Books, 1995.

Terkel, Studs, *The "Good War."* New York: The New Press, 1997. Oral history of World War II.

### VIDEOS

*America, the Way We Were: The Home Front.* IVN Entertainment, Inc., 1987. A three-tape series on behavior, attitudes, and popular culture.

*Zoot Suit.* Universal Home Studios, 1981. Mexican and Anglo cultures clash in 1940s California.

### SOFTWARE

*D-Day: 100 Days of Destiny.* Educorp, 7434 Trade Street, San Diego, CA.

*Powers of Persuasion: The Art of Propaganda in World War II.* Fife and Drum Software, 316 Soapstone Lane, Silver Spring, MD 20905.

562 CHAPTER 17

# OBJECTIVES

**1** Explain how the United States expanded its armed forces in World War II.

**2** Describe the wartime mobilization of industry, labor, scientists, and the media.

**3** Trace the efforts of the U.S. government to control the economy and deal with alleged subversion.

## SKILLBUILDERS

· Interpreting Graphs, p. 564
· Interpreting Visual Sources, p. 566

## CRITICAL THINKING

· Contrasting, p. 564
· Forming Generalizations, p. 565
· Summarizing, p. 567
· Identifying Problems, p. 568
· Analyzing Events, p. 568
· Analyzing Visual Sources, p. 568

# Focus & Motivate

Ask students to put themselves in the place of a high school junior in December 1941 and think how the news of war will impact their lives.

# Instruct

## Instruct: Objective **1**

### Americans Join the War Effort
TAKS SS11 3(US14.A)

· What was the Selective Service System and how did it help the United States meet manpower needs?

· What contributions did women and minorities make to the military effort?

 **In-Depth Resources: Unit 5**
· Guided Reading, p. 22

 **Electronic Library of Primary Sources**
· "What Can I Do?" by the Office of Civilian Defense

---

SECTION **1**

# Mobilizing for Defense

| MAIN IDEA | WHY IT MATTERS NOW | Terms & Names |
|---|---|---|
| Following the attack on Pearl Harbor, the United States mobilized for war. | Military industries in the United States today are a major part of the American economy. | • George Marshall<br>• Women's Auxiliary Army Corp (WAAC)<br>• A. Philip Randolph<br>• Manhattan Project • Office of Price Administration (OPA)<br>• War Production Board (WPB)<br>• rationing |

**TEKS** U.S. History 6A, 6B, 6C, 8A, 14A, 15B, 20D, 21D, 22B, 24A, 24B, 24C, 24H, 25A, 25B, 25C, 25D

### One American's Story

Charles Swanson looked all over his army base for a tape recorder on which to play the tape his wife had sent him for Christmas. "In desperation," he later recalled, "I had it played over the public-address system. It was a little embarrassing to have the whole company hear it, but it made everyone long for home."

**A PERSONAL VOICE** MRS. CHARLES SWANSON

" **Merry Christmas, honey. Surprised? I'm so glad I have a chance to say hello to you this way on our first Christmas apart. . . . About our little girl. . . . She is just big enough to fill my heart and strong enough to help Mommy bear this ache of loneliness. . . . Her dearest treasure is her daddy's picture. It's all marked with tiny handprints, and the glass is always cloudy from so much loving and kissing. I'm hoping you'll be listening to this on Christmas Eve, somewhere over there, your heart full of hope, faith and courage, knowing each day will bring that next Christmas together one day nearer.** "

—quoted in *We Pulled Together . . . and Won!*

▲ Mrs. Charles Swanson and her daughter, Lynne, with a picture of her husband.

As the United States began to mobilize for war, the Swansons, like most Americans, had few illusions as to what lay ahead. It would be a time filled with hard work, hope, sacrifice, and sorrow.

---

## **1** Americans Join the War Effort

The Japanese had attacked Pearl Harbor with the expectation that once Americans had experienced Japan's power, they would shrink from further conflict. The day after the raid, the *Japan Times* boasted that the United States, now reduced to a third-rate power, was "trembling in her shoes." But if Americans were trembling, it was with rage, not fear. Uniting under the battle cry "Remember Pearl Harbor!" they set out to prove Japan wrong.

**562** CHAPTER 17

---

# PROGRAM RESOURCES

 **In-Depth Resources: Unit 5**
· Guided Reading, p. 22
· Building Vocabulary, p. 26
· Skillbuilder Practice: Analyzing Assumptions and Bias, p. 27
· Reteaching Activity, p. 28
· Primary Sources: War Ration Stamps, p. 37
· American Lives: Oveta Culp Hobby, p. 43

 **Reading Study Guide** (English and Spanish), pp. 171–172

 **Access for Student Acquiring English/ESL**
· Guided Reading (Spanish), p. 189
· Skillbuilder Practice, p. 193

 **Formal Assessment**
· Section Quiz, p. 316

 **Integrated Assessment**
· Rubrics

**INTEGRATED TECHNOLOGY**

 Electronic Library of Primary Sources

 classzone.com

**TEXAS RESOURCES**

 TAKS Spiraled Content Review

 TAKS Practice Tests

TAKS Practice Transparencies TT95

TAKS Online Test Practice

## SELECTIVE SERVICE AND THE GI

After Pearl Harbor, eager young Americans jammed recruiting offices. "I wanted to be a hero, let's face it," admitted Roger Tuttrup. "I was havin' trouble in school. . . . The war'd been goin' on for two years. I didn't wanna miss it. . . . I was an American. I was seventeen."

Even the 5 million who volunteered for military service, however, were not enough to face the challenge of an all-out war on two global fronts—Europe and the Pacific. The Selective Service System expanded the draft and eventually provided another 10 million soldiers to meet the armed forces' needs.

The volunteers and draftees reported to military bases around the country for eight weeks of basic training. In this short period, seasoned sergeants did their best to turn raw recruits into disciplined, battle-ready GIs.

According to Sergeant Debs Myers, however, there was more to basic training than teaching a recruit how to stand at attention, march in step, handle a rifle, and follow orders.

**Background**
The initials *GI* originally stood for "galvanized iron" but were later reinterpreted as "government issue," meaning uniforms and supplies. In time, the abbreviation came to stand for American soldiers.

▲ In March 1941, a group of African-American men in New York City enlisted in the United States Army Air Corps. This was the first time the Army Air Corps opened its enlistment to African Americans.

### A PERSONAL VOICE SERGEANT DEBS MYERS

" The civilian went before the Army doctors, took off his clothes, feeling silly; jigged, stooped, squatted, wet into a bottle; became a soldier. He learned how to sleep in the mud, tie a knot, kill a man. He learned the ache of loneliness, the ache of exhaustion, the kinship of misery. He learned that men make the same queasy noises in the morning, feel the same longings at night; that every man is alike and that each man is different. "

—quoted in *The GI War: 1941–1945*

**EXPANDING THE MILITARY** The military's work force needs were so great that Army Chief of Staff General **George Marshall** pushed for the formation of a **Women's Auxiliary Army Corps (WAAC).** "There are innumerable duties now being performed by soldiers that can be done better by women," Marshall said in support of a bill to establish the Women's Auxiliary Army Corps. Under this bill, women volunteers would serve in noncombat positions.

Despite opposition from some members of Congress who scorned the bill as "the silliest piece of legislation" they had ever seen, the bill establishing the WAAC became law on May 15, 1942. The law gave the WAACs an official status and salary but few of the benefits granted to male soldiers. In July 1943, after thousands of women had enlisted, the U.S. Army dropped the "auxiliary" status, and granted WACs full U.S. Army benefits. WACs worked as nurses, ambulance drivers, radio operators, electricians, and pilots—nearly every duty not involving direct combat.

**Tracing Themes**
WOMEN AND POLITICAL POWER

### Women in the Military

In addition to the WAACs, many women served in the WAVES (Navy), and the SPAR (Coast Guard). Female pilots served in the Women's Auxiliary Ferrying Squadron (WAFS) and the Women's Air Force Service Pilots (WASP). The performance of these women led General Dwight D. Eisenhower to admit that "when this project [women in the military] was proposed
. . . like most old soldiers, I was violently against it . . . Every phase of the record they compiled during the war convinced me of the error of my first reaction."

📖 In-Depth Resources: Unit 5
· American Lives: Oveta Culp Hobby, p. 43

NOW & THEN

### WOMEN IN THE MILITARY

A few weeks after the bill to establish the Women's Auxiliary Army Corps (WAAC) had become law, Oveta Culp Hobby (shown, far right) a Texas newspaper executive and the first director of the WAAC, put out a call for recruits. More than 13,000 women applied on the first day. In all, some 350,000 women served in this and other auxiliary branches during the war.

The WAC remained a separate unit of the army until 1978 when male and female forces were integrated. In 2001, almost 200,000 women served in the United States armed forces.

### NOW & THEN

### Women in the Military

**Drawing Conclusions** Ask students: Now that women have been integrated into combat forces, do you think that women should be drafted into the armed forces, along with men? (*Some may answer if men are going to be drafted, it is only fair that women be subject to the draft as well. Others might suggest women may be in the military, but not in combat. Still others might suggest that women may volunteer for the military but should not be drafted.*)

*The United States in World War II* **563**

---

 **BLOCK SCHEDULING**

### Eyewitness Testimony

**Class Time** 45 minutes

**Task** Preparing interview questions about World War II experiences

**Purpose** To understand the experience of the war

**Directions** To find willing interviewees, contact local veterans' organizations or retirement homes to identify veterans or people who lived through the war on the home front. Have groups of students prepare questions for different categories of interviewees: combat veterans, women in the military, people who lived through the war as adults, people who lived through the war as children. Arrange for the groups to complete their interviews and report their findings.

## Tracing Themes

### CIVIL RIGHTS

#### Chinese Exclusion

In 1942, sociologist Rose Hum Lee wrote an article on Chinese-American participation in the war effort. In it she noted that the Chinese exclusion laws still banned immigration from China to the United States and that Chinese immigrants already in America were not allowed to become naturalized citizens. "To be fighting for freedom and democracy in the Far East . . . and to be denied equal opportunity in the greatest of democracies seems the height of irony." The irony was not lost on President Roosevelt, who persuaded Congress to repeal the Chinese exclusion laws in 1943.

## Instruct: Objective ❷

### A Production Miracle
TAKS SS11 3(US14.A)

· How did American industry contribute to the war effort?

· How did the war create new job opportunities for women and minorities?

· How did scientists help the war effort?

· How did the mass media contribute to the war effort?

 In-Depth Resources: Unit 5
· Guided Reading, p. 22

 Mini-Lesson 3:
SS11 3(US14.A)

**RECRUITING AND DISCRIMINATION** For many minority groups—especially African Americans, Native Americans, Mexican Americans, and Asian Americans—the war created new dilemmas. Restricted to racially segregated neighborhoods and reservations and denied basic citizenship rights, some members of these groups questioned whether this was their war to fight. "Why die for democracy for some foreign country when we don't even have it here?" asked an editorial in an African-American newspaper. On receiving his draft notice, an African American responded unhappily, "Just carve on my tombstone, 'Here lies a black man killed fighting a yellow man for the protection of a white man.'"

**DRAMATIC CONTRIBUTIONS** Despite discrimination in the military, more than 300,000 Mexican Americans joined the armed forces. While Mexican Americans in Los Angeles made up only a tenth of the city's population, they suffered a fifth of the city's wartime casualties.

About one million African Americans also served in the military. African-American soldiers lived and worked in segregated units and were limited mostly to noncombat roles. After much protest, African Americans did finally see combat in the last year of the war.

Asian Americans took part in the struggle as well. More than 13,000 Chinese Americans, or about one of every five adult males, joined the armed forces. In addition, 33,000 Japanese Americans put on uniforms. Of these, several thousand volunteered to serve as spies and interpreters in the Pacific war. "During battles," wrote an admiring officer, "they crawled up close enough to be able to hear [Japanese] officers' commands and to make verbal translations to our soldiers."

Some 25,000 Native Americans enlisted in the armed services, too, including 800 women. Their willingness to serve led *The Saturday Evening Post* to comment, "We would not need the Selective Service if all volunteered like Indians."

## A Production Miracle

Early in February 1942, American newspapers reported the end of automobile production for private use. The last car to roll off an automaker's assembly line was a gray sedan with "victory trim,"—that is, without chrome-plated parts. This was just one more sign that the war would affect almost every aspect of life.

**THE INDUSTRIAL RESPONSE** Within weeks of the shutdown in production, the nation's automobile plants had been retooled to produce tanks, planes, boats, and

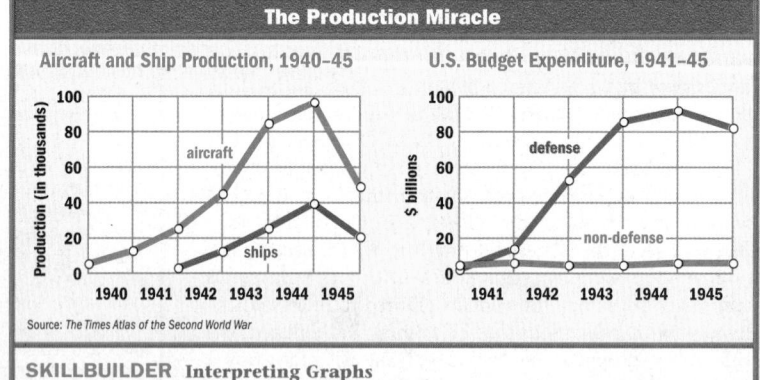

### The Production Miracle

**Aircraft and Ship Production, 1940–45**

Source: *The Times Atlas of the Second World War*

**U.S. Budget Expenditure, 1941–45**

**SKILLBUILDER** Interpreting Graphs

1. Study the first graph. In what year did aircraft and ship production reach their highest production levels?
2. How does the second graph help explain how this production miracle was possible?

**MAIN IDEA**

Contrasting

Ⓐ How did the American response to the Japanese raid on Pearl Harbor differ from Japanese expectations?

*A. Answer*
The Japanese expected the United States to act like a defeated nation. Instead enraged Americans mobilized for war.

*Skillbuilder Answers*
1. 1944
2. The U.S. budget expenditure was highest in 1944.

---

### Analyzing Bias

**Explaining the Skill** Bias can be used to demean the subject or, ironically, it can even appear in what was intended as praise. To detect bias, look for words or phrases that may convey a positive or a negative point of view.

**Applying the Skill** On the board write the following quotation about Native American soldiers. "The red soldier is tough. . . . He has lived outdoors all his life and lived by his senses; he is a natural Ranger. He takes to Commando fighting with gusto. Why not? His ancestors invented it." *American Legion Magazine*

Tell students that while the quote was written in praise, it stereotypes Native Americans. Ask students to rewrite the quote in a way that removes the stereotypes.

 In-Depth Resources: Unit 5
· Skillbuilder Practice: Analyzing Assumptions and Bias, p. 27

command cars. They were not alone. Across the nation, factories were quickly converted to war production. A maker of mechanical pencils turned out bomb parts. A bedspread manufacturer made mosquito netting. A soft-drink company converted from filling bottles with liquid to filling shells with explosives.

Meanwhile, shipyards and defense plants expanded with dizzying speed. By the end of 1942, industrialist Henry J. Kaiser had built seven massive new shipyards that turned out Liberty ships (cargo carriers), tankers, troop transports, and "baby" aircraft carriers at an astonishing rate. Late that year, Kaiser invited reporters to Way One in his Richmond, California, shipyard to watch as his workers assembled *Hull 440*, a Liberty ship, in a record-breaking four days. Writer Alyce Mano Kramer described the first day and night of construction.

### A PERSONAL VOICE ALYCE MANO KRAMER

" At the stroke of 12, Way One exploded into life. Crews of workers, like a champion football team, swarmed into their places in the line. Within 60 seconds, the keel was swinging into position. . . . *Hull 440* was going up. The speed of [production] was unbelievable. At midnight, Saturday, an empty way—at midnight Sunday, a full-grown hull met the eyes of graveyard workers as they came on shift. "

—quoted in *Home Front, U.S.A.*

Before the fourth day was up, 25,000 amazed spectators watched as *Hull 440* slid into the water. How could such a ship be built so fast? Kaiser used prefabricated, or factory-made, parts that could be quickly assembled at his shipyards. Equally important were his workers, who worked at record speeds.

**LABOR'S CONTRIBUTION** When the war began, defense contractors warned the Selective Service System that the nation did not have enough workers to meet both its military and its industrial needs. They were wrong. By 1944, despite the draft, nearly 18 million workers were laboring in war industries, three times as many as in 1941.

More than 6 million of these new workers were women. At first, war industries feared that most women lacked the necessary stamina for factory work and were reluctant to hire them. But once women proved they could operate welding torches or riveting guns as well as men, employers could not hire enough of them—especially since women earned only about 60 percent as much as men doing the same jobs.

Defense plants also hired more than 2 million minority workers during the war years. Like women, minorities faced strong prejudice at first. Before the war, 75 percent of defense contractors simply refused to hire African Americans, while another 15 percent employed them only in menial jobs. "Negroes will be considered only as janitors," declared the general manager of North American Aviation. "It is the company policy not to employ them as mechanics and aircraft workers." **B**

During the war, women took many jobs previously held by men. In this 1943 photo, a young woman is seen operating a hand drill in Nashville, Tennessee.

*B. Answer*
Women and minorities faced discrimination. Some defense plants refused to hire blacks. Women were not paid as much as men.

**MAIN IDEA**

**Forming Generalizations**
**B** What difficulties did women and minorities face in the wartime work force?

*The United States in World War II* **565**

**More About . . .**

### Henry J. Kaiser

Kaiser (1882-1967) was an industrial pioneer. He first proved his genius in organizing the construction companies that were involved in the construction of the Boulder, Bonneville, and Grand Coulee Dams. He revolutionized production with his shipyards in California during the war. By 1945, his shipyards were launching one ship a day.

**More About . . .**

### Economic Effects of World War II

World War II greatly impacted the home front economy by bringing about the end of the Great Depression. Massive military orders in 1942 almost instantly soaked up the idle industrial capacity of the still-lingering Depression. Millions of men and women went to work in well-paying defense jobs. From 1939 to 1945, the total value of goods produced by American workers more than doubled, and unemployment virtually came to an end. The economic boom during the war continued after the war. In the post-war years, America became more affluent than most Americans could have imagined before the war. Ask, How did World War II end the Great Depression? *(The massive defense industry provided jobs to millions of Americans.)*

**More About . . .**

### Women in Defense Industries

During World War II, women were actively recruited into what had been non-traditional work for women, including such jobs as welding, machinist, construction, and bus and truck driving. The image of "Rosie the Riveter" was used to encourage women to join the workforce.

---

### Comparing

Have students compare the treatment of women with the treatment of minorities in the workforce as explained in the section Labor's Contribution. List examples of prejudicial treatment on two side-by-side lists on the board or a wall chart. See the example at the right.

| Women | Minorities |
|---|---|
| paid less | not hired at all |
| not promoted | menial jobs only |
|  |  |
|  |  |

## More About . . .

### A. Philip Randolph

American labor and civil rights leader Asa Philip Randolph (1889-1979) was the son of a minister. After attending college in New York, he organized the Brotherhood of Sleeping Car Porters in 1925. It was the first union composed of mostly black workers to be granted a charter by the American Federation of Labor. In 1955, Randolph was elected a vice president of the merged AFL-CIO. In 1963, he was one of the organizers of the March on Washington.

To protest such discrimination both in the military and in industry, **A. Philip Randolph,** president and founder of the Brotherhood of Sleeping Car Porters and the nation's most respected African-American labor leader, organized a march on Washington. Randolph called on African Americans everywhere to come to the capital on July 1, 1941, and to march under the banner "We Loyal Colored Americans Demand the Right to Work and Fight for Our Country."

▲ A. Philip Randolph in 1942.

Fearing that the march might provoke white resentment or violence, President Roosevelt called Randolph to the White House and asked him to back down. "I'm sorry Mr. President," the labor leader said, "the march cannot be called off." Roosevelt then asked, "How many people do you plan to bring?" Randolph replied, "One hundred thousand, Mr. President." Roosevelt was stunned. Even half that number of African-American protesters would be far more than Washington—still a very segregated city—could feed, house, and transport.

In the end it was Roosevelt, not Randolph, who backed down. In return for Randolph's promise to cancel the march, the president issued an executive order calling on employers and labor unions "to provide for the full and equitable participation of all workers in defense industries, without discrimination because of race, creed, color, or national origin."

## History Through *Film*

### World War II Era Films

People did tire of the earnest propaganda films churned out by a patriotic Hollywood. Though it wasn't a smash hit in its day, comedian Charlie Chaplin's 1940 film *The Great Dictator,* a spoof of Hitler's dreams of world conquest, was prophetic and a true work of art. If possible, show the film or a portion of it to students.

### SKILLBUILDER ANSWERS

1. The Nazis are portrayed as brutally cruel, as one Nazi official whips a bound prisoner.
2. Audiences might have become enraged at the cruelty of the Nazis. This might have united them in their desire to defeat Germany.

## History Through **Film**

### HOLLYWOOD HELPS MOBILIZATION

In the aftermath of Pearl Harbor, Hollywood churned out war-oriented propaganda films. Heroic movies like *Mission to Moscow* and *Song of Russia* glorified America's new wartime ally, the Soviet Union. On the other hand, "hiss-and-boo" films stirred up hatred against the Nazis. In this way, movies energized people to join the war effort.

As the war dragged on, people grew tired of propaganda and war themes. Hollywood responded with musicals, romances, and other escapist fare designed to take filmgoers away from the grim realities of war, if only for an hour or two.

▲ *Hitler, Beast of Berlin*, produced in 1939, was one of the most popular hiss-and-boo films. Viewing audiences watched in rage as the Nazis conducted one horrible act after another.

▲ Moviemakers also turned out informational films. The most important of these films—the *Why We Fight* series—were made by the great director Frank Capra. Capra is shown (*right*) consulting with Colonel Hugh Stewart (commander of the British Army film unit) in a joint effort in the making of *Tunisian Victory,* the first official film record of the campaign that expelled Germany from North Africa.

### SKILLBUILDER  Interpeting Visual Sources

1. How does the image from *Hitler, Beast of Berlin* portray the Nazis?
2. How might audiences have responded to propaganda films?

📁 **SEE SKILLBUILDER HANDBOOK, PAGE R23.**

---

**DIFFERENTIATING INSTRUCTION**   **GIFTED AND TALENTED**

### Comparing Presidential Responses to Popular Pressure

Roosevelt's backing down from Randolph stands in stark comparison to an event nine years earlier, Hoover's reaction to the Bonus Marchers. In both cases, the president was faced with popular pressure. Ask students to research both situations. Make sure that they take into account the context of both situations—Depression and brink of war. Then ask them to write a short paper that compares and contrasts each president's response to popular pressure.

**Rubric**

The compare and contrast paper should. . . .
· outline the main points of popular pressure
· identify the similarities of the presidential responses
· clearly illustrate differences in presidential responses

 Integrated Assessment
· Rubrics 1, 5

**MOBILIZATION OF SCIENTISTS** That same year, in 1941, Roosevelt created the Office of Scientific Research and Development (OSRD) to bring scientists into the war effort. The OSRD spurred improvements in radar and sonar, new technologies for locating submarines underwater. It encouraged the use of pesticides like DDT to fight insects. As a result, U.S. soldiers were probably the first in history to be relatively free from body lice. The OSRD also pushed the development of "miracle drugs," such as penicillin, that saved countless lives on and off the battlefield.

The most significant achievement of the OSRD, however, was the secret development of a new weapon, the atomic bomb. Interest in such a weapon began in 1939, after German scientists succeeded in splitting uranium atoms, releasing an enormous amount of energy. This news prompted physicist and German refugee Albert Einstein to write a letter to President Roosevelt, warning that the Germans could use their discovery to construct a weapon of enormous destructive power.

Roosevelt responded by creating an Advisory Committee on Uranium to study the new discovery. In 1941, the committee reported that it would take from three to five years to build an atomic bomb. Hoping to shorten that time, the OSRD set up an intensive program in 1942 to develop a bomb as quickly as possible. Because much of the early research was performed at Columbia University in Manhattan, the **Manhattan Project** became the code name for research work that extended across the country.

**MAIN IDEA**

**Summarizing**
**C** Why did President Roosevelt create the OSRD, and what did it do?

*C. Answer*
To bring scientists into the war effort; it developed improvements in radar and sonar, pesticides, and "miracle drugs." It also launched the Manhattan project to create an atomic bomb.

## The Federal Government Takes Control ❸

As war production increased, there were fewer consumer products available for purchase. Much factory production was earmarked for the war. With demand increasing and supplies dropping, prices seemed likely to shoot upwards.

**ECONOMIC CONTROLS** Roosevelt responded to this threat by creating the **Office of Price Administration (OPA).** The OPA fought inflation by freezing prices on most goods. Congress also raised income tax rates and extended the tax to millions of people who had never paid it before. The higher taxes reduced consumer demand on scarce goods by leaving workers with less to spend. In addition,

| The Government Takes Control of the Economy, 1942–1945 | |
|---|---|
| **Agencies and Laws** | **What the Regulations Did** |
| Office of Price Administration (OPA) | • Fought inflation by freezing wages, prices, and rents<br>• Rationed foods, such as meat, butter, cheese, vegetables, sugar, and coffee |
| National War Labor Board (NWLB) | • Limited wage increases<br>• Allowed negotiated benefits, such as paid vacation, pensions, and medical insurance<br>• Kept unions stable by forbidding workers to change unions |
| War Production Board (WPB) | • Rationed fuel and materials vital to the war effort, such as gasoline, heating oil, metals, rubber, and plastics |
| Department of the Treasury | • Issued war bonds to raise money for the war effort and to fight inflation |
| Revenue Act of 1942 | • Raised the top personal-income tax rate to 90%<br>• Added lower- and middle-income Americans to the income-tax rolls |
| Smith-Connally Labor Disputes Act (1943) | • Limited the right to strike in industries crucial to the war effort<br>• Gave the president power to take over striking plants |

*The United States in World War II* **567**

**CHAPTER 17 · SECTION 1**

**More About . . .**

**Albert Einstein**
Although Einstein was a firm opponent of the atomic bomb, his scientific work was influential in its development. His theories paved the way for splitting the atom. Then, in 1939, Niels Bohr and others persuaded a hesitant Einstein to write to Roosevelt, warning of the danger of the German attempt to create an atomic bomb. Einstein was always firmly committed to peace and worked for nuclear disarmament.

**Instruct: Objective ❸**

**The Federal Government Takes Control**
TAKS SS11 3(US14.A)
· How did the Federal government act to control the economy?
· How did government actions affect everyday life?

📖 In-Depth Resources: Unit 5
· Guided Reading, p. 22

**HISTORY from VISUALS**

**Interpreting a Chart**
The chart shows how the war touched the lives of every single American. Discuss with students the importance of winning political support for this degree of control over American life. Ask students how they think Americans might have responded if they were not convinced the war was vitally important and the national security was at stake.
*(Americans might reject so much government intrusion and control over the nation's economy.)*

---

**DIFFERENTIATING INSTRUCTION** | **LESS PROFICIENT READERS**

**Government Regulations**

Help less proficient readers understand how the economic regulations listed in the chart on this page affected the lives of Americans. Have pairs of students use the chart to list the effects of each regulation on employers, workers, and consumers.

| | Regulation | Effect |
|---|---|---|
| Employers | | |
| Workers | | |
| Consumers | WPB rationing | Less food and fuel |

*The United States in World War II* **567**

## Assess & Reteach

### SECTION 1 ASSESSMENT

Have students work in pairs to answer questions. One student should work on questions 1 and 3 and the other on questions 2 and 4.

 Formal Assessment
· Section Quiz, p. 316

### SELF-ASSESSMENT

Have students exchange papers and discuss how they would modify each other's answers to make them more complete.

### RETEACH

Create a class web on the board indicating the ways that America prepared for war in 1941–1942. Use students' answers to question 2 as the basis for the web.

 In-Depth Resources: Unit 5
· Reteaching Activity, p. 28

▲
Boys using pots and pans as helmets and drums encourage New Yorkers to donate aluminum to the war effort

the government encouraged Americans to use their extra cash to buy war bonds. As a result of these measures, inflation remained below 30 percent—about half that of World War I—for the entire period of World War II.

Besides controlling inflation, the government needed to ensure that the armed forces and war industries received the resources they needed to win the war. The **War Production Board (WPB)** assumed that responsibility. The WPB decided which companies would convert from peacetime to wartime production and allocated raw materials to key industries. The WPB also organized nationwide drives to collect scrap iron, tin cans, paper, rags, and cooking fat for recycling into war goods. Across America, children scoured attics, cellars, garages, vacant lots, and back alleys, looking for useful junk. During one five-month-long paper drive in Chicago, schoolchildren collected 36 million pounds of old paper—about 65 pounds per child. **D**

**RATIONING** In addition, the OPA set up a system for **rationing,** or establishing fixed allotments of goods deemed essential for the military. Under this system, households received ration books with coupons to be used for buying such scarce goods as meat, shoes, sugar, coffee, and gasoline. Gas rationing was particularly hard on those who lived in western regions, where driving was the only way to get around. First Lady Eleanor Roosevelt sympathized with their complaints. "To tell the people in the West not to use their cars," she observed, "means that these people may never see another soul for weeks and weeks nor have a way of getting a sick person to a doctor."

Most Americans accepted rationing as a personal contribution to the war effort. Workers carpooled or rode bicycles. Families coped with shortages of everything from tires to toys. Inevitably, some cheated by hoarding scarce goods or by purchasing them through the "black market," where rationed items could be bought illegally without coupons at inflated prices.

While people tightened their belts at home, millions of other Americans put their lives on the line in air, sea, and land battles on the other side of the world.

**MAIN IDEA**

**Identifying Problems**

**D** What basic problems were the OPA and WPB created to solve?

*D. Answer*
Controlling inflation, managing shortages, and making sure that the armed forces and war industries got the resources they needed.

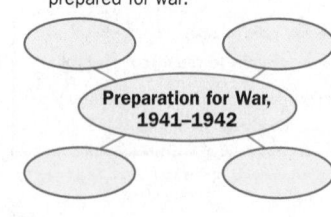

**SECTION 1 ASSESSMENT**

## 1. TERMS & NAMES For each term or name, write a sentence explaining its significance.
- George Marshall
- Women's Auxiliary Army Corp (WAAC)
- A. Philip Randolph
- Manhattan Project
- Office of Price Administration (OPA)
- War Production Board (WPB)
- rationing

### MAIN IDEA

**2. TAKING NOTES**
Re-create the web below on your paper, and fill in ways that America prepared for war.

Preparation for War, 1941–1942

### CRITICAL THINKING

**3. ANALYZING EVENTS**
How did government regulations impact the lives of civilians?

**4. ANALYZING VISUAL SOURCES**
What is the message of the World War II poster to the right? Why was this message important?

When you ride ALONE you ride with Hitler !

Join a Car-Sharing Club TODAY !

**568** CHAPTER 17

**SECTION 1 ASSESSMENT** Answers

### 1. TERMS & NAMES
George Marshall, p. 563
Women's Auxiliary Army Corps (WAAC), p. 563
A. Philip Randolph, p. 566
Manhattan Project, p. 567
Office of Price Administration (OPA), p. 567
War Production Board (WPB), p. 568
rationing, p. 568

### 2. TAKING NOTES
Industries to wartime production; employment of women in the war industry; creation of OSRD; establishment of OPA

### 3. ANALYZING EVENTS
Rationing forced people to use resources wisely, carpool or walk to work, and to do without some goods. A "black market" developed that illegally sold scarce goods.

### 4. ANALYZING VISUAL SOURCES
The poster stresses the importance of gas rationing at home. Gas rationing was important because overseas forces needed gas for vehicles that carried supplies and moved troops.

# The War for Europe and North Africa

| MAIN IDEA | WHY IT MATTERS NOW | Terms & Names |
|---|---|---|
| Allied forces, led by the United States and Great Britain, battled Axis powers for control of Europe and North Africa. | During World War II, the United States assumed a leading role in world affairs that continues today. | •Dwight D. Eisenhower •D-Day •Omar Bradley •George Patton •Battle of the Bulge •V-E Day •Harry S. Truman |

**TEKS U.S. History**
1B, 1C, 6B, 6C, 8A, 8B, 9A, 19A, 19B, 19C, 24A, 24B, 24C, 25A, 25B, 25C, 25D, 26A, 26B

### One American's Story

It was 1951, and John Patrick McGrath was just finishing his second year in drama school. For an acting class, his final exam was to be a performance of a death scene. McGrath knew his lines perfectly. But as he began the final farewell, he broke out in a sweat and bolted off the stage. Suddenly he had a flashback to a frozen meadow in Belgium during the Battle of the Bulge in 1945. Three German tanks were spraying his platoon with machine-gun fire.

**A PERSONAL VOICE** JOHN PATRICK MCGRATH

" Only a few feet away, one of the men in my platoon falls. . . . He calls out to me. 'Don't leave me. Don't. . . .' The tanks advance, one straight for me. I grab my buddy by the wrist and pull him across the snow. . . . The tank nearest to us is on a track to run us down. . . . When the German tank is but 15 yards away, I grab my buddy by the wrist and feign a lurch to my right. The tank follows the move. Then I lurch back to my left. The German tank clamors by, only inches away. . . . In their wake the meadow is strewn with casualties. I turn to tend my fallen comrade. He is dead. "

—*A Cue for Passion*

Like countless other soldiers, McGrath would never forget both the heroism and the horrors he witnessed while fighting to free Europe.

▲ Private John P. McGrath carried this bullet-riddled letter in a pack that saved his life. In 1990, he visited Anzio, where members of his company were buried.

## 1 The United States and Britain Join Forces

"Now that we are, as you say, 'in the same boat,'" British Prime Minister Winston Churchill wired President Roosevelt two days after the Pearl Harbor attack, "would it not be wise for us to have another conference . . . and the sooner the better." Roosevelt responded with an invitation for Churchill to come at once. So began a remarkable alliance between the two nations.

*The United States in World War II* **569**

## OBJECTIVES

**1** Summarize the Allies' plan for winning the war.

**2** Identify events in the war in Europe.

**3** Describe the liberation of Europe.

### SKILLBUILDERS
· Geography Skillbuilder: place, movement, p. 572; place, human-environment interaction, p. 575

### CRITICAL THINKING
· Analyzing Causes, p. 570
· Synthesizing, p. 571
· Summarizing, p. 572
· Analyzing Effects, pp. 573, 576
· Evaluating, p. 574
· Evaluating Decisions, p. 577
· Analyzing Primary Sources, p. 577

## Focus & Motivate

Ask students to recall a time when they felt they were in danger. How did it feel? How do they think they would react if they were soldiers marching into battle?

## Instruct

### Instruct: Objective **1**

**The United States and Britain Join Forces**

TAKS SS11 1(US6.B)

· To what did Roosevelt and Churchill agree early in the war?

· Why was winning the Battle of the Atlantic so crucial to the fortunes of the Allies?

📄 In-Depth Resources: Unit 5
· Guided Reading, p. 23

🖥 Humanities Transparencies HT24
· Flying Fortresses Taking Off

🖥 Critical Thinking Transparencies CT25
· U.S. Joins the Allies in World War II

## PROGRAM RESOURCES

📄 **In-Depth Resources: Unit 5**
· Guided Reading, p. 23
· Reteaching Activity, p. 29
· Geography Application: Thunderclap, pp. 32–33
· Outline Map: Crisis in Europe, pp. 34–35
· Primary Sources: War Dispatch from Ernie Pyle, p. 38
· American Lives: George S. Patton, p. 44

📄 **Reading Study Guide** (English and Spanish), pp. 173–174
📄 **Access for Student Acquiring English/ESL**
· Guided Reading (Spanish), p. 190
· Geography Application, pp. 194–195
· Outline Map, pp. 196–197
📄 **Formal Assessment**
· Section Quiz, p. 317
📄 **Integrated Assessment**
· Rubrics

### INTEGRATED TECHNOLOGY

🖥 **Critical Thinking Transp. CT25**
· U.S. Joins the Allies in World War II

🖥 **Geography Transp. GT25**
· Battle of the Bulge

🖥 **Humanities Transp. HT24**
· Flying Fortresses Taking Off

👁 **Electronic Library of Primary Sources**

ⓘ classzone.com

### TEXAS RESOURCES

📄 TAKS Spiraled Content Review

📄 TAKS Practice Tests

🖥 TAKS Practice Transparencies TT95

ⓘ TAKS Online Test Practice

**Roosevelt and Churchill**
Roosevelt and Churchill had many things in common. Both came from upper-class backgrounds. Both had served in civilian defense posts during World War I. Both had battled adversity: Roosevelt, a debilitating illness and Churchill, numerous political setbacks. Their genuine affection for each other helped facilitate a strong alliance between their two nations that continued after the war.

**HISTORY from VISUALS**

**Interpreting the Photograph**
Ask students to put themselves in the role of a German U-Boat commander looking through his periscope at a nearby Allied convoy. How would the convoy appear as both a target and a threat to the U-Boat commander? *(The convoy changed the odds; a U-Boat might successfully sink an Allied ship but faced likely destruction if it dared attack.)*

**WAR PLANS** Prime Minister Churchill arrived at the White House on December 22, 1941, and spent the next three weeks working out war plans with President Roosevelt and his advisors. Believing that Germany and Italy posed a greater threat than Japan, Churchill convinced Roosevelt to strike first against Hitler. Once the Allies had gained an upper hand in Europe, they could pour more resources into the Pacific War.

By the end of their meeting, Roosevelt and Churchill had formed, in Churchill's words, "a very strong affection, which grew with our years of comradeship." When Churchill reached London, he found a message from the president waiting for him. "It is fun," Roosevelt wrote in the message, "to be in the same decade with you."

**THE BATTLE OF THE ATLANTIC** After the attack on Pearl Harbor, Hitler ordered submarine raids against ships along America's east coast. The German aim in the Battle of the Atlantic was to prevent food and war materials from reaching Great Britain and the Soviet Union. Britain depended on supplies from the sea. The 3,000-mile-long shipping lanes from North America were her lifeline. Hitler knew that if he cut that lifeline, Britain would be starved into submission.

For a long time, it looked as though Hitler might succeed in his mission. Unprotected American ships proved to be easy targets for the Germans. In the first four months of 1942, the Germans sank 87 ships off the Atlantic shore. Seven months into the year, German wolf packs had destroyed a total of 681 Allied ships in the Atlantic. Something had to be done or the war at sea would be lost.

▲
A convoy of British and American ships ride at anchor in the harbor of Hvalfjord, Iceland.

The Allies responded by organizing their cargo ships into convoys. Convoys were groups of ships traveling together for mutual protection, as they had done in the First World War. The convoys were escorted across the Atlantic by destroyers equipped with sonar for detecting submarines underwater. They were also accompanied by airplanes that used radar to spot U-boats on the ocean's surface. With this improved tracking, the Allies were able to find and destroy German U-boats faster than the Germans could build them. In May 1943, Admiral Karl Doenitz, the commander of the German U-boat offensive, reported that his losses had "reached an unbearable height."

At the same time, the United States launched a crash shipbuilding program. By early 1943, 140 Liberty ships were produced each month. Launchings of Allied ships began to outnumber sinkings.

By mid-1943, the tide of the Battle of the Atlantic had turned. A happy Churchill reported to the House of Commons that June "was the best month [at sea] from every point of view we have known in the whole 46 months of the war." Ⓐ

*A. Answer*
The Allies had succeeded in using convoys; the United States had greatly increased the production of ships.

**MAIN IDEA**

**Analyzing Causes**
Ⓐ Why had the tide turned in the Battle of the Atlantic by mid-1943?

**570** CHAPTER 17

---

**DIFFERENTIATING INSTRUCTION** | **STUDENTS ACQUIRING ENGLISH/ESL**

**Understanding Idioms**

Have students work in pairs to find the following idioms and other expressions in the text above. Have them read the sentence in context. Then have them explain in their own words what the idiom or expression means.

· Hitler knew if he cut that lifeline, Britain would be starved.
· by organizing their cargo ships into convoys
· mutual protection
· escorted across the Atlantic by destroyers equipped with sonar for detecting submarines
· reached an unbearable height

## ② The Eastern Front and the Mediterranean

By the winter of 1943, the Allies began to see victories on land as well as sea. The first great turning point came in the Battle of Stalingrad.

**THE BATTLE OF STALINGRAD** The Germans had been fighting in the Soviet Union since June 1941. In November 1941, the bitter cold had stopped them in their tracks outside the Soviet cities of Moscow and Leningrad. When spring came, the German tanks were ready to roll.

In the summer of 1942, the Germans took the offensive in the southern Soviet Union. Hitler hoped to capture Soviet oil fields in the Caucasus Mountains. He also wanted to wipe out Stalingrad, a major industrial center on the Volga River. (See map, page 572.)

The German army confidently approached Stalingrad in August 1942. "To reach the Volga and take Stalingrad is not so difficult for us," one German soldier wrote home. "Victory is not far away." The Luftwaffe—the German air force—prepared the way with nightly bombing raids over the city. Nearly every wooden building in Stalingrad was set ablaze. The situation looked so desperate that Soviet officers in Stalingrad recommended blowing up the city's factories and abandoning the city. A furious Stalin ordered them to defend his namesake city no matter what the cost.

For weeks the Germans pressed in on Stalingrad, conquering it house by house in brutal hand-to-hand combat. By the end of September, they controlled nine-tenths of the city—or what was left of it. Then another winter set in. The Soviets saw the cold as an opportunity to roll fresh tanks across the frozen landscape and begin a massive counterattack. The Soviet army closed around Stalingrad, trapping the Germans in and around the city and cutting off their supplies. The Germans' situation was hopeless, but Hitler's orders came: "Stay and fight! I won't go back from the Volga."

The fighting continued as winter turned Stalingrad into a frozen wasteland. "We just lay in our holes and froze, knowing that 24 hours later and 48 hours later we should be shivering precisely as we were now," wrote a German soldier, Benno Zieser. "But there was now no hope whatsoever of relief, and that was the worst thing of all." The German commander surrendered on January 31, 1943. Two days later, his starving troops also surrendered.

In defending Stalingrad, the Soviets lost a total of 1,100,000 soldiers—more than all American deaths during the entire war. Despite the staggering death toll, the Soviet victory marked a turning point in the war. From that point on, the Soviet army began to move westward toward Germany. **Ⓑ**

*B. Answer* Stalin's decision to defend the city and Hitler's decision to besiege it no matter what the cost.

> **MAIN IDEA**
>
> **Synthesizing**
> **Ⓑ** What two key decisions determined the final outcome at Stalingrad?

Dazed, starved, and freezing, these German soldiers were taken prisoner after months of struggle. But they were the lucky ones. More than 230,000 of their comrades died in the Battle of Stalingrad.

▼

**Instruct: Objective ②**

**The Eastern Front and the Mediterranean**
TAKS SS11 5(WH26.C)
· Why was the Battle of Stalingrad so important?
· What happened in the war in North Africa?
· What happened after the Allies invaded Italy?

📰 In-Depth Resources: Unit 5
· Guided Reading, p. 23
· Primary Sources: War Dispatch from Ernie Pyle, p. 38

> **More About . . .**
>
> **Stalingrad**
> Stalingrad has gone through several name changes. It was originally known as Tsaritsyn, or the "tsarina's city." With its strategic location on the Volga, it grew into an important trading city, and under the Soviets, an industrial one. In 1918, Stalin led the defense of the city in the civil war against White Army troops, and the city was renamed in his honor. As a result of the de-Stalinization process undergone by the Communist Party, the Soviet Union renamed the city Volgograd in 1961.

**ACTIVITY** | **LINK TO HUMANITIES / THE ARTS** | **Ⓑ** **BLOCK SCHEDULING**

### Creative Response to War

**Class Time** 30 minutes

**Task** Creating artwork or a literary expression that reflects the suffering of war

**Purpose** To describe the human suffering of war

**Directions** Have students study the text and photograph on page 571 of defeated German soldiers. Students can then create either art work, a song, a poem, or dance movement to express their reaction to what they have read.

**Rubric**

The creative work should . . .
· focus on an aspect of war
· reflect a personal emotion or response
· clearly communicate the creator's response to the viewing audience

📰 Integrated Assessment
· Rubrics 3, 4

## More About . . .

### Erwin Rommel

After D-Day, Rommel tried to convince Hitler that the war was lost and he should sue for peace. On July 20, 1944, there was a failed assassination attempt on Hitler. In the subsequent investigation, Rommel's name came to light, although he did not participate in the attempt. Rommel's popularity in Germany was so high that Hitler did not want to accuse him in public. Instead, he sent two generals to Rommel with poison and the promise that Rommel's participation would be kept secret and his family protected. Rommel took the poison, died, and was buried with full military honors.

## HISTORY from VISUALS

### Interpreting a Map

Ask students to use the map to answer the following question: How did the Axis surrender in North Africa make the invasion of Sicily possible? *(Control of North Africa removed Axis presence from around Sicily and made the invasion possible.)*

📖 In-Depth Resources: Unit 5
· Outline Map: Crisis in Europe, pp. 34–35

American journalist Ernie Pyle, shown here in 1944, was one of the most famous war correspondents of World War II. ▼

**THE NORTH AFRICAN FRONT** While the Battle of Stalingrad raged, Stalin pressured Britain and America to open a "second front" in Western Europe. He argued that an invasion across the English Channel would force Hitler to divert troops from the Soviet front. Churchill and Roosevelt didn't think the Allies had enough troops to attempt an invasion on European soil. Instead, they launched Operation Torch, an invasion of Axis-controlled North Africa, commanded by American General **Dwight D. Eisenhower.**

In November 1942, some 107,000 Allied troops, the great majority of them Americans, landed in Casablanca, Oran, and Algiers in North Africa. From there they sped eastward, chasing the Afrika Korps led by General Erwin Rommel, the legendary Desert Fox. After months of heavy fighting, the last of the Afrika Korps surrendered in May 1943. British general Harold Alexander sent a message to Churchill, reporting that "All enemy resistance has ceased. We are masters of the North African shores." American war correspondent Ernie Pyle caught the mood of the victorious troops. **C**

**C. Answer**
The defeat of Hitler's troops.

**MAIN IDEA**
**Summarizing**
**C** What was the outcome of the North African campaign?

### A PERSONAL VOICE ERNIE PYLE

" This colossal German surrender has done more for American morale here than anything that could possibly have happened. Winning in battle is like winning at poker or catching lots of fish. . . . As a result, the hundreds of thousands of Americans in North Africa now are happy men."

—*Ernie's War: The Best of Ernie Pyle's World War II Dispatches*

*Skillbuilder Answers*
1. Ireland, Spain, Portugal, Saudi Arabia, Turkey, Sweden, Switzerland
2. Operation Torch

## World War II: Europe and Africa, 1942–1944

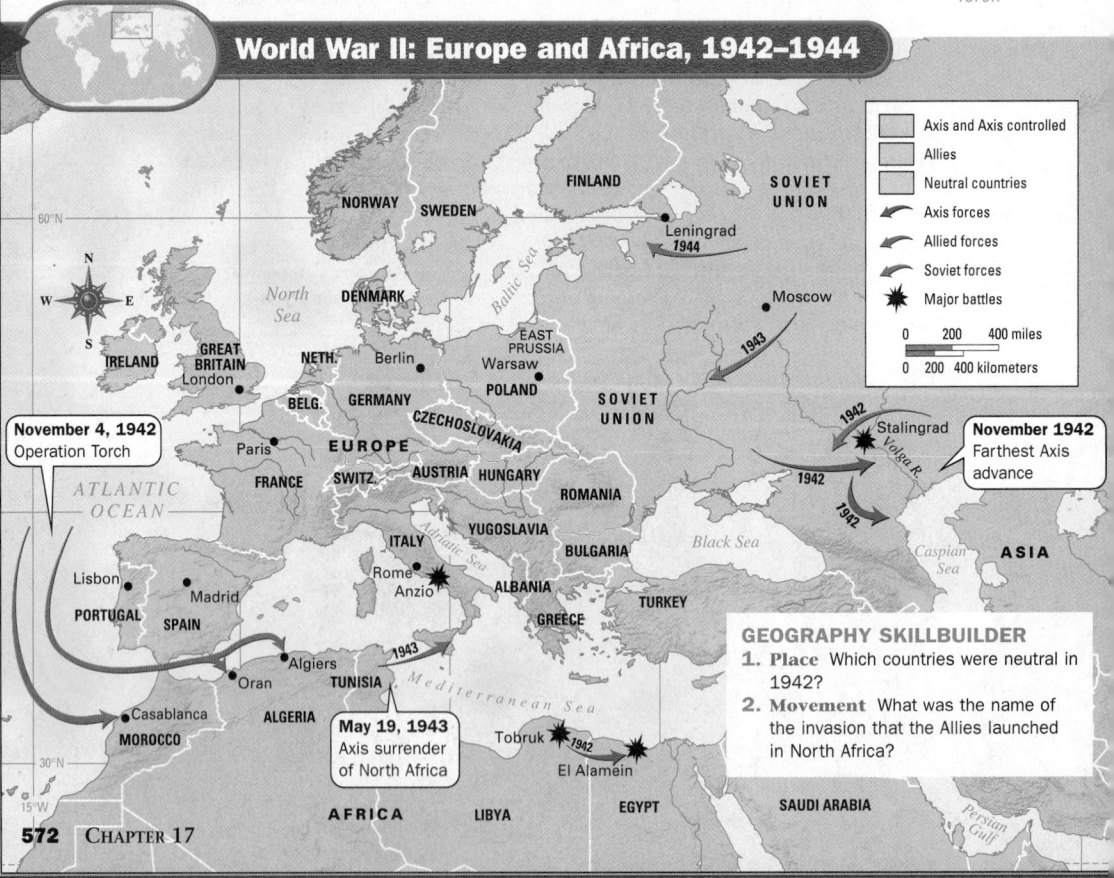

**November 4, 1942**
Operation Torch

**November 1942**
Farthest Axis advance

**May 19, 1943**
Axis surrender of North Africa

Legend:
- Axis and Axis controlled
- Allies
- Neutral countries
- Axis forces
- Allied forces
- Soviet forces
- Major battles

0  200  400 miles
0  200  400 kilometers

**GEOGRAPHY SKILLBUILDER**
1. **Place** Which countries were neutral in 1942?
2. **Movement** What was the name of the invasion that the Allies launched in North Africa?

---

**DIFFERENTIATING INSTRUCTION** | **GIFTED AND TALENTED**

### The Enigma Machine

The German Enigma cipher machine was an electro-mechanical coder that was produced commercially in the 1920s and became the standard code machine of the German military and secret police. Have students research the story of how Alan Turing and other British cryptographers unlocked the secrets of the Enigma machine and helped turn the tide of war in favor of the Allies. Have students describe the machine and explain how it worked to the class.

**Rubric**
The enigma machine report should . . .
· include pictures or diagrams of the machine
· explain how cryptographers cracked the code
· evaluate the impact of decoding German secrets

 Integrated Assessment
· Rubric 3

**THE ITALIAN CAMPAIGN** Even before the battle in North Africa was won, Roosevelt, Churchill, and their commanders met in Casablanca. At this meeting, the two leaders agreed to accept only the unconditional surrender of the Axis powers. That is, enemy nations would have to accept whatever terms of peace the Allies dictated. The two leaders also discussed where to strike next. The Americans argued that the best approach to victory was to assemble a massive invasion fleet in Britain and to launch it across the English Channel, through France, and into the heart of Germany. Churchill, however, thought it would be safer to first attack Italy.

The Italian campaign got off to a good start with the capture of Sicily in the summer of 1943. Stunned by their army's collapse in Sicily, the Italian people forced dictator Benito Mussolini to resign. On July 25, 1943, King Victor Emmanuel III summoned *Il Duce* (Italian for "the leader") to his palace, stripped him of power, and had him arrested. "At this moment," the king told Mussolini, "you are the most hated man in Italy." Italians began celebrating the end of the war.

Their cheers were premature. Hitler was determined to stop the Allies in Italy rather than fight on German soil. One of the hardest battles the Allies encountered in Europe was fought less than 40 miles from Rome. This battle, "Bloody Anzio," lasted four months—until the end of May 1944—and left about 25,000 Allied and 30,000 Axis casualties. During the year after Anzio, German armies continued to put up strong resistance. The effort to free Italy did not succeed until 1945, when Germany itself was close to collapse. **D**

**HEROES IN COMBAT** Among the brave men who fought in Italy were pilots of the all-black 99th Pursuit Squadron—the Tuskegee Airmen. In Sicily, the squadron registered its first victory against an enemy aircraft and went on to more impressive strategic strikes against the German forces throughout Italy. The Tuskegee Airmen won two Distinguished Unit Citations (the military's highest commendation) for their outstanding aerial combat against the German Luftwaffe.

Another African-American unit to distinguish itself was the famous 92nd Infantry Division, nicknamed the Buffaloes. In just six months of fighting in Europe, the Buffaloes won 7 Legion of Merit awards, 65 Silver Stars, and 162 Bronze Stars for courage under fire.

Like African Americans, most Mexican Americans served in segregated units. Seventeen Mexican-American soldiers were awarded the Congressional Medal of Honor. An all-Chicano unit—Company E of the 141st Regiment, 36th Division became one of the most decorated of the war.

Japanese Americans also served in Italy and North Africa. At the urging of General Delos Emmons, the army created the 100th Battalion, which consisted of 1,300 Hawaiian Nisei. (The word *Nisei* refers to American citizens whose parents had emigrated from Japan.) The 100th saw brutal combat and became known as the Purple Heart Battalion. Later the 100th was merged into the all-Nisei 442nd Regimental Combat Team. It became the most decorated unit in U.S. history.

> **MAIN IDEA**
>
> *Analyzing Effects*
> **D** What were the results of the Italian campaign?
>
> *D. Answer*
> The Allies freed Italy despite Hitler's efforts at the Battle of Anzio. Mussolini was removed from power.

On May 31, 1943, the 99th Squadron, the first group of African-American pilots trained at the Tuskegee Institute, arrived in North Africa. ▼

## More About . . .

### Mussolini's Last Days

Rather than leave Italy after his ouster, Mussolini stayed in Italy in hopes of regaining power. Finally, in April 1945, he attempted to sneak across the border into Austria with his mistress. He was recognized by Communist partisans who captured them and killed them. Their bodies were hung upside down in a plaza in Milan. Italians did not mourn him. Instead, there was jubilation at his death and the end of the war.

## More About . . .

### The Tuskegee Airmen

At the beginning of the war, it was thought that African Americans did not have the intelligence, ability, or loyalty to be a soldier, never mind a pilot. However, the 99th Pursuit Squadron posted a training period grade point average that was never equaled.

The crew was called the "Red Tails" because of the distinctive red tail section on its aircraft. In addition to the Presidential Unit citation, the highly decorated squadron earned over 100 Distinguished Flying Crosses, a Legion of Merit, and other commendations.

*The United States in World War II* **573**

---

**ACTIVITY** | **COOPERATIVE LEARNING** |  **classzone.com**

## Combat Heroes

**Class Time** Two class periods

**Task** Researching war heroes

**Purpose** To better understand the heroics of combat veterans

**Directions** Ask student groups to choose a war hero or military unit, such as Eisenhower, Marshall, Bradley, Patton, Congressional Medal of Honor winners, or decorated units like the Tuskegee Airmen, Company E of the 141st Regiment, 36th Division and the 442nd Regimental Combat Team. Have students use research materials or the Internet to look up information on the group or person they selected. Then have student groups prepare a multimedia presentation on the subject of their research.

📝 Integrated Assessment
· Rubric 6

## Instruct: Objective ③

### The Allies Liberate Europe
TAKS SS11 1(US6.03)

· What was D-Day?

· What happened at the Battle of the Bulge?

· What did Allied troops find in Germany?

· What happened to Hitler?

📰 In-Depth Resources: Unit 5
· Guided Reading, p. 23

🗺 Geography Transparencies GT25
· Battle of the Bulge

### KEY PLAYER

#### Dwight D. "Ike" Eisenhower
#### 1890-1969
Eisenhower was a master planner. For D-Day, he knew that he needed to surprise the Germans. He also needed to destroy the Germans' ability to move troops on the French railroad in northern France. Eisenhower insisted that bombers be diverted from bombing runs into Germany to destroy the railroad in a wide area so as not to give away Normandy as the landing target.

### More About . . .

#### Omar Bradley and George Patton
Eisenhower once called Omar Bradley "the best all around combat leader" in the U.S. army. Bradley helped lead U.S. forces to victory in the Tunisian campaign, and later in the war, forces under Bradley's command helped turn the tide in the Battle of the Bulge. Bradley was a gifted tactician and a respected battlefield leader. He was also a strong-willed commander capable of directing General Patton, whose fiery temper and battlefield initiative more often than not got him into trouble with his superiors. Bradley's firm, direct method of dealing with Patton allowed the men to work together toward the common goal of defeating the Nazis.

## ③ The Allies Liberate Europe

Even as the Allies were battling for Italy in 1943, they had begun work on a dramatic plan to invade France and free Western Europe from the Nazis. The task of commanding Operation Overlord, as it was called, fell to American General Dwight D. ("Ike") Eisenhower.

**D-DAY** Under Eisenhower's direction in England, the Allies gathered a force of nearly 3 million British, American, and Canadian troops, together with mountains of military equipment and supplies. Eisenhower planned to attack Normandy in northern France. To keep their plans secret, the Allies set up a huge phantom army with its own headquarters and equipment. In radio messages they knew the Germans could read, Allied commanders sent orders to this make-believe army to attack the French port of Calais—150 miles away—where the English Channel is narrowest. As a result, Hitler ordered his generals to keep a large army at Calais.

The Allied invasion, code-named **D-Day** or Operation Overlord, was originally set for June 5, but bad weather forced a delay. Banking on a forecast for clearing skies, Eisenhower gave the go-ahead for the next day—June 6, 1944. Shortly after midnight, three divisions parachuted down behind German lines. They were followed in the early morning hours by thousands upon thousands of seaborne soldiers—the largest land-sea-air operation in army history.

Despite the massive air and sea bombardment by the Allies, German retaliation was brutal, particularly at Omaha Beach. "People were yelling, screaming, dying, running on the beach, equipment was flying everywhere, men were bleeding to death, crawling, lying everywhere, firing coming from all directions," soldier Felix Branham wrote of the scene there. "We dropped down behind anything that was the size of a golf ball."

**THE ALLIES GAIN GROUND** Despite heavy casualties, the Allies held the beachheads. After seven days of fighting, the Allies held an 80-mile strip of France. Within a month, they had landed a million troops, 567,000 tons of supplies, and 170,000 vehicles in France. On July 25, General **Omar Bradley** unleashed massive air and land bombardment against the enemy at St. Lô, providing a gap in the German line of defense through which General **George Patton** and his Third Army could advance. On August 23, Patton and the Third Army reached the Seine River south of Paris. Two days later, French resistance forces and American troops liberated the French capital from four years of German occupation. Parisians were delirious with joy. Patton announced this joyous event to his commander in a message that read, "Dear Ike: Today I spat in the Seine."

By September 1944, the Allies had freed France, Belgium, and Luxembourg. This good news—and the American people's desire not to "change horses in midstream"—helped elect Franklin Roosevelt to an unprecedented fourth term in November, along with his running mate, Senator Harry S. Truman. **Ⓔ**

### KEY PLAYER

#### DWIGHT D. "IKE" EISENHOWER
#### 1890–1969
When Army Chief of Staff General George Marshall chose modest Lieutenant General Dwight David Eisenhower to become the Supreme Commander of U.S. forces in Europe, he knew what he was doing. Ike was a superb planner and possessed a keen mind for military tactics.

More important, Eisenhower had an uncommon ability to work with all kinds of people, even competitive and temperamental allies. After V-E Day, a grateful Marshall wrote to Ike, saying, "You have been selfless in your actions, always sound and tolerant in your judgments and altogether admirable in the courage and wisdom of your military decisions. You have made history, great history for the good of mankind." In 1953, Dwight D. Eisenhower became president of the United States.

**Background**
American paratroopers on D-Day carried a simple signaling device to help them find one another in the dark. Each had a metal toy cricket to click. No German radio operators could intercept these messages.

*Skillbuilder Answers*
**1.** This is the narrowest part of the channel. **2.** It was complex, involving five separate landings in France.

*E. Answer*
Yes. On D-Day, the Allies penetrated the beaches along the Normandy Coast. Despite heavy losses, they held the beachheads and began moving inland.

**MAIN IDEA**

**Evaluating**
**Ⓔ** Was the Allied invasion of Europe successful? Explain your answer.

---

**DIFFERENTIATING INSTRUCTION** **LESS PROFICIENT READERS**

#### Sequencing
To help students understand the events on pages 574–577, have them construct an annotated time line beginning with D-Day (June 6, 1944) and ending with V-E Day (May 8, 1945). The time line should include all events referred to in the section.

After the students have constructed the time line, assign one event to each student and have them create a "living" time line in which they stand in the correct sequence and identify and explain their event.

| June 6, 1944 D-Day | August 25, 1944 Paris Liberated | | April 25, 1945 Russian Army storms Berlin |
| July 25, 1944 St. Lô | | October–November 1944 Battle of the Bulge | May 8, 1945 V-E Day |

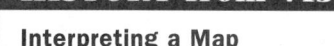

On D-Day morning, a platoon of American infantry wade ashore to Omaha Beach.

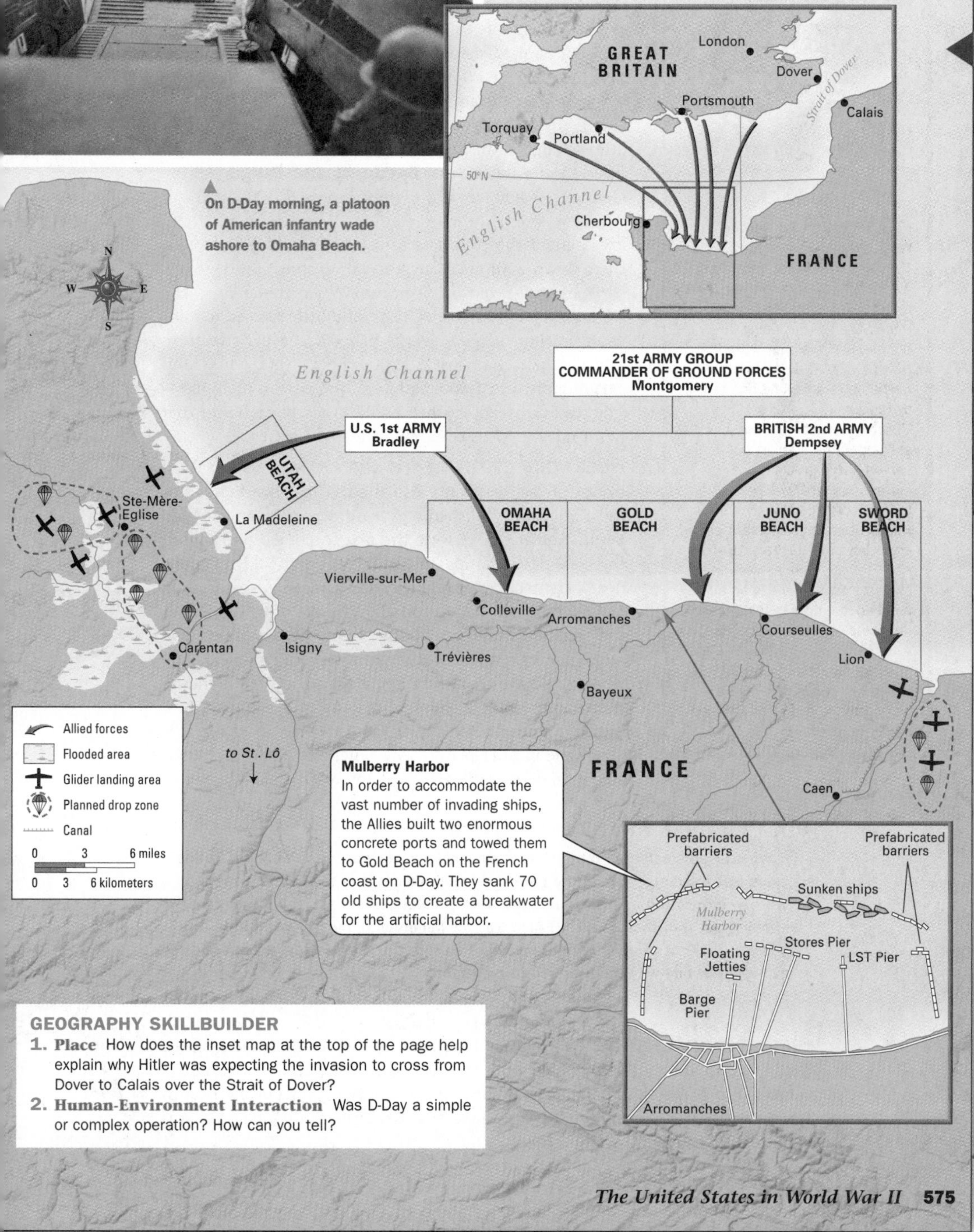

**GREAT BRITAIN**

London
Dover
Portsmouth
Torquay
Portland
Calais
*Strait of Dover*
50°N
*English Channel*
Cherbourg
**FRANCE**

*English Channel*

**21st ARMY GROUP**
**COMMANDER OF GROUND FORCES**
Montgomery

**U.S. 1st ARMY**
Bradley

**BRITISH 2nd ARMY**
Dempsey

UTAH BEACH

Ste-Mère-Eglise
La Madeleine

**OMAHA BEACH**
**GOLD BEACH**
**JUNO BEACH**
**SWORD BEACH**

Vierville-sur-Mer
Colleville
Arromanches
Courseulles
Lion

Carentan
Isigny
Trévières
Bayeux
Caen

**FRANCE**

to St. Lô

Legend:
- Allied forces
- Flooded area
- Glider landing area
- Planned drop zone
- Canal

0   3   6 miles
0   3   6 kilometers

**Mulberry Harbor**
In order to accommodate the vast number of invading ships, the Allies built two enormous concrete ports and towed them to Gold Beach on the French coast on D-Day. They sank 70 old ships to create a breakwater for the artificial harbor.

Prefabricated barriers
Prefabricated barriers
Sunken ships
*Mulberry Harbor*
Floating Jetties
Stores Pier
LST Pier
Barge Pier
Arromanches

**GEOGRAPHY SKILLBUILDER**
1. **Place** How does the inset map at the top of the page help explain why Hitler was expecting the invasion to cross from Dover to Calais over the Strait of Dover?
2. **Human-Environment Interaction** Was D-Day a simple or complex operation? How can you tell?

## HISTORY from VISUALS

### Interpreting a Map
Help students use the information provided to understand there was much more to the invasion than landing soldiers on the beach. Have them identify the paratrooper landings, the construction of a harbor, and the bombing campaigns that preceded the invasion. Tell them that the success of the bombing campaign was crucial. Taking out bridges and rail lines impeded the Germans' ability to move troops from the Calais area where they had been massed to meet the expected invasion. Have them use the map to determine which of the armies shown might have had the greatest challenge in communication and coordination. *(Bradley's 1st Army, split between Omaha and Utah Beaches, might have had the greatest communication and coordination challenge.)*

## More About . . .

### D-Day
The key to the success of D-Day was the military's ability to deliver so many men to the invasion point at the same time. A great armada of ships, including 1,200 fighting ships, 4,126 landing craft, 804 transport ships, and many other special purpose ships, delivered 132,500 soldiers across the English Channel from several ports. The Allies used 10,000 planes. World War II was the first war in which parachutists were used in such a tactical manner. Twenty-three thousand airborne troops were used. Ten thousand American paratroopers were dropped into France in the early morning of the invasion.

 In-Depth Resources: Unit 5
· Geography Application: Thunderclap, pp. 32–33

---

**ACTIVITY** | **LINK TO WORLD HISTORY**  **classzone.com**

### D-Day

**Class Period** 45 minutes

**Task** Researching the planning and execution of Operation Overlord

**Purpose** To better understand the international cooperation of D-Day operations

 Mini-Lesson 1: SS11 1(US6.B)

**Directions** Have student groups choose between the planning of Operation Overlord or the actual attack on D-Day, and use library and Internet resources to find out more about the participation of British and Canadian forces. Have students construct a multimedia presentation of their findings.

Integrated Assessment
· Rubric 6

## HISTORICAL SPOTLIGHT

### Audie Murphy

Audie Murphy leveraged his fame as a soldier into an acting career in which he appeared in more than 40 movies. Perhaps the pinnacle of his acting career was the 1955 movie about his life, *To Hell And Back*, which dramatized Murphy's battlefield heroics.

Murphy was also a successful songwriter. His songs were recorded by such artists as Dean Martin, Charley Pride, and Porter Waggoner. Murphy died in an airplane accident in 1971. Ask: Why do you think Audie Murphy became an American hero? *(Murphy rose above the level of the common soldier and did something extraordinary.)*

## More About . . .

### Survivors of Concentration Camps

Israel Lau was just eight years old when an American Jewish Chaplain, smiling and weeping, embraced him in Buchenwald on April 11, 1945. "'How old are you, my child?' he asked. 'What difference does it make. I'm older than you,' I answered. 'Why do you think you are older than me?' he asked. 'Because you cry and laugh as a child. And I can't even cry. So I must be older than you.'"

---

### HISTORICAL SPOTLIGHT

**AUDIE MURPHY**

Near the end of the Second World War, Audie Murphy became famous as the most decorated American soldier of the war. He received 24 medals from the United States—including the Congressional Medal of Honor. He was also awarded three medals by France and one more by Belgium.

Born in Kingston, Texas, Murphy enlisted in the army in 1942. He served in North Africa and Europe, and in 1944 he rose to the rank of second lieutenant. His most impressive act of bravery occurred in January 1945 near Colmar, France, when in the midst of a furious German attack, he jumped onto a burning tank destroyer and killed about 50 Axis troops with his machine gun. Although wounded in the leg, he rallied his troops to retake the ground the Germans had gained earlier in the day.

---

**THE BATTLE OF THE BULGE** In October 1944, Americans captured their first German town, Aachen. Hitler responded with a desperate last-gasp offensive. He ordered his troops to break through the Allied lines and to recapture the Belgian port of Antwerp. This bold move, the Führer hoped, would disrupt the enemy's supply lines and demoralize the Allies.

On December 16, under cover of dense fog, eight German tank divisions broke through weak American defenses along an 80-mile front. Hitler hoped that a victory would split American and British forces and break up Allied supply lines. Tanks drove 60 miles into Allied territory creating a bulge in the lines that gave this desperate last-ditch offensive its name, the **Battle of the Bulge.** As the Germans swept westward, they captured 120 American GIs near Malmédy. Elite German troops—the SS troopers—herded the prisoners into a large field and mowed them down with machine guns and pistols.

The battle raged for a month. When it was over, the Germans had been pushed back, and little seemed to have changed. But, in fact, events had taken a decisive turn. The Germans had lost 120,000 troops, 600 tanks and assault guns, and 1,600 planes in the Battle of the Bulge—soldiers and weapons they could not replace. From that point on, the Nazis could do little but retreat. **F**

**LIBERATION OF THE DEATH CAMPS** Meanwhile, Allied troops pressed eastward into the German heartland, and the Soviet army pushed westward across Poland toward Berlin. Soviet troops were the first to come upon one of the Nazi death camps, in July 1944. As the Soviets drew near a camp called Majdanek in Poland, SS guards worked feverishly to bury and burn all evidence of their hideous crimes. But they ran out of time. When the Soviets entered Majdanek, they found a thousand starving prisoners barely alive, the world's largest crematorium, and a storehouse containing 800,000 shoes. "This is not a concentration camp," reported a stunned Soviet war correspondent, "it is a gigantic murder plant." The Americans who later liberated Nazi death camps in Germany were equally horrified.

> **Vocabulary**
> **elite:** a small and privileged group

> **MAIN IDEA**
>
> **Analyzing Effects**
> **F** Why was the Battle of the Bulge important?
>
> *F. Answer*
> The Germans lost men and equipment that they could not replace. The battle weakened their offense.

### A PERSONAL VOICE ROBERT T. JOHNSON

" We started smelling a terrible odor and suddenly we were at the concentration camp at Landsberg. Forced the gate and faced hundreds of starving prisoners. . . . We saw emaciated men whose thighs were smaller than wrists, many had bones sticking out thru their skin. . . . Also we saw hundreds of burned and naked bodies. . . . That evening I wrote my wife that 'For the first time I truly realized the evil of Hitler and why this war had to be waged.' "

—quoted in *Voices: Letters from World War II*

**UNCONDITIONAL SURRENDER** By April 25, 1945, the Soviet army had stormed Berlin. As Soviet shells burst overhead, the city panicked. "Hordes of soldiers stationed in Berlin deserted and were shot on sight or hanged from the nearest tree," wrote Claus Fuhrmann, a Berlin clerk. "On their chests they had placards reading, 'We betrayed the Führer.'"

---

### Eyewitness Journal

**Class Time** 30 minutes

**Task** Writing journal entries for eyewitness discovery of the death camps

**Purpose** To deepen understanding of the experience of soldiers who liberated death camps

**Directions** Ask students to put themselves in the role of Robert T. Johnson (quoted in A Personal Voice) or other soldiers who discovered the death camps. While persecution of the Jews was a part of Nazi propaganda, no one had any idea of the deadly efficiency with which the Nazis had transformed words into deeds. Ask students to write a journal entry or letter based on what they discover. Have students share their writing with the class.

 Integrated Assessment
· Rubric 5

In his underground headquarters in Berlin, Hitler prepared for the end. On April 29, he married Eva Braun, his longtime companion. The same day, he wrote out his last address to the German people. In it he blamed the Jews for starting the war and his generals for losing it. "I die with a happy heart aware of the immeasurable deeds of our soldiers at the front. I myself and my wife choose to die in order to escape the disgrace of . . . capitulation," he said. The next day Hitler shot himself while his new wife swallowed poison. In accordance with Hitler's orders, the two bodies were carried outside, soaked with gasoline, and burned.

**Vocabulary**
capitulation: surrender

A week later, General Eisenhower accepted the unconditional surrender of the Third Reich. On May 8, 1945, the Allies celebrated **V-E Day**—Victory in Europe Day. The war in Europe was finally over.

**ROOSEVELT'S DEATH** President Roosevelt did not live to see V-E Day. On April 12, 1945, while posing for a portrait in Warm Springs, Georgia, the president had a stroke and died. That night, Vice President **Harry S. Truman** became the nation's 33rd president.

▲
New Yorkers celebrate V-E Day with a massive party that began in Times Square and went on for days at sites throughout the city.

## 2 ASSESSMENT

1. **TERMS & NAMES** For each term or name, write a sentence explaining its significance.
   - •**Dwight D. Eisenhower**
   - •**D-Day**
   - •**Omar Bradley**
   - •**George Patton**
   - •**Battle of the Bulge**
   - •**V-E Day**
   - •**Harry S. Truman**

### MAIN IDEA

2. **TAKING NOTES**
   Create a time line of the major events influencing the fighting in Europe and North Africa.

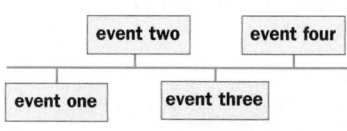

   Write a paragraph indicating how any two of these events are related.

### CRITICAL THINKING

3. **EVALUATING DECISIONS**
   Do you agree with the decision made by Roosevelt and Churchill to require unconditional surrender by the Axis powers? Why or why not?
   **Think About:**
   • the advantages of defeating a foe decisively
   • the advantages of ending a war quickly
   • how other conflicts, such as the Civil War and World War I, ended

4. **ANALYZING PRIMARY SOURCES**
   When President Roosevelt's body was brought by train to Washington, Betty Conrad was among the servicewomen who escorted his casket.

   " **The body in the casket was not only our leader but the bodies of all the men and women who had given their lives for freedom. They must not and will not have died in vain.** "

   What did Roosevelt's body symbolize to Betty Conrad?

## OBJECTIVES

1. Identify key turning points in the war in the Pacific.

2. Describe the Allied offensive against the Japanese.

3. Explain both the development of the atomic bomb and debates about its use.

4. Describe the challenges faced by the Allies in building a just and lasting peace.

### SKILLBUILDERS

· Geography Skillbuilder: movement, human-environment interaction, p. 580
· Interpreting Visual Sources, p. 582

### CRITICAL THINKING

· Comparing, p. 579
· Drawing Conclusions, pp. 581, 583, 587
· Analyzing Motives, p. 585
· Evaluating Decisions, pp. 585, 587
· Summarizing, pp. 585, 586
· Developing Historical Perspective, p. 587

## Focus & Motivate

Ask students to look at a map of the western Pacific and then think about how different it would be to fight a war in Japan rather than in Europe.

## Instruct

### Objective 1

**The Allies Stem the Japanese Tide**
TAKS SS11 1(US6.03)
· How extensive were the Japanese conquests?
· What American actions surprised the Japanese?
· What was the importance of the Battle of Midway?
· What strategy did the United States adopt in fighting Japan?

📖 In-Depth Resources: Unit 5
· Guided Reading, p. 24

# The War in the Pacific

| MAIN IDEA | WHY IT MATTERS NOW | Terms & Names |
|---|---|---|
| In order to defeat Japan and end the war in the Pacific, the United States unleashed a terrible new weapon, the atomic bomb. | Countries of the modern world struggle to find ways to prevent the use of nuclear weapons. | • Douglas MacArthur<br>• Chester Nimitz<br>• Battle of Midway<br>• kamikaze<br>• J. Robert Oppenheimer<br>• Hiroshima<br>• Nagasaki<br>• Nuremberg trials |

 U.S. History 1B, 1C, 6B, 6C, 8A, 8B, 9A, 19A, 19B, 22B, 24A, 24B, 24F, 24H, 25A, 25B, 25C, 25D, 26A, 26B

### One American's Story

The writer William Manchester left college after Pearl Harbor to join the marines. Manchester says that, as a child, his "horror of violence had been so deep-seated that I had been unable to trade punches with other boys." On a Pacific island, he would have to confront that horror the first time he killed a man in face-to-face combat. Manchester's target was a Japanese sniper firing on Manchester's buddies from a fisherman's shack.

**A PERSONAL VOICE** WILLIAM MANCHESTER

" My mouth was dry, my legs quaking, and my eyes out of focus. Then my vision cleared. I . . . kicked the door with my right foot, and leapt inside. . . . I . . . saw him as a blur to my right. . . . My first shot missed him, embedding itself in the straw wall, but the second caught him dead-on . . . . A wave of blood gushed from the wound. . . . He dipped a hand in it and listlessly smeared his cheek red. . . . Almost immediately a fly landed on his left eyeball. . . . A feeling of disgust and self-hatred clotted darkly in my throat, gagging me. "

—from *Goodbye Darkness: A Memoir of the Pacific War*

The Pacific War was a savage conflict fought with raw courage. Few who took part in that fearsome struggle would return home unchanged.

▲ American soldiers on Leyte help retake the Philippine Islands in late 1944.

## 1 The Allies Stem the Japanese Tide

While the Allies agreed that the defeat of the Nazis was their first priority, the United States did not wait until V-E Day to move against Japan. Fortunately, the Japanese attack on Pearl Harbor in 1941 had missed the Pacific Fleet's submarines. Even more importantly, the attack had missed the fleet's aircraft carriers, which were out at sea at the time.

**578** CHAPTER 17

---

**JAPANESE ADVANCES** In the first six months after Pearl Harbor, the Japanese conquered an empire that dwarfed Hitler's Third Reich. On the Asian mainland, Japanese troops overran Hong Kong, French Indochina, Malaya, Burma, Thailand, and much of China. They also swept south and east across the Pacific, conquering the Dutch East Indies, Guam, Wake Island, the Solomon Islands, and countless other outposts in the ocean, including two islands in the Aleutian chain, which were part of Alaska.

In the Philippines, 80,000 American and Filipino troops battled the Japanese for control. At the time of the Japanese invasion in December 1941, General **Douglas MacArthur** was in command of Allied forces on the islands. When American and Filipino forces found themselves with their backs to the wall on Bataan, President Roosevelt ordered MacArthur to leave. On March 11, 1942, MacArthur left the Philippines with his wife, his son, and his staff. As he left, he pledged to the many thousands of men who did not make it out, "I shall return."

**DOOLITTLE'S RAID** In the spring of 1942, the Allies began to turn the tide against the Japanese. The push began on April 18 with a daring raid on Tokyo and other Japanese cities. Lieutenant Colonel James Doolittle led 16 bombers in the attack. The next day, Americans awoke to headlines that read "Tokyo Bombed! Doolittle Do'od It." Pulling off a Pearl Harbor–style air raid over Japan lifted America's sunken spirits. At the same time, it dampened spirits in Japan.

**BATTLE OF THE CORAL SEA** The main Allied forces in the Pacific were Americans and Australians. In May 1942 they succeeded in stopping the Japanese drive toward Australia in the five-day Battle of the Coral Sea. During this battle, the fighting was done by airplanes that took off from enormous aircraft carriers. Not a single shot was fired by surface ships. For the first time since Pearl Harbor, a Japanese invasion had been stopped and turned back.

**THE BATTLE OF MIDWAY** Japan's next thrust was toward Midway, a strategic island which lies northwest of Hawaii. Here again the Allies succeeded in stopping the Japanese. Americans had broken the Japanese code and knew that Midway was to be their next target.

Admiral **Chester Nimitz,** the commander of American naval forces in the Pacific, moved to defend the island. On June 3, 1942, his scout planes found the Japanese fleet. The Americans sent torpedo planes and dive bombers to the attack. The Japanese were caught with their planes still on the decks of their carriers. The results were devastating. By the end of the Battle of Midway, the Japanese had lost four aircraft carriers, a cruiser, and 250 planes. In the words of a Japanese official, at Midway the Americans had "avenged Pearl Harbor." **A**

The **Battle of Midway** was a turning point in the Pacific War. Soon the Allies began "island hopping." Island by island they won territory back from the Japanese. With each island, Allied forces moved closer to Japan.

**Background**
General MacArthur held out against 200,000 invading Japanese troops for four months on the Bataan Peninsula. Hunger, disease, and bombardments killed 14,000 Allied troops and wounded 48,000.

**A. Answer**
Both were surprise naval attacks that resulted in substantial destruction of the enemy's fleet.

**MAIN IDEA**

**Comparing**
**A** In what ways were the American victory at Midway and the Japanese triumph at Pearl Harbor alike?

## HISTORICAL SPOTLIGHT

### NAVAJO CODE TALKERS

On each of the Pacific islands that American troops stormed in World War II, the Japanese heard a "strange language gurgling" in their radio headsets. The code seemed to have Asian overtones, but it baffled everyone who heard it. In fact, the language was Navajo, which was spoken only in the American Southwest and traditionally had no alphabet or other written symbols. Its "hiddenness" made it a perfect candidate for a code language.

Though the Navajo had no words for combat terms, they developed terms such as *chicken hawk* for *divebomber* and *war chief* for *commanding general.* Throughout the Pacific campaign—from Midway to Iwo Jima—the code talkers were considered indispensable to the war effort. They finally received national recognition in 1969.

▲
Four hundred Navajo were recruited into the Marine Corps as code talkers. Their primary duty was transmitting telephone and radio messages.

## HISTORICAL SPOTLIGHT

### Navajo Code Talkers

Philip Johnston, the son of a missionary to the Navajo and one of the few non-Navajo people fluent in the Navajo language, was the man responsible for using Navajo in this crucial role. Johnston approached a Marine commander who arranged a test. The Navajo so out-performed all other code machines that the commander was impressed and began the Code Talker program immediately. Navajo Code Talkers provided indispensable service in every Marine assault in the Pacific from 1942 to the end of the war. Ask: Why do you think it took so long for Navajo Code Talkers to receive national recognition? *(General prejudice and a tendency to overlook the contributions of non-whites is a probable reason.)*

## More About . . .

### The Battle of Midway

Despite catching the Japanese carriers unprepared at Midway, the battle at first went disastrously for the Americans. Speedy Japanese fighters cut down the slow torpedo bombers as they approached the Japanese carriers. But persistence paid off. Thirty six dive-bombers made it through the Japanese defenses and scored direct hits on carriers. A fourth carrier was later crippled, resulting in an overwhelming defeat for the Japanese navy.

*The United States in World War II* **579**

---

**ACTIVITY** | **COOPERATIVE LEARNING** | **BLOCK SCHEDULING**

### Creating a Code

**Class Time** 30 minutes

**Task** Creating a code

**Purpose** To gain an understanding of cryptology

**Directions** Divide students into small groups. Ask them to create a code using numbers as indicators. Have them write a sentence in their code. Then give each group a chance to crack the other's code.

## HISTORY from VISUALS

### Interpreting a Map

Ask students to use the map to help them predict how the course of the war might have been different had the Japanese won the Battle of Midway. *(Midway's location near Hawaii is crucial. If the Japanese had won the Battle of Midway, they might have attempted an invasion of Hawaii. Certainly they would have delivered a crippling blow to the U.S. Navy and a discouraging one to the American people. This may have been so great a blow that the United States might have been forced to sue for peace in the Pacific.)*

### More About . . .

#### Island Hopping

The map illustrates the American strategy in fighting an ocean war with Japan. Remind students that, just as in Europe, if not more so, the geography of the war put enormous pressure on the United States to supply forces thousands of miles from home. A strong navy, and the quick building of bases on newly conquered islands, complete with port facilities and airfields, is what enabled the United States to wage a successful war, despite the geographic challenge.

## War in the Pacific and in Europe

**PACIFIC**

- U.S. surrenders Bataan in the Philippines.
- Allies turn back Japanese fleet in Battle of the Coral Sea.
- U.S. declares war on Japan.
- Allies defeat Japan in Battle of Midway.
- U.S. marines land on Guadalcanal.

1941   Apr   Jun    Dec   **1942**    Apr   May   Jun   Aug     Nov    **1943**   Feb     May

**EUROPE**

- Germany invades the Soviet Union.
- Germany invades Greece and Yugoslavia.
- Germany and Italy declare war on the United States.
- Hitler orders attack on Stalingrad.
- Allies land in North Africa.
- Germans surrender at Stalingrad.
- Axis forces surrender in North Africa.

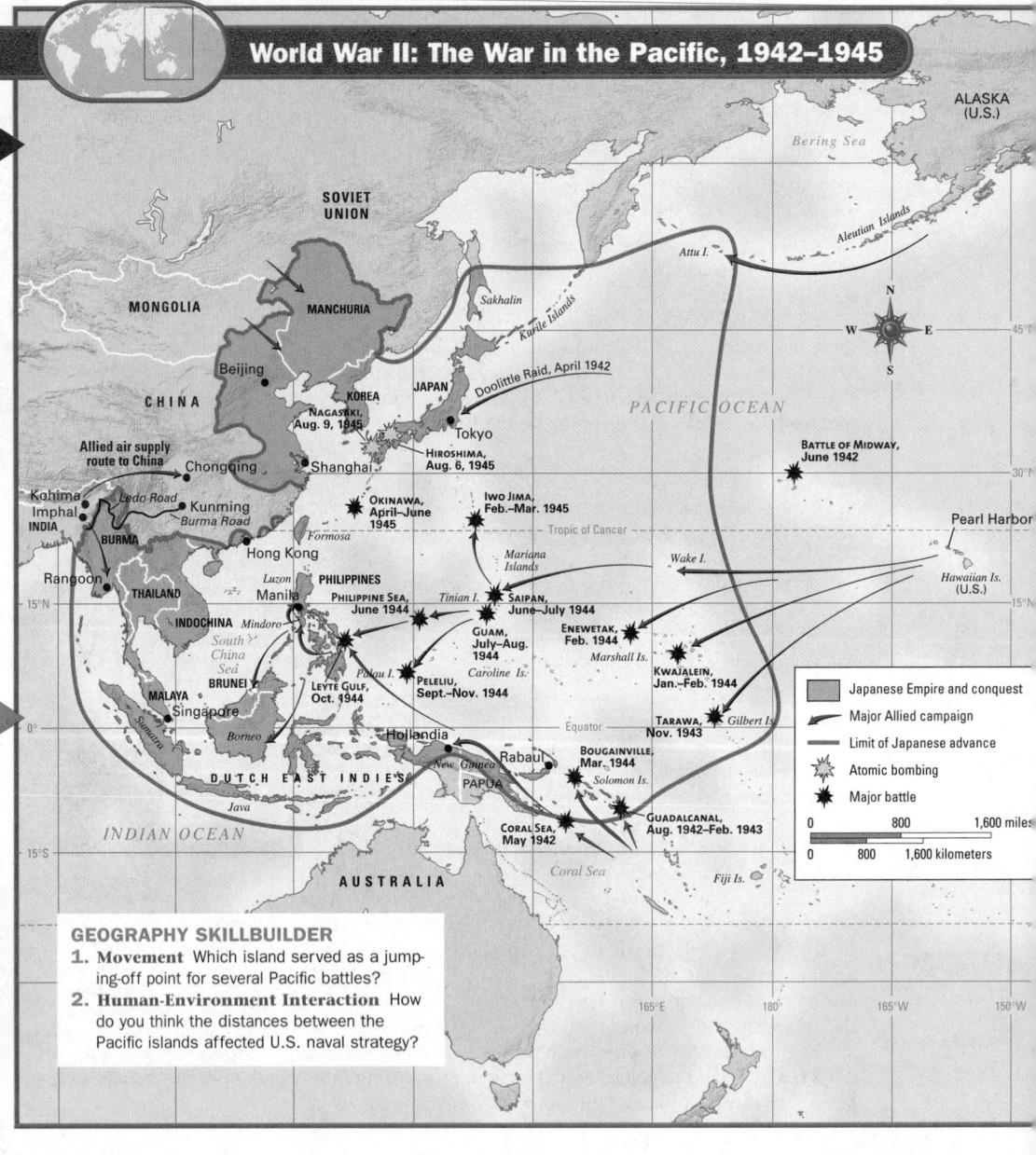

### World War II: The War in the Pacific, 1942–1945

**GEOGRAPHY SKILLBUILDER**

1. **Movement** Which island served as a jumping-off point for several Pacific battles?
2. **Human-Environment Interaction** How do you think the distances between the Pacific islands affected U.S. naval strategy?

## DIFFERENTIATING INSTRUCTION    LESS PROFICIENT READERS

### Map Reading

Reading a map involves different spatial and visual skills than reading text. Students may need assistance reading a complicated map such as the one on this page. Have students work in pairs to analyze the map on page 580.

· Find each map key item on the map.
· List the major battles shown on the map.
· Find the discussion of each battle in the text, or list each battle discussed in the text and find it on the map.

It might be helpful for students to refer to the map as they create a time line for the war in the Pacific. Students may benefit from seeing a chronology for the battles shown on the map.

**Timeline:**

Allies win Battle of the Philippine Sea.
Allies win Battle of Leyte Gulf.
Allies capture Iwo Jima.
Allies capture Okinawa.
U.S. drops atomic bombs on Hiroshima and Nagasaki.
Japan surrenders.

Jul   Sep   **1944** May   Jun Jul Aug   Oct   Dec   **1945**   Mar Apr May Jun   Aug Sep   **1946**

Allies invade Sicily.
Italy secretly surrenders to Allies.
Allies liberate Paris.
Soviets first liberate death camps.
Allies invade Europe on D-Day.
"Bloody Anzio" ends.
Germans attack Allies in Battle of the Bulge.
V-E Day ends war in Europe.
Italians execute Mussolini.
Hitler commits suicide.

## ② The Allies Go on the Offensive

The first Allied offensive began in August 1942 when 19,000 troops stormed Guadalcanal in the Solomon Islands. By the time the Japanese abandoned Guadalcanal six months later, they called it the Island of Death. To war correspondent Ralph Martin and the troops who fought there, it was simply "hell."

### A PERSONAL VOICE   RALPH G. MARTIN

" Hell was red furry spiders as big as your fist, giant lizards as long as your leg, leeches falling from trees to suck blood, armies of white ants with bites of fire, scurrying scorpions inflaming any flesh they touched, enormous rats and bats everywhere, and rivers with waiting crocodiles. Hell was the sour, foul smell of the squishy jungle, humidity that rotted a body within hours, . . . stinking wet heat of dripping rain forests that sapped the strength of any man. "

—The GI War

Guadalcanal marked Japan's first defeat on land, but not its last. The Americans continued leapfrogging across the Pacific toward Japan, and in October 1944, some 178,000 Allied troops and 738 ships converged on Leyte Island in the Philippines. General MacArthur, who had left the Philippines two years earlier, waded ashore and announced, "People of the Philippines: I have returned."

**THE JAPANESE DEFENSE** The Japanese threw their entire fleet into the Battle of Leyte Gulf. They also tested a new tactic, the **kamikaze** (kä′mĭkä′zē), or suicide-plane, attack in which Japanese pilots crashed their bomb-laden planes into Allied ships. (*Kamikaze* means "divine wind" and refers to a legendary typhoon that saved Japan in 1281 by destroying a Mongol invasion.) In the Philippines, 424 kamikaze pilots embarked on suicide missions, sinking 16 ships and damaging another 80.

Americans watched these terrifying attacks with "a strange mixture of respect and pity" according to Vice Admiral Charles Brown. "You had to admire the devotion to country demonstrated by those pilots," recalled Seaman George Marse. "Yet, when they were shot down, rescued and brought aboard our ship, we were surprised to find the pilots looked like ordinary, scared young men, not the wide-eyed fanatical 'devils' we imagined them to be."

Despite the damage done by the kamikazes, the Battle of Leyte Gulf was a disaster for Japan. In three days of battle, it lost 3 battleships, 4 aircraft carriers, 13 cruisers, and almost 500 planes. From then on, the Imperial Navy played only a minor role in the defense of Japan. **B**

Japanese kamikaze pilots receive a briefing on the mission that would be their last. ▼

*Skillbuilder Answers*
1. Guam.
2. The distances meant that the Allies had to leapfrog from one island to another, causing great difficulties in transporting goods and men.

**B. Answer**
The battle was a disaster for Japan. From then on, the Imperial Navy played only a minor role in the defense of Japan.

**MAIN IDEA**

**Drawing Conclusions**
**B** Why was the Battle of Leyte Gulf so crucial to the Allies?

---

**Instruct: Objective ②**

**The Allies Go on the Offensive**
TAKS SS11 5(US24.A)
· What were *kamikazes*?
· Why did the Japanese fight so hard on Iwo Jima?
· Why did the Allies believe Okinawa was a foretaste of an invasion of Japan?

📖 In-Depth Resources: Unit 5
· Guided Reading, p. 24

**More About . . .**

**Guadalcanal**
Japanese strategy on Guadalcanal was to wage a guerrilla war of attrition in the jungle. The Japanese questioned American resolve and tested it severely. The hand-to-hand combat on Guadalcanal was a trial of American grit and also a preview of what the land war in the island-hopping campaign was to be like for the remainder of the war.

**More About . . .**

**Japanese Kamikaze Pilots**
At first, young Japanese airmen considered it a great honor to volunteer for suicide missions. The pilots' farewell letters were filled with passionate patriotism. One young man wrote his family, "Think kindly of me and consider it my good fortune to have done something so praiseworthy." Another left this final entry in his diary: "Like cherry blossoms / In the spring / Let us fall / Clean and radiant."

---

**DIFFERENTIATING INSTRUCTION**   **LESS PROFICIENT READERS**

### Sequencing

Help students see the sequence of events that brought the war to a close. Ask them to write July, August, and September as heads for three columns on the page. Then give them the following dates to enter under the correct heads, leaving space after each date: July 15, 1945; August 9, 1945; July 25, 1945; September 2, 1945; August 6, 1945.

Help students enter the correct event next to each date:

· First test of atomic bomb
· Truman orders military to make plans to use bomb
· Hiroshima bombed
· Nagasaki bombed
· Japan surrenders

## History Through *Photojournalism*

### Interpreting the Photograph

After the first flag raising, Marine battalion commander, Lt. Col. Chandler Johnson told 2nd Lt. Albert Tuttle to go down to a ship and get a large battle flag, "large enough that the men at the other end of the island can see it. It will lift their spirits also." Tuttle found such a flag, 96 inches by 56 inches, on a ship. Later investigations revealed that the flag had been salvaged from a ship at Pearl Harbor. Rosenthal climbed the mountain shortly after the flag raising detail and nearly missed the shot when a Marine cameraman distracted him.

### SKILLBUILDER
#### Interpreting Visual Sources

1. Rosenthal's image shows six men strongly united in the effort of raising the flag. The flag is in the process of being raised, thus symbolizing the difficulty of the struggle.

2. unity, cooperation, courage, triumph against odds

---

## History Through *Photojournalism*

### RAISING THE FLAG ON IWO JIMA

On February 19, 1945, the war in Europe was nearing its end, but in the Pacific one of the fiercest battles of World War II was about to erupt. On that day, 70,000 marines converged on the tiny, Japanese-controlled island of Iwo Jima. Four days later, they had captured Mount Suribachi, the island's highest point, but the battle for Iwo Jima would rage on for four more weeks.

Photographer Lou Lowery documented the men ▶ of "Easy Company" hoisting an American flag on a makeshift pole atop Mount Suribachi. But the original flag was soon taken down to be kept as a souvenir by the commanding officer.

 Six marines were sent to replace the flag with an even larger one. Joe Rosenthal, a wire-service photographer, saw the second flag raising, grabbed his camera, and clicked off a frame without even looking through his viewfinder. Rosenthal's photo appeared the next morning on the front pages of American newspapers. In the minds of Americans, it immediately replaced the gloomy, blurred images of Pearl Harbor going up in flames.

#### SKILLBUILDER  Interpeting Visual Sources

1. One of the Mount Suribachi images became one of the most recognized, most reproduced images of World War II. Study the details and point of view in each photo. Explain why you think Rosenthal's image, rather than Lowery's, became important.

2. What human qualities or events do you think Rosenthal's photograph symbolizes?

 SEE SKILLBUILDER HANDBOOK, PAGE R23.

---

**ACTIVITY**   LINK TO HUMANITIES                    BLOCK SCHEDULING

### Iconic Images

**Class Time**  45 minutes

**Task**  Explaining the meaning of a patriotic image or song

**Purpose**  To understand the power of art and images to communicate beyond their literal meaning

**Directions**  Explain to students that Rosenthal's famous photograph has become an American icon. To Americans who grew up during or after the war, it is in indelible patriotic image. Ask students to think about other pictures, artworks, or songs that have that inspirational power for Americans, and have them bring in an example to show and explain what meaning they think Americans find in the work.

**IWO JIMA** After retaking much of the Philippines and liberating the American prisoners of war there, MacArthur and the Allies turned to Iwo Jima, an island that writer William Manchester later described as "an ugly, smelly glob of cold lava squatting in a surly ocean." Iwo Jima (which means "sulfur island" in Japanese) was critical to the United States as a base from which heavily loaded bombers might reach Japan. It was also perhaps the most heavily defended spot on earth, with 20,700 Japanese troops entrenched in tunnels and caves. More than 6,000 marines died taking this desolate island, the greatest number in any battle in the Pacific to that point. Only 200 Japanese survived. Just one obstacle now stood between the Allies and a final assault on Japan—the island of Okinawa.

**THE BATTLE FOR OKINAWA** In April 1945, U.S. marines invaded Okinawa. The Japanese unleashed more than 1,900 kamikaze attacks on the Allies during the Okinawa campaign, sinking 30 ships, damaging more than 300 more, and killing almost 5,000 seamen.

Once ashore, the Allies faced even fiercer opposition than on Iwo Jima. By the time the fighting ended on June 21, 1945, more than 7,600 Americans had died. But the Japanese paid an even ghastlier price—110,000 lives—in defending Okinawa. This total included two generals who chose ritual suicide over the shame of surrender. A witness to this ceremony described their end: "A simultaneous shout and a flash of the sword . . . and both generals had nobly accomplished their last duty to their Emperor."

The Battle for Okinawa was a chilling foretaste of what the Allies imagined the invasion of Japan's home islands would be. Churchill predicted the cost would be a million American lives and half that number of British lives. **C**

---

**MAIN IDEA**

**Drawing Conclusions**
**C** Why was Okinawa a significant island in the war in the Pacific?

*C. Answer*
It was the last island that stood between the Allies and a final assault on Japan. The battle itself was a foretaste of what the Allies imagined the final invasion of Japan would be.

---

## The Atomic Bomb Ends the War **3**

The taking of Iwo Jima and Okinawa opened the way for an invasion of Japan. However, Allied leaders knew that such an invasion would become a desperate struggle. Japan still had a huge army that would defend every inch of homeland. President Truman saw only one way to avoid an invasion of Japan. He decided to use a powerful new weapon that had been developed by scientists working on the Manhattan Project—the atomic bomb.

**THE MANHATTAN PROJECT** Led by American scientist **J. Robert Oppenheimer,** the development of the atomic bomb was not only the most ambitious scientific enterprise in history, it was also the best-kept secret of the war. At its peak, more than 600,000 Americans were involved in the project, although few of them knew its ultimate purpose. Even Truman did not learn about the project until he became president.

The first test of the new bomb took place on the morning of July 16, 1945, in an empty expanse of desert near Alamogordo, New Mexico. A blinding flash, which was visible 180 miles away, was followed by a deafening roar as a tremendous shock wave rolled across the trembling desert. Otto Frisch, a scientist on the project, described the huge mushroom cloud that rose over the desert as "a red-hot elephant standing balanced on its trunk." The bomb worked!

---

**KEY PLAYER**

**DOUGLAS MACARTHUR**
**1880–1964**

Douglas MacArthur was too arrogant and prickly to be considered a "regular guy" by his troops. But he was arguably the most brilliant Allied strategist of World War II. For every American soldier killed in his campaigns, the Japanese lost ten.

He was considered a real hero of the war, both by the military and by the prisoners on the Philippines, whom he freed. "MacArthur took more territory with less loss of life," observed journalist John Gunther, "than any military commander since Darius the Great [king of Persia, 522–486 B.C.]."

---

**KEY PLAYER**

**Douglas MacArthur**
MacArthur's most lasting achievement may have been his role in rebuilding Japan after the war. He implemented a complete reform of the Japanese economic and political institutions. What made his work so successful was his ability to adapt Japanese traditions to a westernized political and economic system. MacArthur had presidential ambitions but failed to gain the Republican nomination. **Ask:** Do you think MacArthur's experience as a general and his work in Japan qualified him to run for president? *(Some students will think the experience was valuable; others may think MacArthur was not political enough for the job.)*

---

**Instruct: Objective 3**

**The Atomic Bomb Ends the War**
TAKS SS11 1(US6.B)
· What was the Manhattan Project?
· How did scientists view using the atomic bomb?
· When was the atomic bomb used?

 In-Depth Resources: Unit 5
· Guided Reading, p. 24

 Electronic Library of Primary Sources
· Statement on the Atomic Bomb by Harry S. Truman

---

**More About . . .**

**First Atomic Bomb Test**
J. Robert Oppenheimer, in describing the first bomb test in New Mexico, recalled, "A few people laughed, a few people cried, most people were silent." Oppenheimer himself said that as he watched the incredible spectacle, he thought of two passages from the ancient Hindu epic *Bhagavad-Gita.* First: "If the radiance of a thousand suns were to burst into the sky, that would be the splendor of the Mighty One." But the second was, "I am become Death, the shatterer of worlds."

---

*The United States in World War II* **583**

---

## More About . . .

### Hiroshima and Nagasaki

The Hiroshima atomic bomb killed an estimated 66,000 people on impact and injured 69,000. In Hiroshima, the bomb destroyed about 67 percent of the city's structures. In Nagasaki, it is estimated that the bomb destroyed about 40 percent of the city. The Nagasaki bomb did less damage because of the geography of the city. It killed more than 39,000 and injured 25,000.

Hiroshima and Nagasaki have become centers for peace movements to ban atomic bombs. Hiroshima houses the Peace Memorial Park, which is located near the center of the atomic blast site. The park contains a museum and a memorial to those who died in the blast.

 In-Depth Resources: Unit 5
· Primary Sources: Bombing of Nagasaki, p. 39

## More About . . .

### The Firebombing of Tokyo

Incredibly, Hiroshima and Nagasaki were not the worst blows absorbed by Japan. On March 9, 1945, 334 B-29 bombers bombed Tokyo, starting many fires which, whipped by high winds, turned into a terrible firestorm. This firestorm destroyed much of the city. The attack left more than 83,000 people dead, 125,000 wounded, and 1.2 million homeless.

President Truman now faced a difficult decision. Should the Allies use the bomb to bring an end to the war? Truman did not hesitate. On July 25, 1945, he ordered the military to make final plans for dropping two atomic bombs on Japanese targets. A day later, the United States warned Japan that it faced "prompt and utter destruction" unless it surrendered at once. Japan refused. Truman later wrote, "The final decision of where and when to use the atomic bomb was up to me. Let there be no mistake about it. I regarded the bomb as a military weapon and never had any doubt that it should be used."

**HIROSHIMA AND NAGASAKI** On August 6, a B-29 bomber named *Enola Gay* released an atomic bomb, code-named Little Boy, over **Hiroshima,** an important Japanese military center. Forty-three seconds later, almost every building in the city collapsed into dust from the force of the blast. Hiroshima had ceased to exist. Still, Japan's leaders hesitated to surrender. Three days later, a second bomb, code-named Fat Man, was dropped on **Nagasaki,** leveling half the city. By the end of the year, an estimated 200,000 people had died as a result of injuries and radiation poisoning caused by the atomic blasts. Yamaoka Michiko was 15 years old and living near the center of Hiroshima when the first bomb hit.

### A PERSONAL VOICE  YAMAOKA MICHIKO

" They say temperatures of 7,000 degrees centigrade hit me. . . . Nobody there looked like human beings. . . . Humans had lost the ability to speak. People couldn't scream, 'It hurts!' even when they were on fire. . . . People with their legs wrenched off. Without heads. Or with faces burned and swollen out of shape. The scene I saw was a living hell. "

—quoted in *Japan at War: An Oral History*

Emperor Hirohito was horrified by the destruction wrought by the bomb. "I cannot bear to see my innocent people suffer any longer," he told Japan's leaders tearfully. Then he ordered them to draw up papers "to end the war." On September 2, formal surrender ceremonies took place on the U.S. battleship *Missouri* in Tokyo Bay. "Today the guns are silent," said General MacArthur in a speech marking this historic moment. "The skies no longer rain death—the seas bear only commerce—men everywhere walk upright in the sunlight. The entire world is quietly at peace."

Hiroshima in ruins following the atomic bomb blast, August 9, 1945 ▶

---

**ACTIVITY**   **COOPERATIVE LEARNING**       **BLOCK SCHEDULING**

### Letters to Truman About Use of Atomic Bomb

**Class Time** 30 minutes

**Task** Writing a letter to President Truman, advising him on what to do with the first two atomic bombs

**Purpose** To build an historical perspective about the reasons for using the bomb against Japan

**Directions** Divide students into small groups. Ask them to review the material they have read about the atomic bomb and then add their own opinions. Then have the group draft a letter, summarizing their reasoning to the president. Dissenting members can file a dissenting opinion.

📄 Integrated Assessment
· Rubric 5

## POINT

**"The only way to end the war against Japan was to bomb the Japanese mainland."**

Many advisors to President Truman, including Secretary of War Henry Stimson, had this point of view. They felt the bomb would end the war and save American lives. Stimson said, "The face of war is the face of death."

Some scientists working on the bomb agreed—even more so as the casualty figures from Iwo Jima and Okinawa sank in. "Are we to go on shedding American blood when we have available a means to a steady victory?" they petitioned. "No! If we can save even a handful of American lives, then let us use this weapon—now!"

Two other concerns pushed Americans to use the bomb. Some people feared that if the bomb were not dropped, the project might be viewed as a gigantic waste of money.

The second consideration involved the Soviet Union. Tension and distrust were already developing between the Western Allies and the Soviets. Some American officials believed that a successful use of the atomic bomb would give the United States a powerful advantage over the Soviets in shaping the postwar world.

## COUNTERPOINT

**"Japan's staggering losses were enough to force Japan's surrender."**

Many of the scientists who had worked on the bomb, as well as military leaders and civilian policymakers, had doubts about using it. Dr. Leo Szilard, a Hungarian-born physicist who had helped President Roosevelt launch the project and who had a major role in developing the bomb, was a key figure opposing its use.

A petition drawn up by Szilard and signed by 70 other scientists argued that it would be immoral to drop an atomic bomb on Japan without fair warning. Many supported staging a demonstration of the bomb for Japanese leaders, perhaps by exploding one on a deserted island near Japan, to convince the Japanese to surrender.

Supreme Allied Commander General Dwight D. Eisenhower agreed. He maintained that "dropping the bomb was completely unnecessary" to save American lives and that Japan was already defeated. Ike told Secretary of War Henry Stimson, "I was against it [the bomb] on two accounts. First the Japanese were ready to surrender and it was not necessary to hit them with that awful thing. Second, I hated to see our country be the first to use such a weapon."

### THINKING CRITICALLY

1. **CONNECT TO HISTORY** **Summarizing** What were the main arguments for and against dropping the atomic bomb on Japan?

    **SEE SKILLBUILDER HANDBOOK, PAGE R4.**

2. **CONNECT TO TODAY** **Evaluating Decisions** Do you think the United States was justified in using the bomb against the Japanese? In a paragraph, explain why or why not.

## ④ Rebuilding Begins

With Japan's surrender, the Allies turned to the challenge of rebuilding war-torn nations. Even before the last guns fell silent, they began thinking about principles that would govern the postwar world.

**THE YALTA CONFERENCE** In February 1945, as the Allies pushed toward victory in Europe, an ailing Roosevelt had met with Churchill and Stalin at the Black Sea resort city of Yalta in the Soviet Union. Stalin graciously welcomed the president and the prime minister, and the Big Three, as they were called, toasted the defeat of Germany that now seemed certain.

For eight grueling days, the three leaders discussed the fate of Germany and the postwar world. Stalin, his country devastated by German forces, favored a harsh approach. He wanted to keep Germany divided into occupation zones—areas controlled by Allied military forces—so that Germany would never again threaten the Soviet Union.

When Churchill strongly disagreed, Roosevelt acted as a mediator. He was prepared to make concessions to Stalin for two reasons. First, he hoped that the Soviet Union would stand by its commitments to join the war against Japan that was still waging in the Pacific. (The first test of the atom bomb was still five months away.) Second, Roosevelt wanted Stalin's support for a new world peace-keeping organization, to be named the United Nations. **D**

*D. Answer*
Roosevelt wanted Soviet help in the war against Japan; He also wanted Soviet cooperation in establishing the United Nations.

**MAIN IDEA**

**Analyzing Motives**
**D** Why was Roosevelt anxious to make concessions to Stalin concerning the fate of postwar Germany?

*The United States in World War II* **585**

## POINT COUNTERPOINT

### Objectives

· To analyze the different views about the ethics of using the atomic bomb

· To understand the political and military pressures to use the bomb

### Instruct

· How did the battles on Iwo Jima and Okinawa influence the decision to use the bomb against Japan?

· What reasons did opponents of using the bomb offer to Secretary Stinson?

### Instruct: Objective ④

**Rebuilding Begins**
TAKS SS11 5(US24.B)

· What plans for peacekeeping did the United States make near the end of the war?

· What did the United States do with the surviving leaders of Germany and Japan?

· What happened to Japan after the war ended?

 In-Depth Resources: Unit 5
· Guided Reading, p. 24

### More About . . .

**The Yalta Conference**
In February 1945, Roosevelt could not see the end of the war in Japan. Stalin's help was needed. Both Roosevelt and Churchill believed Stalin would keep his word about elections in Eastern Europe. Russian domination of those countries had begun. As the Red Army rolled across Eastern Europe, it not only killed Nazis, but also inserted Commissars into local politics.

### THINKING CRITICALLY: ANSWERS

1. **CONNECT TO HISTORY** **Pro Arguments:** prevent additional Allied casualties; if the project were dropped, people would regard it as a great waste of money; success would give the United States an advantage over the Soviet Union. **Con Arguments:** immoral to drop the bomb on Japan without fair warning; unnecessary to drop the bomb because Japan was already defeated

2. **CONNECT TO TODAY**
   **Rubric**
   The paragraph should . . .
   · clearly state the writer's position and provide facts or examples to support the position
   · draw a conclusion that is supported by valid reasons
   · show an understanding of the moral implication as well as the costs and benefits of the action taken

The historic meeting at Yalta produced a series of compromises. To pacify Stalin, Roosevelt convinced Churchill to agree to a temporary division of Germany into four zones, one each for the Americans, the British, the Soviets, and the French. Churchill and Roosevelt assumed that, in time, all the zones would be brought together in a reunited Germany. For his part, Stalin promised "free and unfettered elections" in Poland and other Soviet-occupied Eastern European countries.

Stalin also agreed to join in the war against Japan. That struggle was expected to continue for another year or more. In addition, he agreed to participate in an international conference to take place in April in San Francisco. There, Roosevelt's dream of a United Nations (UN) would become a reality. **E**

**THE NUREMBERG WAR TRIALS** Besides geographic division, Germany had another price to pay for its part in the war. The discovery of Hitler's death camps led the Allies to put 24 surviving Nazi leaders on trial for crimes against humanity, crimes against the peace, and war crimes. The trials were held in the southern German town of Nuremberg.

At the **Nuremberg trials,** the defendants included Hitler's most trusted party officials, government ministers, military leaders, and powerful industrialists. As the trial began, U.S. Supreme Court Justice Robert Jackson explained the significance of the event.

> **A PERSONAL VOICE** ROBERT JACKSON
>
> " The wrongs which we seek to condemn and punish have been so calculated, so malignant and so devastating, that civilization cannot tolerate their being ignored because it cannot survive their being repeated. . . . It is hard now to perceive in these miserable men . . . the power by which as Nazi leaders they once dominated much of the world and terrified most of it. Merely as individuals, their fate is of little consequence to the world. What makes this inquest significant is that these prisoners represent sinister influences that will lurk in the world long after their bodies have returned to dust. They are living symbols of racial hatreds, of terrorism and violence, and of the arrogance and cruelty of power. . . . Civilization can afford no compromise with the social forces which would gain renewed strength if we deal ambiguously or indecisively with the men in whom those forces now precariously survive. "
>
> —quoted in opening address to the Nuremberg War Crimes Trial

**MAIN IDEA**

Summarizing
**E** What decisions did Roosevelt, Churchill, and Stalin make at the Yalta Conference?

**E. Answer**
They agreed to a temporary division of Germany into four zones; Stalin promised that Soviet-occupied Eastern European countries would have free elections; Stalin agreed to send troops to defeat Japan; Stalin agreed to the establishment of the United Nations.

## More About . . .

### The Nuremberg War Trials

The Nuremberg trials (1945–1946) were conducted by the International Military Tribunal under authority from the London Agreement (1945), and negotiated by representatives of the United States, Great Britain, France and the Soviet Union. Among those tried and convicted were Joachim von Ribbentrop, Hitler's Foreign Minister, who negotiated the Hitler-Stalin Pact of 1939; Rudolf Hess, Hitler's Vice Chancellor; Hermann Goering, head of the Luftwaffe; and Albert Speer, Hitler's chief architect.

## More About . . .

### Rudolf Hess

Hess was an early associate of Hitler's whose loyalty earned him promotions in the Nazi hierarchy until he became Vice Chancellor, or the number-two man in the Nazi Party. In 1941, Hess, feeling his prestige falling, undertook a peace mission. He flew to Scotland and parachuted into the country with peace proposals. The British treated Hess as a prisoner of war and ignored his peace proposals. Hitler rejected Hess, saying he was suffering from "pacifist delusions." After the war, Hess was brought to Germany, tried, and convicted. He served a life sentence, dying in prison in 1987.

**War Criminals on Trial, 1945–1949**

Each defendant at the Nuremberg trials was accused of one or more of the following crimes:

• **Crimes Against the Peace**—planning and waging an aggressive war

• **War Crimes**—acts against the customs of warfare, such as the killing of hostages and prisoners, the plundering of private property, and the destruction of towns and cities

• **Crimes Against Humanity**—the murder, extermination, deportation, or enslavement of civilians

---

**DIFFERENTIATING INSTRUCTION**  **GIFTED AND TALENTED STUDENTS**  **classzone.com**

### Human Rights Law

The Nuremberg Trials played a part in the development of international law that sanctions human rights. Ask students to research the Internet to find information on the foundations of human rights in international law. Then have them identify one place where human rights organizations have been effective in bringing attention to the breaking of international law.

**Rubric**

The research report should . . .

· identify specific international laws regarding human rights
· list specific examples of successful human rights organization activities
· include a list of all resources used

 Integrated Assessment
· Rubric 1

In the end, 12 of the 24 defendants were sentenced to death, and most of the remaining were sent to prison. In later trials of lesser leaders, nearly 200 more Nazis were found guilty of war crimes. Still, many people have argued that the trials did not go far enough in seeking out and punishing war criminals. Many Nazis who took part in the Holocaust did indeed go free.

Yet no matter how imperfect the trials might have been, they did establish an important principle—the idea that individuals are responsible for their own actions, even in times of war. Nazi executioners could not escape punishment by claiming that they were merely "following orders." The principle of individual responsibility was now firmly entrenched in international law.

> *"I was only following orders."*
>
> **DEFENDANTS AT THE NUREMBERG TRIALS**

**THE OCCUPATION OF JAPAN** Japan was occupied by U.S. forces under the command of General Douglas MacArthur. In the early years of the occupation, more than 1,100 Japanese, from former Prime Minister Hideki Tojo to lowly prison guards, were arrested and put on trial. Seven, including Tojo, were sentenced to death. In the Philippines, in China, and in other Asian battlegrounds, additional Japanese officials were tried for atrocities against civilians or prisoners of war.

During the seven-year American occupation, MacArthur reshaped Japan's economy by introducing free-market practices that led to a remarkable economic recovery. MacArthur also worked to transform Japan's government. He called for a new constitution that would provide for woman suffrage and guarantee basic freedoms. In the United States, Americans followed these changes with interest. The *New York Times* reported that "General MacArthur . . . has swept away an autocratic regime by a warrior god and installed in its place a democratic government presided over by a very human emperor and based on the will of the people as expressed in free elections." The Japanese apparently agreed. To this day, their constitution is known as the MacArthur Constitution.

## ASSESSMENT

**1. TERMS & NAMES** For each term or name, write a sentence explaining its significance.

- Douglas MacArthur
- Chester Nimitz
- Battle of Midway
- kamikaze
- J. Robert Oppenheimer
- Hiroshima
- Nagasaki
- Nuremberg trials

### MAIN IDEA

**2. TAKING NOTES**
Using a chart such as the one below, describe the significance of key military actions in the Pacific during World War II.

| Military Action | Significance |
|---|---|
| 1. | |
| 2. | |
| 3. | |
| 4. | |
| 5. | |

Which military action was a turning point for the Allies?

### CRITICAL THINKING

**3. DEVELOPING HISTORICAL PERSPECTIVE**
At the trials, many Nazis defended themselves by saying they were only following orders. What does this rationale tell you about the German military? Why was it important to negate this justification?

**4. DRAWING CONCLUSIONS**
Explain how the United States was able to defeat the Japanese in the Pacific.

**5. EVALUATING DECISIONS**
Is it legitimate to hold people accountable for crimes committed during wartime? Why or why not?
**Think About:**
- the laws that govern society
- the likelihood of conducting a fair trial
- the behavior of soldiers, politicians, and civilians during war

*The United States in World War II* **587**

---

*The United States in World War II* **587**

## TRACING THEMES

### Objectives

· Explain the connection between military technology and subsequent civilian technological developments.

· Describe civilian applications of selected military technologies.

### Focus & Motivate

**Making Predictions** Ask student how technology has changed their lives in the last five years. *(Students may cite wireless technology and the ability to receive and send messages and entertainment from any place in the world.)* Then ask students how they think technology will change life in the next ten years. *(Answers will vary.)*

### More About . . .

**Supersonic Flight**

Flight faster than the velocity of sound is called supersonic. The speed of sound, referred to as Mach 1, is 760 miles per hour. The first supersonic flight was taken by Air Force Major Charles E. Yeager on October 14, 1947. Most supersonic military aircraft fly at about Mach 2.5. The first and only commercial supersonic aircraft is the Concorde. The Concorde cruises at Mach 2 in its 3 hour and 50 minute trip from London to New York. The Concorde was grounded in 2000 after an accident.

# Science and Technology

Radar, guided missiles, nuclear submarines, reconnaissance satellites, atomic bombs—the inventions of the 20th century seem intended mainly for war, with the usual dreaded results. But these technological developments have also had far-reaching applications in peacetime. Because the innovations were originally intended for the battlefield, they were developed quickly and with a narrow purpose. However, their applications during peacetime have led to life-enhancing benefits that will extend far into the 21st century.

## 1914–1918 WORLD WAR I

**FIGHTER PLANES TO COMMUTER FLIGHTS ▼**

Airplanes were first used to gather military information but were soon put to work as fighters and bombers. The *Sopwith Camel* (*shown at right*), was one of the most successful British fighter planes, bringing down almost 1,300 enemy aircraft during World War I. The development of flight technology eventually led to sophisticated supersonic aircraft. Today, non-military aircraft are primarily used for travel and cargo transport. Jumbo jets carry hundreds of passengers with each takeoff.

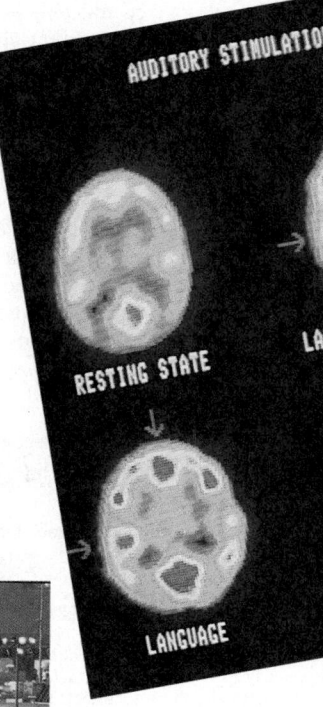

588

---

## RECOMMENDED RESOURCES

### BOOKS FOR TEACHERS

Buderi, Robert. *The Invention That Changed the World.* New York: Simon and Schuester, 1996. Radar launches a technological revolution.

Campbell-Kelly, Martin. *Computer: A History of the Information Machine.* New York: Basic, 1996. Story of the machine that changed modern life.

Elder, Donald C. *Out from Behind the Eight-Ball.* San Diego: American Astronomical Society, 1995. A history of Project Echo, a landmark in the development of satellite communications.

Watson-Watt, Sir Robert Alexander. *The Pulse of Radar.* New York: Dial, 1959. An autobiographical account by a British pioneer of radar.

### VIDEOS

*A Is for Atom.* Coronet/MTI. An exploration of nuclear energy and how science harnessed it.

*The Age of Flight.* MPI Home Video, 1991. A history of aviation.

*Distant Voices.* BBC and Time-Life, 1979. Part 3 of the Connections series explores technological change in warfare and related developments.

*Echoes of War.* Vestron Video, 1989. An episode for PBS' *Nova* series tracing the development of radar in World War II.

*Wings: The Jet Age.* Pacific Arts Video, 1989. The evolution of civil and military jets from World War II to the late 1980s.

# 1939–1945 WORLD WAR II

## ▼ ATOM BOMBS TO BRAIN SCANS

Faced with alarming rumors of work on a German atomic bomb, America mobilized some of the finest scientific minds in the world to create its own atomic bomb. The energy released by its nuclear reaction was enough to kill hundreds of thousands of people, as evidenced by the destruction of Hiroshima and Nagasaki. But the resulting ability to harness the atom's energy also led to new technologies for diagnosing and treating human diseases. Techniques such as positron emission tomography (PET) now reveal the inner workings of the human brain itself.

| Applications of World War II Technology | | |
| --- | --- | --- |
| **TECHNOLOGY** | **MILITARY USE** | **PEACETIME USE** |
| Semiconductors | Navigation | Transistors, radios, electronics |
| Computers | Code breaking | Software programs, video games |
| Freeze-dried food | Soldiers' rations | TV dinners, space-shuttle rations |
| Synthetic materials | Parachutes, weapons parts, tires | Telephones, automobile fenders, pacemakers |
| Radar | Tracking and surveillance | Weather tracking, air traffic control, archaeological digs |

# 1945–1991 THE COLD WAR

### ▼ SATELLITES TO CELLULAR PHONES

The Soviet Union launched *Sputnik*, the first successful artificial space satellite, in 1957. As the United States raced to catch up with the Soviets in space, both countries eventually produced satellites that have improved life for people around the world. Satellites not only track weather patterns and control air traffic but also link the continents in a vast communications network.

---

**THINKING CRITICALLY**

**CONNECT TO HISTORY**
1. **Hypothesizing** Do you think that peacetime technologies would have been developed without the stimulus provided by war? Support your answer.

 **SEE SKILLBUILDER HANDBOOK, PAGE R13.**

**CONNECT TO TODAY**
2. **Evaluating Technological Impact** What invention or technological breakthrough do you think has had the greatest impact on American society? Write a paragraph to explain your answer. Stage a debate with your classmates in which you defend your choice.

 **RESEARCH LINKS** CLASSZONE.COM

---

*The United States in World War II* **589**

## Instruct

1. Ask students to evaluate the importance of the inventions and applications discussed on pages 588–589. Then have the class rank the developments based on their usefulness.
2. Discuss civilian applications of the technologies discussed on pages 588–589. (*airplane—crop dusting, cloud seeding; nuclear power—generation of electricity; satellites—satellite TV, the Internet*)

### MAKING PERSONAL CONNECTIONS

Make sure students understand the significance of digital technology and how it has changed the American economy from an industrial economy to an information economy. Help students understand that digital technology will change the way they will earn a living. While their grandparents and even parents could make a decent living with a minimum of education and even technology, their prospects are likely to rise and fall with the technical skills and education they acquire.

## More About . . .

### Cellular Phones and Wireless Technology

Cellular telephones are an addition to the telephone company in industrialized countries. But in the Third World, where the basic infrastructure for telephones and even electricity is nonexistent or of uncertain reliability, cellular telephones have enabled countries to leapfrog over an era of technology and create a working phone system with relatively little investment.

---

## THINKING CRITICALLY: ANSWERS

1. **CONNECT TO HISTORY Yes** Peacetime inventions of the past or the motives such as profit, fame, and the desire to benefit humanity. **No** The funding for or drive to do the research arose only because of wartime emergencies, Cold War competition, and threats to the nation's survival.

2. **CONNECT TO TODAY**
**Rubric**
Paragraphs should . . .
· identify a specific invention or technological breakthrough
· explain why it is important
· support opinions with accurate facts and examples

**590** CHAPTER 17

# The Home Front

| MAIN IDEA | WHY IT MATTERS NOW | Terms & Names |
|---|---|---|
| After World War II, Americans adjusted to new economic opportunities and harsh social tensions. | Economic opportunities afforded by World War II led to a more diverse middle class in the United States. | • GI Bill of Rights<br>• James Farmer<br>• Congress of Racial Equality (CORE)    • Internment<br>• Japanese American Citizens League (JACL) |

 U.S. History
6B, 6F, 7A, 7B, 8A, 8B, 10A, 14A, 18A, 21A, 21D, 24B, 25A, 25B, 25C, 25D, 26A, 26B

### One American's Story

The writer and poet Maya Angelou was a teenager living in San Francisco when the United States got involved in World War II. The first change she noticed was the disappearance of the city's Japanese population. The second change was an influx of workers, including many African Americans, from the South. San Franciscans, she noted, maintained that there was no racism in their city by the bay. But Angelou knew differently.

**A PERSONAL VOICE** MAYA ANGELOU

" A story went the rounds about a San Franciscan white matron who refused to sit beside a Negro civilian on the streetcar, even after he made room for her on the seat. Her explanation was that she would not sit beside a draft dodger who was a Negro as well. She added that the least he could do was fight for his country the way her son was fighting on Iwo Jima. The story said that the man pulled his body away from the window to show an armless sleeve. He said quietly and with great dignity, 'Then ask your son to look around for my arm, which I left over there.' "
—I Know Why the Caged Bird Sings

At the end of the war, returning veterans—even those who weren't disabled—had to begin dealing with the very real issues of reentry and adjustment to a society that offered many opportunities but still had many unsolved problems.

## 1 Opportunity and Adjustment

In contrast to the Great Depression, World War II was a time of opportunity for millions of Americans. Jobs abounded, and despite rationing and shortages, people had money to spend. At the end of World War II, the nation emerged as the world's dominant economic and military power.

**TWICE A PATRIO**

EX-PRIVATE OBIE BARTLETT LOST LEFT ARM—PEARL RELEASED: DEC, 1941—NOW AT WORK WELDING IN A WEST COAST SHIPYARD...

▲ Like many minority veterans, Obie Bartlett was twice a patriot— and was still regarded as a second-class citizen.

---

---

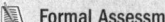

**ECONOMIC GAINS** The war years were good ones for working people. As defense industries boomed, unemployment fell to a low of 1.2 percent in 1944. Even with price and wage controls, average weekly paychecks rose 35 percent during the war. And although workers still protested long hours, overtime, and night shifts, they were able to save money for the future. Some workers invested up to half their paychecks in war bonds.

Farmers also prospered during the war. Unlike the depression years, when farmers had battled dust storms and floods, the early 1940s had good weather for growing crops. Farmers benefited from improvements in farm machinery and fertilizers and reaped the profits from rising crop prices. As a result, crop production increased by 50 percent, and farm income tripled. Before the war ended, many farmers could pay off their mortgages.

Women also enjoyed employment gains during the war, although many lost their jobs when the war ended. Over 6 million women had entered the work force for the first time, boosting the percentage of women in the total work force to 35 percent. A third of those jobs were in defense plants, which offered women more challenging work and better pay than jobs traditionally associated with women, such as as waitressing, clerking, and domestic service. With men away at war, many women also took advantage of openings in journalism and other professions. "The war really created opportunities for women," said Winona Espinosa, a wife and mother who became a riveter and bus driver during the war. "It was the first time we got a chance to show that we could do a lot of things that only men had done before."

**POPULATION SHIFTS**
In addition to revamping the economy, the war triggered one of the greatest mass migrations in American history. Americans whose families had lived for decades in one place suddenly uprooted themselves to seek work elsewhere. More than a million newcomers poured into California between 1941 and 1944. Towns with defense industries saw their populations double and even triple, sometimes almost overnight. As shown in the map to the right, African Americans left the South for cities in the North in record numbers. **A**

"THE GIRL HE LEFT BEHIND" IS STILL BEHIND HIM
She's a **WOW**
WOMAN ORDNANCE WORKER

▲
The war gave women the chance to prove they could be just as productive as men. But their pay usually did not reflect their productivity.

---

**African-American Migration, 1940–1950**

West Coast
Mountain and Plains States
Midwest
Middle Atlantic
New England
South
+26,300
+523,200
+386,800
+24,900
+283,600
−1,244,800

**GEOGRAPHY SKILLBUILDER**
1. **Movement** To which geographic region did the greatest number of African Americans migrate?
2. **Movement** How did the wartime economy contribute to this mass migration?

---

*Skillbuilder Answers*
1. The Midwest.
2. There were defense jobs in northern factories.

**Vocabulary**
**migration:** the act of moving from one country or region to another

*A. Answer*
In towns and cities with defense plants, population increased. African Americans left the South for factory jobs in the North.

**MAIN IDEA**

**Analyzing Causes**
**A** How did World War II cause the U.S. population to shift?

---

---

TAKS Mini-Lesson 2:
SS11 2(US10.A)      *The United States in World War II* **591**

---

## Tracing Themes
### ECONOMIC OPPORTUNITY

**The GI Bill of Rights**
The GI Bill of Rights made the American dream a reality for millions of World War II veterans by providing them with education and unemployment allowances, and home, farm, and business loans. The GI Bill programs continue to cover men and women who served in the armed forces, including those who served in the Persian Gulf War and those serving in the Reserves and Army and Air National Guard.

## More About . . .

**GI Bill of Rights**
The GI Bill offered free education to returning veterans. It was estimated that the bill produced 450,000 engineers; 238,000 teachers; 91,000 scientists; 67,000 doctors; 22,000 dentists; and more than a million other college-trained men and women. The World War II program cost the government approximately $14.5 billion.

## Instruct: Objective ❷

**Discrimination and Reaction / Internment of Japanese Americans**
TAKS SS11 1(US6.B)
· How were African Americans treated at home and in the military?
· How did Americans react to progress in acceptance of African Americans?
· Why were Japanese Americans placed in internment camps?
· How were Japanese Americans compensated for internment?

 In-Depth Resources: Unit 5
· Guided Reading, p. 25

Attending Pennsylvania State College under the GI Bill of Rights, William Oskay, Jr., paid $28 a month for the trailer home in which you see him working. ▶

**SOCIAL ADJUSTMENTS** Families adjusted to the changes brought on by war as best they could. With millions of fathers in the armed forces, mothers struggled to rear their children alone. Many young children got used to being left with neighbors or relatives or in child-care centers as more and more mothers went to work. Teenagers left at home without parents sometimes drifted into juvenile delinquency. And when fathers finally did come home, there was often a painful period of readjustment as family members got to know one another again.

The war helped create new families, too. Longtime sweethearts—as well as couples who barely knew each other—rushed to marry before the soldier or sailor was shipped overseas. In booming towns like Seattle, the number of marriage licenses issued went up by as much as 300 percent early in the war. A New Yorker observed in 1943, "On Fridays and Saturdays, the City Hall area is blurred with running soldiers, sailors, and girls hunting the license bureau, floral shops, ministers, blood-testing laboratories, and the Legal Aid Society."

In 1944, to help ease the transition of returning servicemen to civilian life, Congress passed the Servicemen's Readjustment Act, better known as the **GI Bill of Rights.** This bill provided education and training for veterans, paid for by the federal government. Just over half the returning soldiers, or about 7.8 million veterans, attended colleges and technical schools under the GI Bill. The act also provided federal loan guarantees to veterans buying homes or farms or starting new businesses. Ⓑ

## ❷ Discrimination and Reaction

Despite the opportunities that opened up for women and minorities during the war, old prejudices and policies persisted, both in the military and at home.

**CIVIL RIGHTS PROTESTS** African Americans made some progress on the home front. During the war, thousands of African Americans left the South. The majority moved to the Midwest, where better jobs could be found. Between 1940 and 1944, the percentage of African Americans working in skilled or semiskilled jobs rose from 16 to 30 percent.

MAIN IDEA

Analyzing Effects
Ⓑ How did the war affect families and personal lives?

*B. Answer*
During the war, mothers became single parents and women took jobs outside the home. The war helped create new families.

---

 **ACTIVITY** COOPERATIVE LEARNING | BLOCK SCHEDULING

**Effect of Demobilization**

**Class Time** 20 minutes

**Task** Predicting the effect on colleges and universities of the GI Bill

**Purpose** To understand the social and political impact of demobilization

**Directions** Help students understand the problems governments are faced with in demobilizing large armies. First ask students to predict what will happen when thousands of military personnel return to the United States after the war. What needs will these individuals have? Ask students to consider the effects of the GI Bill on colleges and universities. Ask them to consider how the GI Bill was a win-win situation for both veterans and the U.S. government.

Wherever African Americans moved, however, discrimination presented tough hurdles. In 1942, civil rights leader **James Farmer** founded an interracial organization called the **Congress of Racial Equality (CORE)** to confront urban segregation in the North. That same year, CORE staged its first sit-in at a segregated Chicago restaurant.

As African-American migrants moved into already overcrowded cities, tensions rose. In 1943, a tidal wave of racial violence swept across the country. The worst conflict erupted in Detroit on a hot Sunday afternoon in June. What started as a tussle between blacks and whites at a beach on the Detroit River mushroomed into a riot when white sailors stationed nearby joined the fray. The fighting raged for three days, fueled by false rumors that whites had murdered a black woman and her child and that black rioters had killed 17 whites. By the time President Roosevelt sent federal troops to restore order, 9 whites and 25 blacks lay dead or dying.

The violence of 1943 revealed to many Americans—black and white alike—just how serious racial tensions had become in the United States. By 1945, more than 400 committees had been established by American communities to improve race relations. Progress was slow, but African Americans were determined not to give up the gains they had made. **C**

**MAIN IDEA**

**Analyzing Causes**
**C** What caused the race riots in the 1940s?

*C. Answer*
Discrimination, racism, concentration of minorities in cities.

**TENSION IN LOS ANGELES** Mexican Americans also experienced prejudice during the war years. In the violent summer of 1943, Los Angeles exploded in anti-Mexican "zoot-suit" riots. The zoot suit was a style of dress adopted by Mexican-American youths as a symbol of their rebellion against tradition. It consisted of a long jacket and pleated pants. Broad-brimmed hats were often worn with the suits.

The riots began when 11 sailors in Los Angeles reported that they had been attacked by zoot-suit-wearing Mexican Americans. This charge triggered two nights of violence involving thousands of servicemen and civilians. Mobs poured into Mexican neighborhoods and grabbed any zoot-suiters they could find. The attackers ripped off their victims' clothes and beat them senseless. The riots lasted more than ten days and resulted in the beating of hundreds of Mexican-American youth and other minorities.

Despite such unhappy experiences with racism, many Mexican Americans believed that their sacrifices during wartime would lead to a better future.

▲
These Mexican Americans, involved in the 1943 Los Angeles riots, are seen here leaving jail to make court appearances.

**A PERSONAL VOICE** MANUEL DE LA RAZA

" This war . . . is doing what we in our Mexican-American movement had planned to do in one generation. . . . It has shown those 'across the tracks' that we all share the same problems. It has shown them what the Mexican American will do, what responsibility he will take and what leadership qualities he will demonstrate. After this struggle, the status of the Mexican Americans will be different."

—quoted in *A Different Mirror: A History of Multicultural America*

*The United States in World War II* **593**

---

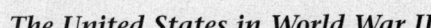

## Japanese Relocation Camps, 1942

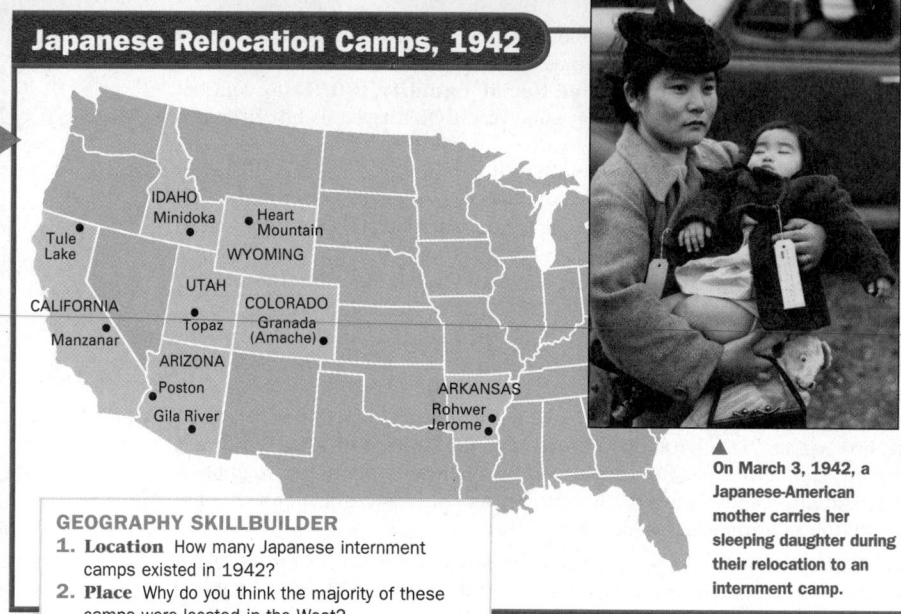

### GEOGRAPHY SKILLBUILDER
1. **Location** How many Japanese internment camps existed in 1942?
2. **Place** Why do you think the majority of these camps were located in the West?

▲ On March 3, 1942, a Japanese-American mother carries her sleeping daughter during their relocation to an internment camp.

---

## More About. . .

### Japanese-American Internment
The following are excerpts from the instructions given to Japanese Americans in California.

The Following Instructions Must Be Observed:

1. A responsible member of each family will report . . . to the Civil Control Station to receive further instructions. This must be done between 8:00 A.M. and 5:00 P.M. on Monday, May 24, 1942, or between 8:00 A.M. and 5:00 P.M. on Tuesday, May 25, 1942.

2. Evacuees must carry with them on departure . . . the following property:
   (a) Bedding and linens (no mattress) for each member of the family;
   (b) Toilet articles for each member of the family;
   (c) Extra clothing for each member of the family;
   (d) Sufficient knives, forks, spoons, plates, bowls and cups for each member of the family;
   (e) Essential personal effects for each member of the family.

3. No pets of any kind will be permitted.

4. No personal items and no household goods will be shipped.

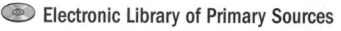 **Electronic Library of Primary Sources**
· Japanese-American Testimony from National Defense Migration Hearings

 **In-Depth Resources: Unit 5**
· Primary Sources: from *Farewell to Manzanar*, p. 36
· Literature: from *Snow Falling on Cedars*, pp. 40–42

---

## Internment of Japanese Americans

Mini-Lesson 4: SS11 3(US12.A)

While Mexican Americans and African Americans struggled with racial tension, the war produced tragic results for Japanese Americans. When the war began, 120,000 Japanese Americans lived in the United States. Most of them were citizens living on the West Coast.

The surprise Japanese attack on Pearl Harbor in Hawaii had stunned the nation. After the bombing, panic-stricken citizens feared that the Japanese would soon attack the United States. Frightened people believed false rumors that Japanese Americans were committing sabotage by mining coastal harbors and poisoning vegetables.

This sense of fear and uncertainty caused a wave of prejudice against Japanese Americans. Early in 1942, the War Department called for the mass evacuation of all Japanese Americans from Hawaii. General Delos Emmons, the military governor of Hawaii, resisted the order because 37 percent of the people in Hawaii were Japanese Americans. To remove them would have destroyed the islands' economy and hindered U.S. military operations there. However, he was eventually forced to order the **internment,** or confinement, of 1,444 Japanese Americans, 1 percent of Hawaii's Japanese-American population.

On the West Coast, however, panic and prejudice ruled the day. In California, only 1 percent of the people were Japanese, but they constituted a minority large enough to stimulate the prejudice of many whites, without being large enough to effectively resist internment. Newspapers whipped up anti-Japanese sentiment by running ugly stories attacking Japanese Americans.

On February 19, 1942, President Roosevelt signed an order requiring the removal of people of Japanese ancestry from California and parts of Washington, Oregon, and Arizona. Based on strong recommendations from the military, he justified this step as necessary for national security. In the following weeks, the army rounded up some 110,000 Japanese Americans and shipped them to ten hastily constructed remote "relocation centers," euphemisms for prison camps.

**594** CHAPTER 17

---

### Japanese Internment

Ask students to use Internet and other research tools to read original articles involving the Japanese population in California in 1941 and 1942. Use the *Los Angeles Times*, *San Francisco Chronicle*, *San Francisco Examiner*, and *Oakland Tribune* between December 8, 1941, and February, 1942, when Roosevelt signed the executive order for internment. Have them report their findings to the rest of the class. Then discuss what the research suggests about the mainstream press and its reporting of the situation.

**Rubric**

The research report should . . .
· trace the events in the specified time period
· include excerpts from newspaper articles
· evaluate the assumptions or biases of the mainstream press reporting

 **Integrated Assessment**
· Rubric 1

**MAIN IDEA**

**Analyzing Motives**

 Why did President Roosevelt order the internment of Japanese Americans?

*D. Answer* Because some people perceived them as a threat to national security

About two-thirds were Nisei, or Japanese Americans who had been born in this country and were thus American citizens. Thousands of Nisei had already joined the armed forces, and to Ted Nakashima, an architectural draftsman from Seattle, the evacuation seemed utterly senseless.

## A PERSONAL VOICE   TED NAKASHIMA

"[There are] electricians, plumbers, draftsmen, mechanics, carpenters, painters, farmers—every trade—men who are able and willing to do all they can to lick the Axis. . . . We're on this side and we want to help. Why won't America let us?"

—from *New Republic* magazine, June 15, 1942

No specific charges were ever filed against Japanese Americans, and no evidence of subversion was ever found. Faced with expulsion, terrified families were forced to sell their homes, businesses, and all their belongings for less than their true value.

Japanese Americans fought for justice, both in the courts and in Congress. The initial results were discouraging. In 1944, the Supreme Court decided, in *Korematsu* v. *United States*, that the government's policy of evacuating Japanese Americans to camps was justified on the basis of "military necessity." (See pages 596–597.) After the war, however, the **Japanese American Citizens League (JACL)** pushed the government to compensate those sent to the camps for their lost property. In 1965, Congress authorized the spending of $38 million for that purpose—less than a tenth of Japanese Americans' actual losses.

The JACL did not give up its quest for justice. In 1978, it called for the payment of reparations, or restitution, to each individual that suffered internment. A decade later, Congress passed, and President Ronald Reagan signed, a bill that promised $20,000 to every Japanese American sent to a relocation camp. When the checks were sent in 1990, a letter from President George Bush accompanied them, in which he stated, "We can never fully right the wrongs of the past. But we can take a clear stand for justice and recognize that serious injustices were done to Japanese Americans during World War II."

## More About . . .

### Fred Korematsu

Korematsu was in his early 20s and living in his hometown of Oakland when the exclusion order was announced in 1942. He tried twice to enlist in the army, but was turned down because of a physical disability. Korematsu was working in a defense plant for a while. He was a loyal, law-abiding citizen who had never been in trouble or arrested. Rather than be separated from his white girlfriend, Korematsu posed as Chinese and took a job in a trailer park. He was arrested in May 1942 and tried and convicted of violating the exclusion order.

## Assess & Reteach

**SECTION 4 ASSESSMENT**
Have students work in groups of four, with each student answering one question.

Formal Assessment
· Section Quiz, p. 319

**SELF-ASSESSMENT**
Have students note the changes made in their answers during group discussion. Ask them how they could improve their answers next time.

**RETEACH**
Use the poster of Obie Bartlett on page 590 as the basis of a class discussion of the social impact of World War II on various groups of Americans.

In-Depth Resources: Unit 5
· Reteaching Activity, p. 31

---

## 4 ASSESSMENT

**1. TERMS & NAMES** For each term or name, write a sentence explaining its significance.
- GI Bill of Rights
- James Farmer
- Congress of Racial Equality (CORE)
- internment
- Japanese Americans Citizens League (JACL)

### MAIN IDEA

**2. TAKING NOTES**
List the advances and problems in the economy and in civil rights during World War II.

|  | Advances | Problems |
|---|---|---|
| Economy |  |  |
| Civil Rights |  |  |

Which of these advances and problems do you think had the most far-reaching effect? Explain your answer.

### CRITICAL THINKING

**3. COMPARING**
How were the experiences of African Americans, Mexican Americans, and Japanese Americans similar during World War II? How were they different?

**4. DEVELOPING HISTORICAL PERSPECTIVE**
Do you think that the government's policy of evacuating Japanese Americans to camps was justified on the basis of "military necessity"? Explain your answer.

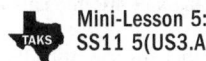 Mini-Lesson 5: SS11 5(US3.A)

**5. ANALYZING EFFECTS**
What effect did World War II have on American families? **Think About:**
- the role of women in families and the economy
- the relationship between the races
- the impact of the federal government on society

---

**Answers** **ASSESSMENT 4**

**1. TERMS & NAMES**
GI Bill of Rights, p. 592
James Farmer, p. 593
Congress of Racial Equality (CORE), p. 593
internment, p. 594
Japanese American Citizens League (JACL), p. 595

**2. TAKING NOTES**
**Economy—Advances:** Low unemployment, rising crop prices, opportunities for women; **Problems:** Shortage of housing and food; rationing
**Civil Rights—Advances:** More equality in the military, founding of CORE; **Problems:** Segregation, discrimination, race riots in Detroit and Los Angeles; internment of Japanese Americans

**3. COMPARING**
**Similar:** All three groups suffered from discrimination. **Different:** Japanese Americans living on the West Coast were forced into internment camps.

**4. DEVELOPING HISTORICAL PERSPECTIVE**
**Yes** The United States government had no way of telling with certainty that Japanese citizens were loyal. **No** There was no proof that Japanese Americans were disloyal to their country.

**5. ANALYZING EFFECTS**
The war changed traditional gender roles as women enlisted in the armed forces and took jobs outside the home. The war also reinforced the country's long-standing policy of discrimination against minorities.

## HISTORIC DECISIONS OF THE SUPREME COURT

### Objectives

· To analyze the Supreme Court case of *Korematsu* v. *United States* in its historical context

· To understand the legal reasoning used to decide the *Korematsu* case

## Focus & Motivate

**Drawing Conclusions** Ask students to remember the military situation immediately following Pearl Harbor. Tell them that previously Americans felt safe from conflict, an ocean away from both aggressors. Pearl Harbor not only shattered the illusion of security, it created the fear of immediate threat. Ask: Would they expect military authorities to make judicious decisions when faced with conflicts about security and liberty? How would racism, fear, and ignorance play into the decision?

## More About . . .

### Military Necessity

Justice Murphy in his dissent challenged the issue of military necessity, writing:

" . . . this forced exclusion was the result in good measure of this erroneous assumption of racial guilt rather than bona fide military necessity. . . . In support of this blanket condemnation of all persons of Japanese descent, however, no reliable evidence is cited to show that such individuals were generally disloyal, or had generally so conducted themselves in this area as to constitute a special menace to defense installations or war industries, or had otherwise by their behavior furnished reasonable ground for their exclusion as a group."

# KOREMATSU v. UNITED STATES (1944)

**ORIGINS OF THE CASE** Following the Japanese attack on Pearl Harbor on December 7, 1941, U.S. military officials argued that Japanese Americans posed a threat to the nation's security. Based on recommendations from the military, President Franklin Roosevelt issued Executive Order 9066, which gave military officials the power to limit the civil rights of Japanese Americans. Military authorities began by setting a curfew for Japanese Americans. Later, they forced Japanese Americans from their homes and moved them into detention camps. Fred Korematsu was convicted of defying the military order to leave his home. At the urging of the American Civil Liberties Union (ACLU), Korematsu appealed that conviction.

**THE RULING** The Court upheld Korematsu's conviction and argued that military necessity made internment constitutional.

## LEGAL REASONING

Executive Order 9066 was clearly aimed at one group of people—Japanese Americans. Korematsu argued that this order was unconstitutional because it was based on race. Writing for the Court majority, Justice Hugo Black agreed "that all legal restrictions which curtail the civil rights of a single racial group are immediately suspect." However, in this case, he said, the restrictions were based on "a military imperative" and not "group punishment based on antagonism to those of Japanese origin." As such, Justice Black stated that the restrictions were constitutional.

" Compulsory exclusion of large groups, . . . except under circumstances of direct emergency and peril, is inconsistent with our basic governmental institutions. But when under conditions of modern warfare our shores are threatened by hostile forces, the power to protect must be commensurate with the threatened danger."

Justice Frank Murphy, however, dissented—he opposed the majority. He believed that military necessity was merely an excuse that could not conceal the racism at the heart of the restrictions.

" This exclusion . . . ought not to be approved. Such exclusion goes 'over the very brink of constitutional power' and falls into the ugly abyss of racism."

Two other justices also dissented, but Korematsu's conviction stood.

### LEGAL SOURCES

#### LEGISLATION

**U.S. CONSTITUTION, FIFTH AMENDMENT (1791)**
"No person shall . . . be deprived of life, liberty, or property, without due process of law."

**EXECUTIVE ORDER 9066 (1942)**
"I hereby authorize and direct the Secretary of War . . . to prescribe military areas in such places and of such extent as he . . . may determine, from which any or all persons may be excluded."

#### RELATED CASES

**HIRABAYASHI v. UNITED STATES (JUNE 1943)**
The Court upheld the conviction of a Japanese-American man for breaking curfew. The Court argued that the curfew was within congressional and presidential authority.

**EX PARTE ENDO (DECEMBER 1944)**
The Court ruled that a Japanese-American girl, whose loyalty had been clearly established, could not be held in an internment camp.

---

## RECOMMENDED RESOURCES

### BOOKS

Alonso, Karen. ***Korematsu v. United States: Japanese American Internment Camps.***

Daniels, Roger and Eric Foner eds. ***Prisoners Without Trial: Japanese Americans in World War II.*** New York: Hill & Wang, 1993.

Maki, Mitchell T., Harry H. L. Kitano, S. Megan Berthold, Roger Daniels. **A*chieving the Impossible Dream: How Japanese Americans Obtained Redress.*** Urbana: U of Illinois P, 1999.

United States Commission on Wartime Relocation and Internment of Civilians, Tetsuden Kashima, ed., ***Personal Justice Denied: Report of the Commission on Wartime Relocation and Internment of Civilians.*** Seattle: U of Washington P, 1997.

### INTEGRATED TECHNOLOGY

For teacher support and more information about the Supreme Court including the full text of the Supreme Court decisions, visit. . . .

 classzone.com

## Instruct

1. What was the key conflict in the *Korematsu* case?

2. What role did the military play in the Court's decision?

3. What did Justice Murphy base his dissent on?

**MAKING PERSONAL CONNECTIONS**

Discuss how the use of wartime propaganda to build support for the war made it difficult, if not impossible, to stop the racial stereotyping and hatred directed toward Japanese Americans.

## WHY IT MATTERED

About 110,000 Japanese Americans were forced into internment camps, as shown above, during World War II. Many had to sell their businesses and homes at great loss. Thousands were forced to give up their possessions. In the internment camps, Japanese Americans lived in a prison-like setting under constant guard.

The Court ruled that these government actions did not violate people's rights because the restrictions were based on military necessity rather than on race. But the government treated German Americans and Italian Americans much differently. In those instances, the government identified potentially disloyal people but did not harass the people it believed to be loyal. By contrast, the government refused to make distinctions between loyal and potentially disloyal Japanese Americans.

## HISTORICAL IMPACT

In the end, the internment of Japanese Americans became a national embarrassment. In 1976, President Gerald R. Ford repealed Executive Order 9066.

▲ President Clinton presents Fred Korematsu with a Presidential Medal of Freedom during a ceremony at the White House on January 15, 1998.

Similarly, the Court's decision in *Korematsu* became an embarrassing example of court sanctioned racism often compared to the decisions on *Dred Scott* (1857) and *Plessy* v. *Ferguson* (1896). In the early 1980s, a scholar conducting research obtained copies of government documents related to the *Hirabayashi* and *Korematsu* cases. The documents showed that the army had lied to the Court in the 1940s. Japanese Americans had not, in fact, posed any security threat to the nation. In 1984, a federal court overturned the convictions of Korematsu and Hirabayashi. Four years later, Congress passed a law ordering reparations payments to surviving Japanese Americans who had been detained in the camps.

## More About . . .

### Politics and the Court

The *Korematsu* case ranks with *Dred Scott* and *Plessy* v. *Ferguson* as one of the low points of the Supreme Court. Hindsight clearly shows the racism and expediency behind the military's thinking. What students of the Court are left to ponder is why a majority on the Court accepted the military's evaluation without question. The politics of the war certainly made questioning the military a risky business. The decision was a case of a Court majority going along with the actions because the political energy to stand by the Constitution in wartime was not there.

---

### THINKING CRITICALLY

**CONNECT TO HISTORY**

1. **Hypothesizing** The internment of Japanese Americans during World War II disrupted lives and ripped apart families. What do you think can be done today to address this terrible mistake? How can the government make amends?

    **SEE SKILLBUILDER HANDBOOK, PAGE R13.**

**CONNECT TO TODAY**

2.  **INTERNET ACTIVITY** CLASSZONE.COM

   Visit the links for Historic Decisions of the Supreme Court to locate the three dissenting opinions in *Korematsu* written by Justices Frank Murphy, Robert Jackson, and Owen Roberts. Read one of these opinions, and then write a summary that states its main idea. What constitutional principle, if any, does the opinion use?

---

### THINKING CRITICALLY: ANSWERS

1. **CONNECT TO HISTORY** Students may refer to the compensations granted by the government in 1984 or may have additional suggestions as to reparations to Japanese Americans.

2. **CONNECT TO TODAY**
   **Rubric**
   The summary should . . .
   · identify which Justice's opinion is being summarized and the constitutional principle cited
   · state the main idea and present supporting evidence of that idea
   · show evidence of the constitutional principle in the opinion of the Justice

## TERMS & NAMES

1. A. Philip Randolph, p. 566
2. Manhattan Project, p. 567
3. rationing, p. 568
4. Dwight D. Eisenhower, p. 572
5. D-Day, p. 574
6. V-E Day, p. 577
7. Douglas MacArthur, p. 579
8. Hiroshima, p. 584
9. GI Bill of Rights, p. 592
10. Congress of Racial Equality, p. 593

## MAIN IDEAS

1. It included large numbers of white, African Americans, Native Americans, Mexican Americans, and Asian Americans.
2. It drafted civilians and established a system of rationing and other economic controls.
3. The media issued propaganda films that stressed the alliance between the United States and the Soviet Union and reinforced the view of Germany as the enemy.
4. They used the convoy system and an accelerated shipbuilding program.
5. Soviets stopped Hitler's eastward expansion, destroyed the German Sixth Army, and diverted German troops from the western front.
6. Germany could not replace the manpower and weapons it lost, and could only retreat.
7. The Allies adopted a policy of leapfrogging from island to island, all the time moving westward toward the Japanese homeland.
8. The United States wanted to avoid the casualties that would result from an invasion of Japan, and to end the war quickly.
9. Unemployment decreased, women took jobs outside the home, and housing and food were in short supply.
10. Racial riots in Detroit, zoot suit riots in Los Angeles, and the internment of Japanese Americans.

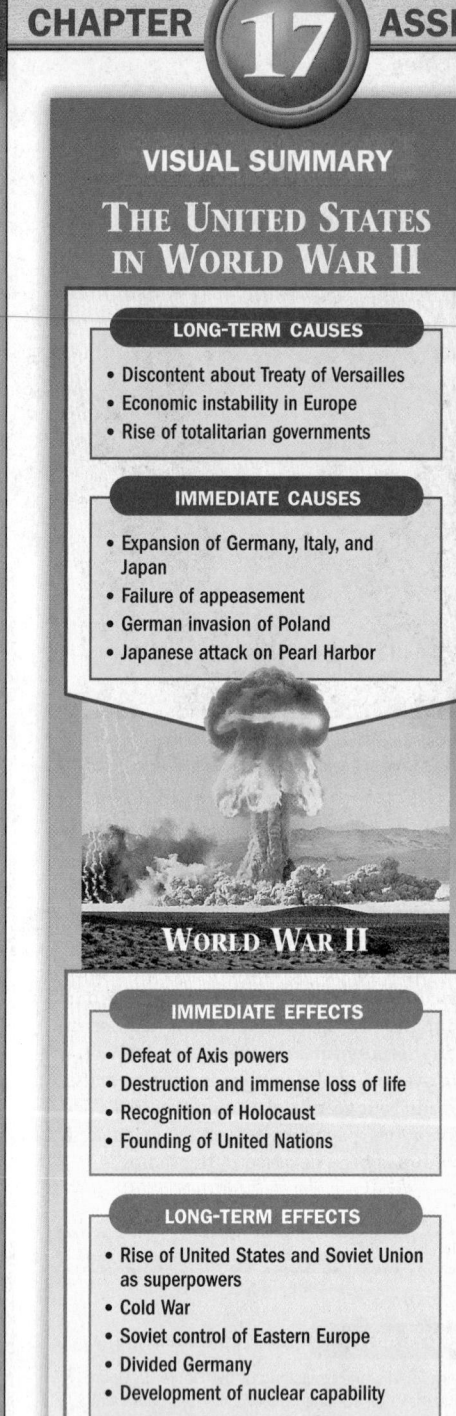

**VISUAL SUMMARY**

### THE UNITED STATES IN WORLD WAR II

**LONG-TERM CAUSES**

- Discontent about Treaty of Versailles
- Economic instability in Europe
- Rise of totalitarian governments

**IMMEDIATE CAUSES**

- Expansion of Germany, Italy, and Japan
- Failure of appeasement
- German invasion of Poland
- Japanese attack on Pearl Harbor

**WORLD WAR II**

**IMMEDIATE EFFECTS**

- Defeat of Axis powers
- Destruction and immense loss of life
- Recognition of Holocaust
- Founding of United Nations

**LONG-TERM EFFECTS**

- Rise of United States and Soviet Union as superpowers
- Cold War
- Soviet control of Eastern Europe
- Divided Germany
- Development of nuclear capability

## TERMS & NAMES

**For each term or name below, write a sentence explaining its connection to World War II.**

1. A. Philip Randolph
2. Manhattan Project
3. rationing
4. Dwight D. Eisenhower
5. D-Day
6. V-E Day
7. Douglas MacArthur
8. Hiroshima
9. GI Bill of Rights
10. Congress of Racial Equality (CORE)

## MAIN IDEAS

**Use your notes and the information in the chapter to answer the following questions.**

**Mobilizing for Defense** (pages 562–568)

1. How did the U.S. military reflect the diversity of American society during World War II?
2. How did the federal government's actions influence civilian life during World War II?
3. What role did the media play in helping the country mobilize?

**The War for Europe and North Africa** (pages 569–577)

4. How did the Allies win control of the Atlantic Ocean between 1941 and 1943?
5. What was the significance of the Battle of Stalingrad?
6. How did the Battle of the Bulge signal the beginning of the end of World War II in Europe?

**The War in the Pacific** (pages 578–587)

7. Briefly describe the island war in the Pacific.
8. Why did President Truman decide to use atomic weapons?

**The Home Front** (pages 590–595)

9. How did the U.S. economy change during World War II?
10. What events show the persistence of racial tensions?

## CRITICAL THINKING

1. **USING YOUR NOTES** In a chart like the one shown, provide causes for the listed effects of World War II.

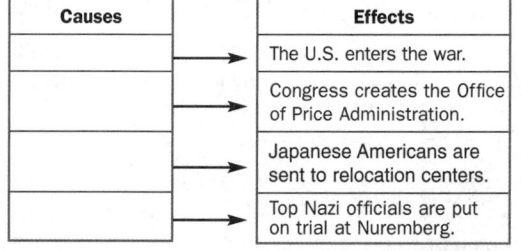

| Causes | | Effects |
|---|---|---|
| | → | The U.S. enters the war. |
| | → | Congress creates the Office of Price Administration. |
| | → | Japanese Americans are sent to relocation centers. |
| | → | Top Nazi officials are put on trial at Nuremberg. |

2. **ANALYZING ISSUES** Would you support the use of nuclear weapons today, and if so, under what circumstances?

3. **INTERPRETING MAPS** Judging from the map on page 572, why was a victory in North Africa essential to an invasion of southern Europe?

## CRITICAL THINKING

1. **USING YOUR NOTES** Cause: Japan bombs Pearl Harbor. Effect: The United States enters the war. Cause: The threat of inflation. Effect: Congress creates the OPA. Cause: Japanese Americans are seen as a security threat. Effect: Japanese Americans are sent to relocation centers. Cause: The Allies discover Hitler's death camps. Effect: Top Nazi officials are put on trial at Nuremberg.

2. **ANALYZING ISSUES** Yes: Use of nuclear weapons is justified to respond to an enemy attack or to prevent an enemy from using them. No: Using atomic weapons is not justified because they kill and maim indiscriminately. The use of nuclear weapons by one country may provoke another country into using them, thus resulting in a nuclear holocaust that would destroy the world.

3. **INTERPRETING MAPS** North Africa and southern Europe are separated only by the Mediterranean Sea. Once the Allies secured North Africa, they could use it as a launching pad to send forces and supplies into southern Europe.

## Standardized Test Practice

**Use the map and your knowledge of U.S. history to answer question 1.**

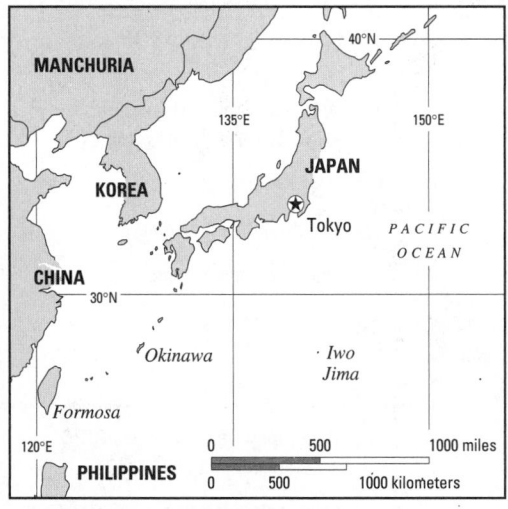

1. Why was it critical for the Allies to take the Japanese-held islands of Iwo Jima and Okinawa?

   A The islands were highly populated areas with little military protection.

   B The islands were critical as bases from which Allied bombers could reach Japan.

   C The islands were centers for Japanese development of a nuclear bomb.

   D The Allies intended to drop atomic bombs on the islands.

2. How did World War II lead to one of the largest population shifts in U.S. history?

   F Service men and women were forced to leave their homes for Europe.

   G The loss of loved ones led people to move in with their families.

   H People moved to states with military bases and factories for better jobs.

   J People moved to the middle of the country to escape wars on both coasts.

3. How did natural geography contribute to Germany's defeat in World War II?

   A Large bodies of water stood between Germany and its enemies.

   B Germany had to fight a war on three fronts: North Africa, Western Europe, and Eastern Europe and the Soviet Union.

   C There were too few rivers to be used for German supplies.

   D Switzerland pledged to remain neutral throughout the war.

**ADDITIONAL TEST PRACTICE, pages S1–S33.**

TEST PRACTICE  CLASSZONE.COM

---

## ALTERNATIVE ASSESSMENT

1. **INTERACT WITH HISTORY**

   Recall your discussion of the question on page 561:

   *How can the United States use its resources to achieve victory?*

   Write a newspaper article in which you describe the ways in which the United States used its resources during World War II. Include information about rationing and about the various offices that the Federal government established to monitor inflation and convert a peacetime economy into a wartime economy.

2. **INTERNET ACTIVITY** CLASSZONE.COM

   Visit the links for Chapter Assessment to find out more about A. Philip Randolph. Write a brief biography of Randolph in which you describe his life-long contributions as a labor leader. Here are some questions to consider:

   • What did he do during his youth that prepared him for his life's work?

   • What role did he play in ending discrimination in the armed services?

   • What union did he organize?

   • What role did he play in the march on Washington in 1963?

---

## Standardized Test Practice

1. The correct answer is letter **B**.
   The locations would better facilitate the Allied attack on main islands of Japan. Letter A is not correct because both areas were heavily defended. Letter C is not correct because Japan was not developing an atomic bomb. Letter D is not correct because the bombs were not dropped on the island but on Hiroshima and Nagasaki.

2. The correct answer is letter **H**.
   The war effort required moves for military purposes and people moved to take advantage of economic opportunities. Letter F is not correct because military duty did not change permanent residence. Letter G is not correct because these losses would not have resulted in such massive movement. Letter J is not correct because with the exception of Alaska there was no fighting in the United States.

3. The correct answer is letter **B**.
   Germany is located in the middle of Europe and chose to fight in Africa to gain access to oil. Letter A is not correct because Germany's continental enemies were next door. Letter C is not correct because Germany has many easily navigated rivers. Letter D is not correct because Switzerland's neutrality was not a factor in the land war.

UNIT PROJECT

**DEBATE**

**Tips for Teaching**

· Review each team's basic arguments and evidence.

· Help each team anticipate the counter-arguments and ways to respond to those challenges.

 Formal Assessment

· Chapter Test, Forms A, B, and C, pp. 320–337

---

## ALTERNATIVE ASSESSMENT

### 1. INTERACT WITH HISTORY

**Rubric**

A newspaper article should . . .

· precisely describe use of resources during World War II

· present information in a clear and unbiased manner

· reflect an understanding of the economic conditions of the time

### 2. INTERNET ACTIVITY

**Rubric**

The summation should . . .

· clearly state the position

· give appropriate background and support for the position

· contain a conclusion that summarizes the main points and reiterates the position

# Cold War Conflicts

| | CHAPTER OVERVIEW | COPYMASTERS | INTEGRATED TECHNOLOGY |
|---|---|---|---|
| **CHAPTER RESOURCES** | *After World War II, tensions between the United States and the Soviet Union lead to a war without direct conflict—the Cold War. Both countries invest heavily in nuclear weapons, and the U.S. enter the Korean War. At home, fear of communism escalates.* | Telescoping the Times · Chapter Summary, pp. 35–36<br><br>Planning for Block Schedules | American Stories video series · "The Cold War Comes Home"<br><br>Power Presentations<br><br>Electronic Teacher Tools<br><br>Online Lesson Planner<br><br>classzone.com |
| **SECTION 1**<br><br>Origins of the Cold War<br><br>pp. 602–608 | **KEY IDEAS**<br><br>*The Allied coalition falls apart as the United States and the Soviet Union find themselves in conflict with each other* | In-Depth Resources: Unit 5 · Guided Reading, p. 45 · Building Vocabulary, p. 49 · Skillbuilder Practice, p. 50 · Reteaching Activity, p. 51 · Geography Application, pp. 55–56 · Primary Sources, p. 57<br><br>Lesson Plans, pp. 143–144 | Geography Transparencies GT26 · The Berlin Airlift: 1948–49<br><br>Critical Thinking Transparencies CT26 · The Cold War<br><br>Electronic Library of Primary Sources · The Truman Doctrine<br><br>classzone.com |
| **SECTION 2**<br><br>The Cold War Heats Up<br><br>pp. 609–615 | *U.S. containment policies and Communist successes in China and North Korea lead to the Korean War.* | In-Depth Resources: Unit 5 · Guided Reading, p. 46 · Reteaching Activity, p. 52 · Primary Sources, pp. 58–59 · American Lives, p. 64<br><br>Lesson Plans, pp. 145–146 | Electronic Library of Primary Sources · Frustration in Korea<br><br>classzone.com |
| **SECTION 3**<br><br>The Cold War at Home<br><br>pp. 616–621 | *The Cold War kindles a fear of Communist influence in the United States.* | In-Depth Resources: Unit 5 · Guided Reading, p. 47 · Reteaching Activity, p. 53 · American Lives, p. 65<br><br>Lesson Plans, pp. 147–148 | American Stories video series · "The Cold War Comes Home"<br><br>Electronic Library of Primary Sources · Statement of Civil Liberties in America<br><br>classzone.com |
| **SECTION 4**<br><br>Two Nations Live on the Edge<br><br>pp. 622–629 | *Tension mounts between the United States and the Soviet Union as both try to spread their influence around the world.* | In-Depth Resources: Unit 5 · Guided Reading, p. 48 · Reteaching Activity, p. 54 · Primary Sources, p. 60 · Literature, p. 61–63<br><br>Lesson Plans, pp. 149–150 | Critical Thinking Transparencies CT26, CT60 · The Cold War · The Space Race<br><br>Humanities Transparencies HT25, HT41 · California bomb shelter, 1951 · Wonder Why We're Not Keeping Pace?<br><br> classzone.com |

| | | | | |
|---|---|---|---|---|
| 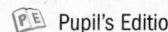 PE | Pupil's Edition |  | Overhead Transparency | 👁 CD-ROM |
| TE | Teacher's Edition | | 🔊 Audio Library | 🌐 Internet |
| 📄 | Copymaster | | | |

## ASSESSMENT OPTIONS

PE Chapter Assessment, pp. 630–631

📄 Formal Assessment
· Chapter Tests, Forms A, B, and C, pp. 342–353

👁 Test Generator

📄 Integrated Assessment Book

🌐 TAKS Online Test Practice

📄 TAKS Spiraled Content Review

TAKS Practice Tests

---

PE Section 1 Assessment, p. 608

TE Self-Assessment, p. 608

📄 Formal Assessment, Quiz, p. 338

📄 Integrated Assessment Book

👁 Test Generator

🔧 TAKS Practice Transparencies TT98

---

PE Section 2 Assessment, p. 615

TE Self-Assessment, p. 615

📄 Formal Assessment, Quiz, p. 339

📄 Integrated Assessment Book

👁 Test Generator

🔧 TAKS Practice Transparencies TT99

---

PE Section 3 Assessment, p. 621

TE Self-Assessment, p. 621

📄 Formal Assessment, Quiz, p. 340

📄 Integrated Assessment Book

👁 Test Generator

🔧 TAKS Practice Transparencies TT100

---

PE Section 4 Assessment, p. 627

TE Self-Assessment, p. 627

📄 Formal Assessment, Quiz, p. 341

📄 Integrated Assessment Book

👁 Test Generator

🔧 TAKS Practice Transparencies TT101

## RESOURCES FOR DIFFERENTIATING INSTRUCTION

### Students Acquiring English/ESL

📄 **Reading Study Guide:** (English and Spanish) pp. 181–190

📄 **Access for Students Acquiring English/ESL:** Spanish Translations, pp. 198–206

🔊 **Chapter Summaries on CD** (English and Spanish)

### Less Proficient Readers

📄 **Reading Study Guide** (English and Spanish) pp. 181–190

📄 **Telescoping the Times** · Chapter Summary, pp. 35–36

🔊 **Chapter Summaries on CD** (English and Spanish)

### Gifted and Talented Students

📄 **In-Depth Resources: Unit 5** · Primary Sources, pp. 57–60 · Literature, pp. 61–63 · American Lives: Douglas MacArthur; p. 64, Margaret Chase, p. 65

👁 **Electronic Library of Primary Sources** · Unit 5, Chapter 18

## CROSS-CURRICULAR CONNECTIONS

### Civics
McGilligan, Paul and Buhle, Paul. *Tender Comrades: A Backstory of the Hollywood Blacklist.* NY: Griffin Trade Paperback, 1999. A compilation of interviews with screenwriters, actors, directors, and others whose careers were interrupted by the blacklist created during the McCarthy era.

### Science
Stwertka, Albert. *The World of Atoms and Quarks.* NY: 21st Century, 1995. A short, understandable overview of the world of atomic energy.

Collins, Martin J, et al. *Space Race: U.S.-U.S.S.R. Competition to Reach the Moon.* Beverly Hills: Pomegranate, 1999. Tells the fascinating story of the struggle between the United States and the Soviet Union to be the first to send a man to the moon.

### McDougal Littell
### Literature Connections

Orwell, George. *1984 (with related readings).* Originally published in 1949, this startling, futuristic indictment of the totalitarian state was the original "big brother."

Bradbury, Ray. *Fahrenheit 451 (with related readings).* Set in a future where the government burns books to keep people from thinking or rebelling, this chilling story, first published in 1953, has powerful meaning today.

Miller, Arthur. *The Crucible (with related readings).* A witch hunt in Puritan New England with overtones of McCarthyism.

## ENRICHMENT ACTIVITIES

PE **Pupil's Edition,** pp. 600–629
Interact with History, pp. 600–601
American Literature, pp. 628–629

📄 **In-Depth Resources: Unit 5**
· Geography Application: The Marshall Plan, pp. 55–56
· Primary Sources: *Letter to His Daughter,* p. 57
· Primary Sources: Farewell to Congress, pp. 58–59
· Primary Sources: Statement on the U-2 Incident, p. 60
· Literature: from *The Nuclear Age,* pp. 61–63
· American Lives: Douglas MacArthur, p. 64
· American Lives: Margaret Chase Smith, p. 65

👁 **Electronic Library of Primary Sources**
· Unit 5, Chapter 18

👁 **Primary Source Explorer**

📹 **American Stories video series**
· "The Cold War Comes Home"

# CHAPTER 18: PACING GUIDE

## BLOCK SCHEDULE LESSON PLAN OPTIONS (90-MINUTE PERIOD)

### DAY 1

**CHAPTER 18 OPENER**
pp. 600–601

**Class Time** 20 minutes

**History from Visuals, p. 600**

**Class Time** 10 minutes

*Options for Pacing and Variety*

· Time Saver Have students study the photograph on page 600. Ask them what information the photograph reveals. **Class Time** 10 minutes

**Interact with History, p. 601**

**Class Time** 10 minutes

*Options for Pacing and Variety*

· Role-Playing Ask students to read the situation and think about the questions posed in Examine the Issues. Then ask them whether or not they would stand by a friend accused of an un-American activity, even if their support would cause suspicion. **Class Time** 10 minutes

**SECTION 1, pp. 602–608**

**Class Time** 35 minutes

*Options for Pacing and Variety*

· Peer Teaching Ask students to read the chart on page 604 comparing U.S. aims vs. Soviet aims in Europe. Have them do the Extension activity in the TE. **Class Time** 15 minutes

### DAY 1 continued

· Time Saver Have students read Winston Churchill's quote on page 605. Discuss the meaning of "iron curtain" from the context of the speech and from the metaphorical import of the phrase that became the commonplace term for the division of Europe. **Class Time** 15 minutes

· Time Saver Ask students to look at the political cartoon on page 608 and have them do the extension in the TE. **Class Time** 15 minutes

**SECTION 2, pp. 602–608**

**Class Time** 35 minutes

*Options for Pacing and Variety*

· Peer Teaching Have students work in small groups to research the career of Mao Zedong. Assign groups to topics such as the Long March, the victory in the civil war, the Cultural Revolution, the "Little Red Book," and Mao's meeting with Nixon. Then have each group give a brief report of their event. Follow with a class discussion of Mao's career. Refer to TE page 610. **Class Time** 35 minutes

· Time Saver Ask students to read "India's Viewpoint" on page 614. Ask them the related question in the TE page. **Class Time** 15 minutes

· Peer Evaluation Have students answer the section assessment questions and then compare answers with another student. Ask the student pairs to find the text passages to support their answers. **Class Time** 20 minutes

### DAY 2

**SECTION 3, pp. 616–621**

**Class Time** 30 minutes

*Options for Pacing and Variety*

· History on Film View the video "The Cold War Comes Home: Hollywood Blacklists the Kahn Family," and discuss its main ideas. **Class Time** 20 minutes

· Time Saver Ask students to read the feature on television on pages 618–619. Have them do the activity in the TE, interviewing relatives and neighbors about televised news events. Have some students share interesting responses that they recorded. **Class Time** 20 minutes

· Peer Teaching Have students work in pairs to discuss the chart on page 621, listing the causes and effects of McCarthyism. **Class Time** 10 minutes

### DAY 2 continued

**SECTION 4, pp. 622–629**

**Class Time** 30 minutes

*Options for Pacing and Variety*

· Time Saver Ask students to study the map on page 624 and answer the questions included. Read the additional information in the TE on the Warsaw Pact. **Class Time** 20 minutes

· Peer Teaching After reading in the text about the arms race, have students read Dr. Suess' allegory, *The Butter Battle Book*. Have them work with a partner to define *allegory*, and make a list of aspects of the book that represent actual events and the message the book tries to convey through its form and subject. **Class Time** 30 minutes

· Internet Ask students to read the feature on pages 628–629, "Science Fiction Reflects Cold War Realities," and complete item 2 of Thinking Critically. **Class Time** 30 minutes

**ASSESSMENT, pp. 630–631**

**Class Time** 30 minutes

*Options for Pacing and Variety*

· Peer Evaluation Ask students to complete Critical Thinking questions 2 and 3 on their own and then read another student's responses and correct or add to them. **Class Time** 15 minutes

· Time Saver Have students complete the Standardized Test Practice on page 631. **Class Time** 15 minutes

---

**TEACHER-TESTED ACTIVITY**      Betsy Fitzgerald, Erskine Academy, South China, Maine

**HEADSTONES FOR PRESIDENT TRUMAN**

**Class Time** 45 minutes

**Task** Designing a headstone for President Harry Truman

**Purpose** To recognize and appreciate President Truman's legacy

**Supplies Needed**
· Poster board
· Markers

**Activity** Remind students that headstone inscriptions are short but significant reminders of a person's life. Have each student design a headstone bearing Truman's name, birth and death dates, and an inscription indicating his legacy. Students should be prepared to support what they wrote. Display the headstones and discuss the inscriptions.

# CHAPTER 18 CORRELATION

 **CORRELATION TO THE TEXAS ESSENTIAL KNOWLEDGE AND SKILLS**

Chapter 18 addresses the following standards of the Texas Essential Knowledge and Skills for U.S. History.

| TEKS | Instruction | Student Question/Activity |
|---|---|---|
| **(1A)** Identify major eras in U.S. history from 1877 to the present and describe their defining characteristics. | **PE 600–601** time line examination of the Cold War era | **TE 600** questions requiring students to interpret the time line |
| **(1C)** Explain the significance of the following date: 1957. | **PE 626** discussion of the launch of the Soviet satellite *Sputnik* and the U.S.-Soviet space race it began | **TE 626** science activity in which students conduct further research on the impact of *Sputnik* on the United States |
| **(6D)** Describe U.S. responses to Soviet aggression after World War II. | **PE 602–608** examination of U.S. responses to the Soviets, including the Truman Doctrine, the Marshall Plan, the North Atlantic Treaty Organization, and the Berlin airlift | **PE 608** Critical Thinking questions about these various Cold War episodes |
| **(6E)** Analyze the conflicts in Korea and describe their domestic and international effects. | **PE 611–615** analysis of the Korean War and its impact on domestic affairs in the United States | **PE 615** Critical Thinking questions about the Korean War |
| **(6F)** Describe the impact of McCarthyism. | **PE 620–621** examination of the rise and fall of McCarthyism | **PE 621** question regarding political cartoon about McCarthyism |
| **(14C)** Describe the impact of the Cold War on the business cycle and defense spending. | **PE 626** graph depicting the increase in defense spending during the Cold War era | **PE 626** Skillbuilder questions that require students to interpret the graph |
| **(20A)** Describe how the characteristics and issues of various eras in U.S. history have been reflected in works of art, music, and literature. | **PE 628–629** American Literature feature on the Cold War's impact on literature | **PE 629** Critical Thinking questions about the feature |

## TAKS MINI-LESSONS

1. **Social Studies Skills: Objective 1 (US6.D):** Describe U.S. responses to Soviet aggression after World War II **Activity** Have students write a brief summary of each of the following: Truman Doctrine, Marshall Plan, North Atlantic Treaty Organization, Berlin airlift.

2. **Social Studies Skills: Objective 1 (US6.E):** Analyze conflicts in Korea and Vietnam and describe their domestic and international effects **Activity** Have students create a cause and effect chart regarding America's involvement in the Korean War.

3. **Social Studies Skills: Objective 1 (US6.F):** Describe the impact of McCarthyism **Activity** Have students answer the Critical Thinking questions about McCarthyism in the Section 3 Assessment.

4. **English Language Arts Skills: Objective 2 (11.A):** Compare and contrast aspects of texts, such as themes, conflicts, and allusions **Activity** Have students write a paragraph summarizing the conflict between Douglas MacArthur and Harry Truman.

5. **English Language Arts Skills: Objective 3 (8.D):** Interpret the possible influences of the historical context on literary works **Activity** Have students answer the questions regarding the American Literature feature on pages 628–629.

## HISTORY from VISUALS

### Interpreting the Photograph

Ask students to study the photograph. Then, ask them what information is revealed by the photograph. *(McCarthy is being sworn in to testify; there is a large audience, which probably means this was an important event; there are several army officers sitting near him; a stenographer is present in the front left.)*

## Time Line Discussion

Tell students that the time line covers events in the United States and the world from the end of World War II until 1960.

· Ask students which wars ended when Eisenhower was president. *(Korean War and the conflict between the French and the Vietnamese)*

· Ask students which events involving spies occurred during this period. *(The Rosenbergs are executed; Powers's U-2 spy plane is shot down.)*

· Ask students who gave a speech about the Iron Curtain. *(Churchill)*

Senator Joseph McCarthy, shown here, charged that Communists had infiltrated many areas of American life.

**1948** Harry S. Truman is elected president.

**1949** United States joins NATO.

**1950** U.S. sends troops to Korea.

**1952** U.S. explodes first hydrogen bomb.

**1952** Dwight D. Eisenhower is elected president.

USA
WORLD

**1945**

**1950**

**1945** United Nations is established.

**1946** Churchill gives his "Iron Curtain" speech.

**1948** Berlin airlift begins.

**1949** China becomes communist under Mao Zedong.

**1950** Korean War begins.

**600** CHAPTER 18

## THEMES IN CHAPTER 18

### ECONOMIC OPPORTUNITY

After World War II, the United States converted to a peacetime economy. It faced the monumental tasks of supplying jobs for returning soldiers and meeting civilian demand for goods that were unavailable during wartime.

**See Teacher's Edition note, p. 604.**

### CIVIL RIGHTS

A major challenge to the Constitution arose during the Cold War. It was the challenge to the rights of free speech and assembly that resulted from Senator Joseph McCarthy's attacks on suspected Communists.

**See Teacher's Edition note, p. 617.**

### SCIENCE AND TECHNOLOGY

The brilliant scientific achievements that led to the creation of the atomic and hydrogen bombs also cast a shadow of impending nuclear holocaust over the 1950s. Despite this fear, many peaceful applications of nuclear energy resulted.

**See Teacher's Edition note, p. 626.**

# INTERACT
## WITH HISTORY

At the end of World War II, Americans begin to be haunted by a new fear. The Soviets have embraced a tightly controlled political system called communism. Many believe it threatens the American way of life. Throughout the nation, suspected communists are called before a House subcommittee for questioning. Anyone accused of un-American activity faces public humiliation and professional ruin.

## *What do you do when a friend is accused?*

### Examine the issues

- Do Americans with communist beliefs pose a threat to the nation?
- What can individual citizens do to protect the rights of all people?
- Should citizens speak out to preserve the rights of others?

 **RESEARCH LINKS** CLASSZONE.COM

Visit the Chapter 18 links for more information about Cold War Conflicts.

# INTERACT
## WITH HISTORY

### Objectives

- To help students understand Americans' fear of Communism
- To help students recognize how the fear of Communism caused abridgments of freedom

### Examine the Issues

1. Have students discuss Americans' reaction to Communism. Encourage them to compare how Americans responded to communism with how European democracies dealt with it.
2. Have students examine the courage it took in the 1950s to speak out against anti-Communist witch-hunts.
3. Ask students what they would do if they saw that the rights of other people were being abridged.

---

**1953** Julius and Ethel Rosenberg are executed as spies.

**1954** Senator Joseph McCarthy alleges Communist involvement in U.S. Army.

**1960** Francis Gary Powers's U-2 spy plane is shot down by the Soviets.

**1960** John F. Kennedy is elected president.

### 1955          1960

**1953** Participants in Korean War agree on cease-fire.

**1954** French are defeated in Vietnam.

**1957** Soviets launch *Sputnik*.

**1959** Fidel Castro comes to power in Cuba.

*Cold War Conflicts* **601**

---

## RECOMMENDED RESOURCES

### BOOKS FOR THE TEACHER

Bundy, McGeorge. *Danger and Survival: The Political History of the Nuclear Weapon.* New York: Random House, 1988.

McCullough, David. *Truman.* New York: Simon, 1996.

Winik, Jay. *On the Brink.* New York: Simon, 1996.

### BOOKS FOR THE STUDENT

Miller, Merle. *Plain Speaking: An Oral Biography of Harry S. Truman.* New York: Berkley, 1986.

Rovere, Richard. *Senator Joe McCarthy.* Berkeley: U of California P, 1996.

### VIDEOS

*Are We Winning, Mommy? America and the Cold War.* First Run Features, 153 Waverly Place, New York, NY 10014.

*Atomic Cafe.* Virginia Beach, VA: Pallisades Home Video, 1995. The history of the atomic bomb.

*On the Beach.* Dir. Stanley Kramer. MGM/UA, 1959.

*McCarthy: Death of a Witch Hunter.* Filmic Archives, The Cinema Center, Botsford, CT 06404, 800-366-1920.

### SOFTWARE

*Trinity and Beyond: A History of Nuclear Weapons.* Heizer Software, P.O. Box 232019, Pleasant Hill, CA 94523.

### INTEGRATED TECHNOLOGY

For teacher support, visit . . .

 classzone.com

# Origins of the Cold War

| MAIN IDEA | WHY IT MATTERS NOW | Terms & Names |
|---|---|---|
| The United States and the Soviet Union emerged from World War II as two "superpowers" with vastly different political and economic systems. | After World War II, differences between the United States and the Soviet Union led to a Cold War that lasted almost to the 21st century. | • United Nations (UN)  • satellite nation  • containment  • iron curtain  • Cold War  • Truman Doctrine   • Marshall Plan  • Berlin airlift  • North Atlantic Treaty Organizat (NATO) |

**TEKS** U.S. History 6D, 8A, 8B, 9A, 9B, 19A, 19B, 24B, 24C, 24H, 25A, 25B, 25C, 25D

### One American's Story

Seventy miles south of Berlin, Joseph Polowsky and a patrol of American soldiers were scouting for signs of the Soviet army advancing from the east. As the soldiers neared the Elbe River, they saw lilacs in bloom. Polowsky later said the sight of the flowers filled them with joy.

Across the Elbe, the Americans spotted Soviet soldiers, who signaled for them to cross over. When the Americans reached the opposite bank, their joy turned to shock. They saw to their horror that the bank was covered with dead civilians, victims of bombing raids.

**A PERSONAL VOICE** JOSEPH POLOWSKY

" Here we are, tremendously exhilarated, and there's a sea of dead. . . . [The platoon leader] was much moved. . . . He said, 'Joe, let's make a resolution with these Russians here and also the ones on the bank: this would be an important day in the lives of the two countries.' . . . It was a solemn moment. There were tears in the eyes of most of us. . . . We embraced. We swore never to forget. "

—quoted in *The Good War*

U.S. and Soviets link up at Elbe River, April

▲ American and Soviet soldiers meet *(top)* at the Elbe River in Germany near the end of World War II. A 1996 postage stamp *(above)* commemorates the historic meeting.

The Soviet and U.S. soldiers believed that their encounter would serve as a symbol of peace. Unfortunately, such hopes were soon dashed. After World War II, the United States and the Soviet Union emerged as rival superpowers, each strong enough to greatly influence world events.

## **1** Former Allies Clash

The United States and the Soviet Union had very different ambitions for the future. These political differences created a climate of icy tension that plunged the two countries into a bitter rivalry.

Under Soviet communism, the state controlled all property and economic activity, while in the capitalistic American system, private citizens controlled almost all economic activity. In the American system, voting by the people elected a president and a congress from competing political parties; in the Soviet Union, the Communist Party established a totalitarian government with no opposing parties.

The United States was furious that Joseph Stalin—the leader of the Soviet Union—had been an ally of Hitler for a time. Stalin had supported the Allies only after Hitler invaded the Soviet Union in June 1941. In some ways, the Americans and Soviets became more suspicious of each other during the war. Stalin resented the Western Allies' delay in attacking the Germans in Europe. Such an attack, he thought, would draw part of the German army away from the Soviet Union. Relations worsened after Stalin learned that the United States had kept its development of the atomic bomb secret. **A**

**THE UNITED NATIONS** In spite of these problems, hopes for world peace were high at the end of the war. The most visible symbol of these hopes was the **United Nations (UN).** On April 25, 1945, the representatives of 50 nations met in San Francisco to establish this new peacekeeping body. After two months of debate, on June 26, 1945, the delegates signed the charter establishing the UN.

Ironically, even though the UN was intended to promote peace, it soon became an arena in which the two superpowers competed. Both the United States and the Soviet Union used the UN as a forum to spread their influence over others.

**TRUMAN BECOMES PRESIDENT** For the United States, the key figure in the early years of conflict with the Soviets was President Harry S. Truman. On April 12, 1945, Truman had suddenly become president when Franklin Roosevelt died. This former Missouri senator had been picked as Roosevelt's running mate in 1944. He had served as vice-president for just a few months before Roosevelt's death. During his term as vice-president, Truman had not been included in top policy decisions. He had not even known that the United States was developing an atomic bomb. Many Americans doubted Truman's ability to serve as president. But Truman had honesty and a willingness to make tough decisions—qualities that he would need desperately during his presidency.

**MAIN IDEA**

**Analyzing Causes**
**A** What caused the tension between the Soviet Union and the United States after the war?

*A. Answer* Different political and economic systems; Soviet Union had been an ally of Germany; Stalin resented Allies' delay in attacking Germans in Europe.

### KEY PLAYERS

**HARRY S. TRUMAN**
**1884–1972**

Harry S. Truman, the son of a Missouri livestock trader and his wife, did not seem destined for greatness. When he graduated from high school in 1901, he drifted from job to job. After WWII, he invested in a men's clothing store, but the business failed.

Discouraged by his business failure, Truman sought a career in politics. As a politician, his blunt and outspoken style won both loyal friends and bitter enemies. As president, his decisiveness and willingness to accept responsibility for his decisions ("The Buck Stops Here" read a sign on his desk) earned him respect that has grown over the years.

**JOSEPH STALIN**
**1879–1953**

As a young revolutionary, Iosif Vissarionovich Dzhugashvili took the name *Stalin*, which means "man of steel" in Russian.

His father was a failed shoemaker and an alcoholic. His mother helped support the family as a washerwoman.

Stalin is credited with turning the Soviet Union into a world power but at a terrible cost to its citizens. He ruled with terror and brutality and saw "enemies" everywhere, even among friends and supporters. He subdued the population with the use of secret police and labor camps, and he is believed to have been responsible for the murder of millions of Soviets.

*Cold War Conflicts* **603**

### Instruct: Objective ❷

**Tension Mounts**

TAKS SS11 1(US6.D)

· What was the essence of the disagreement between the United States and the Soviet Union in Europe?

· How were the United States and the Soviet Union different?

· What action did the Soviet Union take in Europe that was opposed by the United States?

 In-Depth Resources: Unit 5
· Guided Reading, p. 45

### Tracing Themes

**ECONOMIC OPPORTUNITY**

**The World Economy**

Economic considerations strongly influenced U.S. foreign policy after World War II. The U.S. government wanted to promote a healthy world economy by making it possible for Europe to rebuild and by encouraging capitalism. At the same time, the United States also wanted to create markets for its goods and materials.

### HISTORY from VISUALS

**Interpreting the Chart**

Remind students to repeat the column head before reading each of the bulleted items. For example: *"The United States wanted to create a new world order . . ."*

**Extension** Have pairs of students each write three sentences. One student will write a sentence summarizing a U.S. aim; the other will write a sentence summarizing the corresponding Soviet aim. Then, have the students collaborate on a sentence explaining the incompatibility of the aims.

---

**THE POTSDAM CONFERENCE** Truman's test as a diplomat came in July 1945 when the Big Three—the United States, Great Britain, and the Soviet Union—met at the final wartime conference at Potsdam near Berlin. The countries that participated were the same ones that had been present at Yalta in February 1945. Stalin still represented the Soviet Union. Clement Attlee replaced Churchill as Britain's representative mid-conference, because Churchill's party lost a general election. And Harry Truman took Roosevelt's place.

At Yalta, Stalin had promised Roosevelt that he would allow free elections— that is, a vote by secret ballot in a multiparty system—in Poland and other parts of Eastern Europe that the Soviets occupied at the end of the war. By July 1945, however, it was clear that Stalin would not keep this promise. The Soviets prevented free elections in Poland and banned democratic parties. **B**

### ❷ Tension Mounts

Stalin's refusal to allow free elections in Poland convinced Truman that U.S. and Soviet aims were deeply at odds. Truman's goal in demanding free elections was to spread democracy to nations that had been under Nazi rule. He wanted to create a new world order in which all nations had the right of self-determination.

**BARGAINING AT POTSDAM** At the Yalta conference, the Soviets had wanted to take reparations from Germany to help repay Soviet wartime losses. Now, at Potsdam, Truman objected to that. After hard bargaining, it was agreed that the Soviets, British, Americans, and French would take reparations mainly from their own occupation zones.

Truman also felt that the United States had a large economic stake in spreading democracy and free trade across the globe. U.S. industry boomed during the war, making the United States the economic leader of the world. To continue growing, American businesses wanted access to raw materials in Eastern Europe, and they wanted to be able to sell goods to Eastern European countries.

**SOVIETS TIGHTEN THEIR GRIP ON EASTERN EUROPE** The Soviet Union had also emerged from the war as a nation of enormous economic and military strength. However, unlike the United States, the Soviet Union had suffered heavy devastation on its own soil. Soviet deaths from the war have been estimated at 20 million, half of whom were civilians. As a result, the Soviets felt justified in their claim to Eastern Europe. By dominating this region, the Soviets felt they could stop future invasions from the west.

---

**MAIN IDEA**

*Analyzing Causes*

**B**  What did Stalin do to make President Truman distrust him?

*B. Answer* Stalin would not allow free elections in Eastern Europe.

---

### U.S. Aims Versus Soviet Aims in Europe

| The United States wanted to . . . | The Soviets wanted to . . . |
|---|---|
| · Create a new world order in which all nations had the right of self-determination<br>· Gain access to raw materials and markets for its industries<br>· Rebuild European governments to ensure stability and to create new markets for American goods<br>· Reunite Germany, believing that Europe would be more secure if Germany were productive | · Encourage communism in other countries as part of the worldwide struggle between workers and the wealthy<br>· Rebuild its war-ravaged economy using Eastern Europe's industrial equipment and raw materials<br>· Control Eastern Europe to balance U.S. influence in Western Europe<br>· Keep Germany divided and weak so that it would never again threaten the Soviet Union |

**SKILLBUILDER Interpreting Charts**
1. Which aims involved economic growth of the United States?
2. Which Soviet aims involved self-protection?

*Skillbuilder Answers*
1. Gaining access to raw materials and markets; rebuilding European governments.
2. Controlling Eastern Europe; keeping Germany divided and weak.

---

**DIFFERENTIATING INSTRUCTION**  **LESS PROFICIENT READERS**

### Clarifying Ideas

Pair less proficient readers with more proficient ones to clarify the main ideas in this section. Have student pairs follow these steps:

1. Read pages 604 and 605 of the text together.
2. Make a list of the causes of tensions between the United States and the Soviet Union as they read.
3. Review their list.

4. Write out unanswered questions they have about the tensions.
5. Review the pages and write answers to the questions.

You could then have different pairs compare their lists of questions and answers.

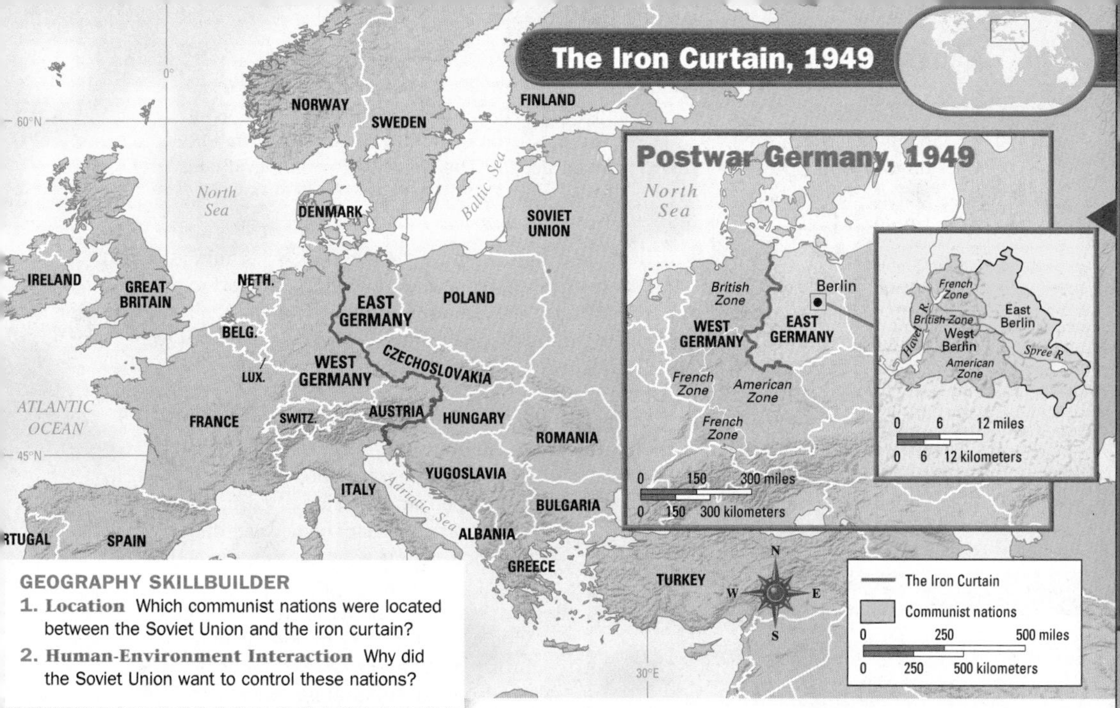


**GEOGRAPHY SKILLBUILDER**

1. **Location** Which communist nations were located between the Soviet Union and the iron curtain?
2. **Human-Environment Interaction** Why did the Soviet Union want to control these nations?

***Skillbuilder Answers***
1. Bulgaria, Romania, Poland, Albania, Hungary, Yugoslavia, Czechoslovakia, East Germany.
2. To protect the Soviet Union from invasion on its eastern front, especially by Germany.

## HISTORY from VISUALS

**Interpreting the Map**
Point out that the squares on this map are called "areas of detail" and that each square conveys a different level of information. In a way, the series of maps functions like a series of enlarged snapshots.

**Extension** Discuss what students know about Berlin today. On November 9, 1989, the wall was breached as the East German Communist regime collapsed. After German reunification in October 1990, the parliament voted to make Berlin the capital of the reunited Germany.

Stalin installed communist governments in Albania, Bulgaria, Czechoslovakia, Hungary, Romania, Yugoslavia, and Poland. These countries became known as **satellite nations,** countries dominated by the Soviet Union. In early 1946, Stalin gave a speech announcing that communism and capitalism were incompatible—and that another war was inevitable.

**UNITED STATES ESTABLISHES A POLICY OF CONTAINMENT** Faced with the Soviet threat, American officials decided it was time, in Truman's words, to stop "babying the Soviets." In February 1946, George F. Kennan, an American diplomat in Moscow, proposed a policy of **containment.** By containment he meant taking measures to prevent any extension of communist rule to other countries. This policy began to guide the Truman administration's foreign policy. C

**MAIN IDEA**

**Analyzing Motives**
C What were Truman's goals in establishing the policy of containment?

*C. Answer*
To stop the spread of Soviet influence.

Europe was now divided into two political regions, a mostly democratic Western Europe and a communist Eastern Europe. In March 1946, Winston Churchill traveled to the United States and gave a speech that described the situation in Europe.

A PERSONAL VOICE WINSTON CHURCHILL

"**A shadow has fallen upon the scenes so lately lighted by the Allied victory. . . . From Stettin in the Baltic to Trieste in the Adriatic, an iron curtain has descended across the Continent. Behind that line lie all the capitals of the ancient states of Central and Eastern Europe. . . . All these famous cities and the populations around them lie in . . . the Soviet sphere, and all are subject in one form or another, not only to Soviet influence but to a very high and . . . increasing measure of control from Moscow.**"

—"Iron Curtain" speech in Fulton, Missouri

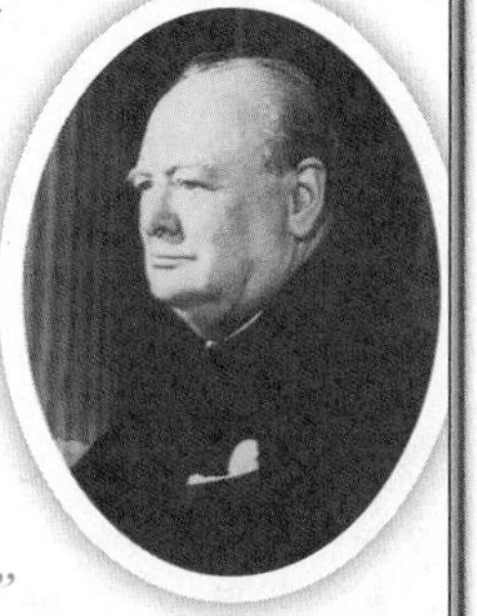

**Winston Churchill, Prime Minister of Great Britain**

The phrase **"iron curtain"** came to stand for the division of Europe. When Stalin heard about the speech, he declared in no uncertain terms that Churchill's words were a "call to war."



## More About . . .

**The Impact of the Cold War**
The United States entered the Cold War in a state of increasing economic strength. In contrast to European nations, whose industrial base had been severely damaged or destroyed by World War II, the United States emerged from the war with its industry intact. Because of this, America grew affluent exporting its products to foreign nations. Although the business cycle continued to produce minor recessions in the years between 1945 and 1970, few of these recessions lasted longer than a year. The strength of the American economy during the early Cold War period led all other currencies to be valued against the American dollar. Ask, To what extent did the Cold War affect the business cycle in the United States? *(Due to a strong economy and industry, the Cold War did not have a lasting effect on the business cycle in the United States.)*

**ACTIVITY** **SKILLBUILDER LESSON**

### Analyzing Motives

**Explaining the Skill** To analyze something is to separate it into its constituent parts. Analysis can be applied to almost anything–a math problem, a sports outcome, or political actions. Analyzing a motive involves separating an event into parts and examining the needs that caused persons or groups to take an action.

**Applying the Skill** Ask students to consider this question, "What were Stalin's reasons for setting up Communist governments in Eastern Europe?" Suggest that students separate the subjects into the following parts–*Stalin's reasons:* Need for buffers against invasion from the west; wartime destruction in the Soviet Union; industrial assets needed for rebuilding. *Truman's reasons:* Soviet actions after World War II; differing ideologies of capitalism and communism.

In-Depth Resources: Unit 5
· Skillbuilder Practice: Analyzing Motives, p. 50

## Instruct: Objective 3

**Cold War In Europe**
TAKS SS11 2(US6.D)
· What was the Truman Doctrine?
· What was the Marshall Plan?

 In-Depth Resources: Unit 5
· Guided Reading, p. 45

👁 Electronic Library of Primary Sources
· The Truman Doctrine, 1947, by H. S. Truman

---

## HISTORY from VISUALS

### Interpreting the Graph

Ask which factors students think determined the amount of aid each nation received. *(The nation's involvement in the war and the damage it incurred.)*

---

## More About . . .

### General George C. Marshall

Marshall (1880–1959) played a central role in American government during World War II and the postwar period. During the war, he was chief of staff of the army. He then served in Truman's cabinet, as secretary of state (1947–1949), and as secretary of defense (1950–1951). Marshall had hoped that by offering aid to the Soviet Union under the Marshall Plan, U.S.-Soviet tensions might be reduced. But Stalin would not accept aid. Still, the Marshall Plan is credited with rebuilding Europe and eliminating the conditions that might have been conducive to the spread of communism in Western Europe. In 1953, Marshall was awarded the Nobel Peace Prize for his work.

---

## 3 Cold War in Europe

The conflicting U.S. and Soviet aims in Eastern Europe led to the **Cold War,** a conflict between the United States and the Soviet Union in which neither nation directly confronted the other on the battlefield. The Cold War would dominate global affairs—and U.S. foreign policy—from 1945 until the breakup of the Soviet Union in 1991.

**THE TRUMAN DOCTRINE** The United States first tried to contain Soviet influence in Greece and Turkey. Britain was sending economic and military support to both nations to prevent communist takeovers. However, Britain's economy had been badly hurt by the war, and the formerly wealthy nation could no longer afford to give aid. It asked the United States to take over the responsibility.

President Truman accepted the challenge. On March 12, 1947, Truman asked Congress for $400 million in economic and military aid for Greece and Turkey. In a statement that became known as the **Truman Doctrine,** he declared that "it must be the policy of the United States to support free peoples who are resisting attempted subjugation by armed minorities or by outside pressures." Congress agreed with Truman and decided that the doctrine was essential to keeping Soviet influence from spreading. Between 1947 and 1950, the United States sent over $400 million in aid to Turkey and Greece, greatly reducing the danger of communist takeover in those nations.

**THE MARSHALL PLAN** Like postwar Greece, Western Europe was in chaos. Most of its factories had been bombed or looted. Millions of people were living in refugee camps while European governments tried to figure out where to resettle them. To make matters worse, the winter of 1946–1947 was the bitterest in several centuries. The weather severely damaged crops and froze rivers, cutting off water transportation and causing a fuel shortage.

In June 1947, Secretary of State George Marshall proposed that the United States provide aid to all European nations that needed it, saying that this move was directed "not against any country or doctrine but against hunger, poverty, desperation, and chaos."

The **Marshall Plan** revived European hopes. Over the next four years, 16 countries received some $13 billion in aid. By 1952, Western Europe was flourishing, and the Communist party had lost much of its appeal to voters.

**Vocabulary**
**subjugation:** bringing under control

Mini-Lesson 1: SS11 1(US6.D)

*Skillbuilder Answers*
**1.** Great Britain and France.
**2.** They had been the staunchest U.S. allies.

**Background**
The Marshall Plan also benefited the United States. To supply Europe with goods, American farms and factories raised production levels. As a result, the American economy continued its wartime boom.

### The Marshall Plan

| | U.S. Aid (in millions of dollars) |
|---|---|
| Great Britain | 2,826 |
| France | 2,445 |
| Italy | 1,316 |
| West Germany | 1,297 |
| Holland | 877 |
| Austria | 561 |
| Belgium/Lux. | 547 |
| Greece | 515 |
| Denmark | 257 |
| Norway | 237 |
| Turkey | 153 |
| Ireland | 146 |
| Sweden | 119 |
| Portugal | 51 |
| Yugoslavia | 33 |
| Iceland | 29 |
| Other | 350 |

Source: *Problemes Economiques*, No. 306

**SKILLBUILDER Interpreting Graphs**
**1.** Which two countries received the most aid?
**2.** Why do you think these countries received so much aid?

---

| ACTIVITY | LINK TO ECONOMICS | |  classzone.com |

### The Marshall Plan

**Class Time** 45 minutes

**Task** Researching how the Marshall Plan helped Western European countries develop capitalist rather than communist economic systems

**Purpose** To evaluate the political and economic forces at work in the postwar world

**Directions** Discuss with students how Communism could become more attractive to people in severe economic circumstances. Then have them work in small groups to research how the Marshall Plan not only helped rebuild Western Europe but also encouraged the growth of capitalism and reduced the appeal of Communism. Then have students write a brief analysis of the effects of the Marshall Plan.

📄 In-Depth Resources: Unit 5
· Geography Application: The Marshall Plan, pp. 55–56

## ④ Superpowers Struggle over Germany

As Europe began to get back on its feet, the United States and its allies clashed with the Soviet Union over the issue of German reunification. At the end of World War II, Germany was divided into four zones occupied by the United States, Great Britain, and France in the west and the Soviet Union in the east. In 1948, Britain, France, and the United States decided to combine their three zones into one nation. The western part of Berlin, which had been occupied by the French, British, and Americans, was surrounded by Soviet-occupied territory. (See map, page 605.)

Although the three nations had a legal right to unify their zones, they had no written agreement with the Soviets guaranteeing free access to Berlin by road or rail. Stalin saw this loophole as an opportunity. If he moved quickly, he might be able to take over the part of Berlin held by the three Western powers. In June 1948, Stalin closed all highway and rail routes into West Berlin. As a result, no food or fuel could reach that part of the city. The 2.1 million residents of the city had only enough food to last for approximately five weeks.

**THE BERLIN AIRLIFT** The resulting situation was dire. In an attempt to break the blockade, American and British officials started the **Berlin airlift** to fly food and supplies into West Berlin. For 327 days, planes took off and landed every few minutes, around the clock. In 277,000 flights, they brought in 2.3 million tons of supplies—everything from food, fuel, and medicine to Christmas presents that the planes' crews bought with their own money.

West Berlin survived because of the airlift. In addition, the mission to aid Berlin boosted American prestige around the world. By May 1949, the Soviet Union realized it was beaten and lifted the blockade. **D**

*D. Answer*
It broke the Soviet blockade, increased American prestige, and reduced Soviet prestige.

**MAIN IDEA**

**Analyzing Effects**
**D** What were the effects of the Berlin airlift?

Beginning in June 1948, planes bringing tons of food and other supplies to West Berlin landed every few minutes.
▼

**Instruct: Objective ④**

**Superpowers Struggle over Germany**
TAKS SS11 1(US6.D)
· What caused Stalin to close access to Berlin?
· How did the Allies get supplies to West Berlin?
· Why was the NATO alliance formed?

📖 In-Depth Resources: Unit 5
· Guided Reading, p. 45

### More About . . .

**The Berlin Airlift**
The Berlin Airlift was an important political event, but it also had a human side. One German child recalled later, "The Americans remembered, as they had many times before to make the children happy. . . . In the afternoon came the surprise. A transport machine landed, and a living camel got out." The camel was part of a "Camel Caravan" organized to collect food and gifts from families in West Germany for the children of Berlin.

⬇ Geography Transparencies GT36
· The Berlin Airlift

---

**ACTIVITY**   **COOPERATIVE LEARNING**

**Charting the Berlin Airlift**

**Class Time** 45 minutes

**Task** Creating a news report about the Berlin Airlift

**Purpose** To analyze the organizational achievement of the Berlin airlift

**Directions** Have students work in small groups, using library or Internet resources to research the Berlin Airlift. Ask students to compile facts about flights, such as tonnage of goods, number of participants, costs, etc. Then have them assemble their findings into a form of a news report on a television news program that would have been broadcast after the airlift ended. Students should play the roles of anchorperson, analyst, and reporters.

📖 Integrated Assessment
· Rubrics 1, 6

🌐 classzone.com

In the same month, the western part of Germany officially became a new nation, the Federal Republic of Germany, also called West Germany. It included West Berlin. A few months later, from its occupation zone, the Soviet Union created the German Democratic Republic, called East Germany. It included East Berlin.

## Assess & Reteach

### SECTION 1 ASSESSMENT
Assign pairs of students to help each other answer the questions.

 Formal Assessment
· Section Quiz, p. 338

### SELF-ASSESSMENT
Have students mark the questions on the Section 1 Assessment that they could not answer. Ask them to locate the portions of the text that best answer each question.

### RETEACH
On the board, create a blank chart like the one on page 604. Have students fill in the aims of the Soviet Union and the United States to test their comprehension of the material.

 In-Depth Resources: Unit 5
· Reteaching Activity, p. 51

This cartoon depicts the nations that signed the North Atlantic Pact, which created NATO in 1949. The nations, shown as hats, are arranged in a pyramid to show the bigger countries on the bottom supporting the smaller, weaker nations on top.

**THE NATO ALLIANCE** The Berlin blockade increased Western European fear of Soviet aggression. As a result, ten Western European nations—Belgium, Denmark, France, Great Britain, Iceland, Italy, Luxembourg, the Netherlands, Norway, and Portugal—joined with the United States and Canada on April 4, 1949, to form a defensive military alliance called the **North Atlantic Treaty Organization (NATO).** (See map, page 624.) The 12 members of NATO pledged military support to one another in case any member was attacked. For the first time in its history, the United States had entered into a military alliance with other nations during peacetime. The Cold War had ended any hope of a return to U.S. isolationism. Greece and Turkey joined NATO in 1952, and West Germany joined in 1955. By then, NATO kept a standing military force of more than 500,000 troops as well as thousands of planes, tanks, and other equipment.

 **ASSESSMENT**

1. **TERMS & NAMES** For each term or name, write a sentence explaining its significance.
   - United Nations (UN)
   - satellite nation
   - containment
   - iron curtain
   - Cold War
   - Truman Doctrine
   - Marshall Plan
   - Berlin airlift
   - North Atlantic Treaty Organization (NATO)

### MAIN IDEA

2. **TAKING NOTES**
Use a graphic organizer like the one below to describe the U.S. actions and the Soviet actions that contributed most to the Cold War.

| U.S. Actions | Soviet Actions |
|---|---|
|  |  |

Write a paragraph explaining which country was more responsible and why you think so.

### CRITICAL THINKING

3. **EVALUATING LEADERSHIP**
People who had served as aides to President Franklin Roosevelt worried that Truman was not qualified to handle world leadership. Considering what you learned in this section, evaluate Truman as a world leader.
**Think About:**
   - his behavior toward Stalin
   - his economic support of European nations
   - his support of West Berlin

4. **MAKING INFERENCES**
Which of the two superpowers do you think was more successful in achieving its aims during the period 1945–1949? Support your answer by referring to historical events.

5. **ANALYZING MOTIVES**
What were Stalin's motives in supporting Communist governments in Eastern Europe?

**608** CHAPTER 18

 **ASSESSMENT** Answers

### 1. TERMS & NAMES
United Nations (UN), p. 603
satellite nation, p. 605
containment, p. 605
iron curtain, p. 605
Cold War, p. 606
Truman Doctrine, p. 606
Marshall Plan, p. 606
Berlin airlift, p. 607
North Atlantic Treaty Organization (NATO), p. 608

### 2. TAKING NOTES
**U.S. Actions**—Marshall Plan, aid to Greece and Turkey, containment, Truman Doctrine, Berlin airlift
**Soviet Actions**—refusal to allow free elections in Poland, control of Eastern Europe, blockade of West Berlin

### 3. EVALUATING LEADERSHIP
Most students probably will think that Truman was an effective leader because he took firm actions to contain Soviet influence and supported the Marshall Plan and Berlin Airlift. Some students might think that he overreacted and was too belligerent.

### 4. MAKING INFERENCES
Some students may say that the Soviets were most successful because they extended their influence into Eastern Europe. Others will say that the United States was more successful because it broke the blockade of West Berlin and helped rebuild Europe.

### 5. ANALYZING MOTIVES
Stalin wanted Eastern Europe as a buffer zone to protect the Soviet Union from an invasion on its western front.

# The Cold War Heats Up

| MAIN IDEA | WHY IT MATTERS NOW | Terms & Names |
|---|---|---|
| After World War II, China became a communist nation and Korea was split into a communist north and a democratic south. | Ongoing tensions with China and North Korea continue to involve the United States. | • Chiang Kai-shek · 38th parallel<br>• Mao Zedong · Korean War<br>• Taiwan |

TEKS U.S. History 1B, 6E, 8A, 8B, 9A, 9B, 19A, 19B, 24B, 24C, 24G, 24H, 25A, 25B, 25C, 25D, 26A, 26B

### One American's Story

First Lieutenant Philip Day, Jr., vividly remembers his first taste of battle in Korea. On the morning of July 5, 1950, Philip Day spotted a column of eight enemy tanks moving toward his company.

**A PERSONAL VOICE** PHILIP DAY, JR.

" I was with a 75-mm recoilless-rifle team. 'Let's see,' I shouted, 'if we can get one of those tanks.' We picked up the gun and moved it to where we could get a clean shot. I don't know if we were poorly trained, . . . but we set the gun on the forward slope of the hill. When we fired, the recoilless blast blew a hole in the hill which instantly covered us in mud and dirt. . . . When we were ready again, we moved the gun to a better position and began banging away. I swear we had some hits, but the tanks never slowed down. . . . In a little less than two hours, 30 North Korean tanks rolled through the position we were supposed to block as if we hadn't been there. "

—quoted in *The Korean War: Pusan to Chosin*

▲ American soldiers fire mortars at communist strongholds near Mundung-ni in Korea.

Only five years after World War II ended, the United States became embroiled in a war in Korea. The policy of containment had led the United States into battle to halt communist expansion. In this conflict, however, the enemy was not the Soviet Union, but North Korea and China.

## ① China Becomes a Communist Country

For two decades, Chinese Communists had struggled against the nationalist government of **Chiang Kai-shek** (chăng′ kī′shĕk′). The United States supported Chiang. During World War II, the American government sent the Nationalists approximately $3 billion in aid.

*Cold War Conflicts* **609**

---

### OBJECTIVES

1 Explain how Communists came to power in China and how the United States reacted.

2 Summarize the events of the Korean War.

3 Explain the conflict between President Truman and General MacArthur.

### SKILLBUILDERS

· Geography Skillbuilder: movement, place, p. 613

### CRITICAL THINKING

· Analyzing Causes, pp. 610, 612
· Analyzing Events, pp. 611, 615
· Comparing, p. 614
· Hypothesizing, p. 615
· Evaluating Decisions, p. 615

## Focus & Motivate

Ask students what they know about the Korean War from relatives or possibly from watching reruns of the 1970s hit television show *M*A*S*H*.

## Instruct

### Instruct: Objective ①

**China Becomes a Communist Country**
TAKS SS11 5(US24.B)

· What precipitated renewed civil war in China?
· What was the outcome of the civil war in China?
· How did the outcome of the Chinese civil war affect American politics?

 In-Depth Resources: Unit 5
· Guided Reading, p. 46

---

## PROGRAM RESOURCES

 **In-Depth Resources: Unit 5**
· Guided Reading, p. 46
· Reteaching Activity, p. 52
· Primary Source: Farewell to Congress, pp. 58–59
· American Lives: Douglas MacArthur, p. 64

 **Reading Study Guide** (English and Spanish), pp. 183–184

 **Access for Students Acquiring English/ESL**
· Guided Reading (Spanish), p. 201

 **Formal Assessment**
· Section Quiz, p. 339

Integrated Assessment
· Rubrics

### INTEGRATED TECHNOLOGY

 Electronic Library of Primary Sources

 classzone.com

### TEXAS RESOURCES

 TAKS Spiraled Content Review

 TAKS Practice Tests

 TAKS Practice Transparencies TT99

 TAKS Online Test Practice

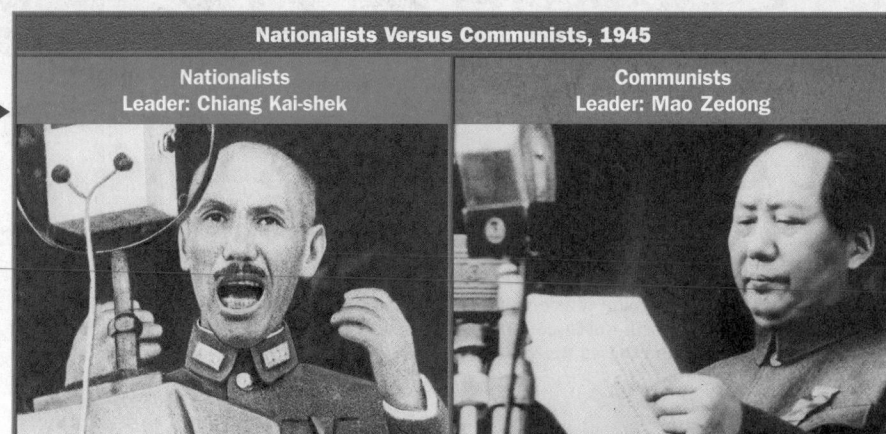

**Nationalists Versus Communists, 1945**

| Nationalists — Leader: Chiang Kai-shek | Communists — Leader: Mao Zedong |
|---|---|
| • Ruled in southern and eastern China<br>• Relied heavily on aid from United States<br>• Struggled with inflation and a failing economy<br>• Suffered from weak leadership and poor morale | • Ruled in northern China<br>• Relied heavily on financial aid from Soviet Union<br>• Attracted peasants with promises of land reform<br>• Benefited from experienced guerrilla army and a highly motivated leadership |

Many Americans were impressed by Chiang Kai-shek and admired the courage and determination that the Chinese Nationalists showed in resisting the Japanese during the war. However, U.S. officials who dealt with Chiang held a different view. They found his government inefficient and hopelessly corrupt.

Furthermore, the policies of Chiang's government undermined Nationalist support. For example, the Nationalists collected a grain tax from farmers even during the famine of 1944. When city dwellers demonstrated against a 10,000 percent increase in the price of rice, Chiang's secret police opened fire on them.

In contrast, the Communists, led by **Mao Zedong** (mou′dzŭ′dŏng′), gained strength throughout the country. In the areas they controlled, Communists worked to win peasant support. They encouraged peasants to learn to read, and they helped to improve food production. As a result, more and more recruits flocked to the Communists' Red Army. By 1945, much of northern China was under communist control.

**RENEWED CIVIL WAR** As soon as the defeated Japanese left China at the end of World War II, cooperation between the Nationalists and the Communists ceased. Civil war erupted again between the two groups. In spite of the problems in the Nationalist regime, American policy favored the Nationalists because they opposed communism.

From 1944 to 1947, the United States played peacemaker between the two groups while still supporting the Nationalists. However, U.S. officials repeatedly failed to negotiate peace. Truman refused to commit American soldiers to back up the nationalists, although the United States did send $2 billion worth of military equipment and supplies.

The aid wasn't enough to save the Nationalists, whose weak military leadership and corrupt, abusive practices drove the peasants to the Communist side. In May 1949, Chiang and the remnants of his demoralized government fled to the island of **Taiwan**, which Westerners called Formosa. After more than 20 years of struggle, the Communists ruled all of mainland China. They established a new government, the People's Republic of China, which the United States refused to accept as China's true government. **A**

*A. Answer* The Nationalists were corrupt and nonsupportive of the peasants. The Communists had strong leadership, and they worked to win peasant support.

**MAIN IDEA**

**Analyzing Causes**
**A** What factors led to the Communist takeover in China?

**AMERICA REACTS TO COMMUNIST TAKEOVER** The American public was stunned that China had become Communist. Containment had failed! In Congress, conservative Republicans and Democrats attacked the Truman administration for supplying only limited aid to Chiang. If containing communism was important in Europe, they asked, why was it not equally important in Asia?

The State Department replied by saying that what had happened in China was a result of internal forces. The United States had failed in its attempts to influence these forces, such as Chiang's inability to retain the support of his people. Trying to do more would only have started a war in Asia—a war that the United States wasn't prepared to fight.

Some conservatives in Congress rejected this argument as a lame excuse. They claimed that the American government was riddled with Communist agents. Like wildfire, American fear of communism began to burn out of control, and the flames were fanned even further by events in Korea the following year.

## ② The Korean War

Japan had taken over Korea in 1910 and ruled it until August 1945. As World War II ended, Japanese troops north of the **38th parallel** (38° North latitude) surrendered to the Soviets. Japanese troops south of the parallel surrendered to the Americans. As in Germany, two nations developed, one communist and one democratic.

In 1948, the Republic of Korea, usually called South Korea, was established in the zone that had been occupied by the United States. Its government, headed by Syngman Rhee, was based in Seoul, Korea's traditional capital. Simultaneously, the Communists formed the Democratic People's Republic of Korea in the north. Kim Il Sung led its government, which was based in Pyongyang. (See map, page 613.) **B**

Soon after World War II, the United States had cut back its armed forces in South Korea. As a result, by June of 1949 there were only 500 American troops there. The Soviets concluded that the United States would not fight to defend South Korea. They prepared to back North Korea with tanks, airplanes, and money in an attempt to take over the entire peninsula.

**NORTH KOREA ATTACKS SOUTH KOREA** On June 25, 1950, North Korean forces swept across the 38th parallel in a surprise attack on South Korea. The conflict that followed became known as the **Korean War.**

Within a few days, North Korean troops had penetrated deep into South Korea. South Korea called on the United Nations to stop the North Korean invasion. When the matter came to a vote in the UN Security Council, the Soviet Union was not there. The Soviets were boycotting the council in protest over the presence of Nationalist China (Taiwan). Thus, the Soviets could not veto the UN's plan of military action. The vote passed.

On June 27, in a show of military strength, President Truman ordered troops stationed in Japan to support the South Koreans. He also sent an American fleet into the waters between Taiwan and China.

### MAIN IDEA

**Analyzing Events**

**B** How did Korea become a divided nation after World War II?

**B. Answer** North Korea surrendered to the Soviets. South Korea surrendered to the United States. Two separate countries emerged: North Korea and South Korea.

---

**WORLD STAGE**

**TAIWAN**

In 1949, Chiang Kai-shek and other Nationalist leaders retreated to the island of Taiwan, which lies about 100 miles off the southeast coast of the Chinese mainland. There the United States helped set up a Nationalist government— the Republic of China. From 1949 through the 1960s, the United States poured millions of dollars of aid into the Taiwanese economy.

During the 1970s, a number of nations, including the United States, decided to end diplomatic relations with Taiwan and established ties with Communist China. With the collapse of Soviet communism in the early 1990s, relations between Taiwan and the United States improved. In 2001, the United States sold weapons to Taiwan to bolster the island nation's defense system.

---

### ON THE WORLD STAGE

**Taiwan**

**Analyzing Effects** Tell students that Taiwan is an active trading partner with the United States. But no country that wants formal diplomatic relations with the People's Republic of China can have an official diplomatic relationship with Taiwan because China considers Taiwan a renegade province. Ask students how this status might affect people living in Taiwan.

### Instruct: Objective ②

**The Korean War**
TAKS SS11 1(US6.E)

· How did Korea become divided into two countries?

· How did the Korean War start?

· Why did the United States go to the aid of South Korea?

 In-Depth Resources: Unit 5
· American Lives: Douglas MacArthur, p. 64

 Electronic Library of Primary Sources
· Frustration in Korea, 1947, by D. MacArthur

### More About . . .

**The North Korean Attack**

The Korean War came as a surprise to much of the world. America's main focus in Asia had been China, where Mao and Chiang were making warlike statements over Taiwan. In January 1950, Secretary of State Dean Acheson gave a speech about American intentions to defend Japan, and the Philippines. No mention was made of Korea or Taiwan. Some historians have speculated that the Russians then gave North Korean leader Kim Il Sung approval to invade the south, because they believed that the United States would not intervene.

*Cold War Conflicts* **611**

---

**ACTIVITY**  **LINK TO GEOGRAPHY**

 **classzone.com**

## Taiwan (Republic of China) and People's Republic of China

**Class Time** 45 minutes

**Task** Comparing Taiwan (Republic of China) and the People's Republic of China

**Purpose** To better understand the differences between the two countries

**Directions** Have students use an almanac or Internet resources to create a comparison chart that contrasts Taiwan and the People's Republic of China. Have students compare such categories as land area, population, capital city, ethnic makeup, gross domestic product, per capita income, exports, imports, literacy rate, type of government, political parties, and other relevant data.

📄 Integrated Assessment
· Rubric 2

## Instruct: Objective ❸

**The United States Fights in Korea**

TAKS SS11 1(US6.E)

· What did MacArthur's counterattack at Inchon accomplish?

· What brought China into the war?

· What caused the disagreement between MacArthur and Truman?

· How did the Korean War end?

📄 In-Depth Resources: Unit 5
· Guided Reading, p. 46

### More About . . .

**U.S. Action in Korea**

Congress never declared war in Korea. Unlike Vietnam, there was no formal Congressional assent to the action, such as the Gulf of Tonkin Resolution. Truman used an executive action to send troops. Thus, technically the United States was never officially at war in Korea, but instead was involved in a United Nations "police action."

### More About . . .

**Beverly Scott**

After Korea, Beverly Scott continued to serve in the U.S. Army in duty stations around the world. During the Vietnam War, he was on the staff of the Army Inspector General in Vietnam. Scott commented about the life of an African-American army officer saying, "There was no better institution in American life . . . than the army for the black man in the forties and fifties. . . . You had more leverage in the army. You always had somebody you could go to and complain about bad treatment. A black man couldn't do that in civilian life."

---

In all, 16 nations sent some 520,000 troops to aid South Korea. Over 90 percent of these troops were American. South Korean troops numbered an additional 590,000. The combined forces were placed under the command of General Douglas MacArthur, former World War II hero in the Pacific.

## ❸ The United States Fights in Korea

At first, North Korea seemed unstoppable. Driving steadily south, its troops captured Seoul. After a month of bitter combat, the North Koreans had forced UN and South Korean troops into a small defensive zone around Pusan in the southeastern corner of the peninsula.

**MACARTHUR'S COUNTERATTACK** MacArthur launched a counterattack with tanks, heavy artillery, and fresh troops from the United States. On September 15, 1950, his troops made a surprise amphibious landing behind enemy lines at Inchon, on Korea's west coast. Other troops moved north from Pusan. Trapped between the two attacking forces, about half of the North Korean troops surrendered; the rest fled back across the 38th parallel. MacArthur's plan had saved his army from almost certain defeat.

The UN army chased the retreating North Korean troops across the 38th parallel into North Korea. In late November, UN troops approached the Yalu River, the border between North Korea and China. It seemed as if Korea was about to become a single country again.

**THE CHINESE FIGHT BACK** The Chinese, however, had other ideas. Communist China's foreign minister, Zhou En-lai, warned that his country would not stand idly by and "let the Americans come to the border"—meaning the Yalu River. In late November 1950, 300,000 Chinese troops joined the war on the side of North Korea. The Chinese wanted North Korea as a Communist buffer state to protect their northeastern provinces that made up Manchuria. They also felt threatened by the American fleet that lay off their coast. The fight between North Korea and South Korea had escalated into a war in which the main opponents were the Chinese communists and the Americans.

By sheer force of numbers, the Chinese drove the UN troops southward. At some points along the battlefront, the Chinese outnumbered UN forces ten to one. By early January 1951, all UN and South Korean troops had been pushed out of North Korea. The Chinese advanced to the south, capturing the South Korean capital, Seoul. "We face an entirely new war," declared MacArthur. **Ⓒ**

For two years, the two sides fought bitterly to obtain strategic positions in the Korean hills, but neither side was able to make important advances. One officer remembered the standoff.

Beverly Scott

**A PERSONAL VOICE** BEVERLY SCOTT

"Our trenches . . . were only about 20 meters in front of theirs. We were eyeball to eyeball. . . . We couldn't move at all in the daytime without getting shot at. Machine-gun fire would come in, grenades, small-arms fire, all from within spitting distance. It was like World War I. We lived in a maze of bunkers and deep trenches. . . . There were bodies strewn all over the place. Hundreds of bodies frozen in the snow."

—quoted in *No Bugles, No Drums: An Oral History of the Korean War*

612 CHAPTER 18

---

🔺TAKS

Mini-Lesson 2: SS11 1(US6.E)

**Vocabulary**
**amphibious:** capable of traveling both on land and on water

*C. Answer*
Just as UN forces had overtaken North Korea, the Chinese entered the war on the side of North Korea and pushed UN troops southward.

**MAIN IDEA**

**Analyzing Causes**
Ⓒ How did the involvement of communist China affect the Korean War?

*Skillbuilder Answers*
1. To Pusan.
2. Other UN troops moved north from Pusan, and the two forces trapped the North Koreans, who were forced to flee north across the border.

---

**DIFFERENTIATING INSTRUCTION** | **STUDENTS ACQUIRING ENGLISH/ESL**

### Clarifying Phrases and Terms

Pair students with native English speakers. Have them review the following terms, phrases, and sentence fragments, putting each into their own words:

· MacArthur launched a *counterattack*
· the rest *fled* back across the 38th parallel
· Zhou Enlai warned that his country would not stand *idly by*
· The Chinese wanted North Korea as a *Communist buffer state*

· By *sheer force of numbers*
· We were *eyeball to eyeball*
· all from within *spitting distance*

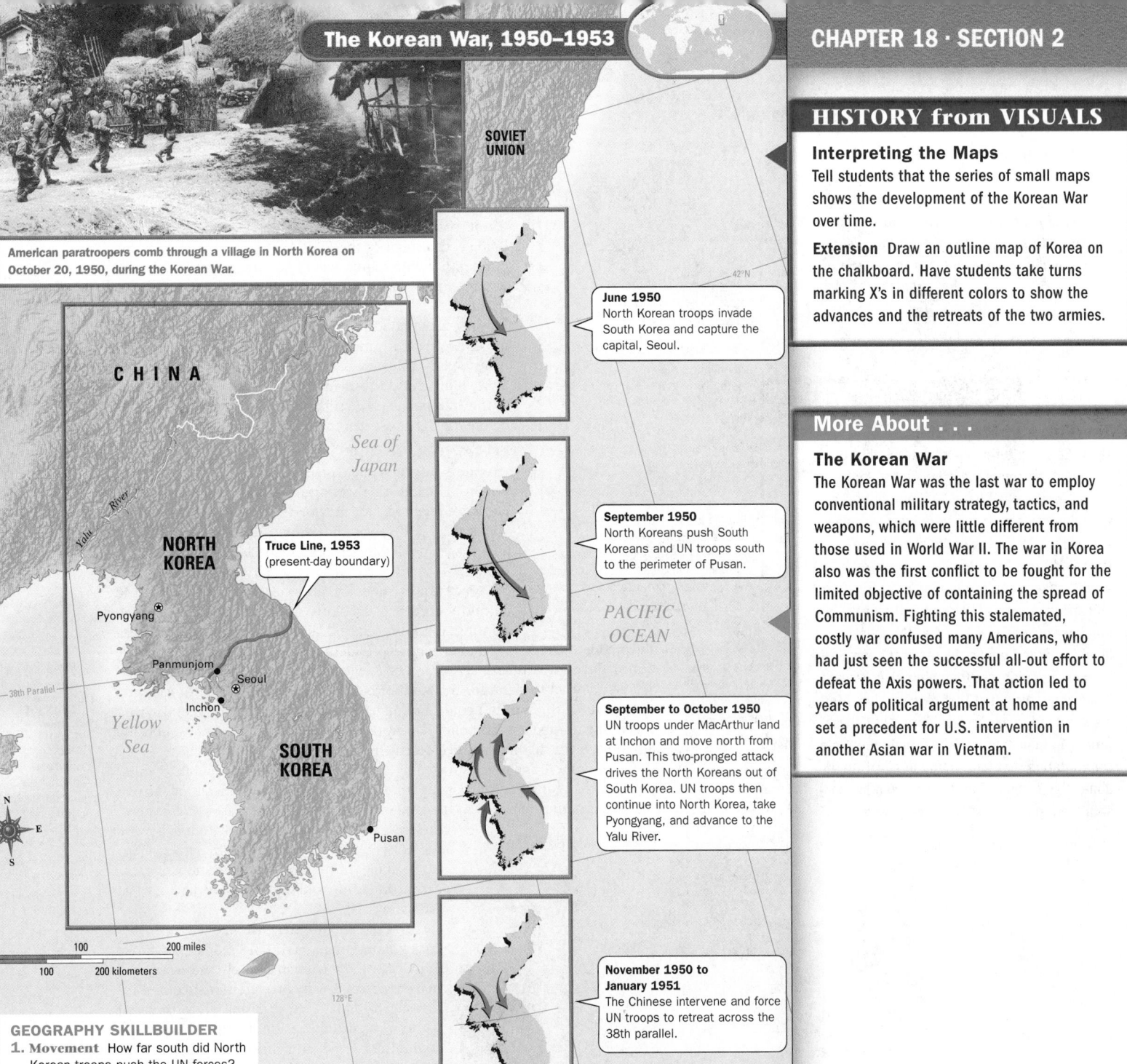

**The Korean War, 1950–1953**

SOVIET UNION

American paratroopers comb through a village in North Korea on October 20, 1950, during the Korean War.

CHINA

Sea of Japan

*Yalu River*

**NORTH KOREA**

Pyongyang ⊛

**Truce Line, 1953** (present-day boundary)

Panmunjom

Seoul ⊛

Inchon

38th Parallel

*Yellow Sea*

**SOUTH KOREA**

Pusan

PACIFIC OCEAN

0   100   200 miles
0   100   200 kilometers

128°E

42°N

30°N

**June 1950**
North Korean troops invade South Korea and capture the capital, Seoul.

**September 1950**
North Koreans push South Koreans and UN troops south to the perimeter of Pusan.

**September to October 1950**
UN troops under MacArthur land at Inchon and move north from Pusan. This two-pronged attack drives the North Koreans out of South Korea. UN troops then continue into North Korea, take Pyongyang, and advance to the Yalu River.

**November 1950 to January 1951**
The Chinese intervene and force UN troops to retreat across the 38th parallel.

**GEOGRAPHY SKILLBUILDER**
1. **Movement** How far south did North Korean troops push the UN forces?
2. **Place** Why do you think MacArthur chose Inchon as his landing place?

*Cold War Conflicts* **613**

## HISTORY from VISUALS

### Interpreting the Maps
Tell students that the series of small maps shows the development of the Korean War over time.

**Extension** Draw an outline map of Korea on the chalkboard. Have students take turns marking X's in different colors to show the advances and the retreats of the two armies.

## More About . . .

### The Korean War
The Korean War was the last war to employ conventional military strategy, tactics, and weapons, which were little different from those used in World War II. The war in Korea also was the first conflict to be fought for the limited objective of containing the spread of Communism. Fighting this stalemated, costly war confused many Americans, who had just seen the successful all-out effort to defeat the Axis powers. That action led to years of political argument at home and set a precedent for U.S. intervention in another Asian war in Vietnam.

---

**classzone.com**

**ACTIVITY**    **LINK TO GOVERNMENT**

### The United Nations

**Class Time** 45 minutes

**Task** Creating a poster showing the structure of the United Nations

**Purpose** To identify the structure of the United Nations and the governing policy of the Security Council

**Directions** Have students use library resources and the Internet to identify the different agencies and the governing policy of the United Nations. Have them pay particular attention to the membership and functions of the Security Council. Ask students to display their research on a poster with text explanations for each UN agency.

ANOTHER
## PERSPECTIVE

### INDIA'S VIEWPOINT

Nonaligned nations such as India were on neither side of the Cold War and had their own perspectives. In 1951, the prime minister of India, Jawaharlal Nehru *(shown above),* had this to say about the Korean War:

"This great struggle between the United States and Soviet Russia is hardly the proper role in this world for those great powers. . . . Their role should be to function in their own territories and not be a threat to others."

General Douglas MacArthur *(left)* and President Truman *(right)* strongly disagreed about how best to proceed in the Korean War.

**MACARTHUR RECOMMENDS ATTACKING CHINA** To halt the bloody stalemate, in early 1951, MacArthur called for an extension of the war into China. Convinced that Korea was the place "where the Communist conspirators have elected to make their play for global conquest," MacArthur called for the use of nuclear weapons against Chinese cities.

Truman rejected MacArthur's request. The Soviet Union had a mutual-assistance pact with China. Attacking China could set off World War III. As General Omar N. Bradley, chairman of the Joint Chiefs of Staff, said, an all-out conflict with China would be "the wrong war, at the wrong place, at the wrong time, and with the wrong enemy."

Instead of attacking China, the UN and South Korean forces began to advance once more, using the U.S. Eighth Army, led by Matthew B. Ridgway, as a spearhead. By April 1951, Ridgway had retaken Seoul and had moved back up to the 38th parallel. The situation was just what it had been before the fighting began.

**MACARTHUR VERSUS TRUMAN** Not satisfied with the recapture of South Korea, MacArthur continued to urge the waging of a full-scale war against China. Certain that his views were correct, MacArthur tried to go over the president's head. He spoke and wrote privately to newspaper and magazine publishers and, especially, to Republican leaders.

MacArthur's superiors informed him that he had no authority to make decisions of policy. Despite repeated warnings to follow orders, MacArthur continued to criticize the president. President Truman, who as president was commander-in-chief of the armed forces and thus MacArthur's boss, was just as stubborn as MacArthur. Truman refused to stand for this kind of behavior. He wanted to put together a settlement of the war and could no longer tolerate a military commander who was trying to sabotage his policy. On April, 1, 1951, Truman made the shocking announcement that he had fired MacArthur. **D**

Many Americans were outraged over their hero's downfall. A public opinion poll showed that 69 percent of the American public backed General MacArthur. When MacArthur returned to the United States, he gave an address to Congress, an honor usually awarded only to heads of government. New York City honored him with a ticker-tape parade. In his closing remarks to Congress, MacArthur said, "Old soldiers never die, they just fade away."

Throughout the fuss, Truman stayed in the background. After MacArthur's moment of public glory passed, the Truman administration began to make its case. Before a congressional committee investigating MacArthur's dismissal, a parade of witnesses argued the case for limiting the war. The committee agreed with them. As a result, public opinion swung around to the view that Truman had done the right thing. As a political figure, MacArthur did indeed fade away.

**SETTLING FOR STALEMATE** As the MacArthur controversy died down, the Soviet Union unexpectedly suggested a cease-fire on June 23, 1951. Truce talks began in July 1951. By the following spring, the opposing sides had agreed on two points: the location of the cease-fire line at the existing battle line and the establishment of a demilitarized zone between the opposing sides. Negotiators spent another year wrangling over the exchange of prisoners. Finally, in July 1953, the two sides signed an armistice ending the war.

At best, the agreement was a stalemate. On the one hand, the North Korean invaders had been pushed back, and communism had been contained without the use of atomic weapons. On the other hand, Korea was still two nations rather than one.

On the home front, the war had affected the lives of ordinary Americans in many ways. It had cost 54,000 American lives and $67 billion in expenditures. The high cost of this unsuccessful war was one of many factors leading Americans to reject the Democratic Party in 1952 and to elect a Republican administration under World War II hero Dwight D. Eisenhower. In addition, the Korean War increased fear of communist aggression and prompted a hunt for Americans who might be blamed for the communist gains.

**Vocabulary**
**demilitarize:** to ban military forces in an area or region

 South Korean President Kim Dae-jung waves to cheering North Koreans on June 13, 2000.

## NOW & THEN

### THE TWO KOREAS

Korea is still split into North Korea and South Korea, even after 50 years. South Korea is booming economically, while North Korea, still communist, struggles with severe shortages of food and energy.

Periodically, discussions about reuniting the two countries resume. In 2000, South Korean President Kim Dae-jung won the Nobel Peace Prize for his efforts to improve ties with North Korea. The two nations met in North Korea for the first time since the nations were established in 1948. Although economic and political differences continue to keep the two countries apart, there is renewed hope that one day Korea will become a united nation.

## NOW & THEN

**The Two Koreas**
**Making Inferences** Ask students to research the current state of relations between North Korea and South Korea. Discuss conditions under which the countries might be united.

## Assess & Reteach

### SECTION 2 ASSESSMENT

Have students answer the questions and then compare their answers with those of another student. Ask the student pairs to find the text passage to support their answers.

📝 Formal Assessment
· Section Quiz, p. 339

### SELF–ASSESSMENT

Have students make a time line of events of the Korean War to illustrate what they have learned. Have them compare those time lines with the ones they created as they read the selection and note any omissions or discrepancies.

### RETEACH

Review the map on page 613 to reinforce students' understanding of the Korean War.

📝 In-Depth Resources: Unit 5
· Reteaching Activity, p. 52

---

## SECTION 2 ASSESSMENT

**1. TERMS & NAMES** For each term or name, write a sentence explaining its significance.
- **Chiang Kai-shek**
- **Mao Zedong**
- **Taiwan**
- **38th parallel**
- **Korean War**

### MAIN IDEA

**2. TAKING NOTES**
On a time line such as the one shown below, list the major events of the Korean War.

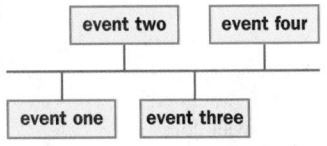

Choose two events and explain how one event led to the other.

### CRITICAL THINKING

**3. HYPOTHESIZING**
What might have happened if MacArthur had convinced Truman to expand the fighting into China? How might today's world be different?

**4. ANALYZING EVENTS**
Many Americans have questioned whether fighting the Korean War was worthwhile. What is your opinion? Why? **Think About:**
- the loss of American lives
- the fear of communism that enveloped the country at the time
- the stalemate that ended the war

**5. EVALUATING DECISIONS**
At the end of China's civil war, the United States refused to accept the communist People's Republic of China as China's true government. What were the advantages of such a policy? What were the disadvantages? Do you agree with this decision? Why or why not?

*Cold War Conflicts* **615**

---

Answers **ASSESSMENT** 2

**1. TERMS AND NAMES**
Chiang Kai-shek, p. 609
Mao Zedong, p. 610
Taiwan, p. 610
38th parallel, p. 611
Korean War, p. 611

**2. TAKING NOTES**
1948: Korea is split into two nations. June 1950: North Korea invades South Korea. June 1950: U.S. supports South Korea. Sept. 1950: North Korea occupies most of Korea. Sept.–Oct. 1950: UN counterattack succeeds. Nov. 1950: China enters the war. July 1953: Armistice is signed.

**3. HYPOTHESIZING**
A third world war might have broken out, resulting in the obliteration of millions by nuclear weapons.

**4. ANALYZING EVENTS**
Some students may say that the war was not worthwhile because Korea remained a divided nation. Others may say that, without the war, all of Korea might Communist.

**5. EVALUATING DECISIONS**
**Advantages**—The United States remained committed to its policy of containment of Communism.
**Disadvantages**—Refusal to recognize the Communist government in China kept the United States from influencing China and drove China into an alliance with the Soviet Union. Answers about agreement or disagreement will vary.

# The Cold War at Home

| MAIN IDEA | WHY IT MATTERS NOW | Terms & Names |
|---|---|---|
| During the late 1940s and early 1950s, fear of communism led to reckless charges against innocent citizens. | Americans today remain vigilant about unfounded accusations. | • HUAC  • Ethel and Julius Rosenberg<br>• Hollywood Ten  • Joseph McCarthy<br>• blacklist  • McCarthyism<br>• Alger Hiss |

 **U.S. History**
TEKS 1B, 6D, 6E, 6F, 8A, 15C, 16A, 19A, 19B, 22A, 22C, 24A, 24B, 24C, 24D, 25A, 25B, 25C, 25D

### One American's Story

Tony Kahn made the neighbors uncomfortable because they thought his father, Gordon Kahn, was a Communist. In 1947, Gordon Kahn was a successful screenwriter. However, when a congressional committee began to investigate Communists in Hollywood, Kahn was blacklisted—named as unfit to hire. Later, in 1951, he was scheduled to testify before the committee himself.

To save himself, Gordon Kahn simply had to name others as Communists, but he refused. Rather than face the congressional committee, he fled to Mexico. Tony Kahn remembers how the Cold War hurt him and his family.

**A PERSONAL VOICE** TONY KAHN

" The first time I was called a Communist, I was four years old. . . . I'll never forget the look in our neighbors' eyes when I walked by. I thought it was hate. I was too young to realize it was fear. "

—from *The Cold War Comes Home*

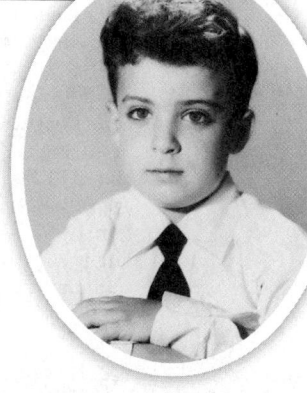

Tony Kahn

**VIDEO**

*THE COLD WAR COMES HOME*
**Hollywood Blacklists the Kahn Family**

The members of the Kahn family were among thousands of victims of the anti-Communist hysteria that gripped this country in the late 1940s and early 1950s. By the end of the period, no one was immune from accusations.

## **1** Fear of Communist Influence

In the early years of the Cold War, many Americans believed that there was good reason to be concerned about the security of the United States. The Soviet domination of Eastern Europe and the Communist takeover of China shocked the American public, fueling a fear that communism would spread around the world. In addition, at the height of World War II, about 80,000 Americans claimed membership in the Communist Party. Some people feared that the first loyalty of these American Communists was to the Soviet Union.

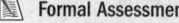

**LOYALTY REVIEW BOARD** Strongly anti-Communist Republicans began to accuse Truman of being soft on communism. Consequently, in March 1947, President Truman issued an executive order setting up the Federal Employee Loyalty Program, which included the Loyalty Review Board. Its purpose was to investigate government employees and to dismiss those who were found to be disloyal to the U.S. government. The U.S. attorney general drew up a list of 91 "subversive" organizations; membership in any of these groups was grounds for suspicion.

From 1947 to 1951, government loyalty boards investigated 3.2 million employees and dismissed 212 as security risks. Another 2,900 resigned because they did not want to be investigated or felt that the investigation violated their constitutional rights. Individuals under investigation were not allowed to see the evidence against them. **A**

**THE HOUSE UN-AMERICAN ACTIVITIES COMMITTEE** Other agencies investigated possible Communist influence, both inside and outside the U.S. government. The most famous of these was the **House Un-American Activities Committee (HUAC).** HUAC first made headlines in 1947, when it began to investigate Communist influence in the movie industry. The committee believed that Communists were sneaking propaganda into films. The committee pointed to the pro-Soviet films made during World War II when the Soviet Union had been a United States ally.

HUAC subpoenaed 43 witnesses from the Hollywood film industry in September 1947. Many of the witnesses were "friendly," supporting the accusation that Communists had infiltrated the film industry. For example, the movie star Gary Cooper said he had "turned down quite a few scripts because I thought they were tinged with Communistic ideas." However, when asked which scripts he meant, Cooper couldn't remember their titles.

Ten "unfriendly" witnesses were called to testify but refused. These men, known as the **Hollywood Ten,** decided not to cooperate because they believed that the hearings were unconstitutional. Because the Hollywood Ten refused to answer questions, they were sent to prison.

**MAIN IDEA**

**Drawing Conclusions**

**A** How did the Loyalty Review Board pose a threat to civil liberties?

**A. Answer** Individuals under investigation were not allowed to see the evidence against them.

**PAUL ROBESON**

Paul Robeson was an all-American football player and Phi Beta Kappa member at Rutgers University. After earning a law degree in 1923, he began a distinguished international career as a singer and actor. He was a vocal civil rights activist, and he was sympathetic to the Soviet culture and political philosophy.

In 1950, when he refused to sign an affidavit indicating whether he had ever been a member of the Communist Party, the State Department revoked his passport for eight years. During that time, he was unable to perform abroad and was blacklisted at home. His income fell from $150,000 a year to $3,000 a year.

**HISTORICAL SPOTLIGHT**

**Paul Robeson**

Ask students to read an account of Paul Robeson's life in a book such as *Paul Robeson Speaks* by Philip S. Foner and then summarize Robeson's strong social and political activism. What parallels do students see in the lives of Gordon Kahn and Paul Robeson?

**Tracing Themes**

**CIVIL RIGHTS**

HUAC's attempts to remove persons with "un-American" views from the entertainment industry raised significant constitutional issues. The investigations by HUAC and later by Senator Joseph McCarthy seemed to clash with the constitutional rights of freedom of speech and freedom of assembly and with the right of accused persons to be fully informed of the nature of accusations against them. The investigations continued despite protests by the Hollywood Ten and other prominent Americans.

👁 **Electronic Library of Primary Sources**
· Statement on Civil Liberties in America, 1956, by P. Robeson

Protesters demonstrate in support of the Hollywood Ten. ▼

EDWARD DMYTRYK IS GOING TO JAIL — FREE THE HOLLYWOOD TEN

ALVAH BESSIE IS GOING TO JAIL — FREE THE HOLLYWOOD 10

DALTON TRUMBO D 10 IS GOING TO JAIL — FREE THE HOLLYWOOD 10

ADRIAN SCOTT IS GOING TO JAIL — FREE THE HOLLYWOOD 10

Albert Mal is going to Jail — FREE the Hollywood Ten

FREE THE HO—

617

classzone.com

**ACTIVITY** **LINK TO HUMANITIES**

**The Arts and Politics**

**Class Time** 45 minutes

**Task** Assessing the impact of politics on the entertainment figures who appeared before HUAC

**Purpose** To analyze the relationship between an artist's work and politics

**Directions** Have students use Internet and library resources to research the HUAC hearings on Hollywood in 1947. Ask them to assess the position of one of the artists who appeared before the committee and especially analyze motivation. Then, have students stage a roundtable discussion in which they present their assessments.

 **Integrated Assessment**
· Rubrics 1, 3

## Instruct: Objective ❷

**Spy Cases Stun the Nation**
TAKS SS11 5(US24.B)

· Why was State Department official Alger Hiss investigated?

· Who were Julius and Ethel Rosenberg?

📖 In-Depth Resources: Unit 5
· Guided Reading, p. 47

In response to the hearings, Hollywood executives instituted a **blacklist**, a list of people whom they condemned for having a Communist background. People who were blacklisted—approximately 500 actors, writers, producers, and directors—had their careers ruined because they could no longer work. **B**

**THE MCCARRAN ACT** As Hollywood tried to rid itself of Communists, Congress decided that Truman's Loyalty Review Board did not go far enough. In 1950, Congress passed the McCarran Internal Security Act. This made it unlawful to plan any action that might lead to the establishment of a totalitarian dictatorship in the United States. Truman vetoed the bill, saying, "In a free country, we punish men for the crimes they commit, but never for the opinions they have." But Congress enacted the law over Truman's veto.

### ❷ Spy Cases Stun the Nation

Two spy cases added to fear that was spreading like an epidemic across the country. One case involved a former State Department official named Alger Hiss.

**ALGER HISS** In 1948, a former Communist spy named Whittaker Chambers accused **Alger Hiss** of spying for the Soviet Union. To support his charges, Chambers produced microfilm of government documents that he claimed had been typed on Hiss's typewriter. Too many years had passed for government prosecutors to charge Hiss with espionage, but a jury convicted him of perjury—for lying about passing the documents—and sent him to jail. A young conservative Republican congressman named Richard Nixon gained fame for pursuing the charges against Hiss. Within four years of the highly publicized case, Nixon was elected vice president of the United States.

Hiss claimed that he was innocent and that Chambers had forged the documents used against him. However, in the 1990s, Soviet cables released by the National Security Agency seemed to prove Hiss's guilt.

### MAIN IDEA

**Analyzing Causes**
**B** Why was Hollywood a target of anti-Communist investigations by Congress?

**B. Answer**
HUAC believed that Hollywood was sneaking propaganda into films. Its members pointed to pro-Soviet films made during the war.

---

## NOW & THEN

**TELEVISION: MAKING NEWS**

Historians of popular culture believe that the early 1950s were the best years of television. Most programs were filmed live and had a fresh, unrehearsed look. Along with variety shows, early television presented some of the best serious drama of the age.

Since the 1950s, television has also become a major vehicle for reporting the news. Not only does television report the news, it also has increasingly helped to shape it.

**1954** In 1954, the Communist-hunting senator Joseph McCarthy, in U.S. Senate hearings that were televised live, accused the U.S. Army of "coddling Communists." As many as 20 million Americans watched the combative senator malign people who had no chance to defend themselves.

**1960** In the 1960 presidential election, a major factor in John Kennedy's victory over Richard Nixon was a series of four televised debates, the first televised presidential debates in history. An estimated 85 million to 120 million Americans watched one or more of the debates, which turned the tide in favor of Kennedy.

**618** CHAPTER 18

---

**ACTIVITY** **COOPERATIVE LEARNING**

ℹ️ classzone.com

### Television and Public Opinion

**Class Time** 45 minutes

**Task** Writing an analysis of the influence of television on important news events

**Purpose** To evaluate television's influence in shaping public opinion and policy

**Directions** Have students work in small groups and use the Internet and other resources to research one of the five events in the feature. Ask students to find out how television covered the event and influenced both public opinion and any subsequent action resulting from public opinion. Have student groups share their reports with the rest of the class so that each event is covered by a report.

📖 Integrated Assessment
· Rubrics 1, 5

**THE ROSENBERGS** Another spy case rocked the nation even more than the Hiss case, partially because of international events occurring about the same time. On September 3, 1949, Americans learned that the Soviet Union had exploded an atomic bomb. Most American experts had predicted that it would take the Soviets three to five more years to make the bomb. People began to wonder if Communist supporters in the United States had leaked the secret of the bomb.

This second spy case seemed to confirm that suspicion. In 1950, the German-born physicist Klaus Fuchs admitted giving the Soviet Union information about America's atomic bomb. The information probably enabled Soviet scientists to develop their own atomic bomb years earlier than they would have otherwise. Implicated in the Fuchs case were **Ethel and Julius Rosenberg**, minor activists in the American Communist Party.

When asked if they were Communists, the Rosenbergs denied the charges against them and pleaded the Fifth Amendment, choosing not to incriminate themselves. They claimed they were being persecuted both for being Jewish and for holding radical beliefs. The Rosenbergs were found guilty of espionage and sentenced to death. In pronouncing their sentence, Judge Irving Kaufman declared their crime "worse than murder." To him, they were directly responsible for one of the deadliest clashes of the Cold War. **C**

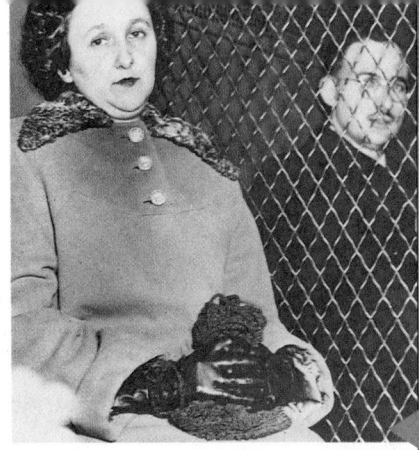

▲ Ethel and Julius Rosenberg were executed in June 1953 despite numerous pleas to spare their lives.

---

**MAIN IDEA**

**Analyzing Causes**

**C** Why did the cases of Alger Hiss and the Rosenbergs heighten the anti-Communist mood of Americans?

*C. Answer*
They added to the impression that the U.S. was being betrayed by Communist spies.

---

**A PERSONAL VOICE** IRVING KAUFMAN

" I believe your conduct in putting into the hands of the Russians the A-bomb years before our best scientists predicted Russia would perfect the bomb has already caused, in my opinion, the Communist aggression in Korea."

—quoted in *The Unquiet Death of Julius and Ethel Rosenberg*

---

**More About . . .**

**The Rosenbergs**
The chief witness against the Rosenbergs was Ethel Rosenberg's brother, David Greenglass, a machinist who had worked on the atomic bomb project in Los Alamos, New Mexico. Greenglass testified that he gave classified information to Julius Rosenberg, information then relayed to the Soviets. It was widely believed by people close to the case that Ethel was innocent and that her arrest and the threat of execution was a government ploy to get her to testify against her husband. But she did not admit to anything and was tried and executed. In 1997, information was released by Russia from Soviet spy files that confirmed Julius' involvement, but there was no evidence that Ethel had engaged in any espionage activities.

---

**More About . . .**

**Espionage**
The end of the Cold War has not meant the end of espionage between the United States and Russia. In 1994, Aldrich Ames, a CIA official, was arrested for long-time espionage activities with the Soviet Union. Ames was a Soviet "mole" inside the CIA. In 2001, a high-ranking FBI official, Robert Hanssen, was arrested and charged with spying for the Soviet Union and, later, Russia.

---

**1967** By 1967, American support for the Vietnam War had plummeted as millions of TV viewers witnessed the horrors of war on the nightly news.

**1974** The Watergate scandal that toppled Richard Nixon's presidency in 1974 played to a rapt TV audience. During the Senate hearings in 1973, the televised testimony of John Dean, the president's counsel, had convinced two out of three Americans that the president had committed a crime.

**2000** During the 2000 presidential election, TV networks first declared Al Gore the winner and then declared George W. Bush the winner. The latter declaration led Al Gore to concede. However, Gore subsequently retracted his concession because the election was too close to call. This "election muddle" blurs even further the already indistinct line between reporting the news and making it.

*Cold War Conflicts* **619**

---

## Analyzing *Political Cartoons*

### "IT'S OK—WE'RE HUNTING COMMUNISTS"

The fear of Communist subversion affected the entire society. People were so suspicious that almost any unusual opinion might be labeled "un-American." The climate of suspicion was most severe in the years 1947–1954, but it lasted throughout the 1950s.

#### SKILLBUILDER Analyzing Political Cartoons

1. What organization does the car represent?
2. What does the cartoon imply about the methods of this organization?

📁 SEE SKILLBUILDER HANDBOOK, PAGE R24.

### Instruct: Objective ③

**McCarthy Launches His "Witch-Hunt"**

TAKS SS11 1(US6.F)

· What was controversial about McCarthy's tactics?
· Why did most Republicans remain silent about McCarthy's "Witch Hunt?"
· What caused McCarthy's downfall?
· What other anti-Communist measures were enacted in the early 1950s?

 In-Depth Resources: Unit 5
· Guided Reading, p. 47

### More About . . .

#### McCarthyism

McCarthy's executive secretary was Mary Brinkley Driscoll, the sister of television news commentator David Brinkley. Years later, Brinkley asked his sister what McCarthy was holding when he made his famous accusation that 205 Communists were working for the State Department. Driscoll told her brother, "He had a few scribbled notes to use in his speech. Nothing about Communists." She confirmed that McCarthy made up the number to get publicity.

 In-Depth Resources: Unit 5
· American Lives: Margaret Chase Smith, p. 65

People from all over the world appealed for clemency for the Rosenbergs. Many considered the evidence and the testimony too weak to warrant the death sentence. The case was appealed to the U.S. Supreme Court, but the Court refused to overturn the conviction. Julius and Ethel Rosenberg died in the electric chair in June 1953, leaving behind two sons. They became the first U.S. civilians executed for espionage.

## ③ McCarthy Launches His "Witch Hunt"

The most famous anti-Communist activist was Senator **Joseph McCarthy**, a Republican from Wisconsin. During his first three years in the Senate, he had acquired a reputation for being an ineffective legislator. By January 1950, he realized that he was going to need a winning issue in order to be reelected in 1952. Looking for such an issue, McCarthy charged that Communists were taking over the government.

**MCCARTHY'S TACTICS** Taking advantage of people's concerns about communism, McCarthy made one unsupported accusation after another. These attacks on suspected Communists in the early 1950s became known as **McCarthyism.** Since that time, McCarthyism has referred to the unfair tactic of accusing people of disloyalty without providing evidence. At various times McCarthy claimed to have in his hands the names of 57, 81, and 205 Communists in the State Department. (He never actually produced a single name.) He also charged that the Democratic Party was guilty of "20 years of treason" for allowing Communist infiltration into the government. He was always careful to do his name-calling only in the Senate, where he had legal immunity that protected him from being sued for slander.

The Republicans did little to stop McCarthy's attacks because they believed they would win the 1952 presidential election if the public saw them purging the nation of Communists. But one small group of six senators, led by Senator Margaret Chase Smith of Maine, did speak out.

**Vocabulary**
**infiltration:** the act of penetrating a group or organization without being noticed for purposes such as spying

> **A PERSONAL VOICE** MARGARET CHASE SMITH
>
> " I speak as a Republican. I speak as a woman. I speak as a United States senator. I speak as an American. . . . I am not proud of the way in which the Senate has been made a publicity platform for irresponsible sensationalism. I am not proud of the reckless abandon in which unproved charges have been hurled from this side of the aisle."
>
> —*Declaration of Conscience*

---

**ACTIVITY** COOPERATIVE LEARNING                          classzone.com

### Investigating Witch Hunts

**Class Time** 45 minutes

**Task** Investigating either McCarthy's crusade against alleged Communists in the 1950s or the witch trials in Salem, Massachusetts, in 1692

**Purpose** To evaluate the impact of widespread public fears and hysteria on the lives of people and institutions

**Directions** Have groups choose to research either McCarthy or Salem witch trials. Tell students to investigate basic facts in each case, concentrating on the veracity of the evidence and the presumption of guilt until proven innocent. Have students present their reports and compare the similarities of each case, drawing conclusions about why waves of fear swept away reason and what could be done to prevent such situations in the future.

 Integrated Assessment
· Rubrics 1, 5

**MCCARTHY'S DOWNFALL** Finally, in 1954, McCarthy made accusations against the U.S. Army, which resulted in a nationally televised Senate investigation. McCarthy's bullying of witnesses alienated the audience and cost him public support. The Senate condemned him for improper conduct that "tended to bring the Senate into dishonor and disrepute." Three years later, Joseph McCarthy, suffering from alcoholism, died a broken man.

**OTHER ANTI-COMMUNIST MEASURES** Others besides Joseph McCarthy made it their mission to root communism out of American society. By 1953, 39 states had passed laws making it illegal to advocate the violent overthrow of the government, even though such laws clearly violated the constitutional right of free speech. Across the nation, cities and towns passed similar laws.

At times, the fear of communism seemed to have no limits. In Indiana, professional wrestlers had to take a loyalty oath. In experiments run by newspapers, pedestrians on the street refused to sign petitions that quoted the Declaration of Independence because they were afraid the ideas were communist. The government investigated union leaders, librarians, newspaper reporters, and scientists. It seemed that no profession was safe from the hunt for Communists.

*Skillbuilder Answers*
1. Soviet domination of Eastern Europe and Soviet development of the bomb heightened fear of communism.
2. McCarthyism led to required loyalty oaths, hesitancy to speak out on public issues, and decreased activism by labor unions.

---

### Causes and Effects of McCarthyism

**Causes**

- Soviets successfully establish Communist regimes in Eastern Europe after World War II.
- Soviets develop the atomic bomb more quickly than expected.
- Korean War ends in a stalemate.
- Republicans gain politically by accusing Truman and Democrats of being soft on communism.

**Effects**

- Millions of Americans are forced to take loyalty oaths and undergo loyalty investigations.
- Activism by labor unions goes into decline.
- Many people are afraid to speak out on public issues.
- Anti-communism continues to drive U.S. foreign policy.

**SKILLBUILDER Interpreting Charts**
1. How did world events help lead to McCarthyism?
2. How did McCarthyism affect the behavior of individual Americans?

---

## Assess & Reteach

**SECTION 3 ASSESSMENT**
Ask students to work in pairs or small groups to answer the questions.

📄 Formal Assessment
· Section Quiz, p. 340

**SELF-ASSESSMENT**
Have students explore their understanding of anti-Communist feelings by creating a two-column chart in which they list the actions taken against suspected Communists and the results of those actions.

**RETEACH**
Review the heads and the subheads of the section, and have students determine whether they can identify the topic of each one.

📄 In-Depth Resources, Unit 5
· Reteaching Activity, p. 53

---

### ASSESSMENT (SECTION 3)

**1. TERMS & NAMES** For each term or name, write a sentence explaining its significance.
- HUAC
- Hollywood Ten
- blacklist
- Alger Hiss
- Ethel and Julius Rosenberg
- Joseph McCarthy
- McCarthyism

#### MAIN IDEA

**2. TAKING NOTES**
Re-create the web below on your paper and fill in events that illustrate the main idea in the center.

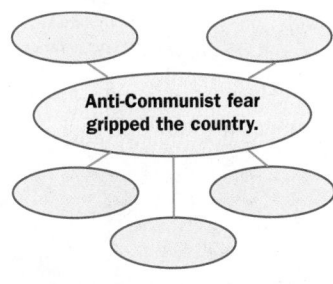

**Anti-Communist fear gripped the country.**

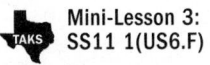

Which event had the greatest impact on the country?

#### CRITICAL THINKING

**3. HYPOTHESIZING**
If you had lived in this period and had been accused of being a Communist, what would you have done? **Think About:**
- the Hollywood Ten, who refused to answer questions
- the Rosenbergs, who pleaded the Fifth Amendment

**4. ANALYZING MOTIVES**
Choose one of the following roles: Harry Truman, a member of HUAC, Judge Irving Kaufman, or Joseph McCarthy. As the person you have chosen, explain your motivation for opposing communism.

**5. ANALYZING VISUAL SOURCES**
What does this cartoon suggest about McCarthy's downfall?

Mini-Lesson 3: SS11 1(US6.F)

*Cold War Conflicts* **621**

---

**1. TERMS AND NAMES**
HUAC, p. 617
Hollywood Ten, p. 617
blacklist, p. 618
Alger Hiss, p. 618
Ethel and Julius Rosenberg, p. 619
Joseph McCarthy, p. 620
McCarthyism, p. 620

**2. TAKING NOTES**
*Events:* HUAC investigates un-American activities in Hollywood; Congress passes the McCarran Act; Spy cases increase fears; McCarthy arouses fear of a Communist conspiracy.

**3. HYPOTHESIZING**
Some students might say that they would have refused to name others because that would have been the honorable course of action. Others might say that they would have shown their loyalty to the United States by answering the committee's questions.

**4. ANALYZING MOTIVES**
Answers will vary, but most students will probably cite loyalty to the United States and fear of Communism.

**5. ANALYZING VISUAL SOURCES**
McCarthy was caught in his own web of deception and lies.

## OBJECTIVES

**1** Explain the policy of brinkmanship.

**2** Describe American and Soviet actions that caused the Cold War to spread around the world.

**3** Summarize the impact of *Sputnik* and the U-2 incident on the United States.

### SKILLBUILDER

· Geography Skillbuilder: region p. 624
· Interpreting Graphs, p. 626

### CRITICAL THINKING

· Analyzing Causes, p. 623
· Summarizing, p. 624
· Analyzing Effects, p. 625
· Comparing, p. 626
· Hypothesizing, p. 627
· Evaluating, p. 627
· Forming Generalizations, p. 627

## Focus & Motivate

Ask students how they react when they feel threatened. Do they think that those same reactions apply to nations? Explain.

## Instruct

### Instruct: Objective **1**

**Brinkmanship Rules U.S. Policy**
TAKS SS11 5(US24.B)

· How does the hydrogen bomb differ from the atomic bomb?
· What was the policy of brinkmanship?

 **In-Depth Resources: Unit 5**
· Guided Reading, p. 48

 **Humanities Transparencies HT25**
· Bomb Shelter Under Construction

# Two Nations Live on the Edge

| MAIN IDEA | WHY IT MATTERS NOW | Terms & Names |
|---|---|---|
| During the 1950s, the United States and the Soviet Union came to the brink of nuclear war. | The Cold War continued into the following decades, affecting U.S. policies in Cuba, Central America, Southeast Asia, and the Middle East. | •H-bomb  •Dwight D. Eisenhower  •John Foster Dulles  •brinkmanship  •CIA  •Warsaw Pact  •Eisenhower Doctrine  •Nikita Khrushchev  •Francis Gary Powers  •U-2 incident |

 **U.S. History**
1C, 6D, 6F, 6H, 8A, 8B, 9B, 14C, 15B, 19C, 22A, 22B, 23A, 24B, 24G, 24H, 25A, 25B, 25D, 26A, 26B

### One American's Story

Writer Annie Dillard was one of thousands of children who grew up in the 1950s with the chilling knowledge that nuclear war could obliterate their world in an instant. Dillard recalls practicing what to do in case of a nuclear attack.

**A PERSONAL VOICE** ANNIE DILLARD

"At school, we had air-raid drills. We took the drills seriously; surely Pittsburgh, which had the nation's steel, coke, and aluminum, would be the enemy's first target. . . . When the air-raid siren sounded, our teachers stopped talking and led us to the school basement. There the gym teachers lined us up against the cement walls and steel lockers, and showed us how to lean in and fold our arms over our heads. . . . The teachers stood in the middle of the room, not talking to each other. We tucked against the walls and lockers. . . . We folded our skinny arms over our heads, and raised to the enemy a clatter of gold scarab bracelets and gold bangle bracelets."

—*An American Childhood*

The fear of nuclear attack was a direct result of the Cold War. After the Soviet Union developed its atomic bomb, the two superpowers embarked on an arms race that enormously increased both the number and the destructive power of weapons.

▲ A father helps his daughter practice getting into a bomb shelter.

## **1** Brinkmanship Rules U.S. Policy

Although air-raid drills were not common until the Eisenhower years (1953–1961), the nuclear arms race began during Truman's presidency. When the Soviet Union exploded its first atomic bomb in 1949, President Truman had to make a terrible decision—whether to develop an even more horrifying weapon.

---

## PROGRAM RESOURCES

 **In-Depth Resources: Unit 5**
· Guided Reading, p. 48
· Reteaching Activity, p. 54
· Literature: from *The Nuclear Age*, pp. 61–63

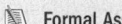 **Reading Study Guide** (English and Spanish), pp. 187–188

 **Access for Students Acquiring English/ESL**
· Guided Reading (Spanish), p. 203

 **Formal Assessment**
· Section Quiz, p. 341

 **Integrated Assessment**
· Rubrics

### INTEGRATED TECHNOLOGY

 **Critical Thinking Transp. CT26, CT60**
· The Cold War
· The Space Race

 **Humanities Transp. HT25, HT41**
· Bomb shelter under construction
· Wonder Why We're Not Keeping Pace?

 **Electronic Library of Primary Sources**

 **classzone.com**

### TEXAS RESOURCES

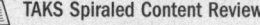 TAKS Spiraled Content Review

TAKS Practice Tests

TAKS Practice Transparencies TT101

TAKS Online Test Practice

**RACE FOR THE H-BOMB** The scientists who developed the atomic bomb had suspected since 1942 that it was possible to create an even more destructive thermo-nuclear weapon—the hydrogen bomb, or **H-bomb.** They estimated that such a bomb would have the force of 1 million tons of TNT (67 times the power of the bomb dropped on Hiroshima). But they argued vehemently about the morality of creating such a destructive weapon.

Despite such concerns, the United States entered into a deadly race with the Soviet Union to see which country would be the first to produce an H-bomb. On November 1, 1952, the United States won the race when it exploded the first H-bomb. However, the American advantage lasted less than a year. In August 1953, the Soviets exploded their own ther-monuclear weapon. **Ⓐ**

**THE POLICY OF BRINKMANSHIP** By the time both countries had the H-bomb, **Dwight D. Eisenhower** was president. His secretary of state, **John Foster Dulles,** was staunchly anti-Communist. For Dulles, the Cold War was a moral crusade against communism. Dulles proposed that the United States could prevent the spread of communism by promising to use all of its force, including nuclear weapons, against any aggressor nation. The willingness of the United States, under President Eisenhower, to go to the edge of all-out war became known as **brinkmanship.** Under this policy, the United States trimmed its army and navy and expanded its air force (which would deliver the bombs) and its buildup of nuclear weapons. The Soviet Union followed suit.

The threat of nuclear attack was unlike any the American people had ever faced. Even if only a few bombs reached their targets, millions of civilians would die. Schoolchildren like Annie Dillard practiced air-raid procedures, and some families built underground fallout shelters in their back yards. Fear of nuclear war became a constant in American life for the next 30 years.

## The Cold War Spreads Around the World ❷

As the nation shifted to a dependence on nuclear arms, the Eisenhower adminis-tration began to rely heavily on the recently formed **Central Intelligence Agency (CIA)** for information. The CIA used spies to gather information abroad. The CIA also began to carry out covert, or secret, operations to weaken or over-throw governments unfriendly to the United States.

**COVERT ACTIONS IN THE MIDDLE EAST AND LATIN AMERICA** One of the CIA's first covert actions took place in the Middle East. In 1951, Iran's prime min-ister, Mohammed Mossadegh, nationalized Iran's oil fields; that is, he placed the formerly private industries (owned mostly by Great Britain) under Iranian control. To protest, the British stopped buying Iranian oil. As the Iranian economy

▲ A dramatic civil defense poster shows the fear of nuclear attack.

### MAIN IDEA

**Analyzing Causes**
Ⓐ How did the U.S. and the Soviet Union start the arms race?

*A. Answer*
By developing more powerful weapons, including the H-bomb.

**Background**
From ancient times until 1935, Iran was known as Persia. Persia once ruled a great empire that stretched from the Mediterranean Sea to India's Indus River.

*Cold War Conflicts* **623**

## HISTORY from VISUALS

### Interpreting the Map

Ask students to recall Stalin's desire to create buffer states to shield the Soviet Union from invasion from the west. Then, ask students to use the map to explain how the creation of the Warsaw Pact fulfilled the goal set out by Stalin after World War II. *(Almost the entire Soviet European border is protected by Warsaw Pact nations. The only non-Warsaw Pact nations sharing a border with the Soviet Union were NATO member Turkey and neutral Finland.)*

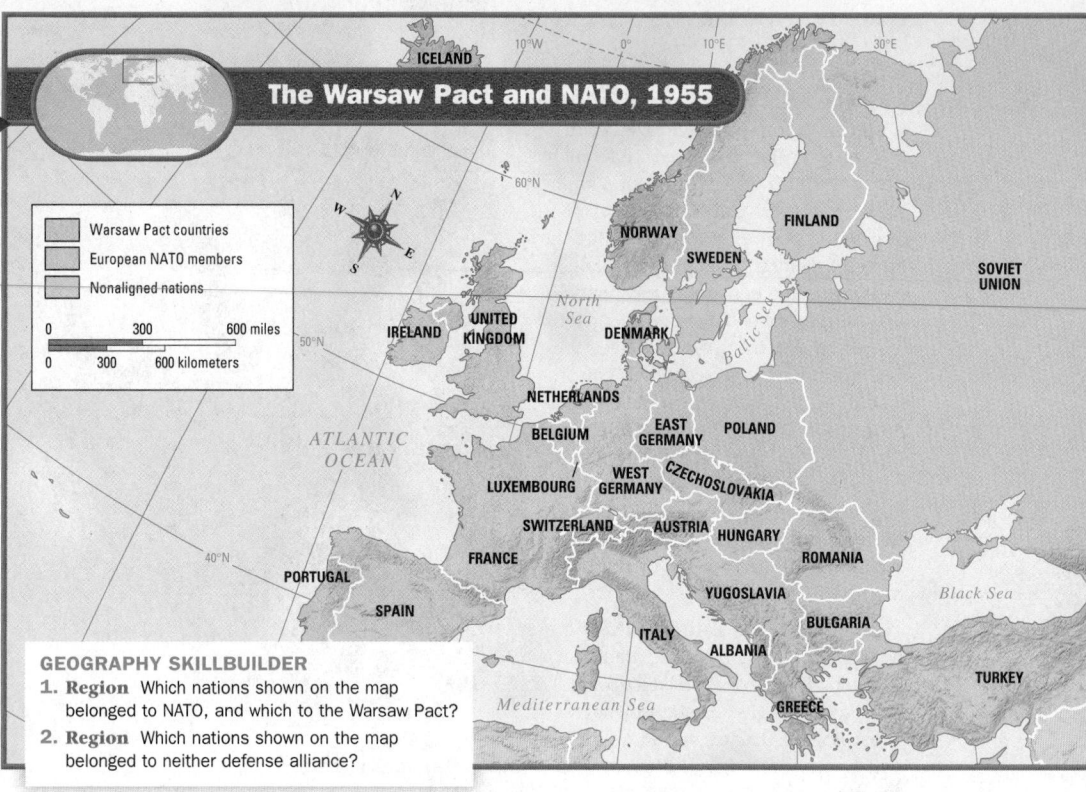

### The Warsaw Pact and NATO, 1955

Warsaw Pact countries
European NATO members
Nonaligned nations

0    300    600 miles
0    300    600 kilometers

**GEOGRAPHY SKILLBUILDER**
1. **Region** Which nations shown on the map belonged to NATO, and which to the Warsaw Pact?
2. **Region** Which nations shown on the map belonged to neither defense alliance?

### More About . . .

### Warsaw Pact

The Warsaw Pact was established by the Warsaw Treaty of Friendship, Cooperation, and Mutual Assistance signed in May 1955. The pact included the following countries: the Soviet Union, Albania, East Germany, Hungary, Poland, Romania, Czechoslovakia, and Bulgaria. It was formed about a week after the admission of West Germany into NATO. The treaty called for a unified military command and the stationing of Soviet military units in all participating countries.

*Skillbuilder Answers*
**1. NATO:** Great Britain, Netherlands, Belgium, France, Luxembourg, West Germany, Denmark, Norway, Greece, Turkey, Portugal, Italy.
**Warsaw Pact:** East Germany, Poland, Czechoslovakia, Hungary, Romania, Bulgaria, Albania, Soviet Union.
**2.** Spain, Switzerland, Austria, Yugoslavia, Sweden, Finland, Ireland.

faltered, the United States feared that Mossadegh might turn to the Soviets for help. In 1953, the CIA gave several million dollars to anti-Mossadegh supporters. The CIA wanted the pro-American Shah of Iran, who had recently been forced to flee, to return to power. The plan worked. The Shah returned to power and turned over control of Iranian oil fields to Western companies.

In 1954, the CIA also took covert actions in Guatemala, a Central American country just south of Mexico. Eisenhower believed that Guatemala's government had Communist sympathies because it had given more than 200,000 acres of American-owned land to peasants. In response, the CIA trained an army, which invaded Guatemala. The Guatemalan army refused to defend the president, and he resigned. The army's leader then became dictator of the country. **B**

**THE WARSAW PACT** In spite of the growing tension between the superpowers, U.S.-Soviet relations seemed to thaw following the death of Joseph Stalin in 1953. The Soviets recognized West Germany and concluded peace treaties with Austria and Japan. However, in 1955, when West Germany was allowed to rearm and join NATO, the Soviet Union grew fearful. It formed its own military alliance, known as the **Warsaw Pact.** The Warsaw Pact linked the Soviet Union with seven Eastern European countries.

**A SUMMIT IN GENEVA** In July 1955, Eisenhower traveled to Geneva, Switzerland, to meet with Soviet leaders. There Eisenhower put forth an "open skies" proposal. The United States and the Soviet Union would allow flights over each other's territory to guard against surprise nuclear attacks. Although the Soviet Union rejected this proposal, the world hailed the "spirit of Geneva" as a step toward peace.

**MAIN IDEA**

**Summarizing**
**B** What was the role of the CIA in the Cold War?

*B. Answer*
To gather intelligences and to carry out secret operations against unfriendly governments.

**624** CHAPTER 18

---

**DIFFERENTIATING INSTRUCTION** | **GIFTED AND TALENTED STUDENTS**

### Researching and Analyzing Covert Action

Have students choose one incident of American covert action in Iran or Guatemala in the 1950s to research. Then, ask students to assess the effects of the covert action and to answer whether such action is compatible with American principles and law. Have students share their work with the rest of the class.

Assessments should . . .

· focus on one covert action
· reflect historical facts accurately
· express a clear point of view about whether the action is compatible with American principles and law

**THE SUEZ WAR** In 1955, the same year in which the Geneva Summit took place, Great Britain and the United States agreed to help Egypt finance construction of a dam at Aswan on the Nile River. However, Gamal Abdel-Nasser, Egypt's head of government, tried to play the Soviets and the Americans against each other, by improving relations with each one in order to get more aid. In 1956, after learning that Nasser was making deals with the Soviets, Dulles withdrew his offer of a loan. Angered, Nasser responded by nationalizing the Suez Canal, the Egyptian waterway that was owned by France and Great Britain. The French and the British were outraged.

Egyptian control of the canal also affected Israel. Nasser refused to let ships bound for Israel pass through the canal, even though the canal was supposed to be open to all nations. Israel responded by sending troops. So did Great Britain and France. The three countries seized the Mediterranean end of the canal. The UN quickly stepped in to stop the fighting. It persuaded Great Britain, France, and Israel to withdraw. However, it allowed Egypt to keep control of the canal. **C**

**MAIN IDEA**

*Analyzing Effects*

**C** What were the results of the Suez War?

**C. Answer** Great Britain, France, and Israel withdrew from the Mediterranean end of the canal and control of the canal passed to Egypt.

**THE EISENHOWER DOCTRINE** The Soviet Union's prestige in the Middle East rose because of its support for Egypt. To counterbalance this development, President Eisenhower issued a warning in January 1957. This warning, known as the **Eisenhower Doctrine**, said that the United States would defend the Middle East against an attack by any Communist country. In March, Congress officially approved the doctrine.

**THE HUNGARIAN UPRISING** Even as fighting was raging in the Middle East, a revolt began in Hungary. Dominated by the Soviet Union since the end of World War II, the Hungarian people rose in revolt in 1956. They called for a democratic government.

Imre Nagy, the most popular and liberal Hungarian Communist leader, formed a new government. He promised free elections, denounced the Warsaw Pact, and demanded that all Soviet troops leave Hungary.

The Soviet response was swift and brutal. In November 1956, Soviet tanks rolled into Hungary and killed approximately 30,000 Hungarians. Armed with only pistols and bottles, thousands of Hungarian freedom fighter threw up barricades in the streets and fought the invaders to no avail. The Soviets overthrew the Nagy government and replaced it with pro-Soviet leaders. Nagy himself was executed. Some 200,000 Hungarians fled to the west.

Although the Truman Doctrine had promised to support free peoples who resisted communism, the United States did nothing to help Hungary break free of Soviet control. Many

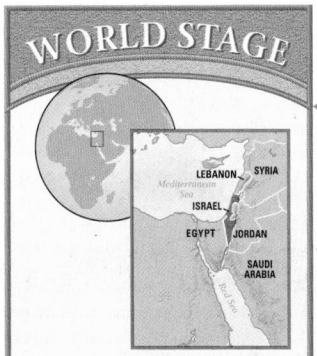

**WORLD STAGE**

**ISRAEL**

On May 14, 1948, the United Nations created the nation of Israel by partitioning Palestine into two states, one Jewish and one Arab. Thousands of Jews had immigrated to Palestine from Europe before and during World War II, and Israel became the "promised land" they had been seeking since biblical times. The creation of Israel was one of the few issues upon which the United States and the Soviet Union agreed, as the world reacted uniformly to the horror that had befallen the Jews in the Holocaust.

**WORLD STAGE**

**Israel**

**Analyzing Events** Have students do outside reading about the current situation in Israel with regard to its conflict with the Palestinians. Then, ask students to identify reasons why the U.S. government has an interest in the events in the area. *(Answers will vary.)*

**More About . . .**

**The Hungarian Uprising**

The Hungarian Uprising had its origins in a February 1956 speech by Nikita Khrushchev, head of the Soviet Communist Party. He publicly criticized his predecessor, Stalin, for having committed crimes against the Soviet people. Such open criticism of the previous regime made people around the world wonder if the Soviet Union was becoming a less repressive country. Some Eastern European nations began to dream of breaking free of Soviet control. Poles rose up against their government in October 1956, and Hungary followed less than a month later. Khrushchev acquiesced to the nationalist government of Wladyslaw Gomulka in Poland. But Nagy, by withdrawing Hungary from the Warsaw Pact, had gone too far for Khrushchev.

Crowds surround a captured Russian tank during the anti-Communist revolution in Hungary.

▼

*Cold War Conflicts* **625**

---

**ACTIVITY**  **COOPERATIVE LEARNING**

**Creating a Political Cartoon**

**Class Time** 45 minutes

**Task** Creating political cartoons that capture the anxiety of the 1950s.

**Purpose** To clarify U.S. motivations and responses in pursuing the Cold War

**Directions** Have groups of three to four students read newspaper and magazine accounts of the Suez crisis, the invasion of Hungary, the launch of *Sputnik*, or the downing of the U-2. They can then brainstorm to create a political cartoon showing some aspect of the U.S. response to the specific event. They might consider the fear of Sputnik as an all-seeing spy, or the U-2 incident, for example.

 **Integrated Assessment**
· Rubrics 1, 4

Hungarians were bitterly disappointed. The American policy of containment did not extend to driving the Soviet Union out of its satellites.

No help came to Hungary from the United Nations either. Although the UN passed one resolution after another condemning the Soviet Union, the Soviet veto in the Security Council stopped the UN from taking any action.

## ❸ The Cold War Takes to the Skies

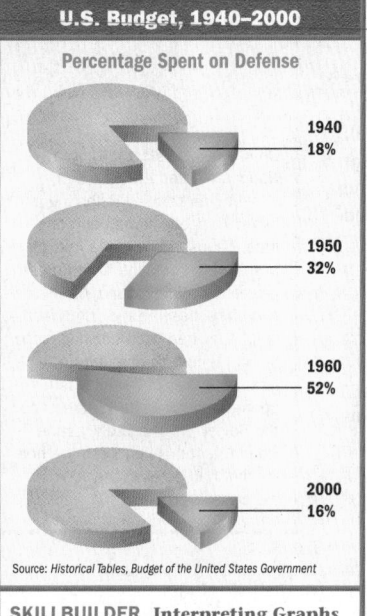

**U.S. Budget, 1940–2000**

**Percentage Spent on Defense**

1940 — 18%

1950 — 32%

1960 — 52%

2000 — 16%

Source: *Historical Tables, Budget of the United States Government*

**SKILLBUILDER Interpreting Graphs**
1. By how much did the percentage of the federal budget for defense increase between 1950 and 1960?
2. Why do you think it increased that much?

After Stalin's death in 1953, the Soviet Union had no well-defined way for one leader to succeed another. For the first few years, a group of leaders shared power. As time went by, however, one man did gain power. That man was **Nikita Khrushchev** (krōōsh'chĕf). Like Stalin, Khrushchev believed that communism would take over the world, but Khrushchev thought it could triumph peacefully. He favored a policy of peaceful coexistence in which two powers would compete economically and scientifically. **Ⓓ**

**THE SPACE RACE** In the competition for international prestige, the Soviets leaped to an early lead in what came to be known as the space race. On October 4, 1957, they launched *Sputnik*, the world's first artificial satellite. *Sputnik* traveled around the earth at 18,000 miles per hour, circling the globe every 96 minutes. Its launch was a triumph of Soviet technology.

Americans were shocked at being beaten and promptly poured money into their own space program. U.S. scientists worked frantically to catch up to the Soviets. The first attempt at an American satellite launch was a humiliating failure, with the rocket toppling to the ground. However, on January 31, 1958, the United States successfully launched its first satellite.

**A U-2 IS SHOT DOWN** Following the rejection of Eisenhower's "open skies" proposal at the 1955 Geneva summit conference, the CIA began making secret high-altitude flights over Soviet territory. The plane used for these missions was the U-2, which could fly at high altitudes without detection. As a U-2 passed over the Soviet Union, its infrared cameras took detailed photographs of troop movement and missile sites.

By 1960, however, many U.S. officials were nervous about the U-2 program for two reasons. First, the existence and purpose of the U-2 was an open secret among some members of the American press. Second, the Soviets had been aware of the flights since 1958, as **Francis Gary Powers**, a U-2 pilot, explained.

**A PERSONAL VOICE** FRANCIS GARY POWERS
" We . . . knew that the Russians were radar-tracking at least some of our flights. . . . We also knew that SAMs [surface-to-air missiles] were being fired at us, that some were uncomfortably close to our altitude. But we knew too that the Russians had a control problem in their guidance system. . . . We were concerned, but not greatly. "
—*Operation Overflight: The U-2 Spy Pilot Tells His Story for the First Time*

**626** CHAPTER 18

---

Finally, Eisenhower himself wanted the flights discontinued. He and Khrushchev were going to hold another summit conference on the arms race on May 15, 1960. "If one of these aircraft were lost when we were engaged in apparently sincere deliberations, it could . . . ruin my effectiveness," he told an aide. However, Dulles persuaded him to authorize one last flight.

That flight took place on May 1, and the pilot was Francis Gary Powers. Four hours after Powers entered Soviet airspace, a Soviet pilot shot down his plane, and Powers was forced to parachute into Soviet-controlled territory. The Soviets sentenced Powers to ten years in prison.

◄ Francis Gary Powers's military identification card

Francis Gary Powers at a Senate committee hearing following his release by the Soviets ▼

**Background**
After 18 months, Francis Gary Powers was released from the Soviet Union in exchange for Soviet agent Rudolf Abel, who had been convicted of spying in the United States.

**RENEWED CONFRONTATION** At first, Eisenhower denied that the U-2 had been spying. The Soviets had evidence, however, and Eisenhower finally had to admit it. Khrushchev demanded an apology for the flights and a promise to halt them. Eisenhower agreed to stop the U-2 flights, but he would not apologize.

Khrushchev angrily called off the summit. He also withdrew his invitation to Eisenhower to visit the Soviet Union. Because of the **U-2 incident,** the 1960s opened with tension between the two superpowers as great as ever.

# Assess & Reteach

**SECTION 4 ASSESSMENT**
Have students work individually to answer the questions. Then, have them share the headlines that they wrote for question 2 with others in the class.

📄 Formal Assessment
· Section Quiz, p. 341

**SELF-ASSESSMENT**
Ask students to review their answers for question 4 on the section assessment. What did they learn from evaluating U.S. actions?

**RETEACH**
Use the cause-and-effect transparency to review the actions and reactions of the two superpowers during the Cold War.

📄 In-Depth Resources, Unit 5
· Reteaching Activity, p. 54

---

## SECTION 4 ASSESSMENT

**1. TERMS & NAMES** For each term or name, write a sentence explaining its significance.

- H-bomb
- Dwight D. Eisenhower
- John Foster Dulles
- brinkmanship
- Central Intelligence Agency (CIA)
- Warsaw Pact
- Eisenhower Doctrine
- Nikita Khrushchev
- Francis Gary Powers
- U-2 incident

### MAIN IDEA

**2. TAKING NOTES**
List Cold War trouble spots in Iran, Guatemala, Egypt, and Hungary. For each, write a newspaper headline that summarizes the U.S. role and the outcome of the situation.

| Trouble Spot | Headline |
|---|---|
|  |  |

Choose one headline and write a paragraph about that trouble spot.

### CRITICAL THINKING

**3. HYPOTHESIZING**
How might the Cold War have progressed if the U-2 incident had never occurred? **Think About:**
 the mutual distrust between the Soviet Union and the United States
 the outcome of the incident

**4. EVALUATING**
Which of the two superpowers do you think contributed more to Cold War tensions during the 1950s?

**5. FORMING GENERALIZATIONS**
Should one nation have the right to remove another nation's head of government from power? If so, when? If not, why?

---

**1. TERMS AND NAMES**
H-bomb, p. 623
Dwight D. Eisenhower, p. 623
John Foster Dulles, p. 623
brinkmanship, p. 623
Central Intelligence Agency (CIA), p. 623
Warsaw Pact, p. 624
Eisenhower Doctrine, p. 625
Nikita Khrushchev, p. 626
Francis Gary Powers, p. 626
U-2 incident, p. 627

**2. TAKING NOTES**
Guatemala: CIA-Trained Army Topples Guatemalan Government
Iran: U.S. Prevents Iranian-Soviet Alliance
Egypt: U.S. Urges Peaceful Suez Solution
Hungary: No U.S. Help for Hungarians as Soviets Put Down Revolt

**3. HYPOTHESIZING**
The U-2 incident greatly increased tension. Had it not happened, the United States and the Soviet Union might have taken steps to resolve their differences.

**4. EVALUATING**
Some may say the Soviets because they took over Eastern Europe, crushed the Hungarian Uprising, and rejected

Eisenhower's "open skies" proposal. Others may say the United States, citing the U-2 incident, the Eisenhower Doctrine, and involvement in Guatemala and Iran. Some may say that both were equally at fault.

**5. FORMING GENERALIZATIONS**
Answers will vary but should be clearly stated.

## AMERICAN LITERATURE

### Objectives

· To explain how the science fiction of the 1950s reflected the anxieties of the age

· To identify the messages in three science fiction excerpts

## Focus & Motivate

**Evaluating** Ask students to think about their favorite or recent science fiction films or TV shows that they might have seen. Ask whether students think science fiction generally conveys political or social messages or is simply entertainment.

## More About . . .

### Ray Bradbury

Because Bradbury rarely writes about space hardware or gadgetry, some critics have been reluctant to call him a science fiction writer. Bradbury himself says, "If you're too good a scientist, you're not a good writer." He goes on to say, "I write for fun. . . .I have fun with ideas. I play with them. I approach my craft with enthusiasm and respect. If my work sparks serious thought, fine. But I don't write with that in mind. I'm not a serious person, and I don't like serious people."

# AMERICAN LITERATURE

# Science Fiction Reflects Cold War Fears

**1950–1959** Many writers of science fiction draw on the scientific and social trends of the present to describe future societies that might arise if those trends were to continue. Nuclear proliferation, the space race, early computer technology, and the pervasive fear of known and unknown dangers during the Cold War were the realities that prompted a boom in science fiction during the 1950s and 1960s.

### THE BODY SNATCHERS

Written in 1955 at the height of the Great Fear, Jack Finney's *The Body Snatchers* (on which the movie *Invasion of the Body Snatchers* was based) tells of giant seed pods from outer space that descend on the inhabitants of a California town. The pods create perfect physical duplicates of the townspeople and lack only one thing—human souls.

"Miles, he looks, sounds, acts, and remembers exactly like Ira. On the outside. But *inside* he's different. His responses"—she stopped, hunting for the word—"aren't *emotionally* right, if I can explain that. He remembers the past, in detail, and he'll smile and say 'You were sure a cute youngster, Willy. Bright one, too,' just the way Uncle Ira did. But there's something *missing*, and the same thing is true of Aunt Aleda, lately." Wilma stopped, staring at nothing again, face intent, wrapped up in this, then she continued. "Uncle Ira was a father to me, from infancy, and when he talked about my childhood, Miles, there was—always—a special look in his eyes that meant he was remembering the wonderful quality of those days for him. Miles, that look, 'way in back of the eyes, is gone. With *this*—this Uncle Ira, or whoever or whatever he is, I have the feeling, the absolutely certain *knowledge,* Miles, that he's talking by rote. That the facts of Uncle Ira's memories are all in his mind in every last detail, ready to recall. But the emotions are not. There *is* no emotion—none—only the pretense of it. The words, the gestures, the tones of voice, everything else—but not the feeling."

Her voice was suddenly commanding: "Miles, memories or not, appearances or not, possible or impossible, that is not my Uncle Ira."

—Jack Finney, *The Body Snatchers* (1955)

## RECOMMENDED RESOURCES

### BOOKS

Benét, Stephen Vincent. **"By the Waters of Babylon,"** in *Selected Works of Stephen Vincent Benét.* New York: Farrar, 1942. A famous coming-of-age story set in New York City long after its total destruction.

Bradbury, Ray. **Fahrenheit 451.** New York: Ballantine, 1996.

A repressive society controls its citizens by burning all books.

Clark, Walter van Tilburg. **"The Portable Phonograph,"** in *The Watchful Gods and Other Stories.* New York: New American, 1961. The survivors of a nuclear war fight over their meager remaining possessions.

### VIDEO

**Fahrenheit 451.** Dir. François Truffaut. MCA Universal Home Video, 1966.

**Invasion of the Body Snatchers.** Dir. Don Siegel. Republic Pictures Home Video, 1956. Chillingly paranoid McCarthy-era classic.

**The Martian Chronicles Parts 1 and 2.** Dir. Jack Gold. Fries Home Video, 1979. Made for television.

**Planet of the Apes.** Dir. Franklin J. Schaffner. CBS Fox Video, 1967. The original *Planet of the Apes* film.

**Ray Bradbury Theater,** Buena Vista Home Video, 1985. Adaptations of Bradbury tales. "The Playground" in Volume 1 is especially creepy.

## THE MARTIAN CHRONICLES

In *The Martian Chronicles*, Ray Bradbury describes how earthlings who have colo-nized Mars watch helplessly as their former planet is destroyed by nuclear warfare.

They all came out and looked at the sky that night. They left their suppers or their washing up or their dressing for the show and they came out upon their now-not-quite-as-new porches and watched the green star of Earth there. It was a move without conscious effort; they all did it, to help them understand the news they had heard on the radio a moment before. There was Earth and there the coming war, and there hundreds of thousands of mothers or grand-mothers or fathers or brothers or aunts or uncles or cousins. They stood on the porches and tried to believe in the existence of Earth, much as they had once tried to believe in the existence of Mars; it was a problem reversed. To all intents and purposes, Earth now was dead; they had been away from it for three or four years. Space was an anesthetic; seventy million miles of space numbed you, put memory to sleep, depopulated Earth, erased the past, and allowed these people here to go on with their work. But now, tonight, the dead were risen, Earth was reinhabited, memory awoke, a mil-lion names were spoken: What was so-and-so doing tonight on Earth? What about this one and that one? The people on the porches glanced sideways at each other's faces.

At nine o'clock Earth seemed to explode, catch fire, and burn.

The people on the porches put up their hands as if to beat the fire out.

They waited.

—Ray Bradbury, *The Martian Chronicles* (1950)

## A CANTICLE FOR LEIBOWITZ

In *A Canticle for Leibowitz*, Walter M. Miller, Jr., portrays the centuries after a nuclear holocaust as a new "Dark Age" for humanity on earth.

He had been wandering for a long time. The search seemed endless, but there was always the promise of finding what he sought across the next rise or beyond the bend in the trail. When he had finished fanning himself, he clapped the hat back on his head and scratched at his bushy beard while blinking around at the landscape. There was a patch of unburned forest on the hillside just ahead. It offered welcome shade, but still the wanderer sat there in the sunlight and watched the curious buzzards. . . .

Pickings were good for a while in the region of the Red River; but then out of the carnage, a city-state arose. For rising city-states, the buz-zards had no fond-ness, although they approved of their eventual fall. They shied away from Texarkana and ranged far over the plain to the west. After the manner of all living things, they replenished the Earth many times with their kind.

Eventually it was the Year of Our Lord 3174.

There were rumors of war.

—Walter M. Miller, Jr., *A Canticle for Leibowitz* (1959)

### THINKING CRITICALLY

1. **Comparing** What themes, or general messages about life or humanity, do you think these three books convey? How might readers' interpretations of these messages today differ from readers' interpretations during the Cold War?

   **SEE SKILLBUILDER HANDBOOK, PAGE R8.**

2.  **INTERNET ACTIVITY** CLASSZONE.COM

   Visit the links for American Literature to learn more about Ray Bradbury and *The Martian Chronicles*. When was *The Martian Chronicles* published? How does it reflect Cold War fears? What does the writing tell you about Ray Bradbury's view of American society at the time?

## Instruct

1. What ideas and realities of the 1950s are contained in the fiction on these pages?
2. What role does technology play in the worlds depicted in these stories?

**MAKING PERSONAL CONNECTIONS**

Ask students about their favorite science fiction stories, movies, or TV shows. Help them analyze the qualities of science fiction they enjoy.

Ask them to analyze the role of technology—often a theme in science fiction—in their favorite stories.

What makes favorite stories scary or threatening? What is the source of the dread?

### More About . . .

**A Canticle for Leibowitz**
Walter Miller used a neo-medieval setting for his best-selling novel. Much the same as the early Roman Catholic monks preserved the learning of the Roman Empire after the fall of Rome, Miller has the Church acting as the preserver of knowledge in a world shattered by nuclear holocaust. The mystery is provided by the main character's uncertainty about what artifacts and ideas really are, how they were used, and what the "old world" was actually about.

## THINKING CRITICALLY: ANSWERS

1. **COMPARING** *The Martian Chronicles:* Even life on Mars is simple, ordinary; people are helpless and sad in the face of nuclear destruction; life goes on. *The Body Snatchers:* As technology advances, we may be in danger of losing our souls. *A Canticle for Leibowitz:* Life in the future may be desolate and violent, filled with scavengers and sadness.
   Readers during the Cold War would have interpreted these works as dire warnings of a terrible future. Readers today would be less afraid of a nuclear holocaust and would treat the works more as adventure stories.

2. **INTERNET ACTIVITY** Student analyses will vary. Each should, how-ever, show an understanding of *The Martian Chronicles* and clearly state the student's opinion. Plot outlines should provide the set-ting, general circumstances of the story, and character descrip-tions, and also contain enough realism when describing imagined events to capture readers' interest.

## TERMS & NAMES

1. containment, p. 605
2. North Atlantic Treaty Organization (NATO), p. 608
3. Mao Zedong, p. 610
4. Korean War, p. 611
5. McCarthyism, p. 620
6. John Foster Dulles, p. 623
7. brinkmanship, p. 623
8. Central Intelligence Agency (CIA), p. 623
9. Nikita Khrushchev, p. 626
10. U-2 incident, p. 627

## MAIN IDEAS

1. To encourage democracy; to gain access to raw materials and markets; to rebuild Europe; to contain Soviet expansion
2. A policy of helping countries resist Communist takeover; strongly supported by Americans
3. To prevent Soviet aggression
4. Communist victory in China; North Korea's attack on South Korea
5. Truman wanted to limit the Korean War to Korea. MacArthur wanted to bomb and invade China.
6. McCarthy's allegation of Communists in government and in the armed forces
7. The Rosenberg case involved transfer of nuclear secrets to the Soviets; Americans feared any Soviet influence in the United States and their possession of nuclear weapons.
8. By sponsoring covert actions to overthrow governments unfriendly to the United States

## VISUAL SUMMARY

### COLD WAR CONFLICTS

**CAUSES**

- Soviet domination of Eastern Europe
- Communist victory in China
- Mutual suspicion between United States and Soviet Union

THE COLD WAR

**IMMEDIATE EFFECTS**

- Truman Doctrine and Marshall Plan
- East-West tensions over Berlin
- Establishment of NATO and Warsaw Pact
- McCarthyism

**LONG-TERM EFFECTS**

- Arms race between superpowers
- Superpower rivalry for world power

## TERMS & NAMES

For each term or name below, write a sentence explaining its significance to the Cold War.

1. containment
2. North Atlantic Treaty Organization (NATO)
3. Mao Zedong
4. Korean War
5. McCarthyism
6. John Foster Dulles
7. brinkmanship
8. Central Intelligence Agency (CIA)
9. Nikita Khrushchev
10. U-2 incident

## MAIN IDEAS

Use your notes and the information in the chapter to answer the following questions.

**Origins of the Cold War** (pages 602–608)

1. What were the goals of U.S. foreign policy in the Cold War?
2. Describe the Truman Doctrine and how America reacted to it
3. What was the purpose of the NATO alliance?

**The Cold War Heats Up** (pages 609–615)

4. What global events led to U.S. involvement in Korea?
5. What issue between General Douglas MacArthur and President Truman eventually cost MacArthur his job?

**The Cold War at Home** (pages 616–621)

6. What actions of Joseph McCarthy worsened the national hysteria about communism?
7. How did the Rosenberg case fuel anti-communist feeling?

**Two Nations Live on the Edge** (pages 622–627)

8. How did the U.S., including the CIA, wage the Cold War in the 1950s?

## CRITICAL THINKING

1. **USING YOUR NOTES** Create a cause-and-effect diagram like the one shown for each of these events: (a) the United States adoption of a policy of containment, and (b) the beginning of the nuclear arms race between the United States and the Soviet Union.

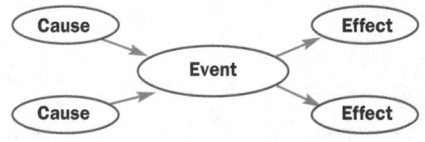

2. **ANALYZING EVENTS** What government actions during the Communist scare conflicted with the Bill of Rights? Explain.

3. **INTERPRETING MAPS** Look carefully at the map on page 605. How did the absence of a natural barrier on the western border of the Soviet Union affect post-World War II Soviet foreign policy? Explain your answer.

## CRITICAL THINKING

1. **Using Your Notes**
   (a) Event—containment
   *Cause*—Soviet aggression in Europe; *Effect*—Truman Doctrine.
   *Cause*—Soviets hold West Berlin hostage; *Effect*—Berlin airlift.
   *Cause*—North Koreans invade South Korea; *Effect*—U.S. enters the Korean War.
   (b) *Event*—nuclear arms race
   *Cause*—Soviets explode atomic bomb. *Effect*—U.S. develops an H-bomb. *Cause*—U.S. tests H-bomb. *Effect*—Soviets develop an H-bomb. *Cause*—U.S. builds nuclear arsenal. *Effect*—Soviets build a comparable arsenal.

2. **Analyzing Events** Loyalty Review Board, HUAC, McCarran Act, McCarthy's unsupported accusations

3. **Interpreting Maps** Some students may say that the lack of a natural barrier caused the Soviets to create buffer nations. Others may argue that the Soviets would have created buffer nations even if they had provided natural protection.

## Standardized Test Practice

Use the quotation below and your knowledge of U.S. history to answer question 1.

> "In 1945 I had ordered the A Bomb dropped on Japan at two places devoted almost exclusively to war production. We were at war. We were trying to end it in order to save the lives of our soldiers and sailors. . . . We stopped the war and saved thousands of casualties on both sides.
>
> In Korea we were fighting a police action with sixteen allied nations to support the World Organization which had set up the Republic of Korea. We had held the Chinese after defeating the North Koreans and whipping the Russian Air Force. I just could not make the order for a Third World War. I know I was *right*."

—*Off the Record: The Private Papers of Harry S. Truman*

1. According to President Truman, what was the main difference between using the atomic bomb on Japan in 1945 and the possibility of using it on China in 1951?

   A Japan was more of a military power in 1945 than China was in 1951.

   B In 1945 we had many allies, but in 1951 we had only two.

   C In 1945 the bomb ended a world war, but in 1951 it would have started one.

   D The Japanese were much fiercer fighters than the Chinese were.

Use the cartoon below and your knowledge of U.S. history to answer question 2.

2. What point of view about the arms race does this 1950 cartoon *best* support?

   F The arms race between "Russia" and the United States is as dangerous as a war.

   G Communism uncontained will spread.

   H The bombs of the United States only threaten countries other than the United States.

   J The United States needs to build up its arsenal in order to compete with "Russia."

ADDITIONAL TEST PRACTICE, pages S1–S33.

 TEST PRACTICE  CLASSZONE.COM

## Standardized Test Practice

1. The correct answer is **C**.

   The bomb was used to bring an end to military actions in World War II. To bomb China during the Korean Conflict would have started a war with the Chinese. Letters A and D are incorrect because China was just as much of a military power as Japan, and the Chinese, too, were fierce fighters. Letter B is incorrect because, in each case, more countries would have been affected by the actions than just the United States and the country that was bombed.

2. The correct answer is **F**.

   The cartoon shows that the arms race threatened the world. Letter G is incorrect because the cartoon does not refer to Communism. Letter H is incorrect because the bombs were a threat to all countries, including the United States. Letter J is incorrect because it shows that the nuclear arsenals of both nations were equally dangerous.

**UNIT PROJECT**

**DEBATE**

**Tips for Teaching**

· Tell students in a formal debate they have a specified time limit to present their argument and a specified time limit in which to respond to the opponents challenges.

· Have students prepare their opening speech.

· Remind students to use evidence to support their arguments.

## ALTERNATIVE ASSESSMENT

1. **INTERACT WITH HISTORY**  Recall your discussion of the question on page 601:

### *What do you do when a friend is accused?*

Suppose your best friend has been accused of being a Communist. You have been called to serve as a character witness for him or her.

Write a speech that you will present to the House Un-American Activities Committee (HUAC). In your speech explain why you feel that your friend's constitutional rights are being violated.

2. **VIDEO  LEARNING FROM MEDIA**  View the *American Stories* video, "The Cold War Comes Home: Hollywood Blacklists the Kahn Family." Discuss the following questions, and then do the activity:

   • How was Gordon Kahn caught up in events beyond his control?

   • What alternatives did Gordon have? Do you think he chose the right path? Explain your opinion.

**Cooperative Learning Activity**  With a small group, create a step-by-step flowchart to show how Gordon Kahn's life, reputation, and career were ruined by blacklisting.

*Cold War Conflicts*  **631**

 Formal Assessment
· Chapter Test, Forms A, B, and C, pp. 342–353

## ALTERNATIVE ASSESSMENT

**1. INTERACT WITH HISTORY**

**Rubrics**

The speech. . .

· should focus on the issue of constitutional rights

· use specific details to support the speaker's position

· employ oral skills and use persuasive techniques

**2. LEARNING FROM MEDIA**

**Rubrics**

The flow chart should. . .

· be organized chronologically

· clearly describe events

· show cause-and-effect relationships

# The Postwar Boom

| | CHAPTER OVERVIEW | COPYMASTERS | INTEGRATED TECHNOLOG |
|---|---|---|---|
| **CHAPTER RESOURCES** | *Postwar America experiences an economic boom fueled by consumer spending that is spurred by the mass media, especially television. But many find themselves mired in poverty and stifled by discrimination.* | 📄 **Telescoping the Times** · Chapter Summary, pp. 37–38  📄 **Planning for Block Schedules** | 🔊 America's Music CD  👁 Power Presentations  👁 Electronic Teacher Tools  ℹ Online Lesson Planner  ℹ classzone.com |
| **SECTION 1** **The Postwar Boom** pp. 634–640 | **KEY IDEAS** *As Americans try to put the nightmare of World War II behind them and begin rebuilding their lives, the economy booms and the country becomes conservative.* | 📄 **In-Depth Resources: Unit 5** · Guided Reading, p. 66 · Building Vocabulary, p. 70 · Reteaching Activity, p. 72 · Primary Sources, p. 78 · American Lives, p. 85  📄 **Lesson Plans**, pp. 151–152 | 💿 Electronic Library of Primary Sources · Desegregation at Central High School by Melba Pattillo Beals · Desegregation at Central High School by Craig Rains  ℹ classzone.com |
| **SECTION 2** **The American Dream in the Fifties** pp. 641–651 | *Many Americans find their dream of material comfort and economic prosperity realized. But some find the cost too high.* | 📄 **In-Depth Resources: Unit 5** · Guided Reading, p. 67 · Reteaching Activity, p. 73 · Geography Application, pp. 76–77 · Primary Sources, p. 79 · Literature, pp. 82–83  📄 **Lesson Plans**, pp. 153–154 | 📥 Geography Transparencies GT27 · Highway Systems, 1950 and 2987  📥 Critical Thinking Transparencies CT61 · Urban-Suburban Growth Rates  📥 Humanities Transparencies HT43 · Highway Construction  👁 Electronic Library of Primary Sources · from *The Feminine Mystique*  ℹ classzone.com |
| **SECTION 3** **Popular Culture** pp. 652–659 | *Mass popular culture booms, largely because of television. While the media generally reflect mainstream middle-class values, a vital counterculture flourishes.* | 📄 **In-Depth Resources: Unit 5** · Guided Reading, p. 68 · Skillbuilder Practice, p. 71 · Reteaching Activity, p. 74 · Literature, p. 84 · American Lives, p. 86  📄 **Lesson Plans**, pp. 155–156 | 🔊 America's Music CD  ℹ classzone.com |
| **SECTION 4** **The Other America** pp. 660–663 | *Many Americans suffer from poverty and racial discrimination, despite unprecedented economic prosperity in the nation.* | 📄 **In-Depth Resources: Unit 5** · Guided Reading, p. 69 · Reteaching Activity, p. 75 · Primary Sources, pp. 80–81  📄 **Lesson Plans**, pp. 157–158 | 📥 Critical Thinking Transparencies CT27 · Postwar Boom  📥 Humanities Transparencies HT26 · "Her World" by Philip Evergood  👁 Electronic Library of Primary Sources · from *The Other America*  ℹ classzone.com |

Key symbols legend:

P.E Pupil's Edition  
TE Teacher's Edition  
Copymaster  
Overhead Transparency  
Audio Library  
CD-ROM  
Internet

## ASSESSMENT OPTIONS

P.E Chapter Assessment, pp. 664–665

Formal Assessment
- Chapter Tests, Forms A, B, and C, pp. 354–369

Test Generator

Integrated Assessment Book

TAKS Online Test Practice

TAKS Spiraled Content Review

TAKS Practice Tests

---

P.E Section 1 Assessment, p. 640

TE Self-Assessment, p. 640

Formal Assessment, Quiz, p. 354

Integrated Assessment Book

Test Generator

TAKS Practice Transparencies TT102

---

P.E Section 2 Assessment, p. 649

TE Self-Assessment, p. 649

Formal Assessment, Quiz, p. 355

Integrated Assessment Book

Test Generator

TAKS Practice Transparencies TT103

---

P.E Section 3 Assessment, p. 657

TE Self-Assessment, p. 657

Formal Assessment, Quiz, p. 356

Integrated Assessment Book

Test Generator

TAKS Practice Transparencies TT104

---

P.E Section 4 Assessment, p. 663

TE Self-Assessment, p. 663

Formal Assessment, Quiz, p. 357

Integrated Assessment Book

Test Generator

TAKS Practice Transparencies TT105

## RESOURCES FOR DIFFERENTIATING INSTRUCTION

### Students Acquiring English/ESL

Reading Study Guide: (English and Spanish) pp. 191–200

Access for Students Acquiring English/ESL: Spanish Translations, pp. 207–215

Chapter Summaries on CD (English and Spanish)

### Less Proficient Readers

Reading Study Guide (English and Spanish) pp. 191–200

Telescoping the Times
- Chapter Summary, pp. 37–38

Chapter Summaries on CD (English and Spanish)

### Gifted and Talented Students

In-Depth Resources: Unit 5
- Primary Sources, pp. 78–81
- Literature, pp. 82–84
- American Lives, pp. 85–86

Electronic Library of Primary Sources
- Unit 5, Chapter 19

## CROSS-CURRICULAR CONNECTIONS

### Civics
Cohen, Daniel. *Joseph McCarthy: The Misuse of Political Power.* Brookfield, CT: Millbrook, 1996. A fair, well-told biography of the most feared man of his era.

### Humanities: Music
Shirley, David. *The History of Rock and Roll.* NY: Watts, 1997. From Elvis to Nirvana, this book provides an overview of the singers and groups that led the rock 'n' roll revolution.

### Humanities: Art
Phillips, Lisa. *The American Century: Art and Culture, 1950–2000.* NY: W.W. Norton, 1999. This catalog for an exhibit at the Whitney Museum of Art provides an overview of American art in the second half of the century. Contains short sidebars on topics such as Hollywood, modern dance, and music.

### Literature
Dillard, Annie. *An American Childhood.* NY: Harper Perennial, 1993. This outstanding autobiography traces the author's development from preschool through her teenage years. It is filled with joyful and humorous memories of growing up in the 1950s.

### McDougal Littell
### Literature Connections

Hansberry, Lorraine. *A Raisin in the Sun (with related readings).* Set in Chicago in the 1950s, this three-act play explores the struggles of an African-American family that dreams of owning a house. The racism they encounter and their own family tensions and anger lead them to examine what is truly important in their lives.

Rivera, Tomás. *. . . And The Earth Did Not Devour Him.* A classic of Chicano literature, this novel offers impressions of a community of South Texas migrant workers who go north to pick crops after World War II.

## ENRICHMENT ACTIVITIES

P.E Pupil's Edition, pp. 632–663
Interact with History, pp. 632–633
Geography Spotlight, pp. 650–651
Daily Life, pp. 658–659

In-Depth Resources: Unit 5
- Geography Application: The Baby Boom, pp. 76–77
- Primary Source: Cartoon, p. 78
- Primary Source: *The Organization Man*, p. 79
- Primary Source: *The Other America*, p. 80
- Primary Source: The Voluntary Relocation Program, p. 81

- Literature: from *The Man in the Gray Flannel Suit* by Sloan Wilson, pp. 82–83
- Literature: from *1959* by Thulani David, p. 84
- American Lives: Jackie Robinson, p. 85
- American Lives: Milton Berle, p. 86

Electronic Library of Primary Sources
- Unit 5, Chapter 19

America's Music CD

## BLOCK SCHEDULE LESSON PLAN OPTIONS (90-MINUTE PERIOD)

### DAY 1

**CHAPTER OPENER**
pp. 632–633

**Class Time** 20 minutes

**History from Visuals, p. 632**

**Class Time** 10 minutes

*Options for Pacing and Variety*

· **Time Saver** Ask students to look at the photograph; ask them the related questions in the TE.
**Class Time** 10 minutes

**Interact with History, p. 633**

**Class Time** 10 minutes

*Options for Pacing and Variety*

· **Role-Playing** Have students read about the postwar period and discuss the questions. Ask students if they think that during the postwar years people's dreams became simpler or more complicated.
**Class Time** 10 minutes

**SECTION 1 pp. 634–640**

**Class Time** 35 minutes

*Options for Pacing and Variety*

· **Peer Teaching** Have students work in pairs to complete the activity on TE page 636 on understanding cause and effect in relation to the economic recovery.
**Class Time** 20 minutes

· **Time Saver** Have students look at the map of the election of 1948 on page 638 and ask them the questions in the PE and TE, including the extension question.
**Class Time** 10 minutes

### DAY 1 continued

· **Peer Evaluation** Have students form groups to share and discuss their answers to the questions in the previous activity.
**Class Time** 20 minutes

**SECTION 2 pp. 641-651**

**Class Time** 35 minutes

*Options for Pacing and Variety*

· **Internet** Have students read from Betty Friedan's *The Feminine Mystique* according to the activity on TE page 644. Then have them conduct Internet or library research to find reviews on the book and its influence. Discuss findings in class.
**Class Time** 30 minutes

· **Peer Teaching** Have students work in pairs to complete the Section Assessment and then work individually to write a paragraph describing the American dream in the 1950s.
**Class Time** 20 minutes

· **Time Saver** Ask students to read the feature on pages 650–651, "Geography Spotlight: The Road to Suburbia." Discuss question 1 of the Thinking Critically questions. Then relate the discussion about public transportation to the advent of the idea that owning a car was a necessary part of family life. Also discuss the questions in Making Personal Connections in the TE.
**Class Time** 15 minutes

### DAY 2

**SECTION 3 pp. 652–659**

**Class Time** 30 minutes

*Options for Pacing and Variety*

· **Time Saver** Ask students to look at the graphs on television ownership and viewership on page 653. Then discuss the Skillbuilder questions along with the discussion question in the TE. **Class Time** 10 minutes

· **Peer Evaluation** Have students work on the Section Assessment on their own and then discuss their answers in groups.
**Class Time** 20 minutes

· **Peer Teaching** Ask students to read the feature on pages 658–659, "Daily Life 1950–1960," and work in small groups to discuss the questions on the second page.
**Class Time** 15 minutes

**SECTION 4 pp. 660–663**

**Class Time** 30 minutes

*Options for Pacing and Variety*

· **Time Saver** Ask students to read both selections of "A Personal Voice." In discussion, compare and contrast the thematic and topical concerns of Baldwin and Harrington, viewpoints, and tone of voice.
**Class Time** 15 minutes

· **Humanities Transparencies** Have students view Humanities Transparency 22, "A relief center in Louisville, Kentucky." Then discuss the irony in the photograph—the contrast between America's propagandized prosperity and the actual lives of the poor. **Class Time** 15 minutes

### DAY 2 continued

· **Peer Teaching** Have students work in pairs to complete the Section Assessment and then discuss questions 3 and 5 with the class.
**Class Time** 25 minutes

**ASSESSMENT**
pp. 664–665

**Class Time** 30 minutes

*Options for Pacing and Variety*

· **Peer Teaching** Have students work in pairs on the Main Ideas questions, as well as on Terms & Names. Ask them to record the page numbers for answers they had to look up. **Class Time** 15 minutes

· **Time Saver** Have students do the Critical Thinking questions for homework and then collect the papers and discuss questions 2 and 3 with the class. In the discussion, ask students whether they feel American culture is still very conformist and have them speculate on the reasons why this is so. Have them think particularly about the reasons why this trend began, about which they read about in Section 2.
**Class Time** 15 minutes

---

**TEACHER-TESTED ACTIVITY**     Suzanne Cook, Scarborough High School, Houston, Texas

**CROSSWORD PUZZLES OF POSTWAR TERMS**

**Class Time** 45 minutes

**Task** Creating a crossword puzzle

**Purpose** To reinforce knowledge of vocabulary associated with the postwar boom

**Supplies Needed**

· Internet access or lined paper

**Activity** Have students use 20 terms and corresponding definitions from Chapter 19 to create a crossword puzzles. Next the students should find a puzzle maker Web site by entering the key word "puzzle" in a search engine. Tell them to enter their terms and definitions. Have students print out their puzzles and exchange them with partners. Students without Internet access may list terms on one side of a sheet of paper and definitions on the other. Partners may use the sheets to quiz each other.

# CHAPTER 19 CORRELATION

## CORRELATION TO THE TEXAS ESSENTIAL KNOWLEDGE AND SKILLS

Chapter 19 addresses the following standards of the Texas Essential Knowledge and Skills for U.S. History.

| TEKS | Instruction | Student Question/Activity |
|---|---|---|
| **(4C)** Evaluate the impact of third parties and their candidates. | **PE 638** discussion of the emergence of the Dixiecrat Party during the 1948 presidential election | **TE 638** civics activity in which students examine more closely the role of third parties |
| **(6F)** Describe the impact of the GI Bill of Rights. | **PE 635** examination of the GI Bill of Rights and how it aided WWII veterans | **TE 635** cooperative learning activity in which students demonstrate the impact of the GI Bill of Rights |
| **(7A)** Trace the historical development of the civil rights movement in the 20th century. | **PE 637–638** analysis of President Truman's efforts to advance civil rights | **PE 640** Critical Thinking question about the differences between presidents Truman and Eisenhower regarding civil rights |
| **(11A)** Identify the effects of population growth on the physical environment. | **PE 643–645** discussion of the baby boom and its effect on the nation's landscape and culture | **PE 643** Skillbuilder questions requiring students to interpret baby boom graph |
| **(20A)** Describe how the characteristics and issues of various eras in U.S. history have been reflected in works of art, music, and literature. | **PE 655–657** examination of the emergence of the beat movement and rock 'n' roll as a backlash against mainstream society | **PE 657** Critical Thinking question about the beat movement and rock 'n' roll |
| **(20D)** Analyze the relationship between culture and the economy and identify examples such as the impact of the entertainment industry on the U.S. economy. | **PE 652–655** discussion of the rise of television and its impact on American society | **TE 653** cooperative learning activity about the impact of television on family life |
| **(21D)** Identify the political, social, and economic contributions of women to American society. | **PE 644–645** examination of women's roles in the 1950s and their increasing entry into the workforce | **TE 644** activity asking students to read and analyze the significant women's book *The Feminine Mystique* |

## TAKS MINI-LESSONS

1. **Social Studies Skills: Objective 1 (US6.F):** Describe the impact of the GI Bill of Rights **Activity** Have students conduct research to find out how many Americans took advantage of the GI Bill.

2. **Social Studies Skills: Objective 3 (US22.A):** Explain the effects of scientific discoveries and technological innovations, such as medical vaccinations **Activity** Have students discuss why Dr. Jonas Salk's polio vaccination was so significant.

3. **Social Studies Skills: Objective 3 (US23.A):** Analyze how scientific discoveries and technological innovations, including those in transportation, have changed the standard of living in the United States **Activity** Have students create a chart detailing how the growth of the automobile simultaneously raised and lowered the standard of living in America.

4. **English Language Arts Skills: Objective 2 (11.E):** Connect literature to historical contexts **Activity** Have students discuss how the excerpt from *On the Road* on page 655 demonstrated a backlash against 1950s society.

5. **English Language Arts Skills: Objective 3 (7.E):** Analyze text structures such as cause/effect to see how they influence meaning **Activity** Have students list the causes and effects of the postwar economic boom from the text and graph on page 636.

# THE POSTWAR BOOM

CHAPTER 19

## HISTORY from VISUALS

### Interpreting the Photograph

Have students examine the photograph. Ask them what backyards provided for homeowners and how suburban families might relax in different ways from city families. (*Backyards provided a place to relax with some privacy. City families would need to sit on front steps or go to a park where they would encounter other people.*)

## Time Line Discussion

Explain to students that the time line covers events in the United States and the world during the postwar years from 1946 to 1960.

· Ask students who was president during most of the 1950s. (*Dwight D. Eisenhower*)

· Ask students which were the last two states to enter the union. (*Alaska and Hawaii*)

· Ask students which two events had a major impact on civil rights in America. (*Jackie Robinson integrating baseball in 1947 and the* Brown v. Board of Education *case in 1954*)

· Ask students what important events occurred in science and technology during these years. (*USSR opens first small nuclear power plant in 1954; Soviets launch Sputnik 1 in 1957; NASA is established in 1958.*)

In the 1950s, the backyard was the perfect place for suburban homeowners to relax.

**1946** Baby boom begins.

**1947** Jackie Robinson integrates major league baseball.

**1948** Harry S. Truman is elected president.

**1950's** Disc jockey Alan Freed is the first to use the term "rock 'n' roll" on the air.

**1952** Dwight D. Eisenhower is elected president.

USA
WORLD

**1946**   **1948**   **1950**   **1952**

**1949** Mao Zedong's Communist forces gain control of China.

**1950** Korean War begins.

## THEMES IN CHAPTER 19

### WOMEN AND POLITICAL POWER

The ideal woman of the 1950s was a wife, mother, and homemaker. Many suburban housewives, however, felt dissatisfied and bored with their lack of identity.

**See Teacher's Edition note, p. 644.**

### ECONOMIC OPPORTUNITY

The economic boom of the postwar years brought prosperity to millions of Americans. However, the nation experienced a recession during 1957-1958, and the national debt rose.

**See Teacher's Edition note, p. 647.**

### SCIENCE AND TECHNOLOGY

The rapid rise of television in the 1950s affected many aspects of American life. Television provided entertainment and information, but critics objected to the stereotypes and violence it presented.

**See Teacher's Edition note, p. 654.**

### DIVERSITY AND NATIONAL IDENTITY

Thousands of Mexican Americans and Native Americans fought for the United States in World War II. After the war, these citizens faced discrimination in a society that ignored the rights of minorities.

**See Teacher's Edition note, p. 662.**

## INTERACT
### WITH HISTORY

You have returned home from serving in World War II to find that your country is changing. The cities have swelled. Outlying suburbs are being built up with almost identical homes. America produces more and cheaper goods. In a booming economy, couples marry and start families in record numbers. As you watch clever ads on TV for the newest labor-saving gadgets, you feel nostalgia for a simpler time.

# What is the American dream of the 1950s?

### Examine the Issues

- How does pressure to conform affect the American dream?
- Who might be excluded from the new prosperity?
- How does advertising promote certain lifestyles and ideals?

**RESEARCH LINKS** CLASSZONE.COM

Visit the Chapter 19 links for more information about The Postwar Boom.

## INTERACT
### WITH HISTORY

### Objectives

· To help students understand the prevailing social values of the postwar period
· To explore the impact of foreign tensions on domestic life in America

### Examine the Issues

1. Have students think about social groups at school and about tastes in clothing, music, and other name-brand merchandise.
2. Ask students if the lifestyle shown on television shows and in advertisements is available to everyone in the United States. Discuss how poor people might feel in an environment of conspicuous consumption.
3. Discuss the subtly persuasive message of television programming and advertising and how it affects the viewer.

---

| | | | |
|---|---|---|---|
| **1953** Korean War ceasefire is signed. | **1954** *Brown v. Board of Education of Topeka* outlaws school segregation. | **1956** Eisenhower is reelected. | **1958** NASA— the National Aeronautics and Space Administration— is established. | **1959** Alaska and Hawaii become the 49th and 50th states. | **1960** John F. Kennedy is elected president. |

**1954**      **1956**      **1958**      **1960**

**1954** U.S.S.R. opens the first small nuclear power plant.

**1956** Soviets crush uprising in Hungary.

**1957** Soviets launch Sputnik 1.

**1959** Fidel Castro comes to power in Cuba.

*The Postwar Boom* **633**

---

## RECOMMENDED RESOURCES

### BOOKS FOR THE TEACHER

Goldman, Eric F. *The Crucial Decade and After.* New York: Knopf, 1965. History of social and political changes.

Halberstam, David. *The Fifties.* New York: Villard, 1993. Study of all aspects of American life and culture.

Katz, Donald. *Home Fires.* New York: Harper Collins, 1992. A real family's adjustment to postwar life and beyond.

### BOOKS FOR THE STUDENT

Barnouw, Erik. *Tube of Plenty.* 2nd ed. New York: Oxford UP, 1990. History of television and its impact.

Kytle, Elizabeth, ed. *Willa Mae.* Athens: U of Georgia P, 1993. An African-American woman recalls segregation.

*The American Dream: The 50s.* New York: Time-Life, 1998. Visual collection of life during the 1950s.

### VIDEOS

*Avalon.* Dir. Barry Levinson. RCA/Columbia Pictures Home Video, 1991. Several generations of immigrants move from poverty to prosperity and adapt to world changes.

*The Best Years of Our Lives.* Dir. William Wyler. 1946. HBO Home Video. Gripping story of GIs returning home.

### SOFTWARE

*American Chronicles Series: Age of Anxiety (1952-1958)* and *Fragile Balance (1955-1961).* CD-ROM. AIMS Media.

### INTEGRATED TECHNOLOGY

For teacher support, visit . . .

 classzone.com

# Postwar America

| MAIN IDEA | WHY IT MATTERS NOW | Terms & Names |
|---|---|---|
| The Truman and Eisenhower administrations led the nation to make social, economic, and political adjustments following World War II. | In the years after World War II, the United States became the economic and military power that it still is today. | • GI Bill of Rights  • Dixiecrat<br>• suburb  • Fair Deal<br>• Harry S. Truman |

 U.S. History 1B, 4C, 6E, 6F, 7A, 7C, 8A, 14B, 17A, 18A, 19A, 19B, 19C, 24B, 24G, 24H, 25A, 25B, 25C, 25D

**One American's Story**

Sam Gordon had been married less than a year when he was shipped overseas in July 1943. As a sergeant in the United States Army, he fought in Belgium and France during World War II. Arriving back home in November 1945, Sam nervously anticipated a reunion with his family. A friend, Donald Katz, described Sam's reactions.

**A PERSONAL VOICE** DONALD KATZ

" Sam bulled through the crowd and hailed a taxi. The cab motored north through the warm autumn day as he groped for feelings appropriate to being back home alive from a terrible war. . . . [He was] nearly panting under the weight of fear. . . . *Back home alive . . . married to a girl I haven't seen since 1943 . . . father of a child I've never seen at all.*"

— Home Fires

▲ GIs returned home to their families after World War II with new hope, but also with new problems.

Sam Gordon met his daughter, Susan, for the first time the day he returned home from the war, and he went to work the next morning. Like many other young couples, the Gordons began to put the nightmare of the war behind them and to return to normality.

## **1** Readjustment and Recovery

By the summer of 1946, about 10 million men and women had been released from the armed forces. Veterans like Sam Gordon—along with the rest of American society—settled down to rebuild their lives.

**634** CHAPTER 19

---

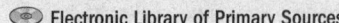

**TAKS**

Mini-Lesson 1:
SS11 1(US6.F)

**THE IMPACT OF THE GI BILL** To help ease veterans' return to civilian life, Congress passed the Servicemen's Readjustment Act, or the **GI Bill of Rights,** in 1944. In addition to encouraging veterans to get an education by paying part of their tuition, the GI Bill guaranteed them a year's worth of unemployment benefits while job hunting. It also offered low-interest, federally guaranteed loans. Millions of young families used these benefits to buy homes and farms or to establish businesses.

**HOUSING CRISIS** In 1945 and 1946, returning veterans faced a severe housing shortage. Many families lived in cramped apartments or moved in with relatives. In response to this housing crisis, developers like William Levitt and Henry Kaiser used efficient, assembly-line methods to mass-produce houses. Levitt, who bragged that his company could build a house in 16 minutes, offered homes in small residential communities surrounding cities, called **suburbs,** for less than $7,000.

▲ The suburbs were a mass phenomenon, even on moving day.

Levitt's first postwar development—rows of standardized homes built on treeless lots—was located on New York's Long Island and named Levittown. These homes looked exactly alike, and certain zoning laws ensured that they would stay the same. Despite their rigid conformity, Americans loved the openess and small-town feel to the planned suburbs. With the help of the GI Bill, many veterans and their families moved in and cultivated a new lifestyle.

**REDEFINING THE FAMILY** Tension created by changes in men's and women's roles after the war contributed to a rising divorce rate. Traditionally, men were the breadwinners and heads of households, while women were expected to stay home and care for the family. During the war, however, about 8 million women, 75 percent of whom were married, entered the paid work force. These women supported their families and made important household decisions. Many were reluctant to give up their newfound independence when their husbands returned. By 1950, more than a million war marriages had ended in divorce.

**ECONOMIC READJUSTMENT** After World War II, the United States converted from a wartime to a peacetime economy. The U.S. government immediately canceled war contracts totaling $35 billion. Within ten days of Japan's surrender, more than a million defense workers were laid off. Unemployment increased as veterans joined laid-off defense workers in the search for jobs. At the peak of postwar unemployment, in March 1946, nearly 3 million people were seeking work.

**Background**
See *unemployment rate* on page R47 in the Economics Handbook.

Rising unemployment was not the nation's only postwar economic problem, however. During the war, the Office of Price Administration (OPA) had halted inflation by imposing maximum prices on goods. When these controls ended on June 30, 1946, prices skyrocketed. In the next two weeks, the cost of consumer products soared 25 percent, double the increase of the previous three years. In some cities, consumers stood in long lines, hoping to buy scarce items, such as sugar, coffee, and beans. Prices continued to rise for the next two years until the supply of goods caught up with the demand.

---

**MAIN IDEA**

**Identifying Problems**
Ⓐ What problems did Americans face after World War II?

*A. Answer* Housing shortages, employment, readjustment to family life, rising inflation and lower wages, and shortages of goods.

While prices spiraled upward, many American workers also earned less than they had earned during the war. To halt runaway inflation and to help the nation convert to a peacetime economy, Congress eventually reestablished controls similar to the wartime controls on prices, wages, and rents. Ⓐ

---

**More About . . .**

**Levittown**
Levitt & Sons' first development consisted of 2,000 homes that the company rented to married veterans at $65 a month. These homes had two bedrooms and a bathroom; a kitchen equipped with a refrigerator, stove, and washing machine; a living room; and an attic that could be made into additional bedrooms.

**More About . . .**

**Postwar Inflation**
The conversion from a war economy to a peacetime economy is never easy. With still-recent memories of the Depression, Americans were badly frightened by the economic dislocations following the end of the war. People were unemployed again, and the cost of living was skyrocketing. But once the conversion was made to a consumer economy, prices leveled off and incomes caught up. A period of tremendous economic growth began. The build-up of the defense budget to meet the challenges of the Cold War helped both to support employment and to increase the national debt.

📄 In-Depth Resources: Unit 5
· Primary Source: Political Cartoon, p. 78

*The Postwar Boom* **635**

---

**Exploring Postwar Life**

**Class Time** 45 minutes

**Task** Creating one of the following items for a museum exhibit about postwar issues: a song, essay, letter, series of fictional journal entries, cartoon, or news report

**Purpose** To understand social and economic issues in the United States after World War II

**Directions** Have groups of students choose one of the following topics: GI Bill, housing shortage, family roles, or economic problems. Each group should use one of the suggested formats to represent the impact of their topic on American society in the postwar era. Students' contributions to the exhibit should include both a visual and a written component.

 **Integrated Assessment**
· Rubric 1

**REMARKABLE RECOVERY** Most economists who had forecast a postwar depression were proved wrong because they had failed to consider consumers' pent-up accumulation of needs and wants. People had gone without many goods for so long that by the late 1940s, with more than $135 billion in savings from defense work, service pay, and investments in war bonds, Americans suddenly had money to spend. They snatched up everything from automobiles to houses. After a brief period of postwar economic readjustment, the American economy boomed. The demand for goods and services outstripped the supply and increased production, which created new jobs. Judging from the graphs (shown left), many Americans prospered in the 1950s in what the economist John Kenneth Galbraith called "the affluent society."

The Cold War also contributed to economic growth. Concern over Soviet expansion kept American defense spending high and people employed. Foreign-aid programs, such as the Marshall Plan, provided another boost to the American economy. By helping nations in Western Europe recover from the war, the United States helped itself by creating strong foreign markets for its exports. **B**

## HISTORY from VISUALS

### Interpreting the Graphs

Ask students to identify the years each indicator grew the most quickly and the most slowly (or fell). *(Homes: quickly 1950–56; slowly 1956–60. Autos: quickly 1952–54; slowly 1954–56. Incomes: quickly 1950–52; slowly 1952–54 or 1956–58. Savings: quickly 1960–62; slowly 1958–60)* Ask students what patterns they see in the growth indicators. What might explain the fast and slow growth? *(Sharp demand for homes and cars after the war reflected the return to a peacetime economy. There were little savings until many homes and cars had been purchased.)*

### Instruct: Objective

**Meeting Economic Challenges**
TAKS SS11 5(US24.B)

· How did Truman handle strikes by miners and railroad workers?

· What caused voters to elect a conservative Republican Congress in 1946?

 In-Depth Resources: Unit 5
· Guided Reading, p. 66

---

### A Dynamic Economy

**Home Ownership**

(Millions of Homeowners: axis 20, 25, 30, 35; years 1950, 1952, 1954, 1956, 1958, 1960)

**Automobile Registrations**

(Millions of Registrations: axis 40, 50, 60, 70; years 1950, 1952, 1954, 1956, 1958, 1960)

**Median Family Income**

(Income in Dollars: axis 3000, 4000, 5000, 6000; years 1950, 1952, 1954, 1956, 1958, 1960)

**Savings Accounts**

(Billions of Dollars: axis 0, 5, 10, 15, 20, 25; years 1950, 1952, 1954, 1956, 1958, 1960, 1962)

Source: *Historical Statistics of the United States, Colonial times to 1970*

#### SKILLBUILDER
**Interpreting Graphs**
1. From 1950 to 1960, by what percentage did each of the economic indicators shown above increase?
2. Which years show the biggest increases for each of the graphs above?

---

## 2 Meeting Economic Challenges

Despite an impressive recovery, Americans faced a number of economic problems. Their lives had been in turmoil throughout the war, and a desire for stability made the country more conservative.

**PRESIDENT TRUMAN'S INHERITANCE** When **Harry S. Truman** suddenly became president after Franklin D. Roosevelt's death in 1945, he asked Roosevelt's widow, Eleanor, whether there was anything he could do for her. She replied, "Is there anything we can do for you? For you are the one in trouble now." In many ways, President Truman was in trouble.

### A PERSONAL VOICE HARRY S. TRUMAN

" I don't know whether you fellows ever had a load of hay fall on you, but when they told me yesterday what had happened [Roosevelt's death], I felt like the moon, the stars, and all the planets had fallen on me."

—excerpt from a speech, April 13, 1945

Despite his lack of preparation for the job, Truman was widely viewed as honorable, down-to-earth, and self-confident. Most important of all, he had the ability to make difficult decisions and to accept full responsibility for their consequences. As the plaque on his White House desk read, "The Buck Stops Here." Truman faced two huge challenges: dealing with the rising threat of communism, as discussed in Chapter 18, and restoring the American economy to a strong footing after the war's end.

---

**MAIN IDEA**

**Analyzing Causes**
**B** What factors contributed to the American postwar economic boom?

**B. Answer** The GI bill, which offered veterans low-interest loans and education benefits; wage, price, and rent controls; the Cold War, military build-up, and foreign aid programs, such as the Marshall Plan; savings, and a desire for consumer products.

*Skillbuilder Answers*
1. Home ownership—38%; Automobile registrations—50%; Income—75%; Savings—400%
2. Home ownership—1952–1954; Automobile Registrations—1952–1954; Median Family Income—1954–1956; Savings Accounts—1960–1962.

---

**DIFFERENTIATING INSTRUCTION** | **LESS PROFICIENT READERS**

### Understanding Cause and Effect

Help students to understand the economic recovery of the postwar era by making a list of causes and effects. Have them draw a line down the page and write *Causes* on the left side and *Effects* on the right. Make *Postwar Recovery* the heading. As the students read the section "Remarkable Recovery," see that they record "pent-up accumulation of needs and wants" and "savings from defense work, service pay, and investments in war bonds" and "American defense spending" as causes. Then, see they record demand for autos, appliances, and housing as effects.

| Postwar Recovery | |
|---|---|
| **Causes** | **Effects** |
| 1. | |
| 2. | |
| 3. | |
| 4. | |

**TRUMAN FACES STRIKES** One economic problem that Truman had to address was strikes. Facing higher prices and lower wages, 4.5 million discontented workers, including steelworkers, coal miners, and railroad workers, went on strike in 1946. Although he generally supported organized labor, Truman refused to let strikes cripple the nation. He threatened to draft the striking workers and to order them as soldiers to stay on the job. He authorized the federal government to seize the mines, and he threatened to take control of the railroads as well. Truman appeared before Congress and asked for the authority to draft the striking railroad workers into the army. Before he could finish his speech, the unions gave in. **C**

**MAIN IDEA**

**Summarizing**
**C** What actions did President Truman take to avert labor strikes?

**C. Answer**
Truman threatened to draft striking workers, keep them on the job as soldiers and to take control of the railroads and mines.

**"HAD ENOUGH?"** Disgusted by shortages of goods, rising inflation, and labor strikes, Americans were ready for a change. The Republicans asked the public, "Had enough?" Voters gave their answer at the polls: in the 1946 congressional elections, the Republican Party won control of both the Senate and the House of Representatives for the first time since 1928. The new 80th Congress ignored Truman's domestic proposals. In 1947, Congress passed the Taft-Hartley Act over Truman's veto. This bill overturned many rights won by the unions under the New Deal.

### ❸ Social Unrest Persists

Problems arose not only in the economy but in the very fabric of society. After World War II, a wave of racial violence erupted in the South. Many African Americans, particularly those who had served in the armed forces during the war, demanded their rights as citizens.

**TRUMAN SUPPORTS CIVIL RIGHTS** Truman put his presidency on the line for civil rights. "I am asking for equality of opportunity for all human beings," he said, ". . . and if that ends up in my failure to be reelected, that failure will be in a good cause." In September 1946, Truman met with African-American leaders who proposed a federal anti-lynching law, abolition of the poll tax as a voting requirement, and the establishment of a permanent body to prevent racial discrimination in hiring.

**Vocabulary**
**discrimination:** treatment based on class or category rather than individual merit

Congress refused to pass these measures, or a measure to integrate the armed forces. As a result, Truman himself took action. In July 1948, he issued an executive order for integration of the armed forces, calling for "equality of treatment and opportunity in the armed forces without regard to race, color, religion, or national origin." In addition, he ordered an end to discrimination in the hiring of government employees. The Supreme Court also ruled that the lower courts could not bar

In 1947, Jackie Robinson joined the ▶ Brooklyn Dodgers, angering some fans but winning the hearts, and respect, of many others.

---

**HISTORICAL**
**SPOTLIGHT**

**JACKIE ROBINSON**

Jackie Robinson took a brave step when he turned the Brooklyn Dodgers into an integrated baseball team in 1947. But he—and the country—had a long way to go.

Unhappy fans hurled insults at Robinson from the stands. Some players on opposing teams tried to hit him with pitches or to injure him with the spikes on their shoes. He even received death threats. But he endured this with poise and restraint, saying,

"Plenty of times, I wanted to haul off when somebody insulted me for the color of my skin but I had to hold to myself. I knew I was kind of an experiment."

In 1949, Robinson was voted the National League's most valuable player. He later became the first African American to be inducted into the Baseball Hall of Fame.

---

**More About . . .**

**Harry S. Truman**
When Truman took office, the nation was in shock from the war and the death of Roosevelt. Next to the urbane, aristocratic Roosevelt, Truman paled in comparison. Though his popularity rose enough to get him elected in 1948, he was for most of the time an embattled president. Years later, his reputation grew. He came to be viewed as an honest, direct leader, who guided the nation through an exceptionally treacherous period.

**HISTORICAL SPOTLIGHT**

**Jackie Robinson**
Jackie Robinson was a complete player—a great hitter and a versatile fielder who started at four different positions in his major league career. But it was his base running that had perhaps the greatest impact. Once on base, Robinson was a master at distracting pitchers. Ask students how they think Robinson managed to contain his emotions when fans and opposing players taunted him. *(He knew that he had to stay composed because he was an experiment.)*

 **In-Depth Resources: Unit 5**
· American Lives: Jackie Robinson, p. 85

**Instruct: Objective ❸**
**Social Unrest Persists**
TAKS SS11 5(WH26.C)
· How did Truman deal with civil rights?
· How did the civil rights issue affect the Democratic Party in the election of 1948?
· What was Truman's Fair Deal and how was it received in Congress?

 **In-Depth Resources: Unit 5**
· Guided Reading, p. 66

---

**ACTIVITY** **COOPERATIVE LEARNING**

 **classzone.com**

**Researching the Negro Leagues**

**Class Time** 45 minutes

**Task** Researching the history of African Americans in baseball before integration

**Purpose** To expand and deepen students' appreciation for the history of African Americans

**Directions** Divide the class into small groups. Have the groups use the Internet to research aspects of the Negro Leagues that flourished before integration, including notable teams and important players, such as Josh Gibson, Satchel Paige, Buck O'Neill, and Cool Papa Bell. Ask students to look into how the National Baseball Hall of Fame honors players from this era.

## HISTORY from VISUALS

### Interpreting the Painting

Help students to see the direct message of the painting. Ask students why they think white Southerners were so resistant to civil rights for African Americans. *(White Southerners felt threatened by any effort that would give full rights to African Americans. It challenged their ideas of racial superiority and threatened their political control.)*

▲
**Wipe Out Discrimination** (1949), a poster by Milton Ackoff, depicts the civil rights consciousness that angered the Dixiecrats.

African Americans from residential neighborhoods. These actions represented the beginnings of a federal commitment to dealing with racial issues. **D**

**THE 1948 ELECTION** Although many Americans blamed Truman for the nation's inflation and labor unrest, the Democrats nominated him for president in 1948. To protest Truman's emphasis on civil rights, a number of Southern Democrats—who became known as **Dixiecrats**—formed the States' Rights Democratic Party, and nominated their own presidential candidate, Governor J. Strom Thurmond of South Carolina. Discontent reigned at the far left of the Democratic spectrum as well. The former vice-president Henry A. Wallace led his supporters out of mainstream Democratic ranks to form a more liberal Progressive Party.

As the election approached, opinion polls gave the Republican candidate, New York Governor Thomas E. Dewey, a comfortable lead. Refusing to believe the polls, Truman poured his energy into the campaign. First, he called the Republican-dominated Congress into a special session. He challenged it to pass laws supporting such elements of the Democratic Party platform as public housing, federal aid to education, a higher minimum wage, and extended Social Security coverage. Not one of these laws was passed. Then he took his campaign to the people. He traveled from one end of the country to the other by train, speaking from the rear platform in a sweeping "whistlestop campaign." Day after day, people heard the president denounce the "do-nothing, 80th Congress."

**STUNNING UPSET** Truman's "Give 'em hell, Harry" campaign worked. He won the election in a close political upset. The Democrats gained control of Congress as well, even though they suffered losses in the South, which had been solidly Democratic since Reconstruction.

| MAIN IDEA |
| --- |
| **Summarizing** **D** How did Truman use his executive power to advance civil rights? |

**D. Answer** Truman issued an executive order integrating the military after Congress refused to act.

*Skillbuilder Answers*
1. Truman—the West, the Midwest, and the South; Dewey—the Northwest, the Northeast, and the Midwest; Thurmond—the South.
2. The Northeast and the South.

## HISTORY from VISUALS

### Interpreting the Map

Tell students that Truman won the election because Thurmond was not able to sweep the South and Dewey did not win enough traditional Republican states in the Midwest and the West.

**Extension** Ask students why they think Truman was able to win despite the desertion of the Dixiecrats and Dewey's lead in the polls. *(Dewey was not a strong campaigner, but Truman was. He was able to convince enough Americans that the problems were the fault of the Republican "do-nothing" Congress.)*

### Presidential Election of 1948

Truman surprised the ▶ newspapers by winning the 1948 election.

\* Tennessee—11 electoral votes for Truman, 1 electoral vote for Thurmond

| Party | Candidate | Electoral Votes | Popular Votes |
| --- | --- | --- | --- |
| Democratic | Harry S. Truman | 303 | 24,179,000 |
| Republican | Thomas E. Dewey | 189 | 21,991,000 |
| States' Rights | J. Strom Thurmond | 39 | 1,176,000 |
| Progressive | Henry A. Wallace | — | 1,157,000 |

**GEOGRAPHY SKILLBUILDER**
1. **Region** In which regions of the country did Truman carry states? Dewey? Thurmond?
2. **Region** In which regions was support for Truman the weakest?

---

| ACTIVITY | LINK TO CIVICS |
| --- | --- |

### Examining the Role of Third Parties

**Class Time** 30 minutes

**Task** Comparing the role third parties played in two elections—1912 and 1948

**Purpose** To help students better understand the electoral process

**Directions** Have students examine the election of 1948 and the election of 1912, which they read about on pages 330 and 331. Ask them to compare how third parties influenced the results in each election. *(In 1912, the split in the Republican Party between Taft and Roosevelt resulted in Wilson's election. But in 1948 Truman was able to prevail despite the desertion of the Dixiecrats.)*

 Integrated Assessment
· Rubric 2

THE FAIR DEAL After his victory, Truman continued proposing an ambitious economic program. Truman's **Fair Deal,** an extension of Roosevelt's New Deal, included proposals for a nationwide system of compulsory health insurance and a crop-subsidy system to provide a steady income for farmers. In Congress, some Northern Democrats joined Dixiecrats and Republicans in defeating both measures.

In other instances, however, Truman's ideas prevailed. Congress raised the hourly minimum wage from 40 cents to 75 cents, extended Social Security coverage to about 10 million more people, and initiated flood control and irrigation projects. Congress also provided financial support for cities to clear out slums and build 810,000 housing units for low-income families.

**MAIN IDEA**

**Evaluating Leadership**

**E** What were some of Truman's achievements as president?

*E. Answer* He led the U.S. to final victory in World War II, dealt with labor disputes, and supported social programs and civil rights legislation.

## Republicans Take the Middle Road ④

Despite these social and economic victories, Truman's approval rating sank to an all-time low of 23 percent in 1951. The stalemate in the Korean War and the rising tide of McCarthyism, which cast doubt on the loyalty of some federal employees, became overwhelming issues. Truman decided not to run for reelection. The Democrats nominated the intellectual and articulate governor Adlai Stevenson of Illinois to run against the Republican candidate, General Dwight D. Eisenhower, known popularly as "Ike."

**I LIKE IKE!** During the campaign, the Republicans accused the Democrats of "plunder at home and blunder abroad." To fan the anti-Communist hysteria that was sweeping over the country, Republicans raised the specter of the rise of communism in China and Eastern Europe. They also criticized the growing power of the federal government and the alleged bribery and corruption among Truman's political allies.

Eisenhower's campaign hit a snag, however, when newspapers accused his running mate, California Senator Richard M. Nixon, of profiting from a secret slush fund set up by wealthy supporters. Nixon decided to reply to the charges. In an emotional speech to an audience of 58 million, now known as the "Checkers speech," he exhibited masterful use of a new medium—television. Nixon denied any wrongdoing, but he did admit to accepting one gift from a political supporter.

◀ Campaign accessories expressed Ike's popularity and voters' desire for a positive political change.

**Vocabulary**
**slush fund:** a fund often designated for corrupt practices, such as bribery

**A PERSONAL VOICE** RICHARD M. NIXON

" You know what it was? It was a little cocker spaniel dog in a crate, that he'd [the political supporter] sent all the way from Texas. Black and white spotted. And our little girl—Tricia, the six-year-old—named it Checkers. And you know the kids, like all kids, love the dog and I just want to say this right now, that regardless of what they say about it, we're going to keep it. "

—"Checkers speech," September 23, 1952

**Instruct: Objective** ④

**Republicans Take the Middle Road**
TAKS SS11 5(US24.A)

· Why did Truman not run for reelection in 1952?

· What kind of leadership style did Eisenhower bring to the presidency?

· What did Eisenhower's reelection in 1956 signify?

 In-Depth Resources: Unit 5
· Guided Reading, p. 66

**More About . . .**

**Election of 1952**
Many issues were working for Eisenhower and against Stevenson in the election. Polls revealed that the nation was tiring of the Korean War. Stevenson supported Truman's policies in Korea, but Eisenhower pledged to end the conflict. Also, Stevenson was victim of the American voters' periodic desire for change. The Democrats had been in power for 20 years. Many voters simply thought it was time for a change.

---

**DIFFERENTIATING INSTRUCTION**    **LESS PROFICIENT READERS**

**Analyzing Issues**

Help students clarify the important issues in the election of 1952, so that they will understand the swing away from the Democrats to the Republicans. Remind them that the Democrats had been in power for 20 years. Then, ask students to identify reasons and list them on the board. *(Issues include: Korean War stalemate; perceived loyalty of federal employees because of the anti-Communist hysteria; Communist victory in China and Eastern Europe; alleged bribery and corruption* *of Truman's political allies)* Review each issue with students and discuss how each one reflected badly on the incumbent party and presented opportunities for the Republicans.

 Integrated Assessment
· Rubric 2

## More About . . .

### Eisenhower and Civil Rights

Eisenhower did not exert strong leadership in the first school integration crisis, in Little Rock, Arkansas in 1957. Governor Orval Faubus had mobilized the Arkansas National Guard to prevent the integration of Little Rock Central High School. Eisenhower took no action until a federal judge ordered Faubus to withdraw the troops. Fearing violence, Eisenhower then sent 1,000 U.S. soldiers to Little Rock and put the Arkansas guardsmen under federal command. Troops patrolled the school for the rest of the year.

 Electronic Library of Primary Sources
· Desegregation at Central High School by Melba Pattillo Beals
· Desegregation at Central High School by Craig Rains

## Assess & Reteach

### SECTION 1 ASSESSMENT

Have students form groups to share and discuss their answers to all questions.

 Formal Assessment
· Section Quiz, p. 354

### SELF-ASSESSMENT

Have students write down the five most interesting things that they have learned from this section. Then, have them compare their lists with those of their classmates.

### RETEACH

Use the Guided Reading worksheet for Section 1 to help review the main ideas of the section.

 In-Depth Resources: Unit 5
· Reteaching Activity, p. 72

▲ Countering slush fund charges, Richard Nixon speaks to TV viewers about his daughters and their dog, Checkers.

Nixon's speech saved his place on the Republican ticket. In November 1952, Eisenhower won 55 percent of the popular vote and a majority of the electoral college votes, while the Republicans narrowly captured Congress.

**WALKING THE MIDDLE OF THE ROAD**
President Eisenhower's style of governing differed from that of the Democrats. His approach, which he called "dynamic conservatism," was also known as "Modern Republicanism." He called for government to be "conservative when it comes to money and liberal when it comes to human beings."

Eisenhower followed a middle-of-the-road course and avoided many controversial issues, but he could not completely sidestep a persistent domestic issue—civil rights—that gained national attention due to court rulings and acts of civil disobedience in the mid-1950s. The most significant judicial action occurred in 1954, when the Supreme Court ruled in *Brown* v. *Board of Education of Topeka* that public schools must be racially integrated. (See page 708.) In a landmark act of civil disobedience a year later, a black seamstress named Rosa Parks refused to give up her seat on a bus to a white man. Her arrest sparked a boycott of the entire Montgomery, Alabama, bus system. The civil rights movement had entered a new era.

Although Eisenhower did not assume leadership on civil rights issues, he accomplished much on the domestic scene. Shortly after becoming president, Eisenhower pressed hard for programs that would bring around a balanced budget and a cut in taxes. During his two terms, Ike's administration raised the minimum wage, extended Social Security and unemployment benefits, increased funding for public housing, and backed the creation of interstate highways and the Department of Health, Education, and Welfare. His popularity soared and he won reelection in 1956.

 **ASSESSMENT**

1. **TERMS & NAMES** For each term or name, write a sentence explaining its significance.
   - GI Bill of Rights
   - suburb
   - Harry S. Truman
   - Dixiecrat
   - Fair Deal

**MAIN IDEA**

2. **TAKING NOTES**
Create a time line of key events relating to postwar America. Use the dates below as a guide.

1946 1947 1948 1949     1952

Write a paragraph describing the effects of one of these events.

**CRITICAL THINKING**

3. **DRAWING CONCLUSIONS**
Do you think Eisenhower's actions reflected his philosophy of dynamic conservatism? Why or why not?
**Think About:**
   • the definition of dynamic conservatism
   • Eisenhower's actions on civil rights policies
   • Eisenhower's accomplishments on other domestic issues

4. **EVALUATING LEADERSHIP**
Why do you think most Americans went along with Eisenhower's conservative approach to domestic policy?

5. **CONTRASTING**
How did presidents Truman and Eisenhower differ regarding civil rights?

**640** CHAPTER 19

---

 **ASSESSMENT** Answers

**1. TERMS & NAMES**
GI Bill of Rights, p. 635
suburb, p. 635
Harry S. Truman, p. 636
Dixiecrat, p. 638
Fair Deal, p. 639

**· 2. TAKING NOTES**
1946—Postwar unemployment peaks; strikes breakout;

Republican Party controls the House and Senate; Truman appoints Committee on Civil Rights.
1947—Congress passes anti-union Taft-Hartley Act.
1948—Truman integrates the armed forces; Dixiecrats form States' Rights Democratic Party; Truman wins presidency.
1949—Jackie Robinson voted National League's Most Valuable Player.
1952—Eisenhower wins presidency.

Answers will differ and should focus on one event and its effects.

**3. DRAWING CONCLUSIONS**
**Yes**—He raised the minimum wage, extended social security and unemployment benefits, and increased funding for public housing. **No**—He did little to support civil rights.

**4. EVALUATING LEADERSHIP**
The Cold War caused many Americans to

seek security in traditional conservative values, and Eisenhower's approach had brought progress and prosperity.

**5. CONTRASTING**
Truman took action. He integrated the military, appointed a committee on civil rights, and had the 1948 Democratic Party's platform emphasize civil rights. Eisenhower did not believe that the federal government had a role to play in desegregation, but did uphold existing laws.

# The American Dream in the Fifties

| MAIN IDEA | WHY IT MATTERS NOW | Terms & Names |
|---|---|---|
| During the 1950s, the economy boomed, and many Americans enjoyed material comfort. | The "American dream," a notion that was largely shaped by the fifties, is still pursued today. | • conglomerate  • consumerism<br>• franchise  • planned obsolescence<br>• baby boom<br>• Dr. Jonas Salk |

**TEKS U.S. History**
1C, 8A, 11A, 14B, 20A, 21D, 22A, 22B, 22C, 23A, 23B, 24A, 24B, 24C, 24D, 24G, 24H, 25A, 25B, 25C, 25D

### One American's Story

Settled into her brand new house near San Diego, California, Carol Freeman felt very fortunate. Her husband Mark had his own law practice, and when their first baby was born, she became a full-time homemaker. She was living the American dream, yet Carol felt dissatisfied—as if there were "something wrong" with her because she was not happy.

**A PERSONAL VOICE** CAROL FREEMAN

" As dissatisfied as I was, and as restless, I remember so well this feeling [we] had at the time that the world was going to be your oyster. You were going to make money, your kids were going to go to good schools, everything was possible if you just did what you were supposed to do. The future was rosy. There was a tremendous feeling of optimism. . . . Much as I say it was hateful, it was also hopeful. It was an innocent time. "

—quoted in *The Fifties: A Women's Oral History*

▲
The dream woman of the 1950s was depicted in advertising and on TV as doing constant housework, but always with a smile.

After World War II ended, Americans turned their attention to their families and jobs. The economy prospered. New technologies and business ideas created fresh opportunities for many, and by the end of the decade Americans were enjoying the highest standard of living in the world. The American dream of a happy and successful life seemed within the reach of many people.

## ① The Organization and the Organization Man

During the 1950s, businesses expanded rapidly. By 1956, the majority of Americans no longer held blue-collar, or industrial, jobs. Instead, more people worked in higher-paid, white-collar positions—clerical, managerial, or professional occupations. Unlike blue-collar workers, who manufactured goods for sale, white-collar workers tended to perform services in fields like sales, advertising, insurance, and communications.

*The Postwar Boom* **641**

---

## OBJECTIVES

1 Explain how changes in business affected workers.

2 Describe the suburban lifestyle of the 1950s.

3 Identify causes and effects of the boom in the automobile industry.

4 Explain the increase in consumerism in the 1950s.

**SKILLBUILDERS**
· Interpreting Graphs, p. 643

**CRITICAL THINKING**
· Comparing, p. 642
· Analyzing Effects, pp. 643, 644, 646, 649
· Contrasting, p. 645
· Analyzing Causes, pp. 646, 648
· Evaluating, p. 649
· Interpreting Visual Sources, p. 649

## Focus & Motivate

Ask students to describe what the American Dream means to them. Do they think their dreams are different from those of their parents?

## Instruct

### Instruct: Objective ①

**The Organization and the Organization Man**
TAKS SS11 3(US22.C)
· What happened to blue-collar jobs in the 1950s?
· How did American business expand in the 1950s?
· How did expectations change from one generation to another?

📖 In-Depth Resources: Unit 5
· Guided Reading, p. 67
· Primary Source: from *The Organization Man*, p. 79
· Literature: from *The Man in the Gray Flannel Suit*, pp. 82–83

---

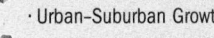
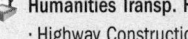

## NOW & THEN

### Franchises

**Comparing** What impact has franchising had on your community? Have students talk with parents or long-time residents of the community and ask them to compare the restaurants that were there 30 to 40 years ago with those that exist today. Ask students whether they would rather patronize a franchised store or restaurant with a national reputation or a little-known, local establishment. *(Answers will vary.)*

## More About . . .

### Ray Kroc

Kroc (1902–1984) was a pioneer of the fast-food industry, who built McDonald's Corporation into a global business. When he was selling commercial food mixers in California in 1954, he visited the McDonald brothers' drive-in restaurant in San Bernardino. Kroc was curious because the McDonalds had purchased several of his mixers to make milk shakes. Kroc saw the potential of their business and joined with the brothers. In 1961, he bought them out for $2.7 million, going on to build a multi-billion-dollar fast-food chain.

## More About . . .

### Social Conformity

In a popular song titled "Little Boxes," folk singer Malvina Reynolds satirized social conformity: "And they all play on the golf course / And drink their martinis dry / And they all have pretty children / And the children go to school / And the children go to summer camp / And then to the university / Where they are put in boxes / And they all come out the same."

**CONGLOMERATES** Many white-collar workers performed their services in large corporations or government agencies. Some of these corporations continued expanding by forming **conglomerates**. (A conglomerate is a major corporation that includes a number of smaller companies in unrelated industries.) For example, one conglomerate, International Telephone and Telegraph (ITT), whose original business was communications, bought car-rental companies, insurance companies, and hotel and motel chains. Through this diversification, or investment in various areas of the economy, ITT tried to protect itself from declines in individual industries. Other huge parent companies included American Telephone and Telegraph, Xerox, and General Electric.

**FRANCHISES** In addition to diversifying, another strategy for business expansion—franchising—developed at this time. A **franchise** is a company that offers similar products or services in many locations. (*Franchise* is also used to refer to the right, sold to an individual, to do business using the parent company's name and the system that the parent company developed.) **A**

Fast-food restaurants developed some of the first and most successful franchises. McDonald's, for example, had its start when the McDonald brothers developed unusually efficient service, based on assembly-line methods, at their small drive-in restaurant in San Bernardino, California. They simplified the menu, featured 15-cent hamburgers, and mechanized their kitchen.

Salesman Ray Kroc paid the McDonalds $2.7 million for the franchise rights to their hamburger drive-in. In April 1955, he opened his first McDonald's in Des Plaines, Illinois, where he further improved the assembly-line process and introduced the golden arches that are now familiar all over the world.

### NOW & THEN

#### FRANCHISES

In the decades since Ray Kroc opened his first McDonald's (shown below), franchising has become all but a way of life in the United States. Today, there are nearly 3,000 franchised companies operating over 500,000 businesses throughout the country. Officials estimate that franchises account for nearly one-third of all U.S. retail sales. American franchises today provide a wide array of goods and services, from car maintenance, to tax services, to hair care.

In an attempt to tap into the international market, hundreds of U.S. companies have established overseas franchises. The franchise with perhaps the greatest global reach is the one that started it all. In addition to its more than 10,000 U.S. franchises, McDonald's now operates over 14,000 franchises in dozens of countries around the world.

> **MAIN IDEA**
>
> **Comparing**
> **A** How were conglomerates and franchises alike and how were they different?
>
> *A. Answer* Both were successful business entities that grew rapidly. The conglomerate grew by diversifying; franchises grew by opening identical stores in new locations.

**A PERSONAL VOICE** RAY KROC

" It requires a certain kind of mind to see the beauty in a hamburger bun. Yet is it any more unusual to find grace in the texture and softly curved silhouette of a bun than to reflect lovingly on the . . . arrangements and textures and colors in a butterfly's wings? . . . Not if you view the bun as an essential material in the art of serving a great many meals fast."

—quoted in *The Fifties*

**SOCIAL CONFORMITY** While franchises like McDonald's helped standardize what people ate, some American workers found themselves becoming standardized as well. Employees who were well paid and held secure jobs in thriving companies sometimes paid a price for economic advancement: a loss of their individuality. In general, businesses did not want creative thinkers, rebels, or anyone who would rock the corporate boat.

**642** CHAPTER 19

---

**ACTIVITY**    **LINK TO ECONOMICS** 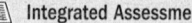 classzone.com

### Franchising

**Class Time** 45 minutes

**Task** Researching how a franchise arrangement works

**Purpose** To better understand a popular business practice

**Directions** Have students work in small groups to research how franchising operations work. Students can use the Internet and other research tools. They also can interview local franchise operators of fast-food and other businesses. Have students use a visual display to present their findings.

📖 Integrated Assessment
· Rubric 4

In *The Organization Man*, a book based on a classic 1956 study of suburban Park Forest, Illinois, and other communities, William H. Whyte described how the new, large organizations created "company people." Companies would give personality tests to people applying for jobs to make sure they would "fit in" the corporate culture. Companies rewarded employees for teamwork, cooperation, and loyalty and so contributed to the growth of conformity, which Whyte called "belongingness." Despite their success, a number of workers questioned whether pursuing the American dream exacted too high a price, as conformity replaced individuality. **B**

## The Suburban Lifestyle ➋

Though achieving job security did take a psychological toll on some Americans who resented having to repress their own personalities, it also enabled people to provide their families with the so-called good things in life. Most Americans worked in cities, but fewer and fewer of them lived there. New highways and the availability and affordability of automobiles and gasoline made commuting possible. By the early 1960s, every large city in the United States was surrounded by suburbs. Of the 13 million new homes built in the 1950s, 85 percent were built in the suburbs. For many people, the suburbs embodied the American dream of an affordable single-family house, good schools, a safe, healthy environment for children, and congenial neighbors just like themselves.

▲ The "organization man" had to step lively to keep up with the Joneses.

**THE BABY BOOM** As soldiers returned from World War II and settled into family life, they contributed to an unprecedented population explosion known as the **baby boom.** During the late 1940s and through the early 1960s, the birthrate (number of live births per 1,000 people) in the United States soared. At the height of the baby boom, in 1957, one American infant was born every seven seconds—a total of 4,308,000 that year. The result was the largest generation in the nation's history.

*Skillbuilder Answer*
1. The birthrate remained almost the same from the beginning of the war until the war ended. Then it increased.
2. It dropped from 24 per 1000 to 19 per 1000.

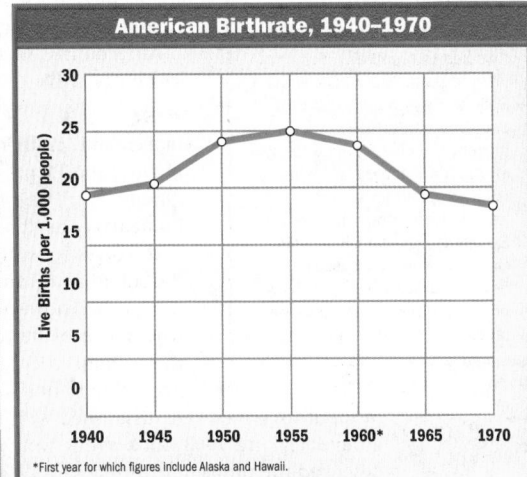

### American Birthrate, 1940–1970

*Live Births (per 1,000 people)* — vertical axis: 0, 5, 10, 15, 20, 25, 30
horizontal axis: 1940, 1945, 1950, 1955, 1960*, 1965, 1970

*First year for which figures include Alaska and Hawaii.
Source: *Historical Statistics of the United States, Colonial Times to 1970*

**SKILLBUILDER** Interpreting Graphs
1. What was the overall trend in the birthrate at the start of World War II, and after the war ended?
2. What was the difference in the birthrate between 1960 and 1970?

◀ Some of the 40 million new Americans who were born during the baby boom.

*The Postwar Boom* **643**

## KEY PLAYER

### Jonas Salk

Salk's research was in response to an acute need. From 1947 to 1951 there were about 34,000 new cases of polio in the U.S., but that number jumped to 60,000 in 1952 alone. Victims could be permanently paralyzed. Understandably, polio was one of the nation's most feared diseases, as evidenced by the 1,830,000 school children who were volunteered by their parents to act as Salk's research subjects. Ask, How did Salk's discovery result from specific needs? *(People were justifiably afraid of polio, which was rampant and could cause permanent paralysis.)*

## Tracing Themes

### WOMEN AND POLITICAL POWER

### Changing Women's Roles

In the 1950s, most women put their husband's success above their own achievement. The percentage of women college students in the 1950s was smaller than in the 1920s. Revealingly, in a 1962 Gallup Poll of 2,300 women, more than 90 percent hoped that their daughters would be better educated and would lead different lives than they had.

Beginning with the 1960s, more and more women did go to college. Women's advocacy groups succeeded in opening new paths for many women. Ask students if they think women are treated equally with men in terms of opportunity and pay today.

 Electronic Library of Primary Sources
· from *The Feminine Mystique* by Betty Friedan

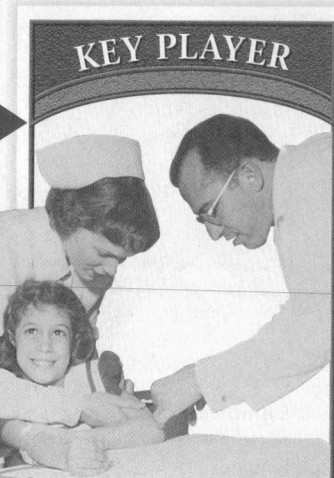

## KEY PLAYER

### JONAS SALK 1914–1995

One of the most feared diseases in the 1950s was polio, the disease that had partially paralyzed President Franklin D. Roosevelt. Polio afflicted 58,000 American children in 1952, killing some and making others reliant on crutches, wheelchairs, or iron lungs (machines that helped people with paralyzed chest muscles to breathe).

In the early 1950s, Dr. Jonas Salk (at right in photo above) developed an effective vaccine to prevent the disease, and the government sponsored a free inoculation program for children. The vaccine was extremely effective. By 1974, thanks to Salk's vaccine and a new oral vaccine developed by Dr. Albert Sabin, only seven new polio cases were reported in the country.

Contributing to the size of the baby-boom generation were many factors, including: reunion of husbands and wives after the war, decreasing marriage age, desirability of large families, confidence in continued economic prosperity, and advances in medicine.

**ADVANCES IN MEDICINE AND CHILDCARE** Among the medical advances that saved hundreds of thousands of children's lives was the discovery of drugs to fight and prevent childhood diseases, such as typhoid fever. Another breakthrough came when **Dr. Jonas Salk** developed a vaccine for the crippling disease poliomyelitis—polio.

Many parents raised their children according to guidelines devised by the author and pediatrician Dr. Benjamin Spock. His *Common Sense Book of Baby and Child Care*, published in 1946, sold nearly 10 million copies during the 1950s. In it, he advised parents not to spank or scold their children. He also encouraged families to hold meetings in which children could express themselves. He considered it so important for mothers to be at home with their children that he proposed having the government pay mothers to stay home.

The baby boom had a tremendous impact not only on child care but on the American economy and the educational system as well. In 1958, toy sales alone reached $1.25 billion. During the decade, 10 million new students entered the elementary schools. The sharp increase in enrollment caused overcrowding and teacher shortages in many parts of the country. In California, a new school opened every seven days. **C**

**WOMEN'S ROLES** During the 1950s, the role of homemaker and mother was glorified in popular magazines, movies, and TV programs such as *Father Knows Best* and *The Adventures of Ozzie and Harriet*. *Time* magazine described the homemaker as "the key figure in all suburbia, the thread that weaves between family and community—the keeper of the suburban dream." In contrast to the ideal portrayed in the media, however, some women, like Carol Freeman, who spoke of her discontentment, were not happy with their roles; they felt isolated, bored, and unfulfilled. According to one survey in the 1950s, more than one-fifth of suburban wives were dissatisfied with their lives. Betty Friedan, author of the groundbreaking 1963 book about women and society, *The Feminine Mystique*, described the problem.

### A PERSONAL VOICE  BETTY FRIEDAN

" For the first time in their history, women are becoming aware of an identity crisis in their own lives, a crisis which . . . has grown worse with each succeeding generation. . . . I think this is the crisis of women growing up—a turning point from an immaturity that has been called femininity to full human identity. "

—*The Feminine Mystique*

The number of women working outside the home rose steadily during the decade. By 1960, almost 40 percent of mothers with children between ages 6 and 17 held paying jobs.

TAKS

Mini-Lesson 2:
SS11 3(US22.A)

*C. Answer*
Creation of youth-centered culture; increased demand for consumer goods and jobs related to rearing and educating children.

**MAIN IDEA**

**Analyzing Effects**
**C** How did the baby boom affect American life in the 1950s?

**Background**
The percentage of women college students in the 1950s was smaller than in the 1920s.

---

## DIFFERENTIATING INSTRUCTION      GIFTED AND TALENTED

### Analyzing *The Feminine Mystique*

Betty Friedan's *The Feminine Mystique* was not the first book written about the role of women in society. But when it appeared in 1963, it had an enormous impact on American women and is often credited with being one of the catalysts for the modern feminist movement in the United States. Have students read passages in the book, or the entire book if they have time. You could also ask them to look for reviews and discussions of the book in mainstream magazines and newspapers of the 1960s. Suggest that students focus on these questions as they read:

· What seems to be Betty Friedan's main points?
· What arguments does Friedan use to support her assertions?
· Do you find her arguments convincing? Why or why not?
· How applicable is Friedan's book to the circumstances women face today?

Have students report back to the class on the impact of the book, both personally and in the larger culture at the time.

But having a job didn't necessarily contribute to a woman's happiness. A woman's career opportunities tended to be limited to fields such as nursing, teaching, and office support, which paid less than other professional and business positions did. Women also earned less than men for comparable work. Although increasing numbers of women attended four-year colleges, they generally received little financial, academic, or psychological encouragement to pursue their goals. **D**

**LEISURE IN THE FIFTIES** Most Americans of the 1950s had more leisure time than ever before. Employees worked a 40-hour week and earned several weeks' vacation per year. People owned more labor-saving devices, such as washing machines, clothes dryers, dishwashers, and power lawn mowers, which allowed more time for leisure activities. *Fortune* magazine reported that, in 1953, Americans spent more than $30 billion on leisure goods and activities.

Americans also enjoyed a wide variety of recreational pursuits—both active and passive. Millions of people participated in such sports as fishing, bowling, hunting, boating, and golf. More fans than ever attended baseball, basketball, and football games; others watched professional sports on television.

Americans also became avid readers. They devoured books about cooking, religion, do-it-yourself projects, and homemaking. They also read mysteries, romance novels, and fiction by popular writers such as Ernest Hemingway, John Steinbeck, Daphne du Maurier, and J. D. Salinger. Book sales doubled, due in part to a thriving paperback market. The circulation of popular magazines like *Reader's Digest* and *Sports Illustrated* steadily rose, from about 148 million to more than 190 million readers. Sales of comic books also reached a peak in the mid-1950s.

**MAIN IDEA**

**Contrasting**
**D** How did women's roles and opportunities in the 1950s differ from women's roles today?

**D. Answer** Most 1950s women were homemakers and had fewer educational and career opportunities than women have today.

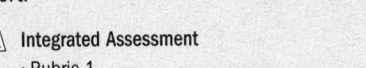

3-D comics and 3-D movies were two ▶ of the many fads that mesmerized the nation in the 1950s.

## History Through *Art*

Tell students that Norman Rockwell (1894-1978) was a painter of small-town America, not of the urban-suburban youth culture that was just beginning to develop in the 1950s. He was a master of realistic detail, who painted real life subjects with a touch of humor. In 1977, President Gerald Ford presented Rockwell with the Presidential Medal of Freedom, an award to civilians for outstanding achievement. *(The familiarity of all the people in the picture refers to a time and place where people knew one another well.)*

## More About . . .

**Entertainment and the Economy**
One example of the impact of culture on the economy is the entertainment industry. At the movie industry's peak in 1955, motion pictures accounted for nearly $1 billion in national income and employed over 200,000 people directly. The additional impact on the economy includes jobs in related industries such as film and film equipment manufacturing. Ask, How do Americans' cultural preferences affect the economy? *(Choices of leisure activities affect how people spend their money and so affect what industries have jobs to offer.)*

**classzone.com**

---

**ACTIVITY** | **COOPERATIVE LEARNING**

### 1950s Amusements

**Class Time** 45 minutes

**Task** Researching 1950s amusements

**Purpose** To deepen students' historical understanding of an era

**Directions** Write the following subjects on the board: comic books, hula hoops, Davy Crockett, televised sports, bowling, and westerns. Divide students into small groups. Ask them to choose a topic and use research materials and the Internet to find out more about it. Have students present their findings to the class in an oral report.

Integrated Assessment
· Rubric 1

## Instruct: Objective ❸
**The Automobile Culture**

· What happened to car sales in the 1950s?
· How did the interstate highway system change the way Americans traveled?
· What opportunities and problems were created by the successes of the automobile industry in the 1950s?

 In-Depth Resources: Unit 5
· Guided Reading, p. 67

### NOW & THEN

**Southern California and the Automobile**
**Making Predictions** California has originated many trends in American culture. Ask students to use the Internet to research the progress in hybrid cars and fuel cells and to predict how cars of the future will be different from today's cars. Ask them if the auto industry is successful in developing electric cars, what other industries might be affected. (*Oil industry, gas stations, auto parts*)

### More About . . .

**The Interstate Highway System**
The construction of the interstate highway system was justified as a national defense issue. It also was a boon to the construction, automobile, oil, and trucking industries. The limited-access highway system changed the landscape of America, by diverting traffic for commercial activity from downtown areas to the cloverleaf on the edge of cities and towns.

 Geography Transparencies GT27
· Federal Highways, 1950; Interstate Highways, 1987
 Humanities Transparencies HT42
· Highway Construction

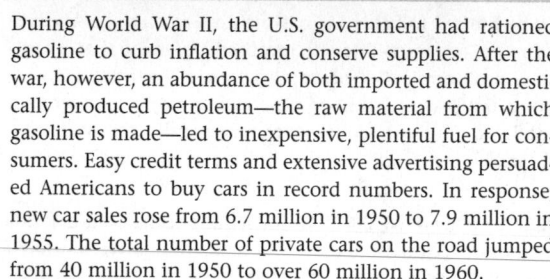

**SOUTHERN CALIFORNIA AND THE AUTOMOBILE**

No state has exemplified automania in the U.S. more than California. By the late 1990s, Californians owned more cars, held more driver's licenses, and traveled more miles on their roads than the people of any other state. The center of this automobile culture is the metropolitan area of Los Angeles.

Contributing to the importance of the automobile is Southern California's suburban lifestyle. This dependence on cars has contributed to problems of air pollution and traffic jams. But, California is addressing these problems by reviving public transportation systems and promoting the use of electric cars that produce no pollution.

## The Automobile Culture ❸

During World War II, the U.S. government had rationed gasoline to curb inflation and conserve supplies. After the war, however, an abundance of both imported and domestically produced petroleum—the raw material from which gasoline is made—led to inexpensive, plentiful fuel for consumers. Easy credit terms and extensive advertising persuaded Americans to buy cars in record numbers. In response, new car sales rose from 6.7 million in 1950 to 7.9 million in 1955. The total number of private cars on the road jumped from 40 million in 1950 to over 60 million in 1960.

**AUTOMANIA** Suburban living made owning a car a necessity. Most of the new suburbs, built in formerly rural areas, did not offer public transportation, and people had to drive to their jobs in the cities. In addition, many of the schools, stores, synagogues, churches, and doctors' and dentists' offices were not within walking distance of suburban homes. **E**

**THE INTERSTATE HIGHWAY SYSTEM** The more cars there were, the more roads were needed. "Automania" spurred local and state governments to construct roads linking the major cities while connecting schools, shopping centers, and workplaces to residential suburbs. The Interstate Highway Act, which President Eisenhower signed in 1956, authorized the building of a nationwide highway network—41,000 miles of expressways. The new roads, in turn, encouraged the development of new suburbs farther from the cities.

Interstate highways also made high-speed, long-haul trucking possible, which contributed to a decline in the commercial use of railroads. Towns along the new highways prospered, while towns along the older, smaller roads experienced hard times. The system of highways also helped unify and homogenize the nation. As John Keats observed in his 1958 book, *The Insolent Chariots*, "Our new roads, with their ancillaries, the motels, filling stations, and restaurants advertising Eats, have made it possible for you to drive from Brooklyn to Los Angeles without a change of diet, scenery, or culture." With access to cars, affordable gas, and new highways, more and more Americans hit the road. They flocked to mountains, lakes, national parks, historic sites, and amusement parks for family vacations. Disneyland, which opened in California in July 1955, attracted 3 million visitors the next year.

**MOBILITY TAKES ITS TOLL** As the automobile industry boomed, it stimulated production and provided jobs in other areas, such as drive-in movies, restaurants, and shopping malls. Yet cars also created new problems for both society and the environment. Noise and exhaust polluted the air. Automobile accidents claimed more lives every year. Traffic jams raised people's stress levels, and heavy use damaged the roads. Because cars made it possible for Americans to live in suburbs, many upper-class and middle-class whites left the crowded cities. Jobs and businesses eventually followed them to the suburbs. Public transportation declined, and poor people in the inner cities were often left without jobs and vital services. As a result, the economic gulf between suburban and urban dwellers and between the middle class and the poor widened. **F**

**MAIN IDEA**
**Analyzing Causes**
**E** Why did auto sales surge in the 1950s?
*E. Answer* Cars were necessary for life in the suburbs, Americans loved cars, and the positive economic factors allowed Americans to buy cars.

**Vocabulary**
**homogenize:** to make the same or similar
*F. Answer* Positive—growth of suburbs, increased mobility. Negative—pollution, deterioration of public transportation.

**MAIN IDEA**
**Analyzing Effects**
**F** What positive and negative effects did the mass availability of the automobile have on American life in the 1950s?

---

**DIFFERENTIATING INSTRUCTION    LESS PROFICIENT READERS**

**Understanding Main Ideas and Details**
Help students to understand what they read. Have them work in small groups to use the web diagram at right to take notes on each topic related to the impact of automobiles on American life.

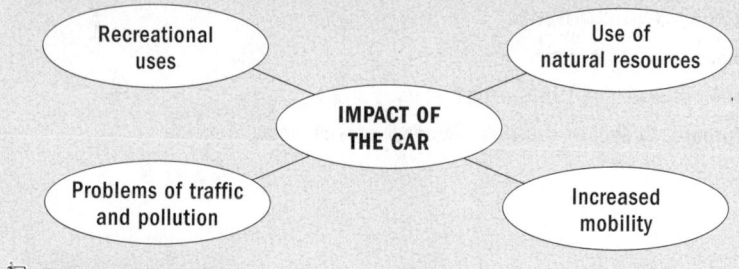

 Integrated Assessment
· Rubric 4

## Americans Hit the Road

In the 1950s Americans loved their cars—big, powerful, and flashy. Some car owners spent their leisure time maintaining their automobiles for the daily commute to work or for the annual family vacation on any one of the nation's 22 new interstate highways.

▲ **The Drive-Thru**
Fast-food restaurants catered to the car culture by offering drive-up service. Waitresses wearing fancy uniforms or roller skates added to the fun of front-seat dining.

▲ **The Drive-In**
Young suburban families piled into their cars to see a movie at one of the country's 5,000 or so drive-in theaters.

**Car Ads** ▶
Not just for transport, cars were marketed for fashion and fun. Car ads used words like "fresh" and "frisky."

◀ **Cruising Teens**
Often teenagers drove around familiar neighborhoods ending up at popular teen meeting places to see and be seen.

NEARLY EVERYONE KNOWS BY NOW—
*Pontiac's Got a Hit!*

## HISTORY from VISUALS

### Interpreting the Photographs
Ask students to look at the people in the photographs on this page. Ask them in what ways the activities shown are similar to or different from those of today. *(The activities such as the drive-thru and cruising and the car advertisements are similar. But there are only a few drive-in movie theaters left in the country.)*

## More About . . .

### Car Ads
One key to the success of the automobile industry was its ability to make cars status symbols in the eyes of the public, rather than simple functional machines. After Henry Ford's Model T, cars were marketed by style, color, and chrome content more than by engineering and performance. Millions of dollars were spent advertising vehicles in print ads and on television.

## Tracing Themes
### ECONOMIC OPPORTUNITY

The prosperity of the postwar era helped turn the automobile, which earlier had only been within reach of middle and upper class Americans, into a necessity. People outside major cities were clearly at an economic disadvantage without a car. Later, the necessity expanded to two cars, if both husband and wife worked in different areas.

*The Postwar Boom* **647**

---

**ACTIVITY**   **LINK TO ECONOMICS**        **BLOCK SCHEDULING**

### Analyzing Automobile Advertising

**Class Time** 45 minutes

**Task** Analyzing car ads to identify the primary appeal to the consumer

**Purpose** To better understand the methods of advertising

**Directions** Ask students to bring in car ads from magazines. Have students work in small groups to analyze how the layout, color, print quality, design, and positioning of the car and people add information to the ad. Have students write a summary of how the manufacturer is trying to sell the car, to whom the ad is directed, and what the message is.

📝 Integrated Assessment
· Rubric 4

## 4 Consumerism Unbound

By the mid-1950s, nearly 60 percent of Americans were members of the middle class, about twice as many as before World War II. They wanted, and had the money to buy, increasing numbers of products. **Consumerism**, buying material goods, came to be equated with success.

**NEW PRODUCTS** One new product after another appeared in the marketplace, as various industries responded to consumer demand. *Newsweek* magazine reported in 1956 that "hundreds of brand-new goods have become commonplace overnight." Consumers purchased electric household appliances—such as washing machines, dryers, blenders, freezers, and dishwashers—in record numbers.

With more and more leisure time to fill, people invested in recreational items. They bought televisions, tape recorders, and the new hi-fi (high-fidelity) record players. They bought casual clothing to suit their suburban lifestyles and power lawn mowers, barbecue grills, swimming pools, and lawn decorations for their suburban homes.

**PLANNED OBSOLESCENCE** In addition to creating new products, manufacturers began using a marketing strategy called **planned obsolescence**. In order to encourage consumers to purchase more goods, manufacturers purposely designed products to become obsolete—that is, to wear out or become outdated—in a short period of time. Carmakers brought out new models every year, urging consumers to stay up-to-date. Because of planned obsolescence, Americans came to expect new and better products, and they began to discard items that were sometimes barely used. Some observers commented that American culture was on its way to becoming a "throwaway society." **G**

**BUY NOW, PAY LATER** Many consumers made their purchases on credit and therefore did not have to pay for them right away. The Diner's Club issued the first credit card in 1950, and the American Express card was introduced in 1958. In addition, people bought large items on the installment plan and made regular payments over a fixed time. Home mortgages (loans for buying a house) and automobile loans worked the same way. During the decade, the total private debt grew from $73 billion to $179 billion. Instead of saving money, Americans were spending it, confident that prosperity would continue.

**THE ADVERTISING AGE** The advertising industry capitalized on this runaway consumerism by encouraging even more spending. Ads were everywhere—in newspapers and magazines, on radio and television, and on billboards along the

In the 1950s, advertisers made "keeping up with the Joneses" a way of life for consumers.

---

---

highways—prompting people to buy goods that ranged from cars to cereals to cigarettes. Advertisers spent about $6 billion in 1950; by 1955, the figure was up to $9 billion. Since most Americans had satisfied their basic needs, advertisers tried to convince them to buy things they really didn't need.

**A PERSONAL VOICE** VANCE PACKARD

" On May 18, 1956, *The New York Times* printed a remarkable interview with a young man named Gerald Stahl, executive vice-president of the Package Designers Council. He stated: 'Psychiatrists say that people have so much to choose from that they want help—they will like the package that hypnotizes them into picking it.' He urged food packers to put more hypnosis into their package designing, so that the housewife will stick out her hand for it rather than one of many rivals.

Mr. Stahl has found that it takes the average woman exactly twenty seconds to cover an aisle in a supermarket if she doesn't tarry; so a good package design should hypnotize the woman like a flashlight waved in front of her eyes. "

—*The Hidden Persuaders*

More and more, ad executives and designers turned to psychology to create new strategies for selling. Advertisers appealed to people's desire for status and "belongingness" and strived to associate their products with those values.

Television became a powerful new advertising tool. The first one-minute TV commercial was produced in 1941 at a cost of $9. In 1960, advertisers spent a total of $1.6 billion for television ads. By 2001, a 30-second commercial during the Superbowl cost an advertiser $2.2 million. Television had become not only the medium for mass transmission of cultural values, but a symbol of popular culture itself.

**More About . . .**

**Advertising**
In the 1957 bestseller *The Hidden Persuaders*, author Vance Packard exposed advertising techniques that appealed to values. For example, Cadillac ads appealed to the desire for status and mouthwash ads held the promise of social acceptance.

## Assess & Reteach

**SECTION 2 ASSESSMENT**
Have students locate parts of the text that answer each question. Discuss answers in class and clarify understandings.

Formal Assessment
· Section Quiz, p. 355

**SELF-ASSESSMENT**
Have students synthesize their understanding of this section by writing a paragraph describing the American dream in the 1950s.

**RETEACH**
Have students write one question for each main heading in Section 2. Then have them exchange questions with another student. Partners should answer each other's questions, and then work together to verify information.

In-Depth Resources: Unit 5
· Reteaching Activity, p. 73

## ASSESSMENT

1. **TERMS & NAMES** For each term or name, write a sentence explaining its significance.
   - conglomerate
   - franchise
   - baby boom
   - Dr. Jonas Salk
   - consumerism
   - planned obsolescence

**MAIN IDEA**

2. **TAKING NOTES**
In a graphic organizer like the one below, list examples of specific goals that characterized the American dream for suburbanites in the 1950s.

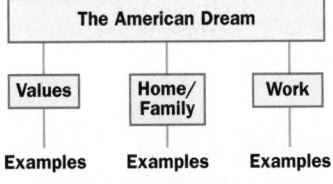

The American Dream
Values — Home/Family — Work
Examples — Examples — Examples

What do you think the most important goal was?

**CRITICAL THINKING**

3. **ANALYZING EFFECTS**
In what ways do you think current environmental consciousness is related to the "throwaway society" of the 1950s? Support your answer.
**Think About:**
- the purchasing habits of 1950s consumers
- the effects of planned obsolescence
- today's emphasis on recycling

4. **EVALUATING**
Do you think that the life of a typical suburban homemaker during the 1950s was fulfilling or not? Support your answer.

5. **INTERPRETING VISUAL SOURCES**
This ad is typical of how the advertising industry portrayed housewives in the 1950s. What message about women is conveyed by this ad?

*The Postwar Boom* **649**

---

Answers **ASSESSMENT**

**1. TERMS & NAMES**
conglomerate, p. 642
franchise, p. 642
baby boom, p. 643
Dr. Jonas Salk, p. 644
consumerism, p. 648
planned obsolescence, p. 648

**2. TAKING NOTES**
*Values*—conformity, material goods implied success; *Home/Family*—two or three children, close family ties, single-family home in suburbia, one or two cars, television; *Work*—man is the breadwinner, who works at a white-collar job; woman takes care of home and children. Answers will differ and should focus on one goal.

**3. ANALYZING EFFECTS**
Today's common practice of recycling discarded items and trash, reusing empty food and other containers, and buying products with long-term warranties might be seen as necessary steps to reverse the "throwaway" trend of the 1950s.

**4. EVALUATING**
*Dream*—had a home in the suburbs, a car, children, material comforts, and did not have to work outside the home; *Nightmare*—tied to her home and family and had no time or encouragement to develop her own interests.

**5. INTERPRETING VISUAL SOURCES**
Women are portrayed as happy waiting on their husbands and children. A woman's world did not extend beyond the home, and what she most wanted was a "pushbutton" stove.

# GEOGRAPHY SPOTLIGHT

# The Road to Suburbia

"Come out to Park Forest where small-town friendships grow—and you still live so close to a big city." Advertisements like this one for a scientifically planned Chicago suburb captured the lure of the suburbs for thousands of growing families in the 1950s. The publicity promised affordable housing, congenial neighbors, fresh air and open spaces, good schools, and easy access to urban jobs and culture. Good transportation was the lifeline of suburban growth a half century ago, and it continues to spur expansion today.

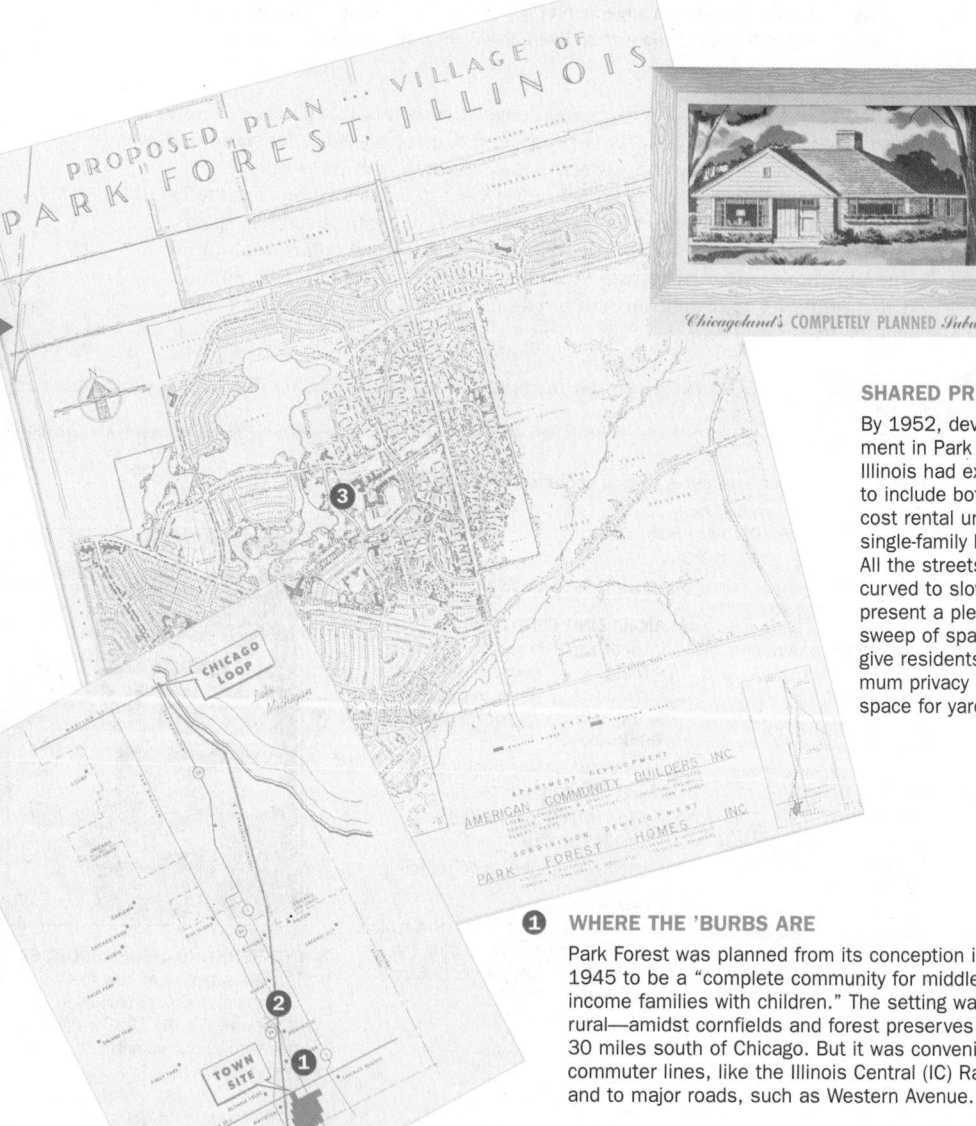

**SHARED PRIVACY ▶**

By 1952, development in Park Forest, Illinois, had expanded to include both low-cost rental units and single-family homes. All the streets were curved to slow traffic, present a pleasing sweep of space, and give residents maximum privacy and space for yards.

**❶ WHERE THE 'BURBS ARE**

Park Forest was planned from its conception in 1945 to be a "complete community for middle-income families with children." The setting was rural—amidst cornfields and forest preserves about 30 miles south of Chicago. But it was convenient to commuter lines, like the Illinois Central (IC) Railroad, and to major roads, such as Western Avenue.

**650** Chapter 19

## RECOMMENDED RESOURCES

### BOOKS

Arnold, Eve. *The Fifties.* New York: Pantheon, 1985. A social history in photographs introduced by John Chancellor.

Baldassare, Mark. *Trouble in Paradise.* New York: Columbia UP, 1986. The suburban transformation in America.

Gans, Herbert J. *The Levittowners.* New York: Pantheon, 1967. A study of life and politics in a then-new suburban community.

Halberstam, David. *The Fifties.* New York: Villard, 1993. A noteworthy recent account of the era.

Jackson, Kenneth T. *Crabgrass Frontier.* New York: Oxford UP, 1985. U.S. suburbanization.

Marling, Karal Ann. *As Seen on TV: The Visual Culture of Everyday Life in the 1950s.* Cambridge: Harvard UP, 1994. Fifties America through the eyes of television.

Wood, Robert Coldwell. *Suburbia: Its People and Their Politics.* Boston: Houghton, 1958. A contemporaneous account.

### VIDEOS

*Suburbs, Arcadia for Everyone.* Dir. Murray Grigor. Films for the Humanities, 1986. The evolution of the suburban ideal in 20th century America.

**2 THE COMMUTER CRUSH**
Men commuted to work on the IC railroad, while their wives usually stayed home to take care of the children, who thrived in Park Forest's safe, wholesome family environment.

**3 SHOPPING CENTERS**
Consumerism became a driving force in the 1950s, and Park Forest kept up with the trend. The central shopping center served the community well until the late 1960s. When Interstate 57 was built, a mammoth mall, built just off the highway, caused the original shopping area to decline. Park Forest is still struggling to revive its central shopping area.

---

**THINKING CRITICALLY**

1. **Analyzing Patterns** How did the availability of transportation influence the creation and ongoing development of Park Forest?

2. **Creating a Database** Pose a historical question about a suburb near you. Collect statistics about changes in population, living patterns, income, and economic development in that suburb. Use those statistics to create a database that will help answer your questions.

 **SEE SKILLBUILDER HANDBOOK, PAGE R33.**

 **RESEARCH LINKS** CLASSZONE.COM

*The Postwar Boom* **651**

# Instruct

1. Why did many Americans move to the suburbs in the postwar eras?
2. What role was played by transportation in the development of suburbs?

**MAKING PERSONAL CONNECTIONS**

Have students discuss why the suburbs might have been so appealing to many Americans in the postwar era. *(Affordable housing, less congested, less polluted, feeling of community, status symbol, more privacy and independence, better schools, less crime, many like to live closer to nature)*

Have students discuss the drawbacks of living in the suburbs. *(Commuting, less variety of people, fewer cultural activities, new developments not always scenic, homes sometimes poorly constructed)*

---

## HISTORY from VISUALS

**Interpreting the Images**
Have students study the graphics.

Where is Park Forest in relation to the downtown part of Chicago known as the Loop? *(Southwest)*

In addition to the IC, or Illinois Central Railroad, how might suburbanites have commuted to downtown Chicago? *(driving on Route 1 or 54)*

---

**THINKING CRITICALLY: ANSWERS**

1. **ANALYZING PATTERNS** Good transportation was necessary to both the creation and ongoing development of the suburb. Working commuters had to have convenient forms of transportation. Commuter railroad lines, such as the Illinois Central Railroad, provided reliable transportation to and from the city, where the jobs were.

2. **CREATING A DATABASE** Students might perform this activity in small groups. In addition to visiting the school library or public library, students may find information through local real estate firms, development housing offices, and/or organizations such as the Chamber of Commerce. Encourage students to discuss how their database might be used when it is complete.

# Popular Culture

| MAIN IDEA | WHY IT MATTERS NOW | Terms & Names |
|---|---|---|
| Mainstream Americans, as well as the nation's subcultures, embraced new forms of entertainment during the 1950s. | Television and rock 'n' roll, integral parts of the nation's culture today, emerged during the postwar era. | • **mass media**  • **beat movement** <br>• **Federal Communications Commission (FCC)**  • **rock 'n' roll** <br> • **jazz** |

**TEKS** U.S. History 8A, 14B, 20A, 20B, 20C, 20D, 21C, 22A, 23A, 23B, 24A, 24B, 24C, 24D, 24G, 24H, 25A, 25B, 25C, 25D

### One American's Story

H. B. Barnum, a 14-year-old saxophone player who later became a music producer, was one of many teenagers in the 1950s drawn to a new style of music that featured hard-driving African-American rhythm and blues. Barnum described the first time he saw the rhythm-and-blues performer Richard Wayne Penniman, better known as Little Richard.

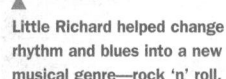

**A PERSONAL VOICE** H. B. BARNUM

" He'd just burst onto the stage from anywhere, and you wouldn't be able to hear anything but the roar of the audience. . . . He'd be on the stage, he'd be off the stage, he'd be jumping and yelling, screaming, whipping the audience on. . . . Then when he finally did hit the piano and just went into di-di-di-di-di-di-di, you know, well nobody can do that as fast as Richard. It just took everybody by surprise. "

—quoted in *The Rise and Fall of Popular Music*

Born poor, Little Richard wore flashy clothes on stage, curled his hair, and shouted the lyrics to his songs. As one writer observed, "In two minutes [he] used as much energy as an all-night party." The music he and others performed became a prominent part of the American culture in the 1950s, a time when both mainstream America and those outside it embraced new and innovative forms of entertainment.

Little Richard helped change rhythm and blues into a new musical genre—rock 'n' roll.

## **1** New Era of the Mass Media

Compared with other **mass media**—means of communication that reach large audiences—television developed with lightning speed. First widely available in 1948, television had reached 9 percent of American homes by 1950 and 55 percent of homes by 1954. In 1960, almost 90 percent—45 million—of American homes had television sets. Clearly, TV was the entertainment and information marvel of the postwar years.

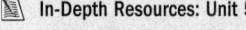
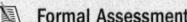

**THE RISE OF TELEVISION** Early television sets were small boxes with round screens. Programming was meager, and broadcasts were in black and white. The first regular broadcasts, beginning in 1949, reached only a small part of the East Coast and offered only two hours of programs per week. Post–World War II innovations such as microwave relays, which could transmit television waves over long distances, sent the television industry soaring. By 1956, the **Federal Communications Commission (FCC)**—the government agency that regulates and licenses television, telephone, telegraph, radio, and other communications industries—had allowed 500 new stations to broadcast.

This period of rapid expansion was the "golden age" of television entertainment—and entertainment in the 1950s often meant comedy. Milton Berle attracted huge audiences with *The Texaco Star Theater,* and Lucille Ball and Desi Arnaz's early situation comedy, *I Love Lucy,* began its enormously popular run in 1951.

At the same time, veteran radio broadcaster Edward R. Murrow introduced two innovations: on-the-scene news reporting, with his program, *See It Now* (1951–1958), and interviewing, with *Person to Person* (1953–1960). Westerns, sports events, and original dramas shown on *Playhouse 90* and *Studio One* offered entertainment variety. Children's programs, such as *The Mickey Mouse Club* and *The Howdy Doody Show,* attracted loyal young fans.

American businesses took advantage of the opportunities offered by the new television industry. Advertising expenditures on TV, which were $170 million in 1950, reached nearly $2 billion in 1960.

Sales of *TV Guide,* introduced in 1953, quickly outpaced sales of other magazines. In 1954, the food industry introduced a new convenience item, the frozen TV dinner. Complete, ready-to-heat individual meals on disposable aluminum trays, TV dinners made it easy for people to eat without missing their favorite shows. **A**

**A. Answer** More households used television for entertainment and people spent an increasing number of hours watching TV. More varied shows were broadcast, and TV dinners were invented to accommodate viewers.

**MAIN IDEA**

**Analyzing Effects**

**A** How did the emergence of television affect American culture in the 1950s?

---

**HISTORICAL SPOTLIGHT**

**TV QUIZ SHOWS**

Beginning with *The $64,000 Question* in 1955, television created hit quiz shows by adopting a popular format from radio and adding big cash prizes.

The quiz show *Twenty-One* made a star of a shy English professor named Charles Van Doren. He rode a wave of fame and fortune until 1958, when a former contestant revealed that, to heighten the dramatic impact, producers had been giving some of the contestants the right answers.

A scandal followed when a congressional subcommittee confirmed the charges. Most of the quiz shows soon left the air.

---

## HISTORICAL SPOTLIGHT

### TV Quiz Shows

The quiz show scandals rocked America. The 1950s were a time of trust—people believed what they were told. Discuss with students how viewers might have been shocked to find out that they were misled into thinking what they saw was real. Would the students be shocked by this type of activity

📃 In-Depth Resources: Unit 5
· American Lives: Milton Berle, p. 86

---

### Glued to the Set

**Households with TV Sets, 1950–2000**

Millions of Households

Source: Nielsen Media Research, 2000

**Average Daily Hours of TV Viewing, 1950–1999**

Hours per Day

Source: Nielson Media Research, 2000

**SKILLBUILDER** Interpreting Graphs
1. During which decade did the number of households with TV sets increase the most?
2. What might account for the drop in TV viewing from 1995–1999?

*Skillbuilder Answers:*
1. 1950–1960
2. People used computers more.

---

## HISTORY from VISUALS

### Interpreting the Graphs

First, help students understand how people spent their leisure time before the appearance of television. Next ask them to imagine how the acquisition of a TV set might change a family's life. Then ask them how life would be different for them if there was not TV at their home.

---

*The Postwar Boom* **653**

---

**ACTIVITY** COOPERATIVE LEARNING

 **BLOCK SCHEDULING**

## The Impact of Television on Family Life

**Class Time** 30 minutes

**Task** Interviewing people who remember the day that their family got their first television set

**Purpose** To deepen understanding of the impact of television on family life

**Directions** Have students work in small groups to devise a questionnaire to use in the interviews. The questions should probe memory of early images, curiosity about the new medium, and the effect on family life. Then, have students find family members, neighbors, and others in their community who remember the day they got their first TV.

📃 Integrated Assessment
· Rubric 3

## Tracing Themes
### SCIENCE AND TECHNOLOGY

### The Role of Television

To Newton Minow, television was a "vast wasteland." Not so to commentator Bill Moyers, a producer of many important documentary programs about political, social, and cultural issues. Moyers once held the same belief as Minow but changed his mind. According to Moyers, "Television can instruct, inform, and inspire, as well as distract, distort, and demean." Have students discuss the positive and negative effects of television.

## More About . . .

### James Dean

Years later, it may be hard to understand the continuing appeal of James Dean. After all, he only starred in three movies before his death in a car accident at age 24. But Dean's role in *Rebel Without a Cause*, a teenager fighting against conformity, struck a nerve with American teenagers. He became a hero and symbol of their own frustrations with conformity in American society. Dean's early death only cemented his romantic hold on the imagination of a generation.

LOOK

Lucille Ball had to fight to have real-life husband, Cuban-born Desi Arnaz, cast in the popular TV series *I Love Lucy*.

James Dean, seen here in the movie *Giant*, had a self-confident indifference that made him the idol of teenagers. He died in a car accident at age 24. ▼

**STEREOTYPES AND GUNSLINGERS** Not everyone was thrilled with television, though. Critics objected to its effects on children and its stereotypical portrayal of women and minorities. Women did, in fact, appear in stereotypical roles, such as the ideal mothers of *Father Knows Best* and *The Adventures of Ozzie and Harriet*. Male characters outnumbered women characters three to one. African Americans and Latinos rarely appeared in television programs at all.

Television in the 1950s portrayed an idealized white America. For the most part, it omitted references to poverty, diversity, and contemporary conflicts, such as the struggle of the civil rights movement against racial discrimination. Instead, it glorified the historical conflicts of the Western frontier in hit shows such as *Gunsmoke* and *Have Gun Will Travel*. The level of violence in these popular shows led to ongoing concerns about the effect of television on children. In 1961, Federal Communications Commission chairman Newton Minow voiced this concern to the leaders of the television industry.

### A Personal Voice NEWTON MINOW

" When television is bad, nothing is worse. I invite you to sit down in front of your television set when your station goes on the air . . . and keep your eyes glued to that set until the station signs off. I can assure you that you will observe a vast wasteland. " **B**

—speech to the National Association of Broadcasters, Washington, D.C., May 9, 1961

**RADIO AND MOVIES** Although TV turned out to be wildly popular, radio and movies survived. But instead of competing with television's mass market for drama and variety shows, radio stations turned to local programming of news, weather, music, and community issues. The strategy paid off. During the decade, radio advertising rose by 35 percent, and the number of radio stations increased by 50 percent.

From the beginning, television cut into the profitable movie market. In 1948, 18,500 movie theaters had drawn nearly 90 million paid admissions per week. As more people stayed home to watch TV, the number of moviegoers decreased by nearly half. As early as 1951, producer David Selznick worried about Hollywood: "It'll never come back. It'll just keep on crumbling until finally the wind blows the last studio prop across the sands."

But Hollywood did not crumble and blow away. Instead, it capitalized on the advantages that movies still held over television—size, color, and stereophonic sound. Stereophonic sound, which surrounded the viewer, was introduced in 1952. By 1954, more than 50 percent of movies were in color. By contrast, color television, which became available that year, did not become widespread until the

**Vocabulary**
**stereotypical:** conventional, formulaic, and oversimplified

**MAIN IDEA**

**Evaluating**
**B** Do you think the rise of television had a positive or a negative effect on Americans? Explain.

*B. Answer*
Positive—informing and entertaining; reinforcing cultural values. Negative—promoting stereotypes of minorities and women; exposing children to images of violence.

**ACTIVITY** | **LINK TO POPULAR CULTURE** | **BLOCK SCHEDULING**

### Analyzing 1950s Television Shows

**Class Time** 45 minutes

**Task** Watching and analyzing 1950s television shows

**Purpose** To deepen cultural understanding of an era

**Directions** There are alternate ways to do this activity. Videos of classic 1950s shows, such as *I Love Lucy*, *The Honeymooners*, or *The Adventures of Ozzie and Harriet*, could be shown to the class. Or, students could be asked to watch these classic shows on cable television. Then, the students should meet in small groups to analyze the shows. They should contrast them with contemporary shows or with shows from other decades with which they are familiar.

**MAIN IDEA**

**Summarizing**
**C** How did radio and movies maintain their appeal in the 1950s?

**C. Answer** They concentrated on what they did best—local news, weather, and music programming on radio; size, color, and stereophonic sound in movies.

next decade. In 1953, 20th Century Fox introduced CinemaScope, which projected a wide-angle image on a broad screen. The industry also tried novelty features: Smell-O-Vision and Aroma-Rama piped smells into the theaters to coincide with events shown on the screen. Three-dimensional images, viewed through special glasses supplied by the theaters, appeared to leap into the audience. **C**

## A Subculture Emerges ❷

Although the mass media found a wide audience for their portrayals of mostly white popular culture, dissenting voices rang out throughout the 1950s. The messages of the beat movement in literature, and of rock 'n' roll in music, clashed with the tidy suburban view of life and set the stage for the counterculture that would burst forth in the late 1960s.

**THE BEAT MOVEMENT** Centered in San Francisco, Los Angeles, and New York City's Greenwich Village, the **beat movement** expressed the social and literary nonconformity of artists, poets, and writers. The word *beat* originally meant "weary" but came to refer as well to a musical beat.

Followers of this movement, called beats or beatniks, lived nonconformist lives. They tended to shun regular work and sought a higher consciousness through Zen Buddhism, music, and, sometimes, drugs.

**D. Answer** Teenagers looking for alternatives to the conformity and consumerism of their parents found a celebration of poverty, unconformity, and art that reflected im-mediate sensory experience.

Many beat poets and writers believed in imposing as little structure as possible on their artistic works, which often had a free, open form. They read their poetry aloud in coffeehouses and other gathering places. Works that capture the essence of this era include Allen Ginsberg's long, free-verse poem, *Howl*, published in 1956, and Jack Kerouac's novel of the movement, *On the Road*, published in 1957. This novel describes a nomadic search across America for authentic experiences, people, and values.

**A PERSONAL VOICE** JACK KEROUAC
" [T]he only people for me are the mad ones, the ones who are mad to live, mad to talk, mad to be saved . . . the ones who never yawn or say a commonplace thing, but burn, burn, burn like fabulous yellow roman candles exploding like spiders across the stars. "

—*On the Road*

▲ Novelist Jack Kerouac's *On the Road*, published in 1957, sold over 500,000 copies.

**MAIN IDEA**

**Analyzing Causes**
**D** Why do you think many young Americans were attracted to the beat movement?

Many mainstream Americans found this lifestyle less enchanting. *Look* magazine proclaimed, "There's nothing really new about the beat philosophy. It consists merely of the average American's value scale—turned inside out. The goals of the Beat are *not* watching TV, *not* wearing gray flannel, *not* owning a home in the suburbs, and especially—*not* working." Nonetheless, the beatnik attitudes, way of life, and literature attracted the attention of the media and fired the imaginations of many college students. **D**

## ❸ African Americans and Rock 'n' Roll

While beats expressed themselves in unstructured literature, musicians in the 1950s added electronic instruments to traditional blues music, creating rhythm and blues. In 1951, a Cleveland, Ohio, radio disc jockey named Alan Freed was among the first to play the music. This audience was mostly white but the music usually was produced by African-American musicians. Freed's listeners responded enthusiastically, and Freed began promoting the new music that grew out of rhythm and blues and country and pop. He called the music **rock 'n' roll,** a name that has come to mean music that's both black and white—music that is American.

*The Postwar Boom* **655**

**Instruct: Objective** ❷
**A Subculture Emerges**
TAKS SS11 5(US24.A)
· How did the beat movement challenge conformity?
· How did the attitude of beat writers toward structure reflect their views about society?

In-Depth Resources: Unit 5
· Guided Reading, p. 68

**More About . . .**

**Jack Kerouac**
Kerouac's geographical and religious wanderings (from Roman Catholicism to Buddhism) provide the background for his novels. *On the Road,* his most famous book, was written in three weeks. It tells the story of Kerouac's travels across the country with his buddy Neal Cassidy in search of meaning and fulfillment. In the 1960s, hounded by hippies and other truth seekers, Kerouac took refuge in Florida with his mother. There, he turned back to Catholicism and the conservative political values of his family. He died in 1969 at age 47.

**Instruct: Objective** ❸
**African Americans and Rock 'n' Roll**
TAKS SS11 3(US21.A)
· How did rock 'n' roll challenge middle class values?
· How did rock 'n' roll get into mainstream culture?
· What was the relationship between African Americans and mainstream culture in the 1950s?

---

**ACTIVITY** **SKILLBUILDER LESSON**

**Primary and Secondary Sources**

**Explaining the Skill** Works created by members of a historical movement (primary sources)—or by critics and analysts looking back at a movement (secondary sources)—can tell historians much about the movement and about the society in which it developed. Such sources often reflect the person's strong feelings and attitudes. Therefore, identifying the writer or speaker of the material and investigating his or her attitudes helps historians assess the value of the source.

 In-Depth Resources: Unit 5
· Skillbuilder Practice, p. 71

**Applying the Skill** Have students read about the beat movement and look at "A Personal Voice" on this page. Then ask these questions:

1. Is Jack Kerouac a good source for information about the beat movement? Why or why not? *(Most will say yes, because he was a leader of the movement and felt passionately about it. He is not objective, but one should not expect him to be.)*
2. What does Kerouac mean by the word mad? *(Passionate, excited)*
3. What is Kerouac's message in this passage? *(Kerouac is bored with traditional society and likes people who feel passionate about life.)*

### Popular American Culture

During the late 1950s and early 1960s, popular American culture had a significant impact on the rest of the world. American television programs and Hollywood movies influenced everything from clothing styles to music in Europe and in other areas of the world. American rock 'n' roll in particular had a profound impact on musical tastes and styles overseas. Many of Britain's most popular bands in the early 1960s, including the Rolling Stones and the Beatles, drew their inspiration from American artists such as Carl Perkins, Elvis Presley, Little Richard, and Buddy Holly. Ask ,Why do you think popular American culture had such an influence on the rest of the world? *(Young people in other countries were drawn to the new sounds, style, and ideas emerging in American culture and were eager to adopt them as their own.)*

## History Through *Music*

### "Hound Dog"— A Rock 'n' Roll Crossover

Rock 'n' roll came out of the rhythm and blues musical tradition. To highlight the problem many adults had with rock 'n' roll, tell them about Presley's famous appearance on the *Ed Sullivan Show.* To avoid Presley's provocative "swivel-hipped" performance, he was only shown from the waist up.

### SKILLBUILDER ANSWERS
#### Developing Historical Perspective
1. Because of racial discrimination
2. Fear of the future, fear of personal violence, concerns about finding a life partner, anger at the establishment

▲ Chuck Berry is as much known for his "duck walk" as for his electric guitar-playing heard on hit records including "Johnny B. Goode" and "Maybellene."

**ROCK 'N' ROLL** In the early and mid-fifties, Richard Penniman, Chuck Berry, Bill Haley and His Comets, and especially Elvis Presley brought rock 'n' roll to a frantic pitch of popularity among the newly affluent teens who bought their records. The music's heavy rhythm, simple melodies, and lyrics—featuring love, cars, and the problems of being young—captivated teenagers across the country.

Elvis Presley, the unofficial "King of Rock 'n' Roll," first developed his musical style by singing in church and listening to gospel, country, and blues music on the radio in Memphis, Tennessee. When he was a young boy, his mother gave him a guitar, and years later he paid four dollars of his own money to record two songs in 1953. Sam Phillips, a rhythm-and-blues producer, discovered Presley and produced his first records. In 1955, Phillips sold Presley's contract to RCA for $35,000.

Presley's live appearances were immensely popular, and 45 of his records sold over a million copies, including "Heartbreak Hotel," "Hound Dog," "All Shook Up," "Don't Be Cruel," and "Burning Love." Although *Look* magazine dismissed him as "a wild troubadour who wails rock 'n' roll tunes, flails erratically at a guitar, and wriggles like a peep-show dancer," Presley's rebellious style captivated young audiences. Girls screamed and fainted when he performed, and boys tried to imitate him. **E**

Not surprisingly, many adults condemned rock 'n' roll. They believed that the new music would lead to teenage delinquency and immorality. In a few cities, rock 'n' roll concerts were banned. But despite this controversy, television and radio exposure helped bring rock 'n' roll into the mainstream, and it became more acceptable by the end of the decade. Record sales, which were 189 million in 1950, grew with the popularity of rock 'n' roll, reaching 600 million in 1960.

*E. Answer* Songs were about love and heartache, and the problems of being young.

**MAIN IDEA**

**Making Inferences**
**E** Based on Elvis Presley's song titles, what do you think were teenagers' concerns in the 1950s?

## History Through *Music*

### "HOUND DOG"— A ROCK 'N' ROLL CROSSOVER

Few examples highlight the influence African Americans had on rock 'n' roll—and the lack of credit and compensation they received for their efforts—more than the story of Willie Mae "Big Mama" Thornton.

In 1953, she recorded and released the song "Hound Dog" to little fanfare. She received a mere $500 in royalties. Only three years later, Elvis Presley recorded a version of the tune, which sold millions of records. Despite her contributions, Thornton reaped few rewards and struggled her entire career to make ends meet.

#### SKILLBUILDER
**Developing Historical Perspective**
1. Why might black musicians have been commercially less successful than white musicians in the 1950s? Explain.
2. What concerns of the current generation are reflected in today's popular music?

SEE SKILLBUILDER HANDBOOK, PAGE R11.

▲ Willie Mae "Big Mama" Thornton is remembered as the first artist to record "Hound Dog."

Elvis Presley recorded ▶ "Hound Dog" in 1956— making it a popular hit.

## ACTIVITY  LINK TO MUSIC

### Examining "Oldies But Goodies"

**Class Time** 30 minutes

**Task** Listening to and analyzing 1950s rock 'n' roll songs

**Purpose** To help students better understand an historical era

**Directions** Bring in 1950s rock 'n' roll songs by such artists as Elvis Presley, Chuck Berry, Fats Domino, Little Richard, Buddy Holly, and Jerry Lee Lewis. Ask students to discuss the characteristics these songs have in common and why the music was so popular among teenagers. Also, ask them to compare and contrast these songs to contemporary music that they enjoy.

 Integrated Assessment
· Rubric 3

**THE RACIAL GAP** African-American music had inspired the birth of rock 'n' roll, and many of the genre's greatest performers were—like Berry and Penniman—African Americans. In other musical genres, singers Nat "King" Cole and Lena Horne, singer and actor Harry Belafonte, and many others paved the way for minority representation in the entertainment fields. Musicians like Miles Davis, Sonny Rollins, Charlie Parker, Dizzy Gillespie, and Thelonius Monk played a style of music characterized by the use of improvisation, called **jazz.** These artists entertained audiences of all races.

But throughout the 1950s, African-American shows were mostly broadcast on separate stations. By 1954, there were 250 radio stations nationwide aimed specifically at African-American listeners. African-American stations were part of radio's attempt to counter the mass popularity of television by targeting specific audiences. These stations also served advertisers who wanted to reach a large African-American audience. But it was the black listeners—who had fewer television sets than whites and did not find themselves reflected in mainstream programming—who appreciated the stations most. Thulani Davis, a poet, journalist, and playwright, expressed the feelings of one listener about African-American radio (or "race radio" as the character called it) in her novel *1959.*

▲ Innovative American jazz trumpeter and composer Miles Davis, shown during a recording session in 1959, continued to blaze musical trails throughout his career.

### A PERSONAL VOICE THULANI DAVIS

" Billie Holiday died and I turned twelve on the same hot July day. The saddest singing in the world was coming out of the radio, race radio that is, the radio of the race. The white stations were on the usual relentless rounds of Pat Boone, Teresa Brewer, and anybody else who couldn't sing but liked to cover songs that were once colored. . . . White radio was at least honest—they knew anybody in the South could tell Negro voices from white ones, and so they didn't play our stuff. "

—*1959*

At the end of the 1950s, African Americans were still largely segregated from the dominant culture. This ongoing segregation—and the racial tensions it fed—would become a powerful force for change in the turbulent 1960s.

## 3 ASSESSMENT

1. **TERMS & NAMES** For each term, write a sentence explaining its significance.
   - mass media
   - Federal Communications Commission (FCC)
   - beat movement
   - rock 'n' roll
   - jazz

### MAIN IDEA

2. **SUMMARIZING**
   Create a "Who's Who" chart of popular culture idols of the 1950s. Identify the art form and major achievements associated with each person.

   | Person | Art Form | Achievements |
   |--------|----------|--------------|
   |        |          |              |
   |        |          |              |

   Why do you think they appealed to the young people of the 1950s?

### CRITICAL THINKING

3. **EVALUATING**
   Do you agree with Newton Minow's statement, on page 654, that TV was "a vast wasteland"? Support your answer with details from the text.

4. **ANALYZING EFFECTS**
   How did radio, TV, and the movies contribute to the success of rock 'n' roll?

5. **COMPARING AND CONTRASTING**
   In what ways were the rock 'n' roll musicians and the beat poets of the 1950s similar and different? Support your answer with details from the text. **Think About:**
   - the values the musicians and poets believed in
   - people's reactions to the musicians, poets, and writers

*The Postwar Boom* **657**

---

**Answers** ASSESSMENT 3

### 1. TERMS & NAMES
mass media, p. 652
Federal Communications Commission (FCC), p. 653
beat movement, p. 655
rock 'n' roll, p. 655
jazz, p. 657

### 2. TAKING NOTES
Some popular culture idols were: Lucille Ball/television/star of *I Love Lucy;* Edward R. Murrow/television/host of *Person to Person;* Elvis Presley/music/rock 'n' roll singer.

### 3. EVALUATING
*Agree*—TV presented idealized white values and ignored the problems of minorities. *Disagree*—TV programs provided needed escape for many people and also portrayed the ideal family life that many valued.

### 4. ANALYZING EFFECTS
They carried images of singers and the sounds of their music to most Americans.

### 5. COMPARING AND CONTRASTING
Both were rebellious, experimental, and innovative; often wore nonconformist clothing; attracted the young, as well as older, middle-class Americans; and performed for live audiences.

## DAILY LIFE 1950–1960

### Objectives

· Describe the broader role of teenagers in postwar America.

· Explain how the new social and economic significance of teenagers helped shape American popular culture.

## Focus & Motivate

Ask students to compare and contrast popular music today with the songs of the 1950s.

## More About . . .

### Rock 'n' Roll

Early in the 1950s, young white audiences seeking something to dance to turned increasingly to rhythm and blues, a lively form of music that originated with African-American musicians. White performers brought an infusion of country music to the mix, and rock 'n' roll was born. Its early stars were both black (Chuck Berry, Fats Domino, Little Richard) and white (Elvis Presley, Buddy Holly, Jerry Lee Lewis). The term *rock 'n' roll* was popularized by Cleveland disc jockey Alan Freed on his radio show.

# DAILY LIFE 1950–1960

# The Emergence of the Teenager

Life after World War II brought changes in the family. For the first time, the teenage years were recognized as an important and unique developmental stage between childhood and adulthood. The booming postwar economy made it possible for teenagers to stay in school instead of working to help support their families, and allowed their parents to give them generous allowances. American business, particularly the music and movie industries, rushed to court this new consumer group.

▲ **TEENS AS CONSUMERS**
Comic books, pimple creams, and soft drinks were just a few of the products aimed at teenagers with money to spend.

---

## RECOMMENDED RESOURCES

### BOOKS

Breines, Wini. *Young, White, and Miserable.* Boston: Beacon, 1992. One person's experience of growing up female in 1950s America.

Crenshaw, Marshall. *Hollywood Rock.* New York: Harper, 1994. The guide to rock 'n' roll films covers most of the movies geared to teens.

Cillet, Charlie. *The Sound of the City.* New York: Da Capo, 1996. The rise of rock 'n' roll.

Horsley, E.M. *The 1950s.* New York: Mallard, 1990. A pictorial history.

Tobler, John. *30 years of Rock.* New York: Exeter, 1985. The story of rock music by a noted rock historian.

### VIDEOS

*American Graffiti.* Dir. George Lucas. 1973. MCA Universal Home Video, 1991. This award-winning, PG-rated film vividly captures the pastimes and music of teens in the early 1960s.

*The Blackboard Jungle.* Dir. Richard Brooks. 1955. MGM/UA Home Video, 1989. Based on an Evan Hunter novel, this famous film about troubled youth

played Bill Haley's "Rock Around the Clock" during the opening credits—the first major use of rock 'n' roll in a movie.

*History of Rock 'n' Roll.* Warner Home Video, 1995. A ten-part series, with the first two parts focusing on fifties music.

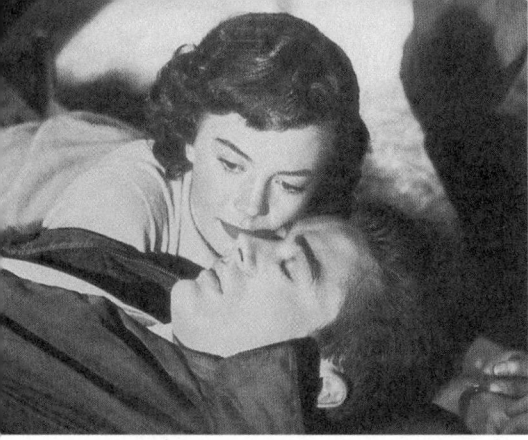

**THE TEEN MOVIE SCENE ▲**

Teenagers with money in their pockets often found themselves at the movies. Hollywood responded by producing films especially for teens. *Rebel Without a Cause* (1955) told the story of a troubled youth driven by anger and fear. It starred teen heart-throbs James Dean and Natalie Wood.

**◄ ROCKING TO A NEW BEAT**

Teenagers seeking a collective identity found it in rock 'n' roll, a fresh form of music that delighted teenagers and enraged their parents. Dick Clark's *American Bandstand* (shown at left) showcased young performers playing music ranging from doo-wop (shown above) to hard-driving rhythm and blues. The songs they sang underscored themes of alienation and heartbreak.

# DATA FILE

### TEENAGE TIDBITS

- A *Life* magazine survey showed that, during the 1950s, teens spent $20 million on lipstick alone.
- In 1956, a total of 42,000 drive-in movie theaters—heavily frequented by teenagers—took in one-quarter of the year's total box-office receipts.
- College enrollments more than doubled between 1946 and 1960.
- A weekly credit payment for a record player was $1.

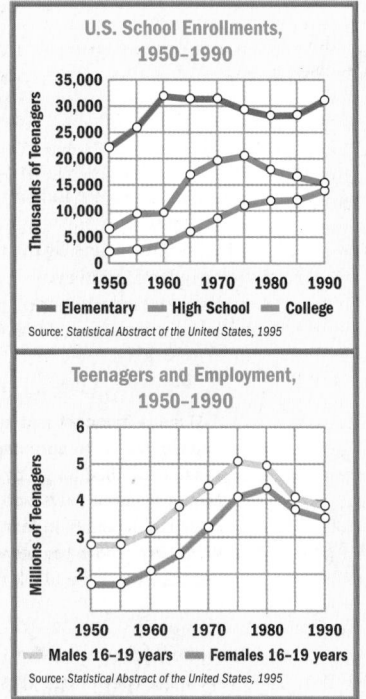

**U.S. School Enrollments, 1950–1990**

Thousands of Teenagers

Elementary ■ High School ○ College

*Source: Statistical Abstract of the United States, 1995*

**Teenagers and Employment, 1950–1990**

Millions of Teenagers

Males 16–19 years ■ Females 16–19 years

*Source: Statistical Abstract of the United States, 1995*

---

**THINKING CRITICALLY**

**CONNECT TO HISTORY**

1. **Interpreting Data** What were some causes of the booming teenage market in the 1950s? To answer the question, review the entire feature, including the Data File.

 **SEE SKILLBUILDER HANDBOOK, PAGE R28.**

**CONNECT TO TODAY**

2. **Analyzing Movies Today** What types of movies do American studios make for the teenage market today? How do these movies differ from those of the 1950s?

 **RESEARCH LINKS** CLASSZONE.COM

## Instruct

1. Why did 1950s teenagers have so much influence?
2. How did teenage consumers affect product development?

**MAKING PERSONAL CONNECTIONS**

- Have students share what they know about teenage lifestyles in the 1950s.
- If possible, bring in a few recordings by fifties rockers such as Elvis Presley, Little Richard, or Buddy Holly. Then have students discuss their reactions to the music.

---

**HISTORY from VISUALS**

**Interpreting Images**
Have students study the photographs and comic book cover.

How would you compare what you know about *American Bandstand* to MTV's teen music shows today? *(Today's shows are much more sophisticated and varied, and show a wide variety of types of music.)*

---

**THINKING CRITICALLY: ANSWERS**

1. **CONNECT TO HISTORY** New social attitudes placed more significance on the teen years and distinguished teenagers from both children and adults; economic affluence allowed parents to give teenagers an allowance, enabled more teenagers to remain in school, and provided part-time and summer jobs; the increase in teens' spending money made them a potent new consumer group.

2. **CONNECT TO TODAY** In identifying types of movies made today, students may mention action, horror, and science fiction films, and films with young stars, among other things. In comparing movies, students might mention more sophisticated special effects, more explicit subject matter, different slang and other dialogue, and changes in viewing venues (viewing on videotape, few drive-ins). Encourage students to pool their ideas orally or on group lists.

## OBJECTIVES

**1** Explain how the white migration to the suburbs created an urban crisis.

**2** Describe the efforts of minorities to gain equal rights and fight poverty.

### SKILLBUILDERS

· Interpreting Graphs, p. 661

### CRITICAL THINKING

· Analyzing Effects, p. 661
· Analyzing Issues, pp. 662, 663
· Evaluating, p. 663
· Drawing conclusions, p. 663

## Focus & Motivate

Ask students to think of a time when they felt left out of a good time or overlooked. Discuss how they would feel if they were so poor that they had to worry about getting enough food to eat, while others may have enough money to spend not only on necessities but also on luxury items.

## Instruct

### Instruct: Objective **1**

**The Urban Poor**

TAKS SS11 5(WH26.C)

· Why did whites leave the cities?
· What was the result of white flight?
· How did urban renewal affect cities?

 **In-Depth Resources: Unit 5**
· Guided Reading, p. 69
· Primary Source: from *The Other America*, p. 80

 **Humanities Transparencies HT26**
· *Her World*

# The Other America

| MAIN IDEA | WHY IT MATTERS NOW | Terms & Names |
|---|---|---|
| Amidst the prosperity of the 1950s, millions of Americans lived in poverty. | America today continues to experience a marked income gap between affluent and nonaffluent people. | • urban renewal • bracero • termination policy |

 **TEKS** U.S. History 6H, 7A, 8A, 10A, 14B, 18A, 21A, 24B, 24H, 25A, 25B, 25C, 25D

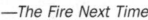 **One American's Story**

James Baldwin was born in New York City, the eldest of nine children, and grew up in the poverty of the Harlem ghetto. As a novelist, essayist, and playwright, he eloquently portrayed the struggles of African Americans against racial injustice and discrimination. He wrote a letter to his young nephew to mark the 100th anniversary of emancipation, although, in his words, "the country is celebrating one hundred years of freedom one hundred years too soon."

**A PERSONAL VOICE** JAMES BALDWIN

" [T]hese innocent and well-meaning people, your countrymen, have caused you to be born under conditions not very far removed from those described for us by Charles Dickens in the London of more than a hundred years ago. . . . This innocent country set you down in a ghetto in which, in fact, it intended that you should perish. . . . You were born where you were born and faced the future that you faced because you were black and *for no other reason.* "

—*The Fire Next Time*

 ▲ James Baldwin

For many Americans, the 1950s were a time of unprecedented prosperity. But not everyone experienced this financial well-being. In the "other" America, about 40 million people lived in poverty, untouched by the economic boom.

## **1** The Urban Poor

Despite the portrait painted by popular culture, life in postwar America did not live up to the "American dream." In 1962, nearly one out of every four Americans was living below the poverty level. Many of these poor were elderly people, single women and their children, or members of minority groups, including African Americans, Latinos, and Native Americans.

**WHITE FLIGHT** In the 1950s, millions of middle-class white Americans left the cities for the suburbs, taking with them precious economic resources and isolating themselves from other races and classes. At the same time, the rural poor migrated to the inner cities. Between the end of World War II and 1960, nearly 5 million African Americans moved from the rural South to urban areas.

**660** CHAPTER 19

## PROGRAM RESOURCES

 **In-Depth Resources: Unit 6**
· Guided Reading, p. 69
· Reteaching Activity, p. 75
· Primary Source: from *The Other America*, p. 80; The Voluntary Relocation Program, p. 81

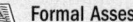 **Reading Study Guide** (English and Spanish), pp. 197–198

 **Access for Student Acquiring English/ESL**
· Guided Reading (Spanish), p. 212

 **Formal Assessment**
· Section Quiz, p. 357

 **Integrated Assessment**
· Rubrics

**INTEGRATED TECHNOLOGY**

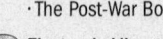 Humanities Transp. HT26
· *Her World*

 Critical Thinking Transp. CT27
· The Post-War Boom

◉ Electronic Library of Primary Sources

ⓘ classzone.com

**TEXAS RESOURCES**

 TAKS Spiraled Content Review

 TAKS Practice Tests

 TAKS Practice Transparencies TT105

 TAKS Online Test Practice

The urban crisis prompted by the "white flight" had a direct impact on poor whites and nonwhites. The cities lost not only people and businesses but also the property and income taxes they had paid. City governments could no longer afford to properly maintain or improve schools, public transportation, and police and fire departments—and the urban poor suffered.

**THE INNER CITIES** While poverty grew rapidly in the decaying inner cities, many suburban Americans remained unaware of it. Some even refused to believe that poverty could exist in the richest, most powerful nation on earth. Each year, the federal government calculates the minimum amount of income needed to survive—the poverty line. In 1959, the poverty line for a family of four was $2,973. In 2000, it was $17,601. **A**

After living among the nation's poor across America, Michael Harrington published a shocking account that starkly illuminated the issue of poverty. In *The Other America: Poverty in the United States* (1962), he not only confirmed that widespread poverty existed but also exposed its brutal reality.

**A PERSONAL VOICE** MICHAEL HARRINGTON

" The poor get sick more than anyone else in the society. . . . When they become sick, they are sick longer than any other group in the society. Because they are sick more often and longer than anyone else, they lose wages and work, and find it difficult to hold a steady job. And because of this, they cannot pay for good housing, for a nutritious diet, for doctors. "

—*The Other America*

**URBAN RENEWAL** Most African Americans, Native Americans, and Latinos in the cities had to live in dirty, crowded slums. One proposed solution to the housing problem in inner cities was **urban renewal.** The National Housing Act of 1949 was passed to provide "a decent home and a suitable living environment for every American family." This act called for tearing down rundown neighborhoods and constructing low-income housing. Later, the nation's leaders would create a new cabinet position, Housing and Urban Development (HUD), to aid in improving conditions in the inner city.

Although dilapidated areas were razed, parking lots, shopping centers, highways, parks, and factories were constructed on some of the cleared land, and there was seldom enough new housing built to accommodate all the displaced people. For example, a *barrio* in Los Angeles was torn down to make way for Dodger Stadium, and poor people who were displaced from their homes simply moved from one ghetto to another. Some critics of urban renewal claimed that it had merely become urban *removal.* **B**

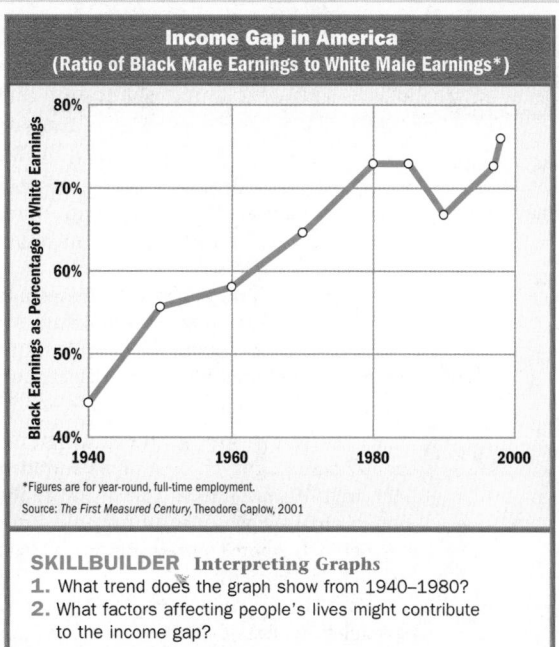

**Income Gap in America**
(Ratio of Black Male Earnings to White Male Earnings*)

*Figures are for year-round, full-time employment.
Source: *The First Measured Century*, Theodore Caplow, 2001

**SKILLBUILDER** Interpreting Graphs
1. What trend does the graph show from 1940–1980?
2. What factors affecting people's lives might contribute to the income gap?

*A. Answer* Loss of people and income leading to decaying ghettos.

**MAIN IDEA**

**Analyzing Effects**
**A** What effect did white flight have on America's cities?

**Background**
See *poverty* on page R43 in the Economics Handbook.

*Skillbuilder Answers:*
1. The ratio of black male earnings to white male earnings increased substantially.
2. Education; occupational training; discrimination.

*B Answer* Because the building boom primarily took place in the suburbs; because of lack of jobs, discrimination, and the impact of white flight.

**MAIN IDEA**

**Analyzing Effects**
**B** Why were attempts at urban renewal viewed as less than successful?

**More About . . .**

**James Baldwin**

In 1948, James Baldwin fled the discrimination he found in the United States by moving to Paris. Though primarily a novelist, Baldwin's nonfiction works, notably *The Fire Next Time* and *Notes of a Native Son*, earned him acclaim as a spokesperson for the civil rights movement. He died in Paris in 1987.

**More About . . .**

**Michael Harrington**

Harrington's book *The Other America* had a galvanizing impact on public awareness of poverty and, ultimately, on social policy. Along with Rachel Carson's environmental classic *Silent Spring*, published the same year, it changed public opinion and governmental policy. The "war on poverty" declared by Lyndon Johnson had its roots in Harrington's book.

**HISTORY from VISUALS**

**Interpreting the Graph**
Have students note that black male earnings were about 43 percent of white male earnings in 1940 and were still less than 80 percent in 2000.

**Extension** Ask students to check a statistical almanac or the Internet to find the differences in earnings between black females and white females.

Critical Thinking Transparencies CT27
· The Post-War Boom

*The Postwar Boom* **661**

---

**DIFFERENTIATING INSTRUCTION** | **LESS PROFICIENT READERS**

**Using Context Clues**

There are constructions and expressions on this page that students might find unfamiliar and may need context clues to understand. Have them work together to use context clues to decode the following terms:

suitable             accommodate

dilapidated          decaying inner cities

razed                white flight

Suggest that students use a chart similar to the one at the right to explore these terms.

| Term | Dictionary Definition | Context Clues | Meaning in Context |
|------|----------------------|---------------|--------------------|
|      |                      |               |                    |
|      |                      |               |                    |
|      |                      |               |                    |
|      |                      |               |                    |
|      |                      |               |                    |

## Instruct: Objective ②

**Poverty Leads to Activism**

TAKS SS11 3(US21.A)
· What role did Mexican Americans play in the development of the Southwest?
· What was the Longoria incident?
· What civil rights efforts were undertaken by Native Americans?
· What was the termination policy?

 In-Depth Resources: Unit 5
· Guided Reading, p. 69

### Tracing Themes
**DIVERSITY AND NATIONAL IDENTITY**

During the 1950s, one-third of the Mexican Americans in the United States lived below the poverty level. Native Americans remained the poorest minority. These groups were part of the invisible poor—those on the other side of the American dream. In the 1960s, Chicano (Mexican-American) activists founded a political organization in California and the Southwest, *La Raza Unida*, to work for economic and political reform.

### More About . . .

**Braceros**

After World War II, the widespread use of irrigation increased the amount of agricultural land, creating a demand for cheap farm labor. In 1951, Congress enacted a temporary work program that permitted Mexican laborers to enter the United States for seasonal work. In 1962, these *braceros* were placed under the protection of the minimum wage law. The *braceros* program ended in 1965.

## ② Poverty Leads to Activism

Despite ongoing poverty, during the 1950s, African Americans began to make significant strides toward the reduction of racial discrimination and segregation. Inspired by the African-American civil rights movement, other minorities also began to develop a deeper political awareness and a voice. Mexican-American activism gathered steam after veterans returned from World War II, and a major change in government policy under Eisenhower's administration fueled Native American protest.

▲ In 1942, Mexican farm workers on their way to California bid farewell to their families.

**MEXICANS SEEK EMPLOYMENT** Many Mexicans had become U.S. citizens during the 19th century, when the United States had annexed the Southwest after the War with Mexico. Large numbers of Mexicans had also crossed the border to work in the United States during and after World War I.

When the United States entered World War II, the shortage of agricultural laborers spurred the federal government to initiate, in 1942, a program in which Mexican **braceros** (brə-sâr′ōs), or hired hands, were allowed into the United States to harvest crops. Hundreds of thousands of braceros entered the United States on a short-term basis between 1942 and 1947. When their employment was ended, the braceros were expected to return to Mexico. However, many remained in the United States illegally. In addition, hundreds of thousands of Mexicans entered the country illegally to escape poor economic conditions in Mexico.

**THE LONGORIA INCIDENT** One of the more notorious instances of prejudice against Mexican Americans involved the burial of Felix Longoria. Longoria was a Mexican-American World War II hero who had been killed in the Philippines. The only undertaker in his hometown in Texas refused to provide Longoria's family with funeral services.

In the wake of the Longoria incident, outraged Mexican Americans stepped up their efforts to stamp out discrimination. In 1948, Mexican-American veterans organized the G.I. Forum. Meanwhile, activist Ignacio Lopez founded the Unity League of California to register Mexican-American voters and to promote candidates who would represent their interests. **Ⓒ**

**NATIVE AMERICANS CONTINUE THEIR STRUGGLE** Native Americans also continued to fight for their rights and identity. From the passage of the Dawes Act, in 1887, until 1934, the policy of the federal government toward Native Americans had been one of "Americanization" and assimilation. In 1924, the Snyder Act granted citizenship to all Native Americans, but they remained second-class citizens.

In 1934, the Indian Reorganization Act moved official policy away from assimilation and toward Native American autonomy. Its passage signaled a change in federal policy. In addition, because the government was reeling from

**Background**
In 1954, the U.S. launched a program designed to find and return undocumented immigrants to Mexico. Between 1953 and 1955, the U.S. deported more than 2 million illegal Mexican immigrants.

**C. Answer**
They were outraged at the discrimination against Mexican-Americans and the incident spurred them on to become more politically active and organized.

**MAIN IDEA**

**Analyzing Issues**
Ⓒ How did the Longoria incident motivate Mexican Americans to increase their political and social activism?

---

**DIFFERENTIATING INSTRUCTION** | **GIFTED AND TALENTED STUDENTS** |  **classzone.com**

**Mexican Immigration**

The emigration of Mexicans to California and the Southwest has been going on for more than three centuries. It is part of the endless movement of people searching for economic opportunity. Illegal immigration is a sensitive issue between Mexico and the United States today as it has been for several decades. Have students use the Internet to research the history of this issue and what proposals currently are being discussed to deal with it. Have students report their findings to the class.

Encourage students to address these questions:
· What are the estimates for illegal immigrants entering the United States?
· What border-control practices are currently in place in the Southwest?
· What U.S. agencies are responsible for controlling the borders of the United States?
· What varying opinions on this issue have received public attention?

 Integrated Assessment
· Rubric 2

**Vocabulary**
**subsidizing:** financial assistance given by a government to a person or group to support an undertaking regarded as being in the public interest

the Great Depression, it wanted to stop subsidizing the Native Americans. Native Americans also took the initiative to improve their lives. In 1944, they established the National Congress of American Indians. The congress had two main goals: (1) to ensure for Native Americans the same civil rights that white Americans had, and (2) to enable Native Americans on reservations to retain their own customs.

During World War II, over 65,000 Native Americans left their reservations for military service and war work. As a result, they became very aware of discrimination. When the war ended, Native Americans stopped receiving family allotments and wages. Outsiders also grabbed control of tribal lands, primarily to exploit their deposits of minerals, oil, and timber.

**THE TERMINATION POLICY** In 1953, the federal government announced that it would give up its responsibility for Native American tribes. This new approach, known as the **termination policy,** eliminated federal economic support, discontinued the reservation system, and distributed tribal lands among individual Native Americans. In response to the termination policy, the Bureau of Indian Affairs began a voluntary relocation program to help Native Americans resettle in cities.

The termination policy was a dismal failure, however. Although the Bureau of Indian Affairs helped relocate 35,000 Native Americans to urban areas during the 1950s, they were often unable to find jobs in their new locations because of poor training and racial prejudice. They were also left without access to medical care when federal programs were abolished. In 1963, the termination policy was abandoned.

▲ Native Americans like the man above received job training from the Bureau of Indian Affairs to help them settle in urban areas.

## ④ SECTION ASSESSMENT

**1. TERMS & NAMES** For each term, write a sentence explaining its significance.
• urban renewal     • bracero     • termination policy

**MAIN IDEA**

**2. TAKING NOTES**
In overlapping circles like the one below, fill in the common problems that African Americans, Mexican Americans, and Native Americans faced during the 1950s.

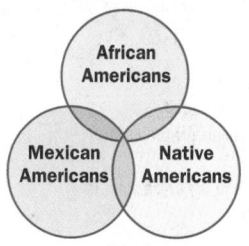

African Americans

Mexican Americans     Native Americans

What do these problems illustrate about life in the 1950s?

**CRITICAL THINKING**

**3. EVALUATING**
Do you think that urban renewal was an effective approach to the housing problem in inner cities? Why or why not? **Think About:**
• the goals of the National Housing Act of 1949
• the claims made by some critics of urban renewal
• the residents' best interest

**4. ANALYZING ISSUES**
How did Native Americans work to increase their participation in the U.S. political process?

**5. DRAWING CONCLUSIONS**
Which major population shift— "white flight," migration from Mexico, or relocation of Native Americans—do you think had the greatest impact on U.S. society? Why? **Think About:**
• the impact of "white flight"
• the influx of "braceros"
• the effects of the termination policy

*The Postwar Boom* **663**

**Assess & Reteach**

**SECTION 4 ASSESSMENT**
Assign questions as homework or as a class activity.

📄 Formal Assessment
· Section Quiz, p. 212

**SELF-ASSESSMENT**
Hold an informal debate in which students take the positions they took in their answer to question 4 in the section assessment. Make sure they make use of references to the text to support their positions.

**RETEACH**
Have students review their main understandings of this section by creating a chart comparing minority groups with middle-class white Americans in the 1950s. Bases of comparison might include living conditions, employment opportunities, and quality of life.

📄 In-Depth Resources: Unit 5
· Reteaching Activity, p. 75

---

**Answers ASSESSMENT**

**1. TERMS & NAMES**
urban renewal, p. 661
bracero, p. 662
termination policy, p. 663

**2. TAKING NOTES**
poverty, inadequate housing, discrimination and social injustice, limited job opportunities, limited social mobility, harsh or ineffective government policies, few advocates among mainstream public, second-class citizenship, exclusion from the American Dream. While white middle-class Americans pursued the "dream" of the 1950s, other Americans lived in a culture of poverty.

**3. EVALUATING**
*Effective*—The ultimate goal was to construct affordable housing for the poor, and it did tear down many bad areas and put up new housing. *Ineffective*—It did not provide enough new housing and displaced many poor people when old housing was torn down.

**4. ANALYZING ISSUES**
Native Americans formed organizations to register voters and protest discrimination.

**5. DRAWING CONCLUSIONS**
Answers will vary. *White flight*—It caused polarization of rich and poor and suburban and urban cultures. *Migration of Mexicans*—They met with opposition because they provided job competition. *Native American relocation*—It displaced an entire group of people.

## TERMS & NAMES

1. suburb, p. 635
2. Dixiecrat, p. 638
3. Fair Deal, p. 639
4. conglomerate, p. 642
5. baby boom, p. 643
6. mass media, p. 652
7. beat movement, p. 655
8. rock 'n' roll, p. 655
9. urban renewal, p. 661
10. *bracero*, p. 662

## MAIN IDEAS

1. Tuition reimbursements provided an incentive for education; a year's unemployment benefits gave financial support for job searches; loans helped them buy homes or farms or establish businesses.
2. The Korean War stalemate, the rise of McCarthyism, the threat of communism, the expanding power of the federal government, alleged corruption among Truman's political allies, inflation, and labor unrest.
3. By 1956, the majority of Americans held white-collar jobs.
4. Suburbia offered affordable single-family houses, good schools, a safe environment for children, and neighbors like themselves.
5. Local programming of news, weather, music, and community issues; targeting specific audiences, such as African Americans.
6. African-American music and performers greatly influenced rock 'n' roll.
7. Many white families moved to the suburbs and the rural poor moved into the cities, which contributed to the economic decline of many large cities.
8. Racial prejudice, inadequate education, lack of jobs, and poor access to medical care.

## TERMS & NAMES

**For each item below, write a sentence explaining its historical significance in the 1950s.**

1. suburb
2. Dixiecrat
3. Fair Deal
4. conglomerate
5. baby boom
6. mass media
7. beat movement
8. rock 'n' roll
9. urban renewal
10. *bracero*

## MAIN IDEAS

**Use your notes and the information in the chapter to answer the following questions.**

**Postwar America** *(pages 634–640)*

1. How did the GI Bill of Rights help World War II veterans?
2. What domestic and foreign issues concerned voters during the 1952 presidential election?

**The American Dream in the Fifties**
*(pages 641–649)*

3. What shift in employment trends had occurred by the mid-1950s?
4. How did life in the suburbs provide the model for the American dream?

**Popular Culture** *(pages 652–657)*

5. What strategies did radio stations use to counteract the mass popularity of television?

6. How did African-American performers influence American popular culture in the 1950s?

**The Other America** *(pages 660–663)*

7. How did many major cities change in the 1950s?
8. What obstacles to improving their lives did Native Americans face in the 1950s?

## CRITICAL THINKING

1. **USING YOUR NOTES** In a web like the one below, show the postwar technological advances you consider most influential.

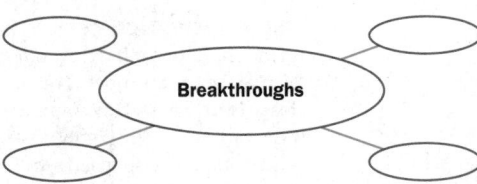

2. **HYPOTHESIZING** During America's first two centuries, the national character was marked by individualism. Why do you think conformity became the norm in the 1950s?

3. **ANALYZING PRIMARY SOURCES** Do you agree or disagree with the following quotation from *Life* magazine on American culture in 1954: "Never before so much for so few"? Support your answer with evidence.

---

**VISUAL SUMMARY** THE POSTWAR BOOM

### SUBURBAN GROWTH

- Baby boom causes population growth.
- Demand for goods exceeds supply.
- Highways and affordable homes make suburban living desirable.

### POLITICS

- Eisenhower's presidency brings prosperity and political conservatism.
- Equal rights remains a problem.
- The Cold War creates fear and anxiety.

## LIFE IN POSTWAR AMERICA
## 1945–1960

### POPULAR CULTURE

- Rock 'n' roll and jazz pave the way for minority representation.
- The beat movement rejects conformity.
- Recreation and consumerism flourish.
- Television portrays an idealized white America.

### UNEQUAL OPPORTUNITIES

- Urban areas fall into decay.
- Minorities experience prejudice and discrimination.
- Minorities establish organizations to improve civil rights.

---

## CRITICAL THINKING

1. **Using Your Notes** High fidelity record players; television sets; Teflon-coated cookware; polyester fabrics; various plastic products; electric household appliances; frozen TV dinners

2. **Hypothesizing** The unsettling effects of the Great Depression and World War II made Americans long for stability and sameness. The business world fostered an environment that rewarded employees who "fit in." The rapid growth of almost identical communities encouraged conformity.

3. **Analyzing Primary Sources**
*Agree*—Many elderly people, single women with children, and members of minority groups lived in poverty, untouched by the general economic boom. *Disagree*—The 1950s were a time of unprecedented prosperity for a growing number of Americans.

## Standardized Test Practice

Use the chart and your knowledge of U.S. history to answer questions 1 and 2.

| Geographic Distribution of U.S. Population, 1930–1970 | | | |
| --- | --- | --- | --- |
| Year | Central Cities | Suburbs | Rural Areas and Small Towns |
| 1930 | 31.8% | 18.0% | 50.2% |
| 1940 | 31.6% | 19.5% | 48.9% |
| 1950 | 32.3% | 23.8% | 43.9% |
| 1960 | 32.6% | 30.7% | 36.7% |
| 1970 | 31.4% | 37.6% | 31.0% |

Source: Adapted from U.S. Bureau of the Census, *Decennial Censuses, 1930–1970*

1. Which of the following statements supports the information in the chart?

   A From 1940–1960, more people lived in cities than in rural areas.

   B In 1960, twice as many people lived in cities as in suburbs.

   C By 1960, suburbs had surpassed cities in total population.

   D From 1930–1970, the precentage of U.S. population in rural areas decreased every decade.

2. From 1940–1970 the distribution doubled —

   F in cities and suburbs.

   G only in suburbs.

   H only in cities.

   J only in rural areas.

Use the song lyric below and your knowledge of U.S. history to answer question 3.

> **"Little Boxes"**
> Little boxes on the hillside,
> Little boxes made of ticky-tacky,
> Little boxes on the hillside,
> Little boxes all the same.
> There's a pink one and a green one
> And a blue one and a yellow one,
> And they're all made out of ticky-tacky
> And they all look just the same.
>
> —Malvina Reynolds

3. This popular song of the era describes —

   A planned obsolescence.

   B urban renewal.

   C suburban communities.

   D beatnik life style.

ADDITIONAL TEST PRACTICE, pages S1–S33.

 **TEST PRACTICE** CLASSZONE.COM

## Standardized Test Practice

1. The correct answer is letter **D**.
   The population in rural areas decreased from 1930 to 1970. Letter A is not correct because more people lived in rural areas than in cities. Letter B is not correct because about an equal percentage of people lived in cities and in suburbs. Letter C is incorrect because the suburbs passed central cities in population in 1970.

2. The correct answer is **G**.
   The population doubled only in suburbs. Letters F and H are incorrect because city population stayed about the same during this time. Letter J is incorrect because the rural population decreased.

3. The correct letter is **C**.
   This song describes houses in suburban communities. Letter A is incorrect because *planned obsolescence* refers to a business marketing strategy. Letter B is incorrect because *urban renewal* refers to a governmental policy in cities. Letter D is incorrect because *beatnik lifestyle* refers to a nonconformist way of life.

**DEBATE**

**Tips for Teaching**
- Remind students to rehearse their speeches.
- Review the basic rules for a formal debate.

**Project Presentation Rubric**
The debate should . . .
- Have a clearly stated proposition that can be divided into two points of view.
- Present logical and reasoned arguments supported by evidence.
- Include a summary speech itemizing the position of the team and its response to challenges by the opposing team.

📖 Formal Assessment
  · Chapter Test, Forms A, B, and C, pp. 358–369

## ALTERNATIVE ASSESSMENT

1.  **INTERACT WITH HISTORY** Recall your discussion of the question on page 631:

   *What is the American dream of the 1950s?*

   Suppose you are a beat poet and have been asked to write an original poem entitled, *A Postwar American Dream*. Use information from Chapter 19 and your knowledge of American history to support your poem. Remember to include a wide range of lifestyles in your poem.

2. 🌐 **INTERNET ACTIVITY** CLASSZONE.COM

   Visit the links for Chapter Assessment to plan and prepare a web page about one aspect of popular culture—music, television, fashion, or the movies—from the 1950s. Include particular events and personalities of that period.

   **Cooperative Learning Activity** Talk to other students in your class to identify those who chose a topic that was different from yours. Then work with those students to plan an electronic presentation that includes all elements of popular culture. Present your complete guide to fifties popular culture to the class.

*The Postwar Boom* 665

## ALTERNATIVE ASSESSMENT

### 1. INTERACT WITH HISTORY
**Rubric**
The poem should . . .
- show an understanding of the beat movement and beat poetry
- use appropriate elements of poetry, such as images and symbolism
- include a wide range of American lifestyles

### 2. INTERNET ACTIVITY
**Rubric**
The electronic presentation should . . .
- show proficiency in the use of technology
- utilize several sources of information
- include particular events and personalities of the 1950s
- reflect many aspects of 50s popular culture, including music, television, fashion, and movies

## Previewing the Unit

Unit 6 describes the social changes in American society from the 1950s through the mid-1970s. During this time Congress passes many new laws in an effort to create a "great society." African Americans launch a powerful movement that gains civil rights and spurs Hispanics, women, and Native Americans to push for rights for themselves. U.S. military involvement in Vietnam sharply divides American society.

### HISTORICAL INQUIRY: LOBBYING CAMPAIGN

Use this project to teach students to explain and apply the use of primary and secondary sources.

### Explaining the Use of Primary and Secondary Sources

Review with students the lesson on "Primary and Secondary Sources," Skillbuilder Handbook, page R22. An author of a primary source, being involved in the events, has a limited perspective; the author of a secondary source may be less biased and generally has a broader perspective. However, secondary sources are often intended to convince or persuade, and so are subject to bias. Ask students to explain the different uses of primary and secondary sources. (secondary sources provide useful background material and help us to interpret primary sources)

*(continued on next page)*

### Lobbying Campaign

This unit covers years of great social and political turmoil. Imagine that you have decided to lobby for—convince government officials to support—a cause or issue that is important to you. Create a plan for lobbying in which you encourage others to support your point of view.

*Civil Rights March, 1965 by James Karales*

666

# Living with Great Turmoil
## 1954–1975

## More About the Image

### The Selma Marches

The distance between Selma and Montgomery was 54 miles. The marchers were marching to the state capitol to appeal to Governor George Wallace to stop police brutality.

The Selma Marches occurred in March of 1965. Actually there were three marches. The first march, on March 7, is sometimes referred to as "Bloody Sunday." Marchers were met by state troopers who used tear gas and batons to disperse the crowd.

The second march occurred on March 9 and was called "Turnback Tuesday" because marchers turned back at the Edmund Pettus Bridge. The final march, held six days after President Johnson sent a voting rights proposal to Congress, took place between March 21 to 25 and was successful.

**Using Primary and Secondary Sources**
Tell students that they should rely as much as possible on primary sources, and should use secondary sources as background. Secondary sources can also suggest interpretations; but students should think critically before accepting someone else's interpretation.

Tell students that they can find primary sources in their textbook and in library materials. Tell them that in planning their lobbying campaign they must use at least four primary sources.

**Rubric**
A Lobbying Campaign should . . .
· identify persons and groups who would be able to bring about the desired legislative action
· reflect an understanding of the historical context in which the lobbying campaign is to be conducted, by including important information on the frames of reference and points of view of the people who are to be lobbied
· demonstrate understanding of the appropriate uses of primary and secondary sources

## HISTORY from VISUALS

### Interpreting the Photograph
New coverage of the civil rights movement had great impact on public opinion. Images of policemen beating civil rights activists aroused outrage. The peaceful, dignified behavior of the civil rights marchers contrasted sharply with their treatment. James Karales took this photograph of one of the marches to Selma that occurred in March of 1965. Ask students what words best describe these marchers. Why do the marchers carry American flags?

**Extension** Using the Internet or library resources, find and read the speech given at the end of the march in Montgomery by Dr. Martin Luther King, Jr.

**The Selma Marchers**

The marchers included many of the biggest names in the civil rights movement, such as A. Phillip Randolph, the head of a labor union with mostly African-American membership; Ralph Bunche, Nobel Peace Prize winner; Dr. Ralph Abernathy, who took over leadership of the SCLU after King's death in 1968; and Dr. Martin Luther King, Jr. and his wife Coretta Scott King.

The marchers included African Americans as well as white protesters. Among the white protesters were priests, ministers, and rabbis. Two Northern whites were killed while participating in the march and a minister was beaten to death on the streets of Selma.

# The New Frontier and the Great Society

| | **CHAPTER OVERVIEW** | **COPYMASTERS** | **INTEGRATED TECHNOLOGY** |
|---|---|---|---|
| **CHAPTER RESOURCES** | *President Kennedy survives major confrontations with the Soviet Union but cannot get his domestic policies past Congress. President Johnson succeeds him and launches an era of liberal activity with a wide-ranging program of new laws.* | Telescoping the Times · Chapter Summary, pp. 39–40<br><br>Planning for Block Schedules | Power Presentations<br><br>Electronic Teacher Tools<br><br>Online Lesson Planner<br><br>classzone.com |
| **SECTION 1**<br>**Kennedy and the Cold War**<br>pp. 670–678 | **KEY IDEAS**<br>*Foreign affairs dominate the presidential campaign of 1960 and the administration of John F. Kennedy. Kennedy faces some of the most dangerous Soviet-American confrontations of the Cold War.* | In-Depth Resources: Unit 6 · Guided Reading, p. 1 · Building Vocabulary, p. 4 · Skillbuilder Practice, p. 5 · Reteaching Activity, p. 6 · Geography Application, pp. 9–10 · Primary Sources, pp. 11–13<br><br>Lesson Plans, pp. 159–160 | classzone.com |
| **SECTION 2**<br>**The New Frontier**<br>pp. 679–685 | *With the stirring phrase "the New Frontier," Kennedy outlines a broad vision for progress, but Congress enacts few of his initiatives. His efforts are ended by his tragic assassination.* | In-Depth Resources: Unit 6 · Guided Reading, p. 2 · Reteaching Activity, p. 7 · Literature, pp. 15–17 · American Lives, p. 18<br><br>Lesson Plans, pp. 161–162 | Geography Transparencies GT28 · Influence of Alliance for Progress<br><br>Humanities Transparencies HT43 · The Nations Mourns<br><br>Electronic Library of Primary Sources · from On the Space Program · from "That Day in Dallas"<br><br>classzone.com |
| **SECTION 3**<br>**The Great Society**<br>pp. 686–695 | *Lyndon B. Johnson drives the most ambitious legislative agenda through Congress since the New Deal. The landmark decisions of the Supreme Court under Chief justice Earl Warren reflect the era of liberal activism.* | In-Depth Resources: Unit 6 · Guided Reading, p. 3 · Reteaching Activity, p. 8 · Primary Sources, p. 14 · American Lives, p. 19<br><br>Lesson Plans, pp. 163–164 | Critical Thinking Transparencies CT28, CT62 · The Great Society · Federal Budget: 1952–1968<br><br>Humanities Transparencies HT44 · Johnson Rag<br><br>Electronic Library of Primary Sources · from Civil Rights Act of 1964 · from Citizen's Guide to the Civil Rights Act of 1964<br><br>classzone.com |

## RESOURCES FOR DIFFERENTIATING INSTRUCTION

### Students Acquiring English/ESL

**Reading Study Guide:**
(English and Spanish)
pp. 201–208

**Access for Students Acquiring English/ESL:**
Spanish Translations,
pp. 216–223

**Chapter Summaries on CD**
(English and Spanish)

### Less Proficient Readers

**Reading Study Guide**
(English and Spanish)
pp. 201–208

**Telescoping the Times**
· Chapter Summary,
  pp. 39–40

**Chapter Summaries on CD**
(English and Spanish)

### Gifted and Talented Students

**In-Depth Resources: Unit 6**
· Primary Sources, pp. 11–14
· Literature, pp. 15–17
· American Lives: Alan
  Shepard, p. 18; Rachel
  Carson, p. 19

**Electronic Library of Primary Sources**
· Unit 6, Chapter 20

## ASSESSMENT OPTIONS

**Chapter Assessment,** pp. 696–697

**Formal Assessment**
· Chapter Tests, Forms A, B, and C, pp. 373–384

**Test Generator**

**Integrated Assessment Book**

**TAKS Online Test Practice**

**TAKS Spiraled Content Review**

**TAKS Practice Tests**

---

**Section 1 Assessment,** p. 678

**Self-Assessment,** p. 678

**Formal Assessment,** Quiz, p. 370

**Integrated Assessment Book**

**Test Generator**

**TAKS Practice Transparencies TT106**

---

**Section 2 Assessment,** p. 683

**Self-Assessment,** p. 683

**Formal Assessment,** Quiz, p. 371

**Integrated Assessment Book**

**Test Generator**

**TAKS Practice Transparencies TT107**

---

**Section 3 Assessment,** p. 693

**Self-Assessment,** p. 693

**Formal Assessment,** Quiz, p. 372

**Integrated Assessment Book**

**Test Generator**

**TAKS Practice Transparencies TT108**

## CROSS-CURRICULAR CONNECTIONS

### Government
Finkelstein, Norman. *Thirteen Days/Ninety Miles: The Cuban Missile Crisis.* NY: Messner, 1994. Using information not available at the time, the author depicts the Cold War crisis as it was seen by both sides.

### Culture
Plissner, Martin. *The Control Room: How Television Calls the Shots In Presidential Elections.* NY: Free Press, 1999. This is an in-depth look at how television has affected the election process, from the first televised convention in the 1950s to the present.

### Pop Culture
Mulvaney, Jay and Dunne, Dominick. *Jackie: The Clothes of Camelot.* NY: St. Martin's Press, 2001. This book focuses on the fashion and style of Jackie Kennedy as an important influence on the culture of the day.

### Literature
Oates, Joyce Carol. *Because It Is Bitter, and Because It Is My Heart.* NY: Plume, 1991. A realistic retelling of life in America during the 1950s and 1960s. Issues of race and family dominate this gritty novel.

Thomas, Maria. *Antonia Saw the Oryx First.* NY: Soho Press, 1987. The experiences of a Peace Corps volunteer in Africa are at the center of this story of a richly complex community, unusual personalities, cultural confusions, and the powerful African landscape.

Wolfe, Tom. *The Right Stuff.* NY: Farrar, Straus, and Giroux, 1991. This is the true story of the first seven astronauts—Alan Shepard, Gus Grissom, John Glenn, Scott Carpenter, Walter Schirra, Gordon Cooper, and Deke Slayton—chosen for the U.S. space program. The story follows them through their selection, training, and daily routines.

**McDougal Littell**
*The Language of Literature*
**American Literature**
Unit 6 , Part 2

## ENRICHMENT ACTIVITIES

**Pupil's Edition,** pp. 668–695
Interact with History, pp. 668–669
Geography Spotlight, pp. 684–685
Point/Counterpoint, p. 692
Supreme Court, pp. 694–695

**In-Depth Resources: Unit 6**
· Geography Application: Divided Germany &
  the Berlin Wall, pp. 9–10
· Primary Source: John F. Kennedy's Inaugural
  Address, pp. 11–12

· Primary Source: Political Cartoon, p. 13
· Primary Source: from *Unsafe at Any Speed*,
  p. 14
· Literature: from *Paper Wings*, pp. 15–17
· American Lives: Alan Shepard, p. 18
· American Lives: Rachel Carson, p. 19

**Electronic Library of Primary Sources**
Unit 6, Chapter 20

## BLOCK SCHEDULE LESSON PLAN OPTIONS (90-MINUTE PERIOD)

### DAY 1

**CHAPTER 20 OPENER**
**pp. 668–669**

**Class Time** 30 minutes

**History from Visuals, p. 668**

**Class Time** 10 minutes

*Options for Pacing and Variety*

· **Time Saver** Have students look at the time line. Then ask them the TE questions for clarification and to test their understanding of why a time line is an important tool for historians. **Class Time** 5 minutes

**Interact with History, p. 669**

**Class Time** 20 minutes

*Options for Pacing and Variety*

· **Role-Playing** Have students read the situation. Then select a few students to act as a panel on a television news discussion show. They should discuss the question "What are the qualities of effective leaders?" **Class Time** 20 minutes

**SECTION 1, pp. 670–678**

**Class Time** 60 minutes

*Options for Pacing and Variety*

· **Time Saver** Ask students to look at the map on page 675 on the Cuban Missile Crisis. Work as a

### DAY 1 continued

class to construct an accurate time line of the events for this event. Refer to the TE activity on page 673. **Class Time** 20 minutes

· **Peer Evaluation** Have students complete the Section Assessment and then trade papers with another student. Review answers as a class. **Class Time** 20 minutes

**SECTION 2, pp. 679–685**

**Class Time** 30 minutes

*Options for Pacing and Variety*

· **Peer Teaching** Have students work in groups to research the foreign-aid programs launched during Kennedy's presidency, including the Peace Corps and the Alliance for Progress. They should find background information on the programs, how they were started, if the programs still exist, and statistics on how many people volunteer today. Share findings with the class. **Class Time** 30 minutes

· **Time Saver** Ask students to read the feature on page 684, "Geographical Spotlight: The Movement of Migrant Workers." Discuss question 1 and additional questions in the TE. **Class Time** 20 minutes

### DAY 2

**SECTION 3, pp. 686–695**

**Class Time** 45 minutes

*Options for Pacing and Variety*

· **Peer Teaching** Divide the class into groups of five and do the activity on page 688, researching presidential campaigns then and now. Each group can present their findings during a class discussion of the topic. **Class Time** 45 minutes (over two days)

· **Internet** As a class, research the effectiveness of Project Head Start, a daycare and school-like program that serves lower-income families. Use the Internet to find background information, statistics, and interviews with former students or former teachers. Utilizing this information, the class should decide how to measure the success of the program and what important factors they included in their determination. **Class Time** 60 minutes (over two days)

· **Time Saver** Ask students to read the feature on pages 690–691, "The Supreme Court: *Miranda* v. *Arizona (1966)*." Have students work in pairs or groups to answer the questions and then discuss them as a class. **Class Time** 30 minutes

### DAY 2 continued

**ASSESSMENT**
**pp. 696–697**

**Class Time** 45 minutes

*Options for Pacing and Variety*

· **Peer Competition** Have students read the Visual Summary on the two presidents in the 1960s. Based on the concerns highlighted in the policies of each, have students infer the political and social climate at the time of each president. Have them enumerate the facts they know and then a list of inferences they can check. Ask for these inferences and put the best ones on the board. Circle the ones that are true or that can be assumed true by historians. **Class Time** 25 minutes

· **Internet** Discuss the issues raised in Alternative Assessment question 2 on page 697 and use the CD-ROM Electronic Library of Primary Sources to read contemporary reactions and speculations about the major events covered. **Class Time** 30 minutes

---

**TEACHER-TESTED ACTIVITY**
**ANALYSIS OF A JOHN F. KENNEDY SPEECH**

Steve Smith, Clayton High School, Clayton, North Carolina

**Class Time** 45 minutes

**Task** Analyzing a presidential speech

**Purpose** To compare and contrast the content of John F. Kennedy's Inaugural Address with events of that time

**Supplies Needed**

· Copies of John F. Kennedy's Inaugural Address

· Recording of John F. Kennedy's Inaugural Address (if possible)

**Activity** Play the speech and have students follow along. (If recording cannot be found, have students take turns reading the speech aloud.) Then lead a discussion, placing the speech within the context of 1960s events. Ask the following questions:

· Was the speech clear in presenting Kennedy's views?
· Did Kennedy leave anything out?
· To whom was he trying to appeal?
· What message was he trying to get across?
· What appeared to worry or concern him?

# CHAPTER 20 CORRELATION

 **CORRELATION TO THE TEXAS ESSENTIAL KNOWLEDGE AND SKILLS**

Chapter 20 addresses the following standards of the Texas Essential Knowledge and Skills for U.S. History.

| TEKS | Instruction | Student Question/Activity |
|---|---|---|
| **(1A)** Identify major eras of U.S. history from 1877 to the present and describe their defining characteristics. | **PE 668–669** time line of key events of the New Frontier and Great Society era | **TE 668** questions requiring students to interpret the time line |
| **(7C)** Evaluate government efforts, including the Civil Rights Act of 1964, to achieve equality in the United States. | **PE 688** discussion of the Civil Rights Act of 1964 | **PE 693** Taking Notes activity about major Great Society measures |
| **(10A)** Analyze the effects of changing demographic patterns resulting from migration within the United States. | **PE 684–685** Geography Spotlight feature on the movement of migrant workers in the United States | **PE 685** Critical Thinking questions about the feature |
| **(17A)** Analyze the effects of 20th-century landmark U.S. Supreme Court cases. | **PE 694–695** feature on the landmark Supreme Court case, *Miranda* v. *Arizona*. | **PE 695** Critical Thinking questions about the feature |
| **(19C)** Identify the contributions of Texans who have been President of the United States | **PE 686–693** examination of the presidency of Lyndon B. Johnson, with an in-depth look at his Great Society program | **PE 693** Critical Thinking questions about Johnson's achievements as president |
| **(23B)** Explain how technological innovations in areas such as space exploration have led to other innovations that affect daily life and the standard of living. | **PE 681** discussion of how space exploration led to the growth of other industries in the United States. | **PE 681** Skillbuilder questions requiring students to interpret a space-race expenditures chart |

## TAKS MINI-LESSONS

1. **Social Studies Skills: Objective 2 (WG1.A):** Analyze the effects of physical and human geographic patterns on events in the past **Activity** Have students answer the questions regarding the Geography Spotlight feature on the movement of migrant workers.

2. **Social Studies Skills: Objective 4 (US17.A):** Analyze the effects of 20th-century landmark U.S. Supreme Court cases **Activity** Have students answer the questions on the feature examining the landmark Supreme Court case, *Miranda* v. *Arizona*, on pages 694–695.

3. **Social Studies Skills: Objective 5 (WH26.C):** Interpret visuals including graphs **Activity** Have students answer the Skillbuilder question regarding the Great Society Programs chart on page 690.

4. **English Language Arts Skills: Objective 1 (8.B):** Read in varied sources such as maps **Activity** Have students answer the Skillbuilder questions regarding the Cuban Missile Crisis map.

5. **English Language Arts Skills: Objective 2 (11.A):** Compare and contrast aspects of texts such as conflicts **Activity** Have students summarize the Cold War conflicts that the Kennedy administration faced.

# CHAPTER 20

# THE NEW FRONTIER AND THE GREAT SOCIETY

## HISTORY from VISUALS

### Interpreting the Photograph

Ask students if they would like to go to outer space. Tell them that the first years of the space program were filled with excitement and drama as humans for the first time left earth. Ask them to put themselves inside the spacesuit of the astronaut shown in the photograph. Ask them how they think they would feel. (Excited, scared, awed)

## Time Line Discussion

Explain to students that the time line covers events in the United States and the world during the years 1960 to 1968. Mention that events involving civil rights and the Vietnam War happened in the years shown but are covered in succeeding chapters. Thus, they are omitted from the time line.

· Ask students who was the first American to orbit the earth and in what year it happened. (John Glenn, 1962)

· Ask who was president during the Cuban missile crisis and in what year it occurred. (John F. Kennedy, 1962)

· Ask students what was significant about Thurgood Marshall's appointment to the Supreme Court. Which president appointed him and in what year? (Marshall was the first African American on the Court. He was appointed by President Johnson in 1967.)

Scientific and technological advances in the early 1960s made possible the first American spacewalk during the Gemini 6 mission on June 3, 1965.

**1960** John F. Kennedy is elected president.

LEADERSHIP for the 60's
KENNEDY ★ JOHNSON

**1961** U.S. launches the Bay of Pigs invasion.

**1962** John Glenn becomes the first American to orbit the earth.

**1962** U.S. and USSR face off in the Cuban missile crisis.

**1963** President Kennedy is assassinated; Lyndon B. Johnson becomes president.

USA
WORLD

**1960** | **1961** | **1962** | **1963**

**1960** Seventeen African countries gain independence.

**1961** Soviet cosmonaut Yuri Gagarin becomes the first human in outer space.

**1962** The drug thalidomide is pulled from the market after it is found responsible for thousands of birth defects in Europe.

**668** CHAPTER 20

## THEMES IN CHAPTER 20

### SCIENCE AND TECHNOLOGY

By the 1960s, the United States and the Soviet Union had built up a stockpile of nuclear weapons. During periods of crisis, including the Cuban missile crisis, the American people feared that these powerful weapons would be used. The United States and the Soviet Union also competed in the space race.

After the Soviet Union successfully launched the first human into space in 1961, President Kennedy announced that it would be America's goal to send a man to the moon by decade's end.

**See Teacher's Notes, pp. 674, 681.**

### ECONOMIC OPPORTUNITY

With the legislative agenda of the Great Society, President Johnson sought to aid the poor and others in need. The Economic Opportunity Act provided funds for job training, education, and the war on poverty.

**See Teacher's Notes, p. 688.**

### IMMIGRATION AND MIGRATION

The Great Society brought profound changes to the nation's immigration laws with passage of the Immigration Act of 1965. This act allowed many non-European immigrants to settle in the United States.

**See Teacher's Notes, p. 691.**

# INTERACT
## WITH HISTORY

Against the backdrop of an intense space race between America and the Soviet Union, the 1960 presidential election approaches. The leading candidates are a young, charismatic senator and the ambitious, experienced vice-president. The new president will face tremendous responsibilities. Abroad, the Soviet Union is stockpiling nuclear weapons. At home, millions suffer from poverty and discrimination.

## *What are the qualities of effective leaders?*

### Examine the Issues

- How can a leader motivate and influence the public?
- What skills are needed to persuade legislators?
- What enables a leader to respond to crises?

**RESEARCH LINKS** CLASSZONE.COM

Visit the Chapter 20 links for more information about The New Frontier and the Great Society.

# INTERACT
## WITH HISTORY

### Objectives

- To help students understand the qualities of effective leadership
- To examine the relationship between reality and perception in politics over a presidential candidate's ability to lead the nation

### Examine the Issues

1. Ask students to discuss the qualities in figures of authority that make the difference in their being given respect, indifference, or disrespect.
2. Discuss the challenge a president faces in winning the support of legislators, even those of the same party, when there are divergent interests.
3. Ask students to examine the role of decisiveness, confidence, and vision in responding to a crisis.

---

**1964** Lyndon B. Johnson is elected president.

**1964** Congress passes the Economic Opportunity Act and Civil Rights Act.

**1965** U.S. troops enter Vietnam.

**1967** Thurgood Marshall becomes the first African-American justice of the Supreme Court.

**1968** Richard M. Nixon is elected president.

**1964**   **1965**   **1966**   **1967**

**1965** Ferdinand Marcos becomes president of the Philippines.

**1966** Indira Gandhi becomes prime minister of India.

**1967** Israel wins Arab territories in the Six Day War.

**1968** Warsaw Pact troops invade Czechoslovakia.

*The New Frontier and the Great Society* **669**

---

## RECOMMENDED RESOURCES

### BOOKS FOR THE TEACHER

Schlessinger, Arthur, Jr. *A Thousand Days.* Boston: Houghton Mifflin, 1965. An account of JFK's administration by a distinguished historian and member of the presidential staff.

Unger, Irwin. *The Best of Intentions.* New York: Doubleday, 1996. Assessment of the Great Society.

### BOOKS FOR THE STUDENT

Morrison, Joan, and Robert K. Morrison, eds. *From Camelot to Kent State.* New York: Oxford UP, 2001. Remembrances of the 1960s.

O'Neill, William. *Coming Apart.* Chicago: Quadrangle, 1971. Informal history of the 1960s.

### VIDEOS

*Crisis: Missiles in Cuba.* Zenger Video, 1987. Social Studies School Service, 800-421-4246. Story of Cuban missile crisis.

*The Fabulous Sixties.* MPI Home Video, 1970. 800-323-0442. Eleven-tape series.

*The Great Debates: John F. Kennedy vs. Richard M. Nixon.* MPI Home Video, 1989.

*Rachel Carson's Silent Spring.* PBS Home Video, 1993. Documentary about environmental activist.

### SOFTWARE

*The Space Race.* CD-ROM. First Educational Publishing, 1995. 211 Congress Street, Boston, MA 02110.

# Kennedy and the Cold War

 **One American's Story**

**John F. Kennedy** became the 35th president of the United States on a crisp and sparkling day in January 1961. Appearing without a coat in freezing weather, he issued a challenge to the American people. He said that the world was in "its hour of maximum danger," as Cold War tensions ran high. Rather than shrinking from the danger, the United States should confront the "iron tyranny" of communism.

**A PERSONAL VOICE** JOHN F. KENNEDY

"Let the word go forth from this time and place, to friend and foe alike, that the torch has been passed to a new generation of Americans, born in this century, tempered by war, disciplined by a hard and bitter peace, proud of our ancient heritage, and unwilling to witness or permit the slow undoing of those human rights to which this nation has always been committed. . . .

Let every nation know, whether it wishes us well or ill, that we shall pay any price, bear any burden, meet any hardship, support any friend, oppose any . . . foe, in order to assure . . . the survival and the success of liberty."

—Inaugural Address, January 20, 1961

The young president won praise for his well-crafted speech. However, his words were put to the test when several Cold War crises tried his leadership.

▲ John F. Kennedy delivers his inaugural address on January 20, 1961.

## **1** The Election of 1960

In 1960, as President Eisenhower's second term drew to a close, a mood of restlessness arose among voters. The economy was in a recession. The USSR's launch of *Sputnik 1* in 1957 and its development of long-range missiles had sparked fears that the American military was falling behind that of the Soviets. Further setbacks including the U-2 incident and the alignment of Cuba with the Soviet Union had Americans questioning whether the United States was losing the Cold War.

◄ John F. Kennedy (*right*) appeared confident and at ease during a televised debate with his opponent Richard M. Nixon.

The Democratic nominee for president, Massachusetts senator John Kennedy, promised active leadership "to get America moving again." His Republican opponent, Vice President Richard M. Nixon, hoped to win by riding on the coattails of Eisenhower's popularity. Both candidates had similar positions on policy issues. Two factors helped put Kennedy over the top: television and the civil rights issue.

**THE TELEVISED DEBATE AFFECTS VOTES** Kennedy had a well-organized campaign and the backing of his wealthy family, and was handsome and charismatic. Yet many felt that, at 43, he was too inexperienced. If elected, he would be the second-youngest president in the nation's history.

**Vocabulary**
**charismatic:** possessing personal charm that attracts devoted followers

Americans also worried that having a Roman Catholic in the White House would lead either to influence of the pope on American policies or to closer ties between church and state. Kennedy was able to allay worries by discussing the issue openly.

One event in the fall determined the course of the election. Kennedy and Nixon took part in the first televised debate between presidential candidates. On September 26, 1960, 70 million TV viewers watched the two articulate and knowledgeable candidates debating issues. Nixon, an expert on foreign policy, had agreed to the forum in hopes of exposing Kennedy's inexperience. However, Kennedy had been coached by television producers, and he looked and spoke better than Nixon. **Ⓐ**

*" That night, image replaced the printed word as the natural language of politics."*
**RUSSELL BAKER**

**MAIN IDEA**

**Predicting Effects**
**Ⓐ** What effect do you think the televised debate would have on American politics?

*A. Possible Answer*
Voters would begin making decisions based on a candidate's perceived image rather than on his or her stand on the issues.

Kennedy's success in the debate launched a new era in American politics: the television age. As journalist Russell Baker, who covered the Nixon campaign, said, "That night, image replaced the printed word as the natural language of politics."

**KENNEDY AND CIVIL RIGHTS** A second major event of the campaign took place in October. Police in Atlanta, Georgia, arrested the Reverend Martin Luther King, Jr., and 33 other African-American demonstrators for sitting at a segregated lunch counter. Although the other demonstrators were released, King was sentenced to months of hard labor—officially for a minor traffic violation. The Eisenhower administration refused to intervene, and Nixon took no public position.

When Kennedy heard of the arrest and sentencing, he telephoned King's wife, Coretta Scott King, to express his sympathy. Meanwhile, Robert Kennedy, his brother and campaign manager, persuaded the judge who had sentenced King to release the civil rights leader on bail, pending appeal. News of the incident captured the immediate attention of the African-American community, whose votes would help Kennedy carry key states in the Midwest and South.

*The New Frontier and the Great Society* **671**

**More About . . .**

**The Kennedy Nixon Debates**
The debate on September 26, 1960 was the first of four televised debates between candidates for president. The debates brought the candidates into American's living room in a brand new way. The candidate could appeal directly to the voters, and scenes of the candidate's presentations could be repeated indefinitely adding to the public's exposure to the candidate's views. As a result, television began to undercut the value of a party structure in drumming up support for a candidate. Running a political campaign now demanded tapping into the power of television to gain an advantage.

**More About . . .**

**The King Arrest**
King's father, a Baptist minister who had supported Nixon, reversed his position after Kennedy contacted his son's wife, Coretta. "Because this man," King, Sr., declared, "was willing to wipe the tears away from my daughter [in-law]'s eyes, I've got a suitcase of votes and I'm going to take them to Mr. Kennedy and dump them in his lap." Across the country, scores of other African-American Protestant ministers followed suit, urging their congregations to set aside "the religious question" (Kennedy's Catholicism was an issue for some American Protestants of all races) in favor of the civil rights question.

---

**ACTIVITY** **SKILLBUILDER LESSON**

## Predicting Effects

**Explaining the Skill** Historians often make predictions about what may happen as a result of a decision or event. They think critically about the event and make realistic predictions about its possible outcomes and consequences.

**Applying the Skill** Many historians believe that Kennedy's success in the televised debates brought fundamental changes to politics. Ask students what role television plays in elections today. *(TV often reduces politics to photo opportunities and sound bites.)* Then have students make predictions about television's role in politics in the future. *(Some may say that TV will become even more important. Others may think there will be a backlash against TV.)*

 In-Depth Resources: Unit 6
· Skillbuilder Practice: Predicting Effects, p. 5

More About . . .

## More About . . .

### Kennedy's Inaugural Address

In his speech, Kennedy appealed to the American people to serve their country. He called on Americans to "struggle against the common enemies of man: tyranny, poverty, disease, and war itself." In a strangely prophetic statement, the new president said, "In your hands, my fellow citizens, more than mine, will rest the final success or failure of our course."

 **In-Depth Resources: Unit 6**
· Primary Source: John F. Kennedy's Inaugural Address, pp. 11–12

## HISTORY from VISUALS

### Interpreting the Photograph

Kennedy was skillful in his use of the press. This photograph shows the Kennedys as a typical American family, despite the wealth and privilege that was part of the background of both the president and his wife. Ask students how a photograph like this may help a president. *(By showing the Kennedys as a regular American family, it makes it easier for voters to think the president is like them and understands their needs and interests.)*

**B. Answers**
The press portrayed the Kennedys as a young, attractive, energetic, and stylish couple; attention to arts and culture; young children; Kennedy's eloquence; television; an admiring press.

---

President and Mrs. Kennedy enjoy time with their children, Caroline and John, Jr., while vacationing in Hyannis Port, Massachusetts. ▼

# 1 The Camelot Years

The election in November 1960 was the closest since 1884; Kennedy won by fewer than 119,000 votes. His inauguration set the tone for a new era at the White House: one of grace, elegance, and wit. On the podium sat over 100 writers, artists, and scientists that the Kennedys had invited, including opera singer Marian Anderson, who had once been barred from singing at Constitution Hall because she was African American. Kennedy's inspiring speech called for hope, commitment, and sacrifice. "And so, my fellow Americans," he proclaimed, "ask not what your country can do for you—ask what you can do for your country."

During his term, the president and his beautiful young wife, Jacqueline, invited many artists and celebrities to the White House. In addition, Kennedy often appeared on television. The press loved his charm and wit and helped to bolster his image.

**THE KENNEDY MYSTIQUE** Critics of Kennedy's presidency argued that his smooth style lacked substance. But the new first family fascinated the public. For example, after learning that JFK could read 1,600 words a minute, thousands of people enrolled in speed-reading courses. The first lady, too, captivated the nation with her eye for fashion and culture. It seemed the nation could not get enough of the first family. Newspapers and magazines filled their pages with pictures and stories about the president's young daughter Caroline and his infant son John.

**Background**
The fictional King Arthur was based on a real fifth- or sixth-century Celt. In literature, Arthur's romantic world is marked by chivalry and magic.

With JFK's youthful glamour and his talented advisers, the Kennedy White House reminded many of a modern-day Camelot, the mythical court of King Arthur. Coincidentally, the musical *Camelot* had opened on Broadway in 1960. Years later, Jackie recalled her husband and the vision of Camelot.

**A PERSONAL VOICE** JACQUELINE KENNEDY

"At night, before we'd go to sleep, Jack liked to play some records and the song he loved most came at the very end of [the *Camelot*] record. The lines he loved to hear were: 'Don't let it be forgot, that once there was a spot, for one brief shining moment that was known as Camelot.' There'll be great presidents again . . . but there'll never be another Camelot again." **B**

—quoted in *Life magazine, John F. Kennedy Memorial Edition*

**MAIN IDEA**

Developing Historical Perspective
**B** What factors help explain the public's fascination with the Kennedys?

**THE BEST AND THE BRIGHTEST** Kennedy surrounded himself with a team of advisers that one journalist called "the best and the brightest." They included McGeorge Bundy, a Harvard University dean, as national security adviser; Robert McNamara, president of Ford Motor Company, as secretary of defense; and Dean Rusk, president of the Rockefeller Foundation, as secretary of state. Of all the advisers who filled Kennedy's inner circle, he relied most heavily on his 35-year-old brother Robert, whom he appointed attorney general.

**672** CHAPTER 20

---

**ACTIVITY** | **LINK TO GOVERNMENT**

 **classzone.com**

### Researching the President's Staff

**Class Time** 45 minutes

**Task** Researching the names and backgrounds of the president's staff

**Purpose** To organize information about members of the executive branch

**Directions** Tell students there are two sets of advisors in the executive branch: the cabinet and the president's White House staff. While cabinet appointments are often made for political reasons, staff members are usually chosen because of their relationship to the president. Have students use the library and the Internet to research the roles and backgrounds of the president's staff, including national security advisor, chief of staff, and others. Then have them put the information in a directory. They should include a list of their sources.

 **Integrated Assessment**
· Rubrics 1, 5

## A New Military Policy

From the beginning, Kennedy focused on the Cold War. He thought the Eisenhower administration had not done enough about the Soviet threat. The Soviets, he concluded, were gaining loyalties in the economically less-developed third-world countries of Asia, Africa, and Latin America. He blasted the Republicans for allowing communism to develop in Cuba, at America's doorstep.

**DEFINING A MILITARY STRATEGY** Kennedy believed his most urgent task was to redefine the nation's nuclear strategy. The Eisenhower administration had relied on the policy of massive retaliation to deter Soviet aggression and imperialism. However, threatening to use nuclear arms over a minor conflict was not a risk Kennedy wished to take. Instead, his team developed a policy of **flexible response.** Kennedy's secretary of defense, Robert McNamara, explained the policy.

**Vocabulary**
**third world:** during the Cold War, the developing nations not allied with either the United States or the Soviet Union

### A PERSONAL VOICE  ROBERT S. MCNAMARA

"The Kennedy administration worried that [the] reliance on nuclear weapons gave us no way to respond to large non-nuclear attacks without committing suicide. . . . We decided to broaden the range of options by strengthening and modernizing the military's ability to fight a nonnuclear war."

—*In Retrospect*

Kennedy increased defense spending in order to boost conventional military forces—nonnuclear forces such as troops, ships, and artillery—and to create an elite branch of the army called the Special Forces, or Green Berets. He also tripled the overall nuclear capabilities of the United States. These changes enabled the United States to fight limited wars around the world while maintaining a balance of nuclear power with the Soviet Union. However, even as Kennedy hoped to reduce the risk of nuclear war, the world came perilously close to nuclear war under his command as a crisis arose over the island of Cuba. **C**

**MAIN IDEA**

**Summarizing**
**C** What was the goal of the doctrine of flexible response?

*C. Answer*
*To allow the U.S. to fight limited wars around the world while maintaining a nuclear balance of power with the Soviets.*

## Crises over Cuba

The first test of Kennedy's foreign policy came in Cuba, just 90 miles off the coast of Florida. About two weeks before Kennedy took office, on January 3, 1961, President Eisenhower had cut off diplomatic relations with Cuba because of a revolutionary leader named **Fidel Castro.** Castro openly declared himself a communist and welcomed aid from the Soviet Union.

**THE CUBAN DILEMMA** Castro gained power with the promise of democracy. From 1956 to 1959, he led a guerrilla movement to topple dictator Fulgencio Batista. He won control in 1959 and later told reporters, "Revolutionaries are not born, they are made by poverty, inequality, and dictatorship." He then promised to eliminate these conditions from Cuba.

The United States was suspicious of Castro's intentions but nevertheless recognized the new government. However, when Castro seized three American and British oil refineries, relations between the United States and Cuba worsened. Castro also broke up commercial farms into communes that would be worked by formerly landless peasants. American sugar companies,

**Vocabulary**
**guerrilla:** a soldier who travels in a small group, harassing and undermining the enemy

**Instruct: Objective**

**A New Military Policy**
TAKS SS11 5(US24.B)

· What was the policy of flexible response?
· Why did Kennedy think it was necessary to develop a new military policy?

📖 In-Depth Resources: Unit 6
· Guided Reading, p. 1

---

**ANOTHER PERSPECTIVE**

**Eisenhower's Warning**
**Evaluating** Ask students what Eisenhower feared might result from the development of a "military-industrial complex." *(Industry and the military would become too powerful, eclipsing the government.)* Ask why Eisenhower believed that some military development was necessary. *(He felt that the military had to be strengthened to counter the Soviet threat.)*

**Instruct: Objective**

**Crises over Cuba**
TAKS SS11 5(WH26.C)

· What political change did Fidel Castro undergo after taking power?
· How did the results of the Bay of Pigs invasion affect Castro and the United States?
· What happened in the Cuban missile crisis?
· Why did Cuban exiles turn against Kennedy and the Democrats?

📖 In-Depth Resources: Unit 6
· Guided Reading, p. 1
· Primary Sources: Political Cartoon, p. 13

*The New Frontier and the Great Society* **673**

---

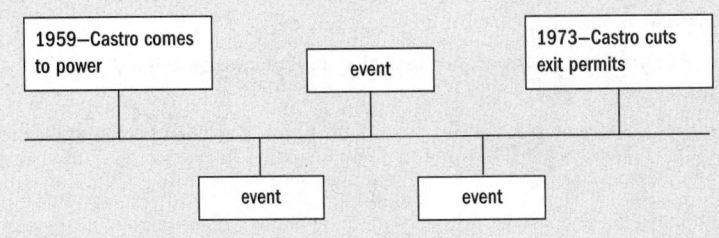

## More About . . .

### The Bay of Pigs Invasion

The Bay of Pigs invasion was a fiasco from the start. The CIA had tried to make the invasion look like an autonomous Cuban operation with no U.S. support. Even U.S. Ambassador to the UN Adlai Stevenson was allowed to address the General Assembly and assert that the U.S. government was not involved. But within days of the failed invasion, the story unraveled. The United States was faced with both a military and major foreign relations disaster from which it took years to recover. In terms of Cuba, the haphazard support given to the invasion created an opening for Khrushchev to send missiles to Castro to defend Cuba and also gave the Soviet leader mixed signals about U.S. resolve.

## Tracing Themes

### SCIENCE AND TECHNOLOGY

By the early 1960s, the United States and the Soviet Union each had built stockpiles of nuclear weapons. Many scientists who had helped develop such weapons warned against their use. But both the United States and the Soviet Union followed a strategy of nuclear deterrence and mutually assured destruction. The idea was that since each side could annihilate the other, this assured destruction would keep each side from launching a first strike.

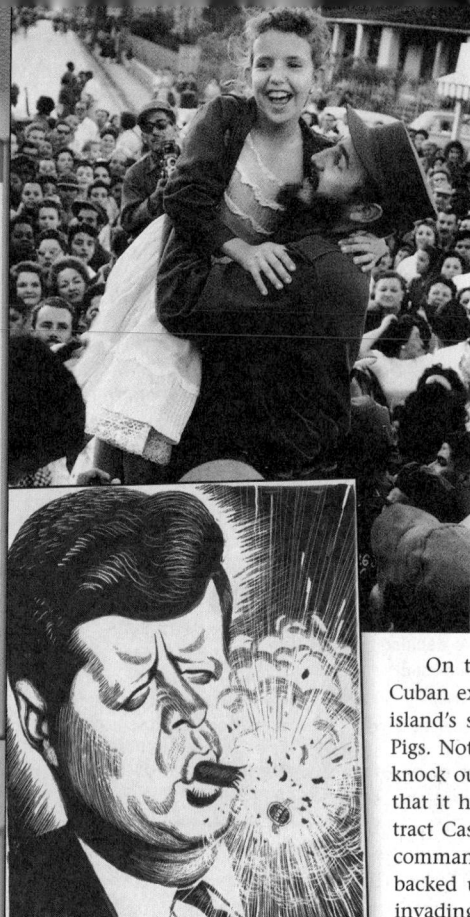

▲ *(top)* Castro celebrates after gaining power in Cuba.
*(above)* The Bay of Pigs mission was said to have blown up in Kennedy's face.

which controlled 75 percent of the crop land in Cuba, appealed to the U.S. government for help. In response, Congress erected trade barriers against Cuban sugar.

Castro relied increasingly on Soviet aid—and on the political repression of those who did not agree with him. While some Cubans were taken by his charisma and his willingness to stand up to the United States, others saw Castro as a tyrant who had replaced one dictatorship with another. About 10 percent of Cuba's population went into exile, mostly to the United States. Within the large exile community of Miami, Florida, a counterrevolutionary movement took shape.

**THE BAY OF PIGS** In March 1960, President Eisenhower gave the CIA permission to secretly train Cuban exiles for an invasion of Cuba. The CIA and the exiles hoped it would trigger a mass uprising that would overthrow Castro. Kennedy learned of the plan only nine days after his election. Although he had doubts, he approved it.

On the night of April 17, 1961, some 1,300 to 1,500 Cuban exiles supported by the U.S. military landed on the island's southern coast at Bahia de Cochinos, the Bay of Pigs. Nothing went as planned. An air strike had failed to knock out the Cuban air force, although the CIA reported that it had succeeded. A small advance group sent to distract Castro's forces never reached shore. When the main commando unit landed, it faced 25,000 Cuban troops backed up by Soviet tanks and jet aircraft. Some of the invading exiles were killed, others imprisoned.

The Cuban media sensationalized the defeat of "North American mercenaries." One United States commentator observed that Americans "look like fools to our friends, rascals to our enemies, and incompetents to the rest." The disaster left Kennedy embarrassed. Publicly, he accepted blame for the fiasco. Privately, he asked, "how could that crowd at the CIA and the Pentagon be this wrong." **D**

Kennedy negotiated with Castro for the release of surviving commandos and paid a ransom of $53 million in food and medical supplies. In a speech in Miami, he promised exiles that they would one day return to a "free Havana." Although Kennedy warned that he would resist further Communist expansion in the Western Hemisphere, Castro defiantly welcomed further Soviet aid.

**THE CUBAN MISSILE CRISIS** Castro had a powerful ally in Moscow: Soviet Premier Nikita Khrushchev, who promised to defend Cuba with Soviet arms. During the summer of 1962, the flow to Cuba of Soviet weapons—including nuclear missiles—increased greatly. President Kennedy responded with a warning that America would not tolerate offensive nuclear weapons in Cuba. Then, on October 14, photographs taken by American planes revealed Soviet missile bases in Cuba—and some contained missiles ready to launch. They could reach U.S. cities in minutes.

On October 22, Kennedy informed an anxious nation of the existence of Soviet missile sites in Cuba and of his plans to remove them. He made it clear that any missile attack from Cuba would trigger an all-out attack on the Soviet Union.

**674** CHAPTER 20

**Vocabulary**
**political repression:** government intimidation of those with different political views

*Skillbuilder Answers*
**1.** Between 10 and 15 minutes
**2.** Because power, resources, and wealth are concentrated in these places.

**MAIN IDEA**

**Analyzing Effects**
**D** What were the consequences of the failed invasion for the United States?

*D. Answers*
Failure to oust Castro, loss of world prestige, embarrassment for JFK, ransom for captured commandos.

---

| ACTIVITY | COOPERATIVE LEARNING | |  BLOCK SCHEDULING |

### Debating the Bay of Pigs

**Class Time** 45 minutes

**Task** Reviewing Kennedy's options in the Bay of Pigs invasion and writing a position paper

**Purpose** To use a problem solving process to suggest a solution to relations with Cuba

**Directions** Divide the class into four smaller groups, two taking the position that the United States should have backed the invasion with more force and commitment and the others that the invasion should have been called off and Castro dealt with diplomatically. The groups should prepare position papers outlining the advantages and risks to their strategies and then debate.

 Integrated Assessment
· Rubrics 3, 5

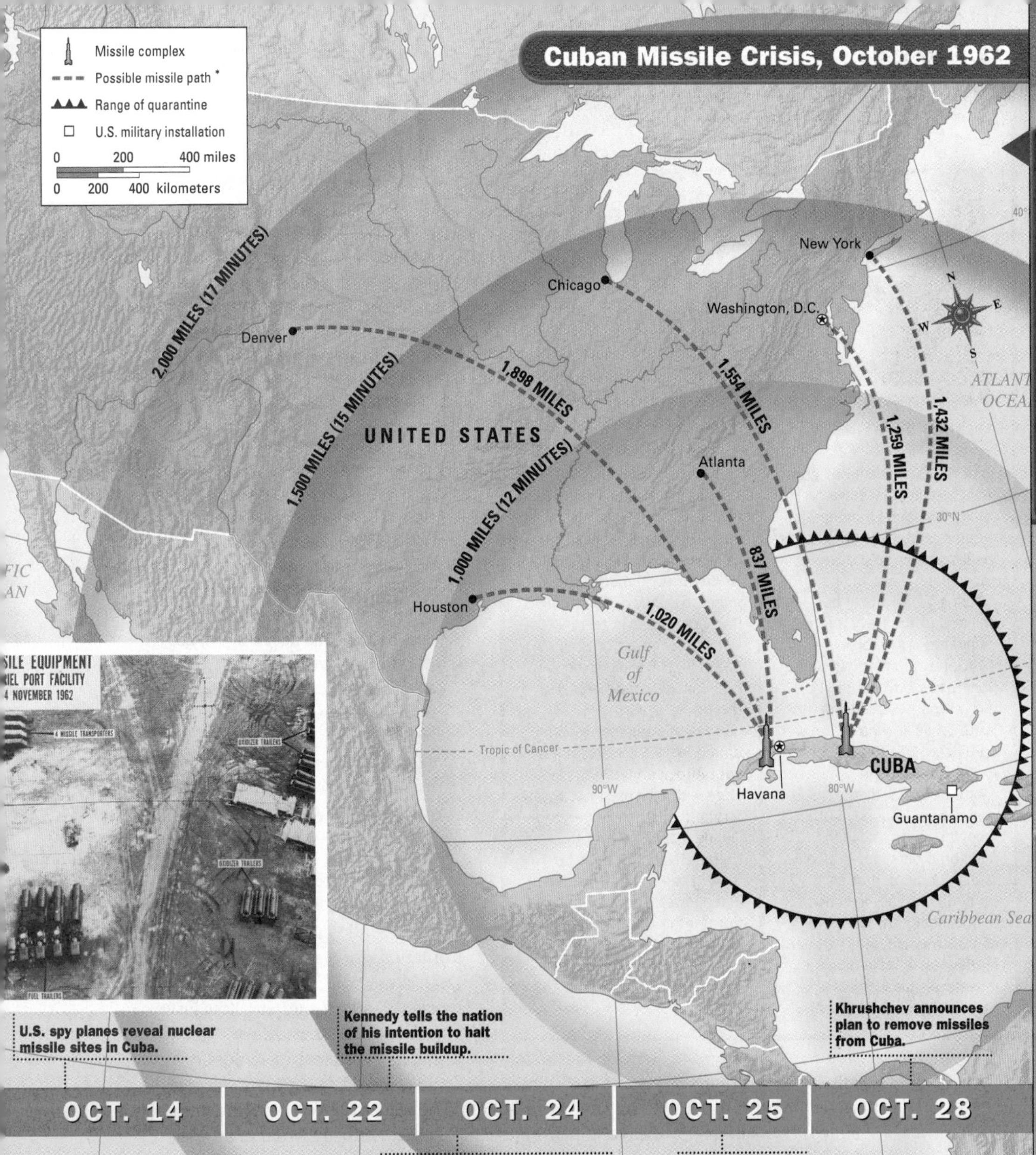
Cuban Missile Crisis, October 1962
Missile complex
Possible missile path *
Range of quarantine
U.S. military installation
0 200 400 miles
0 200 400 kilometers
UNITED STATES
New York
Chicago
Washington, D.C.
Denver
Atlanta
Houston
Havana
CUBA
Guantanamo
Gulf of Mexico
Caribbean Sea
ATLANTIC OCEAN
Tropic of Cancer
90°W
80°W
30°N
40°N
2,000 MILES (17 MINUTES)
1,500 MILES (15 MINUTES)
1,000 MILES (12 MINUTES)
1,898 MILES
1,554 MILES
1,259 MILES
1,432 MILES
837 MILES
1,020 MILES
SILE EQUIPMENT
IEL PORT FACILITY
4 NOVEMBER 1962
U.S. spy planes reveal nuclear missile sites in Cuba.
Kennedy tells the nation of his intention to halt the missile buildup.
Khrushchev announces plan to remove missiles from Cuba.
OCT. 14
OCT. 22
OCT. 24
OCT. 25
OCT. 28
Kennedy implements a naval "quarantine" of Cuba, blocking Soviet ships from reaching the island. (*below*) A U.S. patrol plane flies over a Soviet freighter.
Soviet ships approaching Cuba come to a halt.

*Missile path times and distances are approximate.

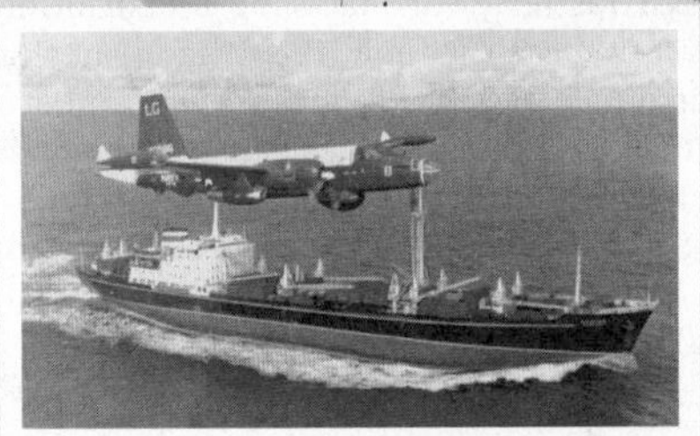

**GEOGRAPHY SKILLBUILDER**

1. **Movement** About how long would it have taken for a missile launched from Cuba to reach New York?
2. **Human-Environment Interaction** Why do you think it may have been important for Soviet missiles to reach the U.S. cities shown above?

*The New Frontier and the Great Society* **675**

## HISTORY from VISUALS

### Interpreting the Map

Tell students that they can use the arcs on the map to calculate how long it would take a Cuban missile to reach an American city. Then ask them how long it would have taken for a missile to reach Los Angeles. *(about 20 minutes)*

**Extension** Ask students why the U.S. range of quarantine extended to the tip of Florida. *(to prevent Soviet ships from entering American waters)*

## More About . . .

### The Cuban Missile Crisis

For a few days, nuclear war and massive destruction was a distinct possibility for every American. In schools, children practiced air raid drills, a common occurrence during the Cold War. People who had built bomb shelters began stocking them with food and other provisions. Millions of Americans listened to their radios and watched their televisions, feeling both fear and helplessness. Even the president called his wife and children, who had been traveling, back to the White House where they could be protected in the presidential nuclear shelter, if necessary.

**ACTIVITY** LINK TO WORLD HISTORY

**BLOCK SCHEDULING**

### Gathering Cuban Missile Crisis Memories

**Class Time** Two class periods

**Task** Creating questions and interviewing people who lived through the Cuban missile crisis

**Purpose** To develop a historical perspective on a crisis that threatened nuclear destruction

**Directions** Ask students to create a list of people to interview. Encourage them to interview individuals who were children, high school students, or adults during that fateful October. Have them develop questions for each. Perhaps, some interviewees could come to class for a videotaped interview. Other interviews could be done as homework assignments.

Integrated Assessment
- Rubric 3

## KEY PLAYERS

**JOHN F. KENNEDY**
**1917–1963**

John F. "Jack" Kennedy grew up in a politically powerful family that helped make his dreams possible. His parents instilled in him the drive to accomplish great things.

During World War II he enlisted in the Navy and was decorated for heroism. In 1946, he won his first seat in Congress from a Boston district where he had never lived. While a senator, he won a Pulitzer Prize for his book *Profiles in Courage*.

Although he radiated self-confidence, Kennedy suffered many ailments, including Addison's disease—a debilitating condition that he treated with daily injections of cortisone. "At least one half of the days that he spent on this earth were days of intense physical pain," recalled his brother Robert.

**NIKITA KHRUSHCHEV**
**1894–1971**

"No matter how humble a man's beginnings," boasted Nikita Khrushchev, "he achieves the stature of the office to which he is elected." Khrushchev, the son of a miner, became a Communist Party organizer in the 1920s. Within four years of Stalin's death in 1953, Khrushchev had consolidated his power in the Soviet Union.

During his regime, which ended in 1964, Khrushchev kept American nerves on edge with alternately conciliatory and aggressive behavior. During a 1959 trip to the United States, he met for friendly talks with President Eisenhower. The next year, in front of the UN General Assembly, he took off his shoe and angrily pounded it on a desk to protest the U-2 incident.

For the next six days, the world faced the terrifying possibility of nuclear war. In the Atlantic Ocean, Soviet ships—presumably carrying more missiles—headed toward Cuba, while the U.S. Navy prepared to quarantine Cuba and prevent the ships from coming within 500 miles of it. In Florida, 100,000 troops waited—the largest invasion force ever assembled in the United States. C. Douglas Dillon, Kennedy's secretary of the treasury and a veteran of nuclear diplomacy, recalled those tension-filled days of October.

### A PERSONAL VOICE
C. DOUGLAS DILLON

" The only time I felt a fear of nuclear war or a use of nuclear weapons was on the very first day, when we'd decided that we had to do whatever was necessary to get the missiles out. There was always some background fear of what would eventually happen, and I think this is what was expressed when people said they feared they would never see another Saturday. "

—quoted in *On the Brink*

The first break in the crisis occurred when the Soviet ships stopped suddenly to avoid a confrontation at sea. Secretary of State Dean Rusk said, "We are eyeball to eyeball, and the other fellow just blinked." A few days later, Khrushchev offered to remove the missiles in return for an American pledge not to invade Cuba. The United States also secretly agreed to remove missiles from Turkey. The leaders agreed, and the crisis ended. "For a moment, the world had stood still," Robert Kennedy wrote years later, "and now it was going around again."

**KENNEDY AND KHRUSHCHEV TAKE THE HEAT** The crisis severely damaged Khrushchev's prestige in the Soviet Union and the world. Kennedy did not escape criticism either. Some people criticized Kennedy for practicing brinkmanship when private talks might have resolved the crisis without the threat of nuclear war. Others believed he had passed up an ideal chance to invade Cuba and oust Castro. (It was learned in the 1990s that the CIA had underestimated the numbers of Soviet troops and nuclear weapons on the island.)

The effects of the crisis lasted long after the missiles had been removed. Many Cuban exiles blamed the Democrats for "losing Cuba" (a charge that Kennedy had earlier leveled at the Republicans) and switched their allegiance to the GOP.

**MAIN IDEA**

**Analyzing Effects**

**E** What were the results of the Cuban missile crisis?

*E. Answers*
Kennedy staved off war; Khrushchev's prestige tarnished; many Cuban exiles blamed Democrats for "losing Cuba" and switched allegiance to GOP; Castro limited exiles' access to Cuba.

Meanwhile, Castro closed Cuba's doors to the exiles in November 1962 by banning all flights to and from Miami. Three years later, hundreds of thousands of people took advantage of an agreement that allowed Cubans to join relatives in the United States. By the time Castro sharply cut down on exit permits in 1973, the Cuban population in Miami had increased to about 300,000. **E**

## Crisis over Berlin 4

One goal that had guided Kennedy through the Cuban Missile Crisis was that of proving to Khruschev his determination to contain communism. All the while, Kennedy was thinking of their recent confrontation over Berlin, which had led to the construction of the **Berlin Wall,** a concrete wall topped with barbed wire that severed the city in two.

**THE BERLIN CRISIS** In 1961, Berlin was a city in great turmoil. In the 11 years since the Berlin Airlift, almost 3 million East Germans—20 percent of that country's population—had fled into West Berlin because it was free from Communist rule. These refugees advertised the failure of East Germany's Communist government. Their departure also dangerously weakened that country's economy.

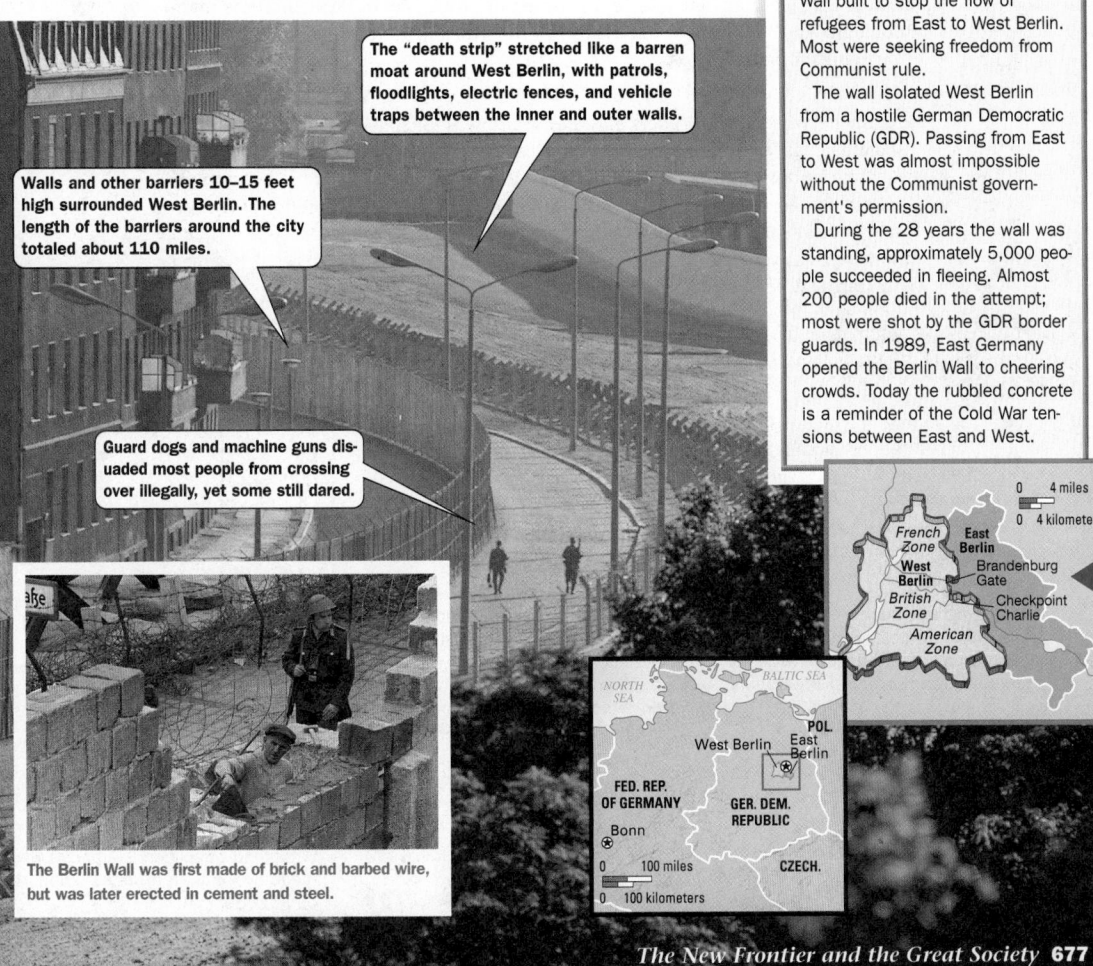

The "death strip" stretched like a barren moat around West Berlin, with patrols, floodlights, electric fences, and vehicle traps between the inner and outer walls.

Walls and other barriers 10–15 feet high surrounded West Berlin. The length of the barriers around the city totaled about 110 miles.

Guard dogs and machine guns disuaded most people from crossing over illegally, yet some still dared.

The Berlin Wall was first made of brick and barbed wire, but was later erected in cement and steel.

### WORLD STAGE

**THE BERLIN WALL, 1961**

In 1961, Nikita Khrushchev, the Soviet premier, ordered the Berlin Wall built to stop the flow of refugees from East to West Berlin. Most were seeking freedom from Communist rule.

The wall isolated West Berlin from a hostile German Democratic Republic (GDR). Passing from East to West was almost impossible without the Communist government's permission.

During the 28 years the wall was standing, approximately 5,000 people succeeded in fleeing. Almost 200 people died in the attempt; most were shot by the GDR border guards. In 1989, East Germany opened the Berlin Wall to cheering crowds. Today the rubbled concrete is a reminder of the Cold War tensions between East and West.

*The New Frontier and the Great Society* **677**

**Crisis Over Berlin**
TAKS SS11 5(WG8.B)
· Why was the Berlin Wall built?
· How did Kennedy and Khrushchev ease tensions between their nations?

In-Depth Resources: Unit 6
· Guided Reading, p. 1

### ON THE WORLD STAGE

**The Berlin Wall, 1961**
At the stroke of midnight on November 9, 1989, thousands of Germans took hammers and chisels and began to tear down the hated wall that divided Berlin. For the first time in 28 years, East and West Germans walked freely between the two zones, embracing each other, crying, and rejoicing.

### HISTORY from VISUALS

**Interpreting the Infographic**
Discuss with students that in building the wall, the East Germans were not just building a security barrier but making a statement. Ask students what they think that statement was. *(The state is all-powerful and can keep someone from leaving.)*

**Extension** Ask students how Berlin's location presented security problems for East Germany. *(Before the wall, people could escape from East Germany by crossing the street to freedom in West Berlin.)*

---

**ACTIVITY** | **LINK TO GEOGRAPHY**

 **classzone.com**

### Mapping Berlin and Germany

**Class Time** 45 minutes

**Task** Mapping the partition of Germany and Berlin

**Purpose** To analyze the geographic problems presented by a divided Berlin in the Cold War

**Directions** Ask students to use the text and library and Internet resources to research the partitioning of Germany and Berlin at the end of World War II. Have students draw maps of both Germany and Berlin that show the partitioning. Ask them to use the maps to explain why the division of Berlin inside East Germany was a continual trouble spot during the Cold War.

Integrated Assessment
· Rubric 2

## More About . . .

### Kennedy and Berlin

One of the highpoints of Kennedy's foreign travels was a trip he made to Berlin in 1963 to dramatize America's commitment to West Berlin and West Germany. In a speech at the Berlin Wall, Kennedy electrified an audience of about 150,000 Germans by stating, *"Ich bin ein Berliner"* (I am a Berliner), thus declaring the solidarity of all free people with the people of West Berlin. Kennedy was enormously popular in Europe, and Europeans mourned his death in 1963.

## Assess & Reteach

### SECTION 1 ASSESSMENT

Have small groups of students get together to discuss and answer the questions.

 Formal Assessment
· Section Quiz, p. 370

### SELF-ASSESSMENT

To document what they have learned, have students create a time line listing the main events of Kennedy's presidency.

### RETEACH

Use the map and accompanying time line on page 675 to review the Soviet-American confrontation during the Cuban missile crisis.

 In-Depth Resources: Unit 6
· Reteaching Activity, p. 6

---

*"I want peace. But, if you want war, that is your problem."*

**SOVIET PREMIER NIKITA KHRUSHCHEV**

*F. Answer* Communists wanted to stop the flow of East German refugees into West Berlin and further isolate the thriving city.

Khrushchev realized that this problem had to be solved. At a summit meeting in Vienna, Austria, in June 1961, he threatened to sign a treaty with East Germany that would enable that country to close all the access roads to West Berlin. When Kennedy refused to give up U.S. access to West Berlin, Khrushchev furiously declared, "I want peace. But, if you want war, that is your problem."

After returning home, Kennedy told the nation in a televised address that Berlin was "the great testing place of Western courage and will." He pledged "[W]e cannot and will not permit the Communists to drive us out of Berlin."

Kennedy's determination and America's superior nuclear striking power prevented Khrushchev from closing the air and land routes between West Berlin and West Germany. Instead, the Soviet premier surprised the world with a shocking decision. Just after midnight on August 13, 1961, East German troops began to unload concrete posts and rolls of barbed wire along the border. Within days, the Berlin Wall was erected, separating East Germany from West Germany.

The construction of the Berlin Wall ended the Berlin crisis but further aggravated Cold War tensions. The wall and its armed guards successfully reduced the flow of East German refugees to a tiny trickle, thus solving Khrushchev's main problem. At the same time, however, the wall became an ugly symbol of Communist oppression. **F**

**SEARCHING FOR WAYS TO EASE TENSIONS** Showdowns between Kennedy and Khrushchev made both leaders aware of the gravity of split-second decisions that separated Cold War peace from nuclear disaster. Kennedy, in particular, searched for ways to tone down his hard-line stance. In 1963, he announced that the two nations had established a **hot line** between the White House and the Kremlin. This dedicated phone enabled the leaders of the two countries to communicate at once should another crisis arise. Later that year, the United States and Soviet Union also agreed to a **Limited Test Ban Treaty** that barred nuclear testing in the atmosphere.

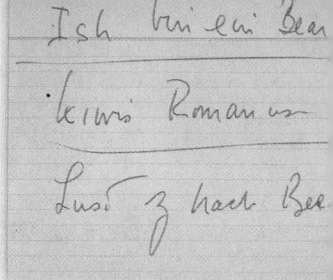

Reading from this note card during a speech in West Berlin, Kennedy proclaimed "Ich bin ein Berliner" ("I am a Berliner").

**MAIN IDEA**

Analyzing Motives
**F** What led Khrushchev to erect the Berlin Wall?

---

### ASSESSMENT

1. **TERMS & NAMES** For each term or name, write a sentence explaining its significance.

- John F. Kennedy
- flexible response
- Fidel Castro
- Berlin Wall
- hot line
- Limited Test Ban Treaty

**MAIN IDEA**

2. **TAKING NOTES**
Using diagrams such as the one below, list two outcomes for each of these events: first Kennedy-Nixon debate, Bay of Pigs invasion, Cuban missile crisis, and construction of the Berlin Wall.

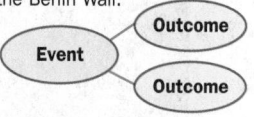

Which of these outcomes led directly to other events listed here or described in this section?

**CRITICAL THINKING**

3. **EVALUATING DECISIONS**
How well do you think President Kennedy handled the Cuban missile crisis? Justify your opinion with specific examples from the text.
**Think About:**
- Kennedy's decision to impose a naval "quarantine" of Cuba
- the nuclear showdown between the superpowers
- Kennedy's decision not to invade Cuba

4. **ANALYZING VISUAL SOURCES**
Examine the cartoon above of Kennedy (*left*) facing off with Khrushchev and Castro. What do you think the cartoonist was trying to convey?

5. **DRAWING CONCLUSIONS**
What kind of political statement was made by the United States' support of West Berlin?

**678** CHAPTER 20

---

### ASSESSMENT   Answers

**1. TERMS & NAMES**
John F. Kennedy, p. 670
flexible response, p. 673
Fidel Castro, p. 673
Berlin Wall, p. 677
hot line, p. 678
Limited Test Ban Treaty, p. 678

**2. TAKING NOTES**
**Debate:** Kennedy won support, TV became important in politics; **Bay of Pigs:** United States embarrassed, Cuba moved closer to Soviets; **Cuban missile crisis:** world at brink of nuclear war, Soviets backed down; **Berlin Wall:** increased Cold War tensions, symbolized Communist oppression.

**3. EVALUATING DECISIONS**
Students giving Kennedy high marks might say that the Cuban missiles were removed, nuclear war was averted, and there was no military engagement. Students giving him low marks might say that he risked nuclear war over the crisis.

**4. ANALYZING VISUAL SOURCES**
The cartoonist was trying to indicate that Kennedy and the United States were in a deadly showdown with Khrushchev and the Soviet Union over Castro's Cuba.

**5. DRAWING CONCLUSIONS**
The United States was telling other nations, the Soviet Union especially, to keep their hands off West Berlin.

# The New Frontier

## MAIN IDEA

While Kennedy had trouble getting his ideas for a New Frontier passed, several goals were achieved.

## WHY IT MATTERS NOW

Kennedy's space program continues to generate scientific and engineering advances that benefit Americans.

## Terms & Names

- New Frontier
- mandate
- Peace Corps
- Alliance for Progress
- Warren Commission

### OBJECTIVES

**1** Summarize the New Frontier domestic and foreign agendas.

**2** Describe the tragic chain of events surrounding Kennedy's assassination.

### SKILLBUILDER
· Interpreting Graphs and Charts, p. 681

### CRITICAL THINKING
· Identifying Problems, p. 680
· Analyzing Motives, pp. 681, 683
· Analyzing Effects, p. 681
· Making Inferences, pp. 682, 683
· Contrasting, p. 683
· Evaluating Leadership, p. 683

 U.S. History
TEKS
7A, 8A, 8B, 19B, 22A, 22B, 23B, 24B, 24D, 25A, 25B, 25C, 25D

### One American's Story

On May 5, 1961, American astronaut Alan Shepard climbed into *Freedom 7*, a tiny capsule on top of a huge rocket booster. The capsule left the earth's atmosphere in a ball of fire and returned the same way, and Shepard became the first American to travel into space. Years later, he recalled his emotions when a naval crew fished him out of the Atlantic.

**A PERSONAL VOICE** ALAN SHEPARD

"Until the moment I stepped out of the flight deck . . . I hadn't realized the intensity of the emotions and feelings that so many people had for me, for the other astronauts, and for the whole manned space program. . . . I was very close to tears as I thought, it's no longer just our fight to get 'out there.' The struggle belongs to everyone in America. . . . From now on there was no turning back."

—*Moon Shot: The Inside Story of America's Race to the Moon*

▲ Astronaut Alan Shepard (*inset*) prepares to enter the space capsule for his *Mercury* flight.

The entire trip—which took only 15 minutes from liftoff to splashdown—reaffirmed the belief in American ingenuity. John F. Kennedy inspired many Americans with the same kind of belief.

## The Promise of Progress **1**

Kennedy set out to transform his broad vision of progress into what he called the **New Frontier.** "We stand today on the edge of a New Frontier," Kennedy had announced upon accepting the nomination for president. He called on Americans to be "new pioneers" and explore "uncharted areas of science and space, . . . unconquered pockets of ignorance and prejudice, unanswered questions of poverty and surplus."

Kennedy had difficulty turning his vision into reality, however. He offered Congress proposals to provide medical care for the aged, rebuild blighted urban areas, and aid education, but he couldn't gather enough votes. Kennedy faced the same conservative coalition of Republicans and Southern Democrats that had

*The New Frontier and the Great Society* **679**

## Focus & Motivate

Ask students whether they can imagine a historical event that so moved them that they would remember exactly where they were and what they were doing for the rest of their lives. Tell them that millions of Americans have such a memory of the moment when they heard that President Kennedy was shot.

## Instruct

### Instruct: Objective **1**
**The Promise of Progress**
TAKS SS11 1(US1.A)
· Why did Kennedy have trouble enacting his New Frontier proposals?
· What was the economic plan of the Kennedy administration?
· How did Kennedy help developing nations?
· What spurred the development of the U.S. space program?
· How were the issues of poverty and civil rights addressed?

 In-Depth Resources: Unit 6
· Guided Reading, p. 2
· American Lives: Alan Shepard, p. 18
Geography Transparencies GT28
· Influence of Alliance for Progress

---

## PROGRAM RESOURCES

 In-Depth Resources: Unit 6
· Guided Reading, p. 2
· Reteaching Activity, p. 7
· Literature: from *Paper Wings*, pp. 15–17
· American Lives: Alan Shepard, p. 18

 Reading Study Guide (English and Spanish), pp. 203–204

 Access for Students Acquiring English/ESL
· Guided Reading (Spanish), p. 219

 Formal Assessment
· Section Quiz, p. 371

 Integrated Assessment
· Rubrics

### INTEGRATED TECHNOLOGY

 Geography Transp. GT28
· Influence of Alliance for Progress

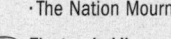 Humanities Transp. HT43
· The Nation Mourns

 Electronic Library of Primary Sources

classzone.com

### TEXAS RESOURCES

 TAKS Spiraled Content Review

 TAKS Practice Tests

 TAKS Practice Transparencies TT107

 TAKS Online Test Practice

## ECONOMIC BACKGROUND

### What Is a Recession?

The functioning definition of a recession used by most economists is a decline in the GDP for two consecutive quarters. A recession is usually characterized by a decline in consumer spending, which sets in motion a chain of events that slows business further. Reductions in consumer spending lead to increased inventories, employee layoffs, and a further decline in consumer confidence. Ask students how they would respond if they thought they were about to lose their job. (reduce spending)

## More About . . .

### The Peace Corps

Kennedy voiced the need for a peace corps during his 1960 campaign. He declared, "There is not enough money in all America to relieve the misery of the underdeveloped world in a giant and endless soup kitchen. But there is enough know-how and knowledgeable people to help those nations help themselves." After his election, he appointed his brother-in-law, R. Sargent Shriver, director of the Peace Corps. Much of the early success of the Peace Corps was attributed to Shriver's leadership.

## ECONOMIC BACKGROUND

### WHAT IS A RECESSION?

A recession is, in a general sense, a moderate slowdown of the economy marked by increased unemployment and reduced personal consumption. In 1961, the nation's jobless rate climbed from just under 6 percent to nearly 7 percent. Personal consumption of several major items declined that year, as people worried about job security and spent less money.

Car sales, for example, dropped by more than $1 billion from the previous year, while fewer people took overseas vacations. Perhaps the surest sign that the country had entered a recession was the admission by government officials of how bleak things were. "We are in a full-fledged recession," Labor Secretary Arthur Goldberg declared in February of 1961. (See *recession* on page R44 in the Economics Handbook.)

blocked Truman's Fair Deal, and he showed little skill in pushing his domestic reform measures through Congress. Since Kennedy had been elected by the slimmest of margins, he lacked a popular **mandate**—a clear indication that voters approved of his plans. As a result, he often tried to play it safe politically. Nevertheless, Kennedy did persuade Congress to enact measures to boost the economy, build the national defense, provide international aid, and fund a massive space program. **A**

**STIMULATING THE ECONOMY** One domestic problem the Kennedy team tackled was the economy. By 1960 America was in a recession. Unemployment hovered around 6 percent, one of the highest levels since World War II. During the campaign, Kennedy had criticized the Eisenhower administration for failing to stimulate growth. The American economy, he said, was lagging behind those of other Western democracies and the Soviet Union.

Kennedy's advisers pushed for the use of deficit spending, which had been the basis for Roosevelt's New Deal. They said that stimulating economic growth depended on increased government spending and lower taxes, even if it meant that the government spent more than it took in.

Accordingly, the proposals Kennedy sent to Congress in 1961 called for increased spending. The Department of Defense received a nearly 20 percent budget increase for new nuclear missiles, nuclear submarines, and an expansion of the armed services. Congress also approved a package that increased the minimum wage to $1.25 an hour, extended unemployment insurance, and provided assistance to cities with high unemployment.

**ADDRESSING POVERTY ABROAD** One of the first campaign promises Kennedy fulfilled was the creation of the **Peace Corps,** a program of volunteer assistance to the developing nations of Asia, Africa, and Latin America. Critics in the United States called the program "Kennedy's Kiddie Korps" because many volunteers were just out of college. Some foreign observers questioned whether Americans could understand other cultures.

◀ A Peace Corps volunteer gives a ride to a Nigerian girl.

Despite these reservations, the Peace Corps became a huge success. People of all ages and backgrounds signed up to work as agricultural advisers, teachers, or health aides or to do whatever work the host country needed. By 1968, more than 35,000 volunteers had served in 60 nations around the world.

A second foreign aid program, the **Alliance for Progress,** offered economic and technical assistance to Latin American countries. Between 1961 and 1969, the United States invested almost

> **MAIN IDEA**
>
> **Identifying Problems**
> **A** Why did Kennedy have difficulty achieving many of his New Frontier goals?
>
> *A. Answer*
> He lacked the votes in Congress and a popular mandate.
>
> **Background**
> See *deficit spending* on page R39 in the Economics Handbook.

---

**ACTIVITY** | **COOPERATIVE LEARNING**

 **classzone.com**

### Writing an Advertisement for the Peace Corps

**Class Time** 45 minutes

**Task** Writing a job description to recruit people to join the Peace Corps

**Purpose** To explore the purpose of the Peace Corps and the dedication of its volunteers

**Directions** Students can use library resources and the Internet to research the work that Peace Corps volunteers do. Then, they should write an ad for a specific job in a specific country, giving a description of the work involved and listing qualifications needed by applicants. If possible, the ad should include photos or drawings of volunteers doing similar work.

📄 Integrated Assessment
· Rubrics 2, 4, 5

MAIN IDEA

Analyzing Motives

**B** Why did Kennedy want to invest in foreign aid?

*B. Answer*
To help developing countries and to create a strong U.S. presence to counter communist influence.

$12 billion in Latin America, in part to deter these countries from picking up Fidel Castro's revolutionary ideas. While the money brought some development to the region, it didn't bring fundamental reforms. **B**

**RACE TO THE MOON** On April 12, 1961, Soviet cosmonaut Yuri A. Gagarin became the first human in space. Kennedy saw this as a challenge and decided that America would surpass the Soviets by sending a man to the moon.

In less than a month the United States had duplicated the Soviet feat. Later that year, a communications satellite called Telstar relayed live television pictures across the Atlantic Ocean from Maine to Europe. Meanwhile, America's National Aeronautics and Space Administration (NASA) had begun to construct new launch facilities at Cape Canaveral, Florida, and a mission control center in Houston, Texas. America's pride and prestige were restored. Speaking before a crowd at Houston's Rice University, Kennedy expressed the spirit of "the space race."

### A PERSONAL VOICE PRESIDENT JOHN F. KENNEDY

" We choose to go to the moon in this decade and do the other things, not because they are easy, but because they are hard, because that goal will serve to organize and measure the best of our energies and skills, because that challenge is one that we are willing to accept, one we are unwilling to postpone, and one which we intend to win, and the others, too. "

—Address on the Nation's Space Effort, September 12, 1962

Seven years later, on July 20, 1969, the U.S. would achieve its goal. An excited nation watched with bated breath as U.S. astronaut Neil Armstrong took his first steps on the moon.

As a result of the space program, universities expanded their science programs. The huge federal funding for research and development gave rise to new industries and new technologies, many of which could be used in business and industry and also in new consumer goods. Space- and defense-related industries sprang up in the Southern and Western states, which grew rapidly. **C**

MAIN IDEA

Analyzing Effects

**C** What effect did the space program have on other areas of American life?

*C. Answer*
It improved education, particularly in science and math, and spurred many businesses and industries.

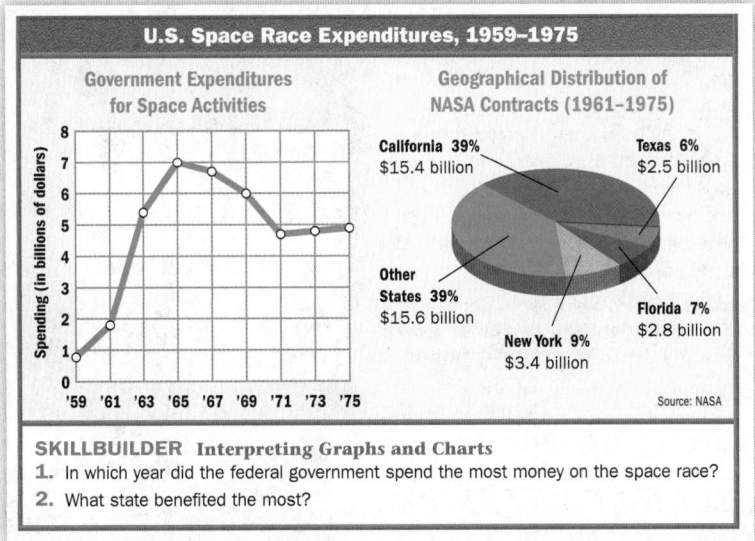

**U.S. Space Race Expenditures, 1959–1975**

**Government Expenditures for Space Activities**

*Spending (in billions of dollars)*
'59 '61 '63 '65 '67 '69 '71 '73 '75

**Geographical Distribution of NASA Contracts (1961–1975)**

California 39% $15.4 billion
Texas 6% $2.5 billion
Other States 39% $15.6 billion
Florida 7% $2.8 billion
New York 9% $3.4 billion

Source: NASA

**SKILLBUILDER** Interpreting Graphs and Charts
**1.** In which year did the federal government spend the most money on the space race?
**2.** What state benefited the most?

*Skillbuilder Answers*
1. 1965
2. California

---

### HISTORICAL SPOTLIGHT

**Johnson and Mission Control**
Ask students what Johnson's actions as chairman of the National Aeronautics and Space Council reveal about the role he envisioned for himself as vice president. *(He was ambitious and unwilling to be a passive vice president.)*

### Tracing Themes
SCIENCE AND TECHNOLOGY

**The Space Program**
Technology developed for the space program greatly influenced the scientific community, the civilian economy, and American life. Computer chips; medical, telecommunication, and aviation advances; and even freeze-dried foods and instant beverages were all developments of the space program.

Electronic Library of Primary Sources
· *from* On the Space Program, 1961, by John F. Kennedy

### HISTORY from VISUALS

**Interpreting the Graph and Charts**
Explain that the line graph shows the amount of money NASA spent per year, while the pie chart shows the total amount of money individual states received from NASA over a period of time. Ask students why the pie chart covers only certain states. *(These are states where space program centers were located.)*

---

**ACTIVITY** LINK TO SCIENCE

 classzone.com

## Charting the U.S. Space Program

**Class Time** 45 minutes

**Task** Charting and discussing U.S. space programs

**Purpose** To evaluate current U.S. commitment to space exploration

**Directions** Ask students to use the Internet to learn about the current American commitment to space exploration. Their research should include names and purposes of space programs, plus information on funding the program. They should chart their findings. Next have a class discussion about the level of space funding and the impact of space technology and exploration on life on earth.

Integrated Assessment
· Rubrics 1, 3

## More About . . .

### Kennedy and Civil Rights

Kennedy's civil rights bill was blocked in Congress by conservative southern Democrats. In August 1963, civil rights organizations held the March on Washington to urge passage of the measure. About 250,000 Americans of all races came to Washington to show their support. Among the speakers on that sweltering August day was Martin Luther King, Jr., who gave his memorable "I Have a Dream" speech.

## Instruct: Objective ➋

### Tragedy in Dallas
TAKS SS11 5(US24.B)
· What were people's reaction to Kennedy's assassination?
· How did television coverage both shock and bring the nation together?
· What was the task of the Warren Commission?

 In-Depth Resources: Unit 6
· Guided Reading, p. 2

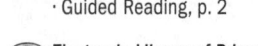 Electronic Library of Primary Sources
· from That Day in Dallas, 1963, by T. Wicker

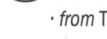 Humanities Transparencies HT43
· The Nation Mourns

**ADDRESSING DOMESTIC PROBLEMS** While progress was being made on the new frontiers of space exploration and international aid, many Americans suffered at home. In 1962, the problem of poverty in America was brought to national attention in Michael Harrington's book *The Other America*. Harrington profiled the 50 million people in America who scraped by each year on less than $1,000 per person. The number of poor shocked many Americans.

While Harrington awakened the nation to the nightmare of poverty, the fight against segregation took hold. Throughout the South, demonstrators raised their voices in what would become some of the most controversial civil rights battles of the 1960s. (See Chapter 21.) Kennedy had not pushed aggressively for legislation on the issues of poverty and civil rights, although he effected changes by executive action. However, now he felt that it was time to live up to a campaign promise.

In 1963, Kennedy began to focus more closely on the issues at home. He called for a "national assault on the causes of poverty." He also ordered Robert Kennedy's Justice Department to investigate racial injustices in the South. Finally, he presented Congress with a sweeping civil rights bill and a proposal to cut taxes by over $10 billion. **D**

## ➋ Tragedy in Dallas

In the fall of 1963, public opinion polls showed that Kennedy was losing popularity because of his advocacy of civil rights. Yet most still supported their beloved president. No one could foresee the terrible national tragedy just ahead.

**FOUR DAYS IN NOVEMBER** On the sunny morning of November 22, 1963, *Air Force One*, the presidential aircraft, landed in Dallas, Texas. President and Mrs. Kennedy had come to Texas to mend political fences with members of the state's Democratic Party. Kennedy had expected a cool reception from the conservative state, but he basked instead in warm waves of applause from crowds that lined the streets of downtown Dallas.

Jacqueline and her husband sat in the back seat of an open-air limousine. In front of them sat Texas Governor John Connally and his wife, Nellie. As the car approached a state building known as the Texas School Book Depository, Nellie Connally turned to Kennedy and said, "You can't say that Dallas isn't friendly to you today." A few seconds later, rifle shots rang out, and Kennedy was shot in the head. His car raced to a nearby hospital, where doctors frantically tried to revive him, but it was too late. President Kennedy was dead.

As the tragic news spread through America's schools, offices, and homes, people reacted with disbelief. Questions were on everyone's lips: Who had killed the president, and why? What would happen next?

▷ John Kennedy, Jr., salutes his father's casket as it is prepared for the trip to Arlington National Cemetery. His uncles, Edward Kennedy and Attorney General Robert Kennedy; his mother; and his sister look on.

*The New York Times.* LATE CITY EDITION

**KENNEDY IS KILLED BY SNIPER AS HE RIDES IN CAR IN DALLAS; JOHNSON SWORN IN ON PLANE**

| MAIN IDEA |
| --- |

**Making Inferences**
**D** In what directions did President Kennedy seem to be taking his administration in 1963?

*D. Answer*
Toward taking more action on domestic problems, including poverty, civil rights, and the economy.

---

**DIFFERENTIATING INSTRUCTION** | **GIFTED AND TALENTED STUDENTS** |  classzone.com

### Researching the Warren Report and Conspiracy Theories

Encourage interested students to research the facts and theories about Kennedy's assassination. Have students use Internet or library resources to get an overview of the Warren Commission report and the theories of the leading critics of the report. They should consider the accuracy of the commission's finding that Lee Harvey Oswald alone was responsible for Kennedy's death. Have students report their findings to the class. Then have the students hold a panel discussion on the lingering doubts about the assassination.

Discussions should . . .
· show evidence of sound research
· cover both the Warren Commission report and the criticism of the report
· demonstrate the involvement of each person in the group

During the next four days, television became "the window of the world." A photograph of a somber Lyndon Johnson taking the oath of office aboard the presidential airplane was broadcast. Soon, audiences watched as Dallas police charged Lee Harvey Oswald with the murder. His palm print had been found on the rifle used to kill John F. Kennedy.

The 24-year-old Marine had a suspicious past. After receiving a dishonorable discharge, Oswald had briefly lived in the Soviet Union, and he supported Castro. On Sunday, November 24, as millions watched live television coverage of Oswald being transferred between jails, a nightclub owner named Jack Ruby broke through the crowd and shot and killed Oswald.

The next day, all work stopped for Kennedy's funeral as America mourned its fallen leader. The assassination and televised funeral became a historic event. Americans who were alive then can still recall what they were doing when they first heard about the shooting of their president.

**UNANSWERED QUESTIONS** The bizarre chain of events made some people wonder if Oswald was part of a conspiracy. In 1963, the **Warren Commission** investigated and concluded that Oswald had shot the president while acting on his own. Later, in 1979, a reinvestigation concluded that Oswald was part of a conspiracy. Investigators also said that two persons may have fired at the president. Numerous other people have made investigations. Their explanations have ranged from a plot by anti-Castro Cubans, to a Communist-sponsored attack, to a conspiracy by the CIA.

What Americans did learn from the Kennedy assassination was that their system of government is remarkably sturdy. A crisis that would have crippled a dictatorship did not prevent a smooth transition to the presidency of Lyndon Johnson. In a speech to Congress, Johnson expressed his hope that "from the brutal loss of our leader we will derive not weakness but strength." Not long after, Johnson drove through Congress the most ambitious domestic legislative package since the New Deal.

*E. Answer*
It declared that Oswald acted alone, while others claimed a conspiracy.

**Vocabulary**
**conspiracy:** an agreement by two or more persons to take illegal political action

---

**MAIN IDEA**

**Contrasting**
**E** How did the Warren Commission's findings differ from other theories?

---

**KENNEDY'S ASSASSINATION**

From the beginning, people have questioned the Warren Commission report. Amateur investigators have led to increasing public pressure on the government to tell all it knows about the assassination.

In response, Congress passed the JFK Records Act in 1992, which created a panel to review government and private files and decide which should be part of the public record.

Since the law was enacted, newly declassified information has added some weight to a body of evidence that JFK was shot from the front (the Warren Commission had concluded that a single bullet struck the president from behind) and that Oswald, thus, could not have acted alone. While such evidence challenges the Warren Commission's report, no information has yet surfaced that conclusively disproves its findings.

---

**NOW & THEN**

**Kennedy's Assassination**
Ask students why the Kennedy assassination continues to fascinate people. Why are some people convinced that there was a conspiracy? *(Some facts have not been adequately explained; people do not want to believe that one individual like Oswald could alter the course of history; people distrust government.)*

## Assess & Reteach

### SECTION 2 ASSESSMENT
Pair more proficient students with less proficient ones to answer the questions.

📄 Formal Assessment
· Section Quiz, p. 371

### SELF-ASSESSMENT
Ask students to make a list of the impressions they had of Kennedy and his presidency before reading Section 2. Then have them note whether their reading has confirmed or contradicted their preconceptions.

### RETEACH
Use the Section Quiz to help students review Section 2.

📄 In-Depth Resources: Unit 6
· Reteaching Activity, p. 7

---

## ② ASSESSMENT

**1. TERMS & NAMES** For each term or name, write a sentence explaining its significance.
- New Frontier
- Peace Corps
- Warren Commission
- mandate
- Alliance for Progress

**MAIN IDEA**

**2. TAKING NOTES**
Re-create the web shown and fill it in with programs of the New Frontier.

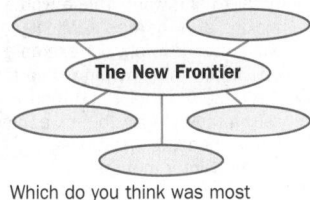

The New Frontier

Which do you think was most successful? Why?

**CRITICAL THINKING**

**3. ANALYZING MOTIVES**
Why do you think Congress was so enthusiastic about allocating funds for the space program but rejected spending in education, social services, and other pressing needs?

**4. MAKING INFERENCES**
Why do you think Kennedy lost popularity for supporting civil rights?

**5. EVALUATING LEADERSHIP**
Do you think President Kennedy was a successful leader? Explain your viewpoint. **Think About:**
- the reasons for his popularity
- the goals he expressed
- his foreign policy
- his legislative record

*The New Frontier and the Great Society* **683**

---

Answers **ASSESSMENT**

**1. TERMS & NAMES**
New Frontier, p. 679
mandate, p. 680
Peace Corps, p. 680
Alliance for Progress, p. 680
Warren Commission, p. 683

**2. TAKING NOTES**
Peace Corps, Alliance for Progress, moon program, tax cut, civil rights bill

**3. ANALYZING MOTIVES**
It was largely a matter of pride, since the Soviets had already sent a cosmonaut into space.

**4. MAKING INFERENCES**
Kennedy lost popularity for supporting civil rights because people in some sections of the country opposed granting civil rights to African Americans.

**5. EVALUATING LEADERSHIP**
Successful: popular, focused on projects that Congress would support, peacefully handled the missile crisis, arranged for the test-ban treaty. Not successful: tended to react to events rather than lead, did not get his legislative program enacted before his death.

GEOGRAPHY
SPOTLIGHT

## Objectives

· To describe the movements of migrant farm workers in the United States

· To identify the role played by climate and growing seasons in migrant workers' movements

## Focus & Motivate

**Making Generalizations** Ask students to think of jobs they have done either at home or for pay that involve manual labor. Ask how they felt at the end of the day. Then, ask why it may be difficult to find people to fill manual labor jobs.

## More About . . .

### Migrant Farm Workers

The children of migrant farm workers often become migrant farm workers themselves. Because migrant families move so often, the children tend to fall behind in their education. In fact, only about one-fifth of all migrant children attend school beyond sixth grade. When these children grow up, they usually find that their education has prepared them for little other than farm work. As a result, generations of migrant families are caught in a cycle of poverty.

## GEOGRAPHY SPOTLIGHT

Mini-Lesson 1:
SS11 2(WG1.A)

# The Movement of Migrant Workers

The nation's 3 million farm workers are responsible for harvesting much of the fruit and vegetables that families eat each day. Most field workers on United States farms remain in one place most of the year. Others are migrant workers, who move with their entire family from one region to the next as the growing seasons change. Nationally, migrant workers make up around 10 percent of hired farm workers, depending on the season and other factors.

As the map shows, there were three major streams of migrant worker movements in the 1960s: the Pacific Coast, the Midwest, and the Atlantic Coast. While these paths may have changed slightly since then, the movement of migrant workers into nearly every region of the nation continues today.

▼ **THE PACIFIC COAST**

The Pacific Coast region's moderate climate allows for year-round harvesting. Most of California's migrant farm workers work on large fruit farms for much of the year. More than 62,000 workers make their way up to Washington each year to pick cherries, apples, and other crops.

▲ **THE MIDWEST**

Workers along the Midwest and East Coast streams, where crops are smaller, must keep moving in order to find work. These workers picking strawberries in Michigan will soon move on. For example, one family may travel to Ohio for the tomato harvest and then return to Michigan to pick apples before heading back to Texas for the winter months.

**684** CHAPTER 20

## RECOMMENDED RESOURCES

### BOOKS

Altman, Linda Jacobs. *César Chávez.* San Diego: Lucent Books, 1996. Biography of the charismatic labor leader who struggled to organize migrant farm workers.

Jiménez, Francisco. "The Circuit." *Cuentos Chicanos: A Short Story*

*Anthology.* Ed. Rodolfo A. Anaya and Antonio Márquez. Rev. ed. Albuquerque: U of New Mexico P, 1984. Short story depicting the plight of migrant children.

Valle, Isabel. *Fields of Toil.* Pullman: Washington State UP, 1994. Traces the journey of a family of migrant farm workers.

### VIDEOS

*César Chávez.* Schlesinger Media, 1995. Visual chronicle of Chávez's 30-year effort to organize migrant farm workers.

*Harvest of Shame.* Ambrose Video Publishing, Inc., 1992. Renowned 1960 documentary on the exploitation of migrant farm workers in the United States.

WASHINGTON
OREGON
IDAHO
MONTANA
NORTH DAKOTA
MINNESOTA
WYOMING
SOUTH DAKOTA
WISCONSIN
MICHIGAN
MAINE
VERMONT
N.H.
NEW YORK
MASS.
R.I.
NEVADA
UTAH
NEBRASKA
IOWA
PENNSYLVANIA
CONN.
N.J.
CALIFORNIA
COLORADO
KANSAS
ILLINOIS
INDIANA
OHIO
WEST VIRGINIA
DELAWARE
MARYLAND
VIRGINIA
ARIZONA
NEW MEXICO
OKLAHOMA
ARKANSAS
MISSOURI
KENTUCKY
TENNESSEE
NORTH CAROLINA
SOUTH CAROLINA
GEORGIA
T E X A S
MISS.
ALABAMA
LA.
FLORIDA

Pacific Coast paths
Midwest paths
Atlantic Coast paths
Year-round work
Migrant base areas

0       250       500 miles
0       250       500 kilometers

▲
The map above shows the three major streams of migrant worker movements in the 1960s.

## THE ATLANTIC COAST

While some workers along the Atlantic Coast stream remain in Florida, like the workers shown here picking beans, others travel as far north as New Hampshire and New York. There, they work from March through September. Due to the winters, migrant workers in most of the Midwest and Atlantic regions can find work for only six months out of the year.

### THINKING CRITICALLY

**CONNECT TO HISTORY**
1. **Analyzing Patterns** Retrace the movement of migrant workers in the three regions. Why do you think migrant workers have to keep moving?

**CONNECT TO TODAY**
2. **Creating a Database** Pose a historical question about the relationship between crops and planting seasons. For example, what types of crops are harvested in Michigan during the fall? Then research and create a database that answers this and other such questions.
   **SEE SKILLBUILDER HANDBOOK, PAGE R44**

  **RESEARCH LINKS** CLASSZONE.COM

*The New Frontier and the Great Society* **685**

## Instruct

1. Where did migrant farm workers travel?
2. Why did workers in the Midwest and on the Atlantic Coast have to travel farther than workers in other regions?
3. Why was California's climate helpful to migrant farm workers?

**MAKING PERSONAL CONNECTIONS**
· Ask students to consider the hardships of migrant workers, including poor living conditions, long hours, and low pay.
· Have students suggest ways to improve the situation of migrant farm workers.

### HISTORY from VISUALS

**Interpreting the Infographic**
Have students study the map and the photographs carefully. Three states offer year-round work—Florida, Texas, and California. What conclusions can students draw about the climates of these states? *(They have warm climates that allow year-round growing seasons.)* Which group of migratory paths shown on the map overlaps the other two groups? *(the Midwest paths)*

**Extension** On the basis of the photos, write four or five words that characterize migrant farm work. *(backbreaking, monotonous, tiring, dirty)*

### THINKING CRITICALLY: ANSWERS

1. **CONNECT TO HISTORY** During the winter months, migrant workers in the Midwest and Atlantic Coast paths seek employment in California, Florida, and Texas. They head north as the weather gets warmer and work in a number of Northern states during the summer and early fall. Once summer begins to fade into autumn, however, the workers once again move south. Migrant workers keep moving because they need year-round employment.

2. **CONNECT TO TODAY**
   **Rubric**
   A database should present . . .
   · a variety of information on agricultural regions, crops, planting and harvesting seasons
   · types of laborers needed
   · clearly identified sources

# The Great Society

| MAIN IDEA | WHY IT MATTERS NOW | Terms & Names |
|---|---|---|
| The demand for reform helped create a new awareness of social problems, especially on matters of civil rights and the effects of poverty. | Reforms made in the 1960s have had a lasting effect on the American justice system by increasing the rights of minorities. | • Lyndon Baines Johnson<br>• Economic Opportunity Act<br>• Great Society | • Medicare and Medicaid<br>• Immigration Act of 1965<br>• Warren Court<br>• reapportionment |

 U.S. History 1B, 6H, 7A, 7C, 7D, 8A, 9B, 11B, 17A, 19A, 19B, 19C, 24A, 24B, 24D, 25A, 25B, 25C, 25D, 26A

### One American's Story

In 1966, family finances forced Larry Alfred to drop out of high school in Mobile, Alabama. He turned to the Job Corps, a federal program that trained young people from poor backgrounds. He learned to operate construction equipment, but his dream was to help people. On the advice of his Job Corps counselor, he joined VISTA—Volunteers in Service to America—often called the "domestic Peace Corps."

Both the Job Corps and VISTA sprang into being in 1964, when President Lyndon B. Johnson signed the Economic Opportunity Act. This law was the main offensive of Johnson's "war on poverty" and a cornerstone of the Great Society.

VISTA assigned Alfred to work with a community of poor farm laborers in Robstown, Texas, near the Mexican border. There he found a number of children with mental and physical disabilities who had no special assistance, education, or training. So he established the Robstown Association for Retarded People, started a parents education program, sought state funds, and created a rehabilitation center. At age 20, Larry Alfred was a high school dropout, Job Corps graduate, VISTA volunteer, and in Robstown, an authority on people with disabilities. Alfred embodied Johnson's Great Society in two ways: its programs helped him turn his life around, and he made a difference in people's lives.

▲ VISTA volunteers worked in a variety of capacities. This woman is teaching art to young pupils.

## ❶ LBJ's Path to Power

By the time **Lyndon Baines Johnson,** or LBJ as he was called, succeeded to the presidency, his ambition and drive had become legendary. In explaining his frenetic energy, Johnson once remarked, "That's the way I've been all my life. My daddy used to wake me up at dawn and shake my leg and say, 'Lyndon, every boy in town's got an hour's head start on you.'"

**FROM THE TEXAS HILLS TO CAPITOL HILL** A fourth-generation Texan, Johnson grew up in the dry Texas hill country of Blanco County. The Johnsons never knew great wealth, but they also never missed a meal.

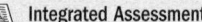

LBJ entered politics in 1937 when he won a special election to fill a vacant seat in the U.S. House of Representatives. Johnson styled himself as a "New Dealer" and spokesperson for the small ranchers and struggling farmers of his district. He caught the eye of President Franklin Roosevelt, who took Johnson under his wing. Roosevelt helped him secure key committee assignments in Congress and steer much-needed electrification and water projects to his Texas district. Johnson, in turn, idolized FDR and imitated his leadership style.

Once in the House, Johnson eagerly eyed a seat in the Senate. In 1948, after an exhausting, bitterly fought campaign, he won the Democratic primary election for the Senate by a margin of only 87 votes out of 988,000.

**A MASTER POLITICIAN** Johnson proved himself a master of party politics and behind-the-scenes maneuvering, and he rose to the position of Senate majority leader in 1955. People called his legendary ability to persuade senators to support his bills the "LBJ treatment." As a reporter for the *Saturday Evening Post* explained, Johnson also used this treatment to win over reporters.

### A PERSONAL VOICE  STEWART ALSOP

"The Majority Leader [Johnson] was, it seemed, in a relaxed, friendly, reminiscent mood. But by gradual stages this mood gave way to something rather like a human hurricane. Johnson was up, striding about his office, talking without pause, occasionally leaning over, his nose almost touching the reporter's, to shake the reporter's shoulder or grab his knee. . . . Appeals were made, to the Almighty, to the shades of the departed great, to the reporter's finer instincts and better nature, while the reporter, unable to get a word in edgewise, sat collapsed upon a leather sofa, eyes glazed, mouth half open."

—"The New President," *Saturday Evening Post*, December 14, 1963

Johnson's deft handling of Congress led to the passage of the Civil Rights Act of 1957, a voting rights measure that was the first civil rights legislation since Reconstruction. Johnson's knack for achieving legislative results had captured John F. Kennedy's attention, too, during Kennedy's run for the White House. To Kennedy, Johnson's congressional connections and his Southern Protestant background compensated for his own drawbacks as a candidate, so he asked Johnson to be his running mate. Johnson's presence on the ticket helped Kennedy win key states in the South, especially Texas, which went Democratic by just a few thousand votes.

## Johnson's Domestic Agenda

In the wake of Kennedy's assassination, President Johnson addressed a joint session of Congress. It was the fifth day of his administration. "All I have I would have given gladly not to be standing here today," he began. Kennedy had inspired Americans to begin to solve national and world problems. Johnson urged Congress to pass the civil rights and tax-cut bills that Kennedy had sent to Capitol Hill.

### MAIN IDEA

**Analyzing Motives**
**A** Why did Kennedy choose Johnson to be his running mate?

*A. Answer*
Johnson brought balance to the ticket because of his experience and influence in Congress and his Southern Protestant background.

---

**KEY PLAYER**

**LYNDON B. JOHNSON**
**1908–1973**

LBJ received his teaching degree from Southwest Texas State Teachers College in 1930. To finance his own education, Johnson took a year off from college to work at a Mexican-American school in Cotulla, Texas. He later taught public speaking and debate at the Sam Houston High School in Houston. At age 26, he became the state director of the National Youth Administration, a New Deal agency.

As president, Johnson pushed hard for the passage of the Elementary and Secondary Education Act. In 1965, he signed the act at the one-room schoolhouse near Stonewall, Texas, where his own education had begun. Johnson later wrote,

"My education had begun with what I learned in that school-room. Now what I had learned and experienced since that time had brought me back to fulfill a dream."

---

*The New Frontier and the Great Society* **687**

---

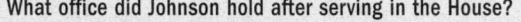

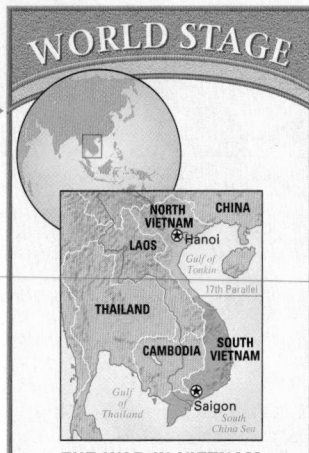

**WORLD STAGE**

**THE WAR IN VIETNAM**

As LBJ pushed through his domestic programs, the U.S. grew more interested in halting the spread of Communism around the world. In Vietnam, anti-Communist nationalists controlled South Vietnam while Communist leader Ho Chi Minh had taken over North Vietnam. The Geneva Accords had temporarily provided peace, dividing Vietnam along the 17th parallel into two distinct political regions. Despite this treaty, the North was supporting Communist rebels who were trying to take over the South.

Though Presidents Eisenhower and Kennedy had provided economic and military aid to South Vietnam, soon the U.S. would be directly involved in fighting the war.

◀ Campaign buttons like this one capitalized on the nation's growing liberal democratic sentiments.

In February 1964 Congress passed a tax reduction of over $10 billion into law. As the Democrats had hoped, the tax cut spurred economic growth. People spent more, which meant profits for businesses, which increased tax revenues and lowered the federal budget deficit from $6 billion in 1964 to $4 billion in 1966.

Then in July, Johnson pushed the Civil Rights Act of 1964 through Congress, persuading Southern senators to stop blocking its passage. It prohibited discrimination based on race, religion, national origin, and sex and granted the federal government new powers to enforce its provisions.

**THE WAR ON POVERTY** Following these successes, LBJ pressed on with his own agenda—to alleviate poverty. Early in 1964, he had declared "unconditional war on poverty in America" and proposed sweeping legislation designed to help Americans "on the outskirts of hope."

In August 1964, Congress enacted the **Economic Opportunity Act** (EOA), approving nearly $1 billion for youth programs, antipoverty measures, small-business loans, and job training. The EOA legislation created:
- the Job Corps Youth Training Program
- VISTA (Volunteers in Service to America)
- Project Head Start, an education program for underprivileged preschoolers
- the Community Action Program, which encouraged poor people to participate in public-works programs. **B**

**THE 1964 ELECTION** In 1964, the Republicans nominated conservative senator Barry Goldwater of Arizona to oppose Johnson. Goldwater believed the federal government had no business trying to right social and economic wrongs such as poverty, discrimination, and lack of opportunity. He attacked such long-established federal programs as Social Security, which he wanted to make voluntary, and the Tennessee Valley Authority, which he wanted to sell.

In 1964, most American people were in tune with Johnson—they believed that government could and should help solve the nation's problems. Moreover, Goldwater had frightened many Americans by suggesting that he might use nuclear weapons on Cuba and North Vietnam. Johnson's campaign capitalized on this fear. It produced a chilling television commercial in which a picture of a little girl counting the petals on a daisy dissolved into a mushroom cloud created by an atomic bomb. Where Goldwater advocated intervention in Vietnam, Johnson assured the American people that sending U.S. troops there "would offer no solution at all to the real problem of Vietnam."

LBJ won the election by a landslide, winning 61 percent of the popular vote and 486 electoral votes, while Senator Goldwater won only 52. The Democrats also increased their majority in Congress. For the first time since 1938, a Democratic president did not need the votes of conservative Southern Democrats in order to get laws passed. Now Johnson could launch his reform program in earnest.

---

**Instruct: Objective** ③

**Building the Great Society**
TAKS SS11 1(US1.A)
· What were the components of LBJ's Great Society?
· How did Great Society legislation affect education, Social Security, housing, and immigration?
· What effect did Great Society programs have on the environment and consumers?

 **In-Depth Resources: Unit 6**
· Guided Reading, p. 3
· Primary Sources: from *Unsafe at Any Speed*, p. 14
· American Lives: Rachel Carson, p. 19

 **Critical Thinking Transparencies CT28**
· The Great Society

# Building the Great Society ③

In May 1964, Johnson had summed up his vision for America in a phrase: the **Great Society.** In a speech at the University of Michigan, Johnson outlined a legislative program that would end poverty and racial injustice. But, he told an enthusiastic crowd, that was "just the beginning." Johnson envisioned a legislative program that would create not only a higher standard of living and equal opportunity, but also promote a richer quality of life for all.

**A PERSONAL VOICE** LYNDON B. JOHNSON

" The Great Society is a place where every child can find knowledge to enrich his mind and to enlarge his talents. It is a place where leisure is a welcome chance to build and reflect, not a feared cause of boredom and restlessness. It is a place where the city of man serves not only the needs of the body and the demands of commerce but the desire for beauty and the hunger for community. It is a place where man can renew contact with nature. It is a place which honors creation for its own sake and for what it adds to the understanding of the race. "

—"The Great Society," May 22, 1964

Like his idol FDR, LBJ wanted to change America. By the time Johnson left the White House in 1969, Congress had passed 206 of his measures. The president personally led the battle to get most of them passed.

**EDUCATION** During 1965 and 1966, the LBJ administration introduced a flurry of bills to Congress. Johnson considered education "the key which can unlock the door to the Great Society." The Elementary and Secondary Education Act of 1965 provided more than $1 billion in federal aid to help public and parochial schools purchase textbooks and new library materials. This was the first major federal aid package for education in the nation's history.

▲ These preschoolers in a Head Start classroom are among the millions of Americans whose daily lives have been affected by Great Society programs.

**More About . . .**

**Education and Government**
Lyndon Johnson considered education the key to unlocking the door to the Great Society. He declared that every child "must have the best education our nation can provide." Issues of race, religion, region, and constitutional debate had long blocked federal money for public education. After Great Society education laws were enacted in 1965, the federal government spent more than $2 billion on education in that year alone. Strong support for educational funding has continued, as evidenced by the political platforms of both presidential candidates in the 2000 election, Al Gore and George W. Bush.

*The New Frontier and the Great Society* **689**

---

**ACTIVITY** **LINK TO GOVERNMENT**

 **classzone.com**

**Researching Project Head Start**

**Class Time** 45 minutes

**Task** Researching the effectiveness of Project Head Start

**Purpose** To evaluate the effectiveness of an early childhood education program

**Directions** Have students use library or Internet resources to research information about Project Head Start—what it is, how many children it has reached, and if it has made a difference in educational performance. Students themselves may have participated in this program or may have younger siblings with more recent memories of it. Have students collect both research and anecdotal material and assemble a wall chart showing their findings.

 Integrated Assessment
· Rubrics 1, 4

## HISTORY from VISUALS

### Interpreting the Chart

Point out that the chart organizes the Great Society programs in distinct categories. Then ask students in which years the greatest number of programs were passed. *(1965)* Ask how this fact is connected to the results of the 1964 election. *(Johnson hurried through a flurry of bills soon after the election to take advantage of his electoral mandate.)*

**Extension** Ask students what the scope of the Great Society programs suggests about the Johnson administration. *(The administration was ambitious, compassionate, liberal.)* Ask why the number of programs dropped off after 1967. *(because Johnson began to focus his energies on the Vietnam War)*

### More About . . .

#### Medicare and Medicaid

Medicare and Medicaid were enacted in 1965 as Titles XVIII and XIX, respectively, to the Social Security Act of 1935. Medicare is partially funded by Social Security taxes; Medicaid is funded by the federal government and the states. Among the benefits of Medicare are hospitalization, nursing-home and skilled-nursing care, and home health care. The pressure of rising health care costs coupled with the aging of the population has put pressure on Medicare and Medicaid funding and resulted in calls for reform of the system.

Mini-Lesson 3: SS11 5(WH26.C)

---

### Great Society Programs, 1964–1967

#### POVERTY

**1964 Tax Reduction Act** cut corporate and individual taxes to stimulate growth.

**1964 Economic Opportunity Act** created Job Corps, VISTA, Project Head Start, and other programs to fight the "war on poverty."

**1965 Medicare Act** established Medicare and Medicaid programs.

**1965 Appalachian Regional Development Act** targeted aid for highways, health centers, and resource development in that economically depressed area.

#### CITIES

**1965 Omnibus Housing Act** provided money for low-income housing.

**1965 Department of Housing and Urban Development** was formed to administer federal housing programs.

**1966 Demonstration Cities and Metropolitan Area Redevelopment Act** funded slum rebuilding, mass transit, and other improvements for selected "model cities."

#### EDUCATION

**1965 Elementary and Secondary Education Act** directed money to schools for textbooks, library materials, and special education.

**1965 Higher Education Act** funded scholarships and low-interest loans for college students.

**1965 National Foundation on the Arts and the Humanities** was created to financially assist painters, musicians, actors, and other artists.

**1967 Corporation for Public Broadcasting** was formed to fund educational TV and radio broadcasting.

#### DISCRIMINATION

**1964 Civil Rights Act** outlawed discrimination in public accommodations, housing, and jobs; increased federal power to prosecute civil rights abuses.

**1964 Twenty-Fourth Amendment** abolished the poll tax in federal elections.

**1965 Voting Rights Act** ended the practice of requiring voters to pass literacy tests and permitted the federal government to monitor voter registration.

**1965 Immigration Act** ended national-origins quotas established in 1924.

#### ENVIRONMENT

**1965 Wilderness Preservation Act** set aside over 9 million acres for national forest lands.

**1965 Water Quality Act** required states to clean up their rivers.

**1965 Clean Air Act Amendment** directed the federal government to establish emission standards for new motor vehicles.

**1967 Air Quality Act** set federal air pollution guidelines and extended federal enforcement power.

#### CONSUMER ADVOCACY

**1966 Truth in Packaging Act** set standards for labeling consumer products.

**1966 National Traffic and Motor Vehicle Safety Act** set federal safety standards for the auto and tire industries.

**1966 Highway Safety Act** required states to set up highway safety programs.

**1966 Department of Transportation** was created to deal with national air, rail, and highway transportation.

---

**SKILLBUILDER** Interpreting Charts
What did the Great Society programs indicate about the federal government's changing role?

---

*Skillbuilder Answer*
*The programs were wide-ranging, which reflected an expanding role for the federal government in addressing certain problems of American society.*

**HEALTHCARE** LBJ and Congress changed Social Security by establishing Medicare and Medicaid. **Medicare** provided hospital insurance and low-cost medical insurance for almost every American age 65 or older. **Medicaid** extended health insurance to welfare recipients. **C**

**HOUSING** Congress also made several important decisions that shifted the nation's political power from rural to urban areas. These include: appropriating money to build some 240,000 units of low-rent public housing and help low- and moderate-income families pay for better private housing; establishing the Department of Housing and Urban Development (HUD); and appointing Robert Weaver, the first African-American cabinet member in American history, as Secretary of HUD.

MAIN IDEA

**Comparing**
**C** How are Medicare and Medicaid similar?

*C. Answer*
*Both provide government-sponsored health insurance.*

---

 **ACTIVITY** COOPERATIVE LEARNING

 BLOCK SCHEDULING

### Outlining Provisions for a Great Society Program

**Class Time** 45 minutes

**Task** Outlining provisions for a Great Society–inspired program that would address a problem today

**Purpose** To use steps of a problem solving model to address a current problem

**Directions** Place students in small groups to discuss some of the major problems that society faces today. Encourage students to use the categories and bills listed in the chart on this page to spark ideas. Students should select a problem that they would like to address and then, using a problem solving model, write an outline describing the problem and a proposed solution. The outline should detail the roles of the individuals and groups involved in the solution.

Integrated Assessment
· Rubrics 1, 2, 5

**IMMIGRATION** The Great Society also brought profound changes to the nation's immigration laws. The Immigration Act of 1924 and the National Origins Act of 1929 had established immigration quotas that discriminated strongly against people from outside Western Europe. The Act set a quota of about 150,000 people annually. It discriminated against southern and eastern Europeans and barred Asians completely. The **Immigration Act of 1965** opened the door for many non-European immigrants to settle in the United States by ending quotas based on nationality. **D**

**THE ENVIRONMENT** In 1962, *Silent Spring*, a book by Rachel Carson, had exposed a hidden danger: the effects of pesticides on the environment. Carson's book and the public's outcry resulted in the Water Quality Act of 1965, which required states to clean up rivers. Johnson also ordered the government to search out the worst chemical polluters. "There is no excuse . . . for chemical companies and oil refineries using our major rivers as pipelines for toxic wastes." Such words and actions helped trigger the environmental movement in the United States. (See Chapter 24.)

**CONSUMER PROTECTION** Consumer advocates also made headway. They convinced Congress to pass major safety laws, including a truth-in-packaging law that set standards for labeling consumer goods. Ralph Nader, a young lawyer, wrote a book, *Unsafe at Any Speed,* that sharply criticized the U.S. automobile industry for ignoring safety concerns. His testimony helped persuade Congress to establish safety standards for automobiles and tires. Precautions extended to food, too. Congress passed the Wholesome Meat Act of 1967. "Americans can feel a little safer now in their homes, on the road, at the supermarket, and in the department store," said Johnson.

## Reforms of the Warren Court **4**

The wave of liberal reform that characterized the Great Society also swept through the Supreme Court of the 1960s. Beginning with the 1954 landmark decision *Brown* v. *Board of Education*, which ruled school segregation unconstitutional, the Court under Chief Justice Earl Warren took an activist stance on the leading issues of the day.

Several major court decisions in the 1960s affected American society. The **Warren Court** banned prayer in public schools and declared state-required loyalty oaths unconstitutional. It limited the power of communities to censor books and films and said that free speech included the wearing of black armbands to school by antiwar students. Furthermore, the Court brought about change in federal and state reapportionment and the criminal justice system.

**CONGRESSIONAL REAPPORTIONMENT** In a key series of decisions, the Warren Court addressed the issue of **reapportionment,** or the way in which states redraw election districts based on the changing number of people in them. By 1960, about 80 percent of Americans lived in cities and suburbs. However, many states had failed to change their congressional districts to reflect this development; instead, rural districts might have fewer than 200,000 people, while some urban districts had more than 600,000. Thus the voters in rural areas had more representation—and also more power—than those in urban areas.

---

**MAIN IDEA**

**Analyzing Effects**
**D** How did the Immigration Act of 1965 change the nation's immigration system?

*D. Answer*
It replaced the nation origins system, which discriminated against people from outside Western Europe.

---

**NOW & THEN**

**MEDICARE ON THE LINE**
When President Johnson signed the Medicare bill in 1965, only half of the nation's elderly had health insurance. Today, thanks largely to Medicare, nearly all persons 65 years or older are eligible.

In 1998, federal spending on Medicare was about $160 billion. In recent years, experts have debated over whether Medicare can be sustained in the face of changing trends: (1) people are living longer, (2) health care continues to become more expensive, and (3) the large baby boomer generation is moving toward retirement age. Though most Americans are not in favor of cutbacks to medicare, the Balanced Budget Act of 1997 reduced federal spending on Medicare from 1998 through 2002 by $112 billion.

---

**CHAPTER 20 · SECTION 3**

**Tracing Themes**
IMMIGRATION AND MIGRATION

**Immigration Legislation**
The major impact of the Immigration Act of 1965 was to greatly boost the number of non-European immigrants. The result of that increase today is that Hispanic Americans and Asian Americans significantly increased their numbers. The Immigration Act of 1990 raised the caps on immigration from individual countries, thus accelerating immigration from Asia, Latin and Central America, and Africa.

---

**NOW & THEN**

**Medicare on the Line**
**Evaluating** Ask students whether they think cutbacks should be made in Medicare. Ask them if Medicare is an entitlement. Have students consider whether other federal programs should be cut to help fund Medicare, or whether Medicare in its present state is too expensive to maintain.

---

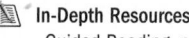

**Instruct: Objective** **4**
**Reforms of the Warren Court**
TAKS SS11 4(US17.A)
· How did the Supreme Court reflect the wave of liberal reform that characterized the Great Society?
· How was political representation affected by the Supreme Court?
· How were the rights of people accused of crimes expanded by the Supreme Court?

 In-Depth Resources: Unit 6
· Guided Reading, p. 3

**Chief Justice Earl Warren**

---

---

**ACTIVITY**   **LINK TO CIVICS**

**classzone.com**

## Researching Consumer Protection

**Class Time** 45 minutes

**Task** Creating a display on federal and state consumer protection laws and agencies

**Purpose** To identify government efforts to protect consumers

**Directions** Have students work in small groups to research state and federal consumer protection agencies and laws in the library or on the Internet. Ask students to create a visual display that illustrates their findings.

**Visual displays should . . .**
· present the information on the agencies clearly through the positioning of pictures, words, and/or symbols
· contain a complete overview
· be neatly presented and creative

E. Answer
Liberals supported the decisions for protecting individual rights, while conservatives criticized the Court for protecting criminal suspects and limiting police power.

*Baker* v. *Carr* (1962) was the first of several decisions that established the principle of "one person, one vote." The Court asserted that the federal courts had the right to tell states to reapportion—redivide—their districts for more equal representation. In later decisions, the Court ruled that congressional district boundaries should be redrawn so that districts would be equal in population, and in *Reynolds* v. *Sims* (1964), it extended the principle of "one person, one vote" to state legislative districts. (See *Reynolds* v. *Sims,* page 774.) These decisions led to a shift of political power throughout the nation from rural to urban areas.

**RIGHTS OF THE ACCUSED** Other Warren Court decisions greatly expanded the rights of people accused of crimes. In *Mapp* v. *Ohio* (1961), the Court ruled that evidence seized illegally could not be used in state courts. This is called the exclusionary rule. In *Gideon* v. *Wainwright* (1963), the justices required criminal courts to provide free legal counsel to those who could not afford it. In *Escobedo* v. *Illinois* (1964), the justices ruled that an accused person has a right to have a lawyer present during police questioning. In 1966, the Court went one step further in *Miranda* v. *Arizona*, where it ruled that all suspects must be read their rights before questioning. (See *Miranda* v. *Arizona,* page 690.)

These rulings greatly divided public opinion. Liberals praised the decisions, arguing that they placed necessary limits on police power and protected the right of all citizens to a fair trial. Conservatives, however, bitterly criticized the Court. They claimed that *Mapp* and *Miranda* benefited criminal suspects and severely limited the power of the police to investigate crimes. During the late 1960s and 1970s, Republican candidates for office seized on the "crime issue," portraying liberals and Democrats as being soft on crime and citing the decisions of the Warren Court as major obstacles to fighting crime.

**MAIN IDEA**

Contrasting
**E** What were the differing reactions to the Warren Court decisions on the rights of the accused?

## More About . . .

### Rights of the Accused

The rulings of the Warren Court on the rights of accused persons were based on the constitutional principles of due process and the assumption of innocence until proven guilty. These decisions were made in an era when the focus was on extending constitutional rights to all Americans, regardless of race, gender, or class.

# POINT COUNTERPOINT

## Objective

To examine contrasting views of the lasting value of the programs of Johnson's Great Society

· What was significant about the way Johnson used government power?

· How did Great Society programs affect awareness of social problems?

· Why was there a conservative backlash to Great Society programs?

---

## POINT

**"The Great Society succeeded in prompting far-reaching social change."**

Defenders of the Great Society contend that it bettered the lives of millions of Americans. Historian John Morton Blum notes, "The Great Society initiated policies that by 1985 had had profound consequences: Blacks now voted at about the same rate as whites, and nearly 6,000 blacks held public offices; almost every elderly citizen had medical insurance, and the aged were no poorer than Americans as a whole; a large majority of small children attended preschool programs."

Attorney Margaret Burnham argues that the civil rights gains alone justify the Great Society: "For tens of thousands of human beings . . . giving promise of a better life was significant . . . . What the Great Society affirmed was the responsibility of the federal government to take measures necessary to bring into the social and economic mainstream any segment of the people [who had been] historically excluded."

## COUNTERPOINT

**"Failures of the Great Society prove that government-sponsored programs do not work."**

The major attack on the Great Society is that it created "big government": an oversized bureaucracy, too many regulations, waste and fraud, and rising budget deficits. As journalist David Alpern writes, this comes from the notion that government could solve all the nation's problems: "The Great Society created unwieldy new mechanisms like the Office of Economic Opportunity and began 'throwing dollars at problems . . . .' Spawned in the process were vast new constituencies of government bureaucrats and beneficiaries whose political clout made it difficult to kill programs off."

Conservatives say the Great Society's social welfare programs created a culture of dependency. Economist Paul Craig Roberts argues that "The Great Society . . . reflected our lack of confidence in the institutions of a free society. We came to the view that it is government spending and not business innovation that creates jobs and that it is society's fault if anyone is poor."

### THINKING CRITICALLY

**CONNECT TO HISTORY**

1. **Evaluating** Do you think the Great Society was a success or a failure? Explain.

   📖 SEE SKILLBUILDER HANDBOOK, PAGE R17.

**CONNECT TO TODAY**

2. **Analyzing Social Problems** Research the most pressing problems in your own neighborhood or precinct. Then propose a social program you think would address at least one of those problems while avoiding the pitfalls of the Great Society programs.

---

## THINKING CRITICALLY: ANSWERS

1. **CONNECT TO HISTORY**

   **Success:** It resulted in great gains in civil rights, reduced the poverty level of many Americans, helped disadvantaged children get a head start in school, and helped develop people's awareness of social problems.

   **Failure:** It fostered the creation of big government, negated the power of the free enterprise system, minimized work incentives, and mired dependents in a cycle of poverty and despair.

2. **CONNECT TO TODAY**

   Rubric
   Social programs should . . .

   · present a practical solution to a problem in students' neighborhoods

   · propose a solution that takes people's needs into account but that also encourages independence

   · not be too costly or involve excessive government interference

# Impact of the Great Society ⑤

The Great Society and the Warren Court changed the United States. People disagree on whether these changes left the nation better or worse, but most agree on one point: no president in the post–World War II era extended the power and reach of the federal government more than Lyndon Johnson. The optimism of the Johnson presidency fueled an activist era in all three branches of government, for at least the first few years.

The "war on poverty" did help. The number of poor people fell from 21 percent of the population in 1962 to 11 percent in 1973. However, many of Johnson's proposals, though well intended, were hastily conceived and proved difficult to accomplish.

Johnson's massive tax cut spurred the economy. But funding the Great Society contributed to a growing budget deficit—a problem that continued for decades. Questions about government finances, as well as debates over the effectiveness of these programs and the role of the federal government, left a number of people disillusioned. A conservative backlash began to take shape as a new group of Republican leaders rose to power. In 1966, for example, a conservative Hollywood actor named Ronald Reagan swept to victory in the race for governor of California over the Democratic incumbent.

Thousands of miles away, the increase of Communist forces in Vietnam also began to overshadow the goals of the Great Society. The fear of communism was deeply rooted in the minds of Americans from the Cold War era. Four years after initiating the Great Society, Johnson, a peace candidate in 1964, would be labeled a "hawk"—a supporter of one of the most divisive wars in recent U.S. history. **F**

"SUNRISE...ALL THE FOREIGN TROUBLE MAKERS GOIN' TO SLEEP AN' ALL THE DOMESTIC ONES WAKIN' UP"

As this cartoon points out, President Johnson had much to deal with at home and abroad. This autographed copy was presented to President Johnson by the cartoonist.

**F. Possible Answers**
Some programs contributed to the budget deficit; federal spending, deficits, and intervention sparked conservative backlash; the Vietnam War drew away funds and attention.

> **MAIN IDEA**
>
> **Identifying Problems**
> **F** What events and problems may have affected the success of the Great Society?

### Instruct: Objective ⑤

**Impact of the Great Society**
TAKS SS11 1(US1.A)
· How did the Great Society expand the power of government?
· How effective was the War on Poverty?
· How did the Great Society contribute to a conservative backlash?

 In-Depth Resources: Unit 6
· Guided Reading, p. 3

## Assess & Reteach

### SECTION 3 ASSESSMENT
After students finish answering the questions, have them discuss their responses to item 2.

 Formal Assessment
· Section Quiz, p. 372

### SELF-ASSESSMENT
Ask students to jot down four or five words or phrases they associate with Johnson and the Great Society. Then have students compare and discuss their list with a partner.

### RETEACH
Use the chart on page 688 to review the achievements of the Great Society.

 In-Depth Resources: Unit 6
· Reaching Activity, p. 8

---

## SECTION 3 ASSESSMENT

**1. TERMS & NAMES** For each term or name, write a sentence explaining its significance.

- Lyndon Baines Johnson
- Economic Opportunity Act
- Great Society
- Medicare and Medicaid
- Immigration Act of 1965
- Warren Court
- reapportionment

**MAIN IDEA**

**2. TAKING NOTES**
List four or more Great Society programs and Warren Court rulings.

| Great Society Programs | Warren Court Rulings |
|---|---|
| 1. | 1. |
| 2. | 2. |
| 3. | 3. |
| 4. | 4. |

Choose one item and describe its lasting effects.

**CRITICAL THINKING**

**3. EVALUATING LEADERSHIP**
Explain how Lyndon Johnson's personal and political experiences might have influenced his actions as president. **Think About:**
- his family's background and education
- his relationship with Franklin Roosevelt
- his powers of persuasion

**4. ANALYZING VISUAL SOURCES**
Look at the political cartoon above. What do you think the artist was trying to convey about the Johnson administration?

*The New Frontier and the Great Society* **693**

---

Answers **ASSESSMENT** ③

**1. TERMS & NAMES**
Lyndon Baines Johnson, p. 686
Economic Opportunity Act, p. 688
Great Society, p. 689
Medicare and Medicaid, p. 690
Immigration Act of 1965, p. 691
Warren Court, p. 691
reapportionment, p. 691

**2. TAKING NOTES**
Great Society programs include Civil Rights Act of 1964, Economic Opportunity Act, Elementary and Secondary Education Act, Medicare, and Medicaid; Warren Court rulings include *Brown* v. *Board of Education*, *Baker* v. *Carr*, *Escobedo* v. *Illinois*, *Miranda* v. *Arizona*.

**3. EVALUATING LEADERSHIP**
Johnson's upbringing might have taught him about the hardships of those in need; as a New Dealer, he learned how the government could help people in need; in Congress, he learned the importance of political connections and clout and the skills to negotiate political deals.

**4. ANALYZING VISUAL SOURCES**
The cartoonist appears to be trying to convey that Johnson felt that his foreign and domestic troubles never seem to end.

## HISTORIC DECISIONS OF THE SUPREME COURT

### Objectives

· To understand the significance of the *Miranda* decision on the criminal justice system and on civil liberties

· To analyze the legal reasoning that the Court used to decide the *Miranda* case

· To describe the historical impact of the *Miranda* ruling

## Focus & Motivate

**Evaluating** Ask student to consider what rights people accused of crimes should have. Remind them that when someone is arrested he or she is innocent until proven guilty. Have students consider the inherent conflict between allowing the police to do their job and protecting the rights of citizens.

## More About . . .

### Warren's Opinion

In writing his opinion, Chief Justice Warren quoted extensively from police interrogation manuals that suggested techniques for winning confessions from suspects. Among the techniques was "Friendly/Unfriendly," where one interrogator is sympathetic and the other aggressive. Warren called it the "Mutt and Jeff Act," after a famous comic strip of the time about two mismatched friends. Warren's point was that the police had numerous techniques for extracting confessions. While a confession expedited the criminal procedure, it did not serve the cause of justice if it was not true.

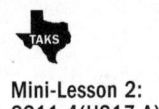

Mini-Lesson 2: SS11 4(US17.A)

### HISTORIC DECISIONS OF THE SUPREME COURT

# *MIRANDA* v. *ARIZONA* (1966)

**ORIGINS OF THE CASE** In 1963, Ernesto Miranda was arrested at his home in Phoenix, Arizona, on charges of kidnapping and rape. After two hours of questioning by police, he signed a confession and was later convicted, largely based on the confession. Miranda appealed. He claimed that his confession was invalid because it was coerced and because the police never advised him of his right to an attorney or his right to avoid self-incrimination.

**THE RULING** The Court overturned Miranda's conviction, holding that the police must inform criminal suspects of their legal rights at the time of arrest and may not interrogate suspects who invoke their rights.

### LEGAL REASONING

Chief Justice Earl Warren wrote the majority opinion in *Miranda* v. *Arizona*. He based his argument on the Fifth Amendment, which guarantees that an accused person cannot be forced "to be a witness against himself" or herself. Warren stressed that when suspects are interrogated in police custody, the situation is "inherently intimidating." Such a situation, he argued, undermines any evidence it produces because "no statement obtained from the defendant [while in custody] can truly be the product of his free choice."

For this reason, the Court majority found that Miranda's confession could not be used as evidence. In the opinion, Chief Justice Warren responded to the argument that police officials might find this requirement difficult to meet.

" Not only does the use of the third degree [harassment or torture used to obtain a confession] involve a flagrant violation of law by the officers of the law, but it involves also the dangers of false confessions, and it tends to make police and prosecutors less zealous in the search for objective evidence. "

▲ Ernesto Miranda (*at right*) converses with attorney John J. Flynn in February 1967.

**694** CHAPTER 20

### LEGAL SOURCES

#### U.S. CONSTITUTION

**U.S. CONSTITUTION, FIFTH AMENDMENT (1791)**
"No person . . . shall be compelled in any criminal case to be a witness against himself, nor be deprived of life, liberty, or property, without due process of law."

#### RELATED CASES

**MAPP v. OHIO (1961)**
The Court ruled that prosecutors may not use evidence obtained in illegal searches (exclusionary rule).

**GIDEON v. WAINWRIGHT (1963)**
The Court said that a defendant accused of a felony has the right to an attorney, which the government must supply if the defendant cannot afford one.

**ESCOBEDO v. ILLINOIS (1964)**
The Court held that a suspect has the right to an attorney when being questioned by police.

## RECOMMENDED RESOURCES

### BOOKS

Cortner, Richard C. *The Supreme Court and Civil Liberties Policy.* Palo Alto: Mayfield Publishing Co., 1975.

Dorsen, Norman *The Rights of Americans.* New York: Random House, 1972.

Ginger, Annfagan *The Law, the Supreme Court, and the People's Rights.* Woodbury, NY: Barron's Publishing, 1977.

Irons, Peter and Guitton, Stephanies, ed. *May It Please the Court.* New York: The New Press / Norton, 1993.

### INTEGRATED TECHNOLOGY

For teacher support and more information about the Supreme Court, including the full text of the Supreme Court opinions, visit . . .

 classzone.com

## WHY IT MATTERED

*Miranda* was one of four key criminal justice cases decided by the Warren Court (see Related Cases). In each case, the decision reflected the chief justice's strong belief that all persons deserve to be treated with respect by their government. In *Miranda,* the Court directed police to inform every suspect of his or her rights at the time of arrest and even gave the police detailed instructions about what to say.

The rights of accused people need to be protected in order to ensure that innocent people are not punished. These protections also ensure that federal, state, or local authorities will not harass people for political reasons—as often happened to civil-rights activists in the South in the 1950s and 1960s, for example.

Critics of the Warren Court claimed that *Miranda* would lead to more crime because it would become more difficult to convict criminals. Police departments, however, adapted to the decision. They placed the list of suspects' rights mentioned in *Miranda* on cards for police officers to read to suspects. The statement of these rights became known as the Miranda warning and quickly became familiar to anyone who watched a police show on television.

As for the defendant, Ernesto Miranda, he was retried and convicted on the basis of other evidence.

*(right)* This card is carried by police officers in order to read suspects their rights. *(far right)* An officer reads a suspect his rights.

## HISTORICAL IMPACT

The *Miranda* decision was highly controversial. Critics complained that the opinion would protect the rights of criminals at the expense of public safety.

Since *Miranda,* the Court has continued to try to strike a balance between public safety and the rights of the accused. Several cases in the 1970s and 1980s softened the *Miranda* ruling and gave law enforcement officers more power to gather evidence without informing suspects of their rights. Even so, conservatives still hoped to overturn the *Miranda* decision.

In 2000, however, the Supreme Court affirmed *Miranda* by a 7-to-2 majority in *Dickerson* v. *United States.* Writing for the majority, Chief Justice William Rehnquist argued, "There is no such justification here for overruling *Miranda. Miranda* has become embedded in routine police practice to the point where warnings have become part of our national culture."

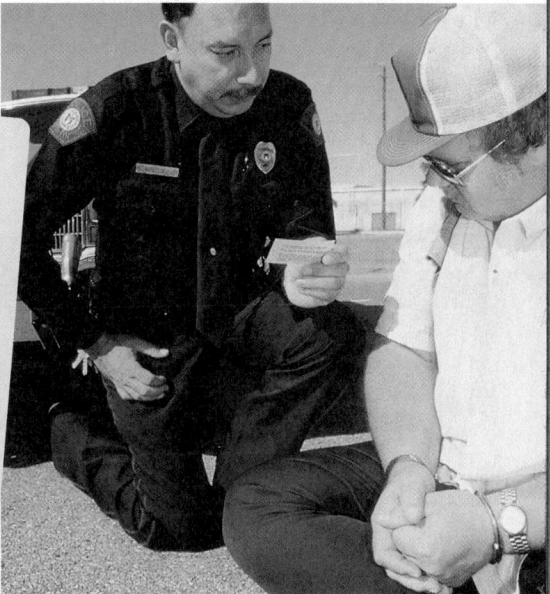

**MIRANDA** WARNING
CUSTODIAL INTERROGATION
JUVENILE & ADULT

*The officer must determine whether the suspect understands the warning and waives his rights.*

1. You have the right to remain silent.
2. Anything you say can be used as evidence against you.
3. You have a right to consult with an attorney before questioning and to have him with you during questioning.
4. If you can not afford an attorney, one will be appointed to represent you free of charge.
5. Knowing these rights, do you want to talk to me without having a lawyer present? You may stop talking to me at any time and you may also demand a lawyer at any time.

### THINKING CRITICALLY

**CONNECT TO HISTORY**
1. **Drawing Conclusions** Critics charged that *Miranda* incorrectly used the Fifth Amendment. The right to avoid self-incrimination, they said, should only apply to trials, not to police questioning. Do you agree or disagree? Why?

 **SEE SKILLBUILDER HANDBOOK, PAGE R18.**

**CONNECT TO TODAY**
2.  **INTERNET ACTIVITY** CLASSZONE.COM

Visit the links for Historic Decisions of the Supreme Court to research laws and other court decisions related to *Mapp* and *Miranda.* Then, prepare a debate on whether courts should or should not set a guilty person free if the government broke the law in establishing that person's guilt.

## TERMS & NAMES

1. John F. Kennedy, p. 670
2. Fidel Castro, p. 673
3. Berlin Wall, p. 677
4. hot line, p. 678
5. New Frontier, p. 679
6. Peace Corps, p. 680
7. Warren Commission, p. 683
8. Great Society, p. 689
9. Medicare and Medicaid, p. 690
10. Warren Court, p. 691

## MAIN IDEAS

1. Kennedy spoke better in the televised debates, and his brother helped get Martin Luther King, Jr., out of jail. He had a well financed and organized campaign.
2. The Soviets removed their missiles from Cuba, and nuclear war was avoided.
3. Kennedy's legislative agenda was based on a broad vision of progress; he faced a conservative coalition in Congress of Republicans and Southern Democrats; and he lacked a popular mandate.
4. The Peace Corps and the Alliance for Progress.
5. The public deeply mourned the fallen leader.
6. They addressed the problem of poverty by providing job corps youth training programs, education programs, small business loans, medical care, and housing programs.
7. By establishing the principle of "one person, one vote," it made district apportionment more fair; it expanded such protections to the accused as free legal counsel, the right to a lawyer, and the requirement to notification of one's rights at the time of arrest.

---

## TERMS & NAMES

For each term or name below, write a sentence explaining its connection to the Kennedy and Johnson administrations.

1. John F. Kennedy
2. Fidel Castro
3. Berlin Wall
4. hot line
5. New Frontier
6. Peace Corps
7. Warren Commission
8. Great Society
9. Medicare and Medicaid
10. Warren Court

## MAIN IDEAS

Use your notes and the information in the chapter to answer the following questions.

### Kennedy and the Cold War  (pages 670–678)

1. Explain the factors that led to Kennedy's victory over Nixon in the 1960 presidential campaign.
2. What were the most significant results of the Cuban missile crisis?

### The New Frontier  (pages 679–683)

3. What was Kennedy's New Frontier? Why did he have trouble getting his New Frontier legislation through Congress?
4. What two international aid programs were launched during the Kennedy administration?
5. How did Kennedy's assassination affect the public?

### The Great Society  (pages 686–693)

6. Describe ways that Great Society programs addressed the problem of poverty.
7. How did the courts increase the political power of people in urban areas and those accused of crimes?

## CRITICAL THINKING

1. **USING YOUR NOTES** Use a Venn diagram to show the major legislative programs of the New Frontier and the Great Society.

NEW FRONTIER          GREAT SOCIETY

Passed under JFK | Proposed by JFK, passed under LBJ | Passed under LBJ

2. **MAKING GENERALIZATIONS** John F. Kennedy said, "[M]y fellow Americans, ask not what your country can do for you—ask what you can do for your country." Do you agree with his view about the relationship between individuals and the country? Explain your opinion.

3. **EVALUATING** Do you think the Great Society helped people achieve their hopes of making life better for themselves and their children? Explain.

---

**VISUAL SUMMARY** THE NEW FRONTIER AND THE GREAT SOCIETY

**JFK**

- Peace Corps
- new "flexible response" strategy for Cold War
- Cuban missile crisis
- Bay of Pigs
- race to the moon
- boosted the economy by increasing government spending
- increased minimum wage to $1.25
- extended unemployment insurance
- provided assistance to cities with high unemployment
- supported civil rights

**LBJ**

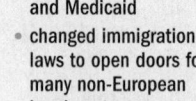
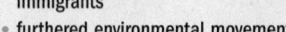

- Great Society reform legislation and federal assistance programs
- war on poverty
- increased protection of individual rights
- pushed civil rights bill through Congress
- EOA, VISTA, Project Head Start
- established Medicare and Medicaid
- changed immigration laws to open doors for many non-European immigrants
- furthered environmental movement
- cut taxes but increased budget deficit

---

## CRITICAL THINKING

1. **USING YOUR NOTES**
   **Passed under JFK:** Peace Corps, Alliance for Progress, space program. **Proposed by JFK, passed under LBJ:** tax cut, antipoverty legislation, civil rights bill. **Passed under LBJ:** Elementary and Secondary Education Act, Medicare and Medicaid, HUD, Immigration Act of 1965, environmental and consumer laws.

2. **MAKING GENERALIZATIONS**
   Students may agree that individuals should show their patriotism by serving their country. Others might disagree, arguing that the government of a nation should serve the citizens.

3. **EVALUATING** Students might defend the Great Society for helping people out of poverty. Others might attack it for increasing government expenditures and causing individuals to rely on outside assistance.

## Standardized Test Practice

Use the quotation and your knowledge of United States history to answer questions 1 and 2.

> "It is our purpose to win the Cold War, not merely wage it in the hope of attaining a standoff. . . . [I]t is really astounding that our government has never stated its purpose to be that of complete victory over the tyrannical forces of international communism. . . . We need a declaration that our intention is victory. . . . And we need an official act, such as the resumption of nuclear testing, to show our own peoples and the other freedom-loving peoples of the world that we mean business."
>
> —Senator Barry Goldwater,
> address to the U.S. Senate, July 14, 1961

1. Based on the quotation, it is reasonable to infer that Senator Goldwater probably opposed —

   A the space race.
   B the Bay of Pigs invasion.
   C the Tax Reduction Act.
   D the Limited Test Ban Treaty.

2. Lyndon Johnson helped to bring about all of the following except —

   F the Voting Rights Act.
   G Head Start.
   H Social Security.
   J Medicare.

Use the graph as well as your knowledge of United States history to answer question 3.

**U.S. Poverty, 1960–1969**

3. Which of the following is true about the graph?

   A Johnson's war on poverty failed.
   B Poverty began to rise again after 1969.
   C Poverty decreased throughout the 1960s.
   D In 1960, the poverty level was about 12%.

ADDITIONAL TEST PRACTICE, pages S1–S33.

 TEST PRACTICE CLASSZONE.COM

## Standardized Test Practice

1. The correct answer is letter **D.**
   Goldwater mentions the resumption of nuclear testing in his speech. The letters A and B are not correct because Goldwater would have wanted to pursue the space race and an invasion of Cuba. The letter C is not correct because his statement has nothing to do with taxation.

2. The correct answer is letter **H.**
   Social Security was begun under Franklin Roosevelt. The letters F, G, and J are incorrect. These programs were started during the Johnson administration.

3. The correct answer is letter **C.**
   The graph shows that poverty decreased throughout the 1960s. The letter A is incorrect because poverty did decrease. The letter B is incorrect because the chart ends at 1969. The letter D is incorrect because the poverty level in 1960 is shown as about 22 percent.

### UNIT PROJECT

**LOBBYING PLAN**

**Tips for Teaching**
· Students should prepare a set of bulleted reasons for support of the action they are lobbying for.
· Have students prepare a position paper to be presented to government officials.
· Students should list ways to gain public support for their cause.

## ALTERNATIVE ASSESSMENT

1. **INTERACT WITH HISTORY** Recall your discussion of the question on p. 667:

   *What are the qualities of effective leaders?*

   Write a job description for "U.S. President." Include a section on "Responsibilities" and one on "Requirements" that lists necessary traits and experience. Think About:
   • Kennedy's and Johnson's (and Nixon's) background and style
   • the role of the media
   • the challenges each leader faced and how he dealt with them
   • the American public's tastes and preferences

2. **LEARNING FROM MEDIA** Use the CD-ROM *Electronic Library of Primary Sources* and other resources for Chapter 20. Discuss the following questions in a small group.

   • Consider key events such as the Bay of Pigs Invasion, the Cuban missile crisis, and the Berlin crisis. What are the dangers of nuclear armament?

   • What are the constitutional responsibilities of the federal government to defend and protect the people of the United States?

   **Cooperative Learning Activity** It is June 1963, and President Kennedy announces his intention to negotiate with the Soviets to limit or halt nuclear testing. What is your reaction to this plan—do you approve or disapprove? Working with a partner, design and create a poster that supports or criticizes President Kennedy's proposal.

 Formal Assessment
· Chapter Test, Forms A, B, and C, pp. 373–384

*The New Frontier and the Great Society* **697**

## ALTERNATIVE ASSESSMENT

### 1. INTERACT WITH HISTORY
**Rubric**
The job description should . . .
· show a deep understanding of the responsibilities and requirements of the office of the presidency
· summarize the required qualities and experience
· employ an interesting and creative style

### 2. LEARNING FROM MEDIA
**Rubric**
A poster should . . .
· demonstrate an understanding of President Kennedy's proposal
· clearly convey the student's position through effective visuals
· use persuasive language in slogans or memorable sentences

# Civil Rights

| | CHAPTER OVERVIEW | COPYMASTERS | INTEGRATED TECHNOLOGY |
|---|---|---|---|
| **CHAPTER RESOURCES** | *After decades of discrimination, African Americans begin a struggle for equality. They make gains against unfair laws in the South, but as the movement reaches northern cities, gains are fewer.* | 📄 **Telescoping the Times** · Chapter Summary, pp. 41–42 <br><br> 📄 **Planning for Block Schedules** | 📹 **American Stories video series** · "Justice in Montgomery" <br> 👁 **Power Presentations** <br> 👁 **Electronic Teacher Tools** <br> ⓘ **Online Lesson Planner** <br> ⓘ **classzone.com** |
| **SECTION 1** <br><br> **Taking on Segregation** <br><br> pp. 700–709 | **KEY IDEAS** <br> *African Americans use strong organization and nonviolent tactics to confront the South's policies of segregation and racial inequality.* | 📄 **In-Depth Resources: Unit 6** · Guided Reading, p. 20 · Building Vocabulary, p. 23 · Skillbuilder Practice, p. 23 · Reteaching Activity, p. 25 · Geography Application, pp. 28–29 · Primary Sources, p. 30 · American Lives, p. 37 <br> 📄 **Lesson Plans,** pp. 165–166 | 📹 **American Stories video series** · "Justice in Montgomery" <br> 📊 **Critical Thinking Transparencies CT29** · Civil Rights Movement <br> 👁 **Electronic Library of Primary Sources** · Desegregation at Central High School by Melba Pattillo Beals · Desegregation at Central High School by Craig Rains · from *Stride Toward Freedom* by Martin Luther King, Jr. <br> ⓘ **classzone.com** |
| **SECTION 2** <br><br> **The Triumphs of a Crusade** <br><br> pp. 710–716 | *Civil rights activists break down numerous racial barriers through continued social protest and prompting of landmark legislation.* | 📄 **In-Depth Resources: Unit 6** · Guided Reading, p. 21 · Reteaching Activity, p. 26 · Primary Sources, pp. 31–33 · Literature, pp. 34–36 · American Lives, p. 38 <br> 📄 **Lesson Plans,** pp. 167–168 | 📊 **Geography Transparencies GT29** · Before and After the Voting Rights Act of 1965 <br> 📊 **Humanities Transparencies HT27** · March on Washington <br> ⓘ **classzone.com** |
| **SECTION 3** <br><br> **Challenges and Changes in the Movement** <br><br> pp. 717–725 | *The civil rights movement turns north, new leaders emerge, and the movement becomes more militant, thus leaving behind a mixed legacy.* | 📄 **In-Depth Resources: Unit 6** · Guided Reading, p. 22 · Reteaching Activity, p. 27 <br> 📄 **Lesson Plans,** pp. 169–170 | 📊 **Critical Thinking Transparencies CT29, CT63** · Civil Rights Movement · African American Educational Attainment <br> 👁 **Electronic Library of Primary Sources** · *from* A Speech to Mississippi Youth by Malcolm X <br> ⓘ **classzone.com** |

## ASSESSMENT OPTIONS

[PE] **Chapter Assessment**, pp. 696–697

[▨] **Formal Assessment**
· Chapter Tests, Forms A, B, and C, pp. 388–405

[◉] **Test Generator**

[▨] **Integrated Assessment Book**

[ⓘ] **TAKS Online Test Practice**

[▨] **TAKS Spiraled Content Review**

**TAKS Practice Tests**

---

[PE] **Section 1 Assessment**, p. 707

[TE] **Self-Assessment**, p. 707

[▨] **Formal Assessment**, Quiz, p. 385

[▨] **Integrated Assessment Book**

[◉] **Test Generator**

[⤓] **TAKS Practice Transparencies TT109**

---

[PE] **Section 2 Assessment**, p. 716

[TE] **Self-Assessment**, p. 716

[▨] **Formal Assessment**, Quiz, p. 386

[▨] **Integrated Assessment Book**

[◉] **Test Generator**

[⤓] **TAKS Practice Transparencies TT110**

---

[PE] **Section 3 Assessment**, p. 723

[TE] **Self-Assessment**, p. 723

[▨] **Formal Assessment**, Quiz, p. 387

[▨] **Integrated Assessment Book**

[◉] **Test Generator**

[⤓] **TAKS Practice Transparencies TT111**

## RESOURCES FOR DIFFERENTIATING INSTRUCTION

### Students Acquiring English/ESL

[▨] **Reading Study Guide:**
(English and Spanish)
pp. 209–216

[▨] **Access for Students Acquiring English/ESL:**
Spanish Translations,
pp. 226–231

[◀)) **Chapter Summaries on CD**
(English and Spanish)

### Less Proficient Readers

[▨] **Reading Study Guide**
(English and Spanish)
pp. 209–216

[▨] **Telescoping the Times**
· Chapter Summary,
pp. 41–42

[◀)) **Chapter Summaries on CD**
(English and Spanish)

### Gifted and Talented Students

[▨] **In-Depth Resources: Unit 6**
· Geography Application,
pp. 28–29
· Primary Sources, pp. 30–33
· Literature, pp. 334–336
· American Lives: Rosa
Parks, p. 37; A. Philip
Randolph, p. 38

[▨] **Historic Supreme Court Decisions**
· *Brown* v. *Board of Education*, pp. 73–78

[◉] **Electronic Library of Primary Sources**
· Unit 6, Chapter 21

## CROSS-CURRICULAR CONNECTIONS

### Civics

Fireside, Harvey and Fuller, Sarah Betsy. *Brown v. Board of Education: Equal Schooling for All.* Hillside, NJ: Enslow Publishers, 1994. Describes the historical context of the landmark Supreme Court decision and provides quotes from the people involved.

Haskins, James. *The March on Washington.* NY: Harper Collins, 1993. The inside story of organizing and participating in the famous 1963 March on Washington.

### Primary Sources

Levine, Ellen. *Freedom's Children: Young Civil Rights Activists Tell Their Own Stories.* NY: Putnam, 1993. Thirty first-person accounts of African-American children who worked for civil rights.

### Humanities: Music

Ferris, Jerri. *What I Had Was Singing: The Story of Marian Anderson.* Minneapolis: Lerner, 1994. Brief, well-researched biography of the African-American opera singer whose career was intertwined with the civil rights movement.

### McDougal Littell *Literature Connections*

Head, Bessie. *When Rain Clouds Gather (with related readings).* Fleeing South Africa in the 1960s, Makhaya comes to a rural village in Botswana as that country approaches independence. The story resonates with the same issues of race, privilege, and identity that drove the civil rights movement in the United States.

Mathabane, Mark. *Kaffir Boy (with related readings).* Born under the hopelessness of apartheid, Mathabane raised himself up from squalor and desperation to win a scholarship to an American university. His extraordinary memoir of life under apartheid is a triumph of the human spirit over hatred.

## ENRICHMENT ACTIVITIES

[PE] **Pupil's Edition**, pp. 698–725
Interact with History, pp. 698–699
Supreme Court, pp. 708–709
Tracing Themes, pp. 724–725

[▨] **In-Depth Resources: Unit 6**
· Geography Application: The *Brown* Decision,
10 Years Later, pp. 28–29
· Primary Source: Crisis in Little Rock, p. 30
· Primary Source: Civil Rights Song, p. 31
· Primary Source: "I Have a Dream," p. 32
· Primary Source: Political Poster, p. 33

· Literature: *And All Our Wounds Forgiven,*
pp. 34–36
· American Lives: Rosa Parks, p. 37
· American Lives: A. Philip Randolph, p. 38

[▨] **Historic Supreme Court Decisions**
· *Brown* v. *Board of Education,* pp. 73–78

[◉] **Electronic Library of Primary Sources**
· Unit 6, Chapter 21

[◉] **Primary Source Explorer**
· Martin Luther King, Jr., *I Have a Dream*
speech 1963

## BLOCK SCHEDULE LESSON PLAN OPTIONS (90-MINUTE PERIOD)

### DAY 1

**CHAPTER OPENER**
pp. 698–699

**Class Time** 30 minutes

**History from Visuals, p. 698**

**Class Time** 15 minutes

*Options for pacing and variety*

· Time Saver Have students look at the photograph, and ask them the discussion questions in the TE. **Class Time** 10 minutes

**Interact with History, p. 699**

**Class Time** 20 minutes

*Options for pacing and variety*

· Role-Playing Before reading the chapter, ask students to give their preliminary opinions of the issues raised in the questions. As a class role play a meeting in a southern city to discuss the issues that seem most important and how to respond to these issues. **Class Time** 15 minutes

**Section 1, pp. 700–709**

**Class Time** 55 minutes

*Options for pacing and variety*

· History on Film View the video, "Justice in Montgomery," about Jo Ann Gibson Robinson and the bus boycott. Discuss the Robinson quote on page 700. **Class Time** 30 minutes

### DAY 1 continued

· Peer Teaching Have students work in groups to research court cases. They could do an opinion piece on *Brown* v. *Board of Education,* or they could choose another court case mentioned in the section (see TE page 700). Have each group work on a different case and then share their information with the class. **Class Time** 40 minutes

· Internet Have students read the spread on pages 708-709, "The Supreme Court: *Brown* v. *Board of Education* (1954)," and have them complete the activity under question 2. Create a chart on the board, and fill it in as a class. **Class Time** 15 minutes

### DAY 2

**SECTION 2, pp. 710–716**

**Class Time** 30 minutes

*Options for pacing and variety*

· Time Saver Have students complete the Instruct questions on TE page 711. **Class Time** 10 minutes

· Time Saver Have students read the "A Personal Voice" features in the section, and write short responses to them. Students should include their emotional responses, as well as their intellectual responses. Ask them what they learned from the quote that they did not know before. **Class Time** 20 minutes

· Time Saver Ask students to read the feature, "I Am A Man, Earnest Withers (1968)," and discuss the questions in both the PE and the TE. **Class Time** 15 minutes

**SECTION 3, pp. 717–725**

Class Time 30 minutes

*Options for pacing and variety*

· Peer Teaching Bring to class some of the primary sources listed in the activity on TE page 719. Read them to the class, and discuss their major themes and the development of the ideas from earlier civil rights leaders, such as W.E.B. DuBois and Booker T. Washington. Students may also refer to the quotations throughout the section in the discussion. **Class Time** 30 minutes

### DAY 2 continued

· Peer Evaluation Have students work in pairs to create questions about the people or the terms and names mentioned in the section. Then have them team up with another pair and quiz each other using the questions. **Class Time** 20 minutes

· Internet Ask students to read the spread on pages 724-725, "Tracing Themes: Civil Rights," and do the Internet activity listed under question 2. Depending on access to the Internet, students may need work in pairs. **Class Time** 35 minutes

**ASSESSMENT**
pp. 726–727

**Class Time** 30 minutes

*Options for pacing and variety*

· Time Saver Assign the Thinking Critically questions for homework, and discuss the responses in class. **Class Time** 10 minutes

· Role-Playing Ask students to work in groups to discuss the initial opinions they expressed the first day during the discussion of Interact with History. Students should then write a personal account of their opinions and how their increased knowledge may have affected changes in the way they view certain issues. **Class Time** 30 minutes

---

**TEACHER-TESTED ACTIVITY**   Steve Ellison, Petaluma High School, Petaluma, California

**"MOST VALUABLE ACTIVIST" AWARD**

**Class Time** 30 minutes

**Task** Creating an award for the most valuable civil rights activist

**Purpose** To recognize the importance of key individuals in the civil rights movement

**Supplies Needed**
· Poster board
· Markers

**Activity** Tell students to select an activist who exemplifies the spirit of the civil rights movement. Have students use poster board to create a plaque naming the "Most Valuable Activist" and listing at least three reasons why the activist should be recognized. Then have students display their work and explain their choices as you list them on the board.

**CORRELATION TO THE TEXAS ESSENTIAL KNOWLEDGE AND SKILLS**

Chapter 21 addresses the following standards of the Texas Essential Knowledge and Skills for U.S. History.

| TEKS | Instruction | Student Question/Activity |
|---|---|---|
| **(1C)** Explain the significance of the date: 1957. | **PE 703–704** discussion of the Little Rock school crisis in the early attempts at school integration | **TE 703** Activity asking students to conduct further research on the "Little Rock Nine" |
| **(6H)** Identify the origins of major domestic and foreign policy issues currently facing the United States. | **PE 722–723** examination of various civil rights policies, including affirmative action, that remain a part of American society today | **TE 722** civics activity in which students study and discuss the issue of race and examine ways of improving race relations |
| **(7A)** Trace the historical development of the civil rights movement in the 20th century. | **PE 700–723** In-depth examination of civil rights movement of the 1950s and 1960s | **PE 726** Main Idea and Critical Thinking questions about the many aspects of the civil rights movement |
| **(7B)** Identify significant leaders of the civil rights movement, including Martin Luther King, Jr. | **PE 704–706** discussion of the emergence of Martin Luther King, Jr. as the leader of the civil rights movement | **PE 705** Main Idea question about the central points of King's philosophy |
| **(7C)** Evaluate government efforts, including the Civil Rights Act of 1964, to achieve equality in the United States. | **PE 714** analysis of the Civil Rights Act of 1964. | **PE 714** Skillbuilder question requiring students to interpret a civil rights acts chart |
| **(7D)** Identify changes in the United States that have resulted from the civil rights movement. | **PE 722–723** discussion of the gains of the civil rights movement, including the increased participation of minorities in the political process | **PE 722** Main Idea question about the accomplishments of the civil rights movement |
| **(17A)** Analyze the effects of 20th-century landmark Supreme Court cases. | **PE 708–709** feature on the landmark case, *Brown v. Board of Education of Topeka*, which struck down the principle of separate but equal | **PE 709** Critical Thinking questions about the feature |

## TAKS MINI-LESSONS

1. **Social Studies Skills: Objective 3 (US7.B):** Identify significant leaders of the civil rights movement, including Martin Luther King, Jr. **Activity** Have students discuss what they feel were the leadership qualities of Martin Luther King, Jr.

2. **Social Studies Skills: Objective 4 (US7.C):** Evaluate government efforts, including the Civil Rights Act of 1964, to achieve equality in the United States **Activity** Have students answer the Analyzing Primary Sources question in the Section 2 Assessment.

3. **Social Studies Skills: Objective 4 (US17.A):** Analyze the effects of 20th-century landmarks U.S. Supreme Court decisions **Activity** Have students complete the questions regarding the feature on the landmark U.S. Supreme Court case, *Brown v. Board of Education of Topeka*.

4. **English Language Arts Skills: Objective 1 (7.F):** Produce summaries of texts by identifying main ideas and their supporting details. **Activity** Have students summarize the legacy of the civil rights movement and support their summary with appropriate details.

5. **English Language Arts Skills: Objective 4 (2.C):** Proofread writing for appropriateness of organization, content, style, and conventions **Activity** Have pairs of students proofread each other's answer to the Section 2 Assessment questions (p. 716).

# CHAPTER 21 · CIVIL RIGHTS

Civil Rights activists lead the 1965 voting rights march from Selma to Montgomery, Alabama.

**1954** *Brown v. Board of Education* decision orders the desegregation of public schools.

**1955** Montgomery bus boycott begins.

**1956** Dwight D. Eisenhower is reelected.

**1957** School desegregation crisis occurs in Little Rock, Arkansas.

**1960** John F. Kennedy is elected president.

USA
WORLD

1955

1960

**1956** Suez Canal crisis occurs in Egypt.

**1957** African nation of Ghana wins independence.

**1959** Fidel Castro assumes power in Cuba.

**698** CHAPTER 21

## HISTORY from VISUALS

### Interpreting the Photograph
Have students identify people they recognize in the photograph. *(Most students will identify Dr. Martin Luther King and his wife, Coretta. Others include A. Philip Randolph; Rev. Ralph Abernathy, who was King's associate at the Southern Christian Leadership Conference; and Ralph Bunche, an African-American scholar and diplomat who won the Nobel Peace Prize in 1950.)*

**Extension** Have students draw conclusions based on the photograph about the significance of the event to the marchers.

## Time Line Discussion

Explain to students that the time line covers the years of the American civil rights movement.

· Ask students what event began a new chapter in the civil rights movement. *(the 1954 Brown v. Board of Education decision)*

· Ask students who was president when the Civil Rights Act was passed. *(Lyndon B. Johnson)*

· Ask students what kinds of activities marked the civil rights movement. *(boycotts, court cases, marches, assassinations)*

## THEMES IN CHAPTER 21

### CIVIL RIGHTS

The civil rights movement exposed the ugly face of racial prejudice and pushed a reluctant federal government to take action on behalf of African Americans. Both Eisenhower and Kennedy used the military to enforce desegregation. Although the Fifteenth Amendment guaranteed voting rights for all citizens regardless of "race, color, or previous condition of servitude," most Southern states restricted African Americans' access to the ballot. The civil rights movement changed that.

**See Teacher's Edition notes**, pp. 711, 715.

### ECONOMIC OPPORTUNITY

There is no explicit right to work guaranteed by the U.S. Constitution, but the rights to "life, liberty, and the pursuit of happiness" stated in the Declaration of Independence make it clear that the opportunity to make a decent living is a basic American right. The civil rights movement addressed the fact that African Americans as well as other Americans had been denied that right.

**See Teacher's Edition note**, p. 718.

## INTERACT
### WITH HISTORY

The year is 1960, and segregation divides the nation's people. African Americans are denied access to jobs and housing and are refused service at restaurants and stores. But the voices of the oppressed rise up in the churches and in the streets, demanding civil rights for all Americans.

## What rights are worth fighting for?

### Examine the Issues

- Are all Americans entitled to the same civil rights?
- What are the risks of demanding rights?
- Why might some people fight against equal rights?

**RESEARCH LINKS** CLASSZONE.COM

Visit the Chapter 21 links for more information about Civil Rights.

## INTERACT
### WITH HISTORY

### Objectives

· To trace the history of the civil rights movement
· To analyze the motivation of proponents and opponents of civil rights

### Examine the Issues

1. Discuss the meaning of *liberty and equality* with students. Ask how liberty and equality are jeopardized when one or more groups of people are denied rights enjoyed by others.
2. Ask students what causes they would fight for when potential violence is involved.
3. Tell students that at various stages of the civil rights movement, some African-American leaders preached the virtues of separatism. Ask students why they think this was so.

1963 Lyndon B. Johnson becomes president upon John F. Kennedy's assassination.

1964 Lyndon B. Johnson is elected president.

1964 Congress passes the Civil Rights Act.

KEEP THE IDEA OF FREEDOM ALIVE — JOIN NAACP

1967 Race riots occur in major U.S. cities.

1968 Richard M. Nixon is elected president.

1968 Martin Luther King, Jr., is assassinated.

1969 U.S. astronauts walk on the moon.

**1965**
**1970**

1962 South African civil rights leader Nelson Mandela is imprisoned.

1966 Cultural Revolution begins in China.

1968 Tet offensive begins in Vietnam.

1970 President Nasser of Egypt dies.

*Civil Rights* **699**

## RECOMMENDED RESOURCES

### BOOKS FOR THE TEACHER

Chafe, William H. *Civilities and Civil Rights: Greensboro, North Carolina, and the Black Struggle for Freedom.* New York: Oxford UP, 1980.

Morris, Aldon D. *The Origins of the Civil Rights Movement.* New York: Free Press, 1986.

Ralph, James R. *Northern Protest: Martin Luther King, Jr., Chicago and the Civil Rights Movement.* Cambridge: Harvard UP, 1993.

### BOOKS FOR THE STUDENT

Goldfield, David. *Black, White, and Southern: Race Relations and Southern Culture, 1940 to the Present.* Baton Rouge: Louisiana State UP, 1990.

Kluger, Richard. *Simple Justice: The History of Brown v. Board of Education and Black America's Struggle for Equality.* New York: Vintage Books, 1977.

### VIDEOS

*At the River I Stand.* Dir. David Appleby. California Newsreel, 1993. Documentary of Martin Luther King's last civil rights campaign.

*Eyes on the Prize.* PBS Home Video, 1986, 1989. 800-424-7963. 14-hour

chronicle of the civil rights movement.

### SOFTWARE

*Prejudice.* Diskettes. Tom Snyder Productions, Inc., 1992. 800-342-0236.

### INTEGRATED TECHNOLOGY

For teacher support visit . . .

 classzone.com

*Civil Rights* **699**

# Taking on Segregation

| MAIN IDEA | WHY IT MATTERS NOW | Terms & Names |
|---|---|---|
| Activism and a series of Supreme Court decisions advanced equal rights for African Americans in the 1950s and 1960s. | Landmark Supreme Court decisions beginning in 1954 have guaranteed civil rights for Americans today. | • Thurgood Marshall • *Brown* v. *Board of Education of Topeka* • Rosa Parks • Martin Luther King, Jr. • Southern Christian Leadership Conference (SCLC) • Student Nonviolent Coordinating Committee (SNCC) • sit-in |

 U.S. History 1C, 7A, 7B, 8A, 8B, 10A, 17A, 18A, 18B, 19A, 19B, 19C, 21D, 24A, 24B, 24D, 24G, 25A, 25B, 25C, 25D

**One American's Story**

Jo Ann Gibson Robinson drew back in self-defense as the white bus driver raised his hand as if to strike her. "Get up from there!" he shouted. Robinson, laden with Christmas packages, had forgotten the rules and sat down in the front of the bus, which was reserved for whites.

Humiliating incidents were not new to the African Americans who rode the segregated buses of Montgomery, Alabama, in the mid-1950s. The bus company required them to pay at the front and then exit and reboard at the rear. "I felt like a dog," Robinson later said. A professor at the all-black Alabama State College, Robinson was also president of the Women's Political Council, a group of professional African-American women determined to increase black political power.

**A PERSONAL VOICE** JO ANN GIBSON ROBINSON

" We had members in every elementary, junior high, and senior high school, and in federal, state, and local jobs. Wherever there were more than ten blacks employed, we had a member there. We were prepared to the point that we knew that in a matter of hours, we could corral the whole city. "

—quoted in *Voices of Freedom: An Oral History of the Civil Rights Movement*

On December 1, 1955, police arrested an African-American woman for refusing to give up her seat on a bus. Robinson promptly sent out a call for all African Americans to boycott Montgomery buses.

**VIDEO**

*JUSTICE IN MONTGOMERY*
**Jo Ann Gibson Robinson and the Bus Boycott**

## ❶ The Segregation System

Segregated buses might never have rolled through the streets of Montgomery if the Civil Rights Act of 1875 had remained in force. This act outlawed segregation in public facilities by decreeing that "all persons . . . shall be entitled to the full and equal enjoyment of the accommodations . . . of inns, public conveyances on land or water, theaters, and other places of public amusement." In 1883, however, the all-white Supreme Court declared the act unconstitutional.

*Skillbuilder Answer*
**Segregated:** The South; **Segregation prohibited:** The Industrial Northeast, the northeastern Midwest, and the Pacific Northwest.

---

**PLESSY V. FERGUSON** During the 1890s, a number of other court decisions and state laws severely limited African-American rights. In 1890, Louisiana passed a law requiring railroads to provide "equal but separate accommodations for the white and colored races." In the *Plessy* v. *Ferguson* case of 1896, the Supreme Court ruled that this "separate but equal" law did not violate the Fourteenth Amendment, which guarantees all Americans equal treatment under the law.

**Background**
See *Plessy* v. *Ferguson* on page 290.

Armed with the *Plessy* decision, states throughout the nation, but especially in the South, passed what were known as Jim Crow laws, aimed at separating the races. These laws forbade marriage between blacks and whites and established many other restrictions on social and religious contact between the races. There were separate schools as well as separate streetcars, waiting rooms, railroad coaches, elevators, witness stands, and public restrooms. The facilities provided for blacks were always inferior to those for whites. Nearly every day, African Americans faced humiliating signs that read: "Colored Water"; "No Blacks Allowed"; "Whites Only!" **A**

**MAIN IDEA**

**Analyzing Effects**
**A** What were the effects of the Supreme Court decision *Plessy* v. *Ferguson*?

**A. Answer** Since the Court ruled that segregation was not unconstitutional, many states, especially in the South, passed segregationist Jim Crow laws.

**SEGREGATION CONTINUES INTO THE 20TH CENTURY**
After the Civil War, some African Americans tried to escape Southern racism by moving north. This migration of Southern African Americans speeded up greatly during World War I, as many African-American sharecroppers abandoned farms for the promise of industrial jobs in Northern cities. However, they discovered racial prejudice and segregation there, too. Most could find housing only in all-black neighborhoods. Many white workers also resented the competition for jobs. This sometimes led to violence.

## WORLD STAGE

### APARTHEID—SEGREGATION IN SOUTH AFRICA

In 1948, the white government of South Africa passed laws to ensure that whites would stay in control of the country. Those laws established a system called apartheid, which means "apartness." The system divided South Africans into four segregated racial groups—whites, blacks, coloreds of mixed race, and Asians. It restricted what jobs nonwhites could hold, where they could live, and what rights they could exercise. Because of apartheid, the black African majority were denied the right to vote.

In response to worldwide criticism, the South African government gradually repealed the apartheid laws, starting in the late 1970s. In 1994, South Africa held its first all-race election and elected as president Nelson Mandela, a black anti-apartheid leader whom the white government had imprisoned for nearly 30 years.

## WORLD STAGE

### Apartheid—Segregation in South Africa

**Comparing** Ask students to compare the South African apartheid laws with Jim Crow laws in the American South. *(The critical link in both sets of laws was the denial of the right to vote. By denying the vote, those in power were ensuring that people of color had no legal recourse to change the system.)*

### U.S. School Segregation, 1952

[Map of the United States showing school segregation status by state]

Wash., Oreg., Mont., Idaho, Wyo., N.Dak., S.Dak., Nebr., Minn., Wis., Iowa, Maine, Vt., N.H., Mass., R.I., Conn., N.Y., Mich., Pa., N.J., Nev., Utah, Colo., Calif., Ariz., N.Mex., Kans., Mo., Ill., Ind., Ohio, W. Va., Va., Del., Md., D.C., Ky., Okla., Ark., Tenn., N.C., Miss., Ala., Ga., S.C., Texas, La., Fla.

☐ Segregation required
☐ Segregation permitted
☐ Segregation prohibited
☐ No specific legislation, or local option

**GEOGRAPHY SKILLBUILDER**
**Region** In which regions were schools segregated by law? In which were segregation expressly prohibited?

These photos of the public schools for white children *(top)* and for black children *(above)* in a Southern town in the 1930s show that separate facilities were often unequal in the segregation era.

## HISTORY from VISUALS

**Interpreting the Map**
Ask students to use their knowledge of American history and the Civil War to account for the information on the map. *(Students should mention the former Confederacy's adherence to segregation, the outlawing of segregation in the older Union states, and the lack of laws on the subject in states in the West, upper Midwest, and northern New England where there were relatively few African Americans.)*

*Civil Rights* **701**

---

classzone.com

**ACTIVITY** **LINK TO WORLD HISTORY**

### Researching the Life of Nelson Mandela

**Class Time** 45 minutes

**Task** Preparing an exhibit on the life and achievements of Nelson Mandela

**Purpose** To evaluate the accomplishments of Nelson Mandela

**Directions** Have students work in small groups and use library and Internet resources to research the life and achievements of Nelson Mandela. Students may write a group report or assemble their findings, perhaps with collage imagery on poster board. As an extension activity, they could compare Mandela's life with that of Martin Luther King, Jr.

📝 Integrated Assessment
· Rubrics 1, 4, 5

*Civil Rights* **701**

## Instruct: Objective ❷

### Challenging Segregation in Court/ Reaction to the *Brown* Decision

TAKS SS11 4(US17.A)

· What issues did the NAACP use to challenge the *Plessy* decision?

· How did Thurgood Marshall help advance the cause of civil rights?

· How did the *Brown* decision affect the cause of civil rights?

· Why did the Supreme Court issue a second ruling enforcing the *Brown* decision?

 In-Depth Resources: Unit 6
· Guided Reading, p. 20
· Geography Application: The Brown Decision, pp. 28–29
· Primary Source: Crisis in Little Rock, p.30

---

### KEY PLAYER

**Thurgood Marshall**

Marshall's grandfather was a slave who fought in the Civil War. His mother was one of the first African Americans to graduate from Columbia University Teachers College. His father was the first African American to serve on a grand jury in Baltimore County in the 20th century. Ask students how Marshall's family's past might have helped prepare him for his role in history. *(From his family, Marshall learned pride and the importance of excelling.)*

---

**A DEVELOPING CIVIL RIGHTS MOVEMENT** In many ways, the events of World War II set the stage for the civil rights movement. First, the demand for soldiers in the early 1940s created a shortage of white male laborers. That labor shortage opened up new job opportunities for African Americans, Latinos, and white women.

Second, nearly one million African Americans served in the armed forces, which needed so many fighting men that they had to end their discriminatory policies. Such policies had previously kept African Americans from serving in fighting units. Many African-American soldiers returned from the war determined to fight for their own freedom now that they had helped defeat fascist regimes overseas.

Third, during the war, civil rights organizations actively campaigned for African-American voting rights and challenged Jim Crow laws. In response to protests, President Roosevelt issued a presidential directive prohibiting racial discrimination by federal agencies and all companies that were engaged in war work. The groundwork was laid for more organized campaigns to end segregation throughout the United States. **B**

### ❷ Challenging Segregation in Court

The desegregation campaign was led largely by the NAACP, which had fought since 1909 to end segregation. One influential figure in this campaign was Charles Hamilton Houston, a brilliant Howard University law professor who also served as chief legal counsel for the NAACP from 1934 to 1938.

**THE NAACP LEGAL STRATEGY** In deciding the NAACP's legal strategy, Houston focused on the inequality between the separate schools that many states provided. At that time, the nation spent ten times as much money educating a white child as an African-American child. Thus, Houston focused the organization's limited resources on challenging the most glaring inequalities of segregated public education.

In 1938, he placed a team of his best law students under the direction of **Thurgood Marshall.** Over the next 23 years, Marshall and his NAACP lawyers would win 29 out of 32 cases argued before the Supreme Court.

Several of the cases became legal milestones, each chipping away at the segregation platform of *Plessy* v. *Ferguson*. In the 1946 case *Morgan* v. *Virginia*, the Supreme Court declared unconstitutional those state laws mandating segregated seating on interstate buses. In 1950, the high court ruled in *Sweatt* v. *Painter* that state law schools must admit black applicants, even if separate black schools exist.

***BROWN* V. *BOARD OF EDUCATION*** Marshall's most stunning victory came on May 17, 1954, in the case known as ***Brown* v. *Board of Education of Topeka.*** (See page 708). In this case, the father of eight-year-old Linda Brown had charged the board of education of Topeka, Kansas, with violating Linda's rights by denying her admission to an all-white elementary school four blocks from her house. The nearest all-black elementary school was 21 blocks away.

In a landmark verdict, the Supreme Court unanimously struck down segregation in schooling as an unconstitutional violation of the Fourteenth Amendment's Equal Protection

---

### KEY PLAYER

**THURGOOD MARSHALL 1908–1993**

Thurgood Marshall dedicated his life to fighting racism. His father had labored as a steward at an all-white country club, his mother as a teacher at an all-black school. Marshall himself was denied admission to the University of Maryland Law School because of his race.

In 1961, President John F. Kennedy nominated Marshall to the U.S. Court of Appeals. Lyndon Johnson picked Marshall for U.S. solicitor general in 1965 and two years later named him as the first African-American Supreme Court justice. In that role, he remained a strong advocate of civil rights until he retired in 1991.

After Marshall died in 1993, a copy of the *Brown* v. *Board of Education* decision was placed beside his casket. On it, an admirer wrote: "You shall always be remembered."

---

**MAIN IDEA**

**Developing Historical Perspective**
**B** How did events during World War II lay the groundwork for African Americans to fight for civil rights in the 1950s?

**B. Answers**
Blacks had experienced better job opportunities; many veterans who had fought racist Germans wanted to resist racist Americans; civil rights groups had staged some successful protests.

---

*Brown* v. *Board of Education*

**Class Time** 45 minutes

**Task** Writing an opinion piece about the significance of the *Brown* case

**Purpose** To gain a deeper understanding of a historic Supreme Court case

**Directions** Have students work in small groups and use library and Internet resources to research the issues in the *Brown* decision. Then have students write an editorial or opinion piece about the decision. Tell students to share their work with the rest of the class.

📓 Historic Supreme Court Cases: *Brown v. Board of Education,* pp. 73–78

**MAIN IDEA**

**Making Inferences**

**C** How did the *Brown* decision affect schools outside of Topeka?

**C. Answer** *Brown* said that segregation has no place in public education, so all public schools must desegregate.

Clause. Chief Justice Earl Warren wrote that, "[I]n the field of public education, the doctrine of separate but equal has no place." The *Brown* decision was relevant for some 12 million schoolchildren in 21 states. **C**

## Reaction to the *Brown* Decision

Official reaction to the ruling was mixed. In Kansas and Oklahoma, state officials said they expected segregation to end with little trouble. In Texas the governor promised to comply but warned that plans might "take years" to work out. In Mississippi and Georgia, officials vowed total resistance. Governor Herman Talmadge of Georgia branded the decision "a flagrant abuse of judicial power" and pledged, "The people of Georgia . . . will map a program to insure . . . permanent segregation of the races."

**RESISTANCE TO SCHOOL DESEGREGATION** Within a year, more than 500 school districts had desegregated their classrooms. In Baltimore, St. Louis, and Washington, D.C., black and white students sat side by side for the first time in history. However, in many areas where African Americans were a majority, whites resisted desegregation. In some places, the Ku Klux Klan reappeared and White Citizens Councils boycotted businesses that supported desegregation.

To speed things up, in 1955 the Supreme Court handed down a second ruling, known as *Brown II,* that ordered school desegregation implemented "with all deliberate speed." Initially President Eisenhower refused to enforce compliance. "The fellow who tries to tell me that you can do these things by force is just plain nuts," he said. Events in Little Rock, Arkansas, would soon force Eisenhower to go against his personal beliefs.

**CRISIS IN LITTLE ROCK** In 1948, Arkansas had become the first Southern state to admit African Americans to state universities without being required by a court order. By the 1950s, some scout troops and labor unions in Arkansas had quietly ended their Jim Crow practices. Little Rock citizens had elected two men to the school board who publicly backed desegregation—and the school superintendent, Virgil Blossom, began planning for desegregation soon after *Brown.*

**D. answer** Some Southern whites and state officials resisted segregation, and neither the president nor Congress forced them to act quickly.

**MAIN IDEA**

**Analyzing Causes**

**D** Why weren't schools in all regions desegregated immediately after the *Brown II* decision?

However, Governor Orval Faubus publicly showed support for segregation. In September 1957, he ordered the National Guard to turn away the "Little Rock Nine"—nine African-American students who had volunteered to integrate Little Rock's Central High School as the first step in Blossom's plan. A federal judge ordered Faubus to let the students into school.

NAACP members called eight of the students and arranged to drive them to school. They could not reach the ninth student, Elizabeth Eckford, who did not have a phone, and she set out alone. Outside Central High, Eckford faced an abusive crowd. Terrified, the 15-year-old made it to a bus stop where two friendly whites stayed with her. **D**

As white students jeer her and Arkansas National Guards look on, Elizabeth Eckford enters Little Rock Central High School in 1957. ▼

 **Electronic Library of Primary Sources**
· Desegregation at Central High School, 1957, by Melba Patlillo Beak
· Desegregation at Central High School, 1957, by Craig Rains

### More About . . .

**Elizabeth Eckford**
The experience at Central High School was difficult for Eckford, who disappeared from public view and refused all interview requests after 1958. In 1996, she was persuaded by some Kansas high school students to be the subject of a video that became a finalist in a National History Day competition.

### STORY from VISUALS

**Interpreting the Photograph**
Discuss the photograph with the students. Ask them to put themselves in the place of Elizabeth Eckford. How do they think they would have felt at the moment that this photograph was taken? (*Students should infer that fear would be the predominant feeling.*)

---

**DIFFERENTIATING INSTRUCTION**    **GIFTED AND TALENTED STUDENTS**

### Researching the "Little Rock Nine"

Ask students to research the "Little Rock Nine" and then write an outline for a documentary about them. Have them include the students' motivation for volunteering to enter the high school, what they experienced upon their arrival, and what impact the experience had on their lives.

The documentary outline should . . .

· show an understanding of the characters and the event

· indicate the use of standard interview techniques

· project an accurate and dramatic portrayal of the experiences of the "Little Rock Nine"

 Integrated Assessment
· Rubrics 1, 6

## Instruct: Objective ③

**The Montgomery Bus Boycott /
Martin Luther King and the SCLC**
TAKS SS11 3(US7.B)

· What caused the Montgomery Bus Boycott?

· How did the boycott end?

· Who inspired Martin Luther King, Jr.?

· How did young people respond to King's leadership?

 In-Depth Resources: Unit 6
· Guided Reading, p. 20
· American Lives: Rosa Parks, p. 37

### KEY PLAYER

**Rosa Parks**

Rosa Parks left Montgomery in 1957 and moved to Detroit. For 23 years, she served on the staff of Michigan Congressman John Conyers. In 1999, she was awarded the Congressional Gold Medal of Honor, the highest honor awarded to an American civilian. Ask students how they would have felt in Parks's place on the Montgomery bus in 1955. *(Students will probably say that they would have felt afraid but also determined to undertake such a significant action.)*

---

The crisis in Little Rock forced Eisenhower to act. He placed the Arkansas National Guard under federal control and ordered a thousand paratroopers into Little Rock. The nation watched the televised coverage of the event. Under the watch of soldiers, the nine African-American teenagers attended class.

But even these soldiers could not protect the students from troublemakers who confronted them in stairways, in the halls, and in the cafeteria. Throughout the year African-American students were regularly harassed by other students. At the end of the year, Faubus shut down Central High rather than let integration continue.

On September 9, 1957, Congress passed the Civil Rights Act of 1957, the first civil rights law since Reconstruction. Shepherded by Senator Lyndon B. Johnson of Texas, the law gave the attorney general greater power over school desegregation. It also gave the federal government jurisdiction—or authority—over violations of African-American voting rights. **E**

### KEY PLAYER

**ROSA PARKS
1913–**

Long before December 1955, Rosa Parks (shown being finger printed) had protested segregation through everyday acts. She refused to use drinking fountains labeled "Colored Only." When possible, she shunned segregated elevators and climbed stairs instead.

Parks joined the Montgomery chapter of the NAACP in 1943 and became the organization's secretary. A turning point came for her in the summer of 1955, when she attended a workshop designed to promote integration by giving the students the experience of interracial living.

Returning to Montgomery, Parks was even more determined to fight segregation. As it happened, her act of protest against injustice on the buses inspired a whole community to join her cause.

## The Montgomery Bus Boycott ③

The face-to-face confrontation at Central High School was not the only showdown over segregation in the mid-1950s. Impatient with the slow pace of change in the courts, African-American activists had begun taking direct action to win the rights promised to them by the Fourteenth and Fifteenth Amendments to the Constitution. Among those on the frontline of change was Jo Ann Robinson.

**BOYCOTTING SEGREGATION** Four days after the *Brown* decision in May 1954, Robinson wrote a letter to the mayor of Montgomery, Alabama, asking that bus drivers no longer be allowed to force riders in the "colored" section to yield their seats to whites. The mayor refused. Little did he know that in less than a year another African-American woman from Alabama would be at the center of this controversy, and that her name and her words would far outlast segregation.

On December 1, 1955, **Rosa Parks,** a seamstress and an NAACP officer, took a seat in the front row of the "colored" section of a Montgomery bus. As the bus filled up, the driver ordered Parks and three other African-American passengers to empty the row they were occupying so that a white man could sit down without having to sit next to any African Americans. "It was time for someone to stand up—or in my case, sit down," recalled Parks. "I refused to move."

As Parks stared out the window, the bus driver said, "If you don't stand up, I'm going to call the police and have you arrested." The soft-spoken Parks replied, "You may do that."

News of Parks's arrest spread rapidly. Jo Ann Robinson and NAACP leader E. D. Nixon suggested a bus boycott. The leaders of the African-American community, including many ministers, formed the Montgomery Improvement Association to organize the boycott. They elected the pastor of the Dexter Avenue Baptist Church, 26-year-old **Martin Luther King, Jr.,** to lead the group. An ordained minister since 1948, King had just earned a Ph.D. degree in theology from Boston University. "Well, I'm not sure I'm the best person for the position," King confided to Nixon, "but if no one else is going to serve, I'd be glad to try."

**MAIN IDEA**

**Making Inferences**
**E** What effect do you think television coverage of the Little Rock incident had on the nation?

*E. Possible Answer* Television allowed people to see the white separatists' cruel treatment of the African-American students.

Mini-Lesson 1:
SS11 3(US7.B)

---

| **ACTIVITY** | **SKILLBUILDER LESSON** |

**Making Inferences**

**Explaining the Skill** Writers do not always explain every aspect of an event in detail. They rely on readers to make inference, or draw conclusions, about the event by using clues in the text and by drawing on their own personal experience, historical knowledge and common sense.

**Applying the Skill** Use the following questions to help students make inferences about the Montgomery Bus Boycott.

· What do clues in the text reveal about the reason for the boycott: *(Buses had a "colored" section and drivers abused African-American riders.)*

· Why did African Americans in Montgomery participate in the boycott? *(They thought it was the only way to change the system)*

· Why was the boycott successful? *(It caused a lawsuit that resulted in Supreme Court order to desegregate the buses)*

 In-Depth Resources: Unit 6
· Skillbuilder Practice: Making Inferences, p. 24

◀ During the bus boycott, Montgomery's black citizens relied on an efficient car pool system that ferried people between more than forty pickup stations like the one shown.

More About . . .

**The Montgomery Bus Boycott**
Before the boycott began, Martin Luther King Jr. thought that if 60 percent of Montgomery's African Americans boycotted the bus system, the boycott would be a success. Instead, 90 percent boycotted the buses. Revenues for the bus system plummeted. Downtown retail business also declined sharply, as many African Americans no longer went downtown to shop. Although white leaders fought back with harassment, conspiracy charges, and outright violence, the boycotters' unity never wavered.

**WALKING FOR JUSTICE** On the night of December 5, 1955, Dr. King made the following declaration to an estimated crowd of between 5,000 and 15,000 people.

*F. Possible Answers*
Parks's refusal to yield her seat to a white man led to a citywide bus boycott; it also brought Martin Luther King, Jr., to prominence.

**A PERSONAL VOICE** MARTIN LUTHER KING, JR.
" There comes a time when people get tired of being trampled over by the iron feet of oppression. . . . I want it to be known—that we're going to work with grim and bold determination—to gain justice on buses in this city. And we are not wrong. . . . If we are wrong—the Supreme Court of this nation is wrong. If we are wrong—God Almighty is wrong. . . . If we are wrong—justice is a lie. "
—quoted in *Parting the Waters: America in the King Years, 1954–63*

**MAIN IDEA**

**Synthesizing**
**F** Why was Rosa Parks's action on December 1, 1955, significant?

King's passionate and eloquent speech brought people to their feet and filled the audience with a sense of mission. African Americans filed a lawsuit and for 381 days refused to ride the buses in Montgomery. In most cases they had to find other means of transportation by organizing car pools or walking long distances. Support came from within the black community—workers donated one-fifth of their weekly salaries—as well as from outside groups like the NAACP, the United Auto Workers, Montgomery's Jewish community, and sympathetic white southerners. The boycotters remained nonviolent even after a bomb ripped apart King's home (no one was injured). Finally, in 1956, the Supreme Court outlawed bus segregation. **F**

## Martin Luther King and the SCLC ❸

*G. answer*
"Soul force," or nonviolent resistance, which included acts of civil disobedience, demonstrations, and adherence to nonviolence.

The Montgomery bus boycott proved to the world that the African-American community could unite and organize a successful protest movement. It also proved the power of nonviolent resistance, the peaceful refusal to obey unjust laws. Despite threats to his life and family, King urged his followers, "Don't ever let anyone pull you so low as to hate them."

**CHANGING THE WORLD WITH SOUL FORCE** King called his brand of nonviolent resistance "soul force." He based his ideas on the teachings of several people. From Jesus, he learned to love one's enemies. From writer Henry David Thoreau he took the concept of civil disobedience—the refusal to obey an unjust law. From labor organizer A. Philip Randolph he learned to organize massive demonstrations. From Mohandas Gandhi, the leader who helped India throw off British rule, he learned to resist oppression without violence. **G**

**MAIN IDEA**

**Summarizing**
**G** What were the central points of Dr. King's philosophy?

"We will not hate you," King said to white racists, "but we cannot . . . obey your unjust laws. . . . We will soon wear you down by our capacity to suffer. And in winning our freedom, we will so appeal to your heart and conscience that we will win you in the process."

👁 Electronic Library of Primary Sources
· from *Stride Toward Freedom*, 1958, by M.L. King, Jr.

*Civil Rights* **705**

---

**DIFFERENTIATING INSTRUCTION**    **LESS PROFICIENT READERS**

### Activating Prior Knowledge

Have less proficient readers define *boycott*. Ask whether any students have participated in a boycott. If so, encourage them to share their experiences.

Ask the following questions, recording responses on the board:

· What motivates a person to defy authority and risk jail?
· Why would a whole community organize a boycott?
· What can happen when enough people defy authority?

Tell students to keep these questions in mind as they read about the Montgomery bus boycott.

### Ella Baker

Ella Baker thought that a charismatic leader was a handicap for oppressed people. Baker explained her position by saying that a charismatic person usually becomes a leader as a result of media attention. She reasoned that if the media could *make* a leader, it could *unmake* one as well.

## KEY PLAYER

### Martin Luther King, Jr.

King was a man of faith and erudition. Both his father and grandfather were Baptist preachers. At Crozer Theological Seminary, King first became acquainted with the ideas of Mohandas Gandhi, which influenced him greatly. At Boston University, he earned a Ph.D. Ask students how they think King's education helped him in his work. (*King assembled his philosophy of nonviolence from ideas encountered during his education.*)

## Instruct: Objective ❹

### The Movement Spreads

TAKS SS11 4(US7.A)

· What was SNCC?
· How did the Congress of Racial Equality (CORE) influence SNCC?
· How did sit-ins advance the cause of the civil rights movement?

📝 In-Depth Resources: Unit 6
· Guided Reading, p. 20

## KEY PLAYER

### MARTIN LUTHER KING, JR.
### 1929–1968

Born Michael Luther King, Jr., King had to adjust to a new name in 1934. In that year, his father—Rev. Michael King, Sr.—returned home from a trip to Europe, where he had toured the site where Martin Luther had begun the Protestant Reformation. Upon his return home, the elder King changed his and his son's names to Martin.

Like Luther, the younger King became a reformer. In 1964, he won the Nobel peace prize. Yet there was a side of King unknown to most people—his inner battle to overcome his hatred of the white bigots. As a youth, he had once vowed "to hate all white people." As leader of the civil rights movement, King said all Americans had to be freed: "Negroes from the bonds of segregation and shame, whites from the bonds of bigotry and fear."

King held steadfast to his philosophy, even when a wave of racial violence swept through the South after the *Brown* decision. The violence included the 1955 murder of Emmett Till—a 14-year-old African-American boy who had allegedly flirted with a white woman. There were also shootings and beatings, some fatal, of civil rights workers.

**FROM THE GRASSROOTS UP** After the bus boycott ended, King joined with ministers and civil rights leaders in 1957 to found the **Southern Christian Leadership Conference (SCLC).** Its purpose was "to carry on nonviolent crusades against the evils of second-class citizenship." Using African-American churches as a base, the SCLC planned to stage protests and demonstrations throughout the South. The leaders hoped to build a movement from the grassroots up and to win the support of ordinary African Americans of all ages. King, president of the SCLC, used the power of his voice and ideas to fuel the movement's momentum.

The nuts and bolts of organizing the SCLC was handled by its first director, Ella Baker, the granddaughter of slaves. While with the NAACP, Baker had served as national field secretary, traveling over 16,000 miles throughout the South. From 1957 to 1960, Baker used her contacts to set up branches of the SCLC in Southern cities. In April 1960, Baker helped students at Shaw University, an African-American university in Raleigh, North Carolina, to organize a national protest group, the **Student Nonviolent Coordinating Committee,** or **SNCC,** pronounced "snick" for short.

It had been six years since the *Brown* decision, and many college students viewed the pace of change as too slow. Although these students risked a great deal—losing college scholarships, being expelled from college, being physically harmed—they were determined to challenge the system. SNCC hoped to harness the energy of these student protesters; it would soon create one of the most important student activist movements in the nation's history. **Ⓗ**

## The Movement Spreads ❹

Although SNCC adopted King's ideas in part, its members had ideas of their own. Many people called for a more confrontational strategy and set out to reshape the civil rights movement.

**DEMONSTRATING FOR FREEDOM** The founders of SNCC had models to build on. In 1942 in Chicago, the Congress of Racial Equality (CORE) had staged the first **sit-ins,** in which African-American protesters sat down at segregated lunch counters and refused to leave until they were served. In February 1960, African-American students from North Carolina's Agricultural and Technical College staged a sit-in at a whites-only lunch counter at a Woolworth's store in Greensboro. This time, television crews brought coverage of the protest into homes throughout the United States. There was no denying the ugly face of racism. Day after day, news reporters captured the scenes of whites beating, jeering at, and pouring food over students who refused to strike back. The coverage sparked many other sit-ins across the South. Store managers called

**MAIN IDEA**

**Evaluating**
**Ⓗ** What was the role of the SCLC?

*H. Answer*
It organized protests and demonstrations to promote civil rights.

---

 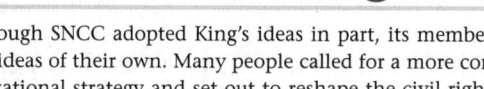
### Civil Rights Organizations

**Class Time** 45 minutes

**Task** Reporting on a civil rights organization

**Purpose** To trace the development and activities of civil rights organizations

**Directions** Have student groups choose one of the following organizations: NAACP, SCLC, CORE, SNCC, Urban League, Montgomery Improvement Association, or the Greensboro Citizens Association. Tell them to use library or Internet resources to research the organization's history, philosophy, leaders, and achievements. Have students report their findings in a written report or in a chart.

📝 Integrated Assessment
· Rubrics 1, 4, 5

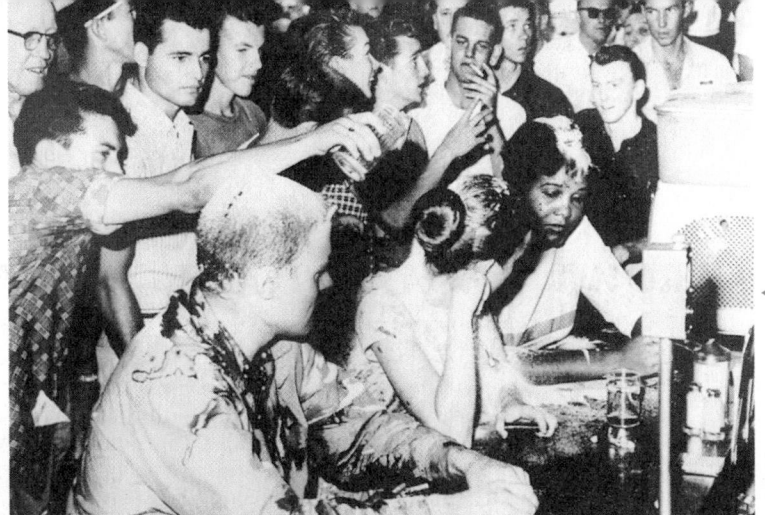

◀ Sit-in demonstrators, such as these at a Jackson, Mississippi, lunch counter in 1963, faced intimidation and humiliation from white segregationists.

in the police, raised the price of food, and removed counter seats. But the movement continued and spread to the North. There, students formed picket lines around national chain stores that maintained segregated lunch counters in the South.

By late 1960, students had descended on and desegregated lunch counters in some 48 cities in 11 states. They endured arrests, beatings, suspension from college, and tear gas and fire hoses, but the army of nonviolent students refused to back down. "My mother has always told me that I'm equal to other people," said Ezell Blair, Jr., one of the students who led the first SNCC sit-in in 1960. For the rest of the 1960s, many Americans worked to convince the rest of the country that blacks and whites deserved equal treatment.

## Assess & Reteach

**SECTION 1 ASSESSMENT**

Have students work in pairs to quiz each other on the questions.

📖 Formal Assessment
· Section Quiz, p. 385

**SELF-ASSESSMENT**

Have students use the people presented in this section to create a game of "Who Am I?" Students should take turns listing the accomplishments of someone covered in the section and then ask, "Who Am I?" Others in the class should write down their answers. Students who are unable to identify the individual being described should write up their own "Who Am I?" description for that person.

**RETEACH**

Use the list of Terms & Names to link each leader with the civil rights organizations and the protest movements with which he or she was involved.

📖 In-Depth Resources: Unit 6
· Reteaching Activity, p. 25

**ASSESSMENT**

**1. TERMS & NAMES** For each term or name, write a sentence explaining its significance.

- •**Thurgood Marshall**
- •*Brown* v. *Board of Education of Topeka*
- •**Rosa Parks**
- •**Martin Luther King, Jr.**
- •**Southern Christian Leadership Conference (SCLC)**
- •**Student Nonviolent Coordinating Committee (SNCC)**
- •**sit-in**

**MAIN IDEA**

**2. TAKING NOTES**

Fill in a spider diagram like the one below with examples of tactics, organizations, leaders, and Supreme Court decisions of the civil rights movement up to 1960.

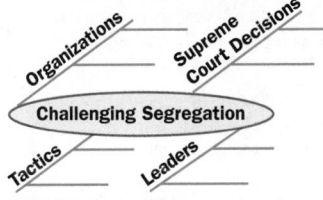

**CRITICAL THINKING**

**3. EVALUATING**

Do you think the nonviolence used by civil rights activists was a good tactic? Explain. **Think About:**

- the Montgomery bus boycott
- television coverage of events
- sit-ins

**4. CONTRASTING**

How did the tactics of the student protesters from SNCC differ from those of the boycotters in Montgomery?

**5. DRAWING CONCLUSIONS**

After the *Brown* v. *Board of Education of Topeka* ruling, what do you think was the most significant event of the civil rights movement prior to 1960? Why? **Think About:**

- the role of civil rights leaders
- the results of confrontations and boycotts
- the role of grassroots organizations

*Civil Rights* **707**

---

### HISTORIC DECISIONS OF THE SUPREME COURT

## Objectives

· To explain the legal reasoning behind the *Brown* decision

· To identify cases related to the *Brown* decision

· To analyze the historical significance and impact of the *Brown* decision

## Focus & Motivate

**Critical Thinking** Have students discuss whether there was any way that separate educational facilities could ever be considered equal. Then ask them how important education is to achieving opportunities.

## More About . . .

### Monroe Elementary School

In 1992, Congress passed a law designating Linda Brown's segregated Topeka school, Monroe Elementary, as a National Historic Site. A museum and a historical exhibit about the *Brown* case have been established in the school building. The current building, constructed in 1926, is the third school building on the site. The school was closed in 1975 and used by the Board of Education for storage facilities until it was taken over by the National Park Service.

## HISTORIC DECISIONS OF THE SUPREME COURT

# BROWN v. BOARD OF EDUCATION OF TOPEKA (1954)

**ORIGINS OF THE CASE** In the early 1950s, the school system of Topeka, Kansas, like all Southern elementary school systems, operated separate schools for "the two races"—blacks and whites. Reverend Oliver Brown protested that this was unfair to his eight-year-old daughter Linda. Although the Browns lived near a "white" school, Linda was forced to take a long bus ride to her "black" school across town.

**THE RULING** The Court ruled that segregated public schools were "inherently" unequal and therefore unconstitutional.

### LEGAL REASONING

While the correctness of the *Brown* ruling seems obvious today, some justices had difficulty agreeing to it. One reason was the force of legal precedent. Normally, judges follow a policy of *stare decisis,* "let the decision stand." The *Plessy* v. *Ferguson* decision endorsing segregation (see page 290) had stood for over 50 years. It clearly stated that "separate but equal" facilities did not violate the Fourteenth Amendment.

Thurgood Marshall, the NAACP lawyer who argued *Brown,* spent years laying the groundwork to chip away at Jim Crow—the local laws that required segregated facilities. Marshall had recently won two Supreme Court decisions in 1950 (*Mclaurin* and *Sweatt;* see Legal Sources at right) that challenged segregation at graduate schools. Then in 1952, the Supreme Court agreed to hear the Browns' case. The Court deliberated for two years deciding how to interpret the Fourteenth Amendment.

In the end, Chief Justice Earl Warren carefully sidestepped *Plessy,* claiming that segregated schools were not and never could be equal. On Monday, May 17, 1954, Warren read the unanimous decision:

> " Does segregation of children in public schools . . . deprive children of . . . equal opportunities? We believe it does. . . . To separate them . . . solely because of their race generates a feeling of inferiority . . . that may affect their hearts and minds in a way unlikely ever to be undone.''
>
> —*Brown v. Board of Education of Topeka*

 Mini-Lesson 3: SS11 3(US17.A)

Linda Brown's name headed a list of five school desegregation cases heard by the Supreme Court. ▶

### LEGAL SOURCES

#### U.S. CONSTITUTION

**FOURTEENTH AMENDMENT, EQUAL PROTECTION CLAUSE (1868)**
"No state shall . . . deny to any person within its jurisdiction the equal protection of the laws."

#### RELATED CASES

**PLESSY v. FERGUSON (1896)**
• Upheld Louisiana's laws requiring that train passengers be segregated by race.

• Established the doctrine of "separate but equal."

**MCLAURIN v. OKLAHOMA STATE (1950)**
Ruled that Oklahoma State University violated the Constitution by keeping its one "Negro" student in the back of the class and the cafeteria.

**SWEATT v. PAINTER (1950)**
Required the University of Texas to admit an African-American student to its previously all-white law school.

## RECOMMENDED RESOURCES

### BOOKS

Kluger, Richard. *Simple Justice: The History of Brown v. Board of Education and Black America's Struggle for Equality.* New York: Knopf, 1975.

Patterson, James T. *Brown v. Board of Education: A Civil Rights Milestone and Its Troubled Legacy.* New York: Oxford UP, 2001.

### VIDEOS

*Simple Justice.* PBS Home Video, 1993. Documentary about *Brown v. Board of Education.*

### INTEGRATED TECHNOLOGY

For teacher support, and more information about the Supreme Court including the full text of the Supreme Court opinions, visit . . .

 classzone.com

## WHY IT MATTERED

The Court's decision in *Brown* had an immediate impact on pending rulings. In a series of cases after *Brown,* the Supreme Court prohibited segregation in housing, at public beaches, at recreation facilities, and in restaurants. Later decisions extended equal access to other groups, including women and resident aliens.

The decision encountered fierce resistance, however. It awakened the old battle cry of States' Rights. Directly following *Brown,* some Congress members circulated the "Southern Manifesto" claiming the right of the states to ignore the ruling. In taking a stand on a social issue, they said, the Court had taken a step away from simply interpreting legal precedents. Critics charged that the Warren Court had acted as legislators and even as sociologists.

The *Brown* case strengthened the Civil Rights movement, however, and paved the way for the end of Jim Crow. The NAACP had fought and won the legal battle and had gained prestige and momentum. Americans got the strong message that the federal government now took civil rights seriously.

## HISTORICAL IMPACT

Three of the parties involved in *Brown*—Delaware, Kansas, and the District of Columbia—began to integrate schools in 1954. Topeka County informed the Court that 123 black students were already attending formerly all-white schools. Even so, the Supreme Court was well aware that its decision would be difficult to enforce. In a follow-up ruling, *Brown II* (1955), the Court required that integration take place with "all deliberate speed." To some this meant quickly. Others interpreted *deliberately* to mean slowly.

Only two Southern states even began to integrate classrooms in 1954: Texas and Arkansas opened one and two districts respectively. By 1960, less than one percent of the South's students attended integrated schools. Many school districts were ordered to use aggressive means to achieve racial balance. Courts spent decades supervising forced busing, a practice that often pitted community against community.

Still, despite the resistance and the practical difficulties of implementation, *Brown* stands today as a watershed, the single point at which breaking the "color barrier" officially became a federal priority.

## Instruct

1. What was the key legal judgment in the *Brown* decision?
2. What was the reaction in the South to the *Brown* decision?
3. What was the historical impact of the *Brown* decision?

📄 Historic Decisions of the Supreme Court
· *Brown v. Board of Education,* pp. 73–78
· *Plessey v Ferguson,* pp. 67–72

### MAKING PERSONAL CONNECTIONS

· Ask students if they know that rejection is a key part of discrimination.
· Ask them to recall a time when they felt rejected by friends or peers.
· Have students discuss feelings associated with rejection, such as pain, helplessness, or confusion.

## More About . . .

### *Brown*

In 1979, the American Civil Liberties Union (ACLU) reopened the *Brown* case, arguing that 13 of Topeka's schools remained segregated because of de facto segregation in housing. In 1992, a federal court sided with the ACLU. Topeka responded by changing school boundaries, setting up a transfer program, and constructing new schools. "It's disheartening that we are still fighting," said Linda Brown Thompson, who was 11 when her parents joined the now famous class-action suit, "but we are dealing with human beings. As long as we are, there will always be those who feel the races should be separate."

▲ Thurgood Marshall was appointed the first African-American Supreme Court justice by President Johnson in 1967.

THE NEW YORK TIMES

HIGH COURT BANS SCHOOL SEGREGATION; 9-TO-0 DECISION GRANTS TIME TO COMPLY

McCarthy Hearing Off a Week as Eisenhower Bars Report

## THINKING CRITICALLY

### CONNECT TO HISTORY

1. **Analyzing Primary Sources** Legal precedents are set not only by rulings, but also by dissenting opinions, in which justices explain why they disagree with the majority. Justice John Marshall Harlan was the one dissenting voice in *Plessy* v. *Ferguson.* Read his opinion and comment on how it might apply to *Brown.*

   📕 **SEE SKILLBUILDER HANDBOOK, PAGE R22.**

### CONNECT TO TODAY

2.  **INTERNET ACTIVITY** CLASSZONE.COM

   Visit the links for Historic Decisions of the Supreme Court to research the Supreme Court's changing opinions on civil rights. Compile a chart or time line to present the facts—date, plaintiff, defendant, major issue, and outcome—of several major cases. Then give an oral presentation explaining the Supreme Court's role in civil rights.

*Civil Rights* **709**

## THINKING CRITICALLY: ANSWERS

1. **CONNECT TO HISTORY** Students' responses should refer to Harlan's statement that the Constitution does not discriminate according to the color of one's skin. *Brown* echoes the point by concluding that separating students on the basis of race is unconstitutional.

2. **CONNECT TO TODAY** Time lines should be in chronological order and chart information clearly presented.
   Oral presentations should . . .
   · summarize the role of the Supreme Court in the civil rights movement
   · support conclusions with information presented in the graph or chart

## OBJECTIVES

1 Identify the goal of the freedom riders.

2 Explain how civil rights activism forced President Kennedy to act against segregation.

3 State the motives of the 1963 March on Washington.

4 Describe the tactics tried by civil rights organizations to secure passage of the Voting Rights Act.

### SKILLBUILDERS

· Interpreting Visual Sources, p. 713
· Interpreting Charts, p. 714

### CRITICAL THINKING

· Analyzing Issues, pp. 711, 716
· Chronological Order, p. 712
· Analyzing Events, p. 714
· Analyzing Motives, p. 715
· Developing Historical Perspective, p. 715
· Comparing, p. 716
· Analyzing Primary Sources, p. 716

## Focus & Motivate

Ask students to recall a time when they, or someone they know, took an unpopular stand. Have volunteers explain the situation, motivation, and results to the class.

## Instruct

### Instruct: Objective 1

**Riding for Freedom**

TAKS SS11 4(US7.A)

· How did freedom riders expose Southern resistance to desegregation rulings?

· How did the violence against the freedom riders affect President Kennedy?

 In-Depth Resources: Unit 6
· Guided Reading, p. 21

---

# The Triumphs of a Crusade

| MAIN IDEA | WHY IT MATTERS NOW | Terms & Names |
|---|---|---|
| Civil Rights activists broke through racial barriers. Their activism prompted landmark legislation. | Activism pushed the federal government to end segregation and ensure voting rights for African Americans. | • freedom riders  • James Meredith  • Civil Rights Act of 1964  • Freedom Summer  • Fannie Lou Hamer  • Voting Rights Act of 1965 |

 **TEKS U.S. History** 1B, 7A, 7B, 7C, 7D, 17B, 18A, 18B, 19B, 19C, 21A, 21D, 24A, 24B, 24D, 25A, 25B, 25C, 25D

### One American's Story

In 1961, James Peck, a white civil rights activist, joined other CORE members on a historic bus trip across the South. The two-bus trip would test the Supreme Court decisions banning segregated seating on interstate bus routes and segregated facilities in bus terminals. Peck and other **freedom riders** hoped to provoke a violent reaction that would convince the Kennedy administration to enforce the law. The violence was not long in coming.

At the Alabama state line, white racists got on Bus One carrying chains, brass knuckles, and pistols. They brutally beat African-American riders and white activists who tried to intervene. Still the riders managed to go on. Then on May 4, 1961—Mother's Day—the bus pulled into the Birmingham bus terminal. James Peck saw a hostile mob waiting, some holding iron bars.

**A PERSONAL VOICE** JAMES PECK

" I looked at them and then I looked at Charles Person, who had been designated as my team mate. . . . When I looked at him, he responded by saying simply, 'Let's go.' As we entered the white waiting room, . . . we were grabbed bodily and pushed toward the alleyway . . . and out of sight of onlookers in the waiting room, six of them started swinging at me with fists and pipes. Five others attacked Person a few feet ahead."

—Freedom Ride

The ride of Bus One had ended, but Bus Two continued southward on a journey that would shock the Kennedy administration into action.

Three days after being beaten unconscious in Birmingham, freedom rider James Peck demonstrates in New York City to pressure national bus companies to support desegregation.

## 1 Riding for Freedom

In Anniston, Alabama, about 200 angry whites attacked Bus Two. The mob followed the activists out of town. When one of the tires blew, they smashed a window and tossed in a fire bomb. The freedom riders spilled out just before the bus exploded.

---

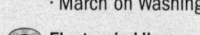
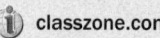

**NEW VOLUNTEERS** The bus companies refused to carry the CORE freedom riders any farther. Even though the determined volunteers did not want to give up, they ended their ride. However, CORE director James Farmer announced that a group of SNCC volunteers in Nashville were ready to pick up where the others had left off.

When a new band of freedom riders rode into Birmingham, policemen pulled them from the bus, beat them, and drove them into Tennessee. Defiantly, they returned to the Birmingham bus terminal. Their bus driver, however, feared for his life and refused to transport them. In protest, they occupied the whites-only waiting room at the terminal for eighteen hours until a solution was reached. After an angry phone call from U.S. Attorney General Robert Kennedy, bus company officials convinced the driver to proceed. The riders set out for Montgomery on May 20.

**ARRIVAL OF FEDERAL MARSHALS** Although Alabama officials had promised Kennedy that the riders would be protected, a mob of whites—many carrying bats and lead pipes—fell upon the riders when they arrived in Montgomery. John Doer, a Justice Department official on the scene, called the attorney general to report what was happening. "A bunch of men led by a guy with a bleeding face are beating [the passengers]. There are no cops. It's terrible. There's not a cop in sight. People are yelling. 'Get 'em, get 'em.' It's awful."

The violence provoked exactly the response the freedom riders wanted. Newspapers throughout the nation and abroad denounced the beatings.

President Kennedy arranged to give the freedom riders direct support. The Justice Department sent 400 U.S. marshals to protect the riders on the last part of their journey to Jackson, Mississippi. In addition, the attorney general and the Interstate Commerce Commission banned segregation in all interstate travel facilities, including waiting rooms, restrooms, and lunch counters.

▲
In May 1967, a mob firebombed this bus of freedom riders outside Anniston, Alabama, and attacked passengers as they tried to escape.

> *"We will continue our journey one way or another. . . . We are prepared to die."*
> JIM ZWERG, FREEDOM RIDER

**MAIN IDEA**

**Analyzing Issues**
Ⓐ What did the freedom riders hope to achieve?

*A. Answer*
They hoped to call attention to the South's refusal to abandon segregation so as to pressure the federal government to enforce the Supreme Court's desegregation rulings.

## Standing Firm ②

With the integration of interstate travel facilities under way, some civil rights workers turned their attention to integrating some Southern schools and pushing the movement into additional Southern towns. At each turn they encountered opposition and often violence.

**INTEGRATING OLE MISS** In September 1962, Air Force veteran **James Meredith** won a federal court case that allowed him to enroll in the all-white University of Mississippi, nicknamed Ole Miss. But when Meredith arrived on campus, he faced Governor Ross Barnett, who refused to let him register as a student.

President Kennedy ordered federal marshals to escort Meredith to the registrar's office. Barnett responded with a heated radio appeal: "I call on every Mississippian to keep his faith and courage. We will never surrender." The broadcast turned out white demonstrators by the thousands.

On the night of September 30, riots broke out on campus, resulting in two deaths. It took thousands of soldiers, 200 arrests, and 15 hours to stop the rioters. In the months that followed, federal officials accompanied Meredith to class and protected his parents from nightriders who shot up their house.

*Civil Rights* **711**

### Tracing Themes
**CIVIL RIGHTS**

Efforts to desegregate the South exposed the longtime unwillingness of federal and state governments to protect African Americans from racial discrimination and violence. Kennedy once said, "the rights of every man are diminished when the rights of one man are threatened." Yet, as a political leader, he faced the challenge of building support for a policy he thought was right. His task was complicated by the fact that much of the Senate leadership was composed of longtime Democratic Senators from Southern segregationist states.

## Instruct: Objective ②

**Standing Firm**
TAKS SS11 4(US7.C)
· How did civil rights organizers integrate Southern campuses and towns?
· Who was James Meredith and what did he do?
· How did television coverage of the Birmingham marchers affect legislation?

📖 In-Depth Resources: Unit 6
· Guided Reading, p. 21

---

**DIFFERENTIATING INSTRUCTION**   **GIFTED AND TALENTED STUDENTS**   🅱 **BLOCK SCHEDULING**

### Divergent Views Within the Movement

Many Americans have forgotten that a host of speakers addressed the crowd at the March on Washington in August 1963. Some of the speakers, such as John Lewis of SNCC and Martin Luther King, Jr., had different views on how to achieve equality most quickly and completely. Have students read King's "I Have a Dream" speech and the original (unaltered) version of Lewis's speech delivered at the March on Washington. Then have them list on a chart the points upon which the two men expressed divergent views. Encourage them to consider possible explanations for why they differed.

| Issue | King | Lewis |
|---|---|---|
| 1. | | |
| 2. | | |
| 3. | | |

News photos and television coverage of police dogs in Birmingham attacking African Americans shocked the nation.

## More About . . .

### The SCLC in Birmingham

Throughout the demonstrations in Birmingham, the SCLC's leadership brought pressure to bear on the city's Chamber of Commerce. The SCLC insisted on greater economic opportunities for Birmingham's African-American citizens. It demanded an immediate upgrading of African-American store employees, a program of non-discriminatory hiring, and the institution of specific programs for the hiring of African-American policemen. Facing ongoing demonstrations, the Chamber of Commerce eventually agreed to the gradual desegregation of stores and public facilities and to a program to upgrade and improve employment opportunities for Birmingham's African American community. Ask students: Why are religious organizations often effective in expanding economic opportunities at the local level? (*religious groups usually have a broad base of support and can therefore influence local businesses and chambers of commerce*)

## More About . . .

### "Letter from a Birmingham Jail"

King wrote his letter on scattered strips of paper that a friend smuggled out of jail. A complicated series of arrows and loops indicated how the strips should be connected. Another friend, Wyatt Walker deciphered King's "chicken-scratch" writing for a secretary. One sentence totaled more than 300 words. The typed version was smuggled back to King and then smuggled out again. The process continued until a 20-page document emerged.

**HEADING INTO BIRMINGHAM** The trouble continued in Alabama. Birmingham, a city known for its strict enforcement of total segregation in public life, also had a reputation for racial violence, including 18 bombings from 1957 to 1963.

Reverend Fred Shuttlesworth, head of the Alabama Christian Movement for Human Rights and secretary of the SCLC, decided something had to be done about Birmingham and that it would be the ideal place to test the power of non-violence. He invited Martin Luther King, Jr., and the SCLC to help desegregate the city. On April 3, 1963, King flew into Birmingham to hold a planning meeting with members of the African-American community. "This is the most segregated city in America," he said. "We have to stick together if we ever want to change its ways."

After days of demonstrations led by Shuttlesworth and others, King and a small band of marchers were finally arrested during a demonstration on Good Friday, April 12th. While in jail, King wrote an open letter to white religious leaders who felt he was pushing too fast.

**A PERSONAL VOICE** MARTIN LUTHER KING, JR.

"I guess it is easy for those who have never felt the stinging darts of segregation to say, 'Wait.' But when you have seen vicious mobs lynch your mothers and fathers at whim; when you have seen hate-filled policemen curse, kick, brutalize and even kill your black brothers and sisters; . . . when you see the vast majority of your twenty million Negro brothers smothering in the air-tight cage of poverty; . . . when you have to concoct an answer for a five-year-old son asking: . . . 'Daddy, why do white people treat colored people so mean?' . . . then you will understand why we find it difficult to wait."

—"Letter from a Birmingham Jail"

On April 20, King posted bail and began planning more demonstrations. On May 2, more than a thousand African-American children marched in Birmingham; Police commissioner Eugene "Bull" Connor's men arrested 959 of them. On May 3, a second "children's crusade" came face to face with a helmeted police force. Police swept the marchers off their feet with high-pressure fire hoses, set attack dogs on them, and clubbed those who fell. TV cameras captured all of it, and millions of viewers heard the children screaming.

Continued protests, an economic boycott, and negative media coverage finally convinced Birmingham officials to end segregation. This stunning civil rights victory inspired African Americans across the nation. It also convinced President Kennedy that only a new civil rights act could end racial violence and satisfy the demands of African Americans—and many whites—for racial justice. **B**

*B. Answer* Days of demonstrations; arrest of King and others; King's "Letter from a Birmingham Jail"; more demonstrations met by arrests and police violence; economic boycott.

**MAIN IDEA**

**Chronological Order**
**B** What events led to desegregation in Birmingham?

---

## Creating News Reports on the Birmingham Protests

**Class Time** Two class periods

**Task** Creating reports for a key event that took place during April-September 1963 in Birmingham

**Purpose** To draw conclusions about the impact of the media on the civil rights movement

**Directions** Have the class work in small groups, with each group researching a different event. Direct students to use news magazines from 1963 such as *Time*, *Newsweek*, or *Life*. Have students create you-are-there type news reports based on the magazine accounts and deliver them to the rest of the class. Follow up with a discussion of how the media brought the brutalities of Birmingham to a national audience and helped create political support for civil rights.

📓 Integrated Assessment
· Rubrics 1, 4

## History Through *Photojournalism*

### ERNEST WITHERS

Born in Memphis in 1922, photographer Ernest Withers believed that if the struggle for equality could be shown to people, things would change. Armed with only a camera, he braved violent crowds to capture the heated racism during the Montgomery bus boycott, the desegregation of Central High in Little Rock, and the 1968 Memphis sanitation workers strike (below) led by Martin Luther King, Jr. The night before the Memphis march, Withers had helped make some of the signs he photographed.

"**G. C. Brown printed those 'I AM A MAN' signs right over there. . . . I had a car and it was snowing, so we went and rented the saw and came back that night and cut the sticks.**"

▲ Withers in 1950

Withers had to be careful about his involvement in groups like the NAACP and COME (Community On the Move for Equality), for he had a wife and children to support. He went to several meetings a night, sometimes taking pictures, other times offering a suggestion. "I always had FBI agents looking over my shoulder and wanting to question me. I never tried to learn any high-powered secrets."

◀ Withers in 1992

**SKILLBUILDER** Interpreting Visual Sources
1. What do the signs tell you about African Americans' struggle for civil rights?
2. What kind of treatment do you suppose these men had experienced? Why do you think so?

**SEE SKILLBUILDER HANDBOOK, PAGE R23.**

### History Through *Photojournalism*

#### SKILLBUILDER ANSWERS
1. African Americans in 1968 felt that they weren't treated with the minimal respect afforded human beings.
2. Some students might answer that the "I AM A MAN" posters seek to convey the treatment of African Americans in the workplace as subhuman, perhaps as evidenced by unequal pay and poor working conditions.

*Civil Rights* **713**

---

**ACTIVITY** | **LINK TO HUMANITIES**

 **classzone.com**

### Presenting Images and Sounds of a Historic Time

**Class Time** Two class periods

**Task** Creating a multimedia presentation

**Purpose** To gain a deeper understanding of the early 1960s

**Directions** Have students assemble collages and recordings of the material pertaining to the era. Direct students to news magazines and Internet resources for photographic images. The Internet will also provide the means to download such songs as Joan Baez singing "We Shall Overcome" and Bob Dylan's "Blowin' in the Wind." Tell students to interview and record or videotape people who lived through the early 1960s, recounting their memories of the period. Have students combine their material into a multimedia presentation.

📄 Integrated Assessment
· Rubrics 1, 6

*Civil Rights* **713**

## Instruct: Objective ③

**Marching to Washington**

TAKS SS11 4(US7.C)

· Why did civil rights activists organize the March on Washington?

· What famous speech was given at the March?

· Did the March achieve its goals?

 In-Depth Resources: Unit 6
· Guided Reading, p. 21
· Primary Source: "I Have a Dream," p. 32

 Humanities Transparencies HT27
· March on Washington

---

## HISTORY from VISUALS

**Interpreting the Chart**

Have students list major goals of the civil rights movement that were achieved by the passage of these laws.

**SKILLBUILDER ANSWER**

the Civil Rights Act of 1964, because it banned discrimination in employment and public accommodations—areas that affect nearly everyone

---

## More About . . .

**Birmingham Church Bombing**

On September 15, 1963, a bomb exploded at the 16th Street Baptist Church, killing four girls—11-year-old Denise McNair and three 14-year-olds—Cynthia Wesley, Carole Robertson, and Addie Mae Collins. It was not until May 2001 that one of the perpetrators of the crime, Thomas Blanton, was brought to justice. Blanton was found guilty of four counts of first-degree murder and sentenced to life imprisonment.

---

*"I say, Segregation now! Segregation tomorrow! Segregation forever!"*

GEORGE WALLACE,
ALABAMA GOVERNOR, 1963

**KENNEDY TAKES A STAND** On June 11, 1963, the president sent troops to force Governor George Wallace to honor a court order desegregating the University of Alabama. That evening, Kennedy asked the nation: "Are we to say to the world—and much more importantly, to each other—that this is the land of the free, except for the Negroes?" He demanded that Congress pass a civil rights bill.

A tragic event just hours after Kennedy's speech highlighted the racial tension in much of the South. Shortly after midnight, a sniper murdered Medgar Evers, NAACP field secretary and World War II veteran. Police soon arrested a white supremacist, Byron de la Beckwith, but he was released after two trials resulted in hung juries. His release brought a new militancy to African Americans. Many demanded, "Freedom now!"

**Background**
Beckwith was finally convicted in 1994, after the case was reopened based on new evidence.

## ③ Marching to Washington

The civil rights bill that President Kennedy sent to Congress guaranteed equal access to all public accommodations and gave the U.S. attorney general the power to file school desegregation suits. To persuade Congress to pass the bill, two veteran organizers—labor leader A. Philip Randolph and Bayard Rustin of the SCLC—summoned Americans to a march on Washington, D.C.

**THE DREAM OF EQUALITY** On August 28, 1963, more than 250,000 people—including about 75,000 whites—converged on the nation's capital. They assembled on the grassy lawn of the Washington Monument and marched to the Lincoln Memorial. There, people listened to speakers demand the immediate passage of the civil rights bill. **C**

When Dr. Martin Luther King, Jr., appeared, the crowd exploded in applause. In his now famous speech, "I Have a Dream," he appealed for peace and racial harmony.

**MAIN IDEA**

**Analyzing Events**
**C** Why did civil rights organizers ask their supporters to march on Washington?

**C. Answer**
To spur passage of the civil rights bill.

**A PERSONAL VOICE** MARTIN LUTHER KING, JR.

"I have a dream that one day this nation will rise up and live out the true meaning of its creed: 'We hold these truths to be self-evident; that all men are created equal.' . . . I have a dream that my four little children will one day live in a nation where they will not be judged by the color of their skin but by the content of their character. . . . I have a dream that one day the state of Alabama . . . will be transformed into a situation where little black boys and black girls will be able to join hands with little white boys and white girls and walk together as sisters and brothers."

—"I Have a Dream"

**MORE VIOLENCE** Two weeks after King's historic speech, four young Birmingham girls were killed when a rider in a car hurled a bomb through their church window. Two more African Americans died in the unrest that followed.

Two months later, an assassin shot and killed John F. Kennedy. His successor, President Lyndon B. Johnson, pledged to carry on Kennedy's work. On July 2, 1964, Johnson signed the **Civil Rights Act of 1964,** which prohibited discrimination because of race, religion, national origin, and gender. It gave all citizens the right to enter libraries, parks, washrooms, restaurants, theaters, and other public accommodations.

---

### Civil Rights Acts of the 1950s and 1960s

**CIVIL RIGHTS ACT OF 1957**
- Established federal Commission on Civil Rights
- Established a Civil Rights Division in the Justice Department to enforce civil rights laws
- Enlarged federal power to protect voting rights

**CIVIL RIGHTS ACT OF 1964**
- Banned most discrimination in employment and in public accommodations
- Enlarged federal power to protect voting rights and speed up school desegregation
- Established Equal Employment Opportunity Commission to ensure fair treatment in employment

**VOTING RIGHTS ACT OF 1965**
- Eliminated voter literacy tests
- Enabled federal examiners to register voters

**CIVIL RIGHTS ACT OF 1968**
- Prohibited discrimination in the sale or rental of most housing
- Strengthened antilynching laws
- Made it a crime to harm civil rights workers

**SKILLBUILDER**
**Interpreting Charts**
Which law do you think benefited the most people? Explain your choice.

---

### Understanding a Speech and Its Impact

Pair ESL students with strong readers and have them read Martin Luther King, Jr.'s "I Have a Dream" speech. If you can obtain a recording of the speech, have students listen to it as they follow along before reading the speech aloud. Then have student pairs identify and discuss examples of imagery that appear in the speech.

Examples include:

· a great beacon light of hope

· seared in the flames of withering injustice

· a joyous day break to end the long night of captivity

In the summer of 1964, college students volunteered to go to Mississippi to help register that state's African-American voters.

## HISTORY from VISUALS

### Interpreting the Photograph

Tell students that the summer of 1964 was a dangerous time for both black and white civil rights activists in Mississippi. Discuss with students how they would have felt in 1964 about civil rights. Would they have volunteered to go to Mississippi?

 **In-Depth Resources: Unit 6**
· Primary Source: Civil Rights Song, p. 31

## Fighting for Voting Rights ④

**D. Answer**
They hoped to call attention to the lack of voting rights in segregationist strongholds and to promote passage of a federal voting rights act.

---

**MAIN IDEA**

**Analyzing Motives**
**D** Why did civil rights groups organize Freedom Summer?

Meanwhile, the right of all African Americans to vote remained elusive. In 1964, CORE and SNCC workers in the South began registering as many African Americans as they could to vote. They hoped their campaign would receive national publicity and that in turn this would influence Congress to pass a voting rights act. Focused in Mississippi, the project became known as **Freedom Summer.**

**FREEDOM SUMMER** To fortify the project, civil rights groups recruited college students and trained them in nonviolent resistance. Thousands of student volunteers—mostly white, about one-third female—went into Mississippi to help register voters. For some, the job proved deadly. In June of 1964, three civil rights workers and one summer volunteer disappeared in Neshoba County, Mississippi. Investigators later learned that Klansmen and local police had murdered three of the men, two of whom were white. Through the summer the racial beatings and murders continued, along with the burning of businesses, homes, and churches. **D**

**A NEW POLITICAL PARTY** African Americans needed a voice in the political arena if sweeping change was to occur. In order to gain a seat in Mississippi's all-white Democratic Party, SNCC organized the Mississippi Freedom Democratic Party (MFDP). **Fannie Lou Hamer,** the daughter of Mississippi sharecroppers, would be their voice at the 1964 Democratic National Convention. In a televised speech that shocked the convention and viewers nationwide, Hamer described how she was jailed for registering to vote in 1962, and how police forced other prisoners to beat her.

### Instruct: Objective ④

**Fighting for Voting Rights**
TAKS SS11 4(US7.A)
· What prevented millions of African Americans from voting in the South?
· How did civil rights workers try to win a voting rights act?
· What did the Voting Rights Act of 1965 guarantee?

 **In-Depth Resources: Unit 6**
· Primary Source: Political Poster, p. 33

**Geography Transparencies GT29**
· Percentage of Registered African Americans of Voting Age

---

**E. Answer**
Because the leaders agreed to a compromise with the Johnson administration that kept most MFDP delegates from the Democratic convention.

---

**MAIN IDEA**

**Developing Historical Perspective**
**E** Why did young people in SNCC and the MFDP feel betrayed by some civil rights leaders?

**A PERSONAL VOICE** FANNIE LOU HAMER

" The first [prisoner] began to beat [me], and I was beat by the first until he was exhausted. . . . The second [prisoner] began to beat. . . . I began to scream and one white man got up and began to beat me in my head and tell me to 'hush.' . . . All of this on account we want to register, to become first-class citizens, and if the Freedom Democratic Party is not seated now, I question America. "

—quoted in *The Civil Rights Movement: An Eyewitness History*

In response to Hamer's speech, telegrams and telephone calls poured in to the convention in support of seating the MFDP delegates. President Johnson feared losing the Southern white vote if the Democrats sided with the MFDP, so his administration pressured civil rights leaders to convince the MFDP to accept a compromise. The Democrats would give 2 of Mississippi's 68 seats to the MFDP, with a promise to ban discrimination at the 1968 convention.

When Hamer learned of the compromise, she said, "We didn't come all this way for no two seats." The MFDP and supporters in SNCC felt that the leaders had betrayed them. **E**

### Tracing Themes

**CIVIL RIGHTS**

The Fifteenth Amendment barred states from depriving citizens of the right to vote "on account of race, color, or previous condition of servitude." It also gave Congress the "power to enforce this article by appropriate legislation." Yet, from the end of Reconstruction, Southern states set up both practical and legal barriers to keep African Americans from voting. While some Americans saw radicalism in the civil rights movement, the historical view was that it was simply advocating that the federal government enforce the Constitution.

*Civil Rights* **715**

---

 **BLOCK SCHEDULING**

### Civil Rights Time Line, 1963–1965

**Class Time** 45 minutes

**Task** Constructing a time line of events in the civil rights movement in the United States from 1963 through 1965

**Purpose** To trace the activities of the civil rights movement during this significant period

**Directions** Divide the class into groups and assign each a segment of the time period. Have students research events in their time period and decide which ones to list. Have each group construct its time line on chart paper. Then students should tape the various sections together to form a time line of the entire period.

 **Integrated Assessment**
· Rubrics 1, 2

## HISTORICAL SPOTLIGHT

### Twenty-Fourth Amendment— Barring Poll Taxes

The Twenty-Fourth Amendment ended a game of Constitutional cat and mouse that had gone on for a century. States used the Tenth Amendment, which reserves all power not given to the federal government for the states, as the basis for making laws that deprived African Americans of their voting rights. Until the civil rights movement created sufficient political pressure, Congress and the courts had supported the status quo despite the flagrant disregard for the provisions of the Fifteenth Amendment. Ask students: How did the civil rights movement create the climate for support of the Twenty-Fourth Amendment? *(The civil rights movement created public sympathy and concern for African Americans. This, in turn, prodded legislators to act to end poll taxes that kept African Americans from voting.)*

## Assess & Reteach

### SECTION 2 ASSESSMENT

Divide students into groups of four and have each group address one point from question 4. Then have them share the answers with each other.

 Formal Assessment
· Section Quiz, p. 386

### SELF-ASSESSMENT

Ask students to review the answers they gave for question 3. How might other factors have shaped opposition to the civil rights movement?

### RETEACH

Use the Guided Worksheet for Section 2 to help review the main ideas of the section.

 In-Depth Resources: Unit 6
· Reteaching Activity, p. 25

---

### HISTORICAL SPOTLIGHT

#### TWENTY-FOURTH AMENDMENT—BARRING POLL TAXES

On January 24, 1964, South Dakota became the 38th state to ratify the Twenty-Fourth Amendment to the Constitution. The key clause in the amendment reads: "The right of citizens of the United States to vote in any primary or other election . . . shall not be denied or abridged by the United States or any State by reason of failure to pay any poll tax or other tax."

Poll taxes were often used to keep poor African Americans from voting. Although most states had already abolished their poll taxes by 1964, five Southern states—Alabama, Arkansas, Mississippi, Texas, and Virginia—still had such laws on the books. By making these laws unconstitutional, the Twenty-Fourth Amendment gave the vote to millions who had been disqualified because of poverty.

---

**THE SELMA CAMPAIGN** At the start of 1965, the SCLC conducted a major voting rights campaign in Selma, Alabama, where SNCC had been working for two years to register voters. By the end of 1965, more than 2,000 African Americans had been arrested in SCLC demonstrations. After a demonstrator named Jimmy Lee Jackson was shot and killed, King responded by announcing a 50-mile protest march from Selma to Montgomery, the state capital. On March 7, 1965, about 600 protestors set out for Montgomery.

That night, mayhem broke out. Television cameras captured the scene. The rest of the nation watched in horror as police swung whips and clubs and clouds of tear gas swirled around fallen marchers. Demonstrators poured into Selma by the hundreds. President Johnson asked Congress for the swift passage of a new voting rights act.

On March 21, 3,000 marchers again set out for Montgomery, this time with federal protection. Soon the number grew to an army of 25,000. **F**

**VOTING RIGHTS ACT OF 1965** Ten weeks after the march, Congress passed the **Voting Rights Act of 1965.** The act eliminated the so-called literacy tests that had disqualified many voters. It also stated that federal examiners could enroll voters who had been denied suffrage by local officials. In Selma, the proportion of African Americans registered to vote rose from 10 percent in 1964 to 60 percent in 1968. Overall the percentage of registered African-American voters in the South tripled.

Although the Voting Rights Act marked a major civil rights victory, some felt that the law did not go far enough. Centuries of discrimination had produced social and economic inequalities. Anger over these inequalities led to a series of violent disturbances in the cities of the North.

---

**MAIN IDEA**

**Comparing**
**F** In what ways was the civil rights campaign in Selma similar to the one in Birmingham?

**F. Answer**
In Both campaigns, civil rights workers encountered a violent response, and in both cases, TV coverage of that violence helped force the federal government to intervene.

---

## 2 ASSESSMENT

1. **TERMS & NAMES** For each term or name, write a sentence explaining its significance.

- freedom riders
- James Meredith
- Civil Rights Act of 1964
- Freedom Summer
- Fannie Lou Hamer
- Voting Rights Act of 1965

**MAIN IDEA**

2. **TAKING NOTES**
In a graphic like the one shown, list the steps that African Americans took to desegregate buses and schools from 1962 to 1965.

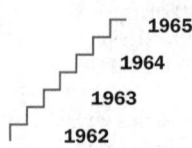

**CRITICAL THINKING**

3. **ANALYZING ISSUES**
What assumptions and beliefs do you think guided the fierce opposition to the civil rights movement in the South? Support your answer with evidence from the text. **Think About:**
- the social and political structure of the South
- Mississippi governor Ross Barnett's comment during his radio address
- the actions of police and some white Southerners

4. **ANALYZING PRIMARY SOURCES**
Just after the Civil Rights Act of 1964 was passed, white Alabama governor George Wallace said,

" It is ironical that this event occurs as we approach the celebration of Independence Day. On that day we won our freedom. On this day we have largely lost it."

What do you think Wallace meant by his statement?

 Mini-Lesson 2: SS11 4(US7.C)

**716** CHAPTER 21

---

 **ASSESSMENT** Answers

**1. TERMS & NAMES**
freedom riders, p. 710
James Meredith, p. 711
Civil Rights Act of 1964, p. 714
Freedom Summer, p. 715
Fannie Lou Hamer, p. 715
Voting Rights Act of 1965, p. 716

**2. TAKING NOTES**
**1962:** A federal court case allows James Meredith to enroll in the University of Mississippi. **1963:** Protests, boycotts, and media coverage force Birmingham to end segregation; Kennedy orders troops to desegregate University of Alabama; March on Washington; **1964:** Johnson signs Civil Rights Act; **1965:** Voting Rights Act passed.

**3. ANALYZING ISSUES**
Many white Southerners considered blacks to be members of an inferior race—an attitude that stemmed from the former use of slaves. Southerners feared a backlash if African Americans gained equal rights. Some, like Governor Barnett, viewed the battle for segregation as a war. Police and others often acted accordingly, with violence.

**4. ANALYZING PRIMARY SOURCES**
Wallace apparently felt that the gaining of equal rights by African Americans would diminish the freedom of Southerners to do as they pleased and to maintain the kind of society and political structure to which they were accustomed.

# Challenges and Changes in the Movement

| MAIN IDEA | WHY IT MATTERS NOW | Terms & Names |
|---|---|---|
| Disagreements among civil rights groups and the rise of black nationalism created a violent period in the fight for civil rights. | From the fight for equality came a resurgence of racial pride for African Americans, a legacy that influences today's generations. | • de facto segregation · de jure segregation · Malcolm X · Nation of Islam · Stokely Carmichael    • Black Power • Black Panthers · Kerner Commission · Civil Rights Act of 1968 · affirmative action |

**U.S. History**
6H, 7A, 7B, 7C, 7D, 19A, 19B, 19C, 21A, 21C, 21D, 24A, 24B, 24D, 24H, 25A, 25B, 25C, 25D

### One American's Story

Alice Walker, the prize-winning novelist, became aware of the civil rights movement in 1960, when she was 16. Her mother had recently scraped together enough money to purchase a television.

**A PERSONAL VOICE** ALICE WALKER

" Like a good omen for the future, the face of Dr. Martin Luther King, Jr., was the first black face I saw on our new television screen. And, as in a fairy tale, my soul was stirred by the meaning for me of his mission—at the time he was being rather ignominiously dumped into a police van for having led a protest march in Alabama—and I fell in love with the sober and determined face of the Movement. "

—*In Search of Our Mothers' Gardens*

▲ Alice Walker during an interview in New York's Central Park in August 1970

The next year, Walker attended the all-black Spelman College. In 1963, Walker took part in the March on Washington and then traveled to Africa to discover her spiritual roots. After returning home in 1964, she worked on voter registration, taught African American history and writing, and wrote poetry and fiction.

Walker's interest in her heritage was part of a growing trend among African Americans in the mid-1960s. But millions of African Americans were still living in poverty. Angry and frustrated over the difficulty in finding jobs and decent housing, some participated in riots that broke out between 1964 and 1966.

## 1 African Americans Seek Greater Equality

What civil rights groups had in common in the early 1960s were their calls for a newfound pride in black identity and a commitment to change the social and economic structures that kept people in a life of poverty. However, by 1965, the

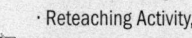
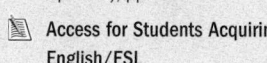

**Tracing Themes**
ECONOMIC OPPORTUNITY

There is no express guarantee in the U.S. Constitution for the right to earn a decent living and for freedom from economic want. Millions of African Americans in the 1960s felt that discrimination in effect denied them their basic economic rights just as it had denied them their right to vote. In the mainstream of American political theory, economic justice is dealt with in terms of equal opportunity and a social safety net for the truly needy. African Americans viewed equal opportunity as the key to a better standard of living and an improved quality of life.

## More About . . .

### The Harlem Riot

In assessing the Harlem riot of 1964, the poet Langston Hughes wrote: "White folks respect us more when they find out we mean business. When they only listen to our speeches or read our writings—if they ever do—they think we are just blowing off steam. But when rioters break the plate glass windows of their stores, they know the steam has some force behind it."

Between 1964 and 1968, more than 100 race riots erupted in major American cities. The worst included Watts in Los Angeles in 1965 *(top)* and Detroit in 1967 *(right)*. In Detroit, 43 people were killed and property damage topped $40 million.

leading civil rights groups began to drift apart. New leaders emerged as the movement turned its attention to the North, where African Americans faced not legal segregation but deeply entrenched and oppressive racial prejudice.

**NORTHERN SEGREGATION** The problem facing African Americans in the North was **de facto segregation**—segregation that exists by practice and custom. De facto segregation can be harder to fight than **de jure** (dē jŏŏr'ē) **segregation,** or segregation by law, because eliminating it requires changing people's attitudes rather than repealing laws. Activists in the mid-1960s would find it much more difficult to convince whites to share economic and social power with African Americans than to convince them to share lunch counters and bus seats. **Ⓐ**

De facto segregation intensified after African Americans migrated to Northern cities during and after World War II. This began a "white flight," in which great numbers of whites moved out of the cities to the nearby suburbs. By the mid-1960s, most urban African Americans lived in decaying slums, paying rent to landlords who didn't comply with housing and health ordinances. The schools for African-American children deteriorated along with their neighborhoods. Unemployment rates were more than twice as high as those among whites.

In addition, many blacks were angry at the sometimes brutal treatment they received from the mostly white police forces in their communities. In 1966, King spearheaded a campaign in Chicago to end de facto segregation there and create an "open city." On July 10, he led about 30,000 African Americans in a march on City Hall.

In late July, when King led demonstrators through a Chicago neighborhood, angry whites threw rocks and bottles. On August 5, hostile whites stoned King as he led 600 marchers. King left Chicago without accomplishing what he wanted, yet pledging to return.

**URBAN VIOLENCE ERUPTS** In the mid 1960s, clashes between white authority and black civilians spread like wildfire. In New York City in July 1964, an encounter between white police and African-American teenagers ended in the death of a 15-year-old student. This sparked a race riot in central Harlem. On August 11, 1965, only five days after President Johnson signed the Voting

MAIN IDEA

**Comparing**
Ⓐ How were civil rights problems in Northern cities similar to those in the South?

*A. Answer*
Both Northern and Southern blacks experienced poverty and inferior schools, and their civil rights demands were met with white anger and violence and police brutality.

---

**DIFFERENTIATING INSTRUCTION**     **LESS PROFICIENT READERS**

### Interpreting Photographs

Remind students that photographs serve as primary sources, or firsthand information, about the past. Have students work in pairs to write down what these photographs say about the urban riots of 1965-1967. Tell students to imagine that these two pictures are part of a photographic history of the civil rights movement. Ask students what captions they would write to summarize their content.

**Rubric**

Captions should . . .

· convey the content of the photograph

· be interesting and effective

· use appropriate form and style

Rights Act into law, one of the worst race riots in the nation's history raged through the streets of Watts, a predominantly African-American neighborhood in Los Angeles. Thirty-four people were killed, and hundreds of millions of dollars worth of property was destroyed. The next year, 1966, saw even more racial disturbances, and in 1967 alone, riots and violent clashes took place in more than 100 cities.

The African-American rage baffled many whites. "Why would blacks turn to violence after winning so many victories in the South?" they wondered. Some realized that what African Americans wanted and needed was economic equality of opportunity in jobs, housing, and education. **B**

Even before the riots in 1964, President Johnson had announced his War on Poverty, a program to help impoverished Americans. But the flow of money needed to fund Johnson's Great Society was soon redirected to fund the war in Vietnam. In 1967, Dr. King proclaimed, "The Great Society has been shot down on the battlefields of Vietnam."

MAIN IDEA

**Analyzing Causes**

**B** What were some of the causes of urban rioting in the 1960s?

*B. Answers* De facto segregation, police brutality, run-down communities and schools, and high unemployment.

## New Leaders Voice Discontent 2

The anger that sent rioters into the streets stemmed in part from African-American leaders who urged their followers to take complete control of their communities, livelihoods, and culture. One such leader, **Malcolm X,** declared to a Harlem audience, "If you think we are here to tell you to love the white man, you have come to the wrong place."

**AFRICAN-AMERICAN SOLIDARITY** Malcolm X, born Malcolm Little, went to jail at age 20 for burglary. While in prison, he studied the teachings of Elijah Muhammad, the head of the **Nation of Islam**, or the Black Muslims. Malcolm changed his name to Malcolm X (dropping what he called his "slave name") and, after his release from prison in 1952, became an Islamic minister. As he gained a following, the brilliant thinker and engaging speaker openly preached Elijah Muhammad's views that whites were the cause of the black condition and that blacks should separate from white society.

**Background** See "Islam" on page 9.

Malcolm's message appealed to many African Americans and their growing racial pride. At a New York press conference in March 1964, he also advocated armed self-defense.

### A Personal Voice MALCOLM X

"**Concerning nonviolence: it is criminal to teach a man not to defend himself when he is the constant victim of brutal attacks. It is legal and lawful to own a shotgun or a rifle. We believe in obeying the law. . . . [T]he time has come for the American Negro to fight back in self-defense whenever and wherever he is being unjustly and unlawfully attacked.**"

—quoted in *Eyewitness: The Negro in American History*

The press gave a great deal of publicity to Malcolm X because his controversial statements made dramatic news stories. This had two effects. First, his call for armed self-defense frightened most whites and many moderate African Americans. Second, reports of the attention Malcolm received awakened resentment in some other members of the Nation of Islam. **C**

*C. Answer* He blamed black poverty and social inferiority on whites and advocated armed resistance to white oppression.

MAIN IDEA

**Synthesizing**

**C** Why did some Americans find Malcolm X's views alarming?

### KEY PLAYER

MALCOLM X
1925–1965

Malcolm X's early life left him alienated from white society. His father was allegedly killed by white racists, and his mother had an emotional collapse, leaving Malcolm and his siblings in the care of the state. At the end of eighth grade, Malcolm quit school and was later jailed for criminal behavior. In 1946, while in prison, Malcolm joined the Nation of Islam. He developed a philosophy of black superiority and separatism from whites.

In the later years of his life, he urged African Americans to identify with Africa and to work with world organizations and even progressive whites to attain equality. Although silenced by gunmen, Malcolm X is a continuing inspiration for many Americans.



## Instruct: Objective 2

**New Leaders Voice Discontent**

TAKS SS11 3(US7.B)

- What was Malcolm X's appeal as a leader to African Americans?
- How did Malcolm X alienate Black Muslims?
- How did the Black Panthers reflect a growing radicalism in segments of the movement?

In-Depth Resources: Unit 6
- Guided Reading, p. 22

### KEY PLAYER

**Malcolm X**

Malcolm X was famous for his controversial ideas and opinions. For example, he provoked considerable discussion with his assessment of the Kennedy assassination, calling it "a case of the chickens coming home to roost." This comment referred to the tradition of violence that whites practiced on blacks. Ask why his comment might have offended whites. Have students discuss other examples of ways in which Malcolm X provoked controversy. Interested students may wish to read *The Autobiography of Malcolm X*, written by Alex Haley and based on interviews he conducted with Malcolm X..

Electronic Library of Primary Sources
- from *A Speech to Mississippi Youth*, 1964, by Malcolm X

**DIFFERENTIATING INSTRUCTION** GIFTED AND TALENTED STUDENTS

### Writing a Book Review

Have students read and write a book review of one of the following: *Where Do We Go from Here: Chaos or Community?* by Martin Luther King, Jr.; *Black Power* by Stokely Carmichael and Charles V. Hamilton; or *The Autobiography of Malcolm X*. Tell students to consider the book from the perspective of the 1960s as they write their reviews. After they have written their reviews, students may want to research compare reviews and commentaries written at the time the books were published. Have students share their work with the rest of the class.

**Rubric**

Book reviews should . . .

- include an introduction that identifies the book and states a response to the work
- support the response with evidence from the book
- consider the book from the perspective of the 1960s

*Civil Rights* **719**

**BALLOTS OR BULLETS?** In March 1964, Malcolm broke with Elijah Muhammad over differences in strategy and doctrine and formed another Muslim organization. One month later, he embarked on a pilgrimage to Mecca, in Saudi Arabia, a trip required of followers of orthodox Islam. In Mecca, he learned that orthodox Islam preached racial equality, and he worshiped alongside people from many countries. Wrote Malcolm, "I have [prayed] . . . with fellow Muslims whose eyes were the bluest of blue, whose hair was the blondest of blond, and whose skin was the whitest of white." When he returned to the United States, his attitude toward whites had changed radically. He explained his new slogan, "Ballots or bullets," to a follower: "Well, if you and I don't use the ballot, we're going to be forced to use the bullet. So let us try the ballot."

Because of his split with the Black Muslims, Malcolm believed his life might be in danger. "No one can get out without trouble," he confided. On February 21, 1965, while giving a speech in Harlem, the 39-year-old Malcolm X was shot and killed.

**BLACK POWER** In early June of 1966, tensions that had been building between SNCC and the other civil rights groups finally erupted in Mississippi. Here, James Meredith, the man who had integrated the University of Mississippi, set out on a 225-mile "walk against fear." Meredith planned to walk all the way from the Tennessee border to Jackson, but he was shot by a white racist and was too injured to continue.

Martin Luther King, Jr., of the SCLC, Floyd McKissick of CORE, and **Stokely Carmichael** of SNCC decided to lead their followers in a march to finish what Meredith had started. But it soon became apparent that SNCC and CORE members were quite militant, as they began to shout slogans similar to those of the black separatists who had followed Malcolm X. When King tried to rally the marchers with the refrain of "We Shall Overcome," many SNCC workers—bitter over the violence they'd suffered during Freedom Summer—began singing, "We shall overrun."

Police in Greenwood, Mississippi, arrested Carmichael for setting up a tent on the grounds of an all-black high school. When Carmichael showed up at a rally later, his face swollen from a beating, he electrified the crowd.

Stokely Carmichael (1968). The slogan "Black Power" became the battle-cry of militant civil rights activists.

### A PERSONAL VOICE   STOKELY CARMICHAEL

"This is the twenty-seventh time I have been arrested—and I ain't going to jail no more! . . . We been saying freedom for six years—and we ain't got nothin'. What we're gonna start saying now is BLACK POWER."

—quoted in *The Civil Rights Movement: An Eyewitness History*

**Black Power,** Carmichael said, was a "call for black people to begin to define their own goals . . . [and] to lead their own organizations." King urged him to stop using the phrase because he believed it would provoke African Americans to violence and antagonize whites. Carmichael refused and urged SNCC to stop recruiting whites and to focus on developing African-American pride.  **D**

**BLACK PANTHERS** Later that year, another development demonstrated the growing radicalism of some segments of the African-American community. In Oakland, California, in October 1966, Huey Newton and Bobby Seale founded a political party known as the **Black Panthers** to fight police brutality in the ghetto. The party advocated self-sufficiency for African-American communities, as well as full employment and decent housing. Members maintained that African Americans should be exempt from military service because an unfair number of black youths had been drafted to serve in Vietnam.

720

**D. Answer** SNCC leaders worried that calls for Black Power would provoke black violence and alienate whites.

**MAIN IDEA**

**Analyzing Motives**
**D** Why did some leaders of SNCC disagree with SCLC tactics?

---

**ACTIVITY**   **LINK TO HUMANITIES**

### Researching Kwanzaa

**Class Time** 45 minutes

**Task** Researching the origins and practices of Kwanzaa

**Purpose** To gain a richer cultural understanding of an African-American cultural celebration

**Directions** Have students use library and Internet resources to research and report on the origin of Kwanzaa and how it is celebrated. Ask any students who are familiar with Kwanzaa to share their knowledge. The report may be a multimedia presentation or a demonstration of the various elements of Kwanzaa.

📄 Integrated Assessment
· Rubrics 1, 4, 6

**MAIN IDEA**

**Making Inferences**
**E** Why was the public reaction to the Black Panthers mixed?

*E. Answer*
Americans feared the Black Panther's rhetoric and their involvement in violence; some poor African Americans benefited from their community programs.

Dressed in black leather jackets, black berets, and sunglasses, the Panthers preached self-defense and sold copies of the writings of Mao Zedong, leader of the Chinese Communist revolution. Several police shootouts occurred between the Panthers and police, and the FBI conducted numerous investigations of group members (sometimes using illegal tactics). Even so, many of the Panthers' activities—the establishment of daycare centers, free breakfast programs, free medical clinics, assistance to the homeless, and other services—won support in the ghettos. **E**

## 1968—A Turning Point in Civil Rights ❸

Martin Luther King, Jr., objected to the Black Power movement. He believed that preaching violence could only end in grief. King was planning to lead a Poor People's March on Washington, D.C. However, this time the people would have to march without him.

**KING'S DEATH** Dr. King seemed to sense that death was near. On April 3, 1968, he addressed a crowd in Memphis, where he had gone to support the city's striking garbage workers. "I may not get there with you but . . . we as a people will get to the Promised Land." He added, "I'm not fearing any man. Mine eyes have seen the glory of the coming of the Lord." The next day as King stood on his hotel balcony, James Earl Ray thrust a high-powered rifle out of a window and squeezed the trigger. King crumpled to the floor.

**REACTIONS TO KING'S DEATH** The night King died, Robert F. Kennedy was campaigning for the Democratic presidential nomination. Fearful that King's death would spark riots, Kennedy's advisers told him to cancel his appearance in an African-American neighborhood in Indianapolis. However, Kennedy attended anyway, making an impassioned plea for nonviolence.

(above) Coretta Scott King mourns her husband at his funeral service.
(below) Robert F. Kennedy

**A PERSONAL VOICE** ROBERT F. KENNEDY

"For those of you who are black—considering the evidence . . . that there were white people who were responsible—you can be filled with bitterness, with hatred, and a desire for revenge. We can move in that direction as a country, in great polarization—black people amongst black, white people amongst white, filled with hatred toward one another.

Or we can make an effort, as Martin Luther King did, to understand and comprehend, and to replace that violence, that stain of bloodshed that has spread across our land, with an effort to understand [with] compassion and love."

—"A Eulogy for Dr. Martin Luther King, Jr."

**Vocabulary**
**polarization:** separation into opposite camps

Despite Kennedy's plea, rage over King's death led to the worst urban rioting in United States history. Over 100 cities exploded in flames. The hardest-hit cities included Baltimore, Chicago, Kansas City, and Washington, D.C. Then in June 1968, Robert Kennedy himself was assassinated by a Jordanian immigrant who was angry over Kennedy's support of Israel.

*Civil Rights* **721**

**Instruct: Objective** ❸

**1968—A Turning Point in Civil Rights**
TAKS SS11 3(US7.B)
· What was Martin Luther King, Jr.'s response to the rhetoric of Black Power?
· Why was King visiting Memphis when he was assassinated?
· What happened in cities across America after King's assassination?

📖 In-Depth Resources: Unit 6
· Guided Reading, p. 22

**More About . . .**

**Martin Luther King, Jr.**
Challenged by younger leaders, King appeared to be reevaluating his political position at the time of his death. In 1967, a time when support for the war in Vietnam was still high among many Americans, King had publicly expressed opposition to the war. His Poor People's Campaign was an attempt to create links to labor and working-class Americans through an agenda that may have been too radical for some of his white middle-class supporters.

---

**ACTIVITY** | **COOPERATIVE LEARNING**

 **BLOCK SCHEDULING**

### Creating a Historical Atlas

**Class Time** One class period

**Task** Preparing a historical atlas on race relations in the United States

**Purpose** To identify events or statistics about race relations in the country during the 20th century

**Directions** Ask pairs of students to create an annotated map that shows important events or statistics about race relations in one state during a single decade in the 20th century. Have students choose states from different regions to avoid duplication. Examples would be a map showing California cities that experienced civil rights protests in the 1960s or a map showing the counties in Mississippi that lost the most African-American migrants during the 1940s.

📖 Integrated Assessment
· Rubrics 2, 4

## ④ Legacy of the Civil Rights Movement

**Instruct: Objective ④**

**Legacy of the Civil Rights Movement**

TAKS SS11 5(WH26.C)

· How successful was the civil rights move-ment in getting rid of de jure segregation?

· How successful was the civil rights move-ment in getting rid of de facto segregation?

· What was the Kerner Commission?

 In-Depth Resources: Unit 6
· Guided Reading, p. 22

 Critical Thinking Transparencies CT29, CT63
· The Civil Rights Movement
· African-American Educational Attainment, 1960–1995

**HISTORICAL SPOTLIGHT**

**Shirley Chisholm**

Chisholm's election to the U.S. House of Representatives was a symbolic victory at a time when there were few African Americans in Congress—none of whom were women. Chisholm was a liberal who supported abor-tion and full-employment programs. She opposed American involvement in Vietnam and the U.S. nuclear weapons policy. Ask stu-dents why Chisholm's election was considered an achievement of the civil rights movement. *(The civil rights movement created the awareness that African Americans, as well as women, were not fairly represented in Congress.)*

**HISTORICAL SPOTLIGHT**

**SHIRLEY CHISHOLM**

African-American women such as Shirley Chisholm exemplified the advances won in the civil rights movement. In 1968, Chisholm became the first African-American woman in the United States House of Representatives.

In the mid-1960s, Chisholm served in the New York state assembly, representing a district in New York City. While there, she supported programs to establish public day-care centers and pro-vide unemployment insurance to domestic workers.

In 1972, Chisholm gained national prominence by running for the Democratic presidential nomination. Despite the fact that she never won more than 10% of the vote in the primaries, she controlled 152 delegates at the Democratic convention in Miami.

On March 1, 1968, the **Kerner Commission,** which President Johnson had appointed to study the causes of urban violence, issued its 200,000-word report. In it, the panel named one main cause: white racism. Said the report: "This is our basic conclusion: Our nation is moving toward two societies, one black, one white—sepa-rate and unequal." The report called for the nation to create new jobs, construct new housing, and end de facto segregation in order to wipe out the destructive ghetto environment. However, the Johnson administration ignored many of the recom-mendations because of white opposition to such sweeping changes. So what had the civil rights movement accomplished?

**CIVIL RIGHTS GAINS** The civil rights movement ended de jure segregation by bringing about legal protection for the civil rights of all Americans. Congress passed the most important civil rights legislation since Reconstruction, including the **Civil Rights Act of 1968,** which ended discrimination in housing. After school segregation ended, the numbers of African Americans who finished high school and who went to college increased significantly. This in turn led to better jobs and business opportunities.

Another accomplishment of the civil rights movement was to give African Americans greater pride in their racial identity. Many African Americans adopted African-influenced styles and proudly displayed symbols of African history and culture. College students demanded new Black Studies pro-grams so they could study African-American history and liter-ature. In the entertainment world, the "color bar" was lowered as African Americans began to appear more frequently in movies and on television shows and commercials.

In addition, African Americans made substantial political gains. By 1970, an estimated two-thirds of eligible African Americans were registered to vote, and a significant increase in African-American elected officials resulted. The number of African Americans holding elected office grew from fewer than 100 in 1965 to more than 7,000 in 1992. Many civil rights activists went on to become political leaders, among them Reverend Jesse Jackson, who sought the democratic nomination for president in 1984 and 1988; Vernon Jordan, who led voter-registration drives that enrolled about 2 million African Americans; and Andrew Young, who has served as UN ambassador and Atlanta's mayor. **F**

**UNFINISHED WORK** The civil rights movement was suc-cessful in changing many discriminatory laws. Yet as the 1960s turned to the 1970s, the challenges for the movement changed. The issues it confronted—housing and job discrim-ination, educational inequality, poverty, and racism—involved the difficult task of changing people's attitudes and behavior. Some of the proposed solutions, such as more tax monies spent in the inner cities and the forced busing of schoolchildren, angered some whites, who resisted further changes. Public support for the civil rights movement declined because some whites were frightened by the urban riots and the Black Panthers.

By 1990, the trend of whites fleeing the cities for the suburbs had reversed much of the progress toward school

*F. Answer*
End of legalized segregation; constitutional and legal pro-tection of civil rights and voting rights; increased pride in racial identity; more African American vot-ers, elected offi-cials, and high school and col-lege graduates. They were secured through the civil rights movement, which helped change national opinion, and through result-ing federal inter-vention and pas-sage of federal laws like the Voting Rights Act of 1965,

**MAIN IDEA**

**Evaluating**
**F** What were some accomplish-ments of the civil rights movement?

---

**ACTIVITY** **LINK TO CIVICS**

 **BLOCK SCHEDULING**

**Discussing Tolerance**

**Class Time** 45 minutes

**Task** Discussing racial attitudes

**Purpose** To analyze viewpoints regarding racial and ethnic understanding

**Directions** In 1992, *Teaching Tolerance*, a biennial publication by the Southern Poverty Law Center polled students on two questions: 1. What causes most racial and ethnic conflicts between people? 2. What do you think individuals can do to bring about greater understanding between racial and ethnic groups? First, have students write a personal response to each question. Then select volunteers to participate in a panel discussion of these issues. Allow ten minutes for the discus-sion of each question, followed by a five-minute period for comments by the remaining student "audience."

integration. In 1996–1997, 28 percent of blacks in the South and 50 percent of blacks in the Northeast were attending schools with fewer than 10 percent whites. Lack of jobs also remained a serious problem for African Americans, who had a poverty rate three times that of whites.

To help equalize education and job opportunities, the government in the 1960s began to promote **affirmative action.** Affirmative-action programs involve making special efforts to hire or enroll groups that have suffered discrimination. Many colleges and almost all companies that do business with the federal government adopted such programs. But in the late 1970s, some people began to criticize affirmative-action programs as "reverse discrimination" that set minority hiring or enrollment quotas and deprived whites of opportunities. In the 1980s, Republican administrations eased affirmative-action requirements for some government contractors. The fate of affirmative action is still to be decided.

Today, African Americans and whites interact in ways that could have only been imagined before the civil rights movement. In many respects, Dr. King's dream has been realized—yet much remains to be done.

**Background**
**quota:**
requirement that a certain number of positions are filled by minorities

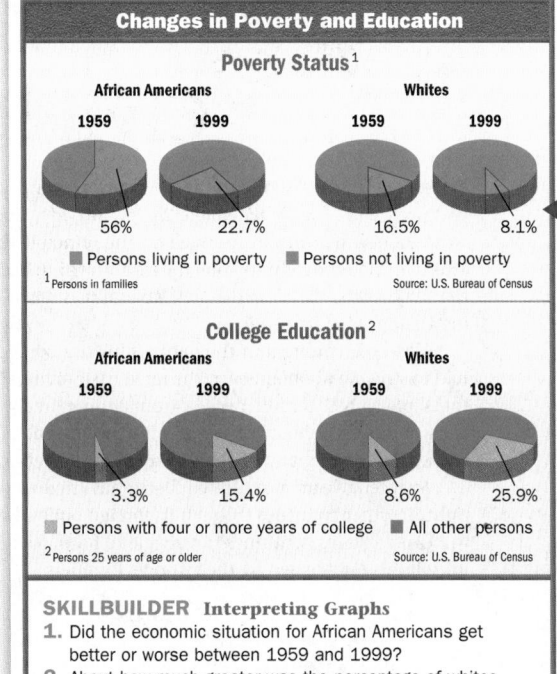

**Changes in Poverty and Education**

**Poverty Status**[1]

| African Americans | | Whites | |
|---|---|---|---|
| 1959 | 1999 | 1959 | 1999 |
| 56% | 22.7% | 16.5% | 8.1% |

■ Persons living in poverty  ■ Persons not living in poverty

[1]Persons in families                Source: U.S. Bureau of Census

**College Education**[2]

| African Americans | | Whites | |
|---|---|---|---|
| 1959 | 1999 | 1959 | 1999 |
| 3.3% | 15.4% | 8.6% | 25.9% |

■ Persons with four or more years of college  ■ All other persons

[2]Persons 25 years of age or older           Source: U.S. Bureau of Census

**SKILLBUILDER** Interpreting Graphs
1. Did the economic situation for African Americans get better or worse between 1959 and 1999?
2. About how much greater was the percentage of whites completing four or more years of college in 1999 than the percentage of African Americans?

## HISTORY from VISUALS

**Interpreting Graphs**
Have students use the graph to answer the following: How much did the percentage of college-educated African Americans increase from 1959 to 1999? *(by more than four times as much)*

**SKILLBUILDER ANSWER**
1. It improved because a smaller percentage were living in poverty.
2. The percentage of whites was nearly two times greater.

## Assess & Reteach

**SECTION 3 ASSESSMENT**
Have students work in groups of four and compare their responses to question 3.

📋 Formal Assessment
· Section Quiz, p. 387

**SELF-ASSESSMENT**
Direct students to write the one question they think should have been included in the Section Assessment but was not.

**RETEACH**
Review the events in the time line in question 2 to reteach the major civil rights events in the section.

📋 In-Depth Resources: Unit 6
· Reteaching Activity, p. 27

---

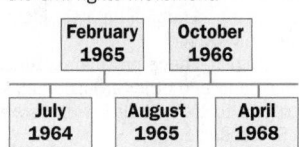 **ASSESSMENT**

**1. TERMS & NAMES** For each term or name, write a sentence explaining its significance.

- de facto segregation
- de jure segregation
- Malcolm X
- Nation of Islam
- Stokely Carmichael
- Black Power
- Black Panthers
- Kerner Commission
- Civil Rights Act of 1968
- affirmative action

**MAIN IDEA**

**2. TAKING NOTES**
Create a timeline of key events of the civil rights movement.

| February 1965 | October 1966 |
|---|---|

| July 1964 | August 1965 | April 1968 |
|---|---|---|

In your opinion, which event was most significant? Why?

**CRITICAL THINKING**

**3. ANALYZING ISSUES**
What factors contributed to the outbreak of violence in the fight for civil rights? **Think About:**
- different leaders' approach to civil rights issues
- living conditions in urban areas
- de facto and de jure segregation

**4. COMPARING AND CONTRASTING**
Compare and contrast the civil rights strategies of Malcolm X and Martin Luther King, Jr. Whose strategies do you think were more effective? Explain and support your response.

*Civil Rights* **723**

---

Answers **ASSESSMENT**

**1. TERMS & NAMES**
de facto segregation, p. 718
de jure segregation, p. 718
Malcolm X, p. 719
Nation of Islam, p. 719
Stokely Carmichael, p. 720
Black Power, p. 720
Black Panthers, p. 720
Kerner Commission, p. 722
Civil Rights Act of 1968, p. 722
affirmative action, p. 723

**2. TAKING NOTES**
**July 1964:** Harlem riots; **February 1965:** Malcolm X assassinated; **August 1965:** Watts riots in Los Angeles; **October 1966:** Black Panthers founded; **April 1968:** Martin Luther King, Jr., assassinated

**3. ANALYZING ISSUES**
Malcolm X, Black Panthers, and others' philosophy of violent protests; African Americans' reaction to the assassination of civil rights leaders; backlash against white racist acts; poor living and working conditions, especially in urban areas; difficulty in eradicating de facto segregation in the North

**4. COMPARING AND CONTRASTING**
Both wanted civil rights and greater opportunities. King preached racial equality. Malcolm X preached black separatism and armed self-defense.
**Effectiveness:** King, because his demonstrations caused civil rights legislation to be passed; Malcolm X, because he urged African Americans to fight back

## Objectives

· To identify civil rights as a significant theme in American history

· To trace the evolution of civil rights

## Focus & Motivate

Ask students for their definition of civil rights. Ask them what is an example of a civil right? Have students consider which documents, laws, and government institutions are important in defining and guaranteeing civil rights.

## More About . . .

### Civil Rights

Although the civil rights struggle focused on the efforts of African Americans to win full civil rights, other groups of Americans have been denied their civil rights as well. Women's rights to control their own property and earnings once were sharply restricted. Women also were denied the right to vote until passage of the Nineteenth Amendment in 1920. Native Americans were denied their land and full participation in society. Hispanics and Asian Americans, as well as Native Americans, have been discriminated against based on race and ethnicity and women, on the basis of gender. Many European immigrant groups also have suffered discrimination.

# Civil Rights

Thomas Jefferson asserted in the Declaration of Independence that "all men are created equal" and are endowed with the "unalienable rights" of "life, liberty, and the pursuit of happiness." With these words, a new nation was founded on the principle that citizens have certain fundamental civil rights. These include the right to vote, the right to enjoy freedom of speech and religion, and others. For more than 200 years, the United States has stood as a worldwide example of a country committed to securing the rights of its people.

However, throughout the nation's history, some Americans have had to struggle to obtain even the most basic civil rights. Laws or customs prevented certain people from voting freely, from speaking their minds on political issues, and from living and going where they wish. Over time, many of these barriers have been torn down.

In recent years, the United States has tried to promote human rights in other countries through its foreign policy. Even as it does so, the United States continues to struggle to fulfill for all Americans the lofty ideals established by the nation's founders.

## 1791

### ▼ BILL OF RIGHTS

During the Constitutional Convention, the question of a bill of rights arose, but none was included. During the process of ratification, many people argued that the Constitution needed to list the basic civil rights and liberties that the federal government could not take away from the people.

Accordingly, the nation ratified ten amendments to the Constitution—the Bill of Rights. It establishes such rights as freedom of speech, religion, and assembly, freedom of the press, and the right to a trial by jury. While these rights have been subject to interpretation over the nation's history, the Bill of Rights serves as the cornerstone of American democracy.

## 1868

### THE FOURTEENTH AMENDMENT ▲

In the engraving above, a crowd of black and white Americans celebrates the passage of the Civil Rights Act of 1866. This act recognized the citizenship of African Americans and granted the same civil rights to all people born in the United States except Native Americans.

The Fourteenth Amendment, ratified two years later, made these changes part of the Constitution. The Amendment declared that states cannot deny anyone "equal protection of the laws" and extended the right to vote to all 21-year-old males, including former slaves.

Despite these provisions, African Americans and other groups would still struggle to claim their full rights as U.S. citizens.

## RECOMMENDED RESOURCES

### BOOKS

Belz, Herman. *Emancipation and Equal Rights: Politics and Constitutionalism in the Civil War Era.* New York: Norton, 1978.

Rutland, Robert. *The Birth of the Bill of Rights, 1776-1791.* Boston: Northeastern UP, 1991.

Totten, Samuel. *Human Rights.* Hillside, NJ: Enslow, 1989. Includes the UN's Universal Declaration of Human Rights.

### VIDEOS

*Bill of Rights, Bill of Responsibilities.* Cambridge Educational, 1995. A fast-paced commentary featuring comedian Bill Maher.

*Fighting for Civil Rights.* Coronet/MTI, 1993. Part 3 of the award-winning In the Land of Jim Crow series.

### SOFTWARE

*African-American History—Slavery to Civil Rights.* CD-ROM. Queue. From the slave trade to recent times; DOS version called *Black American History.*

*Amnesty Interactive.* CD-ROM. Voyager, 1994. Traces human rights from ancient to modern times.

# 1950s & 1960s

### THE CIVIL RIGHTS MOVEMENT ▶

Despite the Fourteenth Amendment and later the Fifteenth Amendment, which forbade states from denying any-one the right to vote on account of race, African Americans continued to live as second-class citizens, especially in the South.

During the 1950s and 1960s, African Americans and other Americans led a powerful movement to fight for racial equality. The movement often met with strong resistance, such as in Birmingham, Alabama, where police sprayed demonstrators with high-pressure fire hoses. *(right)* Nevertheless, it succeeded in securing for African Americans the civil rights promised by the Constitution and the Declaration of Independence. The civil rights move-ment has also been the basis for other groups gaining equal rights, including other minori-ties, women, and people with disabilities.

# 1970s

### HUMAN RIGHTS ▶

President Jimmy Carter considered human rights an important foreign policy issue. Human rights are what Americans think of as their civil rights, including the right to vote and to receive a fair trial. The Carter administration tried to encourage greater freedom abroad by taking such steps as cutting off military aid to countries with poor human rights records.

While these efforts met with mixed results, the issue of human rights has continued to influence U.S. foreign policy. In the 1990s, for example, the U.S. government tried to push China toward increasing human rights while keeping alive its trade ties with that country.

As a private citizen, Jimmy Carter has also continued to champion human rights causes. In 1982, he and his wife, Rosalynn, founded the Carter Center, whose programs seek to end human rights abuses and promote democracy worldwide.

---

## THINKING CRITICALLY

### CONNECT TO HISTORY

1. **Analyzing Issues** The Fourteenth and Fifteenth Amendments both provided for the voting rights of African Americans. Based on what you have read in the chapter, how were these rights denied African Americans? How were they finally secured?

📁 **SEE SKILLBUILDER HANDBOOK, PAGE R14.**

### CONNECT TO TODAY

2. **Writing About Rights** Have you or anyone you've known had their civil rights denied them in any way? Research a current day instance of an alleged civil rights injustice. Write an account of the issue and share it with your class.

ℹ️ **RESEARCH LINKS** CLASSZONE.COM

*Civil Rights* **725**

## Instruct

1. How did the Declaration of Independence and the Bill of Rights lay a foundation for civil rights in America?
2. What are the provisions of the Fourteenth Amendment?
3. How did the civil rights movement attack de facto segregation in the South?
4. Why is human rights an important issue for American foreign policy?

### MAKING PERSONAL CONNECTIONS

· Ask students to name the civil rights they enjoy.
· Ask them what full rights they are denied as minors.
· Do they think the denial of their full rights is appropriate? Why or why not?

### More About . . .

### Civil Rights and Persons With Disabilities

The Civil Rights movement gave impetus to the disability movement. Disabled persons and their supporters organized to seek civil rights protections for individuals with disabilities. The result was the passage of the Americans With Disabilities Act of 1990. This law guaranteed disabled persons equal opportunity in employment, public accommodations, transportation, state and local government services, and telecommunications.

---

## THINKING CRITICALLY: ANSWERS

1. **CONNECT TO HISTORY** **Denied:** through poll taxes, unevenly applied literacy tests, other unfair voting qualifications (for example, you could not vote if your grandfather had not voted), and intimidation of potential African-American voters. **Secured:** through the civil rights movement, which helped change national opinion, and through resulting federal intervention and legislation.

2. **CONNECT TO TODAY** Accounts should meet the following criteria:
· Identify the individuals involved and the time and place of the incident;
· Clarify the specific right or rights being violated;
· Indicate the reasons for the violation, if known;
· Describe the victim's feelings;
· Describe action taken to improve the situation.

## TERMS & NAMES

1. *Brown v. Board of Education,* p. 702
2. Rosa Parks, p. 704
3. Martin Luther King, Jr., p. 704
4. Student Nonviolent Coordinating Committee, p. 706
5. freedom riders, p. 710
6. Civil Rights Act of 1964, p. 714
7. Fannie Lou Hamer, p. 715
8. de facto segregation, p. 718
9. Malcolm X, p. 719
10. Black Power, p. 720

## MAIN IDEAS

1. Jim Crow laws, passed in the South, were aimed at separating the races. Application of these laws included separate schools, streetcars, and public restrooms.
2. King's beliefs were rooted in Jesus' teachings to love one's enemies, Thoreau's concept of civil disobedience, Randolph's techniques for organizing massive demonstrations, and Gandhi's use of nonviolent resistance.
3. Meredith won a federal court case allowing him to enroll in the University of Mississippi.
4. Fannie Lou Hamer was beaten trying to register to vote; a bomb in a Birmingham church killed four African-American girls; Klansmen, with the support of local police, murdered three civil rights activists in Mississippi.
5. Black nationalism, self-determination, racial pride, self-respect, the use of self-defense.
6. Leaders felt that the slogan "black power" antagonized whites.

---

# CHAPTER 21 ASSESSMENT

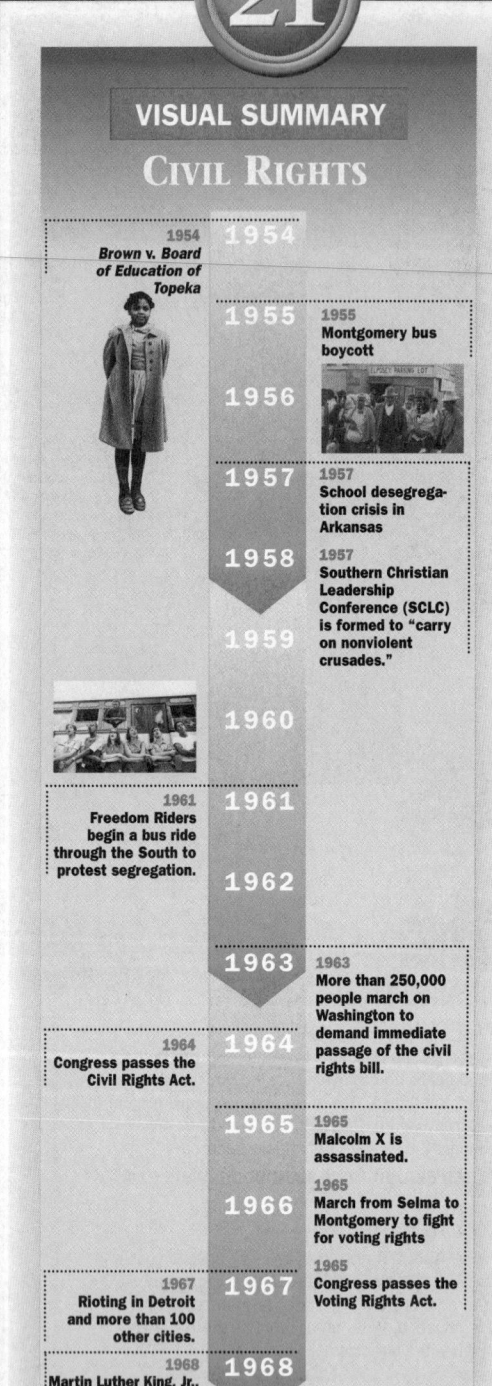

**VISUAL SUMMARY**

## CIVIL RIGHTS

**1954**
*Brown v. Board of Education of Topeka*

**1954**

**1955**
1955 Montgomery bus boycott

**1956**

**1957**
1957 School desegregation crisis in Arkansas

**1958**
1957 Southern Christian Leadership Conference (SCLC) is formed to "carry on nonviolent crusades."

**1959**

**1960**

**1961**
1961 Freedom Riders begin a bus ride through the South to protest segregation.

**1962**

**1963**
1963 More than 250,000 people march on Washington to demand immediate passage of the civil rights bill.

**1964**
1964 Congress passes the Civil Rights Act.

**1965**
1965 Malcolm X is assassinated.

**1966**
1965 March from Selma to Montgomery to fight for voting rights

**1967**
1965 Congress passes the Voting Rights Act.

1967 Rioting in Detroit and more than 100 other cities.

**1968**
1968 Martin Luther King, Jr., is assassinated.

---

## TERMS & NAMES

For each term or name below, write a sentence explaining its connection to the civil rights movement.

1. *Brown v. Board of Education of Topeka*
2. Rosa Parks
3. Martin Luther King, Jr.
4. Student Nonviolent Coordinating Committee
5. freedom rider
6. Civil Rights Act of 1964
7. Fannie Lou Hamer
8. de facto segregation
9. Malcolm X
10. Black Power

## MAIN IDEAS

Use your notes and the information in the chapter to answer the following questions.

### Taking on Segregation (pages 700–707)

1. What were Jim Crow laws and how were they applied?
2. What were the roots of Martin Luther King, Jr.'s beliefs in nonviolent resistance?

### The Triumphs of a Crusade (pages 710–716)

3. What was the significance of the federal court case won by James Meredith in 1962?
4. Cite three examples of violence committed between 1962 and 1964 against African Americans and civil rights activists.

### Challenges and Changes in the Movement (pages 717–723)

5. What were some of the key beliefs advocated by Malcolm X?
6. Why did some civil rights leaders urge Stokely Carmichael to stop using the slogan "black power"?

## THINKING CRITICALLY

1. **USING YOUR NOTES** On your own paper, draw a cluster diagram like the one shown below. Then, fill it in with four events from the civil rights movement that were broadcast on nationwide television and that you find the most compelling.

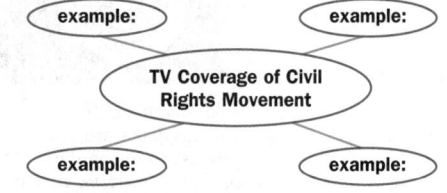

example:   example:

**TV Coverage of Civil Rights Movement**

example:   example:

2. **HISTORICAL PERSPECTIVE** Overall, would you characterize the civil rights struggle as a unified or disunified movement? Explain.

3. **INTERPRETING MAPS** Look carefully at the map of U.S. school segregation on page 701. What regional differences do you think spurred civil rights activists to target the South before the North?

---

## CRITICAL THINKING

1. **Using Your Notes** the crisis at Central High School in Little Rock, Arkansas (1957); the sit-in at Greensboro, North Carolina (1960); Fannie Lou Hamer's speech to the Democratic National Convention (1964); the Selma march (1965)

2. **Historical Perspective**
   **Unified:** All civil rights activists shared the same goals—freedom, justice, and equality; gender and age differences were surmounted; the March on Washington was a powerful display of unity.
   **Disunified:** Violent versus nonviolent methods created divisiveness; Northern blacks and Southern blacks had different needs.

3. **Interpreting Maps** As the map shows, schools segregated by law were predominant in the Southern states. The legal racism—de jure segregation—of the South was easier to tackle than de facto segregation—the more subtle form of racism predominant in the North.

## Standardized Test Practice

Use the diagram and your knowledge of United States history to answer question 1.

**Civil Rights Strategies and Actions, 1954-1968**

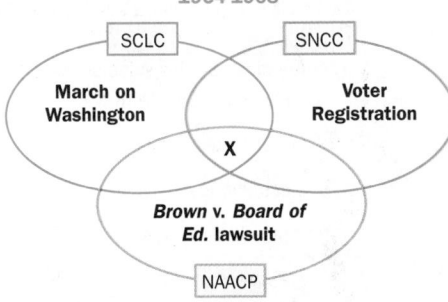

1. The Venn diagram is partially filled in with the strategies of various civil rights groups in the 1960s. Which of the following could be added to the area of the diagram labeled **X**?

   A provide social services to the needy

   B boycotts

   C nonviolent demonstrations

   D armed self-defense

Use the quotation as well as your knowledge of United States history to answer question 2.

"An illegal attack, an unjust attack, and an immoral attack can be made against you by any one. Just because a person has on a [police] uniform does not give him the right to come and shoot up your neighborhood. No, this is not right, and my suggestion would be that as long as the police department doesn't use those methods in white neighborhoods, they shouldn't come . . . and use them in our neighborhood. . . ."

—MALCOLM X, "Prospects for Freedom in 1965"

2. Which of the following events justifies Malcolm X's concerns about police brutality?

   F the Rosa Parks incident in 1965

   G the 1963 Birmingham demonstrations

   H the desegregation of Little Rock's Central High in 1957

   J the first sit-ins in 1942

**ADDITIONAL TEST PRACTICE, pages S1–S33.**

 **TEST PRACTICE** CLASSZONE.COM

---

## Standardized Test Practice

1. The correct answer is letter **C**.
   Remind students that each of the three organizations on the diagram advocated nonviolence. The March on Washington was a nonviolent demonstration; tactics used to register voters and to desegregate schools were also nonviolent. Letters A, B, and D are incorrect because they are not directly relevant to all three strategies and actions shown on the diagram.

2. The correct answer is letter **G**.
   Letters F, H, and J are not correct because police brutality was not an issue in these situations; instead, African Americans were subjected to other forms of abuse.

### LOBBYING PLAN

**Tips for Teaching**

· Have students begin to put together materials to raise awareness and support for their cause.

· Letters to government officials should be drafted and reviewed

· Review students' position papers and make suggestions for changes.

---

## ALTERNATIVE ASSESSMENT

1.  Recall your discussion of the question on page 699:

   *What rights are worth fighting for?*

   Choose one participant in the civil rights movement. From that person's perspective, write a speech in which you evaluate your role in the movement. Consider these questions:

   • What civil rights did you work for?

   • Why are these rights important?

   • How successful were you?

   • What were the costs of your struggle?

2. **VIDEO** **LEARNING FROM MEDIA** View the *American Stories* video, "Justice in Montgomery." Discuss the following questions with a small group of classmates. Then do the activity.

   • What role did Jo Ann Gibson Robinson and the African-American women of Montgomery play in the boycott?

   • What responsibilities do you think individuals have to stop injustice?

   **Cooperative Learning Activity** You have just seen an account of the Montgomery bus boycott through the eyes of one person, Jo Ann Gibson Robinson. With your group, decide how you would teach people about the boycott—from what perspective and with what materials. Create a multimedia presentation to give to the class.

 **Formal Assessment**
· Chapter Test, Forms A, B, and C, pp. 388–405

*Civil Rights* **727**

---

## ALTERNATIVE ASSESSMENT

### 1. INTERACT WITH HISTORY

**Rubric**

The student's speech should . . .

· reflect an understanding of the role of the individual in the civil rights movement

· explain the individual's commitment to civil rights

· place the individual's role within the proper historic context

· capture the interest of the audience with a lively presentation

### 2. VIDEO LEARNING FROM MEDIA

**Rubric**

The multimedia presentation should . . .

· show a clear understanding of the event and issues involved

· include appropriate historical background

· convey the motivations and feelings of the boycotters

· explain the outcome of the boycott

# The Vietnam War Years

| | CHAPTER OVERVIEW | COPYMASTERS | INTEGRATED TECHNOLOGY |
|---|---|---|---|
| **CHAPTER RESOURCES** | *The United States enters a war in Vietnam, which results in the deaths of tens of thousands of U.S. soldiers, the division of American society into bitterly opposed camps, and a lasting impact on U.S. foreign policy.* | 📄 Telescoping the Times · Chapter Summary, pp. 43–44  📄 Planning for Block Schedules | 📼 American Stories video series · "Matters of Conscience"  👁 Power Presentations  👁 Electronic Teacher Tools  🖐 Online Lesson Planner  🖐 classzone.com |
| **SECTION 1** Moving Toward Conflict pp. 730–735 | **KEY IDEAS** *America slowly involves itself in the war in Vietnam as it seeks to halt the spread of communism.* | 📄 In-Depth Resources: Unit 6 - Guided Reading, p.39 · Building Vocabulary, p. 44 · Reteaching Activity, p. 46  📄 Lesson Plans, pp. 171–172 | ⚒ Critical Thinking Transparencies CT30 · The War in Vietnam  👁 Electronic Library of Primary Sources · The Tonkin Gulf Resolution  🖐 classzone.com |
| **SECTION 2** U.S. Involvement and Escalation pp. 736–741 | *The United States sends troops to fight in Vietnam, but the war quickly turns into a stalemate.* | 📄 In-Depth Resources: Unit 6 · Guided Reading, p. 40 · Skillbuilder Practice, p. 45 · Reteaching Activity, p. 47 · Primary Sources, p. 55 · American Lives, p. 62  📄 Lesson Plans, pp. 173–174 | ⚒ Geography Transparencies GT30 · Vietnam War: 1964–1975  👁 Electronic Library of Primary Sources · from "Peace Without Conquest" by Lyndon B. Johnson  🖐 classzone.com |
| **SECTION 3** A Nation Divided pp. 742–747 | *An antiwar movement emerges in the United States, pitting those who oppose the government's war policy against those who support it.* | 📄 In-Depth Resources: Unit 6 · Guided Reading, p. 41 · Reteaching Activity, p. 48 · Primary Sources, pp. 56–57  📄 Lesson Plans, pp. 175–176 | 📼 American Stories video series · "Matters of Conscience"  🖐 classzone.com |
| **SECTION 4** 1968: A Tumultuous Year pp. 748–753 | *A shocking enemy attack in Vietnam, two assassinations, and a chaotic political convention help make 1968 the most explosive year of the decade.* | 📄 In-Depth Resources: Unit 6 - Guided Reading, p. 42 · Reteaching Activity, p. 49 · Geography Application, pp. 51–52 · Primary Sources, p. 58 · American Lives, p. 63  📄 Lesson Plans, pp. 177–178 | ⚒ Critical Thinking Transparencies CT64 · Impact of the TET Offensive  👁 Electronic Library of Primary Sources · from *The Strategy of Confrontation*  🖐 classzone.com |
| **SECTION 5** 1968: The End of the War and Its Legacy pp. 754–763 | *The nation's longest war ends after nearly ten years and leaves a lasting impact on U.S. policy and American society.* | 📄 In-Depth Resources: Unit 6 - Guided Reading, p. 43 · Reteaching Activity, p. 50 · Outline Map, pp. 53–54 · Literature, pp. 59–61  📄 Lesson Plans, pp. 179–180 | ⚒ Critical Thinking Transparencies CT30 · The War in Vietnam  ⚒ Geography Transparencies GT30 · Vietnam War: 1964–1975  ⚒ Humanities Transparencies HT28, HT45 · Fall of Saigon · The Blind Leading the Blind  👁 Electronic Library of Primary Sources · Kent State  🖐 classzone.com |

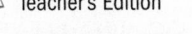

| | | |
|---|---|---|
| PE | Pupil's Edition | |
| TE | Teacher's Edition | |
| Copymaster | | |

| | |
|---|---|
| Overhead Transparency | |
| Audio Library | |

| | |
|---|---|
| CD-ROM | |
| Internet | |

## ASSESSMENT OPTIONS

- PE **Chapter Assessment,** pp. 764–765
- **Formal Assessment**
  · Chapter Tests, Forms A, B, and C, pp. 411–422
- **Test Generator**
- **Integrated Assessment Book**
- **TAKS Online Test Practice**
- **TAKS Spiraled Content Review**
- **TAKS Practice Tests**

---

- PE **Section 1 Assessment,** p. 735
- TE **Self-Assessment,** p. 735
- **Formal Assessment,** Quiz, p. 406
- **Integrated Assessment Book**
- **Test Generator**
- **TAKS Practice Transparencies TT112**

---

- PE **Section 2 Assessment,** p. 741
- TE **Self-Assessment,** p. 741
- **Formal Assessment,** Quiz, p. 407
- **Integrated Assessment Book**
- **Test Generator**
- **TAKS Practice Transparencies TT113**

---

- PE **Section 3 Assessment,** p. 747
- TE **Self-Assessment,** p. 747
- **Formal Assessment,** Quiz, p. 408
- **Integrated Assessment Book**
- **Test Generator**
- **TAKS Practice Transparencies TT114**

---

- PE **Section 4 Assessment,** p. 753
- TE **Self-Assessment,** p. 753
- **Formal Assessment,** Quiz, p. 409
- **Integrated Assessment Book**
- **Test Generator**
- **TAKS Practice Transparencies TT115**

---

- PE **Section 5 Assessment,** p. 761
- TE **Self-Assessment,** p. 761
- **Formal Assessment,** Quiz, p. 410
- **Integrated Assessment Book**
- **Test Generator**
- **TAKS Practice Transparencies TT116**

## RESOURCES FOR DIFFERENTIATING INSTRUCTION

### Students Acquiring English/ESL

- **Reading Study Guide:** (English and Spanish) pp. 217–226
- **Access for Students Acquiring English/ESL:** Spanish Translations, pp. 234–243
- **Chapter Summaries on CD** (English and Spanish)

### Less Proficient Readers

- **Reading Study Guide** (English and Spanish) pp. 217–226
- **Telescoping the Times**
  · Chapter Summary, pp. 43–44
- **Chapter Summaries on CD** (English and Spanish)

### Gifted and Talented Students

- **In-Depth Resources: Unit 6**
  · Primary Sources, pp. 55–58
  · Literature, pp. 59–61
  American Lives: Robert McNamara, p. 62; John Lewis, p. 63
- **Electronic Library of Primary Sources**
  · Unit 6, Chapter 22

## CROSS-CURRICULAR CONNECTIONS

### Primary Sources
Denenberg, Barry. *Voices from Vietnam.* NY: Scholastic, 1995. A compilation of quotes from soldiers, officers, politicians, celebrities, and reporters about the difficulty of understanding the Vietnam War.

### Civics
Brown, Gene. *The Nation in Turmoil: Civil Rights and the Vietnam War, (1960–1973).* NY: 21st Century Books, 1995. Presents primary source material outlining major events of the 1960s.

### Humanities: Art
Ashabranner, Brent and Ashabranner, Jennifer (photographer). *Their Names to Life: What the Vietnam Memorial Means to Americans,* NY: 21st Century, 1998. Photographs show the powerful reactions of visitors to the wall.

### Literature
Whelan, Gloria. *Goodbye, Vietnam.* NY: Random House, 1993. Mai and her family must leave Vietnam, and they make the dangerous journey along the Mekong delta to the sea and then by boat to Hong Kong.

### McDougal Littell
*Literature Connections*

Myers, Walter Dean. *Fallen Angels (with related readings).* This novel presents the experiences of a small group of men who come of age during the Vietnam War. Richie Perry enlists in the army mainly to escape his problems at home and finds himself in the middle of a war that is more traumatic and confusing than the life he fled.

Ho, Mingfong. *The Clay Marble.* Set in a Cambodian refugee camp in the early 1980s, this novel describes how a young girl is helped through the ordeal by stories and a special marble.

## ENRICHMENT ACTIVITIES

- PE **Pupil's Edition,** pp. 730–763
  Interact with History, pp. 730–731
  American Literature, pp. 762-763
- **In-Depth Resources: Unit 6**
  · Geography Application: The Ho Chi Minh Trail., pp. 51–52
  · Outline Map: The Vietnam War, pp. 53–54
  · Primary Source: Letters from a Soldier in Vietnam, p. 55
  · Primary Source: Protest Buttons, p. 56
  · Primary Source: The New Left, p. 57
  · Primary Source: LBJ on Vietnam and Reelection, p. 58
  · Literature: from *In Country,* pp. 59–61
  · American Lives: Robert McNamara, p. 62
  · American Lives: John Lewis, p. 63
- **AMERICAN STORIES video series**
  · "Matters of Conscience"
- **Electronic Library of Primary Sources**
  · Unit 6, Chapter 22

## BLOCK SCHEDULE LESSON PLAN OPTIONS (90-MINUTE PERIOD)

### DAY 1

**CHAPTER OPENER**
pp. 728–729

**Class Time** 20 Minutes

**History from Visuals, p. 728**

**Class Time** 10 minutes

*Options for Pacing and Variety*

· Peer Teaching Have students read the time line on pages 728–729 and then work in pairs to create a different way of organizing the information given, such as a chart. Students should also add any important information not included in the time line. **Class Time** 10 minutes

**Interact with History, p. 729**

**Class Time** 10 minutes

*Options for Pacing and Variety*

· Internet Have students read the situation in the text and research. Using the Internet, have students find the number of people who went to Canada to evade the draft, the professions that were exempted from the draft, and how many people the exemption affected. **Class Time** 10 minutes

**SECTION 1, pp. 730–735**

**Class Time** 35 minutes

*Options for Pacing and Variety*

· Peer Evaluation Have students work in pairs to create questions for the terms and names of Section 1. Then have them quiz another

### DAY 1 continued

pair of students. **Class Time** 25 minutes

· Peer Teaching Have students look at the headline for *The New York Times* on page 735 and ask them how they might go about researching the other views of the Gulf of Tonkin incident and the U.S. response. Have them work in groups to begin a search based on the discussion. **Class Time** 35 minutes

**SECTION 2, pp. 736–741**

**Class Time** 35 minutes

*Options for Pacing and Variety*

· Time Saver Ask students to read the Tim O'Brien quote on page 736 and discuss the experiences and feelings that soldiers might have had. Ask students what O'Brien is talking about and what his attitude toward the situation is. Ask students how they think the men coped with the work they had to do. **Class Time** 15 minutes

· Peer Teaching Ask students to help each other answer the questions in the Section Assessment. **Class Time** 15 minutes

### DAY 2

**SECTION 3, pp. 742–747**

**Class Time** 50 minutes

*Options for Pacing and Variety*

· History on Film View the video "Matters of Conscience: Stephan Gubar and the Vietnam War" and discuss it. **Class Time** 25 minutes

· Internet Ask students to use the Internet to research the racial statistics of American troops in Vietnam and racial tensions in the U.S. Army. **Class Time** 30 minutes

· Peer Teaching Have student pairs discuss and answer the Main Ideas questions on page 746. Have them compare and contrast the arguments for and against the resistance movement. **Class Time** 20 minutes

**SECTION 4, pp. 748–753**

**Class Time** 40 minutes

*Options for Pacing and Variety*

· Peer Teaching Ask students to work in pairs to create a time line or cause-and-effect chart of the important events in this section. **Class Time** 20 minutes

· Internet Ask students to research the Chicago protests, including first-person accounts, and write a page citing direct and indirect causes of the tension surrounding the 1968 election. **Class Time** 20 minutes

### DAY 3

**SECTION 5, pp. 754–763**

**Class Time** 45 minutes

*Options for Pacing and Variety*

· Time Saver Have students read the quotation from Nixon on page 755 and discuss how Nixon used his image to his advantage during the Vietnam War. **Class Time** 10 minutes

· Time Saver Ask students to look at the famous photograph on page 757 and discuss the questions included. **Class Time** 5 minutes

· Internet Ask students to read the feature on pages 762–763, "Literature of the Vietnam War," and use the Internet to research question 2 in Thinking Critically. **Class Time** 30 minutes

**ASSESSMENT**
pp. 764–765

**Class Time** 45 minutes

*Options for Pacing and Variety*

· Peer Teaching Ask student pairs to quiz each other on the Main Ideas questions from the chapter. **Class Time** 25 minutes

· Time Saver Discuss the Critical Thinking questions as a class and create the chart for item 1 on the board. **Class Time** 15 minutes

---

**TEACHER-TESTED ACTIVITY**
**ILLUSTRATED TIME LINE**

**Class Time** 45 minutes

**Task** Creating an illustrated time line

**Purpose** To document U.S. involvement in Vietnam

**ACTIVITY John Seeley, Westminster High School, Westminster, California**

**Supplies Needed**
· Large rolls of paper
· Internet and library resources
· Markers
· Glue

**Activity** Have students work in small groups to create pictorial time lines of America's involvement in Southeast Asia. Tell them at the beginning of the chapter to begin collecting information and appropriate visual materials. They also may incorporate written statements reflecting their views of events. Display the time lines for comparison and discussion.

# CHAPTER 22 CORRELATION

## CORRELATION TO THE TEXAS ESSENTIAL KNOWLEDGE AND SKILLS

Chapter 22 addresses the following standards of the Texas Essential Knowledge and Skills for U.S. History.

| TEKS | Instruction | Student Question/Activity |
|---|---|---|
| **(1A)** Identify major eras in U.S. history from 1877 to the present and describe their defining characteristics. | **PE 728–729** time line highlighting significant events of the Vietnam era | **TE 728** question that require students to interpret the time line |
| **(6E)** Analyze the conflicts in Korea and Vietnam and describe their domestic and international effects. | **PE 730–761** in-depth examination of America's involvement in the Vietnam War | **PE 764** Main Idea and Critical Thinking questions about the many aspects of the war |
| **(9A)** Analyze the effects of physical and human geographic features on major events. | **PE 738–740** discussion of the jungle terrain in Vietnam and the difficulty it presented to U.S. troops | **PE 739** Main Idea question about the difficulties U.S. troops encountered in Vietnam |
| **(16A)** Evaluate the impact of events, including the Gulf of Tonkin Resolution and the War Powers Act, on the relationship between the legislative and executive branches of government. | **PE 735, 761** discussion of the Gulf of Tonkin Resolution and the War Powers Act and what each meant with regard to the relationship between Congress and the President | **PE 735** Critical Thinking question about passage of the Tonkin Gulf Resolution |
| **(19C)** Identify the contributions of Texans who have been President of the United States. | **PE 736–738; 745–747; 750** examination of President Johnson's handling of the Vietnam War, from his decision to escalate America's involvement to his decision to seek an end to the war | **PE 753** Critical Thinking questions about events that prompted Johnson to seek an end to the fighting in Vietnam |
| **(20A)** Describe how the characteristics and issues of various eras in U.S. history have been reflected in works of art, music, and literature. | **PE 762–763** American Literature feature on the literature of the Vietnam War | **PE 763** Critical Thinking questions about the American Literature feature |

## TAKS MINI-LESSONS

1. **Social Studies Skills: Objective 1 (US1.B):** Apply absolute and relative chronology through the sequencing of significant events **Activity** Have students create a time line of significant events—domestic and abroad—surrounding the Vietnam War.

2. **Social Studies Skills: Objective 1 (US6.E):** Analyze the conflicts in Korea and Vietnam and describe their domestic and international effects **Activity** Have students discuss the reasons why the United States entered the Vietnam War and what impact U.S. involvement eventually had on the home front.

3. **Social Studies Skills: Objective 5 (WH26.C):** Interpret visuals including graphs, charts, time lines, and maps **Activity** Have students answer the skill-builder questions about the map of the Tet Offensive on page 749.

4. **English Language Arts Skills: Objective 3 (8.D):** Interpret possible influences of the historical context on literary works **Activity** Have students discuss how the literature examined on pages 762–763 reflected the nation's feelings about the Vietnam War.

5. **English Language Arts Skills: Objective 4 (19.B):** Analyze ideas as represented in various media **Activity** Have students answer the question regarding the visual source in the Section 3 Assessment on page 747.

CHAPTER 22 · OBJECTIVE

To understand the military and political events of the Vietnam War in Southeast Asia and its impact on life in the United States

# CHAPTER 22
# THE VIETNAM WAR YEARS

U.S. troops on patrol with helicopter support in Vietnam, 1965.

## HISTORY from VISUALS

### Interpreting the Photograph

Have students examine the photograph. Ask them why they think the soldiers are patrolling. What kind of support do they think the helicopters can provide? *(The soldiers are probably looking for enemy soldiers. Helicopters can move troops in and out of an area. They also may be able to spot danger from the air that soldiers on the ground cannot see.)*

### Time Line Discussion

Explain to students that the time line covers events in the United States and the world during the years 1954–1975. Ask students to use the time line to answer the following questions:

· What years were American combat troops in South Vietnam? *(1965–1973)*
· Who was the first president to send American combat troops to South Vietnam? *(Johnson)*
· What other examples of political upheaval in Asia appear on the time line? *(The Cultural Revolution in China; Marcos declares martial law in the Philippines; Six-Day War.)*

**USA**
**WORLD**

**1960**
**1965**

1960 John F. Kennedy is elected president.

1963 Kennedy is assassinated; Lyndon B. Johnson becomes president.

1964 Lyndon B. Johnson is elected president.

1965 First major U.S. combat units arrive in Vietnam.

1960 The National Liberation Front forms in South Vietnam.

1962 The African nation of Uganda becomes independent.

1966 Mao Zedong begins the Cultural Revolution in China.

1967 Israel captures Gaza Strip and West Bank in Six-Day War.

## THEMES IN CHAPTER 22

### AMERICA IN WORLD AFFAIRS

America's mission in Vietnam was to halt the spread of communism—a threat to democracy. Ironically, the South Vietnamese regimes that the U.S. supported were not very democratic themselves.

**See Teacher's Edition notes, pp. 731, 734.**

### CIVIL RIGHTS

Initially, mainstream civil rights leaders were reluctant to criticize the Vietnam War, fearing they would jeopardize President Johnson's support for their cause. When the war threatened Great Society reforms, Dr. Martin Luther King, Jr., and other civil rights leaders voiced their opposition.

**See Teacher's Edition note, p. 743.**

### DIVERSITY AND NATIONAL IDENTITY

Many Vietnamese refugees seeking a homeland in the United States at the end of the war developed a cultural identity that was a blend of two traditions—Vietnamese and American.

**See Teacher's Edition note, p. 760.**

# INTERACT
## WITH HISTORY

In 1965, America's fight against communism has spread to Southeast Asia, where the United States is becoming increasingly involved in another country's civil war. Unable to claim victory, U.S. generals call for an increase in the number of combat troops. Facing a shortage of volunteers, the president implements a draft.

## Who should be exempt from the draft?

### Examine the Issues

- Should people who believe the war is wrong be forced to fight?
- Should people with special skills be exempt?
- How can a draft be made fair?

**RESEARCH LINKS** CLASSZONE.COM

Visit the Chapter 22 links for more information about The Vietnam War Years.

# INTERACT
## WITH HISTORY

### Objectives

· To understand the political, social, and cultural issues of the draft in the Vietnam War
· To analyze the social implications when draft exemptions are offered to certain categories of people

### Examine the Issues

1. Discuss with students the difference between objecting to war in general and objecting to a particular war. What might happen to someone who is unwilling to fight because he believes war is wrong?
2. Tell students that a number of physicists were exempt from World War II because the government needed them to develop the atomic bomb. Have students give examples of others who, in their opinion, might reasonably be exempted from the draft.
3. Ask students to consider the fairness of drafting men only.

**1968** Martin Luther King, Jr., and Robert Kennedy are assassinated.

**1968** Richard M. Nixon is elected president.

**1969** U.S. troops begin their withdrawal from Vietnam.

**1970** Ohio National Guard kills four students at Kent State University.

**1972** Richard M. Nixon is reelected.

**1973** United States signs cease-fire with North Vietnam and Vietcong.

**1974** Gerald R. Ford becomes president after Richard M. Nixon resigns.

**1970**

**1975**

**1972** Ferdinand Marcos declares martial law in the Philippines.

**1975** Communists capture Saigon; South Vietnam surrenders.

*The Vietnam War Years* **729**

## RECOMMENDED RESOURCES

### BOOKS FOR THE TEACHER
Goldman, Eric F. *The Tragedy of Lyndon Johnson.* New York: Knopf, 1969. Johnson's presidency, including the Vietnam War.

Karnow, Stanley. *Vietnam.* New York: Penguin Books, 1997. Thorough survey of the Vietnam War.

Wells, Tom. *The War Within.* New York: Holt, 1996. Polarization of American society over Vietnam.

### BOOKS FOR THE STUDENT
Caputo, Philip. *A Rumor of War.* New York, Ballantine, 1996. Compelling combat memoir.

McNamara, Robert. *In Retrospect.* New York: Vintage, 1996. Former secretary of defense's later thoughts on war.

Terry, Wallace. *Bloods.* New York: Ballantine, 1984. African-American veterans' oral histories of the Vietnam War.

### VIDEOS
*Chicago 1968.* PBS Home Video, 1995. Story of Democratic convention.

*Fall of Saigon.* Discovery Channel Home Video, 1995. Last days of South Vietnam.

*No Time for Tears: Vietnam; The Women Who Served.* West End Films, 1993. Documentary about women's experiences in Vietnam.

### SOFTWARE
*Passage to Vietnam.* CD-ROM. Against All Odds/Interval Research, 1995.

*The Wall.* CD-ROM. Interactive, 1995.

*The War in Vietnam: A Multimedia Chronicle.* CD-ROM. Macmillan Digital, 212-654-8500.

### INTEGRATED TECHNOLOGY
For teacher support, visit . . .

 classzone.com

# OBJECTIVES

**1** Summarize Vietnam's history as a French colony and its struggle for independence.

**2** Examine how the United States became involved in the Vietnam conflict.

**3** Describe the expansion of U.S. military involvement under President Johnson.

## SKILLBUILDER
· Geography Skillbuilder: movement, location, p. 733

## CRITICAL THINKING
· Synthesizing, p. 731
· Analyzing Motives, p. 732
· Forming Generalizations, p. 734
· Developing Historical Perspective, p. 735
· Making Inferences, p. 735
· Synthesizing, p. 735
· Evaluating, p. 735

# Focus & Motivate

Ask students how they would respond if, in attempting to solve a problem, they found more complications instead of a solution.

# Instruct

## Instruct: Objective **1**

### America Supports France In Vietnam
TAKS SS11 5(US24.A)
· When did France rule Vietnam?
· Who were the Vietminh and what were they fighting for?
· What happened at Dien Bien Phu?
· What did the Geneva Accords do to Vietnam?

 In-Depth Resources: Unit 6
· Guided Reading, p. 39

# Moving Toward Conflict

| MAIN IDEA | WHY IT MATTERS NOW | Terms & Names |
|---|---|---|
| To stop the spread of communism in Southeast Asia, the United States used its military to support South Vietnam. | The United States' support role in Vietnam began what would become America's longest and most controversial war in its history. | • Ho Chi Minh  • Ngo Dinh Diem<br>• Vietminh  • Vietcong<br>• domino theory  • Ho Chi Minh Trail<br>• Dien Bien Phu  • Tonkin Gulf<br>• Geneva Accords  Resolution |

**TEKS** U.S. History 6E, 8A, 8B, 9A, 16A, 19A, 19B, 19C, 24B, 24C, 25A, 25B, 25C, 25D

## One American's Story

On the morning of September 26, 1945, Lieutenant Colonel A. Peter Dewey was on his way to the Saigon airport in Vietnam. Only 28, Dewey served in the Office of Strategic Services, the chief intelligence-gathering body of the U.S. military and forerunner of the Central Intelligence Agency. Dewey was sent to assess what was becoming an explosive situation in Vietnam, a Southeast Asian country that had recently been freed from Japanese rule as a result of the allied victory in World War II. (See map on page 733.)

Before the war, France had ruled Vietnam and the surrounding countries; now it sought—with British aid—to regain control of the region. The Vietnamese had resisted Japanese occupation; now they were preparing to fight the French. Dewey saw nothing but disaster in France's plan. "Cochinchina [southern Vietnam] is burning," he reported, "the French and British are finished here, and we [the United States] ought to clear out of Southeast Asia."

On his way to the airport, Dewey encountered a roadblock staffed by Vietnamese soldiers and shouted at them in French. Presumably mistaking him for a French soldier, the guards shot him in the head. Thus, A. Peter Dewey, whose body was never recovered, was the first American to die in Vietnam.

Unfortunately, Dewey would not be the last. As Vietnam's independence effort came under communist influence, the United States grew increasingly concerned about the small country's future. Eventually, America would fight a war to halt the spread of communism in Vietnam. The war would claim the lives of almost 60,000 Americans and more than 2 million Vietnamese. It also would divide the American nation as no other event since the Civil War.

▲ Lieutenant Colonel A. Peter Dewey

## **1** America Supports France in Vietnam

America's involvement in Vietnam began in 1950, during the French Indochina War, the name given to France's attempt to reestablish its rule in Vietnam after World War II. Seeking to strengthen its ties with France and to help fight the spread of communism, the United States provided the French with massive economic and military support.

**730** CHAPTER 22

---

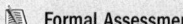

**FRENCH RULE IN VIETNAM** From the late 1800s until World War II, France ruled most of Indochina, including Vietnam, Laos, and Cambodia. French colonists, who built plantations on peasant land and extracted rice and rubber for their own profit, encountered growing unrest among the Vietnamese peasants. French rulers reacted harshly by restricting freedom of speech and assembly and by jailing many Vietnamese nationalists. These measures failed to curb all dissent, and opposition continued to grow.

The Indochinese Communist Party, founded in 1930, staged a number of revolts under the leadership of **Ho Chi Minh.** Although the French condemned Ho Chi Minh to death for his rebellious activity, he fled Vietnam and orchestrated Vietnam's growing independence movement from exile in the Soviet Union and later from China.

In 1940 the Japanese took control of Vietnam. The next year, Ho Chi Minh returned home and helped form the **Vietminh,** an organization whose goal it was to win Vietnam's independence from foreign rule. When the Allied defeat of Japan in August 1945 forced the Japanese to leave Vietnam, that goal suddenly seemed a reality. On September 2, 1945, Ho Chi Minh stood in the middle of a huge crowd in the northern city of Hanoi and declared Vietnam an independent nation.

**FRANCE BATTLES THE VIETMINH** France, however, had no intention of relinquishing its former colony. French troops moved back into Vietnam by the end of 1945, eventually regaining control of the cities and the country's southern half. Ho Chi Minh vowed to fight from the North to liberate the South from French control. "If ever the tiger pauses," Ho had said, referring to the Vietminh, "the elephant [France] will impale him on his mighty tusks. But the tiger will not pause, and the elephant will die of exhaustion and loss of blood."

In 1950, the United States entered the Vietnam struggle—despite A. Peter Dewey's warnings. That year, President Truman sent nearly $15 million in economic aid to France. Over the next four years, the United States paid for much of France's war, pumping nearly $1 billion into the effort to defeat a man America had once supported. Ironically, during World War II, the United States had forged an alliance with Ho Chi Minh, supplying him with aid to resist the Japanese. But by 1950, the United States had come to view its one-time ally as a communist aggressor. **A**

**THE VIETMINH DRIVE OUT THE FRENCH** Upon entering the White House in 1953, President Eisenhower continued the policy of supplying aid to the French war effort. By this time, the United States had settled for a stalemate with the communists in Korea, which only stiffened America's resolve to halt the spread of communism elsewhere. During a news conference in 1954, Eisenhower explained the **domino theory,** in which he likened the countries on the brink of communism to a row of dominoes waiting to fall one after the other. "You have a row of dominoes set up," the president said. "You knock over the first one, and what will happen to the last one is the certainty that it will go over very quickly."

Despite massive U.S. aid, however, the French could not retake Vietnam. They were forced to surrender in May of 1954, when the Vietminh overran the French outpost at **Dien Bien Phu,** in northwestern Vietnam.

*The Vietnam War Years* **731**

---

**Vocabulary**
**peasant:** a member of the class of agricultural laborers

**MAIN IDEA**
**Synthesizing**
**A** How and why did the United States support France's Vietnam War efforts?

*A. Answer* The United States provided France with economic and military support. The goals were to keep France as an ally and to keep communism from spreading.

---

## KEY PLAYER

**HO CHI MINH**
**1890–1969**

Born Nguyen Tat Thanh to a poor Vietnamese family, Ho Chi Minh (which means "He Who Enlightens") found work as a cook on a French steamship. This allowed him to visit such cities as Boston and New York.

Ho Chi Minh based the phrasing of the Vietnamese Declaration of Independence on the U.S. Declaration of Independence. His admiration for the United States turned to disappointment, however, after the government chose to support France rather than his nationalist movement.

The Communist ruler's name lived on after his death in 1969. In 1975, the North Vietnamese Army conquered South Vietnam and changed the name of the South's capital from Saigon to Ho Chi Minh City.

---

## KEY PLAYER

**Ho Chi Minh**
Ho Chi Minh lived in France from 1917 to 1923. There he became a socialist and organized Vietnamese émigrés living in France. In 1919, he addressed the Paris Peace Conference at Versailles, where he demanded equal rights for France's colonial subjects in Indochina. His demand went unheeded. Have students discuss how this action was consistent with the role he later played in Vietnam.

---

## Tracing Themes
### AMERICA IN WORLD AFFAIRS

**America and the Cold War**
The U.S. decision to assist France in its fight to retake Vietnam stemmed from American global concerns during the Cold War era. As the Iron Curtain descended in eastern Europe, the United States could not afford to antagonize France, an important European ally against Soviet encroachments in that region. In Asia, the fall of China to communism in the late 1940s intensified Western fears of the growing threat of Communist power worldwide, and the spread of communism to North Korea gave additional support to the domino theory.

---

**ACTIVITY** | **LINK TO WORLD HISTORY**

 **BLOCK SCHEDULING**

### Chinese Influence in Vietnam

**Class Time** 45 minutes

**Task** Documenting and preparing a feature article on the influence of China and France on Vietnam

**Purpose** To analyze the effects of foreign domination on Vietnamese culture

**Directions** Have students research and write a report giving basic facts (such as dates of conquest and eventual independence) regarding the conquest of Vietnam by China and by France and the impact of foreign cultures on that of Vietnam. Students should also look for evidence regarding the effect of foreign domination on Vietnamese desire to be independent. Then have students work in small groups to combine their findings into a feature article.

📖 Integrated Assessment
· Rubrics 1, 5

From May through July 1954, the countries of France, Great Britain, the Soviet Union, the United States, China, Laos, and Cambodia met in Geneva, Switzerland, with the Vietminh and with South Vietnam's anticommunist nationalists to hammer out a peace agreement. The **Geneva Accords** temporarily divided Vietnam along the 17th parallel. The Communists and their leader, Ho Chi Minh, controlled North Vietnam from the capital of Hanoi. The anticommunist nationalists controlled South Vietnam from the capital and southern port city of Saigon. An election to unify the country was called for in 1956.

## ❷ The United States Steps In

In the wake of France's retreat, the United States took a more active role in halting the spread of communism in Vietnam. Wading deeper into the country's affairs, the Eisenhower and the Kennedy administrations provided economic and military aid to South Vietnam's non-Communist regime.

**DIEM CANCELS ELECTIONS** Although he directed a brutal and repressive regime, Ho Chi Minh won popular support in the North by breaking up large estates and redistributing land to peasants. Moreover, his years of fighting the Japanese and French had made him a national hero. Recognizing Ho Chi Minh's widespread popularity, South Vietnam's president, **Ngo Dinh Diem** (ngō′ dĭn′ dē-ĕm′), a strong anti-Communist, refused to take part in the countryside election of 1956. The United States also sensed that a countrywide election might spell victory for Ho Chi Minh and supported canceling elections. The Eisenhower administration promised military aid and training to Diem in return for a stable reform government in the South. **B**

Diem, however, failed to hold up his end of the bargain. He ushered in a corrupt government that suppressed opposition of any kind and offered little or no land distribution to peasants. In addition, Diem, a devout Catholic, angered the country's majority Buddhist population by restricting Buddhist practices.

By 1957, a Communist opposition group in the South, known as the **Vietcong,** had begun attacks on the Diem government, assassinating thousands of South Vietnamese government officials. Although the political arm of the group would later be called the National Liberation Front (NLF), the United States continued to refer to the fighters as the Vietcong.

Ho Chi Minh supported the group, and in 1959 began supplying arms to the Vietcong via a network of paths along the borders of Vietnam, Laos, and Cambodia that became known as the **Ho Chi Minh Trail.** (See map on page 733.) As the fighters stepped up their surprise attacks, or guerrilla tactics, South Vietnam grew more unstable. The Eisenhower administration took little action, however, deciding to "sink or swim with Ngo Dinh Diem."

**KENNEDY AND VIETNAM** The Kennedy administration, which entered the White House in 1961, also chose initially to "swim" with Diem. Wary of accusations that Democrats were "soft" on communism, President Kennedy increased financial aid to Diem's teetering regime and sent thousands of military advisers to help train South Vietnamese troops. By the end of 1963, 16,000 U.S. military personnel were in South Vietnam.

Meanwhile, Diem's popularity plummeted because of ongoing corruption and his failure to respond to calls for land reform. To combat the growing Vietcong presence in the South's countryside, the Diem administration initiated the strategic hamlet program, which meant moving all villagers to protected areas.

---

## Instruct: Objective ❷
### The United States Steps In
TAKS SS11 1(US6.E)
· Why did Diem cancel elections?
· Why did Kennedy decide to support Diem?
· Why did Diem's popularity plummet?

 In-Depth Resources: Unit 6
· Guided Reading, p. 39

---

### More About . . .

#### Vietcong
The Vietcong was a classic guerrilla force, with its members organized into cells, or small groups, that included men, women, and children. Many of its members fulfilled ordinary roles in society and then, at night, slipped off to fight or sabotage South Vietnamese installations. Villagers knew who was in the Vietcong but refused to identify them to South Vietnamese and American authorities, either out of loyalty to the Communists, fear, or both.

---

### HISTORY from VISUALS

#### Interpreting the Propaganda Poster
Discuss how propaganda is used in wartime to build support for government policy. Ask students whether they think that the use of propaganda is acceptable. Then ask how the poster on page 732 might have generated support for the Vietcong. *(It suggests that the Vietnamese people must fight the United States for their freedom or become oppressed.)*

---

Mini-Lesson 2:
SS11 1(US6.E)

The Vietcong saw the United States and South Vietnam as oppressors. This Vietcong propaganda poster reads, "Better death than slavery."

越南必胜！美国必败！

---

*B. Answer* Because it appeared that Ho Chi Minh would win the election and possibly unify Vietnam under communism.

**MAIN IDEA**

**Analyzing Motives**
**B** Why did the United States support canceling elections?

**Background**
The Buddhist religion is based on the teachings of Siddhartha Gautama, also known as Shakyamuni, an Indian mystic who believed that spiritual enlightenment could be obtained through right conduct.

*Skillbuilder Answers*
**1.** Laos and Cambodia.
**2.** Since China borders North Vietnam, it could easily deliver military and other supplies to North Vietnam.

---

 **BLOCK SCHEDULING**

### Division of Vietnam

**Class Time** 30 minutes

**Task** Creating a chart, map, and summary of the changes in Indochina as a result of the Geneva Accords

**Purpose** To draw conclusions about the effect of the Geneva Accords on Indochina

**Directions** Have pairs of students research and chart the changes in the governments of the countries in Indochina as a result of the Geneva Accords. Next they should create a map showing the territorial changes that resulted from the Accords. Finally, they should write a summary statement identifying the effects of the Geneva Accords on the region.

**Indochina, 1959**

CHINA

Red River

NORTH VIETNAM

Dien Bien Phu • Hanoi
• Haiphong

LAOS

Gulf of Tonkin

BURMA

Vientiane ⊕

Mekong River

THAILAND

17th Parallel

Hue •
Da Nang •
My Lai •

Bangkok ⊕

CAMBODIA

Ho Chi Minh Trail

SOUTH VIETNAM

Phnom Penh ⊕

Cam Ranh Bay •

Saigon •

Gulf of Thailand

South China Sea

105°E

0   300   300 miles
0   300   300 kilometers

N W E S

Equator

After parachuting into the mountains north of Dien Bien Phu, South Vietnamese troops await orders from French officers in 1953.

## HISTORY from VISUALS

### Interpreting Maps

Explain that *parallel* refers to a line of latitude. Why is the 17th parallel labeled on the map? *(to indicate the provisional border between North Vietnam and South Vietnam)*

**Extension** Explain that many Vietnamese think that the shape of their country resembles two rice baskets dangling from a bamboo pole. Ask students to discuss the possible significance of this comparison.

## More About . . .

### Ho Chi Minh Trail

The Ho Chi Minh Trail, initiated in 1959, was made up of a series of mountain roads and jungle paths. The trail was used to move North Vietnamese troops and supplies from the north to the south. The trip took about a month. It followed a system of trails that moved along the mountains that divide Vietnam from Laos and Cambodia. By the late 1960s, heavy trucks actually operated on the trails, and there were underground depots that supplied fuel, weapons, supplies, and even medical help.

The swampy terrain of South Vietnam made for difficult and dangerous fighting. This 1961 photograph shows South Vietnamese Army troops in combat operations against Vietcong guerrillas.

Rivers serve as places to bathe and wash clothing.

### GEOGRAPHY SKILLBUILDER

1. **Movement** Through which countries did the Ho Chi Minh Trail pass?
2. **Location** How might North Vietnam's location have enabled it to get aid from its ally, China?

*The Vietnam War Years* **733**

---

**ACTIVITY** | **LINK TO GEOGRAPHY**

**Class Time** 45 minutes

**Task** Researching and creating a chart showing the relationship between climactic and topographical features and the U.S. military effort in Vietnam

**Purpose** To identify problems posed by the environment to the U.S. military in Vietnam

**Directions** Have students work in small groups. Tell them to use atlases and other resources to determine topographical features, climactic conditions, and types of vegetation that placed U.S. soldiers at a disadvantage. Have them copy the chart at right and add to it. Compile a composite chart using an oversized sheet of paper or posterboard.

**BLOCK SCHEDULING**

| Climate/Topography | Military Disadvantage |
|---|---|
| monsoons—heavy seasonal rains | reduced visibility, slippery terrain, washed-out roads |
| | |
| | |

A Buddhist monk sets himself on fire in a busy Saigon intersection in 1963 as a protest against the Diem regime. ▶

## History Through *Photojournalism*

### Interpreting a Photograph

Tell students that Buddhist monks practiced self-immolation (setting oneself on fire) as a means of protest.

Ask students to speculate on how this photograph and similar images affected the American public. *(Most people were horrified. It was an extreme method for bringing the plight and concerns of Vietnamese Buddhists to the forefront.)*

## Instruct: Objective ❸

### President Johnson Expands the Conflict

TAKS SS11 1(US6.E)

· Why did South Vietnam become increasingly unstable?

· What was the Gulf of Tonkin Resolution?

· What did President Johnson do in response to a Vietcong attack in February 1965?

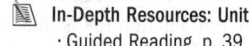 In-Depth Resources: Unit 6
· Guided Reading, p. 39

 Electronic Library of Primary Sources
· The Tonkin Gulf Resolution, 1964, by U.S. Congress

## Tracing Themes

### AMERICA IN WORLD AFFAIRS

U.S. involvement in Vietnam was a mission to halt the spread of Communism, which was perceived as a threat to democracy and free market economies. Le Ly Hayslip, who grew up in Central Vietnam, saw the struggle from a different perspective. In her autobiography, *When Heaven and Earth Changed Places*, she wrote, "For you [American GI's], it was a simple thing: democracy against communism. For us, that was not our fight at all. How could it be? We knew little democracy and even less about communism. For most of us, it was a fight of independence—like the American Revolution."

Many Vietnamese deeply resented being moved from their home villages where they had lived for generations and where ancestors were buried.

Diem also intensified his attack on Buddhism. Fed up with continuing Buddhist demonstrations, the South Vietnamese ruler imprisoned and killed hundreds of Buddhist clerics and destroyed their temples. To protest, several Buddhist monks and nuns publicly burned themselves to death. Horrified, American officials urged Diem to stop the persecutions, but Diem refused. **C**

It had become clear that for South Vietnam to remain stable, Diem would have to go. On November 1, 1963, a U.S.-supported military coup toppled Diem's regime. Against Kennedy's wishes, Diem was assassinated. A few weeks later, Kennedy, too, fell to an assassin's bullet. The United States presidency—along with the growing crisis in Vietnam—now belonged to Lyndon B. Johnson.

### ❸ President Johnson Expands the Conflict

Shortly before his death, Kennedy had announced his intent to withdraw U.S. forces from South Vietnam. "In the final analysis, it's their war," he declared. Whether Kennedy would have withdrawn from Vietnam remains a matter of debate. However, Lyndon Johnson escalated the nation's role in Vietnam and eventually began what would become America's longest war.

**THE SOUTH GROWS MORE UNSTABLE** Diem's death brought more chaos to South Vietnam. A string of military leaders attempted to lead the country, but each regime was more unstable and inefficient than Diem's had been. Meanwhile, the Vietcong's influence in the countryside steadily grew.

President Johnson believed that a communist takeover of South Vietnam would be disastrous. Johnson, like Kennedy, was particularly sensitive to being perceived as "soft" on communism. "If I . . . let the communists take over South Vietnam," Johnson said, "then . . . my nation would be seen as an appeaser and we would . . . find it impossible to accomplish anything . . . anywhere on the entire globe."

**THE TONKIN GULF RESOLUTION** On August 2, 1964, a North Vietnamese patrol boat fired a torpedo at an American destroyer, the U.S.S. *Maddox*, which was patrolling in the Gulf of Tonkin off the North Vietnamese coast. The torpedo missed its target, but the *Maddox* returned fire and inflicted heavy damage on the patrol boat.

**MAIN IDEA**

**Forming Generalizations**
**C** Why was the Diem regime unpopular?

**Vocabulary**
**coup:** a sudden appropriation of leadership; a takeover

*C. Answer*
Corruption, repressive tactics, and persecution of Buddhists.

**734** CHAPTER 22

---

**ACTIVITY** **COOPERATIVE LEARNING**

 **classzone.com**

### Researching Buddhism

**Class Time** 45 minutes

**Task** Researching and evaluating the role of Buddhist monks in opposing the Diem regime

**Purpose** To evaluate the political effect of Buddhists' opposition to the Diem regime

**Directions** Tell students that Buddhist monks were some of the strongest opponents of the Diem regime. Have pairs of students use library and Internet resources to research the causes, manifestations, and results of Buddhist opposition. Then they should write an evaluation of the political effects of the opposition.

 Integrated Assessment
· Rubrics 1, 2, 5

# The New York Times.

"All the News That's Fit to Print"

LATE CITY EDITION

VOL. CXIII—No. 38,910.

NEW YORK, WEDNESDAY, AUGUST 5, 1964.

TEN CENTS

## U.S. PLANES ATTACK NORTH VIETNAM BASES; PRESIDENT ORDERS 'LIMITED' RETALIATION AFTER COMMUNISTS' PT BOATS RENEW RAIDS

Two days later, the *Maddox* and another destroyer were again off the North Vietnamese coast. In spite of bad weather that could affect visibility, the crew reported enemy torpedoes, and the American destroyers began firing. The crew of the *Maddox* later declared, however, that they had neither seen nor heard hostile gunfire.

The alleged attack on the U.S. ships prompted President Johnson to launch bombing strikes on North Vietnam. He asked Congress for powers to take "all necessary measures to repel any armed attack against the forces of the United States and to prevent further aggression." Congress approved Johnson's request, with only two senators voting against it, and adopted the **Tonkin Gulf Resolution** on August 7. While not a declaration of war, it granted Johnson broad military powers in Vietnam.

Johnson did not tell Congress or the American people that the United States had been leading secret raids against North Vietnam. The *Maddox* had been in the Gulf of Tonkin to collect information for these raids. Furthermore, Johnson had prepared the resolution months beforehand and was only waiting for the chance to push it through Congress.

In February of 1965, President Johnson used his newly granted powers. In response to a Vietcong attack that killed eight Americans, Johnson unleashed "Operation Rolling Thunder," the first sustained bombing of North Vietnam. In March of that year the first American combat troops began arriving in South Vietnam. By June, more than 50,000 U.S. soldiers were battling the Vietcong. The Vietnam War had become Americanized. **D**

A 1964 newspaper headline announces the U.S. military's reaction to the Gulf of Tonkin incident.

**D. Answer** It gave Johnson broad authority to widen America's role in the war.

**MAIN IDEA**

Developing Historical Perspective
**D** How did the Tonkin Gulf Resolution lead to greater U.S. involvement in the Vietnam War?

---

**Tonkin Gulf Resolution**
During the debate over this resolution, Senator Wayne Morse of Oregon (one of only two senators to oppose the resolution) predicted, "I believe that history will record that we have made a great mistake in subverting and circumventing the Constitution of the United States, article 1, section 8 thereof [which gives Congress the power to declare war] by means of this resolution . . ." Morse's words were prophetic. In 1973, Congress passed the War Powers Act to curb the president's war-making powers.

## Assess & Reteach

**SECTION 1 ASSESSMENT**
Students might work in pairs to respond to the questions.

 Formal Assessment
· Section Quiz, p. 406

**SELF-ASSESSMENT**
To assess what they have learned, students can write their own questions, exchange them with partners, and try to answer one another's questions.

**RETEACH**
Use the map and other marginal features in Section 1 to help review the main ideas of this section.

 In-Depth Resources: Unit 6
· Reteaching Activity, p. 46

---

## SECTION 1 ASSESSMENT

**1. TERMS & NAMES** For each term or name, write a sentence explaining its significance.

- Ho Chi Minh
- Vietminh
- domino theory
- Dien Bien Phu
- Geneva Accords
- Ngo Dinh Diem
- Vietcong
- Ho Chi Minh Trail
- Tonkin Gulf Resolution

### MAIN IDEA

**2. TAKING NOTES**
In a chart like the one below, cite the Vietnam policy for each of the following presidents: Truman, Eisenhower, Kennedy, and Johnson.

| President | Vietnam Policy |
|-----------|----------------|
|           |                |
|           |                |

Choose one of the four presidents and explain his goals in Vietnam.

### CRITICAL THINKING

**3. MAKING INFERENCES**
How did the United States become more involved in the war? Explain your answer in a short paragraph.

**4. SYNTHESIZING**
In what ways was America's support of the Diem government a conflict of interests? Cite examples to support your answer.

**5. EVALUATING**
Do you think Congress was justified in passing the Tonkin Gulf Resolution? Use details from the text to support your response.
**Think About:**
- the questionable report of torpedo attacks on two U.S. destroyers
- the powers that the resolution would give the president
- the fact that the resolution was not a declaration of war

*The Vietnam War Years* **735**

---

Answers ASSESSMENT

**1. TERMS & NAMES**
Ho Chi Minh, p. 731
Vietminh, p. 731
domino theory, p. 731
Dien Bien Phu, p. 731
Geneva Accords, p. 732
Ngo Dinh Diem, p. 732
Vietcong, p. 732
Ho Chi Minh Trail, p. 732
Tonkin Gulf Resolution, p. 735

**2. TAKING NOTES**
Policies: Truman–economic aid to France; Eisenhower–economic and military aid to South Vietnam; Kennedy–economic aid and military advisers; Johnson–stepped-up U.S. military involvement. Goals: Truman–containing communism; Eisenhower–preventing domino theory; Kennedy–avoiding appearing "soft" on communism; Johnson–preventing control of Vietnam by Communists.

**3. MAKING INFERENCES**
The United States provided France with support when France was trying to reestablish its rule in Vietnam. After the French were forced to surrender, the United States began supplying aid directly to South Vietnam's noncommunist regime.

**4. SYNTHESIZING**
The Diem government was corrupt and unstable. Diem cancelled elections and attacked Buddhism. Nonetheless, the United States continued to support the regime.

**5. EVALUATING**
Yes–Presidential authority should be broadened in response to emergency situations. No–The circumstances surrounding the North Vietnamese attack were not adequately verified.

# U.S. Involvement and Escalation

| MAIN IDEA | WHY IT MATTERS NOW | Terms & Names |
|---|---|---|
| The United States sent troops to fight in Vietnam, but the war quickly turned into a stalemate. | Since Vietnam, Americans are more aware of the positive and negative effects of using U.S. troops in foreign conflicts. | • Robert McNamara • Dean Rusk • William Westmoreland • Army of the Republic of Vietnam (ARVN) • napalm • Agent Orange • search-and-destroy mission • credibility gap |

 U.S. History 6E, 8A, 9A, 22B, 24B, 25A, 25B, 25D

### One American's Story

Tim O'Brien is a novelist who has written several books about his experience in Vietnam and its lasting effects. Drafted at the age of 21, O'Brien was sent to Vietnam in August 1968. He spent the first seven months of his nearly two-year duty patrolling the fields outside of Chu Lai, a seacoast city in South Vietnam. O'Brien described one of the more nerve-racking experiences of the war: walking through the fields and jungles, many of which were filled with land mines and booby traps.

**A PERSONAL VOICE** TIM O'BRIEN

" You do some thinking. You hallucinate. You look ahead a few paces and wonder what your legs will resemble if there is more to the earth in that spot than silicates and nitrogen. Will the pain be unbearable? Will you scream and fall silent? Will you be afraid to look at your own body, afraid of the sight of your own red flesh and white bone? . . .

It is not easy to fight this sort of self-defeating fear, but you try. You decide to be ultra-careful—the hard-nosed realistic approach. You try to second-guess the mine. Should you put your foot to that flat rock or the clump of weeds to its rear? Paddy dike or water? You wish you were Tarzan, able to swing on the vines. You trace the footprints of the men to your front. You give up when he curses you for following too closely; better one man dead than two. "

—quoted in *A Life in a Year: The American Infantryman in Vietnam 1965–1972*

Deadly traps were just some of the obstacles that U.S. troops faced. As the infiltration of American ground troops into Vietnam failed to score a quick victory, a mostly supportive U.S. population began to question its government's war policy.

▲ Vietnam's terrain was often treacherous, such as the thick jungles and rivers these U.S. soldiers encountered in 1966.

## **1** Johnson Increases U.S. Involvement

Much of the nation supported Lyndon Johnson's determination to contain communism in Vietnam. In the years following 1965, President Johnson began sending large numbers of American troops to fight alongside the South Vietnamese.

**STRONG SUPPORT FOR CONTAINMENT** Even after Congress had approved the Tonkin Gulf Resolution, President Johnson opposed sending U.S. ground troops to Vietnam. Johnson's victory in the 1964 presidential election was due in part to charges that his Republican opponent, Barry Goldwater, was an anti-Communist who might push the United States into war with the Soviet Union. In contrast to Goldwater's heated, warlike language, Johnson's speeches were more moderate, yet he spoke determinedly about containing communism. He declared he was "not about to send American boys 9 or 10,000 miles away from home to do what Asian boys ought to be doing for themselves."

However, in March of 1965, that is precisely what the president did. Working closely with his foreign-policy advisers, particularly Secretary of Defense **Robert McNamara** and Secretary of State **Dean Rusk,** President Johnson began dispatching tens of thousands of U.S. soldiers to fight in Vietnam. Some Americans viewed Johnson's decision as contradictory to his position during the presidential campaign. However, most saw the president as following an established and popular policy of confronting communism anywhere in the world. Congress, as well as the American public, strongly supported Johnson's strategy. A 1965 poll showed that 61 percent of Americans supported the U.S. policy in Vietnam, while only 24 percent opposed.

There were dissenters within the Johnson administration, too. In October of 1964, Undersecretary of State George Ball had argued against escalation, warning that "once on the tiger's back, we cannot be sure of picking the place to dismount." However, the president's closest advisers strongly urged escalation, believing the defeat of communism in Vietnam to be of vital importance to the future of America and the world. Dean Rusk stressed this view in a 1965 memo to President Johnson. **Ⓐ**

### A PERSONAL VOICE DEAN RUSK

" The integrity of the U.S. commitment is the principal pillar of peace throughout the world. If that commitment becomes unreliable, the communist world would draw conclusions that would lead to our ruin and *almost certainly to a catastrophic war.* So long as the South Vietnamese are prepared to fight for themselves, we cannot abandon them without disaster to peace and to our interests throughout the world."

—quoted in *In Retrospect*

**THE TROOP BUILDUP ACCELERATES** By the end of 1965, the U.S. government had sent more than 180,000 Americans to Vietnam. The American commander in South Vietnam, General **William Westmoreland,** continued to request more troops. Westmoreland, a West Point graduate who had served in World War II and Korea, was less than impressed with the fighting ability of the South Vietnamese Army, or the **Army of the Republic of Vietnam (ARVN).** The ARVN "cannot stand up to this pressure without substantial U.S. combat support on the ground," the general reported. "The only possible response is the aggressive deployment of U.S. troops." Throughout the early years of the war, the Johnson administration complied with Westmoreland's requests; by 1967, the number of U.S. troops in Vietnam had climbed to about 500,000.

---

**MAIN IDEA**

**Contrasting**
Ⓐ What differing opinions did Johnson's advisers have about Vietnam?

*A. Answer*
Some argued for U.S. escalation in Vietnam, claiming it was vital to stop the spread of communism. George Ball argued against escalation, believing it would be easier to get into the Vietnam War than to get out.

---

## KEY PLAYER

**GENERAL WILLIAM WESTMORELAND (1914– )**

General Westmoreland retired from the military in 1972, but even in retirement, he could not escape the Vietnam War.

In 1982, CBS-TV aired a documentary entitled *The Uncounted Enemy: A Vietnam Deception.* The report, viewed by millions, asserted that Westmoreland and the Pentagon had deceived the U.S. government about the enemy's size and strength during 1967 and 1968 to make it appear that U.S. forces were winning the war.

Westmoreland, claiming he was the victim of "distorted, false, and specious information . . . derived by sinister deception," filed a $120 million libel suit against CBS. The suit was eventually settled, with both parties issuing statements pledging mutual respect. CBS, however, stood by its story.

---

## KEY PLAYER

**General William Westmoreland**
Vietnam was the first American war in which the press and television had access to first-hand information that was not censored relative to its use. Though journalists tried to balance their reports, it soon became clear that there was a discrepancy between the optimistic claims made by the U.S. military and the reality of the situation. Ask: If Westmoreland did indeed manipulate numbers, what might have been his motive in doing so? *(to boost the morale of his troops and the American public and to maintain the political support he needed to continue fighting the war)*

---

### More About . . .

**Army of the Republic of Vietnam (ARVN)**
The United States trained and equipped ARVN, which included many talented officers and well-armed and trained fighting men. Yet ARVN never was able to stand on its own. Despite all the military advantages provided by the United States, ARVN failed to develop the commitment and will necessary to persevere and win a war.

*The Vietnam War Years* **737**

---

ACTIVITY  SKILLBUILDER LESSON

## Distinguishing Fact From Opinion

**Explaining the Skill** Remind students that facts include events, dates, statistics, and statements that are verifiable. Opinions are personal judgments or beliefs.

**Applying the Skill** Have students work in small groups to make lists of statements of fact and of opinion that appear on page 737. Remind them that poll results reflect opinions. *(Facts: After the Tonkin Gulf Resolution, Johnson voiced opposition for sending ground troops to Vietnam. In March 1965, Johnson sent tens of thousands of U.S. soldiers to Vietnam. George Ball opposed escalation. By the end of 1965, there were more than 180,000 Americans in Vietnam.*

*Westmoreland continued to request more troops. Opinions: Some Americans viewed Johnson's actions as contradictory. The president's closest advisors believed the defeat of communism to be of vital importance. Westmoreland believed that ARVN "cannot stand up to this pressure . . .")*

In-Depth Resources: Unit 6
· Skillbuilder Practice: Distinguishing Fact from Opinion, p. 45

## Instruct: Objective

### Fighting in the Jungle

TAKS SS11 2(US29.A)

· What tactics did the Vietcong use?

· What results did the Vietcong achieve?

· Why did U.S. troops have morale problems?

· How did the conduct of the South Vietnamese government affect the way the war was conducted?

 In-Depth Resources: Unit 6
· Guided Reading, pp. 40

##  Fighting in the Jungle

The United States entered the war in Vietnam believing that its superior weaponry would lead it to victory over the Vietcong. However, the jungle terrain and the enemy's guerrilla tactics soon turned the war into a frustrating stalemate.

**AN ELUSIVE ENEMY** Because the Vietcong lacked the high-powered weaponry of the American forces, they used hit-and-run and ambush tactics, as well as a keen knowledge of the jungle terrain, to their advantage. Moving secretly in and out of the general population, the Vietcong destroyed the notion of a traditional front line by attacking U.S. troops in both the cities and the countryside. Because some of the enemy lived amidst the civilian population, it was difficult for U.S. troops to discern friend from foe. A woman selling soft drinks to U.S. soldiers might be a Vietcong spy. A boy standing on the corner might be ready to throw a grenade.

Adding to the Vietcong's elusiveness was a network of elaborate tunnels that allowed them to withstand airstrikes and to launch surprise attacks and then disappear quickly. Connecting villages throughout the countryside, the tunnels became home to many guerrilla fighters. "The more the Americans tried to drive us away from our land, the more we burrowed into it," recalled Major Nguyen Quot of the Vietcong Army.

In addition, the terrain was laced with countless booby traps and land mines. Because the exact location of the Vietcong was often unknown, U.S. troops laid land mines throughout the jungle. The Vietcong also laid their own traps, and disassembled and reused U.S. mines. American soldiers marching through South

## HISTORY from VISUALS

### Interpreting the Illustration

Have students study the illustration carefully. Discuss any prior experiences they have had with tunnels, such as observing ant farms or making sand tunnels at the beach. Then ask them to consider the efficacy of the Vietcong's adaptation to the superior firepower of the United States. Ask students to describe the technology each side brought to the struggle and which side's technology was better suited to the terrain and type of war that was fought. *(The very low-tech Vietcong response to American higher technology and firepower was better suited to the terrain and terms of warfare.)*

### Tunnels of the Vietcong

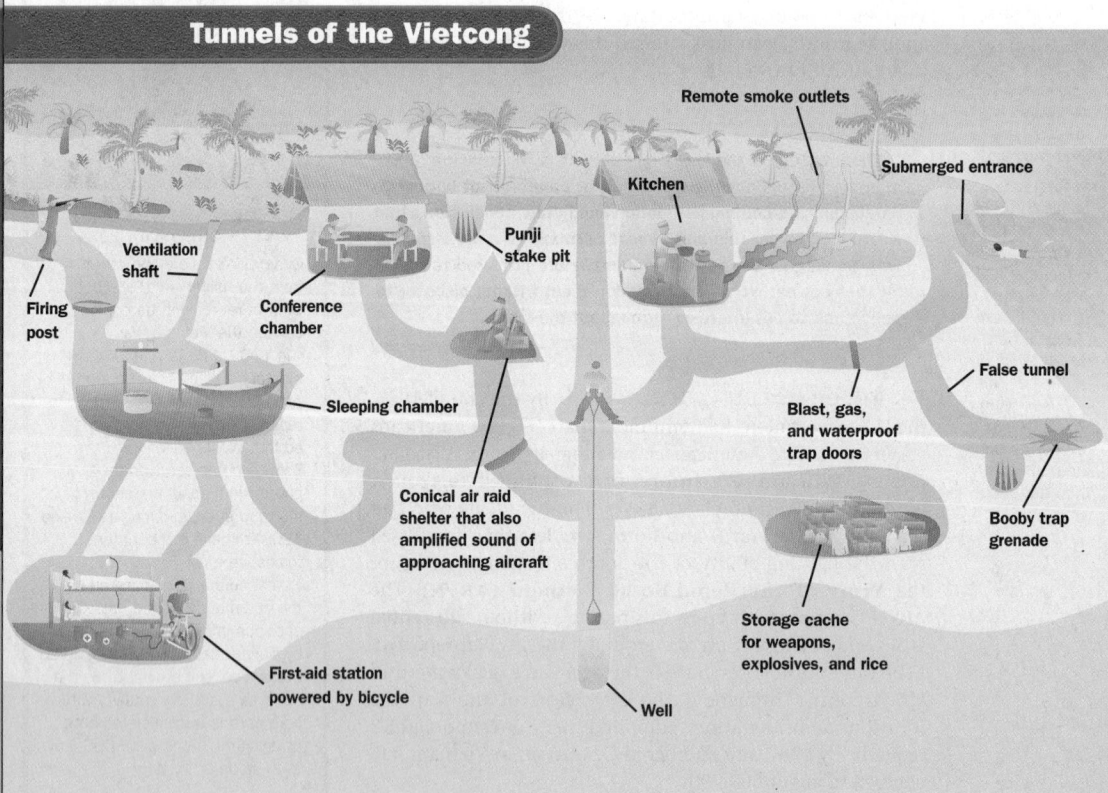

Remote smoke outlets

Submerged entrance

Kitchen

Ventilation shaft

Punji stake pit

Firing post

Conference chamber

Sleeping chamber

False tunnel

Blast, gas, and waterproof trap doors

Conical air raid shelter that also amplified sound of approaching aircraft

Booby trap grenade

Storage cache for weapons, explosives, and rice

First-aid station powered by bicycle

Well

---

**ACTIVITY** LINK TO WORLD HISTORY

 classzone.com

### Guerilla Warfare

**Class Time** 45 minutes

**Task** Comparing the tactics and circumstances of guerilla warfare to conventional warfare

**Purpose** To draw conclusions about use of guerilla warfare as a strategy in Vietnam

**Directions** Have students work in small groups and use library and Internet resources to research the tactics and circumstances of guerilla warfare. Then have them draw up a chart comparing and contrasting guerrilla warfare to conventional warfare. Have them use information in their textbooks about World War II as a reference for conventional warfare. Have groups present their charts to the class. Hold a class discussion about the advantages of using guerilla warfare in Vietnam.

 Integrated Assessment
· Rubrics 1, 2

**MAIN IDEA**

**Drawing Conclusions**
**B** Why did the U.S. forces have difficulty fighting the Vietcong?

*B. Answer* The Vietcong's guerrilla tactics and their superior knowledge of the terrain.

Vietnam's jungles and rice paddies not only dealt with sweltering heat and leeches but also had to be cautious of every step. In a 1969 letter to his sister, Specialist Fourth Class Salvador Gonzalez described the tragic result from an unexploded U.S. bomb that the North Vietnamese Army had rigged. **B**

**A PERSONAL VOICE** SALVADOR GONZALEZ

" **Two days ago 4 guys got killed and about 15 wounded from the first platoon. Our platoon was 200 yards away on top of a hill. One guy was from Floral Park [in New York City]. He had five days left to go [before being sent home]. He was standing on a 250-lb. bomb that a plane had dropped and didn't explode. So the NVA [North Vietnamese Army] wired it up. Well, all they found was a piece of his wallet.** "

—quoted in *Dear America: Letters Home from Vietnam*

**A FRUSTRATING WAR OF ATTRITION** Westmoreland's strategy for defeating the Vietcong was to destroy their morale through a war of attrition, or the gradual wearing down of the enemy by continuous harassment. Introducing the concept of the body count, or the tracking of Vietcong killed in battle, the general believed that as the number of Vietcong dead rose, the guerrillas would inevitably surrender.

However, the Vietcong had no intention of quitting their fight. Despite the growing number of casualties and the relentless pounding from U.S. bombers, the Vietcong—who received supplies from China and the Soviet Union—remained defiant. Defense Secretary McNamara confessed his frustration to a reporter in 1966: "If I had thought they would take this punishment and fight this well, . . . I would have thought differently at the start."

General Westmoreland would say later that the United States never lost a battle in Vietnam. Whether or not the general's words were true, they underscored the degree to which America misunderstood its foe. The United States viewed the war strictly as a military struggle; the Vietcong saw it as a battle for their very existence, and they were ready to pay any price for victory. **C**

**MAIN IDEA**

**Making Inferences**
**C** In what way did the United States underestimate the Vietcong?

*C. Answer* The United States believed the Vietcong would give up the fight due to the massive number of casualties.

**THE BATTLE FOR "HEARTS AND MINDS"** Another key part of the American strategy was to keep the Vietcong from winning the support of South Vietnam's rural population. Edward G. Lansdale, who helped found the fighting unit known as the U.S. Army Special Forces, or Green Berets, stressed the plan's importance. "Just remember this. Communist guerrillas hide among the people. If you win the people over to your side, the communist guerrillas have no place to hide."

The campaign to win the "hearts and minds" of the South Vietnamese villagers proved more difficult than imagined. For instance, in their attempt to expose Vietcong tunnels and hideouts, U.S. planes dropped **napalm**, a gasoline-based bomb that set fire to the jungle. They also sprayed **Agent Orange,** a leaf-killing toxic chemical. The saturation use of these weapons often wounded civilians and left villages and their surroundings in ruins. Years later, many would blame Agent Orange for cancers in U.S. veterans of Vietnam.

U.S. soldiers conducted **search-and-destroy missions,** uprooting civilians with suspected ties to the Vietcong, killing their livestock, and burning villages. Many villagers fled into the cities or refugee camps, creating by 1967 more than 3 million refugees in the South. The irony of the strategy was summed up in February 1968 by a U.S. major whose forces had just leveled the town of Ben Tre: "We had to destroy the town in order to save it."

*The Vietnam War Years* **739**

---

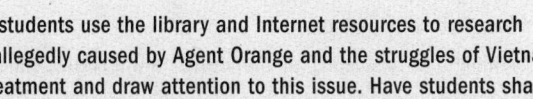

## NOW & THEN

### LAND MINES

Around 3.5 million armed mines remain in Vietnam, causing 160 civilian casualties each month. Worldwide, more than 25,000 civilians are killed or maimed by land mines each year.

The 1997 Mine Ban Treaty bans production and use of antipersonnel mines worldwide. As of 2000, 139 nations had agreed to the treaty, with the notable exceptions of the United States, Russia, and China. In 1998, President Clinton declared that the United States would sign the treaty by 2006, if "suitable alternatives" to land mines had been developed, and asked the military to begin working toward this goal.

The United States has been a big financial contributor to humanitarian land mine clearance. Contributions in 2003–2004 are expected to reach $105 million.

---

## NOW & THEN

### Land Mines

Refer students back to novelist Tim O'Brien's description on page 736 of an infantryman's fear of land mines and booby traps. Tell students that because land mines are relatively cheap, armies and guerilla fighters have made great use of them—especially when retreating. Ask students why land mines continue to be a problem during peacetime in many places in the world. *(Land mines continue to kill people long after a war is over.)*

---

## More About . . .

### Agent Orange

Long-term illnesses affecting soldiers, as well as birth defects in their children, have been attributed to the dioxins contained in Agent Orange. However, the Department of Veteran Affairs has stated that to date there is no real evidence that exposure to Agent Orange has contributed to birth defects in children.

---

**ACTIVITY** **LINK TO SCIENCE**

 **classzone.com**

### Agent Orange

**Class Time** 45 minutes

**Task** Researching and preparing a report on how Agent Orange has affected Vietnam veterans

**Purpose** To evaluate the effects of and responses to health problems attributed to Agent Orange.

**Directions** Have students use the library and Internet resources to research health problems allegedly caused by Agent Orange and the struggles of Vietnam veterans to get treatment and draw attention to this issue. Have students share their findings in an oral or written report.

📖 Integrated Assessment
· Rubrics 1, 3, 5

▲
A soldier with the 61st Infantry Division wears symbols of both war and peace on his chest.

## More About . . .

### Philip Caputo

After returning from Vietnam in 1967, Caputo worked briefly as a corporate publicist and then became a reporter with the *Chicago Tribune*. In 1973, he won a Pulitzer Prize for his reporting on primary election fraud. Four years later, he won literary acclaim with his Vietnam memoir, *A Rumor of War* (see page 763). Since then, Caputo has published several novels, often set in war-torn lands, as well as *Means of Escape* (1991), a fictionalized memoir based on his experiences as a war correspondent.

## Instruct: Objective ❸

### The Early War At Home

TAKS SS11 5(US24.B)

· How did the cost of the war effect the U.S. economy?

· How did TV broadcasts from Vietnam affect support for the war?

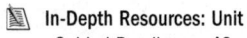 In-Depth Resources: Unit 6
· Guided Reading, p. 40

**SINKING MORALE** The frustrations of guerrilla warfare, the brutal jungle conditions, and the failure to make substantial headway against the enemy took their toll on the U.S. troops' morale. Philip Caputo, a marine lieutenant in Vietnam who later wrote several books about the war, summarized the soldiers' growing disillusionment: "When we marched into the rice paddies . . . we carried, along with our packs and rifles, the implicit convictions that the Vietcong could be quickly beaten. We kept the packs and rifles; the convictions, we lost."

As the war continued, American morale dropped steadily. Many soldiers, required by law to fight a war they did not support, turned to alcohol, marijuana, and other drugs. Low morale even led a few soldiers to murder their superior officers. Morale would worsen during the later years of the war when soldiers realized they were fighting even as their government was negotiating a withdrawal. **D**

Another obstacle was the continuing corruption and instability of the South Vietnamese government. Nguyen Cao Ky, a flamboyant air marshal, led the government from 1965 to 1967. Ky ignored U.S. pleas to retire in favor of an elected civilian government. Mass demonstrations began, and by May of 1966, Buddhist monks and nuns were once again burning themselves in protest against the South Vietnamese government. South Vietnam was fighting a civil war within a civil war, leaving U.S. officials confused and angry.

**FULFILLING A DUTY** Most American soldiers, however, firmly believed in their cause—to halt the spread of communism. They took patriotic pride in fulfilling their duty, just as their fathers had done in World War II.

Most American soldiers fought courageously. Particularly heroic were the thousands of soldiers who endured years of torture and confinement as prisoners of war. In 1966, navy pilot Gerald Coffee's plane was shot down over North Vietnam. Coffee spent the next seven years—until he was released in 1973 as part of a cease-fire agreement—struggling to stay alive in an enemy prison camp.

> **A PERSONAL VOICE** GERALD COFFEE
>
> " My clothes were filthy and ragged. . . . With no boots, my socks—which I'd been able to salvage—were barely recognizable. . . . Only a few threads around my toes kept them spread over my feet; some protection, at least, as I shivered through the cold nights curled up tightly on my morguelike slab. . . . My conditions and predicament were so foreign to me, so stifling, so overwhelming. I'd never been so hungry, so grimy, and in such pain. "
>
> —*Beyond Survival*

### ❸ The Early War at Home

The Johnson administration thought the war would end quickly. As it dragged on, support began to waver, and Johnson's domestic programs began to unravel.

---

> **MAIN IDEA**
>
> Analyzing Causes
>
> **D** What factors led to the low morale of U.S. troops?
>
> *D. Answer* Frustrations of guerilla warfare, the jungle conditions, and the continuing instability of the South Vietnamese government.

---

**ACTIVITY** · COOPERATIVE LEARNING  BLOCK SCHEDULING

### Simulating a TV Interview

**Class Time** Two class periods

**Task** Creating and conducting an interview by a war correspondent of a U.S. soldier in Vietnam

**Purpose** To gain insight into journalists' and soldiers' perspectives on the Vietnam War

**Directions** Partners should decide which role each student will play. The student posing as a journalist should prepare a list of interview questions based on information in this section and in other sources. The student portraying the soldier should research firsthand accounts of combat experiences during the war. The pair should then collaborate on writing a script of the interview, using a question-and-answer format. Allow time for partners to rehearse interviews before conducting them for the class. Students can present live interviews or create videotapes or audiotapes.

**THE GREAT SOCIETY SUFFERS** As the number of U.S. troops in Vietnam continued to mount, the war grew more costly, and the nation's economy began to suffer. The inflation rate, which was less than 2 percent through most of the early 1960s, more than tripled to 5.5 percent by 1969. In August of 1967, President Johnson asked for a tax increase to help fund the war and to keep inflation in check. Congressional conservatives agreed, but only after demanding and receiving a $6 billion reduction in funding for Great Society programs. Vietnam was slowly claiming an early casualty: Johnson's grand vision of domestic reform.

**THE LIVING-ROOM WAR** Through the media, specifically television, Vietnam became America's first "living-room war." The combat footage that appeared nightly on the news in millions of homes showed stark pictures that seemed to contradict the administration's optimistic war scenario.

Quoting body-count statistics that showed large numbers of communists dying in battle, General Westmoreland continually reported that a Vietcong surrender was imminent. Defense Secretary McNamara backed up the general, saying that he could see "the light at the end of the tunnel."

The repeated television images of Americans in body bags told a different story, though. While communists may have been dying, so too were Americans—over 16,000 between 1961 and 1967. Critics charged that a **credibility gap** was growing between what the Johnson administration reported and what was really happening.

One critic was Senator J. William Fulbright, chairman of the powerful Senate Foreign Relations Committee. Fulbright, a former Johnson ally, charged the president with a "lack of candor" in portraying the war effort. In early 1966, the senator conducted a series of televised committee hearings in which he asked members of the Johnson administration to defend their Vietnam policies. The Fulbright hearings delivered few major revelations, but they did contribute to the growing doubts about the war. One woman appeared to capture the mood of Middle America when she told an interviewer, "I want to get out, but I don't want to give in." **E**

By 1967, Americans were evenly split over supporting and opposing the war. However, a small force outside of mainstream America, mainly from the ranks of the nation's youth, already had begun actively protesting the war. Their voices would grow louder and capture the attention of the entire nation.

*E. Answer* The continued reports of American casualties, television coverage, and the Johnson administration's credibility gap.

**MAIN IDEA**

**Analyzing Effects**
**E** What led to the growing concern in America about the Vietnam War?

First used in World War I, dog tags were stamped with personal identification information and worn by U.S. military personnel.

**More About . . .**

**J. William Fulbright**
Fulbright, a senator from Arkansas, is remembered for initiating an international scholarship program that bears his name. He also served as a mentor to the young Bill Clinton.

## Assess & Reteach

### SECTION 2 ASSESSMENT
Have pairs of students evaluate each other's responses.

📄 Formal Assessment
· Section Quiz, p. 407

### SELF-ASSESSMENT
Have students add to the time line on pages 728–729. Tell them to trace U.S. involvement in Vietnam from the Truman administration through the Johnson administration. Then have them identify events that they find difficult to understand.

### RETEACH
Use the Guided Reading worksheet for Section 2 to help review the main ideas of the section.

📄 In-Depth Resources: Unit 6
· Reteaching Activity, p. 47

---

## ② ASSESSMENT

1. **TERMS & NAMES** For each term or name, write a sentence explaining its significance.
   - Robert McNamara
   - Dean Rusk
   - William Westmoreland
   - Army of the Republic of Vietnam (ARVN)
   - napalm
   - Agent Orange
   - search-and-destroy mission
   - credibility gap

**MAIN IDEA**

2. **TAKING NOTES**
   Re-create the chart below. Then, show key military tactics and weapons of the Vietcong and Americans.

   |          | Vietcong | U.S. |
   |----------|----------|------|
   | **Tactics**  |          |      |
   | **Weapons**  |          |      |

   Which weapons and tactics do you think were most successful? Explain.

**CRITICAL THINKING**

3. **DRAWING CONCLUSIONS**
   Why did Americans fail to win the "hearts and minds" of the Vietnamese?

4. **CONTRASTING**
   In a paragraph, contrast the morale of the U.S. troops with that of the Vietcong. Use evidence from the text to support your response.

5. **FORMING GENERALIZATIONS**
   What were the effects of the nightly TV coverage of the Vietnam War? Support your answer with examples from the text. **Think About:**
   - television images of Americans in body bags
   - the Johnson administration's credibility gap

*The Vietnam War Years* **741**

---

Answers **ASSESSMENT** ②

**1. TERMS & NAMES**
Robert McNamara, p. 737
Dean Rusk, p. 737
William Westmoreland, p. 737
Army of the Republic of Vietnam (ARVN), p. 737
napalm, p. 739
Agent Orange, p. 739
search-and-destroy mission, p. 739
credibility gap, p. 741

**2. TAKING NOTES**
Vietcong tactics: ambushes, hit-and-run attacks; weapons: booby traps, land mines; U.S. tactics: large-scale bombing, search-and-destroy missions; weapons: napalm, Agent Orange, bombers; most successful: booby traps and land mines, which killed and wounded many soldiers and undermined morale of U.S. soldiers.

**3. DRAWING CONCLUSIONS**
Use of napalm and Agent Orange, harmed the rural Vietnam; U.S. search-and-destroy missions uprooted civilians and burned their villages, creating millions of refugees.

**4. CONTRASTING**
U.S. troops were frustrated by the jungle terrain of Vietnam, guerilla-style warfare, and by the instability of the South Vietnamese government. The Vietcong were fighting on familiar terrain, and were determined to win, whatever the cost.

**5. FORMING GENERALIZATIONS**
Watching the graphic TV images of the Vietnam war caused many Americans to question the war. They began to doubt the Johnson administration's reports that the enemy was near defeat.

*The Vietnam War Years* **741**

## OBJECTIVES

1. Explain the draft policies that led to the Vietnam War becoming a working-class war.

2. Trace the roots of opposition to the war.

3. Describe the antiwar movement and the growing divisions in U.S. public opinion about the war.

### SKILLBUILDER
· Interpreting Graphs, p. 743

### CRITICAL THINKING
· Synthesizing, p, 743
· Making Inferences, p. 744
· Summarizing, p. 745
· Analyzing Issues, p. 746
· Evaluating, pp. 746, 747
· Developing Historical Perspective, p. 747
· Interpreting Visual Sources, p. 747

## Focus & Motivate

Ask students how they would feel if student privileges at their school—the best classes, schedules, parking—were awarded according to the wealth or prominence of the student's family.

## Instruct

### Instruct: Objective 1

**The Working Class Goes to War**
TAKS SS11 5(WH26.C)
· How was the draft unfair?
· What issues did Vietnam raise for African-Americans?
· What did women in the military do in Vietnam?

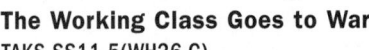 In-Depth Resources: Unit 6
· Guided Reading, p. 41

---

# A Nation Divided

| MAIN IDEA | WHY IT MATTERS NOW | Terms & Names |
|---|---|---|
| An antiwar movement in the U.S. pitted supporters of the government's war policy against those who opposed it. | The painful process of healing a divided nation continues today. | • draft • New Left • Students for a Democratic Society (SDS) • Free Speech Movement • dove • hawk |

 **U.S. History** 6E, 8A, 18A, 19B, 19C, 20A, 24A, 24B, 24C, 24D, 24G, 24H, 25A, 25B, 25C, 25D, 26B

### One American's Story

In 1969, Stephan Gubar was told to report for possible military service in Vietnam. Gubar, 22, a participant in the civil rights movement, had filed as a conscientious objector (CO), or someone who opposed war on the basis of religious or moral beliefs. He was granted 1-A-O status, which meant that while he would not be forced to carry a weapon, he still qualified for noncombatant military duty. That year, Gubar was drafted—called for military service.

As did many other conscientious objectors, Gubar received special training as a medic. He described the memorable day his training ended.

**A PERSONAL VOICE** STEPHAN GUBAR

" The thing that stands out most was . . . being really scared, being in formation and listening to the names and assignments being called. The majority of COs I knew had orders cut for Vietnam. And even though I could hear that happening, even though I could hear that every time a CO's name came up, the orders were cut for Vietnam, I still thought there was a possibility I might not go. Then, when they called my name and said 'Vietnam,'. . . I went to a phone and I called my wife. It was a tremendous shock. "

—quoted in *Days of Decision*

**VIDEO**

*MATTERS OF CONSCIENCE*
Stephan Gubar and the Vietnam War

While many young Americans proudly went off to war, some found ways to avoid the draft, and others simply refused to go. The growing protest movement sharply divided the country between supporters and opponents of the government's policy in Vietnam.

## 1 The Working Class Goes to War

The idea of fighting a war in a faraway place for what they believed was a questionable cause prompted a number of young Americans to resist going to Vietnam.

**A "MANIPULATABLE" DRAFT** Most soldiers who fought in Vietnam were called into combat under the country's Selective Service System, or **draft**, which had been established during World War I. Under this system, all males had to register with their local draft boards when they turned 18. All registrants were screened, and unless they were excluded—such as for medical reasons—in the event of war, men between the ages of 18 and 26 would be called into military service.

---

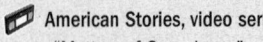

As Americans' doubts about the war grew, thousands of men attempted to find ways around the draft, which one man characterized as a "very manipulatable system." Some men sought out sympathetic doctors to grant medical exemptions, while others changed residences in order to stand before a more lenient draft board. Some Americans even joined the National Guard or Coast Guard, which often secured a deferment from service in Vietnam.

One of the most common ways to avoid the draft was to receive a college deferment, by which a young man enrolled in a university could put off his military service. Because university students during the 1960s tended to be white and financially well-off, many of the men who fought in Vietnam were lower-class whites or minorities who were less privileged economically. With almost 80 percent of American soldiers coming from lower economic levels, Vietnam was a working-class war.

**AFRICAN AMERICANS IN VIETNAM** African Americans served in disproportionate numbers as ground combat troops. During the first several years of the war, blacks accounted for more than 20 percent of American combat deaths despite representing only about 10 percent of the U.S. population. The Defense Department took steps to correct that imbalance by instituting a draft lottery system in 1969.

Martin Luther King, Jr., had refrained from speaking out against the war for fear that it would divert attention from the civil rights movement. But he could not maintain that stance for long. In 1967 he lashed out against what he called the "cruel irony" of American blacks dying for a country that still treated them as second-class citizens.

### A PERSONAL VOICE DR. MARTIN LUTHER KING, JR.

" We were taking the young black men who had been crippled by our society and sending them eight thousand miles away to guarantee liberties in Southeast Asia which they had not found in Southwest Georgia and East Harlem. . . . We have been repeatedly faced with the cruel irony of watching Negro and white boys on TV screens as they kill and die together for a nation that has been unable to seat them together in the same schools. "

—quoted in *America's Vietnam War: A Narrative History*

Racial tension ran high in many platoons, and in some cases, the hostility led to violence. The racism that gripped many military units was yet another factor that led to low troop morale in Vietnam. Ⓐ

**Vocabulary**
deferment: the act or instance of delaying

*Skillbuilder Answer*
1965 through 1968.

*A. Answer*
African Americans were fighting and dying for a country that still discriminated against them.

**MAIN IDEA**

**Synthesizing**
Ⓐ Why did King call African Americans' fighting in Vietnam an "irony"?

▲ A *Life* magazine cover shows new draft inductees arriving for training at Fort Knox, Kentucky.

**U.S. Military Personnel in Vietnam***

536,000

Troops (in thousands): 600, 500, 400, 300, 200, 100, 0

Years: 1963, 1964, 1965, 1966, 1967, 1968, 1969, 1970, 1971, 1972

Source: *Statistical Abstract of the United States, 1985;* Encyclopedia Americana    *Year-end figures

**SKILLBUILDER** Interpreting Graphs
What years signaled a rapid increase in the deployment of U.S. troops?

Despite racial tensions, black and white soldiers fought side by side in Vietnam. ▼

▶ Two U.S. nurses rest at Cam Ranh Bay, the major entry point in South Vietnam for American supplies and troops.

**WOMEN JOIN THE RANKS** While the U.S. military in the 1960s did not allow females to serve in combat, 10,000 women served in Vietnam—most of them as military nurses. Thousands more volunteered their services in Vietnam to the American Red Cross and the United Services Organization (USO), which delivered hospitality and entertainment to the troops.

As the military marched off to Vietnam to fight against communist guerrillas, some of the men at home, as well as many women, waged a battle of their own. Tensions flared across the country as many of the nation's youths began to voice their opposition to the war.

## ❷ The Roots of Opposition

Even before 1965, students were becoming more active socially and politically. Some participated in the civil rights struggle, while others pursued public service. As America became more involved in the war in Vietnam, college students across the country became a powerful and vocal group of protesters.

**THE NEW LEFT** The growing youth movement of the 1960s became known as the **New Left.** The movement was "new" in relation to the "old left" of the 1930s, which had generally tried to move the nation toward socialism, and, in some cases, communism. While the New Left movement did not preach socialism, its followers demanded sweeping changes in American society.

Voicing these demands was one of the better-known New Left organizations, **Students for a Democratic Society (SDS),** founded in 1960 by Tom Hayden and Al Haber. The group charged that corporations and large government institutions had taken over America. The SDS called for a restoration of "participatory democracy" and greater individual freedom.

In 1964, the **Free Speech Movement** (FSM) gained prominence at the University of California at Berkeley. The FSM grew out of a clash between students and administrators over free speech on campus. Led by Mario Savio, a philosophy student, the FSM focused its criticism on what it called the American "machine," the nation's faceless and powerful business and government institutions. **B**

**CAMPUS ACTIVISM** Across the country the ideas of the FSM and SDS quickly spread to college campuses. Students addressed mostly campus issues, such as dress codes, curfews, dormitory regulations, and mandatory Reserved Officer

*B. Answer* Corporations and government institutions were growing too dominant and were inhibiting personal freedom.

**MAIN IDEA**

**Making Inferences**
**B** What concerns about American democratic society did the New Left voice?

---

**DIFFERENTIATING INSTRUCTION**  **LESS PROFICIENT READERS**

### Questioning Techniques

To help students build their comprehension skills, have students work in pairs and use the following suggestions for reading pages 744-747. Have students change the headings and subheadings into questions using the familiar "five *w*'s"—*who, what, when, where,* and *why*. Sample questions:

· What were the roots of opposition to the Vietnam War?
· Who joined the New Left movement?
· Why did campus activism spread?

Have students begin by going through the pages to formulate the questions. Then have them answer each question as they read the appropriate portion of the text.

Training Corps (ROTC) programs. At Fairleigh Dickinson University in New Jersey, students marched merely as "an expression of general student discontent."

With the onset of the Vietnam War, students across the country found a galvanizing issue and joined together in protest. By the mid-sixties, many youths believed the nation to be in need of fundamental change.

## The Protest Movement Emerges ③

Throughout the spring of 1965, groups at a number of colleges began to host "teach-ins" to protest the war. At the University of Michigan, where only a year before President Johnson had announced his sweeping Great Society Program, teachers and students now assailed his war policy. "This is no longer a casual form of campus spring fever," journalist James Reston noted about the growing demonstrations. As the war continued, the protests grew and divided the country.

**THE MOVEMENT GROWS** In April of 1965, SDS helped organize a march on Washington, D.C., by some 20,000 protesters. By November of that year, a protest rally in Washington drew more than 30,000. Then, in February of 1966, the Johnson administration changed deferments for college students, requiring students to be in good academic standing in order to be granted a deferment. Campuses around the country erupted in protest. SDS called for civil disobedience at Selective Service Centers and openly counseled students to flee to Canada or Sweden. By the end of 1969, SDS had chapters on nearly 400 campuses.

Youths opposing the war did so for several reasons. The most common was the belief that the conflict in Vietnam was basically a civil war and that the U.S. military had no business there. Some said that the oppressive South Vietnamese regime was no better than the Communist regime it was fighting. Others argued that the United States could not police the entire globe and that war was draining American strength in other important parts of the world. Still others saw war simply as morally unjust. **C**

The antiwar movement grew beyond college campuses. Small numbers of returning veterans began to protest the war, and folk singers such as the trio Peter, Paul, and Mary, and Joan Baez used music as a popular protest vehicle. The number one song in September 1965 was "Eve of Destruction," in which singer Barry McGuire stressed the ironic fact that in the 1960s an American male could be drafted at age 18 but had to be 21 to vote:

> The Eastern world, it is explodin',
> Violence flaring, bullets loadin',
> You're old enough to kill, but not for votin',
> You don't believe in war, but what's that gun you're totin'?

**FROM PROTEST TO RESISTANCE** By 1967, the antiwar movement had intensified, with no sign of slowing down. "We were having no effect on U.S. policy," recalled one protest leader, "so we thought we had to up the ante." In the spring of 1967, nearly half a million protesters of all ages gathered in New York's Central Park. Shouting "Burn cards, not people!" and "Hell, no, we won't go!" hundreds tossed their draft cards into a bonfire. A woman from New Jersey told a reporter, "So many of us are frustrated. We want to criticize this war because we think it's wrong, but we want to do it in the framework of loyalty."

**MAIN IDEA**

**Summarizing**
**C** For what reasons did the protesters oppose the Vietnam War?

**C. Answer**
Protesters felt that America had no business in Vietnam; the war was draining American strength from other parts of the world; the war was morally unjust.

**HISTORICAL SPOTLIGHT**

**"THE BALLAD OF THE GREEN BERETS"**

Not every Vietnam-era pop song about war was an antiwar song. At the top of the charts for five weeks in 1966 was "The Ballad of the Green Berets" by Staff Sergeant Barry Sadler of the U.S. Army Special Forces, known as the Green Berets:

> Fighting soldiers from the sky,
> Fearless men who jump and die,
> Men who mean just what they say,
> The brave men of the Green Beret.

The recording sold over a million copies in its first two weeks of release and was *Billboard* magazine's song of the year.

**Instruct: Objective ③**

**The Protest Movement Emerges**
TAKS SS11 1(US6.E)

· What issue fueled campus protests?
· How did draft-eligible Americans respond to the draft?
· How did the American public respond to the protests against the war?

📖 In-Depth Resources: Unit 6
 · Guided Reading, p. 41
 · Primary Source: Protest Buttons, p. 56

**HISTORICAL SPOTLIGHT**

**"The Ballad of the Green Berets"**
Tell students that the song "The Ballad of the Green Berets" was featured in the 1968 movie, *The Green Berets*, starring John Wayne, an actor famous for his heroic cowboy roles. Explain that some movie critics dismissed the film as propaganda. Ask students if the song lyrics quoted on this page, in the context of the highly polarized debate about the Vietnam War, might also be considered propaganda. (*Students should see the lyrics as idealizing the soldiers. In the political context of the time, an assessment of the lyrics as propaganda would be a fair one.*)

*The Vietnam War Years* **745**

**ACTIVITY** **LINK TO MUSIC**

**Composing "Hawk" or "Dove" Lyrics**

**Class Time** 45 minutes

**Task** Composing and performing songs supporting or protesting the Vietnam War

**Purpose** To discover how popular music can effectively convey political ideas

**Directions** Have small groups of student write lyrics for a "hawk" or a "dove" song. Encourage musically talented students to compose original music to accompany their group's lyrics. Other students may write lyrics to a familiar tune, or rap the lyrics to a rhythm they devise. Students may perform their songs live or tape them. Have students distribute copies of their song lyrics so that classmates can follow along as they listen to the performances.

📖 Integrated Assessment
 · Rubric 3

**BLOCK SCHEDULING**

## DIFFICULT DECISIONS

### Resist the Draft or Serve Your Country?

1. The decision to serve or resist was made by many young men according to both their conscience and to enormous social pressure. Peer pressure generally took the form of resistance, while families and communities often supported the obligation to serve.

2. Probably. For example, many young men were eager to volunteer during World War II because the enemy was perceived as a potential threat to freedom in the Western world.

---

### DIFFICULT DECISIONS

#### RESIST THE DRAFT OR SERVE YOUR COUNTRY?

As the fighting in Vietnam intensified, young men of draft age who opposed the war found themselves considering one of two options: register with the draft board and risk heading off to war, or find a way to avoid military service. Ways to avoid service included medical and educational deferments. But a great many men did not qualify for these. The choices that remained, such as fleeing the country, going to jail, or giving in and joining the ranks, came with a high price. Once a decision was made, there was no turning back.

1. Imagine you oppose the war and are called to serve in Vietnam. What decision would you make? Would you feel guilty if you avoided the draft? If you chose to serve, how would you view those who did not serve your country?

2. Do you think more young men would have been willing to serve had this been a different war? Explain.

---

This sign reflects the view of many Americans that the antiwar protests undermined the war effort in Vietnam. ▶

**746**

---

Others were more radical in their view. David Harris, who would spend 20 months in jail for refusing to serve in Vietnam, explained his motives.

**A PERSONAL VOICE** DAVID HARRIS

"Theoretically, I can accept the notion that there are circumstances in which you have to kill people. I could not accept the notion that Vietnam was one of those circumstances. And to me that left the option of either sitting by and watching what was an enormous injustice . . . or [finding] some way to commit myself against it. And the position that I felt comfortable with in committing myself against it was total noncooperation—I was not going to be part of the machine."

—quoted in *The War Within*

Draft resistance continued from 1967 until President Nixon phased out the draft in the early 1970s. During these years, the U.S. government accused more than 200,000 men of draft offenses and imprisoned nearly 4,000 draft resisters. (Although some were imprisoned for four or five years, most won parole after 6 to 12 months.) Throughout these years, about 10,000 Americans fled, many to Canada. **D**

In October of 1967, a demonstration at Washington's Lincoln Memorial drew about 75,000 protesters. After listening to speeches, approximately 30,000 demonstrators locked arms for a march on the Pentagon in order "to disrupt the center of the American war machine," as one organizer explained. As hundreds of protesters broke past the military police and mounted the Pentagon steps, they were met by tear gas and clubs. About 1,500 demonstrators were injured and at least 700 arrested.

**WAR DIVIDES THE NATION** By 1967, Americans increasingly found themselves divided into two camps regarding the war. Those who strongly opposed the war and believed the United States should withdraw were known as **doves.** Feeling just as strongly that America should unleash much of its greater military force to win the war were the **hawks.** Despite the visibility of the antiwar protesters, a majority of American citizens in 1967 still remained committed to the war. Others, while less certain about the proper U.S. role in Vietnam, were shocked to see protesters publicly criticize a war in which their fellow Americans were fighting and dying. A poll taken in December of 1967 showed that 70 percent of Americans believed the war protests were "acts of disloyalty." A firefighter who lost his son in Vietnam articulated the bitter feelings a number of Americans felt toward the antiwar movement.

**A PERSONAL VOICE**

"I'm bitter. . . . It's people like us who give up our sons for the country. . . . The college types, the professors, they go to Washington and tell the government what to do. . . . But their sons, they don't end up in the swamps over there, in Vietnam. No sir. They're deferred, because they're in school. Or they get sent to safe places. . . . What bothers me about the peace crowd is that you can tell from their attitude, the way they look and what they say, that they don't really love this country."

—a firefighter quoted in *Working-Class War*

---

**MAIN IDEA**

**Evaluating**

**D** Do you think it was right for the government to imprison draft resisters? Explain.

*D. Possible Answers* **Yes:** It was fair, since resisting the draft was a serious offense. **No:** it was unfair; people should not be forced into war.

---

MAIN IDEA

**Evaluating**

 What were the key issues that divided America?

*E. Answer*
Those who supported America's involvement in the war thought the U.S. should take an even more powerful stance to win the war. Those who opposed wanted U.S. troops to withdraw immediately.

Responding to antiwar posters, Americans who supported the government's Vietnam policy developed their own slogans: "Support our men in Vietnam" and "America—love it or leave it."

**JOHNSON REMAINS DETERMINED** Throughout the turmoil and division that engulfed the country during the early years of the war, President Johnson remained firm. Attacked by doves for not withdrawing and by hawks for not increasing military power rapidly enough, Johnson was dismissive of both groups and their motives. He continued his policy of slow escalation.

**A PERSONAL VOICE** LYNDON B. JOHNSON

"There has always been confusion, frustration, and difference of opinion in this country when there is a war going on. . . . You know what President Roosevelt went through, and President Wilson in World War I. He had some senators from certain areas . . . that gave him serious problems until victory was assured. . . . We are going to have these differences. No one likes war. All people love peace. But you can't have freedom without defending it."

—quoted in *No Hail, No Farewell*

However, by the end of 1967, Johnson's policy—and the continuing stalemate—had begun to create turmoil within his own administration. In November, Defense Secretary Robert McNamara, a key architect of U.S. escalation in Vietnam, quietly announced he was resigning to become head of the World Bank. "It didn't add up," McNamara recalled later. "What I was trying to find out was how . . . the war went on year after year when we stopped the infiltration [from North Vietnam] or shrunk it and when we had a very high body count and so on. It just didn't make sense."

As it happened, McNamara's resignation came on the threshold of the most tumultuous year of the sixties. In 1968 the war—and Johnson's presidency—would take a drastic turn for the worse.

I WANT OUT

**More About . . .**

**Robert McNamara**
McNamara served as Secretary of Defense for both Kennedy and Johnson. A former president of Ford Motor Company, he was famous for reorganizing the sprawling defense department along corporate lines. McNamara was a key advisor to Johnson in escalating U.S. involvement. After leaving public service, he underwent a period of introspection. McNamara emerged as a spokesman for nuclear disarmament in the 1980s. In 1995, he wrote *In Retrospect*, a memoir in which he admitted that he had been wrong about Vietnam, analyzed the reasons for his mistakes, and conveyed a strong sense of guilt and regret over Vietnam.

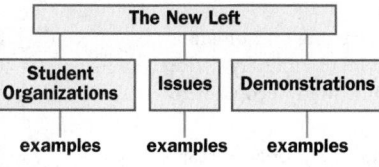

**ASSESSMENT**

1. **TERMS & NAMES** For each of the following, write a sentence explaining its significance.

- draft
- New Left
- Students for a Democratic Society (SDS)
- Free Speech Movement
- dove
- hawk

**MAIN IDEA**

2. **TAKING NOTES**
Re-create the tree diagram below on your paper. Then fill it in with examples of student organizations, issues, and demonstrations of the New Left.

| The New Left | | |
|---|---|---|
| Student Organizations | Issues | Demonstrations |
| examples | examples | examples |

**CRITICAL THINKING**

3. **DEVELOPING HISTORICAL PERSPECTIVE**
Imagine it is 1967. Do you think you would ally yourself with the hawks or the doves? Give reasons that support your position.

4. **EVALUATING**
Do you agree that antiwar protests were "acts of disloyalty"? Why or why not?

5. **ANALYZING VISUAL SOURCES**
This antiwar poster is a parody of the World War I Uncle Sam poster (shown on page 382), which states, "I want you for the U.S. Army." Why might the artist have chosen this American character to express the antiwar message?

**Assess & Reteach**

**SECTION 3 ASSESSMENT**
Have students work individually to answer the questions. Then have them share with the class their tree diagrams for item 2.

📖 Formal Assessment
· Section Quiz, p. 408

**SELF-ASSESSMENT**
Have each student make a two-column chart with the headings "Hawks" and "Doves" and fill in each group's arguments about the war.

**RETEACH**
Use the headings of the section to review the main ideas covered.

📖 In-Depth Resources: Unit 6
· Reteaching Activity, p. 48

*The Vietnam War Years* **747**

---

Answers **ASSESSMENT**

**1. TERMS & NAMES**
draft, p. 742
New Left, p. 744
Students for a Democratic Society, p. 744
Free Speech Movement, p. 744
dove, p. 746
hawk, p. 746

**2. TAKING NOTES**
Student Organizations: Students for a Democratic Society, Free Speech Movement. Issues: Vietnam War, abolition of college deferments, campus issues. Demonstrations: march on Washington, protest rally in Washington, civil disobedience at Selective Service Centers.

**3. DEVELOPING HISTORICAL PERSPECTIVE**
Hawks: The way to win is to increase U.S. military strength. The U.S. must stop the spread of communism. Doves: The U.S. should not fight another country's war.

**4. EVALUATING**
Agree: Americans have the patriotic duty to support soldiers fighting for their country; protests demoralized U.S.

soldiers and the American public. Disagree: The people condemning the protesters did not examine the reasons for fighting the war; suppressing dissent is undemocratic.

**5. INTERPRETING VISUAL SOURCES**
The poster is a direct mockery of army recruiting posters and implies that the United States wants out of Vietnam.

## OBJECTIVES

1 Describe the Tet offensive and its effect on the American public.

2 Explain the domestic turbulence of 1968.

3 Describe the 1968 presidential election.

### SKILLBUILDERS

· Geography Skillbuilder: location, p. 749
· Interpreting Charts, p. 753

### CRITICAL THINKING

· Analyzing Issues, pp. 749, 751
· Analyzing Motives, p. 750
· Summarizing, p. 752
· Analyzing Events, p. 753
· Making Inferences, p. 753

## Focus & Motivate

Ask students to remember a time when they or a friend or family member was dealing with a problem that just seemed to get worse no matter how hard they tried to solve it.

## Instruct

### Instruct: Objective 1

**The Tet Offensive Turns the War**
TAKS SS11 1(US6.E)
· What was the Tet Offensive?
· How did the Tet Offensive change American public opinion about the war?
· How did the Tet Offensive change President Johnson's popularity?

 In-Depth Resources: Unit 6
· Guided Reading, p. 42
· Primary Source: LBJ on Vietnam and Reelection, p. 58

 Critical Thinking Transparencies CT64
· The Impact of the Tet Offensive

---

# 1968:
# A Tumultuous Year

| MAIN IDEA | WHY IT MATTERS NOW | Terms & Names |
|---|---|---|
| An enemy attack in Vietnam, two assassinations, and a chaotic political convention made 1968 an explosive year. | Disturbing events in 1968 accentuated the nation's divisions, which are still healing in the 21st century. | · Tet offensive    · Eugene McCarthy<br>· Clark Clifford    · Hubert Humphrey<br>· Robert Kennedy    · George Wallace |

**TEKS U.S. History**
1B, 4C, 6E, 7B, 8B, 9A, 16A, 18A, 19B, 19C, 24B, 24C, 24G, 24H, 25A, 25C, 25D

### One American's Story

On June 5, 1968, John Lewis, the first chairman of the Student Nonviolent Coordinating Committee, fell to the floor and wept. Robert F. Kennedy, a leading Democratic candidate for president, had just been fatally shot. Two months earlier, when Martin Luther King, Jr., had fallen victim to an assassin's bullet, Lewis had told himself he still had Kennedy. And now they both were gone. Lewis, who later became a congressman from Georgia, recalled the lasting impact of these assassinations.

**A PERSONAL VOICE** JOHN LEWIS

"There are people today who are afraid, in a sense, to hope or to have hope again, because of what happened in . . . 1968. Something was taken from us. The type of leadership that we had in a sense invested in, that we had helped to make and to nourish, was taken from us. . . . Something died in all of us with those assassinations."

—quoted in *From Camelot to Kent State*

John Lewis

These violent deaths were but two of the traumatic events that rocked the nation in 1968. From a shocking setback in Vietnam to a chaotic Democratic National Convention in Chicago, the events of 1968 made it the most tumultuous year of a turbulent decade.

## 1 The Tet Offensive Turns the War

The year 1968 began with a daring surprise attack by the Vietcong on numerous cities in South Vietnam. The simultaneous strikes, while ending in military defeat for the Communist guerrillas, stunned the American public. Many people with moderate views began to turn against the war.

**A SURPRISE ATTACK** January 30 was the Vietnamese equivalent of New Year's Eve, the beginning of the lunar new year festivities known in Vietnam as Tet.

---

 **In-Depth Resources: Unit 6**
· Guided Reading, p. 42
· Reteaching Activity, p. 49
· Geography Application: The Ho Chi Minh Trail, pp. 51–52
· Primary Sources: LBJ on Vietnam and Reelection, p. 58
· American Lives: John Lewis, p. 63

 **Reading Study Guide** (English and Spanish), pp. 223–224

 **Access for Students Acquiring English/ESL**
· Guided Reading, p. 237
· Geography Application, pp. 241–242

**Formal Assessment**
· Section Quiz, p. 409

**Integrated Assessment**
· Rubrics

### INTEGRATED TECHNOLOGY

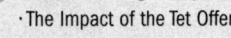 **Geography Transp. GT30**
· The Vietnam War

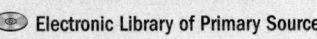 **Critical Thinking Transp. CT64**
· The Impact of the Tet Offensive

◉ **Electronic Library of Primary Sources**

ⓘ **classzone.com**

### TEXAS RESOURCES

 TAKS Spiraled Content Review

 TAKS Practice Tests

 TAKS Practice Transparencies TT115

 TAKS Online Test Practice

Throughout that day in 1968, villagers—taking advantage of a weeklong truce proclaimed for Tet—streamed into cities across South Vietnam to celebrate their new year. At the same time, many funerals were being held for war victims. Accompanying the funerals were the traditional firecrackers, flutes, and, of course, coffins.

The coffins, however, contained weapons, and many of the villagers were Vietcong agents. That night the Vietcong launched an overwhelming attack on over 100 towns and cities in South Vietnam, as well as 12 U.S. air bases. They even attacked the U.S. embassy in Saigon, killing five Americans. The **Tet offensive** continued for about a month before U.S. and South Vietnamese forces regained control of the cities.

General Westmoreland declared the attacks an overwhelming defeat for the Vietcong, whose "well-laid plans went afoul." From a purely military standpoint, Westmoreland was right. The Vietcong lost about 32,000 soldiers during the month-long battle, while the American and ARVN forces lost little more than 3,000.

However, from a psychological—and political—standpoint, Westmoreland's claim could not have been more wrong. The Tet offensive greatly shook the American public, which had been told repeatedly and had come to believe that the enemy was close to defeat. The Johnson administration's credibility gap suddenly widened to a point from which it would never recover. Daily, Americans saw the shocking images of attacks by an enemy that seemed to be everywhere.

**TET CHANGES PUBLIC OPINION** In a matter of weeks, the Tet offensive changed millions of minds about the war. Despite the years of antiwar protest, a poll taken just before Tet showed that only 28 percent of Americans called themselves doves, while 56 percent claimed to be hawks. After Tet, both sides tallied 40 percent. The mainstream media, which had reported the war in a skeptical but generally balanced way, now openly criticized the war. One of the nation's most respected journalists, Walter Cronkite, told his viewers that it now seemed "more certain than ever that the bloody experience of Vietnam is to end in a stalemate." **Ⓐ**

Minds were also changing at the White House. To fill the defense secretary position left vacant by Robert McNamara's resignation, Johnson picked **Clark Clifford**, a friend and supporter of the president's Vietnam policy. However, after settling in and studying the situation, Clifford concluded that the war was unwinnable. "We seem to have a sinkhole," Clifford said. "We put in more—they match it. I see more and more fighting with more and more casualties on the U.S. side and no end in sight to the action."

*A. Answer* The enemy seemed much stronger and more numerous than Americans had thought.

MAIN IDEA

**Analyzing Issues**
**Ⓐ** Why did American support for the war change after the Tet offensive?

## Tet Offensive, Jan. 30–Feb. 24, 1968

NORTH VIETNAM
Khe Sanh
Quang Tri
Hue
Da Nang
Hoi An
Chu Lai
Kon Tum
Plei Ku
Quin Hon
Ban Me Thuot
Nha Trang
Cam Ranh Bay
Bien Hoa
Saigon
Ben Tre
Vinh Long
Can Tho
LAOS
THAILAND
CAMBODIA
Phnom Penh
Mekong River
Ho Chi Minh Trail
SOUTH VIETNAM
South China Sea
17th Parallel
110°E
15°N
10°N
105°E

★ Major battle
□ U.S. base
▭ Demilitarized zone

0 75 150 miles
0 75 150 kilometers

### GEOGRAPHY SKILLBUILDER
**Location** What were the geographical destinations of the Tet offensive attacks? What does this suggest about the Vietcong forces?

## HISTORY from VISUALS

### Interpreting the Map
Remind students that the Ho Chi Minh Trail was the main North Vietnamese supply route to the Vietcong and to North Vietnamese troops in South Vietnam. Point out the numerous star-shaped symbols on the map, representing the major battle sites of the Tet Offensive.

**Extension** Ask students to use the map to explain why the North Vietnamese would have used this route. *(The route followed a flatter area than if it had come straight down through the Central Highlands region of Vietnam. By using the territory of Laos and Cambodia, the North Vietnamese were creating international issues for the U.S. and deflecting bombing of their own territory.)*

📖 In-Depth Resources: Unit 6
· Geography Application: The Ho Chi Minh Trail, pp. 51–52

A *Life* magazine cover shows the capture of a Vietcong guerrilla during the Tet offensive.

## More About . . .

### The Tet Offensive and Public Opinion
Westmoreland's frustration at losing the public relations battle over Tet provides a good example of how guerrilla warfare defies conventional military logic. By any military standards, Tet was a devastating defeat for the North Vietnamese. Westmoreland, relying on his body count statistics, concluded that he had dealt the enemy a crippling defeat. But the war was waged on political as well as military fronts. On the political front, Tet was the decisive battle in American public opinion. It exposed the "credibility gap" between military and civilian assessments of the war.

*The Vietnam War Years* **749**

---

**ACTIVITY** **COOPERATIVE LEARNING**

🅘 classzone.com

## Images of War

**Class Time** 45 minutes

**Task** Creating a collage of photographs of the Tet Offensive

**Purpose** To gain an understanding of how the Tet Offensive affected the American public

**Directions** Tell students that because the Tet Offensive was fought in the cities of South Vietnam, journalists were right in the middle of the battle. They were able to capture shocking images that Americans saw on television and in their daily newspapers. Have students use library resources and the Internet to locate photographs of the Tet Offensive. Students may photocopy or download and print the photos in order to assemble them in a collage on poster board. Then have students discuss how they think the images might have affected Americans—especially those who favored the war and believed the optimistic assessments coming from government and military officials.

## Instruct: Objective ②

### Days of Loss and Rage

TAKS SS11 1(US6.E)

· How did Eugene McCarthy change the race for president in 1968?

· What prompted Robert Kennedy to enter the race for president?

· Why did President Johnson decide not to seek reelection?

· What was the reaction to the assassinations of Martin Luther King, Jr. and Robert Kennedy?

 In-Depth Resources: Unit 6
· Guided Reading, p. 42
· American Lives: John Lewis, p. 63

### More About . . .

#### Robert Kennedy

Kennedy's candidacy attracted the support of African Americans and Latinos, whose causes he had championed in the past. It divided the anti-war ranks between McCarthy backers, who saw Kennedy's late entry into the race as opportunism, and Kennedy backers, who saw their candidate as more likely to be elected. Kennedy previously had served as an attorney for Senator Joseph McCarthy's Senate committee and then as Attorney General under his brother, President John F. Kennedy. At the end of his life, Robert Kennedy was perceived by many as a man who demonstrated great compassion for the poor and who held a vision for the healing of America.

---

Following the Tet offensive, Johnson's popularity plummeted. In public opinion polls taken at the end of February 1968, nearly 60 percent of Americans disapproved of his handling of the war. Nearly half of the country now felt it had been a mistake to send American troops to Vietnam.

> *"If I've lost Walter [Cronkite], then it's over. I've lost Mr. Average Citizen."*
> LYNDON B. JOHNSON

War weariness eventually set in, and 1968 was the watershed year. Johnson recognized the change, too. Upon learning of Cronkite's pessimistic analysis of the war, the president lamented, "If I've lost Walter, then it's over. I've lost Mr. Average Citizen."

## ② Days of Loss and Rage

The growing division over Vietnam led to a shocking political development in the spring of 1968, a season in which Americans also endured two assassinations, a series of urban riots, and a surge in college campus protests.

▲ The Vietnam War and the divisiveness it caused took its toll on President Johnson.

**JOHNSON WITHDRAWS** Well before the Tet offensive, an antiwar coalition within the Democratic Party had sought a Democratic candidate to challenge Johnson in the 1968 primary elections. **Robert Kennedy,** John F. Kennedy's brother and a senator from New York, decided not to run, citing party loyalty. However, in November of 1967, Minnesota senator **Eugene McCarthy** answered the group's call, declaring that he would run against Johnson on a platform to end the war in Vietnam.

McCarthy's early campaign attracted little notice, but in the weeks following Tet it picked up steam. In the New Hampshire Democratic primary in March 1968, the little-known senator captured 42 percent of the vote. While Johnson won the primary with 48 percent of the vote, the slim margin of victory was viewed as a defeat for the president. Influenced by Johnson's perceived weakness at the polls, Robert Kennedy declared his candidacy for president. The Democratic Party had become a house divided.

In a televised address on March 31, 1968, Johnson announced a dramatic change in his Vietnam policy—the United States would seek negotiations to end the war. In the meantime, the policy of U.S. escalation would end, the bombing would eventually cease, and steps would be taken to ensure that the South Vietnamese played a larger role in the war.

The president paused and then ended his speech with a statement that shocked the nation. Declaring that he did not want the presidency to become "involved in the partisan divisions that are developing in this political year," Lyndon Johnson announced, "Accordingly, I shall not seek, and I will not accept, the nomination of my party for another term as your president." The president was stepping down from national politics, his grand plan for domestic reform done in by a costly and divisive war. "That . . . war," Johnson later admitted, "killed the lady I really loved—the Great Society." **B**

**VIOLENCE AND PROTEST GRIP THE NATION** The Democrats—as well as the nation—were in for more shock in 1968. On April 4, America was rocked by the assassination of Martin Luther King, Jr. Violence ripped through more than 100 U.S. cities as enraged followers of the slain civil rights leader burned buildings and destroyed neighborhoods.

Just two months later, a bullet cut down yet another popular national figure. Robert Kennedy had become a strong candidate in the Democratic primary, drawing support from minorities and urban Democratic voters. On June 4, Kennedy won the crucial California primary. Just after midnight of June 5, he gave a victory

**B. Answer** He believed that seeking a second term would cause further turmoil and divisiveness within the Democratic Party.

**MAIN IDEA**

Analyzing Motives

**B** Why did President Johnson decide not to run again?

---

| ACTIVITY | LINK TO POLITICS |

 **classzone.com**

### Writing Editorials

**Class Time** Two class periods

**Task** Writing a newspaper editorial or opinion piece about an issue related to the Vietnam War after 1968

**Purpose** To voice an opinion on a controversial issue

**Directions** Have students work in groups and choose a topic covered on pages 757–759. Examples: the My Lai massacre, invasion of Cambodia, student slayings at Kent State and Jackson State, publication of the Pentagon Papers, Kissinger's "peace is at hand" announcement, or the Christmas bombings of 1972. Have students gather facts about their issue, choose a position, create an outline, and draft an editorial or opinion piece. Have students share their work with the rest of the class. As an extensions activity, have student groups that have taken opposing positions on the same issue debate it in class.

speech at a Los Angeles hotel. On his way out he passed through the hotel's kitchen, where a young Palestinian immigrant, Sirhan Sirhan, was hiding with a gun. Sirhan, who later said he was angered by Kennedy's support of Israel, fatally shot the senator.

Jack Newfield, a speechwriter for Kennedy, described the anguish he and many Americans felt over the loss of two of the nation's leaders.

### A PERSONAL VOICE JACK NEWFIELD

" Things were not really getting better . . . we shall not overcome. . . . We had already glimpsed the most compassionate leaders our nation could produce, and they had all been assassinated. And from this time forward, things would get worse: Our best political leaders were part of memory now, not hope. "

—quoted in *Nineteen Sixty-Eight*

Meanwhile, the nation's college campuses continued to protest. During the first six months of 1968, almost 40,000 students on more than 100 campuses took part in more than 200 major demonstrations. While many of the demonstrations continued to target U.S. involvement in the Vietnam War, students also clashed with university officials over campus and social issues. A massive student protest at Columbia University in New York City held the nation's attention for a week in April. There, students protesting the university's community policies took over several buildings. Police eventually restored order and arrested nearly 900 protesters.

Recalling the violence and turmoil that plagued the nation in 1968, the journalist and historian Garry Wills wrote, "There was a sense everywhere . . . that things were giving way. That [people] had not only lost control of [their] history, but might never regain it." **C**

## A Turbulent Race for President ③

The chaos and violence of 1968 climaxed in August, when thousands of antiwar demonstrators converged on the city of Chicago to protest at the Democratic National Convention. The convention, which featured a bloody riot between protesters and police, fractured the Democratic Party and thus helped a nearly forgotten Republican win the White House.

**TURMOIL IN CHICAGO** With Lyndon Johnson stepping down and Robert Kennedy gone, the 1968 Democratic presidential primary race pitted Eugene McCarthy against **Hubert Humphrey,** Johnson's vice president. McCarthy, while still popular with the nation's antiwar segment, had little chance of defeating Humphrey, a loyal party man who had President Johnson's support. During the last week of August, the Democrats met at their convention in Chicago, supposedly to choose a candidate. In reality, Humphrey's nomination had already been determined, a decision that upset many antiwar activists.

As the delegates arrived in Chicago, so too did nearly 10,000 protesters. Led by men such as SDS veteran Tom Hayden, many demonstrators sought to pressure the Democrats into adopting an antiwar platform. Others came to voice their

### MAIN IDEA

**Analyzing Issues**
**C** Why was 1968 characterized as a year of "lost control" in America?

*C. Answer*
Antiwar demonstrations, student takeovers of universities, and the assassinations of two of the country's leaders were unprecedented; people did not know how to control such events.

**Vocabulary**
**platform:** a formal declaration of the principles on which a political party makes its appeal to the public

Hotel busboy Juan Romero was the first person to reach Robert Kennedy after he was shot June 5, 1968. Kennedy had just won the California Democratic primary.

### More About . . .

**1968**
The United States was not the only country to undergo social unrest in 1968. In Paris, French students took to the streets to protest university issues and policies of the French government. Unions joined forces with students. In Mexico City, hundreds of students protesting political issues were killed by Mexican troops.

### Instruct: Objective ③

**A Turbulent Race for President**
TAKS SS11 1(US6.E)
· Why did riots occur at the Democratic National Convention in Chicago?
· Why was Humphrey unpopular with many Democrats?
· How did George Wallace affect the outcome of the 1968 election?
· Why was Nixon's election in 1968 considered a great political comeback?

📄 In-Depth Resources: Unit 6
· Guided Reading, p. 42

### More About . . .

**Hubert Humphrey**
Humphrey campaigned vigorously for the presidency in 1968, but was saddled with both his ties to Johnson's Vietnam policy and—given his ties to Mayor Daley and the party regulars—the debacle of the Chicago convention. Humphrey first came to national prominence at the Democratic National convention in 1948. At that time mayor of Minneapolis, Humphrey led the charge for a strong civil rights platform. Humphrey had a distinguished career in the Senate as a liberal leader for reform.

*The Vietnam War Years* **751**

---

**DIFFERENTIATING INSTRUCTION**    **LESS PROFICIENT READERS**

### Tracking Presidential Candidates

To help students better understand the 1968 presidential candidates, put the following chart on the chalkboard and have students fill in the missing information as they read pages 751–753.

| Presidential Candidates | Party | Career Highlights | Views |
|---|---|---|---|
| Hubert Humphrey | | | |
| Richard Nixon | | | |
| George Wallace | | | |

Chicago police attempt to disperse antiwar demonstrators at the 1968 Democratic convention. Protesters shouted, "The whole world is watching!" ▶

displeasure with Humphrey's nomination. Still others, known as Yippies (members of the Youth International Party), had come hoping to provoke violence that might discredit the Democratic Party. Chicago's mayor, Richard J. Daley, was determined to keep the protesters under control. With memories of the nationwide riots after King's death still fresh, Daley mobilized 12,000 Chicago police officers and over 5,000 National Guard. "As long as I am mayor," Daley vowed, "there will be law and order."

Order, however, soon collapsed. On August 28, as delegates cast votes for Humphrey, protesters were gathering in a downtown park to march on the convention. With television cameras focused on them, police moved into the crowd, sprayed the protesters with Mace, and beat them with nightsticks. Many protesters tried to flee, while others retaliated, pelting the riot-helmeted police with rocks and bottles. "The whole world is watching!" protesters shouted, as police attacked demonstrators and bystanders alike. **D**

The rioting soon spilled out of the park and into the downtown streets. One nearby hotel, observed a *New York Times* reporter, became a makeshift aid station.

### A PERSONAL VOICE J. ANTHONY LUKAS

"Demonstrators, reporters, McCarthy workers, doctors, all began to stagger into the [hotel] lobby, blood streaming from face and head wounds. The lobby smelled from tear gas, and stink bombs dropped by the Yippies. A few people began to direct the wounded to a makeshift hospital on the fifteenth floor, the McCarthy staff headquarters."

—quoted in *Decade of Shocks*

Disorder of a different kind reigned inside the convention hall, where delegates bitterly debated an antiwar plank in the party platform. When word of the riot filtered into the hall, delegates angrily shouted at Mayor Daley, who was present as a delegate himself. Daley returned their shouts with equal vigor. The whole world indeed was watching—on their televisions. The images of the Democrats—both inside and outside the convention hall—as a party of disorder became etched in the minds of millions of Americans.

**MAIN IDEA**

Summarizing
**D** What were the reasons protesters demonstrated in Chicago?

*D. Answer*
Some wanted to pressure Democrats to adopt an antiwar platform, others were displeased with Humphrey's nomination, and Yippies came to provoke violence to discredit the Democratic Party.

---

**NIXON TRIUMPHS** One beneficiary of this turmoil was Republican presidential candidate Richard M. Nixon, who by 1968 had achieved one of the greatest political comebacks in American politics. After his loss to Kennedy in the presidential race of 1960, Nixon tasted defeat again in 1962 when he ran for governor of California. His political career all but dead, Nixon joined a New York law firm, but he never strayed far from politics. In 1966, Nixon campaigned for Republican candidates in congressional elections, helping them to win back 47 House seats and 3 Senate seats from Democrats. In 1968, Nixon announced his candidacy for president and won the party's nomination.

During the presidential race, Nixon campaigned on a promise to restore law and order, which appealed to many middle-class Americans tired of years of riots and protests. He also promised, in vague but appealing terms, to end the war in Vietnam. Nixon's candidacy was helped by the entry of former Alabama governor **George Wallace** into the race as a third-party candidate. Wallace, a Democrat running on the American Independent Party ticket, was a longtime champion of school segregation and states' rights. Labeled the "white backlash" candidate, Wallace captured five Southern states. In addition, he attracted a surprisingly high number of Northern white working-class voters disgusted with inner-city riots and antiwar protests.

In the end, Nixon defeated Humphrey and inherited the quagmire in Vietnam. He eventually would end America's involvement in Vietnam, but not before his war policies created even more protest and uproar within the country.

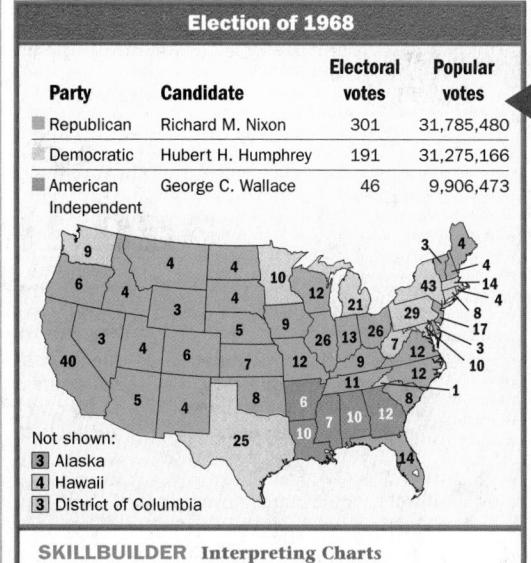

### Election of 1968

| Party | Candidate | Electoral votes | Popular votes |
|---|---|---|---|
| ■ Republican | Richard M. Nixon | 301 | 31,785,480 |
| ▨ Democratic | Hubert H. Humphrey | 191 | 31,275,166 |
| ■ American Independent | George C. Wallace | 46 | 9,906,473 |

Not shown:
3 Alaska
4 Hawaii
3 District of Columbia

**SKILLBUILDER** Interpreting Charts
1. In what region did Wallace carry states?
2. By how many electoral votes did Nixon defeat Humphrey?

*Skillbuilder Answers*
1. The South.
2. 110 votes.

## HISTORY from VISUALS

**Interpreting Charts**
Tell students that Nixon paid attention to the Wallace vote and crafted his policies to win Wallace supporters in his bid for reelection. Ask students how they think Nixon fared in 1972. *(He won in a landslide.)*

## Assess & Reteach

### SECTION 4 ASSESSMENT
Have pairs of students work together to find evidence in the text to support their answers.

📖 Formal Assessment
· Section Quiz, p. 409

### SELF-ASSESSMENT
Have students create multiple-effects charts showing the short- and long-term consequences of the Tet Offensive. Ask them to refer to their completed charts as they review their answers for item 3. Do they have new ideas to add?

### RETEACH
Use the time lines students created for item 2 to review the turbulent events in the first half of 1968.

📖 In-Depth Resources: Unit 6
· Reteaching Activity, p. 49

---

## SECTION 4 ASSESSMENT

1. **TERMS & NAMES** For each term or name, write a sentence explaining its significance.
   - Tet offensive
   - Robert Kennedy
   - Hubert Humphrey
   - Clark Clifford
   - Eugene McCarthy
   - George Wallace

### MAIN IDEA

2. **TAKING NOTES**
   Create a time line of major events that occurred in 1968. Use the months already plotted on the time line below as a guide.

   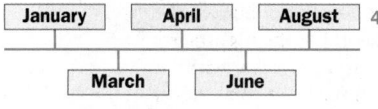

   | January | April | August |
   |---|---|---|
   | | March | June |

   Which event do you think was most significant? Explain.

### CRITICAL THINKING

3. **ANALYZING EVENTS**
   Why do you think the Tet offensive turned so many Americans against the war? Support your answer with reasons.

4. **MAKING INFERENCES**
   Refer to President Johnson's quote on page 750. What do you think he meant when he said "If I've lost Walter [Cronkite], then it's over. I've lost Mr. Average Citizen"? Explain.

5. **MAKING INFERENCES**
   Do you think there might have been a relationship between the violence of the Vietnam War and the growing climate of violence in the United States during 1968? Why or why not?

*The Vietnam War Years* **753**

---

Answers **ASSESSMENT** 4

**1. TERMS & NAMES**
Tet offensive, p. 749
Clark Clifford, p. 749
Robert Kennedy, p. 750
Eugene McCarthy, p. 750
Hubert Humphrey, p. 751
George Wallace, p. 753

**2. TAKING NOTES**
January–Tet Offensive; March–Johnson's withdrawal from presidential race; April–King's assassination; June–Robert Kennedy's assassination; August–Democratic National Convention.

**3. ANALYZING EVENTS**
It widened the Johnson administration's credibility gap and prompted mainstream media to criticize the war.

**4. MAKING INFERENCES**
Johnson believed that once Cronkite took a pessimistic stance on the war, any remaining supporters in the viewing audience would lose faith in Johnson's Vietnam policy.

**5. MAKING INFERENCES**
Yes–People were angry about U.S. involvement in the war and protests became increasingly violent. Much of the violence in the United States was sparked by the assassinations of King and Robert Kennedy. No–There is no cause-and-effect relationship between the two kinds of violence.

*The Vietnam War Years* **753**

# The End of the War and Its Legacy

| MAIN IDEA | WHY IT MATTERS NOW | Terms & Names |
|---|---|---|
| President Nixon instituted his Vietnamization policy, and America's longest war finally came to an end. | Since Vietnam, the United States considers more carefully the risks to its own interests before intervening in foreign affairs. | • Richard Nixon • Kent State • Henry Kissinger University • Vietnamization • Pentagon Papers • silent majority • War Powers Act • My Lai |

**U.S. History** 6E, 6H, 8A, 15C, 16A, 19B, 24B, 25A, 25B, 25C, 25D

## One American's Story

Alfred S. Bradford served in Vietnam from September 1968 to August 1969. A member of the 25th Infantry Division, he was awarded several medals, including the Purple Heart, given to soldiers wounded in battle. One day, Bradford's eight-year-old daughter, Elizabeth, inquired about his experience in Vietnam. "Daddy, why did you do it?" she asked. Bradford recalled what he had told himself.

**A PERSONAL VOICE** ALFRED S. BRADFORD

" Vietnam was my generation's adventure. I wanted to be part of that adventure and I believed that it was my duty as an American, both to serve my country and particularly not to stand by while someone else risked his life in my place. I do not regret my decision to go, but I learned in Vietnam not to confuse America with the politicians elected to administer America, even when they claim they are speaking for America, and I learned that I have a duty to myself and to my country to exercise my own judgment based upon my own conscience. "

—quoted in *Some Even Volunteered*

The legacy of the war was profound; it dramatically affected the way Americans viewed their government and the world. Richard Nixon had promised in 1968 to end the war, but it would take nearly five more years—and over 20,000 more American deaths—to end the nation's involvement in Vietnam.

▲ A U.S. soldier sits near Quang Tri, Vietnam, during a break in the fighting.

## **1** President Nixon and Vietnamization

In the summer of 1969, newly elected president **Richard Nixon** announced the first U.S. troop withdrawals from Vietnam. "We have to get rid of the nightmares we inherited," Nixon later told reporters. "One of the nightmares is war without end." However, as Nixon pulled out the troops, he continued the war against North Vietnam, a policy that some critics would charge prolonged the "war without end" for several more bloody years.

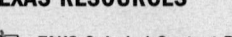
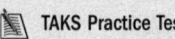
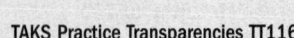
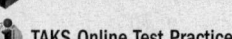

**THE PULLOUT BEGINS** As President Nixon settled into the White House in January of 1969, negotiations to end the war in Vietnam were going nowhere. The United States and South Vietnam insisted that all North Vietnamese forces withdraw from the South and that the government of Nguyen Van Thieu, then South Vietnam's ruler, remain in power. The North Vietnamese and Vietcong demanded that U.S. troops withdraw from South Vietnam and that the Thieu government step aside for a coalition government that would include the Vietcong.

In the midst of the stalled negotiations, Nixon conferred with National Security Adviser **Henry Kissinger** on a plan to end America's involvement in Vietnam. Kissinger, a German emigrant who had earned three degrees from Harvard, was an expert on international relations. Their plan, known as **Vietnamization,** called for the gradual withdrawal of U.S. troops in order for the South Vietnamese to take on a more active combat role in the war. By August of 1969, the first 25,000 U.S. troops had returned home from Vietnam. Over the next three years, the number of American troops in Vietnam dropped from more than 500,000 to less than 25,000. Ⓐ

**"PEACE WITH HONOR"** Part of Nixon and Kissinger's Vietnamization policy was aimed at establishing what the president called a "peace with honor." Nixon intended to maintain U.S. dignity in the face of its withdrawal from war. A further goal was to preserve U.S. clout at the negotiation table, as Nixon still demanded that the South Vietnamese government remain intact. With this objective—and even as the pullout had begun—Nixon secretly ordered a massive bombing campaign against supply routes and bases in North Vietnam. The president also ordered that bombs be dropped on the neighboring countries of Laos and Cambodia, which held a number of Vietcong sanctuaries. Nixon told his aide H. R. Haldeman that he wanted the enemy to believe he was capable of anything.

**A PERSONAL VOICE** RICHARD M. NIXON

" I call it the madman theory, Bob. . . . I want the North Vietnamese to believe I've reached the point where I might do anything to stop the war. We'll just slip the word to them that 'for God's sake, you know Nixon is obsessed about Communists. We can't restrain him when he's angry—and he has his hand on the nuclear button' —and Ho Chi Minh himself will be in Paris in two days begging for peace. "

—quoted in *The Price of Power*

**A. Answer** Vietnamization drastically cut America's involvement in Vietnam and allowed for thousands of U.S. troops to come home.

**MAIN IDEA**

**Synthesizing**
Ⓐ What was the impact of Vietnamization on the United States?

**Skillbuilder Answers**
**1.** Bombing was on a steady increase until 1968. It decreased after 1968 as U.S. troops began to withdraw from Vietnam.
**2.** *Possible Answer* The U.S. relied heavily on bombing to demoralize and defeat the Vietcong.

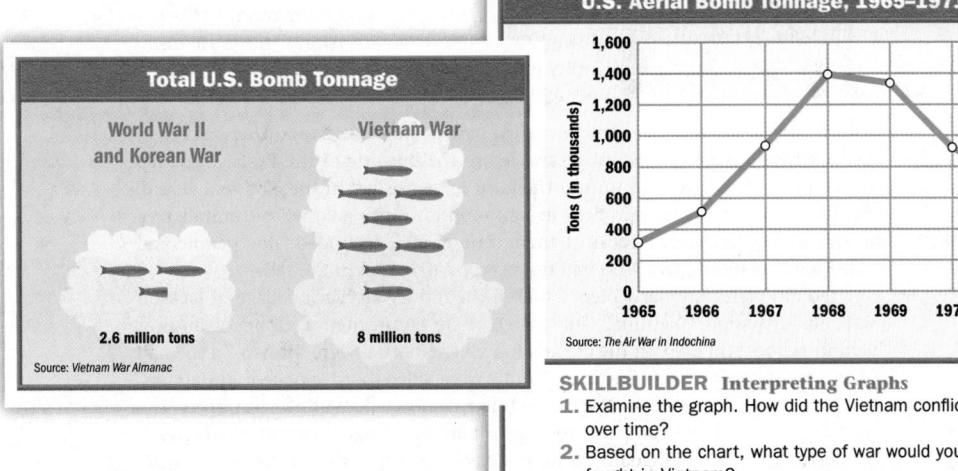

**Total U.S. Bomb Tonnage**

World War II and Korean War — 2.6 million tons
Vietnam War — 8 million tons

Source: *Vietnam War Almanac*

**U.S. Aerial Bomb Tonnage, 1965–1971**

Tons (in thousands) — 1965, 1966, 1967, 1968, 1969, 1970, 1971

Source: *The Air War in Indochina*

**SKILLBUILDER** Interpreting Graphs
1. Examine the graph. How did the Vietnam conflict change over time?
2. Based on the chart, what type of war would you say was fought in Vietnam?

**Interpreting Charts**
Ask students to briefly contrast the Vietnam War to World Wars I and II and the Korean War. Then ask them whether they think aerial bombing would have been as effective a strategy in Vietnam as it was in the other wars. *(In a guerrilla war, aerial bombing is of limited value and may be counterproductive to the degree that it hurts and alienates the populace, whose loyalty and support are critical to winning the war.)*

**More About . . .**

**Vietnamization**
Vietnamization was a plausible policy to many Americans. But its success was dependent on the ability of ARVN to defend South Vietnam and of the South Vietnamese government to command the loyalty of its people. Subsequent events proved that both ARVN and the government of President Thieu failed. In the end, Vietnamization prolonged the war and provided a political cover for American withdrawal.

*The Vietnam War Years* 755

---

**DIFFERENTIATING INSTRUCTION**   **LESS PROFICIENT READERS**

**Chronological Order**

As students read pages 755–759, have them identify events that mark the end of the war. Then place the events on a time line similar to the one shown on the right. Finally, have students review the steps toward peace.

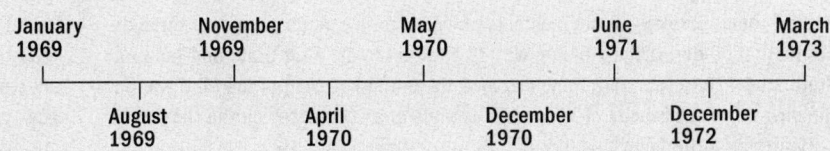

January 1969 — November 1969 — May 1970 — June 1971 — March 1973

August 1969 — April 1970 — December 1970 — December 1972

## Instruct: Objective

### Trouble Continues on the Home Front

TAKS SS11 1(US6.E)

· What happened at My Lai?

· Why did students and others protest Nixon's invasion of Cambodia?

· What happened at Kent State and Jackson State that prompted nationwide protests on college campuses all across America?

· What were the Pentagon Papers?

 In-Depth Resources: Unit 6
· Guided Reading, p. 43

---

### More About . . .

#### Kent State

Over the years the ROTC had become a principal target of campus antiwar protests. Some wanted to ban the ROTC in order to create a manpower shortage in the U.S. military, since many officers were graduates of ROTC programs. Ironically, William Schroeder, one of the four students killed at Kent State, was an ROTC cadet. The killings at Kent State added fuel to a national student strike already scheduled in protest of the Cambodia invasion. In fact, it was at a protest connected with this strike that the Jackson State killings occurred.

👁 Electronic Library of Primary Sources
· On the Kent State Tragedy, 1970, by the Presidential Commission on Campus Unrest

---

## ② Trouble Continues on the Home Front

Seeking to win support for his war policies, Richard Nixon appealed to what he called the **silent majority**—moderate, mainstream Americans who quietly supported the U.S. efforts in Vietnam. While many average Americans did support the president, the events of the war continued to divide the country.

**THE MY LAI MASSACRE** In November of 1969, Americans learned of a shocking event. That month, *New York Times* correspondent Seymour Hersh reported that on March 16, 1968, a U.S. platoon under the command of Lieutenant William Calley, Jr., had massacred innocent civilians in the small village of **My Lai** (mē′ lī′) in northern South Vietnam. Calley was searching for Vietcong rebels. Finding no sign of the enemy, the troops rounded up the villagers and shot more than 200 innocent Vietnamese—mostly women, children, and elderly men. "We all huddled them up," recalled 22-year-old Private Paul Meadlo. "I poured about four clips into the group. . . . The mothers was hugging their children. . . . Well, we kept right on firing."

The troops insisted that they were not responsible for the shootings because they were only following Lieutenant Calley's orders. When asked what his directive had been, one soldier answered, "Kill anything that breathed." Twenty-five army officers were charged with some degree of responsibility, but only Calley was convicted and imprisoned.

**THE INVASION OF CAMBODIA** Despite the shock over My Lai, the country's mood by 1970 seemed to be less explosive. American troops were on their way home, and it appeared that the war was finally winding down.

▲ President Nixon points to a map of Cambodia during a televised speech on April 30, 1970.

On April 30, 1970, President Nixon announced that U.S. troops had invaded Cambodia to clear out North Vietnamese and Vietcong supply centers. The president defended his action: "If when the chips are down, the world's most powerful nation acts like a pitiful, helpless giant, the forces of totalitarianism and anarchy will threaten free nations . . . throughout the world."

Upon hearing of the invasion, college students across the country burst out in protest. In what became the first general student strike in the nation's history, more than 1.5 million students closed down some 1,200 campuses. The president of Columbia University called the month that followed the Cambodian invasion "the most disastrous month of May in the history of . . . higher education."

**VIOLENCE ON CAMPUS** Disaster struck hardest at **Kent State University** in Ohio, where a massive student protest led to the burning of the ROTC building. In response to the growing unrest, the local mayor called in the National Guard. On May 4, 1970, the Guards fired live ammunition into a crowd of campus protesters who were hurling rocks at them. The gunfire wounded nine people and killed four, including two who had not even participated in the rally.

Ten days later, similar violence rocked the mostly all-black college of Jackson State in Mississippi. National Guardsmen there confronted a group of antiwar demonstrators and fired on the crowd after several bottles were thrown. In the hail of bullets, 12 students were wounded and 2 were killed, both innocent bystanders.

In a sign that America still remained sharply divided about the war, the country hotly debated the campus shootings. Polls indicated that many Americans supported the National Guard; respondents claimed that the students "got what

**Background**
Calley was imprisoned only a short time before President Nixon granted him house arrest. Calley was paroled in 1975, having served less than four years.

---

**DIFFERENTIATING INSTRUCTION** | **GIFTED & TALENTED STUDENTS**

#### Violence on Campus

Have students investigate the incidents of violence on college campuses throughout the nation during the Vietnam war. In addition to the Kent State and Jackson State student protests, they may also investigate the bombing of the Mathematics Building on the University of Wisconsin campus or disturbances on the University of California at Berkeley campus.

Students may put together their findings in a multimedia presentation or as a news broadcast reviewing the topic of violence on campus. After their presentation ask students if they think the student demonstrations were a factor in Nixon's move toward peace.

 Integrated Assessment
· Rubrics 3, 6

## History Through *Photojournalism*

### KENT STATE

Photographer John Filo was a senior at Kent State University when anti-war demonstrations rocked the campus. When the National Guard began firing at student protesters, Filo began shooting pictures, narrowly escaping a bullet himself.

As he continued to document the horrific scene, a girl running to the side of a fallen student caught his eye. Just as she dropped to her knees and screamed, Filo snapped a photograph that would later win the Pulitzer Prize and become one of the most memorable images of the decade.

Mary Ann Vecchio grieves over the body of Jeffrey Glenn Miller, a student shot by National Guard troops at Kent State. In the original photograph, a fence post appeared behind the woman's head. It is believed that someone manipulated the image in the early 1970s to make it more visually appealing.

**SKILLBUILDER Analyzing Visual Sources**
1. Why do you think this photograph remains a symbol of the Vietnam War era today? Explain your answer with specific details of the photograph.
2. What do you think is the most striking element of this photograph? Why?

📁 **SEE SKILLBUILDER HANDBOOK, PAGE R23.**

### History Through *Photojournalism*

**Interpreting a Photograph**

This famous photograph made an important statement in the growing division about the Vietnam War. Nixon and Agnew and their supporters were successful in characterizing student protesters as spoiled and destructive young people, not worthy of serious consideration. Ask students how the picture may have challenged those perceptions. *(Students should see that it pictures young people who probably looked no different than other young people of the time and who are undeserving of the brutal response of the National Guard.)*

**SKILLBUILDER ANSWERS**
1. The photograph shows the reality of the violence that erupted across the country during the Vietnam War. It shows that the war was not something that happened only overseas, but also on American soil.
2. The most striking element is the look of pain on the woman's face as she falls to her knees by the wounded student. Her outstretched arms seem to beg for an answer as to why this act of violence occurred.

---

**MAIN IDEA**

**Analyzing Issues**

**B** How did the campus shootings demonstrate the continued divisions within the country?

*B. Answer* The shootings sparked heated debate as well as the resurgence of "hardhats."

they were asking for." The weeks following the campus turmoil brought new attention to a group known as "hardhats," construction workers and other blue-collar Americans who supported the U.S. government's war policies. In May of 1970, nearly 100,000 members of the Building and Construction Trades Council of New York held a rally outside city hall to support the government. **B**

**THE PENTAGON PAPERS** Nixon and Kissinger's Cambodia policy, however, cost Nixon significant political support. By first bombing and then invading Cambodia without even notifying Congress, the president stirred anger on Capitol Hill. On December 31, 1970, Congress repealed the Tonkin Gulf Resolution, which had given the president near independence in conducting policy in Vietnam.

Support for the war eroded even further when in June of 1971 former Defense Department worker Daniel Ellsberg leaked what became known as the **Pentagon Papers.** The 7,000-page document, written for Defense Secretary Robert McNamara in 1967–1968, revealed among other things that the government had drawn up plans for entering the war even as President Lyndon Johnson promised that he would not send American troops to Vietnam. Furthermore, the papers showed that there was never any plan to end the war as long as the North Vietnamese persisted.

For many Americans, the Pentagon Papers confirmed their belief that the government had not been honest about its war intentions. The document, while not particularly damaging to the Nixon administration, supported what opponents of the war had been saying.

### More About . . .

**The Pentagon Papers**

The Pentagon Papers revealed U.S. involvement with Vietnam going back to the Truman administration's military aid to France in its war against the Vietminh. They showed that the Eisenhower administration was directly involved in preventing the 1956 elections in Vietnam. Because the Pentagon Papers revealed a detailed history of diplomatic secrets kept from the American people, Nixon went to extraordinary lengths to keep them from being published.

*The Vietnam War Years* **757**

---

### Understanding Idioms

Have students work with native English speakers to review the following words and phrases that appear on this page: After they have reviewed the list have them find the sentences in the text where the words or phrases appear. Have them read the sentence aloud and explain what concept the sentence conveys.

campus turmoil
hardhats
blue-collar Americans
rally
support for the war eroded
had drawn up plans

## Instruct: Objective ③

**America's Longest War Ends**

TAKS SS11 1(US6.E)

· What announcement did Kissinger make one week before the election?

· What happened with peace talks after Nixon's reelection?

· What were the terms of the cease-fire agreement?

· What was the final resolution of the Vietnam War?

 **In-Depth Resources: Unit 6**
· Guided Reading, p. 43

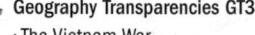 **Geography Transparencies GT30**
· The Vietnam War

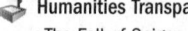 **Humanities Transparencies HT28**
· The Fall of Saigon

---

### KEY PLAYER

#### Henry Kissinger

Kissinger was the architect of foreign policy during a pivotal period. Perhaps his greatest achievement was creating the opening with China that culminated in Nixon's visit with Mao Zedong in 1972. Kissinger was attempting to resolve crises in Chile, Russia, and the Middle East, where he was active in "shuttle diplomacy." In 1973, he and Le Duc Tho, the North Vietnamese negotiator, were jointly awarded the Nobel Peace Prize.

---

### KEY PLAYER

**HENRY KISSINGER
1923–**

Henry Kissinger, who helped negotiate America's withdrawal from Vietnam and who later would help forge historic new relations with China and the Soviet Union, held a deep interest in the concept of power. "You know," he once noted, "most of these world leaders, you wouldn't want to know socially. Mostly they are intellectual mediocrities. The thing that is interesting about them is . . . their power."

At first, Kissinger seemed an unlikely candidate to work for Richard Nixon. Kissinger declared, "That man Nixon is not fit to be president." However, the two became trusted colleagues.

---

## America's Longest War Ends ③

In March of 1972, the North Vietnamese launched their largest attack on South Vietnam since the Tet offensive in 1968. President Nixon responded by ordering a massive bombing campaign against North Vietnamese cities. He also ordered that mines be laid in Haiphong harbor, the North's largest harbor, into which Soviet and Chinese ships brought supplies. The Communists "have never been bombed like they are going to be bombed this time," Nixon vowed. The bombings halted the North Vietnamese attack, but the grueling stalemate continued. It was after this that the Nixon administration took steps to finally end America's involvement in Vietnam.

**"PEACE IS AT HAND"** By the middle of 1972, the country's growing social division and the looming presidential election prompted the Nixon administration to change its negotiating policy. Polls showed that more than 60 percent of Americans in 1971 thought that the United States should withdraw all troops from Vietnam by the end of the year.

Henry Kissinger, the president's adviser for national security affairs, served as Nixon's top negotiator in Vietnam. Since 1969, Kissinger had been meeting privately with North Vietnam's chief negotiator, Le Duc Tho. Eventually, Kissinger dropped his insistence that North Vietnam withdraw all its troops from the South before the complete withdrawal of American troops. On October 26, 1972, days before the presidential election, Kissinger announced, "Peace is at hand."

**THE FINAL PUSH** President Nixon won reelection, but the promised peace proved to be elusive. The Thieu regime, alarmed at the prospect of North Vietnamese troops stationed in South Vietnam, rejected Kissinger's plan. Talks broke off on December 16. Two days later, the president unleashed a ferocious bombing campaign against Hanoi and Haiphong, the two largest cities in North Vietnam. In what became known as the "Christmas bombings," U.S. planes dropped 100,000 bombs over the course of eleven straight days, pausing only on Christmas Day.

At this point, calls to end the war resounded from the halls of Congress as well as from Beijing and Moscow. Everyone, it seemed, had finally grown weary of the war. The warring parties returned to the peace table, and on January 27, 1973, the United States signed an "Agreement on Ending the War and Restoring Peace in Vietnam." Under the agreement, North Vietnamese troops would remain in South Vietnam. However, Nixon promised to respond "with full force" to any violation of the peace agreement. On March 29, 1973, the last U.S. combat troops left for home. For America, the Vietnam War had ended. **ⓒ**

**THE FALL OF SAIGON** The war itself, however, raged on. Within months of the United States' departure, the cease-fire agreement between North and South Vietnam collapsed. In March of 1975, after several years of fighting, the North Vietnamese launched a full-scale invasion against the South. Thieu appealed to the United States for help. America provided economic aid but refused to send troops. Soon thereafter, President Gerald Ford—who assumed the presidency after the Watergate scandal forced President Nixon to resign—gave a speech in which he captured the nation's attitude toward the war:

*C. Answer* Kissinger dropped his insistence that the North Vietnamese withdraw all troops from the South before complete withdrawal of U.S. troops. The Thieu regime rejected Kissinger's plan. Nixon unleashed a bombing campaign on North Vietnam. Peace talks resumed and the warring parties signed an agreement to end the war.

**MAIN IDEA**

**Chronological Order**

**ⓒ** Summarize what led to the agreement to end the war in Vietnam.

---

### Creating a Vietnam War Poster

**Class Time** 45 minutes

**Task** Creating a poster that visually communicates a theme or time period of the Vietnam War

**Purpose** To help students better understand a particular aspect of the war or its impact

**Directions** Tell pairs of students to decide on a theme or a time period. Allow them time to look through print sources, including their textbook, for ideas and appropriate images. Tell them to create a thumbnail sketch of what their poster will look like. They may photocopy images, download them from the Internet, or draw them. Students may also choose to use a slogan. Display the posters in the classroom. You may also initiate a class discussion of the completed posters.

 Integrated Assessment
· Rubric 4

MAIN IDEA

**Evaluating Decisions**

**D** Why might the United States have refused to reenter the war?

*D. Answer*
Because of the war's divisive effect on the country, as well as the desire to heal and rebuild after massive casualties and expense.

"America can regain its sense of pride that existed before Vietnam. But it cannot be achieved by refighting a war that is finished as far as America is concerned." On April 30, 1975, North Vietnamese tanks rolled into Saigon and captured the city. Soon after, South Vietnam surrendered to North Vietnam. **D**

## The War Leaves a Painful Legacy ❹

The Vietnam War exacted a terrible price from its participants. In all, 58,000 Americans were killed and some 303,000 were wounded. North and South Vietnamese deaths topped 2 million. In addition, the war left Southeast Asia highly unstable, which led to further war in Cambodia. In America, a divided nation attempted to come to grips with an unsuccessful war. In the end, the conflict in Vietnam left many Americans with a more cautious outlook on foreign affairs and a more cynical attitude toward their government.

**AMERICAN VETERANS COPE BACK HOME** While families welcomed home their sons and daughters, the nation as a whole extended a cold hand to its returning Vietnam veterans. There were no brass bands, no victory parades, no cheering crowds. Instead, many veterans faced indifference or even hostility from an America still torn and bitter about the war. Lily Jean Lee Adams, who served as an army nurse in Vietnam, recalled arriving in America in 1970 while still in uniform.

> **A PERSONAL VOICE** LILY JEAN LEE ADAMS
>
> " In the bus terminal, people were staring at me and giving me dirty looks. I expected the people to smile, like, 'Wow, she was in Vietnam, doing something for her country—wonderful.' I felt like I had walked into another country, not my country. So I went into the ladies' room and changed. "
>
> —quoted in *A Piece of My Heart*

Many Vietnam veterans readjusted successfully to civilian life. However, about 15 percent of the 3.3 million soldiers who served developed post-traumatic stress disorder. Some had recurring nightmares about their war experiences, while many suffered from severe headaches and memory lapses. Other veterans became

◄ Lieutenant Colonel Robert Stirm, a returning POW, receives a warm welcome from his family in 1973. The longest-held Vietnam POW was Lieutenant Everett Alvarez, Jr., of California. He was imprisoned for more than eight years.

---

**Instruct: Objective ❹**

**The War's Painful Legacy**
TAKS SS11 1(US6.E)

· What kind of reception did Vietnam veterans receive when they came home?
· What happened in Southeast Asia after the Vietnam War?
· What is the legacy of the Vietnam War?
· How does the war still influence American politics and foreign policy?

📖 In-Depth Resources: Unit 6
· Guided Reading, p. 43

🗂 Critical Thinking Transparencies CT30
· The War in Vietnam

**More About . . .**

**Returning Veterans**
Vietnam veterans faced a very different homecoming than that given veterans of previous wars. Since most soldiers did a year's rotation "in country," they returned home individually, not as a unit. As a result, there was little public recognition of their effort. Many war protesters blamed soldiers for the war. Some veterans tried to slip back into civilian life and put the experience behind them. Others formed their own protest organizations and staged demonstrations against the war.

---

**ACTIVITY** **LINK TO POLITICS**

**MIA's**

**Class Time** 45 minutes

**Task** Writing a letter asking for information on MIA's

**Purpose** To analyze the issue of American MIA's

**Directions** Have students research the number of Americans Missing in Action (MIA's). Have students use library and Internet resources to document the numbers of MIA's and the reasons why the MIA issue remains alive for some Americans. Have students draft a letter to the government of Vietnam asking for information on MIA's.

📖 Integrated Assessment
· Rubrics 1, 5

 classzone.com

▲ Each year, over two million people visit the Vietnam Veterans Memorial. Many leave remembrances that are collected nightly by park rangers and stored in a museum. Inscribed on the memorial are over 58,000 names of Americans who died in the war or were then still listed as missing in action.

## HISTORICAL SPOTLIGHT

### Maya Lin and The Wall

Maya Lin has continued to make a name for herself as an accomplished architect and sculptor. She designed the Civil Rights Memorial in Montgomery, Alabama, as well as other large-scale installations. In 1995, a documentary film about her, *Maya Lin: A Strong, Clear Vision,* won an Oscar for Best Documentary. Ask students how Lin's design helped acknowledge all who died in Vietnam. *(By listing the names of all 58,000 people who died, the Wall commemorates each individual in a personal way.)*

## Tracing Themes
### DIVERSITY AND NATIONAL IDENTITY

Many of the Vietnamese refugees who fled to the United States after the war have developed a new and unique cultural identity. As Hien Duc Do remarked, "Having left Vietnam at an early age [14], I have realized that I can never truly be a Vietnamese, and, at the same time not having grown up in the United States, I can never fully be an American. In the final analysis, my life experience will be . . . Vietnamese-American. I need to merge the world of my parents with the opportunities, experiences, and hopes that America has to offer."

## HISTORICAL SPOTLIGHT

### VIETNAM VETERANS MEMORIAL: THE WALL

In 1981, a national competition was held to determine the Vietnam memorial's design. Maya Ying Lin, above, a 21-year-old architecture student of Chinese descent, submitted the winning design—two long, black granite walls on which are etched the names of the men and women who died or are missing in action.

"I didn't want a static object that people would just look at," Lin said, "but something they could relate to as on a journey, or passage, that would bring each to his own conclusions." Lin's design became known simply as "the Wall."

highly apathetic or began abusing drugs or alcohol. Several thousand even committed suicide.

In an effort to honor the men and women who served in Vietnam, the U.S. government unveiled the Vietnam Veterans Memorial in Washington, D.C., in 1982. Many Vietnam veterans, as well as their loved ones, have found visiting the memorial a deeply moving, even healing, experience.

**FURTHER TURMOIL IN SOUTHEAST ASIA** The end of the Vietnam War ushered in a new period of violence and chaos in Southeast Asia. In unifying Vietnam, the victorious Communists initially held out a conciliatory hand to the South Vietnamese. "You have nothing to fear," declared Colonel Bui Tin of the North Vietnamese Army.

However, the Communists soon imprisoned more than 400,000 South Vietnamese in harsh "reeducation," or labor, camps. As the Communists imposed their rule throughout the land, nearly 1.5 million people fled Vietnam. They included citizens who had supported the U.S. war effort, as well as business owners, whom the Communists expelled when they began nationalizing the country's business sector.

Also fleeing the country was a large group of poor Vietnamese, known as boat people because they left on anything from freighters to barges to rowboats. Their efforts to reach safety across the South China Sea often met with tragedy; nearly 50,000 perished on the high seas due to exposure, drowning, illness, or piracy.

The people of Cambodia also suffered greatly after the war. The U.S. invasion of Cambodia had unleashed a brutal civil war in which a communist group known as the Khmer Rouge, led by Pol Pot, seized power in 1975. In an effort to transform the country into a peasant society, the Khmer Rouge executed professionals and anyone with an education or foreign ties. During its reign of terror, the Khmer Rouge is believed to have killed at least 1 million Cambodians.

---

 **BLOCK SCHEDULING**

### Honoring the Returning Vietnam Veteran

**Class Time** Two class periods

**Task** Creating and performing a ceremony welcoming a returning Vietnam veteran

**Purpose** To gain an understanding of how others can facilitate readjustment to civilian life

**Directions** Tell students that various tribal ceremonies helped many Native American veterans recover from the trauma of Vietnam. For example, one Kiowa veteran was honored as a warrior by his people in a ritual ceremony. He said he felt pride "because that's the way the Kiowa people tell you that you've done well." Have students work in small groups to create and perform a welcoming ceremony. Tell them that the returning veteran may be real (such as a family member who served) or fictitious. In either case, they should explain who is being honored, that person's role in the war (such as soldier or nurse), and any symbolism involved in the ceremony.

**THE LEGACY OF VIETNAM** Even after it ended, the Vietnam War remained a subject of great controversy for Americans. Many hawks continued to insist that the war could have been won if the United States had employed more military power. They also blamed the antiwar movement at home for destroying American morale. Doves countered that the North Vietnamese had displayed incredible resiliency and that an increase in U.S. military force would have resulted only in a continuing stalemate. In addition, doves argued that an unrestrained war against North Vietnam might have prompted a military reaction from China or the Soviet Union.

The war resulted in several major U.S. policy changes. First, the government abolished the draft, which had stirred so much antiwar sentiment. The country also took steps to curb the president's war-making powers. In November 1973, Congress passed the **War Powers Act,** which stipulated that a president must inform Congress within 48 hours of sending forces into a hostile area without a declaration of war. In addition, the troops may remain there no longer than 90 days unless Congress approves the president's actions or declares war.

In a broader sense, the Vietnam War significantly altered America's views on foreign policy. In what has been labeled the Vietnam syndrome, Americans now pause and consider possible risks to their own interests before deciding whether to intervene in the affairs of other nations.

Finally, the war contributed to an overall cynicism among Americans about their government and political leaders that persists today. Americans grew suspicious of a government that could provide as much misleading information or conceal as many activities as the Johnson and Nixon administrations had done. Coupled with the Watergate scandal of the mid-1970s, the war diminished the optimism and faith in government that Americans felt during the Eisenhower and Kennedy years.

---

**MAIN IDEA**

**Contrasting**
 Contrast the two viewpoints regarding the legacy of the Vietnam War.

**E. Answer**
Hawks: The, U.S. could have won if greater military power had been used; protest movements damaged American morale. Doves: An increase in military power would have resulted in a continuing stalemate.

**Mini-Lesson 1: SS11 1(US1.B)**

---

## NOW & THEN

### U.S. RECOGNITION OF VIETNAM

In July of 1995, more than 20 years after the Vietnam War ended, the United States extended full diplomatic relations to Vietnam. In announcing the resumption of ties with Vietnam, President Bill Clinton declared, "Let this moment . . . be a time to heal and a time to build." Demonstrating how the war still divides Americans, the president's decision drew both praise and criticism from members of Congress and veterans' groups.

In an ironic twist, Clinton nominated as ambassador to Vietnam a former prisoner of war from the Vietnam War, Douglas Peterson, a congress member from Florida. Peterson, a former air force pilot, was shot down over North Vietnam in 1966 and spent six and a half years in a Hanoi prison.

---

## NOW & THEN

**U.S. Recognition of Vietnam**
**Summarizing** Tell students that Vietnam has become a tourist destination for many Americans. Have each student find and read an article about American veterans who have returned to Vietnam. Tell them to present an oral summary of the article to the class.

## Assess & Reteach

### SECTION 5 ASSESSMENT
Have students work in small groups to discuss the questions and assess one another's responses.

Formal Assessment
· Section Quiz, p. 410

### SELF ASSESSMENT
Have students explore their understanding of the Vietnam War's legacy by listing in a chart the war's effects on each of the following: Vietnam veterans, Southeast Asia, U.S. policies, and U.S. attitudes.

### RETEACH
Have students construct a time line that identifies the key events of the war.

In-Depth Resources: Unit 6
· Reteaching Activity, p. 50

---

## 5 ASSESSMENT

1. **TERMS & NAMES** For each term or name, write a sentence explaining its significance.
   - Richard Nixon
   - Henry Kissinger
   - Vietnamization
   - silent majority
   - My Lai
   - Kent State University
   - Pentagon Papers
   - War Powers Act

**MAIN IDEA**

2. **TAKING NOTES**
In a web like the one shown, list the effects of the Vietnam War on America.

Vietnam War's Effect on America

Choose one effect to further explain in a paragraph.

**CRITICAL THINKING**

3. **ANALYZING EFFECTS**
In your opinion, what was the main effect of the U.S. government's deception about its policies and military conduct in Vietnam? Support your answer with evidence from the text. **Think About:**
   - the contents of the Pentagon Papers
   - Nixon's secrecy in authorizing military maneuvers

4. **MAKING INFERENCES**
How would you account for the cold homecoming American soldiers received when they returned from Vietnam? Support your answer with reasons.

5. **SYNTHESIZING**
In the end, do you think the United States' withdrawal from Vietnam was a victory for the United States or a defeat? Explain your answer.

---

Answers **ASSESSMENT**

**1. TERMS & NAMES**
Richard Nixon, p. 754
Henry Kissinger, p. 755
Vietnamization, p. 755
silent majority, p. 756
My Lai, p. 756
Kent State University, p. 756
Pentagon Papers, p. 757
War Powers Act, p. 761

**2. TAKING NOTES**
Thousands of Americans killed or wounded; many Americans developed a more cautious outlook on foreign affairs; many Americans became cynical about the government; anti-war demonstrations resulted in violence and even deaths; policy changes were made, such as War Powers Act and abolition of draft.

**3. ANALYZING EFFECTS**
Americans became increasingly distrustful of the government. Examples include responses to the Pentagon Papers; Congressional repeal of the Gulf of Tonkin Resolution.

**4. MAKING INFERENCES**
Some Americans blamed the war's failure on the soldiers; the My Lai

massacre might have tarnished the image of all U.S. soldiers.

**5. SYNTHESIZING**
Victory–The United States withdrew on its own terms. U.S. withdrawal curtailed American military and economic losses. Defeat–The United States was unable to claim victory because North Vietnam did not surrender.

AMERICAN LITERATURE

## AMERICAN LITERATURE

### Objectives

· To explain the Vietnam War's influence on literature

· To identify the perceptions of the Vietnam War expressed in three literary excerpts

## Focus & Motivate

Ask students to identify books they have read or movies they have seen that have given them a picture of the Vietnam War.

· What ideas about the war have they gotten from these books and/or films?

· How do the literary and film images compare with those of books and movies set in other 20th century wars?

### More About . . .

**Tim O'Brien**

A gifted writer about the Vietnam War, Tim O'Brien was drafted just after graduating from Macalester College in 1968. A Minnesota native, he was deeply troubled by the war and even considered avoiding service. Instead, he fought valiantly in Vietnam and earned a Purple Heart. He completed his tour of duty in 1970 and won acclaim in 1973 for his semifictional memoir, *If I Die in a Combat Zone, Box Me Up and Ship Me Home.* Another book he wrote, *Going After Cacciato* received the National Book Award.

# Literature of the Vietnam War

Throughout history, soldiers as well as citizens have written about the traumatic and moving experiences of war. The Vietnam War, which left a deep impression on America's soldiers and citizens alike, has produced its share of literature. From the surreal fantasy of *Going After Cacciato* to the grim realism of *A Rumor of War,* much of this literature reflects the nation's lingering disillusionment with its involvement in the Vietnam War.

Going After Cacciato
A NOVEL BY
TIM O'BRIEN

WINNER OF THE NATIONAL BOOK AWARD
"A MAJOR ACHIEVEMENT." — *The New York Times Book Review*

**762** CHAPTER 22

**GOING AFTER CACCIATO**

In *Going After Cacciato*, Vietnam veteran Tim O'Brien tells the story of Paul Berlin, a newcomer to Vietnam who fantasizes that his squad goes all the way to Paris, France, in pursuit of an AWOL soldier.

"How many days you been at the war?" asked Alpha's [Alpha Company's] mail clerk, and Paul Berlin answered that he'd been at the war seven days now.

The clerk laughed. "Wrong," he said. "Tomorrow, man, that's your first day at the war."

And in the morning PFC [Private First Class] Paul Berlin boarded a resupply chopper that took him fast over charred pocked mangled country, hopeless country, green skies and speed and tangled grasslands and paddies and places he might die, a million possibilities. He couldn't watch. He watched his hands. He made fists of them, opening and closing the fists. His hands, he thought, not quite believing. *His* hands.

Very quickly, the helicopter banked and turned and went down.

"How long you been at the war?" asked the first man he saw, a wiry soldier with ringworm in his hair.

PFC Paul Berlin smiled. "This is it," he said. "My first day."

—Tim O'Brien, *Going After Cacciato* (1978)

---

## RECOMMENDED RESOURCES

### BOOKS

Hayslip, Le Ly. *When Heaven and Earth Changed Places.* New York: Doubleday, 1989. A first-person account of a Vietnamese woman's experiences in the war.

O'Brien, Tim. *The Things They Carried.* Boston: Houghton: 1990. Interrelated stories capturing the Vietnam War era. (Note: contains strong language.)

Wyatt, David. *Out of the Sixties.* Cambridge UP: 1993. A study of storytelling and the Vietnam War generation.

### VIDEOS

*A Rumor of War.* Dir. Richard T. Heffron. USA Home Video, 1984. Acclaimed made-for-TV movie based on Caputo's book.

*Vietnam: Chronicle of a War.* CBS/FOX Video, 1981. Retrospective of the Vietnam War based on CBS news broadcasts featuring Walter Cronkite and others.

### SOFTWARE

*USA Wars: Vietnam.* CD-ROM. Quanta Press. Brings the war to life with articles, images, facts, statistics, and the entire Vietnam Veterans Memorial database.

*Vietnam: A Visual Investigation.* CD-ROM. Medio, 1994.

**A RUMOR OF WAR**

In *A Rumor of War*, considered to be among the best nonfiction accounts of the war, former marine Philip Caputo reflects on his years as a soldier in Vietnam.

At the age of twenty-four, I was more prepared for death than I was for life. . . . I knew how to face death and how to cause it, with everything on the evolutionary scale of weapons from the knife to the 3.5-inch rocket launcher. The simplest repairs on an automobile engine were beyond me, but I was able to field-strip and assemble an M-14 rifle blindfolded. I could call in artillery, set up an ambush, rig a booby trap, lead a night raid.

Simply by speaking a few words into a two-way radio, I had performed magical feats of destruction. Summoned by my voice, jet fighters appeared in the sky to loose their lethal droppings on villages and men. High-explosive bombs blasted houses to fragments, napalm sucked air from lungs and turned human flesh to ashes. All this just by saying a few words into a radio transmitter. Like magic.

—Philip Caputo,
*A Rumor of War* (1977)

**FALLEN ANGELS**

Richie Perry, a 17-year-old Harlem youth, describes his harrowing tour of duty in Vietnam in Walter Dean Myers's novel *Fallen Angels*.

The war was about us killing people and about people killing us, and I couldn't see much more to it. Maybe there were times when it was right. I had thought that this war was right, but it was only right from a distance. Maybe when we all got back to the World and everybody thought we were heroes for winning it, then it would seem right from there. . . . But when the killing started, there was no right or wrong except in the way you did your job, except in the way that you were part of the killing.

What you thought about, what filled you up more than anything, was the being scared and hearing your heart thumping in your temples and all the noises, the terrible noises, the screeches and the booms and the guys crying for their mothers or for their wives.

—Walter Dean Myers,
*Fallen Angels* (1988)

---

**THINKING CRITICALLY**

1. **Comparing** What similar views about war do you think these books convey?

   **SEE SKILLBUILDER HANDBOOK, PAGE R8.**

2.  **INTERNET ACTIVITY** CLASSZONE.COM

   Visit the links for American Literature to research personal accounts of the Vietnam War, such as interviews, letters, and essays. Copy several excerpts you find particularly interesting or moving and assemble them in a book. Write an introduction to your collection explaining why you chose them. Share your book with the class.

## Instruct

1. How do the authors depict the war?
2. What is different about the characterization of the Vietnam War compared to the way wars are traditionally depicted?
3. How do the authors deal with moral concerns?

**MAKING PERSONAL CONNECTIONS**

Remind students that many of the soldiers in Vietnam were only a few years older than the students are now. Ask them to put themselves in the place of young men during the Vietnam War era. What would they have done? Would they have tried to avoid being drafted? If drafted, would they have served in Vietnam? How would they feel about risking their lives in a war that had such conflicting aims and troublesome tactics?

**More About . . .**

**African-American Soldiers in Vietnam**

African Americans served in disproportionate numbers in Vietnam (12.6 and 15% of armed forces; 10% of population). Added to that injustice were the pressing issues at home involving African Americans—the struggles of the civil rights movement, the assassination of Martin Luther, King, Jr., and urban riots that left African-American communities burned and ruined.

*The Vietnam War Years* **763**

---

**THINKING CRITICALLY: ANSWERS**

1. **COMPARING** The grim reality of war; they paint portraits of disillusionment, horror, violence, fear, inhumanity, and senselessness.

2. **INTERNET ACTIVITY**
   **Rubric**
   The collected accounts should . . .
   · include a variety of accounts
   · have an introduction
   · be organized in an interesting manner

CHAPTER 22 ASSESSMENT

## TERMS & NAMES

1. Ho Chi Minh, p. 731
2. Ngo Dinh Diem, p. 732
3. Vietcong, p. 732
4. William Westmoreland, p. 737
5. credibility gap, p. 741
6. Tet offensive, p. 749
7. Robert Kennedy, p. 750
8. Henry Kissinger, p. 755
9. Vietnamization, p. 755
10. Pentagon Papers, p. 757

## MAIN IDEAS

1. The resolution granted President Johnson broad war-making powers that allowed him to escalate U.S. involvement in the Vietnam War.
2. Countries on the brink of communism were like a row of dominoes. If one fell, the rest would follow in a chain reaction.
3. They believed that the spread of communism jeopardized democracy.
4. Americans became aware of the credibility gap between what was really happening and what they were being told. U.S. troops were frustrated by the conditions in Vietnam and by the elusiveness of their enemy.
5. A disproportionately high number of African Americans served and died; racial tensions existed in many platoons.
6. Doves staged massive anti-war demonstrations; hawks urged a greater use of military force in Vietnam.
7. Johnson's high disapproval rating in public-opinion polls after the Tet offensive; the divisions within the Democratic Party.
8. the assassinations of Dr. Martin Luther King, Jr., and Robert Kennedy; the riots at the Democratic National Convention
9. The war raged on; the cease-fire agreement between North and South Vietnam collapsed.
10. Immediate: U.S. policy changes, including abolishment of the draft and enactment of the War Powers Act. More lasting: American public's cynicism about the government and its increasingly cautious attitude regarding foreign affairs.

**VISUAL SUMMARY**

### THE VIETNAM WAR YEARS

**1964**
**1964** Congress passes the Tonkin Gulf Resolution, giving the president broad military powers in Vietnam.

**1965**
**1965** First major U.S. combat troops arrive in Vietnam to fight the Vietcong and North Vietnamese Army.

**1966**

**1967**
**1967** Antiwar protests in the United States intensify.

**1968**
**1968** Vietcong launch massive Tet offensive on numerous South Vietnamese cities.

**1969**
**1969** Paris peace talks begin in earnest; President Nixon announces Vietnamization of war—gradual withdrawal of U.S. troops.

**1970**
**1970** President Nixon orders invasion of Cambodia to destroy enemy supply bases; American college campuses erupt in protest.

**1971**

**1972**
**1972** Nixon unleashes "Christmas bombings" on North Vietnamese cities after peace talks break off.

**1973**
**1973** United States and North Vietnam sign a truce; the U.S. withdraws the last of its troops from Vietnam.

**1974**

**1975**

## TERMS AND NAMES

For each term or name below, write a sentence explaining its connection to the Vietnam War years.

1. Ho Chi Minh
2. Ngo Dinh Diem
3. Vietcong
4. William Westmoreland
5. napalm
6. Tet offensive
7. Robert Kennedy
8. Henry Kissinger
9. Vietnamization
10. Pentagon Papers

## MAIN IDEAS

Use your notes and the information in the chapter to answer the following questions.

### Moving Toward Conflict (pages 730–735)

1. How did the Tonkin Gulf Resolution lead to greater U.S. involvement in Vietnam?
2. What was President Eisenhower's explanation of the domino theory?

### U.S. Involvement and Escalation (pages 736–741)

3. Why did so much of the American public and many in the Johnson administration support U.S. escalation in Vietnam?
4. Why did the war begin to lose support at home? What contributed to the sinking morale of the U.S. troops?

### A Nation Divided (pages 742–747)

5. What race-related problems existed for African-American soldiers who served in the Vietnam War?
6. Summarize the ways in which the United States was sharply divided between hawks and doves.

### 1968: A Tumultuous Year (pages 748–753)

7. What circumstances set the stage for President Johnson's public announcement that he would not seek another term as president?
8. What acts of violence occurred in the United States during 1968 that dramatically altered the mood of the country?

### The End of the War and Its Legacy (pages 754–761)

9. Briefly describe the military conflict in Vietnam soon after the last U.S. combat troops departed in 1973.
10. List the immediate effects and the more lasting legacies of America's involvement in the Vietnam War.

## CRITICAL THINKING

1. **USING YOUR NOTES** Create a cause-and-effect diagram like the one below for each of these congressional measures: **a.** Tonkin Gulf Resolution (1964), **b.** repeal of the Tonkin Gulf Resolution (1970), **c.** War Powers Act (1973).

cause → Congressional Measure → effect

2. **DEVELOPING HISTORICAL PERSPECTIVE** Why do you think so many young Americans became so vocal in their condemnation of the Vietnam War?

## CRITICAL THINKING

1. **Using Your Notes (a) Causes–** North Vietnamese torpedo boats allegedly attack U.S. destroyers. **Effects–**Johnson administration escalates U.S. military involvement in Vietnam. **(b) Causes–**Nixon's policy of bombing and invading Cambodia without notifying Congress; **Effects–**President's autonomy becomes limited in conducting Vietnam policies; Congress regains power in shaping Vietnam policies. **(c) Causes–**The outcome of the Vietnam War; fears that Nixon was setting a dangerous precedent of unchecked presidential power; **Effects–**President's war-making powers curbed.

2. **Developing Historical Perspective** Since the draft board called men between the ages of 18 and 26 into military service, the Vietnam War directly affected young Americans; the war would take its greatest toll on this generation and would have a tremendous impact on shaping their lives; the tragedies at Kent State revealed that students could, in a sense, also become casualties of war.

## Standardized Test Practice

Use the cartoon and your knowledge of U.S. history to answer question 1.

REDUCED STRIKE ZONE

1. Which of the following was a reason the U.S. had difficulty winning the war in Vietnam?

   **A** The Vietcong hid in small villages throughout the country and were difficult to find.

   **B** Vietcong troops outnumbered U.S. troops.

   **C** The U.S. had to fight two enemy armies at the same time: the South Vietnamese and the North Vietnamese.

   **D** The U.S. could not use its tanks because they could not be transported across the Pacific.

Use the quotation and your knowledge of U.S. history to answer question 2.

> " Perhaps the place to start looking for a credibility gap is not in the offices of the government in Washington, but in the studios of the networks in New York. "
>
> —Spiro T. Agnew

2. During the Vietnam War, the term "credibility gap" referred to the American people's lack of trust in —

   **F** Presidents Johnson and Nixon.

   **G** television news reporters.

   **H** antiwar protesters.

   **J** Ho Chi Minh.

3. What happened to Vietnam after the U.S. pullout in 1973?

   **A** The North and South remained divided and at peace.

   **B** The North and South remained enemies, separated by a United Nations-controlled demilitarized zone.

   **C** The North became a Chinese puppet state; the South experienced continual violent rebellions.

   **D** The North defeated the South and incorporated it under a communist government.

**ADDITIONAL TEST PRACTICE, pages S1–S33.**

 **TEST PRACTICE** CLASSZONE.COM

## Standardized Test Practice

1. The correct answer is letter **A**.

   Letter B is not correct because the number of Vietcong was unknown. Letter C is not correct because the South Vietnamese were allies of the United States. Letter D is not correct because tanks would have been of little use against guerrilla fighters.

2. Letter **F** is correct.

   Letter G is not correct because Americans generally believed what was reported to them by the news media. Letters H and J were not correct because the credibility gap referred to erroneous information provided by the Johnson and Nixon administrations.

3. Letter **D** is correct.

   Letters A, B, and C are not correct because they do not reflect what happened to Vietnam after the U.S. pullout in 1973.

## LOBBYING PLAN

**Tips for Teaching**

· Students should finalize position papers, pamphlets, advertising, posters, or other promotional material.

· Review the overall lobbying plan and make suggestions for changes.

**Project Presentation Rubrics**

The Lobbying Plan should . . .

· state the desired government action and reasons for it

· outline specific steps to raise awareness in supporters and government officials

· include samples of position papers, pamphlets, advertising, posters or other promotional material

📝 Formal Assessment

   · Chapter Test, Forms A, B, and C, pp. 411–422

## ALTERNATIVE ASSESSMENT

1. **INTERACT WITH HISTORY** Recall your discussion of the question on page 729:

   *Who should be exempt from the draft?*

   What lessons do you think can be learned from the ways in which Americans reacted to the draft? Write a paragraph expressing and giving reasons for your judgments. Think About:

   • how the draft affected Americans' views on the Vietnam War

   • how the draft affected Americans' participation in the Vietnam War

   • how draft protests affected other Americans

2. **VIDEO** LEARNING FROM MEDIA  View the *American Stories* video "Matters of Conscience." Discuss the following questions in a group; then do the activity.

   • What different views about the Vietnam War were expressed in the video?

   • Why does Gubar say he feels guilt about having served in the war?

   **Cooperative Learning Activity**  Organize two teams for debate. One team should argue for the side of the hawks, and the other team should argue on behalf of the doves. Research the arguments put forth by both sides and debate the issue before the class.

## ALTERNATIVE ASSESSMENT

### 1. INTERACT WITH HISTORY

**Rubric**

Paragraphs should . . .

· clearly state the student's opinion

· include evidence from the Vietnam era to support the opinion

· follow the rules of spelling, punctuation, and grammar

### 2. LEARNING FROM MEDIA

**Rubric**

Debating students should . . .

· support their position with facts and well-thought-out arguments

· respond appropriately to each other's statements

· speak clearly so that everyone in the room can hear them

# An Era of Social Change

| | CHAPTER OVERVIEW | COPYMASTERS | INTEGRATED TECHNOLOGY |
|---|---|---|---|
| **CHAPTER RESOURCES** | *The civil rights movements inspires Latinos, Native Americans, and women to seek equality in American society. At the same time, the nation's young people adopt values that conflict with mainstream culture.* | 📖 Telescoping the Times<br>· Chapter Summary, pp. 45–46<br><br>📖 Planning for Block Schedules | 💿 Primary Source Explorer<br>👁 Power Presentations<br>💿 Electronic Teacher Tools<br>🖥 Online Lesson Planner<br>🖥 classzone.com |
| **SECTION 1**<br><br>Latinos and Native Americans Seek Equality<br><br>pp. 768–775 | **KEY IDEAS**<br>*The nation's Latinos and Native Americans demand greater equality.* | 📖 In-Depth Resources: Unit 6<br>· Guided Reading, p. 64<br>· Building Vocabulary, p. 67<br>· Reteaching Activity, p. 69<br>· Primary Sources, pp. 74–75<br>· Literature, pp. 78–80<br>· American Lives, p. 81<br><br>📖 Lesson Plans, pp. 181-182 | 🗺 Geography Transparencies GT31<br>· Latino and Native American Population Centers, 1970<br>🗺 Humanities Transparencies HT29<br>· Mural in Los Angeles<br>💿 Electronic Library of Primary Sources<br>· *The Birth of La Causa* by César Chávez<br>🖥 classzone.com |
| **SECTION 2**<br><br>Women Fight for Equality<br><br>pp.776–780 | *A new feminist movement emerges during the 1960s, as women fight to improve their opportunities and status in society.* | 📖 In-Depth Resources: Unit 6<br>· Guided Reading, p. 65<br>· Reteaching Activity, p. 70<br>· Geography Application, pp. 72–73<br>· Primary Sources, p. 76<br>· American Lives, p. 82<br><br>📖 Lesson Plans, pp. 183-184 | 🗺 Critical Thinking Transparencies CT31, CT65<br>· The Women's Movement<br>· Percentage of All Women Who Are Working<br>💿 Electronic Library of Primary Sources<br>· from *The Feminine Mystique* by Betty Friedan<br>· *from* NOW's Statement of Purpose<br>🖥 classzone.com |
| **SECTION 3**<br><br>Culture and Counterculture<br><br>pp. 781–787 | *Groups of disillusioned youths shun the social activism of the time and choose instead to "drop out" of society and establish their own way of life.* | 📖 In-Depth Resources: Unit 6<br>· Guided Reading, p. 66<br>· Skillbuilder Practice, p. 68<br>· Reteaching Activity, p 71<br>· Primary Sources, p. 77<br><br>📖 Lesson Plans, pp. 185-186 | 🖥 classzone.com |

| | Pupil's Edition | | Overhead Transparency | | CD-ROM |
| | Teacher's Edition | | Audio Library | | Internet |
| | Copymaster | | | | |

## ASSESSMENT OPTIONS

Chapter Assessment, pp. 460–461

Formal Assessment
· Chapter Tests, Forms A, B, and C, pp. 426–437

Test Generator

Integrated Assessment Book

TAKS Online Test Practice

TAKS Spiraled Content Review

TAKS Practice Tests

---

Section 1 Assessment, p. 773

Self-Assessment, p. 773

Formal Assessment, Quiz, p. 423

Integrated Assessment Book

Test Generator

TAKS Practice Transparencies TT117

---

Section 2 Assessment, p. 780

Self-Assessment, p. 780

Formal Assessment, Quiz, p. 424

Integrated Assessment Book

Test Generator

TAKS Practice Transparencies TT118

---

Section 3 Assessment, p. 787

Self-Assessment, p. 787

Formal Assessment, Quiz, p. 425

Integrated Assessment Book

Test Generator

TAKS Practice Transparencies TT119

## RESOURCES FOR DIFFERENTIATING INSTRUCTION

### Students Acquiring English/ESL

**Reading Study Guide**
(English and Spanish)
pp. 229–234

**Access for Students Acquiring English/ESL:**
Spanish Translations,
pp. 246–251

**Chapter Summaries on CD**
(English and Spanish)

### Less Proficient Readers

**Reading Study Guide**
(English and Spanish)
pp. 229–234

**Telescoping the Times**
· Chapter Summary,
pp. 45–46

**Chapter Summaries on CD**
(English and Spanish)

### Gifted and Talented Students

**In-Depth Resources: Unit 6**
· Primary Sources,
pp. 74–77
Literature, pp. 78–80
· American Lives: César
Chávez, p. 81; Betty
Friedan, p. 82

**Electronic Library of Primary Sources**
· Unit 6, Chapter 23

## CROSS-CURRICULAR CONNECTIONS

### Primary Sources
Dog, Mary Crow. *Lakota Woman.* NY: Weidenfeld, 1990. The autobiography of a Native American who participated in the struggle to attain equal rights in the 1960s and 1970s.

Duplessis, Rachel Blau (editor) et al. *The Feminist Memoir Project: Voices from Women's Liberation.* NY: Crown Publishing, 1998. Assembled accounts of the feminist movement in the 1960s and 1970s. These stories inspire and amuse.

### Civics
Ferriss, Susan, et al. *The Fight in the Fields: César Chávez and the Farmworkers Movement.* NY: Harcourt Brace, 1997. As the founder of the United Farm Workers Union, this Hispanic American from humble means leads immigrant workers through a nonviolent struggle to achieve basic human rights.

### Humanities: Music
Heylin, Clinton. *Bob Dylan: Behind the Shades.* NY: William Morrow & Co., 2001. An in-depth look at the man that helped unleash the counterculture through his music and lyrics.

### Humanities: Art
Broude, Norma and Garrad, Mary D. (editors). *The Power of Feminist Art: The American Movement of the 1970s, History and Impact.* NY: Harry N. Abrams, 1996. A compilation of the history of American feminist art—art that depicts the experience of the female as a result of gender-role restrictions.

### Literature
McDougall Littell
Nextext
*Latino Writers in the U.S.*

## ENRICHMENT ACTIVITIES

**Pupil's Edition**, pp. 766–787
Interact with History, pp. 766–767
Supreme Court, pp. 774–775
Daily Life, pp. 786–787

**In-Depth Resources: Unit 6**
· Geography Application: The Equal Rights
Amendment, pp. 72–73
· Primary Source: The Farm Workers
Movement, p.74
· Primary Source: United Farm Workers
Poster, p. 75

· Primary Source: *The Feminine Mystique*, p. 76
· Primary Source: Popular Song, p. 77
· Literature: from *Los Vendidos*, pp. 78–80
· American Lives: César Chávez, p. 81
· American Lives: Betty Friedan, p. 82

**Electronic Library of Primary Sources**
· Unit 6, Chapter 23

**Primary Source Explorer**
· César Chávez, *An Open Letter,* 1969

## BLOCK SCHEDULE LESSON PLAN OPTIONS (90-MINUTE PERIOD)

### DAY 1

**CHAPTER OPENER**
pp. 766–767

**Class Time** 35 minutes

**History from Visuals, p. 766**

**Class Time** 10 minutes

*Options for Pacing and Variety*

· Time Saver Ask students to examine the photograph carefully. Ask them what they think is happening in the photograph and what visual details led them to that conclusion. **Class Time** 10 minutes

**Interact with History, p. 767**

**Class Time** 25 minutes

*Options for Pacing and Variety*

· Role-Playing Have students divide into groups of four. Within these small groups, have two students think of arguments for radical social change and two students think of arguments for a change occurring within the rules of society. Then have each group create a chart listing their arguments. Combine the small group lists into a class list of arguments for and against radical change and discuss as a class. **Class Time** 25 minutes

**SECTION 1, pp. 768–775**

**Class Time** 55 minutes

*Options for Pacing and Variety*

· Peer Teaching Divide the class into pairs and have them do the activity, creating a cluster diagram for clarifying ideas on TE page 769. **Class Time** 20 minutes

### DAY 1 continued

· Time Saver After they read pages 771–773, ask students why they think Native Americans resisted assimilation. Ask students where they have heard the term *assimilation* before, and if they have not, discuss the term and its positive and negative connotations. **Class Time** 15 minutes

· Peer Teaching Ask students to read the time line on Native American Legal Victories on page 773 and have them work in groups to research one of the instances of Native American victories, including the protest activities and the political debate leading up to the victory. Have students share their findings with the class. **Class Time** 50 minutes

· Time Saver Ask students to read the feature "The Supreme Court: *Reynolds* v. *Sims* (1964)" on pages 774–775. Then ask them to answer the questions on TE 775. **Class Time** 15 minutes

### DAY 2

**SECTION 2, pp. 776–780**

**Class Time** 30 minutes

*Options for Pacing and Variety*

· Peer Teaching Have students read the features "A Personal Voice," throughout the section and discuss them as a class. Ask students how each story affected them and what each made them think about. Which one did they find most thought provoking? Encourage students to think of their own experiences and relate those experiences to the features. **Class Time** 30 minutes

· Internet Have students work in groups to research the number of women in the national government since 1960. They should make a line graph to show the changes in women's visibility in government. They can also break down the numbers of women by percentages in the House of Representatives, in the Senate, on the White House staff, and in state government. **Class Time** 35 minutes

**SECTION 3, pp. 781–787**

**Class Time** 30 minutes

*Options for Pacing and Variety*

· Time Saver After reading the section, ask students why they think the hippie movement was short-lived. Students should cite political events and later changes in the cultural climate. Also ask them what they know of the term *counterculture* and if there is any counterculture that they can think of in our society today. **Class Time** 15 minutes

### DAY 2 continued

· Time Saver Ask students to read the feature on page 784, "History Through Music: Protest Songs of the Sixties." Discuss these and other songs students can think of and also discuss the questions included. **Class Time** 15 minutes

· Internet Ask students to read the feature "Daily Life: Signs of the Sixties" on pages 786–787. Then have students work in small groups to complete question 2. **Class Time** 15 minutes

**ASSESSMENT pp. 788–789**

**Class Time** 30 minutes

*Options for Pacing and Variety*

· Peer Evaluation Ask students to work in pairs to quiz each other on the Main Ideas questions on page 788. **Class Time** 20 minutes

· Time Saver Have students read the visual summary on page 788. Then ask them which of the points they see reflected in our society today and which they do not. Ask them to think about the political context of the time—how did the actions and beliefs of the hippies reflect the political atmosphere and what were they trying to express that spoke for the whole era? **Class Time** 15 minutes

**TEACHER-TESTED ACTIVITY**
**PROTEST SIGNS**

**Class Time** 30 minutes

**Task** Creating protest signs

**Purpose** To consider anti-establishment protests during the 1960s

**Dominic Fruscello, West Genesee High School, Camillus, New York**

**Supplies Needed**
· Poster board
· Paint stir sticks
· Markers
· Glue or staplers

**Activity** Review with students the major issues of the 1960s, including civil rights, women's rights, Native American rights, environmental concerns, and the Vietnam War. Have each student create a protest sign relevant to one of the issues. Display the signs and lead a discussion regarding the significance of protest and its effectiveness.

# CHAPTER 23 CORRELATION

 **CORRELATION TO THE TEXAS ESSENTIAL KNOWLEDGE AND SKILLS**

Chapter 23 addresses the following standards of the Texas Essential Knowledge and Skills for U.S. History.

| TEKS | Instruction | Student Question/Activity |
|---|---|---|
| **(4B)** Evaluate the impact of reform leaders on American society. | **PE 770** examination of the efforts by César Chávez to win work reforms for nation's farm workers | **TTE 770** questions based on the biography of Chávez |
| **(7A)** Trace the civil rights movement in the 20th century. | **PE 768–773** examination of the effort by Latinos and Native Americans to gain greater civil rights | **PE 773** Critical Thinking questions that explore the civil rights efforts by these groups |
| **(7D)** Identify changes in the United States that have resulted from the civil rights movement such as increased participation of minorities in the political process. | **PE 770–771** discussion of efforts by Latinos to organize politically to gain a greater voice in the political process | **PE 773** Critical Thinking question about Latino's emerging political power |
| **(10B)** Analyze the effects of changing demographic patterns resulting from immigration to the United States. | **PE 768–769** analysis of the growth of the Latino population through immigration and its effect on American society | **TE 769** activity in which students summarize the key factors in the rise of the Latino population |
| **(17A)** Analyze the effects of 20th-century landmark U.S. Supreme Court decisions. | **PE 774–775** feature on the landmark Supreme Court case *Reynolds* v. *Sims,* which upheld the principle of "one person, one vote" | **PE 775** Critical Thinking questions based on the feature |
| **(20C)** Identify examples of American art, music, and literature that transcend American culture and convey universal themes. | **PE 786–787** Daily Life feature on the art and music movements of the 1960s that influenced the nation | **PE 787** Critical Thinking questions based on the feature |
| **(21D)** Identify the political, social, and economic contributions of women to American society. | **PE 776–780** examination of the women's movement, as well as the contributions women have made economically, socially, and politically | **PE 780** Critical Thinking questions about the women's movement |

## TAKS MINI-LESSONS

1. **Social Studies Skills: Objective 3 (US21.A):** Explain actions taken by people from various racial, ethnic, and religious groups to expand economic opportunities and political rights in American society **Activity** Have students complete the economic activity about the grape boycott led by the United Farm Workers Union on TE page 770.

2. **Social Studies Skills: Objective 3 (US21.B):** Identify the political, social, and economic contributions of women to American society **Activity** Have students make a list of the legal, social, employment, and political gains made by women during the 1960s and 1970s.

3. **Social Studies Skills: Objective 5 (US24.A):** Explain and apply different methods that historians use to interpret the past, including the use of primary and secondary sources **Activity** Have students summarize the feelings expressed in "A Personal Voice" on page 777.

4. **English Language Arts Skills: Objective 2 (10.B):** Use elements of text to defend, clarify, and negotiate responses and interpretations **Activity** Have students use elements of the text to answer the Critical Thinking questions in the Section 1 Assessment on page 773.

5. **English Language Arts Skills: Objective 3 (7.G):** Draw inferences such as conclusions and support them with text evidence **Activity** Have students discuss what conclusions they can make about the desire by many Native Americans to choose their own way of life.

To understand the sweeping social protest movements of the 1960s and the quest for radical change initiated by Latinos, Native Americans, women, and young people

## CHAPTER 23

# AN ERA OF SOCIAL CHANGE

Hippies gather in El Rito, New Mexico, at a Fourth of July parade in 1969.

## HISTORY from VISUALS

### Interpreting the Photograph

Ask students to examine the photograph carefully. Ask them what they think is happening in the photograph and what visual details lead them to that conclusion. *(Young people are involved in some kind of party. The details are the relaxed body language, the long hair, the elaborate and eccentric clothing, and the painted school bus.)*

## Time Line Discussion

Explain to students that the time line covers events in the United States and the world in the 1960s and early 1970s.

· Ask students who founded the National Farm Workers Association and in what year? *(César Chávez and Dolores Huerta; 1962)*
· Ask students what success did farm workers have and in what year? *(In 1970, a successful boycott of grapes forced growers to sign contracts with the United Farm Workers Organizing Committee.)*
· Ask students what group staged a protest at Wounded Knee? *(Native Americans)* Using their knowledge of American history, ask them what was significant about the location of the protest? *(It was the site of a famous massacre of Native Americans in 1890.)*

**1962** César Chávez and Dolores Huerta found the National Farm Workers Association.

**1964** Lyndon B. Johnson is elected president.

**1966** National Organization for Women (NOW) is formed.

USA
WORLD

| 1960 | 1962 | 1964 | 1966 |

**1962** Chinese forces invade India.

**1963** Civil war breaks out between Greeks and Turks on Cyprus.

**1967** Six-Day War between Israel and Arab nations.

## THEMES IN CHAPTER 23

### IMMIGRATION AND MIGRATION

During the 1960s, the Latino population in the United States grew from three million to more than nine million. Most Latinos settled in large cities, where they often encountered discrimination. At this time, Latinos also began organizing politically.

See Teacher's Edition note, p. 769.

### CIVIL RIGHTS

The 1960s witnessed the struggle of Native Americans for greater equality. Impatience with the slow pace of reform, however, led to the formation of the American Indian Movement, which actively confronted the government.

See Teacher's Edition note, p. 771.

### WOMEN AND POLITICAL POWER

For American women, the 1960s and 1970s were a time of consciousness-raising about "a woman's place." Many women struggled to find fulfillment beyond the bounds of home and family life.

See Teacher's Edition note, p. 777.

### DIVERSITY AND NATIONAL IDENTITY

In the 1960s, members of the counter-culture rejected the American dream and chose to drop out of mainstream society. Hippies sought to redefine the American dream by creating a society based on love.

See Teacher's Edition note, 783.

## INTERACT
### WITH HISTORY

In the late 1960s, a new breed of youth known as the counterculture rejects the fashions, traditions, and morals of American society. Minority groups assert their equal rights, demanding changes to longstanding practices and prejudices. Women protest forms of oppression and male privileges that have "always," it seems, been taken for granted. Many Americans begin to feel as if the whole nation has been turned on its side.

## How much can a society change?

### Examine the Issues

- Does every individual have a responsibility to follow the unwritten rules of society?
- What are the positive and negative aspects of change?

**RESEARCH LINKS** CLASSZONE.COM

Visit the Chapter 23 links for more information about An Era of Social Change.

## INTERACT
### WITH HISTORY

### Objectives

- To help students understand the challenge to mainstream society in the 1960s
- To motivate students to learn more about the discontent that led to social protest

### Examine the Issues

1. Have students discuss the cost of social conformity to the individual and the price of dissent to society as a whole.
2. Discuss the problems protest groups have with getting their message heard and the disruption that social protest causes to society as a whole.

---

**1968** Richard M. Nixon is elected president.

**1970** Political party La Raza Unida is formed.

**1970** Grape boycott forces growers to sign contracts with United Farm Workers.

BOYCOTT NON-UFW GRAPES

**1972** Richard M. Nixon is reelected.

**1973** Native Americans stage protest at Wounded Knee, South Dakota.

## 1968    1970    1972    1974

**1969** President Charles de Gaulle of France resigns.

**1970** Anwar el-Sadat becomes president of Egypt.

**1972** Earthquake kills 10,000 in Nicaragua.

*An Era of Social Change* **767**

---

## RECOMMENDED RESOURCES

### BOOKS FOR THE TEACHER

Matthiessen, Peter. *In the Spirit of Crazy Horse.* New York: Viking, 1992. FBI conflict with the American Indian Movement recounted by noted American novelist and journalist.

Takaki, Ronald. *A Different Mirror.* Boston: Little, 1994. History of African Americans, Latinos, and Asian Americans in the United States.

### BOOKS FOR THE STUDENT

Friedan, Betty. *The Feminine Mystique.* Updated edition. New York: Norton, 2001. Includes her thoughts 30 years after the original publication.

Mankiller, Wilma, and Michael Wallis. *Mankiller.* New York: St. Martins, 2000. Life of a woman who was a Cherokee chief.

Shorris, Earl. *Latinos.* New York: Norton, 1992. Describes diverse Latino communities in the United States.

### VIDEOS

*America: The Second Century: The American Indian; Black Americans; Hispanic Americans; Women in America.* GPN, 402-472-2007.

*American Indians, Yesterday and Today.* Altschul Group, 847-328-6700.

### SOFTWARE

*Her Heritage.* CD-ROM. Pilgrim New Media, 800-997-5476.

### INTEGRATED TECHNOLOGY

For teacher support, visit . . .

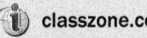 classzone.com

SECTION 1

# Latinos and Native Americans Seek Equality

| MAIN IDEA | WHY IT MATTERS NOW | Terms & Names |
|---|---|---|
| Latinos and Native Americans confronted injustices in the 1960s. | Campaigns for civil rights and economic justice won better representation and opportunity for Latinos and Native Americans. | • César Chávez<br>• United Farm Workers Organizing Committee<br>• La Raza Unida<br>• American Indian Movement (AIM) |

 U.S. History 1B, 4B, 7A, 7B, 7C, 7D, 8A, 10B, 14D, 15C, 18A, 18B, 19A, 21A, 24A, 24B, 24C, 25A, 25B, 25D

### One American's Story

Jessie Lopez de la Cruz's life changed one night in 1962, when **César Chávez** came to her home. Chávez, a Mexican-American farm worker, was trying to organize a union for California's mostly Spanish-speaking farm workers. Chávez said, "The women have to be involved. They're the ones working out in the fields with their husbands." Soon Jessie was in the fields, talking to farm workers about the union.

**A PERSONAL VOICE** JESSIE LOPEZ DE LA CRUZ

"Wherever I went to speak . . . I told them about . . . how we had no benefits, no minimum wage, nothing out in the fields—no restrooms, nothing. . . . I said, 'Well! Do you think we should be putting up with this in this modern age? . . . We can stand up! We can talk back! . . . This country is very rich, and we want a share of the money those growers make [off] our sweat and our work by exploiting us and our children!'"

—quoted in *Moving the Mountain: Women Working for Social Change*

The efforts of Jessie Lopez de la Cruz were just part of a larger rights movement during the turbulent and revolutionary 1960s. As African Americans were fighting for civil rights, Latinos and Native Americans rose up to assert their own rights and improve their lives.

▲ Carrying signs that say "Strike" (*huelga*), Mexican-American farm workers protest poor working conditions.

## **1** The Latino Presence Grows

Latinos, or Americans of Latin American descent, are a large and diverse group. During the 1960s, the Latino population in the United States grew from 3 million to more than 9 million. Today the Latino population includes people from several different areas, primarily Mexico, Puerto Rico, Cuba, the Dominican Republic, Central America, and South America. Each of these groups has its own history, its

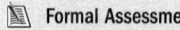

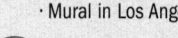
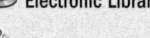

◄ In the 1920s, thousands of Mexican people came to the U.S. and settled in *barrios.* Shown here, Hispanic men gather in a park in California.

own pattern of settlement in the United States, and its own set of economic, social, cultural, and political concerns.

**LATINOS OF VARIED ORIGINS** Mexican Americans, the largest Latino group, have lived mostly in the Southwest and California. This group includes descendants of the nearly 100,000 Mexicans who had lived in territories ceded by Mexico to the United States in 1848. Another million or so Mexicans came to the United States in the 1910s, following Mexico's revolution. Still others came as *braceros,* or temporary laborers, during the 1940s and 1950s. In the 1960s close to half a million Mexicans immigrated, most in search of better paying jobs.

Puerto Ricans began immigrating to the United States after the U.S. occupation of Puerto Rico in 1898. As of 1960, almost 900,000 Puerto Ricans were living in the continental United States, including almost half a million on New York City's West Side.

Large Cuban communities also formed in New York City and in Miami and New Jersey. This is because hundreds of thousands of Cubans, many of whom were academics and professionals, fled to the United States in 1959 to escape Fidel Castro's Communist rule. In addition, tens of thousands of Salvadorans, Guatemalans, Nicaraguans, and Colombians immigrated to the United States after the 1960s to escape civil war and chronic poverty.

Wherever they had settled, during the 1960s many Latinos encountered ethnic prejudice and discrimination in jobs and housing. Most lived in segregated *barrios,* or Spanish-speaking neighborhoods. The Latino jobless rate was nearly 50 percent higher than that of whites, as was the percentage of Latino families living in poverty. **A**

## Latinos Fight for Change ❷

As the presence of Latinos in the United States grew, so too did their demand for greater representation and better treatment. During the 1960s, Latinos demanded not only equal opportunity, but also a respect for their culture and heritage.

**MAIN IDEA**

**Identifying Problems**
**A** What problems did different groups of Latino immigrants share?

*A. Answer*
Prejudice, job and housing discrimination, high unemployment, and poverty.

### Tracing Themes
**IMMIGRATION AND MIGRATION**

#### The Latino Population
The growing Latino population enriched American society. Latinos spread their culture, including language, literature, cuisine, and music. The influx of Latinos also had negative effects—overcrowding in cities, increased crime, and higher unemployment. Recognizing their disadvantaged position in society, Latinos began to organize in the 1960s.

## HISTORICAL SPOTLIGHT

### HISTORICAL SPOTLIGHT

#### DESPERATE JOURNEYS
In the 1960s and 1970s, thousands of poor Mexicans illegally crossed the 2,000-mile border between the United States and Mexico each year. The journey these illegal aliens undertook was often made more difficult by "coyotes," guides who charged large amounts of money to help them cross the border, but who often didn't deliver on their promises.

Illegal immigrants' problems didn't end when they entered the United States, where they were denied many social services, including unemployment insurance and food stamps. In addition, the Immigration and Naturalization Service urged businesses to refrain from hiring them. As a result, some owners stopped employing people with Latino names, including legal immigrants.

#### Desperate Journeys
Illegal immigration from Mexico has remained a controversial domestic and foreign relations issue. American authorities have recognized that economic conditions in Mexico drive poor Mexicans to emigrate. The North American Free Trade Agreement has spurred Mexican-American cooperation. In 2001, the presidents of both countries, Vicente Fox and George W. Bush, pledged to work together on the problem. Ask students what steps the United States should take to reduce illegal immigration.

### Instruct: Objective ❷

**Latinos Fight for Change**
TAKS SS11 3(US21.A)
· Who was César Chávez, and what did he do to help Latinos?
· What did Latino "brown power" movements advocate?
· What did Latinos do to enhance their political power?

📄 In-Depth Resources: Unit 6
· American Lives: César Chávez, p. 81
· Primary Source: The Farm Worker Movement, p. 74

*An Era of Social Change* **769**

**THE FARM WORKER MOVEMENT** As Jessie Lopez de la Cruz explained, thousands working on California's fruit and vegetable farms did backbreaking work for little pay and few benefits. César Chávez believed that farm workers had to unionize, that their strength would come from bargaining as a group. In 1962, Chávez and Dolores Huerta established the National Farm Workers Association. Four years later, this group merged with a Filipino agricultural union (also founded by Huerta) to form the **United Farm Workers Organizing Committee** (UFWOC).

*"To us, the boycott of grapes was the most near-perfect of nonviolent struggles."*
CÉSAR CHÁVEZ

Chávez and his fellow organizers insisted that California's large fruit and vegetable companies accept their union as the bargaining agent for the farm workers. In 1965, when California's grape growers refused to recognize the union, Chávez launched a nationwide boycott of the companies' grapes. Chávez, like Martin Luther King, Jr., believed in using nonviolence to reach his goal. The union sent farm workers across the country to convince supermarkets and shoppers not to buy California grapes. Chávez then went on a three-week fast in which he lost 35 pounds. He ended his fast by attending Mass with Senator Robert F. Kennedy. The efforts of the farm workers eventually paid off. In 1970, Huerta negotiated a contract between the grape growers and the UFWOC. Union workers would finally be guaranteed higher wages and other benefits long denied them. **B**

**CULTURAL PRIDE** The activities of the California farm workers helped to inspire other Latino "brown power" movements across the country. In New York, members of the Puerto Rican population began to demand that schools offer Spanish-speaking children classes taught in their own language as well as programs about their culture. In 1968, Congress enacted the Bilingual Education Act, which provided funds for schools to develop bilingual and cultural heritage programs for non-English-speaking children.

Young Mexican Americans started to call themselves Chicanos or Chicanas—a shortened version of "Mexicanos" that expressed pride in their ethnic heritage. A Chicano community action group called the Brown Berets formed under the leadership of David Sanchez. In 1968, the Brown Berets organized walkouts in East Los Angeles high schools. About 15,000 Chicano students walked out of class demanding smaller classes, more Chicano teachers and administrators, and programs designed to reduce the high Latino dropout rate. Militant Mexican-American students also won the establishment of Chicano studies programs at colleges and universities.

**POLITICAL POWER** Latinos also began organizing politically during the 1960s. Some worked within the two-party system. For example, the Mexican American Political Association (MAPA) helped elect Los Angeles politician Edward Roybal to the House of Representatives. During the 1960s, eight Hispanic Americans served in the House, and one Hispanic senator was elected—Joseph Montoya of New Mexico.

Others, like Texan José Angel Gutiérrez, sought to create an independent Latino political movement. In 1970, he established **La Raza Unida** (Mexican-Americans United). In the 1970s, La Raza Unida ran Latino candidates in five states and won races for mayor, as well as positions on school boards and city councils.

### KEY PLAYER

**CÉSAR CHÁVEZ
1927–1993**

César Chávez spoke from experience when he said, "Many things in farm labor are terrible."

As a teenager, Chávez moved with his family from farm to farm, picking such crops as grapes, apricots, and olives. "The worst crop was the olives," Chávez recalled. "The olives are so small you can never fill the bucket."

The seeds of protest grew early in Chávez. As a teenager, he once went to see a movie, only to find that the theater was segregated—whites on one side of the aisle and Mexicans on the other side. "I really hadn't thought much about what I was going to do, but I had to do something," Chávez recalled. The future union leader sat down in the whites-only section and stayed there until the police arrived and arrested him.

---

Still other Latinos took on a more confrontational tone. In 1963, one-time evangelical preacher Reies Tijerina founded the Alianza Federal de Mercedes (Federal Alliance of Land Grants) to help reclaim U.S. land taken from Mexican landholders in the 19th century. He and his followers raided the Rio Arriba County Courthouse in Tierra Amarilla, New Mexico, in order to force authorities to recognize the plight of New Mexican small farmers. They were later arrested.

## Native Americans Struggle for Equality ③

**Vocabulary**
**homogeneous:** uniform or similar throughout

As are Latinos, Native Americans are sometimes viewed as a single homogeneous group, despite the hundreds of distinct Native American tribes and nations in the United States. One thing that these diverse tribes and nations have shared is a mostly bleak existence in the United States and a lack of autonomy, or ability to control and govern their own lives. Through the years, many Native Americans have clung to their heritage, refusing to assimilate, or blend, into mainstream society. Native American nationalist Vine Deloria, Jr., expressed the view that mainstream society was nothing more than "ice cream bars and heart trouble and . . . getting up at six o'clock in the morning to mow your lawn in the suburbs."

**NATIVE AMERICANS SEEK GREATER AUTONOMY** Despite their cultural diversity, Native Americans as a group have been the poorest of Americans and have suffered from the highest unemployment rate. They have also been more likely than any other group to suffer from tuberculosis and alcoholism. Although the Native American population rose during the 1960s, the death rate among Native American infants was nearly twice the national average, while life expectancy was several years less than for other Americans.

In 1954, the Eisenhower administration enacted a "termination" policy to deal with these problems, but it did not respect Native American culture. Native Americans were relocated from isolated reservations into mainstream urban American life. The plan failed miserably. Most who moved to the cities remained desperately poor.

In 1961, representatives from 61 Native American groups met in Chicago and drafted the Declaration of Indian Purpose, which stressed the determination of Native Americans to "choose our own way of life." The declaration called for an end to the termination program in favor of new policies designed to create economic opportunities for Native Americans on their reservations. In 1968, President Lyndon Johnson established the National Council on Indian Opportunity to "ensure that programs reflect the needs and desires of the Indian people." **C**

---

**MAIN IDEA**

**Analyzing Motives**
**C** Why did Native Americans resist assimilation?

**C. Answer** Some viewed white culture as shallow and meaningless.

---

**VOICES OF PROTEST** Many young Native Americans were dissatisfied with the slow pace of reform. Their discontent fueled the growth of the **American Indian Movement (AIM)**, an often militant Native American rights organization. While AIM began in 1968 largely as a self-defense group against police brutality, it soon branched out to include protecting the rights of large Native American populations in northern and western states.

**NOW & THEN**

**BEN NIGHTHORSE CAMPBELL**

Whereas many Native Americans rejected assimilation, Ben Nighthorse Campbell has chosen to work within the system to improve the lives of Native Americans. Campbell's father was a North Cheyenne, and his great-grandfather, Black Horse, fought in the 1876 Battle of the Little Bighorn—in which the Cheyenne and the Sioux defeated Lieutenant Colonel George Custer.

In 1992, Campbell was elected to the U.S. Senate from Colorado, marking the first time since 1929 that a Native American had been elected to the Senate. Campbell stated that while his new job covered the entire nation, the needs of Native Americans would always remain a high priority.

---

**Instruct: Objective** ③

**Native Americans Struggle for Equality**
TAKS SS11 3(US21.A)
· What was the American Indian Movement, and what did it advocate?
· How did the American Indian Movement engage the government?
· What successes did Native Americans attain?

📖 In-Depth Resources: Unit 6
· Guided Reading, p. 64

**Tracing Themes**
CIVIL RIGHTS

**Equality for Native Americans**
Native Americans had been denied basic rights for generations. Their goals in the 1960s were to win more control over their own lives, new economic opportunities, rights to lands taken by the government, improved living conditions on reservations, and more say in the education of their children.

---

**NOW & THEN**

**Ben Nighthorse Campbell**
**Making Inferences** Ask students whether they think Native Americans can achieve their goals by working within the system as Campbell did. *(Yes, as a U.S. senator he is in a position to help his people. Campbell also serves as a role model for Native Americans. No, he is only one senator and has to represent all the people of Colorado to get reelected.)* Have students research Campbell's Senate career and assess how effective he has been in helping Native Americans.

*An Era of Social Change* **771**

---

**DIFFERENTIATING INSTRUCTION** **GIFTED AND TALENTED STUDENTS**  **classzone.com**

**Researching AIM**

Have students research the current and past activities of the American Indian Movement (AIM). Ask students to consider the group's principles and its conflicts with the federal government. Have students make a poster that illustrates what they have found and share it with the class.

As an extension activity, you could ask them to compare the activities of AIM with those of Senator Ben Nighthorse Campbell on behalf of Native Americans. Have students attempt to evaluate whose activities have been more effective, AIM's or Senator Campbell's.

AIM leader Dennis ▶ Banks speaks at the foot of Mount Rushmore, in South Dakota, during a 1970s rally.

### More About . . .

**The Trail of Broken Treaties**

When the Native Americans who took part in the Trail of Broken Treaties arrived in Washington, they did not plan to occupy the BIA building. The protesters first approached the BIA for help in finding a place to stay while they tried to make appointments with government officials. As Mary Crow Dog, who was one of the demonstrators, recalled, "Somebody suggested, 'Let's all go to the BIA.' It seemed a natural thing to do . . . They would have to put us up. It was 'our' building, after all." The AIM demonstrators left seven days later, when the Nixon administration promised to study their demands. "Morally, it had been a great victory," wrote Mary Crow Dog.

For some, this new activism meant demanding that Native American lands, burial grounds, and fishing and timber rights be restored. Others wanted a new respect for their culture. Mary Crow Dog, a Lakota Sioux, described AIM's impact.

**A PERSONAL VOICE** MARY CROW DOG

"My first encounter with AIM was at a pow-wow held in 1971. . . . One man, a Chippewa, stood up and made a speech. I had never heard anybody talk like that. He spoke about genocide and sovereignty, about tribal leaders selling out. . . . He had himself wrapped up in an upside-down American flag, telling us that every star in this flag represented a state stolen from the Indians. . . . Some people wept. An old man turned to me and said, 'These are the words I always wanted to speak, but had kept shut up within me.'"

—*Lakota Women*

**CONFRONTING THE GOVERNMENT** In its early years, AIM, as well as other groups, actively—and sometimes violently—confronted the government. In 1972, AIM leader Russell Means organized the "Trail of Broken Treaties" march in Washington, D.C., to protest the U.S. government's treaty violations throughout history. Native Americans from across the country joined the march. They sought the restoration of 110 million acres of land. They also pushed for the abolition of the Bureau of Indian Affairs (BIA), which many believed was corrupt. The marchers temporarily occupied the BIA building, destroyed records, and caused $2 million in property damage.

*"If the government doesn't start living up to its obligations, armed resistance . . . will have to become a regular thing."*
**CHIPPEWA PROTESTER**

A year later, AIM led nearly 200 Sioux to the tiny village of Wounded Knee, South Dakota, where the U.S. cavalry had massacred a Sioux village in 1890. In protest against both tribal leadership and federal policies, the Sioux seized the town, taking hostages. After tense negotiations with the FBI and a shootout that left two Native Americans dead and others wounded, the confrontation ended with a government promise to reexamine Native American treaty rights. **D**

**NATIVE AMERICAN VICTORIES** Congress and the federal courts did make some reforms on behalf of Native Americans. In 1972, Congress passed the Indian Education Act. In 1975, it passed the Indian Self-Determination and Education

*D. Answer*
AIM used confrontational and sometimes violent tactics, such as occupying the Bureau of Indian Affairs and taking hostages during a protest at Wounded Knee.

**MAIN IDEA**

**Summarizing**
**D** What tactics did AIM use in its attempts to gain reforms?

---

**ACTIVITY**  **COOPERATIVE LEARNING**

🌐 classzone.com

**Listing Native American Demands**

**Class Time** 45 minutes

**Task** Creating a list of issues raised by Native American groups

**Purpose** To analyze issues that are a part of the Native American struggle for equality

**Directions** Have students research the 1973 demonstration and identify the conditions that caused the protest. Then, ask them to determine whether any of the 1973 issues have been resolved and if other issues have been added. Students should create a list showing all the issues. The list should include actions taken to resolve the issue and the current status of the issue.

**1970**
Taos of New Mexico regain possession of Blue Lake as well as surrounding forestland.

**1971**
Alaska Native Claims Settlement Act gives Alaskan natives 44 million acres and more than $962 million.

**1979**
Maine Implementing Act provides $81.5 million for native tribes, including Penobscot and Passamaquoddy, to buy back land.

**1980**
U.S. awards Sioux $106 million for illegally taken land in South Dakota.

**1988**
U.S. awards Puyallup tribe $162 million for land claims in Washington.

Assistance Act. These laws gave tribes greater control over their own affairs and over their children's education.

Armed with copies of old land treaties that the U.S. government had broken, Native Americans went to federal court and regained some of their rights to land. In 1970, the Taos of New Mexico regained possession of their sacred Blue Lake, as well as a portion of its surrounding forestland. Land claims by natives of Alaska resulted in the Alaska Native Claims Settlement Act of 1971. This act gave more than 40 million acres to native peoples and paid out more than $962 million in cash. Throughout the 1970s and 1980s, Native Americans won settlements that provided legal recognition of their tribal lands as well as financial compensation.

While the 1960s and the early 1970s saw a wave of activism from the nation's minority groups, another group of Americans also pushed for changes. Women, while not a minority group, were in many ways treated like second-class citizens, and many joined together to demand equal treatment in society.

## ASSESSMENT

**1. TERMS & NAMES** For each term or name, write a sentence explaining its significance.
- **César Chávez**
- **United Farm Workers Organizing Committee**
- **La Raza Unida**
- **American Indian Movement (AIM)**

### MAIN IDEA

**2. TAKING NOTES**
Create a Venn diagram like the one below to show the broad similarities between the issues faced by Latinos and Native Americans during the 1960s, as well as the unique concerns of the two groups.

**Issues Faced by Latinos and Native Americans**

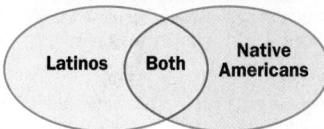

Which group do you think had more to gain by fighting for what they wanted?

### CRITICAL THINKING

**3. EVALUATING**
How would you judge whether an activist organization was effective? List criteria you would use, and justify your criteria. **Think About:**
- UFWOC, MAPA, and La Raza Unida
- AIM
- the leaders and activities of these organizations

**4. ANALYZING EFFECTS**
In what ways did the Latino campaign for economic and social equality affect non-Latino Americans?

**5. ANALYZING PRIMARY SOURCES**
Vine Deloria, Jr., said,

> "When you get far enough away from the reservation, you can see it's the urban man who has no identity."

What do you think he meant by this?

*An Era of Social Change* **773**

---

**HISTORIC DECISIONS OF
THE SUPREME COURT**

### Objectives

· To explain the legal reasoning behind the *Reynolds* decision

· To analyze the political implications and historical impact of the *Reynolds* decision

## Focus & Motivate

Ask students what would happen if some legislative districts had more people than others. Given that different regions of a state can have different interests, how would the unequal population of legislative districts influence the legislative agenda of a state?

### More About . . .

#### Warren's Majority Opinion

Warren's opinion was very clear and direct. He wrote: "Legislators are elected by voters, not farms or cities or economic interests. As long as ours is a representative form of government, the right to elect legislators in a free and unimpaired fashion is a bedrock of our political system. . . . And, if a State should provide that the votes of citizens in one part of the State should be given two times, or five times, or ten times the weight of votes of citizens in another part of the State, it could hardly be contended that the right to vote of those residing in the disfavored areas had not been effectively diluted."

# HISTORIC DECISIONS OF THE SUPREME COURT

## *REYNOLDS v. SIMS* (1964)

**ORIGINS OF THE CASE**  In 1901, seats in the Alabama state legislature were apportioned, or assigned to districts, based on population. By the early 1960s, each Alabama county still had the same number of representatives as it did in 1901, even though the populations of the counties had changed. A group of voters sued to make representation proportional to the changed populations. When the suit succeeded, state legislators who were threatened with losing their seats appealed to the Supreme Court.

**THE RULING**  The Supreme Court upheld the principle of "one person, one vote" and ruled that the equal protection clause required representation in state legislatures to be based on population.

### LEGAL REASONING

Prior to *Reynolds*, the Court had already applied the "one person, one vote" principle to federal congressional elections (see Legal Sources). In *Reynolds*, Chief Justice Earl Warren extended this principle to state legislatures. He argued that when representation does not reflect population, some people's votes are worth more than others'.

> " The fundamental principle of representative government in this country is one of equal representation for equal numbers of people, without regard to . . . place of residence within a State. . . . Legislators represent people, not trees or acres. Legislators are elected by voters, not farms or cities or economic interests. "

Warren concluded that Alabama's apportionment scheme discriminated against people because of where they live.

For these reasons, the Court ruled that any acceptable apportionment plan must provide an equal number of legislative seats for equally populated areas. A plan that does not is unconstitutional because it denies some voters the equal protection of the laws.

#### LEGAL SOURCES

##### U.S. CONSTITUTION

**U.S. CONSTITUTION, FOURTEENTH AMENDMENT (1868)**
"No state shall . . . deprive any person of life, liberty, or property, without due process of law; nor deny to any person within its jurisdiction the equal protection of the laws."

##### RELATED CASES

***BAKER v. CARR* (1962)**
The Court decided that federal courts could settle issues of apportionment. Previously, federal courts had refused to address such issues on the grounds that they were political issues.

***GRAY v. SANDERS* (1963)**
The Court ruled that states must follow the principle of "one person, one vote" in primary elections.

***WESBERRY v. SANDERS* (1964)**
The Court applied the "one person, one vote" rule to congressional districts.

◄ The Warren Court, 1962–1965

**774**  CHAPTER 23

---

### RECOMMENDED RESOURCES

#### BOOKS

Cortner, Richard. *Apportionment Cases.* New York: W.W. Norton, 1972.

Grofman, Bernard N. *Voting Rights, Voting Wrongs: The Legacy of Baker v. Carr.* New York, The Century Foundation, 1990.

McKay, R.B. *Reapportionment: The Law and Politics of Equal Representation.* Gemantown, NY: Periodicals Service Co., 1965.

Schwab, Larry M. *The Impact of Congressional Reapportionment and Redistricting.* Lanham, MD: University Press of America, 1988.

#### INTEGRATED TECHNOLOGY

For teacher support and more information about the Supreme Court including the full text of the Supreme Court opinions . . .

 classzone.com

## WHY IT MATTERED

The voters who initiated the suit against Alabama's apportionment were part of America's tremendous urban growth in the 20th century. During and after World War II, tens of thousands of Americans—including large numbers of African Americans—moved from rural areas to cities and suburbs. Voters in Alabama's more urban areas found that they were underrepresented. Likewise, before *Reynolds*, urban residents as a whole paid far more in taxes than they received in benefits. A great deal was at stake.

The "one person, one vote" principle increased the influence of urban residents by forcing legislatures to create new election districts in the cities to reflect their large populations. As more legislators representing urban and suburban needs were elected, they were able to change funding formulas, funneling more money into their districts. In addition, minorities, immigrants, and professionals, who tend to make up a large proportion of urban populations, gained better representation.

On the other hand, the power of farmers was eroded as election districts in rural areas were combined and incumbents had to campaign against each other for a single seat.

## HISTORICAL IMPACT

The Warren Court's reapportionment decisions in *Baker* v. *Carr*, *Gray* v. *Sanders*, *Wesberry* v. *Sanders*, and *Reynolds* were a revolution in U.S. politics. The lawsuit that culminated in the *Reynolds* decision was also part of a broader movement in the 1960s to protect voting rights. Largely because of the Voting Rights Act of 1965, voter registration among African Americans in Mississippi, for instance, climbed from 6.7 percent to 59.8 percent. Viewed together, the combination of increased protection of voting rights and acceptance of the "one person, one vote" principle brought the United States several steps closer to fulfilling its democratic ideals.

In the 1990s, the Court revisited reapportionment. A 1982 act of Congress had required states to create districts with "minority majorities" in order to increase the number of nonwhite representatives. As a result, following the 1990 census, a record number of African Americans were elected to Congress. But opponents contended that defining districts by race violated equal protection and "one person, one vote." In a series of decisions, the Court agreed and abolished minority districting.

## Instruct

1. What was the key legal principle in *Reynolds*?
2. How were politics affected by the decision?
3. What was the long-term historical impact of the decision?

### MAKING PERSONAL CONNECTIONS

Have students consider how voting is the core action available to citizens in a democracy.

· Ask them to recall a time when they felt their opinions were disregarded.
· How do they feel as young people who do not enjoy the full rights of citizenship because of their age?

## More About . . .

### Population Disparities

Alabama was not the only state with population disparities in legislative districts. Urbanization and social change left a trail of unevenly represented districts. For example, in Vermont, one assembly district had 33,000 residents, while another had only 238. In California, one Los Angeles state senate district had 6 million residents, while one rural district had only 14,000.

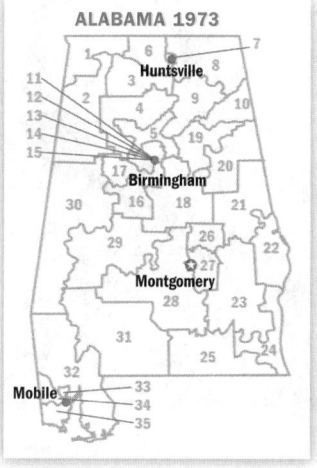

**ALABAMA 1901** — **ALABAMA 1973**

These two apportionment maps show Alabama's 35 state senatorial districts in 1901 *(left)* and 1973 *(right)*. The 1973 map shows how the districts were redrawn after the *Reynolds* decision, based on the 1970 census. Notice how the 1973 map reflects the growth of Alabama cities.

## THINKING CRITICALLY

### CONNECT TO TODAY

1. **Analyzing Maps** Obtain a map of the state legislative districts in your state. Then compare the map created following the 2000 census with the map based on the 1990 census. Study the differences in the size and location of the districts. Write a paragraph explaining which regions of the state gained representatives and which lost representatives.

 **SEE SKILLBUILDER HANDBOOK, PAGE R26.**

### CONNECT TO HISTORY

2. **INTERNET ACTIVITY** CLASSZONE.COM

Visit the links for Historic Decisions of the Supreme Court to research minority redistricting decisions such as *Shaw* v. *Hunt* (1996). Write a summary of the rulings and how they have affected elections.

## THINKING CRITICALLY: ANSWERS

1. **CONNECT TO TODAY** The students' paragraphs should contain references to both the 1990 and 2000 maps. They should also clearly present the students' findings based on comparing the legislative districts.

2. **CONNECT TO HISTORY** The summary should show a deep understanding of the rulings. It also should clearly state the impact of the rulings on elections.

## Focus & Motivate

Ask students if they think women are discriminated against or have equal opportunities. To stimulate discussion, ask why there has not been a woman president or why so few heads of major corporations are women.

## Instruct

### Instruct: Objective **1**

**A New Women's Movement Arises**
TAKS SS11 3(US21.D)

· What kinds of discrimination did women encounter at their jobs in the 1960s?
· How did women's experiences in civil rights and antiwar protests increase their awareness of sexism?
· What was the impact of Betty Friedan's book *The Feminine Mystique?*

 **In-Depth Resources: Unit 6**
· Guided Reading, p. 65
· Primary Source: from *The Feminine Mystique*, pg. 76
· American Lives: Betty Friedan, p. 82

 **Critical Thinking Transparencies, CT31**
· The Women's Movement

# Women Fight for Equality

### One American's Story

During the 1950s, writer **Betty Friedan** seemed to be living the American dream. She had a loving husband, healthy children, and a house in the suburbs. According to the experts—doctors, psychologists, and women's magazines—that was all a woman needed to be fulfilled. Why, then, wasn't she happy? In 1957, after conducting a survey of her Smith College classmates 15 years after graduation, she found she was not alone. Friedan eventually wrote a book, *The Feminine Mystique,* in which she addressed this "problem that has no name."

**A PERSONAL VOICE** BETTY FRIEDAN

" **The problem lay buried, unspoken. . . . It was a strange stirring, a sense of dissatisfaction, a yearning that women suffered in the middle of the twentieth century in the United States. Each suburban wife struggled with it alone. As she made the beds, shopped for groceries, matched slipcover material, ate peanut butter sandwiches with her children, chauffeured Cub Scouts and Brownies, lay beside her husband at night—she was afraid to ask even of herself the silent question—'Is this all?'** "

—*The Feminine Mystique*

**Betty Friedan, November 1967**

During the 1960s, women answered Friedan's question with a resounding "no." In increasing numbers they joined the nation's African Americans, Latinos, and Native Americans in the fight for greater civil rights and equality in society.

## **1** A New Women's Movement Arises

The theory behind the women's movement of the 1960s was **feminism,** the belief that women should have economic, political, and social equality with men. Feminist beliefs had gained momentum during the mid-1800s and in 1920 won women the right to vote. While the women's movement declined after this achievement, it reawakened during the 1960s, spurred by the political activism of the times.

## Women in the Workplace, 1950–2000

### Working Women and Percent of Labor Force

### Median Incomes for Working Women and Men

= $2000

| | 1950 | | 1970 | | 2000 | |
|---|---|---|---|---|---|---|
| | Women | Men | Women | Men | Women | Men |
| | $953 | $2,570 | $2,237 | $6,670 | $25,532 | $33,592 |

**SKILLBUILDER** Interpreting Graphs
1. For each year shown, what percentage of men's income did women make?
2. About how many more women were working in 1990 than in 1960?

📁 **SEE SKILLBUILDER HANDBOOK, PAGE R28.**

This 1960s pin displays a slogan used by Betty Friedan at the National Women's Political Caucus.

WOMEN MAKE POLICY NOT COFFEE

---

*Skillbuilder Answers*
1. 1950: 37 percent; 1970: 33 percent; 19—: xx percent.

**WOMEN IN THE WORKPLACE** In 1950, only one out of three women worked for wages. By 1960, that number had increased to about 40 percent. Still, during this time, certain jobs were considered "men's work" and women were shut out. The jobs available to women—mostly clerical work, domestic service, retail sales, social work, teaching, and nursing—paid poorly.

The country largely ignored this discrimination until President Kennedy appointed the Presidential Commission on the Status of Women in 1961. In 1963, the commission reported that women were paid far less than men, even when doing the same jobs. Furthermore, women were seldom promoted to management positions, regardless of their education, experience, and ability. These newly publicized facts awakened many women to their unequal status in society.

**WOMEN AND ACTIVISM** Ironically, many women felt the sting of discrimination when they became involved in the civil rights and antiwar movements—movements that toted the ideological banner of protecting people's rights. Within some of these organizations, such as SNCC and SDS, men led most of the activities, while women were assigned lesser roles. When women protested this arrangement, the men usually brushed them aside.

*Vocabulary*
**ideological:** concerned with a certain set of ideas

Such experiences led some women to organize small groups to discuss their concerns. During these discussions, or "consciousness-raising" sessions, women shared their lives with each other and discovered that their experiences were not unique. Rather, they reflected a much larger pattern of sexism, or discrimination based on gender. Author Robin Morgan delineated this pattern. **Ⓐ**

**MAIN IDEA**

*Analyzing Effects*
**Ⓐ** What effects did the civil rights and the antiwar movements have on many women?

*A. Answer* They spurred women to demonstrate for equality by both inspiring them to act and opening their eyes to their unequal treatment.

*"Move on little girl; we have more important issues to talk about here than women's liberation."*
**A MALE ANTIWAR ACTIVIST**

**A PERSONAL VOICE** ROBIN MORGAN

"It makes you very sensitive—raw, even, this consciousness. Everything, from the verbal assault on the street, to a 'well-meant' sexist joke your husband tells, to the lower pay you get at work (for doing the same job a man would be paid more for), to television commercials, to rock-song lyrics, to the pink or blue blanket they put on your infant in the hospital nursery, to speeches by male 'revolutionaries' that reek of male supremacy—everything seems to barrage your aching brain. . . . You begin to see how all-pervasive a thing is sexism."

—quoted in *Sisterhood Is Powerful: An Anthology of Writings from the Women's Liberation Movement*

**TAKS**
Mini-Lesson 3: SS11 5(US24.C)

---

📐 **HISTORY from VISUALS**

**Reading the Graphs**
Ask students why the number of women in the workforce and women's median income increased after 1970. *(because of gains and reforms that resulted from the work of the women's movement)*

⚒ Critical Thinking Transparencies CT65
· Percentage of All Women Who Are Working, 1950–1955

**Tracing Themes**
WOMEN AND POLITICAL POWER

**The Women's Movement**
Many women worked in the civil rights movement. Working for equality for African Americans raised their consciousness about their own disadvantaged position. This was not the first time this situation occurred. Women such as Elizabeth Cady Stanton and Susan B. Anthony had been active in the abolitionist movement. When they tried to assert women's rights, they were rejected by the male leaders of the abolitionist movement. Unlike male abolitionists, many civil rights leaders lent their support to the women's movement.

*An Era of Social Change* **777**

---

**ACTIVITY** COOPERATIVE LEARNING

 **BLOCK SCHEDULING**

### Surveying the Workplace

**Class Time** 45 minutes

**Task** Creating a survey about the gender of workplace managers

**Purpose** To interpret data on women in business management

**Directions** Ask students to put together a brief questionnaire on women's representation in management structure in the workplace that they can use to survey each other, parents, and neighbors. Have students pool their surveys and discuss the implications of their findings.

📄 Integrated Assessment
· Rubric 2

## Instruct: Objective ❷

**The Movement Experiences Gains and Losses**

TAKS SS11 5(US24.A)

· What were the National Organization for Women's goals?

· What factions formed in NOW?

· What was *Roe* v. *Wade,* and why was it important to women?

· What happened to the Equal Rights Amendment?

 In-Depth Resources: Unit 6
· Geography Application: The Equal Rights Amendment, pp. 72-73

👁 Electronic Library of Primary Sources
· from NOW's Statement of Purpose, 1966, by NOW.

### More About . . .

**The Feminine Mystique**

Betty Friedan spoke about the obsession she felt with her writing: "I wrote every day, on the dining-room table, while the children were in school, and after they went to bed at night." Her central thesis was that sexism was a pervasive form of discrimination, in which women were victimized by false values that kept them from gaining access to equal roles in society.

👁 Electronic Library of Primary Sources
· from *The Feminine Mystique,* 1963, by B. Friedan

### KEY PLAYER

**Gloria Steinem**

As a successful writer and advocate for her cause, Steinem was skilled at phrasing pithy feminist quotations, such as "I have yet to hear a man ask for advice on how to combine marriage and a career." Also, tell students that "Ms." was coined so that women, too, would have a title that did not convey marital status. Ask students why this was important. *(Women did not want be defined by their relationship to men.)*

---

**THE WOMEN'S MOVEMENT EMERGES** *The Feminine Mystique,* which captured the very discontent that many women were feeling, quickly became a bestseller and helped to galvanize women across the country. By the late 1960s, women were working together for change. "This is not a movement one 'joins,'" observed Robin Morgan. "The Women's Liberation Movement exists where three or four friends or neighbors decide to meet regularly . . . on the welfare lines, in the supermarket, the factory, the convent, the farm, the maternity ward."

## ❷ The Movement Experiences Gains and Losses

As the women's movement grew, it achieved remarkable and enduring political and social gains for women. Along the way, however, it also suffered setbacks, most notably in its attempt to ensure women's equality in the Constitution.

**THE CREATION OF NOW** The women's movement gained strength with the passage of the Civil Rights Act of 1964, which prohibited discrimination based on race, religion, national origin, and gender and created the Equal Employment Opportunity Commission (EEOC) to handle discrimination claims. By 1966, however, some women argued that the EEOC didn't adequately address women's grievances. That year, 28 women, including Betty Friedan, created the **National Organization for Women (NOW)** to pursue women's goals. "The time has come," the founders of NOW declared, "to confront with concrete action the conditions which now prevent women from enjoying the equality of opportunity . . . which is their right as individual Americans and as human beings." **B**

NOW members pushed for the creation of child-care facilities that would enable mothers to pursue jobs and education. NOW also pressured the EEOC to enforce more vigorously the ban on gender discrimination in hiring. NOW's efforts prompted the EEOC to declare sex-segregated job ads illegal and to issue guidelines to employers, stating that they could no longer refuse to hire women for traditionally male jobs.

**A DIVERSE MOVEMENT** In its first three years, NOW's ranks swelled to 175,000 members. A number of other women's groups sprang up around the country, too. In 1968, a militant group known as the New York Radical Women staged a well-publicized demonstration at the annual Miss America Pageant. The women threw bras, girdles, wigs, and other "women's garbage" into a "Freedom Trash Can." They then crowned a sheep "Miss America." Around this time, **Gloria Steinem,** a journalist, political activist, and ardent supporter of the women's liberation movement, made her voice heard on the subjects of feminism and equality. Steinem's grandmother had served as president of the Ohio Woman's Suffrage Association from 1908 to 1911; Steinem had inherited her passion and conviction. In 1971, Steinem helped found the National Women's Political Caucus, a moderate group that encouraged women to seek political office. In 1972, she and other women created a new women's magazine, *Ms.,* designed to treat contemporary issues from a feminist perspective.

**LEGAL AND SOCIAL GAINS** As the women's movement progressed, women began to question all sorts of gender-based distinctions. People protested that a woman's physical

### KEY PLAYER

**GLORIA STEINEM
1934–**

Gloria Steinem became one of the more prominent figures of the women's movement after she and several other women founded *Ms.* magazine in 1972. The magazine soon became a major voice of the women's movement. Steinem said that she decided to start the feminist magazine after editors in the mainstream media continually rejected her stories about the women's movement:

"Editors who had assumed I had some valuable biological insight into food, male movie stars, and textured stockings now questioned whether I or other women writers were biologically capable of writing objectively about feminism. That was the beginning."

 **MAIN IDEA**

**Analyzing Causes**
**B** What prompted women to establish NOW?

*B. Answer*
Their dissatisfaction with the EEOC and the need for a more organized effort to combat sexism.

---

**DIFFERENTIATING INSTRUCTION** | **STUDENTS ACQUIRING ENGLISH/ESL**

### Decoding Idioms

Pair students with a native English speaker and have them review the phrases to the right. Have the students work together to explain the phrase by investigating the literal meaning of the words and how they are being used in this specific context.

· *galvanizing women*
· *gender discrimination*
· *concrete action*
· *sex-segregated job ads*
· *militant group*

◄ Thousands of women march through the streets of New York City during the summer of 1970 to promote women's equality.

appearance was often considered a job qualification. Girls' exclusion from sports such as baseball and football came into question. Some women began using the title Ms., instead of the standard Miss or Mrs., and refused to adopt their husband's last name upon marriage.

These changes in attitude were paralleled by numerous legal changes. In 1972, Congress passed a ban on gender discrimination in "any education program or activity receiving federal financial assistance," as part of the Higher Education Act. As a result, several all-male colleges opened their doors to women. That same year, Congress expanded the powers of the EEOC and gave working parents a tax break for child-care expenses. **C**

**ROE v. WADE** One of the more controversial positions that NOW and other feminist groups supported was a woman's right to have an abortion. In 1973, the Supreme Court ruled in *Roe* v. *Wade* that women do have the right to choose an abortion during the first three months of pregnancy. Some thought the ruling might "bring to end the emotional and divisive public argument." However, the issue still divides Americans today.

**THE EQUAL RIGHTS AMENDMENT (ERA)** In what seemed at first to be another triumph for the women's movement, Congress passed the **Equal Rights Amendment (ERA)** in 1972. The amendment then needed ratification by 38 states to become part of the Constitution. First introduced to Congress in 1923, the ERA would guarantee that both men and women would enjoy the same rights and protections under the law. It was, many supporters said, a matter of "simple justice."

The amendment scared many people, and a Stop-ERA campaign was launched in 1972. Conservative **Phyllis Schlafly,** along with conservative religious groups, political organizations, and many anti-feminists, felt that the ERA would lead to "a parade of horribles," such as the drafting of women, the end of laws protecting homemakers, the end of a husband's responsibility to provide for his family, and same-sex marriages. Schlafly said that radical feminists "hate men, marriage, and children" and were oppressed "only in their distorted minds."

### A PERSONAL VOICE  PHYLLIS SCHLAFLY

" The U.S. Constitution is not the place for symbols or slogans, it is not the proper device to alleviate psychological problems of personal inferiority. Symbols and slogans belong on bumper strips—not in the Constitution. It would be a tragic mistake for our nation to succumb to the tirades and demands of a few women who are seeking a constitutional cure for their personal problems. "

— quoted in *The Equal Rights Amendment: The History and the Movement*

**THE NEW RIGHT EMERGES** In order to combat the ERA and the pro-abortion supporters, conservatives built what they called a new "pro-family" movement. In the 1970s, this coalition—which focused on social, cultural, and moral problems—came to be known as the New Right. The New Right and the women's movement debated family-centered issues such as whether the government should pay for daycare, which the New Right opposed. Throughout the 1970s, the New Right built grassroots support for social conservatism. It would later play a key role in the election of Ronald Reagan to the presidency in 1980. **D**

**MAIN IDEA**

**Making Generalizations**
**C** What sort of gains did the women's movement make by the early 1970s?

**C. Possible Answers** Women were treated more equally in jobs and education; new laws protected women's equality; gender became a less significant fact about a person.

**D. Answer** Fear of change and the perceived drastic effects the amendment might have had on traditional family life.

**MAIN IDEA**

**Analyzing Motives**
**D** What concerns motivated those who opposed the ERA?

### Connections Across Time
**1973 AND TODAY**

#### Roe v. Wade
Abortion continues to pull at society and serve as a political wedge issue. Opponents have organized controversial vigils at abortion centers. Some have resorted to violence, bombing abortion centers and killing doctors who perform abortions. Supporters of a woman's right to choose have counter-organized to fight the protests. In the political arena, candidates for office are often forced to declare their position on the issue.

### More About . . .

#### Phyllis Schlafly
Schlafly was a leading conservative thinker who led the resistance to the Equal Rights Amendment. In doing so, she moved the debate from political and economic issues to cultural ones by implying that feminists were attacking the social order. According to Schlafly, "If young women think that there are greater career satisfactions in being elected to important positions, traveling to exciting faraway places . . . or earning a financial fortune than there are in having a baby, they are wrong. None of those measures of career success can compare with the thrill, the satisfaction, and the fun of having and caring for babies, and watching them respond and grow. . . ."

Phyllis Schlafly

*An Era of Social Change*  **779**

---

**ACTIVITY**   **LINK TO GOVERNMENT**

 **classzone.com**

### Equal Rights Amendment

**Class Time** 45 minutes

**Task** Debating the advisability of adopting an Equal Rights Amendment to the U.S. Constitution

**Purpose** To compare the arguments made by each side in the equal rights amendment debate

**Directions** Divide the class into small groups. Ask pairs of students in each group to choose a side and research debating points on the Equal Rights Amendment. Have each group stage a debate. Then, discuss possible reasons why the proposed amendment has not been ratified.

📝 Integrated Assessment
· Rubric 3

### Instruct: Objective ③

**The Movement's Legacy**

TAKS SS11 3(US21.D)

· How successful was the women's movement in expanding opportunities for women?

· How did the women's movement change the way society looks at work and careers for women?

 In-Depth Resources: Unit 6
· Guided Reading, p. 65

 Critical Thinking Transparencies, CT31
· The Women's Movement

## Assess & Reteach

### SECTION 2 ASSESSMENT

Ask students to work independently to answer the questions. Then, have them meet in small groups to discuss their answers.

 Formal Assessment
· Section Quiz, p. 424

### SELF-ASSESSMENT

Ask students to make a list of impressions that they had about the women's movement before they read Section 2. Then, have them note whether their reading has confirmed or contradicted their preconceptions.

### RETEACH

Use the graphs on page 777 to review the progress women have made in the workplace since 1970.

 In-Depth Resources: Unit 6
· Reteaching Activity, p. 70

---

 **The Movement's Legacy**

The New Right and the women's movement clashed most dramatically over the ERA. By 1977 it had won approval from 35 of the 38 states needed for ratification, but the New Right gained strength. By June of 1982—the deadline for ratification—not enough states had approved the amendment. The ERA went down in defeat.

Despite ERA's defeat, the women's movement altered society in countless ways, such as by transforming women's conventional roles and their attitudes toward career and family. Interviews with women graduates at Stanford University reflect the change. Of graduates in 1965, 70 percent planned not to work at all when their children were of preschool age. When the class of 1972 was surveyed, only 7 percent said they would stop working to raise children.

The women's movement also succeeded in expanding career opportunities for women. For instance, as of 1970, 8 percent of all medical school graduates and 5 percent of all law school graduates were women. By 1998, those proportions had risen to 42 and 44 percent, respectively. Yet many women ran into a "glass ceiling"—an invisible, but very real, resistance to promoting women into top positions.

By 1983 women held 13.5 percent of elected state offices as well as 24 seats in the U.S. Congress. More importantly, as historian Sara Evans has noted, by 1980 "feminist concerns were firmly on the national political agenda and clearly there to stay." Most of all, the women's movement helped countless women open their lives to new possibilities. "For we have lived the second American revolution," wrote Betty Friedan in 1976, "and our very anger said a 'new YES' to life."

As this poster shows, women have made significant political strides by being elected to the U.S. Congress. ▼

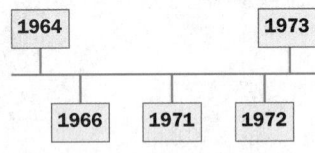

A WOMAN'S PLACE IS IN THE HOUSE... ...AND ALSO IN THE SENATE!

---

 **ASSESSMENT**

**1. TERMS & NAMES** For each term or name, write a sentence explaining its significance.

- Betty Friedan
- feminism
- National Organization for Women (NOW)
- Gloria Steinem
- Equal Rights Amendment (ERA)
- Phyllis Schlafly

#### MAIN IDEA

**2. TAKING NOTES**
Create a time line of key events relating to the women's movement.

| 1964 | | 1973 |
|------|--|------|
| 1966 | 1971 | 1972 |

Explain which event you think best demonstrates progressive reform.

Mini-Lesson 2:
SS11 3(US21.B)

#### CRITICAL THINKING

**3. HYPOTHESIZING**
What if the Equal Rights Amendment had been ratified? Speculate on how women's lives might have been different. Use reasons to support your answer.

**Think About:**
- rights addressed by the amendment
- legal support that the amendment might have provided
- possible reactions from groups opposing the amendment

**4. ANALYZING VISUAL SOURCES**
Examine the drawing on this 1972 cover of *Ms.* The woman shown has eight arms and is holding a different object in each hand. What do you think these objects symbolize in terms of women's roles? What do you think this drawing says about women in the 1960s? Explain.

**780** CHAPTER 23

---

**1. TERMS & NAMES**
Betty Friedan, p. 776
feminism, p. 776
National Organization for Women (NOW), p. 778
Gloria Steinem, p. 778
Equal Rights Amendment (ERA), p. 779
Phyllis Schlafly, p. 779

**2. TAKING NOTES**
1964—Congress passes the Civil Rights Act of 1964. 1966—National Organization for Women is formed. 1971—National Women's Political Caucus is organized. 1972—*Ms.* is founded; Congress passes Equal Rights Amendment (ERA) and bans sex discrimination in federally assisted educational programs and activities. 1973—Supreme Court's ruling in *Roe* v. *Wade* legalizes abortion.

**3. HYPOTHESIZING**
Women might have won more sex-discrimination lawsuits; the "glass ceiling" phenomenon might have been less of a problem for professional women; ratification might have spurred a powerful male backlash; Phyllis Schlafly and other opponents of the ERA might have formed organizations to undermine the amendment.

**4. ANALYZING VISUAL SOURCES**
It captures the notion that women's roles are multi-faceted; many are forced to juggle their responsibilities in society and in the family.

# Culture and Counterculture

| MAIN IDEA | WHY IT MATTERS NOW | Terms & Names |
|---|---|---|
| The ideals and lifestyle of the counterculture challenged the traditional views of Americans. | The music, art, and politics of the counterculture have left enduring marks on American society. | • counterculture  • the Beatles<br>• Haight-Ashbury  • Woodstock |

U.S. History 6E, 6H, 8A, 18C, 20A, 20B, 20C, 21C, 24B, 25A, 25B, 25D

### One American's Story

In 1966, Alex Forman left his conventional life in mainstream America and headed to San Francisco. Arriving there with little else but a guitar, he joined thousands of others who were determined to live in a more peaceful and carefree environment. He recalled his early days in San Francisco's Haight-Ashbury district, the hub of hippie life.

**A PERSONAL VOICE** ALEX FORMAN

" It was like paradise there. Everybody was in love with life and in love with their fellow human beings to the point where they were just sharing in incredible ways with everybody. Taking people in off the street and letting them stay in their homes. . . . You could walk down almost any street in Haight-Ashbury where I was living, and someone would smile at you and just go, 'Hey, it's beautiful, isn't it?'. . . It was a very special time. "

—quoted in *From Camelot to Kent State*

▲ Members of the counterculture relax in a California park.

Forman was part of the **counterculture**—a movement made up mostly of white, middle-class college youths who had grown disillusioned with the war in Vietnam and injustices in America during the 1960s. Instead of challenging the system, they turned their backs on traditional America and tried to establish a whole new society based on peace and love. Although their heyday was short-lived, their legacy remains.

## 1 The Counterculture

In the late 1960s, the historian Theodore Roszak deemed these idealistic youths the counterculture. It was a culture, he said, so different from the mainstream "that it scarcely looks to many as a culture at all, but takes on the alarming appearance of a barbarian intrusion."

*An Era of Social Change* **781**

## OBJECTIVES

1 Describe the flowering and decline of the counterculture in the 1960s.

2 Summarize the impact of the counterculture on art, fashion, music, and attitudes.

3 Explain the conservative response to the counterculture.

**CRITICAL THINKING**

· Analyzing Causes, p. 782
· Making Inferences, pp. 783, 785
· Forming Generalizations, p. 785
· Developing Historical Perspective, p. 785
· Analyzing Issues, p. 785

## Focus & Motivate

Ask students what images come to mind when they hear the word "hippie." What do they know about the music of the 1960s and how it influenced the growth of the popular music business?

## Instruct

### Instruct: Objective 1

**The Counterculture**
TAKS SS11 5(US24.B)

· How did members of the counterculture relate to mainstream culture?
· What were the primary components of hippie life?
· What happened to the counterculture?

📖 In-Depth Resources: Unit 6
· Guided Reading, p. 66

## PROGRAM RESOURCES

📖 In-Depth Resources: Unit 6
· Guided Reading, p. 66
· Skillbuilder Practice: Comparing; Contrasting, p. 68
· Reteaching Activity, p. 71
· Primary Source: Popular Song, p. 77

📖 Reading Study Guide (English and Spanish), pp. 233–234

📖 Access for Students Acquiring English/ESL
· Guided Reading (Spanish), p. 248
· Skillbuilder Practice, p. 249

 Formal Assessment
· Section Quiz, p. 425

📖 Integrated Assessment
· Rubrics

**INTEGRATED TECHNOLOGY**

🔵 classzone.com

**TEXAS RESOURCES**

 TAKS Spiraled Content Review

 TAKS Practice Tests

 TAKS Practice Transparencies TT119

 TAKS Online Test Practice

## More About . . .

### Hippie Speak

In addition to "flower power" and "do your own thing," the counterculture created a whole lexicon of "hip" language. Among the words and phrases used by hippies to express approval were *far out, groovy, right on,* and *out of sight.* Other terms, such as *hang up, freak out,* and *bummer,* were used to express disapproval. The counterculture also coined a number of behavioral injunctions, including "Let it all hang out" and "Get your act together."

## More About . . .

### Communes

Many hippies rejected mainstream society by living together in communes with shared property and money and rather flexible and loose relationships. Communal living flourished in both cities and the country. Most communes were short-lived, but those that lasted years had a significant social and economic impact on the surrounding area. This is how Harvard Business School professor Rosabeth Moss Kanter recalled her communal experience: "The things that make up community are terribly subtle; it's the little things . . . making dinner with a crew once a week, remembering who's a vegetarian and needs a special meal. Expanded consciousness of others . . . nothing big and spectacular. The scenes that move me are the little things about our life together."

**"TUNE IN, TURN ON, DROP OUT"** Members of the counterculture, known as hippies, shared some of the beliefs of the New Left movement. Specifically, they felt that American society—and its materialism, technology, and war—had grown hollow. Influenced by the nonconformist beat movement of the 1950s, hippies embraced the credo of Harvard psychology professor and counterculture philosopher Timothy Leary: "Tune in, turn on, drop out." Throughout the mid- and late 1960s, tens of thousands of idealistic youths left school, work, or home to create what they hoped would be an idyllic community of peace, love, and harmony.

*"How does it feel to be without a home . . . like a rolling stone?"*
**BOB DYLAN**

**HIPPIE CULTURE** The hippie era, sometimes known as the Age of Aquarius, was marked by rock 'n' roll music, outrageous clothing, sexual license, and illegal drugs—in particular, marijuana and a new hallucinogenic drug called LSD, or acid. Timothy Leary, an early experimenter with the drug, promoted the use of LSD as a "mind-expanding" aid for self-awareness. Hippies also turned to Eastern religions such as Zen Buddhism, which professed that one could attain enlightenment through meditation rather than the reading of scriptures.

Hippies donned ragged jeans, tie-dyed T-shirts, military garments, love beads, and Native American ornaments. Thousands grew their hair out, despite the fact that their more conservative elders saw this as an act of disrespect. Signs across the country said, "Make America beautiful—give a hippie a haircut."

Hippies also rejected conventional home life. Many joined communes, in which the members renounced private property to live communally. By the mid-sixties, **Haight-Ashbury** in San Francisco was known as the hippie capital, mainly because California did not outlaw hallucinogenic drugs until 1966.

**DECLINE OF THE MOVEMENT** After only a few years, the counterculture's peace and harmony gave way to violence and disillusionment. The urban communes eventually turned seedy and dangerous. Alex Forman recalled, "There were ripoffs, violence . . . people living on the street with no place to stay." Having dispensed with society's conventions and rules, the hippies had to rely on each other. Many discovered that the philosophy of "do your own thing" did not provide enough guidance for how to live. "We were together at the level of peace and love," said one disillusioned hippie. "We fell apart over who would cook and wash dishes and pay the bills." By 1970, many had fallen victim to the drugs they used, experiencing drug addiction and mental breakdowns. The rock singer Janis Joplin and the legendary guitarist Jimi Hendrix both died of drug overdoses in 1970.

As the mystique of the 1960s wore off, thousands of hippies lined up at government offices to collect welfare and food stamps—dependent on the very society they had once rejected. **Ⓐ**

*A. Answer*
The dark side of the drug and music scene, and the hippies' inability to exist outside mainstream America.

**MAIN IDEA**

**Analyzing Causes**
Ⓐ What events and other factors hastened the decline of the counterculture movement?

A prominent symbol of the counterculture movement was bright colors. ▶

782

---

**ACTIVITY   SKILLBUILDER LESSON**

### Comparing; Contrasting

**Explaining the Skill** Finding similarities and differences between events, social or political groups, and movements can help historians understand the past more completely. For example, comparing the lifestyles and values of different groups can help historians identify trends or universal human needs.

**Applying the Skill** Make two columns on the chalkboard: "Hippies" and "Establishment." Ask students to list as many differing characteristics of hippie and establishment, or mainstream, culture as they can find on this page. Point out that they may need to infer some establishment characteristics from descriptions by hippies. Also ask students if they find any similarities. Examples—Hippies: long hair, rock 'n' roll music, freedom to "do your own thing," outrageous clothes, communes; Establishment: short hair, other kinds of music, respect for social conventions, traditional home life.

📖 In-Depth Resources: Unit 6
· Skillbuilder Practice: Comparing; Contrasting, p. 68

## A Changing Culture ❷

Although short-lived, some aspects of the counterculture—namely, its fine arts and social attitudes—left a more lasting imprint on the world.

**ART** The counterculture's rebellious style left its mark on the art world. The 1960s saw the rise of pop art (popular art). Pop artists, led by Andy Warhol, attempted to bring art into the mainstream. Pop art was characterized by bright, simple, commercial-looking images often depicting everyday life. For instance, Warhol became famous for his bright silk-screen portraits of soup cans, Marilyn Monroe, and other icons of mass culture. These images were repeated to look mass-produced and impersonal, a criticism of the times implying that individual freedoms had been lost to a more conventional, "cookie-cutter" lifestyle.

**ROCK MUSIC** During the 1960s, the counterculture movement embraced rock 'n' roll as its loud and biting anthem of protest. The music was an offshoot of African-American rhythm and blues music that had captivated so many teenagers during the 1950s. **B**

> **MAIN IDEA**
>
> **Making Inferences**
> **B** What did rock 'n' roll symbolize for American youth?

The band that, perhaps more than any other, helped propel rock music into mainstream America was **the Beatles.** The British band, made up of four youths from working-class Liverpool, England, arrived in America in 1964 and immediately took the country by storm. By the time the Beatles broke up in 1970, the four "lads" had inspired a countless number of other bands and had won over millions of Americans to rock 'n' roll.

One example of rock 'n' roll's popularity occurred in August 1969 on a farm in upstate New York. More than 400,000 showed up for a free music festival called "**Woodstock** Music and Art Fair." This festival represented, as one songwriter put it, "the '60s movement of peace and love and some higher cultural cause." For three days, the most popular bands and musicians performed, including Jimi Hendrix, Janis Joplin, Joe Cocker, Joan Baez, the Grateful Dead, and Jefferson Airplane. Despite the huge crowd, Woodstock was peaceful and well organized. However, Tom Mathews, a writer who attended the Woodstock festival, recalled his experience there as less than blissful.

▲ The Beatles, shown here in 1967, influenced fashion with their long hair and psychedelic clothing.

### A PERSONAL VOICE  TOM MATHEWS

" The last night of the concert I was standing in a narrow pit at the foot of the stage. I made the mistake of looking over the board fence separating the pit from Max Yasgur's hillside. When I peered up I saw 400,000 . . . people wrapped in wet, dirty ponchos, sleeping bags and assorted, tie-dyed mufti slowly slipping toward the stage. It looked like a human mud slide. . . . After that night I couldn't get out of there fast enough. "

—"The Sixties Complex," *Newsweek*, Sept. 5, 1988

**CHANGING ATTITUDES** While the counterculture movement faded, its casual "do your own thing" philosophy left its mark. American attitudes toward sexual behavior became more casual and permissive, leading to what became known as the sexual revolution. During the 1960s and 1970s, mass culture—including TV, books,

*An Era of Social Change*  **783**

### Instruct: Objective ❷

**A Changing Culture**
TAKS SS11 5(US24.A)
· What influence did hippies have on art and fashion?
· What did rock music mean to hippies?
· How did the counterculture change American social attitudes?

📰 In-Depth Resources: Unit 6
· Guided Reading, p. 66
· Primary Source: Popular Song, p. 77

### More About . . .

**Woodstock**
Woodstock represented the high water mark of the hippie culture. The 400,000 young people who gathered on farmer Max Yasgur's 600-acre dairy farm in August 1969 called themselves the Woodstock Nation. For its three-day existence, Woodstock considered itself a peaceful kingdom—united by love, peace, and music. The music and the experience of the festival were captured in a popular documentary titled *Woodstock* (1970).

### Tracing Themes
**DIVERSITY AND NATIONAL IDENTITY**

**The Counterculture**
The counterculture rejected mainstream society. Hippies especially renounced materialism, conventional home life, and success in the workplace. For them, the American dream revolved around peace, love, communal living, and personal exploration. While many in the counterculture thought they were inventing a whole new world, their ideas were part of a American tradition of utopian communities, scores of which flourished in the 1800s.

 **classzone.com**

---

## ACTIVITY    LINK TO MUSIC

### Classic Rock

**Class Time** 45 minutes

**Task** Creating a multimedia presentation on the beginnings of the rock music industry

**Purpose** To analyze the roots and development of a major cultural industry

**Directions** Have students work in groups and choose one of the following topics to research: rock albums, FM rock radio, or rock concerts. Have students use the Internet and other research materials to learn about the beginnings of these cultural institutions. Ask students share their findings with the rest of the class in a multimedia presentation.

 Integrated Assessment
· Rubrics 1, 6

## History Through *Music*

### PROTEST SONGS OF THE SIXTIES

During the turbulent climate of the sixties, hippies and other activists used music as a vehicle for political expression. In bus terminals, in the streets, and on the White House lawn, thousands united in song, expressing their rejection of mainstream society, their demand for civil rights, and their outrage over the Vietnam War. Musicians like Bob Dylan stirred up antiwar sentiment in songs like "The Times They Are A-Changin'," while Joan Baez and Pete Seeger popularized the great African-American spiritual "We Shall Overcome," which became the anthem of the Civil Rights Movement.

**We Shall Overcome**
**(African-American Spiritual)**

We shall overcome,
We shall overcome,
We shall overcome some day.
(*Chorus*) Oh, deep in my heart
I do believe:
We shall overcome some day.

We'll walk hand in hand. . . .
We shall all be free. . . .
We are not afraid. . . .
We are not alone. . . .
The whole wide world around. . . .
We shall overcome. . . .

▲ Joined in harmony, African-American students in Selma, Alabama, gather on the steps of the Tabernacle Baptist Church to sing "We Shall Overcome." (1963)

Joan Baez, 1965

Bob Dylan, 1966 ▶

*from* **The Times They Are A-Changin' (Bob Dylan, 1962)**

Come senators, congressmen
Please heed the call
Don't stand in the doorway
Don't block up the hall
For he that gets hurt
Will be he who has stalled
There's a battle outside
And it is ragin'.
It'll soon shake your windows
And rattle your walls
For the times they are a-changin'.

Come mothers and fathers
Throughout the land
And don't criticize
What you can't understand
Your sons and your daughters
Are beyond your command
Your old road is
Rapidly agin'.
Please get out of the new one
If you can't lend your hand
For the times they are a-changin'.

magazines, music, and movies—began to address subjects that had once been prohibited, particularly sexual behavior and explicit violence.

While some hailed the increasing permissiveness as liberating, others attacked it as a sign of moral decay. For millions of Americans, the new tolerance was merely an uncivilized lack of respect for established social norms. Eventually, the counterculture movement would lead a great many Americans to more liberal attitudes about dress and appearance, lifestyle, and social behavior; yet in the short run, it produced largely the opposite effect.

**784** CHAPTER 23

---

## ③ The Conservative Response

In the late 1960s, many believed that the country was losing its sense of right and wrong. Increasingly, conservative voices began to express people's anger. At the 1968 Republican convention in Miami, candidate Richard M. Nixon expressed that anger.

**A PERSONAL VOICE** RICHARD NIXON

" As we look at America we see cities enveloped in smoke and flame. We hear sirens in the night. We see Americans hating each other at home. . . . Did we come all this way for this? . . . die in Normandy and Korea and Valley Forge for this? "

—Speech at Republican Convention, 1968

▲ In contrast to the 1968 Democratic Convention in Chicago, the Republican convention was orderly and united—particularly in the delegates' opposition to the counterculture.

**CONSERVATIVES ATTACK THE COUNTERCULTURE** Nixon was not the only conservative voice expressing alarm. FBI Director J. Edgar Hoover issued a warning that "revolutionary terrorism" was a threat on campuses and in cities. Other conservative critics warned that campus rebels posed a danger to traditional values and threatened to plunge American society into anarchy. Conservatives also attacked the counterculture for what they saw as its decadent values. In the view of psychiatrist Bruno Bettelheim, student rebels and members of the counterculture had been pampered in childhood; as young adults, they did not have the ability for delayed gratification. According to some conservative commentators, the counterculture had abandoned rational thought in favor of the senses and uninhibited self-expression. **C**

The angry response of mainstream Americans caused a profound change in the political landscape of the United States. By the end of the 1960s, conservatives were presenting their own solutions on such issues as lawlessness and crime, the size of the federal government, and welfare. This growing conservative movement would propel Nixon into the White House—and set the nation on a more conservative course.

*C. Possible Answer*
They believed the counterculture movement was threatening the American way of life.

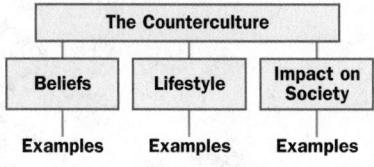

**MAIN IDEA**

**Forming Generalizations**
**C** Why were conservatives angry about the counterculture?

**CHAPTER 23 · SECTION 3**

**Instruct: Objective ③**

**The Conservative Response**
TAKS SS11 5(US24.A)
· Why did conservatives object to the counterculture?
· How did the counterculture help contribute to the conservative backlash?

📰 In-Depth Resources: Unit 6
· Guided Reading, p. 66

**More About . . .**

**Conservative Backlash**
Conservatives made no distinction between what was becoming a generally apolitical cultural movement and a smaller radical political movement that was making increasingly violent attacks on the government. Within the counterculture, it was known that most hippies, while harboring anti-establishment attitudes, had little inclination to act on them.

**Assess & Reteach**

**SECTION 3 ASSESSMENT**
Have students work in small groups to answer the questions.

📰 Formal Assessment
· Section Quiz, p. 425

**SELF-ASSESSMENT**
Have students share the diagrams that they created for Item 2 in a class discussion of the counterculture movement.

**RETEACH**
Use the Guided Reading worksheet for Section 3 to review the main concepts.

📰 In-Depth Resources: Unit 6
· Reteaching Activity, p. 71

---

③ **ASSESSMENT**

1. **TERMS & NAMES** For each term or name, write a sentence explaining its significance.
   • counterculture          • Haight-Ashbury          • the Beatles          • Woodstock

**MAIN IDEA**

2. **TAKING NOTES**
Re-create the tree diagram below on your paper. Then fill in examples that illustrate the topics in the second row of boxes.

**The Counterculture**

| Beliefs | Lifestyle | Impact on Society |

Examples      Examples      Examples

Which example do you think had the biggest impact on society? Why?

**CRITICAL THINKING**

3. **DEVELOPING HISTORICAL PERSPECTIVE**
A stereotype is a generalization made about a group. What stereotype do you think hippies might have formed about mainstream Americans? What stereotype do you think mainstream Americans might have formed about hippies? Why? **Think About:**
• Alex Forman's comments in "A Personal Voice" (page 781)
• hippies' values and lifestyle
• mainstream Americans' values and lifestyle

4. **MAKING INFERENCES**
In your opinion, why didn't the hippies succeed?

5. **ANALYZING ISSUES**
What role did the counterculture and antiwar movement play in helping Richard Nixon win the presidency?

*An Era of Social Change* **785**

---

Answers **ASSESSMENT** ③

**1. TERMS & NAMES**
counterculture, p. 781
Haight-Ashbury, p. 782
the Beatles, p. 783
Woodstock, p. 783

**2. TAKING NOTES**
Beliefs—rejection of mainstream society's materialism and technology; opposition to war; vision of a society filled with peace, love, and harmony. Lifestyle—rock 'n' roll music; outrageous clothing; drug use; communal living. Impact on society—pop art; men's and women's fashions, especially blue jeans; rock 'n' roll music; conservative movement.

**3. DEVELOPING HISTORICAL PERSPECTIVE**
Stereotypes of mainstream Americans—greedy and materialistic; old-fashioned and narrow-minded; insensitive and intolerant; pro-war and ultraconservative. Stereotypes of hippies—flamboyant and shallow; lawless and immoral; self-absorbed and unrealistic; radical, violent, and disruptive.

**4. MAKING INFERENCES**
Student answers will vary but should show a clear understanding of the factors that prevented success.

**5. ANALYZING ISSUES**
Frightened by the discontent in the country, mainstream society voted for Nixon, the candidate who they thought would restore order.

DAILY LIFE
1960–1970

## Objectives

· To identify some of the ways the social changes of the 1960s effected teenagers

· To summarize the types of music and movies popular in the 1960s

## Focus & Motivate

Ask students what, if any, music or movies from the 1960s they like. What do they know about the 1960s? Remind them of political events and cultural changes they have read about and discuss what it must have been like to be a teenager in the 1960s.

## More About . . .

### Music of the 1960s

By the early 1960s, some of the energy of early rock 'n' roll had begun to dissipate. Elvis Presley had been drafted; Chuck Berry jailed (on charges that many deemed racially motivated); and Jerry Lee Lewis disgraced for marrying his 13-year–old cousin. Little Richard had left pop music to join the ministry, and plane and car crashes had claimed the lives of Buddy Holly, Ritchie Valens, the Big Bopper, and Eddie Cochran and injured two other early rockers, Carl Perkins and Gene Vincent. Then, in 1964, the Beatles began the British invasion that breathed new life into rock 'n' roll.

---

DAILY LIFE
1960–1970

# Signs of the Sixties

The wave of social change that swept across America during the 1960s affected everyone, but especially the nation's teenagers. Abandoning the conservative and "clean-cut" look of the 1950s, many teens experimented with new and different appearances. In a declaration of their individuality and desire for more freedom, they also embraced a variety of new music and films during the 1960s.

**FASHION: A NEW LOOK ▶**

During the 1960s, many youths wore a wide range of unconventional clothing. While most Americans did not adopt the outlandish look of hippies, many came out of the sixties wearing longer hair and blue jeans, which became a staple in nearly every wardrobe. Bright colors and psychedelic patterns also became wildly popular.

**◀ THE RISE OF SOUL MUSIC**

Rock 'n' roll's popularity continued to soar as teenagers listened to a wider variety of sounds in the 1960s. African-American soul artists, whose music had inspired the more popular white rock 'n' roll performers of the 1950s, grew widely popular themselves during the 1960s. During this decade, Detroit's Motown label produced the most popular and successful African-American artists, including Marvin Gaye, Stevie Wonder, and the Supremes (left).

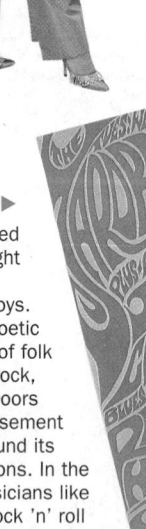

**A DIVERSE MUSIC SCENE ▶**

Scores of teenagers also tuned to surf music, a harmonic, light sound made popular by a California band, the Beach Boys. Other teens listened to the poetic and socially conscious lyrics of folk rock. Heavy, or psychedelic, rock, sung by bands such as the Doors (whose 1967 concert advertisement appears to the right), also found its way into many album collections. In the later part of the decade, musicians like Jimi Hendrix (far right) took rock 'n' roll in a new direction.

---

## RECOMMENDED RESOURCES

### BOOKS

Howard, Gerald, ed. *The Sixties.* New York: Paragon, 1991. Art, politics, and the media in an explosive decade.

O'Neil, Doris C., ed. *Life—The 60s.* Boston: Little, 1989. A pictorial history.

Polsgrove, Carol. *It Wasn't Pretty Folks, but Didn't we Have Fun?* New York: Norton, 1995. The 1960s as depicted in *Esquire* magazine.

### VIDEOS

*Berkeley in the Sixties.* Dir. Mark Kitchell. 1990. First Run Features, 1996. The Free Speech Movement, antiwar protests, and counterculture at the University of California.

*Breaking Boundaries, Testing Limits.* PBS Video, 1991. The youth rebellion and counterculture.

*Flashing on the Sixties.* Lisa Law Productions, 1994. Surveys some of the people, places, events and ideals that helped shape the 1960s.

*The History of Rock 'n' Roll.* Time-Life, 1995. A ten-part series of rock music from rhythm and blues to rap.

**GOING TO THE SHOW** ▲

As the nation's movie industry grew, more and more teenagers flocked to the cinema. Teens took in such diverse films as the counterculture classic *Easy Rider* and the science fiction classic *2001: A Space Odyssey* (above), which tells the story of HAL, a spaceship computer that develops a mind of its own.

**POP ART** ▲

Andy Warhol created this image of movie actress and popular icon Marilyn Monroe. A leader of the pop art movement, Warhol attempted to criticize the conventional lifestyle of the mass culture through commercial-looking images that depicted the loss of individuality.

---

## DATA FILE

**POPULAR SONGS**
- "Blowin' in the Wind" (1962)
- "Surfin' USA" (1963)
- "Where Did Our Love Go?" (1964)
- "California Dreamin'" (1966)
- "Light My Fire" (1967)
- "Mrs. Robinson" (1967)
- "Aquarius/Let the Sunshine In" (1968)
- "Come Together" (1969)
- "Everyday People" (1968)

**POPULAR TV SHOWS**
- *The Dick Van Dyke Show* (1962–1966)
- *The Beverly Hillbillies* (1962–1971)
- *Green Acres* (1965–1971)
- *The Addams Family* (1964–1966)
- *The Man from U.N.C.L.E.* (1964–1968)
- *Mission: Impossible* (1966–1973)
- *Laugh-In* (1968–1973)
- *Bonanza* (1959–1973)

**1960** — 1960: Alfred Hitchcock's *Psycho* terrifies movie audiences across the nation.

**1962** — 1962: Wilt Chamberlain scores 100 points in a basketball game.

**1963** — 1963: The movie *Cleopatra*, produced for $37 million, is the most expensive film to date.

1963: Graphic Artist Harvey Ball invents the smiley face for an ad campaign aimed at boosting workers' morale.

**1964** — 1964: The Beatles arrive in America.

**1965** — 1965: The miniskirt is introduced.

**1966** — 1966: The National Association of Broadcasters instructs disc jockeys to screen records for obscene or hidden meanings.

**1967** — 1967: The Green Bay Packers defeat the Kansas City Chiefs in the first Super Bowl.

**1968** — 1968: The government mandates that all new cars must be equipped with seat belts.

**1969** — 1969: Pantsuits become acceptable for everyday wear by women.

### THINKING CRITICALLY

**CONNECT TO HISTORY**

1. **Drawing Conclusions** What conclusions can you draw about teenagers in the 1960s from the images and information in this feature?

   **SEE SKILLBUILDER HANDBOOK, PAGE R18.**

**CONNECT TO TODAY**

2. **The Role of Culture** Do the arts merely *reflect* social change, or can art, music, fashion, etc. help to *bring about* social change? Think about how music and fashions affect your actions and opinions. Discuss your thoughts with a small group of classmates.

 **RESEARCH LINKS** **CLASSZONE.COM**

*An Era of Social Change* **787**

---

## Instruct

1. How did teenagers influence popular culture?
2. What was unique about 1960s fashion?
3. What was surf music?
4. Was there a distinctive 1960s style of art?

**MAKING PERSONAL CONNECTIONS**

Many musicians from the 1960s are still active today. Discuss with students their view of 50-to-60-year-old rockers, such as Bob Dylan, Mick Jagger, Rod Stewart, Neil Young, Eric Clapton, Paul Simon, Tina Turner, Aretha Franklin, and others, performing today. Ask students to consider what rock music means to people of their parents' and grandparents' generations.

### More About . . .

**Pop Art**

Andy Warhol became one of the most famous artists of the international Pop Art movement that flourished during the 1960s. Like other Pop artists, Warhol's work was inspired by images used in advertising and the mass media. Warhol even used mass production techniques, such as silkscreen printing, to make his pictures of food products and celebrities resemble the printed images found in magazines or on billboards. Even though Warhol focused on uniquely American products and celebrities, his art actually transcended American culture, becoming a criticism of Western consumer society in general. By presenting pictures of movie stars or canned goods as objects of veneration, Warhol challenged the values of international consumer culture. Ask, How did Andy Warhol's art transcend American culture? *(By commenting on the values of Western consumer society.)*

---

### THINKING CRITICALLY: ANSWERS

1. **CONNECT TO HISTORY** Teenagers were rebellious and wanted to express their individuality. They also were wild, self-confident, self-important, fun-loving, and naive. Although teenagers thought they were being different, their appearance showed little individuality, as they conformed to an accepted "in" look. Teenage tastes dominated culture.

2. **CONNECT TO TODAY** The discussion should be focused on the role of the arts in social change, and each student should share an opinion with the group.

## TERMS & NAMES

1. César Chávez, p. 768
2. La Raza Unida, p. 770
3. American Indian Movement (AIM), p. 771
4. feminism, p. 776
5. Betty Friedan, p. 776
6. Equal Rights Amendment (ERA), p. 779
7. Phyllis Schlafly, p. 779
8. counterculture, p. 781
9. Haight-Ashbury, p. 782
10. Woodstock, p. 783

## MAIN IDEAS

1. Nonviolence; he launched a boycott to pressure California grape growers to recognize the United Farm Workers Organizing Committee.
2. The demands were restoration of 110 million acres of land to Native American tribes and abolition of the Bureau of Indian Affairs.
3. The creation of more childcare facilities, better educational opportunities for women, and EEOC enforcement of the ban on sex discrimination in hiring
4. That women had the right to choose an abortion during the first three months of pregnancy
5. A counterculture guru, Leary popularized the credo "tune in, turn on, drop out" and promoted the use of LSD.
6. It inspired a conservative backlash among mainstream Americans that led to a wave of Republican election victories.

## TERMS & NAMES

**For each term or name below, write a sentence explaining its connection to the 1960s.**

1. César Chávez
2. La Raza Unida
3. American Indian Movement (AIM)
4. feminism
5. Betty Friedan
6. Equal Rights Amendment (ERA)
7. Phyllis Schlafly
8. counterculture
9. Haight-Ashbury
10. Woodstock

## MAIN IDEAS

**Use your notes and the information in the chapter to answer the following questions.**

### Latinos and Native Americans Seek Equality
(pages 768–773)

1. What strategies did both César Chávez and the UFWOC use to achieve their goals? How did they successfully apply these tactics?
2. What were the demands of the American Indian Movement (AIM) organizers who staged "The Trail of Broken Treaties" march on Washington in 1972?

### Women Fight for Equality (pages 776–780)

3. Name three changes that members of the National Organization of Women (NOW) advocated.
4. What was the Supreme Court's decision in the *Roe* v. *Wade* case?

### Culture and Counterculture (pages 781–785)

5. Briefly explain the role Timothy Leary played in the counterculture movement.
6. What unintended impact did the counterculture have on many mainstream Americans?

## CRITICAL THINKING

1. **USING YOUR NOTES** Re-create the diagram shown below. Then fill in the appropriate areas with key individual and shared achievements of Latinos, Native Americans, and feminists.

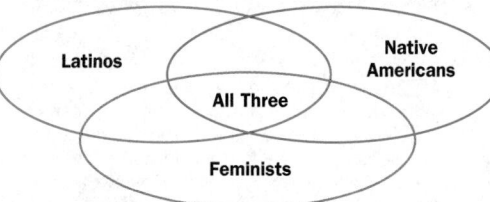

2. **DEVELOPING HISTORICAL PERSPECTIVE** Consider the organizations that Latinos, Native Americans, and women formed during the 1960s. Which do you think was the most influential? Why?
3. **ANALYZING PRIMARY SOURCES** Reread the song lyrics of Bob Dylan's "The Times They Are A-Changin'" on page 784. How do you think this song captured the main message of the counterculture movement?

## VISUAL SUMMARY   AN ERA OF SOCIAL CHANGE

**POLITICAL**
- protests against Vietnam War
- NOW fuels feminism
- the New Right emerges
- ERA defeated
- *Roe* v. *Wade*
- more women in the work force
- AIM wins reforms and land rights
- La Raza Unida and MAPA fight for more rights for Latinos
- bilingual education
- Latino farm workers unionize

**SOCIAL**
- hippies reject mainstream society
- more communal living
- new fashion trends reflect freedom of expression
- traditional forms of worship rejected in favor of Eastern religious teachings
- more drug use
- women and minorities seek equality
- more permissive sexual behavior
- books, magazines, and movies show explicit violence

**CHANGES BROUGHT ABOUT BY THE COUNTERCULTURE**

**MUSIC**
- music as political expression
- Motown label produces African-American artists
- rock music; the Beatles; Woodstock festival

**ART AND FASHION**
- pop art movement
- long hair as rebellion
- hippies popularize bright, colorful clothing, beads, and blue jeans

788

## CRITICAL THINKING

1. **USING YOUR NOTES** Individual achievements: *Latinos*—Bilingual Education Act; Chicano studies programs. *Native Americans*—Indian Education Act; Indian Self-Determination and Education Assistance Act. *Feminists*—Higher Education Act; increased numbers of women in law and medicine. Shared achievements: *All groups*—Education reform; greater political presence. *Latinos and Native Americans*—Stronger cultural identity. *Latinos and feminists*—Greater assimilation into mainstream society.

2. **DEVELOPING HISTORICAL PERSPECTIVE** United Farm Workers Organizing Committee, American Indian Movement (AIM), and National Organization for Women (NOW)

3. **ANALYZING PRIMARY SOURCES** The main message was that change was needed, and "The Times They Are A-Changin'" was telling public officials, parents, and others not to stand in the way.

## Standardized Test Practice

Use the flowchart and your knowledge of U.S. history to answer question 1.

| 1. UFWOC organizes a boycott of grapes. |
|---|

↓

| 2. Growers lose money. |
|---|

↓

| 3. UFWOC signs new contracts with growers. |
|---|

↓

| 4. |
|---|

1. Which event accurately completes the cause-and-effect chain?

   A EEOC rules that unhealthful working conditions amount to illegal discrimination.

   B UFWOC disbands.

   C Grape boycott is extended to apricots and olives.

   D Working conditions for migrant farmworkers are improved.

2. In the 1960s, women fought in Congress, in the courts, and in their everyday lives for treatment as political and social equals. Today, job discrimination against women is illegal because of —

   F the Fourteenth Amendment.

   G the ERA.

   H the Civil Rights Act of 1964.

   J the *Roe* v. *Wade* decision.

3. Which of the following statements is a fact?

   A Hippies believed that everyone should love each other.

   B Hippies spoiled the Woodstock Festival.

   C The hippie movement failed because the hippies' beliefs were too radical.

   D Hippies invented rock music in Liverpool, England.

4. The women's rights movement largely grew out of—

   F the counterculture movement.

   G the civil rights movement.

   H the movement to organize farmworkers.

   J reaction to the Warren Court decisions.

**ADDITIONAL TEST PRACTICE, pages S1–S33.**

 **TEST PRACTICE** CLASSZONE.COM

## Standardized Test Practice

1. The correct answer is letter **D.**
   The letter A is not correct because the EEOC was not involved. The letter B is incorrect because the UFWOC continued. The letter C is incorrect because there was no need for a boycott extension.

2. The correct answer is **H.**
   The letter F is incorrect because it has not been used in job discrimination cases. The letter G is incorrect because the ERA was not ratified. The letter J is incorrect because it refers to abortion rights.

3. The letter **A** is correct.
   The letter B is incorrect because they did not spoil Woodstock. The letter C is incorrect because most hippies were not radicals. The letter D is incorrect because rock music developed in the United States.

4. The letter **G** is correct.
   The letters F, H, and J are incorrect because they did not play a large role in the women's rights movement.

## LOBBYING PLAN

### Tips for Teaching

· Have students organize their materials in file folders for position papers, promotional materials, and over all lobbying plan.

· Give students a copy of evaluation rubrics to self-assess their project

### Project Presentation Rubrics

The Lobbying Plan should. . . .

· state the desired government action and reasons for it

· outline specific steps to raise awareness in supporters and government officials

· include samples of position papers, pamphlets, advertising, posters or other promotional material

📓 Formal Assessment
· Chapter Test, Forms A, B, and C, pp. 426–437

## ALTERNATIVE ASSESSMENT

1. **INTERACT WITH HISTORY**  Recall your discussion of the question on page 767:

### *How much can a society change?*

Write a script in which five people debate the question: a Native American activist, a Latino activist, a feminine activist, a hippie, and a conservative politician who wants to preserve the status quo in 1964. If you work in a group, be sure that each group member considers several points of view.

2. 🌐 **INTERNET ACTIVITIY** CLASSZONE.COM

Visit the links for Chapter Assessment to find examples of 1960s culture, such as songs, paintings, posters, clothing, cars, and so on. Prepare a paper or electronic museum exhibit of several artifacts that display a trend or theme discussed in the chapter. Write captions for the artifacts explaining their historical context and relating them to your chosen theme.

*An Era of Social Change* **789**

## ALTERNATIVE ASSESSMENT

### 1. INTERACT WITH HISTORY
**Rubric**

The script should . . .

· include the viewpoints of all five people: Native American activist, Latino activist, feminist, hippie, and conservative politician

· clearly state the views of each of the five

· use correct grammar, spelling, and punctuation

### 2. INTERNET ACTIVITY
**Rubric**

The museum exhibit should . . .

· clearly demonstrate the 1960s trend or theme

· include a variety of artifacts

· contain accurate and well-described textual information

## Previewing the Unit

Unit 7 describes the turbulent presidency of Richard Nixon and the failure of his successors to fix the economic problems of the 1970s. A growing conservatism in the American public in the 1980s accompanies economic change and the end of the Cold War. In the 1990s, vast social changes reshape Americans' lives while the challenges and opportunities of a new century emerge.

### UNIT PROJECT

### HISTORICAL INQUIRY: CAMPAIGN SCRAPBOOK

Use this project to teach students to explain and apply the use of historical context.

**Explaining the Use of Historical Context**
Tell students that when events are understood with reference to the actors's points of view and frames of reference, then people and events can be placed in historical context. This means they can be related to other events and ideas that occurred at the same time. Explain that this is a main goal of any historical inquiry: to understand why events happened as they did and how events affected and were effected by other events.

**Applying Historical Context**
Review with students what they have learned about point of view and frame of reference. Explain that for this project, they will need to understand and exhibit the points of view and frames of reference of the voters to

(continued on next page)

---

## UNIT 7

### UNIT PROJECT

*Campaign Scrapbook*

As you read this unit, choose a candidate for political office whom you think you would have supported. Create a fictional but realistic scrapbook that recounts your experiences on the campaign trail.

Exhibit at the Ellis Island Immigration Museum, design by MetaForm; portraits in flag by Pablo Delano

790

---

# Passage to a New Century 1968–2001

1

2

---

## More About the Image

**1 Ellis Island**

More than 12 million immigrants passed through the reception facility on Ellis Island in New York Harbor from the time it opened in 1892. More than 40 percent of all Americans alive today have an ancestor who passed through the facility.

Abandoned in 1954, Ellis Island became part of the Statue of Liberty National Monument in 1965. The statue was restored in 1986 on its hundredth anniversary. This step revived interest in Ellis Island, and it was reopened to the public in 1990 after being renovated.

**2 Construction of the flag**

The flag is composed of clear plastic prisms that are mounted on a metal frame. On the two outer faces of each prism is a photographic portrait of an American.

whom their candidate will make appeals. Ask what sorts of information they could include to do this. *(state of the economy and how it affected various economic groups; major events such as wars; social issues; special interest groups; positions of opposing candidates)*

## Tips for Scrapbooks
Have students work in small groups to brainstorm ideas about what artifacts their scrapbooks might include, such as diary entries; text of their candidate's speeches, brochures, and press releases; campaign strategy notes, itineraries, and budgets; polling results; and newspaper reports, analyses, and editorials.

### Rubric
A Campaign Scrapbook should . . .
· present a clear picture of the candidate's positions on important issues
· reflect an understanding of the historical context in which the campaign would have been conducted, by including important information on the frames of reference and points of view of potential supporters and opponents

### Follow-up
Ask students to explain how placing events in historical context helped them to understand those events better.

## HISTORY from VISUALS

### Interpreting the Exhibit
Photographer Pablo Delano took hundreds of photographs that were assembled to create this image. It acts as both a symbol of America and a profound representation of the diversity of Americans. Ask students if this image is a good way to symbolize the United States. Then ask what other images have been used to represent the United States.

**Extension** Ask students how, in the future, Americans will deal with the social diversity revealed by the faces in this flag.

**3 Immigration museum**
In 1990, the Ellis Island Immigration Museum opened. The museum includes photographs, passports, and the belonging of immigrants; exhibits on how immigrants were processed at Ellis Island; and other films, images, and objects that reveal the immigrant experience.

**4 The faces**
Delano took 754 photographs of Americans representing all ages, both genders, all races and all ethnic groups. Half were taken with a dark background and half with a light background to help create the red and white stripes of the flag.

**5 "The Peopling of America"**
The flag is one exhibit in a section of the museum called, "The Peopling of America." This section includes displays that vividly provide data on immigration, including country-of-origin statistics.

# An Age of Limits

| | CHAPTER OVERVIEW | COPYMASTERS | INTEGRATED TECHNOLOG |
|---|---|---|---|
| **CHAPTER RESOURCES** | *Richard Nixon takes office as president, slowing down the growth of federal power and changing foreign policy. He resigns in disgrace during his second term, and his successors are unable to fix growing economic problems* | 📄 **Telescoping the Times** · Chapter Summary, pp. 47–48 <br><br> 📄 **Planning for Block Schedules** | 📹 **American Stories, video series** · "Poisoned Playground" <br> 👁 **Power Presentations** <br> 👁 **Electronic Teacher Tools** <br> 🎧 **Online Lesson Planner** <br> 🎧 **classzone.com** |
| **SECTION 1** <br><br> **The Nixon Administration** <br><br> pp. 794–801 | **KEY IDEAS** <br> *President Richard M. Nixon attempts to move the country in a more conservative direction and to ease Cold War tensions throughout the world.* | 📄 **In-Depth Resources: Unit 7** · Guided Reading, p. 1 · Building Vocabulary, p. 5 · Reteaching Activity, p. 7 · Primary Sources, p. 13 · American Lives, p. 20 <br><br> 📄 **Lesson Plans,** pp. 187–188 | 🎧 **classzone.com** |
| **SECTION 2** <br><br> **Watergate: Nixon's Downfall** <br><br> pp. 802–809 | *Richard Nixon's involvement in the cover-up of a campaign burglary forces him to resign from office— the only president to do so.* | 📄 **In-Depth Resources: Unit 7** · Guided Reading, p. 2 · Reteaching Activity, p. 8 · Primary Sources, p. 14 · American Lives, p. 21 <br><br> 📄 **Lesson Plans,** pp. 189–190 | 🖥 **Critical Thinking Transparencies CT32, CT66** · The Watergate Scandal · Shift in Presidential Politics <br> 🖥 **Humanities Transparencies HT46** · "I am the Law" <br> 💿 **Electronic Library of Primary Sources** · Articles of Impeachment <br> 🎧 **classzone.com** |
| **SECTION 3** <br><br> **The Ford and Carter Years** <br><br> pp. 810–819 | *In the wake of Watergate, Presidents Ford and Carter try to restore faith in America's leadership as they battle the worst economic crisis in decades.* | 📄 **In-Depth Resources: Unit 7** · Guided Reading, p. 3 · Reteaching Activity, p. 9 · Geography Application, pp. 11–12 · Literature. pp. 17–19 <br><br> 📄 **Lesson Plans,** pp. 191–192 | 🖥 **Geography Transparencies GT32** · OPEC <br> 🖥 **Humanities Transparencies HT30** · Bicentennial celebration <br> 💿 **Electronic Library of Primary Sources** · On Energy by Jimmy Carter · from "Victim-Victimizer: Why Excel?" by Rev. Jessie L. Jackson <br> 🎧 **classzone.com** |
| **SECTION 4** <br><br> **Environmental Activism** <br><br> pp. 820–825 | *Americans, struck by their sense of limitations, begin to address a growing number of environmental concerns.* | 📄 **In-Depth Resources: Unit 7** · Guided Reading, p. 4 · Skillbuilder Practice, p. 6 · Reteaching Activity, p.10 · Primary Sources, pp. 15–16 <br><br> 📄 **Lesson Plans,** pp. 193–194 | 📹 **American Stories video series** · "Poisoned Playground" <br> 💿 **Electronic Library of Primary Sources** · "Principles of Environmental Justice" <br> 🎧 **classzone.com** |

## ASSESSMENT OPTIONS

PE Chapter Assessment, pp. 826–827

Formal Assessment
· Chapter Tests, Forms A, B, and C, pp. 442–453

Test Generator

Integrated Assessment Book

TAKS Online Test Practice

TAKS Spiraled Content Review

TAKS Practice Tests

---

PE Section 1 Assessment, p. 801

TE Self-Assessment, p. 801

Formal Assessment, Quiz, p. 438

Integrated Assessment Book

Test Generator

TAKS Practice Transparencies TT120

---

PE Section 2 Assessment, p. 809

TE Self-Assessment, p. 809

Formal Assessment, Quiz, p. 439

Integrated Assessment Book

Test Generator

TAKS Practice Transparencies TT121

---

PE Section 3 Assessment, p. 817

TE Self-Assessment, p. 817

Formal Assessment, Quiz, p. 440

Integrated Assessment Book

Test Generator

TAKS Practice Transparencies TT122

---

PE Section 4 Assessment, p. 825

TE Self-Assessment, p. 825

Formal Assessment, Quiz, p. 441

Integrated Assessment Book

Test Generator

TAKS Practice Transparencies TT123

## RESOURCES FOR DIFFERENTIATING INSTRUCTION

### Students Acquiring English/ESL

Reading Study Guide:
(English and Spanish)
pp. 237–244

Access for Students
Acquiring English/ESL:
Spanish Translations,
pp. 254–260

Chapter Summaries on CD
(English and Spanish)

### Less Proficient Readers

Reading Study Guide
(English and Spanish)
pp. 237–244

Telescoping the Times
· Chapter Summary,
pp. 47–48

Chapter Summaries on CD
(English and Spanish)

### Gifted and Talented Students

In-Depth Resources: Unit 7
· Primary Sources,
pp. 13–16
· Literature, pp. 17-19
· American Lives: Henry
Kissinger, p. 20; Barbara
Jordan, p. 21

Electronic Library of
Primary Sources
· Unit 7, Chapter 24

## CROSS-CURRICULAR CONNECTIONS

### Government

Bernstein, Carl and Woodward, Bob. *All the President's Men.* NY: Touchstone Books, 1994. This book by two young reporters for *The Washington Post* covers their investigation of the Watergate break-in.

### Culture

Stewart, Gail, editor. *The 1970s.* San Diego: Lucent Books, 1999. An overview of the people, places, trends, and events of the decade.

### Economics

Brown, Paul. *Energy and Resources.* NY: Franklin Watts, 1998. This book discusses the aims of the 1992 Earth Summit and its plan for attaining sustainable development.

### Science

Kluger, Jeffrey and Lovell, James A. *Lost Moon: The Perilous Voyage of Apollo 13.* Boston: Houghton Mifflin, 1994. A space capsule on the way to the moon is rocked by an explosion and loses the oxygen it needs for power and water. Can the three astronauts on board be brought back to Earth safely? The crisis brings out the best in hundreds of engineers and technicians on the ground and in the three astronauts, who must remain calm and clearheaded.

### Literature

Updike, John. *Memories of the Ford Administration.* NY: Fawcett, 1993. When a history professor is asked to record his impressions of the Ford administration, he uses that turbulent time—following the resignation of Richard Nixon—to recall a piece of turbulent personal history: his unfinished book on the 19th-century president James Buchanan.

Klass, David. *California Blue.* NY: Scholastic, 1994. Seventeen-year-old John Rodgers loves his local redwood forest. John's discovery of a rare butterfly in the forest creates conflicts with his logger father's job. Powerfully written.

## ENRICHMENT ACTIVITIES

PE Pupil's Edition, pp. 792–825
Interact with History, pp. 792–793
Daily Life, pp. 808–809
Supreme Court, pp. 818–819
Science & Technology, p. 823

In-Depth Resources: Unit 7
· Geography Application: Oil Consumption in the 1970s, pp. 11–12
· Primary Source: Newspaper Front Page, p. 13
· Primary Source: *All the Presidents Men,* p. 14

· Primary Source: *Love Canal: My Story,* p. 15
· Primary Source: *Silent Spring,* p. 16
· Literature: from *Memories of the Ford Administration,* pp. 17–19
· American Lives: Henry Kissinger, p. 20
· American Lives: Barbara Jordan, p. 21

Electronic Library of Primary Sources
Unit 7, Chapter 24

American Stories video series
· "Poisoned Playground"

## BLOCK SCHEDULE LESSON PLAN OPTIONS (90-MINUTE PERIOD)

### DAY 1

**CHAPTER 24 OPENER**
pp. 792–793
**Class Time** 20 minutes

**History from Visuals, p. 792**
**Class Time** 10 minutes
*Options for Pacing and Variety*

· **Role-Playing** Ask students to look at the photograph and the caption. Then discuss President Nixon's public expression and the private feelings he might have had at that moment. Ask students why Nixon might have portrayed a different expression than he was feeling. **Class Time** 10 minutes

**Interact with History, p. 793**
**Class Time** 10 minutes
*Options for Pacing and Variety*

· **Time Saver** Ask students to read the page and discuss the questions. Then have them make a list of ways a president can misuse power and what the relative seriousness of that misuse of power is. **Class Time** 10 minutes

**SECTION 1, pp. 794–801**
**Class Time** 35 minutes
*Options for Pacing and Variety*

· **Peer Teaching** Ask students to look at the political cartoon on page 795 after they have finished reading about Nixon's legislative accomplishments. Have students work in pairs to make a list of Nixon presidential goals and of examples of the legislation that forwarded each of those goals. Refer to the activity and information on the TE page 795. **Class Time** 15 minutes

### DAY 1 continued

· **Peer Competition** Read the information on busing on TE page 797 to the class. Divide the class into two groups, one that supports the issue and another one that opposes it. Have each group prepare for a debate on the issue, finding facts to support their side, and addressing why they do not support the other side. **Class Time** 35 minutes

· **Peer Teaching** Have students work in pairs to find the meanings of the words on TE page 797. **Class Time** 15 minutes

**SECTION 2 pp. 802–809**
**Class Time** 35 minutes
*Options for Pacing and Variety*

· **Time Saver** Have students read the "Historical Spotlight on Woodward and Bernstein" on page 804. Read the additional information on TE page 803 and ask them what they think about journalistic reliance on anonymous sources. **Class Time** 15 minutes

· **Peer Teaching** Ask groups of students to work together to answer the Section Assessment questions. Have each group share their response to question 3. **Class Time** 20 minutes

· **Time Saver** Ask the class to read the feature on pages 808–809, "Television Reflects Daily Life," and discuss the Connect to History question on page 809. **Class Time** 15 minutes

### DAY 2

**SECTION 3, pp. 810–819**
**Class Time** 30 minutes
*Options for Pacing and Variety:*

· **Time Saver** Have the class do the inflation experiment on TE page 812. **Class Time** 10 minutes

· **Internet** Have students read the sidebar on the Soviet-Afghanistan War and ask them the questions in the TE. Have them work in groups and do an Internet search for U.S. policy in Afghanistan at the time. Students should make a list of Web sites that had relevant and reliable information. **Class Time** 30 minutes

· **Internet** Ask students to read the feature on the Supreme Court case *Regents of the University of California* v. *Bakke* (1978) on pages 818–819. Then have them visit **classzone.com** to read about Proposition 209. Discuss whether they think the law will have a positive or negative long-term effect. Refer to item 2 on page 819. **Class Time** 20 minutes

### DAY 2 continued

**SECTION 4 pp. 820–825**
**Class Time** 30 minutes
*Options for Pacing and Variety*

· **History on Film** View the video "Poisoned Playground," the story of Lois Gibbs and the Love Canal crisis, and discuss the issues she raises in the film. **Class Time** 30 minutes

· **Peer Competition** Ask students to read page 823 about the accident at Three Mile Island. Hold a class debate, using the TE page activity "Nuclear Energy Pro and Con." **Class Time** 30 minutes

**ASSESSMENT, pp. 826–827**
**Class Time** 30 minutes
*Options for Pacing and Variety:*

· **Peer Teaching** Have students work in small groups to complete item 1 under Critical Thinking. As a class, discuss why they think the impact of each development is negative or positive. **Class Time** 20 minutes

· **Time Saver** Ask students to complete Main Ideas questions 1, 4, 5, and 6 for homework. Review the answers in class. **Class Time** 10 minutes

· **Peer Evaluation** Have students work in pairs to complete all the questions in the Critical Thinking section. Then exchange papers with another pair to evaluate their answers. **Class Time** 15 minutes

---

**TEACHER-TESTED ACTIVITY**

**NIXON ON TRIAL**

**Class Time** Two class periods

**Task** Creating and presenting the framework of a Watergate trial

**Purpose** To consider Nixon's involvement in Watergate

**Gloria Remijio, Del Valle High School, El Paso, Texas**

**Supplies Needed**
· Textbooks
· Internet and library resources

**Activity** Have students work in small groups to research Watergate as if they were preparing to try President Nixon. Tell them to do the following: state the charge(s); select one to three key witnesses (and explain their choices); and outline the prosecution's major points and the defense's responses. Have groups present their work orally to their classmates, who will serve as a jury.

# CHAPTER 24 CORRELATION

 **CORRELATION TO THE TEXAS ESSENTIAL KNOWLEDGE AND SKILLS**

Chapter 24 addresses the following standards of the Texas Essential Knowledge and Skills for U.S. History.

| TEKS | Instruction | Student Question/Activity |
|---|---|---|
| **(6H)** Identify the origins of major domestic and foreign policy issues currently facing the United States. | **PE 820–825** examination of the emergence of the environmental movement that continues in the United States today | **PE 825** Critical Thinking questions about various aspects of the movement |
| **(11B)** Trace the development of the conservation of natural resources. | **PE 822** discussion of the efforts to conserve much of Alaska's land in the wake of a significant oil discovery there | **PE 822** question about environmental actions taken by the Nixon administration |
| **(15C)** Evaluate the effects of political incidents such as Watergate on the views of U.S. citizens concerning the role of the federal government. | **PE 806–807** discussion of how the Watergate scandal increased the public's cynicism toward elected officials | **PE 826** question about the effects of Watergate |
| **(17A)** Analyze the effects of 20th-century landmark Supreme Court decisions. | **PE 818–819** feature on the landmark Supreme Court case *Regents of the University of California* v. *Bakke,* in which the court ruled that racial quotas were unconstitutional | **PE 819** Critical Thinking questions based on the feature |
| **(18B)** Evaluate the contributions of significant political and social leaders. | **PE 812–817** examination of how effective Jimmy Carter was in battling the energy crisis, advancing civil rights, and dealing with foreign affairs | **PE 817** Critical Thinking questions about Carter's policies |
| **(22A)** Explain the effects of petroleum-based products on the development of the United States. | **PE 812–813** discussion of how America's dependence on oil helped lead to an energy crisis during the 1970s | **PE 813** question about Jimmy Carter's efforts to remedy the energy crisis |
| **(24H)** Use appropriate mathematical skills to interpret social studies information such as maps and graphs. | **PE 813** graph depicting the course of unemployment and inflation during the 1970s | **PE 813** Skillbuilder questions that require students to interpret the graph |

# TAKS MINI-LESSONS

1. **Social Studies Skills: Objective 3 (US14.E):** Describe the dynamic relationship between U.S. international trade policies and the U.S. free enterprise system **Activity** Have students summarize the text under the heading "A Changing Economy" on page 814.

2. **Social Studies Skills: Objective 4 (US18.B):** Evaluate various means of achieving equality of political rights, including the 26th amendment **Activity** Have students answer the question about the 26th amendment on TE page 798.

3. **Social Studies Skills: Objective 5 (WG8.B):** Compare ways that humans depend on, adapt to, and modify the physical environment **Activity** Have student complete the Link to Science activity on TE page 821.

4. **English Language Arts Skills: Objective 3 (19.B):** Analyze ideas as represented in various media **Activity** Have students answer the Interpreting Primary Sources question in the Section 4 Assessment on page 825.

5. **English Language Arts Skills: Objective 6 (2.C):** Proofread writing for appropriateness of organization, content, style, and conventions **Activity** Have pairs of students proofread each other's answers to the Section 3 Assessment questions on page 817.

## CHAPTER 24 · AN AGE OF LIMITS

### Time Line Discussion

Explain to students that this time line spans the years 1968 through 1979. Ask the following:

· What events took place involving the Middle East? *(1972: Israeli athletes at Munich Olympics killed by terrorists; 1973: Yom Kippur War; 1978: Camp David Accords; 1979: Ayatollah Khomeni seizes power in Iran)*
· How did Gerald R. Ford become president? *(Nixon resigned)*
· What caused gasoline prices to soar? *(Energy crisis)*
· What event marked a triumph for American science and technology? *(1969: Neil Armstrong walked on the moon)*

Richard Nixon leaves the White House after resigning as President on Friday, August 9, 1974.

**1968** Richard M. Nixon is elected president.

**1969** Astronaut Neil Armstrong becomes the first person to walk on the moon.

EARTH DAY APRIL 22

**1970** America celebrates the first Earth Day.

**1972** Nixon visits China and the Soviet Union.

**1972** Nixon is reelected.

**1973** Energy crisis begins, and gasoline prices soar.

USA
WORLD  **1968   1969   1970   1971   1972   1973**

**1972** China gives the U.S. two pandas.

**1972** Terrorists kill eleven Israeli athletes at the XX Olympiad in Munich.

**1973** War breaks out in the Middle East when seven Arab states attack Israel on Yom Kippur.

### THEMES IN CHAPTER 24

**ECONOMIC OPPORTUNITY**

In the 1970s, the United States was faced with its worst economic crisis in years. Unemployment, inflation, and economic stagnation frustrated the administrations of Richard Nixon, Gerald Ford, and Jimmy Carter.

**See Teacher's Edition notes, pp. 799.**

**SCIENCE AND TECHNOLOGY**

Advances in computer technology were a mixed blessing. Certain jobs were becoming obsolete as new technologies were introduced. Scientific discoveries were offering new ways to address the nation's problem of dwindling natural resources.

**See Teacher's Edition notes, pp. 814, 821.**

**AMERICA IN WORLD AFFAIRS**

Human rights as an underpinning of foreign policy came to the fore in Jimmy Carter's administration. The issue of human rights as a part of foreign policy was controversial. Some of

America's allies in the cold War were notorious violators of human rights within their own countries, yet their support was needed to battle Communism.

**See Teacher's Edition Notes, p. 815.**

# INTERACT
## WITH HISTORY

The date is August 9, 1974. You are serving your country as an honor guard at the White House. As a member of the military, you've always felt patriotic pride in your government. Now the highest officer of that government, President Richard M. Nixon, is stepping down in disgrace. The trust you once placed in your leaders has been broken.

## *In what ways can a president misuse power?*

### Examine the Issues

- What are some powers granted to the president?
- What systems exist to protect against abuse of power?
- How can a president lose or restore the nation's trust?

**RESEARCH LINKS** CLASSZONE.COM

Visit the Chapter 24 links for more information related to An Age of Limits.

# INTERACT
## WITH HISTORY

### Objectives

- To analyze the political and social impact of the Watergate scandal
- To explain the role of the Constitution in the Watergate crisis

### Examine the Issues

1. Discuss with students the powers granted to the president by Article II of the Constitution.
2. Analyze the governmental system of checks and balances and the role of the media in influencing public opinion.
3. Discuss with students the respect the president commands with the American public, and how that respect is won or lost.

**1974** Vice President Gerald R. Ford becomes president after the Watergate scandal forces President Nixon to resign.

**1976** President Jimmy Carter is elected president.

**1976** Americans celebrate the nation's bicentennial.

**1977** The movie *Saturday Night Fever* inspires disco fashion.

**1979** A nuclear power accident occurs at Three Mile Island in Pennsylvania.

| 1974 | 1975 | 1976 | 1977 | 1978 | 1979 |

**1978** Egyptian and Israeli leaders meet and sign the Camp David Accords with President Carter.

**1979** Ayatollah Khomeini seizes power in Iran.

*An Age of Limits* **793**

## RECOMMENDED RESOURCES

### BOOKS FOR THE TEACHER

Bernstein, Carl and Bob Woodward. *The Final Days.* New York: Simon, 1994. A detailed look at the final days of the Nixon presidency.

Carter, Jimmy. *Keeping Faith: Memoirs of a President.* New York: Bantam, 1982.

Villaseñor, Victor. *Rain of Gold.* New York: Dell, 1992. A Mexican family's long history—similar to *Roots*.

### BOOKS FOR THE STUDENT

Lawson, Don. *America Held Hostage: The Iran Hostage Crisis and the Iran-Contra Affair.* New York: Watts, 1991.

Lazzari, Marie. *Environmental Viewpoints.* Detroit: Gale Research, Inc., Vol. 1, 1992, Vol. 2, 1993.

### VIDEOS

*All the President's Men.* Dir. Alan J. Pakula. Warner Home Video, 1976. Portrayal of Watergate investigation from Woodward-Bernstein book.

*America Held Hostage.* MPI Home Video, 1989. 800-323-0442. ABC Reports of Iran hostage crisis.

*Apollo 13.* Dir. Ron Howard. MCA Universal Home Video., 1995, PG. Story of the ill-fated moon mission.

### SOFTWARE

*Environment.* Diskette. Tom Snyder Productions, Inc., 800-342-0236.

### INTEGRATED TECHNOLOGY

for teacher support visit...

 classzone.com

SECTION
1

# The Nixon Administration

| MAIN IDEA | WHY IT MATTERS NOW | Terms & Names |
|---|---|---|
| President Richard M. Nixon tried to steer the country in a conservative direction and away from federal control. | American leaders of the early 1970s laid the foundations for the broad conservative base today. | •Richard M. Nixon  •New Federalism  •revenue sharing  •Family Assistance Plan  •Southern strategy  •stagflation |
| | | •OPEC (Organization of Petroleum Exporting Countries)  •realpolitik  •détente  •SALT I Treaty |

 U.S. History 7A, 8A, 14D, 14E, 15D, 16A, 16B, 17B, 18A, 18B, 19B, 23B, 24A, 24B, 24C, 24D, 24F, 25A, 25B, 25C, 25D, 26B

### One American's Story

In November of 1968, **Richard M. Nixon** had just been elected president of the United States. He chose Henry Kissinger to be his special adviser on foreign affairs. During Nixon's second term in 1972, as the United States struggled to achieve an acceptable peace in Vietnam, Kissinger reflected on his relationship with Nixon.

**A PERSONAL VOICE** HENRY KISSINGER

"I . . . am not at all so sure I could have done what I've done with him with another president. . . . I don't know many leaders who would entrust to their aide the task of negotiating with the North Vietnamese, informing only a tiny group of people of the initiative."

—quoted in *The New Republic*, December 16, 1972

President Nixon (right) confers with Henry Kissinger.

Nixon and Kissinger ended America's involvement in Vietnam, but as the war wound down, the nation seemed to enter an era of limits. The economic prosperity that had followed World War II was ending. President Nixon wanted to limit the federal government to reduce its power and to reverse some of Johnson's liberal policies. At the same time, he would seek to restore America's prestige and influence on the world stage—prestige that had been hit hard by the Vietnam experience.

## 1 Nixon's New Conservatism

President Richard M. Nixon entered office in 1969 determined to turn America in a more conservative direction. Toward that end, he tried to instill a sense of order into a nation still divided over the continuing Vietnam War.

## Analyzing *Political Cartoons*

**"DOMESTIC LIFE"**
Pulitzer-Prize winning cartoonist Paul Szep frequently used Nixon as the subject of his cartoons. Although President Nixon focused his domestic policy on dismantling a number of Great Society social programs, his chief interest was foreign policy.

**SKILLBUILDER**
Analyzing Political Cartoons
1. What does the cartoonist suggest about Nixon by showing him leaving with his bags packed?
2. Whom do the children represent in this cartoon?

📁 SEE SKILLBUILDER HANDBOOK, PAGE R24.

### Analyzing *Political Cartoons*

**SKILLBUILDER ANSWERS**

1. The cartoon suggests Nixon is abandoning his home and children—the nation.

2. The children represent American citizens who were dependent on domestic programs; Nixon is leaving them to fend for themselves.

---

**MAIN IDEA**

**Summarizing**
Ⓐ What was the goal of Nixon's New Federalism?

*A. Answer* To shrink the size and responsibility of the federal government by distributing some of its power to state and local governments.

**NEW FEDERALISM** One of the main items on President Nixon's agenda was to decrease the size and influence of the federal government. Nixon believed that Lyndon Johnson's Great Society programs, by promoting greater federal involvement with social problems, had given the federal government too much responsibility. Nixon's plan, known as **New Federalism,** was to distribute a portion of federal power to state and local governments. Ⓐ

To implement this program, Nixon proposed a plan to give more financial freedom to local governments. Normally, the federal government told state and local governments how to spend their federal money. Under **revenue sharing,** state and local governments could spend their federal dollars however they saw fit within certain limitations. In 1972, the revenue-sharing bill, known as the State and Local Fiscal Assistance Act, became law.

**WELFARE REFORM** Nixon was not as successful, however, in his attempt to overhaul welfare, which he believed had grown cumbersome and inefficient. In 1969, the president advocated the so-called **Family Assistance Plan (FAP).** Under the FAP, every family of four with no outside income would receive a basic federal payment of $1,600 a year, with a provision to earn up to $4,000 a year in supplemental income. Unemployed participants, excluding mothers of preschool children, would have to take job training and accept any reasonable work offered them.

Nixon presented the plan in conservative terms—as a program that would reduce the supervisory role of the federal government and make welfare recipients responsible for their own lives. The House approved the plan in 1970. However, when the bill reached the Senate, lawmakers from both parties attacked it. Liberal legislators considered the minimum payments too low and the work requirement too stiff, while conservatives objected to the notion of guaranteed income. The bill went down in defeat.

**NEW FEDERALISM WEARS TWO FACES** In the end, Nixon's New Federalism enhanced several key federal programs as it dismantled others. To win backing for his New Federalism program from a Democrat-controlled Congress, Nixon supported a number of congressional measures to increase federal spending for some social programs. Without fanfare, the Nixon administration increased Social

### More About . . .

**Nixon's Legislative Accomplishments**
Nixon was dedicated to shrinking the size of the federal government. At the same time, however, he increased the scope of federal responsibility. During his administration, Nixon proposed legislation that created such agencies as the Environmental Protection Agency (EPA) and the Occupation Safety and Health Administration (OSHA). He also substantially increased funding for the Equal Employment Opportunity Commission (EEOC).

*An Age of Limits* **795**

---

**DIFFERENTIATING INSTRUCTION** | **LESS PROFICIENT READERS**

### Summarizing

As students read pages 794-796, have them write a sentence to summarize components of Nixon's "New Conservatism." Use the following list as a guide:

· Nixon's New Federalism called for. . . .

· Under the revenue sharing plan, state and local governments could. . . .

· Under the Family Assistance Plan, poor families would. . . .

· Nixon's New Federalism enhanced. . . .

· An example of New Federalism's two faces is. . . .

· Nixon's impoundment of funds resulted in. . . .

## More About . . .

**Neil Armstrong**
Neil Armstrong was born in 1930 in Wapakoneta, Ohio. By the age of 16, he had earned his pilot's license. In 1947, he became a naval air cadet. He studied aeronautical engineering at Purdue University. By 1950, Armstrong was a decorated veteran of the Korean War. In 1955, Armstrong went to work for the organization that became the National Aeronautics and Space Administration.

## Instruct: Objective ❷

**Nixon's Southern Strategy**
TAKS SS11 4(US17.A)
· How did Nixon appeal to Southern Democrats?
· What actions did Nixon take to slow desegregation?
· Why did Nixon attempt to stop school busing?
· What was Nixon's approach to choosing Supreme Court Justices?

 **In-Depth Resources: Unit 7**
· Guided Reading, p. 1

---

## HISTORICAL SPOTLIGHT

### AMERICANS WALK ON THE MOON

Not all was political war during the Nixon administration. On July 20, 1969, one of America's long-held dreams became a reality.

Nearly ten years after John F. Kennedy challenged America to put a person on the moon, astronaut Neil Armstrong climbed down the ladder of his lunar module and stepped onto the surface of the moon. "That's one small step for man," Armstrong said, "one giant leap for mankind." Americans swelled with pride and accomplishment as they watched the historic moon landing on their televisions. Speaking to the astronauts from the White House, President Nixon said, "For every American, this has to be the proudest day of our lives."

▲
**Neil Armstrong's photograph of Buzz Aldrin on the moon**

Security, Medicare, and Medicaid payments and made food stamps more accessible.

However, the president also worked to dismantle some of the nation's social programs. Throughout his term, Nixon tried unsuccessfully to eliminate the Job Corps program that provided job training for the unemployed and in 1970 he vetoed a bill to provide additional funding for Housing and Urban Development. Confronted by laws that he opposed, Nixon also turned to a little-used presidential practice called impoundment. Nixon impounded, or withheld, necessary funds for programs, thus holding up their implementation. By 1973, it was believed that Nixon had impounded almost $15 billion, affecting more than 100 federal programs, including those for health, housing, and education.

The federal courts eventually ordered the release of the impounded funds. They ruled that presidential impoundment was unconstitutional and that only Congress had the authority to decide how federal funds should be spent. Nixon did use his presidential authority to abolish the Office of Economic Opportunity, a cornerstone of Johnson's antipoverty program. **B**

**LAW AND ORDER POLITICS** As President Nixon fought with both houses of Congress, he also battled the more liberal elements of society, including the antiwar movement. Nixon had been elected in 1968 on a dual promise to end the war in Vietnam and mend the divisiveness within America that the war had created. Throughout his first term, Nixon aggressively moved to fulfill both pledges. The president de-escalated America's involvement in Vietnam and oversaw peace negotiations with North Vietnam. At the same time, he began the "law and order" policies that he had promised his "silent majority"—those middle-class Americans who wanted order restored to a country beset by urban riots and antiwar demonstrations.

To accomplish this, Nixon used the full resources of his office—sometimes illegally. The FBI illegally wiretapped many left-wing individuals and the Democratic Party offices at the Watergate office building in Washington, D.C. The CIA also investigated and compiled documents on thousands of American dissidents—people who objected to the government's policies. The administration even used the Internal Revenue Service to audit the tax returns of antiwar and civil rights activists. Nixon began building a personal "enemies list" of prominent Americans whom the administration would harass.

Nixon also enlisted the help of his combative vice president, Spiro T. Agnew, to denounce the opposition. The vice president confronted the antiwar protesters and then turned his scorn on those who controlled the media, whom he viewed as liberal cheerleaders for the antiwar movement. Known for his colorful quotes, Agnew lashed out at the media and liberals as "an effete [weak] corps of impudent snobs" and "nattering nabobs of negativism."

## ❷ Nixon's Southern Strategy

Even as President Nixon worked to steer the country along a more conservative course, he had his eyes on the 1972 presidential election. Nixon had won a slim majority in 1968—less than 1 percent of the popular vote. As President, he began

**MAIN IDEA**

**Analyzing Issues**
**B** In what ways did Nixon both strengthen and weaken federal programs?

**B. Answer**
He increased several federal programs, including Social Security, Medicare, and Medicaid, while he dismantled other programs, most notably the Office of Economic Opportunity.

---

 **classzone.com**

**Walk on the Moon**

**Class Time** 45 minutes

**Task** Creating a multimedia presentation on people's memories of the first moon landing

**Purpose** To analyze the historical impact of the mission to the moon

**Directions** Have students put together a collection of people's memories of the first lunar landing. Encourage them to interview family members and neighbors and to use the Internet and library resources. Have students create a multimedia presentation for the class based on their findings.

 Integrated Assessment
· Rubrics 3, 6

working to forge a new conservative coalition to build on his support. In one approach, known as the **Southern strategy,** Nixon tried to attract Southern conservative Democrats by appealing to their unhappiness with federal desegregation policies and a liberal Supreme Court. He also promised to name a Southerner to the Supreme Court.

**A NEW SOUTH** Since Reconstruction, the South had been a Democratic stronghold. But by 1968 many white Southern Democrats had grown disillusioned with their party. In their eyes, the party—champion of the Great Society and civil rights—had grown too liberal. This conservative backlash first surfaced in the 1968 election, when thousands of Southern Democrats helped former Alabama governor George Wallace, a conservative segregationist running as an independent, carry five Southern states and capture 13 percent of the popular vote.

Nixon wanted these voters. By winning over the Wallace voters and other discontented Democrats, the president and his fellow Republicans hoped not only to keep the White House but also to recapture a majority in Congress. **C**

**NIXON SLOWS INTEGRATION** To attract white voters in the South, President Nixon decided on a policy of slowing the country's desegregation efforts. In September of 1969, less than a year after being elected president, Nixon made clear his views on civil rights. "There are those who want instant integration and those who want segregation forever. I believe we need to have a middle course between those two extremes," he said.

Throughout his first term, President Nixon worked to reverse several civil rights policies. In 1969, he ordered the Department of Health, Education, and Welfare (HEW) to delay desegregation plans for school districts in South Carolina and Mississippi. Nixon's actions violated the Supreme Court's second *Brown* v. *Board of Education* ruling—which called for the desegregation of schools "with all deliberate speed." In response to an NAACP suit, the high court ordered Nixon to abide by the second Brown ruling. The president did so reluctantly, and by 1972, nearly 90 percent of children in the South attended desegregated schools—up from about 20 percent in 1969.

In a further attempt to chip away at civil rights advances, Nixon opposed the extension of the Voting Rights Act of 1965. The act had added nearly one million African Americans to the voting rolls. Despite the president's opposition, Congress voted to extend the act. **D**

**CONTROVERSY OVER BUSING** President Nixon then attempted to stop yet another civil rights initiative—the integration of schools through busing. In 1971, the Supreme Court ruled in *Swann* v. *Charlotte-Mecklenburg Board of Education* that school districts may bus students to other schools to end the pattern of all-black or all-white educational institutions. White students and parents in cities such as Boston and Detroit angrily protested busing. One South Boston mother spoke for other white Northerners, many of whom still struggled with the integration process.

### A PERSONAL VOICE
"I'm not against any individual child. I am not a racist, no matter what those high-and-mighty suburban liberals with their picket signs say. I just won't have my children bused to some . . . slum school, and I don't want children from God knows where coming over here."
—A South Boston mother quoted in *The School Busing Controversy, 1970–75*

A demonstrator in Boston protests court-ordered school busing during the early 1970s. ▼

---

**MAIN IDEA**

**Forming Generalizations**
**C** Why had many Democratic voters in the South become potential Republican supporters by 1968?

*C. Answer* They were unhappy with the Democratic leadership's desegregation policies, as well as the liberal leanings of the Supreme Court.

**MAIN IDEA**

**Analyzing Motives**
**D** Why did President Nixon oppose the extension of the Voting Rights Act?

*D. Answer* It was part of his "Southern strategy" to attract the support of white Southerners.

---

---

**DIFFERENTIATING INSTRUCTION** | **STUDENTS ACQUIRING ENGLISH/ESL**

## Understanding Idioms

Pair non-native English speaking students with native speakers. Have them review the phrases below. Suggest that students use a dictionary to look up the meaning of each word. Then have them interpret the meaning of the words in the specific context on the text narrative.

· Democratic stronghold
· conservative backlash
· discontented Democrats
· desegregation efforts
· instant integration
· chip away at Civil Rights advances

## HISTORICAL SPOTLIGHT

### The 26th Amendment

The impetus for the 26th Amendment was born out of Vietnam War protests. Students pointed out that they could be drafted and sent to war but that they could not vote. Despite political objections, Republicans reluctantly supported the amendment, which passed easily. Ask students if they think they are mature enough to vote and to serve in the armed forces at 18. (Some students will agree. Others will say that perhaps students are not mature enough until 21.)

 Mini-Lesson 3: SS11 4(US18.B)

## More About . . .

### Warren Burger

Nixon's appointment of Burger as Chief Justice is fraught with historical irony. It was Burger who wrote the Supreme Court opinion denying Nixon's claim to executive privilege and ordering him to turn over the Watergate tapes. The decision had a profound effect on the President. "I thought that the United States had lost," Nixon wrote. "I felt that the presidency itself was a casualty of this ruling."

### Instruction: Objective ❸

**Confronting a Stagnant Economy**
TAKS SS11 5(US24.B)
· What is stagflation?
· What economic factors caused stagflation?
· What steps did Nixon take to battle stagflation?

 In-Depth Resources: Unit 7
· Guided Reading, p. 1

**HISTORICAL SPOTLIGHT**

**THE TWENTY-SIXTH AMENDMENT**

During President Nixon's first term, the Twenty-sixth Amendment was ratified in 1971, extending voting rights to Americans 18 years or older. The amendment was one example of efforts in the 1960s and 1970s to expand opportunities to participate in government.

At the time, liberals supported the amendment because they believed that young people were more likely to be liberal. Conservatives opposed it because they didn't want to extend the vote to more liberals.

Opponents also argued that the amendment would be too expensive for states to administer and that 18-year-olds were not mature enough for the responsibility. Many Americans, however, considered it unfair to be asked to fight and die for their country in Vietnam without being allowed to vote.

Nixon also opposed integration through busing and went on national television to urge Congress to halt the practice. While busing continued in some cities, Nixon had made his position clear to the country—and to the South.

**A BATTLE OVER THE SUPREME COURT** During the 1968 campaign, Nixon had criticized the Warren Court for being too liberal. Once in the White House, Nixon suddenly found himself with an opportunity to change the direction of the court. During Nixon's first term, four justices, including chief justice Earl Warren, left the bench through retirement. President Nixon quickly moved to put a more conservative face on the Court. In 1969, the Senate approved Nixon's chief justice appointee, U.S. Court of Appeals judge Warren Burger.

Eventually, Nixon placed on the bench three more justices, who tilted the Court in a more conservative direction. However, the newly shaped Court did not always take the conservative route—for example, it handed down the 1971 ruling in favor of racially integrating schools through busing. **E**

## ❸ Confronting a Stagnant Economy

One of the more pressing issues facing Richard Nixon was a troubled economy. Between 1967 and 1973, the United States faced high inflation and high unemployment—a situation economists called **stagflation.**

**THE CAUSES OF STAGFLATION** The economic problems of the late 1960s and early 1970s had several causes. Chief among them were high inflation—a result of Lyndon Johnson's policy to fund the war and social programs through deficit spending. Also, increased competition in international trade, and a flood of new workers, including women and baby boomers, led to stagflation. Another cause of the nation's economic woes was its heavy dependency on foreign oil. During the 1960s, America received much of its petroleum from the oil-producing countries of the

**MAIN IDEA**

**Summarizing**
**E** What was Nixon's Southern strategy and how did he implement it?

*E. Answer* It involved winning over disgruntled Southern Democrats by appealing to their unhappiness with integration and a liberal Supreme Court. To win these voters, Nixon slowed integration policies and attempted to appoint Supreme Court justices who were more conservative. **Dependant on foreign oil, Americans in 1979 wait in line for gas during the oil embargo.** ▼

## Confirming a Supreme Court Justice

**Class Time** 45 minutes

**Task** Reporting on the process for confirming a Supreme Court justice

**Purpose** To analyze the process of appointing Supreme Court justices

**Directions** Have students work in small groups to research the process of nomination and confirmation of Supreme Court justices. Ask students to investigate the role of the president, the Senate Judiciary Committee, and the full Senate.

Have students find recent articles regarding the current Supreme Court. Then have students prepare a brief summary and report their findings to the class.

 Integrated Assessment
· Rubric 5

**Vocabulary**
**cartel:** a bloc of independent business organizations that controls a service or business

**Background**
See *embargo* on page R40 in the Economics Handbook.

Middle East. Many of these countries belonged to a cartel called **OPEC (Organization of Petroleum Exporting Countries).** During the 1960s, OPEC gradually raised oil prices. Then in 1973, the Yom Kippur War broke out, with Israel against Egypt and Syria. When the United States sent massive military aid to Israel, its longtime ally, the Arab OPEC nations responded by cutting off all oil sales to the United States. When OPEC resumed selling its oil to the United States in 1974, the price had quadrupled. This sharp rise in oil prices only worsened the problem of inflation.

**NIXON BATTLES STAGFLATION** President Nixon took several steps to combat stagflation, but none met with much success. To reverse deficit spending, Nixon attempted to raise taxes and cut the budget. Congress, however, refused to go along with this plan. In another effort to slow inflation, Nixon tried to reduce the amount of money in circulation by urging that interest rates be raised. This measure did little except drive the country into a mild recession, or an overall slowdown of the economy.

In August 1971, the president turned to price and wage controls to stop inflation. He froze workers' wages as well as businesses' prices and fees for 90 days. Inflation eased for a short time, but the recession continued.

**MAIN IDEA**

**Analyzing Causes**
**F** What factors brought on the country's economic problems in the late 1960s and early 1970s?

*F. Answer*
Inflation prompted by Johnson's deficit spending, increased competition in international trade, too many new workers, and the OPEC oil embargo.

## Nixon's Foreign Policy Triumphs ❹

Richard Nixon admittedly preferred world affairs to domestic policy. "I've always thought this country could run itself domestically without a president," he said in 1968. Throughout his presidency, Nixon's top priority was gaining an honorable peace in Vietnam. At the same time, he also made significant advances in America's relationships with China and the Soviet Union.

**KISSINGER AND REALPOLITIK** The architect of Nixon's foreign policy was his adviser for national security affairs, Henry Kissinger. Kissinger, who would later become Nixon's secretary of state, promoted a philosophy known as **realpolitik,** from a German term meaning "political realism." According to realpolitik, foreign policy should be based solely on consideration of power, not ideals or moral principles. Kissinger believed in evaluating a nation's power, not its philosophy or beliefs. If a country was weak, Kissinger argued, it was often more practical to ignore that country, even if it was Communist.

*G. Answer*
Foreign policy should be based solely on considerations of power, not on ideals or moral principles.

Realpolitik marked a departure from the former confrontational policy of containment, which refused to recognize the major Communist countries. On the other hand, Kissinger's philosophy called for the United States to fully confront the powerful nations of the globe. In the world of realpolitik, however, confrontation largely meant negotiation as well as military engagement.

**MAIN IDEA**

**Summarizing**
**G** What was the philosophy of realpolitik?

Nixon shared Kissinger's belief in realpolitik, and together the two men adopted a more flexible approach in dealing with Communist nations. They called their policy **détente**—a policy aimed at easing Cold War tensions. One of the most startling applications of détente came in early 1972 when President Nixon—who had risen in politics as a strong anti-Communist—visited Communist China.

**THE YOM KIPPUR WAR**
On October 6, 1973, Syria and Egypt invaded Israel on Yom Kippur, the most sacred Jewish holiday. The war—the climax of years of intense border disputes—was short but brutal. Even though fighting lasted only three weeks, as many as 7,700 Egyptians, 7,700 Syrians, and 4,500 Israelis were killed or wounded.

Although the United States supplied massive amounts of military aid to Israel, U.S. officials also worked to broker a cease-fire between the warring nations. In what became known as "shuttle diplomacy," Secretary of State Henry Kissinger traveled back and forth between Middle Eastern countries in an attempt to forge a peace agreement. Kissinger's diplomatic efforts finally paid off. Israel signed an official peace accord with Egypt in January 1974. Four months later in May, Israel signed a cease-fire with Syria.

*An Age of Limits* **799**

---

**Tracing Themes**
**ECONOMIC OPPORTUNITY**

The economic downswing that gripped the nation during the Nixon administration would last for roughly a decade and frustrate other administrations as well. Throughout the 1970s, as inflation and unemployment rose and dipped, millions of American grew anxious about their economic opportunities. Playing a key role in the decade-long downturn was the rising cost of oil.

**WORLD STAGE**

**The Yom Kippur War**
**Evaluating** Ask students why the United States worked to bring about a cease-fire between the warring nations in the Yom Kippur War, even though it supplied military aid to its ally Israel. (Although the United States wanted to support its ally Israel, it also did no want to further alienate the oil-producing nations of the region.)

**Instruct: Objective ❹**

**Nixon's Foreign Policy Triumphs**
TAKS SS11 5(US24.B)
· How did Nixon's philosophy of realpolitik differ from the idea of containment?
· What was the policy of détente?
· What was the significance of Nixon's trip to China?
· What were the provisions and significance of the SALT I Treaty?

📃 In-Depth Resources: Unit 7
· Guided Reading, p. 1
· American Lives: Henry Kissinger, p. 20

---

**DIFFERENTIATING INSTRUCTION** | **GIFTED AND TALENTED STUDENTS**

**Evaluating an Autobiographic Source**

Not long after leaving government, Henry Kissinger wrote two books about his White House experiences: *White House Years* (1979) and *Years of Upheaval* (1982). Ask students to read selections in these books that relate to the decision to improve relations with China and the Soviet Union. Then have them write a brief report on what special insights Kissinger's account provides. In addition, have students indicate whether they would rely on such autobiographies as their main source of historical information? Why or why not?

◀ President Nixon tours the Great Wall as part of his visit to China in 1972.

### More About . . .

**Nixon in China**

The first-ever meeting between Nixon and Chinese leader Mao Zedong was marked by its light-heartedness. Mao joked that in his mind he had voted for Nixon. "I like rightists," the Chairman quipped. "I am comparatively happy when these people on the right come into power." Less friendly to Nixon was Mao's wife. "She obviously did not approve of the visit," Nixon wrote. "She said to me sharply, 'Why did you not come to China before now?'"

### KEY PLAYER

**RICHARD M. NIXON**
**1913-1994**

Nixon was remarkably resilient, coming back from defeats. Ask students what personality traits of Richard Nixon are revealed in the profile. *(hard-working, determined, intelligent, driven)*

## KEY PLAYER

**RICHARD M. NIXON**
**1913–1994**

The hurdles that Richard Nixon overcame to win the presidency in 1968 included his loss in the 1960 presidential race and a 1962 defeat in the race for governor of California.

Nixon faced many obstacles from the start. As a boy, he rose every day at 4 A.M. to help in his father's grocery store. Nixon also worked as a janitor, a bean picker, and a barker at an amusement park.

The Nixon family suffered great tragedy when one of Nixon's brothers died from meningitis and another from tuberculosis.

None of these traumatic experiences, however, dulled the future president's ambition. Nixon finished third in his law class at Duke University, and after serving in World War II, he launched his political career.

After winning a seat in Congress in 1946, Nixon announced, "I had to win. That's the thing you don't understand. The important thing is to win."

**NIXON VISITS CHINA** Since the takeover of mainland China by the Communists in 1949, the United States had not formally recognized the Chinese Communist government. In late 1971, Nixon reversed that policy by announcing to the nation that he would visit China "to seek the normalization of relations between the two countries."

By going to China, Nixon was trying, in part, to take advantage of the decade-long rift between China and the Soviet Union. China had long criticized the Soviet Union as being too "soft" in its policies against the West. The two Communist superpowers officially broke ties in 1960. Nixon had thought about exploiting the fractured relationship for several years. "We want to have the Chinese with us when we sit down and negotiate with the Russians," he told a reporter in 1968. Upon his arrival at the Beijing Airport in February, 1972, Nixon recalls his meeting with Chinese premier Zhou En-lai.

**A PERSONAL VOICE** RICHARD M. NIXON

" I knew that Zhou had been deeply insulted by Foster Dulles's refusal to shake hands with him at the Geneva Conference in 1954. When I reached the bottom step, therefore, I made a point of extending my hand as I walked toward him. When our hands met, one era ended and another began. "

—*The Memoirs of Richard Nixon*

*H. Answer*
Nixon opened friendly diplomatic and economic relations with China.

Besides its enormous symbolic value, Nixon's visit also was a huge success with the American public. Observers noted that it opened up diplomatic and economic relations with the Chinese and resulted in important agreements between China and the United States. The two nations agreed that neither would try to dominate the Pacific and that both would cooperate in settling disputes peacefully. They also agreed to participate in scientific and cultural exchanges as well as to eventually reunite Taiwan with the mainland.

**NIXON TRAVELS TO MOSCOW** In May 1972, three months after visiting Beijing, President Nixon headed to Moscow—the first U.S. president ever to visit the

**MAIN IDEA**

**Analyzing Effects**
**H** How did Nixon's trip change the United States relationship with China?

---

**ACTIVITY**     **LINK TO GOVERNMENT**                       classzone.com

## Mao Zedong Rule

**Class Time** 45 minutes

**Task** Preparing a historical analysis for an oral presentation

**Purpose** To analyze Mao Zedong's rule of China

**Directions** Have students work in groups. Suggest that they use library and Internet resources to research Mao's rule of China after the Communists came to power. Then ask them to consider both negative and positive aspects. Ask students to develop oral presentations based on their research.

📄 Integrated Assessment
· Rubrics 1, 3

◄ A 1973 military parade in Moscow displays the Soviet Union's arsenal, components of which were frozen at 1972 levels as a result of the Salt I Treaty.

Soviet Union. Like his visit to China, Nixon's trip to the Soviet Union received wide acclaim. After a series of meetings called the Strategic Arms Limitation Talks (SALT), Nixon and Brezhnev signed the **SALT I Treaty.** This five-year agreement limited the number of intercontinental ballistic missiles (ICBMs) and submarine-launched missiles to 1972 levels.

The foreign policy triumphs with China and the Soviet Union and the administration's announcement that peace "is at hand" in Vietnam helped reelect Nixon as president in 1972.

But peace in Vietnam proved elusive. The Nixon administration grappled with the war for nearly six more months before withdrawing troops and ending America's involvement in Vietnam. By that time, another issue was about to dominate the Nixon administration—one that would eventually lead to the downfall of the president.

### More About . . .

### SALT I

The Strategic Arms Limitation Talks were scheduled to open in Helsinki in November 1969. Gerard Smith, director of the Arms Control and Disarmament Agency (ACDA), was appointed to lead the U.S delegation. He represented the United States in the first series of SALT I negotiations. The talks were private to ensure an atmosphere, in which both countries could freely express their views on sensitive issues. In 1972, President Nixon traveled to the Soviet Union where he and Brezhnev signed the SALT I Treaty.

## Assess & Reteach

### SECTION 1 ASSESSMENT

Have students work together to answer the Section Assessment questions. Recreate the chart from question 2 and complete it as a class.

📖 Formal Assessment
· Section Quiz, p. 438

### SELF-ASSESSMENT

Have students grade Nixon on his overall performance as president. Ask them to share their opinions with the class and offer examples to support their evaluations.

### RETEACH

Use the Section 1 Guided Worksheet to review main ideas.

📖 In-Depth Resources: Unit 7
· Reteaching Activity, p. 7

---

## ASSESSMENT

**1. TERMS & NAMES** For each term or name, write a sentence explaining its significance.

- Richard M. Nixon
- New Federalism
- revenue sharing
- Family Assistance Plan
- Southern strategy
- stagflation
- OPEC
- realpolitik
- détente
- SALT I Treaty

### MAIN IDEA

**2. TAKING NOTES**
In a two-column chart similar to the one shown, list the policies of Richard Nixon that promoted change and those that slowed it down.

| Promoted Change | Slowed Change |
|-----------------|---------------|
| Policies: | Policies: |
| | |

In what ways do you think Nixon was most conservative? In which way was he least conservative? Explain.

### CRITICAL THINKING

**3. ANALYZING EFFECTS**
What were the effects of the Arab OPEC oil embargo on the United States?

**4. DRAWING CONCLUSIONS**
Why was the timing of Nixon's foreign policy achievements particularly important? Relate his achievements to other events.

**5. EVALUATING DECISIONS**
In your opinion, did Nixon's policy of détente help solve the country's major foreign policy problems? Support your answer with evidence from the text. **Think About:**

- the definition and origin of détente
- the effect of détente on U.S. dealings with Communist countries
- the effect of détente on the American public

*An Age of Limits* **801**

---

### 1. TERMS & NAMES
Richard M. Nixon, p. 794
New Federalism, p. 795
revenue sharing, p. 795
Family Assistance Plan, p. 795
Southern strategy, p. 797
stagflation, p. 798
OPEC, p. 799
realpolitik, p. 799
détente, p. 799
SALT I Treaty, p. 801

### 2. TAKING NOTES
Promoted Change: revenue sharing program; Family Assistance Plan; China visit; Soviet Union visit; SALT I Treaty; Slowed Change: Impounded federal funds; abolished Office of Economic Opportunity; opposed school busing; appointed conservatives to the Supreme Court.

### 3. ANALYZING EFFECTS
increased fuel prices, fuel conservation, inflation, factories and businesses closed

### 4. DRAWING CONCLUSIONS
Nixon's achievements helped him win reelection in 1972.

### 5. EVALUATING DECISIONS
Yes: improved relations between the Soviet Union and China; enhanced Nixon's world image; opened up diplomatic and economic relations with the Chinese. No: did nothing to help the situation in Vietnam.

*An Age of Limits* **801**

# Watergate: Nixon's Downfall

| MAIN IDEA | WHY IT MATTERS NOW | Terms & Names |
|---|---|---|
| President Richard Nixon's involvement in the Watergate scandal forced him to resign from office. | The Watergate scandal raised questions of public trust that still affect how the public and media skeptically view politicians. | · **impeachment** · **Watergate** · H. R. Haldeman · John Ehrlichman · John Mitchell · Committee to Reelect the President · John Sirica · Saturday Night Massacre |

**U.S. History**
1B, 6H, 15C, 16A, 17A, 19A, 24A, 24B, 24C, 24D, 24F, 25A, 25B, 25C, 25D

 **One American's Story**

On July 25, 1974, Representative Barbara Jordan of Texas, a member of the House Judiciary Committee, along with the other committee members, considered whether to recommend that President Nixon be impeached for "high crimes and misdemeanors." Addressing the room, Jordan cited the Constitution in urging her fellow committee members to investigate whether impeachment was appropriate.

**A PERSONAL VOICE** BARBARA JORDAN

" 'We the people'—it is a very eloquent beginning. But when the Constitution of the United States was completed . . . I was not included in that 'We the people'. . . . But through the process of amendment, interpretation, and court decision, I have finally been included in 'We the people'. . . . Today . . . [my] faith in the Constitution is whole. It is complete. It is total. I am not going to sit here and be an idle spectator in the diminution, the subversion, the destruction of the Constitution. . . . Has the President committed offenses . . . which the Constitution will not tolerate? "

—quoted in *Notable Black American Women*

▲ U.S. Representative Barbara Jordan, 1974.

The committee eventually voted to recommend the **impeachment** of Richard Nixon for his role in the Watergate scandal. However, before Congress could take further action against him, the president resigned. Nixon's resignation, the first by a U.S. president, was the climax of a scandal that led to the imprisonment of 25 government officials and caused the most serious constitutional crisis in the United States since the impeachment of Andrew Johnson in 1868.

## **1** President Nixon and His White House

The **Watergate** scandal centered on the Nixon administration's attempt to cover up a burglary of the Democratic National Committee (DNC) headquarters at the Watergate office and apartment complex in Washington, D.C. However, the

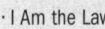

Watergate story began long before the actual burglary. Many historians believe that Watergate truly began with the personalities of Richard Nixon and those of his advisers, as well as with the changing role of the presidency.

**AN IMPERIAL PRESIDENCY** When Richard Nixon took office, the executive branch—as a result of the Great Depression, World War II, and the Cold War—had become the most powerful branch of government. In his book *The Imperial Presidency*, the historian Arthur Schlesinger, Jr., argued that by the time Richard Nixon became president, the executive branch had taken on an air of imperial, or supreme, authority.

President Nixon settled into this imperial role with ease. Nixon believed, as he told a newspaper reporter in 1980, that "a president must not be one of the crowd. . . . People . . . don't want him to be down there saying, 'Look, I'm the same as you.'" Nixon expanded the power of the presidency and gave little thought to constitutional checks, as when he impounded funds for federal programs he opposed, or when he ordered troops to Cambodia without congressional approval.  **A**

**THE PRESIDENT'S MEN** As he distanced himself from Congress, Nixon confided in a small and fiercely loyal group of advisers. They included **H. R. Haldeman,** White House chief of staff; **John Ehrlichman,** chief domestic adviser; and **John Mitchell,** the attorney general. These men had played key roles in Nixon's 1968 election victory and now helped the president direct White House policy.

These men also shared President Nixon's desire for secrecy and the consolidation of power. Critics charged that these men, through their personalities and their attitude toward the presidency, developed a sense that they were somehow above the law. This sense would, in turn, prompt President Nixon and his advisers to cover up their role in Watergate, and fuel the coming scandal.

## The Drive Toward Reelection

**The Inner Circle**

H.R. Haldeman
Chief of Staff

John Ehrlichman
Chief Domestic Advisor

John N. Mitchell
Attorney General

John W. Dean III
Presidential Counsel

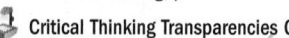

**2**

Throughout his political career, Richard Nixon lived with the overwhelming fear of losing elections. By the end of the 1972 reelection campaign, Nixon's campaign team sought advantages by any means possible, including an attempt to steal information from the DNC headquarters.

**A BUNGLED BURGLARY** At 2:30 A.M., June 17, 1972, a guard at the Watergate complex in Washington, D.C., caught five men breaking into the campaign headquarters of the DNC. The burglars planned to photograph documents outlining Democratic Party strategy and to place wiretaps, or "bugs," on the office telephones. The press soon discovered that the group's leader, James McCord, was a former CIA agent. He was also a security coordinator for a group known as the **Committee to Reelect the President** (CRP). John Mitchell, who had resigned as attorney general to run Nixon's reelection campaign, was the CRP's director.  **B**

*An Age of Limits* **803**

Just three days after the burglary, H. R. Haldeman noted in his diary Nixon's near obsession with how to respond to the break-in.

**A PERSONAL VOICE** H. R. HALDEMAN

" The P[resident] was concerned about what our counterattack is. . . . He raised it again several times during the day, and it obviously is bothering him. . . . He called at home tonight, saying that he wanted to change the plan for his press conference and have it on Thursday instead of tomorrow, so that it won't look like he's reacting to the Democratic break-in thing. "

—*The Haldeman Diaries*

**Woodward and Bernstein**

The mystery surrounding the identity of "Deep Throat" continues to this day. Use of anonymous sources in journalism continues to be controversial. Courts have, at times, ordered reporters to name their sources. Many journalists have refused, claiming it would undermine their ability to gather information from future sources. Ask students what they think about journalists using anonymous sources. (Students may say it is unfair to use anonymous sources when it prevents people from facing their accusers. Others may note that anonymous sources are vital to freedom of the press.)

 **In-Depth Resources: Unit 7**
· Primary Sources: *All the Presidents men*, p.14

---

**Instruct: Objective** ❸

**The Cover-Up Unravels**

TAKS SS11 5(US24.B)

· What event triggered the Watergate investigation?

· What was important about testimony given by John Dean and Alexander Butterfield?

· What was the Saturday Night Massacre?

· Why did Spiro Agnew resign as Vice President?

 **In-Depth Resources: Unit 7**
· Guided Reading, p. 2

 **Critical Thinking Transparencies CT32**
· The Watergate Scandal

**HISTORICAL SPOTLIGHT**

**WOODWARD AND BERNSTEIN**

Bob Woodward and Carl Bernstein of the *Washington Post* seemed an unlikely team. Woodward, 29 (at right in the photo above), had graduated from Yale, while the 28-year-old Bernstein was a college dropout.

As the two men dug deeper into the Watergate scandal, a mysterious inside source known only as Deep Throat helped them to uncover the scandal. Nearly 30 years later, the reporters still refuse to identify their famous source.

While people lauded the two reporters for their dogged determination, some Nixon officials remain bitter toward them.

"I really believe [they] were on a personal crusade to bring down a president," said Gerald Warren, Nixon's deputy press secretary. Woodward denied that charge, saying, "We tried to do our job and, in fact, if you look at it, our coverage was pretty conservative."

The cover-up quickly began. Workers shredded all incriminating documents in Haldeman's office. The White House, with President Nixon's consent, asked the CIA to urge the FBI to stop its investigations into the burglary on the grounds of national security. In addition, the CRP passed out nearly $450,000 to the Watergate burglars to buy their silence after they were indicted in September of 1972. **Ⓒ**

Throughout the 1972 campaign, the Watergate burglary generated little interest among the American public and media. Only the *Washington Post* and two of its reporters, Bob Woodward and Carl Bernstein, kept on the story. In a series of articles, the reporters uncovered information that linked numerous members of the administration to the burglary. The White House denied each new *Post* allegation. Upon learning of an upcoming story that tied him to the burglars, John Mitchell told Bernstein, "That's the most sickening thing I ever heard."

The White House reaction proved effective. Casting himself as a "global peacemaker"—in light of his China and Soviet Union summits and his promise of peace in Vietnam—Richard Nixon soundly defeated George S. McGovern, a liberal senator from South Dakota. Even as Nixon savored his presidential landslide victory, the storm clouds of Watergate gathered on the horizon.

**The Cover-Up Unravels** ❸

In January 1973, the trial of the Watergate burglars began. The trial's presiding judge, **John Sirica,** made clear his belief that the men had not acted alone. On March 20, a few days before the burglars were scheduled to be sentenced, James McCord sent a letter to Sirica, in which he indicated that he had lied under oath. He also hinted that powerful members of the Nixon administration had been involved in the break-in.

**THE SENATE INVESTIGATES WATERGATE** McCord's revelation of possible White House involvement in the burglary aroused public interest in Watergate. President Nixon moved quickly to stem the growing concern. On April 30, 1973, Nixon dismissed White House counsel John Dean and announced the resignations of Haldeman and Ehrlichman. All three men had been involved in the Watergate affair. The president then went on television and denied any attempt at a cover-up. He announced that he was

**MAIN IDEA**

**Chronological Order**

**Ⓒ** What steps did the White House take to cover up its involvement in the Watergate break-in?

*C. Answer* Officials shredded documents, attempted to obstruct the investigation, and paid the Watergate burglars to remain silent.

---

**Creating a Time Line**

To help students keep track of the twists and turns of the Watergate scandal, have them create a time line. Suggest they begin their time lines with the burglary and end with Ford's pardon of Nixon.

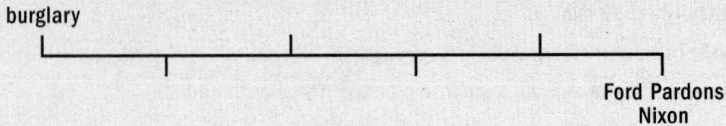

burglary

Ford Pardons Nixon

appointing a new attorney general, Elliot Richardson, and was authorizing him to appoint a special prosecutor to investigate Watergate. "There can be no whitewash at the White House," Nixon said.

The president's reassurances, however, came too late. In May 1973, the Senate began its own investigation of Watergate. A special committee, chaired by Senator Samuel James Ervin of North Carolina, began to call administration officials to give testimony. Throughout the summer millions of Americans sat by their televisions as the "president's men" testified one after another.

*"Divine right went out with the American Revolution and doesn't belong to White House aides."*

SENATOR SAM ERVIN

**STARTLING TESTIMONY** John Dean delivered the first bomb. In late June, during more than 30 hours of testimony, Dean provided a startling answer to Senator Howard Baker's repeated question, "What did the president know and when did he know it?" The former White House counsel declared that President Nixon had been deeply involved in the cover-up. Dean referred to one meeting in which he and the president, along with several advisers, discussed strategies for continuing the deceit.

The White House strongly denied Dean's charges. The hearings had suddenly reached an impasse as the committee attempted to sort out who was telling the truth. The answer came in July from an unlikely source: presidential aide Alexander Butterfield. Butterfield stunned the committee when he revealed that Nixon had taped virtually all of his presidential conversations. Butterfield later claimed that the taping system was installed "to help Nixon write his memoirs." However, for the Senate committee, the tapes were the key to revealing what Nixon knew and when he knew it. **D**

**THE SATURDAY NIGHT MASSACRE**
A year-long battle for the "Nixon tapes" followed. Archibald Cox, the special prosecutor whom Elliot Richardson had appointed to investigate the case, took the president to court in October 1973 to obtain the tapes. Nixon refused and ordered Attorney General Richardson to fire Cox. In what became known as the **Saturday Night Massacre,** Richardson refused the order and resigned. The deputy attorney general also refused the order, and he was fired. Solicitor General Robert Bork finally fired Cox. However, Cox's replacement, Leon Jaworski, proved equally determined to get the tapes. Several months after the "massacre," the House Judiciary Committee began examining the possibility of an impeachment hearing. **E**

The entire White House appeared to be under siege. Just days before the Saturday Night Massacre, Vice President Spiro Agnew had resigned after it was revealed that he had accepted bribes from Maryland engineering firms, as governor of Maryland, and during his term as vice president. Acting under the Twenty-fifth

*D. Answer* The tapes of Nixon's private conversations would provide clear and convincing evidence as to what Nixon knew about Watergate and when he knew it.

*E. Answer* Attorney General Richardson refused to obey Nixon's order to fire the special prosecutor, Archibald Cox, after he asked him to hand over the secret tapes. Richardson resigned. The deputy attorney general also refused to fire Cox. Nixon then turned to Solicitor General Robert Bork, who agreed to fire Cox.

**MAIN IDEA**

**Drawing Conclusions**
**D** What was significant about the revelation that Nixon taped his conversations?

**MAIN IDEA**

**Summarizing**
**E** What events led to the Saturday Night Massacre?

**More About . . .**

**Senate Watergate Hearings**
The Senate Watergate hearings were televised, and the drama gripped the nation. John Dean, Alexander Butterfield, senators, and committee staff members became instant celebrities. Fred Thompson, a Tennessee lawyer, served as an aide to Republican committee members. He later won election to the Senate from Tennessee. Another committee staff member, Hillary Rodham, went on to become First Lady as the wife of President Bill Clinton and, later, U.S. Senator from New York.

**More About . . .**

**Spiro T. Agnew**
The scandals of the Nixon administration began with Agnew. While serving as governor of Maryland, Agnew was accused of extortion, accepting bribes, and income tax violation. Agnew fought the accusations, but with Nixon under investigation, Republican forces prevailed on him to resign. He was the first Vice President to resign under duress. Agnew later pleaded *nolo contendere*, or not contest, to felony charges, although he continued to maintain his innocence.

▲
The Watergate hearings, chaired by Senator Sam Ervin, shown *(top left)* with Sam Dash, chief counsel to the Senate Watergate Committee, made headlines throughout the summer of 1973.

*An Age of Limits* **805**

---

**ACTIVITY** **COOPERATIVE ACTIVITY**

 **classzone.com**

**Writing an Editorial about the Saturday Night Massacre**

**Class Time** 30 minutes

**Task** Writing an editorial

**Purpose** To evaluate President Nixon's actions in the Saturday Night Massacre

**Directions** Have students work in small groups to research the events leading up to the Saturday Night Massacre and the events of that night. Have students use the Internet and library resources to conduct their search. Ask students to write an editorial based on their findings.

Integrated Assessment
· Rubrics 1, 5

Amendment, Nixon nominated the House minority leader, Gerald R. Ford, as his new vice president. Congress quickly confirmed the nomination.

## Instruct: Objective ④

**The Fall of a President**

TAKS SS11 4(8.16D)

· What actions did the House Judiciary Committee take in the Watergate scandal?

· What did the White House tapes reveal?

· Why did Nixon resign?

· What were the effects of Watergate?

 In-Depth Resources: Unit 7
· American Lives. Barbara Jordan, p. 21

 Electronic Library of Primary Sources
· Articles of Impeachment, 1973, by the House Judiciary Committee

---

### More About . . .

**The Tapes**

From January 1971 to July 1973, Nixon secretly recorded conversations between himself, staff, and visitors in the Oval Office, the Cabinet Room, and other White House locations and also at Camp David, the presidential retreat in Maryland. About 3700 hours of recordings were made. The tapes are in the possession of the National Archives and are being transcribed and periodically released to the public. Some already-released tapes show that Nixon considered destroying the tapes in April 1973 before their existence would be made known but changed his mind. The tapes also reveal many abuses of government power by the Nixon administration.

---

### Analyzing *Political Cartoons*

**SKILLBUILDER ANSWERS**

1. There was no privacy. All conversations were recorded

2. The White House

 Humanities Transp. HT46
· I Am the Law

---

## ④ The Fall of a President

In March 1974, a grand jury indicted seven presidential aides on charges of conspiracy, obstruction of justice, and perjury. The investigation was closing in on the president of the United States.

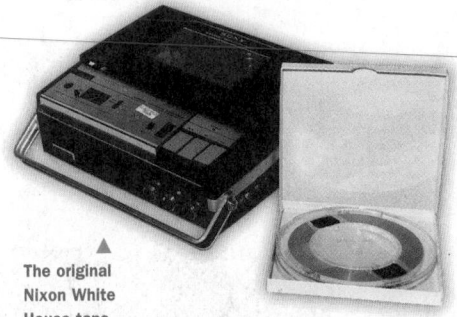

▲
The original Nixon White House tape recorder and tape from the 1970s.

**NIXON RELEASES THE TAPES** In the spring of 1974, President Nixon told a television audience that he was releasing 1,254 pages of edited transcripts of White House conversations about Watergate. Nixon's offering failed to satisfy investigators, who demanded the unedited tapes. Nixon refused, and the case went before the Supreme Court. On July 24, 1974, the high court ruled unanimously that the president must surrender the tapes. The Court rejected Nixon's argument that doing so would violate national security. Evidence involving possible criminal activity could not be withheld, even by a president. President Nixon maintained that he had done nothing wrong. At a press conference in November 1973, he proclaimed defiantly, "I am not a crook."

**THE PRESIDENT RESIGNS** Even without holding the original tapes, the House Judiciary Committee determined that there was enough evidence to impeach Richard Nixon. On July 27, the committee approved three articles of impeachment, charging the president with obstruction of justice, abuse of power, and contempt of Congress for refusing to obey a congressional subpoena to release the tapes.

**Background**
Although historians sued for access to thousands of hours of tapes, it was not until some 21 years later, in 1996, that an agreement was made for over 3,700 hours of tape to be made public.

---

### Analyzing *Political Cartoons*

**THE WHITE HOUSE TAPES**

During the Watergate hearings a bombshell exploded when it was revealed that President Nixon secretly tape-recorded all conversations in the Oval Office. Although Nixon hoped the tapes would one day help historians document the triumphs of his presidency, they were used to confirm his guilt.

**SKILLBUILDER**
**Analyzing Political Cartoons**

1. What does this cartoon imply about privacy during President Nixon's term in office?

2. What building has been transformed into a giant tape recorder?

 **SEE SKILLBUILDER HANDBOOK, PAGE R24.**

AUTH copyright © Philadelphia Inquirer. Reprinted with permission of Universal Press Syndicate. All rights reserved.

---

**ACTIVITY** | **LINK TO GOVERNMENT**

 classzone.com

**Gerald Ford's Succession to the Presidency**

**Class Time** 45 minutes

**Task** Tracing Gerald Ford's succession to the presidency.

**Purpose** To analyze the political implications of Ford's succession to the presidency

**Directions** Have students work in small groups, using library and Internet resources, to research the constitutional and political issues surrounding Gerald Ford's vice-presidential appointment and succession to the presidency. Lead a class discussion based on students' findings.

On August 5, Nixon released the tapes. They contained many gaps, and one tape revealed a disturbing 18½-minute gap. According to the White House, Rose Mary Woods, President Nixon's secretary, accidentally erased part of a conversation between H. R. Haldeman and Nixon. More importantly, a tape dated June 23, 1972—six days after the Watergate break-in— that contained a conversation between Nixon and Haldeman, disclosed the evidence investigators needed. Not only had the president known about his administration's role in the burglary, he had agreed to the plan to cover up and obstruct the FBI's investigation.

The evidence now seemed overwhelming. On August 8, 1974, before the full House vote on the articles of impeachment began, President Nixon announced his resignation from office. Defiant as always, Nixon admitted no guilt. He merely said that some of his judgments "were wrong." The next day, Nixon and his wife, Pat, returned home to California. A short time later, Gerald Ford was sworn in as the 38th president of the United States.

**THE EFFECTS OF WATERGATE** The effects of Watergate have endured long after Nixon's resignation. Eventually, 25 members of the Nixon Administration were convicted and served prison terms for crimes connected to Watergate. Along with the divisive war in Vietnam, Watergate produced a deep disillusionment with the "imperial" presidency. In the years following Vietnam and Watergate, the American public and the media developed a general cynicism about public officials that still exists today. Watergate remains the scandal and investigative story against which all others are measured.

▲
With wife Pat looking on, Richard Nixon bids farewell to his staff on his final day as president. Nixon's resignation letter is shown above.

### More About . . .

**Nixon's Resignation**
The major difference between Nixon's resignation and the impeachments of Andrew Johnson and Bill Clinton was the fact that the actions against Johnson and Clinton were highly partisan. The Radical Republicans felt Johnson was impeding their legislative agenda and dealing too leniently with the South. Republican opponents of Democrat Clinton's polices were the driving force behind his impeachment. On the other hand, Nixon's opposition was bi-partisan. After the House Judiciary Committee voted to send an impeachment bill to the House, Republican Senator Barry Goldwater went to see the President. He informed Nixon that the Republican Party would no longer support him, and that they would vote in favor of his impeachment.

## Assess & Reteach

### SECTION 2 ASSESSMENT
Ask groups of students to work together to answer the section assessment questions. Have one member from each group share the group's answer to question 3 with the class.

📄 Formal Assessment
· Section Quiz p. 439

### SELF-ASSESSMENT
Have students write a brief essay explaining what they think President Nixon could have done differently in regard to Watergate.

### RETEACH
As a class, reexamine the key events of the Watergate scandal.

📄 In-Depth Resources: Unit 7
· Reteaching Activity, p. 8

## 2 · ASSESSMENT

**1. TERMS & NAMES** For each term or name, write a sentence explaining its significance.

- impeachment
- Watergate
- H. R. Haldeman
- John Ehrlichman
- John Mitchell
- Committee to Reelect the President
- John Sirica
- Saturday Night Massacre

### MAIN IDEA

**2. TAKING NOTES**
Use a time line like the one below to trace the events of the Watergate scandal.

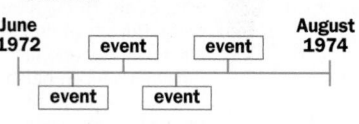

Which event made Nixon's downfall certain?

### CRITICAL THINKING

**3. HYPOTHESIZING**
If Nixon had admitted to and apologized for the Watergate break-in, how might subsequent events have been different? Explain.
**Think About:**
- the extent of the cover-up
- the impact of the cover-up
- Nixon's public image

**4. ANALYZING EVENTS**
How did the Watergate scandal create a constitutional crisis?

**5. EVALUATING**
Do you think that Nixon would have been forced to resign if the tapes had not existed? Explain your answer.

*An Age of Limits* **807**

---

Answers  ASSESSMENT  2

**1. TERMS & NAMES**
impeachment, p. 802
Watergate, p. 802
H. R. Haldeman, p. 803
John Ehrlichman, p. 803
John Mitchell, p. 803
Committee to Reelect the President, p. 803
Judge John Sirica, p. 804
Saturday Night Massacre, p. 805

**2. TAKING NOTES**
June 1972: Watergate break-in; May 1973: Senate investigates; June 1973: John Dean testifies before Senate; October 1973: Saturday Night Massacre; July 1974: Judiciary Committee votes to impeach Nixon; August 1974: President Nixon resigns.

**3. HYPOTHESIZING**
Nixon's public image would not have been as badly damaged; Americans might have respected him for his honesty; he probably would have lost some of the American people's trust.

**4. ANALYZING EVENTS**
During the scandal, Nixon abused his power and obstructed justice. The crisis centered on the issue of how the nation

would handle a president's alleged criminal misconduct.

**5. EVALUATING**
Yes: There may have been other ways of bringing the pertinent information to light. No: Nixon could have continued to maintain his innocence, and without proper evidence, he would not have been impeached.

# DAILY LIFE

## Objectives

· Analyze the growing realism of American television in the 1970s.

· Describe popular television programs of the 1970s.

## Focus & Motivate

Ask students to think about realistic television shows that are currently popular. What is it about these shows that make them so true-to-life?

## More About . . .

### Alex Haley

In 1965, Haley published the critically acclaimed classic, *The Autobiography of Malcolm X*, based on interviews he had conducted with the Black Muslim leader. However, it was Haley's book *Roots: The Saga of an American Family*, that made him a household name. Haley said he began writing *Roots* after listening to his maternal grandmother talk about the family's history. He spent 12 years researching the book. *Roots* earned Haley numerous accolades, including a Pulitzer Prize.

---

## DAILY LIFE 1968–1980

# Television Reflects American Life

From May until November 1973, the Senate Watergate hearings were the biggest daytime TV viewing event of the year. Meanwhile, television programming began to more closely reflect the realities of American life. Shows more often addressed relevant issues, more African-American characters appeared, and working women as well as homemakers were portrayed. In addition, the newly established Public Broadcasting System began showing many issue-oriented programs.

**▼ DIVERSITY**

*Chico and the Man* was the first series set in a Mexican-American barrio, East Los Angeles. The program centered on the relationship between Ed Brown, a cranky garage owner, and Chico Rodriguez, an optimistic young mechanic Brown reluctantly hired.

**▲ EDUCATIONAL PROGRAMMING**

Public television devoted much of its programming to quality children's television. Shows such as *Sesame Street* and *Zoom!* made it fun for children to learn. They were deliberately fast-paced to appeal to the new generation of "television babies."

**◄ SOCIAL VALUES**

*All in the Family* was the most popular series of the 1970s. It told the story of a working-class family, headed by the bigoted Archie Bunker and his long-suffering wife, Edith. Through the barbs Bunker traded with his son-in-law and his African-American neighbor, George Jefferson, the show dealt openly with the divisions in American society.

---

## RECOMMENDED RESOURCES

### BOOKS

Alley, Robert S. et al. *Love is All Around.* New York: Dell, 1989. A book about the making of The Mary Tyler Moore Show.

Esslin, Martin. *The Age of Television.* San Francisco: Freeman, 1981. Written soon after the close of the 1970s, this study focuses on societal aspects of television.

Lesser, Gerald S. *Children and Television.* New York: Random, 1974. Lessons from Sesame Street detailed in a book published not long after the show's creation.

Reiss, David S. *M*A*S*H.* Indianapolis: Bobbs-Merrill, 1980. An inside look at the popular TV show with a forward by star Alan Alda.

### VIDEOS

*All in the Family 20th Anniversary Special.* Columbia Pictures Home Video, 1991. A retrospective featuring the stars of the show and its creator, Norman Lear.

*On Television.* Films Inc., 1988. An exploration of TV as a social institution, hosted by Edwin Newman.

*Roots* vol. 1. Dir. David Greene. Warner Home Video, 1977. The original six-part miniseries.

◄ **INDEPENDENT WOMEN**

*The Mary Tyler Moore Show* depicted Mary Richards, a single woman living in Minneapolis and working as an assistant manager in a local TV news department. Mary symbolized the young career woman of the 1970s.

▼ **CULTURAL IDENTITY**

The miniseries *Roots*, based on a book by Alex Haley, told the saga of several generations of an African-American family. The eight-part story began with Kunta Kinte, who was captured outside his West African village and taken to America as a slave. It ended with his great-grandson's setting off for a new life as a free man. The groundbreaking series, broadcast in January 1977, was one of the most-watched television events in history.

# DATA FILE

**TV EVENTS OF THE 1970s**

- A congressional ban on TV cigarette commercials took effect in 1971.

- ABC negotiated an $8-million-a-year contract to televise *Monday Night Football*, first broadcast in September 1970.

- In 1972, President Nixon, accompanied by TV cameras and reporters from the major networks, made a groundbreaking visit to China.

- *Saturday Night Live*—a show that would launch the careers of Dan Aykroyd, Jane Curtin, Eddie Murphy, and many other comic actors—premiered in October 1975.

- WTCG-TV (later WTBS) in Atlanta, owned by Ted Turner, became the basis of the first true satellite-delivered "superstation" in 1976.

- In November 1979, ABC began broadcasting late-night updates on the hostage crisis in Iran. These reports evolved into the program *Nightline* with Ted Koppel.

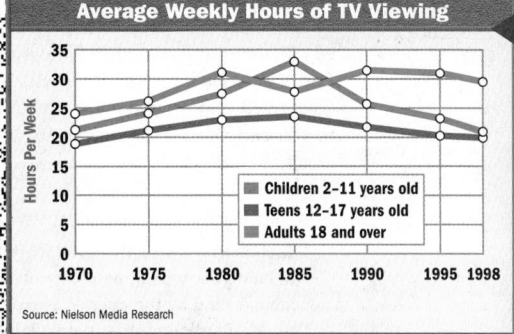

**Average Weekly Hours of TV Viewing**

Hours Per Week

35
30
25
20
15
10
5
0

1970  1975  1980  1985  1990  1995 1998

■ Children 2–11 years old
■ Teens 12–17 years old
■ Adults 18 and over

Source: Nielson Media Research

**THINKING CRITICALLY**

**CONNECT TO HISTORY**

1. **Analyzing Causes** In what ways did television change to reflect American society in the 1970s? What factors might have influenced these changes?

 **SEE SKILLBUILDER HANDBOOK, PAGE R7.**

**CONNECT TO TODAY**

2. **Creating a Graph** Use the Internet or an almanac to find data on the number of televisions owned in the United States and the number of hours of TV watched every day. Make a graph that displays the data.

 **RESEARCH LINKS** CLASSZONE.COM

## Instruct

1. How did television change in the 1970s?
2. What shows centered around ethnic and cultural differences?
3. What types of shows did the Public Broadcasting System focus on?

**MAKING PERSONAL CONNECTIONS**

· Ask students if they are familiar with any of the classic 1970s television programs referred to in these pages.
· Ask them how television shows have changed since the 1970s.

**HISTORY from VISUALS**

**Interpreting the Graph**
Have students note the time span of the graph—more than quarter of a century, from 1970 to 1998. Ask them to observe the fluctuations in the viewing habits of each group.
**Extension** Have students create graphs comparing their own average weekly hours of television viewing with those of their parents, friends, and siblings.

---

**THINKING CRITICALLY: ANSWERS**

1. **CONNECT TO HISTORY** Television shows were becoming more inclusive, urban, working class, and multicultural. Programs were more realistic and addressed social issues.

2. **CONNECT TO TODAY**
**Rubrics**
Student graphs should . . .
· include data relevant over a specific time period
· highlight the number of television sets owned in the United States and the hours of TV watched
· be clearly labeled and display accurate historical details from their research

**810** CHAPTER 24

# The Ford and Carter Years

<table>
<tr><td>MAIN IDEA</td><td>WHY IT MATTERS NOW</td><td>Terms & Names</td></tr>
</table>

| MAIN IDEA | WHY IT MATTERS NOW | Terms & Names |
|---|---|---|
| The Ford and Carter administrations attempted to remedy the nation's worst economic crisis in decades. | Maintaining a stable national economy has remained a top priority for every president since Ford and Carter. | • Gerald R. Ford  • Camp David<br>• Jimmy Carter    Accords<br>• National Energy Act  • Ayatollah Ruholla<br>• human rights    Khomeini |

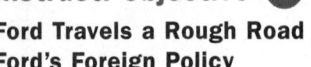 U.S. History
1B, 6H,
8A, 8B, 9B, 17A,
19A, 19B, 20D,
22A, 22C, 24A,
24B, 24C, 24D,
24G, 24H, 25A,
25B, 25C, 25D,
26B

### One American's Story

James D. Denney couldn't believe what he was hearing. Barely a month after Richard Nixon had resigned amid the Watergate scandal, President **Gerald R. Ford** had granted Nixon a full pardon. "[S]omeone must write, 'The End,'" Ford had declared in a televised statement. "I have concluded that only I can do that." Denney wrote a letter to the editors of *Time* magazine, in which he voiced his anger at Ford's decision.

**A PERSONAL VOICE** JAMES D. DENNEY

" Justice may certainly be tempered by mercy, but there can be no such thing as mercy until justice has been accomplished by the courts. Since it circumvented justice, Mr. Ford's act was merely indulgent favoritism, a bland and unworthy substitute for mercy. "

—*Time*, September 23, 1974

James Denney's feelings were typical of the anger and the disillusionment with the presidency that many Americans felt in the aftermath of the Watergate scandal. During the 1970s, Presidents Gerald Ford and Jimmy Carter sought to restore America's faith in its leaders. At the same time, both men had to focus much of their attention on battling the nation's worsening economic situation.

▲ Two women protest President Ford's pardon of Richard Nixon.

## ① Ford Travels a Rough Road

Upon taking office, Gerald R. Ford urged Americans to put the Watergate scandal behind them. "Our long national nightmare is over," he declared. The nation's nightmarish economy persisted, however, and Ford's policies offered little relief.

---

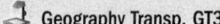
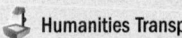

**"A FORD, NOT A LINCOLN"** Gerald Ford seemed to many to be a likable and honest man. Upon becoming vice president after Spiro Agnew's resignation, Ford candidly admitted his limitations. "I'm a Ford, not a Lincoln," he remarked. On September 8, 1974, President Ford pardoned Richard Nixon in an attempt to move the country beyond Watergate. The move cost Ford a good deal of public support.

**FORD TRIES TO "WHIP" INFLATION** By the time Ford took office, America's economy had gone from bad to worse. Both inflation and unemployment continued to rise. After the massive OPEC oil-price increases in 1973, gasoline and heating oil costs had soared, pushing inflation from 6 percent to over 10 percent by the end of 1974. Ford responded with a program of massive citizen action, called "Whip Inflation Now" or WIN. The president called on Americans to cut back on their use of oil and gas and to take other energy-saving measures.

In the absence of incentives, though, the plan fell flat. Ford then tried to curb inflation through a "tight money" policy. He cut government spending and encouraged the Federal Reserve Board to restrict credit through higher interest rates. These actions triggered the worst economic recession in 40 years. As Ford implemented his economic programs, he continually battled a Democratic Congress intent on pushing its own economic agenda. During his two years as president, Ford vetoed more than 50 pieces of legislation.

---

**MAIN IDEA**

**Making Inferences**
Ⓐ Why was Ford's call for voluntary actions to help the economy unsuccessful?

*A. Answer*
Many Americans had little faith in their government and so were less likely to make personal sacrifices at government suggestion.

---

## Ford's Foreign Policy ❶

Ford fared slightly better in the international arena. He relied heavily on Henry Kissinger, who continued to hold the key position of secretary of state.

**CARRYING OUT NIXON'S FOREIGN POLICIES** Following Kissinger's advice, Ford pushed ahead with Nixon's policy of negotiation with China and the Soviet Union. In November 1974, he met with Soviet premier Leonid Brezhnev. Less than a year later, he traveled to Helsinki, Finland, where 35 nations, including the Soviet Union, signed the Helsinki Accords—a series of agreements that promised greater cooperation between the nations of Eastern and Western Europe. The Helsinki Accords would be Ford's greatest presidential accomplishment.

**ONGOING TURMOIL IN SOUTHEAST ASIA** Like presidents before him, Ford encountered trouble in Southeast Asia. The 1973 cease-fire in Vietnam had broken down. Heavy fighting resumed and Ford asked Congress for over $722 million to help South Vietnam. Congress refused. Without American financial help, South Vietnam surrendered to the North in 1975. In the same year, the Communist government of Cambodia seized the U.S. merchant ship *Mayagüez* in the Gulf of Siam. President Ford responded with a massive show of military force to rescue 39 crew members aboard the ship. The operation cost the lives of 41 U.S. troops. Critics argued that the mission had cost more lives than it had saved.

---

**DIFFICULT DECISIONS**

**PARDONING PRESIDENT NIXON**

President Ford's pardon of Richard Nixon outraged many Americans. But President Ford argued that the pardon of Richard Nixon was in the country's best interest. In the event of a Watergate trial, Ford argued, "ugly passions would again be aroused. . . . And the credibility of our free institutions . . . would again be challenged at home and abroad." Ford called the pardon decision "the most difficult of my life, by far."

In 2001, after more than 25 years, Ford received the John F. Kennedy Profiles in Courage Award for his courageous decision in the face of public opposition.

1. How might the country have been affected if a former United States president had gone on trial for possible criminal wrongdoing?

2. If you had been in President Ford's position, would you have pardoned Richard Nixon? Why or why not?

---

**DIFFICULT DECISIONS**

**Pardoning President Nixon**

1. Students might say that some Americans would have felt that justice had been done. Others might have felt ashamed that the nation's president was on trial.

2. Yes: Students might say that pardoning Nixon allowed the nation to move forward. No: Students might point out that not even the president is above the law.

Ford's pardon of Nixon was fiercely debated. It had a profound impact on Ford's political future. Many Americans voted against Ford because of it in the 1976 election.

---

**More About . . .**

**Ford and Presidential Vetoes**
Had Gerald Ford served longer, his combative relationship with Congress may have led him to veto even more bills. Franklin Roosevelt, who served longer than any other president (12 years), vetoed the most bills, with a total of 635. Grover Cleveland, who served two terms, was second with 584. In third place was Harry Truman, who vetoed 250 bills sent to him during his more than seven years in office. From the presidencies of George Washington through Bill Clinton, more than 2,500 vetoes were cast. Slightly more than 100, or about 4 percent were overridden by Congress.

---

*An Age of Limits* **811**

---

**ACTIVITY**    **LINK TO CIVICS**

 **classzone.com**

### Debating the Nixon Pardon

**Class Time** 45 minutes

**Task** Debating the topic of Ford's pardon of Nixon

**Purpose** To analyze the social and political impact of Ford's decision to pardon Richard Nixon

**Directions** Have students work in small groups. Direct them to use text, library, and Internet resources to research the political impact of Ford's pardon of Nixon. Have students choose opposing sides and prepare their arguments. Organize a class debate.

📄 Integrated Assessment
· Rubrics 1, 3

## Instruct: Objective ❷

**Carter Enters the White House**
TAKS SS11 5(US24.A)

· What political factors weakened the Republicans in 1976?
· How did Carter reach out to the American people?
· What were Carter's relations with Congress?

 In-Depth Resources: Unit 7
· Guided Reading, p. 3

### KEY PLAYER

**Jimmy Carter**

Carter used his down-to-earth charm to gain the American people's approval. Being an outsider with a fresh face helped him win the presidential election. In office, however, Carter's charm was not enough to sway Congress. Ask students why they think Carter was reluctant to make deals and play the "insider" game in Washington. *(Carter had his own way of doing things; he was reluctant to compromise in order to appease Congress. As a result, he failed to gain support from legislators.)*

## Instruct: Objective ❸

**Carter's Domestic Agenda**
TAKS SS11 4(US17.A)

· How did Carter deal with the energy crisis?
· How successful was Carter in dealing with the nation's economic problems?
· How did economic issues affect Carter's political support?
· What were Carter's accomplishments in regard to civil rights?

 In-Depth Resources: Unit 7
· Guided Reading, p. 3

 Electronic Library of Primary Sources
· On Energy and National Goals, 1979, by J. Carter

### KEY PLAYER

**JIMMY CARTER**
**1924–**

James Earl Carter, Jr., was born into relative prosperity. His father, Earl Carter was a disciplinarian who tried to instill a sense of hard work and responsibility in his son.

To earn money for himself, Carter undertook a variety of jobs selling peanuts, running a hamburger and hot dog stand, collecting newspapers and selling them to fish markets, and selling scrap iron.

Before entering politics, Carter joined the navy, where he excelled in electronics and naval tactics. In 1952, he joined a select group of officers who helped develop the world's first nuclear submarines. The group's commander was Captain Hyman G. Rickover. Carter later wrote that Rickover "had a profound effect on my life—perhaps more than anyone except my own parents. . . . He expected the maximum from us, but he always contributed more."

This 1976 ► campaign toy exaggerates Jimmy Carter's well-known smile and parodies his occupation as a peanut farmer.

**812** CHAPTER 24

## Carter Enters the White House ❷

Gerald Ford won the Republican nomination for president in 1976 after fending off a powerful conservative challenge from former California governor Ronald Reagan. Because the Republicans seemed divided over Ford's leadership, the Democrats confidently eyed the White House. "We could run an aardvark this year and win," predicted one Democratic leader. The Democratic nominee was indeed a surprise: a nationally unknown peanut farmer and former governor of Georgia, **Jimmy Carter.**

**MR. CARTER GOES TO WASHINGTON** During the post-Watergate era, cynicism toward the Washington establishment ran high. The soft-spoken, personable man from Plains, Georgia, promised to restore integrity to the nation's highest office, "I will never tell a lie to the American people."

Throughout the presidential campaign, Carter and Ford squared off over the key issues of inflation, energy, and unemployment. On Election Day, Jimmy Carter won by a narrow margin, claiming 40.8 million popular votes to Ford's 39.1 million. **Ⓑ**

From the very beginning, the new first family brought a down-to-earth style to Washington. After settling into office, Carter stayed in touch with the people by holding Roosevelt-like "fireside chats" on radio and television.

Carter failed to reach out to Congress in a similar way, refusing to play the "insider" game of deal making. Relying mainly on a team of advisers from Georgia, Carter even alienated congressional Democrats. Both parties on Capitol Hill often joined to sink the president's budget proposals, as well as his major policy reforms of tax and welfare programs.

## Carter's Domestic Agenda ❸

Like Gerald Ford, President Carter focused much of his attention on battling the country's energy and economic crises but was unable to bring the United States out of its economic slump.

**CONFRONTING THE ENERGY CRISIS** Carter considered the energy crisis the most important issue facing the nation. A large part of the problem, the president believed, was America's reliance on imported oil. On April 18, 1977, during a fireside chat, Carter urged his fellow Americans to cut their consumption of oil and gas.

**A PERSONAL VOICE** JIMMY CARTER
" The energy crisis . . . is a problem . . . likely to get progressively worse through the rest of this century. . . . Our decision about energy will test the character of the American people. . . . This difficult effort will be the 'moral equivalent of war,' except that we will be uniting our efforts to build and not to destroy. "
—quoted in *Keeping Faith*

> **MAIN IDEA**
>
> **Analyzing Causes**
> **Ⓑ**  What factors played a significant role in Carter's election?
>
> **B. Answer**
> Carter's personality and sense of morality, as well as his direct campaign style.

In addition, Carter presented Congress with more than 100 proposals on energy conservation and development. Representatives from oil- and gas-producing states fiercely resisted some of the proposals. Automobile manufacturers also lobbied against gas-rationing provisions. "It was impossible for me to imagine the bloody legislative battles we would have to win," Carter later wrote.

Out of the battle came the **National Energy Act**. The act placed a tax on gas-guzzling cars, removed price controls on oil and natural gas produced in the United States, and extended tax credits for the development of alternative energy. With the help of the act, as well as voluntary conservation measures, U.S. dependence on foreign oil had eased slightly by 1979. **C**

**THE ECONOMIC CRISIS WORSENS** Unfortunately, these energy-saving measures could do little to combat a sudden new economic crisis. In the summer of 1979, renewed violence in the Middle East produced a second major fuel shortage in the United States. To make matters worse, OPEC announced another major price hike. In 1979 inflation soared from 7.6 percent to 11.3 percent.

Faced with increasing pressure to act, Carter attempted an array of measures, none of which worked. Carter's scatter-shot approach convinced many people that he had no economic policy at all. Carter fueled this feeling of uncertainty by delivering his now-famous "malaise" speech, in which he complained of a "crisis of spirit" that had struck "at the very heart and soul of our national will." Carter's address made many Americans feel that their president had given up.

By 1980, inflation had climbed to nearly 14 percent, the highest rate since 1947. The standard of living in the United States slipped from first place to fifth place in the world. Carter's popularity slipped along with it. This economic downswing—and Carter's inability to solve it during an election year—was one key factor in sending Ronald Reagan to the White House.

### Vocabulary
**lobby:** a special-interest group that tries to influence the legislature

---

**MAIN IDEA**

**Summarizing**
**C** How did the National Energy Act help ease America's energy crisis?

**C. Answer**
The act placed a tax on gas-guzzling cars, encouraged the development of alternative energy sources, and removed price controls on oil and natural gas produced in the United States.

---

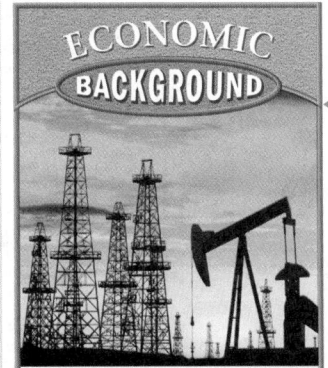

**THE 1980s TEXAS OIL BOOM**

The economic crisis that gripped the country in the late 1970s was largely caused by the increased cost of oil. The OPEC cartel raised the price of oil by agreeing to restrict oil production. The resulting decrease in the supply of oil in the market caused the price to go up.

Most Americans were hurt by the high energy prices. However, in areas that produced oil, such as Texas, the rise in prices led to a booming economy. Real-estate values—for land on which to drill for oil, as well as for office space in cities like Houston and Dallas—increased greatly. (See *supply and demand* on page R45 in the Economics Handbook.)

---

## ECONOMIC BACKGROUND

### The 1980s Texas Oil Boom
In the 1980s, rising prices for imported oil led to increasing demand for domestic oil. As oil prices declined throughout the 1990s, the oil economy fell into a temporary slump. Oil prices were again driven upwards in the late 1990s, when OPEC restricted production. Point out to students that when the price of oil drops, oil producers have less incentive to drill for new oil. Ask students how they think the economy influences the energy choices made by Americans. *(Consumers have limited choices, unless they are willing to pay for more-expensive cleaner or renewable energy.)*

**Electronic Library of Primary Sources**
· *From* Victim–Victimizer: Why Excel?, 1977, by Rev. J. Jackson

---

### Unemployment and Inflation, 1970–1980

*Graph: Percent (0–15) by year 1970–1980, showing Unemployment Rate and Inflation Rate.*

Source: *Statistical Abstract of the United States, 1980, 1995*

■ Unemployment Rate  ■ Inflation Rate

**SKILLBUILDER Interpreting Graphs**
1. What trends did the economy experience during the Carter years?
2. Which year of the Carter administration saw the greatest stagflation (inflation plus unemployment)?

### Skillbuilder Answers
1. The inflation rate rose; the unemployment rate dipped and then began to rise again.
2. 1980.

---

## HISTORY from VISUALS

### Interpreting the Graph
Ask students to use the graph to determine what year saw the least stagflation (inflation plus unemployment). (1972: just under 9 percent, with inflation at about 3 percent and unemployment slightly less than 6 percent)

Ask students what role the economy plays in a presidential election. Then have students determine the stagflation rates for the election years of 1972, 1976, and 1980 and whether the incumbent president was reelected or defeated. (1972: just under 9 Percent; Nixon reelected. 1976: more than 13 percent; Ford defeated. 1980: nearly 21 percent; Carter defeated.)

---

*An Age of Limits* **813**

---

**ACTIVITY** **LINK TO ECONOMICS**

 **BLOCK SCHEDULING**

## Unemployment and Inflation

**Class Time** 30 minutes

**Task** Charting unemployment and inflation rates

**Purpose** To analyze recent economic statistics

**Directions** Have students work in small groups. Using the current Statistical Abstract of the United States, have students make a line graph of the last five years. Suggest they use the chart on page 813 as an example. Have students create a second graph that substitutes state unemployment figures for the national ones. Display the finished charts and interpret the data as a class.

**Integrated Assessment**
· Rubric 2

## HISTORY from VISUALS

### Interpreting Graphs

Ask students to consider the implications of the data shown on the charts. Then have them discuss how they are personally affected by the changing economy.

Ask students what they think jobs are like in the service industry. Have them talk about their own experience. (*Many entry-level service jobs pay around the minimum wage; good for part-time work; hard to support a family. Answers will vary.*)

Mini-Lesson 1: SS11 3(US14.E)

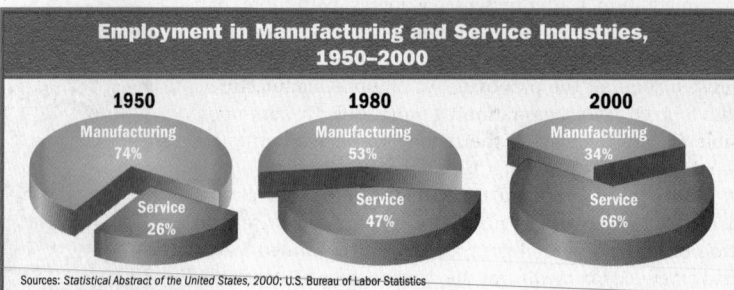

**Employment in Manufacturing and Service Industries, 1950–2000**

| 1950 | 1980 | 2000 |
|------|------|------|
| Manufacturing 74% | Manufacturing 53% | Manufacturing 34% |
| Service 26% | Service 47% | Service 66% |

Sources: *Statistical Abstract of the United States, 2000;* U.S. Bureau of Labor Statistics

**SKILLBUILDER** Interpreting Graphs
1. How much greater was the percentage of employment in service industries in 1980 than in 1950?
2. What additional change is shown by the year 2000? Do you think the trend will continue?

*Skillbuilder Answers*
1. 21% more; 26% in 1950, 47% in 1980.
2. 19% more; 47% in 1980, 66% in 2000: Yes. the service industries will continue to grow as more manufacturing occurs outside the United States.

### Tracing Themes
#### SCIENCE AND TECHNOLOGY

In the midst of the economic crisis of the 1970s, a new technology was being implemented that would revive the the US economy. The microchip gave rise to a new technology industry and changed the face of business. Microchips have gotten smaller and more powerful over the years. This technology is used to power everything from video games, digital watches, and computers, to medical instruments and microwave ovens.

### More About . . .

#### Andrew Young

Andrew Young (1932–) is a minister who first gained notice in the civil rights movement as Martin Luther King, Jr.'s associate in the Southern Christian Leadership Conference. Young was elected to Congress in 1972 and was twice reelected. He accepted appointment to the post of ambassador to the United Nations in 1977. He served as mayor of Atlanta in the 1980s.

**A CHANGING ECONOMY** Many of the economic problems Jimmy Carter struggled with resulted from long-term trends in the economy. Since the 1950s, the rise of automation and foreign competition had reduced the number of manufacturing jobs. At the same time, the service sector of the economy expanded rapidly. This sector includes industries such as communications, transportation, and retail trade.

The rise of the service sector and the decline of manufacturing jobs meant big changes for some American workers. Workers left out of manufacturing jobs faced an increasingly complex job market. Many of the higher-paying service jobs required more education or specialized skills than did manufacturing jobs. The lower-skilled service jobs usually did not pay well.

Growing overseas competition during the 1970s caused further change in America's economy. The booming economies of West Germany and countries on the Pacific Rim (such as Japan, Taiwan, and Korea) cut into many U.S. markets. Many of the nation's primary industries—iron and steel, rubber, clothing, automobiles—had to cut back production, lay off workers, and even close plants. Especially hard-hit were the automotive industries of the Northeast. There, high energy costs, foreign competition, and computerized production led companies to eliminate tens of thousands of jobs. **D**

**MAIN IDEA**

**Analyzing Causes**
**D** What factors played a role in America's economic stagnation?
*D. Answer* The technological revolution and growing overseas competition.

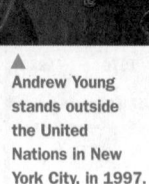
▲ Andrew Young stands outside the United Nations in New York City, in 1997.

**CARTER AND CIVIL RIGHTS** Although Carter felt frustrated by the country's economic woes, he took special pride in his civil rights record. His administration included more African Americans and women than any before it. In 1977, the president appointed civil rights leader Andrew Young as U.S. ambassador to the United Nations. Young was the first African American to hold that post. To the judicial branch alone, Carter appointed 28 African Americans, 29 women (including 6 African Americans), and 14 Latinos.

However, President Carter fell short of what many civil rights groups had expected in terms of legislation. Critics claimed that Carter—preoccupied with battles over energy and the economy—failed to give civil rights his full attention. Meanwhile, the courts began to turn against affirmative action. In 1978, in the case of *Regents of the University of California* v. *Bakke*, the Supreme Court decided that the affirmative action policies of the university's medical school were unconstitutional. The decision made it more difficult for organizations to establish effective affirmative action programs. (See *Regents of the University of California* v. *Bakke,* page 818.)

---

**DIFFERENTIATING INSTRUCTION** **GIFTED AND TALENTED STUDENTS**  **classzone.com**

### Economics and Society

Have students use the Internet and the resources of the library or local historical society to research community businesses of the 1970s. Ask them to answer the following questions:

· Who were the top employers?
· Which companies are still in business?
· How has the business climate changed over the years?

Then have students compile their findings in a chart and share their work with the rest of the class.

Jimmy Carter rejected the philosophy of realpolitik—the pragmatic policy of negotiating with powerful nations despite their behavior—and strived for a foreign policy committed to human rights.

**ADVANCING HUMAN RIGHTS** Jimmy Carter, like Woodrow Wilson, sought to use moral principles as a guide for U.S. foreign policy. He believed that the United States needed to commit itself to promoting **human rights**—such as the freedoms and liberties listed in the Declaration of Independence and the Bill of Rights—throughout the world.

Putting his principles into practice, President Carter cut off military aid to Argentina and Brazil, countries that had good relations with the United States but had imprisoned or tortured thousands of their own citizens. Carter followed up this action by establishing a Bureau of Human Rights in the State Department.

Carter's philosophy was not without its critics. Supporters of the containment policy felt that the president's policy undercut allies such as Nicaragua, a dictatorial but anti-Communist country. Others argued that by supporting dictators in South Korea and the Philippines, Carter was acting inconsistently. In 1977, Carter's policies drew further criticism when his administration announced that it planned to give up ownership of the Panama Canal. **E**

**YIELDING THE PANAMA CANAL** Since 1914, when the United States obtained full ownership over the Panama Canal, Panamanians had resented having their nation split in half by a foreign power. In 1977, the two nations agreed to two treaties, one of which turned over control of the Panama Canal to Panama on December 31, 1999.

In 1978, the U.S. Senate, which had to ratify each treaty, approved the agreements by a vote of 68 to 32—one more vote than the required two-thirds. Public opinion was also divided. In the end, the treaties did improve relationships between the United States and Latin America.

**THE COLLAPSE OF DÉTENTE** When Jimmy Carter took office, détente—the relaxation of tensions between the world's superpowers—had reached a high point. Beginning with President Nixon and continuing with President Ford, U.S. officials had worked to ease relations with the Communist superpowers of China and the Soviet Union.

However, Carter's firm insistence on human rights led to a breakdown in relations with the Soviet Union. President Carter's dismay over the Soviet Union's treatment of dissidents, or opponents of the government's policies, delayed a second round of SALT negotiations. President Carter and Soviet premier Leonid Brezhnev finally met in June of 1979 in Vienna, Austria, where they signed an agreement known as SALT II. Although the agreement did not reduce armaments, it did provide for limits on the number of strategic weapons and nuclear-missile launchers that each side could produce.

The SALT II agreement, however, met sharp opposition in the Senate. Critics argued that it would put the United States at a military disadvantage. Then, in December 1979, the Soviets invaded the neighboring country of Afghanistan. Angered over the invasion, President Carter refused to fight for the SALT II agreement, and the treaty died. **F**

---

**MAIN IDEA**

**Identifying Problems**

**E** What criticisms were made of Carter's foreign-policy philosophy?

**E. Answer** It undercut Cold War alliances and was inconsistent in its treatment of dictators.

---

**F. Answer** Carter's concern over the Soviets' human rights violations and their invasion of Afghanistan.

**MAIN IDEA**

**Analyzing Causes**

**F** What led to the collapse of détente with the Soviet Union?

---

## WORLD STAGE

**SOVIET–AFGHANISTAN WAR**

Afghanistan, an Islamic country along the southern border of the Soviet Union, had been run by a pro-Soviet government for a number of years. However, a strong Muslim rebel group was intent on overthrowing the Afghan government. Fearing a rebel victory in Afghanistan, the Soviet Union sent troops to Afghanistan in late 1979.

While the Soviets had superior weaponry, the rebels fought the Soviets to a stalemate by using guerrilla tactics and knowledge of the country's mountainous terrain.

After suffering thousands of casualties, the last Soviet troops pulled out of Afghanistan in February 1989. Fighting between rival factions continued for years. The Taliban, a radical Muslim faction, eventually gained control of the country and imposed harsh rule based on its version of Islamic fundamentalism.

---

**Instruct: Objective 4**

**A Human Rights Foreign Policy**
TAKS SS11 5(WH26.C)
· What was the role of human rights in Carter's foreign policy?
· Why did Carter agree to relinquish control of the Panama Canal?
· Why was Carter unsuccessful in dealing with the Soviet Union?

📖 In-Depth Resources: Unit 7
· Guided Reading, p. 3

**Tracing Themes**

**AMERICA IN WORLD AFFAIRS**

The basic principles of a nation's foreign policy are usually based on maintaining friendly relations with other nations in the world to promote peace and often to create economic opportunity. As such, domestic policies within a nation are not considered the business of another nation and may be ignored. The inclusion of human rights as a factor in foreign policy marked a shift in United States priorities in dealing with other nations of the world.

**ON THE WORLD STAGE**

**The Soviet-Afghanistan War**

**Analyzing Effects** During the Soviet-Afghanistan War, American intelligence operatives armed Afghan rebels and trained them in terrorist tactics. Years later, some of these rebels turned against the United States. They used their terrorist tactics to target American interests. Ask students to consider why the Afghan rebels would target the United States. *(angry that America did not fully support their cause; United States wielded too much world power)*

*An Age of Limits* **815**

---

**ACTIVITY** **LINK TO GOVERNMENT**

**Human Rights and Foreign Policy**

**Class Time** Two class periods

**Task** Writing a position paper on foreign policy

**Purpose** To analyze the national and ethical issues dictating foreign policy

**Directions** Ask students to work in small groups to discuss the contrasting foreign policies of Nixon/Ford and Carter. They should consider such foreign policy concerns as American economic interests and the ethics of human rights. Then ask each student to write a position paper, in which they analyze and recommend how the president should conduct foreign policy for the United States.

📖 Integrated Assessment
· Rubrics 1, 5

**B** **BLOCK SCHEDULING**

**Middle East, 1978–1982**

## HISTORY from VISUALS

### Interpreting the Maps

Have students study the map. Ask them why the conflict between Egypt and Israel was so potentially dangerous. *(proximity)*

**Extension** Have students research current events in the Middle East. Ask them to write a brief essay comparing and contrasting past and present conflicts in the region.

### Instruct: Objective 5

**Triumph and Crisis in the Middle East**

TAKS SS11 5(US24.B)

· What were the Camp David Accords?

· Why did Iranian revolutionaries take Americans hostage?

 In-Depth Resources: Unit 7
· Guided Reading, p. 3

 Geography Transp. GT32
· OPEC (Organization of Petroleum Exporting Countries)

**Map legend:**
- Israel
- Israeli-occupied land
- Israeli conquests returned to Egypt, 1979–1982
- OPEC Member

### GEOGRAPHY SKILLBUILDER

1. **Location** What OPEC countries are shown on the map?
2. **Human-Environment Interaction** How does Israel's location contribute to its conflicts?

*Skillbuilder Answers*
**1.** Algeria, Libya, Iraq, Iran, Kuwait, Saudi Arabia, Qatar, United Arab Emirates.
**2.** It is located at the crossroads of 3 continents and 2 seas. It is located centrally to many oil producing nations.

### More About . . .

#### Anwar el-Sadat

In the West, Sadat won public praise. He shared the Nobel Peace Prize with Begin in honor of their peacemaking efforts. In much of the Arab world, however, Anwar el-Sadat was seen as a traitor for making peace with Israel. Worsening economic conditions in Egypt and anger at the Camp David accords, erupted in political dissent. In Cairo, on October 6, 1981, Anwar el-Sadat was assassinated during a military parade.

## 5 Triumph and Crisis in the Middle East

*President Carter, President Anwar el-Sadat, and Prime Minister Menachem Begin reach a peace agreement in 1978.*

Through long gasoline lines and high energy costs, Americans became all too aware of the troubles in the Middle East. In that area of ethnic, religious, and economic conflict, Jimmy Carter achieved one of his greatest diplomatic triumphs—and suffered his most tragic defeat.

**THE CAMP DAVID ACCORDS** Through negotiation and arm-twisting, Carter helped forge peace between long-time enemies Israel and Egypt. In 1977, Egyptian president Anwar el-Sadat and Israeli prime minister Menachem Begin met in Jerusalem to discuss an overall peace between the two nations. In the summer of 1978, Carter seized on the peace initiative. When the peace talks stalled, he invited Sadat and Begin to Camp David, the presidential retreat in Maryland.

After 12 days of intense negotiations, the three leaders reached an agreement that became known as the **Camp David Accords.** Under this first signed peace agreement with an Arab country, Israel agreed to withdraw from the Sinai Peninsula, which it had seized from Egypt during the Six-Day War in 1967. Egypt, in turn, formally recognized Israel's right to exist. Still, many issues were left unresolved. **G**

*G. Answer* It was the first signed agreement between Israel and an Arab country.

**MAIN IDEA**

**Summarizing**
**G** What was the significance of the Camp David Accords?

---

**ACTIVITY** | **LINK TO WORLD HISTORY**

 **classzone.com**

### Creation of the State of Israel

**Class Time** Two class periods

**Task** Creating a multimedia presentation on the creation of the State of Israel

**Purpose** To analyze the reasons for and the impact of the creation of the State of Israel

**Directions** Have students work in groups to research the creation of the State of Israel. Suggest they use the Internet and library resources to find articles, photographs, and facts on the subject. Ask students to put together a multimedia presentation for the class.

 Integrated Assessment
· Rubrics 1, 6

Joking at the hard work ahead, Carter wrote playfully in his diary, "I resolved to do everything possible to get out of the negotiating business!" Little did the president know that his next Middle East negotiation would be his most painful.

**THE IRAN HOSTAGE CRISIS** By 1979, the shah of Iran, an ally of the United States, was in deep trouble. Many Iranians resented his regime's widespread corruption and dictatorial tactics.

In January 1979, revolution broke out. The Muslim religious leader **Ayatollah Ruhollah Khomeini** (ī′yə-tō′lə rōō-hō′lə kō-mā′nē) led the rebels in overthrowing the shah and establishing a religious state based on strict obedience to the Qur'an, the sacred book of Islam. Carter had supported the shah until the very end. In October 1979, the president allowed the shah to enter the United States for cancer treatment, though he had already fled Iran in January 1979.

The act infuriated the revolutionaries of Iran. On November 4, 1979, armed students seized the U.S. embassy in Tehran and took 52 Americans hostage. The militants demanded that the United States send the shah back to Iran in return for the release of the hostages.

Carter refused, and a painful yearlong standoff followed, in which the United States continued quiet but intense efforts to free the hostages. The captives were finally released on January 20, 1981, shortly after the new president, Ronald Reagan, was sworn in as president. Despite the hostages' release after 444 days in captivity, the crisis in Iran seemed to underscore the limits that Americans faced during the 1970s. Americans also realized that there were limits to the nation's environmental resources. This realization prompted both citizens and the government to actively address environmental concerns.

▲ U.S. hostages were blindfolded and paraded through the streets of Tehran.

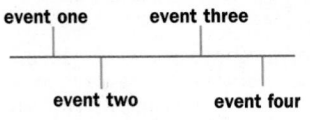

## ASSESSMENT

**1. TERMS & NAMES** For each term or name, write a sentence explaining its significance.

- Gerald R. Ford
- Jimmy Carter
- National Energy Act
- human rights
- Camp David Accords
- Ayatollah Ruhollah Khomeini

### MAIN IDEA

**2. TAKING NOTES**
Create a time line of the major events of the Ford and Carter administrations, using a form such as the one below.

event one    event three

event two    event four

Which two events do you think were the most important? Why?

### CRITICAL THINKING

**3. EVALUATING DECISIONS**
Do you think that Ford made a good decision in pardoning Nixon? Explain why or why not.

**4. COMPARING**
How were the actions taken by Presidents Ford and Carter to address the country's economic downturn similar? How did they differ?

**5. ANALYZING ISSUES**
Do you agree with President Carter that human rights concerns should steer U.S. foreign policy? Why or why not? **Think About:**
- the responsibility of promoting human rights
- the loss of good relations with certain countries
- the collapse of détente with the Soviet Union

*An Age of Limits* **817**

**1. TERMS & NAMES**
Gerald R. Ford, p. 810
Jimmy Carter, p. 812
National Energy Act, p. 813
human rights, p. 815
Camp David Accords, p. 816
Ayatollah Ruhollah Khomeini, p. 817

**2. TAKING NOTES**
1974: Ford pardons Nixon. 1975: Helsinki Accords signed. 1977: U.S. and Panama sign canal treaties. March 1979: Anwar el-Sadat and Begin sign peace treaty. Nov. 4, 1979: Iranians seize U.S. hostages. Dec. 1979: Soviets invade Afghanistan. 1980: almost 14 percent inflation.

**3. EVALUATING DECISIONS**
Good Decision: Ford needed to prevent the country from enduring a trial and restore confidence in the presidency. Bad Decision: Nixon should be held accountable; he never publicly admitted guilt.

**4. COMPARING**
Both emphasized energy conservation and battled Congress; Ford put more emphasis on voluntary citizen action, whereas Carter emphasized government action.

**5. ANALYZING ISSUES**
Agree: U.S. has a duty to stand up for human rights. Disagree: too strict a policy might alienate allies.

*An Age of Limits* **817**

## HISTORIC DECISIONS OF THE SUPREME COURT

### Objectives

· To understand the significance of the *Bakke* case for affirmative action

· To analyze the legal reasoning the Court used to decide the *Bakke* case

· To describe the historical impact of the *Bakke* case

## Focus & Motivate

**Making Decisions** Have students consider the complexities of equality. Ask them how far they think the government should be willing to go to correct past discrimination and abuses.

### More About . . .

**The Politics of Affirmative Action**
In the late 1990s, opposition to affirmative action solidified in Congress. The Republican-controlled Senate rejected Bill Lann Lee's appointment as assistant Attorney General, because Lee supported affirmative action. Rejection of Lee's appointment demonstrated the political division over the issue.

## HISTORIC DECISIONS OF THE SUPREME COURT

# REGENTS OF THE UNIVERSITY OF CALIFORNIA v. BAKKE (1978)

**ORIGINS OF THE CASE** In 1973, Allan Bakke applied to the University of California at Davis medical school. The school had a quota-based affirmative-action plan that reserved 16 out of 100 spots for racial minorities. Bakke, a white male, was not admitted to the school despite his competitive test scores and grades. Bakke sued for admission, arguing that he had been discriminated against on the basis of race. The California Supreme Court agreed with Bakke, but the school appealed the case.

**THE RULING** The Court ruled that racial quotas were unconstitutional, but that schools could still consider race as a factor in admissions.

### LEGAL REASONING

The Court was closely divided on whether affirmative-action plans were constitutional. Two different sets of justices formed 5-to-4 majorities on two different issues in *Bakke*.

Five justices agreed the quota was unfair to Bakke. They based their argument on the equal protection clause of the Fourteenth Amendment. Justice Lewis Powell, writing for the majority, explained their reasoning.

▲ Allan Bakke receives his degree in medicine from the medical school at U.C. Davis on June 4, 1982.

" The guarantee of equal protection cannot mean one thing when applied to one individual and something else when applied to a person of another color. If both are not accorded the same protection, then it is not equal."

The four justices that joined Powell in this part of the decision said race should *never* play a part in admissions decisions. Powell and the other four justices disagreed. These five justices formed a separate majority, arguing that "the attainment of a diverse student body . . . is a constitutionally permissible goal for an institution of higher education." In other words, schools could have affirmative-action plans that consider race as *one* factor in admission decisions in order to achieve a diverse student body.

### LEGAL SOURCES

#### LEGISLATION

**U.S. CONSTITUTION, FOURTEENTH AMENDMENT (1868)**
"No state shall . . . deprive any person of life, liberty, or property, without due process of law; nor deny to any person within its jurisdiction the equal protection of the laws."

#### RELATED CASES

**UNITED STEELWORKERS OF AMERICA v. WEBER (1979)**
The Court said a business could have a short-term program for training minority workers as a way of fixing the results of past discrimination.

**ADARAND CONSTRUCTORS v. PENA (1995)**
The Court struck a federal law to set aside 10 percent of highway construction funds for minority-owned businesses. The Court also said that affirmative-action programs must be focused to achieve a compelling government interest.

## RECOMMENDED RESOURCES

### BOOKS

Bowen, William and Derek Bok. *The Shape of the River.* Princeton: Princeton UP, 2000. A study of the long-term consequences of considering race in college admissions.

Curry, George and Cornel West eds. *The Affirmative Action Debate.* New York: Perseus Press, 1996.

Ezorsky, Gerturde. *Racism and Justice: The Case for Affirmative Action.* Ithaca: Cornell UP, 1991

Sowell, Thomas. *Civil Rights: Rhetoric or Reality.* New York: William Morrow Press, 1985.

### INTEGRATED TECHNOLOGY

For teacher support and more information about the Supreme Court including the full text of the Supreme Court decisions, visit . . .

 classzone.com

On October 8, 1977, protestors march in support of affirmative action at a park in Oakland, California.

## Instruct

1. Why was affirmative action started?
2. What did the Court say about the constitutionality of affirmative action programs?
3. What rights did the Court grant university admissions programs?

**MAKING PERSONAL CONNECTIONS**

Ask students to consider the various sides of the affirmative action debate. Have students share their own opinions on the issue and explain their reasoning.

### WHY IT MATTERED

Many people have faced discrimination in America. The struggle of African Americans for civil rights in the 1950s and 1960s succeeded in overturning Jim Crow segregation. Even so, social inequality persisted for African Americans, as well as women and other minority groups. In 1965, President Lyndon Johnson explained why more proactive measures needed to be taken to end inequality.

> " You do not take a person who for years has been hobbled by chains and . . . bring him up to the starting line of a race and then say, 'you are free to compete with all the others' and still justly believe that you have been completely fair. "

As a result, Johnson urged companies to begin to take "affirmative action" to hire and promote African Americans, helping them to overcome generations of inequality. Critics quickly opposed affirmative action plans as unfair to white people and merely a replacement of one form of racial discrimination with another.

University admissions policies became a focus of the debate over affirmative action. The Court's ruling in *Bakke* allowed race to be used as one factor in admissions decisions. Schools could consider a prospective student's race, but they could not use quotas or use race as the *only* factor for admission.

### HISTORICAL IMPACT

Since *Bakke,* the Court has ruled on affirmative action several times, usually limiting affirmative-action plans. For example, in *Adarand Constructors* v. *Pena* (1995), the Court struck a federal law to set aside "not less than 10 percent" of highway construction funds for businesses owned by "socially and economically disadvantaged individuals." The Court said that affirmative-action programs must be narrowly focused to achieve a "compelling government interest."

On cases regarding school affirmative-action plans, the Supreme Court has chosen not to act. The Court refused to hear a case challenging a California law banning the consideration of race or gender for admission to the state's universities. Similarly, the Court refused to hear an appeal of a 1996 lower court ruling that outlawed any consideration of race for admission to the University of Texas law school. In December of 2000, however, supporters of affirmative action won a victory in the federal court. A federal judge ruled that a University of Michigan affirmative action plan was constitutional. He noted that *Bakke*—not the Texas case—was the law of the land, and schools still had the right to consider race in admissions decisions.

In recent years, some states have found new ways of helping minority students enter state universities. For instance, California, Florida, and Texas have enacted plans guaranteeing admittance to state universities for top students from each high school graduating class.

### More About . . .

**Affirmative Action and the Supreme Court**

Opponents of affirmative action have continued to push for a reversal of the options granted to university admissions offices under the *Bakke* case. In May 2001, however, the Supreme Court rejected the appeal of three white applicants to the University of Washington Law school, who claimed they had been denied admission because of their race.

---

### THINKING CRITICALLY

**CONNECT TO HISTORY**

1. **Evaluating** Research articles about *Bakke* in the library or on the Internet. Read the articles and write a paragraph for each one explaining the writer's point of view on the case. Conclude by telling which article gives the best discussion of the case. Cite examples to support your choice.

 **SEE SKILLBUILDER HANDBOOK, PAGE R16.**

**CONNECT TO TODAY**

2.  **INTERNET ACTIVITY** CLASSZONE.COM

Visit the links for Historic Decisions of the Supreme Court to research and read about Proposition 209, California's 1996 law banning affirmative action at state universities. Prepare arguments for an in-class debate about whether the law will have a positive or negative long-term effect.

---

### THINKING CRITICALLY: ANSWERS

**1. CONNECT TO HISTORY**

**Rubrics**

Students' paragraphs should . . .

· explain the author's point of view on the case
· summarize the main points of the article
· draw a conclusion about which article offers the best discussion of the *Bakke* case
· support the conclusion with specific examples

**2. CONNECT TO TODAY**

**Rubrics**

Students' arguments should . . .

· be based on their reading of the text and on independent research
· clearly support a point of view about the long-term impact of Proposition 209
· include examples to support students' reasoning

# Environmental Activism

| MAIN IDEA | WHY IT MATTERS NOW | Terms & Names |
|---|---|---|
| During the 1970s, Americans strengthened their efforts to address the nation's environmental problems. | The nation today continues to struggle to balance environmental concerns with industrial growth. | • Rachel Carson  • Earth Day  • environmentalist  • Environmental Protection Agency (EPA)  • Three Mile Island |

**TEKS U.S. History** 6H, 8A, 11A, 11B, 20D, 21D, 22A, 24A, 24B, 24C, 24D, 24F, 25A, 25B, 25D

### One American's Story

In 1972, Lois Gibbs and her family moved to Niagara Falls, New York. Underneath this quiet town, however, was a disaster in the making. In the 1890s, the Love Canal had been built to provide hydroelectric power for the Niagara Falls area. Chemical companies were dumping hazardous waste into the canal. In 1953, bulldozers filled in the canal. Shortly thereafter, a school and rows of homes were built nearby.

In 1977, when Lois Gibbs's son fell sick, she decided to investigate. She eventually uncovered the existence of the toxic waste and mobilized the community to demand government action. In 1980, President Carter authorized funds for many Niagara Falls families to move to safety. Years later, Lois Gibbs wrote a book detailing her efforts.

**A PERSONAL VOICE** LOIS GIBBS

" I want to tell you our story—my story—because I believe that ordinary citizens—using the tools of dignity, self-respect, common sense, and perseverance—can influence solutions to important problems in our society. . . . In solving any difficult problem, you have to be prepared to fight long and hard, sometimes at great personal cost; but it can be done. It must be done if we are to survive . . . at all. "

—*Love Canal: My Story*

**VIDEO**

**POISONED PLAYGROUND** Lois Gibbs and the Crisis at Love Canal

Lois Gibbs's concerns about environmental hazards were shared by many Americans in the 1970s. Through the energy crisis, Americans learned that their natural resources were limited; they could no longer take the environment for granted. Americans—from grassroots organizations to the government—began to focus on conservation of the environment and new forms of energy.

## **1** The Roots of Environmentalism

The widespread realization that pollution and overconsumption were damaging the environment began in the 1960s. One book in particular had awakened

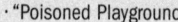

America's concerns about the environment and helped lay the groundwork for the activism of the early seventies.

**RACHEL CARSON AND SILENT SPRING** In 1962, **Rachel Carson**, a marine biologist, published a book entitled *Silent Spring*. In it, she warned against the growing use of pesticides—chemicals used to kill insects and rodents. Carson argued that pesticides poisoned the very food they were intended to protect and as a result killed many birds and fish.

Carson cautioned that America faced a "silent spring," in which birds killed off by pesticides would no longer fill the air with song. She added that of all the weapons used in "man's war against nature," pesticides were some of the most harmful.

### A PERSONAL VOICE RACHEL CARSON

" These sprays, dusts, and aerosols . . . have the power to kill every insect, the 'good' and the 'bad,' to still the song of birds and the leaping of fish in the streams, to coat the leaves with a deadly film, and to linger on in soil—all this though the intended target may be only a few weeds or insects. Can anyone believe it is possible to lay down such a barrage of poisons on the surface of the earth without making it unfit for all life? "

—*Silent Spring*

Within six months of its publication, *Silent Spring* sold nearly half a million copies. Many chemical companies called the book inaccurate and threatened legal action. However, for a majority of Americans, Carson's book was an early warning about the danger that human activity posed to the environment. Shortly after the book's publication, President Kennedy established an advisory committee to investigate the situation.

With Rachel Carson's prodding, the nation slowly began to focus more on environmental issues. Although Carson would not live to see the U.S. government outlaw DDT in 1972, her work helped many Americans realize that their everyday behavior, as well as the nation's industrial growth, had a damaging effect on the environment. **A**

**MAIN IDEA**

**Analyzing Effects**

**A** What effects did Rachel Carson's book have on the nation as a whole?

*A. Answer* It heightened Americans' awareness that many of their activities were potentially harmful to the environment.

## Environmental Concerns in the 1970s ❷

During the 1970s, the administrations of Richard Nixon and Jimmy Carter confronted such environmental issues as conservation, pollution, and the growth of nuclear energy.

**THE FIRST EARTH DAY** The United States ushered in the 1970s—a decade in which it would actively address its environmental issues—fittingly enough with the first **Earth Day** celebration. On that day, April 22, 1970, nearly every community

KEY PLAYER

**RACHEL CARSON**
**1907–1964**

The marine biologist Rachel Carson was born far from the sea, in the small town of Springdale, Pennsylvania.

Carson was a sickly child who often had to remain at home, where her mother tutored her. Throughout her youth and into her college years, Carson was a studious, but quiet and aloof, person.

Carson entered college intent on becoming a writer. During her sophomore year, she took a biology class to fulfill her science requirement and quickly fell in love with the study of nature. By the next year Carson switched her major from English to zoology—the study of animals.

A flag celebrating the first Earth Day in 1970.

## More About . . .

### The Environmental Protection Agency (EPA)

The EPA was created to administer federal environmental legislation. The Clean Air Act (1970) was the agency's first mandate, followed by legislation such as the Federal Environmental Pesticide Control Act and the Clean Water Act. To clean up toxic waste sites, the EPA put forth the Comprehensive Environmental Response, Compensation, and Liability Act. The EPA fostered an agreement with the automobile industry, whereby catalytic converters to reduce hydrocarbon emissions would be installed in cars.

## More About . . .

### Trans-Alaska Pipeline

Environmentalists opposed the construction of the Trans-Alaska pipeline. One fear was that a spill from the pipeline would damage the tundra. In October 2001, bullets were fired into the pipeline causing a leak of 285,000 gallons of oil. The oil was contained in an area of about two acres by a series of dikes. Although there was no evidence that any wildlife was affected, decontamination of the trees, brush, and tundra will take years. Another spill happened in 1978 when about 670,000 gallons were spilled near Fairbanks Alaska.

in the nation and more than 10,000 schools and 2,000 colleges hosted some type of environmental-awareness activity and spotlighted such problems as pollution, the growth of toxic waste, and the earth's dwindling resources. The Earth Day celebration continues today. Each year on April 22, millions of people around the world gather to heighten public awareness of environmental problems.

**THE GOVERNMENT TAKES ACTION** Although President Nixon was not considered an **environmentalist,** or someone who takes an active role in the protection of the environment, he recognized the nation's growing concern about the environment. In an effort to "make our peace with nature," President Nixon set out on a course that led to the passage of several landmark measures. In 1970, he consolidated 15 existing federal pollution programs into the **Environmental Protection Agency (EPA).** The new agency was given the power to set and enforce pollution standards, to conduct environmental research, and to assist state and local governments in pollution control. Today, the EPA remains the federal government's main instrument for dealing with environmental issues.

In 1970 Nixon signed a new Clean Air Act that added several amendments to the Clean Air Act of 1963. The new act gave the government the authority to set air standards. Following the 1970 Clean Air Act, Congress also passed the Endangered Species Act, in addition to laws that limited pesticide use and curbed strip mining—the practice of mining for ore and coal by digging gaping holes in the land. Some 35 environmental laws took effect during the decade, addressing every aspect of conservation and clean-up, from protecting endangered animals to regulating auto emissions. **B**

**BALANCING PROGRESS AND CONSERVATION IN ALASKA** During the 1970s, the federal government took steps to ensure the continued well-being of Alaska, the largest state in the nation and one of its most ecologically sensitive.

The discovery of oil there in 1968, and the subsequent construction of a massive pipeline to transport it, created many new jobs and greatly increased state revenues. However, the influx of new development also raised concerns about Alaska's wildlife, as well as the rights of its native peoples. In 1971, Nixon signed the Alaska Native Claims Settlement Act, which turned over millions of acres of land to the state's native tribes for conservation and tribal use. In 1978, President Carter enhanced this conservation effort by setting aside an additional 56 million acres in Alaska as national monuments. In 1980, Congress added another 104 million acres as protected areas.

**THE DEBATE OVER NUCLEAR ENERGY** As the 1970s came to a close, Americans became acutely aware of the dangers that nuclear power plants posed to both humans and the environment. During the 1970s, as America realized the drawbacks to its heavy dependence on foreign oil for energy, nuclear power seemed to many to be an attractive alternative.

Opponents of nuclear energy warned the public against the industry's growth. They contended that nuclear plants, and the wastes they produced, were potentially dangerous to humans and their environment.

**THREE MILE ISLAND** In the early hours of March 28, 1979, the concerns of nuclear energy opponents were validated. That morning, one of the nuclear reactors at a plant on **Three Mile Island** near Harrisburg, Pennsylvania, malfunctioned. The reactor overheated after its cooling system failed, and fear quickly arose that radiation might escape and spread over the region. Two days later,

The Trans-Alaska Pipeline, stretching across hundreds of miles of tundra, was completed in 1977. ▼

**Vocabulary**
**toxic:** capable of causing injury or death, especially by chemical means; poisonous

**MAIN IDEA**

**Summarizing**
**B** What were the environmental actions taken during the Nixon administration?

**B. Answer** In 1970 Nixon signed a new Clean Air Act. Congress passed the Endangered Species Act, and additional laws limiting pesticide use and curbing strip mining were passed.

---

### Analyzing Assumptions

**Explaining the Skill** People often make decisions based on their assumptions. Examining the context in which decisions are made allows historians to analyze underlying assumptions.

**Applying the Skill** Refer students to the section "The Government Takes Action." Ask them to analyze the assumptions behind the following actions:

· Creation of the Environmental Protection Agency. (Government has a role in protecting the environment.)

· Passage of the Clean Air Act of 1970, Clean Water Act, and Endangered Species Act. (Industries should be held accountable for the pollution they produce.)

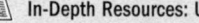 In-Depth Resources: Unit 7
· Skillbuilders Practice: Analyzing Assumptions, p. 6

## Science & *Technology*

### THE ACCIDENT AT THREE MILE ISLAND

A series of human and mechanical errors that caused the partial meltdown of the reactor core brought the Three Mile Island nuclear power plant to the brink of disaster. The accident at Three Mile Island caused widespread concern about nuclear power throughout the American public.

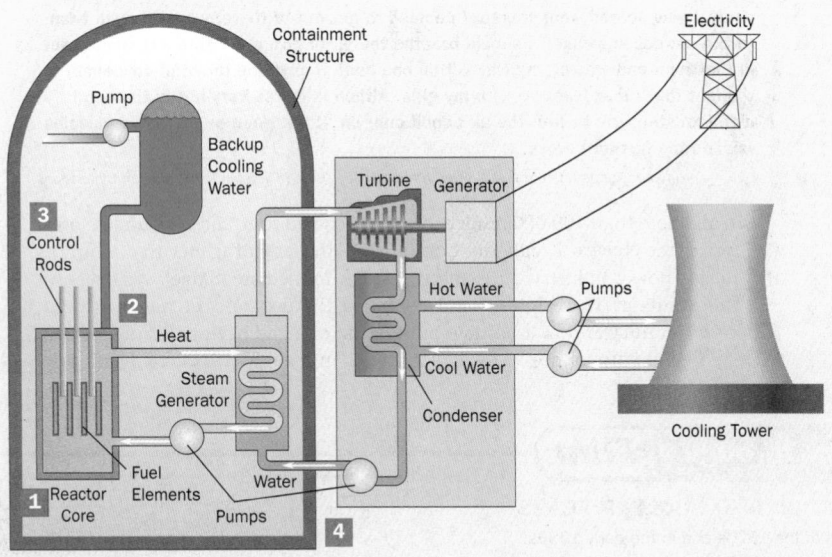

### REACTOR MELTDOWN

1. The radioactive reactor core generates heat as its atoms split during a controlled chain reaction.
2. An inoperative valve releases thousands of gallons of coolant from the reactor core.
3. Half of the 36,816 exposed fuel rods melt in temperatures above five thousand degrees.
4. The melted material burns through the lining of the reactor chamber and spills to the floor of the containment structure.

More than 20 years after the accident, clean-up at Three Mile Island continues. The final 'clean-up bill' could soar to more than $3 billion. The TMI-2 reactor was dangerously contaminated and could not be entered for two years. All the materials in the containment structure, along with anything used in the clean-up, had to be decontaminated. Because the reactor will never be completely free of radioactivity, it will one day be entombed in cement.

### Science & *Technology*

**Nuclear Energy**

A major cause of people's concern about nuclear energy is how to properly dispose of radioactive waste. In 1995, the nation's nuclear power plants continued to store their waste on site. The construction of safe disposal sites has long been in the works. Even with the possible construction of such sites, safe transportation of spent nuclear material remains an issue. Environmentalists are concerned about the likelihood of spills resulting from accidents.

### More About . . .

**Nuclear Accidents**

The world's worst nuclear accident occurred on April 26, 1986, at the Chernobyl nuclear plant in Ukraine, a part of the Soviet Union. An explosion released large amounts of radiation into the air. Soviet officials reported 31 deaths and hundreds of injuries. But the deaths and destructive effects continue to this day, with increased cancer and other illnesses in people of the surrounding area and in continuing levels of radiation on the ground and in the air.

*An Age of Limits* **823**

---

### Nuclear Energy Pro and Con

**Class Time** 45 minutes

**Task** Debating the ongoing use of nuclear energy

**Purpose** To analyze the scientific, environmental, and political issues surrounding the use of nuclear energy

**Directions** Have students work in small groups to research the controversy surrounding the use of nuclear power. Have them pay particular attention to how the power shortage in California in 2001 influenced public opinion about nuclear power. Ask students to take a stand on the issue and prepare arguments. Then hold a class debate.

 **Integrated Assessment**
· Rubrics 1, 3

low-level radiation actually did escape from the crippled reactor. Officials evacuated some residents, while others fled on their own. One homemaker who lived near the plant recalled her desperate attempt to find safety.

**Background**
The U.S. government does not expect to have a permanent burial site for nuclear waste until 2010. A proposed site is beneath the Yucca Mountains in southern Nevada about 100 miles northwest of Las Vegas.

### A PERSONAL VOICE

" On Friday, a very frightening thing occurred in our area. A state policeman went door-to-door telling residents to stay indoors, close all windows, and turn all air conditioners off. I was alone, as were many other homemakers, and my thoughts were focused on how long I would remain a prisoner in my own home. . . . Suddenly, I was scared, real scared. I decided to get out of there, while I could. I ran to the car not knowing if I should breathe the air or not, and I threw the suitcases in the trunk and was on my way within one hour. If anything dreadful happened, I thought that I'd at least be with my girls. Although it was very hot in the car, I didn't trust myself to turn the air conditioner on. It felt good as my tense muscles relaxed the farther I drove. "

—an anonymous homemaker quoted in *Accident at Three Mile Island: The Human Dimensions*

In all, more than 100,000 residents were evacuated from the surrounding area. On April 9, the Nuclear Regulatory Commission, the federal agency that monitors the nuclear power industry, announced that the immediate danger was over.

The events at Three Mile Island rekindled the debate over nuclear power. Supporters of nuclear power pointed out that no one had been killed or seriously injured. Opponents countered by saying that chance alone had averted a tragedy.

---

## History Through *Film*

**Three Mile Island and *The China Syndrome***

The movie *The China Syndrome* got its name from the notion that, in a core meltdown, the entire nuclear power plant would burn through the earth and emerge in China. The film was highly publicized and received much critical acclaim.

**SKILLBUILDER ANSWERS**

1. People can identify with the experiences shown in the movie.
2. They educated people about the dangers of nuclear energy.

---

## History Through *Film*

### HOLLYWOOD AND NUCLEAR FEARS

At the end of the 1970s and in the early 1980s, Hollywood responded to Americans' concerns over nuclear power by making pointed social-awareness films exposing dangers in the nuclear industry. These films alerted the public to the importance of regulations in the relatively new field of atomic energy.

In 1979, *The China Syndrome*, starring Jane Fonda and Jack Lemmon, became the movie everyone was talking about. Only 12 days after the film's release, a serious accident similar to the one portrayed in the movie occurred at the Three Mile Island nuclear power plant. ▶

◀ In 1983, on her way to meet with a reporter from the *New York Times*, Karen Silkwood, a worker at a nuclear power facility, was hit and died in a car crash. In the film dramatization, *Silkwood* (1983), Meryl Streep played Karen, and Kurt Russell and Cher, her co-workers.

**SKILLBUILDER** Interpreting Visual Sources

1. Why do you think movies based on real events are popular with the general public?
2. How do you think these films influenced present-day nuclear energy policy?

 **SEE SKILLBUILDER HANDBOOK, PAGE R23.**

---

**ACTIVITY**  **LINK TO SCIENCE**  classzone.com

## Researching Chernobyl

**Class Time** 45 minutes

**Task** Researching the environmental impact of the Chernobyl nuclear accident

**Purpose** To analyze the effects of the nuclear accident at Chernobyl

**Directions** Have students research the damage caused by the Chernobyl nuclear accident. Students can use the Internet to download pictures of the devastation caused by the accident. Have them compile a visual display of pictures, charts, and reports on the impact of Chernobyl.

 Integrated Assessment
· Rubrics 1, 4

They demanded that the government call a halt to the construction of new power plants and gradually shut down existing nuclear facilities.

While the government did not do away with nuclear power, federal officials did recognize nuclear energy's potential danger to both humans and the environment. As a result of the accident at Three Mile Island, the Nuclear Regulatory Commission strengthened its safety standards and improved its inspection procedures. **C**

## A Continuing Movement ③

Although the environmental movement of the 1970s gained popular support, opponents of the movement also made their voices heard. In Tennessee, for example, where a federal dam project was halted because it threatened a species of fish, local developers took out ads asking residents to "tell the government that the size of your wallet is more important than some two-inch-long minnow." When confronted with environmental concerns, one unemployed steelworker spoke for others when he remarked, "Why worry about the long run, when you're out of work right now."

The environmental movement that blossomed in the 1970s became in the 1980s and 1990s a struggle to balance environmental concerns with jobs and progress. In the years since the first Earth Day, however, environmental issues have gained increasing attention and support.

**HISTORICAL**
**SPOTLIGHT**

**PRIVATE CONSERVATION GROUPS**

As concerns about pollution and the depletion of nonrenewable resources grew, so did membership in private, nonprofit organizations dedicated to the preservation of wilderness and endangered species. Many of these groups lobbied government for protective legislation. Some filed lawsuits to block projects such as road or dam construction or logging that would threaten habitats. The Environmental Defense Fund (today Environmental Defense) brought lawsuits that led to the bans on DDT and on leaded gasoline.

Radical groups also emerged. Members of Greenpeace risked their lives at sea to escort whales and protect them from commercial hunters.

### SECTION 4 — ASSESSMENT

**1. TERMS & NAMES** For each term or name, write a sentence explaining its significance.

- **Rachel Carson**
- **Earth Day**
- **environmentalist**
- **Environmental Protection Agency (EPA)**
- **Three Mile Island**

**MAIN IDEA**

**2. TAKING NOTES**

Re-create the web below on your paper and fill in events that illustrate the main idea in the center.

Concern for the environment grew in the United States.

**CRITICAL THINKING**

**3. ANALYZING CAUSES**

How much should the United States rely on nuclear power as a source of energy? Explain your view.

**Think About:**
- the safety of nuclear power
- the alternatives to nuclear power
- U.S. energy demands

**4. ANALYZING VISUAL SOURCES**

What message does this 1969 poster from the Environmental Protection Agency give about the government's role in pollution?

Clean air is a product of the United States Environmental Protection Agency.

*An Age of Limits* **825**

---

**Answers** ASSESSMENT ④

**1. TERMS & NAMES**

Rachel Carson, p. 821
Earth Day, p. 821
environmentalist, p. 822
Environmental Protection Agency (EPA), p. 822
Three Mile Island, p. 822

**2. TAKING NOTES**

Rachel Carson publishes *Silent Spring, 1962;* in 1970, the first Earth Day is held; Nixon creates the EPA; Three Mile Island accident in 1979 raises concerns about nuclear power. People struggle to balance environmental with economic concerns.

**3. ANALYZING CAUSES**

Supporters may say that nuclear power should be used, since it is cleaner than coal or oil, and is plentiful and cheap. Opponents may say that nuclear power is dangerous, nuclear waste is difficult to contain, and the risks outweigh the benefits.

**4. INTERPRETING VISUAL SOURCES**

The government is responsible for stopping or slowing pollution. The government's role as regulator should be recognized for the resulting clean air and healthy environment.

## TERMS & NAMES

1. Richard M. Nixon, p. 794
2. stagflation, p. 798
3. OPEC, p. 799
4. SALT I Treaty, p. 801
5. Watergate, p. 802
6. Saturday Night Massacre, p. 805
7. Camp David Accords, p. 816
8. Ayatollah Ruhollah Khomeini, p. 817
9. Rachel Carson, p. 821
10. Environmental Protection Agency (EPA), p. 822

## MAIN IDEAS

1. He tried to lessen the federal government's responsibilities through revenue sharing and welfare reform.
2. He tried to raise taxes, cut the budget, raise interest rates, and impose wage-and-price controls.
3. They shredded incriminating evidence, paid off the burglars, lied under oath, and attempted to stall the burglary investigation.
4. Nixon resigned as president, and many people lost faith in the government.
5. Ford helped the nation move beyond Watergate and also negotiated the Helsinki Accords.
6. Carter asked Americans to reduce energy consumption and pushed the National Energy Act through Congress.
7. The publication of Carson's *Silent Spring*, Earth Day celebrations, and the incident at Three Mile Island increased environmental concerns.
8. It caused the government to strengthen its safety standards and to improve inspection procedures of nuclear facilities.

## TERMS & NAMES

For each term or name below, write a sentence explaining its significance to the Nixon, Ford, or Carter administrations.

1. Richard M. Nixon
2. stagflation
3. OPEC (Organization of Petroleum Exporting Countries)
4. SALT I Treaty
5. Watergate
6. Saturday Night Massacre
7. Camp David Accords
8. Ayatollah Ruhollah Khomeini
9. Rachel Carson
10. Environmental Protection Agency (EPA)

## MAIN IDEAS

Use your notes and the information in the chapter to answer the following questions.

### The Nixon Administration (pages 794–801)

1. In what ways did President Nixon attempt to reform the federal government?
2. How did Nixon try to combat stagflation?

### Watergate: Nixon's Downfall (pages 802–807)

3. In what ways did the participants in Watergate attempt to cover up the scandal?
4. What were the results of the Watergate scandal?

### The Ford and Carter Years (pages 810–817)

5. What were Gerald Ford's greatest successes as president?
6. How did President Carter attempt to solve the energy crisis?

### Environmental Activism (pages 820–825)

7. What factors increased Americans' concerns about environmental issues during the 1960s and 1970s?
8. What was the impact of the Three Mile Island incident?

## CRITICAL THINKING

1. **USING YOUR NOTES** In a chart like the one shown, identify one major development for each issue listed that occurred between 1968 and 1980. Indicate whether you think the impact of the development was positive (+) or negative (–).

| Issue | Development | Impact |
|---|---|---|
| Economic conditions | | |
| Democratic government | | |
| Efficient energy use | | |
| Environmental protection | | |

2. **ANALYZING EVENTS** Between 1972 and 1974 Americans were absorbed by the fall of President Nixon in the Watergate scandal. What might Americans have learned about the role of the executive office? Explain.

3. **INTERPRETING GRAPHS** Study the graph on page 813. Describe the changes in unemployment as compared to inflation from 1970 to 1980.

## VISUAL SUMMARY  AN AGE OF LIMITS

| THE NIXON ADMINISTRATION | THE FORD ADMINISTRATION | THE CARTER ADMINISTRATION |
|---|---|---|
| • Revenue sharing<br>• Law-and-order politics<br>• Integration delays<br>• Inflation, recession, and unemployment<br>• Opening to China<br>• Détente with the Soviet Union<br>• Watergate scandal<br>• Nixon resignation | • Unelected president<br>• Nixon pardon<br>• Whip Inflation Now program<br>• Economic recession<br>• Mayagüez incident<br>• Helsinki Accords | • Energy crisis<br>• Worsening inflation<br>• Panama Canal Treaties<br>• Camp David Accords<br>• Nuclear power<br>• Iran hostage crisis |

Special Issue
TIME
THE HEALING BEGINS

## CRITICAL THINKING

1. **Using Your Notes** Economic conditions: high inflation and unemployment rates (-); Democratic government: Watergate scandal (-); Efficient energy use: Carter's energy conservation measures (+); Environmental protection: Clean Air Acts, Endangered Species Act, ban on DDT (+)

2. **Analyzing Events** A president can expand his power without giving any thought to constitutional checks; a president can become corrupt; no one person is above the law.

3. **Interpreting Graphs** Unemployment rose slightly from 1970 to 1980, but inflation more than doubled.

## Standardized Test Practice

**Use the two graphs below and your knowledge of U.S. history to answer question 1.**

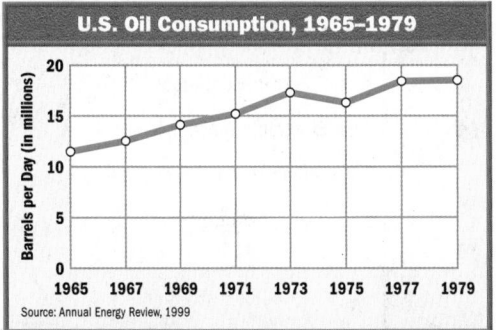

U.S. Oil Consumption, 1965–1979

Source: Annual Energy Review, 1999

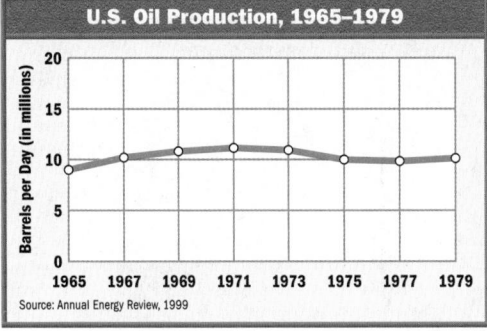

U.S. Oil Production, 1965–1979

Source: Annual Energy Review, 1999

1. The OPEC oil embargo hit the United States so hard in 1973 because —

   **A** domestic oil production slowed and people immediately consumed less.
   **B** domestic oil consumption and production slowed causing an economic slump.
   **C** the United States consumed increasingly more oil while producing less.
   **D** the United States increased oil consumption dramatically that year.

2. How did Watergate affect the presidents who followed after Richard Nixon?

   **F** It caused them to be less trusted and less powerful.
   **G** It made them reluctant to oppose Congress.
   **H** It made them more popular with the media.
   **J** It caused them to rely less on the counsel of cabinet members.

3. Which of the following is a contribution made by Rachel Carson to the American environmental movement?

   **A** Carson researched "cleaner" sources of energy.
   **B** Carson lobbied for the passage of the National Energy Act.
   **C** Carson lobbied for making April 22, 1970 the first Earth Day.
   **D** Carson published a book on the hazards of pesticide use.

**ADDITIONAL TEST PRACTICE, pages S1–S33.**

 **TEST PRACTICE** CLASSZONE.COM

## ALTERNATIVE ASSESSMENT

1. **INTERACT WITH HISTORY** Recall your discussion of the question on page 793:

   *In what ways can a president misuse power?*

   Now that you've learned how your country's highest office holder, President Nixon, lost the nation's trust after the Watergate scandal, would you change your response? Discuss your suggestions with a small group. Then create a list, ranking the misuses from least to most severe.

2. **VIDEO** **LEARNING FROM MEDIA** View the *American Stories* video "Poisoned Playground." Discuss the following questions in a group; then do the activity.

   • How did Lois Gibbs's struggle affect her personal life?
   • What finally prompted the government to evacuate the residents of Love Canal?

   **Cooperative Learning Activity** In a small group, discuss possible environmental problems in each group member's neighborhood, listing them on a sheet of paper. Compare lists with other groups to determine the most common problems. List possible solutions for each problem.

*An Age of Limits* **827**

## Standardized Test Practice

1. The correct answer is letter **D.** Consumption increased while production did not. Letter A is not correct because consumption did not drop. Letter B is not correct because neither consumption or production slowed. Letter C is not correct because oil production was stable.

2. The correct answer is letter **F.** Watergate left Americans with a lack of faith in government. Letter G is not correct because presidents were not reluctant to oppose Congress. Letter H is not correct because it did not make subsequent presidents more popular. Letter J is not correct because presidents still relied on the counsel of their cabinets.

3. The correct answer is letter **D.** Carson's book Silent Spring exposed the dangers of pesticide use. Letter B is not correct because it did not research new sources of energy. Letter C is not correct because Carson was not a lobbyist. Letter C is not correct because Carson was not involved in Earth Day.

**CAMPAIGN SCRAPBOOK**

**Tips for Teaching**

· Tell students to select two or three issues of the campaign to highlight with candidate position papers.
· Help students find Internet links or library resources that contain the position papers of the candidate they selected.

📄 Formal Assessment
· Chapter Test, Forms A, B, and C, pp. 442–453

## ALTERNATIVE ASSESSMENT

### 1. INTERACT WITH HISTORY
**Rubrics**

Students' discussion should . . .
· center on their various opinions about the Watergate scandal
· include opinions supported by details in the text and from independent research
· produce a list ranking the misuses of presidential power

### 2. LEARNING FROM PRIMARY SOURCES
**Rubrics**

Students' lists should . . .
· identify a neighborhood or area with environmental problems
· include specific environmental problems in the area that students believe need to be addressed
· propose to possible solutions or courses of action

# The Conservative Tide

| | CHAPTER OVERVIEW | COPYMASTERS | INTEGRATED TECHNOLOGY |
|---|---|---|---|
| **CHAPTER RESOURCES** | *A growing conservatism brings Ronald Reagan and George Bush to the presidency. Their policies affect the American economy, while other forces transform American society and changes reshape the world.* | 📄 Telescoping the Times<br>· Chapter Summary, pp. 49–50<br><br>📄 Planning for Block Schedules | 👁 Power Presentations<br>💿 Electronic Teacher Tools<br>🕹 Online Lesson Planner<br>🕹 classzone.com |
| **SECTION 1**<br><br>A Conservative Movement Emerges<br><br>pp. 830–833 | **KEY IDEAS**<br>*The new conservatism begins with the defeat of Barry Goldwater in 1964 and triumphs with the election of Ronald Reagan in 1980.* | 📄 In-Depth Resources: Unit 7<br>· Guided Reading, p. 22<br>· Building Vocabulary, p. 26<br>· Reteaching Activity, p. 28<br><br>📄 Lesson Plans, pp. 195–196 | 🕹 classzone.com |
| **SECTION 2**<br><br>Conservative Policies Under Reagan and Bush<br><br>pp. 834–838 | *President Reagan puts in place conservative policies that affect the nation's budget and the federal government.* | 📄 In-Depth Resources: Unit 7<br>· Guided Reading, p. 23<br>· Skillbuilder Practice, p. 27<br>· Reteaching Activity, p. 29<br>· Primary Sources, pp. 36–37<br>· Literature pp. 40–41<br>· American Lives, p. 43<br><br>📄 Lesson Plans, pp. 197–198 | 🔨 Critical Thinking Transparencies CT33, CT67<br>· The Conservative 1980s<br>· Theory of Supply-Side Economics<br><br>👁 Electronic Library of Primary Sources<br>· On the Program for Economic Recovery by Ronald Reagan<br><br>🕹 classzone.com |
| **SECTION 3**<br><br>Social Concerns of the 1980s<br><br>pp. 839–847 | *Social issues of many kinds continue to concern the nation during the conservative backlash.* | 📄 In-Depth Resources: Unit 7<br>· Guided Reading, p. 24<br>· Reteaching Activity, p. 30<br>· Geography Application, pp. 32–33<br>· Primary Sources, p. 38<br>· Literature. p. 42<br><br>📄 Lesson Plans, pp. 199–200 | 👁 Electronic Library of Primary Sources<br>· Why Fear Spanish? by Carlos Montaner<br><br>🕹 classzone.com |
| **SECTION 4**<br><br>Foreign Policy After the Cold War<br><br>pp. 848–855 | *Major changes throughout the world have a great impact on the direction of U.S. foreign policy.* | 📄 In-Depth Resources: Unit 7<br>· Guided Reading, p. 25<br>· Reteaching Activity, p. 31<br>· Outline Map, pp. 34–35<br>· Primary Sources, p. 39<br>· American Lives, p. 44<br><br>📄 Lesson Plans, pp. 201–202 | 🔨 Geography Transparencies CT33<br>· The Cold War Ends, 1989–1990<br><br>🔨 Humanities Transparencies CT47<br>· "Jobs That May Be Lost"<br><br>👁 Electronic Library of Primary Sources<br>· from Setting Limits by Jeane Kirkpatrick<br><br>🕹 classzone.com |

## ASSESSMENT OPTIONS

P E  **Chapter Assessment,** pp. 856–857

**Formal Assessment**
· Chapter Tests, Forms A, B, and C, pp. 458–469

**Test Generator**

**Integrated Assessment Book**

**TAKS Online Test Practice**

**TAKS Spiraled Content Review**

**TAKS Practice Tests**

---

P E  **Section 1 Assessment,** p. 833

T E  **Self-Assessment,** p. 833

**Formal Assessment,** Quiz, p. 454

**Integrated Assessment Book**

**Test Generator**

**TAKS Practice Transparencies TT124**

---

P E  **Section 2 Assessment,** p. 838

T E  **Self-Assessment,** p. 838

**Formal Assessment,** Quiz, p. 455

**Integrated Assessment Book**

**Test Generator**

**TAKS Practice Transparencies TT125**

---

P E  **Section 3 Assessment,** p. 845

T E  **Self-Assessment,** p. 845

**Formal Assessment,** Quiz, p. 456

**Integrated Assessment Book**

**Test Generator**

**TAKS Practice Transparencies TT125**

---

P E  **Section 4 Assessment,** p. 852

T E  **Self-Assessment,** p. 852

**Formal Assessment,** Quiz, p. 457

**Integrated Assessment Book**

**Test Generator**

**TAKS Practice Transparencies TT126**

## RESOURCES FOR DIFFERENTIATING INSTRUCTION

### Students Acquiring English/ESL

**Reading Study Guide**
(English and Spanish)
pp. 247–254

**Access for Students Acquiring English/ESL:**
Spanish Translations, pp. 261–266

**Chapter Summaries on CD**
(English and Spanish)

### Less Proficient Readers

**Reading Study Guide**
(English and Spanish)
pp. 247–254

**Telescoping the Times**
· Chapter Summary, pp. 49–50

**Chapter Summaries on CD**
(English and Spanish)

### Gifted and Talented Students

**In-Depth Resources: Unit 7**
· Primary Sources, pp. 36–39
· Literature, pp. 40–42
· American Lives: Sandra Day O'Connor, p. 43; Daniel Inouye, p. 44

**Electronic Library of Primary Sources**
· Unit 7, Chapter 25

##  CROSS-CURRICULAR CONNECTIONS

### Culture
Fernandez-Shaw, Carlos M. *The Hispanic Presence in North America from 1492 to Today.* NY: Facts on File, 1991. A valuable reference tool includes a general historical overview and a state-by-state study.

### Economics
O'Toole, Thomas. *Global Economics.* Minneapolis: Lerner, 1991. Emphasizes the contrasts between overdeveloped and underdeveloped countries.

### Humanities: Music
McCoy, Judy. *Rap Music in the 1980s.* Lanham, MD: Scarecrow Press, 1992. A comprehensive bibliography of articles, news items, and reviews that were published about rap music in the 1980s.

### Literature
Russo, Richard. *Nobody's Fool.* NY: Vintage, 1994. In this quietly funny and moving novel, Russo follows the lives of quirky, flawed, and yet likable characters in a deadbeat, upstate New York town.

Wolfe, Tom. *The Bonfire of the Vanities.* NY: Bantam, 1990. We see New York City from the perspective of Wall Street wizards, lawyers, mayors, civil rights leaders, journalists, and anyone who gets in between.

Lutzeier, Elizabeth. *The Wall.* NY: Holiday House, 1992. Two teenage girls come together as friends in East Germany and become involved in the turbulent events just before the fall of the Berlin Wall.

## ENRICHMENT ACTIVITIES

P E  **Pupil's Edition,** pp. 828–855
Interact with History, pp. 828–829
Geography Spotlight, pp. 846–847
Point/Counterpoint, p. 853

**In-Depth Resources: Unit 7**
· Geography Application: Latino Population in the 1980s, pp. 32–33
· Outline Map: U.S. Attention on the Middle East, pp. 34–35
· Primary Source: Political Cartoon, p. 36
· Primary Source: Reagan's Farewell Address, p. 37

· Primary Source: Civil Rights in the 1980s, p. 38
· Primary Source: The First Day of Desert Storm, p. 39
· Literature: from *The Bonfire of the Vanities,* pp. 40–41
· Literature: from "Salvador Late or Early," p. 42
· American Lives: Sandra Day O'Connor, p. 43
· American Lives: Daniel Inouye, p. 44

**Electronic Library of Primary Sources**
· Unit 7, Chapter 25

## BLOCK SCHEDULE LESSON PLAN OPTIONS (90-MINUTE PERIOD)

### DAY 1

**CHAPTER OPENER**
pp. 828–829

**Class Time** 25 minutes

**History from Visuals, p. 828**

**Class Time** 10 minutes

*Options for Pacing and Variety*

· Time Saver Have students read the time line on page 828 for an overview of the significant events of the time. **Class Time** 5 minutes

**Interact with History, p. 829**

**Class Time** 15 minutes

*Options for Pacing and Variety*

· Role-Playing Have students imagine they are running for office in the political atmosphere of the 1980s. Discuss which aspects of their beliefs and personalities they would want to be displayed in campaign material.
**Class Time** 15 minutes

**SECTION 1, pp. 830–833**

**Class Time** 30 minutes

*Options for Pacing and Variety*

· Peer Teaching Have students work in pairs to define the terms in the TE activity on page 831.
**Class Time** 10 minutes

· Time Saver Have students read the chart on page 831. Have them write an example of how each goal was reflected in policy choices and government actions.
**Class Time** 10 minutes

### DAY 1 continued

· Peer Evaluation Have students work on their own to answer the Section Assessment questions. Then ask them to trade papers with another student to compare answers. **Class Time** 20 minutes

**SECTION 2, pp. 834–838**

**Class Time** 35 minutes

*Options for Pacing and Variety*

· Time Saver Ask students to read the sidebar on the trickle-down theory on page 835. Read them the additional information in the TE and ask them whether they think the theory had a factual basis or if it was a rationalization. If they believe it was a rationalization, ask them to think of reasons why governments might want to give more money to the wealthy.
**Class Time** 20 minutes

· Peer Teaching Pair less proficient readers with more proficient ones to make a chart of the effects of Reaganomics. Use the model in the TE activity on page 835.
**Class Time** 20 minutes

· Peer Teaching Have students work in small groups to research Supreme Court cases and rulings made by Supreme Court appointees of Reagan and George H. W. Bush. Refer to the activity on TE page 836. **Class Time** 45 minutes

### DAY 2

**SECTION 3, pp. 839–847**

**Class Time** 30 minutes

*Options for Pacing and Variety*

· Peer Teaching Have students work in groups to research school issues and to develop a plan of action for a particular issue. Refer to the TE activity on page 841.
**Class Time** 30 minutes

· Internet Ask students to review the chart detailing men's and women's average yearly earnings for a variety of careers on page 842. Using the Internet or the library, have students research some of these statistics for the year 2000. Have them use the source cited in the chart to get started. **Class Time** 30 minutes

· Time Saver Have students read "Geography Spotlight: Sunbelt, Rustbelt, Ecotopia" on pages 846–847. As a class, discuss Thinking Critically item 1.
**Class Time** 15 minutes

**SECTION 4, pp. 848–855**

**Class Time** 30 minutes

*Options for Pacing and Variety*

· Peer Teaching Divide the class into four groups and assign each group a region to research. Have each group create a foreign-affairs time line for their region. Refer to the TE activity on page 849.
**Class Time** 30 minutes

### DAY 2 continued

· Time Saver Ask students to look at the map on page 851 and discuss the Skillbuilder questions. Then ask them the additional questions in the TE. **Class Time** 10 minutes

· Peer Teaching Have students read Point/Counterpoint on page 853 and discuss question 1. Then have students work in groups to answer question 2. **Class Time** 20 minutes

**ASSESSMENT**
pp. 856–857

**Class Time** 30 minutes

*Options for Pacing and Variety*

· Time Saver Ask students to read the visual summary on page 856 and suggest a further effect on government or society for each item listed under "Effects."
**Class Time** 10 minutes

· Peer Evaluation Ask students to work in groups to complete Thinking Critically questions 2 and 3. As a class, discuss the answers, evaluating each group's responses.
**Class Time** 20 minutes

---

**TEACHER-TESTED ACTIVITY**
**DISCUSSION OF REAGANOMICS**

**ACTIVITY Craig T. Grace, Lanier High School, West Austin, Texas**

**Class Time** 45 minutes

**Task** Analyzing Reagan's economic policies

**Purpose** To understand the economic and social consequences of tax cuts and military spending

**Supplies Needed**
· Internet or library resources

**Activity** Organize students into four groups. One group should consider reasons for reducing taxes and another group the reasons against. A third group should consider the pros of increased military spending and a fourth group the cons. Students should use the Internet or library to research their positions. Have one student from each group summarize the group's findings. Then have students discuss the effects of implementing both a tax cut and an increase in military spending at the same time.

# CHAPTER 25 CORRELATION

## CORRELATION TO THE TEXAS ESSENTIAL KNOWLEDGE AND SKILLS

Chapter 25 addresses the following standards of the Texas Essential Knowledge and Skills for U.S. History.

| TEKS | Instruction | Student Question/Activity |
|---|---|---|
| **(6G)** Analyze reasons for the Western victory in the Cold War and the challenge of changing relationships among nations. | **PE 848–852** examination of U.S. foreign policy after the Cold War and the reason for the collapse of the Soviet Union | **PE 855** Critical Thinking questions on the end of the Cold War and changes in U.S. foreign policy |
| **(6H)** Identify the origins of major domestic and foreign policy issues currently facing the United States. | **PE 839-841; 852–855** discussion of domestic issues such as health, education, and cities, as well as foreign issues such as turmoil in the Middle East, that still occupy the nation | **PE 845** Critical Thinking questions about various social concerns of the 1980s |
| **(8B)** Pose and answer questions about geographic distribution patterns shown on maps, graphs, charts, models, and databases. | **PE 846–947** Geographic Spotlight feature on the population shift to the western, southern, and southwestern regions of the country | **PE 847** Critical Thinking questions about the feature |
| **(14C)** Describe the impact of the Cold War on the business cycle and defense spending. | **PE 835** examination of the increased defense spending during the Reagan administration | **TE 835** activity in which students create a chart and summarize Reagan's economic policies, including defense spending |
| **(19B)** Evaluate the contributions of significant political and social leaders in the United States. | **PE 834–838** discussion of Ronald Reagan's leadership during the 1980s. | **PE 838** Critical Thinking questions about various aspects of Reagan's presidency |
| **(21A)** Explain actions taken by people from racial, ethnic, and religious groups to expand economic opportunities and political rights in American society. | **PE 843–845** analysis of the 1980s struggle by minorities to gain greater rights and opportunities | **TE 844** activity examining the growth rate and distribution pattern of the nation's minority groups |
| **(21D)** Identify the political, social, and economic contributions of women to American society. | **PE 842–843** examination of women's continuing efforts to make economic and social gains | **PE 842** Skillbuilder questions on chart about pay inequities for men and women |

## TAKS MINI-LESSONS

1. **Social Studies Skills: Objective 1 (US1.A):** Identify the major eras of U.S. history from 1877 to the present and describe their defining characteristics **Activity** Have students summarize the key goals of the conservative movement and how its leaders sought to achieve those goals.

2. **Social Studies Skills: Objective 2 (US10.A):** Analyze the effects of changing demographic patterns resulting from migration within the United States **Activity** Have students answer the questions regarding the Geography Spotlight feature on pages 846–847.

3. **Social Studies Skills: Objective 5 (WH26.C):** Interpret visuals, including graphs, charts, time lines, and maps **Activity** Have students answer the Geography Skillbuilder questions about the map of the Persian Gulf War on page 854.

4. **English Language Arts Skills: Objective 3 (12.B):** Evaluate the credibility of information sources, including how a writer's motivation may affect that credibility **Activity** Have students discuss what opinions are being expressed in the Personal Voice on page 832 and how the opinions affect the speaker's credibility.

5. **English Language Arts Skills: Objective 6 (2.C):** Proofread writing for appropriateness of organization, content, style, and conventions **Activity** Have pairs of students proofread each other's answers to the Critical Thinking question in the Section 2 on page 838.

# CHAPTER 25

# THE CONSERVATIVE TIDE

Ronald Reagan addresses the 1980 Republican Convention.

**1980** Ronald Reagan is elected president.

**1981** Sandra Day O'Connor becomes the first woman appointed to the Supreme Court.

**1982** Equal Rights Amendment fails to win ratification.

**1984** President Reagan is reelected.

USA
WORLD

**1980**   **1982**   **1984**

**1980** Zimbabwe claims independence.

**1982** Great Britain and Argentina go to war over the Falkland Islands.

**1984** South African Bishop Desmond Tutu receives the Nobel Peace Prize.

## THEMES IN CHAPTER 25

### WOMEN AND POLITICAL POWER

The Supreme Court was at the center of two events affecting women: the appointment of the first female justice, Sandra Day O'Connor, to the Supreme Court and a hearing on charges of alleged sexual harassment committed by a court nominee.

See Teacher's Edition Note, p. 836.

### CIVIL RIGHTS

A number of groups (African Americans, Latinos, Native Americans, Asian Americans, women, and gays and lesbians) struggled to achieve equal rights in the 1980s during the Reagan and Bush administrations.

See Teacher's Edition Note, p. 844.

### DIVERSITY AND NATIONAL IDENTITY

President Reagan set the upholding of traditional values as a major goal. But whose values are the traditional values? Some values indeed may be common to many of the diverse cultures found in this country. Other values vary by gender and ethnicity.

See Teacher's Edition Note, p. 845.

# INTERACT
## WITH HISTORY

It is the autumn of 1980. You are a campaign manager for Republican presidential candidate, Ronald Reagan, former film star and past governor of California. Reagan must defeat President Jimmy Carter, who has lost support. Carter has failed to bring home the hostages in Iran and to revive the economy. Reagan, an optimist, pledges to do both. He also plans to cut taxes and cut back on government programs.

## What campaign slogan will you create?

### Examine the Issues

- What qualities in your candidate will win support?
- What issues are important?
- How can you present Reagan as a winner?

**RESEARCH LINKS** CLASSZONE.COM

Visit the Chapter 25 links for more information about The Conservative Tide.

# INTERACT
## WITH HISTORY

### Objectives

· To analyze a political campaign slogan
· To identify key campaign issues and candidates' strengths and weaknesses

### Examine the Issues

1. Discuss with students how to analyze a candidate's strengths.
2. Ask students to describe how they would identify issues that are important to voters.
3. Ask students how far a campaign should go to present the opposition in a negative light.

**1986** Iran arms deal is revealed.

**1987** President Reagan and Soviet leader Mikhail Gorbachev sign the Intermediate-Range Nuclear Forces Treaty.

**1988** George Bush is elected president.

**1988** Reverend Jesse Jackson runs for the Democratic presidential nomination.

**1991** Persian Gulf War breaks out.

**1985** The Soviet Union suffers a disastrous accident at the Chernobyl nuclear power plant.

**1989** The Chinese government kills student protesters in Tiananmen Square.

**1989** Germans dismantle the Berlin Wall.

**1991** Soviet Union breaks apart.

1986    1988    1990

*The Conservative Tide*  **829**

---

## RECOMMENDED RESOURCES

### BOOKS FOR THE TEACHER

Ash, Timothy. *The Magic Lantern.* New York: Vintage, 1993. End of Cold War.

Cannon, Lou. *Ronald Reagan.* New York: Public Affairs, LLC, 2001. Reagan's presidency.

Smith, Hedrick. *The Power Game.* New York: Ballantine, 1996. Inner workings of Washington.

### BOOKS FOR THE STUDENT

Peirce, Neil R., and Jerry Hagstrom. *The Book of America: Inside Fifty States Today.* New York: Warner Books, 1984. Life in the 1980s.

Terkel, Studs. *The Great Divide.* New York: Avon, 1989. Oral history of the American Dream as seen in 1980s.

### VIDEOS

*America in Search of Itself.* AIMS Multimedia, 800-367-2467. Reagan wins presidency.

*Colin Powell: A Soldier's Campaign.* A&E Home Video, 1998. Biography.

*One Thousand Days of the Reagan Presidency.* MPI Home Video, 1983. 800-777-2223.

### SOFTWARE

*Desert Storm: The War in the Persian Gulf.* CD-ROM. Time Warner Interactive, 800-482-3766.

### INTEGRATED TECHNOLOGY

For teacher support, visit . . .

 classzone.com

# A Conservative Movement Emerges

| MAIN IDEA | WHY IT MATTERS NOW | Terms & Names |
|---|---|---|
| Conservatism reached a high point with the election in 1980 of President Ronald Reagan and Vice-President George Bush. | In the early 21st century, conservative views strongly influenced both major political parties. | • entitlement program  • conservative coalition<br>• New Right  • Moral Majority<br>• affirmative action  • Ronald Reagan<br>• reverse discrimination |

 **U.S. History 8A,** 18C, 19A, 19B, 24B, 24C, 24H, 25A, 25B, 25C, 25D

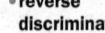 **One American's Story**

Peggy Noonan grew up with a strong sense of social and political justice. As a child, she idolized the liberal Kennedys; as a teenager, she devoured articles on social and political issues. After college, Noonan went to work for CBS.

Over the years, Noonan's political views became increasingly conservative. She eventually won a job as a speechwriter for Ronald Reagan, whose commitment to his conservative values moved her deeply. Noonan recalled that her response to Reagan was not unusual.

**A PERSONAL VOICE** PEGGY NOONAN

" The young people who came to Washington for the Reagan revolution came to make things better. . . . They looked at where freedom was and . . . where freedom wasn't and what that did, and they wanted to help the guerrilla fighters who were trying to overthrow the Communist regimes that had been imposed on them. . . . The thing the young conservatives were always talking about, . . . was freedom, freedom:

*we'll free up more of your money,*
*we'll free up more of the world,*
*freedom freedom freedom—*

It was the drumbeat that held a disparate group together, the rhythm that kept a fractious, not-made-in-heaven alliance in one piece. "

—*What I Saw at the Revolution*

Peggy Noonan

Like millions of other Reagan supporters, Noonan agreed with the slogan that was the heart of Reagan's political creed: "Government is not the solution to our problem. Government is the problem."

## **1** The Conservative Movement Builds

Ever since Senator Barry Goldwater of Arizona had run for president in 1964, conservatives had argued that state governments, businesses, and individuals needed freedom from the heavy hand of Washington, D.C. In 1980, one out of every

three households in America was receiving benefits from government programs. Many Americans resented the cost of these federal **entitlement programs**— programs that guaranteed and provided benefits to particular groups.

In addition, some people had become frustrated with the government's civil rights policies. Congress had passed the Civil Rights Act of 1964 in an effort to eliminate racial discrimination. Over the years, however, judicial decisions and government regulations had broadened the reach of the act. A growing number of Americans viewed with skepticism what had begun as a movement toward equal opportunity. Although many people had rejected separate schools for blacks and whites as unfair and unequal, few wanted to bus their children long distances to achieve a fixed ratio of black and white students.

**THE NEW RIGHT** As the 1970s progressed, right-wing grass-roots groups across the country emerged to support and promote single issues that reflected their key interests. These people became known as the **New Right.** The New Right focused its energy on controversial social issues, such as opposing abortion, blocking the Equal Rights Amendment, and evading court-ordered busing. It also called for a return to school prayer, which had been outlawed by the Supreme Court in 1962.

Many in the New Right criticized the policy of **affirmative action.** Affirmative action required employers and educational institutions to give special consideration to women, African Americans, and other minority groups, even though these people were not necessarily better qualified. Many conservatives saw affirmative action as a form of **reverse discrimination,** favoring one group over another on the basis of race or gender. To members of the New Right, liberal positions on affirmative action and other issues represented an assault on traditional values. **A**

**THE CONSERVATIVE COALITION** Beginning in the mid-1960s, the conservative movement in the United States grew in strength. Eventually conservative groups formed the **conservative coalition**—an alliance of business leaders, middle-class voters, disaffected Democrats, and fundamentalist Christian groups.

Conservative intellectuals argued the cause of the conservative coalition in newspapers such as *The Wall Street Journal* and magazines such as the *National Review,* founded in 1955 by conservative William F. Buckley, Jr. Conservative think tanks, such as the American Enterprise Institute and The Heritage Foundation, were founded to develop conservative policies and principles that would appeal to the majority of voters.

**THE MORAL MAJORITY** Religion, especially evangelical Christianity, played a key role in the growing strength of the conservative coalition. The 1970s had brought a huge religious revival, especially among fundamentalist sects. Each week, millions of Americans watched evangelist preachers on television or listened to them on the radio. Two of the most influential televangelists were Jerry Falwell and Pat Robertson. Falwell formed an organization called the **Moral Majority.** The Moral Majority consisted mostly of evangelical and fundamentalist Christians who interpreted

▲ Several high school students in New York hold a prayer meeting in 1973.

**TAKS**

**Mini-Lesson 1:** SS11 1(US1.A)

---

**MAIN IDEA**

**Analyzing Issues**
**A** What was the agenda of the New Right?

*A. Answer*
The New Right focused its agenda on controversial social issues, such as opposing abortion and blocking the Equal Rights Amendment.

---

**More About . . .**

**Peggy Noonan**
Noonan wrote some of Reagan's, and later George Bush's, most memorable speeches. She went on to a career as a political commentator for *The Wall Street Journal*. After the *Challenger* disaster, she wrote, "We will never forget them, nor the last time we saw them—this morning, as they prepared for their journey, and waved good-bye, and 'slipped the surly bonds of earth' to 'touch the face of God.'" For Bush, she originated the campaign slogans: "read my lips, no new taxes" and "a thousand points of light."

**More About . . .**

**Liberals v. Conservatives**
From 1932 to 1976, Democrats won 8 of the 12 presidential elections. The two Republican presidents, Eisenhower and Nixon, had democratic Congresses that prevented them from asserting a conservative agenda. By 1980, the conservative coalition had gained enough support to not only elect Reagan, but also to change the political direction of the nation.

---

**Goals of the Conservative Movement**

- Shrink the size of the federal government and reduce spending
- Promote family values and patriotic ideals
- Stimulate business by reducing government regulations and lowering taxes
- Strengthen the national defense

*The Conservative Tide* **831**

---

**DIFFERENTIATING INSTRUCTION**    **LESS PROFICIENT READERS**

**Clarifying Conservatism**

To understand the concept of conservatism, students might begin by studying some key terms. Ask students to define each of the following terms and suggest an example:

· **big government**—*Government that is involved in many aspects of public life. Example: desegregation of public schools by government order*
· **entitlements**—*Government programs that guaranteed and provided benefits to certain groups. Example: Social Security*

· **affirmative action**—*A government program requiring employers and educational institutions to give special consideration to women, African Americans, and other minority groups. Examples: quotas for hiring African Americans and women*
· **special-interest group**—*A group that supports a particular issue or cause and is committed to influencing public opinion and government policy. Examples: The National Rifle Association; Mothers Against Drunk Driving*

## Instruct: Objective ❷

**Conservatives Win Political Power**

TAKS SS11 5(WH26.C)

· Who were Ronald Reagan and George Bush?

· What was Reagan's appeal to voters?

· How did a Republican Senate help Republicans change the legislative agenda?

📖 In-Depth Resources: Unit 7
· Guided Reading, p. 22

### KEY PLAYER

**Ronald Reagan**

Reagan was a staunch conservative. During his two terms as Governor of California, he clashed with left-wing radicals and liberal Democrats. Reagan campaigned vigorously for the presidential nomination in 1976. The Republican Party, however, was shaken by the Watergate scandal and was not prepared to discard a sitting president. As a result, Reagan lost the nomination to Gerald Ford. Ask students how Reagan's former career as an actor might have helped and hurt his political campaign. *(helped—communicate clearly with voters; make the public feel that he understood them; hurt—insincere; only an act; not qualified for the presidency)*

---

the Bible literally and believed in absolute standards of right and wrong. They condemned liberal attitudes and behaviors and argued for a restoration of traditional moral values. They worked toward their political goals by using direct-mail campaigns and by raising money to support candidates. Jerry Falwell became the spokesperson for the Moral Majority. **B**

**A PERSONAL VOICE** REVEREND JERRY FALWELL

❝ Our nation's internal problems are the direct result of her spiritual condition. . . . Right living must be reestablished as an American way of life. . . . Now is the time to begin calling America back to God, back to the Bible, back to morality. ❞

As individual conservative groups formed networks, they created a movement dedicated to bringing back what they saw as traditional "family values." They hoped their ideas would help to reduce the nation's high divorce rate, lower the number of out-of-wedlock births, encourage individual responsibility, and generally revive bygone prosperity and patriotic times.

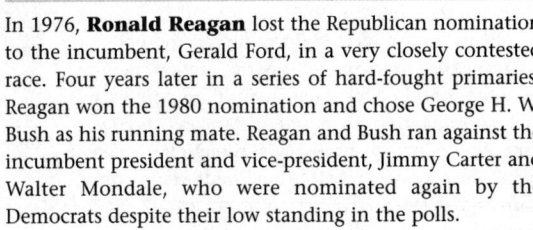

**KEY PLAYER**

**RONALD REAGAN**
**1911–**

Ronald Wilson Reagan was born in 1911 in Tampico, Illinois. He grew up in Dixon, Illinois, graduated from nearby Eureka College, and then worked as a sports announcer in Iowa. In 1937, Reagan moved to Hollywood and became a movie actor, eventually making 53 films. As president of the Screen Actors Guild, he worked actively to remove alleged Communist influences from the movie industry.

Reagan had the ability to express his ideas in simple and clear language that the average voter could understand. When he proposed a 10 percent cut in government spending on social programs, he stated, "We can lecture our children about extravagance until we run out of voice and breath. Or we can cure their extravagance by simply reducing their allowance."

## Conservatives Win ❷ Political Power

In 1976, **Ronald Reagan** lost the Republican nomination to the incumbent, Gerald Ford, in a very closely contested race. Four years later in a series of hard-fought primaries, Reagan won the 1980 nomination and chose George H. W. Bush as his running mate. Reagan and Bush ran against the incumbent president and vice-president, Jimmy Carter and Walter Mondale, who were nominated again by the Democrats despite their low standing in the polls.

**REAGAN'S QUALIFICATIONS** Originally a New Deal Democrat, Ronald Reagan had become a conservative Republican during the 1950s. He claimed that he had not left the Democratic Party but rather that the party had left him. As a spokesman for General Electric, he toured the country making speeches in favor of free enterprise and against big government. In 1964, he campaigned hard for Barry Goldwater, the Republican candidate for president. His speech nominating Goldwater at the 1964 Republican convention made Reagan a serious candidate for public office. In 1966, Reagan was elected governor of California, and in 1970, he was reelected.

**THE 1980 PRESIDENTIAL ELECTION** In 1980, Reagan ran on a number of key issues. Supreme Court decisions on abortion, pornography, the teaching of evolution, and prayer in public schools all concerned conservative voters, and they rallied to Reagan. The prolonged Iranian hostage crisis and the weak economy under Carter, particularly the high rate of inflation, also helped Reagan.

Thanks in part to his acting career and his long experience in the public eye, Reagan was an extremely effective candidate. In contrast to Carter, who often seemed stiff and nervous, Reagan was relaxed, charming, and affable. He loved making quips: "Recession is when your neighbor loses his job. Depression is when you lose yours. And recovery is

**MAIN IDEA**

Summarizing
**B** What were the main concerns of the Moral Majority?

*B. Answer*
To restore traditional family values, reduce the divorce rate, reduce the number of unmarried couples, and increase individual responsibility.

**Background**
See *free enterprise* on page R41 in the Economics Handbook.

---

**ACTIVITY** | **LINK TO POLITICAL SCIENCE**

**B** **BLOCK SCHEDULING**

### Tracing Shifts to and from Conservatism

**Class Time** 45 minutes

**Task** Creating an annotated time line focusing on the rise and fall of conservatism during the 1920s–1980s

**Purpose** To trace the shifts to and from conservatism during the 20th century

**Directions** Have students work in small groups and use text and library resources to review each decade from the 1920s to the 1980s. Ask students to examine such issues as federal spending, business regulation, taxes, national defense spending, and family values. As a class, create a time line and have students fill in the specifics from their research. Discuss the changing role of conservatism throughout the decades.

when Jimmy Carter loses his." Reagan's long-standing skill at simplifying issues and presenting clear-cut answers led his supporters to call him the Great Communicator. Also, his commitment to military and economic strength appealed to many Americans.

Only 52.6 percent of American voters went to the polls in 1980. Reagan won the election by a narrow majority; he got 44 million votes, or 51 percent of the total. His support, however, was spread throughout the country, so that he carried 44 states and won 489 electoral votes. Republicans also gained control of the Senate for the first time since 1954. As Reagan assumed the presidency, many people were buoyed by his genial smile and his assertion that it was "morning again in America." **C**

Now, conservatives had elected one of their own—a true believer in less government, lower taxes, and traditional values. Once elected, Reagan worked to translate the conservative agenda into public policy.

**MAIN IDEA**

**Analyzing Causes**
**C** What factors led to Reagan's victory in 1980?

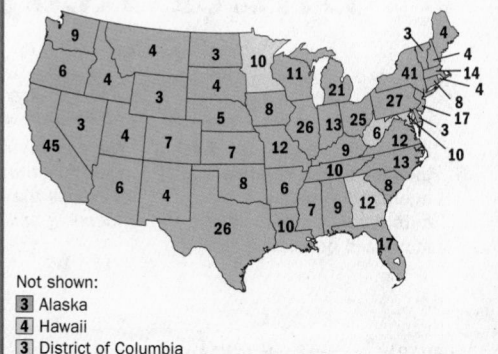

**Presidential Election of 1980**

| Party | Candidate | Electoral Votes | Popular Votes |
|-------|-----------|-----------------|---------------|
| Republican | Ronald Reagan | 489 | 43,904,153 |
| Democratic | Jimmy Carter | 49 | 35,483,883 |
| Independent | John Anderson | | 5,720,060 |

Not shown:
3 Alaska
4 Hawaii
3 District of Columbia

**GEOGRAPHY SKILLBUILDER**
1. **Location** Which states and/or district voted for Jimmy Carter in 1980?
2. **Region** Which region of the country—North, South, East, or West—voted exclusively for Ronald Reagan?

**HISTORY from VISUALS**

**ELECTION OF 1980**
**Interpreting the Map**
Point out to students that all of the green colored states voted for Ronald Reagan. The yellow states went to Jimmy Carter. Ask students what the numbers on each state represent. *(the number of electoral votes for that state)*

## Assess & Reteach

**SECTION 1 ASSESSMENT**
Have students work on their own to answer the Section Assessment questions. Then ask them to trade papers with another student to compare answers.

📝 Formal Assessment
· Section Quiz, p. 454

**SELF-ASSESSMENT**
Ask students to reread the text and review the answers to the Section Assessment questions.

**RETEACH**
Use the Guided Reading worksheet for this section to review the main ideas.

📝 In-Depth Resources: Unit 7
· Reteaching Activity, p. 28

---

## SECTION 1 ASSESSMENT

1. **TERMS & NAMES** For each term or name below, write a sentence explaining its significance.
   - **entitlement program**
   - **New Right**
   - **affirmative action**
   - **reverse discrimination**
   - **conservative coalition**
   - **Moral Majority**
   - **Ronald Reagan**

**MAIN IDEA**

2. **TAKING NOTES**
Use a cluster diagram to record the issues that conservatives strongly endorsed.

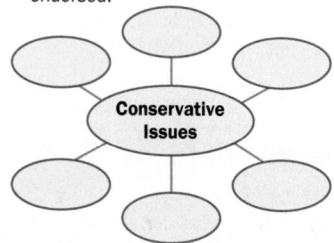

Conservative Issues

Choose one issue and explain in a paragraph the conservative position on that issue.

**CRITICAL THINKING**

3. **ANALYZING MOTIVES**
How did the leaders of the conservative movement of the 1980s want to change government?
**Think About:**
- the difference between the conservative view of government and the liberal view
- the groups that made up the conservative coalition
- conservatives' attitudes toward existing government programs

4. **ANALYZING EFFECTS**
What role did the Moral Majority play in the conservative movement of the 1970s and early 1980s?

5. **EVALUATING LEADERSHIP**
What personal qualities in Ronald Reagan helped him to win election as president in 1980?

---

Answers **ASSESSMENT**

**1. TERMS & NAMES**
entitlement program, p. 831
New Right, p. 831
affirmative action, p. 831
reverse discrimination, p. 831
conservative coalition, p. 831
Moral Majority, p. 831
Ronald Reagan, p. 832

**2. TAKING NOTES**
Conservative issues—reduce entitlement programs; end affirmative action; reduce the size of the federal government; end busing; stop the regulation of guns; eliminate legal abortions; defeat the ERA; prayer in school

**3. ANALYZING MOTIVES**
Conservatives wanted to reduce the size of federal government; lower taxes; end gun control, affirmative action, and busing; increase defense spending; and promote traditional family values.

**4. ANALYZING EFFECTS**
The Moral Majority represented a religious revival that stressed a literal interpretation of the Bible and argued for restoration of traditional values.

**5. EVALUATING LEADERSHIP**
Reagan, known as the Great Communicator, had the ability to simplify issues and offer clear-cut answers.

## OBJECTIVES

1 Summarize Reagan's economic programs.

2 Describe the changes that occurred in the makeup and decisions of the Supreme Court.

3 Identify results of deregulation of the savings and loan industry and of cutting the budget of the Environmental Protection Agency.

4 Analyze the presidential elections of 1984 and 1988.

### SKILLBUILDER

· Analyzing Political Cartoons, p. 836

### CRITICAL THINKING

· Summarizing, p. 835
· Analyzing Effects, p. 836
· Analyzing Causes, p. 838
· Analyzing Motives, p. 838
· Evaluating, p. 838
· Analyzing Primary Sources, p. 838

## Focus & Motivate

Ask students to consider a time when they felt that someone else had control over their lives (parents, teachers, friends). Was the perception a valid one? How did they handle the situation?

## Instruct

### Instruct: Objective 1

**"Reaganomics" Takes Over**
TAKS SS11 5(US24.B)

· What were Reagan's beliefs about government?

· What did Reagan hope to accomplish by cutting taxes?

· What was the result of the Reagan tax cut?

In-Depth Resources: Unit 7
· Guided Reading, p. 23

Electronic Library of Primary Sources
· On the Program for Economic Recovery, 1981, by R. Reagan

# Conservative Policies Under Reagan and Bush

| MAIN IDEA | WHY IT MATTERS NOW | Terms & Names |
|---|---|---|
| Presidents Reagan and Bush pursued a conservative agenda that included tax cuts, budget cuts, and increased defense spending. | The conservative views of Reagan and Bush created policies and priorities that affect government spending and budgeting today. | •Reaganomics •supply-side economics •Strategic Defense Initiative •Sandra Day O'Connor | •deregulation •Environmental Protection Agency •Geraldine Ferraro •George Bush |

 U.S. History 6H, 8A, 14C, 19B, 19C, 21D, 24A, 24B, 24C, 24D, 25A, 25B, 25C, 25D

**One American's Story**

Throughout the 1980 presidential campaign and in the early days of his administration, President Reagan emphasized the perilous state of the economy during the Carter administration. In a speech to the nation on February 5, 1981—his first televised speech from the White House—Reagan announced his new economic program. He called for a reduction in income tax rates for individuals and a big reduction in government spending.

**A PERSONAL VOICE** RONALD REAGAN

" I'm speaking to you tonight to give you a report on the state of our nation's economy. I regret to say that we're in the worst economic mess since the Great Depression. . . . It's time to recognize that we've come to a turning point. We're threatened with an economic calamity of tremendous proportions, and the old business-as-usual treatment can't save us. Together, we must chart a different course. "

—televised speech to the nation, February 5, 1981

President
Ronald Reagan

President Reagan would deal with these problems by consistently stressing a sweeping package of new economic policies. These economic policies, dubbed **"Reaganomics,"** consisted of three parts: (1) budget cuts, (2) tax cuts, and (3) increased defense spending.

## 1 "Reaganomics" Takes Over

As soon as Reagan took office, he worked to reduce the size and influence of the federal government, which, he thought, would encourage private investment. Because people were anxious about the economy in 1980, their concern opened the door for new approaches to taxes and the federal budget.

---

## PROGRAM RESOURCES

 In-Depth Resources: Unit 7
· Guided Reading, p. 23
· Skillbuilder Practice: Analyzing Political Cartoons, p. 27
· Reteaching Activity, p. 29
· Primary Sources: Political Cartoon, p. 36; from Ronald Reagan's Farewell Address, p. 37
· Literature: from *The Bonfire of the Vanities*, pp. 40–41

· American Lives: Sandra Day O'Connor, p. 43
 Reading Study Guide (English and Spanish), pp. 249–250
 Access for Students Acquiring English/ESL
· Guided Reading (Spanish), p. 264
· Skillbuilder Practice, p. 267
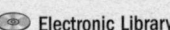 Formal Assessment
· Section Quiz, p. 455

 Integrated Assessment
· Rubrics

### INTEGRATED TECHNOLOGY

Critical Thinking Transp. CT33, CT67
· The Conservative 1980s
· Theory of Supply-Side Economics

Electronic Library of Primary Sources

classzone.com

### TEXAS RESOURCES

 TAKS Spiraled Content Review

 TAKS Practice Tests

 TAKS Practice Transparencies TT125

 TAKS Online Test Practice

**BUDGET CUTS** Reagan's strategy for downsizing the federal government included deep cuts in government spending on social programs. Yet his cuts did not affect all segments of the population equally. Entitlement programs that benefited the middle class, such as Social Security, Medicare, and veterans' pensions, remained intact. On the other hand, Congress slashed by 10 percent the budget for programs that benefited other groups: urban mass transit, food stamps, welfare benefits, job training, Medicaid, school lunches, and student loans.

**TAX CUTS** "Reaganomics" rested heavily upon **supply-side economics.** This theory held that if people paid fewer taxes, they would save more money. Banks could then loan that money to businesses, which could invest the money in resources to improve productivity. The supply of goods then would increase, driving down prices. At Reagan's urging, Congress lowered income taxes by 25 percent over a three-year period. Reagan based his ideas for supply-side economics on the work of economists such as George Gilder and Arthur Laffer. **A**

**A PERSONAL VOICE** ARTHUR LAFFER

" The most debilitating act a government can perpetrate on its citizens is to adopt policies that destroy the economy's production base, for it is the production base that generates any prosperity to be found in the society. U.S. tax policies over the last decade have had the effect of damaging this base by removing many of the incentives to economic advancement. It is necessary to restore those incentives if we are to cure our economic palsy. "

—*The Economics of the Tax Revolt: A Reader*

**INCREASED DEFENSE SPENDING** At the same time, Reagan authorized increases in military spending that more than offset cuts in social programs. Between 1981 and 1984, the Defense Department budget almost doubled. Indeed, the president revived two controversial weapons systems—the MX missile and the B-1 bomber. In 1983, Reagan asked the country's scientists to develop a defense system that would keep Americans safe from enemy missiles. Officially called the **Strategic Defense Initiative,** or SDI, the system quickly became known as Star Wars, after the title of a popular movie. The Defense Department estimated that the system would cost trillions of dollars.

**RECESSION AND RECOVERY** While Reagan was charting a new course for the American economy, the economy itself was sinking into recession. Lasting from July 1981 until November 1982, it was the most severe recession since the Great Depression. However, early in 1983, an economic upturn began as consumers went on a spending spree. Their confidence in the economy was bolstered by tax cuts, a decline in interest rates, and lower inflation. The stock market surged, unemployment declined, and the gross national product went up by almost 10 percent. The stock market boom lasted until 1987, when the market crashed, losing 508 points in one day. This fall was due in large part to automated and computerized buying and selling systems. However, the market recovered and then continued its upward climb.

**THE NATIONAL DEBT CLIMBS** Beneath the surface of recovery lay problems that continued to plague the economy. Tax cuts had helped the rich, while social welfare cuts had hurt the poor. Despite large reductions in parts of the

---

**Background**
See *supply-side economics* on page R46 in the Economics Handbook.

**MAIN IDEA**

**Summarizing**
**A** What are the main ideas of supply-side economics?

*A. Answer* If people paid fewer taxes, they would save more money, which banks could loan to businesses for investment in improved productivity. The increased supply of goods would force prices down.

**Background**
See *recession* on page R44 in the Economics Handbook.

**Background**
See *national debt* on page R43 in the Economics Handbook.

---

**ECONOMIC BACKGROUND**

**THE "TRICKLE-DOWN" THEORY**

Ronald Reagan's budget director, David Stockman, used supply-side economics to draft the Economic Recovery Tax Act of 1981. His tax package cut income taxes and business taxes by an average of 25 percent; the largest tax cuts went to those with the highest incomes. Administration officials defended the plan by claiming that as prosperity returned, the profits at the top would trickle down to the middle class and even the poor.

Despite Reagan's "trickle-down" theory, the wealthy gained the most from these tax cuts. In the 1980s, the rich got richer as poverty deepened for many others.

---

**More About . . .**

**The Laffer Curve**
Economist Arthur Laffer was sitting in a Washington restaurant explaining his ideas about tax rates and revenues to a group of journalists and politicians. To explain his idea about how tax rates affect tax revenues, Laffer sketched a curve on a napkin. The Laffer curve illustrated the idea that lower tax rates would ultimately generate high tax revenues as a result of economic growth. It is a basic tenet of supply-side economics. History did not prove Laffer's assumption to be valid but the ideas became part of Ronald Reagan's economic policies.

**ECONOMIC BACKGROUND**

**The "Trickle-Down Theory"**
One effect of the tax rate cut in Reagan's supply-side economics was less tax revenue, not more. Revenue from personal income taxes fell by nine percent even though the average income grew by four percent. In 1986 tax revenues were lower than they were when Reagan instituted his tax rate reduction in 1981. In the years of Reagan's administration the federal government ran large budget deficits.

---

*The Conservative Tide* **835**

---

**DIFFERENTIATING INSTRUCTION** | **LESS PROFICIENT READERS**

## Charting Reaganomics

Pair less proficient readers with more proficient ones to make a chart of the effects of Reaganomics. After students have read pages 834–836, have them draw up a chart that lists each of the subheads on those pages. Then, after each subhead, list one example of Reagan's economic policy. The uncompleted chart might look like this:

| Economic Policy | Example |
|---|---|
| Budget cuts | |
| Tax cuts | |
| Increased defense spending | |
| Recession and recovery | |
| The national debt climbs | |

## Analyzing *Political Cartoons*

### SKILLBUILDER ANSWERS

1. The wheel is labeled "Deficits," so its flying off suggests that the federal deficit is spinning out of control.
2. The American people

## Analyzing *Political Cartoons*

### "THE INFLATION STAGECOACH"

During Reagan's first term, federal spending far outstripped federal revenue and created a huge budget deficit. In this cartoon, Reagan (with budget director David Stockman sitting beside him on the inflation stagecoach) sees something that "shouldn't be there."

### SKILLBUILDER
**Analyzing Political Cartoons**
1. What is the meaning of the wheel flying off the stagecoach?
2. Whom do the passengers inside the stagecoach represent?

 SEE SKILLBUILDER HANDBOOK, PAGE R24.

## Instruct: Objective ❷

### Judicial Power Shifts to the Right
TAKS SS11 5(US24.B)

· Which justices did Reagan and Bush appoint to the Supreme Court?
· Why was the nomination of Clarence Thomas to the Court controversial?
· How did the Reagan and Bush appointees change the direction of the Court?

 In-Depth Resources: Unit 7
· Guided Reading, p. 23
· American Lives: Sandra Day O'Connor, p. 43

## Tracing Themes

### WOMEN AND POLITICAL POWER

During the Reagan and Bush administrations, the Supreme Court played a central role in the discussion of women's roles in social, political, and business affairs. The first woman justice—Sandra Day O'Connor—was appointed to the Supreme Court. The testimony of Anita Hill in the sexual harassment hearings, although it exposed negative aspects of women's struggle for equality in the workplace, pushed the issue to the forefront of the nation's consciousness.

budget, federal spending still outstripped federal revenue. Budget deficits were growing. Even though Reagan backed away from supply-side economics in 1982 and imposed new taxes, they were not enough to balance the budget. By the end of his first term, the national debt had almost doubled. **B**

## ❷ Judicial Power Shifts to the Right

*Anita Hill and Clarence Thomas testify before the Senate Judiciary Committee in October 1991.* ▼

One the most important ways in which Reagan accomplished his conservative goals was through his appointments to the Supreme Court. Reagan nominated **Sandra Day O'Connor,** Antonin Scalia, and Anthony M. Kennedy to fill seats left by retiring judges. O'Connor was the first woman to be appointed to the Court. He also nominated Justice William Rehnquist, the most conservative justice on the court at the time, to the position of chief justice.

President Bush later made the Court even more conservative when David H. Souter replaced retiring justice William Brennan. Bush also nominated Clarence Thomas to take the place of Thurgood Marshall. However, controversy exploded when law professor Anita Hill testified that Thomas had sexually harassed her when she worked for him in the 1980s. During several days of televised Senate hearings, committee members questioned Thomas, Hill, and witnesses for each side. Thomas eventually won approval by a final vote of 52 to 48.

The Reagan and Bush appointments to the Supreme Court ended the liberal control over the Court that had begun under Franklin Roosevelt. These appointments became increasingly significant as the Court revisited constitutional issues related to such topics as discrimination, abortion, and affirmative action. In 1989, the Court, in a series of rulings, restricted a woman's right to an abortion. The Court also imposed new restrictions on civil rights laws that had been designed to protect the rights of women and minorities. During the 1990–1991 session, the Court narrowed the rights of arrested persons.

**MAIN IDEA**

Analyzing
**Effects**
**B** What were some of the effects of "Reaganomics"?

**B. Answer** It encouraged growth, lowered inflation, and decreased unemployment. It also created a large budget deficit.

---

**ACTIVITY** | **SKILLBUILDER LESSON**

**B** **BLOCK SCHEDULING**

## Analyzing Political Cartoons

**Explaining the Skill** Political cartoons utilize signs, symbols, and irony to express a point of view. If the cartoon has a title, students should study it and relate it to the cartoon as a whole. They also should identify important symbols and details in the cartoon and then interpret the cartoon's message.

**Applying the Skill** Look at the cartoon at the top of this page. Answer the following questions:

· What is the title of the cartoon? *(The Inflation Stagecoach)*
· Who are the figures riding on top of the stage? *(President Reagan and Budget Director David Stockman)*
· Who is represented inside the stage? *(the American public)*
· What is Reagan trying to do? *(Slow down runaway inflation)*
· What is the meaning of the wheel flying off the coach? *(Deficits are creating additional danger.)*

 In-Depth Resources: Unit 7
· Skillbuilder Practice: Analyzing Political Cartoons, p. 27

## Deregulating the Economy

Reagan achieved one of his most important objectives—reducing the size and power of the federal government—in part by cutting federal entitlement programs but also through **deregulation,** the cutting back of federal regulation of industry. As part of his campaign for smaller government, he removed price controls on oil and eliminated federal health and safety inspections for nursing homes. He deregulated the airline industry (allowing airlines to abandon unprofitable air routes) and the savings and loan industry. One of the positive results of this deregulation was that it increased competition and often resulted in lower prices for consumers.

In a further effort at deregulation, President Reagan cut the budget of the **Environmental Protection Agency (EPA),** which had been established in 1970 to fight pollution and conserve natural resources. He ignored pleas from Canada to reduce acid rain and appointed opponents of the regulations to enforce them. For example, James Watt, Reagan's secretary of the interior, sold millions of acres of public land to private developers—often at bargain prices. He opened the continental shelf to oil and gas drilling, which many people thought posed environmental risks. Watt also encouraged timber cutting in national forests and eased restrictions on coal mining.

## Conservative Victories in 1984 and 1988

It was clear by 1984 that Reagan had forged a large coalition of conservative voters who highly approved of his policies. These voters included the following:

- *businesspeople*—who wanted to deregulate the economy
- *Southerners*—who welcomed the limits on federal power
- *Westerners*—who resented federal controls on mining and grazing
- *Reagan Democrats*—who agreed with Reagan on limiting federal government and thought that the Democratic Party had drifted too far to the left

THE 1984 PRESIDENTIAL ELECTION In 1984, Reagan and Bush won the Republican nominations for reelection without challenge. Walter Mondale, who had been vice president under President Carter, won the Democratic Party's nomination and chose Representative **Geraldine Ferraro** of New York as his running mate. Ferraro became the first woman on a major party's presidential ticket.

In 1984 the economy was strong. Reagan and Bush won by a landslide, carrying every state but Mondale's home state of Minnesota and the District of Columbia.

### HISTORICAL SPOTLIGHT

**AN ASSASSINATION ATTEMPT**

On March 30, 1981, President Reagan and other members of his staff were shot by a mentally unbalanced man named John Hinckley, Jr. While being wheeled into surgery to have a bullet removed, the president said to his wife, "Honey, I forgot to duck" (a line first used by boxer Jack Dempsey in the 1920s, after being knocked out in a bout). In the operating room, Reagan said to the team of surgeons, "I hope you fellas are Republicans." Reagan recovered speedily and his popularity grew.

▲ President Reagan is pushed into a presidential limousine after being shot by a deranged man.

**Instruct: Objective**

**Deregulating the Economy**
TAKS SS11 5(US24.B)
· What specific actions did Reagan take to cut back on government regulations?
· How did Reagan handle the Environmental Protection Agency?

📖 In-Depth Resources: Unit 7
· Guided Reading, p. 23

### HISTORICAL SPOTLIGHT

**An Assassination Attempt**
The four men wounded in the assassination attempt—President Reagan, Presidential Press Secretary James Brady, Secret Service Agent Timothy McCarthy, and Metropolitan Police Officer Thomas Delahanty—all survived the attack. The most seriously wounded was Jim Brady, who suffered severe head wounds. Although left permanently disabled, Brady, along with his wife, Sarah, later led a successful campaign for gun control that resulted in the passage of the Brady Handgun Violence Prevention Act of 1993.

**Instruct: Objective**

**Conservative Victories in 1984 and 1988**
TAKS SS11 5(US24.B)
· Where did Reagan's support come from in the 1984 election?
· How did "attack ads" influence the election of 1988?

📖 In-Depth Resources: Unit 7
· Guided Reading, p. 23
· Primary Sources: from Ronald Reagan's Farewell Address, p. 37

*The Conservative Tide* **837**

---

**ACTIVITY** COOPERATIVE LEARNING

 classzone.com

### Researching Supreme Court Cases

**Class Time** One class period

**Task** Summarizing rulings made by Reagan and Bush Supreme Court appointees

**Purpose** To analyze the shifting political philosophy of the U.S. Supreme Court

**Directions** Have students work in small groups to research the opinions of Supreme Court Justices appointed by Reagan and Bush. Have students research prominent cases pertaining to such issues as abortion, affirmative action, and discrimination. Ask each group to write a report summarizing the justices' decisions that they researched. Then, have students share their findings with the class. Discuss the Court as a whole.

◄ George Bush announces his presidential candidacy at a rally in 1987.

### Connections Across Time
#### 1988 AND 2000—BUSH PRESIDENCY

In 1988, Bush rode the crest of the conservative wave in his presidential campaign. The Moral Majority were staunch supporters of Reagan, and it was not difficult for Bush to win their votes. Ask students to compare the presidential campaigns of George H. W. Bush, in 1988, and his son, George W. Bush, in the year 2000. Have students consider the wax and wane of conservatism in the United States over time. *(Both father and son appealed to Republican voters, conservatives, and the Moral Majority; Bush, the father, built on Reagan's legacy; his son won a contested election that found the country about equally divided between Democrats and Republicans.)*

*"Read my lips: no new taxes."*
GEORGE BUSH

### THE 1988 PRESIDENTIAL ELECTION

In 1988, a majority of Americans were economically comfortable, and they attributed their comfort to Reagan and Bush. When Michael Dukakis, the Democratic governor of Massachusetts, ran for the presidency in 1988 against **George Bush**, Reagan's vice-president, most voters saw little reason for change.

George Bush simply built on President Reagan's legacy by promising, "Read my lips: no new taxes" in his acceptance speech at the Republican convention. He stressed his commitment to the conservative ideas of the Moral Majority. Though Bush asserted that he wanted a "kinder, gentler" nation, his campaign sponsored a number of negative "attack ads" aimed at his opponents. He told audiences that Dukakis was an ultraliberal whose views were outside the mainstream of American values. In particular, Bush suggested that Dukakis was soft on crime and unpatriotic.

Some commentators believed that the negative ads contributed to the lowest voter turnout in 64 years. Only half of the eligible voters went to the polls in 1988. Fifty-three percent voted for George Bush, who won 426 electoral votes. Bush's electoral victory was viewed, as Reagan's had been, as a mandate for conservative social and political policies. **C**

**C. Answer** Reagan put together a winning coalition of businesspeople, southern and western voters, and disaffected Democrats. Bush ran when the economy was healthy. He built on Reagan's legacy by promising no new taxes.

**MAIN IDEA**

Analyzing Causes
**C** What factors contributed to Reagan's victory in 1984 and Bush's victory in 1988?

## Assess & Reteach

### SECTION 2 ASSESSMENT

Have students answer the Section Assessment questions and make note of the page references where answers can be found.

📖 Formal Assessment
· Section Quiz, p. 455

### SELF-ASSESSMENT

Have students identify questions with which they had difficulty. Then, have students work with partners to locate the text passages that contain the answers.

### RETEACH

Ask students to identify concepts that they found difficult. Review the material as a class.

📖 In-Depth Resources: Unit 7
· Reteaching Activity, p. 29

### ② ASSESSMENT

**1. TERMS & NAMES** For each term or name below, write a sentence explaining its significance.
- •Reaganomics
- •supply-side economics
- •Strategic Defense Initiative
- •Sandra Day O'Connor
- •deregulation
- •Environmental Protection Agency
- •Geraldine Ferraro
- •George Bush

#### MAIN IDEA

**2. TAKING NOTES**
Use a diagram like the one below to explore the effects of "Reaganomics."

| DEFINITION OF REAGANOMICS |
|---|

↓

| Short-Term Effects |
|---|

↓

| Long-Term Effects |
|---|

Explain in a paragraph whether you think "Reaganomics" was good or bad for the economy.

#### CRITICAL THINKING

**3. ANALYZING MOTIVES**
Why did President Reagan and President Bush think it was important to appoint conservative justices to the Supreme Court?

**4. EVALUATING**
In your opinion was Reagan's first term a success? **Think About:**
- how his tax cuts impacted the rich and the poor
- the economy
- the federal budget

**5. ANALYZING PRIMARY SOURCES**
Read the following excerpt from Ronald Reagan's speech at the 1992 Republican Convention.

"We mustn't forget . . . the very different America that existed just 12 years ago; an America with 21 percent interest rates and . . . double-digit inflation; an America where mortgage payments doubled, paychecks plunged, and motorists sat in gas lines; an America whose leaders told us . . . that what we really needed was another good dose of government control and higher taxes."

What picture did Reagan paint of the Carter administration?

**838** CHAPTER 25

### ② ASSESSMENT  Answers

**1. TERMS & NAMES**
Reaganomics, p. 834
supply-side economics, p. 835
Strategic Defense Initiative, p. 835
Sandra Day O'Connor, p. 836
deregulation, p. 837
Environmental Protection Agency, p. 837
Geraldine Ferraro, p. 837
George Bush, p. 838

**2. TAKING NOTES**
Definition—policy advocating tax cuts to bolster private investments, leading to increased national supply of goods and services
Short-Term—Falling interests rates, decreased inflation, economic growth
Long-Term—Increased national debt, budget deficit, trade imbalance, higher taxes

**3. ANALYZING MOTIVES**
The Supreme Court decides which laws are constitutional. Both Reagan and Bush had conservative agendas and wanted the Supreme Court to support those agendas.

**4. EVALUATING**
Reagan's first term was a mix of success and failure—stopped the growth of inflation but the federal deficit rose.

**5. ANALYZING PRIMARY SOURCES**
That high interest rates, high inflation, gas lines, and too much government marked Carter's administration.

# Social Concerns in the 1980s

**MAIN IDEA**

Beneath the surge of prosperity that marked the conservative era of the 1980s lay serious social problems.

**WHY IT MATTERS NOW**

Issues involving health care, education, civil rights, and equal rights for women continue to challenge American society.

**Terms & Names**

- AIDS (acquired immune deficiency syndrome)
- pay equity
- L. Douglas Wilder
- Jesse Jackson
- Lauro Cavazos
- Antonia Coello Novello

TEKS

U.S. History 6H, 7A, 7B, 7C, 7D, 18A, 21A, 21D, 23B, 24B, 24G, 24H, 25A, 25B, 25C, 25D, 26A, 26B

### One American's Story

Trevor Ferrell lived an ordinary life in Gladwyne, an affluent suburb 12 miles from downtown Philadelphia. Trevor had brothers and sisters, his own room, a favorite pillow, a fondness for video games, and a bike. In short, he seemed like a typical 11-year-old boy until he watched a television news report about homeless people.

Trevor was astonished. "Do people really live like that?" he asked his parents. "I thought they lived like that in India, but not here, I mean in America." Trevor convinced his parents to drive downtown that night, where he gave a pillow and a blanket to the first homeless man he saw. Soon he and his family were collecting food and clothes to give to the homeless.

**A PERSONAL VOICE** TREVOR FERRELL

" They have to live on the streets, and right after you see one of them, you see someone in a limousine pull up to a huge, empty mansion. It's such a difference. Some people can get anything they want, and these other people couldn't get a penny if they needed one. "

—quoted in *Trevor's Place*

Trevor Ferrell listens to a homeless person on the corner of 12th and Chestnut streets in Philadelphia.

As Trevor saw, the restored American economy of the 1980s did not mean renewed prosperity for everyone. As presidents Reagan and Bush pursued conservative domestic policies, people disagreed about the impact of these policies.

## Health, Education, and Cities in Crisis ❶

In the 1980s, both in the cities and in rural and suburban areas, local governments strove to deal with crises in health, education, and safety. Americans directed their attention to issues such as AIDS, drug abuse, abortion, and education.

*The Conservative Tide* **839**

## Focus & Motivate

Ask students to identify school and community problems. How might the government address these issues? Ask students if they think the government is doing enough to help.

## Instruct

### Instruct: Objective ❶

**Health, Education, and Cities in Crisis**

TAKS SS11 5(US24.B)
· What were some of the major health-care issues in the 1980s?
· How did Reagan and Bush approach the problem of drugs in America?
· What did Americans think about the quality of education that their children were receiving?
· What challenges did most American cities face in the 1980s?

 In-Depth Resources: Unit 7
· Guided Reading, p. 24

## More About . . .

### AIDS Memorial Quilt

In 1985, Cleve Jones, a dedicated gay rights activist from San Francisco, came up with the idea for a memorial AIDs quilt. In June, 1987, Jones and a small group of activists organized the NAMES Project Foundation. The Quilt, made up of individual panels commemorating those who had lost their lives to AIDS, elicited immediate public support. Today, the Quilt consists of more than 44,000 panels, in memory of individuals around the globe. In 1989, the Quilt was nominated for a Nobel Peace Prize.

## NOW & THEN

### AIDS Worldwide

**Summarizing** Ask students which of the 2000 statistics about AIDS most surprised them. Have students write several sentences summarizing what they learned.

## NOW & THEN

### AIDS WORLDWIDE

In the year 2000, it was estimated that 5.3 million people worldwide became infected with HIV/AIDS. Impoverished countries that lie in sub-Saharan Africa remain hardest hit by the deadly pandemic, accounting for an estimated 3.8 million, or 72 percent, of new cases during the year. At the end of December 2000, the number of adults and children living with HIV/AIDS worldwide was estimated at 36.1 million people, of whom the proportions of males and females were almost equal.

▲ The AIDS quilt was displayed on the National Mall in Washington, D.C., in 1987. Each panel honors a person who died of AIDS.

**HEALTH ISSUES** One of the most troubling issues that concerned Americans in the 1980s was **AIDS (acquired immune deficiency syndrome).** Possibly beginning as early as the 1960s, AIDS spread rapidly throughout the world. Caused by a virus that destroys the immune system, AIDS weakens the body so that it is prone to infections and normally rare cancers.

AIDS is transmitted through bodily fluids, and most of the early victims of the disease were either homosexual men or intravenous drug users who shared needles. However, many people also contracted AIDS through contaminated blood transfusions, and children acquired it by being born to infected mothers. As the 1980s progressed, increasing numbers of heterosexuals began contracting AIDS. As the epidemic grew, so did concern over prevention and cure.

**ABORTION** Many Americans were concerned about abortion in the 1980s. Abortion had been legal in the United States since 1973, when the Supreme Court ruled in *Roe* v. *Wade* that first-trimester abortions were protected by a woman's right to privacy. Opponents of legalized abortion quickly organized under the pro-life banner. They argued that human life begins at conception and that no woman has the right to terminate a human life by her individual decision. Proponents of legalized abortion described themselves as pro-choice. They argued that reproductive choices were personal health-care matters and noted that many women had died from abortions performed by unskilled people in unsterile settings before the procedure was legalized.

In July 1989, the Supreme Court ruled in *Webster* v. *Reproductive Health Care Services* that states had the right to impose new restrictions on abortion. As a result, abortion restrictions varied from state to state. Ⓐ

***A. Answer***
Those in favor of legalized abortion argue that abortion is protected by a woman's right to privacy. Opponents of legalized abortion argue that human life begins at conception and that no woman has the right to terminate a human life by her individual decision.

**MAIN IDEA**

**Contrasting**
Ⓐ What are the two viewpoints on legalized abortion?

**840** CHAPTER 25

---

**DIFFERENTIATING INSTRUCTION**    **LESS PROFICIENT READERS**

### Outlining Social Issues

Have students create an outline with the heading, "Health, Education, and Cities in Crisis." Begin by using the heading and subheads as the basic outline structure. *(See the example at the right.)* As students read the text on pages 839–841, have them fill in supporting ideas for each subhead.

**Example**

I. Health Issues
   A.
   B.
   C.

II. Abortion
   A.
   B.
   C.

III. Drug Abuse
   A.
   B.
   C.

IV. Education
   A.
   B.
   C.

V. The Urban Crisis
   A.
   B.
   C.

**DRUG ABUSE** Battles over abortion rights sometimes competed for public attention with concerns about rising drug abuse. A few people argued that drugs should be legalized to reduce the power of gangs who made a living selling illegal drugs. Others called for treatment facilities to treat addictions. The Reagan administration launched a war on drugs and supported moves to prosecute users as well as dealers. First Lady Nancy Reagan toured the country with an antidrug campaign that admonished students to "Just say no!" to drugs.

> *"Just say no!"*
> NANCY REAGAN, SLOGAN
> IN THE WAR ON DRUGS

**EDUCATION** Education became another issue that stirred people's concerns. In 1983, a federal commission issued a report on education titled *A Nation at Risk*. The report revealed that American students lagged behind students in most other industrialized nations. In addition, the report stated that 23 million Americans were unable to follow an instruction manual or fill out a job application form.

The commission's findings touched off a debate about the quality of education. The commission recommended more homework, longer school days, and an extended school year. It also promoted increased pay and merit raises for teachers, as well as a greater emphasis on basic subjects such as English, math, science, social studies, and computer science.

In April 1991, President Bush announced an education initiative, "America 2000." He argued that choice was the salvation of American schools and recommended allowing parents to use public funds to send their children to schools of their choice—public, private, or religious. First Lady Barbara Bush toured the country to promote reading and writing skills. **B**

**THE URBAN CRISIS** The crisis in education was closely connected to the crisis in the cities. Many undereducated students lived in cities such as Baltimore, Chicago, Detroit, Philadelphia, and Washington, D.C. During the 1970s, the United States had become increasingly suburbanized as more and more white families responded to the lure of new homes, big lawns, shopping malls, and well-equipped schools outside the cities. Businesses moved, too, taking jobs and tax revenue with them.

Poor people and racial minorities were often left in cities burdened by high unemployment rates, crumbling infrastructures, inadequate funds for sanitation and health services, deteriorating schools, and growing social problems. By 1992, thousands of people were homeless, including many families with children. Cities were increasingly divided into wealthy neighborhoods and poverty-stricken areas.

One poverty-stricken area, south-central Los Angeles (which had erupted in violence in 1965 and 1968) erupted again in 1992. Four white police officers had been videotaped beating an African-American man named Rodney King, who had been fleeing from the officers in a speeding car. An all-white jury found the officers not guilty on charges of brutality. This verdict resulted in riots that lasted five days and caused the deaths of 53 people.

**MAIN IDEA**

**Identifying Problems**

**B** What problems in education emerged during the 1980s?

**B. Answer** American students lagged behind students in most other industrialized nations. Twenty-three million Americans were not able to follow an instructional manual or fill out a job application.

---

**DIFFICULT DECISIONS**

**SENDING MONEY INTO SPACE**

Under the Reagan administration, the government shifted the emphasis of the space program from scientific to military and commercial applications.

Beginning in 1981, NASA directed a series of space shuttle flights. The agency hoped to establish a space station and have the shuttle ferry workers and materials to it.

The explosion of the space shuttle *Challenger* in 1986 in which the crew was killed *(crew shown above)* caused a reexamination of ventures into space. Many people thought the money spent on space should be spent on social needs.

1. Should the federal government spend money on space exploration when so many American citizens require basic assistance?

2. If you were a legislator being asked to vote in favor of funding space exploration today, how would you vote? Why?

---

**Connections Across Time**

**1991 AND 2001**

**Presidential Education Plans**

The issue of improving schools has not disappeared as a focus of presidential concerns. Despite George Bush's, "American 2001" plan, education levels in the United States did not improve. Like his father, George W. Bush announced a plan to improve education in America. The plan titled "No Child Left Behind" features a seven point blueprint to improve performance in schools. Federal dollars will be linked to specific performance goals to ensure improved results.

**DIFFICULT DECISIONS**

**Sending Money Into Space**

The *Challenger* disaster made many Americans reevaluate the space program. The death of a civilian schoolteacher, Christa McAuliffe, brought the dangers of space travel close to home. The revelation that substandard equipment and human error may have caused the explosion raised questions about the decision-making processes at NASA.

**ANSWERS**

1. Students might say that with so many social and environmental problems, the money would be better spent on these issues. Others might say that space research and exploration is essential to the future of humanity.

2. Most students will probably support continued funding; some will not.

*The Conservative Tide* **841**

---

**ACTIVITY** **COOPERATIVE LEARNING**

 **classzone.com**

**Developing a Plan for Better Schools**

**Class Time** 45 minutes

**Task** Researching topics related to school reform and developing a plan of action for a local school

**Purpose** To identify problems facing public schools

**Directions** Have students work in groups to research school issues, such as national standards, national testing, financing of public education, and technology and education. Have each group focus on one topic and develop a proposal on how to address the issue. Ask students to prepare their proposals as if they had been asked to present their ideas to an audience of parents, teachers, and administrators.

📄 Integrated Assessment
· Rubrics 1, 2, 4, 5

## 2 The Equal Rights Struggle

2 The Equal Rights Struggle

Within this environment of dwindling resources and social struggle, women worked to achieve economic and social gains.

**POLITICAL LOSSES AND GAINS** During the early 1980s, women's rights activists worked to obtain ratification of the Equal Rights Amendment (ERA). Although Congress had passed the amendment in 1972, it had not yet been ratified, or approved, by three-fourths of the states. Supporters of the amendment had until June 30, 1982, to gain ratification from 38 states. They obtained only 35 of the 38 ratifications they needed, and the ERA did not become law. With the failure of the Equal Rights Amendment, women's organizations began to concentrate on electing women to public office. More women candidates began to run for office, and in 1984 the Democrats chose Geraldine Ferraro as their vice-presidential candidate. She had spoken of the necessity for women to continue working for equal opportunities in American society.

### A PERSONAL VOICE   GERALDINE FERRARO

"It is not just those of us who have reached the top who are fighting this daily battle. It is a fight in which all of us—rich and poor, career and home oriented, young and old—participate, simply because we are women."

—quoted in *Vital Speeches of the Day*

In the November 1992 election, the number of women in the House of Representatives increased from 23 to 47, and the number of women senators tripled—from two to six. President Reagan also had earlier named two women to his cabinet: In 1983, Elizabeth Dole became secretary of transportation, and Margaret Heckler became secretary of health and human services. Nevertheless, women remained underrepresented in political affairs. **C**

**INEQUALITY** Several factors contributed to what some called the "feminization of poverty." By 1992, 57.8 percent of the nation's women were part of the work force, and a growing percentage of women worked as professionals and managers. However, in that year women earned only about 76 cents for every dollar men earned. Female college graduates earned only slightly more than male high-school graduates. Also, about 31 percent of female heads of households lived in poverty, and among African-American women, the poverty rate was even higher. New trends in divorce settlements aggravated the situation. Because of no-fault divorce, fewer women won alimony payments, and the courts rarely enforced the meager child support payments they awarded.

To close the income gap that left so many women poor, women's organizations and unions proposed a system of **pay equity.** Jobs would

Geraldine Ferraro speaks at the 1984 Democratic Convention.

### Women's and Men's Average Yearly Earnings in Selected Careers, 1982

| Career | Women | Men |
|---|---|---|
| Accountant | $19,916 | $25,272 |
| Advertising Manager | 19,396 | 32,292 |
| Computer Operator | 13,728 | 17,992 |
| Cook | 8,476 | 9,880 |
| Engineer | 26,052 | 31,460 |
| Financial Manager | 19,136 | 30,004 |
| High School Teacher | 18,980 | 21,424 |
| Insurance Salesperson | 15,236 | 22,152 |
| Lawyer | 30,264 | 34,008 |
| Personnel Specialist | 17,836 | 26,832 |
| Physician | 21,944 | 26,884 |
| Police/ Detective | 15,548 | 20,072 |
| Real Estate Salesperson | 16,432 | 24,076 |
| Registered Nurse | 20,592 | 20,696 |
| Retail Sales Worker | 8,736 | 13,728 |
| Social Worker | 15,600 | 20,436 |
| University Professor | 20,748 | 26,832 |

*Source: Bureau of Labor Statistics, Current Population Survey, 1983–1989.*

**SKILLBUILDER Interpreting Charts**
1. Name one career that paid men and women almost equally.
2. What conclusion can you draw from this chart?

---

**Instruct: Objective 2**

**The Equal Rights Struggle**

TAKS SS11 3(US21.D)

· What was the outcome of the campaign to adopt an Equal Rights Amendment?
· How did women respond to the fact they were underrepresented in public office?
· What were the legislative issues for which women campaigned?
· Who was Geraldine Ferraro?

 In-Depth Resources: Unit 7
· Guided Reading, p. 24

## More About . . .

### Geraldine Ferraro

Geraldine Ferraro (b. 1935) was the first woman to receive a major party nomination for high government office. Prior to her nomination, she had served three terms in Congress, representing a district in Queens, one of New York City's five boroughs. Ferraro built up a record of supporting women's issues, the elderly, and labor, and of opposing restrictions on abortion. After the election, she remained active in Democratic politics. During the Clinton administration, Ferraro headed the U.S. delegation to the UN Human Rights Commission.

**MAIN IDEA**

**Summarizing**
**C** What steps did women take to help them move forward after the ERA failed to pass?

*C. Answer* They concentrated on electing women to public office.

*Skillbuilder Answers*
1. nursing
2. In the early 1980s, men made more money than women for the same job.

---

**DIFFERENTIATING INSTRUCTION** | **LESS PROFICIENT READERS**

### Identifying Main Ideas and Supporting Details

Pair less proficient readers with more proficient ones to identify the main ideas and supporting details presented in this section on the equal rights struggle. Have students read the text on pages 842–843 and list the main idea for each paragraph on a chart similar to the one at the right. Then have them go back to identify details that support each of the main ideas and list them.

| Main Idea | Supporting Details |
|---|---|
|  |  |
|  |  |
|  |  |
|  |  |
|  |  |

be rated on the basis of the amount of education they required, the amount of physical strength needed to perform them, and the number of people that an employee supervised. Instead of relying on traditional pay scales, employers would establish pay rates that reflected each job's requirements. By 1989, 20 states had begun adjusting government jobs to offer pay equity for jobs of comparable worth.

Women also fought for improvements in the workplace. Since many working women headed single-parent households or had children under the age of six, they pressed for family benefits. Government and corporate benefit packages began to include maternity leaves, flexible hours and workweeks, job sharing, and work-at-home arrangements. Some of these changes were launched by individual firms, while others required government intervention. Yet the Reagan administration sharply cut the budget for daycare and other similar programs. **D**

## The Fight for Rights Continues **3**

Cuts in government programs and the backlash against civil rights initiatives, such as affirmative action, affected other groups as well.

**AFRICAN AMERICANS** African Americans made striking political gains during the 1980s, even though their economic progress suffered. By the mid-1980s, African-American mayors governed many cities, including Los Angeles, Detroit, Chicago, Atlanta, New Orleans, Philadelphia, and Washington, D.C. Hundreds of communities in both the North and the South had elected African Americans to serve as sheriffs, school board members, state legislators, and members of Congress. In 1990, **L. Douglas Wilder** of Virginia became the nation's first African-American governor. The Reverend **Jesse Jackson** ran for the Democratic presidential nomination in 1984 and 1988.

Middle-class African Americans often held professional and managerial positions. But the poor faced an uncertain future of diminishing opportunities. In 1989, the newly conservative Supreme Court handed down a series of decisions that continued to change the nation's course on civil rights. In the case of *Richmond* v. *J. A. Croson Company*, for example, the Court further limited the scope of affirmative action, policies that were designed to correct the effects of discrimination in the employment or education of minority groups or women. Other decisions by the Court outlawed contracts set aside for minority businesses. Sylvester Monroe, an African-American correspondent for *Newsweek* magazine, commented on the way many African Americans saw the backlash against affirmative action. **E**

▲
Jesse Jackson campaigns for the Democratic presidential nomination in 1984.

**A PERSONAL VOICE** SYLVESTER MONROE

"There's a finite pie and everybody wants his piece. Everybody is afraid of losing his piece of the pie. That's what the fight against affirmative action is all about. People feel threatened. As for blacks, they're passé. They're not in anymore. Nobody wants to talk about race."

—quoted in *The Great Divide*

*The Conservative Tide* **843**

Tracing Themes
CIVIL RIGHTS

During years of the Reagan and Bush administrations, the conservative agenda was center stage. The political climate limited advances in civil rights for minorities, but minority groups continued to organize and lobby for change. The issue of equal opportunity for all Americans, regardless of race, ethnicity, or gender, became established in the political mainstream. Political debate followed over how equal opportunity might be achieved. Despite obstacles, each group mentioned in this section—women, African Americans, Latinos, Native Americans, Asian Americans, and gay men and lesbians, made strides.

**In-Depth Resources: Unit 7**
· Geography Application: Latino Population in the 1980s, pp. 32–33

**Electronic Library of Primary Sources**
· Why Fear Spanish?, 1988, by C.A. Montaner

# NOW & THEN

## Affirmative Action

**Evaluating** Have students research the current status of affirmative action, taking into account pending court challenges and statements on the subject by the president. Ask students what they think about the affirmative action debate. *(Some students might say affirmative action should be continued because it is an effective means to account for past discrimination; others might say it is a reverse form of discrimination.)*

▲ Dr. Antonia Coello Novello served as surgeon general under President Bush.

**GAINS FOR LATINOS** Latinos became the fastest growing minority during the 1980s. By 1990, they constituted almost nine percent of the population, and demographers estimated that Latinos would soon outnumber African Americans as the nation's largest minority group. About two out of three Latinos were Mexican Americans, who lived mostly in the Southwest. A Puerto Rican community thrived in the Northeast, and a Cuban population was concentrated in Florida. Like African Americans, Latinos gained political power during the 1980s. Toney Anaya became governor of New Mexico, while Robert Martinez became governor of Florida. In August 1988, President Reagan appointed **Lauro Cavazos** as secretary of education. In 1990, President Bush named Dr. **Antonia Coello Novello** to the post of surgeon general.

Many Latinos supported bilingual education. They feared that abandoning Spanish would weaken their distinctive culture. In the words of Daniel Villanueva, a television executive, "We want to be here, but without losing our language and our culture. They are a richness, a treasure that we don't care to lose." The Bilingual Education Act of 1968 and the 1975 amendent to the Voting Rights Act enabled Spanish speakers to attend school and vote in their own language, but by the mid-1980s opposition to bilingualism was rising. Critics argued that it slowed the rate at which Spanish-speaking people entered mainstream American life. They also feared that the nation would become split between English speakers and Spanish speakers.

**Vocabulary**
**demographer:** a person who studies the characteristics of human population, such as growth, density, and distribution

## NOW & THEN

### AFFIRMATIVE ACTION

Affirmative action refers to the effort to provide employment opportunities for women and minority groups, including Latinos, African Americans, and Native Americans. The federal government instituted affirmative action policies under the Civil Rights Acts of 1964.

Presidents Reagan and Bush actively opposed affirmative action and racial quotas throughout the 1980s. In the 1990s, President Clinton supported affirmative action. Despite his support, in 1996, voters in California approved a referendum that did away with state affirmative action programs.

In 2001, President George W. Bush expressed support for affirmative access to open the doors of opportunity through programs such as the Texas 10 percent plan which gives those who graduate in the top 10 percent of their class automatic admission to any state college or university.

**NATIVE AMERICANS SPEAK OUT** Native Americans also became more self-conscious of their dignity and more demanding of their rights. In the 1970s, they organized schools to teach young Native Americans about their past. They also began to fight for the return of ancestral lands wrongfully taken from them.

During the 1980s, the Reagan administration slashed aid to Native Americans for health, education, and other services. Driven to find new sources of revenue, Native Americans campaigned for gambling casinos on their land as a way to bring in money. After the Supreme Court ruled in favor of Native Americans, many tribes opened Las Vegas-style casinos, which provided additional funding for the tribes that operated them. Nonetheless, the long-term problems faced by Native Americans have not been solved by gambling casinos, although the new wealth has helped to some extent. **F**

**AN EXPANDING ASIAN-AMERICAN POPULATION** Asian Americans were the second fastest growing minority in the United States during the 1980s. By 1992, the U.S. population included about 8.3 million Asian Americans and Pacific Islanders. Asian Americans constituted 3.25 percent of the population.

In 1976, an organization named Asian Women United (AWU) was founded. The AWU seeks to generate awareness of Asian culture. It sponsors activities that build networks of Asian-American and Pacific-American women. It also seeks to expose and eliminate racist views about Asian Americans and to present an accurate picture of Asian culture.

*F. Answer* The Reagan administration slashed aid to Native Americans for health, education, and other services. Native Americans were forced to find new sources of revenue through the establishment of gambling casinos on their native lands.

**MAIN IDEA**

**Identifying Problems**
**F** What problems did Native Americans face in the 1980s?

---

ACTIVITY    COOPERATIVE LEARNING

## Minority Population Growth and Distribution

**Class Time** Parts of two class periods

**Task** Charting the growth rates and distribution patterns of minority groups

**Purpose** To analyze the value of census data and how it reveals a picture of a changing America

**Directions** The 2000 census revealed the growth of the Latino and Asian American populations, showing that Latinos will soon make up the largest minority group in the United States. Have students work in groups to compare census data from 1990 and 2000. Then, have them create a bar graph illustrating the population change for African Americans, Latinos, Asian Americans, and Native Americans.

 **Integrated Assessment**
· Rubrics 1, 2

◄ A gay rights march
in Washington, D.C.,
October 1987

**THE GAY RIGHTS MOVEMENT ADVANCES** During the 1970s and 1980s, gay men and lesbians emerged from political invisibility to fight openly for civil rights. While the gay rights movement suffered a setback during the early 1980s in the face of conservative opposition and the AIDS crisis, by the late 1980s and early 1990s a new surge of gay activism was under way in the country. Direct action groups sprang up throughout the country, calling for an end to anti-gay discrimination. Although several speakers at the 1992 Republican National Convention condemned gay activism, these speakers were unable to slow the pace of change. By the year 1993, seven states and 110 communities had outlawed such discrimination.

## Tracing Themes
### DIVERSITY AND NATIONAL IDENTITY

Discuss with students the cultural diversity represented by the groups discussed on pages 843–845. Ask students which traditional values upheld by presidents Reagan and Bush are held in common by all the groups. (*Some students may respond that broad values such as honesty, care for children, and a stable family life are accepted by all groups. Students may also observe that some issues, such as civil rights, cut across minority lines, with some members in favor and some members in opposition.*)

## Assess & Reteach

### SECTION 3 ASSESSMENT
Have students focus on question 4 in the Section Assessment, which elicits a good overview of the section.

  Formal Assessment
  · Section Quiz, p. 456

### SELF-ASSESSMENT
Ask students to list issues particular to each minority group mentioned in this section. Have them note specific goals and achievements.

### RETEACH
Review question 2 in the Section Assessment by drawing the graphic organizer on the chalkboard.

  In-Depth Resources: Unit 7
  · Reteaching Activity, p. 30

---

## 3 ASSESSMENT

**1. TERMS & NAMES** For each term or name below, write a sentence explaining its significance.
- **AIDS (acquired immune deficiency syndrome)**
- **pay equity**
- **L. Douglas Wilder**
- **Jesse Jackson**
- **Lauro Cavazos**
- **Antonia Coello Novello**

### MAIN IDEA

**2. TAKING NOTES**
Use a chart like the one below to list some of the social problems of the Reagan and Bush years and how the government responded to them.

| Social Problems | Government Responses |
|-----------------|----------------------|
|                 |                      |

Choose one issue and write other responses the government might have made.

### CRITICAL THINKING

**3. PREDICTING EFFECTS**
How might improvements in the educational system help solve other social problems? **Think About:**
- the impact education might have on health-related problems
- the impact that education might have on urban problems
- the impact that education might have on unemployment

**4. COMPARING**
Compare the political gains and losses experienced by various groups during the Reagan and Bush administrations.

**5. FORMING GENERALIZATIONS**
Why might a widening gap between the richest and poorest citizens of a country be a cause for concern about that country's future?

*The Conservative Tide* **845**

---

Answers ASSESSMENT 3

**1. TERMS & NAMES**
AIDS, p. 840
pay equity, p. 842
L. Douglas Wilder, p. 843
Jesse Jackson, p. 843
Lauro Cavazos, p. 844
Antonia Coello Novello, p. 844

**2. TAKING NOTES**
abortion—Supreme Court restrictions; drug abuse—"Just say No!" campaign; education—America 2000 education initiative; women's rights—day care budget cuts; pay equity in some states; equal rights for minorities—Supreme Court reversal of affirmative-action decision.

**3. PREDICTING EFFECTS**
Education might help discourage unsafe sex and drug use. Education would lead to future job opportunities and lower unemployment rates.

**4. COMPARING**
More jobs and political opportunities for women and minorities; Native Americans gained support for gambling

casinos on their native lands; Asian Americans were the second fastest-growing minority population; several states outlawed anti-gay discrimination.

**5. FORMING GENERALIZATIONS**
Some students might say that a widening economic gap could lead to a permanently divided society.

### Objectives

· To describe regional population shifts in America in recent decades

· To analyze the tremendous population growth in the South and Southwest, or Sunbelt

## Focus & Motivate

**Making Decisions** Ask students to consider the different parts or regions of the United States.

· What do they especially like about where they live?

· Where in the United States would they live, if they had their choice?

## More About . . .

### Las Vegas, Nevada

Located in Nevada's southeastern corner, Las Vegas is considered one of the cities of the Sunbelt. In recent years, it has experienced unprecedented expansion. In fact, according to the U.S Bureau of the Census, Las Vegas was the fastest-growing city in America in the 1900s. The city boasts one of the largest residential real estate markets in the nation. A warm, sunny city surrounded by desert stretches, Las Vegas began growing after gambling was legalized in the state in 1931 and construction of nearby Hoover Dam was completed five years later.

## GEOGRAPHY SPOTLIGHT

# Sunbelt, Rustbelt, Ecotopia

In the 1970s, people on the move created new names for areas to which they moved. The West was sometimes called *Ecotopia* because of its varied scenery and ecological attractions. The South and Southwest were called the *Sunbelt* because of their warm climate. The North Central and Northeast regions were called the *Rustbelt* because many of their aging factories had been closed.

As a geographical term, *region* is used to designate an area with common features or characteristics that set it apart from its surroundings. For example, the Mississippi Valley is a large physical region; Warren Woods is a small physical region. The term is often used for groups of states that share an area and certain characteristics.

As people move from state to state, and from region to region, they gradually transform the balance of political and economic power in the nation. Each census in recent times has recorded how certain states have gained population and others have lost population. If the gains or losses are large enough, a state's representation in the U.S. House of Representatives will increase or decrease commensurately.

**Americans on the Move, 1970s**

311,000

NORTHEAST

NORTH CENTRAL

67,000

WEST

472,000

964,000

790,000

75,000

SOUTH

Source: Bernard L. Weinstein and Robert E. Firestine, *Regional Growth and Decline in the United States* (1978)

**Regional Internal Migration, 1982–1998**

Gain / Loss (axis: 600, 400, 200, 0, −200, −400, −600)

Years: 1982 1984 1986 1988 1990 1992 1994 1996 1998

— West  — Midwest  — South  — Northeast

Source: U.S. Census Bureau

**846** CHAPTER 25

### REGIONAL EXCHANGES

Between 1970 and 1975, the population center of the United States, which had generally moved westward for 17 decades, suddenly moved southward as well. The arrows show the net number of Americans who migrated and their patterns of migration in the early 1970s. The West gained 311,000 from the Northeast plus 472,000 from the North Central region, for a total of 783,000 people. However, it also lost 75,000 people to the South. During the 1980s and 1990s the southward and westward shift continued.

## RECOMMENDED RESOURCES

### BOOKS

Abbot, Carl. *The New Urban America.* Chapel Hill: U of North Carolina P, 1981. A study of Sunbelt cities and the political ramifications of their growth.

Bernard, Richard M., and Bradley R. Rice. *Sunbelt Cities.* Austin: U of Texas P, 1983. Growth and politics of Sunbelt cities since World War II.

Herbers, John. *The New Heartland.* New York: Times Books, 1986. A study of American migration beyond the suburbs and how it is changing the nation.

*Population Trends in the 1980s.* Washington, D.C.: Bureau of the Census, U.S. Department of Commerce, 1992. Pamphlet of statistics on national and state populations trends and trends in internal migration.

Preston, Richard. *American Steel.* New York: Prentice, 1991. An account of efforts to resurrect America's Rustbelt by revitalizing the steel industry.

### VIDEOS

*Top Ten Retirement Locations in the Sunbelt.* Leisure Living, 1990. A tour of ten popular Sunbelt retirement communities.

## Americans on the Move, 1990-2000

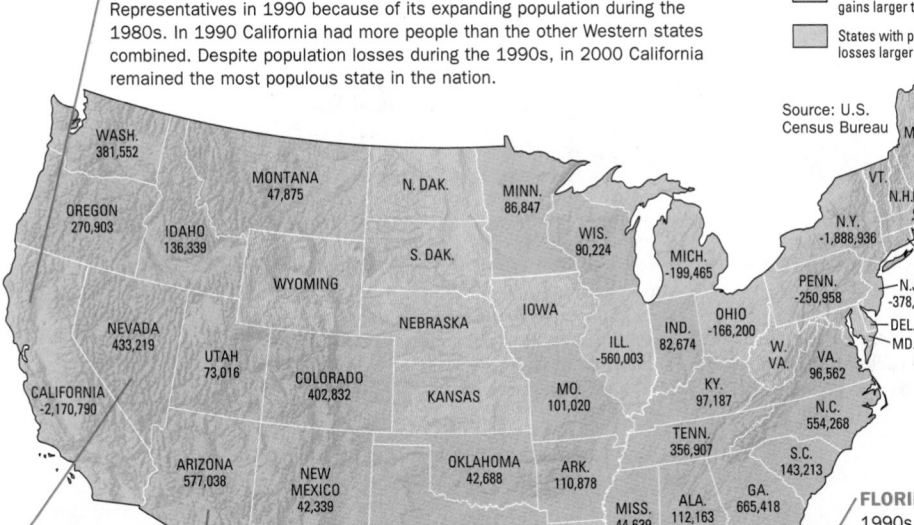

**CALIFORNIA** The state of California gained seven seats in the House of Representatives in 1990 because of its expanding population during the 1980s. In 1990 California had more people than the other Western states combined. Despite population losses during the 1990s, in 2000 California remained the most populous state in the nation.

States with population gains larger than 40,000

States with population losses larger than 110,000

Source: U.S. Census Bureau

WASH. 381,552

OREGON 270,903

MONTANA 47,875

N. DAK.

MINN. 86,847

MAINE

VT.

N.H.

MASS. -244,494

IDAHO 136,339

WYOMING

S. DAK.

WIS. 90,224

N.Y. -1,888,936

R.I.

CONN.

NEVADA 433,219

UTAH 73,016

NEBRASKA

IOWA

MICH. -199,465

PENN. -250,958

N.J. -226,370

-378,495

DEL.

MD.

CALIFORNIA -2,170,790

COLORADO 402,832

KANSAS

ILL. -560,003

IND. 82,674

OHIO -166,200

W. VA.

VA. 96,562

MO. 101,020

KY. 97,187

N.C. 554,268

ARIZONA 577,038

NEW MEXICO 42,339

OKLAHOMA 42,688

ARK. 110,878

TENN. 356,907

S.C. 143,213

TEXAS 569,957

MISS. 44,639

ALA. 112,163

GA. 665,418

LA. -139,704

FLA. 1,108,514

**NEVADA** There has been such a large influx of people since 1945 that building houses for newcomers has become a major industry in Nevada.

**ARIZONA** Much of the population gain in Arizona has been concentrated in Phoenix. By 2000, the population of Phoenix had reached over three million, up 45 percent from 1990.

**TEXAS** During the 1990s, Texas eclipsed New York to become the nation's second most populous state behind California. Sixty percent of the Texas increase has been driven by Hispanic growth.

**FLORIDA** During the 1990s, Florida's population increased 23.5 percent making it the nation's fourth largest state behind California, Texas, and New York. With so many new residents, Florida gained two additional House seats, bringing its congressional delegation to 25.

*(below left)* Housing development near Danville, California, 1990; *(inset)* Housing construction, Rohnert Park, California, 1991

### THINKING CRITICALLY

1. **Analyzing Distributions** Which states lost the most people between 1990 and 2000? Which states gained the most people?

2. **Creating a Graph** Choose one of the most populous states and then pose a historical question about population in that state. Create a graph or graphs that show various aspects of population for the state you have chosen. Be sure that the graph(s) help to answer the question you posed. Then display the graph(s) and the question in the classroom.

**SEE SKILLBUILDER HANDBOOK, PAGE R28.**

**RESEARCH LINKS** CLASSZONE.COM

*The Conservative Tide* **847**

## OBJECTIVES

**1** Identify changes in the Communist world that ended the Cold War.

**2** Summarize U.S. actions taken to influence Central American and Caribbean affairs.

**3** Describe the events leading up to the Iran-Contra scandal.

**4** Analyze U.S. involvement in the Persian Gulf War.

### SKILLBUILDER

· Geography Skillbuilder: location, region, p. 851; region, movement, p. 854

### CRITICAL THINKING

· Evaluating Leadership, p. 849
· Analyzing Events, p. 850
· Comparing, p. 852
· Drawing Conclusions, p. 855
· Analyzing Causes, p. 855
· Forming Generalizations, p. 855
· Hypothesizing, p. 855

## Focus & Motivate

Ask students how they might react if a feud between two people they know suddenly ended.

## Instruct

### Instruct: Objective **1**

**The Cold War Ends**

TAKS SS11 1(US1.A)
· What did Gorbachev do to change politics and life in the Soviet Union?
· What caused the end of the Cold War?
· What caused the reunification of Germany?
· What changes occurred in China?

 In-Depth Resources: Unit 7
· Guided Reading, p. 25

 Geography Transparencies GT33
· The Cold War Ends, 1989–1990

# Foreign Policy After the Cold War

| MAIN IDEA | WHY IT MATTERS NOW | Terms & Names |
|---|---|---|
| The end of the Cold War, marked by the breakup of the Soviet Union in 1991, led to a redirection of many U.S. goals and policies. | After the Cold War, the United States provided and continues to provide substantial economic support to the new capitalistic and democratic nations. | • Mikhail Gorbachev<br>• *glasnost*<br>• *perestroika*<br>• INF Treaty<br>• Tiananmen Square<br>• *Sandinistas*<br>• *Contras*<br>• Operation Desert Storm |

 U.S. History 1B, 6G, 6H, 8A, 8B, 19A, 19B, 19C, 24B, 24C, 24G, 25A, 25, 25C, 25D, 26A, 26B

 **One American's Story**

Colin Powell did not start out in life with any special privileges. He was born in Harlem and raised in the Bronx, where he enjoyed street games and tolerated school. Then, while attending the City College of New York, he joined the Reserve Officer Training Corps (ROTC). He got straight A's in ROTC, and so he decided to make the army his career.

Powell served first in Vietnam and then in Korea and West Germany. He rose in rank to become a general; then President Reagan made him national security adviser. In this post, Powell noted that the Soviet Union was a factor in all the administration's foreign policy decisions.

**A PERSONAL VOICE** COLIN POWELL

" Our choosing sides in conflicts around the world was almost always decided on the basis of East-West competition. The new Soviet leader, Mikhail Gorbachev, however, was turning the old Cold War formulas on their head. . . . Ronald Reagan . . . had the vision and flexibility, lacking in many Cold Warriors [participants in the Cold War between the U.S. and the USSR], to recognize that Gorbachev was a new man in a new age offering new opportunities for peace. "

—*My American Journey*

General Colin Powell

Though U.S. foreign policy in the early 1980s was marked by intense hostility toward the Soviet Union, drastic economic problems in the Soviet Union destroyed its ability to continue the Cold War standoff.

## **1** The Cold War Ends

In March of 1985, **Mikhail Gorbachev** became the general secretary of the Communist Party in the Soviet Union. His rise to power marked the beginning of a new era in the Soviet Union.

---

## PROGRAM RESOURCES

 In-Depth Resources: Unit 7
· Guided Reading, p. 25
· Reteaching Activity, p. 31
· Outline Map: U.S. Attention on the Middle East, pp. 34–35
· Primary Source: The First Day of Desert Storm, p. 39
· American Lives: Daniel Inouye, p. 44

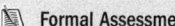 **Reading Study Guide** (English and Spanish), pp. 253–254

 Access for Students Acquiring English/ESL
· Guided Reading (Spanish), p. 266
· Outline Map, pp. 270–271

Formal Assessment
· Section Quiz, p. 457

Integrated Assessment
· Rubrics

### INTEGRATED TECHNOLOGY

 Geography Transp. GT33
· The Cold War Ends, 1989–1990

 Humanities Transp. HT47
· "Jobs That May Be Lost"

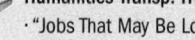 Electronic Library of Primary Sources

 classzone.com

### TEXAS RESOURCES

 TAKS Spiraled Content Review

 TAKS Practice Tests

 TAKS Practice Transparencies TT127

 TAKS Online Test Practice

**GORBACHEV INITIATES REFORM** Gorbachev had inherited a host of problems in the Soviet Union. Many of them revolved around the stagnant Soviet economy. But in fact the entire Soviet system suffered from gross inefficiency and recession.

An imaginative, skilled diplomat and political leader, Gorbachev advocated a policy known as *glasnost* (Russian for "openness"). He allowed open criticism of the Soviet government and took some steps toward freedom of the press. In 1987, he outlined his plans for *perestroika*, a restructuring of Soviet society. He called for less government control of the economy, the introduction of some private enterprise, and steps toward establishing a democratic government in the Soviet Union. His plan of action reflected the failure of the Communist system.

Gorbachev recognized that better relations with the United States would allow the Soviets to reduce their military spending and reform their economy. As a result, he initiated a series of arms-control meetings that led to the **INF Treaty (Intermediate-Range Nuclear Forces Treaty)** signed on December 8, 1987. The United States Senate ratified the treaty five months later in May 1988. The treaty eliminated two classes of weapons systems in Europe and allowed each nation to make on-site inspections of the other's military installations. **Ⓐ**

**THE SOVIET UNION DECLINES** Gorbachev's introduction of democratic ideals led to a dramatic increase in nationalism on the part of the Soviet Union's non-Russian republics. The pressure for complete change was overwhelming. In December 1991, 14 non-Russian republics declared their independence from the Soviet Union. Muscled aside by Russian reformers who thought he was working too slowly toward democracy, Gorbachev himself lost power and resigned as Soviet president. After 74 years, the Soviet Union dissolved.

A loose federation known as the Commonwealth of Independent States (CIS) took the place of the Soviet Union. In February 1992, President George Bush and Russian president Boris Yeltsin issued a formal statement declaring an end to the Cold War that had plagued the two nations and divided the world since 1945. The statement marked the beginning of a new era of "friendship and partnership" between the two nations. In January 1993, Yeltsin and Bush signed the START II pact, designed to cut both nations' nuclear arsenals by 75 percent.

**THE COLLAPSE OF COMMUNIST REGIMES** Before his resignation, Gorbachev had encouraged the people of East Germany and Eastern Europe to go their own ways. In 1988, when the Soviet Union was still intact, he reduced the number of Soviet troops in Eastern Europe and allowed non-Communist parties to organize in satellite nations, such as East Germany and Poland. He encouraged the satellite nations to move toward democracy. The impoverished Soviet Union would no longer support unpopular Communist regimes.

In October 1989, East Germans startled the world by repudiating their Communist government. On November 9, 1989, East Germany opened the Berlin Wall, allowing free passage between the two parts of the city for the first time in

---

**MAIN IDEA**

**Evaluating Leadership**
Ⓐ Which evidence in the text supports the viewpoint that Gorbachev was a skilled politician and diplomat?

*A. Answer* Gorbachev recognized that the Soviet economy and political system were in disarray. Rather than trying to heal these systems, he offered new plans for government and the economy through glasnost and perestroika.

---

WORLD STAGE

**DEMOCRATIC ELECTIONS IN RUSSIA**

After the Soviet Union dissolved in 1991, Boris Yeltsin continued as president of Russia. Yeltsin ended price controls and increased private business ownership. The Russian parliament opposed Yeltsin's policies, even after a 1993 referendum showed that the majority of voters supported them.

In December 1993, Russian voters installed a new parliament and approved a new constitution, parts of which resembled the U.S. Constitution. The election results heralded an era of increasing democracy in Russia. In 1996, Yeltsin won reelection as president of Russia. He was succeeded in 2000 by Vladimir Putin.

---

**More About . . .**

*Perestroika*
When Gorbachev took over as general secretary of the Communist Party in 1985, the Soviet Union was in crisis. He perceived the need for immediate action and initiated a program of economic and political restructuring called *perestroika*. Gorbachev described *perestroika* as "the decisive defeat of the process of stagnation, . . . the creation of a reliable and effective mechanism for increasing the pace of social-economic development. The main idea of our strategy is to unite the achievements of the scientific-technical revolution with a planned economy and to bring into action the entire potential of socialism."

---

**WORLD STAGE**

**Democratic Elections in Russia**
Ask students why they think the Russian parliament continued to oppose Yeltsin's policies even after a majority of people voted for them. *(Old parliament was reluctant to give up power; persistence of strongly held beliefs.)*

---

👁 Electronic Library of Primary Sources

· from *The United States and the World: Setting Limits*, 1986, by J. Kirkpatrick

---

*The Conservative Tide* **849**

---

### More About . . .

**Eastern Europe and the Treaty of Versailles**

The events that occurred after the fall of communism in Eastern Europe demonstrate the historical impact of the 1919 Treaty of Versailles. Yugoslavia, Czechoslovakia, Austria, Hungary, and other countries were cobbled together amidst the dismantling of the Austro-Hungarian and Ottoman empires. In Czechoslovakia, two major ethnic groups, the Czechs and Slovaks, managed to separate peacefully, creating the Czech Republic and Slovakia. In Yugoslavia, however, the transition was fraught with ethnic conflict.

### More About . . .

**Tiananmen Square**

Ironically, *Tiananmen* means the "Gate of Heavenly Peace." The gate itself overlooks the square, which has often been a place of national celebrations with parades and fireworks. The students who began holding rallies in the square for a more democratic China were joined by tens of thousands. As the situation spiraled out of control, the government called in military units from distant provinces. On June 3, the military mobilized and attacked the unarmed protesters, killing hundreds. Thousands more were arrested in the days that followed.

▲ A demonstrator pounds away on the Berlin Wall as East German border guards look on from above at the Brandenberg Gate, on November 11, 1989.

28 years. East German border guards stood by and watched as Berliners pounded away with hammers and other tools at the despised wall. In early 1990, East Germany held its first free elections, and on October 3 of that year, the two German nations were united.

Other European nations also adopted democratic reforms. Czechoslovakia withdrew from the Soviet bloc. The Baltic states of Latvia, Estonia, and Lithuania declared their independence from the Soviet Union. Hungary, Bulgaria, and Romania made successful transitions from communism. **B**

Yugoslavia, however, collapsed. Four of its six republics seceded. Ethnic rivalries deteriorated into a brutal war among Muslims, Orthodox Serbs, and Roman Catholic Croats, who were dividing Yugoslavia, each claiming parts of it. Serbia backed Serb minorities that were stirring up civil unrest in Croatia and Bosnia.

**COMMUNISM CONTINUES IN CHINA** Even before perestroika unfolded in the Soviet Union, economic reform had begun in China. Early in the 1980s, the Chinese Communist government loosened its grip on business and eliminated some price controls. Students in China began to demand freedom of speech and a greater voice in government.

In April 1989, university students in China held marches that quickly grew into large demonstrations in Beijing's **Tiananmen** (tyän′än′mĕn′) **Square** and on the streets of other cities. In Tiananmen Square, Chinese students constructed a version of the Statue of Liberty to symbolize their struggle for democracy.

China's premier, Li Peng, eventually ordered the military to crush the protesters. China's armed forces stormed into Tiananmen Square, slaughtering unarmed students. The world's democratic countries watched these events in horror on television. The collapse of the pro-democracy movement left the future in China uncertain. As one student leader said, "The government has won the battle here today. But they have lost the people's hearts."

**MAIN IDEA**

**Analyzing Events**
**B** What signs signaled that the Cold War had come to an end?

*B. Answer* The Soviet Union dissolved. East Germany and West Germany were unified. Several Eastern European countries adopted democratic governments.

A Chinese protester defies the tanks in Tiananmen Square in 1989. ▷

**850** CHAPTER 25

---

 **classzone.com**

### Creating a Foreign Affairs Time Line

**Class Time** One class period

**Task** Creating a foreign affairs time line for the years 1980–1992

**Purpose** To examine the chronology and the significance of issues pertaining to foreign affairs

**Directions** Divide the class into four groups and assign each group one of the following regions: Europe, Asia, Middle East, Central America/Caribbean. Ask each group to research the foreign affairs issues specific to their region from 1980–1992. Have each group record their research findings on a class time line. Encourage students to find out about events that are not covered in the text.

📄 **Integrated Assessment**
· Rubric 2

## Central America and the Caribbean, 1981–1992

**Guatemala Dec. 1990**
U.S. suspends military aid because of regime's civil rights abuses.

**Honduras 1982–1990**
Military aid includes 100 military advisers. Country is a base for Nicaraguan Contras.

**El Salvador 1981–1992**
U.S. expands economic and military aid; sends advisers, including Green Berets, to help government combat leftist guerrillas.

**Nicaragua 1982–1990** Opposed to military buildup of Sandinista government and its aid to leftist rebels in El Salvador, U.S. trains and aids Nicaraguan Contra rebels.

**Panama Dec. 20, 1989**
In Operation Just Cause, 22,000 U.S. troops overthrow General Manuel Noriega.

**Grenada Oct. 25, 1983**
In first large-scale invasion in region since 1965, 1,200 marines and 700 Army Rangers restore law and order after overthrow of Bishop government.

Gulf of Mexico · Nassau · ATLANTIC OCEAN · BAHAMAS · Havana · Tropic of Cancer · CUBA · DOMINICAN REPUBLIC · Port-au-Prince · HAITI · Santo Domingo · San Juan · PUERTO RICO (U.S.) · Kingston · JAMAICA · Caribbean Sea · Belmopan BELIZE · Guatemala City · Tegucigalpa · San Salvador · Managua · San José · COSTA RICA · Panama City · COLOMBIA · VENEZUELA · MEXICO

0   200   400 miles
0   200   400 kilometers

### GEOGRAPHY SKILLBUILDER
1. **Location** Which Central American and Caribbean countries experienced an actual U.S. invasion of their territory during the 1980s?
2. **Region** Besides direct attack, what other techniques did the United States employ to influence countries in the Caribbean and Central American regions?

*Skillbuilder Answers*
1. Grenada and Panama.
2. Providing economic and military aid, as well as dispatching military advisors.

## Central American and Caribbean Policy ❷

Cold War considerations during the Reagan and Bush administrations continued to influence affairs in Central America and the Caribbean. In these places, the United States still opposed left-leaning and socialist governments in favor of governments friendly to the United States.

**NICARAGUA** The United States had had a presence in Nicaragua ever since 1912, when President Taft sent U.S. marines to protect American investments there. The marines left in 1933, but only after helping the dictator Anastasio Somoza come to power.

The Somoza family ruled Nicaragua for 42 years. To keep control of its business empire, the family rigged elections and assassinated political rivals. Many people believed that only a revolution would end the Somoza dictatorship.

Between 1977 and 1979, Nicaragua was engulfed in a civil war between Somoza's national guard and the **Sandinistas,** rebels who took their name from a rebel leader named Sandino who had been killed in 1934. When Sandinista rebels toppled the dictatorship of Somoza's son in 1979, President Carter recognized the new regime and sent it $83 million in economic aid. The Soviet Union and Cuba sent aid as well.

In 1981, however, President Reagan charged that Nicaragua was a Soviet outpost that was "exporting revolution" to other Central American countries. Reagan cut all aid to the Sandinista government and threw his support to guerrilla forces known as the **Contras** because they were "against" communism. By 1983, the Contra army had grown to nearly 10,000 men, and American officials from the CIA had stationed themselves to direct operations—without congressional approval. In response, Congress passed the Boland Amendment, banning military

*The Conservative Tide* **851**

### Nicaragua and the United States

Explain to students that the United States has had a strategic interest in Nicaragua since the mid-19th century. Have students use library resources and the Internet to research the history of the relationship between the United States and Nicaragua. Ask students why the United States has been interested in Nicaragua, and what form this interest has taken. Have students assess how the United States has influenced the development of the Nicaraguan nation. Have students write a brief history of U.S.–Nicaraguan relations.

**Rubric**
The history report should . . .
· trace relations from the mid-19th century to the present
· identify U.S. interests in Nicaragua
· analyze U.S. influence on Nicaraguan economic and political development

## Instruct: Objective ❸

### Middle East Trouble Spots

TAKS SS11 5(WH26.C)

· What was the Iran-Contra scandal?

· What prompted the United States to take action in the Middle East?

· How did the United States respond to Iraqi aggression?

 **In-Depth Resources: Unit 7**
· Guided Reading, p. 25
· Outline Map: U.S. Attention on the Middle East, pp. 34–35
· Primary Sources: The First Day of Desert Storm, p. 39
· American Lives: Daniel Inouye, p. 44

### More About . . .

**Iran-Contra Affair**

Both Oliver North and his boss, Rear Admiral John Poindexter, head of the National Security Council, lost their jobs and were prosecuted. Their convictions were appealed and over-turned. The appeals court ruled that the testimony they gave before Congress under a grant of limited immunity had been used against them in court. Among other Reagan administration officials indicted was former Defense Secretary Caspar Weinberger. He was one of the principals pardoned by Bush in 1992 before he left office. In a final report on his investigation, Special Prosecutor Walsh criticized Presidents Reagan and Bush for their roles in events relating to the scandal but did not file criminal charges against them.

---

aid to the Contras for two years. However, Reagan's administration still found ways to negotiate aid to the Contras.

On February 25, 1990, Nicaraguan president Daniel Ortega held free elections, and Violeta de Chamorro, a Contra supporter, was elected the nation's new president. Chamorro's supporters and the Sandinistas agreed to work together to rebuild Nicaragua.

**GRENADA** On the tiny Caribbean island of Grenada, the United States used direct military force to accomplish its aims. After noting that the island was developing ties to Communist Cuba, President Reagan sent approximately 2,000 troops to the island in 1983. There they overthrew the pro-Cuban government, which was replaced by one friendlier to the United States. Eighteen American soldiers died in the attack, but Reagan declared that the invasion had been necessary to defend U.S. security.

**PANAMA** Six years later, in 1989, President Bush sent more than 20,000 soldiers and marines into Panama to overthrow and arrest General Manuel Antonio Noriega on charges of drug trafficking. Noriega had been receiving money since 1960 from the CIA, but he was also involved in the international drug trade. After he was indicted by a Miami grand jury, Noriega was taken by force by the American military and flown to Miami to stand trial. In April 1992, Noriega was convicted and sentenced to 40 years in prison. Many Latin American governments deplored the "Yankee imperialism" of the action. However, many Americans—and Panamanians—were pleased by the removal of a military dictator who supported drug smuggling. **Ⓒ**

### ❸ Middle East Trouble Spots

Results favorable to U.S. interests were more difficult to obtain in the Middle East. Negotiating conflicts between ever-shifting governments drew the United States into scandal and its first major war since Vietnam.

▲ President Reagan's message to television audiences about selling arms to Iran differed greatly from what was going on behind the scenes.

**THE IRAN-CONTRA SCANDAL**
In 1983, terrorist groups loyal to Iran took a number of Americans hostage in Lebanon. Reagan denounced Iran and urged U.S. allies not to sell arms to Iran for its war against Iraq. In 1985, he declared that "America will never make concessions to terrorists." Therefore, Americans were shocked to learn in 1986 that President Reagan had approved the sale of arms to Iran. In exchange for those sales, Iran promised to win the release of seven American hostages held in Lebanon by pro-Iranian terrorists. What's more, members of Reagan's staff sent part of the

**MAIN IDEA**

**Comparing**
**Ⓒ** Between 1980 and 1992, how did U.S. policies regarding Central America differ from those regarding Europe?

*C. Answer* The government used direct intervention in Central America and diplomacy in Europe.

---

**ACTIVITY** | **LINK TO GOVERNMENT**

ⓘ classzone.com

## THE IRAN-CONTRA AFFAIR AND THE U.S. CONSTITUTION

**Class Time** 45 minutes

**Task** Charting details of the Iran-Contra scandal

**Purpose** To analyze a constitutional conflict between the president and Congress

**Directions** Have students use library and Internet resources to research the background and details of the Iran-Contra scandal. Have students identify the key figures in the affair and the specific constitutional conflict between the president and Congress. Then create a chart as a class based on students' research findings.

 **Integrated Assessment**
· Rubrics 1, 4

profits from those illegal arms sales to the Contras in Nicaragua—in direct violation of the Boland Amendment. President Reagan held a press conference to explain what had happened.

### A PERSONAL VOICE  RONALD REAGAN

"I am deeply troubled that the implementation of a policy aimed at resolving a truly tragic situation in the Middle East has resulted in such controversy. As I've stated previously, I believe our policy goals toward Iran were well founded."

—presidential press conference, November 25, 1986

In the summer of 1987, special committees of both houses of Congress conducted a dramatic inquiry into the Iran-Contra affair during a month of joint televised hearings. Among those testifying was Lieutenant Colonel Oliver North, a member of the National Security Council staff who played a key role in providing aid to the Contras. North appeared in military uniform adorned with medals. In defending his actions, North talked about patriotism and love of country. He asserted that he thought he was carrying out the president's wishes and that the end of helping the Contras justified almost any means.

After a congressional investigation, Special Prosecutor Lawrence E. Walsh, early in 1988, indicted various members of the Reagan administration who were involved in the scandal. Oliver North was found guilty of taking part in the cover-up. He was sentenced to pay a stiff fine and perform community service. On Christmas Eve of 1992, President Bush pardoned a number of Reagan officials.

**THE PERSIAN GULF WAR** Regardless of the scandal surrounding the Iran-Contra affair, conflict with Iraq (Iran's long-standing enemy) and its leader, Saddam Hussein, soon eclipsed U.S. problems with Iran. During the 1980s, Iran and Iraq had fought a prolonged war, and Hussein found himself with enormous war debts to pay. Several times, Hussein had claimed that the oil-rich nation of Kuwait was part of Iraq. On August 2, 1990, Iraqi troops invaded a disputed area claimed by Kuwait. The Iraqi invaders looted Kuwait, then headed toward Saudi Arabia and

## More About . . .

### Persian Gulf War

There were several notable facts about the Persian Gulf War. The first was the deliberate manner in which Bush and Baker built an international coalition to oppose Iraq. The second notable fact was the televised Congressional debate over whether or not to go to war with Iraq. The end of the Cold War allowed Congressmen and Senators to express reservations about going to war without being attacked for being "soft on communism." A third historic fact was the courageous service of women in the military, who were stationed in combat zones for the first time in U.S. history.

## POINT / COUNTERPOINT

### POINT

**"The United States must occasionally intervene militarily in regional conflicts."**

Proponents of U.S. military intervention abroad agreed with General Norman Schwarzkopf that "as the only remaining superpower, we have an awesome responsibility to . . . the rest of the world."

"The United States must take the lead in promoting democracy," urged Morton H. Halperin, former director of the ACLU (American Civil Liberties Union). "To say 'Let the UN do it' is a cop-out," stated adviser Robert G. Neumann.

Political scientist Jane Sharp expressed a similar sentiment. She asked, "Can any nation that has taken no action in Bosnia to stop the Serbian practice of ethnic cleansing continue to call itself civilized?"

### COUNTERPOINT

**"The United States should not intervene militarily in regional conflicts."**

A foreign-policy analyst at the Cato Institute, Barbara Conry, stated that "intervention in regional wars is a distraction and a drain on resources." What's more, she argued, "It does not work." Recalling the presence of American troops in Lebanon, Conry argued that intervention not only jeopardized American soldiers, it often obstructed what it sought to achieve.

"The internal freedom of a political community can only be achieved by members of that community," agreed Professor Stephen R. Shalom. He added that "using [military action] encourages quick fix solutions that ignore the underlying sources of conflict."

### THINKING CRITICALLY

1. **CONNECT TO TODAY  Comparing and Contrasting** What do you think are the strongest arguments for and against military intervention in regional conflicts?

   **SEE SKILLBUILDER HANDBOOK, PAGE R8.**

2. **CONNECT TO HISTORY  Hypothesizing** With at least one partner, research the events leading up to U.S. involvement in one of these countries: Lebanon, Grenada, Panama, or Kuwait. Then negotiate to resolve the conflict.

## POINT COUNTERPOINT

### Objectives

· To analyze the issues concerning U.S. military intervention in other countries

· To evaluate the responsibilities the United States faces as the only remaining superpower

· To draw conclusions about motives for military intervention

*The Conservative Tide*  **853**

### THINKING CRITICALLY: ANSWERS

1. **CONNECT TO TODAY** Arguments for military intervention: only U.S. can promote democracy; U.S. must oppose injustice and evil such as genocide. Arguments against military intervention: may not work; drain on resources; distraction from domestic problems

2. **CONNECT TO HISTORY**
   **Rubric**
   Student conflict negotiations should . . .
   · concentrate on a specific country
   · be fueled by discussions of their research
   · propose resolutions

## More About . . .

### Women in the Gulf War

About 37,000 women served in the military in the Persian Gulf War. For the first time, women's roles in the armed forces were expanded to include many combat-related occupations, such as ammunition technicians, helicopter pilots, and commanders. One Marine officer commented, "They [women] endured the same living conditions, duties, and responsibilities." Although women were not deployed in direct combat missions, often combat came to them. Reportedly, five female Army soldiers were killed in action, and many were wounded. Women accounted for seven percent of the total forces in Operation Desert Storm.

## HISTORY from VISUALS

### Interpreting the Map

Ask students to use the map to point out Kuwait's strategic importance in the Middle East. *(The oil fields and location on the Persian Gulf gave Kuwait importance; also, balance of power in the Middle East might be disrupted if Iraq annexed Kuwait.)*

 Mini-Lesson 3: SS11 5(WH26.C)

## The Persian Gulf War, 1990–1991

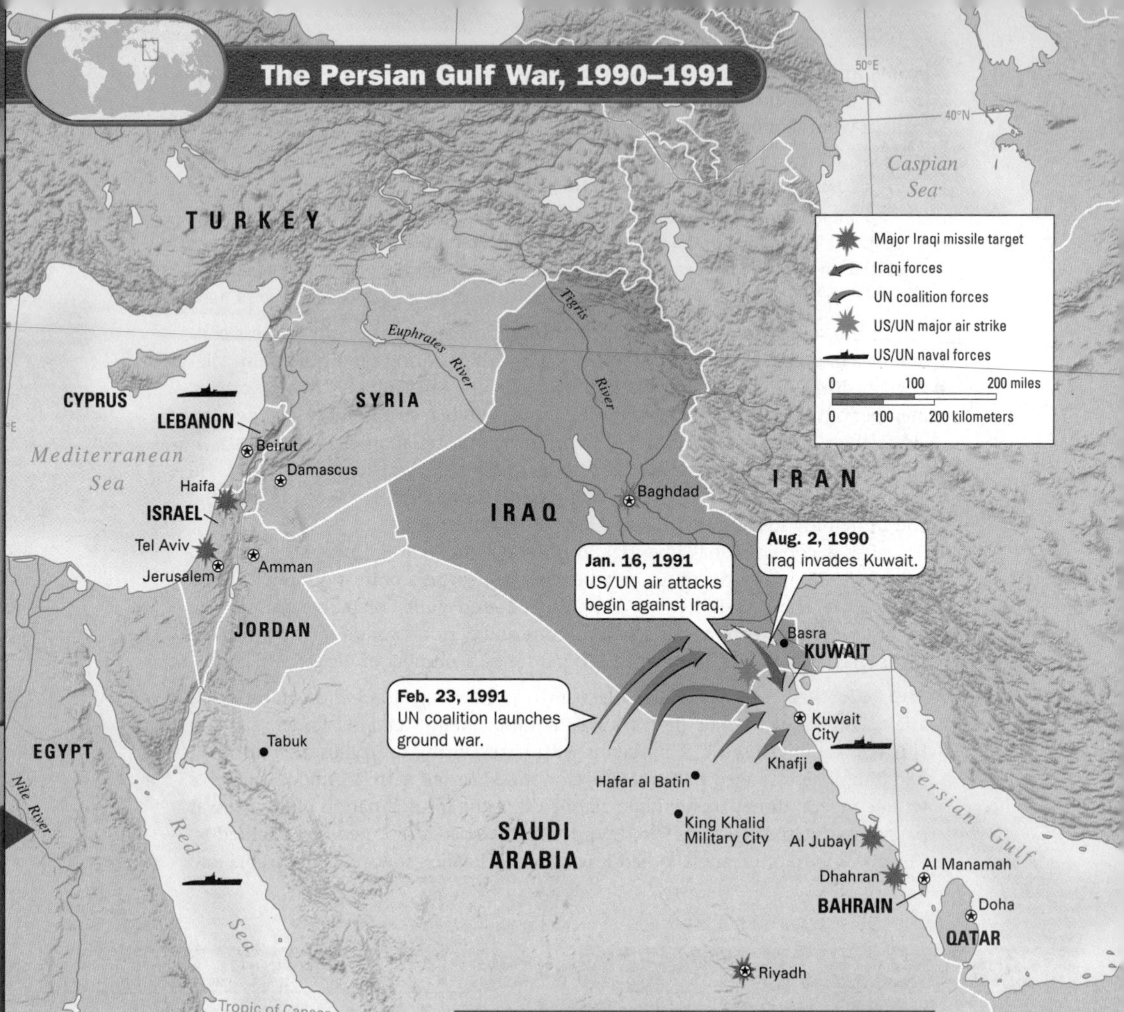

Major Iraqi missile target
Iraqi forces
UN coalition forces
US/UN major air strike
US/UN naval forces

0    100    200 miles
0    100    200 kilometers

**Aug. 2, 1990** Iraq invades Kuwait.

**Jan. 16, 1991** US/UN air attacks begin against Iraq.

**Feb. 23, 1991** UN coalition launches ground war.

Women served along with men in the military during the Gulf War *(right)*. Massive oil fires started by the Iraqis burned in Kuwait *(below)*.

### GEOGRAPHY SKILLBUILDER

1. **Region** What did UN coalition forces probably hope to achieve by moving forces into southern Iraq?
2. **Movement** How did the movements of coalition ground forces show that the intention of the coalition in the Gulf War was ultimately defensive, not offensive?

## ACTIVITY    COOPERATIVE LEARNING

## BLOCK SCHEDULING

### Interviewing Gulf War Veterans

**Class Time** Two class periods

**Task** Interviewing Gulf War veterans about their experiences in the war

**Purpose** To interpret the experiences of Gulf War veterans and analyze the legacy of the war

**Directions** Have students contact local veterans organizations to identify local Gulf War veterans who might be willing to be interviewed. Have students prepare a list of questions regarding war experiences and Gulf War Syndrome. Have students ask permission to record the interviews. Ask students to give a short presentation to the class, summarizing their findings.

 Integrated Assessment
· Rubric 3

KEY PLAYER

**H. NORMAN SCHWARZKOPF**
**1934–**

In 1988, Norman Schwarzkopf, shown above, became commander in chief of forces in Asia and Africa. During the Persian Gulf War, more than 540,000 men and women served under the command of "Stormin' Norman." Schwarzkopf said of Saddam Hussein that he was "neither a strategist, nor is he schooled in the operational arts, nor is he a tactician, nor is he a general, nor is he a soldier. Other than that, he is a great military man."

**MAIN IDEA**

**Drawing Conclusions**

 What issue led to the conflict in the Middle East?

*Skillbuilder Answers*
1. By securing the area, coalition forces were probably hoping to cut Iraq off from further land access to Kuwait and also to isolate Iraqi forces already in Kuwait.
2. Coalition forces did not strike deep into Iraq, only going far enough to protect Kuwait.

**D. Answer**
Control over the oil in the region.

its oil fields. If Iraq conquered Saudi Arabia as well as Kuwait, it would control one-half of the world's known oil reserves, which would severely threaten U.S. oil supplies.

For several months, President Bush and Secretary of State James Baker organized an international coalition against Iraqi aggression. With the support of Congress and the UN, President Bush launched **Operation Desert Storm** to liberate Kuwait from Iraqi control. On January 16, 1991, the United States and its allies staged a massive air assault against Iraq. On February 23, they launched a successful ground offensive from Saudi Arabia. On February 28, 1991, President Bush announced a cease-fire. Operation Desert Storm was over. Kuwait was liberated.

Millions of Americans turned out for the victory parades that greeted returning soldiers. After the debacle in Vietnam, they were thrilled the war was over, with fewer than 400 casualties among UN coalition forces. (However, there were subsequent reports that Gulf veterans were suffering from disabilities caused by chemicals used in the war.) By contrast, Iraq had suffered an estimated 100,000 military and civilian deaths. During the embargo that followed, many Iraqi children died from outbreaks of cholera, typhoid, enteritis, and other diseases.

**BUSH'S DOMESTIC POLICIES** Despite his great achievement in the Persian Gulf War, President Bush was not as successful on the domestic front. He was hurt by rising deficits and a recession that began in 1990 and lasted through most of 1992. Bush was forced to raise taxes despite his campaign pledge. His approval rating had dropped to 40 percent by 1992. The weak economy and the tax hike doomed Bush's reelection campaign, and 12 years of Republican leadership came to an end.

## SECTION 4 ASSESSMENT

**1. TERMS & NAMES** For each term or name, write a sentence explaining its meaning.
- Mikhail Gorbachev
- *perestroika*
- Tiananmen Square
- *Contras*
- *glasnost*
- INF Treaty
- *Sandinistas*
- Operation Desert Storm

**MAIN IDEA**

**2. TAKING NOTES**
Use a chart like the one below to explain U.S. foreign policy toward world regions.

| U.S. Foreign Policy |
| --- |
| Europe |
| Central America and Caribbean |
| Middle East |

Now write a paragraph in which you describe a trouble spot in one of these regions.

**CRITICAL THINKING**

**3. ANALYZING CAUSES**
What factors caused the end of the Cold War? **Think About:**
- events in the Soviet Union
- events in Germany and Eastern Europe
- how U.S. leaders responded to those events

**4. FORMING GENERALIZATIONS**
What factors do you think determined whether or not the United States intervened militarily in other nations?

**5. HYPOTHESIZING**
Is it possible for an authoritarian government to make economic reforms without also making political reforms? Support your answer with details from the text.

---

## KEY PLAYER

**H. Norman Schwarzkopf**
Saddam Hussein was still in power after the Persian Gulf War. Some critics have faulted Schwarzkopf for not continuing the war to Baghdad and ousting Saddam Hussein. Others have pointed out that the international coalition of Desert Storm was defensive rather than offensive in nature, and Schwarzkopf followed that battle plan. Ask students to give examples from the Persian Gulf War that illustrate the idea that the lasting impact of events is not always evident. *(Iraq suffered an overwhelming military defeat; Saddam Hussein remained in power; Gulf War Syndrome.)*

## Assess & Reteach

### SECTION 4 ASSESSMENT
Have students answer the Section Assessment questions and then compare answers with another student. Ask the pairs to locate text passages that support their answers.

📄 Formal Assessment
· Section Quiz, p. 457

### SELF-ASSESSMENT
Ask students to identify events covered in this chapter that they found difficult to understand. Have them formulate questions, and review the text to find the answers.

### RETEACH
Review the maps on pages 845 and 848, which provide insight into the central content of the chapter.

📄 In-Depth Resources: Unit 7
· Reteaching Activity, p. 31

---

**1. TERMS & NAMES**
Mikhail Gorbachev, p. 848
*glasnost*, p. 849
*perestroika*, p. 849
INF Treaty, p. 849
Tiananmen Square, p. 850
*Sandinistas*, p. 851
*Contras*, p. 851
Operation Desert Storm, p. 855

**2. TAKING NOTES**
Europe: INF Treaty; START II Pact; Cold War ends. Central America and Caribbean: cut aid to Sandinistas; send aid to Contras; invasion of Grenada. Middle East: Iran-Contra affair; Operation Desert Storm.

**3. ANALYZING CAUSES**
Collapse of Soviet economy, Gorbachev's reforms in the Soviet Union, unification of East and West Germany

**4. FORMING GENERALIZATIONS**
The United States intervened when essential United States interests and assets—American lives, democracy, oil— were at stake.

**5. HYPOTHESIZING**
Some students may say no and use the Soviet Union as an example. Others may say yes and point to China.

## TERMS & NAMES

1. entitlement program, p. 831
2. affirmative action, p. 831
3. Moral Majority, p. 831
4. Ronald Reagan, p. 832
5. supply-side economics, p. 835
6. Geraldine Ferraro, p. 837
7. AIDS, p. 840
8. Mikhail Gorbachev, p. 848
9. *Contras*, p. 851
10. Operation Desert Storm, p. 855

## MAIN IDEAS

1. frustration over entitlement programs, inflation, high taxes, criticism of affirmative action, religious revival
2. Reagan's views on key issues; prolonged Iranian hostage crisis; weak economy; high rate of inflation
3. cutting social programs, lowering taxes, increasing defense spending
4. removal of government regulations on industries; deregulation increased competition and resulted in lower prices for consumer
5. African Americans made political gains, although economic progress lagged; Latinos became fastest growing minority, gaining political and economic power; Native Americans faced long-term problems in health, education, and employment; Asian Americans became second fastest growing minority; gay men and lesbians openly fought for civil rights
6. Ferraro's 1984 vice presidential candidacy; increase in number of women in Congress; push for pay equity
7. economic problems and nationalism in non-Russian republics
8. United States organized international coalition against Iraqi aggression; Bush launched Operation Desert Storm in which the United States and allies staged massive air assault against Iraq, followed by a successful ground offensive

## TERMS & NAMES

**For each term or name below, write a sentence explaining its significance.**

1. entitlement program
2. affirmative action
3. Moral Majority
4. Ronald Reagan
5. supply-side economics
6. Geraldine Ferraro
7. AIDS
8. Mikhail Gorbachev
9. *Contras*
10. Operation Desert Storm

## MAIN IDEAS

**Use your notes and the information in the chapter to answer the following questions.**

### A Conservative Movement Emerges
*(pages 830–833)*

1. What caused the conservative revolution of the early 1980s?
2. What factors led to Ronald Reagan's victory in 1980?

### Conservative Policies Under Reagan and Bush *(pages 834–838)*

3. What principles formed the basis of "Reaganomics"?
4. What is deregulation, and how did it affect certain industries in the 1980s?

### Social Concerns in the 1980s *(pages 839–845)*

5. What progress and obstacles did different minority groups experience in the 1980s?
6. What were some gains that women achieved in the 1980s?

### Foreign Policy After the Cold War
*(pages 848–855)*

7. What caused the downfall of the Soviet Union and the founding of the Commonwealth of Independent States?
8. Summarize the U.S. response to Iraq's invasion of Kuwait.

## CRITICAL THINKING

1. **USING YOUR NOTES** Choose two events from each of the sections of the chapter and place them in chronological order on a timeline like the one below.

| Ronald Reagan becomes president. | |
|---|---|
| | George Bush is defeated. |

2. **EVALUATING** Review the goals of the conservative movement and the actions of the government under Reagan and Bush. Evaluate how well the goals had been achieved by the end of Bush's term.

3. **INTERPRETING MAPS** Look at the map on page 851. Between 1982 and 1992, the United States intervened in Latin America many times. How might the presence of a Communist government on the island of Cuba have influenced U.S. actions?

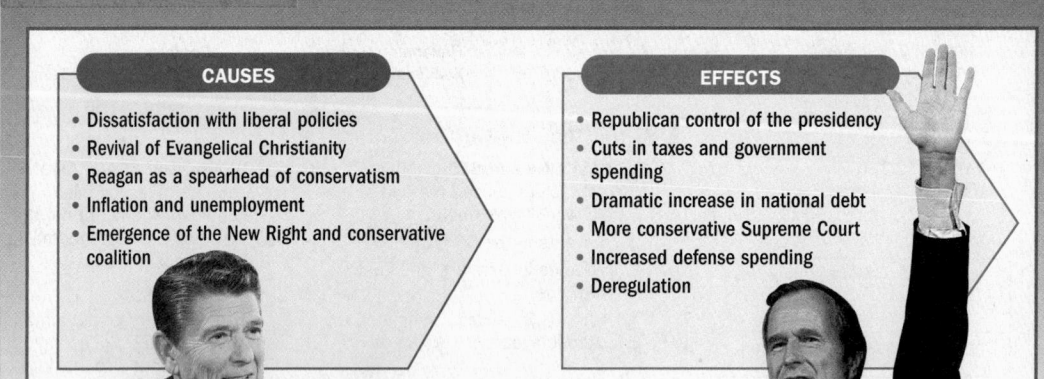

**VISUAL SUMMARY** **THE CONSERVATIVE TIDE**

**CAUSES**
- Dissatisfaction with liberal policies
- Revival of Evangelical Christianity
- Reagan as a spearhead of conservatism
- Inflation and unemployment
- Emergence of the New Right and conservative coalition

**EFFECTS**
- Republican control of the presidency
- Cuts in taxes and government spending
- Dramatic increase in national debt
- More conservative Supreme Court
- Increased defense spending
- Deregulation

## CRITICAL THINKING

1. **Using Your Notes** 1982: ERA failed to pass; 1983: Reagan proposes Strategic Defense Initiative; invasion of Grenada; 1984: Geraldine Ferraro runs for Vice President; Reagan and Bush win election; 1989: Supreme Court ruling on abortion; 1991: Operation Desert Storm; Anita Hill/Clarence Thomas hearings.

2. **Evaluating** Goals achieved: government deregulation of business; cuts in taxes and social programs. Failures: rise of inflation; increased national deficit; problems caused by weakening of environmental and social agencies; failure to win the war on drugs.

3. **Interpreting Maps** During this time period, the United States feared the spread of communism from Cuba.

## Standardized Test Practice

Use the passage and your knowledge of U.S. history to answer question 1.

> "The system has never failed us, but, for a time, we failed the system. We asked things of government that government was not equipped to give. We yielded authority to the national government that properly belonged to states or to local governments or to the people themselves. We allowed taxes and inflation to rob us of our earnings and savings and watched the great industrial machine that had made us the most productive people on Earth slow down and the number of unemployed increase."
>
> —Ronald Reagan, Second Inaugural Address, 1985

1. The passage suggests that President Ronald Reagan supported which point of view?

   **A** There should be an end to all social welfare programs.

   **B** The role of the federal government should be reduced.

   **C** The role of the federal government should be increased.

   **D** The federal government should raise taxes.

2. Which of the following events signaled the end of the Cold War?

   **F** Operation Desert Storm

   **G** Iran-Contra Scandal

   **H** collapse of the Soviet Union

   **J** protests at Tiananmen Square

Use the graph and your knowledge of U.S. history to answer question 3.

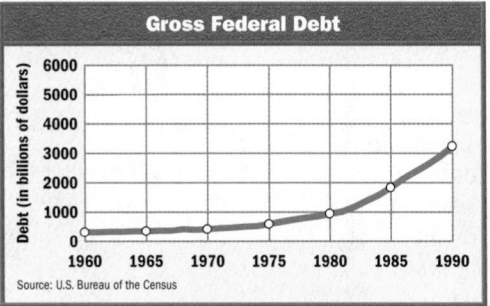

**Gross Federal Debt**

Source: U.S. Bureau of the Census

3. The graph shows that the gross federal debt —

   **A** stayed the same during the Reagan and Bush years.

   **B** greatly increased during the Reagan and Bush years.

   **C** greatly decreased during the Reagan and Bush years.

   **D** did not exist during the Reagan and Bush years.

4. Which of the following was *not* a goal of the conservative movement of the 1980s?

   **F** strengthen the national defense

   **G** reduce government regulations

   **H** promote family values and patriotic ideals

   **J** increase taxes

**ADDITIONAL TEST PRACTICE, pages S1–S33.**

**TEST PRACTICE** CLASSZONE.COM

## Standardized Test Practice

1. The correct answer is letter **B.**
   Letter A is not correct because he is not referring to social welfare programs. Letter C is not correct because Reagan does not want to increase the federal government's power. Letter D is not correct because he did not want to raise taxes.

2. The correct answer is letter **H.**
   Letter F is not correct because Operation Desert Storm took place after the Cold War. Letter G is not correct because the Iran-Contra affair was part of the Cold War. Letter J is not correct because the protests in Tiananmen Square did not affect the Cold War.

3. The correct answer is letter **B.**
   Letters A, C, D are not correct because the graph shows an increase.

4. The correct answer is letter **J.**
   Letter F is not correct because each wanted to strengthen the national defense. Letter G is not correct because government regulations were reduced. Letter H is not correct because family values and patriotic ideals were supported.

### UNIT PROJECT

**CAMPAIGN SCRAPBOOK**

**Tips for Teaching**

· Have students do an Internet search for pictures of campaign literature or buttons that could be included in their scrapbook.

· Students may want to include video clips of campaign ads or speeches in their scrapbooks.

Formal Assessment
· Chapter Test, Forms A, B, and C, pp. 458–469

## ALTERNATIVE ASSESSMENT

1. **INTERACT WITH HISTORY** Recall your discussion of the question on page 829:

   *What campaign slogan will you create?*

   As a speechwriter for Ronald Reagan in 1980, write an effective speech that contains your campaign slogan and presents reasons why people should vote for Reagan. Present your speech to the class.

2.  **INTERNET ACTIVITY** CLASSZONE.COM

   Visit the links for Chapter Assessment to find out more about Saddam Hussein's rise to power in Iraq. Write a short (3 to 5 paragraphs) biography. What tactics did he use to become dictator? Why is he often compared to Germany's Adolf Hitler? How do his policies affect the people of Iraq? Describe his present relationship with the United States.

*The Conservative Tide* **857**

## ALTERNATIVE ASSESSMENT

### 1. INTERACT WITH HISTORY
**Rubric**

Student speeches should . . .

· include a campaign slogan

· be persuasive and explain why people should vote for Reagan

· identify Reagan's position on critical issues

### 2. INTERNET ACTIVITY
**Rubric**

Student paragraphs should . . .

· provide biographical information about Saddam Hussein

· explain Saddam's rise to power, dictatorial tactics, and governmental policies

· identify the reasons why Saddam Hussein has been compared to Hitler

· include details and examples to support conclusions

# The United States in Today's World

| | CHAPTER OVERVIEW | COPYMASTERS | INTEGRATED TECHNOLOGY |
|---|---|---|---|
| **CHAPTER RESOURCES** | President Bill Clinton locks horns with a Republican Congress, and George W. Bush becomes president following the contested 2000 election. Americans face economic, technological, and demographic changes that are reshaping their lives and redefining the main issues that concern citizens. | Telescoping the Times<br>· Chapter Summary, pp. 51–52<br><br>Planning for Block Schedules | Power Presentations<br>Electronic Teacher Tools<br>Online Lesson Planner<br>classzone.com |
| **SECTION 1**<br><br>The 1990s and the New Millennium<br><br>pp. 860–868 | **KEY IDEAS**<br><br>*Bill Clinton is elected and moves the nation's politics toward the center. The second Clinton term is marred by scandal and an impeachment. George W. Bush wins the Presidency amid controversy over balloting in several states.* | In-Depth Resources: Unit 7<br>· Guided Reading, p. 45<br>· Building Vocabulary, p. 49<br>· Reteaching Activity, p. 51<br>· Primary Sources, pp. 57–58<br><br>Lesson Plans, pp. 203–204 | Geography Transparencies GT34<br>· Eligible Votes Cast, 1996<br>Critical Thinking Transparencies CT34, CT68<br>· Federal Government Shutdown<br>· Federal Budget, 1945–1995<br>Electronic Library of Primary Sources<br>· Clinton's First Inaugural Address<br>· A Contract with America<br>· Bush's Inaugural Address<br>classzone.com |
| **SECTION 2**<br><br>The New Global Economy<br><br>pp. 869–875 | *Workers face new challenges to their economic security as the U.S. economy evolves.* | In-Depth Resources: Unit 7<br>· Guided Reading, p. 46<br>· Reteaching Activity, p. 52<br>· Geography Application, pp. 55–56<br>· Primary Source, p. 59<br>· American Lives, p. 63<br><br>Lesson Plans, pp. 205–206 | classzone.com |
| **SECTION 3**<br><br>Technology and Modern Life<br><br>pp. 876–881 | *New opportunities and challenges arise from technological developments in many industries, especially computers and communications.* | In-Depth Resources: Unit 7<br>· Guided Reading, p. 47<br>· Reteaching Activity, p. 53<br><br>Lesson Plans, pp. 207–208 | Electronic Library of Primary Sources<br>· from *Being Digital* by Nicholas Negroponte<br>classzone.com |
| **SECTION 4**<br><br>The Changing Face of America<br><br>pp. 882–889 | *Demographic changes in the United States have significant implications for American society at the outset of the 21st century.* | In-Depth Resources: Unit 7<br>· Guided Reading, p. 48<br>· Skillbuilder Practice, p. 50<br>· Reteaching Activity, p. 54<br>· Primary Source, p. 60<br>· American Lives, p. 64<br><br>Lesson Plans, pp. 109–110 | Humanities Transparencies HT48<br>· This Isn't Exactly the Sort of Active Retirement I Hoped For . . .<br>Electronic Library of Primary Sources<br>· from Mission Statement by the Organizing Committee of the Million Man March<br>· from *My American Century* by Studs Terkel<br>classzone.com |

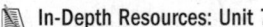
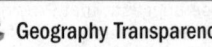

## ASSESSMENT OPTIONS

PE Chapter Assessment, pp. 890–891

Formal Assessment
· Chapter Tests, Forms A, B, and C, pp. 474–491

Test Generator

Integrated Assessment Book

TAKS Online Test Practice

TAKS Spiraled Content Review

TAKS Practice Tests

---

PE Section 1 Assessment, p. 868

TE Self-Assessment, p. 868

Formal Assessment, Quiz, p. 470

Integrated Assessment Book

Test Generator

TAKS Practice Transparencies TT128

---

PE Section 2 Assessment, p. 873

TE Self-Assessment, p. 873

Formal Assessment, Quiz, p. 471

Integrated Assessment Book

Test Generator

TAKS Practice Transparencies TT129

---

PE Section 3 Assessment, p. 879

TE Self-Assessment, p. 879

Formal Assessment, Quiz, p. 472

Integrated Assessment Book

Test Generator

TAKS Practice Transparencies TT130

---

PE Section 4 Assessment, p. 887

TE Self-Assessment, p. 887

Formal Assessment, Quiz, p. 473

Integrated Assessment Book

Test Generator

TAKS Practice Transparencies TT131

---

## RESOURCES FOR DIFFERENTIATING INSTRUCTION

### Students Acquiring English/ESL

**Reading Study Guide:** (English and Spanish) pp. 257–264

**Access for Students Acquiring English/ESL:** Spanish Translations, pp. 272–273

**Chapter Summaries on CD** (English and Spanish)

### Less Proficient Readers

**Reading Study Guide** (English and Spanish) pp. 257–264

**Telescoping the Times** · Chapter Summary, pp. 51–52

**Chapter Summaries on CD** (English and Spanish)

### Gifted and Talented Students

**In-Depth Resources: Unit 7** · Primary Sources, pp. 57–60 · Literature, pp. 61–62 · American Lives: Bill Gates, p. 63; Wilma Mankiller, p. 64

**Electronic Library of Primary Sources** · Unit 7, Chapter 26

---

## CROSS-CURRICULAR CONNECTIONS

### Science

Wunch, Susi Trautmann. *The Adventures of Sojourner: The Mission to Mars That Thrilled the World.* NY: Mikaya Press, 1998. Wonderful story of the voyage and the breathtaking photographs it supplied.

Gore, Al. *Earth in the Balance: Ecology and the Human Spirit.* Boston: Houghton Mifflin, 1992. As a senator from Tennessee, Al Gore makes his case for protecting the environment before the risks to air, water, and soil destroy the earth for good.

### Sociology

Allison, Anthony. *Hear These Voices: Youth at the Edge of the Millennium.* NY: Dutton, 1999. Mesmerizing testimonies from teenagers around the world who have endured addiction, AIDS, neglect, and abuse. The book also contains interviews with adults who have intervened to help.

### World History

Andryszewki, Tricia. *Kosovo: The Splintering of Yugoslavia.* Brookfield, CT: Millbook Press, 1999. Reviews the history of the area and reports on both the success and failure of mediations.

### Literature

Buckley, Christopher. *Thank You for Smoking.* NY: Harper, 1995. This wickedly funny novel about the adventures of a spokesman for the tobacco lobby who will do anything to sell his product.

### McDougal Littell

*The Language of Literature* Unit 8, parts 1, 2

*Literature Connections*

Soto, Gary. *Taking Sides.* A Mexican-American youth has trouble adjusting after he moves from the inner city to the suburbs.

---

## ENRICHMENT ACTIVITIES

PE **Pupil's Edition,** pp. 858–889
Interact with History, pp. 858–859
American Literature, pp. 874–875
Science & Technology, pp. 880–881
Tracing Themes, pp. 888–889

**In-Depth Resources: Unit 7**
· Geography Application: The U.S. Trade in Goods, pp. 55–56
· Primary Source: Contract with America, p. 57

· Primary Source: "A Bridge to the Future," p. 58
· Primary Source: *The Road Ahead,* p.59
· Primary Source: Road Sign, p. 60
· Literature: Selected Poems, pp. 61–62
· American Lives: Bill Gates, p. 63
· American Lives: Wilma Mankiller, p. 64

**Electronic Library of Primary Sources**
· Unit 7, Chapter 26

## BLOCK SCHEDULE LESSON PLAN OPTIONS (90-MINUTE PERIOD)

### DAY 1

**CHAPTER 26 OPENER**
**pp. 858–859**
**Class Time** 30 minutes

**History from Visuals, p. 858**
**Class Time** 10 minutes
*Options for Pacing and Variety*
· Class Discussion Have students study the photograph and describe the scene. Have them discuss their own volunteering experiences. Ask them to consider why people do volunteer work. **Class Time** 15 minutes

**Interact with History, p. 859**
**Class Time** 20 minutes
*Options for Pacing and Variety*
· Role-Playing Have students read the situation and discuss how a national news program would present the issues raised. **Class Time** 15 minutes

**SECTION 1, pp. 860–868**
**Class Time** 30 minutes
*Options for Pacing and Variety*
· Time Saver After students have read the section, ask them the Objective 3 questions on TE page 863. **Class Time** 10 minutes

· Peer Teaching Have students work in groups to make a time line of the events in one of the subheadings in the section. **Class Time** 20 minutes

### DAY 1 continued

· Internet Have students work in groups to research the effects of the 2000 elections. Have each group use the Internet or library to research a different part of the situation. Refer to the activity on page 867 TE. **Class Time** 30 minutes

**SECTION 2, pp. 869–875**
**Class Time** 30 minutes
*Options for Pacing and Variety*
· Internet Have students use library resources and the Internet to research American trade with China and Japan. Refer to the TE activity on page 872. Have them present their findings to the class. **Class Time** 30 minutes

· Time Saver Ask students to read the sidebar on economics and immigration on page 873. Read them the additional information in the TE and discuss the questions in the TE. **Class Time** 20 minutes

· Team Teaching Ask students to read pages 874-875, "Women Writers Reflect American Diversity." If possible, ask an English literature teacher to visit your class to discuss these and other women writers, the importance of the context in which they write, writing from a woman's perspective, and writing from an immigrant perspective. **Class Time** 30 minutes

### DAY 2

**SECTION 3, pp. 876–881**
**Class Time** 30 minutes
*Options for Pacing and Variety*
· Time Saver Ask students to look at the political cartoon on page 873 and discuss the Skillbuilder questions as a class. **Class Time** 15 minutes

· Peer Teaching Ask students to work in pairs on the Section Assessment. **Class Time** 20 minutes

**SECTION 4, pp. 882–889**
**Class Time** 30 minutes
*Options for Pacing and Variety*
· Peer Teaching Explain to students the meaning of the term *gentrification* (see TE page 883). Then have them work in groups to complete the research activity on local demographic change on TE page 883. **Class Time** 30 minutes

· Peer Evaluation Have students answer the Section Assessment questions individually. Then have them compare answers with another student. Ask students to locate text passages that support their answers. **Class Time** 25 minutes

· Time Saver Ask students to read the feature on pages 888–889, "Immigration and Migration," and discuss and complete the Thinking Critically questions. **Class Time** 25 minutes

### DAY 2 continued

**ASSESSMENT**
**pp. 890–891**
**Class Time** 30 minutes
*Options for Pacing and Variety*
· Peer Evaluation Have students work in small groups to answer the Critical Thinking questions. Then have them trade answers with another group and evaluate their responses. **Class Time** 20 minutes

· Time Saver Have students revisit their responses to the Interact with History questions at the beginning of the chapter. Ask them how they would respond differently and what aspects of their reading influenced these changes. **Class Time** 15 minutes

---

**TEACHER-TESTED ACTIVITY**     Mark A. Van Hecke, Anchor Bay High School, New Baltimore, Michigan
**CHART OF U.S. PRESIDENTS AND MAP OF HOME STATES**

**Class Time** 40 minutes
**Task** Completing a chart and an outline map
**Purpose** To understand how migration to the Sunbelt has affected presidential selection in the last half of the 20th century

**Supplies Needed**
· Transparency showing 10-row chart with 4 column heads: "President;" "Years in Office;" "Home State;" "Political Party"
· Blank transparency outline map of the United States, including the states

**Activity** Beginning with John F. Kennedy, assign a different U.S. president to pairs or small groups of students. Tell them to use the textbook to find the information listed on the chart. Then as a class, fill in the chart and label the home states (states of residence at the time of election) on the map. Have students discuss the impact of the Sunbelt.

# CHAPTER 26 CORRELATION

 **CORRELATION TO THE TEXAS ESSENTIAL KNOWLEDGE AND SKILLS**

Chapter 26 addresses the following standards of the Texas Essential Knowledge and Skills for U.S. History.

| TEKS | Instruction | Student Question/Activity |
|---|---|---|
| **(4C)** Evaluate the impact of third parties and their candidates such as H. Ross Perot. | **PE 861** discussion of the impact of third party candidate H. Ross Perot on the 1992 presidential election | **PE 868** writing activity asking students to demonstrate their understanding of the significance of H. Ross Perot |
| **(6G)** Analyze the reasons for the Western victory in the Cold War and the challenges of changing relationships among nations. | **PE 863–864** examination of foreign policy under President Clinton and the challenge of the post-Cold War world | **TE 863** activity in which students prepare an oral report of the roots of ethnic conflict in the Balkans |
| **(6H)** Identify the origins of major domestic and foreign policy issues currently facing the United States. | **PE 869–873** analysis of the growth of the service sector, high-tech industry, and the global economy | **PE 873** Critical Thinking questions about America's transformed economy |
| **(10A)** Analyze the effects of changing demographic patterns resulting from migration within the United States. | **PE 888–889** Tracing Themes features on the impact of immigration to and migration within the United States | **PE 889** Critical Thinking questions about the feature |
| **(13E)** Analyze how various New Deal agencies and programs continue to affect the lives of U.S. citizens. | **PE 884–885** discussion of the growing importance of Social Security as the number of elderly Americans increases | **PE 885** Main Idea question about the future of social security |
| **(14E)** Describe the dynamic relationship between U.S. international trade policies and the U.S. free enterprise system. | **PE 872–873** discussion of the rise of a global economy and its impact on the United States | **PE 872** Skillbuilder questions about World Trading Blocs map |
| **(20A)** Describe how characteristics and issues of various eras in U.S. history have been reflected in works of art, music, and literature. | **PE 874–875** American Literature feature on how the growing voices of minority writers reflect the nation's growing diversity | **PE 875** Critical Thinking questions about the feature |
| **(22A)** Explain the scientific discoveries and technological innovations on the development of the United States. | **PE 876-881** examination of the computer-driven communications revolution, as well as significant scientific and medical break-throughs | **PE 881** Critical Thinking questions about the significant discoveries and innovations of the 1990s |

## TAKS MINI-LESSONS

1. **Social Studies Skills: Objective 3 (US14.E):** Describe the dynamic relationship between U.S. international trade policies and the U.S. free enterprise system **Activity** Have students write a paragraph summarizing the text under the heading "Change and the Global Economy" on page 872.

2. **Social Studies Skills: Objective 3 (US21.A):** Explain actions taken by people from racial, ethnic, and religious groups to expand economic opportunities and political rights in American society **Activity** Have students summarize the actions taken by Native Americans in recent years to improve their status in the United States.

3. **Social Studies Skills: Objective 3 (US23.A):** Analyze how scientific discoveries and technological innovations, including those in transportation and communication, have changed the standard of living in the United States **Activity** Have students answer the skillbuilder questions about the political cartoon on page 877.

4. **English Language Arts Skills: Objective 1 (7.F):** Produce summaries of texts by identifying main ideas and their supporting details **Activity** Have students summarize the events surrounding the presidential election of 2000 in a paragraph with a topic sentence and supporting details.

5. **English Language Arts Skills: Objective 6 (2.C):** Proofread writing for appropriateness of organization, content, style, and conventions **Activity** Have pairs of students proofread each other's answers to Section 1 Assessment questions on page 868.

# CHAPTER 26

# THE UNITED STATES IN TODAY'S WORLD

## HISTORY from VISUALS

**Interpreting the Photograph**
Have students study the photograph and describe the scene. Have them discuss their own volunteering experiences. Ask them to consider why so many Americans do volunteer work. *(to contribute to causes; to help others in need; to foster community awareness; to raise funds)*

## Time Line Discussion

Explain to students that the time line covers the decade of the 1990s and the start of the new millennium. Ask:

· What was unique about Madeline Albright's appointment as Secretary of State? *(She was the first woman to fill the position.)*
· What important political event happened during President Clinton's second term? *(Clinton impeached and acquitted)*
· What was significant about the presidential election in South Africa? *(the first all-race election; Nelson Mandela elected)*

Participants at the Walk For Hunger, held annually in Massachusetts, help to support local and emergency food programs.

**1992** Twenty-seventh Amendment prohibits midterm congressional pay raises.

**1992** William Jefferson Clinton is elected president.

**1994** Republicans gain control of both houses of Congress.

**1995** "Million Man March" held in Washington, D.C.

**1996** President Clinton is reelected.

USA
WORLD

**1992**          **1994**          **1996**

**1993** Russia and United States sign START-II treaty reducing warheads and ICBMs.

**1994** In South Africa's first all-race election, Nelson Mandela is elected president.

**1995** Israeli prime minister Yitzhak Rabin is assassinated.

**858** CHAPTER 26

## THEMES IN CHAPTER 26

### ECONOMIC OPPORTUNITY

The federal government's pursuit of international trade agreements was fueled by a desire to expand foreign markets. At issue was the impact of such agreements on jobs at home.

**See Teacher's Edition note, p. 870.**

As the 21st century began, economic problems threatened Americans' sense of financial security. Many wondered if the American dream would survive.

**See Teacher's Edition note, pp. 862.**

### SCIENCE AND TECHNOLOGY

Technological advances in medicine, communications, and entertainment affected many aspects of American life. These new technologies drew praise as well as criticism.

**See Teacher's Edition note, p. 880.**

### IMMIGRATION AND MIGRATION

Cultural demographics in the United States were shifting. Immigration policies sparked controversy. Opinions were divided about how to handle the increased influx of illegal immigrants.

**See Teacher's Edition note, p. 886.**

# INTERACT
## WITH HISTORY

You are a high school senior who is active in student government and community service. You have been chosen from among thousands of students nationwide to address an international youth symposium on global issues and reforms. As a U.S. delegate to the event, you address the crowd, confident that young people will be able to change the future.

## What are the most important issues that affect the world today?

### Examine the Issues

- What makes nations increasingly dependent on one another?
- How does technology affect society worldwide?
- What are the ways to foster cooperation among nations?

**RESEARCH LINKS** **CLASSZONE.COM**

Visit the Chapter 26 links for more information about The United States in Today's World.

**1997** Madeleine Albright is the first woman to become secretary of state.

**1998** President Clinton is impeached.

**1999** Senate acquits President Clinton.

**2000** George W. Bush is elected 43rd president.

**2001** On September 11, terrorists attack New York's World Trade Center and the Pentagon with hijacked jets.

**1998**                **2000**                **2002**

**1997** Scottish scientist clones "Dolly" the sheep.

**1998** Northern Ireland, the Irish Republic, and the United Kingdom sign peace agreements.

**2000** The dreaded "Y2K" bug proves harmless to computer systems globally.

**2001** Serbian president Slobodan Milosevic is brought before the UN war crimes tribunal.

*The United States in Today's World* **859**

---

## INTERACT
### WITH HISTORY

### Objectives

· To help students understand future challenges they might face
· To help students understand the impact of globalism on their everyday lives

### Examine the Issues

1. Have with students consider how technology and the international movement of capital connect nations in new ways.
2. Ask students to analyze how a government's ability to control access to information might be impaired by technology.
3. Have students describe the advantages of contact with many different cultures.

---

## RECOMMENDED RESOURCES

### BOOKS FOR THE TEACHER

Bell, Derek. *And We Are Not Saved.* New York, Basic, 1989. Race in America.

Woodward, Bob. *The Agenda.* New York: Pocket, 1995. First two years of Clinton White House.

### BOOKS FOR THE STUDENT

Costello, Cynthia, and Barbara Kivimae Krimgold. *The American Woman, 1996–1997.* New York, Norton, 1996. Women at work.

Morrison, Joan, and Charlotte Fox Zabusky. *American Mosaic.* U of Pittsburgh, PA, 1993. The immigrant experience.

### VIDEOS

*Becoming American.* Dir. Ken Levine. New Day Films, 1983. Hmong immigrants adapt to life in the United States.

### SOFTWARE

*Clinton: Portrait of a Victory.* CD-ROM. Time Warner Interactive. Speeches, music, narration, and more than 300 photographs.

*CNN Time Capsule 1994.* CD-ROM. Vicarious, Inc. More than 1,000 articles and photographs.

### INTEGRATED TECHNOLOGY

For teacher support, visit . . .

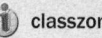 classzone.com

# OBJECTIVES

1. Summarize the issues of the 1992 presidential campaign.
2. Describe Clinton's stand on domestic issues.
3. Analyze Clinton's approach to foreign policy.
4. Explain the political events surrounding Clinton's impeachment trial.
5. Analyze the events of the 2000 election.
6. Describe the first months of the Bush administration.

## SKILLBUILDER
· Geography Skillbuilder; region, human-environment interaction, p. 862

## CRITICAL THINKING
· Analyzing Causes, pp. 861, 864, 865
· Summarizing, pp. 862, 864
· Analyzing Effects, p. 866
· Analyzing Motives, p. 867
· Analyzing Issues, p. 867
· Evaluating, p. 868
· Analyzing Visual Sources, p. 868

## Focus & Motivate

Ask students how they think age might affect a candidate's chance of winning a presidential election.

## Instruct

### Instruct: Objective 1

**Clinton Wins the Presidency**
TAKS SS11 5(US24.B)
· What was the major issue of the 1992 election?
· How did Clinton move the Democratic Party toward the political center?

📄 In-Depth Resources: Unit 7
· Guided Reading, p. 45

👁 Electronic Library of Primary Sources
· from First Inaugural Address, 1993 by B. Clinton

---

SECTION 1

# The 1990s and the New Millennium

| MAIN IDEA | WHY IT MATTERS NOW | Terms & Names |
|---|---|---|
| The Democrats gained control of the White House by moving their party's platform toward the political center. | As the Democratic and Republican parties move closer in agenda, the extreme liberal or conservative viewpoints are less popular. | • William Jefferson Clinton  • H. Ross Perot  • Hillary Rodham Clinton  • NAFTA  • Newt Gingrich  • Contract with America  • Kenneth Starr  • Al Gore  • George W. Bush |

**TEKS U.S. History** 1B, 4C, 6G, 6H, 8A, 8B, 9B, 14D, 15C, 15D, 16A, 16B, 19B, 19C, 24A, 24B, 24C, 24D, 24H, 25A, 25B, 25C, 25D, 26B

### One American's Story

On January 20, 1993, poet Maya Angelou was honored as the first woman and the first African American to read her work at a presidential inauguration. Bill Clinton asked Angelou to compose and deliver a poem. Angelou expressed the optimism of the day, recalling the dream of Martin Luther King, Jr., as she recited her poem "On the Pulse of Morning."

**A PERSONAL VOICE** MAYA ANGELOU

" Lift up your faces, you have a piercing need
For this bright morning dawning for you.
History, despite its wrenching pain,
Cannot be unlived, but if faced
With courage, need not be lived again.

Lift up your eyes
Upon this day breaking for you.
Give birth again
To the dream. "
—"On the Pulse of Morning"

Maya Angelou

Moments later, William Jefferson Clinton was inaugurated as the 42nd president of the United States. Clinton entered the presidency at a time when America was at a turning point. A severe economic recession had made many Americans uneasy about the future. They looked to Clinton to lead a government that would be more responsive to the people.

## 1 Clinton Wins the Presidency

Governor **William Jefferson Clinton** of Arkansas became the first member of the baby-boom generation to win the presidency. He captured the White House, at the age of 46, by vowing to strengthen the nation's weak economy and to lead the Democratic Party in a more moderate direction.

---

 In-Depth Resources: Unit 7
· Guided Reading, p. 45
· Building Vocabulary, p. 49
· Reteaching Activity, p. 51
· Primary Sources: from the Contract with America, p. 57; from "A Bridge to the Future", p.58

Reading Study Guide (English and Spanish), pp. 257–258

 Access for Students Acquiring English/ESL
· Guided Reading (Spanish), p. 274

Formal Assessment
· Section Quiz, p. 470

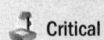 Integrated Assessment
· Rubrics

**INTEGRATED TECHNOLOGY**

 Geography Transp. GT34
· Percentage of Eligible Votes Cast, 1996 Presidential Election

 Critical Thinking Transp. CT34, CT68
· Shutdown of the Federal Government
· Budget and Federal Debt, 1945–1995

 Electronic Library of Primary Sources

 classzone.com

**TEXAS RESOURCES**

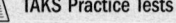 TAKS Spiraled Content Review

TAKS Practice Tests

TAKS Practice Transparencies TT128

TAKS Online Test Practice

**THE ELECTION OF 1992** After the U.S. victory in the Persian Gulf War in 1991, Republican president George Bush's popularity had climbed to an 89 percent approval rating. Shortly after the war ended, however, the nation found itself in the grips of a recession. In early 1992, Bush's approval rating nose-dived to 40 percent. In his run for reelection, President Bush could not convince the public that he had a clear strategy for ending the recession and creating jobs. **A**

Throughout the presidential race, Bill Clinton campaigned as the candidate to lead the nation out of its economic crisis. So did a third-party candidate—Texas billionaire **H. Ross Perot.** Perot targeted the soaring federal budget deficit as the nation's number one problem. A budget deficit occurs when the federal government borrows money to meet all its spending commitments. "It's time," Perot declared in his usual blunt style, "to take out the trash and clean up the barn."

Election Day results, however, demonstrated that Clinton's center-of-the-road strategy had the widest appeal. Though Clinton won, he captured only 43 percent of the popular vote. Bush received 38 percent, while Perot managed an impressive 19 percent.

**A "NEW" DEMOCRAT** Bill Clinton won the presidency in part by promising to move away from traditional Democratic policies. He also emphasized the need to move people off welfare and called for growth in private business as a means to economic progress.

In office, Clinton worked to move the Democratic Party toward the political center by embracing both liberal and conservative programs. According to an ally, Clinton hoped "to modernize liberalism so it could sell again." By doing so, he sought to create a "new" and more inclusive Democratic Party.

## Moderate Reform and Economic Boom ❷

President Clinton demonstrated his willingness to pursue both liberal and conservative policies on health care, the budget deficit, crime, and welfare.

**HEALTH CARE REFORM** Clinton had pledged to create a plan to guarantee affordable health care for all Americans, especially for the millions of Americans who lacked medical insurance. Once in office, Clinton appointed First Lady **Hillary Rodham Clinton,** a skilled lawyer and child-welfare advocate, to head the team creating the plan. The president presented the health care reform bill to Congress in September 1993.

Congress debated the plan for a year. Intense lobbying and Republican attacks on the plan for promoting "big government" sealed its doom. In the end, Congress never even voted on the bill. **B**

**MAIN IDEA**

Analyzing Causes

**A** What factors accounted for Bush's decline in popularity?

**A. Answer** The country was experiencing a recession and Bush did not have a strategy to end it or to create additional jobs.

**B. Answer** Intense lobbying against it; the public viewed the plan as one that would increase the size of government.

**MAIN IDEA**

Analyzing Causes

**B** What factors led to the defeat of Clinton's health care plan?

### KEY PLAYER

**WILLIAM JEFFERSON CLINTON, 1946–**

Born in Hope, Arkansas, at the beginning of the baby boom, Bill Clinton had wanted to be president most of his life. As a college student in the 1960s, he had opposed the Vietnam War and pulled strings to avoid being drafted.

After studying in England as a Rhodes scholar and graduating from Yale law school, Clinton returned to Arkansas. He taught at the University of Arkansas School of Law and dived into politics, becoming governor in 1979 at the age of thirty-two.

Hillary Rodham Clinton explains the health care reform plan to a Senate subcommittee.

### KEY PLAYER

**Bill Clinton**
The lasting historical legacy of Clinton's presidency has yet to be determined. What stands out was the President's ability to communicate with the American people. Despite scandal and an impeachment vote by the Republican-controlled House of Representatives, Clinton maintained high voter approval ratings. Ask students how important they think it is for the President of the United States to be able to communicate with the American people? *(Most students will say it is very important)*

### Instruct: Objective ❷

**Moderate Reform and Economic Boom / Crime and Terrorism**
TAKS SS11 5(US24.B)
· On which issues did Hillary Rodham Clinton focus her energies?
· What did President Clinton accomplish in terms of the budget?
· How did President Clinton reform the welfare system?
· What acts of terrorism in the 1990s shocked Americans?

Critical Thinking Transparencies, CT68
· Budget and Federal Debt, 1945–1995

### More About . . .

**Hillary Rodham Clinton**
Hillary Rodham Clinton grew up in the Chicago area. She was a Barry Goldwater supporter in high school in 1964. Influenced by the events of the 1960s, she became a political liberal. She married her law school classmate Bill Clinton, and after his election as president, she became one of the most influential First Ladies since Eleanor Roosevelt. In 2000, she was elected to the U.S. Senate from New York.

*The United States in Today's World* **861**

---

**DIFFERENTIATING INSTRUCTION** | **LESS PROFICIENT READERS**

### Finding Main Ideas

To help students identify main ideas in a text, have them restate subheadings in the form of questions. Ask students to read "Moderate Reform and Economic Boom" on pages 861–862.

Have them form questions from the subheadings. *(How did President Clinton work toward health care reform? In what ways did the country experience an economic boom? How was welfare reformed?)* Then have students find the answers in the text.

**Background**
See *national debt*
on page R43 in
the Economics
Handbook.

**BALANCED BUDGET AND AN ECONOMIC BOOM** President Clinton was more successful in his efforts to reduce the federal budget deficit. Clinton and the Republican-controlled Congress agreed in 1997 on legislation to balance the federal budget by the year 2002. The bill cut spending by billions of dollars, lowered taxes to win Republican support, and included programs aimed at helping children and improving health care.

A year later, Clinton announced that—for the first time in nearly 30 years—the federal budget had a surplus. That is, the government took in more than it spent. Surpluses were used, in part, to pay down the nation's debt, which had soared to around $5.5 trillion.

Perhaps the most effective tool in generating a surplus was the booming economy. About the time Clinton took office, the economy rebounded. Unemployment fell and the stock market soared to new heights. As a result, the government's tax revenues rose, and fewer people received public aid. These factors helped slash the federal debt.

**REFORMING WELFARE** Clinton and the congressional Republicans cooperated to reform the welfare system. In 1996, a bill was proposed to place limits on how long people could receive benefits. It also put an end to a 61-year federal guarantee of welfare, and instead gave states "block grants"—set amounts of federal money they could spend on welfare or for other social concerns.

Although liberal Democrats feared the effects of eliminating the federal safety net for the poor, the president backed the bill. Over the next few years, states moved millions of people from welfare to jobs. Because of the strong economy, the transition was more successful than some had been predicting.

## Crime and Terrorism

The improved economy—along with enlargement of police forces—combined to lower crime rates in the 1990s. However, fears were raised among Americans by acts of violence and terrorism around the country.

A shocking crime occurred April 1999 when two students at Columbine High School, in Colorado, killed 12 and wounded 23 classmates and a teacher, and then shot themselves. Americans were appalled at copycat crimes that began to occur. Some called for tougher gun control, while others argued that exposure to violent imagery should be curtailed. Violence had pervaded television news throughout the decade.

In 1993, terrorists had exploded bombs in the World Trade Center in New York City. This was closely followed by a 1995 blast that destroyed a nine-story federal office building in Oklahoma City, killing 168 children, women, and men. Timothy McVeigh, an American veteran of the Gulf War, was found guilty in the Oklahoma bombing. He was executed in 2001, the first use of the federal death penalty in 38 years. Although American embassies and military targets abroad were subject to sporadic and deadly terrorist attacks during the decade, the U.S. was in no way prepared for a devastating attack that took place on its own soil on the morning of September 11, 2001.

Injured victims after the April 1995 bombing of the Alfred P. Murrah Federal Building in Oklahoma City, Oklahoma. ▼

---

### Tracing Themes
#### ECONOMIC OPPORTUNITY

While millions of Americans benefited from the rising stock market, many social critics were concerned about the widening gap between rich and poor. Americans without savings or retirement funds had little access to the wealth generated by increased stock values. The economic boom, however, did contribute to a marked decrease in unemployment. In fact, employers were soon faced with a shortage of qualified workers. As a temporary solution, businesses recruited retirees and students, offering flexible work schedules and attractive benefits packages.

### More About . . .

#### Crime Rate

In the 1990s, the United States expanded "get tough" policies on crime and sharply increased expenditures on prisons. The crime rate in the 1990's dropped significantly in most serious crime categories. The murder rate dropped 30 percent; rape decreased 14 percent; robbery dropped 29 percent; and burglary down 18 percent. Many analysts attributed this decline to an increased likelihood of going to prison and serving more time for those crimes. Some other studies suggest that an economy with little unemployment also contributed to the drop in crime rates.

---

  **ACTIVITY**    **LINK TO CIVICS**

 **classzone.com**

### School Policies

**Class Time** 45 minutes

**Task** Creating a multimedia presentation on how the eruption of violence in American schools has affected school policies

**Purpose** To analyze the cause and effect of changes in school policies

**Directions** Discuss students' reactions to the school shootings in the United States. Ask them to consider how school policies have changed in the wake of such violence. Ask students to investigate the issue by reading articles, talking to teachers, and doing research on the Internet. Have students put together a multimedia presentation for the class.

 Integrated Assessment
· Rubrics 1, 6

In a coordinated effort, two hijacked commercial jets struck the twin towers of the World Trade Center in New York City, one crashing just minutes after the other. The jets exploded on impact and subsequently leveled the tallest buildings of New York's skyline, the symbolic center of American finance. Almost an hour later, a third plane tore into the Pentagon building, the U.S. military headquarters outside Washington, D.C. Air travel ceased almost immediately; across the nation planes in the air were ordered to land. During the evacuation of Washington, D.C., and the New York financial district, a fourth hijacked plane crashed near Pittsburgh, Pennsylvania.

Everyone on board all four planes was killed. Close to 200 people lost their lives in the Pentagon attack, while over 3000 in New York— including hundreds of rescue workers—were killed in the collapse of the World Trade Center and surrounding structures. (See "The War on Terrorism," begining on page US2.)

▲ A view across the Brooklyn Bridge shows the devastating impact of two jets used by terrorists as missiles to destroy the World Trade Center.

## New Foreign Policy Challenges ❸

**Vocabulary**
**globalization:** to make worldwide in scope or application

Conflicts and confused alliances grew in the wake of the Cold War. The question of U.S. intervention overseas, and the globalization of the economy presented the United States with a host of new challenges.

**RELATIONS WITH FORMER COLD WAR FOES** Maintaining strong relations with Russia and China became major goals for the Clinton administration. Throughout the 1990s, the U.S. and Russia cooperated on economic and arms-control issues. Still, Russia criticized U.S. intervention in Yugoslavia, where a bloody civil war raged. Meanwhile, U.S. officials protested against Russian attacks on rebels in the Russian region of Chechnya.

U.S. relations with China were strained as well. Clinton had stressed that he would lean on China to grant its citizens more democratic rights. As president, however, he put greater emphasis on increasing trade with China. Despite concerns that Chinese spies had stolen U.S. defense secrets, Clinton supported a bill—passed in 2000—granting China permanent trade rights.

**TROOPS ABROAD** With the Cold War over, the United States turned more of its attention to regional conflicts. President Clinton proved willing to use troops to end conflicts overseas. In 1991, military leaders in Haiti forced the elected president from office. Thousands of refugees fled the military leaders' harsh rule. In 1994, President Clinton dispatched American troops to Haiti, and the military rulers were forced to step down.

Other interventions occurred in the former Communist country of Yugoslavia. In 1991, Yugoslavia broke apart into five nations. In Bosnia, one of the newly independent states, Serbs began "ethnic cleansing," killing or expelling from their homes people of certain ethnic groups. In 1995, the United States helped negotiate a peace agreement in Bosnia. Clinton sent U.S. troops to join NATO troops to help ensure the deal. About three years later, Serb forces attacked ethnic Albanians in the Serb province of Kosovo. The U.S. and its NATO allies launched air strikes against Serbian targets in 1999, forcing the Serbs to back down. Again, American troops followed up by participating in an international

### Instruct: Objective ❸
**New Foreign Policy Challenges**
TAKS SS11 3(US14.E)
· What foreign policy challenges did Bill Clinton face?
· What did the United States do in Kosovo?
· What is NAFTA and why did it spark controversy?
· What events took place in the Pacific Rim, in the late 1990s that affected the United States?

 In-Depth Resources: Unit 7
· Guided Reading, p. 45

### More About . . .

**The Conflict in Kosovo**
The U.S.-led NATO campaign against Serb forces in Kosovo lasted from March 24 to June 9, 1999. It consisted mainly of aerial bombardment by American planes and submarine-launched missiles. After Serbia agreed to sign a UN-approved peace agreement with NATO on June 9, a UN peacekeeping force, which included U.S. troops, was deployed in Kosovo. The UN Mission in Kosovo (UNMIK) was to secure the peace, aid in resettlement of the nearly 900,000 refugees driven out of Kosovo by the Serbs, and prepare the Kosovars for democratic government. The United States pledged more than $500 million in humanitarian aid to the people of Kosovo.

*The United States in Today's World* **863**

---

**DIFFERENTIATING INSTRUCTION**  **GIFTED AND TALENTED STUDENTS**

 **classzone.com**

### Researching the Roots of the Struggle in Yugoslavia

Have students research the historical roots of the ongoing conflict between the Serbs and other ethnic groups in the former Republic of Yugoslavia. Ask them to consider such issues as: the Balkans under the Ottoman Turks; the formation of Yugoslavia under the Treaty of Versailles; Tito's rule; Milosevic's rule. Ask them to prepare a brief oral report focusing on the roots of ethnic conflict for the class.

The oral report should . . .

· show evidence of sound research using multiple sources
· reflect the student's understanding of the basic concepts underlying the ethnic rivalry
· be clear and organized

## Instruct: Objective **4**

### Partisan Politics and Impeachment
TAKS SS11 5(US24.B)

· What happened in 1994 that changed the balance of power in Washington?

· Who was Newt Gingrich?

· Why did the House vote to impeach President Clinton?

 In-Depth Resources: Unit 7
· Guided Reading, p. 45
· Primary Sources: from "A Bridge to the Future"

▲ American workers protest against the North American Free Trade Agreement (NAFTA).

peace-keeping force. In both Bosnia and Kosovo, the administration promised early withdrawal. However, the U.S. troops stayed longer than had been intended, drawing criticism of Clinton's policies. **D**

**TRADE AND THE GLOBAL ECONOMY** Seeing flourishing trade as essential to U.S. prosperity and to world economic and political stability, President Clinton championed the **North American Free Trade Agreement (NAFTA).** This legislation would bring Mexico into the free-trade zone that the United States and Canada already had formed. Supporters said NAFTA would strengthen all three economies and create more American jobs. Opponents insisted that NAFTA would transfer American jobs to Mexico, where wages were lower, and harm the environment because of Mexico's weaker antipollution laws. Congress rejected these arguments, and the treaty was ratified by all three countries' legislatures in 1993. Once the treaty took effect, on January 1, 1994, trade with Mexico increased.

Critics of free trade and the global economy remained vocal, however. In late 1999, the World Trade Organization (WTO), an organization that promotes trade and economic development, met in Seattle. Demonstrators protested that the WTO made decisions with little public input and that these decisions harmed poorer countries, the environment, and American manufacturing workers.

Subsequent anti-globalization protests have been held worldwide. Violent clashes erupted between police and demonstrators at the April 2001 third Summit of the Americas, held in Quebec City, Canada. Nevertheless, the activists failed to halt plans to launch, by 2006, the Free Trade Area of the Americas (FTAA)—an enlarged version of NAFTA covering the 34 countries in the Western Hemisphere, except Cuba.

## **4** Partisan Politics and Impeachment

While Clinton and Congress worked together on deficit reduction and NAFTA, relations in Washington became increasingly partisan. In the midst of political wrangling, a scandal rocked the White House, and Bill Clinton became the second president in U.S. history to be impeached.

**REPUBLICANS TAKE CONTROL OF CONGRESS** In mid-1994, after the failure of President Clinton's health care plan and recurring questions regarding his leadership, Republican congressman **Newt Gingrich** began to turn voters' dissatisfaction with Clinton into support for Republicans. He drafted a document called the **Contract with America**—ten items Republicans promised to enact if they won control of Congress. They included congressional term limits, a balanced-budget amendment, tax cuts, tougher crime laws, and welfare reform. **E**

In the November 1994 election, the Republicans handed the Democrats a humiliating defeat. Voters gave Republicans control of both houses of Congress for the first time since 1954. Chosen as the new Speaker of the House, Newt Gingrich was jubilant.

**A PERSONAL VOICE** NEWT GINGRICH

"I will never forget mounting the rostrum . . . for the first time. . . . The whole scene gave me a wonderful sense of the romance of America and the magic by which Americans share power and accept changes in government."

—*To Renew America*

---

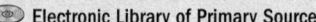
### Analyzing the Contract with America

**Class Time** 45 minutes

**Task** Summarizing main points of the Republican's Contract with America and identifying possible voter support of the contract

**Purpose** To analyze the Contract with America and its appeal to voters

**Directions** Divide the class into groups. Have each group use library and Internet resources to research the provisions of the 1994 Republican campaign document, "Contract with America." Have students analyze the document, point by point, and consider how it might have appealed to voters. Ask each group to summarize its findings in chart form. Then discuss the issues as a class.

👁 **Electronic Library of Primary Sources**
· *A Contract with America,* 1994 by N. Gingrich   ·

President Clinton and the Republican-controlled Congress clashed. Clinton opposed Republican budgets that slowed entitlements—federal programs which provide for basic human needs—such as Social Security, and Medicaid. Clinton and Congress refused to compromise, and the Republicans refused to pass the larger budgets he wanted. As a result, the federal government shut down for almost a week in November 1995, and again for several weeks in the next two months.

**THE 1996 REELECTION** The budget standoff helped Clinton, as did the strong economy and passage of the welfare reform law of 1996, which suggested an improved working relationship with Congress. As a result, voters reelected Clinton in November 1996. With 49 percent of the popular vote, he outpolled the Republican nominee, U.S. Senator Bob Dole, and the Reform Party candidate, H. Ross Perot. Still, the Republicans maintained control of the House and Senate. Both President Clinton and Republican leaders pledged to work more cooperatively. Soon however, the president faced his most severe problems yet. **F**

**THE PRESIDENT IS INVESTIGATED** During the late 1970s, President Clinton was involved in a land deal with the Whitewater Development Company in Arkansas. He was later accused of improperly using some of the land money to fund his 1984 gubernatorial reelection campaign. In August 1994, a federal court appointed **Kenneth Starr** as the independent counsel to investigate the matter. (By September 2000, Starr's replacement as independent counsel, Robert Ray, cleared the Clintons of wrongdoing in this matter.)

During his investigation, Starr had expanded his probe of Bill Clinton to matters unrelated to Whitewater. He learned the president had had an improper relationship with a young White House intern. Furthermore, Clinton allegedly had lied under oath about the affair. In August 1998, Clinton admitted in a national address that he had engaged in an improper relationship with the intern. Nevertheless, he denied lying about the incident under oath or attempting to obstruct the investigation.

**CLINTON IMPEACHED** The majority of Americans approved of Clinton's job performance. Nevertheless, in December 1998, the House of Representatives voted to impeach him. The House approved two articles of impeachment, charging the president with perjury and obstruction of justice. With the House vote, Clinton became only the second president—and the first in 130 years—to face a trial in the Senate.

The Senate opened its trial of President Clinton in January 1999. A month later, the Senate fell short of the 67 votes—a two thirds majority—required to convict him. Clinton remained in office and apologized for his actions.

During Clinton's remaining two years as president, bitter political partisanship impeded the passage of much-needed legislation. Meanwhile, the campaign to elect a new president began in earnest.

**MAIN IDEA**

**Analyzing Causes**
**F** What factors contributed most to Clinton's reelection?
*F. Answer* The strong economy and legislative victories over Congress.

**More About . . .**

**Impeachment**
Before Bill Clinton was impeached in 1998, Andrew Johnson was the only U.S. president impeached by the House of Representatives. There are similarities in the two episodes. In both cases, the relationship between the president and Congress was bitter. In both cases, the public turned against Congress's efforts at impeachment, and the Senate refused to remove the president from office, although Johnson came within one vote of conviction.

**More About . . .**

**Bill Clinton**
Despite the impeachment, Clinton maintained his popularity with the American public. He spent much time during his last year in office working to further peace negotiations between Israel and the Palestinians. After leaving office, he planned to write his memoirs and to establish the Clinton Presidential Library in Little Rock. He also moved to New York, the state from which his wife, Hillary, had won election to the Senate in November 2000.

◄ Chicago newspaper headlines leave no doubt about President Clinton's impeachment.

**865**

---

**ACTIVITY**  **COOPERATIVE ACTIVITY**

 **classzone.com**

## Graphing Election Results

**Class Time** 45 minutes

**Task** Graphing, and comparing the results of the 1996 and 2000 presidential elections

**Purpose** To interpret election results

**Directions** Have students work in small groups and use Internet and library resources to gather data on the 1996 presidential election. Ask them to gather information on electoral votes, popular votes, and voter turnout. Have students create a graph of the 1996 electoral and popular votes, and compare that data with the 2000 election results shown on page 862.

 Integrated Assessment
· Rubrics 1, 2

## Instruct: Objective ⑤

**The Race for the White House**

TAKS SS11 5(WH26.C)

· What caused the confusion over final results on election night?

· What were the issues in the dispute in Florida?

· What role did the U.S. Supreme Court play in the election?

📓 In-Depth Resources: Unit 7
· Guided Reading, p. 45

### More About . . .

**Elections and Accuracy**

Disputes over accuracy raged following the 2000 Presidential election. But the chance of achieving 100 percent accuracy in a contest involving over 100 million votes was impossible. The election results brought to light the problem of statistical anomalies. Dealing with these anomalies is a part of some election reform proposals.

### HISTORY from VISUALS

**Interpreting the Map**

Tell students that Al Gore is from Tennessee. Ask them which candidate won Tennessee and how many electoral votes were at stake. *(Bush; 11)*

---

## ⑤ The Race for the White House

In the 2000 presidential race, the Democrats chose Vice President **Al Gore** to succeed Bill Clinton. The Republicans nominated **George W. Bush,** governor of Texas and the son of the former president. Ralph Nader, a long-time consumer advocate, ran for the Green Party, which championed environmental causes and promoted an overall liberal agenda. On the eve of the election, polls showed the race to be one of the tightest in recent memory. The election proved one of the closest in U.S. history. Determining a winner would take over a month.

**ELECTION NIGHT CONFUSION** As election night unfolded, Al Gore appeared to take the lead. The television networks projected that Gore would win Florida, Pennsylvania, and Michigan—states rich in electoral votes—which would ultimately decide the winner of the race. Then, in a stunning turn of events, the TV networks recanted their original projection about Gore's victory in Florida and proclaimed the state "too close to call."

As midnight passed, it became clear that whoever won Florida would gain the 270 electoral votes needed to win the election. About 2 A.M., the networks predicted Bush the winner of Florida—and thus the presidency. Gore called the Texas governor to congratulate him and prepared to deliver a concession speech. **G**

As the final votes in Florida rolled in, Bush's lead shrank considerably and the state again became too close to call. As a result, Gore phoned Bush again and took back his concession. By the next day, Al Gore had won the popular vote by more than 500,000 votes out of 105 million cast. Meanwhile, all eyes turned to Florida, as George Bush's razor-thin victory there triggered an automatic recount to determine the true winner of the state—and the presidency.

*Skillbuilder Answers*
**1.** Gore was strong in the Northeast, West Coast, northern Midwest; Bush captured the South, Midwest, and the Northwest.
**2.** The party received no electoral votes while the popular vote the party received could have changed the outcome of the election.

*G. Answer*
The networks named Gore the projected winner and then recanted their projection, as well as declared the race too close to call.

**MAIN IDEA**

**Analyzing Effects**
**G** How did television reporting add to the chaos and confusion on election night?

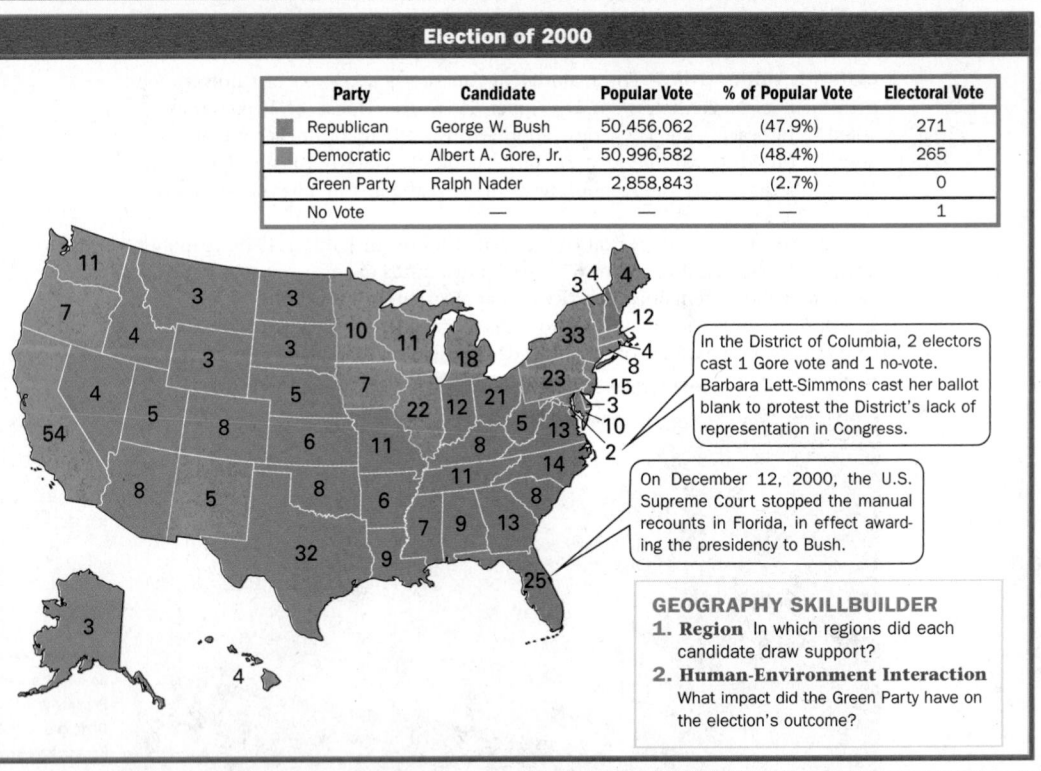

### Election of 2000

| Party | Candidate | Popular Vote | % of Popular Vote | Electoral Vote |
|---|---|---|---|---|
| Republican | George W. Bush | 50,456,062 | (47.9%) | 271 |
| Democratic | Albert A. Gore, Jr. | 50,996,582 | (48.4%) | 265 |
| Green Party | Ralph Nader | 2,858,843 | (2.7%) | 0 |
| No Vote | — | — | — | 1 |

In the District of Columbia, 2 electors cast 1 Gore vote and 1 no-vote. Barbara Lett-Simmons cast her ballot blank to protest the District's lack of representation in Congress.

On December 12, 2000, the U.S. Supreme Court stopped the manual recounts in Florida, in effect awarding the presidency to Bush.

**GEOGRAPHY SKILLBUILDER**

1. **Region** In which regions did each candidate draw support?
2. **Human-Environment Interaction** What impact did the Green Party have on the election's outcome?

---

**ACTIVITY**   **LINK TO JOURNALISM**

 classzone.com

**Examining Television News and Elections**

**Class Period** 45 minutes

**Task** Creating a report on the controversy surrounding the media's role in the election process

**Purpose** To analyze the media's role in the election process

**Directions** Have students work in small groups to research the controversy surrounding the media's announcement of election results. Ask students to consider the time zone differences across the United States. Have them analyze the impact a premature announcement of results might have on voter turnout and the election. Ask students to present their findings to the class in an oral report.

📓 Integrated Assessment
· Rubrics 1, 2, 3

**DISPUTE RAGES IN FLORIDA** In the weeks following the election, lawyers and spokespersons went to Florida to try to secure victory. The recount of the state's ballots gave Bush a win by just over 300 votes—but the battle for the presidency did not end there. After the election, the public learned of voting irregularities in several counties in Florida—a state where George's brother Jeb Bush was governor. Most prominently, voters in Palm Beach County claimed that a confusing ballot design had caused thousands to mistakenly vote for a different candidate or to punch two names, thus invalidating their ballots.

Prompted by these problems, as well as by the belief that voting machines had misread numerous ballots, the Gore campaign requested manual recounts in four mostly Democratic counties. "All we are seeking is this: that the candidate who the voters preferred become our president," declared Gore campaign chairman William Daley. Bush representatives opposed the manual recounts. James A. Baker III, former secretary of state and leader of the Bush team in Florida, argued that such recounts would raise the possibility of political mischief. **H**

▲ *Time* magazine's cover on November 20, 2000, almost two weeks after the election.

**A PERSONAL VOICE** JAMES A. BAKER III

" Human error, individual subjectivity and decisions to 'determine the voters' intent' would replace precision machinery."

—quoted in *The New York Times*, November 12, 2000

By May 2001, Florida had voted to outlaw punch-card ballots. Other states also instituted their own election reforms, hoping not to repeat the chaos.

**THE BATTLE MOVES TO THE COURTS** As the manual recounting began on November 12, the Republicans sued to stop the recounts; a month-long court fight followed. The battle ultimately reached the Supreme Court. On December 12, a divided court voted 5 to 4 to stop the recounts—thus awarding the Florida electoral votes and the presidency to Bush. The justices argued that manual recounts lacked uniform standards and, therefore, violated equal protection for voters. The next night, in back-to-back televised speeches, Vice President Gore conceded and Governor Bush accepted victory. Five weeks after election day, one of the most divisive elections in history had ended. **I**

**THE AFTERMATH OF THE ELECTION** In the wake of the divisive presidential election, President Bush encountered an equally divided Congress. The 2000 elections produced a 50-50 Republican-Democratic split in the Senate and a slim nine-vote Republican majority in the House of Representatives. Critics across the nation predicted years of legislative gridlock.

*H. Answer*
The Gore campaign believed that voting machines had misread numerous ballots, while the Bush campaign believed that manual counting might lead to further inaccuracies and even political misconduct.

**MAIN IDEA**

**Analyzing Motives**
**H** Why did the Gore campaign support manual recounts in Florida and the Bush campaign oppose them?

*I. Answer*
**Weaknesses:** lack of uniform and fair voting practices, partisan arguing and claims of favoritism among the Supreme Court justices; **Strengths:** the government continuing to function; election reforms that emerged from the chaos.

**MAIN IDEA**

**Analyzing Issues**
**I** How did the election of 2000 highlight both the weaknesses and the strengths of America's election process?

**ANOTHER PERSPECTIVE**

**NADER AND THIRD PARTY IMPACT**

Like most third-party candidates, Ralph Nader of the Green Party claimed to speak for those citizens disillusioned with the nation's two main parties. Nader accused both Democrats and Republicans of catering to wealthy special interest groups rather than to average citizens.

Despite winning less than 3 percent of the popular vote, Nader played what many observers felt was a significant role in the 2000 presidential election. He picked up almost 100,000 votes in Florida, votes that might have enabled Al Gore to capture Florida—and the presidency.

After the election, Nader dismissed the notion that he had hurt the Democrats, and he called for the continuation of third parties in American politics.

*The United States in Today's World* **867**

---

## Instruct: Objective ⑥

### The Bush Administration Begins Anew

TAKS SS11 5(US24.B)

· What did President Bush do in his first six months in office to further his political agenda?

 In-Depth Resources: Unit 7
· Guided Reading, p. 45

👁 Electronic Library of Primary Sources
· Inaugural Address, 2001 by George W. Bush

## Assess & Reteach

### SECTION 1 ASSESSMENT

Have students work individually to answer the Section Assessment questions. Then ask students to trade papers and compare answers.

 Formal Assessment
· Section Quiz, p. 470

### SELF-ASSESSMENT

Ask students to identify passages in the text that helped them answer each question.

### RETEACH

Use the Section 1 Geography transparency to review voter turnout for each state in the 1996 election.

📄 In-Depth Resources: Unit 7
· Reteaching Activity, p. 51

---

## ⑥ The Bush Administration Begins Anew

After the protests and legal actions subsided, George W. Bush was inaugurated as the 43rd president of the United States on January 20, 2001. Many people questioned how effectively a president who had not won the popular majority would govern. Nevertheless, Bush inherited a favorable situation, a large budget surplus and a period of relative economic stability. At the six-month mark, public support for the president remained steady.

During his first months as president, Bush began to advance his political agenda, presenting a budget that included $1.6 trillion worth of tax cuts—reduced by the Senate to $1.35 trillion—over 11 years. He also declared plans to reform the federal role in education and to privatize Social Security, and had an early success in resolving a standoff with China over a downed U.S. spy plane. However, many environmentalists protested his reversal of a campaign pledge to limit carbon dioxide emissions, as well as his plans to increase "sensitive drilling" for oil at the Arctic National Wildlife Refuge.

Adding to Bush's political woes, in May 2001 Republican senator Jim Jeffords of Vermont, disillusioned by the administration's extreme, conservative policies, left his party to become an Independent. Control of the Senate reverted back to the Democrats. Bush now faced an uphill battle in working to pass many of his legislative initiatives.

The political landscape changed dramatically, however, after the September 11 terrorist attacks. The Bush administration, now with the overwhelming support of Congress and the American people, shifted its energy and attention to combating terrorism. Bush's main efforts were to create an Office of Homeland Security and to authorize anti-terrorist military operations overseas. He also proposed $125 billion in additional tax cuts and emergency spending.

Thus, even before the close of 2001, it had become clear to Americans that the events of September 11 and the administration's response to them would determine the nation's future as few other events have.

TAX RELIEF FOR AMERICA

▲ President George W. Bush signs a $1.35 trillion tax cut bill on June 7, 2001, at the White House.

---

### ① ASSESSMENT

**1. TERMS & NAMES** For each term or name, write a sentence explaining its significance.
- William Jefferson Clinton
- H. Ross Perot
- Hillary Rodham Clinton
- NAFTA
- Newt Gingrich
- Contract with America
- Kenneth Starr
- Al Gore
- George W. Bush

**MAIN IDEA**

**2. TAKING NOTES**
Create a time line of President Clinton's major actions during his two terms, Use a form such as the one below.

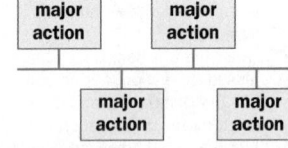

Explain whether each action was a success or a failure for Clinton.

**CRITICAL THINKING**

**3. EVALUATING**
What event or trend during the Clinton administration do you think will have the most lasting impact on the United States? Why?

**4. ANALYZING VISUAL SOURCES**
How might the design of the "butterfly ballot" have confused voters?

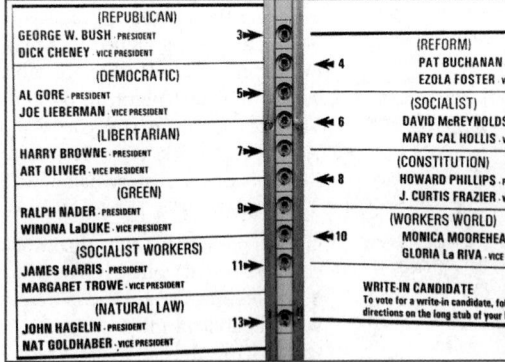

---

 **① ASSESSMENT** Answers

### 1. TERMS & NAMES
William J. Clinton, p. 860
H. Ross Perot, p. 861
Hillary Rodham Clinton, p. 861
NAFTA, p. 864
Newt Gingrich, p. 864
Contract with America, p. 854
Kenneth Starr, p. 865
Al Gore, p. 866
George W. Bush, p. 866

### 2. TAKING NOTES
September 1993: health care bill to Congress; November 1993: NAFTA; 1995: American peace-keeping force in Bosnia; 1996: signed welfare reform bill; 1997: signed budget agreement; 1999: authorized U.S. participation in NATO bombing of Serbia. *(Evaluations of success or failure may vary.)*

### 3. EVALUATING
Welfare reform: shift in policy regarding poverty. Clinton's impeachment: one of only two Presidents to have faced impeachment. Balancing the budget: helped strengthen the economy. *(Answers will vary.)*

### 4. ANALYZING VISUAL SOURCES
Because the holes for both pages were in the center, some voters may have become confused and unwittingly voted for a different candidate than they had intended.

# The New Global Economy

## MAIN IDEA

Because of technological advances and new trade laws, the U.S. economy underwent a boom during the late 20th century.

## WHY IT MATTERS NOW

New types of business have meant new work environments and new challenges for American workers.

## Terms & Names

- service sector
- downsize
- Bill Gates
- NASDAQ
- dotcom
- General Agreement on Tariffs and Trade (GATT)

 **U.S. History** 6G, 6H, 8A, 8B, 14D, 14E, 20D, 22C, 23A, 24B, 24H, 25A, 25B, 25C, 25D, 26A

### One American's Story

As Bill Clinton took office in 1993, some regions of the nation, particularly the Northeast, were still in an economic recession. Near Kennebunkport, Maine, the John Roberts clothing factory faced bankruptcy. With help from their union, the factory workers were able to turn their factory into an employee-owned company.

Ethel Beaudoin, who worked for the company for more than 30 years, was relieved that the plant would not be closing.

 ▲ Workers at the John Roberts clothing factory

**A PERSONAL VOICE** ETHEL BEAUDOIN

" It's a nice feeling to be part of the process . . . of deciding what this company buys for machinery and to know the customers more intimately. They're our customers, and it's a nicer feeling when the customers know that the coat that we put out is made by owners. "

—quoted in *Divided We Fall*

Beaudoin's experience offered one example of the economic possibilities in America. A new global economy—brought about by new technologies, increased international competition, and the end of the Cold War—changed the nation's economic prospects.

## The Shifting Economy

Americans heard a great deal of good news about the economy. Millions of new jobs were created between 1993 and 1999. By the fall of 2000, the unemployment rate had fallen to the lowest it had been since 1970.

---

## OBJECTIVES

1 Describe changes in the American workplace.
2 Explain increased competition for domestic and international markets.

### SKILLBUILDERS

- Interpreting Charts, p. 871
- Geography Skillbuilder: location, p. 872

### CRITICAL THINKING

- Summarizing, p. 870
- Analyzing Effects, pp. 870, 873
- Analyzing Issues, p. 873
- Drawing Conclusions, p. 873

## Focus & Motivate

Ask students if they know where everyday objects, such as clothing, shoes, computers, and CD players, are manufactured. Have them consider why it might be important to know where these items are made. Ask students how they are affected by the global economy.

## Instruct

### Instruct: Objective

**The Shifting Economy**

TAKS SS11 3(US14.E)

- What has happened to the income gap between rich and poor?
- What are the disadvantages of temporary job positions?
- What impact have the economic changes of the decade had on younger workers?
- How has technology impacted the national economy?

📄 In-Depth Resources: Unit 7
  · Guided Reading, p. 46
  · Primary Source: from *The Road Ahead*, p. 59
  · American Lives: Bill Gates, p. 63

---

## ECONOMIC BACKGROUND

### Greenspan and the Fed

In 2001, Alan Greenspan, once deemed the "guru" of the American economy, became the target of some criticism. Stock prices plummeted, so the Fed cut interest rates. Critics found fault with the Fed early, claiming that the economic slowdown in 2001 was due to the Fed's interest rate hike in 2000. Greenspan was also criticized for supporting Bush's tax cut plan. Ask students if they agree, or disagree, that the Fed chairman is more powerful than the President. *(Agree: Strong economy is central to the government's operation; American lives impacted by the Fed's decisions. Disagree: Economy is not the only issue; president has the power to declare war.)*

### Tracing Themes
#### ECONOMIC OPPORTUNITY

In the pursuit of international trade agreements, such as NAFTA, the government was concerned with the United States economy as a whole. This concern outweighed consideration of the effect on businesses or employees. The overall assumption on NAFTA was that the expansion of U.S. foreign markets would benefit everyone. One result would be providing cheaper goods to American consumers. However, another result would be the loss of jobs in certain industries especially those requiring many less skilled workers.

**ECONOMIC BACKGROUND**

**GREENSPAN AND THE FED**
Alan Greenspan has been chairman of the Federal Reserve System (the Fed) since 1987, when he was appointed by President Ronald Reagan. The Fed has been described as the economic pacemaker of the United States because it helps determine how much money there will be in the American economy.

Before being elected president in 2000, George W. Bush made it a point to meet with Alan Greenspan before meeting with anyone else in Washington. (See *interest rate* in the Economics Handbook, page R41.)

But there was alarming news as well. Wage inequality between upper- and lower-income Americans—the income gap—widened. Median household income began to drop. Although economists disagreed about the reasons for the economy's instability, most everyone agreed it was undergoing significant changes.

**MORE SERVICE, LESS SECURITY** Chief among the far-reaching changes in the workplace of the 1990s was the explosive growth of jobs in the **service sector,** the part of the economy that provides services to consumers. By 2000, nearly 80 percent of American workers were teachers, medical professionals, lawyers, engineers, store clerks, waitstaff, and other service workers.

Low-paying jobs, such as sales and fast-food, grew fastest. These positions, often part-time or temporary, offered limited benefits. Many corporations, rather than invest in salaries and benefits for full-time staff, instead hired temporary workers, or temps, and began to **downsize**—trim payrolls to streamline operations and increase profits. Manpower, Inc., a temporary services agency, became the largest U.S. employer, earning $2 billion in 1993 when fully 640,000 Americans cashed its paychecks. In 1998, over one-fourth of the nation's workforce worked in temporary or part-time positions. **A**

Of those cut in downsizing, younger workers suffered higher rates of unemployment. In 1999, an average 11 percent of workers aged 16 to 24 were unemployed—more than double the national rate. Three out of four young Americans expected to earn less money as adults than their parents did.

**FARMS AND FACTORIES** The nation's shift to a service economy came at the expense of America's traditional workplaces. Manufacturing, which surpassed farming midcentury as the largest job sector, experienced a sharp decline in the 1980s and 1990s. In 1992, for example, 140,000 steelworkers did the same work that 240,000 had accomplished ten years earlier. Larry Pugh talked about the downsizing of a farm equipment factory in his hometown of Waterloo, Iowa.

**A PERSONAL VOICE** LARRY PUGH

" There used to be 17,500 people working here. . . . Now there are 6000. Those people spent their money. They bought the cars. They bought the houses. They were replaced by people that are at the minimum wage—seven or eight dollars an hour, not 15 or 20 dollars an hour. These people can hardly eke out a living at today's wages. "

—quoted in *Divided We Fall*

The decline in industrial jobs contributed to a drop in union membership. In 1945, 35 percent of American workers belonged to unions; by 1998, only 14 percent were union members. In the 1990s, unions had trouble organizing. High-tech and professional workers felt no need for unions, while low-wage service employees feared losing their jobs in a strike. Some workers saw their incomes decline. The increased use of computer-driven robots to make manufactured goods eliminated many jobs, but it also spurred a vibrant high-tech economy. Those with advanced training and specialized technical skills or a sense of entrepreneurial risk-taking saw their salaries rise and their economic security expand. **B**

**MAIN IDEA**

**Summarizing**
**A** How did the change from an industrial economy to a service economy affect Americans' economic security?

*A. Answer*
Unlike factory jobs, most jobs in the service sector paid low wages. Also, many service jobs provided only contract or part-time work.

*B. Answer*
It led to higher unemployment, particularly in farms, factories, and in cities. It also resulted in the hiring of more temporary workers.

**MAIN IDEA**

**Analyzing Effects**
**B** How did downsizing affect people?

### Understanding Expressions

Have students work in pairs to decode the meaning of the following expressions. Ask students to use a dictionary to look up the meaning of each italicized word. Then, have them analyze what each word means in context.

· *alarming* news
· *explosive* growth
· *streamline* operations
· *suffer* high rates
· *expense* of America's traditional workplaces

| Persons Employed in Three Economic Sectors* | | | |
|---|---|---|---|
| Year | Farming | Manufacturing | Service Producing |
| 1900 | 11,050 | 7,252 | 6,832 |
| 1950 | 6,001 | 18,475 | 20,721 |
| 2006 (projected) | 3,618 | 24,451 | 111,867 |

*numbers in millions
Sources: *Historical Statistics of the United States, Colonial Times to 1970*;
*Statistical Abstracts of the United States, 1953, 1954, 1999*

**SKILLBUILDER** Interpreting Charts
1. What sector of the U.S. economy has seen the greatest decline in workers over the past century?
2. In terms of employee participation, by roughly what percent is the service sector expected to grow between 1950 and 2006?

*Skillbuilder Answers:*
1. farming
2. 500 percent

**HIGH-TECH INDUSTRIES** In the late 1990s, entrepreneurs turned innovative ideas about computer technology into huge personal fortunes, hoping to follow in the footsteps of **Bill Gates,** the decade's most celebrated entrepreneur. In 1975, Gates saw the advent of personal computers as a promising opportunity. He founded the software company Microsoft with his friend Paul Allen. In 2000, it had made him the wealthiest individual in the world, with assets estimated at about $60 billion.

A frenetic outcropping of new businesses accompanied the explosive growth of the Internet late in the decade. The **NASDAQ** (National Association of Securities Dealers Automated Quotation System), a technology-dominated stock index on Wall Street, rose dramatically as enthusiasm grew for high-tech businesses. These businesses were known as **dotcoms,** a nickname derived from their identities, or addresses, on the World Wide Web, which often ended in ".com." The dotcoms expanded rapidly and attracted young talent and at times excessive investment funding for such untested fledgling companies. While many people were drawn into the startup Internet-based companies, others profited from quitting previous jobs to become day traders and exchange stock online. As technology sales accelerated and stock prices rose, personal fortunes increased for some. The euphoria of a seemingly unstoppable economy caused memories of recession to fade.

Even industry giants, such as Microsoft and America Online, could not predict the speed with which the general public would adopt these new technologies. Thousands of smaller businesses were quick to anticipate the changes that the Internet would bring. Suddenly companies could work directly with consumers or with other companies. Many predicted that the price of doing business would fall dramatically and that overall worldwide productivity would jump dramatically, a combination not seen since the Industrial Age of the 19th century. The boom of new business was termed "The New Economy."

Highly overvalued, the NASDAQ fell sharply in 2000, however, and many personal fortunes evaporated. Nevertheless, the fast-growing technology sector gave birth to new fields of enterprise—web security, wireless communication, robotic engineering, and multimedia programming.

**Background**
See *e-commerce* on page R40 in the Economics Handbook.

At 18 years old, Shawn Fanning started a free music downloading service on the Internet called Napster. He became a multi-millionaire after forming an alliance with a German media company. ▼

*The United States in Today's World* **871**

---

## World Trading Blocs, 2000

## World Trading Blocs, 2000

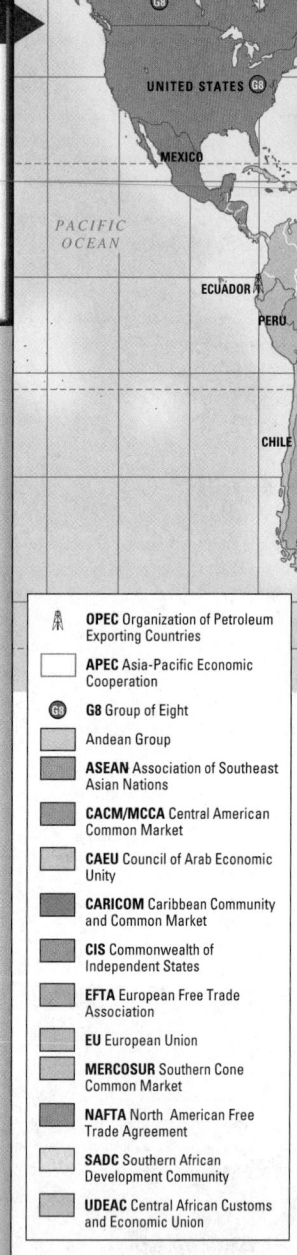

### Interpreting the Map

Help students read the map by asking them to identify the members of the G7. *(United States, Canada. United Kingdom, France, Germany, Italy, Japan)* Ask them to name the countries that belong to both of the following trade groups: G7, EU. *(United Kingdom, France, Italy, Germany)*

## Instruct: Objective ❷

### Change and the Global Economy

TAKS SS11 3(US14.E)

· How did President Clinton propose to match foreign competition?

· Why were labor organizations opposed to international trade agreements such as NAFTA?

 In-Depth Resources: Unit 7

· Geography Application, pp. 55–56

---

| | |
|---|---|
|  | **OPEC** Organization of Petroleum Exporting Countries |
| | **APEC** Asia-Pacific Economic Cooperation |
| G8 | **G8** Group of Eight |
| | Andean Group |
| | **ASEAN** Association of Southeast Asian Nations |
| | **CACM/MCCA** Central American Common Market |
| | **CAEU** Council of Arab Economic Unity |
| | **CARICOM** Caribbean Community and Common Market |
| | **CIS** Commonwealth of Independent States |
| | **EFTA** European Free Trade Association |
| | **EU** European Union |
| | **MERCOSUR** Southern Cone Common Market |
| | **NAFTA** North American Free Trade Agreement |
| | **SADC** Southern African Development Community |
| | **UDEAC** Central African Customs and Economic Union |

---

**GEOGRAPHY SKILLBUILDER**

1. **Location** What is the only G-8 country located outside Europe and North America?
2. **Location** To which world trade organizations does the United States belong?

*Skillbuilder Answers:*
1. Japan.
2. G8; NAFTA; APEC.

## Change and the Global Economy ❷

In 1900, airplanes hadn't yet flown and telephone service was barely 20 years old. U.S. trade with the rest of the world was worth about $2.2 billion (roughly 12 percent of the economy). Nearly a century later, New Yorkers could hop a supersonic jet and arrive in London within three hours, information traveled instantly by fax machines and computers, and U.S. trade with other countries approached $2 trillion (more than 25 percent of the economy). As American companies competed for international and domestic markets, American workers felt the sting of competing with workers in other countries.

**INTERNATIONAL TRADE** The expansion of U.S. trade abroad was an important goal of President Clinton's foreign policy, as his support of NAFTA had shown. In 1994, in response to increasing international economic competition among trading blocs, the United States joined many other nations in adopting a new version of the **General Agreement on Tariffs and Trade (GATT)**. The new treaty lowered trade barriers, such as tariffs, and established the World Trade Organization (WTO) to resolve trade disputes. As President Clinton announced at the 1994 meeting of the Group of Seven, (the world's seven leading economic powers, which later became the Group of Eight when Russia joined in 1996), "[T]rade as much as troops will increasingly define the ties that bind nations in the twenty-first century."

 TAKS

Mini-Lesson 1:
SS11 3(US14.E)

---

**ACTIVITY** | **LINK TO ECONOMICS**  classzone.com

### Analyzing Foreign Trade

**Class Time** One class period

**Task** Creating a database on American foreign trade

**Purpose** To analyze the impact of foreign trade on the American economy

**Directions** Have students use library resources and the Internet to research American trade with China, Japan, and selected other countries. Have students compile the most recent import and export figures for each country and specify the types of trade goods. Ask students to put together a multimedia presentation database for the class using graphs, charts, or photographs.

 Integrated Assessment

· Rubrics 1, 6

**INTERNATIONAL COMPETITION** International trade agreements caused some American workers to worry about massive job flight to countries that produced the same goods as the United States but at a lower cost.

**Background**
"Job flight" had occurred in the 1970s, when cheap but quality auto imports from Japan and Germany forced many U.S. workers out of high-paying jobs.

In the 1990s, U.S. businesses frequently moved their operations to less economically advanced countries, such as Mexico, where wages were lower. After the passage of NAFTA, more than 100,000 low-wage jobs were lost in U.S. manufacturing industries such as apparel, auto parts, and electronics. Also, competition with foreign companies caused many U.S. companies to maintain low wages.

*C. Answer*
International trade agreements opened new markets, but companies exported work to countries with lower wages, costing Americans jobs.

Less economically advanced countries also offered some businesses an opportunity to evade the strict environmental regulations legislated in such developed nations as the United States. Just south of the U.S. border with Mexico, for example, foreign-owned *maquiladoras*, or assembly plants, were accused of operating irresponsibly, dumping poisonous chemical wastes on Mexican soil.

To remain competitive, many U.S. businesses felt the need to make their operations more global in order to produce goods as economically as possible. Indeed, the shipping label for a product of one American electronics company reads: "Made in one or more of the following countries: Korea, Hong Kong, Malaysia, Singapore, Taiwan, Mauritius, Thailand, Indonesia, Mexico, Philippines. The exact country of origin is unknown." **C**

▲
In Montreal, Canada on March 29, 2001, protesters demonstrate at a summit on globalization and the Free Trade Area of the Americas (FTAA).

**MAIN IDEA**

**Analyzing Effects**
**C** What were some of the effects of NAFTA and GATT?

With the U.S. economy undergoing such extensive change at the turn of the 21st century, feelings of insecurity were inevitable. Many Americans in all sectors of the economy feared being left behind by the rapid change. Other Americans, however, saw great opportunities for progress—especially from the endless stream of new technology.

**More About . . .**

**International Competition**
In 1996, the U.S.–Mexican border crossing between San Diego and Tijuana was one of the busiest in the world. Every day, some 40,000 people crossed the border there legally to work, shop, or visit. Many others crossed illegally elsewhere along the border. It was suggested that creating more jobs in Mexico would be a sound way to prevent illegal immigration to the United States. Carlos de Orduna, an executive at a Mexican assembly plan owned by a foreign company, said that few of his workers attempted to emigrate illegally. He argued, "If you have a job that allows you to live reasonably well, . . . why should you go to the United States?"

## Assess & Reteach

**SECTION 2 ASSESSMENT**
Have students work in pairs to compare the cluster diagrams that they created for question 2.

📖 Formal Assessment
· Section Quiz, p. 471

**SELF-ASSESSMENT**
Ask students to review their responses to question 4 in the Section Assessment. Have them expand on their answers with additional ideas about how workers might prepare for the future job market.

**RETEACH**
Have students work in groups and compile their answers to question 2. Ask them to create a cluster diagram based on the groups' responses.

📖 In-Depth Resources: Unit 7
· Guided Reading, p. 52

---

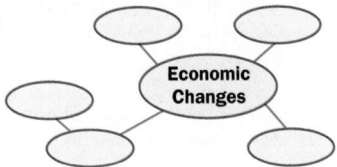 **ASSESSMENT**

**1. TERMS & NAMES** For each term or name, write a sentence explaining its significance.

- **service sector**
- **downsize**
- **Bill Gates**
- **NASDAQ**
- **dotcom**
- **General Agreement on Tariffs and Trade (GATT)**

**MAIN IDEA**

**2. TAKING NOTES**
In a cluster diagram like the one below, record the major changes that occurred in the U.S. economy during the 1990s.

```
      (    )        (    )
          Economic
          Changes
  (    )      (    )      (    )
```

Which change has affected you the most? Explain.

**CRITICAL THINKING**

**3. ANALYZING EFFECTS**
Explain who was negatively affected by the changes in the economy and what negative effects they suffered.
**Think About:**
- who had the highest unemployment rates
- what types of jobs were eliminated
- what other negative effects there were

**4. ANALYZING ISSUES**
How do you explain some Americans' fears over the international trade agreements?

**5. DRAWING CONCLUSIONS**
Considering the economic changes described in this section, how do you think workers can best prepare themselves for the future?

*The United States in Today's World* **873**

---

 Answers **ASSESSMENT** 2

**1. TERMS & NAMES**
service sector, p. 870
downsize, p. 870
Bill Gates, p. 871
NASDAQ, p. 871
dotcom, p. 871
General Agreement on Tariffs and Trade (GATT), p. 872

**2. TAKING NOTES**
expanding service sector; contract workers; downsizing; NASDAQ; dotcoms; high unemployment; decline in industrial work; drop in union membership; high-tech industry; global economy; international trade; GATT.

**3. ANALYZING EFFECTS**
Young people, factory workers, and unskilled workers lost jobs; large corporations hired temporary employees; Many workers received only small wage increases and experienced cuts in benefits.

**4. ANALYZING ISSUES**
Americans feared job security would be threatened. Companies would move

operations to other countries to take advantage of cheap labor and lower production costs.

**5. DRAWING CONCLUSIONS**
self-employment; good job-hunting skills; education; technology skills; learn foreign languages; be flexible; acquire new skills

## AMERICAN LITERATURE

### Objectives

· To explore the literary styles of three contemporary American women writers.

· To examine cultural diversity in the United States.

### Focus & Motivate

**Making Inferences** Ask students to think about the gender, ethnicity, and personal background of writers they have read.

· How would these factors influence the issues and themes a writer chose to explore?

· Which of these factors would have the most influence on his or her work?

### More About . . .

#### Nikki Giovanni

Nikki Giovanni came of age during the civil rights movement. In the late 1960s, she was committed to the Black Power movement. Her first books were passionate calls to arms. After she became a mother in the 1970s, Giovanni focused her writing on children, family, and the struggle of single mothers. During the Reagan administration, Giovanni displayed her eloquence by speaking out against the rising tide of conservatism in the nation. For more than 30 years, Nikki Giovanni has continued to create poetry that speaks directly to the issues of the day.

# Women Writers Reflect American Diversity

**1978–2000** The broadening of opportunities for American women that began in the 1970s is as evident in literature as it is in other fields. Toni Morrison, Mary Oliver, Nikki Giovanni, Amy Tan, Anne Tyler, Alice Walker, Marge Piercy, Sandra Cisneros—these are just a few of the talented women novelists and poets who reflect the multicultural nature of the American identity. These women's writing shares a common characteristic—that of conveying the American experience through the exploration of personal memories, nature, childhood, and family.

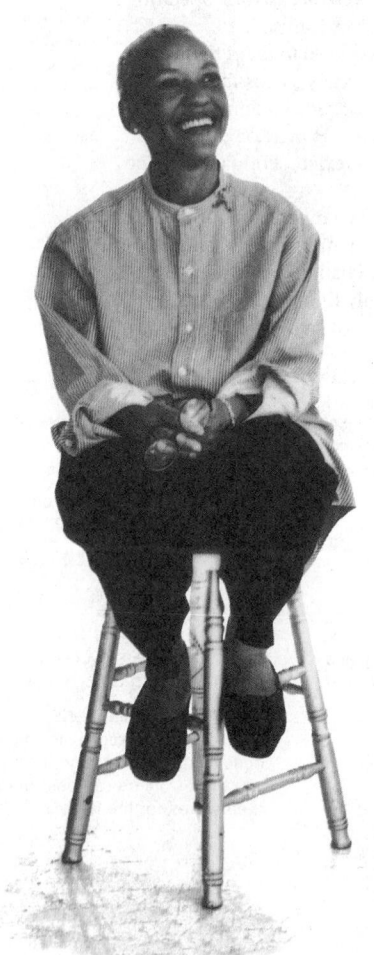

◄ **NIKKI GIOVANNI**

In the late 1960s, Nikki Giovanni won instant attention as an African American poet writing about the Black Power movement. Since then her poetry has often focused on childhood, family ties, and other personal concerns. In the following poem, Giovanni deals with individual empowerment—even under less than ideal circumstances.

### Choices

if i can't do
what i want to do
then my job is to not
do what i don't want
to do

it's not the same thing
but it's the best i can
do

if i can't have
what i want then
my job is to want
what i've got
and be satisfied
that at least there
is something more
to want

since i can't go
where i need
to go then i must go
where the signs point
though always understanding
parallel movement
isn't lateral

when i can't express
what i really feel
i practice feeling
what i can express
and none of it is equal
i know
but that's why mankind
alone among the mammals
learns to cry

—Nikki Giovanni,
"Choices," from *Cotton Candy on a Rainy Day* (1978)

## RECOMMENDED RESOURCES

### BOOKS

Cisneros, Sandra. *The House on Mango Street.* New York: Vintage Books, 1991.

Erdrich, Louise. *The Beet Queen.* New York: Harperperennial Library, 1998.

Giovanni, Nikki. *Blues For All The Changes: New Poems.* New York: William Morrow & Co., 1999.

Tan, Amy. *The Joy Luck Club.* New York: Ivy Books, 1994.

Tan, Amy. *The Kitchen God's Wife.* New York: Ballentine Books, 2001.

### SOUND RECORDINGS

Angelou, Maya. *I Know Why the Caged Bird Sings.* New York: Random House, 1996. An abridgment of Angelou's autobiography read by the author.

Cisneros, Sandra. *The House on Mango Street.* New York: Random House, 1998. Taped abridgement read by the author.

### VIDEOS

*Breathing Lessons.* Dir. John Erman. Republic Pictures, 1994. Film version of the novel by Anne Tyler.

*The Joy Luck Club.* Dir. Wayne Wang. Hollywood Pictures Home Video, 1993. The film based on the Amy Tan novel.

**AMY TAN**

A native of Oakland, California, Amy Tan draws on personal experiences in *The Joy Luck Club*, a series of interconnected stories about four Chinese-American daughters and their immigrant mothers. The four mothers establish a club for socializing and playing the game of mahjong.

My mother started the San Francisco version of the Joy Luck Club in 1949, two years before I was born. This was the year my mother and father left China with one stiff leather trunk filled only with fancy silk dresses. There was no time to pack anything else, my mother had explained to my father after they boarded the boat. Still his hands swam frantically between the slippery silks, looking for his cotton shirts and wool pants.

When they arrived in San Francisco, my father made her hide those shiny clothes. She wore the same brown-checked Chinese dress until the Refugee Welcome Society gave her two hand-me-down dresses, all too large in sizes for American women. The society was composed of a group of white-haired American missionary ladies from the First Chinese Baptist Church. And because of their gifts, my parents could not refuse their invitation to join the church. Nor could they ignore the old ladies' practical advice to improve their English through Bible study class on Wednesday nights and, later, through choir practice on Saturday mornings. This was how my parents met the Hsus, the Jongs, and the St. Clairs. My mother could sense that the women of these families also had unspeakable tragedies they had left behind in China and hopes they couldn't begin to express in their fragile English. Or at least, my mother recognized the numbness in these women's faces. And she saw how quickly their eyes moved when she told them her idea for the Joy Luck Club.

—Amy Tan, *The Joy Luck Club* (1989)

**SANDRA CISNEROS** ▶

Sandra Cisneros is one of many Chicana writers to win fame in recent years. In *The House on Mango Street*, she traces the experiences of a poor Hispanic girl named Esperanza (Spanish for *hope*) and her warm-hearted family. Nenny is her sister.

**Four Skinny Trees**

They are the only ones who understand me. I am the only one who understands them. Four skinny trees with skinny necks and pointy elbows like mine. Four who do not belong here but are here. Four raggedy excuses planted by the city. From our room we can hear them, but Nenny just sleeps and doesn't appreciate these things.

Their strength is secret. They send ferocious roots beneath the ground. They grow up and they grow down and grab the earth between their hairy toes and bite the sky with violent teeth and never quit their anger. This is how they keep.

Let one forget his reason for being, they'd all droop like tulips in a glass, each with their arms around the other. Keep, keep, keep, trees say when I sleep. They teach.

When I am too sad and too skinny to keep keeping, when I am a tiny thing against so many bricks, then it is I look at trees. When there is nothing left to look at on this street. Four who grew despite concrete. Four who reach and do not forget to reach. Four whose only reason is to be and be.

—Sandra Cisneros
*The House on Mango Street* (1989)

**THINKING CRITICALLY**

1. **Comparing** From these selections, what can you infer about women's experiences in American life today? Cite passages to support your response.

   **SEE SKILLBUILDER HANDBOOK, PAGE R8.**

2. **INTERNET ACTIVITY** CLASSZONE.COM

   Visit the links for American Literature to find and choose selections for an anthology of writing by three contemporary American women. Write a "capsule biography" summarizing each writer's background and achievements.

## Instruct

1. What are the common themes expressed by the three women writers featured on these pages?

2. How do a writer's family and childhood memories help readers recall their own early memories?

**MAKING PERSONAL CONNECTIONS**

What do you think you will tell your children about your childhood memories? How might your memories be different from those of your classmates? your parents? the writers in this feature?

**More About . . .**

**Amy Tan**

Amy Tan, was born in Oakland, California, and grew up in California and Switzerland. She went to college in California and soon after began a successful career as a freelance business writer. In 1987, Tan took her mother to China. While there, Tan began to explore her roots. She met her relatives and learned about her mother's life. Upon returning to the United States, Tan wrote her first novel, *The Joy Luck Club* (1989). The book became a best seller and was turned into a movie in 1993.

**THINKING CRITICALLY: ANSWERS**

**1. COMPARING**

**Rubrics**

Student responses should . . .

· express an understanding of the reading

· draw conclusions about women's experiences as described in the writing

· cite passages to support their conclusions

**2. INTERNET ACTIVITY**

**Rubrics**

Student biographies should . . .

· focus on three American women writers

· contain brief sketches that highlight the background and significant achievements of each author

· include quotes or other factual evidence to support their findings

# Technology and Modern Life

| MAIN IDEA | WHY IT MATTERS NOW | Terms & Names |
|---|---|---|
| Advances in technology have increased the pace but also the comfort of many Americans' daily lives. | Providing access to the new technology and regulating its use are two current challenges facing 21st-century America. | • information superhighway<br>• Internet<br>• telecommute<br>• Telecommunications Act Of 1996<br>• genetic engineering |

 U.S. History 8A, 11A, 22A, 22B, 22C, 23A, 23B, 24A, 24B, 25A, 25B, 25C, 25D

### One American's Story

The crowds stand four-deep cheering for 12-year-old Rudy Garcia-Tolson as he captures a new national record for his age group at the San Diego half-marathon. Despite the loss of his legs, Rudy competes in sports and is headed for the 2004 paralympics.

For years, Rudy was confined to a wheelchair. After undergoing a double amputation he was fitted with carbon fiber prostheses—artificial replacements for missing body parts. These light-weight, strong and durable new legs now make many things possible for Rudy.

**A PERSONAL VOICE** RUDY GARCIA-TOLSON

"I told them to cut my legs off. I saw pictures of people running with prosthetic legs. I didn't want to stay in a wheelchair. . . . My legs won't stop me. Nothing stops me. . . . I like to show kids that there's no limitations—kids or challenged people or adults, there's no limitations to what a person can do. . . . My motto is, if you have a brave heart, that's a powerful weapon."

—quoted in *Press-Enterprise*, January 1, 2000

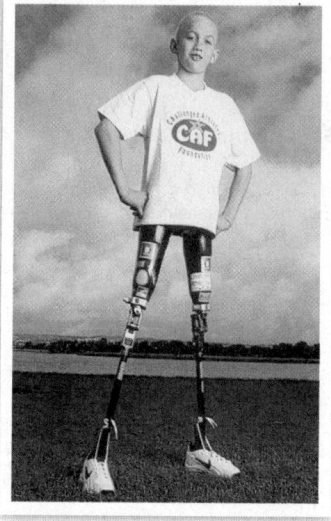

Rudy Garcia-Tolson, 2001

Advances in medical technology have permitted Rudy to live a more fully active life. Throughout the 20th century and into the 21st, technological developments helped Americans become more active in many ways.

## **1** The Communications Revolution

The computer industry transformed the 1980s. Instead of giant mainframes and minicomputers, desktop workstations now ruled business. Home computers became widely available, and many thousands of people joined online subscription services that provided electronic mail and magazine-style information.

**876** CHAPTER 26

 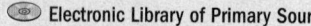

## Analyzing *Political Cartoons*

### "VACATION, 2000"

By the end of the 20th century, millions of Americans owned any number of personal communication devices. People were able to speak to or correspond with each other instantaneously almost anytime, almost anywhere. The cartoon suggests that Americans are dependent on their communication devices, and that the once relaxing and peaceful family vacation has given way to the hustle and bustle of constant access.

### SKILLBUILDER
**Analyzing Political Cartoons**

1. What modern-day communication devices are being used in this cartoon?
2. In what ways do the characters in this cartoon seem trapped by modern-day communications technology?

 **SEE SKILLBUILDER HANDBOOK, PAGE R24.**

VACATION, 2000

### Analyzing *Political Cartoons*

**SKILLBUILDER ANSWERS**

1. email, cellular phone, pager
2. The family is supposed to be on vacation, and yet, these new communication devices do not allow them to escape the office or everyday life.

---

**Mini-Lesson 3:**
**SS11 3(US23.A)**

**ENTERING THE INFORMATION AGE** The **information superhighway**—a network of communication devices linking people and institutions across the nation and the world—promised to advance the revolution that had begun with the personal computer. In 1994, Vice President Al Gore began to oversee the government's participation in developing this superhighway. Even though private industries would build the superhighway, the government would keep access democratic, ensure affordable service for everyone, protect privacy and property rights, and develop incentives for investors.

The 1990s enjoyed explosive growth of the **Internet,** an international network linking computers and allowing almost instant transmittal of text, images, and sound. Originally developed in the late 1960s by the U.S. Department of Defense for defense research, the Internet drew early popularity at universities. By the mid-1990s *Internet* became a household word. Use of the network was further popularized by the World Wide Web, which provided a simple visual interface for words and pictures to be seen by an unlimited audience. As businesses, schools, and organizations began to use the Web as a primary form of communication, new forms of social interaction emerged. Users developed "electronic presence" in virtual worlds, fantasy environments created with electronics.

**Vocabulary**
**interface:**
the point of communication between a computer and any other entity, such as a printer or human operator

**NEW TOOLS, NEW MEDIA** Through an electronic connection, such as a TV cable or phone line, users accessed an array of media, from streaming video to research archives, from on-line shopping catalogs to customized news broadcasts. Users could interact with each other across the world. By 2000, as many as 97 million Americans used the Internet regularly to send email (electronic notes and messages), to share music, or to browse or search through "pages" on the Web. During the 1990s, classrooms across the nation increasingly used computer networking. Long-distance video and audio transmissions also linked American students. Some content was delivered not on networks but stored on a CD-ROM (Compact Disc Read-Only Memory), which evolved from music CDs that contained code for sound waves. CD-ROMs also carry digital code for pictures, text, and animation to be played on a computer.

### More About . . .

**Internet Access**

As more and more people gained access to the Internet it became more difficult to log on to the Internet. To meet the demands of customers who wanted faster service, three high-speed access technologies were developed: digital subscriber lines (DSL), which uses existing telephone lines, cable modems from cable companies, and satellite downloads using home satellite dishes. These high-speed access technologies allowed users to download information at speeds up to 1.5 million bits per second compared to ordinary speeds of 56,000 bits per second.

*The United States in Today's World* **877**

---

**DIFFERENTIATING INSTRUCTION** | **LESS PROFICIENT READERS**

### Outlining

Help students understand the section, "Telecommunications Act of 1996" on page 878. Suggest that they create an outline to organize the information presented in the passage. Write a sample outline on the board as a reference. Use the following example:

I. Impact of computer and communication technology
   A. On society
   B. On home offices
   C. On entertainment

II. Growth of communications companies
   A. Federal regulations
   B. Benefits of competition

III. Implications of new technology
   A. Federal response
   B. Auction of air waves
   C. The Communications Decency Act
   D. Public response

## Instruct: Objective ❷

**Scientific Advances Enrich Lives**
TAKS SS11 2(WH23.A)
· How has technology affected American life?
· Which technological advances caused controversy?

 **In-Depth Resources: Unit 7**
· Guided Reading, p. 47

The late 20th century advances in computers and communications have had an impact on American society and business comparable to the industrial developments of the late 1800s. Americans now have more entertainment options, as cable service has multiplied the number of television channels available and greater bandwidth offers the possibility for high-definition television. Because of cellular phones, fax machines, the Internet, and overnight shipping, people can more readily **telecommute,** or work out of their homes instead of going to an office every day. Ⓐ

**LEGISLATING TECHNOLOGY** In the 1980s, the government was slow to recognize the implications of the new communications technology. In 1994, however, the Federal Communications Commission (FCC) began to auction the valuable rights to airwaves and collected over $9 billion. Then, with the rapid growth in the communications industry, the federal government took several steps to ensure that consumers received the best service. Congress passed the **Telecommunications Act of 1996**, removing barriers that had previously prevented one type of communications company from starting up or buying another related one. While it increased competition in the industry, the law also paved the way for major media mergers. When Capital Cities/ABC Inc. joined the Walt Disney Company, industry watchdogs noted that this reflected the trend toward concentrating media influence in the hands of a few powerful conglomerates.

The passage of the Telecommunications Act won applause from the communications industry but only mixed reviews from the public. Consumer activists worried that the law would fail to ensure equal access to new technologies for rural residents and poor people. Civil rights advocates contended that the Communications Decency Act (part of the Telecommunications Act) restricted free speech because it barred the transmission of "indecent" materials to minors via the Internet. In addition, Congress also called for a "V-chip" in television sets—a computer chip that would enable parents to block TV programs that they deemed inappropriate for their children. Parts of these laws were later struck down in court. Ⓑ

**MAIN IDEA**

**Summarizing**
Ⓐ Explain the revolutionary nature of communicating via the Internet.

*A. Answer*
Communicating via the Internet provides nearly instantaneous transmission of text, image, and sound from a worldwide data network.

**MAIN IDEA**

**Predicting Effects**
Ⓑ How might the Telecommunications Act affect consumers?

*B. Answer*
Consumers will probably enjoy increased choice and a greater variety of services.

## ❷ Scientific Advances Enrich Lives

▲ At NASA Langley Research Center in Virginia, an aerospace engineer wearing stereo glasses sees a 3-D view of a space station simulation, as shown in the background.

The exciting growth in the telecommunications industry in the 1990s was matched by insights that revolutionized robotics, space exploration, and medicine. The world witnessed marvels that for many of the "baby boom generation," people born in the late 1940s and the 1950s, echoed science fiction.

**SIMULATION, ROBOTICS, AND MACHINE INTELLIGENCE** Visual imaging and artificial intelligence (a computer's ability to perform activities that require intelligence) were combined to provide applications in industry, medicine, and education. For example, virtual reality began with the flight simulators used to train military and commercial pilots. Today, with a headset that holds tiny video screens and earphones, and with a data glove that translates hand movements to a computer screen, a user can navigate a "virtual landscape." Doctors have used virtual reality to take

---

a computerized tour of a patient's throat and lungs to check for medical problems. Surgeons have performed long-distance surgery through telepresence systems—gloves, computers, and robotic elements specially wired so that a doctor can operate on a patient hundreds of miles away. Architects and engineers have used virtual reality to create visual, rather than physical, models of their buildings, cars, and other designs. Modeling also affected the nightly newscast. Using supercomputers and improved satellite data, meteorologists could offer three-day weather forecasts that reached the accuracy of one-day forecasts of 1980.

As technology became more sophisticated, computers increased in capability. IBM's Deep Blue defeated chess champion Garry Kasparov in 1997. Computational linguists steadily improved natural language understanding in computers, thus fine-tuning the accuracy of voice recognition systems.

Robots grew more humanlike as engineers equipped them with high-capacity chips simulating brain function. By the year 2000, robots had the ability to walk on two legs, interact with people, learn taught behaviors, and express artificial feelings with facial gestures.

**SPACE EXPLORATION** In the 1990s, astronomy expanded our view of the universe. In 1997, NASA's *Pathfinder* and its rover *Sojourner* transmitted live pictures of the surface of Mars to millions of Internet users.

Shuttle missions, meanwhile, concentrated on scientific research and assembly, transport, and repair of orbiting objects, paving the way to possible human missions to Mars and other space travel in the coming century. NASA concentrated on working with other nations to build the *International Space Station (ISS)*. The *ISS* promised to offer scientists a zero-gravity laboratory for research in medicine, space mechanics and architecture, and long-term living in space. Ellen Ochoa, part of the first shuttle crew to dock to the *ISS*, hoped to inspire young students:

**Background**
The *International Space Station* was established by joining and expanding upon the Russian station, *Mir*, and the American *Spacelab*.

**A PERSONAL VOICE** ELLEN OCHOA

" I'm not trying to make everyone an astronaut, but I want students to think about a career and the preparation they'll need. . . . I tell students that the opportunities I had were a result of having a good educational background. Education is what allows you to stand out."

—quoted in *Stanford University School of Engineering Annual Report*, 1997-98.

Dr. Ellen Ochoa

Another shuttle crew in 1993 aboard the *Endeavour* repaired the Hubble Space Telescope, which returns dazzling intergalactic views. In late 1995, astronomers using observatories discovered a planet orbiting the fourth closest star to Earth, the first planet to be detected outside our own solar system. Since then dozens more have been detected. Astronomers back on Earth have also spent considerable effort tracking asteroids and comets whose paths might collide with our planet. Astrobiologists hailed the discovery on Antarctica of a small meteorite that traveled to Earth from Mars about 15 million years ago.

**BIOTECHNOLOGY** The most profound insight into the book of life came from the field of biotechnology. The Human Genome Project, an international effort to map the genes of the human body, and Celera, a private company in molecular biology, simultaneously announced in 2000 that they had sequenced nearly all of the human genome only a decade after the research began. Cooperation via the Internet and access to computerized databases by multiple research groups vastly accelerated the scientists' ability to identify and order over three billion chemical

**More About . . .**

**Virtual Reality**
One application of virtual reality, developed in England, enables viewers to assess their chances of escaping from a fire in a simulated structure. The program is called VEGAS, which stands for virtual egress analysis and simulation. Users can program the software so that the several dozen virtual occupants will respond as if they were children or elderly or handicapped persons. Programs can duplicate any existing structure. The results show possible structural flaws or places where bottlenecks will form during escape, the speed of smoke flow, and poor escape strategies of the occupants.

**More About . . .**

**Dr. Ellen Ochoa**
Ellen Ochoa became the first Hispanic-American woman in space in April 1993, when she served as a mission specialist aboard the Space Shuttle Discovery. She has a doctorate in electrical engineering from Stanford and holds three patents for optical engineering systems. It was her interest in optics and computer hardware that first brought her to the attention of the National Aeronautics and Space Administration. On three space flights in the 1990s, Ochoa logged more than 719 hours in orbit. She has also been involved in the development of the international space station.

*The United States in Today's World* **879**

---

**DIFFERENTIATING INSTRUCTION**     **GIFTED AND TALENTED STUDENTS**      classzone.com

**Researching the Human Genome**

The mapping of the human genome was among the most outstanding scientific achievements of the past few years. Have students use the Internet and library resources to research the human genome project and its implications for future generations. Ask students to prepare a multimedia presentation for the class.

 Integrated Assessment
· Rubrics 1, 6

## Tracing Themes
### SCIENCE AND TECHNOLOGY

Advances in the fields of science and technology have had a significant impact on American life during the 20th century. These advances had had both the positive and negative effects on society. The value of new technologies will differ depending upon one's perspective, for technology itself is morally neutral. The application of a particular technology will ultimately determine its negative or positive impact.

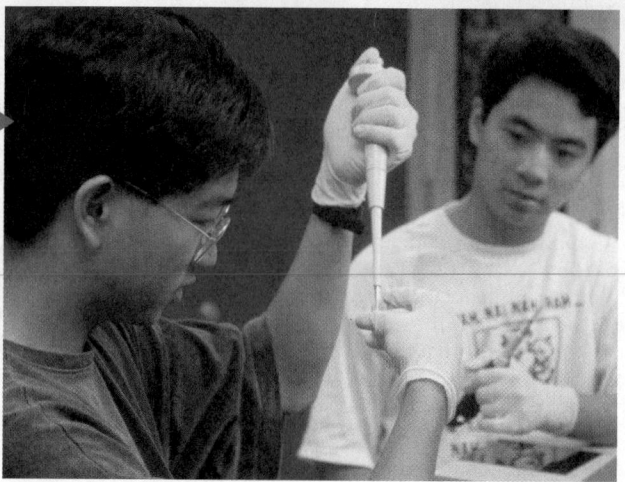

▲ High-school students Li-Ho (*left*) and Yu-Fong Hong (*right*), among the youngest scientists to have worked on the Human Genome Project, are shown at a San Ramon, California, laboratory.

## More About . . .

### Genetic Engineering

Advances in genetic engineering have sparked heated debate. Some scientists emphasize the myriad of possible applications for this new technology, while others fear the unknown consequences. Public opinion is sharply divided about genetically engineered crops. Advocates claim such crops are hardier, resistant to pests, and can be harvested in a variety of climates. Critics point out the adverse effects that genetically engineered crops might have on human beings and the environment.

"letters" of the genetic code of DNA. Molecular biologists hoped that this genetic map would offer the key to treating many inherited diseases and diagnosing congenital disabilities, and that drug makers could one day design pharmaceuticals for each patient's particular profile.

DNA had been in the spotlight before the breakthrough announcement. In well publicized legal proceedings, prosecutors relied on DNA evidence to help prove the guilt of defendants who may have left behind a single hair at a crime scene. Others, wrongly imprisoned, were released when genetic analysis proved their innocence.

But different opinions arose over some of the new "biotechnology." Some speculated that technological progress outpaced social evolution and society's ability to grapple with the consequences. In 1997, Scottish researchers cloned Dolly the sheep from one cell of an adult sheep. Shortly thereafter, two Rhesus monkeys were cloned in Oregon, and many wondered whether human cloning was next. Firms sought to patent genes used for medical and research applications, using the principle of invention and property. Advances such as these, as well as gene therapy, artificial human chromosomes, and testing embryos for genetic defects all sparked heated debates among scientists, ethicists, religious leaders, and politicians.

The use of **genetic engineering**—the artificial changing of the molecular biology of organisms' cells to alter an organism—also aroused public concern. However, the Federal Department of Agriculture (FDA) holds that genetically engineered foods are safe and that they require no extra labeling. Scientists in the late 1990s modified corn and rice to provide resistance to pests and increase nutritional value. In 1996, the European Union limited the importation of such products in response to consumer pressure, allowing only those clearly labeled as having been genetically modified.

**MEDICAL PROGRESS** People suffering from some diseases benefited from advances in medicine in the 1990s. Cancer survival rates improved drastically as clinicians explored the use of gene therapy, genetically engineered antibodies, and immune system modulation. Improvements in tracking the spread of HIV—the virus that causes AIDS (acquired immune deficiency syndrome)—through the body made researchers better prepared to find a cure. AIDS patients were treated with combination therapies, and public health officials advocated abstinence and "safer sex" practices to control the spread of HIV.

Improved technology for making medical diagnoses offered new hope as well. Magnetic resonance imaging (MRI), for example, was used to produce cross-sectional images of any part of the body. Advances that will make the MRI procedure ten times faster will also make MRI more widely available and cheaper to use. Medical researchers look ahead to using fleets of tiny "nanosensors" one-thousandth the width of a human hair to find tumors and to deploying "nanobots" to repair tissues and even genes. **C**

**Background**
In 1998, less than 13,500 Americans died from AIDS, roughly one-third the 1992 number.

*C. Answer*
It improved diagnosis.

**MAIN IDEA**
**Summarizing**
**C** Describe how technology affected health care.

---

## Analyzing the Digital World

**Class Time** 45 minutes

**Task** Demonstrating differences in analog and digital devices

**Purpose** To evaluate the impact of digital technology

**Directions** Have students use the Internet and instruction manuals for digital devices to research the ways in which digital technology has improved retail appliances. Ask students to compare analog and digital devices of such items as visual recording devices, a 35mm camera, and telephones. Then have students give a brief class presentation that includes a demonstration.

📰 Integrated Assessment
· Rubrics 1, 3

## Science & Technology

### ALTERNATIVE CARS

In an effort to reduce the nation's dependence on fossil fuels, researchers have been working to develop a "cleaner" car, or one that runs on something other than gasoline. Such alternative models include an electric car, which uses a rechargable battery and gas power, and a vehicle that runs on compressed natural gas.

POWERED BY VEGETABLE OIL

▶ Carl Bielenberg of Calais, Vermont, holds a container of seeds of the jatropha plant. He runs his compact car on vegetable oil that is made from the seed.

▲ A solar-powered car built by high school students from Saginaw, Michigan, makes its way through busy traffic.

### More About . . .

#### Hybrid Cars

In the year 2000, two automobile companies began marketing a hybrid car. The car has both an electric engine powered by batteries and a small gasoline engine. Instead of needing to recharge the batteries by plugging into a power source, the gasoline engine cuts in to charge the batteries when the power runs low. Furthermore, the batteries capture the energy generated when the brakes are applied. The cars are quiet, able to run well at highway speeds, and average 40–65 miles per gallon in gasoline consumption.

**ENVIRONMENTAL MEASURES** With the spreading use of technology came greater concern about the impact of human activities on the natural environment. Scientists have continued examining ways to reduce American dependence on pollution-producing fossil fuels. Fossil fuels such as oil provided 85 percent of the energy in the United States in the 1990s but also contributed to poor air quality, acid rain, and global warming. Many individuals have tried to help by reducing consumption of raw materials. By the early 1990s, residents set out glass bottles and jars, plastic bottles, newspapers, phone books, cardboard, and aluminum cans for recycling at curbsides, and consumers purchased new products synthesized from recycled materials.

## SECTION 3 ASSESSMENT

1. **TERMS & NAMES** For each term or name, write a sentence explaining its significance.
   - •information superhighway
   - •Internet
   - •telecommute
   - •Telecommunications Act of 1996
   - •genetic engineering

### MAIN IDEA

2. **TAKING NOTES**
   On a chart like the one shown, list four of the technological changes described in this section and explain how each change has affected your life.

   | Technological Change | Effect on Me |
   | --- | --- |
   | 1. | |
   | 2. | |
   | 3. | |
   | 4. | |

### CRITICAL THINKING

3. **MAKING INFERENCES**
   Explain how government, business, and individuals are important to the existence of the information superhighway. **Think About:**

   - the costs of developing the superhighway
   - the equipment and personnel needed to maintain it
   - who uses the superhighway and why they use it

4. **ANALYZING ISSUES**
   Why is genetic engineering a source of controversy?

5. **EVALUATING**

   Which area of technological change described in this section do you think was the most important one for the country? Explain.

---

## Assess & Reteach

### SECTION 3 ASSESSMENT

Ask students to identify passages in the text that helped them answer the questions in the Section Assessment.

📄 Formal Assessment
· Section Quiz, p. 472

### SELF-ASSESSMENT

Have students review their answer to question 4 in the Section Assessment. Ask them to elaborate on their original answer and to fill in any missing details.

### RETEACH

Conduct a class debate about the pros and cons of technological change. Ask students to support their positions with details from this section.

📄 In-Depth Resources: Unit 7
· Reteaching Activity, p. 53

---

Answers ASSESSMENT 3

**1. TERMS & NAMES**
information superhighway, p. 877
Internet, p. 877
telecommute, p. 878
Telecommunications Act of 1996, p. 878
genetic engineering, p. 880

**2. TAKING NOTES**
Technological changes: Internet; e-mail; V-chip; MRI; artificial limbs; virtual reality; CD-ROMs; air bags; Global Positioning System; electric cars; genetically engineered food

**3. MAKING INFERENCES**
Government provides regulation, financial support, incentives for businesses; companies provide goods, services,

advertising, upgrades; individual consumers support businesses; all three groups contribute information, research, and participation in global communications

**4. ANALYZING ISSUES**
The possibility that genetic engineering may be used to control people's appearance or behavior has created controversy about its applications.

**5. EVALUATING**
Communications: global proliferation of information, improved education. Transportation: safety and efficiency. Health care: new medical technologies saved lives, better quality of life. Entertainment: fun, leisure activities. Environment: technology to aid in solving the pollution problem.

## OBJECTIVES

**1** Identify causes of urban flight.

**2** Analyze the impact of the aging of America.

**3** Describe changing migration patterns and immigration policies.

**4** Explain challenges and opportunities Americans may face in the 21st century.

### SKILLBUILDER

· Interpreting Visual Sources, p. 883
· Interpreting Charts, p. 884
· Geography Skillbuilder: movement, p. 885

### CRITICAL THINKING

· Analyzing Causes, p. 883
· Predicting Effects, p. 885
· Comparing, pp. 886, 887
· Drawing Conclusions, p. 887

## Focus & Motivate

Ask students to think about where they live and describe what they do and do not like about it. Ask students if they would move to another place if they had the chance?

## Instruct

### Instruct: Objective **1**

**Urban Flight**
TAKS SS11 5(US24.B)

· What caused people to move out of American cities?
· How were cities benefited by gentrification?
· What was the impact of population growth on the suburbs?

 In-Depth Resources: Unit 7
· Guided Reading, p. 48

# The Changing Face of America

| MAIN IDEA | WHY IT MATTERS NOW | Terms & Names |
|---|---|---|
| At the end of the 20th century, the U.S. population grew more diverse both in ethnic background and in age. | Americans of all backgrounds share common goals: the desire for equal rights and economic opportunity. | • urban flight    • Proposition 187<br>• gentrification |

 **TEKS** U.S. History 8A, 8B, 10A, 10B, 11A, 13E, 21B, 21C, 24B, 24G, 24H, 25A, 25B, 25C, 25D, 26A

 **One American's Story**

Every ten years the United States conducts a census, or head count of its population. The results of the census determine, among other things, how billions of federal dollars are spent for housing, health care, and education over the coming decade. The Census Bureau estimates that the 1990 census undercounted Latinos by more than five percent. This undercount resulted in a loss of millions of dollars of aid to municipalities with large Latino populations, as well as denying Latinos political representation in all levels of government.

During the latest census conducted in 2000, Antonia Hernandez, President and General Counsel of the Mexican American Legal Defense and Education Fund (MALDEF), spearheaded the national *¡Hágase Contar!* Make Yourself Count! campaign. MALDEF workers canvassed neighborhoods urging residents to complete the census. They stressed that all information was confidential and discussed the high stakes of being counted.

**A PERSONAL VOICE** ANTONIA HERNANDEZ

" The census not only measures our growth and marks our place in the community, but it is the first and indispensable step toward fair political representation, equal distribution of resources, and enforcement of our civil rights. "

—Public statement for *¡Hágase Contar!* campaign, 2000

Antonia Hernandez, MALDEF's president

Data from the 2000 census revealed that the Hispanic population had grown by close to 58 percent since 1990, reaching 35.3 million. The 2000 census also confirmed a vast increase in what were once ethnic minorities.

## **1** Urban Flight

One of the most significant socio-cultural changes in American history has been the movement of Americans from the cities to the suburbs. The years after World War II through the 1980s saw a widespread pattern of **urban flight,** the process in which Americans left the cities and moved to the suburbs. At mid-century, the population of cities exceeded that of suburbs. By 1970, the ratio became even.

**882** CHAPTER 26

---

## PROGRAM RESOURCES

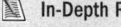 **In-Depth Resources: Unit 7**
· Guided Reading, p. 48
· Skillbuilder Practice: Hypothesizing, p. 50
· Reteaching Activity, p. 54
· Primary Source: Road Sign, p. 60
· Literature, pp. 61–62
· American Lives: Wilma Mankiller, p. 64

 **Reading Study Guide** (English and Spanish), pp. 263–264

 **Access for Students Acquiring English/ESL**
· Guided Reading (Spanish), p. 277
· Skillbuilder, p. 278

 **Formal Assessment**
· Section Quiz, p. 473

 **Integrated Assessment**
· Rubrics

**INTEGRATED TECHNOLOGY**

 **Humanities Transparencies HT48**
· This Isn't Exactly the Sort of Active Retirement I Hoped For . . .

 **Electronic Library of Primary Sources**

**classzone.com**

**TEXAS RESOURCES**

· TAKS Spiraled Content Review
· TAKS Practice Tests
· TAKS Practice Transparencies TT131
· TAKS Online Test Practice

In the year 2000, after decades of decline, some major cities across the country had increased their populations while others slowed or halted declines. The transformation of the United States into a nation of suburbs had intensified the problems of the cities.

CAUSES OF URBAN CHANGE Several factors contributed to the movement of Americans out of the cities. Because of the continued movement of job-seeking Americans into urban areas in the 1950s and 1960s, many urban American neighborhoods became overcrowded. Overcrowding in turn contributed to such urban problems as increasing crime rates and decaying housing.

During the 1970s and early 1980s, city dwellers who could afford to do so moved to the suburbs for more space, privacy, and security. Often, families left the cities because suburbs offered newer, less crowded schools. As many middle-class Americans left cities for the suburbs, the economic base of many urban neighborhoods declined, and suburbs grew wealthy. Following the well-educated labor force, more industries relocated to suburban areas in the 1990s. The economic base that provided tax money and supported city services in large cities such as New York, Detroit, and Philadelphia continued to shrink as people and jobs moved outward.

In addition, many downtown districts fell into disrepair as suburban shoppers abandoned city stores for suburban shopping malls. According to the 1990 census, the 31 most impoverished communities in the United States were in cities. **Ⓐ**

By the mid-1990s, however, as the property values in the nation's inner cities declined, many people returned to live there. In a process known as **gentrification,** they purchased and rehabilitated deteriorating urban property, oftentimes displacing lower income people. Old industrial sites and neighborhoods in locations convenient to downtown became popular, especially among young, single adults who preferred the excitement of city life and the uniqueness of urban neighborhoods to the often more uniform environment of the suburbs.

---

**MAIN IDEA**

**Analyzing Causes**
**Ⓐ** List the factors that influenced middle-class residents to leave cities for suburbs.

*A. Answer*
Overcrowding; crime; better schools in the suburbs.

---

**More About . . .**

**The Effects of Population Distribution**
All over the world, people are now more aware of the need to balance economic progress with conservation. For example, city planners now take into consideration the impact on new construction—both residential and commercial—on the physical environment. Car companies in the United States and many other countries are working to develop pollution-free vehicles. And, beginning in the 1990s, Americans are planting more than two million acres of new trees each year. In the decades to come, state, federal, and local agencies will have to work together to protect the environment from the harmful effects of an increasing population on vanishing resources. Ask, What are some other ways in which the environment can be protected from future encroachment? *(responsible planning for growth; stronger legislation for protection of wildlife; responsible use of technology in everyday life)*

---

**History Through  *Architecture***

**REBUILDING THE RIVERFRONTS**
As part of the effort to revitalize cities, a number of architects, landscape architects, and urban planners have focused on enhancing what for many urban centers had become a neglected eyesore—their waterfronts. In Pittsburgh, landscape architects turned a dreary strip of concrete and parking lot into Allegheny Riverfront Park, an inviting stretch of natural walkways and recreation areas.

**SKILLBUILDER**
**Interpreting Visual Sources**
1. Why might landscape architects consider improving riverfronts to be a key part of revitalizing cities?
2. In what other ways could architects and urban designers make city living more attractive?

   **SEE SKILLBUILDER HANDBOOK, PAGE R23.**

▲ Allegheny Riverfront Park in 1999

◀ The Allegheny River waterfront in 1984

*The United States in Today's World* **883**

---

**History Through *Architecture***

**SKILLBUILDER ANSWERS**
1. A vibrant waterfront would attract visitors and businesses to the downtown area.
2. more parks and trees; variety of architectural shapes; scenic views

---

**ACTIVITY    COOPERATIVE ACTIVITY**

classzone.com

**Predicting Local Demographic Changes**

**Class Time** 45 minutes

**Task** Researching and reporting on local demographic changes and predicting future trends

**Purpose** To analyze local population trends

**Directions** Have students work in groups and use the Internet and library resources to research local population trends. Encourage them to gather anecdotal evidence from parents, neighbors, and their own experiences. Ask students to create a profile of recent population changes in their neighborhood or community. Then have them present their findings to the class and make predictions about future trends.

## Instruct: Objective ❷

**The Aging of America**

TAKS SS11 5(US24.B)

· What are the causes of the aging of America?

· How does the aging of the population impact health services and Social Security?

 **Humanities Transparencies HT48**
· This Isn't Exactly the Sort of Active Retirement I Hoped For . . .

**Electronic Library of Primary Sources**
· My American Century, 1997 by S. Terkel

---

## HISTORY from VISUALS

### Interpreting the Charts

Have students look at the graph to see the numbers of Americans 65 and older projected in the 21st century. During what decade does the projected number of older Americans begin to increase significantly? *(in the 2010s—a projected 16 million increase as compared to a less than 3 million increase projected in the 2000s)*

---

## More About . . .

### Senior Power

There are advantages to being part of the majority in a democratic country. The Baby Boom generation dominated the market as teenagers and young adults, just as the aging means a shift in economic power to older Americans. Increasingly, advertising dollars are being spent to market products geared toward senior citizens. The government is concentrating more resources on programs for the elderly. The highest percentage of voters in the country is older Americans. Politicians might need to adjust their agendas to earn the votes of their older constituents.

---

**SUBURBAN LIVING** While many suburbanites continued to commute to city jobs during the 1990s, increasing numbers of workers began to telecommute, or use new communications technology, such as computers, modems, and fax machines, to work from their homes. Another notable trend was the movement of minority populations to the suburbs. Nationwide, by the early 1990s, about 43 percent of the Latino population and more than half of the Asian-American population lived in suburbs.

Suburban growth led to intense competition between suburbs and cities, and among the suburbs themselves, for business and industry. Since low-rise suburban homes yielded low tax revenues, tax-hungry suburbs offered tax incentives for companies to locate within their borders. These incentives resulted in lower tax revenues for local governments—meaning that less funds were available for schools, libraries, and police departments. Consequently, taxes were often increased to fund these community services as well as to build the additional roads and other infrastructure necessary to support the new businesses.

The shift of populations from cities to suburbs was not the only significant change in American life in the 1990s. The American public was also growing older, and its aging raised complex issues for American policymakers.

*Skillbuilder Answers:*
1. 2020 and 2030.
2. About 125%.

**Vocabulary**
**infrastructure:** the basic facilities, services, and installations needed for the functioning of a community or society

### The Graying of America, 1990–2030

| Year | Number of Americans 65 and older* | Percent of U.S. population |
|------|-----------------------------------|----------------------------|
| 1990 | 31,081 | 12.4 |
| 2000 | 34,837 | 12.7 |
| 2010 | 37,385** | 13.2** |
| 2020 | 53,733** | 16.5** |
| 2030 | 70,319** | 20** |

*numbers in thousands
**projected totals

Source: U.S. Census Bureau; *Statistical Abstract of the United States 2000*

**SKILLBUILDER Interpreting Charts**
1. Between what years is America's elderly population expected to grow the most?
2. By roughly what percentage is America's elderly population expected to increase between 1990 and 2030?

## The Aging of America ❷

The 2000 census documents that Americans were older than ever before, with a median age of 35.3—two years older than a decade prior. Increased longevity and the aging of the baby boom generation were the primary reasons for the rising median age.

Behind the rising median age lie several broad trends. The country's birthrate has slowed slightly, and the number of seniors has increased as Americans live longer because of advances in medical care and living healthier lifestyles. The number of people over 85 has increased at a faster rate than any other segment of the population, to 4.3 million in the year 2000.

The graying of America has placed new demands on the country's programs that provide care for the elderly. These programs accounted for only 6 percent of the national budget in 1955. It was projected that the programs would consume about 39 percent of the budget by 2005.

The major programs that provide care for elderly and disabled people are Medicare and Social Security. Medicare, which pays medical expenses for senior citizens, began in 1965, when most Americans had lower life expectancies. By 2000, the costs of this program exceeded $200 billion.

◀ **Senior Athletes compete at the first U.S. National Senior Olympics held in St. Louis, Missouri, in 2000.**

---

**ACTIVITY** SKILLBUILDER LESSON

### Hypothesizing

**Explaining the Skill** Hypothesizing about the future involves analyzing statistics and other data and making predictions. Reaching one's own conclusions, based on the information available, can help foster a deeper understanding of a subject.

**Applying the Skill** Ask students to read the information in this section about the aging of America and Social Security. Encourage them to consider the facts from the chapter and their own knowledge of the subject to hypothesize about the future of Social Security. *(Students might say that Social Security needs to be reformed. Evidence: increasing number of retirees, longer life expectancy, increasing costs, and fewer workers to support Social Security.)*

 **In-Depth Resources: Unit 7**
· Skillbuilder Practice: Hypothesizing, p. 50

Social Security, which pays benefits to retired Americans, was designed to rely on continued funding from a vast number of younger workers who would contribute taxes to support a small number of retired workers. That system worked well when younger workers far outnumbered retirees and when most workers didn't live long after retirement.

In 1996, it took Social Security contributions from three workers to support every retiree. By 2030, however, with an increase in the number of elderly persons and an expected decline in the birthrate, there will be only two workers' contributions available to support each senior citizen. Few issues loomed as large in the 2000 presidential election as what to do about Social Security. If President Bush and Congress do not restructure the system, Social Security will eventually pay out more money than it will take in. Some people suggest that the system be reformed by raising deductions for workers, taxing the benefits paid to wealthier Americans, and raising the age at which retirees can collect benefits. **B**

> **MAIN IDEA**
>
> **Predicting Effects**
> **B** What are the factors that will force an eventual restructuring of Social Security?
>
> *B. Answer*
> Increased life expectancy; the huge baby-boom generation; declining birthrate.

## The Shifting Population ❸

In addition to becoming increasingly suburban and elderly, the population of the United States has also been transformed by immigration. Between 1970 and 2000, the country's population swelled from 204 million to more than 284 million. Immigration accounted for much of that growth. As the nation's newest residents yearned for U.S. citizenship, however, other Americans debated the effects of immigration on American life.

**A CHANGING IMMIGRANT POPULATION** The most recent immigrants to the United States differ from immigrants of earlier years. The large numbers of immigrants who entered the country before and just after 1900 came from Europe.

*Skillbuilder Answers:*
1. Iowa and Mississippi.
2. The map shows immigrants are moving to the Midwest and Northwest, but does not show the absolute numbers.

### CHAPTER 26 · SECTION 4

**Instruct: Objective ❸**
**The Shifting Population**
TAKS SS11 3(US21.A)
· How are ethnic and racial demographics changing in the United States?
· Why is illegal immigration a controversial issue?
· What have some state governments done to control immigration?
· What changes have Native Americans made in recent decades?

📖 In-Depth Resources: Unit 7
  · Guided Reading, p. 48
  · Primary Source: Road Sign, p. 60
  · Literature, pp. 61–62
  · American Lives: Wilma Mankiller, p. 64

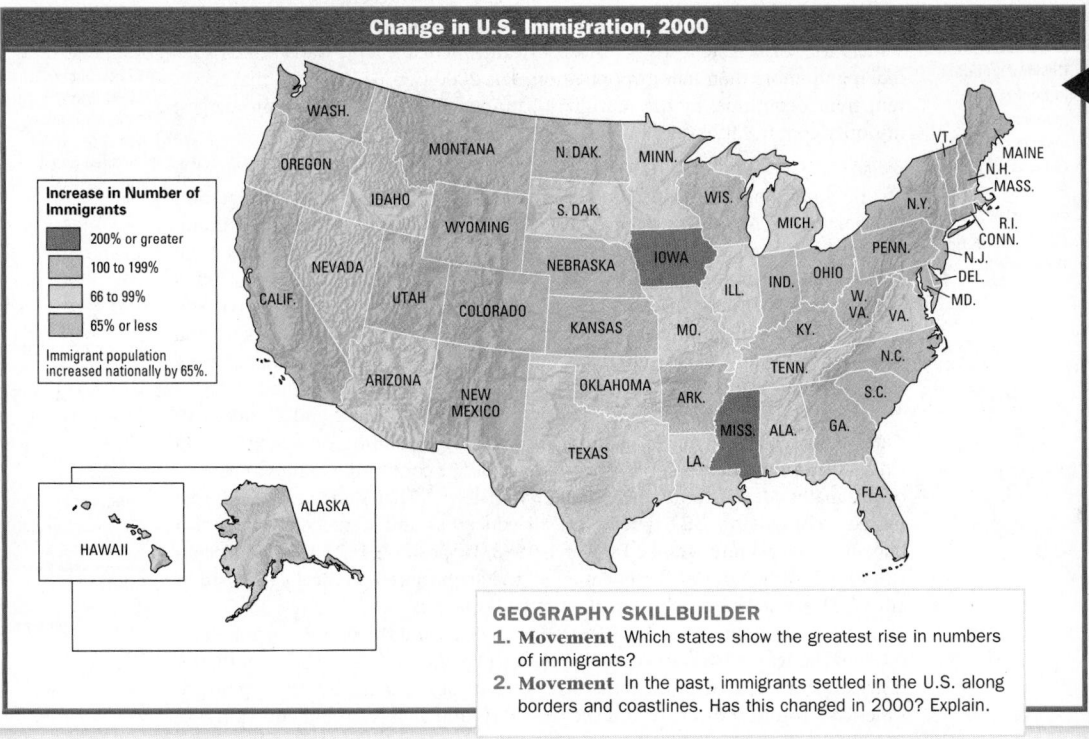

**Change in U.S. Immigration, 2000**

**Increase in Number of Immigrants**
- 200% or greater
- 100 to 199%
- 66 to 99%
- 65% or less

Immigrant population increased nationally by 65%.

**GEOGRAPHY SKILLBUILDER**
1. **Movement** Which states show the greatest rise in numbers of immigrants?
2. **Movement** In the past, immigrants settled in the U.S. along borders and coastlines. Has this changed in 2000? Explain.

### HISTORY from VISUALS

**Interpreting the Map**
Ask students to study the map. Have them identify the states in blue with the fewest number of immigrants. *(Maine, Vermont, West Virginia, Mississippi, North Dakota, South Dakota, Wyoming, Montana, Alaska.)* Ask students to suggest reasons why these particular states might not have attracted many immigrants. *(Many of these states share a harsh, northern climate; remote location; fewer job opportunities.)*

*The United States in Today's World* **885**

---

**ACTIVITY**  **LINK TO GEOGRAPHY**   **BLOCK SCHEDULING**

### Mapping the Immigrant Population

**Class Time** 45 minutes

**Task** Mapping the immigrant population

**Purpose** To identify and locate immigrant populations in a selected state

**Directions** Ask students to study the map above and make a list of all states that had a more than 100 percent increase in immigration. Have each student select one state and research the immigrant populations in that state. Ask students to determine from where the immigrants have come and where they now reside within the state. Then have students create a map of the state they selected and indicate where the immigrants are living.

📖 Integrated Assessment
  · Rubric 2

TAKS

Mini-Lesson 2:
SS11 3(US21.A)

## Tracing Themes
### IMMIGRATION AND MIGRATION

Throughout the nation's history, U.S. immigration policies have been influenced by the political and economic climate of the time. National immigration policy in the United States has a history of fluctuation with periods of time during which the country followed a restrictive immigration policy, usually followed by years characterized by less restrictive policy.

## More About . . .

### Proposition 187

The California Supreme Court struck down Proposition 187. In the court's opinion, the federal government has sole jurisdiction over immigration law. Passing Proposition 187 would be usurping federal authority. Several provisions of the law were declared to be in violation of the Fourteenth Amendment, specifically those that called for expulsion of illegal immigrants without a hearing. This would be considered denial of due process. In addition, denying public education to the children of illegal immigrants would also be in violation of due process.

▲
Lowe Shee Miu, of Oakland, California, stands in front of a monument commemorating Chinese immigrants at Angel Island—the Ellis Island of the West.

In contrast, about 45 percent of immigrants since the 1960s have come from the Western Hemisphere, primarily Mexico, and 30 percent from Asia.

In Mexico, for example, during three months in 1994–1995, the Mexican peso was devalued by 73 percent. The devaluation made the Mexican economy decline. As a result, almost a million Mexicans lost their jobs. Many of the unemployed headed north in search of jobs in the United States.

This search for a better opportunity continues today as more than 2,000 legal immigrants and refugees arrive daily. Another 5,000 newcomers enter the U. S. illegally each day. About 4,000 of those who enter illegally are deported to Mexico shortly after crossing the U.S.-Mexico border. To help those seeking more opportunity in America, in July 2001, President Bush's administration proposed a temporary guest worker program for the 3 million Mexicans residing illegally in the United States.

Based on the 2000 Census, it was reported that patterns of immigration are changing the country's ethnic and racial makeup. By 2001, for example, California had become a majority minority state, with Asian Americans, Latinos, African Americans, and Native Americans making up more than half its population. The 2000 Census indicated that if current trends continue, by the year 2050 Latinos will become the nation's largest minority community overall.

**DEBATES OVER IMMIGRATION POLICY** The presence of such a large number of immigrants has also added to the continuing debate over U.S. immigration policies. Many Americans believe that their country can't absorb more immigrants. By the early 1990s, an estimated 3.2 million illegal immigrants from Mexico, El Salvador, Guatemala, and Haiti had made their way to the United States. Many illegal immigrants also arrived from Canada, Poland, China, and Ireland. They took jobs many Americans turned down, as farm workers and domestic servants—often receiving the minimum wage or less and no benefits. By 2001, between 5 and 6 million illegal immigrants resided in the United States.

Hostility toward illegal immigration peaked in California and Florida, two states with high percentages of immigrants. In 1994, Florida Governor Lawton Chiles filed suit against the U.S. government for "its continuing failure to enforce or rationally administer its own immigration laws." That same year, California passed **Proposition 187,** which cut all education and nonemergency health benefits to illegal immigrants. By March 1998, Proposition 187 was ruled unconstitutional. Although never implemented, the law inspired political participation among Hispanic voters, who saw themselves as targets.

As more immigrants make their way to the U.S. and the nation's ethnic composition changes, debates about immigration will continue. Those who favor tighter restrictions argue that immigrants take desired jobs. Others, however, point to America's historical diversity and the new ideas and energy immigrants bring. Ⓒ

**Background**
The U.S. Census has asked a race question on every census since the first survey in 1790. Since 1890, the categories and definitions have changed nearly every census.

*C. Answer*
Americans fear job competition with immigrants who would work for low wages and the high social welfare expenses of immigrants.

MAIN IDEA

**Comparing**
Ⓒ How are current arguments against immigration similar to those used in the past?

---

ACTIVITY  LINK TO CIVICS

 classzone.com

## Conducting an Immigration Debate

**Class Time** Two class periods

**Task** Debating U.S. immigration policies

**Purpose** To analyze U.S. immigration policy

**Directions** Divide the class into groups to research U.S. immigration policies. Then have students choose a position on immigration and conduct a class debate. Conclude the session by asking students to share their personal opinions about U.S. immigration policies.

📝 Integrated Assessment
· Rubrics 1, 3

**NATIVE AMERICANS CONTINUE LEGAL BATTLES** As the nation debated its immigrant policies, the ancestors of America's original inhabitants continued to struggle. The end of the 20th century found most members of this minority enduring extremely difficult lives. In 2001, about 32 percent of Native Americans lived below the poverty line, more than three times the poverty rate for white Americans. Furthermore, Native Americans endured a suicide rate that was 72 percent higher than that of the general population and an alcoholism rate seven times greater.

In the face of such hardships, Native Americans strived to improve their lives. Throughout the 1990s, dozens of tribes attained greater economic independence by establishing thriving gaming resorts. Although controversial for promoting gambling, reservation gaming—a nearly $10 billion a year industry by 2000—provided Native Americans with much-needed money for jobs, education, social services, and infrastructure. Over the past decades, Native Americans have used the courts to attain greater recognition of their tribal ancestry and land rights. In 1999, for example, the U.S. Supreme Court ruled that the Chippewa Indians of Minnesota retained fishing and hunting rights on some 13 million acres of land that were guaranteed to them in an 1837 treaty. Across the nation, a number of other tribes have had similar land rights affirmed.

## America in a New Millennium

As the 21st century begins, Americans face both new problems and old ones. Environmental concerns have become a global issue and have moved to center stage. Furthermore, poverty remains a problem for many Americans in the late 20th century, as does the increasing threat that terrorist acts pose to Americans at home and abroad.

It is clear that the new century America faces will bring changes, but those changes need not deepen divisions among Americans. With effort and cooperation, the change could foster growth and tolerance. The 20th century brought new ways of both destroying and enriching lives. What will the 21st bring? Much will depend on you—the dreamers, the decision makers, and the voters of the future.

## ASSESSMENT

**1. TERMS & NAMES** For each term or name, write a sentence explaining its significance.
- urban flight
- gentrification
- Proposition 187

### MAIN IDEA

**2. TAKING NOTES**
Demography is the study of statistics about human populations. Use a table like the one below to summarize the demographic changes occurring in the United States.

| Demographic Changes | |
| --- | --- |
| Urban distribution | |
| Age | |
| Ethnic and racial makeup | |

### CRITICAL THINKING

**3. HYPOTHESIZING**
As urban problems become more common in the suburbs, how might the residents of suburbs respond? Base your answer on existing behavior patterns. **Think About:**
- the spread of suburbs farther and farther from the city
- the new ability to telecommute
- the tax problems that suburbs face

**4. COMPARING AND CONTRASTING**
How was the immigration that occurred in the years 1990–2000 similar to and different from earlier waves of immigration?

**5. DRAWING CONCLUSIONS**
How do disagreements over immigration policy reflect the benefits and challenges of a diverse population?

## Instruct: Objective

**America in a New Millennium**
TAKS SS11 1(US1.A)
- What are some of American's concerns about the environment?
- What economic challenges will Americans face in the years ahead?

 In-Depth Resources: Unit 7
· Guided Reading, p. 48

## Assess & Reteach

### SECTION 4 ASSESSMENT
Have students answer the Section Assessment questions individually. Then have them compare answers with another student. Ask students to locate text passages that support their answers.

 Formal Assessment
· Section Quiz, p. 473

### SELF-ASSESSMENT
Ask students to identify events from the chapter that they found hard to understand. Then have them formulate one question about the reading that they would like to have answered.

### RETEACH
Organize a group roundtable. Have students discuss their responses to question 4, "What will be the biggest challenge facing the United States in the new millennium?" Ask students to suggest ways to handle the challenge.

 In-Depth Resources: Unit 7
· Guided Reading, p. 54

---

**Answers** ASSESSMENT

**1. TERMS & NAMES**
urban flight, p. 882
gentrification, p. 883
Proposition 187, p. 886

**2. TAKING NOTES**
Urban distribution: more suburban, less urban. Age: more senior citizens. Ethnic and racial makeup: more Asians and Hispanics.

**3. HYPOTHESIZING**
Some people move to different suburbs farther away. Others might return to the cities.

**4. COMPARING AND CONTRASTING**
Similar: desire for economic opportunity, democratic freedom. Different: 1990–2000 immigrants from a wider variety of countries.

**5. DRAWING CONCLUSIONS**
The disagreements show that in a diverse culture there are differing ideas on immigration policy and that society allows freedom of speech on the issue.

## TRACING THEMES

### Objectives

· To explain how war and other factors affected immigration to and migration within the United States

· To analyze the impact of the various waves of immigration and migration

## Focus & Motivate

**Evaluating** Ask students to consider the effects of immigration on American society.

· What changes have taken place in American society in the last four or five years as a result of recent immigration?

· What role do you think ethnic heritage should play in today's America?

## More About . . .

### Anti-Immigrant Feelings

Among the challenges facing immigrants, prejudice is perhaps one of the most insidious. In the early 1900s, Senator Henry Cabot Lodge said that immigrants were inferior peoples. Such discrimination has been a constant in the American consciousness. Immigrants have long been involved in the struggle for equality. As the American population grows increasingly diverse, the need for fair and equal treatment for all citizens becomes even greater.

## TRACING THEMES

# Immigration and Migration

Immigrants to the United States have been part of a worldwide movement pushing people away from traditional means of support and pulling them toward better opportunities. Most immigrants have left their homelands because of economic problems, though some have fled oppressive governments or political turmoil.

War has often been the deciding factor for people to immigrate to the United States or to migrate within the country. Others have migrated to escape poverty, religious persecution, and racial violence. But the chief lure in coming to the United States or migrating within its borders continues to be the opportunity to earn a living.

## 1840s

**MIGRATING TO THE WEST ▶**

Throughout the 19th century, Americans continued their movement westward to the Pacific Ocean. Victory in the War with Mexico in 1848 greatly increased the amount of land under American control, and thousands of Americans moved out West to take advantage of it.

Two important consequences emerged from this movement. First, following the discovery of gold in California, hundreds of thousands of people from around the world rushed in to strike it rich. Within a year, there were enough residents in California to qualify it for statehood. Second, Americans disagreed over whether the new lands should be open to slavery. That disagreement fueled the fires that led to the Civil War.

## 1910–1920

**◀ ADAPTING TO AMERICAN WAYS**

With hope and apprehension, millions of foreign immigrants poured into America's pulsing cities during the early 20th century. Bringing with them values, habits, and attire from the Old World, they faced a multitude of new experiences, expectations, and products in the New World.

Many native-born Americans feared that the new immigrants posed a threat to American culture. Instead of the immigrants being allowed to negotiate their existence by combining the old with the new they were pressured to forget their old cultures, languages, and customs for more "American" ways.

**888** CHAPTER 26

## RECOMMENDED RESOURCES

### BOOKS

Chermayeff, Ivan et al. *Ellis Island; An Illustrated History of the Immigrant Experience.* New York: Maxwell Macmillan, 1991. Text by Mary J. Shapiro.

Orth, Samuel Peter. *Our Foreigners.* St. Clair Shores, MI: Scholarly Press, 1970. A period account of immigration.

Pan, Lynn. *Sons of the Yellow Emperor.* NY: Kodansha International, 1994. A history of the Chinese Diaspora.

Portes, Alejandro. *Immigrant America: A Portrait.* Berkeley: U of California P, 1990. A study of immigrants and the process of their Americanization.

### VIDEOS

*Ellis Island: Gateway to America.* Sterling Educational Media, 1991. History of Ellis Island.

*The Immigrant Experience: The Long, Long Journey.* Dir. Joan M. Silver. Coronet/MTI Film and Video, 1972. Experiences of one turn-of-the-century immigrant family.

### SOFTWARE

*Ellis Island.* Diskette. Educational Activities, 1994. Students role-play an Italian teenager who immigrates to America in 1892.

# 1940s

**MIGRATING FOR JOBS ▶**

Throughout the 20th century African Americans migrated across the United States. In the Great Migration of the early 20th century, they left their homes in the rural South. Of the millions of African Americans who left, most moved to cities, usually in the North.

The Second Migration, sparked by World War II, allowed African Americans to take industrial jobs—many formerly held by whites—to support the war effort. This migration had lasting consequences for the civil rights movement. Many African Americans who remained in the South moved to cities, where they developed organizations that helped them fight segregation.

# 1970–2000

**▼ IN SEARCH OF A NEW LIFE**

In 1964, 603 Vietnamese lived in the United States. A decade later, as the Vietnam War ended, hundreds of thousands of Vietnamese refugees fled their homeland for other nations, including the United States. Vietnamese immigration to America continued, and by 1998 there were nearly one million Vietnamese-born persons living in the United States.

The men and women who made this long and arduous journey from Vietnam are part of the changing face of U.S. immigration. Beginning in the 1970s, Asians and Latin Americans replaced Europeans as the two largest immigrant groups in the United States. Between 1970 and 1990 about 1.5 million Europeans journeyed to America's shores. During that same period, roughly 5.6 million Latin Americans and 3.5 million Asians arrived. This trend continued into the 1990s, as the largest immigrant groups in the United States in 1995 hailed from Mexico, the Philippines, Vietnam, and China. These most recent arrivals to America have come for largely the same reasons—greater freedom and economic opportunity and the chance to begin a new life.

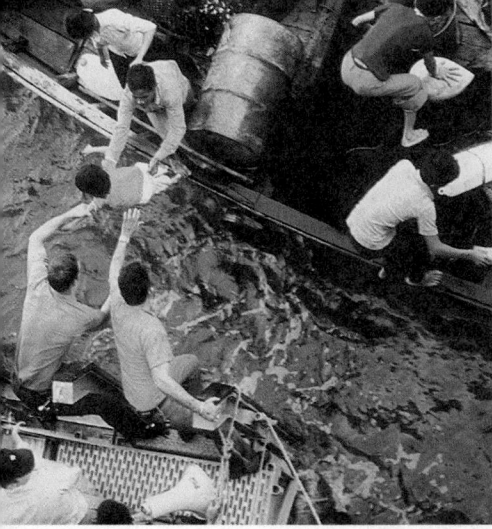

## THINKING CRITICALLY

**CONNECT TO HISTORY**

1. **Forming Generalizations** Based on what you have read about immigration, what generalizations can you make about the causes that led to a rise in the number of immigrants to the U.S.? How have wars affected the flow of immigration? How does this affect economic change?

 **SEE SKILLBUILDER HANDBOOK, PAGE R21.**

**CONNECT TO TODAY**

2. **Research** Interview family members and people in your community to find out how immigration and migration have shaped your current surroundings. Try to record specific stories and events that compare a recent immigration with one in the more distant past.

 **RESEARCH LINKS** CLASSZONE.COM

*The United States in Today's World* **889**

## Instruct

1. What obstacles have immigrants faced in establishing a new life in America?
2. What was the Great Migration?
3. What was the primary cause of Vietnamese immigration to the United States?

### MAKING PERSONAL CONNECTIONS

· Ask students if they, or someone they know, have moved to a new community, or country?
· Ask them to recall their thoughts and feelings at the time.
· Have them consider what it might be like to move to a place where they don't speak the language and are not familiar with the customs. Ask students how they might go about making a new life for themselves.

## More About . . .

### Vietnamese Refugees

Vietnamese refugees faced many difficulties in getting out of their home country. After the triumph of the North Vietnamese, citizens were forbidden to leave the country. Millions who had worked or fought for the South Vietnamese government were imprisoned or sent to reeducation camps. People escaped on makeshift boats, floating out into the South China Sea, braving the elements, sharks, and government patrol boats. Many died. By the time the survivors reached the United States, the worst was over.

## THINKING CRITICALLY: ANSWERS

1. **CONNECT TO HISTORY** War has often been the catalyst for people to flee their homelands. People have been forced to find new homes when their own homes have been destroyed.

2. **CONNECT TO TODAY**
   **Rubrics**
   Student interviews should . . .
   · focus on the subject's experiences and recollections
   · provide informative details about how immigration and migration have shaped current surroundings
   · compare current and past immigration and migration experiences

## TERMS & NAMES

1. William Jefferson Clinton, p. 860
2. NAFTA, p. 864
3. Contract with America, p. 864
4. George W. Bush, p. 866
5. service sector, p. 870
6. GATT, p. 872
7. Telecommunications Act of 1996, p. 878
8. genetic engineering, p. 880
9. urban flight, p. 882
10. Proposition 187, p. 886

## MAIN IDEAS

1. The House passed two articles of impeachment—for perjury and obstruction of justice. At the trial, the Senate did not find Clinton guilty.
2. close election; third-party candidacy of Ralph Nader; U.S. Supreme Court decision; TV networks announced Gore's victory prematurely. Bush won the Florida election. victory triggered a recount. Gore's campaign requested a manual recount. The Supreme Court declared it unconstitutional. Bush was elected.
3. Service-sector and high-tech industries grew; manufacturing and agriculture declined.
4. to resolve trade disputes
5. Internet links people to government agencies, library databases, news media, entertainment, and global information.
6. Positive: improvements in medicine; entertainment; education; automobile safety; the environment. Negative: people spent less time socializing with peers and more time on-line.
7. urban poverty; suburban sprawl; more problems with crime
8. environmental problems, poverty, global terrorism, cultural diversity

## TERMS & NAMES

**For each term or name below, write a sentence explaining its significance.**

1. William Jefferson Clinton
2. NAFTA
3. Contract with America
4. George W. Bush
5. service sector
6. General Agreement on Tariffs and Trade (GATT)
7. Telecommunications Act of 1996
8. genetic engineering
9. urban flight
10. Proposition 187

## MAIN IDEAS

**Use your notes and the information in the chapter to answer the following questions.**

### The 1990s and The New Millennium
(pages 860–868)

1. What happened following the investigation of President Clinton?
2. What factors led George W. Bush to victory in 2000?

### The New Global Economy (pages 869–873)

3. Summarize which parts of the economy grew during the 1990s and which declined.
4. Why was the World Trade Organization founded?

### Technology and Modern Life (pages 876–881)

5. What resources did the Internet make available?
6. What were the positive and negative influences that technology had on American lives in the 1990s?

### The Changing Face of America (pages 882–887)

7. How has urban flight changed both cities and suburbs?
8. What challenges do experts think the United States will face in the future?

## CRITICAL THINKING

1. **USING YOUR NOTES** Create a time line of important events from the 2000 election, using a form like the one below.

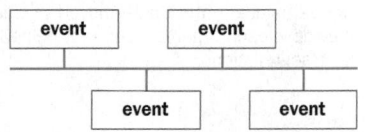

Which event do you think was the turning point? Explain.

2. **PREDICTING EFFECTS** Compile a list of technological innovations of the late 20th century described in the chapter. Then predict what kinds of technological advancements might change American life during the 21st century.

3. **INTERPRETING MAPS** Look carefully at the map on page 885. What might account for the high percentage change in numbers of immigrants in Iowa and Mississippi, compared with more traditional destinations—such as California and New York?

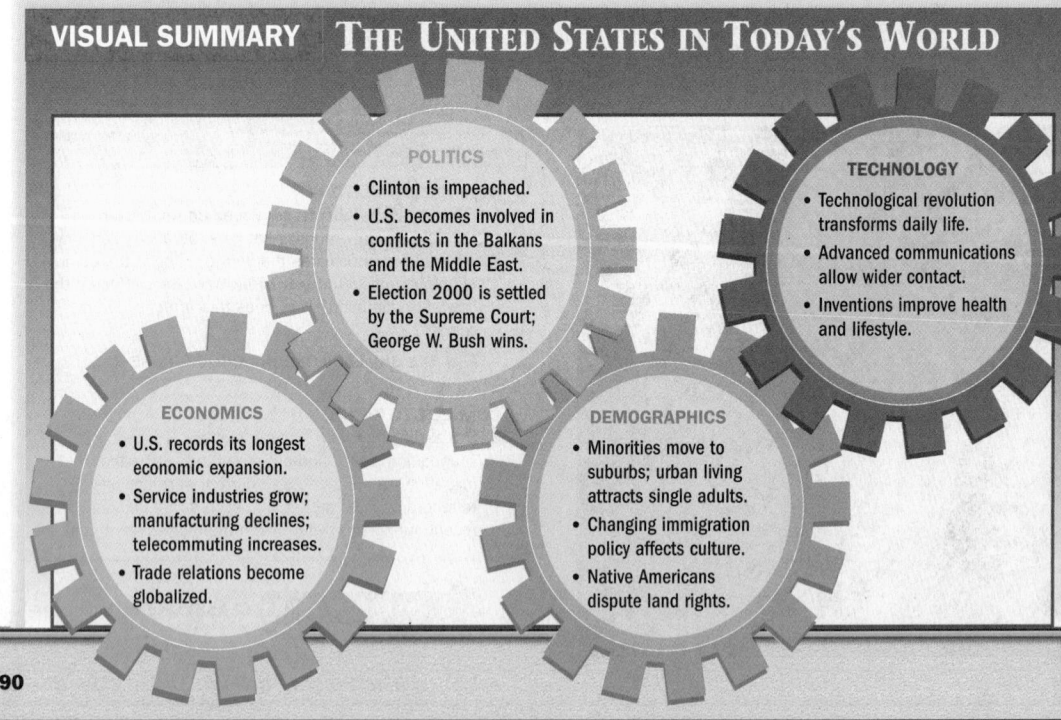

**VISUAL SUMMARY** **THE UNITED STATES IN TODAY'S WORLD**

**POLITICS**
- Clinton is impeached.
- U.S. becomes involved in conflicts in the Balkans and the Middle East.
- Election 2000 is settled by the Supreme Court; George W. Bush wins.

**TECHNOLOGY**
- Technological revolution transforms daily life.
- Advanced communications allow wider contact.
- Inventions improve health and lifestyle.

**ECONOMICS**
- U.S. records its longest economic expansion.
- Service industries grow; manufacturing declines; telecommuting increases.
- Trade relations become globalized.

**DEMOGRAPHICS**
- Minorities move to suburbs; urban living attracts single adults.
- Changing immigration policy affects culture.
- Native Americans dispute land rights.

890

## CRITICAL THINKING

1. **Using Your Notes** First: TV networks recanted Gore victory announcement. Bush declared in Florida; Second: automatic recount; Third: Gore's campaign requested a manual recount of selected counties; Supreme Court stopped the recount; Fourth: Bush took office

2. **Predicting Effects** Late-20th century innovations: Internet; CD-ROMs; fax machines; MRI; prosthetics; GPS; Hubble telescope; International Space Station. Possible advancements for the 21st century: widespread use of electric cars; integration of the television and the Internet; continued advances in engineering and medicine.

3. **Interpreting Maps** Immigrants moving to less populated areas where opportunities might be greater.

## Standardized Test Practice

Use the graph below and your knowledge of U.S. history to answer questions 1 and 2.

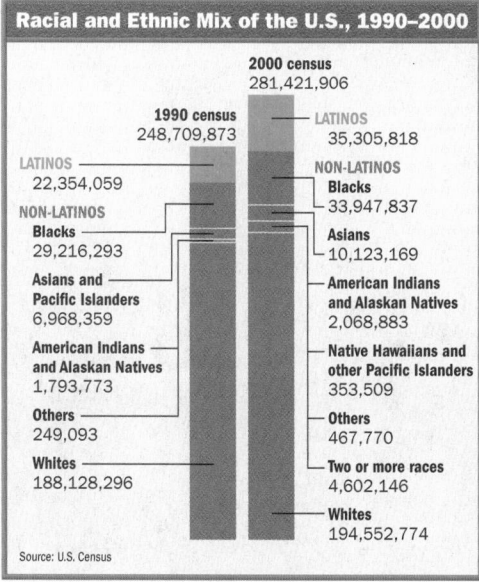

**Racial and Ethnic Mix of the U.S., 1990–2000**

**2000 census**
281,421,906

**1990 census**
248,709,873

LATINOS
35,305,818

NON-LATINOS

LATINOS
22,354,059

NON-LATINOS

Blacks
33,947,837

Blacks
29,216,293

Asians
10,123,169

Asians and
Pacific Islanders
6,968,359

American Indians
and Alaskan Natives
2,068,883

American Indians
and Alaskan Natives
1,793,773

Native Hawaiians and
other Pacific Islanders
353,509

Others
249,093

Others
467,770

Whites
188,128,296

Two or more races
4,602,146

Whites
194,552,774

Source: U.S. Census

**1.** Which U.S. population increased the most between 1990 and 2000?

A Latinos
B Native Americans
C whites
D blacks

**2.** What change is shown in the 2000 census data, compared with the data from 1990?

F The data shows more immigrants in the Midwest.
G The 2000 census data shows a decline in the population of non-Latino whites.
H The 2000 census data reflects a broader range of categories.
J The 2000 census data shows that immigration has slowed.

**3.** Which of the following is *false* about the 2000 presidential election?

A At first the television networks declared Al Gore the winner in Florida.
B The design of the butterfly ballot caused some voters to vote incorrectly.
C The Supreme Court voted that a manual recount of the Florida vote was unnecessary.
D George W. Bush won the national popular vote.

**4.** Which country was not a member of the G8 in 2000?

F China
G Japan
H Italy
J United States

ADDITIONAL TEST PRACTICE, pages S1–S33.

TEST PRACTICE  CLASSZONE.COM

## Standardized Test Practice

1. The correct answer is letter **A**.
   Latinos had the largest increase. Letters B, C, and D are not correct because neither Native Americans, Whites, nor the black population showed the greatest increase.

2. The correct answer is letter **H**.
   Letters F, G, and J are not correct because no data is shown from the Midwest; non-Latino whites increased; and the data does not show immigration.

3. The correct answer is letter **D**.
   Bush did not win the popular vote.

4. The correct answer is letter **F**.
   China was not a member of the G8 in 2000. Letters G, H, and I are not correct because Japan, Italy, and the United States were members in 2000.

UNIT PROJECT

**CAMPAIGN SCRAPBOOK**
**Tips for Teaching**
· Have students prepare their journal entry or entries summarizing their campaign experiences.
· Ask students to begin to assemble the various parts of their scrapbook.
· Remind students that their scrapbook should be historically accurate.

**Project Presentation Rubrics**
The campaign scrapbook should . . .
· include position papers, campaigning memorabilia, and a journal entry
· reflect the experiences and the activities of a political campaign
· use correct grammar, usage, capitalization, punctuation, and spelling in the written text

 Formal Assessment
· Chapter Test, Forms A, B, and C, pp. 474–491

## ALTERNATIVE ASSESSMENT

**1.** INTERACT WITH HISTORY  Recall your discussion of the question on page 859:

*What are the most important issues that affect the world today?*

As a "think tank" director who researches and analyzes future issues, you are asked to write a concise summary of the five most important issues facing Americans in the 21st century. Present and distribute your summary to the class.

**2.** INTERNET ACTIVITY  CLASSZONE.COM

Visit the links for Chapter Assessment to research the results of the 2000 Census. What are some important facts and trends? Consider the following:

• What significant changes took place in the United States during the 1990s?
• What states increased the most in population? the least?
• What changes took place in your state?

Present your findings in an organized poster.

*The United States in Today's World* **891**

## ALTERNATIVE ASSESSMENT

### 1. INTERACT WITH HISTORY
**Rubrics**

Student summaries should . . .
· identify the most important issues facing Americans in the 21st century
· explain why the issues are crucial
· provide supporting evidence

### 2. INTERNET ACTIVITY
**Rubrics**

Student poster should . . .
· use visuals and text to answer the posed questions about the results of the 2000 census
· be well organized and visually appealing
· incorporate supporting statistical evidence

# The War on Terrorism

## Reporter's Notes

By Kevin McCoy

NEW YORK— First came a deep rumble. Then a roar like a giant speeding train. But the sound came crashing from the sky, not along steel tracks. In an instant, a warm, sunny September morning at the World Trade Center in Lower Manhattan became a darkened moonscape of choking cement dust and swirling paper, wailing sirens and screaming victims.

"I heard the rumbling and I looked up, and one of the towers was coming down," said Sergeant Moises Cruz, a New York City police officer who ran for his life with other survivors of the most horrible terrorist attack in U.S. history. Lower Broadway, normally a bustling checkerboard of financial traders, government officials, businessmen and tourists, lay silenced under a three-inch carpet of gritty gray dust.

"I can't even describe it, it was so awful," said Wilbert, a 50-year-old elevator maintenance worker. "All I could do was run."

News reporters who covered the attacks knew instinctively this was the most significant story of a lifetime.

**The twin towers of the World Trade Center in New York City, before (inset) and after the terrorist attacks of September 11, 2001**

# The Attack on America

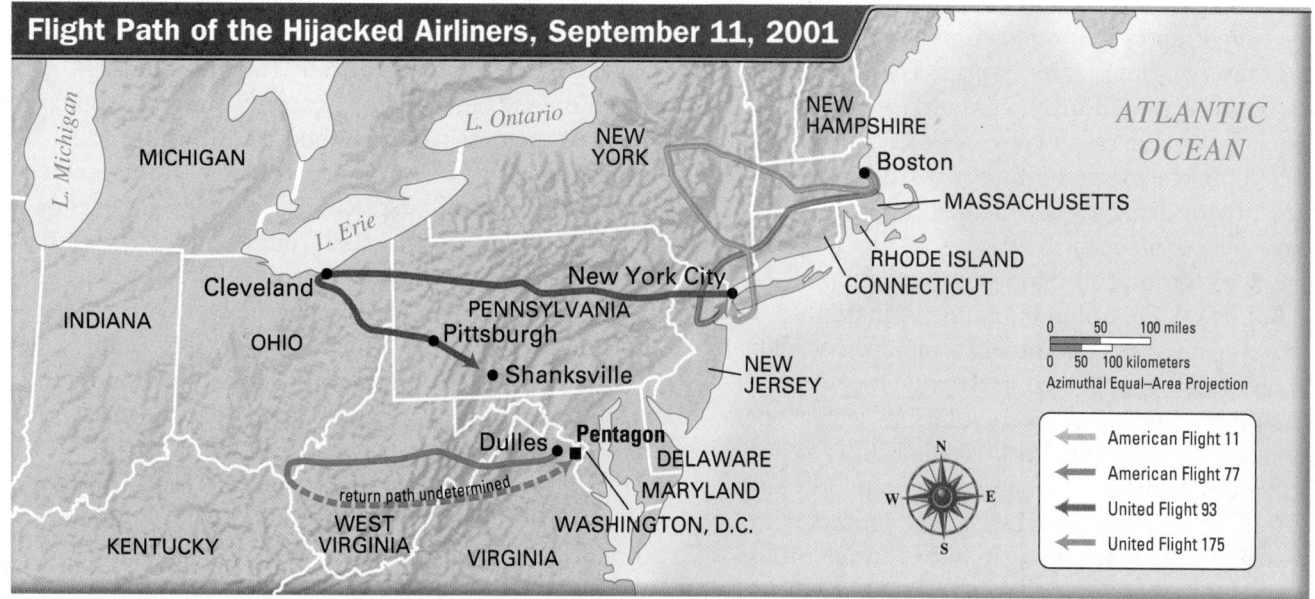

**Flight Path of the Hijacked Airliners, September 11, 2001**

MICHIGAN
L. Michigan
L. Ontario
NEW YORK
NEW HAMPSHIRE
ATLANTIC OCEAN
Boston
MASSACHUSETTS
L. Erie
Cleveland
RHODE ISLAND
CONNECTICUT
New York City
PENNSYLVANIA
INDIANA
Pittsburgh
OHIO
Shanksville
NEW JERSEY
0  50  100 miles
0  50  100 kilometers
Azimuthal Equal–Area Projection
Dulles
Pentagon
DELAWARE
return path undetermined
MARYLAND
WEST VIRGINIA
WASHINGTON, D.C.
KENTUCKY
VIRGINIA
N W E S

American Flight 11
American Flight 77
United Flight 93
United Flight 175

McCoy's reporter's instincts were right. Before the day was over, there would be more than 3,000 victims of the most destructive act of terrorism in modern history. **Terrorism** is the calculated use of, or threatened use of, violence against individuals or property for the purpose of intimidating or causing fear for political or social ends.

The terrorist attacks on September 11 were aimed at well-known symbols of the economic and military power of the United States. But what they mainly destroyed was something Americans value much more—the lives of thousands of individual citizens.

## UNIMAGINABLE HORROR

On the morning of September 11, 2001, many New Yorkers were heading for work or school when 19 Arab terrorists hijacked four airliners from East Coast airports. The first plane crashed into the upper floors of the north tower of the World Trade Center and exploded into flames. About 20 minutes later, the second plane sliced into the south tower.

Desks, chairs, paper—and people—blew out of the windows of the twin towers. People on the streets below watched in horror as more than a dozen workers on the upper floors jumped from the blazing buildings to their deaths. Other workers poured out of the towers to escape the fire.

Less than an hour after the twin towers were hit, the third hijacked plane rammed into the southwest side of the Pentagon in Arlington, Virginia. It tore a 75-foot gash in the five-sided, five-story building.

That crash site, too, immediately became engulfed in flames. Meanwhile, passengers on the fourth hijacked plane had used their cell phones and had heard about the other plane crashes. Some of the passengers rushed the hijackers and prevented them from striking their intended target, thought to be either the White House or the Capitol.

Because of these heroic efforts, the plane crashed not into a crowded building but into an empty field in Pennsylvania. No one will ever know how many lives the passengers saved as they gave up their own.

Recovery efforts continue on the collapsed section of the Pentagon's southwest side two days after the attack.

**The Destruction** The planes were loaded with fuel. They became destructive missiles when they crashed into the World Trade Center and the Pentagon. As one investigator noted, the hijackers "couldn't carry

anything—other than an atom bomb—that could be as bad as what they were flying."

The explosions and fires so weakened the damaged skyscrapers that they crumbled to the ground less than two hours after impact. The fire and raining debris caused nearby buildings to collapse as well. Nine buildings in New York City's financial district completely or partially collapsed. Six others suffered major damage. The disaster area covered 16 acres. The damage at the Pentagon, though extensive, was confined to one wing of the building.

But it was the toll in human lives that most grieved Americans and others around the world. About 3,000 people died in the attacks. All passengers on the four planes were killed, as well as workers and visitors in the World Trade Center and the Pentagon. The dead included more than 300 New York City firefighters and 40 police officers who rushed to the scene and were buried in the rubble when the skyscrapers collapsed.

**Grieving Families and Companies** "Please tell the children I love them," said a father of three from the World Trade Center before the phone line went dead. From the burning towers and the hijacked planes, men and women used their last moments to call and to speak with their families for the last time.

In the first hours and days after the September 11 attacks, family members and friends of people in the World Trade Center frantically tried to find their loved ones. They checked hospitals and posted pictures of the missing on lampposts and walls. The thousands of people who escaped before the towers collapsed were reunited with their families. But only a few survivors were pulled from the wreckage of the buildings. For thousands of people, loved ones never returned home. Also, several businesses with offices in the towers lost large numbers of employees.

The horror of September 11 has haunted more than just the survivors and witnesses of the attacks, although they were the hardest hit. Millions of Americans watched the events on television shortly after they occurred. They, too, would have difficulty forgetting those horrifying images.

### RESCUE EFFORTS

Amidst the brutal destruction at the World Trade Center, the courage, selflessness, and noble actions of New York City's firefighters, police officers, and rescue workers stood as a testament. Many of the first

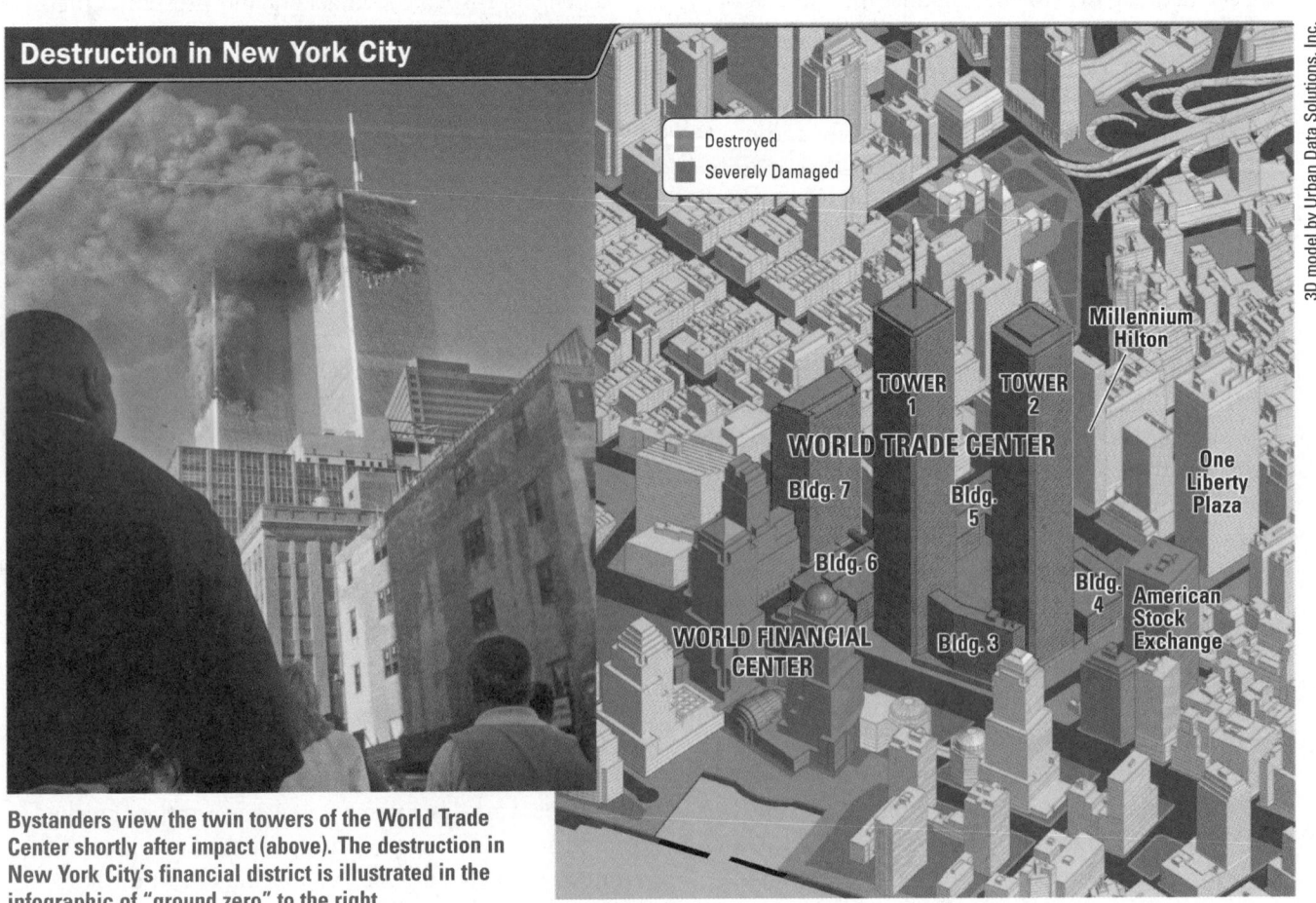

Destruction in New York City

Destroyed
Severely Damaged

Millennium Hilton

TOWER 1    TOWER 2

WORLD TRADE CENTER

Bldg. 7    Bldg. 5

One Liberty Plaza

Bldg. 6

Bldg. 4    American Stock Exchange

WORLD FINANCIAL CENTER    Bldg. 3

3D model by Urban Data Solutions, Inc.

**Bystanders view the twin towers of the World Trade Center shortly after impact (above). The destruction in New York City's financial district is illustrated in the infographic of "ground zero" to the right.**

**USA TODAY**

first appeared in print 9/25/2001

# How the debris is removed

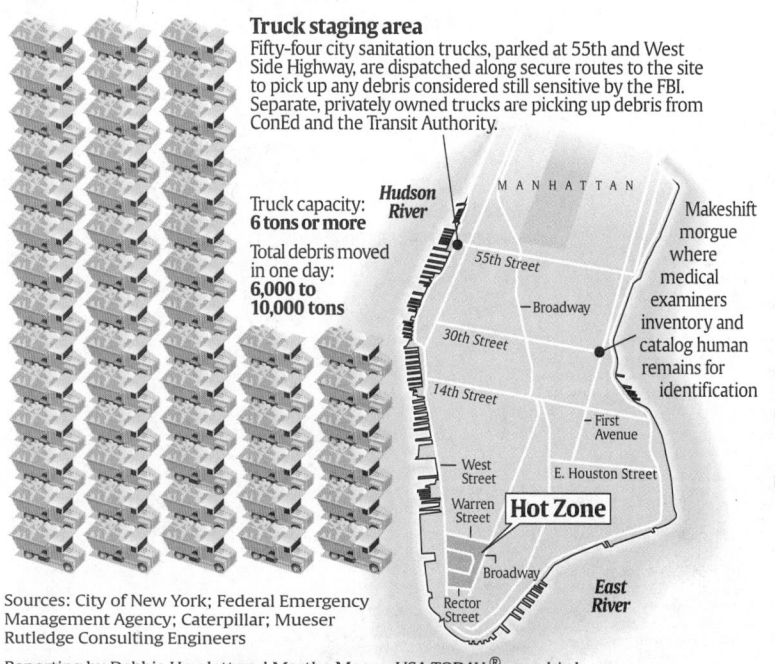

**Truck staging area**
Fifty-four city sanitation trucks, parked at 55th and West Side Highway, are dispatched along secure routes to the site to pick up any debris considered still sensitive by the FBI. Separate, privately owned trucks are picking up debris from ConEd and the Transit Authority.

Truck capacity:
**6 tons or more**

Total debris moved in one day:
**6,000 to 10,000 tons**

Sources: City of New York; Federal Emergency Management Agency; Caterpillar; Mueser Rutledge Consulting Engineers

Reporting by Debbie Howlett and Martha Moore, USA TODAY ®; graphic by Frank Pompa, Robert Ahrens, Adrienne Lewis and Dave Merrill, USA TODAY ®

**1** Trucks are loaded at the site and driven to marine transfer stations, where debris is loaded onto barges.

**2** The barges carry 600 tons of debris on each trip.

**3** Trucks carrying the heaviest debris, such as steel beams, make the trip by flatbed trucks via the Battery Tunnel and across the Verrazano Narrows Bridge.

**At the landfill site**

**4** Two piles are created, one that is considered debris...

**5** ...and the other, which may yield more evidence. The workers have created a grid system on the ground; these truckloads are dumped into a checkerboard that is then sifted through in large, table-like trays with mesh-screen bottoms. FBI investigators are searching for clues, such as those that led to the cracking of the Oklahoma City bombing case when they found the Ryder truck axle with the vehicle identification number on it.

---

firefighters at the scene disappeared into the burning buildings to help those inside and never came out again. Entire squads were lost. New York City Fire Department chaplain, Father Mychal Judge, was killed by falling debris just after giving the last rites of the Catholic Church to a firefighter at the scene.

Firefighters worked around the clock trying to find survivors in the wreckage. They had to contend with shifting rubble and smoky, ash-filled air. Medical workers from the area rushed to staff the city's trauma centers. But after the first wave of injured, there were few survivors to treat. One emergency medical technician said, "We were set up for any emergency. It was a great site, full of surgeons. But we were treating firemen and police who needed their eyes washed."

A flood of volunteers assisted rescue workers. Ironworkers helped cut through steel beams, while high school students helped provide water and food for the rescue workers. From around the country, people sent donations of blood, food, and money to New York City. The city kept functioning in the hours and days that followed the attack under the direction of its mayor, Rudy Giuliani.

**The Cleanup** After the first few days, the work at "ground zero," the World Trade Center disaster site, shifted to recovering bodies and removing the massive amount of debris. The twin towers alone contained more than 200,000 tons of steel, 425,000 cubic yards of concrete, and 14 acres of glass—an estimated 2 billion pounds.

## SEARCH FOR TERRORISTS BEGINS

In the weeks that followed, the U.S. government organized a massive effort to identify those responsible for the attacks. Officials concluded that Osama bin Laden, a Saudi Arabian millionaire, directed the terrorists. He had been exiled from his native country because of suspected terrorist activities. Bin Laden was hiding in Afghanistan, protected there by the strict Islamic government known as the Taliban. The effort to bring him to justice would lead the United States to begin military action against Afghanistan in October, as the next section explains.

**Thinking Critically**

**CURRENT EVENTS** CLASSZONE.COM

- Why were the specific targets of the September attacks selected by the terrorists?

- What might cause individuals to use terrorist tactics to attempt to change situations they think are a problem?

Thinking Critically Answers
- They were symbols of American economic and military power.
- They feel that they are unable to change a situation through regular channels.

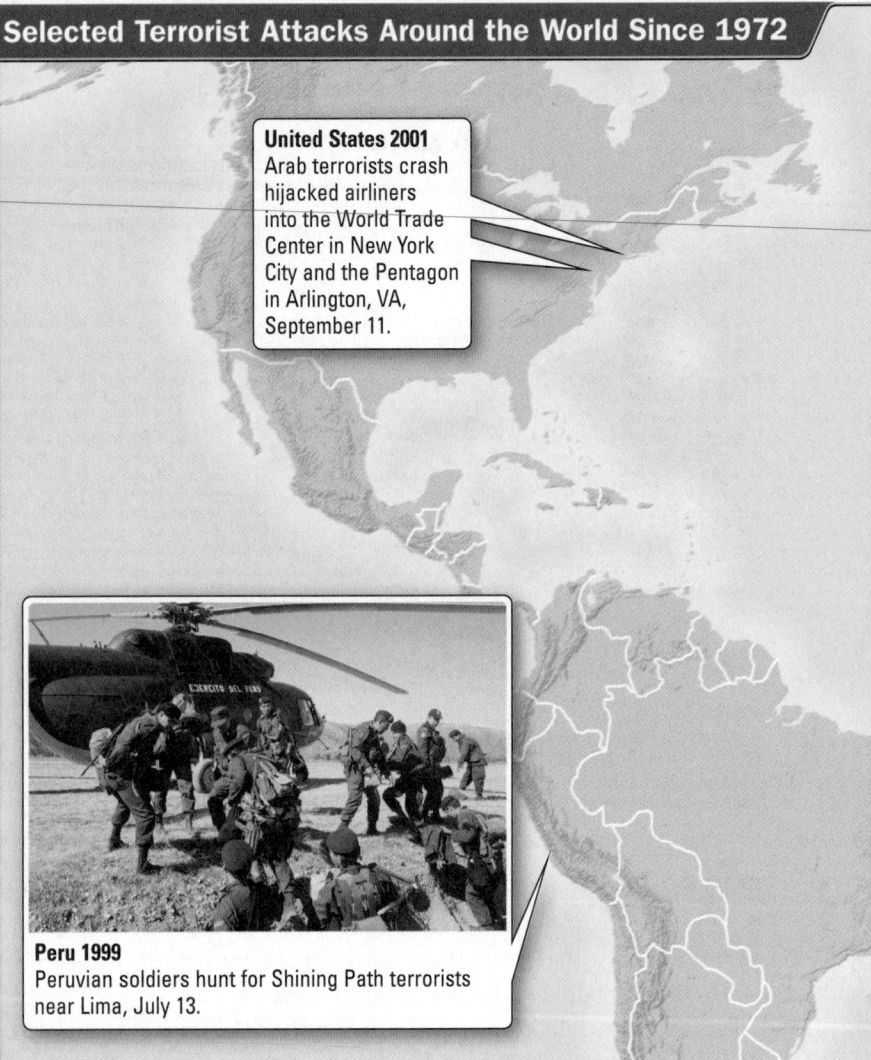
## Reporter's Notes
By Tim Friend

AFGHANISTAN— I entered Afghanistan from the north on an aging ferry boat at dusk on October 22. All I could see in the encroaching darkness were silhouettes of Northern Alliance fighters with Kalishnikov weapons slung loosely on their shoulders. My passport was stamped in a small mud hut under a dim lantern, then I was off to the village of Hoja Baddahuin, where the Northern Alliance had set up headquarters after the Taliban had taken over most of the country.

The United States had entered the war in Afghanistan after the terrorist attacks on September 11, 2001. Covering the war in Afghanistan has been the single most challenging experience of my career as a reporter at USA TODAY.

The most dangerous part of the experience was traveling through the front lines as I made my way to Kabul. My jeep had to cross minefields and the most narrow mountain roads imaginable. At Taloqan, the first city to be restored to the Northern Alliance, I wrote my stories while gunfire erupted outside my walled compound. I paid two men to stay inside with their machine guns and to answer the door should someone come knocking. Taliban fighters were still hiding out in houses just down the street. Through it all, I learned to stay calm by doing the best I could to ensure both my safety and the safety of my team, and to leave the rest to a healthy dose of faith.

**United States 2001**
Arab terrorists crash hijacked airliners into the World Trade Center in New York City and the Pentagon in Arlington, VA, September 11.

**Peru 1999**
Peruvian soldiers hunt for Shining Path terrorists near Lima, July 13.

# Hunting for the Terrorists

Terrorism is not new. Reporters like Tim Friend have been covering terrorist attacks across the globe for the last three decades. Throughout history, individuals, small groups, and governments have used terror tactics to try to achieve political or social goals— whether it be to bring down a government, eliminate opponents, or promote a cause.

In recent times, however, terrorism has become an international problem. Since the late 1960s, more than 14,000 terrorist attacks have occurred worldwide. International terrorist groups have carried out increasingly destructive, high-profile attacks to attract global attention. Many countries also face domestic terrorists who oppose their governments' policies or have special interests to promote.

The reasons for modern terrorism are many. The traditional motives, such as gaining independence, expelling foreigners, or changing society, still drive various terrorist groups around the world. These terrorists use violence to force concessions from their enemies, usually the governments in power. But other kinds of terrorists, driven by radical religious motives, began to emerge in the late 20th century.

The goal of these terrorists is the destruction of what they consider the forces of evil. This evil might be located in their own countries or in other parts of the world. These terrorists often threaten to use weapons of mass destruction, such as chemical, biological, or nuclear weapons, to kill their enemies.

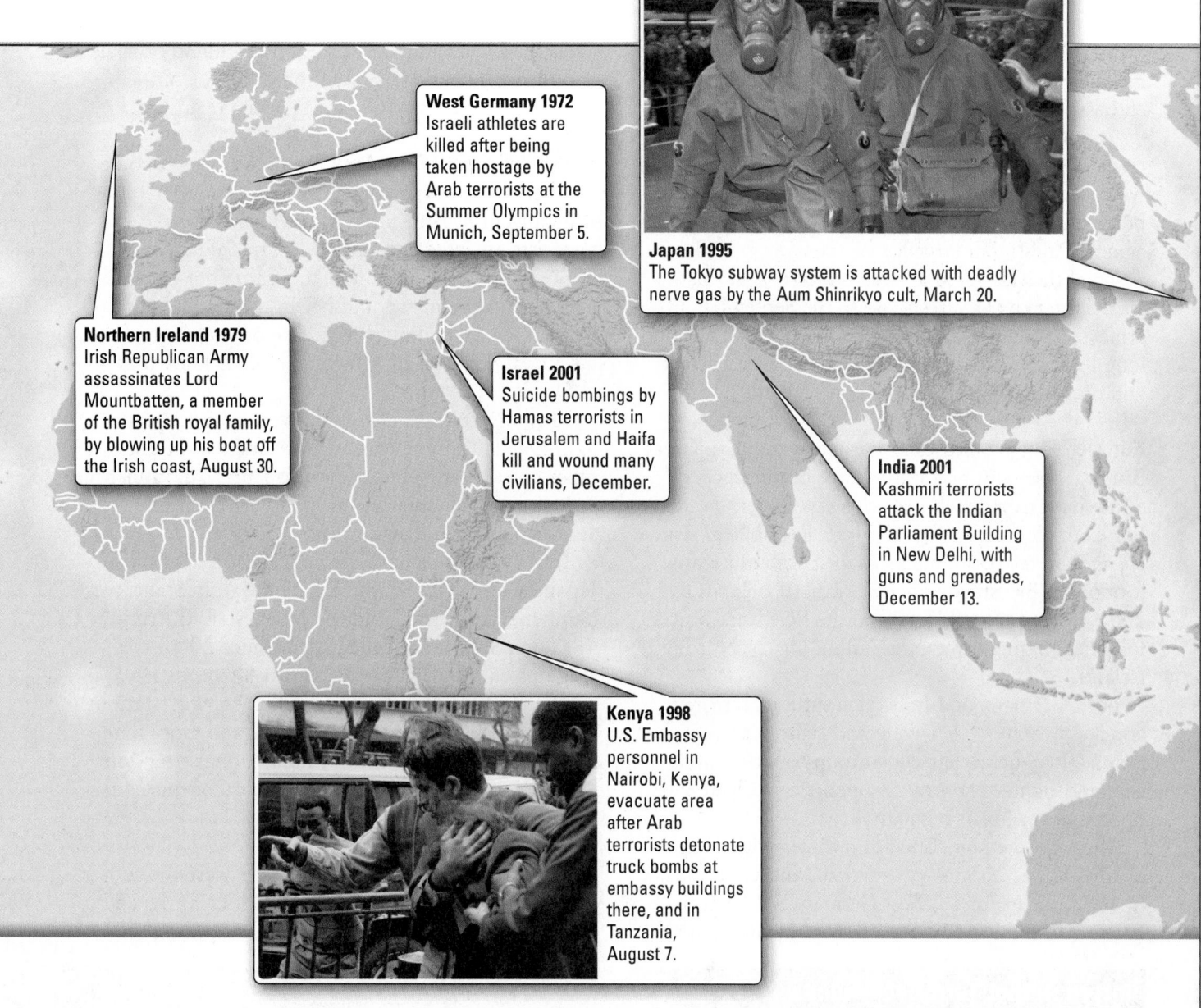

**West Germany 1972**
Israeli athletes are killed after being taken hostage by Arab terrorists at the Summer Olympics in Munich, September 5.

**Japan 1995**
The Tokyo subway system is attacked with deadly nerve gas by the Aum Shinrikyo cult, March 20.

**Northern Ireland 1979**
Irish Republican Army assassinates Lord Mountbatten, a member of the British royal family, by blowing up his boat off the Irish coast, August 30.

**Israel 2001**
Suicide bombings by Hamas terrorists in Jerusalem and Haifa kill and wound many civilians, December.

**India 2001**
Kashmiri terrorists attack the Indian Parliament Building in New Delhi, with guns and grenades, December 13.

**Kenya 1998**
U.S. Embassy personnel in Nairobi, Kenya, evacuate area after Arab terrorists detonate truck bombs at embassy buildings there, and in Tanzania, August 7.

## TERRORISM AROUND THE WORLD

The problem of international terrorism first came to world attention in a shocking way during the 1972 Summer Olympic Games in Munich, Germany (then West Germany). Eight members of a Palestinian terrorist group called Black September killed two Israeli athletes and took nine others hostage. Five of the terrorists, all the hostages, and a police officer were later killed in a bloody gun battle. The attack became known as the Munich Massacre. Since then, few regions of the world have been spared from terrorist attacks.

**The Middle East** Like Black September, many terrorist organizations have their roots in the Israeli-Palestinian conflict over land in the Middle East.

("Middle East" is the political term for the geographic region of Southwest Asia.) Arab terrorist groups such as the Palestine Islamic Jihad, Hamas, and Hizballah have sought to prevent a peace settlement between Israel and the Palestinians. They want a homeland for the Palestinians on their own terms, with the most extreme among them denying Israel's right to exist. In a continual cycle of violence, the Israelis retaliate after each terrorist attack, and the terrorists attack again.

Among Muslims in the Middle East, the Israeli-Palestinian violence has bred widespread Arab anger at Israel—and at the United States for supporting Israel. For example, the Lebanese-based group Hizballah seeks to eliminate all non-Islamic influences in Muslim countries. It is thought to have been

responsible for bombing the U.S. embassy and marine barracks in Beirut in 1983 and the U.S. embassy annex in Beirut in 1984.

In December 2001, terrorist attacks on Israeli civilians in Jerusalem and Haifa killed 27 people and wounded more than 200. Hamas claimed responsibility, and the Israelis responded with military strikes against Palestinian targets.

Israel then declared a "war on terrorism," patterned after the U.S. response to the September 11 attacks. Moderates in the region believe that the only long-term solution is a compromise between Israel and the Palestinians over the issue of land.

**Europe** Many countries in Europe—including Great Britain, Germany, and Italy—have been targets of domestic terrorists who oppose government policies. For example, for decades the Irish Republican Army engaged in terrorist attacks against Britain because it opposed British control of Northern Ireland. By 2001, however, the British and the IRA were peacefully negotiating for greater autonomy for Northern Ireland.

Both Germany and Italy have suffered terrorist attacks by extreme left-wing and right-wing domestic groups. In general, left-wing groups oppose capitalism, and right-wing groups support capitalism and oppose government regulation.

These groups sometimes join forces with other terrorist organizations when it suits their purposes. In 1975, for example, West Germany's Red Army Faction and Italy's Red Brigades cooperated with the Palestine Liberation Organization to kidnap officials at a meeting of the Organization of Petroleum Exporting Countries (OPEC) in Vienna, Austria.

**South Asia and East Asia** South Asia has become another hotbed of terrorism in recent years. Afghanistan became a haven for international terrorists after the extremist Muslim Taliban came to power in 1996. In that year, Osama bin Laden moved to Afghanistan and began using mountain hideouts in that country as a base of operations for his global network of Muslim terrorists known as al-Qaeda.

Muslim extremists from all over the world came to al-Qaeda training camps. Bin Laden and these other extremists were opposed to American influence in Muslim lands. Bin Laden called for terrorist attacks against Americans and U.S. allies.

Terrorist groups have arisen in East Asia, as well. Japanese terrorist groups include the Aum Shinrikyo (Supreme Truth Sect) and the Japanese Red Army. The Aum Shinrikyo (called Aleph since 2000) is a religious cult that wants to control Japan. In 1995, it released sarin, a deadly nerve gas, in subway stations in Tokyo. Twelve people were killed and more than 5,700 injured. This attack brought global attention to the threat of biological and chemical agents as terrorist weapons.

**Africa** Civil unrest and regional wars were the root causes of most terrorist activity in Africa at the end of the 20th century. But al-Qaeda cells operated in

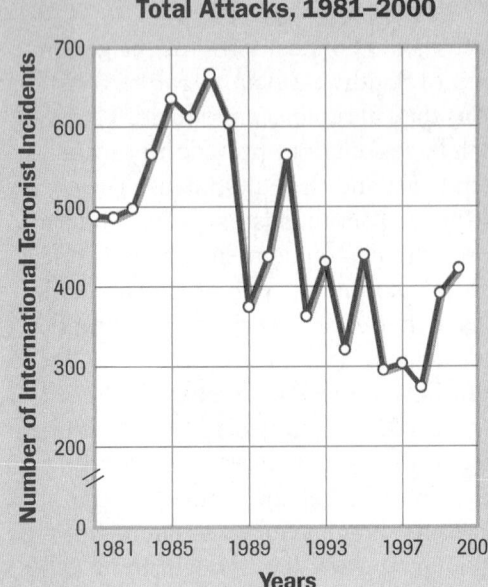

## International Terrorist Attacks

### Total Attacks, 1981–2000

### International Casualties of Terrorism, 1995–2000

| | Africa | Asia | Euroasia | Latin America | Middle East | North America | Western Europe |
|---|---|---|---|---|---|---|---|
| 1995 | 8 | 5369 | 29 | 46 | 445 | 0 | 287 |
| 1996 | 80 | 1507 | 20 | 18 | 1097 | 0 | 503 |
| 1997 | 28 | 344 | 27 | 11 | 480 | 7 | 17 |
| 1998 | 5379 | 635 | 12 | 195 | 68 | 0 | 405 |
| 1999 | 185 | 690 | 8 | 9 | 31 | 0 | 16 |
| 2000 | 102 | 898 | 103 | 20 | 69 | 0 | 4 |
| Totals | 5782 | 9713 | 199 | 299 | 2190 | 7 | 1232 |

Source: U.S. Department of State

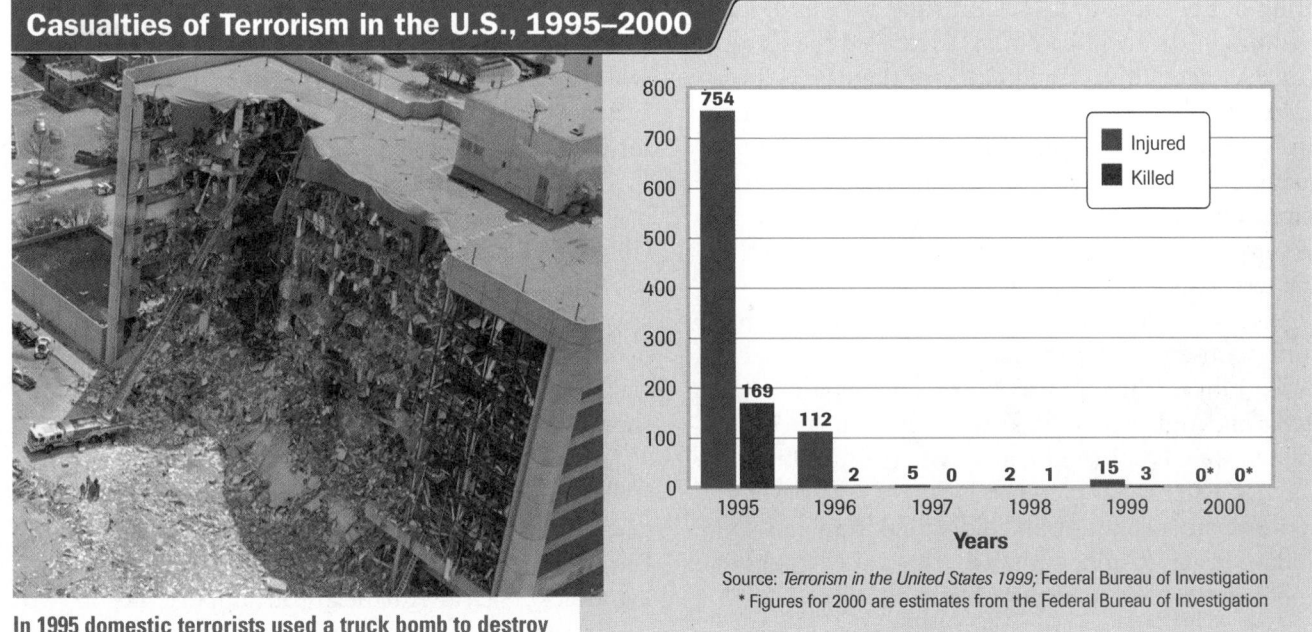

## Casualties of Terrorism in the U.S., 1995–2000

In 1995 domestic terrorists used a truck bomb to destroy the Murrah Federal Building in Oklahoma City, Oklahoma.

Source: *Terrorism in the United States 1999;* Federal Bureau of Investigation
* Figures for 2000 are estimates from the Federal Bureau of Investigation

many African countries, and several major attacks against U.S. personnel and facilities in Africa were linked to al-Qaeda.

For example, a 1993 attack on U.S. soldiers in Somalia killed 18. In 1998, bombings at the U.S. embassies in Kenya and Tanzania left 301 dead and more than 5,000 people injured. The United States responded to these attacks with missile strikes on suspected terrorist facilities in Afghanistan, and in Sudan where bin Laden was based from 1991 to 1996.

**Latin America** In 2000, more terrorist attacks occurred in Latin America than in any other region of the world. Terrorist activity was particularly heavy in Colombia, a country where powerful narcotics organizations have frequently turned to violence. The Revolutionary Armed Forces of Colombia (FARC) is a left-wing guerrilla group responsible for numerous bombings, hijackings, and kidnappings of Colombians and foreign citizens. It has attacked Colombian political, military, and economic targets, as well as those with American ties. FARC is linked to narcotics traffickers.

The region where the borders of Argentina, Brazil, and Paraguay meet has become a center of Islamic extremism and terrorist financing. The Israeli embassy in Buenos Aires, Argentina, was bombed in 1992, and another Israeli target was hit in 1994.

**The United States** Before September 11, the most destructive act of terrorism on American soil had been the 1995 truck bombing of the Murrah Federal Building in Oklahoma City, Oklahoma. That attack killed 168 people, but it was an act of domestic terrorism. It was carried out by an antigovernment extremist named Timothy McVeigh. Such domestic terrorists are motivated by the belief that the government has too much power to regulate people's lives.

The longest-lasting terrorist campaign by an individual in U.S. history was conducted by Theodore Kaczynski, who was known as the Unabomber. From 1978 to 1995, Kaczynski mailed bombs to business executives and scientists because he opposed the effects of modern technology on society. He killed 3 people and injured 23 others.

The attack on the World Trade Center on September 11 was not the first to have occurred there. A previous attack took place in 1993, when a van filled with explosives was detonated in the center's parking garage. Six people died and more than 1,000 were injured. The person responsible, Ramzi Yousef, was captured and imprisoned, but Osama bin Laden was suspected of being part of the plot. Another bin Laden-linked attack was the bombing of the destroyer USS *Cole* in Yemen in October 2000.

## FINDING THOSE RESPONSIBLE

Immediately after the September 11 attacks, the Bush administration launched the largest criminal investigation in U.S. history. The FBI searched across the country—and the world—for clues to the identities of the suicide hijackers and those who aided them.

In an address to Congress and the nation, President George W. Bush pledged, "Whether we

bring our enemies to justice or bring justice to our enemies, justice will be done." He called the terrorist attacks "acts of war" and declared that the United States would wage a war to end global terrorism. He vowed that as a part of that war, "We will pursue nations that provide aid or safe haven to terrorism. Every nation in every region now has a decision to make. Either you are with us, or you are with the terrorists."

Seven nations were on a U.S. government list of state sponsors of terrorism in 2001—Iran, Iraq, Syria, Libya, Cuba, North Korea, and Sudan. In addition, Afghanistan, Pakistan, Lebanon, and Yemen were considered major centers of terrorist activity. After the September 11 attacks, however, some of these countries, including Pakistan and Sudan, began to cooperate with the United States in hunting down those responsible.

The investigation into the September 11 attacks soon showed that top leaders in the al-Qaeda network were responsible for planning the attacks. The U.S. government then undertook a worldwide hunt for terrorists linked to al-Qaeda.

The United States built an international coalition, or alliance, to fight the war on terrorism. Canada, China, Great Britain, Pakistan, Russia, and many other nations joined the coalition. They agreed to share intelligence information, to arrest terrorists operating within their borders, and to seize the financial assets of terrorist groups. The coalition also gave support to U.S. military action in Afghanistan.

Great Britain took an especially active role in the coalition. One Londoner left a card at the U.S. embassy that reflected the surge of support that the United States received immediately after the devastating attacks: "Dear America, You supported us in two world wars. We stand with you now."

### The War in Afghanistan

The U.S. government first focused its military response on Afghanistan, because that country was the home base of Osama bin Laden's al-Qaeda network. The strict Islamic regime that controlled most of Afghanistan—the Taliban—had harbored bin Laden and al-Qaeda since 1996. In return, bin Laden helped keep the Taliban in power by providing fighters in their civil war against the Northern Alliance, a coalition of anti-Taliban Afghan groups.

The United States demanded that the Taliban turn over bin Laden. After they refused, the United States began military action. The U.S. goals were to find bin Laden, to destroy al-Qaeda, and to end Taliban rule.

**USA TODAY** first appeared in print 10/16/2001

# The corporate structure of Terror Inc.

Osama bin Laden's terrorist organization, al-Qaeda, is organized like a business. Here is a flow chart of its structure, as of the terrorist attacks on September 11, 2001:

**Emir**
Osama bin Laden

A key member of the military committee is Muhammad Atef, also known as Abu Hafs el Masry. The second-ranking person in al-Qaeda, he was indicted in the U.S. embassy bombings in Kenya and Tanzania in 1998. Atef was killed during the bombing of Afghanistan.

**Shura council**
A policymaking council of about 30 top aides, business associates and religious scholars.

**Ayman al-Zawahri**

A key member of the shura council is Ayman al-Zawahri, bin Laden's top aide. The Egyptian-born surgeon, sentenced to death for terrorism in his native country, reportedly slipped into the United States in 1995 as Abdel Moez for a fundraising tour. He supplied $250,000 in 1991 for the purchase of a farm for al-Qaeda in Sudan.

**Atef**

**Military committee**
Responsible for training, weapons acquisition and planning attacks.

**Money/business committee**
Runs al-Qaeda business operations. Key members include Abu Fadhl al Makkee and Abu Hammam al Saudi.

**Media committee**
Ran now-defunct al-Qaeda newspaper, Newscast, and did public relations.

**Islamic study/ fatwah committee**
Issues fatwahs, or religious edicts, such as an edict in 1998 telling Muslims to kill Americans.

**Travel office**
Provides plane tickets and fake passports.

**Payroll office**
Pays al-Qaeda members.

**Management office**
Oversees money-making businesses (banks, farms).

Abu Fadhl and Abu Hammam managed the business operations and deployed assets and al-Qaeda members. Abu Fadhl was identified in court papers as "the man who bought bin Laden a salt farm in Sudan." Abu Hammam did advance work on the move to Sudan.

Source: Reported by Dennis Cauchon, USA TODAY®

By Dave Merrill, USA TODAY®

Secretary of Defense Donald Rumsfeld addresses U.S. troops in Afghanistan.

**The War Against Terrorism, Afghanistan 2001**

TURKMENISTAN

TAJIKISTAN

Mazar-e Sharif KONDOZ Feyzabad
JOWZJAN BALKH Konduz TAKHAR BADAKHSHAN

Meymaneh SAR-E-POL Baghlan Taloqan
BAGHLAN LAGHMAN
FARYAB SAMANGAN KAPISA KONAR
BADGHIS PARVAN KABUL

Herat Bamian BAMIAN VARDAK Kabul Jalalabad INDIA
HERAT NANGARHAR Islamabad
GHOWR LOWGAR
Shindand AFGHANISTAN PAKTIA
FARAH ORUZGAN GHAZNI Khowst

Farah PAKTIKA
ZABOL PAKISTAN

Qandahar

IRAN NIMRUZ HELMAND

QANDAHAR

Estimated area of Northern Alliance control
■ Suspected training camps/militia bases
◆ Taliban army bases
✈ Military and/or civilian airfields
Province boundaries

0    100    200 miles
0  100   200 kilometers
Conformal Conic Projection

In October 2001, the United States began bombing Taliban air defenses, airfields, and command centers, as well as al-Qaeda training camps. On the ground, the United States relied on anti-Taliban groups—first, the Northern Alliance and later, the Eastern Alliance—to do most of the fighting against the Taliban. These Afghan groups were assisted by U.S. air strikes against Taliban military positions and by a small number of U.S. special-forces troops and marines.

In December, the Taliban were driven from power, but the fight to destroy al-Qaeda continued. Meanwhile, the United Nations worked with the Northern Alliance and other Afghan groups to establish an interim government to replace the Taliban.

A number of nations in the antiterrorism coalition actively assisted the United States in Afghanistan, including Pakistan. The Pakistanis shared intelligence information and allowed the United States to stage military operations from their country.

Pakistan, a Muslim country, took a political risk by giving support to the United States. The Pakistani government's actions were opposed by groups within Pakistan who believed the antiterrorism campaign to be anti-Islamic.

The United States tried to make it clear to Muslim nations that the antiterrorism campaign was *not* anti-Islamic and that Americans respected the religion of Islam. For the United States, maintaining the support of moderate Muslim leaders was important to the long-term success of the war against terrorism—a war that in its next phase would target other nations that supported international terrorism.

**Thinking Critically**  **CURRENT EVENTS CLASSZONE.COM**

• How will the graph on page US8 change when the statistics for the year 2001 are added?

• What are some of the reasons for domestic terrorism in the various regions of the world?

## Reporter's Notes

**By Blake Morrison**

WASHINGTON, D.C.—A month after the September 11 terrorist hijackings, the pilot of US Airways Flight 62 stepped from the cockpit just before takeoff, an ax in his hand. "These are extraordinary times," he told passengers over the jet's public address system. The cabin quieted. Then he rattled off three scenarios in the event of a terrorist attack aboard the San Francisco-to-Charlotte flight.

"One, someone stands up and says 'bomb,' " the pilot said. "If they tell you that, it's a lie." Second, someone pretends to be an air marshal. "We don't have an armed marshal on this flight," he said, still holding the ax. Third, someone might threaten to release some sort of biological agent. Don't be afraid, he told passengers. Pilots would land the plane before any lasting harm could be done.

In any case, the pilot advised, passengers should not back down. "Throw your shoes at them. A couple of you get up and tackle him. Beat him. I don't care." As for the ax he was holding, standard on jets in case of emergency? It's kept in the cockpit, he said. "It's very sharp. I can shave with it. For anyone to try to break into this cockpit would be a very bad idea." Then the pilot paused. "Having said all this, I'd like you all to sit back, relax, and enjoy the trip." Some passengers chuckled. Almost everyone clapped.

The stunning announcement illustrates just how much flying changed in the wake of the September 11 terrorist attacks—and how quickly Americans have grown to accept the new reality.

# The Impact on American Life

 first appeared in print 9/18/2001

## Airport security tightens up

As the nation's 400 airports get back to business, passengers around the country are finding tighter security. Since the Sept. 11 hijacking of four U.S. airliners, the procedures from ticket counter to gate are stiffer. Airlines are recommending that passengers arrive between two and four hours early for flights. Security measures and wait times varied widely, according to USA TODAY® reporters.

**Security**
Passengers, and their families and friends, could all go to the gate. Keys, cell phones and change could be dropped into plastic dishes or cups to one side of the metal detectors. Hand-held sensors were used if metal still detected, or sometimes a manual pat-down.

**Check in**
Photo ID required. Ticket agent asks "Have your bags been in your possession since you packed them?"

Curb-side luggage check-in permitted

No curb-side luggage check permitted.

**Carry-on**
Bags are placed on a conveyor belt and contents displayed on a screen. Security employees are trained to spot suspicious objects.

Increased use of bomb-sniffing dogs. Dogs and police officers were highly visible at Newark International.

**Security**
Only passengers beyond this point. Cell phones, keys, pagers and other loose objects have to be put on the conveyor belts, where they are screened, according to passengers at San Francisco and Chicago airports Monday. Knives and cutting tools prohibited. Overhead metal detectors are being used in addition to hand-held units. In Baltimore, some bags were checked for bomb dust.

**Before security checkpoint**
Passengers asked to show tickets and photo IDs again.

**Before the Sept. 11 attack**

**After the attack**

**Check in**
Baggage checked randomly. Photo ID required. In some cases, passengers had to exchange e-tickets for paper tickets. Passengers still asked if they have had their bags in their possession since packing.

Sources: FAA; reporting by Jack Gruber, Debbie Howlett, Martin Kasindorf, USA TODAY®; and Reed Stacey

By Frank Pompa, USA TODAY®

---

After the September 11 attacks, many Americans reported feeling that everything had changed—that life would never be the same. Before, Americans had viewed war as something that happened in other countries. Now they felt vulnerable, and the threat of terrorism began to affect many aspects of American life—as the experience of those on Flight 62 showed.

## THE AIRLINES AND THE ECONOMY

In the wake of the terrorist attacks, the Federal Aviation Administration (FAA) shut down all airports in the United States for the first time in the nation's history. They did so to prevent any other hijackings. When the airports reopened and flights resumed a few days later, the airlines had few passengers. Some people did not feel safe flying, and others did not want to face the delays caused by tighter airport security.

The number of passengers dropped 43 percent in the days after flights resumed. The airline industry lost an estimated $5 billion in September and cut more than 100,000 jobs to reduce their costs. Congress quickly passed a $15-billion-aid package to help the industry get through the crisis. After September, airline business partially recovered. But even months later, the passenger airfleet was still flying well below capacity.

Industries related to the airlines also suffered. Travel agents, hotels, resorts, and theme parks all lost business. Also hard hit was the insurance industry, which would have to pay billions in death and property loss claims due to the attacks.

The New York Stock Exchange and other stock markets closed after the attacks and did not reopen until the following Monday. The last time the New York exchange had shut down for more than three days was in 1914, at the start of World War I. After the stock markets reopened, the Dow Jones Industrial Average suffered its biggest weekly drop since the Great Depression—14.3 percent.

Over the next few weeks, the markets began to rebound, but the economy continued to decline. Consumers spent less, and unemployment rose. Experts believed that the attacks had only worsened an economic slowdown that had begun early in 2001. They agreed that the nation was in a recession.

### THE ANTHRAX THREAT

Not long after September 11th, terrorism struck America again, but in a different form. Letters containing spores of a bacterium that causes the disease anthrax were sent to persons in the news media and to members of Congress in Washington, D.C.

Anthrax bacteria can cause illness when they come in contact with skin or when inhaled. The skin form of anthrax is usually not fatal. But if anthrax bacteria are inhaled, the poisons they produce can damage body tissues. If not treated quickly, inhalation anthrax can cause death.

**The threat of biological warfare became real when letters containing the anthrax bacterium (right) were sent to some members of the U.S. Congress in Washington D.C. (below) and persons in the news media after the September 11 attacks.**

Five people who came in contact with spores from the tainted letters died of inhalation anthrax. Two were postal workers. Many others contracted the skin form of the disease. Thousands who were exposed to anthrax were treated with antibiotics.

The anthrax scare frightened many Americans. The U.S. Postal Service warned Americans to be suspicious of mail without return addresses or in strange packages and to wash their hands after handling mail. Many businesses began taking precautions.

Investigators did not immediately find a link between the anthrax letters and the September 11 attacks. Some experts believed that the anthrax letters might be the work of a lone terrorist rather than an organized group. The anthrax scare not only made Americans fearful of the mail but also of the threat of other biological or chemical weapons, such as the smallpox virus or the nerve gas sarin.

### ANTITERRORISM MEASURES

The federal government warned Americans that additional terrorist attacks were likely. It then took actions to prevent such attacks. The Office of Homeland Security was created to coordinate national efforts against terrorism. Antiterrorism measures included a search for terrorists in the United States, the passage of an antiterrorism law, and the adoption of new aviation security regulations.

**Searching for Terrorists** The al-Qaeda network was able to carry out its terrorist attacks partly through the use of "sleepers." These are agents who move to a country, blend into a community, and then, when directed, secretly prepare for and carry out terrorist acts. A search to find any al-Qaeda terrorists who remained in the United States was started. Officials began detaining and questioning Arabs whose behavior was considered suspicious or who had violated immigration regulations.

Because the hijackers had been Arabs, the government held that the actions were justified. But some critics charged that detaining these men was unfair to the innocent and violated their civil rights. In one incident, Mohammed Irshaid, a Jordanian-born civil engineer who had lived in the United States for more than 20 years, was jailed for three weeks without being charged. His three children were American citizens. Although the incident humiliated him, he said that it "doesn't change my love of America."

President George W. Bush discusses the war against terrorism with advisers, including Vice President Dick Cheney (left) and Secretary of State Colin Powell (right).

More than three million Arab Americans live in the United States, and many were viewed with distrust by other Americans after the September 11 attacks. In one incident, three Arab Americans were taken off a plane when other passengers refused to fly with them. After questioning the men, officials allowed them to take a later flight.

Such incidents sparked debate about the need to respect civil rights while conducting searches for terrorists. The government argued that it was not unusual to curtail civil liberties during wartime in order to protect national security. This argument was also used to justify a proposal to try some terrorist suspects in military tribunals rather than in criminal courts.

### Antiterrorism Law
On October 26, 2001, President Bush signed into law an antiterrorism bill. The law allowed the government to

- detain foreigners suspected of terrorism for seven days without charging them with a crime
- tap all phones used by suspects and monitor their e-mail and Internet use
- make search warrants valid across states
- order U.S. banks to investigate sources of large foreign accounts
- prosecute terrorist crimes without any time restrictions or limitations

Again, critics warned that these measures would let the government infringe on people's civil rights.

### Aviation Security
The federal government also increased its involvement in aviation security. The Federal Aviation Administration ordered airlines to install bars on cockpit doors to prevent passengers from gaining control of planes, as the hijackers had done. Sky marshals were assigned to fly on planes; National Guard troops began patrolling airports.

In November 2001, a new aviation-security law made airport security the responsibility of the federal government. Previously, individual airports had been responsible. The law provided for a federal security force that would inspect passengers and carry-on bags. It also required the screening of checked baggage.

Airline and government officials debated these and other measures for making air travel more secure. Major concerns were long delays at airports and respect for passengers' privacy. It also became clear that public debate over security measures would continue as long as the United States fights terrorism and tries to balance national security with civil rights.

## Thinking Critically

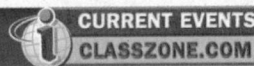
CURRENT EVENTS
CLASSZONE.COM

- Is it important for the U.S. government to respect people's civil rights as it wages a war against terrorism? Why or why not?

- What has been the greatest impact of terrorism on American life, aside from the tragic deaths caused by the September 11 attacks?

Thinking Critically Answers
- Some will say that civil rights always must be respected; others, that defeating terrorism is more important.
- Answers might include the continued fear of terrorism, the limitations on civil rights caused by increased security, or the economic costs of security measures.

# RAND McNALLY
# World Atlas

# CONTENTS

## Complete Legend for Physical and Political Maps

### Symbols

 Lake

 Salt Lake

 Seasonal Lake

 River

\ Waterfall

— Canal

△ Mountain Peak

▲ Highest Mountain Peak

### Cities

■ **Los Angeles**   City over 1,000,000 population

▣ Calgary   City of 250,000 to 1,000,000 population

• Haifa   City under 250,000 population

⊛ *Paris*   National Capital

★ Vancouver   Secondary Capital (State, Province, or Territory)

### Type Styles Used to Name Features

**CHINA**   Country

O N T A R I O   State, Province, or Territory

**PUERTO RICO (U.S.)**   Possession

A T L A N T I C  O C E A N   Ocean or Sea

*A l p s*   Physical Feature

*Borneo*   Island

### Boundaries

 International Boundary

 Secondary Boundary

### Land Elevation and Water Depths

**Land Elevation**

| Meters | | Feet |
|---|---|---|
| 3,000 and over -- | | -- 9,840 and over |
| 2,000 - 3,000 -- | | -- 6,560 - 9,840 |
| 500 - 2,000 -- | | -- 1,640 - 6,560 |
| 200 - 500 -- | | -- 656 - 1,640 |
| 0 - 200 -- | | -- 0 - 656 |

**Water Depth**

| | | |
|---|---|---|
| Less than 200 -- | | -- Less than 656 |
| 200 - 2,000 -- | | -- 656 - 6,560 |
| Over 2,000 -- | | -- Over 6,560 |

ARCTIC OCEAN

GREENLAND (Den.)

Baffin Bay

Arctic Cir

ICELAND

FAROE (Den

RUSSIA

ALASKA

Yukon (U.S.)

Anchorage

Aleutian Islands

CANADA

Hudson Bay

Vancouver

Missouri

Montréal

Ottawa

Newfoundland

IRELAND

Chicago

UNITED STATES

New York

Washington D.C.

Azores (Port.)

PORTUGAL

Los Angeles

Colorado

Casablanca

MIDWAY IS. (U.S.)

Houston

Canary Islands (Sp.)

ATLANTIC

Tropic of Cancer

MEXICO

Gulf of Mexico

BAHAMAS

W. SAHARA

Hawaiian Islands (U.S)

Mexico City

CUBA

HAITI

DOM. REP.

PUERTO RICO (U.S.)

CAPE VERDE

MAURITAN

BELIZE

JAMAICA

Caribbean Sea

SENEGAL

PACIFIC

GUAT.

HOND.

GAMBIA

EL. SAL.

NIC.

GUINEA-BISSAU

GUINEA

COSTA RICA

Caracas

TRINIDAD AND TOBAGO

SIERRA LEONE

PANAMA

VENEZUELA

GUYANA

LIBERIA

COLOMBIA

SURINAME

FRENCH GUIANA

Equator

Galapagos Islands (Ecuador)

ECUADOR

Amazon

KIRIBATI

PERU

Lima

BRAZIL

OCEAN

OCEAN

SAMOA

AMERICAN SAMOA

BOLIVIA

ST. HELENA (U.K.)

COOK ISLANDS (N.Z.)

TONGA

FRENCH POLYNESIA

PARAGUAY

Rio de Janeiro

Tropic of Capricorn

Easter Island (Chile)

ARGENTINA

URUGUAY

Santiago

Buenos Aires

N

0        1000        2000 Miles

0    1000    2000    3000 Kilometers

Copyright by Rand McNally & Co.
Robinson Projection

FALKLAND IS. (U.K.)

South Georgia (U.K.)

South Orkney Is. (U.K.)

Antarctic Circle

South Shetland Is. (U.K.)

Weddell Sea

ARCTIC OCEAN

Franz Josef
Land

Novaya
Zemlya

FINLAND

SWEDEN    EST.
LAT.
LITH.
MANY   POLAND   BELARUS
CZ.  SLVK.
AUS. HUNG.   UKRAINE
CRO.   MOLD.
ROM.
BOS.
ALB. MA-.   BUL.
GREECE

TUNISIA

Crete   CYPRUS   LEB.
ISRAEL
Cairo   JORDAN

LIBYA   EGYPT

NGER   CHAD   SUDAN

ERIA

CENTRAL
AFRICAN
CAMEROON   REPUBLIC

GABON   UGANDA

RWANDA   KENYA
DEM. REP.
OF CONGO   BURUNDI
TANZANIA

ANGOLA

ZAMBIA   ZIMBABWE

NAMIBIA

BOTSWANA

SWAZILAND

SOUTH   LESOTHO
AFRICA

ape Town

Moscow

Volga

Black Sea

GEO.
ARM. AZER.
TURKEY
SYRIA   IRAQ
KUWAIT

SAUDI   QATAR
ARABIA   U.A.E.

YEMEN

DJIBOUTI
Addis
Ababa
ETHIOPIA

SOMALIA

COMOROS

MADAGASCAR   MAURITIUS

REUNION
(Fr.)

Yenisey

RUSSIA

Novosibirsk

KAZAKHSTAN

UZBEKISTAN
KYRG.
TURKMENISTAN   TAJIK.

AFGHANISTAN

IRAN

PAKISTAN

OMAN

Mumbai
(Bombay)

Arabian
Sea

MALDIVES

SEYCHELLES

INDIAN

OCEAN

Kerguelen
Islands
(Fr.)

Lena

MONGOLIA

Beijing

CHINA

NEPAL
Ganges

INDIA

Kolkata
(Calcutta)   BNGL.

MYANMAR

Bay of
Bengal

THAILAND

SRI LANKA

Bangkok

Sea of Okhotsk

NORTH
KOREA   Sea of Japan
SOUTH
KOREA

Chang Jiang
(Yangtze)

Shanghai

Guangzhou   TAIWAN

Bering
Sea

JAPAN
Tokyo

PACIFIC

Tropic of Cancer

NORTHERN
MARIANA ISLANDS
(U.S.)

WAKE ISLAND
(U.S.)

South China
Sea   PHILIPPINES   GUAM (U.S.)   O C E A N

LAOS

VIETNAM

CAMBODIA

BRUNEI

MALAYSIA

SINGAPORE
Borneo

Sumatra

Jakarta
Java   INDONESIA

PALAU

FED. STATES OF
MICRONESIA

New Guinea
PAPUA
NEW GUINEA

EAST TIMOR

MARSHALL
ISLANDS

Equator

SOLOMON
ISLANDS

Darwin

Coral Sea

AUSTRALIA

Perth

Melbourne

Tasmania

Darling

VANUATU

NEW CALEDONIA
(Fr.)

FIJI

Tropic of Capricorn

Sydney

NEW ZEALAND
Wellington

Antarctic Circle

ANTARCTICA

30°   45°   60°   75°   90°   105°   120°   135°   150°   165°   180°

ARCTIC OCEAN

Baffin
Bay

Greenland

Baffin
Island

Arctic

Iceland

Yukon

Mackenzie

Canadian Shield

Faro

Mt. McKinley △
20,320 Ft.
6,194m

NORTH

Hudson
Bay

Aleutian Islands

Rocky Mountains

Great Plains

AMERICA

St. Lawrence

Newfoundland

Vancouver

Appalachian Mts.

Azores

Los Angeles

Colorado

Washington D.C.

Mississippi

Cape Hatteras

ATLANTIC

Midway Is.

Baja
California

Gulf of Mexico

Canary
Islands

Tropic of Cancer

Hawaiian
Islands

Yucatan
Peninsula

Cuba

Hispaniola

Puerto Rico

Cape
Verde
Islands

Jamaica

Caribbean
Sea

Cape Verde

PACIFIC

Trinidad

Orinoco

OCEAN

Palmyra

Galapagos Islands

Amazon

Amazon
Basin

SOUTH

Equator

Kiribati

AMERICA

Marquesas Is.

Andes

Samoa
Islands

Mato Grosso
Plateau

St. Helena

Tonga
Is.

Cook
Islands

Tahiti

Tropic of Capricorn

Easter Island

Andes

Paraná

Rio de Janeiro

N

△ Mt. Aconcagua
22,831 Ft.
6,959m

Buenos Aires

Chatham Is.

Archipiélago
Juan Fernández

Patagonia

Falkland Is.

South
Georgia

| 0 | | 1000 | | 2000 Miles |

| 0 | 1000 | 2000 | 3000 Kilometers |

Copyright by Rand McNally & Co.
Robinson Projection

Tierra del Fuego

Cape Horn

South
Sandwich Is.

South
Orkney Is.

Antarctic Circle

South
Shetland Is.

Antarctic
Peninsula

Weddell
Sea

Ross
Sea

Marie
Byrd
Land

△ Vinson Massif
16,066 Ft.
4,897m

ARCTIC OCEAN

Spitsbergen
Franz Josef
Land
North Cape
Novaya
Zemlya
Scandinavian
Peninsula

Siberia

Yenisey
Lena

Bering
Sea of Okhotsk
Sea

EUROPE
Moscow
Volga
Don
Ural Mts.
Ob'
Altai Mts.
ASIA
Aral
Sea
Gobi Desert
Beijing
Sakhalin
Kamchatka
Peninsula

Sea of Japan
Hokkaidō
Honshū

Alps
Balkan
Peninsula
Caucasus
Mt. Elbrus
18,510 Ft.
5,642m
Black Sea
Pamir
Caspian Sea
Plateau
of
Tibet
Himalayas
Huang
Yangtze
East
China
Sea
Kyūshū

Sicily
Crete
Cyprus
inia
Zagros Mts.
Indus
Ganges
Mt. Everest
29,035 Ft.
8,850m
Mekong
Taiwan

PACIFIC

Cairo
Mediterranean Sea
Red Sea

ra Desert
Arabian
Peninsula
Tropic of Cancer
Hainan
Island
Mariana
Islands
Wake
Island

hel
Nile
AFRICA
Mumbai
(Bombay)
Arabian
Sea
Deccan
Plateau
South China
Sea
Luzon
Guam

OCEAN

Socotra
Lakshadweep
Bay of
Bengal
Mindanao
Palau
Islands
Caroline
Islands
Marshall
Islands

Ethiopian
Plateau
Sri Lanka
Malay
Peninsula

Congo
Congo
Basin
Rift Valley
Kilimanjaro
19,340 Ft.
5,895m
Maldive
Islands
Borneo
Celebes
New Guinea
Solomon
Islands
Equator

Seychelles
Sumatra
Java
Timor

Zambezi
INDIAN
Cocos
Island
New
Hebrides
Coral Sea
New Caledonia
Fiji
Is.

Madagascar
Mauritius
Reunion
Great
Sandy
Desert
Tropic of Capricorn

Kalahari
Desert
OCEAN
AUSTRALIA

Cape Town
of Good Hope
Cape Leeuwin
Darling
Great Dividing Range
Sydney
North Island

Aoraki
(Mt. Cook)
12,316 Ft.
3,754m
Tasmania
Kerguelen
Islands
South Island

OCEAN

60

Antarctic Circle

Maud
nd
Enderby
Land
Wilkes Land
Victoria Land

ANTARCTICA

BRITISH COLUMBIA
ALBERTA
SASKATCHEWAN
Lake Manitoba
CA
MANIT

Bellingham
Seattle
Olympia
Tacoma
WASHINGTON
Columbia
Spokane
Yakima
Coeur d'Alene
Kennewick
Flathead Lake
Missouri
Milk
Great Falls
MONTANA
Fort Peck Lake
Minot
NORTH DAKOTA
Gran
Portland
Columbia
Pendleton
Lewiston
Missoula
Butte
Helena
Billings
Yellowstone
Miles City
Bismarck
Salem
Corvallis
Bend
Eugene
OREGON
Salmon
Snake
IDAHO
Bozeman
Powder
Jam

Medford
Klamath Falls
Goose Lake
Nampa
Boise
Idaho Falls
American Falls Res.
Snake
Twin Falls
Pocatello
Yellowstone Lake
Sheridan
WYOMING
Lake Oahe
Abe

Eureka
Shasta Lake
Sacramento
Winnemucca
Humboldt
Elko
Great Salt Lake
Logan
Ogden
Rock Springs
Casper
Laramie
Rapid City
Pierre
SOUTH DAKOTA
Lake Francis Case
Niobrara
Scottsbluff
North Platte
NEBRASKA
Nor

Santa Rosa
Sacramento
Pyramid Lake
Reno
Lake Tahoe
Carson City
NEVADA
Salt Lake City
Provo
Green
Fort Collins
Cheyenne
North Platte
Grand Island
Platte

Oakland
San Francisco
San Jose
Stockton
Modesto
Ely
UTAH
Colorado
Moab
Grand Junction
Boulder
Denver
Colorado Springs
COLORADO
Republican

Monterey
Fresno
San Joaquin
CALIFORNIA
Cedar City
St. George
Lake Powell
Durango
Farmington
Pueblo
Trinidad
Smoky Hill
Arkansas
Dodge City
Hutchinson
KANSAS
Salina
Wichit

Las Vegas
Lake Mead
Colorado
Bakersfield
Santa Barbara
Little Colorado
Flagstaff
Prescott
Gallup
Santa Fe
Albuquerque
Canadian
Amarillo
Oklahoma City
Stillw
OKLAHO

Los Angeles
Long Beach
San Bernardino
Riverside
San Diego
Salton Sea
Colorado
Gila
ARIZONA
Salt
Phoenix
NEW MEXICO
Clovis
Rio Grande
Roswell
Lubbock
Red
Lawton
Wichita Falls

Tijuana
Yuma
Tucson
Nogales
Las Cruces
Alamogordo
Hobbs
El Paso
Odessa
Midland
Fort Worth
TEXAS

PACIFIC OCEAN

San An
Del Rio
Nueces

Laredo
Rio Grande
MEXICO
McAllen
Br

Niihau
Kalaheo
Kauai
Kauai Channel
Oahu
Wahiawa
Molokai
Hawaiian Islands
Honolulu
Lanai
Maui
N
0 50 Miles
0 50 Kilometers
Kahoolawe
Mauna Kea 13,796 Ft. 4,205m
Hawaii
HAWAII
Mauna Loa 13,679 Ft. 4,169m
Hilo
PACIFIC OCEAN
© RMcN

ARCTIC OCEAN
Barrow
Beaufort Sea
Chukchi Sea
Arctic Circle
RUSSIA
Kotzebue
NORTHWEST TERRITORIES
Bering Strait
Nome
ALASKA
Yukon
Fairbanks
Yukon
YUKON
CANADA
Saint Lawrence Island
Kuskokwim
Whitehorse
Bethel
Anchorage
Valdez
BRITISH COLUMBIA
N
Seward
Gulf of Alaska
Juneau
Bering Sea
Kodiak
Sitka
0 100 200 300 Miles
0 200 400 Kilometers
Aleutian Islands
Dutch Harbor
PACIFIC OCEAN
© RMcN

D A

ONTARIO

QUÉBEC

NEW BRUNSWICK

Lake Nipigon

International Falls

Lake of the Woods

*Duluth*

Isle Royale

Lake Superior

Sault Ste. Marie

MAINE

Moosehead Lake

Bangor

NESOTA

Marquette

MICHIGAN

Montréal

Ottawa

*Augusta*

Cloud

*St. Paul*

Eau Claire

Green Bay

Lake Huron

Georgian Bay

Lake Champlain

VERMONT

Burlington

Montpelier

NEW HAMPSHIRE

Concord

Portland

Gulf of Maine

neapolis

Rochester

WISCONSIN

Appleton

OshKosh

Sheboygan

Saginaw

Traverse City

Flint

Watertown

Lake Ontario

NEW YORK

Rochester

Syracuse

Manchester

MASSACHUSETTS

Boston

Worcester

kankato

Milwaukee

Madison

Racine

Grand Rapids

Lansing

Toronto

Buffalo

Albany

Binghamton

CONNECTICUT

Hartford

Providence

R.I.

Nantucket Island

Des Moines

Waterloo

Dubuque

Cedar Rapids

Rockford

Kalamazoo

Ann Arbor

Detroit

Lake Erie

Erie

Scranton

Bridgeport

Long Island

IOWA

Davenport

Moline

Aurora

Chicago

Gary

South Bend

Toledo

Cleveland

Akron

Youngstown

PENNSYLVANIA

Oil City

Allentown

Trenton

New York

Newark

es Moines

Fort Wayne

Lima

OHIO

Pittsburgh

Harrisburg

Philadelphia

NEW JERSEY

Peoria

Bloomington

INDIANA

Muncie

Columbus

Susquehanna

Wilmington

Dover

Illinois

Springfield

Decatur

Indianapolis

Dayton

Springfield

Ohio

Baltimore

Washington D.C.

Annapolis

DELAWARE

Delaware Bay

St. Joseph

Terre Haute

Cincinnati

MARYLAND

ILLINOIS

Bloomington

WEST VIRGINIA

Columbia

Kansas City

Missouri

St. Louis

Jefferson City

Louisville

Frankfort

Lexington

Huntington

Charleston

VIRGINIA

Richmond

Newport News

Wabash

Evansville

Owensboro

Roanoke

Norfolk

Virginia Beach

MISSOURI

Springfield

Cape Girardeau

KENTUCKY

Albemarle Sound

Roanoke

Clarksville

Cumberland

Johnson City

Winston-Salem

Greensboro

Durham

Raleigh

ria

Kentucky Lake

Nashville

Knoxville

Asheville

NORTH CAROLINA

uskogee

Fayetteville

Jonesboro

TENNESSEE

Chattanooga

Greenville

ATLANTIC OCEAN

Fort Smith

Memphis

Huntsville

Charlotte

Wilmington

Little Rock

SOUTH CAROLINA

ARKANSAS

Pine Bluff

Athens

Columbia

70°

xarkana

Birmingham

Atlanta

Augusta

Greenville

Ouachita

Tombigbee

Tuscaloosa

Macon

Savannah

Charleston

MISSISSIPPI

ALABAMA

Columbus

GEORGIA

Altamaha

Savannah

N

Shreveport

Monroe

Montgomery

Chattahoochee

Albany

Toledo Bend Res.

Red

Mississippi

Jackson

Dothan

LOUISIANA

Hattiesburg

Mobile

Pensacola

Tallahassee

Jacksonville

100   200   300 Miles

am

rn

Lake Charles

Baton Rouge

Gulfport

New Orleans

0   100   200   300   400 Kilometers

Copyright by Rand McNally & Co.
Alber's Conic Equal Area Projection

Lafayette

Gainesville

Daytona Beach

ouston

Galveston

Orlando

GULF OF MEXICO

Tampa

Lakeland

St. Petersburg

FLORIDA

Lake Okeechobee

West Palm Beach

19°   ATLANTIC OCEAN   67°   66°

Fort Myers

Fort Lauderdale

Miami

N

Arecibo

San Juan

Mayagüez

Caguas

Ponce

Key West

18°   PUERTO RICO (U.S.)

Caribbean Sea

0   25   50 Miles

0   25   50 Kilometers

© RMcN.

BRITISH COLUMBIA
ALBERTA
SASKATCHEWAN
MANITO
CA

ROCKY

WASHINGTON

Cape Flattery
Olympic Mts.
Mt. Olympus 7,965 Ft. 2,428m
Seattle
Puget Sound
Columbia

Columbia
Clark Fork
Flathead Lake
Marias
Milk
Missouri

Mt. Rainier 14,410 Ft. 4,392m

Mt. Saint Helens 8,364 Ft. 2,549m

Columbia

MONTANA
Fort Peck Lake
Yellowstone

Lake Sakakawea
Sheyenne

NORTH DAKOT

James

Mt. Hood 11,239 Ft. 3,426m

Blue Mts.

Snake

Bitterroot Range

Salmon
Salmon River Mountains

IDAHO

Borah Peak 12,662 Ft. 3,859m

Absaroka Range

Granite Peak 12,799 Ft. 3,901m

Tongue
Powder

Yellowstone

Moreau

Lake Oahe

SOUTH DAKOT

OREGON

Cascade Range

Cape Blanco

Harney Basin

Mt. McLoughlin 9,495 Ft. 2,894m

Goose Lake

American Falls Res.

Snake

Grand Teton 13,770 Ft. 4,197m

Yellowstone Lake

Bighorn Mts.
Bighorn

Cloud Peak 13,167 Ft. 4,013m

Cheyenne

Black Hills

Harney Peak 7,242 Ft. 2,207m

White Lake Francis Case

Mt. Shasta 14,162 Ft. 4,317m

Coast Ranges

Cape Mendocino

Shasta Lake

Humboldt

Pyramid Lake

Great Salt Lake

WYOMING

Great Divide Basin

North Platte

Niobrara
North Loup

NEBRASKA

Mis

Sierra Nevada

San Francisco

Lake Tahoe

Great NEVADA Basin

Utah Lake

Flaming Gorge Res.

Wasatch Range

Uinta Mts.

Kings Peak 13,528 Ft. 4,123m

Green

Front Range

Longs Peak 14,255 Ft. 4,345m

Colorado

Denver

South Platte
Platte
Republican

UNITE

Wheeler Peak 13,064 Ft. 3,982m

UTAH

COLORADO

Smoky Hill

KANSA

Central Valley
San Joaquin

Mt. Whitney 14,494 Ft. 4,418m

Death Valley

Lake Powell

Colorado Plateau

San Juan

Mt. Elbert 14,433 Ft. 4,399m

Pikes Pk. 14,110 Ft. 4,301m

Arkansas

Point Arguello

Telescope Peak 11,050 Ft. 3,368m

CALIFORNIA

Coast Ranges

Mojave Desert

Lake Mead

Colorado

Grand Canyon

Little Colorado

Humphreys Peak 12,633 Ft. 3,851m

Sangre de Cristo Mountains

San Juan Mts.

Wheeler Peak 13,161 Ft. 4,011m

Cimarron

Los Angeles

Channel Islands

Salton Sea

Colorado

ARIZONA

Salt

Phoenix

Gila

Baldy Peak 11,404 Ft. 3,476m

Mt. Taylor 11,301 Ft. 3,445m

NEW MEXICO

Canadian

OKLAHO

Red

PACIFIC

OCEAN

Pelomcillo Mts.

Rio Grande

Sacramento Mts.

Llano Estacado

Stockton Plateau

Edwards Plateau

Guadalupe Pk. 8,749 Ft. 2,667m

Pecos

Dalla

TEXAS

Emory Peak 7,825 Ft. 2,385m

Nueces

Rio Grande

MEXICO

**Alaska inset:**

ARCTIC OCEAN
Point Barrow
Prudhoe Bay
Beaufort Sea
NORTHWEST TERRITORIES

Chukchi Sea
Arctic Circle
RUSSIA
Brooks Range

Bering Strait

Kobuk

ALASKA

Nome
Saint Lawrence Island

Yukon
Fairbanks

Yukon

CANADA

YUKON

Mt. McKinley 20,320 Ft. 6,194m

Kuskokwim

Tanana

Alaska Range

Valdez

Anchorage

Kenai Pen.

BRITISH COLUMBIA

Juneau

Gulf of Alaska

0  100  200  300 Miles

0  200  400 Kilometers

N

Bering Sea
Bristol Bay
Kodiak Island
Aleutian Islands
Alaska Peninsula

PACIFIC OCEAN

©RMN.

**Hawaii inset:**

Niihau  Kauai
Kalaheo
Oahu  Wahiawa
Honolulu  Molokai
Lanai  Maui
Kahoolawe
Mauna Kea 13,796 Ft. 4,205m
Hawaii
Hilo
Mauna Loa 13,679 Ft. 4,169m

Hawaiian Islands
Kauai Channel
N

0  50 Miles
0  50 Kilometers

HAWAII

PACIFIC OCEAN

©RMN.

CANADA

ONTARIO

Lake of the Woods

Lake Nipigon

QUEBEC

St. Lawrence

NEW BRUNSWICK

Montréal

Mt. Katahdin 5,268 Ft. △1,606m

MAINE

Moosehead Lake

Kennebec

MINNESOTA

Minneapolis

Isle Royale

Keweenaw Peninsula

Whitefish Point

Lake Superior

Great Lakes

Upper Peninsula

MICHIGAN

Bruce Peninsula

Georgian Bay

Lake Huron

Saginaw Bay

WISCONSIN

Chippewa

Lake Winnebago

Wisconsin

Muskegon

Lower Peninsula

Grand

Lake Michigan

Detroit

Lake Erie

Maumee

Lake Champlain

VERMONT

△Mt. Washington 6,288 Ft. 1,917m

White Mts.

Adirondack Mountains

NEW HAMPSHIRE

Green Mts.

Gulf of Maine

NEW YORK

Connecticut

MASS. ★Boston

Cape Cod

CONNECTICUT R.I.

Nantucket Island

Toronto ★

Lake Ontario

Niagara Falls

Catskill Mts.

Hudson

Allegheny Plateau

Allegheny Mountains

Long Island

New York

IOWA

Des Moines

Iowa

Mississippi

Illinois

Chicago

INDIANA

OHIO

Scioto

PENNSYLVANIA

Susquehanna

Philadelphia

NEW JERSEY

Delaware Bay

DELAWARE

UNITED STATES

ILLINOIS

White

Wabash

Ohio

Ohio

WEST VIRGINIA

Washington D.C.

MARYLAND

Chesapeake Bay

Lake of the Ozarks

Missouri

St. Louis

MISSOURI

Ozark Plateau

KENTUCKY

Green

Lake Cumberland

Cumberland

Appalachian Mountains

VIRGINIA

James

Roanoke

Albemarle Sound

Cape Hatteras

Boston Mts.

White

Arkansas

Kentucky

Kentucky Lake

Mt. Mitchell 6,684 Ft. △2,037m

Blue Ridge

Piedmont

NORTH CAROLINA

Pamlico Sound

Cape Lookout

Ouachita Mts.

ARKANSAS

Ouachita

Mississippi

Cumberland Plateau

TENNESSEE

Tennessee

Appalachian

Clarks Hill Lake

SOUTH CAROLINA

Pee Dee

Santee

Cape Fear

Cape Fear

ATLANTIC OCEAN

Yazoo

Atlanta ★

Savannah

Coastal Plain

Sea Islands

Toledo Bend Res.

Red

MISSISSIPPI

ALABAMA

Tombigbee

Pearl

Alabama

GEORGIA

Altamaha

Flint

Chattahoochee

LOUISIANA

Houston

New Orleans

Atchafalaya Bay

Mississippi Delta

Cape San Blas

Apalachee Bay

Suwannee

Cape Canaveral

GULF OF MEXICO

Tampa Bay

FLORIDA

Lake Okeechobee

The Everglades

Miami

Cape Sable

Florida Keys

N

0      100      200      300 Miles
0   100   200   300   400 Kilometers

Copyright by Rand McNally & Co.
Alber's Conic Equal Area Projection

ATLANTIC OCEAN

19°

San Juan

Arecibo

N

Mayagüez

Ponce

Caguas

18°

67°

66°

25°

PUERTO RICO (U.S.)

0   25   50 Miles
0   25   50 Kilometers

Caribbean Sea

© RMN

ASIA

RUSSIA

ARCTIC OCEAN

North Pole

Bering Strait

Point Hope

Point Barrow

Beaufort Sea

Cape Bathurst

Queen Elizabeth Islands

Ellesmere Island

GREENLAND (Denmark)

Ice Cap

Arctic Circle

ICELAND

Norwegian

Bering Sea

Aleutian Islands

Alaska Peninsula

Anchorage

Alaska Range

U.S.

Brooks Range

Yukon

Kuskokwim

Mt. McKinley 20,320 ft. 6,194m

Mt. Logan 19,551 ft. 5,959m

Gulf of Alaska

Prudhoe Bay

Cape

Banks Island

Victoria Island

Devon Island

Baffin Bay

Cape Adair

Baffin Island

Cape Mercy

Cape Farvel

Mackenzie

Whitehorse

Great Bear Lake

Great Slave Lake

Foxe Basin

Hudson Bay

Péninsule d'Ungava

PACIFIC OCEAN

Queen Charlotte Islands

Vancouver Island

Coast Mountains

Peace

Edmonton

CANADA

Saskatchewan

Lake Athabasca

Churchill

Nelson

Lake Winnipeg

Albany

James Bay

Canadian Shield

Newfoundland

Cape Blanco

Cape Mendocino

Rocky Mountains

Vancouver

Range

Cascades

Columbia

Coast Ranges

Sierra Nevada

Snake

Great Salt Lake

Great Basin

Great Plains

Missouri

Lake Superior

Great Lakes

Lake Michigan

Lake Huron

Lake Erie

Lake Ontario

Niagara Falls

St. Lawrence

Montréal

Ottawa

Gulf of St. Lawrence

Cape Cod

New York

UNITED STATES

Mt. Whitney 14,494 Ft. 4,418m

Denver

Colorado

Arkansas

Colorado Plateau

Los Angeles

Red

Ohio

Ozark Plateau

Mississippi

Chicago

Appalachian Mts.

Washington D.C.

Coastal Plain

Cape Hatteras

BERMUDA

ATLANTIC OCEAN

Tropic of Cancer

MEXICO

Sierra Madre Occidental

Gulf of California

Rio Grande

Houston

Cape Canaveral

GULF OF MEXICO

The Everglades

Miami

BAHAMAS

Tropic of Cancer

Sierra Madre Oriental

Cabo San Lucas

Gulf of Campeche

Yucatán Peninsula

Havana

CUBA

DOMINICAN REPUBLIC

HAITI

PUERTO RICO

Mexico City

GUATEMALA

BELIZE

HONDURAS

JAMAICA

CARIBBEAN SEA

EL SALVADOR

NICARAGUA

Lago de Nicaragua

COSTA RICA

PANAMA

Golfo de Panamá

VENEZ

COLOMBIA

PACIFIC OCEAN

SOUTH AMERICA

N

0    200   400   600   800   1000 Miles

0   300   600   900  1200  1500 Kilometers

Copyright by Rand McNally & Co.
Lambert Azimuthal Equal Area Projection

Equator

GULF OF MEXICO
90°
80°
CUBA
70°
60°
DOMINICAN REPUBLIC
HAITI
50°
40°
20°
Greater Antilles
Lesser Antilles
NORTH AMERICA
JAMAICA
BELIZE
Gulf of Honduras
HONDURAS
MEXICO
GUATEMALA
EL SALVADOR
NICARAGUA
PUERTO RICO (U.S.)
CARIBBEAN SEA
ATLANTIC OCEAN
COSTA RICA
Gulf of Panama
PANAMA
Cristóbal Colón Peak △ 18,948 Ft. 5,775m
⊛ Caracas
TRINIDAD AND TOBAGO
-10°
Llanos
Orinoco
VENEZUELA
GUYANA
FRENCH GUIANA
⊛ Bogotá
SURINAME
Cape Orange
COLOMBIA
Magdalena
ECUADOR
△ Chimborazo 20,703 Ft. 6,310m
Putumayo
Japurá
Negro
Manaus ■
Amazon
Ilha de Marajó
Belém ■
Galapagos Islands (Ec.)
Equator
0°
Amazon
Amazon
Amazon Basin
Tapajós
Tocantins
Juruá
Madeira
B R A Z I L
Selvas
Ucayali
PERU
Mt. Huascarán 22,133 Ft. 6,746m △
Recife ■
-10°
Mato Grosso Plateau
São Francisco
Andes
Lima ⊛
Mt. Illampu 21,066 Ft. 6,421m △
Lake Titicaca
BOLIVIA
Brasília ⊛
Serra do Espinhaço
Cordillera Oriental
△ Mt. Sajama 21,463 Ft. 6,542m
Atacama Desert
Gran Chaco
PARAGUAY
Paraná
São Paulo ■
Rio de Janeiro ■
-20°
Isla San Ambrosio (Chile)
Tropic of Capricorn
Tropic of Capricorn
Mt. Ojos del Salado 22,615 Ft. 6,893m
Isla San Felix (Chile)
Paraná
N
CHILE
ARGENTINA
Andes
URUGUAY
-30°
Archipiélago Juan Fernández (Chile)
Mt. Aconcagua 22,831 Ft. 6,959m
Santiago ⊛
Buenos Aires ⊛
Rio de la Plata
PACIFIC OCEAN
Pampas
110°
100°
San Matías Gulf
Chiloé
Península Valdés
-40°
Patagonia
San Jorge Gulf
ATLANTIC OCEAN
Point Medanoso
Grand Bay
West Falkland
FALKLAND ISLANDS (U.K.)
Strait of Magellan
East Falkland
-50°
Tierra del Fuego
Cape Horn
South Georgia (U.K.)
0    200   400   600   800   1000 Miles
0   300   600   900   1200   1500 Kilometers
Copyright by Rand McNally & Co.
Lambert Azimuthal Equal Area Projection
Drake Passage
South Shetland Islands (U.K.)
South Orkney Islands (U.K.)
South Sandwich Islands (U.K.)
60°
50°
40°
30°
20°
10°

**A11**

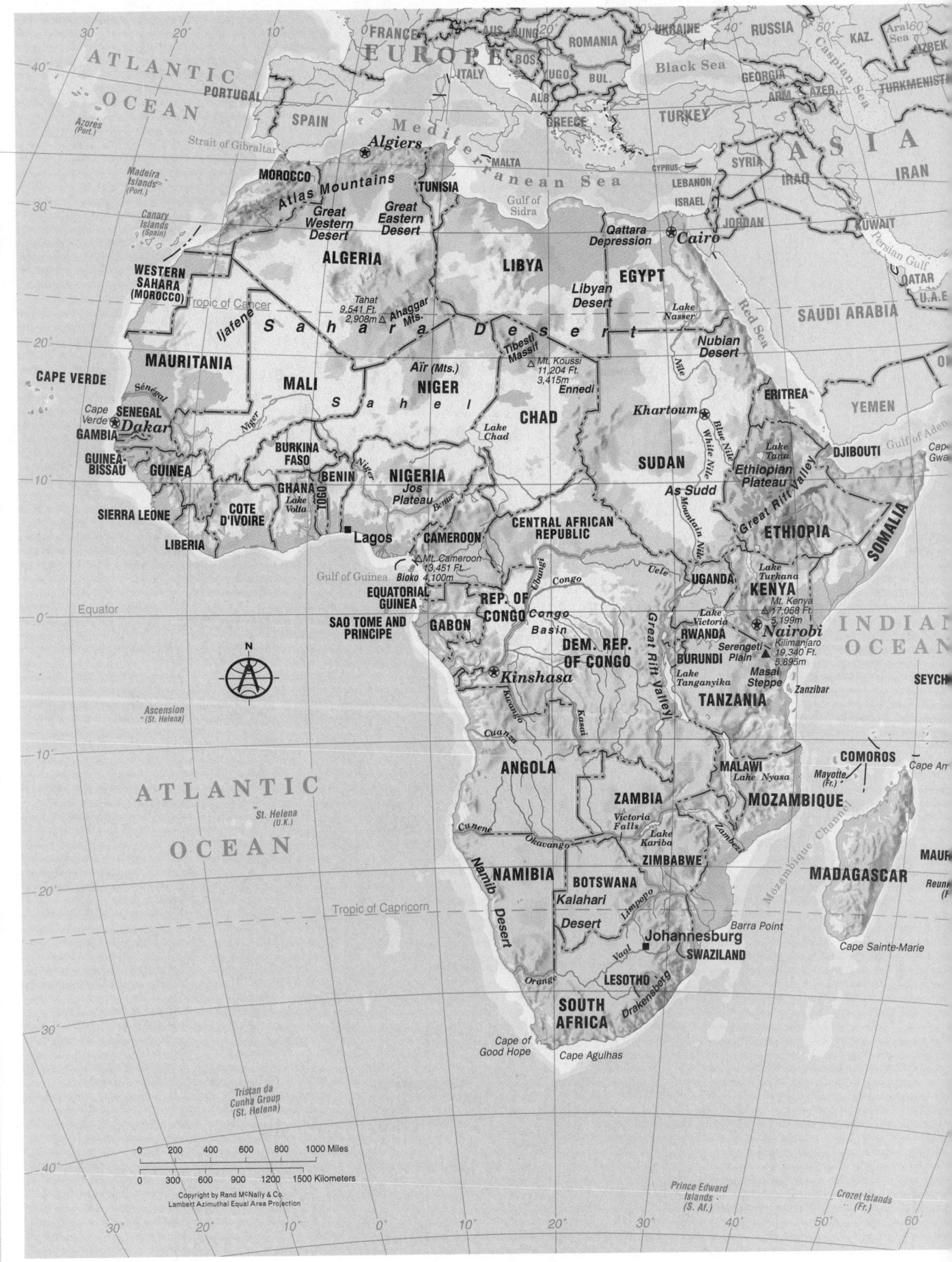

ATLANTIC OCEAN

PORTUGAL

Azores (Port.)

Strait of Gibraltar

Madeira Islands (Port.)

Canary Islands (Spain)

Tropic of Cancer

WESTERN SAHARA (MOROCCO)

Ijafene

CAPE VERDE

Cape Verde

Dakar
SENEGAL
GAMBIA
GUINEA-BISSAU
GUINEA
SIERRA LEONE
LIBERIA

EUROPE

FRANCE
SPAIN
ITALY
Mediterranean Sea
MALTA
Algiers
MOROCCO
Atlas Mountains
TUNISIA
Great Western Desert
Great Eastern Desert
Gulf of Sidra
ALGERIA
LIBYA
Tahat 9,541 Ft. 2,908m △
Ahaggar Mts.
Saïr (Mts.)
MAURITANIA
MALI
NIGER
S a h a r a   D e s e r t
Tibesti Massif
Mt. Koussi 11,204 Ft. 3,415m △
Ennedi
Sénégal
Niger
S a h e l
Lake Chad
CHAD
BURKINA FASO
BENIN
NIGERIA
GHANA
Lake Volta
COTE D'IVOIRE
Jos Plateau
Benue
Lagos
CAMEROON
Mt. Cameroon 13,451 Ft. 4,100m △
Bioko
EQUATORIAL GUINEA
Gulf of Guinea
SAO TOME AND PRINCIPE
GABON
Equator
Ascension (St. Helena)

CENTRAL AFRICAN REPUBLIC

REP. OF CONGO
Ubangi
Congo
Congo Basin
DEM. REP. OF CONGO
Kinshasa
Kwango
Kasai
Cuanza

BOS.
YUGO.
ALB.
GREECE
ROMANIA
BUL.
Black Sea
UKRAINE
RUSSIA
GEORGIA
ARM. AZER.
KAZ.
Caspian Sea
TURKMENISTAN
UZBEK.
Aral Sea
CYPRUS
SYRIA
LEBANON
ISRAEL
TURKEY
IRAQ
IRAN
JORDAN
KUWAIT
QATAR
U.A.E.
SAUDI ARABIA
Qattara Depression
Cairo
EGYPT
Libyan Desert
Lake Nasser
Nubian Desert
Red Sea
Nile
Khartoum
SUDAN
White Nile
Blue Nile
As Sudd
Mountain Nile
ERITREA
YEMEN
DJIBOUTI
Gulf of Aden
Cape Gwa
Lake Tana
Ethiopian Plateau
ETHIOPIA
SOMALIA
Great Rift Valley
UGANDA
Uele
Lake Victoria
RWANDA
BURUNDI
KENYA
Mt. Kenya 17,058 Ft. 5,199m △
Nairobi
Serengeti Plain
Kilimanjaro 19,340 Ft. 5,895m ▲
Masai Steppe
Lake Turkana
Great Rift Valley
Lake Tanganyika
TANZANIA
Zanzibar
ASIA
Persian Gulf
INDIAN OCEAN
SEYCH.

N

ATLANTIC

St. Helena (U.K.)

OCEAN

ANGOLA
Cunene
ZAMBIA
Victoria Falls
Lake Kariba
Zambezi
ZIMBABWE
MALAWI
Lake Nyasa
COMOROS
Mayotte (Fr.)
Cape An
MOZAMBIQUE
Mozambique Channel
MADAGASCAR
MAUR
Reun (F

Tropic of Capricorn

NAMIBIA
Namib Desert
Okavango
Kalahari Desert
BOTSWANA
Limpopo
Johannesburg
SWAZILAND
Barra Point
Cape Sainte-Marie

Orange
Vaal
LESOTHO
SOUTH AFRICA
Drakensberg
Cape of Good Hope
Cape Agulhas

Tristan da Cunha Group (St. Helena)

0 200 400 600 800 1000 Miles

0 300 600 900 1200 1500 Kilometers

Copyright by Rand McNally & Co.
Lambert Azimuthal Equal Area Projection

Prince Edward Islands (S. Af.)

Crozet Islands (Fr.)

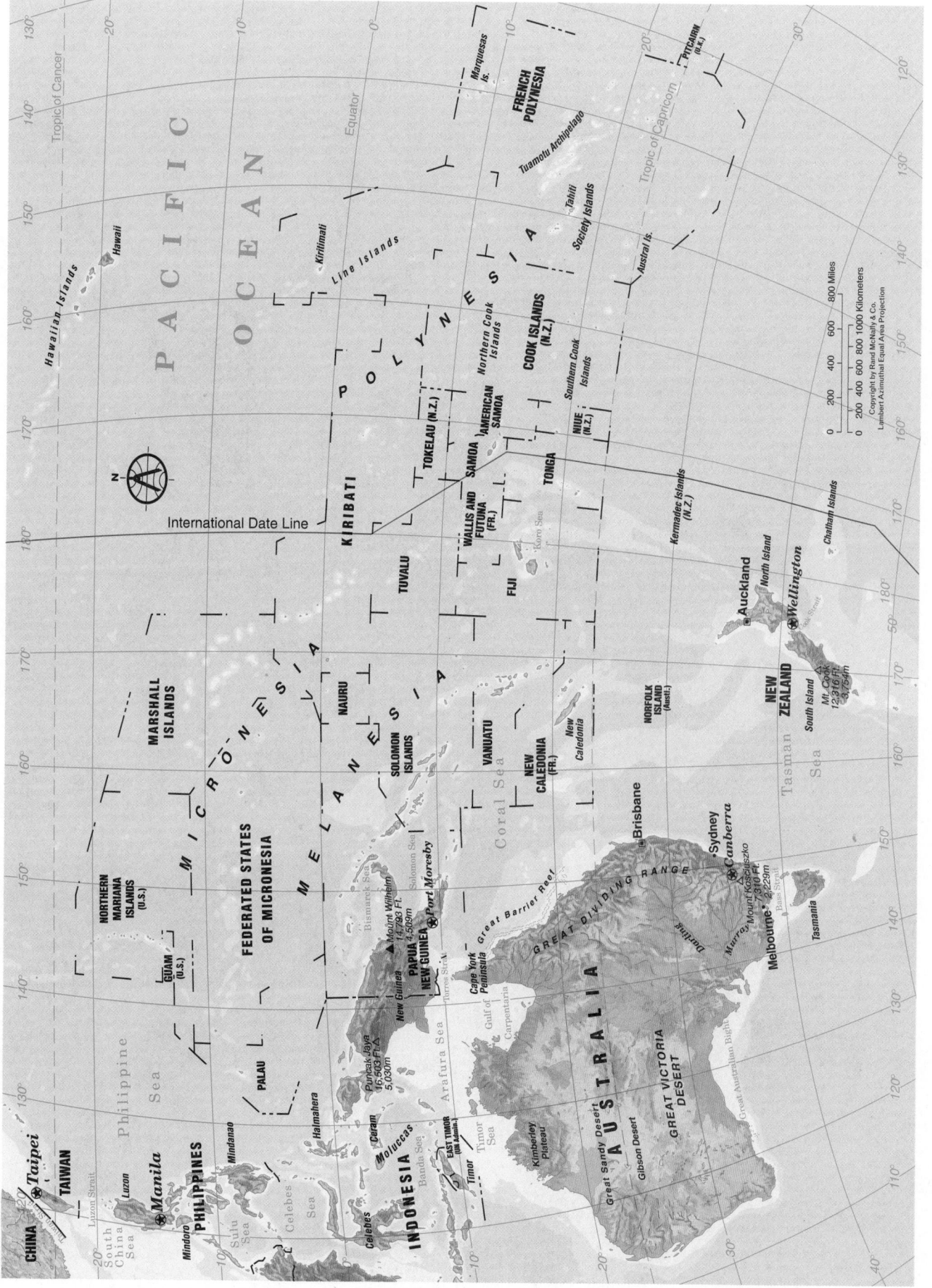

## Australia and Oceania

**PACIFIC OCEAN**

Tropic of Cancer

130°  140°  150°  160°  170°  180°  170°  160°  150°  140°  130°  120°

20°

Hawaiian Islands
Hawaii

10°

Equator

Marquesas Is.

Kiritimati

**FRENCH POLYNESIA**

Line Islands

Tuamotu Archipelago

Tahiti
Society Islands

Tropic of Capricorn

Austral Is.

**PITCAIRN** (U.K.)

20°

**P O L Y N E S I A**

Northern Cook Islands

**COOK ISLANDS** (N.Z.)

Southern Cook Islands

**NIUE** (N.Z.)

800 Miles
0  200  400  600  800  1000 Kilometers
0  200  400  600  800 1000
Copyright by Rand McNally & Co.
Lambert Azimuthal Equal Area Projection

**TOKELAU** (N.Z.)

N

**AMERICAN SAMOA**

**SAMOA**

**KIRIBATI**

International Date Line

**WALLIS AND FUTUNA** (FR.)

**TONGA**

Koro Sea

Kermadec Islands (N.Z.)

Chatham Islands

**TUVALU**

**FIJI**

**M I C R O N E S I A**

**MARSHALL ISLANDS**

**NAURU**

**M E L A N E S I A**

**VANUATU**

**NEW CALEDONIA** (FR.)

New Caledonia

**NORFOLK ISLAND** (Austl.)

Auckland
North Island

Wellington

**NEW ZEALAND**

South Island
Mt. Cook
12,316 Ft.
3,754m

Tasman Sea

Cook Strait

**NORTHERN MARIANA ISLANDS** (U.S.)

**FEDERATED STATES OF MICRONESIA**

**SOLOMON ISLANDS**

Bismarck Sea

Solomon Sea

Coral Sea

Brisbane

Sydney
Canberra

**GUAM** (U.S.)

Mount Wilhelm
14,793 Ft.
4,509m

**PAPUA NEW GUINEA**

Port Moresby

Cape York Peninsula

Great Barrier Reef

**GREAT DIVIDING RANGE**

Mount Kosciuszko
7,310 Ft.
2,229m

Melbourne

Murray

Darling

Bass Strait

Tasmania

**PALAU**

New Guinea

Puncak Jaya
16,503 Ft.
5,030m

Torres Strait

Gulf of Carpentaria

**A U S T R A L I A**

Great Sandy Desert

Kimberley Plateau

**GREAT VICTORIA DESERT**

Gibson Desert

Great Australian Bight

**CHINA**

Taipei
**TAIWAN**

Luzon Strait

Manila
**PHILIPPINES**

Luzon

Mindoro

Mindanao

South China Sea

Sulu Sea

Philippine Sea

Celebes Sea

Halmahera

Ceram

Moluccas

**EAST TIMOR** (UN Admin.)

**INDONESIA**

Celebes

Banda Sea

Timor

Timor Sea

Arafura Sea

A T L A N T I C

O C E A N

ICELAND

*Horn*

*Fontur*

*Surtsey*

Arctic Circle

NORWEGIAN
SEA

*Lofoten Islands*

△Kebnekaise
6,926 Ft.
2,111m

FAROE ISLANDS
(Den.)

Scandinavian
Peninsula

NORWAY   SWEDEN

Galdhøpiggen △
8,100 Ft.
2,469m

*Hebrides*

*Orkney
Islands*

*Grampian
Mts.*

*Cheviot
Hills*

UNITED

KINGDOM

IRELAND

*Irish
Sea*

Great
Britain

*Thames*

⊛ London

N O R T H
S E A

*Skagerrak*

Stockholm ⊛

*Vänern*

*Vättern*

*Öland*

DENMARK

*Bornholm
(Den.)*

Northern  Eu

*Dalälven*

Berlin
⊛

*Elbe*

*Oder*

GERMANY

POLAND

NETHERLANDS

BELGIUM

*Rhine*

LUX.

*St. George's Channel*

English  Channel

*Strait of Dover*

CZECH
REPUBLIC

SLOVAK

*Bohemian
Forest*

*Danube*

⊛ Paris
Paris
Basin

*Seine*

*Saône*

*Jura*

*Black
Forest*

*Loire*

FRANCE

Bay of Biscay

*Cantabrian Mts.*

*Duero*

*Iberian Mts.*

*Dordogne*

Massif
Central

Mt. Blanc
15,771 Ft.
4,808m

SWITZERLAND  LIECH.

*Po*

AUSTRIA

HUNGARY

*Drava*

Great Hun

Great Plai

SLOVENIA

CROATIA

BOSNIA AND
HERZEGOVINA

Bal

YUGOS

*Pyrenees*

ANDORRA

*Rhône*

*Apennines*

SAN
MARINO

*Adriatic Alps*

ADRIATIC SEA

PORTUGAL

*Duero*

Iberian
Peninsula

*Tagus*

SPAIN

Lisbon ⊛

*Ebro*

MONACO

*Corsica
(Fr.)*

Rome ⊛

ITALY

ALBANIA

Pir

Sierra Morena

Balearic Islands

*Minorca*

*Ibiza*

*Majorca*

*Sardinia
(It.)*

△Vesuvius
4,190 Ft.
1,277m

TYRRHENIAN
SEA

IONIAN
SEA

*Strait of Gibraltar*

GIBRALTAR
(U.K.)

M E D I T E R R A N

⊛ Algiers

Mt. Etna
10,902 Ft.
3,323m△

*Sicily*

MOROCCO

A F R I C A

ALGERIA

TUNISIA

MALTA

0   100   200   300   400 Miles
0   200   400   600 Kilometers

Copyright by Rand McNally & Co.
Lambert Conformal Conic Projection

Murmansk

Kola
Peninsula
*Ponoy*

WHITE SEA

*Timan Ridge*

*Pechora*

*Ob'*

*Irtysh*

*Mezen*

*Onega*

Northern Dvina

*Sukhona*

Northern Uvals
(Uplands)

*Kama*

Ural Mountains

AND

Lake
Onega

Lake
Ladoga

...sinki

...nland

Lake
Peipus

Rybinsk
Res.

RUSSIA

ASIA

LA

ATVIA

Valdai
Hills

Moscow

*Oka*

... Plain

*Neman*

Central
Russian
Upland

*Don*

*Khopër*

*Ural*

KAZAKHSTAN

*Syr Darya*

Aral Sea

ANIA

BELARUS

*Pripyat*

Dnieper

Lowland

Donets Basin

Caspian Depression

UZBEKISTAN

*Amu Darya*

Kiev

UKRAINE

*Dnieper*

*Volga*

...ster

MOLDOVA

Sea of Azov

TURKMENISTAN

...ian Mts

ANIA

Crimean
Peninsula

CASPIAN SEA

...ian Alps

*Danube*

BLACK SEA

Mt. Elbrus
18,510 Ft.
5,642m

Caucasus

GEORGIA

Baku

...nsula

AZERBAIJAN

BULGARIA

ARMENIA

AZER.

Istanbul

Tehran

IRAN

...mpus

TURKEY

...EAN SEA

...ECE

Rhodes

NORTH
CYPRUS

SYRIA

*Euphrates*

IRAQ

Crete

SEA

CYPRUS

LEBANON

*Tigris*

ATLANTIC
OCEAN

ICELAND

ARCTIC OCE

Arctic Circle

FAROE ISLANDS (Den.)

IRELAND

UNITED KINGDOM

London

NORTH SEA

NORWAY

SWEDEN

Barents Sea

Novaya Zemlya

Kara Sea

Yamal Pen.

PORTUGAL

SPAIN

MOROCCO

GIBRALTAR

FRANCE

DENMARK

NETH.

GERMANY

POLAND

BELARUS

LITH.

LATVIA

ESTONIA

FINLAND

Moscow

Ural Mountains

West Siberian Lowland

Novosi

Ob

ALGERIA

TUNISIA

ITALY

AUSTRIA

HUNGARY

SLOVAKIA

CZECH REP.

SWITZ.

SLOVENIA

CROATIA

BOS.

YUGO.

ALB.

MAC.

ROMANIA

BULGARIA

MOLDOVA

UKRAINE

Volga

Astana

KAZAKHSTAN

Irtysh

Ishim

Ob

Mediterranean Sea

GREECE

Black Sea

Ankara

TURKEY

GEORGIA

Caucasus

ARM.

AZER.

Caspian Depression

Aral Sea

Caspian Sea

Ust-Urt Plateau

UZBEKISTAN

Syr Darya

Lake Balkhash

Tian Shan

LIBYA

N. CYPRUS

CYPRUS

LEBANON

ISRAEL

SYRIA

Mount Ararat 16,940 ft. 5,165m

Tigris

Euphrates

Tehran

Dasht-e Kavir

IRAN

Kara Kum (Desert)

Amu Darya

TURKMENISTAN

KYRGYZSTAN

TAJIKISTAN

Pamirs

Tarim Basin

K2 (Qogir Feng) 28,250 Ft. 8,611m

Kunlu

Alt

EGYPT

Nile

Sinai Pen.

JORDAN

IRAQ

KUWAIT

Zagros Mts.

Hindu Kush

AFGHANISTAN

CHAD

An-Nafud

SAUDI ARABIA

BAHRAIN

QATAR

Persian Gulf

U.A.E.

Gulf of Oman

PAKISTAN

New Delhi

Indus

Great Indian Desert

NEPAL

HIMALAYA

Mt. E 29,

SUDAN

Red Sea

Arabian Peninsula

Rub Al-Khali

OMAN

Ganges

Cairo

ERITREA

YEMEN

Gulf of Aden

Socotra (Yem.)

INDIA

Mumbai (Bombay)

Godavari

DEM. REP. OF THE CONGO (ZAIRE)

DJIBOUTI

ETHIOPIA

Arabian Sea

Lakshadweep (India)

Deccan Plateau

Western Ghats

Eastern Ghats

B

Bo

RWANDA

BURUNDI

UGANDA

KENYA

SOMALIA

N

SRI LANKA

TANZANIA

MALDIVES

INDIAN OCEAN

ZAMBIA

MALAWI

MOZAMBIQUE

0   200   400   600   800 Miles

0   200  400  600  800  1000 Kilometers

Copyright by Rand McNally & Co.
Lambert Azimuthal Equal Area Projection

RAND McNALLY

RUSSIA

New Siberian Islands

East Siberian Sea

Laptev Sea

Kolyma

Indigirka

Verkhoyansk Mts.

Lena

Stanovoy Range

Central ...berian ...nds

...r Peninsula

Amur

Lake Baikal

Greater Khingan Range

... Mountains

...i Mts.

MONGOLIA

Gobi Desert

Beijing

Qilian Shan

CHINA

Qinling Shandi

Chang (Yangtze)

Xi

...aputra

Irrawaddy

Salween

Red

Gulf of Tonkin

MYANMAR

LAOS

THAILAND

Bangkok

CAMBODIA

VIETNAM

Mekong

Andaman Sea

Gulf of Thailand

MALAY PENINSULA

MALAYSIA

Str. of Malacca

Singapore

Sumatra

Greater Sunda Islands

Jakarta

Java

Java Sea

INDONESIA

Borneo

BRUNEI

MALAYSIA

Celebes

Celebes Sea

Ceram

Banda Sea

Moluccas

New Guinea

PAPUA NEW GUINEA

Arafura Sea

Gulf of Carpentaria

Coral Sea

AUSTRALIA

Timor Sea

EAST TIMOR (UN Admin.)

Timor

Sea of Okhotsk

Kamchatka Peninsula

Sakhalin

Kuril Islands

Tatar Strait

Sikhote-Alin Mts.

Hokkaido

Sea of Japan

Honshu

Tokyo

JAPAN

Mt. Fuji 12,388 Ft. 3,776m

Shikoku

Kyushu

NORTH KOREA

SOUTH KOREA

Yellow Sea

Shanghai

East China Sea

TAIWAN

Luzon Strait

Luzon

Hainan Island

South China Sea

Manila

PHILIPPINES

Mindanao

Sulu Sea

Bering Sea

Aleutian Islands (U.S.)

PACIFIC OCEAN

Tropic of Cancer

NORTHERN MARIANA ISLANDS (U.S.)

Philippine Sea

GUAM (U.S.)

FEDERATED STATES OF MICRONESIA

PALAU

Equator

70 60 50 40 30 170 180 20 10 150 140 130 120 100

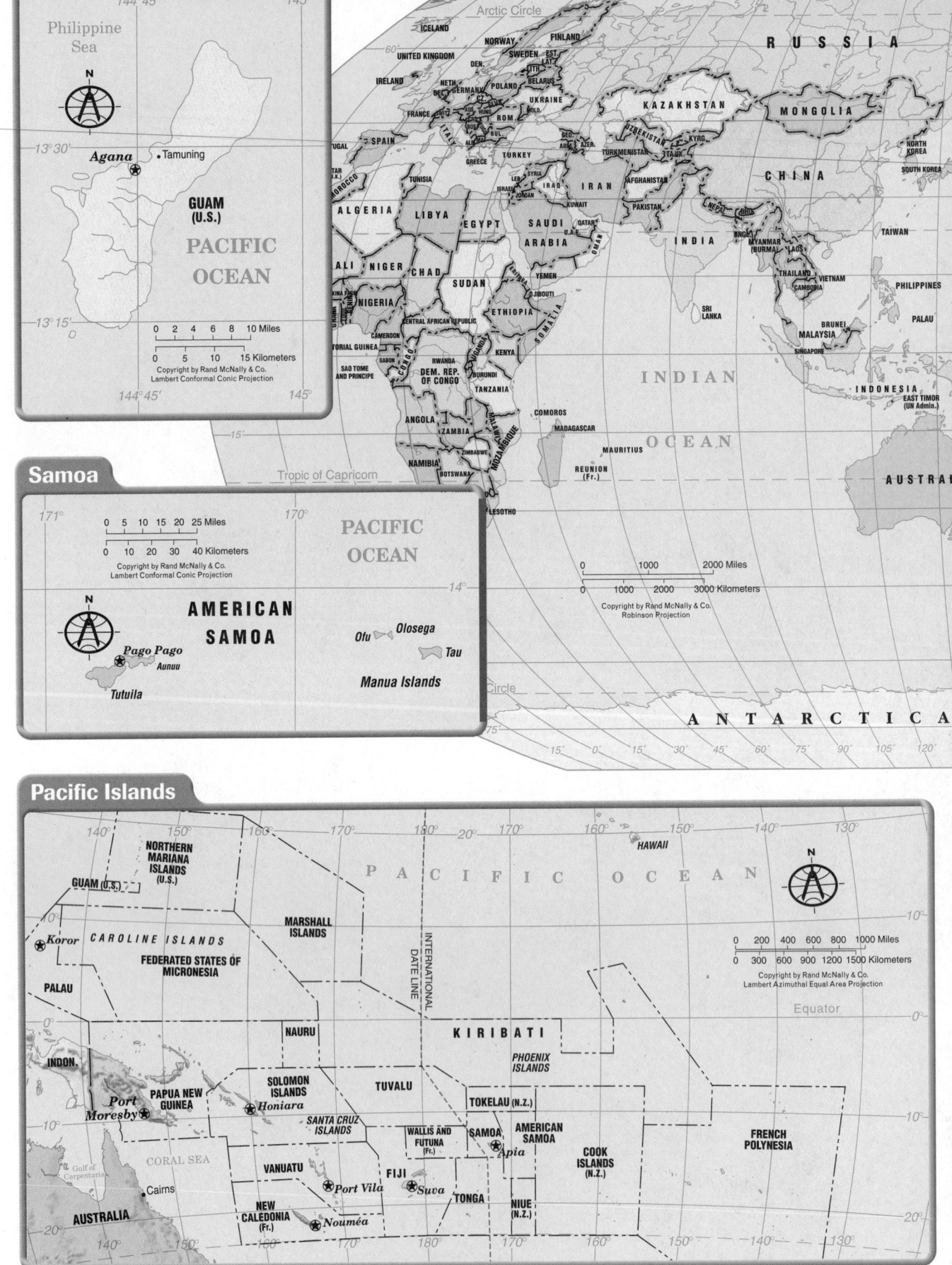

## Guam

Philippine Sea

N

144°45'    145°

13°30'    • Agana    • Tamuning

GUAM
(U.S.)

PACIFIC

OCEAN

13°15'

0  2  4  6  8  10 Miles

0   5    10    15 Kilometers
Copyright by Rand McNally & Co.
Lambert Conformal Conic Projection

144°45'    145°

## Samoa

171°    170°

0  5  10  15  20  25 Miles

0   10   20   30   40 Kilometers
Copyright by Rand McNally & Co.
Lambert Conformal Conic Projection

PACIFIC

OCEAN

14°

N

AMERICAN
SAMOA

Ofu ⊃⊂ Olosega
Tau

Pago Pago
Aunuu

Manua Islands

Tutuila

## Pacific Islands

140°    150°    160°    170°    180°   20°   170°    160°    150°    140°    130°

PACIFIC    OCEAN

HAWAII

N

NORTHERN
MARIANA
ISLANDS
(U.S.)

GUAM (U.S.)

0°

MARSHALL
ISLANDS

0  200  400  600  800  1000 Miles

0  300  600  900  1200  1500 Kilometers
Copyright by Rand McNally & Co.
Lambert Azimuthal Equal Area Projection

⊛ Koror    CAROLINE ISLANDS

FEDERATED STATES OF
MICRONESIA

INTERNATIONAL DATE LINE

10°

PALAU

Equator    0°

NAURU    KIRIBATI

INDON.    PHOENIX
ISLANDS

Port    PAPUA NEW    SOLOMON    TUVALU    TOKELAU (N.Z.)
Moresby ⊛  GUINEA    ISLANDS
⊛ Honiara
SANTA CRUZ
ISLANDS    WALLIS AND
FUTUNA    SAMOA    AMERICAN
(Fr.)    SAMOA    COOK
ISLANDS    FRENCH
POLYNESIA
(N.Z.)

Gulf of
Carpentaria    ⊛ Apia

CORAL SEA    VANUATU
Cairns    FIJI
⊛ Port Vila    ⊛ Suva    NIUE
(N.Z.)
AUSTRALIA    NEW
CALEDONIA    TONGA
(Fr.)    ⊛ Nouméa

140°    150°    160°    170°    180°    170°    160°    150°    140°    130°

Arctic Circle
ICELAND
UNITED KINGDOM    NORWAY    SWEDEN    FINLAND    EST.
IRELAND    DEN.    LITH. LAT.
NETH.    GERMANY    POLAND    BELARUS    RUSSIA
FRANCE    AUS.    CZ.    UKRAINE    KAZAKHSTAN    MONGOLIA
ITALY    ROM.    KYRG.
PORTUGAL    SPAIN    GEO.    UZBEKISTAN    NORTH
GREECE    TURKEY    ARM. AZER.    TURKMENISTAN    TAJIK.    CHINA    KOREA
MOROCCO    SYRIA    IRAQ    IRAN    AFGHANISTAN    SOUTH KOREA
TUNISIA    ISRAEL    JORDAN    PAKISTAN    NEPAL    TAIWAN
ALGERIA    LIBYA    EGYPT    SAUDI    QATAR    INDIA    MYANMAR    LAOS
ARABIA    U.A.E.    OMAN    (BURMA)    PHILIPPINES
MALI    NIGER    CHAD    SUDAN    YEMEN    THAILAND    VIETNAM    PALAU
NIGERIA    DJIBOUTI    CAMBODIA    BRUNEI
SRI    MALAYSIA
ETHIOPIA    LANKA    SINGAPORE    INDONESIA
CENTRAL AFRICAN REPUBLIC    EAST TIMOR
EQUATORIAL GUINEA    CAMEROON    KENYA    INDIAN    (UN Admin.)
SAO TOME    GABON    DEM. REP.    RWANDA    SOMALIA
AND PRINCIPE    OF CONGO    BURUNDI    UGANDA
CONGO    TANZANIA    OCEAN
ANGOLA    ZAMBIA    COMOROS    AUSTRAL
ZIMBABWE    MADAGASCAR
Tropic of Capricorn    MAURITIUS
NAMIBIA    MOZAMBIQUE    REUNION
BOTSWANA    (Fr.)
LESOTHO

0    1000    2000 Miles

0   1000   2000    3000 Kilometers
Copyright by Rand McNally & Co.
Robinson Projection

Circle

75°

ANTARCTICA

15°  0°  15°  30°  45°  60°  75°  90°  105°  120°

ARCTIC OCEAN

GREENLAND (Den.)

Arctic Circle

CANADA

UNITED STATES

ATLANTIC

BERMUDA (U.K)

OCEAN

Tropic of Cancer

MEXICO

CUBA

BAHAMAS

DOM. REP.
HAITI
PUERTO RICO
U.S. VIRGIN ISLANDS

BELIZE
GUAT. HOND.
EL. SAL. NIC.
JAMAICA

Navassa
Island

International Date Line

MIDWAY ISLANDS

WAKE ISLAND

Johnston Atoll

PACIFIC

N

COSTA
RICA
PANAMA

TRINIDAD AND TOBAGO

VENEZUELA
GUYANA
SURINAME
FRENCH GUIANA

MARSHALL ISLANDS

Palmyra Atoll    Kingman Reef

COLOMBIA

ATES

ESIA

NAURU    KIRIBATI

Howland Island
Baker Island    Jarvis Island

Equator

ECUADOR

0°

OCEAN

SOLOMON ISLANDS

TUVALU

TOKELAU (N.Z.)

PERU

BRAZIL

SAMOA

NEW
EDONIA
FR.)

VANUATU

AMERICAN SAMOA

BOLIVIA

FIJI

NIUE (N.Z.)

COOK ISLANDS (N.Z.)

FRENCH POLYNESIA

PARAGUAY

TONGA

Tropic of Capricorn

NORFOLK ISLAND (Austl.)

ARGENTINA

URUGUAY

NEW ZEALAND

FALKLAND ISLANDS (U.K)

Antarctic Circle

## Puerto Rico and the U.S. Virgin Islands

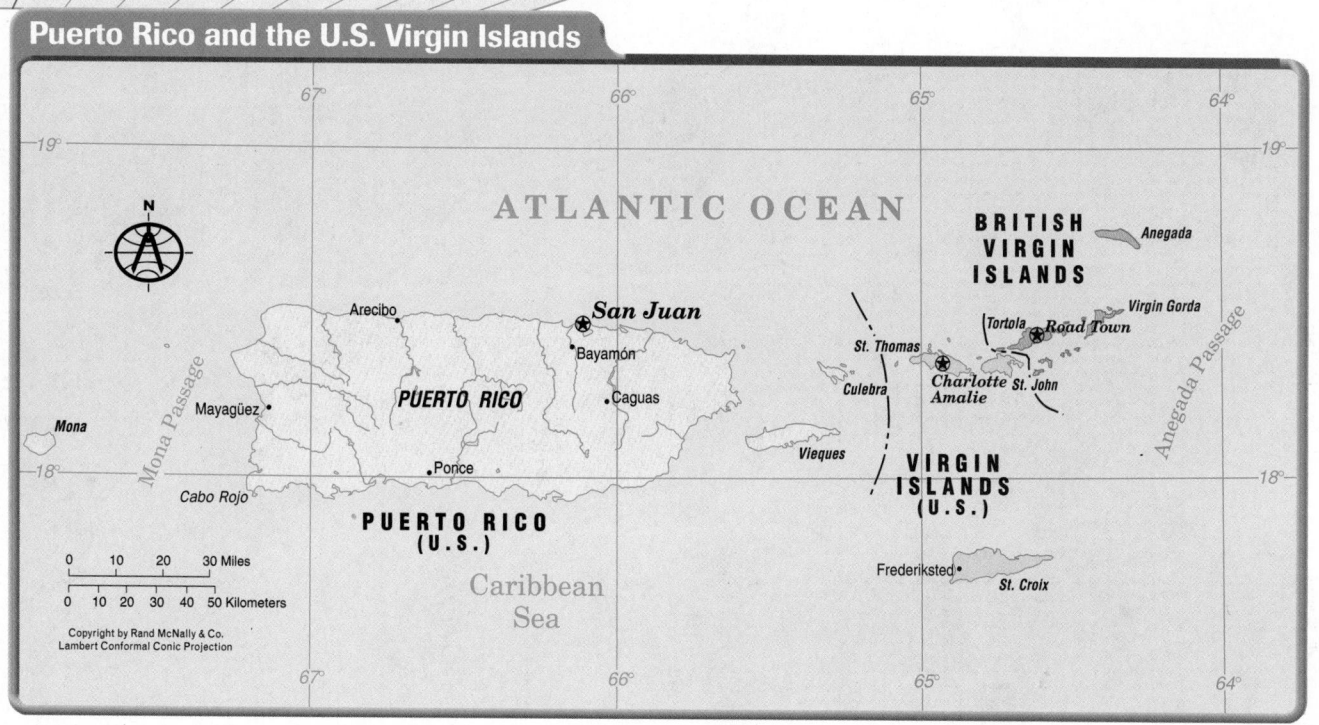

ATLANTIC OCEAN

BRITISH VIRGIN ISLANDS

Anegada

N

Arecibo

San Juan

Bayamón

Virgin Gorda

Tortola    Road Town

St. Thomas

Mona

Mayagüez

PUERTO RICO

Caguas

Culebra

Charlotte
Amalie    St. John

Mona Passage

Ponce

Vieques

VIRGIN ISLANDS (U.S.)

Anegada Passage

Cabo Rojo

PUERTO RICO (U.S.)

Caribbean
Sea

Frederiksted    St. Croix

0    10    20    30 Miles
0    10    20    30    40    50 Kilometers

Copyright by Rand McNally & Co.
Lambert Conformal Conic Projection

RAND McNALLY

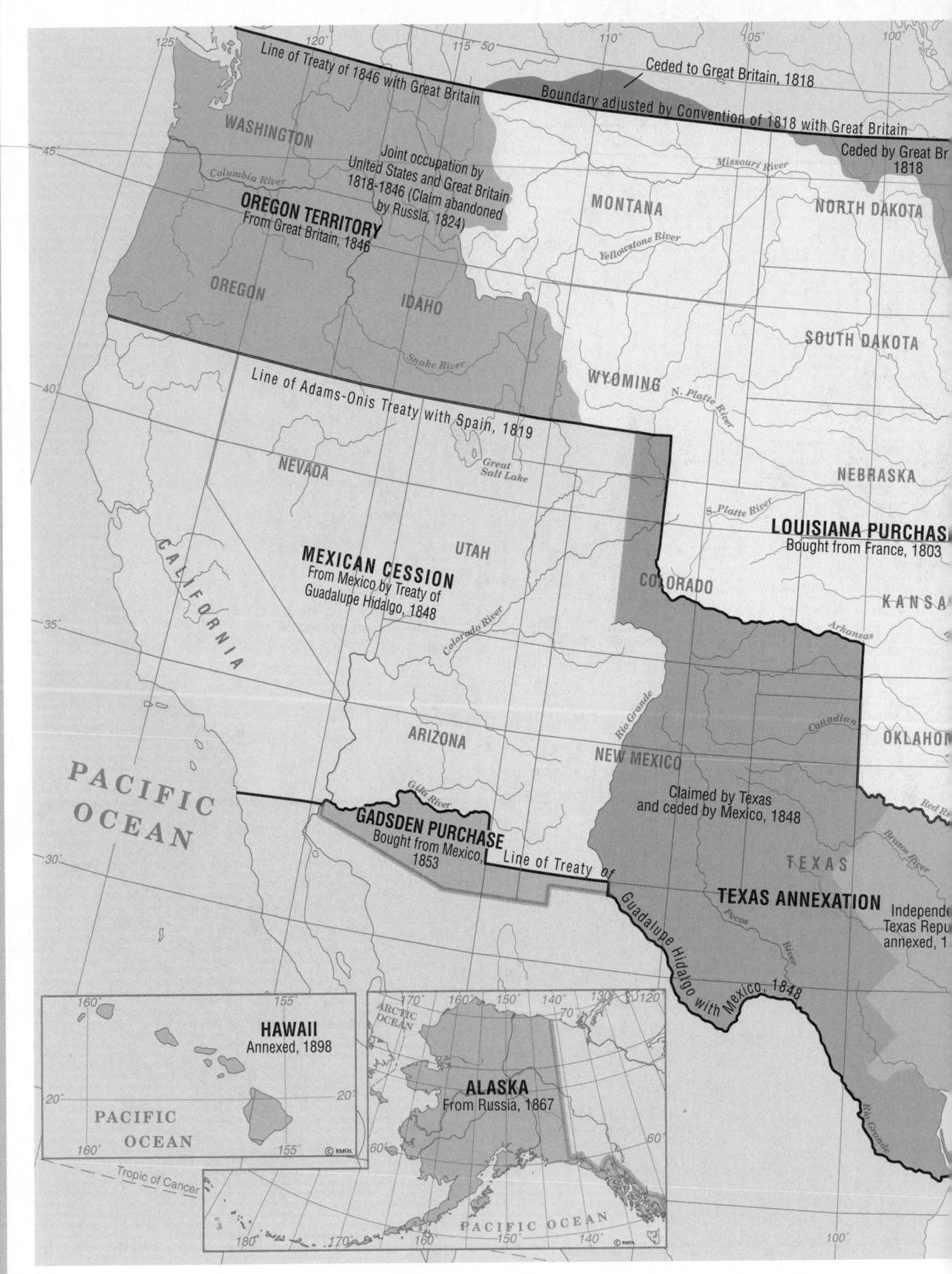

Line of Treaty of 1846 with Great Britain

Ceded to Great Britain, 1818

Boundary adjusted by Convention of 1818 with Great Britain

Ceded by Great Br
1818

WASHINGTON

MONTANA

NORTH DAKOTA

Columbia River

Missouri River

Joint occupation by
United States and Great Britain
1818-1846 (Claim abandoned
by Russia, 1824)

**OREGON TERRITORY**
From Great Britain, 1846

Yellowstone River

OREGON

IDAHO

Snake River

SOUTH DAKOTA

WYOMING

Line of Adams-Onis Treaty with Spain, 1819

N. Platte River

NEVADA

Great
Salt Lake

NEBRASKA

S. Platte River

**LOUISIANA PURCHAS**
Bought from France, 1803

UTAH

**MEXICAN CESSION**
From Mexico by Treaty of
Guadalupe Hidalgo, 1848

COLORADO

KANSA

Colorado River

Arkansas

PACIFIC
OCEAN

ARIZONA

NEW MEXICO

Gila River

Rio Grande

Canadian

OKLAHOM

**GADSDEN PURCHASE**
Bought from Mexico,
1853

Line of Treaty of

Claimed by Texas
and ceded by Mexico, 1848

Red R

TEXAS

Brazos River

**TEXAS ANNEXATION**

Independe
Texas Repu
annexed, 1

Guadalupe Hidalgo with Mexico, 1848

Pecos

River

Rio Grande

160°    155°

**HAWAII**
Annexed, 1898

ARCTIC
OCEAN

170°  160° 150° 140°

70°

130°  120°

PACIFIC
OCEAN

20°

**ALASKA**
From Russia, 1867

PACIFIC
OCEAN

160°    155°

60°

60°

Tropic of Cancer

180°    170°    160°    150°    140°

PACIFIC OCEAN

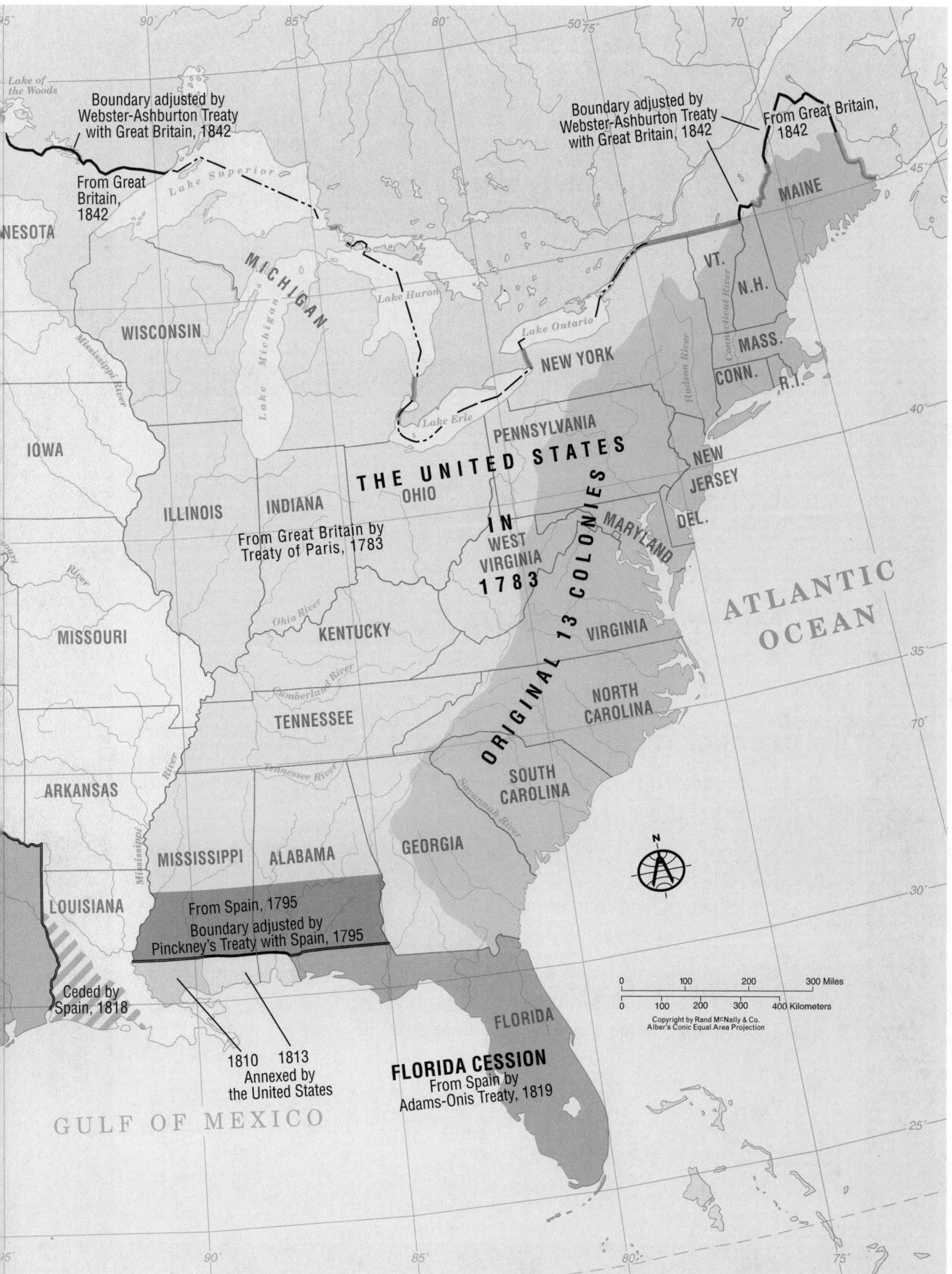

Boundary adjusted by
Webster-Ashburton Treaty
with Great Britain, 1842

From Great
Britain,
1842

Boundary adjusted by
Webster-Ashburton Treaty
with Great Britain, 1842

From Great Britain,
1842

MAINE

*Lake of
the Woods*

*Lake Superior*

NESOTA

MICHIGAN

*Lake Huron*

WISCONSIN

*Lake Michigan*

VT.

N.H.

*Connecticut River*

MASS.

CONN.

R.I.

*Lake Ontario*

NEW YORK

*Hudson River*

IOWA

*Lake Erie*

PENNSYLVANIA

THE UNITED STATES

*Mississippi River*

ILLINOIS

INDIANA

OHIO

NEW
JERSEY

DEL.

IN

From Great Britain by
Treaty of Paris, 1783

WEST
VIRGINIA

MARYLAND

*River*

*Ohio River*

1783

ORIGINAL 13 COLONIES

ATLANTIC
OCEAN

MISSOURI

KENTUCKY

VIRGINIA

*Cumberland River*

TENNESSEE

*Tennessee River*

NORTH
CAROLINA

ARKANSAS

*Mississippi River*

SOUTH
CAROLINA

*Savannah River*

MISSISSIPPI

ALABAMA

GEORGIA

From Spain, 1795

LOUISIANA

Boundary adjusted by
Pinckney's Treaty with Spain, 1795

Ceded by
Spain, 1818

1810    1813
Annexed by
the United States

FLORIDA

FLORIDA CESSION
From Spain by
Adams-Onis Treaty, 1819

GULF OF MEXICO

N

0        100        200        300 Miles
0    100    200    300    400 Kilometers
Copyright by Rand McNally & Co.
Alber's Conic Equal Area Projection

# The AMERICANS
### Reconstruction to the 21st Century

## REFERENCE SECTION

# SKILLBUILDER HANDBOOK

# 1.1 Finding Main Ideas

### DEFINING THE SKILL

**Finding main ideas** means identifying words that sum up the single most important thought in an entire paragraph or section. To find the main idea of a passage, identify the topic. Then, as you read, ask, What central idea do the many details explain or support?

### APPLYING THE SKILL

This excerpt from President Richard M. Nixon's memoirs is about wiretapping, or bugging—planting a concealed microphone to get information. The diagram that follows identifies and organizes information in the passage.

### HOW TO FIND MAIN IDEAS

**Strategy** ❶ Identify the topic by looking at the title, or by looking for key words. This passage repeats the words *bugged, bugging, tapped,* and *wiretap.*

**Strategy** ❷ Look for a topic sentence. Ask whether any one sentence sums up the point of the whole passage. In this passage, the second sentence states Nixon's attitude toward bugging.

**Strategy** ❸ Look for details or examples. The many examples support the attitude that wiretapping was a common practice.

> **NIXON ON WIRETAPPING ❶**
>
> I had been in politics too long, and seen everything from dirty tricks to vote fraud. ❷ I could not muster much moral outrage over a political ❶ bugging.
>
> Larry O'Brien [director of the Democratic National Committee] might affect astonishment and horror, but he knew as well as I did that political bugging had been around nearly since the invention of the wiretap. ❸ As recently as 1970 a former member of Adlai Stevenson's [Democratic candidate for president in 1952 and 1956] campaign staff had publicly stated that he had tapped the [John F.] Kennedy organization's phone lines at the 1960 Democratic convention. ❸ Lyndon Johnson felt that the Kennedys had had him tapped; ❸ Barry Goldwater said that his 1964 campaign had been bugged; ❸ and Edgar Hoover [director of the FBI, 1924–1972] told me that in 1968 Johnson had ordered my campaign plane bugged.
>
> Source: Richard Nixon, *The Memoirs of Richard Nixon* (New York: Grosset & Dunlap, 1978), pp. 628–629.

### Make a Diagram

State the topic and list the supporting details in a chart. Use the information you record to help you state the main idea.

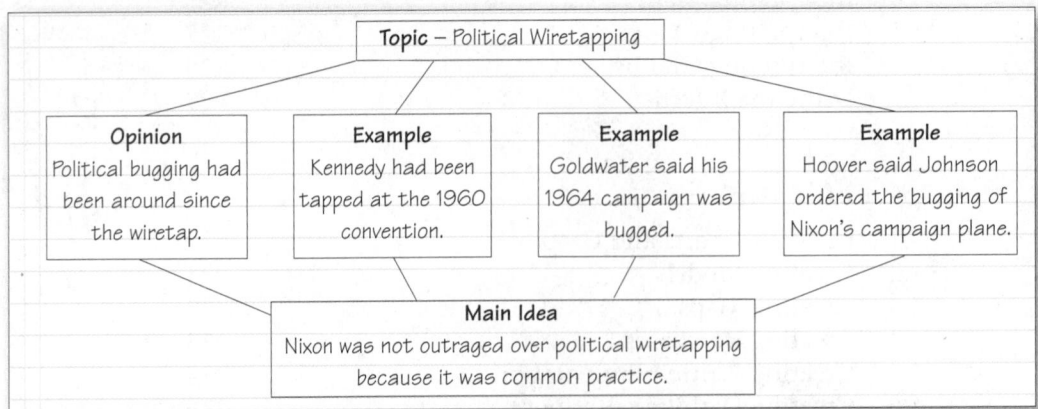

### PRACTICING THE SKILL

Turn to Chapter 26, Section 3, p. 879 and read the passage headed "Space Exploration." Make a diagram, like the one above, to identify the topic, the most important details, and the main idea of the passage.

# 1.2 Following Chronological Order

## DEFINING THE SKILL

**Chronological order** is "time order"—the sequence of events in time. Chronology may be either relative or absolute. Relative chronology relates one event to another. This helps historians to see causes, effects, and other relationships between events. Absolute chronology ties events to an exact time or date, pinpointing dates in one universal framework—the passage of time.

## APPLYING THE SKILL

The following paragraph is about several events leading up to the Watergate scandal that brought down the Nixon administration. The time line that follows puts the events of the passage in chronological order.

## HOW TO FOLLOW CHRONOLOGICAL ORDER

**Strategy** ① Look for clue words about time. These are words like *initial*, *first*, *next*, *then*, *before*, *after*, *finally*, and *by that time*.

**Strategy** ② Use specific dates provided in the text.

**Strategy** ③ Watch for references to previous historical events that are included in the background. Usually a change in verb tense will indicate a previous event.

> ### The Pentagon Papers
>
> The ① initial event that many historians believe led to Watergate took place on ② June 13, 1971, when the *New York Times* began publishing articles called the Pentagon Papers, which divulged government secrets about the U.S. involvement in Vietnam. The information had been leaked by a former Defense Department official, Daniel Ellsberg. The Justice Department asked the courts to suppress publication of the articles, but on ② July 30, 1971, the Supreme Court ruled that the information could be published. ① Two months later, in September, a group of special White House agents known as the plumbers burglarized the office of Ellsberg's psychiatrist in a vain attempt to find evidence against Ellsberg. President Nixon ③ had authorized the creation of the plumbers in 1971, after the Pentagon Papers were published, to keep government secrets from leaking to the media and to help ensure his reelection in November 1972.

## Make a Time Line

If the events in a passage are numerous and complex, make a time line to represent them. The time line here lists the events from the passage above in time order.

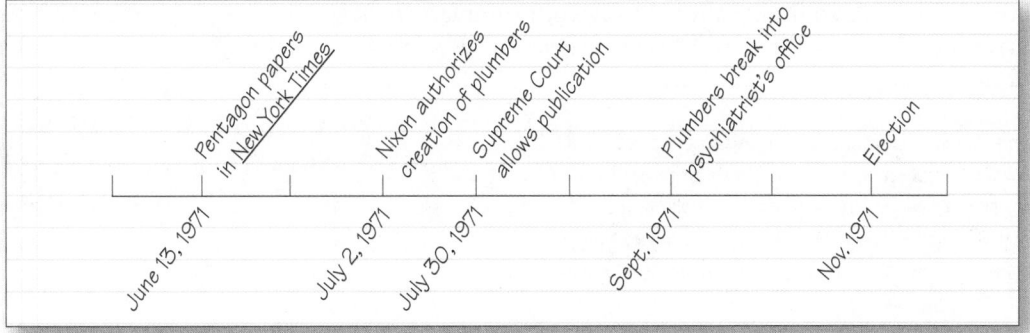

## PRACTICING THE SKILL

Skim, Chapter 21, Section 2, p. 710 "The Triumphs of a Crusade," to find out how the civil rights movement helped end segregation in the South. Make a list of the important dates you find, starting with the freedom ride in May 1961 and ending with the passage of the Voting Rights Act of 1965. Use the model above to help you create your own time line, showing what happened on each date.

# 1.3 Clarifying; Summarizing

### DEFINING THE SKILL

**Clarifying** means checking to be sure you clearly understand what you have read. One way to do this is by asking yourself questions. In your answers, you might restate in your own words what you have read.

When you **summarize,** you condense what you have read into fewer words, stating only the main idea and the most important supporting details. It is important to use your own words in a summary.

### APPLYING THE SKILL

The excerpt below describes a major oil spill. Following the excerpt is a summary that condenses the key information in the passage into a few sentences.

### HOW TO SUMMARIZE

**Strategy 1** Look for topic sentences stating the main ideas. These are often at the beginning of a section or paragraph. In a summary, rewrite the main ideas in your own words.

**Strategy 2** Include only the most important facts and statistics. Pay attention to numbers, dates, quantities, and other data.

**Strategy 3** Clarify understanding by asking questions. Also, look up any words you do not recognize.

---

**THE EXXON VALDEZ OIL SPILL**

**1** In March 1989, the oil tanker *Exxon Valdez* ran aground in Prince William Sound along the coast of Alaska, dumping about **2** 11 million gallons of crude oil into the sea. Within days, 1,800 miles of coastline were fouled with thick black oil that coated rocks and beaches. At least 10 percent of the area's birds, sea otters, and other animals were killed, and commercial fisheries estimated that they would lose at least 50 percent of the season's catch.

The captain of the *Exxon Valdez* was found guilty of **3** negligence, and attempts were made to clean up the spill. **2** Four years later, however, scientists found that pools of oil buried in coves were still poisoning shellfish, otters, and ducks, while several bird species failed to reproduce.

**2** Between 1989 and 1994, Exxon spent about $2.1 billion in efforts to clean up Prince William Sound. In the meantime, some 34,000 commercial fishers and other Alaskans sued the company for damages, claiming that the oil spill had ruined their livelihoods.

---

### Write a Summary

You can write your summary in a paragraph. The paragraph below summarizes the passage about the *Exxon Valdez* oil spill. After writing your summary, review it to see that you have included only the most important details.

> In 1989, the *Exxon Valdez* ran aground off the Alaskan coast, spilling 11 million gallons of oil. The water and coastline for hundreds of miles were badly polluted, and many animals died. Alaskans sued the oil company for lost income. Exxon spent $2.1 billion for a cleanup effort and was subject to litigation from people who lost their livelihoods because of the spill.

### PRACTICING THE SKILLS

Turn to Chapter 14, Section 1, p. 464 and read the passage headed "Economic Troubles on the Horizon." Make notes of the main ideas. Look up any words you don't recognize. Then write a summary of the passage, using the model above as your guide.

**R4** SKILLBUILDER HANDBOOK

# 1.4 Identifying Problems

## DEFINING THE SKILL

**Identifying problems** means recognizing and understanding difficulties faced by particular people or groups at particular times. Being able to focus on specific problems helps historians understand the motives for actions and the forces underlying historical events.

## APPLYING THE SKILL

The following passage tells about the experience of newcomers to Northern cities, like Boston and Philadelphia, in the late 1800s. Below the passage is a chart that organizes the information the passage contains.

## HOW TO IDENTIFY PROBLEMS

**Strategy 1** Look for problems that are implied but not stated. Problems are sometimes stated indirectly. This sentence implies that many immigrants settled in the cities because of limited opportunities elsewhere.

**Strategy 2** Look for difficulties people faced.

**Strategy 3** Evalute solutions to problems.

**Strategy 4** Recognize that sometimes the solution to one problem may cause another problem.

### IMMIGRANT LIFE IN THE CITIES

1 The lure that drew many immigrants to America and its cities often was the same one that had attracted settlers to the West—opportunity. In the nation's industrialized centers people saw a chance to 2 escape poverty, find work, and carve out a better life.

Cities offered unskilled laborers steady jobs in mills and factories and provided the social support of neighborhoods of people with the same ethnic background. 3 Living among people who shared their background enabled the newcomers to speak their own language while learning about their new home. 4 Overcrowding soon became a problem, however—one that was intensified by the migration of people from America's rural areas.

## Make a Chart

The chart below summarizes the problems and solutions in the passage. The chart details what the problems were, what steps people took to solve the problems, and how those solutions affected them.

| Problems | Solutions | Outcomes |
|---|---|---|
| poverty | coming to U.S. cities | jobs available |
| lack of opportunity | coming to U.S. cities | jobs, housing, communities |
| lack of work skills | factory and mill jobs requiring low level of training | enough jobs for the time being |
| unfamiliarity with language | living in ethnic communities | community but overcrowding |

## PRACTICING THE SKILL

Turn to Chapter 23, Section 2, p. 776 and read the passage headed "Women Fight for Equality." Note the social and economic problems many women faced in the 1960s and 1970s. Then make a chart, like the one above, in which you summarize the information you found in the passage. Be sure to read to the end of the section so that you can evaluate the solutions attempted and their outcomes.

# 1.5 Analyzing Motives

## DEFINING THE SKILL

**Analyzing motives** in history means examining the reasons why a person, group, or government took a particular action. These reasons often go back to the needs, emotions, and prior experiences of the person or group, as well as their plans, circumstances, and objectives.

## APPLYING THE SKILL

The following paragraphs tells how the early Mormons were treated and why they moved west in the mid-1800s. The diagram below the passage summarizes the Mormons' motives for that journey.

## HOW TO ANALYZE MOTIVES

**Strategy** **1** Look for different kinds of motives. Some motives are negative, and others are positive.

**Strategy** **2** Look for the influence of important individuals or leaders in motivating others.

**Strategy** **3** Look for basic needs and human emotions as powerful motivators. Such needs and emotions include food and shelter, greed, ambition, compassion, and fear.

### The Mormon Migration

Some of the Mormons' beliefs alarmed and angered other Americans. **1** Plagued by persecution and violence and seeking to convert Native Americans, Mormon church founder Joseph Smith led his followers west from New York to a small community in Illinois. Conflict soon developed again when Smith allowed male members to have more than one wife. This idea infuriated many of Smith's neighbors, and he was eventually murdered by a mob.

**2** The Mormons rallied around a new leader, Brigham Young, who urged them to move farther west. There they encountered a desert area near a salt lake, just beyond the moutains of what was then part of Mexico. The salty water was useless for crops and animals. Because the land was not desirable to others, **3** Young realized that his people might be safe there. The Mormons began to build Salt Lake City.

### Make a Diagram

In the center of the diagram, list the important actions from the passage. Around it, list motives in different categories.

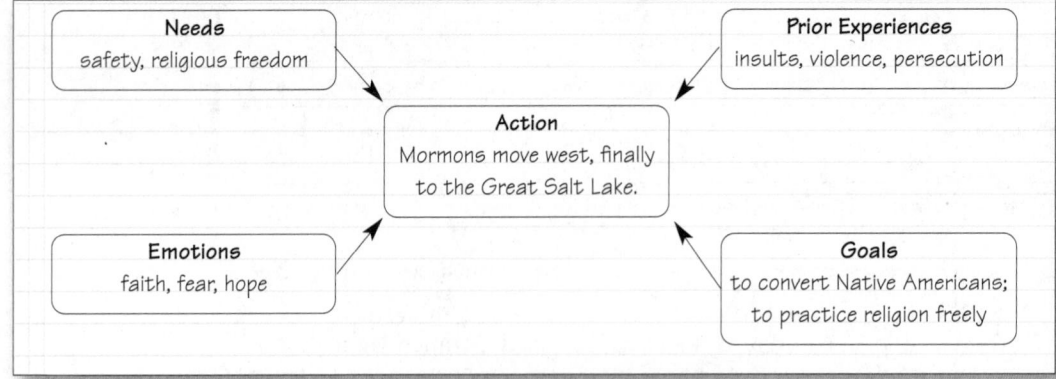

| Needs | | Prior Experiences |
| --- | --- | --- |
| safety, religious freedom | | insults, violence, persecution |

Action
Mormons move west, finally to the Great Salt Lake.

| Emotions | | Goals |
| --- | --- | --- |
| faith, fear, hope | | to convert Native Americans; to practice religion freely |

## PRACTICING THE SKILL

Turn to Chapter 17, Section 3, p. 583 and read the passage headed "The Atomic Bomb Ends the War." Take notes about President Truman's motives in dropping atomic bombs on Japan. Then create a diagram similar to the one shown here.

# 1.6 Analyzing Causes and Effects

## DEFINING THE SKILL
A **cause** is an action in history that prompts something to happen. An **effect** is a historical event or condition that is the result of the cause. A single event may have several causes. It is also possible for one cause to result in several effects. Historians identify cause-and-effect relationships to help them understand why historical events took place.

## APPLYING THE SKILL
The following paragraphs describe the early events leading to the Battle of Little Bighorn. The diagram that follows the passage summarizes the chain of causes and effects.

## HOW TO IDENTIFY CAUSES AND EFFECTS

**Strategy ❶** Look for reasons behind the events. Here the discovery of gold motivated white Americans to move into Sioux territory.

**Strategy ❷** Look for clue words indicating cause. These include *because, due to, since,* and *therefore.*

**Strategy ❸** Look for clue words indicating consequences. These include *brought about, led to, as a result, thus, consequently,* and *responded.* Remember that a cause may have several effects.

### Broken Treaties
The Treaty of 1868 had promised the Sioux that they could live forever in Paha Sapa, the Black Hills area of what is now South Dakota and Wyoming. The area was sacred to the Sioux. It was the center of their land and the place where warriors went to await visions from their guardian spirits.

Unfortunately for the Sioux, the Black Hills contained large deposits of gold. ❶ As soon as white Americans learned that gold had been discovered, they poured into the Native Americans' territory and began staking claims.

❷ Because the Sioux valued their land so highly, they appealed to the government to enforce the treaty terms and remove the miners. The government ❸ responded by offering to purchase the land from the Sioux. When the Sioux refused, the government sent in the Seventh Cavalry to remove the Native Americans.

## Make a Cause-and-Effect Diagram
Starting with the first cause in a series, fill in the boxes until you reach the end result.

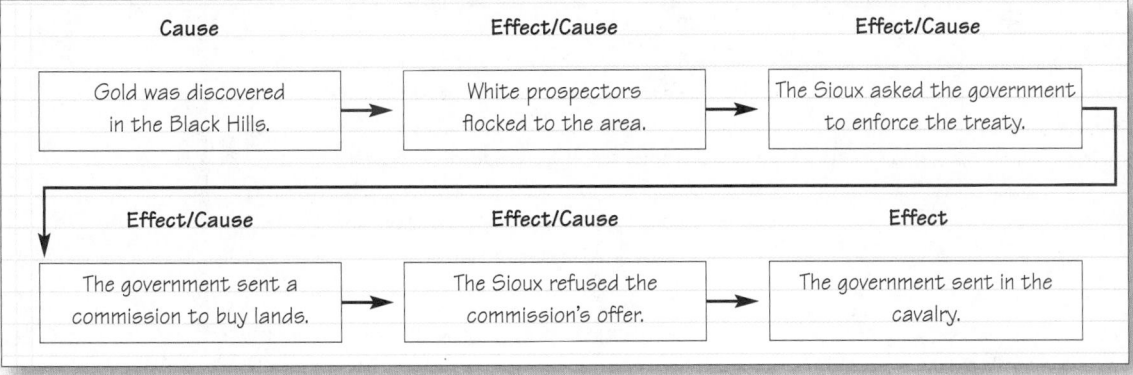

## PRACTICING THE SKILL
Turn to Chapter 11, Section 3, p. 392 and read the passage headed "African Americans and the War." Take notes about the causes and effects of African-American migration. Make a diagram, like the one shown above, to organize the information you find.

# 1.7 Comparing; Contrasting

## DEFINING THE SKILL

**Comparing** involves looking at the similarities and differences between two or more things. **Contrasting** means examining only the differences between them. Historians might compare and contrast events, personalities, beliefs, institutions, works of art, or many other types of things in order to give them a context for the period of history they are studying.

## APPLYING THE SKILL

The following passage describes life in colonial America during the last half of the 1600s. The Venn diagram below shows the similarities and differences between the Northern and Southern colonies.

## HOW TO COMPARE AND CONTRAST

**Strategy ①** Look for clue words that show how two things differ. Clue words include *different, differ, unlike, by contrast, however,* and *on the other hand.*

**Strategy ②** Look for clue words indicating that two things are alike. Clue words include *both, all, like, as, likewise,* and *similarly.*

**Strategy ③** Look for features that two things have in common.

### Life in the Early American Colonies

Not long after the English colonies were established, it became apparent that two very ① different ways of life were developing in the Northern and Southern colonies. In the South, both ② rich plantation owners and poorer frontier farmers sought land. Virginia and Maryland became known as the tobacco colonies. ③ Large farms, but few towns, appeared there.

Slavery existed in ③ all the colonies, but it became a vital source of labor in the South. ① By contrast, the New England and middle colonies did not rely on slave labor or single staple crops, such as tobacco or rice. Most people were farmers, but they grew a wide variety of crops. The New England colonies traded actively with the islands of the West Indies. In addition to foods, they exported all kinds of other items, ranging from barrels to horses. In return, they imported sugar and molasses. ③ All this trade resulted in the growth of small towns and larger port cities.

## Make a Venn Diagram

Use the two ovals to contrast the Northern and Southern colonies and the overlapping area to show what the two regions have in common.

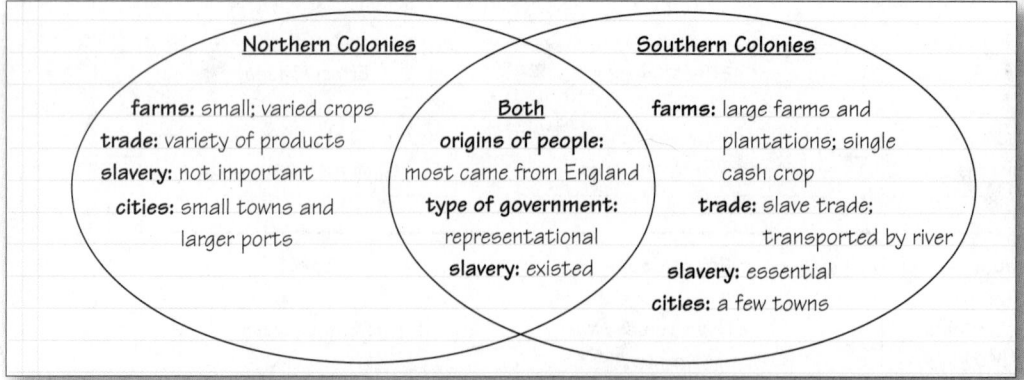

Northern Colonies

**farms:** small; varied crops
**trade:** variety of products
**slavery:** not important
**cities:** small towns and larger ports

Both

**origins of people:** most came from England
**type of government:** representational
**slavery:** existed

Southern Colonies

**farms:** large farms and plantations; single cash crop
**trade:** slave trade; transported by river
**slavery:** essential
**cities:** a few towns

## PRACTICING THE SKILL

Turn to Chapter 5, Section 1, pp. 202, 203 and read the passages headed "The Culture of the Plains Indians" and "Settlers Push Westward." Pay special attention to descriptions of the American settlers and Native Americans on the Great Plains. Make a Venn diagram showing what the two groups had in common and what made them different.

**R8** SKILLBUILDER HANDBOOK

# 1.8 Distinguishing Fact from Opinion

## DEFINING THE SKILL
**Facts** are dates, statistics, and accounts of events, or they are statements that are generally known to be true. Facts can be checked for accuracy.
**Opinions** are the judgments, beliefs, and feelings of a writer or speaker.

## APPLYING THE SKILL
The following excerpt describes the 1886 Haymarket affair in Chicago. The chart summarizes the facts and opinions.

## HOW TO DISTINGUISH FACT FROM OPINION

**Strategy ❶** Look for specific events, dates, and statistics that can be verified.

**Strategy ❷** Look for assertions, claims, hypotheses, and judgments. Here a speaker at the event is expressing an opinion.

**Strategy ❸** Look for judgments the historian makes about events. Here the writer states the opinion that the event was a disaster and then backs up this opinion by explaining the negative consequences of the event.

### The Haymarket Affair
❶ At ten o'clock another speaker stepped forward, the main burden of his address being that ❷ there was no hope of improving the condition of workingmen through legislation; it must be through their own efforts.

The speaker hurried to a conclusion, but at that point 180 police officers entered the square and headed for the speakers' platform. The captain in charge called on the meeting to disperse.

❶ At that moment someone threw a bomb into the ranks of the policemen gathered about the speakers. In response, the police opened fire on the crowd. One policeman had been killed by the bomb, and more than 60 injured. One member of the crowd was killed by police fire, and at least 12 were wounded. . . .

❸ In almost every . . . way Haymarket was a disaster. It vastly augmented [increased] the already considerable paranoia of most Americans in regard to anarchists, socialists, communists, and radicals in general. It increased hostility toward foreigners. And it caused a serious impairment of freedom of speech in every part of the country.

Source: Page Smith, *The Rise of Industrial America* (New York: Penguin, 1990), pp. 244–256.

## Make a Chart
List the facts you learn in a passage as well as the opinions that are expressed.

| Facts | Opinions |
|---|---|
| Just after 10:00, as a speaker was finishing up, someone threw a bomb into the group of 180 policemen surrounding the speakers. More than 60 police were injured, and about 13 civilians were injured or killed when police fired into the crowd. | speaker: Workers must improve their own situations since legislation can't do it for them. <br><br> historian: Nothing good came of the Haymarket affair; and in fact it had many negative consequences: <br> • increased paranoia about radicals <br> • increased hostility toward foreigners <br> • impaired freedom of speech |

## PRACTICING THE SKILL
Read Chapter 7, Section 3, p. 267, "The Emergence of Political Machines."
Make a chart in which you list some facts about political machines and some opinions on graft expressed in the passage.

# 1.9 Making Inferences

### DEFINING THE SKILL

**Making inferences** from a piece of historical writing means drawing conclusions based on facts, examples, opinions, and the author's use of language. To make inferences, use clues in the text and your own personal experience, historical knowledge, and common sense.

### APPLYING THE SKILL

The following passage is from a speech by President Ronald Reagan promoting his economic program. The chart below lists some inferences that can be drawn from the first paragraph.

### HOW TO MAKE INFERENCES

**Strategy** ❶ From the facts in the text and historical knowledge, you can infer that Reagan is blaming the Democrats for the poor economy.

**Strategy** ❷ Look for clues about the writer's opinion. From Reagan's language and the goals of his program, you can infer that he sees government spending and taxation as a major cause of the economic crisis.

**Strategy** ❸ Note opinionated language. You can infer from words such as *exaggerated* and *inaccurate* that Reagan disagrees with criticism of his plan.

> **On the Program for Economic Recovery**
>
> ❶ All of us are aware of the punishing inflation which has for the first time in 60 years held to double-digit figures for 2 years in a row. Interest rates have reached absurd levels of more than 20 percent and over 15 percent for those who would borrow to buy a home. . . . Almost 8 million Americans are out of work. . . .
>
> ❷ I am proposing a comprehensive four-point program . . . aimed at reducing the growth in government spending and taxing, reforming and eliminating regulations which are unnecessary and unproductive or counterproductive, and encouraging a consistent monetary policy aimed at maintaining the value of the currency.
>
> Now, I know that ❸ exaggerated and inaccurate stories about these cuts have disturbed many people. . . . Those who, through no fault of their own, must depend on the rest of us—the poverty stricken, the disabled, the elderly, all those with true need—can rest assured that the social safety net of programs they depend on are exempt from any cuts.

### Make a Chart

Record clues in the text as well as what you know about the topic on the basis of you own experience, knowledge, and common sense.

| Clues in the Text: Facts, Examples, Language | Personal Experience, Historical Knowledge, Common Sense | Inference |
|---|---|---|
| • inflation in double digits<br>• Interest rates over 20%<br>• 8 million unemployed<br>• Inflation is "punishing"<br>• Inflation rates "absurd" | • Reagan defeated Democratic incumbent Jimmy Carter in the 1980 election. | Reagan blames the Democrats for the current economic problems. |

### PRACTICING THE SKILL

Turn to Chapter 10, Section 3, p. 356 and read the passage headed "The Impact of U.S. Territorial Gains." Create a chart like the one above, making inferences based on clues in the text and on your own personal experience, historical knowledge, and common sense.

# 2.1 Developing Historical Perspective

## DEFINING THE SKILL

**Historical perspective** is an understanding of events and people in the context of their times. Using historical perspective can help you avoid judging the past solely in terms of present-day norms and values.

## APPLYING THE SKILL

The following passage is the opening portion of an address by President Theodore Roosevelt. Below it is a chart that summarizes the information from a historical perspective.

## HOW TO DEVELOP HISTORICAL PERSPECTIVE

**Strategy** **1** Identify any historical figures, occasions, events, and dates.

**Strategy** **2** Notice words, phrases, and settings that reflect the period. Here the language used by the president reflects the optimism of the Progressive Era.

**Strategy** **3** Explain how people's actions and words reflect attitudes, values, and passions of the era. Here Roosevelt equates a strong nation with "manly virtues."

### Write a Summary

In a chart, list key words, phrases, and details from the passage, and then write a short paragraph summarizing the basic values and attitudes it conveys.

> **1** **INAUGURAL ADDRESS, 1905**
> **President Theodore Roosevelt**
>
> My fellow-citizens, no people on earth have more cause to be thankful than ours, and this is said . . . with gratitude to the Giver of Good who has blessed us with the conditions which have enabled us to achieve so large a measure of well-being and happiness. To us as a people it has been granted to lay the foundations of our national life in a **2** new continent. We are the **2** heirs of the ages, and yet we have had to pay few of the penalties which in old countries are exacted by the dead hand of a bygone civilization. We have not been obliged to fight for our existence against any alien race; and yet our life has called for the **3** vigor and effort without which the manlier and hardier virtues wither away. . . . [The] success which we confidently believe the future will bring, should cause in us no feeling of vainglory, but rather a deep and abiding realization of all which life has offered us; a full acknowledgment of the repsonsibility which is ours; and a fixed determination to show that under a free government a mighty people can thrive best, alike as regards the things of the body and the things of the soul.

| Key Phrases | Attitudes | Roosevelt's Inaugural Address |
|---|---|---|
| • Giver of Good<br>• blessed us<br>• heirs of the ages<br>• bygone civilization<br>• manlier and hardier virtues<br>• mighty people<br>• things of the body and things of the soul | • belief in God<br>• optimistic about the future<br>• grateful for the past | Theodore Roosevelt reveals a strong and resilient optimism about the American nation. His confidence is grounded in deep religious faith in God (the "Giver of Good") and God's plan for the nation. Roosevelt clearly believes in the ability of the American people to solve whatever problems they face as they move into a bright future. Roosevelt's faith and appeal to the manly virtues reflects typical attitudes and values of the 19th- and early 20th-century Americans. |

## PRACTICING THE SKILL

Turn to Chapter 8, Section 2, p. 282 and read the One American's Story feature, which discusses ideas about educational reform in the late 19th century. Use historical perspective to summarize those ideas in a chart like the one above.

# 2.2 Formulating Historical Questions

### DEFINING THE SKILL

**Formulating historical questions** entails asking questions about events and trends—what caused them, what made them important, and so forth. The ability to formulate historical questions is an important step in doing research. Formulating questions will help you to guide and focus your research as well as to understand maps, graphs, and other historical sources.

### APPLYING THE SKILL

At a women's rights convention in the mid-1800s, the delegates adopted a "Declaration of Sentiments" that set forth a number of grievances. The following passage is a description of that event. Below is a web diagram that organizes historical questions about the event.

### HOW TO FORMULATE HISTORICAL QUESTIONS

**Strategy 1** Ask about the basic facts of the event. Who were the leaders? What did they do? Where and when did the event take place?

**Strategy 2** Ask about the cause of an event. Why did an event take place?

**Strategy 3** Ask about historical influences on a speaker or event. What other historical events was it similar to? How was it different?

**Strategy 4** Ask about the results produced by various causes. What were the results of the event?

---

**Seneca Falls, 1848**

**1** Elizabeth Cady Stanton and Lucretia Mott decided to act on their resolution to hold a women's rights convention. In 1848, more than 300 women and men convened at Seneca Falls, New York, the small town that gave the convention its name. Before the convention, Stanton and Mott spent a day composing an agenda and a **2** detailed statement of grievances. Stanton carefully modeled this "Declaration of Sentiments" on the **3** Declaration of Independence. **4** The participants approved all measures unanimously, except for one: women's right to vote. This measure passed by a narow margin due to Stanton's insistence. The franchise for women, though it passed, remained a controversial topic.

---

### Make a Web Diagram

Using a web diagram, ask a broad question about the event described above. Then ask specific questions to help you explore the first.

### PRACTICING THE SKILL

Turn to Chapter 22, Section 1, p. 734 and read the passage headed "The Tonkin Gulf Resolution." Use a web diagram to write a historical question about the passage, as well as more specific questions that could guide your research into the topic.

**R12** SKILLBUILDER HANDBOOK

# 2.3 Hypothesizing

## DEFINING THE SKILL

**Hypothesizing** means developing a possible explanation for historical events. A hypothesis is a tentative assumption about what happened in the past or what might happen in the future. A hypothesis takes available information, links it to previous experience and knowledge, and comes up with a possible explanation, conclusion, or prediction.

## APPLYING THE SKILL

As the Cold War came to an end, people offered various hypotheses to explain why the Soviet Union broke up and to predict what would replace it. Read this passage and form your own hypothesis. Below the passage is a chart that presents a hypothesis and the facts used to support it.

## HOW TO FORM AN HYPOTHESIS

**Strategy 1** Identify the events, pattern, or trend you want to explain. Develop a hypothesis that might explain the event. You might hypothesize that Gorbachev's new policies would deeply affect politics in the Soviet Union and Eastern Europe.

**Strategy 2** Determine what facts you have about the situation. These facts support various hypotheses about how Gorbachev's policies affected politics both inside and outside the Soviet Union.

### The Cold War Ends

In March 1985, Mikhail Gorbachev became the general secretary of the Communist Party in the Soviet Union. **1** He initiated a new policy of openness and reform within the USSR, putting an end to the collective ownership of resources, most government censorship, and controlled elections. **2** A dramatic increase in nationalism on the part of the non-Russian republics followed the open elections, and in December 1991, all 14 republics declared independence. **2** The USSR was replaced by a loose federation of 12 republics called the Commonwealth of Independent States. **2** Gorbachev's new policies led to massive changes in Eastern Europe, as the satellite states, with his encouragement, moved toward democracy.

## Make a Chart

Use a chart to summarize your hypothesis about Gorbachev's reforms and the facts that support it. Then you can see what additional information you need to help prove or disprove it.

| Hypothesis | Facts that support the hypothesis | Additional information needed |
|---|---|---|
| Gorbachev's new policies would help lead to Western victory in the Cold War. | • increase in nationalism in non-Russian republics<br>• USSR replaced by a loose federation<br>• Satellite states moved towards democracy | • Were democratic reforms put into effect?<br>• Did free elections result in greater stability?<br>• Did the end of collective ownership advance private enterprise? |

## PRACTICING THE SKILL

Turn to Chapter 24, Section 2, p. 803 and read the passage headed "A Bungled Burglary." Make a chart in which you hypothesize about the consequences of the burglary at the Democratic National Committee headquarters. Then list facts and indicate whether they support your hypothesis.

# 2.4 Analyzing Issues

### DEFINING THE SKILL

**Analyzing issues** in history means taking apart complicated issues to identify the different points of view in economic, social, political, or moral debates.

### APPLYING THE SKILL

The following passage describes working conditions in U.S. factories in the late 1800s and early 1900s. Notice how the cluster diagram below it helps you to analyze the issue of child labor.

### HOW TO ANALYZE ISSUES

**Strategy** **1** Identify the central point of view and how it is defended.

**Strategy** **2** Look for facts and statistics. The numbers supplied by facts and statistics can help you decide on a position.

**Strategy** **3** Look for the other side to an issue. You need to look at all sides of an issue before deciding what you think.

> ### Children at Work
>
> **1** Wages for most factory workers were so low that many families could not survive unless all their members, including children, worked. **2** Between 1890 and 1910, 20 percent of boys and 10 percent of girls under age 15—some as young as five years old—held full-time jobs. **2** A typical work week was 12 hours a day, six days a week. Many of these children worked from dawn to dusk, wasted by hunger and exhaustion that made them prone to crippling accidents. With little time or energy left for school, child laborers gave up their futures to help their families make ends meet.
>
> **3** Nonetheless, factory owners and some parents praised child labor for keeping children out of mischief. They believed that idleness for children was bad and that work provided healthy occupation. Meanwhile, the reformer Jacob Riis and others worked for decent conditions, better wages, and laws that restricted child labor.

### Make a Cluster Diagram

In order to better analyze an issue, make a diagram and distinguish the facts as well as the different points of view.

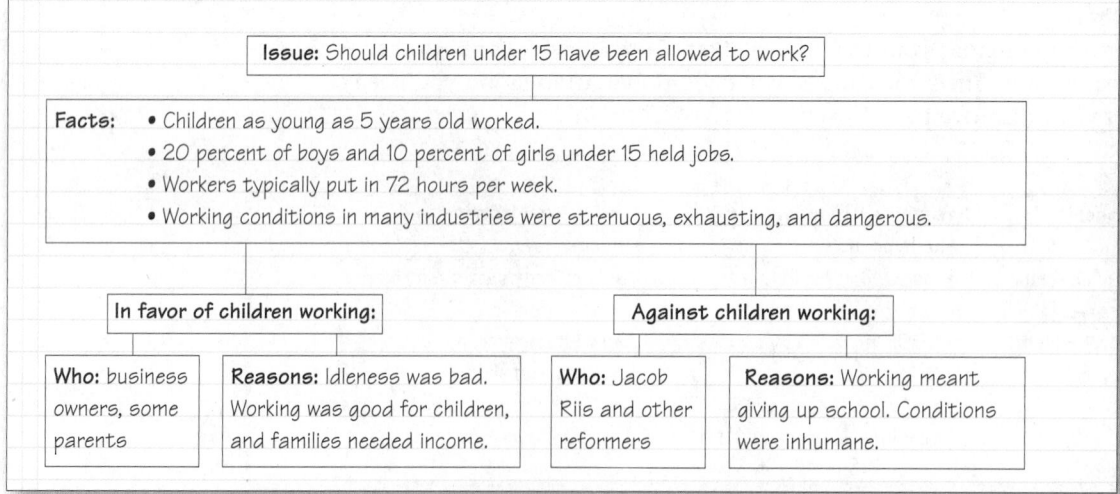

### PRACTICING THE SKILL

Read the passages headed "The Equal Rights Amendment (ERA)" and "The New Right Emerges" in Chapter 23, Section 2, p. 779. Make a cluster diagram to analyze the central issue and the positions of the people involved.

# 2.5 Analyzing Assumptions and Biases

## DEFINING THE SKILL

An **assumption** is a belief or an idea that is taken for granted. Some assumptions are based on evidence; some are based on feelings. A **bias** is a prejudiced point of view. Historical accounts that are biased reflect the personal prejudices of the author or historian and tend to be one-sided.

## APPLYING THE SKILL

The following passage is from *The Americans at Home* by the Scottish minister David Macrae, who wrote the book after visiting the United States in the 1860s. The chart below the excerpt helps to summarize information about the writer's assumptions and biases.

## HOW TO ANALYZE ASSUMPTIONS AND BIASES

**Strategy ①** Identify the author and information about him or her. Does the author belong to a special-interest group, religious organization, political party, or social movement that might promote a one-sided or slanted viewpoint on the subject?

**Strategy ②** Examine the evidence. Is what the author relates consistent with other accounts or supported by factual data?

**Strategy ③** Look for words, phrases, statements, or images that might convey a positive or negative slant, and thus reveal the author's bias.

---

**The Americans at Home**
**①** by David Macrae
[T]he American girls are very delightful. **②** And in one point they fairly surpass the majority of English girls—they are all educated and well informed. . . . The admirable educational system . . . covering the whole area of society, has given them education whether they are rich or poor, has furnished them with a great deal of information, and has quickened their desire for more. . . .
**③** Their tendency is perhaps to talk too much, and . . . it seemed to me sometimes to make no perceptible difference whether they knew anything of the subject they talked about or not. But they usually know a little of everything; and their general intelligence and vivacity make them very delightful companions.

---

## Make a Chart

For each of the heads listed on the left-hand side of the chart, summarize what information you can find in the passage.

| David Macrae's Impression of American Girls | |
|---|---|
| speaker | David Macrae |
| date | 1860s |
| occasion | Macrae's visit to the United States |
| tone | humorous, light-hearted |
| assumptions | The author assumes that girls are to be measured by companionship abilities. |
| bias | The author seems to have a prejudice that girls are inferior to boys or men. |

## PRACTICING THE SKILL

Look at the opinions expressed by A. Mitchell Palmer in the feature A Personal Voice in Chapter 12, Section 1, p. 413. Summarize his underlying assumptions and biases in a chart like the one shown above.

# 2.6 Evaluating Decisions and Courses of Action

### DEFINING THE SKILL

**Evaluating decisions** means making judgments about the decisions that historical figures made. Historians evaluate decisions on the basis of their moral implications and their costs and benefits from different points of view. **Evaluating alternative courses** of action means carefully judging the choices that historical figures had in order to better understand why they made the decisions they did.

### APPLYING THE SKILL

The following passage describes the decisions President John F. Kennedy had to make when he learned of Soviet missile bases in Cuba. Below the passage is a chart in which one possible alternative decision is analyzed.

### HOW TO EVALUATE DECISIONS

**Strategy ❶** Look at decisions made by individuals or by groups. Notice the decisions Kennedy made in response to Soviet actions.

**Strategy ❷** Look at the outcome of the decisions.

**Strategy ❸** Analyze a decision in terms of the alternatives that were possible. Both Kennedy and Khrushchev faced the alternatives of either escalating or defusing the crisis.

### Make a Chart

Make a chart evaluating an alternative course of action regarding the Cuban missile crisis based on its possible pros and cons.

---

**The Cuban Missile Crisis**

During the summer of 1962, the flow of Soviet weapons into Cuba—including nuclear missiles—greatly increased. ❶ President Kennedy responded cautiously at first, issuing a warning that the United States would not tolerate the presence of offensive nuclear weapons in Cuba.

❶ On the evening of October 22, after the president learned that the Soviets were building missile bases in Cuba, he delivered a public ultimatum: any missile attack from Cuba would trigger an all-out attack on the Soviet Union. Soviet ships continued to head toward the island, while the U.S. military prepared to invade Cuba. To avoid confrontation, ❷ the Soviet premier, Khrushchev, offered to remove the missiles from Cuba in exchange for a pledge not to invade the island. Kennedy agreed, and the crisis ended.

❸ Some people criticized Kennedy for practicing brinkmanship when private talks might have resolved the crisis without the threat of nuclear war. Others believed he had been too soft and had passed up an ideal chance to invade Cuba and to oust its communist leader, Fidel Castro.

---

| alternative | pros | cons | evaluation |
|---|---|---|---|
| Negotiate a settlement quietly without threatening nuclear war. | 1. Avoid the threat of nuclear war 2. Avoid frightening U.S. citizens | 1. The U.S. would not look like a strong world leader. 2. The government would lose favor with Cuban exiles living in the U.S. | your answer: Would this have been a good choice? Why or why not? |

### PRACTICING THE SKILL

Turn to Chapter 17, Section 3, p. 583 and read the passage headed "The Atomic Bomb Ends the War." Evaluate the U.S. decision to drop the bomb. Make a chart like the one shown to summarize the pros and cons of an alternative decision, and then write an evaluation of that decision.

# 2.7 Forming Opinions (Evaluating)

## DEFINING THE SKILL

**Forming opinions,** or evaluating, means deciding what your own thoughts or feelings are and making judgments about events and people in history. Opinions should be supported with facts and examples.

## APPLYING THE SKILL

The following passage includes comments on the French Revolution by Gouverneur Morris, one of the participants in the Constitutional Convention, and by Thomas Jefferson.

## HOW TO FORM AN OPINION AND SUPPORT IT WITH FACTS

**Strategy 1** Decide what you think about a subject after reading all the information available to you. After reading this description, you might decide that political causes either do or do not sometimes justify violence.

**Strategy 2** Support your opinion with facts, quotations, and examples, including references to similar events in other historical eras.

**Strategy 3** Look for the opinions of historians and other experts. Consider their opinions when forming your own.

### A Scene of Mob Violence

Gouverneur Morris was a visitor to Paris during the early days of the French Revolution. In the following journal entry he describes a scene of revolutionary mob violence: **1** "The head and body of Mr. de Foulon are introduced in triumph. . . . His crime [was] to have accepted a place in the Ministry. This mutilated form of an old man of seventy-five is shown to Bertier, his son-in-law, the intend't. [another official] of Paris, and afterwards **2** he also is put to death and cut to pieces. . . ." Such violence was common during the French Revolution and shocked a good many Americans. **3** However, Thomas Jefferson was a supporter of the Revolution, saying, "The liberty of the whole earth was depending on the issue of the contest, and . . . rather than it should have failed, I would have seen half the earth desolated."

## Make a Chart

Summarize your opinion and supporting information in a chart. List facts, quotations, and examples.

**Opinion:** The French Revolution was especially violent and cruel.

| facts: | quotations: | examples: |
|---|---|---|
| • Violence escalated. <br> • Jacobins launched Reign of Terror. <br> • Moderates sent to guillotine. <br> • Jacobins declared war on other countries. | "he also is put to death and cut to pieces" | Jacobins beheaded Louis XVI |

## PRACTICING THE SKILL

Read the Point/Counterpoint feature in Chapter 15, Section 5, p. 516. Form your own opinion about the success or failure of the New Deal. Record your opinion in a chart like the one shown, and provide supporting information to back it up.

# 2.8 Drawing Conclusions

### DEFINING THE SKILL

**Drawing conclusions** involves considering the implications of what you have read and forming a final statement about its meaning or consequences. To draw conclusions, you need to look closely at facts and then use your own experience and common sense to decide what those facts mean.

### APPLYING THE SKILL

The following passage tells about employment trends in the 1990s. The highlighted text indicates information from which conclusions can be drawn. In the diagram below, the information and conclusions are organized in a clear way.

### HOW TO DRAW CONCLUSIONS

**Strategy** ❶ Use the facts to draw a conclusion. Conclusion: In general, the economy was good in the mid-1990s.

**Strategy** ❷ Read carefully to understand all the facts. Conclusion: Income expectations were lower.

**Strategy** ❸ Ask questions of the material. How did the use of temporary workers affect job security? (It reduced it.) What did employment statistics for young people indicate? (Jobs were harder for young people to find.)

**Make a Diagram**

Summarize the data and your conclusion about the above passage in a diagram.

> ### Job Outlook in the Mid-1990s
>
> Several trends emerged in the workplace of the 1990s. ❶ Inflation was at its lowest level since the 1960s, and 10 million new jobs created between 1993 and 1996 helped lower the unemployment rate to 5.1 percent in 1996. ❷ Median household income adjusted for inflation, however, declined from $33,585 to $31,241, even though there were many households in which both parents worked.
>
> In addition, ❸ many jobs once done by permanent employees of a company were done by temporary workers, who were paid only for the time they were needed and who typically received no benefits. Three out of four young Americans thought they would earn less in their lifetimes than their parents did. Unemployment in their age group continued at the same rate, while the unemployment rate for other adults had fallen. ❸ In 1993, about one in seven workers between the ages of 16 and 25 was out of work, double the national average.

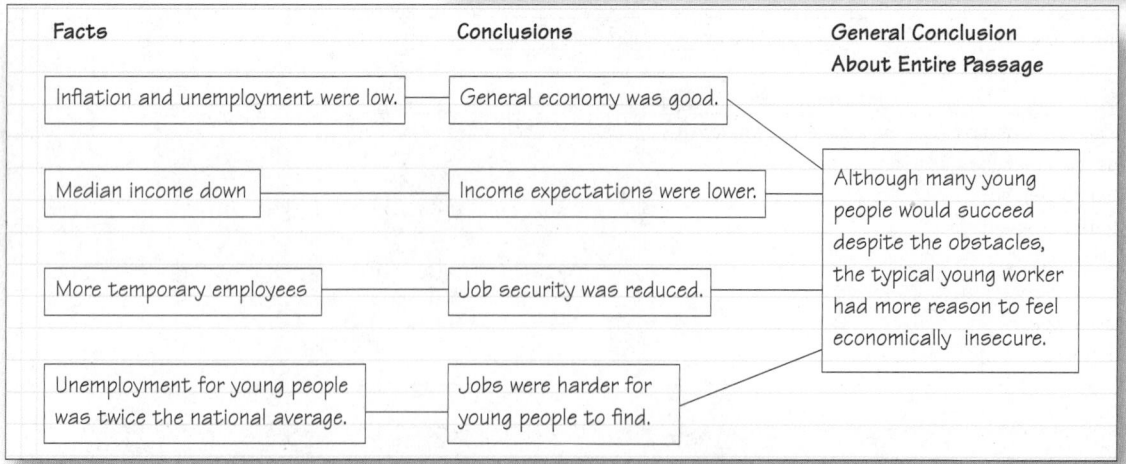

### PRACTICING THE SKILL

Turn to Chapter 26, Section 4, p. 884 and read the passage headed "The Aging of America." Draw conclusions based on the facts in the passage. Using the model as a guide, create your own diagram, showing the facts and conclusions you have used to arrive at a general conclusion.

# 2.9 Synthesizing

## DEFINING THE SKILL

**Synthesizing** is the skill historians use in developing interpretations of the past. Like detective work, synthesizing involves putting together clues, information, and ideas to form an overall picture of a historical event.

## APPLYING THE SKILL

The following passage describes the earliest inhabitants of the Americas. The high-lighted text indicates how some information leads toward a synthesis—an overall picture.

## HOW TO SYNTHESIZE

**Strategy** ❶ Read carefully to understand the facts.

**Strategy** ❷ Look for explanations that link the facts together. This assertion is based on the evidence provided in the next couple of sentences.

**Strategy** ❸ Consider what you already know in order to accept statements as reasonable.

**Strategy** ❹ Bring together the information you have gathered to arrive at a new understanding of the subject.

### The First Americans

From the ❶ discovery of chiseled arrowheads and charred bones at ancient sites, it appears that the earliest Americans lived as big-game hunters. ❷ People gradually shifted to hunting smaller game and gathering available plants. They collected nuts and wild rice. They invented snares, as well as bows and arrows, to hunt small animals, and they wove nets to catch fish.

Between 10,000 and 15,000 years ago, a revolution took place in what is now central Mexico. ❸ People began to raise plants as food. Maize may have been the first domesticated plant. Agriculture eventually spread to other regions.

The rise of agriculture brought tremendous changes to the Americas. Agriculture made it possible for people to remain in one place. It also enabled them to accumulate and store surplus food. As their surplus increased, people had the time to develop skills and more complex ideas about the world. ❹ From this agricultural base rose larger, more stable, and increasingly complex societies.

### Make a Cluster Diagram

Use a cluster diagram to organize the facts, opinions, examples, and interpretations that you have brought together to form a synthesis.

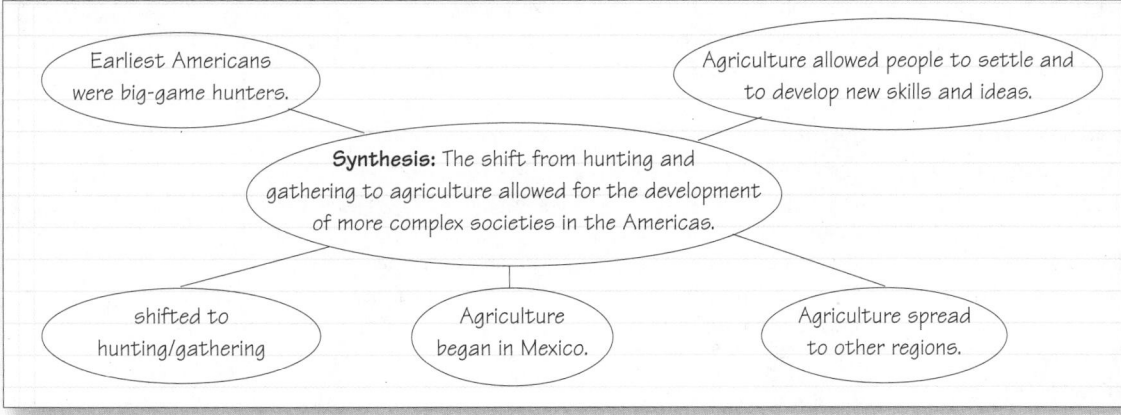

- Earliest Americans were big-game hunters.
- Agriculture allowed people to settle and to develop new skills and ideas.
- **Synthesis:** The shift from hunting and gathering to agriculture allowed for the development of more complex societies in the Americas.
- shifted to hunting/gathering
- Agriculture began in Mexico.
- Agriculture spread to other regions.

## PRACTICING THE SKILL

Turn to Chapter 13, Section 2, p. 441 and read "Women Shed Old Roles at Home and at Work." Look for information to support a synthesis about the fundamental changes in the family brought about by women's new opportunities.

# 2.10 Making Predictions

### DEFINING THE SKILL

**Making predictions** entails identifying situations that leaders or groups face or have faced in the past, and then suggesting what course of action they might take as well as what might happen as a result of that action. Making predictions about the effects of past events helps you to understand how events in the past shape the future. Making predictions about the effects of proposed actions, such as proposed legislation, helps you to evaluate possible courses of action.

### APPLYING THE SKILL

The following passage discusses the central weaknesses of the Treaty of Versailles, which ended World War I. Below the passage is a chart that lists decisions made by those who framed the treaty, along with alternative decisions and predictions of possible outcomes.

### HOW TO MAKE PREDICTIONS

**Strategy** ❶ Identify the decisions.

**Strategy** ❷ Decide what other decisions might have been made.

**Strategy** ❸ Predict the outcomes of the alternative decisions.

**Make a Chart**
Record decisions made as well as alternative decisions and possible outcomes.

**Weaknesses of the Treaty of Versailles**

❶ First, the treaty humiliated Germany. The war-guilt clause, which forced Germany to accept blame for the war and pay financial reparations, caused Germans of all political viewpoints to detest the treaty.

❷ Second, Russia, which had fought with the Allies, was excluded from the peace conference. Russia had suffered almost the same number of casualties as Germany—the two countries had by far the highest casualty rates of the war. Russia lost more territory than Germany did. The Union of Soviet Socialist Republics, as Russia was called after 1922, grew determined to regain its lost territory.

❸ Third, the treaty ignored the claims of colonized people for self-determination. For example, the Allies dismissed the claims of the Vietnamese, who wanted freedom from French colonial rule.

| Decision: The treaty included a war-guilt clause. | Decision: Russia was excluded from the peace conference. | Decision: Treaty ignored the claims of colonized peoples. |
|---|---|---|
| Alternative decision: The treaty had no war-guilt clause. | Alternative decision: Russia was included in the peace negotiations. | Alternative decision: The treaty respected the claims of colonized peoples. |
| Possible outcome: Germany rebuilds. World War II does not occur. | Possible outcome: Tension between the Soviet Union and the West decreases. | Possible outcome: Tensions are reduced worldwide; Vietnam War is averted. |

### PRACTICING THE SKILL

Turn to Chapter 26, Section 1, p. 862 and read the passage "Reforming Welfare." Make a chart like the one above in which you identify provisions of the welfare reform law, alternative provisions that might have been included, and their possible outcomes. Consider how the effects of each law might change depending on the health of the nation's economy.

# 2.11 Forming Generalizations

## DEFINING THE SKILL

**Forming generalizations** means making broad judgments based on the information in texts. When you form generalizations, you need to be sure they are valid. They must be based on sufficient evidence, and they must be consistent with the information given.

## APPLYING THE SKILL

The following three excerpts deal with Herbert Hoover and his relation to the Great Depression. Notice how the information in the web diagram below supports the generalization drawn.

## HOW TO FORM GENERALIZATIONS

**Strategy ❶** Determine what information the sources have in common. All the sources suggest that people blamed Hoover for the Great Depression.

**Strategy ❷** State your generalization in sentence form. A generalization often needs a qualifying word, such as *most*, *many*, or *some*, to make it valid.

**Make a Web Diagram**
Use a web diagram to record relevant information and make a valid generalization.

---

**On President Hoover and the Great Depression**

❶ "By 1930, people were calling the shantytowns in American cities Hoovervilles. . . . Homeless people called the newspapers in which they wrapped themselves 'Hoover blankets.' Empty pockets turned inside out were 'Hoover flags.'"

—*The Americans*

"[My aunt] told me . . . . ❶ People were starving because of Herbert Hoover. My mother was out of work because of Herbert Hoover. Men were killing themselves because of Herbert Hoover."

—Russell Baker

❶ "If someone bit an apple and found a worm in it, Hoover would get the blame."

—Will Rogers

---

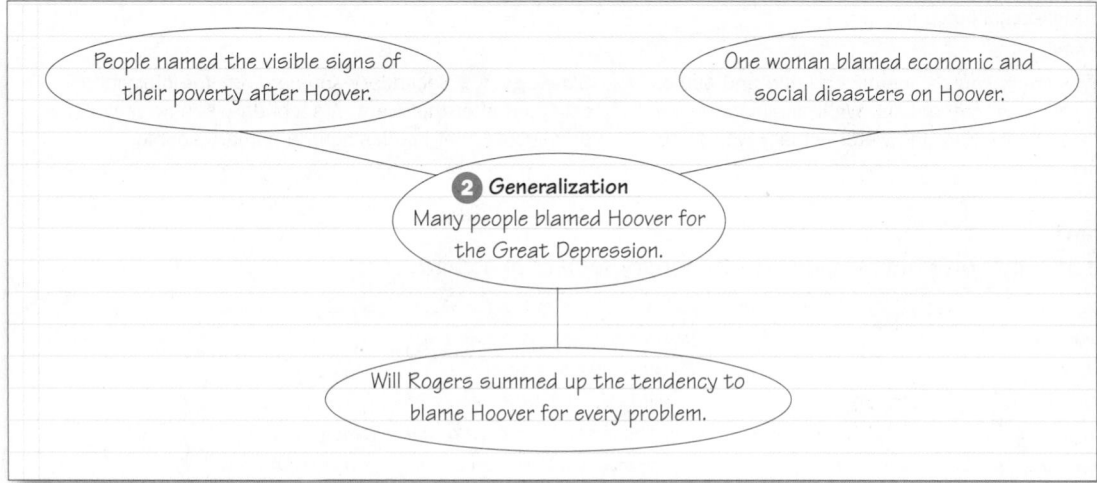

People named the visible signs of their poverty after Hoover.

One woman blamed economic and social disasters on Hoover.

❷ Generalization
Many people blamed Hoover for the Great Depression.

Will Rogers summed up the tendency to blame Hoover for every problem.

## PRACTICING THE SKILL

Study the Daily Life feature "Signs of the Sixties" in Chapter 23, p. 786. Create a diagram like the one above to make a generalization about teenagers during the sixties. Use information from textual and visual sources to support your generalization.

# 3.1 Primary and Secondary Sources

## DEFINING THE SKILL

**Primary sources** are accounts written or created by people who were present at historical events, either as participants or as observers. These include letters, diaries, journals, speeches, some news articles, eyewitness accounts, government data, statutes, court opinions, and autobiographies.

**Secondary sources** are based on primary sources and are produced by people who were not present at the original events. They often combine information from a number of different accounts. Secondary sources include history books, historical essays, some news articles, and biographies.

## APPLYING THE SKILL

The following passage describes the explosion of the first atomic bomb in 1945. It is mainly a secondary source, but it quotes an eyewitness account that is a primary source.

## HOW TO LOCATE AND IDENTIFY PRIMARY AND SECONDARY SOURCES

**Strategy** ❶ Locating sources: The catalog in your school library or a local public library lists resources alphabetically by subject, title, and author. Most of these are secondary sources but may contain copies or excerpts of primary sources. Articles in a general encyclopedia such as *World Book* or *Encyclopedia Americana* can give you an overview of a topic and usually provide references to additional sources.

**Strategy** ❷ Secondary source: Look for information collected from several sources.

**Strategy** ❸ Primary source: Identify the title and author and evaluate his or her credentials. What qualifies the writer to report on the event? Here the writer actually worked on developing the bomb.

### ❶ The First Atomic Bomb

As the time to test the bomb drew near, the air around Los Alamos crackled with rumors and fears. ❷ At one end of the scale were fears that the bomb wouldn't work at all. At the other end was the prediction that the explosion would set fire to the atmosphere, which would mean the end of the earth.

On July 16, 1945, the first atomic bomb was detonated in the desert near Alamogordo, New Mexico. ❸ In his book *What Little I Remember*, Otto Frisch, a Manhattan Project scientist, described what happened next:

"[T]hat object on the horizon which looked like a small sun was still too bright to look at. . . . After another ten seconds or so it had grown and . . . was slowly rising into the sky from the ground, with which it remained connected by a lengthening grey stem of swirling dust. . . ."

❹ That blinding flash was followed by a deafening roar as a tremendous shock wave rolled across the trembling desert. The bomb not only worked, but it was more powerful than most had dared hope.

**Strategy** ❹ Secondary source: Look for information collected after the event. A secondary source provides a perspective that is missing in a primary source.

## Make a Chart

Summarize information from primary and secondary sources in a chart.

| Primary Source | Secondary Source |
|---|---|
| Author: Otto Frisch | Author: unknown |
| Qualifications: scientist working on Manhattan Project | Qualifications: had access to multiple accounts of the time leading up to and following event |
| Information: detailed description, sensory observations, feeling of awe | Information: description of range of points of view and of information available only after event |

## PRACTICING THE SKILLS

Turn to Chapter 25, Section 1, p. 830, and read the One American's Story feature, which includes a quotation. Use a chart like the one above to summarize information from the primary and secondary sources.

## 3.2 Visual, Audio, Multimedia Sources

### DEFINING THE SKILL

**Visual sources** can be paintings, illustrations, photographs, political cartoons, and advertisements. **Audio sources** include recorded speeches, interviews, press conferences, and radio programs. Movies, CD-ROMs, television, and computer software are the newest kind of historical sources, called **multimedia sources.** These sources are rich with historical details and sometimes convey the feelings and points of view of an era better than words do.

### APPLYING THE SKILL

The following photograph shows a group of college students and civil rights activists joined in song as they protest unfair voting laws in 1964.

**1** In the summer of 1964, college students volunteered to go to Mississippi to help register that state's African-American voters.

### HOW TO INTERPRET VISUAL SOURCES

**Strategy 1** Identify the subject and the source. A title or caption often gives a description of a photo or other visual source. This photograph shows volunteers who worked in the 1964 voting rights drive in Mississippi.

**Strategy 2** Identify important visual details. In this photograph, white and black college students are holding hands and singing. Behind them is a bus.

**Strategy 3** Make inferences from the visual details. Holding hands and singing together suggest fellowship and unity—the students are showing solidarity in the fight for civil rights.

### Make a Chart

Summarize your interpretation of the photograph in a simple chart.

### PRACTICING THE SKILL

Turn to the photograph in Chapter 21, Section 2, p. 712, showing police dogs in Birmingham, Alabama, attacking African Americans. Use a chart like the one at the right to analyze and interpret the photograph.

| Subject | A diverse group of college students. |
|---|---|
| Details | Bus, joined hands, white and black Americans side by side, singing |
| Inferences | The subjects share a belief in racial equality, freedom, and solidarity. Some or all of the group may have traveled to Mississippi together on the bus. |

# 3.3 Analyzing Political Cartoons

### DEFINING THE SKILL

**Political cartoons** use humor to make a serious point. Political cartoons often express a point of view on an issue better than words do. Understanding signs and symbols will help you to interpret political cartoons.

Like many text sources that express a point of view, cartoons are often **biased,** or unfairly weighted toward one point of view. To identify a cartoon's bias, look for exaggerations and caricature. Try to restate the message of the cartoon in words, then identify overgeneralizations and opinions stated as facts.

### APPLYING THE SKILL

The following political cartoon shows President Calvin Coolidge playing the saxophone while big business dances. The chart below it summarizes historical information gained from interpreting the visual source.

### HOW TO INTERPRET VISUAL SOURCES

**Strategy** ① Identify the subject. This cartoon deals with President Calvin Coolidge's relationship with big business.

**Strategy** ② Identify important symbols and details. Big business is shown as a carefree flapper of the twenties. The president's saxophone is labeled "Praise," suggesting his positive attitude toward the fun-loving flapper.

**Strategy** ③ Interpret the message. The image implies that serving big business interests is important to the president.

**Strategy** ④ Analyze the point of view. The cartoonist suggests that the relationship between the president and big business is too cozy.

**Strategy** ⑤ Identify bias. The president is caricatured by being depicted engaging in frivolity and at the service of big business. The cartoon charges that the president does not take his responsibilities seriously.

### Make a Chart

Summarize your interpretation of the cartoon in a simple chart.

| Subject: Coolidge's Relationship with big business | | |
| --- | --- | --- |
| Point of View | Symbols/Details | Message |
| Satirical of the Coolidge administration and of big business | Flapper: big business, carefree and overgrown | Big business and the president are too close. |
| | President: playing a tune for business | Business is having too good a time—with the president's help. |

### PRACTICING THE SKILL

Turn to the political cartoon on p. 426, which presents an opinion about Franklin D. Roosevelt's New Deal programs. Use a chart like the one above to analyze and interpret the cartoon.

**R24** SKILLBUILDER HANDBOOK

# 3.4 Interpreting Maps

### DEFINING THE SKILL

**Maps** are representations of features on the earth's surface. Historians use maps to locate historical events, to demonstrate how geography has influenced history, and to illustrate patterns and distributions of human activity and its environmental effects.

**Political maps** show political units, from countries, states, and provinces to counties, districts, and towns. **Physical maps** show mountains, hills, plains, rivers, lakes, and oceans. They may include elevations of land and depths of water. **Historical maps** illustrate such things as economic activity, political alliances, migrations, battles, and population density. While reading maps, historians pose questions and use the following features to find answers:

A **compass rose** indicates the map's orientation on the globe. It may show all four cardinal directions (N, S, E, W) or just one, north.

**Lines** indicate boundaries between political areas, roads and highways, routes of exploration or migration, and rivers and other waterways. Lines may vary in width and color.

**Symbols** or icons represent real objects or events. Cities, towns, and villages often appear as dots. A capital city is often shown as a star within a circle. An area's products or resources may be indicated by symbols. Battles are often shown by starbursts, troop movements by arrows.

**Labels** designate key places, such as cities, states, bodies of water, and events.

**Lines of longitude and latitude** appear on maps to indicate the absolute location of the area shown. Lines of latitude show distance north or south of the equator, measured in degrees. Lines of longitude show distance in degrees east or west of the prime meridian, which runs through Greenwich, England.

A **legend or key** is a small table in which the symbols, types of lines, and special colors that appear in the map are listed and explained.

Sometimes **colors** are used to indicate areas under different political or cultural influence. Colors and **shading** are also used to show distributions, patterns, and such features as altitudes.

A **map's scale** shows the ratio between a unit of length on the map and a unit of distance on the earth. A typical scale shows a one-inch segment and indicates the number of miles that length represents on the map. A map on which an inch represents 500 miles has a scale of 1:31,680,000.

*Continued on page R26.*

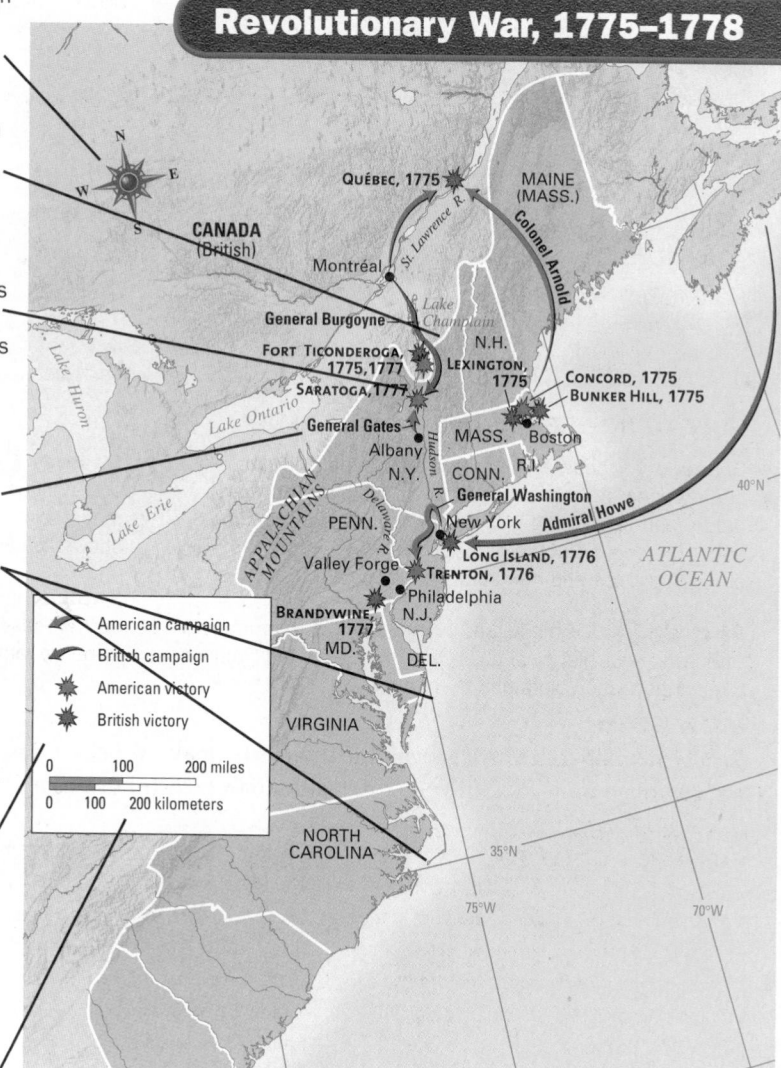

**Revolutionary War, 1775–1778**

Distributions on a map are where certain symbols, such as those for cities, fall. Sometimes distributions show patterns, such as a cluster, a line, or a wide circle. On this map, for example, the battle symbols show a pattern of being fought near rivers or ports.

The historical maps below show land claims in Europe in 1915 and after 1919. Together they show the political effects of World War I.

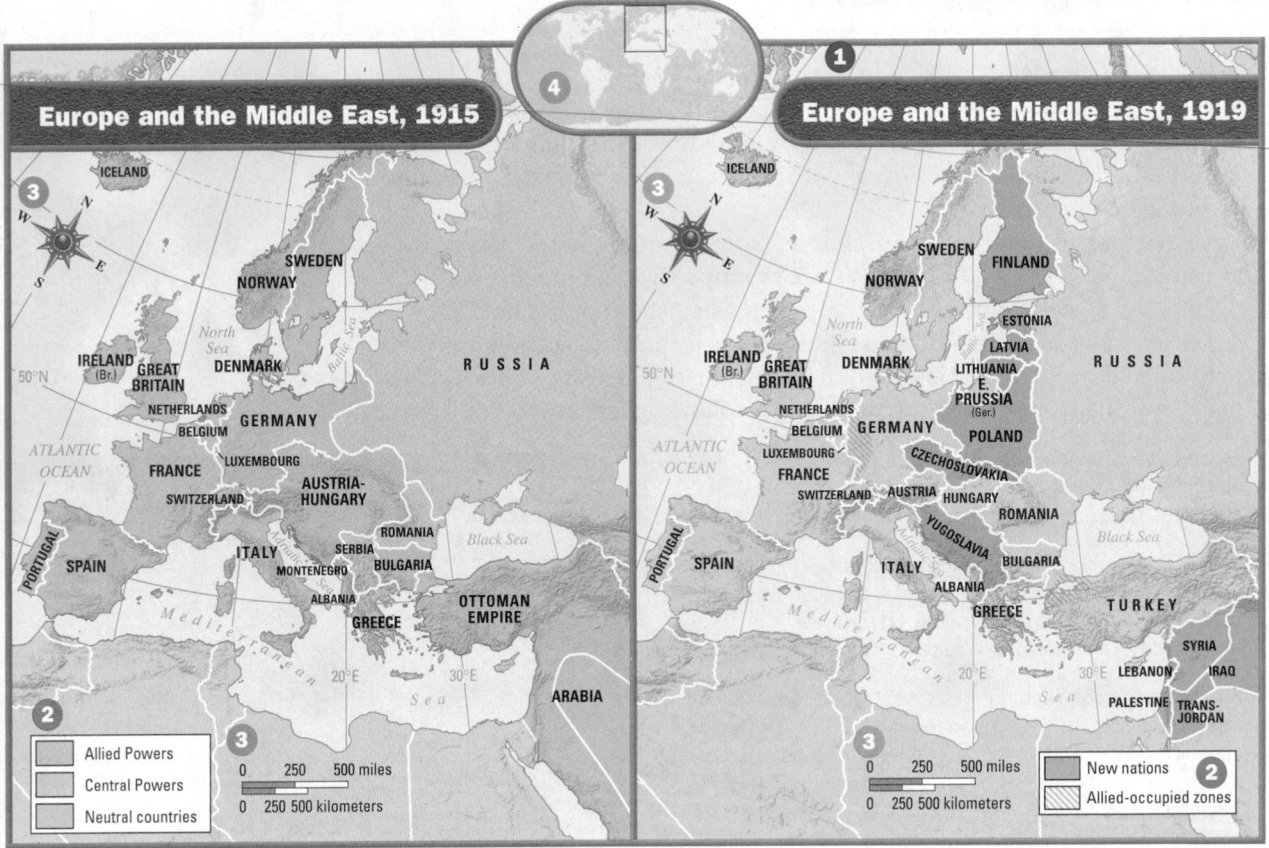

### HOW TO INTERPRET A HISTORICAL MAP

**Strategy** ❶ Look at the map's title to learn the subject and purpose of the map. Here the maps show Europe before and after World War I. Pose a historical question about the subject of the map, such as "How were old empires divided and new countries formed?"

**Strategy** ❷ Use the legend to interpret the map in order to answer your historical question. The legend tells you what the symbols and colors on the map mean.

**Strategy** ❸ Look at the scale and compass rose. The scale shows you what distances are represented. On these maps, 1.4 cm represents 500 miles. The compass rose shows you which direction on the map is north.

**Strategy** ❹ Find where the map area is located on the earth. These maps span a large area from the Arctic Circle to below latitude 30° N, and from 10° to 40° E.

### Make a Chart

Relate the map to the five geographic themes by making a chart. The five themes are described on p. xxx. In your chart, also analyze distributions and find patterns.

| Location: | Place: | Region: | Movement: | Human-Environment Interaction: |
|---|---|---|---|---|
| Europe and the Middle East; from the Arctic Circle to below 30° North and from 10° West to 40° East | A continent that is a peninsula surrounded by the Mediterranean Sea, the Atlantic Ocean, the North Sea, as well as western-most Asia | The old empires of the Central Powers are distributed within Central Europe and the Middle East. The new nations are in Eastern Europe and the Middle East. | Political boundaries shifted after the war. The Treaty of Versailles established nine new nations. | The new boundaries fall along rivers, bodies of water, and mountain ranges. There is a pattern. The pattern shows that the new countries form a narrow strip from North to South. |

### PRACTICING THE SKILL

Study the maps titled "D-Day, June 6, 1944" on p. 575. Make a chart, like the one shown above, in which you summarize what the maps show.

# 3.5 Interpreting Charts

## DEFINING THE SKILL

**Charts** are visual presentations of material. Historians use charts to organize, simplify, and summarize information in a way that makes it more meaningful or memorable.

   **Simple charts** are used to consolidate or compare information. **Tables** are used to organize numbers, percentages, or other information into columns and rows for easy reference. Diagrams provide visual clues to the meaning of the information they contain. Illustrated diagrams are sometimes called **infographics.**

## APPLYING THE SKILL

The following diagram gives a visual representation of how the economy functions. The paragraph below summarizes the information contained in the diagram.

## HOW TO INTERPRET CHARTS

**Strategy ❶** Identify the symbols. Here the symbols represent individuals, producers, government, and the product market.

**Strategy ❷** Look for the main idea. The arrows show the cycle of supply and demand in a free enterprise system of economy. Here, individuals are at the top of the chart indicating that they begin the cycle by creating a demand for goods and services.

**Strategy ❸** Follow the arrows to study the chart. Read the description of each image in the diagram. Together, the images show the flow of economic activity from producers to individuals and back. The government affects the cycle by regulating and stabilizing economic activity.

## Write a Summary

Write a paragraph to summarize what you learned from the diagram.

> Individuals want or need products or services. Producers try to fulfill that demand by hiring workers (labor) to produce the good or service. Producers then make the goods and services available for sale on the market. During this process, the government regulates economic activity and equalizes the distribution of wealth, among other functions. Once goods are sent to stores or other distribution centers, people must be hired (labor) to sell the goods.

## PRACTICING THE SKILL

Turn to Chapter 6, Section 3, p. 242, and study the chart titled "Vertical and Horizontal Integration." Write a paragraph in which you summarize what you learned from the chart. Tell how the process of vertical integration works, and describe how it is different from horizontal integration.

# 3.6 Interpreting Graphs

## DEFINING THE SKILL

**Graphs** show statistical information in a visual manner. Historians use graphs to visualize and compare amounts, ratios, economic trends, and changes over time.

**Line graphs** typically show quantities on the vertical axis (up the left side) and time in various units on the horizontal axis (across the bottom). **Pie graphs** are useful for showing relative proportions. The circle represents the whole and the slices represent the parts belonging to various subgroups. **Bar graphs** are commonly used to display information about quantities.

## PRACTICING THE SKILL

The image below shows a double line graph. The lines show the rate of inflation as compared with the rate of unemployment during the 1970s.

## HOW TO INTERPRET A GRAPH

**Strategy** ❶ Read the title to identify the main idea of the graph. When two subjects are shown, such as unemployment and inflation, the graph will probably show a relationship between them.

**Strategy** ❷ Read the vertical and horizontal axes of the graph. The horizontal axis shows years, and the vertical axis gives percents.

**Strategy** ❸ Look at the legend. Find out what each symbol in the graph represents. In this graph the gold line represents the inflation rate and the purple line represents the unemployment rate.

**Strategy** ❹ Summarize the information shown in each part of the graph. What trends do you see in the line graph over certain years? When did unemployment rise and fall? What about inflation? What can you infer from the patterns?

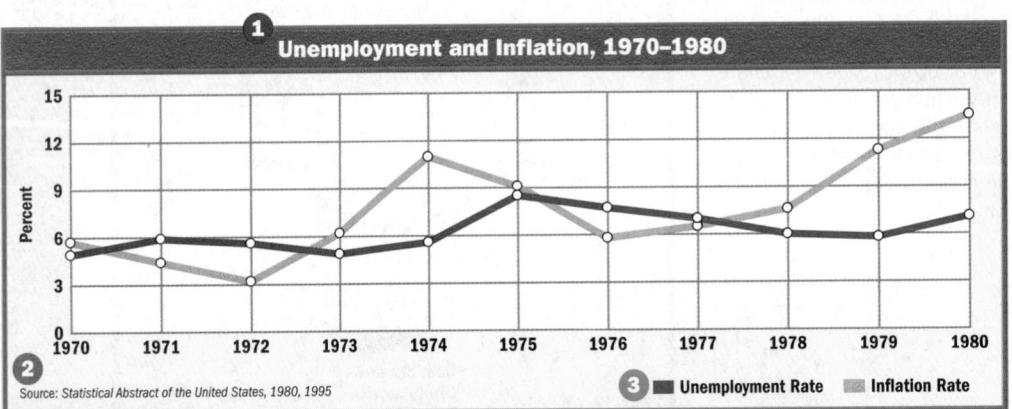

Source: Statistical Abstract of the United States, 1980, 1995

### Write a Summary

Write a paragraph to summarize what you learned from the graph.

> Unemployment declined between 1976 and 1979 but rose between 1974 and 1975, while inflation declined between 1975 and 1976 and rose in the periods 1973–1974 and 1977–1980. From the graph it appears that unemployment rises or falls following inflation rate changes, but less dramatically.

## PRACTICING THE SKILL

Turn to Chapter 19, Section 3, p. 653, and look at the two graphs titled "Glued to the Set." Study the graphs and write a paragraph in which you summarize what you learned from them. Explain how the two line graphs work together.

# 3.7 Using the Internet

## DEFINING THE SKILL

The **Internet** is a network of computers associated with universities, libraries, news organizations, government agencies, businesses, and private individuals worldwide. Every page of information on the Internet has its own address, or **URL.**

The international collection of sites known as the **World Wide Web** is a source of information about current events as well as research on historical subjects. This textbook contains many suggestions for using the World Wide Web. You can begin by entering the URL for McDougal Littell's site: www.classzone.com.

## APPLYING THE SKILL

The computer screen below shows the home page of the Library of Congress.

## HOW TO USE THE INTERNET

**Strategy 1** Go directly to a web page. If you know the address of a particular web page, type the address in the strip at the top of the screen and press RETURN. After a few seconds, that page will appear on your screen.

If you want to research the Web for information on a topic, visit a general search site such as www.google.com or www.yahoo.com. The following sites have information that may be useful in your research:

Library of Congress—www.loc.gov

National Archives and Records Administration—
www.nara.gov

Smithsonian Institution—www.si.org

PBS—www.pbs.org

National Geographic—www.nationalgeographic.com

**Strategy 2** Learn about the page. Click on one of the topics across the top of the page to learn more about the Library of Congress and how to use its Web site.

**Strategy 3** Explore the features of the page. Click on any one of the images or topics to find out more about a specific subject.

## PRACTICING THE SKILL

Turn to Chapter 21, Section 2, p. 710, "The Triumphs of a Crusade." Read the section, making a list of topics you would like to research. If you have a computer with Internet access, go to the McDougal Littell site, www.classzone.com. There you will be able to search the Chapter 21 Research Links and other features to explore a variety of historical topics.

# 4.1 Creating Charts and Graphs

### DEFINING THE SKILL

**Charts** and **graphs** are visual representations of information. (See Skillbuilders 3.5 and 3.6.) Three types of graphs are **bar graphs, line graphs,** and **pie graphs.** Use a bar graph to display information about quantities and to compare related quantities. Use a line graph to show a change in a single quantity over time. Use a pie graph to show relative proportions among parts of a single thing. Charts can be used to condense and organize written information or lists.

### APPLYING THE SKILL

The following passage includes data about American commuting choices between 1960 and 1990. The bar graph below shows how the information in the passage might be represented.

### HOW TO CREATE A BAR GRAPH

**Strategy ❶** Use a title that sums up the information; include a time span.

**Strategy ❷** Note dates and the percentages. Dates will form the horizontal axis of your graph; percentages will form the vertical axis.

**Strategy ❸** Organize the data. Group numbers that provide information about the same year.

**Strategy ❹** Decide how best to represent the information. Sketch a graph and a legend, denoting the meanings of any colors and symbols.

> **American Commuting Choices, 1960–1990**
>
> In 1960, 64% of the population traveled to work by car, truck, or van; 12% took public transportation; 7% worked at home; and 17% got to work by other means. In 1990, 87% traveled to work by car, truck, or van; 5% took public transportation; 3% worked at home; and 5% went to work by other means.

### Create a Bar Graph

Clearly label vertical and horizontal axes. Draw bars accurately. Include a legend.

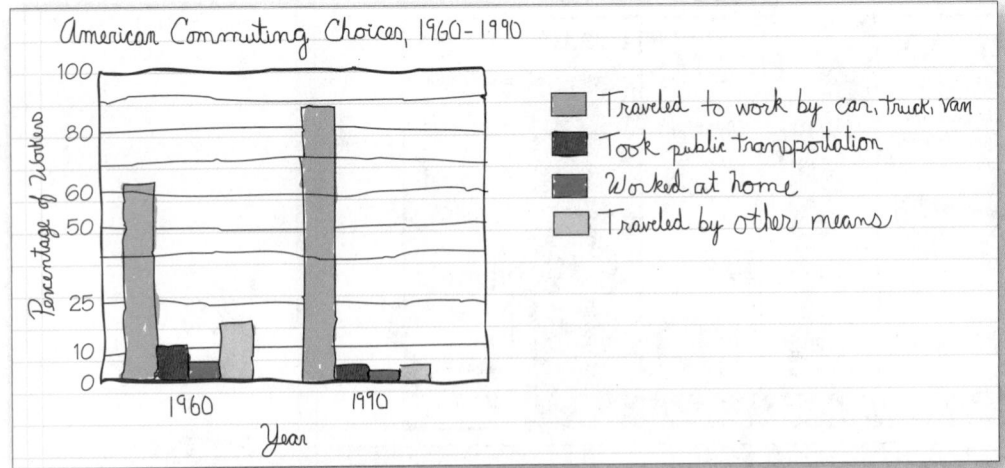

### PRACTICING THE SKILL

Turn to Chapter 26, Section 4, p. 585, and read the passage headed "A Changing Immigration Population." Use a pie graph to show percentages of ethnic distribution of the American population in 1990.

# 4.2 Creating Models

## DEFINING THE SKILL

**Models,** like maps, are visual representations of information. Historians make models of geographical areas, villages, cities, inventions, buildings, and other physical objects of historical importance. A model can be a two-dimensional representation, such as a poster or a diagram that explains how something happened. It also can be a three-dimensional representation or even a computer-created image.

## APPLYING THE SKILL

The following image is a two-dimensional model of the tunnel system used by the Vietcong during the Vietnam War. Examine the strategies used in making this model to learn how to create your own.

## HOW TO CREATE A MODEL

**Strategy ❶** Gather the information you need to understand the situation or event. Here the creator has gathered information about the tunnel system from various reference sources.

**Strategy ❷** Think about symbols you may want to use. Since the model should give information in a visual way, think about ways you can use color, pictures, or other visuals to tell the story.

**Strategy ❸** Gather the supplies you will need to create the model. For this model, the creator might have used computer software or colored markers or pencils.

**Strategy ❹** Visualize and sketch an idea for your model. Once you have created a picture in your mind from either written text or other images, make an actual sketch to plan how your model might look.

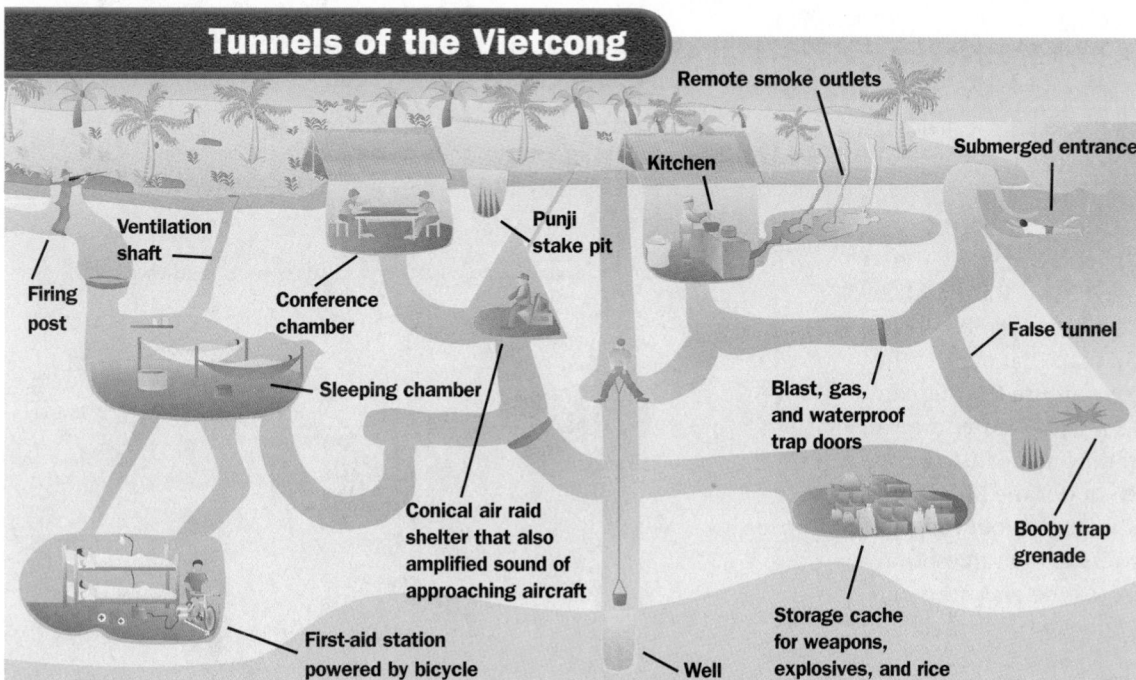

**Tunnels of the Vietcong**

Remote smoke outlets
Submerged entrance
Kitchen
Ventilation shaft
Punji stake pit
Firing post
Conference chamber
False tunnel
Sleeping chamber
Blast, gas, and waterproof trap doors
Booby trap grenade
Conical air raid shelter that also amplified sound of approaching aircraft
First-aid station powered by bicycle
Well
Storage cache for weapons, explosives, and rice

## PRACTICING THE SKILL

Turn to Chapter 6, Section 3, p. 244, and read the text under the heading "Labor Unions Emerge." Use the information to create a model of a "sweatshop" factory during the turn of the century. Use the process described above as a guide.

# 4.3 Creating Maps

### DEFINING THE SKILL

Maps are scale representations, usually of land surfaces. (See Skillbuilder 3.4.) Creating a map involves representing geographical data visually. When you draw a map, it is easiest to use an existing map as a guide. You can include data on climate and population and on patterns or distributions of human activity.

### APPLYING THE SKILL

The following chart shows the numbers of 1995 immigrants who planned to settle in the southwestern states of the United States. The map below depicts the data given in the chart.

| Immigrants, by State of Intended Residence, 1995 | | | | | |
|---|---|---|---|---|---|
| Arizona | 7,700 | Nevada | 4,306 | Texas | 49,963 |
| California | 166,482 | New Mexico | 2,758 | Utah | 2,831 |
| Colorado | 7,713 | | | | |

### HOW TO CREATE A MAP

**Strategy ❶** Determine what map you should use as a guide. Find a map of the southwest that you can re-create.

**Strategy ❷** Decide how best to show the data. These data can be grouped in three broad categories of numbers: more than 100,000; 10,000 to 100,000; and less than 10,000.

**Strategy ❸** Select a title that identifies the geographical area and the map's purpose. Include a date or time span.

**Strategy ❹** Draw and label the lines of latitude and longitude. Use the guide map's scale and a ruler to help you correctly space the lines of latitude and longitude.

**Strategy ❺** Draw the subject of your map, following your guide map carefully. Color or mark the map to show its purpose. Use each color or symbol to represent similar information.

**Strategy ❻** Include a key or legend explaining colors, symbols, or shading. Reproduce the scale and compass rose from the map you used as a guide.

### PRACTICING THE SKILL

Turn to p. 606 and study the graph titled "The Marshall Plan." Use the process described above to draw a map that depicts the data. (You can use the map on p. 605 as a guide.) After drawing the map pose some historical questions about the Marshall Plan. How might your map convey answers to your questions? Write one of the questions and its answer below your map.

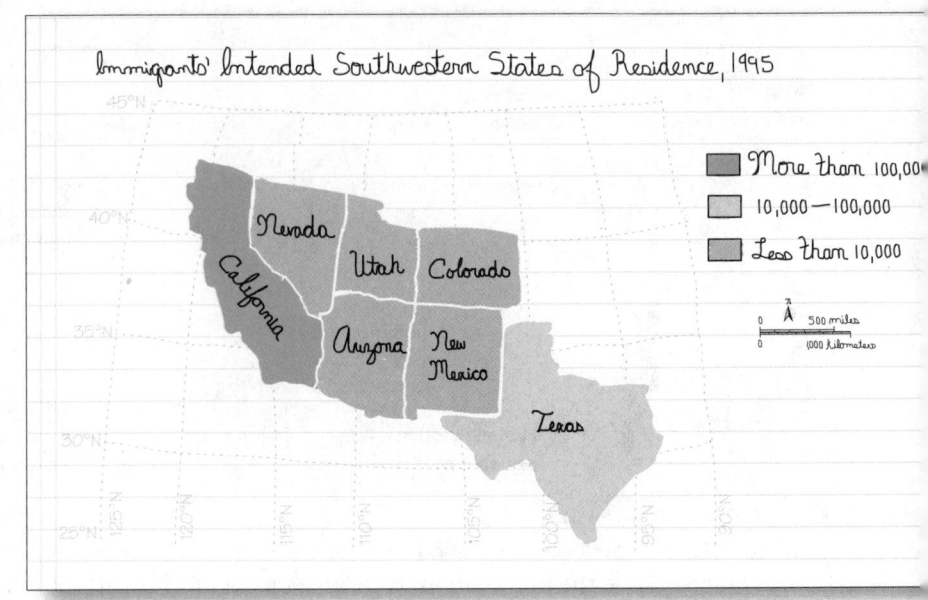

Immigrants' Intended Southwestern States of Residence, 1995

More than 100,000
10,000—100,000
Less than 10,000

# 4.4 Creating Databases

### DEFINING THE SKILL

A **database** is a collection of data, or information,. that is organized so that you can find and retrieve information on a specific topic quickly and easily. Once a computerized database is set up, you can search it to find specific information without going through the entire database. The database will provided a list of all stored information related to your topic. Learning how to use a database will help you learn how to create one.

### APPLYING THE SKILL

The chart below is a database for some of the significant legislation passed during President Johnson's Great Society program.

| 1 Significant Great Society Legislation | | |
|---|---|---|
| 2 Legislation | Date | Significance |
| 3 Economic Opportunity Act | 1964 | 4 created Job Corps and other programs to help the poor |
| Civil Rights Act | 1964 | outlawed discrimination in public accomodations |
| Medical Care Act | 1965 | 4 established Medicare and Medicaid programs to help the elderly and the poor |
| Higher Education Act | 1965 | provided low-interest loans for college students |
| Truth in Packaging Act | 1966 | set standards for labeling consumer products |
| Highway Safety Act | 1966 | required states to set up highway safety programs |
| Metropolitan Development Act | 1966 | 4 provided funds to rebuild poor neighborhoods |
| Air Quality Act | 1967 | set federal air pollution guidelines |

### HOW TO CREATE A DATABASE

**Strategy** 1 Identify the topic of the database. The keywords, or most important words, in the title are "Great Society" and "Legislation." These words were used to begin the research for this database.

**Strategy** 2 Identify the kind of data you need to enter in your database. These will be the column headings—or categories—of your database. The keywords "Legislation," "Date," and "Significance," were chosen to categorize this research.

**Strategy** 3 Once you find the data you want to include, identify the entries under each heading.

**Strategy** 4 Use the database to help you find the information quickly. For example, in this database you could search by the word "poor" for programs related to anti-poverty measures.

### PRACTICING THE SKILL

Turn to Chapter 11, "The First World War," and create a database of key battles of World War I. Use a format like the one above for your database and include the following column headings: "Battle," "Date," "Location," and "Signficance." You can create your database using computer software or by setting up a 4-column chart on paper.

# 4.5 Creating Written Presentations

### DEFINING THE SKILL

**Written presentations** are in-depth reports on a topic in history. Often, written presentations take a stand on an issue or try to support a specific conclusion. To successfully report on an event or make a point, your writing needs to be clear, concise, and supported by factual details.

### APPLYING THE SKILL

The following is a written presentation about the main goals of progressivism. Use the strategies listed below to help you learn to create a written presentation.

### HOW TO CREATE A WRITTEN PRESENTATION

**Strategy** ❶ Identify a topic that you wish to research, focusing on one or more questions that you hope to answer about the topic. Then research the topic using library resources and the Internet.

**Strategy** ❷ Formulate a hypothesis. This will serve as the main idea, or thesis, of your presentation. Analyze the information in your sources and develop a hypothesis that answers your questions about the topic.

**Strategy** ❸ Organize the facts and supporting details around your main idea. These facts and examples should be presented in a way that helps you build a logical case to prove your point.

**Strategy** ❹ To express your ideas clearly, use standard grammar, spelling, sentence structure, and punctuation. Proofread your work to make sure it is well-organized and grammatically correct.

For more on how to create a historical research paper and other written presentations, see the **Writing for Social Studies** handbook.

### Make an Outline

Creating an outline like the one shown here will help you organize your ideas and produce an effective written presentation.

❶ The Goals of Progressivism
I. ❷ All progressive reforms had one of four goals.
  A. Protecting Social Welfare
  ❸ 1. Social Gospel movement sought to help the poor.
    2. Settlement houses provided aid to poor city dwellers.
  B. Promoting Moral Improvement
    1. Reformers sought to improve Americans' personal behavior.
    2. WCTU worked for prohibition.
  C. Creating Economic Reform
    1. Writers criticized capitalism.
    2. American Socialist Party formed.
    3. Muckrakers exposed corruption in business and government.
  D. Fostering Efficiency
    1. Emergence of scientific management in the workplace
    2. Development of the assembly line

### The Goals of Progressivism

As America approached the 20th century a number of citizens tried to reform society. Their efforts formed what became known as the progressive movement. Progressive reformers had the following four goals: social welfare, moral improvement, economic reform, and efficiency.

> Use punctuation marks for their correct purposes. A colon precedes a list.

Many reformers sought to promote social welfare—especially in the crowded, run-down, and unhealthy areas of the cities. The Social Gospel movement inspired followers to erect churches in poor communities. It also persuaded business leaders to treat workers more fair. Other reformers established settlement house in slum neighborhoods which provided educational, cultural, and social services to people—especially to immigrants.

> Use the correct parts of speech. An adverb modifies a verb.
>
> Check for common agreement errors. Subjects and verbs must agree in person and number.

Another group of reformers felt that the lives of poor people could be improved through moral instruction. These reformers offered programs to improve personal behavior. The Women's Christian Temperance Union, for instance, promoted prohibition. It believed that alcohol was the root of many of society's problems.

> Use consistent verb tense. Use past tense for events in the past.

> Check spelling with both an electronic spell checker and a dictionary.

Other progressives, such as Henry George and Edward Bellamy, blamed the competitive nature of capitalism for creating a large underclass. Some Americans, especially workers, embraced socialism. In 1900, Eugene Debs helped organize the american socialist party. This organization Advocated communal living and a classless society. During the early 20th century, journalists exposed the corrupt side of business and politics known as muckrakers.

> Capitalize all proper nouns, including names of political parties.

> Use correct sentence structure. Every sentence needs a subject and a verb.

> Be sure sentence structure leads clearly from one phrase to the next. Correct misplaced modifiers.

Meanwhile, some tried to make American society more efficient. Frederick Winslow Taylor popularized scientific management, the effort to improve efficiency in the workplace by applying scientific principles. Out of this concept emerged the assembly line, which required workers to perform the same task over and over, and thus speed up production.

Through their hard work, the progressives reformed many levels of society and helped Americans live better lives.

## PRACTICING THE SKILL

Create a two-page written presentation on a topic of historical importance that interests you. Use the strategies and sample outline and draft to help you create your presentation.

# 4.6 Creating Oral Presentations

### DEFINING THE SKILL

An **oral presentation** is a speech or talk given before an audience. Oral presentations can be given to inform an audience about a certain topic or persuade an audience to think or act in a certain way. You can learn how to give effective oral presentations by examining some of the more famous ones in history.

### APPLYING THE SKILL

The following is an excerpt from a student's speech supporting Southern secession. Use the strategies listed below to help you learn to create an oral presentation.

### HOW TO CREATE AN ORAL PRESENTATION

**Strategy ❶** Choose one central idea or theme and organize your presentation to support it. Here, the writer calls for the United States government to allow the Southern states to secede.

**Strategy ❷** Use words or images to persuade your audience. In this speech, the writer has used a metaphor of family conflict to express the antagonism between North and South.

**Strategy ❸** Make sure your arguments support your central idea or theme. In this speech, the writer's arguments all support the main theme.

> ❶ The Southern states should be allowed to secede. ❸ Since it was the states that helped create the national government, surely the states have the right to declare their independence from that government.
>
> The industrial North will never understand the needs of the farmers and plantation owners of the South. ❷ The South and the North are like two brothers whose lives and attitudes have become so different that they can no longer live under the same roof. Why should they be forced to remain together?

### Giving an Oral Presentation

When you give an oral presentation, make sure to
- maintain eye contact with your audience.
- use gestures and body language to emphasize your main points and to help express your ideas.
- pace yourself. Do not rush to finish your presentation.
- vary your tone of voice to help bring out the meaning of your words.

### PRACTICING THE SKILL

Turn to Chapter 16, Section 4, p. 552, and study the Point/Counterpoint feature about U.S. involvement in WWII. Choose a side and create an outline for a speech that supports that side. Use the strategies to help you make an oral presentation.

# 4.7 Creating Visual Presentations

### DEFINING THE SKILL

A **visual presentation** of history uses visual sources to explain a particular historical event. Such sources could include paintings, maps, charts and graphs, costume drawings, photographs, political cartoons, and advertisements. Movies, CD-ROMs, television, and computer software are the newest kind of visual sources, called multimedia sources because they also include sound. (See Skillbuilder 3.2.) Visual sources can provide much insight into various eras and events of the past. Creating a visual presentation will help you to become more familiar with the many differents sources of historical information available.

### APPLYING THE SKILL

The image below shows a student using a computer to create a visual presentation. Use the strategies listed below to help you plan out the steps needed to compile a clear, engaging, and informative presentation.

### HOW TO CREATE A VISUAL PRESENTATION

**Strategy** ❶ Identify the topic of your presentation and decide which types of visuals will most effectively convey your information. For example, you might want to use slides and posters along with a map. If you want to include multimedia sources, you could use documentary film or television footage of an event.

**Strategy** ❷ Conduct research to determine what visual sources are available. Some topics, such as wars, may have more visual source material than others. You can create your own visual sources, such as a graph or chart, to accompany what you find.

**Strategy** ❸ Write a script for the presentation. A narration of events to accompany the visuals will tie the various sources together and aid you in telling the story.

**Strategy** ❹ Videotape the presentation. Videotaping the presentation will preserve it for future viewing and allow you to show it to different groups of people.

### PRACTICING THE SKILL

Turn to Chapter 5, Section 1, p. 210, and read "A Day in the Life of a Cowboy," or choose another section in the chapter. Use the strategies above to create a visual presentation of the topic.

# ECONOMICS HANDBOOK

**NOTE:** *Boldfaced words are terms that appear in this handbook.*

**BOYCOTT** *A refusal to have economic dealings with a person, a business, an organization, or a country.* The purpose of a boycott is to show disapproval of particular actions or to force changes in those actions. A boycott often involves an economic act, such as refusing to buy a company's goods or services.

African Americans in Montgomery, Alabama (shown below), organized a bus boycott in 1955 to fight segregation on city buses. The boycotters kept many buses nearly empty for 381 days. The boycott ended one month after the Supreme Court outlawed bus segregation.

American labor unions have sometimes used boycotts to win concessions for their members. Consumer groups, too, have organized boycotts to win changes in business practices.

**BUSINESS CYCLE** *A pattern of increases and decreases in economic activity.* A business cycle generally consists of four distinct phases—expansion, peak, contraction, and trough, as shown in the graph in the next column.

An expansion is marked by increased business activity. The **unemployment rate** falls, businesses produce more, and consumers buy more goods and services. A peak is a transition period in which expansion slows. A contraction, or **recession,** occurs when business activity decreases. The unemployment rate rises, while both production and consumer spending fall. A deep and long-lasting contraction is called a **depression.** Business activity reaches its lowest point during a trough. After time, business activity starts to increase and a new cycle begins.

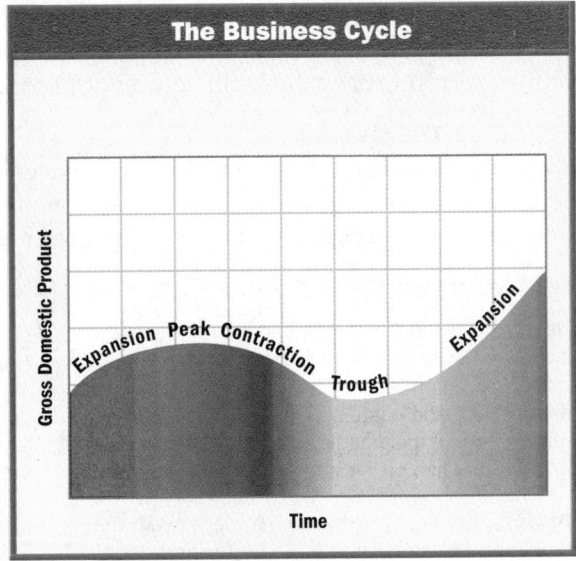

**CAPITALISM** *An economic system in which there is private ownership of natural resources and capital goods.* The basic idea of capitalism is that producers are driven by the desire to make a profit —the money left over after costs have been subtracted from revenues. This desire for profit motivates producers to provide consumers with the goods and services they desire. Prices and wages are determined by **supply and demand.**

Along with the opportunity to earn a profit there is a risk. Businesses tend to fail if they don't produce goods people want at prices they are willing to pay. Because anyone is free to start a business or enterprise, a capitalist system is also known as a **free enterprise** system.

Capitalism contrasts with **socialism,** an economic system in which the government owns and controls capital and sets prices and production levels. Critics of capitalism argue that it allows decisions that ought to be made democratically to be made instead by powerful business owners and that it allows too-great disparities in wealth and well-being between the poor and the rich.

**COMMUNISM** *An economic system based on one-party rule, government ownership of the means of production, and decision making by centralized authorities.* Under communism there is little or no private ownership of property and little or no political freedom. Government planners make economic decisions, such as which and how many goods and services should be produced. Individuals have little say in a communist economy. Such a system, communists believe, would end inequality. For more information on the ideas on which communism is based, read the Economic Background on page 413.

During the 20th century, most communist economies failed to achieve their goals. Economic decisions frequently were made to benefit only Communist Party officials. Also, government economic planning was inefficient, often creating shortages of goods. Those goods that were available were often of poor quality.

People became discontented with the lack of prosperity and political freedom and began to call for change. These demands led in the late 1980s and early 1990s to the collapse of communist governments in the Soviet Union and Eastern Europe.

Even governments that clung to communism introduced elements of **free enterprise.** Some communist countries—such as China—have experienced economic growth but have not granted more political freedom to their citizens.

**CONSUMER PRICE INDEX (CPI)** *A measure of the change in cost of the goods and services most commonly bought by consumers.* The CPI notes the prices of over 200 goods and services bought by average urban consumers on a regular basis. Items on which consumers spend a good deal of their income—such as food and housing—are given more weight in the CPI than items on which consumers spend less.

Price changes are calculated by comparing current prices with prices at a set time in the past. In 2001, for example, the CPI used the period from 1982 to 1984 as this base. Prices for this period are given a base value of 100. The prices for subsequent years are expressed as percentages of the base. Therefore, a CPI of 160 means that prices have risen by 60 percent since 1982–1984. The graph below illustrates changes in the CPI from 1960 to 2000.

Consumer Price Index, 1960–2000

Source: Bureau of Labor Statistics

**DEFICIT SPENDING** *A situation in which a government spends more money than it receives in revenues.* For the most part, the government engages in deficit spending when the economy is in a contraction phase of the **business cycle.** The government borrows or issues money to finance deficit spending.

In theory, the extra funds should stimulate business activity, pushing the economy into an expansion phase. As the economy recovers, revenues should increase, providing the government with a budget surplus. The government then can use the surplus to pay back the money it borrowed. For more information on deficit spending, read the Economic Background on page 492.

ECONOMICS HANDBOOK **R39**

**R39**

**DEPRESSION** *A very severe and prolonged contraction in economic activity.* During a depression, consumer spending, production levels, wages, prices, and profits fall sharply. Many businesses fail, and many workers lose their jobs.

The United States has experienced several economic depressions in its history. The worst was the Great Depression, which started in 1929 and lasted throughout the 1930s. Between 1929 and 1932, business activity in the United States decreased by an average of 10 percent each year. During the same period, some 40 percent of the country's banks failed, and prices for farm products dropped more than 50 percent. By 1933, the worst year of the Great Depression, 30 percent of American workers were unemployed—some, like the man shown below, were reduced to selling apples on the street.

For a personal account of life during the Great Depression, view the *American Stories* video "Broke but Not Broken: Ann Marie Low Remembers the Dust Bowl." For information about the effects of war on a depression, read the Economic Background on page 557.

**E-COMMERCE** *All forms of buying and selling goods and services electronically.* Short for "electronic commerce," e-commerce refers to business activity on the Internet and on private computer networks. There are two main types of e-commerce: business-to-consumer and business-to-business.

Consumer-related e-commerce includes sales to the public over the computer, usually through a seller's Web site. Many business transactions can be completed wholly electronically, such as sales of computer software, which can be paid for with a credit card number and delivered over the Internet directly to the buyer's computer. A growing proportion of financial transactions are also moving online, such as electronic banking and **stock market** trading, or e-trading. The convenience of online shopping has turned it into a booming enterprise. Between 1998 and 1999, for instance, U.S. consumer spending online grew from about $7.7 billion to more than $17 billion.

Business-to-business e-commerce is growing at an even greater rate, reaching nearly $177 billion in 1999. Much of that business includes Web site design and servicing and online advertising. Businesses also use networked computers to purchase supplies and merchandise and to access information from subscription services.

For many businesses, e-commerce is not only convenient but also cost-effective. On average, corporations spend $100 on paperwork alone each time they make a purchase. Moving those transactions online could save companies millions of dollars annually.

**EMBARGO** *A government ban on trade with another nation, commonly backed by military force.* In a civil embargo the nation imposing an embargo prevents exports to or imports from the country against which it has declared the embargo. A hostile embargo involves seizing the goods of another nation.

The major purpose of an embargo is to show disapproval of a nation's actions. For example, in 1980 the United States imposed a civil embargo on grain sales to the Soviet Union to protest the December 1979 Soviet invasion of Afghanistan.

**FREE ENTERPRISE** *An economic system based on the private ownership of the means of production, free markets, and the right of individuals to make most economic decisions.* The free enterprise system is also called the free market system or **capitalism.** The United States has a free enterprise economic system.

In a free enterprise system, producers and consumers are motivated by self-interest. To maximize their profits, producers try to make goods and services that consumers want. Producers also engage in competition—through lowering prices, advertising their products, and improving product quality—to encourage consumers to buy their goods. Consumers serve their self-interest by purchasing the best goods and services for the lowest price.

Government plays a limited, but important, role in most free-enterprise economies:

- It regulates economic activity to ensure there is fair competition, such as by preventing and prosecuting fraud and barring **monopolies.**

- It produces certain necessary goods and services that private producers consider unprofitable, such as roadways.

- It protects the public health and safety, such as through building codes, environmental protection laws, and labor laws.

- It provides economic stability, such as by regulating banks, coining money, and supervising unemployment insurance programs.

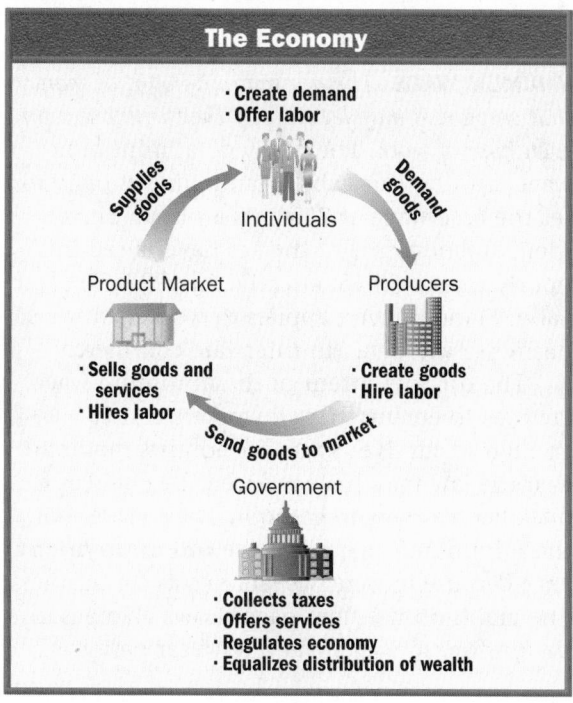

**GOLD STANDARD** *A monetary system in which a country's basic unit of currency is valued at, and can be exchanged for, a fixed amount of gold.* The gold standard tends to curb **inflation,** since a government cannot put more currency into circulation than it can back with its gold supplies. This gives people confidence in the currency.

This advantage is also a weakness of the gold standard. During times of **recession,** a government may want to increase the amount of money in circulation to encourage economic growth. Economic disruption during the Great Depression of the 1930s caused most nations to abandon the gold standard. The United States moved to a modified gold standard in 1934 and abandoned the gold standard completely in 1971.

**GROSS DOMESTIC PRODUCT (GDP)** *The market value of all the goods and services produced in a nation within a specific time period, such as a quarter (three months) or a year.* It is the standard measure of how a nation's economy is performing. If GDP is growing, the economy is probably in an expansion phase. If GDP is not increasing or is declining, the economy is probably in a contraction phase.

GDP is calculated by adding four components: spending by individual consumers on goods and services; investment in such items as new factories, new factory machinery, and houses; government spending on goods and services; and net exports—the value of exports less the value of imports. GDP figures are presented in two ways. Nominal GDP is reported in current dollars. Real GDP is reported in constant dollars, or dollars adjusted for **inflation.**

**INFLATION** *A sustained rise in the average level of prices.* Since more money is required to make purchases when prices rise, inflation is sometimes defined as a decrease in the purchasing value of money. Economists measure price changes with indexes. The most widely used index in the United States is the **consumer price index (CPI).**

Inflation may result if the demand for goods increases without an increase in the production of goods. Inflation may also take place if the cost of producing goods increases. Producers pass on increased costs, such as higher wages and more expensive raw materials, by charging consumers higher prices.

**INTEREST RATE** *The cost of borrowing money.* Interest is calculated as a yearly percentage, or rate, of the money borrowed. A 10 percent interest rate, therefore, would require a borrower to pay $10 per year for every $100 borrowed.

When interest rates are low, people will borrow more, because the cost of borrowing is lower. However, they will save and invest less, because the return on their savings or investment is lower. With high interest rates, people save and invest more but borrow less. Because interest rates affect the economy, the government takes steps to control them through the Federal Reserve System, the nation's central banking system. The graph below shows the relationship between the rate of **inflation** and interest rates over time.

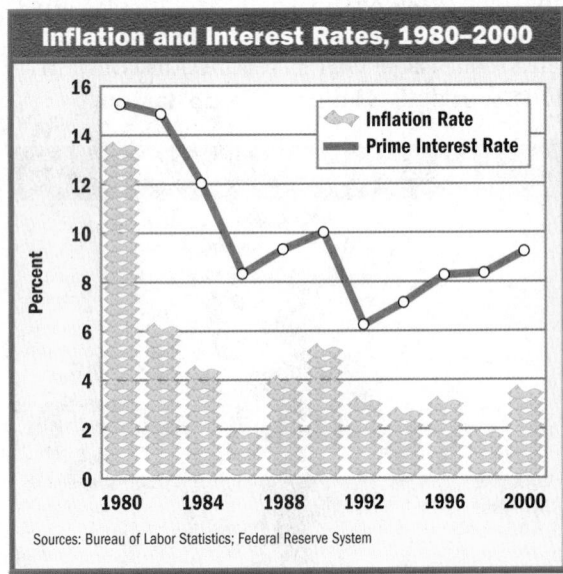

**Inflation and Interest Rates, 1980–2000**

Percent

— Inflation Rate
— Prime Interest Rate

1980   1984   1988   1992   1996   2000

Sources: Bureau of Labor Statistics; Federal Reserve System

**KEYNESIAN ECONOMICS** *The use of government spending to encourage economic activity by increasing the demand for goods.* This approach is based on the ideas of British economist John Maynard Keynes (shown below). In a 1936 study, Keynes pointed out that during economic downturns, more people are unemployed and have less income to spend. As a result, businesses cut production and lay off more workers.

Keynes's answer to this problem was for government to increase spending and reduce **taxes.** This would stimulate demand for goods and services by replacing the decline in consumer demand. Government would want goods and services for its new programs. More people would be working and earning an income and, therefore, would want to buy more goods and services. Businesses would increase production to meet this new demand. As a result, the economy would soon recover.

Critics maintain, however, that Keynesian economics has led to the growth of government and to high taxes, inflation, high unemployment, and low economic growth. For an example of Keynesian economics at work, read the Economic Background on page 557.

**MINIMUM WAGE** *The minimum amount of money that employers may legally pay their employees for each hour of work.* The first federal minimum wage law, the Fair Labor Standards Act of 1938, set the base wage at 25 cents an hour. Since then, amendments to the act have raised this hourly rate to $5.15, effective in 1997. The Fair Labor Standards Act applies to workers in most businesses involved in interstate commerce.

The original intent of the minimum wage law was to ensure that all workers earned enough to survive. Some economists maintain that the law may have reduced the chances for unskilled workers to get jobs. They argue that the minimum wage raises the **unemployment rate** because it increases labor costs for business. The graph on the next page shows changes in the minimum wage over a ten-year period.

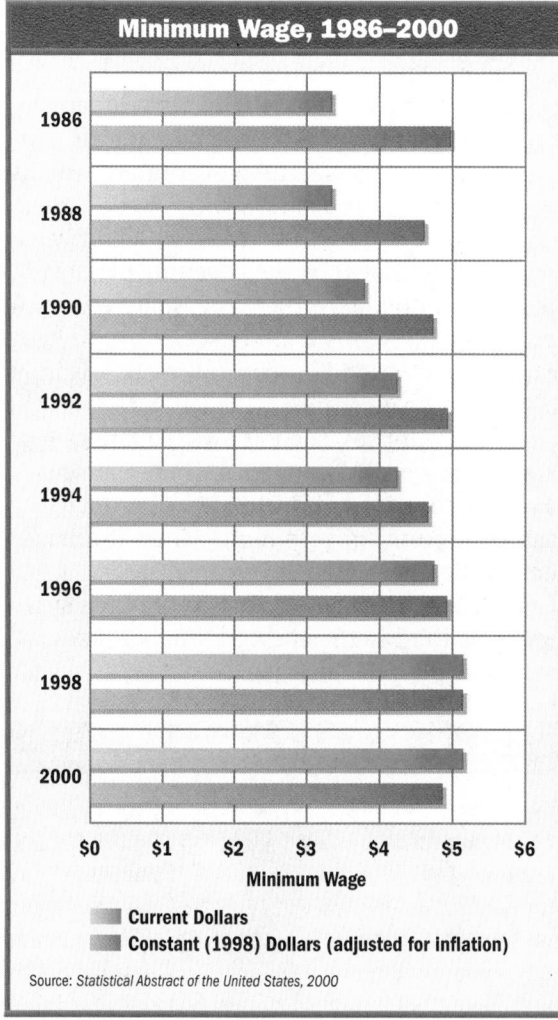

**Minimum Wage, 1986–2000**

| | |
| --- | --- |
| 1986 | |
| 1988 | |
| 1990 | |
| 1992 | |
| 1994 | |
| 1996 | |
| 1998 | |
| 2000 | |

$0   $1   $2   $3   $4   $5   $6
**Minimum Wage**

■ Current Dollars
■ Constant (1998) Dollars (adjusted for inflation)

Source: *Statistical Abstract of the United States, 2000*

**MONOPOLY** *A situation in which only one seller controls the production, supply, or pricing of a product for which there are no close substitutes.* In the United States, basic public services such as electrical power distributors and cable television suppliers operate as local monopolies. This way of providing utilities is economically more efficient than having several competing companies running electricity or cable lines in the same area.

Monopolies, however, can be harmful to the economy. Since it has no competition, a monopoly does not need to respond to the wants of consumers by improving product quality or by charging fair prices. The government counters the threat of monopoly either by breaking up or regulating the monopoly.

**NATIONAL DEBT** *The money owed by a national government.* During wartime, during economic recession, or at other times, the government may employ **deficit spending.** However, the government may not pay back all the money it has borrowed to fund this policy. Each year's federal budget deficit adds to the national debt. By 2000, the national debt of the United States stood at $5.67 trillion, or about $20,000 for each citizen.

The rapid growth of the U.S. national debt since 1980 has prompted many Americans to call for changes in government economic policies. Some suggest that the government raise taxes and cut spending to reduce the debt. Others recommend a constitutional amendment that would require the government to have a balanced budget, spending only as much as it takes in.

**POVERTY** *The lack of adequate income to maintain a minimum* **standard of living.** In the United States, this adequate income is referred to as the poverty line. In 1999, the poverty threshold for a family of four was $17,029. That year, the poverty rate dropped to 11.8 percent—the lowest rate since 1979, and more than 32 million Americans lived in poverty.

While poverty rates have remained relatively steady over the last 30 or so years, inequality in the distribution of income has grown. Between 1970 and 2000, the share of income received by the wealthiest 20 percent of families increased from 43.3 percent to 56.7 percent. In the same period, the poorest 20 percent of families' share of income fell from 4.1 percent to 2.7 percent.

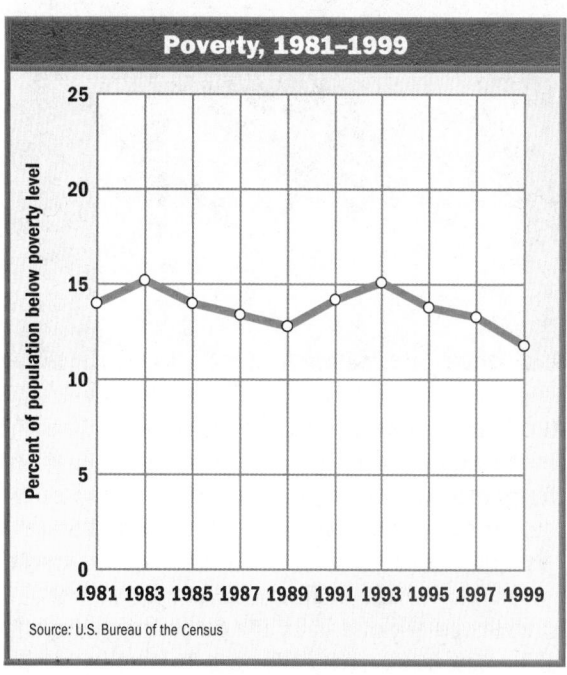

**Poverty, 1981–1999**

Percent of population below poverty level

25
20
15
10
5
0

1981 1983 1985 1987 1989 1991 1993 1995 1997 1999

Source: U.S. Bureau of the Census

**PRODUCTIVITY** *The relationship between the output of goods and services and the input of resources.* Productivity is the amount of goods or services that a person can produce at a given time. It is closely linked to economic growth, which is defined as an increase in a nation's real **gross domestic product (GDP)** from one year to the next. A substantial rise in productivity means the average worker is producing more, a key factor in spurring economic expansion. Between 1995 and 2000, for example, worker productivity in the United States increased about 3 percent each year. This increase, along with other economic factors, helped the nation's real GDP grow an average of about 4 percent during those years.

A number of elements affect productivity, including available supplies of labor and raw materials, education and training, attitudes toward work, and technological innovations. Computer technology, for instance, is believed to have played a significant role in bolstering productivity during the 1990s by allowing workers to do their jobs more quickly and efficiently. Conversely, a lack of adequate training and fewer innovations were thought to be behind the meager productivity growth rates of the 1970s and 1980s—when productivity rose at an annual rate of less than 1 percent.

**RECESSION** *A period of declining economic activity.* In economic terms, a recession takes place when the **gross domestic product** falls for two quarters, or six months, in a row. The United States has experienced several of these **business-cycle** contractions in its history. On average, they have lasted about a year. If a recession persists and economic activity plunges, it is called a **depression.** For more information on recessions, read the Economic Background on page 680.

**SOCIALISM** *An economic system in which the government owns most of the means of production and distribution.* Like **communism,** the goal of socialism is to use the power of government to reduce inequality and meet people's needs. Under socialism, however, the government usually owns only major industries, such as coal, steel, and transportation. Other industries are privately owned but regulated by the government. Government and individuals, therefore, share economic decision-making. Also, under socialism, the government may provide such services as reasonably priced health care.

Some countries, such as Sweden, are called democratic socialist countries. These nations have less government ownership of property than communist governments. They also have democratically elected governments.

Critics of socialism maintain that this system leads to less efficiency and higher taxes than does the **free enterprise** system.

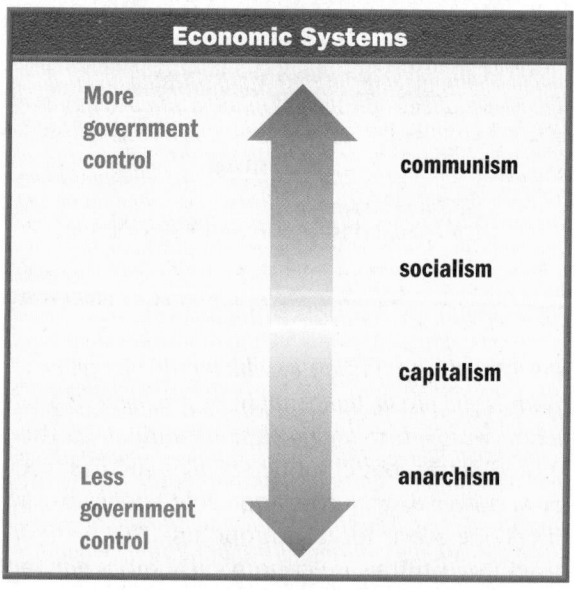

**STANDARD OF LIVING** *The overall economic situation in which people live.* Economists differ on how best to measure the standard of living. Some suggest average personal income, while others propose per capita **gross domestic product**—the GDP divided by the population. Another possible measure is the value of the goods and services bought by consumers during a year. In general terms, the nation's standard of living rises as these measures rise. Some people argue that measuring the quality of life also requires consideration of noneconomic factors such as pollution, health, work hours, and even political freedom.

**STOCK MARKET *or* STOCK EXCHANGE** *A place where stocks and bonds are bought and sold.* Since stocks and bonds together are known as securities, a stock market is sometimes called a securities market.

Large companies often need extra money to fund expansion and to help cover operating costs. To raise money, they sell stocks, or shares of ownership, in their companies or borrow by issuing bonds, or certificates of debt, promising to repay the money borrowed, plus interest.

Individuals invest in securities to make a profit. Most stockholders receive dividends, or a share of the company's profits. Bondholders receive interest. Investors may also make a profit by selling their securities. This sale of securities takes place in the stock exchange.

Stocks and bonds are traded on exchanges. The largest and most important exchange in the United States is the New York Stock Exchange (pictured below; for more information on the New York Stock Exchange, read the Now & Then on page 468). Activity on this and other exchanges often signals how well the economy is doing. A bull market—when stock prices rise—usually indicates economic expansion. A bear market—when stock prices fall—usually indicates economic contraction.

A rapid fall in stock prices is called a crash. The worst stock market crash in the United States came in October 1929. To help protect against another drastic stock market crash, the federal government set up the Securities and Exchange Commission (SEC), which regulates the trading of securities.

| Selected World Stock Exchanges | |
| --- | --- |
| **Exchange** | **Products** |
| New York Stock Exchange (NYSE) | stocks, bonds |
| American Stock Exchange (AMEX) (New York) | stocks, bonds |
| National Association of Securities Dealers Automated Quotations (NASDAQ) | over-the-counter stocks |
| London Stock Exchange | stocks |
| Tokyo Stock Exchange | stocks, bonds, futures, options |
| Hong Kong Stock Exchange | stocks, bonds, mutual funds |
| German Stock Exchange (Frankfurt) | stocks |

**STRIKE** *A work stoppage by employees to gain higher wages, better working conditions, or other benefits.* Strikes are also sometimes used as political protests. A strike is usually preceded by a failure in collective bargaining—the negotiation of contracts between labor unions and employers. Union members may decide to call a strike if they believe negotiations with the employer are deadlocked. Collective bargaining and strikes are regulated by the NLRA, or Wagner Act, of 1935, administered by the National Labor Relations Board (NLRB). There are also wildcat strikes, which do not involve unions.

When strikes do occur, union representatives and employers try to negotiate a settlement. An outside party is sometimes asked to help work out an agreement.

For a personal account of a strike, view the *American Stories* video, "A Child on Strike: The Testimony of Camella Teoli, Mill Girl."

**SUPPLY AND DEMAND** *The forces that determine prices of goods and services in a market economy.* Supply is the amount of a good or service that producers are willing and able to produce at a given price. Demand is the amount of a good or service consumers are willing and able to buy at a given price. In general, producers are willing to produce more of a good or service when prices are high; conversely, consumers are willing to buy more of a good or service when prices are low.

The table and graph below show supply and demand for a certain product. The line *S* shows the amount of the good that producers would be willing to make at various prices. The line *D* shows the amount that consumers would be willing to buy at various prices. Point *E*, where the two lines intersect, is called the equilibrium price. It is the price at which the amount produced and the amount demanded would be the same.

When the equilibrium price is the market price, the market operates efficiently. At prices above the equilibrium price, consumers will demand less than producers supply. Producers, therefore, will have to lower their prices to sell the surplus, or excess, products. At prices below equilibrium, consumers will demand more. Producers will be able to raise their prices because the product is scarce, or in short supply.

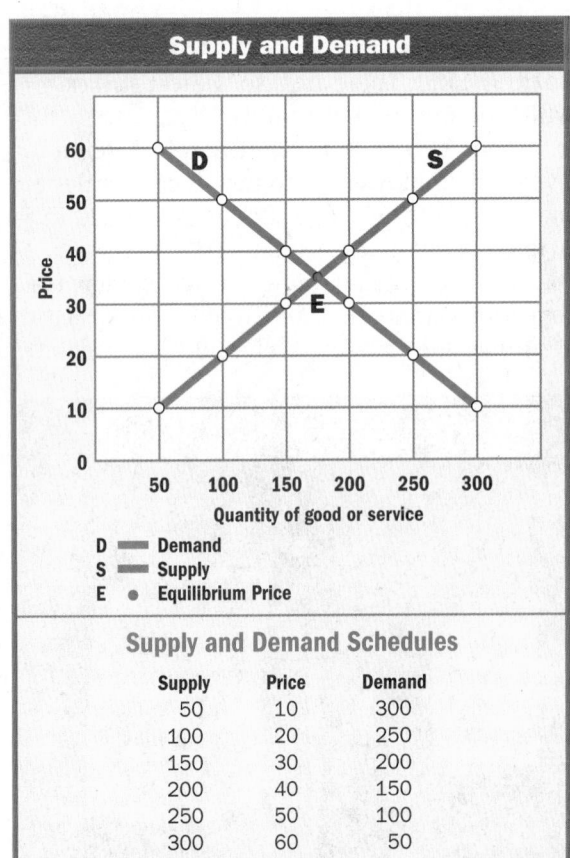

**Supply and Demand**

| Supply | Price | Demand |
|--------|-------|--------|
| 50 | 10 | 300 |
| 100 | 20 | 250 |
| 150 | 30 | 200 |
| 200 | 40 | 150 |
| 250 | 50 | 100 |
| 300 | 60 | 50 |

D ▬ Demand
S ▬ Supply
E ● Equilibrium Price

**Supply and Demand Schedules**

**SUPPLY-SIDE ECONOMICS** *Government policies designed to stimulate the production of goods and services, or the supply side of the economy.* Supply-side economists developed these policies in opposition to **Keynesian economics.**

Supply-side policies call for low tax rates particularly in income from investments. Lower taxes mean that people keep more of each dollar they earn. Therefore, supply-side economists argue, people will work harder in order to earn more. They will then use their extra income to save and invest. This investment will fund the development of new businesses and, as a result, create more jobs. For more information on supply-side economics, read the Economic Background on page 835.

**TARIFF** *A fee charged for goods brought into a state or country from another state or country.* Beginning in 1789, Congress created tariffs to raise revenue and to protect American products from foreign competition. Soon, however, special interest groups used tariffs to protect specific industries and increase profits.

**Trade** without tariffs is called free trade. In recent decades, a growing number of U.S. economists have favored free trade policies because they believe that such policies will help increase U.S. exports to other countries. In 1994, the North American Free Trade Agreement (NAFTA) established a free-trade zone among the United States, Canada, and Mexico.

**TAXATION** *The practice of requiring persons, groups, or businesses to contribute funds to the government under which they reside or transact business.* All levels of government—federal, state, and local—collect many kinds of taxes. Income taxes are the chief source of revenue for the federal government and an important revenue source for many states. Both corporations and individuals pay income tax, or taxes on earnings. Since its inception in 1913, the federal income tax has been a progressive tax, one that is graduated, or scaled, such that those with greater incomes are taxed at a greater rate.

Sales taxes are another important source of income for state governments.

Property taxes are the main source of funds for local governments. Property tax is calculated as a percentage of the assessed value of real estate —land and improvements such as buildings.

**TRADE** *The exchange of goods and services between countries.* Almost all nations produce goods that other countries need, and they sell (export) those goods to buyers in other countries. At the same time, they buy (import) goods from other countries as well. For example, Americans sell goods such as wheat to people in Japan and buy Japanese goods such as automobiles in return.

Nations that trade with one another often become dependent on one another's products. Sometimes this brings nations closer together, as it did the United States, Great Britain, and France before World War I. Other times it causes tension among nations, such as that between the United States and Arab oil-producing countries in the 1970s. For an example of how trade influences foreign policy, read the Economic Background on page 377.

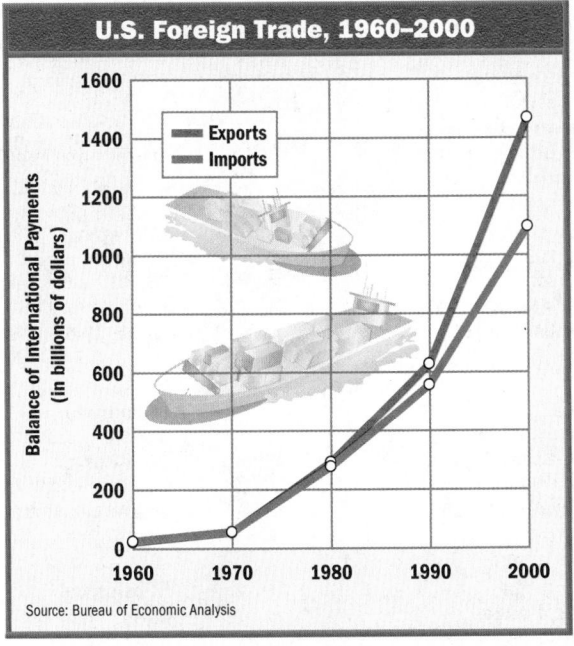

**U.S. Foreign Trade, 1960–2000**

Source: Bureau of Economic Analysis

**TRUST** *A form of business merger in which the major stockholders in several corporations turn over their stock to a group of trustees.* The trustees then run the separate corporations as one large company, or trust. In return for their stock, the stockholders of the separate corporations receive a share of the trust's profits.

American business leaders of the late 1800s used trusts to stifle competition and take control of entire industries, as in a **monopoly.** Trusts were outlawed by the Sherman Antitrust Act of 1890. However, business leaders eventually found other ways to merge corporations in an industry.

**UNEMPLOYMENT RATE** *The percentage of the labor force that is unemployed but actively looking for work.* The labor force consists of all civilians 16 years of age and older who are employed or who are unemployed but actively looking and available for work. The size of the labor force and the unemployment rate are determined by surveys conducted by the U.S. Bureau of the Census.

The unemployment rate provides an indicator of economic health. Rising unemployment rates signal a contraction in the economy, while falling rates indicate an economic expansion. The graphs below show two different methods of portraying unemployment in the United States.

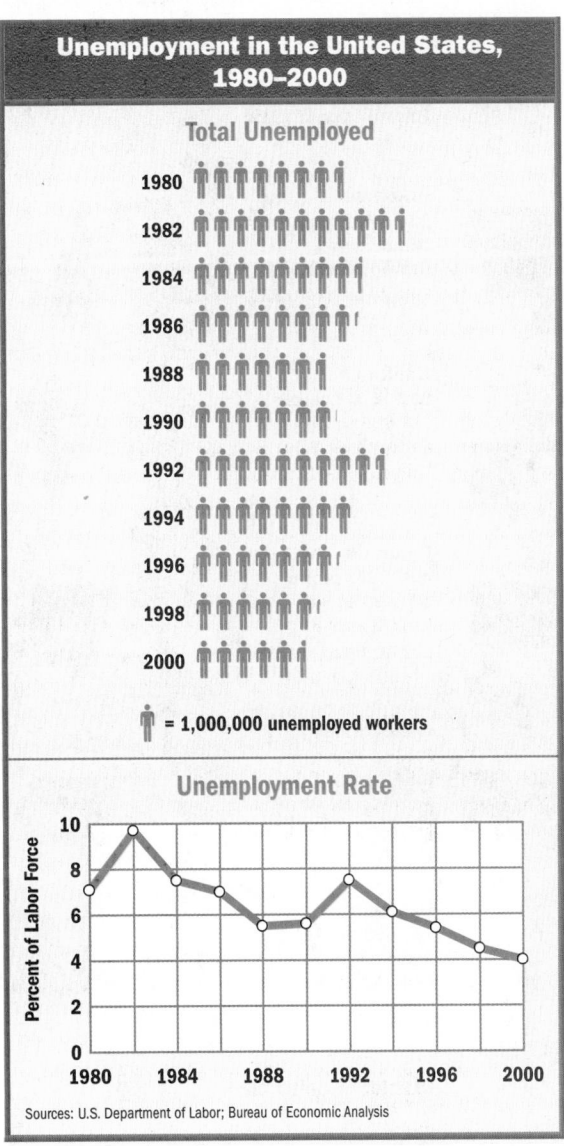

**Unemployment in the United States, 1980–2000**

Total Unemployed

= 1,000,000 unemployed workers

Unemployment Rate

Sources: U.S. Department of Labor; Bureau of Economic Analysis

# FACTS ABOUT THE STATES

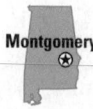
**Alabama**
4,447,000 people
52,237 sq. mi.
Rank in area: 30
Entered Union in 1819

**Florida**
15,982,378 people
59,928 sq. mi.
Rank in area: 23
Entered Union in 1845

**Louisiana**
4,468,976 people
49,651 sq. mi.
Rank in area: 31
Entered Union in 1812

**Alaska**
626,932 people
615,230 sq. mi.
Rank in area: 1
Entered Union in 1959

**Georgia**
8,816,453 people
58,977 sq. mi.
Rank in area: 24
Entered Union in 1788

**Maine**
1,274,923 people
33,741 sq. mi.
Rank in area: 39
Entered Union in 1820

**Arizona**
5,130,632 people
114,006 sq. mi.
Rank in area: 6
Entered Union in 1912

**Hawaii**
1,211,537 people
6,459 sq. mi.
Rank in area: 47
Entered Union in 1959

**Maryland**
5,296,486 people
12,297 sq. mi.
Rank in area: 42
Entered Union in 1788

**Arkansas**
2,673,400 people
53,182 sq. mi.
Rank in area: 28
Entered Union in 1836

**Idaho**
1,293,953 people
83,574 sq. mi.
Rank in area: 14
Entered Union in 1890

**Massachusetts**
6,349,097 people
9,241 sq. mi.
Rank in area: 45
Entered Union in 1788

**California**
33,871,648 people
158,869 sq. mi.
Rank in area: 3
Entered Union in 1850

**Illinois**
12,419,293 people
57,918 sq. mi.
Rank in area: 25
Entered Union in 1818

**Michigan**
9,938,444 people
96,705 sq. mi.
Rank in area: 11
Entered Union in 1837

**Colorado**
4,301,261 people
104,100 sq. mi.
Rank in area: 8
Entered Union in 1876

**Indiana**
6,080,485 people
36,420 sq. mi.
Rank in area: 38
Entered Union in 1816

**Minnesota**
4,919,479 people
86,943 sq. mi.
Rank in area: 12
Entered Union in 1858

**Connecticut**
3,405,565 people
5,544 sq. mi.
Rank in area: 48
Entered Union in 1788

**Iowa**
2,926,324 people
56,276 sq. mi.
Rank in area: 26
Entered Union in 1846

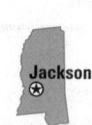
**Mississippi**
2,844,658 people
48,286 sq. mi.
Rank in area: 32
Entered Union in 1817

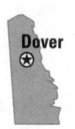
**Delaware**
783,600 people
2,396 sq. mi.
Rank in area: 49
Entered Union in 1787

**Kansas**
2,688,418 people
82,282 sq. mi.
Rank in area: 15
Entered Union in 1861

**Missouri**
5,595,211 people
69,709 sq. mi.
Rank in area: 21
Entered Union in 1821

**District of Columbia**
572,059 people
68 sq. mi.

**Kentucky**
4,041,769 people
40,411 sq. mi.
Rank in area: 37
Entered Union in 1792

**Montana**
902,195 people
147,046 sq. mi.
Rank in area: 4
Entered Union in 1889

*Population figures are according to the 2000 decennial census.*

**Nebraska**
1,711,263 people
77,359 sq. mi.
Rank in area: 16
Entered Union in 1867

**Oregon**
3,421,399 people
97,832 sq. mi.
Rank in area: 10
Entered Union in 1859

**Utah**
2,233,169 people
84,904 sq. mi.
Rank in area: 13
Entered Union in 1896

**Nevada**
1,998,257 people
110,567 sq. mi.
Rank in area: 7
Entered Union in 1864

**Pennsylvania**
12,281,054 people
46,058 sq. mi.
Rank in area: 33
Entered Union in 1787

**Vermont**
608,827 people
9,615 sq. mi.
Rank in area: 43
Entered Union in 1791

**New Hampshire**
1,235,786 people
9,283 sq. mi.
Rank in area: 44
Entered Union in 1788

**Rhode Island**
1,048,319 people
1,231 sq. mi.
Rank in area: 50
Entered Union in 1790

**Virginia**
7,078,515 people
42,326 sq. mi.
Rank in area: 35
Entered Union in 1788

**New Jersey**
8,414,350 people
8,215 sq. mi.
Rank in area: 46
Entered Union in 1787

**South Carolina**
4,012,012 people
31,189 sq. mi.
Rank in area: 40
Entered Union in 1788

**Washington**
5,894,121 people
70,637 sq. mi.
Rank in area: 19
Entered Union in 1889

**New Mexico**
1,819,046 people
121,598 sq. mi.
Rank in area: 5
Entered Union in 1912

**South Dakota**
754,844 people
77,121 sq. mi.
Rank in area: 17
Entered Union in 1889

**West Virginia**
1,808,344 people
24,231 sq. mi.
Rank in area: 41
Entered Union in 1863

**New York**
18,976,457 people
53,989 sq. mi.
Rank in area: 27
Entered Union in 1788

**Tennessee**
5,689,283 people
42,146 sq. mi.
Rank in area: 36
Entered Union in 1796

**Wisconsin**
5,363,675 people
64,599 sq. mi.
Rank in area: 22
Entered Union in 1848

**North Carolina**
8,049,313 people
52,672 sq. mi.
Rank in area: 29
Entered Union in 1789

**Texas**
20,851,820 people
267,277 sq. mi.
Rank in area: 2
Entered Union in 1845

**Wyoming**
493,782 people
97,819 sq. mi.
Rank in area: 9
Entered Union in 1890

**North Dakota**
642,200 people
70,704 sq. mi.
Rank in area: 18
Entered Union in 1889

**Ohio**
11,353,140 people
44,828 sq. mi.
Rank in area: 34
Entered Union in 1803

**Oklahoma**
3,450,654 people
69,903 sq. mi.
Rank in area: 20
Entered Union in 1907

---

## United States: Major Dependencies (as of 1999)

**American Samoa** 63,781 people; 90 sq. mi.

**Guam** 151,968 people; 217 sq. mi.

**Commonwealth of Puerto Rico** 3,889,507 people; 3,508 sq. mi.

**Virgin Islands of the United States** 119,615 people; 171 sq. mi.

# PRESIDENTS OF THE UNITED STATES

Dates given are for term in office.

## Here are some little-known facts about the presidents of the United States:

- First president born in the new United States: **Martin Van Buren** (8th president)
- Only president who was a bachelor: **James Buchanan**
- First left-handed president: **James A. Garfield**
- Largest president: **William Howard Taft** (6 feet, 2 inches; 332 pounds)
- Youngest president: **Theodore Roosevelt** (42 years old)
- Oldest president: **Ronald Reagan** (77 years old when he left office in 1989)
- First president born west of the Mississippi River: **Herbert Hoover** (born in West Branch, Iowa)
- First president born in the 20th century: **John F. Kennedy** (born May 29, 1917)

**1** George Washington
**1789–1797**
*No Political Party*
Birthplace: Virginia
Born: February 22, 1732
Died: December 14, 1799

**2** John Adams
**1797–1801**
*Federalist*
Birthplace: Massachusetts
Born: October 30, 1735
Died: July 4, 1826

**3** Thomas Jefferson
**1801–1809**
*Democratic-Republican*
Birthplace: Virginia
Born: April 13, 1743
Died: July 4, 1826

**4** James Madison
**1809–1817**
*Democratic-Republican*
Birthplace: Virginia
Born: March 16, 1751
Died: June 28, 1836

**5** James Monroe
**1817–1825**
*Democratic-Republican*
Birthplace: Virginia
Born: April 28, 1758
Died: July 4, 1831

**6** John Quincy Adams
**1825–1829**
*Republican*
Birthplace: Massachusetts
Born: July 11, 1767
Died: February 23, 1848

**7** Andrew Jackson
**1829–1837**
*Democrat*
Birthplace: South Carolina
Born: March 15, 1767
Died: June 8, 1845

**8** Martin Van Buren
**1837–1841**
*Democrat*
Birthplace: New York
Born: December 5, 1782
Died: July 24, 1862

**9** William H. Harrison
**1841**
*Whig*
Birthplace: Virginia
Born: February 9, 1773
Died: April 4, 1841

**10** John Tyler
**1841–1845**
*Whig*
Birthplace: Virginia
Born: March 29, 1790
Died: January 18, 1862

**11** James K. Polk
**1845–1849**
*Democrat*
Birthplace: North Carolina
Born: November 2, 1795
Died: June 15, 1849

**12** Zachary Taylor
**1849–1850**
*Whig*
Birthplace: Virginia
Born: November 24, 1784
Died: July 9, 1850

**13** **Millard Fillmore**
**1850–1853**
*Whig*
Birthplace: New York
Born: January 7, 1800
Died: March 8, 1874

**14** **Franklin Pierce**
**1853–1857**
*Democrat*
Birthplace: New Hampshire
Born: November 23, 1804
Died: October 8, 1869

**15** **James Buchanan**
**1857–1861**
*Democrat*
Birthplace: Pennsylvania
Born: April 23, 1791
Died: June 1, 1868

**16** **Abraham Lincoln**
**1861–1865**
*Republican*
Birthplace: Kentucky
Born: February 12, 1809
Died: April 15, 1865

**17** **Andrew Johnson**
**1865–1869**
*Democrat*
Birthplace: North Carolina
Born: December 29, 1808
Died: July 31, 1875

**18** **Ulysses S. Grant**
**1869–1877**
*Republican*
Birthplace: Ohio
Born: April 27, 1822
Died: July 23, 1885

**19** **Rutherford B. Hayes**
**1877–1881**
*Republican*
Birthplace: Ohio
Born: October 4, 1822
Died: January 17, 1893

**20** **James A. Garfield**
**1881**
*Republican*
Birthplace: Ohio
Born: November 19, 1831
Died: September 19, 1881

**21** **Chester A. Arthur**
**1881–1885**
*Republican*
Birthplace: Vermont
Born: October 5, 1829
Died: November 18, 1886

**22 24** **Grover Cleveland**
**1885–1889, 1893–1897**
*Democrat*
Birthplace: New Jersey
Born: March 18, 1837
Died: June 24, 1908

**23** **Benjamin Harrison**
**1889–1893**
*Republican*
Birthplace: Ohio
Borna: August 20, 1833
Died: March 13, 1901

**25** **William McKinley**
**1897–1901**
*Republican*
Birthplace: Ohio
Born: January 29, 1843
Died: September 14, 1901

**26** **Theodore Roosevelt**
**1901–1909**
*Republican*
Birthplace: New York
Born: October 27, 1858
Died: January 6, 1919

**27** **William H. Taft**
**1909–1913**
*Republican*
Birthplace: Ohio
Born: September 15, 1857
Died: March 8, 1930

**28** **Woodrow Wilson**
**1913–1921**
*Democrat*
Birthplace: Virginia
Born: December 29, 1856
Died: February 3, 1924

**29** **Warren G. Harding**
**1921–1923**
*Republican*
Birthplace: Ohio
Born: November 2, 1865
Died: August 2, 1923

**30 Calvin Coolidge**
**1923–1929**
*Republican*
Birthplace: Vermont
Born: July 4, 1872
Died: January 5, 1933

**31 Herbert C. Hoover**
**1929–1933**
*Republican*
Birthplace: Iowa
Born: August 10, 1874
Died: October 20, 1964

**32 Franklin D. Roosevelt**
**1933–1945**
*Democrat*
Birthplace: New York
Born: January 30, 1882
Died: April 12, 1945

**33 Harry S. Truman**
**1945–1953**
*Democrat*
Birthplace: Missouri
Born: May 8, 1884
Died: December 26, 1972

**34 Dwight D. Eisenhower**
**1953–1961**
*Republican*
Birthplace: Texas
Born: October 14, 1890
Died: March 28, 1969

**35 John F. Kennedy**
**1961–1963**
*Democrat*
Birthplace: Massachusetts
Born: May 29, 1917
Died: November 22, 1963

**36 Lyndon B. Johnson**
**1963–1969**
*Democrat*
Birthplace: Texas
Born: August 27, 1908
Died: January 22, 1973

**37 Richard M. Nixon**
**1969–1974**
*Republican*
Birthplace: California
Born: January 9, 1913
Died: April 22, 1994

**38 Gerald R. Ford**
**1974–1977**
*Republican*
Birthplace: Nebraska
Born: July, 14, 1913

**39 James E. Carter, Jr.**
**1977–1981**
*Democrat*
Birthplace: Georgia
Born: October 1, 1924

**40 Ronald W. Reagan**
**1981–1989**
*Republican*
Birthplace: Illinois
Born: February 6, 1911

**41 George H. W. Bush**
**1989–1993**
*Republican*
Birthplace: Massachusetts
Born: June 12, 1924

**42 William J. Clinton**
**1993–2001**
*Democrat*
Birthplace: Arkansas
Born: August 19, 1946

**43 George W. Bush**
**2001–**
*Republican*
Birthplace: Connecticut
Born: July 6, 1946

# GLOSSARY

The Glossary is an alphabetical listing of many of the key terms from the chapters, along with their meanings. The definitions listed in the Glossary are the ones that apply to the way the words are used in this textbook. The Glossary gives the part of speech of each word. The following abbreviations are used:

*adj.* = adjective    *n.* = noun    *v.* = verb

## PRONUNCIATION KEY

| Symbol | Examples | Symbol | Examples | Symbol | Examples |
|--------|----------|--------|----------|--------|----------|
| ă | **a**t, g**a**s | m | **m**an, see**m** | v | **v**an, sa**v**e |
| ā | **a**pe, d**ay** | n | **n**ight, mitte**n** | w | **w**eb, t**w**ice |
| ä | f**a**ther, b**a**rn | ng | si**ng**, a**ng**er | y | **y**ard, law**y**er |
| âr | f**air**, d**are** | ŏ | **o**dd, n**o**t | z | **z**oo, rea**s**on |
| b | **b**ell, ta**b**le | ō | **o**pen, r**oa**d, gr**ow** | zh | trea**s**ure, gara**g**e |
| ch | **ch**in, lun**ch** | ô | **aw**ful, b**ough**t, h**or**se | ə | **a**wake, **e**ven, penc**i**l, |
| d | **d**ig, bore**d** | oi | c**oi**n, b**oy** | | pil**o**t, foc**u**s |
| ĕ | **e**gg, t**e**n | ŏŏ | l**oo**k, f**u**ll | | |
| ē | **e**vil, s**ee**, m**ea**l | ōō | r**oo**t, gl**ue**, thr**ough** | ər | p**er**form, lett**er** |
| f | **f**all, lau**gh**, **ph**rase | ou | **ou**t, c**ow** | | |
| g | **g**old, bi**g** | p | **p**ig, ca**p** | **Sounds in Foreign Words** | |
| h | **h**it, in**h**ale | r | **r**ose, sta**r** | KH | *German* i**ch**, au**ch**; |
| hw | **wh**ite, every**wh**ere | s | **s**it, fa**ce** | | *Scottish* lo**ch** |
| ĭ | **i**nch, f**i**t | sh | **sh**e, ma**sh** | N | *French* e**n**tre, bo**n**, fi**n** |
| ī | **i**dle, m**y**, tr**i**ed | t | **t**ap, hopp**ed** | œ | *French* f**eu**, c**oeu**r; |
| îr | d**ear**, h**ere** | th | **th**ing, wi**th** | | *German* sch**ö**n |
| j | **j**ar, **g**em, ba**dge** | *th* | **th**en, o**th**er | ü | *French* **u**tile, r**ue**; |
| k | **k**eep, **c**at, lu**ck** | ŭ | **u**p, n**u**t | | *German* gr**ü**n |
| l | **l**oad, ratt**le** | ûr | f**ur**, **ear**n, b**ir**d, w**or**m | | |

## STRESS MARKS

′  This mark indicates that the preceding syllable receives the primary stress. For example, in the word *lineage*, the first syllable is stressed: [lĭn′ē-ĭj].

′  This mark is used only in words in which more than one syllable is stressed. It indicates that the preceding syllable is stressed, but somewhat more weakly than the syllable receiving the primary stress. In the word *consumerism*, for example, the second syllable receives the primary stress, and the fourth syllable receives a weaker stress: [kən-sōō′mə-rĭz′əm].

Adapted from *The American Heritage Dictionary of the English Language, Fourth Edition;* Copyright © 2000 by Houghton Mifflin Company. Used with the permission of Houghton Mifflin Company.

# A

**abolition** *n.* movement to end slavery. (p. 144)

**affirmative** [ə-fûr′mə-tĭv] **action** *n.* a policy that seeks to correct the effects of past discrimination by favoring the groups who were previously disadvantaged. (pp. 723, 831)

**Agent Orange** *n.* a toxic leaf-killing chemical sprayed by U.S. planes in Vietnam to expose Vietcong hideouts. (p. 739)

**Agricultural Adjustment Act (AAA)** *n.* a law enacted in 1933 to raise crop prices by paying farmers to leave a certain amount of their land unplanted, thus lowering production. (p. 491)

**AIDS** [ādz] **(acquired immune deficiency syndrome)** *n.* a disease caused by a virus that weakens the immune system, making the body prone to infections and otherwise rare forms of cancer. (p. 840)

**Alamo, the** [ăl′ə-mō′] *n.* a mission and fort in San Antonio, Texas, where Mexican forces massacred rebellious Texans in 1836. (p. 134)

**Alien and Sedition** [ā′lē-ən] [sĭ-dĭsh′ən] **Acts** *n.* a series of four laws enacted in 1798 to reduce the political power of recent immigrants to the United States. (p. 78)

**Alliance** [ə-lī′əns] **for Progress** *n.* a U.S. foreign-aid program of the 1960s, providing economic and technical assistance to Latin American countries. (p. 680)

**Allies** [ăl′īz] *n.* **1.** in World War I, the group of nations—originally consisting of Great Britain, France, and Russia and later joined by the United States, Italy, and others—that opposed the Central Powers (p. 373). **2.** in World War II, the group of nations—including Great Britain, the Soviet Union, and the United States—that opposed the Axis powers. (p. 554)

**American Expeditionary** [ĕk′spĭ-dĭsh′ə-nĕr′ē] **Force (AEF)** *n.* the U.S. forces, led by General John Pershing, who fought with the Allies in Europe during World War I. (p. 384)

**American Federation of Labor (AFL)** *n.* an alliance of trade and craft unions, formed in 1886. (p. 245)

**American Indian Movement (AIM)** *n.* a frequently militant organization that was formed in 1968 to work for Native American rights. (p. 771)

**Americanization** [ə-mĕr′ĭ-kə-nĭ-zā′shən] **movement** *n.* education program designed to help immigrants assimilate to American culture. (p. 263)

**American System** *n.* a pre-Civil War set of measures designed to unify the nation and strengthen its economy by means of protective tariffs, a national bank, and such internal improvements as the development of a transportation system. (p. 122)

**anarchist** [ăn′ər-kĭst] *n.* a person who opposes all forms of government. (p. 413)

**Anasazi** [ä′nə-sä′zē] *n.* a Native American group that lived on the mesa tops, cliff sides, and canyon bottoms of the Four Corners region (where the present-day states of Arizona, New Mexico, Colorado, and Utah meet) from about A.D. 100 to 1300. (p. 5)

**Antifederalist** [ăn′tē-fĕd′ər-ə-lĭst] *n.* an opponent of a strong central government. (p. 69)

**appeasement** [ə-pēz′mənt] *n.* the granting of concessions to a hostile power in order to keep the peace. (p. 538)

**Appomattox** [ăp′ə-măt′əks] **Court House** *n.* town near Appomatox, Virginia, where Lee surrendered to Grant on April 9, 1865. (37°N 79°W) (p. 181)

**arbitration** *n.* a method of settling disputes in which both sides submit their differences to a mutually approved judge. (p. 245)

**armistice** [är′mĭ-stĭs] *n.* a truce, or agreement to end an armed conflict. (p. 387)

**Army of the Republic of Vietnam (ARVN)** *n.* the southern Vietnamese soldiers with whom U.S. troops fought against communism and forces in the North during the Vietnam War. (p. 737)

**Articles of Confederation** [kən-fĕd′ə-rā′shən] *n.* a document, adopted by the Second Continental Congress in 1777 and finally approved by the states in 1781, that outlined the form of government of the new United States. (p. 67)

**Ashcan School** *n.* a group of early twentieth-century American artists who often painted realistic pictures of city life—such as tenements and homeless people—thus earning them their name. (p. 295)

**assimilation** [ə-sĭm′ə-lā′shən] *n.* a minority group's adoption of the beliefs and way of life of the dominant culture. (p. 206)

**Atlantic Charter** *n.* a 1941 declaration of principles in which the United States and Great Britain set forth their goals in opposing the Axis powers. (p. 554)

**Axis** [ăk′sĭs] **powers** *n.* the group of nations—including Germany, Italy, and Japan—that opposed the Allies in World War II. (p. 551)

**Aztec** [ăz′tĕk′] *n.* a Native American people that settled in the Valley of Mexico in the 1200s A.D. and later developed a powerful empire. (p. 5)

## B

**baby boom** *n.* the sharp increase in the U.S. birthrate following World War II. (p. 643)

**Battle of the Bulge** *n.* a month-long battle of World War II, in which the Allies succeeded in turning back the last major German offensive of the war. (p. 576)

**Battle of Midway** *n.* a World War II battle that took place in early June 1942. The Allies decimated the Japanese fleet at Midway, an island lying northwest of Hawaii. The Allies then took the offensive in the Pacific and began to move closer to Japan. (p. 579)

**Battle of Wounded Knee** [wōōn′dĭd nē′] *n.* the massacre by U.S. soldiers of 300 unarmed Native Americans at Wounded Knee Creek, South Dakota, in 1890. (pp. 207–208)

**Beatles, the** [bēt′lz] *n.* a British band that had an enormous influence on popular music in the 1960s. (p. 783)

**beat movement** *n.* a social and artistic movement of the 1950s, stressing unrestrained literary self-expression and nonconformity with the mainstream culture. (p. 655)

**Benin** [bə-nĭn′] *n.* a West African kingdom that flourished in the Niger Delta region (in what is now Nigeria) from the 14th to the 17th century. (p. 9)

**Berlin airlift** [bûr-lĭn′ âr′lĭft′] *n.* a 327-day operation in which U.S. and British planes flew food and supplies into West Berlin after the Soviets blockaded the city in 1948. (p. 607)

**Berlin Wall** *n.* a concrete wall that separated East Berlin and West Berlin from 1961 to 1989, built by the Communist East German government to prevent its citizens from fleeing to the West. (p. 677)

**Bessemer** [bĕs′ə-mər] **process** *n.* a cheap and efficient process for making steel, developed around 1850. (p. 231)

**Bill of Rights** *n.* the first ten amendments to the U.S. Constitution, added in 1791 and consisting of a formal list of citizens' rights and freedoms. (p. 70)

**bimetallism** [bī-mĕt′l-ĭz′əm] *n.* the use of both gold and silver as a basis for a national monetary system. (p. 222)

**blacklist** [blăk′lĭst′] *n.* a list of about 500 actors, writers, producers, and directors who were not allowed to work on Hollywood films because of their alleged Communist connections. (p. 618)

**Black Panthers** *n.* a militant African-American political organization formed in 1966 by Huey Newton and Bobby Seale to fight police brutality and to provide services in the ghetto. (p. 720)

**Black Power** *n.* a slogan used by Stokely Carmichael in the 1960s that encouraged African-American pride and political and social leadership. (p. 720)

**Black Tuesday** *n.* a name given to October 29, 1929, when stock prices fell sharply. (p. 468)

**blitzkrieg** [blĭts′krēg′] *n.* from the German word meaning "lightning war," a sudden, massive attack with combined air and ground forces, intended to achieve a quick victory. (p. 539)

**bonanza** [bə-năn′zə] **farm** *n.* an enormous farm on which a single crop is grown. (p. 218)

**Bonus** [bō′nəs] **Army** *n.* a group of World War I veterans and their families who marched on Washington, D.C., in 1932 to demand the immediate payment of a bonus they had been promised for military service. (p. 482)

**bootlegger** [boot′lĕg′ər] *n.* a person who smuggled alcoholic beverages into the United States during Prohibition. (p. 437)

**Boston Massacre** [bô′stən măs′ə-kər] *n.* a clash between British soldiers and Boston colonists in 1770, in which five of the colonists were killed. (p. 48)

**Boston Tea Party** *n.* the dumping of 18,000 pounds of tea into Boston Harbor by colonists in 1773 to protest the Tea Act. (p. 49)

**Boulder** [bōl′dər] **Dam** *n.* a dam on the Colorado River—now called Hoover Dam—that was built during the Great Depression as part of a public-works program intended to stimulate business and provide jobs. (p. 480)

**Boxer Rebellion** *n.* a 1900 rebellion in which members of a Chinese secret society sought to free their country from Western influence. (p. 357)

**bracero** [brə-sâr′ō] *n.* a Mexican laborer allowed to enter the United States to work for a limited period of time during World War II. (p. 662)

**bread line** *n.* a line of people waiting for free food. (p. 473)

**brinkmanship** [brĭngk′mən-shĭp′] *n.* the practice of threatening an enemy with massive military retaliation for any aggression. (p. 623)

***Brown* v. *Board of Education of Topeka*** *n.* a 1954 case in which the Supreme Court ruled that "separate but equal" education for black and white students was unconstitutional. (p. 702)

**Bull Moose Party** *n.* a name given to the Progressive Party, formed to support Theodore Roosevelt's candidacy for the presidency in 1912. (p. 330)

**buying on margin** [mär′jĭn] *n.* the purchasing of stocks by paying only a small percentage of the price and borrowing the rest. (p. 467)

## C

**cabinet** [kăb′ə-nĭt] *n.* the group of department heads who serve as the president's chief advisers. (p. 75)

**Camp David Accords** [ə-kôrdz′] *n.* historic agreements between Israel and Egypt, reached in negotiations at Camp David in 1978. (p. 816)

**carpetbagger** [kär′pĭt-băg′ər] *n.* a Northerner who moved to the South after the Civil War. (p. 186)

**Central Powers** *n.* the group of nations—led by Germany, Austria-Hungary, and the Ottoman Empire—that opposed the Allies in World War I. (p. 374)

**checks and balances** *n.* the provisions in the U.S. Constitution that prevent any branch of the U.S. government from dominating the other two branches. (p. 69)

**Chinese Exclusion Act** *n.* a law, enacted in 1882, that prohibited all Chinese except students, teachers, merchants, tourists, and government officials from entering the United States. (p. 259)

**Chisholm** [chĭz′əm] **Trail** *n.* the major cattle route from San Antonio, Texas, through Oklahoma to Kansas. (p. 209)

**chlorination** *n.* a method of purifying water by mixing it with chemical chlorine. (p. 264)

**Christianity** [krĭs′chē-ăn′ĭ-tē] *n.* a religion based on the life and teachings of Jesus Christ. (p. 10)

**CIA** *n.* the Central Intelligence Agency—a U.S. agency created to gather secret information about foreign governments. (p. 623)

**Civilian Conservation Corps** [kôr] **(CCC)** *n.* an agency, established as part of the New Deal, that put young unemployed men to work building roads, developing parks, planting trees, and helping in erosion-control and flood-control projects. (p. 491)

**Civil Rights Act of 1964** *n.* a law that banned discrimination on the basis of race, sex, national origin, or religion in public places and most workplaces. (p. 714)

**Civil Rights Act of 1968** *n.* a law that banned discrimination in housing. (p. 722)

**civil service** *n.* the nonmilitary branches of government administration. (p. 270)

**Clayton Antitrust** [klāt′n ăn′tē-trŭst′] **Act** *n.* a law, enacted in 1914, that made certain monopolistic business practices illegal and protected the rights of labor unions and farm organizations. (p. 333)

**Cold War** *n.* the state of hostility, without direct military conflict, that developed between the United States and the Soviet Union after World War II. (p. 606)

**Columbian Exchange** [kə-lŭm′bē-ən ĭks-chānj′] *n.* the transfer—beginning with Columbus's first voyage—of plants, animals, and diseases between the Western Hemisphere and the Eastern Hemisphere. (p. 15)

**Committee to Reelect the President** *n.* an organization formed to run President Nixon's 1972 reelection campaign, which was linked to the break-in at the Democratic National Committee headquarters that set off the Watergate scandal. (p. 803)

***Common Sense*** *n.* a pamphlet by Thomas Paine, published in 1776, that called for separation of the colonies from Britain. (p. 52)

***Commonwealth*** [kŏm′ən-wĕlth′] **v. *Hunt*** *n.* an 1842 case in which the Massachusetts Supreme Court upheld workers' right to strike. (p. 143)

**communism** [kŏm′yə-nĭz′əm] *n.* an economic and political system based on one-party government and state ownership of property. (p. 413)

**concentration** [kŏn′sən-trā′shən] **camp** *n.* a prison camp operated by Nazi Germany in which Jews and other groups considered to be enemies of Adolf Hitler were starved while doing slave labor or were murdered. (p. 546)

**Confederacy** [kən-fĕd′ər-ə-sē] *n.* the Confederate States of America, a confederation formed in 1861 by the Southern states after their secession from the Union. (p. 165)

**conglomerate** [kən-glŏm′ər-ĭt] *n.* a major corporation that owns a number of smaller companies in unrelated businesses. (p. 642)

**Congress of Industrial Organizations (CIO)** *n.* a labor organization expelled from the American Federation of Labor in 1938. (p. 508)

**Congress of Racial Equality** [rā′shəl ĭ-kwŏl′ĭ-tē] **(CORE)** *n.* an interracial group founded in 1942 by James Farmer to work against segregation in Northern cities. (p. 593)

***conquistador*** [kŏng-kē′stə-dôr′] *n.* one of the Spaniards who traveled to the Americas as an explorer and conqueror in the 16th century. (p. 16)

**conscientious objector** [kŏn′shē-ĕn′shəs ŏb-jĕk′tər] *n*. a person who refuses, on moral grounds, to participate in warfare. (p. 386)

**conscription** [kən-skrĭp′shən] *n*. the drafting of citizens for military service. (p. 173)

**conservation** [kŏn′sûr-vā′shən] *n*. the planned management of natural resources, involving the protection of some wilderness areas and the development of others for the common good. (p. 323)

**conservative coalition** [kən-sûr′və-tĭv kō′ə-lĭsh′ən] *n*. an alliance formed in the mid-1960s of right-wing groups opposed to big government. (p. 831)

**consolidation** [kən-sŏl′ĭ-dā′shən] *n*. the act of uniting or combining. (p. 240)

**consumerism** [kən-soo′mə-rĭz′əm] *n*. a preoccupation with the purchasing of material goods. (p. 648)

**containment** [kən-tān′mənt] *n*. the blocking of another nation's attempts to spread its influence—especially the efforts of the United States to block the spread of Soviet influence during the late 1940s and early 1950s. (p. 605)

**Contract** [kŏn′trăkt′] **with America** *n*. a document that was drafted by Representative Newt Gingrich and signed by more than 300 Republican candidates in 1994, setting forth the Republicans' conservative legislative agenda. (p. 864)

***Contras*** [kŏn′trəz] *n*. Nicaraguan rebels who received assistance from the Reagan administration in their efforts to overthrow the Sandinista government in the 1980s. (p. 851)

**convoy** [kŏn′voi′] **system** *n*. the protection of merchant ships from U-boat—German submrine—attacks by having the ships travel in large groups escorted by warships. (p. 383)

**counterculture** [koun′tər-kŭl′chər] *n*. the culture of the young people who rejected mainstream American society in the 1960s, seeking to create an alternative society based on peace, love, and individual freedom. (p. 781)

**credibility** [krĕd′ə-bĭl′ĭ-tē] **gap** *n*. a public distrust of statements made by the government. (p. 741)

**credit** [krĕd′ĭt] *n*. an arrangement in which a buyer pays later for a purchase, often on an installment plan with interest charges. (p. 466)

**Crédit Mobilier** [krĕd′ĭt mō-bēl′yər] *n*. a construction company formed in 1864 by owners of the Union Pacific Railroad, who used it to fraudulently skim off railroad profits for themselves. (p. 238)

## D

**Dawes** [dôz] **Act** *n*. a law, enacted in 1887, that was intended to "Americanize" Native Americans by distributing reservation land to individual owners. (p. 206)

**D-Day** *n*. a name given to June 6, 1944—the day on which the Allies launched an invasion of the European mainland during World War II. (p. 574)

**debt peonage** [dĕt′ pē′ə-nĭj] *n*. a system in which workers are bound in servitude until their debts are paid. (p. 289)

**Declaration** [dĕk′lə-rā′shən] **of Independence** *n*. the document, written by Thomas Jefferson in 1776, in which the delegates of the Continental Congress declared the colonies' independence from Britain. (p. 53)

**de facto segregation** [dĭ făk′tō sĕg′rĭ-gā′shən] *n*. racial separation established by practice and custom, not by law. (p. 718)

**deficit** [dĕf′ĭ-sĭt] **spending** *n*. a government's spending of more money than it receives in revenue. (p. 492)

**de jure segregation** [dē jŏor′ē sĕg′rĭ-gā′shən] *n*. racial separation established by law. (p. 718)

**Democratic-Republican** *n*. political party known for its support of strong state governments, founded by Thomas Jefferson in 1792 in opposition to the Federalist Party. (pp. 76, 112)

**deregulation** *n*. the cutting back of federal regulation of industry. (p. 837)

**détente** [dā-tänt′] *n*. the flexible policy, involving a willingness to negotiate and an easing of tensions, that was adopted by President Richard Nixon and his adviser Henry Kissinger in their dealings with communist nations. (p. 799)

**direct relief** [rĭ-lēf′] *n*. the giving of money or food by the government directly to needy people. (p. 475)

**Dixiecrat** [dĭk′sē-krăt′] *n*. one of the Southern delegates who, to protest President Truman's civil rights policy, walked out of the 1948 Democratic National Convention and formed the States' Rights Democratic Party. (p. 638)

**dollar diplomacy** [dĭ-plō′mə-sē] *n*. the U.S. policy of using the nation's economic power to exert influence over other countries. (p. 363)

**domino theory** [dŏm′ə-nō′ thē′ə-rē] *n*. the idea that if a nation falls under communist control, nearby nations will also fall under communist control. (p. 731)

**dotcom** *n*. a business related to or conducted on the Internet. (p. 871)

**double standard** *n*. a set of principles granting greater sexual freedom to men than to women. (p. 441)

**dove** [dŭv] *n*. a person who opposed the Vietnam War and believed that the United States should withdraw from it. (p. 746)

**Dow Jones** [dou′ jōnz′] **Industrial Average** *n*. a measure based on the prices of the stocks of 30 large companies, widely used as a barometer of the stock market's health. (p. 467)

**downsize** [doun′sīz′] *v*. to dismiss numbers of permanent employees in an attempt to make operations more efficient and save money. (p. 870)

**draft** *n*. required enrollment in the armed services. (p. 742)

**Dust Bowl** *n*. the region, including Texas, Oklahoma, Kansas, Colorado, and New Mexico, that was made worthless for farming by drought and dust storms during the 1930s. (p. 474)

## E

**Earth Day** *n*. a day set aside for environmental education, celebrated annually on April 22. (p. 821)

**Economic Opportunity Act** *n*. a law, enacted in 1964, that provided funds for youth programs, antipoverty measures, small-business loans, and job training. (p. 688)

**egalitarianism** [ĭ-găl′ĭ-târ′ē-ə-nĭz′əm] *n*. the belief that all people should have equal political, economic, social, and civil rights. (p. 63)

**Eisenhower Doctrine** [ī′zən-hou′ər dŏk′trĭn] *n*. a U.S. commitment to defend the Middle East against attack by any communist country, announced by President Dwight D. Eisenhower in 1957. (p. 625)

**Emancipation Proclamation** [prŏk′lə-mā′shən] *n.* an executive order issued by Abraham Lincoln on January 1, 1863, freeing the slaves in all regions behind Confederate lines. (p. 172)

**encomienda** [ĕng-kô-myĕn′dä] *n.* a system in which Spanish authorities granted colonial landlords the service of Native Americans as forced laborers. (p. 16)

**Enlightenment** [ĕn-līt′n-mənt] *n.* an 18th-century intellectual movement that emphasized the use of reason and the scientific method as means of obtaining knowledge. (p. 35)

**entitlement** [ĕn-tīt′l-mənt] **program** *n.* a government program—such as Social Security, Medicare, or Medicaid—that guarantees and provides benefits to a specific group. (p. 831)

**entrepreneur** [ŏn′trə-prə-nûr′] *n.* a person who organizes, operates, and assumes the risk for a business venture. (p. 140)

**environmentalist** [ĕn-vī′rən-mĕn′tl-ĭst] *n.* a person who works to protect the environment from destruction and pollution. (p. 822)

**Environmental Protection Agency (EPA)** *n.* a federal agency established in 1970 for the regulation of water and air pollution, toxic waste, pesticides, and radiation. (p. 837)

**Equal Rights Amendment (ERA)** *n.* a proposed and failed amendment to the U.S. Constitution that would have prohibited any government discrimination on the basis of sex. (p. 779)

**Espionage and Sedition** [ĕs′pē-ə-näzh′ ənd sĭ-dĭsh′ən] **Acts** *n.* two laws, enacted in 1917 and 1918, that imposed harsh penalties on anyone interfering with or speaking against U.S. participation in World War I. (p. 392)

**exoduster** [ĕk′sə-dŭs′tər] *n.* an African American who migrated from the South to Kansas in the post-Reconstruction years. (p. 215)

**extortion** *n.* illegal use of one's official position to obtain property or funds. (p. 269)

# F

**Fair Deal** *n.* President Harry S. Truman's economic program—an extension of Franklin Roosevelt's New Deal—which included measures to increase the minimum wage, to extend social security coverage, and to provide housing for low-income families. (p. 639)

**Family Assistance Plan** *n.* a welfare-reform proposal, approved by the House of Representatives in 1970 but defeated in the Senate, that would have guaranteed an income to welfare recipients who agreed to undergo job training and to accept work. (p. 795)

**Farmers' Alliances** *n.* groups of farmers, or those in sympathy with farming issues, who sent lecturers from town to town to educate people about agricultural and rural issues. (p. 221)

**fascism** [făsh′ĭz′əm] *n.* a political philosophy that advocates a strong, centralized, nationalistic government headed by a powerful dictator. (p. 530)

**Federal Communications Commission (FCC)** *n.* an agency that regulates U.S. communications industries, including radio and television broadcasting. (p. 653)

**Federal Deposit Insurance Corporation (FDIC)** *n.* an agency created in 1933 to insure individuals' bank accounts, protecting people against losses due to bank failures. (p. 517)

**Federal Home Loan Bank Act** *n.* a law, enacted in 1931, that lowered home mortgage rates and allowed farmers to refinance their loans and avoid foreclosure. (p. 481)

**federalism** *n.* a political system in which a national government and constituent units, such as state governments, share power. (p. 68)

**Federalist** [fĕd′ər-ə-lĭst] *n.* a supporter of the Constitution and of a strong national government. (p. 69)

**Federal Reserve System** *n.* a national banking system, established in 1913, that controls the U.S. money supply and the availability of credit in the country. (p. 334)

**Federal Securities** [sĭ-kyŏŏr′ĭ-tēz] **Act** *n.* a law, enacted in 1933, that required corporations to provide complete, accurate information on all stock offerings. (p. 490)

**Federal Trade Commission (FTC)** *n.* a federal agency established in 1914 to investigate and stop unfair business practices. (p. 333)

**feminism** [fĕm′ə-nĭz′əm] *n.* the belief that women should have economic, political, and social equality with men. (p. 776)

**Fifteenth Amendment** *n.* an amendment to the U.S. Constitution, adopted in 1870, that prohibits the denial of voting rights to people because of their race or color or because they have previously been slaves. (p. 186)

**flapper** *n.* one of the free-thinking young women who embraced the new fashions and urban attitudes of the 1920s. (p. 441)

**flexible response** [flĕk′sə-bəl rĭ-spŏns′] *n.* a policy, developed during the Kennedy administration, that involved preparing for a variety of military responses to international crises rather than focusing on the use of nuclear weapons. (p. 673)

**Foraker** [fôr′ə-kər] **Act** *n.* legislation passed by Congress in 1900, in which the U.S. ended military rule in Puerto Rico and set up a civil government. (p. 353)

**Fordney-McCumber Tariff** [fôrd′nē mə-kŭm′bər tăr′ĭf] *n.* a set of regulations, enacted by Congress in 1922, that raised taxes on imports to record levels in order to protect American businesses against foreign competition. (p. 420)

**Fourteen Points** *n.* the principles making up President Woodrow Wilson's plan for world peace following World War I. (p. 399)

**Fourteenth Amendment** *n.* an amendment to the U.S. Constitution, adopted in 1868, that makes all persons born or naturalized in the United States—including former slaves—citizens of the country and guarantees equal proection of the laws. (p. 185)

**franchise** [frăn′chīz′] *n.* a business that has bought the right to use a parent company's name and methods, thus becoming one of a number of similar businesses in various locations. (p. 642)

**Freedmen's Bureau** [frēd-mĕnz byŏŏr′ō] *n.* a federal agency set up to help former slaves after the Civil War. (p. 184)

**freedom rider** *n.* one of the civil rights activists who rode buses through the South in the early 1960s to challenge segregation. (p. 710)

**Freedom Summer** *n.* a 1964 project to register African-American voters in Mississippi. (p. 715)

**free enterprise** [ĕn′tər-prīz′] *n.* the economic system in which private businesses and individuals control the means of production. (p. 140)

**Free Speech Movement** *n.* an antiestablishment New Left organization that originated in a 1964 clash between students and administrators at the University of California at Berkeley. (p. 744)

**French and Indian War** *n.* a conflict in North America, lasting from 1754 to 1763, that was a part of a worldwide struggle between France and Britain and that ended with the defeat of France and the transfer of French Canada to Britain. (p. 37)

**Fundamentalism** [fŭn′də-měn′tl-ĭz′əm] *n.* a Protestant religious movement grounded in the belief that all the stories and details in the Bible are literally true. (p. 438)

## G

**General Agreement on Tariffs and Trade (GATT)** [găt] *n.* an international agreement first signed in 1947. In 1994, the U.S. and other countries adopted a new version of GATT. This treaty lowered trade barriers, such as tariffs, and created the World Trade Organization, which resolves trade disputes. (p. 872)

**genetic engineering** [jə-nět′ĭk ěn′jə-nîr′ĭng] *n.* the alteration of the molecular biology of organisms' cells in order to create new varieties of bacteria, plants, and animals. (p. 880)

**Geneva Accords** [jə-nē′və ə-kôrdz′] *n.* a 1954 peace agreement that divided Vietnam into Communist-controlled North Vietnam and non-Communist South Vietnam until unification elections could be held in 1956. (p. 732)

**genocide** [jĕn′ə-sīd′] *n.* the deliberate and systematic extermination of a particular racial, national, or religious group. (p. 544)

**Gentlemen's Agreement** *n.* a 1907–1908 agreement by the government of Japan to limit Japanese emigration to the United States. (p. 259)

**gentrification** [jĕn′trə-fĭ-kā′shən] *n.* the process of restoring deteriorated urban property by middle-class people, which often results in the displacement of lower-income residents. (p. 883)

**Gettysburg Address** [gĕt′ēz-bûrg′ ə-drĕs′] *n.* a famous speech delivered by Abraham Lincoln in November 1863, at the dedication of a national cemetery on the site of the Battle of Gettysburg. (p. 177)

**ghetto** [gĕt′ō] *n.* a city neighborhood in which a certain minority group is pressured or forced to live. (p. 545)

**GI Bill of Rights** *n.* a name given to the Servicemen's Readjustment Act, a 1944 law that provided financial and educational benefits for World War II veterans. (pp. 592, 635)

**glasnost** [gläs′nəst] *n.* the open discussion of social problems that was permitted in the Soviet Union in the 1980s. (p. 849)

**Glass-Steagall** [glăs′ stē′gəl] **Act** *n.* the 1933 law that established the Federal Deposit Insurance Corporation to protect individuals' bank accounts. (p. 490)

**gold standard** *n.* a monetary system in which the basic unit of currency is defined in terms of a set amount of gold. (p. 222)

**Gone with the Wind** *n.* a 1939 movie dealing with the life of Southern plantation owners during the Civil War—one of the most popular films of all time. (p. 511)

**graft** *n.* the illegal use of political influence for personal gain. (p. 269)

**grandfather clause** *n.* a provision that exempts certain people from a law on the basis of previously existing circumstances—especially a clause formerly in some Southern states' constitutions that exempted whites from the strict voting requirements used to keep African Americans from the polls. (p. 287)

**Grange** [grānj] *n.* the Patrons of Husbandry—a social and educational organization through which farmers attempted to combat the power of the railroads in the late 19th century. (p. 221)

**Grapes of Wrath, The** *n.* a novel by John Steinbeck, published in 1939, that deals with a family of Oklahomans who leave the Dust Bowl for California. (p. 514)

**Great Awakening** *n.* a revival of religious feeling in the American colonies during the 1730s and 1750s. (p. 35)

**Great Depression** *n.* a period, lasting from 1929 to 1940, in which the U.S. economy was in severe decline and millions of Americans were unemployed. (p. 469)

**Great Migration** [mĭ-grā′shən] *n.* the large-scale movement of African Americans from the South to Northern cities in the early 20th century. (p. 393)

**Great Plains** *n.* the vast grassland that extends through the central portion North America, from Texas northward to Canada, east of the Rocky Mountains. (p. 202)

**Great Society** *n.* President Lyndon B. Johnson's program to reduce poverty and racial injustice and to promote a better quality of life in the United States. (p. 689)

## H

**Haight-Ashbury** [hāt′ ăsh′bĕr-ē] *n.* a San Francisco district that became the "capital" of the hippie counterculture during the 1960s. (p. 782)

**Harlem Renaissance** [här′ləm rĕn′ĭ-säns′] *n.* a flowering of African-American artistic creativity during the 1920s, centered in the Harlem community of New York City. (p. 454)

**hawk** *n.* a person who supported U.S. involvement in the Vietnam War and believed that the United States should use increased military force to win it. (p. 746)

**Hawley-Smoot Tariff** [hô′lē smōōt′ tăr′ĭf] **Act** *n.* a law, enacted in 1930, that established the highest protective tariff in U.S. history, worsening the depression in America and abroad. (p. 471)

**H-bomb** *n.* the hydrogen bomb—a thermonuclear weapon much more powerful than the atomic bomb. (p. 623)

**Ho Chi Minh** [hō′ chē′ mĭn′] **Trail** *n.* a network of paths used by North Vietnam to transport supplies to the Vietcong in South Vietnam. (p. 732)

**Hollywood Ten** *n.* ten witnesses from the film industry who refused to cooperate with the HUAC's investigation of Communist influence in Hollywood. (p. 617)

**Holocaust** [hŏl′ə-kôst′] *n.* the systematic murder—or genocide—of Jews and other groups in Europe by the Nazis before and during World War II. (p. 542)

**Homestead** [hōm′stĕd′] **Act** *n.* a U.S. law enacted in 1862, that provided 160 acres in the West to any citizen or intended citizen who was head of household and would cultivate the land for five years; a law whose passage led to record numbers of U.S. settlers claiming private property which previously had been reserved by treaty and by tradition for Native American nomadic dwelling and use; the same law strengthened in 1889 to encourage individuals to exercise their private property rights and develop homesteads out of the vast government lands. (p. 215)

**horizontal integration** [hôr′ĭ-zŏn′tl ĭn′tĭ-grā′shən] *n.* the merging of companies that make similar products. (p. 242)

**hot line** *n.* a communication link established in 1963 to allow the leaders of the United States and the Soviet Union to contact each other in times of crisis. (p. 678)

**House Un-American Activities Committee (HUAC)** [hyōō′ăk′] *n.* a congressional committee that investigated Communist influence inside and outside the U.S. government in the years following World War II. (p. 617)

**human rights** *n.* the rights and freedoms, such as those named in the Declaration of Independence and the Bill of Rights, to which all people are entitled. (p. 815)

## I

**immigration** [ĭm'ĭ-grā'shən] *n.* coming and settling in a country of which one is not a native. (p. 142)

**Immigration Act of 1965** *n.* a law that increased the number of immigrants allowed to settle in the United States. (p. 691)

**impeachment** *n.* the process of accusing a public official of wrongdoing. (p. 802)

**imperialism** [ĭm-pîr'ē-ə-lĭz'əm] *n.* the policy of extending a nation's authority over other countries by economic, political, or military means. (p. 342)

**impressment** [ĭm-prĕs'mənt] *n.* the forcible seizure of men for military service. (p. 114)

**incandescent** [ĭn'kən-dĕs'ənt] *adj.* giving off visible light as a result of being heated. (p. 232)

**income tax** *n.* a tax on earnings. (p. 174)

**indentured** [ĭn-dĕn'chərd] **servant** *n.* a person who has contracted to work for another for a limited period, often in return for travel expenses, shelter, and sustenance. (p. 23)

**Industrial Workers of the World (IWW)** *n.* a labor organization for unskilled workers, formed by a group of radical unionists and socialists in 1905. (p. 246)

**inflation** [ĭn-flā'shən] *n.* an increase in prices or decline in purchasing power caused by an increase in the supply of money. (p. 60)

**information superhighway** [sōō'pər-hī'wā] *n.* a computer communications network linking people and institutions throughout the world, providing individuals with services such as libraries, shopping, movies, and news. (p. 877)

**INF Treaty** *n.* the Intermediate-Range Nuclear Forces Treaty—a 1987 agreement between the United States and the Soviet Union that eliminated some weapons systems and allowed for on-site inspection of military installations. (p. 849)

**initiative** [ĭ-nĭsh'ə-tĭv] *n.* a procedure by which a legislative measure can be originated by the people rather than by lawmakers. (p. 312)

**installment** [ĭn-stôl'mənt] **plan** *n.* an arrangement in which a purchaser pays over an extended time, without having to put down much money at the time of purchase. (p. 426)

**Internet** [ĭn'tər-nĕt'] *n.* a worldwide network, originally developed by the U.S. Department of Defense, that links computers and allows almost immediate communication of texts, pictures, and sounds. (p. 877)

**internment** *n.* confinement or a restriction in movement, especially under wartime conditions. (p. 594)

**Interstate** [ĭn'tər-stāt'] **Commerce Act** *n.* a law, enacted in 1887, that reestablished the federal government's right to supervise railroad activities and created a five-member Interstate Commerce Commission to do so. (p. 239)

**iron curtain** [ī'ərn kûr'tn] *n.* a phrase used by Winston Churchill in 1946 to describe an imaginary line that separated Communist countries in the Soviet bloc of Eastern Europe from countries in Western Europe. (p. 605)

**Iroquois** [ĭr'ə-kwoi'] *n.* a group of Native American peoples inhabiting the woodlands of the Northeast. (p. 6)

**Islam** [ĭs-läm'] *n.* a religion founded in Arabia in A.D. 622 by the prophet Muhammad; its believers are called Muslims. (p. 9)

**isolationism** [ī'sə-lā'shə-nĭzm] *n.* opposition to political and economic entanglements with other countries. (p. 412)

## J

**Jacksonian democracy** [jăk-sō'nē-an dĭ-mŏk'rə-sē] *n.* Jackson's political philosophy, based on his belief that common people were the source of American strength. (p. 123)

**Japanese American Citizens League (JACL)** *n.* an organization that pushed the U.S. government to compensate Japanese Americans for property they had lost when they were interned during World War II. (p. 595)

**jazz** *n.* a style of music characterized by the use of improvisation. (p. 657)

**Jeffersonian republicanism** [jĕf'ər-sō'nē-ən rĭ-pŭb'lĭ-kə-nĭz'əm] *n.* Jefferson's theory of government, which held that a simple government best suited the needs of the people. (p. 113)

**Jim Crow laws** *n.* laws enacted by Southern state and local governments to separate white and black people in public and private facilities. (p. 287)

**joint-stock companies** *n.* businesses in which investors pool their wealth for a common purpose. (p. 21)

**judicial review** *n.* the Supreme Court's power to declare an act of Congress unconstitutional. (p. 113)

**Judiciary** [jōō-dĭsh' ē-ĕr'ē] **Act of 1789** *n.* a law that established the federal court system and the Supreme Court and that provided for the appeal of certain state court decisions to the federal courts. (p. 74)

**Jungle, The** *n.* a novel by Upton Sinclair, published in 1906, that portrays the dangerous and unhealthy conditions prevalent in the meatpacking industry at that time. (p. 317)

## K

**kamikaze** [kä'mĭ-kä'zē] *adj.* involving or engaging in the deliberate crashing of a bomb-filled airplane into a military target. (p. 581)

**Kent State University** *n.* an Ohio university where National Guardsmen opened fire on students protesting the Vietnam War on May 4, 1970, wounding nine and killing four. (p. 756)

**Kerner** [kûr'nər] **Commission** *n.* a group that was appointed by President Johnson to study the causes of urban violence and that recommended the elimination of de facto segregation in American society. (p. 722)

**King Philip's War** *n.* a conflict, in the years 1675–1676, between New England colonists and Native American groups allied under the leadership of the Wampanoag chief Metacom. (p. 25)

**Kongo** [kŏng'gō] *n.* a group of small kingdoms along the Zaire River in West-Central Africa, united under a single leader in the late 1400s. (p. 9)

**Korean** [kə-rē'ən] **War** *n.* a conflict between North Korea and South Korea, lasting from 1950 to 1953, in which the United States, along with other UN countries, fought on the side of the South Koreans and China fought on the side of the North Koreans. (p. 611)

**Kristallnacht** [krĭ-stäl′näkн t′] *n.* "night of broken glass," a name given to the night of November 9, 1938, when gangs of Nazi storm troopers attacked Jewish homes, businesses, and synagogues in Germany. (p. 543)

**Ku Klux Klan** [kōō′ klŭks klăn′] **(KKK)** *n.* a secret organization that used terrorist tactics in an attempt to restore white supremacy in Southern states after the Civil War. (p. 188)

## L

**La Raza Unida** [lä rä′sä ōō-nē′dä] *n.* a Latino political organization founded in 1970 by José Angel Gutiérrez. (p. 770)

**League of Nations** *n.* an association of nations established in 1920 to promote international cooperation and peace. (p. 399)

**Lend-Lease Act** *n.* a law, passed in 1941, that allowed the United States to ship arms and other supplies, without immediate payment, to nations fighting the Axis powers. (p. 552)

**Limited Test Ban Treaty** *n.* the 1963 treaty in which the United States and the Soviet Union agreed not to conduct nuclear-weapons tests in the atmosphere. (p. 678)

**long drive** *n.* the moving of cattle over trails to a shipping center. (p. 210)

**longhorn** [lông′hôrn′] *n.* a breed of sturdy, long-horned cattle brought by the Spanish to Mexico and suited to the dry conditions of the Southwest. (p. 208)

**Louisiana Purchase** *n.* the 1803 purchase by the United States of France's Louisiana Territory—extending from the Mississippi River to the Rocky Mountains—for $15 million. (p. 114)

**Lowell textile** [lō′əl tĕks′tĭl′] **mills** *n.* 19th-century mills for the manufacture of cloth, located in Lowell, Massachusetts, that mainly employed young women. (p. 142)

**Loyalist** [loi′ə-lĭst] *n.* a colonist who supported the British government during the American Revolution. (p. 59)

**Lusitania** [lōō′sĭ-tā′nē-ə] *n.* a British passenger ship that was sunk by a German U-boat in 1915. (p. 378)

## M

**mandate** [măn′dāt′] *n.* the authority to act that an elected official receives from the voters who elected him or her. (p. 680)

**Manhattan Project** [măn-hăt′n prŏj′ĕkt′] *n.* the U.S. program to develop an atomic bomb for use in World War II. (p. 567)

**manifest destiny** [măn′ə-fĕst′ dĕs′tə-nē] *n.* the 19th-century belief that the United States would inevitably expand westward to the Pacific Ocean and into Mexican territory. (p. 131)

**Marbury v. Madison** [măr′bar-ē vûr′səs măd′ĭ-sən] *n.* an 1803 case in which the Supreme Court ruled that it had the power to abolish legislative acts by declaring them unconstitutional; this power came to be known as judicial review. (p. 113)

**market revolution** *n.* the major change in the U.S. economy produced by people's beginning to buy and sell goods rather than make them for themselves. (p. 139)

**Marshall** [măr′shəl] **Plan** *n.* the program, proposed by Secretary of State George Marshall in 1947, under which the United States supplied economic aid to European nations to help them rebuild after World War II. (p. 606)

**mass media** [mē′dē-ə] *n.* the means of communication—such as television, newspapers, and radio—that reach large audiences. (p. 652)

**mass transit** *n.* transportation systems designed to move large numbers of people along fixed routes. (p. 264)

**McCarthyism** [mə-kär′thē-ĭz′əm] *n.* the attacks, often unsubstantiated, by Senator Joseph McCarthy and others on people suspected of being Communists in the early 1950s. (p. 620)

**Meat Inspection Act** *n.* a law, enacted in 1906, that established strict cleanliness requirements for meatpackers and created a federal meat-inspection program. (p. 320)

**Medicaid** [mĕd′ĭ-kād′] *n.* a program, established in 1965, that provides health insurance for people on welfare. (p. 690)

**Medicare** [mĕd′ĭ-kâr′] *n.* a federal program, established in 1965, that provides hospital insurance and low-cost medical insurance to Americans aged 65 and over. (p. 690)

**melting pot** *n.* a mixture of people from different cultures and races who blend together by abandoning their native languages and cultures. (p. 258)

**mercantilism** [mûr′kən-tē-lĭz′əm] *n.* an economic system in which nations seek to increase their wealth and power by obtaining large amounts of gold and silver and by establishing a favorable balance of trade. (p. 28)

**mestizo** [mĕs-tē′zō] *adj.* of mixed Spanish and Native American ancestry. (p. 16)

**middle passage** *n.* the transportation of slaves from Africa to the West Indies. (p. 32)

**militarism** [mĭl′ĭ-tə-rĭz′əm] *n.* the policy of building up armed forces in aggressive preparedness for war and their use as a tool of diplomacy. (p. 373)

**Missouri Compromise** [kŏm′prə-mīz′] *n.* a series of agreements passed by Congress in 1820–1821 to maintain the balance of power between slave states and free states. (p. 122)

**Monroe Doctrine** [mən-rō′ dŏk′trĭn] *n.* a policy of U.S. opposition to any European interference in the affairs of the Western Hemisphere, announced by President Monroe in 1823. (p. 117)

**Moral Majority** [môr′əl mə-jôr′ĭ-tē] *n.* a political alliance of religious groups, consisting mainly of evangelical and fundamentalist Christians, that was active in the 1970s and 1980s, condemning liberal attitudes and behavior and raising money for conservative candidates. (p. 831)

**Morrill** [môr′əl] **Acts** *n.* laws enacted in 1862 and 1890 to help create agricultural colleges by giving federal land to states. (p. 217)

**muckraker** [mŭk′rā′kər] *n.* one of the magazine journalists who exposed the corrupt side of business and public life in the early 1900s. (p. 308)

**Munn v. Illinois** [mŭn′ vûr′səs ĭl′ə-noi′] *n.* an 1877 case in which the Supreme Court upheld states' regulation of railroads for the benefit of farmers and consumers, thus establishing the right of government to regulate private industry to serve the public interest. (p. 239)

**My Lai** [mē′ lī′] *n.* a village in northern South Vietnam where more than 200 unarmed civilians, including women and children, were massacred by U.S. troops in May 1968. (p. 756)

**N**

**NAACP** [ĕn′ dŭb′əl ā′ sē′ pē′] *n.* the National Association for the Advancement of Colored People—an organization founded in 1909 to promote full racial equality. (p. 325)

**NACW** *n.* the National Association of Colored Women—a social service organization founded in 1896. (p. 315)

**NAFTA** [năf′tə] *n.* the North American Free Trade Agreement—a 1993 treaty that lowered tariffs and brought Mexico into the free-trade zone established by the United States and Canada. (p. 864)

**napalm** [nā′päm′] *n.* a gasoline-based substance used in bombs that U.S. planes dropped in Vietnam in order to burn away jungle and expose Vietcong hideouts. (p. 739)

**NASDAQ** [năz′dăk′] *n.* the National Association of Securities Dealers Automated Quotation System—a stock exchange for over-the-counter sales, comprised largely of technology companies. (p. 871)

**National Energy Act** *n.* a law, enacted during the Carter administration, that established a tax on "gas-guzzling" automobiles, removed price controls on U.S. oil and natural gas, and provided tax credits for the development of alternative energy sources. (p. 813)

**National Industrial Recovery Act (NIRA)** *n.* a law enacted in 1933 to establish codes of fair practice for industries and to promote industrial growth. (p. 491)

**nationalism** *n.* a devotion to the interests and culture of one's nation. (p. 373)

**National Labor Relations Board (NLRB)** *n.* an agency created in 1935 to prevent unfair labor practices and to mediate disputes between workers and management. (p. 518)

**National Organization for Women (NOW)** *n.* an organization founded in 1966 to pursue feminist goals, such as better child-care facilities, improved educational opportunities, and an end to job discrimination. (p. 778)

**National Trades' Union** *n.* the first national association of trade unions, formed in 1834. (p. 143)

**National Youth Administration** *n.* an agency that provided young Americans with aid and employment during the Great Depression. (p. 499)

**Nation of Islam** [ĭs-läm′] *n.* a religious group, popularly known as the Black Muslims, founded by Elijah Muhammad to promote black separatism and the Islamic religion. (p. 719)

**nativism** [nā′tĭ-vĭz′əm] *n.* favoring the interests of native-born people over foreign-born people. (pp. 258, 412)

**Navigation** [năv′ĭ-gā′shən] **Acts** *n.* a series of laws enacted by Parliament, beginning in 1651, to tighten England's control of trade in its American colonies. (p. 28)

**NAWSA** *n.* the National American Woman Suffrage Association—an organization founded in 1890 to gain voting rights for women. (p. 316)

**Nazism** [nät′sĭz′əm] *n.* the political philosophy—based on extreme nationalism, racism, and militaristic expansionism—that Adolf Hitler put into practice in Germany from 1933 to 1945. (p. 531)

**Neutrality Acts** *n.* a series of laws enacted in 1935 and 1936 to prevent U.S. arms sales and loans to nations at war. (p. 535)

**New Deal** *n.* President Franklin Roosevelt's program to alleviate the problems of the Great Depression, focusing on relief for the needy, economic recovery, and financial reform. (p. 489)

**New Deal Coalition** [kō′ə-lĭsh′ən] *n.* an alliance of diverse groups—including Southern whites, African Americans, and unionized workers—who supported the policies of the Democratic Party in the 1930s and 1940s. (p. 507)

**New Federalism** [fĕd′ər-ə-lĭz′əm] *n.* President Richard Nixon's program to turn over part of the federal government's power to state and local governments. (p. 795)

**New Frontier** *n.* President John F. Kennedy's legislative program, which included proposals to provide medical care for the elderly, to rebuild blighted urban areas, to aid education, to bolster the national defense, to increase international aid, and to expand the space program. (p. 677)

**New Left** *n.* a youth-dominated political movement of the 1960s, embodied in such organizations as Students for a Democratic Society and the Free Speech Movement. (p. 744)

**New Right** *n.* a late-20th-century alliance of conservative special-interest groups concerned with cultural, social, and moral issues. (p. 831)

**Niagara Movement** *n.* founded by W. E. B. Du Bois in 1905 to promote the education of African Americans in the liberal arts. (p. 285)

**Nineteenth Amendment** *n.* an amendment to the U.S. Constitution, adopted in 1920, that gives women the right to vote. (p. 335)

**nomadic** *adj.* having no fixed home, moving from place to place according to seasons and availability of food and water. (p. 5)

**"no man's land"** *n.* an unoccupied region between opposing armies. (p. 376)

**nonaggression** [nŏn′ə-grĕsh′ən] **pact** *n.* an agreement in which two nations promise not to go to war with each other. (p. 539)

**North Atlantic Treaty Organization (NATO)** *n.* a defensive military alliance formed in 1949 by ten Western European countries, the United States, and Canada. (p. 608)

**Northwest Ordinance** [ôr′dn-əns] **of 1787** *n.* a law that established a procedure for the admission of new states to the Union. (p. 67)

**nullification** [nŭl′ə-fĭ-kā′shən] *n.* a state's refusal to recognize an act of Congress that it considers unconstitutional. (p. 79)

**Nuremberg** [nŏŏr′əm-bûrg′] **trials** *n.* the court proceedings held in Nuremberg, Germany, after World War II, in which Nazi leaders were tried for war crimes. (p. 586)

**O**

**Office of Price Administration (OPA)** *n.* an agency established by Congress to control inflation during World War II. (p. 567)

**Ohio gang** *n.* a group of close friends and political supporters whom President Warren G. Harding appointed to his cabinet. (p. 420)

**OPEC** [ō′pĕk′] *n.* the Organization of Petroleum Exporting Countries—an economic association of oil-producing nations that is able to set oil prices. (p. 799)

**Open Door notes** *n.* messages sent by Secretary of State John Hay in 1899 to Germany, Russia, Great Britain, France, Italy, and Japan, asking the countries not to interfere with U.S. trading rights in China. (p. 356)

**Operation Desert Storm** [dĕz′ərt stôrm′] *n.* a 1991 military operation in which UN forces, led by the United States, drove Iraqi invaders from Kuwait. (p. 855)

**Oregon Trail** *n.* a route from Independence, Missouri, to Oregon City, Oregon, used by pioneers traveling to the Oregon Territory. (p. 131)

## P

**Panama Canal** [păn′ə-mä′ kə-năl′] *n.* an artificial waterway cut through the Isthmus of Panama to provide a shortcut between the Atlantic and Pacific oceans, opened in 1914. (p. 360)

**parity** [păr′ĭ-tē] *n.* a government-supported level for the prices of agricultural products, intended to keep farmers' incomes steady. (p. 518)

**Patriot** [pā′trē-ət] *n.* a colonist who supported American independence from Britain. (p. 59)

**patronage** [pā′trə-nĭj] *n.* an officeholder's power to appoint people—usually those who have helped him or her get elected—to positions in government. (p. 270)

**pay equity** [ĕk′wĭ-tē] *n.* the basing of an employee's salary on the requirements of his or her job rather than on the traditional pay scales that have frequently provided women with smaller incomes than men. (p. 842)

**Payne-Aldrich Tariff** [pān′ ôl′drĭch tăr′ĭf] *n.* a set of tax regulations, enacted by Congress in 1909, that failed to significantly reduce tariffs on manufactured goods. (p. 329)

**Peace Corps** *n.* an agency established in 1961 to provide volunteer assistance to developing nations in Asia, Africa, and Latin America. (p. 680)

**Pendleton** [pĕn′dl-tən] **Civil Service Act** *n.* a law, enacted in 1883, that established a bipartisan civil service commission to make appointments to government jobs by means of the merit system. (p. 270)

**Pentagon** [pĕn′tə-gŏn′] **Papers** *n.* a 7,000-page document—leaked to the press in 1971 by the former Defense Department worker Daniel Ellsberg—revealing that the U.S. government had not been honest about its intentions in the Vietnam War. (p. 757)

*perestroika* [pĕr′ĭ-stroi′kə] *n.* the restructuring of the economy and the government instituted in the Soviet Union in the 1980s. (p. 849)

**planned obsolescence** [ŏb′sə-lĕs′əns] *n.* the designing of products to wear out or to become outdated quickly, so that people will feel a need to replace their possessions frequently. (p. 648)

**Platt** [plăt] **Amendment** *n.* a series of provisions that, in 1901, the United States insisted Cuba add to its new constitution, commanding Cuba to stay out of debt and giving the United States the right to intervene in the country and the right to buy or lease Cuban land for naval and fuelling stations. (p. 354)

*Plessy* v. *Ferguson* [plĕs′ē vûr′səs fûr′gə-sən] *n.* an 1896 case in which the Supreme Court ruled that separation of the races in public accommodations was legal, thus establishing the "separate but equal" doctrine. (p. 287)

**political machine** *n.* an organized group that controls a political party in a city and offers services to voters and businesses in exchange for political and financial support. (p. 268)

**poll** [pōl] **tax** *n.* an annual tax that formerly had to be paid in some Southern states by anyone wishing to vote. (p. 287)

**popular sovereignty** [sŏv′ər-ĭn-tē] *n.* a system in which the residents vote to decide an issue. (p. 157)

**Populism** [pŏp′yə-lĭz′əm] *n.* a late-19th-century political movement demanding that people have a greater voice in government and seeking to advance the interests of farmers and laborers. (p. 221)

**price support** *n.* the maintenance of a price at a certain level through government intervention. (p. 465)

**Proclamation** [prŏk′lə-mā′shən] **of 1763** *n.* an order in which Britain prohibited its American colonists from settling west of the Appalachian Mountains. (p. 39)

**progressive** [prə-grĕs′ĭv] **movement** *n.* an early-20th-century reform movement seeking to return control of the government to the people, to restore economic opportunities, and to correct injustices in American life. (p. 307)

**prohibition** [prō′ə-bĭsh′ən] *n.* the banning of the manufacture, sale, and possession of alcoholic beverages. (p. 307)

**Prohibition** [prō′ə-bĭsh′ən] *n.* The period from 1920–1933 during which the Eighteenth Amendment forbidding the manufacture and sale of alcohol was in force in the United States. (p. 436)

**propaganda** [prŏp′ə-găn′də] *n.* a kind of biased communication designed to influence people's thoughts and actions. (p. 390)

**Proposition 187** *n.* a bill passed in California in 1994 that ended all education and nonemergency health benefits to illegal immigrants. (p. 886)

**protective tariff** [prə-tĕk′tĭv tăr′ĭf] *n.* a tax on imported goods that is intended to protect a nation's businesses from foreign competition. (p. 76)

**protectorate** [prə-tĕk′tə-rĭt] *n.* a country whose affairs are partially controlled by a stronger power. (p. 354)

**Pueblo** [pwĕb′lō] *n.* a group of Native American peoples—descendants of the Anasazi—inhabiting the deserts of the Southwest. (p. 6)

**Pure Food and Drug Act** *n.* a law enacted in 1906 to halt the sale of contaminated foods and drugs and to ensure truth in labeling. (p. 322)

**Puritan** [pyoor′ĭ-tn] *n.* a member of a group that wanted to eliminate all traces of Roman Catholic ritual and traditions in the Church of England. (p. 24)

## Q

**Quaker** [kwā′kər] *n.* a member of the Society of Friends, a religious group persecuted for its beliefs in 17th-century England. (p. 26)

**quota** [kwō′tə] **system** *n.* a system that sets limits on how many immigrants from various countries a nation will admit each year. (p. 415)

## R

**ratification** [răt′ə-fĭ-kā′shən] *n.* the official approval of the Constitution, or of an amendment, by the states. (p. 69)

**rationing** [răsh′ə-nĭng] *n.* a restriction of people's right to buy unlimited amounts of particular foods and other goods, often implemented during wartime to ensure adequate supplies for the military. (p. 568)

**Reaganomics** [rā′gə-nŏm′ĭks] *n.* the economic policies of President Ronald Reagan, which were focused on budget cuts and the granting of large tax cuts in order to increase private investment. (p. 834)

**realpolitik** [rā-äl′pō′lĭ-tēk′] *n.* a political philosophy, advocated by Henry Kissinger in the Nixon administration, that involves dealing with other nations in a practical and flexible way rather than according to a rigid policy. (p. 799)

**reapportionment** [rē′ə-pôr′shən-mənt] *n.* the redrawing of election districts to reflect changes in population. (p. 691)

**recall** [rĭ-kôl′] *n.* a procedure for removing a public official from office by a vote of the people. (p. 312)

**Reconstruction** [rē′kən-strŭk′shən] *n.* the period of rebuilding that followed the Civil War, during which the defeated Confederate states were readmitted to the Union. (p. 184)

**Reconstruction Finance** [fə-nǎns′] **Corporation (RFC)** *n.* an agency established in 1932 to provide emergency financing to banks, life-insurance companies, railroads, and other large businesses. (p. 481)

**referendum** [rĕf′ə-rĕn′dəm] *n.* a procedure by which a proposed legislative measure can be submitted to a vote of the people. (p. 312)

**Reformation** [rĕf′ər-mā′shən] *n.* a religious movement in 16th-century Europe, growing out of a desire for reform in the Roman Catholic Church and leading to the establishment of various Protestant churches. (p. 10)

**Renaissance** [rĕn′ĭ-säns′] *n.* a period of European history, lasting from about 1400 to 1600, during which renewed interest in classical culture led to far-reaching changes in art, learning, and views of the world. (p. 11)

**reparations** [rĕp′ə-rā′shənz] *n.* the compensation paid by a defeated nation for the damage or injury it inflicted during a war. (p. 400)

**republic** [rĭ-pŭb′lĭk] *n.* a government in which the citizens rule through elected representatives. (p. 67)

**Republic of California** *n.* the nation proclaimed by American settlers in California when they declared their independence from Mexico in 1846. (p. 136)

**revenue** [rĕv′ə-nōō] **sharing** *n.* the distribution of federal money to state and local governments with few or no restrictions on how it is spent. (p. 795)

**reverse discrimination** [dĭ-skrĭm′ə-nā′shən] *n.* an unfair treatment of members of a majority group—for example, white men—resulting from efforts to correct discrimination against members of other groups. (p. 831)

**rock 'n' roll** [rŏk′ən-rōl′] *n.* a form of American popular music that evolved in the late 1940s and 1950s out of rhythm and blues, country, jazz, gospel, and pop; the American musical form characterized by heavy rhythms and simple melodies which has spread worldwide having significant impacts on social dancing, clothing fashions, and expressions of protest. (p. 655)

**Roosevelt Corollary** [rō′zə-vĕlt′ kôr′ə-lĕr′-ē] *n.* an extension of the Monroe Doctrine, announced by President Theodore Roosevelt in 1904, under which the United States claimed the right to protect its economic interests by means of military intervention in the affairs of Western Hemisphere nations. (p. 362)

**Rough Riders** *n.* a volunteer cavalry regiment, commanded by Leonard Wood and Theodore Roosevelt, that served in the Spanish-American War. (p. 350)

**rural free delivery (RFD)** *n.* the free government delivery of mail and packages to homes in rural areas, begun in 1896. (p. 297)

**SALT I** [sôlt′ wŭn′] **Treaty** *n.* a five-year agreement between the United States and the Soviet Union, signed in 1972, that limited the nations' numbers of intercontinental ballistic missiles and submarine-launched missiles. (p. 801)

**Sandinista** [sǎn′dĭ-nēs′tə] *adj.* belonging to a leftist rebel group that overthrew the Nicaraguan government in 1979. (p. 851)

**Santa Fe** [sǎn′tə fā′] **Trail** *n.* a route from Independence, Missouri, to Santa Fe, New Mexico, used by traders in the early and mid-1800s. (p. 131)

**satellite** [sǎt′l-īt′] **nation** *n.* a country that is dominated politically and economically by another nation. (p. 605)

**Saturday Night Massacre** [mǎs′ə-kər] *n.* a name given to the resignation of the U.S. attorney general and the firing of his deputy in October 1973, after they refused to carry out President Nixon's order to fire the special prosecutor investigating the Watergate affair. (p. 805)

**scalawag** [skǎl′ə-wǎg′] *n.* a white Southerner who joined the Republican Party after the Civil War. (p. 186)

**scientific management** *n.* the application of scientific principles to increase efficiency in the workplace. (p. 308)

**Scopes** [skōps] **trial** *n.* a sensational 1925 court case in which the biology teacher John T. Scopes was tried for challenging a Tennessee law that outlawed the teaching of evolution. (p. 438)

**search-and-destroy mission** [sûrch′ ənd′ dĭ-stroi′ mĭsh′ən] *n.* a U.S. military raid on a South Vietnamese village, intended to root out villagers with ties to the Vietcong but often resulting in the destruction of the village and the displacement of its inhabitants. (p. 739)

**secession** [sĭ-sĕsh′ən] *n.* the formal withdrawal of a state from the Union. (p. 157)

**Securities and Exchange** [sĭ-kyŏŏr′ĭ-tēz ənd ĭks-chānj′] **Commission (SEC)** *n.* an agency, created in 1934, that monitors the stock market and enforces laws regulating the sale of stocks and bonds. (p. 517)

**segregation** [sĕg′rĭ-gā′shən] *n.* the separation of people on the basis of race. (p. 287)

**Selective** [sĭ-lĕk′tĭv] **Service Act** *n.* a law, enacted in 1917, that required men to register for military service. (p. 382)

**Seneca Falls** [sĕn′ĭ-kə fôlz′] **Convention** *n.* a women's rights convention held in Seneca Falls, New York, in 1848. (p. 149)

**service sector** [sĕk′tər] *n.* the part of the economy that provides consumers with services rather than goods. (p. 870)

**settlement house** *n.* a community center providing assistance to residents—particularly immigrants—in a slum neighborhood. (p. 266)

**Seventeenth Amendment** *n.* an amendment to the U.S. Constitution, adopted in 1913, that provides for the election of U.S. senators by the people rather than by state legislatures. (p. 312)

**shantytown** [shǎn′tē-toun′] *n.* a neighborhood in which people live in makeshift shacks. (p. 473)

**sharecropping** [shâr′krŏp′ĭng] *n.* a system in which landowners give farm workers land, seed, and tools in return for a part of the crops they raise. (p. 188)

**Shays's** [shā′zəz] **Rebellion** *n.* an uprising of debt-ridden Massachusetts farmers protesting increased state taxes in 1787. (p. 67)

**Sherman Antitrust** [shûr′mən ăn′tē-trŭst′] **Act** n. a law, enacted in 1890, that was intended to prevent the creation of monopolies by making it illegal to establish trusts that interfered with free trade. (p. 244)

**silent majority** [mə-jôr′ĭ-tē] n. a name given by President Richard Nixon to the moderate, mainstream Americans who quietly supported his Vietnam War policies. (p. 756)

**sit-in** n. a form of demonstration used by African Americans to protest discrimination, in which the protesters sit down in a segregated business and refuse to leave until they are served. (p. 706)

**Social Darwinism** [sō′shəl där′wĭ-nĭz′əm] n. an economic and social philosophy—supposedly based on the biologist Charles Darwin's theory of evolution by natural selection—holding that a system of unrestrained competition will ensure the survival of the fittest. (p. 242)

**Social Gospel** [gŏs′pəl] **movement** n. a 19th-century reform movement based on the belief that Christians have a responsibility to help improve working conditions and alleviate poverty. (p. 266)

**Social Security Act** n. a law enacted in 1935 to provide aid to retirees, the unemployed, people with disabilities, and families with dependent children. (p. 501)

**soddy** [sŏd′ē] n. a home built of blocks of turf. (p. 216)

**soup kitchen** n. a place where free or low cost food is served to the needy. (p. 473)

**Southern Christian Leadership Conference (SCLC)** n. an organization formed in 1957 by Dr. Martin Luther King, Jr., and other leaders to work for civil rights through nonviolent means. (p. 706)

**Southern strategy** n. President Nixon's attempt to attract the support of Southern conservative Democrats who were unhappy with federal desegregation policies and the liberal Supreme Court. (p. 797)

**speakeasy** [spēk′ē′zē] n. a place where alcoholic drinks were sold and consumed illegally during Prohibition. (p. 436)

**speculation** [spĕk′yə-lā′shən] n. an involvement in risky business transactions in an effort to make a quick or large profit. (p. 467)

**Square Deal** n. President Theodore Roosevelt's program of progressive reforms designed to protect the common people against big business. (p. 319)

**stagflation** [stăg-flā′shən] n. an economic condition marked by both inflation and high unemployment. (p. 798)

**Stamp Act** n. a 1765 law in which Parliament established the first direct taxation of goods and services within the British colonies in North America. (p. 47)

**Strategic Defense Initiative** [strə-tē′jĭk dĭ-fĕns′ ĭ-nĭsh′ə-tĭv] **(SDI)** n. a proposed defense system—popularly known as Star Wars—intended to protect the United States against missile attacks. (p. 835)

**strike** n. a work stoppage intended to force an employer to respond to demands. (p. 142)

**Student Nonviolent Coordinating** [nŏn-vī′ə-lənt kō-ôr′dn-ā′tĭng] **Committee (SNCC)** [snĭk] n. an organization formed in 1960 to coordinate sit-ins and other protests and to give young blacks a larger role in the civil rights movement. (p. 706)

**Students for a Democratic Society (SDS)** n. an antiestablishment New Left group, founded in 1960, that called for greater individual freedom and responsibility. (p. 744)

**suburb** [sŭb′ûrb′] n. a residential town or community near a city. (p. 635)

**suffrage** [sŭf′rĭj] n. the right to vote. (p. 315)

**Sugar Act** n. a trade law enacted by Parliament in 1764 in an attempt to reduce smuggling in the British colonies in North America. (p. 47)

**supply-side economics** n. the idea that a reduction of tax rates will lead to increases in jobs, savings, and investments, and therefore to an increase in government revenue. (p. 835)

**T**

**Taino** [tī′nō] n. a Native American people of the Caribbean islands—the first group encountered by Columbus and his men when they reached the Americas. (p. 14)

**Teapot Dome scandal** [skăn′dl] n. Secretary of the Interior Albert B. Fall's secret leasing of oil-rich public land to private companies in return for money and land. (p. 421)

**Telecommunications** [tĕl′ĭ-kə-myōō′nĭ-kā′shənz] **Act of 1996** n. a law enacted in 1996 to remove barriers that had previously prevented communications companies from engaging in more than one type of communications business. (p. 878)

**telecommute** [tĕl′ĭ-kə-myōōt′] v. to work at home for a company located elsewhere, by using such communications technologies as computers, the Internet, and fax machines. (p. 878)

**tenement** [tĕn′ə-mənt] n. a multifamily urban dwelling, usually overcrowded and unsanitary. (p. 264)

**Tennessee Valley Authority (TVA)** n. a federal corporation established in 1933 to construct dams and power plants in the Tennessee Valley region to generate electricity as well as to prevent floods. (p. 519)

**termination** [tûr′mə-nā′shən] **policy** n. the U.S. government's plan, announced in 1953, to give up responsibility for Native American tribes by eliminating federal economic support, discontinuing the reservation system, and redistributing tribal lands. (p. 663)

**Tet offensive** [tĕt′ ə-fĕn′sĭv] n. a massive surprise attack by the Vietcong on South Vietnamese towns and cities early in 1968. (p. 749)

**Texas Revolution** n. the 1836 rebellion in which Texas gained its independence from Mexico. (p. 134)

**Thirteenth Amendment** n. an amendment to the U.S. Constitution, adopted in 1865, that has abolished slavery and involuntary servitude. (p. 183)

**Tiananmen** [tyän′än′mĕn′] **Square** n. the site of 1989 demonstrations in Beijing, China, in which Chinese students demanded freedom of speech and a greater voice in government. (p. 850)

**Tonkin Gulf** [tŏn′kĭn′ gŭlf′] **Resolution** n. a resolution adopted by Congress in 1964, giving the president broad powers to wage war in Vietnam. (p. 735)

**totalitarian** [tō-tăl′ĭ-târ′ē-ən] adj. characteristic of a political system in which the government exercises complete control over its citizens' lives. (p. 529)

**Trail of Tears** [tûrz] n. the marches in which the Cherokee people were forcibly removed from Georgia to the Indian Territory in 1838–1840, with thousands of the Cherokee dying on the way. (p. 124)

**transcendentalism** [trăn′sĕn-dĕn′tl-ĭz′əm] *n.* a philosophical and literary movement of the 1800s that emphasized living a simple life and celebrated the truth found in nature and in personal emotion and imagination. (p. 145)

**transcontinental** [trăns′kŏn-tə-nĕn′tl] **railroad** *n.* a railroad line linking the Atlantic and Pacific coasts of the United States, completed in 1869. (p. 237)

**Treaty of Fort Laramie** *n.* the treaty requiring the Sioux to live on a reservation along the Missouri River. (p. 204)

**Treaty of Guadalupe Hidalgo** [gwäd′l-ōōp′ hĭ-däl′gō] *n.* the 1848 treaty ending the U.S. war with Mexico, in which Mexico ceded California and New Mexico to the United States. (p. 136)

**Treaty of Paris (1783)** *n.* the treaty that ended the Revolutionary War, confirming the independence of the United States and setting the boundaries of the new nation. (p. 62)

**Treaty of Paris (1898)** *n.* the treaty ending the Spanish-American War, in which Spain freed Cuba, turned over the islands of Guam and Puerto Rico to the United States, and sold the Philippines to the United States for $20 million. (p. 350)

**Treaty of Tordesillas** [tôr′də-sē′əs] *n.* the 1494 treaty in which Spain and Portugal agreed to divide the lands of the Western Hemisphere between them. (p. 15)

**Treaty of Versailles** [vər-sī′] *n.* the 1919 peace treaty at the end of World War I which established new nations, borders, and war reparations. (p. 400)

**trench warfare** *n.* military operations in which the opposing forces attack and counterattack from systems of fortified ditches rather than on an open battlefield. (p. 376)

**triangular** [trī-ăng′gyə-lər] **trade** *n.* the transatlantic system of trade in which goods and people, including slaves, were exchanged between Africa, England, Europe, the West Indies, and the colonies in North America. (p. 32)

**Truman Doctrine** [trōō′mən dŏk′trĭn] *n.* a U.S. policy, announced by President Harry S. Truman in 1947, of providing economic and military aid to free nations threatened by internal or external opponents. (p. 606)

**Tuskegee** [tŭs-kē′gē] **Normal and Industrial Institute** *n.* founded in 1881, and led by Booker T. Washington, to equip African Americans with teaching diplomas and useful skills in the trades and agriculture. (p. 285)

**two-party system** *n.* a political system dominated by two major parties. (p. 76)

## U

**Underground Railroad** *n.* a system of routes along which runaway slaves were helped to escape to Canada or to safe areas in the free states. (p. 158)

**Unitarian** [yōō′nĭ-târ′ē-ən] *n.* member of a religious group that emphasizes reason and faith in the individual. (p. 145)

**United Farm Workers Organizing Committee (UFWOC)** *n.* a labor union formed in 1966 to seek higher wages and better working conditions for Mexican-American farm workers in California. (p. 770)

**United Nations (UN)** *n.* an international peacekeeping organization to which most nations in the world belong, founded in 1945 to promote world peace, security, and economic development. (p. 603)

**urban** [ûr′bən] **flight** *n.* a migration of people from cities to the surrounding suburbs. (p. 882)

**urbanization** [ûr′bə-nĭ-zā′shən] *n.* the growth of cities. (p. 262)

**urban renewal** [rĭ-nōō′əl] *n.* the tearing down and replacing of buildings in rundown inner-city neighborhoods. (p. 661)

**urban sprawl** [sprôl′] *n.* the unplanned and uncontrolled spreading of cities into surrounding regions. (p. 424)

**U.S.S. *Maine*** *n.* a U.S. warship that mysteriously exploded and sank in the harbor of Havana, Cuba, on February 15, 1898. (p. 348)

**U-2 incident** *n.* the downing of a U.S. spy plane and capture of its pilot by the Soviet Union in 1960. (p. 627)

## V

**V-E Day** *n.* a name given to May 8, 1945, "Victory in Europe Day" on which General Eisenhower's acceptance of the unconditional surrender of Nazi Germany marked the end of World War II in Europe. (p. 577)

**vertical integration** [vûr′tĭ-kəl ĭn′tĭ-grā′shən] *n.* a company's taking over its suppliers and distributors and transportation systems to gain total control over the quality and cost of its product. (p. 242)

**Vietcong** [vē-ĕt′kŏng′] *n.* the South Vietnamese Communists who, with North Vietnamese support, fought against the government of South Vietnam in the Vietnam War. (p. 732)

**Vietminh** [vē-ĕt′mĭn′] *n.* an organization of Vietnamese Communists and other nationalist groups that between 1946 and 1954 fought for Vietnamese independence from the French. (p. 731)

**Vietnamization** [vē-ĕt′nə-mĭ-zā′shən] *n.* President Nixon's strategy for ending U.S. involvement in the Vietnam War, involving the gradual withdrawal of U.S. troops and their replacement with South Vietnamese forces. (p. 755)

**Voting Rights Act of 1965** *n.* a law that made it easier for African Americans to register to vote by eliminating discriminatory literacy tests and authorizing federal examiners to enroll voters denied at the local level. (p. 716)

## W

**Wagner** [wăg′nər] **Act** *n.* a law—also known as the National Labor Relations Act—enacted in 1935 to protect workers' rights after the Supreme Court declared the National Industrial Recovery Act unconstitutional. (p. 499)

**war-guilt** [wôr′ gĭlt′] **clause** *n.* a provision in the Treaty of Versailles by which Germany acknowledged that it alone was responsible for World War I. (p. 400)

**War Industries Board (WIB)** *n.* an agency established during World War I to increase efficiency and discourage waste in war-related industries. (p. 389)

**War Powers Act (WPA)** *n.* a law enacted in 1973, limiting a president's right to send troops into battle without consulting Congress. (p. 761)

**War Production Board (WPB)** *n.* an agency established during World War II to coordinate the production of military supplies by U.S. industries. (p. 568)

**Warren** [wôr′ən] **Commission** *n.* a group, headed by Chief Justice Earl Warren, that investigated the assassination of President Kennedy and concluded that Lee Harvey Oswald was alone responsible for it. (p. 683)

**Warren Court** *n.* the Supreme Court during the period when Earl Warren was chief justice, noted for its activism in the areas of civil rights and free speech. (p. 691)

**Warsaw** [wôr′sô′] **Pact** *n.* a military alliance formed in 1955 by the Soviet Union and its Eastern European satellites. (p. 624)

**Watergate** [wô′tər-gāt′] *n.* a scandal arising from the Nixon administration's attempt to cover up its involvement in the 1972 break-in at the Democratic National Committee headquarters in the Watergate apartment complex. (p. 802)

**Women's Auxiliary** [ôg-zĭl′yə-rē] **Army Corps (WAAC)** *n.* U.S. army unit created during World War II to enable women to serve in noncombat positions. (p. 563)

**Woodstock** [woŏd′stŏk′] *n.* a free music festival that attracted more than 400,000 young people to a farm in upstate New York in August 1969. (p. 783)

**Works Progress Administration (WPA)** *n.* an agency, established as part of the Second New Deal, that provided the unemployed with jobs in construction, garment making, teaching, the arts, and other fields. (p. 498)

**XYZ Affair** *n.* a 1797 incident in which French officials demanded a bribe from U.S. diplomats. (p. 78)

**yellow journalism** [jûr′nə-lĭz′əm] *n.* the use of sensationalized and exaggerated reporting by newspapers or magazines to attract readers. (p. 347)

**Zimmermann** [zĭm′ər-mən] **note** *n.* a message sent in 1917 by the German foreign minister to the German ambassador in Mexico, proposing a German-Mexican alliance and promising to help Mexico regain Texas, New Mexico, and Arizona if the United States entered World War I. (p. 379)

# SPANISH GLOSSARY

**abolition** [abolición] *s.* movimiento para acabar con la esclavitud. (p. 144)

**affirmative action** [acción afirmativa] *s.* medidas para corregir los efectos de la discriminación anterior; favorecen a grupos que estaban en desventaja. (pp. 723, 831)

**Agent Orange** [Agente Naranja] *s.* químico tóxico exfoliante que fumigaron las tropas estadounidenses en Vietnam para poner al descubierto refugios del Vietcong. (p. 739)

**Agricultural Adjustment Act** [Ley de Ajustes Agrícolas] *s.* ley de 1933 que elevó el precio de las cosechas al pagarle a los granjeros para que no cultivaran cierta porción de sus tierras, reduciendo así la producción. (p. 491)

**AIDS (acquired immune deficiency syndrome)** [SIDA, síndrome de inmunodeficiencia adquirida] *s.* enfermedad causada por un virus que debilita el sistema inmunológico y hace que el cuerpo sea vulnerable a infecciones y formas poco comunes de cáncer. (p. 840)

**Alamo, the** [El Álamo] *s.* misión y fuerte situado en San Antonio, Texas, en donde fuerzas mexicanas masacraron a rebeldes texanos en 1836. (p. 134)

**Alien and Sedition Acts** [Leyes de Extranjeros y de Sedición] *s.* cuatro leyes aprobadas en 1798 para reducir el poder político de los nuevos inmigrantes a EE.UU. (p. 78)

**Alliance for Progress** [Alianza para el Progreso] *s.* programa de los sesenta para ofrecer ayuda económica a los países latinoamericanos. (p. 680)

**Allies** [Aliados] *s.* 1. en la I Guerra Mundial, naciones aliadas en un tratado contra Alemania y las otras Potencias Centrales; originalmente Gran Bretaña, Francia y Rusia; más adelante se unieron Estados Unidos, Japón, Italia y otros. (p. 396) 2. en la II Guerra Mundial, naciones asociadas contra el Eje, en particular Gran Bretaña, la Unión Soviética y Estados Unidos. (p. 554)

**American Expeditionary Force (AEF)** [Fuerza Americana de Expediciones] *s.* fuerzas dirigidas por el general John Pershing, quien lucho con los aliados en Europa durante la Primera Guerra Mundial. (p. 384)

**American Federation of Labor (AFL)** [Federación Norteamericana del Trabajo] *s.* sindicato de trabajadores calificados creado en 1886 y dirigido por Samuel Gompers. (p. 245)

**American Indian Movement (AIM)** [Movimiento Indígena Americano] *s.* organización con frecuencia militante creada en 1968 con el fin de luchar por los derechos de los amerindios. (p. 771)

**Americanization movement** [movimiento de americanización] *s.* programa educativo ideado para facilitar la asimilación de los inmigrantes a la cultura estadounidense. (p. 263)

**American System** [Sistema Americano] *s.* programa económico previo a la Guerra Civil diseñado para fortalecer y unificar a Estados Unidos por medio de aranceles proteccionistas, un banco nacional y un sistema de transporte eficiente. (p. 122)

**anarchist** [anarquista] *s.* persona que se opone a toda forma de gobierno. (p. 413)

**Anasazi** *s.* grupo amerindio que vivió cerca de la región de Four Corners —donde Arizona, New Mexico, Colorado y Utah se unen— de los años 100 a 1400 d.C., aproximadamente. (p. 5)

**Antifederalist** [antifederalista] *s.* oponente de la Constitución y de un gobierno central fuerte. (p. 69)

**appeasement** [apaciguamiento] *s.* política de ceder a las demandas de una potencia hostil con el fin de mantener la paz. (p. 538)

**Appomattox Court House** *s.* pueblo cerca de Appomatox, Virginia, donde Lee se rindió a Grant el 9 de abril de 1865. (37°N 79°O) (p. 181)

**arbitration** [arbitraje] *s.* método de resolver disputas en el cual ambos lados someten sus diferencias a un juez elegido por las dos partes. (p. 245)

**armistice** [armisticio] *s.* tregua o acuerdo para terminar un conflicto armado. (p. 387)

**Army of the Republic of Vietnam (ARVN)** [Ejército de la República de Vietnam] *s.* soldados del sur de Vietnam que lucharon junto a soldados estadounidenses contra el comunismo y las fuerzas del norte de Vietnam durante la Guerra de Vietnam. (p. 737)

**Articles of Confederation** [Artículos de la Confederación] *s.* documento aprobado por el Segundo Congreso Continental en 1777 y ratificado por los estados finalmente en 1781. Detallaba la forma del gobierno de los nuevos Estados Unidos. (p. 67)

**Ashcan School** *s.* grupo de artistas estadounidenses de principios del siglo XX que a menudo pintaban escenas realistas de la vida urbana —como arrabales y gente sin hogar— ganándose así el nombre de la escuela del basurero. (p. 295)

**assimilation** [asimilación] *s.* adopción, por parte de un grupo minoritario, de las creencias y estilo de vida de la cultura dominante. (p. 206)

**Atlantic Charter** [Carta del Atlántico] *s.* declaración de principios de 1941 en que Estados Unidos y Gran Bretaña establecieron sus objetivos contra las Potencias del Eje. (p. 554)

**Axis powers** [Potencias del Eje] *s.* países unidos contra los Aliados en la II Guerra Mundial, que incluyeron a Alemania, Italia y Japón. (p. 551)

**Aztec** [azteca] *s.* pueblo amerindio que colonizó el Valle de México en 1200 A.C. y desarrolló un gran imperio. (p. 5)

**baby boom** *s.* marcado aumento en el índice de natalidad en Estados Unidos después de la II Guerra Mundial. (p. 643)

**Battle of the Bulge** [Batalla del Bolsón] *s.* batalla de un mes de duración en la II Guerra Mundial durante la cual los Aliados rompieron la última gran ofensiva alemana de la guerra. (p. 576)

**Battle of Midway** [Batalla de Midway] *s.* batalla de la Segunda Guerra Mundial que ocurrió a principios de junio en 1942. Los aliados redujeron la flotilla japonesa en Midway, una isla al Noreste de Hawai. A partir de esta batalla los aliados tomaron la ofensiva y comenzaron a moverse a Japón. (p. 579)

**Battle of Wounded Knee** [Batalla de Wounded Knee] *s.* masacre de 300 indígenas desarmados en Wounded Knee Creek, South Dakota, en 1890. (p. 208)

**Beatles, the** *s.* conjunto inglés que tuvo gran influencia en la música popular en los años 60. (p. 783)

**beat movement** [movimiento beat] *s.* movimiento social y literario de los años 50 que enfatizó la expresión literaria sin reglas y la disconformidad. (p. 655)

**Benin** *s.* reino de África occidental que existió en la actual Nigeria; floreció en los bosques del delta del Níger del siglo 14 al 17. (p. 9)

**Berlin airlift** [puente aéreo de Berlín] *s.* operación de 327 días de duración, en la que aviones estadounidenses y británicos llevaron alimentos y provisiones a Berlín Occidental después de que la Unión Soviética bloqueó la ciudad en 1948. (p. 607)

**Berlin Wall** [Muro de Berlín] *s.* muro de concreto que separó Berlín Oriental y Occidental de 1961 a 1989; construido por Alemania Oriental para impedir que sus ciudadanos se escaparan al occidente. (p. 677)

**Bessemer process** [método Bessemer] *s.* técnica más eficiente y barata de fabricar acero, desarrollada hacia 1850. (p. 231)

**Bill of Rights** [Carta de Derechos] *s.* primeras diez enmiendas a la Constitución que identifican los derechos de los ciudadanos; se adoptaron en 1791. (p. 70)

**bimetallism** [bimetalismo] *s.* sistema monetario nacional que utiliza el oro y la plata para respaldar la moneda. (p. 222)

**blacklist** [lista negra] *s.* lista de unos 500 actores, escritores, productores y directores a quienes no se permitía trabajar en películas de Hollywood debido a sus supuestos vínculos comunistas. (p. 618)

**Black Panthers** [Panteras Negras] *s.* organización política afroamericana militante formada por Huey Newton y Bobby Seale en 1966 para luchar contra la violencia de la policía y suministrar servicios en el ghetto. (p. 720)

**Black Power** [Poder Negro] *s.* consigna usada por Stokely Carmichael en los años 60, que pedía poder político y social para los afroamericanos. (p. 720)

**Black Tuesday** [Martes Negro] *s.* octubre 29 de 1929, día en que los precios de las acciones bajaron drásticamente. (p. 468)

**blitzkrieg** *s.* proveniente de la palabra alemana que significa "guerra relámpago". Repentina ofensiva de fuerzas aéreas y terrestres a gran escala con el fin de obtener una victoria rápida. (p. 539)

**bonanza farm** [granja de bonanza] *s.* extensa granja dedicada a un solo cultivo. (p. 218)

**Bonus Army** *s.* grupo de veteranos de la I Guerra Mundial que marcharon en Washington, D.C., en 1932 para exigir bonos prometidos a cambio de su servicio militar. (p. 482)

**bootlegger** *s.* persona que contrabandeaba bebidas alcohólicas durante la época de Prohibición. (p. 437)

**Boston Massacre** [Masacre de Boston] *s.* choque entre soldados británicos y colonos en Boston en 1770, durante el cual cinco colonos fueron asesinados. (p. 48)

**Boston Tea Party** [Motín del Té de Boston] *s.* protesta en 1773 contra el impuesto británico sobre el té; los colonos arrojaron 18,000 libras de té al puerto de Boston. (p. 49)

**Boulder Dam** [Presa de Boulder] *s.* presa del río Colorado construida durante la Depresión con fondos federales para estimular la economía; ahora llamada Presa Hoover. (p. 480)

**Boxer Rebellion** [Rebelión de los Boxer] *s.* rebelión encabezada en 1900 por los Boxer, sociedad secreta de China, para detener la difusión de la influencia occidental. (p. 357)

**bracero** *s.* trabajador mexicano que laboró temporalmente en Estados Unidos durante la Segunda Guerra Mundial. (p. 662)

**bread line** [cola para comer] *s.* fila de personas que esperan comida gratis. (p. 473)

**brinkmanship** *s.* práctica de amenazar al enemigo con represalias militares extremas ante cualquier agresión. (p. 623)

***Brown* v. *Board of Education of Topeka*** *s.* decisión de la Suprema Corte en 1954 que declaró que la segregación de estudiantes negros y blancos era inconstitucional. (p. 702)

**Bull Moose Party** [Partido Bull Moose] *s.* apodo del Partido Progresista, bajo el que Theodore Roosevelt aspiró, sin éxito, a la presidencia en 1912. (p. 330)

**buying on margin** [compra con margen] *s.* compra de acciones en la que se paga sólo una porción del valor de la acción al vendedor o corredor de bolsa, y se presta el resto. (p. 467)

**C**

**cabinet** [gabinete] *s.* jefes de departamentos que son asesores directos del presidente. (p. 75)

**Camp David Accords** [Acuerdos de Camp David] *s.* acuerdos de paz históricos entre Israel y Egipto, negociados en Camp David, Maryland, en 1978. (p. 816)

**carpetbagger** *s.* norteños que se trasladaron al Sur después de la Guerra Civil. (p. 186)

**Central Powers** [Potencias Centrales] *s.* en la I Guerra Mundial, el grupo de naciones —Alemania, Austro-Hungría y el imperio otomano— que se opuso a los Aliados. (p. 374)

**checks and balances** [control y compensación de poderes] *s.* sistema en el cual cada rama del gobierno controla o restringe a las demás ramas. (p. 69)

**Chinese Exclusion Act** [Ley de Exclusión de Chinos] *s.* ley de 1882 que prohibía la inmigración de ciudadanos chinos, con la excepción de estudiantes, maestros, comerciantes, turistas y funcionarios gubernamentales. (p. 259)

**Chisholm Trail** [Sendero Chisholm] *s.* la ruta principal de ganado que iba desde San Antonio, Texas, por Oklahoma hasta Kansas. (p. 209)

**chlorination** [cloración] *s.* purificación del agua al mezclarla químicamente con cloro. (p. 264)

**Christianity** [cristianismo] *s.* religión basada en la vida y las enseñanzas de Jesucristo. (p. 10)

**CIA** *s.* Central Intelligence Agency (Agencia Central de Inteligencia), agencia gubernamental establecida para espiar y realizar operaciones secretas en países extranjeros. (p. 623)

**Civilian Conservation Corps (CCC)** [Cuerpo Civil de Conservación] *s.* agencia establecida como parte del New Deal con el fin de ocupar a jóvenes desempleados en trabajos como la construcción de carreteras y el cuidado de parques nacionales y ayudar en situaciones de emergencia. (p. 491)

**Civil Rights Act of 1964** [Ley de Derechos Civiles de 1964] *s.* ley que prohíbe la discriminación en lugares públicos, en la educación y en los empleos por cuestión de raza, color, sexo, nacionalidad o religión. (p. 714)

**Civil Rights Act of 1968** [Ley de Derechos Civiles de 1968] *s.* ley que prohíbe la discriminación en la vivienda. (p. 722)

**civil service** [servicio civil] *s.* cualquier servicio gubernamental en el que se obtiene un cargo mediante exámenes públicos. (p. 270)

**Clayton Antitrust Act** [Ley Antitrust Clayton] *s.* ley de 1914 que declaraba ilegales ciertas prácticas empresariales injustas y protegía el derecho de los sindicatos y organizaciones agrícolas. (p. 333)

**Cold War** [Guerra Fría] *s.* estado de hostilidad, sin llegar a conflictos armados, entre Estados Unidos y la Unión Soviética tras la II Guerra Mundial. (p. 606)

**Columbian Exchange** [Transferencia Colombina] *s.* transferencia —iniciada con el primer viaje de Colón a las Américas— de plantas, alimentos, animales y enfermedades entre el Hemisferio Occidental y el Hemisferio Oriental. (p. 15)

**Committee to Reelect the President** [Comité de Reelección del Presidente] *s.* grupo que dirigió la campaña para la reelección del presidente Nixon en 1972, cuya conexión con el allanamiento de la Sede Nacional del Partido Demócrata hizo estallar el escándalo Watergate. (p. 803)

**Common Sense** [Sentido común] *s.* folleto escrito en 1776 por Thomas Paine que exhortaba la separación de las colonias británicas. (p. 52)

**Commonwealth v. Hunt** *s.* caso judicial de 1842 en el cual la Suprema Corte de Massachusetts ratificó el derecho de los obreros a la huelga. (p. 143)

**communism** [comunismo] *s.* sistema económico y político basado en un gobierno de un solo partido y en la propiedad estatal. (p. 413)

**concentration camp** [campo de concentración] *s.* campamento de presos operado por la Alemania nazi para judíos y otros grupos que consideraba enemigos de Adolfo Hitler; a los presos los mataban o los hacían morir de hambre y a causa de trabajos forzados. (p. 546)

**Confederacy** [Estados Confederados de América] *s.* confederación formada en 1861 por los estados del Sur después de que se separaron de la unión. (p. 165)

**conglomerate** [conglomerado] *s.* corporación grande que posee compañías más pequeñas dedicadas a negocios diversos. (p. 642)

**Congress of Industrial Organizations** [Congreso de Organizaciones Industriales] *s.* organización sindical expulsada de la Federación Norteamericana del Trabajo en 1938. (p. 508)

**Congress of Racial Equality (CORE)** [Congreso de Igualdad Racial] *s.* grupo interracial, fundado por James Farmer en 1942, que luchaba contra la segregación en ciudades del Norte. (p. 593)

**conquistador** *s.* explorador y colonizador español de las Américas en el siglo 16. (p. 16)

**conscientious objector** [objetor de conciencia] *s.* persona que se opone a toda guerra por principio de conciencia. (p. 386)

**conscription** [conscripción] *s.* servicio militar obligatorio de ciertos miembros de la población. (p. 173)

**conservation** [conservación] *s.* práctica de preservar algunas zonas naturales y desarrollar otras por el bien común. (p. 323)

**conservative coalition** [coalición conservadora] *s.* alianza de grupos de ultraderecha opuestos a la ingerencia del gobierno formada a mediados de los años sesenta. (p. 831)

**consolidation** [consolidación] *s.* acto de unir o combinar. (p. 240)

**consumerism** [consumismo] *s.* gran interés en la compra de bienes materiales. (p. 648)

**containment** [contención] *s.* política estadounidense de formar alianzas con países más pequeños y débiles con el fin de bloquear la expansión de la infuencia soviética tras la II Guerra Mundial. (p. 605)

**Contract with America** [Contrato con América] *s.* documento elaborado por el representante Newt Gingrich y firmado por 300 candidatos republicanos el 27 de septiembre de 1994, que presentaba sus planes legislativos conservadores. (p. 864)

**Contras** [la contra] *s.* fuerzas anticomunistas nicaragüenses que recibieron asistencia de la administración Reagan para derrocar al gobierno sandinista de Nicaragua. (p. 851)

**convoy system** [flotilla de escolta] *s.* medio de proteger los buques mercantes del ataque de submarinos alemanes al hacer que viajaran con una escolta de destructores. (p. 383)

**counterculture** [contracultura] *s.* cultura de la juventud de los años 60 que rechazaba la sociedad tradicional y buscaba paz, amor y libertad individual. (p. 781)

**credibility gap** [falta de credibilidad] *s.* desconfianza del público en las declaraciones oficiales del gobierno. (p. 741)

**credit** [crédito] *s.* acuerdo en el que se compran artículos en el presente para ser pagados en el futuro mediante un plan de cuotas con intereses. (p. 466)

**Crédit Mobilier** *s.* compañía constructora formada en 1864 por los dueños de la Union Pacific Railroad; quienes la usaron ilegalmente para obtener ganancias. (p. 238)

## D

**Dawes Act** [Ley Dawes] *s.* ley aprobada por el Congreso en 1887 para "americanizar" a los indígenas distribuyendo a individuos la tierra de las reservaciones. (p. 206)

**D-Day** [Día D] *s.* junio 6 de 1944, día en que los Aliados emprendieron una invasión por tierra, mar y aire contra el Eje. (p. 574)

**debt peonage** [deuda por peonaje] *s.* sistema de servidumbre en el que una persona es obligada a trabajar para pagar una deuda. (p. 289)

**Declaration of Independence** [Declaración de Independencia] *s.* documento escrito por Thomas Jefferson en 1776 en el cual los delegados del Congreso Continental declaron la independencia de las colonias de Gran Bretaña. (p. 53)

**de facto segregation** [segregación *de facto*] *s.* segregación racial impuesta por la práctica y la costumbre más que por las leyes. (p. 718)

**deficit spending** [gasto deficitario] *s.* práctica por parte de un gobierno de gastar más de lo que recibe por concepto de rentas públicas. (p. 492)

**de jure segregation** [segregación *de jure*] *s.* segregación racial impuesta por la ley. (p. 718)

**Democratic-Republican** [Demócrata-Republicano] *s.* partido político conocido por su apoyo a un fuerte gobierno estatal. Fue fundado por Thomas Jefferson en 1792 en oposición al Federalist Party [Partido Federalista]. (p. 76, 112)

**deregulation** [liberalización] *s.* acción de limitar el alcance de la regulación federal sobre la industria. (p. 837)

**détente** [distensión] *s.* política flexible con la intención de negociar y disminuir tensiones; fue adoptada por Richard Nixon y su consejero Henry Kissinger para tratar con países comunistas. (p. 799)

**direct relief** [ayuda directa] *s.* alimentos o dinero que el gobierno da directamente a los necesitados. (p. 475)

**Dixiecrat** *s.* delegado sureño que se retiró de la convención del Partido Demócrata en 1948 para protestar la plataforma del Presidente Truman sobre derechos civiles y formó un grupo denominado States' Rights Democratic Party. (p. 638)

**dollar diplomacy** [diplomacia del dólar] *s.* política de usar el poder económico o la influencia económica de Estados Unidos para alcanzar sus objetivos de política exterior en otros países. (p. 363)

**domino theory** [teoría del dominó] *s.* teoría que supone que si una nación se vuelve comunista, las naciones vecinas inevitablemente se volverán comunistas también. (p. 731)

**dotcom** [puntocom] *s.* negocio relacionado con el Internet o conducido a través de éste. (p. 871)

**double standard** [doble moral] *s.* conjunto de principios que permite mayor libertad sexual al hombre que a la mujer. (p. 441)

**dove** [paloma] *s.* persona que se oponía a la Guerra de Vietnam y creía que Estados Unidos debía retirarse. (p. 746)

**Dow Jones Industrial Average** [Promedio Industrial Dow Jones] *s.* medida que computa el valor de las acciones de 30 compañías grandes; se usa como barómetro de los mercados bursátiles. (p. 467)

**downsize** [recortar] *v.* despedir trabajadores de una organización con el fin de hacer las operaciones más eficientes y ahorrar dinero. (p. 870)

**draft** [reclutamiento] *s.* requisito de matrícula en las fuerzas armadas. (p. 742)

**Dust Bowl** *s.* región que incluye Texas, Oklahoma, Kansas, Colorado, y New Mexico que quedó inservible para la agricultura debido a la sequía y a las tormentas de arena durante los años 30. (p. 474)

## E

**Earth Day** [Día de la Tierra] *s.* día dedicado a la educación ambiental que desde 1970 se celebra el 22 de abril de cada año. (p. 821)

**Economic Opportunity Act** [Ley de Oportunidades Económicas] *s.* ley promulgada en 1964, que adjudicó fondos a programas para la juventud, medidas para combatir la pobreza, préstamos para pequeños negocios y capacitación laboral. (p. 688)

**egalitarianism** [igualitarismo] *s.* creencia de que todas las personas deben tener igualdad de derechos políticos, económicos, sociales y civiles. (p. 63)

**Eisenhower Doctrine** [Doctrina Eisenhower] *s.* advertencia del presidente Eisenhower en 1957 de que Estados Unidos defendería el Oriente Medio contra el ataque de cualquier país comunista. (p. 625)

**Emancipation Proclamation** [Proclama de Emancipación] *s.* orden ejecutiva de Abraham Lincoln el 1º de enero de 1863 que abolía la esclavitud en los estados confederados. (p. 172)

**encomienda** *s.* institución colonial de España en las Américas que repartía indígenas a los conquistadores para hacer trabajos forzados. (p. 16)

**Enlightenment** [Ilustración] *s.* movimiento intelectual del siglo 18 que enfatizaba la razón y los métodos científicos para obtener conocimientos. (p. 35)

**entitlement program** [programa de subvención] *s.* programa gubernamental, como Social Security, Medicare y Medicaid, que brinda beneficios a grupos específicos. (p. 831)

**entrepreneur** [empresario] *s.* persona que organiza, opera y asume todo el riesgo de una ventura de negocios. (p. 140)

**environmentalist** [ambientalista] *s.* persona que procura proteger el medio ambiente de la destrucción y de la contaminación. (p. 822)

**Environmental Protection Agency (EPA)** [Agencia de Protección Ambiental] *s.* agencia federal establecida en 1970 para la regulación de la contaminación del agua y el aire, los desperdicios tóxicos, los pesticidas y la radiación. (p. 837)

**Equal Rights Amendment (ERA)** [Enmienda de Igualdad de Derechos] *s.* enmienda propuesta pero rechazada que hubiese prohibido la discriminación del gobierno en razón del sexo de una persona. (p. 779)

**Espionage and Sedition Acts** [Leyes de Espionaje y Sedición] *s.* dos leyes aprobadas en 1917 y 1918, que castigaban fuertemente a quienes criticaran o bloquearan la participación de Estados Unidos en la II Guerra Mundial. (p. 392)

**exoduster** *s.* afroamericano que emigró del Sur a Kansas después de la Reconstrucción. (p. 215)

**extortion** [extorsión] *s.* uso ilegal de un cargo público para obtener dinero o propiedad. (p. 269)

# F

**Fair Deal** s. plan económico del presidente Truman que expandió el New Deal de Roosevelt; aumentó el salario mínimo, amplió el seguro social y le dio vivienda a familias de bajos recursos, entre otras medidas. (p. 639)

**Family Assistance Plan** [Plan de Asistencia Familiar] s. propuesta de reforma a los programas de beneficencia, aprobada por la Cámara de Representantes en 1970 pero rechazada por el Senado, que garantizaba un ingreso a los beneficiarios de ayuda pública que aceptaran capacitarse y emplearse en un oficio. (p. 795)

**Farmers' Alliances** [Alianzas de granjeros] s. grupos de granjeros o simpatizantes de éstos, que enviaban a oradores a viajar de pueblo a pueblo para educar a la gente sobre cuestiones agrarias y rurales. (p. 221)

**fascism** [fascismo] s. filosofía política que propone un gobierno fuerte, centralizado, nacionalista, caracterizado por una rígida dictadura unipartidista. (p. 530)

**Federal Communications Commission (FCC)** [Comisión Federal de Comunicaciones] s. agencia del gobierno que regula la industria de comunicaciones en EE.UU., incluso la transmisión de radio y televisión. (p. 653)

**Federal Deposit Insurance Corporation (FDIC)** [Corporación Federal de Seguros de Depósitos] s. agencia creada en 1933 para garantizar depósitos bancarios individuales cuando un banco quiebra. (p. 517)

**Federal Home Loan Bank Act** [Ley Federal para Préstamos de Vivienda] s. ley aprobada en 1931 que redujo las cuotas hipotecarias y permitió a los agricultores refinanciar sus préstamos para prevenir juicios hipotecarios. (p. 481)

**federalism** [federalismo] s. sistema político gubernamental en el cual el poder se comparte entre un gobierno nacional y las entidades que lo constituyen, como los gobiernos estatales. (p. 68)

**Federalist** [federalista] s. partidario de la Constitución y de un gobierno nacional fuerte. (p. 69)

**Federal Reserve System** [Sistema de la Reserva Federal] s. sistema bancario nacional establecido por Woodrow Wilson en 1913 que controla el dinero circulante del país. (p. 334)

**Federal Securities Act** [Ley Federal de Valores] s. ley de 1933 que obliga a las corporaciones a suministrar información completa y fidedigna sobre sus ofertas de acciones. (p. 490)

**Federal Trade Commission (FTC)** [Comisión Federal de Comercio] s. agencia federal establecida en 1914 para investigar y parar prácticas empresariales injustas. (p. 333)

**feminism** [feminismo] s. creencia de que la mujer debe tener igualdad económica, política y social con respecto al hombre. (p. 776)

**Fifteenth Amendment** [Enmienda 15] s. enmienda a la Constitución, adoptada en 1870, que establece que a nadie puede negársele el derecho al voto por motivos de raza, color o por haber sido esclavo. (p. 186)

**flapper** s. jovencita típica de los años 20 que actuaba y se vestía de manera atrevida y nada convencional. (p. 441)

**flexible response** [respuesta flexible] s. doctrina, desarrollada durante la administración Kennedy, de prepararse para una variedad de respuestas militares, en vez de concentrarse en las armas nucleares. (p. 673)

**Foraker Act** [Ley Foraker] s. legislación que el Congreso aprobó en 1900 para acabar con el gobierno militar en Puerto Rico y autorizar un gobierno civil. (p. 353)

**Fordney-McCumber Tariff** [Arancel Fordney-McCumber] s. serie de reglas, aprobada por el Congreso en 1922, que elevó a niveles sin precedentes los impuestos a las importaciones en 1922 para proteger las compañías estadounidenses de la competencia extranjera. (p. 420)

**Fourteen Points** [los catorce puntos] s. plan del presidente Wilson en pro de la paz mundial tras la I Guerra Mundial. (p. 399)

**Fourteenth Amendment** [Enmienda 14] s. enmienda a la constitución adoptada en 1868 que hace ciudadano a toda persona nacida o naturalizada en Estados Unidos, incluso a antiguos esclavos, y garantiza igualdad de protección bajo la ley. (p. 185)

**franchise** [franquicia] s. forma de negocio en la que individuos compran el derecho a usar el nombre y los métodos de una compañía matriz, con lo que la compañía se multiplica. (p. 642)

**Freedmen's Bureau** [Oficina de libertos] s. agencia federal formada después de la Guerra Civil para ayudar a personas que habían sido esclavos antes. (p. 184)

**freedom rider** s. activista de derechos civiles que viajó en autobús a través del Sur a comienzos de los años 60 para protestar contra la segregación. (p. 710)

**Freedom Summer** s. campaña de registro de votantes afroamericanos en el verano de 1964 en Mississippi. (p. 715)

**free enterprise** [libre empresa] s. sistema económico en el que compañías privadas e individuos controlan los medios de producción. (p. 140)

**Free Speech Movement** [Movimiento de Libre Expresión] s. movimiento activista de los años 60 que surgió a raíz de un enfrentamiento entre los estudiantes y la administración de la Universidad de California en Berkeley en 1964. (p. 744)

**French and Indian War** [Guerra contra Franceses e Indígenas] s. guerra librada en Norteamérica (1757-1763) como parte de un conflicto mundial entre Francia y Gran Bretaña; finalizó con la derrota de Francia y el traspaso del Canadá francés a Gran Bretaña. (p. 37)

**Fundamentalism** [fundamentalismo] s. movimiento religioso protestante basado en la interpretación textual, o palabra por palabra, de las escrituras. (p. 438)

# G

**General Agreement on Tariffs and Trade (GATT)** [Acuerdo General de Aranceles y Comercio] s. acuerdo internacional firmado inicialmente en 1947. En 1994, EE.UU. y otros países del mundo adoptaron una nueva versión de GATT. Este tratado redujo las barreras de comercio y los aranceles, como las tarifas, y creó la Organización Mundial de Comercio. (p. 872)

**genetic engineering** [ingeniería genética] s. alteración de la biología molecular de las células de un organismo para crear nuevas variedades de bacterias, plantas o animales. (p. 880)

**Geneva Accords** [Acuerdos de Ginebra] *s.* plan de paz de Indochina en 1954 en el que Vietnam fue dividido temporalmente en Vietnam del Norte y Vietnam del Sur, mientras se celebraban las elecciones de 1956. (p. 732)

**genocide** [genocidio] *s.* exterminio deliberado y sistemático de un grupo de personas por su raza, nacionalidad o religión. (p. 544)

**Gentlemen's Agreement** [Acuerdo de Caballeros] *s.* acuerdo concertado durante 1907 y 1908, mediante el cual el gobierno de Japón limitó la emigración a Estados Unidos. (p. 259)

**gentrification** [aburguesamiento] *s.* restauración de propiedades urbanas por personas de la clase media que a menudo resulta en la pérdida de vivienda para personas de medios escasos. (p. 883)

**Gettysburg Address** [Discurso de Gettysburg] *s.* famoso discurso de Abraham Lincoln durante la Guerra Civil al inaugurar un cementerio nacional en el campo de batalla de Gettysburg, Pennsylvania, el 19 de noviembre de 1863. (p. 177)

**ghetto** [gueto] *s.* tipo de vecindario urbano donde cierto grupo minoritario es obligado o forzado a vivir. (p. 545)

**GI Bill of Rights** [Carta de Derechos de los Veteranos] *s.* nombre dado a la Ley de Reajuste de Militares de 1944, que ofrecía beneficios financieros y educativos a los veteranos de la II Guerra Mundial. (pp. 592, 635)

**glasnost** *s.* la discusión abierta de problemas sociales que se dio en la Unión Soviética durante los años 80. (p. 849)

**Glass-Steagall Banking Act** [Ley Bancaria Glass-Steagall] *s.* ley de 1933 que aseguró los depósitos bancarios mediante la Corporación Federal de Seguros de Depósitos. (p. 490)

**gold standard** [patrón de oro] *s.* sistema monetario en el cual la unidad básica de moneda se define en relación a una cantidad fija de oro. (p. 222)

**Gone with the Wind** [Lo que el viento se llevó] *s.* película de 1939 sobre la vida de los dueños de plantaciones del Sur durante la Guerra Civil; una de las más populares de todos los tiempos. (p. 511)

**graft** [corrupción] *s.* uso ilegal de un cargo político con el fin de ganacia personal. (p. 269)

**grandfather clause** [cláusula del abuelo] *s.* estipulación que exime de cumplir una ley a ciertas personas por circunstancias previas; específicamente, cláusula de la constitución de algunos estados sureños que eximía a los blancos de los estrictos requisitos que impedían que los afroamericanos votaran. (p. 287)

**Grange** [la Granja] *s. The Patrons of Husbandry*—organización de granjeros que intentaron, a partir de la década de 1870, combatir el poder de los ferrocarriles. (p. 221)

**Grapes of Wrath, The** [Las uvas de la ira] *s.* novela de John Steinbeck, publicada en 1939, sobre una familia de Oklahoma que se va de la región del Dust Bowl a California. (p. 514)

**Great Awakening** [Gran Despertar] *s.* serie de grandes asambleas religiosas en las décadas de 1730 y 1750. (p. 35)

**Great Depression** [Gran Depresión] *s.* período de 1929 a 1940 en el que la economía estadounidense quebró y millones quedaron sin empleo. (p. 469)

**Great Migration** [Gran Migración] *s.* movimiento de cientos de miles de afroamericanos sureños a ciudades del Norte a principios del siglo 20. (p. 393)

**Great Plains** [Grandes Praderas] *s.* vasta pradera que se extiende a través de Norteamérica, de Texas a Canadá en dirección Norte y hacia el este de las Montañas Rocosas. (p. 202)

**Great Society** [Gran Sociedad] *s.* ambicioso programa legislativo del presidente Lyndon B. Johnson para reducir la pobreza y la injusticia racial, y mejorar el nivel de vida. (p. 689)

## H

**Haight-Ashbury** *s.* distrito de San Francisco, "capital" de la contracultura hippie durante los años 60. (p. 782)

**Harlem Renaissance** [Renacimiento de Harlem] *s.* período de sobresaliente creatividad afroamericana durante los años 20 y 30, en la zona de Harlem en New York City. (p. 454)

**hawk** [halcón] *s.* persona que respaldaba la Guerra de Vietnam y creía que Estados Unidos debía incrementar su fuerza militar para ganarla. (p. 746)

**Hawley–Smoot Tariff Act** [Ley de Aranceles Hawley-Smoot] *s.* ley de 1930 que estableció los más altos aranceles proteccionistas en la historia estadounidense, afectando negativamente el comercio internacional y empeorando le depresión mundial y doméstica. (p. 471)

**H-bomb** [bomba de hidrógeno] *s.* bomba de hidrógeno, o termonuclear, mucho más poderosa que la bomba atómica. (p. 623)

**Ho Chi Minh Trail** [Sendero de Ho Chi Minh] *s.* red de caminos por la que Vietnam del Norte abastecía al Vietcong en Vietnam del Sur. (p. 732)

**Hollywood Ten** [los Diez de Hollywood] *s.* diez testigos de la industria cinematográfica que se negaron a cooperar con la investigación de influencia comunista en Hollywood. (p. 617)

**Holocaust** [Holocausto] *s.* asesinato sistemático o genocidio de judíos y de otros grupos en Europa por los nazis antes y durante la II Guerra Mundial. (p. 542)

**Homestead Act** [Ley de la Heredad] *s.* ley aprobada en 1862 que otorgaba 160 acres de tierra en el Oeste a cualquier ciudadano or ciudadano futuro que fuera cabeza de familia y que cultivara la tierra por cinco años; ley cuya aprobación llevó a un gran número de colonos estadounidenses a reclamar como propiedad privada tierra que había sido reservada por tratados y tradiciones para la vivienda de indígenas americanos; la misma ley, reforzada en 1889, dio incentivos para que los individuos ejercieran su derecho de propiedad privada y desarrollaran viviendas. (p. 215)

**horizontal integration** [integración horizontal] *s.* proceso mediante el cual compañías que fabrican productos similares se unen y reducen la competencia. (p. 242)

**hot line** [línea de emergencia] *s.* línea directa de comunicación establecida en 1963 para que los líderes de Estados Unidos y la Unión Soviética pudieran hablarse durante una crisis. (p. 678)

**House Un-American Activities Committee (HUAC)** [Comité de la Cámara de Representantes sobre Actividades Antiamericanas] *s.* comité del Congreso creado en 1938 que investigó la influencia comunista dentro y fuera del gobierno durante los años que siguieron la II Guerra Mundial. (p. 617)

**human rights** [derechos humanos] *s.* derechos y libertades considerados básicos, como los que establece la Declaración de Independencia y la Carta de Derechos. (p. 815)

**I**

**immigration** [inmigración] *s.* llegada a un país distinto al país natal para vivir en él. (p. 142)

**Immigration Act of 1965** [Ley de Inmigración de 1965] *s.* ley que abrió las puertas a más inmigrantes. (p. 691)

**impeachment** [acusación] *s.* proceso por el cual se acusa a un funcionario público de delitos. (p. 802)

**imperialism** [imperialismo] *s.* política de controlar países por medios económicos, políticos o militares. (p. 342)

**impressment** [leva] *s.* práctica de reclutar hombres a la fuerza para prestar servicio militar. (p. 114)

**incandescent** [incandescente] *adj.* que emite luz visible como resultado de haber sido calentado (p. 232)

**income tax** [impuesto sobre la renta] *s.* impuesto que retiene un porcentaje específico de ingresos. (p. 174)

**indentured servant** [sirviente por contrato] *s.* inmigrante que, a cambio de un pasaje para las Américas, era contratado a trabajar por un periodo límite. (p. 23)

**Industrial Workers of the World (IWW)** *s.* sindicato de trabajadores de mano de obra no calificada creado en 1905. (p. 246)

**inflation** [inflación] *s.* fenómeno económico en el que hay un aumento constante en los precios por el incremento del dinero circulante; reduce el poder adquisitivo. (p. 60)

**information superhighway** [supercarretera de información] *s.* red de comunicación por computadoras para unir a personas e instituciones por todo el mundo y suministrar a individuos servicios de bibliotecas, compras, cines y noticias. (p. 877)

**INF Treaty** [Tratado sobre Fuerzas Nucleares Intermedias] *s.* tratado entre Estados Unidos y la Unión Soviética firmado en 1987, que eliminó algunas armas y permitió la inspección directa de emplazamientos de misiles. (p. 849)

**initiative** [iniciativa] *s.* reforma gubernamental que permite a los ciudadanos presentar proyectos de ley en el Congreso o en cuerpos legislativos estatales. (p. 312)

**installment plan** [pago a plazos] *s.* práctica de comprar a crédito mediante pagos regulares durante determinado período de tiempo. (p. 426)

**Internet** *s.* red mundial, originalmente diseñada por el Departamento de Defensa, que une computadores y permite una comunicación casi instantánea de textos, ilustraciones y sonidos. (p. 877)

**internment** [confinamiento] *s.* restricción de movimiento, en especial durante condiciones de guerra. (p. 594)

**Interstate Commerce Act** [Ley de Comercio Interestatal] *s.* ley de 1887 que restablecía el derecho del gobierno federal a supervisar los ferrocarriles; creó una Comisión de Comercio Interestatal de cinco miembros. (p. 239)

**iron curtain** [cortina de hierro] *s.* frase usada por Winston Churchill en 1946 para describir una línea imaginaria que separaba los países comunistas que estaban en la parte soviética al este de Europa de los países en Europa occidental. (p. 605)

**Iroquois** [iroqueses] *s.* grupo de pueblos amerindios que vivían en los bosques del Noreste. (p. 6)

**Islam** [islamismo] *s.* religión fundada en Arabia por el profeta Mahoma en el año 622; a sus seguidores se les llama musulmanes. (p. 9)

**isolationism** [aislacionismo] *s.* política que se opone a participar en conflictos políticos y económicos con otros países. (p. 412)

**J**

**Jacksonian democracy** [democracia Jacksoniana] *s.* filosofía política de Jackson, basada en su creencia de que la gente común y corriente era la fuente de la fortaleza nacional. (p. 123)

**Japanese Americans Citizens League (JACL)** [Sociedad de Ciudadanos Americano-Japoneses] *s.* organización que presionó al gobierno a compensar a los estadounidenses de origen japonés por las propiedades que perdieron al ser internados durante la II Guerra Mundial. (p. 595)

**jazz** *s.* estilo de música caracterizado por la improvisación. (p. 657)

**Jeffersonian republicanism** [republicanismo Jeffersoniano] *s.* teoría de gobierno de Jefferson; sostenía que un gobierno sencillo correspondía a las necesidades del pueblo. (p. 113)

**Jim Crow laws** [leyes Jim Crow] *s.* leyes impuestas por los gobiernos estatales y municipales del Sur con el fin de separar a blancos y afroamericanos en instalaciones públicas y privadas. (p. 287)

**joint-stock company** [sociedad de capitales] *s.* institución empresarial tipo corporación en la que inversionistas unen riquezas con un fin común; se usaron para financiar la exploración de las Américas. (p. 21)

**judicial review** [revisión judicial] *s.* poder de la Suprema Corte de declarar inconstitucional una ley del Congreso. (p. 113)

**Judiciary Act of 1789** [Ley Judicial de 1789] *s.* ley que estableció el sistema de tribunales federales y la Suprema Corte que permitió la apelación a cortes federales de ciertas decisiones tomadas por cortes estatales. (p. 74)

**Jungle, The** [La jungla] *s.* novela publicada en 1906 por el periodista Upton Sinclair que denunciaba la insalubridad de la industria de carne en aquella época; llevó a reformas nacionales. (p. 317)

**K**

**kamikaze** *adj.* que estrellaba deliberadamente un avión bombardero contra un blanco militar. (p. 581)

**Kent State University** [Universidad Estatal de Kent] *s.* universidad de Ohio donde guardias militares abrieron fuego contra estudiantes durante una protesta contra la Guerra de Vietnam el 4 de mayo de 1970, hiriendo a nueve de ellos y matando a cuatro. (p. 756)

**Kerner Commission** [Comisión Kerner] *s.* grupo designado por el presidente Lyndon B. Johnson para estudiar las causas de la violencia urbana; recomendó eliminar la segregación de facto en la sociedad estadounidense. (p. 722)

**King Philip's War** [Guerra del Rey Felipe] *s.* conflicto, en los años 1675 y 1676, entre los colonos de Nueva Inglaterra y grupos amerindios aliados bajo la dirección del cacique Metacom de los wampanoagas. (p. 25)

**Kongo** *s.* serie de pequeños reinos unidos bajo un líder a finales del siglo 15 en las selvas tropicales a lo largo del río Zaire (Congo) en África Central-Occidental. (p. 9)

**Korean War** [Guerra de Corea] *s.* guerra de 1950 a 1953 entre Corea del Norte y Corea del Sur; China respaldó a Corea del Norte y las tropas de las Naciones Unidas, integradas en su mayoría por soldados estadounidenses, apoyaron a Corea del Sur. (p. 611)

**Kristallnacht** *s.* "noche del cristal quebrado", noviembre 9 de 1938, noche en que milicianos nazis atacaron viviendas, negocios y sinagogas judías en Alemania. (p. 543)

**Ku Klux Klan** *s.* sociedad secreta de hombres blancos en los estados sureños después de la Guerra Civil que desató terror para restaurar la supremacía blanca. (p. 188)

**La Raza Unida** *s.* organización política latina establecida en 1969 por José Ángel Gutiérrez. (p. 770)

**League of Nations** [Liga de las Naciones] *s.* organización internacional establecida en 1920 para promover la cooperación y la paz internacional. (p. 399)

**Lend-Lease Act** [Ley de Préstamo y Alquiler] *s.* ley aprobada en 1941, que autorizó al gobierno a mandar armas y otros productos, sin pago inmediato, a las naciones que luchaban contra el Eje. (p. 552)

**Limited Test Ban Treaty** [Tratado de Limitación de Pruebas Nucleares] *s.* tratado de 1963 en que Estados Unidos y la Unión Soviética acordaron no realizar pruebas de armas nucleares en la atmósfera. (p. 678)

**long drive** [arreo de ganado] *s.* proceso mediante el cual los vaqueros llevaban por tierra ganado hacia el mercado. (p. 210)

**longhorn** *s.* resistente raza de ganado vacuno de cuernos largos llevada por los españoles a México, muy apta para las condiciones de esa región. (p. 208)

**Louisiana Purchase** [Compra de Louisiana] *s.* compra de terrenos a Francia por 15 millones de dólares en 1803 de las tierras desde el río Mississippi hasta las montañas Rocosas. (p. 114)

**Lowell textile mills** [fábrica de textiles de Lowell] *s.* talleres para la fabricación de tela de Lowell, Massachusetts, del siglo 19; empleaban principalmente a trabajadoras jóvenes. (p. 142)

**Loyalist** [realista] *s.* colono que apoyaba al gobierno británico durante la Revolución Norteamericana. (p. 59)

**Lusitania** *s.* barco británico de pasajeros que se hundió cerca de costas irlandesas el 7 de mayo de 1915, tras ser atacado por un submarino alemán. (p. 378)

**mandate** [mandato] *s.* conquista de una porción suficientemente grande del voto, que indica que un líder elegido tiene apoyo popular para sus programas. (p. 680)

**Manhattan Project** [Proyecto Manhattan] *s.* programa estadounidense que se inició en 1942 con el fin de diseñar una bomba atómica para la II Guerra Mundial. La primera detonación atómica completa ocurrió en Alamogordo, New Mexico, el 16 de julio de 1945. (p. 567)

**manifest destiny** [destino manifiesto] *s.* término usado en la década de 1840 para describir la creencia de que Estados Unidos estaba inexorablemente destinado a adquirir más territorio, especialmente mediante su expansión hacia el oeste. (p. 131)

**Marbury v. Madison** *s.* caso de 1803 en que la Suprema Corte decidió que tenía el poder de abolir decretos legislativos declarándolos inconstitucionales; ese poder se conoce como revisión judicial. (p. 113)

**market revolution** [revolución mercantil] *s.* gran cambio económico que llevó a comprar y vender productos en lugar de hacerlos en el hogar. (p. 139)

**Marshall Plan** [Plan Marshall] *s.* plan formulado por el Secretario de Estado George Marshall en 1947, mediante el que se ofreció ayuda a países europeos con el fin de reparar los daños de la II Guerra Mundial. (p. 606)

**mass media** [medios informativos] *s.* medios de comunicación — tales como televisión, prensa y radio— que llegan a grandes audiencias. (p. 652)

**mass transit** [transporte público] *s.* sistemas de transporte diseñados para llevar grandes números de personas por rutas fijas. (p. 264)

**McCarthyism** [macartismo] *s.* ataques, a menudo sin respaldo, del senador Joseph McCarthy y otros contra presuntos comunistas en los años 50. (p. 620)

**Meat Inspection Act** [Ley de Inspección de la Carne] *s.* ley de 1906 que establecía estrictos requisitos sanitarios en las empacadoras de carne, así como un programa federal de inspección de carnes. (p. 320)

**Medicaid** *s.* programa federal que se inició en 1965 para brindar atención médica a las personas que reciben ayuda pública. (p. 690)

**Medicare** *s.* programa federal que se inició en 1965 para brindar seguros médicos y de hospitalización a bajo costo a los mayores de 65 años. (p. 690)

**melting pot** [crisol de culturas] *s.* mezcla de personas de diferentes culturas y razas que se amalgaman y abandonan su idioma y cultura natal. (p. 258)

**mercantilism** [mercantilismo] *s.* sistema económico en que un país aumenta su riqueza y poder al incrementar su posesión de oro y plata, y al exportar más productos de los que importa. (p. 28)

**mestizo** *adj.* con mezcla de español e indígena. (p. 16)

**middle passage** [travesía intermedia] *s.* tramo de África a las Antillas; parte del triángulo comercial de esclavos. (p. 32)

**militarism** [militarismo] *s.* política de mantener una sólida organización militar como preparación agresiva para la guerra y su empleo como herramienta diplomática. (p. 373)

**Missouri Compromise** [Acuerdo de Missouri] *s.* serie de acuerdos aprobados por el Congreso en 1820–1821 para mantener un equilibrio seccional entre los estados esclavistas y los estados libres. (p. 122)

**Monroe Doctrine** [Doctrina Monroe] *s.* declaración del presidente Monroe en 1823 que establecía que Estados Unidos no permitiría la interferencia europea en los asuntos del Hemisferio Occidental. (p. 117)

**Moral Majority** [Mayoría Moral] *s.* coalición política de organizaciones religiosas conservadoras en los años 70 y 80 que recaudó dinero para respaldar agendas y candidatos conservadores, y condenó actitudes y comportamientos liberales. (p. 831)

**Morrill Acts** [Leyes Morrill] *s.* leyes aprobadas en 1862 y 1890 que otorgaban tierras federales a los estados para financiar universidades agrícolas. (p. 217)

**muckraker** *s.* uno de los reporteros de revistas que desenmascaraban el lado corrupto de las empresas y de la vida pública a principios del siglo 20. (p. 308)

**Munn v. Illinois** *s.* caso de la Suprema Corte en 1877; estableció el derecho del gobierno federal a regular la industria privada en beneficio del interés público. (p. 239)

**My Lai** *s.* pueblo del norte de Vietnam del Sur, donde más de 200 civiles desarmados, incluso mujeres y niños, fueron masacrados por las tropas de EE.UU. en mayo de 1968. (p. 756)

## N

**NAACP** *s.* National Association for the Advancement of Colored People (Asociación Nacional para el Avance de la Gente de Color), organización fundada en 1909 y dedicada a la igualdad racial. (p. 325)

**NACW** *s.* National Association of Colored Women (Asociación Nacional de Mujeres de Color), organización de servicio social fundada en 1896. (p. 315)

**NAFTA** *s.* North American Free Trade Agreement (Tratado de Libre Comercio, TLC), tratado de 1993 que redujo aranceles e incorporó a México en la zona de libre comercio ya vigente entre Estados Unidos y Canadá. (p. 864)

**napalm** *s.* sustancia incendiaria de gasolina que lanzaban los aviones estadounidenses en Vietnam, con el fin de incendiar la selva y revelar los escondites del Vietcong. (p. 739)

**NASDAQ** *s.* sigla de National Association of Securities Dealers Automated Quotation System, una bolsa de valores de venta directa dominada por companías tecnológicas. (p. 871)

**National Energy Act** [Ley Nacional de Energía] *s.* ley promulgada durante la administración Carter para aliviar la crisis energética; aplicó impuestos a los autos que usan gasolina de manera ineficiente y suspendió el control de precios del petróleo y el gas natural estadounidenses. (p. 813)

**National Industrial Recovery Act (NIRA)** [Ley Nacional de Recuperación Industrial] *s.* ley aprobada en 1933 que establecía agencias para supervisar industrias y suministrar empleos. (p. 491)

**nationalism** [nacionalismo] *s.* devoción a los intereses y la cultura de la nación propia. (p. 373)

**National Labor Relations Board (NLRB)** [Junta Nacional de Relaciones Laborales] *s.* agencia creada en 1935 con el fin de prevenir prácticas laborales injustas y mediar en disputas laborales. (p. 518)

**National Organization for Women (NOW)** [Organización Nacional de la Mujer] *s.* organización fundada en 1966 con el fin de impulsar metas feministas, tales como mejores guarderías, mayores oportunidades educativas y el fin de la discriminación laboral. (p. 778)

**National Trades' Union** [Unión Nacional de Sindicatos] *s.* primera asociación nacional de sindicatos, creada en 1834. (p. 143)

**National Youth Administration** [Administración Nacional de Recursos para la Juventud] *s.* programa que suministraba ayuda y empleos a jóvenes durante la Depresión. (p. 499)

**Nation of Islam** [Nación del Islam] *s.* grupo religioso, popularmente conocido como musulmanes negros, fundado por Elijah Muhammad para promover el separatismo negro y la religión islámica. (p. 719)

**nativism** [patriotería] *s.* favoritismo de los intereses de las personas nacidas en un lugar sobre los de las personas extranjeras. (pp. 258, 412)

**Navigation Acts** [Leyes de Navegación] *s.* serie de leyes aprobadas a partir de 1651 que imponían un control más rígido del comercio en las colonias inglesas. (p. 28)

**NAWSA** *s.* National American Woman Suffrage Association (Asociación Nacional Americana del Sufragio Femenino), creada en 1890 para obtener derechos electorales para la mujer. (p. 316)

**Nazism** [nazismo] *s.* movimiento político basado en un extremo nacionalismo, racismo y expansionismo militar; instituido en Alemania como sistema de gobierno por Adolfo Hitler en 1933. (p. 531)

**Neutrality Acts** [Leyes de Neutralidad] *s.* serie de leyes aprobadas por el Congreso en 1935 y 1936 que prohibieron la venta y el alquiler de armas a naciones en guerra. (p. 535)

**New Deal** *s.* medidas económicas y políticas adoptadas por el presidente Franklin Roosevelt en los años 30 para promover recuperación económica, ayuda a los necesitados y reforma financiera. (p. 489)

**New Deal Coalition** [Coalición del New Deal] *s.* alianza temporal de distintos grupos, tales como blancos sureños, afroamericanos y sindicalistas, que apoyaban al Partido Demócrata en los años 30 y 40. (p. 507)

**New Federalism** [Nuevo Federalismo] *s.* programa del presidente Richard Nixon para distribuir una porción del poder del gobierno federal a gobiernos estatales y locales. (p. 795)

**New Frontier** [Nueva Frontera] *s.* agenda legislativa del presidente John F. Kennedy; tenía medidas de atención médica para ancianos, renovación urbana y apoyo a la educación, que fueron rechazadas por el Congreso, así como medidas que sí se aprobaron de defensa nacional, ayuda internacional y programas espaciales. (p. 677)

**New Left** [Nueva Izquierda] *s.* movimiento político juvenil de los años 60 con organizaciones como Students for a Democratic Society (Estudiantes por una Sociedad Democrática) y el Free Speech Movement (Movimiento de Libre Expresión). (p. 744)

**New Right** [Nueva Derecha] *s.* alianza política de grupos conservadores de fines del siglo 20, con énfasis en asuntos culturales, sociales y morales. (p. 831)

**Niagara Movement** [Movimiento Niágara] *s.* fundado en 1905 por W. E. B. Du Bois para promover la enseñanza de humanidades entre los afroamericanos. (p. 285)

**Nineteenth Amendment** [Enmienda 19] *s.* enmienda a la Constitución adoptada en 1920 que le otorga a la mujer el derecho de votar. (p. 335)

**"no man's land"** [tierra de nadie] *s.* en la I Guerra Mundial, extensión baldía de tierra entre trincheras de ejércitos enemigos. (p. 376)

**nomadic** [nómade] *adj.* que no tiene hogar fijo, que se muda de un lugar a otro según las estaciones y la disponibilidad de comida y agua. (p. 5)

**nonaggression pact** [pacto de no agresión] *s.* acuerdo entre dos naciones de no luchar entre sí. (p. 539)

**North Atlantic Treaty Organization (NATO)** [Organización del Tratado del Atlántico Norte] *s.* alianza militar defensiva formada en 1949 por diez países de Europa del oeste, Estados Unidos y Canadá. (p. 608)

**Northwest Ordinance of 1787** [Ordenanza del Noroeste de 1787] *s.* procedimiento para la admisión de nuevos estados a la Unión. (p. 67)

**nullification** [anulación] *s.* rechazo de un estado a reconocer cualquier ley del Congreso que considere inconstitucional. (p. 79)

**Nuremberg trials** [juicios de Nuremberg] *s.* juicios llevados a cabo en Nuremberg, Alemania, inmediatamente después de la II Guerra Mundial, a líderes nazis por sus crímenes de guerra. (p. 586)

**O**

**Office of Price Administration (OPA)** [Oficina de Administración de Precios] *s.* agencia establecida por el Congreso durante la II Guerra Mundial con facultad para combatir la inflación al congelar los precios de la mayoría de los artículos. (p. 567)

**Ohio gang** [pandilla de Ohio] *s.* amigos y partidarios políticos del presidente Warren G. Harding, a quienes éste nombró a su gabinete. (p. 420)

**OPEC** *s.* Organization of Petroleum Exporting Countries (Organización de Países Exportadores de Petróleo, OPEP), alianza económica para ejercer influencia sobre los precios del petróleo. (p. 799)

**Open Door notes** [notas de Puertas Abiertas] *s.* notas que el Secretario de Estado John Hay envió a Gran Bretaña, Francia, Alemania, Italia, Japón y Rusia, instándolos a no interponerse entre el comercio de Estados Unidos y China. (p. 356)

**Operation Desert Storm** [Operación Tormenta del Desierto] *s.* operación militar en la que fuerzas de las Naciones Unidas, encabezadas por Estados Unidos, liberaron a Kuwait y derrotaron al ejército iraquí. (p. 855)

**Oregon Trail** [Sendero de Oregon] *s.* camino que va de Independence, Missouri, a la ciudad de Oregon, Oregon. (p. 131)

**P**

**Panama Canal** [canal de Panamá] *s.* canal artificial construido a través del istmo de Panamá para abrir paso entre los océanos Atlántico y Pacífico; se abrió en 1914. (p. 360)

**parity** [paridad] *s.* regulación de precios de ciertos productos agrícolas, apoyada por el gobierno, con el fin de mantener estables los ingresos agrícolas. (p. 518)

**Patriot** [patriota] *s.* colono que apoyaba la independencia norteamericana de Gran Bretaña. (p. 59)

**patronage** [clientelismo] *s.* sistema de otorgar empleos a personas que ayudan a la elección de un candidato. (p. 270)

**pay equity** [equidad salarial] *s.* sistema que basa el salario de un empleado en los requisitos del trabajo y no en escalas salariales tradicionales, que normalmente pagan menos a la mujer. (p. 842)

**Payne-Aldrich Tariff** [Arancel Payne-Aldrich] *s.* serie de reglamentos de impuestos, aprobados por el Congreso en 1909, que no logró reducir mucho los aranceles de productos manufacturados. (p. 329)

**Peace Corps** [Cuerpo de Paz] *s.* programa fundado en 1965 bajo iniciativa del presidente Kennedy, que envía voluntarios a las naciones en desarrollo de Asia, África y Latinoamérica para ayudar en escuelas, clínicas y otros proyectos. (p. 680)

**Pendleton Act** [Ley Pendleton] *s.* ley de 1883 que autorizaba nombrar empleados del servicio civil por mérito. (p. 270)

**Pentagon Papers** [Documentos del Pentágono] *s.* documento de 7,000 páginas que dejó filtrar a la prensa en 1971 el antiguo funcionario del Departamento de Defensa Daniel Ellsberg, donde se revela que el gobierno mintió sobre sus planes en la Guerra de Vietnam. (p. 757)

***perestroika*** *s.* palabra rusa para designar la reestructuración económica y burocrática de la Unión Soviética que ocurrió en los años 80. (p. 849)

**planned obsolescence** [obsolencia planeada] *s.* diseño de artículos que se desgastan o pasan de moda muy pronto, para crear la necesidad de remplazarlos con frecuencia. (p. 648)

**Platt Amendment** [Enmienda Platt] *s.* serie de medidas implantadas por Estados Unidos en 1901, las cuales debieron ser incluidas por Cuba en su nueva constitución para quedar libre de su deuda y por las que Estados Unidos obtenía el derecho a intervenir el país y a comprar o alquilar el territorio cubano para establecer estaciones navales y de combustible. (p. 354)

***Plessy* v. *Ferguson*** *s.* caso de 1896 en que la Suprema Corte declaró legal la separación de razas en instalaciones públicas y estableció la doctrina de "separados aunque iguales". (p. 287)

**political machine** [maquinaria política] *s.* grupo organizado que controla un partido político en una ciudad y ofrece servicios a los votantes y negocios a cambio de apoyo político y financiero. (p. 268)

**poll tax** [impuesto para votar] *s.* impuesto anual que los ciudadanos debían pagar en algunos estados sureños para poder votar. (p. 287)

**popular sovereignty** [soberanía popular] *s.* sistema en el cual los ciudadanos votan para decidir sobre un tema. (p. 157)

**Populism** [populismo] *s.* movimiento político de finales del siglo 19 que exigía la voz popular en el gobierno y que representaba los intereses de los granjeros y promovía una reforma del sistema monetario. (p. 221)

**price support** [apoyo de precios] *s.* apoyo de los precios de ciertos artículos al valor del mercado o por encima, algunas veces mediante la compra de excedentes por parte del gobierno. (p. 465)

**Proclamation of 1763** [Proclama de 1763] *s.* decreto británico que prohibía que los colonos se instalaran al oeste de los montes Apalaches. (p. 39)

**progressive** [progresista] *s.* que favorece el avance hacia mejores condiciones o nuevas ideas. (p. 258)

**progressive movement** [movimiento progresista] *s.* movimiento reformista de comienzos del siglo 20 cuyos objetivos eran mejorar el bienestar social, promover la moralidad, incrementar la justicia económica y devolver a la ciudadanía el control del gobierno. (p. 307)

**prohibition** [prohibición] *s.* prohibición de bebidas alcohólicas. (p. 307)

**Prohibition** [Ley Seca] *s.* período entre 1920 y 1933 durante el cual, por medio de la decimoctava enmienda, se prohibió la producción y la venta de alcohol en Estados Unidos. (p. 436)

**propaganda** *s.* comunicación prejuiciada diseñada para influir los pensamientos y actos de la gente. (p. 390)

**Proposition 187** [Propuesta 187] *s.* proyecto de ley aprobado en California en 1994, el cual canceló todos los beneficios educativos y de salud que no fueran emergencias a los inmigrantes ilegales. (p. 886)

**protective tariff** [arancel proteccionista] *s.* impuesto aplicado a productos importados para proteger las empresas nacionales de la competencia extranjera. (p. 76)

**protectorate** [protectorado] *s.* nación cuyo gobierno y asuntos son controlados por una potencia más fuerte. (p. 354)

**Pueblo** *s.* amerindios descendientes de los anasazi; viven en los desiertos del Suroeste. (p. 6)

**Pure Food and Drug Act** [Ley de Pureza de Alimentos y Drogas] *s.* ley de 1906 que paró la venta de alimentos y drogas contaminadas y demandó etiquetas fidedignas. (p. 322)

**Puritan** [puritano] *s.* miembro de la Iglesia Anglicana que deseaba eliminar las tradiciones católicas y simplificar los servicios religiosos. (p. 24)

**Quaker** [cuáquero] *s.* miembro de una secta religiosa considerada radical en el siglo 17, también conocida como Sociedad de Amigos. (p. 26)

**quota system** [sistema de cuotas] *s.* sistema que limita el número de inmigrantes de varios países que pueden ser admitidos a Estados Unidos cada año. (p. 415)

**ratification** [ratificación] *s.* aprobación oficial de la Constitución, o de una enmienda, por parte de los estados. (p. 69)

**rationing** [racionamiento] *s.* medida tomada durante tiempos de guerra para limitar la cantidad de ciertos alimentos y otros productos que cada persona puede comprar. (p. 568)

**Reaganomics** [reaganomía] *s.* nombre dado a la política económica del presidente Reagan, que abogaba por recortes presupuestarios y por una gran reducción en los impuestos con el fin de incrementar la inversión privada y por consiguiente expandir el suministro de productos y servicios. (p. 834)

***realpolitik*** *s.* enfoque de política exterior, identificado con Henry Kissinger y Richard Nixon, que propone hacer lo que resulte realista y práctico en lugar de seguir una política al pie de la letra. (p. 799)

**reapportionment** [nueva repartición] *s.* redistribución de distritos electorales cuando cambia el número de personas en un distrito. (p. 691)

**recall** [destitución] *s.* reforma gubernamental que permite a los votantes deponer a funcionarios públicos elegidos. (p. 312)

**Reconstruction** [Reconstrucción] *s.* período de reconstrucción después de la Guerra Civil y readmisión a la Unión de los estados de la Confederación que habían sido derrotados; de 1865 a 1877. (p. 184)

**Reconstruction Finance Corporation (RFC)** [Corporación Financiera de la Reconstrucción] *s.* organización establecida en 1932 para dar financiación de emergencia a bancos, aseguradoras de vida, compañías ferroviarias y otras empresas grandes. (p. 481)

**referendum** [referendo] *s.* procedimiento que permite someter al voto popular propuestas legislativas. (p. 312)

**Reformation** [Reforma] *s.* movimiento religioso en la Europa de comienzos del siglo 16, encaminado a reformar la Iglesia Católica Romana; condujo a la formación del protestantismo. (p. 10)

**Renaissance** [Renacimiento] *s.* período de la historia europea, que se extendió aproximadamente desde 1400 a 1600, durante el cual un renovado interés en la cultura clásica originó cambios trascendentales en las artes, el aprendizaje y la visión del mundo. (p. 11)

**reparations** [reparación] *s.* compensación que paga una nación derrotada en una guerra por las pérdidas económicas del vencedor o por crímenes cometidos contra individuos. (p. 400)

**republic** [república] *s.* gobierno en el que los ciudadanos mandan por medio de sus representantes elegidos. (p. 67)

**Republic of California** [República de California] *s.* nación proclamada por los colonos estadounidenses en California, al declarar éstos su independencia de México en 1846. (p. 136)

**revenue sharing** [distribución de rentas] *s.* plan puesto en práctica en 1972 que faculta a los gobiernos estatales y locales a invertir el dinero federal a su conveniencia. (p. 795)

**reverse discrimination** [discriminación a la inversa] *s.* tratamiento injusto de los miembros de un grupo mayoritario, típicamente hombres blancos, como resultado de los esfuerzos por remediar la discriminación contra otros grupos. (p. 831)

**rock 'n' roll** *s.* forma de música popular estadounidense que evolucionó a finales de los 40 y durante los 50, a partir del rhythm and blues, el country, el jazz, el gospel y el pop; forma musical estadounidense caracterizada por ritmos fuertes y melodías simples, la cual se ha expandido por todo el mundo y ha tenido impactos significativos en el baile social, la moda de la vestimenta y las expresiones de protesta. (p. 655)

**Roosevelt Corollary** [Corolario de Roosevelt] *s.* declaración de 1904 del presidente Theodore Roosevelt en que advertía que Estados Unidos intervendría militarmente en los asuntos de cualquier nación del Hemisferio Occidental para proteger sus intereses económicos si fuera necesario. (p. 362)

**Rough Riders** *s.* regimiento de caballería voluntario comandado por Leonard Wood y Theodore Roosevelt en la Guerra Española-Norteamericana-Cubana. (p. 350)

**rural free delivery (RFD)** [correo rural gratuito] *s.* entrega gubernamental gratis de correo y paquetes a zonas rurales; se inició en 1896. (p. 321)

**SALT I Treaty** [Tratado Salt I] *s.* acuerdo de cinco años entre Estados Unidos y la Unión Soviética que surgió de las Conversaciones sobre Limitación de Armas Estratégicas de 1972; limitó el número de misiles balísticos intercontinentales y de misiles de submarinos. (p. 801)

**Sandinista** *adj.* relativo a las fuerzas izquierdistas rebeldes que derrocaron al gobierno nicaragüense en 1979; el presidente Reagan, quien respaldaba a la contra anticomunista, se les opuso. (p. 851)

**Santa Fe Trail** [Sendero de Santa Fe] *s.* camino que va de Independence, Missouri, a Santa Fe, New Mexico. (p. 131)

**satellite nation** [nación satélite] *s.* país dominado política y económicamente por otro. (p. 605)

**Saturday Night Massacre** [Masacre de Sábado en la Noche] *s.* nombre dado a la renuncia del procurador general y al despido de su comisionado el 20 de octubre de 1973, después de haberse negado a acatar la orden del presidente Nixon de despedir al fiscal especial en el caso Watergate. (p. 805)

**scalawag** *s.* término despectivo para referirse a los sureños blancos que se unieron al Partido Republicano y apoyaron la Reconstrucción después de la Guerra Civil. (p. 186)

**scientific management** [administración científica] *s.* aplicación de principios científicos para simplificar y facilitar las tareas laborales. (p. 308)

**Scopes trial** [juicio de Scopes] *s.* sensacional juicio de 1925 en el que el maestro de biología John T. Scopes fue juzgado por desafiar una ley de Tennessee que prohibía la enseñanza de la evolución. (p. 438)

**search-and-destroy mission** [misión de búsqueda y destrucción] *s.* ataque militar estadounidense a aldeas de Vietnam del Sur con el fin de erradicar al Vietcong, que solía resultar en la destrucción de la aldea y el desplazamiento de sus habitantes. (p. 739)

**secession** [secesión] *s.* retiro formal de un estado de la Unión federal. (p. 157)

**Securities and Exchange Commission (SEC)** [Comisión de Valores y Cambios] *s.* agencia creada en 1934 para controlar el mercado bursátil y hacer cumplir las leyes que rigen la venta de acciones y bonos. (p. 517)

**segregation** [segregación] *s.* separación de la gente según su raza. (p. 287)

**Selective Service Act** [Ley de Servicio Selectivo] *s.* ley aprobada por el Congreso en mayo de 1917 que ordena que todos los hombres se inscriban para el servicio militar obligatorio. (p. 382)

**Seneca Falls Convention** [convención de Seneca Falls] *s.* convención de derechos femeninos celebrada en 1848 en Seneca Falls, New York. (p. 149)

**service sector** [sector de servicios] *s.* renglón de la economía que ofrece servicios en vez de productos. (p. 870)

**settlement house** [casa de beneficencia] *s.* centro comunitario en un barrio pobre que ayudaba a los residentes, particularmente a los inmigrantes. (p. 266)

**Seventeenth Amendment** [Enmienda 17] *s.* enmienda a la Constitución adoptada en 1913; dispone que los senadores federales sean elegidos por los votantes y no por cuerpos legislativos estatales. (p. 312)

**shantytown** [tugurio] *s.* vecindario en donde la gente vivía en chozas temporales. (p. 473)

**sharecropping** [aparcería] *s.* sistema en el cual se da a los agricultores tierra, semillas, herramientas y alimentos para vivir, así como una parte de la cosecha, por cultivar la tierra. (p. 188)

**Shays's Rebellion** [Rebelión de Shays] *s.* sublevación de granjeros endeudados de Massachusetts en 1787, en protesta por los impuestos estatales. (p. 67)

**Sherman Antitrust Act** [Ley Antitrust Sherman] *s.* ley contra los monopolios de 1890 que declaró ilegal la formación de consorcios que obstruyeran el libre comercio. (p. 244)

**silent majority** [mayoría silenciosa] *s.* nombre dado por el presidente Richard Nixon a los estadounidenses moderados que apoyaban silenciosamente su involucramiento en la Guerra de Vietnam. (p. 756)

**sit-in** *s.* forma de protesta —iniciada por el Congreso de Igualdad Racial en los años 40 y empleada con frecuencia en los años 60— en la que afroamericanos ingresaban a un lugar segregado, tal como el mostrador de un restaurante, y se negaban a salir hasta que se les sirviera. (p. 706)

**Social Darwinism** [darvinismo social] *s.* conjunto de creencias políticas y económicas basadas en la teoría del biólogo Charles Darwin sobre la selección natural o supervivencia del más apto; favorecía una competencia libre, no regulada, y creía que los individuos o grupos triunfaban porque eran genéticamente superiores. (p. 242)

**Social Gospel movement** [movimiento del Evangelio Social] *s.* movimiento de reforma del siglo 19 basado en la noción de que los cristianos tenían la responsabilidad social de mejorar las condiciones laborales y aliviar la pobreza urbana. (p. 266)

**Social Security Act** [Ley de Seguro Social] *s.* ley aprobada en 1935 para ayudar a los jubilados, desempleados, incapacitados y familias con niños dependientes. (p. 501)

**soddy** [choza de tepe] *s.* casa provisional hecha de césped, muy común en las llanuras, donde la madera era escasa. (p. 216)

**soup kitchen** [comedor de beneficencia] *s.* lugar donde se sirven alimentos gratis o a bajo costo a los necesitados, muy común durante la Depresión. (p. 473)

**Southern Christian Leadership Conference (SCLC)** [Conferencia de Líderes Cristianos del Sur] *s.* organización formada en 1957 por el doctor Martin Luther King, Jr., y otros líderes para promover los derechos civiles sin violencia. (p. 706)

**Southern strategy** [estrategia sureña] *s.* estrategia del presidente Nixon de apelar a los demócratas conservadores sureños que estaban descontentos con la integración y con una Suprema Corte liberal. (p. 797)

**speakeasy** *s.* lugar donde se vendían bebidas alcohólicas ilegalmente, como ocurrió durante la Prohibición. (p. 436)

**speculation** [especulación] *s.* transacciones de alto riesgo con el fin de obtener ganancias rápidas o grandes. (p. 467)

**Square Deal** *s.* programa de reformas progresistas del presidente Theodore Roosevelt para proteger a la gente común y corriente de las grandes empresas. (p. 319)

**stagflation** [estanflación] *s.* situación económica en la que hay niveles altos de inflación y desempleo simultáneamente. (p. 798)

**Stalwart** *s.* republicano seguidor del "jefe" de New York City, Roscoe Conkling, quien favorecía el sistema de prebendas y se oponía a la reforma al servicio civil. (p. 292)

**Stamp Act** [Ley del Timbre] *s.* primer impuesto directo aplicado en 1765 por Gran Bretaña a una variedad de artículos y servicios, tales como documentos legales y periódicos. (p. 47)

**Strategic Defense Initiative (SDI)** [Iniciativa para la Defensa Estratégica] *s.* sistema de defensa propuesto en los años 80, popularmente conocido como la Guerra de las Galaxias, cuyo fin era proteger a Estados Unidos de ataques de misiles. (p. 835)

**strike** [huelga] *s.* interrupción del trabajo para presionar a un patrono a responder a ciertas demandas. (p. 142)

**Student Nonviolent Coordinating Committee (SNCC)** [Comité Coordinador de Estudiantes no Violentos] *s.* organización fundada en 1961, conocida como SNCC, para coordinar sit-ins y otras protestas, y para darles a los jóvenes negros mayor participación en el movimiento de derechos civiles. (p. 706)

**Students for a Democratic Society (SDS)** [Estudiantes por una Sociedad Democrática] *s.* grupo activista de los años 60, conocido como SDS, que urgía una mayor libertad y responsabilidad individual. (p. 744)

**suburb** [suburbio] *s.* pueblo o comunidad residencial cerca de una ciudad. (p. 635)

**suffrage** [sufragio] *s.* derecho a votar. (p. 315)

**Sugar Act** [Ley del Azúcar] *s.* ley británica de 1764 que aplicó un impuesto comercial a la melaza, el azúcar y otras importaciones para reducir el contrabando en las colonias. (p. 44)

**supply-side economics** [economía de oferta] *s.* teoría económica, practicada por el presidente Ronald Reagan, que sostiene que recortar los impuestos de los ricos beneficia a todos pues aumenta empleos, ahorros e inversiones. (p. 835)

# T

**Taino** [taíno] *s.* pueblo amerindio que Colón y su tripulación vieron al arribar a la isla hoy conocida como San Salvador, el 12 de octubre de 1492. (p. 14)

**Teapot Dome scandal** [escándalo de Teapot Dome] *s.* escándalo generado cuando Albert Fall, Secretario del Interior del presidente Warren G. Harding, concedió en secreto valiosas reservas de petróleo en Wyoming y California a compañías privadas a cambio de dinero y tierras. (p. 421)

**Telecommunications Act of 1996** [Ley de Telecomunicaciones] *s.* ley de 1996 que retiró las barreras que impedían que un tipo de compañía de comunicaciones ingresara a otro tipo de negocio en el mismo campo. (p. 878)

**telecommute** *v.* trabajar desde la casa para una compañía ubicada en otra parte, mediante la nueva tecnología de comunicaciones, como computadoras, Internet y máquinas de fax. (p. 878)

**tenement** [casa de pisos] *s.* vivienda urbana de varias familias, usualmente sobrepoblada y poco sanitaria. (p. 264)

**Tennessee Valley Authority (TVA)** [Autoridad del Valle de Tennessee] *s.* corporación federal creada en 1933 para construir presas y centrales eléctricas en la región del valle de Tennessee con el objeto de generar electricidad así como prevenir inundaciones. (p. 519)

**termination policy** [política de terminación] *s.* programa del gobierno federal en 1953 de cesar su responsabilidad hacia las naciones amerindias y eliminar el apoyo económico federal, suspender el sistema de reservaciones y redistribuir las tierras tribales. (p. 663)

**Tet offensive** [ofensiva de Tet] *s.* sorpresivo ataque masivo del Vietcong a pueblos y ciudades de Vietnam del Sur a comienzos de 1968; la batalla, de un mes de duración, convenció a muchos estadounidenses de que no era posible ganar la guerra. (p. 749)

**Texas Revolution** [Revolución de Texas] *s.* rebelión de 1836 con la que Texas se independizó de México. (p. 134)

**Thirteenth Amendment** [Enmienda 13] *s.* enmienda a la Constitución, ratificada en 1865, que ha abolido la esclavitud y la servidumbre involuntaria. (p. 183)

**Tiananmen Square** [plaza Tianamen] *s.* lugar de protestas estudiantiles en 1989 en Beijing, China, por la falta de libertades democráticas, donde el gobierno atacó a los estudiantes. (p. 850)

**Tonkin Gulf Resolution** [Resolución del Golfo de Tonkin] *s.* resolución aprobada por el Congreso en 1964 que le otorgaba al presidente Johnson amplios poderes para la Guerra de Vietnam. (p. 735)

**totalitarian** [totalitario] *adj.* característico de un sistema político en que el gobierno ejerce completo control sobre la vida de los ciudadanos. (p. 529)

**Trail of Tears** [Sendero de las Lágrimas] *s.* marcha obligada del pueblo cherokee desde Georgia hasta el Territorio Indio entre 1838 y 1840, durante la cual murieron miles de ellos. (p. 124)

**transcendentalism** [trascendentalismo] *s.* movimiento filosófico y literario que proponía llevar una vida sencilla y celebrar la verdad implícita de la naturaleza, la emoción personal y la imaginación. (p. 145)

**transcontinental railroad** [ferrocarril transcontinental] *s.* línea férrea finalizada en 1869 que unía la costa Atlántica y la costa Pacífica. (p. 237)

**Treaty of Fort Laramie** [Tratado del Fuerte Laramie] *s.* tratado que requería que los sioux vivieran en una reservación a lo largo del río Missouri. (p. 204)

**Treaty of Guadalupe Hidalgo** [Tratado de Guadalupe Hidalgo] *s.* tratado de 1848 que puso fin a la guerra entre Estados Unidos y México, mediante el cual Estados Unidos obtuvo enormes tierras en el Oeste y el Suroeste. (p. 136)

**Treaty of Paris (1783)** [Tratado de París] *s.* tratado que puso fin a la Guerra Revolucionaria Norteamericana y estableció las fronteras de la nueva nación. (p. 62)

**Treaty of Paris (1898)** [Tratado de París] *s.* tratado el cual puso fin a la guerra entre España y Estados Unidos. Por medio de este tratado España liberó a Cuba, cedió las islas de Guam y Puerto Rico a Estados Unidos y vendió las Filipinas a este país por 20 millones de dólares. (p. 350)

**Treaty of Tordesillas** [Tratado de Tordesillas] *s.* tratado de 1494 que dividió las Américas entre España y Portugal mediante una línea vertical imaginaria en el Atlántico; cada país tenía poder sobre un lado de la línea. (p. 15)

**Treaty of Versailles** [Tratado de Versalles] *s.* tratado de paz firmado en 1919 al finalizar la I Guerra Mundial, el cual establecía nuevas naciones, fronteras y reparaciones de guerra. (p. 400)

**trench warfare** [guerra de trincheras] *s.* guerra en que los combatientes atacan desde un sistema de zanjas fortificadas y no en un campo abierto de batalla. (p. 376)

**triangular trade** [triángulo comercial de esclavos] *s.* sistema transatlántico de comercio en el cual la mercancía, incluidos los esclavos, se intercambiaba entre África, Inglaterra, Europa, las Indias Occidentales y las colonias de Norteamérica. (p. 32)

**Truman Doctrine** [Doctrina Truman] *s.* declaración del presidente Truman en 1947, que establecía que Estados Unidos debía dar apoyo económico y militar para liberar a naciones amenazadas por fuerzas internas o externas. (p. 606)

**Tuskegee Normal and Industrial Institute** [Instituto Normal e Industrial Tuskegee] *s.* fundado en 1881 y dirigido por Booker T. Washington para otorgar diplomas de magisterio y enseñar destrezas comerciales y agrícolas a los afroamericanos. (p. 285)

**two-party system** [bipartidismo] *s.* sistema político dominado por dos partidos. (p. 76)

**Underground Railroad** [Ferrocarril Subterráneo] *s.* red secreta de personas que ayudaban a los esclavos fugitivos a escapar a lo largo de diversas rutas hacia Canadá o hacia zonas seguras en los estados libres. (p. 158)

**Unitarian** [unitario] *s.* miembro de un grupo religioso que destaca la razón y la fe en el individuo. (p. 145)

**United Farm Workers Organizing Committee (UFWOC)** [Comité Organizador de Trabajadores Agrícolas Unidos] *s.* sindicato establecido en 1966 por César Chávez para mejorar los salarios y las condiciones laborales de los trabajadores agrícolas. (p. 770)

**United Nations (UN)** [Naciones Unidas] *s.* organización internacional promotora de la paz a la que pertenecen la mayoría de naciones, fundada en 1945 para fomentar la paz, la seguridad y el desarrollo económico del mundo. (p. 603)

**urban flight** [huida urbana] *s.* migración de las ciudades a los suburbios aledaños. (p. 882)

**urbanization** [urbanización] *s.* movimiento de personas a una ciudad. (p. 262)

**urban renewal** [renovación urbana] *s.* práctica que se inició con la Ley Nacional de Vivienda de 1949, de remplazar vecindarios urbanos decaídos por viviendas nuevas para gente de bajos recursos. (p. 661)

**urban sprawl** [explosión urbana] *s.* expansión desordenada y desmedida de las ciudades a las áreas contiguas. (p. 424)

**U.S.S. *Maine*** *s.* buque de guerra estadounidense que explotó y naufragó misteriosamente el 15 de febrero de 1898 en el puerto de La Habana, Cuba. (p. 348)

**U-2 incident** [incidente del U-2] *s.* derribo en 1960 de un avión espía estadounidense U-2 en suelo soviético; complicó las conversaciones de paz entre Estados Unidos y la Unión Soviética. (p. 627)

**V-E Day** [Día V-E] *s.* mayo 8 de 1945, día de la victoria europea, cuando el general Eisenhower aceptó la rendición incondicional de Alemania; puso fin a la II Guerra Mundial en Europa. (p. 585)

**vertical integration** [integración vertical] *s.* proceso mediante el cual una compañía se adueña de sus proveedores y distribuidores así como de los sistemas de transporte, con lo que obtiene control total sobre la calidad y el costo de su producción. (p. 242)

**Vietcong** *s.* rebeldes comunistas de Vietnam del Sur apoyados por Vietnam del Norte a partir de 1959. (p. 73)

**Vietminh** [Vietmin] *s.* organización de comunistas vietnamitas y otros grupos nacionalistas que luchó contra los franceses por la independencia de Vietnam de 1946 a 1954. (p. 731)

**Vietnamization** [vietnamización] *s.* plan del presidente Nixon de retiro gradual de las tropas estadounidenses de Vietnam y su remplazo por el ejército vietnamita. (p. 755)

**Voting Rights Act of 1965** [Ley de Derechos Electorales de 1965] *s.* ley para facilitarles a los afroamericanos inscribirse para votar; eliminó las pruebas discriminatorias de lectura y escritura, y autorizó a los examinadores federales inscribir votantes rechazados a nivel local. (p. 716)

**Wagner Act** [Ley Wagner] *s.* ley—también conocida como Ley Nacional de Relaciones Laborales—promulgada en 1935 para proteger los derechos de los trabajadores después de que la Corte Suprema consideró que la Ley Nacional de Recuperación Industrial (NIRA) era inconstitucional. (p. 499)

**war-guilt clause** [cláusula de culpabilidad] *s.* cláusula del Tratado de Versalles que obligaba a Alemania a reconocer que había sido totalmente responsable por la I Guerra Mundial. (p. 400)

**War Industries Board (WIB)** [Junta de Industrias Bélicas] *s.* junta establecida en 1917 que animaba a las compañías a usar técnicas de producción en masa para mejorar la eficiencia durante la I Guerra Mundial. (p. 389)

**War Powers Act (WPA)** [Ley de Poderes de Guerra] *s.* ley aprobada en 1973 tras la Guerra de Vietnam que limitaba el derecho de un presidente a enviar tropas a combatir sin consultar con el Congreso. (p. 761)

**War Production Board (WPB)** [Junta de Producción Bélica] *s.* agencia establecida durante la II Guerra Mundial para coordinar la producción de suministros militares por la industria nacional. (p. 578)

**Warren Commission** [Comisión Warren] *s.* grupo encabezado por Earl Warren, presidente de la Suprema Corte, que realizó la investigación oficial del asesinato del presidente Kennedy y concluyó que Lee Harvey Oswald había actuado por su cuenta. (p. 683)

**Warren Court** [la Corte Warren] *s.* la Suprema Corte de la que fue presidente Earl Warren, que se destacó por sus actividades en torno a los derechos civiles y la libre expresión. (p. 691)

**Warsaw Pact** [Pacto de Varsovia] *s.* alianza militar formada en 1955 por la Unión Soviética y las naciones satélite de Europa del este. (p. 624)

**Watergate** *s.* serie de escándalos en que el presidente Nixon trató de encubrir la participación de su comité de relección en el allanamiento de la sede del Partido Demócrata en los apartamentos Watergate en 1972. (p. 802)

**Women's Auxiliary Army Corps (WAAC)** [Unidad Auxiliar de Mujeres (WAAC)] *s.* unidad del Ejército de EE.UU. creada durante la Segunda Guerra Mundial para permitir que las mujeres colaboraran en puestos que no fueran de combate. (p. 563)

**Woodstock** *s.* festival gratuito de música que atrajo a más de 400,000 jóvenes a una granja del estado de New York en agosto de 1969. (p. 782)

**Works Progress Administration (WPA)** [Administración para el Progreso de Obras] *s.* agencia gubernamental del New Deal que empleó a personal desocupado en construcción de escuelas y hospitales, reparación de carreteras, enseñanza, escritura y artes. (p. 498)

## X

**XYZ Affair** [Asunto XYZ] *s.* incidente diplomático de 1797 en el que funcionarios franceses trataron de sobornar a funcionarios estadounidenses para entrevistarse con un alto ministro francés. (p. 78)

## Y

**yellow journalism** [prensa amarillista] *s.* uso de métodos sensacionalistas en periódicos o revistas para atraer o influenciar lectores. (p. 347)

## Z

**Zimmermann note** [nota Zimmermann] *s.* mensaje enviado por el canciller alemán en 1917 al canciller mexicano en el que prometía a México los estados de Texas, New Mexico y Arizona si se aliaba a Alemania en contra de Estados Unidos en la I Guerra Mundial. (p. 379)

# INDEX

An *i* in italics preceding a page number refers to an illustration on the page. An *m* or a *c* in italics preceding a page number refers to a map or chart on the page.

## A

**AAA.** *See* Agricultural Adjustment Act.
**Abilene, Kansas,** 209–210, 238
*Ableman* v. *Booth*, 166
**abolitionists.** *See* antislavery movement.
**abortion rights,** 97, 779, 840
*Abrams* v. *United States*, 396–397
**ACLU.** *See* American Civil Liberties Union.
**acquired immune deficiency syndrome (AIDS),** 840, 880, R53
**Adams, Abigail,** 56, *i* 56
**Adams, John,** 56, 62, 77–78, *i* 77, 79, 86, 112–113, 118–119, R50
**Adams, John Quincy,** 116, 123, R50
**Adams, Samuel,** 47
**Adams-Onís Treaty,** 116, *m* 116
*Adarand Constructors* v. *Pena*, 818, 819
**Addams, Jane,** 266, *i* 266, 337, 358, 394
**Adena culture,** 6
*Adventures of Huckleberry Finn, The* (Twain), 296
**advertising,** 297, 425–426, 648–649
**AEF.** *See* American Expeditionary Force.
**affirmative action,** 429, 818–819, 843, 844, R53
  reverse discrimination and, 831, R63
**Afghanistan,** 815, US5, US6, US10–11, *m* US11, R40
**AFL.** *See* American Federation of Labor.
**Africa,** 13, 144, 343. *See also* North Africa; West Africa.
  slave trade and, 10, 15, 32–33
*Africana*, 456
**African Americans,** *c* 147, 182–183, 260, 324–325, 452–454, 473, 505–506, 843. *See also* antislavery movement; civil rights; exodusters; segregation; slavery; slaves; *names of specific individuals.*
  in business, 187–188
  churches of, 145, 187–188
  in cities, 187, 263, 266, 288, 393–394, 435, 452–453, 454, 455, *i* 455, 718
  in Civil War, 173
  in Congress, 188, 722
  as cowboys, 210
  discrimination against, 71, 173, 286–288, 564, 565–566
  education of, 148, 184, 187, 188, 283, 284–285, *i* 285, 701, *c* 701, 702–703, 722, 723, *c* 723, 900
  Farmers' Alliances and, 220–221
  female, 148, 149, 314, 315
  Harlem Renaissance and, 454, 455, *i* 455, 456
  in labor force, 215, 314, 565–566
  in labor movement, 245, 418, 565–566
  migrations of, 204, 215, *i* 215, 393–394, 452–453, 591, *m* 591,

701, 889
  music of, 298, 299, 655–657, 786
  in Philippine-American War, 355
  popular culture and, 655–656, *i* 656
  race riots and, 288, 394, 453, 841
  Reconstruction and, 184, 185–188, 189
  in Revolutionary War, 59, 61
  in Spanish-American War, 350, *i* 350
  as U.S. citizens, 166–167
  in Vietnam War, 743
  voting rights of, 71, 102, 104, 185–186, 187, 286–287, 315, 637, 715–716
  in World War I, 382, 392–394
  in World War II, 563, *i* 563, 564, 573, *i* 573, 702, 889
**Africans, in American colonies,** 15, 23, 32–33
**Afrika Korps,** 572
**Agee, James,** 514
**Agent Orange,** 739
*Age of Innocence, The* (Wharton), 451
**Agnew, Spiro T.,** 796, 805, 811
**Agricultural Adjustment Act (AAA),** 491, 496
**agriculture.** *See also* farmers.
  education in, 217
  in English colonies, 23, 31–32, 34
  farm worker movement and, 770
  inventions for, 121, 141, 217, *c* 217, 232, 263
  in Midwest, 141
  migrant workers and, 684–685, *i* 684, *i* 685, *m* 685
  of Native Americans, 5, 6, 25
  New Deal and, 518
  plantation, 15, 31–32, 146, *i* 147
  in South, 121–122, 141, 182, 187–188
  in Soviet Union, 529
  water projects and, 256, 289, 324
**Aguinaldo, Emilio,** 349, 355
**AIDS.** *See* acquired immune deficiency syndrome.
**AIM.** *See* American Indian Movement.
**airlines,**
  deregulation of, 837
  hijackings, 863, US3, *m* US3
**airplane(s)**
  airmail and, 280, *i* 280, 281
  commercial use of, 424, *i* 424, 588, *i* 588
  famous flights of, 449, *m* 449
  first flight of, 279, 280, *i* 280
  in World War I, 381, 384–385, *i* 384, 588
  in World War II, 539, 540–541
**airports,** security at, US13, *c* US13, US15
**Alabama,** 165, 704–705, 716, 774

facts about, R48
**Alamo,** 134–135, *i* 134, R53
**Alaska,** 5, 6, 116, 117, 212, 773, *c* 773, 822 1857, *m* 45
  facts about, R48
  U.S. purchase of, 344
**Alaska Native Claims Settlement Act,** 773, 822
**Alaskan Pipeline,** 822, *i* 822
**Albany, New York,** 60, 120, 139, 140
**Alcott, Louisa May,** 174
**Alexander II (czar of Russia),** 116–117
**Alexander, Harold,** 572
**Alien and Sedition Acts,** 78–79, 392
**Allen, Frederick Lewis,** 469, 475
**Allen, Gracie,** 511, *i* 512
**Alliance for Progress,** 680–681, R54
**Allies,** R54
  in World War I, 373–374, 376, 377, 378, *i* 386
  in World War II, 554
**al-Qaeda,** US8, US10, *c* US10, US14–15
**Álvarez de Piñeda, Alonso,** 18
**Amendments to Constitution.** *See specific number.*
**American Civil Liberties Union (ACLU),** 438
**American Colonization Society,** 145
**American Expeditionary Force (AEF),** 384, R54
**American Federation of Labor (AFL),** 245–246, 333, 417, 508, R54
*American Gothic* (Wood), 513, *i* 513
**American Independent Party,** 753
**American Indian Movement (AIM),** 771–772
**American Indians.** *See* Native Americans.
**Americanization movement,** 263, R54
**American Liberty League,** 493
**American Missionary Associaton,** 187
**American Protective Association,** 258
**American Railway Union (ARU),** 246, 248
**American Revolution.** *See* Revolutionary War.
**American Socialist Party,** 309
**American System,** 122, R54
**America Online (AOL),** 871
**Ameringer, Oscar,** 478
**Amnesty Act,** 189
**amusement parks,** 292–293
**analyzing causes,** 11, 13, 23, 39, 121, 127, 208, 211, 215, 220, 222, 247, 256, 270, 271, 277, 296, 310, 314, 356, 373, 439, 451, 457, 475, 512, 530, 534, 535, 554, 570, 591, 593, 603, 604, 610, 612, 618, 619, 623, 636, 646, 648, 655, 703, 715, 716, 719, 740, 778, 799, 809, 812, 814, 815, 825, 809, 833, 838, 855, 861, 864, 865, 883, R7
**analyzing distributions,** 73, 521, 847, R25, R32

**Civil War,** 94, 168–174, *m* 170–171, *i* 173, 175–181, 184, 888
    effects of, 181–183, 186–187, 244
    photographs of, 178, *i* 178
    resources of North and South, *c* 169
**Civil Works Administration (CWA),** 488, *i* 488, 491, *c* 500
**clarifying,** R4. *See also* summarizing.
**Clark, William,** 114
**Clay, Henry,** 122, 123, 126, 157–158, *i* 157
**Clayton Antitrust Act,** 333, R55
**Clean Air Act,** 822
**Clemenceau, Georges,** 399, *i* 399
**Clemens, Samuel (Mark Twain),** 224, 267, 294, 296, 358, *i* 358
*Clermont,* 120, 140
**Cleveland, Grover,** 248, 258, 271, 330, 345, 358, R51
**Cleveland, Ohio,** 231, 234–235, 264, 307, 310
**Clifford, Clark,** 749
**Clinton, Bill,** 85, *i* 597, 844, 860–868, *i* 861, R52
    Bosnia and, 863–864
    Congress and, 862, 864–865
    foreign policy of, 863–864
    GATT and, 872
    health-care reform and, 861
    impeachment and, 865
    NAFTA and, 864, 872
    Russia and, 863
    welfare reform and, 862
**Clinton, Henry,** 62
**Clinton, Hillary Rodham,** 861, *i* 861
**cloning,** 880
**CNLU.** *See* Colored National Labor Union.
**coal,** 231, *m* 231, 237, 465
    mining of, *i* 321
**Coca-Cola,** 293
**Cody, William F. "Buffalo Bill"**
    Wild West Show of, 206, 211
*Cohens* v. *Virginia,* 118
**Coit, Stanton,** 266
**Cold War,** 405, 589, 606, R55. *See also* Soviet Union.
    arms race and, 622–623, 670, 849
    Berlin and, 677–678
    communism in China and, 609–610
    communism in U.S. and, 616–621
    covert actions in, 623–624
    Cuba and, 673–674, 676
    defense spending in, *c* 626
    development of, 602–605
    effects of end of, 848–850
    end of, 848–849
    in Europe, 606
    flexible response in, 673, R57
    Geneva summit and, 624
    hot line in, 678, R58
    impact on business cycle, 604, 606, 611
    Kennedy and, 671–674, 676–678
    Korean War and, 611–612, 614–615
    McCarthyism and, 620–621
    Nixon and, 799–800
    reasons for Western victory in, 849–850
    science fiction and, 628–629

    Truman Doctrine and, 606
    U-2 incident in, 626, *i* 627, 670
    U.S. foreign policy and, 622–623
**Colfax, Schuyler,** 238
**collective bargaining,** 246
**Collier, John,** 507, *i* 507
**Colombia,** 360
**colonial America,** *m* 25, *m* 29. *See also* Revolutionary War; Spain, American colonies of; *names of specific colonies.*
    courtship in, 40–41, *i* 40, *i* 41
    governments in, 30
    life in, 32, 33–36
    meetinghouses, *i* 27
    relations with Britain in, 28, 30, 39, 46–53, *c* 48, *c* 49, 55, 56, 58, 59, 64
    relations with Native Americans in, 23, 25–26, 37, 39, 53
    settlement of, 21, 23–30
    slaves in, 23, 28, 32–33, 34, 53
    women in, 32, 34, 41, 53, 64
**Colorado,** 137, 204, 204
    facts about, R48
**Colored Farmers' National Alliance,** 221
**Colored National Labor Union (CNLU),** 245
**Colton, Walter,** 137
**Columbian Exchange,** 15, *m* 15, R55
**Columbian Exposition,** *i* 274–275, 279
**Columbus, Christopher,** 10, 12, 13, 14–16, *i* 14, *m* 17
**Comanche,** 206
**Committee on Public Information,** 390
**committees of correspondence,** 49
**Committee to Reelect the President (CRP),** 803–804
*Common Sense* **(Paine),** 52, *i* 52
**Commonwealth of Independent States (CIS),** 849
*Commonwealth* v. *Hunt,* 143
**communications, advances in,** 140, *c* 140–141, 141, 279, 589, 876–878. *See also* telegraph; telephone; television.
**Communications Decency Act,** 878
**communism,** 246, 412, 413, R39, *c* R44, R55. *See also* Cold War.
    in China, 609–610, *c* 610, 616, 799–800, 850, R39
    in Eastern Europe, 605, 677–678, 849–850, R39
    Hollywood and, 616, 617–618, *i* 617
    roots of, 413
    in Soviet Union, 413, 529, 603, 800, 848–849, R39
    in United States, 412, 413, 417, 456, 616–621
    in Vietnam, 688, 730, 731, 732
*Communist Manifesto* **(Marx and Engels),** 413
**Community Action Program,** 688
**comparing,** 9, 42, 119, 163, 182, 211, 272, 285, 289, 322, 358, 397, 417, 426, 445, 459, 468, 558, 579, 595, 614, 626, 642, 690, 716, 763, 817, 827, 845, 852, 875, 886, 889, R8. *See also* contrasting.

**comparing and contrasting,** 27, 41, 42, 178, 195, 225, 327, 365, 441, 477, 516, 657, 659, 723, 853, 887, R8
**Compromise of 1850,** 157–158, 160, *m* 160
**computers,** 140, 141, 429, 871, 872, 876–878
    using, 3, 43, 108, 369, 697, R29, R33, R37. *See also* Internet, using for research
**concentration camps,** *i* 548, R55
    in Cuba, 347
    in World War II, 546–549, *i* 546–547, 576
**conclusions, drawing.** *See* drawing conclusions.
**Concord, Battle of,** *c* 49, 50, 52
**Coney Island,** 292–293, *i* 292
**Confederate States of America, or Confederacy,** R55. *See also* Civil War.
    formation of, 165, 168–169
    life in, 174, 180
**Conflict in Korea.** *See* Korean War.
**Conflict in Vietnam.** *See* Vietnam War.
**Congdon, Don,** 510
**Congress,** 74–75, 84–90, *c* 87, 353, 691, 862, 864–865, 867. *See also* House of Representatives; Senate; *names of specific acts.*
    African Americans in, 188, 722
    under Articles of Confederation, 67, 69
    plans for, in Constitutional Convention, 68, 69, *c* 69
    powers of, 71, 88–90, 116–117, 166–167, 502–503
    role of, in New Deal, 489–490, 492, 493, 496, 497, 498–499, 502, 503
    role of, in Reconstruction, 185–186, 189
    women in, 65, 372, 722
**Congress of Industrial Organizations (CIO),** 508
**Congress of Racial Equality (CORE),** 593, 706, 710–711, 715, R55
**Conkling, Roscoe,** 268, 270
**Connally, John,** 682
**Connecticut**
    facts about, R48
    settlement of, 25
**Connor, Bull,** 712
*conquistadores,* 16, R55
**conscientious objector,** 386, R56
**conscription.** *See* draft.
**consequences.** *See* analyzing effects; evaluating effects.
**conservation.** *See* environment, protection of.
**Conservative Coalition,** 831, R56
**conservatives,** 794, 830–833, 838. *See also* Contract with America; Reagan, Ronald.
**Constitution,** 74, 75, 77, 82–83, 104, 113, 124, 128
    amendments to, 69–70, 94–95, 96–103. *See also specific amendments by number.*
    Bill of Rights in, 70–71, 89, 96–97, 724
    drafting of, 68–69

effects, predicting. *See* predicting effects.
egalitarianism, 63, R56
Egypt, 625, 799, 816
Ehrlichman, John, 803, *i* 803, 804
1868, Treaty of, 204, 206
Eighteenth Amendment, 100, 434, 436, 437
Eighth Amendment, 97
Einstein, Albert, 567
Eisenhower, Dwight D., 585, 615, *i* 638, 639–640, 670, R52
    Bonus Army and, 483
    civil rights and, 640
    Cold War and, 623–624, 626–627
    farewell address of, 673
    at Geneva summit, 624
    U-2 incident and, 626–627
    Vietnam and, 688, 731
    as World War II general, 572, 574, *i* 574
Eisenhower Doctrine, 625, R56
election, presidential
    of 1796, 77
    of 1800, 98, 112–113
    of 1824, 123
    of 1828, 123
    of 1836, 127
    of 1840, 127
    of 1852, 161
    of 1856, 162
    of 1860, 163
    of 1864, 181
    of 1868, 186
    of 1876, 189
    of 1880, 270
    of 1884, 271
    of 1888, 271
    of 1892, 271, 330
    of 1896, 222
    of 1908, 328
    of 1912, 330–331, *c* 331
    of 1916, 379
    of 1920, 419
    of 1928, 466
    of 1932, 488–489
    of 1936, 496
    of 1940, 551
    of 1948, 638, *c* 638
    of 1952, 640
    of 1960, 670–671
    of 1964, 688
    of 1968, 751–752, *c* 753
    of 1972, 804
    of 1976, 812
    of 1980, 832–833, *c* 833
    of 1984, 837
    of 1988, 838
    of 1992, 861
    of 1996, 865
    of 2000, 619, *i* 619, 866–868, *c* 866
Electoral College, 69, 90, 113, 866
electricity, 35, 232–233
    conveniences and, 425, *c* 425, *i* 425
    transportation and, 277
electronic commerce. *See* e-commerce.
Elementary and Secondary Education Act, 689
Eleventh Amendment, 98
Elijah Muhammad, 719–720

Eliot, T. S., 451
Elkins Act, 320
Ellington, Edward Kennedy "Duke," 457, *i* 457
Ellis Island, 256–257
Ellsberg, Daniel, 757
e-mail, 141, 877
emancipation, 122, 145–146, 172–173, 260
Emancipation Proclamation, 172–173, 183, 260, *i* 260, R57
embargo, 555, R40
Emergency Banking Relief Act, 490, *c* 500
Emergency Quota Act, 415, 416
Emerson, Ralph Waldo, 145
*encomienda*, 16, R57
energy, alternative sources of, 881, *i* 881
Enforcement Acts, 188–189
Engels, Friedrich, 413
England, 11, 13, 20. *See also* Great Britain.
    American colonies of, 20, 21, 23–28, *c* 29, *m* 29, 30
    civil war and Restoration in, 26
    English Bill of Rights, 52, 86, 97
    Magna Carta, 52, 97
Enlightenment, 34–35, 36, 52, R57
Enola Gay, 584
entertainment. *See* leisure activities;
    motion pictures; music; radio;
    sports; television.
entitlement programs, 831, 865, R57
entrepreneurs, 140, 243, 244, 429, R57
environment, protection of, 216, 322–324, 328, 329, 519, 691, 820–822, 824, 825, 837, 868, 881 *See also* pollution.
Environmental Protection Agency (EPA), 822, 837
EOA. *See* Economic Opportunity Act.
EPA. *See* Environmental Protection Agency.
Equal Employment Opportunity Commission (EEOC), 778, 779
Equal Rights Amendment (ERA), 65, 779, 780, 842, R57
Equiano, Olaudah, 33, *i* 33
ERA. *See* Equal Rights Amendment.
eras
    Cold War, 405, 606, 894
    Colonial Era, 21, 23–26, *m* 25, 28, *m* 29, 30, 31–39, *i* 34, 40–41, *i* 40–41
    globalization, 872–873, 895
    Great Depression, *i* 462–463, 464–469, *c* 470, 471, 472–477, 478–483, *i* 478, 488
    Great Society, 689–691, *c* 690, 719, 741
    Industrial Age, 120–121, 141, 230–233, 234–235, 236–238, 241–243
    New Deal, 488–494, 506–507
    post–Cold War, 848–852, 894
    Progressive Era, 306–312, 313–316, 317–320, 322–325, 326–327, 328–331, 332–337, 419
    Roaring Twenties, 434–439, 440–443, 444–445, *i* 444–445, 446–451, 452–454, 455–457

Vietnam War era, 91, 103, 619, *i* 619, 730–732, *m* 733, 734–741, *i* 736, 742–747, *c* 743, *i* 744, 748–753, *m* 749, *i* 750, 754–755, 801
Watergate era, 619, *i* 619, 758, 802–807, *i* 805, *i* 807
World War I, 374, 375–380, *m* 375, 381–387, 388–391, 588, *i* 588
World War II, 536–541, *m* 538, 542–549, 550–555, *m* 556, 557, 562–568, 569–574, *m* 572, *m* 575, 576–577, 578–579, *m* 580, 581, 583–585, 590–595, *i* 602
Erie, Lake, 139, 234
Erie Canal, 139, *i* 139, 141
Erie Railroad, 221
Ervin, Sam J., Jr., 805, *i* 805
*Escobedo* v. *Illinois*, 692, 694
Espionage and Sedition Acts, 392, 396, 397, R57
Ethiopia, 533
ethnic groups. *See* specific groups.
European societies of 1400s, 10–11
evaluating, 30, 50, 53, 62, 63, 71, 80, 106, 117, 127, 138, 145, 149, 152, 181, 218, 223, 244, 259, 266, 272, 281, 308, 325, 331, 334, 345, 358, 395, 418, 429, 439, 441, 443, 451, 460, 492, 494, 499, 506, 509, 516, 539, 574, 589, 627, 649, 654, 657, 663, 681, 692, 706, 722, 735, 746, 747, 773, 807, 819, 838, 856, 868, 881, R17, R20
    decisions, 113, 365, 482, 501, 541, 549, 557, 577, 585, 587, 615, 678, 759, 801, 817, R16
    effects, 53, 125, 190, 223, 238, 269, 358, 421, 497, 509, 519, 592, 621, 640, 704, 761, 838, 881, 889. *See also* analyzing effects.
    leadership, 79, 117, 165, 249, 271, 420, 490, 494, 519, 608, 639, 640, 683, 693, 833, 849
Evans, Walker, 514
events, analyzing. *See* analyzing events.
Evers, Medgar, 714
Ewuare, 9
examining issues. *See* issues, examining.
executive branch, 69, 75, 90–92, 803
Executive Order 9066, 596–597
exodusters, 215, *i* 215, R57
expansionism, 343–344, 346–347, 350–351, 353, *i* 354, *m* 356
exploration by Europeans
    of Africa, 12–13
    of Americas, 14–15, 16, *m* 17, 18–19, 26
ex post facto law, 89

F

fact from opinion, distinguishing. *See* distinguishing fact from opinion.
factories, 121, 142, 870
    conditions in, 142, 233, 244–245, 248–249, 306, 309
Fair Deal, 639, 680, R57
Fair Labor Standards Act, 499, *c* 500, 518, R42

**Homestead Act,** 215, 428, R58
**homesteaders,** 215, 428
**Homestead strike,** 247–248
**Hoover, Herbert,** 422, 466, *i* 466, 478–480, *i* 478, 481, 489, R52
    Bonus Army and, 482–483
    Food Administration and, 389–390
    Great Depression and, 471, 478–480
    philosophy of government of, 479
    as secretary of commerce, 420
**Hoover Dam.** *See* Boulder Dam.
**Hope, Bob,** 511
**Hopewell culture,** 5
**Hopkins, Harry,** 492, 498, 512
**Hopper, Edward,** 450
*Hopwood* v. *Texas,* 901
**horizontal integration,** 242, R58
**horses**
    Native Americans and, 203
    Spanish and, 203, 208
**House, Edward M.,** 398, *i* 398
**House Judiciary Committee,** 802, 805, 806
**House of Burgesses,** 23
**House of Representatives,** 68, 84–85, 86, 186, 330, 846, 847, 865. *See also* Congress.
    election of 1800 and, 98, 113
**House Un-American Activities Committee (HUAC),** 617, R58
**housing,** 465
    in cities, 264, 883
    Great Society and, 690
    New Deal and, 492
    after World War II, 635
**Housing and Urban Development, Department of (HUD),** 690
**Houston, Sam,** 134–135, *i* 135
**Howard, Ebenezer,** 279
**Howe, Julia Ward,** 316
**HUAC.** *See* House Un-American Activities Committee.
**Hubble Space Telescope,** 879
**HUD.** *See* Housing and Urban Development, Department of.
**Hudson, Henry,** *m* 17, 26
**Hudson River,** 26, 120
**Huerta, Dolores,** 770
**Huerta, Victoriano,** 363
**Hughes, Charles Evans,** 379, 419
**Hughes, Langston,** 454, 456, 459, *i* 459
**Hull, Cordell,** 552
**Hull House,** 266
**human-environment interaction,** xxx, 231, 239, 323, 345, 356, 575, 580, 605, 675, 816, 866. *See also* geographic factors, human.
**Human Genome Project,** 879
**human rights,** 725, 815, 895
    in China, 863, R59
**Humphrey, Hubert,** 751–752, 753
**Humphrey, R. M.,** 221
**Hundred Days,** 489, 495
**Hungary,** 625–626
**hunting and gathering,** 5, 6
**Hupa,** 6
**Hurston, Zora Neale,** 452, *i* 452, 453, 456, 514
**Hussein, Saddam,** 853
**Hutchinson, Anne,** 25

**hypothesizing,** 165, 233, 249, 271, 281, 285, 331, 368, 403, 468, 494, 514, 589, 597, 615, 621, 627, 664, 773, 807, 853, 855, 887, R13, R34

**ICC.** *See* Interstate Commerce Commission.
**Ice Age,** 4–5
**Idaho,** 316
    facts about, R48
**identifying bias.** *See* bias, identifying.
**identifying problems.** *See* problems, identifying.
**ILGWU.** *See* International Ladies' Garment Workers' Union.
**Illinois,** 131, 162, 163, 166, 231
    facts about, R48
*I Love Lucy,* 653, *i* 654
**immigrants,** 78, *i* 143, 885–886, 888. *See also* immigration.
    at Angel Island, 257, *i* 258
    Chinese, 204, 215, *i* 237, 254, 255, *c* 255, 257, 258–259, *i* 258, *i* 259, 289
    in cities, 262–263, 266, 435
    Cuban, 844
    difficulties of, 256–258
    education of, 284
    at Ellis Island, 256–257
    European, 32, 34, 142, *i* 143, 255, 415, *i* 416, 428
    female, 314
    German, 32, 34, 204, *c* 255, 391–392
    illegal, 769, 886, 897
    Irish, 142, 215, 237, *c* 255, 263
    Italian, *c* 255, 415
    Japanese, 255, *c* 255, 259, 415
    Jewish, 34, 255, 258, 284
    Mexican, 256, *c* 256, *i* 416, 769, 886
    nativism and, 258–259, 414–415, 896
    origins of, 255–256, *c* 255, *c* 416, 885–886
    political machines and, 268
    Scandinavian, 34, *c* 255
    Scottish and Scots-Irish, 32, 34
    Vietnamese, 889, *i* 889
    West Indian, 256
    World War I and, 391–392, 393
**immigration,** 142, 254–259, 260, *i* 260, 428, 691, 885–886, *m* 885. *See also* immigrants.
    patterns of, *c* 255, *c* 416
    restrictions on, 258–259, 414–415, 417
    westward expansion and, 204, 215, 138, 888, *i* 888
**Immigration Acts of 1924 and 1965,** 691, R59
**Immigration Restriction League,** 258
**impeachment,** 85, 92, 186, 806, 807, 864–865, R59
**imperialism,** R59
    Asian, 343
    European, 342, 343, 373
    U.S., 342, 343, 346–347, 350–351, 353, *i* 354, *m* 356
**imperial presidency,** 803

*Imperial Presidency, The* (Schlesinger), 803
**impressment,** 114, R59
**Inca,** 5, 18
**income**
    difference between men's and women's, *c* 842
    uneven distribution of, *c* 466, 471, *c* 661
**income tax,** 100, 174, 182, 221, 390, 334, *c* 334, 423, 567, R59
**inferences, making.** *See* making inferences.
**indentured servants,** 23, 34, R59
**Independence, Missouri,** 131
**Indian,** 15. *See also* Native Americans; Plains Indians.
**Indiana,** 231
    facts about, R48
**Indian Affairs, Bureau of,** 772
**Indian Education Act,** 772
**Indian Removal Act,** 124, *m* 125
**Indian Reorganization Act,** 662–663
**Indian Self-Determination and Education Assistance Act,** 772–773
**Indian Territory,** 124
**Indochina,** 579, 731, *m* 733. *See also* Cambodia; Laos; Vietnam.
**Industrial Revolution,** 121
**Industrial Workers of the World (IWW),** 246, *i* 246, 392, *i* 392, 413, R59
**industry,** 28, 33, 120–121, 141, 244, *c* 814, 870–871. *See also* business; factories; inventions; railroads; steel industry; textile industry.
    electricity and, 232–233
    expansion of, in late 19th century, 231–232, 241–244
    natural resources and, 230–232, *m* 231
    in 1920s, 464, 465
    pollution and, 234–235, 820
    railroads and, 237–238
    in World War II, 564–565, *c* 564
**inferences, making,** R10
**inflation,** 60, 567–568, 798, 811, 813, *c* 813, R41, R42, R59
*Influence of Sea Power upon History, 1660–1783, The* (Mahan), 344
**information superhighway,** 877, R59
**INF Treaty.** *See* Intermediate-Range Nuclear Forces Treaty.
**Ingram, David,** 8
**initiative,** 312, R59
**installment plan,** 425–426, R59
**interacting with history.** *See* history, interacting with.
**interest rate,** 811, *c* R42
**Interior, Department of the,** 216, 421
**Intermediate-Range Nuclear Forces Treaty (INF Treaty),** 849, R59
**Internal Revenue Service,** 796
**International Ladies' Garment Workers' Union (ILGWU),** 248–249, 508
**international relations.** *See* foreign affairs and foreign policy.
**International Space Station (ISS),** 879
**Internet,** 140, 141, 429, 877, R59. *See also* computers, using; researching.

King, Rodney, 841
King Philip. *See* Metacom.
King Philip's War, 25–26, R59
Kiowa, 206, 225
Kissinger, Henry, 758, *i* 758, 794, *i* 794, 799, 811
Klein, Gerda Weissmann, 542, *i* 542, 549
Knights of Labor, 245, 246
Know-Nothing Party, 161–162
Knox, Henry, 75
Kodak camera, 281, *i* 281
Kongo, 9, R59
Kopecki, Lilli, 548
Koran. *See* Qur'an.
Korea, 360, 611. *See also* Korean War.
Korean War, 91, 609, *i* 609, 611–615, *m* 613, 731, R59
　domestic effects of, 611, 615
　international effects of, 612, 615
*Korematsu* v. *United States*, 595, 596–597
Kramer, Alyce Mano, 565
*Kristallnacht*, 543, *i* 543, R60
Ku Klux Klan, 188, 415, *i* 415, R60
Kuwait, 853, *i* 854, 855
Kwakiutl, 6

labor force, 246, 642–643, *c* 814, 842–843, 869–871, *c* 871. *See also* economy; industry; labor movement; unions; working conditions.
　children in, *i* 244, 245, 248, 306, 310–311, *i* 311, 321, *i* 321
　in factories, 142, 233, 244–245, 306, 309
　New Deal and, 499, 503, 518
　unemployment and, 127, 222, 240, 469, *c* 470, *c* 517, *c* 813, R40, R47
　women in, 142, *i* 142, 233, 244–245, 307, 311, 313–314, 388, 441–442, *c* 442, *i* 442, 565, *i* 565, 591, *i* 591, 777, *c* 777, *i* 869, 869
　in World War II, 565–566
labor movement, 142–143, 244–249, 389, 412, 417, 418. *See also* labor force; strikes; unions.
　African Americans in, 245, 418, 565–566
　agricultural workers and, 246, 768, 770
　women in, 248–249, *i* 417, 777, 842–843
labor unions. *See* unions.
bin Laden, Osama, US8, US9, US10, *i* US10
Lafayette, Marquis de, 61, 62
Laffer, Arthur, 835
La Flesche, Susette, 313, *i* 313
La Follette, Robert M., 310
laissez faire doctrine, 242
land mines, 182, 739
Landon, Alfred, 496
Land Ordinance of 1785, 67, 72, *m* 72
Lange, Dorothea, 495, *i* 496, 497
Laos, 732, *m* 733, 755
La Raza Unida, 770, R60
La Salle, Sieur de (Robert Cavelier), *m* 17

Latin America, 362, 680–681, 768–769. *See also* Panama Canal; *names of specific nations.*
　and Alliance for Progress, 680–681
　Good Neighbor Policy in, 534
Latinos, 473, 768–771, 844, 882, 884, 886. *See also* Mexican Americans; Puerto Ricans.
Lawrence, Joseph D., 383, *i* 383
Lazarus, Emma, 261
League of Nations, 398, 399, 401, 402, 412, 531–533, R60
learning new vocabulary. *See* vocabulary, learning new.
Lease, Mary Elizabeth, 219, *i* 219, 221
Le Duc Tho, 758
Lee, Richard Henry, 52, 70
Lee, Robert E., 170–171, 175–177, 180, *i* 180, 181, *i* 181, 183
legislative branch, 69, 84–90. *See also* Congress.
Leigh, Vivian, *i* 511
leisure activities, 293–294, 298–299, 645. *See also* entertainment; sports.
Lend-Lease Act, 552, 553, R60
Lenin, Vladimir I., *i* 405, 411, 413, 529
"Letter from a Birmingham Jail" (King), 712
*Letters from the Federal Farmer* (Lee), 70
*Letters on the Equality of the Sexes and the Condition of Woman* (Grimké), 148
*Let Us Now Praise Famous Men* (Agee and Evans), 514, *i* 514
Lewis, John, 748, *i* 748
Lewis, John L., 418, *i* 418, 508
Lewis, Meriwether, 114
Lewis, Sinclair, 450
Lewis and Clark expedition, 112, 114, *m* 115
Lexington, Battle of, *c* 49, 50, *i* 50, 52
Leyte Gulf, Battle of, 581
*Liberator, The*, 145–146, *i* 145
Liberty League. *See* American Liberty League.
Liberty Party, 162
light bulb, 232, 233
Liliuokalani, 342, *i* 342, 345
Limited Test Ban Treaty, 678
Lin, Maya, 760, *i* 760
Lincoln, Abraham, 163, *i* 163, 164, 168, 172, *i* 172, *i* 183, R51
　assassination of, 91, 183, *i* 183
　in Civil War, 169, 172, 173, 177, 180, 181, 260
　Reconstruction and, 184–185, 186
Lindbergh, Charles, 424, 449, *i* 449, 552
Li Peng, 850
literacy test, 258, 287
literature
　beat movement and, 655
　Harlem Renaissance and, 454, 456, 458, 459
　in 1920s, 450–451, 458–459
　in 1930s, 514
　science fiction, 628–629
　at turn of century, 296
　of Vietnam War, 762–763
　of West, 224–225

women and, 459, 874–875
Little Bighorn, Battle of, 204, *m* 205, 206
Little Rock, Arkansas, 703–704, *i* 703
Livingston, Robert, 114
Lloyd George, David, 399, *i* 399
lobbying, 109, 666, 895
location, xxx, 7, 25, 59, 136, 159, 176, 179, 205, 345, 349, 356, 375, 386, 400, 530, 532, 538, 594, 605, 733, 749, 816, 833, 851, 872
Locke, Alain, 454, 457
Locke, John, 52, 53, 54
Locust Street Social Settlement, 266
Lodge, Henry Cabot, Sr., 401
London, Jack, 265, 296
Long, Huey, 494, *i* 494
long drive. *See* cattle drive. R60
longhorn cattle, 208, 210, R60
longhouse, *i* 7
Longoria, Felix, 662
Looking Glass, Chief, *i* 150
Lopez de la Cruz, Jessie, 768
Los Angeles, California, 719, 841, 843
Lost Generation, 451
Louis XIV (king of France)
Louisiana, 165, 185, 494, 701
　facts about, R48
　French, Spanish, and U.S. territory of, 114, 122
Louisiana Purchase, 114, *i* 115, 157, R60
Love Canal, 820
Low, Ann Marie, 472, *i* 472
Lowell, Massachusetts, 142, R60
Loyalists, in Revolutionary War, 59, R60
Loyalty Review Board, 617
Lucas, Anthony F., 230
Luftwaffe, 539, 540–541
*Lusitania*, *m* 375, 378, *i* 378, R60
Lyon, Mary, 148

MacArthur, Douglas, 483, 579, 581, 583, *i* 583, 587, 612, 614–615, *i* 614
Madero, Francisco, 363
Madison, James, 68, *i* 68, 70, *i* 70, 75, 113, 114, 116, 118–119, 122, R50
magazines, 279, 441, 447
Maginot Line, 540, *i* 540
Magna Carta, 52, 97
magnetic resonance imaging (MRI), 880
Mahan, Alfred T., 343, *i* 343
mahjong, 448
Mahpiua Luta. *See* Red Cloud.
mail-order catalogs, 297, *i* 297
Maine, 94, 122, 133, 681, *c* 773
　facts about, R48
*Maine*, U.S.S., 340, 348, *i* 348, 404
main ideas, finding, 327, 829, 835, R2, R27
making decisions, 109, 129, 329, 586
*Making Do* (Westin), 475
making inferences, 8, 10, 13, 33, 39, 52, 67, 69, 113, 142, 146, 149, 169, 170, 179, 186, 211, 223, 233, 240, 293, 316, 351, 379, 389, 393, 395, 402, 421, 450, 471, 481, 552, 608, 656, 682, 683, 704, 721, 735, 739,

*Monitor*, 183

Monmouth, Battle of, 61, *i* 61

monopoly, 243, 330–331, 333, 356, R43

Monroe, James, 114, 116–117, *i* 117, 363, R50

Monroe, Sylvester, 843

Monroe Doctrine, 116–117, *i* 351, 362, 363, 404, R60

Montana
    facts about, R48

Montezuma, 16

Montgomery, Alabama, 165
    bus boycott in, 700, 704–705, *i* 705, R38

Montgomery Ward, 297

moon landing, 796, *i* 796

Moral Majority, 831–832, 838, R60

Morgan, J. P., 240, 243

*Morgan v. Virginia*, 702

Mormons, 131, 133

Morrill Act, 217, R60

Morris, Robert, 61

Morrison, Blake, US12

Morse Code, 140

Morse, Samuel F. B., 140

motion pictures, 294, 299, *i* 299, 402, 450, 510–511, *i* 510, 566, *i* 566, 654–655, 787, 824

motives, analyzing. *See* analyzing motives.

Mott, Lucretia, 64, 148

Mount Holyoke Female Seminary, 148

movement (geographic theme), xxx, 17, 62, 115, 125, 132, 159, 176, 179, 205, 239, 255, 263, 423, 474, 532, 556, 572, 580, 591, 613, 675, 733, 854, 885

movies. *See* motion pictures.

MRI. *See* magnetic resonance imaging.

muckrakers, 308, 326–327, R60

Muhammad, 9

Muir, John, 323, 329

*Muller v. Oregon*, 311

Muncie, Indiana, 209

*Munn v. Illinois*, 239, R60

Muñoz Rivera, Luis, 352, *i* 352

Murphy, Audie, 576, *i* 576

Murray, Patty, 65

Murrow, Edward R., 653

music
    jazz, 456–457, 657
    popular, 652
    ragtime, 299
    rock 'n' roll, 655–656, *i* 656, 786, R63
    soul, 786
    surf, 786

Muslims, 9, 10, 850. *See also* Islam.

Mussolini, Benito, 530, *m* 530, 531, *i* 531, 573

*My Ántonia* (Cather), 451

Myers, Deb, 563

Myers, Walter Dean, 763

My Lai massacre, 756, R60

NAACP. *See* National Association for the Advancement of Colored People.

NACW. *See* National Association of Colored Women.

Nader, Ralph, 691
    Green Party and, 866, 867

NAFTA. *See* North American Free Trade Agreement.

Nagasaki, Japan, 584

napalm, 739, R61

Napoleon. *See* Bonaparte, Napoleon.

NASA. *See* National Aeronautics and Space Administration.

NASDAQ. *See* National Association of Securities Dealers Automated Quotation System.

Nasser, Gamal Abdel, 625

Nast, Thomas, 269

Nation, Carry, *i* 307

National Aeronautics and Space Administration (NASA), 681, 879

National American Woman Suffrage Association (NAWSA), 316, 332, 335 , R61

National Association for the Advancement of Colored People (NAACP), 288, 291, 325, 335–336, 453, R61

National Association of Colored Women (NACW), 315, R61

National Association of Securities Dealers Automated Quotation System (NASDAQ), 871, R61

national bank. *See* Bank of the United States; Second Bank of the United States.

National Child Labor Committee, 310

National Council of Indian Opportunity, 771

national debt, 75, *c* 76, 835–836, 862, R43

National Energy Act, 813, R61

National Farm Workers Association, 770

National Housing Act, 492

National Industrial Recovery Act (NIRA), 491–492, 499, R61

nationalism, 116, 373, 528, *m* 530, R61

National Labor Relations Act (Wagner Act), 499, *c* 500, 502–503, 507, R65

National Labor Relations Board (NLRB), 499, 500, 502, 517, R61

National Labor Union (NLU), 245

National Organization for Women (NOW), 778, R61

National Origins Act, 691

National Park System. *See also* Yellowstone National Park; Yosemite National Park.
    establishment of, 323

National Reclamation Act, 256, 289, 323–324

National Recovery Administration (NRA), 492, *c* 500

National Republican Party, 123

National Security Council, 853

National Trades' Union, 143, R61

National War Labor Board, 389

National Youth Administration (NYA), 499, *i* 499, *c* 500, 505, R61

*Nation at Risk, A*, 841

Nation of Islam, 719–720, R61

Native Americans, 4–5, 6, 71, 114, 216, 224, 231, 260, 288, 313, 844, 886–887. *See also* names of specific individuals and peoples.
    ancient cultures of, 4–5, *i* 6, 260
    assimilation of, 206–207, 662–663, 771
    buffalo and, 203, 207
    colonial Americans and, 23, 25–26, 37, 38, 39, 53, 428
    diseases and, 15, 26, 39
    education of, 772–773, 887
    in 1400s, *i* 2–3, 6, *m* 7, 8–9
    French and, 37, 39
    horses and, 203
    land claims of, 67, 77, *m* 204, 507, 772–773, 887
    land use of, 8, 25, 203, 428
    New Deal and, 507
    religious beliefs of, 7, 8, 203
    removal of, 124, 428
    in Revolutionary War, 59, 61, 63
    social organization of, 8
    Spanish and, 14–15, 16, 18–20
    struggle for rights of, 105, 662–663, 771–773, 886–887
    trading networks of, *m* 7, 8
    westward expansion and, 39, 77, 131, 203–204, 428
    white settlers and, *i* 200–201
    World War II and, 564, 579, *i* 579

nativism, 161, 258–259, 412, 414–415, R61

NATO. *See* North Atlantic Treaty Organization.

Navajo, *i* 132, 579, *i* 579

Navigation Acts, 28, 30, R61

Navy, U.S., 113, 169, 343, 348, 383, 570, 579, 735

NAWSA. *See* National American Woman Suffrage Association.

Nazism and Nazis, *i* 526–527, 530, 543, 545, R61. *See also* Germany; Nuremberg trials; World War II.

Nebraska, 160, 215
    facts about, R49

Nehru, Jawaharlal, 614, *i* 614

Netherlands, the, 540

Neutrality Acts, 535, 550, R61

Nevada, 137, 847
    facts about, R49

New Amsterdam, 26

New Deal, 488–494, 506–507, R61. *See also* Great Depression.
    agencies of, *c* 500
    banking relief, 490
    Civilian Conservation Corps in, 491, *i* 491, 505, 519
    Civil Works Administration in, 488, *i* 488, 491
    effects of, 488–493, 495–496, 498–499, *c* 500, 501, 503, 504–509, 518
    effects on state governments, 491, 492, 493, 499, 502–503, 518
    Fair Labor Standards Act and, 499, 518
    farmers under, 491, 496, 498, 518
    Federal Deposit Insurance Corporation, 490, 517, 518
    Hundred Days, 489
    labor unions and, 502–503, 507–509

National Labor Relations Act and, 499, 518

National Recovery Administration and, 492, 499

opposition to, 493–494, 516

Public Utilities Holding Company Act and, 501

Public Works Administration and, 491

Second, 495–501

Securities and Exchange Commission, 490, 518, R45

Social Security system and, 501, 518

Supreme Court and, 493, 496, 499

Tennessee Valley Authority and, 519, m 520–521

women and, 504–505

Works Progress Administration and, 498–499, 512–513

**New Deal Coalition,** 507, R61

**"New Democrats,"** 861

**New England,** 59, 60, 121

colonies in, 24–26, m 25, c 29, m 29, 34, 35, 50

**New Federalism,** 795, R61

**New France,** 37

**New Frontier,** 679, R61

**New Hampshire,** 25

facts about, R49

**New Jersey,** 26, 101, 423

facts about, R49

**New Jersey Plan,** 68

**Newlands Act.** *See* National Reclamation Act.

**New Left,** 744, R61

**Newman, Pauline,** 248–249

**New Mexico,** 18, 136, 137, 157, 160

facts about, R49

Mexican province of, 131, 135, 136

Spanish settlement of, 18, 20, 203

***New Negro, The*** (Locke), 454

**New Netherland,** 26

**New Orleans, Louisiana,** 38, 77, 170

**New Orleans, Battle of,** 114

**New Right,** 779, 780, 831, R61

**New South,** 797

**New Spain,** 18, 20

**newspapers,** 279, 294–295, 346, 347, 447

**New Sweden,** 26

**Newton, Huey,** 720

**Newton, Isaac,** 34–35

**New York,** 26, 34, 60, 95, 249, 847

**New York City,** 120, 140, 141, 209, 232, 249, 264, 265, 276, 277, 288, 318, 435, 509

colonial, 26, 33, 47

draft riot in, 173

facts about, R49

immigrants in, i 143, 262, 263, m 263

political machines and, 268, 269

in Revolutionary War, 59, 60, 62

tenements in, 262, 264

terrorism in, 862, 863, US2–4, i US4, US5, m US5

urban planning and, 277–278

**New York Stock Exchange,** 467, 468, i 468, R45

**Nez Perce,** 150, 208

**Ngo Dinh Diem,** 732, 734

**Niagara Falls Conference,** i 324, 325

**Niagra Movement,** 285, R61

**Nicaragua,** 360, 362–363, 851–852

**Nicholas II (czar of Russia),** 360

**Nimitz, Chester,** 579

***Niña,*** 14

**Nineteenth Amendment,** 64, 101, 105, 335, R61

**Ninth Amendment,** 70, 97

**NIRA.** *See* National Industrial Recovery Act.

**Nixon, Richard M.,** 91, 639–640, i 640, 746, 753, i 792–793, i 794, 800, 803–804, R52

"Checkers speech" of, 639–640

civil rights and, 796–797

détente and, 799, 815

environment and, 821–822

foreign policy of, 799–801, 815

impeachment and, 806, 807

New Federalism and, 795

pardon of, 810, 811

resignation of, 806–807, i 807

SALT I Treaty and, 800–801

Saturday Night Massacre and, 805–806

Southern strategy of, 796–797, R64

stagflation and, 798–799

Vietnam War and, 754–758, 794, 796

visit to China of, 800–801, i 800

Watergate scandal and, 623, i 623, 802–807

welfare reform and, 795

**NLRB.** *See* National Labor Relations Board.

***NLRB* v. *Jones and Laughlin Steel Corp.,*** 502–503

**NLU.** *See* National Labor Union.

**Nobel Peace Prize,** 360

**nonaggression pact,** 539, R61

**Noonan, Peggy,** 830, i 830

**Nootka,** 6

**Noriega, Manuel,** 852

**Normandy invasion,** 574

**North, Frederick,** 48, 49

**North, Oliver,** 853

**North Africa,** 9

in World War II, 572, m 572

**North American Free Trade Agreement (NAFTA),** 864, i 864, R61

**North Atlantic Treaty Organization (NATO),** 608, i 608, 624, m 624, 863, R46, R61

**North Carolina,** 28, 32, 52, 104, 169, 706

facts about, R49

**North Dakota,** 474

facts about, R49

**Northern colonies,** 30, 33–34. *See also* middle colonies; New England, colonies in.

**Northern Pacific Railroad,** 221

**Northern Securities Company,** 319

***North Star, The,*** 146

**Northwest Coast, Native Americans of,** 6, m 7

**Northwest Ordinance of 1787,** 67, 72, 167, R61

**Northwest Territory,** 67, m 72, 77, 130

**notes, using,** 42, 80, 152, 190, 226, 250, 272, 300, 338, 369, 406, 430, 460, 522, 558, 598, 630, 664, 696, 726, 764, 788, 826, 856, 890

**note-taking.** *See* taking notes.

**Novello, Antonia Coello,** 844, i 844

**NOW.** *See* National Organization for Women.

**NRA.** *See* National Recovery Administration.

**nuclear energy,** 822, 824–825

**Nuclear Regulatory Commission,** 824

**nuclear weapons,** 622, 623–624, 670, 678, 849

Limited Test Ban Treaty and, 678, R60

**nullification,** 79, 124, 125, 128, R61

**Nuremberg Laws,** 543

**Nuremberg trials,** 586–587, i 586, R61

**NYA.** *See* National Youth Administration.

**Nye, Gerald,** 534

## O

**Oakley, Annie,** 211

**oba,** 9

**Obregón, Alvaro,** 365

**O'Brien, Tim,** 736, 763

**Ochoa, Ellen,** 879

**O'Connor, Sandra Day,** i 93, 836

**Oettinger, Hank,** 488

**Office of Alien Property,** 421

**Office of Economic Opportunity,** 796

**Office of Price Administration (OPA),** 567, 635, R61

**Office of Scientific Research and Development (OSRD),** 567

**Oglethorpe, James,** 28

**Ohio,** 73, 77, 131, 231

facts about, R49

**Ohio gang,** 420, R61

**Ohio River,** 37, 165

**oil,** 231, m 231, 243

in Alaska, 822

energy crisis and, 812–813

Organization of Petroleum Exporting Countries and, 799, 811

Persian Gulf War and, 853–854

in Texas, 230, 231, 813

**O'Keeffe, Georgia,** 450

**Okinawa,** 583

**Oklahoma,** 18, 215

facts about, R49

**Olmec culture,** 5

**Olive Branch Petition,** 51, 52

**Oliver, Joe "King,"** 456

**Olmsted, Frederick Law,** 277

**Omaha, Nebraska,** 215, 221

**Omaha Beach,** 574, i 575

**Onís, Luis de,** 116

***On the Road*** (Kerouac), 655

**OPA.** *See* Office of Price Administration.

**OPEC.** *See* Organization of Petroleum Exporting Countries.

**Open Door notes,** 356, 357, 359, R61

**Open Door policy,** 356, 357

**open-hearth process,** 232

**Operation Desert Storm,** 855, R61

**Operation Overlord,** 574

**Operation Rolling Thunder,** 735

**Operation Torch,** 572

opinions, forming. *See* forming opinions.
**Oppenheimer, J. Robert,** 583
**oral presentations, creating,** R36
**Oregon,** 131, 208
  facts about, R49
**Oregon Territory,** 116, *m* 116, 133
**Oregon Trail,** 131, *m* 132, 150,
  *m* 150–151, R62
*Organization Man, The* (Whyte), 643
**Organization of Petroleum Exporting**
  **Countries (OPEC),** 799, 811, 813,
  R62
*Origin of Species, On The* (Darwin), 242
**Orlando, Vittorio,** 399
**Ortega, Daniel,** 852
**Oswald, Lee Harvey,** 683
**Osage,** 203
**OSRD.** *See* Office of Scientific Research
  and Development.
*Other America, The* (Harrington), 681
**Ottoman Empire,** 374, *m* 375
**outline, creating a,** R35, R36

## P

**Paine, Thomas,** 52
painting. *See* art.
**Pakistan,** US11
**Palestinians,** 816, US7–8
**Palmer, A. Mitchell,** 413
**Palmer raids,** 413
**Panama,** 360–361, 367, 815, 852
**Panama Canal,** 353, 359, *i* 359, 360–361,
  *i* 361, 366–367, *m* 366–367, 815,
  R62
**panic of 1837,** 127, 131
**panic of 1873,** 189
**panic of 1893,** 221–222, 240, 248
**Pankhurst, Emmeline,** 335, *i* 335
**Paris, Treaty of,** R65
  of 1763, 38
  of 1783, 62, 63
  of 1898, 350–351, 353, 355
**parity,** 518, R62
**Parker, Dorothy,** 450
**Parks, Gordon,** 464, *i* 464
**Parks, Rosa,** 291, *i* 291, 704, *i* 704
**Parliament (British),** 26, 28, 47, 49, 51, 55
**Parrish, Essie,** 4, *i* 4
**participation, political,** 744–746, 756–757.
  *See also* lobbying; Vietnam War,
  protests against; voting rights.
  of minorities, 64–65,105, 148–149,
  286–288, 314–316, 332, 334–335,
  637, 715–716
  Supreme Court and, 775, 844
**Paterson, William,** 68
*Pathfinder,* 879
**Patman, Wright,** 482
**Patman Bill,** 482
**Patriots, in Revolutionary War,** 59, 60, R62
**patronage,** 270, R62
**Patrons of Husbandry.** *See* Grange.
patterns, analyzing. *See* analyzing patterns.
patterns, geographic. *See* geographic
  patterns.
**Patton, George S.,** 574
**Paul, Alice,** 332, 335
**Payne-Aldrich Tariff,** 329, 330, R62

**Peace Corps,** 680, *i* 680, R62
**Pearl Harbor,** 344, 555–557, *i* 555, *i* 556,
  *m* 556, *i* 560–561, 562, 578, 579
**Peck, James,** 710, *i* 710
**Pendergast, James "Big Jim,"** 268
**Pendleton Civil Service Act,** 270–271, R62
**Penn, William,** 26, 28
**Pennsylvania,** 26, 28, 60, 104, 176, 822, 866
  facts about, R49
**Pentagon Papers,** 757, R62
**People's Party.** *See* Populist Party.
**Peralta, Pedro de,** 18
*perestroika,* 849, R62
**Perkins, Frances,** 501, 504–505, *i* 505
**Perot, H. Ross,** 861, 865
**Pershing, John J.,** 364–365, 384, *i* 384, 386
**Persian Gulf War,** 853, *m* 854, 855, 861
**Personal Responsibility and Work**
  **Opportunity Act,** 907
perspective, developing historical. *See*
  historical perspective, developing.
**Pétain, Philippe,** 540
**petroleum-based product,** 231. *See also* oil;
  gasoline.
**Philadelphia, Pennsylvania,** 60, 61, 435,
  509, 839, 843
  colonial, 33, 34, 47, 49
**Philadelphia and Reading Railroad,** 221
**Philippine-American War,** 355, *i* 355
**Philippines**
  independence of, 355
  rebellion in, 355
  in Spanish-American War, 349
  as Spanish colony, 346, 349
  U.S. annexation of, 350–351, 355
  war with U.S., 355, *i* 355
  World War II and, *i* 578, 579, 581
**Photography**
  inventions in, 281
  journalism and, 178, 311, 497, 582,
  713, 757
**Pierce, Franklin,** 137, 161, R51
**Pilgrims,** 24
**Pinchot, Gifford,** 323, 328, *i* 328, 329
**Pinckney, Thomas,** 77
**Pinckney Treaty,** 77
**Pingree, Hazen,** 310
**Pinkerton Detective Agency,** 247–248
*Pinta,* 14
**Pitt, William,** 38
**Pitcher, Molly.** *See* Hays, Mary Ludwig.
**Pittsburgh, Pennsylvania,** 231, *m* 231
**Pizarro, Francisco,** 17, 18
**place,** xxx, 17, 38, 59, 62, 116, 125, 134,
  159, 160, 170, 209, 263, 375, 386,
  423, 572, 575, 594, 613
**Plains Indians,** *m* 7
  battles with, 204, *m* 205, 206,
  207–208
  culture of, 202–203
  restriction of, 204, 207–208
**Plains of Abraham,** 38
**planned obsolescence,** 648, R62
plantation. *See* agriculture.
**Platt Amendment,** 354, R62
**Plessy, Homer A.,** 290
*Plessy* v. *Ferguson,* 287, 290–291, 701,
  702–703, 708–709, R62

points of view. *See* historical perspective,
  developing.
**Poland,** 604–605, 849
  in World War II, 538, 539, *i* 539, 542,
  551, 576
political cartoons, analyzing. *See* analyzing
  political cartoons.
**political machines,** 267–268, R62
**Polk, James K.,** 135–136, R50
**poll tax,** 102, 287, 637, 716, R62
**pollution**
  of air, 824
  automobiles and, 881
  DDT and, 821
  industrial, 234–235, 820
  Love Canal and, 820
**Polo, Marco,** 12
**Ponca,** 313
**Ponce de León, Juan,** *m* 17, 18
**Pontiac,** 39
**Popé,** 20
**popular American culture,** 298–299,
  444–445, 658–659, 786–787,
  808–809. *See also* art, literature,
  motion pictures, music, radio,
  television.
  impact on world culture, 299, R63
**popular sovereignty,** 157, 160, 163, R62
**population.** *See also* migration.
  changes, effects of, 591, 846–847, 434
  growth, 591
  shifts in, 591, 846–847
**Populism,** 221, R62
**Populist Party,** 221, 222, 223
**Port Hudson, Louisiana,** 170, 179
**Portsmouth, Treaty of,** 360
**Portugal,** 10, 11, 13, 15, 116–117
posing questions. *See* questions, posing.
**Post Office, U.S.,** 297
**Potomac, Army of the,** 175, *i* 178, 179
**Potomac River,** 171, 176
**Potsdam conference,** 604
**Pound, Ezra,** 451
**poverty,** 266, 660–661, 681, 688, *c* 723,
  842, *c* R43
**Powell, Colin,** 848, *i* 848
**Powers, Francis Gary,** 626–627, *i* 627
**Powhatan,** 23
**pow wow,** *i* 6
**predicting effects,** 124, 26, 30, 117, 131,
  261, 331, 427, 557, 671, 845, 878,
  885, 890, R20
  of legislation, 862, 878, R20
**predictions, making,** R20
**Prescott, Samuel,** 50
**presentations, creating,** 43, 153, 213, 273,
  339, 397, 408, 523, 552, 665, 727,
  857, 891
  oral, 108, 109, 167, 198, 369, 709,
  857, R36
  visual, 225, R37
  written, 108, 109, 725, R34–35
**president,** 69, 78, 85, 87, 90–92. *See also*
  *names of specific presidents.*
**Presidential Commission on the Status of**
  **Women,** 777
**Presley, Elvis,** 656, *i* 656
**Preuss, Charles,** 150

716, 731, 735, 743, 755, 761, R11, R19

**Szilard, Leo,** 585

# ACKNOWLEDGMENTS

## TEXT ACKNOWLEDGMENTS

**CHAPTER 5, page 225:** Excerpt from "El Corrido de Gregorio Cortez," from *With His Pistol in His Hands: A Border Ballad and Its Hero* by Américo Paredes. Copyright © 1958, renewed 1986. Reprinted by permission of the author and the University of Texas Press.

**CHAPTER 7, page 257:** Excerpt from "The Reminiscences of Edward Ferro," from *I Was Dreaming to Come to America: Memories from the Ellis Island Oral History Project*, page 24. Selected and illustrated by Veronica Lawlor; forward by Rudolph W. Giuliani. Copyright © 1995 by Viking.

**CHAPTER 13, page 459:** "First Fig," from *Collected Poems* by Edna St. Vincent Millay, published by HarperCollins. Copyright © 1922, 1950 by Edna St. Vincent Millay. Reprinted by permission of Elizabeth Barnett, literary executor.

"Dream Variations," from *The Collected Poems of Langston Hughes* by Langston Hughes. Copyright © 1994 by the Estate of Langston Hughes. Used be permission of Alfred A. Knopf, a division of Random House, Inc.

**CHAPTER 14, pages 473, 483:** Excerpts from "A. Everette McIntyre" and "Herman Shumlin," from *Hard Times* by Studs Terkel. Copyright © 1970. Reprinted by permission of Donadio & Olson, Inc.

**CHAPTER 15, page 513:** Excerpt from "Dust Bowl Refugee," words and music by Woody Guthrie. Copyright © 1960 (renewed) and 1963 (renewed) by Ludlow Music, Inc., New York, New York. Used by permission.

**CHAPTER 16, page 542:** Excerpt from Gerda Weissmann Klein's interview in the film *One Survivor Remembers*, a production of Home Box Office and the United States Holocaust Museum. By permission of Gary Greenberg for Gerda Weissmann Klein.

**CHAPTER 17, page 562:** Excerpts from "Wife's Recorded Message Made Many Long for Home," from *We Pulled Together . . . and Won!* by Charles Swanson (Reminisce Books). Reprinted by permission of the Estate of Charles Swanson.

**CHAPTER 18, page 628:** Excerpt from *The Body Snatchers* by Jack Finney. Copyright © 1955 by Jack Finney. Copyright © renewed 1983 by Jack Finney. Reprinted by permission of Don Congdon Associates.

**page 629:** Excerpt from *The Martian Chronicles* by Ray Bradbury. Copyright © 1945 by Street and Smith. Copyright © renewed 1972 by Ray Bradbury. Reprinted by permission of Don Congdon Associates.

**CHAPTER 22, page 739:** Excerpt from *Dear America: Letters Home from Vietnam*, edited by Bernard Edelman for the New York Vietnam Veterans Memorial Commission. Published in 1985 by W. W. Norton & Company. Copyright © 1985 by the New York Vietnam Veterans Memorial Commission. Reprinted by permission of Bernard Edelman.

**page 745:** Excerpt from "Eve of Destruction," words and music by P. F. Sloan. Copyright © 1965 by Duchess Music Corporation. Sole selling agent MCA Music Publishing, a division of MCA Inc. International copyright secured. All rights reserved. Excerpt from "Ballad of the Green Berets" by Barry Sadler. Reprinted by permission of Estaboga Music.

**Page 762:** Excerpt from *Going After Cacciato* by Tim O'Brien. Copyright © 1978 by Tim O'Brien. Reprinted by permission of Dell Publishing, a division of Random House, Inc.

**Page 763:** Excerpt from *A Rumor of War* by Philip Caputo. Copyright © 1977 by Philip Caputo. Reprinted by permission of Henry Holt and Company, L.L.C. Excerpt from *Fallen Angels* by Walter Dean Myers. Copyright © 1988 by Walter Dean Myers. Used by permission of Scholastic. Hardcover, a trademark of Scholastic, Inc.

**CHAPTER 25, page 846:** "Migration Patterns: Where Americans Are Going," from *Regional Growth and Decline in the United States*. Copyright © 1985 by Bernard L. Weinstein, Harold T. Gross, and John Rees. Reprinted by permission of Bernard L. Weinstein, University of North Texas, Denton, Texas.

**CHAPTER 26, page 860:** Excerpt from "On the Pulse of the Morning" by Maya Angelou. Copyright © 1993 by Maya Angelou. Used by permission of Random House, Inc.

**page 874:** "Choices," from *Cotton Candy on a Rainy Day* by Nikki Giovanni. Copyright © 1978 by Nikki Giovanni. Used by permission of HarperCollins Publishers, Inc.

**page 875:** Excerpt from *The Joy Luck Club* by Amy Tan. Copyright © 1989 by Amy Tan. Used by permission of G. P. Putnam's Sons, a division of Penguin Putnam, Inc. "Four Skinny Trees," from *The House on Mango Street* by Sandra Cisneros. Copyright © 1984 by Sandra Cisneros. Published by Vintage Books, a division of Random House, Inc., and in hardcover by Alfred A. Knopf. Reprinted by permission of Susan Bergholz Literary Services, New York. All rights reserved.

McDougal Littell Inc. has made every effort to locate the copyright holders for selections used in this book and to make full acknowledgment for their use. Omissions brought to our attention will be corrected in a subsequent edition.

## ART CREDITS

### COVER AND FRONTISPIECE

**Jane Addams:** Copyright © Bettmann/Corbis
**Ben Nighthorse Campbell:** AP/Wide World Photos
**César Chávez:** Copyright © 1990 Lisa Quinones/Black Star/PNI
**Lyndon B. Johnson:** Copyright © Corbis
**Barbara Jordan:** AP/Wide World Photos
**Martin Luther King, Jr.:** Copyright © Flip Schulke/Black Star
**Gerda Weissman Klein:** Photograph by Scott Wachter, courtesy of Gerda Weissman Klein/HBO
**Queen Liliuokalani:** The Granger Collection, New York
**Maya Lin:** Copyright © 1993 Richard Howard/Black Star/PNI

**Sandra Day O'Connor:** Copyright © Roger Ressmeyer/Corbis
**Ronald Reagan:** Copyright © Bettmann/Corbis
**Franklin Delano Roosevelt:** Hulton Archive by Getty Images

**Maps:** MapQuest.com, Inc.
7, 17, 22, 25, 29, 38, 59, 62, 72, 73, 115, 116, 125, 132, 134, 136, 150, 159, 160, 170, 176, 179, 205, 209, 231, 234, 239, 255, 263, 278, 323, 331, 345, 349, 356, 366, 375, 386, 400, 416, 423, 449, 455, 474, 521, 530, 532, 538, 556, 572, 575, 580, 591, 594, 605, 611, 613, 624, 625, 638, 650, 675, 677, 685, 688, 701, 733, 749, 753, 775, 815, 816, 833, 846, 847, 851, 854, 866, 872, 885, R25, R26

The presidential seal is used throughout by permission of The Office of the Counsel to the President, The White House, Washington, D.C. Photo provided by The Granger Collection, New York.

**vi** *top to bottom* The Granger Collection, New York; *Battle of Lexington* (c. 1850), Alonzo Chappel. Photograph Copyright © Bettmann/Corbis; Photograph by Richard Strauss, 1994. Collection of the Supreme Court Historical Society; **vii** *top to bottom* National Museum of American History, Smithsonian Institution [75-2348]; Matthew Brady Studio (1864), Hulton Archive by Getty Images; The Granger Collection, New York; **viii** *top to bottom, Portrait of a Sioux Man and Woman* (date unknown), Gertrude Käsebier. Photographic History Collection, National Museum of American History, Smithsonian Institution; National Museum of American History, Smithsonian Institution; Culver Pictures; **ix** *all* Copyright © Bettmann/Corbis; **x** *top to bottom* Culver Pictures; Beinecke Rare Book and Manuscript Library, Yale University; Underwood Photo Archives; **xi** *top to bottom* Courtesy of Gerda Weissman Klein; Copyright © Bettmann/Corbis; Courtesy of Republic Entertainment, Inc.; **xii** *top to bottom* Hulton Archive by Getty Images; Courtesy of Arthur L. Freeman; Copyright © 1995 Paul Fusco/Magnum Photos; **xiii** *top* cartoon by Tony Auth. Copyright © Universal Press Syndicate; *bottom* AP/Wide World Photos; **xiv** *top* Copyright © Bettmann/Corbis; *bottom* National Archives; **xvi** *top* Illustration by Matthew Pippin; *center* Panel no. 1: *During the World War There Was a Great Migration North by Southern Negroes*, from the Migration of the Negro mural series (1940–1941), Jacob Lawrence. Tempera on masonite, 12″ × 18″. Acquired through Downtown Gallery, 1942. The Phillips Collection, Washington, D.C.; *bottom* Joe Rosenthal AP/Wide World Photos; **xvii** *top* Copyright © Stock Montage; *bottom* Copyright © Seny Norasingh/Light Sensitive; **xviii** Dale Atkins AP/Wide World Photos; **xix** The Granger Collection, New York; **xx** *top* from *Puerto Rico: A Political and Cultural History*, Arturo Morales Carrion; *bottom* Copyright © The Dorothea Lange Collection, Oakland Museum of California, City of Oakland. Gift of Paul S. Taylor; **xxi** *top* Hulton Archive by Getty Images; *bottom* Copyright © Flip Schulke/Black Star; **xxii** *top* Copyright © Donald J. Weber; *bottom* Copyright © 1993 Jim Stratford/Black Star; **xxiv** Copyright © UPI/Corbis-Bettmann; **xxv** National Archives; **xxviii** *top* National Aeronautics and Space Administration; *bottom* Copyright © Reuters NewMedia Inc./ CORBIS; **xxix** *top* The Granger Collection, New York; *center* H. Armstrong Roberts; *bottom* Photo by Howard Sochurek/*Life* Magazine. Copyright © Time, Inc.; **xxx** Copyright © 1991 Woodward Payne.

**Chapter 1**
**1** *across Signing of the Constitution*, Howard Chandler Christy. Art Resource, New York; **2–3** *across* The Granger Collection, New York; **2** *bottom left* Copyright © Nik Wheeler/Corbis; *bottom right* Museo del Templo Mayor, Mexico City, D.F., Mexico, Michel Zabé/Art Resource, New York; **3** *bottom left, The Mayflower in Plymouth Harbor* (late 19th century) William Halsall. Copyright © Burstein Collection/Corbis; *bottom right* Copyright © Bettmann/Corbis; **4** *top right* Copyright © Library of Congress/Corbis; *center right* Phoebe A. Hearst Museum of Anthropology, University of California at Berkeley; **5** *top* Courtesy Arizona State Museum, University of Arizona, Tucson, Arizona. Photograph Copyright © 1996 Jerry Jacka; *bottom* Reconstruction of the Valley of the Valley of Mexico, Lake Texcoco, and Great Tenochtitlan. Museum of Mexico City. Copyright © C. Lenars/Photo Researchers; **6** Copyright © Mike Zens/Corbis; **7** *top* Hulton Getty/Getty News Services; *center left* Edward S. Curtis, 1900. Copyright © Corbis; *center right* Copyright © Nathan Benn-Corbis; **8** Copyright © Stock Montage; **10** The Granger Collection, New York; **11** *June* from *Tres Riches Hueres du Duc de Berry* (early 15th century), Limbourg Brothers. Musée Conde, Chantilly, France. Giraudon/Art Resource, New York; **12** Matthew Pippin; **14** *top right* Copyright © Library of Congress/Corbis; *center right, Portrait of a Man Called Christopher Columbus* (1519), Sebastiano del Piombo. Oil on canvas, 42″ × 34¾″. The Metropolitan Museum of Art, New York. Gift of J. Pierpont Morgan, 1900. Copyright © 1979 The Metropolitan Museum of Art; **16, 17** *inset* Copyright © The Granger Collection, New York; **19** *bottom left* Copyright © Ted Streshinsky/Corbis; *bottom right* Illustration by Lawrence Ormsby. Reprinted by permission from *Spanish Colonial Missions* by Gloria Giffords. Published by Southwest Parks and Monuments Association. Copyright © 1988; **21** *top right* Copyright © Library of Congress/Corbis; *center left* The Granger Collection, New York; **22** *top right, top inset* Courtesy of the Association for the Preservation of Virginia Antiquities; *bottom* Hulton Getty/Getty News Services; **24** Pilgrim Society, Plymouth, Massachusetts; **27** Matthew Pippin **31** *top right* Copyright © Library of Congress/Corbis; *center right* Copyright © Taylor Lewis. Courtesy Catherine Fallin, Kerhonkson, New York; **32** Library of Congress, Prints and Photographs Division [LC-USZ62-44000]; **33** The Granger Collection, New York; **34** *left* Photograph by John Chew. Courtesy of Cliveden of the National Trust; *right* Copyright © Lee Snider/Corbis; **35** The Granger Collection, New York; **36** *left, Benjamin Franklin* (c. 1785), Joseph Siffred Duplessis. Oil on canvas, 28½″ × 23½″. National Portrait Gallery, Smithsonian Institution, gift of the Morris and Gwendolyn Cafritz Foundation/Art Resource, New York; **36** *right,* **37** The Granger Collection, New York; **40** *bottom left, Celebrating Couple: General Jackson and His Lady* (date unknown), Reverend H. Young. Pen and watercolor, 10¼″ × 7⅝″. Courtesy, Museum of Fine Arts, Boston, gift of Maxim Karolik; **40–41** *across,* **41** *top* Abby Aldrich Rockefeller Folk Art Center, Williamsburg, Virginia; **41** *bottom* Library of Congress, Prints and Photographs Division [LC-USZ62-33939]; **43** Copyright © Corbis.

**Chapter 2**
**44–45** *across* The Granger Collection, New York; **44** *bottom left* Copyright © Leonard de Selva/Corbis; *bottom right* Copyright © Leif Skoogfors/Corbis; **45** *bottom center* Engraving after Gilbert Stewart, 1789. Copyright © Corbis; *bottom* Copyright © Paul Almasy/Corbis; **46** *top right* Detail of *Washington Crossing The Delaware* (1851), Emanuel Gottlieb Leutze. Photograph Copyright © Bettmann/Corbis; *center right* Copyright © Stock Montage; **48** *top* Rare Books and Manuscripts Division, The New York Public Library, Astor, Lenox and Tilden Foundations; *bottom, The Boston Massacre (The Bloody Massacre)* (1770), Paul Revere. Hand-colored engraving, 10¼″ × 9⅛″. The Metropolitan Museum of Art, New York. Gift of Mrs. Russell Sage, 1909. Copyright © 1979 The Metropolitan Museum of Art, New York; **49** American Antiquarian Society; **50** *Battle of Lexington* (c. 1850), Alonzo Chappel. Photograph Copyright © Bettmann/Corbis; **51** *Attack on Bunker's Hill, with the Burning of Charles Town* (c. 1783), unknown artist. Oil on canvas, 23⅞″ × 30½″ × 1½″ framed. Copyright © 1996 Board of Trustees, National Gallery of Art, Washington, D.C. Gift of Edgar William and Bernice Chrysler Garbisch; **52** Library of Congress, Prints and Photographs Division [LC-USZ62-10658]; **54** *signature* National Archives; *portrait* The Granger Collection, New York; **55** Photograph by Sharon Hoogstraten; **56** Massachusetts Historical Society; **57** *top* Photograph by Sharon Hoogstraten; *signature, top* The Granger Collection, New York; *other signatures* National Archives; *center right* Copyright © Bettmann/Corbis;

**58** *top right* Detail of *Washington Crossing The Delaware* (1851), Emanuel Gottlieb Leutze. Photograph Copyright © Bettmann/Corbis; *center right* Collection of Mrs. Jackson C. Boswell, Arlington, Virginia. Courtesy of the Frick Art Reference Library; **59** *top, bottom* David Kamerman; **60** The Granger Collection, New York; **61** *Molly Pitcher at the Battle of Monmouth,* (1854) Dennis Malone Carter. Oil on canvas, 42″ × 56″. Gift of Herbert P. Whitlock, 1913. Courtesy of Fraunces Tavern Museum, New York City; **63** Image by courtesy of the Trustees of the Wedgwood Museum, Barlaston, Staffordshire, England **64** *top, Governor and Mrs. Mifflin,* J.S. Copley. The Historical Society of Pennsylvania; *center left* Courtesy of Seneca Falls (New York) Historical Society; **64–65** *across* The Granger Collection, New York; **65** *top* Photograph by Sharon Hoogstraten; *top right* Copyright © Reuters NewMedia Inc./Corbis; **66** *top right* Detail of *Washington Crossing The Delaware* (1851), Emanuel Gottlieb Leutze. Photograph Copyright © Bettmann/Corbis; *center right* Detail of *John Dickinson* (c. 1835), James Barton Longacre, after Charles Wilson Peale. Sepia watercolor on artist board, $11\frac{5}{8}'' \times 8\frac{7}{8}''$. National Portrait Gallery, Smithsonian Institution/Art Resource, New York; **68, 70, 71** The Granger Collection, New York; **72** Copyright © Stone; **73** *Township VII, Range XIV, Ohio Company* (1787), Rufus Putnam. Clements Library, University of Michigan; **74** *top right* Detail of *Washington Crossing The Delaware* (1851), Emanuel Gottlieb Leutze. Photograph Copyright © Bettmann/Corbis; *center right* The Granger Collection, New York; **75** *left, Alexander Hamilton* (c. 1796), James Sharples, the elder. Pastel on paper. National Portrait Gallery, Smithsonian Institution/Art Resource, New York; *right* Copyright © Bettmann/Corbis; **76** *Taking of the Bastille, 14 July 1789* (late 1700s), unknown artist, Chateau Versailles, France. Giraudon/Art Resource, New York; **77** Copyright © Bettmann/Corbis; **78** The Granger Collection, New York; **80** *top, bottom* David Kamerman; **81** Library of Congress, Prints and Photographs Division [LC-USZ62-9487] **82** The Granger Collection, New York; **83** Bettmann/Corbis; **92** *top* Joe Marquette/AP/Wide World Photos; *bottom* The Granger Collection, New York; **93** Photograph by Richard Strauss, 1994. Collection of the Supreme Court Historical Society; **97** *The Federal Edifice: On the Erection of the Eleventh Pillar,* cartoon from *The Massachusetts Centinel,* August 2, 1788. Courtesy of the New-York Historical Society, New York City; **99** HWG/AP/Wide World Photos; **100** Copyright © Bettmann/Corbis; **103** AP/Wide World Photos; **104** *left* Copyright © Bettmann/Corbis; *right* Detail of *Daniel Boardman* (1789), Ralph Earl. Oil on canvas, $81\frac{5}{8}'' \times 55\frac{1}{4}''$. Copyright © 1996, Board of Trustees, National Gallery of Art, Washington, D.C. Gift of Mrs. W. Murray Crane; **105** *top* FPG International; *bottom* AP/Wide World Photos; **106** The Granger Collection, New York; **107** from *Straight Herblock* (Simon & Schuster, 1964); **108** *top* Photograph by Sharon Hoogstraten; *bottom* Copyright © David Young-Wolff/PhotoEdit; **109** Copyright © Photo Edit.

**Chapter 3**

**110–111** *across,* **110** *bottom left, bottom center* Copyright © Bettmann/Corbis; *bottom right* Library of Congress, Prints and Photographs Division [LC-USZ62-116232]; **111** *bottom left* Copyright © Bettmann/Corbis; *bottom center* Copyright © Corbis; *bottom right* The Granger Collection, New York; **112** *top right* Undated colored woodcut by F. O. C. Darley. Copyright © Bettmann/Corbis; *center right* Courtesy of Mrs. V. James Taranik; **113** Detail of *John Marshall, Chief Justice of the United States* (c. 1832), William James Hubard, National Portrait Gallery, Smithsonian Institution/Art Resource, New York; **115** *top left* US Mint/AP/Wide World Photos; *top right, Mandan Village* (c. 1834), Karl Bodmer. From *Travels in the Interior of North America* by Maximilian Prince zu Wied. Yale Collection of Western Americana, Beinecke Rare Book and Manuscript Library, Yale University; *bottom left* American Philosophical Society Library; *bottom right* National Museum of American History, Smithsonian Institution [75-2348]; **117** Copyright © Bettmann/Corbis; **118** *Portrait of Chief Justice John Marshall,* Rembrandt Peale. Courtesy of the Supreme Court of the United States; **119** *Portrait of Chief Justice William Marbury* (c. 1820–1830), Rembrandt Peale. Photographer: Vic Boswell, National Geographic Society. Courtesy of the Supreme Court of the United States; **120** *top right* Undated colored woodcut by F.O.C. Darley. Copyright © Bettmann/Corbis; *center right, Telegraph,* James Bard, The Mariners' Museum; **121** National Museum of American History, Smithsonian Institution, [73-11287]; **123** *top, Portrait of Andrew Jackson, 1767–1845, Seventh President of the United States* (1820), James Barton Longacre. Hand-colored stipple engraving, 37.2 cm × 30 cm. National Portrait Gallery, Smithsonian Institution/Art Resource, New York; *bottom* The Granger Collection, New York; **124** *The Trail of Tears,* Troy Anderson/Sun Valley Photography; **125** *top left* Smithsonian Institution; *top right* The Granger Collection, New York; *bottom* Detail of *Trail of Tears* (date unknown), Robert Lindneux, Woolaroc Museum, Bartlesville, Oklahoma; **126** Library of Congress, Prints and Photographs Division [LC-USZ62-1562]; **128** *bottom left* The Granger Collection, New York; *center* The Library Company of Philadelphia; **128–129** *top across* Copyright © Bettmann/Corbis; **129** Copyright © 1957 Burt Glinn/Magnum Photos; **130** *top right* Undated colored woodcut by F. O. C. Darley. Copyright © Bettmann/Corbis; **131** Courtesy, Colorado Historical Society; **132** *top* National Archives; *bottom left* Edward S. Curtis (c. 1904), Library of Congress, Prints and Photographs Division [LC-USZ62-97089]; *bottom right* Edward S. Curtis (c. 1904)/Library of Congress, Prints and Photographs Division [LC-USZ62-103498]; **134** *inset* The Granger Collection, New York; **135** *top left* Copyright © Bettmann/Corbis; *top right* The Granger Collection, New York; **137** California State Library; **138** The Bancroft Library, University of California, Berkeley; **139** *top right* Undated colored woodcut by F. O. C. Darley. Copyright © Bettmann/Corbis; *center right* The Granger Collection, New York; **140** *bottom left* Courtesy of the Smithsonian Institution, Washington, D.C.; *bottom center* Copyright © H. Armstrong Roberts; **140** *bottom right,* **141** *bottom left* Copyright © UPI/Bettmann/Corbis; **141** *bottom center* Copyright © Charles E. Rotkin/Corbis; *bottom right* School Division, Houghton Mifflin Company; *bottom right, screen image* Martha Granger/EDGE Productions; **142** Jack Naylor Collection/PRC Archive; **143** The Granger Collection, New York; **144** *top right* Undated colored woodcut by F. O. C. Darley. Copyright © Bettmann/Corbis; *center right* Historical Society of Pennsylvania, Leon Gardiner Collection; **145** North Wind Picture Archives; **146** The Granger Collection, New York; **147** *top* Matthew Pippin; *inset* Collection of the New-York Historical Society, neg. 48169; **148, 149** The Granger Collection, New York; **150** *bottom left* Courtesy of the Smithsonian Institution; **150–151** *center across* National Archives; **151** *top* Idaho State Historical Society. Photograph number 1254-D-1; *bottom* Copyright © Ric Ergenbright Photography; **152** *bottom left* Courtesy of the Smithsonian Institution, Washington, D.C.; *bottom center* National Museum of American History, Smithsonian Institution [75-2348]; **152** *bottom right,* **153** The Granger Collection, New York.

**Chapter 4**

**154–155** *across* Engraving, 1859. Copyright © Corbis; **154** *bottom left, above time line* From the Collection of Edith Hariton/Antique Textile Resource. Picture Research Consultants and Archives; *bottom left, below time line* Copyright © Hulton-Deutsch Collection/Corbis; *bottom right* Copyright © Tria Giovan/Corbis; **155** *bottom* Copyright © Corbis; **156** *top right, Battle of Gettysburg* (1884). Color illustration. Copyright © Hulton Archive by Getty Images; *center right* Daguerreotype, Mathew Brady Studio, 1848–1849/The Granger Collection, New York; **157** The Granger Collection, New York; **159** C.T. Weber, 1893. Copyright © Bettmann/Corbis; **161, 162** The Granger Collection, New York; **163** *bottom left, Stephen Douglas* (c. 1860), Mathew Brady Studio. Photograph, albumen silver print, $3\frac{1}{8}'' \times 2\frac{1}{8}''$. National Portrait Gallery, Smithsonian Instiitution/Art Resource, New York; *bottom right* The Granger Collection, New York; **164** *John Brown Going to His Hanging* (1942), Horace Pippin. Oil on canvas, $24\frac{1}{8}'' \times 30\frac{1}{4}''$. Courtesy of the Museum of American Art of the Pennsylvania Academy of the Fine Arts, Philadelphia, Pennsylvania. John Lambert Fund; **166** Copyright © Bettmann/Corbis; **167** Library of Congress, Prints and Photographs Division [US-0989-46]; **168** *top right, Battle of Gettysburg* (1884). Color illustration. Copyright © Hulton Archive by Getty Images; *center right* Beverley R. Robinson Collection, United States Naval Academy Museum, Annapolis,


R110

Maryland. Accession number 51.7.667; **169** *top left* George Eastman House; *top right* Library of Congress, Prints and Photographs Division [LC-B8184-10374]; **171** The Granger Collection, New York; **172** *top left, Portrait of Abraham Lincoln,* (1864), William Willard, National Portrait Gallery, Smithsonian Institution/Art Resource, New York; *top right* Copyright © Bettmann/Corbis; **173** Mathew Brady Studio (1864). The Granger Collection, New York; **174** *top* The Granger Collection, New York; *bottom* Copyright © Tria Giovan/Corbis; **175** *top right, Battle of Gettysburg* (1884). Color illustration. Copyright © Hulton Archive by Getty Images; *center right, Mary Boykin Chesnut* (1854), Samuel Osgood. On loan from Serena Willliams Miles Van Rensselaer. National Portrait Gallery, Smithsonian Institution/Art Resource, New York; **178** *top* Mathew Brady Studio (1864). Copyright © Hulton Archive by Getty Images; *bottom* Mathew Brady Studio/Library of Congress, Prints and Photographs Division [LC-B8171-1214]; **180** *top left* Library of Congress, Prints and Photographs Division [LC-USZ62-115549]; *top right* Library of Congress, Prints and Photographs Division [504790 LC U5260-20244]; **181** Copyright © Tom Lovell/NGS Image Collection; **182** The Granger Collection, New York; **183** Illinois State Historical Library; **184** *top right, Battle of Gettysburg* (1884). Color illustration. Copyright © Hulton Archive by Getty Images; *center right* Copyright © 1956, 1978 by Pauli Murray. Reprinted by permission of Frances Collin, literary agent; **185** *A Burial Party: Civil War, Cold Harbor, Virginia* (1865), Alexander Gardner. Photograph. Chicago Historical Society; **186, 187** *top* The Granger Collection, New York; **187** *bottom* Indianapolis Children's Museum; **188** The Granger Collection, New York; **189** Copyright © Bettmann/Corbis; **192** Copyright © Sylvain Grandadam/Photo Researchers, Inc.; **193** The Granger Collection, New York; **194** *top, Taking of the Bastille, 14 July 1789* (late 1700's), unknown artist, Chateau Versailles, France. Giraudon/Art Resource, New York; **195** *top* Beverley R. Robinson Collection, United States Naval Academy Museum, Annapolis, Maryland. Accession number 51.7.667; *bottom* The Granger Collection, New York; **196** *top* The Granger Collection, New York; *bottom* Copyright © Bettmann/Corbis; **197** California State Library.

## Chapter 5

**198–199,** *Champions of the Mississippi,* The Currier & Ives, lithograph. Scala/Art Resource, New York; **200** *bottom left to right* Copyright © Bettmann/Corbis; The Granger Collection, New York; Hulton Archive by Getty Images; **200–201** National Anthropological Archives, National Museum of Natural History, Smithsonian Institution; **201** *bottom left to right* Copyright © Bettmann/Corbis; Hulton Archive by Getty Images; **202** *top right, And So, Unemotionally, There Begun One of the Wildest and Strangest Journeys Ever Made in Any Land* (date unknown), William Henry David Koerner. Oil on canvas, 22¼" × 72¼". Buffalo Bill Historical Center, Cody Wyoming; *center right* Courtesy of Brigham Young University; **203** *top right, Portrait of a Sioux Man and Woman* (date unknown), Gertrude Käsebier. Photographic History Collection, National Museum of American History, Smithsonian Institution; *bottom* Copyright © The Detroit Institute of Arts, Founders Society Purchase with funds from Flint Ink Corporation; **204** The Granger Collection, New York; **205** The Granger Collection, New York; **206** *top right* Buffalo Bill Historical Center, Cody Wyoming. Gift Olin Corporation, Winchester Arms Collection; *center left* The Granger Collection, New York; *bottom right* American Museum of Natural History, New York. Photograph by Lee Boltin; **207** *bottom left to right* T. Ulrich/H. Armstrong Roberts; Copyright © Steven Fuller/Animals, Animals; Copyright © Marilyn "Angel" Wynn/Native Stock; **208** *top* Marilyn "Angel" Wynn/Native Stock; *bottom, Vaqueros in a Horse Coral* (1887), James Walker. Oil on canvas, 24¼" × 40". Gilcrease Museum.; **210** *top, The Stampede* (date unknown), Frederic Remington. Oil on canvas, 27" × 40". Gilcrease Museum; **211** The Granger Collection, New York; **212** *bottom left* Photograph by E.A. Hegg. Special collections division, University of Washington Libraries, Seattle. Negative number 1312; **212** *top* The Granger Collection,

New York; **213** *top left, Miners Underground* (1897), unknown photographer. Glass plate negative. Colorado Historical Society; **213** *bottom* Photograph by J.G Wilson. Denver Public Library, Western History Department Collection; *top right* Chuck Lawliss; **214** *top right, And So, Unemotionally, There Begun One of the Wildest and Strangest Journeys Ever Made in Any Land* (date unknown), William Henry David Koerner. Oil on canvas, 22¼" × 72¼". Buffalo Bill Historical Center, Cody Wyoming; *center right, Pioneer Woman* (date unknown), Harvey Dunn. Hazel L. Meyer Memorial Library, De Smet, South Dakota; **215** *top* Kansas State Historical Society, Topeka; *bottom* Library of Congress; **216** The Granger Collection, New York; **217** *left to right* The Granger Collection, New York; 1999, North Wind Pictures; The Granger Collection, New York; North Wind Pictures; *background* James Schuebel/ Panoramic Images; **218** State Historical Society of North Dakota; **219** *top right, And So, Unemotionally, There Begun One of the Wildest and Strangest Journeys Ever Made in Any Land* (date unknown), William Henry David Koerner. Oil on canvas, 22¼" × 72¼". Buffalo Bill Historical Center, Cody Wyoming; *center* Kansas State Historical Society, Topeka; **220** Culver Pictures; **222** Courtesy of Chicago Tribune/Chicago American Photo File., Copyright © KMTV; **223** The Granger Collection, New York; **224** The Granger Collection, New York; **225** *top right* Detail of *Vaquero* (modeled 1980/cast 1990), Luis Jimenez. Cast fiber glass and epoxy. Courtesy of the National Museum of Art, Smithsonian Institution, Washington D.C./Art Resource, New York. Gift of Judith and Wilbur L. Ross, Jr.; *left* Photograph by William Stinson Soule, Archives & Manuscripts Division of the Oklahoma Historical Society. Courtesy of the Oklahoma Historical Society (neg. no. 3969); **226** *clockwise from top left* American Museum of Natural History, New York. Photograph by Lee Boltin; The Granger Collection, New York; Northwind Pictures; The Granger Collection, New York; Copyright © Steve Fuller/Animals/Animals.

## Chapter 6

**228** *bottom left to right* Underwood Photo Archives, San Francisco; National Museum of American History/Smithsonian Institution; **228–229** California State Railroad Museum; **229** *bottom left and right* The Granger Collection, New York; **230** *top right* The Granger Collection, New York; Reproduced from *Prospectus: The True History of the Beaumont Oil Fields* by Pattillo Higgins. 1902 Pattillo Higgins. Courtesy of the estate of Pattillo Higgins; **232** The Granger Collection, New York; **233** Copyright © Corbis; **234** *top left* From the *Atlas of Cuyahoga County, Ohio,* Titus, Simmons and Titus; *bottom* Western Reserve Historical Society, Cleveland; **234–235** From the *Atlas of Cuyahoga County, Ohio,* Titus, Simmons and Titus; **235** *top right* Copyright © Cleveland Public Library/Bettmann/Corbis; **236** *top right* The Granger Collection, New York; *center* Historic Pullman Foundation Archives, Chicago; **237** *right* Copyright © Jake Lee; **238** The Granger Collection, New York; **240** The Granger Collection, New York; **241** *both,* The Granger Collection, New York; **242** The Granger Collection, New York; **243** *top, bottom* Library of Congress; **244** Courtesy of George Eastman House; **246** Copyright © Bettmann/Corbis; **248** *left* Eugene Debs Collection/Tamiment Institute Library, New York University; *right* The Granger Collection, New York; **249** Copyright © Bettmann/Corbis; **250** Western Reserve Historical Society, Cleveland, Ohio.

## Chapter 7

**252** *bottom left* Copyright © Bettmann/Corbis; *bottom center, right* The Granger Collection, New York; **252–253** The Granger Collection, New York; **253** The Granger Collection, New York; **254** *top right* Copyright © Corbis; *center* Courtesy of the Fong See Family; **256** National Park Service/Statue of Liberty National Monument; **257** *top left* Culver Pictures; top right New York Academy of Medicine Library; **258** The Granger Collection, New York; **259** Copyright © Bettmann/Corbis; **260** *left to right, Mission Francisco Solano de Sonoma* (date unknown), Oriana Day. Fine Arts Museum of San Francisco (California), gift of Eleanor

Martin, 37573; Culver Pictures, Inc.; From *An Illustrated History of the Civil War* by Miller and Pohankas, *Time-Life*; **261** *top right* The Granger Collection, New York; *bottom left* Copyright © Bettmann/Corbis; **262** *top right* Copyright © Corbis; *center* The Granger Collection, New York; **264** Library of Congress; **265** *bottom left* The Granger Collection, New York; *bottom right* Copyright © Bettman/Corbis; **266** University of Illinois at Chicago Library, the Jane Addams Memorial Collection; **267** *top right* Copyright © Bettmann/Corbis; *center right* The Granger Collection, New York; **268** Copyright © Bettmann/Corbis; **269** *center, bottom* The Granger Collection, New York; **270** *all* The Granger Collection, New York; **273** *top* Harper's Weekly, August 19, 1871.

### Chapter 8

**274** *bottom left* The Granger Collection, New York; **274–275** Stock Montage; **275** *bottom left to right* Copyright © Bettmann/Corbis Copyright © Charles & Josette Lenars/Corbis; Hulton Archive by Getty Images; **276** *top right* The Granger Collection, New York; *center right* Library of Congress; **277** Library of Congress; **278** *top, Plan of the Center of the City, Showing the Present Street and Boulevard System*, plate 111 from *Plan of Chicago* (1909), Daniel H. Burnham and Edward H. Bennett, Chicago partnership 1903–1912. Ink and watercolor on paper, 131.1cm × 102.4 cm. On permanent loan to the Art Institute of Chicago, 19.148.1966. Photograph, The Art Institute of Chicago. All rights reserved; *bottom* The Granger Collection, New York; **279** Copyright © Bettmann/Corbis; **280** *top* Copyright © John Batchelor/World Wide Publishing Solutions; *center* Copyright © Smithsonian Institution; *bottom* National Archives and Records Administration; **281** *top* Copyright © Bettmann/Corbis; *bottom* Copyright © Eastman Kodak Company; **282** *top right* The Granger Collection, New York; *center* Culver Pictures; **284** Copyright © 1991 Stephen Frisch/Stock Boston; **285** *top right* Moorland-Spingarn Research Center, Howard University Archives; **286** *top right, center* The Granger Collection, New York; **287** Hulton Archive by Getty Images; **289** Sacramento Archives and Museum Collection Center; **290** The Granger Collection, New York; **291** *top* Copyright © 1965 Danny Lyon/Magnum Photos; *bottom* Copyright © Reuters NewMedia, Inc./Corbis; **292** *top right* The Granger Collection, New York; *center* Culver Pictures; **294** National Baseball Hall of Fame; **295** *bottom, The Champion Single Sculls (Max Schmitt in a Single Scull)* (1871), Thomas Eakins. Oil on canvas, 32¼" × 46¼". The Metropolitan Museum of Art, purchase, The Alfred N. Punnett Endowment Fund George D. Pratt Gift, 1934 (34.92); **296** The Granger Collection, New York; **297** *both* Courtesy Sears, Roebuck and Co.; **298** *left* Archive Photos; *right* The Granger Collection, New York; **299** *top right* Hulton Archive by Getty Images; *bottom right* The Granger Collection, New York; **300** *bottom* The Granger Collection, New York.

### Chapter 9

**302–303** *The Statue of Liberty* (date unknown), Francis Hopinkson Smith. Oil on canvas. 11" × 15" (27.9 cm × 38.1 cm). Courtesy of Christie's Images; **304–305** *across* Copyright © Bettmann/Corbis; *bottom left* Copyright © Michael Maslin Historic Photographs/Corbis; *bottom right* Copyright © Bettmann/Corbis; **305** *bottom left* Copyright © Bettmann/Corbis; *bottom center* Peter Ruhe/Hulton Archive by Getty Images; *bottom right* The Granger Collection, New York; **306** *top right, center right* Copyright © Bettmann/Corbis; **307** *top* Copyright © UPI/Bettmann/Corbis; *bottom* Hulton Archive by Getty Images; **309** Copyright © Bettmann/Corbis; **310** Archives & Information Services Division, Texas State Library, Austin; **311** *center left* Lewis W. Hine (1912), Courtesy George Eastman House; *top right* Lewis W. Hine (1908), Copyright © Bettmann/Corbis **312** Hulton Archive by Getty Images; **313** *top right* Copyright © Bettmann/Corbis; *center right* The Granger Collection, New York **314** Copyright © Bettmann/Corbis; **315** Copyright © Corbis; **316, 317** *top right, center right* Copyright © Bettmann/Corbis; **318** *top left* National Museum of American History, Smithsonian Institution; **318** *bottom,* **319** Copyright © Bettmann/Corbis; **321** *illustration* Matthew Pippin; *inset, top right* Lewis W. Hine (1909), Copyright © George Eastman House/Hulton Archive by Getty Images; *inset, center* Hulton Archive by Getty Images; **322** *top* Copyright © UPI/Bettmann/Corbis; *bottom*

*left* The Granger Collection, New York; **324** *top left* Copyright © Bill Ross/Corbis; *bottom* The Granger Collection, New York; **325** Hulton Getty/Getty News Services; **326, 327** *top right* The Granger Collection, New York; **327** *bottom left* Jacket from *The Jungle*. Used by permission of University of Illinois Press. Cover art from the Chicago Historical Society; **328** *top right* Copyright © Bettmann/Corbis; *center right* The Granger Collection, New York; **329** Copyright © Bettmann/Corbis **330** The Granger Collection, New York; **332** *top right, center right,* **335** Copyright © Bettmann/Corbis; **336** *center left* Ezra Stoller, Copyright © Esto; *top right* Copyright © Michael T. Sedam/Corbis.

### Chapter 10

**340** *bottom, left to right* Copyright © Bettmann/Corbis; Hulton Archive by Getty Images; **340–341** Copyright © Corbis; **341** *bottom, left to right* Panama Canal Company; Copyright © Corbis; **342** *top right* Library of Congress, Prints and Photographs Division (LC-USZC4-5232); *center* Copyright © Bettmann/Corbis; **343** *top* Culver Pictures; *bottom* The Granger Collection, New York; **346** *top right* Library of Congress, Prints and Photographs Division (LC-USZC4-5232); *center* Copyright © Bettmann/Corbis; **347** The Granger Collection, New York; **348** Copyright © Bettmann/Corbis; **350** Copyright © Corbis; **351** Copyright © Bettmann/Corbis; **352** *top right* Library of Congress, Prints and Photographs Division (LC-USZC4-5232); *center, From Puerto Rico: A Political and Cultural History,* Arturo Morales Carrion; **353** Copyright © AFP/Corgis; **354** The Granger Collection, New York; **355** Keystone-Mast Collection (24039), UCR/California Museum of Photography, University of California, Riverside; **357** Copyright © The British Museum; **358** Copyright © Bettmann/Corbis; **359** *top right* Library of Congress, Prints and Photographs Division (LC-USZC4-5232); *center* UPI/Corbis-Bettmann; **360** The Granger Collection, New York; **361** Copyright © Corbis; **362** *top* The Granger Collection, New York; *bottom* Theodore Roosevelt Collection, Harvard College Library; **364** *Zapatistas Marching,* Jose Clemente Orozco. Private Collection/Index/Bridgeman Art Library, Copyright © Estate of Jose Clemente Orozco/Licensed by Vaga, New York, NY; **365** The Granger Collection, New York; **366** *top* Panama Canal Company; *bottom* Copyright © Will and Deni McIntyre/Stone; **367** *top* Copyright © The Mariner's Museum/Corbis; *bottom* Courtesy of The Historic New Orleans Collection, New Orleans, LA; **368** Copyright © Corbis; **369** *left* Culver Pictures; *right* Michelle Hlubinka.

### Chapter 11

**370** *bottom, left to right* Copyright © Bettmann/Corbis; Copyright © Dorling Kindersley; Copyright © Underwood & Underwood/Corbis; **370–371** Copyright © Bettmann/Corbis; **371** *bottom, left to right* San Francisco Chronicle; The Granger Collection, New York; **372** *top* Copyright © PhotoDisc, Inc; Photograph by Michael Vines, from the collection of the Old Rhinebeck Aerodrome; *center* Copyright © Corbis; **373** Copyright © Corbis; **374** AP Photo/Rikard Larma; **376** Illustrations by Chris Costello, *inset* Copyright © Corbis; **378** *top* Hulton Archive by Getty Images; *right* The Granger Collection, New York; **379** Culver Pictures; **381** *top* Copyright © PhotoDisc, Inc; Photograph by Michael Vines, from the collection of the Old Rhinebeck Aerodrome; *center* Copyright © Bettmann/Corbis; **382** *top* Copyright © Corbis; *left* The Granger Collection, New York; **384** *top* The Granger Collection, New York; *bottom center* Photograph by Michael Vines, from the collection of the Old Rhinebeck Aerodrome; **384–385** Hulton Archive by Getty Images; **385** *bottom center* Copyright © Dorling Kindersley; *bottom right* Hulton Archive by Getty Images; **386** Copyright © Bettmann/Corbis; **387** Library of Congress, Prints and Photographs Division; **388** *top* Copyright © PhotoDisc, Inc; Photograph by Michael Vines, from the collection of the Old Rhinebeck Aerodrome; *center* Brown Brothers; **390** *top* Copyright © Bettmann/Corbis; *left* The Granger Collection, New York; **390** *top left* Copyright © Bettmann/Corbis; **391** Copyright © Corbis; **392** *left* Courtesy of The Industrial Workers of the World; *bottom* Copyright © Bettmann/Corbis; **393** Panel no. 1: *During the World War There Was a Great Migration North by Southern Negroes,* from the Migration of the Negro mural series (1940–1941), Jacob Lawrence. Tempera on masonite, 12" × 18". Acquired through

Downtown Gallery, 1942. The Phillips Collection, Washington, D.C.; **394** Copyright © UPI/Corbis-Bettmann; **395** Copyright © Bettmann/Corbis; **396** *top* Copyright © PhotoDisc, Inc; *bottom* Copyright © Bettmann/Corbis; **397** *both* Copyright © Bettmann/Corbis; **398** *top* Copyright © PhotoDisc, Inc; Photograph by Michael Vines, from the collection of the Old Rhinebeck Aerodrome; *center left* Hulton Archive by Getty Images; **399** *top* The Granger Collection, New York; *bottom* Copyright © Corbis; **402** *top right* Photofest; *top center* Photofest; *top left* Photofest; *bottom left* From *Frankenstein* (1931), Universal, Courtesy of The Kobal Collection; **404** *both* The Granger Collection, New York; **405** *top left* Copyright © Reuters/Corbis-Bettmann; *top right* Copyright © 1968 Philip Jones Griffiths/Magnum Photos; *bottom* Photograph by George Rodger/*Life* Magazine; **407** Michelle Hlubinka.

**Chapter 12**
**408–409** *Drouth Stricken Area* (1934), Alexandere Hogue. Oil on canvas, 30″ × 42¼″. Dallas Museum of Art, Dallas Art Association Purchase; **410** *bottom, left to right* Copyright © David J. & Janice L. Frent Collection/Corbis; Photograph by Martin Plomer, Copyright © Dorling Kindersley; **410–411** Copyright © Bettmann/Corbis; **411** *bottom, left to right* Hulton Archive by Getty Images; Copyright © UPI/Corbis-Bettmann; Copyright © Bettmann/Corbis; **412** *top right* Copyright © Bettmann/Corbis; *center* From *The Jewish Americans*, Copyright © 1982 by Milton Meltzer. Thomas Y. Crowell Junior Books/Harper Collins Childrens' Books; **414** *Sacco and Vanzetti* (1932), Ben Shahn. Tempera 21″ × 48″. Private Collection. Photograph courtesy of Kennedy Galleries, New York. Copyright © Estate of Ben Shahn/Licensed by VAGA, New York, NY; **415** Copyright © UPI/Corbis-Bettmann; **416** Library of Congress, Prints and Photographs Division (LC-USZ4-5584); **417** Library of Congress, Prints and Photographs Division; **418** Copyright © UPI/Corbis-Bettmann; **419** *top right* Copyright © Bettmann/Corbis; *center* Detail of *Warren Gamaliel Harding* (about 1923), Margaret Lindsay William. National Portrait Gallery, Smithsonian Institution/Art Resource, New York; **420** Hulton Archive by Getty Images; **421** Stock Montage; **422** *top right* Copyright © Bettmann/Corbis; *center* H. Armstrong Roberts; **423** *both* Brown Brothers; **424** *bottom,* courtesy of United Airlines; **425** Copyright © Camerique Stock Photos; **426** Culver Pictures; **428** *top* Library of Congress, Prints and Photographs Division (LC-USZC4-2635); *bottom* Library of Congress, Prints and Photographs Division (LC-B2-3982); **429** *top* Pittsburgh Courier Archives/Hulton Archive by Getty Images; *bottom* FPG Internatonal; **430** *top* Copyright © American Stock/Hulton Archive by Getty Images; *bottom* Copyright © Dan McCoy/Rainbow; **431** Daniel Fitzpatrick, courtesy of the State Historical Society of Missouri, Columbia, Missouri.

**Chapter 13**
**432–433** *across* Frank Driggs Collection/Hulton Archive by Getty Images; *bottom left, above time line* Hulton Archive by Getty Images; *bottom left, below time line* Copyright © Bettmann/Corbis; *bottom right* TimePix; *bottom left* Copyright © Bettmann/Corbis; *bottom center* Copyright © UPI/Bettmann/Corbis; **434** *top right, center right* Copyright © Bettmann/Corbis; **435** Aaron Douglas, *Aspects of Negro Life: Song of the Towers* (1934). Oil on canvas, 9′ × 9′. Schomburg Center for Research in Black Culture, Art & Artifacts division, the New York Public Library, Astor, Lenox and Tilden Foundations; **436** *bottom, left and right* Copyright © Underwood and Underwood/Bettmann/Corbis; **437** Copyright © Underwood and Underwood/Corbis; **438** Copyright © UPI/Bettmann/Corbis; **439** The Granger Collection, New York; **440** *top right* Copyright © Bettmann/Corbis; **440** *center right,* **441** Hulton Archive by Getty Images; **442** Lewis W. Hine/Courtesy George Eastman House; **444** *bottom left* Brown Brothers; *bottom right* Frank Driggs Collection/Hulton Archive by Getty Images **444–445** *center across* Copyright © Minnesota Historical Society/Corbis; **445** *top* National Archives; *bottom* Copyright © Bettmann/Corbis; **446** *top right* Copyright © Bettmann/Corbis; *center right* Copyright © UPI/Bettmann/Corbis;

**447** *bottom left, bottom center* Copyright © Underwood and Underwood/Corbis; *bottom right* Copyright © Hulton-Deutsch Collection/Corbis; **448** *bottom left* National Baseball Hall of fame, Cooperstown, NY; *center* Copyright © UPI/Bettmann/Corbis; *top right* New York Times Co./Hulton Archive by Getty Images; *bottom right* Hulton Archive by Getty Images; **449** *top, center left* Copyright © UPI/Bettmann/Corbis; *center right* Copyright © Bettmann/Corbis; **450** *Radiator Building—Night, New York* (1927), Georgia O'Keefe. Oil on canvas. The Alfred Stieglitz Collection, Fisk University Art Galleries, Nashville, Tennessee. Photograph by Vando Rogers; **451** Hulton Archive by Getty Images; **452** *top right* Copyright © Bettmann/Corbis; *center right* Brown Brothers; **453** Fisk University, Nashville, Tennessee; **454** Copyright © UPI/ Bettmann/Corbis; **455** *map* Karen Minot; *inset, top left* Frank Driggs Collection/Hulton Archive by Getty Images; *inset, center right* Copyright © Hulton-Deutsch Collection/Corbis; **455** *bottom,* **456, 457** Frank Driggs Collection/Hulton Archive by Getty Images; **458** Jacket cover of the first edition of THE GREAT GATSBY by F. Scott Fitzgerald (New York: Scribner, 1925). Reproduced by permission of Simon & Schuster; **459** *top left, Edna St. Vincent Millay* (1930), unknown photographer, National Portrait Gallery, Smithsonian Institution/Art Resource; *center right Langston Hughes* (c. 1920), Winold Reiss. National Portrait Gallery, Smithsonian Institution/Art Resource **460** *top* Photofest; *2nd from top* Frank Driggs Collection/Hulton Archive by Getty Images; *3rd from top* Copyright © Underwood and Underwood/ Corbis; *bottom* Copyright © UPI/Bettmann/Corbis; **461** Culver Pictures.

**Chapter 14**
**462** *bottom, left to right* © "Vanity Fair," The Condé Nast Publications, Inc., "Vanity Fair," October 1, 1933 cover; Copyright © Bettmann/Corbis; Copyright © UPI/Corbis-Bettmann; **462–463** Hulton Archive by Getty Images; **463** *bottom, left to right* Copyright © Bettmann/Corbis; Courtesy of The Chicago Historical Society; **464** *top right* Hulton Archive by Getty Images; *center* AP/Wide World Photos; **465** Copyright © Arthur Rothstein/Corbis; **466** Hulton Archive by Getty Images; **467** *Dies Irae* (October 29, 1929), James Naumburg Rosenberg. National Museum of American Art, Washington, D.C./Art Resource, New York; **468** *top* Copyright © Bettmann/Corbis; *bottom* Copyright © Reuters NewMedia Inc./Corbis; **469** Conservative Research Department, Conservative Party, London; **470** *background* Library of Congress, Prints and Photographs Division (LC-USF34-028362-D); *inset, both* Copyright © Underwood Photo Archives; **472** *top right* Hulton Archive by Getty Images; *center* Reproduced from *Dust Bowl Diary* by Ann Marie Low, by permission of the University of Nebraska Press. Copyright © 1984 by the University of Nebraska Press; **473** Franklin D. Roosevelt Library and UPI/Corbis-Bettmann; **474** Library of Congress, Prints and Photographs Division (LC-USZCA-4840, LC-USZ62-11491); **476** National Archives (119-CAL-11); **477** Farm Security Administration; **478** *top right* Hulton Archive by Getty Images; *center* Library of Congress, Prints and Photographs Division; **479** Detail of *Herbert Clark Hoover* (1931), Douglas Chandor. Oil on Canvas. National Portrait Gallery, Smithsonian Institution/Art Resource, New York; **480** Copyright © Lake County Museum/Corbis; **481** Reprinted from The Albany Evening News, June 7, 1931, with permission of the Times Union, Albany, New York; **483** Copyright © Bettmann/Corbis.

**Chapter 15**
**486–487** *across* Franklin D. Roosevelt Library/National Archives; **486** *bottom left* Copyright © Corbis; *bottom center* Copyright © Bettmann/Corbis; *bottom right,* Leon Carlin/© "Vanity Fair," The Condé Nast Publications, Inc., "Vanity Fair," October 1, 1933; **487** *bottom center* The Granger Collection, New York; *bottom right* MGM/The Kobal Collection; **488** *top right, Construction of the Dam* (1937), by William Gropper. Mural study done for the Department of the Interior, Washington D.C. National Museum of American Art, Washington, D.C./Art Resource, New York; *center right* Copyright © 1984 John Gutmann; **489** *center left,*

*Franklin Delano Roosevelt* (1935), Henry Salem Hubbell, National Portrait Gallery, Smithsonian Institution/ Art Resource, New York; *center right* Detail of *Anna Eleanor Roosevelt* (1949), Douglas Chandor. Oil on canvas. 49½" × 38¼". White House Historical Association;
**490** *Franklin D. Roosevelt at Hilltop Cottage with Ruthie Bie and Fala* (1941), Margaret Suckley. Photograph, Franklin D. Roosevelt Library; **491** National Archives; **492** AP/Wide World Photos; **493** *top right* Jay N. "Ding" Darling. Copyright © 1937 by the Des Moines Register and Tribune Company. Reprinted with permission/Stock Montage; **493** *bottom right,* **494** Copyright © Bettmann/Corbis; **495** *top right, Construction of the Dam* (1937), by William Gropper. Mural study done for the Department of the Interior, Washington D.C. National Museum of American Art, Washington, D.C./Art Resource, New York; *center right* Copyright © The Dorothea Lange Collection, Oakland Museum of California, City of Oakland. Gift of Paul S. Taylor; **496** *top left* Copyright © Underwood and Underwood/Corbis; *bottom left* Photofest; **497** *top, Migrant Mother, Nipomo, California* (1936), Dorothea Lange/Library of Congress [LC-USZ62- 95653]; *bottom* Dorothea Lange/Library of Congress [LC-USZ62-58355]; **498** Margaret Bourke-White/ TimePix; **499** Copyright © UPI/Bettmann/Corbis; **500** *center left* Copyright © Bettmann/Corbis; *top right* The Granger Collection, New York; *center right* National Archives; **501** Lester Beall/Library of Congress, Prints and Photographs Division [U.S. B415.3]; **502, 503** Copyright © Bettmann/Corbis; **504** *top right, Construction of the Dam* (1937), by William Gropper. Mural study done for the Department of the Interior, Washington D.C. National Museum of American Art, Washington, D.C./Art Resource, New York; **505** *top right* Copyright © UPI/Bettmann/ Corbis; *bottom right* Detail of *Mary McLeod Bethune (1875–1955), Educator* (1943–1944), Betsy Graves Reyneau. National Portrait Gallery, Smithsonian Institution/Art Resource, New York; **506** Pictorial Parade/Hulton Archive by Getty Images; **507** Copyright © UPI/Bettmann/Corbis; **508** *top left* AP/Wide World Photos; *top inset* The Granger Collection, New York; *top right* Copyright © UPI Bettmann/Corbis; **509** Carl Linde/Courtesy of the Illinois Labor History Society; **510** *top right, Construction of the Dam* (1937), by William Gropper. Mural study done for the Department of the Interior, Washington D.C. National Museum of American Art, Washington, D.C./Art Resource, New York; *center right* Russell Lee (1941)/Library of Congress, Prints and Photographs Division [USF34-38814-D]; **511** *top right, bottom right,* **512** *top left* Photofest; **512** *bottom, Industries of California* (1934), Ralph Stackpole. Photograph courtesy of the San Francisco (California) Art Commission. Photograph by Malcolm Kimberlin; **513** *top right American Gothic* (1930), Grant Wood. Oil on beaver board. 74.3 cm × 62.4 cm. All rights reserved. The Art Institute of Chicago, Friends of American Art Collection. 1930.934/VAGA. New York, NY; *bottom right* Courtesy of the Woody Guthrie Foundation and Archives; **514** Walker Evans (1935)/Library of Congress, Prints and Photographs Division [LC-USF342-008138-A]; **515** *top right, Construction of the Dam* (1937), by William Gropper. Mural study done for the Department of the Interior, Washington D.C. National Museum of American Art, Washington, D.C./Art Resource, New York; *center right* Franklin D. Roosevelt Library and AP/Wide World Photos; **517** Dorothea Lange (1936)/Library of Congress, Prints and Photographs Division [LC-USF34- 009669-E]; **518** Library of Congress, Prints and Photographs Division [LC-USZC4-4890]; **519** Courtesy of the Franklin D. Roosevelt Library; **520** Chris Costello; **521** *bottom left* Lewis W. Hine (1933)/Courtesy of the Tennessee Valley Authority; *top right* Courtesy of the Tennessee Valley Authority.

**Chapter 16**
**524–525** *Dawn Patrol of Launching* (1942), Paul Sample. Army Art Collection, Washington DC; **526** *bottom, left to right* Copyright © M. Howell/Camerique/H. Armstrong Roberts; Library of Congress, Prints and Photographs Division; **526–527** Copyright © Corbis; **527** *bottom, left to right* Library of Congress, Prints and Photographs Division (LC-USZ62-45002); Hulton Archive by Getty Images; **528** *top right* Hulton Archive by Getty Images; *center* Copyright © Bettmann/Corbis; **529** *left* Hulton Archive by Getty Images; *right* Copyright © Archivo Iconografico, S.A./Corbis;

**531** *left to right* Copyright © Bettmann/Corbis; Copyright © Hulton-Deutsch Collection/Corbis; Hulton Archive by Getty Images; **533** *both* Hulton Archive by Getty Images; **534** Copyright © The Washington Post. Reprinted with permission; **536** *top right* Hulton Archive by Getty Images; *center* Copyright © Bettmann/ Corbis; **537** Hulton Archive by Getty Images, J.D. Hackett; **539** *top* Hulton Archive by Getty Images; *bottom* AP/Wide World Photos; **540** *bottom* Copyright © John Topham/Black Star; **541** Woodfin Camp; **542** *top right* Hulton Archive by Getty Images; *center* Courtesy of Gerda Weissman Klein; **543** *left* Hulton Archive by Getty Images; *right* Yad Vashem Archives; **544** *Albert Einstein Among Other Immigrants* (date unknown), Ben Shahn. Scala/Art Resource, New York/licensed by VAGA, New York, NY; **546** *bottom* Copyright © UPI/Corbis-Bettmann; **546–547** U.S. Army Military History Institute; **547** KZ Gedenkstaette Dachau, courtesy of USHMM Photo Archives; **548** Main Commission for the Prosecution of the Crimes against the Polish Nation, courtesy of USHMM Photo Archives; **549** Magnum Photos; **550** *both* Hulton Archive by Getty Images; **551** National Archives; **553** National Archives (NWDNS-080-G-43376); **554** AP/WideWorld Photos; **555** *left* Library of Congress, Prints and Photographs Division (LC-USF34-71206-D); *right* Reprinted by permission of the Honolulu Star Bulletin;
**556** Copyright © UPI/Corbis-Bettmann; **559** Library of Congress, Prints and Photographs Division (CD1 Shoemaker, no. 2 (B size).

**Chapter 17**
**560** *bottom* Copyright © Corbis; **560–561** Copyright © Corbis; **561** *bottom, second from left* Martha Swope/TimePix; *all others* Hulton Archive by Getty Images; **562** *top right* Copyright © PhotoDisc, Inc.; *center* Courtesy of Charles Swanson; **563** *top* Copyright © Bettmann/Corbis; *bottom* Al Aumuller/Library of Congress, Prints and Photographs Division (LC-USZ62-118263); **565** Library of Congress, Prints and Photographs Division (LC-USW361-295); **566** *top* Library of Congress, Prints and Photographs Division (LC-USW3-11696-C); *bottom left, right* Photofest; **568** *top* AP/Wide World Photos; **569** *top right* Copyright © PhotoDisc, Inc.; *center (both),* Courtesy of Adrienne McGrath; **570** Copyright © Corbis; **571** Copyright © UPI/Corbis-Bettmann; **572** Copyright © Bettmann/Corbis; **573** *top* Copyright © Bettmann/Corbis; *bottom* Alan B. Taylor Collection; **574** AP/Wide World Photos; **575** Robert F. Sargent/Library of Congress, Prints and Photographs Division (LC-USZC4-4731); **576** Copyright © UPI/Corbis-Bettmann; **577** New York Daily News Photo; **578** *top right* Copyright © PhotoDisc, Inc. *center* Copyright © UPI/Corbis-Bettmann; **579** Copyright © Corbis; **581** Courtesy of the U.S. Navy/PhotoAssist, Inc./Woodfin Camp; **582** *top* AP/Wide World Photos; *bottom* AP/Wide World Photos; **583** Copyright © Bettmann/Corbis; **584** *top* Courtesy of the Air Force Administration/PhotoAssist, Inc./Woodfin Camp; *bottom* Copyright © Bernard Hoffman/TimePix; **586** National Archives; **588** *top* Copyright © Dan McCoy/Rainbow; *bottom* Copyright © 1999 Russell Munson/The Stock Market; **588–589** Copyright © Hank Morgan/Rainbow; **589** *top* AP/Wide World Photos; *center* Sovfoto/Eastfoto; *bottom* Copyright © 1993 Larry Mulvehill/ Rainbow; **590** *top right* Copyright © PhotoDisc, Inc.; *center, Twice a Patriot* (1943), unknown artist. Lithograph. Amistad Foundation Collection at the Wadsworth Atheneum, Hartford, Connecticut; **591** Photograph courtesy of the Franklin D. Roosevelt Library; **592** Copyright © Bettmann/Corbis; **593** Library of Congress, Prints and Photographs Division (LC-USZ62-48275); **594** Copyright © Seattle Post-Intelligencer Collection; Museum of History and Industry/Corbis; **597** *top* Copyright © Eliot Elisofon/TimePix; *right* Dennis Cook/ AP/Wide World Photos; **598** AP/Wide World Photos; **599** Michelle Hlubinka.

**Chapter 18**
**600** *bottom, left to right* Copyright © PhotoDisc, Inc.; Copyright © Bettmann/Corbis; **600–601** AP/Wide World Photos; **601** *bottom, left to right* Copyright © Aereo Graphics, Inc./Corbis; Sovfoto/ Eastfoto; **602** *top right* Hulton Archive by Getty Images; *center top* Copyright © Bettmann/Corbis; *center bottom* Copyright © United States Postal Service; **603** *both* Hulton Archive by Getty Images; **605** Hulton Archive by Getty Images; **606** Copyright © UPI/

Corbis-Bettmann; **607** AP/Wide World Photos; **608** Library of Congress, Prints and Photographs Division (LC-USZ62-53089); **609** *both* Hulton Archive by Getty Images; **610** *left* AP/Wide World Photos; *right* Hsinhua News Agency/AP/Wide World Photos; **612** Courtesy of Beverly Scott; **613** AP/Wide World Photos; **614** *both* Copyright © Bettmann/Corbis; **615** Yonhap/POOL/AP/Wide World Photos; **616** *top right* Hulton Archive by Getty Images; *center* Courtesy of Tony Kahn; **617** *top* Library of Congress, Prints and Photographs Division (LC-USF34-013363-C); *bottom* Photofest; **618** *left* Copyright © Bettmann/Corbis; *right* Photofest; **619** *top* Photofest; *bottom, left to right* AP/Wide World Photos; Copyright © AFP/Corbis; AP/Wide World Photos; **620** from *The Herblock Book* (Beacon Press, 1952); **621** from *Herblock's Here & Now* (Simon & Schuster, 1955); **622** *top right* Hulton Archive by Getty Images; *center* AP/Wide World Photos; **623** The American Civil Defense Association, photograph courtesy of Eric Green; **625** Copyright © Bettmann/Corbis; **627** *top* Sovfoto/Eastfoto; *bottom* Hulton Archive by Getty Images; **628** Courtesy of Republic Entertainment, Inc.; **629** *left* Courtesy of Bantam Books; *right* Courtesy of Bantam Doubleday Books; **631** Copyright © Corbis.

**Chapter 19**

**632** *bottom, left to right* Copyright © Bettmann/Corbis; Copyright © Dorling Kindersley; Copyright © George Lepp/Corbis; **632–633** Copyright © 1957 SEPS: The Curtis Publishing Company, Agent; **633** *bottom, left to right* National Aeronautics and Space Administration; Copyright © SuperStock, Inc.; **634** *top right* Copyright © 2001 Ken Whitmore/Stone; *center* Harold M. Lambert/Hulton Archive by Getty Images; **635** Copyright © J.R. Eyerman/TimePix; **637** Culver Pictures; **638** *top, Wipe Out Discrimination* (1949), Milton Ackoff. Offset lithograph, printed in color, 43⅞" × 32¾". The Museum of Modern Art, New York. Gift of the Congress of Industrial Organizations. Photography Copyright 1999 the Museum of Modern Art, New York; *bottom* Copyright © UPI/Corbis-Bettmann; **639** *top to bottom* Cousley Historical Collections. Photograph by Stephen Mays, New York; Cousley Historical Collections. Photograph by Stephen Mays, New York; Blank Archives/Hulton Archive by Getty Images; **640** Copyright © George Silk/TimePix; **641** *top right* Copyright © 2001 Ken Whitmore/Stone; *center* Copyright © SuperStock, Inc.; **642** Copyright © Bettmann/Corbis; **643** *top* Copyright © Harold M. Lambert/Hulton Archive by Getty Images; *bottom* The Image bank; **644** Copyright © Bettmann/Corbis; **645** *top, After the Prom* (September 1957). Printed by permission of the Norman Rockwell Family Trust. Copyright © 1957 the Norman Rockwell Family trust. Photograph courtesy of The Norman Rockwell Museum at Stockbridge; *bottom* Copyright © UPI/Corbis-Bettmann; **646** Copyright © Aldo Torelli/Stone; **647** *background* Copyright © PhotoDisc, Inc.; *clockwise from top right* Copyright © Alfred Eisenstaedt/TimePix; The Granger Collection, New York; Copyright © Carl Iwasaki/TimePix; Copyright © Francis Miller/TimePix; **648** *both* The Granger Collection, New York; **649** Hulton Archive by Getty Images/Michael Barson Collection; **650** *both* Courtesy of The Park Forest Historical Society; **650–651** Courtesy of The Park Forest Historical Society; **651** *center* Courtesy of The Park Forest Historical Society; *top right* Copyright © Dab Weiner, courtesy Sandra Weiner; **652** *top right* Copyright © 2001 Ken Whitmore/Stone; *center* Michael Ochs Archives; **653** Copyright © TimePix; **654** *top left* Robert Vose/Library of Congress Prints and Photographs Division (LC-USZ4-4889); *bottom* Photofest; **655** Hulton Archive by Getty Images; **656** *top left* Frank Driggs Collection/Hulton Archive by Getty Images; *bottom left* Hulton Archive by Getty Images; *bottom right* Copyright © Bettmann/Corbis; **657** Hulton Archive by Getty Images; **658** *center left* Copyright © 2001 Archie Comic Publications. Reprinted by permission of the copyright holder, Archie Comic Publications; *center right* Equinox Archives; *bottom left* Blank Archives/Hulton Archive by Getty Images. Photograph by Sharon Hoogstraten; **658–659** Copyright © Paul Schutzer/TimePix; **659** *top left* Photofest; **659** *center* Copyright © Paul Schutzer/TimePix; **660** *top right* Copyright © 2001 Ken Whitmore/Stone; *center*

The Granger Collection, New York; **662** Copyright © William Shrout/TimePix; **663** *Milwaukee (Wisconsin) Journal/Milwaukee Sentinel.*

**Chapter 20**

**666–667** *Civil Rights March, May 1965,* Copyright © James H. Karales. **668** *bottom, left to right* Blank Archive/Hulton Archive by Getty Images; Hulton Archive by Getty Images; **668–669** National Aeronautics and Space Administration; **669** *bottom, left to right* Copyright © Marilyn Silverstone/Magnum Photos; Copyright © Bettmann/Corbis; **670** Copyright © 1961 Black Star; **671** Copyright © Bettmann/Corbis; **672** Courtesy of John F. Kennedy Library; **674** *top left* Burt Glinn/Magnum Photos; *bottom, Kennedy and Exploding Cuban Cigar.* Leslie Illingsworth, Apr. 21, 1961. Courtesy of National Library of Wales; **675** *left* Copyright © Bettmann/Corbis; *bottom* Hulton Archive by Getty Images; **676** *both* Copyright © Bettmann/Corbis; **677** *background* Copyright © 1976 Leonard Freed/Magnum Photos; *inset* Kreusch/AP/Wide World Photos; **678** *top* John F. Kennedy Library, Boston; *bottom* Library of Congress; **679** *both* National Aeronautics and Space Administration; **680** Copyright © Bettmann/Corbis; **682** *left* Copyright © 1963,1964 by The New York Times Company. Reprinted by permission; *right, New York Daily News* photograph; **684** *left* Copyright © T Resource/Stone; *right* Copyright © Bruce Forster/Stone; Copyright © Richard Elliot/Stone; **687** Hulton Archive by Getty Images; **686** AP/Wide World Photos; *inset* Copyright © Bettmann/Corbis; **688** Museum of American Political Life, University of Hartford, West Hartford, Connecticut. Photograph by Sally Anderson-Bruce; **689** Copyright © Paul Conklin/P hoto Edit; **691** Copyright © Bettmann/Corbis; **693** LBJ Library; **694** Copyright © Bettmann/Corbis; **695** *left* Photograph by Sharon Hoogstraten, *right* Copyright © Bob Daemmrich/Stock Boston; **696** *clockwise from top left* Copyright © 1961 Black Star; Hulton Archive by Getty Images; Copyright © Paul Conklin/PhotoEdit; Hulton Archive by Getty Images.

**Chapter 21**

**698** *bottom, left to right* Copyright © Archive Photos/Express Newspaper by Getty Images; Copyright © Hulton Deutsch/Bettmann/Corbis; Copyright © Bettmann/Corbis; **698–699** Copyright © Ivan Massar/Black Star; **699** *left to right* Hulton Archive by Getty Images; AP/Wide World Photos; **700** *top right* Francis Miller/TimePix; *center* Courtesy of Arthur L. Freeman; **701** *both* Library of Congress; **702** Copyright © Archive Photos/Consolidated News by Getty Images; **703** Copyright © UPI/Bettmann/Corbis; **704** AP/Wide World Photos; **705** Dan Weiner/Courtesy of Sandra Weiner; **706** Copyright © Flip Schulke/Bettmann/Corbis; **707** AP/Wide World Photos; **708** Carl Iwasaki/TimePix; **709** *left* Copyright © Bettmann/Corbis; *right* The Granger Collection, New York; **710** *top right* Francis Miller/TimePix; *center* Copyright © UPI/Corbis-Bettmann; **711** Copyright © UPI/Corbis-Bettmann; **712** *top* AP/Wide World Photos; **713** *All* Photographs by Ernest C. Withers. Courtesy of Panopticon Gallery; **715** *top* Copyright © 1964 Steve Shapiro/Black Star; **717** *top right* Francis Miller/TimePix; *center* Copyright © UPI/Corbis-Bettmann; **718** *left* Photograph by J.R. Eyerman/*Life* Magazine; *right* Copyright © UPI/Corbis-Bettmann; **719** Copyright © 1964 John Launois/Black Star; **720** *left* Photograph by Sharon Hoogstraten; *right* Ken Regan/Camera 5; **721** *top* Black Star; *bottom* Copyright © Bettmann/Corbis; **722** Copyright © Leif Skoogfors/Bettmann/Corbis; **724** *both* The Granger Collection, New York; **725** *top right* Copyright © 1963 Charles Moore/Black Star; *center* UPI/Corbis-Bettmann; **726** *top left* Carl Iwasaki/TimePix; *top right* Dan Weiner/Courtesy of Sandra Weiner; *center* Copyright © 1964 Steve Shapiro/Black Star; *bottom* AP/Wide World Photos.

**Chapter 22**

**728** *bottom left* Copyright © Corbis; *bottom right* Copyright © SuperStock, Inc.; **728–729** Copyright © Tim Page/Corbis; **729** *bottom left* Photograph by V. Merritt. Copyright © Time, Inc.;

730 *top right* Copyright © PhotoDisc, Inc.; 731 AP/Wide World Photos; 733 *top* Hulton Archive by Getty Images; *bottom left* Copyright © Corbis; *bottom right* Scott Swanson Collection, Hulton Archive by Getty Images; 734 AP/Wide World Photos; 735 Copyright © 1963, 1964, by The New York Times Company. Reprinted by permission; 736 *top right* Copyright © PhotoDisc, Inc.; *center* U.S. Army/Hulton Archive by Getty Images; 737 Copyright © Bettmann/Corbis; 740 The Granger Collection, New York; 741 Photograph by Sharon Hoogstraten; 742 *top right* Copyright © PhotoDisc, Inc.; *center* Courtesy of Stephan Gubar; 743 *top* Photograph by Mark Kauffman/*Life* Magazine. Copyright © 1965 Time, Inc.; *bottom* Copyright © 1967 James Pickerell/Black Star; 744 AP/Wide World Photos; 746 Copyright © 1995 Burt Glinn/Magnum Photos; 747 Peter Newark's Pictures; 748 *top right* Copyright © PhotoDisc, Inc.; *center* Copyright © 1996 Danny Lyon/Magnum Photos; 749 Copyright © Time, Inc.; 750 Courtesy of Jack Kightlinger; 751 Photogaph by Bill Eppridge/*Life* Magazine. Copyright © Time, Inc.; 752 Copyright © Jeffrey Blankfort/Jereboam; 754 *top right* Copyright © PhotoDisc, Inc.; *center* Copyright © Donald J. Weber; 756 Copyright © Bettmann/Corbis; 757 Copyright © John Paul Filo; 758 Copyright © UPI/Corbis-Bettmann; 759 AP/Wide World Photos; 760 *top left* Copyright © Seny Norasingh/Light Sensitive; *top right* Copyright © Wolfgang Kaehler/Corbis; *center left* Copyright © 1993 Richard Howard/Black Star/PNI; 762 *left* From *Going after Cacciato* (jacket cover) by Tim O'Brien. Used by permission of Delacorte Press/Seymour Lawrence, a division of Bantam Doubleday Dell Publishing Group Inc.; 762–763 *background* Copyright © UPI/Corbis-Bettmann; 763 cover of *A Rumor of War* by Philip Caputo, copyright 1996 by Henry Holt and Co. Reprinted by permission of Henry Holt and Company, LLC. Cover photograph copyright © Don McCullin/Magnum Photos; *bottom* Cover illustration by Jim Dietz from *Fallen Angels* by Walter Dean Myers. Illustration Copyright © 1988 by Jim Dietz. Reprinted with permission of Scholastic, Inc.; 764 *top* Photo by Mark Kauffman/*Life* Magazine. Copyright © 1965 Time, Inc.; *center* Copyright © UPI/Corbis-Bettmann; *bottom* Peter Newark's Pictures; 765 Copyright © by Karl Hubenthal - All Rights Reserved.

**Chapter 23**
766 *bottom left to right* Copyright © UPI/Bettmann/Corbis; Liaison by Getty Images; Copyright © 1980 Arnold Zann/Black Star; 766–767 Lisa Law/The Image Works; 767 *bottom left to right* Sahm Doherty/TimePix; Jon Hammer/Archive Photos by Getty Images; UPI/Corbis-Bettmann; 768 Copyright © Paul Fusco/Magnum Photos; 769 Copyright © Underwood Photo Archives; 770 photograph by Arthur Schatz/*Life* Magazine. Copyright © TIME, Inc.; 771 Copyright © Liaison by Getty Images; 772 Copyright © Rick Smolan; 774 Photograph by Harris and Ewing, collection of the Supreme Court of the United States; 775 Data courtesy of Alabama State Archives; 776 Copyright © UPI/Bettmann/Corbis; 778 Copyright © Mark Klamkin/Black Star; 779 *top* Copyright © Werner Wolf/Black Star; *bottom* Copyright © Lynda Gordon/Liaison by Getty Images; 780 *left* Library of Congress; *right* Courtesy MS. Magazine; 781 *center* Copyright © Bob Fitch/Black Star; 782 *top* Photograph by Sharon Hoogstraten; *bottom* Copyright © Bettmann/Corbis; 783 © 1967 Hulton-Deutsch Collection/Corbis; 784 *center left* Copyright © Danny Lyon/Magnum Photos; *center right* Copyright © Bettmann/Corbis; *bottom left* Agence France Presse/Archive Photos by Getty Images; 785 *top* Copyright © UPI/Bettmann/Corbis; 786 *clockwise, top left* Photofest Copyright © Coni Kaufman/Southern Stock/PNI; Copyright © Joel Axelrod/Michael Ochs Archives; Poster #75 Bonnie Maclean; 787 *top* Photofest; *Marilyn Monroe* (1967), Andy Warhol. Screenprint on white paper, 36″ × 36″. The Andy Warhol Foundation, Inc./Art Resource, New York;

**Chapter 24**
790–791 Statue of Liberty National Monument/National Park Service/photograph copyright © Norman McGrath, all rights reserved; 792 *bottom, left to right* Photograph by Sharon Hoogstraten; Copyright © Bettmann/Corbis; 792–793 AP/Wide World Photos; 793 *bottom, left to right* Courtesy of the Jimmy Carter Library; Copyright © Charles E. Rotkin/Corbis; Copyright © Bettmann/Corbis; 794 *top right* Copyright © PhotoDisc, Inc.; *center* Copyright © UPI/Corbis-Bettmann; 795 Courtesy of Paul Szep; 796 National Aeronautics and Space Administraton; 797 Copyright © Ira Wyman/Sygma; 798 *both* Copyright © Bettmann/Corbis; 799 AP/Wide World Photos; 800 Copyright © Bettmann/Corbis; 801 AP/Wide World Photos; 802 *top right* Copyright © PhotoDisc, Inc.; *center* AP/Wide World Photos; 803 *background* H. Armstrong Roberts; *top left, top right* J.P. Laffront/Sygma; *bottom left, bottom right* AP/Wide World Photos; 804 Copyright © 1973 Dennis Brack/ Black Star; 805 *top* Copyright © Wally McNamee/Corbis; 806 *top* National Archives/AP/Wide World Photos; *bottom* Cartoon by Tony Auth. Copyright © Universal Press Syndicate; 807 *top* Copyright © 1974 Harry Benson; *bottom* National Archives; 808 *top left* Courtesy of TV Guide; *center, bottom* PhotoFest; 809 *top* Photofest; *center* Copyright © 1977 ABC/Warner TV/MPTV; 810 *top right* Copyright © PhotoDisc, Inc.; *center* Bill Pierce/Time Magazine.; 811 Copyright © 1974 Time, Inc. Reprinted by permission; 812 *top* Copyright © Owen Franken/Sygma; *bottom* Museum of American Political Life, University of Hartford, West Hartford, Connecticut. Photograph by Sally Anderson-Bruce; 813 Copyright © Bill Ross/Corbis; 814 Copyright © 1977 Alex Webb/Magnum Photos; 816 Courtesy of the Jimmy Carter Library; 817 Copyright © Alain Mingam/ Liaison Agency, Inc.; 818 AP/Wide World Photos; 819 Copyright © Bettmann/Corbis; 820 *top right* Copyright © PhotoDisc, Inc.; *center* Copyright © UPI/Corbis-Bettmann; 821 *top* Copyright © 1962 Eric Hartmann/Magnum Photos; *bottom* Hulton Archive by Getty Images; 822 Copyright © Leonard Lee Rue III/Stock Boston; 823 Copyright © 1994 John McGrail; 824 *left* 20th Century Fox (courtesy The Kobal Collection); *right* COLUMBIA (courtesy The Kobal Collection); 825 Library of Congress, Prints and Photographs Division (LC-USZ62-102359). Source: U.S. EPA; 826 *left to right* Copyright © Bettmann/Corbis; Copyright © 1974 Time, Inc. Reprinted by permission; Museum of American Political Life, University of Hartford, West Hartford, Connecticut. Photograph by Sally Anderson-Bruce.

**Chapter 25**
828 *bottom, left to right* Hulton Archive by Getty Images; Copyright © Wally McNamee/Corbis; Hulton Archive by Getty Images; 828–829 Copyright © Robert Maass/Corbis; 829 *bottom, left to right* Copyright Copyright © Giles Bassignac/Liaison Agency, Inc.; Copyright © Owen Franken/Corbis; 830 *top right* Copyright © Corbis; *center* Copyright © 1988 Dennis Brack/Black Star; 831 Copyright © Bettmann/Corbis; 832 Copyright © 1991 Dennis Brack/Black Star; 834 *top right* Copyright © Corbis; *center* Copyright © Wally McNamee/Corbis; 836 *top* Cartoon by Pat Oliphant. Copyright © Universal Press Syndicate; *bottom, both* Copyright © 1991 Dennis Brack/Black Star; 837 AP/WideWorld Photos; 838 Copyright © 1987 Dennis Brack/Black Star; 839 *top right* Copyright © Corbis; *center* From *Trevor's Place: The Story of the Boy Who Brings Hope to the Homeless*. Copyright © 1985 by Frank and Janet Ferrell; 840 Copyright © Brad Markel/Liaison Agency, Inc.; 841 National Aeronautics and Space Administration; 842 Copyright © Wally McNamee/Corbis; 843 Copyright © 1994 P.F. Bentley/Black Star; 844 Copyright © 1991 Dennis Brack/Black Star; 845 Copyright © Lee Snider/Corbis; 847 *left* Copyright © Bob Rowan/Progressive Images/Corbis; *right* Copyright © Dewitt Jones/Corbis; 848 *top right* Copyright © Corbis; *center* Reuters/Stephen Jaffe/Hulton Archive by Getty Images; 849 Copyright © 1989 by National Review, Inc., 215 Lexington Avenue, New York, NY 10016. Reprinted by Permission; 850 *top* Reuters/David Brauchli/ Hulton Archive by Getty Images; *bottom* AP/Wide World Photos; 852 from *Herblock at Large* (Pantheon, 1987); 854 *left* AP/Wide World Photos; *right* Copyright © David & Peter Turnley/Corbis; 855 AP/Wide World Photos; 856 *left* Copyright © 1991 Dennis Brack/Black Star; *right* Copyright © 1987 Dennis Brack/Black Star.

**Chapter 26**

858 *bottom left* Copyright © US Air Force/TimePix; *bottom right* Steve Helber/AP/Wide World Photos; 858–859 Copyright © Nancy Sheehan/PhotoEdit; 859 *bottom, left to right* Copyright © Robert Maass/CORBIS; John Chadwick/AP/Wide World Photos; Copyright © Kevin Lamarque/Reuters/TimePix; 860 *top right* Copyright © PhotoDisc, Inc.; *center* Copyright © 1993 Jim Stratford/Black Star; 861 *top* Copyright © Reuters/Corbis-Bettmann; *bottom* John Duricka/AP/Wide World Photos; 862 *top* Copyright © 1995 David Longstreath/AP/Wide World Photos; *bottom* AP/Wide World Photos; 863 Steve Ludlum/The New York Times; 864 Copyright © Reuters/Corbis-Bettmann; 865 Michael S. Green/AP/Wide World Photos; 867 Time Magazine, Copyright © TIME Inc.; 868 *top* Ron Edmonds/AP/Wide World Photos; *bottom* Gary I. Rothstein/AP/Wide World Photos; 869 *top right* Copyright © PhotoDisc, Inc.; *center* Courtesy of Mike Cavanaugh/UNITE; 870 Copyright © UPI/Corbis-Bettmann; 871 Copyright © Lou Dematteis/Reuters/TimePix; 873 Copyright © Shaun Best/Reuters/TimePix; 874 Copyright © Barron Claiborne/Outline; 875 *top* Jacket from *The Joy Luck Club*. Used by permission of G.P. Putnam Sons. Cover illustration Copyright © Gretchen Shields; *bottom* Copyright © Greg Smith/SABA; 876 *top right* Copyright © PhotoDisc, Inc.; *center* Courtesy of Challenged Athletes Foundation, photograph by Tim Mantoani; 877 Courtesy of Gary Brookins/Richmond Times-Dispatch; 878 Adrin Snider/Daily Press/AP/Wide World Photos; 879 Copyright © Corbis; 880 Copyright © James A. Sugar/Corbis; 881 *left* Toby Talbot/AP/Wide World Photos; *right* Dale Atkins/AP Wide World Photos; 882 *top right* Copyright © PhotoDisc, Inc.; *center* Courtesy of MALDEF; 883 *both* Courtesy of Michael Van Valkenburgh Associates, Inc., and Ann Hamilton. Photograph by Ed Massery; 884 Copyright © Joseph Sohm; Chromosohm, Inc./Corbis; 886 Paul Sakuma/AP/Wide World Photos; 888 *left* Hulton Archive by Getty Images; *right* Library of Congress, Prints and Photographs Division (LC-USZC4-4580, LC-USZ62-20359); 889 *top* Copyright © Sam Shere/TimePix; *bottom* National Archives (WDNS -428-K-108890).

**The War on Terrorism**

**Cover** Photograph by FEMA/Getty Images; **US2** Copyright © AFP/Corbis; *inset* Copyright © John Annerino/TimePix; **US3** *top* Copyright © MapQuest.com; *bottom* Susan Walsh/AP/Wide World Photos; **US4** *left* AP/Wide World Photos; *right* Copyright © MapQuest.com; **US5** USA TODAY®; **US6–US7** Copyright © MapQuest.com; **US6** *inset* Copyright © Reuters NewMedia Inc./Corbis; **US7** *top inset* Katsumi Ksashara/AP/Wide World Photos; *bottom inset* Sayyid Azim/AP/Wide World Photos; **US9** *left* AP/Wide World Photos; **US10** USA TODAY®; *top inset* AP/Wide World Photos; *middle inset* Al-Jazeera/AP/Wide World Photos; *bottom inset* AP/Wide World Photos; **US11** *top* Copyright © David Hume Kennerly/Corbis Sygma; *bottom* Copyright © MapQuest.com; **US12** Copyright © Jeff Christensen/Reuters/TimePix; *inset* Copyright © Greg Mathieson/MAI/TimePix; **US13** USA TODAY®; **US14** *left* Copyright © Digital Stock/Corbis; *top inset* Copyright © Kent Wood/Photo Researchers; *bottom* FBI/AP/Wide World Photos; *bottom inset* Justice Department/AP/Wide World Photos; **US15** Copyright © Eric Draper/The White House/TimePix

**Reference Section**

**R23** Copyright © Steve Schapiro/Black Star; **R24** Culver Pictures; **R37** Kindra Clineff; **R38** *Life* Magazine. Copyright © 1956 Time, Inc.; **R39** Copyright © 1989 by National Review, Inc.; 215 Lexington Avenue, New York, NY 10016. Reprinted by Permission; **R40** *left* Copyright © UPI/Corbis-Bettmann; *right* Copyright © Luc Beziat/Stone; **R42** AP/WideWorld Photos; **R44** Copyright © H. David Seawell/CORBIS; **R45** *left* Copyright © Reuters NewMedia, Inc./CORBIS; *right* Copyright © Reuters/John Sommers II/ TimePix.

# REVIEWERS (continued)